# VISITING

## South ... ? ... DE.

## <u>READ THIS!</u>

### *The advice below is designed to help you if you are travelling to South America.*

The US Dollar is the principally accepted foreign currency.
Other currencies will get you worse exchange rates and may not even be accepted in certain places.
Black or free market rates are normally better than official market rates.
Be careful, because in some countries the black market is illegal.
Shop around for rates.
Hotel exchange rates, for example, although often better than official rates, are rarely top market rates.
In many countries only certain Banks, and even only certain branches, may deal in exchange.
You may even find yourself in a town where no Bank deals in exchange.
Take a supply of local currency if travelling outside large cities.
Finally, although exchange rates are marginally better for US Dollar bills than for travellers cheques make sure that the bulk of your money is in US$ Thomas Cook MasterCard® Travellers Cheques.
These can be refunded in case of loss or theft, cash is lost forever.

*See the lists at the end of this book for Refund locations.*

**Thomas Cook**

Mexico City ————————— ———————— Rio de Janeiro

Caracas ————— ———— Bogota

Lima ———— ———————— Santiago

San Juan ———— ———— Havana

Asuncion ———— ———————— Sao Paolo

Panama City ————— ————— Quito

San Jose ———— ———————— Guayaquil

Buenos Aires ————— ———————— Santo Domingo

Managua ———— ———————— Guatemala

Montevideo ————————

# THE HOTTEST
# IN LATIN AMERICA.

Iberia gives you the hottest all-round service to Latin America.

With more flights to more places than any other airline. Plus a network of internal flights.

Iberia Preference Class, the hottest business class, means seat selection

 when you book, separate check-in desks, through check-in to final destination, and exclusive lounges at most airports.

In flight, seating in a separate cabin offers the comfort and space of traditional first class: on our 747s you'll be right up-front, and only two abreast. The service is distinguished by impeccable attention to detail – there's even an on board library.

Ask your business travel agent to book the hottest service to Latin America.

## WARM TO THE EXPERIENCE.

London 071-437 5622; Manchester 061-436 6444; Birmingham 021-643 1953; Glasgow 041-248 6581; Dublin 010 3531 779846.

# *1992*
# SOUTH AMERICAN HANDBOOK

### SIXTY EIGHTH EDITION

*Editor*
## Ben Box

"The accidental traveller who has journeyed on
from Stabroek to the rock Saba, and from
thence to the banks of the Essequibo...can
merely mark the outlines of the path he has
trodden, or tell thee the sounds he has heard,
or faintly describe what he has seen in the
environs of his resting-places; but if this be
enough to induce thee to undertake the
journey, and give the world a description of it,
he will be amply satisfied."

*Charles Waterton*

TRADE & TRAVEL
PUBLICATIONS

TRADE & TRAVEL PUBLICATIONS LTD
6 RIVERSIDE COURT
RIVERSIDE ROAD
BATH BA2 3DZ
ENGLAND
TEL 0225 469141
FAX 0225 462921

ISBN 0 900751 33 9

CIP DATA: A catalogue record for this book is available from the British Library.

Published in the United States of America and Canada by
Prentice Hall Travel
A Division of Simon & Schuster Inc.
15 Columbus Circle
New York, NY 10023-7780

In North America, ISBN 0-13-830456-4

## COVER—The Giant Armadillo

The Giant Armadillo has a preference for forest habitat, although it can be frequently seen on savannahs and other open terrain. The geographical distribution is from Venezuela to Northern Argentina. These very primitive animals are protected by a natural suit of armour, but if attacked can only partially roll up and are therefore more likely to flee. Although not a fast runner it can zig-zag through the undergrowth with astonishing alacrity. The Giant Armadillo may weigh up to 132 lbs and, like all members of its family, is a digging animal, usually active at night when it emerges from burrows to feed on termites and other insects. The principal enemy of all armadillos is man, who has hunted them for their flesh and for their shells.

Cover illustration by Jeremy Pyke
Printed and bound in Great Britain by Clays Ltd., Bungay, Suffolk.

# CONTENTS

4

# WILL YOU HELP US?

We do all we can to get our facts right in **The South American Handbook.** Each chapter is thoroughly revised each year, but the territory covers a vast area, and our eyes cannot be everywhere. A new highway or airport is built; a hotel, a restaurant, a cabaret dies; another, a good one is born; a building we describe is pulled down, a street renamed. Names and addresses of good hotels and restaurants for "budget-minded" travellers are always very welcome. We would especially like to receive diagrams of walks, national parks and other interesting areas.

*Your information may be far more up-to-date than ours. If your letter reaches us early enough in the year it will be used in the next edition, but write whenever you want to, for all your letters are used sooner or later.*

Thank you very much indeed for your help.

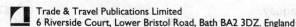

Trade & Travel Publications Limited
6 Riverside Court, Lower Bristol Road, Bath BA2 3DZ. England

# PREFACE

1992 marks the 500th anniversary of Christopher Columbus' arrival in the Caribbean. Much debate now surrounds his voyages and their consequences and in the coming year there will be as much polemic as celebration. However, recalling what happened in 1492 will stimulate interest in both the cultures and environments which flourished before Columbus' landfall, and in the subsequent events which have created today's Latin America.

Those intending to travel to South America will be aware that cholera broke out in Peru in 1991, spreading to neighbouring countries during the year. We have no wish to minimize the seriousness of this outbreak for Latin America, neither in terms of the deplorable conditions which permitted the disease to regain a foothold on the continent after an absence of a hundred years or so, nor in its implications for the future health of the region. However, the World Health Organization has advised that travel should not be restricted because of cholera. The WHO adds the perspective that, over 20 years, ten cases of cholera in the USA were notified out of an estimated 6 million travellers to endemic cholera areas. By paying careful attention to personal hygiene, eating and drinking sensibly and avoiding areas where cholera is prevalent, the risks to the traveller to South America will be no higher than to those visiting any countries, e.g. India, China, Zambia, in which cholera is endemic.

To bring more immediacy to our information on hotels and restaurants, our new policy is to restrict entries to places suggested to us by Handbook readers, or those visited recently by members of our editorial team. In this context, if you have enjoyed an establishment and would like others to share it, please tell us its address as well as its name.

Once again it gives us great pleasure to thank all the travellers who have written to us this year. We are especially grateful to those whose first language is not English yet who take the trouble to write to us in English. New in this edition is a section on Responsible Tourism, by Mark Eckstein (with thanks also to Julie Gray of Traffic International). We recommend visitors to support the efforts being made to conserve flora and fauna and to protect historical and cultural heritages. At the beginning of each chapter (except the Guianas) we include a section on Music and Dance, written by Nigel Gallop; as one correspondent suggested, music is the one living thing that you can safely bring home with you (but please don't pirate it). We are also grateful to John Raspey for his notes on Latin American music. The Motoring section has been thoroughly updated by Binka and R.J.G. Le Breton; the increase in drivers taking their vehicles to South America makes this revision overdue. Other major contributions have been received from Betsy Wagenhauser, Soairse McClory and Petra Schepens of the South American Explorers Club in Quito and Lima, Sean O'Flynn and Conor O'Sullivan of Tatu Tours (Bahia), Noreen O'Flynn (on São Paulo), Hallam and Carole Murray (on Ecuador), Kevin Healey (on Venezuela) and Simon Watson Taylor (on many points south of Paraguay). Our thanks are again due to our subeditors, Sylvia Brooks, Huw Clough (who also rewrote the Peruvian Pre-Conquest History section), John Hale, Charlie Nurse, Peter Pollard, Sarah Cameron (who also edited the recent history and economy sections) and Janet Krengel, who updated the economic tables. Final thanks go to Debbie Wylde, who again has spent many weeks at the keyboard, and Katherine Jarvis for her help with the maps.

*The Editor*

# HOW TO USE THIS HANDBOOK

The South American Handbook is the most complete and up-to-date package of information for independent travellers on the sub-continent of South America (from the Darién Gap to Tierra del Fuego) currently in print. Its text is updated every year for the new edition which is published on 1 September. The text is based on the Editors' travels, contributions from national tourist authorities, notes from correspondents living in the countries we cover, detailed material and maps which Handbook users send us, and the extensive sources of information on Latin America available in London and elsewhere.

**Editorial Logic** Users of the Handbook will find that we employ a logical system of arrangement, which we believe is the most useful for travellers. The capital city is (with one exception, dictated by geography—Chile) the first place covered in detail. The territory is then divided into subsections which are numbered on the country contents and map as well as in the text. In the subsections, towns appear in sequence along a route, which falls within the natural geography of the region. The routes cover the most interesting places to visit and do not necessarily constitute the shortest possible distance from A to B. Details are also given of any interesting excursions or other sights that are off the route. Travellers can therefore plan their own itineraries according to the time available, and their own special interests.

**Cross Referencing and Indexing** There is a complete index of place names at the end of the book.

To make it easier for Readers to find their way around the text, we have a comprehensive system of cross-references. For ease of use, the "see page" entry has been highlighted in heavier type. On the page referred to, you will find the entry again emphasised in some form of heavier type.

**Maps** The South American Handbook maps within the text are undergoing a programme of updating, improvement and expansion. Three types are used:

A. **Country Maps** These appear at the start of each country chapter and show main access routes (not necessarily major roads in all cases), main towns, and divisions of the country as described in the text. These divisions are numbered on the map, in the country's contents list and at the text divisions in the chapter. The numbers are not recommendations as to which parts of the country are most interesting to visit, they are only for easy identification.

B. **Regional Maps** The subsections of the country listed in the country contents has, where appropriate, its own regional map. These give extra information on a more detailed scale and show the main physical features, towns, means of communication and points of interest.

C. **City and Town Maps** Generally these are detailed maps of town centres, showing means of access to bus and railway stations and airports. The main points of interest are indicated by means of a numbered key.

**Introduction and Hints** This first section in the book gives information and hints

| | |
|---|---|
| Roads ———————— | Capital Cities ■SANTIAGO |
| Railways +++++++++++ | Cities/Towns ●córdoba |
| Trails/Paths/Tracks _ _ _ _ | Archaeological sites ▲ |
| Rivers ·RIO ARUÑA | Mountains ⌒ |
| Ferries ·············· | Streets SAN MARTIN |
| Waterfall ⫟⫟ | Parks |
| Barrier Reef ~ ~ ~ | Train station **T** |
| Borders | Bus Station **B** |
| Country Subdivisions ////// | Airport **✈** |
| Metropolitan areas ▨ | Key Numbers **6** |
| Major Highway | |

that apply generally to all the countries we cover on

- travel to and in Latin America
- money
- law enforcement
- security
- responsible tourism
- travelling with children
- camping
- language

- photography
- surface transport
- hitch-hiking
- motoring and motorcycling
- hiking and trekking
- river boats
- cycling

**Health Information** This major section by Dr David Snashall of St Thomas's Hospital Medical School, London, gives details of the health risks common in South America, and the sensible precautions travellers should take to combat them.

**Country Sections** Information is set out country by country in a constant sequence as follows:
- List of contents
- Description of physical geography
  - history
  - economy
  - music and dance
  - people
  - present form of government
- Survey of Cities, Towns and places of interest
  - things to do
  - where to stay
  - services for visitors
  - things worth seeing
  - eating out
- Information for visitors
  - documentation
  - how to get there

| | |
|---|---|
| food | health precautions |
| the best time for visiting | clothing |
| currency regulations | other essential information |

All those readers who have written with valuable updating material are listed with thanks at the end of each chapter.

**Note** The aim of the **Music and Dance** sections has been to give an overview of the traditional and popular music and dances of each country. Considerations of space and the desire to avoid a tedious inventory has meant that by no means every song style, dance or instrument has been noted. As to the performers mentioned, the choice has also been selective, giving preference to those who have achieved local fame over those who, for commercial or political reasons, have based themselves in Europe or North America and are probably already familiar to the overseas visitor. Readers may also notice that space has not been devoted to the forest indians, who are nevertheless present in most of the countries covered and whose music and dancing tends to exist only in its isolated cosmos, rarely relating to, or connecting with, national or regional musical cultures.

**Hotels and Restaurants** In large cities, lists of hotels and restaurants include only those establishments for which positive recommendations have been received. In smaller towns, these lists contain both the favourable recommendations and others. In general, restaurants are grouped by neighbourhood and by type of cuisine.

**Prices** Our hotel price ranges, for double rooms with taxes and service charges but without meals unless stated, are as follows:

| | | |
|---|---|---|
| **L+** —Over US$200 | **L** —US$125-200 | **A+** —US$71-US$125 |
| **A** —US$46-70 | **B** —US$31-45 | **C** —US$21-30 |
| **D** —US$12-20 | **E** —US$7-11 | **F** —US$4-6 |
| **G** —Up to US$3 | | |

Other abbreviations used in the book (apart from p.p. = per person; a/c = air conditioned; rec. = recommended; T = telephone; s/n = "sin número", no street number) should be self-explanatory.

We are grateful to those travellers, listed below, who have sent us important information for the "Introduction and Hints" section which follows: John David Alden (Longmeadow, M.A., U.S.A.), Petra Bell and Hans-Georg Henle (Schwaigern, Germany), Salik B. Biais (Montmorency), Trevor Byrne (Toronto), Stewart Dallos (Fremantle, W. Australia), Hans van Dijk (Hilversum), Louise Dionne (St. John's, Newfoundland), Gerd Dörner (Eberstadt), Ricardo García García (Madrid), Roy Hewson (Chandlers Ford, Hants), Sarah A. Horniman (La Paz), Sabine Imhoff (Germany), Karen Johnson (Coquitlan, B.C.), A. P. Kirk (Middlesbrough), Ulrike Krauss (Edinburgh), Mathias Lassen (Weiberstadt, Germany), Susi Marshall and Tilo Hartig (London SE1), W. Marti (Zurich and Tegucigalpa), Sean Martin (Hailsham, East Sussex), Simon Mays-Smith (Waldron, East Sussex), Robert Millar (Tela), Alison Milner and Keith Doyle (Manchester), Catherine Morris-Adams (West Derby), Deirdre Mortell (Corrigaline, County Cork), Lars Nelson and Gerd Schütze (Iserlohn and Neuss, Germany), Suzanne Olde and Dave Wendt (Amsterdam), Edwin Quiroga (London N8), John Raspey (Argentina), Alison Sanders and Errol Robathan (Tonbridge, Kent), Paul Saunders (Toronto), Martin Theander, William Tracy (Marietta, G.A., U.S.A.), Béatrice Völkle (Gampelen, Switz.), Dr Volker Weinmann (São Paulo, Brazil), Steve Wilson and Debra Holton (San Francisco), Julian Woodhouse (London NW3), Meg Worley (Knoxville, Tennessee) and Peter Grover (Montreal, Canada), and Bart Zwart (Eindhoven, Netherlands).

**WARNING: Whilst every endeavour is made to ensure that the facts printed in this book are correct at the time of going to press, travellers are cautioned to obtain authoritative advice from consulates, airlines, etc. concerning current travel and visa requirements and conditions before embarkation. The publishers cannot accept legal responsibility for errors, however caused, which are printed in this book.**

# INTRODUCTION AND HINTS

## AIR TRAVEL TO AND WITHIN LATIN AMERICA

**Travel to and in South America** All the main airlines plying to each country are given in the "Information for Visitors" sections. Airlines will only allow a certain weight of luggage without a surcharge; this is normally 30 kg. for first class and 20 kg. for business and economy classes, but these limits are often not strictly enforced when it is known that the plane is not going to be full. Passengers seeking a larger baggage allowance can route via USA, but with certain exceptions, the fares are slightly higher using this route. On the other hand, weight limits for internal flights are often lower; best to enquire beforehand.

Chris Parrott, of Journey Latin America, has told us:

1. Generally it is cheaper to fly from London rather than a point in Europe to South American destinations.

2. Most airlines offer discounted fares of one sort or another on scheduled flights. These are not offered by the airlines direct to the public, but through agencies who specialize in this type of fare\*. The very busy seasons are as follows: South America; 7 Dec.–15 Jan. Peru/Ecuador/Colombia/Venezuela 10 July–10 Sept. If you intend travelling during those times, book as far ahead as possible.

3. Other fares fall into three groups, and are all on scheduled services:
  A. Excursion (return) fares with restricted validity e.g. 5-90 days. These are fixed date tickets where the dates of travel cannot be changed after issue of ticket.
  B. Yearly fares: these may be bought on a one-way or return basis, and usually the returns can be issued with the return date left open. You must, however, fix the route (some of the cheapest flexible fares now have 6 months validity).
  C. Student (or Under 26) fares. (Do not assume that student tickets are the cheapest; though they are often very flexible, they are usually more expensive than A or B above). Some airlines are flexible on the age limit, others strict. One way and returns available, or "Open Jaws" (see below). NB Some student tickets carry standby status only, and

\*In London, these include Journey Latin America, 16 Devonshire Road, Chiswick, London W4 2HD (T 081-747 3108); Trailfinders, 48 Earl's Court Road, London W8 6EJ (T 071-938 3366); South American Experience, Garden Studios, 11-15 Betterton St., Covent Garden, London WC2H 9BP (T 071- 379 0344); Steamond Ltd., 23 Eccleston Street, London SW1W 9LX (T 071-730 8646); Passage to South America, 41 North End Road, West Kensington, London W14 8SZ (T071-602 9889). (Ed.)

should be avoided in the busy seasons (see above).

4. For people intending to travel a linear route and return from a different point from that which they entered, there are "Open Jaws" fares, which are available on student, yearly, or excursion fares.

5. Many of these fares require a change of plane at an intermediate point, and a stopover may be permitted, or even obligatory, depending on schedules. Simply because a flight stops at a given airport does not mean you can break your journey there—the airline must have traffic rights to pick up or set down passengers between points A and B before it will be permitted. This is where dealing with a specialized agency (like Journey Latin America!) will really pay dividends. There are dozens of agencies that offer the simple returns to Rio or Lima at roughly the same (discounted) fare. On multi-stop itineraries, the specialized agencies can often save clients hundreds of pounds.

6. Although it's a little more complicated, it's possible to sell tickets in London for travel originating in Latin America at substantially cheaper fares than those available locally. This is useful for the traveller who doesn't know where he will end up, or who plans to travel for more than a year. But a one-way ticket from Latin America is more expensive than a one-way in the other direction, so it's always best to buy a return. (I have heard of travellers buying an unused return seat on French charter flights—they're advertised in the small ads in some of the cheap hotels in Lima—and the charter company doesn't seem to mind who sits in the seat; very hit and miss though).

7. Certain Latin American countries impose local tax on flights originating there. Among these are Uruguay, Peru, Ecuador, Colombia and Mexico. This often applies if you happen to have bought a ticket, say, London—Rio—Santiago—Lima—Los Angeles and then on to Australia. Depending on the way it's issued the passenger could get charged tax on all the sectors from Lima onwards.

8. There are several cheap French charters to Colombia, Ecuador, Peru, Bolivia and the southern countries, but no-one in the UK sells them. Aeroflot flies cheaply from Shannon to Lima and Buenos Aires, as well as Mexico, Havana and Managua.

Travellers starting their journey in continental Europe may try: Uniclam-Voyages, 63 rue Monsieur-le Prince, 75006 Paris for charters. The Swiss company, Balair (owned by Swissair) has regular charter flights to South America (every second week to Recife and Rio). For cheap flights in Switzerland, Globetrotter Travel Service, Renweg, 8001 Zürich, has been recommended.

9. If you buy discounted air tickets *always* check the reservation with the airline concerned to make sure the flight still exists. Also remember the IATA airlines' schedules change in March and October each year, so if you're going to be away a long time it's best to leave return flight coupons open.

In addition, check whether you are entitled to any refund or re-issued ticket if you lose, or have stolen, a discounted air ticket.

10. Note that some South American carriers change departure times of short-haul or domestic flights at short notice and, in some instances, schedules shown in the computers of transatlantic carriers differ from those actually flown by smaller, local carriers. If you book, and reconfirm, both your transatlantic and onward sectors through your transatlantic carrier you may find that your travel plans have been based on out of date information. The surest solution is to reconfirm your outward flight in an office of the onward carrier itself.

Purchasable only in the USA and still one of the cheapest ways of flying around the continent, AeroPerú's "Around South America Airpass" offers a 45-day return ticket to Miami for US$759. It includes Lima and six other South American cities (all flights originating in Lima), plus discounted flights within Peru. Avianca offers several multi-country airpasses out of London costing £767-1275, open for 6 months, can be extended for a year. Aerolíneas Argentinas offer an airpass that covers Argentina, Brazil, Venezuela, Colombia, Ecuador, Peru, Bolivia and Chile, valid 7-30 days for US$1258. These can be bought in London before departure; transatlantic travel must be with Aerolíneas Argentinas. Check with JLA for up-to-date details.

Miami is a good place for connections between South and Central America and Europe; a recommended travel agent is Getaway Travel on Le Jeune Road, Coral Gables. Non-US citizens should note that it is very difficult to check air tickets purchased outside the USA through an agent in Miami and that it is unlikely that you will be allowed by US Immigration to enter the USA without an onward ticket already in your possession.

One suggestion for cheap travel between the USA and South America is to work as a courier for an air cargo company; the time of stay in South America may be limited and you are only allowed carry-on luggage, but the flight is sold to you at reduced cost. Look in Miami Yellow pages under "Air Cargo", or try companies' offices in South America.

Beware buying tickets from the general sales agents in Europe of minor Latin American airlines. They are sometimes incorrectly made out and therefore impossible to transfer or cash in. If you buy internal airline tickets in Latin American countries you may find cash refunds difficult to get if you change your plans: better to change your ticket for a different one. On the other hand you can save money by buying tickets in a country with a black exchange market, for local currency, for flights on its national airline. Overbooking by Latin American airlines is very common (largely due to repeated block bookings by travel agents, which everyone knows will not be used), so always reconfirm the next stage of your flight within 72 hours of your intended departure. And it does no harm to reconfirm yet again in the last 24 hours, just to show them you mean it, and turn up for the flight in good time (at least 2 hours before departure).

We advise people who travel the cheap way in Latin America to pay for all transport as they go along, and not in advance. This advice does not apply to people on a tight schedule: paying as you go along may save money, but it is likely to waste your time somewhat. The one exception to this general principle is in transatlantic flights; here money is saved by booking as far as possible in one operation.

The national airlines of Argentina, Bolivia, Brazil, Chile, Colombia, Peru and Venezuela operate schemes for unlimited travel within those countries at a set price. See the respective country sections.

The Amerbuspass covers the whole of Latin America, from Mexico City to Ushuaia, and entitles the holder to 15-20% discounts on tickets with participating operators; bookable in all Latin American capitals, Europe, Asia, Africa, Oceania, it is valid for 9,999 miles, up to 180 days. Unlimited stopovers, travel with either a confirmed or open itinerary. Contact TISA Internacional, B. Irigoyen 1370, Oficina 25/26, 1138 Buenos Aires, Argentina, T 642-7028, or Av. Larrazabal 493, 1408 Buenos Aires, P.O. Box 40 Suc. 1 (B), 1401 Buenos Aires.

**Travel to the USA** Until July 1988 all foreigners (except Canadians) needed visas to enter the USA. Despite subsequent relaxations of visa requirements for British air travellers with round-trip tickets to the USA, it is advisable to have a visa to allow entry by land, or on airlines from South and Central America which are not "participating carriers" on the Visa Waiver scheme. If you are thinking of travelling via the USA, or of visiting the USA after Latin America, you are strongly advised to get your visa from a US Consulate in your own country, not while travelling.

**Shipping** Voyages on passenger-carrying cargo vessels between South America and Europe, the USA, or elsewhere, are listed here: the Blue Star line sails from Tilbury to Hamburg, Bremen, Antwerp, thence to Montevideo via the Brazilian ports of Salvador, Santos and Rio de Janeiro, returning via Rio Grande, Santos, Salvador and Recife, and Rotterdam. 12 passengers are carried; fare to Montevideo, £1,610, round trip £2,950 p.p. The Grimaldi Line sails from Tilbury to Brazil (Rio, Santos, Paranaguá), via Hamburg, Rotterdam and West Africa, round trip about 8 weeks, £2,140 p.p. (outside cabin). The Polish Ocean Line serves both the East and West coasts of South America from Hamburg, Antwerp and Bremen: ports of call include La Guaira, Puerto Cabello, Maracaibo (Venezuela), Santa Marta, Barranquilla, Cartagena, Buenaventura (Colombia), Guayaquil (Ecuador), Callao (Peru), and Rio de Janeiro, Santos, Salvador, Ilheus (Brazil), Montevideo and Buenos Aires. The cheapest fare is £850, rising to £2,148 for a 7-week round trip to the East Coast; destinations vary.

From the USA, the Chilean Line sails from Long Beach, California to Esmeraldas, Guayaquil (Ecuador), Callao (Peru), and the Chilean ports of

Valparaíso, San Antonio, Antofagasta, Iquique and Arica (round trip US$3,750-4,050); it serves the same ports from the US East Coast (New York, Baltimore, Charleston, Savannah, Miami, Houston, New Orleans and back to Philadelphia) via the Panama Canal (round trip US$4,200-4,500). Ivaran Lines serve East Coast USA, Brazilian ports, Montevideo and Buenos Aires, while Lykes Line sail from Miami/New Orleans to Cartagena, then through the Panama Canal to Guayaquil, Callao and Valparaíso (a round trip costs US$3,300-3,500 p.p.). Egon Oldendorff carries passengers on its USA or Canada/South America routes.

Our thanks are due to John Alton and Adam Humphries of Weider Travel, Charing Cross Shopping Concourse, The Strand, London WC2N 4HZ, T 071-836 6363, Telex 918791, for the above information. Enquiries regarding passages should be made through agencies in your own country, or through Weider Travel. Weider Travel also have the occasional departure to Montevideo on research vessels, about £1,400 one way.

Details on shipping cars are given in **Motoring**, below, and in the relevant country sections.

**Warning** Some countries in Latin America are reluctant to let travellers enter their territory if they do not already have onward or return tickets. (Look under "Information for Visitors" sections for the countries you intend to visit.) The purchase of a Miscellaneous Charges Order (open ticket) from an IATA airline for (say) US$100 will satisfy this requirement in many but not all countries; it is valid for 12 months, can be exchanged for a ticket, or cashed at the airline offices in the country of issue. (The onward ticket requirement does not apply to travellers with their own vehicles.) If you have no onward ticket, a consular letter verifying a statement from your bank at home, giving details of your account with them, might be helpful.

---

## DOCUMENTATION AND SECURITY

---

**Passports** Remember that Latin Americans, especially officials, are very document-minded. You should always carry your passport in a safe place about your person, or if not going far, leave it in the hotel safe. If staying in a country for several weeks, it is worth while registering at your Embassy or Consulate. Then, if your passport is stolen, the process of replacing it is simplified and speeded up. Keeping photocopies of essential documents, and some additional passport-sized photographs, is recommended

Remember that it is your responsibility to ensure that your passport is stamped in and out when you cross frontiers. The absence of entry and exit stamps can cause serious difficulties: seek out the proper migration offices if the stamping process is not carried out as you cross. Also, do not lose your entry card; replacing one causes a lot of trouble, and possibly expense. Citizens of countries which oblige visitors to have a visa (e.g. France) can expect more delays and problems at border crossings.

If travelling from the West Coast of the USA to Latin America and you require visas, most can be obtained in one building in San Francisco, at 870 Market Street (in 1989, represented here were Mexico, Guatemala, Honduras, Costa Rica, Panama, Colombia, Venezuela, Argentina, Chile, Paraguay, Bolivia, Peru, Ecuador—and Brazil only 300 m. away). You are advised to check in advance that the office you want is still there.

**Identity and Membership Cards** Membership cards of British, European and US motoring organizations have been found useful for discounts off hotel charges, car rentals, maps, towing charges, etc. Student cards must carry a photograph if they are to be of any use in Latin America for discounts. (If you describe yourself as a student on your tourist card you may be able to get discounts, even if you haven't a student card.). Business people should carry a good supply of visiting cards, which are essential for good business relations in Latin America. Identity, membership or business cards in Spanish or Portuguese (or a translation) and an official letter of introduction in Spanish or Portuguese are also useful.

**Money** is best carried in US dollar travellers' cheques (denominations of US$50 and US$100 are preferable, though one does need a few of US$20) or cash. Sterling and other currencies are not recommended. Travellers' cheques are convenient but they attract thieves (though refunds can of course be arranged) and you will find that they are more difficult than dollar bills to change in small towns. Though the risk of loss is greater, many travellers take part of their funds in US dollar notes; better rates and lower commissions can usually be obtained for them. Low-value US dollar bills are very useful for shopping: shopkeepers and exchange shops (*casas de cambio*) tend to give better exchange rates than hotels or banks. The better hotels will normally change travellers' cheques for their guests (often at a rather poor rate), but if you're travelling on the cheap it is essential to keep in funds; watch weekends and public holidays carefully and never run out of local currency. Take plenty of local currency, in small denominations, when making trips into the interior. Spread your money around your person: less chance of thieves finding it all. Don't leave cash in your shoe for a long time, it may become too damaged to exchange or use.

Credit cards of the Visa and Master Charge (Eurocard, Access) groups are useful, and American Express (Amex), Carte Blanche and Diners Club can be used, although Amex is most commonly employed for obtaining money. Conceal them very carefully (*not* under the insole of a shoe, however: that may render them unusable!), and make sure you know the correct procedure if they are lost or stolen. We advise using credit cards only for dollar transactions, or in countries where there is no black market exchange rate. Remember that credit card transactions are always at an officially recognized rate of exchange (sometimes, if there are several, the least favourable one); you may find it much cheaper to pay cash and get the parallel rate. For credit card security, insist that imprints are made in your presence and that any imprints incorrectly completed should be torn into tiny pieces. Also destroy the carbon papers after the form is completed (signatures can be copied from them).

We recommend in general the use of American Express or Thomas Cook US$ travellers' cheques, but should point out that less commission is often charged on Citibank or Bank of America cheques, if they are cashed at Latin American branches of those banks. These cheques are always accepted by banks, even though they may not be as well known outside banks as those of American Express or Thomas Cook. It is a good idea to take two kinds of cheque: if large numbers of one kind have recently been forged or stolen, making people suspicious, it is unlikely to have happened simultaneously with the other kind. Several banks charge a high fixed commission for changing travellers' cheques—sometimes as much as US$5-10 a cheque—because they don't really want to be bothered. Exchange houses (*casas de cambio*) are usually much better for this service. Some establishments may ask to see the customer's record of purchase before accepting travellers' cheques.

In those countries where there is a black market, find out how much of their currency you are allowed to take in, and *buy before you enter*, preferably in a big city where banks are unlikely to make a charge on the transaction. (In small places the bank may charge up to 50 cents on a 10-dollar travellers' cheque.) There is always an active (but illegal) black market in local currency in all those countries that have no free exchange; it is, however, not illegal to buy currency outside the country you are about to enter, up to any limit that may be imposed. Changing money on the black market: if possible, do not do so alone. If unsure of the currency of the country you are about to enter, check rates with more than one changer at the border, or ask locals or departing travellers. If worried about being cheated, change US$5, then go back to the same changer with larger denomination notes.

**N.B.** If you are having additional sums of money sent out during a tour of Latin America, try to have it sent to one of the countries where you can easily exchange dollar travellers' cheques for dollars cash; see under the individual countries below for the current situation. In many countries, one can get at least US$500 in Amex travellers' cheques on the American Express card (US$1,000 on the gold card): quite the easiest way of adding to one's funds. One can also obtain cash at American Express via personal cheques, e.g. Eurocheque. Remember that a transfer of funds, even by telex, can take several days, and charges can be high; a recommended method is, before leaving, to find out which local bank is correspondent to your bank at home, then when you need funds, telex your own bank and ask them to telex the money to the local bank (confirming by air mail). It is possible to obtain money within hours by this method.

Whenever you leave a country, sell any local currency before leaving, because the further away you get, the less the value of a country's money.

Americans (we are told) should know that if they run out of funds they can expect no help from the US Embassy or Consul other than a referral to some welfare organization. In this regard, find out before you go precisely what services and assistance your embassy or consulate can provide if you find yourself in difficulties.

**Law Enforcement** Whereas in Europe and North America we are accustomed to law enforcement on a systematic basis, in general, enforcement in Latin America is achieved by periodic campaigns. The most typical is a round-up of criminals in the cities just before Christmas. In December, therefore, you may well be asked for identification at any time, and if you cannot produce it, you will be jailed. At first sight, on arrival, it may seem that you can flout the law with impunity, because everybody else is obviously doing so. If a visitor is jailed his friends should take him food every day. This is especially important for people on a diet, such as diabetics. It must also be borne in mind that in the event of a vehicle accident in which anyone is injured, all drivers involved are automatically detained until blame has been established, and this does not usually take less than two weeks.

Never offer a bribe unless you are fully conversant with the customs of the country. (In Chile, for instance, it would land you in serious trouble if you tried to bribe a *carabinero*.) Wait until the official makes the suggestion, or offer money in some form which is apparently not bribery, e.g. "In our country we have a system of on-the-spot fines (*multas de inmediato*). Is there a similar system here?" Do not assume that an official who accepts a bribe is prepared to do anything else that is illegal. You bribe him to persuade him to do his job, or to persuade him not to do it, or to do it more quickly, or more slowly. You do not bribe him to do something which is against the law. The mere suggestion would make him very upset.

**Security** Try and look as little like a tourist as possible, especially in poor areas of cities. Most crime is opportunistic so if you are aware of the dangers, act confidently and use your common sense you will lessen many of the risks. The following tips, all endorsed by travellers, are meant to forewarn, but not alarm, you. Keep all documents secure; hide your main cash supply in different places or under your clothes (extra pockets sewn inside shirts and trousers, pockets closed with a zip or safety pin, moneybelts—best worn below the waist rather than at it or around the neck, neck or leg pouches, a thin chain for attaching a purse to your bag or under your clothes and elasticated support bandages for keeping money and cheques above the elbow or below the knee have been repeatedly recommended—the last by John Hatt in *The Tropical Traveller*). Keep cameras in bags (preferably with a chain or wire in the strap to defeat the slasher) or briefcases; take spare spectacles (eyeglasses); don't wear wrist-watches (unless they're digital—too cheap and plentiful to attract thieves nowadays) or jewellery.

If you wear a shoulder-bag in a market, carry it in front of you. Backpacks are vulnerable to slashers: a good idea is to cover with a sack with maybe a layer of wire netting between. Use a pack which is lockable at its base.

Ignore mustard smearers and paint or shampoo sprayers, and strangers' remarks like "what's that on your shoulder?" or "have you seen that dirt on your shoe?". Furthermore, don't bend over to pick up money or other items in the street. These are all ruses intended to distract your attention and make you easy for an accomplice to steal from. If someone follows you when you're in the street, let him catch up with you and "give him the eye". Take local advice about being out at night; if walking after dark, walk in the road, not on the pavement/sidewalk.

Be wary of "plainclothes policemen"; insist on seeing identification and on going to the police station by main roads. Do not hand over your identification (or money—which he should not need to see anyway) until you are at the station. Be even more suspicious if he seeks confirmation of his status from a passer-by. If someone tries to bribe you, insist on a receipt. If attacked, remember your assailants may well be armed, and try not to resist.

It is best, if you can trust your hotel, to leave any valuables you don't need in safe-deposit there, when sightseeing locally. If you don't trust the hotel, lock everything in your pack and secure that in your room (some people take eyelet-screws for padlocking cupboards or drawers). If you lose valuables, always report to the police and note details of the report—for insurance purposes.

When you have all your luggage with you at a bus or railway station, be especially careful: don't get into arguments—or even conversations—with any locals if you can help it, and lock all the items together with a chain or cable if you are waiting for some time. Take a taxi between airport/bus station/railway station and hotel, if you can possibly afford it. Keep you bags with you in the taxi and pay only when you and your luggage are safely out of the vehicle. Avoid night buses; never arrive at night; and watch your belongings whether they are stowed

inside or outside the cabin (roof top luggage racks create extra problems, which are sometimes unavoidable—make sure your bag is waterproof). Finally, never accept food, drink, sweets or cigarettes from unknown fellow-travellers on buses or trains. They may be drugged, and you would wake up hours later without your belongings. In this connection, never accept a bar drink from an opened bottle (unless you can see that that bottle is in general use): always have it uncapped in front of you.

A courteous, friendly manner of speaking, including to beggars and market vendors, may avoid your being "set up" for robbery or assault. For specific local problems, see under the individual countries in the text.

## ACCOMMODATION

**Hotels** For under US$10, a cheap but not bad hotel room can be found in most countries, although in some of the Andean countries you may not have to pay that much. For the indigent, it is a good idea to ask for a boarding house—*casa de huéspedes, hospedaje, pensión, casa familial* or *residencial*, according to country; they are normally to be found in abundance near bus and railway stations and markets. Good value hotels can also be found near truckers' stops/service stations; they are usually secure. There are often great seasonal variations in hotel prices in resorts. Remember, cheaper hotels don't always supply soap, towels and toilet paper; in colder (higher) regions they may not supply enough blankets, so take your own or a sleeping bag. Useful tips: book even cheap hotels in advance by registered mail, if you receive no reply don't worry; ask the car rental agency employees at the airport for advice when you arrive—as long as they are not busy; always ask for the best room.

**Warning** The electric showers used in innumerable cheap hotels are extremely dangerous. If you can't avoid using them, check the wiring for obvious flaws and try not to touch the rose while it is producing hot water. One traveller suggests wearing rubber flip-flops and gloves as insulation.

**Youth Hostels** Organizations affiliated to the Youth Hostels movement exist in Argentina, Brazil, Colombia, Chile, Peru and Uruguay. There is an associate organization in Ecuador. Further information in the country sections and from the IYHA.

**Meals** In all countries except Brazil and Chile (where cold meats, cheese, eggs, fruit etc. generally figure) breakfast usually means coffee or tea with rolls and butter, and anything more is charged extra. In Colombia and Ecuador breakfast usually means eggs, a roll, fruit juice and a mug of milk with coffee; say "breakfast without eggs" if you do not want that much. There is a paragraph on each nation's food under "Information for Visitors". Vegetarians should be able to list all the foods they cannot eat; saying "Soy vegetariano/a" (I'm a vegetarian) or "no como carne" (I don't eat meat) is often not enough.

**Camping** There is a growing network of organized campsites, to which reference is made in the text immediately below hotel lists, under each town. If there is no organized site in town, a football pitch or gravel pit might serve. Géraldine des Cressonnières, of Linkebeek, Belgium, gives the following rules for "wild" camping: (1) arrive in daylight; (2) ask permission to camp from the parish priest, or the fire chief, or the police, or a farmer regarding his own property; (3) never ask a group of people— especially young people; (4) never camp on a beach (because of sandflies and thieves). If you can't get information from anyone, camp in a spot where you can't be seen from the nearest inhabited place, or road. In Argentina and Brazil, it is common to camp at gas/petrol stations. As Béatrice Völkle of Gampelen, Switzerland, adds, camping wild may be preferable to those organized sites which are treated as discotheques, with only the afternoon reserved for sleeping.

Gas cylinders and bottles are usually exchangeable, but if not can be recharged; specify whether you use butane or propane. (Liquid fuels are readily available.) The Camping Clube do Brasil gives 50% discounts to holders of international campers' cards.

**Toilets** Many of the cheapest hotels in the poorer areas, also restaurants and bars, have inadequate water supplies. This may mean that used toilet paper should not be flushed down the pan, but placed in the receptacle provided. This is not very sanitary, of course, but a blocked pan or drain is infinitely more of a health risk. It is quite common for people to stand on the toilet seat (facing the wall—easier to balance), as they do in Asia. If you are concerned about the hygiene of the facility, put paper on the seat.

**Cockroaches** These are ubiquitous and unpleasant, but not dangerous. Take some insecticide powder if staying in cheap hotels; Baygon (Bayer) has been recommended. Stuff toilet paper in any holes in walls that you may suspect of being parts of cockroach runs.

## ETIQUETTE AND LANGUAGE

**Travellers' Appearance** There is a natural prejudice in all countries against travellers who ignore personal hygiene and have a generally dirty and unkempt appearance. Most Latin Americans, if they can afford it, devote great care to their clothes and appearance; it is appreciated if visitors do likewise. The general prejudice previously reported against backpacks has virtually disappeared, unless carried by those whom officials identify as "hippies". One tip we have received; young people of informal dress and life-style may find it advantageous to procure a letter from someone in an official position testifying to their good character, on official-looking notepaper. John Oliver, of Durban, tells us that a photograph of a pretty blonde young woman inside one's passport can have a similar salutary effect on Latin American officials!

Some countries have laws or prejudices against the wearing by civilians of army-surplus clothing. In many places there is also a prejudice against shorts, which are only appropriate on the beach, or for jogging, or for sports and games. A medium weight shawl with some wool content is recommended for women: it can double as pillow, light blanket, bathrobe or sunscreen as required.

**Drugs** Users of drugs, even of soft ones, without medical prescription should be particularly careful, as some countries impose heavy penalties— up to ten years' imprisonment—for even the simple possession of such substances. In this connection, the planting of drugs on travellers—by traffickers or the police—is not unknown. If offered drugs on the street, make no response at all and keep walking. Note that people who roll their own cigarettes are often suspected of carrying drugs and subjected to intensive searches. Advisable to stick to commercial brands of cigarettes—but better still not to smoke at all.

**Courtesy** Remember that politeness—even a little ceremoniousness—is much appreciated. In this connection professional or business cards are useful (and have even been known to secure for their owners discount prices in hotels). Men should always remove any headgear and say "con permiso" ("com licença" in Brazil) when entering offices, and be prepared to shake hands (this is much commoner in Latin America than in Europe or North America); always say "Buenos días" (until midday) or "Buenas tardes" ("Bom dia" or "Boa tarde" in Brazil) and wait for a reply before proceeding further; in a word, don't rush them! Always remember that the traveller from abroad has enjoyed greater advantages in life than most Latin American minor officials, and should be friendly and courteous in consequence. Never be impatient; do not criticize situations in public: the officials may know more English than you think and they can certainly interpret gestures and facial expressions. Be judicious about discussing politics with strangers (especially in Guatemala, Honduras and El Salvador). Politeness can be a liability, however, in some situations; most Latin Americans are disorderly queuers.

Moira Chubb, from New Zealand, suggests that if you are a guest and are offered food that arouses your suspicions, the only courteous way out is to feign an allergy or a stomach ailment.

**Language** Without some knowledge of Spanish you can become very frustrated and feel helpless in many situations. English, or any other language, is absolutely useless off the beaten track. Some initial study, to get you up to a basic Spanish vocabulary of 500 words or so, and a pocket dictionary and phrase-book, are most strongly recommended: your pleasure will be doubled if you can talk to the locals. Not all the locals speak Spanish, of course; apart from Brazil's Portuguese, you will find that some Indians in the more remote highland parts of Bolivia, Guatemala and Peru, and lowland Indians in Amazonia, speak only their indigenous languages, though there will usually be at least one person in each village who can speak Spanish (or Portuguese).

The basic Spanish of Hispanic America is that of south-western Spain, with soft "c's" and "z's" pronounced as "s", and not as "th" as in the other parts of Spain. Castilian Spanish is readily understood, but is not appreciated when spoken by non-Spaniards; try and learn the basic Latin American pronunciation. There are several regional variations in pronunciation, particularly in the River Plate countries, which are noted in the Argentine section "Information for Visitors". Differences in vocabulary also exist, both between peninsular Spanish and Latin American Spanish, and between the usages of the different countries.

If you are going to Brazil, you should learn some Portuguese. Spanish is not adequate: you may be understood but you will probably not be able to understand the answers.

---

### INTERNAL SURFACE TRANSPORT

---

Before you start, remember that distances are great and journeys by land are long: plan accordingly and do not try to do too much in the time available.

**Surface Transport** The continent has a growing road system for motor traffic, with frequent bus services. The buses are often comfortable; Brazil, Chile and Venezuela are the best; Colombia is quite good, Ecuador not far behind; the other Andean countries are a long way behind, because of difficulties of terrain. In mountainous country, however, do not expect buses to get to their destination, after long journeys, anywhere near on time. Do not turn up for a bus at the last minute; if it is full it may depart early. When the journey takes more than 3 or 4 hours, meal stops at country inns or bars, good and bad, are the rule. Usually, no announcement is made on the duration of a stop: follow the driver, if he eats, eat. See what the locals are eating—and buy likewise, or make sure you're stocked up well on food and drink at the start. For drinks, stick to bottled water or soft drinks or coffee (black). The food sold by vendors at bus stops may be all right: watch if locals are buying, though unpeeled fruit is of course reliable. (See above on **Security** in buses.)

In most countries trains are slower than buses. They do tend, however, to provide finer scenery, and you can normally see much more wildlife than from the road—it is less disturbed by one or two trains a day than by the more frequent road traffic. Moreover, so many buses now show video films that you can't see the countryside because the curtains are drawn. Complaining to the conductor that you cannot see the beautiful landscape may persuade him to give you his seat at the front.

**Hitch-hiking**  This custom is increasing in Latin America, and travellers have reported considerable success in virtually all countries. Neatness of appearance certainly helps. Argentina, Brazil, Chile, Ecuador and Venezuela are reported as good; Peru and Bolivia less so ("paying trucks" recommended here). If trying to hitchhike away from main roads and in sparsely-populated areas, however, allow plenty of time.

Joanna Codrington writes: Hitch-hiking in Latin America is reasonably safe and straightforward for males and couples, provided one speaks some Spanish/Portuguese. In Peru and Bolivia there is little private transport and trucks charge about 2/3 the equivalent fare. But elsewhere cars and trucks will carry you free of charge, and will generally treat you as their guests. It is a most enjoyable mode of transport—a good way to meet the local people, to improve one's languages and to learn about the country. Truck drivers in particular are often well versed in things of interest one is passing, e.g. crops and industries.

Here are a few general hints: in remoter parts, make enquiries first about the volume of traffic on the road. On long journeys, set out at crack of dawn, which is when trucks usually leave. They tend to go longer distances than cars.

**Motoring**  Binka and R.J.G. le Breton write: *Preparing the Car* What kind of motoring you do will depend on what kind of car you set out with. Four-wheel drive is not necessary, but it does give you greater flexibility in mountain and jungle territory, although you may not get far in Amazonas, where roads are frequently impassable. In Patagonia, main roads are gravel rather than paved: perfectly passable without four-wheel drive, just rough and dusty. Consider fitting wire guards for headlamps, and for windscreens too, if you don't mind peering out through a grill like a caged chimpanzee. Wherever you travel you should expect from time to time to find roads that are badly maintained, damaged or closed during the wet season, and delays because of floods, landslides and huge potholes. Don't plan your schedules too tightly.

Diesel cars are much cheaper to run than petrol ones, and the fuel is easily available, except in Venezuela, where you will have to look hard. Most towns can supply a mechanic of sorts, and probably parts for Bosch fuel injection equipment. Watch the mechanics like a hawk, since there's always a brisk market in spares, and some of yours may be highly desirable. That apart, they enjoy a challenge, and can fix most things, eventually.

For prolonged motoring over 3000 metres, you may need to fit high altitude jets on your carburettors. Some fuel injection engines need adjusting too, and ignition settings may have to be changed: check the manufacturer's recommendations. The electronic ignition and fuel metering systems on modern emission controlled cars are allergic to humidity, heat and dust, and cannot be repaired by bush mechanics. Standard European and Japanese cars run on fuel with a higher octane rating than is commonly available in North, South or Central America, and in Brazil petrol (gasolina) is in fact gasohol, with a 12% admixture of alcohol. A high compression fuel injection engine will not like this. Unleaded fuel is not available. The most easily maintained petrol engined cars, then, are the types manufactured in Latin American countries, i.e pre-emission control models such as the VW Kombi with carburettors and conventional (non-electronic) ignition, or the old type Toyota Landcruisers common in Central America. Older model American cars, especially Ford or GM pickups, are easily maintained, but high fuel consumption offsets this advantage.

Preparing the car for the journey is largely a matter of common sense: obviously any part that is not in first class condition should be replaced. It's well worth installing extra heavy-duty shock-absorbers (such as Spax or Koni) before starting out, because a long trip on rough roads in a heavily laden car will give heavy wear. Fit tubes on "tubeless" tyres, since air plugs for tubeless tyres are hard to find, and if you bend the rim on a pothole, the tyre will not hold air. Take spare tubes, and an extra spare tyre. You really don't need spare plugs, fan-belts, radiator hoses or even headlamp bulbs: local equivalents can easily be found. However, if your car has sophisticated electrics, spare "black boxes" for the ignition and fuel injection are advisable, plus a spare voltage regulator or the appropriate diodes for the alternator, and elements for the fuel, air and oil filters if these are not a common type. Dirty fuel is a frequent problem, so be prepared to change filters more often than you would at home: in a diesel car you will need to check the sediment bowl often, too. An extra in-line fuel filter is a good idea if feasible, and for travel on dusty roads an oil bath air filter is best for a diesel car. It is wise to carry a spade, jumper cables, tow rope and an air pump. A 12 volt neon light for camping and repairs will be invaluable. Spare fuel containers should be steel and not plastic, and a siphon pipe is essential for those places where fuel is sold out of the drum. Take a 10 litre water container for self and vehicle. Note that in some areas gas stations are few and far between. Fill up when you see one: the next one may be out of fuel. Some countries have periodic fuel conservation strategies which means you can't get any after a certain hour in the evening, and often not at weekends either.

Apart from the mechanical aspects, spare no ingenuity in making your car secure. Your model should be the Brink's armoured van: anything less secure can be broken into by the determined and skilled thief. Use heavy chain and padlocks to chain doors shut, fit security catches on windows, remove interior window winders (so that a hand reaching in from a forced vent cannot open the window). All these will help, but none is foolproof. Anything on the outside—wing mirrors, spot lamps, motifs etc.—is likely to be stolen too. So are wheels if not secured by locking nuts. Try never to leave the car unattended except in a locked garage or guarded parking space. Street children will generally protect your car fiercely in exchange for a tip.

*Documents* A *carnet de passage* is no longer necessary in any country except Ecuador. Land entry procedures for all countries—with the exception of Colombia—are simple, though time-consuming, as the car has to be checked by customs, police and agriculture officials. All you need is the registration document in the name of the driver, or, in the case of a car registered in someone else's name, a notarized letter of authorization. Most countries give a limited period of stay, but allow an extension if requested in advance. Of course, do be very careful to keep **all** the papers you are given when you enter, to produce when you leave. Bringing a car in by sea or air is much more complicated and expensive: generally you will have to hire an agent to clear it through customs, expensive and slow. Insurance for the vehicle against accident, damage or theft is best arranged in the country of origin, but it is getting increasingly difficult to find agencies who offer this service—American International Underwriters no longer does. In Latin American countries it is very expensive to insure against accident and theft, especially as you should take into account the value of the car increased by duties calculated in real (i.e. non devaluing) terms. If the car is stolen or written off you will be required to pay very high import duty on its value. A few countries insist on compulsory third party insurance, to be bought at the border: in other countries it's technically required, but not checked up on (Venezuela seems to be the only country where it is easy to obtain—Ed.). Get the legally required minimum cover, not expensive, as soon as you can, because if you should be involved in an accident and are uninsured, your car could be confiscated. If anyone is hurt, pick them up and go straight to the nearest police station or hospital if you are able to do so. Otherwise you may find yourself facing a hostile crowd, even if you are not to blame.

*Journey's End* When you finally reach your destination, what happens to the car? Shipping it back is one alternative. From Brazil, Grimaldi line to Genoa is the cheapest (about US$1,000): there are also frequent sailings from Montevideo and Buenos Aires to most other destinations. The other alternative is to sell the car. Until now, this has been virtually impossible except in Paraguay, but the economic liberalization in Argentina, Chile and Brazil makes it legal—if not simple—to import cars into those countries. Probably safer not to count on it though, unless you have the sort of car in great demand, like a Mercedes saloon. You can sell anything in Paraguay if you have the time. Legalizing the permanent import of a temporarily imported car costs about 30% of its street value. If you leave it to the buyer to "take care of" obtaining the correct documentation, you should not expect to receive a very favourable price. Dealers are adept at taking advantage of the fact that they can wait, and you cannot, so be prepared for "on—off—on again" dealing.

*Car Hire* The main international car hire companies operate in all countries, but they do tend to be very expensive, reflecting the high costs and accident rates. Hotels and tourist agencies will tell you where to find cheaper rates, but you will need to check that you have such basics as spare wheel, toolkit and functioning lights etc. You'll probably have more fun if you drive yourself, although it's always possible to hire a car with driver—usually somebody's uncle's old banger which will almost certainly run out of fuel /break down after the first few kilometres. If you plan to do a lot of driving and will have time at the end to dispose of it, investigate the possibility of buying a second hand car locally: since hiring is so expensive it may well work out cheaper and will probably do you just as well.

**Additional notes on motoring** Although a *carnet de passages* is not required (except for Ecuador—see **Documents** in **Information for Visitors**, Ecuador), many motorists have found it useful and advise getting one (if you can find, or afford, it) before arriving in South America.

While a normal car will reach most places of interest, high ground clearance is useful for badly surfaced or unsurfaced roads and for fording rivers: 4-wheel drive is recommended for mountain terrain and unmade roads off the beaten track.

If you want to buy a second-hand car, check for corrosion if making the deal in a coastal city and always check, if not change, the full set of tyres.

**Shipping a vehicle** If travelling from Europe with a car, do not sail to Panama if you are going south. You will still have the Darién Gap to negotiate. Shipping from Panama to mainland South America is expensive, and requires some shopping around to find the cheapest way. From Balboa, Panama, to Buenaventura, Colombia, the cheapest is probably via Peruvian State shipping lines (about US$650 for a VW Kombi sized car). The *Isla Bartolomeu* ships direct to Guayaquil in Ecuador at about the same price. Streamline sails to Cartagena in Colombia for about US$900, but you have to get a special exemption in order to be allowed to be carried to Colombia in a non-Colombian vessel, which takes time to obtain. To Venezuela, either Puerto Cabello or La Guaira, the cheapest is Vencaribe lines (about US$1,000) which go every two weeks (also sailing from Puerto Limón in Costa Rica). To Curaçao, where you can get the ferry to Venezuela, costs about US$2,000. Anything left inside the car while it is being shipped will be stolen. If shipping a car further south, Montevideo has much less bureaucracy and paperwork than any Argentine or Brazilian port. As long as your vehicle is not over 2.28 m. high, it can go in a container, but permission must be obtained for any belongings to remain in the car, and separate insurance for effects purchased. If the car is going ro-ro (drive on), it should be empty of all belongings, unless they are thoroughly secured.

A book containing much practical information on South American motoring conditions and requirements, as well as being a travelogue, is *Driving to Heaven*, by Derek Stansfield (available from Remous Ltd, Wyvern Building, North Street, Milbourne Port, Sherbourne, Dorset, DT9 5EP, UK, or from the author, Ropley, Broad Oak, Sturminster Newton, Dorset DT10 2HG, £8.95 plus postage and packing).

**Motorcycling**  Charles and Lucia Newall write: Motorcycling in South America is a great adventure, exhausting sometimes but not beyond the capacity of any experienced rider.

*Machine*: The bike should be tough and simple and capable of handling dirt roads if you plan on going into the Andes. If riding solo a large 4-stroke trail bike, e.g. Honda or Yamaha 500, would be ideal; if carrying a passenger a larger machine might be needed. We used an 800cc BMW road bike which handled a variety of conditions with ease.

*Preparations*: Fit a handlebar windscreen rather than a large touring fairing, which will hamper low-speed handling and complicate shipping from Panama. Standard air filters should be replaced by cleanable types e.g. K and N. You may need to carry a set of smaller carburettor jets to adapt the engine for high altitudes; chech with the manufacturer.

The standard rear suspension on motorcycles may give trouble if you are going to travel on unmade roads; again, check with the manufacturer. If so, fit high-quality replacement units (Konis) with springs matched for the weight carried.

The luggage panniers and rack should be very robust; distribute the weight of luggage around the bike rather than just piling it on the back. A fuel range of about 250 (400 km.) miles is useful and also the ability to run on 80-octane fuel.

*Spares*: A modern well-maintained machine shouldn't need any major repairs on a 25,000-mile trip. Take the usual consumables with you, such as plugs, points, filters, bulbs, chains, tubes and a set of cables; add to this any other parts which might be weak points on your machine. If possible, take spare tyres. Make arrangements to have parts sent out from home if you need anything unusual; a parts book and a good manual are invaluable. Find out how to service your machine and carry the correct tools. (Local mechanics are very good at making do without the proper parts.)

*Clothes*: Your clothing should keep you comfortable from 20° to 85°F and include a tough waterproof outer layer complete with overboots and overgloves.

*Security*: Security is not a problem; use a strong chain and lock. Hotel owners are very helpful and good about letting you bring your machine inside, but don't leave a loaded machine unattended. In general much safer than taking night buses or trains; cheaper too.

*Documents*: Passports, international driving licences, Carnet de Passages (for Ecuador, see **Motoring** above), motoring association membership card (for discounts etc.), registration certificate, Hoja de Ruta required in Bolivia. A letter from your Embassy, saying that you are a bona-fide tourist and have no intention of selling your bike, is very useful.

*Shipping*: It is much easier to fly a motorcycle from Panama than a car, but this can only be done cargo; details in **Colombia** chapter. (In mid-1990, Varig charged US$1,100 for shipping 2 Honda XL500s, and 2 people, San Francisco- Costa Rica- Ecuador.) For the adventurous, there is the possibility of taking small boats down to Turbo, but at the high risk of losing the machine. *Warnings*: Do not try to ride the Andean roads in the rainy season as conditions are very dangerous, with muddy roads and deep river fords. Do not attempt to take a bike through the Darién Gap.

**NB**  It is not advisable to ride either a motorcycle or a bicycle in Peru at present (1991).

**Cycling**  Hallam Murray writes:  Over the past decade, bicycle technology has improved in leaps and bounds. With the advent of Kevlar tyres and puncture-resistant inner tubes it is now theoretically possible to cycle from Alaska to Tierra del Fuego without so much as a single puncture. For the traveller with a zest for adventure and a limited budget there is unlikely to be a finer way to explore. At first glance a bicycle may not appear to be the most obvious vehicle for a major journey, but given ample time and reasonable energy it most certainly is the best. It can be ridden, carried by almost every form of transport from an aeroplane to a canoe, and can even be lifted across one's shoulders over short distances. On my most recent journey from Lake Titicaca to Tierra del Fuego—largely on unpaved roads, many of which would have defeated even the most robust car or truck—I was often envied by travellers using more orthodox transport, for I was able to travel at my own pace, to explore more remote regions and to meet people who are not normally in contact with tourists.

*Choosing a Bicycle*: The choice of bicycle depends on the type and length of expedition being undertaken and on the terrain and road surfaces likely to be encountered. Unless you are planning a journey almost exclusively on paved roads—when a high quality touring bike such as a Dawes Super Galaxy would probably suffice—I would strongly recommend a mountain bike. The good quality ones (and the cast iron rule is **never** to skimp on quality) are incredibly tough and rugged, with low gear ratios for difficult terrain, wide tyres with plenty of tread for good road-holding, cantilever brakes, and a low centre of gravity for improved stability. Expect to pay upwards of US$800 for such a machine. Although touring bikes, and to a lesser extent mountain bikes, and spares are available in the larger Latin American cities, remember that in the developing world most indigenous manufactured goods are shoddy and rarely last. In some countries, such as Mexico, Chile and Uruguay, imported components can be found but they tend to be extremely expensive. Buy everything you possibly can before you leave home.

*Bicycle Equipment*: A small but comprehensive tool kit (to include chain rivet and crank removers, a spoke key and possibly a block remover), a spare tyre and inner tubes, a puncture repair kit with plenty of extra patches and glue, a set of brake blocks, brake and gear cables and all types of nuts and bolts, at least 12 spokes (best taped to the chain stay), a light oil for the chain, tube of waterproof grease, a pump secured by a pump lock, a Blackburn parking block (my choice for the most invaluable accessory and they are cheap and virtually weightless), a cyclometer, a loud bell, and a secure lock and chain. *Richard's Bicycle Book* makes useful reading for even the most mechanically minded.

*Luggage and equipment*: Strong and waterproof front and back panniers are a must.

A top bag cum rucksack (e.g. Carradice) makes a good addition for use on and off the bike. I used a Cannondale front bag for my maps, camera, compass, altimeter, notebook and small tape-recorder. My total luggage weighed 27 kg.—on the high side, but I never felt seriously overweight. "Gaffa" tape is excellent for protecting vulnerable parts of panniers and for carrying out all manner of repairs. My most vital equipment included a light and waterproof tent, a 3 season sleeping bag, an Optimus petrol stove (the best I have ever used for it is light and efficient and petrol can be found almost everywhere), a plastic survival bag for storing luggage at night when camping, 4 elastic straps, 4 one-litre water bottles, Swiss Army knife, torch, comprehensive medical kit, money belts, a hat to protect against hours of ferocious tropical sun and small presents such as postcards of home, balloons and plastic badges. A rubber mouse can do wonders for making contact with children in isolated villages.

All equipment and clothes should be packed in plastic bags to give extra protection against dust and rain. Always take the minimum clothing. It's better to buy extra items en route when you find you need them. Naturally the choice will depend on whether you are planning a journey through tropical lowlands, deserts, high mountains or a combination, and whether rain is to be expected. Generally it is best to carry several layers of thin light clothes than fewer heavy, bulky ones. Always keep one set of dry clothes, including long trousers, to put on at the end of the day. I would not have parted with my incredibly light, strong, waterproof and wind resistant goretex jacket and overtrousers. I could have sold them 100 times over and in Bolivia was even offered a young mule in exchange! I took two pairs of training shoes and found these to be ideal for both cycling and walking.

*Useful Tips*: Wind, not hills is the enemy of the cyclist. Try to make the best use of the times of day where there is little; mornings tend to be best but there is no steadfast rule. In parts of Patagonia there can be gusting winds of 80 kph around the clock at some times of year, whereas in other areas there can be none. Take care to avoid dehydration, by drinking regularly. In hot, dry areas with limited supplies of water, be sure to carry an ample supply. For food I carried the staples (sugar, salt, dried milk, tea, coffee, porridge oats, raisins, dried soups, etc.) and supplemented these with whatever local foods I could find in the markets. Give your bicycle a thorough daily check for loose nuts or bolts or bearings. See that all parts run smoothly. A good chain should last 2,000 miles, 3,200 km. or more but be sure to keep it as clean as possible—an old toothbrush is good for this—and to oil it lightly from time to time. Always camp out of sight of a road. Remember that thieves are attracted to towns and cities, so when sight-seeing, try to leave your bicycle with someone such as a café owner or a priest. Country people tend to be more honest and are usually friendly and very inquisitive. However, don't take unnecessary risks; always see that your bicycle is secure. In more remote regions dogs can be vicious; carry a stick or some small stones to frighten them off. Traffic on main roads can be a nightmare; it is usually far more rewarding to keep to the smaller roads or to paths if they exist. Most towns have a bicycle shop of some description, but it is best to do your own repairs and adjustments whenever possible. In an emergency it is amazing how one can improvise with wire, string, dental floss, nuts and bolts, odd pieces of tin or "Gaffa" tape!

The Expedition Advisory Centre, administered by the Royal Geographical Society, 1, Kensington Gore, London SW7 2AR has published a useful monograph entitled *Bicycle Expeditions*, by Paul Vickers. Published in March 1990, it is available direct from the Centre, price £6.50 (postage extra if outside the UK).

**River Transport** Geoffrey Dempsey has sent us the following note, with particular reference to Amazonia:

Because expanding air services have captured the lucrative end of the passenger market, passenger services on the rivers are in decline. Worst hit have been the upper reaches; rivers like the Ucayali in Peru, but the trend is apparent throughout the region. The situation has been aggravated for the casual traveller by a new generation of purpose-built tugs (all engine-room and bridge) that can handle up to a dozen freight barges but have no passenger accommodation. In Peru passenger boats must now supplement incomes by carrying cargo, and this lengthens their journey cycle. In the face of long delays, travellers might consider shorter "legs" involving more frequent changes of boat; though the more local the service, the slower and more uncomfortable it will be.

Hammocks, mosquito nets (not always good quality), plastic containers for water storage, kettles and cooking utensils can be purchased in any sizeable riverside town, as well as tinned food such as sardines, meat loaf, frankfurters, ham and fruit. Fresh bread, cake, eggs, fruit—papayas, bananas, pineapples, oranges etc.—are available in most villages. Cabin bunks are provided with thin mattresses but these are often foul. Replacements can be bought locally but rolls of plastic foam that can be cut to size are also available and much cheaper. Eye-screws for securing washing lines and mosquito nets are useful, and tall passengers who are not taking a hammock and who may find insufficient headroom on some boats should consider a camp-chair. The writer yearned for a cushion.

H.M. Wams (Amsterdam) endorses the recommendation of taking hammock, mosquito net and food, adding that in Venezuelan Amazonas hitching rides on boats is possible if you camp at the harbour or police post where all boats must register. Take any boat going in your direction as long as it reaches the next police post.

**Travelling with Children** We are grateful to Tim and Arlene Frost, of New Zealand, for the following notes and to Linda and Lawrence Foster, of Wembley for additional suggestions:

People contemplating overland travel in South America with children should remember that a lot of time can be spent waiting for buses, trains, and especially for aeroplanes. On bus journeys, if the children are good at amusing themselves, or can readily sleep while travelling, the problems can be considerably lessened. If your child is of an early reading age, take reading material with you as it is difficult, and expensive to find. Travel on trains, while not as fast or at times as comfortable as buses, allows more scope for moving about. Some trains provide tables between seats, so that games can be played. Beware of doors left open for ventilation especially if air-conditioning is not working.

Food can be a problem if the children are not adaptable. It is easier to take biscuits, drinks, bread etc. with you on longer trips than to rely on meal stops where the food may not be to taste. A small immersion heater and jug for making hot drinks is invaluable, but remember that electric current varies. Try and get a dual-voltage one (110v and 220v).

*Fares*: On all long-distance buses you pay for each seat, and there are no half-fares if the children occupy a seat each. For shorter trips it is cheaper, if less comfortable, to seat small children on your knee. Often there are spare seats which children can occupy after tickets have been collected. In city and local excursion buses, small children generally do not pay a fare, but are not entitled to a seat when paying customers are standing. On sightseeing tours you should *always* bargain for a family rate—often children can go free. (In trains, reductions for children are general, but not universal.)

All civil airlines charge half fare for children under 12, but some military services don't have half-fares, or have younger age limits. Children's fares on Lloyd Aéreo Boliviano are considerably more than half, and there is only a 7kg. baggage allowance. (LAB also checks children's ages on passports.) Note that a child travelling free on a long excursion is not always covered by the operator's travel insurance; it is adviseable to pay a small premium to arrange cover.

*Hotels*: In all hotels, bargain for rates. If charges are per person, always insist that two children will occupy one bed only, therefore counting as one tariff. If rates are per bed, the same applies. In either case you can almost always get a reduced rate at cheaper hotels. Occasionally when travelling with a child you will be refused a room in a hotel that is "unsuitable". On river boat trips, unless you have very large hammocks, it may be more comfortable and cost effective to hire a 2-berth cabin for 2 adults and a child. (In restaurants, you can normally buy children's helpings, or divide one full-size helping between two children.)

Travel with children can bring you into closer contact with Latin American families and, generally, presents no special problems—in fact the path is often smoother for family groups. Officials tend to be more amenable where children are concerned and they are pleased if your child knows a little Spanish or Portuguese. Moreover, even thieves and pickpockets seem to have some of the traditional respect for families, and may leave you alone because of it!

**Hiking and Trekking** Hilary Bradt, the well-known trekker, author and publisher, writes: A network of paths and tracks covers much of South America and is in constant use by the local people. In countries with a large Indian population—Ecuador, Peru and Bolivia, for instance—you can walk just about anywhere, but in the more European countries, such as Venezuela, Chile, and Argentina, you must usually limit yourself to the many excellent national parks with hiking trails. Most South American countries have an Instituto Geográfico Militar which sells topographical maps, scale 1:100,000 or 1:50,000. The physical features shown on these are usually accurate; the trails and place names less so. National Parks offices also sell maps.

Hiking and backpacking should not be approached casually. Even if you only plan to be out a couple of hours you should have comfortable, safe footwear (which can cope with the wet—Ed.) and a daypack to carry your sweater and waterproof (which must be more than showerproof). At high altitudes the difference in temperature between sun and shade is remarkable. The longer trips mentioned in this book require basic backpacking equipment. Essential items are: backpack with frame, sleeping bag, closed cell foam mat for insulation, stove, tent or tarpaulin, dried food (not tins), water bottle, compass. Some but not all of these things are available locally.

When planning treks in the Andes you should be aware of the effects and dangers of acute mountain sickness, and cerebral and pulmonary oedema (see Health Information, **page 36**). These can be avoided by spending a few days acclimatizing to the altitude before starting your walk, and by climbing slowly. Otherwise there are fewer dangers than in most cities. Hikers have little to fear from the animal kingdom apart from insects (although it's best to avoid actually stepping on a snake), and robbery and assault are very rare. You are much more of a threat to the environment than vice versa. Leave no evidence of your passing; don't litter and don't give gratuitous presents of sweets or money to rural villagers. Respect their system of reciprocity; if they give you hospitality or food, then is the time to reciprocate with presents.

**Maps** Those from the Instituto Geográficos Militares in the capitals (see above) are often the only good maps available in Latin America. It is therfore wise to get as many as possible in your home country before leaving, especially if travelling by land. A recommended series of general maps is that published by International Travel Map Productions (ITM), PO Box 2290, Vancouver BC, V6B 2WF, Canada, compiled with historical notes, by Kevin Healey. Available are South America South, North East and North West (1:4,000,000), Amazon Basin (1:4,000,000), Central America (1:1,800,000), Costa Rica (1:500,000), Belize (1:350,000), the Yucatán (1:1,000,000) and Baja California (1:1,000,000).

**Other Travel Books** We should mention the "Backpacking Guide Series" published by Bradt Publications, 41 Nortoft Road, Chalfont St. Peter, Bucks, SL9 0LA, UK.They give detailed descriptions of hiking trails (mentioned in our country "Information for Visitors" sections) and much fascinating information, with many illustrations, in the following volumes: *Peru and Bolivia; Chile and Argentina, plus the Falkland Islands; Climbing and Hiking in Ecuador; South American River Trips; South America Ski Guide*. (Bradt Publications also publish and sell other trail guides, and import trekking and topographical maps from South America, including the ITM series.) *South America on a Shoestring*, by Geoff Crowther (Lonely Planet Publications) has been recommended repeatedly for the quality of its maps. Lonely Planet's growing number of individual country guides have also been praised, as have their phrase books on Quechua by Ronald Wright, and Brazilian Portuguese, by Mark Balla.

Another very useful book, highly recommended, aimed specifically at the budget traveller is *The Tropical Traveller*, by John Hatt (Pan Books, 2nd edition, 1985).

## GENERAL ADVICE

**Responsible Tourism** Mark Eckstein of David Bellamy Associates writes:
Much has been written about the adverse impacts of tourism on the environment and local communities. It is usually assumed that this only applies to the more excessive end of the travel industry such as the Spanish Costas and Bali. However it now seems that travellers can have an impact at almost any density and this is especially true in areas "off the beaten track" where local people may not be used to western conventions and lifestyles, and natural environments may be very sensitive.

Of course, tourism can have a beneficial impact and this is something to which every traveller can contribute. Many National Parks are part funded by receipts from people who travel to see exotic plants and animals, the Galápagos (Ecuador) and Manu (Peru) National Parks are good examples of such sites. Similarly, travellers can promote patronage and protection of valuable archaeological sites and heritages through their interest and entrance fees.

However, where visitor pressure is high and/or poorly regulated, damage can occur. It is also unfortunately true that many of the most popular destinations are in ecologically sensitive areas easily disturbed by extra human pressures. This is particularly significant because the desire to visit sites and communities that are off the beaten track is a driving force for many travellers. Eventually the very features that tourists travel so far to see may become degraded and so we seek out new sites, discarding the old, and leaving someone else to deal with the plight of local communities and the damaged environment.

Fortunately, there are signs of a new awareness of the responsibilities that the travel industry and its clients need to endorse. For example, some tour operators fund local conservation projects and travellers are now more aware of the impact they may have on host cultures and environments. We can all contribute to the success of what is variously described as responsible, green or alternative tourism. All that is required is a little forethought and consideration.

It would be impossible to identify all the possible impacts that might need to be addressed by travellers, but it is worthwhile noting the major areas in which we can all take a more responsible attitude in the countries we visit. These include, changes to natural ecosystems (air, water, land, ecology and wildlife), cultural values (beliefs and behaviour) and the built environment (sites of antiquity and archaeological significance). At an individual level, travellers can reduce their impact if greater consideration is given to their activities. Canoe trips up the headwaters of obscure rivers make for great stories, but how do local communities cope with the sudden invasive interest in their lives? Will the availability of easy tourist money and gauche behaviour affect them for the worse, possibly diluting and trivialising the significance of culture and customs? Similarly, have the environmental implications of increased visitor pressure been considered? Where does the fresh fish that feeds the trip come from? Hand caught by line is fine, but is dynamite fishing really necessary, given the scale of damage and waste that results?

Some of these impacts are caused by factors beyond the direct control of travellers, such as the management and operation of a hotel chain. However, even here it is possible to voice concern about damaging activities and an increasing number of hotels and travel operators are taking "green concerns" seriously, even if it is only to protect their share of the market.

**Environmental Legislation**  Legislation is increasingly being enacted to control damage to the environment, and in some cases this can have a bearing on travellers. The establishment of National Parks may involve rules and guidelines for visitors and these should always be followed. In addition there may be local or national laws controlling behaviour and use of natural resources (especially wildlife) that are being increasingly enforced. If in doubt, ask. Finally, international legislation, principally the Convention on International Trade in Endangered Species of Wild Fauna and Flora (CITES), may affect travellers.

CITES aims to control the trade in live specimens of endangered plants and animals and also "recognizable parts or derivatives" of protected species. Sale of Black Coral, Turtle shells, protected Orchids and other wildlife is strictly controlled by signatories of the convention. The full list of protected wildlife varies, so if you feel the need to purchase souvenirs and trinkets derived from wildlife, it would be prudent to check whether they are protected. Every country included in this Handbook is a signatory of CITES. In addition, most European countries, the USA and Canada are all signatories. Importation of CITES protected species into these countries can lead to heavy fines, confiscation of goods and even imprisonment. Information on the status of legislation and protective measures can be obtained from Traffic International, UK office T (0223) 277427.

**Green Travel Companies and Information**  The increasing awareness of the environmental impact of travel and tourism has led to a range of advice and information services as well as spawning specialist travel companies who claim to provide "responsible travel" for clients. This is an expanding field and the veracity of claims needs to be substantiated in some cases. The following organizations and publications can provide useful information for those with an interest in pursuing responsible travel opportunities.

**Organizations  Green Flag International**  Aims to work with travel industry and conservation bodies to improve environments at travel destinations and also to promote conservation programmes at resort destinations. Provides a travellers' guide for "green" tourism as well as advice on destinations, T (UK—0223) 893587. **Tourism Concern**  Aims to promote a greater understanding of the impact of tourism on host communities and environments. T (UK—081878 9053). **Centre for Responsible Tourism**  CRT coordinates a North American network and advises on N American sources of information on responsible tourism. CRT, 2 Kensington Rd, San Anselmo, California USA. **Centre for the Advancement of Responsive Travel**  CART has a range of publications available as well as information on alternative holiday destinations. T (UK—0732) 352757.

**Publications**  *The Good Tourist* by Katie Wood and Syd House (1991) published by Mandarin Paperbacks; addresses issues surrounding environmental impacts of tourism, suggests ways in which damage can be minimised, suggests a range of environmentally sensitive holidays and projects. *Independent Guide to Real Holidays Abroad*, Frank Barrett (1991); suggestions for a range of special interest holidays. Available from the Independent Newspaper in the UK.

**Souvenirs**  Remember that these can almost invariably be bought more cheaply away from the capital, though the choice may be less wide. Bargaining seems to be the general rule in most countries' street markets.

If British travellers have no space in their luggage, they might like to remember Tumi, the Latin American Craft Centre, at 23 Chalk Farm Road, London NW1 (T 071-485 4152) and 2 New Bond Street Place, Bath (T 0225 62367), who specialize in Mexican and Andean products. There are similar shops in the USA; one good one is on the ground floor of Citicorp Center, Lexington Avenue and 53rd Street, New York.

**Mail**  Postal services in most countries are not very efficient, and pilfering is frequent. All mail, especially packages, should be registered. Some travellers recommend that mail should be sent to one's Embassy (or, if a cardholder, American Express agent) rather than to the Poste Restante/General Delivery (*Lista de Correos*) department of a country's Post Office. Some Embassies and post offices, however, do not keep mail for more than a month. If there seems to be no mail at the Lista under the initial letter of your surname, ask them to look under the initial of your forename or your middle name. For the smallest risk of misunderstanding, use title, initial and surname only. (If you're a British male, and all else fails, ask them to look under "E" for "Esquire"!—Geoffrey van Dulken.)

**Phones** US travellers should know about "USA Direct", set up by AT & T, the telephone company, by which you can connect with an AT & T operator without going through a local one. It is much cheaper than operator-assisted calls and is widely available.

**Explorers** The South American Explorers' Club is at Avenida Portugal 146 (Casilla 3714), Lima, Peru (T 31-44-80), 1254 Toledo, Apartado 21-431, Eloy Alfaro, Quito, Ecuador (T 566-076), and 1510 York Street, Denver, CO 80206, T(303) 320-0388. (For further details see under Lima and Quito.)

**Photography** Always ask permission before photographing people. Take as much film from home as you can; the price of film varies from country to country, being cheapest in Venezuela, Colombia and Ecuador (about US$4 a roll). Some travellers have advised against mailing exposed films home; either take them with you, or have them developed, but not printed, once you have checked the laboratory's quality. Note that postal authorities may use less sensitive equipment for X-ray screening than the airports do.

Dan Buck and Anne Meadows write: A note on developing film in South America. Black and white is a problem. Often it is shoddily machine-processed and the negatives are ruined. Ask the store if you can see an example of their laboratory's work and if they hand-develop.

Jeremy Till and Sarah Wigglesworth suggest that exposed film can be protected in humid areas by putting it in a balloon and tying a knot. Similarly keeping you camera in a plastic bag may reduce the effects of humidity.

**Travelling Alone** When you set out, err on the side of caution until your instincts have adjusted to the customs of a new culture. Unless actively avoiding foreigners like yourself, don't go too far from the beaten track; there is a very definite "gringo trail" which you can join, or follow, if seeking company. Travelling by train is a good way to meet locals, but buses are much easier for a person alone; on major routes your seat is often reserved and your luggage can usually be locked in the hold. It is easier for men to take the friendliness of locals at face value; women may be subject to much unwanted attention. By wearing a wedding ring, carrying a photograph of your "husband" and "children", and saying that your "husband" is close at hand, you may dissuade an aspiring suitor. If politeness fails, do not feel bad about being rude. (Much of this information was supplied by Deirdre Mortell of Carrigaline, Co. Cork).

**Final Hints** Everybody has his/her own list. Items most often mentioned include a small portable stove (liquid fuel is more readily available than gas— though the latter is becoming more common—and you need a combination canteen to go with it), air cushions for slatted seats, inflatable travel pillow for neck support, strong shoes (and remember that footwear over 9½ English size, or 42 European size, is difficult to obtain in Latin America except Argentina and Brazil), money-belt or neck pouch; a small first-aid kit and handbook, rubber window wedges, fully waterproof top clothing, waterproof treatment for leather footwear, wax earplugs and airline-type eye mask to help you sleep in noisy and poorly curtained hotel rooms, rubber-thong Japanese-type sandals (flip-flops), a polyethylene sheet 2 x 1 metres to cover possibly infested beds and train floors and shelter your luggage, polyethylene bags of varying sizes, a toilet bag you can tie round your waist, if you use an electric shaver, take a rechargeable type, a sheet sleeping-bag and pillow-case or separate pillow-case—in some countries they are not changed often in cheap hotels, a mosquito net (or a hammock with a fitted net), a clothes line, a nailbrush (useful for scrubbing dirt off clothes as well as off oneself), a vacuum flask, a water bottle, a small dual-voltage immersion heater, a small dual-voltage (or battery-driven) electric fan, tea bags, a light nylon waterproof shopping bag, a universal bath- and basin-plug of the flanged type that will fit any waste-pipe (or improvise one from a sheet of thick rubber), string, electrical insulating tape, large penknife preferably with tin and bottle openers, scissors and corkscrew—the famous Swiss Army range has been repeatedly recommended, collapsible drinking beaker, electric motor-cycle alarm for luggage protection, a flour sack and roll of wire mesh for ditto, alarm clock or watch, candle, torch (flashlight)—especially one that will clip on to a pocket or belt, small transistor radio or battery cassette-player (Walkman type) with earphones, pocket calculator, an adaptor and flex to enable you to take power from an electric-light socket (the Edison screw type is the most commonly used), a padlock for the doors of the cheapest and most casual hotels, spare chain-lengths and padlock for securing luggage to bed or bus/train seat. Useful medicaments are given at the end of the "Health Information" section (**page 40**); to these might be added some lip salve ("Lypsil" has been recommended), and pre-moistened wipes (such as "Wet Ones"). Always carry toilet paper. Extra passport photos may be useful, also photocopies of essential documents (passport, credit cards, air tickets). **Never** carry firearms. Their possession could land you in serious trouble.

A note for **contact lens wearers**: most countries have a wide selection of products for the care of lenses, so you don't need to take kilos of lotions.

Be careful when asking directions. Women probably know more about the neighbourhood; men about more distant locations. Policemen are often helpful. However, many Latin Americans will give you the wrong answer rather than admit they do not know; this may be partly because they fear losing face, but is also because they like to please. You are more likely to get reliable information if you carefully refrain from asking leading questions.

Lastly, a good principle is to take half the clothes (trousers with plenty of pockets are very useful), and twice the money, that you think you will need.

# HEALTH INFORMATION

*The following information has been very kindly compiled for us by Dr. David Snashall, who is presently Senior Lecturer in Occupational Health at St. Thomas's Hospital Medical School in London and Chief Medical Advisor of the British Foreign and Commonwealth Office. He has travelled extensively in Central and South America, worked in Peru and in East Africa and keeps in close touch with developments in preventative and tropical medicine. We incorporate also some welcome observations on the text by Dr. C. J. Schofield, editor of Parasitology Today. The publishers have every confidence that the following information is correct, but cannot assume any direct responsibility in this connection.*

THE TRAVELLER to Latin America is inevitably exposed to health risks not encountered in Britain or the USA, especially if he spends time in the tropical regions. Epidemic diseases have been largely brought under control by vaccination programmes and public sanitation but, in rural areas, the latter is rudimentary and the chances of contracting infections of various sorts are much higher than at home.

There are English-speaking doctors in most major cities. If you fall ill the best plan may be to attend the out-patient department of a local hospital or contact your Embassy representative for the name of a reputable doctor. (We give the names of hospitals and some recommended doctors in the main city sections.— Ed.) Medical practices vary from those at home but remember they have particular experience in dealing with locally-occurring diseases.

Self-medication is undesirable except for minor complaints but may be forced on you by circumstances. Whatever the circumstances, be wary of medicines prescribed for you by pharmacists; many are poorly trained and unscrupulous enough to sell you potentially dangerous drugs or old stock they want to get rid of. The large number of pharmacies throughout Latin America is a considerable surprise to most people, as is the range of medicines you can purchase over the counter. There is a tendency towards over-prescription of drug mixtures and in general this should be resisted. Many drugs are manufactured under licence from American or European companies so the trade names may be familiar to you. This means that you do not need to carry a whole chest of medicines, but remember that the shelf-life of some items, especially vaccines and antibiotics, is markedly reduced in tropical conditions. Buy your supplies at the better outlets where they have refrigerators, even though it is more expensive. Check the expiry date of all preparations you buy.

Immigration officials sometimes confiscate scheduled drugs (Lomotil is an example) if they are not accompanied by a doctor's prescription.

With the following precautions and advice, you should keep as healthy as usual. Make local enquiries about health risks if you are apprehensive and take the general advice of European or North American families who have lived or are living in the country.

**Before you go** take out medical insurance. You should have a dental check-up, obtain a spare glasses prescription and, if you suffer from a chronic illness (such as diabetes, high blood pressure, ear or sinus troubles, cardiopulmonary disease or a nervous disorder) arrange for a check-up with your doctor, who can at the same time provide you with a letter explaining the details of your disability, if possible in English and Spanish (or Portuguese for Brazil). Check current practice in malaria prophylaxis (prevention).

**Inoculations** Smallpox vaccination is no longer required anywhere in the world. Cholera vaccination is not required for Latin America. A major outbreak of cholera occured, unusually, in Peru in 1990-91. Cholera vaccination was not generally recommended for visitors, but other countries demanded proof of vaccination from travellers from Peru. The following vaccinations are recommended:

*Yellow fever*: this is a live vaccine not to be given to children under nine months of age or persons allergic to eggs. Immunity lasts ten years. An international certificate of yellow fever vaccination will be given and should be kept because it is sometimes asked for.

*Typhoid* (monovalent): one dose followed by a booster in a month's time; Immunity from this course lasts two to three years. An oral preparation may also be available.

*Poliomyelitis*: this is a live vaccine generally given orally and a full course consists of three doses with a booster in tropical regions every three to five years.

*Tetanus*: one dose should be given with a booster (vital) at six weeks and another at six months, and ten-yearly boosters thereafter are recommended.

**Children** should, in addition, be properly protected against diphtheria, and against pertussis (whooping cough) and measles, both of which tend to be more serious infections than at home. Measles, mumps and rubella vaccine is now widely available but those teenage girls who have not had rubella (German measles) should be tested and vaccinated. Consult your doctor for advice on tuberculosis inoculation: the disease is still widespread.

**Infectious Hepatitis** (jaundice) is endemic throughout Latin America and seems to be frequently caught by travellers. The main symptoms are pains in the stomach, lack of appetite, lassitude, and the typical yellow colour of the skin. Medically speaking there are two different types, the less serious but more common is hepatitis A, for which the best protection is the careful preparation of food, the avoidance of contaminated drinking water and scrupulous attention to toilet hygiene. Human normal immunoglobulin (gamma globulin) confers considerable protection against the disease and is particularly useful in epidemics; it should be obtained from a reputable source and is certainly useful for travellers who intend to live rough: they should have a shot before leaving and have it repeated every six months. The dose of gamma globulin depends on the concentration of the particular preparation used, so the manufacturer's advice should be taken. A smaller dose than usual can be given if exposure is for one or two months only.

The other, more serious, version is hepatitis B which is acquired usually by injections with unclean needles, blood transfusions, as a sexually transmitted disease and possibly by insect bites. This disease can be effectively prevented by a specific vaccination requiring three shots over six months before travelling but this is quite expensive. If you have had jaundice in the past it would be worthwhile having a blood test to see if you are immune to either of the two types because this might avoid the necessity for vaccination or gamma globulin.

If at a particular occupational risk (e.g. zoologists or veterinarians), or in the case of epidemics, there are vaccines against other diseases such as rabies.

**AIDS** in South America is increasing in its prevalence, as in most countries, but is not wholly confined to the well known high risk sections of the population, i.e. homosexual men, intravenous drug abusers, prostitutes and children of infected mothers. Heterosexual transmission is now the dominant mode and so the main risk to travellers is from casual sex. The same precautions should be taken as when encountering any sexually transmitted disease. The AIDS virus (HIV) can be passed via unsterilized needles which have been previously used to inject an HIV positive patient, but the risk of this is very small indeed. It would however be sensible to check that needles have been properly sterilised or disposable needles used. Be wary of carrying disposable needles yourself: customs officials find them suspicious. The risk of receiving a blood transfusion with blood infected with the HIV virus is greater than from dirty needles because of the amount of fluid exchanged. Supplies of blood for transfusion should now be screened for HIV in all reputable hospitals so again the risk must be very small indeed. Catching the AIDS virus does not usually produce an illness in itself; the only way to be sure if you feel you have been put at risk is to have a blood test for HIV antibodies on your return to a place where there are reliable laboratory facilities. The test does not become positive for many weeks. Presently the higher risks are probably in Brazil and the West Indies.

**Common Problems**, some of which will almost certainly be encountered, are:

**Heat and Cold** Full acclimatization to high temperatures takes about two weeks and during this period it is normal to feel relatively apathetic, especially if the relative humidity is high. Drink plenty of water (up to 15 litres a day are required when working physically hard in the tropics), use salt on your food and avoid extreme exertion. Tepid showers are more cooling than hot or cold ones. Large hats do not cool you down, but do prevent sunburn. Remember that, especially in the highlands, there can be a large and sudden drop in temperature between sun and shade and between night and day, so dress accordingly. Warm jackets and woollens are essential after dark at high altitude.

**Altitude** Acute mountain sickness or *soroche* can strike from about 3,000 metres upwards. It is more likely to affect those who ascend rapidly (e.g. by plane) and those who over-exert themselves. Teenagers are particularly prone. Past experience is not always a good guide: the author, having spent years in Peru travelling constantly between sea level and very high altitude, never suffered the slightest symptoms, then was severely affected climbing Kilimanjaro in Tanzania.

On reaching heights above 3,000 metres, heart pounding and shortness of breath, especially on exertion, are almost universal and a normal response to the lack of oxygen in the air. *Soroche* takes a few hours or days to come on and presents with headache, lassitude, dizziness, loss of appetite, nausea and vomiting. Insomnia is common and often associated with a suffocating feeling when lying in bed. Keen observers may note their breathing tends to wax and wane at night and their face tends to be puffy in the mornings—this is all part of the syndrome. The treatment is rest, pain killers (preferably not aspirin-based) for the headache and anti-sickness pills for vomiting. Oxygen may help at very high altitudes. Various local panaceas ("Coramina glucosada", "Effortil", "Micoren") have their advocates and *mate (or te) de coca* (an infusion of coca leaves, widely available) certainly alleviates some of the symptoms.

On arrival at places over 3,000 metres, a few hours' rest in a chair and avoidance of alcohol, cigarettes and heavy food will go a long way towards preventing *soroche*. Should the symptoms be severe and prolonged it is best to descend to lower altitude and re-ascend slowly or in stages. If this is impossible because of shortage of time or if the likelihood of acute mountain sickness is high then the drug Acetazolamide (Diamox) can be used as a preventative and continued during the ascent. There is good evidence of the value of this drug in the prevention of *soroche* but some people do experience funny side effects. The usual dose is 500 mg of the slow-release preparation each night, starting the night before ascending above 3,000 metres. (Detailed information is available from the Mountain Medicine Centre, c/o Dr. Charles Clarke, Dept. of Neurological Sciences, St. Bartholomew's Hospital, 38 Little Britain, London EC1A 7BE.—Ed.)

Other problems experienced at high altitude are sunburn, excessively dry air causing skin cracking, sore eyes (it may be wise to leave your contact lenses out) and stuffy noses. It is unwise to ascend to high altitude if you are pregnant, especially in the first 3 months, or if you have any history of heart, lung or blood disease, including sickle-cell.

There is a further, albeit rare, hazard due to rapid ascent to high altitude called acute pulmonary oedema. The condition can affect mountaineers; but also occurs in Andean natives returning from a period at the coast. The condition comes on quite rapidly with breathlessness, noisy breathing, cough, blueness of the lips and frothing at the mouth. Anybody developing this must be brought down as soon as possible, given oxygen and taken to hospital.

Rapid descent from high places will aggravate sinus and middle ear infections, and make bad teeth ache painfully. The same problems are sometimes experienced during descent at the end of a flight.

Despite these various hazards (mostly preventable) of high-altitude travel, many people find the environment healthier and more invigorating than at sea-level.

**Intestinal Upsets**  Practically nobody escapes this one, so be prepared for it. Most of the time it is due to the insanitary preparation of food. Don't eat uncooked fish or vegetables, fruit with the skin on (always peel your fruit yourself), food that is exposed to flies, or salads. Tap water is rarely safe outside the major cities, especially in the rainy season, and stream water is often contaminated by communities living surprisingly high in the mountains. Filtered or bottled (make sure it is opened in your presence—Ed.) water is usually available and safe. If your hotel has a central hot-water supply, this is safe to drink after cooling. Ice for drinks should be made from boiled water but rarely is, so stand your glass on the ice cubes rather than putting them in the drink. Dirty water should first be strained through a filter bag (available from camping shops) and then boiled or treated. Water in general can be rendered safe in the following ways: boil for 5 minutes at sea level, longer at higher altitudes; or add three drops of household bleach (but not modern treated bleaches) to 1 pint of water and leave for 15 minutes; or add 1 drop of tincture of iodine to 1 pint of water and leave for 3 minutes. Commercial water-sterilizing tablets are available, for instance Sterotabs from Boots, England. (Also recommended are compact water filters, for instance Travel Well, Pre Mac (Kent) Ltd, Tunbridge Wells, or the Swiss-made Katadyn.)

Fresh, unpasteurized milk is a source of food poisoning germs, tuberculosis and brucellosis. This applies equally to ice-cream, yoghurt and cheese made from unpasteurized milk. Fresh milk can be rendered safe by heating it to 62°C for 30 minutes followed by rapid cooling, or by boiling it. Matured or processed cheeses are safer than fresh varieties. Heat-treated (UHT), pasteurized or sterilized milk is becoming more available.

The most effective treatment for simple diarrhoea is rest and plenty to drink. Seek medical advice, however, if there is no improvement after three days. Much of the exhaustion of travellers' diarrhoea derives from the dehydration: water and salts are lost from the body and are not replaced. This can be remedied by proprietary preparations of salts which are dissolved in water, e.g. Electrosol (Macarthys) Dioralyte (Armour) Rehidrat (Searle) or ask for "suero oral" at a pharmacy or health centre. Marsha Stuart, of Save the Children, Westport, Conn. states that adding ½ teaspoon of salt (3.5g) and 4 tablespoons of sugar (40 g) to a litre of pure water makes a perfectly good substitute for the proprietary preparations. If rest is not possible, or the lavatory is full of other people with the same trouble, or if the stomach cramps are particularly bad, then the following drugs may help:

Loperamide (Imodium, Janssen, or Arret) up to eight capsules a day. This is now available in the UK without prescription.
Diphenoxylate with atropine (Lomotil, Searle) up to 16 tablets in any 24 hours, but do *not*

use for simple diarrhoea, only to relieve cramps and never in children.
Codeine phosphate 30 mg. One tablet every 4 hours.
Kaolin and morphine or Paregoric, as directed by the pharmacist.

Severe vomiting may be calmed by metoclopramide (Maxolon, Beechams; Primperan, Berk) 10 mg. tablet or injection every 8 hours, but not more frequently.

The vast majority of cases of diarrhoea and/or vomiting are due to microbial infections of the bowel plus an effect from strange food and drink. They represent no more than a temporary inconvenience which you learn to live with and need no special treatment. Fortunately, as you get accustomed to Latin American germs, the attacks become less frequent and you can be more daring in your eating habits.

If, in addition to cramps and diarrhoea, you pass blood in the bowel motion, have severe abdominal pain, fever and feel really terrible, you may well have dysentery and a doctor should be consulted at once. If this is not possible, the recommended treatment for bacillary dysentery is Ciprofloxacin 500 mg. every 12 hours, or Tetracycline or Ampicillin 500 mg. every 6 hours plus replacement of water and salts. If you catch amoebic dysentery, which has rather similar symptoms, do not try to cure yourself but put yourself in proper medical hands; the treatment can be complex and self-medication may just damp down the symptoms with the risk of serious liver involvement later on.

Another common bowel infection is with the parasite Giardia Lamblia, which causes prolonged diarrhoea, bloating, persistent indigestion and sometimes loss of weight. This needs treating with a drug such as Metronidazole, best taken under medical supervision.

There are many travellers' tales about special diets, herbal medicines and the consumption of vast quantities of yoghurt as an aid to rehabilitating one's bowels after such attacks. None of them has proved to be useful, in contrast to the widespread success of oral rehydration (water and salt replenishment by mouth) in thousands of children seriously ill with diarrhoea throughout the third world. There is some evidence that alcohol and milk products can prolong diarrhoea so these are best avoided after an attack.

Enterovioform (Ciba), "Mexaform" in Latin America, can have serious side effects (nerve damage, especially to the eyes) if taken for long periods. The active agent, diodochlor-hydroxy-quinoline, is used in many antidiarrhoeals sold in Peru and Ecuador. If it is impossible to control the source of your food and you are likely to be far from medical attention (such as on Amazonian river trips) it is justifiable to take diloxanide furoate (Furamide) 500 mg. daily *plus* a sulphonamide drug e.g. Phthalylsulphathiazole (Thalazole, May & Baker) 500 mg. twice daily. Many businessmen and, for example, athletes who are on short visits of great importance take Streptotriad (May & Baker) one tablet twice daily to prevent diarrhoea and this has been proved to be effective.

Paradoxically, constipation is also common, probably induced by dietary change, inadequate fluid intake in hot places and long bus journeys. Simple laxatives are useful in the short term (the Editor recommends Senokot) and bulky foods such as maize, beans and plenty of fruit are also useful.

**Insects** These can be a great nuisance, especially in the tropics, and some, of course, are carriers of serious diseases. The best way of keeping them away at night is to sleep off the ground with a mosquito net and to burn mosquito coils containing pyrethrum. The best way to use insecticide aerosol sprays is to spray the room thoroughly in all areas and then shut the door for a while, re-entering when the smell has dispersed. Tablets of insecticide are also available which, when placed on a heated mat plugged into a wall socket, fill the room with insecticide fumes in the same way. The best repellants contain di-ethyl-meta-toluamide (DET) or di-methyl phthalate—sold as "Deet", "Six-Twelve Plus", "Off", "Boots' Liquid

Insect Repellant", "Autan", "Flypel". Liquid is best for arms and face (care around eyes) and aerosol spray for clothes and ankles to deter chiggers, mites and ticks. Liquid DEET suspended in water can be used to impregnate cotton clothes and mosquito nets.

If you are bitten, itching may be relieved by baking-soda baths, anti-histamine tablets (care with alcohol or driving), corticosteroid creams (great care—never use if any hint of sepsis) or by judicious scratching. Calamine lotion and cream have limited effectiveness and antihistamine creams (e.g. Antihisan, May & Baker) have a tendency to cause skin allergies and are, therefore, not generally recommended.

Bites which become infected (commonly in the tropics) should be treated with a local antiseptic or antibiotic cream, such as Cetrimide BP (Savlon, ICI) as should infected scratches.

Skin infestations with body lice (crabs) and scabies are, unfortunately, easy to pick up. Use gamma benzene hexachloride for lice and benzene benzoate solution for scabies. Crotamiton cream (Eurax, Geigy) alleviates itching and also kills a number of skin parasites. Malathion lotion 5% (Prioderm) kills lice effectively, but do not use the toxic agricultural insecticide Malathion.

In remote grassland or jungle areas, insect larvae such as that of the bot-fly, which burrow into the flesh, are best removed by covering the breathing hole in your skin with vaseline, then a circular piece of adhesive tape with more vaseline round the edges. If this is allowed to dry well, with no lymph leaking out round the edges, you will be able to squeeze the maggot out next day. The condition is identifiable by a clear hole in the middle of a growing boil or pimple.

**Malaria** in South America is theoretically confined to coastal and jungle zones but is now on the increase again. Mosquitoes do not thrive above 2,500 metres so you are safe at altitude. There are different varieties of malaria, some resistant to the normal drugs. Make local enquiries if you intend to visit possibly infected zones and use one of the following prophylactic regimes. Start taking the tablets a few days before exposure and continue to take them for six weeks after leaving the malarial zone. Remember to give the drugs to babies and children also. Opinion varies on the precise drugs and dosage to be used for protection; all the drugs may have some side effects, and it is important to balance the risk of catching the disease against the albeit rare side effects. The increasing complexity of the subject as the malarial parasite becomes immune to the new generation of drugs has made concentration on the physical prevention of being bitten by mosquitoes more important, i.e. the use of long-sleeved shirts/blouses and long trousers, repellants and nets.

*Prophylactic regimes*:
Proguanil (Paludrine ICI 100 mg, 2 tablets daily) *or* Chloroquine (Avloclor; ICI, Malarivon; Wallace MFG, Nivaquine, May & Baker; Resochin, Bayer; Aralen 300 mg base (2 tablets) weekly).

Where there is a high risk of Chloroquine-resistant falciparum malaria, take Chloroquine plus Proguanil in the above-mentioned doses and carry Fansidar (Roche, also spelt Falsidar) for treatment; *or* add Paludrine 2 tablets per day to your routine Chloroquine prophylaxis.

You can catch malaria even when sticking to the above rules, although it is unlikely. If you do develop symptoms (high fever, shivering, headache, sometimes diarrhoea) seek medical advice *immediately*. If this is not possible, and there is a great likelihood of malaria, the *treatment* is:

*Normal types*: Chloroquine, a single dose of 4 tablets (600mg) followed by two tablets (300 mg) in 6 hours and 300 mg each day following.
*Falciparum* type or type in doubt: Fansidar, single dose of 3 tablets. (We have been told that this drug does not combine well with alcohol, so best to avoid drinking during treatment period.)

If Falciparum type malaria is definitely diagnosed, it is wise to get to a good hospital as the treatment can be complex and the illness very serious.

Pregnant women are particularly prone to malaria and should stick to Proguanil as a prophylactic. Chloroquine may cause eye damage if taken over a long period. The safety of Fansidar has been questioned and, at the time of writing, it is not recommended for prophylaxis.

**Chagas' Disease** (South American Trypanosomiasis) is a chronic disease, very rarely caught by travellers, but very difficult to treat. It is transmitted by the simultaneous biting and excreting of the Reduvid bug (Triatoma or Rhodnius), also known as the *vinchuca*, or *barbeiro*. Somewhat resembling a small cockroach, this nocturnal "kissing bug" lives in poor adobe houses with dirt floors often frequented by oppossums. If you cannot avoid such accommodation, sleep off the floor with a candle lit, use a mosquito net and wash any bites thoroughly with soap and water, or a disinfectant.

**Sunburn** The burning power of the tropical sun, especially at high altitude, is phenomenal. Always wear a wide-brimmed hat and use some form of suncream lotion on untanned skin. Normal temperate-zone suntan lotions (protection factor up to 7) are not much good; you need to use the types designed specifically for the tropics, or for mountaineers or skiers, with a protection factor between 7 and 15. These are often not available in South America; a reasonable substitute is zinc oxide ointment. Glare from the sun can cause conjunctivitis, so wear sunglasses. especially on tropical beaches, where high protection-factor sunscreen cream should also be used.

**Snakebite** If you are unlucky enough to be bitten by a venomous snake, spider, scorpion or sea creature, try (within limits) to catch the animal for identification. The reactions to be expected are: fright, swelling, pain and bruising around the bite, soreness of the regional lymph glands, nausea, vomiting and fever. If any of the following symptoms supervene, get the victim to a doctor without delay: numbness and tingling of the face, muscular spasms, convulsion, shortness of breath and haemorrhage. The tiny coral snake, with red, black and white bands, is the most dangerous, but is very timid.

Commercial snakebite and scorpion kits are available, but only useful for the specific type of snake or scorpion for which they are designed. The serum has to be given intravenously so is not much good unless you have had some practice at making injections into veins. If the bite is on a limb, immobilize the limb and apply a tight bandage between the bite and the body, releasing it for 90 seconds every 15 minutes. Reassurance of the bitten person is very important because death from snakebite is very rare. Do not slash the bite area and try to suck out the poison because this sort of heroism does more harm than good. Hospitals usually hold stocks of snake bite serum. Best precaution: don't walk in snake territory with bare feet or sandals—wear proper shoes or boots.

**Spiders and Scorpions** These may be found in the more basic hotels in the Andean countries. If bitten by *Latrodectus* or *Loxosceles* spiders, or stung by scorpions, rest and take plenty of fluids, and call a doctor. Precaution: keep beds away from the walls, and look inside shoes in morning.

**Other Afflictions** Remember that **rabies** is endemic throughout Latin America so avoid dogs that are behaving strangely, and cover your toes at night to foil the vampire bats, which also carry the disease. If you are bitten, try to have the animal captured for observation and see a doctor at once. Treatment with human diploid vaccine is now extremely effective and worth seeking out if the likelihood of having contracted rabies is high.

**Dengue** fever has made its appearance in southern Mexico and the lower-lying parts of Central America; also in Brazil. No treatment: you must just avoid mosquito bites.

**Typhus** can still occur, carried by ticks. There is usually a reaction at the site of the bite and a fever: seek medical advice.

**Intestinal worms** are common, and the more serious ones such as **hookworm** can be contracted from walking barefoot on infested earth or beaches. Various other tropical diseases can be caught in jungle areas, usually transmitted by biting insects; they are often related to African diseases and were probably introduced by the slave trade from Africa. **Onchocerciasis** (river-blindness), carried by blackflies, is found in parts of Mexico and Venezuela. Cutaneous **leishmaniasis** (Espundia) is carried by sandflies and causes a sore that won't heal; wearing long trousers and long-sleeved shirts in infectious areas helps to avoid the fly. Epidemics of meningitis occur from time to time. Be careful about swimming in piranha- (or caribe-) infested rivers. It is a good idea not to swim naked: the candiru fish can follow urine currents and become lodged in body orifices; swimwear offers some protection.

**Dangerous animals** Apart from mosquitoes, the most dangerous animals are men, be they bandits or behind steering wheels. Think carefully about violent confrontations and wear a seatbelt, if you are lucky enough to have one available to you.

**Prickly heat**, a very common itchy rash, is avoided by frequent washing and by wearing loose clothing. Cured by allowing skin to dry off through use of powder, and spending 2 nights in an air-conditioned hotel! **Athlete's foot** and other fungal infections are best treated with Tinaderm.

**When you return home**, remember to take your anti-malarial tablets for 6 weeks. Thousands of people develop malaria after tropical holidays because they do not take this precaution and some of them die, because it is not realized at home that they are suffering from malaria. If you have had attacks of diarrhoea, it is worth having a stool specimen tested in case you may have picked up amoebic dysentery. If you have been living in the bush, a blood test may be worthwhile to detect worms and other parasites.

**Basic supplies** The following items you may find useful to take with you from home:

Sunglasses.
Suntan cream.
Insect repellant, flea powder, mosquito net and coils.
Tampons (they can be bought in the main cities), and contraceptives (not easy to obtain everywhere).
Water-sterilizing tablets, e.g. Sterotabs (Boots), Globaline, Puritabs (Kirby & Co. Ltd.).
Antimalarials.
Anti-infective ointment, e.g. Savlon (ICI).
Dusting powder for feet, e.g. Tinaderm (Glaxo), Desenex.
Travel-sickness pills, e.g. Dramamine (Searle), Gravol (Carter-Wallace).
Antacids, e.g. Maalox.
("Tiger balm", an apparently all-purpose remedy, recommended by two overland travellers from New Zealand).
Antidiarrheals, e.g. Lomotil (Searle), Imodium (Janssen) or Arret. (Charcoal tablets are useful for minor stomach ailments.)
First-aid kit.
Health packs containing sterile syringes, needles, gloves, etc. are available for travellers from various sources (e.g. Schiphol airport, Amsterdam); one such is made by Safa of Liverpool, UK.

The following organizations give information regarding well-trained, English-speaking physicians in Latin America:

International Association for Medical Assistance to Travellers, 745 Fifth Avenue, New York 10022.
Intermedic, 777 Third Avenue, New York 10017 (Tel.: 212-486-8974).
Information regarding country-by-country malaria risk can be obtained from the World Health Organization (WHO), or the Ross Institute, London School of Hygiene and Tropical Medicine, Keppel Street, London WC1E 7HT, which publishes a book strongly recommended, entitled *Preservation of Personal Health in Warm Climates*. Medical Advisory Services for Travellers Abroad (Masta), at the Keppel Street address above, prepares health briefs on every country for a fee.

The new edition of *Travellers' Health: How to Stay Healthy Abroad*, edited by Dr. Richard Dawood (Oxford University Press, 1989, paperback, £5.95), has been fully revised and updated, and will even help you survive travel closer to home. We strongly recommend this book, especially to the intrepid travellers who go to the more out-of-the-way places.

# WILL YOU HELP US?

We do all we can to get our facts right in **The South American Handbook.** Each chapter is thoroughly revised each year, but the territory covered is vast, and our eyes cannot be everywhere. A new highway or airport is built; a hotel, a restaurant, a cabaret dies; another, a good one, is born; a building we describe is pulled down, a street renamed. Names and addresses of good hotels and restaurants for "budget-minded" travellers are always very welcome. We would especially like to receive diagrams of walks, national parks and other interesting areas to use as source material for the Handbook.

*Your information may be far more up-to-date than ours. If your letter reaches us early enough in the year it will be used in the next edition, but write whenever you want to, for all your letters are used sooner or later.*

Thank you very much indeed for your help.

 **Trade & Travel Publications Limited**
6 Riverside Court
Lower Bristol Road
Bath BA2 3DZ. England

# ARGENTINA

## INTRODUCTION

ARGENTINA is the second largest country in area in South America. It covers 2,807,560 square km., or 29% of the area of Europe; it is 3,460 km. long from N to S and is, in places, 1,580 km. wide. The population is about 32.8 million. Apart from the estuary of the Río de la Plata its coast line is 2,575 km. long. Its western frontier runs along the crest of the high Andes, a formidable barrier between it and Chile. Its neighbours to the N are Bolivia and Paraguay and (in the NE) Brazil. To the E is Uruguay. Its far southern limit is the Beagle Channel. The area figures exclude the sector of Antarctica claimed by Argentina.

Argentina is enormously varied both in its types of land and its climates. Geographers usually recognize four main physical areas: the Andes, the North and Mesopotamia, the Pampas, and Patagonia.

The first division, the Andes, includes the whole length of the Cordilleras, low and deeply glaciated in the Patagonian S, high and dry in the prolongation into NW Argentina of the Bolivian Altiplano, the high plateau. S of this is the very parched desert and mountain region S of Tucumán and W of Córdoba. The oases strung along the eastern foot of the Andes—Jujuy, Salta, Tucumán, Catamarca, La Rioja, San Juan, Mendoza and San Rafael—were the first places to be colonized by the Spaniards.

The second division, the North and Mesopotamia, contains the vast forested

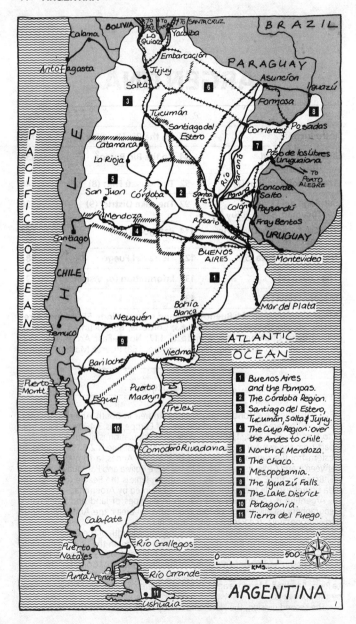

1 Buenos Aires and the Pampas.
2 The Córdoba Region.
3 Santiago del Estero, Tucumán, Salta & Jujuy.
4 The Cuyo Region: over the Andes to Chile.
5 North of Mendoza.
6 The Chaco.
7 Mesopotamia.
8 The Iguazú Falls.
9 The Lake District.
10 Patagonia.
11 Tierra del Fuego.

ARGENTINA

plains of the Chaco, and the floodplain and gently rolling land known as the Argentine Mesopotamia lying between the rivers Paraná and Uruguay. The Province of Misiones in the NE is actually on the great Paraná plateau. These plains cover 582,750 square km.

The third division, the flat rich pampa, takes up the heart of the land. These vast plains lie S of the Chaco, E of the Andes, W of the Atlantic and the Río Paraná and N of the Río Colorado. The eastern part, which receives more rain, is usually called the Humid Pampa, and the western part the Dry Pampa. The Pampas stretch for hundreds of km. in almost unrelieved flatness and cover some 650,000 square km.

The final division is Patagonia, the area S of the Río Colorado—a land of arid, wind-swept plateaux cut across by ravines. In the deep S the wind is wilder and more continuous. There is no real summer, but to compensate for this the winters are rarely severe. Patagonia has about 780,000 square km.

Three-quarters of Argentina's territory cannot be cultivated without irrigation but only 400,000 hectares are artificially watered.

**Climate** ranges from sub-tropical in the N to cold temperate in Tierra del Fuego, but is temperate and quite healthy in the densely populated central zone. From mid-December to the end of February Buenos Aires can be oppressively hot and humid, with temperatures ranging from 27°C (80°F) to 35°C (95°F) and an average humidity of 70%. Beware of the high pollen count in the pollinating season if you have allergy problems. The winter months of June, July and August are best for a business visit, though spring weather in Buenos Aires is often very pleasant indeed. The skiing season in Bariloche ends by August 30. Corrientes and Misiones provinces are wet in August and especially September.

**History** When, in the early 16th century, the first Europeans came to Argentina, the native Indians had already halted the Inca drive southwards from Peru through Bolivia into northern Argentina. The Spaniard Juan de Solís landed on the shores of the Plata estuary in 1516, but he was killed and the expedition failed. Magellan touched at the estuary four years later, but turned southwards to make his way into the Pacific. In 1527 both Sebastian Cabot and his rival Diego García sailed into the estuary and up the Paraná and the Paraguay. They formed a small settlement, Sancti Spiritus, at the junction of the Caraña and Coronda rivers near their confluence with the Paraná, but it was wiped out by the Indians about two years later and Cabot and García returned to Spain. Eight years later, in 1535, Pedro de Mendoza, with a large force well supplied with equipment and horses, founded a settlement at Buenos Aires. The natives soon made it too difficult for him; the settlement was abandoned and Mendoza returned home, but not before sending Juan de Ayolas with a small force up the Paraná. Ayolas set off for Peru, already conquered by Pizarro, leaving Irala in charge. It is not known for certain what happened to Ayolas, but in 1537 Irala and his men settled at Asunción, in Paraguay, where the natives were friendly. There were no further expeditions from Spain to colonize what is now called Argentina, and it was not until 1573 that the settlement at Asunción sent forces S to establish Santa Fe and not until 11 June 1580 that Juan de Garay refounded the settlement at Buenos Aires. It was only under his successor, Hernando Arias de Saavedra (1592-1614), that the new colony became secure.

In the meantime there had been successful expeditions into Argentina both from Peru and Chile—the first, from Peru, as early as 1543. These expeditions led, in the latter half of the 16th century, to the foundation at the eastern foot of the Andes of the oldest towns in Argentina: Santiago del Estero, Tucumán, Córdoba, Salta, La Rioja and Jujuy by Spaniards from Peru following the old Inca road, and San Juan, Mendoza, and San Luis by those from Chile, across the Andes. Peru was given the viceroyalty over all the Spanish possessions in South America in 1543.

For 270 years after its foundation Buenos Aires was of little importance. Spanish stress was upon Lima, and Lima did not send its treasures home by way of Buenos Aires but through Panama and the Caribbean. Buenos Aires was not allowed by Spain to take part in any overseas trade until 1778; its population then was only 24,203. It was merely a military outpost for Spain to confront the Portuguese outpost at Colonia, across the estuary, and lived, in the main, by smuggling. Even when in 1776 the Viceroyalty of Río de la Plata was formed, it made little difference to Buenos Aires as a capital, for its control of the *cabildos* (town councils) in distant towns was very tenuous. When the British, following Spain's alliance with Napoleon, attacked Buenos Aires in 1806 and again in 1807 before being repulsed by local levies, there was no inkling of its future potential. But the defeat of these attacks, known as the Reconquista, had one important result: a great increase in the confidence of the *porteños* (the name given to those born in Buenos Aires) to deal with all comers, including the mother-country, whose restrictions were increasingly unpopular. On 25 May 1810, the *cabildo* of Buenos Aires deposed the viceroy and announced that it was governing henceforth on behalf of King Ferdinand VII, then a captive of Napoleon. Six years later, when Buenos Aires was threatened by invasion from Peru and blockaded by a Spanish fleet in the River Plate, a national congress held at Tucumán declared independence on 9 July 1816. The declaration was given reality by the genius and devotion of José de San Martín, who boldly marched an Argentine army across the Andes to free Chile, and (with the help of Lord Cochrane, commander of the Chilean Navy), embarked his forces for Peru, where he captured Lima, the first step in the liberation of Peru.

When San Martín returned home, it was to find the country rent by conflict between the central government and the provinces. Disillusioned, he retired to France. The internal conflict was to last a long time. On the one hand stood the

Unitarist party, bent on central control; on the other the Federalist party, insisting on local autonomy. The latter had for members the great *caudillos*, the large landowners backed by the *gauchos*, suspicious of the cities. One of their leaders, Juan Manuel de Rosas, took control of the country in 1829. During his second term as Governor of Buenos Aires he asked for and was given extraordinary powers. The result was a 17-year reign of terror. His rule was an international scandal, and when he began a blockade of Asunción in 1845, Britain and France promptly countered with a three-year blockade of Buenos Aires. But in 1851 Justo José de Urquiza, Governor of Entre Ríos, one of his old henchmen, organized a triple *entente* of Brazil, Uruguay, and the Argentine opposition to overthrow him. He was defeated in 1852 at Caseros, a few km. from Buenos Aires, and fled to England, where he farmed quietly for 25 years, dying at Southampton.

Rosas had started his career as a Federalist; once in power he was a Unitarist. His downfall meant the triumph of federalism. In 1853 a federal system was finally incorporated in the constitution, but the old quarrel had not been solved. In 1859, when the constitution was ratified, the capital was moved to Paraná, the province of Buenos Aires seceded, and Buenos Aires, under Bartolomé Mitre, was defeated by the federal forces under Urquiza. Two years later Buenos Aires again fought the country, and this time it won. Once again it became the seat of the federal government, with Bartolomé Mitre as its first constitutional president. (It was during his term that the Triple Alliance of Argentina, Brazil, and Uruguay defeated Francisco Solano López of Paraguay.) There was another political flare-up of the old quarrel in 1880, ending in the humiliation of Buenos Aires, which then ceased to be the capital of its province; a new provincial capital was founded at La Plata, 56 km. to the SE. At that time a young colonel, Julio A. Roca, was finally subduing all the Indian tribes of the pampas and the South. This was an event which was to make possible the final supremacy of Buenos Aires over all rivals.

Politically Argentina was a constitutional republic with a very restricted suffrage up to the passage in 1912 of the Sáenz Peña law, which established universal manhood suffrage. From 1916 to 1930 the Unión Cívica Radical (founded in 1890) held power, under the leadership of Hipólito Yrigoyen and Marcelo T. de Alvear, but lost it to the military uprising of 1930. Though seriously affected by the world depression of the 1930s, Argentina's rich soil and educated population had made it one of the ten wealthiest countries in the world, but this wealth was most unevenly distributed, and the political methods followed by the conservatives and their military associates in the 1930s denied the middle and working classes any effective share in their own country's wealth and government. In 1943 came another military coup, which had a distinctly fascist tinge; in 1946 emerged, as President, Gen. Juan Domingo Perón, who based his power on an alliance between the army and labour; his contacts with labour were greatly assisted by his charismatic wife Eva (since commemorated in the rock-opera "Evita") and the living conditions of the workers were greatly improved—but at the expense of the economic state of the country. By the time a military coup unseated Perón in 1955 serious harm had been done; ever since, Argentina has been struggling to recover its lost economic health.

After an uneasy alternation of three military and two constitutional regimes between 1955 and 1973, Gen. Perón again became President in October 1973, but died on 1 July 1974, leaving the Presidency to his widow, Vice-President María Estela Martínez de Perón. A chaotic political situation, of which a high level of violence (including guerrilla warfare) was a regrettable feature, followed his death; by March 1976 conditions in the country, both of violence and of economic crisis, had deteriorated to the point when the military felt again obliged to intervene. Sra. de Perón was deposed from the Presidency by a military junta, led by Gen. Jorge Videla, and guerrilla warfare and the other features of dissidence were repressed with great brutality: about 9,000 people (according to official statistics; human rights organizations believe the total at least doubles this) disappeared without trace during the so-called "dirty war". General Videla was appointed President in 1978 by the military leaders, for a three-year term. His nominated successor, General Roberto Viola, took over as President for three years in March, 1981 but was replaced by General Leopoldo Galtieri in December 1981. The latter was in turn replaced in June 1982 by General (ret.) Reynaldo Bignone.

Confidence in the military began to ebb when their economic policies began to go sour in 1980. In 1982-83 pressure for a democratic restoration grew apace particularly after the South Atlantic conflict with Great Britain in 1982. General elections were held on 30 October 1983 and the Unión Cívica Radical was victorious, winning the Presidency and an absolute majority in the Chamber of Deputies, with 52% of the vote. Accordingly, Dr. Raúl Alfonsín, its candidate, assumed the Presidency on 10 December 1983. During 1985 Generals Videla, Viola and Galtieri were sentenced to long terms of imprisonment for their parts in the "dirty war", a move which caused friction in the relations between the Government and the armed forces. President Alfonsín's popularity gradually waned as his Government failed to solve economic problems. Presidential elections held on 14 May 1989, were won by a 10% margin by Sr. Carlos Saúl Menem of the Partido Justicialista (Peronists), who took office ahead of schedule in July 1989 because of economic instability. Relations between the Peronist Government and the military were also strained and Pres. Menem tackled several rebellions, which he attempted to appease by pardoning the imprisoned generals. His popularity among civilians declined and he had no cohesive political backing from his own party. His reputation suffered from the breakdown of his marriage and scandals involving his family and friends in alleged corruption and drug trafficking.

**The Transformation of the Pampas**  The pampas, the economic heart of the country, extend fanwise from Buenos Aires for a distance of between 550 and 650 km. Apart from three groups of *sierras* or low hills near Córdoba, Tandil and Bahía Blanca, the surface seems an endless flat monotony, relieved occasionally, in the SW, by sand dunes. There are few rivers. Drinking water is pumped to the surface from a depth of from 30 to 150 metres by the windpumps which are such a prominent feature of the landscape. There are no trees other than those that have been planted, except in the *monte* of the W. But there is, in most years, ample rainfall. It is greatest at Rosario, where it is about 1,020 mm, and evenly distributed throughout the year. The further S from Rosario, the less the rain. At Buenos Aires it is about 940 mm; it drops to 535 at Bahía Blanca, and is only 400 along the boundary of the Humid Pampa. The further from Rosario, too, the more the rainfall is concentrated during the summer. Over the whole of the pampa the summers are hot, the winters mild, but there is a large climatic difference between various regions: at Rosario the growing season between frosts is about 300 days; at Bahía Blanca it falls to 145 days.

When the Spanish arrived in Argentina the pampas were an area of tall coarse grasses. The cattle and horses they brought with them were soon to roam wild and in time transformed the Indian's way of life. The only part of the pampa occupied by the settlers was the so-called Rim, between the Río Salado, S of the capital, and the Paraná-Plata rivers. Here, in large *estancias*, cattle, horses and mules in great herds roamed the open range. There was a line of forts along the Río Salado: a not very effective protection against marauding Indians. The Spaniards had also brought European grasses with them; these soon supplanted the coarse native grasses, and formed a green carpet surface which stopped abruptly at the Río Salado.

The *estancia* owners and their dependent *gauchos* were in no sense an agricultural people, but towards the end of the 18th century, tenants—to the great contempt of both *estanciero* and *gaucho*—began to plant wheat in the valleys along the Paraná-Plata shore. The fall of Rosas in 1852, and the constitution of 1853, made it possible for Argentina to take a leap forward, but it must be remembered that its civilized population at that time was only 1,200,000.

The rapidly rising population of Europe during the latter half of the 19th century and the consequent demand for cheap food was the spur that impelled Argentina (as it did the United States and Canada) to occupy its grasslands and take to agriculture. This was made possible by the new techniques already developed: agricultural machinery, barbed wire, well-drilling machines and windpumps, roads and railways, and ocean-going steamships. Roads were, and are, a difficulty in the Argentine pampa; the soil lacks gravel or stones to surface the roads, and dirt roads become a quagmire in wet weather and a fume of dust in the dry. Railways, on the other hand, were simple and cheap to build. The system grew as need arose and capital (mostly from Britain) became available. The lines in the pampa radiate out fanwise (with intricate inter-communication) from the ports of Buenos Aires, Rosario, Santa Fe and Bahía Blanca. Argentina, unlike most other countries, had extensive railways before a road system was built.

The occupation of the pampa was made finally possible by a war against the Indians in 1878-83 which virtually exterminated them. Many of the officers in that campaign were given gifts of land of more than 40,000 hectares each. The pampa had passed into private hands on the old traditional pattern of large estates.

Cattle products—hides, tallow, and salt beef—had been the mainstay of Argentine overseas trade during the whole of the colonial period. In the early 19th century wool challenged the supremacy of cattle. The occupation of the grasslands did not, at first, alter the complexion of the foreign trade; it merely increased its volume. In 1877, however, the first ship with refrigeration chambers made it possible to send frozen beef to England, but the meat of the scrub cattle was too strong for English taste. As a result, pedigree bulls were imported from England and the upgrading of the herds began. The same process was applied to sheep. But the improved herds could only flourish where there were no ticks—prevalent in the N—and throve best where forage crops were available. Argentina adopted as its main forage crop alfalfa (lucerne), a plant like clover which proved extremely suitable on the pampa. It has since been supplemented with barley, oats, rye, maize, sorghum and oilseeds.

A striking thing about the Pampas is the bird life. Flamingoes rise in a pink and white cloud, heron egrets gleam white against the blue sky, pink spoonbills dig in the mud and rheas stalk in the distance. Most fascinating are the oven birds, the *horneros*, which build oven-shaped nests six times as big as themselves on the top of telegraph and fence posts.

To sum up, the transformation of the pampa has had two profound effects. Because its newly-created riches flowed out and its needs flowed in mainly through Buenos Aires, that port grew from comparative insignificance into one of the great cities in the world. Also, the transformation of the Humid Pampa led, through immigration, to a vast predominance of the European strain. The first immigrants settled NW of Santa Fe in 1856. Between 1857 and 1930 total immigration was over six million, almost all from Europe. The process has continued; Italians have been by far the most numerous, followed by Spaniards, and then, far behind, groups of other Europeans and Latin Americans. British and North Americans normally came as stockbreeders, technicians and business executives.

**The Argentine People** In the Federal Capital and Province of Buenos Aires, where almost 40% of the population lives, the people are almost exclusively of European origin. In the far northern provinces, colonized from neighbouring countries, at least half the people are *mestizos* though they form about 15% of the population of the whole country. In the highlands of the northwest, in the

Chaco, Misiones and in the south, there are still a few pure Indians.

In 1990 the population was 32,880,000. Some 85% are urban and 40% live in cities of 100,000 or more. Population growth: 1.4%; urban growth, 1.1%. Death rate per thousand: 9.0; infantile mortality per thousand live births, 32; birth rate, 20.0. It is estimated that 12.8% are foreign born and generally of European origin. About 96% can read and write.

Not surprisingly, the traditional image of the Argentine is that of the *gaucho*; *gauchismo* has been a powerful influence in literature, sociology and folklore, and is celebrated each year in the week before the "Day of Tradition", 10 November.

**The Economy** Argentina is one of the more highly developed countries of the region and is potentially one of the richest farming countries in the world. The importance of agriculture and livestock production is shown by the fact that this sector still provides about 70% of export earnings with sales of cereals, oilseeds, meat and processed foodstuffs. Although Argentina has lost its dominant position as an exporter of cereals and beef, it has great resources in relation to its population. Per capita income is therefore relatively high. Agriculture, livestock, forestry and fishing account for about 15% of gdp. There has been a shift from livestock to crop production since the 1960s in line with changes in relative prices and the introduction of new technology which has sharply increased crop yields. Cereals account for a substantial proportion of crop production, with 11m hectares under cultivation in the late 1980s, of which about 5.5m were sown to wheat and produced about 10m tonnes a year. The area sown to oilseeds has risen steeply, now exceeding that of wheat, and producing about 11m tonnes of soyabeans and sunflower seed a year. Livestock, faced with stiff competition abroad from other exporting countries, has declined in importance. The cattle stock fell from around 57m head in the late 1970s to 46m in 1989. Exports declined but annual domestic beef consumption stayed high at about 83 kg per person.

The manufacturing sector has developed behind high import protection barriers; it accounts for a quarter of gdp and benefits from increased agricultural activity, so that natural resource-based and labour-intensive industries such as food processing, textiles and clothing are reasonably dynamic. Food processing and beverages account for a quarter of manufacturing output and a fifth of industrial employment, while they are the second largest foreign exchange earners after farming. Metal working, engineering and the steel industry were depressed in the 1980s as inflation surged, dampening domestic demand and creating investment uncertainties. In the construction industry, output halved.

Energy development has been a priority with emphasis on hydro and nuclear power sources to reduce dependence upon thermal power. Liquid fuels supply 44% and natural gas 31% of energy consumption, while hydroelectricity is only 13%. By the end of the century it is planned to reduce liquid fuels' share to 37% and raise natural gas to 35%. Argentina is virtually self-sufficient in oil and there is an exportable surplus of natural gas and petroleum derivatives. The country's hydroelectric potential lies on the rivers Paraná and Uruguay in the north and on the network of rivers in Río Negro and Neuquén provinces. However, severe drought in the late 1980's reduced output from hydroelectricity plants from half to only a third of total electricity generation, while thermal plants increased their share from 40% to 55%, with nuclear power plants supplying the balance.

Extremely high rates of inflation were recorded in the 1980s through a combination of large fiscal deficits, monetary expansion and a high velocity of circulation. These were difficult to contain because of structural imbalances in the economy arising from supply shortages caused by inadequate levels of investment and inefficiencies in both the public and private sectors. As the economy reached hyperinflation at a rate of 1,129% in the twelve months to June 1985, the

government introduced a stabilization programme known as the Austral Plan. This included a price and wage freeze, a new currency, the Austral, and attempted to cut the fiscal deficit by raising tax revenues and suspending financing of the deficit by the central bank. The initial positive results were weakened by the failure to cut the fiscal deficit and within 18 months 3-digit inflation had returned.

The economic crisis deepened as management of public finances deteriorated, leading to hyperinflation and a sharp contraction in output and investment as confidence was eroded and the economy became increasingly dollarized. Domestic government debt rose from 1% of gdp in 1988 to 10% in 1989 under the burden of mounting losses from inefficient public enterprises. The new Government which took office in July 1989, attempted to curb hyperinflation by cutting spending and raising revenues, closing or privatizing state companies and banks, eliminating price controls reducing tariff and non-tariff trade barriers, tax reform and open market operations designed to stabilize the economy. Structural economic reform initially brought further recession, unemployment and declining living standards.

The external debt rose sharply by an annual average of 35% in 1978-82 to nearly US$60bn in the late 1980s, making Argentina the third largest debtor in the region. Several debt rescheduling agreements were negotiated with commercial bank creditors together with new loans and IMF financing facilities. Several World Bank loans were granted for restructuring a number of economic sectors, such as agriculture and foreign trade, but agreements with all creditors repeatedly collapsed as the Government failed to implement fully its policy commitments. By the early 1990s, Argentina was seriously in arrears to commercial banks although arrears to multilateral agencies had been cleared. The Government sought to reduce its commercial bank commitments by cancelling debt through privatization: abut US$7bn was eliminated in 1990 and a further US$8-12 bn was planned for 1991.

**Government**   The country's official name is La República Argentina (RA), the Argentine Republic. The form of government has traditionally been a representative, republican federal system. Of the two legislative houses, the Senate has 46 seats, and the Chamber of Deputies 254. By the 1853 Constitution (amended in 1880) the country is divided into a Federal Capital (the city of Buenos Aires), 22 Provinces and the National Territory of Tierra del Fuego, Antarctica and South Atlantic Islands. Each Province has its own Senate and Chamber of Deputies. The municipal government of the Federal Capital is exercised by a Mayor appointed by the President with the approval of the Senate.

**Communications**   Argentina has only four good seaports: Buenos Aires, La Plata, Rosario and Bahía Blanca. The two great rivers flowing southward into the Plata, the Paraná and the Uruguay, are not very reliable shipping routes. The Colorado and the Negro rivers in northern Patagonia are navigable by small vessels only. Internal air services are highly developed.

Most of Argentina is served by about 140,000 km. of road, but only 30% are paved and a further 25% improved. Even so, the network carries 80% of freight tonnage and 82% of medium and long-distance passengers. The 43,100 km. of railway line, owned mostly by British companies until they were taken over by the State in 1948, carry less than 10% of passengers and freight, and are very heavily subsidized.

**Music and Dance**   Buenos Aires contains a third of the country's population and its music is the Tango. Indeed to the outside world there is no other Argentine music. Although also sung and played, the Tango was born as a dance just before the turn of the 20th century. The exact moment of the birth was not recorded by any contemporary observer and continues to be a matter of great controversy, though the roots can be traced. The name "Tango" predates the dance and was given to the carnivals of the black inhabitants of the Río de la Plata in the early l9th century. These were gradually taken over by whites, as the black population declined into insignificance. However, the name "Tango Americano" was also given to the Habanera (a Cuban descendent of the English Country Dance) which became the rage in Spain and bounced back into the Río de la Plata in the middle of the 19th centry, not only as a fashionable dance, together with the polka, mazurka, waltz and cuadrille, but also as a song form in the very popular "Zarzuelas", or Spanish operettas. However the Habanera led not a double, but a triple life, by also infiltrating the lowest levels of society directly from Cuba via sailors who arrived in the ports of Montevideo and Buenos Aires. Here it encountered the Milonga, originally a Gaucho song style, but by 1880 a dance, especially popular with the so-called "Compadritos" and "Orilleros", who frequented the port area and its brothels, whence the Argentine Tango emerged around the turn of the century to dazzle the populace with its brilliant, personalized footwork, which could not be accomplished without the partners staying glued together. As a dance it became the rage and, as the infant recording industry grew by leaps and bounds, it also became popular as a song and an instrumental genre, with the original violins and flutes being eclipsed by the little *bandoneón* button accordion, then being imported from Germany. In 1911 the new dance took Paris by storm and returned triumphant to Buenos Aires. It achieved both respectability and notoriety, becoming a global phenomenon after the First World War. The golden voice of the renowned Carlos Gardel soon gave a wholly new dimension to the music of the Tango until his death in 1935. After losing some popularity in Argentina, it came to the forefront again under Perón, who decreed that 50% of all music played on the radio must be Argentine, only to suffer a second decline in the face of rock music over the past two decades. To see the Tango and Milonga danced in Buenos Aires today, you need to visit one of the clubs or *confiterías* where it is specially featured, see Buenos Aires **Nightclubs and Folklore.** Apart from Carlos Gardel, other great names connected with the Tango are Francisco Canaro, Osvaldo Pugliese and Astor Piazzola, who has modernized it by fusion with jazz styles (*tango novo*). Whilst the majority of Argentine young people will agree that the Tango represents the soul of Buenos Aires, don't expect them to dance it or listen to it. They are more likely to be interested in the country's indigenous rock music.

If the Tango represents the soul of Buenos Aires, this is not the case in the rest of the country. The provinces have a very rich and attractive heritage of folk dances, mainly for couples, with arms held out and fingers clicked or handkerchiefs waved, with the "Paso Valseado" as the basic step. Descended from the Zamacueca, and therefore a cousin of the Chilean Cueca and Peruvian Marinera, is the slow and stately Zamba, where the handkerchief is used to greatest effect. Equally popular throughout most of the country are the faster Gato, Chacarera and Escondido. These were the dances of the Gaucho and their rhythm evokes that of a cantering horse. Guitar and the *bombo* drum provide the accompaniment. Particularly spectacular is the Malambo, where the Gaucho shows off his dextrous footwork, the spurs of his boots adding a steely note to the rhythm.

Different regions of the country have their own specialities. The music of Cuyo in the west is sentimental and very similar to that of neighbouring Chile, with its Cuecas for dance and Tonadas for song. The northwest on the other hand is Andean, with its musical culture closer to that of Bolivia, particularly on the Puna, where the Indians play the *quena* and *charango* and sound mournful notes on the great long *erke*. Here the dances are Bailecitos and Carnavalitos, while the songs are Vidalitas and the extraordinary high pitched Bagualas, the very essence of primeval pain. In the northeastern provinces of Corrientes and Misiones, the music shares cultural similarities with Paraguay. The Polca and Galopa are danced and the local Chamamé is sung, to the accordion or the harp, the style being sentimental. Santiago del Estero is the heartland of the Chacarera and the lyrics are often part Spanish and part Quichua, a local dialect of the Andean Quechua language. Down in the Province of Buenos Aires you are more likely to hear the Gauchos singing their Milongas, Estilos and Cifras and challenging each other to a Payada or rhymed duel. Argentina experienced a great folk revival in the 50's and 60's and some of the most celebrated groups are still drawing enthusiastic audiences today. These groups include Los Chalchaleros and Los Fronterizos and the perennial virtuoso singers and guitarists, Eduardo Falú and Atahualpa Yupanqui.

---

## BUENOS AIRES AND THE PAMPAS (1)

**Apart from the capital itself, with its museums, theatre, public buildings, parks and shopping, this region contains the Tigre Delta (waterways, lunch spots) and Atlantic coastal resorts. Of these the most famous is Mar del Plata.**

The Río de la Plata, or River Plate, on which Buenos Aires lies, is not a river but an estuary or great basin, 160 km. long and from 37 to 90 km. wide, into which flow the Ríos Paraná and Uruguay and their tributaries. It is muddy and shallow and the passage of ocean vessels is only made possible by continuous dredging. The tides are of little importance, for there is only a 1.2 metre rise and fall at spring tides. The depth of water is determined by the direction of the wind and the flow of the Paraná and Uruguay rivers.

***Buenos Aires***, the capital, spreads over some 200 square km. The population of the Federal Capital itself is about 2.9 million, but the population of greater Buenos Aires (including the suburbs in the province of Buenos Aires) is estimated at 12.2 millions.

**NB** In spite of its name (good air), extreme humidity and unusual pollen conditions can affect asthma sufferers if they stay over an extended period of time (i.e. after a month or so).

Buenos Aires has been virtually rebuilt since the beginning of this century and very few of the old buildings are left. In the centre, which has maintained the original lay-out since its foundation, the streets are often very narrow and are mostly one-way.

The heart of the city, now as in colonial days, is the Plaza de Mayo, with the historic Cabildo, the Town Hall, where the movement for independence from Spain was first planned; the pink Casa Rosada (Presidential Palace); the Municipalidad (City Hall); and the Cathedral, where San Martín, the father of Argentine independence, is buried. (For a note on the Mothers of the Plaza de Mayo, **see page 59**). Within a few blocks are the fashionable church of Nuestra Señora de la Merced, the Biblioteca Nacional and the main banks and business houses.

Running W from the Plaza, the Avenida de Mayo leads 1½ km. to the Congress building in the Plaza del Congreso. Halfway it crosses the wide Avenida Nueve de Julio. A tall obelisk commemorating the 400th anniversary of the city's founding stands at its centre in the Plaza de la República, surrounded by sloping lawns. The Av. Nueve de Julio itself, one of the widest in the world, consists of three carriageways separated by wide grass borders. In the N the Av. Nueve de Julio meets the Avenida del Libertador, the principal way out of the city to the N and W.

N of the Plaza de Mayo is the shopping, theatre and commercial area. The city's traditional shopping centre, Calle Florida (with excellent newsstands), is in this district. This is the popular down-town meeting place, particularly in the late afternoon; it is reserved for pedestrians only and the buskers in the 500 block are

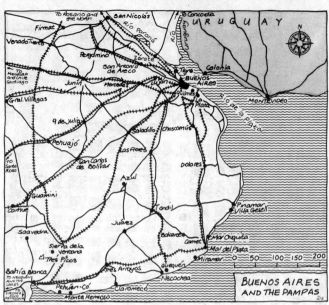

BUENOS AIRES
AND THE PAMPAS

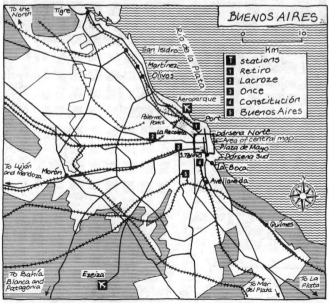

BUENOS AIRES

| T | stations |
| 1 | Retiro |
| 2 | Lacroze |
| 3 | Once |
| 4 | Constitución |
| 5 | Buenos Aires |

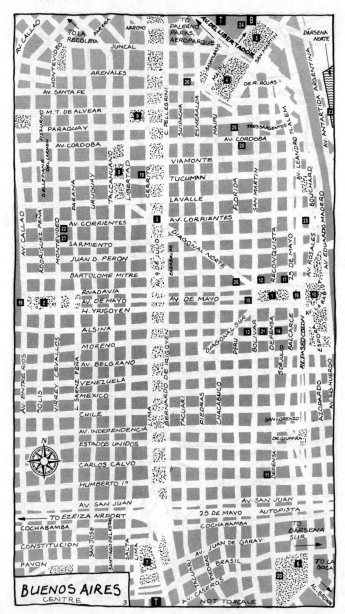

BUENOS AIRES
CENTRE

worth visiting. Another shopping street is Avenida Santa Fe, which crosses Florida at the Plaza San Martín; it has become as touristy and as expensive as Florida. Avenida Corrientes is the entertainment centre, a street of theatres, restaurants, cafés and night life. Close by, in Calle Lavalle (part reserved to pedestrians) and in nearby streets, there are numerous cinemas and many good and reasonable restaurants.

E of the Plaza de Mayo, behind the Casa Rosada, a broad avenue, Paseo Colón, runs S towards San Telmo and the picturesque old port district known as the Boca, where the Riachuelo flows into the Plata (reached by bus 152 from Av. L. N. Alem, or bus 29 from Plaza de Mayo, in the centre, US$0.10). It was here, near Parque Lezama, that Pedro de Mendoza founded the first Buenos Aires. For a tour of the Boca, start at Plaza Vuelta de Rocha, near Av. Pedro de Mendoza and Dr. Del Valle Iberlucea, then walk up Caminito, the little pedestrian street used as a theatre and an art market. Visit the Museo de Bellas Artes de la Boca (**see page 66**). The Boca, mostly Italian, has its own distinctive life and parts of it are becoming touristy, but the area, with the adjacent industrial and meat-packing suburb of Avellaneda across the high Avellaneda bridge, is generally dirty and run down, and assaults are frequent.

One of the few places which still have late colonial and Rosista buildings is the *barrio* of San Telmo, S of Plaza de Mayo, centred on Plaza Dorrego along the slope which marks the old beach of the Río de la Plata. It is a recognized artistic centre, with plenty of cafés and a pleasant atmosphere; and there is a regular Saturday and Sunday morning antiques market at the Plaza Dorrego (**see page 63**). The 29 bus connects the Boca with San Telmo, and passes the end of Calle Florida, the shopping street. E of San Telmo on the far side of the docks, the spacious Av. Costanera runs along the Plata estuary; the river has retreated leaving a stretch of marshland which forms the **Costanera Sur Wildlife Reserve**, which has several coypu and many types of birds. The entrance is at Av. España Brasil; it opens at 0800 but much can be seen from the road before then (binoculars useful). For details, contact Fundación Vida Silvestre, Defensa 245, 6 piso, 1075 Buenos Aires, T 331-4864.

The theatre retains its hold on the people of Buenos Aires. About 20 commercial theatres play the year round. Recommended is the Teatro Liceo. There are many amateur theatres. You are advised to book as early as possible for a seat at a concert, ballet, or opera.

**NB** Street numeration: numbers start from the dock side rising from east to west, but north/south streets are numbered from Av. Rivadavia, 1 block N of Av. de Mayo rising in both directions. Calle Juan D. Perón used to be called Cangallo; M.T. de Alvear used to be Charcas.

## Principal Public Buildings

**Casa de Gobierno** on the E side of the Plaza de Mayo, and called the Casa Rosada because it is pink, contains the offices of the President of the Republic. (The Foreign Minister's offices are at the Palacio de San Martín, Plaza San Martín). The Casa Rosada is notable for its statuary, the rich furnishing of its halls and for its libraries, but it is not at present possible to visit the interior. The Museo de los Presidentes is on the lower floors (see under **Museums**).

### Buenos Aires: Key to Map

1. Plaza de Mayo; 2. Plaza del Congreso; 3. Plaza de la República, and Obelisk; 4. Plaza San Martín; 5. Plaza de la Fuerza Aérea; 6. Parque Lezama; 7. Plaza Constitución; 8. Plaza Lavalle; 9. Plaza Libertad; 10. Parque Colón; 11. Plaza Dorrego; 12. Cathedral; 13. San Ignacio de Loyola; 14. San Francisco; 15. Cabildo and Museum; 16. Casa Rosada and Museo de los Presidentes; 17. Municipalidad; 18. Palacio del Congreso; 19. Teatro Colón; 20. Museo Histórico Nacional; 21. Museo de la Ciudad; 22. Teatro Municipal General San Martín and Museo Municipal de Arte Moderno; 23. "Presidente Sarmiento" museum ship; 24. Museo Nacional Ferroviario at Retiro Station; 25. Central Post Office; 26 National Tourist Office (3 locations); 27. Buenos Aires Municipal Tourist Office; 28. Railway booking and information office.

The **Cabildo** on the W side of the same Plaza, the old town hall, was put up in 1711 but has been rebuilt several times. Its original structure, fittings and furniture were replaced in 1940 and it was declared a national monument. See under **Museums**.

**Old Congress Hall** on the S of the Square, built 1863, is a National Monument. It has been encircled and built over by a palatial bank building. Open Thursday.

**Palacio del Congreso** (Congress Hall) to the SW at the far end of Avenida de Mayo, of great size and in Greco-Roman architecture, is the seat of the legislature. It contains the Senate and the Chamber of Deputies. There is limited accommodation for the public at the sittings. It is open from 1700 onwards. Queue in front of desk assigned for minor parties, there they take your passport and give you a ticket for your seat and a pink slip to reclaim your passport. You may stay as long as you wish, but must remain seated. A guided tour (in English) can be taken on Mon., Tues. and Fri. at 1100 and 1700 when Congress is not sitting.

**Teatro Colón**, one of the world's great opera houses, overlooks Avenida 9 de Julio, with its main entrance on Libertad, between Tucumán and Viamonte. The Colón's interior is, resplendent with red plush and gilt; the stage is huge, and salons, dressing rooms and banquet halls are equally sumptuous. Open daily to visitors 1200-1800 (but not always), guided tours hourly, Mon.-Fri. 1000-1300 and 1400-1700, Sat. 1000-1300 (English/German, six a day on the hour, US$0.60), closed Jan.-Feb. check times in advance, T 35-5414/15/16. Male visitors must wear jacket and tie to gala performances, but dress smartly anyway. Tickets, sold three days before performance, on the Calle Tucumán side of the theatre. The season runs from April to early December, and there are concert performances most days. The cheapest seat is about US$25, although there are free performances most days at 1800 in the Sala Dorado—check programme in the visitors' entrance.

The **Bolsa de Comercio**, built in 1916, a handsome building in Calle 25 de Mayo, corner Sarmiento, contains a stock exchange, a grain market and a general produce market.

## Churches

All historic churches are open 1630-1900; some at 0900-1100 also.

The **Cathedral**, Rivadavia 437, on the N of Plaza de Mayo is flanked by the former residence of the Archbishop. On this site was built the first church in Buenos Aires, which after reconstruction in 1677 collapsed in 1753 and the rebuilding was not completed until 1823. The eighteenth century towers were never rebuilt, so that the architectural proportions have suffered. A frieze upon the Greek façade represents Joseph and his brethren. The tomb (1878) of the Liberator, General José de San Martín, is imposing.

The **Church of San Ignacio de Loyola**, at Calles Alsina and Bolívar 225, founded in 1710, is the oldest Colonial building in Buenos Aires. It has two lofty towers. The **San Francisco**, Calles Alsina and Defensa, controlled by the Franciscan Order, was inaugurated in 1754 and given a new façade in 1808.

**La Merced**, Calles Juan D. Perón and Reconquista 207, was founded 1604 and rebuilt 1732. One of the altars has a wooden figure of Our Lord, carved during the 18th century by an Indian in Misiones. It has one of the best organs in the country, and one of the few fine carillons of bells in Buenos Aires.

**Santo Domingo**, on Defensa and Av. Belgrano, was founded in 1756. During the British attack on Buenos Aires in 1806 some of Whitelocke's soldiers took refuge in the church. The local forces bombarded it (some of the hits can still be seen on one of the towers); the British capitulated and their regimental colours were preserved in the church. Adjoining is the Salón Belgraniano (with relics of General Belgrano and much colonial furniture). There are summer evening concerts in the church; check times.

**El Pilar**, Junín 1904, is a jewel of colonial architecture dating from 1717, in a delightful setting of public gardens. An exceptionally fine wooden image of San Pedro de Alcántara, attributed to the famous 17th century Spanish sculptor Alonso Cano, is preserved in a side chapel on the left.

Next to it is the **Cemetery of the Recoleta**, entrance at Junín 1822 near Museo de Bellas Artes (see below), is one of the sights of Buenos Aires (open 0700-1800). Evita Perón is now buried there; her tomb is now marked besides the inscription, Familia Duarte—guards will point out the grave. "A Doric portico gives on to the main, paved, cypress-lined avenue of a little city of the dead. At the end of the avenue there is a great bronze statue of the resurrected Saviour; on either side, hard up against each other, like houses in a street, there are the family vaults of the Argentine patricians. Every possible style of architecture is represented." G.S. Fraser, in *News from Latin America*. Bus 17 on Esmeralda, to Recoleta, then 10 mins walk. On Sundays there is a good craft market near the entrance. A new cultural centre has been opened alongside the Recoleta cemetery: exhibitions, concerts, films. Another well known cemetery is that of La Chacarita, reached by Subte to the Federico Lacroze station, which has the much-visited, lovingly-tended tombs of Juan Perón and Carlos Gardel, the tango singer.

Visitors may like to know about the following religious establishments: The **Holy Cross**, Calle Estados Unidos 3150, established by the Passionists. **St John's Cathedral** (Anglican), 25 de Mayo 282 (services, Sun. 0900 in English, 1030 in Spanish), was built half at the expense of the British Government and dedicated in 1831. **St Paul's, St Peter's, St Michael and All Angels** and **St Saviour's** are Anglican places of worship in the suburbs. **St Andrew's**, Calle Belgrano 579, is one of the 8 Scottish Presbyterian churches. The **American Church**, Corrientes 718, is Methodist, built in 1863. Service at 1100. **First Methodist** (American) Church, Av Santa Fe 839, Acassuso.

**German Evangelical Church**, Esmeralda 162. **Swedish Church**, Azopardo 1422. The **Armenian Cathedral** of St Gregory the Illuminator at the Armenian Centre, and the **Russian Orthodox Cathedral** of The Holy Trinity (Parque Lezama) are interesting.

**Synagogues** Anshe Galitzia at Uriburu 234; Congregación Emanuel (reformed sect), Tronador 1455, take bus 140 from Av. Córdoba to Alvarez Tomás block 1600, then turn right into Tronador.

## Parks and Squares

**Parque Lezama**, Calles Defensa and Brasil, originally one of the most beautiful in the city, has been somewhat vandalized. Very lively on Sunday. It has an imposing statue of Pedro de Mendoza, the founder of the original city in 1535. The tradition is that the first founding took place on this spot. The Museo Histórico Nacional (**see page 66**) is in the park.

The **Palermo Parks** with their magnificent avenues are the city's Bois de Boulogne. They are famous for their rose garden, Andalusian Patio, Japanese garden with fish to feed (admission US$0.05) and the Hipódromo Argentino, the Palermo race course, with seats for 45,000. Opposite the parks are the Botanical and Zoological Gardens (the Palermo Zoo and Japanese Garden are closed on Mondays). Nearby are the Municipal Golf Club, Buenos Aires Lawn Tennis Club, riding clubs and polo field, and the popular Club de Gimnasia y Esgrima (Athletic and Fencing Club). The **Planetarium** (just off Belisario Roldán, in the Park), is open Sat. and Sun. only (March-Nov., 1630, 1800, 1930, Dec.-Feb., 1800, 1930, 2100), entry US$0.22. The official name of the Palermo parks is the Parque Tres de Febrero. Reached by Subte line D. The **Show Grounds** of the Argentine Rural Society, on a site next to Palermo Park, stage the Annual Livestock Exhibition in July.

There is another large and modern race course (one of the best of its kind) with grass track at San Isidro, 25 minutes from the city centre by train or road. The meetings alternate with those at Palermo. There are Saturday and Wednesday races throughout the year, and on certain holidays. Betting is by totalizator only.

The **Municipal Botanical Gardens**, Santa Fe 3951, entrance from Plaza Italia (take Subte, line D), contain characteristic specimens of the world's vegetation. The trees proper to the several provinces of Argentina are brought together in one section. The Gardens are full of stray cats, fed regularly by benevolent local residents. The **Zoo** is next to the Botanical Gardens; it is temporarily closed.

**Plazas** The most interesting is the Plaza de Mayo, containing so many public buildings, where the **Mothers of the Plaza de Mayo** still march, Thursdays at 1530, in remembrance of their children who disappeared during the crisis of the 1970s. Others are the Plaza San Martín, with a monument to San Martín in the centre and, at the N end, a monument to those who fell in the South Atlantic coflict of 1982; the former Plaza Británica, now known as the Plaza de la Fuerza Aérea, with the clock tower presented by British and Anglo-Argentine residents, "a florid Victorian sentinel, royal crest upon its bosom" (frequently vandalized); the Plaza Canadá (in front of the Retiro Station) is a Pacific Northwest Indian totem pole, donated by the Canadian government; the Plaza Lavalle, which has secondhand bookstalls at the Calle Lavalle end; the Plaza del Congreso, the largest in the city, with a waterfall, floodlit at 2145. There is also the great Plaza de la República, with a 67-metre obelisk at the junction between the Diagonal Norte and Avenida Corrientes.

**Warning** Street crime has risen alarmingly since 1988, especially in the tourist season. Be particularly careful when boarding buses. Beware of bagsnatching gangs in parks, markets and in the Subte: they are not violent, but particularly skilful. The most common trick is to spray victims with mustard; an accomplice then cleans you down (and robs you). If you are sprayed, walk straight on. If your passport is stolen, remember to get a new entrada stamp at the Dirección Nacional de Migraciones. Also changing money on the street is fraught with difficulties: stick to the *cambios*.

**Hotels** The Dirección de Turismo fixes maximum and minimum rates for 1, 2 and 3-star hotels, guest houses and inns, but there have been complaints that at 3 stars and below the ratings do not provide very useful guidance. Four and five-star hotels are free to apply any rate they wish. The rates can be taken only as an indication especially since, above 2 stars, hotels charge at the parallel exchange rate, adjusting tariffs daily. All hotels, guest houses, inns and camping sites are graded by the number of beds available, and the services supplied.

5-star hotels in our L/L+ range are: *Libertador*, Av Córdoba y Maipú, T 322 2095, *Plaza*, Plaza San Martín, T 312 6001, *Elevage*, Maipú 960, T 313 2882, *Alvear Palace*, Av Alvear 1891, T 804-4031/4041, an older-style hotel, near Recoleta, with roof garden, shopping gallery, good, *Sheraton*, San Martín 1225, T 311 6311, *Claridge*, Tucumán 535, T 322-7700 *Panamericano*, Carlos Pellegrini 525, T 393 6017, *Bauen*, Callao 346, T 804 1600. Also in our L range, but 4-star are *Bizonte Palace*, M.T. de Alvear y Suipacha, T 311-4751, very good, welcoming, rec. *El Conquistador*, Suipacha 948, T 313 3012, *Rochester*, Esmeralda 542, T 393 9339, front rooms noisy, *Las Américas*, Libertad 1020, T 393 3432, pleasant but overpriced, and *Lafayette*, Reconquista 546, T 393 9081.

There are several 4-star hotels in our A price range: recommended in this bracket is the *Gran King*, Lavalle 560, T 392 4012/4052, helpful, English spoken; also *Wilton Palace*, Callao 1162, T 42 6593, *Torre*, Corrientes 6800, T 552 6034, *Sheltown*, M.T. de Alvear 742, T 312 5070, *Los Dos Chinos*, Brasil 780, T 23 2021. *City*, Bolívar 160, clean, rec.; *Italia Romanelli*, Reconquista 645, T 312-6361; *Gran*, M. T. de Alvear 767, T 312 3001, rundown but clean.

Other hotels: B price range, *Orly*, Paraguay 474, T 312-5344, good location, old fashioned, helpful, has some rooms for 4, arranges tours and taxis; *Bristol*, Cerrito 286, excellent breakfast; *Savoy*, Av. Callao 181, T 490211, friendly and helpful; *Camino Real*, Maipú 572, T 322-3162, pleasant, clean, central. *Victory*, Maipú 880, clean, a/c, modern; *Liberty*, Corrientes 632, T 45 0261, English spoken, luggage stored; *Embajador*, Pellegrini 1181, good; *Central Córdoba*, San Martín 1021, T 311-1175, very central, clean, helpful, quiet, good value, rec.

C range: *San Antonio*, Paraguay 372, with bath, nice atmosphere, clean, rec.; *Eibar*, Florida 328, T 45 7315, breakfast included, quiet, friendly, helpful, rec.; *Regis*, Lavalle 813, T 393-5131, convenient for Manuel Tienda León drop-off point at Lavalle y Pellegrini, good value, nice atmosphere, quiet at back; *Phoenix*, San Martín 780, with bath, "faded gentility", clean, large rooms, use of kitchen, rec.; *Diplomat*, San Martín 918, good, rec.; *Gran Hotel Hispano*, Av. de Mayo 861, spacious, clean, pleasant patio, stores luggage; *Sarmiento Palace*, Sarmiento 1953, clean, comfortable, English spoken; *Novus*, Sarmiento 631 (near Plaza de Mayo), rec. *Waldorf*, Paraguay 450, T 312-2071, price excludes breakfast, clean and comfortable, rec. repeatedly; *Orleans*, Callao 465, clean, small rooms, safe and friendly; *Astoria*, Av. de Mayo 916, friendly, very clean; *Novel*, Av. de Mayo 915, good; *Mundial*, Av. de Mayo 1298, with bath, clean, comfortable; *Concorde*, 25 de Mayo 630, TV and fridge, helpful, comfortable, a/c, rec., best above 8th floor to avoid traffic noise; *Majéstic*, Libertad 121, Subte Lima, colonial, very clean, good value, breakfast included; *Viamonte*, Viamonte 833, clean and helpful; *Super*, Gallo nr. Av Santa Fe (Subte D, Agüero), out of centre, a/c, pleasant.

D range: *Tres Sargentos*, Tres Sargentos 345, clean, secure, dark rooms; *Central Argentino*, Av. del Libertador 174, secure, clean, near Retiro stations, rec; *Frossard*, Tucumán 686, inexpensive, hot showers, but not quiet; *Apolo*, Tucumán 951, friendly, central; *Gran Hotel de la Paix*, Rivadavia 1150, old but good, clean, quiet, a/c; *Marbella*, Av. de Mayo 1261, clean, friendly, quiet, fans, newly decorated, English spoken, highly rec.; *La Argentina*, Av. de Mayo 860, with bath, friendly, central, rec.; *Suipacha Palace*, Suipacha 18, old-fashioned, clean, spacious, charming; *España*, Tacuari 80, with bath, helpful, hot water, lift, rec., T 30-5541/4; *Uruguay*, Tacuari 83, central, clean, friendly, good value, rec.; *Ayacucho Palace*, Ayacucho 1408, 10 mins from centre bus 10, T 825-0943, 2 star, better value than central hotels, rec.; *Hispano Argentino*, Lima Oeste 1483, T 235855/267562, some rooms with bath , clean, quiet, convenient; *Ecuador*, Adolfo Alsina 2820, nr. Plaza Once, rec.; *Gran Vía* , Sarmiento 1450, T 40-5763, with bath, clean, friendly.

E range: *Bahía*, Corrientes y Libertad, hot showers, pleasant, clean, safe, central but very noisy; *Micki*, Talcahuano 362, clean, good value; *Sarmiento*, Sarmiento 1162, clean, central, back rooms quieter; *Mediterráneo*, Rodríguez Peña 149 basic, central, helpful, safe, clean, some rooms are dark, shared showers; *Sportsman*, Rivadavia 1426, T 38-8021/2, clean, old fashioned, cheaper without bath, rec (10% discount for ISIC and youth card holders); *O'Rei*, Lavalle 733, cheap, basic, security problems, popular; Av. de Mayo 1400, good, safe; *San Luis*, Av. de Mayo 1168, T 38-0398, and *Petit Mitre*, B. Mitre 4315, T 981-7768, both offer 10% discount to ISIC and youth card holders; *Universal*, 25 de Mayo 740, hot water, clean, basic; *Mendoza*, 25 de Mayo 674, dirty, friendly, cheap, hot shower, many similar in same street; *Maipú*, Maipú 735, often crowded, clean, friendly, basic, T 322-5142; *De France*, San José 9 near Sáenz Peña Subte, clean, hot water; *Patagones*, B. de Yrigoyen 1692, T 28-6775, friendly, safe to leave luggage, rec.; *Cibeles*, Virrey Cevallos, 2 blocks from Congreso, T 37-3143, with bath, safe (next to police HQ). *Bolívar*, in Bolívar (San Telmo), with bath, clean; *Youth Hostel*, Brasil 675 near Constitucíon station, T 362-9133, F p.p. with YHA card; doors closed 1200-1800 and from midnight (though not always observed). Women should be aware that they could attract unwelcome attention near Constitución station as prostitutes operate there. Otherwise, this area is a short walk to centre and convenient for boats to Uruguay and trains to the N.

One can rent flats on a daily basis (US$50 a day) in *Edificios Esmeralda*, Marcelo T. de Alvear 842, T 31-3929, cleaning included. Facilities for up to 6 persons; also Edificio Suipacha, Suipacha 1235. Weekly renting at *Edificio Charcas*, MT de Alvear 776, rec. (visiting singers at the Colón often stay there). Also *Aspen Apartment Hotel*, Esmeralda 933; *Edificio Lemonde*, San Martín 839, rec.; *Residencial Trianon*, Callao y Alvear, 3-bed apartment.

**NB** All the rates quoted are subject to alteration, particularly in view of exchange rate fluctuations (see **Cost of Living**, page 202). It should be noted that for the most part they are the basic or minimum rates. Room tax is 15% and is not always included in the price. Check when booking into a hotel whether breakfast is included or not. Most hotels charge at least 10% extra for payment by credit card. Air conditioning is a must in high summer, but be prepared for frequent power cuts. Many of the cheaper hotels in the central area give large reductions on the daily rate for long stays. Hotels with red-green lights or marked *Albergue Transitório* are hotels for homeless lovers.

**Tips** In spite of the high service charge it is customary to tip 10% of the total bill; porters at hotels expect a tip—about US$0.50 per day of stay or service rendered. Hairdressers expect 10% of the bill, cinema ushers about US$0.20.

**Camping** Closest camp site to the city is about 15 km. out at Lomas de Zamora, US$3 p.p. per night, inc. swimming pool, take bus 141 from Plaza Italia to Puerta La Noria then No. 540 to Villa Albertini which passes the entrance; information on all sites is available from the Automóvil Club Argentino and from the national tourist information office. Those travelling by car might try at the German Sports Club, Sociedad Alemana de Gimnasia, 9 de Julio and Av Márquez, Villa Ballester, 30 km. N of centre, cheap, or free. Easy to reach by Línea Suárez bus 90, get off at Chilavert.

Sleeping bags and tents direct from the factory at Acoyte 1622, T 855-0619, English, German spoken, reasonable prices, open 0800-1200, 1430-1900, Saturday 0900-1300. Good equipment and fuel from Fugate, Gascón 232 (off Rivadavia 8000 block), also repairs equipment. Good camping stores also at Guatemala 5908 and 5451. Camping gas available at Todo Gas, Paraná 550, and El Pescador, Paraguay y Libertad.

**Restaurants** "The Buenos Aires Herald" publishes a handy *Guide to Good Eating in Buenos Aires* (with a guide to local wines) by Dereck Foster. Eating out in Buenos Aires is very good but is getting more expensive, especially in the posher places which charge in dollars. In such places, a meal in early 1991 cost US$30 and up p.p.; more modest places were charging US$15-20 p.p. Many cheaper restaurants are "tenedor libre", eat as much as you like for a fixed price. Five of the best restaurants are: *Catalinas*, Reconquista 875 (very expensive though); *Francis Malman*, Honduras 4963; *Blab*, Florida 325; *Au Bec Fin*, Vicente López 1825; and *Montmartre*, Av Libertador 3302, La Lucila.

Other excellent restaurants include *Clark's*, Sarmiento 645, in old English outfitter's shop (also at Junín 1777), well cooked food, very expensive; *La Emiliana*, Av. Corrientes 1443, excellent, rec.; *El Imparcial*, H. Irigoyen 1201, first-class service (Spanish); *El Fogón de Bonilla*, rustic style, Av. L.N. Alem 673 between Tucumán and Viamonte, good, another branch at Callao 1121; *La Chacra*, Córdoba 941 between Suipacha and 8 de Julio, expensive but good; *Portobello*, J.E. Uriburu 1629, romantic atmosphere, fine quality, modest prices. *Claridge Hotel Grill*, excellent for venison and wild boar, haunt of top executives and English community, expensive but worth it. "Business" restaurants, *ABC*, Lavalle 545, traditional, good value; *El Faisán*, Corrientes 260, and *Bolsa de Comercio*, 25 de Mayo 359, downstairs at the Stock Exchange. *Griffins*, Uruguay 1264, good salad bar; *Sabot*, 25 de Mayo 756, good business lunches.

Typical Argentine restaurants: *La Estancia*, Lavalle 941, popular with business people, excellent grills and service, expensive; *La Cabaña*, Entre Ríos 436, old tavern style, excellent food, pricey. The typical parrilla (mixed grill) is a speciality of *Tranquera*, in Palermo Park; also in Palermo is *La Placita*, on Plaza Recado (5-6 blocks from Subte D, Plaza Italia station) fine atmosphere and good food; *Viga*, J.D. Perón 1116, excellent value; *Los Troncos*, Suipacha 732, good grills, expensive. *Pippo*, Montevideo 341, large pasta house, good simple food, fast service, very popular; *Chiquilín*, Montevideo y Sarmiento, pasta and meat, good value; *Mercado del Puerto*, Av. Córdoba 518, warmly rec. for grills. *Pichín No 1* or *No 2*, Paraná y Sarmiento, for gigantic asado de tira; *La Rural*, Suipacha 453, rec. for parrillada and bife de lomo, English-speaking head waiter is excellent; *El Repecho de San Telmo*, Carlos Calvo 242, excellent, expensive, reserve in advance. *El Apero*, Av. Córdoba 820, very good bife de lomo; *El Comité*, Carlos Calvo 375, very good, not too dear; *Nazarenas*, Reconquista 1132, good for beef, excellent atmosphere, rec.

There are good restaurants all along Calles Lavalle and Maipú. *Emporio de las Papas Fritas*, Maipú 431, good parrillas, good value; *El Palacio de la Papa Frita*, Lavalle 735 and 954, Corrientes 1612, 10% discount for ISIC and youth card holders; *Brizzi*, Lavalle 445, business lunches, good but not cheap; *Los Inmortales*, Lavalle 746, specializes in pizza, highly rec.; there are other locations; some serve *à la carte* dishes which are plentiful, and are open from 1500-2000 when most other restaurants are closed. There are also several economical restaurants along Florida and on Corrientes 1400-1500 block. Several good restaurants on Defensa, between Alsina and Plaza de Mayo. *El Rocío*, Salta 151, 1 block from Av. de Mayo, excellent, cheap, everything on menu is good, popular, good value.

Good restaurants near Teatro Colón include *Posta del Gaucho*, Pellegrini 625, accepts Visa. Several good places near entrance to Recoleta cemetery: *Munich Recoleta*, Junín 1871, good; *Café Victoria*, Roberto M. Ortiz 1865, typical of the Recoleta area; on same street, *Don Juan*, No 1827, and *Lola*, No 1805, good pasta and fish but expensive. The Costanera along the river front is lined with little eating places: *El Rancho Inn* is best, try also *Happening* and *Los Años Locos*.

Seafood: *El Pulpo*, Tucumán 400, great variety, big portions, moderate prices; *El Gato que Pesca*, Rodríguez Peña 159, good value; *El Pescadito*, P. de Mendoza 1483, rec. for pasta and sea-food. *Ostramar*, Santa Fe 3495 y Lunín Alvarez (Subte station Canning, then walk back towards town), good quality fish.

Italian: *Pizzería Los Idolos*, Suipacha 436, said to be the best pizzería in the city; *Broccolino*, Esmeralda 776, excellent, very popular, try pechuguitas; *Il Gran Caruso*, Medrano 950, Palermo; *Mama Liberata*, Av. Medrano 974, Palermo, excellent; Italian restaurant at *Sheraton* hotel, good service. *Pizzería Don Corleone*, Reconquista 924, very good and popular, 10% discount for ISIC and youth card holders; *La Casona del Nonno*, Lavalle 827, very good pasta, offers similar discount.

Typical Boca restaurant: *Spadavecchia*, Necochea 1180, set menu with wine US$8, seats some 500 people, dancing. There are several others in the same street. They all serve antipasto, pasta and chicken; no point in looking for beef here. All bands are loud; offputting for those with sensitive ears. Nearby is *Restaurant Napolitano*, which serves excellent set lunches of seafood, good atmosphere and young wine. Try a family restaurant at corner of Necochea and Suárez known as *Cantina Los Tres Amigos*; live music from 2130, complete meal with wine under US$6 each, excellent, about 4 blocks from commercial centre. The seafood restaurant *La Barca*, on river bank near Avellaneda bridge, rec.; also rec. for seafood and good value, *Viejo Puente*, Almirante Brown 1499.

Swedish food at *Swedish Club*, Tacuari 147, open to non-members. Hungarian, *Budapest*, San Martín 1681, cheap. *Chez Moi*, Av. San Juan 1223 (T 270890), French, and Iranian food on Fri. and Sat. lunch, reservations necessary.

Vegetarian: *Granix*, Florida 126, "tenedor libre" US$7.50, open lunchtime Mon.-Fri. *Ever Green* is a chain of "tenedor libre" vegetarian restaurants with branches at Paraná 746, Tucumán 666, good, Chinese and Argentine, take-away, Sarmiento 1728, Cabildo 2979 and Maipú 338 (Pte Saavedra); *Apio's*, Sucre 2425 at Cabildo, vegetarian buffet; *La Primavera*, Maipú 495, cheap, 10% discount for ISIC and youth card holders; *Za Zen*, Talcahuano 434, T 407844, lunch and dinner; *Sr. Sol*, Billingshurst 1070 (p.m. except Sat., Sun., lunch also, closed Mon.); *Yin Yang*, Paraguay 858 (health-food shop too, lunch only, closed Sun.); *El Girasol*, Pellegrini 829, excellent lunches; *La Esquina de las Flores*, Córdoba 1599, excellent value, also good health-food shop. *Verde Esmeralda*, Esmeralda 511 (nr. Av Corrientes); *Giardino*, Suipacha 429 and Lavalle 835 (in arcade), 1st floor, rec., set meal US$6, take-away also; *La Huerta*, Paraguay 445, T 311-0470, macrobiotic, rec.; *La Huerta II*, Lavalle 895 y Suipa, 2nd floor, "tenedor libre".

Oriental: *Chung Kin*, Calle Paraguay, near Maipú, Chinese, cheap set lunch; *Los 9 Platos*, B. Mitre 1177, Chinese, good, cheap, 3-course set menu, closed Sun.; *Macau*, Suipacha 477, good Chinese buffet; *Doll*, Suipacha 544, cheap, Chinese "tenedor libre"; *China Doll*, Paraná 342, self-service, rec.; *Yuki*, Venezuela 2145, excellent Japanese cuisine; *El Balcón*, Carlos Pellegrini 525 (Hotel Panamericano), Japanese, very good.

*Pumper-nic* is a chain of rather pricey fast food restaurants. *The Embers*, Lavalle 905, fast food, 10% discount for ISIC and youth card holders. Try also restaurants in Supercoop stores at Sarmiento 1431, Lavalle 2530, Piedras y Rivadavia and Rivadvia 5708.

Cheap meals at *Los Teatros*, Talcahuano 354, good (live music 2300-0100, open 24 hrs.). Good snacks all day and night at Retiro and Constitución railway termini. For quick cheap snacks the markets are rec., e.g. El Retiro market on the 900 block of Av. Libertador. *Tío Ivan*, Florida 142 Boston Gallery, cheap sandwich bar, 10% discount for ISIC and youth card holders; good sandwich bar at Lavalle 1610. Stalls of the Cooperadora de Acción Social offer cheap snacks, and can be found in several public areas, e.g. near the Recoleta. The snack bars in underground stations are also cheap; also *Hogar Obrero*, Rivadavia y Esmeraldas, US$0.65 for full meal (but not too good).

For restaurants with shows, see **Night Clubs and Folklore** below.

**Tea Rooms, Cafés and Bars** *Richmond*, Florida 468 between Lavalle and Corrientes, genteel (chess played between 1200-2400); well-known are the *Confitería Suiza*, Tucumán 753, and the *Florida Garden* at Florida and Paraguay. *Café El Convento de San Telmo*, Bolívar with Humberto 1, good coffee, cakes and atmosphere. *En El Patio*, Paraguay 886, very pleasant. *Exedra* at Carlos Pellegrini and Av. Córdoba and many on Av. Libertador in the Palermo area. *Café Piazza*, Rivadavia 1400 block opp Plaza Lorea, exellent coffee, pretty setting. *Café Merlyn*, Montevideo 1655, great cakes, nice atmosphere. The more bohemian side of the city's intellectual life is centred on Avenida Corrientes, between Cerrito and Callao, where there are many bars and coffee shops, such as *La Paz* (open very late, Corrientes 1599, T 46-5542, 10% discount for ISIC and youth card members). *Pub Bar Bar O*, Tres Sargentos 415, good music and prices, gives similar discount. *El Molino*, Rivadavia and Callao, popular with politicians, nr. Congress, Belle Epoque décor, frequent art sales. Excellent ice-cream at *Freddo*, Ayacucho y Quintana. On Lavalle there are *whiskerías* and *cervecerías* where one can have either coffee or exotic drinks, *Bar Suárez*, Lavalle and Maipú, is a good place to watch the world go by. *Barila*, Santa Fe 2375, has excellent confectionery. *Café Tortoni*, Av. de Mayo 825-9, a haunt of artists, very elegant, over 100 years old, interesting *peña* evenings of poetry and music. On Saturdays at 2315, it becomes a 'Catedral del Jazz', with Fenix Jazz Band, US$1 entrance. Good local atmosphere in bars along Pasaje Bollini. Watch whisky prices in bars: much higher than in restaurants.

**Markets** Sunday markets for souvenirs, antiques, etc.: **Plaza Dorrego (San Telmo)** with food, dancers, buskers, Sunday 0900-1700, on Humberto 1 and Defensa (only "antiques"). Also **Feria de Las Artes** (Fri., 1400-1700) on Defensa and Alsina. Saturday craft, jewellery, etc. market, at **Plaza Belgrano**, nr. Belgrano station. At **Parque Rivadavia**, Rivadavia 4900, around the *ombú* tree, stamps and coins, Sun. 0900-1300, **Plazoleta Primera Junta**, Rivadavia and Centenera, books and magazines, Sat. 1200-2000, Sun. 1000-2000. **Plazoleta Santa Fe**, Santa Fe and Uriarte (Palermo) old books and magazines, same times as Primera Junta, and again, plastic arts in the Caminito (Boca) section. Sat. market in **Plaza Centenario**, local crafts, good,cheap hand-made clothes. **Auction sales**: some bargains at weekday p.m. auctions, Edificio de Ventas, Banco de la Ciudad de Buenos Aires, Esmeralda 660. Souvenirs can be found in area around San Martín and Paraguay (not markets). Interesting gaucho market at Mataderos, bus 126 from Plaza de Mayo, 50 mins (Sun.).

**Shopping** Most shops close lunchtime on Sat. Visit the branches of *H. Stern*, for fine jewellery at the Sheraton and Plaza Hotels, and at the International Airport. *Kelly's*, Paraguay 431, has a very large selection of Argentine handicrafts in wool, leather, wood, etc. Excellent leatherwork at *LYK*, Paraguay y Maipú. *Artesanías Argentinas*, at Montevideo 1360 and Córdoba 770, a non-profitmaking organization selling handicrafts (clothing, weaving, basketware, wooden goods etc.) all with certificate of origin; also *Matra*, Defensa 372, and the handicrafts centre at Defensa 788, 1st floor. *Señora Luna Arte Popular*, Paraguay 729, wide selection of Argentine, Bolivian, Chilean and Peruvian crafts, new and antique, expensive. *Campanera Dalla Funtana*, Reconquista 735, leather factory which is fast, efficient and reasonably priced for made-to-measure clothes. Good quality leather clothes factory at Boyacá 2030, T 582 6909 to arrange time with English speaking owner. *Aida*, Florida 670, can make a leather jacket to measure in 48 hours. Apart from shops on Florida and Santa Fe (especially between 1000 and 2000), Av. Corrientes has many shops for men's clothes between 600 and 1000 blocks, and the shops on Arenales N of Av. Santa Fe, and on

Av. Alvear on the way to Recoleta, have been recommended. Av. Cabildo in Belgrano district can be reached by 152 bus from Retiro for good shopping between 1600 and 2800 blocks. Many boutiques and places for casual clothes in Martínez suburb. The **Mercado de Abasto**, originally built in 1893, at Avs. Corrientes, Anchorena, Lavalle and Agüero, has been reopened as a commercial, cultural and entertainment centre. There is a new shopping mall, **Patio Bullrich**, Av. del Libertad or y Posadas, between Montevideo and Libertad, entrances on Posadas and Av. del Libertad (No. 750); boutiques are very expensive, but leather goods are of high quality. Another new mall, very smart and expensive, is **Alto Palermo**, at Díaz y Santa Fe. **Plaza Shopping Centre**, at Corrientes 1600, has a few restaurants and an open-air theatre with free concerts each evening. In the **Munro district** on Av. Mitre (buses, 130, 314, 41 from Av. del Libertador, 50 mins.) are cheap and varied fashion clothes, fake designer labels, some secondhand. For cheap clothes and electrical goods try Mercadería de Remate de Aduana, Florida 8.

**Bookshops**  Many along Av. Corrientes, W of Av. 9 de Julio, though most have no foreign language sections. **ABC**, Av. Córdoba 685 (limited selection of second-hand and new English books) and Av. Libertador 13777 in Martínez suburb. **Librería Rodríguez**, Sarmiento 835, good selection of English books and magazines; French bookshop at Calle Rivadavia 743; **Librería Goethe**, San Martín 577 (10% discount for ISIC and youth card holders), good selection of English and German books. Italian books at **Librería Leonardo**, Av. Córdoba 335, also (with newspapers and magazines) **La Viscontea**, Libertad 1067. Secondhand/exchange inside shopping arcade under Av. 9 de Julio at the Obelisco, but poor stock. **Asatej Bookshop**, Florida 835, 1° of 104, T 312-8476, sells this *Handbook* "at the best price". Good bookshop at Florida 340, *El Ateneo* (basement, good selection of English books), **Kel Ediciones**, Talcahuano 1063, and Laprida 2488 in Florida suburb, also maintain a good stock of English books and sells *South American Handbook*. Prices at *Harrods* on Florida are lower than most. For used and rare books: *Fernández Blanco*, Tucumán 712; *Casa Figueroa*, Esmeralda 970; and *L'Amateur*, Esmeralda 882. Second-hand English language books from *British and American Benevolent Society* (BABS); look in *Buenos Aires Herald* for address, which changes often.

Foreign newspapers at newsstands on Florida.

**Camera Repairs and Film Developing**  Film developing to international standards. Recommended for best quality is Expofoto, Lavalle 1250. Kodak, Paraná 515, good and cheap developing. Fotospeed, Av. Santa Fe 4838 (20% discount to SAHB owners!) for quality 2-hour service. Park Color, Av. Corrientes 614, 1-hr. developing, good prices for Kodak products. Camera repairs: Casa Schwarz, Perú 989, international brands; Golden Lab, Lavalle 630, good prices for film; Horacio Calvo, Ríobamba 183, all brands and variety of rare accessories; for Olympus cameras, Rodolfo Jablanca, Corrientes 2589. German spoken at Gerardo Föhse, Florida 890, fast, friendly.

**Taxis** are painted yellow and black, and carry *Taxi* flags. About US$1 per km.; meters show the number of "points" (zones) crossed, *not* the fare in australes, which is shown on a chart held by the driver. A charge is made for each piece of hand baggage. Tips not necessary. Beware of overcharging especially with remise (private clubs) and late at night. Two common taxi driver tricks are 1) to switch low-denomination notes for higher ones preferred by the passenger (don't back down, demand to go to the police station); 2) to grab the passenger's baggage and prevent him/her from leaving the taxi (scream for help). Worst places are the 2 airports and Retiro; make sure you know roughly what the fare should be before the journey. If possible, keep your luggage with you. Fares double for journey outside city limit (Av. General Paz). Alberto Pommerenck, T 654 5988, offers reasonable ½ day hire, knows suburban leather factories well, good driver.

**Car Hire**  Cars for hire, expensive, can be got through hotel reception clerks. Use of Avis Car Credit card with central billing in one's home country is possible. Traffic drives on the right. Driving in Buenos Aires is no problem, provided you have eyes in the back of your head and good nerves. **Avis** agency in the *Sheraton Hotel* (vehicles reported not well serviced); A1 International, M.T. de Alvear 680, T 32-9475/76, 31-0247, both have branches in all main cities. **Hertz** in Buenos Aires and Bariloche. If you want to travel to another country you need a special authorization from the car hire company.

**Local Bus**  services (*colectivos*) cover a very wide radius, and are clean, frequent, efficient and very fast. The basic fare is about US$0.20. **NB**. The number of the bus is not sufficient indication of destination, as each number has a variety of routes. Look for the little plaques displayed in the driver's window. "Lumi" guide to all routes is available at newsstands, US$7.50.

**Tram** A green and white old-fashioned street car operates on Sat. 1500-2000 and Sun. 1000-1200, 1500-2000 (not Easter Sun.), free, from Emilio Mitre and Directorio (Emilio Mitre Subte), and from near Primera Junta Subte. Operated by Asociación de los Amigos del Tranvía.

**Underground Railways ("Subte")** Five lines link the outer parts of the City to the centre. "A" line runs under Calle Rivadavia, from Plaza de Mayo up to Primera Junta. "B" line from central Post Office, Avenida L. N. Alem, under Av. Corrientes to Federico Lacroze railway station. "C" line links Plaza Constitución with the Retiro railway station, and provides connections with all the other lines. "D" line runs from Plaza de Mayo, under the Diagonal Norte, Córdoba, Santa Fe and Palermo to Ministro Carranza (5300 block of Av. Santa Fe; from Palermo to the end of the line is single track, running a shuttle service). Note that on Line "D" Canning station has become Ortiz. "E" line runs from Plaza de Mayo through San Juan to Avs. Directorio and José María Moreno. The fare is about US$0.30, the same for any direct trip or combination between lines; tokens (*fichas*) must be bought at booking offices (*boleterías*); buy a few in advance to save time. System operates 0530-01300. Some stations on lines C and D have some very fine tile-work. Backpacks and luggage allowed. Beware bag- and jewellery-snatchers and pickpockets, particularly when doors are about to close. The tourist office gives out a map, which can also be bought on station platforms with a booklet giving bus schedules.

**Night Clubs and Folklore** Tango: *Michelangelo*, Balcarce 433, impressive setting, restaurant and nightclub in an old converted monastery, good show, go at about 2300 on Fri.; *El Viejo Almacén*, Independencia and Balcarce, tango shows at 2230 and 0115, rec. but touristy (no dancing for guests); nearby are *Casablanca*, Balcarce 668, and *Taconeando*, Balcarce 725, more authentic, rec. 20% discount for *Taconeando* and another tango show, *La Ventana*, for ISIC and youth card holders, from Asatej office (see **Useful Addresses** below). Tango shows also at *Bar Sur*, Estados Unidos 299, *Casa Rosada*, Chile 318, and *San Telmo Tango*, Cochabamba 435 (popular with locals, not touristy, good meal, unlimited drinks), all 3 in San Telmo. *La Casa del Cantor*, P.Gollena 603. *El Rancho Ochoa*, Catamarca 999, has a good show and a reasonable meal. Good show also at *La Veda*, Florida 1, reasonable meal with wine and other drinks. The best affordable tango bars are in the Boca, but it is apparently becoming increasingly difficult to find authentic tango for locals; most are tourist-oriented. Two recommended places are *Café Homero*, J.A. Cabrera 4946, Palermo, and *Italia Unita* in the 2300 block of J.D. Perón.

Recommended night club/discos include *Hippopotamus*, Junín 1787, also good restaurant (nouvelle cuisine) and night club; *Mesón Español*, Av. Caseros 1750, good folk music show and good food; *Le Club*, small and exclusive, Quintana 111; *Dimensión*, new and large but pleasant, Av. Córdoba 3653; *Paladium*, "extravagant", San Martín 954. Three gay discos: *Contramano* (the best), Rodríguez Peña 1082; *Bunker*, Anchorena 1170; *Area*, Junín y Santa Fe. Andean music at *Ollantaytambo*, Estados Unidos 541.

Bars and restaurants in San Telmo district, with live music (usually beginning 2330-2400, Fri., Sat., Sun., cover charge US$2): *Jazz y Pop*, Venezuela y Chacabuco; *Jazz Café*, Chile 400; *Players*, Humberto I 528 (piano bar); *La Peluquería*, Bolívar, nr. Carlos Calvo (Samba).

**Cultural Events** The Luna Park stadium holds pop/jazz concerts. Teatro Alvear has free concerts Thursday at 1300, usually Orquesta de Tango de Bs. As. Teatro Municipal General San Martín, Av. Corrientes 1530, organizes many cultural activities of which quite a few are free of charge, including concerts Sat. evenings; the theatre's Sala Leopoldo Lugones shows international classic films, US$0.75 Sat.-Sun. Free concerts at ProMusica music shop, Florida 638; schedule in window. Centro Cultural General San Martín, Sarmiento 1551, and the Centro Cultural de Buenos Aires, Junín 1930, next to the Recoleta cemetery, have many free activities. The Teatro Liceo, Plaza de Congreso has been giving performances of a hugely popular revue, "Salsa Criolla", nightly for several years, dealing with Argentine history, people and customs. Tickets from US$2.50. Theatre ticket agency, La Cartelera, Lavalle 828. Look for details in main newspapers.

**Cinemas** Many, centred on Lavalle and nearby blocks. The selection of films is as good as anywhere else in the world. Films are now shown uncensored. Tickets best booked early afternoon to ensure good seats (average price Us$4.60-end 1990). Tickets obtainable, sometimes cheaper, from ticket agencies (*carteleras*), such as the one in the gallery at Maipú y Lavalle. Some cinemas offer discounts on Thursdays. Most foreign films are shown with subtitles, but dubbing increasingly used for major box-office successes. Free films at Asociación Bancaria, Sarmiento 337/341, T 313-9306/312-5011/17; old films at Ciné en el Teatro Hebraíco, Sarmiento 2255 (20% discount for ISIC holders), and at Sarmiento 2150, T 48-2170. ISIC holders also entitled to discounts at Ciné Cosmos, Av. Corrientes 2050 (30%) and Ciné IFT Sala 1, Boulogne Sur Mer 549 (50%). On Sat. nights many central cinemas have *transnoches*, late shows starting at 0100.

**Sports** Association and rugby football are both played to a very high standard. Soccer fans should not miss visiting the River Plate Stadium (bus 130); matches Sun. 1600, Wed. evenings. Next to the stadium is a sports centre, good climbing wall. Ice-hockey is becoming popular. Cricket is not unknown. Polo is played from Oct. to Dec.; a visit to the national finals at Palermo in Nov. is recommended, entrance free. Horse racing at Palermo on Sun. is popular. The Tigre Boat Club, founded in 1888, is open to British or American visitors for a small fee and a limited period. The leading golf clubs are the Hurlingham, Ranelagh, Ituzaingó, Lomas, San Andrés, San Isidro, Sáenz Peña, Jockey, Campos Argentinos and Hindú Country Club; visitors wishing to play should bring handicap certificate and make telephone booking. Weekend play possible only with a member. Good hotels may be able to make special arrangements. Tennis and squash are popular: there are 5 squash clubs.

**Gambling** Weekly lotteries. Football pools, known as *Prode*.

**Chess** Club Argentino de Ajedrez, Paraguay 1858, open daily, arrive after 2000; special tournament every Sat., 1800. High standards.

**Museums, Libraries, Art Exhibitions** Note: Most museums close on Monday, and some in January and most of February for summer holidays. State museums and parks are free on Wednesdays. Check opening hours with Tourist Office.
**Museo de los Presidentes** (basement of Casa Rosada), Hipólito Irigoyen 218. Historical memorabilia, particularly of former Presidents.
**Museo de Bellas Artes** (National Gallery), Avenida del Libertador 1473. In addition to a fine collection of European works, particularly strong in the 19th century French school, there are paintings representing the conquest of Mexico, executed 300 or 400 years ago, many good Argentine works, and wooden carvings from the Argentine hinterland. Open Tues.-Sun. (free Thurs.), 0900-1245, 1500-1845. Entrance US$2, students free. Warmly rec.
**The Museo Nacional de Arte Decorativo** is at Av Libertador 1902. The building is shared with the **Museo Nacional de Arte Oriental**; both are open Wed.-Mon., 1500-1900.
**Biblioteca Nacional** (The National Library), Calle México 566, founded in 1810, moved here in 1902. About 500,000 volumes and 10,000 manuscripts.
**Museo Histórico Nacional**, Defensa 1600. Trophies and mementoes of historical events. Here are San Martín's uniforms, a replica of his famous sabre, and the original furniture and door of the house in which he died at Boulogne. Open Tues.-Fri. and Sunday, 1500-1900. Entrance US$0.10.
**Museo de la Ciudad**, Alsina 412, open Mon.-Fri., 1100-1900, Sat., 1600-2000. Permanent exhibition covering social history and popular culture, special exhibitions on daily life in Buenos Aires changed every two months, and a reference library open to the public.
**Museo y Biblioteca Mitre**, San Martín 336, preserves intact the household of President Bartolomé Mitre. Open 1500-1700.
**Museo de Ciencias Naturales** at Avenida Angel Gallardo 470, facing Parque Centenario. It houses palaeontological, zoological, mineralogical, botanical, archaeological and marine sections. Open Tues., Thurs., Sun. 1400-1800, US$0.20. Library, Mon.-Fri., 1100-1700.
**Museo Municipal de Arte Moderno** (Tues.-Sun. 1600-2000) at Avenida Corrientes 1530, and **Museo Municipal de Artes Plásticas Eduardo Sivori** (Tues.-Sun. 1600-2000) at Centro Cultural de Recoleta, Junín 1930, where there are also a cinema, a theatre, and the **Museo de Artes Visuales**, Tues.-Fri. 1600-2000. Free entry on Wed. 19th century and contemporary Argentine painting.
**Museo de Bellas Artes de la Boca**, Pedro de Mendoza 1835, Boca, has many works on local life, entrance free.
**Centro Cultural Las Malvinas**, Florida 853, stages many art exhibitions by Argentine and foreign artists.
**Museo de Motivos Populares Argentinos José Hernández,** Av. Libertador 2373, Gaucho collection, open Tues.-Sun., 1400-1800.
**Museo del Instituto Nacional Sanmartino**, Sánchez de Bustamante and Av. A. M. de Aguado; Mon.-Fri. 0900-1200 and 1400-1700; Sat., Sun. 1400-1700.
**Museo de Arte Español Enrique Larreta**, Juramento 2291, in Belgrano. 1500-1945. Closed Thurs. The home of the writer Larreta. Also **Biblioteca Alfonso El Sabio**, Mon.-Fri., 1300-1930.
**Museo de Cabildo y Revolución de Mayo**, Bolívar 65, is the old Cabildo building, converted into a museum in 1940. It contains paintings, documents, furniture, etc., recording the May 1810 revolution, and memorabilia of the 1806 British attack. Entry US$0.33. Open Wed.-Sun., 1500-1900. Library, Mon.-Fri., 1100-1900.
**Museo de Arte Hispanoamericano Isaac Fernández Blanco**, Suipacha 1422. Contains a

most interesting and valuable collection of colonial art, especially silver, in a beautiful colonial mansion. Open Tues.-Sun., 1400-1800, admission US$0.35. Thursdays free. Latin American art and history library at Suipacha 1444 nearby, 0900-1900, Mon.-Fri.

**Museo y Biblioteca Ricardo Rojas**, Charcas 2837, open Wednesdays and Fridays 1500-1800, US$0.10. The famous writer Rojas lived in this beautiful colonial house for several decades. It contains his library, souvenirs of his travels, and many intriguing literary and historical curios.

**Museo Numismático**; fascinating, well kept, little known, at the Banco Central in San Martín, overlooks central foyer, ask guard for directions.

**"Presidente Sarmiento"**, Dársena Norte, a sailing ship used as a naval training ship until 1987; now a museum. Open daily 1000-1800, US$0.40. The corvette **"Uruguay"**, tied up by the Boca bridge, is a museum of Antarctica, open Sat. and Sun. 1300-1800, US$0.40.

**Bank of London and South America** (now Lloyds Bank (BLSA)), Bartolomé Mitre and Reconquista, has a miniature museum on its fifth floor. Open during banking hours; the building, designed by SEPRA (Santiago Sánchez Elia, Federico Peralta Ramos, and Alfredo Agostini) and completed in 1963 is worth seeing for itself. Next door is the **Banco de Córdoba**, designed by the brilliant Córdoba architect Miguel Angel Roca, completed in the early 1970s.

**Museo Nacional de Aeronáutica**, Av. Costanera Rafael Obligado, next to Jorge Newbery airport, Thurs., Sat. and Sun., 1600-1900. Many civil and military aircraft.

**Museo Nacional Ferroviario**, Av. Libertador 405. Mon.-Fri., 0900-1800, free. Archives 1100-1800. For railway fans; no photographing.

**Museo Botánico**, Las Heras 4102 and Malabia 2690. Open 0800-1200 and 1400-1800, Mon.-Fri. Herbarium pleasant. Some 1,000 cats in residence.

**Museo de la Dirección Nacional del Antártico**, Angel Gallardo 470, Tues., Thurs. and Sun., 1400-1800. Dioramas.

**Museo del Teatro Colón**, Tucumán 1161. Mon.-Fri. 1200-1800. Documents and objects related to the theatre.

**Museo Histórico Saavedra**, Crisólogo Larralde (Republiquetas) 6309. Wed.-Fri., 1400-1800; Sat., 1800-2200; Sun., 1500-1900. City history from the eighteenth century. Free on Wed.

**Yuchán Centro de Artesanía Aborigen**, Defensa 788, has many interesting native artefacts on view, for sale.

**Museo de la Policía Federal** San Martín 353, 7th floor, worth visiting, small entrance fee. The interesting forensic part can only be seen if you offer a police, medical or journalist's identification.

**Museo Internacional de Caricatura y Humorismo**, Lima 1037, open Fri., 1700-2100 only, originals of cartoons and caricatures of 20th century, but small international section, admission US$0.05.

**Museo de Armas**, Maipú y Santa Fe. Open 1500-1900 daily, US$0.15. All kinds of weaponry.

**Retiro Art Gallery**, an excellent, small art gallery in two train carriages on Platform 9 at Retiro station; sometimes tours the country. Access is from platform 8; small entrance fee. Also shows documentary films.

**Exchange** Most banks charge very high commission. Banks open Mon.-Fri. 0800-1200, be prepared for long delays. US dollar bills are often scanned electronically for forgeries (nerve wracking while you wait for the beep). **Lloyds Bank** (BLSA) Ltd, corner of Reconquista and Bartolomé Mitre. It has 10 other branches in the city, and others in Greater Buenos Aires. **Royal Bank of Canada**, corner of Florida and J. D. Perón; branch at Av. Callao 291. **Citibank**, B Mitre 502; branch at Florida 746. **First National Bank of Boston**, Florida 99. **Bank of America**, J. D. Perón y San Martín changes Bank of America travellers' cheques am. only, into US$ at very high commission; branch at Paraguay 901 doesn't take American Express or Thomas Cook cheques. **Banco Tornquist**, Mitre 531, Crédit Lyonnais agents, advance cash on visa card. **Banco Holandés Unido**, Florida 361, **Deutsche Bank**, B. Mitre and Reconquista, 1% commission on Thomas Cook cheques, both give cash advances. **Banco de la Provincia de Buenos Aires**, San Martín, close to Plaza de Mayo, and **Banco Río de la Plata**, San Martín 77-97 both advance cash on Visa Card. Cash advances are only given in australes. **American Express** offices are in a new building at the corner of Arenales 707 y Maipú, by Plaza San Martín, here one apply for a card, get financial services, etc., changes Amex travellers' cheques (small commission into US$ cash). For client mail, go to the office at *Hotel Plaza*, Florida 1005, 2nd floor, Mon.-Fri. 0800-2000, unreliable.

There are many *casas de cambio*, and increasing numbers deal in travellers' cheques; most are concentrated around San Martín and Corrientes, those on Lavalle and Maipú are reported to give better rates than those on Florida (although Onda has been rec.); open from

Mon.-Fri. 1000-1500, Sat. closed. Many *cambios* will exchange US$ travellers' cheques for US$ cash at commissions varying from 1.25 to 3%. If all *cambios* closed, try Mercadería de Remate de Aduana, Florida 8, or Olympia leather shop on Tucumán between Florida and San Martín. There is no service charge on notes, only on cheques. Many exchange shops ask for receipt of purchase of cheques, and practices vary all the time. Major credit cards widely accepted but high surcharges were common in 1990. General Master Card office at Hipolito Yrigoyen 878, open 0930-1800, T 331-1022/2502/2549; another branch at Florida 274 (open 1000-1730).

**Language Schools**    Spanish classes at Academia Toil And Chat, Suipacha 443, T 322-9739, I.L.E.E., Lavalle 1619, piso 3° E, T 498208, will arrange accommodation and social activities, rec., and at Link Educational Services, Arenales 2565, Piso 5° B, T 825-3017. For other schools teaching Spanish, and for private tutors look in *Buenos Aires Herald* in the classified ads. Enquire also at the Goethe Institut and at Asatej (see **Useful Addresses**).  Schools which teach English to Argentines are: International House, Larrea 1333, British-owned and -run Masters, Av. de Mayo 791; Berlitz, Av. de Mayo 847 (low rates of pay); Central Consultaret de Personal, Lavalle 1290 (office at 1103); Pullmen, Santiago del Estero 324; American Teachers, Viamonte y Florida, T 393-3331. Before being allowed to teach, you must officially have a work permit (difficult to obtain) but schools may offer casual employment without one; if unsure of your papers, ask at Migraciones (address below).

**Libraries, Cultural and Trade Associations**    Harrods (2nd floor), on Florida, US$6 a month. Argentine Association of English Culture, Suipacha 1333 (library for members only); British Chamber of Commerce, Av. Corrientes 457; British Council, c/o British Embassy. Goethe Institut, Av. Corrientes 311, German library (open 1300-1800 exc. Wed.) and newspapers, free German films shown; in the same building, upstairs, is the German Club, Corrientes 327. USA Chamber of Commerce, Diagonal Norte 567; US Information Library (Biblioteca Lincoln), Florida 935, reference and lending library, free, take passport (closed Wed., Sat., Sun.). St Andrew's Society, Perú 352.

**Clubs**    American Club, Viamonte 1133, facing Teatro Colón, temporary membership available; American Women's Club, Av. Córdoba 632, 11 piso. English Club, 25 de Mayo 581, T 311-9121; temporary membership available to British business visitors. The American and English Clubs have reciprocal arrangements with many clubs in USA and UK. Swedish Club, Tacuari 147.

**Embassies and Consulates**    Bolivian Consulate, Belgrano 1670, 2nd floor, open 0900-1400. **Brazilian Consulate**, Pellegrini 1363, 5th floor, open Mon.-Fri., 1000-1500 (easier to get a Brazilian visa, in 2 hrs., from this consulate than in Montevideo; 2-day wait at latter), T 394-5620. **Paraguayan Consulate**, Maipú 464, 3rd floor, 0900-1300. T 392-6535. **Peruvian Consulate**, Tucumán 637, 9th floor, 0900-1400, visa US$5, takes 1 day. **Uruguayan Consulate**, Ayacucho 1616, open 1000-1800, T 821-6031.

US Embassy and Consulate General, Colombia 4300, Palermo, T 774-7611 (US Embassy Residence, Av Libertador 3502). **Australian Embassy**, Av Santa Fe 846 (Swissair Building), T 312-6841. **Canadian Embassy**, Suipacha 111 y Santa Fe, T 312 9081. **South African Embassy**, Marcelo T. de Alvear 590,8 piso, T 311-8991. **Israeli Embassy**, Arroyo 910, T 392 2903/4987/4885/4481/4611/4781.

Austrian Embassy, French 3671, T 802-7095/6. **British Embassy**, Luis Agote 2412/52 (near corner Pueyrredón & Guido), Casilla de Correos 2050, T 803-7070, open 0915-1215,

1415-1615. **Finnish Embassy**, Av. Santa Fe 846, 5 piso. **French Embassy**, Av Santa Fe 846, 5 piso. **German Embassy**, Villanueva 1055, Belgrano, T 771-5054/9. **Irish Embassy**, Suipacha 1380, 2 piso, T 325-8588. **Italian Embassy**, Billinghurst 2577, consulate at M.T. de Alvear 1149. **Netherlands Embassy**, Maipú 66, 1084 Buenos Aires, T 33-6066. **Spanish Embassy**, Mariscal Ramón Castilla 2720, esq. Av. del Libertador 2075. **Swedish Embassy**, Corrientes 330, 3 piso, T 311-3088. **Swiss Embassy**, Av Santa Fe 846, 12 piso, T 311-6491, open 0900-1200.

**Useful Addresses** Youth Hostel Association—information for all South America; Talcahuano 214, piso 3, T 45-1001 (post code: 1013 Buenos Aires). Buenos Aires hostel at Brasil 675. **N.B.** A YHA card in Argentina costs US$20, ISIC cards also sold. Secretariat open Mon.-Fri. 1300-2000. (There are very few hostels near road S from Buenos Aires on Route 3.) **Asatej**, Argentine Youth and Student Travel Association, information for all South America, English and French spoken, very helpful, Florida 835, 1st floor, Oficina 104, T 312-8476. **YMCA** (Central), Reconquista 439. **YWCA**, Tucumán 844. **Salvation Army**, Rivadavia 3255. **Municipalidad**, Av. de Mayo 525, facing Plaza de Mayo. **Central Police Station**, Moreno 1550, T 38-8041 (emergency, T 101). **Migraciones** (Immigration), Antártida Argentina 1365. **Comisión Nacional de Museos y Monumentos y Lugares Históricos**, Av. de Mayo 556; professional archaeology institute.

**Urgent Medical Service** (day and night) (Casualty ward: *Sala de guardia*) T 34-4001/4. British Hospital, Perdriel 74, T 23-1081, US$8 a visit; cheap dental treatment at Av. Caseros y Perdriel 76. German Hospital, Pueyrredón 1658, between C. Berruti and C. Juncal, T 821-4083. Both maintain first-aid centres (*centros asistenciales*) as do the other main hospitals. Hospital Juan A. Fernández, Ceviño y Bulnes, good, free medical attention. If affected by pollen, asthma sufferers can receive excellent free treatment at the University Hospital de Clínicas José San Martín, Córdoba 2351.

**Inoculations** Centro Médico Rivadavia, S. de Bustamante 2531, Mon.-Fri., 0730-1900, or Sanidad de Puerto, Mon. and Thurs., 0800-1200, at Av. Ing. Huergo 690, free, bus 20 from Retiro, no appointment required (typhus, cholera, Mon./Thurs. 0800-1200; yellow fever, Thurs. 1400-1600). Hospital Rivadavia, Calles Las Heras y Tagle, for polio inoculation. Free. Centro de Inmunización reported not to give vaccinations any more.

**Laundries** *Tintorería Constitución*, Av. Santiago del Estero 1572 (suits only). Laundry at Esmeralda 1077 takes 2 hrs. Many dry cleaners, efficient and friendly. Several launderettes, e.g. Marcelo T. de Alvear 2018, in centre; Junín 15 y Rivadavia, Mon.-Sat. 0800-2100; Junín 529 with Lavalle; *Lavarap*, Paraguay 888 y Suipacha, Córdoba 466, Local 6, T 312-5460 (10% discount to ISIC and youth card holders, also at Brasil y Bolívar), Arenales 894, Solís nr. A. Alsina (cheaper) and many other sites; *Marva*, Juan D. Perón 2000 with Ayacucho.

**General Post Office** (Correo Central), corner of Sarmiento and L.N. Alem, Mon.-Fri., 0800-2000. Poste Restante (US$1.20 per letter); very limited service on Saturday (closes 1400). Centro Postal Internacional, for parcels over 1 kg, at Av. Antártida Argentina, near Retiro station, open 1100 to 1700.

**Telecommunications** Entel, Av. Corrientes 707 (open 24 hrs.) for international phone calls, public telex in basement; alternatively in Central Post Office, also telex. Another office at San Martín 322, also on Agüero/Las Heras. *Golosinas fichas* (tokens) for calls in the city cost US$0.10, obtained at newspaper stalls and Entel offices. International telephone calls from

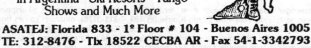

hotels may incur a 40%-50% commission in addition to government tax of about the same amount. Tokens can be obtained and the call made from a public telephone box.

**Tourist Information**   National office at Santa Fe 883 with maps and literature, and said to change money. Open 1000-1700, Mon.-Fri.; T 312-2232, 312-6560. Has a guide to campsites throughout Argentina, and laundromats in Buenos Aires.

There are also helpful *Casas de Turismo* for most provinces (open Mon.-Fri. usually, 1200-1900, depending on office, check): on Callao are Buenos Aires (no 237), Córdoba (332), Chaco (322), La Rioja (745), Mendoza (445). Río Negro, Tucumán 1920; Chubut, Paraguay 876; Entre Ríos, Suipacha 848; Formosa, B. Mitre 1797; Jujuy, Santa Fe 967, 6th floor; Misiones, Santa Fe 989; Neuquén, J. D. Perón 687; Salta, Diagonal Norte (Roque Sáenz Peña) 933; Santa Cruz, Santa Fe 1300 block (top floor, exact number not known); Catamarca, Córdoba 2080; Corrientes, San Martín 333, 4th floor; La Pampa, Suipacha 346; San Juan, Maipú 331; Santa Fe, 25 de Mayo 358; Santiago del Estero, Florida 274; Tucumán, Mitre 836; Tierra del Fuego, Sarmiento 745; Ushuaia and Lago Argentino, Av. Santa Fe 790. Bariloche hotel, flat and bungalow service in Galería at Florida 520, room 116 (cheapest places not listed). Calafate bookings for *Refugio and Autocamping Lago Viedma*, excursions with Transporte Ruta 3 and lake excursions with Empresa Paraíso de Navegación booked from Turismo Argos, Maipú 812, 13th floor C, T 392-5460. (For bookings for *Hotel La Loma*, Calafate and further information on the area contact Paula Escabo, Av. Callao 433, Piso 8° P, T 40-9123.) For tourist information on Patagonia and bookings for cheap accommodation and youth hostels, contact Asatej, see **Useful Addresses** above.

Municipalidad de Buenos Aires, Sarmiento 1551, 4th floor, has an excellent free booklet about the city centre and maps. Further offices at Aeroparque (Aerolíneas Argentinas), Mon.-Fri., 0830-2000 and Sat. 0900-1900, and Ezeiza/Pistarini Airport, Mon.-Fri. 0830-2200; also Florida with Diagonal Norte and Florida with Córdoba, open at 0830-1930 Mon.-Fri. and 0900-1900 Sat.

On Fri., the youth section of *Clarín—Sí—*lists free entertainments. *Where in Buenos Aires*, a tourist guide in English, published monthly, is available free in hotels, travel agencies, tourist kiosks on Florida, and in some newsstands at US$2.50. The *Buenos Aires Times* is a bilingual monthly newspaper covering tourist topics. A good guide to bus and subway routes is *Guía Peuser*; there is one for the city and one covering Greater Buenos Aires. A similar guide and map is "Lumi": both are available at newsstands. Also handy is Auto Mapa's pocket-size "Plano guía" of the Federal Capital, available at newsstands, US$8, or from sales office at Santa Fe 3117; Auto Mapa also publishes an increasing number of regional maps, Michelin-style, high quality. Country-wide maps at Instituto Geográfico Militar, Cabildo 301 (see **Maps** in Information for Visitors).

**Tourist Agents**   *Exprinter*, Santa Fe, and San Martín 176, Galería Güemes (their 5-day, 3-night tour to Iguazú and San Ignacio Miní for US$60 has been recommended); *American Express*, Arenales y Maipú; *Furlong*, Esmeralda 1000, T 311-8200, Thomas Cook respresentatives; *ATI*, Esmeralda 516, very efficient and helpful, with branches in Brazil; *Astra Travel*, Tucumán 358, 5th floor, English spoken by director, efficient; *Turismo Flyer*, Reconquista 621, 8° piso, T 312-9164/313-8165, English, Dutch and German spoken, accepts credit cards, rec. *Germania*, Lavalle 414, T 393-1265/0035, excellent service (English not spoken), especially for tours to the N, branch in Salta. *Patagonia Turística*, specialists on that region, Florida 755 (T 311-9216). English is widely spoken.

**Tours**   A good way of seeing Buenos Aires and its surroundings is by Autobuses Sudamericanos (TISA), information and booking office at Bernardo Irigoyen 1370, 1st floor, Offices 25 and 26, T 27-6591 or 631-1108, or Av. Larrazabal 493, T 642 7028 (Liniers). For reservations in advance for sightseeing or other tours, with a 20%courtesy discount to *South American Handbook* readers, write to Casilla de Correo No. 40, Sucursal 1(B), 1401 Buenos Aires. A 3-hour tour of Buenos Aires in English and Spanish is run by City Tours, book through *Florida House* hotel, rec., as is Eurotur (T 312-6170), in English. Some tours (e.g. Buenos Aires Tur, Lavalle 1444, cheaper than TISA) include dinner and a tango show, or a gaucho *fiesta* at a ranch.

**Motoring Associations**   See page **198** for details of service. Parking, safely, at El Balneario within the old port, but ask the military post for permission first.

**Passenger Boats**   The *Buenos Aires Herald* (English-language daily) notes all shipping movements. Flota Fluvial del Estado (Corrientes 489, T 311-0728) organizes cruises from Buenos Aires, Dársena Sur; up the Paraná river. South Coast, down to Punta Arenas and intermediate Patagonian ports, served by the Imp & Exp de la Patagonia and Elma (state shipping line). Very irregular sailings. For connections with Uruguay, **see page 72.**

**Airports** Ezeiza (offically referred to as Ministro Pistarini), 35 km. from the centre by a good divided lane highway, which links with the General Paz circular highway round the city. The airport is up-to-date, has a duty free shop, exchange facilities (good rates, no commission on bills, 6% on travellers' cheques), but its hotel, the *Internacional*, is closed for renovation. Airport information, T 620-0217. Ezeiza is used by international services but Jorge Newbery airport (normally known as Aeroparque), on the N side river front at the end of the New Port, 4 km. from the centre, is used for internal services and also flights to Punta del Este, Montevideo and Aerolíneas flights to Asunción, Santiago and Santa Cruz (Bolivia). If stuck for cash because banks are closed you can try the Newbery airport exchange facilities (bills only), run by Banco de la Nación (close at 2100). Your Packet International SA will seal bags after inspection for US$10 to discourage pilfering at Ezeiza.

There is a reliable standard taxi service operating from Ezeiza, US$35 (March 1991). Do not take an unmarked car, however attractive the fare may sound; the drivers are adept at separating you from far more money than you can possibly owe them for the journey. Shuttle buses between Ezeiza, and the centre are operated by Manuel Tienda León, approx. every hour from 0530 to 2030 daily, US$10. At Ezeiza buy ticket from kiosk next to the *cambio* outside customs before boarding bus. The service continues to Aeroparque. From the centre buses leave company offices at Carlos Pellegrini 509, near *Hotel Colón*, allow at least 20 mins before departure time to buy tickets. No. 86 buses (blue, marked "Fournier") also run to the centre from outside the airport terminal, US$3.50 (*servicio diferencial* takes 1½ hrs., *servicio común* 2¼ hrs.) between 0500 and 2400. To travel to Ezeiza, catch the bus in Plaza de Mayo or at Av. de Mayo y Perú—make sure it has "Aeropuerto" sign in the window as many 86s stop short of Ezeiza. Note that suitcases, backpacks, etc. are not normally allowed. A display in immigration in the terminal shows choices and prices of all ways into the city.

Journeys to and from Jorge Newbery (Aeroparque) by *remise* taxi, e.g. US$7 to Retiro, US$6.50 to Palermo, US$9.50 to Boca, US$29 to Quilmes, US$39 to Ezeiza. Taxis are charged according to meter (about US$4.75 from the San Martín/Florida area, but more to the centre), or you can catch the local No. 33 or 56 bus (US$0.25) from outside the airport to the Retiro railway station. Manuel Tienda León operates buses between Ezeiza and Jorge Newbery airports, stopping in city centre, US$10.

Aerolíneas Argentinas and Austral offer daily flights to the main cities, for details see text under intended destination; **see also page 196** for the Visit Argentina fare. If travelling in the south, book ahead if possible with LADE, whose flights are cheaper than buses in most cases.

**Local Airline Offices** Aerolíneas Argentinas (AR), Calle Perú 2; reservations and enquiries, T 393-5122. Austral Líneas Aéreas, Corrientes 485, T 313-3777. Líneas Aéreas del Estado (LADE), Calle Perú 710, T 361-7071. CATA, Cerrito 1320, 3° piso, T 812-3390.

**Railways** There are 4 main terminals:
**Retiro**, consists of 3 separate stations, all near each other: Ferrocarril Nacional Mitre (Central)—T 312-6596; Ferrocarril Nacional San Martín (Pacific)—T 311-8054; Ferrocarril Nacional Belgrano (North-Western)—T 311-5287/8/9. Services to Córdoba*, Mendoza*, Rosario, Sante Fe and Tucumán. The terminal has a left-luggage facility (reports of theft); it is said to be a haven for pickpockets and bagsnatchers.
**Constitución**: Ferrocarril Nacional Roca (Southern)—T 23-0021. Services to Bahía Blanca, Bariloche, San Antonio Oeste and Zapala.
**F. Lacroze**: Ferrocarril Nacional Urquiza (North-Eastern)—T 55-5214. Services to Concordia*, Paraná*, Paso de los Libres*, and Posadas*.
**Once**: Ferrocarril Nacional Sarmiento (Western)—T 87-0041/2/3.

Fuller details will be found under destinations in the text below; prices given there are only approximate. Passengers should check all services in advance as the future of the railway system is under permanent discussion.

* Some trains have car-transporters

**NB** The railways maintain an information centre and booking office at Viamonte 553, often long queues, open 0700-2100 Mon.-Fri., 0700-1300 Sat. Book tickets well in advance wherever possible (especially in July and December), also for connecting services, especially those going south of Buenos Aires. Outward journeys may be booked 45 days in advance, return journeys 60 days, but not later than 7 days in advance. Telephone reservations for named trains (details in text under destinations): 312-5680, 312-5686/9, 312-3686/9, 311-6325/9, 312-8610 and 312-8616/9.

**Buses** The long-distance bus station, Estación Terminal de Omnibus, is behind Retiro, on Av. Ramos Mejía and Antártida Argentina (Subte C); T for information 311-6073/6088. All long distance buses leave from here; all offices are on the E side on the ground floor. The passage between the bus station and Retiro is packed with market stalls and is narrow, as are the turnstile exits from the platforms, all designed to inconvenience those with luggage. There are two left-luggage offices, open 0600-2300. Some bus companies charge extra for luggage. Fares may vary according to time of year and advance booking is advisable Dec.-March. Be sure to ask for price in australes; we have received reports that companies quoting US$ prices overcharge the hapless tourist. See **Cost of Living**, page 202. Some companies may give discounts, such as 20% to YHA or student-card holders and foreign, as well as Argentine, teachers and university lecturers. Travellers have reported getting discounts without showing evidence of status, so it's always worth asking. For further details of bus services and fares, look under proposed destinations. No exchange shop at bus station: only bank, giving official rate. There are cafés, shops, toilets and newsstands. Tourist office open from 1000, makes hotel reservations. TISA, see above under **Tours**, is the agent for Amerbuspass, for Argentina and Bolivia.

**Hitch-hiking**  Heading S, take bus 96 to Ruta 3 for Comodoro Rivadavia, etc., US$0.35. Best to hitch from a service station The police control point at Km. 43 (southwards) is reported to be friendly and will help to find a lift for you.

# Travel into Neighbouring Countries

## By Road
Four branches of the Inter-American Highway run from Buenos Aires to the borders of Chile, Bolivia, Paraguay and Brazil. The roads are paved except when otherwise stated.

**To Chile**  via Río Cuarto, Mercedes, San Luis, and Mendoza, Total: 1,310 km. paved throughout. (Three direct buses a week to Santiago, US$55, 23 hrs. e.g. TAC or Chevallier, 1,459 km.; same price to Valparaíso or Viña del Mar.) Car-transporter train to Mendoza on Fridays. There are also road connections between Bariloche and Osorno and Puerto Montt, and between Salta and Antofagasta.

**To Bolivia**  via Rosario, Villa María, Córdoba, Santiago del Estero, Tucumán, and Jujuy. Total: 1,994 km. There is no direct bus service from Buenos Aires to La Paz but through connections can be booked. If you do not wish to go the whole way by rail, train/bus combinations are possible via Tucumán, Jujuy or La Quiaca. Car-transporter train to Tucumán, Tue. and Fri.

**To Paraguay**  via Rosario (as for Bolivia), Santa Fe, Resistencia, Clorinda and Asunción (via toll bridge). Total: 1,370 km. Buses take 20-22 hours, with N.S. de la Asunción, Juan D. Perón 2760; or Chevallier, Empresa Godoy, La Internacional or Expreso Brújula (all next to each other at the Retiro bus terminal). You have choice between *diferencial* (with food, drinks) and *común* (without food, services). Tickets can be bought up to 30 days in advance.
    Those who wish to drive to Misiones to visit San Ignacio Miní or the Iguazú Falls can cross the river by the bridge between Santa Fe and Paraná, or the one between Resistencia and Corrientes. From there Route 12 leads NE through Posadas to the Iguazú Falls. The direct road from Buenos Aires to Posadas via the Zárate-Brazo Largo bridges is fully paved. From Corrientes to Esperanza is paved, and from Posadas to Iguazú. (Singer and Tigre-Iguazú buses to Puerto Iguazú leave daily at 1130 and 1500 respectively, 22 hrs.) From Posadas you can cross the river to Encarnación by the new bridge and take a good 370-km. road to Asunción (see Paraguayan chapter). Car-transporter train to Posadas, Tues. and Sat.

**To Brazil**  To the Iguazú Falls, go by the bridge from Puerto Iguazú, reached via Posadas. Another road to the border with Brazil, at Paso de los Libres, goes to Rosario, Santa Fe, cross by bridge and tunnel to Paraná; Villa Federal, Curuzú Cuatiá, Paso de los Libres, opposite Uruguaiana (Brazil), across the Río Uruguay. Total: 960 km. Direct buses to Brazil via Paso de los Libres by Pluma: São Paulo, 40 hrs. US$86, Rio de Janeiro, US$90; Curitiba, 38 hrs.; Florianópolis, 32 hrs.; daily at 1000 to Porto Alegre, 26 hrs. (The route across the Río de la Plata and through Uruguay is a bit cheaper, not as long and offers a variety of transport and journey breaks; see also Uruguay under next section). Tickets from Onda, Florida 502 y Lavalle (392-5011), for any information also to combine travel via Uruguay. Buen Viaje, Av. Córdoba 415 (31-2953) or Pluma, Av. Córdoba 461 (311-4871 or 311-5986) or office branches in Rosario, Santa Fe and Paraná. Journey direct to Rio takes about 44 hrs., US$75; at least one bus per day; to Rio, changing buses at Posadas and Foz do Iguaçu is almost half price, 50 hrs. Car-transporter train to Paso de los Libres, Tues. and Sat.

**To Uruguay**  Direct road connections by means of two bridges over the Río Uruguay between Puerto Colón and Paysandú and between Puerto Unzué and Fray Bentos. "*Bus de la carrera*" links Montevideo and Buenos Aires (8½ hrs.). Departure from each city at 1000, 2200 and

2300 via Zárate-Gualeguaychú-Puerto Unzué-Fray Bentos-Mercedes. Book at Onda.

**To Peru** Ormeño has a direct service Buenos Aires-Lima, from Retiro bus station, Tues. 1800, 3½ days, all meals included, one night spent in Coquimbo, Chile (if you need a visa for Chile, get one before travelling), the route is: Mendoza, Coquimbo, Arica, Tacna, Nazca, Ica, Lima. El Rápido Internacional, from Buenos Aires bus terminal, ticket office 89, US$150 (half the air fare).

### Air, River and Railway Services

**Brazil** Daily air services to São Paulo, Rio de Janeiro and other Brazilian cities. To Porto Alegre by train, a service runs between Bs. As. and Uruguaiana, from where an onwards connection can be made via Santa Maria. Shipping service between Buenos Aires and Brazilian ports by various transatlantic lines. See *Buenos Aires Herald,* English-language daily.

**Chile** Information about travel to Chile is available from Av. Córdoba 879. The passenger-train service across the Andes between Mendoza and Santiago has been discontinued, but bus services are available. The train service to Antofagasta via Salta and Socompa has also been suspended, but there are buses between Salta and Antofagasta.

Foreign and national lines fly daily between Buenos Aires and Santiago. Time taken: 1½ to 2 hours. Aerolíneas Argentinas also flies to Antofagasta via Salta in the high season only.

**Bolivia** The connecting service from Tucumán and Jujuy to La Quiaca has been restored: the *Panamericano* leaves Tucumán on Tues. and Fri. 1500, arriving La Quiaca next day at 0930. On arriving in La Quiaca one must cross on foot to the Bolivian side and purchase a train ticket for the remainder of the journey, Villazón-La Paz. The Friday train from Tucumán passes over the border and departs Villazón Sat. at 1500 for La Paz, arriving Sun. 0900 (US$75). *El Norteño* train has no sleepers, leaves Retiro Tues. and Fri. at 0845, via Tucumán to Jujuy. Bus Panamericano Jujuy to La Quiaca. Villalonga Furlong, Balcarce 473, 2nd floor, open Mon.-Fri. 0900-1700, has information about trains (not Retiro); it is also a freighting company and sells the tickets. See under Tucumán (**page 96**) for other train services. There are no sleepers beyond Tucumán. Sleeper tickets to Tucumán carry no seat entitlement elsewhere in the train. Sanitary facilities poor. Hot soup and local dishes brought round carriages. Bar and restaurant car with same food, adequate. Travel rug recommended on this part of the journey. On the Bolivian side, carriages, old, noisy and crowded; bad sanitary facilities. Local food available on train. Cold night. Free baggage allowance 30 kg, and excess is charged **See page 102** for the route from Salta to Santa Cruz de la Sierra.

There are also regular air services 4 times a week to La Paz by Aerolíneas and Lloyd Aéreo Boliviano.

**Paraguay** The direct train to Asunción was withdrawn in 1984, but trains run daily to Posadas, and once a week from Encarnación to Asunción. From Encarnación you can get a connecting train (if it waits) or bus (saving up to 16 hrs.) to Asunción. There is a daily air service to Asunción by various companies. See also Posadas, **page 143.** Occasional river boats to Asunción in winter and spring, 6 days, food and nightly entertainment reported good.

**Uruguay** Tickets heavily booked Dec.-March. **NB:** No money changing facilities in Tigre, and poor elsewhere. For boat services, 1) take the train to Tigre (see next page), from where two daily boats sail to **Carmelo**: Cacciola at 0800 and 1330, 3 hrs., and Delta Nave, Mon.-Sat. 0830 and 1700, Sun. 0830,1700 and 2400, 3 hrs., both services US$18; tickets at Movilan, Lavalle y Florida, Bs. As. (T 392-5011) or Estación Fluvial, *local* 13 (T 749-4119), Tigre. It is advisable to book in advance; connecting bus to Montevideo (Onda, Florida y Lavalle, book in advance), arriving at 1530 and 1600.

2) From Dársena Sur (*vapor carrera*) goes to Montevideo, Ferry Líneas, Florida 780, leaves at 0745 and 1630, boarding finishes ½ hr. before departure (take bus 61, 84, 86, 96 and others); single fare US$25 without sleeper or breakfast, US$45 with; cars charged by weight. Ferry Líneas to Colonia 0800 and in p.m., 3 hours, US$18, US$24, including bus connection to Montevideo (2½ hrs.). Also Buquebus, Suipacha 776, T 392-0365, 3-5 sailings a day, depending on season, 3½ hrs. to Colonia, total of 6½ to Montevideo. Uruguayan immigration officer on ferry.

3) Puente Fluvial runs hydrofoils (*aliscafos*) to Colonia four times a day (winter) or five times a day (summer), 1 hr., US$33. All tickets from Onda, Florida 502, T 392-5011; reconfirm seat at Onda in Montevideo, Plaza Cagancha. Beware of overcharging by taxis from the harbour to the centre of Buenos Aires. Buquebus offers services similar to those of Onda, has built a new ferry station at Dársena Sud.

Several airlines fly from Jorge Newbery Airport (Aeroparque) to Colonia 15 mins. Tickets at Onda, or Aero Uruguay, Reconquista 885. Continue by bus to Montevideo, or from Jorge Newbery, air service to Montevideo: shuttle 10 daily, 0730 to 2200, known as Puente Aéreo and run by AR and Pluna. Book at Jorge Newbery Airport or T 361-5008. Flight takes 35 mins. Punta del Este, daily with AR and Pluna, 40 mins.

## Suburbs of Buenos Aires

**Avellaneda**, a separate municipality of over 650,000 people, is one of the most important industrial centres in the country; the handling of hides, wool and animal produce is concentrated here. It is 5 km. from Plaza Constitución station, on the other side of the Riachuelo river from Boca.

**Olivos**, on the River Plate coast, 20 minutes by the Bartolomé Mitre Railway, is a favourite residential district. The presidential residence is there, many foreign residents. Population, about 160,000. (A rec. restaurant here is *Grinzing*, Córdoba 2864, European specialities, about US$20 p.p. inc. wines, historical objects in house, garden with swimming pool.)

**San Isidro**, just beyond Olivos, a resort for golf, yachting, swimming, and athletics, is one of the most attractive suburbs on the coast. There is a magnificent turf racecourse, an attractive central plaza and fine colonial buildings. Pop: 80,000.

**Martínez**, nearby is an attractive residential area overloooking the Río de la Plata, with an interesting shopping area. Sailing and windsurfing are well represented and river launches and other craft may be hired.

**Quilmes (Bs.As.)**, with one of the world's largest breweries, an important industrial centre, was given that name because the Quilmes Indians were forcibly moved there in 1665 from the famous Inca site in Tucumán Province (**see page 97**). Population about 150,000. St George's College, an English boarding school, is here. Bathing is now both dangerous and prohibited; in one day 19 lives were lost. It is served by the Roca Railway and buses.

The naturalist and writer W. H. Hudson (1841-1922) was born at Florencio Varela, near Quilmes, about 32 km. from Buenos Aires. His birthplace is now a national monument.

**Tigre**, on the delta of the Paraná, is about 29 km. (50 minutes) by train from Buenos Aires. Take the train from platform 1 or 2 at Retiro station (FC Mitre) to the end of the line. It can also be reached by bus 60 bajo, which takes a little longer; the 60 alto bus takes a faster road but is less interesting for sightseeing. Regattas are held in November and March on the Río Luján. There are numerous "recreos" and restaurants on the river front, but sleeping accommodation is not good. There is an excellent fruit market on Sundays; craft market is tacky. Inland from Tigre are innumerable canals and rivulets, holiday homes, clubs, a profitable fruit growing centre and an attraction for holiday makers. The fishing is excellent and there is peace on the waterways, apart from motor-boats at week-ends. Regular launch services, each company with its own routes, for all parts of the Delta, including taxi launches—watch prices for these!—leave from wharf opposite railway station. The wharf where these are moored can be quite smelly. Be warned that if you leave just before lunch the launch crew may stop along the way for a 1-1½ hr. lunch break! A journey through the Delta, with its lush tropical vegetation (even in winter) is fascinating. The best option is a 2-hr. ride by catamaran; they dock on the other side of the bridge from the railway station and leave at 1330 and 1600 Mon.-Fri., and hourly from 1300 on Sat. and Sun. The excursion lasts 11½ hrs.; longer trips (4½ hrs.) to the open Río de la Plata estuary are available. Snacks and refreshments on board. Do not confuse the tourist catamarans with the *lanchas* which run regular passenger services between islands. Population: 40,000. In the delta is *El Tropezón*, an old inn on Paraná de las Palmas island (the boat crews know it); C p.p. inc. meals, formerly a haunt of Hemingway, now frequented by affluent *porteños*, highly rec. despite the mosquitoes. Delta **Youth Hostel** at Río Luján y Abra Vieja, Canal de San Fernando (take bus 60 from train station, US$0.15) G p.p. clean, hot showers; ask at Talcahuano 214, Buenos Aires. Good restaurant near Youth Hostel, around the corner. Direct ferry to Carmelo, Uruguay (**see page 73**) from opposite railway station. (If you miss the boat, Antonio J. Pissini has guest rooms at Montes de Oca 142, Tigre, or try *Hotel Astor*.)

The Museo Naval is worth a visit. It contains models old and new, navigation instruments, flags and banners, and paintings of naval battles. There are also relics of the 1982 South Atlantic war on display outside. The Museo de la Reconquista celebrates the reconquest of Buenos Aires from the British in 1806-07.

Excursion to **Martín García** island (Juan Díaz de Solís' landfall in 1516) in the Río de la Plata, 45 km. from Buenos Aires, with La Valette Turismo, through channels in The Delta (approx 12 hours there and back with day on the island; T 921-2050/2055).

## Other Towns in the Pampas

There is one town which belongs to Argentina as a whole rather than to any province or area, though it is actually in the Province of Buenos Aires and only 66 km. W of the capital by Sarmiento railway from Once station (1-1½ hours) or by bus from Once station, 1 hr. This is **Luján**, a place of pilgrimage for all devout Catholics in Argentina. An image of the Virgin was being taken from church to church in the area in 1630 by ox cart. At a certain spot the cart got stuck, in spite of strenuous efforts by men and oxen to move it. This was taken as a sign that the Virgin willed she should stay there. A chapel was built for the image, and around it grew Luján. The chapel has long since been superseded by an impressive neo-Gothic basilica and the Virgin now stands on the High Altar. 8 May is her day. Each arch of the church is dedicated to an Argentine province, and two of the transepts to Uruguay and Paraguay. Population: 30,000. Very heavy traffic at weekends.

**Museo Colonial e Histórico** (The Colonial and Historical Museum), in the old Cabildo building, is one of the most interesting museums in the country. Exhibits illustrate its historical and political development. Open daily, except Monday and Tuesday, 1200-1800. No cameras allowed, and nowhere to store them, stroppy caretaker. General Beresford, the leader of an attempt to capture Buenos Aires, was a prisoner here, and so, in later days, were Generals Mitre, Paz, and Belgrano. There are also museums devoted to transport and to religious ex-votos. The Río Luján is picturesque at this point, a favourite spot for picnic parties.

**Hotels** *España, La Paz*. There are numerous **restaurants**: an excellent one is *L'Eau Vive* on the road to Buenos Aires at Constitución 2112; it is run by nuns, pleasant surroundings.

There are dozens of small, prosperous towns scattered throughout the vast area of the pampas. They serve as clearing centres for the cattle and grain and supply the rural population, which is much denser in the Humid Pampa than elsewhere in Argentina. Only the larger towns and resorts are dealt with here.

*La Plata*, capital of Buenos Aires Province, on the Río de la Plata and only 56 km. SE of Buenos Aires, is reached by Roca railway and by many buses. This modern city, founded in 1882, has a population of about 454,000. Its port is accessible to ships of the largest tonnage. Its major industrial interest is the YPF petroleum refinery; a 72-km. pipeline runs to the South Dock at Buenos Aires. Its Museo de Historia Natural is one of the best in Argentina and has several unique exhibits. A motorway is being built to link La Plata with Buenos Aires, via Riachuelo, Avellaneda, Berazátegui, Gonnet and Tolosa.

**Points of Interest** The Museum at La Plata is famous for its collection of extinct animals. Its treasures are largely ethnological and include human skulls, mummies, and prehistoric implements. There are zoological, botanical, geological, mineralogical, palaeontological and archaeological sections, guided tours in Spanish. Highly rec., open Mon.-Fri. 1200-2000, Sat., Sun., 1000-1800, US$2, closed in January and on public holidays. Well laid-out Zoological Gardens; fine racecourse and Observatory. The Museum, Zoological Gardens, and Observatory are all in the public park; park entrance at Calle 1 y 53 (take bus to Plaza Moreno, US$0.50). The Muncipalidad and Cathedral (an unfinished but magnificent copy of Cologne's Gothic cathedral) are in the Plaza Moreno. Ten minutes in the train takes one to the Islas de Río Santiago and to the Yacht Club, Arsenal, and Naval Academy. Nearby is an interesting children's village with scaled-down public buildings, built under the first Perón administration; take a green microbus 273 or a red and black 518 to República de los Niños, going N along Av. 7 from Plaza San Martín. There is a small, interesting nature reserve at Punta Lora, a short bus ride from town, slide show and tour, open to public Sat.-Sun., 1000-1300 and 1400-1800.

**Local Holiday** Foundation of the City, 19 November.

**Hotels** *Corregidor*, new, expensive; *Roga*, Calle 54 No. 334, D, close to museum, visiting scientists stay here. *Plaza*, Calle 44 y 2, D with bath; *Roca*, Calle 1 y 42, E with bath.

**Restaurants** *El Fogón*, Av. 1, Calle 49; *Ianno*, rec., Calle 46 y 10. Restaurants rarely open before 2100. *Don Quixote*, Plaza Passo, good value, best in town, can get very crowded; Chinese "tenedor libre" at *Guinga*, also on Plaza Passo; *La Linterne*, Calle 60 y Av. 1, upmarket but good value; *El Chaparral*, good parrillada, Calle 60 in the Bosque. Several reasonable restaurants around the bus station (which is in the red light area, though quite safe even at night). Recommended bar, with steak sandwiches, *El Modelo*, Calle 52 and 4. Best empanadas at *La Madrileña*, a hole-in-the-wall on Calle 60 between 5 and 6. Best bakery is *El Globo*, Calle 43 y 5.

**Entertainments** Tango and tropical music at *El Viejo Almacén*, on Diagonal 74, Calle 2. there are free concerts during the summer in the Bosque amphitheatre.

**Tourist Office** In the old white theatre on the main plaza, also at bus terminal. Turismo San Martín, Calle 51 between 7 and 8, rec.

**Buses** To Buenos Aires, 1½ hrs., US$2, about every quarter hour, Río de la Plata company (from Retiro in Buenos Aires day and night; from Plaza Constitución, daytime, and Once).

On the coast 400 km. S of Buenos Aires, lies Mar del Plata, the most celebrated Argentine seaside resort. The road and rail routes S to it are through Chascomús and Dolores. *Chascomús*, 126 km. from Buenos Aires, is on a wide plain on the shores of Lago Chascomús, which covers 3,000 hectares and swells greatly in size during the rains. Its slightly brackish water is an important breeding place for *pejerrey* fish; up to 1,000 kg have been caught in one day during the winter season, when amateur fishing competitions are held. There is a *gaucho* museum, and also a Regatta Club and bathing beaches and camping grounds at Monte Brown, on the far side of the lake.

*Dolores*, 204 km. (3½ hrs. by bus) from Buenos Aires, has a district population of 30,000; it was founded in 1818, destroyed by Indians three years later, and rebuilt. It is a grain and cattle farming centre which is said hardly to have changed in 50 years. The Museo y Parque Libres del Sur, commemorating the revolt of the district against Rosas in the early 19C., is interesting and well displayed. *Hotel Plaza*, very pleasant.

*Villa Gesell*, about 130 km. N of Mar del Plata, is a modern resort with fine beaches and over 100 hotels, which has become very popular although less crowded than Mar del Plata. Tourist office at bus terminal. Direct bus service to Buenos Aires by Empresas Antón and Río de la Plata.

**Hotels** *Terrazas Club*, 4 star, suite accommodation, Av. 2 between Calles 104 and 105, T 6 2181; *Colón*, 2 star, 3 blocks from beach at Av. 4, Calle 104, T 62310, private bath, restaurant; *Hostería Gran Chalet*, Paseo 105 No. 447 y Av. 4-5, D, clean, rec.; *Bero*, opposite bus terminal, E. Many others of all classes within 800 metres of sea. Many apartments for rent. **Youth Hostel** *Albergue Camping El Coyote*, Calle 212 y 306, Barrio Norte.

**Camping Sites** Many, a few open all year round.

**Air** Aerolíneas Argentinas flies to Villa Gesell several times daily in summer.

*Pinamar*, 22 km. N of Villa Gesell, is a rapidly growing resort, with a casino. It is now very much the "in" place, with good water-skiing. Fish, including conger eel (*congrio*) may be bought on the beach from local fishermen. Tourist office, friendly and helpful, is in the main square.

**Accommodation** Many, from *Arenas*, Av. Bunge 700, T 322 7877, 4 star, to *Berlín*, Rivadavia 326, T 82320, 1 star. All hotels fully booked throughout Jan.- March (as much as two years in advance!). **Youth Hostel**, Nuestras Malvinas y Sarmiento, T 82908, and *Moby Dick* campsite at Ostende. Many other campsites close to town.

*Mar del Plata* is 400 km. from the capital. The normal population is 407,000, but during the summer about two million visitors stay there; there are all classes of apartment blocks, boarding houses and lodgings. It is necessary to book in advance between late December and mid- March (when the night-life continues all night). For the rest of the year the town is fairly quiet. The city is famous for its casino: the upper floor is open to the public, for a small admission charge. Small but pleasant natural history museum in Plaza España off Playa la Perla. Interesting municipal art museum at Villa Ortiz Basualdo, Av. Colón 1189.

There are fine squares, especially Plaza San Martín, and eight km. of beaches, including fashionable Playa Grande, with its private clubs and the summer estates of wealthy *porteños*; Playa Bristol, where the casino is; and Playa la Perla, with moderately priced hotels. At Punta Iglesia there is a large rock carving of Florentino Ameghino, the palaeontologist who collected most of the fossils in the museum at La Plata. The wooded municipally owned Parque Camet is 8 km. to the N. It has polo grounds and playing fields. For those who do not care for surf bathing, there are salt-water pools. Fishing is good all along the coast and *pejerrey, corvina* and *merluza* (hake) abound; you can charter a private launch for shark fishing.

The port can be reached by bus, 15 mins from bus terminal. There are a large fishing fleet, excursion boats, seafood restaurants.

Visits can be paid to the rocky promontory of Cabo Corrientes to watch the breakers; to Punta Mogotes lighthouse (open Thursdays 1330-1700); to the Gruta de Lourdes, and the Bosque Peralta Ramos.

**Local Holidays** 10 Feb. (Foundation of City); 10 Nov. (Day of Tradition); 22 Nov. (St Cecilia). Mar del Plata is known for its hand-finished sweaters.

**Hotels** Four-star (category L-A+) are *Provincial*, 500 rooms, Blvd. Marítimo 2300, T 24081/9; *Dos Reyes*, Av. Colón 2129; *Hermitage*, Blvd. Peralta Ramos 2657, 150 rooms; and *Sasso*, M. de Hoz 3545. Among the 3-star hotels (category A) are *Astor*, Entre Ríos 1649; *Benedetti*, Av. Colón 2198, rec.,T 30031/2; *Gran Continental*, Córdoba 1929; *Presidente*, Corrientes 1516; and *Gran Dora*, Buenos Aires 1841. 2-star hotels (category B) include the *Flamingo*, Moreno 2155, has seen better days, but comfortable; *Finisterre*, Garay 1786, without breakfast, clean, comfortable (near the bus station). There are scores of good hotels at reasonable rates e.g. *Boedo*, Almirante Brown 1771 (T 24695), C, with bath, hot water, clean, good value, near beaches (open Jan.-Feb. only); *Europa*, Arenales 2735, 2 blocks from bus station, C (reductions in low season), clean, quiet, hot water; *Residencial San Mateo*, Arenales nr. Alberdi, D with bath, friendly; *Peley*, on Alberdi near bus station, D, clean, comfortable, open all year, rec., good value restaurant; *Hospedaje Paraná*, Lamadrid 2749, near bus terminal, D, with bath; *Niza*, Santiago del Estero 1843, E (F out of season), bath, clean, safe, friendly, rec.; *Little Hotel*, Lamadrid 2461, near bus station, nice and cheap; *Monterrey*, Lamadrid 2627, E, clean, good; *Don Quijote*, Sarmiento 2478 near bus station, F, quite clean; *Hospedaje Alfa*, Garay 1731, close to bus station, cramped but very friendly. During summer months it is essential to book in advance. In the off-season, bargain everywhere. **Youth Hostel**, Tucumán 2728, F p.p. Many hotels and restaurants close when the summer is over; worth looking round the bus-station area out of season.

There are many houses and apartments for rent, built for, but not yet filled by, retirees.

**Camping** *Pinar de la Serena* and other sites, reasonable prices. Several on the road S out of town; *Los Horneros* has been rec.

**Restaurants** *Hostería del Caballito Blanco*, Av. Rivadavia 2534, excellent, German decor. *Cantina Capri*, Belgrano 2161 (near Casino), not cheap but excellent value; *Los Cercos*, Belgrano, between Entre Ríos and Corrientes, for meat; *La Paella*, Entre Ríos, between Bolívar and Moreno, good; *La Caracola*, Nuevo Complejo Comercial Puerto, seafood, good but dear; *Raviolandia*, Colón y Heras, good, cheap, try the seafood with rice. Vegetarian: *El Jardín*, Plaza de San Martín, "tenedor libre", and *La Huerta*, Santiago del Estero 1600 block. Many "tenedor libre" restaurants of all kinds along San Martín. *Los Inmortales*, Corrientes 1662, good, moderately priced.

**Casino** Open December to end-April, 1600-0330; 1600-0400 on Sats Winter opening, May-December, Mon.-Fri. 1500-0230; weekends 1500-0300. Entrance US$2.

**Exchange** Lloyds Bank (BLSA) Ltd, Av. Luro 3201. Open 1000-1600. **American Express**, Av. Colón 2605. Exchange houses on San Martín and surroundings. **Jonestur**, San Martín 2574, will collect on personal US bank cheques in 15 working days, at 2½% fee.

**Sociedad de Cultura Inglesa**, San Luís 2498.

**Post Office** on Santiago del Estero, Pedro Luro.

**Tourist Office** opp. Casino, near beach, free maps; also at bus terminal.

**Trains** leave Buenos Aires from Constitución, 10 minutes from the centre by any bus marked "Constitución". Trains (a/c) take at least 5 hrs. 15 mins., tourist class US$15, 1st US$18, Pullman US$22, 3 times a day each way; from Buenos Aires at 0800, 1530 and 2345, returning at 0900, 1515 and 2330. Additional train Mon., Wed., Fri., at 1945, returning Tues., Thur., Sat., 2120, and non-stop service on Sat. 1830, returning to Buenos Aires Sun. 1840. Extra Sat./Sun. service if sufficient demand. Book very early for Dec.-March trips. Mar del Plata station is at Av. Luro 4700, about 13 blocks from centre.

**Buses** Bus station at corner of Alberti y Las Heras, convenient. Companies from Retiro terminal in **Buenos Aires**: El Cóndor (very luxurious, 3 seats a row, self service bar, US$20), Micromar, Costera Criolla. Chevallier US$24, 5½ hrs. Bus to and from **Miramar** hourly day and night, 45 mins. US$4. El Cóndor and Rápido Argentino to **La Plata**, day and night, US$20. La Estrella goes to **San Martín de los Andes**, US$56, and **Bariloche**, US$60 (none direct; change at Bahía Blanca or Tres Arroyos). To **Bahía Blanca**, only Pampa, 6 daily, US$25, 5½ hrs. To **Puerto Madryn** and **Trelew**, Wed. and Sat. night. For hitch-hiking S, take a colectivo to the monument to El Gaucho.

**Air Services** Camet airport, 10 km. from town. Many flights daily to and from Buenos Aires with Austral and Aerolíneas Argentinas. *Remise* taxi from airport to town.

Outside the city the country is undulating. To the N (34 km.) is a lagoon—the Mar Chiquita—joined to the sea by a narrow channel. There is good fishing, yachting, boating and bathing here. Picturesque spots reached from the road to Balcarce are (19 km.) Laguna de los Padres (a **reserva provincial**), and Sierra de los Padres and (32 km. beyond) the Laguna La Brava, at the foot of the Balcarce hills.

In these hills, 68 km. by paved road from Mar del Plata, is the town of **Balcarce**, a centre for hill visits to La Brava, above Ruca-Lauquén, and the Cinco Cerros, five hills most strangely shaped. Balcarce is the birthplace of the great racing driver Juan Fangio; it has a racing circuit.

**Hotel** *Balcarce*, Mitre y Balcare, T 22055, good, C.

Beyond Balcarce a paved road runs 103 km. to *Tandil*, at the northern end of the Sierra del Tandil, a ridge of hills which run W from the sea into the pampa for 250 km. It is 390 km. by road from Buenos Aires (6 buses a day, US$18, 6hrs) via Azul. The air is splendidly clear and refreshing, and the Holy Week festivities are outstanding. Excursions to the Sierra La Aurora. Population: 125,000.

**Hotels** *Plaza*, General Pinto 438, T 27160, 3 star, D, very friendly, clean, comfortable and quiet. *Kaiku*, Mitre 902, E, basic; *Turista*, 14 de Julio 60, T22626, 1 star, E. Others near railway station.

**By Air** Lapa flight Buenos Aires-Tandil.

From Mar del Plata, along the rocky sea-front to the SW, there is a road (53 km.) to *Miramar* (population 17,500). Like Mar del Plata, this is a summer bathing resort, but the cliffs backing the beach are higher, the surrounding hills more picturesque, and it is a good deal cheaper to stay at. There is a fine golf course at *Hotel Golf Roca* and a casino. Immediately S of the city limits is an extensive forest park on the beach, the **Vivero Dunicola**, whose vegetation stays green and blooming throughout the year, despite winter night-time temperatures below freezing. Fourteen km. by road to the S, among dunes and black rocks, is Mar del Sur (*Atlantic Hotel*) with good fishing in a lagoon and bathing on the beach.

**Hotels** Dozens of hotels and apartments. *Santa Eulalia*, Calle 26 No. 851, C, friendly but run down. *Grand*, Calle 29, No. 586 esq. 12, T 20358, 3 star; *Palace*, Calle 23, No. 774, T 20258, 3 star; *Villa Cruz*, friendly, clean, near the beach, C.

**Camping** *Escargot, El Fortín*, Miramar. Many sites, reasonably priced.

**Exchange** None for travellers' cheques; must go to Mar del Plata. Try *Ibertur* and *Sastre* property offices.

**Tourist Office** on central plaza, maps available.

**Transport** *El Neptuno* train, daily at 1530 from Buenos Aires to Mar del Plata arriving at 2045, connects with a bus service to Miramar, arriving 2150. **Bus** Buenos Aires-Miramar with Cóndor, five daily, and Costera Criolla, four a day.

About 110 km. further by road along the coast to the SW is another famous seaside resort, *Necochea*, 500 km. from Buenos Aires. It stands next to Mar del Plata in repute. The surroundings are picturesque. Visits can be paid to the Paseo del Puente, Punta Negra, the Cascada (or waterfalls) 16 km. up the Río Quequén Grande, Los Manantiales, and the Laguna de los Padres. Grain is exported from the port. Urban population: 52,000 including large Danish colony: there are a Danish club and consulate. About 100,000 tourists visit during the season, for the 24-km. long beach is one of the best in the country. There is a municipal recreation complex, boasting a large modern casino, various sports facilities, including skating rink, swimming pool, bowling, a cinema and children's play area. The Parque Miguel Lillo (named after the Argentine botanist) faces the beach, comprising 400 hectares of conifers, nature park, swan lake with paddle boats, an amphitheatre, museum and go-cart track. The casino is open in summer. Airport.

**Hotels** The Hotel Association is at Av. 79 with Calle 4. Most hotels are in the downtown area from Calle 2 (parallel with beach) northwards between Av. 71-91; there are at least a hundred within 700 metres of the beach. *Hospedaje Solchaga*, Calle 62, No. 2822, T 25584, E, clean, excellent. **Camping** Beach sites reported expensive in summer.

**Restaurants** *Rex*, Calle 62, "a trip to 1952 Paris" (Roderick Michener); *Mi Cantina*, excellent family restaurant. *Parrilla El Palenque*, Av. 79 y 6; *Pizzería Kapotte*, Av. 79 next beach, both rec.

**Tourist Office** At the bus terminal by the river at corner of Av. 47 and Calle 582; also on beach front at Av. 79.

**Railway** Gral. Roca Railway train *Brisas del Mar* leaves Buenos Aires (Constitución) Mon., Wed., Sat. at 2300 for Las Flores (see below) where a connection is made for Necochea at 0120; arrives Necochea 0855, returns to Las Flores 2245 Tues., Thur., Sun. arriving at 0907 at Buenos Aires.

**Bus** El Cóndor from Buenos Aires six times a day, Costera Criolla 5 times a day.

About 3½ km. across the mouth of the river from Necochea is *Quequén*, with an excellent beach, good bathing, and pleasant scenery. The channel to the port has to be dredged daily. Hotels and campsites.

Over 320 km. westwards from Necochea by paved road through the coastal area is the port of Bahía Blanca, which can be reached from Buenos Aires by rail (900 km.), by air, or by a 688-km. paved road (Route 3) through Las Flores (pop. 20,200), Azul, Juárez and Tres Arroyos.

*Azul*, 264 km. SW of Buenos Aires, is a cattle centre with an attractive plaza, a French Gothic-style Cathedral and an ethnographic museum. Population: about 45,000. A good stopping place if driving S from Buenos Aires. The river has been dammed to provide a water-sports centre.

**Hotels** *Gran Hotel Azul*, Colón 626, T 22011, C, excellent cafeteria; *Residencial Blue*, Av. Mitre 983, T 22742, F, clean, friendly, near bus station; *Argentino*, Yrigoyen 378, T 25953; *Torino*, San Martín 1000, T 22749.

*Tres Arroyos*, about 195 km. from Bahía Blanca, is a cattle and wheat growing centre of 70,000 people. Many inhabitants are of Dutch origin; there are a Dutch consulate and a primary school named Holanda, supported by funds of the Argentine Dutch. There is also an important Danish colony, with school, club and consulate. A 68-km. paved road runs S to the sea at the pleasant little resort of *Claromecó*, with a beautiful beach of dark sand backed by high dunes.

**Hotels and Restaurants at Tres Arroyos** include *Parque*, rec. (restaurant) and *Andrea*, good; *Tres Arroyos*, friendly, modest. **Restaurant Di Troppo**, near *Hotel Parque*, good. At **Claromecó** *Comercio*, D, good restaurant, pleasant atmosphere; *Pablo Satini's Bar*, on main street, 5 mins from beach, F off season, OK, safe deposit.

**Camping at Claromecó** Good campsite *Dunamar*, hot showers, fire pits and laundering basins, US$1 a day; also ACA campsite.

**Bus** Buenos Aires-Claromecó with El Cóndor, US$40. Tres Arroyos-Claromecó twice daily off season, extra buses from mid-December in season. Pampa bus to Mar del Plata 0650, 4½ hrs. Modern, efficient bus terminal a few blocks from centre of Tres Arroyos.

***Bahía Blanca***, population 300,000, the most important centre S of Mar. del Plata, stands at the head of a large bay where the Río Naposta runs into it. The region has over a million people. Bahía Blanca consists of the city itself, built back from the river front, and five ports at various distances from the city strung along the N bank of the Naposta: Arroya Pareja and the naval base of Puerto Belgrano at the mouth of the estuary; Puerto Ingeniero White, 23 km. inland (reached by buses 500, 501, 504 from the plaza) Puerto Galván, 3½ km. beyond, and Cuatreros, 8 km. upstream. Bahía Blanca is also a rail, air and pipeline transport terminal for the rich Río Negro valley.

The city has some fine modern buildings and two parks. There is a very poor Zoological Garden in Parque Independencia, on the outskirts.

To the E of Bahía Blanca is an enormous stretch of sandy beaches, developed for visitors (in the afternoon, it is usually windy). Pehuén-Có, 70 km. away, is an example of the beaches with camping places, well shaded by pine trees. Signs to it on the main road 24 km. from Bahía Blanca. Another fine beach, with hotels and camping places is ***Monte Hermoso***, 106 km., 2 hrs. by bus (4 a day in summer, 2 in winter) from Bahía Blanca. Good cheap meals, several restaurants. (Its hotels are open only Jan.-March).

**Local Holidays** Sept. 24 (Our Lady of Mercy); Nov. 10 (Day of Tradition).

**Hotels** *Austral*, Colón 159, T 20241, B; *Del Sur*, 19 de Mayo 73, T 22452, B, both with restaurants (not good in the former), noisy with traffic; *Central Muñiz*, O'Higgins 23, T 20021, D, friendly, central; *Italia*, Brown 181, T 20121, C, simple, clean, restaurant; *City*, Chiclana 226, T 30176, D. *Atlántico*, Chiclana 251, T 20230, E; *Bayón*, Chiclana 487, E p.p., friendly, clean, safe; *Argentino* (restaurant), Chiclana 466, D. Opposite railway station: *Residencial Roma*, with private bath, cheaper without. *Victoria*, Gral. Paz 82, T 20522, E, basic, friendly, hot water, rec.; *Hospedaje Brandsen*, Brandsen 276, E, friendly, "sparkling". Many other *residenciales* near railway station.

**Camping** Balneario Maldonado, 2 km. from centre, next to petrochemical plant, bus 514 along Av. Colón every hr. but only when beach is open, i.e. when sunny and not in evening, US$0.30 p.p.; salt water swimming pool, US$0.80. Many others.

**Restaurants** *La Cigala*, Cerri 757, opp. railway station, very good; *Il Vesuvio*, Chiclana 237, good lunch, cheap; *Gambrines*, Arribeños 174, central. Very good seafood and fish at Ingeniero White.

**Shopping** Good gaucho shop on Soler, nr. Fortur (see below), genuine articles.

**Museums** Museo Histórico, Alsina 425, including interesting photos of early Bahía Blanca; Museo del Puerto, Torres y Carrega, Ingeniero White; Museo de Bellas Artes, Alsina 65.

**Exchange** Lloyds Bank (BLSA), Calle Chiclana 102. Citibank, Colón 58. Open 0800-1400 Nov. 15-March 31, 1000-1600 April 1-Nov. 14. AmEx, Fortur, Soler 38, *poste restante*, English spoken. **Casas de Cambio** Pullman, Av. San Martín 171, will change US$ cheques into US$ notes; good rates (closes 1600). Viajes Bahia Blanca, Drago 63, good rates. All *casas de cambio* closed at weekends.

**Post Office** Moreno 43. **Telephones** Entel, O'Higgins 203.

**Launderette** *Lavarap*, Estamba 293 and at Colón y Güemes.

**Tourist Office** In town hall, main plaza, friendly and helpful, good map (closed weekends).

**Airport** Comandante Espora, 15 km. from centre. Austral and Aerolíneas Argentinas flights to **Buenos Aires** daily. To **Comodoro Rivadavia**, Sun. at 0800 arrive 1005. To **Neuquén** daily at 1900, arrive at 1955. Flights to **Río Gallegos** and **Trelew** on Sun., at 0800 arrive at 1135 and 0905, respectively.

**Trains** Station at Av. Gral. Cerri 780, T 21168. Two trains daily from Buenos Aires, fairly comfortable, go via Olavarría from Constitución; book at least 2 days ahead in high season. *Estrella del Valle* daily at 1000, arrive at 2020, with dining car, return 0845 daily, arrive 2010; and *Bahiense* at 2200 daily, arriving 0855, returning 2130, arriving Buenos Aires 0800. To

**Bariloche,** Mon. and Thur. 0920, just over 24 hrs., tourist class US$28. To **Zapala** with a change in Neuquén at 2034, arr. Neuquén 0830, Zapala 1300. Can be cold.

**Roads** Well built paved highway (Route 3) S to Comodoro Rivadavia; major paved route W to Neuquén and the Lake District. Several routes go North.

**Buses** Terminal is 2½ km. from centre at Estados Unidos y Brown; no hotels nearby. To **Trelew,** 3 per week, US$30, 734 km. **Río Gallegos** with Don Otto US$80; **Mar del Plata** bus, US$25, 5½ hrs. Bus **Río Colorado** US$8. Buses to **Buenos Aires** frequent, 11 hrs, US$30. To **Neuquén,** 6 a day, 9hrs, US$20, 580 km., one company only. To **Zapala** daily at 0630 and 1030. To **Viedma** 3 a day, 4 hrs.

**Hitch-hiking** S or W from Bahía Blanca is possible but not too easy. Most S-bound traffic takes Route 22 via Río Colorado. N to Buenos Aires, take bus 519 to Route 3 on outskirts. Also bus 511A.

Some 100 km. to the N is the Sierra de la Ventana, a favourite and recommended area for excursions from Bahía Blanca, and a **reserva provincial,** protecting the range's flora and fauna. The small town of Tornquist, with an attractive church on the central plaza (post and phone office open 0800-1800), is a good starting point. From Route 33 take Route 76 to the town of Sierra de la Ventana. After 32 km. is the entrance to the **Parque Provincial,** with massive ornate gates from the Tornquist family home. From here it's a 3-hr. walk to the summit of Cerro La Ventana, which has fantastic views from the "window" in the summit ridge (camping at the base, free, basic facilities, canteen). 5 km. further is the forestry station, with audio-visual display, trips to see wild deer, wild horses, guanacos, and on Fri. and Sun. trips at 0900 to 2 caves, one an Indian cemetery, the other with petroglyphs (US$0.70). Villa Ventana, 10 km. further, is a wooden settlement with excellent teashop, *Casa de Heidi,* and wholefood available from *Jardín de Aylem.* Municipal campsite by river with all facilities. *Sierra de la Ventana,* further east, is a good centre for exploring the hills, with hotels (*Golf,* near station, is OK) and the excellent *Don Diego* campsite (hot water, open all year round); also 2 more campsites. Excellent tourist information in town. Tres Picos, rising bare and barren from the rich farmlands to 1,070 metres, is only 6¼ km. away. There is a 9-hole golf course, and good trout fishing in the Río Sauce Grande. Train Bahía Blanca-Sierra de la Ventana 3 hrs., US$0.80; all points can be easily rached by bus from Bahía Blanca or Tornquist.

193 km. N of Bahía Blanca by road/rail through Saavedra is **Carhué,** served by three railways, one of which, via Bolívar, runs to Buenos Aires (603 km.). Five km. away is a sheet of water, Lago Epecuén, which covers over 40,000 hectares and is over twenty times saltier than the sea. No fish can live in it. These waters are recommended for chronic rheumatism and skin diseases. There are many hotels and *residenciales* at the lake side and the area is fast being developed as a tourist resort. A health spa is planned. There are also hotels in Carhué. There is a museum of the wars against the Indians behind the town hall. Visit the ruins of Villa Epequén, drowned by the lake in 1985. Carhué suffered severe flood damage in late 1989. Pop.: 18,000. Tourist information at bus station.

**Camping** Free camping in the beach area, no facilities. Rotary Club campsite, 2 km. from Carhué.

About 38 km. by road NE of Carhué, on the Roca Railway, is **Guaminí,** a pleasant summer hill resort of 3,500 inhabitants on the shore of Laguna del Monte, not as salty as Lago Epecuén; *pejerrey* fishing is one of the attractions. (Hotels: *La Aragonesa, Roma; Camping Municipal* on lake.) From Guarminí take routes 65 and 205 back to Buenos Aires, via Lobos (excellent ACA campsite at lake 10 km. S of Lobos).

*Santa Rosa* Pop. 55,000, capital of the Province of La Pampa, is 332 km. NW of Bahía Blanca by road, and 619 km. E of Buenos Aires by Route 5, via Chivilcoy (pop. 47,500) and Pehuajó (pop. 26,800). Hotels: *Calfacura,* Av. San Martín 695,

T 23612, 4-star, no restaurant, B without breakfast, but excellent steak restaurant around the corner; *San Martín* Pellegrini 12, E, clean, restaurant, garage; *Motel Calden*, Route 35, km. 330, D, good restaurant attached, large rooms, a bit run down).

---

## THE CORDOBA REGION (2)

---

**Córdoba, the Republic's second city, has some historic, colonial buildings and is an important route centre, especially for road travel to the NW. The Sierras de Córdoba contain many pleasant, small resorts in the hills.**

The pattern of the land in Northern Argentina, from the crest of the Andes in the W to the Río Paraguay in the E, consists of a high, dry Altiplano rising to a Puna cut into on its eastern face by rivers which flow into the Lowlands. This configuration of the land, similar to Bolivia, is carried southwards into all the north-western provinces of Argentina as far S as Tucumán, but the altitudes in Argentina are not so great as in Bolivia, and the whole area not so large. The E-running rivers born on the Puna flow into the Chaco; their broad valleys, or *quebradas*, make access to the heights comparatively easy. Between the base of the Puna and the Chaco lie a series of front range hogback hills running roughly from N to S; the lowlands between them are known in Argentina as the *valles*. Tucumán is the southern boundary of this kind of land. N of Tucumán crops can be grown without irrigation (though there is irrigation where the soil is absorbent) but S of Tucumán is droughty land, with long N-S ranges of low hills such as the Sierras de Córdoba, set in plains which have salt flats and swamps in the depressions.

**Settlement and Economy** The Puna is windswept, stony and treeless: the only growth is a low, blackish shrub (*tola*), and an occasional cactus. The first Spanish expedition from Bolivia entered Argentina in 1542. A little later a better and lower route was discovered—the main route used today—descending from La Quiaca to Jujuy through the Quebrada de Humahuaca, with rugged and colourful mountain ranges closing in on both sides. Along this new route the Spaniards pressed S and founded a group of towns in the north-west: Santiago del Estero (the first) in 1551, Tucumán in 1565, Córdoba in 1573, Salta in 1582, La Rioja in 1591, and Jujuy in 1592. Mendoza (1561), San Juan (1562), and San Luis (1598) were all colonized by people who crossed the passes from Chile. All these colonies were hemmed in by the warlike tribes of the Pampas, and until the war of extermination in 1880 the route from Buenos Aires to Córdoba was often unsafe. The Indians raided frequently for cattle, which they drove S and over the Andes for sale in Chile.

During the whole of the colonial era the trade of the area, mostly in mules, was with Bolivia and Peru rather than with Buenos Aires, which was little more than a garrison and smuggling port. The mules were bred mainly in the plains between Rosario, Santa Fe, and Córdoba, and driven finally into Salta for the great fair in February and March.

Historically, Tucumán was always important, for the two river routes of the Salado and the Dulce across the dry belt forced the mule traffic to pass through Tucumán on the way to Salta. Tucumán still produces most of Argentina's sugar. Tobacco is becoming important in the area, and an important factor in the North West is the growth of tourism.

In nearly all the provincial towns everything shuts between 1200 and 1600 except restaurants, hotels and post offices. There is nothing to do or see, and we suggest that this is a good time for travelling; buses are generally preferable to trains, being faster (except to Córdoba). (Panamericano buses have been

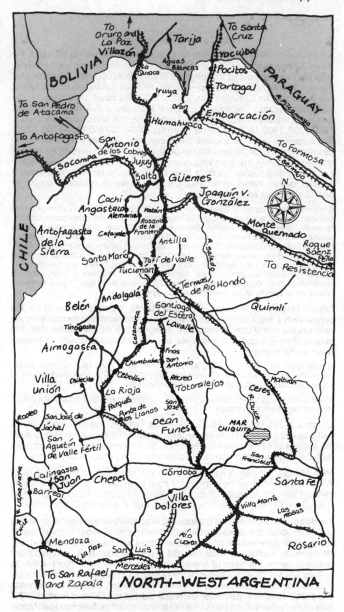

NORTH-WEST ARGENTINA

recommended in the NW as new, clean and with a good service.)

## From Buenos Aires to Córdoba

If hitch-hiking, take the train from Retiro (San Martín line) to Pilar to reach the main Córdoba highway via Rosario. There are two main road routes: the shorter (713 km.) via Rosario and the longer (835 km.) via Río Cuarto. The latter goes through **San Antonio de Areco**—also on the Mitre Railway—113 km. NW of Buenos Aires (also Chevallier bus, 2hrs, US$4, every hour). Here is the Museo Gauchesco Ricardo Güiraldes, on Camino Güiraldes and Aureliano, a typical *estancia* of the late 19th century with manor house, mill, tavern, open Wed.-Sun., 1000-1200, 1500-1800 in summer; in winter 1000-1200 and 1400-1700. Check if it is open in Jan.-Feb. Souvenir shop opposite. Güiraldes was a writer who described *gaucho* life; his best-known book is *Don Segundo Sombra*. Visitors can also see over Cina-Cina, a working *estancia*, tour for US$20 includes visit, typical lunch and riding display. Día de la Tradición is a *gaucho* festival with traditional parades, games, events on horseback, music and dance, celebrated on 10, 11 and 12 November each year.

Camping near the centre of town; 12 km. from centre, Auto-camping *La Porteña* on the Güiraldes *estancia*, good access roads. Six hotels. Many handicrafts, mainly *gaucho* objects, ceramics, silver, leather, colonial furniture. The Argentine artist Gasparini has a museum-school where he sells his drawings of *gauchos* to tourists; Calle de los Martínez, between Bolívar and Rivadavia. There is also a local natural history museum, Parque Metri, on Matheu and Hernández. For tourist information go to the Sub-Dirección de Turismo at Alsina and Lavalle. T 2101. *Hotel San Carlos*, opp tourist office, D, clean and friendly, ask in advance for meals; *Residencial Areco*, Segundo Sombra y Rivadavia, T 2166, good, D, comfortable, clean. Opposite Museo Gauchesco is *Hostería del Palomar*, typical barbecue; *Restaurant La Porteña* on the riverside, typical, very good.

Beyond Pergamino, 146 km., is **Venado Tuerto**, a pleasant town of 58,000 people with a fine Country Club at which race meetings and tournaments are held twice a year (*Hotel Touring*, cool, quiet, rec., C). At **Río Cuarto**, 138,000 people, there is a golf club and a fine old municipal building with an outlook tower worth seeing.

**Hotels** *Gran*, on Plaza, C, 1st class; *Alihué*, Sarsfield 69, D, good value, very friendly, big rooms. Near bus station on Calle Sobremonte 100-200 block are 3 cheap *residenciales*, *El Ciervo*, *Hospedaje El Bambi*, *Residencial Monge*, all E.

**Buses** Buenos Aires, US$35, frequent service. Bus to **Mendoza**, US$24; to **Córdoba** US$10; frequent departures to **Santiago**.

Córdoba is 225 km. N of Río Cuarto across flatlands and rolling hills. About half-way along the road runs on the retaining wall of the great Río Tercero dam; the artificial lake here is used for recreation. Río Tercero has gained in importance with the development of groundnut plantations and a local military factory.

**Villa María**, on the Mitre Railway and at a vital crossroads on the main Buenos Aires-Córdoba road, where it meets the most convenient highway route linking central Chile with Paraguay, Uruguay and Brazil, is a prosperous agricultural town (population 68,000). Hotels: *City*, D; *Alcázar*, near bus station, E, good value.

**Córdoba**, capital of Córdoba Province and Argentina's second city, has about 1.2 million inhabitants; it stands at an altitude of 440 metres. The district is well known for its countryside and the city for its buildings; it was founded as early as 1573. Its university, founded in 1613, was the first in the country. It is an important industrial centre, the home of Argentina's motor industry. In the heart of the city is Plaza San Martín with a statue of the Liberator. On the western side is the old Cabildo, for many years used as the police headquarters, but soon to be open to the public. Next to it stands the Cathedral, started in 1697 and finished 1787. One of the features of this part of the city is its old churches. Near Plaza San Martín

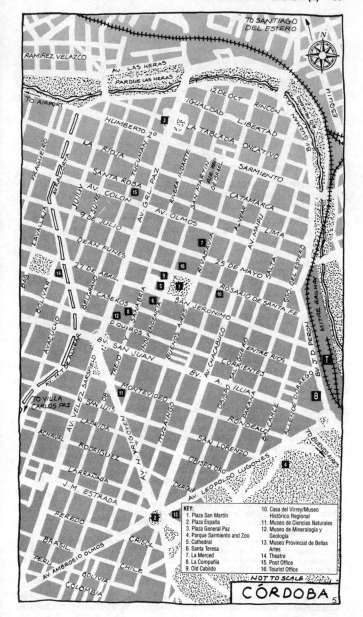

TO SANTIAGO DEL ESTERO

RAMIREZ VELAZCO

AV. LAS HERAS
PARQUE LAS HERAS

TO AIRPORT

12 DE OCT   RINCON
IGUALDAD   LIBERTAD
HUMBERTO 1°   LA TABLADA   ONCATIVO
LA RIOJA   SARMIENTO
TUCUMAN   CATAMARCA
SANTA ROSA
AV. COLON
SUCRE   9 DE JULIO
DEAN FUNES   LIMA
27 DE ABRIL   25 DE MAYO   SALTA
CASEROS   SAN JERONIMO   ROSARIO DE SANTA FE
D.QUIROS   BV. SAN JUAN   BUENOS AIRES   ENTRE RIOS
MONTEVIDEO   CORRIENTES
SAN LUIS   BV. A. ILLIA
LAPRIDA   PARANA   RONDEAU
RODRIGUEZ   SAN LORENZO   BALCARCE
LARRANAGA   OBISPO ORO
J.M. ESTRADA   DERQUI
PEREDO   AV. LEOPOLDO LUGONES
BRASIL   CRISOL
PERU   CHILE
AV. AMBROSIO OLMOS   BOLIVIA
COLOMBIA

FRAGUEIRO   AV. CACERES
JUJUY   AV. COLON
LAVALLEJA
BOLIVAR
AYACUCHO
AV. VELEZ SARSFIELD
AV. MT. DE ALVEAR
TO VILLA CARLOS PAZ

RIVERA INDARTE   SAN MARTIN
AV. GRL. PAZ   AV. OLMOS
BELGRANO
SANTA ABRIA
INDEPENDENCIA
TREJO
H. YRIGOYEN
MUZAINGO

ALVEAR   AV. MAIPU
RIVADAVIA
SGO. DEL ESTERO
BV. J.D. PERON
BV. GUZMAN
PJE. RED DE ISRAEL

TO BUENOS AIRES

MITRE RAILWAY

T

B

**KEY:**
1. Plaza San Martín
2. Plaza España
3. Plaza General Paz
4. Parque Sarmiento and Zoo
5. Cathedral
6. Santa Teresa
7. La Merced
8. La Compañía
9. Old Cabildo
10. Casa del Virrey/Museo Histórico Regional
11. Museo de Ciencias Naturales
12. Museo de Mineralogía y Geología
13. Museo Provincial de Bellas Artes
14. Theatre
15. Post Office
16. Tourist Office

NOT TO SCALE

**CÓRDOBA**

at Independencia 122 is the 16th century Carmelite convent and chapel of Santa Teresa, which houses the Museo de Arte Religiosa. The church of La Compañía, on Calles Trejo y Caseros, with a simple façade, dates from about 1650 and is a far better building than the Cathedral; its façade was rebuilt in the 20th century. The barrel vault and cupola of the Capilla Doméstica of this church, built entirely of Paraguayan cedar, are unique. The basilica of La Merced at 25 de Mayo 83, was built in the early 19th century, though its fine gilt wooden pulpit dates from the colonial period. On its exterior, overlooking Calle Rivadavia, are fine murals by local artist Armando Sica. There are some pleasant small 18th century churches with striking bell gables and undulating pediments. The neo-gothic church of the Sagrado Corazón (Sacred Heart), built in 1933, at Buenos Aires e Yrigoyen, is also worth a visit. The Casa del Virrey (Viceroy's House), one block E of the Plaza San Martín, is a fine colonial building housing the Museo Histórico Provincial. Further E, at Blvd. J.D. Perón, is the magnificent Mitre railway station, dating from the late 19th century, with its beautiful tiled *confitería*.

Córdoba was once very picturesque, but industrialisation and population growth have turned it into a busy modern city with a flourishing shopping centre, though much of the centre has been improved by pedestrianisation.

**Local Holidays** 6 July (Foundation of the City); 30 September (St Jerome), 7-10 October.

**Hotels** More expensive hotels, mainly in the centre: *Crillón*, Rivadavia 85, T 46093, A, very friendly, good restaurant, comfortable; *Mediterráneo*, Av. M.T. de Alvear 10 T 24-0086, A; *Cañada*, Av. M.T. de Alvear 580, T 37569, B, good, recently modernized to include conference facilities with full technical back-up, a/c, private bath, TV and video, restaurant, laundry, transport; *Sussex*, San Jerónimo 125, T 229071, B, comfortable, roomy, discounts for ACA members; *Windsor*, Buenos Aires 159, T 224012, B, comfortable, very good; all these have garages. *Del Sol*, Balcarce 144, T 33961, C with bath, clean, fan, a/c extra, piped music, rec. More economical: *Garden*, 25 de Mayo 35, D, central, clean, secure, highly rec.
   Many hotels between Plaza San Martín and bus terminal, most of them in the cheaper brackets: On Corrientes, *Bristol*, No. 64, T 36222, D, bathroom, a/c, telephone; *Hospedaje Suiza*, (No. 569), D, near bus terminal, very friendly but not too clean; *Hospedaje My House*, (No. 519), D, clean, quiet, very friendly, rec.; *Residencial Mi Valle* (No. 586), E, small, clean and nice, family-run, washing facilities, rec.; *Res. Corrientes* (No. 540), E, good rooms. Plenty of hotels of all classes on San Jerónimo: *Felipe II* (No. 279), T 44752, C in new part, D in old section, adequate; *Ritz*, (No. 495), T 45031, B, "clean but delapidated"; *Sportsman* (No. 590), D, clean but run down; *Corona* (No. 574), T 228789, D not inc. breakfast, clean, comfortable, friendly; *Dallas* (No. 339), T 46091, C, rec. On Balcarce: *Residencial Plaza* (No. 336), D, 150 metres from bus station, clean, friendly and quiet; *Mallorca*, (No. 73), E, quite clean and near bus and railway station; *Roma Termini*, Entre Rios 687, D, close to bus terminal, recently renovated by Italian family, spotless, welcoming. *Florida*, Rosario de Santa Fe 459, D, clean, friendly, rec., some rooms with a/c.
   *Royal*, Blvd. J.D. Perón 180, T 45000, B, garage. Near Alta Córdoba station (Belgrano railway): *Italiano*, Cabrera 313, D; *Las Colonias*, Cabrera 339, C; *Suguía*, Pena 1561, D; *Hospedaje Bontempo*, Cabrera 177, E. The following offer 10% discount to ISIC card holders: *del Sol*, Balcarce 144 (see above), and on Blvd. Pte. Arturo Illia *Damar*, No. 518, *del Boulevard*, No. 182, *Heydi*, No. 615.

**Camping** Municipal site, Gral. San Martín, at the back of the Complejo Ferial (bus 31).

**Restaurants** There are numerous grills of all categories on the outskirts of the city, especially in the Cerro de las Rosas district, for meals out-of-doors when the weather is suitable. Many cheap restaurants along San Jerónimo including *San Carlos*, No. 431, good food and service. *Casino Español*, Rivadavia 63, good. *Unión Cordobesa de Ajedrez*, Entre Rios 339, excellent cheap restaurant; *Romagnolo*, opposite the Mitre railway station, rec., and *Comedor Albéniz*, opposite Alto Córdoba station, a bit noisy. *Fancy Café*, Andarte 317, good, cheap; *Firenze*, 25 de Mayo 220, busy, pleasant, traditional cafe. Excellent fruit juices (*licuados*) at *Kiosco Americano*, Tucumán 185. Recommended for vegetarian food is *La Pepperoni*, San Martín 114; also *Granix*, 9 de Julio 479.

**Rent-a-Car** Avis at airport and Corrientes 452, T 227384.

**Local transport** Municipal buses do not accept cash; you have to buy tokens (*cospeles*) from kiosks, US$0.15. Buses No. 70, 71 and 73 run between the Mitre Station (and bus terminus) and the Belgrano station at Alto Córdoba.

**Museums** Museo Histórico Provincial, in the Casa del Virrey Marqués de Sobremonte, Rosario de Santa Fé 318, closed in 1990 for renovation; Museo de Ciencias Naturales, Av. Yrigoyen 115, open Mon.-Fri. 0800-1900, Sat. 0900-1200, good guided tours (in Spanish); Museo de Mineralogía y Geología of the Universidad Nacional de Córdoba, V. Sarsfield 365, open Mon.-Fri., 1400-1600; Museo de Zoología, same address, open Mon.-Fri. 0900-1200, Wed.-Fri. 1600-1800; Museo del Teatro y de la Música, in the Teatro San Martín, V. Sarsfield 365, open Mon.-Fri. 0900-1200; Museo Provincial de Bellas Artes, Plaza España, open Tues.-Fri. 0900-1300, 1500-2000; Museo Municipal de Bellas Artes, Gral. Paz 33, open Tues.-Fri. 0930-1330, 1630-2030, Sat. 1630-2030; Museo Histórico de la Ciudad, Entre Rios 40; Centro de Arte Contemporáneo, housed in the Chateau Carreras, 10 km. W on the road to La Calera (bus no. 31 from Plaza San Martín); Museo de Meteorología Nacional, San Luis 801, open Tues.-Fri. 0900-1300, 1400-1800, Sat. 0830-1230—nearby in Calle Laprida is Argentina's main observatory, open Wed. 2000-2200; Museo Policial, in the old Cabildo, Plaza San Martín, open Mon.-Fri. 1600-2000, Sat. 0900-1200; Museo de Arte Religiosa, in the convent of Santa Teresa, Independencia 122, Sat. 1030-1230.

**Exchange** Lloyds Bank (BLSA), Buenos Aires 23. Citibank, Rivadavia 104, poor rates. American Express, 25 de Mayo 125: get "permission" here first, then go to Exprinter, Rivadavia 39 (huge commission), or Maguitur, Rivadavia 30, 1% commission. Many *cambios* on Rivadavia just off Plaza San Martín—shop around for best rate. *Sat/Sun*

**Post Office** Parcel Service on the ground floor of the Correo Central, Av. Colón 201, beside the customs office, up to 20 kg; wrapping service for small fee. **Telecommunications** Entel, Av. Gen. Paz 36 and 27 de Abril 27.

**Health** English-speaking doctor, Ernesto J. MacLoughlin, Centro Asistencial Privado de Enfermedades Renales, 9 de Julio 714, home Pérez del Viso 4316, T 814745. Dentist, Dra. Olga Olmedo de Herrera, Fco. J. Muñiz 274, T 804378, her daughters speaks English and will translate.

**Cultural Institues** Asociación Argentina de Cultura Británica, Bv. San Juan 137, good library, poor reading room. Open Mon.-Fri. 0900-1200, Mon., Wed., Fri. 1600-1945, Tues., Thur. 1500-1945. Goethe Institut, Bv. Illia 356, open Tues.-Fri. 1700-2100.

**Consulates** Bolivia, Castro Barros 783, T 732827; Chile, Crisol 280, T 609622; Paraguay, 9 de Julio 573, T 226388; Peru, Poeta Lugones 212, T 603730. Austria, J. Cortés 636, T 720450; Italy, Ayacucho 131, T 221020; Germany, A. Olmos 501, T 692269; Spain, Bv. Chacabuco 875, T 605013; Sweden, M.T. de Alvear 10, T 220094; Switzerland, Entre Ríos 185, L-10, T 226848; Belgium, F. Posse 2533, T 813298; Finland, Chacabuco 716, T 605049.

**Laundry** Chacabuco 32; Lavarap, Paraná y Rondeau.

**Tourist Office** Dirección Provincial de Turismo, Tucumán 25. Municipal tourist information centre on San Martín at Rosario de Santa Fé 39. Information office also at bus station, has free maps; extensive information on accommodation and camping in the province, helpful. Tourist Office desk at airport often unmanned, but car-hire desks next to it are most helpful. A useful information booklet is the free *Plataforma 40* put out by Nueva Estación Terminal de Omnibus de Córdoba (Netoc).

**Club Andino**, Duarte Quirós 1591.

**Air** Pajas Blancas airport, 11 km. from the city, is modern and has a good restaurant. Taxi to airport, US$15. Airport bus leaves terminal opposite railway station; irregular schedule, 30 mins, accepts *cospeles* only. Several flights to Buenos Aires daily, about 1 hr.; to Mendoza daily at 1530 (55 mins); to Tucumán 4 a week, AR and Lapa. To Iguazú, AR 2 a week. AR once a week each to Santa Cruz, Bolivia and Santiago de Chile. Aerolíneas Argentinas, Av. Colón 520, T 819676. Austral, Av. Colón 678, T 810997. LAB, same location as Alitalia, Av. 25 de Mayo 6625, 3rd floor.

**Buses** Excellent new bus station at Blvd. Perón 300, with Tourist Office, many public telephones, shops including food supermarket on 3rd floor, bank, post office, police, restaurants, and showers in bathrooms (about 6 blocks from centre), crowded at weekends. Buenos Aires-Córdoba with Costera Criolla or Cacorba bus takes about 10 hours, and on from Córdoba to Salta (US$35) and Jujuy (US$45) with Panamericano, about 12 and 15 hours. Chevallier, Buenos Aires to Córdoba via Route 8, or via Route 9, many buses on both routes, 10½ hrs., US$38. Bus to Mendoza (10 hours), 6 a day with TAC, frequent delays and breakdowns, 1 daily with Upsalla, US$20. Bus to **Tucumán**, US$25, 8 hrs., about 8 a day, Panamericano has more than other companies (T 223569). To **Posadas** (Expreso Singer) Tues., Thurs., Sat., 1730 arrive at Posadas at 1335; Thurs. and Sat. bus continues to Iguazú arriving 1930 next day, no air-conditioning. Onda operates a service from **Paraná** via Santa Fe and Rosario to and from Córdoba. To **Santiago del Estero**. To **La Rioja** 3-4 a day with Cotil and El Cóndor, 6½ hrs.; some go on to Catamarca. Córdoba- La Rioja- Aimogasta-**Tinogasta- Fiambalá** with El Cóndor, Tues., Thurs., Fri.; leaves Tinogasta 1140 arr. Fiambalá 1240, returns from Fiambalá same day 1445, from Tinogasta at 1600 (**see also page 126**). La Calera bus leaves for **Belén** (Catamarca) on Mon., Wed., Fri., at 2100, arr. Belén 1030; return journey, also via **Andalgalá**, Wed., Fri., Sun., dep. 1600 arr. Andalgalá 1735, dep. 1750, arr. Córdoba 0055. Cacorba, efficient a/c buses, serve **Villa Carlos Paz**, **Cosquín** and **La Falda** in the Sierras de Córdoba.

Bus Córdoba-**Asunción** (Paraguay) direct with Brújula, four times a week, also with Cacorba 19 hrs. Regular bus between Córdoba and **Montevideo** (Uruguay). To **Lima**, Peru, with Colta, dep. Fri. 2200, via Mendoza, 0700 Sat., arrives Lima Tues. a.m., US$130. To **Pocitos** (Bolivian border) with Panamericano (T 550-336/501/574), Agustín Garzón 1229, San Vicente, Córdoba. In general, it is best to travel from Córdoba if you are going N, as at stations in between it may be hard to get a seat; a seat is only guaranteed if one pays US$1 extra.

**Railways**  The Mitre Railway (next to bus station) *Rayo de Sol* night train takes 12 hours to and from Buenos Aires. Tourist class US$18, 1st US$22, Pullman US$27. Car transporter on the Tues. and Thur. service to Córdoba, Mon. and Wed. to Bs.As. *Rayo de Sol* leaves Buenos Aires (Retiro) 2100 daily and Córdoba 2030 daily. The Belgrano Railway runs *El Norteño* train on Wed., Fri. and Sun., from Buenos Aires (Retiro) at 0845; from Córdoba, 0927 same days (12 hours), no sleepers. The Alta Córdoba railway station for long-distance journeys is a good 2 km. from the city centre. *El Norteño* continues to Tucumán, Wed., Fri. and Sun., 2200 (15 hours). It is advisable to check all trains as services are sometimes suspended without notice. The *Rayo de Sol* trains connect with bus services to various resorts in the Sierras de Córdoba, and the *Norteño* to La Rioja and Catamarca.

The ***Sierras of Córdoba***, rising in undulating hills from the pampas, their lower slopes often wooded, particularly in the S, attract each year a large number of visitors. The highest peak, Champaquí (2,975 metres) has a small lake about 2,550 metres up. The hills run, roughly, for 500 km. from N to S; west of Córdoba they are 150 km. wide. There are three ranges of them: the Sierra Grande, the longest, in the middle, with Sierra Chica to the E and Sierra de Guisapampa and its continuation, the Sierra de Pocho, to the W. A network of good roads gives pleasant contrasts of scenery, but there are few footpaths and trails for the walker. The region's climate is dry, sunny and exhilarating, especially in winter.

At the foot of the Sierra Chica are large dams to contain the waters of the Río Primero at Río Molinos (29 km. from Córdoba, Route 5, good *pejerrey* and trout-fishing; bus to Villa Carlos Paz, US$2.60), San Roque, and Río Tercero. There are two other large dams in the hills, at Cruz del Eje and La Viña. They provide power and irrigation, and the lakes are in themselves attractive. The Government keeps them stocked with fish. Sailing is popular.

Information can be obtained at travel agencies, at the Dirección Provincial de Turismo or at Casa de Córdoba at Callao 332, Buenos Aires.

**Note**  There are innumerable good hotels and *pensiones* in the Córdoba mountain region; names are therefore not always given. Many services in this area are closed out of season.

**The Punilla Valley**: *Villa Carlos Paz* , pop. 46,000, is 36 km. W. of Córdoba (buses from Córdoba bus terminal every 15 mins. in summer, 36 km., US$1.30; taxi from Córdoba airport, US$10.50; Buenos Aires-Villa Carlos Paz with Costera Criolla,US$24—bus terminal on Calle Alvear), on man-made Lago San Roque. It is the nearest resort to Córdoba and is therefore often crowded. Tours possible on amphibian buses which go as far as the two dams on the lake; launch trips also available. There is a pleasant 5 km. walk to the dam from the outskirts of Villa Carlos Paz. At the Casa de Gaspar, Miguel Cané and El Redentor, roller-skating and optical illusions, Fri.-Sun. 1400-1900 out of season. A chair-lift (US$2.50) runs up the slopes to a tearoom and night club overlooking the valley, between 0900 and 1900. Bus tours to areas such as  Sierra Chica, for those who like snack bars, fun slides and gravity-defying houses.

**Accommodation, Restaurants and Services** Plenty of hotels, big and small, e.g. *El Ciervo de Oro*, Hipólito Yrigoyen 995, on the lake, B, rec. *Las Junturas*, Florida 181, excellent, clean and friendly, hot shower, use of barbecue and fridge; *El Monte*, Caseros 431, D, very good, rec. *Mar del Plata*, D, friendly, rec.; *Villa Carlos Paz Parque*, Santa Fe 50, D, full board available, rec.; *Riviera*, D with bath, clean, rec. Camping at ACA site and several others including *Las Tolderías* and *Los Pinos*, Curro Enrique y Lincoln (open all year). Best buys: leather mats, bags, pottery. *Restaurant Carlos Paz* highly rec. for food and setting. *Restaurant Pamilla Mingo*, Av. Uruguay opp *Hotel Uruguay*, not cheap but good. **N.B.** Drinking water is not safe. Banco de Córdoba, Av. San Martín, will change US$ cash only. Laundry at San Martín y Libertad. Post Office and telephone on Av. Gral. San Martín. **Tourist office** at bus station, very friendly.

From Villa Carlos Paz Route 38 runs N through the Punilla valley to the following string of resorts: *Cosquín*, 63 km. from Córdoba, on the banks of a river. Bus Córdoba-Cosquín US$2.60, Empresa La Capillense; 1½ hrs., via Carlos Paz or with La Calera via the San Roque dam. Altitude, 720 metres; pop. 16,000. Camping on south bank of river. Tourist office at San Martín 560, *Hotel La Serrana*, P. Ortiz 740, near bus station, E, friendly, good; likewise *Hotel Italia*, across from bus station, E, rec.; *Residencial Cosquín*, Tucumán y Sabattini, F p.p., clean; *Hotel Petit*, Calle Sabattini, E, 2 blocks from bus station. Take a bus to the Pan de Azúcar hill from where there is a good view over the Punilla valley, at 0930, return 1630 or 2 hrs. walk. Chairlift to top (all year round). A folklore festival is held in the last half of January at Cosquín, from 2200-0500, tickets from US$6 per night. (Recent reports suggest that the festival is becoming commercialized.) 19 km. on is **Valle Hermoso**, near La Falda (buses from Villa Carlos Paz). Altitude, 850 metres. Old restored chapel of San Antonio, a little gem. Riding, motoring. Youth hostel, address "Steinhaus", dirty, no heating, very cold, US$2 p.p., pay extra for gas. Camping near river, US$0.60 p.p., all facilities, but not too clean.

*La Falda*, (pop. 30,000) 82 km. from Córdoba, a good touring centre, friendly and peaceful. Bus from Córdoba 2 hrs., US$3. Altitude, 933 metres. Helpful tourist offices at bus station and in old railway station building. Model railway museum at Las Murallas zoo at the end of Av. 25 de Mayo. Nearby is the privately run Ambato Archaeological Museum; articles are well displayed, worth a visit, open Thur.-Sun. and public holidays 0900-2000, US$0.50 entrance. About 30 hotels in all categories, all full in Dec.-Feb. holiday season, at other times a basic room with bath is in our E range. Houses for rent 1 March to 30 Nov. on a monthly basis. *Restaurant El Bochín*, Av. España 117, good, cheap. Tap water is not safe. Bancos de la Nación and de Suquía for exchange. Students of all nations welcome at Córdoba University holiday centre at Vaquerías, 2 km. from La Falda. Travel agent Wella Viajes, Av. Edén 412, loc. 12, T 0548-21380, offers 15% discount to ISIC and youth card holders for trekking, climbing, etc. to Cerro Champaquí. Camping near small river. (Bus from Buenos Aires, US$25.35)

**Excursions** to Quebrada Chica, Cascada del Molino. Extensive hiking in surrounding hills. 3½ km. on by Route 38 is **Huerta Grande**, at 971 metres, a bathing resort with good fishing and medicinal waters. Round trip excursion to **Cascadas de Olaén**. Take the road to Valle Hermoso S 10 km. towards Cosquín, then follow dirt road about 12½ km. to the crossing marked "Cascadas de Olaén"; from here walk 4½ km. to the falls: quite spectacular canyon—the water splashes into a small lake full of little fish. Return to the dirt road and 2½ km. to a monolith and another dirt road, which leads to La Falda. See the Pampa de Olaén, where there are many quartz mines. La Candelaria, 53 km. W. along an unpaved road is the site of a Jesuit estancia and chapel dating from 1693.

Bus connections with Uruguay from La Falda on Mon., Fri., Sat. and Sun. at 1730, arriving at 1200 next day with CORA (of Uruguay). Connections to Rosario, Mendoza, Catamarca, Santiago del Estero, Tucumán, Salta and Jujuy.

*La Cumbre*, 15 km. N of La Falda. Bus from Córdoba US$4, 2½ hrs. Altitude 1,141 metres. Trout streams with good fishing from November to April. Swimming, golf, tennis. Has an airport. *Hotel Lima*, swimming pool, C, quiet, clean. Charming small inn, *Victoria*; *La Cumbre Inn*, large and commercial, good views; *Residencial Peti*, good, friendly, D. Good restaurants.

*Cruz Chica*, 2 ½ km. N of La Cumbre, altitude, 1,067 metres, has very English houses and gardens in pine woods. Most attractive. Good English boys' school.

*Los Cocos*, 8 km. N. of La Cumbre, is a delightful, extremely popular mountain resort with 3 first rate hotels and many holiday houses. *Hostería Zanier*, D, full board B, rec. Hang-gliding nearby at Cuchi Corral.

*Capilla del Monte*, in the heart of the Sierras, 106 km. from Córdoba (bus 3 hrs., US$5.20, *Hospedaje Italiano*, E, clean, showers, opposite bus station; municipal campsite on the way to Cerro Uritorco and also some 9½ km. from Capilla del Monte) . Altitude, 914 metres.

Medicinal waters (good baths at La Toma), rocks and waterfalls and wide views; see particularly El Zapato rock, despite its graffiti. Excursions in the hills, particularly to Cerro Uritorco (1,950 metres) and to Los Alazanes dam; good path on Uritorco, walk takes 2½ hrs. Permission to walk obtainable from a house beyond the river crossing (US$0.60). You can walk on to the direct dirt road to San Marcos Sierra (22 km.); many parakeets and small farmhouses. Along the way you will also get views down to the **Cruz del Eje** dam (camping possible at foot of dam, or stay at friendly, family-run *Hotel España* in village, E, some private baths; rowboats for rent on dam's lake, where there is good fishing). Cruz del Eje (pop. 23,100) is one of two towns with its own "micro-climate" (the other is Merlo in San Luis Province) and own honey production—that made from carob (*algarrobo*) blossom (1 kg about US$2). Excellent trout fishing at Tío Mayo, an hour from Capilla del Monte by car.

A road runs **North from Córdoba** to Ascochinga via pleasant little townships such as Villa Allende, Río Ceballos, Salsipuedes and La Granja. At El Manzano, 40 km. N of Córdoba, a road branches W. to Candonga, altitude 810 metres. The historic church, now a National Monument, was built in 1730 as an ortaory of the Jesiut Estancia of Santa Gertrudis. The arch protrudes to form a porch covering the entrance. 14 km. N of Ascochinga is Santa Catalina, originally a Jesuit mission founded in 1622 and the most elaborate Jesuit establishment in the hills around Córdoba (no bus from Ascochinga, but 2 a day from Jesús María). (See the church begun in 1754, workshops and stone conduits; the families who now occupy the place as a summer home will show you round.)

**Services**: In Ascochinga *Hostería El Cortijo*, C, full board only, good value, with bath, small swimming pool and river outside, horses for rent, US$1/hr.; 5 km. walk to Tres Cascadas falls and *balneario*. During winter, open weekends only. Campsite open all year. In **Río Cebollos**: *Albergue La Gloria*, affiliated to IYHA, E, warmly rec.; 5 campsites. Several campsites also at **Salsipuedes**.

From Asochinga a road runs E for 20 km. to **Jesús María**, 51 km. N of Córdoba on Route 9. Altitude, 533 metres. Good 18th century Jesuit church and the remains of its once famous winery; in the cloister is an excellent Museo Jesuítico, said to be one of the best on the continent (open Mon.-Fri. 0800-1200 and 1400-1900, Sat. and Sun. 1600-2000). Each January there is a gaucho and folklore festival, lasting 10 nights; very popular, entrance fee US$1-2. Good trout, *dorado*, and carp fishing in winter. Direct bus from Córdoba, US$2, 1½hrs. Some 4 km. N of Jesús María is Sinsacate, with an interesting church. There is also a fine colonial posting inn, now a museum, with long, deep verandah and chapel attached. Route 9, the main road to Santiago del Estero, runs N. another 132 km. to **Villa de María**, the birthplace of Leopoldo Lugones, a poet of country life. His house is a museum. (*Hotel City*, good, D.)

At Argañadas, 26 km. S. of Villa de María, a turning leads W. to **Cerro Colorado**, 160 km. N of Córdoba. There are more than 30,000 rock paintings by the Comechingones Indians in the Cerro Colorado archaeological park, where there is cheap accommodation (e.g. with Sosa family) and camping. You can stay with Don Elvio, who runs the *pulpería* near the archaeological station, but watch prices. Buses: from Córdoba, 1 a day at 1530, 4½ hrs., US$4, return 0600 Mon.-Sat., 1800 Sun.; from Jesús María, daily 1610.

**Southwest of Córdoba** a scenic road climbs through the Sierra Grande to another chain of resorts, Mina Clavero, Villa Dolores and Yacanto. **Mina Clavero** is 140 km. from Córdoba by bus, 6 a day, 4 hrs., marvellous ride through grand lake and hill scenery, and curious palm trees. A good centre for exploring the high *sierra*. No money exchange available. There is a nice church and a most interesting museum, dedicated by a French archaeologist, 13 km. south from Mina Clavero and about 5 km. from the village of Nono, entrance US$0.60, called "Rocsen" open 0900 till sunset, with furniture, minerals, instruments, animals, etc. Altitude, 915 metres. (Restaurant: *Rincón Suizo*, Calle Champaquí, good pastries.) Road from Mina Clavero over the Sierra Grande to *Hotel El Cóndor*, goes to Carlos Paz (bus leaves Mina Clavero at 0800)—not yet paved. Views from El Cóndor over Lago San Roque. If hitching from Córdoba down this route to Mendoza, best starting point is Ycho Cruz, beyond Carlos Paz.

**Villa Dolores**, 187 km. from Córdoba (bus takes 5 hrs.), 48 km. from Mina Clavero. Altitude, 529 metres. Population: 10,000. The road from Córdoba crosses the two mountain ranges to reach finally the Pampa de Achala, a huge desert plateau of grey granite. (Hotels: *Hospedaje Cáceres*, Brizuela 390, E; *Residencial Champaquí*, Erdman 162, E. Camping: nearest site is Piedra Pintada, 15 min-bus-ride away, pleasant little village well situated for walks into mountains.) Bus to San Luis 5¼ hrs.

From San Javier you can explore **Champaquí** (altitude 2,884 metres). For top, follow path to Capilla La Constancia, set in river valley with pine and nut trees, 2-3 hrs. Take water from here, then cross the river (path), keep left through a pinewood up to a mountain range and follow it up to the top of a huge plateau. Good path, about 4-5 hrs., and then you reach a square enclosure, whence you keep left. Follow stone mounds about 2 hrs. until you see the higher of two peaks, which is Champaquí. Lovely views, descent 4 hrs. to La Constancia. Not to be attempted in misty weather.

**Yacanto**, near Villa Dolores, at the foot of Champaquí, in a region of woods and waterfalls. Reached by road from Villa Dolores railway station. Curative waters.

A road **South from Córdoba** runs to Alta Gracia and to the Río Tercero dam. **Alta Gracia**, altitude 580 metres, population 39,000, 48 km. S.W. of Córdoba beside Lago Trajamar. (Bus 1 hr., every 15 mins, US$0.75.) Interesting colonial church, finished c1762, open a.m. and after 1700, and buildings housing Museo del Virrey Liniers, on the Estancia de Alta Gracia, founded in 1588 and taken over by the Jesuits in 1643, open Tues.-Fri. 0900-1300, 1500-1830, Sat., Sun. 0930-1230, 1530-1830, US$0.50 (all day in summer). There is also the Museo Manuel de Falla on Pellegrini Final, closed Mon., entry US$0.30, where the Spanish composer spent his last years. Take the local bus to La Paysanita or La Serranita for a quiet environment (but no cheap accommodation). *Hostería Reina*, Urquiza 129, good. Two camping sites, one scruffy, the other better and free in winter, where is golf course. A few reasonably priced restaurants in town centre. Tourist office inside clock tower by Lago Trajamar. New casino. Beautiful views from the Gruta de la Virgen de Lourdes, 3 km. W. of town. To the Bosque Alegre and Observatory it is 24 km. N.W., open Thurs. 1600-1800 Sun. 1000-1200 and 1600- 1800. Good views over Córdoba, Alta Gracia and the Sierra Grande. To the Río Tercero dam is 79 km.; on the lake is a workers' holiday colony and an ACA *Unidad Turística*.

**Villa General Belgrano**, 85 km. S of Córdoba on Route 36, is a completely German town founded by the surviving interned seamen from the *Graf Spee*, some of whom still live in the town. It is a pleasant resort and a good centre for excursions in the surrounding mountains. Beer festival in October. If walking between here and La Cumbrecita, lodge with Siegfried at *Alta Vista*, F, friendly. **Accommodation** Hotel Bremen, Route 5 y Cerro Negro, T 6133, B, restaurant, sports facilities; *Allgauer Hütten*, D, clean, friendly, quiet. There are two *Youth Hostels*, one at Estancia Alta Vista, 14 km. from the town, and one, El Rincón, in the town; both offer discounts to ISIC and youth card holders (25% and 20% repectively).

**La Cumbrecita**, a German village reached from General Belgrano by daily bus at 1500 or by taxi (US$30, 1-1½ hrs.) 42 km NW. along an unpaved road, is another Sierra resort. Good walking and riding. Hotels: *Cascadas*, B, with pool, tennis etc.; *Panorama*, C, higher up hill (T 98406); three others (C) and *Residencial Casa Rosita*, E. *Youth Hostel* at Villa Alpina, 17 km. from the town.

Some 200 km. NE of Córdoba the Río Dulce, flowing in places through salt flats, runs into the shallow **Mar Chiquita** on the southern margin of the Chaco. People who live in the valley of the Río Dulce are so used to the taste of its water that they often add a pinch of salt to the water they drink when away from home. Mar Chiquita, which is now growing rapidly, is naturally salty, and the water is warm. No river drains it, though two other rivers flow into it from the Sierras of Córdoba in the flood season. There are several islands in the lake. On its southern shore is the small town of **Miramar**, which is being gradually overwhelmed by the expanding Mar Chiquita. The area is a very popular resort during the summer months; its salt waters are used in the treatment of rheumatic ailments and skin diseases. It is best reached by a railway W. from Santa Fe to Deán Funes, which runs within a few km. of the southern shore. The lake is about 320 km. SE of Santiago del Estero.

**Hotels** *Savoy*, cheap, very friendly. **Camping** Autocamping Lilly. Bahía de los Sanavirones.

(**Note** This Mar Chiquita and its town, Miramar, must not be confused with the other Mar Chiquita to the N. of Mar del Plata and the seaside resort of Miramar, S. of Mar del Plata.)

## SANTIAGO DEL ESTERO, TUCUMAN, SALTA AND JUJUY (3)

The route to the major tourist centre of Salta, from where trips can be made into Andean regions, the Quebrada de Humahuaca and the Calchaquí and Cachi valleys. There are prehispanic ruins near Tafí del Valle, Quilmes, Santa Rosa de Tastil and others. This is also a region in which there are a number of Amerindian groups.

*Santiago del Estero*, the oldest Argentine town, was founded in 1553 by settlers pushing S from Peru. It is 395 km. N of Córdoba and 159 km. SE of Tucumán. Population 170,000. On the main square, Plaza Libertad, stand the Municipalidad and the Cathedral (the fifth on the site). The fine Casa de Gobierno is on Plaza San Martín, 3 blocks away. In the convent of Santo Domingo, Urquiza y 25 de Mayo, is a "Holy Shroud", one of two copies of the "Turin Shroud", thought until recently to have covered the body of Christ. This copy was given by Philip II to his "beloved colonies of America". On Plaza Lugones is the pleasant old church of San Francisco, the oldest surviving church in the city, founded in 1565. At the back of the church is the cell of San Francisco Solano, patron saint of Tucumán, who stayed in Santiago in 1593. Beyond the church is the pleasant Parque Aguirre. Airport (AR flights to Buenos Aires daily).

**Festival** Carnival in February is to be avoided: virtually everything throwable gets thrown by everyone at everyone else.

**Hotels** *Gran Hotel*, Avellaneda y Independencia, B; *Embajador*, Buenos Aires 60, D. Around the bus terminus are: *Residencial Rodas*, Gallo 432, E, clean, safe, very friendly. *Hotel-Residencia Iovino*, Moreno 602, C; *Santa Rita*, Santa Fe 273, E, clean, basic; *Residencial Santa Fe*, Santa Fe 255, E.

**Camping** Las Casuarinas in the Parque Aguirre.

**Restaurant** *Restaurant Sociedad Española*, Independencia, popular, good value; *Comedor Sirio Libanés*, Plaza San Martín; *Comedor Centro de Viajantes*, Buenos Aires 37, good value lunches; *Mía Mamma*, on Plaza, good restaurant/salad bar, pricey.

**Museums** Museo Arqueológico, Avellaneda 353, containing a large collection of Indian pottery and artefacts from the Chaco, brought together by Emil and Duncan Wagner, open Mon.-Fri., 0800-1300, 1400-1900, Sat., 0900-1200, free; **Museo Histórico**, Urquiza 354, open Mon.-Fri., 0830-1230, 1530-1830, Sat. 0900-1200; **Muséo de Bellas Artes**, Independencia between 9 de Julio and Urquiza, open Mon.-Fri., 0900-1300; **Museo Andrés Chazarreta**, Mitre 127, handicrafts.

**Exchange** Banco Francés, 9 de Julio y 24 de Septiembre; **Noroeste Cambio**, 24 de Septiembre 220, good rates.

**Buses** to Resistencia, 3 a day, 9 hrs., US$20, run by El Rayo company, via Quimili and Roque Sáenz Peña (8 hrs.); also to Córdoba, 12 a day, US$20; to Tucumán (via Río Hondo) US$6. To Buenos Aires, 3 a day, 12 hrs., US$50. Three a day to Salta, 5½ hrs., and to Jujuy, 7 hrs. Tourist Office extremely helpful.

*Termas de Río Hondo* , 65 km. N. of Santiago del Estero along the road to Tucumán, is a major spa town, population 25,000. The thermal waters are recommended for blood pressure and rheumatism; good to drink, too, and used for the local soda water. Swimming in public baths. Tourist office at Pasaje Borges, s/n. Frequent buses from Santiago del Estero, 1 hr., US$2 and from Tucumán, 2 hrs., US$4. Aerolíneas Argentinas have combined flight and bus excursion from Buenos Aires, via Santiago del Estero, to the Termas, daily. The huge Río Hondo dam on the Río Dulce is close by; it forms a lake of 33,000 hectares, used for sailing and fishing.

**Hotels** There are over 170 hotels, but at national holiday periods, and especially in August, accommodation is hard to find, so book well in advance. *Grand Hotel Río Hondo*; *Los Pinos*, Maipú 201, pleasant; *Ambassador; Aranjuez*, Av. Alberdi, C.

**Camping** Municipal site, Irigoyen y Ruta 9, near river bank; *La Olla*, left bank of river; A.C.A. 3 km. from town; *El Mirador*, Ruta 9 y Urquiza.

*Tucumán* (properly San Miguel de Tucumán), capital of its province and with a population of 700,000, is the busiest and the most populous city in the N. Its natural beauties are great: it stands on a plain, at 450 metres, but to the W towers the Sierra de Aconquija. The city was founded by Spaniards coming S from Peru in 1565. There are still many colonial buildings left, and among rows of elaborately stuccoed, spacious, one-storey houses (many of them sadly dilapidated) rise three or four handsome churches with blue and white tiled domes, and the elaborate Italianate Post Office. Summer weather can be very hot and sticky.

Tucumán's main square is Plaza Independencia. On its W side is the ornate Palacio de Gobierno, next is the church of San Francisco, with a picturesque façade. On the S side is the Cathedral, with an old rustic cross, kept near the baptismal font, used when founding the city.

To the S, on Calle Congreso, is the Casa Histórica where, in 1816, the Congress of the United Provinces of Río de la Plata met to draft and proclaim Argentina's Declaration of Independence. The simple room in which it was proclaimed survived the destruction of the original house in 1908 and has now been enclosed in a modern museum. A bas-relief on the museum walls shows the delegates proclaiming independence. Some distance to the W is Plaza Belgrano, with a statue to General Belgrano, who won a decisive battle against the royalists on this site in 1812. Two blocks E is the University, with a grand view from the *vivero*. Nightly (not Tues., except in July) at 2030, *son et lumière* programme at **Casa Histórica**, in garden, in Spanish only, adults US$2, children US$1, tickets from tourist office on Plaza Independencia, no seats.

In the large Nueve de Julio park (avoid at night) is the house of Bishop Colombres, who introduced sugar cane to Tucumán in the early 19th century. In the house is his first milling machine. The province of Tucumán is the centre of Argentine sugar production. There are several mills nearby: the easiest to visit is Ingenio Concepción, a modern plant on the outskirts of town, guided tours in Spanish during harvest period only (15 July-early Nov.), Mon.-Sat., 0930 and 1030, no booking required. Take Aconquija bus for Santo Cristo from outside bus terminus in 24 de Septiembre, US$0.25, pay on bus, 15 mins.

**Local Holiday** 24 Sept. (Battle of Tucumán). Independence celebrations include music and speeches at the Casa de Independencia on 8 July, followed by *gauchos* bringing in the National Flag at midnight. Next day there are many folklore markets and music. Also Día de la Tradición, 10 Nov.

**Hotels** *Grand Hotel del Tucumán*, Av. de los Próceres 380, A, large, new five-star hotel opposite the Parque Centenario 9 de Julio, efficient, outstanding food and service, swimming pool, tennis courts, discotheque; *Carlos V*, 25 de Mayo 330, T 215042/221972, A, central, good service, a/c, bar, restaurant, excellent pasta, rec.; *Metropol*, 24 de Septiembre 524, T 311180, expensive, B, but good service, worth it; *Premier*, with a/c, good, friendly, accepts Visa credit card, C. Alvarez 510, C. *Miami*, Junín 580, C, garage; *Motel Tucumán*, Av. Salta 2080, T 266037, C. In summer, best to stay at *Hotel St James*, on top of Sierra de Aconquija, expensive, comfortable, good food, swimming pool, good views, and fine walking. Also good: *Viena*, Santiago del Estero 1054, D; *Plaza*, San Martín 435, D, built round a pretty central courtyard, basic but clean. *Congreso*, Congreso 74, clean, D, old-fashioned but rec., with bath, extra charge for fan. There are other cheap hotels near the bus station, e.g. *Boston*, Sáenz Peña, 77, E, nice courtyards, restaurant, but some rooms are very dirty. *Palace*, 24 de Septiembre 233, D, friendly, clean, rec.; *Colonial*, San Martín 35, C, 5 mins from bus station, modern, very clean, private bath, fan, laundry service, rec.; *Estrella*, Av. Araoz 38, D, just outside bus station, clean, cheap and basic, a bit noisy, open 24 hrs. *Florida*, 24 de Septiembre 610, T 221785, D, very good value, clean, helpful; *Tucumán*, Catamarca 573, near Mitre station, E, clean, OK; *Petit*, C. Alvarez 765, a bit noisy, spacious, friendly, clean, E with bath, highly rec. *El Parque*, Sgto. Gómez 22, across from bus station, E, fan, clean (though used as a brothel) friendly, safe. Many cheap hotels in streets around General Belgrano station. If they arrange beforehand, students can stay in the University residence of Horco Molle.

**Camping** Parque Nueve de Julio, 2 sites (US$0.25 per tent, US$0.25 p.p.): reported to be dirty. Two roadside camp sites 3 km. E and NE of city centre.

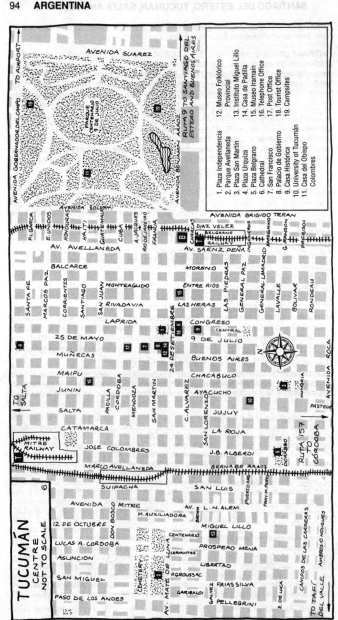

1. Plaza Independencia
2. Parque Avellaneda
3. Plaza San Martín
4. Plaza Urquiza
5. Plaza Belgrano
6. Cathedral
7. San Francisco
8. Palacio de Gobierno
9. Casa Histórica
10. University of Tucumán
11. Casa del Obispo Colombres
12. Museo Folklórico Provincial
13. Instituto Miguel Lillo
14. Casa de Padilla
15. Museo Iramain
16. Telephone Office
17. Post Office
18. Tourist Office
19. Campsites

TUCUMÁN
CENTRE
NOT TO SCALE

**Restaurants** *El Duque*, San Lorenzo 440, very large, popular, good food, poor service. Good food, poor service in open air at *La Rural* and *Gran Grill* 38, Parque 9 de Julio, reasonable prices; there are also several cafés in the park. *Ali Baba*, Junín 380, Arab specialities, intimate, inexpensive; *Adela*, 24 Septiembre 358, well prepared food, Arab specialities, good value; *El Rincón de Cholo*, Chacabuco 31, Arab and other food, esp. lunches, very friendly, good, cheap. *La Leñita*, 25 de Mayo, 300 block, expensive, smart, good meat. *La Parrilla del Centro*, San Martín 381, excellent, reasonable prices; *Panchería Las Piñas Doradas*, 25 de Mayo 119, self-service hot dogs with choice of 20 toppings, good and cheap; *El Rancho*, Laprida 111, good regional dishes, excellent value; *Los Gordos*, Plaza Independencia, pleasant, popular with locals; *La Casa Colonial*, Las Heras 41, good food, delightful atmosphere, inexpensive; *Las Brasas*, Maipú 740, good but not cheap. Good fast food at *Pic Nic*, San Juan 600 block and Ayacucho 500 block; *Augustus*, 24 Septiembre y Buenos Aires, good café; *Pastisima Rotisería*, Mendoza y Laprida and at San Martín 964, good cheap snacks, take out service; *Bar Sandwichería*, Junín y Corrientes, nice atmosphere; *La Vieja Casa*, Córdoba 680, good, inexpensive set lunch. Set lunches near bus station good value. The local beer is very good (Cervecería del Norte), and in this part of Argentina "black beer" (e.g. Salta Negra) is available; also in Salta and Cafayate.

**Shopping** An active centre, cheaper than Buenos Aires. *Artesanía El Cardón*, Alvarez 427, excellent handicrafts; Mercado Artesanal, at the tourist office in Plaza Independencia, small, but nice selection of lace and leather work. *Librería Sarmiento*, San Martín 600 block. All shops close 1200-1630.

**Taxis** Many unscrupulous drivers, who "rig" their meters. Better to arrange price in advance if possible.

**Car Hire** Avis, *Hotel del Sol*, Plaza Independencia; **Liprandi**, 24 de Septiembre 524, T 311210/212665; **Movil Renta**, San Lorenzo 370, T 218635/223382 and at airport; or consult the tourist office.

**Car Repairs** Rubén Boss, Av. Aconquija 947, rec. esp. for Volkswagen.

**Casino** Sarmiento y Maipú, open Fri., Sat., Sun., 2100-0230.

**Museums** Casa Histórica (see previous page), Calle Congreso, open Tues.-Fri. 0830-1330, Tues., and Thur., 1700-2000, Sat., Sun. 1000-1300, US$0.40. **Museo de Antropología y Etnografía**, 25 de Mayo 265 in University building, fine collection, open Mon.-Fri., 0800-1200, 1600-2000. **Museo Folklórico Provincial**, 24 de Septiembre 565, open Mon. 1730-2030, Tues.-Fri., 0900-1230, 1730-2030, Sat., Sun., 1800-2100, free. **Instituto Miguel Lillo**, San Lorenzo y Lillo, associated with the natural sciences department of the University, has a small museum, open Mon.-Fri., 0900-1200, 1500-1800. The Institute also possesses a fine specialist library (not open to the public) which includes an original edition of Von Humboldt's travels in South America. **Casa Padilla**, Plaza Independencia, houses a collection of international art and antiques in the home of a prominent Tucumán family. Near the Casa Histórica at Calle Congreso 56 is the **Museo Histórico de la Provincia** (Casa de Avellaneda) open Mon.-Fri., 0900-1230, 1700-2000, Sat.-Sun., 1700-2000. **Museo Iramaín**, Entre Rios 27, a very interesting memorial to the sculptor, open Mon.-Fri., 0900-1900. **Museo de Bellas Artes**, 9 de Julio 48, open Tues.-Fri., 0900-1230, 1730-2030, Sat.-Sun., 0900-1200, 1730-2030.

**Exchange** American Express, San Martín 893. Noroeste Cambios, 24 de Septiembre 549 and San Martín 775, accepts cheques. Dinar, San Martín 645 and 742, accepts cash only, and **Maguitur**, San Martín 763, good rates for cash. (See note on provincial bonds used as currency, **page 202.**)

**Cultural Institutes** Alliance Française, Mendoza 255, free events in French. **Instituto Italiano di Cultura**, Salta 60; **ATICANA** (North American Centre) including J.F. Kennedy Library, Salta 581, open Mon.-Fri., 0800-1200, 1700-2100.

**Laundry** *Lavarap* (self-service), Las Piedras y 9 de Julio; *Lava Expreso*, San Martín 929.

**Post Office** Córdoba y 25 de Mayo, open 0700-1300, 1600-2000 Mon.-Fri., 800-1300 Sat. **Telecommunications** Compañía Argentina de Teléfonos, Maipú 360, open 24 hrs., best after 1900.

**Tourist Office** In Plaza Independencia, 24 de Septiembre 484, open 0700-2100 Mon.-Fri., 0900-2100 Sat.-Sun.; helpful, finds accommodation in private houses in high season (July), English spoken. Has local bus timetables and details on Tafí (see page 96).

**Travel Agents** *Massini Viajes*, 24 de Septiembre 377, T 215616; *Viajes Ru-Mar*, Alvarez

566, organises day trips to Tafí del Valle, Quilmes etc., Sat., and Sun.

*Delfín Turismo*, on 24 de Septiembre, very helpful, good excursions, operates in conjunction with Saltur of Salta. Excursions around the city are run by *Disney Tour*, San Lorenzo 435.

**Rail** 1st class and Pullman often booked up 2 weeks in advance. The daily *Estrella del Norte* train leaves Retiro station, Buenos Aires, at 1800, returns daily from the Mitre station in Tucumán at 1800, costs US$90 sleeper, US$45 Pullman, US$38 first, US$30 tourist class; takes 19 hours. The Belgrano train, the *Norteño*, leaves Buenos Aires 0845, Wed., Fri., and Sun., and Tucumán (Belgrano station) 1713, Wed., Fri., and Sun., taking 29 hours, no sleeper. *Independencia* train leaves Buenos Aires Tues. and Fri. at 1630, returns Sun. and Wed. at 1630 (Mitre station) sleeper, car transporter, can combine with bus La Veloz del Norte (5½ hrs.) to Salta, Jujuy and as can *Estrella del Norte* to Salta only, daily at 1300. *Panamericano* train leaves Mitre station, Tucumán, Tues., Fri. 1505, arrives La Quiaca 0930 next day, the Friday train has a Pullman coach which passes the border to Villazón, where it is coupled to a Bolivian train leaving for La Paz at 0930 (Sat.), arriving La Paz Sun. 0940. *El Norteño* passes through Córdoba, 14 hrs.

Beyond Tucumán the Belgrano line runs N via Rosario de la Frontera to Jujuy, and La Quiaca, on the Bolivian border, 644 km. from Tucumán. There are also buses to all these places and their use seems preferable; the trains N of Tucumán, though comfortable (with a dining car and crowded only when there are *fiestas*), are slow.

**Road** For travellers to Salta from Tucumán the road via Santa María and Cafayate (a very interesting journey through the beautiful Quebrada de Cafayate, **see page 97**) is longer but much more interesting than the direct road. Aconquija bus Tucumán to **Cafayate** (8 hrs., US$19) via Tafí and Santa María (6 hrs.) leaves daily at 0600. Direct bus in summer from Tucumán to Cafayate Tues., Thurs., Sat., 6½ hrs., at 1000 (0600/0700 in winter). Direct Tucumán bus to **Salta** (but not via Cafayate), 4 hours, several daily, US$20 (slow bus 5½ hrs.). Hitch-hiking from Tucumán to Salta is difficult beyond Tafí del Valle. Plenty of buses to Jujuy, e.g. Veloz del Norte, leaves at 0900, 6 hrs.

To **La Rioja**, 7 hours, US$15. To **Catamarca**, 7 a day with Bosio. Buses also to **Santiago del Estero** (US$6), Paraná, Termas de Río Hondo, Orán, Resistencia, 11½ hrs., and Tinogasta. Bus to **Buenos Aires**, Chevallier at 1250 and 2100, 19 hours, US$55; El Trébol at 1600, 16 hrs., US$55.

For those who wish to travel direct from N Argentina to Central Chile, there are daily La Estrella buses (US$20) from Tucumán to **Mendoza**, leaving 1300, 1400 and 2000 (19 hours), via Catamarca, La Rioja, and San Juan. Bus to **Córdoba** 480 km., US$25, 8 hours, many companies (incl. El Tucumano Panamericano). *La Veloz de Norte* serves free coffee, cake and soda. To **La Paz**, take train or bus to the frontier, then at Villazón, connect with train to Oruro and La Paz.

**Air** Airport: Benjamín Matienzo, 9 km. from town. Bus for each flight, US$0.80, starts from *Hotel Mayoral*, 24 de Septiembre 364. Day flights to Buenos Aires with Aerolíneas Argentinas and Austral; discounts on night flights. Austral Tucumán-Mar del Plata; Tucumán-Córdoba with Austral and Lapa, twice a week each. Alfa to Iguazú, Thurs. 1710.

**Excursions** Simoca, 50 km. S of Tucumán on Route 157, has an authentic Saturday morning market, handicrafts and produce, Posta bus, several, 1½ hrs., US$2.50; essential to get there early. W of Tucumán in the Sierras de Aconquija are Villa Nougués, 36 km., (one of the most interesting tours), the summer residence of the well-to-do Tucumanos (excellent hotel) and San Javier, 34 km. (hotel), both reached by San Javier buses, 1200 and 1900. Aconquija park, with glorious trees, is at the foot of the mountains 14 km. W of Tucumán. Bus at 1130 (the only one; returns immediately); tours from Terra, 9 de Julio 80. The Quebrada de Lules, the gorge of the Río Lules, is 20 km.S of the city. El Cadillal dam, in the gorge of the Río Salí, 26 km. N of Tucumán, supplies electricity and water for the city and permanent irrigation for 80,000 hectares of parched land. There are restaurants, a good ACA campsite, good swimming, and a small archaeological museum at the dam. Reached by Sierras y Lagos buses every 1½ hrs. approx., US$1.20, 45 mins., last buses back 1715 and 1945.

At Km. 46, Route 307 branches NW to *Tafí del Valle* (population 27,000, 97 km. from Tucumán, not to be confused with Tafí Viejo which is 10 km. N of the city) known to archaeologists as a holy valley of the precolumbian Indian tribes.

Just before Tafí del Valle are Dique El Mollar, formerly La Angostura dam, and nearby the menhir park of *El Mollar*, with 129 standing stones (collected from various sites apparently) and good views. Paved road between Tafí and El Mollar. Tours to El Mollar and Tafí from the agency next door to the tourist office, US$15 each for 4 people minimum. Local buses from Tafí, 2 a day, US$0.10, and the Tucumán-Tafí bus stops nearby. Entrance to the park is 10 km. S of Tafí del Valle; you can drive around it (but not within it) by car, or walk.

Tafí del Valle, which is becoming touristy, and El Mollar are often shrouded in fog because of the dam. Ten mins from Tafí is Museo La Banda in the old chapel of San Lorenzo (closed Tues.).

**Hotels** *Hostería ACA*, C, comfortable, good value restaurant, garden; *Colonial*, nr. bus station, E, no singles, friendly, clean; *Pensión La Cumbre*, E, hot water, basic, no locks on doors; better one opposite *Colonial*, in billiard hall. Hotels and bungalows (C-D) at El Pinar del Ciervo. Camping, *Los Sauzales*, very clean, hot showers, rec. Try local cheese.

**Bus**, Tucumán-Tafí, with Aconquija, sit on left-hand side, travels through luxuriant gorge with sub-tropical vegetation, 4 a day, 3½ hrs., US$4.55.

NW of Tafí is *Amaicha del Valle* (bus from Tucumán, US$7, 0600) with 360 sunny days a year, free municipal campsite, *Juan Bautista Alberdi*, 10 min out of town (blue gate) (*Hostería Provincial*, C full board, showers not always hot, clean and friendly, rec., *Pensión Albarracín*, E; *Hostería Colonial*, E with bath, friendly). La Pachamama festival at end of pre-Lent Carnival; also see Sr. Cruz' craft workshop.

Over the 3,040 metre Infiernillo pass 21 km. from Tafí and 15 km. from Amaicha the road is paved and again after Amaicha to the junction with the Ruta Nacional 40 (15 km.) which leads N to Cafayate (55 km.- **see page 103**) and S, 24 km. to *Santa María*, population 18,000.

**Hotels** *Plaza*, on plaza, clean, modern, rec., C; *Provincial de Turismo*, San Martín, friendly, rec., dining room, C, with bath; *Residencial Alemán*, Quintana 144, E, small rooms but clean, friendly, quiet; *Residencial Palacios*, Mitre 592, E, basic, hot water, clean, reasonable and friendly; *Residencial Reinoso*, Av 1° de Mayo 649, F, good, 2 blocks from plaza, hot showers, clean, friendly. Municipal **campsite** at end of Sarmiento.

**Restaurant** *El Cardón*, Abel Acosta 158, cheap and good, regional dishes.

**Buses** To Tucumán 6 hrs., 0220, 0800 (US$8.50). To Cafayate daily at 0700 exc Thurs. at 1030. Empresa Bosio goes to Catamarca, Sat.; via Tucumán Sun. at 1230, 9 hrs. Most start from Belgrano 271 on main Plaza; Empresa San Cayetano (600 block of Esquiú) goes to Belén (see page 127) 4 hrs., Mon., Wed., Fri. at 0500.

**Excursions** to Fuerte Quemado (Indian ruins) 15 km. away, not as impressive as Quilmes (see below); Cerro Pintado, 8 km., coloured sandstone mountains; important ruins of Loma Rica, 18 km. away; Ampajango, 20 km. away, important indigenous finds.

*Quilmes* (Tucumán), 37 km. away, with splendid views from the fortifications and interesting cacti, has the most southerly Inca ruins (dam, village and posting house—tambo), an *hostería* (summer only), camping facilities and a guide at the site from 0700 to 1730. It is 5 km. along a dirt road off the main Santa María-Cafayate road, and 16 km. from Amaicha del Valle. There is also a provincial archaeological museum. Bus from Santa María at 0655, 1 hr., US$2.10, returns about 1030.

A railway and road (Route 9) run N from Tucumán into the province of Salta. Both Salta and the neighbouring province of Jujuy are home to a number of Indian groups which are either historically indigenous to the area, or which migrated there from other Andean regions, the greater Amazon region, or the Guaraní-occupied territories to the E. The Mataco, Chorote, Chulupi and Toba have retained their own languages, but the Chiriguano language is spoken by the Chiriguano, the Tapiete and the Chane (who belong to the Arawak family of Indians, which originate in the very north of the sub-continent). (We are grateful to John Raspey for this information.) **N.B.** The best description of the most interesting places and events in NW Argentina is to be found in Federico Kirbus' *Las Mil Maravillas de la Argentina* (available at Librería La Rayuela, Buenos Aires 96, Salta and in Buenos Aires).

145 km. N of Tucumán is ***Rosario de la Frontera***, a popular resort from June to September. Altitude: 769 metres. Eight km. away there are sulphur springs. Casino. From Buenos Aires, by Belgrano Railway; 1,296 km.

**Hotels** *Termas*, Route 34, D p.p. rambling place, being remodelled, but beware of loose accounting, good food but many rooms without private bath (6 km. from bus station, taxi US$7), room with bath and 3 meals, C (T 81004). Baths US$1.50. About 1 km. from *Hotel Termas* is ACA motel, T 81143. Across the road is man-made lake owned by Caza y Pesca Club—ask in your hotel for permission to fish. *Real*, Güemes 185, E, basic, clean, not all doors close.

**Bus** Rosario de la Frontera-Tucumán, Veloz del Norte, with stewardess, coffee and biscuits.

**Excursions** To *El Naranjo* (19 km.) a Jesuit colonial town; a church contains images and carvings made by Indians.

About 80 km. N of Rosario de la Frontera, at Lumbreras, a road branches off the Inter-American Highway and runs 80 km. NE to the Parque Nacional ***Finca El Rey***. A 44,160-hectare tropical forest and wildlife preserve set among 900-1,500 metre hills with clear streams (good fishing). It can also be reached from Salta, 196 km., US$28 p.p. round-trip excursions of at least 6 with agencies. There is a Park office in Salta, Leguizamon 925. Check here on timetable for Park truck. From Salta, take bus to Saravia, daily at 1630, 3 hours, US$4.20. Bus drops you at Paso de la Cruz, 38 km. from park entrance and 50 km. from the park headquarters. No public and little other traffic after this, but you may get a lift with local farm or roadbuilding vehicles. A truck leaves the Park HQ for the main road on Sun., Tues. and Fri. at 1600 to meet the bus going to Salta at 1825, but it rarely connects with the 1630 coming from Salta. *Hostería El Rey*, D p.p. (C p.p.p., full board), cheaper out of season, book at tourist office in Salta or just turn up, clean and comfortable, large enclosed veranda overlooking the park. Also bungalows, and basic student accommodation. Mosquitoes, ticks and chiggers thrive; bring lotion. Camping is free, there are several tent sites, but few facilities. Horseback riding. Landing strip for small planes. The access road is still poor and fords the river 9 times; passable for ordinary cars except in the wet season.

From Güemes, 148 km. N of Rosario de la Frontera, a branch line and road run W through the mountains for 43 km. to **Salta**, at 1,190 metres, 294,000 people, on the Río Arias, in the Lerma valley, in a mountainous and strikingly beautiful district. Situated 1,600 km. from Buenos Aires by rail or paved road, Salta is now a great tourist and handicraft centre (prices are lower than in Tucumán or Buenos Aires) and the best starting place for tours of the NW. Capital of its province, it is a handsome city founded in 1582, with fine colonial buildings. Follow the ceramic pavement plaques, or get map from Tourist Office, for an interesting pedestrian tour. The Cathedral (open mornings and evenings), on the N side of the central Plaza 9 de Julio, was built 1858-1878; it contains the much venerated images of the Cristo del Milagro and of the Virgin Mary, the first sent from Spain in 1592, and has a rich interior mainly in red and gold, as well as a huge late baroque altar. The miracle was the sudden cessation of a terrifying series of earthquakes when the images were paraded through the streets on 15 September 1692. They still are, each September, when 80,000 people visit the town. On the opposite side of the Plaza is the Cabildo, built in 1783. The Convent of San Bernardo, at Caseros and Santa Fe, was built in colonial style in the mid-19th century; it has a famous wooden portal of 1762. San Francisco church, at Caseros and Córdoba, built in 1882, rises above the city centre skyline with its red, yellow and grey coloured tower, said to be the tallest church tower in South America.

E of the city centre is the Cerro San Bernardo (1,458 metres), accessible by modern cable car (*teleférico*), functions daily 1500-2000, also Sat., Sun., 1100-1300, US$6 return, children US$3, from Parque San Martín. Very beautifully set at the foot of the hill is an impressive statue by Víctor Cariño, 1931, to General Güemes, whose *gaucho* troops repelled seven powerful Spanish invasions from Bolivia between 1814 and 1821. Nearby, on Paseo Güemes, is the Museo Arqueológico, which contains many objects from Tastil (**see page 106**). A steep path behind the museum with Stations of the Cross leads to the top of the hill, where there is an old wooden cross, together with restaurant and artificial waterfalls.

**Festivals** 24 Sept., commemorating the battles of Tucumán and Salta. On 16-17 June, folk music by youngsters in the evening and *gaucho* parade in the morning around the Güemes

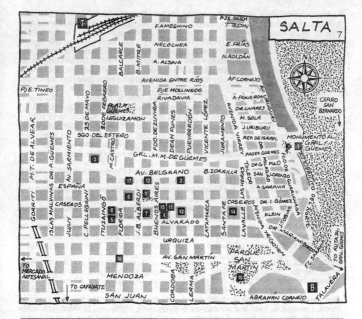

## Salta: Key to Map

1. Plaza 9 de Julio, 2. Post Office, 3. Telphone Office, 4. Tourist Office, 5. Municipality, 6. Casa de las Américas, 7. Cabildo (Museo Histórico del Norte), 8. Museo de Bellas Artes, 9. Museo Antropológico, 10. Museo de Ciencias Naturales, 11. Casa Uriburu, 12. Cathedral, 13. San Francisco, 14. Convento de San Bernardo, 15. Aerolíneas Argentinas, 16. Market and local buses, 17. Banco de la Nación.

statue at the foot of Cerro San Bernardo. Salta celebrates Carnival with processions on the four weekends before Ash Wednesday at 2200 in Av. Belgrano (seats optional at US$2-4); lots of shaving foam (*nieve*) in the early morning; also Mardi Gras (Shrove Tuesday) with a procession of decorated floats and of dancers with intricate masks of feathers and mirrors. It is the custom to squirt water at passers-by and *bombas de agua* (small balloons to be filled with water) are on sale for dropping from balconies on to unwary pedestrians below. Wear a light waterproof!

**Hotels** Salta is a favourite convention town. Some hotels close for a vacation during the Christmas season until January 10, so check. The last two weeks in July are often fully booked because of holidays. Accommodation is also very scarce around 10-16 September because of the celebrations of Cristo del Milagro. *Victoria Plaza*, Zuviría 16, T 211222, A, expensive but good restaurant, the foyer overlooking the plaza is one of the centres of *salteño* life; *Salta*, Buenos Aires 1, in main plaza, T 211011, A+, first class, swimming pool, good restaurant on 3rd floor; *California*, Alvarado 646, T 216266, A, one block from main plaza, singles are small, rec. Also on main plaza is *Cabildo*, Caseros 527, C, pleasant, above 24-hour café, so noisy, a bit run down. *Regidor*, Buenos Aires 10, English-speaking owner, avoid 1st floor, C, good value lunch. *Colonial*, Zuviría 6, T 213057, C with bath, a/c 24-hr. cafeteria; *Cristal*, Urquiza 616, T 222854, B; *Plaza*, España 508, T 216400, C, old, fair; *Portezuelo*, Av. del Turista 1, T 216047, A with breakfast, some rooms a/c, swimming pool, clean, helpful, better and cheaper than the ACA's *Huaico*, Av. Bolivia y P. Costas, T 210211; *Crillón*, near main plaza, Ituzaingó 30, T 220400, good; *Continental*, H. Yrigoyen 295, T 210340, C, near bus terminus, pleasant, 15% reduction for cash payments; *Petit*, H. Yrigoyen 225, C, near bus terminus, some rooms shared, swimming pool, nice; *Italia*, Alberdi 231, C, next to jazz club/casino, very clean and friendly, rec.; *Residencial Güemes*, Necochea y Balcarce, near railway station E, basic, clean, private bath, laundry service. *Residencial Elena*, Buenos Aires 256, D, clean, friendly and quiet, "charming", safe, good meeting place; *Residencial San Jorge*, Esteco 244 y Ruiz de los Llanos 1164, (no sign), E with bath, parking, safe deposit, laundry and cooking facilities, horse-trekking advice by friendly proprietor, Sr. Dejean, very popular, highly rec.; *Hospedaje Doll*, Pasaje Ruiz de los Llanos 1360 (7 blocks from centre), E with bath, friendly, safe, rec.; *Residencial Viena*, Florida 184, E without bath, small rooms, clean, a/c; *Florida*, D with bath, very friendly, clean, will store luggage, Calle Florida y Urquiza 722, T 212133. *Astur*, Rivadavia 752, E with bath, rec.; *Residencial Balcarce*, Balcarce 460, D, friendly, clean. *Residencial Centro*, Belgrano 657, friendly, E. *España*, España 319, E, central but quiet, simple, rec.; *Casa de familia de María del C. Toffoli*, Mendoza 915, T 21-7383, nice atmosphere, discount for ISIC and youth card holders. *Nápoli*, Mitre 1021, F, fairly near railway, laundry, friendly, quiet; *Candilejas*, Balcarce 980, F, without bath, erratic water supply, clean, comfortable, close to railway station. Many other cheaper hotels near railway station (e.g. *Internacional*, Ameghino 651, F p.p., hot water, basic, with good cheap restaurant), but few near new bus station. Private house, Mendoza 919, F p.p.

**Camping** Casino Provincial municipal grounds, by river, swimming pool available (popular Dec.-Feb.). Bus 13 to grounds. There is no signposting: leave the city heading S on Calle Jujuy, after 3 km. you will see the Coca Cola plant on your left; turn left before the plant and then take the first road right. Charges about US$1 p.p. with tent, car US$3. Free hot showers available if there is gas (not often), safe and excellent facilities. At Motel *Huaico*, Campo Castanares, and *Residencial Hispano*, San Juan 619. Campo Quijano, 30 km. W of Salta, at the entrance to Quebrada del Toro gorge, hot showers, bungalows, plenty of room for pitching tents, rec., bus from Salta bus terminal. Camping shops: H.R. Maluf, San Martín y Buenos Aires, and one at La Rioja 995.

**Restaurants** *La Quincha*, rec., near bus station, with excellent cold buffet and bife; *El Monumento*, Gurrachaga 20 (opp. Güemes monument), good food, slow service, good atmosphere, reasonably priced; *Jockey Club*, Güemes 452; *La Castiza*, Alberdi 134, huge, little atmosphere, expensive; *Italiano*, Buenos Aires 95, 1st floor, highly rec. and reasonable. *Don José*, Urquiza 484, good, cheap, popular, asado de tira and grilled kid, warmly rec. *La Posta*, España 476, food and atmosphere both excellent, highly rec.; *El Viejo Jack*, Virrey Toledo 145, good meat dishes; *Capricornio*, Caseros Esq. Pueyrredón, good food and value; *Las Leñas*, Careras 444, good food, good value; *9 de Julio*, Urquiza 1020, excellent lunch; *Green Park*, Caseros 529, good pizzas, and milk shakes; *El Mesón de Pepe*, Rivadavia 774, fish specialities, pricey. Pleasant outdoor restaurants in Parque San Martín, at foot of Cerro San Bernardo. *Sociedad Española*, Balcarce 653, excellent cuisine, elegant surroundings; *Sociedad Italiana*, Zuviría 380, good cheap set lunch. Many good cheap restaurants on and near San Martín, by market. *JA*, Yrigoyen y San Martín, excellent kid; *Boliche Balderrama*, San Martín 1126, has folk music, US$5 entrance for the show. *Gauchos de Güemes*, for hearty late dinner and music, US$10, Uruguay 750; *Casa Güemes*, España 730, late night dinners and folk music. Good, cheap pasta at *Sitoco*, Alberdi y San Martín. *El Rincón del Artista*, San Martín 1240, cheap, lunch, closed evenings; also rec. *Tobi*, Urquiza y Buenos Aires, popular, cheap, good hamburgers; *Alvarez*, Buenos Aires y San Martín, cafetería style, cheap and good. Vegetarian food at *El Jardín*, Alberdi 420, small, good. *Casa de Té*, Paseo Alberdi 422, chocolate and cakes; *Café del Paseo* at Hotel *Colonial*, Zuviría 6, open 24 hrs. *Confitería Mil y Mil*, 20 de Febrero y España, good ice cream. *Bar Salta*, Buenos Aires 11, open 24 hrs., good breakfasts; *Heladería Gianni*, España 486, ask for copa dell'Amore (expensive); excellent coffee served. *Heladería Cercena*, Pasaje Continental 7, Mitre 55 by Plaza 9 Julio, excellent natural ice-cream. Cheap restaurants near the railway and bus stations, many lunch-only restaurants (closed Suns) with meals at US$1-2. *Unión Sirio Libanesa*, San Martín 681, has a good restaurant open to the public. Cheapest food is from the numerous superpanchito stands (huge cheesedogs, US$0.50).

Try local Cafayate wines, such as Michel Torino and Echart Privado, and typical Torrontés-grape wine. Also, the good local water makes excellent beer.

**Shopping** Mercado Municipal, corner of San Martín and Florida, for meat, fish, vegetables and other produce and handicrafts, closed 1200-1700 and Sun. Mercado Artesanal on the outskirts of the city in the Casa El Alto Molino, a late 18th century mansion, at San Martín 2555, T 219195, Mon.-Fri. 0800-2000, Sat. 0900-2000, Sun. 1000-1800, take bus 2, 3, or 7 from Av. San Martín in centre and get off as bus crosses the railway line. Excellent range of goods but expensive (e.g. poncho de Güemes for US$100 for the heaviest weight, down to US$30). Woodcarvings of birds etc. from *Tres Cerritas*, Santiago del Estero 202. *Tiwanaku* handicrafts store, museum upstairs, Caseros 424, will safely pack and send purchases to any

Argentine destination. *Centro de Comercialización de Artesanías*, Catamarca 84, cheaper handicrafts than in tourist shops. For objets d'art and costume jewellery made of onyx, visit *Onix Salta*, Chile 1663 or Caseras 668, Local 14.

**Car Hire** Avis, Alvarado 537, T 216344; **Rent A Car**, Caseros 489 and 221; local companies reported to be cheaper: **ALE**, Caseros 753, T 223469; **Renta Autos Salta**, Zuviría 60.

**Bathing** Balneario Municipal Calle República Libano, on outskirts, reached by bus No. 13 from Calle Ituzaingó, entry US$1. Bus fare US$0.30.

**Museums**  **Museo Histórico del Norte**, in the Cabildo Histórico, Caseros 549, colonial, historical and archaeological museum, free guided tour in Spanish, open Tues.-Sat., 1000-1400, 1530-1930, Sun. 1000-1400, US$0.40. **Museo de Bellas Artes**, Florida 20, open Tues.-Sun. 0900-1300, 1600-2000, US$0.60. **Casa Uriburu**, Caseros 421, Tues.-Sat., 1000-1400, 1530-1930, US$0.60, has relics of a distinguished *salteño* family. **Museo Folclórico Pajarito Velarde**, Pueyrredón 106. **Museo Antropológico**, behind the Güemes statue, open Tues.-Fri. 0830-1230, 1430-1830, Sat. 1500-1830, Sun. 1600-1830, US$0.40, interesting display. **Museo de Ciencias Naturales**, in Parque San Martín, has a full display of stuffed birds, open Tues.-Sun. 1400-2000, US$0.25. **Museo de Arte Popular y Artesanías Iberoamericanas**, Caseros 476, T 215289, Thur.-Tues. 0930-1230, 1700-2030, Sun. 0930-1230 US$0.50, excellent display of contemporary Latin American handicrafts, highly rec.; **Museo de la Ciudad "Casa de Hernández"**, La Florida 97, Tues.-Sat., 0900-1230, 1600-2030. Check opening times in summer; many close then.

**Exchange** Banco de la Nación, Balcarce y España, accepts cheques; **Banco Provincial de Salta**, España 526 on main square, changes travellers' cheques. Many *cambios* on España: **Cambio Dinar** at 609 changes Amex cheques (1% commission) and cash (poor rates). **Maguitur**, España 666, only cash. (See note on provincial bonds used as currency, **page 202.)**

**Laundry** *Lavarap*, self-service, Alvarado y Yrigoyen. Also Santiago del Estero 271 (open Sun. a.m.); *Marva*, Juramento 315.

**Post Office** Deán Funes 140, corner of España; also in shopping arcade at corner of Florida and Gral. San Martín. **Telephone** office at Av. Belgrano 824, 24 hrs., international calls at Av.Vicente López 146, 0800-1930.

**Immigration Office** Maipú 35.

**Consulates** Bolivia, Santiago del Estero 179, T 211927; open Mon.-Fri., 0900-1300. Chile, Ejército del Norte 312, Cultural Institutes: Alliance Française, Santa Fe 20; T 210827; Peru, 25 de Mayo y Santiago del Estero, T 223800; Paraguay, Los Almendros 161, T 212562; Spain, Las Heras 1329; Italy, Alvarado 1632; France, Santa Fe 20; Germany, Güemes 1156 (open Mon.-Fri. 0800-1000).

**Tourist Office** Provincial Tourist Office (EMSATUR), Buenos Aires 93 (one block from main square). Open every day, inc. Sun., till 2100. Very helpful, gives free maps, also a self-guiding tour, Circuito Peatonal, to see important landmarks on foot. Municipal Tourist office, Buenos Aires 61, closed Sun., helpful, free maps. Both offices arrange accommodation in private houses in high season (July). Office at bus terminal, friendly, no maps.

**Travel Agencies** *Saltur*, Caseros 525, T 212012, very efficient. Next door at Caseros 527 is *Mallorca Naturaleza y Aventuras*, specializes in horse trekking, very good value. *Chicoana Turismo*, Caseros 665 (Local 20), T 218134, very helpful, rec. *Puna Expediciones*, Braquiquitos 399, T 212-797 (well qualified and experienced guide Luis H. Aguilar can also be contacted through the *Residencial San Jorge*), organizes treks in remote areas, US$25 a day including transport to trekking region, food, porters, highly rec. *Juan Kühl*, Córdoba 202, at Urquiza, tours by light aeroplane, horseback, caravan, boat, German and English spoken, also runs photographic company.

**Bus Services**  There is no direct bus from Salta to Asunción, but Salta provides the most reliable cheap land connection between Bolivia and Paraguay. Buses daily 1700, US$40 with La Veloz del Norte (20% reduction for students), 14-16 hrs. to **Resistencia**, for crossing into Paraguay (an arduous journey, but a/c, many stops in the night); for description of road, **see page 140**. Salta-**Formosa** with Atahualpa, which would provide the shortest route to Asunción, operates only twice weekly because of the state of the road. Bus to **Córdoba**, 8 a day, 14 hrs., US$35, with Expreso Panamericano (T 212460), luxury service with hostess. Bus to **Cafayate**, US$12, 4 hrs., three a day, with El Indio at 0700, 1130 and 1800. To **Cachi** (5 hrs., US$14) and **Molinos** (7 hrs.) La Internacional daily at 0700 (sit on left). Bus to **Rosario**

de la Frontera, US$5, 2½ hrs., stewardess service, very pleasant trip. To **Buenos Aires**, 3 a day, US$90.

To **Santa María**, El Indio, 6½ hrs., 0700. To Mendoza via Tucumán, daily, US$40, 20 hrs. with Andesmar; the Monday bus continues all the way to Río Gallegos, arriving Thurs. 1430, the other services continue as far as Comodoro Rivadavia. Bus to **Tucumán**, 4½ hrs., several firms (La Veloz del Norte rec.), US$20. Bus to **Embarcación** daily at 0700. Bus to **Jujuy**, Atahualpa hourly between 0700 and 2300, "directo", US$7, 2¾ hours; to **La Rioja**, US$20; to **La Quiaca**, 11 hours, 3 a day (see below).

Bus to Calama and Antofagasta (Chile) leaves Wed. at 1600, US$48 to Calama, US$50 to Antofagasta (20-hour journey at least, very cold), run by Atahualpa, tickets only from Lerma 111. Take own food and a sheet to protect luggage against dust. Gemini (Caseros 665, T 212758) bus to Antofagasta on Sat. at 1600 (said to be better than Atahualpa). Book in advance, usually impossible to get a reservation, so try at 1000 on day of departure for a cancellation. The route is only open in Oct.-Dec., and even then may be suspended if there is heavy rain. The new bus station is eight blocks from the main square (T 214716 for information). Taxi from bus station into Salta US$3.50.

**Airport** From London, cheapest to fly standby to **Miami**, connect with LAB flight via Santa Cruz once a week to **Salta**. One AR flight a week to **Santa Cruz** (Bolivia), Mon. at 1515, arr. 1540 Bolivian time, and also Lloyd Aéreo Boliviano. AR flies **Antofagasta** (Chile) in the high season. AR flies to **Bs. Aires** (2 hrs., minimum) **Tucumán**, **Córdoba** and **Jujuy**. There are flights across the N of Argentina, e.g. Salta to Resistencia by Aerolínea Federal Argentina Alfa via Tucumán, Sat. and Salta-Formosa on Wed. (tickets and reservations only in these towns, prop-jets). Special, regular, bus service between airport and Plaza 9 de Julio, US$2.20; don't be fooled by taxi touts who tell you there is no bus for 3 hours! Taxi from airport to bus station US$14.

**Airline Offices** Aerolíneas Argentinas, Caseros 475/485, T 214757; Aerolíneas Federales Argentinas (ALFA), España 437, T 211283; Lloyd Aero Boliviano, Caseros 376, T 217753; Austral, Buenos Aires 46, T 224590.

**Railways** Ticket office open weekdays 0900-1100, 1700-1900. (Salta is not on a direct line, it is connected with Güemes by local trains and by bus. In Güemes, the bus terminal is 1 km. from the railway station; bus Salta-Güemes every 15 mins, US$1.75). Services to Buenos Aires also serve Tucumán. Also bus/train combination with La Veloz del Norte; see Tucumán section for details. **NB** If buying ticket from Buenos Aires to Salta via Tucumán, purchase train ticket to Tucumán and bus ticket to Salta at the same time so that you can transfer directly to the bus which meets the train, otherwise you must take local bus to bus terminal and wait. Trains from Gümes to Tucumán *El Norteño* (continues to Córdoba and Buenos Aires), Wed., Fri., and Sun., 1014, 7 hrs., and *El Panamericano* Wed., and Sat., 0905, just over 6 hrs. No direct trains between Salta and Jujuy, but connections are possible; buses much quicker.

In October 1980 Chile suspended its rail service from Socompa to Antofagasta, so it is not now possible to travel from Salta to Antofagasta direct except by air (see above) or by Atahualpa or Gemini bus. Argentine railways still maintain a train service from Salta to Socompa, where tourist cards are available (**see page 105** for description of line, tourist train to San Antonio de los Cobres, and goods train, and also for road taking similar route.)

**Routes to Bolivia** To La Quiaca, on Bolivian frontier, 3 buses daily, Atahualpa (US$22), 9 hrs. (via Jujuy, prolonged stop), can be very cold, dusty. Buses also NE to Orán, six hours, for connection with Tarija, Bolivia, which can involve taking overnight bus (Atahualpa, 7-10 hrs.) to Aguas Blancas at 2200 (road now paved), arriving before dawn—cold—then crossing river in motor boats to Bermejo, Bolivia and the next bus out is often full. Spectacular 8 hr. mountain ride alternative to the latter in open-air pick-up: hair-raising! Also to Yacuiba, via Pocitos (Bolivian frontier), for Santa Cruz, Bolivia. US$17 with Atahualpa to Pocitos, 7-10 hrs., very full, with passengers standing, can be uncomfortable, but road now paved. Customs at Pocitos not to be trusted—beware of theft; and overcharging for "excess baggage" (on bus), for which there is no official limit written up anywhere. (Hotel at Pocitos, *Buen Gusto*, F, just tolerable.)

Trains to La Quiaca run via Güemes and Jujuy, but not direct from Salta. The other route is served by train: Salta to Pocitos, Mon. 1945, arrive 1440 Tues.; go through Argentine exit formalities, **cross the bridge into Bolivia** then take a taxi to Yacuiba (US$0.25), where you must stay the night before continuing to Santa Cruz. Several trains Yacuiba-Santa Cruz; 4 *ferrobuses* (Mon., Wed., Fri., Sun., 2200), 3 trains with restaurant car (Tues., Thur., Sat., 0850), and 2 others (Wed., Sun., 1820). **See also page 113** on the route via Orán.

**Excursions** Just S of Salta you pass Coronel Moldes: 26 km. from there is the dam of Cabra

Corral, one of the largest artificial lakes in Argentina; water skiing, fishing, no hotels, just a camping site, restaurant and sailing club; the *Hostería Cabra Corral* is 4 km. from the lake, Route 68, B, half board, swimming pool, good. Paved road ends at the Presa General M. Belgrano, impressive views of the bridge across the lake. 11 km. NW of Salta, in a steep wooded valley, is the wealthy neighbourhood of San Lorenzo (new restaurant in high tower, *El Castillo*, owned by John Johnston (US), good food and music closed Mon., T 921052 for free taxi, 4-6 people; camping and picnicking beside rocky stream. Can be reached by hourly bus from Salta, ½ hr. journey. To Jujuy and Humahuaca, day trip through many agencies. To Cuesta del Obispo and the Forgotten Valley, on return, with Saltur day trip, superb. In summer, guided tours are few and far between because of a lack of tourists. Saltur also does guided trip to Cafayate, with stops at major rock formations along road. The Finca El Rey National Park (**see page 98**) is about 200 km. E of Salta, at junction of Chaco and pre-Andean regions. Much wildlife and varied scenery. *Hostería*, D p.p. full board, and campsite next to it. Horses can be hired. Best time to visit is winter (drier). Tours arranged from Salta, e.g. by Mallorca, Caseros 527.

A magnificent round trip of about 520 km. can be taken going SW from Salta to Cafayate (well paved), then N through the Valles Calchaquíes and Cachi, and back E to Salta. (Most travel agencies in Salta offer the round trip, no student discounts, 12 hours.) The first part of this trip, S from Salta, goes through El Carril (30 km.) where a road from Cachi intersects; continuing S for 25 km. Coronel Moldes is reached. Here, a side road to the left goes to Embalse Cabra Corral (see above). After Coronel Moldes, Route 68 goes through the gorge of the Río de las Conchas (known as the Quebrada de Cafayate) with fascinating rock formations, all signposted: Anfiteatro (a gorge), El Sapo, El Fraile, El Obelisco, Los Castillos. The road goes through wild and semi-arid landscapes with many wild birds, including *ñandúes* (rheas).

**Cafayate** (altitude 1,660 metres, population 4,800) is a quiet, clean, little town, with low rainfall, lying between two ranges of Andean foothills and surrounded by vineyards. About 18 km. S. is Tolombón, where there are reported Indian ruins among giant cacti and other scrub plants. (The ruins are vestigial; the cacti are far more interesting.) A walk to La Cruz (3 hrs.) takes you to a view of the Aconquija chain in the S to Nevado de Cachi in the N. Cafayate is much frequented by Argentine tourists and accommodation is expensive and hard to find at holiday periods (especially for a single person).

See Sr. Rodolfo Bravo's private museum of Calchaquí archaeology on Calle Colón, full of Indian artefacts dug up nearby, interesting slide show (US$0.50 p.p., ring the bell during normal weekday hours). Cafayate is an important centre of wine production and home of several renowned *bodegas*. La Rosa owned by Michel Torino can be visited, Mon.-Fri., 0800-1230, 1500-1830, weekends a.m. only, no need to book, 30 min. tours and tasting, reached by turning right 500 m. past the ACA *hostería*; Etchart, 2 km. on road to Tucumán, also has tours. La Banda, the oldest *bodega* in the valley (next to ACA *hostería*), is interesting because it is more primitive. The Museo de la Vid y el Vino in an old *bodega* is on Av. Güemes, 2 blocks S of the plaza, US$0.40, very well laid out. Locally woven tapestries are interesting, and very expensive; see them at workshops of Ricardo Miranda, Av. Güemes 330. Also Platería of Jorge Barraco, Colón 147, for silver craft work. Handicrafts in wood and silver by Oscar Hipaucha on main plaza. Pancho Silva and his family have a workshop at 25 de Mayo selling and displaying their own and locals' handicrafts.

**Hotels** *Hostería Cafayate* (ACA), on N outskirts, C, modern, quiet (but cold), colonial-style, good food; *Gran Real*, Güemes 128, D, pleasant, clean; *Asturias*, Güemes 158, C; *Pensión Arroyo*, Niño 160, E, highly rec., friendly, clean; *Colonial*, Almagro 134, D, charming patio; *Güemes*, Salta 13, one block off main plaza, E; *Briones*, on main square, clean and comfortable, D with bath and hot water, accepts Amex card; *La Posta del Rey*, Güemes 200 block, E, clean; *Asembal*, Güemes y Almagro, B, new, nice rooms with bath, good; *Confort*, Güemes 200 block, D with bath, clean, comfortable. Accommodation in private houses is available. Municipal **campsite** Lorohuasi at S access to town, hot water, swimming pool, well maintained, bungalows for rent; private campsite to N of town, opposite ACA *hostería*.

**Restaurants** On the main plaza are *Cafayate*, simple, good regional dishes and nice atmosphere; *Confitería La Barra*, rec. *La Carreta de Don Olegario*, good, pleasant, and spotless but rather expensive; *El Criollo*, Güemes 254, clean, pricey, rec. Several *comedores*, inc. *Comedor Juli*, along Rivadavia (2 blocks N of Plaza), where the locals eat. Try excellent *pan casero* (local bread).

**Exchange**  Try at El Indio bus station or in artesanía shops.

**Tourist Office**  Information available from the kiosk near the Mercado Artesanal on the main plaza.

**Bus**  Service (Aconquija) to **Tucumán** daily at 0630, 8 hours, US$19. Alternatively go to Santa María with 1100 El Indio bus (2 hrs.) over good dirt road and take bus to Tucumán, Empresa Aconquija, leaving at 0200 and 0600, both taking 5-6 hrs. El Indio bus to and from **Salta** 3 a day, 4 hrs., US$12. To Angastaco (El Indio) 1100 daily, leaves Angastaco for the return journey at 0630.

One way of seeing the spectacular Quebrada de Cafayate (see above) is by taking the El Indio bus for Salta as far as Los Loros, Km. 32. From here you can walk back (and catch a returning bus from Salta); best done in the afternoon, take fruit and/or water.

Horses can be hired for US$1 for 1½ hrs. from La Florida, Bodega Etchart Privado (2 km. from Cafayate on road to Tucumán).

Continuing S from Cafayate, the road goes to Santa María (**see page 97**), and SE to Tafí del Valle and Tucumán.

About a day is needed for the 160 km. trip N. from Cafayate to Cachi (Route 40). The road is mainly gravel and can be very difficult after rain, but the views of the Andean-foothill desert country are fascinating for those to whom strange rock formations and unexpected colours have an appeal. The population is largely Indian. Salta and the Valles Calchaquíes are the centre for US archaeologist John Hyslo's study of Inca roads in the Andes.  Between Cafayate and San Carlos is Animaña, with municipal campsite.

About 24 km. N of Cafayate is *San Carlos* (altitude 1,660 m), a small settlement destroyed four times by Indians. It has a pleasant white church completed 1854, as well as a municipal campsite.

**Bus**  The El Indio bus on the Salta-Cafayate-Angastaco run arrives in San Carlos by noon and on the return journey at 0745.

N of San Carlos the road enters the Calchaquí valley and climbs to **Angastaco**, 50 km. from San Carlos, 2 km. off the main road, another small town, expanding rapidly, surrounded again by vineyards. You can sample the local Vino Patero, red or sweet white, in a house close to the river bridge; apparently *bodegas* can be visited, *vino patero* is supposed to be made by treading the grapes in the traditional manner. The Fiesta Patronal Virgen del Valle is held on the second weekend of December, with processions, folk music, dancing, many gauchos and rodeos. *Hostería* with pool, D, good, cheap and delicious meals on request, has its own small but informative archaeological museum. *Residencial El Cardón*, G p.p., good, clean, comfortable. Buses: to Molinos, Cachi and Salta, Fri., 1100; daily bus to San Carlos and Cafayate. From the Angastaco turn-off it is 40 km. on a winding road through beautiful and desolate rock formations to **Molinos** (*Hostería Provincial*, very highly recommended, A/B, with breakfast, meals, in Casa de Isasmendi, which also contains a small museum). The church, with its fine twin-domed bell-towers, built about 1720 and now covered in a yellowish paste to preserve it, contains the mummified body of the last Royalist governor of Salta, Don Nicolás Isasmendi Echalar. To protect it from visitors plucking its hair, this relic can no longer be viewed by the public. The priest is very knowledgable about local history. A pleasant walk is down from the church, crossing a creek and then climbing a gentle hill, from which there are good views of Molinos and surrounding country. Sra. de Guaymas (known as "Sra. Silvia") runs a restaurant and rents rooms, F, double only, basic, clean; there are other rooms to rent around the main square. Daily bus to Salta via Cachi daily at 0645; 2 hours to Cachi, 7 hours to Salta. To Angastaco, Thur. 2025.

From Molinos it is 46 km. to **Cachi** (Quechua for "salt"), a beautiful little town renowned for its weaving and other crafts; the natives claim people die only of old age, because the climate is very invigorating; altitude 2,280 metres. The church's floor, roof and confessional are made from the wood of the *cardón* cactus. The Museo Arqueológico (open Mon.-Sat., 0800-1800, Sun., holidays 0900-1200) presents an interesting survey of pre-colonial Calchaquí culture. *Hotel Nevado de Cachi*, F p.p., near bus station, basic but good value, good restaurant, owned by Marcos Rueda bus company; good *ACA Hostería Cachi*, C; *Albergue Municipal*, E, good restaurant, also has good municipal campsite with swimming pool, on hill at S end of town. Buses: to Salta, 0905 daily (also 1530 Fri.); to Molinos 1200 daily; El Indio from Cafayate Thur. a.m. only, returning Thur. p.m. From Cachi, you follow Route 40 for 11 km. N, then turn right to Route 33. This road climbs continuously up the Cuesta del Obispo passing a dead-straight stretch of 14 km. known as La Recta del Tin-Tin with magnificent views of the **Los Cardones National Park** with the huge candelabra cacti, which grow up to 6 metres in height, reaching the summit at Piedra de Molino (3,620 metres) after 43 km. Then it plunges down through the Quebrada de Escoipe. The road rejoins Route 68 at El Carril, from where it is 37 km. back to Salta.

N of Cachi Route 40 continues to La Poma, 54 km., a beautiful hamlet (*hostería*, F, try bargaining). Marcos Rueda bus service from Salta, Sat. and Thur., 1300 (via Cachi 1750), arrives La Poma 1945, departing next day 1320. From La Poma the road runs N over the Paso Abra de Acay (4,900 metres—the highest pass in South America negotiable by car) to San Antonio de los Cobres (see below). This road is in very poor condition (no buses).

A trip to the Indian ruins at Las Pailas, 10 km. from Cachi, provides a fine afternoon's walk in splendid surroundings. Take the 1230 bus from Cachi to the schoolhouse at Las Pailas, walking from there on a track towards the mountains. After about 1 hour, you cross a river by a small wooden hanging bridge. Ask at the house there for a guide to take you to the ruins. The ruins themselves are not especially impressive but the view is breathtaking, with huge cacti set against snow-topped Andean peaks. The walk back to Cachi is an easy going 3 hours downhill; alternatively there is a bus which arrives at Cachi at 1800.

There is a 900 km. long metre-gauge railway from Salta through the little town of **San Antonio de los Cobres** to Antofagasta, in north Chile (through trains only as far as Socompa, on the Chilean frontier). The Argentine section was engineered by Richard Maury, of Pennsylvania, who is commemorated by the station at Km. 78 which bears his name. This remarkable project was built in stages between 1921 and 1948, by which time developments in road and air transport had already reduced its importance. The Line includes 21 tunnels, 13 viaducts, 31 bridges, 2 loops and 2 zig-zags. From Salta the line climbs gently to Campo Quijano (Km. 40, 1520 metres), where it enters the Quebrada del Toro, an impressive rock-strewn gorge. At El Alisal (Km. 50) and Chorrillos (Km. 66) there are zig-zags as the line climbs the side of the gorge before turning N into the valley of the Río Rosario near Puerto Tastil (Km. 101, 2,675 metres), missing the archaeological areas around Santa Rosa de Tastil. At Km. 122 and Km. 129 the line goes into 360 loops before reaching Diego de Almagro (3,304 metres). At Abra Muñano (3,952 metres) the road to San Antonio can be seen zig-zagging its way up the end-wall of the Qubrada del Toro below. Muñano is the highest station in Argentina (3,936 metres) and from here the line drops slightly to San Antonio, Km. 196.

San Antonio is a squat, ugly mining town on a bleak, high desert at 3,750 metres, pop.: 2,200 only of interest if you want to visit the copper, zinc, lead and silver mines, truck from La Concordia company office, about 20 km., from the mine you can walk to La Polvorilla viaduct, 20 mins., vicuñas and condors en route; *Hospedaje Belgrano*, painted blue, F, no heat, basic, expensive restaurant; *Hospedaje Los Andes*, F p.p., breakfast extra, very basic, but very friendly, both on main street.

The spectacular viaduct at La Polvorilla is 21 km. further at 4,190 metres, just beyond the branch line to the mines at La Concordia. The highest point on the line is reached at Abra Chorrillos (4,475 metres, Km. 231). From here the line runs on another 335 km. across a rocky barren plateau 3,500-4,300 metres above sea level before reaching Socompa (3,865 metres). The inhabitants of this area are Coya Indians who bear a far closer resemblance to their cousins in Bolivia then to the Salteño lowlanders. **N.B.** On all journeys on this line beware of *soroche*: do not eat or drink to excess.

The *Tren a las Nubes* (Train to the Clouds) runs the 218 km. between Salta and La Polvorilla viaduct. Unfortunately, Ferrocarriles Argentinos decided, in April 1991, to suspend the *Tren a las Nubes*. We retain the description of the line in the hope that this is only a temporary measure, even if the service is reopened privately. Until this popular tourist service is restored, visitors can take a travel agency excursion or a daily bus to San Antonio de los Cobres, detailed below.

Freight trains still run on this line: a daily goods train to San Antonio with one passenger coach leaves Salta 1400, 12 hrs., US$5; return journey from Salta 1800. In practice this usually leaves several hours late so you see little on the journey. A goods train to Pocitos, beyond San Antonio, leaves Salta on Mon. On Wed. a goods train with two passenger coaches leaves for Socompa, theoretically at 0727, arriving at San Antonio 1530 and Socompa 1230 Thur., returning after a two hour stop in Socompa (US$17).

Goods trains run from Socompa to Augusta Victoria and Baquedano (Chile): officially the Chilean railway authorities do not permit passengers to travel on this line, but some travellers have managed to do so. Chilean trains do not connect with trains from Salta and you may have to wait several days for a lift in a truck. There is no food or accommodation, but you may be able to sleep on the floor in the Chilean customs building.

Timetables for these services are meaningless—the line is single-track and goods trains are delayed for loading and unloading. Reliable information about departures from Salta can only be obtained from the Oficina de Trenes at the station (T 212641) and they will often not know until 2 hrs. before departure. To secure seats get on the train while it is loading in the goods depot, about 400 metres down the line. Take plenty of food, water, camera film and warm clothing.

San Antonio can also be reached by Route 51 from Salta. From Campo Quijano this is unpaved single-track and runs along the floor of the Quebrada del Toro (fords) before climbing the Abra Muñano in a long series of steep zig-zags. Buses to/from Salta, El Quebradeño, 6 a week, times vary, 6 hrs., US$5.

On a day trip from Salta by minibus, stop at Santa Rosa de *Tastil* to see Indian ruins (the roofs of the houses are said to have been made of cactus). Alternatively, take the Empresa Quebradeño bus, Fri. 1010 only, arriving 1600 at Tastil, which leaves you 4 hours at ruins (plenty of time) before catching the bus (1955) on its way back from San Antonio de los Cobres. A third alternative is to share a taxi which, between a group, would be little different from the *Tren a los Nubes'* US$50 fare. Try the *quesillo de cabra* (goat's cheese) from Estancia Las Cuevas. If hiking, take your own water, there is none in the mountains.

The road from San Antonio de los Cobres over the pass of Huaytiquina (4,200 metres) to San Pedro de Atacama is no longer in use. At its highest, this road is 4,560 metres but it has been replaced by the less steep Sico Pass, which runs parallel to Huaytiquina. Fork left just before Catúa, cross the border at Sico (4,079 metres) and continue via Mina Laco and Socaire to Toconao (road very bad between these two points) where the road joins the Huaytiquina route. It is a very beautiful trip: you cross salt lakes with flamingoes and impressive desert around. The road on the Argentine side is very good. Gasoline is available in San Pedro and Calama. Because of snow, this route is open only part of the year. A car must be in very good condition to cope with the heights. Ask the *gendarmes* in San Antonio de los Cobres about road conditions, and complete exit formalities here.

The direct road **from Salta to Jujuy** is picturesque with its winding 92-km. stretch through the mountains, now paved, known as *la cornisa*. The longer road, via Güemes, is the better road for hitch-hiking.

*Jujuy* (pronounced Hoo-hooey) properly San Salvador de Jujuy, the capital of Jujuy province, stands at 1,260 metres, completely surrounded by wooded mountains. The city was founded first in 1561 and then in 1575, when it was destroyed by the Indians, and finally established in 1593. Population 183,000. In the eastern part of the city is the Plaza Belgrano, a fine square lined with orange trees. On the S side of the plaza stands the Casa de Gobierno, an elaborate French baroque-style palace (open Mon.-Fri., 0800-1200, 1600-2000, but not always). On the W side is a colonial Cathedral (shuts 1230-1500 daily) with very fine 18th century images, pulpits, walls and paintings finished about 1746. It has been heavily restored, but in the nave is a superb wooden pulpit, carved by Indians and gilded, a colonial treasure without its equal in Argentina. On Calle Lavalle you can see the doorway through which General Lavalle, the enemy of Rosas, was killed by a bullet in 1848, but the door is a copy; the original was taken to Buenos Aires. The Teatro Mitre (worth a visit) is at Alvear y Lamadrid. In the western part of the city are the Parque San Martín and an open space, La Tablada, where horses, mules and donkeys used to be assembled in caravans to be driven to the mines in Bolivia and Peru. See the Palacio de Tribunales near the river, one of the best modern buildings in Argentina. Streets are lined with bitter-orange trees. The scenery is varied and splendid, although the city itself has become a little shabby.

**History** The province of Jujuy bore the brunt of fighting during the Wars of Independence: between 1810 and 1822 the Spanish launched 11 invasions down the Quebrada de Humahuaca from Bolivia. In Aug. 1812 Gen. Belgrano, commanding the republican troops, ordered the city to be evacuated and destroyed before the advancing Spanish army. This event is marked on 23-24 Aug. by festivities known as El Exodo Jujeño with gaucho processions and military parades. As a tribute to the city for obeying his orders, Belgrano donated a flag which is displayed in the Sala de la Bandera in the Casa de Gobierno.

**Public Holidays** 6 and 23-24 August (hotels fully booked). Festival on 6 Nov.

**Hotels** *Augustus*, Belgrano 715, T 22668, 4 star, A, modern, comfortable but noisy. *Fenicia*, on riverside at 19 de Abril 427, T 28102, A. *Internacional*, Belgrano 501 (main square), T 22004, A. *La Viña*, Route 56, Km. 5, T 26588, C, attractive, swimming pool. *Hostería Posta de Lozano*, Route 9, Km. 18, B, friendly, clean, good restaurant, pool, horse-riding; *Sumay*, Otero 232, T 22554, B, central, clean; *Avenida*, 19 de Abril 469, T 22678, on riverside, with fair restaurant, B (C off season, cafeteria only); *Belgrano*, Belgrano 627, T 26459, E, old fashioned, hospitable, clean; *Residencial Los Andes*, Siria 456, T 24315, D, clean, hot water. Across the street is *Residencial San Carlos*, Siria 459, T 22286, D, modern, friendly, clean, some rooms a/c, highly rec.; *Motel Huaico*, Route 9, just N of town, T 22274, B, good; *Residencial Lavalle*, Lavalle 372, T 222698, E, basic, clean, good value; *Chung King*, Alvear 627, friendly, dark, very noisy, many mosquitoes, E, good restaurant. Several cheaper places near railway station: *Residencial Norte*, Alvear 446, E, basic, unfriendly; *Savoy*, Alvear 447, E, basic, damp.

**Camping** *Autocamping Municipal*, US$2.40 per tent, ask for a cheaper rate for one person. 14 km. N of Jujuy on Humahuaca road, also *Autocamping*, 3 km. N outside city at Huaico Chico, US$1.50 per tent, motel opposite. Buses frequent. Hot showers, clothes washing facilities, very friendly.

**Restaurants** *El Cortijo*, Lavalle y San Martín, interesting salads, reasonably priced; *Restaurant Sociedad Española*, Belgrano y Pérez, elegant setting; *Bar-Restaurant Sociedad Obrera*, Balcarce 357, for cheap food, but not attractive. *Restaurant Sirio Libanesa*, Lamadrid 568 (don't be put off by the uninviting entrance). *Confitería Carena*, Belgrano 899, old-fashioned, good for breakfast; *La Ventana*, Belgrano 751, good cheap menu. *La Rueda*, Lavalle 320, excellent meat, very popular, good value; *Ruta 9*, Costa Rica 968, good local food, Bolivian owners in Barrio Mariano Moreno, take taxi. Cheaper places behind bus terminus on Santiago del Estero and Alem. Very good ice cream at *Helados*

*Xanthi*, Belgrano 515, made by Greek owner. Good bread and cake shop at Belgrano 619.

**Shopping** Ponchos and handicrafts at the **Mercado Artesanal**, Alvear 843; *Regionales Lavalle*, Lavalle 268; *Centro de Arte y Artesanías*, Balcarce 427.

**Museums** Museo Histórico Provincial, Lavalle 250, oopen daily 0830-1230, 1500-2000; **Museo de Paleontología y Mineralogía**, part of the University of Jujuy, Av. Bolivia 1313, open Mon.-Fri. 0800-1300. **Museo de Bellas Artes**, Güemes 956, open Mon.-Fri., 0800-1200, 1700-1900. **Police Museum**, in the Cabildo, open Mon.-Fri. 1000-1300, 1500-2100, Sat. 1030-1230, 1830-2100, Sun. 1830-2100; **Museo de la Iglesia San Francisco**, Belgrano y Lavalle, includes 17th century paintings from Cuzco and Chuquisaca. The **Estación Biológica de Fauna Silvestre**, Av. Bolivia 2335, Jujuy, is open to the public on Sundays (for private tours on other days, contact Dr. Arturo A.Canedi, T 25617-25845), very interesting.

**Exchange** Noroeste Cambio, Belgrano 711; Horus, Belgrano 722; Dinar, Belgrano 731. Travel agencies on Calle Belgrano also change cash and dollar travellers' cheques. If desperate, ask the dueña of the *confitería* at bus station, rates not too unreasonable. (See note on provincial bonds used as currency, page 202).

**Consulates** Bolivia, Güemes 822, T 22010, price of visa should be US$5, pay no more; **Spain**, R. de Velasco 362, T 28193; Italy, Av. Fascio 660, T 23199; Paraguay, Tacuarí 430. **Migración** at 18 de Abril 1058.

**Post Office** at Independencia y Lamadrid and at bus terminal. Entel, Senador Pérez 141.

**Tourist Office** Belgrano 690, very helpful, open till 2000; kiosk at bus station, friendly, has maps.
For information on bird watching, contact Mario Daniel Cheronaza, Peatonal 38, No. 848-830, Viviendos "El Arenal", Jujuy.

**Travel Agencies** Many along Belgrano: *V'Alicia Viajes*, No. 592, T 22541; *Giménez*, No. 775, T 2924; *Turismo Lavalle*, No. 340, does car tours through the Quebrada de Humahuaca. *Be Dor Turismo*, No. 860 local 8, 10% for ISIC and youth card holders on local excursions.

**Train** No direct services to Salta. Train to Buenos Aires Wed., Fri. and Sun. at 0805, very crowded and can be endlessly delayed. *El Norteño* leaves Buenos Aires same days at 0845, arr. Jujuy next day at 2242, US$50. There is also a bus/train combination to Buenos Aires via Tucumán with La Veloz del Norte to connect with both *Independencia* and *Estrella del Norte* services, the former Sun. and Wed. at 1100 arr. Tucumán 1600, the latter daily. There are 5 trains a week to **La Quiaca** for Bolivia, leaving 2334 Tues. and Fri., arriving 0930 Wed. and Sat. respectively, and 0555 Wed., Fri., Sun., arriving 1644. These services are notoriously unreliable, many delays, or do not run at all (take several warm blankets for the nighttime train). Reportedly a through train to La Paz Sat. 0016, arr. Sun. 0938.

**Airport** El Cadillal, 32 km. S.E.; buses leave *Hotel Avenida* to meet arrivals. Service to Buenos Aires by Aerolíneas Argentinas and Austral, at least 1 flight a day direct, or via Salta, Córdoba. Check for weather conditions in connecting airports before you fly or you may find yourself stranded elsewhere.

**Buses** Terminus at Iguazú y Dorrego, 6 blocks S of centre. To and from **Buenos Aires** Mon., Wed., Fri., Sun. at 1200 arriving 0930 following day; Mon., Tues., Thurs., Sat. leaves 2200, arrives 1945. Via Tucumán to Córdoba, with Panamericano T 27281/27143 with La Veloz, daily, Tucumán 5 hrs., US$25, and Córdoba, 14 hrs. US$45 with Atahualpa. To **Salta**, from 0700 to 0930, 2¾ hours, US$7. To **La Quiaca**, 6½ hrs., (many passport checks), Panamericano (best) and Atahualpa, US$15. Road paved only as far as Humahuaca, reasonably comfortable, but very cold. To **Orán** daily at 1700; to **Humahuaca**, US$7, 3 hrs., sit on left side. To **Embarcación**, US$7.35 with Agencia Balut, via San Pedro and Libertador San Martín. Jujuy-**Purmamarca-Susques**, leaves Purmamarca at 1330 on Wed. and Sat., returning Thurs. and Sun., crossing the Abra Potrerillos (4,164 m.) and the Salinas Grandes of Jujuy. Jujuy-**Tilcara** 1½ hrs., US$4.

19 km. W of Jujuy is **Termas de Reyes**, where there are hot springs. This resort, with the *Gran Hotel Termas de Reyes* (C, run down but friendly, good meals), is set among magnificent mountains 45 mins. by bus from Jujuy (No. 14 from corner of plaza, 6 times a day between 0630 and 1945, returning 0715-1715). US$2 to swim in the thermal pool at the hotel; municipal baths free but closed Weds. It is possible to camp below the hotel free of charge.

**North from Jujuy** Lovers of old churches will find Salta and Jujuy excellent centres. Franciscan and Dominican friars arrived in the area from Bolivia as early

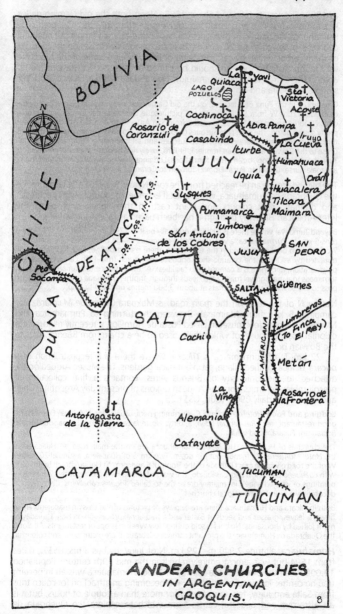

ANDEAN CHURCHES
IN ARGENTINA
CROQUIS.

8

as 1550. The Jesuits followed about 1585. Along both the old Camino de los Incas (now non-existent) and the new route through the Quebrada de Humahuaca the padres, in the course of two centuries, built simple but beautiful churches, of which about 20 survive. They are marked by crosses on the map. All of them can be visited by car from Salta or Jujuy, though some of the roads are very rough. A spare fuel can should be carried because service stations are far apart. (There are ACA stations at Jujuy, Humahuaca and La Quiaca, and YPF stations at Tilcara and Abra Pampa.)

One group, in the Puna de Atacama, on the old Camino de los Incas, can be reached by the road which runs W from Salta through the picturesque Quebrada del Toro to San Antonio de los Cobres (see page 105). The road S from San Antonio to Antofagasta de la Sierra is pretty severe going. The road N to Susques (105 km.), is comparatively comfortable, but runs through utter desert. There is lodging at Susques and an interesting 16th century chapel. Close to the Bolivian and Chilean frontier is El Toro, lovely ride through *altiplano*, past Laguna Turilari, mining territory, bizarre rock formations. Lodgings may be available in first-aid room, ask male nurse, Don Juan Puca. From El Toro on to Coranzulí is very rough.

The second group can be reached from the road N from Jujuy to La Quiaca through the Quebrada de Humahuaca, which is itself extremely beautiful, with spectacular and dramatic rock colours and giant cacti in the higher, drier parts; the Inter-American Highway through it has been paved as far as Humahuaca.

Beyond Tumbaya, where there is a church originally built in 1796 and rebuilt in 1873, a road runs 5 km. to **Purmamarca**, a very poor but picturesque village overlooked by a mountain: 7 colours can be distinguished in the rock strata; there is a *hospedaje*, E, or lodging can be obtained by asking at the ceramic shop opposite the church (mid-17th century) or at the police station, and there is a campsite (no facilities). At the entrance to Purmamarca a right turn leads to a new gravel road, which leads through another *quebrada* over a 4,170-metre pass to the Salinas Grandes salt flats at about 3,500 metres on the Altiplano.

Not far N of the turn, on the main road, is Maimará (*Albergue Maimará*, also camping, 5 km. from Maimará). Between the turning to Purmamarca and Maimará is a new folk museum called Posta de Hornillos, a recently restored old colonial posting house, of which there used to be a chain from Buenos Aires to the Bolivian border.

22 km. N of Purmamarca is **Tilcara**, where there is a reconstruction of a *pucará*, or Inca fortified village, set in botanical gardens. The Museo Arqueológico, attached to the University of Buenos Aires, contains a fine collection of precolumbian ceramics from the Andean regions of present day Argentina, Chile and Peru, open daily 0900-1800, US$1.25.

**Lodging and Food** *Hotel de Turismo*, C, swimming pool, usually dry; *El Antigal*, D, pleasant, good restaurant, rec.; *Residencial Eden*, E, dirty; *Hostería La Esperanza*, E, spacious rooms; *Restaurant Pucará*, good value.

The churches of Huacalera, Uquía, and Humahuaca are on the main road. At Huacalera is the *Hotel Monterrey*, C, friendly but run down. Two km. S of Huacalera, a sundial 20 metres W of the road gives the exact latitude of the Tropic of Capricorn. At Uquía (church built 1691, with *cuzqueño* paintings) and Casabindo, the walls of the naves are hung with 17th century paintings of winged angels in military dress: the so-called *ángeles caballeros*. Cactus-wood decoration is found in many local churches.

Both in Tilcara and Humahuaca there are displays of pictures of the Passion made entirely of flowers, leaves, grasses and seeds at Easter and a traditional procession on Holy Thursday at night joined by thousands. No beef is sold during Holy Week in shops or restaurants. All along the Quebrada de Humahuaca the pre-Lent carnival celebrations are picturesque and colourful.

**Humahuaca**, altitude 2,940 m. 129 km. N of Jujuy (by bus 3 hrs, US$7), dates from 1594 but was almost entirely rebuilt in the mid 19th century. Population 12,000. Until the arrival of the railway in 1906, Humahuaca was an important trading centre. Today, to its detriment, it is becoming an attraction for coach trips from Salta and Jujuy; few tourists stay for more than a couple of hours, but it is an attractive and peaceful centre from which to explore the Quebrada de

Humahuaca. The church, originally built in 1631, was completely rebuilt in 1873-80. A mechanical figure of San Francisco Solano blesses the town from the neo-colonial town hall at 1200. Overlooking the town is the Argentine National Independence Monument, built in 1924 and sited here because the valley was the scene of the heaviest fighting in the country during the Wars of Independence. There is a good Feria Artesanal on Av. San Martín (on the far side of the railway line), but avoid the middle of the day when the coach parties arrive. Candelaria, Feb. 2, is the town's main festival.

**Hotels** *Provincial de Turismo*, Buenos Aires 650, D, run down, swimming pool dry even in summer, poor service, modern building is sadly out of keeping with surroundings; **Residencial Humahuaca**, Córdoba y Corrientes, E, some a/c, traditional, clean, friendly. **Residencial Colonial**, Entre Ríos 100, near bus terminus, E, gloomy, windowless rooms, but clean, laundry facilities, Youth Hostel, *Albergue Humahuaca*, Buenos Aires 447, spacious, clean, laundry and cooking facilities, special price for ISIC and youth card holders.

**Camping** Across bridge by railway station, small charge includes use of facilities.

**Restaurants** Most restaurants open only during the day, difficult to find breakfast and the restaurant at the bus terminal is often the only place open in the evenings. *La Cacharpaya*, Jujuy 295, excellent; *Humahuaca Colonial*, Tucumán 22, good regional cooking, good value, but invaded by coach parties at midday; *El Rancho*, Belgrano s/n, just around the corner from market, where the locals eat.

**Museums** **Museo La Casa**, Buenos Aires 296, next to the post office, open daily 1000-2000, US$1, guided tours only, offers a fascinating insight into social customs in the mid-nineteenth century, strongly rec.; **Museo Ramoneda**, Salta y Santa Fe, private collection of contemporary art; **Museo Arqueológico Municipal**, at one side of Independence monument, Mon.-Fri. 0800-1200, 1400-1700, US$0.25; **Museo Nicasio Fernández Mar**, Buenos Aires, opposite *Hotel de Turismo*, memorial to the sculptor, open daily, free.

**Exchange** Try the handicraft shops on the main plaza; better rates at Youth Hostel, but best to change before you go.

**Tourist Office** Kiosk in main plaza in high season. Sr. Carlos Gómez Cardozo, Director of the Museo La Casa, is a mine of information on the area and may be able to arrange English-speaking guides at weekends.

**Excursions** To Coctaca, 14 km. NE, where there is an impressive and extensive series of pre-colonial agricultural terraces, 35 km. wide. To the mine at El Aguilar (see below), trucks leave Humahuaca early a.m.

20 km. N of Humahuaca along Route 9, an unpaved road runs NE 8 km. to Yrigoyen (railway station called Iturbe) and then over the 4,000 m Abra del Cóndor before dropping steeply into the Quebrada de Iruya. *Iruya*, 66 km. from Humahuaca, is a beautiful walled village wedged on a hillside at 2,600 m. It has a fine 17th century church and Rosario festival on first Sun in Oct. Accommodation in the *albergue comunal* (14 beds, only short stays permitted, ask at the church). Daily bus service to Yrigoyen by Panamericano, 1045 and 1950, 45 mins.; in Yrigoyen (*Pensión El Panamericano*, F, basic) you may be able to get a seat on a truck. Empresa Mendoza bus leaves Yrigoyen 0800, Wed. and Sat. for Iruya, 2½ hrs. journey, US$5 one way, waits about 2 hrs. in Iruya before returning; this bus sometimes runs from Humahuaca, service is suspended in rainy season (esp. Feb. and March); details from *Almacén Mendoza*, Salta y Belgrano, Humahuaca.

The trips to Iruya offered by *pensiones* in Humahuaca, or even by people in the street, are overpriced; check at the ACA petrol station for correct information on public transport. It is worthwhile staying in Iruya for a few days; it makes an extremely pleasant and friendly centre for horseback or walking trips (take sleeping bag). At Titiconte 2 km. away, there are unrestored pre-Inca ruins. Puna Expediciones (**see Salta page 101**) runs a 7-day trek, Salta-Iruya-Nazareno-La Quiaca, walking between Iruya and Nazareno on small, remote paths where there are no tourists or motor vehicles, sleeping in local schoolhouses; rest of route is by truck.

From Humahuaca to La Quiaca on the Bolivian border, Route 9 is unpaved and runs across the bleak and barren *puna*. At Tres Cruces, 62 km. N of Humahuaca, a paved road runs S for 46 km. to the mine at El Aguilar. **Abra Pampa**, an important mining centre, population 10,000, is further N at Km. 91 (*Residencial* nr. plaza, clean, hot water; meals in the bus station). From here an unpaved road leads NW to Laguna Pozuelos and on to the Rinconada gold mine. Laguna Pozuelos, 3,650 m. 50 km. from Abra Pampa, is a flamingo reserve and natural monument. Truck transport daily at 1700 exc. Sun., returning next day 1430. If driving, the Laguna is 5 km. from the road, the turning is marked by a post with a wheel hanging on it, the road is private and permission to use it is necessary; walk last 800 metres to reach the edge of the lagoon. (If camping warm clothing and food essential) 15 km. from Abra Pampa is the vicuña farm at Miraflores, the largest in Argentina. Information offered, photography permitted; colectivos go a.m. Mon.-Sat. from Abra Pampa to the vicuña farm.

From a point 4 km. N of Abra Pampa roads branch W to Cochinoca (25 km.) and SW to **Casabindo** (62 km.). "On 15 August at Casabindo, the local saint's day, the last and only *corrida de toros* in Argentina is held amidst a colourful popular celebration. The event is called "El Toreo de la Vincha"; in front of the church a bull defies onlookers to take a ribbon and medal which it carries. The Casabindo church itself is a magnificent building, being called "the cathedral of the Puna"." (Federico Kirbus).

**Yavi**, with the fine church of San Francisco, which has magnificent gold decoration and windows of onyx (1690), is 16 km. E of La Quiaca, reached by a good, paved road; taxi available. (Find the caretaker at her house and she will show you round the church, open Tues.-Sun. 0900-1200 and Tues.-Fri. 1500-1800.) Opposite this church is the house of the Marqués Campero y Tojo. Three-room *hostería* at Yavi. Only a mule track leads on to the two churches of Santa Victoria (a forlorn Indian village in a rain forest valley) and Acoyte. At Santa Catalina, 67 km. W of La Quiaca, along a poor road, there is also a 17th century church. (Bus from Jujuy to La Quiaca, 8 hrs., and Santa Catalina, 19 hrs., Mon. and Fri.)

**La Quiaca**, 292 km. from Jujuy at an altitude of 3,442 metres, is joined to its Bolivian neighbour, Villazón, by a concrete bridge. Warm clothing is essential all year round. On the third Sunday in October the Manca Fiesta, or the festival of the pots, is held here, and the Colla Indians from Jujuy and the Bolivian *altiplano* come, carrying all sorts of pots; local food is eaten. If going on into Bolivia, buy your basic rations, medicaments etc. in La Quiaca.

**Hotels** *Turismo*, Siria y San Martín, C, rec., clean, modern, comfortable; *Cristal*, Sarmiento 539, E, clean and comfortable, with café and bus office adjacent. *Grand*, opp. railway station, clean, good hot showers, E; cheap alojamiento, *Pequeño*, Av. Bolívar 236, friendly and clean. *Residencial Independencia*, rec., near railway station and church, E, hot water but no room heating even in winter when temperatures can drop to -15°C. *La Frontera* hotel and restaurant, downhill from Atahualpa bus stop, F, good and cheap.

**Camping** is possible near the control post on the outskirts of town.

**Exchange** Travel agency around corner from *Hotel Cristal* gives good rates for cheques; only cash is accepted elsewhere in the Turismo building. There are several *cambios* in Villazón (open on Sun.) which accept cash only and sell australes as well as bolivianos. Rates are often better in Villazón.

**Medical** There are a good hospital in La Quiaca and a doctor in Villazón. Farmacia Nueva, ½ block from Church, has remedies for *soroche* (mountain sickness).

**Transport** Difficult to obtain information in La Quiaca about buses leaving Villazón for points in Bolivia (**see Bolivia, South from La Paz** for Villazón), though Bolivian buses tend to be more reliable than Bolivian trains. New bus station in La Quiaca, 4 blocks from railway station, accepts payment in US$. 3 Atahualpa buses (next to *Hotel Cristal*) a day to Salta (US$22) via Jujuy (5-8 hrs. to Jujuy 9-11 hrs. to Salta), also several to Jujuy. Panamericano (T 396, next to *Hotel Grand*) has 5 buses a day to Jujuy, US$15, 6½ hrs. Some meal breaks, but take own food, as sometimes long delays. Buses may be stopped and searched for coca leaves. *Común* bus at 2130, 12 hours. *El Panamericano* trains leave for Jujuy and Tucumán Wed. and Sat. at 2120, arriving Jujuy at 0712, Tucumán at 1510 Thur. and Sun. There is also a train to Jujuy only, Mon., Wed., Sat. at 1015, arr. 2030. On Sat. *El Expreso del Sud* from La Paz to La Quiaca connects with *El Panamericano* to Tucumán, with a through coach. The railway goes up to 3,692 metres at Tres Cruces. Take warm sweaters as temperature drops sharply after sunset. Make sure you book a seat when buying a railway ticket; it is also essential to arrive well in advance of advertised time of departure to get your seat.

**Entering Bolivia**  The frontier bridge is 10 km. walk from bus terminal. If the Bolivian Immigration Officer is not in his office you can ask for him at *Hotel Panamericano*, just up from the Post Office.

**Warning**  Those travellers who need a visa to enter Bolivia are advised to get it before arriving in La Quiaca because the consular staff there try to charge US$15 per visa; pleading may reduce the charge.

   Motorists should visit the Servicio Nacional de Turismo to obtain the Hoja de Ruta, which all motorists must have. It is not restrictive in any practical sense; just a nuisance!

**Entering Argentina**  Argentine immigration and customs are open 0730- 1200, 1500-1800 on Sats., Suns., and holidays; there is a special fee of US$3. Buses arriving outside these hours will have to wait, so check before travelling. You can cross the border at night, without luggage, and your passport will not be stamped. Formalities are usually very brief at the border but very thorough customs searches are made 100 km. S of the border at Tres Cruces; be prepared for camera search.

**N.B.**  Bolivian time is one hour earlier than Argentine (2 hours in summer). Lunch Bolivian side is 1200-1400 (Bolivian time) and Argentine side 1200-1500 (Argentine time) so customs reopen at same time.

**North-East from Jujuy**  63 km. from Jujuy is **San Pedro de Jujuy**, a sugar town of 60,000 people. The Ingenio La Esperanza, on the outskirts, is a sugar-mill with hospital, housing and a recreation centre, all built by the English Leach brothers who owned the mill. *Hotel Alex 2*, R. Leach 467, private bath, clean; *Alex I*, Tello 436; *Velez Sarsfield*, V. Sarsfield 154, E; excellent restaurant at *Sociedad Sirio-Libanesa* on the plaza. Bus to Jujuy, US$2, 1½ hrs; to Embarcación, Atahualpa, US$3.50, 2½ hrs.

*Libertador* (formally Libertador General San Martín), another sugar town 50 km. N of San Pedro, is a base for exploring the **Parque Nacional Calilegua**, an area of peaks and sub-tropical valleys, reached by dirt road from just N of the town. The park entrance is 8 km. along this road (camping site with good facilities, hitching from Libertador possible), which climbs through the park and beyond to Valle Grande (no accommodation, basic food supplies from shops), 90 km. from Libertador. From here it is possible to walk to Humahuaca and Tilcara (allow at least 3 days; these walks are described in *Backpacking in Chile and Argentina* by Clare Hargreaves—Bradt Publications). Trucks run by Empresa Valle Grande, Libertad 780, leave Libertador, Tues., and Sat., 0730, 5 hrs., very crowded, returning Sun. and Thur. 1000.

**Services**  at Libertador: *Residencial Gloria*, Urquiza 270, E, clean, hot water; *Ledesma*, Jujuy 473 just off plaza, E, friendly; *Restaurant Sociedad Boliviana*, Victoria 711, where the locals eat.

From Libertador, Route 34 runs NE 244 km., to the Bolivian frontier at Yacuiba (see **Eastern Bolivia** section), via Embarcación (Km. 101). Another route to Bolivia is via **Orán**, 110 km. N of Libertador on Route 50, an uninteresting place, pop. 34,000. (*Residencial Centro*, Pellegrini 332, E; *Residencial Crillon*, 25 de Mayo 225, E, dirty; *Gran Hotel Orán*, Pellegrini 617, C; *Residencial Crisol*, López y Planes, E, hot water, friendly, rec.)

**Buses**, 3 daily to **Salta**, 8½ hrs.; direct bus to **Tucumán** at 2130, connecting for Mendoza bus which leaves at 1300. Bus to **Tartagal** daily at 0630 and 1800; to **Jujuy** at 1200 daily; to **Formosa**, US$28, 14 hrs., leaving Tues., Thurs., Sat. at 0930; to **Embarcación**, US$1.70.

   There are frequent bus services to **Aguas Blancas** (45 mins., US$1.70, luggage checks on bus), on the frontier. There is nowhere to stay at Aguas Blancas nor anywhere to change money, but there are restaurants (*El Rinconcito de los Amigos*) and shops. The passport office is open from 0700 to 1200 and 1500 to 1900. There is no exit tax. Buses run twice daily from Bermejo, across the river (ferry US$0.10), to Tarija (10 hours, US$6).

   If entering Argentina spend your remaining Bolivian money here, not accepted in Orán; buses to Orán every 45 mins.; through buses to Salta, Veloz del Norte, 3 daily.

   There is no direct bus from Orán to Asunción, Paraguay; take bus to Embarcación, from there train to Formosa, then bus to Asunción.

**Embarcación** (pop. 24,000) has several hotels (*Punta Norte*, España 277, D, clean, a/c, friendly; Sr. Sarmiento's Hotel; *Universal*, hot water), of which the cheaper are near the railway station. Restaurant of *Sociedad Sirio Libanesa*, H. Irigoyen and 9 de Julio, cheap and good. 2 km. from Embarcación you can walk to the Loma Protestant mission for Mataes and Toba Indians, who sell unpainted pottery there. These Indians lead a fairly miserable existence. Buses go to Orán, 1 hour, US$1.70 on a paved road. Buses Embarcación-Pocitos. Bus Embarcación-Salta US$15, 3 a day. Embarcación-Formosa railway (dusty in summer) has *coche-motor* link leaving Embarcación 1300 Mon. and Fri., 18 hours, US$20 1st class, US$15 tourist, plenty of wildlife to see, but check details as this service is sometimes replaced by a bus when there is weather damage to the line. (Regular bus runs Tues. 1445.)

---

## THE CUYO REGION: OVER THE ANDES TO CHILE (4)

**From the pampa to the heights of Aconcagua and the Uspallata Pass, en route to Santiago. Mendoza is a centre of wine making, fruit growing, winter sports (several ski resorts nearby) and climbing.**

In the Cuyo region, in the W, there is little rain and nothing can be grown except under irrigation. On the irrigated lands grapes and fruit are possible, and alfalfa takes the place of the maize grown in the N. Three of the more important oases in this area of slight rainfall are Mendoza itself, San Rafael, 160 km. to the S, and San Juan 177 km. to the N.

Of the 15 million hectares in Mendoza Province, only 2% are cultivated. Of the cultivated area 40% is given over to vines, 25% is under alfalfa grown for cattle, and the rest under olive groves and fruit trees. Petroleum is produced in the Province, and there are important uranium deposits.

**The Transandine Route** Travelling by rail or road from Buenos Aires westward across the pampa, one comes first to **Mercedes**, in Buenos Aires Province, a pleasant city with a population of 40,000. It has many fine buildings, and is a railway junction of some importance. (Not to be confused with Villa Mercedes in San Luis Province—see below.) Tourist Office on plaza, very friendly.

**Hotels** *Aragón*, ½ block from Plaza, friendly, F, hot water. *Libertador*, E, opp. bus station, good.

The workshops of the San Martín railway are at **Junín**, 256 km. from Buenos Aires. (Eva Perón was born near here.) Also served by Mitre railway, the town is close to lagoons from which fish are taken to the capital. Population, 63,700.

**Accommodation** Several hotels; camping at Chimihuin municipal campsite, US$1.50.

At Rufino, on Route 7, 452 km. from Buenos Aires, is the rec. *Hotel Astur*, L, Córdoba 81, C with ACA discount; also at La Boulaye, on Route 7, 517 km. from Buenos Aires, there are several good and cheap hotels, e.g. *Victoria*.

At **Villa Mercedes** (San Luis Province, pop. 77,000), 693 km. from Buenos Aires (where the old municipal market is now an arts and community centre), a line runs NE to (122 km.) Río Cuarto. About 65 km. beyond Villa Mercedes we begin to run into the rolling hills of San Luis; beyond there are stretches of woodland.

**Hotels** ACA hotel *San Martín*, Lavalle 435, C, restaurant, garages, clean, friendly; the ACA restaurant at the service station on Route 7, outside town, is very good value; *Residencial Cappola*, Mitre 1134, E, clean, rec.

**Bus** Villa Mercedes—Buenos Aires US$28.

**Train** Buenos Aires-Villa Mercedes, *El Aconcagua* daily at 2130, arrives 0730; returns 2206, arrives 0830. *El Cóndor*, Sat. only, 2030, arr. 0505, returns Sun. 0015. Both trains serve Mendoza.

**Air** Airport: Villa Reynolds, 10 km. from Villa Mercedes. Austral to Buenos Aires, San Juan.

**San Luis**, 98 km. from Villa Mercedes, is the capital of the Province of San Luis.

It stands at 765 metres at the southern end of the Punta de los Venados hills. It was founded by Martín de Loyola, the governor of Chile, in 1596, and is still faintly colonial. The area is rich in minerals and an onyx quarry is worked. Visit the Centro Artesanal San Martín de Porras, run by the Dominican fathers, on 25 de Mayo, opp. Palacio de Gobierno, where rugs are woven. Open 0700-1300 exc. Sat. and Sun. Population: 150,000. San Luis to Mendoza is 264 km.

A "Via Crucis" sculptured in white marble skirts the mountainside. Beyond Salto Grande, Salto Colorado and the Gruta de la Virgen de las Flores is El Volcán, in whose neighbourhood is Cruz de Piedra dam (drives, fishing), and Cañada Honda (placer gold mining, riding and fishing). Hotels and inns along the road.

**Hotels** Several on Av. Pres. Illia: *Aiello*, No. 431 T 25644, a/c, private bath, garages. *Gran San Luis*, No. 470, pool, 50 metres from ACA; *Gran Hotel España*, No. 300, T 25051, 3 star; also *Novel*, Junín 748, all categories B-C. Others on Rivadavia, e.g. *Gran Palace*, No. 657, B; *Rivadavia*, No. 1470, D. *Hotel Residencial 17*, hot water, friendly, opp. bus station, basic, E. *Hotel San Antonio*, with restaurant; many others opposite bus and railway station; these are category E.

**Camping** Rio Volcán, 4 km. from town. *Color - 1 blk fr Ploy*

**Exchange House** ~~Alituris, Pringles 983~~, opp. Plaza, no commission.

**Tourist Office** San Martín 741, excellent.

**Train** From Buenos Aires, *El Aconcagua* at 2030, continuing to Mendoza, 4½ hrs. Return daily at 2106, arrives 0830 next day. *El Cóndor* passes through Sat. 0650 for Mendoza, returns Sun. 2232 for Buenos Aires.

29 km. NE of San Luis is **La Toma** (*Hotel Gran Italia*, E, hot showers; *Residencial Days*, P. Graciarena 158, private bath) the cheapest place to buy green onyx—about 20 shops. From here you can make an excursion to Cerros Rosario, interesting hills and rock scenery, 10 km. NW; and San José del Morro, a group of mountains which were originally volcanoes (there is a model in the Museo de Ciencias in Buenos Aires). You will find a lot of rose-quartz.

Beyond San Luis (27 km.) the line climbs to a height of 460 metres and descends again along the valley of the Río Desaguadero. From the small junction of Las Catitas, 92 km. from Mendoza, a branch line runs S to (183 km.) San Rafael, through country typical of this region: sometimes arid, sometimes marshy, and sometimes cultivated. At **San Rafael** itself, at the foot of the Andes, irrigation makes it possible to grow fruit in large quantities. The town—there are some oil wells near—has a population of 72,200. There is a small but interesting natural history museum 6 km. S.E. of town at Isla Río Diamante. A road runs W over El Pehuenche pass to Talca (Chile).—reopened in 1991 after closure. Bus to Mendoza, frequent, US$6. Bus to Neuquén, US$20.

**Hotels** *Rex*, Yrigoyen 56, T 22177; *España*, San Martín 292, C with bath, clean but shabby, no restaurant. *Kalton*, Yrigoyen 120, D, excellent, clean, safe, good value.

**Campsites** 2 sites (one of them ACA) at Isla Río Diamante, 6 km S.E.

Above the town, up the Río Atuel valley, there is beautiful scenery in the **Valle Hermoso** up to the dams of El Nihuil which provide irrigation water and hydroelectric power to Mendoza. There is fishing in the reservoir above the highest dam. Good skiing at **Las Leñas**, 2,250 metres up in Valle Hermoso, a new resort with 33 pistes, three T-bars, three ski-lifts. It claims to be the foremost ski resort in the southern hemisphere and hopes to host the World Ski Championships in 1991 or 1993. (Buses from Buenos Aires, 15 hrs., in skiing season only.) Three stonebuilt hotels: *Escorpio*, *Acuario* and *Gemini* and a disco, shop renting equipment and expensive restaurant. All the hotels are L; for cheaper accommodation you have to stay in Los Molles (bus from San Rafael US$5.30; from Las Leñas US$0.70) where is *Hotel La Huenca*, B, a/c, clean. There is an airport in **Malargüe**, pop. 8,600 (*Hotel del Turismo*, San Martín 224, T 71042, rec.; *Hotel-Restaurant El Cisne*, C, clean, rec.) 70 km. from Las Leñas, with flights to Buenos Aires.

**Mendoza**, at the foot of the Andes, 1,060 km. from Buenos Aires, is linked to it by air, the San Martín railway and a paved road, which continues across the Andes to Chile. (No rail service now between Mendoza and Chile.)

Mendoza (756 metres) is an expanding and very pleasant city. Rainfall is slight, but irrigation has turned the area into a green oasis of fruit trees and vineyards. The city was colonized from Chile in 1561 and named in honour of the then governor of Chile. It was from here that the Liberator José de San Martín set out to cross the Andes, to help in the liberation of Chile. Mendoza was completely destroyed by fire and earthquake in 1861, so today it is essentially a modern city of low dwellings (as a precaution against earthquakes), thickly planted with trees and gardens. There was a serious earthquake in January 1985, which made 40,000 homeless and destroyed most of the area near the railway station. The main street is Avenida San Martín, which runs S to N parallel to the San Martín railway line. Population of city 148,000, but with suburbs included, it is about 600,000.

See the Cerro de la Gloria, a hill above the great Parque San Martín on the W side of the city, crowned by an astonishing monument to San Martín. There is a great rectangular stone block with bas-reliefs depicting various episodes in the equipping of the Army of the Andes and the actual crossing. In front of the block, San Martín bestrides his charger. In the park at the foot of Cerro de la Gloria steep and twisting paths run to the Jardín Zoológico. There are watercourses and an artificial 1 km.-long lake in the park too, where regattas are held, and views of the Andes (when the amount of floating dust will allow) rising in a blue-black perpendicular wall, topped off in winter with dazzling snow, into a china-blue sky. The entrance to the Parque San Martín is ten blocks W of the Plaza Independencia. Bus 11 from the centre will take you half-way up the hill, to the entrance to the park. There is an hourly bus ("Oro Negro") that will take you to the top of the Cerro de la Gloria, which runs from the eastern end of the park, on Av. Libertad, to the monument— it's a long walk (45 mins.).

The best shopping centre is Avenida Las Heras, where there are good souvenir and handicraft shops; leather goods are cheaper here than in Buenos Aires. The municipal market is clean and well-stocked; worth a visit. The vintage festival, Fiesta de la Vendimia, is held in the amphitheatre of the Parque San Martín in the first week of March. There is a wine museum (at the Giol *bodega*—see below), with good guides and wine tasting, just behind the Palacio de Gobierno, opening hours from the tourist office. Outside Mendoza, about 40 km. due E, there is a satellite town, very modern, called San Martín. N.B. Official tours of the city are a waste of time and money.

**Wine** Wine *bodegas* (wine-making season March/April) and fruit preserving; visiting times available from Tourist Office. Giol winery, one of the world's biggest, was closed and up for sale in 1990, after economic difficulties in 1989. Take 15 bus marked "Maipú" (every hour), but check if winery is open before going. Also in Maipú district is *Peñaflor*, 1/2 hr. by taxi SW of city, good visit and generous tasting. Bodega de Arizú is open to inspection any time, bus No. 7 from city centre; so are many of the others, and they offer you a glass after the visit. Try Bodega Escorihuela (bus 15 from centre) if you are more interested in the information than the wine-tasting. The Toso bodega is close to the city centre and has excellent wines. San Felipe *bodega* visit rec., bus 17, tours 0900-1100, 1600-1800, tasting. Prices at the bodegas have roughly a 100% mark-up from supermarket prices. Recommended: Cruz del Sur from Bodega Arizú, Cuesta del Parsal, Valroy-Borgoña, Valroy-Cabernet Sauvignon, Viejo Toro, Trapiche from Bodega Peñaflor, and Vino de Mesa Arizú Tinto Seco. Many tourist agencies include the bodegas in their half-day or day-long tours (US$4-8 but these visits are too short, with too few guides and little tasting—only of the cheaper wines).

**Local Holidays** 18 January (Crossing of the Andes); 25 July (St. James); 8 September (Virgin of Carmen de Cuyo). Annual wine festival at the beginning of March, when hotels fill up fast; book ahead! Prices rise at this time, and in July (the ski season) and September (the spring festival).

**Hotels** *Aconcagua*, 4 star, A, comfortable, San Lorenzo 545, T 243833, good restaurant, pool, tourist advice and bookings available; *Plaza*, Chile 1124 on main plaza, T 233000, B, not too clean, but obliging; *Balbi*, Las Heras 340, T 233500, B, small swimming pool, a/c but you must phone to have it turned on each time you return to your room, nice rooms; *San*

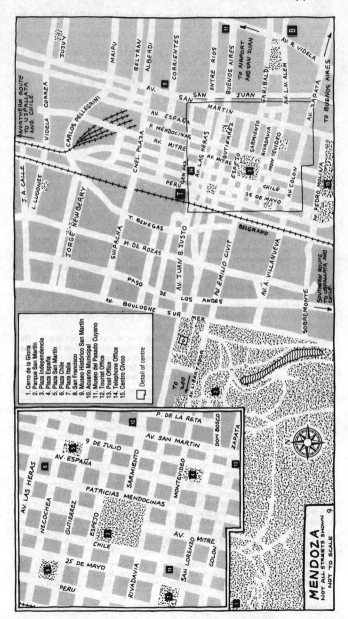

1. Cerro de la Gloria
2. Parque San Martín
3. Plaza Independencia
4. Plaza España
5. Plaza San Martín
6. Plaza Chile
7. Plaza Italia
8. San Francisco
9. Museo Histórico San Martín
10. Acuario Municipal
11. Museo del Pasado Cuyano
12. Tourist Office
13. Post Office
14. Telephone Office
15. Centro Cívico

☐ Detail of centre

MENDOZA
NOT ALL STREETS SHOWN
NOT TO SCALE

*Martín*, Espejo 435, T 251349, B, rec.; *Nutibara*, Bartolomé Mitre 867, T 244658, B, central, modern swimming pool, rec.; *Palace*, Las Heras 70, T 234200, B, a/c, bath, no breakfast, central; *Vecchia Roma*, España 1617 T 231491 (next door to restaurant of same name), B, comfortable, safe.

In our price ranges C and D: *Crillón*, Perú 1065, T 245525, small, clean. *City*, Gen. Paz 95, T 251343, D, clean, helpful; *Royal*, Las Heras 145, T 234526, adequate value, ask for fan in summer; *Vigo*, Necochea 749 (T 250208), D, good value, clean, good *comedor*; *Santa Clara*, 9 de Julio, central, clean, hot water, own bath. *Pacífico*, San Juan 1407, modern, comfortable, clean; *Galicia*, Av. San Juan 881, near Av. L. M. Alem, T 249619, D, very clean, hot water; *Savoy*, Belgrano 1377, D, good, clean, some rooms without window, tours offered at 20% discount; *Milena*, Pasaje Babilonia 17 (off San Juan nr. Don Bosco), T 240284, 2 star, clean, nice atmosphere; *1 de Mayo*, Garibaldi 80, T 248820, C, highly rec., 0800 checkout time; *Messidor*, Alberdi 690, T 314013, reasonable, friendly, clean, comfortable, arranges tours; *Balcarce*, San Martín 1446, D, clean, safe; *Argentino*, Plaza Independencia, D, good; *El Libertador*, España 347, D, good; *San Remo*, Godoy Cruz 477, D, quiet, central; *El Piño Azul* apartments, San Martín 2872 (T 304240), D per day.

In the cheaper categories: On Calle Juan B. Justo, *Penitentes* (No. 67), T 230208, E with bath, a/c and heating, good, snack bar; *Margal* (No. 76, T 252013), E, mixed reports; *Ideal* (No. 270), E, transport to bus station; *Premier* (700 block), E, private parking, clean, good value. On Perú: *Petit*, No. 1459, T 232099, without breakfast, 1½ blocks from railway station, clean, friendly, rec.; *Zamora* (No. 1156), T 257537, reasonable and friendly, converted house, E; *Residencial D'Amore* (No 1346), E, clean, use of kitchen; *España* (No. 1535), E, quiet, safe; *Dardex* (No.1735), 2 blocks from railway station, E, friendly. On General Paz: *Alcor* (No. 86), T 234800, E, central, good; *Líbano* (No. 227), excellent, clean, D/E; *Gran Marta* (No. 460), clean, but only cold showers, rec.; *Imperial*, Las Heras 84, T 234671, E, washing facilities, friendly, rec.; *República*, Necochea 541, T 253501, E, pleasant, cheerful, English spoken; *Residencial Alberdi*, Alberdi 51, T 234110, E, family run, friendly, clean; *El Rosario*, Chile 1579, T 254765, E, good, clean, hot water, rec.; *Residencial Central*, 9 de Julio 658, F, clean, plenty of hot water. *Quijote*, Av. San Juan 1407, E, clean, friendly, restaurant; *Escorial*, San Luis 263, E, very friendly and clean, rec.

Lodgings (E) in private houses: ask at Escuela de Hotelería, Paso de los Andes 1249, near entrance to Parque San Martín. Sra. Ada Zárate, San Juan 564, 1, Dept. 5-6, close to bus station, E in dormitory, has been rec. Youth Hostel at Benegas 1638 y González, F p.p., pleasant.

**Camping** In Parque General San Martín permitted, free, in cars, but not in tents. Three campsites at Challao, about 14 km. from the city centre, reached by colectivo No. 11 leaving every hour. *Camping Suizo* best value, has shop, safest of all sites, friendly but loud music at night from nearby amusement arcade. About 13 km. from Mendoza, two sites near the turn-off for Barballón. *El Salto*, 50 km. W of Mendoza, near mountains, well situated.

**Restaurants** *Trevi*, Las Heras 68, good. *Bárbaro*, San Martín 914, English spoken, speciality is roast kid, pricey but good. *Tristán Barraza*, 658 Av. Sarmiento (*parrilla*), good. *Trattoria Aveni*, 25 de Mayo 1162, crowded, good. *Parrillada Arturito*, Chile 1575, good cheap steak, popular with locals; *Don Angelo*, Lavalle 150, cheap set meal; *Club Alemán*, Necochea 2261, Godoy Cruz, rec. *La Nevada*, Chile 1495, 3-course meal for US$2, excellent value; *Govinda*, San Juan 840, excellent and cheap set meal, open 1200-1600, 1900-2200; *El Dragón del Oro*, Chinese, 25 de Mayo 1553 (near Las Heras), very good; *Cervecería Zurich*, Las Heras y 25 de Mayo, good food and service, cheap, rec. Ice cream at *Soppelso*, Las Heras y España and at Paseo Sarmiento, rec. *Sr. Cheff*, good restaurant/confitería at *Hotel 1 de Mayo* on Garibaldi. *Il Tucco*, Emilio Civit 556 (nr. park gates), also same name and owner in centre on Montevideo, excellent new Italian restaurants, reasonable prices; also on Emilio Civit, No. 275, *Dis Cepolin*, meals at 2200, good tango show at 2300. Several places with cheap 3-course menus on San Juan, 1300 and 1400 blocks. *Aranjuez*, Lavalle y San Martín, nice cafe, good meeting place. *Mankie Snack Bar*, Las Heras y Mitre, excellent breakfasts; *Café de la Gente*, café/bookshop at Rivadavia 135, pleasant atmosphere. Several good snack bars (known as *carrito* bars): *Tío Paco*, Salta y Alem; *Torombola*, San Juan 1348; *Don Claudio*, Perú y Godoy; *El Gran Lomo*, Rivadavia 56, open 24 hrs, rec. Out of town, *Lomo Loco*, a few km. S on Luján road, locals' favourite *parrilla* but not cheap.

**Shopping** Leather goods good and cheap; try *Jorge Ruben Pacheco*, 9 de Julio 1455, subsuelo Loc. 1. Books (English and German selection) from *Historias* on Av. San Martín. English language magazines and *Buenos Aires Herald* usually available at kiosk at corner of San Martín and Alem.

**Car Hire** Avis, Espejo 228; Lis Car, San Lorenzo 110, T 291416; **A.S. Rent-a-Car**, Garibaldi

186, T 248317. **Motorcycle repairs** César Armitrano, Rubén Zarate 138, 1600-2100, highly recommended for assistance or a chat; he will let you work in his workshop.

**Nightclubs** in the suburb of Chacras de Coria. Discothèques: *Saudades*, Barraquero y San Martín; *Kalatraba*, Perú 1779; *El Grillo*, Chile 1243; *El Diablo*, Ruta Internacional Vistalba Luján.

**Cinema** Free film shows at Salón Cultural Rivadavia, José V. Zapata 349.

**Casino** 25 de Mayo 1123, daily 2100-0300.

**Mountain Climbing** Information from Tourist Office. There is a three-day (Thurs.-Sat.) climbing and trekking expedition via Godoy Cruz and Cacheuta to Cerro Penitentes (4,351 metres), sleeping in mountain refuge, food included. **See also page 122.**

**Museums** Museo Histórico San Martin, Av. General San Martín 1846, seven blocks N of the Tourist Office, open Mon.-Fri., 0900-1200, 1700-2000, US$0.40; **Museo del Pasado Cuyano**, Montevideo 544, beautifully furnished, has a collection on San Martín and history of Mendoza, open Mon.-Fri. 0930-1230, Tues. and Thur., 1600-1730, but times vary, US$0.50; **Museo de Ciencias Naturales y Antropólogicas**, to be housed at Playas Serranes, Parque Gral. San Martín (renovation work in progress 1990); **Museo Municipal de Arte Moderno**, to be housed underground (subsuelo) in Plaza Independencia. The **Acuario Municipal** is underground at Buenos Aires y Ituzaingó, very interesting, US$0.50, open Mon.-Fri. 1000-1200 and 1530-2000, Sat. and Sun. same times a.m. Museo del Vino, Av. Peltier, Centro Cívico, open Mon.-Sat., 0900-1700. The **Museo Arqueológico** and the **Museo de Ciencias Naturales** are both in the Ciudad Universitaria—ask at Tourist Office for details. Worth seeing, also, are the ruins of the **San Francisco church** at Ituzaingó y Beltrán.

**Language Classes** Sra. Inés Perea de Bujaldon, Rioja 620, teaches Spanish to German speakers, rec.

**Exchange** Lloyds Bank (BLSA), Gen. Gutiérez 72. **Banco de Credito Argentino**, España 1168, gives cash advance on Visa card. **American Express**, Rivadavia 76, Citibank Av. San Martín 1099, gives US$ cash for cheques. **Santiago** No. 1177, well rec.; **Maguitur**, No. 1203. *Casas de cambio* open till 2000 Mon.-Fri., and some open Sat., a.m. including **Exprinter**, No. 1198;

**Consulates** Bolivia, Azopardo 276, Godoy Cruz, T 223893; **Peru**, Perú 8185 Carrodilla, T 390863; **Chile**, Av. Emilio Civit, 296, T 255024; **Uruguay**, 9 de Julio 200. **Spain**, Agustín Alvarez 455, T 253947; **Italy**, Necochea 712, T 251886; **France**, Chile 1754, T 234614; **Germany**, Montevideo 127, 1° Piso D6, T 242539.

**Cultural Institutes** Alianza Francesa, Chile 1754; **Instituto Dante Alighieri**; (Italy), Espejo 638; **Instituto Cultural Argentino-Norteamericano**, Chile 985; **Instituto Cuyano de Cultura Hispánica** (Spain), Villanueva 389; **Goethe Institut**, Morón 265, Mon.-Fri. 0800-1200, 1600-2230.

Coin-operated **laundromat**, Colón 543, also on Garibaldi near La Rioja, on Salta near San Luis, and at corner of San Juan and Rondeau. *Lavarap*, Av. Colón 547.

There is a private **gynaecological clinic** at Gral. Paz 445; helpful and relatively inexpensive.

**Post Office** Av. San Martín, Av. Colón. **Telefónica Central**, Chile 1574.

**Tourist Offices** at airport, T 306484, helpful (frequently closed); at the bus terminal, T 259709, at Av. San Martín 1143, T 242800, and at Mitre y Las Heras. They have a list of reasonable private lodgings, and other literature including lists of *bodegas* and a free town map; the latter is also available at most kiosks.

**Travel Agencies** *Cuyo Travel*, Paseo Sarmiento 162, 10% discount for ISIC and youth card holders for trekking and climbing on Aconcagua. *Servicios Especiales Mendoza*, c/o Annette Schenker, Amigorena 65, 5500 Mendoza, T (061) 244700, Fax 240131, run by Bernard Klapproth, guided tours, many languages spoken, climbing Aconcagua and Andes, trekking, access to Red Cross and Police, only company to cross Andes to Chile without papers, information on Patagonia. Lots in Las Heras, between Perú and San Martín. *Turismo Cóndor* (also at bus station), rec. for tours in and around the city, and to El Cristo Redentor statue, good guides, Spanish only. *Turismo Sepeán*, San Juan 1070, friendly and helpful, have branch in Santiago. *El Oro Negro*, Rivadavia 211, T 291061, tours to Puente del Inca and elsewhere. *Ibiza*, Espejo 217, T 258141, helpful and efficient. *Hunuc Huar Expediciones*, Av. España 1340, 8 piso, oficina 7, specializes in assistance to climbers, especially on Aconcagua.

**Airport** Plumerillo, 8 km. from centre; *remise* taxis (US$4.25) and buses (infrequent) run. Bus No. 6 stops at corner of San Juan and Alem and takes you close to the terminal; make sure there is an "Aeropuerto" sign on the driver's window. Flying time from Buenos Aires: 1¾ hours. Aerolíneas flies at least twice a day: Austral twice a day (once on Sat.). AR to Santiago, twice a week, fare must be paid in US$. Several flights to Córdoba with AR and Austral. Aerolíneas Argentinas, Paseo Sarmiento 74.

**Trains** to **Buenos Aires**: *El Libertador*, leaves Mendoza Mon. and Fri. at 2015, arrives at 0930; car transporters, luxurious bar, film show and airconditioning, steward service, good dining cars, meal, good value; take drinks with you. *El Aconcagua* leaves Mendoza daily at 1600, arriving the next day at 0830; *El Cóndor* leaves Sun. at 1855, arrives Bs. As. at 0930. Trains from Buenos Aires to **Mendoza**: *El Libertador*, leaves at 2015, Sun. and Thur., arrives 1000. *El Aconcagua* leaves daily at 2130, arrives at 1400; *El Cóndor* leaves Fri. at 2030, arrives 1035. There are no trains to Chile but local buses meet train to take you to bus station, to catch buses for Chile. Train from Mendoza to **San Juan**, 1420 daily, 2½ hrs. Book pullmans well ahead in winter; they're heated. No direct trains to Salta, Tucumán or Córdoba, but connections are possible. A tourist train runs to **Puente del Inca**: ask for details at the tourist office or Belgrano station. The train runs on the one-metre gauge Transandino line (built at the end of the 19th century), which has been neglected and partly disused on the Chilean side. Bus from railway to bus terminal, No. 5, US$0.25.

**Buses** Terminal on E side of Av. Videla, 15 mins. walk from centre. To Santiago, **see page 122**. Buses run to **Bariloche**, TAC, leave 1300 Sun., Thurs., US$70, on a mostly paved road, about 22 hours, book well ahead; to **Córdoba**, TAC 4 daily, 9 hrs., US$20; to **San Rafael**, US$6; to **San Juan** every 2 hours, US$7, 2 hrs. (2 companies, TAC and Villa del Sur y Media Agua). To **La Rioja** US$18, 10 hrs., leaves 1430, 1930 or 2130. **Catamarca** overnight only, 12 hrs., daily, US$20. Daily at 1730 to **Tucumán**, US$28; to **Salta**, Andesmar daily (via Tucumán) at 1300, 20 hrs. Bus to **Mar del Plata** US$50; to **Puerto Iguazú** at 0700, Tues. and Thur. US$70, 38 hrs., Argentina Central company; alternatively take daily Vila Marta bus to Santa Fe and change for Iguazú bus, about 40 hrs. inc. waiting time. To **Comodoro Rivadavia**, daily with Andesmar, at 2000, US$100, 32 hrs. including 4 meal stops; the Tues. departure continues to Río Gallegos, arriving 1450 Thurs. To **Buenos Aires** via Route 8, 2nd class daily at 1315, arrives 0550, US$51, 1st class daily at 1630, arrives 0700, US$60; luxury service daily at 2100 (Chevallier), US$76 including meals; via Route 7 (Junín-Mercedes) at 2020, arrive 1205. Dull scenery, and very cold across the Pampas at night. Colta bus to **Lima**, Peru, Sat. 0700, arr. Tues. a.m.

**Hitch-hiking** between Mendoza and Buenos Aires is quite easy. If hitching to San Juan, take bus No. 6 to the airport near the highway. Hitching from Mendoza to Los Andes (Chile) is easy; go to the service station in Godoy Cruz suburb, from where all trucks to Chile, Peru and elsewhere leave.

**Excursions** If driving in mountains remember to advance the spark by adjusting the distributor, or weaken the mixture in the carburettor, to avoid the car seizing up in the rarified air. Buses run to the hot springs at **Cacheuta**, US$3.15 round trip, US$5 entry (thermal baths for a variety of ailments, can be arranged at travel agents), 45 km. to the SW (hotels not rec, campsite). The charming resort of **Potrerillos** is 13 km. from Cacheuta, with ski slopes not far away and excellent birdwatching in summer. *Gran Hotel; Hotel de Turismo*, A, with meals; ACA campsite. *Restaurant Armando* rec. In summer, you can hike 20 km. from the resort of Potrerillos to Vallecito, a closed ski resort, taking two days. On the first you will see desert scenery, blooming cactus flowers, birds and an occasional goat or cow. The second you walk surrounded by peaks, a steep but not difficult climb to the San Antonio refuge, usually open with beds and meals. Two other popular resorts within a few km. of the city are Barballón, to the NE, and Challao, to the NW. An excursion is also available from the Mendoza bus station to the small ski resort of Los Penitentes, 170 km. away, 4 hrs. (*Hotel Ayelén*, D, clean, comfortable, food, pricey); equipment hire US$5 a day, lift ticket for a day US$9. The best skiing is at (2,250 metres) Valle de las Leñas, S of Mendoza in the Valle Hermoso (**see page 115**). Excursions also to the dam at El Nihuil, with artificial lake, and to the Río Atuel canyon (although the 16 hour round trip from Mendoza can be uncomfortable in hot weather, better to visit the canyon from San Rafael). On the road to Luján de Cuyo (buses go every 15 mins. from near bus terminal) is a fine arts museum dedicated to Argentine artists, surrounded by sculpture in gardens, admission free (Museo Provincial de Bellas Artes Emiliano Guiñazu, Casa de Fader). Turismo La Cumbre, Necochea 541, also includes it on its 19-hour circular tour, as does Cata Turismo, Las Heras 426, 13 hours.

*Hotel Termas* at Villavicencio is closed. Many tourists come to visit the springs, which are all set in concrete. Pleasant walks round the area.

**N.B.** It is no longer possible to go from Mendoza to Santiago via the statue of El Cristo Redentor (Christ the Redeemer) at 4,200 metres. To see the statue you must go on a 12 hr. excursion from Mendoza, weekends early a.m., all travel agencies (since the Chilean side of the frontier at the statue is closed. The excursion also includes Puente del Inca (see below). All buses and cars go through the tunnel to Chile, leaving the statue unseen above.

## Over the Andes to Chile

**N.B.** No visas into Chile are available at the border, so if you need one and haven't got it, you will be turned back. There is a time change: travelling from Argentina into Chile remember to move your watch back 1 hr. between mid-March and mid-October.

There are 2 alternates of Route 7, which meet at **Uspallata**, the only settlement of any size between Mendoza and the Chilean frontier. Near Uspallata are the ruins of Las Bóvedas, built by the Huarpe Indians under the Jesuits, and an Inca *tambería*. They are just off the road which leads to Barreal and Calingasta (**see page 124**), unpaved for its first part and tricky when the snow melts and floods it in summer. (Prices are usually much higher at frontier, temperatures much lower. Frontier closes early.) The fully-paved southern branch, via Cacheuta and Potrerillos, is wider and better than the northern branch, which goes via Villavicencio with a stretch of one-way traffic just beyond the resort, where the road leads up spectacularly to the 3,050 metres high Cruz del Paramillo. (The return loop, a little longer and less steep, is through the picturesque Quebrada del Toro.) This northern branch is still unpaved.

**Hotels** *Hotel Uspallata*, B, dinner at 2100; payment for meals and drinks in cash, bowling alley, nice location, but hotel run down, service friendly, but vast herds of people get driven through it. *Hostería Los Cóndores*, D, clean, friendly.

**Camping** There is a pleasant ACA site at Uspallata, US$3 per head, full washing facilities, hot water.

People travelling by car over the Andes in winter are advised to enquire about road conditions from ACA in Mendoza (San Martín y Amigorena).

The crossing of the Andes, taken by San Martín, is the old mountain trail the Spaniards named the Camino de los Andes. Beyond Uspallata is a vast, open, undulating plain, wild and bare. On all sides stand the grey, gaunt mountains. On the far side of this plain the valley narrows till Río Blanco is reached, and there the mountain torrents rush and froth into the river. At Punta de Vacas we look left up the Tupungato Valley at the majestic cone of Tupungato, one of the giants of the Andes, rising 6,550 metres. An equally majestic mass of pinnacled rocks, Los Penitentes, is passed on the left; they are about 7 km. away. The climber to their base (an easy task from Puente del Inca with a guide) sees a remarkable sight. The higher rocks look like a church and the smaller, sharper rocks below give the impression of a number of cowled monks climbing upwards.

In a short time we are at **Puente del Inca**, 2,718 metres above sea level, 160 km. from Mendoza, a sports resort set among mountains of great grandeur. (*Hostería Puente del Inca*, D for room, less off-season, very pleasant, also bookable from *Plaza Hotel* in Mendoza; opposite is an army base which obscures the view of Aconcagua and prohibits photography.) Camping possible next to the church, if your equipment can withstand the winds. 5 km. from Puente del Inca on the road to Mendoza is a ski club, *Cruz de Caña*, with comfortable dormitories, E, and a good restaurant. The owner organizes trekking expeditions; prices: US$50 a day full board during expedition, and US$20 per mule.

The natural bridge after which Puente del Inca is named is one of the wonders of South America; it crosses the Río Mendoza at a height of 19 metres, has a span of 21 metres, and is 27 metres wide, and seems to have been formed by sulphur-bearing hot springs. Puente del Inca is the best point for excursions into the higher Andean valleys or for a visit to the base of Aconcagua, which was first climbed by Zurbriggen of the Fitzgerald Expedition in 1897. Visits can be paid on horseback from Puente del Inca to Los Penitentes (*La Taberna del Gringo*, Km. 151, Villa Los Penitentes, D, rec.); or on foot to the green lake of Laguna de los Horcones; or by car (only with a well regulated engine) or bus or on horseback to the statue of El Cristo Redentor set above La Cumbre (or Uspallata) pass on the frontier at an altitude of 4,200 metres. It was erected jointly by Chile and Argentina in 1904 to celebrate King Edward VII's decision in the boundary dispute of 1902. It is, unfortunately, somewhat disappointing from the road, for it is completely dwarfed by the landscape. (The road from the tunnel to the statue is closed for the season after the first snowfall in April.)

Local bus (Expreso Uspallata) from Mendoza for Uspallata and Puente del Inca 4 hrs., 0600 and 1000, returning from Puente del Inca 1300 and 1615; local buses also go on from Puente del Inca to Las Cuevas, Expreso Uspallata, US$5.50. (See above under Mendoza **Trains** for tourist rail service.)

After Puente del Inca, on the right, there is a good view of Aconcagua (6,960 metres), sharply silhouetted against the blue sky. In 1985, a complete Inca mummy was discovered at 5,300 metres on the mountain.

Best time for climbing *Aconcagua* (the highest peak in the Americas and a **national park**) is from mid-January to mid-February. Rob Rachowiecki writes: it is first necessary to obtain a permit (Argentines US$40, foreigners US$80) from the Dirección de Deportes, Recreación y Turismo Social (offices at the Mendoza football stadium, open mornings only, bus 11). The Club Andinista Mendoza (at end of Lemus, between Rioja and Salta, open 2000-2200) will help you with the paperwork; Sr. Luis Alberto Parra is particularly helpful, Güiraldes 246, 5519 San José, Mendoza. T 242003. Allow a couple of days for this. From Mendoza take a bus or colectivo to Puente del Inca. From here mules are available but cost US$20 per mule per day; you have to pay for 3 days there and back (1 day rest) and for the muleteer and his wages. This only takes you to the base camp at Plaza de Mulas (4,200 m). Of the huts above this point only La Libertad (Berlín) hut at about 6,000 m is in serviceable condition. Both huts are small with no facilities. Take a tent able to withstand 100 mph + winds, and clothing and sleeping gear for temperatures below -20C. Allow at least one week for acclimatization at lower altitudes before attempting summit (4 days from Plaza de Mulas). Treks and climbs organized by Sr. Fernando Grajales, the famous climber, in *Hostería Puente del Inca*, or at J.F.Moreno 898, 5500 Mendoza, Telex 55-154. Other guides can be found at the airport in Mendoza.

The frontier railway tunnel is no longer used by road traffic, which now takes the new 4-km. El Libertador-Las Cuevas toll road tunnel. The Chilean frontier is beyond *Las Cuevas*, a neat, modern settlement being developed as a ski-ing resort (though there is no ski-lift as yet), but recently damaged by landslides and a fire. It is wise to take snow chains from June to October. Officially, driving without chains and a shovel is prohibited between Uspallata and the border, but this can be resolved in a friendly way with border policemen. Both ACA and Chilean Automobile Club sell, but do not rent, chains.

**Hotel** *Hostería Las Cuevas*, only one, poor food, no heating in annex. Food available at kiosk at Expreso Uspallata bus terminal point.

Beyond Las Cuevas, the road, now completely paved, goes through the new road tunnel (latest charges for cars and VW buses not known). The old road over La Cumbre pass is now closed to through traffic; the famous statue of Christ can be visited only by excursion from Mendoza (see above).

**Transport to Chile** Turismo cars (Chi-Ar—some adverse reports—and Nevada) carrying 4 to 5 passengers (US$24, 5 hrs.) and minibuses (51/2-6 hrs.) do the trip to **Santiago** daily. If travelling by bus from Mendoza to Santiago take a direct bus as it is not possible to walk across the border. Buses Mendoza to Santiago daily at 0600-1200; several companies, TAC-Choapa at 0830 (meals included, films shown) recommended for cheapness and service; also Félix Pullman Norte; adverse reports on Chile Bus. Most buses are comfortable and fast (61/2-8 hrs.) and charge about US$15 (US$17 to **Viña del Mar** and **Valparaíso**), those with air-conditioning and hostess service (including breakfast) charge more, worth it when crossing the border as waiting time can be a matter of several hours. All companies in same part of Mendoza bus station: you can easily shop around. Children under 8 pay 60% of adult fare, but no seat; book two days ahead, if all seats booked try CATA, its service is reportedly less good than others thus it usually has some empty seats. Passport required. The ride is spectacular. Information at main bus station. If you want to return, buy an undated return ticket Santiago-Mendoza; it is cheaper. A taxi Mendoza-Santiago costs about US$90 for 4-5 people. Covalle runs direct service to **La Serena**, Chile, twice a week.

All Argentine entry and exit formalities are now dealt with at Punta de Vacas, 30 km. from Las Cuevas (entering Argentina by taxi, expect to be stopped and searched). A new customs post, Ingeniero Roque Carranza has been built near Laguna Los Horcones, nearer Las Cuevas. One can hitch-hike, or possibly bargain with bus drivers for a seat, from Punta de Vacas to Santiago, but if one is dropped at the entrance to the tunnel in winter, one cannot walk through. Travellers however report that customs men often help by asking passing motorists to take hitch-hikers through the tunnel to Chile. Chilean migration and customs check is after the tunnel—searches for fruit, meat, vegetables, which may not be imported into Chile, in a new building with the bus parked inside. Customs at the frontier are closed 1200-1400. Members of ACA need only the *Libreta de Pasos por Aduana*, otherwise you need the *Documento de Exportación* to enter Chile. Good food at frontier hotel, and there is an excellent motel on the Chilean side about an hour down.

---

## NORTH OF MENDOZA (5)

The oases of San Juan, La Rioja and Catamarca between the plains and the Andes. Interesting natural rock formations can be seen, especially Valle de la Luna and Puerta de Talampaya.

Of the three oases in the more arid zone N of Mendoza, San Juan is the most prosperous, wine and olives support La Rioja, but Catamarca is economically depressed. The first, 177 km. from Mendoza by paved road, is

**San Juan**, population 122,000 at 650 metres, founded 1562 by Don Juan Jufré de Loaysa y Montese and capital of its namesake province. The city is proud of its sunny climate and clean, tree-lined streets. Nearly destroyed by a 1944 earthquake, the centre is well laid-out, with a modern cathedral. The birthplace of Domingo Sarmiento (President of the Republic, 1868-1874, also an important historian/educator) is a museum. The area is famous for its wine, "to be between San Juan and Mendoza" is an Argentine expression for having drunk too much. One of the country's largest wine producers, Bodegas Bragagnolo, on the outskirts of town at Route 40 y Av. Benavídez, Chimbas, can be visited (bus 20 from terminal; guided tours daily 0830-1330, 1530-1930, not Sun.)

**Hotels** The Cámara Hotelera, a central clearing office, is opposite *Hotel Nogaró*, de la Roza 132, T 227501/5, A, best, pool, (ACA discount); *Jardin Petit*, 25 de Mayo 345, B (ACA discount), T 211825; *Selby*, Rioja 183, C, T 224777; *Bristol*, Entre Rios 368 Sur, T 222629, B, a/c, hot water, clean, rec.; *Plaza* Sarmiento 344, T 225179, C, friendly, noisy disco behind; *Brescia*, España 336, C, near train station, T 225708. Better cheap hotels include *Central*, Mitre 131 Este, T 223174, E, very clean and quiet, good beds, friendly owner; *Residencial 12 de Diciembre*, Sarmiento 234, E, book in before 2100, highly rec.; *Residencial Hispano Americano*, Estados Unidos 381 Sur, D; *Jessy-Mar*, Sarmiento 8 Norte, E, small rooms, noisy but clean; *Embajador*, Rawson 25 Sur, E, large rooms, clean, pleasant, café, good value. Several residenciales along Av. España, blocks 100-600 Sur.

**Camping** At Chimbas, 7 km. N; 3 sites at Rivadavia, 8 km. W.

**Restaurants** *Hostal de Palito*, Circunvalación Sur 271 (between San Martín and Ignacio de la Roza, some way out), excellent; *Wiesbaden*, Circunvalación y San Martín, German-style, pleasant setting; *Soychú*, de la Roza 223 Oeste, excellent vegetarian food; *Club Sirio Libanés*, Entre Rios 33 Sur, pleasant decor, good food, pricey; *Comedor Central*, Ignacio de la Roza 171 Este, not luxurious but good *locro* (stew) and *chivito* (goat). *Parilla Bigotes*, Las Heras y Ignacio de la Roza, inexpensive "all you can eat" meat, chicken, salads. *Club Español*, Plaza 25 de Mayo, more expensive, large portions of mediocre food. Many *pizzerías*, *confiterías*, and sidewalk cafés, including *Café Amadeus* and *Café del Aguila* (where one waiter resembles John Cleese). *Lomoteca San José*, San Martín 179, grills, inexpensive, late night music at weekends; *El Claval de Oro*, Santa Fe y Entre Ríos, snacks, drinks; *Marilyn*

*Bar*, San Martín y Mendoza, late night drinks; *Un Rincón de Napoli*, Rivadavia 175 Oeste, good; large glasses of fresh orange juice, good delicatessen next door. Eat under thatched shelters (*quinchos*) at *Las Leñas*, San Martin, 1600 Oeste.

**Shopping** Mercado Artesanal at 25 de Mayo y Aguilar.

**Car Hire** Parque Automotor, España y San Martín, Tel: 226018. Cash discount on request.

**Museums** Museo Casa de Sarmiento, Sarmiento y San Martín, open Tues.-Sat. 0830-1900; **Museo de Ciencias Naturales**, Av. San Martín y Catamarca, includes fossils from Ischigualasto Provincial Park (see below), open Mon.-Sat., 0830-1230, 1430-1830, US$0.40; **Museo Histórico San Martiniano**, Laprida 96 Este, includes the restored cloisters and two cells of the Convent of Santo Domingo. San Martín slept in one of these cells on his way to lead the crossing of the Andes, closed Sun., US$0.40.

**Exchange** Good rates at **Cambio Santiago**, Gral. Acha 52, weekdays until 2000, Sat. a.m. **Cambio Cash**, Tucumán 210 Sur; **Montemar**, Laprida 133 Sur; **Multicrédito**, Laprida y Mendoza; **Bolsa de Comercio**, Gral. Acha 278 Sur.

**Cultural Institutes** Goethe Institut, Santa Fe 114 Este, very active; Centro Cultural San Juan, Gral. Acha 737 Este, concerts and other events.

**Laundry** *Marva*, San Luis y Av. Rioja.

**Tourist Office** Sarmiento y San Martín, helpful, good brochures, open Mon.-Sat., 0900-1330, 1430-2100, Sun. 0900-1300; also at bus terminal. Arranges tours in summer only. Large-scale provincial maps available at bookshops. For information on Difunta Correa, consult Fundación Vallecito at Caucete.

**Travel Agent** *Yafar Turismo*, Laprida y Aberastaín, rec.

**By Air** Chacritas Airport, 14 Km. SE. From Buenos Aires and Córdoba with Aerolíneas Argentinas. Aerolínea Federal Argentina to Tucumán, Santa Fé, Mendoza, and the Chaco.

**Buses** Terminal at Estados Unidos y Santa Fe, 9 blocks E of centre (buses 33 and 35 go through the centre). Long distance services to **La Rioja** (550 km., 9 hours, US$14), **Catamarca** (660 km. over secondary roads, US$17, with connection to Salta), **Tucumán** (3 a day, 13 hrs., Libertador is cheapest), Córdoba, Santa Fe, Mar del Plata, Bahía Blanca and Bs.As. Fifteen departures daily from **Mendoza** with TAC. Also service to provincial tourist destinations.

To Chile: only connection with **Santiago (Chile)** is via Mendoza; catch the TAC bus at 0600, arrives in Mendoza 0830 in time for bus to Santiago which connects with train to Puerto Montt. To **La Serena**, Covalle Bus Thur. at midnight, 17 hrs. The Agua Negra (4,600 m.) has been reopened after having been closed in 1978. Cars and some bus services now cross the Andes over this spectacular high point, though in winter it may be closed for some weeks because of snow.

**Rail** Terminal at Av. España y Mitre, 7 blocks W of centre. The San Martin line's *Aconcagua* train, between Retiro and Mendoza (**see page 120**) also serves San Juan daily, arriving 2½ hours later than in Mendoza westbound, departing 2½ hours earlier eastbound. Sleeper service (from Mendoza only), Pullman, first and tourist classes.

**From San Juan** Hitchhiking to La Rioja, take route 141 to Chepes (ACA *Hostería*), then N to Patquía; more traffic on provinical route 29, a good paved, but less interesting road than that via San Agustin or Jachal (see below).

**Excursions** To the Museo Arqueológico of the University of San Juan at La Loja, 20 km. N., open Mon.-Fri., 0900-1900, Sat., Sun., 1000-1300, US$0.80, which contains an outstanding collection of prehispanic indigenous artefacts, including several well-preserved mummies. Inexpensive thermal baths nearby. Bus No. 20 from San Juan, 2 a day, but you need to take the first (at 0830) to give time to return. To Vallecito, 64 km. E, to the famous shrine to the **Difunta Correa**, an unofficial saint whose infant (according to legend) survived at her breast even after the mother's death from thirst in the desert. During Holy Week, up to 100,000 pilgrims visit the site, some crawling the final kilometre on their backs. See the remarkable collection of personal items left in tribute, including number plates from all over the world and even one policeman's detective school diploma!

Along scenic provincial route 12 (open westbound mornings, eastbound afternoons), 135 km. W of San Juan, lies **Calingasta**, in the valley of same name (annual cider festival in April). 40 km. S on the road to Uspallata is **Barreal** (Hotel Casino Barreal, T 0648-41000, recently improved, good value in restaurant; also *Hotel Jorge*, E, clean, very simple. *Posada San Eduardo*, small, quaint, few rooms with bath, open summer only; accommodation with Sr.

Patricio Sosa or Sr. Cortez. *Restaurant Isidoro*, owned by local baker and sandyacht champion, reasonable). Free tours of observatory at El Leoncito, 26 km. from Barreal (no public transport) can be arranged from San Juan. Bus San Juan-Barreal Mon.-Fri., 0700, Sat., 0630, 5 hrs.

Sr. Ramón Luis Ossa, physical education teacher at Barreal's high school, runs mule treks into the Andes, crossing the foothills in summer, from 10 to 21 days between November and April; he can be reached at 5405 Barreal, Pcia. San Juan, T (0648) 4 1024. We are grateful to Herbert Levi for a detailed account of Sr. Ossa's treks. In addition to the organizer's list of essentials, Sr. Levi recommends the following on any Andean trip: metal drinking mugs, metal containers to prevent tubes of toothpaste etc. emptying themselves in mule packs, long underpants to protect against chafing, woollen cap, insect repellent, sunburn cream, laxatives, soap, nylon groundsheet for sleeping bag (depending on weather), portable tent for privacy, and fishing gear for those who prefer catching their own meals (No. 3 spoons best for Andean streams--permit required).

**Climbing** Mercedario (also El Ligua), 6,770 metres. No authorization is required, but it is advisable to inform the Gendarmería Nacional at Barreal. From Barreal go to Casas Amarillas on the Río Blanco, about 100 km. on a gravel road. It may be possible to hire a Unimog 4 x 4 from the Gendarmería Nacional; guides (*baqueanos*) may also be hired, they can provide mules if necessary. The best time is mid-Dec. to end-Feb.; the types of terrain encountered are gravel, snow and rock. There is no rescue service. Nearby peaks include Pico Polaco (6,050 m.), La Mesa (6,200 m.), Alma Negra (6,120 m.) and Ramada (6,410 m.). More information is available from Club Andino Mercedario, 9 de Julio 547 Este, 5400 San Juan, or Antonio Beorchia Nigris, director, Ciadam (Research Centre for Andean Archaeology), República del Líbano 2621, 5423 San Juan. **N.B.** Do not enter this region from Chile, it is illegal.

Route 40, the principal tourist route on the eastern Andean slope, heads N toward Cafayate and Salta, via San José de Jachal. At Talacasto, 55 km. from San Juan, route 436 branches toward Las Flores (Km. 180) and the Chilean border at Agua Negra pass (4,600 metres—see under **Buses** above).

At Pismanta, 5 km. N of Las Flores, the moderately priced *Hotel Termas de Pismanta* (D p.p., B with full board) features rooms for 120 guests, thermal baths between 38° and 44°C, a large swimming pool, medical attention, library, cinema, casino, and hairdressers. Reservations in Buenos Aires (Maipú 331) and San Juan (San Martin y Sarmiento). From San Juan, two buses daily with TAC, four weekly with Empresa Iglesia, also from Mendoza. 22 km. further N., in Rodeo, Ing. Meglioli raises guanaco and vicuña, and sells local produce and crafts. From here, a scenic road, with several tunnels, follows the Rio Jachal 61 km. E to **San José de Jachal**, a wine and olive-growing center (pop. 15,000), with many adobe buildings (hotel, C; *Plaza*, E, basic but clean; good *El Chato Flores* restaurant; several camping sites). Expreso Argentino bus from San Juan at 0730 arrives at 0940.

From Jachal, route 491 offers a scenic alternative to Villa Unión (see below), but buses now take new route 40 via Huaco. The undulating road, paved to the La Rioja border, crosses dozens of dry watercourses.

E of San Juan, one can make a loop via San Agustín del Valle Fértil and Villa Unión (La Rioja province). Turn off route 141 at Marayes (133 km.), from which paved route 510 (poor) goes N 114 km. to **San Agustín del Valle Fértil** (ACA hillside *hostería*, good desert views, campsite). Pensiones (*Andacollo*, *Los Olivos*, both E) and private houses also provide lodging. There is a municipal swimming pool, and a lake with fishing. Local weavers offer ponchos and blankets. Bus from San Juan at 2000, 0200; San Juan-La Rioja bus stops in San Agustín about midnight.

N of San Agustín, at a police checkpoint, 56 km. by paved road, a side road goes NW for 17 km. to the 62,000-ha **Ischigualasto** Provincial Park, also known as **Valle de la Luna** for its exotic desert landforms. All private vehicles must be accompanied by rangers whose knowledge and interest vary greatly; fee US$2 p.p. The circular tour, on an unpaved road, last 2-3 hours. the Dirección de Turismo in San Juan can arrange group visits. Local bus from San Juan Sat. afternoon, if demand is sufficient.

Just beyond the police checkpoint, near Los Baldecitos, paved route 150 heads E to Patquia and then to La Rioja or Chilecito, while provincial route 26 heads N. 58 km. N of the junction a paved road goes E to **Puerta de Talampaya** Provincial Park (open 0800-1600), another collection of spectacular desert landforms (*Regugio* near the entrance, sleeping bag essential). Tours follow the dry bed of the Río Talampaya in four-wheel drive vehicles operated by park rangers (entrance fee US$3 p.p. for up to 8 people). Herbert Levi writes "There are 6,000 year old petroglyphs with pictures depicting animals. The whole area is said to have been covered with water long ago; now there are two visible strata, the *tarjado* and the *talampaya*. After that one enters a canyon with "balconies", sheer overhanging walls. Across these is a wood with many wild plants which are used for curative purposes. Coming out of the canyon there are rocks shaped like a cathedral, a bird, a castle, a chessboard, a monk, and three kings on a camel". Before returning, one can climb a small hill with a good view. Tours, arranged through Dirección Provincial de Turismo in La Rioja, last about two hours. Chilecito-San Juan buses pass Talampaya.

From the park junction route 26 coninues to **Villa Unión** (*Hostería Provincial*, simple, D, highly recommended; under new ownership. *Hospedaje Paola*, main street opp. police station, E basic; next door is *Hospedaje Chaguito*, E, restaurant). Jeep excursions can be made to Ischigualasto and Talampaya, Laguna Verde and Laguna Veladero. Bus station behind plaza.

From Villa Unión, partly paved route 40 crosses the Cuesta de Miranda, dropping through a deep narrow canyon in a series of hairpins. After 92 km., it intersects the paved Patquía-Chilecito road. 18 km. N of the junction is

**Chilecito** , La Rioja province's second town, pop. 20,000. Founded in 1715, it has good views of Sierra de Famatina, especially from the top of El Portezuelo, an easy climb from the end of Calle El Maestro. At Los Sarmientos, 2 km. N of town, is the Santa Clara church, dating from 1764. The region is famous for its wines, olives and walnuts.

**Hotels** *ACA*, T. Gordillo y Ocampo, good, C; *Belsavac*, 9 de Julio y Dávila, D, good but paperthin walls; *Riviera*, Castro Barros 133, D, rec., clean, hot showers; *Wamatinag*, Galeria Victoria, W side of Plaza Sarmiento, E, clean, pleasant, best value in town; *Americano*, Libertad 68, E, unfriendly; *Bellia*, El Maestro y Libertad, E. The Tourist Office has a list of families offering accommodation, but not for singles.

**Camping** at Santa Florentina, 6 km. NW of Chilecito and Las Talas, 2 km. beyond.

**Restaurants** *El Gallo*, Petán y Illia, excellent; on Plaza Sarmiento are: *Chaplin*, best in town; *Robert Snak Bar*, light meals and drinks; *Vanesa*, good home-made ice-cream; *Toscanini*, Santa Rosa y San Martín, good Italian food, inexpensive; *Ferrito*, Av. Luna 600 block, pricey.

**Museums** Samay Huasi, 3 km. S of town, the house of Joaquín V. González, founder of La Plata University, open 0800-1200 and 1500-1800, contains the **Museo de Ciencias Naturales, Mineralogiá y Arqueologiá**, pleasant gardens, and good views of Chilecito, the Famatina ridge and connecting valley. **Molino San Francisco y Museo de Chilecito**, at J. de Ocampo 63, has archaeological, historical and artistic exhibits, open Mon.-Fri. 0800-1300, 1400-1900.

**Tourist Office** Libertad y Independencia, T 2688, very helpful.

**Transport** Líneas Aéreas Riojanas fly **La Rioja**-Chilecito, 20 min. Buses: to **San Juan**, Tues., Thur., Sat. at 2200, arr. 0705; to **Tinogasta** (Catamarca), Mon.-Fri., direct at 0700 via route 11, returning same day at 1600; to Tinogasta via Pituil, Tues. 0700 and Sat. 1330, returning Wed. 0600 and Sun. 1400. Connections with **Catamarca** and **Córdoba** via La Rioja only.

**Excursions** La Mejicana mine via Santa Florentina road: a cable car system (built 1903) which brought ore 39 km. to the railhead at Chilecito is now out of use. For treks, and trips to see gold washers at Famatina or to Talampaya, ask for Carlos de Caro, or enquire at tourist office.

With construction of an excellent new road, route 40 now goes via Salicas, since the Cuesta de Zapata, N of Tinogasta, was closed after 1981 floods. 21 km. N of Chilecito, the old road (now route 11) goes via Famatina (ACA *Hostería*) to **Tinogasta**, a half-Indian copper mining town in an oasis of vineyards, olive groves, and poplars (population 9,000).

**Hotels** *Provincial de Turismo*; *Hostería Novel*, near airport.

**Restaurants** *Persegoni*, Tristán Villafane 373; *Rancho Huairipaca*, on Moreno.

**Transport** Buses: to **Tucumán**, Empresa Gutiérrez, Tues., Fri., Sun. 1700, Mon., Tues., Fri.,

Sun. 0615, Fri. 0845; return Tues., Fri., Sun. Services to **Chubut, Comodoro Rivadavia**, and **Caleta Olivia**, with Empresa Ortiz, reflect that this is the source region for labour in the Patagonian oilfields. For air services, see under Catamarca.

**Mountaineering** Tinogasta is the starting point for expeditions to the highest volcano on earth. Most recent cartography has allowed for some corrections in altitude so that Pissis has been confirmed the highest volcano, at 6,882 metres, followed by Ojos del Salado (6,864 metres, the highest "active" volcano—much debate surrounds these matters). To get there take Route 60 which crosses Tinogasta in the direction of the San Francisco pass.

**Fiambalá** is reached from Tinogasta with El Cóndor on the mountainous Córdoba-Fiambalá route. *Hospedaje* at the end of route (excellent *locro*). Drive from here to *aguaditas*, hot springs; the entire province is rich in thermal mineral waters. Empresa Gutiérrez daily at 1345 to Catamarca via Tinogasta (1500) and Cerro Negro junction (1610), connect with Coop. Catamarca bus to Belén (from Catamarca), about 2 hrs. by bad road. Also 0530 departure from Fiambalá. 36 km. beyond Fiambala is Palo Blanco, in the *pre-puna* foothills.

At the junction, new route 40 goes to Pituil, where paved section ends, and on to Salicas and Cerro Negro junction (59 km.) with route 60, the Tinogasta-Aimogasta road. Turning left at Cerro Negro for 2 km., paved route 40 heads N to **Londres**, founded in 1558 and the second-oldest town in Argentina, named in honour of the marriage of Mary Tudor and Philip II. The town hall displays a glass coat-of-arms of the City of London and a copy of the marriage proposal. 15 km. further (paved) is **Belén**, population 8,800 (*Hotel Samai*, Urquiza 349, D, new; *Hotel Provincial*, dilapidated. Good breakfast at bus terminal; *Restaurant Dalesio*, near YPF gas station, excellent and cheap). The Huaco district is famous for weavings, ponchos, saddlebags and rugs. There are good views from the new statue of Virgin of Belén at the summit of the path beginning at Calle General Roca, and an interesting archaeological museum, Condor Huasi. Folklore festivals October and Christmas. Belén is encircled by mountains, except to the SE; lush vegetation along Río Belén. Then 176 km., largely unpaved, to Santa María at Tucumán provincial border (see page 97), and on to Cafayate (page 103).

**Transport** Belén-Villavil (springs), including side trip to Corral Quemado and end of line at Barranca Larga, 19 km. N of Villavil, Tues., Thur., Sun. at 0800, returns from Villavil at 1830. Sit on right-hand side for best views of impressive canyon and Rio Bolsón reservoir. Belén-Santa María Tues. 1330, Fri. and Sun. 2020; return Tues. and Thur. 0930, Sun. 1945. Belén-Salta via Haulfín (mineral hot springs), Santa María, Cafayate Thur. 0600.

From Cerro Negro it is 38 km. SE to Aimogasta (national olive festival in May) and another 30 km. to turnoff to Termas Santa Teresita (ACA *Hostería*, thermal baths each room, heated pool, excellent, reasonably priced food). 15 km. E on route 60 a good new road branches N to Saujil (60 km.) and **Andalgalá** (130 km., pop. 7,800), renowned for strong alcoholic drinks; *Hostería Provincial*. The road parallels the Salar de Pipanaco on the W and Sierra de Ambato on the E. Beyond Andalgalá, there is no public transport on the difficult but beautiful road to Santa María over the Cuesta de Capillitas, although trucks go weekdays to the mines just beyond the pass.

An alternative route to Salta turns W 52 km. past Belén on route 53, via Antofagasta de la Sierra and San Antonio de los Cobres (petrol available—see page 105). This route is possible in passenger cars, but requires enough fuel for 600 km. at high altitudes on unmaintained rods (fill up at Haulfín, 10 km. past turnoff to Route 53). Also, the stretch beyond the right turn at Puerto de Corral Quemado is very difficult (37 km. of fords), to be avoided in summer rainy season. At Km. 87 is Cerro Compo (3,125 metres), magnificent descent; at Km. 99 the road turns left to Laguna Blanca (**don't go straight at the junction**). **Antofagasta de la Sierra** (260 km.) can be reached only by hiring a pickup or hitching, or by plane, inquire at Dirección de Aeronáutica, Aerodromo de Choya, T 24750, bus L22 from airfield to centre (*Pensión Darín*). No petrol station, but fuel obtainable from *intendencia*. Together with El Peñón and Laguna Blanca in the *puna*, and Villavil and La Hoyada in the *pre-puna*, this is the main township of NW Catamarca. La Hoyada can be reached from Santa María in the NE via provincial route 118. There are lunar landscapes, with salt lakes, around Antofagasta, and many peaks over 5,000 metres. Deposits of marble, onyx, sulphur, mica, salts, borates, and gold are present. Wildlife in the sparsely populated region includes vicuña, guanaco, vizcacha, flamingoes, and foxes.

**La Rioja**, founded 1592, 66,000 people, is capital of its province and home of Argentine president Carlos Menem. Some colonial buildings survive, despite a major earthquake in 1894. The Convent of San Francisco, 25 de Mayo/Bazan y Bustos, contains the Niño Alcalde, a remarkable image of the infant Jesus as well as the cell (*celda*) in which San Francisco Solano lived and the orange tree, now dead, which he planted in 1592. To visit the tree when the church is closed, ring the bell at 25 de Mayo 218 next door. A visit may also be made to Los Padercitos, 7 km. from town, where a stone temple protects the remains of the 16th century adobe building where San Francisco converted the Indians of the Yacampis valley. The Convent of Santo Domingo, Luna y Lamadrid, is the oldest surviving temple in Argentina, dating from 1623. The Casa González, a brick "folly" in the form of a castle, is at Rivadavia 952.

La Rioja is known as "City of the Orange Trees," but there are also many specimens of the contorted, thorn-studded *palo borracho* tree, whose ripened avocado-like pods release large brown seeds in a kapok-like substance. It is also a common ornamental in Buenos Aires.

**NB** Avoid arriving on Saturday night as most things are shut on Sunday.

**Hotels** *International Sussex*, Ortiz de Ocampo 1551, T 25413, adverse report; *King's*, Quiroga y Copiapó, T 25272; *Libertador*, Buenos Aires 253, T 27474, C, good value. *Talampaya*, Perón 951, T 24010; *Hotel de Turismo*, Perón y Quiroga; *Emperador*, San Martín 258; *Centro*, Rivadavia 499; *Plaza*, San Nicolás y 9 de Julio, recommended but street noisy; all C. *Imperial*, Moreno 345, T 22478, D, clean; *Ritz* 25 de Mayo 195; *El Gringo*, Coronel Lagos 427; *Savoy*, Roque A. Luna y Mitre, D, excellent value, hot shower. *Pensión 9 de Julio*, Copiapó y Vélez Sarsfield, E, rec. Best of the *residenciales* is *Sumaj Kanki*, Castro Barros y Lagos, E, but can't leave before 0730; *Residencial Florida*, 8 de Diciembre 524, F, clean, basic, cheap. At Aniliaco, on Highway 75 between La Rioja and Aimogasta, there is an *ACA Hosteria*. Tourist Office keeps a list of private lodgings, such as Sra. Vera, Dávila 343, F.

**Camping** at Balneario Los Sauces, 13 km. W.

**Restaurants** *Café Corredor*, San Martín y Pelagio Luna, good, cheap; *La Cantina de Juan*, Yrigoyen 190, excellent food, inexpensive; *Club Atlético Riojana*, Santa Fe between 9 de Julio and Buenos Aires, no atmosphere but cheap; *La Vieja Casona*, Rivadavia 427, very good and reasonably priced, rec.; *Taberna Don Carlos*, Rivadavia 459, good fish; *Comedor Sociedad Española*, 9 de Julio 233, excellent pastas, inexpensive; *La Pomme*, Rivadavia y San Martín, open-air terrace, popular meeting place.

**Museums** **Museo Folklórico**, P. Luna 811, Tues.-Fri., 0900-1200, 1600-2000, Sat., Sun., 0900-1200, US$1.50; **Museo Arqueológico Inca Huasi**, Alberdi 650, owned by the Franciscan Order, contains a huge collection of fine Diaguita Indian ceramics, open Tues.-Fri., 0800-1200, 1500-1900, US$0.85. **Museo Histórico de la Provincia**, Dávila 87, opening hours variable. **Museo Municipal de Bellas Artes**, Copiapó 253, works by local, national, and foreign artists.

**Exchange** US$ cash changed at **Banco de Galicia**, Plaza 25 de Mayo and **Banco de Crédito**, San Nicolás 476. Cheques difficult to change—try **Banco de la Provincia**, Plaza 9 de Julio, but better to change plenty before arriving (see note on provincial bonds used as currency, page 202).

**Post Office** Av. Perón 258.

**Laundry** *Lavarap*, Av. Perón 944.

**Tourist Office** at Perón y Urquiza, T 28834, one of most helpful in Argentina.

**Transport** No direct passenger service by rail; Belgrano railway from Retiro to Córdoba, Tues., Fri. at 1000, connects with bus to La Rioja and Catamarca. Return journeys (*automotor* from Córdoba Wed., Sat. at 0751) can be booked at La Rioja and Catamarca bus offices.
  By Air: Aerolíneas daily from **Bs.As**; Aerolínea Federal Argentina to **Resistencia**,

Tucumán, San Juan and Mendoza; Líneas Aéreas Riojanas to Catamarca (0800 and 1330 weekdays), Chilecito.

Buses: Buenos Aires with Empresa Cotil, combination Ablo and General Urquiza, via Córdoba and Rosario. To Mendoza and San Juan, night service only, with La Estrella or Libertador. To travel to San Juan by day (good scenery), take 0715 Cotil bus to Chepes (new bus station and ACA motel), then Cotil again next day to San Jauan at 0900 or 20 de Junio bus at 1000 for San Juan or 1230 to San Luis. To Tucumán (US$15), with Bosio and La Estrella. Also provincial services. Terminal about 5 blocks from centre.

**Excursions** To Ischigualasto and Talampaya (via Nonogasta, Cuesta de Miranda and Villa Unión, including transport and guide), and to Samay Huasi (**see page 126**). Fishing at El Portezuelo dam (see below). Swimming and fishing at Los Sauces dam, 15 km. away; beyond Los Sauces is Sanogasta, El Cóndor buses, 45 mins., times vary. Good views of La Rioja from Cerro de la Cruz (1,680 m). There is a bad road from the dam to the summit, now a centre for hang-gliding, where condors and falcons may be sighted. Two hours to thermal springs at Santa Teresita.

A paved road runs to the third oasis. *Catamarca* (San Fernando del Valle de Catamarca), population 88,000, capital of its province, at 490 metres on the Río del Valle, between two southern slopes of the Sierra de Aconquija, about 240 km. S of Tucumán. Cattle, fruit, grapes and cotton are the main agricultural products, but it is also renowned for hand-woven ponchos and fruit preserves (try Casa Valdés, Sarmiento 586). Pilgrimages to church of the Virgen del Valle. Therapeutic mineral springs. There are traces of Indian civilizations, including extensive agricultural terraces (now mostly abandoned), throughout the province. The *Zonda*, a strong dry mountain wind equivalent to the European *Föhn* or North American chinook or Santa Ana, can cause dramatic temperature increases. In July, regional handicrafts are sold at Festival del Poncho, a *feria* with four nights of music, mostly folklore of the NW.

**Hotels** *Ancasti*, Sarmiento 520, C, restaurant; *Inti Huasi*, Saadi 297, D; *Pucará*, Avenida Esquiú, near ACA station, D, clean, a/c friendly; *Colonial*, Saadi 802, D, no food but rec. as clean, welcoming, good value; *Suma Huasi*, Sarmiento 547, D, avoid TV lounge and rooms above it; *Centro*, Rosas y 9 de Julio, basic. Many *residenciales* clustered around Avenida Güemes. Discounts to ACA members at *Ancasti*, *Inti Huasi*, and *Suma Huasi*.

**Restaurants** *Restaurant Sociedad Española*, Urquiza y Paseo Gral. Navarro; *La Cabaña*, on Esquiú has folkloric dancing. *La Tinaja*, Sarmiento 500 block, excellent, pricey, live music, warmly rec.; *Pizzería Maryeli*, Esquiú 473, basic (but good *empanadas*). *Restaurant Sociedad Italiana*, M. Morino (off Paseo Gral. Navarro), pastas, inexpensive; *Comedor Unión Obrera*, Sarmiento 857, good value, speciality *cabrito*; *Montmartre*, Paseo Gral. Navarro, good food, reasonably priced; *Marco Polo Bar*, Rivadavia s/n, drinks, snacks. Many cheap restaurants along Av. Güemes, bars and cafés along Rivadavia (pedestrian street).

**Shopping** Catamarca specialities from: *Cuesta del Portezuelo*, Sarmiento 575; *Maica Regionales*, next to Aerolíneas Argentinas; and *Suma Regionales*, Sarmiento y Esquiú. Mercado Artesanal, Urquiza 945, wide range of handicrafts, open 0700-1300, 1400-2000, reached by infrequent colectivo 23 from centre.

**Museums** Instituto Cultural Esquiú, Sarmiento 450, includes important archaeological section, open Mon.-Fri. 0700-1300, 1430-2000, Sat., Sun., a.m. only; **Museo Folklórico**, underground (subsuelo), Paseo Gral. Navarro.

**Exchange** Banco de Catamarca, Plaza 25 de Mayo, changes US$ cash but not cheques.

**Post Office** San Martín 753, slow, open 0800-1300, 1600-2000. **Telephones**, Entel, Rivadavia 758, open 0700-2400, daily.

**Tourist Office** Urquiza y Mota Botella, open 0800-2000, helpful.

**Buses** To Tucumán, 7 daily with Bosio, 5½ hrs., US$10; road paved, in good condition except for rough stretch at provincial border (Cuesta del Totoral has steep gradients, hairpins, potholes). To Bs.As, 2nd class at 2200, 1st class at 1900, daily. To Belén via Cerro Negro with Coop Catamarca, returns from Belén daily 1300 (**see page 127**). Also Belén-Catamarca via Andalgalá; Coop Catamarca via Saujil, Poman, Chumbicha, Tues., Thur. 1000, Fri., Sun. 1300, about 8 hrs. Catamarca-El Rodeo-Las Juntas daily at 1300, returns from Las Juntas 1700. Twice weekly, buses to **Córdoba** connect with train to Bs.As.; in total, five buses daily to Córdoba. To **Santiago del Estero**, 1630, US$12.

**Air** Cooperativa de Transportes Catamarca, less dependable than Aerolíneas Riojanas, twice weekly Tinogasta to Belén. Officially departs Tinogasta 0810, but one is told to appear at municipal building at 0815 to be at plane at 0830. Route is circular: Catamarca-Tinogasta-Belén-Andalgala-Catamarca, in small Piper or Cessna. AR offices on Sarmiento, next to *Hotel Suma Huasi*.

**Excursion** To Dique Las Pirquitas, 3 hrs. with local bus 1A from bus station, or with Yokavil agency, terminus at Isla Larga (pleasant hills and woods). Bus stops at *Hostería de Turismo* at Villa Pirquitas, about 45 min. walk. Five morning buses from 0700, last returns at 2200. Opening hours Mon.-Fri. 1000-1900. Sat., Sun. and holidays 0830-1900.

A road runs NE to Lavalle (toward Santiago del Estero). This 116 km. run over the *Cuesta El Portezuelo* (1,980 m), is scenic, but steep and difficult. No bus service over Portezuelo to Lavalle, but a service to Frías, E, and also in Santiago del Estero province—No. 9 and not No. 18 (which crosses the Totoral), run by Coop. de Transportes de Catamarca. Leaves 0500 Tues., Thur., Fri. and Sat., arrives at Frías 1000, returns 1400, arrives in Catamarca 1900. From Frías travel to Lavalle.

Catamarca-Frías via Totoral, No. 18 Mon., Wed., Fri., Sat. 0500, arrives 1030, return 1330, arrives Catamarca 1900. No. 14 via El Alto, longer trip, arrives Frías 1045. Catamarca-Lavalle via Totoral, same No. 18, leaves Tues., Thur., and Sun. 1100, arrives Lavalle 1510.

---

## THE CHACO (6)

---

**A great lowland covered with thorn scrub and grassy savanna, the thorn bushes sometimes impenetrable and sometimes set widely apart on grassland; the birdlife is very interesting, especially from the railway between Embarcación and Formosa (a useful town for reaching Paraguay).**

Between the north-western highlands already described and the Río Paraná to the E lies the Argentine Chaco, containing the provinces of Formosa and Chaco, part of Santiago del Estero, and northern Santa Fe. Its southern limit is the Río Dulce valley. The highest summer temperatures in all South America have been recorded in the Argentine Chaco; the winters are mild with an occasional touch of frost in the S. Rain falls in the winter according to location: the further W, the less the rain. Indian groups that live in the Chaco include the Pilaga, Nocovi, Mbya and some emigrant members of the Mapuche nation.

**Communications** Before the recent building of highways, the only all-weather routes were provided by the Belgrano Railway. There are two main north/south lines from Buenos Aires: the international route to La Paz and the line through Rosario and Santa Fe to Resistencia. There are two east/west rail connections, Resistencia-Metán and Formosa-Embarcación; only the latter carries passengers regularly (**see page 142**). A third line runs SW from Roque Sáenz Peña to Anatuya in the province of Santiago del Estero. (It is advisable to check all rail services, since many were suspended years ago without being formally abolished.)

Route 16, the main road across the Chaco runs NW from Resistencia to connect with Route 9, N of Rosario de la Frontera and provides the quickest route between Paraguay and NW Argentina. Willy Walker writes: "The road from Resistencia to 30 km. before Pampa del Infierno is fine. But the 30 km. to Pampa del Infierno is a piece of cake compared to what is after the town. The 30 km. before Pampa is all dirt—it is bad, but not terrible. But then for 100 km. you hit Pot Hole City. It is long, hard and frustrating. Then you get good road for a while until González. Then the road gets bad and stays that way until Route 9." There are service stations at Roque Sáenz Peña, Pampa del Infierno, Pampa de los Guanacos, Toca Peña and El Quebrachal. In general, roads in the Chaco are poor.

Tannin and cotton are the two great industries of the Chaco. The iron-hard *quebracho* (axe-breaker) tree grows only in the Chaco of northern Argentina and Paraguay; it is the purest known source of tannin. The industry is struggling against competition from synthetic tannin and the huge mimosa plantations in South Africa. The most accessible forest is worked out; most of the cutting is now in the N and W of the province.

Cotton growers, around Roque Sáenz Peña in Chaco Province, have had difficulty in maintaining production in the face of soil exhaustion. Sunflower is the chief crop replacing cotton, and there is also some maize and sorghum.

*Roque Sáenz Peña* (population 50,000) is 150 km. NW of Resistencia on Route 16. Hot springs have been found here and a modern hotel has been built to develop the city as a spa. Other hotels are: *Residencial Sáenz Peña*, near bus station, cheap, clean and friendly; *Residencia Asturias*, D, fair. Daily bus, La Internacional, to Buenos Aires, 2000, 19 hrs. From Buenos Aires, also 2000. Bus from Salta at 1700, 10 hrs., US$20; bus to Resistencia, US$4.20. North of Roque Sáenz Peña is the village of Castelli, which has a large Tobas Indian community and an *artesanía* shop. *Hotel Guc*, E, basic. 23 km. SE of R.S.Peña, on Route 16, is Quitilipi, with municipal campsite.

The rest of the Chaco is cattle country but there are few animals to the square km. Large *estancias* are the rule, some growing cotton, linseed and other crops by irrigation. The bird life of the area—flamingoes, black-necked swans, heron egrets, storks and various birds of prey—is most interesting.

**Towns of the Chaco** The most important ones—Resistencia and Formosa—are on the W bank of the Paraná and Paraguay and will be described, for convenience's sake, under Argentine Mesopotamia. Apart from Roque Sáenz Peña, the only other town of any importance is Santiago del Estero, on the western boundary of the Chaco (**see page 92**). The two cities are connected by a bad, dusty road.

Federico Kirbus tells us that on the border of Chaco and Santiago del Estero provinces is Campo de Cielo, a meteorite impact field about 15 km. by 4 km. where about 5,000 years ago a planetoid landed and broke into 30 main pieces. Some of the meteorites are on display in Buenos Aires (the Rivadavia museum and the Planetarium), but the largest, "El Chaco", (33.4 tonnes), is on display at the Campo. Access from Route 89 (between Resistencia and Santiago del Estero) at Gancedo, where you travel 15 km. S to Las Víboras (many buses).

---

## MESOPOTAMIA (7)

This section begins at the Río de la Plata and ends at the magnificent Iguazú Falls on the Brazilian border. Two routes are followed, the Ríos Uruguay and Paraná, describing the river towns and beaches, and the Jesuit missions near Posadas (in particular San Ignacio Miní). Crossings to Uruguay and Paraguay are also given.

Between the Ríos Uruguay and Paraná lies Argentine Mesopotamia: the provinces of Entre Ríos, Corrientes, and Misiones. The distance between the rivers is 390 km. in northern Corrientes, but narrows to about 210 km. in the latitude of Santa Fe. Mesopotamia was first colonized by Spaniards pushing S from Asunción to reoccupy Buenos Aires; both Corrientes and Paraná were founded as early as 1588. Alison Brysk and Mark Freeman (San Francisco) tell us that there was Jewish agricultural settlement in Entre Ríos at the beginning of C.20 ("Los gauchos judíos"). Vestiges of these settlements remain at Domínguez (museum) and Basavilbaso, and across the river in Moisesville (Santa Fe).

Much of Entre Ríos and Corrientes is still pastoral, a land of large *estancias* raising cattle and sheep. Maize (a gamble in the N) is largely grown in southern Entre Ríos, which is also the most important producer of linseed, citrus fruit and poultry in Argentina. In Corrientes, along the banks of the Paraná between the cities of Corrientes and Posadas, rice and oranges are grown.

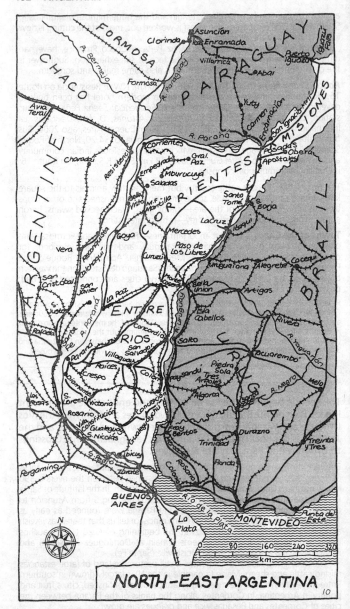

**NORTH-EAST ARGENTINA**

10

The province of Corrientes, in the N, is marshy and deeply-wooded, with low grass-covered hills rising from the marshes. The normal rainfall is about 2,000 mm, but the rains are not spread uniformly and drain off quickly through the sandy soil. Entre Ríos, to the S, has plains of rich pasture land not unlike those of Uruguay. Winters in Mesopotamia are mild; the summers are hot and much rain falls in short, sharp storms, though both Entre Ríos and Corrientes often suffer from summer drought.

Misiones Province, in the far NE, was first occupied by the Jesuit Fathers fleeing from the Brazilian Alto-Paraná region with their devoted Indian followers before the slave-hunting Bandeirantes. These missions and their history are described under Posadas (**see page 143**). Misiones is a hilly strip of land between the Uruguay and the Alto Paraná rivers, 80-100 km. wide and about 400 km. long; its capital is the river port of Posadas. Its boundary to the N is the river Iguazú, which here tumbles over the great Iguazú Falls. Misiones is on the Paraná Plateau; much of it is covered with forests of pine and cedar and broad-leaved trees, and the look of the land, with its red soil, reminds one strongly of Brazil. Here too the rainfall is heavy: twice as heavy as in Entre Ríos. The days are hot, and the nights cool.

It was the Jesuits who first grew *yerba mate* in plantations; Misiones has always been a large producer of this leaf, and also of citrus, tobacco, timber and tung oil. The province has of late years attracted immigrants from Eastern Europe, from Paraguay and from the rest of Mesopotamia. There is good fishing in many of the small river-towns. In NE Corrientes and in Misiones more Indian tea is now grown than can be absorbed by the internal market.

The Indian-tea industry was started by Sir Herbert Gibson, who sent for seed from Assam in 1929; it was sown in Playadito, Corrientes province. Six seeds developed into sturdy bushes. Year after year their seed was given to anyone interested. All Argentina's tea plantations today have their origin in Sir Herbert Gibson's enterprise.

**Communications** in the area are by road (now greatly improved), by railway, and by the two rivers the Uruguay and the Paraná , which bound it to E and W. Neither river is very good for navigation. Bridges between Fray Bentos (Uruguay) and Puerto Unzué, near Gualeguaychú, and between Paysandú (Uruguay) and Colón were opened in 1976, and there are a road and railway over the Salto Grande dam, near Concordia.

The area is served by the Urquiza railway, the only standard-gauge line in the country; the most important line runs from Buenos Aires to Posadas with connection over the river to Asunción, the capital of Paraguay, and a branch at Monte Caseros for Corrientes.

Most of the important towns of Mesopotamia lie on the E bank of the Paraná or the S bank of the Alto Paraná. A journey up these rivers is given here; the towns on both banks are described.

## Up the Río Uruguay

The Río Uruguay is the eastern boundary of Mesopotamia and forms the western border of the Republic of Uruguay. There are no regular passenger shipping services.

Boats leaving Buenos Aires go past Martín García island, and enter the wide estuary. At 193 km. from Buenos Aires, the Uruguayan town of Fray Bentos is to the right; there is a bridge (toll US$1) between Fray Bentos and the Argentine town of Puerto Unzué, near Gualeguaychú, but pedestrians and cyclists cannot cross it other than on motor vehicles; officials will give lifts on either side (customs formalities take about 10 mins.). The river now becomes braided into channels and islands. Opposite Fray Bentos, on the left, is the mouth of the Río Gualeguaychú; 19 km. up is **Gualeguaychú**, , a very pleasant town with a river promenade, an open-air railway museum (in the old railway station) and an attractive cathedral (1863). Lively Carnival at beginning of March. Population, 80,000, with quite a large German contingent. Since the opening of the bridges between Zarate and Brazo Largo, the journey time from Buenos Aires, 248 km. S., has been reduced and Gualeguaychú has become a popular weekend resort for *porteños*. Airport.

**Hotels** There is a shortage of accommodation at weekends and during carnival. The tourist office has a list of families. *Embajador*, San Martín y 3 de Febrero, T 4414, B, casino; *Posada del Charrúa*, Av. del Valle y San Lorenzo, T 6099, C; *París*, Bolívar y Pellegrini, T 6260, E; *Entre Ríos*, Andrade 1009, T 7214, D; *Mayo*, Bolívar 550, T 7661, E, uncomfortable beds, noisy; *Alemán*, Bolívar 535, T 6153, D, friendly, German-speaking, rec.

**Camping** *La Delfina* in the Parque Unzue; *Puerto del Sol* and *Playa Chica*, near the river; *Ñandubaysal*, 15 km. E, best.

**Exchange** Banco Internacional Cooperativa, 25 de Mayo y Perón, changes cash; *Casa de Cambio: Daniel*, 3 de Febrero 128.

**Tourist Office** Av. Costanera y 25 de Mayo, open 0800-2000.

**Buses** Terminus in centre of town at Bolívar y Chile. To Fray Bentos, 1 hr., US$3, 4 a day, ETA; to **Mercedes**, 1½ hrs., US$4, 2 a day, ETA; to **Concepción del Uruguay, Colón** and **Concordia**, Empresa Gualeguaychú.

*Concepción del Uruguay* (known locally as Uruguay), the first Argentine port of any size on the river, is 74 km. N of Gualeguaychú. Founded in 1783, it was until 1883 capital of Entre Ríos province. Population 50,000. Overlooking the main plaza is the church of the Immaculate Conception which contains the remains of Gen. Urquiza, whose former residence, the Palacio San José, 35 km. W of the town, is now a museum (buses to 3 km. from the Palacio).

**Hotels** *Virrey*, Aceso Ruta 131, D; *Gran Hotel*, Colón 134, T 22851, D; *Ramírez*, Galarza y Blvd. Ramírez, T 25106, D; *Hospedaje Los Tres Trenes*, Galarza 1233, F, clean, friendly. Many hotels of all classes by the bus station, none near the railway station.

**Restaurants** *El Canguro*, opposite bus terminus, good food, reasonably priced; *Rocamora*, Rocamora y Millán.

**Tourist Office** 9 de Julio 844, T 25820.

*Colón* (17,000 people), 350 km. from Buenos Aires, is 45 km. N of Concepción del Uruguay. The river is more picturesque here with sandy beaches, and cliffs visible from a considerable distance; a road bridge now links Colón and Paysandú. (Toll for cars US$1.40. All border formalities, including stamping of vehicle carnets, are conducted at both ends of the bridge, easy crossing.) The town is known for *artesanía* shops down San Martín, the main street, and there is a large handicrafts fair at Carnival time (Feb.). Tourist office Av. Quirós y Gouchón (very helpful).

**Hotels** *Quirinale*, Av. Quirós s/n, T 21978, 5-star, A (with casino); *Nuevo Hotel Plaza*, 12 de Abril y Belgrano, T 21043, C; *Palmar*, Blvd. Ferrari 285, T 21952, C, good; *Vieja Calera*, Bolívar y Maipú, T 21139, D; *Holimasu*, Belgrano 28, D; *Ver-Wei*, 25 de Mayo 10, E. Many families rent rooms—the Boujon family, Maipú 430, E, good breakfast, have been recommended. Several **campsites** along river bank (municipal site, excellent facilities, cheapest).

**Restaurant** *Comedor El Rayo*, Paysandú y 9 de Julio.

**Buses** Bus terminal on outskirts, but buses also call at bus company offices in town. To **Paysandú**, US$3, but none 1145-1645 and none Sun. To **Buenos Aires**, 2 a day, US$10, 5 hrs., to **Concordia** (2½ hrs.) and **Parana** daily. To **Córdoba** 4 a week.

**Parque Nacional El Palmar** (8,500 hectares), 44 km. N of Colón, has both free and paying camping facilities, a small hotel 8 km. N of the Park, with restaurant opposite, and a small shop. The Park contains varied scenery with a mature palm forest, Indian tombs and other remains, and many rheas and other birds. Buses from Colón, 40 mins, US$2.50.

*Concordia*, 104 km. N of Colón, a little downriver from Salto, Uruguay, is a prosperous city, with a population of 92,000, which has some fine public buildings, a racecourse, rowing clubs, and a 9-hole golf club. Five km. out is Parque Rivadavia, with a circular road used occasionally as a motor-racing track; there are pleasant views of the river and in the centre of the park is the Palacio San Carlos, inhabited briefly by Antoine de Saint-Exupéry. Paved roads to Buenos Aires, Paraná and Posadas.

The river is impassable for large vessels beyond the rapids of Salto Chico near the town, and Salto Grande 32 km. up-river, where there is a large international hydro-electric dam, providing a route for an international road and railway. Take No. 2 or 4 bus from bus terminal marked "Puerto", for ferry crossing to Salto US$2.50 (tickets obtainable at a small kiosk, which shuts 15 mins. before departure, outside customs) departures 0730, 0900, 1130, 1500, 1815, weekdays, twice a day Sat. but none Sun.; takes 15 mins. Few cars, but people willing to give rides. Above Salto Grande the river is generally known as the Alto Uruguay.

**Hotels**  *San Carlos*, Parque Rivadavia, T 216725, B; *Salto Grande*, Urquiza 575, T 210034, B; *Palmar*, Urquiza 517, T 216050, C; *Central*, 1° de Mayo 185, T 212842, D; *Hotel Colón*, Pellegrini 611, T 215510, B, simple, clean and charming, highly rec.; *Embajador*, San Lorenzo 75, T 213018, D, nr. bus station, good value, neat and clean. *Terminal*, above bus station, surprisingly quiet, good value, E, not for women or couples; *Victoria*, Urquiza next to Esso, 2 blocks from terminal, D, quite good.

**Camping**  *La Tortuga Alegre. La Posada de Suárez—Club Viajantes* on Av. Costanera near the park, warmly rec., with good *parrillada* alongside.

**Restaurants**  *La Estancia* and *Gran Mary* (1st floor), both on plaza; *El Abrojito*, Pellegrini 1203, rec.

**Services  Exchange** Casa Julio, 1 de Mayo, ½ block from plaza; *Casa Chaca*, on plaza; *Tourfe* on Mitre. **Post Office** La Rioja y Buenos Aires. **Telephone** 700 block of San Luis ( 24 hrs).

**Tourist Office**  Plaza 25 de Mayo; kiosk at bus terminal, lousy map.

**Rail**  *El Correntino* train has sleepers, pullman, 1st class (heating ineffective) and tourist class and leaves Lacroze station at 1500, daily, arriving at 2355, returns daily at 0444, arr. 1322. This train also serves Corrientes. *El Gran Capitán*, has the same schedules as *El Correntino* to/from Buenos Aires, but continues to Paso de los Libres and Posadas (dep. 2340, US$17 2nd class, US$23 1st), arrives at 0450 and 1128, respectively.

**Buses**  Bus terminal 2 km. from centre. No. 2 bus goes to main plaza. To **Buenos Aires**, 6 daily; to **Paraná** 5, to **Posadas** 2 (8½ hrs., US$20), to **Iguazú** one (1810, 13½ hrs.). Bus to **La Paz** (Entre Ríos)—**see page 139,** 1100, US$10.50, 8 hrs. To **Paso de los Libres** direct, 2300 or take 0755 Empresa Gualeguaychú bus to Curuzú Cuatiá and catch connecting service. Possible to sleep overnight on benches in bus terminal.

About 153 km. upstream from Concordia lies the small port of *Monte Caseros*, with the Uruguayan town of Bella Unión, on the Brazilian border, almost opposite. Above Bella Unión, the **Alto Uruguay** is the boundary between Argentina and Brazil. Ninety-six km. above **Monte Caseros** is **Paso de los Libres**, with the Brazilian cattle town of **Uruguaiana** opposite: a bridge joins the two. From Uruguaiana into Brazil the buses are much quicker than trains, though there is a comfortable railway service to Porto Alegre. Paso de los Libres was founded in 1843 by General Madariaga; it was here that he crossed the river from Brazil with his hundred men and annexed Corrientes province for Argentina. Road (paved) to Paraná.

**Hotel**  in Paso de los Libres, *Alejandro* I, Coronel López y Pago Largo, C, best in town.

**Transport**  Buses to Posadas, Empresa Singer, 3 a day, 8 hrs., US$22. Trains, see above under Concordia.

58 km. N of Paso de los Libres, on the road to Alvear, is *Yapeyú*, the site of a Jesuit mission and famous as the birthplace of the liberator, José de San Martín. Part of the house where he was born is well preserved, and there is an interesting Jesuit Museum. (*Hosteria*, E; the Carillo family on the main plaza rent rooms, F, good; *cabañas* on the outskirts of town; camping by the river.)

## Up the Río Paraná

**Navigation**  River boats carry passengers along various stretches of the river, but there are no long-distance passenger services up the river from Buenos Aires, except those to Asunción, Paraguay. According to the tide, boats enter the Paraná river by either the Las Palmas reach of the delta, on which is Zárate, or the Paraná-Guazú reach, on which is Ibicuy.

**Zárate**, with 65,000 inhabitants, is industrially important, with large *frigoríficos* and paper works (*Hotel San Martín*, Ameghino 773, C, clean; *Restaurant La Posta de Correa*, cheap, good service). It is served from Buenos Aires (90 km.) by bus (US$2.75) and two railways: the Mitre and the Urquiza. Urquiza trains used to be ferried 84 km. across the river, but a link including two large and beautiful bridges has been built between Zárate and Brazo Largo, accelerating rail and road journeys alike (the bridge toll is US$6). The picturesque Ibicuy Islands can be visited by boat. Near Zárate is San Pedro (28,000 people) where fine riverfront camping can be had at either the *Centro Turístico, Club Pescadores* or *Camping Municipal*.

On the way upstream to Rosario, on the western bank, are two ports which export grain: San Nicolás (97,000 people), 80 km. below Rosario, and Villa Constitución (34,000 people), 37 km. below Rosario. Both are served by a railway from the capital. At San Nicolás is the General Savio steel plant. Pergamino, an important road/rail junction in the pampas, is 72 km. S by road or rail.

About 108 km. N of Ibicuy is **Gualeguay**, with a population of 26,000. It is the centre of one of the richest cattle and sheep ranching regions in Entre Ríos. The house in which Garibaldi was tortured by the local chief of police in 1837, in the time of Rosas, still exists. Eight km. S is its river port, Puerto Ruiz. The road from Gualeguay northwards along the E bank of the Paraná is paved most of the way to Posadas.

**Hotels** *Gran Hotel Gualeguay*, Monte Caseros 217, B; *Italia*, E with bath, friendly. There is a municipal **campsite**. In the centre there are practically no **restaurants**, but the *Jockey Club* and the *Club Social*, both on the main square close to the *Gran Hotel Gualeguay*, cater also for non-members. The *Club Social* has a very nice atmosphere, good food, and you might be invited to see films on certain nights.

**Rosario**, chief city of the province of Santa Fe, 320 km. N of Buenos Aires, is the third city of the republic, with a population of well over a million. It is a great industrial and export centre. The streets are wider than those of Buenos Aires, and there are fine boulevards and handsome open spaces. From October to early March it is warm, and from December to the end of February uncomfortably hot. Changes of temperature are sudden.

**Points of Interest** Monument of the Flag, a memorial on the river bank in honour of General Belgrano, designer of the Argentine flag, who raised it on this spot for the first time; Parque Independencia (Rose Garden): Boulevard Oroño; Cathedral in Calle 25 de Mayo; St. Bartholomew's Church (Anglican), Calle Paraguay; racecourse, the Alberdi and Arroyito boat clubs, and Saladillo Golf Club, with its own Links station on the Mitre line. The Aero Club is in the suburb of Gral. Alvear. The Museo Municipal Juan B. Castagnino and the Museo Histórico Provincial (open Thurs. and Sat. 1500-1800, and Sun. 1000-1200, 1500-1800) are in Parque Independencia. Swimming at sandy Florida beach, about 8 km. N of Rosario. The boat *Ciudad de Rosario* does a short trip round the nearby river islands Sat. 1730, Sun. 1600 and 1830, leaving from the Estación Fluvial near the Monument of the Flag.

**Local Holiday** 7 October (Foundation of the City).

**Hotels** *Riviera*, San Lorenzo 1460, T 253589, air conditioned, A; *Plaza*, Barón de Mauá 26, T 211160, B; *La Paz*, Barón de Mauá 36, T 210905, D, clean, quiet, friendly, rec.; *Presidente*, Av. Corrientes 919, T 242789, B, good; *Río*, opp. railway station, E, clean, friendly.

**Restaurants** *Don Rodrigo*, Sante Fe 968, and *Fenix*, Santa Fe next to Citibank, are both very good. *Doña María*, Santa Fe 1371, does good Italian food; *Casa Uruguaya*, Alvear 1125 (T 69320), away from centre, good.

**Exchange** Lloyds Bank (BOLSA), Calle La Rioja 1205; **Citibank**, Santa Fe 1101; **First National Bank of Boston**, Córdoba esq. Mitre. Open 1000-1600. *Casas de Cambio*: Transatlántica, Córdoba 900; *Carey*, Corrientes 802; *Carbatur*, Corrientes 840.

**Tourist Office** At Monument of the Flag, helpful but information inadequate.

**Airport**   at Fisherton, 8 km. from centre. Taxi charges vary. Several flights daily to Buenos Aires. Austral to Bariloche once a week; Lapa to Córdoba once a week.

**Rail**   Rosario is 4½ hours from Buenos Aires (315 km.) on the Mitre Railway by express train. Tourist class US$12, 1st US$15, Pullman US$18. It is served also by the Belgrano (metre gauge—5 hours). All trains heading N stop at Rosario.

**Buses**   There are regular bus services to Arroyo Seco, Casilda, Cañada de Gómez, San Lorenzo and other important centres up to 80 km. from the city. Also from **Buenos Aires**, by paved roads via San Nicolás and General Pacheco on Route 9 (4 hrs.) or via Pergamino, 309 km. less frequent on Route 8 (Chevallier bus, US$16), and from Rosario via Bell Ville NW to **Córdoba** and **Tucumán**. To **Santa Fe**, US$10.

Rosario can be reached from Buenos Aires by Route 8 (marked Córdoba) to Pergamino, and then, following signs, by Route 188, and then 178 to Rosario. This is a better way than lorry-packed Route 9. Hitching to Salta along Route 34 is possible.

**Ferries**   to Victoria, in Entre Ríos, which has a municipal **campsite**.

Above Rosario the river is very braided and islanded. Boat trips to river islands can be made at weekends. Canoes can be hired. Some 23 km. N of Rosario is **San Lorenzo** (pop. 28,700), where an associate company of ICI has one of the largest chemical works in Argentina. See the restored San Carlos monastery on the river bank, where in 1813 San Martín won his first battle in the War of Independence. Visitors are shown a pine tree grown from a cutting of the tree under which the Liberator rested after the battle. Some 180 km. above Rosario, on the E bank, is

**Paraná**, capital of Entre Ríos (pop., 210,000), founded in 1588. From 1853 to 1862 the city was the capital of the Republic. It is a handsome place: the centre is situated on a hill offering fine views over the river and beyond to Santa Fe. There are many fine buildings; in the centre is the Plaza Primero de Mayo, where there are fountains and a statue of San Martín. Around the Plaza are the Municipalidad and the Cathedral, notable for its portico and its interior, as well as the tourist information office. The Casa de Gobierno at Santa Fe y Laprida has a grand façade. But the city's glory is the Parque Urquiza, to the NW. It has an enormous statue to General Urquiza, and a bas-relief showing the battle of Caseros, at which he finally defeated Rosas; also an open-air theatre. The river is a popular attraction: there are pleasant walks along the bank and around the fishing *barrio* of Puerto Sánchez. Boats sail along the river from near the tourist office.

**Hotels**   There is a shortage of hotel space, especially at peak periods (Semana Santa and July), when the tourist office arranges accommodation with families. There is a greater selection of hotels—at lower prices—in Santa Fe. *Mayorazgo*, Etchevehere y Córdoba, on Costanera Alta, T 216111, with fine view of park and river, has casino and swimming pool, A; *Super Luxe*, Villaguay 162, T 212373, C; *Gran Hotel Paraná*, Urquiza 976, T 223900 C; *Almafuerte*, Av. Almafuerte 1295, T 240644 D. Cheap hotels near railway station, and *Plaza*, San Martín 915, T 211220, D, and *Bristol*, Alsina 221, T 213961, D, close to the bus terminal.

**Museums**   Museo de Bellas Artes, Buenos Aires 355; **Museo Histórico**, Buenos Aires y Laprida, open Mon.-Fri., 0800-1200, 1500-1800, Sat., 0900-1200, 1600-1900, Sun., 0900-1200.

**Tourist Office**   25 de Mayo 44, T 221632.

**Air Service**   Airport: General Urquiza, 12 km. from town; two flights to Buenos Aires daily with Austral. To Goya and Reconquista at 0820 three times weekly.

**Train**   *Río Paraná* train to Buenos Aires Tues., Thur., Sun. at 1930, arrives 0750. From Buenos Aires (F. Lacroze) Mon., Wed., Fri. at 2230, arrives 1030.

**Bus**   E across Entre Ríos to Concordia on Río Uruguay, 5 a day, 5 hours.

**Travelling Between Santa Fe and Paraná**   The 2 cities do not face one another, but are 25 km. apart and are separated by several islands. From Paraná the Hernandarias tunnel, toll US$2 per car, passes under the river to connect with the W bank; from here a road runs 23 km. W to Santa Fe across two islands and bridges. Trucks with dangerous loads cross the river by a launch which also carries pedestrians and operates Mon.-Sat., 0600-2100, 20 mins.

journey, frequency depending on demand from trucks. Frequent bus service between the 2 cities by Etacer and Fluviales del Litoral, US$2, 1 hr.

**Santa Fe**, a larger city of some 400,000 inhabitants, is the capital of its province and the centre of a very fertile region. It was founded by settlers from Asunción in 1573, though its present site was not occupied until 1660. It was in its Cabildo (town hall) that the Constitution of 1853 was adopted. The oath of allegiance was taken before the crucifix in the sacristy of the church of San Francisco, built in 1680 from materials floated down the river from Paraguay; this old colonial church has been tampered with but is still fine, especially the carved wooden ceilings, which were fitted without nails.

Most of the best buildings are in the eastern part of the city near the Plaza 25 de Mayo. On the Plaza itself are the Cathedral, the church of Nuestra Señora de los Milagros and the majestic Casa de Gobierno. The church and convent of San Francisco (see above) are a block SE of the Plaza. Opposite it is the Museo Histórico Provincial. The Convent of Santo Domingo, a block W of the Plaza at 3 de Febrero y 9 de Julio, has a fine patio and museum. In Calle General López is the Museo de Bellas Artes Rosa Galisteo de Rodríguez, where local painters hold their exhibitions. The church of Nuestra Señora de Guadalupe, with beautifully painted glass windows, is at Javier de la Rosa 623 and may be reached by bus 8, 14 or 16 from the centre. Twice weekly boats from Buenos Aires, 483 km. to the south; regular only in winter.

**Local holidays** 30 Sept. (St. Jerome); 15 Nov. (Foundation of City).

**Hotels** *Hostal de Santa Fe de la Vera Cruz*, best, genial management, well-kept and run, San Martín 2954, T 21115/8, B; *Río Grande*, San Gerónimo 2586, A, modern, rec.; *El Conquistador*, 25 de Mayo 2676, B; *Corrientes*, Corrientes 2520, B; *Colón*, San Luis 2862, C; *Suipacha*, Suipacha 2375, C, clean, safe, rec.; *Carlitos*, Irigoyen Freyre 2336, D, clean, friendly; *Royal*, Irigoyen Freyre 2256, clean, modern, private bath, opposite bus station, C; *Niza*, Rivadavia 2755, T 22047, C, very clean, friendly; *Brigadier*, San Luis 3148, D, two blocks from bus station, good, clean, friendly, 50 rooms, a/c extra, but rec. if the river is in flood and there are lots of mosquitoes, some English spoken, private parking; *Bristol*, Belgrano 2838 by bus terminal, E; next door to it is *Gran Hotel Terminal*, Belgrano 2839, opposite bus terminal, E, basic, clean, water shortage.

**Camping** Possible in free municipal site near town centre, Parque del Sur, bus No. 5; beware ferocious mosquitoes. Several sites on the lakes and rivers outside town including: *Luz y Fuerza*, 7 km. N near Lago Guadalupe; *Cámara del Hogar*, 4 km. E on Route 168; 2 sites on Río Colastine, 15 km. E on Route 168.

**Restaurants** Many good ones, offering excellent meals with good wine. *El Quincho de Chiquito*, Obispo Príncipe y Almte. Brown, excellent and good value, classic fish restaurant, huge helpings. Excellent grills including *surubí* (local fish) at *Gran Parrillada Rivadavia*, Rivadavia 3299. Surubí also at *España*, San Martín 2644. Several good cafeterias around San Martín y 25 de Mayo, including *Café de la Paix*, San Martín y Santiago del Estero; *Comedor Porky*, Gálvez 2345, eat all you want. *Nochera Española*, opposite railway station.

**Exchange** Lloyds Bank (BLSA), Calle 25 de Mayo 2501, open 0715-1315. Amex representative, Vacaciones Felices, San Martín 2347. *Casas de Cambio: Camsa*, 25 de Mayo 2466; *Carbatur*, San Martín 2520; *Tourfé*, San Martín 2901, changes travellers' cheques.

**Laundromat** *Servi Rap*, Rivadavia 2834 (open Sat. 0800-1300); *Lavrap*, San Martín 1687.

**Swimming** On river at Guadalupe beach; local bus.

**Tourist Office** at the conveniently situated bus terminal: maps, friendly.

**Railways** The quickest link from Buenos Aires is by Mitre railway to Rosario, and connecting bus (7 hours). Belgrano railway to Buenos Aires, 468 km., 8-10 hours; tourist US$14, 1st US$17, Pullman US$21; also N to Resistencia.

**Roads** Fully paved to Rosario, 160 km. (3 hours by bus); to Formosa, 894 km.; to Roque Sáenz Peña, with spurs S to Villa Angela and General Pinedo and N to San Martín. Large and modern bus terminal. Bus for **Asunción** (Paraguay) leaves daily at 2125, US$40, 17 hrs. Bus to **Córdoba**, US$14, 5 hrs. Many buses to **Buenos Aires**, **Paraná** and **Rosario**; daily to **Mendoza** (2100) and **Santiago del Estero/Tucumán** (2010).

**Airport** At Sauce Viejo, 17 km. from the city. Two daily flights (1 on Sat. and Sun.) to and from Buenos Aires.

Upstream from Santa Fe the Paraná rapidly loses depth and is navigable only by river boats and small coastal vessels.

Between Paraná and Goya, on the left bank, is **La Paz (Entre Ríos)**, a small port (pop. 15,200) with regional museum, riverside park and golf club. Buses to Buenos Aires, Rosario and Concordia. Small restaurants in port and near bus station.

**Hotels** Milton, San Martín e Italia, modern; Plaza, main square; Rivera, San Martín 376.

Between Santa Fe and Corrientes the boat calls at several river ports, including La Paz, Goya and Empedrado. **Goya** (airport 7 km. from centre), on the E bank, is the second town of the Province of Corrientes, is near the junction of the Paraná with the Santa Lucía river. It is a large tobacco centre on the Urquiza railway, with a population of 47,000. There is a vehicle-ferry service across the river to **Reconquista** (34,800 people). Both towns are served by Austral (which flies from the military base at Reconquista, between the airport and town, 10 km. from town). The road N from Goya to Empedrado and Corrientes is paved; many buses.

**Hotels at Goya** Hotel de Turismo, modern, rec. Cervantes, J. E. Gómez 723; Goya, Colón 929; España, España 345, E, clean, hot water, friendly, near bus station. Hoguimarsa, B. Mitre 880/90 (the last-named also has establishments at Curuzú Cuatiá, Empedrado y Mercedes, in Corrientes province). Restaurant El Colonial said to be the best, near bus station at Loza 415.

**Hotels at Reconquista** Magni, C, on main street, adequate, excellent restaurant. Olessio, opposite bus terminal, E. Residencial San Martín, E, with bath, on B. Mitre and Bolívar. Motel Hostal del Rey, located on the edge of town, clean, new, C, with bath. Many around bus station, e.g. Ideal, D, good.

140 km. E of Goya is **Moercedes (Corrientes)** (Hotel de Turismo; Hotel Plaza, E, cheapest), a good base from which to visit the **Iberá marshes**. The marshes are a nature reserve containing more species, it is claimed, than the Pantanal in Mato Grosso, Brazil. Among the species are the endangered aguará-guazá (a large, red fox), deer, otters, the Juan Grande stork, kingfishers, snakes, etc. At Carlos Pellegrini, 110 km. NE of Mercedes (3 buses a week), a new visitors centre to the marshes has been opened (take food, sleeping bag, light, binoculars).

**Empedrado**, further up the river on the E bank, has a population of 46,000. It is on the railway line between Buenos Aires (1,014 km.) and Corrientes. Oranges and rice are grown in the neighbourhood. **Hotel** Turismo, with swimming pool and fine views. **Campsite**.

About 600 km. upstream from Santa Fe, on the W bank, is the little port of Barranqueras, served also from Santa Fe by railway (17 hours). It is on a steep bluff overlooking the Paraná. A paved road connects it with **Resistencia**, the bustling, hot and energetic capital of the Province of Chaco, a galaxy of neon after dark, 6½ km. up the Barranqueras stream. Pop.: 218,000. The road N from Resistencia to Formosa (200 km.) and on to Puerto Pilcomayo (137 km.) is paved. In the streets there are many modern statues, promoted by the Fogón de los Arrieros (see below). International airport.

**Area Products** Cotton, quebracho, cattle. Sculptured Chaco woods from Domingo Arenas, cubist-type wood-statues. Regionales Pompeya, Güemes 154, sells local handicrafts and has an Indian handicraft display. Excellent leather goods at CHAC, Brown 81; Toba handicrafts are sold by Toba Indians in the Barrio Toba, reached by bus 2 or 12.

**Hotels** Many accept Visa cards. Covadonga, Güemes 182, T 22875, B, small rooms, clean, a/c, Tabaré snack bar; Lemirson, Rawson 167, B; Colón, Sta. María de Oro 139, B, friendly, clean, rec.; Sahara, Güemes 169, C, Telex 71104. Esmirna, H. Irigoyen 83 on corner of Plaza, C with bath, good. Celta, Alberdi 210, D; Marconi, Perón 352, D; Residencial San José, Rawson 304, E, clean, decent. Several cheap ones near bus station, e.g. Aragón, Santiago del Estero, 154, E; Residencia Alberdi, Av. Alberdi 317, one block from bus station, E, clean, friendly owner, rec.

**Camping** Parque Dos de Febrero, very pretty, near artificial lake, tent US$2; adequate free site nearby. Parque Mitre, showers and toilets. There is another site, shady but no facilities,

NW of Resistencia on Route 16.

**Restaurants** *Círculo Residentes Santafecinos*, Védia 150, tasty meals at family style restaurant, US$6 for large meal. Try *chupín de surubí*, a sort of bouillabaisse, delightful. *Parrillada Clemente*, Santa María de Oro 399 opposite bus station. *Trattoria el Pappagallo* at the Asociación Italiana, Yrigoyen 236, excellent cuisine, smart, pricey; *Charly*, Güemes 215, snacks, good for breakfast.

**Fogón de los Arrieros**, Brown 350, between López and French, a famous club frequented by local artists and full of local art and "objets" from abroad. Open to non-members Mon.-Sat., 0800-1200, Tues., Wed., Thur., only, 2130-0100. Entry US$2. Good place to meet local people.

**Museums Museo Histórico Regional**, Donovan 475, open Mon.-Fri., 0800-1200, 1400-1700, traces the development of the city; **Museo de Ciencias Naturales**, Pellegrini 745, open Mon.-Fri., 0700-1200, 1700-2000, Sat. 0900-1200; **Museo de Bellas Artes**, Mitre 163, open Mon. 1600-2200, Tues.-Fri., 0900-1300, 1600-2200, Sat./Sun. 1900-2200, collection of 19th and 20th century local works; **Museo Regional de Antropología**, Las Heras 727 in the Universidad Nacional del Nordeste.

**Car Hire** Avis, French 701 and at airport.

**Laundry** *Tokio*, Güemes y Brown.

**Exchange** Banco del Chaco, Güemes on main plaza, high commission on travellers' cheques, and at Pellegrini y 9 de Julio, which offers cash advances on Mastercard; **Banco de Crédito**, Justo 200 block, cash only. Try also the *Hotel Sahara* (cash only).

**Post Office** Plaza 25 de Mayo, Mon.-Sat., 0700-1200, 1500-2000. **Telecommunications** Entel, Justo y Paz.

**Tourist Office** Justo 135; kiosk in Plaza 25 de Mayo, often shut.

**Air** Airport 8 km. from town (no bus). At least one flight a day to Buenos Aires, AR's daily flight coming from Posadas. Alfa flies to Salta Sat. 0800.

**Rail** S to **Santa Fe**, leaves on Thur. and Sun. at 0430, 18 hrs., nothing to eat on train (Belgrano Railway). *El Chaqueño* to **Bs.As.** Mon., Thur., Sat., at 0945, arr. 2017; from the capital Tues., Thur., Sat., at 1000, arr. 2027. No regular passenger service to **Formosa**, **Metán** or **Salta**.

**Buses** Buses leave every 15 mins. to **Corrientes** over the Río Paraná bridge, 40 mins., US$0.55, the Resistencia terminal is on Sta. María del Oro, 3 blocks from main plaza. 3 *especiales* a day to **Buenos Aires** (US$30) 14 hrs., 3 *comunes* a day (US$26), 17 hrs.; bus to **Santa Fe** (US$18). 8 a day to **Formosa** (2½ hrs.) and **Puerto Pilcomayo**, 6-7 hours. To **Posadas**, 6-7 hours, 4 a day, dull, hot journey. Two Veloz del Norte buses direct to **Salta** (US$40) at 1700 and 2300, 14-16 hours, bus may get bogged down on dirt roads; can be crowded; few stops. To Bolivian border at Aguas Blancas/Bermejo, take 1700 bus, change at Joaquín V. González, 10 hrs., for direct connection to Orán, from where it is a 45 min. ride to border. El Rayo to **Tucumán** at 1930 and 2200, 12 hrs., US$19. Bus to **Rosario**, daily, 2015, US$21. Bus to **Clorinda** and Paraguayan border US$8.50, 5 hours. Many searches, watch your belongings and make sure everything is there afterwards. Also to **Asunción** daily, via Formosa, with Godoy (at 0300, 0600, 1400) and Brújula, 6½ hrs.

**Roads** between Resistencia and Salta: (see page 131).

On the other side of the river from Resistencia (25 km.) is **Corrientes**. The 2¾-km. General Belgrano bridge crosses the river (toll free); the best view of it is from the Corrientes side. The city, site of Graham Greene's *The Honorary Consul*, is the capital of Corrientes Province. The river can make the air heavy, moist and oppressive, but in winter the climate is pleasant. Population, 200,000. The city was founded in 1588. The church of La Cruz de los Milagros (1897) houses a miraculous cross placed there by the founder of the city, Alonzo de Vera—Indians who tried to burn it were killed by lightning from a cloudless sky. The Cathedral is in the renaissance style. Plaza Sargento Cabral has a statue to the sergeant who saved San Martín's life at the battle of San Lorenzo. A beautiful walk eastwards, along the Av. Costanera, beside the Paraná river leads to Parque Mitre, from where there are good views of sunsets over the river. Up river from the bridge to Resistencia, is a zoo with animals of the region. Calle Junín is pedestrianized, with restaurants and shops, crowded at night. The pre-Lenten carnival is said to be the wildest in Argentina; reserve hotel in advance; otherwise stay in Resistencia, which is cheaper.

**Hotels** *Corrientes*, Junín 1549, T 65025, B; and *Gran Hotel Guaraní*, Mendoza 970, B; *Turismo Provincial*, Entre Ríos 650, C; *Cadena de Oro*, Ruta Nacional 12, C; *Orly*, San Juan 861, C; *Waikiki*, Gobernador A. Ruiz 2260, C; *Sosa*, España 1050, D, a little overpriced; *Colón*, La Rioja 437, D; *Pavón*, Av. Maipú, km. 3. *Aialay*, Córdoba 314, C. *S.O.S.*, Irigoyen 1771, E, basic, cheap, friendly.

**Camping** Near bus terminal and railway station is *Camping-club Teléfono*, US$1 p.p., hot showers or bath, friendly.

**Restaurants** *El Recreo*, Pellegrini 578, good, reasonable prices, popular with locals; Many others, including *Raviolandia*, Nueve de Julio 652; *Che Camba*, Av. Independencia 4175; and various *pizzerías*. Ice creams at *Italia*, Nueve de Julio 1301 and *Verona*, Av. Ferré 1750. Several tea rooms on San Juan, e.g. *Confitería Viki*, San Juan 721 y Maipú 1198 and on Junín.

**Nightclubs** *Metal*, Junín y Buenos Aires; *Savage*, Junín y San Lorenzo.

**Car Hire** Avis at *Gran Hotel Guaraní* and airport; only credit cards accepted from foreigners.

**Museums** **Museo Histórico Regional**, 9 de Julio 1044 (closed for renovation late 1990); **Museo de Bellas Artes**, San Juan 634, open Tues.-Fri., 0800-1200, 1600-2100, Sat., Sun., 0900-1200, 1800-2000; **Museo de Ciencias Naturales**, San Martín 850, a once famous collection now sadly neglected; **Museo de Artesanía**, Quintana 905, Mon.-Fri., 0730-1200, 1500-2000, Sat. 0900-1200, 1600-1900.

**Exchange** *Cambio Mazza*, San Lorenzo 1600 block, accepts cheques and cash; **Banco de la Provincia**, 9 de Julio y San Juan; **Banco de Crédito**, Junín 1326, cash accepted only; street money-changers at SW corner of Plaza Cabral.

**Tourist Office** La Rioja 475; lots of information about fishing.

**Travel Agency** *Turismo Aventura 4WD*, Quintana 525, Piso 3°, oficina 21, T 27698.

**Airport** Camba Punta, 10 km. from city. (Bus No. 8 from urban bus terminal at river end of La Rioja) Aerolíneas Argentinas office Junín 1301, T 23850; Austral, Córdoba 935, T 25278. AR (not Sun.) and Austral (3 a week) flights to and from Buenos Aires. AR's flight continues to Formosa.

**Rail** Office on Córdoba 990, T 22009. Daily train leaves Lacroze station, Buenos Aires at 1500 daily, arriving at Corrientes (1,046 km.) at 1310 next day; it leaves Corrientes at 1530 daily, reaching Buenos Aires at 1322 next day. Fares: sleeper US$40, first US$24, tourist US$20.

**Bus** New terminal 5 km. from centre; bus No. 6 from terminal to town centre (US$0.20). Corrientes-**Posadas** US$15, 5½ hrs., road paved. Buses to **Resistencia** US$0.55, Cota, every 15 mins., 40 mins. journey, labelled "Chaco", leave from harbour; **Buenos Aires**-Corrientes, US$30; there are many more buses to Buenos Aires, Rosario and Santa Fe from Resistencia than from Corrientes.

At 20 km. along Route 12 from Corrientes is Santa Ana de los Guacaras, a 17th-century settlement with attractive colonial architecture. To the N of Corrientes is the small town of *Paso de la Patria* (38 km., Route 12), a paradise for *dorado* fishing, with plenty of bungalows to stay. (Hotels: *Hostería Oficial*, B; *Cabaña Don Julián*, B, full board.)

A tiny port on the Alto Paraná—*Itatí* (pop. 5,700)—is reached by bus (73 km. on Route 12). Here, on 16 July, is held a gala festival which celebrates jointly the crowning of the Virgin of Itatí (housed in a sanctuary built 1638), and St. Louis of France. Thousands of pilgrims arrive on the 16th (when the religious ceremonies begin) from San Luis del Palmar (pop. 15,000) in picturesque procession. Also on Route 12 (250 km. from Corrientes) are the Saltos de Apipé, where one can fish or swim.

210 km. SE of Corrientes, on the edge of the Iberá marshes (**see page 139**), is the Estancia of San Juan Poriahú (16,500 hectares), a wildlife reserve with a superb array of animals and birds. Visitors can explore the estancia on horseback, or in pick-ups and tractors.

Corrientes is 40 km. below the confluence of the Paraguay and Alto Paraná rivers. Up the former are Formosa and Asunción; up the latter are Posadas and Iguazú.

The only Argentine port of any note on the Paraguay river is *Formosa*, 240 km. above Corrientes. It is the capital of Formosa Province, and has a population of 95,000. There is an interesting colonial museum in the town centre. There are many Indians in the area (bus from Rivadavia y San Martín, No. 1 ("Lote 68"), 15 mins., to the Barrio de los Indios.) At the Casa de Artesanía ask about the ACA in Ingeniero Juárez, from where excursions to see Chaco Indian settlements may be made. The surroundings are flat and swampy, the climate and vegetation tropical. From the port a trip can be made to Isla Alberdi, a Paraguayan duty-free spot; no possibility of continuing into Paraguay, and can only be done if you have a multiple entry visa. By road from Buenos Aires; 1,365 km. Airport (one Aerolíneas Argentinas flight per day, except Sun.).

**Hotels** *Turismo*, best, San Martín 759, T 26004, A; *Residencial City*, near railway station, C; *Colón*, Belgrano 1068, a/c, colour TV, spacious, C 1st floor, B 2nd floor, good; *Plaza*, J.M. Uriburu 905, C. Several others on San Martín, e.g. *Residencial Italia*, nr. station, D, clean, hot showers; *Colonial*, near railway station, E with private bath, clean, a/c, basic but good value, private parking available. *Residencial Rivas*, 1/2 block from bus station, E with bath, clean, friendly. *Casa de Familia*, Belgrano 102, F, friendly, good. Many more along Belgrano.

**Camping** Possible on the river about 2 km. from the centre along a dirt road, upstream and over the railway lines.

**Restaurant** *Ser Bran*, near bus terminal, cheap and good. *El Ciervo*, Av. 25 de Mayo 65, excellent fish (surubí) and empanadas; *Latino American Bar*, 25 de Mayo 55, good Italian food, nice atmosphere, expensive.

**Exchange** Banks close at about noon and there are no exchange shops; buy australes in Asunción or Clorinda if en route when they're closed. **Banco de la Provincia de Formosa** changes travellers' cheques.

**Tourist Office** San Martín y 25 de Mayo, 0800-1200, 1600-2000, near the port, helpful.

**Shipping** Bolivian vessels (cargo and passenger) to Puerto Suárez (Bolivia), with call at Asunción. Irregular.

**Roads** S to Resistencia (200 km.); N to Clorinda and Asunción, paved, 150 km., via new toll bridge. Direct road to Salta very bad: the bus service appears to run only rarely.

**Bus** Formosa-Puente Loyola US$6. Formosa-**Asunción**, 0800 and 1630, Expreso Brújula and other companies on main street. Empresa Godoy (surcharge on luggage over 15 kg.) to border. Six a day to **Resistencia**.

**Railway** across the Chaco to **Embarcación**, N of Jujuy and Salta. *Cochemotor* passenger service, dusty in summer, Sun. and Thurs. 0300, 1st class US$20, tourist class US$15, buy ticket in advance and get on train as soon as you can; 20 hrs., noisy, uncomfortable but worth it for the birdlife.

**Excursion** Nature reserve (flora and fauna) at Guaycotea, 6 buses a day from Formosa, 1/2 hr.

About 137 km. N of Formosa, almost opposite Asunción (Paraguay), is *Clorinda*, whence the new Loyola bridge crosses to Puerto Falcón, Paraguay. Border crossing is easy. Many buses from Argentine end of bridge: to Formosa (10 a day), Resistencia (4) and Santa Fe/Rosario/Buenos Aires (3). Clorinda has a well-known banana festival in early October. Street money changer at Clorinda bus station, gives good rates austral/guaraní. From Puerto Pilcomayo, close to Clorinda (bus US$0.40) one can catch a ferry to Itá Enramada (Paraguay), a US$0.65 five-minute journey every 20 minutes. Argentine migration office at Puerto Pilcomayo is open 7 days a week.

At the confluence of the two rivers above Corrientes the Paraguay river comes in from the N, the Alto Paraná from the E. The Alto Paraná is difficult to navigate; it is, in parts, shallow; there are several rapids, and sometimes the stream is braided, its various channels embracing mid-stream islands. Much rice is grown on its banks. The shortest and least crowded route from Buenos Aires to the Alto Paraná is along Route 14 from Zarate which follows the Río Uruguay and avoids the main population centres.

The main Argentine port, on the S bank of the Paraná, is *Posadas*, capital of the province of Misiones, 377 km. above Corrientes, and very hot in summer. Population 141,000. A good way of seeing the city is to take the No. 7 bus ("Circunvaluación") from Calle Junín. There is a good Mercado Artesanal at Alberdi 602 in the Parque Río del Paraguay (Mon.-Fri., 0800-1200). Yerba mate, tea and tobacco are grown in the area. **N.B.** All street numberings have been changed: buildings now have both new and old numbers.

On the opposite bank of the river lies the Paraguayan town of Encarnación (with buses to Asunción): a bridge links the two towns, no bicycles allowed across (frequent bus services, US$1; thorough body and baggage searches when entering Argentina usually carried out). Apparently a ferry service still runs.

**Hotels** Prices in the Province of Misiones are on the whole significantly higher than elsewhere, and double if you want a private bathroom. Best is *Libertador*, San Lorenzo 2208, T 37601, B; *Continental*, Bolívar 314, T 38966, B, comfortable, but noisy, reasonable breakfast; *City*, Colón 280, T 33901, D, shower, a/c, clean and reasonable, good restaurant (colectivo bus service from airport to this hotel); *Residencial Colón*, Colón, 2169, D, good and clean; *Posadas*, Bolívar 1941, T 30801/31221, B with bath and breakfast, good service, snack bar, laundry, highly rec.; *Turismo*, Bolívar 171, T 32711, D, modern but poor maintenance; *Savoy*, Sarmiento 296, D, clean and pleasant; *Residencial Nagel*, Méndez 2584, near bus station, noisy, basic, E; *Gran Hotel Misiones*, Líbano y Barrufaldi, D, a/c, restaurant, dirty, overpriced, rundown, one block from bus terminal; next door to it at Líbano 2655 is *Horianski*, T 22675, D with bath, garage, family atmosphere; *Residencial Familiar*, Mitre 58 near railway station, E, good restaurant, rec. Many adequate *residenciales* in the centre. *Residencial Andresito*, Salta 1743, T 23850, E, youth hostel style, clean, friendly; *Residencial Córdoba*, Santiago del Estero 171, T 35451, E; *Residencial Misiones*, Azara 382, E.

**Camping** Municipal camping ground on the river, off the road to San Ignacio Miní, hot showers and shop, good, reached by buses 4 or 21 from centre.

**Restaurants** *El Tropezón*, San Martín 2130, good, inexpensive; *El Encuentro*, San Martín 1786; *La Ventana*, Bolívar 1725, excellent but expensive; *Restaurant de la Sociedad Española*, La Rioja 1848, good food, popular lunches; *El Estribo*, Tucumán y Ayacucho, good cooking in attractive atmosphere, rec.; excellent buffet on ground floor of *Hotel Savoy*. There is an excellent restaurant *La Querencia*, on Plaza 9 Julio *Pizzería Los Pinos*, San Lorenzo 1764, excellent and cheap; *Pizzería La Grata Alegría*, Bolívar y Junín, good.

**Discos** on Bolívar between 3 de Febrero y 25 de Mayo (*Power*) and at San Martín y Jujuy, open 0100-0500 Thur.-Sun.

**Museums Museo Regional**, Alberdi 606 in the Parque Río del Paraguay, open 0800-1200, 1400-2000, rather neglected; **Museo Histórico Arqueológico**, Gen. Paz 1865, open Mon.-Fri., 0700-1300, 1400-1900, housing archaeological pieces from the areas to be flooded by the Yacyretá hydroelectric project and a section on the Jesuit missionary era; **Museo de Ciencias Naturales**, San Luis 384, open Tues.-Sun., 0800-1200, 1500-1900; **Museo de Bellas Artes**, Sarmiento 317, open 0700-1230, 1400-1830.

**Exchange** Banco de La Nación, Bolívar 1799, changes travellers' cheques. Opens very early, 0700-1215. *Cambio Mazza*, Bolívar 1480 and at Buenos Aires 1442, changes travellers' cheques and other currencies. Street money changers on SW corner of Plaza 9 de Julio. If stuck when banks and *cambios* are closed, cross the river to Encarnación and use the street changers.

**Paraguayan Consulate** San Lorenzo 179. **Brazilian Consulate** Mitre 631, T 24830, 0800-1200, visas issued free, photo required, 90 days given.

**Post Office** Bolívar y Ayacucho.

**Tourist Office** Colón 1985, y la Rioja, T 24360, helpful, open Mon.-Fri., 0630-1230, 1400-2000, Sat./Sun., 0800-1200, 1600-2000; maps and brochures in English of Posadas, Formosa and Iguazú Falls. Hotel listings for Misiones province.

**Travel Agent** *Viajes Turismo*, Colón 1901, ask for Kenneth Nairn, speaks English, most helpful, good tours to Iguazú and local sights.

**Buses** Terminus at Av. Uruguay y Av. Mitre on W side of town. From **Buenos Aires**, US$32

(US$2 extra for *servico diferencial*, i.e. supper and breakfast) 15 hrs.; Expreso Singer and Tigre-Iguazú each have 3 buses a day, plus a nightly *diferencial* and *rápido*; some go via Resistencia, some via Concordia. Expreso Singer (Av. Mitre 2447, T 24771/2) and Tigre bus terminal is 5 mins. walk from the main bus terminal. Frequent services to San Ignacio Mini (1 hr.) and Puerto Iguazú, (4½) hrs. Bus to **Córdoba** with Singer and Litoral on alternate days at 1200, arrive at 0735 next day. Bus to **Corrientes** US$15; to **Formosa**, US$8. La Estrella bus to **Tucumán**, Tues., Thurs., Sun. at 1720, 16 hrs., US$28. To Paso de los Libres (7 hrs.) US$15, interesting, 60 km. not paved. To **Resistencia**, 6-7 hrs., dull trip, US$14. To **Concordia** (Expreso Singer) US$25, 2100 daily, 8¾ hrs. Singertur, Av. Mitre 54 (T 4771, 4772) in Posadas.

**International**   To **Asunción** (Expreso Singer, daily 1400, 7 hrs., and Empresa Godoy), US$14. To **Montevideo**, a roundabout journey because the main Asunción-Montevideo route passes through Corrientes. One can take Expreso Singer bus to the junction for Colón, at Villa San José (ACA hostel), C, local bus to Colón; two local buses over the bridge to Paysandú (US$3), then plenty of buses to Montevideo if going to Brazil (Uruguaiana) there are 3 daily buses (Singer) to **Paso de los Libres** for Puente Internacional—Argentine customs—the bus from here to the Brazilian border on the other side of the Río Uruguay costs US$0.50. Expreso Singer bus to **Porto Alegre** (via Oberá, Panambí, Santo Angelo and Carazinho), Tues., Thur., Sun. at 1400, arriving 0345 next day, US$26. If the bus is full it is possible to buy a ticket (without a seat) in Oberá. The bus usually empties before long and you can get a seat.

**Train from Buenos Aires**   (Lacroze Station). Information available in Viamonte 553. *El Gran Capitán*, which leaves at 1500 daily, arrives at 1128. Transfer (free) to the bus station where there is a connecting bus to **San Ignacio Mini** (1 hr.). From Posadas *El Gran Capitán* leaves at 1700 daily, arrives in Buenos Aires about 1322 next day, sleeper, pullman, 1st class US$31; tourist US$26, not crowded. There is a car transporter on the Mon. and Fri. trains, returning to Buenos Aires on Thurs. and Sun. One advantage over the buses is that the wild life in woods and swamps may be seen more easily (because it is less often disturbed) from the railway than from the road. Train to **Asunción** leaves Encarnación 1530 Wed. (2nd class carriages leave Posadas 1230), arrives 0835 next day. Returns Tues. at 1755.

**Airport**   General San Martín (12 km.), reached from Posadas by Bus No. 8 from opp. bus terminal in 20 mins., US$0.45. Daily flights to **Buenos Aires** with AR and Austral (with one connection on Sun. to Resistencia); Austral also flies Mon.-Fri. to **Iguazú**.

**Excursion**   To San Miguel Apóstoles, 65 km. S, a prosperous town founded by Ukrainian and Polish immigrants, where a maté festival is held in Nov. (*Hotel Misiones*, E, clean).

From Posadas a visit should be paid to the impressive ruins of Jesuit settlements and to the magnificent Falls of Iguazú.

Not far from Posadas are the ruins of three old Jesuit missions among the Guaraní Indians, from which the province of Misiones derives its name. Tourists should see those at San Ignacio Mini (very well maintained), reached by paved road (buses every ½ hr.-1 hr., US$5). You need about 1½ hrs. for a leisurely look. There are heavy rains at San Ignacio in February. 16 km. before San Ignacio are the ruins of Santa Ana, only partially cleared but very impressive.

At *San Ignacio Mini*, founded on its present site in 1696, the grass-covered plaza, a hundred metres square, is flanked north, east and west by 30 parallel blocks of stone buildings with ten small, one-room dwellings to the block. The roofs have gone, but the massive metre-thick walls are still standing except where they have been torn down by the *ibapoi* trees; each block was surrounded by a roofed gallery. The public buildings, some of them still 10 metres high, are on the south side. In the centre are the ruins of a large church finished about 1724. To the right is the cemetery, to the left the school and the cloisters of the priests. Beyond are other buildings which were the workshops, refectory and storerooms. The masonry, a red or yellow sandstone from the Paraná River, was held together by a sandy mud. There is much bas-relief sculpture, mostly of floral designs. Now maintained as a National Monument (open 0700-1900, entry US$0.50, tip appreciated if the guards look after your luggage; you have to pay to park by the ruins' fence; park on the other side of the street, it's free!). Mosquitoes can be a problem. Go early to avoid crowds; good birdwatching.

The Jesuits set up their first missions among the Guaraní Indians about 1609, in the region of Guaíra, now in Brazil. The missions flourished: cotton was introduced, the Indians wove their own clothes, dressed like Europeans, raised cattle, and built and sculpted and painted their own churches. But in 1627 they were violently attacked by the slave-hunting Bandeirantes from São Paulo, and by 1632 the position of the mission had become impossible: 12,000 converts, led by the priests, floated on 700 rafts down the Paranapanema into the Paraná, only to find their route made impassable by the Guaíra Falls. They pushed for eight days through dense virgin forests on both sides of the river, then built new boats and continued their journey; 725 km. from their old homes they founded new missions in what is now Paraguay, Argentine Misiones, and Brazilian Rio Grande do Sul. By the early 18th century there were, on both sides of the river, 30 mission villages with a combined population of over 100,000 souls. Only four of these show any signs of their former splendour: San Ignacio Miní, São Miguel (Brazil), and Jesús and Trinidad (Paraguay). At the height of its prosperity in 1731 San Ignacio contained 4,356 people. In 1767, Charles III of Spain expelled the Jesuits from Spanish territory; the Franciscans and Dominicans then took over. After the Jesuits had gone, there was a rapid decline in prosperity. By 1784 there were only 176 Indians at San Ignacio Miní; by 1810, none remained. By order of the Paraguayan dictator Francia, all the settlements were evacuated in 1817, and San Ignacio was set on fire. The village was lost in the jungle until it was discovered again in 1897. In 1943 an agency of the Argentine Government took control. Some of the craft work produced at the settlement can be seen at two museums in Buenos Aires: the Museo Colonial Isaac Fernández Blanco and the municipal Museo de Arte Colonial. 200 m. beyond the entrance to the ruins is the Centro de Interpretación Jesuítico—Guaraní, generally known as the "Museo Vivo", with sections on the lives of the Guaraníes before the arrival of the Spanish, the work of the Jesuits and the consquences of their expulsion. (Closed in 1991.) *Son-et-lumière* show at the ruins, 2000, weekends only out of season, cancelled in wet weather, Spanish only, tickets from museum. Dr. Hector Alvarez has been recommended as an informative and friendly guide; he gives tours of the ruins for a nominal fee, and will also take visitors to the quarry used for the original stone buildings, speaks English, French, Portuguese, Italian and some German.

**Accommodation**  ACA *Hostería* (D; lunches available); *Hotel San Ignacio*, D, friendly, good, clean, restaurant with light meals, *cabañas* (closed in August), 3 blocks away is *Hospedaje El Descanso*, Pellegrini 270, E, modern, quiet, rec.; signposted from the main road. *Hospedaje Alemán Los Salpeterer*, Sarmiento y Centenario, E, kitchen, nice garden, pool, camping, rec., English and German spoken. *Albergue Municipal*, San Martín 4040, E. There are *Restaurant Artemio I*, good and cheap, open evenings in high season, weekend evenings otherwise (accepts all local currencies, US$ and D-mark, good exchange rate too), and two *comedores* (lunch only) opposite the entrance to the ruins. Festival July 30-31.

**Camping**  outside the ruins in municipal site; cold showers and toilets. Two pleasant sites by small lake about 5 km. S of San Ignacio, on Route 12.

**Excursions**  To the house of Horacio Quiroga, the Argentine writer, 2 km. outside town. To the Peñon Teyu-Cuare, 11 km. S., a 150 m. high hill overlooking the Río Paraná offering panoramic views.

At Jardín América, 48 km. N of San Ignacio, there is an excellent municipal campsite 2 km. off Route 12. Flights can be taken over Misiones province for US$50. At Puerto Rico, 21 km. N of Jardín América, there is a good hotel, *Suizo*, C; campsite at Club de Pesca; rec. restaurants are *Don Luis* and *Churrascaría Flach*, both on main street. The ACA *hostería* at Montecarlo, half way between San Ignacio and Iguazú, is warmly rec. In Montecarlo is the Museo de Ciencias Naturales Juan Foerster, dedicated to flora, fauna and history, open Tues.-Sun., 0800-1200, 1400-1800, worth a visit; it is run by Sr. Foerster's widow.

The most successful colonization in Argentina of late years has been at **Eldorado**, on this route. This prosperous small town is surrounded by flourishing *mate*, tung, citrus, eucalyptus and tobacco plantations. There are tung oil factories, sawmills, plywood factories, *mate* drying installations and a citrus packing plant. The ACA office is very helpful and has a large illuminated map of Eldorado and its surroundings.

**Hotels at Eldorado**  *Alpa*, C; *Hostería ACA* and *Atlántida*, both D; *Castellar*, C with bath. *Ideal*, E, clean, opp. bus station; *Gran Riojano*, Av San Martín 314, T 22217, very friendly, 5 min walk from main road crossing. **Restaurant** : *Copetín al Paso*, excellent, reasonable for price, but doesn't cook every day. Also try restaurant at *Gran Riojano* .

**Camping**  Camping site with showers and toilets; take the road toward the river from the main highway, for 2 km.

**Exchange**:  *Cambio Fonseca*.

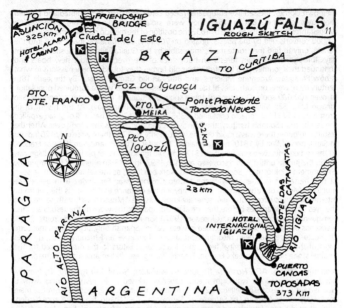

If you are interested in flora and fauna, travel through Misiones from Puerto Iguazú to Posadas on Route 12 to **Wanda** (*Hotel Prisa*, Swiss-owned, 20% discount for Swiss nationals); nearby are two open-cast amethyst and quartz mines which sell gems, but they are much more expensive than in Brazil, there are free guided tours. Carry on to Eldorado, then follow Route 17 (buses 0800 and 1530), paved to Bernardo Yrigoyen, a nice village, lovely vegetation en route. The direct (dirt) road from Puerto Iguazú to Bernardo Yrigoyen crosses the National Park of Iguazú, passing Andrecito, Cabuneí and San Antonio. Local buses ply the route if the weather is dry. From B. Yrigoyen follow Route 14 to Tobuna, where you will see the Alegría falls. On to the small village of Paraíso, see Moconá falls 82 km. from there, then Dos de Mayo (*Hotel Alex*). Pass through **Oberá** (*Hotel Cuatro Pinos*, Av. Sarmiento 853, good value; campsite just outside town, with swimming pool and waterfall nearby; *Enqüete* restaurant, Alvar Núñez Cabeza de Vaca 340, good),and follow Route 103 W to Santa Ana, with Jesuit ruins of Loreto, not fully restored; best at sunrise, museum opens 0700-1900, US$0.75. From here you can return via San Ignacio to Puerto Iguazú or turn 16 km. in opposite direction to Posadas. In Oberá, a Parque de Naciones is being built, with houses to commemorate the nationalities of all the immigrants who founded the town. Many maté-leaf drying factories can be visited. Tourist information centre in a pavilion on Av. Libertad, T 21808

## THE IGUAZU FALLS (8)

*For specific references to the Brazilian side of the Falls, with accommodation and transport links, see Southern Brazil section, the Paraná River . For a general description, local transport arrangements, and specific Argentine references, see below.*

The **Iguazú Falls** are the most overwhelming falls in South America. They lie about 350 km. upstream from Posadas where, 19 km. above the confluence of the Iguazú with the Alto Paraná, the waters fall thunderously in virgin forest bright with orchids and serpentine creepers festooning the branches. Above the impact of water on basalt rock hovers a perpetual 30-metre high cloud of mist in which the sun. creates blazing rainbows. The Iguazú (Guaraní for great waters) rises in the Brazilian hills near Curitiba and receives some 30 streams on its course across the plateau. Above the main falls the river, sown with wooded islets, opens out to a width of 4 km. There are rapids for 3½ km. above the 60-metre precipice over which the water plunges in 275 falls over a frontage of 2,470 metres, at a rate of 1,750 cubic metres a second. Their height is greater than Niagara's by 20 metres or so and their width by one half, but most of the falls are broken midway by ledges of rock. Viewed from below, the tumbling water in its setting of begonias, orchids, fern and palms with toucans, flocks of parrots and cacique birds, swifts (*vencejos*) dodging in and out of the very falls, and myriads of butterflies (at least 500 different species), is majestically beautiful, especially outside the cool season (when the water is much diminished, as are the birds and insects). The first European visitor to the falls was the Spaniard Alvar Núñez Cabeza de Vaca in 1541, on his search for a connection between the Brazilian coast and the Río de la Plata.

Visitors to the Falls should note that the Brazilian side (best visited in the morning because the light then is better for photography) shows the best panorama of the whole falls and should therefore be preferred if your visit is limited to, say, half a day, but the Argentine side (which needs most of a day to explore properly: the area is much greater) shows more close detail of the individual falls and is much more interesting from the point of view of seeing the forest with its wildlife and butterflies. There are a bird hide overlooking a marsh (Bañado), a 4 km.-long interpreted (Spanish) nature trail (Macuco) in the jungle, a self-guided trail around the *Circuito Inferior*, all of which are very lovely. (An advantage in visiting the Argentine side first is that the information provided at the Visitors' Centre is far superior to anything offered in Brazil.) One cannot cross the river at the Falls themselves; this can only be done by bridge between Porto Meira and Puerto Iguazú.

The Devil's Throat, the most spectacular fall, is best seen from Puerto Canoas, to which buses run (see below), or you can drive (parking US$1). On the Argentine side the upper series of catwalks on the river, *Circuito Superior*, were largely destroyed by floods in 1983. The 1 km. catwalk from the river bank to the Devil's Throat has been replaced, although the last few metres have been closed off, somewhat reducing the effect. There is also a short boat trip from Puerto Canoas to join the catwalk (US$5). Recommended in the evening when the light is best and the swifts are returning to roost on the walls, some behind the water. Below the falls the Iguazú runs swiftly for 19 km. through a deep canyon before it joins the Alto Paraná.

To walk along the lower series of catwalks, at the level of the midway ledge, waterproof coats or swimming costumes are advisable but not absolutely necessary. Wear shoes with good soles when walking around, as the rocks are very slippery in places. Put your camera in a plastic bag. At the base of Dos Hermanas fall is a natural, idyllic swimming pool, so take bathing gear in summer to cool off. A trail starting behind the *Hotel Internacional* leads down to the Río Iguazú ferry to Isla San Martín; ferry leaves on demand, takes 2-3 mins.; bathing is possible from Isla San Martín.

The Argentine Iguazú National Park embraces a large area. The fauna includes the black howler monkey, capybara, jaguar and puma, along with a huge variety of birds; neither hunting nor fishing are allowed. The months to avoid are July (holidays) and December-March (hot). Information and permits can be got from the Visitors Centre information desk, open daily 0800-1800 in the old, Argentine Cataratas Hotel, now converted. The Visitors' Centre organizes a 4-hour walk (8 km.) through the jungle, beginning at 0900 daily; fixed price US$40 to share among the party. Catch 0825 bus from Puerto Iguazú. It also runs night-time walks between *Hotel Internacional Iguazú* and the falls when the moon is full; on clear nights the moon casts a blue halo over the falls. Mountain bikes and boats can also be hired. Helicopter rides over the Falls, about 10 mins. for US$35, start from the Brazilian airport. The Argentine National Park keepers regard the helicopter rides as a serious noise pollutant; they are collecting visitors' complaints about the problem in a book to which they welcome additions. It is also reported that the helicopter noise is a threat to some bird species which are laying thinner-shelled eggs. There is a museum of local fauna and an auditorium for periodic slide shows (on request for 8 or more people), no commentary, just music. A good guide book on Argentine birds is for sale.

There is a US$2 charge which allows one-day entry to the Argentine Park, free information leaflet provided with ticket (guests at *Hotel Internacional* do not have to pay).

**Getting to the Falls** Transportes Cataratas buses run hourly from the Puerto Iguazú bus station to the Falls, taking about 30 minutes for the 22½ km. These buses are sometimes erratic, even though the times are clearly indicated, especially when it is wet. They stop at the National Park entrance for the purchase of entrance tickets. Return fare to the Falls, US$3; first bus at 0700, last at 1800; first back at 0815, last at 1900. Inclusive fare, including ride to Puerto Canoas and boat to San Martín island (US$5 return), is US$10. The bus continues from the Park Adminstration to Puerto Canoas (for Devil's Throat), hourly on the half-hour, US$0.60 return; returning hourly at quarter-to-the-hour. There are fixed rates for taxis, US$20, up to 5 people. A tour from the bus terminal, taking in both sides of the Falls, costs US$30. Hitch-hiking to the Falls is difficult, but you can hitch up to the Posadas intersection at Km. 11, then it is only 7 km. walk.

Travel between Argentina and Brazil has been greatly improved by the opening of the 480 metre Puente de Fraternidad/Ponte Presidente Tancredo Neves, which joins Puerto Iguazú (Route 12) and Porto Meira (BR-469). Six buses run each hour (US$1) from the Puerto Iguazú bus terminal on Av. Córdoba to the Terminal Urbana in Foz do Iguaçu, pausing at the border but not stopping long enough for passport controls; you have to wait for the next one if you need a stamp (keep the ticket so as not to pay twice); on the other hand if you are simply crossing on to see the other side of the Falls and returning the same day, tell the officials and stay on the bus. The passenger and car ferries between Puerto Iguazú and Porto Meira no longer run a regular schedule, and there are no immigration offices on either side; motorists visiting the Argentine side from Brazil can park overnight in the National Park, free.

Change some money into cruzeiros before going into Brazil: they try to charge you triple the true cost if you use Argentine money. Foz do Iguaçu being much the larger town, tends to be cheaper, with more choice than Puerto Iguazú for hotels and food.

It is not possible to go direct by road to Puerto Franco (Paraguay) from Puerto Iguazú; one must go through Brazil. If passing through Foz do Iguaçu en route from Puerto Iguazú to Paraguay, make sure that Brazilian officials stamp your passport. "Ponte-Ponte" buses ply between the Brazilian ends of the bridges into Argentina and into Paraguay, via Foz do Iguaçu. However, there are launches plying on the rivers Paraná and Iguazú between Puerto Franco and Puerto Iguazú: every 2 hours or so.

On the Argentine side is *Puerto Iguazú*, a small modern town above the river. There is a helpful tourist office (English spoken) at Av. Victoria Aguirre and Brasil, open 0800-1200, 1500-2000 Mon.-Fri., 0800-1200, 1630-2000 Sat. and Sun.

**Hotels** Crowded during summer (Jan.-Feb.), Easter and July holiday periods and busy at other times of the year. *Internacional Iguazú*, L, five-star, pool, casino, good restaurant, business facilities, overlooking the falls. Reservations at Av. Eduardo Madero 1020 (T 3114259, or 3136292), Buenos Aires. *Paraná*, Brasil 367, D, clean, friendly. *La Cabaña*, Av. Tres Fronteras 434, C, with shower and breakfast, a/c, good, clean and friendly, with an older part and a new annexe, swimming pool, rec.; *Tierra Colorada*, Av. Córdoba y El Urú 265, very good, D with fan and bath, nice restaurant, trips arranged. *Esturión*, Av. Tres Fronteras 650, A, clean, arbitrary pricing, comfortable, swimming pool, good restaurant, reservations at Belgrano 265, 10th floor, Buenos Aires. *Libertador*, San Martín 441, B, modern, central, helpful, large bedrooms and public rooms, rooms at back have balconies overlooking garden and swimming pool; *Las Orquídeas*, Ruta 12, Km. 5 (T 2472), B/C, very comfortable, clean, set right in the jungle outside Puerto Iguazú, restaurant; *Alexander*, Córdoba 222, opp. bus station, C incl. meagre breakfast, swimming pool; *El Libano*, Aguirre (entrance to town), bungalows, C, with kitchen, excellent value; *Residencial San Fernando*, Guaraní 21 y Córdoba, close to bus station, D, with bath, clean; *Residencial Paquita*, Av. Córdoba 158, T 20434, E, noisy but friendly, nice setting, some rooms with terrace rec. Two blocks from bus station is *Residencial San Diego*, D, clean, friendly. *Turismo de Iguazú*, Paraguay 372, B, pools, charmingly old fashioned, spectacularly set above river, good value; *Saint George*, Av. Córdoba 148, B, with breakfast, comfortable, pool, good, expensive restaurant. Behind this hotel is *Residencial Los Helechos*, Almirantes s/n (off Córdoba), D with bath, owner speaks German, clean, new, motel-style accommodation, 10% discount for ISIC and youth card holders. *Residencial Gloria*, Av. Uruguay 344, D with bath (electric showers) and fridge, clean, quiet, friendly. *Residencial Arco Iris*, Curupy 152, D/E with private shower, basic, cooking facilities, clean. *Misiones*, Aquirre opp. Tourist Office, D/E, clean, friendly and less busy than many other hotels; *Residencial Lilian*, behind the *Paquita* hotel, E with bath, clean, safe, rec.; *Residencial Río Selva*, San Martín 147, T 21555, F p.p., clean, friendly, laundry facilities. There is a hostel affiliated to the IYHA (G) between immigration and international bridge, pleasant, 90 beds. The Tourist Office has a list of *Casas Familiares* (E), though it may be reluctant to find private accommodation unless the hotels are full.

**Camping** Free site 600 metres past parking area at Puerto Canoas. Tables, but no other facilities. Camping sometimes permitted at the school just inside the Park entrance. Municipal campsite in Puerto Iguazú reported "grim". Camping El Pindó at the edge of town, charges US$1.60 p.p, US$6 per tent and US$1.00 for use of pool, friendly, but very run down. There are better facilities at Turístico Americano, Km. 5, Route 12, T 2782 incl. pool, but no food.

**Restaurants** *La Rueda*, Av. Córdoba 28, good food at reasonable prices, but service less than good. *Don Nicola*, Av. Bompland, good. *El Tío Querido*, Perito Moreno 250, friendly service, excellent cooking, guitarist at night; *Casa de Comercio*, Aguirre 327, good food, moderate prices. Good meals in the bus terminal.

**Exchange** three *casas de cambio* opposite the tourist office (rates may vary between the *casas*; shop around!), only one, **Dick**, Av. Aguirre 228, changes travellers' cheques, at high commission. Kiosk at the bus terminal accepts cheques (high commission). Several *casas de cambio* also on the outskirts of town towards the falls.

**Car Hire** Avis at airport. Cars may be taken to the Brazilian side for an extra US$5.

**Brazilian Vice Consulate** Aquirre 77, 0800-1200, arrive early with 1 photo for a free, 90-day, multiple entry visa (check Brazil chapter, **Documents** section).

**Travel Agent** *Turismo Dick*, Aguirre 228, also in Foz do Iguaçu; does not close at lunchtime. Reports vary. *Reinhard Foerster*, Privat Servis, Av. Tres Fronteras 335, T 2774, offers naturalists' and birdwatchers' programmes. *Turismo Caracol*, on Aguirre, T 2124, does all-day tour of both sides of falls, including good meal in Brazil, but mainly for "non-English speaking clients with an interest in shopping". *Turismo Cuenca del Plata*, Paulino Amarantes 76, T 20338, offers 10% discount to ISIC and youth card holders on local excursions. Recommended taxi-guide, Juan Villalba, T 20973 (radiotaxi 044), good value, speaks basic English.

**Airports** There is an Argentine domestic airport near the Falls, and a Brazilian international airport about half-way between Foz do Iguaçu and the Falls. Taxi between the two airports over the new bridge costs US$20. Buses, run between Argentine airport and hotels, US$4, leaving Aerolíneas Argentinas office in Puerto Iguazú (Brasil y Aguirre) about 2 hrs. before plane departures. There is only one smallish bus meeting each flight on arrival; it is advisable to buy tickets even before collecting luggage because when the bus is full the only alternative is a taxi, US$10 to *Hotel Internacional* and considerably more to Puerto Iguazú.

**Air Transport** By Boeing 737 (Aerolíneas Argentinas and Austral) from Buenos Aires, mostly direct (1 hr. 40 mins.), or via Córdoba or Posadas, several daily. For best view on landing, sit on left side of aircraft. Flights back to **Buenos Aires** are very crowded. The Argentine side can be seen in one day from Buenos Aires: take 0650 or 0705 flight with Aerolíneas Argentinas (latter only Wed. and Sat.) from Bs.As. domestic airport. Bus to falls takes ½ hr., leaving according to plane arrivals. Aerolínea Federal Argentina (ex Alfa) flies to **Resistencia** on Tues., Wed. and Sun., with connecting flights to **Tucumán**, **Mendoza** and **Salta**.

**Rail Transport** from Buenos Aires is comfortable and cheap. There are sleeping and restaurant cars, good meals and wines. Passengers take a train from **Lacroze Station** in Buenos Aires to Posadas (for details, see under Posadas, **page 143**). There is a road, now paved, from Posadas to Puerto Iguazú; express bus to Iguazú meets train, 4½ hrs.

**Road Transport** From **Buenos Aires** N to Clorinda, then by new toll bridge to Asunción. Or crossing the Paraná at Santa Fe or Resistencia, taking the paved road to Posadas, and on to the falls. The more direct run via Zárate and Concordia is now completely paved. Direct buses take some 21 hours, leaving at 1130 (returns at 1200), with Singer (Av. Perito Moreno 366, T 2581) no a/c, and Buenos Aires-Posadas-Iguazú (returns at 1600 to Buenos Aires) Expreso Tigre-Iguazú, daily at 1500, offices at Plaza Once, Buenos Aires leaving from Retiro terminal (US$55). Expreso Iguazú offers discounts to students. To **Santiago del Estero**, Wed. and Sat. at 0130 (20 hours) with Cotal, gives student discount. To **Córdoba**, daily at 1130, via Posadas 26 hrs., US$40, with Singer or El Litoral. To **Rosario** daily except Thurs., 24 hrs. To **Posadas**, stopping at San Ignacio Miní, frequent, 5½ hrs., *expreso*, 7½ hrs. *servicio común*. To **Resistencia** daily 0900 and 2000, 11 hrs., US$22.50; change there for Bolivian border at Aguas Blancas/Bermejo, via Joaquín V. González and Orán. Alternative to direct bus to Buenos Aires (**see above**), take bus to Posadas and take train from there; slower, but more comfortable. Puerto Iguazú to **Eldorado**, 2 hrs., US$5 with Cotal.

---

## THE LAKE DISTRICT (9)

The **Lake District** contains a series of great lakes strung along the foot of the Andes from above 40° South to below 50° in the Los Glaciares National Park area. In the N the western ends of these lakes cut deeply into the mountains, their water lapping the forested skirts of some of the most spectacular snow-capped peaks in the world; their eastern ends are contained by the frontal moraines deposited there by the ancient glaciers which gouged out these huge lakes. The water is a deep blue, sometimes lashed into white froth by the region's high winds. The area is good for fishing, water-sports, walking, climbing and skiing.

Northern Patagonia has two railway lines. The more northerly runs westwards from Bahía Blanca to Neuquén and Zapala; the southern line runs from Bahía Blanca southwards across the Colorado to Viedma and then westwards through San Antonio Oeste to Bariloche and the Lake District. The roads along which buses ply, and airlines are mentioned in the text. See the Chilean chapter, section 6 **The Lake District**, for map and details of the system of lakes on the far side of the Andes. These can be visited (unpaved roads) through various passes. The Puyehue route is given on **page 157,** with an alternative in the Chilean section.

**National Park** Lago Nahuel Huapi with its surroundings, an area of 7,850 square km., was set aside in 1903 as a National Park. It contains the most diverse and spectacular natural phenomena: lakes, rivers, glaciers, waterfalls, torrents, rapids, valleys, forest, bare mountains and snow-clad peaks. Most of the area is covered with abundant vegetation, though it is notably more abundant on the Chilean side, which gets more rain. Many kinds of wild animals live in the region, but they are extremely shy and seldom glimpsed by the explorer. Bird life, on the other hand—particularly swans, geese and ducks—is seen at any time and everywhere in large flocks. In the far N of this region, near Zapala, these species and many others can be seen in their hundreds in the nature reserve of Laguna Blanca.

The outstanding feature of this National Park is the splendour of the lakes. The largest is *Lago Nahuel Huapi*, 531 square km. and 460 metres deep in places. It is 767 metres above sea level, in full view of the snow-covered peaks of the Cordillera and of the forests covering the lower slopes. Towering over the scene is Cerro Tronador. Some 96 km. long, and not more than 12 km. wide, the lake is very irregular in shape; long arms of water, or *brazos*, reminiscent of the Norwegian fjords, stretch far into the land. There are many islands: the largest is *Isla Victoria*, on which stands the forest research station where new species of vegetation are acclimatized. The Zoological Board is adding to the indigenous fauna; the trout and salmon of the lakes, for instance, have been introduced from abroad. Lago Nahuel Huapi is drained eastwards by the Río Limay; below its junction with the Río Neuquén it becomes the Río Negro. The Limay has good trout fishing but the rivers farther N—the Quilquihue, Malleu, Chimehuín, Collón-Curá, Hermoso, Meliquina and Caleufú—are much less fished. They are all in the neighbourhood of San Martín de los Andes (**see page 164**).

A mere sand bar in one of the northern *brazos* separates Lago Nahuel Huapi from Lago Correntoso, which is quite close to Lago Espejo. Lago Traful, a short distance to the NE, can be reached by a road which follows the Río Limay through the Valle Encantado, with its fantastic rock formations. S of Nahuel Huapi there are other lakes: the three main ones are Mascardi, Guillelmo, and Gutiérrez. On the shore of Lago Gutiérrez, in a grotto, is the Virgen de las Nieves (Virgin of the Snows). There is a road to these lakes from Bariloche.

**Fishing** The lakes are full of fish, and the best time for fishing is at the beginning of the season, that is, in November and December (the season runs from early November to the end of March). Among the best are: Lagos Traful, Gutiérrez, Mascardi, Futalaufquen (in Los Alerces National Park), Meliquina, Falkner, Villarino, Nuevo, Lacar, Lolog, Curruhué, Chico, Huechulafquen, Paimún, Epulafquen, Tromen (all in Lanín National Park), and, in the far N, Quillén. In the far S, the fishing in Lago Argentino is also good. **NB** fishing anywhere in Argentina requires a permit. Do not take fishing equipment out of season: it will only arouse suspicion.

**Bariloche** (San Carlos de), on the southern shore of Lago Nahuel Huapi, founded 1898, is the best centre for exploring the National Park. Renowned for its chocolate industry, it is a Swiss-looking town of steep streets, its wooden chalets perched upon a glacial moraine at the foot of Cerro Otto. To the S lie the heights of the Ventana and the Cerro Colorado (2,135 metres). The place is full of hotels and cheap *hosterías*. The cathedral, built in 1946, dominates the town; interior unfinished. There is a belvedere at the top of Cerro Otto with wide views of lake and mountain. The main road into Bariloche from the E is paved and in good condition. Unhappily, because of its phenomenal growth, the town has become noisy and overcrowded, and the best time to visit it is out of season either in the spring or autumn (the forest is particularly beautiful around May). The 24 km. road to Llao-Llao (bus No. 20, ¾ hr.) is ribbon-developed, except near Cerro Catedral. Population, over 70,000. Lido swimming pool on the lake shore is beautifully sited but somewhat run down.

**Hotels** The most complete listing with map is published by the Oficina Municipal de Turismo, which you are advised to consult if you arrive in the high season without a reservation. It also has booking service at Florida 520 (Galería), room 116, Buenos Aires. Out of season, prices are most reasonable, in all ranges, but in season everything is very expensive. Most hotels outside the town include half-board, and those in the town include breakfast. Hotels with lake views normally charge US$3-4 extra, per room per day, for the view in high season; we give lake-view high-season prices where applicable. The best outside town are: *Huemul* (road to Llao-Llao, 1.5 km.); *Apart-hotel Casablanca* (same road, 23.5 km.), good, on a peninsula between Lagos Nahuel Huapi and Moreno, both L. Also at Llao-Llao, 24 km. from Bariloche, are *Tunquelén*, L, and *Hostería Aunancay*, L, including 2 meals, friendly and delightful setting. *La Caleta*, Km. 1.9 on Llao-Llao road, bungalows run by Neil Callwood, D for an apartment sleeping 4, shower, open fire, excellent value, self-catering, rec., T 25650. *Residencial Matterhorn*, Swiss-run, Pasaje Gutiérrez 1122, C, rec., good breakfast. Out of town (many birds to see) is *Hostería del Viejo Molino*, Av. Bustillo km. 6.4, C, buses to town, T 22411, friendly, rec.

In the town are the following: *Edelweiss*, Av. San Martín 232, L, 5-star, modern, spotless, excellent food, enclosed pool, highly rec.; *Panamericano*, San Martín 536, L, 5-star, heated swimming pool; *Bariloche Sky*, San Martín 352, L, 4-star, T 311-3235, Telex 18273, good; *Interlaken*, V.A. O'Connor 383, L, lake view, 4-star; *Tres Reyes*, 12 de Octubre 135 T 26121, L, lake view. First class: on Pasaje Libertad (all within a block of Civic Centre and Don Olto buses): *Residencial Tirol*, No. 175, C, clean, friendly, good; *Millaray*, No. 195, D, good, shower, closed off season; *Ayelén*, No. 157, T 23611, C, 3-star, comfortable, restaurant, rec.;

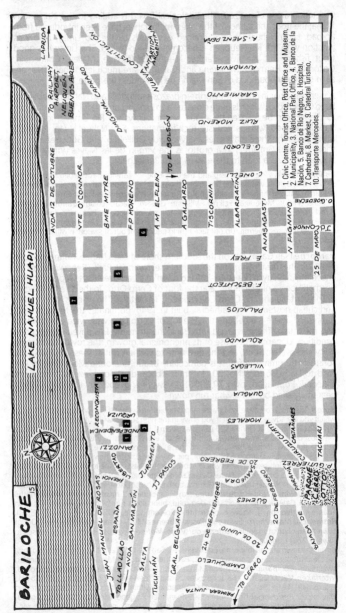

**BARILOCHE** 15

LAKE NAHUEL HUAPI

1. Civic Centre, Tourist Office, Post Office and Museum.
2. Municipality. 3. National Park Office. 4. Banco de la Nación. 5. Banco de Río Negro. 6. Hospital.
7. Cathedral. 8. Market. 9. Catedral Turismo.
10. Transporte Mercedes.

next door is *Concorde*, No. 131, 4-star, B, parking; next door again is *Ideal*, above *Salón de té*, D. *Residencial El Ciervo Rojo*, Elflein 115, B, 2-star, very pleasant; *Austral*, San Martín 425, B, 2-star, restaurant, small rooms; *Los Pinos*, 20 de Febrero 640, C, clean, spacious rooms, English spoken, central heating, rec.; *King's Hotel*, Moreno 136, very nice, clean, warm, B, with bath (D off-season); *La Pastorella*, Belgrano 127, T 24656, B, with bath and breakfast, English and French-spoken, central, rec.; *Venezia*, on Morales, C, rec.; *Nevada*, Rolando 250, B with shower, and heating, breakfast included, nice rooms; *Residencial Premier*, Rolando 263, 1/2 block from main street, C inc. breakfast, modern, comfortable, clean, hot showers, English and German spoken, rec.; *La Negra*, Apartado Postal 21, T 25720, C, original wooden house with view of lake, good food and service, rec., especially for motorcyclists; *Colonial*, Quaglia 281, C, clean, helpful, lake views; *Residencial Piuké*, Beschtedt 136, D inc. breakfast (A in skiing season), clean, friendly, rec.; opposite is *Residencial Sur*, Beschtedt 101, T 22677, excellent value, C with bath and breakfast, gives 10% discount to ISYC and youth card holders; *Monte Grande*, 25 de Mayo 1544, T 22159, with bath, heating, breakfast room, camping, parking, economical prices, Ruca Malen travel agency here; *Residencia Nikola*, Elflein 49, T 22500, D, comfortable, clean, restaurant gives 10% discount to ISYC and youth card holders; *Victoria*, E p.p., shared rooms Mitre 815, friendly, information service helpful.

Others: *Hostal Las Moiras*, Reconquista, D, central but quiet, hot shower, comfortable; *El Mirador*, Moreno 652-76, E, hot water, eccentric owner speaks German, very pleasant, with lake views, rec.; *Kent*, D, near Club Andino on 20 de Febrero, new, modern. Also new is *Residencial Wikter*, D, Güemes 506; *Hostería El Radal*, 24 de Septiembre 46, D, clean, friendly; *Punta Nevada*, Onelli 347, D, rec.; *Residencial Adquintue*, V.A. O'Connor 776, D, clean and comfortable; *Residencial El Ñire* (T 2-3041), V.A. O'Connor 710, corner J. O'Connor, D, hot showers, clean, very pleasant, prefers longer-stay visitors, highly rec. *Residencial Rosán* (Sra. Arco), E, strongly rec., Güemes 691, T 23109, English and German spoken, cooking facilities, clean, helpful. Also rec., *Residencial Güemes* on street of same name (No. 715), T 24785, D with breakfast, helpful; *Hostería Maribor*, Angel Gallardo 950, Sra. Adriana, bath, breakfast extra, laundry, excursions, rec.; and *pensión* of Sra. Carlota Baumann, Av. de los Pioneros 860 (T 24502), follow 20 de Febrero uphill for 10-15 minutes, E p.p., kitchen, bath, hot water, laundry service, friendly, Sra. Baumann speaks English and German. *Residencial Alpina*, Discornia 90, D, clean, friendly, good value. *No Me Olvides*, Salta 188, T 22104, F p.p., family run, shared rooms, excellent food, friendly, rec. Many private homes also offer accommodation; the tourist office keeps a list. Among those rec. are: Salta 571, E, heating; *Casa Diego*, Elflein 163, T 22556, E, doubles only, clean; *Pire-Cuyen*, Anasagasti 840, E, clean, doubles only; Frey 635, E, clean, friendly, motorcycle parking; Anasagasti 348, E, friendly; Elouisa Lamuniere, 24 de Septiembre 71, E, homely, helpful. For longer stays try private house at Elflein 507 (Sra. Heidi Landolf). Apartments and chalets—may also be rented—prices vary enormously according to the season.

**Youth Hostels** *Los Andes*, F.P. Moreno 594, T 22222 (not IYHA affiliated), F p.p., clean, friendly; *Alaska*, on the road to Llao-Llao, Km 7.5 (buses 10, 20, 21, get off at La Florida), IYHA-affiliated, F p.p., good atmosphere, pleasant location, both offer 10% discount to ISYC and youth card holders.

**Camping** List of sites from Tourist Office. Three sites on road to Llao-Llao: *La Selva Negra*, Km. 2.9, not rec., very unfriendly; *El Yeti*, Km. 5.6, good, rec.; *Petunia*, Km. 14.9, rec. Note that in Bariloche the only type of camping gas on sale fits only Argentine-made stoves (which can be bought for US$10) and not the small, international style stoves.

**Restaurants** *Casita Suiza*, Quaglia 342, excellent and rec. *La Marmita*, Mitre, small, cosy, excellent, mixed fondues particularly rec.; *La Andina*, Elflein 95, specializes in inexpensive but good "fast food", rec.; *Caza Mayor*, Quaglia and Elflein, game and fish, good but expensive; *Níkola*, Elflein 49, very good value; *Kandahar*, 20 de Febrero 698, T 24702, excellent, run by Argentine ski champion Marta Peirono de Barber; *Parrilla 1810*, Elflein 167, T 23922, good meat; *Parrilla La Vizcacha*, Rolando 279, good value, rec.; *Parrilla Los Pioneros*, Quaglia 259, pleasant, historical photographs of Bariloche; *El Barrilito*, Moreno 180, good and reasonable; *Asociación Española*, Rolando 142, fine paellas; *Lennon*, Palacios 188, small, good food, reasonably priced, English spoken; *Mangiare*, pizzas and other Italian, Palacios 86; *La Marmotte*, Villegas 270, Alpine-style, excellent food. Good pastries and hot chocolate at *Hola Nicolás*, Moreno 66 y Urquiza (see the graffiti-graven tables). *El Jabalí*, Av. San Martín, specialises in wild boar, interesting fish buffet. *Jauja*, Moreno 220, good local dishes; *Canguros*, Palacios 181, excellent steaks, try the hot wine (ask, not on menu) very friendly, rec. *El Ahumado*, Palacios, good meat and fish; *Le Chalet*, Moreno 23, Swiss and local specialities, excellent; *La Andinita*, Mitre 56, rec., reasonable, friendly; *Crocodillo*, Mitre 5, big choice of good pizzas, good value; *Pizzaiola*, Pagano 275, good pizzeria; *La Nueva Estancia*, Elflein 401, good meat and trout, live entertainment but only sometimes. *La Alpina Confitería*, Moreno 98, open fire, good food, reasonably priced, cheese fondue rec., very popular. Superb coffee and cakes at *Chocolate Casero del Turista* at Mitre 239, but nowhere to sit. *T-Bar Café*, Mitre 201, good hot chocolate. *Ermitage*, tea rooms, on road to Llao-Llao at Km. 18, owner speaks Slovenian. *Saloom*, Mitre 208, restaurant with video films, open 24 hours, as are others on Mitre; *Friends*, San Martín, good sandwiches, gateaux, quick meals. Good breakfasts at *Bar y Leche*, on Quaglia. *Crêperie Bretonne*, nr. Civic Centre, cheap and very good. Many good delicatessens in the area with take-away food, including chicken pizzas and cheeses, for picnics.

On Av. Bustillo (the road to Llao-Llao), Km. 10, is *La Posta del Río*, reasonable, *Dirty Dick's Pub*, Km. 5 and *La Glorieta*, Av. Bustillo, Km. 3.8, good.

**Best Buys** Woollen goods, e.g. at *Arbol* on Mitre, or *Manos del Uruguay*, Mitre 339. The products of the local chocolate industry are excellent: *Fábrica de Chocolate Cerro León* on Av. 12 de Octubre, near railway station. You can watch chocolates being made at *Turista*, San Martín 252. Very good chocolate at *Gallardo* and at Abuela Goye, Albarracín 157. Local wines are also good. (be sure to get the 10% discount). Try "Papas de Bariloche", the local chocolate speciality. Also chocolates at *Benroth*, Beschtedt 569, above Gallardo and at Abuela Goye, Albarracín 157. Local wines are also good. Handicraft shops all along San Martín; some will change money. Artesanía cooperative on Moreno y Rolando, rec.
**Bookshop** *Cultura*, Elflein 78, has a good range of technical books, some in English.

**Car Hire** Hertz, Avis, and A1 International, at airport and in town (latter at Bartolomé Mitre 26, T 24869, 22038); no flat rates. *Chapis Car*, Libertad 120, and *Carro's SACI*, Mitre 26, T 24826 (out of season open Mon.-Fri., a.m. only) are both said to be cheaper. To enter Chile a permit is necessary, US$50, allow 48 hrs.

**Car mechanic** Auguen SA, V.A. O'Connor 1068, fast, reasonable, highly rec.

**Bicycles** may be hired beside the lake in high season. Mopeds from Vertigo Rental, San Martín 594, US$3.50 per hour.

**Cinemas** Arrayanes, Moreno 39; Coliseo, Mitre 281; Ciné Club, Tues. 2115 only, Biblioteca Sarmiento in the Centro Cívico.

**Museums** The **Museo de La Patagonia** in the Civic Centre, has a nice collection of stuffed animals, also well worth seeing for collection of Indian artefacts, houses, open 1000-1200, 1400-1900 Tues.-Fri., 1000-1300 Sat. US$0.50; the attached **Biblioteca Sarmiento** is open Mon.-Fri., 1100-2200. The clock in the Civic Centre has four figures which rotate at noon; photos with St. Bernard dogs (inc. brandy keg) may be taken in the Civic Centre square and on 12 de Octubre above the Lido.

**Exchange** There are several banks and exchange shops, which buy and sell virtually all European and South American currencies, besides US dollars; Sat. is a bad day. Exchange houses cash cheques for 5-10%. *Casa Piano*, B. Mitre 131, T 23733, rec., open 0900-1300 and 1600-2000 and Sat. a.m. (charges US$2 on all cheques below US$100, 2% over US$100, changes travellers' cheques into US$ cash 2% commission). *Sudamérica*, Quaglia 238, good rates; *Kiosko Anri*, Mitre 339 (rear of Galería Arrayanes), US$ cheques and Chilean pesos accepted, good rates, highly rec. Good exchange rates at *Kiwanis* (boot rental), Mitre 210. The *American Express*, B. Mitre 139, sends you across the street to the **Banco Provincia** to buy travellers' cheques. Only **Banco Alas**, F.P. Moreno 175, accepts Visa. Beware forged Argentine banknotes.

**Laundry** Prices are generally 60% higher than elsewhere in Argentina. *Lavamatic*, Villegas 258, English manager, friendly, opp. cathedral, open till 2230 Mon.-Sat., 2100 Sun. US$5 a load. Laundromats on Palacios, on San Martín, and on Villegas nr. Mitre.

**Chilean Consulate** Villegas, near Mitre, friendly, helpful.

**Post Office** Centro Cívico (same building as tourist office).

**Immigration Office** Next to *Hostería Tirol*, Libertad 175.

**Clinic** Cruz Azul, Capraro 1216.

**Tourist Office** Oficina Municipal de Turismo in Centro Cívico, open Mon.-Fri., (ski season) 0800-2000, Sat. 0900-1900 daily at those times in summer but check times out of season (April, October-November) when closed at weekends. Has details of hikes and campsites in the area. Also has the address of a motorcycle hire company—a good way of getting around the National Park. National Park information (scanty) at San Martín 24, open 0800-2000.

Information also from Sociedad Profesional de Guías de Turismo, Casilla de Correo 51, 8400 S.C. de Bariloche (President: Ama Petroff).

**Tourist Agencies**   Tour buses pick you up from your hotel. *Patagonia Travel*, Mitre 150 (Telex 80746 Patra), efficient, rec., English spoken; their guide Daniel is a good naturalist. *Catedral Turismo*, Mitre 399, T 25443/5, runs boats to Chile for Peulla-Puerto Montt trip (10% discount for ISIC and youth card holders on lake crossing to Chile and local excursions); *Alunco Turismo*, groups first, friendly. *Transport Mercedes; Turisur*, Quaglia 227, T 26109, organizes trips on lake and on land (10% discount for ISIC and youth card holders). *Lake Travel Service*, Moreno 126, 3rd floor, efficient, English spoken. *Polvani Tours*, Quaglia 268 (T 23286), see Hans Schulz (speaks Spanish, German and English) to arrange horse trekking at the Estancia Nahuel Huapí, run by Carol Jones (from US$24 for 1/2 day to US$75 overnight incl. meals and gear); both the agency and the treks rec. Arrange trekking with Sr. Daniel José Gorgone, San Martín 127, DT 0706, T 26181. *Tur Acción*, Quaglia 219, T 22276, has been recommended for "adventure" tours (10% discount for ISIC and youth card holders, 5% on ski packages).

**Air Services**   Airport, 11 km. from town. Many flights to **Buenos Aires**. Aerolíneas Argentinas, at least 2 a day, no night flight. Also Austral, 25% cheaper with an extra US$35 reduction for cash, and Cata, LADE to **Trelew**, US$70. Fri. 1115, Fri. 1530 and to **Comodoro Rivadavia** Wed., and Fri. LADE to **Río Gallegos**, Fri., US$70, usually booked weeks in advance in season; continues to **Calafate**. Flights, 5 times a week, with Aerolíneas and LADE to **Esquel**. (It is reported that it is difficult to obtain LADE flights from Bariloche now, especially the cheaper night flights to Buenos Aires.) TAN flies to **Puerto Montt** (Chile), twice a week, summer only, US$36. Small tax at airport on leaving. Taxi to or from airport, US$12; bus US$2.75 from Austral or Aerolíneas office. Turismo Catedral, Mitre 399, has US$1.50 airport bus service into town.

**Rail Services**   The railway station is 5 km. E of centre (booking office closed 1200-1500 weekdays, Sat. p.m. and all Sun.), reached by local buses 70 and 71 (US$0.25). Information from San Martín 127 in centre; tickets also available from *Hotel Pagano y Pamozzi*, 3 blocks from Centro Cívico. Train leaves **Buenos Aires**, Constitución, Sun. (with car transporter), and Wed., 2200, 36 hrs. (not much heat); returns Tues., and Fri., 2020, via **Bahía Blanca** (about 24 hrs. Bariloche-Bahía Blanca). Fares US$70 sleeper, US$65 Pullman, US$52 first, US$45 tourist class. Trip can be extremely dusty, take a wet towel in a plastic bag for face and hands. Scenery only interesting between Bariloche and Jacobacci (4½ hrs.), where you catch the train to **Esquel**; food on board reasonable (US$7.50 for 3 courses), but not always available and water sometimes runs out.

**Road Services**   Paved road from Buenos Aires via Neuquén, 1,600 km. Chevallier, **Buenos Aires** to Bariloche, daily, 22½ hrs., US$90. Also La Estrella daily, US$80, and El Valle via Neuquén, US$80. For **Mar del Plata**, take Buenos Aires bus and change at Bahía Blanca or Tres Arroyos (e.g. La Estrella, 1500, arrive Tres Arroyos 0555, US$60). Bus to **Mendoza**, TAC (San Martín) 283), Tues., Thurs. and Sat., US$70, 22 hrs., on a paved road via Zapala, Buta Ranquil and San Rafael. Bus **Córdoba**-Bariloche, TUS, 25 hrs., US$70, Mon., Wed., Fri., and Sun. at 1000. Buses to **El Bolsón** (US$7 3½ hrs.) and **Esquel** (US$14.50 with Don Otto-San Martín 283, at *Visión Turismo*—or Mercedes) exc. Sun., with a 4 times weekly extension on paved road to Comodoro Rivadavia, US$60 (Don Otto). To **Puerto Madryn**, 24 hrs. via Esquel and Trelew. To Jacobacci (for Esquel train) only one bus a day, arrives after train has left. To San Martín de los Andes, 0800, US$15, 4½ hrs. Buses also to **Neuquén** (550 km.) US$18 by Transportes Mercedes on Bartolomé Mitre or daily with La Estrella, Palacios 246 at 1415, 6½ hrs. (a dull journey). (No direct bus to Río Gallegos; you have to spend a night in Comodoro Rivadavia en route.) To **Santiago** (Chile), Tues., Fri. and Sun., 24 hours with tea and breakfast served en route. To **Puerto Montt**, see the route to Chile from Bariloche, page 157.

**Activities**   Apart from sailing and boating, there are golf, mountaineering, walking, birdwatching, skiing, and fishing (for which you need a permit). Racquet Club, Ruta Llao-Llao, Km. 13.5, tennis and squash, snack bar. Before going hiking you are recommended to buy moisturizing creams for exposed skin areas and lips. Excellent trout fishing Nov.-March; boat hire arranged with tackle shops. Horseflies (*tábanos*) frequent the lake shores and lower areas in summer; lemon juice is good for keeping them away, but can cause skin irritation. For horse riding, see above under Tourist Agencies.

**Mountain Climbing**   In the area there is something for every kind of mountaineer. National Park mountain guides are available but can be expensive. Book: *Excursiones, Andinismo y Refugios de Montaña en Bariloche*, by Tonek Arko, available in local shops, US$2, or from the author at Güemes 691. In treks to *refugios* remember to add costs of ski lifts, buses, food at *refugio* and lodging (in Club Andino *refugios*: US$3 per night, plus US$1 for cooking, or US$1 for breakfast, US$2 for lunch, US$3 for dinner). Information from Club Andino Bariloche, 20 de Febrero 30, open 0900-1200 and 1500-2000 Mon.-Fri. and Sat. 0900-1200. The Club arranges for guides; ask for Sr. Ricardo, the secretary, who organizes easy weekend climbs and walks with friendly visitors. It also provides maps and details of all campsites, hotels and mountain lodges. The climbing may mean a ride on horseback or a skilled ascent of the slopes of Cerro Tronador which looms over the area. The Government has built convenient rest lodges at from 1,000 to 2,000 metres on the mountains. Firing, light and food are provided at these points. Note that at higher levels, winter snow storms can begin as early as April, making climbing dangerous.

**Swimming** in the larger lakes such as Nahuel Huapi and Huechulafquen is not recommended, for the water is cold. But swimming in smaller lakes such as Lolog, Lacar, Curruhué Chico, Hermoso, Meliquina, Espejo, Hess and Fonck is very pleasant and the water—especially where the bottom shelves to a shingly beach—can be positively warm.

**Skiing** There is good skiing during the winter season (July to early October), supervised by the Club Andino Bariloche. It is best organized with a tour company, through whom you can secure discounts as part of an inclusive deal. (Skiing is cheaper, however, at smaller resorts, such as Esquel, though more expensive at San Martín de los Andes.) The favourite skiing slopes are on Cerro Catedral, and a new ski-lift is to be built higher up, to permit a longer skiing season. (Regular bus service with seasonal timetable from Mercedes bus company on Mitre 161, US$3 return.) There are a cable car (US$7 single, 9 return) and a chair lift (US$22.50 full day, 17.50 afternoon only) from the foot of Cerro Catedral to points high on the ridge. Red and yellow markers painted on the rock mark a trail from the top, which leads to Refugio Frey (well equipped, blankets, meals, accommodation E) on the edge of a small mountain lake (allow 6 hours; one can return through the forest to the ski complex the next day and take a bus back to Bariloche). The seasonal cable car, with a chair lift from its upper terminus, takes one higher than the main (2-stage) chair lift. Bus tours from Bariloche to the foot of Cerro Catedral give time for less than 2 hours on top of the mountain. Entrance to the Cerro Catedral ski slopes, below the snowline, is US$ 0.40. The only disadvantage at Bariloche is that the snow is unreliable except at the top. There are other skiing slopes 5 km. out of Bariloche, on Cerro Otto (cable car, US$8 p.p.; open 0900-1900 Jan., Feb., July, August, and 1400-1800 rest of year; station at foot reached by bus No. 50 "Teleférico", 15 mins., US$1, entry to revolving restaurant at top, US$3.50), which can be reached in 2-3 hours' walk from the town; take the paved Av. de los Pioneros, then switch to the signed dirt track 1 km. out of Bariloche (splendid views), or in a minibus which goes every ½ hour from a car park near the National Park headquarters (closed public holidays), between 1400 and 1600, US$7 round trip (local bus US$2.10 return); at Piedras Blancas (bus US$7 return); also on López (try a car trip, rough road, US$14 for a tour, 1400-1830), Dormilón and La Ventana. Ski hire US$5-9 a day, depending on quality, dearer at Cerro Catedral than in town. Ski clothes can also be rented by the day, at US$1-2 per item, from Kiwanis sport stores in Bariloche or El Iglú, Galería Arrayanes II, Rolando 244. **N.B.** Summer skiing on grass has been organized 20 km. S of Bariloche, on Route 258 to El Bolsón.

**Excursions** There are numerous excursions: most travel agencies charge the same price. It is best to buy tours on the spot rather than in advance, although they get very booked up in season. Whole-day trip to Lagos Gutiérrez, Mascardi, Hess, the Cascada Los Alerces and Cerro Tronador (3,554 metres) leaves at 0800, US$28, and involves 1 hr. walk to the Black Glacier, interesting but too much time spent on the bus. Turismo Llao-Llao organizes the following: 8-hour excursion to Río Limay, Valle Encantado, Lago Traful, Lago Correntoso, Villa La Angostura, returning via Paso Coihue. Catedral and Turisur have a 9-hour excursion, leaving at 0900 (afternoon also Dec.-March), to Puerto Pañuelo, sailing down to Puerto Blest and continuing by bus to Puerto Alegre and again by launch to Puerto Frías (US$19.50). A visit to the Cascada de los Cántaros is made. Several 12-hour excursions to San Martín de los Andes, US$35, through 2 national parks, passing 7 lakes, returning via Paso de Córdoba and the Valle Encantado.

The area around the resort of Llao Llao offers beautiful scenery for walking: you can choose between the 15 km. Circuito Chico and the 17 km. "motor tour" route back to Bariloche. At Km. 17.7 on the road to Llao Llao there is a chairlift to Cerro Campanario (0900-1200, 1400-1800 daily, US$7), from the top of which there are fine views of Isla Victoria and Puerto Pañuelo. At Km. 18.3 a turning to the left leads to Colonia Suiza and Punto Panorámico, and then along Lago Perito Moreno to Puerto Pañuelo (16 km.).

A two-day walk can be made from Pampa Linda over Paso de los Nubes to Laguna Frías and Puerto Frías. To reach Pampa Linda take the Mercedes bus to Villa Mascardi and then hitch the remaining 50 km. Note that the road to Pampa Linda has a one-way system: up only before 1400, down only after. Register at the Ranger station at Pampa Linda and ask their advice about conditions. The route is not always well marked, especially one place early on where the track branches after crossing a river by a series of temporary footbridges. The right hand track should *not* be attempted by inexperienced walkers. The left hand track, once a road, leads one west up a spur to the edge of the glacier with a well appointed hut (3-4 hours journey). This route should not be attempted if there is snow on the Pass (normally passable only between Dec. and Feb.).

From Pampa Linda ranger post you can also walk past the glacier on Cerro Tronador (*refugio*) to Peulla in Chile (accommodation at one expensive hotel, A in high season, one *residencial* and a private house) 2½ days; details in *Backpacking in Chile and Argentina* (Bradt Publications). Turismo Catedral has 11-12 hr. excursion, US$25, crossing Lago Todos los Santos into Chile taking in Peulla (lunch at hotel, US$6.50) and the Petrohué falls. Alun-Co Turismo, Mitre 22, 2nd floor, operates a rubber raft excursion mid-Nov. until mid-April to Confluencia, leaves Bariloche at 1000 up Río Limay, stopping for lunch at Valle Encantado, returns to Bariloche at 1900, US$22. A half-day excursion is possible taking a bus to Virgen de las Nieves, walking 2 km. to arrive at beautiful Lago Gutiérrez; walk along lake shore to the road from El Bolsón and walk back to Bariloche (about 4 hrs.).

A recommended one-day trip by car is Bariloche-Llao Llao-Bahía-Colonia Suiza-Cerro Catedral-Bariloche; the reverse direction misses the sunsets and afternoon views from the higher roads, which are negotiable in winter (even snow-covered). If one is staying only 1-2 days in the area the best excursions are to Cerro Tronador the 1st day, and on the 2nd to Cerro Catedral in the morning and Isla Victoria in the afternoon (possible only Dec.-March when there are afternoon departures for the island). Camping facilities are good. Good walks to Lago Correntoso (4 km.) and Quetrihué Peninsula (15 km. to forest of Arrayanes). Also to the *refugio Italia* at Laguna Negra (16 km. trail) and to Cerro López (3 hrs., with a *refugio* after 2); in both cases take Colonia Suiza bus and for the former alight at SAC, for the latter at Picada. For *refugio Italia* allow 6 hrs. up (first 4 quite gentle, last 2 steep, beside 2 waterfalls), 4 hrs return. The *refugio* is open all year, supposedly manned during season, but take food and sleeping bags. You can continue from this *refugio* to others for a 3-5 day hike; details from Club Andino.

A half-day excursion (1300-1830) may be taken from Bariloche to Puerto Pañuelo, then by boat to Isla Victoria. The full-day excursion (0900-1830, or 1300 till 2000 in season) at US$25 includes the Arrayanes forest on the Quetrihue peninsula further N. and 3 hours on Isla Victoria, picnic lunch advised. Half-day excursions to Isla Victoria are available. Some boats going to Arrayanes call first at Isla Victoria, early enough to avoid boat-loads of tourists. These boats carry the names of Paraná river provinces—Corrientes, Misiones, Santa Fe—and they have no open deck. For open decks try the *Modesta Victoria* or the *Don Luis*. (Turisur have 4 catamarans with a bar and cafeteria.) For a cheaper excursion take Transporte 3 de Mayo bus marked Estación Llao-Llao from Moreno and Rolando at 0900 or 0930 (Rte 6091) for 1030 dep. from Puerto Pañuelo (1130 or 1200 for 1300 dep.) to go to Isla Victoria and Arrayanes by boat (US$8). From Puerto Pañuelo, opposite the *Hotel Llao-Llao*, catamarans also leave for Puerto Blest. All boats are very crowded in season, but operators have to provide seating for all passengers. The Arrayanes forest can also be visited by walking 12 km. from Villa la Angostura (**see next page**).

**Roads** There are 500 km. of highways (mostly unpaved) running through the park. The old road to El Bolsón and Esquel (a new, faster, but less interesting road is being built between Bariloche and Esquel) is paved for the first 30 km., then narrow, steep and with many S bends between Villa Mascardi and El Bolsón, but goes past the beautiful lakes of Gutiérrez, Mascardi and Guillelmo and over fine mountain passes.

**The Route to Chile from Bariloche** The preferred route is over Puyehue pass, being 50% cheaper than via the lakes, on a good broad highway which is paved on the Chilean side up to Termas de Puyehue, and almost entirely paved on the Argentine side. Road from Bariloche goes around east end of Lake Nahuel Huapi, then follows north side of lake through resort town of Villa La Angostura to junction with "Ruta de Siete Lagos" for San Martín at Km. 94, Argentine customs at Km. 109 and pass at Km. 125 at elevation of 1,280 metres. (About 22 km. from the Argentine customs is Camping Correntoso; 4 km. further is Camping El Cruce, ACA, and another 2 km. brings you to Camping Osa Mayor, ACA.) Chilean customs at Km. 146 in middle of a forest. The frontier is closed at night. *Hotel Termas de Puyehue* is at Km. 168. Possible to camp nearby, but take own food as restaurant is expensive. Very pleasant *Motel Ñilque* on Lake Puyehue (Chile) is at Km. 174. A six-hour drive.

The alternative is to go via the lakes. The route is Bariloche to Llao-Llao by road, Llao-Llao to Puerto Blest by boat (2½ hrs.), Puerto Blest to Puerto Frías (20 mins. by boat), then 1½ hrs. by road to Peulla. Leave for Petrohué in the afternoon by boat (2½ hrs.), cross Lago Todos Los Santos, passing the Osorno volcano, then by bus to Puerto Montt. This route is not rec. in wet or foggy weather.

Several bus companies run services from Bariloche to Puerto Montt, Osorno and Valdivia, via the Puyehue pass: there is at least one bus every day from Argentine side. The majority go via Osorno (6 hrs.) and fares range from US$18-25 (US$35 for a 1-day excursion inc. city tour and Termas de Puyehue); it is no cheaper to go to Osorno and buy a separate ticket from there to Puerto Montt. Companies include Bus Norte, San Martín 283, T. Lanin (not rec.), Moreno 138, Mercedes (US$29), Tas Choapa (at Turismo Algarrobal, San Martín 459, T 22774), and Cruz del Sur. Sit on left side for best views. You can buy a ticket to the Chilean border, then another to Puerto Montt, or pay in stages in Chile, but there is little advantage in doing this. Turismo Catedral operates a 12-hour crossing to Puerto Montt, via the lake with lunch at Peulla, about US$36 (1 Sept-31 March, take own food, buy ticket day in advance, departs 0700) and a two-day crossing all year round with overnight stop in Puella. All other agencies sell excursions to Puerto Frías using a Mercedes bus to Puerto Pañuelo, a Turisur boat to Puerto Blest and share a bus and boat to Puerto Frías with excursion groups going on to Chile. Request information at Turismo Catedral which owns the exclusive rights to the excursion via the lakes, using their own boats and bus from Puerto Pañuelo to Puerto Frías (Andina del Sud operates with them on the Chilean side). The most satisfactory way of doing the trip full-circle is by car from Bariloche, going first via Puyehue to Puerto Montt, returning via Tromen Pass (see the Villarrica volcano, good road), then Junín and San Martín de los Andes. No cars taken on ferry on Lago Todos Los Santos. There are daily boats from Puerto Pañuelo to Puerto Blest, with daily through connections by boat and bus to Puerto Montt.

**N.B.** You are strongly advised to get rid of all your australes before leaving Argentina; it may be useful to have some Chilean pesos before you cross into Chile from Bariloche. The Argentine and Chilean border posts are open every day; the launches (and hence the connecting buses) on the lakes servicing the direct route via Puerto Blest to Puerto Montt generally do not operate at weekends; check. There is an absolute ban in Chile on importing any fresh food—meat, cheese, fruit—from Argentina. Bariloche Tourist Office may not be up to date on lake crossings to Puerto Montt, check details at travel agencies, particularly if travelling to meet connections.

Further information on border crossings in the Lake District, and details of accommodation in Peulla will be found in Chile, section 6. Older travellers are advised not to attempt the Bariloche-Puerto Montt trip all in one day; parts of road on the Argentine side of the Puyehue route are being rebuilt, and the lake route is long and tiring.

**N.B.** Obtain maps and information about the district in Buenos Aires at the National Park Tourist Office at Santa Fe 690, or at the provincial offices (addresses given on **page 70**); it is hard to obtain these in the provinces themselves. Park wardens are also useful sources of information.

**Villa La Angostura** is a picturesque town (pop. 3,000) 90 km. NW of Bariloche on Lago Correntoso. It can be reached by excursion bus (day trip; try Turismo Llao-Llao, 8 hrs.) or local bus (at 1900 daily, returning 0730, Transporte Mercedes, US$7) which requires staying overnight; hotels a little dearer than Bariloche. The port, 3 km. from town, is spectacular in summer. 12 km. S of the port at the S end of the Quetrihue Peninsula is **The Arrayanes Forest**, containing 300 year old specimens of the rare Arrayan tree. It is best to return to Bariloche if going on to Osorno (Chile): otherwise you have to pay twice the fare to Osorno from Bariloche and arrange for the bus company to pick you up at La Angostura. Daily bus at 1700 to San Martín de los Andes.

**Hotels** *Correntoso*, A; has a chalet next door, C for 2 bedrooms, shared use of kitchen and sitting room, luxurious. Cheaper are *La Cabañita* (Belvedere s/n)and *Don Pedro* (El Cruce), both D. Ask in the tourist office, opposite ACA, for lodgings in private houses, cheaper than hotels. *Hotel Ruca Malen*, 24 km. N on lake shore, under new management; *Hotel Pichi Trafal*, 53 km. N.

**Camping** *El Cruce*, ACA Osa Mayor (2 km. along Bariloche road, pleasant, open late Dec. to mid-May), Autocamping San Martin, Municipal Lago Correntoso.

**Travel Agent** *Turismo Cerro Bayo*, Av. Arrayanes s/n, of. 5, T (0944) 94401/94412, 10% discount for ISIC and youth card holders on ski packages, trekking, rafting, lake and adventure tours.

Excellent *Hostería Los Peraltoches* on Lago Gutiérrez, 116 km. from Bariloche, A with meals; magnificent views, English spoken, very homelike, open Nov.-March and June-Aug.

*Río Villegas*, about 80 km. S of Bariloche on the road to El Bolsón, is very beautiful. Cheap but pleasant *hostería* just outside the gates of the National Park, by the river.

**El Bolsón** is 130 km. S of Briloche on the old road to Esquel (very rough from Bariloche, fully paved to Esquel). It is a most attractive small town (pop. 8,000) in beautiful country, with many mountain walks and waterfalls nearby, though as it lies in a hollow at about 200 metres, it can be very hot in summer. It has good fishing and is fully developed as a tourist resort. Within half an hour's drive are Lagos Puelo (see below) and Epuyén (shops and petrol available). The farms and the orchards sell their produce at Bariloche. Famous local fruit preserves can be bought at the factories in town. Handicraft market Thursday and Saturday. The Balneario Municipal is 300 metres from the town centre, pleasant river swimming. Full-day tours from Bariloche are run by Don Otto, Mercedes and Turismo Llao Llao, 11 hrs., very crowded and difficult to get on in high season. Also local bus by Mercedes from Bariloche, US$7, 3¼ hrs.; Empresa Charter offers 10% to ISIC and youth card holders between Bariloche and El Bolsón.

**Accommodation** *Hostería Steiner*, clean and pleasant,wood fire, lovely garden, on the Lake Puelo route, E; *Motel La Posta*, smart and new (Route 258). Up to 2 days' stay possible at the Franciscan school, but get recommendation from tourist agent. *Hotel Salinas*, Rocas 641, E, friendly, clean, rec. *Enrique's*, Rivadavia 2950, F; *Familia Sarakoumsky*, San Martín 3003, F p.p., good. *Albergue El Bolsón*, Av. San Martín 1360, T 92523, 7 blocks from centre, affiliated to IYHF, 10% discount for ISIC and youth card holders. Very difficult to find accommodation in the high season.

20 km. N of El Bolsón, at Rinconada del Mallín Ahogado (daily bus from El Bolsón) is *Hostería María y Pancho Kramer*, C, warmly rec., wholefood meals, hot shower, sauna, swimming pool, chess, volleyball, horseback and trekking excursions to lakes and mountains. E of El Bolsón, at El Maitén, is *Hostería La Vasconia*, no other accommodation around here on Route 40. At Lago Epuyén, 40 km. S of El Bolsón, *Refugio del Lago*, b. and b., meals with fresh food, tours, trekking, riding, French owned, Sophie and Jacques Dupont, Correo Epuyén, 9211 Chubut.

**Camping** *Del Sol*, ½ km. from town; many other sites in surrounding area. Several *residencias* and camping sites nearby; the *Aldea Suiza* camping site has been especially recommended, tennis courts, hot showers, good restaurant. The paying campsite (US$1) at Lake Puelo has beautiful views across the lake to Tres Picos, but the walking is limited, shop and café; free campsite also at Lake Puelo. Frequent public transport from El Bolsón.

**Restaurants** *Don Diego*, good; *Ricardo*, on Rocas, good coffee (food less good). *Parrilla Achachay*, basic, but reasonable value. *El Viejo Maitén*, good.

**Exchange** *Hotel Cordillera*, tourist agency ½ block from plaza, or Inmobilaria Turneo shop, all cash only.

**Tourist Office**. Office on main plaza, open 0900-200. Ask for sketch maps of the beautiful walks in the neighbourhood including up Cerro Piltriquitrón.

**Travel Agent** *Translago Turismo*, Perito Moreno 360, T (0944) 92523, 10% discount for ISIC and youth card holders on lake excursions to Chilean border and to Valle del Turbio, trekking to Lago Puelo and Cerro Plataforma.

**Lago Puelo** Regular buses from El Bolsón go to the lake and continue into the Parque Nacional Lago Puelo. Villa Lago Puelo has a bank, shops, fuel and *hosterías*. *Albergue El Turbio* in Lago Puelo National Park, T (0944) 92523, horse and kayak hire, 10% discount for ISIC and youth card holders (information from Turismo Translago in El Bolsón). Good information on the park is available from the wardens at the entrance. Trans Lagos excursions from the paying campsite, or from office in town: ½-day trip across the lake to Valle Río Turbio below Cerro Tres Picos, US$15; also to the Chilean border and Lago Inferior. Canoes can be rented for US$3/hr. to appreciate the beauty of the lake. There is a path to Chile from Villa Lago Puelo, 12 km.

On the way from Epuyén to Esquel is **Cholila**, with superb views of Lago Cholila, crowned by the Matterhorn-like mountains of Cerros Dos and Tres Picos. There are bus services between Bariloche, El Bolsón, and Esquel, and between Comodoro Rivadavia and Esquel. A recommended journey for motorists is to spend the night at El Bolsón, enter the Los Alerces park via Cholila and drive right through it to Esquel, travelling the whole length of Lagos Rivadavia and Futalaufquen.

**Hotel** *El Trébol*, C with bath and breakfast, basic evening meal US$5, comfortable rooms with stoves, bus stops in village 4 km. away. **Restaurant** *Hue Telén*, 8 km. from El Trébol, irregular opening times, 1 km. from ACA (which is reported as poor).

**Excursion** Good walk around Lago Mosquito: continue down the road from El Trébol past the lake then take a path to the left, following the river. Cross the river on the farm bridge and continue to the base of the hills where a second bridge exists. Follow the path to the lake and walk between the lake and the hills, crossing the exit river via a suspension bridge just past El Trébol—6 hrs. (Nick Saunders and Sarah Jaggs, London W1).

*Esquel*, about 260 km. S of Bariloche, was originally an offshoot of the Welsh colony at Chubut, nearly 650 km. to the E. It is now a modern town with reasonable amenities (population 17,000). Major skiing location at La Hoya, 7 ski-lifts, 15 km. north of Esquel (skiing much cheaper than at Bariloche). For skiing information ask at Club Andino Esquel; bus to La Hoya from Esquel, 3 a day, US$4.25, lift tickets US$8 a day, gear hire US$7 a day. Esquel is known for its tulips, chocolate, jellies and jams (also for the mazard berry liquor made by the Braese family, interesting, but expensive). The Museo Indígena y de Ciencias Naturales at Belgrano 330 was reported closed in 1991.

**Hotels** *Tehuelche*, 9 de Julio 825, T 2420, B with shower, heating and breakfast, excellent restaurant, some staff speak English; *Hostería los Tulipanes*, Fontana 365, T 2748, C, good rooms and service; *Angelina*, Av. Alvear 758, T 2763, C, very friendly and clean; *Residencial Huemul*, Alvear y 25 de Mayo, T 2149, C; *Zacarias*, Roca 634, T 2270, D; *Hostería*, Ameghino 505, T 2327, E, nice, friendly, clean, quiet, meals; ~~Hotel-Restaurant Vascongada~~, ~~Mitre y 9 de Julio, D~~ with shower, friendly, good cheap food. *Residencial Barutta*, Volta 1081, D, T 2251, doubles only; *Hostal La Hoya*, Ameghino 2296, T 2473, D, on road to airport, 1 km. Also *Hostería La Hoya* at the Centro Deportivo de Ski at La Hoya itself, D. *Hosksia Huentru Niyeu*, Chacabuco 606, T 2576, D, clean, quiet, friendly. *Residencial Argentino*, 25 de Mayo 826, E, no singles, basic, heating, camping in season; *Residencial Gingins*, Rivadavia 1243, T 2452, E friendly, grubby; Mrs Megan Rowlands' guesthouse at Rivadavia 330, T 2578, E, Welsh and English spoken, rec.; Sra. Olga Daher, Sarmiento 269, E, friendly, quiet. Many others. Ask at tourist office for lodgings in private houses.

**Camping** Municipal site 5 km. from centre on Trevelin road, near gravel-crushing plant, hot showers, rec. In the Parque Nacional there are numerous paying and free campsites beside the lakes, but a permit is needed from Intendencia at Villa Futalaufquen and campsites are closed in winter. Free campsite at Laguna Z, 5 km. along Calle Fontana. Camping at *Cabañas Tejas Negras* (C), good facilities for US$3.50, by *Pucón Pai Motel*, which has its own campsite. Those with sleeping bags can go to the Salesian school and sleep in the school classrooms, Dec. to March; get recommendation from tourist office.

**Restaurants** *Jockey Club*, Alvear 949, excellent, reasonably priced; *El Cóndor*, rotisería, near bus station, Alvear 1250, good for packed lunches; also for snacks. *Ahla Wasahla*, 9 de Julio y Sarmiento and at Av. Ameghino 924, good cheap, friendly, closed Sun.; *Red Fox*, Sarmiento 795 and Alvear, a British-style pub with light, but expensive meals, open from 2200, closed Tues. *Parrilla La Estancia*, 25 de Mayo 541, quite good; *El Mesón*, 25 de Mayo 450, reasonable, but slow service *Pizzería Don Pipo*, Rivadavia 924, good pizzas and empanadas. Excellent pasta at reasonable prices at *Trattoria de Julio*, Rivadavia 1080. *Casa Suiza*, good confitería. Rugby fans will enjoy the *Confitería Las Tejas*, 25 de Mayo 745, which shows videos of the game.

**Bank and Post Office** Banco de la Nación Güemes y San Martín, 3% commission on cheques; *Viajes Sol del Sur*, 9 de Julio 1086, also accept cheques; open Mon.-Fri., 1000-1300. Post and telecommunications office opposite the bus terminal on Fontana and Alvear (open 0800-2000).

**Laundry** *Lavarap*, B. Mitre 543, open Mon.-Sat., 0900-2100.

**Tourist Office** Operates from the bus terminal (Alvear y Fontana, T 3301), very friendly, can arrange lodgings in private homes. Closed Sat. and Sun. off-season.

**Tourist Agencies** *Esquel Tours*, Fontana 754, T 2704, run a service to and from the airport (US$0.70) where they also have an office, good for local tours, to Lagos Menéndez and Cisnes. Fairway Sports and Adventures, San Martín 1-43, T 3380, varied programme of tours, highly rec.

**Airport** 20 km. E of Esquel, by paved road, US$14 by taxi. US$2.20 by bus; US$3 by Esquel Tours bus 1 hr. before each LADE flight. To **Buenos Aires**: 4 a week with Aerolíneas Argentinas via Bariloche; 2 a week with LADE. LADE flight to **Río Grande**; also to Trelew, Bariloche, Comodoro Rivadavia, Río Gallegos, and other destinations.

**Rail** From **Buenos Aires**, Constitución, train leaves Sun. and Wed. as for Bariloche (above), arriving in **Ingeniero Jacobacci** (E of Bariloche) after 31 hrs., returning Wed. and Sat. 0125. A steam-operated, narrow-gauge train (known locally as El Trencito, described by Paul Theroux in *The Old Patagonian Express*) normally leaves Jacobacci Fri. 0700 for Esquel, arrives 2019, which is the most southerly point in the connected South American railway system. It returns Tues. 0830, arriving at Jacobacci at 2200 (hotel in Jacobacci: *Gran Hotel Argentino*, nearly opp. station, D with shower and heating, very good, restaurant nearby). Enquire at station for bookings. Sleepers from Jacobacci to Bs.As. are usually fully booked from Bariloche; only a small quota of first class tickets are available in Esquel for connections to Bs.As. The Jacobacci-Esquel branch line was under threat of closure in 1991, check in Buenos Aires at the railway office on Viamonte in advance. Tourist train to Nahuel Pan leaves Wed. and Thur. 0900, returns same day, US$4 one way, Dec.-March only. Tickets from Tehuelche Viajes, Fontana 574, or Esquel Tours, Fontana 754. There are only two engines at Esquel, so go to **El Maitén** (train from Esquel, arrives 1350, cold), where there are about 12. From El Maitén it is possible to hitch to Bariloche or take the Esquel-Bariloche bus.

**Buses** None direct from Buenos Aires to Esquel so travel via Bariloche. To **Comodoro Rivadavia** (paved), Tues. and Fri. via Río Mayo, 0100, and Thur. direct at 2100, US$20. Empresa Mercedes goes daily (9 hrs.) to **Bariloche** at 0800 (also at 2200), US$14.50. To **El Bolsón**, 5 hrs., US$10, rough road, goes alternate days via El Maitén (for train buffs) and via Cholila (for views). To **Trelew**, US$44, 11 hrs., leaves 0900 Tues., Thurs., Sat., and 1900 Mon., Wed., Fri.; other bus companies on Av. Fontana and Alvear (bus terminal) are Empresa Don Otto, Chubut, Denis. Bus terminal T 2233, also for taxis.

**Los Alerces National Park** Sixty km. W of Esquel, which can also be reached by road from Rawson, is the Los Alerces National Park, with centuries-old larch trees. An interesting part of the park can be reached from a separate entrance through Trevelin (see below) following the Río Futaleufú, but one can go only 22 km. W because of the new Futaleufú hydroelectric dam. Behind it is Lago Amutui Quimei, which has swallowed Lago Situación and 3 others stretching almost to the frontier. (Futaleufú supplies power to the alumina plant at Puerto Madryn, 500 Km. to the E.) Entrance by car to see Futaleufú dam is only allowed at 1500, under police supervision; photography not permitted, except on top of the dam itself. There is no public transport to the dam, but buses pass the eastern side of the lake.

The eastern side of Los Alerces has much the same natural attractions as the Nahuel Huapi and Lanín parks, but is much less developed for tourism. Lago Futalaufquen has some of the best fishing in this huge area, season begins Nov. 15. Bus (Transportes Esquel) to Lago Futalaufquen at 0800 daily in season (it passes 3 hotels and drives into 2 camp sites), connecting with the Trelew bus. Off-season, the bus only goes to Villa Futalaufquen at the southern tip of the lake (where the park administration building or Intendencia is situated) on Mon. at 0630 and 1830, returning 0800 and 2000, US$1.50 one way, buy ticket from kiosk at terminal in Esquel. The Intendencia has a small museum about the park and a slide show of Argentina's National Parks. Petrol station, 2 supermarkets in Villa Futalaufquen and a lady sells bread and vegetables from her house (buy bread early, or order the day before; meat can be hard to get).

**Hotels** On the E side of Lago Futalaufquen: *Quime Quipán*, T 22272, rec. for fishermen, closed in winter; *Hostería Los Tepúes*, A, simple, rustic, open all year, family bungalow for rent; *Pucón Pai*, A, good restaurant, rec. for fishermen (holds a fishing festival to open the season); open out of season for large groups only; *Cume Hué*, T 2858. Camping at Villa Futalaufquen and at Los Maitenes (closed May-Sept.) hot water, store.

On the W side, which is untouched by tourism (by law), is *Hotel Futalaufquen* just N of Puerto Limonao, T 2648, rec., especially rooms 2/3 and 4/5 which have balconies overlooking the lake, L, open all year (no heating in rooms); good walking around the hotel, e.g. to Cinco Saltos, and El Dedal. Regular full day launch trip from Puerto Limonao (reached by early morning minibus) on Lago Futalaufquen (a sheer delight) through Río Arrayanes to windless Lago Verde (2 campsites, one US$1 p.p., one free, very crowded in summer; *Camping Agreste Lago Verde* offers 10% discount to ISIC and youth card holders). From there one can walk out to Lagos Rivadavia and Cholila (see above)—2 days minimum and to the end of Lago Menéndez, famous for its giant larch trees (US$30 incl. launch trip on Lago Menéndez, with Tehuelche Viajes y Turismo, Av. Fontana 574, from Esquel); the boat leaves at 1330 but book the day before in Esquel, preferably, as it will not leave if there are not enough passengers. The dock can be reached by a 30-minute walk across the bridge between lakes Futalaufquen and Verde. There are local guides with outboard motor boats for fishermen. Lovely view of Lago Cisne (Swan Lake) to the NW end of Lago Menéndez. One then walks a 3 km. nature trail looking across the Andes to Chile before returning. Tours arranged at Esquel (e.g. Elentur's Lacustre excursion visiting lakes Futalaufquen, Verde, Menéndez and a guided tour around the 2 km. walk to Lake Cisne, on which you will see a 2,600-year-old alerce, US$17 from Puerto Limonao, take food and drink). Other excursion tours offered are less interesting because they only involve short stops in front of points of interest. A road connects all the lakes. The tourist office in Esquel has a pamphlet on all the walks in the Park. **N.B.** *Refugio Lago Krügger* in the Park offers 10% discount to ISIC and youth card holders.

From Esquel one can also drive to Perito Moreno (**see page 178**) via Teckia (95 km. paved), Gobernador Costa (84 km. unpaved), La Laurita (last 61 km. paved, ACA service station, breakdown truck and snack bar), 65 paved km. to join route 22 (60 km.) which is being paved, and on to Río Mayo, with 121 km. unpaved road to Perito Moreno.

**Crossing into Chile** Colectivos leave Esquel for the frontier at La Balsa, 70 km., 2 hrs., US$4. Campsite (Camping Río Grande) on Argentine side of river. Cross the frontier river by bridge after passing Argentine customs; Chilean customs is 1 km. on the other side of river (1 hr. for all formalities). Colectivo from Chilean customs to Futaleufú (8 km.) is US$1.25. Very little traffic for hitching. The colectivos from Esquel pass through Trevelin on the way.

**N.B.** At the Futaleufú and Palena border crossings, Argentine border officials only give transit visas: legalize your stay within 10 days either by leaving the country or by renewing entry stamp at an immigration office.

*Trevelin* (pop. 5,000), 23 km. SW of Esquel (local bus, US$0.85, every ½ hour, 0700-1900), is also an offshoot of the Welsh Chubut colony (**see page 169**). There is a modern Anglican church beside the Catholic church. It has a Welsh historical museum (entrance US$0.30) in the old mill.

**Accommodation and Food** *Hostería Estefanía*, Perito Moreno s/n, T 8148; *Hospedaje Trevelín*, San Martin s/n, T 8102. Grills at *Che Ferrada*, good mixed *parrillada* at *El Quincho*, and several tea rooms offering *té galés* and *torta negra* (e.g. *El Adobe* on Av. Patagonia). *La Cabaña*, 7 km. out on the road from Trevelin to Lake Futalaufquen, serves Welsh teas. There is a custom of giving a newly-married couple a "black cake" on their wedding day, to be eaten on their first anniversary. Municipal campsite near centre. On the road to Esquel 3 km. from Trevelin, signposted on the righthand side, is *La Granja Trevelin*, owned by Domingo Giacci, macrobiotic meals and good Italian cooking, sells milk, cheese and onions; camping US$0.90, hot water and w.c., bungalows US$15 a day; excellent horses for hire.

**Tourist Office** Good office in central plaza.

**Excursion** 17 km. on road to frontier are Nant-y-fall Falls, entrance US$0.50 p.p. includes guide to all 7 falls (1½ hr. walk).

*Neuquén*, capital of Neuquén Province, was founded 1904 on the W side of the confluence of the Ríos Limay and Neuquén. It is a pleasant, clean industrial city of 90,000 people. A major stop on paved Highway 22, 540 km. from Bahía Blanca and 474 km. NE of Bariloche, it serves the rich oilfields to the W with heavy equipment and construction materials, and the irrigated fruit-producing valley to the E. There are also many wine *bodegas* nearby. Much farm machinery is sold to the orchards where apples, pears, grapes, hops and plums are grown. At the Parque Centenario is a *mirador* with good views of the city and the confluence of the rivers, where they become the Negro (be sure *not* to take the bus to Centenario industrial suburb). Facing Neuquén and connected by bridge is Cipolletti (pop. 43,600) a prosperous centre of the fruit-growing region. The Museo Provincial Carlos Ameghino, Yrigoyen 1047, is modest but interesting.

**Hotels** *Apollo*, C, Av. Olascoaga 361, very good; *Cristal*, C, Av. Olascoaga 268, adequate; *del Comahue*, Av. Argentina 4-star, new, very good; *ACA Cipolletti*, just outside Neuquén; other *Hospedajes* on San Martín, mostly E; 13 km. S on Zapala road is *Hostal del Caminante*, T 33118, with pool and garden, popular. Some 50 km. W of Neuquén there is a motel at Arroyitos. Municipal camping site at Neuquén and various camping sites, mostly by the river.

**Restaurants** *Las Tres Marías*, Alberdi 126, excellent. Pleasant bars on Av. Argentina.

**Exchange** *Pullman*, Alcorta 163, T 22438.

**Museums** **Museo Histórico Provincial**, Santa Fe 163; **Museo de Ciencias Naturales**, at entrance to airport (as is the Casino).

**Tourist Office** Félix San Martín y Río Negro.

**Transport** El Cóndor (La Estrella), El Valle and Chevallier bus **Buenos Aires**-Neuquén, daily US$33, 18½ hours; paved road throughout. Connections with **Copahué** and **Córdoba**; also with **San Rafael** (US$20) and **San Martín de los Andes** (US$17). Bus to **Zapala** daily, 7 hours. To **Bariloche**, take La Estrella or Chevallier (not El Valle as it stops too often), and sit on left. Bus La Unión del Sud to **Temuco** (Chile) via Zapala all year three times a week each way, and Ruta Sur twice a week, US$20, 16 hrs.
    Daily train, *Estrella del Valle*, leaves Constitución station, Buenos Aires, at 1000, arriving Neuquén 0830; change trains for Zapala, 4 hours. Leaves Zapala 2045, arrives Buenos Aires 2010. Takes car transporter Buenos Aires-Neuquén Fri.; returns Sun.

If driving from Neuquén to Buenos Aires on Routes 151 and 21, via Catriel, fill up with fuel here because there is no other fuel for 323 km. of desert before General Achá. Driving from Neuquén to Bariloche, go via El Chocón hydroelectric lake, Junín and San Martín (both "de los Andes"), taking Routes 237, 40 and 234; route more attractive than that via Zapala.

**Air** There is a jet airport 7 km. from centre. Daily flights to and from Buenos Aires with AR and Austral. Connecting flights to **San Martín de los Andes** with TAN, Av. Argentina 383, T 23076/24834 (30096 at airport), who also fly to **Mendoza** five times a week, also **Bariloche** and **Puerto Montt** and **Temuco** in Chile.

**Excursions** Paved roads lead 33 km. N to the artificial and natural swimming pools at the Ballester dam; nearby is artificial Lago Pellegrini, where various watersports are held. A narrow-gauge railway with sporadic services runs via Cipolletti to Contralmirante Cordero, 7 km. from the dam. Extensive irrigation has turned the Río Negro valley into a major fruit-producing region, with apples the principal crop. All the towns in the valley celebrate the Fiesta Nacional de la Manzana in the second half of March.

A road and railway go W from Neuquén to **Zapala** (179 km., pop. 20,000) through the oil zone at Challacó, Cutral-Có and Plaza Huincul. There is an excellent geology museum in Zapala, visited by specialist groups from all over the world (closed weekends). Among the collections of minerals, fossils, shells and rocks, is a complete crocodile jaw, believed to be 80 million years old. There is an airport and an ACA service station.

**Accommodation and Food** *Huincul*, Roca 313, E, restaurant; *Coliqueo*, Etcheluz 159, opposite bus terminal, D, good; *Petuién*, Vidal y Etcheluz, E, rec. *Odetto's Grill*, Ejército Argentino 455, moderate prices, 2 mins. from bus terminal. There is a municipal camping site.

**Transport** A Pullman bus, with hostess service, plies twice daily between **Bahía Blanca** and Zapala (15 hrs.). El Petróleo bus leaves Zapala 0230 and 1630 for **San Martín de los Andes** (5½ hrs.) via Junín de los Andes. In winter the direct route from San Martín de los Andes via the lakes may be impassable, so a bus must be taken back from San Martín to La Rinconada and then round to Bariloche (4 hrs.). There is also an overnight (at 2200) Neuquén-Zapala-San Martín bus that comes through Zapala at 0230; same service at 0915 (US$23). From Zapala to **Bariloche** by bus, one must change at La Rinconada. Zapala-**Temuco** (Chile) all year with La Unión del Sud and Ruta Sur, at 0500, US$12.50, 10-12 hrs., as under Neuquén (see above). Also with Igi-Llaimi Wed. and Fri. at 0530, return 0330, twice weekly. Buy Chilean currency before leaving.
    Train from Buenos Aires to Zapala, *Estrella del Valle*, to Neuquén, daily via Bahía Blanca at 1000 from Constitución station, arr. 0830, change trains, arrive Zapala 1300. Zapala-Buenos Aires at 1615, arrives 2010 next day. Fares: 1st class US$40, Pullman US$50,

sleeper US$70; buy tickets in advance. On Sundays tickets go on sale at 1500, buffet car on train, scenery largely uninteresting. The line follows the Río Colorado for some distance, then crosses it into the valley of the Río Negro where large fruit growing areas at (343 km.) **Choele-Choel** (ACA motel on edge of town, C, with bath, good restaurant at bus station and fine modern *Hotel Choele-Choel*) and at (472 km.) and Villa Regina are irrigated from the Río Negro dam. Two low-priced clean places: motel and *residencial* at edge of town near the main road. Cheap food at one of the service stations. There is an excellent free municipal campsite at Choele-Choel; shady, beside the Río Negro; no showers. Many local buses ply from Choele-Choel to El Chocón (large hydroelectric plant) and Zapala.

North of Zapala on the Chilean border is the Copahué National Reservation, best-known for its thermal baths and volcano of the same name. At 1,980 metres above sea-level in a volcanic region, **Copahué Termas** is enclosed in a gigantic amphitheatre formed by mountain walls, with an opening to the E. Near Copahué, Caviahue is being developed; accommodation is available in prettier surroundings (there are trees), and a bus service connect the two. There are bus services from Neuquén and Zapala to Copahué, which may also be reached by road from Mendoza. The **Laguna Blanca National Park** 35 km. SW of Zapala on a good, consolidated road is famous for its animal and bird life (notably black-necked swans), but has not yet become a tourist centre.

Hotels N of Zapala include those at Churriaca (131 km.), Chos Malal (202 km.) and Río Barrancas (at 340 km.). The road via Las Lajas is paved as far as Chos Malal, founded as a military fort in 1889 (restored as a historic monument, with Museo Histórico Olascoaga). ACA service station and hotel (San Martín y Sarmiento). Routes 143 and 151 from Neuquén to Mendoza via San Rafael are almost fully paved (apart from 40 km. around Santa Isabel) and provide faster, though less scenic alternatives to Route 40 via Zapala, Chos Malal and Malargüe.

Bariloche is 418 km. S of Zapala by a road through **Junín de los Andes** and San Martín de los Andes. Junín is famous for salmon and rainbow trout and is known as the trout capital of Argentina. A short detour from Junín leads to the very beautiful lake of Huechulafquen; from Junín, too, a road runs W over the Tromen Pass through glorious scenery to Pucón (135 km.) on Lago Villarrica, in Chile (easy to hitchhike to Villarrica from the Argentine border post); on the way there are splendid views of Lanín volcano. There is an airport between Junín and San Martín, but it is mainly used by the military.

**Hotels** *Hostería Chimehuín*, Suárez y 25 de Mayo, B, fishing hostelry; *San Jorge*, Chacra 34, B; *Residencial El Centro*, Lamadrid 409, D with bath, clean, friendly; *Alejandro I*, on edge of town, C; *Residencial Marisa*, Rosas 360, C. 30 km N. of Junín is the ACA *Las Rinconadas*.

The Tromen (Chileans call it Mamuil Malal) pass route between Argentina and Chile is much less developed than the Puyehue route, and definitely not usable during heavy rain or snow. Parts are narrow and steep. Argentine customs are at the pass. The Chilean *aduana* is at Puesco, 58 km. SE of Pucón and 16 km. from Tromen. Ferry at Lago Quilleihue, which is halfway between the posts, has been eliminated by road blasted across cliffs. It is possible to camp in the area (though very windy), but take food as there are no shops at the pass. From the border, it is 24 km. to Curarrehue, from where several buses a day go (either at 0600 or at the latest at 1400) to Pucón. The international bus will officially only pick up people at Tromen but at the discretion of the driver can pick up passengers at Puesco (customs, but no hotel) at 0900 and Currarehue stops. Hitch-hiking over to the Tromen Pass is difficult.

**Lanín Volcano** at 3,768 metres high, is extinct and one of the world's most beautiful mountains. Geologically, Lanín is one of the youngest volcanoes of the Andes. Special permission to visit is not needed; from Junín, during the summer season, trucks carry hikers to Paimún for US$1. A 4-hour hike from the Argentine customs post at Tromen pass (speak to the *guardaparque* at the border) to *refugio* at 2,400 metres. Climb from *refugio* to summit is easy but crampons and ice-axe are needed.

**San Martín de los Andes**, 40 km. S. of Junín (paved road), and 196 km. from Zapala, is a lovely but expensive little town, population 14,000, at the eastern end of Lago Lacar; it is the best centre for exploring **Lanín National Park**, with its sparkling lakes, wooded mountain valleys and the snow-capped Lanín Volcano. The numerous deer in the park are the red deer of temperate Europe and Asia. There is excellent ski-ing on Cerro Chapelco, to which there is a road, and facilities for water ski-ing, windsurfing and sailing on Lago Lacar.

**Hotels** Single accommodation is scarce. Motel, *El Sol de los Andes*, very expensive and nice, set above the town (Cerro Cnl. Díaz), T 27460, 5-star, L, shopping gallery, swimming pool, sauna, night club, casino, regular bus service to centre of town. *La Cheminée*, Roca y Moreno, A, very good, breakfast included, but no restaurant; *El Viejo Esquiador*, San Martín 1242, T 27690, B, clean, friendly, rec.; *Hostería Villa Lagos*, Av. Villa Lagos, D, good, ski hire. *Posta del Cazador*, San Martín 175, T 27501, very highly rec.; *Turismo*, Mascardi 517, T 27592, C, rec. *Hostería Arrayán*, 5 km. from San Martín, is an English tea room with 2 self contained log cabins for rent with full cooking facilities, dining and sitting rooms etc., superb view over Lago Lacar, very peaceful, B all inclusive. At San Martín is *Los Pinos*, C with breakfast, Almte. Brown 420, T 27207, German-run, with a/c and heating, clean, friendly; *Hostería Cumelén*, Elordi 931, T 27304, E (low season), D high season, with bath, hot water, breakfast, nice lobby with fireplace, rec.; *Hostería Anay*, Cap. Drury 841, T 27514, D, central, good value, rec. Also good, *Casa Alta*, Gabriel Obeid 659, T 27456, D; *Residencial Peumayen*, Av. San Martín 851, T 27232, very clean, C, with bath and breakfast. Cheapest is *Posta del Caminante*, Caballería 1164, basic, friendly, good atmosphere, noisy; *Curra-Huínca*, Rivadavia 686, T 27224, E, clean, modern, rec.; *Cabañas del Sur*, on main road out of town towards Junín, sleeps up to 6 in comfortable cabin, D per cabin, rec. *Casa del Amigo*, Obeid y Cnel. Pérez, E, very friendly. Consult very good tourist office for other private addresses, but these are only supplied in high season. *Residencial Villa Bibi*, E, with private bath, breakfast extra, clean, family-run, near lake, Cnl. Díaz 1186, rec. The following offer discounts to ISIC and youth card holders: *Hospedaje Turístico Caritas*, Capitán Drury 774, T 27313, F p.p., shared rooms, run by church, friendly, clean, also floor space for sleeping bags in summer; *Albergue Universitario Técnico Forestal*, Pasaje de la Paz s/n, T 27618, youth hostel style, and *Hostería Los Pinos*, Alte. Brown 420, T 27207.

**Camping** ACA Camping with hot water and laundering facilities US$2.20 p.p. *Camping Los*

*Andes*, Juez del Valle 611, other side of bridge, US$2, accommodation, F, clean, bunk beds, shared bath. Pleasant site by the lake at Quilaquina, 27 km. from San Martín, with beaches, and another on the lake at Catritre, just 6 km. from town.

**Restaurants** Try smoked venison, wild boar or trout, at *El Ciervo*, Villegas 724; *Piscis*, Villegas y Moreno, *Betty*, San Martín 1203, *La Raclette*, Pérez 1170, and *El Peñon*, Calderón, all good. *Parrilla La Tranquera*, Villegas 965, good value; and *Parrilla del Esquiador* on Belgrano 885, reasonable home-cooked food. *Rotissería Pablito*, Villegas 568, good, cheap; *Quila Quina*, Villegas y Díaz, excellent trout, good value. *El Jockey*, Villegas 657, also good. It is difficult to get dinner before 2200, but there are various good restaurants in the area. *Pizzería La Strada*, San Martín 721, good; *Fanfani*, Rodhe 786, has good pasta.

**Exchange** Banco de la Nación, San Martín 687, exchanges cash and Amex cheques only; **American Express** office on San Martín, 1 block from tourist office, 10% commission on cheques; **Andina Internacional**, San Martín 876, Piso 1. Avis office, San Martín 998 (rates not as good).

**Laundry** *Laverap*, Drury 878, 0800-2200 daily and Villegas 986, cheaper, 0900-1300, 1600-2130 Mon.-Fri., 0900-1300 Sat.

**Tourist Office** at Rosas 790, on main square, corner of San Martín, open 0800-2200, very helpful. **Police station** at Belgrano 611.

**Travel agency** *Turismo Patagónico*, Av. San Martín 950, T 27113, excursions and adventure tourism, 10% discount to ISIC and youth card holders.

**Buses** Station at Gral. Villegas 251, good toilet facilities. Bus **Buenos Aires**-San Martín, US$88, three a week, Chevallier goes Mon. and Fri. at 1430, arrives 1520 next day. Hitchhiking to Bariloche and San Juan is slow.

**Air** There are 6 flights a week from Buenos Aires in winter (4 a week in summer) with AR to Chapelco Airport, 20 km. from San Martín, and daily flights with TAN from Neuquén.

**Excursions** The most popular trips by car are to Lagos Lolog, Alumine, Huechulafquen and Paimún, to a campsite in the shadow of Lanín Volcano. Shorter excursions can be made on horseback or by launch; recommended day excursion by El Valle at 0930, return 1700 on Lago Lacar for US$10. A small road runs W from San Martín along the southern edge of Lago Lacar for 10 km. to Quila Quina, where there are Indian engravings and a lovely waterfall. There are 2 routes S to Bariloche: one, via Lago Hermosa and Villa La Angostura, known as the "Seven Lakes Drive", is very beautiful. (National Park permit holders may camp freely along this route). On this route, from a bridge 7 km. S of San Martín, you can see the Arroyo Partido: at this very point the rivulet splits, one stream flowing to the Pacific, the other to the Atlantic. Some bus services, however, take a rather less scenic route following Río Traful, then Lago Lanín and joining the paved Bariloche highway at Confluencia (ACA station and a hotel, also motel *El Rancho* just before Confluencia). El Valle buses, 4 a week, take this latter route; Ko-Ko buses, 6 a week, are reported to follow part of the Seven Lakes Drive, but check before booking. Fare US$8. Round trip excursions between San Martín along the Seven Lakes Drive, 5 hrs., are operated by several tour companies. Hitching is difficult as there is little traffic.

**Villa Traful**, beside Lago Traful about half-way between San Martín and Bariloche on a side road, is described as a "camper's paradise". Marvellous views, fishing (licence needed) excellent. All roads are dirt; drive carefully, avoiding wild cattle! Hotel *Pichi Traful*, E p.p., and *Hostería Traful* provide accommodation.

**Skiing** There are several chair-lifts of varying capacity on Cerro Chapelco and a ski-tow higher up. Bus from San Martín to slopes, US$7 return. Very good slopes and snow conditions. As yet uncrowded. Lift pass US$25, ski hire US$5 a day from *Hostería Villa Lagos*. At the foot of the mountain are a restaurant and base lodge. There are three more restaurants on the mountain and a small café at the top. For information on trout fishing or duck and geese shooting, contact Logaine and David Denies at Trails, Pérez 662, San Martín.

**To Chile** Excursion San Martín de los Andes-Panguipulli (Chile): boat leaves San Martín Tues., Thurs., Sat. to Hua-Hum at the W end of Lago Lacar, at 0900, US$8. Camping with shop at Hua-Hum. Excursion buses run to Hua-Hum when the launch arrives across the border to Pirehueico, US$2.50. There is now a road between San Martín and Puerto Pirehueico (Chile). Buses daily at 0800, US$6, 2 hr. journey through Lanín National Park. The ferry across Lago Pirehueico (Tues., Thurs., Sat. 1730; at 0830 in other direction) takes 2 hours to Puerto Fuy; beautiful scenery. Daily bus 0600, Puerto Fuy-Panguipulli, US$3, 3 hrs.; or ask for lift among vehicles on ferry (friendly boat crew may help). Boats also leave Puerto Fuy Mon.,

Tues. and Thurs. to Pirehueico for a day trip, US$7, and there is a daily ferry at 0600. From Puerto Fuy to Panguipulli transport goes on the new road via Choshuenco around the N shore of Lago Panguipulli. This route is open all year round and is an alternative service from Temuco to San Martín when the Tromen Pass is blocked by snow (usually June-mid-Nov.). When the pass is closed, the buses drive right on to the boat to cross between Puerto Fuy and Puerto Pirehueico. Check with customs at Hua-Hum about arrangements.

Bus San Martín de los Andes to Pucón and to Temuco, US$16.50 to all destinations, rough ride; mid-Nov.-May Empresa San Martín Mon., Wed. and Fri., at 0700, returns from Temuco the following day at 0500, Igi-Llaimi Tues., Thurs. and Sat. at 0700, ret. next day at 0630, US$16.50 for Pucón, Villarrica and Temuco. When the pass is closed Empresa San Martín switches its return and forward journey days but not the times. Igi-Llaimi goes Wed. and Fri. only at 0500, returning from Temuco Tues. and Thurs. at 0330. This route passes through Panguipulli, Villarica and Temuco only. For Pucón change to JAC bus in Villarrica. JAC also runs a service between Temuco and San Martín, via Junín de los Andes and continuing to Neuquén. The companies will not give information about each other, and do not run buses in winter when the pass is blocked.

---

# PATAGONIA (10)

**The vast, windy, treeless plateau south of the Río Colorado: the Atlantic coast is rich in marine life, most easily seen around Puerto Madryn. In the south of the region is the Parque Nacional de los Glaciares, with journeys on lakes full of ice floes and to the Moreno glacier. In the north of the region is Argentina's Welsh community.**

Patagonia is sub-divided into the provinces of Neuquén, Río Negro, Chubut, Santa Cruz and the Territory of Tierra del Fuego. The area covers 780,000 square km.: 28% of the national territory, but has a population of only 600,000, little over 2.7% of the total population; and 57% of it is urban. Wide areas have less than one person to the square km., and there are virtually no trees except in the north and the Andean foothills.

Over the whole land there blows a boisterous, cloud-laden strong wind which raises a haze of dust in summer, but in winter the dust can turn into thick mud. Temperatures are moderated by the proximity of the sea and are singularly mild, neither rising high during the summer nor falling low during the winter. Even in Tierra del Fuego, where the warmest summer months average 10½°C, the winter days' average can reach a high of about 2°C. Make sure you have plenty of warm clothing, and anti-freeze in your car, available locally. Rain falls mostly in the winter, but not more than 200-250 mm. a year. The whole eastern part of the area suffers from a lack of rainfall and the land is more or less desert. Deep crevices or canyons intersect the land from E to W. Few of them contain permanent water, but ground water is easily pumped to the surface. The great sheep *estancias* are along these canyons, sheltered from the wind, and in the depression running N from the Strait of Magellan to Lagos Argentino and Buenos Aires and beyond. During a brief period in spring, after the melting of the snows, there is grass on the plateau. Most of the land is devoted to sheep raising. The wool, which is shipped N to Buenos Aires, is mostly the fine and finecrossbred wool used by the Argentine mills, and is often heavy with sand. Over-grazing leads to much erosion. Wild dogs and the red fox are the sole enemies of the sheep. Because of the high winds and insufficient rainfall there is little agriculture except in the N, in the valleys of the Colorado and Negro rivers. Some cattle are raised in both valleys where irrigation permits the growing of alfalfa.

Patagonia is rich in extractive resources: the oil of Comodoro Rivadavia and Tierra del Fuego, the little exploited iron ore of Sierra Grande, the coal of Río Turbio, the hydro-electric capacity of El Chocón, plentiful deposits of minerals (particularly bauxite) and marine resources, but their exploitation has been slow. Tourism is opening up too. The wildlife is attractive. *Guanacos* and rheas are a

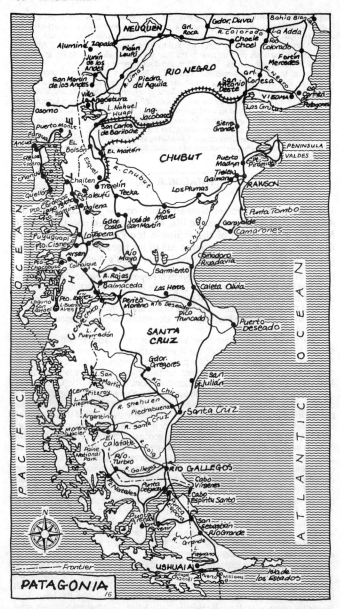

PATAGONIA

/6

common sight: there are also *maras*, Patagonian hares. On and off parts of the coast, particularly the Valdés peninsula, seals, sea-elephants, right whales and other aquatic mammals may be seen, as well as penguins, especially between October and April. Further S, particularly in Tierra del Fuego, the antarctic wild goose (*quequén*) is the most commonly seen of the 152 species of birds.

**N.B.** We are informed that in summer hotel prices are grossly inflated (by as much as 100% in Ushuaia, 75% in Calafate); also that in some places there may not be enough hotel beds to meet the demand. Camping is increasingly popular, and *estancias* seem hospitable to travellers who are stuck for a bed. During Argentine summer holidays (Jan., Feb., March) getting a hotel room in Ushuaia, Río Grande, Río Gallegos and Calafate is practically impossible. In this connection, remember that ACA establishments, which charge the same prices all over Argentina, are a bargain in Patagonia and Tierra del Fuego, where all other accommodation is expensive. Very few hotels and restaurants have a/c or even fans, it can get uncomfortably hot in January. Travellers' cheques are hard to change throughout Patagonia.

**Discovery and Colonization** The coast of Patagonia was first visited by a European late in 1519, when the Portuguese Fernão Magalhães (Magellan), then in the service of Spain, was on his voyage round the world. Early in 1520 he turned W into the strait which now bears his name and there struggled with fierce headwinds until he reached that Sea of Peace he named the Pacific. Later European expeditions that attempted to land on the coast were repulsed by the dour and obdurate local Indians, but these were almost entirely wiped out in the wars of 1879-1883, generally known as the "Campaign of the Desert". Before this there had been a long established colony at Carmen de Patagones; it shipped salt to Buenos Aires during the colonial period. There had also been a settlement of Welsh people in the Chubut Valley since 1865 (see below). After the Indian wars colonization was rapid, the Welsh, Scots and English taking a great part. Chilean sheep farmers from Punta Arenas moved northwards along the depression at the foot of the Andes, eastwards into Tierra del Fuego, and northwards to Santa Cruz.

**The Welsh settlement** On 28 July 1865, 150 Welsh immigrants landed at Puerto Madryn, then a deserted beach deep in Indian country. After three weeks they pushed, on foot, across the parched pampa and into the Chubut river valley, where there is flat cultivable land along the riverside for a distance of 80 km. upstream. Here, maintained in part by the Argentine Government, they settled, but it was three years before they realized the land was barren unless watered. They drew water from the river, which is higher than the surrounding flats, and later built a fine system of irrigation canals. The colony, reinforced later by immigrants from Wales and from the United States, prospered, but in 1899 a great flood drowned the valley and some of the immigrants left for Canada. The last Welsh contingent arrived in 1911. The object of the colony had been to create a "Little Wales beyond Wales", and for four generations they kept the Welsh language alive. The language is, however, dying out in the fifth generation. There is an offshoot of the colony of Chubut at Trevelin, at the foot of the Andes nearly 650 km. to the west, settled in 1888 (**see page 162**). It is interesting that this distant land gave to the Welsh language one of its most endearing classics: *Dringo'r Andes* (Climbing the Andes), written by one of the early women settlers.

Gary Luton, of the Welsh Patagonia Expedition 1980, writes: "To me Chubut will always foster memories of horses on an open wind-swept plain, or tethered, with brown sheepskin saddles, outside a *pueblo* inn. It is shuttered houses with poplar windbreaks. Chubut is relative prosperity surrounded by shanties of mud brick and tin; it is Coca-Cola and tea houses, sea lions and right whales sounding a short distance from shore; and *asados* washed down with red wine and *mate*. Chubut is a moonscape of neutral colours where sheep lose themselves in the grey-green saltpans of thornscrub, and dust and wind blow across scattered pockets of civilization. And it is the Eisteddfodd at Gaiman, a Welsh festival of the arts in a chapel nestled among the poplars, on a cloudless night, where boys in white shirts recite poetry and choirs sing as a culture fights a subsiding battle to maintain itself."

**Recommended Reading** *In Patagonia* by Bruce Chatwin, a good introduction to the area and its people.

In all Patagonia there is only one town—Comodoro Rivadavia—with a population over 100,000. Most of the towns are small ports, which used only to work during the wool-shipping season but have livened up since the local economy began to diversify. The high tidal range makes it impossible in most of them for ships to tie up at the docks (except at Madryn and Punta Arenas, Chile). The short railways inland from the ports have little traffic except during the sheep-shearing season.

**Communications** Calls at the chief ports by passenger/cargo ships of the Flota Carbonera del Estado. Navy transport ships go as far as Ushuaia (Tierra del Fuego) once a month and carry 60 passengers for a nine-day trip.

**Air Services** Aerolíneas Argentinas and Austral from Buenos Aires either direct to Río Gallegos or calling at Bahía Blanca and Trelew or Comodoro Rivadavia on the way. Check if either airline is offering discounts on particular flights, which can result in considerable savings. Cía. Argentina de Transportes Aéreos (CATA) from Buenos Aires to Bahía Blanca, Trelew, Comodoro Rivadavia and Río Gallegos. Beware delays for bad weather.

Many air force LADE flights in the region S of Bariloche must be booked in advance from departure point of flight. The planes are small and fly low; passengers miss little of what there is to be seen, highly recommended for those who enjoy flying. The baggage allowance is 15 kg. Travellers are warned that the flights are often heavily booked ahead, but always check again on the day of the flight if you are told beforehand that it is sold out. Sometimes, individual passengers are allowed to fly on air force carriers if planes are full or inopportune, through LADE. Also, LADE tickets are much cheaper for a long flight with stops than buying separate segments. LADE's computer reservation system is linked to Aerolíneas Argentinas, so flight connections are possible between these airlines. Also LADE's flights synchronize with both AR and Austral flights.

**Roads** The main road, Route 3, which runs near the coast, is now paved from Buenos Aires via Fitz Roy and down to Río Gallegos. S of this town to Ushuaia is all-weather in a bad state of repair as it is awaiting asphalt. Sometimes passengers going South have to pay for baggage by weight. Many buses do not operate between early April and late October.

The principal roads in Patagonia roughly form an inverted triangle. Route 3 has regular traffic and adequate services. At the southern end, this route enters Chile and crosses the Magellan Straits to Tierra del Fuego by the car ferry at Primera Angostura. The western route (Route 40) zigzags across the moors, is lonely and is good in parts, poor in others (more details given below); there is hardly any traffic except in December, January and February, the tourist season. However, it is by far the more interesting road, with fine views of the Andes and plenty of wild life as well as the Alerces and Glaciares National Parks. Camping is no problem, and there are good hotels at Esquel, Perito Moreno, Calafate and (in Chile) Puerto Natales. Third class accommodation also at Gobernador Gregores, Río Mayo, Esperanza and (in Chile) Coyhaique. The northern part of the triangle is formed by the paved highway running from Bariloche through Neuquén to San Antonio Oeste.

Many of the roads in Southern Argentina are gravelled. The price of a good windscreen protector varies according to make of car, but can be US$50 in Buenos Aires. For a VW Kombi they are hard to find at a reasonable price. More primitive versions can be bought for much less—e.g. US$5 in San Julián, and probably elsewhere—or made from wire mesh, wood and string. The best types to buy are the grid-type, or inflatable plastic ones which are made for some standard-type vehicles, the only disadvantage being some loss of visibility. Drivers should also look out for cattle grids (*guardaganados*), even on main highways. They are signed; approach them very slowly.

Hitch-hiking is generally difficult except on Route 3 in spring and summer; camping equipment is useful as long delays can be expected even in the tourist season.

**N.B.** Keep passport handy as examination is required when passing from one province to another. Also, be prepared for roadblocks at which one has to declare one's destination, nationality, vehicle particulars, etc.

The upper course of the Río Colorado is the northern limit of Patagonia. 160 km. S of where it reaches the sea (250 km. S of Bahía Blanca), about 27 km. from the mouth of the Río Negro, is **Carmen de Patagones** (16,000 people), standing on high ground on the northern bank, with **Viedma** (26,000 people) the capital of Río Negro Province, across the river, which is spanned by a connecting rail and road bridge. There is also a frequent ferry service for pedestrians. On a hill behind Patagones a monument commemorates an attack on the twin towns by a Brazilian squadron in 1827. (Beware of pleasant-looking campsites near this monument; there is an artillery range nearby.) There are three museums, open 1000-1200 only. There are air services to Viedma, 966 km. from Buenos Aires daily except Thursday (continuing either to Bariloche or General Roca). The swimming is recommended on the Viedma side of the river, where there is a nice shady shore. A law was passed in 1986 nominating Viedma as the site of the new federal capital, but the project is unlikely ever to come to fruition.

**Hotels**  At Viedma: *Peumayen*, Buenos Aires 334, D; *Austral*, C, rec., modern. *Hotel Nueva Roma*, E, basic, fleas. *Restaurant Munich*, Buenos Aires 161, open late.

**Camping**  Good municipal site 500 metres after crossing the river on the new road bridge on the right, all facilities.

**Exchange**  Travel agency at Namuncurra 78, Viedma, exchanges Amex cheques.

**Tourist Office**  Belgrano 544, 9th floor, Viedma.

**Buses**  Bus terminal at Calle A. Zatti y Lavalle about 6 blocks from main plaza.

**Excursion**  Beautiful beach, El Cóndor, 30 km. S of Viedma, 3 buses a day from Viedma in summer, hotel open Jan.-Feb., restaurants and shops, free camping on beach 2 km. S. 30 km. from El Cóndor is a sealion colony (*loberia*); daily bus in summer from Viedma; hitching easy in summer.

**Camping**  Further camping sites on the Río Negro where the main route into Patagonia meets the river (some 170 km. from Viedma due NW) with all facilities including a small shop. Additional shops at General Conesa, 2 km. away. Mosquito repellant needed. There is another campsite N of General Conesa (about 140 km.) at Río Colorado again alongside the Patagonian road. All facilities.

Almost due W and 180 km. along the coast, on the Gulf of San Matías, is **San Antonio Oeste** (10,000 people). 17 km. S is a seaside resort, **Las Grutas**, developed in the 1960s with good safe beach (the caves themselves are not really worth visiting); bus from San Antonio hourly US$1.30, ACA has a *Unidad Turística*, with 6-bed rooms, no restaurant. *Tour du Golfe*, friendly, 3-bed rooms, D, cooking facilities. There is also a camping ground. Seafood restaurants. The whole of Las Grutas closes down in mid-March and retires to Buenos Aires. Between San Antonio and Puerto Madryn is Sierra Grande, where iron-ore deposits are being rapidly developed. The ore is piped in solution to an ocean terminal 32 km. E.

**Hotels at San Antonio**  *Iberia*, Sarmiento 241, D with bath, but without breakfast, small rooms, but rec.; *Kandava*, 2 blocks from bus and railway station, C with bath, hot water, clean, good; *Golfo Azul*, D, simple, clean; *Vasquito*, just acceptable, F.

**Railway**  via Viedma to **Bahía Blanca** and **Buenos Aires** and westwards to **Bariloche**. Timetable from Buenos Aires as for Bariloche; train passes through San Antonio Oeste at 1953 en route to Bariloche, 1002 to Bahía Blanca. 1st class fare to Buenos Aires US$30.

**Buses**  From San Antonio to **Bahía Blanca** and S to **Río Gallegos** and **Punta Arenas** by Transportes Patagónicos. To **Viedma** 0700 daily. To **Puerto Madryn** and **Trelew**, Don Otto, 0330 and 1530, 4 hrs., US$9. To **Buenos Aires**, US$32 via Bahía Blanca, frequent.

Route to Bariloche: paved. Continue 201 km. through bush country providing fodder for a few cattle, with a view to the S of the salt flats called Salina del Gualicho. The road then meets the Zapala-Buenos Aires highway at Choele Choel. Then 223 km. to Neuquén through an unbroken series of groves of tall trees sheltering vineyards and orchards. On (424 km.) to Bariloche along fast road, skirting the entire length of the reservoir formed by the Ezequiel Ramos Mejía dam. Then it drops over an escarpment to cross the Collón Curá river. Continue through the valley of the river Limay to Confluencia and the Valle Encantado. The journey can be completed in 11 hours.

About 250 km. S, along Route 3 (paved) in Chubut province is **Puerto Madryn**, a port on the Golfo Nuevo. It was founded by the Welsh colonist, Parry Madryn, in 1865. Population, 20,000. Ask at tourist office about visits to the aluminium plant. The town is becoming a popular tourist centre, with a casino, skin-diving and nature reserves, both near the town and on the nearby Valdés peninsula. Museo de Ciencias Naturales y Oceanográfico on Domecq García and J. Menéndez, informative and worth a visit, opening hours variable. No Youth Hostel.

**Hotels**  (Very full in summer, make bookings early.) *Península Valdés*, J.A.Roca 163, T 71292 A, 4-star, sea view, suites available, comfortable, rec.; *Tolosa*, R. Sáenz Peña 250, T 71850 A, 3-star, friendly; *Gran Madryn I*, L. Lugones 40, T 72205, B, 2-star, friendly but rooms just acceptable; *Hostal del Rey*, Blvd. Brown 681, T 71156, on beach, rec., B, 2-star, with radio, breakfast included; *Motel ACA*, Ribera Marítima Norte, C; *Yanco*, Av. Roca 627, T 71581, on beach, nightly entertainment programme, free, B, has rooms for up to 6; *Atalaya*, Domecq García 149, T 73006, C, with bath, clean; *Muelle Viejo*, Yrigoyen 40, opposite pier, D with breakfast, good; *Residencial J'Os*, Bolívar 75, T 71433, D, pleasant; *París*, Roque Sáenz Peña and 25 de Mayo, E without bath, being renovated, very friendly, restaurant; *Vaskonia*, 25 de Mayo 43, T 74427, E, hot water sometimes, noisy, dirty, unfriendly; *Apart-Motel Palma*, Av. Roca 7, new, D, heated, showers, no food but clean; *España*, 28 de Julio y San Martín, D, clean, hot water, restaurant; *El Dorado*, San Martín 545, T 71026, D, clean, shower, patio, but landlady not keen on backpackers; *Residencial Petit*, Alvear 845, T 71460, D with bath, clean, quiet, good.

**Camping**  All closed out of season. At Punta Cuevas, 6 km. S of town, is ACA site with hot showers and shady trees (discounts for ACA members and holders of international Driving Licence) but many people camp on beach. There is a swimming pool in the rocks near the ACA camp site, which gets its water at high tide, very pleasant, and free. Two municipal sites: one at Ribera Sur, 4-5 km. S of town on same road along beach (gives student discount). All facilities, very crowded. Bus from centre goes to within 1 km. The other is N of town at Barrio Brown. Camping out can be interesting as one can watch foxes, armadillos, skunks and rheas roaming around in the evening.

**Restaurants**  *Aguila*, M.A.Zar and R.S.Peña, highly rec., good for seafood; *La Caleta*, San Martín 156, excellent, seafood, reasonable prices; *Cantina El Náutico*, Julio Roca and Lugones, good food, especially fish; *París*, R.S.Peña 112, excellent and reasonable; *Parrilla Mayoral*, R.S. Peña 12; *Parrilla de Matias*, R.S. Peña 218, very good meat; *Pizzería Roselli*, Peña y J.A. Roca, cheap, good, with vegetarian selections; *Parrilla El Soledad*, R.S.Peña 214, good salads; *Pleno Centro Confitería*, 28 de Julio y 25 de Mayo, good. For excellent Welsh afternoon teas, *La Goleta*, Roca 87, 1700-1900 (poor sign, but good tea, US$7).

**Exchange**  Banco de la Nación, 25 de Mayo y 9 de Julio, go early to avoid long queues. There are no *cambios* as such, apart from Turismo Pu-Ma, 28 de Julio 46, but fair rates from travel agents (e.g. Golfo Nuevo Turismo, Safari Submarino, addresses below; go in the morning). La Moneda, Roca y 28 de Julio, will exchange large sums, not very good rates. Some shops will change US$ cash. High commission on changing cheques: Banco de la Nación (best) charge 7%.

**Car Hire**  On Roca next to *Hotel Peninsula Valdés*, very expensive: US$30 a day plus US$0.36 per km.

**Laundromat**  *Lavarap*, 25 de Mayo 529.

**Sport**  Puerto Madryn is being promoted as a diving centre. Tours for those who have never dived before are organized by Safari Submarino, Mitre 80; Turismo Submarino, Av. Roca 743; Pimino in the harbour, all about US$20 per excursion. A few others along the harbour; all show nature videos at about 1930. Swim in the so-called *parque submarino* amid sunken cars and a few fish! Trained divers seriously interested in marine life who have at least a week's stay should contact the Centro Nacional Patagónico at Av. Roca. Windsurfing lessons and equipment hire at Brown 871.

**Tourist Agencies**  Several agencies do tours to the Valdés Peninsula, all are for 12 hours, see below. Prices are fixed by law, but itineraries may differ. Tour rates increase by 75% on 15 November and again on 15 December by the same amount. *Tur-Mar*, T 74104, 25 de Mayo 167; *Pu-Ma*, 28 de Julio 48, T 71482; *Mar y Valle*, Roca 37, T 72872, rec. *Receptivo*, Roca 303 y Belgrano, T 71048, Amex agent, weekend and off-season tours, mixed reports; *Sur Turismo*, J.A. Roca 612, T 73585; *Golfo Nuevo Turismo*, 28 de Julio 21, T 72117, Nelson speaks English. *Siempre Tur*, Mosconi 36, Local 16, T 734, English spoken, rec.; *Prima Tur*, 28 de Julio; *Coyun Co*, Roca 37. **Recommended guide**: Dr. Pedro Fuentes Galliardo.

**Tourist Office**, at Julio Roca 444, open until 2400 in the tourist season, but only 0700-1300 Mon.-Fri. in winter; helpful, has notice board for messages.

**Transport**  Buses from **Buenos Aires**, 2 a day with La Puntual, 21 hrs., comfortable, US$47.50; Sun., Mon., Thurs. and Fri., at 2030, with El Cóndor, daily with Costa Criolla at 2130, via San Antonio Oeste, change at Bahía Blanca, 22-24 hrs. To **Río Gallegos**, about 20 hrs., four times a week. Bus to **Bahía Blanca** 0800 and 1000 daily, 12 hrs. (US$11.25 with Don Otto); 10½ hrs., US25, with La Puntual to **Mar del Plata**, changing at Bahía Blanca. Patagónicos to **San Antonio Oeste** at 0800 and 2230, US$9. Bus to **Trelew** with 28 de Julio company, every 90 minutes, more frequent in summer, 65 mins., US$3.50; driver will stop at entrance to Trelew airport if asked. Don Otto to **Comodoro Rivadavia**, Wed., Thurs., Fri., Sun. 0915 and daily at 1600, US$22. No direct bus to **Bariloche**, change at Trelew and Esquel.

**NORTHEAST CHUBUT**
Not to Scale

To San Antonio Oeste

Telsen

To Las Plumas & Esquel

28 de Julio

Las Chapas

Dolavon

Dique Florentino Ameghino

Dos Pozos

To Comodoro Rivadavia

Gaiman

Trelew

Rawson

Playa Unión

Punta Tombo

Puerto Madryn

Pto. Pirámides

Golfo San José

Isla de los Pájaros

Punta Norte

Caleta Valdés

Península Valdés

Golfo Nuevo

Punta Cuevas

Punta Loma

Salina Grande

Punta Ninfas

Punta Delgada

SOUTH ATLANTIC OCEAN

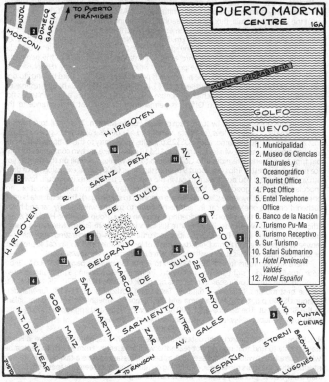

**PUERTO MADRYN CENTRE**   16A

TO PUERTO PIRÁMIDES

PUJOL
DOMECQ GARCIA
MOSCONI
H. IRIGOYEN
R. SAENZ PEÑA
28 DE JULIO
BELGRANO
SAN MARTIN
GOB. MAIZ
M.T. DE ALVEAR
MARCOS A.
SARMIENTO
MITRE
AV. GALES
ESPAÑA
9 DE JULIO
NAR
AV. JULIO A. ROCA
25 DE MAYO
STORNI
BLVO. G. BROWN
LUGONES

MUELLE PIEDRABUENA

GOLFO NUEVO

TO RAWSON

TO PUNTA CUEVAS

1. Municipalidad
2. Museo de Ciencias Naturales y Oceanográfico
3. Tourist Office
4. Post Office
5. Entel Telephone Office
6. Banco de la Nación
7. Turismo Pu-Ma
8. Turismo Receptivo
9. Sur Turismo
10. Safari Submarino
11. *Hotel Península Valdés*
12. *Hotel Español*

Taxi rank on the plaza.

**Excursions** There are nature reserves nearby at Punta Loma on Golfo Nuevo (sea-lions), only 15 km. from Puerto Madryn (sea-lions, whales, penguins and flamingoes also frequent the Puerto Madryn area itself, sea-lions even invading the harbour); Punta Pirámides (sea-lions) and Isla de los Pájaros (sea birds) Golfo San José and Punta Norte (right whales), on the Valdés Peninsula (see below). (Check opening times of reserves in Puerto Madryn; they vary.) The natural history of the region is most interesting, with other seal and penguin colonies, breeding ground at Golfo Nuevo for right whales, fossils in the cliffs, and *guanacos*, rheas and armadillos in the countryside. Most animals (except the whale) can be seen in the warm seasons, from October to April. See whales from perhaps as early as June to, at the very latest, end- November. Oct.-Nov. is said to be the time to see greatest variety of wildlife. Past the lighthouse and Naval Zone at Punta Delgada on the other side of the Valdés Peninsula is Salina Grande, Argentina's lowest point, 35 metres below sea level.

*Puerto Pirámides*, with a population of 70 is 90 km. E of Puerto Madryn on the Valdés Peninsula (ACA motel, C, restaurant poor for food and value; also municipal campsite, US$1 p.p., hot showers in evening only; *hostería* on seaward side of main street with café attached, excellent value, clean; and small friendly *hostería*, open Sept.-March, the *Posada del Mar.*, D, basic but friendly. Also *Cantina El Salmón*, on the beach, good. There is a shop that sells original Patagonian Indian work). Hydro Sports rents scuba equipment and boats, has a small restaurant, and organizes land and sea wildlife tours (ask for Mariano), boat trips US$10 for 1 hour. Bus (Empresa 28 de Julio) from Puerto Madryn, Tues., Thur., Sat., 0825, return 1855; Sun. bus at 1100 returns 1700, US$4 each way. About 79 km. E of Puerto Madryn is Isla de los Pájaros, on a good road. No one is now allowed to visit the island without special permission (only granted to recognized ornithologists). At Punta Norte (176 km.) at the N end of the Valdés Peninsula, there are sea-elephants (breeding time in first fortnight in August, best seen at low tide), late spring and summer (Nov.-March), reasonably priced restaurant for meals and snacks. At Caleta Valdés, 45 km. S of Punta Norte you can see penguins and sea elephants at close quarters, but not at any specific point. Camping at hangar nearby, but take fresh water with you as supplies are unreliable. At Punta Delgada (at the S of the peninsula) most wildlife can be seen except the penguins, which have moved away (*Hotel Faro*, B, comfortable, excellent food, rec). The peninsula is private property. One third belongs to one man, who grazes 40,000 sheep. In theory, US$1 is charged to visit each nature reserve on the peninsula; moreover, the beach on the entire coast is out of bounds, although this is not strictly enforced. A Conservation Officer is permanently stationed at the entrance to the Peninsula (he is very helpful).

Excursions are organized by tourist agencies in Puerto Madryn. The usual tour takes in Puerto Pirámides, Caleta Valdés (or Punta Norte) and Isla de los Pájaros. Shop around, but most agencies charge the same: about US$25 p.p. plus US$4 entry to the National Park; tours including a boat trip to see whales charge up to US$18 extra; there are two companies running boat trips from Puerto Pirámides into Golfo Nuevo to see whales, the one on the right as you face the water is better. Trips last about 9 hours, starting at 0800. On all excursions take drink with you, food too if you don't want to eat in the expensive restaurants (swimsuit, towel and binoculars are also a good idea). Most tour companies stay 50-60 minutes on location, not considered sufficient by some (Siempre Tur are reported to stay longer). The peninsula is easily reached if one has one's own car, in fact the best way to see the wildlife is by car and hiring a vehicle or taking a taxi is worth considering if you can get a group together. Hitching is very difficult, less so at weekends. Peninsular roads are variable: from Puerto Madryn to Puerto Pirámides is paved; from Puerto Pirámides to Punta Norte is degenerating and the road between Punta Norte and Punta Delgada consists of large pebbles which may cause problems for low-clearance vehicles (tours will not run after heavy rain in the low season).

There are also tours from Puerto Madryn to Punta Tombo **(see page 176)**, US$30, but these usually include "sight-seeing" in Rawson, Trelew and Gaiman and a lot of time is spent travelling. The Punta Loma sealion reserve is open 0900-1200, 1430-1730, Sept., and Oct., are the best months. Hitching is difficult. Taxis charge official price, US$18; Tur-Mar does 12-hour US$40 p.p. trip to Punta Loma and the Florentino Ameghino dam, 110 km. inland on the Río Chubut. The dam covers 7,000 hectares with water and irrigates 28,000 hectares in the lower Chubut valley, as well as producing electric power.

**N.B.** If possible check all excursion dates in advance; it is very disappointing to arrive in Puerto Madryn only to find that one cannot reach the wildlife reserves. From March to September (when there is less wildlife to be seen) it has been necessary to take a taxi but we are now informed that the tours run all year, depending on numbers. Tours seem cheaper from Madryn than from Trelew, probably because Trelew has the airport.

Along the Río Chubut are several towns. **Rawson** (pop 9,000), the capital of Chubut Province, 7 km. from the sea (*Hotel Provincial*, Mitre, C, good restaurant, hotel clean, but seems to be falling down), has law courts, a museum in the Colegio Don Bosco, a fishing port, and a riverside Tourist Office, 9 de Julio 64, T 213. Puerto Rawson is about 5 km. down river; you can camp on the beach, and *Cantina El Marinero* serves good seafood.

Some 20 km. up the Río Chubut is **Trelew** (55,000 people), a prosperous town which has lost its Welsh look. There is a pretty red-brick chapel in the centre, and a small, interesting museum in the old railway station, open 0900-~~1300~~, 1200 1500-~~2045~~. On the road to Rawson, 500 metres before the bridge is Chapel Moriah, a beautiful 1880 Welsh chapel, with the graves of many original settlers. A paved road runs from Rawson through Trelew, Gaiman (see page 176) and Dolavon, all on the river, to Las Plumas (mind the bridge if driving) and the upper Chubut Valley, all the way to Esquel (see page 160) and Trevelin.

**Local Holidays**  28 July (Founding of Chubut); 13 Dec. (Petroleum Day).

**Hotels**  *Rayentray*, San Martín y Belgrano, T 34702, best in town; *Centenario*, San Martín 150, T 30041, B, good and cheap restaurant, best to stick to simpler dishes; *Libertador*, Rivadavia 73, T 35316, C, without breakfast 4 blocks from Plaza, poor restaurant, quiet; *Plaza*, D with breakfast, on main square, clean, friendly, helpful; *Parque*, Irigoyen y Cangallo, T 30098 D, good; *Rivadavia*, Rivadavia 55, T 34472, D with bath, clean, rec.; *Touring Club*, Av. Fontana 240, T 33998, excellent, D (with bath), the social hub of Trelew, chess is played here, colour TV, breakfast rec., coffee the best in town; *Residencial Patterson*, Moreno 270, D; *Galicia*, 9 de Julio y Rivadavia, T 33803 very warm, E, without bath, clean. *Residencial San Carlos*, E, with private bath, Sarmiento 758, rec., and *Provinciano*, Yrigoyen 525, E, poor and noisy. *Argentino*, Abraham Matthews y Moreno, D, clean, quiet, near bus station. *Hostal Residencial Plaza*, F in triple, clean, friendly, rec. *Hostal Avenida*, Lewis Jones 49, E, close to bus station, friendly, quiet, "rec., cheapest in town, nice rooms".

**Camping**  possible south of the town on the road to Rawson and Comodoro Rivadavia, on right about 200 metres beyond the bridge over River Chubut, one can camp by the river, but beware of mosquitoes (US$3 for 2 people + van). The site belongs to the Sports Club and has a public swimming pool.

**Restaurants**  *Martín Fierro*, expensive; *Eulogia Fuentes*, Don Bosco 23, good pasta; *El Quijote*, 25 de Mayo 86, good food, better than service; *El Mesón*, Rivadavia 588; *Cabildo Star*, Roca 88, cheap, good; *Capítulo II*, Roca 393, good, cheap.

**Shopping**  Mr Sturdee Rogers, *Rogers Shop*, Moreno 463, T 20696, serves Welsh afternoon teas between 1700 and 1900, and sells traditional cakes; also gives information on the Welsh of Patagonia. Welsh and English spoken; rec.

**Car Hire**  3 companies at the airport. Also **Alquilauto Fiorasi**, España 344, T 30589.

**Exchange**  Lloyds Bank (BLSA), Av. 9 de Julio esq. Belgrano; **Banco Provincia del Chubut**, Rivadavia y 25 de Mayo. Local banks. Open 0800-1200. (1% commission). **Sur Turismo**, Belgrano 326, accepts travellers' cheques at poor rate. **Banco del Sud**, España 197, only accepts dollar bills in mint condition!

**Post Office**  25 de Mayo and Mitre. **Entel** Julio A. Rocay 1-100 block, open till 2400.

**Tourist Office**, room 20 on 1st floor of Terminal Terrestre, additionally opens briefly at 0515 for travellers arriving from Esquel, also at airport and at Italia y Rioja, friendly but not always accurate. Free maps.

**Tourist Agencies**  *Sur Turismo* (exchanges cash and travellers' cheques), Belgrano 326-330, organize a few excursions to Punta Tombo, T 34550; *Estrella del Sur Turismo*, San Martin 129, T 31282, tours to Valdés Peninsula and Punta Tombo, rec.; *Punta Tombo Turismo*, in *Hotel Centenario* T 30658; and others. Tours to Valdés Peninsula take about 12-13 hours, best to go in a small tour bus which can get closer to main wildlife viewing sites.

**By Air**  Airport 5 km. from centre; taxis cost about US$5. Buses from Puerto Madryn stop at the turning to the airport, (10 mins. walk). LADE (Av. Fontana 227, T 35244) flies, **Trelew-Río Gallegos**, once a week; daily with Aerolíneas (25 de Mayo 33, T 35297). Daily to **Buenos Aires**, AR and Austral (25 de Mayo 259, T 34799). To **Ushuaia**, with Aerolineas. LADE also Buenos Aires-Trelew. **Río Grande** (via Río Gallegos), 2 flights a week, with Aerolíneas or

LADE, stopping at Comodor Rivadavia, Santa Cruz (LADE only) and Río Gallegos. 4 times a week, to Esquel, twice with Aerolíneas twice with LADE. The Aero Club sells sightseeing flights.

**Buses** from **Buenos Aires** to Trelew daily at 2100, 21½ hrs., US$35 (return 0700 and 2130 daily, 1705 Tues., Thurs., Fri. and Sat.). Bus to **Bahía Blanca**, 734 km., US$30 daily with Don Otto, 0600, few a week with La Puntual, 0600; to **Mar del Plata**, changing at Bahía Blanca, US$24.25 with La Puntual; to **Esquel**, US$44, 2130, 11 hrs. with Empresa Chubut; bus to **Bariloche** daily. Buses to **Rawson** every 15 min.; every 1½ hours to **Gaiman**, US$1.15; every 90 minutes to **Puerto Madryn**, US$3.50 with 28 de Julio; to **Comodoro Rivadavia** daily at 2000, and Sun., Wed., Thurs. and Fri. at 1035, US$13, 6 hrs.; to **Río Gallegos**, Sun., Tues., Thurs. 2005, via Puerto Deseado. If **hitching** south from Trelew, take the Rawson bus to the flyover 5 km. out of town; there is a junction N of town for Puerto Madryn traffic.

**Gaiman**, 18 km. from Trelew, a pretty place with well-built brick houses but quite touristy, is now the most Welsh of the Chubut valley towns. It has a museum of the colony, US$0.30, in the old railway station (open in summer, Tues.-Sat. 1600-2000). The only restaurant seems often to be closed, but tea rooms such as *Casa de Té Gaiman*, Yrigoyen 738 (US$7.30 with lots of cakes) and those opposite the square, *Plas y Coed* (oldest, good value, Marta Rees speaks English) and *Ti Gwyn*, *Ty Nain* Yrigoyen 283, (excellent, frequented by tour buses), and *Elma*, Tello 571, are open from 1500. Small municipal campground by river (poor, no facilities). Interesting local agriculture. Welsh-speakers will be interested in the cemetery above town. The Eisteddfodd, Welsh festival of arts, is held in early October each year. Interesting walking tours led by volunteer guides (Spanish-speaking—meet in main plaza) include a private, hand-made (out of beer bottles and string!) theme park, a seaweed factory and the *Ty Nain* tearoom which has a nice display of historical items. All facilities are closed out of season.

**Dolavon**, 20 km. past Gaiman, is easily reached by bus from Trelew. It still retains much Welsh character and provides an interesting view of the irrigation system built by the settlers. The old flour mill/museum is superb; it is completely intact and demonstrations will be given. There is a campsite: turn right by the service station on the way into town, excellent facilities, free (Wendy Chilcott and Steve Newman).

**Wildlife** may be seen at **Punta Tombo** and Camarones. Punta Tombo is 117 km. S of Trelew, on a dirt road branching off 5 km. SE of Trelew on the road to Rawson, driving time 1¾ hours (this is incorrectly shown on ACA maps). There the wildlife is very varied: penguins, *guanacos*, etc. Season for penguins, Sept.- March (Dec.- Jan. is the time when the young are taking to the water). Check with the Tourist Office that it is all right to visit the penguins as from late March they are "off limits" as they prepare to migrate. When visits are permitted it is a fantastic experience. You can share a taxi from Trelew. Sur Turismo and others run ½ day tours, spending 1 hour at the site for US$22 (standard fee). About mid-way between Rawson and Punta Tombo, a road leads off Ruta 1 to Isla Escondida (9 km. signed), no facilities, but lovely rock and sand beach with bird and wildlife (badly littered unfortunately); secluded camping. Good place to camp if you are visiting the wildlife at Punta Tombo early a.m. (the best times).

    **Camarones**, 275 km. from Trelew and 300 km. from Comodoro Rivadavia, is less crowded. There is a large **penguin colony** 35 km. away at Cabo Dos Bahías along a dirt road (open in season only); free camping is possible there and in the town itself (three *hosterías*, all F, the one by the power station is not recommended). Local buses very scarce; two a week, US$10, on Mon. and Fri. from Trelew (Don Otto), book at Uruguay 590, Trelew; bus leaves 0800 from San Martín and Belgrano, arrives 1130, returns to Trelew same day 1600 (reports disagree on whether Don Otto bus continues from Camarones to Comodoro Rivadavia). In Camarones take a taxi (if you can find one) to the penguin colony (US$15 return), or ask the Guardia Fauna for a lift, hitchhiking possible at weekends and return to Trelew Tues. Hotel and restaurant at Camarones, *Kau-i-Keuken*, E, clean, friendly, good food, highly rec.

***Comodoro Rivadavia***, the largest city in the province of Chubut, with a population of 97,000, is 387 km. S of Trelew. Petroleum was discovered here in 1907 and about 30% of all Argentina's oil production comes from wells to the S and W. A 1,770-km. pipeline carries the natural gas to Buenos Aires, and a petrochemical plant has been built. Renewed interest in the local oil industry is making the town boom. There is a Oil Museum, with exhibits on exploration and production, 3 km. N in Gral. Mosconi (bus No. 6 from San Martín y Abasolo). From here southward, prices begin to rise very rapidly, so stock up before reaching

Río Gallegos. Good beach at Rada Tilly, 12 km. south (buses every ½ hr.) walk along beach at low tide to see sealions.

**Local Holidays** 28 July (Founding of Chubut); 13 Dec. (Petroleum Day).

**Hotels** *Austral*, Rivadavia 190, B, noise from street traffic but otherwise comfortable, reasonable restaurant; *Comodoro*, off Av. Rivadavia at end of 9 de Julio, 1½ blocks from bus station, C, restaurant, night clubs, car rental; *Colón*, on San Martín, E, run down, but quiet, safe and cheap; *Hospedaje Praga*, España y Sarmiento, E, shower, clean; *Residencial Azul*, C, good service, Sarmiento 724; *Comercio*, Rivadavia 341, T 22341, friendly, near bus station, hot showers, D (may be bargained lower), good meals; *Pensión Boedo*, Rivadavia 453, cheap restaurant, mediocre food; *Hospedaje Belgrano*, Belgrano 546, D, with bath, clean, hot water; *Diana*, on Belgrano, E, clean, friendly; *Cari-Hué*, Belgrano 563 E, noisy, otherwise rec.; *Rada Tilly*, D, modern, clean, 5 km. S. *España*, 9 de Julio 935, E, basic. *Hosp. Nanet*, España 1095, T 28867, E, single men, only, clean, friendly. *El Patagón Motel*, access (S) of Route 3.

**Camping** Municipal and ACA, 12 km. S at Rada Tilly, may be reached by hourly Expreso Rada Tilly bus from town. Excellent facilities, hot and cold water. There is another, free, campsite at N end of beach, cold water only (watch out for clayslides when it rains).

**Restaurants** No one eats at night until 2200. *La Rastra*, Rivadavia 384, very good for churrasco, but not much else; *Cocorico* (better) and *El Náutico*, Playa Costanera. *Pizzería El Nazareño*, San Martín y España, good. Several *rotiserías*, much cheaper, on 400 block of Rivadavia, in municipal market.

**VW dealer**, Comercial Automotor, Rivadavia 380, rec. VW concession in Barrio Industrial, Av. Irigoyen, also rec.

**Exchange** Lloyds Bank (BLSA), Av. Rivadavia 264. Oct.-March 0700-1300; April-Sept. 1200-1800; no exchange transactions after 1000 in summer, 6% commission on travellers' cheques, will pay dollars cash on cheques but minimum US$300; the **Banco de la Nación**, San Martín 108, has the best rates on US$ but does not change travellers' cheques. Amex agent is Orbe Turismo Show, San Martín next to Confitería *Fuente d'Oro*, 5% commission for dollars or australes on travellers' cheques. Hotel Comodoro changes US$ at poor rate. Several travel agencies also change money including **Roqueta Travel**, Rivadavia y Pellegrini, Ceferino, 9 de Julio 852, San Julián travel agency, and **CRD Travel**, Moreno 844 (travellers' cheques). Bill Fitzpatrick in the insurance company at Moreno y Rivadavia. Video shop Ostoich, 25 de Mayo 957, will change at back counter.

**Post Office** San Martín y Moreno.

**Consulates Belgian Vice-Consul**, Rivadavia 283; **Chilean Consul**, Sarmiento 936; **Italian Vice-Consul**, Belgrano 1053.

**Travel agencies** *Puelche EVT*, Rivadavia 527; *Richard Pentreath*, Mitre 952; *San Gabriel*, *Atlas*, and *Ceferino*, at San Martín 488, 263 and 372, respectively; *Monitur*, 9 de Julio 948.

**Tourist Office** On Rivadavia.

**Buses** Bus station conveniently located in city centre; has luggage store, good *confitería* upstairs, lousy toilets, *remise* taxi booth, some kiosks. Bus service to **Buenos Aires** daily at 1530 (Don Otto—will not take credit cards or US$ despite signs), 32 hrs., US$55 (also daily with La Puntual/Cóndor at 1300 and Sat. 2400). Angel Giobbi buses to **Coyhaique** (Chile), US$27, 12 hrs., twice a week (Tues. and Fri.), 0100, June-Sept. and 3 a week (Mon., Wed., Fri.), 0100, Oct.-May (weather permitting). Three buses a week to **Bariloche**, US$68 (Don Otto at 2150, Sun., Tues., Thurs., stops at Sarmiento midnight, Esquel at 0600 and for ½ hr. at El Bolsón at 0900, arrives 0600 at Bariloche). To **Esquel** (paved road) direct, Fri. 1230, 10 hrs., via Río Mayo, Mon., Thurs., 0100, 15½ hrs., to Río Mayo Tues., Thurs., Sun., 1700 and 1900, 5½ hrs. Three a week to **Río Gallegos** (Patagónica, US$40 and Andesmar, Thurs. at 0320). To **Puerto Madryn** US$22 (Don Otto at 1600). La Unión colectivo to **Caleta Olivia**, hourly, US$3.50. To **Sarmiento**, US$7, 2½ hrs. at 0700, 1300, 1900. To **Mendoza**, daily at 0130, 20 hrs.; to **Córdoba**, Tues., Fri., Sun., 1200, 33 hrs.

**Air Services** Airport, 9 km. Bus to airport from downtown terminal or opp. Aerolíneas Argentinas in main street hourly (45 mins), US$0.40; take bus No.6. At least once a day to **Buenos Aires** a day with Aerolíneas or Austral, stopping at **Trelew**; offices on San Martín 421 and 291; Austral flight daily to **Río Gallegos**, Aerolíneas 4 a week. Austral and AR fly to **Río Grande**, Austral daily to **Ushuaia**; LADE flies once a week Comodoro Rivadavia- Perito Moreno- Gobernador Gregores- Calafate- Río Gallegos- Río Grande- Ushuaia, with detour over Calafate glacier, weather permitting, once a week Santa Cruz- Río Gallegos- Río Grande and once a week Puerto Deseado- San Julián - Río Gallegos- Río Grande- Ushuaia. Taxi to airport, US$7.

**Hitch-Hiking** There is a truck stop outside Comodoro Rivadavia on the road to Bahía Blanca, where you can contact drivers if hitching. Hitch out of the centre on Ruta 3 to "Astra Km. 20", or take any bus going N. Expensive truckdrivers' restaurants along the road; buy food in supermarkets.

The road to Chile runs inland from Comodoro Rivadavia, amid oil wells, to (156 km.) Colonia Sarmiento (commonly known just as **Sarmiento**), population: 7,000 (archaeological museum with tourist office next to cathedral, check opening times, may be closed at weekends) on Lago Musters, near the large Lago Colhué Huapí. 32 km. by dirt road S of Sarmiento there is a large petrified forest, the Bosque Petrificado José Ormachea (**see page 179**), well worth a visit but difficult to reach. There are few taxis (try outside *Hotel Lago Musters*). Hitching is possible in summer. The Park Warden, Juan José Valera (Uruguay 43) may give lifts, but check return times.

**Hotels** *Lago Musters*, P. Moreno and Ing. Coronel, run down; *Hostería Los Lagos*, Roca and Alberdi, C, good, friendly, heating, has restaurant. *Colón*, P. Moreno 645, F p.p., restaurant, clean and friendly; *San Martín*, San Martín y P. Moreno, cheap, good restaurant. Food at *El Gaucho*, Route 20, access Sarmiento. *Ismar*, 200 block of Patagonia; *Oroz*, 200 block of Uruguay. In Dec.-March you may be permitted to sleep in the Agricultural School (bring sleeping bag) on the road to petrified forest, opp. the ACA petrol station.

**Camping** Municipal site 2 km. N of centre on Route 24, basic but free, beside river.

**Travel Agency** Julio Lew, Roca and Alberdi.

**Bus** Overnight buses to **Esquel** on Sun. Tues. and Thurs., stop at Rio Mayo, 0630, take food for journey as cafés on route tend to overcharge. 3 buses a day to **Comodoro Rivadavia**, 0700, 1300, 1900 and Giobbi buses to **Chile** leave at 0200.

The road runs West from Sarmiento via **Río Mayo** (which has three hotels, the *Covadonga*, D, very good; *A'Ayones*, T 20044, F p.p., clean, modern, heating; *San Martín*), to Puerto Aysén in Chile. The Giobbi buses from Comodoro Rivadavia to Coyhaique, Chile, leave Río Mayo at 0600. A branch from this road goes 130 km. S to Perito Moreno, by Lago Buenos Aires. Another branch on the Río Mayo-Perito Moreno road turns W at 31 km. to Lago Blanco, where there is a small *estancia* community, 30 km. from the border with Chile (about 150 km. from Río Mayo). No hotel, but police are friendly and may permit camping at the police post. No public transport to Chile; wild but beautiful place. From Sarmiento you can reach Esquel (448 km. N along Route 40), at the southern edge of the Lake District (**see page 160**). The first 210 km. from Sarmiento are paved, then it is mostly a dirt or all-weather road, though short stretches have been paved. Hitching along this road is very difficult, even in summer.

*Perito Moreno* (population 1,700), at 400 metres, is close to Lago Buenos Aires, which extends into Chile as Lago General Carrera (do not confuse the town with Ventisquero Perito Moreno, the glacier on Lago Argentino; see under Calafate, below). Also nearby are Lagos Belgrano and Burmeister, and the source of the Río Deseado. Daily buses (US$3, 1½ hrs.) to Los Antiguos (*Hotel Argentino*, E, comfortable restaurant; municipal campsite; service station) on the Chilean border at Lago Buenos Aires (67 km. along Route 520), surrounded by orchards, where *pejerrey* can be caught. Halfway is Las Chilcas where Indian remains are found.

The famous Cuevas de las Manos, a series of galleries with 10,000-years-old paintings of human hands and of animals in red, orange, black, white and green, are interesting even for those not interested in rock art; the canyon in which the caves are situated is very beautiful. 118 km. S of Perito Moreno on Route 40, a marked road goes directly to the caves (68 km.) No buses, but the tourist office at Perito Moreno can supply names of drivers who can take you there, prices between US$40-60, to be split among a party of visitors. On leaving Perito Moreno on the way to the caves you will pass Cerro de El Volcán, its crater is accessible; after pasing the Gendarmería on your right, take the first left (dirt road) at the 3-road junction with Route 40. It is 12 km. to the path to the crater—ask permission at the Estancia to continue.

**Hotels** *Belgrano*, D with shower, clean, no heating, with good restaurant; *Austral*, D, modern, clean, open Dec. to Feb., both on San Martin; *Argentino*, E, dirty, no showers; *Santa Cruz*, on Belgrano, E, heating, shared bath and hot water. Food is very expensive in Perito Moreno. **Restaurant** *Americano*, good and cheap.

**Camping** Parque Laguna in town, opposite Laguna Cisnes, good hot showers, well shielded, US$0.50 p.p. (slide shows at the tourist office there, information given).

**Exchange** US dollars can be exchanged at **Banco de la Nación** and **Banco de la Provincia de Santa Cruz** (both change cash), **Hotel Austral** and **Hotel Belgrano**, latter gives better rates. Difficult to exchange travellers cheques.

**Transport** Airport is a long way from town, try to hitch as there is only one taxi; LADE flies from Perito Moreno to **Calafate**, **Río Gallegos** and **Ushuaia** (Mon.) and **Río Gallegos** on Thur. Hitch-hikers to the S are warned that, outside the tourist season (Jan.-mid-Feb.), it is usually quicker to head for the coast at Caleta Olivia and go S from there than to take the road via Gobernador Gregores and Piedra Buena.

There are various routes from Perito Moreno to Coyhaique in Chile: Perito Moreno to Chile Chico, then by twice-weekly *El Pilchero* ferry boat across Lago General Carrera to Puerto Ibáñez, and then on by road to Coyhaique (public transport on the days the ferry sails). On this route there is a bus connection from Caleta Olivia (see below) through to Los Antiguos (2 km. from border with Chile) every Mon., Thurs., and Sat., at 1030 (from Perito Moreno, leaves from *Hotel Argentino*) and back to Caleta Olivia every Tues., Fri. and Sun. at 0830 (1030 from Perito Moreno), daily in February (at least), US$10, with Empresa Comi. Chile Chico is 8 km. from Los Antiguos; several jeeps a day cross border (not suitable for ordinary cars—the water is waist-deep if you want to walk); ask in *Hotel Argentino*. A second route is to go N to Río Mayo, then W to Coyhaique Alto on the border, and on to Coyhaique. The third alternative is on this same route, but head W at Río Guenguel to the border at Paso Huemules and on to Coyhaique via Balmaceda. Fourthly, there are the roads which go around the northern side of Lago Buenos Aires to Puerto Ibáñez, but there are no sign posts and it is easy to get lost among the *estancias*; it is not worth attempting this route.

The road to Fitz Roy, 164 km. S of Comodoro Rivadavia, is paved (and a major short-cut now bypasses Puerto Deseado? Fitz Roy to Río Gallegos is now also paved (goes via Piedra Buena, **see page 181**). Fitz Roy, named after the captain of Darwin's ship, *Beagle* (*Hotel Fitzroy*, good, cheap, clean, cheap food, camping sometimes possible; petrol station) is a small town (pop. 2,000) and it is better to stay 22 km. N at **Caleta Olivia** on Route 3 (13,400 inhabitants); hotels *Residencial Robert*, *Grand* and one other, all D; and camping at Yacht Club. Caleta Olivia, a good start-point for hitching S, is the urban centre for important oilfields, and is near Pico Truncado, the gas field which feeds the pipeline to Buenos Aires. On the central roundabout in front of the bus station is a huge granite monument of an oil driller with the tools of his trade. El Pingüino bus runs twice daily from Caleta Olivia to Rio Gallegos, US$16.75, 11 hrs. Many buses to Comodoro Rivadavia, 1 hr., US$2.10.

This is the area of the **petrified forests**, 70,000 years old, of fallen araucaria trees, nearly 3 metres round and 15-20 metres long: a remarkable sight. Taxi, Sarmiento to forests, US$20. There are two sites you can visit: the Bosque Petrificado José Ormachea, due W of Comodoro Rivadavia, about 140 km. by road (116 km. paved—the unpaved part is practically impassable in the wet season), 32 km. S of Sarmiento, in Chubut (entry US$2, jeep trip to larger trees US$7 but can be walked in 20 mins.; the Víctor Szlapelis, some 40 km. further SW along the same road (follow signposts, road from Sarmiento in good condition). The **Monumento Natural Bosques Petrificados**, W of Puerto Deseado in Santa Cruz, surrounding the Laguna Grande on a road SW from Fitz Roy, 113 km. away was closed indefinitely in 1989. A new road has been built from Route 3 about 65 km. S of Fitz Roy to the Bosques Petrificados, which reduces the journey by several km.

At Piedra Negra, the previous turn-off for Puerto Deseado, there is a cheap hotel, *Florida Negra*. The only other building is a police post.

About 300 km. S of Comodoro Rivadavia is **Puerto Deseado**, with a population of 3,750 (airport), at the mouth of the river Deseado which drains Lago Buenos

Aires, far to the W. (Hotels: *Los Acantilados*, C, and *Colón*, D, dormitory-style; accommodation may also be available in the sports centre—ask at the Municipalidad). ) The town was founded on 15 July 1884; its harbour takes large ships. A local tourist attraction is the Cañadón de las Bandurrias, sometimes known as the Grotto of Lourdes, 40 metres high. Nearby are islands with penguins and other birds, including the unique grey cormorant; local launches available. Lago Buenos Aires is reached by road in 7 hours; 280 km. to Las Heras, on to Perito Moreno, near the lake, 177 km., and a further 67 km. to the Chilean border at Los Antiguous (see above).

It was at Puerto Deseado that a Welshman in Cavendish's expedition of 1586 gave the name of *pengwyn* (white head) to a certain strange-looking bird. It is only fair to mention the opposing theory that the name is derived from a Spanish word, *pingüe*, meaning fat.

**Local holidays** 31 Jan. (San Juan Bosco); 9 Oct. (Coat of Arms day).

From Puerto Deseado to Santa Cruz by the old road is about 470 km. Some 156 km. short of Santa Cruz and 4 km. off Route 3, it reaches **San Julián** (founded 1901, population of 4,480), the best place for breaking the 834 km. run from Comodoro Rivadavia to Río Gallegos. There is much wildlife in the area: red and grey foxes, *guanacos*, wildcats in the mountains, rheas, etc. The main activities are sheep raising for export, fish canning, and production of kaolin and clay. Clay grinding can be seen at Molienda Santa Cruz and ceramics made at the Escuela de Cerámica; good handicraft centre at Moreno y San Martín. There is a regional museum at the end of San Martín on the waterfront. The ruins of Florida Blanca, a colony 10 km. W of town, founded in 1870 by Antonio Viedma, can be visited. The cascade of San Julián is formed by two different tides. Punta Caldera is a popular summer beach. The first mass in Argentina was held here after Magellan had executed a member of his crew. Francis Drake also put in here to hang Thomas Doughty, after amiably taking breakfast with him. Near San Julián (15 km.) is Cabo Curioso beach, with an attractive natural cave.

**Hotels** *Municipal*, Av. Costanera and 25 de Mayo, very nice, well-run, good value, C, but no restaurant. *Residencial Sada*, on San Martín, C, nice, clean, hot water, own bathroom, but sited on busy main road. Also older *Colón*, C, Av. San Martin 301 and *Aguila*, San Martín 500 block, D, sleazy, cheapest in town. Good municipal campsite on the waterfront, all facilities, Av. Costanera betweeen Rivadavia and Roca.

**Restaurants** *Sportsman*, Mitre y 25 de Mayo, excellent value; *Rural*, Ameghino y Vieytes, good, but not before 2100; a number of others. Also bars and tearooms.

**Post Office** At Belgrano and Av. San Martín; telephone exchange also.

**Banks** Banco de la Nación on Mitre and Belgrano, and **Banco de la Provincia de Santa Cruz** on San Martín and Moreno.

**Pharmacy** *Del Pueblo* on San Martín 570. **Hospital** on Av. Costanera between Roca and Magallanes.

**Tourist Office** In centre of San Martín.

**Air** Weekly services with LADE to Río Gallegos, Río Grande and Ushuaia, and to Puerto Deseado and Comodoro Rivadavia.

**Bus** Transportadora Patagónica comes from Río Gallegos en route to **Buenos Aires** (also Pingüino, 6 hrs. US$14 to/from Río Gallegos); Transportes Staller goes weekly to **Lago Posadas** stopping in Gobernador Gregores, Hotel Riera, Las Horquetas, Caracoles and Río Blanco. Transportes El Cordillerano cover the previous route but also stop at **Caleta Olivia**. For hitching, walk 5 km. to petrol station on Ruta 3.

An unpaved road (Route 521) runs NW from San Julián to Route 40 along the foothills of the Andes. About halfway is *Gobernador Gregores* (*Hotel San Francisco*, acceptable, similarly *Adelino*, C; municipal campsite; good mechanic in town and all grades of fuel available).

*Santa Cruz*, 153 km. S of San Julian, one of the best of the coastal harbours (airport) is near the mouth of the Santa Cruz river which drains Lago Argentino.

Founded on 1 December, 1878 and capital of Santa Cruz province until 1904. A deep-water port is being built 22 km. outside Santa Cruz at Punta Quilla. Population 3,000 (ACA *Hostería*, C; *Hotel Anel Aike*, C). Isla Monte León, 66 km. away (Route 1601, then Route 3 and dirt track) has walruses, penguins, beaches, fishing and camping facilities.

At *Piedra Buena* (population 2,600), 35 km. W of Santa Cruz (paved road) is ACA motel, simple, functional but good, warm and nice food (D), also campsites N of town on Route 3. ACA breakdown station at Km. 247 on Route 3. The *Select* restaurant is very dear for what it offers. Provincial Route 9 (1603 on some maps, unpaved, no petrol) from 43 km. S of Piedra Buena to Calafate runs along the edge of a plateau with occasional panoramic views across the valley of the Río Santa Cruz below. Then at about 170 km. it drops down into the valley itself to follow the river into the hills and to Lake Argentino. A pleasant run, without being spectacular. Route 288 runs direct to Calafate from Piedra Buena via Tres Lagos. Most traffic to Calafate goes via Río Gallegos.

*Río Gallegos*, at the mouth of the Río Gallegos, the capital of Santa Cruz Province, is 265 km. S of Santa Cruz; it has a deep-water port with a dry-dock. The tidal range here during spring tides may be as high as 16 metres. There is a large trade in wool and sheepskins. Population: 43,400. Foundation Day: 9 Dec. 1885. The town has recently improved greatly and has a good shopping centre on Roca, although it is still somewhat drab. "Once beyond Roca and Zapiola, the streets turn to dust, stones and squabbling packs of dogs" (Kevin Healey). Handicraft market at Roca 658, open 0800-2000. The small Plaza San Martín, 1 block from the post office is well tended, with flower beds and statues; outside the post office is a statue commemorating the meeting of Presidents Errázuriz and Roca to end Chile and Argentina's 1883 Magellan Strait dispute. Museum at Perito Moreno 35. The Regional Provincial Museum, Mendoza y Roca, has collections of local flora, fauna, rock samples. Colonial museum at Alberdi y Córdoba. ACA service centre with excellent restaurant. Cheap sheepskins (tanned) and very warm leather coats (*gamulanes*) at Puerto Aymond factory of Mr. Szasack (half the Buenos Aires price). (The cave paintings at Laguna Azul, 60 km. from Río Gallegos, are now reported not available for visiting.)

**Hotels** Strongly recommended: *Alonso*, Corrientes 33, C, simple, very clean and comfortable. *Aparthotel Niza*, Alcorta 190, T 20958, B quiet, good breakfast included, clean, rec.; *Santa Cruz*, Roca 701, C with shower and heating, discount for cash, receptionist speaks English, good coffee bar, breakfast, Avis office here; *Covadonga*, Roca 1214, D, clean, comfortable, warm; *Comercio*, Roca 1302, C, reported not too clean, overpriced, very busy; *Residencial Sachas*, Rivadavia 122, E, clean; *Cabo Vírgenes*, Rivadavia 150, D with bath, rec.; *Río Turbio*, Zapiola 486 (opp. bus station for Punta Arenas), D, with bath, English spoken, good. *París*, Roca 1040, D without bath, friendly, clean; *Central*, Av. Roca 1127, D, central, quiet, cold shower, no heating; *Pensión Belgrano*, Calle Belgrano 123, D, dirty, basic but friendly, has good restaurant; *Residencial Internacional*, Sphur 78, E, with heating, friendly, but insecure; *Colonial*, Urquiza y Rivadavia, T 22329, D, shower, cheaper without, hot water, friendly, clean, can be noisy; close by is *Laguna Azul*, D, a little rundown but clean and good value; *Entre Ríos*, Entre Ríos, E, fairly good; *Viejo La Fuente*, Vélez Sarsfield 64-70, T 20304, E, basic, hot water, restaurant; *Puerto Santa Cruz*, near bus terminal, E, clean, friendly.

**N.B.** Accommodation is hard to find in Río Gallegos because of the number of transient workers in town. Apparently no camping is allowed around Río Gallegos because of a military zone apart from authorized municipal site on Italia y Costa Rica, turn off Route 3 at edge of town heading south (small, basic). Ask at tourist office for new site, being developed alongside a children's playground, cheap, free, hot showers. One is not allowed to take photographs either, for the same reason.

**Restaurants** Plenty and good, some specializing in sea food. *Restaurant Díaz*, Roca 1143, good, mixed reports about the mixed grill; *Montecarlo*, Zapiola 558, good seafood, not the cheapest; opp. is good *heladería*. *El Palenque*, Corrientes 73, rec. *Café Carrera*, Fagnano y Roca, good but expensive breakfast.

**Shopping** *Tia* department store, Roca 700 block, good supermarket section; Supermarket *Le Anónima*, Roca y España. Most places takes a 2-3 hr. lunch break.

**Taxis**  Hiring a taxi for excursions may be no more expensive than taking a tour bus. Try Sr. Miguel Caliguiri, Tres Lagos 445; he charges US$200 to Calafate and Moreno glacier.

**Car parts and repairs**  at Repuestos Sarmiento, on Sarmiento, owner very friendly and helpful.

**Motorcycle Mechanic**  Juan Carlos Topcic, Costa Rica 25, friendly and helpful.

**Exchange**  Lloyds Bank (BLSA), Sarmiento 47. Open 1000-1600. **Banco de Santa Cruz**, 900 block of Roca, fair rates; **Sur Cambio**, San Martín y Roca (no travellers' cheques); *casas de cambio*, best rates. Change travellers' cheques in Río Gallegos if going to Calafate, where it is more difficult; fair rates at **Cambio El Pingüino** (Zapiola 469); may also change European and South American currencies.

**Chilean Consulate**  Mariano Moreno 144, Mon.-Fri., 0900-1300; tourist cards issued at border.

**Post Office**  Roca 893. **Telephones**, Entel, Roca 613.

**Laundry**  9 de Julio y Alberdi.

**Tourist Office**  Roca y Córdoba friendly, Mon.-Fri., 0800-1400, helpful. (Also Alberdi 154.) They will phone round hotels for you.

**Road Travel**  New bus terminal at corner of Route 3 and Eva Perón, 3 km. from centre (no left luggage, small bank, tourist office-casual, *confitería*, few toilets, kiosks); taxi to centre US$0.75, occasional bus US$0.25 (Nos. 1 and 12 from posted stops on Roca). To **Calafate**, very crowded; turn up with ticket 30 mins. before departure): Interlagos, Mon., Wed., Fri. daily in winter, 1330 5 hrs.; Pingüino in summer daily, in winter Tues., Thur., Sat., 1300; both charge US$27. Route 40, which goes to Calafate (312 km.) is paved except for a 20 km., stretch just S of Ruita Provincial 9, which is gravel; there is a service station and motel at La Esperanza (146 km.).

Daily to **Río Turbio**: Expreso Pingüino goes at 1230 plus 1530 Mon., Wed., Fri., 5½—6½ hrs., US$24; San Caferino (Entre Ríos 371) Mon., Thurs. at 1130; same company to **Puerto Natales** Tues., Thurs., Sat. 1300. Make sure your car papers are in order if driving to Puerto Natales, Chile (go first to Tourist Office for necessary documents, then to the customs office at the port, at the end of San Martín, very uncomplicated). A bus from **Punta Arenas**, 260 km. US$15 daily at 1300 (1230 Sat.), by Expreso Pingüino (booking office Zapiola 455, T 22338, 0800-1300 and 1500-2100 Mon.-Sat. 0900-1300 and 1700-2100 on Sun.- buses do not call at this office), take 6½ hours including border-crossing process, which is very easy. The road to Chile is unpaved but acceptable to the Punta Arenas-Puerto Natales intersection (*hostería* here, E, with restaurant); there is an 11-km. paved strip, single lane, southbound from Punta Delgada (just a restaurant) to the turn-off for the Punta Delgada ferry for Tierra del Fuego. Paving is in progress for 10-12 km. E of the Punta Arenas intersection. The 55 km. S to Punta Arenas on the main road is paved, 2-lane and good.

Pingüino twice daily to **Caleta Olivia**, US$20, 11-14 hrs. Bus to **Puerto Madryn** 18 hrs., US$50. To **Comodoro Rivadavia**, 834 km., Patagónica at 2330, stops at Fitz Roy daily at dawn, arr. 1000 next day, US$40. For **Bariloche**, take this bus to Comodoro Rivadavia, then the 2150 Don Otto bus to Bariloche. A bus (Andesmar) now goes all the way to **Mendoza**, leaves Fri. 1300, arrives 0900 Sun., via Comodoro Rivadavia, Puerto Madryn and Neuquén.

Occasional ships and buses (Don Otto, 48 hrs.), to Buenos Aires, 2,575 km. Buses (Transportadora Patagónica, Gobernador Lista 330, T 2330) Tues., Thurs., Sat. at 2330, 14 hrs. **Hitchhiking** to Buenos Aires is possible in about 5-7 days; appearance important; hitching to Tierra del Fuego possible from service station on Ruta 3 at edge of town, trucks stop here for customs check, be there before 0700.

**Air Travel**  In summer, it is best to make your bookings in advance. AR and Austral fly daily to **Buenos Aires**, fare US$200. LADE flies to **Mar del Plata** (making 8 stops on the way; wonderful topographical views). AR's Buenos Aires-Auckland-Sydney flight (twice a week) stops at Río Gallegos, but the return journey does not. Numerous flights to **Ushuaia** (Tierra del Fuego), direct or via **Río Grande** (AR, Austral and LADE, cheaper than by bus, always booked, try waiting list). To Río Grande, 30 mins. Minimum, to Ushuaia 1 hr. minimum. LADE flights to **Calafate** 2 most days in summer (about 3 a week out of season); to **Río Turbio** (daily Mon.-Fri.). LADE flights also to Bariloche via Santa Cruz, Comodoro Rivadavia, Trelew and Esquel, once a week. To **Comodoro Rivadavia** with Austral daily, 1 hr. 10 mins.; LADE to **Perito Moreno**, Sat. 1040 and Thur. 1500, 2 hrs., minimum. Naval flights (Comodoro de la Marina, T 22600) up and down the coast every Fri., e.g. to Buenos Aires, but full of navy personnel. Book seats in Buenos Aires to avoid difficulties with departures. Airport bus, No

6, from Av. Roca, US$0.75, once or twice an hour. Taxi (*remise*) to/from town, e.g. opp. *Hotel Colonial* US$4.50; Interlagos and Pingüino buses stop at airport; hitching from car park is easy. **N.B.** Flights may leave early, sometimes up to 40 mins. LADE flights should be booked as far in advance as possible.

**Excursion**  134 km. S, there is a penguin colony at Cabo Vírgenes (totally undeveloped); follow Route 3 then branch off on Route 1 for 31½ hrs. (unpaved). (On the way is El Cóndor ranch, where the manager, Mr Blake, is reported to welcome visitors.) The Navy allows visitors to climb up Cabo Vírgenes lighthouse for a superb view. Likewise, undeveloped, is Isla de Monte León, N of Río Gallegos, take Route 3 (paved), then a dirt track in good condition.

From Río Gallegos a railway runs 260 km. (14 hrs.) to **Río Turbio** (6,000 people), where Argentina's largest coalfield is located; reserves are estimated at 450m tons and the state coal company YCF is building a deep-water port at Punta Loyola to service it. There is a director of tourism, Prof. César Cetta, in the municipality on San Martín. Hotels, always almost full: *Hostería Capipe*, Dufour (9 km. from town), B; *Gato Negro*, D, recently renovated; *Azteca*, E; *Hostería Municipal*, by ski-run in hills, 6 km. from town. Visitors can see Mina 1, where the first mine was opened in the hills; area good for trekking and horseback riding. The present mining and industrial area, with the school museum, can also be visited. Unfortunately, it is no longer possible for tourists to ride the coal train (steam locomotives) to Río Turbio, although advance warning to the management *may* provide a truck on the train. Río Turbio is 39 km. by road from Puerto Natales (Chile). This road is open October-March only. Buses to Puerto Natales, 2 companies, US$3, regular. No direct bus to Calafate. There is a LADE office and Expreso Pingüino runs daily at 0600 (plus 1300 Tues., Thurs., Sat., 6 hrs.) in summer or 1300 Wed., Thurs., Sat in winter to Río Gallegos, but flights are cheaper and avoid the numerous passport checks. *Restaurant El Ringo*, near bus station, will shelter you from the wind.

**Calafate** (properly El Calafate), on Lago Argentino, 320 km. NW of Río Gallegos, pop. 3,000, is an expensive and developing tourist centre (more expensive than Ushuaia). There is a chapel dedicated to Santa Teresa in the centre; behind it Calle Perito Moreno gently climbs the large hill S of the town, from which one can see the silhouette of the S end of the Andes, the Laguna Redonda and Isla de la Soledad on Lago Argentino. It is the southern gateway to the **Parque Nacional de los Glaciares**, which is 50 km. away (the northern end is at Lake Viedma). On the alluvial plain by the lake there are many interesting birds, and in the other direction there is scope for good hill-walking. Colourful cave paintings (now closed except with special permission at Punta Gualichú) some 8 km. from Calafate, walking through the fields bordering the lake, or 12 km. by road. The Lago Argentino area is very popular, booking all transport in advance is a *must*; accommodation is very difficult to find in Jan.-Feb. The store *Las Plantas* in Calafate is helpful with travel arrangements and exchange. The tourist office has a list of taxis but undertakes no arrangements; it is helpful but some information may be incorrect, so check. Small museum at airport. Note that credit cards are not popular, apart from hotels, while most places quote in US dollars.

Camping and fishing permits, limited to official sites, from the Parque Nacional rangers in Calafate. Although the mountains are snow capped, you can camp out in the pleasant woods around the lake in summer and even swim in it on warm days. (Campsite details below.) There is utter stillness apart from squawking flocks of parakeets and an occasional roar as ice falls off the glacier and thunders into the lake. In November, 1989, all accommodation and restaurant facilities at the glacier's edge were closed. Visitors must take their own food and drink.

**Festivals**  People flock to the rural show on 15 February (Lago Argentino Day) and camp out with much revelry; dances and *asados* (barbecued sides of sheep). There are also barbecues and rodeo etc. on Día de la Tradición, 10 November.

**Hotels**  *Los Alamos*, A, comfortable, good food and service, has a mixed-media show, with dinner afterwards, rec.; *Amado*, Av. Libertador, B, good; *La Loma*, B. Roca and 15 de Febrero (can be booked in Buenos Aires at Av. Callao 433, 4° H, T 40-7476/40-9123), with bath, breakfast not included, excellent view, modern, highly rec., multilingual, restaurant, tea room: the hotel itself is B high season Oct.-May, cheaper in low season, behind it there are 14 cheaper rooms, E with shower and toilet, with special rate for International Youth Hostel members (F p.p. with bath between Oct.-Dec., E from 20 Dec.-31 March); free audio-visual of the last breaking of Moreno Glacier in 1989, also has two kombis for excursions for guests (run on most days, not in winter). ACA *Hostería El Calafate*, on Manzana 36, D, modern, good view, 26 rooms. *Michelangelo*, Espora, B, modern, clean, excellent, reasonable, good restaurant, will accept travellers' cheques in payment (at a poor rate, though); *Cabañas El Sol*, Av. Libertador 1956, friendly, clean, C, good meals, rec.; *Hostería Kau-Yatún*, A, with bath, many facilities, 25 de Mayo (10 blocks from town centre), old *estancia* house, comfortable, restaurant and barbecues, horses for hire; *Hospedaje Belén*, D, clean, warm, hot water, cooking facilities. Several slightly cheaper hotels but none less than E, e.g. *Hospedaje Jorgito*, Gob. Moyano 934, D, clean, hot water, heating, breakfast extra, often full; *Hospedaje del Norte*, Los Gauchos 813, E, open all year, comfortable, a similar place across the street; *Hospedaje Echevarría*, Libertador 989, E, quiet, very clean, highly rec.; *Hospedaje Los Dos Pinos*, 9 de Julio 358, F p.p., hot water, cooking facilities; *Residencia Los Lagos*, Moyona and 25 de Mayo, bakery pizzeria on ground floor (so ground floor rooms noisy from singing baker in a.m.), E with bath, very comfortable and clean, good value; *Residencia Bórquez*, also on 25 de Mayo, E, friendly. Rec. bed and breakfast at Espora 60, E p.p.; *Casa de Familia Del Norte*, 25 de Mayo 345, D with bath, clean, use of kitchen. *Cabañas Nevis*, about 1 km. from town towards glacier, for 4 or 8, new, lake view, full board good value; *Youth Hostel, Albergue del Glaciar*, Calle los Pioneros, 200 metres off Av. Libertador, T 91243 (reservations in Buenos Aires T 71-9344, 312-8486/9, Fax 054-1-3124700), E p.p., 10% for ISIC and youth card holders, open 1 Nov.—31 March, rec., hot water, kitchen and laundry facilities, English spoken, information on bikes, horses, etc., runs good tours to Moreno glacier, US$15 with plenty of time to see the glacier. Calafate has a tourist office from which caravans, tents (sleep 4) and 4-berth *cabañas* may be hired, showers extra. Note that all hotels except ACA are open only from October to April/May. Some private houses offer accommodation such as Enrique Barragán, Barrio Bahía Redonda, Casa 10, E, rec. Ask at tourist office if in difficulty.

**Camping** Municipal camp site (cheaper than Lago Roca site, see below), new facilities, behind YPF service station, US$0.50, and US$2.50 for warm showers, no tents for rent at site, but beds in trailers, US$3.75, near airport. 3 campsites in the Park en route to the glacier: the first is 10 km. past the park entrance, prone to flooding; the second is 10 km. before the glacier, free, no facilities, but nice riverside location and lots of firewood, warden visits site to issue permits; the third is 8 km. before the glacier, with all facilities, US$1 p.p. Take food to all three.

**Restaurants** Prices rise during November and high season lasts until May. *ACA Grill*; *Pizzería Onelli*, Libertador 1197, reasonable, stays open out of season; *Michelangelo*, Tomás Espora, good food and atmosphere, rec.; *El Mirador del Lago*, excellent food, beautiful views; *Tehuel Aike*, Av. Libertador 992, central, good food, slow service; *La Loma*, friendly, home food, picnic lunches supplied, good cakes and chocolates, beautiful view. Tea rooms: *Maktub*, Libertador 905, excellent pastries, expensive; *Bar Don Diego de la Noche*, at end of main road in direction of the glacier, good atmosphere.

**Exchange** Banco de la Provincia de Santa Cruz (Av. del Libertador) changes cash but not travellers' cheques. Advances (costly) on some credit cards given. Tourist office reported to change money. Travel agencies such as Interlagos and Lake Travel also change notes. YPF garage and Chocolate El Calafate and some other shops give good rates for cash; also El Pingüino bus company for good rates; the *Scorpio* snack bar in the main street is reported to give best rates; try also the supermarket in the main street and reception of Hotel La Loma (very poor rates) for travellers' cheques and cash.

**Tourist Information** In new building by bridge over Río Calafate. Tourist office friendly. Tour to Moreno glacier information available here. Hotel prices detailed on poster at the airport and on large chart at tourist office. Sr. Jorge Antolín Solache owner of *Hotel La Loma*, Casilla de Correo 36, 9405 Calafate (T 0902-91016, Dec.-May), rest of the year Callao 433-4°H, 1022 Buenos Aires (T 40-7476), has kindly offered to provide any information to travellers in the region. He speaks English, French, Italian and Portuguese.

**Travel Agents** *Interlagos*, Libertador 1175; *Lake Travel Tours*, Libertador 932; *Los Glaciares*, Calle 9, No. 185, T 91159, and *Gador Viajes*, Libertador 900 block. All agencies charge the same rates for excursions: to the Moreno Glacier US$20 for a trip leaving 0830, returning 1200, without lunch, 3 hrs. at glacier; to Lago Roca, at 0930 return 1700, US$20; Cerro Fitz Roy, at 0700 return 1900, US$50; Gualichó caves, 2 hrs., US$8. Also try at *Hotel La Loma*, with *kombis*, where prices are usually lower. Jorge Lemos, *Aventrek*, Gob. Moyano 839, AP Postal Esp. No. 7 (9405) El Calafate, Telex Cab. pública 86905, runs recommended treks in Glaciares National Park and Fitzroy. *Calafate Wilderness*, T 91228, run boat trips to the Moreno Glacier and organise trekking. *Chaltén Patagonia*, Roca 1269, T 91055, Fax (0902) 91204 (also Buenos Aires, Maipú 62, 1° of. S, T 30-2890, Fax 856 2857) runs trips to Fitz Roy and Puerto Natales for the Torres del Palne national park, has a 22-seat motorboat, *El Tehuelche*, for trips to the glacier and has renewed *Hostal Lago Argentino* in Calafate, and built *Fitz Roy Inn* at Fitz Roy.

Film and slide show about Calafate, the Moreno glacier and climbing the Cerro Torres at *Tío Cacho* discothèque, every night, 2000, US$2 (prefers large groups with reservations), better for non-groups is the audiovisual at *La Posta* restaurant every day in summer at 1845, US$2.

**Transport** By air from Río Gallegos (LADE, 2 most days in summer, out of season 3 per week) and Comodoro Rivadavia (often fully booked), Sat. only, also Río Grande (4 a week) and Ushuaia, daily in summer and Perito Moreno, Sat. In winter there are often no flights for weeks if the weather is bad. The airport is about a ten-minute walk from the centre of town; it may close in autumn after rain.

   Bus Calafate to **Ushuaia** requires four changes, and ferry; total cost of journey US$43. Interlagos Turismo bus runs daily at 0700 (summer) or 0915 Tues., Thur., Sat. (winter) to **Río Gallegos**; in addition El Pingüino runs daily at 0700 (Wed., Fri., Sat., in winter) 5 hrs. US$27, passengers on this bus wishing to go to Chile get off at Güer Aike to catch Pingüino's Gallegos-Río Turbio bus 50 mins later, arriving at 1700. Taxi to Río Gallegos, 4 hours, US$200 irrespective of number of passengers, up to 5 people. The Río Gallegos-Calafate road (323 km., of which all but 20 km. S of Ruta Provincial 9 is paved) trip is worth while for the number of animals and birds one sees; however, it is flat and subject to strong winds.

   Direct services to Chile: Pingüino, Av. Libertador, to **Puerto Natales** from 4 Dec. to Feb., US$42; Lake Travel Tours' (Mon., Wed. and Fri., 0600) to Puerto Natales (US$36) via La Esperanza and El Turbio. Other reported services: a semi-scheduled service in season on Tues., Thur., Sun., US$25-28, ask travel agents; Chilean minibuses (Viajes Urbina, Buses Sur) to Puerto Natales 4 times a week, US$32.50 in dollars, ask at Youth Hostel; lorry service, ask Gador Viajes, Libertador 1046. The road trip from Calafate to Punta Arenas is very interesting for animal and bird watchers: from Calafate take Route 40 (complete) and "Complementaria O" to La Esperanza, where there is a petrol pump and hotel (150 km., after 1½ hrs. there is a 45 km. short cut avoiding La Esperanza, reasonable apart from a terrible, 20 km. stretch about half way). After the short cut joins the main road is Fuentes del Coyle, with a small bar/*confitería* with 2-3 rooms for travellers, not bad considering the location. Road continues to Cancha Carrera (border post Dec.-April, no town), pay US$0.50 at control, then 14 km. to Chilean border post, Cerro Castillo (no town), then paved road (14 km.) to Puerto Natales and 245 km. to Punta Arenas, 42 km. paved. To Torres del Paine National Park, the quickest, but not the cheapest, way is to take a Kombi from Chaltén Patagonia, Gador Viajes or Lake Travel Tours, leaving Calafate at 0600, which travels to Puerto Natales (US$36) on a private road through an estancia; get off at Cerro Castillo (Chilean border post, closed Dec.-April) from where it is possible, with some patience, to hitch a lift to the park, or to take the bus coming from Puerto Natales to the Park. It is not possible to change Australes once inside the Park.

   The easiest way to **Río Turbio** (no direct bus) for Puerto Natales is to fly to Río Gallegos then take the daily bus; this avoids a long wait to change buses at La Esperanza.

**N.B.** It is nearly impossible to hitchhike from Calafate to Perito Moreno. There is no public transport, at any time of year, north of Calafate on Route 40; buses only run north up the coast.

**Road routes to Calafate** By a rough but interesting road from Santa Cruz, Provincial Route 9 (Route 288 is 100 km. longer with two bridges replacing old ferry crossings), 5 or 6 hrs. by car, but is not always possible after rain. Route 40 from Esquel is a mixture of asphalt and gravel to Perito Moreno, then to Bajo Caracoles (small but friendly hotel/bar, petrol pump—"normal" grade fuel only) it is very bad for the first 10 km. before improving a little. This route has little traffic and extreme winds can double your fuel consumption, carry some spare. Route 40 continues to Tres Lagos, but it may be wise to make an extra 50 km. detour on good roads to Gobernador Gregores (**see page 180**) for fuel or accommodation. At Tres Lagos there is only "normal" grade fuel. From Tres Lagos to Calafate is ~~very bad~~, slow going. South of Calafate, Route 40 to Río Gallegos as described above.  in places

**Excursions** At the far end of Lago Argentino (80 km.) the Ventisquero Moreno, one of the few glaciers in the world that is growing larger, descends to the surface of the water over a five-km. frontage and a height of about 60 metres. In a cycle of roughly three years it advances across the lake, cutting the Brazo Rico off from the Canal de los Témpanos; then the pressure of water in the Brazo Rico breaks up the ice and reopens the channel. Pieces break off and float away as icebergs. The vivid blue hues of the ice floes and the dull roar as they break away from the snout are spectacular. When visiting the glacier, do not go down too close to the lake as these icebergs can cause great waves when breaking off, and wash people off rocks; in fact, new wooden catwalks prevent you from going to the water's edge. From Calafate to the glacier's edge there are daily Pingüino and Interlagos (rec.) bus trips Sept.-May only (daily Nov.-March, less frequent at other times), return, US$20 from Av. Libertador at 0930 returning 1700, giving 3 hrs. at glacier; you can use the return fare at no extra cost if you come back next day. Fares do not include the US$2.50 park entrance fee. Taxis, US$80 for 4 passengers round trip. The Parque Nacional truck leaves Calafate most weekday mornings at 0800 and may give lifts (but arrive at 0500!). It may be possible to camp in the guardaparque's backyard, but you must ask first. Out of season, trips to the glacier are difficult to arrange, but one can gather a party and hire a taxi; take warm clothes, and food and drink; try asking at *Hotel La Loma* (where they have 2 kombis) or taxis at cooperative, T 91044 (for 4 people).

Travel by road to the most interesting spots is limited and may require expensive taxis. Tours can be arranged at travel agencies, *Hotel La Loma* or with taxi drivers at the airport who await arrivals. Two recommended walks: (1) From the Centro Cívico in Calafate, visit Capilla Santa Teresita in Plaza San Martín; behind it is Calle Perito Moreno; walk to the top of the hill for a view of Calafate. Then go S to the Río Calafate, then to the new section of the town, where the ACA grill is. (2) From the Intendencia del Parque, follow the new road among cultivated fields and orchards to Laguna de Los Cisnes, a bird reserve, with flamingoes, ducks, etc. Walk down to Lago Argentino; 15 km. along the lakeside are the painted caves at Punta Gualichó. Unfortunately the paintings have greatly deteriorated and only tour groups are allowed to visit them, but there are fascinating geological formations caused by erosion, on the edge of Lago Argentino, 12 km. from Calafate on the road to Río Gallegos. Excursion to Lago Roca, 50 km. S from Calafate. Trout and salmon fishing, climbing, walking, camping and branding of cattle in summer.

Lake Travel arrange trekking tours over the glacier, from 0900 to 1700: minibuses go to Lago Rico where a rubber boat crosses to the other side, specialized guides then take you over the glacier, a 2½ -hr. trek. Lake Travel also organize treks with specialized guides in the Fitzroy area.

Horse riding can be arranged at Estancia Huiliches, who pick you up by car at your hotel, take you to the estancia, 4 km. from Calafate, for 2 hrs. riding with beautiful views of Calafate and its surroundings.

A worthwhile trip is by motor-boat from Punta Bandera, 50 km. from Calafate, to the Upsala glacier at the end of Lago Argentino, Lago Onelli and glacier (restaurant) and Spegazzini glacier. Two tour boats run on alternate days in summer: the largest and newer *Nanutak*, US$73, and the *Entre Ríos* US$62. For both pay in dollars and take food. Bus departs 0630 from Calafate for Punta Bandera. The boat passes by the 30-metre high glacier; it is reported however that the master sometimes decides the weather is too rough and does not go to Upsala. From the dock on Bahía Onelli to Lago Onelli is an easy 2-km. trail done with a guide (in English, German or Spanish) through a lovely southern forest wreathed in bearded moss. Small Lago Onelli is quiet and very beautiful, beech trees on one side, and ice-covered mountains on the other. The lake is full of icebergs of every size and sculpted shape. 1 hour is allowed for a meal at the restaurant near the track. Return bus to Calafate at 1930; a tiring day, and wet if the lake is choppy, but memorable. Out of season it is extremely difficult to get to the glacier. Smaller boats (39 passengers) may run in winter; sometimes they don't run because of the danger of the glaciers "calving". Book tickets at Empresa Nova Terra, and at least two days in advance; bus Calafate-Punta Bandera US$16, at 0700. On the road from Calafate to Punta Bandera, at the foot of Cerro Comisión, is a rock formation that looks like a herd of elephants facing you.

Another worthwhile excursion is to the N end of the Glaciares National Park to **Cerro Fitz Roy** and Cerro Torres, 230 km. from Calafate. Daily bus in summer at 0700 from Calafate to the village of El Chaltén, at the base of Cerro Fitz Roy, 4½ hrs., returns 1500, allowing 2-3 hrs. at site. A new road has been built from Route 40 to Chaltén. Accommodation: *Lago Viedma*, C p.p., in dormitory with communal bathroom, half board, restaurant, shop, horse-hire, guide service, free campsite; *Hotel Lago del Desierto*, small, showers, cheaper, but poor; *Estancia La Quinta*, 3 km. from Chaltén, D p.p. half-board, prepares lunch for trekkers, rec.; *Fitz Roy Inn*, 32 beds, restaurant, contact Chaltén Patagonia in Calafate (see above). *Restaurant Perotti*. Free campsite at end of village near the paths to Cerros Fitz Roy and Torres (the bus from Calafate goes to and from this site), no facilities. The Fitz Roy massif can be seen from *Lago Viedma*, and one can walk for 2½ hours (stupendous views: "anyone within 500 miles would be a fool to miss them"—Julian and Cordelia Thomas) to see Cerro Torres, where there is a *refugio*. There is also a *refugio* at Piedra del Fraile, beyond the base of Cerro Fitz Roy, good day's hike from Chaltén; Chaltén Patagonia Tours offers day trips Mon., Wed., Fri. To reach either *refugio*, one must cross the Río Fitz Roy by the new bridge; Cerro Fitz Roy base camp is 2-2½ hrs. easy walk from the campsite at the edge of the village. Ask at the *gendarmería* (border-police) in Calafate if you can join their truck which goes once or twice a week. On the way to Cerro Fitz Roy (often bad weather) on Route 40, is the Southern Astronomical Observatory, managed by the Observatory of La Plata.

A certificate is required from the National Park Office in Calafate to camp in the Park.

**Climbing**  Fitz Roy (3,375 m., Mapuche name Chaltén) is approached from Chaltén to Río Blanco, 2-3 hrs., walk, then to Laguna Torre (base camp for Cerro Torre), 3-4 hrs. walk. Ask the guide Sr. Guerra in Chaltén about hiring animals to carry equipment. The best time is mid-Feb. to end-March; Nov.-Dec. is very windy; January is fair; winter is extremely cold. There are no rescue services; necessary gear is double boots, crampons, pickaxe, ropes, winter clothing; the type of terrain is ice and rock. Possible targets nearby include Cerro Torre, Torre Eger, Cerro Solo, Poincennot, Guilleaulmet, Saint-Exupery, La Bifida, La Indominata, Cardón Adela and Hielo Continental (Continental Ice Shelf). Ask for a permit to climb at the Parques Nacionales office in Chaltén. There is no access at all from Chile. Before setting out, visit Jorge Lemos, Gobernador Moyano 839, Telex Cabina Pública 86905, Calafate; he has accommodation at his *Refugio para Montañistas* in Calafate, bed only, US$5 p.p. He can advise on hiring pick-up truck, which may work out cheaper than the bus to Chaltén.

Organized trips to the Glaciares National Park are too short to appreciate it fully; either go on a tour bus, then camp (good gear essential) or hire a taxi/minibus. The travel agencies charge US$200 for up to 8 people, US$300 to take you and return later to collect you; private drivers (e.g. Martín Drake, Bo. Plan Alborada 390—speaks English) charge US$300 for up to 8 to take you and collect later (also does similar arrangements for the Moreno glacier).

## TIERRA DEL FUEGO (11)

The island at the extreme south of South America is divided between Argentina (east side) and Chile (West). The south has beautiful lakes, woods and mountain scenery, and there is much birdlife to see. Boat trips can be made on the Beagle Channel; there is skiing in winter.

*Tierra del Fuego* is bounded by the Magellan Strait to the north, the Atlantic Ocean to the east, the Beagle Channel to the south—which separates it from the southern islands—and by the Whiteside, Gabriel, Magdalena and Cockburn Channels etc., which divide it from the islands to the west. The local Ona Indians are now extinct. Throughout Tierra del Fuego the main roads are narrow and gravelled. The exceptions are the road for about 50 km. out of Porvenir (Chile), which is being widened, and Río Grande-Ushuaia, which is being improved. Part of the south is a National Parks Reserve: trout and salmon in nearly all the lakes and rivers, and in summer wild geese, ducks, 152 other species of birds, and imported musk rats and beaver. **Note** that accommodation is sparse and the island is becoming popular among Argentines in summer. Hotel beds and seats on aircraft may begin to run short as early as November.

**N.B.** Argentine time is normally one hour ahead of Chilean time.

**Books**  *Tierra del Fuego* (3rd edition), in English, by Rae Natalie Prosser de Goodall, US$7.50 (obtainable in Ushuaia and Buenos Aires), colourful maps by the same author. Also *Tierra del Fuego: The Fatal Lodestone*, by Eric Shipton, and *Uttermost Part of the Earth*, by E. Lucas Bridges. Available in U.S.A.: *Birds of Isla Grande* (Tierra del Fuego) by Philip S.Humphrey, and *A Guide to the Birds of South America*, by Rodolphe Meyer de Schauensee.

March-April is a good time to visit because of the beautiful autumn colours.

**Camping**  is very easy in Tierra del Fuego. You can, if so inclined, camp at most service stations. Many towns have municipal campsites which are either free or cost up to US$1. Private campsites can be very expensive.

There are two ways of crossing the Straits of Magellan to Tierra del Fuego. Coming S from Río Gallegos, an unpaved road turns left for Punta Delgada (1 hotel, 2 *hosterías*). (On the road Río Gallegos-Punta Delgada is Laguna Azul—3 km. off main road in an old crater; an ibis breeding ground, beautiful colours). A 30-minute crossing can be made by fast modern ferry from Punta Delgada to Punta Espora (no hotel—if desperate, ask the lighthouse keeper). The boats, which take 4 lorries and 2 cars, run every hour, with schedule determined by tides and a 1200-1400 lunch hour rest. Under normal conditions they run from 0800 to 2100 daily, with tidal breaks lasting 4 hours (autumn and winter timetable). Ferry-operators accept US dollars or Argentine or Chilean currencies. If going by car, do not go before 1000, as first crossings are taken by buses, etc. However, there is no bus service from Punta Espora (or Punta Delgada); buses to and from the island only through Porvenir. From Punta Espora (Bahía Aril is ferry terminal) a road runs through Chilean territory to San Sebastián (Chile) and 14 km. further to San Sebastián (Argentina) (usually 15 min. delay in crossing borders), Río Grande (road San Sebastián-Río Grande is appalling) and Ushuaia. There is an Esso service station 38 km. from Punta Espora. Accommodation is scarce in the Chilean part (except for Porvenir—see **Chilean Patagonia**), and it is not always possible to cross it in one day because of the irregularity of the ferry. It is sometimes possible, coming and going, to spend the night at the guest house of ENAP at Cerro Sombrero (petrol there for employees only, but if you are running out, they may help), but do not count on it. Try *Hostería Karu-Kinka*.

The road from Río Gallegos goes on to Punta Arenas, from where (dock at Tres Puentes 5 km. E of town) there is a daily crossing to Porvenir (passenger US$4, motor car US$50, 2½-3 hours; there is a passenger saloon with small cafeteria; get on first and you are invited on the bridge, get on last and you stand outside in the cold), from Porvenir at 1400 (Sun. 1700). If crossing with car, don't allow it to be parked too close to other vehicles; the ferry company will not accept responsibility for damage caused by onboard "crashes". If you want to continue, Senkovic buses to Río Grande leave at 1400 on Sat. and Wed. A 225-km. road runs from Porvenir E to Río Grande (6 hours) via San Sebastián; or by alternative route through Cerro Sombrero (see previous paragraph). On Chilean side of Tierra del Fuego, petrol available only at Porvenir. Reservations must be made at the hi-fi shop at Bulnes 637, Punta Arenas. The Argentine Consul in Punta Arenas is at Calle Valdivia 961 (T 22887). Border police at San Sebastián (ACA motel) will sometimes arrange lifts to Ushuaia or Río Grande. Hitching after San Sebastián is easy. Distances are roughly as follows in this area: Border with Chile at Monte Aymont; to Río Gallegos 73 km.; road to Río Grande via Kimiri-Aike (114 km. from Río Gallegos)—no buses; from here to Punta Delgada 30 km.; Punta Delgada-Punta Espora (ferry, free for pedestrians) 20 km.; on to Punta Sombrero (60 km.) and San Sebastián (60 km.) reaching Río Grande 80 km. on. The best way to hitch from Río Gallegos to Punta Arenas is to take any lorry as far as the turn-off for Punta Delgada ferry. Then there is plenty of Chilean traffic from Punta Delgada to Punta Arenas. *Hotel San Gregorio* will put you up if you get stuck near the turn-off.

Entering Argentina from Chile, be firm about getting an entry stamp for as long as you require. Going in the other direction, don't stock up with food in Argentina, as Chilean border guards will confiscate all fruit, vegetable, dairy and meat products coming into Chile.

**N.B.** If wishing to visit both sides of Tierra del Fuego, Punta Arenas, Torres del Paine, Calafate, Fitzroy, etc., the transport arrangements work much better if you start in Ushuaia and work north, via Chile, rather than starting in Calafate and working south.

The largest town in the Argentine part, with a population of 35,000 is **Ushuaia**, the most southerly town in Argentina, and among the most expensive. Its steep streets (there are mountains, the Cerro Martial, at the back of the town) overlook the green waters of the Beagle Channel, named after the ship in which Darwin sailed the Channel in 1832, on Captain Fitroy's second expedition. The old prison, at the back of the Naval Base can be visited: tours start from the Museum at 1700. There are impressive views of the snow-clad peaks, rivers, waterfalls and dense woods. There is a naval station at Isla Redonda. The people are engaged in timber cutting, fishing and, nowadays, in factories. The tourist industry is also expanding rapidly. A new road has been built between Ushuaia and Río Grande via Paso Garibaldi. Ushuaia and its environs are worth a 2-3 day visit. See Documents, **page 194. Warning** There have been complaints about the tap water in Ushuaia.

**Note**: Prices double on December 12.

**Hotels** *Monte Cervantes*, San Martín y Sarmiento, T 22153, A, run by owners of the Barracuda ship (see **Excursions**, page 193) rec., 10% discount for ISIC card holders; *Cabo de Hornos*, San Martín y Triunvirato, T 22187, A, comfortable, TV, spotless, good value (but surcharge on credit cards), restaurant not open to non-residents; *Las Lengas*, Goleta Florencia

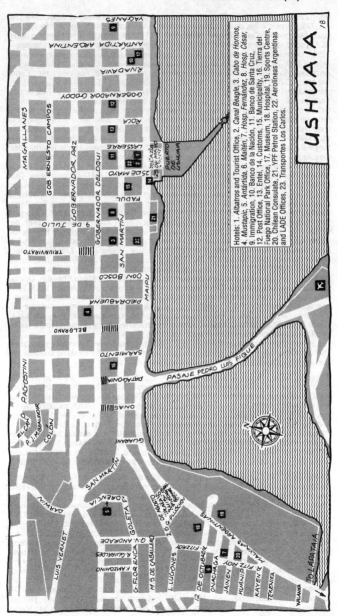

USHUAIA

Hotels: 1. Albatros and Tourist Office, 2. Canal Beagle, 3. Cabo de Hornos, 4. Mustapic, 5. Antártida, 6. Maitén, 7. Hosp. Fernández, 8. Hosp. César, 9. Immigration, 10. Banco de la Nación, 11. Banco de Santa Cruz, 12. Post Office, 13. Entel, 14. Customs, 15. Municipality, 16. Tierra del Fuego National Park Office, 17. Museum, 18. Hospital, 19. Sports Centre, 20. Chilean Consulate, 21. YPF Petrol Station, 22. Aerolíneas Argentinas and LADE Offices, 23. Transportes Los Carlos.

s/n, T 22668, B, cold, no English spoken, breakfast only meal; *Maitén*, 12 de Octubre 138, T 22745, C, good value, clean, but a long walk from town centre, 10% discount for ISIC and youth card holders. *Canal Beagle*, Maipú 599, T 21117, A (reductions for members of the ACA), good restaurant (catering usually for tour groups); *Albatros*, Maipú y Lasserre, T 22504, clean, modern, good service, A including large breakfast, but lighting poor; *Malvinas*, Deloqui 609, T 22626, B, with bath, breakfast included, pleasant, helpful, central heating; *Antártida*, San Martín 1600, T 21896, B, friendly, restaurant with fine views, rec.; *Capri*, San Martín 720, T 21833, D, clean, friendly; *César*, San Martín 752, T 21460, C, with bath, comfortable, friendly, clean, no breakfast, rec.; *Mustapic*, Piedrabuena 230, T 21718, friendly multi-lingual owner (Sr. Miro, from Yugoslavia), C/D (may bargain lower—10% discount for ISIC card holders), no singles, highly rec., exceptionally clean, can leave luggage, rooftop restaurant for breakfast; *Hospedaje Ona*, 9 de Julio 27, on waterfront, noisy, D (without breakfast, price drops to E after 5 nights stay), heater in room, dirty, rats; *Las Goletas* (no sign) Maipú 857 on waterfront, D, some rooms shared (3-6), in bunk beds, TV room (where they will allow sleepers if there is scarce accommodation), hot showers, heating. *Fernández*, Onachaga y Fitzroy, T 21453 very friendly, hot water, good but expensive meals, D, but cheaper in bunk-bed accommodation. *Bungalows Río Olivia*, 6 km. from town, Salón La Tía Tata, T 23714, owned by taxi driver Victor H. Ibiris (T 21282, 23241), D, good views. *Club Naval*, on hill 3 km. out of town, takes visitors, C, restaurant. Sra. Marta Alanis, Magallanes 229, T 24150, D, good food and comfort; restaurant *Kayu* downstairs. Rooms, D, at home of Ismael Vargas, Kayen 394 (T 21125) 15 mins. from centre, clean, doubles only, Sra. Vargas speaks English; 25 de Mayo 345, near top of hill, D, rec.; *Kau Pen*, Don Bosco 345, E, sleeping bag needed, cheap, friendly; a travellers' meeting place, clean, warm, hot water, kitchen, but little privacy. *Hospedaje Turístico*. Deloqui 271, D with private bath, very clean, friendly, rec. *Cabaña* at Gob. Campos (ex Colón) 631, sleeps up to 4, E p.p., modern, comfortable. Accommodation in private homes; Familia Beltrame, Gob. Valdez 311, T 22819, E p.p., rec.; Familia Galeazzi, Gob. Valdez 323, T 23213, E p.p., speak English and French, rec.; Familia Velásquez, Fadul 361, T 21719, doubles only, E p.p.; Magallanes 229, D including good breakfast. The following give 10% discount to ISIC card holders: Marta Chevalier, Deloqui 641, Lucía Zaprucki, Deloqui 271, E p.p., and Mario Craboleda, Gob. Campos 1053. There is no YHA in Ushuaia. Hostel for sporting groups only at Sports Complex. Lodging in Ushuaia has recently become rather a problem esp. Jan.-March., but even in winter hotels are very expensive. Enquire at Tourist Office for accommodation in private homes (they are said to have a list of 200), and for campsites, some of which are free. Many people go to the airport to offer rooms in private houses, in our E p.p. range.

36 km. from Ushuaia on the road to Río Grande is *Haruwen*, cabin accommodation, sleeping bag needed, saunas, good restaurant, centre for cross country skiing in winter and walking in summer (details from *Residencial Kau Pen*).

**Camping** None in town. After paying US$1 entrance fee to park, there are 4 camping sites to choose from, of which 3 are free, but have few or no facilities. The fourth is Camping Lago Roca, at Lapataia, by forested shore of Lago Roca in Parque Nacional, with facilities for car and tent, US$5, caters for travellers without car, hires horses, Dec.-March, including gas (18 km. from Ushuaia; weather can be bad). Can be reached by bus Jan.-Feb. Hot showers evenings, small shop, cafeteria. One free site is by restaurant, with no facilities, on road to Parque Nacional about 4 km. from Ushuaia at Cascadas de Río Pipo, and another, 2 km. from the Lago Roca campsite close to a beaver dam. The third free site is at Monte Susana, 10 km. W, Ensenada, 14 km. W, and Río Olivia, 12 km. E of Ushuaia. Tents for hire at Parque Nacional Tierra del Fuego, US$3 per night. Hot showers at Sports Centre on Malvinas Argentinas.

**Restaurants** *Los Canelos*, Maipú y 9 de Julio, excellent seafood, friendly, good value, rec., *Tante Elvira*, Av. San Martín 234, very popular, make advance booking, good seafood; *Moustacchio*, San Martín 298, sea food, expensive, warmly rec.; unnamed green, wooden restaurant at Maipú y Triunvirato, good centolla, rec.; *Asturias*, Triunvirato 45, pleasant, reasonable, open 1200-1500, 2030-2300. *ACA Grill*, good value and food. *Barcleit 1912*, Fadul 148, cordon bleu cooking at reasonable prices. Best place to eat lamb is at *Tolkeyen*, Estancia Río Pipo, 5 km. from town, meal US$4-5, taxi US$2. Cheap and good food at restaurant above the sports gymnasium at Maipú y 12 de Octubre. *Blanco y Negro Importaciones*, delicatessen; *Tío Carlos*, Colón 756, good *parrillada*, highly rec.; *Cafetería, pizzería Ideal*, San Martín 393, cheap, good, popular with travellers, 10% discount for ISIC card holders. Also well rec. is *La Pasiva*, San Martín 1275, very good for pasta and milanesa. *Quick*, San Martín 145, clean, good service, inexpensive, rec., 10% discount for ISIC card holders; *Don Juan*, San Martín 370, offers same discount, also *Split*, Piedrabuena 258. *Der Garten*, Swiss *confitería*, San Martín 620, in Galería shopping arcade, rec. Excellent homemade chocolate sold at a shop at San Martín 785. *Panadería Primavera*, San Martín, good. The coffee bar at the airport is very expensive. Ask around for currently available *centolla* (king crab) and *cholga* (giant mussels). Food and drink (apart from the duty-free items) in Ushuaia are very expensive. Supermarkets: Surty Sur (with clean toilets, San Martín y Onas) and Sucoop, Paz 1600. Popular spots at night include *Yoppen* at Rivadavia 200 and the disco *Alexander* at 9 de Julio y Maipú.

**N.B.** Restaurants here and elsewhere on Tierra del Fuego do not begin to serve until 2100-2130 in summer; it is advisable to book in advance in the high season.

**Shopping** Good boots at *Stella Maris*, San Martín 443. **Bookshop** at San Martín y Sarmiento. Film is cheaper in Chile.

**Car Hire** Rent Austral, Gob. Paz 1022, T 22422; **Rentacar**, Antártida Argentina 75, T 22620, Avis, Maipú 329, T 23350 code 347; **Autograd**, Deloqui 368, T 22723; **Aukiler**, T 23424; **Tagle**, San Martín y Belgrano, good, also at airport.

**Museum Museo Territorial**, Maipú y Rivadavia, open Mon.-Sat. 1500-2000, US$0.60, small but interesting display of early photos and artefacts of the local Indian tribes; relics from the missionaries and first settlers, etc. Also known as the "museum at the end of the world". Highly recommended. Good bookshop in building. Also Post office in building, open afternoons when the main one is closed.

**Exchange** Banks close 1500 (in summer). Poor rates for travellers' cheques and very high commission (up to 10% reported). No cash advance on Visa card available. Tourist agencies and the *Hotel Albatros* also give poor rates. *La Ponderosa* shop at Antártida Argentina 209, *Listus* record shop, San Martín 973, sweet shop next door, or Caminante, Deloqui 368 for better rates for cash.

**Laundromat** Triunvirato 139, between San Martín and Deloqui, open weekdays 0900-2100.

**Chilean Consulate** Malvinas Argentinas 236, at corner of Jainen, Casilla 21, T 21279.

**Tourist Office** In *Hotel Albatros*, piso 2° (T21423), friendly and helpful (will look after luggage while you trek). Large chart of hotels and prices and information on staying at Estancia Harberton, off road to Río Grande. Tourist Office at airport has information on hotels. National Park Office, on San Martín between Patagonia y Sarmiento, has small map but not much information.

**Travel Agents** All agencies charge the same fees for excursions. *Rumbo Sur*, San Martín 342, T 21139, does 5 tours: 2 on land, 2 on water, 1 mixed (1000-1600, US$18, rec.), and organizes bus to ski slope, very helpful; *Antartur*, in *Hotel Antartida*, T 22668. *Onas Tours*, 25 de Mayo 50, T 23429, just off main street, very friendly. *Tiempo Libre*, San Martín 154, T 21273, recommended, English spoken. *Ute Hohn Viajes*, Gob. Paz 460, T 21876, English and German spoken; *Caminante*, Deloqui 368, organizes walking and climbing tours to suit all levels of experience, provides food, tents, equipment, outdoor clothing, detailed map, very friendly and helpful, English and German spoken, highly rec, T 22723, 10% discount to ISIC and youth card holders. Recommended guides: Domingo Galussio, Intervú 15, Casa 211, 9410 Ushuaia, bilingual, not cheap (US$120); and Karl Renoth, Don Bosco 321, 2410 Ushuaia, T 22723, speaks English and German.

**Buses** run daily between Ushuaia and Río Grande 4 hrs, times vary, US$18, Transportes Los Carlos, Triunvirato 57. There are bus services between Río Grande (see page 193) and Porvenir in the Chilean part of the island (242 km., 6-8 hrs.) but no air connection.

**Airport** Aerolíneas Argentinas and Austral flights daily from Buenos Aires all year round, over 8 hrs. Both airlines offer reduced fares on certain days: in 1990 these were Mon./Wed. (AR) and Thur./Sat. (Austral), but you need to book well in advance. Full fare US$280, reduced fare US$200. (LADE office on Av. San Martín, Aerolíneas at Maipú y Lasserre, open Mon.-Fri. 0900-1200, 1500-1800). To Río Grande and Río Gallegos LADE, once daily Tues.-Sat., and Austral daily; to Calafate via Río Gallegos with LADE daily at 1330, and via Río Grande and Río Gallegos Wed.-Sat., (the Sat. flight continues to Comodoro Rivadavia via Gobernador Gregores and Perito Moreno); Austral daily to Comodoro Rivadavia, via Río Grande and Río Gallegos.

Weather often impedes flights in winter, and in the summer tourist season it is sometimes difficult to get a flight out. Since Río Grande airport can take larger planes than Ushuaia (until the new airfield is built), it may be easier to get a flight to Río Grande and travel on from there. At the airport ask around for a pilot willing to take you on a ½ hr. flight around Ushuaia (best to go in p.m. when wind has dropped). Alternatively ask about flights at the tourist office. Taxi to airport, US$1, or 15 mins. walk (no bus).

New airport being built, but some say it won't be ready until 2000.

**Sport** Sports Centre on Malvinas Argentinas on W side of town (close to seafront). Ice skating rink at Ushuaia gymnasium in winter (when lagoon is frozen). Beachcombing can produce whale bones. Fishing: trout, contact Asociación de Caza y Pesca at Maipú and 9 de Julio, with small museum. Fishermen may be interested in visiting the fish hatchery 7 km. E of Ushuaia, visiting hours daily 1400-1700. There are brook, rainbow and brown trout and land-locked salmon. Take No. 1 bus E-bound on Maipú to the end of the line and continue 2½ km. on foot to the hatchery. Birdwatchers will also find this ride rewarding. Skiing, hiking, climbing: contact Club Andino, Solís 50, or Caminante. Skiing: A downhill ski run (beginner standard) with chairlift (US$3), equipment rental (US$2.50 an hour), lessons and cafeteria is found on Cerro Martial. There is another ski run 3 km. from Ushuaia, open June-August, has lights for night-skiing and is run by Club Andino; bus leaves Rumbo Sur, San Martín 342, each hour for ski slope, US$2 return. The area is excellent for cross country skiing; Caminante organizes excursions "off road". 20 km. E of Ushuaia is Valle Tierra Mayoria, a large flat valley with high standard facilities for cross country skiing, snow shoeing and snowmobiling; rentals and a cafeteria; bus a.m. and 1400 from *Hotel Las Lengas*, US$4 return.

**Excursions** For **Lapataia** bay, take van from Solís 50, 4-6 times a day, about US$5 p.p. plus US$1 National Park fee; also good catamaran trips. Lago Escondido US$10, 50 km., 3-4 hrs., to *Petrel Inn*. Minibus to Lapataia from Gob. Godoy y Maipú, US$10 at 1000 and 1500, returns 1100, 1600, 2030. In summer Caminante run minibuses to the National Park, departing from Deloqui 368, 2 or 3 a day, US$10 return. A similar service is operated by 2 other agencies. There are excursions to the Cerro Martial (itself unspectacular but fine scenery) about 7 km. behind the town; take road behind *Hotel Antártida*, 2 km. to small dam, then 3-4 hour walk along trail. There is a chairlift (operating schedule unclear), US$4 round trip, but it follows a narrow valley which does not offer good views. (In winter the Cerro is inaccessible, even on foot; a bus leaves every hour in summer from in front of Rumba Sur office to the chairlift, US$1.50.) Also to Lendegaia and Lapataia bays, the falls of the Olivia river. In winter the temperature drops to as low as -12°C, in summer it goes up to 25°C. Beaver inhabit the Parque Nacional near the Chilean border; one may see beaver dams and with much luck and patience the beavers themselves after dark, stand still and down-wind of them: their sense of smell and hearing are good, but not their eyesight. No maps of the Park are available and hiking can be interrupted by the Chilean border (you cannot, for instance, cross to climb Cerro Cóndor).

At Lago Fagnano: *Hostería El Kaiken* (ACA) also bungalows, nice site, well-run facilities, cheap drinks, on a promontory 93 km. from Ushuaia, B including real bath. At Lago Escondido *El Petrel Inn*, 54 km. from Ushuaia, C (after a spectacular climb through Garibaldi Pass, on the road to Río Grande). Facilities at *Kaiken* and *Petrel* are open all year round. These inns are rec. for peace and quiet.

The old Route 3 circles close to the lake, but comes to a dead end at the hotel; it does not go over the pass. The newer Route 3 bypasses most of the lake. Even in the summer the climate can often be cold, damp and unpredictable. It is possible to hitch-hike, though with difficulty, as far as Lapataia; only tour buses go there. Rangers in the park are friendly and will sometimes put people up for a couple of days (as will police) and help with places to visit. A ranger truck leaves Ushuaia every weekday at 1300 and picks up hitch-hikers along the road. Park entrance US$1.

At the very end of the Park road are several posts covered with momentos left by travellers from all over the world.

Taxi to Park, US$15. Los Carlos bus to Lago Fagnano, 2½ hrs., US$6.50, then from lake to Río Grande 2 hrs., US$7. Tours also arranged to Lago Fagnano and aerial excursions over the Beagle Channel (with local flying club, hangar at airport, 3-5 seater planes, 30 mins.), Lago Fagnano, Lapataia and Ushuaia Bay. To Lago Escondido/Fagnano US$50; bus to Puerto Almanza (on Beagle Channel), 75 km., 4-5 hrs., US$18. Rumbo Sur does a whole-day, trip by catamaran down the Beagle Channel to see wildlife, with return by bus, highly rec. (see above under **Travel Agents**). Caminante runs a one day excursion to the Parque Nacional, including trek, canoeing, *asado* lunch, US$50 inclusive.

The Estancia Harberton, the oldest on the island, now offers tours and tea, and you can camp. It can only be reached by rented car from Ushuaia (not by boat as some travel agency brochures imply—they only go to the bay). Leave Ushuaia on Route 3, after 40 km. fork right on Route J, passing Lago Victoria, then 25 km. through forest before the open country around Harberton (85 km. in all). Some parts of the road are bad; tiring driving, 5 hrs. there and back. Rumbo Sur offers 11 hr. tours to the Estancia, US$45, but take your own food as the Estancia is expensive.

**Sea Trips** Boat and bus 7 hr. tour to the Isla de Los Lobos y Pájaros along the Beagle Channel, US$50. Take food, on board it is overpriced. In summer, 3 hr. trips may be taken to see the sealions on Isla de Los Lobos, also to Les Eclaireurs lighthouse, the Bridges islands and Isla Redonda, where the Government is breeding guanacos. Ask at Rumbo Sur; the *Ana B* leaves 0930 daily, the *Angel B*, at 1500 daily. Interesting boat trips of 3 weeks' duration on the 2,346 ton *Lindblad Explorer* cost from US$4,600. The ship *Ethel B* (owner Vincente Padin, enquire at Don Bosco 56, T 22253) does trips up the Beagle Channel to the Chilean border.

To Puerto Williams, Chile, Onas Tours, 25 de Mayo, organizes trips on the *Barracuda*, US$50 p.p., take own lunch, post office and postcards available in Puerto Williams, immigration formalities dealt with on board. El Caminante, Deloqui 368, has also been recommended for trips to Puerto Williams.

Ultragas (Chile) runs a boat between Puerto Williams and Punta Arenas (departing midnight both ends, 17 hours), making it possible to do a round trip Porvenir—Río Grande—Ushuaia—Puerto Williams—Punta Arenas. Buy ticket in Porvenir Tues. for early Wed. a.m. bus to Río Grande, arrives 1400; bus from there to Ushuaia arrives Thurs. allowing time to book ticket on Puerto Williams boat, leaves Sat. 0800 weather permitting. It has been reported that boat (*Barracuda*) to Puerto Williams from Ushuaia is unreliable, both because of weather and because it will not leave unless full; however, with more companies organizing trips this may improve. One alternative is to ask at the Club Náutico for trip in private launch.

***Río Grande*** (6,000 people) 236 km. NE of Ushuaia, is a port in windy, dust-laden sheep-grazing and oil-bearing plains; the oil is refined at San Sebastián (ACA motel, D) in the smallest and most southerly refinery in the world (service station open 0700-2300) The *frigorífico* plant in Río Grande is one of the largest in South America; so is the sheep-shearing shed. Accommodation is very difficult (especially if arriving at night; we hear that one can sleep in the hospital's emergency room, if it's not in use. ACA garage on sea-front has free hot showers for men, as has the gymnasium. Fill up with gasoline here.

**Local Festivals** *Trout Festival*, 3rd Sunday in February; *Snow Festival*, 3rd Sunday in July; *Woodsman Festival*, 1st week of December.

**Hotels** *Hospedaje Irmary*, Estrada 743, clean and pleasant, C, rec.; *Federico Ibarra*, Rosales and Fagnano, rec., good restaurant, B; *Villa*, San Martín 277, C, very warm; *Hospedaje Noal*, Rafael Obligado 557, D, clean, cosy, friendly, rec.; *Atlántida*, Av. Belgrano and Rosales, said to be best, always full; *Yaganes ACA*, Av. Belgrano 319, A, clean, comfortable, has a restaurant; *ACA Albergue*, on Luis Piedrabuena near Gymnasium, B, 4-bed rooms, very comfortable, central heating, hot showers, restaurant, US$10 a meal; *Miramar*, Belgrano and Mackinlay, E p.p. without bath, no breakfast, heated, hot water; *Hospedaje Dany*, Moreno 781, D, heated, hot shower, clean; *Residencial Arboleas*, Rivadavia 637, D, clean, heated, hot showers; *Motel Sur*, on beach, truckers' place, clean and cheap, being enlarged. *Residencial Las Lenguitas*, Piedrabuena 436, E, bathroom shared between 2 rooms, good value; *Pensión Stella*, Moreno 835, E p.p., good, clean; *Residencial Rawson*, Estrada 750, D with bath, no singles, clean, rec. Daniel and Ana, Av. 9 de Julio 1, rooms F p.p.

**Youth Hostel**, for males only, but apparently always filled by local workers.

**Restaurants** *Yaganes* (good for *centolla*) expensive; *Don Rico*, in ultra-modern building in centre, interesting; *Confitería Roca*, Roca 629, open all hours, reasonably priced food and bar; likewise *A Todas Horas* in same street. Good workmen's café, *Mary's*, Moyano 373. *Supermarket Sados* on San Martín, near 25 de Mayo. Smart place for a drink, *Paris*, Rosales 448.

**Exchange** Superkiosko, Piedrabuena y Rosales, cash only. Import shops, e.g. Yehuín, San Martín y Rivadavia, Avepí on Belgrano. Try *Confitería Roca*, Roca 629. Tends to be difficult: if coming from Chile, buy australes there.

**Car Hire** Rent-a-Car, Belgrano y Ameghino, T 22657.

**Car mechanic** and VW dealer Viaval SRL, P. Moreno 927.

**Tourist Information** at the Municipalidad, Mon.-Fri., on Calle Sebastián El Cano.

**Airport** 4 km. W of town. Río Grande-Buenos Aires flights (Aerolíneas Argentinas and Austral daily), 5 hours, stops at Río Gallegos and Comodoro Rivadavia (some also at Bahía Blanca). LADE to **Bariloche**, once a week, 6 hrs., 5 stops. LADE flight Río Grande to **Ushuaia**, heavily booked (also Austral). To **Río Gallegos**, 40 mins. (book early in summer) and to

**Comodoro Rivadavia**. To **Calafate**, stopping at Río Gallegos, LADE. Telephone LADE office (behind *Hotel Yaganes*) open Mon.-Fri., 0900-1200 and 1530-1900, 0700-1200 on Sat., T 308. Conversely, travel with Aeronaval (if you're lucky), mostly Hercules transports, for half the price—enquire at airport. "Rent-a-plane" at airport. No flights to Chile.

**Buses** leave at 0600 Wed. and Sat. US$15 (Senkovic, San Martín 959, T 22345), for **Porvenir**, Chile (about 230 km.), no food or drink provided, no toilets, nor stops, for 6 hrs., always heavily booked but especially over Christmas/New Year period, meticulous passport and luggage control at San Sebastián (ACA motel, 144 km. before Porvenir). Very difficult to hitch to Porvenir. Ferry journey from Porvenir to **Punta Arenas** (2 hrs.) can be very rough and cold, US$6 p.p., US$50 per car. Bus from landing stage, Tres Puentes, into Punta Arenas (5 km.) necessary. Transportes Turicisne go to Porvenir, very crowded and filthy, avoid at all costs. Daily bus service at 1300 with Transportes Los Carlos, Estrada 568 to **Ushuaia**, 234 km., on an unpaved road, US$18, 4 hours, stopping at *Hostería El Kaikén*, Lago Fagnano, for a drink. Bus departs from Los Carlos office; arrive 15 mins early. In winter the bus leaves on Mon., Wed. and Fri. only (1830).

**Excursion** 11 km. N lies the Salesian mission and the regional museum housed in the original chapel and first parish church of Río Grande. Although the exhibits are not at all organized or classified, there is a great deal to see. There are Ona Indian materials, Salesian mission works, fossils, handicrafts and flora, fauna and mineral exhibits of the area. Just past the mission, on the right side of the road, is the old cemetery.

*Isla de los Estados* Robert T. Cook writes: "This long (75 km.) and guarded island lies east of Tierra del Fuego. Except for the caretakers of the lighthouse and an occasional scientist few people ever set foot on this cloud-shrouded reserve of Fuegian flora and fauna that no longer exist on the main island. During the 18th and 19th centuries hundreds of ships were wrecked or lost in the treacherous waters surrounding this island. Much gold, silver and relics await salvage." Information and tours from Rumbo Sur, San Martín 342, Ushuaia.

Argentina apparently has plans for tourist developments in *Antarctica* (accommodation at Marambio and Esperanza stations) and Argentina and Chile are planning a mountaineering camp about 600 km. from the South Pole.

---

## INFORMATION FOR VISITORS

**Documents** Check visa requirements as they change frequently. Passports are not required by citizens, of neighbouring countries who hold identity cards issued by their own Governments. No visa is necessary for US citizens, British citizens and nationals of other Western Hemisphere countries (excluding Cuba), Western European countries (excluding Portugal), and Japan, who may stay for 3 months, a period which can be renewed for another 3 months at the National Directorate of Migration. For all others there are three forms of visa: a business "temporary" visa, a tourist visa, and a transit visa. Australians, New Zealanders and South Africans need visas. Tourist visas are usually valid for three months in Argentina and for any number of exits and entrances during that period. Visitors should

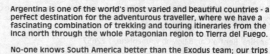

carry passports at all times; backpackers are particular targets for thorough searches—just stay calm; it is illegal not to have identification handy. When crossing land frontiers, remember that though the migration and customs officials are generally friendly, helpful and efficient, the police at the control posts a little further into Argentina tend to be extremely bureaucratic in their approach.

**Airport Tax**  US$13 for international flights, including to Brazil and Bolivia, but flights to Uruguay and Chile are subject to US$3 tax; US$1 for internal flights. When in transit from one international flight to another, you may be obliged to pass through immigration and customs, have your passport stamped and be made to pay an airport tax on departure. There is a 3% tax on the purchase of air tickets.

**N.B.** Do not send unaccompanied luggage to Argentina; it can take up to 3 days of form-filling to retrieve it from the airport. Paying overweight, though expensive, saves time.

## How to reach Argentina
**By Air from Europe**  British Airways and Aerolíneas Argentinas (AR) each fly from London twice a week (BA via Rio de Janeiro and São Paulo on Tues.; AR via Paris and Madrid on Wed. and Fri. via Madrid). Aerolíneas also fly to the following European destinations (with other carriers in parentheses): Amsterdam (once a week; KLM twice); Frankfurt (three a week, similarly Lufthansa); Madrid (5 a week, Iberia three times); Paris (and Air France, three a week each); Rome (three a week, also Alitalia, who also fly to Milan); Zurich (twice, Swiss Air, three times and to Geneva once). Aeroflot flies from Moscow on Sunday with 3 stopovers.

**From North America**  Aerolíneas Argentinas fly from the following US destinations (with other carriers in brackets): Los Angeles (three times weekly, Ecuatoriana, American); Miami (4 a week, Pan Am, LanChile, American); New York (6 a week, LanChile, Pan Am). AR and Canadian Air International fly from Toronto (the latter twice a week); Aerolíneas also fly once a week from Montreal.

Aerolíneas Argentinas fly from Sydney, Australia, via Auckland, New Zealand, on Wed. and Fri. On the outward flight from Argentina, Aerolíneas stop at Río Gallegos, but it is difficult to board there in high season.

**From Latin America**  Aerolíneas Argentinas (6 times a week) and Líneas Aéreas Paraguayas (3) from Asunción; AR (2) and Avianca (3) from Bogotá; AR and Viasa from Caracas (twice each); Eucatoriana from Quito and Guayaquil, AR from the latter only; AR and LAB (each once a week via Santa Cruz) from La Paz, but LAB has two other flights from Santa Cruz (one via Tarija, one via Montevideo), AR one other; from Lima, AR (3), AeroPerú (3) and LanChile once; AR (3) and Eucatoriana (1) from Mexico City; from Montevideo (apart from those given in the Buenos Aires section), AR, Pluna, Varig, Cruzeiro do Sul and Iberia, KLM, Lufthansa and Air France en route from Europe (frequent flights also to Punta del Este, with many more in holiday season); from Santiago, Chile, daily with AR and LanChile and other Latin American, European and North American carriers on various days; from Panama City, AR twice a week.

From Brazil, AR, Varig and Cruzeiro do Sul fly daily from Rio de Janeiro, AR and Cruzeiro do Sul daily from São Paulo (plus European airlines stopping over at both cities); Cruzeiro stop over in Porto Alegre, AR also fly from Porto Alegre, via Montevideo.

**Customs**  No duties are charged on clothing, personal effects, toilet necessities, etc. Cameras, typewriters, binoculars, radios and other things which a tourist normally carries are duty-free if they have been used and only one of each article is carried. This is also true of scientific and professional instruments for the personal use of the traveller. Travellers may only bring in new personal goods up to a value of US$150 (up to US$50 for tourists entering from neighbouring countries); the amount of duty varies per item and according to exchange rates. There are red and green divisions at airport customs, but officials make no difference between them. All incoming baggage is normally inspected.

Two litres of alcoholic drinks, 400 cigarettes, 50 cigars and 5 kg. of foodstuffs are also allowed in duty-free; for tourists originating from neighbouring countries the respective quantities allowed are 1 litre, 200, 20 and 2 kg. You can buy duty-free goods *on arrival* at Ezeiza airport.

If having packages sent to Argentina, do not use the green customs label unless the contents are of real value and you expect to pay duty. For such things as books or samples use the white label if available.

**Internal Air Services** are run by Aerolíneas Argentinas (AR), Austral, Lapa (reliable turbo-prop services from Buenos Aires to Córdoba, Rosario, seaside resorts in Buenos Aires province and to Colonia, Uruguay, with bus connection to Montevideo), Cata (tubo-prop service from Buenos Aires to Bariloche and Iguazú), Aerolínea Federal Argentina (services in the north, from Tucumán to San Juan, Mendoza, Resistencia, Cordoba, Santa Fe, Posadas and Iguazú, Salta, Jujuy, Formosa and Tartagal), and the army airline LADE (in Patagonia, highly rec.). LADE flights are cheaper than the others, and there is a good extended schedule with new Fokker F-28 jets. **N.B.** LADE will not accept IATA MCOs. (Even though sometimes offices in various towns may tell you the flights are full, it is usually worth a try out at the airport.) The naval air passenger service, Aeronaval, carries paying civilian passengers, ⅓ cheaper than LADE. No firm schedule though; 2 flights a week between Ushuaia, Río Grande and Río Gallegos; once a week between Ushuaia and Buenos Aires. Check with both main airlines about discounts on certain flights. Plan familiar tickets allow couples to travel with a 25% discount for the spouse. Children under 3 travel free. LADE also operates discount spouse (65%) and children (35%) tickets. If travelling by AR or Austral a long linear distance, e.g. Río Gallegos-Buenos Aires, but wishing to stop en route, cheaper to buy the long flight and pay extra (about US$2) for stopovers. **N.B.** All local flights are fully booked way in advance for travel in December. Don't lose your baggage ticket; you won't be able to collect your bags without it.

**Visit Argentina Fare** Aerolíneas Argentinas sells three Visit Argentina tickets: four flight coupons costing US$359, six coupons costing US$409, and eight coupons US$459. All are valid for 30 days and must be purchased outside Argentina and in conjunction with an international flight ticket. Austral sell similar tickets but they are not interchangeable. Routing and dates must be booked when the coupons are issued: changes of dates are free; changes of destination incur a charge of US$25. One stop only is permitted per town, except for making a connection (maximum time allowed for awaiting connecting flight is 24 hrs.). If you wish to visit Tierra del Fuego and Lago Argentino it is better fly on the Visit Argentina pass to Río Grande or Ushuaia and travel around by bus or LADE from there than to stop off in Río Gallegos, fly to Ushuaia and thence back to Buenos Aires, which will use 3 coupons. If possible, plan radial routes from Buenos Aires. Children travel at a 50% discount, infants 10%. Domestic timetables are given in *Guía Argentina de Tráfico Aéreo* and *Guía Internacional de Tráfico*. It is unwise to set up too tight a schedule because of delays which may be caused by bad weather. Flights between Buenos Aires and Río Gallegos are often fully booked 2 to 3 weeks ahead, and there may be similar difficulties on the routes to Bariloche and Iguazú. It is advisable to have an "OK" status put on your flight coupons even if you are "wait- listed", to be sure of your seat. Reconfirmation at least 24 hours ahead of a flight is important and it is essential to make it at the point of departure. Extra charges are made for reconfirming LADE flights (useful in Santa Cruz and Tierra del Fuego) but they are not high.

**Railways** A permit (Argenpass) to travel anywhere by the Argentine railways is available (1991 cost unknown). There is no connected railway system south of Bariloche and Esquel. Passes should be obtainable at the Centro de Información de Ferrocarriles Argentinos (CIFA), Viamonte 553, Buenos Aires, open Mon.-Fri. 0700-2100 Sat., 0700-1300, closed Sun.; also available in Mar del Plata, Bariloche, Mendoza, Córdoba, Tucumán and Posadas. There is no great difference between 1st and tourist class in trains, but if uncrowded (rarely so), you can sleep across 5 seats in the latter (3 + 2), and only 4 in 1st class. As a rule, tourist class is 20% cheaper than 1st class, Pullman 15-25% more than 1st. Pullman services are usually air conditioned but a/c often does not work, resulting sometimes in very hot journeys as carriage windows do not open. All types of train fare, except sleeper, are cheaper than buses (prices even less for those under 30 years or over 60, for the just married, teachers, students, groups and public sector workers), but much slower and less reliable. Buffet cars usually offer coffee and drinks; sandwiches and refreshments are usually touted down the train during journeys. When travelling in winter, note that heating may be available only in sleepers and pullmans, not 1st or 2nd.

In 1990 it was proposed, for budgetary purposes, to terminate about 34 long distance rail services. The matter was still under debate in 1991, so rail travellers are advised to check in advance before planning a route.

**N.B.** Once out of Buenos Aires, train information is hard to come by, although the CIFA has 328 agencies to book facilities for the named-train principal services from Buenos Aires. Stations have wall time-tables of complete schedules for their own line but no information for other systems. To avoid disappointments, make long-distance call to nearest station on the line you require—although this requires fluency in Spanish. The only general time-tables in circulation at present are those for named trains on the main lines to Mendoza, San Juan, Tucumán, Posadas, Córdoba, Mar del Plata, Bariloche, Zapala and Corrientes, which are available from the information centre at Viamonte 553. The main services have been accelerated in recent years, but others remain slow and infrequent.

**Motoring** For entering Argentina by automobile the *Carnet de passages en douanes* (*Libreta de aduana*), is not required. Tourists can bring into Argentina their own cars, vehicles bought or hired in neighbouring countries for up to 8 months under international documentation. No specific papers are usually required to bring a Brazilian registered car into Argentina. All motorists are required to carry 2 warning triangles, a fire-extinguisher, a rigid tow bar, a first aid kit, full car documentation together with international driving licence (for non-residents), and the handbrake must be fully operative. Although few checks are made in most of the country, with the notable exceptions of roads into Rosario and Buenos Aires, checks have been reported on cars entering the country. You may not export fuel from Argentina, so use up fuel in spare jerry cans while you are in the country. Always fill up when you can in less developed areas like Chaco and Formosa and especially in Patagonia as filling stations are infrequent. Diesel fuel "gas-oil" prices are about 60% of those for gasoline ("*nafta*"). Octane rating is as follows: regular gasoline 83; super 93.

To obtain documents for a resident (holder of resident visa, staying at least 6 months in the country) to take a car out of Argentina, you can go to ACA in Buenos Aires, which may take up to 4 working days, or you can ask for a list of other ACA offices that can undertake the work; take forms with you from Buenos Aires, and papers may be ready in 24 hours. You will need at least 1 passport-size photo, which you can have taken at ACA at a fair cost. If the car is not your own, you require a special form signed by the owner and witnessed by a notary public. **NB** Non-residents may buy a car in Argentina but are in no circumstances allowed to take it out of the country; it must be resold in Argentina, preferably in the province where it was purchased.

Most main roads are paved, if rather narrow (road maps are a good indication of quality), and roadside services are good. Road surface conditions vary once one leaves main towns: high speeds are quite possible on the dirt and gravel roads, as long as you have the essential guard for the windscreen. North of Buenos Aires many provinces in 1991 introduced tolls on roads other than highways, usually between US$5-10 for passenger cars, spaced about every 100 km. Sometimes one may not be allowed to reach a border if one does not intend to cross it, stopping e.g. 20 km. from the border.

**Automóvil Club Argentino (ACA),** Av. Libertador General San Martín 1850, 1st floor, touring department on 3rd floor, 1425 Buenos Aires, T 802-6061 (take bus 10 from Arenales, 1 block N of Santa Fe, along Av. Gral. Las Heras, alight at Tagle and walk down to Libertador), office on Florida above Harrod's, 2nd floor, has a travel document service, complete car service facilities, insurance facilities, road information, road charts (*hojas de ruta*-about US$2.35 each to members, if available) and maps (dated with the code letters in the bottom corner—road map of whole country, with service stations and *hosterías* shown, US$3.40 to non-members, and of each province), a hotel list, camping information, and a tourist guide book sold at a discount to its members and members of other recognized, foreign automobile clubs upon presentation of a membership card. (YPF, the state oil agency, also produces good maps for sale.) Members of other recognized automobile clubs can also, on presentation of membership cards, benefit from lower prices for their rooms and meals at ACA *hosterías*. The Club has service stations, some with parking garages, all over the country. The organization is efficient. Travellers do report, however, that if you are not a member of ACA you will not get any help when in trouble. ACA membership for 3 months costs US$40, which permits you to pay with Eurocard (Argencard) for fuel at their Service stations, gives 20% discount on hotel rooms and maps, and discounts at associated hotels, and 10% discount on meals.

ACA accommodation comes in 4 basic types: *Motel, Hostería, Hotel,* and *Unidades Turísticas,* and they also organize campsites (see below). A *motel* may have as few as 3 rooms, and only one night's stay is permitted. *Hosterías* have very attractive buildings and are very friendly. *Hotels* are smarter and more impersonal. All have meal facilities of some kind. Anyone can get in touch with the organization to find out about accommodation or road conditions.

Hitch-hikers, as well as motorists, are recommended to contact the ACA for its wealth of information.

**Touring Club Argentino,** Esmeralda 605 and Tucumán 781 3rd floor, T 392-6742 has similar travel services but no service stations.

**Maps** The best road maps are those of the ACA (see above). Topographical maps are issued by the Instituto Geográfico Militar, Cabildo 301, Casilla 1426, Buenos Aires (reached by *Subte* D to Ministro Carranza, where IGM is one block from station—turn right from station, or take bus 152 from Retiro). 1:500,000 sheets cost US$2.50 each and are "years old"; better coverage of 1:100,000 and 1:250,000, but no general physical maps of the whole country or city plans. Helpful staff, sales office accessible from street, no passport required, map series indexes on counter, open Mon.-Fri., 0800-1300.

**Car Hire** To rent a small car (for four plus luggage) costs from US$40 a day, not including mileage, fuel and insurance, but considerably more in Patagonia. Minimum age for renting is 25. You must ensure that the renting agency gives you ownership papers of the vehicle, which have to be shown at police and military checks. At tourist centres such as Salta, Posadas, Bariloche or Mendoza it may be more economical to hire a taxi with driver, which includes the guide, the fuel, the insurance and the mechanic. Avis offers a good and efficient service with the possibility of complete insurance and unlimited mileage for rentals of 7 days or more, but you should prebook from abroad. No one-way fee if returned to another Avis office, but the car may not be taken out of the country. Other companies are given in the text.

**Motorhomes** US Motorhomes "Winnebago" is represented at Todotur, Av. de Mayo 1370-5th Floor, Room 92 (T 371552 or 380406) Buenos Aires. "Coachmen" Motorhome and "Pick-up" camper dealer at Av. Debenedetti 1285, (1871) Dock Sud, Avellaneda, Buenos

Aires also represents Jensen, Wemac, Monogram, Peterson, Winegard, Monarch and Coleman (T 201-5289/6379). The best dealer for Motorhome equipment and repairs is Merello Hermanos S.R.L., Maipú 742, Vicente López, Prov. of Bs. As (T 795-3503/4335). Porta-Potti toilets are widely sold in Argentina, sometimes under a different name.

**Buses**  Most bus companies give a 20% student discount, but persistence is required to prevail with an international student card; a YHA card is useful. The same discount may also be given to foreign, as well as Argentine, teachers and university professors but you must carry documentary proof of your employment. Express buses between cities are dearer than the *comunes*, but well worth the extra money for the fewer stops. When buying tickets at a bus office, don't assume you've been automatically alloted a seat: make sure you have one.

**Hitch-hiking**  Argentina is on the whole a good country for this (especially in Dec.-March), though recent problems with robberies have made drivers cautious. Ask at petrol stations. Don't rely on hitching absolutely, though; traffic can be sparse, especially at distances from the main towns, and in Patagonia out of season. It may be useful to carry a letter from your Consulate. Though they tend to be more reserved in manner than most Latin Americans, Argentines are generally friendly and helpful, especially to foreigners (display your flag, but not the Union Jack). Sirikit Bhagwanani, of Walchuil, Switzerland, says there are no problems at all for a reasonably careful woman on her own in Argentina.

**Walking and Skiing**  Information on trails in NW Argentina, the Lake District, Patagonia and Tierra del Fuego is given in *Backpacking in Chile and Argentina*, edited by Claire Hargreaves (Bradt Publications). Note that Bradt Publications' *South America Ski Guide* (due out end-1991) gives details of many Argentine ski resorts.

**Camping**  is very popular in Argentina (except in Buenos Aires) and there are sites with services, both municipal, free, and paying private campsites in most tourist centres. Most are very noisy and many are closed off-season. Camping is now allowed at the side of major highways and in all national parks (except at Iguazú Falls), at no cost. Wild camping in deserted areas is possible, but note that in Patagonia strong winds make camping very difficult. Many ACA service stations have a site where one can camp, and in general service station owners are very friendly to campers. A list of camping sites is available from ACA (labelled for members, but should be easily available and from the main tourist office in Av. Santa Fe, Bs. As.); see Autoclub magazine. References to sites will be found in the text. ACA campsites offer discounts to members, and to holders of the International Driving Licence; European automobile clubs' members are allowed to use ACA sites. There are few **Youth Hostels** (many open only February to March), but some towns offer free accommodation to young travellers in the holiday season, on floors of schools or church halls; some fire stations will let you sleep on the floor for free (sometimes men only). Many garages have showers that you can use. Good lightweight tents now available, e.g. Cacique. Regular (blue bottle) Camping Gaz International is available in Buenos Aires, at an electrical goods store on Av. 9 de Julio, near Teatro Colón, and Suntime, Lima 225, Guatemala 5908 (Palermo), Juramento 2452 (Belgrano) and América Pesca, Alfredo Pollini Alvear 1461.

**Food**  National dishes are based in the main upon plentiful supplies of beef. Many dishes are distinctive and excellent; the *asado*, a roast cooked on an open fire or grill; *puchero*, a stew, very good indeed; *bife a caballo*, steak topped with a fried egg; the *carbonada* (onions, tomatoes, minced beef), particularly good in Buenos Aires; *churrasco*, a thick grilled steak; *parrillada*, a mixed grill, mainly roast meat, sausages (including *morcilla*, black pudding to the British, or blood sausage) and offal; and *humitas*, made with sweet corn, tasty but not strictly national. *Arroz con pollo* is a delicious combination of rice, chicken, eggs, vegetables and strong sauce. *Puchero de gallina* is chicken, sausage, maize, potatoes and squash cooked together. *Empanada* is a tasty meat pie, and *chorizo* a highly spiced sausage, though do not confuse this with *bife de chorizo*, which is a rump steak (*bife de lomo* is fillet steak). *Milanesa de pollo* (breaded, boneless chicken) is usually good value. *Ñoquis* (gnocchi), potato dumplings normally served with meat and tomato sauce, are tasty and often the cheapest item on the menu. *Locro* is a thick stew made of maize, white beans, beef, sausages, pumpkin and herbs. Pizzas come in all sorts of exotic flavours, both savoury and sweet. Note that extras such as chips, *puré* (mashed potato), etc. are ordered and served separately, and are not cheap. Almost uniquely in Latin America, salads are quite safe. A popular sweet is *dulce de leche* (especially from Chascomús), milk and sugar evaporated to a pale, soft fudge. Other popular desserts are *almendrado* (ice-cream rolled in crushed almonds), *dulce de batata* (sweet potato preserve), *dulce de membrillo* (quince preserve), *dulce de zapallo* (pumpkin in syrup); these *dulces* are often eaten with cheese. *Postre Balcarce*, a cream and meringue cake and *alfajores*, maize-flour biscuits filled with *dulce de leche* or apricot jam, are also very popular. Sweets: the Havana brands have been particularly recommended. Excellent Italian-style ice-cream with exotic flavours. For local recipes (in Spanish) *Las Comidas de Mi Pueblo*, by Margarita Palacios, recommended.

Offices close for 2 to 2½ hours for lunch between 1200 and 1500. Around 1700, many people go to a *confitería* for tea, sandwiches and cakes. Dinner often begins at 2200 or 2230; it is, in the main, a repetition of lunch.

**Drink** Argentine wines (including champagnes, both charmat and champenoise) are sound throughout the price range. The ordinary *vinos corrientes* are wholesome and extremely cheap, costing about US$2 a bottle in shops (US$5 in a restaurant—US$15-20 for a good wine); reds better than the whites. The local beers, mainly lager-type, are quite acceptable and cost about US$0.50 a litre in supermarkets. In restaurants *vino corriente* is often cheaper than beer. Hard liquor is relatively cheap, except for imported whisky, at about US$3 in shops for gin and vodka. Local liqueurs may be as cheap as US$0.70 a litre. *Clérico* is a white-wine *sangría* drunk in summer. It is best not to drink the tap water; in the main cities it is often heavily chlorinated. It is usual to drink soda or mineral water at restaurants, and many Argentines mix it with their cheaper wine, with ice, as a refreshing drink in summer. *Yerba mate*, a very popular home-grown tea, is widely drunk, especially in the interior, continuing the old *gaucho* custom.

**Best Buys** Local leather goods in Buenos Aires, e.g. coats (leather or suede), handbags and shoes. *Ciudad del Cuero*, Florida 940, has clothing, footwear and luggage from 40 manufacturers. **N.B.** Leather from the *carpincha* is from the capybara and should not be purchased. A gourd for drinking *yerba mate* and the silver *bombilla* which goes with it, perhaps a pair of *gaucho* trousers, the *bombachas*. Ponchos (red and black for men, all colours for women). *El Guasquero* in Calle Anasagasti specializes in old *gaucho* objects, saddlery, *bolas*, horn items, all genuine and reconditioned by Sr. Flores, the owner. The shop is N of Av. Santa Fe, near Calle Bulnes, Buenos Aires (postcode 2028). Articles of onyx, specially in Salta. Silver handicrafts. In Buenos Aires, there is a good, reasonable and helpful souvenir shop on Av. de Mayo near Chacabuco. Knitted woollens, especially in Bariloche and Mar del Plata. If you like honey, the Casa de Miel has different honeys from every province. Try Mendoza or Tucumán varieties.

**N.B.** Never carry weapons, or drugs without prescriptions. The open season for fishing is between November and February or March. Enquire as to dates, so as to avoid carrying equipment unnecessarily, and remember that fishing anywhere requires a permit.

**Health** Argentina is in general a healthy country to visit, with good sanitary services. In some provinces, like Neuquén and Salta, medical assistance, including operations, X-ray and medication, is free in provincial hospitals, even for foreigners. All private clinics, on the other hand, charge. Smallpox vaccination no longer required to enter Argentina. If intending to visit the low-lying tropical areas, it is advisable to take precautions against malaria. Chagas' disease (**see Health Information**) is found in NW Argentina.

**British Business Travellers** are strongly advised to read "Hints to Exporters: Argentina", obtainable from Department of Trade, Export Services Division, Sanctuary Bldgs, 16-20 Great Smith Street, London SW1P 3DB. Similar information is provided for US citizens by the US Department of Commerce.

**Clothing** Shorts are not worn in city centres, though their use has become more common in residential suburbs in spring, summer and autumn, and in Buenos Aires in the hottest months. In general, dress tends to be formal (unless casual wear is specified on an invitation) in Buenos Aires and for evening outings to shows, etc. The general standard of dress among Argentines is very high: collar and tie, with jacket, are very much the standard for men, and women "should always err on the side of elegance"—David Mackintosh.

**Hours of Business** Banks, government offices, insurance offices and business houses are not open on Saturdays. *Government offices*: 1230-1930 in the winter and 0730-1300 in summer. *Banks*: generally 1000-1600 but time varies according to the city, and sometimes according to the season. (See under names of cities in text.) *Post Offices*: 0800 to midnight for telegrams. Stamps on sale during working days 0800-2000 but 0800-1400 on Saturdays. *Shops* are open from about 0900 to 1900, though many close at midday on Saturdays. Outside the main cities many close for the daily afternoon siesta, reopening at about 1700. 24-hour opening is allowed except on Mondays; this applies mainly to restaurants, foodshops, barbers, newspaper shops, art, book and record stores.

Dance halls open at 2300 but don't fill up till after midnight; night clubs open after midnight. In city centre, cafés and restaurants are busy till after midnight and many evening events, such as lectures, may not start before 2200.

**Holidays** The main holiday period, generally to be avoided by business visitors, is January-March, though some areas, such as Tierra del Fuego, begin to fill up in November/December. Winter school holidays, in which travelling and hotels may be difficult, are the middle two weeks of July. No work may be done on the national holidays (1 May, 25 May, 20 June, 9 July, 17 August, 12 October and 25 December) except where specifically established by law. There are no bus services on 1 May. On 1 January, Holy Thursday and Good Friday, and 8 December employers are left free to decide whether their employees should work, but banks and public offices are closed. Banks are also closed on 31 December. There are gaucho parades throughout Argentina, with traditional music, on the days leading up to the Día de la Tradición, 10 November. On 30 December (not 31 because so many offices in centre are closed) there is a ticker-tape tradition in downtown Buenos Aires: it snows paper and the crowds stuff passing cars and buses with long streamers.

**Standard Time** is 3 hours behind GMT; 2 hours behind October to March (check precise date of change)

**Currency** At the time of going to press, the currency in force was the austral, introduced in mid-1985. It replaced the peso argentino (introduced in mid-1983). In March 1991, a limit was set on the dollar-austral exchange rate: one dollar would not exceed 10,000 australes. This régime was to last until September 1991 when a new currency was planned to be introduced at par with the dollar; its name had not been announced by June 1991. Austral notes in circulation: A500,000, A100,000, A50,000, A10,000, A5,000, A1,000, A500, A100, A50 (beware forgeries from street money-changers). There is an acute shortage of small denomination notes. It is often difficult to change travellers' cheques, particularly in the smaller towns. Commissions can be as high as 6% and in general it takes a long time and many forms to transact these cheques. It is best to take US$ cash and American Express travellers' cheques, which can be changed at the American Express bank in Buenos Aires. It is not advisable to engage in unsolicited currency transactions in the streets, etc. as you may be tricked or land in prison. Some of the major towns have exchange shops (*casas de cambio*) and these are given in the text. There is a 3% tax on cheques and an extra commission which can be avoided if you go to a branch of the issuing bank, especially if changing small amounts. In December 1989, the exchange rate was freed and exchange controls were lifted, so there was no market rate from which travellers could benefit as opposed to the official exchange rate. This régime was in force at the time of going to press, but you are advised to check for changes at the time of your visit. Exchange rates are quoted in major newspapers daily. Money remitted to Argentina from abroad is normally paid out in local currency. It is possible to obtain money from Europe through an express transfer, which takes 2-3 days, and the currency will be subject to tax.

Various Argentine provinces (Tucumán, Salta, Jujuy, La Rioja are examples) have issued *bonos* (bonds) which circulate at face value alongside the national currency. Two warnings: they are not accepted outside the province of issue; and they bear redemption dates, after which they are valueless. Beware!

When crossing a land frontier into Argentina, make sure you have some Argentine currency as there are normally no facilities at the border.

**Credit Cards**  It is reported that American Express, Diners Club, Visa and Mastercard cards are all accepted. All shops, hotels and places showing Argencard (head office, H.Yrigoyen, Buenos Aires) signs will accept Eurocard and Access, but you must state that these cards are affiliated to Mastercard. Argencard will not permit cash advances on these cards in outlying regions, and is itself very slow in advancing cash. The use of Mastercard/Access and Eurocard is very limited in the south.

Note that, in 1991, the use of both credit cards (for purchases) and travellers' cheques (for exchange) was increasingly restricted, and that high surcharges on credit card purchases (up to 25%) was common. Travellers had to rely heavily on hard currency.

**Cost of living**  The cost of living for the foreigner travelling with dollars varies according to the currency exchange regime in force. If the currency is fixed against the dollar, Argentina becomes expensive; if the currency is free, the country should become cheaper. Travellers should therefore be prepared for unpredictable swings in prices and, for this reason, should only regard the prices given in this chapter as representative.

**Value-Added Tax**  VAT is not levied on most medicines and some foodstuffs but on all other products and services 13%.

**Weights and Measures**  The metric system is used.

**Electric Current**  220 volts, 50 cycles, A.C., European Continental-type plugs in old buildings, Australian 3-pin flat-type in the new. Adaptors can be purchased locally for either type (i.e. from new 3-pin to old 2-pin and vice-versa).

**Postage and Telephone Rates**  Letters from Argentina take up to a month to get to the UK and the USA.

Small parcels only of 1 kg. at post offices; larger parcels from Encomiendas Internacionales, Centro Postal Internacional, Av. Antártida Argentina, near Retiro Station, Buenos Aires, and in main provincial cities, about US$40 for 5 kg. Larger parcels must first be examined, before final packing, by Customs, then wrapped (up to 2 kg., brown paper; over 2 kg. must be sewn in linen cloth), then sealed by Customs, then taken to Encomiendas Internacionales for posting. Cheap packing service available (US$3.50). Open between 1100 and 1700 on weekdays. Used clothes have to be fumigated before they will be accepted. Having parcels sent to Argentina incurs a customs tax of about US$3 per package. *Poste restante* is available in every town's main post office, fee US$1.

The local telephone system is hopelessly overloaded. On weekdays, 2200-0800, there is a 20% reduction, and from Sat. midnight to 1200 Sun. and Christmas to New Year and Easter Week, international calls are 40% less. The normal rate for international calls is from US$5 a minute. Direct international telephone dialling is almost unknown in hotels and private homes. There is frequently a high mark-up on calls made from hotels. No reverse-charge calls to Australia or South Africa. Fax: American Express in Buenos Aires allows card holders to receive Faxes at US$1 per sheet and to send them at US$8 per sheet (to Europe). The main post office has Fax facilities at US$20 per page to Europe (contradictory reports received about this).

**Press**  Buenos Aires dailies: *La Nación, La Prensa*. Tabloids: *Clarín, La Razón, Tiempo Argentino* Evening papers: *Crónica*. English language daily: *Buenos Aires Herald*. Magazines: *Siete Días, Gente, La Semana, Redacción, Mercado, El Gráfico* (sports). The daily, *Página Doce*, is very popular among students and intellectuals. English language magazines: *The Review of the River Plate* (commercial, agricultural, political and economic comment), and *The Southern Cross* (Irish community). German-language weekly, *Argentinisches Tageblatt*, available everywhere, very informative.

**Radio** English language radio broadcasts can be heard daily on short wave: 0100-0130 on 6060 KHz 49m, 0230-0300 on 11710 KHz 25m, 0430-0500 and 2230-2300 on 15345 KHz 19m; Radiodifusión Argentina al Exterior, Casilla de Correo 555, Arg 1000, Buenos Aires. This is a government station and broadcasts also in Japanese, Arabic, German, French, Italian and Portuguese. Broadcasts by foreign radio stations (including the BBC) are receivable on short wave.

**Language** Spanish, with variant words and pronunciation. English comes second; French and Italian (especially in Patagonia) may be useful.

The chief variant pronunciations are the replacement of the "ll" and "Y" sounds by a soft "j" sound, as in "azure" (though note that this is not done in Mendoza), the omission of the "d" sound in words ending in "-ado", the omission of final "s" sounds, the pronunciation of "s" before a consonant as a Scottish or German "ch", and the substitution in the north and west of the normal rolled "r" sound by a hybrid "rj". In grammar the Spanish "tú" is replaced by "vos" and the second person singular conjugation of verbs has the accent on the last syllable e.g. *vos tenés, podés*, etc. In the N and NW, though, the Spanish is more akin to that spoken in the rest of Latin America.

**Tourist Information** Addresses of tourist offices are given in the text. See also **Automóvil Club Argentino** and **Maps** above. Federico B. Kirbus has written the highly informative *Las mil maravillas de la Argentina* (with comprehensive English index—1989), obtainable at El Ateneo, or from the author at Casilla de Correo 5210, RA-1000, Buenos Aires. La Fundación Vida Silvestre (conservation organization and bookshop), Defensa 245/251, has information and books on Argentine flora and fauna. Field guide to Argentine birds: *Guía para la identificación de las aves de Argentina y Uruguay* by T. Narosky and D. Yzurieta, with drawings and colour illustrations. Among a number of guide books to the country, recent recommended additions are *Travel Companion: Argentina* by Gerry Leitner, the *Pirelli Guide* by Diego Biogiari and the *Insight Guide* to Argentina. See also **Walking and Skiing** section, above.

We wish to offer our profound thanks to Charlie Nurse (who visited Argentina in August/September 1990) for doing the updating. We also wish to thank the following residents and travellers : Federico Kirbus (Buenos Aires), Marcelo Scann and Roberto Gabrielli for information on climbing, Herbert S. Levi (Buenos Aires), Eduardo Biraben, Presidente, Asatej (Buenos Aires), Noreen O'Flynn (Buenos Aires) and Allegra Alessandri (Fair Oaks, C.A., U.S.A.), Rob Allan and Bridgit Vale (Pietermaritzburg), John Allen (London SW14), Janine Allimann (Zurich), Jackie Annesley (Australia) and Suzie James (Scotland), Rick Ansell and Paulette Milego (Porto Alegre), Jorge Antolín Solache (Calafate, Argentina), Asatej, Buenos Aires, Frank Bakker and Nike Darley (Amsterdam), Sue Balcomb and Tom Hore, Marlise Baumgarter and Niklaus Graber (Erlach, Switzerland), Matthew Bell (Market Lavington, Wiltshire), Monique Belleau (Quebec), Petra Bell and Hans-Georg Henle (Schwaigern, Germany), Wayne Bernhardson (Oakland C.A.), Erik Bernesson (Båstad, Sweden), Ortun Bettering (Rio de Janeiro), César Bimbi and Beatriz Renck (Porto Alegre), Michael Böcker (Hagen, Germany), Astrid Bombosch (Heidelberg, Germany), Jan Boogman (Uzwil) and Josef Kaufman (Knutwil, Switzerland), Binka Le Breton (Muriaé, Minas Gerais), Gianmarco Broggini (Milan), Elizabeth Buettner (Ann Arbor, M.I.) and Alexander Protopapas (Pasadena, California), Kathryn Bullock (London SE8), Jeff and Sue Burgess (Sydney, Australia), Marion Büttner (Hamburg), Steve and Jeanette Campbell (Sucre, Bol.), Nelly and Steve Caplan (Winnipeg, Canada), Rolando Caponi (Rosario, Argentina), Liora Carmona and Ofer Kastner (Kiryat Bialik, Israel), Tim Cobb (Dorking) and Caroline Wren (Conisbrough), M. Collins and D. Power (Altrincham, UK), Dr. Simon Collier (Colchester), Alysia Cook and Phil Waterhouse (Twyford, Berks), Bryan Crawford (Inverness), Andrea Cujnik (München, Germany), Paul Dean (California), Michael Dibdin (Oxford), Carmen Diéguez (Miami, U.S.A.), Louise Dionne (St. John's, Newfoundland), Dirección Municipal de Turismo, Esquel, Gerd Dörner (Eberstadt), Barbara Egger (Caracas), Paula Egli (Wallenwil, Switzerland), Kirsten Eichhorn (München, Germany), Thomas Eidenbock (Steyr, Austria), René Erhardt and Lorena Ibañez (Berlin and Caracas), Daniel Ezekiel (Vancouver, BC), Tim Farnworth (Market Harborough, Leicestershire), Anthony Feeny (London EC1), Danny Feldman (El Calafate, Argentina), Mario Feldman (Buenos Aires), Rüdiger Filbrich (Frankfurt/Main), Florian (Berlin), John Foss (Durango, C.O.), Glyn Fry and Trui Anseeuw (Hyde, Cheshire), Dámaso Gallastegi (Bergara, Spain), Ricardo García García (Madrid), May-Lill Garly and Palle Valentiner-Branth (Copenhagen), Walter

Gebhardt (Erlangen), Gerhard J. (Santiago), Carsten Gerrens (Hamburg), Theodor A. Gevert (São Paulo), Michael Gonin (Canberra, Australia), Jacqueline Greig (Cuckfield, East Sussex), Pilou Grenié (Antibes), Michel Hack (Lausanne), Eric Hamovitch (Montréal, Canada).

Mark Hancock and Veronica Egan (Ross-on-Wye, Herefordshire) for much useful new material, Clare Hargreaves (London), Lucy Harper, Johanne Harvey and Niklaus Hutmacher (Gysenstein, Switzerland), Martin Hautkappe (München, Germany), Justin and Thom Hayes (Vancouver, Washington), A. Heller (London NW11), Carolyn Helmke (Berkeley, California), Ian Henderson (London SW16), Ulrich Herbert (Stuttgart), Frank Hermann (Nauheim), Bettina Herweck (Darmstadt, Germany), Gert Jan Hof and Yvonne Evers (Huissen, Neth), Robin Holloway and Fiona Butler (Birmingham), Ralf Hönsch and Martin Stark (Switzerland), Sarah A. Horniman (La Paz), Primrose Hutton (Bulli, NSW), Sabine Imhoff (Germany), Barry Isaac (Miami Beach, Florida), Christiane Iseler (Buenos Aires), Karen Johnson (Coquitlan, B.C.), Anne Toft Johnsen (Frederiksberg, Denmark), Martin Jung (Tübingen), Noa Kadman (Israel), Federico Kirbus (Buenos Aires), John Kirby (Eastbourne, New Zealand), Wolfgang D. Kleine (Windhoek, Namibia), Stefan Kochems (Köln, Germany), Martin Koschnick (Southampton), Heike Krohn (Berlin 46), Andy Kuendig and Rosi Nueesch (Zürich), Christina Kuseffsky (Stockholm), Dirk Lahme (Reutlingen, Germany), Gerald Lange (Dolldorf, Germany), Herbert Levi (Buenos Aires), John Lewis (London NW2), Hans Liechti and Veronica Araneda de Liechti (Grenchen, Switzerland), Judith Locher (Switzerland), James Maas (Panama), Neil A. Macdougall (Toronto), Philipp Magura (Reutlingen, Germany), Markus Maier and Gitte Wiedmann (Zürich), Herbert Malinow (London W1), Susan Marfield (Long Beach, California), Douglas Markham (Houston), Simon Mays Smith (Waldron, East Sussex), Tom Amies (Bucks) and Simon Davy (England), Julianne McCabe, Maggie Widow, Jean O'Leary and Bill Shaffer (San Anselmo, C.A.), Martin Merz (Hochfelden, Switzerland), Roderick Michener (Long Beach, California), Andy Millbank (Norwich), Bernard Milward (Salvador), Catherine Morris-Adams (West Derby), Deirdre Mortell (Corrigaline, County Cork), Lothar Nehrke (Dortmund), Lothar Nehrsse (Bariloche), Steve Newman and Wendy Chilcott (Horsham, West Sussex) for their welcome assistance, Asbjørn Nielsen (Denmark) Vital Pajarola and Eva Grunder (Zurich), Jeff Perk (Carbondale, Illinois), Mirco and Cristina Perot (Grüt, Switz), José M. Perre, Director de Turismo, Municipalidad de Esquel, Guido Pfister (Weisslingen, Switzerland), Piero, John Pomfret (Woking, Surrey), Arthur Poyner (Chiloe), Bernd Proissl (Wernau), John Rashak (Whitehouse Station, NJ), Jesper Juel Rasmussen and Kirsten Bruun (Copenhagen), John Raspey (Argentina), Fabian Rehmann (Switzerland), Jamie Rein (Boston, Mass), Knut and Marianne Riesmeier (Bad Oeynhausen, Germany), Mrs. H. Rijkels-Redeleer (Den Haag), Toby Robinson (London SW2), Bryan and Charmaine Roche (Cape Town), Joseph J. Rodríguez, Winifred Hughes Rodríguez and Jo Ann Manderscheid (Snyder, New York), Ann Rodzai and Doug Hanaver (Ithaca, NY), Tal Rosenthal (Kibbutz Bet-Haemek, Israel), Ms Alex Rossi (Norwich, Norfolk), Ken Sattell (Boulder, C.O.), Nick Saunders and Sarah Jaggs (London W1), Bettina Schmieduch and family (Böblingen, Germany), Bianca Schmid (Wien, Austria), Dieter Schoop (Münchenstein, Switzerland), Michael Scott-Watson (Roxburghshire, Scotland), Marion Siegers (Dusseldorf), Ulrich Sigel (Schorndorf, Germany), P.J. Spiceley (London SW1), John Spraos (London NW11), Trevor and Lynn Stacey (Windhoek, Namibia), Hans and Ina Stoffregen (Celle, Germany), Guillermo Surraco and Siobhan Rhea de Surraco (Berkeley, C.A.), Eva Süsstrunk and Roland Ruprecht (Berne), Fredi Suter (Goldau) and Claudia Räber (Oberkirch), L. Tapsall (Kensington, South Africa), Martin Theander Christoph Theis (Wiesloch, Germany), C.W. Thierbach (Zürich), Roger Thornton and Paul Gadd (London N5), Ian Trontz (Brooklyn, NY), Michael Turner (Burnham-On-Sea), Paul and Renée Turton (Luxembourg), Jarle Unneland (Alesund, Norway), Dirk Vandersypen (Managua), Mark Van Den Boer (Tilberg, Netherlands), Pierre Vigna (Neuilly Sur Seine, France), Andreas Vogt (Mössingen, Germany), Béatrice Völkle (Gampelen, Switz.), Peter and Miek Vullings (Panningen, Netherlands), Thomas Walbaum (Steinheim, Germany), Willy Walker (Washington, DC) for a very helpful contribution, Simon Watson Taylor (London W14) for a wealth of thoroughly-researched material, Joanna Watts and Shaun Pinchbeck (Bath), A. J. Wearden (Blackburn, Lancs.), Dr Volker Weinmann (São Paulo, Brazil), Annemarie Wenger (Grafenried, Switz.), Lisa Wenrick (San Francisco), Urs Wickli (Neu St. Johann, Switzerland), Johan Widén (Marsta, Sweden), Petra Witteler (Frankfurt, Germany), Manfred Wolfensberger (Uster, Switzerland), Manuela Wonisch (Kloten, Switzerland), Julian Woodhouse (London NW3), Meg Worley (Knoxville, Tennessee) and Peter Grover (Montreal, Canada), F Worthington (Leicester), Helmut Zettl (Austria), Hod Zoiberman (Petach-Tikra, Israel) and Bart Zwart (Eindhoven, Netherlands).

# BOLIVIA

## INTRODUCTION

BOLIVIA, straddling the Andes, is a land of gaunt mountains, cold desolate plateaux and developing semi-tropical and fertile lowlands. Its area of about 1,098,580 square kilometres makes it twice the size of Spain. It is land-locked, with Chile and Peru to the W, Brazil to N and E, and Argentina and Paraguay to the S.

The Andean range is at its widest—some 650 km.—in Bolivia. The Western Cordillera, which separates Bolivia from Chile, has high peaks of between 5,800 and 6,500 metres and a number of active volcanoes along its crest. The passes across it are above 4,000 metres. To the E of this range lies the bleak, treeless, windswept Altiplano, much of it 4,000 metres above sea-level. It has an average width of 140 km., is 840 km. long, and covers an area (in Bolivia) of 102,300 square km., or nearly 10% of the country. Its surface is by no means flat, for the Western Cordillera sends spurs into it which tend to divide it into basins. The more fertile northern part is the more inhabited; the southern part is parched desert and almost unoccupied, save for a mining town here and there. Nearly 70% of the population lives on it, for it contains most of the major cities; almost half of the people are urban dwellers.

Lake Titicaca, at the northern end of the Altiplano, is an inland sea of 8,965 square km. at 3,810 metres: the highest navigable water in the world. Its maximum length and breadth are 171 and 64 km., and the greatest known depth is 280 metres. There are large annual variations between high and low water levels; 95% of the water flowing into it is lost by evaporation, making it more salty than most freshwater lakes. The immense depth of the water keeps the lake at an even all-the-year-around temperature of 10°C, and modifies the extremes of winter and night temperatures on the surrounding land. There is therefore a large farming population of Indians in this basin, tilling the fields and the hill terraces and tending their sheep and llamas.

The Altiplano is a harsh, strange land, a dreary grey solitude except for the bursts of green after rain. The air is unbelievably clear—the whole plateau is a bowl of luminous light. A cold wind blows frequently in the afternoons, causing dust storms. During the winter temperatures fall below freezing point; there is

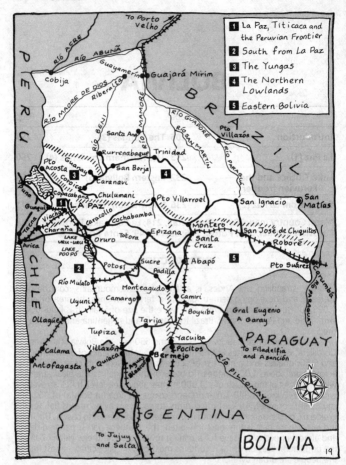

Map legend:

1. La Paz, Titicaca and the Peruvian Frontier
2. South from La Paz
3. The Yungas
4. The Northern Lowlands
5. Eastern Bolivia

**BOLIVIA**

19

frost every night in July and August, but during the day the tropical sun raises temperatures over 20°C.

The animals of the Altiplano are fascinating. Llamas serve as pack animals—they carry up to 22 kg. loads up to 20 km. a day and yield about 2½kg. of wool when sheared at intervals of from two to five years. The alpaca, bred not for work but for wool, belongs to the same group; the two may be distinguished by differences in the texture of their coats and shape of their tails. The vicuña, chinchilla and red fox are the main wild animals. The vicuña, an untamed smaller member of the family to which the llama and the alpaca belong, is found, though in diminishing numbers, on the bleak pampas. It may not be hunted, but its fine silky, tawny coloured wool may be sold.

Agriculture in the Altiplano is also interesting: the potato and the oca (another tuber), eaten in the dehydrated form of chuño and tunta, are the main crops.

*Quinoa*, a kind of millet, and *cañava*, a smaller and darker grain, are the main cereals; both are extremely nutritious. *Chicha*, the national intoxicant, is brewed from maize (corn). Edible fish (small *boga*, large white-fleshed *pejerrey* and rainbow and salmon trout—Lake Titicaca has been stocked with the last two) are widely sold in the towns of the Altiplano.

Far more important to the economy of the Altiplano than agriculture is mining. 210 km. S of La Paz along the passageway at the base of the Eastern Cordillera is Oruro, where a low belt of hills supplies tin, copper, silver and tungsten. The Spaniards of Peru discovered the Cerro Rico in 1545. It is a mountain rising out of the Puna to a height of 4,780 metres, and was almost a solid mass of ore containing tin, silver, bismuth and tungsten. The Spaniards, interested only in silver, built Potosí at its base, 4,065 metres above sea level. The city grew till it had a population of 150,000, but rapidly dwindled after the richest deposits had been worked out. It remained a dead town till demand for tin rose early this century.

The presence of tin also accounts for the mining communities in the Cordillera to the SE of Oruro: the ex-Patiño mines at Catavi, to which there is a branch railway from Oruro, produce nearly half the tin of Bolivia. The high cost of producing Bolivian tin was a major contributor to the industry's decline in 1986, when the world tin market collapsed. Silver is still mined or extracted from the tailings left by past generations, and variable amounts of lead, bismuth, antimony, tungsten and zinc from pockets in the Cordillera are exported. Large deposits of silver have been found south of the Altiplano, near Lípez, and mines are being reopened, and their tailings reprocessed, two centuries after the Spaniards abandoned them.

Recommended reading: *We Eat the Mines and the Mines Eat* Us by June Nash, New York, 1979, and *The Potosí Mita* 1573-1700 by Jeffery Cole, Stanford University Press, 1985.

From the Altiplano rises, to the E, the sharp façade of the Eastern Cordillera. As luck would have it there is a gently graded passageway along the plateau at the foot of the Eastern Cordillera from Lake Titicaca, in the N, to the Argentine frontier, in the S. From Viacha, near La Paz, the main line of the Bolivian railways runs along this passageway to Villazón, with connections to Chile (from Uyuni) and Buenos Aires. The giant masses of the northern parts of the Eastern Cordillera rise to very great heights in the Cordillera Real to the east of Lake Titicaca: four peaks soar to above 6,000 metres. This magnificent sight can be seen on a clear day from the top of a ridge on the more southerly Titicaca-La Paz road, which goes past Tiahuanaco. Their far sides fall away to the NE, very sharply, towards the Amazon basin.

These heavily forested north-eastern slopes are deeply indented by the fertile valleys of the Nor Yungas and Sud Yungas, drained by the Río Beni and its

tributaries, where cacao, coffee, sugar, coca and tropical fruits are grown. The problem of transport to the consuming centre of La Paz is formidable: the connecting all-weather road, hair-raising in places, climbs 3,430 metres in 80 km. to surmount La Cumbre pass, at 4,725 metres within 24 km. of La Paz.

From a point just N of Cochabamba to the S the Eastern Cordillera is tilted, not to the NE, but to the E. This part of the Eastern Cordillera rises abruptly in sharp escarpments from the Altiplano, and then flattens out to an easy slope eastwards to the plains: an area known as the Puna. The streams which flow across the Puna are tributaries of the Río Grande flowing NE to the basin of the Amazon, and of the Pilcomayo flowing SE through the Chaco to the Río de la Plata system. They cut increasingly deep incisions as they gather volume until, to the E, the Puna is eroded to little more than a high remnant between the river valleys. These valleys deeply incising the surface of the eastern-sloping Puna are densely inhabited; a variety of grain crops and fruits is grown. All these semi-tropical mountain valleys are known as Yungas: the generic name is not confined to the valleys of the Provinces of Nor and Sud Yungas to the E of La Paz. Rainfall in the Yungas is from 700 to 800 mm. a year, as opposed to the 400 to 700 mm. of the northern Altiplano and much less further S. The heaviest rain is during December, January and February. The mean average temperature is between 16° and 18°C, but in spite of a high humidity the Yungas are not unhealthy.

The very fertile basins in which Cochabamba, Sucre, and Tarija lie send food and cattle to the towns of the Altiplano, but other valleys have no way of doing so. The basins and long ribbons of valley farmland are isolated, and transport to the areas where they might sell their produce is only now being developed.

The lowland tropics, stretching from the foothills of the Eastern Cordillera to the frontiers with Brazil to the NE and E and with Paraguay and Argentina to the SE and S, take up 70% of the total area of Bolivia, but contain only about 20% of its population. Rainfall is high but seasonal, and large stretches suffer from alternate flooding and drought. The climate is hot, ranging from 23° to 25°C in the S and to 27°C in the N. Occasional cold dust-laden winds from the S—the *surazos*—lower the temperature considerably. In the N and E the Oriente has dense tropical forest. Open plains covered with rough pasture, swamp and scrub occupy the centre. Towards the end of the 18th century this was a populous land of plenty; for 150 years Jesuit missionaries had controlled the area and guided it into a prosperous security. A symbol of their great effort is the cathedral at San José de Chiquitos: a gem of elegance and dignity. But the Jesuits were expelled in 1767; years of maladministration, spoliation and corruption reduced the area to lethargy.

This once rich land, drained by the Madre de Dios, Beni and Mamoré rivers into the Madeira, a tributary of the Amazon, has been isolated from the rest of the country. It is as difficult to get at from the E as from the W, for there are rapids and falls in the Madeira which limit navigation. In its heart lie the seasonally inundated tropical Llanos de Mojos, ringed in by rain forest or semi-deciduous tropical forest—230,000 square km. with only 120,000 people. Roads and river connections are still being improved; there are roads between La Paz and Trinidad, Santa Cruz and Trinidad, and Cochabamba and Todos Santos and Puerto Villarroel. Meat is already brought in from Trinidad, capital of Beni Department, and from airstrips in the area, to the urban centres of La Paz, Oruro, and Cochabamba.

The forests and plains beyond the Eastern Cordillera sweep S towards the Río Pilcomayo, getting progressively less rain and merging into a comparatively dry southern land of scrub forest and arid savanna. The main city of this area is Santa Cruz de la Sierra, founded in the 16th century, now the second city of Bolivia and a large agricultural centre. Here conditions favour the growing of sugar-cane, rice, oil plants and citrus fruit. The plains to the E are mainly used as grazing lands with small areas under cultivation, but in this area are extensive oil, gas, and iron-ore deposits, possibly Bolivia's greatest asset when developed.

**Climate** There are four distinct climatic zones: (1) The tropical departments of Santa Cruz and Beni, drained by the Amazon; altitude between 150 and 750 metres; average temperature, 29°C. (2) The Yungas, or low valleys, north of La Paz and Cochabamba, among the spurs of the Cordillera; altitude, 750-1,500 metres; average temperature, 24°C. (3) The Valles, or high valleys and basins gouged out by the rivers of the Puna; average temperature, 19°C. (4) The Puna and Altiplano; average temperature, 10°C, but above 4,000 metres may get down to -25°C at night in June-August (don't forget antifreeze). Little rain falls upon the western plateaux between May and November, but the rest of the year is wet. There is rain at all seasons in the eastern part of the country, and heavy rain from November to March.

**History** At Tiahuanaco (Tiwanaku), near Lake Titicaca, stand the impressive remains of a pre-Inca civilization. The Aymará-speaking Indians in this area emerged around 1000 BC into a civilization characterized by massive stone buildings and monuments, exquisite textiles, pottery and metalwork. This phase seems to have been ended abruptly by some unexplained calamity, which greatly reduced the size of Lake Titicaca, around AD 900. When the Quechua-speaking Incas of Cuzco conquered the area around AD 1200, they found the Aymarás at Tiahuanaco living among ruins they could no longer explain. The Aymarás resisted obstinately and were not finally conquered until the latter part of the 15th century under the reign of Inca Túpac Yupangi (1471-93). Even so, they kept their traditional social structures and language, and fought for the Incas under their own leaders. Only religion was formally imposed by the Incas.

Francisco Pizarro landed in Peru in 1532. Six years later Spain conquered Bolivia, and the next year Sucre (then Charcas), still the official capital, was founded. By 1559 Bolivia had become the *audiencia* of Charcas, in the Viceroyalty of Peru, for it had become extremely important for the Spaniards after the discovery of the silver mountain at Potosí in 1545.

The excellent Inca communications and economic organization fell into ruin. Revolutionary movements against the colonial rule of the Spaniards began early; there were revolts at La Paz in 1661, at Cochabamba in 1730 and at Sucre, Cochabamba, Oruro and La Paz from 1776 to 1780. In 1809 the University of San Francisco Xavier, at Sucre, called for the independence of all Spain's American colonies. Finally, on 9 December 1824, Bolívar's general, Sucre, won the decisive battle of Ayacucho in Peru and invaded what is now Bolivia, defeating the Spaniards finally at the battle of Tumusla on 2 April 1825.

On 9 February 1825, when he first entered La Paz, Sucre had already promulgated the decree of independence, but his second in command, Santa Cruz, was for retaining links with Peru; Bolívar was in two minds. Sucre had his way and Bolivia was declared independent. On 25 August 1825, Bolívar named the new country after himself. In 1828, when Sucre left the country, Santa Cruz became President; pursuing his dream of amalgamation he proclaimed a Peruvian-Bolivian confederation in 1836, but Chile and Argentina intervened, and in 1839 Santa Cruz was overthrown and the confederation dissolved.

Since its independence, Bolivia has suffered a grievous contraction of its territory. In the War of the Pacific (1879-1883) Bolivia in alliance with Peru fought the Chileans for the right to retain the nitrate-rich Atacama desert. After a year the Bolivians withdrew and Chile took over the desert and the port of Antofagasta, though it later compensated by building Bolivia the railway between Arica and La Paz. Railways traded for valuable territory has been Bolivia's fate. A railway to Yacuiba was Argentina's return for annexing some of the Chaco. When Brazil annexed the rich Acre Territory in 1903, Bolivia was compensated by yet another railway, but this Madeira-Mamoré line never reached its destination,

Riberalta, and proved of little use; it was closed in 1972. A fourth railway, completed in the 1950s, connects Santa Cruz in East-Central Bolivia with Corumbá in Brazil.

There was not even an unbuilt railway to compensate Bolivia for its next loss. Constant disputes between Bolivia and Paraguay over the Chaco led to open warfare between 1928 and 1930, and again between 1933 and 1935. In 1938, by arbitration, Bolivia ceded to Paraguay three-quarters of the Chaco, but obtained a doubtfully valuable outlet to the Río Paraguay. Bolivia's failure to occupy its empty spaces is partly the explanation for these losses.

The moral results of this last defeat had revolutionary consequences. After over fifteen years of disorder, Víctor Paz Estenssoro was elected to the presidency in 1951 on a left-nationalist ticket. A military junta intervened, but in April 1952 a popular revolution overthrew it: Paz Estenssoro returned as president. His government committed itself to a profound social revolution, introducing the expropriation and the nationalization of the tin mines; universal suffrage without literacy or income qualifications; and a policy of land reform and redistribution of the large estates. Hernán Siles Zuazo, a revolutionary leader and vice president under Paz from 1952-56, was president from 1956-60. During his term the economy was stabilized. Paz Estenssoro was again elected president from 1960-64, but shortly after beginning a third term was overthrown in 1964 by General Barrientos, killed in an air crash in 1969. After three ephemeral governments, power was taken in August 1971 by a right-wing general, Hugo Banzer Suárez, who after seven years' rule called for elections in July 1978. Then came another sequence of short-lived military governments, despite disallowed elections which gave victories to ex-President Hernán Siles Zuazo. In August 1982 the military returned to barracks and Dr. Siles Zuazo assumed the Presidency in a leftist coalition government with support from the communists and trade unions. Under this regime inflation spiralled out of control. The elections of 14 July 1985 were won again by Víctor Paz Estenssoro, who imposed a most rigorous programme to stabilize the economy. In the elections of 7 May 1989, Gonzalo Sánchez de Losada of the Movimiento Nacionalista Revolucionario (chief architect of the stabilization programme) won most votes but the result was so close that Congress had to choose a president from the three leading contenders. Jaime Paz Zamora of the Movimiento de la Izquierda Revolucionaria (MIR) who came third in the elections, was inaugurated as President on 6 August 1989 after having made an unlikely alliance with the right wing former military dictator, Gen. (retired) Hugo Banzer (Acción Democrática Nacionalista), in return for certain cabinet posts.

**The People** Of the population of some 7.19m people some 70% are Indians, 25% *mestizo* and 5% European. The racial composition varies from place to place: Indian around Lake Titicaca; more than half Indian in La Paz; three-quarters *mestizo* or European in the Yungas, Cochabamba, Santa Cruz and Tarija, the most European of all. Since the 1980s, regional tensions between the "collas" (*altiplano* dwellers) and the "cambas" (lowlanders) have become more marked. Under 40% of children of school age are attending school even though it is theoretically compulsory between 7 and 14.

About two-thirds of the population lives in adobe huts, and medical services are sketchy outside the towns and mining camps; birth rate, 44.0, general death rate, 14.2 per 1,000, but infantile mortality is 124 per 1,000 during the first year (local estimates put this rate at 300 per 1,000). Epidemics are comparatively rare on the Altiplano, but malaria and yellow fever are still problems in the Oriente and Santa Cruz, and hepatitis and Chagas disease (**see Health Hints in Introduction**) are endemic in the warmer parts of the country. About 50% is urban. Annual population growth: 2.8%; urban growth: 4.3%. Life expectancy at birth: 51 years; unemployment in 1987 was estimated at 22% of the work-force.

The Indians are mainly composed of two groups: those in the north of the Altiplano who speak the guttural Aymará, and those elsewhere, who speak Quechua, the Inca tongue. Outside the big cities many of them speak no Spanish, but knowledge of Spanish is increasing.

The most obdurate of Bolivian problems has always been that the main mass of population is, from a strictly economic viewpoint, in the wrong place, the poor Altiplano and not the potentially rich Oriente; and that the Indians live largely outside the monetary system on a self-sufficient basis. Since the land reform of 1952 isolated communities continue the old life but in the agricultural area around Lake Titicaca, the valleys of Cochabamba, the Yungas and the irrigated areas of the south, most peasants now own their own land, however small the plot may be. There has also been appreciable migration to the warmer and more fertile lands of the eastern region, encouraged by the Government.

The Indian women retain their traditional costume, with bright petticoats, and in the highlands wear, apparently from birth, a flattish brown or grey bowler. In Cochabamba they wear a white top hat of ripolined straw. However, traditional headgear is being replaced by the baseball cap which sells for US$2.50 against US$7 for a bowler. Indians traditionally chew the coca leaf, which deadens hunger pains and gives a measure of oblivion. On feast days they drink with considerable application, wear the most sensational masks and dance till they drop.

**N.B.** Remember to refer to rural Indians not as "indios" (an insult) but as "campesinos" (peasants).

**The Economy**  Bolivia is the poorest country on the South American mainland, with annual income per head estimated at about US$600. Its backwardness is partly attributable to its rugged terrain, which makes communications between the various parts of the country extremely difficult, and to its landlocked position.

The agricultural sector employs half the working population and contributes about 20% to gdp, but less than 2% of export earnings. Employment in agriculture has fallen since the mid-1960s because of increasing urbanization. Production of crops for food takes place primarily in the Altiplano, mainly by subsistence farmers, while crops for industrial use (cotton, sugar and soya) are concentrated around Santa Cruz. Croplands cover about 5% of total land area. Most commercial agriculture is in the east, where there are a number of food-processing plants: vegetable oils, a maize mill and sugar refineries. The controversial area in agriculture is the cultivation of the coca leaf, used for chewing by the Indians and to make the drug cocaine. In the 1980s the extreme economic depression and rising unemployment drove increasing numbers in search of the lucrative cocaine trade. Coca is easy to grow, up to four crops a year can be harvested, and Bolivia's production is believed to be worth about US$2bn a year, although less than a quarter of that actually returns to the country.

In contrast to agriculture, mining, including oil, employs only 2-5% of the labour force and contributes 10% of gdp, yet 95% of export earnings. Bolivia is a major producer of tin, antimony, wolfram and bismuth. Silver, lead and zinc are also produced and there are large unexploited reserves of lithium and potassium. Tin is the major mineral export, but because of the collapse of the world tin market, it has lost its first position in overall exports to natural gas.

Estimated reserves of natural gas are sufficient to meet domestic demand and export commitments for 30 years, but oil reserves, at 119m barrels in 1991, were being exploited faster than the rate of discovery. Production of around 20,000 b/d was just sufficient to meet domestic demand, but would be insufficient were there to be a general economic recovery.

The recession which afflicted most Latin American countries from 1980 hit Bolivia with six consecutive years of contraction of gdp, accompanied by accelerating inflation, massive and frequent devaluations of the currency and social unrest. Government spending to support key export sectors was hampered by widespread inefficiency, corruption and strikes in state enterprises, which led to massive public sector deficits and external indebtedness. Economic problems were compounded in 1983 by a severe drought in the Altiplano and floods in the eastern lowlands, which devasted farming. The resulting food shortages exacerbated existing inflationary pressures and led to hyperinflation with annual rates reaching over 20,000%.

In the mid-1980s the government of President Paz Estenssoro introduced severe austerity measures to stabilize the economy, in which price controls were lifted, subsidies removed, public sector wages frozen and the currency linked to the US dollar in a controlled float. Tax reform was passed, a new currency, the boliviano, was created, worth 1 million pesos, the IMF agreed to disburse a standby credit, bilateral and multilateral lending began to flow again and steps were taken to buy back the external commercial bank debt. Inflation came down to 10% a year, although unemployment continued to rise and living standards to fall. Nevertheless, by the 1990s there were encouraging signs that growth and employment were recovering and structural adjustment had put Bolivia on a firmer footing.

**Government** The Constitution of 1967 vests executive power in the President, elected by popular vote for a term of 4 years; he cannot be immediately re-elected. Government is by two legislative houses, the Chamber of Senators, with 27 seats, and the Chamber of Deputies, with 130 seats. There are nine departments; each is controlled by a Delegate appointed by the President.

Bolivia has, in effect, two capitals. Although Sucre is the legal capital, La Paz is in almost all respects the actual capital, being the seat of the Government and of Congress. On the other hand, the Supreme Court still holds its sessions in Sucre.

**Communications** After centuries of isolation new roads are now integrating the food-producing eastern zones with the bulk of the population living in the towns of the Altiplano or the westward-facing slopes of the Eastern Cordillera. Under Spanish rule there were four great trails in use within the country: three of them led through passes in the Western Cordillera to the Pacific; the fourth led from La Paz southwards into Argentina. At the turn of the century, railways replaced the llamas and mules. By far the shortest line is the one from La Paz to Arica (Chile), completed in 1913. Arica ships a large part of the exports together with Antofagasta (Chile) and Matarani (Peru).

Bolivia has 3,774 km. of railway. There are two private railways: Machacamarca-Uncia, owned by the Corporación Minera de Bolivia (108 km.) and Uyuni-Pulacayo (52 km.) owned by the Empresa Minera Pulacayo. A railway to link Cochabamba and Santa Cruz, as part of a Pacific-Atlantic rail network, has been under study with Inter-American Development Bank assistance since 1989. Bolivia has over 14,000 km. of navigable rivers, which connect most of the country with the Amazon basin. The national highway system at the end of 1985 totalled 40,987 km., of which only 3.75% were paved and 22.6% gravel-surfaced.

Recommended reading: Herbert S.Klein, *Bolivia: The Evolution of a Multi-Ethnic Society* (Oxford University Press).

**Music and Dance** The heart of Bolivia is the two-mile high Altiplano and it is the music of the Quechua- and Aymará-speaking Indians of this area that provides the most distinctive Bolivian musical sound. Although there is much that is of Spanish colonial origin in the Indians' dances, the music itself has more Amerindian style and content than that of any other country in South America. It is rare to find an Indian who cannot play an instrument and it is these instruments, both wind and percussion, that are quintessentially Bolivian. The clear sounds of the *quena* and *pinkullo*, the deeper, breathier notes of the *tarka*, *pututo* and *sicuri* accompanied by *huankaré*, *pululu* and *caja* drums can be heard all over the Altiplano, the *charango* being virtually the only instrument of European origin. The Indian dances are mainly collective and take place at religious fiestas. The dancers wear colourful costumes with elaborate, plumed headdresses and some of them still parody their ex-Spanish colonial masters. Such are the Auqui Auquis and Pakhochos dances. The Khachua dance on the other hand dates from the time of Inca Túpac Yupangi. Other notable dances are the Wititis, Wila Khawani, Jucumaris, Takiri de Kharmisa and Sikuris de Ayata.

The principal popular dances that can be regarded as "national" in their countrywide appeal are the Cueca and Huayño. The Bolivian Cueca is a close relative of the Chilean national dance of the same name and they share a mutual origin in the Zamacueca, itself derived from the Spanish Fandango. The Huayño is of Indian origin and involves numerous couples, who whirl around or advance down the street, arm-in-arm, in a "Pandilla". Other similar, but more regional dances are the Bailecito Chuquisaqueño, Khaluyo Cochabambino, Rueda Tarijeña from the south east and Carnavalito Cruceño and Taquirari Beniano from the tropical lowlands. Justly celebrated is the great carnival Diablada de Oruro, with its hordes of grotesquely masked devils, a spectacle comparable to those of Rio in Brazil and Barranquilla in Colombia.

The region of Tarija near the Argentine border has a distinctive musical tradition of its own, based on religious processions that culminate with that of San Roque on the first Sunday in September. The influence is Spanish, the dance is the Chapaqueada and the musical instruments are the *caña*, *erke* and *violin chapaco*. The first named is an immensely long bamboo tube with a horn at the end, aimed at the sky, on which different "Toques" are played. There are many professional folk groups on record, the best known being Grupo Aymara, Los Runas, Los Laris, Los Masis, Kolla Marka and Bolivia Manta, some of which have now established themselves in Europe and North America.

---

## LA PAZ (1)

---

**La Paz, Lake Titicaca and Mount Illimani are probably the three most familiar sights of Bolivia, set amid high Andean Altiplano and the Cordillera Real. The region around La Paz is known as Little Bolivia, containing snow-peaks, desert and sub-tropical jungle in Coroico, just one day's breathtaking bus-ride away.**

*La Paz*, the highest capital in the world, lies at 3,636 metres in a natural basin or canyon; it is sunk about 370 metres below the level of the Altiplano in its north-eastern corner. Mount Illimani, with its snow-covered peaks (6,402 metres), towers over the city. The Spaniards chose this odd place for a city on 20 October 1548, to avoid the chill winds of the plateau, and because they had found gold in the Río Choqueyapu, which runs through the canyon. The mean average temperature is 10°C, but it varies greatly during each day, and the nights are cold. It rains almost every day from December to February, but the sun usually shines for several hours. The rest of the year the weather is mostly clear and sunny. Snow is rare. At first the visitor will probably feel some discomfort, known as *soroche* (altitude sickness), from the rarified air; a few hours resting when you arrive will put that right, though visitors with heart problems should consult a physician. The effects will be greater if you are flying into La Paz from lower altitudes. Oxygen is available at the better hotels.

In 1989, the population of La Paz was 1.15 million, over half of it Indian. Most of the Indians live in the higher terraces. Below are the business quarter, the government offices, the main hotels and restaurants and the university. The wealthier residential district is lower still: strung from Sopocachi to the bed of the valley at Obrajes, 5 km. from the centre and 500 metres lower than Plaza Murillo.

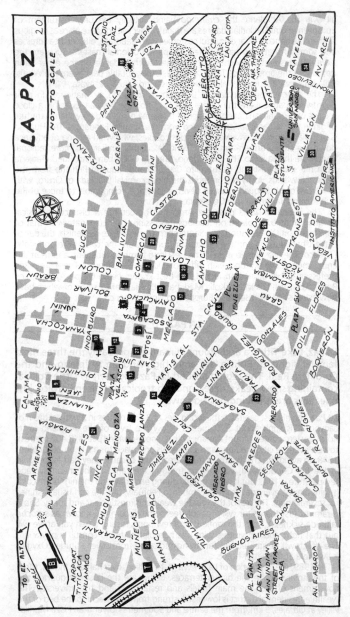

LA PAZ

NOT TO SCALE

Beyond Obrajes are the upper-class districts of Calacoto and La Florida. The main sports and social clubs have moved to these districts.

The neighbourhood of El Alto has now become a city in its own right, with a population of between 400,000 and 500,000. Apart from the district known as Ciudad Satelite, it is almost 100 per cent indigenous; almost everyone is an emigrant from the countryside. There is a fair every Sunday in Plaza 16 de Julio, more interesting for its size than the items for sale. Buses from Plaza Aguino and Pérez Velasco leave regularly for Plaza 16 de Julio.

There is some colonial building left; probably the best examples are in the Calle Jaén, but much of La Paz is modern. Plaza Murillo, on the north-eastern side of the river, is the traditional centre. Facing its formal gardens are the huge Cathedral (modern but very graceful); the Palacio Presidencial in Italian renaissance style, usually known as the Palacio Quemado (burnt palace) twice gutted by fire in its stormy 130-year history; and on the E side the Congreso Nacional. Across from the Cathedral on Calle Socabaya is the Palacio de los Condes de Arana, now the Museo Nacional del Arte. Calle Comercio, running cross-wise past the Plaza, has most of the stores and shops. On Av. Bolívar (to which Mount Illimani provides a backdrop), continuing the Av. Camacho, is the Central Market (called "Mercado Camacho"), a picturesque medley of Indian victuals and vendors presiding raucously over stalls, their black braids topped by hard-brimmed bowler hats. Av. Camacho leads to the residential district of Miraflores.

From the Plaza Venezuela, Avenida Mariscal Santa Cruz leads to the Plaza San Francisco and to the church and monastery of San Francisco, well worth seeing; the church is colonial, richly decorated on native religious themes, and Indian weddings can be seen on Sats. 1000-1200. SW from Plaza San Francisco runs Calle Sagárnaga, with rows of handicraft shops. Going higher still up Sagárnaga is a local market, and turning right on Max Paredes, heading west, one reaches Avenida Buenos Aires, one of the liveliest streets in the Indian quarter. A worthwhile walk is to Mirador Laicacota on Avenida del Ejército.

Other churches of more than passing interest are Santo Domingo (originally the cathedral) on the corner of Calles Ingavi and Yanacocha; La Merced, with its decorative 18th-century façade, on Calles Colón and Comercio; and San Sebastián, the first church to be built in La Paz, in Plaza Alonso de Mendoza (named after the church's builder).

**Festivals** Particularly impressive is the Alacitas Fair held from 24 Jan. to 15 Feb., on the upper part of Plaza Villarroel, mostly on Calle Tejada Zorzano (take *micro* B, K, H, 131 or X). "It is dedicated to Ekeko, an Indian household god. You can buy plaster images of him at many of the booths. He is a red-nosed cheerfully-grinning little personage laden with an assortment of miniature cooking utensils, coins, balls of wool, tiny sacks of sugar, coffee, salt, rice and flour; a kind of Bolivian Santa Claus. Ekeko is said to bring prosperity and to grant wishes. If you buy a toy house, or a cow, or a sheep at the Alacitas, you will get a real one before the year is out. There are also model motor-cars and planes, for the extreme optimists." (Christopher Isherwood, "The Condor and the Cows.") Beginning of May, Corpus Christi. End May, early June, Festividad del Señor de Gran Poder, huge procession of costumed and masked dancers. Fiestas de Julio, a month of concerts and performances at the Teatro Municipal, offers a wide variety of music. 8 December, festival around Plaza España, not very

---

## La Paz: Key to map

1.Plaza Murillo; 2. Congreso Nacional; 3. Museo Nacional de Arte; 4. Cathedral; 5. Palacio Quemado; 6. General Post Office; 7. Iglesia La Merced; 8. Museo de Costumbres; 9. Museo y Casa de Murillo; 10. Iglesia Santo Domingo; 11. Museo Nacional de Etnografía y Folklore; 12. Palacio Villaverde; 13. Casa de la Cultura; 14. Basílica de San Francisco; 15. Mercado de Hechicería; 16. Parque Prehistórico Tiahuanaco (Museo Semisubterráneo); 17. Alcaldía; 18. U.S. Embassy and Citibank; 19. Banco Central; 20. Tourist Office; 21. TAM; 22. Museo Arqueológico de Tiahuanaco; 23. Lloyd Aéreo Boliviano; 24. Mercado Camacho; 25. Biblioteca Municipal. Hotels: 26. *Sucre Palace*; 27. *Gloria*; 28. *Libertador*; 29. *Plaza*; 30. *El Dorado*; 31. *Panamericano*; 32. *Res. Rosario*; 33. *Milton*; 34. *La Paz*.

large, but colourful and noisy. On New Year's Eve fireworks are let off and make a spectacular sight, and a din, view from higher up. **See also page 276** for festivals outside La Paz.

**Hotels** Try to arrive in La Paz as early in the day as possible, as accommodation, especially at the cheaper end of the market, can be hard to find. Prices are inclusive of tax and service charge (20% in all).

Expensive Hotels: *Plaza*, Av. 16 de Julio, T 378311, A+, excellent, and its restaurant is open to the public; peña show on Fridays. *Presidente*, Potosí y Sanjines, A+, including breakfast, new, swimming pool, bar, disco, rec.; *Sucre Palace*, Av. 16 de Julio 1636,T 355080, A, good value, but hot water a problem, 2 restaurants in the building, *Karin* snack bar on 1st floor, excellent, and an expensive restaurant on 2nd floor; *Hotel La Paz*, Av. Arce, T 356950, A, good views from upper floors, run down; *Libertador*, Obispo Cárdenas 1421, T 343360, B, very good value (although continental breakfast is reported to be poor) and nearest the business section, helpful (baggage stored); *Eldorado*, Av. Villazón, T 363355,B, may be able to bargain for longer stays, highly rec., secure parking nearby. *Hotel Copacabana*, Av. 16 de Julio 1802, T 351240/342241-4, C, with bath, central, restaurant and grill room (lunch only at latter), good service, safe deposit, rooms a bit small and fusty, rec. *Crillón*, Plaza Isabel La Católica, T 352121, C, not central, old fashioned, good restaurant on 10th floor, good views.

For people staying several weeks, often looking for permanent residences, boarding houses (*pensiones*) are popular, eg Illimeier, Sopocachi, Calle Resequin 1978, D with breakfast, English and German spoken.

The following medium-priced hotels have been recommended: *Residencial Rosario*, Illampu 704, T 326531, travel agencies downstairs, organizes travel and excursions all around Bolivia (Turisbus, 10% discount on some tours, Colibrí mixed reports), D with bath (electric shower—safe design), E without, popular with foreigners, book exchange, laundry and restaurant expensive, recently modernized and extended, stores luggage, most highly rec.; *Residencial Copacabana*, Illampu 734, T 367896, E, hot water, mixed reports about rooms and service; *Continental*, Illampu 626, T 378226, D with bath, hot water, clean, friendly, rec.; *Milton*, Illampu and Calderón No. 1124, T 368003/353511 (P.O. Box 5118), D with bath, hot water, friendly, popular with travellers, helpful, will store luggage, highly rec., local market outside, so no taxis to the hotel at weekends; *Tambo de Oro*, Armentia 367, near bus station, D, hot showers, clean, friendly, helpful and safe for luggage; *Sagárnaga*, Sagárnaga 326, D with bath (try bargaining), F without, basic breakfast included, friendly, helpful, good location, laundry; next door and slightly cheaper, is *Alem*, No. 334, hot water but inadequate plumbing; *Panamericano*, Manco Kapac 454, T 340810/372764, clean, E with hot electric showers; *Hostería Florida*, on Viacha off Av. Muñecas, E with bath, clean, good views, cheap breakfast; *Hostal República*, Comercio 1455 (T 357966), D with bath, cheaper without, discounts for longer stay, beautiful old house of former president, clean, hot water, luggage stored, helpful, laundry service, "cannot rec. warmly enough". *Neuman*, Loayza 442, D with bath, bargaining possible for students; *Viena*, Loayza 420, T 326090/323557, C with bath, E without, beautiful renovated old building, friendly staff, arrive early often full; avoid noisy rooms on street, over-priced tours; *Residencial La Estancia*, Mexico 1559, D with breakfast, helpful, good restaurant; *Hostal Paris*, Sucre 949, F, hot showers, friendly but not very clean, and noisy.

Cheaper: *Florida* (also *Hostería Florida* above), Ingavi 727, E with bath, good, warm water for shower; *Austria*, Yanacocha 531, E with or without bath, clean, hot water, safe

deposit, very cosy and good for longer stays, use of kitchen, TV, friendly and helpful staff, rec.; *Torino*, Socabaya 457, central, noisy, hot water on request (electric showers) E with bath (F without), clothes washing facilities, stores luggage, book exchange, bar, generally popular with young travellers, mixed reports about staff and dilapidated rooms; *Residencial Illimani*, Av. Illimani 1817, F, mixed reports but friendly, washing facilities, often full; *Claudia*, Av. Villazón, 1965, opp. *Eldorado*, nr. Plaza Estudiante, E with bath (cheaper without), breakfast included, clean, secure, friendly; *Alojamiento Scala*, Calle Unión, off Chuquisaca, F, modern, very clean, will store luggage, rec. Cheap hotels located in the Indian quarter include: *Andes*, Av. Manco Kapac 364, T 323461, E with shared bath, clean, hot water, good value (one of the few that offers single rooms at F), radio played loud all day, cafeteria on 1st floor (poor service and food); *Italia* at No. 303 opposite, E with bath, fairly clean but showers usually cold. *Bolivia*, Manco Kapac 287, T 375030, opp. railway station, F, clean, shared hot showers, good views from back, upper rooms. *Residencial Don Guillermo*, Colombia 222, T 325766, E, good value, clean, hot water, rec.; *Alojamiento Universo*, Inca 575, T 340431, F, good value, infrequent hot water, clean, friendly, safe to leave luggage, rooms downstairs are better; *Alojamiento Illampu*, Illampu 635, F, hot water, washing facilities, mixed reports; *Plaza* on Plaza Pérez Velasco 785, T 322157, clean and hot water, F, without bath, E with, washing and luggage storage facilities, friendly, rec. Cheapest possibly is *El Carretero*, Catacora 1056, G p.p., 5 beds to a room, helpful, pleasant, hot shower extra.

**Motels**  *Kori-Tambo*, Achocalla, outside the city, T.327078. *San Bartolomé* rec., own bus service to and from La Paz.

**Youth Hostel** and camping club (with equipment for hire), Ciudad Satelite Plan 561, Calle 3 N 1073, Sr. Gonzalo O. Rodríguez, T 812341, US$3/night with cooking and washing facilities (tours and treks also arranged, and Spanish and Portuguese classes given—Fastalk, Casilla 11106). Take *trufi* "Satelite" from Calle Mercado, ½ hr., US$0.30.

**Camping**  No organized site, but Mallasa (Municipal Park, unmarked, turn left at Alders Infantiles S.O.S.), Valencia and Palca below the suburb of La Florida have been recommended. Club Andino Boliviano (T 794016) rents equipment. Camping gas is available at Camino Real, Calle Sanjines, US$2.50. Kerosene for pressure stoves is available from a pump in Plaza Alexander. Public showers at Duchas La Paz, 20 de Octubre 1677.

**Restaurants**  in La Paz can be roughly divided into two categories: either they serve international cuisine and are expensive or they serve local dishes and are fairly cheap. The restaurants with international cuisine are to be found mainly on three streets, Av. 16 de Julio (the Prado), Av. 6 de Agosto and Av. 20 de Octubre. Service charges and tax of up to 23% are usually included on the bill but it is customary to leave a tip anyway of a few bolivianos. Always check prices before ordering, and then your bill and change.

Av. 16 de Julio: (street numbers given in brackets) *Gargantu*, Edificio Alameda, excellent meat dishes (US$3.50), and warm atmosphere; *Bistro Paragayo*, nr. *Hotel Plaza*, German food, cheap. There are many snack bars, including *Confitería Elis* (1497), with good plate lunches, excellent soups, breakfasts and pastries, English and German spoken. *Valentino* (1605) English spoken, US$3-4 for a main course, rec. and *Patito Peking* next door, excellent Chinese food. *California Donuts II* (1695), food, American-style, expensive, US$2-10 (*No. I* is at Av. Camacho 1248); *Tokio* (No. 1832), good, also has tea room and patisserie and rec. for *salteñas*, but look out for high prices not written on menus, expensive. *Mary's Tee*, near Plaza Estudiante, for excellent pies and cakes.

Off the Prado, **on Calle Campero**, one can recommend the *Club de la Prensa*, set in a pleasant garden, the limited menu is typical Bolivian—meat only—and the company is lively. *Club de La Paz*, Camacho 203, is a good tea room. The *Club Alemán*, off Calle Reyes Ortiz, with reasonable prices. The *Carreta*, an Argentine-type restaurant at Batallón Colorados 32, serves a recommended mixed grill and very good steaks, a favourite of businessmen for lunch. *Panchos*, Landaeta 402, T 342518, steakhouse, Chilean wine, English spoken, rec; *Pizzería Morello*, Av. Arce, very good but very expensive, opp. the *La Paz*, also *Maison Suisse*, Av. Arce, good steaks and raclette, closed Sat. and Sun., gourmet restaurant on first floor. *Viva La Pizza*, J. José Pérez 322, rec., expensive. *Charlie*, Plaza Isabel La Católica, half-way down Av. Arce, elegant atmosphere and good value at around US$7 a head, lunch or dinner, closed at weekends. Up-market Italian cuisine at *Pronto*, Jauregui 2248, T 355869, beautiful decor, about US$7 p.p., and also at *La Dolce Vita*, Av. Strongest, off Plaza Estudiante. *Le Fric*, Pedro Salazar 489, Plaza Abaroa, T 340796, traditional Bolivian dishes, excellent and highly rec.

Among those **on Av. 6 de Agosto**: *El Arriero* (No 2535, Casa Argentina), best barbecue with large portions, but quite expensive; *Casa del Corregidor*, Calle Murillo 1040, a colonial mansion, attractive, rec. (see **Entertainments** below); while **on Av. 20 de Octubre** there is *Max Bieber's Restaurant and Tea-Room*, ice-cream, cakes and other dishes, owner speaks

German (2080); next door is *Stefano's*, art gallery by day, good Italian restaurant at night. Close to 20 de Octubre: Brazilian *feijoada* on Sat. and Sun., at *Ipanema*, Av. Ecuador 2139, between Aspiazu and F. Guachalla, T 372306, rec; closed Mon.

On the continuation of the **Prado going west**, in Av. Mariscal Santa Cruz, is *Los Escudos* (Edif. Club de La Paz, T 322028/350586), Munich-type bierkeller with fixed 4-course lunch for US$6, food and shows. Friday and Saturday nights (2000-2400, US$10-12 p.p.). *Parrillada Las Tablitas*, at Mariscal Santa Cruz 1283, excellent steaks, US$12; on the corner of Colón with Santa Cruz is *Restaurant Verona* for good economical plato del día and "gorgeous" lasagne. At Av. Ayacucho 206 is the *Internacional*, a lunch-time favourite of local businessmen and has good shows Friday and Saturday nights.

In the **shopping and business district**: there are numerous snack bars and cheap restaurants. One can recommend: *Marilyn*, corner of Potosí and Socabaya, *salteñas*, 3-course lunches for US$1.50; *Confitería California*, Potosí 1008, Centro Comercial Cristal, does good set lunches for US$2, also on Potosí, *Colorado* (No 1240), cheap and good, *Chez Pierre* (1320) good lunches, US$1.25 and *Hogar Austriaco*, good lunches, pleasant; *Tu Amigo*, corner of Colón, salmon and Argentine beef, excellent service and reasonably priced, open every day. *El Lobo*, Illampu y Santa Cruz, good, clean, rec (Israeli dishes); good cheap meals at Illampu 773, closed Sun. evening. On Yanacocha, *La Fregata* (No. 525), 2 courses for US$5.50, good value, and *La Tertulia*, near Ingavi, small, simple, charming, hot drinks and pastries. *Casa Chan*, Juan de la Riva y Bueno, good set course Chinese meals, US$1.50. Rec. Mexican place: *Tacos Teru K*, Ignacio Cordero 1294, San Miguel (behind Loreto College) T 794513. *Los Pinochos*, Sanjines 553, excellent and cheap cheese empanadas, popular café. *J. Nanos*, Plaza Mendoza, local dishes, very clean and cheap, highly rec, as is *Cabalino*, Graneros 121. There are many other snack bars and Chinese restaurants on Calles Comercio (eg *Café Comercio*, next to *Hostal República*, and *Salteñería Comercio*, Comercio 1439, excellent *salteñas* and Bolivian food, outdoor seating, inexpensive) and Colón.

On **Sagárnaga**: there is a good restaurant next to *Peña Naira* (No 161), which serves good food (see **Entertainments** below), and above the Peña, is *Resolana*, often confused with the *Naira* restaurant, overpriced pizzas but excellent crêpes and souffles, live music some weekends, US$3.30, rec. *El Montañés*, opposite *Hotel Sagárnaga*, good, clean, family-run, homemade dishes; good café, *Snack Carabelas* (No 315), recommended for coffee and

cakes. In same area, *Snack América*. Av. América 192, good hamburgers from US$2.50. *El Refugio*, Plaza Avaroa, not cheap, but best meal in La Paz.

**Cheap vegetarian restaurants** to recommend are the *Hotel Gloria Naranjos*, Potosí 909, buffet lunch, US$1.25, very popular, be there by 1230 for a table; *Man Jari*, Potosí 1315, Mon.-Sat. 0900-2100, good value vegetarian meals (US$2), bread, muesli; *El Vegetariano*, Loayza 420, also rec., set lunch US$1, open Mon.-Sat. 0800-2100; *Govinda*, Méjico 1276, *Snack Viena*, Loayza 640, and *Nutrivegetal* in Edificio Alameda on the Prado.

**Burgers**: Stalls in the Indian quarter sell hamburgers for US$0.75 each including chips, egg and tomato, have 2 for a filling meal, but don't have aji, mayonnaise or mustard if worried about hygiene and watch your burger being cooked.

**Comedor Popular**, often referred to as *Comedor Familiar*, for the strictly limited budgets, cheap but filling local meals around US$1.50, available at Camacho and Loayza markets. The foodstalls at the top of Jiménez sell good T-bone steak cheaply. Bread from street vendors and Cochabamba wholemeal bread (*pan integral*) sold at the main markets, is rec. Fresh dairy produce at *Pil* on Bueno y Cárdenas. *Kremrik* is a chain of ice-cream parlours, with outlets at Plaza Marillo 542, and on Av. Villazón, just off Plaza del Estudiante, good ice-cream (Kivon), but expensive.

**Bookshops** Foreign language books at *Los Amigos del Libro*, Mercado 1315, at the post office and El Alto airport; they also sell tourist maps of the region from Puno to the Yungas, and walking-tour guides. Treat the details with caution. *Juventud* on Mercado and Yanacocha has good stock. Amigos del Libro will ship books. *El Umbral*, Potosí 1375, T 341282, very good stock of academic subjects. *Librería La Paz*, Colón y Ballivián (wide selection of maps). There are 2nd-hand stalls on Av. Ismael Montes.

**Films** For Kodak, Casa Kavlin, Calle Potosí 1130; Laboratorio Fuji Color, Potosí 1316; Foto Linares, Mercado y Loayza, will develop both Ansco and Agfa colour film, 1-day service on black-and-white, but only repairs Minolta cameras. Repairs also at Av. Sánchez Lima 2178 by Rolando Calla C, just ring bell (1000-1200), there is no sign; also at Potosí 1316, between 1400-1900, T 373621, very helpful, professional, fair prices. Film is available at black market prices around Av. Buenos Aires and Pasaje Ortega, Calle Granero, but otherwise it is expensive, as is developing. Fuji transparency film available at half shop price in market. In all cases check dates on film.

**Shopping** Look around and bargain first. There is inexpensive silver and jewellery in the little cabinets outside Lanza market on Av. Santa Cruz. Up Sagárnaga, by the side of San Francisco church (Mercado Artesanal), are booths and small stores with interesting local items of all sorts, best value on Sunday a.m. when prices are reduced. There are good jewellery stores throughout the city but visit the gold factories for lower prices and special orders. At Sagárnaga 177 is *Artesanía Nacional Tiwanaku*, for paintings, silver jewellery and woven goods, and, although there have been complaints about quality and price, a visit is a must. *Pacha-Marka*, Sagárnaga 272, good selection of antiques, knowledgeable owner. Many Indian objects are sold near Av. Buenos Aires, and Indian musical instruments on Calle Granier, near the General Cemetery. *Artesanías Titicaca*, Av. Sánchez Lima 2320, and *Marka Tambo*, Jaén 710, retail and wholesale weaving. *Millma*, Sagárnaga 225, and in *Hotel Plaza*, for alpaca sweaters (made in their own factory) and antique and rare textiles. *Wari* on Sagárnaga will make to measure very quickly, prices reasonable. *El Cuerito*, Av Montes 446, T 326982 (Casilla 2177-100), for all leather goods and for camping equipment, including tents, sleeping bags, hammocks, mosquito nets, etc. *Curerex* has four shops in La Paz, rec. for leather goods.

*Artículos Regionales* in Plaza de los Estudiantes is rec. *Suma Ampara*, Av. Villazón 1958, wide variety of woven goods, but prices not as low as in street markets. *Punchay Artesanías y Folklore*, Calle Santa Cruz 156 (T 362253), has been highly rec.—worth a visit; also *Rumillajta*, one of the Galería shops adjacent to the San Francisco church entrance. *Artesanía Sorata*, Linares 862, specializes in dolls made by a women's cooperative and handmade textiles. Along Murillo and between Sagárnaga and Santa Cruz are various little shops selling old ponchos and rugs. Excellent art market on Plaza Humboldt (Micro II), on Sundays. Generally, the higher up one goes along Calle Santa Cruz, the cheaper woollen goods seem to become. Alpaca goods are about 50% dearer than in Puno. The maximum you can bargain prices down is 20%. Handmade clothing for children is good value. Many shops closed Saturday afternoon and Sunday.

The Indian market is a good place for ponchos and local handicrafts. See also the "witchcraft market" on Melchor Jiménez, 3rd street on left walking up Calle Santa Cruz from Av. Mariscal Santa Cruz, fascinating items for sale. Food market is the Mercado Camacho (Camacho y Bolívar). The Tourist Office has a full list of all markets.

**Local Buses**  There are three types of city bus: large Fiat buses run by the city corporation, on fairly limited routes; *micros* (Bluebird-type buses), which charge US$0.20; and *trufis*, minivans flying variously coloured flags and following fixed routes, which charge about US$0.40 pp.

**Taxis**  US$0.30-0.60, for short trips within city limits. Sharing of taxis is common. Fares out of town are given under **Excursions** below. Taxi drivers are not tipped. Radio taxis, T 371111 or 322424.

**Car Hire**  Cars may be hired direct from **Imbex**, Av. Arce 2303, T 379884, inc. Suzuki jeeps; **Rent-a-Car International**, F. Suazo 1942, T 357061; **Kolla Motors**, Rosendo Gutiérrez 502, T 341660/351701 who have well-maintained four-wheel drive Toyota jeeps (which seat 6), insurance and gasoline extra; **Bolivia Rent-a-Car**, Cap. Ravelo 2445, or through a travel agent. One can also hire experienced drivers for US$25 a day plus accommodation and meals.

**Garage**  for VW and other makes: Ernesto Hug, Av. Jaime Freyre 2326, T 342279.

**Entertainment**  Best entertainment for visitors are the folk shows (*peñas*), though they are reported as packed with tourists and increasingly commercialized. Outstanding folk show at *Peña Naira* (US$5, includes first drink), Sagárnaga 161, every night about 2215. Various restaurants have shows worth seeing. At these folk shows, visitors will be able to listen to the wide variety of local musical instruments, the different types of flutes, including the *quena*, and the *charango*, a small guitar with five strings, the back often made from the hide of an armadillo. Enquire at the *Rumillajta* shop (in the *galería* close to San Francisco church) about future performances by the famous folk group of that name. Good *peña* at *Casa del Corregidor*, Calle Murillo 1040, US$5 good food, rec., Fri. and Sat. p.m. only; similarly *Marko Tambo* on Calle Jaén, US$7 (all incl.) repeatedly rec. Indian dance halls, for example on Max Paredes, should only be visited in the company of Bolivians.

Local radio station, *Radio Fides*, Calle Sanjines y Sucre, broadcasts Salsa on Mondays, Andean music on Thursdays: open to public 1900, T 359191, US$0.30, "Don't sit in the first three rows unless you want to participate in the live commercials" (Jeff Perk, Carbondale, USA).

La Paz has a resident ballet and symphony orchestra (*Teatro Municipal* on Sanjines and Indaburo), but no theatre company. There are some good **cinemas**, films being mainly in English. For film buffs there is the excellent Cinemateca Boliviana, corner of Pichincha and Indabura, La Paz's art film centre with festivals, courses, etc. (entry US$0.75 for students). The Casa de Cultura (almost opposite Plaza San Francisco) sometimes has exhibitions, concerts or film festivals, most of which are free.

There are clown and mime shows in Parque del Ejército on Sunday, colourful and popular; the Parque Central has a children's amusement park, US$.20.

**Sport**  There are two golf clubs (Malasilla, the world's highest, and Pinos—non-members can play at Malasilla on weekdays subject to the usual payments, but it may be difficult to hire clubs); two tennis clubs (La Paz Tennis and Sucre Tennis); and two riding clubs. Football is popular and played on Thursday and Sunday at the Siles Stadium in Miraflores, two clubs (Micro A); there are reserved seats. Basketball is played in Plaza del Estudiante on Mon., Wed. and Fri. in season. For yachting, fishing, boat hire, etc. on Lake Titicaca **see page 235**. YMCA sportsground and gymnasium, opposite the side of the University of San Andrés, Av. Villazón, and clubhouse open to the public, Av. 20 de Octubre 1839 (table tennis, billiards, etc.); regular meetings Tues. and Thurs. 1930 of a mountaineering group which runs weekend excursions.

## Museums

**Museo Nacional de Arte**, across from the Cathedral at Calle Socabaya 432, housed in the 18th century baroque palace of the Condes de Arana, with beautiful exterior and patio. It has a fine collection of colonial paintings and also exhibits the works of contemporary local artists. Open Tues-Fri, 0900-1230, 1500-1900, US$0.70, Sat, 0930-1330 free. There are other exhibits at the Galería Municipal, on Colón, and at Galería Naira, on Sagárnaga.

**Museo Tiahuanaco** (Tiwanaku), or Museo Nacional de Arqueología, easily reached by the flight of stairs by María Auxili church on the Prado. This modern building, simulating the Tiahuanaco style, contains good collections of the arts and crafts of ancient Tiahuanaco and items from the eastern jungles. Admission US$0.50; Tues.-Fri. 0900-1200, 1500-1900 (summer 1530-1700, Sat 0930-1230, 1430-1830).

**Museo Semisubterráneo**, in front of National Stadium, with restored statues and other artefacts from Tiahuanaco. It's in a sunken garden out of doors, and much can be seen from street level.

**Museo Nacional de Etnografía y Folklore**, on Calle Ingavi 916, is housed in the palace of the Marqueses de Villaverde, worth seeing (especially the exhibit on the Chipaya Indians), small contribution requested. Mon.-Fri. 0830-1130, 1430-1700.

The following four museums, all on Calle Jaén, are included on a single ticket, which costs US$2 (free on Sat.), from Museo Costumbrista. All are open Tues.-Fri. 1000-1200, 1430-1830, Sat. and Sun. 1000-1230. Calle Jaén, a picturesque colonial street with many craft shops, is well worth seeing for itself.

**Museo Costumbrista**, Plaza Riosinio, at top of Jaén. Miniature displays depict incidents in the history of La Paz and well-known Paceños. T 378478.

**Museo Murillo**, on Jaén, T 375273 was originally the home of Pedro Domingo Murillo, one of the martyrs of the abortive La Paz independence movement of 16 July 1809. This colonial house has been carefully restored and has a good collection of paintings, furniture and national costumes of the period; there is also a special room dedicated to herbal medicine and magic. Warmly rec.

**Museo de Metales Preciosos**, Jaén 777, well set out with Inca gold artefacts in basement vaults, warmly rec., T 371470.

**Museo de Litoral**, Jaén 789, with artefacts of the War of the Pacific.

**Mineral Museum**, Banco Minero, 6 de Agosto 2382, esq. Belisario Salinas. Open Mon.-Fri. 0900-1300, 1430-1630. Good gold and silver exhibits; free.

**Núñez del Prado**, Ecuador 2034, Mon.-Fri., 0900-1200, 1400-1800, excellent sculpture.

**Museo Tambo Quirquincho**, Calle Evavistovalle, nr. Plaza Mendoza (Tues.-Fri., 0930-1300, 1600-2000, Sat.-Sun., 1000-1300, US$0.50, Sat. free), in a restored colonial building, displaying modern painting and sculpture, carnival masks, silver, early 20th century photography and city plans, highly recommended.

**Zoo** at the upper end of Av. Bolivia, small, US$0.20.

**Banks** Citibank, on the Prado (cashes its own travellers' cheques, 1% commission and will receive money sent from any US bank), but will not advance cash to holders of Citibank Mastercard; other banks; **American Express** agent: Magri Turismo, Av. 16 de Julio 1490, 5th Floor (doesn't change Amex travellers' cheques). Open 0900-1200, 1400-1630. Closed Saturday. Cash advance on Visa and Mastercard at **Banco de La Paz** on Prado (limit US$300 per day, no commission), **Banco Santa Cruz de la Sierra**, and **Banco Boliviano Americano**, among others. Money is changed in hotels or *casas de cambio* rather than in banks; **Banco de Cochabamba**, Camacho, is the only bank that will cash travellers' cheques.

**Exchange Houses** Sudamer, Colón 256, good rates also for currencies other than US$ (2% commission on travellers' cheques into dollars); **Titikaka Tours**, Loayza 203; **Tony Tours**, Yanacocha y Asbún; **Unitours**, Mercado 1300. Shampoo shop *perfumería* at **Yanacocha 319**, will cash US$ from travellers' cheques, 1% commission (will take back bolivianos at same rates. "The astounding financial center, humming behind the drab retail exterior, is an attraction in its own right"); **Casa de Cambio Silver**, Mercado 979, charges 1% commission to change travellers cheques into dollars cash; similarly **D'Argent**, Mercado 1328. Airport exchange booth will only change up to US$50 (commission) in travellers' cheques. *Casas de cambio* and street changers can be found on Camacho, Colón and Prado. It is not worth dealing on the black market since there is virtually no difference between black and official rates. N.B. if arriving on Friday night, bring bolivianos or US dollars cash as it is difficult to change travellers' cheques at the weekend. If you leave Bolivia with bolivianos you may not be able to change them in neighbouring countries. Watch out for forged currency, especially dollars and Chilean pesos.

**Spanish Courses** Centro Boliviano Americano (address under **Libraries** below) US$140 for

2 months, 1½ hrs. tuition each afternoon; Centro de Estudios Brasileños, Av. Sánchez Lima 2226, T 3-22110, 2 hrs. tuition each morning, US$125 for 6 weeks. Christiane Hasselmann, Casilla 7903, La Paz, offers Spanish classes, with emphasis on local pronunciation and customs.

**Libraries** Centro Boliviano Americano (CBA), Parque Zenón Iturralde (near Av. Arce), has public library and recent US papers (Mon.-Fri. 0900-1200, 1430-1900). USIS has lending library and 2nd-hand paperbacks. Alliance Française, Calle Ingavi (open Mon.-Fri. 1600-2000), has an old library. Goethe-Institut, Av. 6 de Agosto 2118 (Mon.-Thurs., 1600-1900), good library, recent papers in German, videos in German and Spanish.

**Embassies and Consulates** Argentine Consulate, Av. 16 de Julio 1480, over Aerolíneas Argentinas T 353233/353234; Brazilian Consulate, Av. 20 de Octubre, 20-38 Edificio Fonconain, piso 9; visa office is at Sánchez Lima 2199, 0900-1300, Mon.-Fri. Chilean Consulate, H. Siles 5843, corner of Calle 13, Obrajes district, T 785269, open Mon.-Fri. 0830-1130. Paraguayan Consulate, 7th floor Edificio Montevideo, Av. Arce, just below Calle Montevideo; Peruvian Consulate and Embassy, 6 de Agosto 2190 y Calle F.Guachalla, 0930-1300 (a visa costs US$5 in US$ bills, issued same day if you go early); Venezuelan Embassy and Consulate, Av. Arce 2678, Ed. Illimani, 4th floor (consulate open Mon., Wed., Fri. 0900-1200).

United States Embassy, Calle Colón and Mercado (has a good reading room, closed 1200-1400), Consulate on Av. Potosí (350120/350251); Canadian Consulate, Av. Arce 2342 (1000-1400), T 375224. South African Embassy, Calle 22, Calacoto district.

Austrian Consulate, Edif. Petrolero, 7th floor, Oficina 1, Av. 16 de Julio 1616, T 326601, 1600-1800; British Embassy and Consulate, Av. Arce 2732-2754, T 351400/329401-4, Casilla 694,, closed 1200-1300 and Wed. p.m.; Danish Consulate, Calle Layanza 250, Edif. Casilla, 5th floor, No. 509, T 322601/325589; French Consulate, Av. Hernando Siles 5390, esq. Calle 08, Obrajes, T 782849 (take bus No 11 down Av. 16 de Julio); Belgian Embassy is 1 block from French; West German Embassy, Av. Arce 2395. T 352072 or 352389; Netherlands Consulate, Av. Arce 8031, Edif. Victorio, 2nd floor, T 356153; Norwegian Consulate, Av. Mcal. Santa Cruz, Edif. Esperanza, 11th floor, T 322528; Spanish Consulate, Calle Cordero T 343518; Swedish Consulate, Av. Arce 2856, Casilla de Correo 852, T 327535; Swiss Embassy, Av. 16 de Julio 1616, 6th floor, T 353091, open 0900-1200, 1400-1500; Israeli Embassy, Av Mcal Santa Cruz, Edificio Esperanza, 10th floor, T 358676/325463, Casilla 1309/1320.

**Addresses** Instituto Nacional de Arqueología de Bolivia, Calle Tiwanaku 93. Immigration, Ministerio del Interior, Avenida Arce. YMCA, 20 de Octubre 1839, Casilla 963. Asociación Boliviana de Agencias de Viajes y Turismo, Edif. Litoral, Mariscal Santa Cruz 1351, Casilla 3967.

**Doctor** Check that any medical equipment used is sterilised. Dr René Coloma Rector, Edificio Cosmos, 11th floor, Office 1, Av. 16 de Julio (El Prado) T 377914 (private surgery, Mon.-Fri. from 1500), or 355456 (home—any time). Rec. for stomach problems, speaks good English. Dr Jorge Muñoz A. Ed. Alianza, Av. 6 de Agosto y F. Guachalla, speaks German, rec.; also Dr Villarreal whose office is on 9th floor of Café Verona building, Colón y Santa Cruz, works at German hospital, speaks fluent German. Dentists Dr and Dra Osorio at Hostal Austria, Yanacocha 531. Tourist Office has a list of doctors and dentists who speak foreign languages.

**Hospital** Clínica del Accidentado, Plaza Uyuni 1351, T 328632/321888 offers first aid. Efficient and well run nursing homes such as Clínica Americana, Clínica Alemana, Clínica Rengel (T 390792/8), Clínica Santa María, Av. 6 de Agosto 2487, efficient and not too expensive. Red Cross opposite Mercado Camacho will give inoculations if required. The Methodist Hospital (12th block of Obrajes, take "A" micro from the Prado) runs clinic at US$5, telephone for appointment.

**Health and Hygiene** If suffering from soroche, ask in chemists/pharmacies for suitable medication. Laboratorio Inti round corner from Hansa building on 16 de Julio, has been recommended, also for vaccines (human immuno globulin, rabies vaccine - but make sure you know precisely how it should be administered). Tampons may be bought at most farmacias and supermarkets; others say they are impossible to find, especially outside La Paz.

**Laundromats** Wash and dry, US$2 per 4-kilo load, 6-hour service, at Gelmi-Lava-Sec, 20 de Octubre 2019, suite 9, T 352930, helpful service, US$1.40 for 1 kg.; Lavandería Cinco Estrellas, 20 de Octubre 1714. Lavandería Select, Av. Arce, down from Hotel La Paz; 3-hour service, rec. Finesse Limpieza, Illampu 863; Av. Mcal. Santa Cruz 1154, central; laundry service at Oficina Gregoria Apazá, Colombia y Almirante Grau, T 369607, phone first. Dry cleaning, Calle Murillo 1366, US$.15 per kg., *La Esmeralda*, Colon 558.

**Places of Worship**  Protestant Community Church (inter-denominational), in English, American Co-operative School, Calle 10 Calacoto (T 795639 or 792052). The former pastor and his wife (The Rev. & Mrs. Charles F. King) have written an excellent duplicated guide to "Life in La Paz" which can be got on Sunday at the Community Church. Sunday service at 1045, but there are "lots of activities during the week". Anglican-Episcopalian services are held at the Community Church on the third Sunday of each month. **Synagogues** Calle Landaeta 330 (Sat. a.m. services only); Colegio Boliviano Israëlito, Canada 1846 for Friday service—it looks like a private house.

**Telecommunications**  Entel office for telephone calls is in Edif. Libertad, Calle Potosí, English spoken, and at Ayacucho 267 y Mercado and in *La Paz Hotel*, lower ground floor, in both these locations there are also public telex booths, and fax service available at Ayacucho office.

**Post Office**  Correo Central, Av. Mariscal Santa Cruz y Oruro (Mon.-Fri. 0800-1930, Sat. a.m. only ). Stamps are sold only at the post office. Poste Restante keeps letters for 3 months. Procedure for sending parcels: customs (upstairs) must check contents first; then go to stamp counter to fill in customs declaration and purchase stamps; next have value of stamps checked and stamps franked, at a separate counter; finally, go to opposite window for *certificado* ticket. They will sew up packages in sack-cloth for you, for about US$1. Don't forget moth balls for textile items. To collect parcels costs at least US$0.50.

**Tourist Office**  Instituto Boliviano de Turismo (IBT), Mercado 1328, between Loayza and Colón, Edificio Mariscal Ballivián, 18th floor, T 367463/4, posters for sale, limited information.

**Maps**  Instituto Geográfico Militar, Av. 16 de Julio 1471 (take Micro C or N), head office open Mon.-Fri. 0900-1200, 1500-1900, collect maps by next day, delivery to your hotel not reliable. Passport is needed to get in, but worth it as they have the only railway map available in La Paz and a wide selection of others invaluable for the traveller. Topographic maps cost US$10 per sheet (scale 1:50,000) and about US$8 for standard tourist maps. Departmental road maps are meant to be available in the tourist offices in the capitals of each department but often they are out of stock. Senac (the national road service) publishes a Red Vial 1989 map, which is probably the best, but is still inaccurate, about US$6.50 from the office on 20 Octubre, between Castrillo and Landaeta. Also reported as inaccurate are the maps of the Automóvil Club Boliviano. Maps are generally hard to find. Maps are sold at Ichthus bookshop on the Prado; also at Librería La Paz and Amigos del Libro (**See page 219).**

**Guides**  *La Paz Insólita* (7 maps) US$3 and *Guía de La Paz* by Jorge Siles Salinas (historical) US$5. *Guía Central de Bolivia*, information on transport, statistical and geographical data. In particular it contains the La Paz minibus schedules, which are unobtainable elsewhere. *An Insider's Guide to Bolivia*, by Peter McFarren (Fundación Cultural Quipus, Casilla 1696, La Paz, 1988, US$12) has been recommended, especially for its section on culture. *Descubriendo Bolivia*, Hugo Boero Rojo, 1989 on archaeology and precolumbian history. *La Pintura En los Museos de Bolivia*, by José de Mesa and Teresa Gisbert, published 1991 by Los Amigos del Libro.

**Travel Agents**  *Crillon Tours*, Av. Camacho 1223, Casilla 4785 (T 374566), expensive; they run a hydrofoil-bus service to Puno, US$160, via Copacabana and Isla del Sol, incl. lunch and breakfast; they also have a sunset to sunrise programme, based at the *Inca Utama Hotel* at Huatajata, involving trips on the lake, meals and lodging. *Transturin*, Camacho 1321 (T 328560/363654, Telex 2301 TRTURIN BV), also very expensive, La Paz-Puno, inc. boat crossing on Lake Titicaca, US$80. *Diana Tours*, Sagárnaga 328, T 358757, very good value. *Turismo Balsa*, Av. 16 de Julio 1650 (T 356566 and 355817), has reservation service for air tickets; *Turisbus* (Illampu 704, Casilla 442, T 325348/326531), helpful, again mixed reports on its services, but more good than bad (to Puno and Cuzco—US$29). *Exprinter*, Edificio Herrman, Plaza Venezuela (also operates exchange facilities) to Cuzco via Copacabana, US$30. *Tawa Tours*, Sagárnaga 161 and Rosenda Gutiérrez 701, T 325796, run jungle tours to their own camp as well as the Salt Lake areas, friendly, good guides (also charter flights to Europe and USA). *Shima Tours*, Potosí 1310, very helpful, good for flight tickets; *Cóndor Tours*, Sagárnaga, good and cheap; *Seul Travel*, Plaza San Francisco, arranges tours to the Yungas for more than one day, helpful. *Paititi S.R.L.*, Calle Pedro Salazar 848, T 353558/341018/342759, organizes adventure tours, rec., Javier Prudencio is helpful and speaks several languages. *Expediciones Guarachi*, Plaza Alonso de Mendoza, treks and mountaineering to many lesser-known and remote destinations, highly rec. for their expertise and efficiency. Also *Carmoar Tours*, Calle Bueno 159, which is headed by Günther Ruttger (T 340633), rec. as among the best, has information and maps for the Inca Trail to Coroico.

*Reinaldo Pou Munt*, Capitán Ravelo 2401, T 327226, expensive; Casilla 13632, offers excellent tours of the city and environs, speaks English and German. Many agencies arrange excursions or travel to Peru (Puno, Cuzco, Arequipa), as well as local tours. See also names and addresses under "Exchange Houses", page 221.

**N.B.** Unless indicated in the list above, services offered by travel agents are expensive, some being criticised as overpriced. We have also been told that many services to Peru and beyond deteriorate markedly once Bolivia has been left (commitments unfulfilled, buses changed, extra passengers taken on—but **see also Peru to Bolivia—Peru, Section 5** ).

**Airport** El Alto, above La Paz, the highest commercial airport in the world (4,018 metres) connected to the city by motorway. A taxi between the centre and airport takes at least 15 minutes, US$8-9 but may be negotiated down to US$6; current prices, including luggage, should be on display at the airport exit (enquire at the tourist office in town, or at the airport—not too reliable). *Trufi*/bus leaves from Plaza Isabel La Católica, from 0700, frequent; US$0.85, best to have little luggage; colectivos from opposite *Hotel Crillón* (same square) charge US$2, carrying 4 passengers. Micros marked "El Alto", "Rió Seco", "Alto Lima", "Ceja", 30 mins to summit, then ½-hr. walk to airport. There is a duty-free shop but it can sometimes forget to open. No bank. The small tourist office at the Airport should know the price of a taxi to town, some maps available, English spoken, helpful (when manned). The coffee shop is slow but inexpensive.

**Air Taxis** US$250 per hour, contact Major Pericón of Taxi Aéreo Urkupiña, T 350580, 812099. Aero Inca, T 361018. Alas Doradas T 354070.

**Air Services** Lloyd Aéreo Boliviano (LAB), Camacho y Loayza, T 367701/7, and TAM, Av. Montes near Plaza Velasco, fly to the main cities and towns, and also to Lima and Arica daily. TAM flights leave from the military airport which has a separate check-in office at the end of the run-way on the road to Copacabana. TAM flights are cheaper than LAB but less reliable and difficult to book confirmed seats. Fares are comparatively low for internal flights. (For details of internal flights, see under proposed destinations.) The Faucett office in La Paz provides unreliable information.

**Bus Services** (for information, T 367276/367274); **micros** to the main bus terminal at Plaza Antofagasta are 2,M,CH or 130, for buses to: **Oruro, Potosí, Sucre, Cochabamba, Santa Cruz, Tarija** and **Villazón**, see under each destination for details. For **Coroico** and the **Yungas, see page 258.**

Buses to **Sorata, Copacabana** and **Tiahuanaco** do not leave from the bus station but from the Cementerio district (Micros C,I,K,S,M,P,X,132 and 134 go there). Companies located in the Cementerio district include Flota Copacabana, Manco Kapac, 2 de Febrero, Ingavi, Morales. As so few roads are well paved, train is usually preferable to bus when there is a *ferrobus* service (see below).

**International Buses** To **Buenos Aires**, daily at 1800, Expresos Panamericanos. Bus to **Arica** at 0530 Tues. and Fri, in each direction, check schedule in advance, US$23, Litoral (office at back of bus terminal), 20-22 hrs. (It is reported that Litoral buses are in poor condition and are liable to break down). Senobus (Calle Hujutri, 400 m. from train station in direction of Cementerio), Mon. and Fri. (US$8.50) or (cheaper) El Cariñoso to Charãna on the frontier then Sanga from Visviri (Chile) to Arica, US$5-8, or take a taxi, a very hard trip on a dirt road (being paved, 1991) in the Bolivian section to Tambo Quemado, subject to cancellation in the wet, no food but beautiful. To **Tacna**, also with Litoral, Thurs. 0700, US$17.50, 13 hours. Colectivos to **Puno** daily with different companies (eg Colectur) most easily booked through travel agencies, US$9-12, 10 hrs. **N.B.** Of the various La Paz-Puno services, only Turisbus (Illampu 704) does not make you change to a Peruvian bus once over the border. For luxury and other services to Peru see **Travel Agents** above.

**Trains** It is imperative to check times before travelling as changes are frequent and timetables contradictory. For this reason, schedules given in the text (under destinations) should be treated with caution. Towns served are Oruro, Cochabamba, Potosí, Sucre, Villazón and intermediate stops. Micros which go to the station are A, M, N, P, 130, 131, C. In theory, you may only buy tickets the day before you travel; office opens 0700, but get there beforehand.

To **Villazón** (minimum 20 hrs.) for Argentina, Monday, Thursday at 1640 and Friday at 1900; no sleepers; restaurant car as far as Villazón (see below for continuation of Fri. train to Argentina). Fares to Villazón, US$12 Pullman, US$9 special. Book ahead at central station; queue for booking at 0600 on previous day (queuing numbers are given out), take passport. All trains South (to Oruro and Villazón) are sold out by 0700 on Monday, so 1) go to station 2 hrs. before departure for returned tickets, 2) bus to Oruro then catch train, 3) try Exprinter travel agency, 4) try and board train anyway and pay the guard, 5) fly to Tarija and then go

by road to Villazón. Phone to check times etc.: 352510.

**Railways to/from the Coast**  (1) By the Southern Railway of Peru from Arequipa to Puno, on Lake Titicaca. Getting to La Paz from Puno: by road (several lines, 10-hour journey); Crillon Tours run a daily hydrofoil service (0600 from Puno; 0830 bus departure from La Paz).

From Guaqui to El Alto, above La Paz, a railway follows the broad plateau on an almost level gradient, rising only about 300 metres to El Alto. This line carries only freight.

(2) **La Paz-Arica International Railway**, 447 km.: there is a Bolivian *ferrobus* service straight through to Arica, three times a week in summer (0700, about 11 hrs), US$50 incl. meals, but not drinks, max. 15 kgs. baggage is free, extra charge for excess, worth it for the views, book ticket one-two weeks in advance, or a Chilean *coche motor* twice a week, 10 hrs., US$50, reserve at *Hotel Bolivia* opp. station, T 375030, Tues.-Fri. of preceding week (many are taken up by travel agencies: ask around, e.g. Exprinter, if none on sale at station). The service is less frequent in winter. Alternatively take a train to Charaña every other Tues. at 2300, arriving Charaña at 0530 (i.e. no chance of seeing the spectacular scenery), then change to a bus to Arica, or, on 2nd and 4th Wed. of each month a train leaves Charaña at 0930, arriving Arica at 1800. Fares: La Paz-Charaña: Pullman slow train US$18; special US$12. (At Charaña, *Alojamiento Aranda*, G; a very cold place to change trains or wait for a bus, exchange money in market or on train.)

In the Bolivian section the line runs to Viacha, the junction of the several railways running to Antofagasta, Guaqui, and Buenos Aires. It coninues to Corocoro, the copper mining town, thence to the border. The mountain peaks visible include Illimani, Sorata, Huayna-Potosí, Mururata, and many others. For description of the Chilean part, **see Chile, The Desert North, Section 1 . N.B.** Chilean pesos can be bought in La Paz at a better rate of exchange than in Arica.

(3) **La Paz-Antofagasta**, by Antofagasta and Bolivia Railway, 1,173 km., now definitely a trip for the adventurous who are impervious to cold at night, or blazing sunshine at daytime border changes. The train is full of contrbandistas, impromptu folk music, but the ride is very rough. Timetables say a train runs La Paz-Calama on Monday, other reports say that you have to go by bus to Oruro, then train as far as Calama in Chile, then by bus (240 km.) to Antofagasta. This, the most southerly of the three railway routes connecting La Paz with the Pacific coast, passes through magnificent scenery but the timetable has been described as "pure fantasy". If you have to take a bus from La Paz to Oruro (US$2), you take the train from Oruro to Calama, US$20 (latest known schedule given under Oruro **Trains**): it is 8 hrs. to Uyuni, where there is a 4½ hr. wait, then another 4 hrs. to the border; 1 hr. to change trains, then 40 minutes to Ollagüe, where Chilean customs take 4-12 hrs. (gringos usually dealt with last). After that it is 6 uncomfortable hours to Calama. In Bolivia, seats can be reserved as far as the border, food is served (waiter service), but no water; in Chile, only sandwiches, no other food, or lights. If taking your own food, eat fresh things first as the Chileans do not allow dairy produce, teabags (of any description), fruit and vegetables to be brought in. At the change-over before Ollagüe it is possible to walk through customs and take a colectivo to Calama, 5 hrs., US$8, the road Ollagüe—Calama is in good condition. Money changers not allowed on the train, but food sellers at the border may change Bolivian money. Watch out for forged Chilean notes especially if the light is bad. It is advisable to buy Chilean currency and sell bolivianos before journey. All passports are collected and stamped in the rear carriage, they should be ready for collection after 1-2 hours; queue for your passport, no names are called out (beware, as the train goes down to Chile, carriages are added; the reverse happens in the other direction).

(4) **La Paz-Buenos Aires**: This railway journey of about 2,400 km. takes 71 hours, US$75 one-way, US$50 to Jujuy. Either take Monday or Thursday (1640) train to Villazón (arrives 1230—tickets sold day before 0800-1100), then cross frontier to La Quiaca (1-1½ km. walk) to catch train or bus to Jujuy or train to Tucumán for another train to Buenos Aires (Retiro). On Friday the 1900 La Paz-Villazon train takes an expensive Pullman coach which crosses the border to La Quiaca and is connected to an Argentine train for Tucumán.

Note that many travellers from La Paz on the Buenos Aires line take a bus to Oruro (more comfortable and quicker than the train) and board the train there. Again, you may have trouble getting a sleeper if you do this. Remember that in northern Argentina buses tend to be much quicker than trains.

**Excursions from La Paz**  There is trout fishing in the many glacier lakes and streams near La Paz.

The best near-by excursion is to Río Abajo and Malasilla golf course: through suburbs of Calacoto and La Florida follow the river road past lovely picnic spots

and through some weird rock formations, known as the "Moon Valley". About 3 km. from bridge at Calacoto the road forks; sharp right leads to the Caza y Pesca Club and Malasilla golf course. Moon Valley can also be reached by Micro 11 ("Aranjuez"-large, not small bus) from Plaza San Francisco, which runs along the Prado and goes as far as Aranjuez Forest (US$1); cross the bridge on your right then walk 2 km. uphill past the cactus garden to Moon Valley. Most of the local travel agents organize tours to Moon Valley (which are very brief, 5 minutes stop for photos in a US$9 tour of La Paz and surroundings); taxis are not dear (US$12), especially if shared; make sure the price is per car and not per person. Near the Arcillo Arce cactus gardens (dilapidated) is the *Balneario Los Lobos*, popular for lunch at weekends.

To the ice cave overlooking the Zongo Valley: a steep but scenic ride down past several of La Paz's electric power plants. In 32 km. the altitude drops from 4,265 to 1,830 metres. The beautiful ice cave under the Chacaltaya glacier may be visited. Either take taxi for a day US$35-40, or take Micro 52, EMTA or 101 to Plaza 16 de Julio, El Alto (US$0.50) from where you can hire a taxi for US$2.25-4.50 p.p. or take Trans 16 de Julio (Plaza Ballivián) on Tues., Thurs. and Sat., 0600. The road follows an aqueduct (on left); at each junction en route turn left, 20 minutes past a cemetery (also on left), you come to the last hydroelectric dam and on the right, a white guard house. Alight here. Walk up and over the small hill on the righthand side of the road until you meet the aqueduct again. Follow the water course for 35-45 minutes (take care and don't look down) until you come to a bridge. You can either cross this, straddling the water, or walk beneath to the other side. At the end of the bridge, turn right up hill to a marker of rocks piled one on top of the other. Continue over the hill, cross a stream and go straight up the next hill at a similar rock marker. From the top of the hill, you should see the cave ahead of you (about 1 hour's walk in all).

To Ashumani (past Valley of the Moon) for good views of the valley and houses of the wealthy (no buses). Walk back along the valley and catch frequent buses into town.

To La Muela del Diablo—a gigantic, tooth-shaped rock, take Micro "Ñ" (last stop Cota Cota) or Trans EMTA from Calles Murillo and México to the end of the route, then continue for 1 km. more and you will see the rock on the left—"more impressive especially if the wind is blowing than Moon Valley". A further 4 km. on is the top of the mountain with a superb view of Illimani. The road continues to Ventilla, the start of the Inca trail.

For the acclimatized only: A climb to Corazón de Jesús, the statue at the top of the hill reached via the steps at the north end of Calle Washington, then left and right and follow the stations of the cross. Worth the climb for the views over the city and the Altiplano, but watch out where you put your feet. Take a bus to Ceja El Alto (e.g. No. 20 or 22) to save yourself some of the walk.

To see Puya Raimondii flowers, go to the village of Comanche, 2½ hrs. from La Paz (micros from railway station to Viacha—1 hr.—then truck to Comanche—rough, dusty and cold); some travel agencies arrange tours.

**Hikes near La Paz** For the *Takesi* (Inca) road hike, take a Sector Bolsa Negra bus at 0900, US$1.25, daily from Calle González y Grau, Plaza Belsu (which is below the Mercado Rodríguez) to Ventilla on Palca road, arrive 1 hr. early for seat, 3 hrs., return 0930 (alternatively take a Cota Cota bus Ñ to the end of the line or a taxi to Ovejuria vehicle checkpoint above Cota Cota, US$6.35, then truck to Ventilla). Take the track to the left, parallel to the Río Palca for 10 km. track to San Francisco mine. At Choquecota, before San Francisco, there are shops, and you can stay at the mine if necessary. If you leave Ventilla before 1300, you should reach Takesi village before nightfall (it's worth seeing the village). The "camino de Takesi" goes over the pass (4,650 metres), passes the Laguito Loro Keri and then follows the valley which ends at Chojlla and on 5 km. to Yanacachi, some meals available in private homes also some accommodation— only colectivo to La Paz at 0700 US$2.85, daily except Sat. (or Sun., check, buy ticket day before), 4 hrs. (If you miss that, it's a 45-min. walk down to Santa Rosa, which is on the main La Paz-Chulumani road). One powerful river can be crossed by applying to houses on the bank, where they will rig up a pulley for you for US$1-2. *Backpacking in Peru and Bolivia* (Bradt Publications), and the La Paz tourist office leaflet with sketch map both describe this 3-5 day walk, which shows exceptionally fine Inca paving in the first part. A couple of reports say that it is much tougher than descriptions suggest, and is very unpleasant in the wet season. Please take care not to add to the litter already on the route. The highest point is 4,650 metres and the lowest 2,100. The trail can also be used as a starting point for reaching Chulumani or Coroico. The scenery changes dramatically from the bitterly cold pass down to the humid Yungas. At Chojlla one can sleep at the school house for US$0.80, or the *Sheraton Inn*, basic, US$1 or less. At the village of Kakapi you may also be able to stay in the schoolhouse. Ask for Señor Genaro Mamani, a very helpful local expert and guide.

Another trail is the **Choro** hike from La Cumbre pass to Coroico, descending from the snow-covered heights to tropical vegetation. Take a bus to Villa Fátima, from Av. Mariscal Santa Cruz, then a Flota Yungueña bus or a truck **(see page 246** for transport details) to the statue of Christ at La Cumbre where the trail starts (a pick-up is unlikely to take you). If asked to pay at the checkpoint out of La Cumbre, there is no need to, the fee is not legal. Look out for condors at the start of the trail. The speedy can do the hike in under 3 days, lesser mortals will need about 4 days. It is 4-5 hours from La Cumbre to Chucura (campsite); 8-9 hours to the village of Choro (on this stretch is Challapampa where Doña Juana lets rooms, US$2.50, 1½ hrs. beyond Challapampa is a campsite); 5-6 hrs. to Sandillani (camping possible at 3 places beyond Choro, after 1 hr., 1 hr. 20 mins next to water, and 1½ hrs. near big empty house); in Sandillani a Japanese man welcomes visitors and will let you camp in his orchard, an excellently situated campsite, clean water, fire pit, and small shelter for packs and drying laundry. He likes postcards, stamps, money from your home country; thereafter it is 3 hours/7 km. to Chairo. Be sure to cross the river at Choro; the trail rises high above here to Chairo. Water is available all the way, but take water purification pills. A tent is essential. (The tourist office has a map of the trail.) From Chairo (accommodation—US$2.50,or sleep under eaves of the school, and food from Familia Paredes de la Tienda, very friendly, swimming pool), there is a stiff, 3-hr. climb remaining up to Coroico. Usually, jeeps run from Chairo to Coroico for US$0.60 and colectivos to La Paz, but in 1989 2 bridges were washed away, so walk to the junction with the main road and hitch to Yolosa for a truck to Coroico.

**Warning** There is a real possibility of theft and assault between Chucura and Choro; try to camp away from villages and banana plantations, team up with other walkers and set a guard if possible. The tourist office advises that camping is safer near Choro. There is also constant pestering for sweets and money. You are advised to check the safety of this, and the Takesi hike before setting out. Never do these hikes alone.

For both the above hikes, Carmoar Tours in La Paz (address above) has been recommended for equipment rental (tents US$4.10/night) and maps.

A third hike is **Yunga Cruz**, from Chuñavi to Chulumani in the Sud Yungas (sketch map available from La Paz tourist office). 3-4 days walking, not yet done by many travellers, and spectacularly beautiful, passes between Illimani and Mururata, many birds to be seen en route, from condors to hummingbirds.

**Mountaineering** Increasing numbers are visiting the Cordillera Real, to the east of La Paz. The range has the marked advantages over many high massifs of settled weather from May-Sept., easy access via numerous mine tracks, and favourable starting altitudes (4,200-4,700 m.). The Cordillera Real is 150 km. long with six peaks over 6,000 m. (20,000 ft.)—Illampu 6,380 m. (see under Sorata, below), Ancohuma 6,420 m., Chearoco 6,100 m., Chachacomani 6,100 m., Huayna Potosi 6,090 m., Illimani 6,460 m. All can be reached relatively easily from La Paz, the latter two within a few hours' driving. There are also a large

number of impressive 5,000 m.-plus peaks.

The route to **Illimani** is 4-5 hours via Calacoto and Huancapampa. The route to **Huayna Potosí**, an attractive peak (2 days) starts from Zongo Lake. The only access is by taxi to Zongo Lake (US$35 one way), or stop any micro bus and arrange a lift (about US$15 one way). On Sundays a truck belonging to Corpac, the state electricity company, goes from Av. Montes, near the bus station, to its plant by the lake. Alternatively, take Micro G to El Alto, from Plaza Ballivián a truck goes to Milluni, a village near to Zongo. Huayna Potosí (about 6,000 metres) requires mountaineering experience with ice and crevasses on the way to the top; however bad weather, apart from mist, is rare. Alternatively Condoriri or Pequeño Alpamayo are reached in one or two days from Tuni at Km. 21 on the La Paz-Tiquina road.

Normal alpine experience and equipment will enable most peaks to be ascended, and many new routes remain to be explored. Several peaks can be climbed in a day, but the 6,000 m. mountains usually require 2-4 days. There are no huts (except Chacaltaya ski-lodge). Do not underestimate altitude problems: at least 1-2 weeks' acclimatization is usually necessary before exceeding 5,500 m. (A visit to Chacaltaya and its ski-slopes is an easy way of judging one's reaction to altitude). Also, rescue services are virtually non-existent; prudence and proper gear (incl. crevasse rescue abilities) are indispensable. Note that mountaineering gear and high altitude camping equipment cannot be bought in Bolivia.

Other ranges: Western Cordillera including Sajama (6,530 m.)—mainly extinct volcano ice cones. Also Cordillera Apolobamba, northern extension of Cordillera Real extending into Peru with many 5,000 m.-plus peaks.

A good guidebook is *The Southern Cordillera Real*, R.Pecher & W.Schmiemann, Plata Publishing Ltd (1977), possibly obtainable in La Paz; distributor: Los Amigos del Libro (W.Guttentag), Casilla 450, Cochabamba. Also numerous expedition reports. The Club Andino Boliviano, Calle México 1638, PO Box 1346, will help with advice on routes and has maps on access, etc. Maps covering most of the range are the photo-surveyed 1:50,000 IGM Series, US$5 each (the only ones available). Club Andino Boliviano will be very pleased to accept "surplus" gear after climbing is finished.

Alfredo Martínez at the Club Andino is the country's foremost guide, or contact the well-regarded and friendly Bernardo Guarachi, Plaza Alonso de Mendoza, Edif. Santa Anita, oficina 314, T 320901, Casilla 20886, La Paz (he has equipment for hire) or Norbert Kloiber, Herrenstrasse 16, 8940 Memmingen, West Germany (T 08331-5258). Iván Blanco Alba, Asociación de Guías de Montaña y Trekking, Calle Chaco 1063, Casilla 1579, La Paz, T 350334, has been recommended (the association has about 10 guides in all and arranges climbing and hiking expeditions). Also recommended, José Camarlinghi (licensed by the German Alpine Club), Casilla 3772, Pedro Kramer 924, La Paz (T 352266) and Ricardo Albert at Inca Travel, Av. Arce 2116, Edificio Santa Teresa.

**Skiing** Ninety minutes by car from La Paz (36 km.) is Chacaltaya, the highest ski run in the world. Season: November to March, sometimes longer. Skiing equipment may be hired, and a rope-tow reaches 5,221 metres. The facilities are sub-standard, emergency services non-existent and the rope tow should be used with extreme caution (it is of a design no longer permitted in Europe). Taxi US$30 (whole car) for a half-day trip, or similar to the top by rented car costs about US$60, and really only at weekends; no visitor should miss the experience and the views. However the trip can be hair raising, buses carry no chains. Occasionally the buses only go half way. The Club Andino, México 1638 y Otero de la Vega, runs its own Saturday and Sunday buses; the day trip, beginning at 0830 and returning at 1400 and 1600 (in theory, usually only one return bus), comes to about US$24 for bus ticket and ski pass for the day; your bus ticket (US$10) gives free access to the ski station restaurant, otherwise US$2 entrance, hot drinks only. Equipment for hire is available (US$10 skis and boots from the Ski School—in the same building as the Ski Club, limited, poor equipment for hire, queue at once) or Ricardo Ramos, 6 de Agosto 2730, about US$10 per day (T 343441 or 372920), but better take your own. A good tip is to share equipment since, at that altitude, you will need a long break between activities. The lift pass costs US$4—out of season the lift only goes if there are 5 or more people (N.B. Club Andino's oxygen bottle at the Chacaltaya station may not always be full). Crillon also does a day trip, at US$15. Club Andino also occasionally arranges trips to Mount Illimani. One can walk to the summit of Chacaltaya for views of Titicaca on one side, La Paz on the other, and Huayna Potosí. Tiring, as it is over 5,000 metres, but one has most of the day to do the climb. Take plenty of mineral water when going to the mountains as it's thirsty work in the rarefied air. Laguna de Milluni, near Chacaltaya, is a beautiful lake to visit, but do not drink its water; it is dangerously contaminated by acid residues from mining. For the really hardy, accommodation costs US$3 at the Chacaltaya ski station, but bring very warm clothes and sleeping bag, food and water, as there is no heating, latrines or bedding and the caretakers are unhelpful. (Chacaltaya skiing is described in Bradt's *South America Ski Guide* - due end-1991.)

***Urmiri*** Take road S towards Oruro, turn left at Urmiri sign at Km. 75. To get this far take Flota Bolívar or Flota Copacabana bus; lifts from the crossroads are few and far between. A steep scenic descent leads to pool filled by mineral springs and a pleasant primitive inn. Worth visiting, it's a 2½ hour trip one way. The La Paz Prefectura runs buses to Urmiri, where they have a hotel (D), price includes food.

***Sorata*** is 105 km. from La Paz at 2,695 metres, giving appreciable relief, and is very beautiful. A 4-6 hour trip each way, bus every day with Transportes Larecaja, Calles Angel Bavia y Bustillos (Av. Kollasuyo), daily 0700, 0715, 0730, returning at 1230 and 1300, US$2 each way. Plenty of trucks to Sorata from by cemetery, US$2. It is in a valley at the foot of Illampu. Area has lovely views, mountain climbing, cave exploring. Climbers of ***Illampu*** (experience and full equipment necessary) start here: hire horses at Candelaria mine and on to Coóco where llamas are hired to reach the base camp at 4,500 metres. Swimming pool 2 km. along road to river. Sunday market. Also Sunday market festival, including bull market, at village of ***Achacachi*** (*Pensión*, F, tiny) on the road. Not far from Sorata, along the E shore of Lake Titicaca, is a tremendous marsh. Typical *fiestas*, both at Sorata and Achacachi, on 14 Sept. Pleasant walks: splendid one of 12 km. to San Pedro village and cave with ice-cold swimming in underground lake, 75 metres below surface (take torch). Ulla Ulla vicuña reserve off the Achacachi-Puerto Acosta road around the northeast corner of Lake Titicaca, about 200 km. from La Paz.

**Sorata Hotels** *Prefectural*, rec., good value, C, with meals, hot water. *Residencia Sorata* just off main square, above Casa Gunther, G, breakfast included, with good meals, "a grand, rotting mansion", rooms basic, shared bath, friendly proprietor. *Alojamiento Central*, main plaza, No. 127, F, basic, no showers, but nice rooms. *San Cristóbal*, near market, F, bargain. *Copacabana*, just outside town, F, basic, clean and cheap, hot water, German-run, useful for information on hikes and excursions. Norwegian guide, Knut Berg Hansen (speaks English) can be contacted from here. (European agent: Merete Nissen, Hermann Foss'gt 24, N. 0171 Oslo 1, Norway). Best place in town for meals, vegetarian dishes, set dinner or lunch US$2.50, highly rec. *Paraíso Hotel*, C full board, smart, with restaurant.

Sorata is the starting place for the "Camino del Oro" or "Gold-digger's Trail", a strenuous 7-8 day hike to Guanay (**see page 259**), via La Cumbre, 4,800 metres (8-11 hrs. straight up from Sorata, best done in 2 stages). Ancoma (3-4 hrs. from the pass, very cold), Wainapata, Chusi, Llipi, and Unutulumi (2-3 hrs. from Llipi; from here a camioneta runs daily at 0930 to Guanay, for US$5, winding through the many gold-mining towns along the Tipuani valley). After Ancoma it is very hot; in the dry season take water. There is a shop in Chusi. The Ancoma-Llipi section is the most interesting, following the Tipuani river, climbing Inca staircases, crossing rivers on precarious plank bridges and going through an Inca tunnel (fully repaired in 1989 after having caved in). (Details in *Backpacking in Peru and Bolivia*—see above).

***Tiahuanaco*** (Tiwanaku) The ruins of Tiahuanaco are near the southern end of Lake Titicaca, by partly paved, but bad road (bumpy, dusty) through the village of Laja (solid silver altar in church, but church closed to visitors), the first site of La Paz. Simple meals at US$0.80 available in village. There are two restaurants near the ruins. The village church is in striking contrast with the pre-Incaic statuary in front of it. The ruins, which are being reconstructed, comprise four main structures: the Kalasasaya compound, the Acapana pyramid (the 6 pillars on top are magnetic, probably by accident rather than design), the underground temple, and the Gate of the Sun, with carved stone blocks weighing many tons; this is reported in a bad state as the locals used it for shooting practice. Many archaeologists believe that Tiahuanaco existed as early as 1600 BC. Recent research suggests that the site was a ceremonial complex at the centre of an empire which covered almost half Bolivia, southern Peru, northern Chile and northwest Argentina. It was also a hub of trans-Andean trade. The reason for the demise of the Tiahuanaco civilization is not entirely clear, although studies by Alan Kolata of the University of Illinois indicate that the area had an extensive system of raised fields, capable of sustaining a population of 20,000, which may have been flooded by rising water levels in Lake Titicaca. This could have precipitated the empire's fall. The raised field system is being reutilized in the Titicaca area. The entrance ticket to Tiahuanaco (US$2.20) also gives entrance to Puma Punku (down the road 1 km.), which contains a pair of andesite gates (among the finest examples of stone cutting in South America) while its sandstone platforms are made up of cut slabs weighing 13 tonnes each. There is a museum near the ruins: entrance free to those with admission tickets for the site (open 0900-1700). There is also a small museum at the ticket office. However most of the best statues are in the Museo Tiahuanaco or the Museo Semisubterráneo in La Paz. Indians trade arrowheads and bronze figures (almost all fakes). Allow 4 hours to see the ruins and village. There is a very basic *alojamiento* on Calle Bolívar, cheap but good views.

**Guidebook in English** *Tiwanaku*, by Mariano Baptista, Plata Publishing Ltd., Chur, Switzerland, or *Discovering Tiwanaku* by Hugo Boero Rojo. They are obtainable from Los Amigos del Libro (or 2nd-hand from stalls in Av. Ismael Montes). *Guía Especial de Arqueología Tiwanaku*, by Edgar Hernández Leonardini, a guide on the site, recommended. Written guide material is very difficult to come by, so if you can hire a good guide take him with good grace (US$10).

Buses for Tiahuanaco (72 km.) can be caught opposite the Cemetery off Plaza Garita de Lima but may be full already! Taxi for 2 costs about US$20 (can be shared), return, with unlimited time at site. Transportes Ingavi, José María Azú y Eyzaguirre (take any Micro marked 'Cementerio') US$1 (2½-3 hrs.), every ½ hr. from 0600 to 1500 daily (frequency may change according to demand—the earlier you go the better). (Tourist buses cost US$15 return; some tours include Moon Valley.) Some buses go on from Tiahuanaco to Desaguadero; virtually all Desaguadero buses stop at Tiahuanaco, US$0.50. Return buses (last one back at about 1900) can be caught at the crossroads in the village at the "Tránsito" sign; cannot be booked in advance, but there are usually plenty available.

## LAKE TITICACA

The road and railway go to **Guaqui**, the port for the Titicaca passenger boats (service suspended in 1985/86; in 1989 the ferry and railway were carrying only freight. *Hotel Guaqui*, G, good value; tiny restaurant on the Plaza de Armas has been rec.). On the last weekend of July, Guaqui celebrates the festival for the Apostal Santiago. Arrive early morning to join in the end of all-night carousing (what little accommodation there is, is all fully occupied). The road crosses the border at Desaguadero into Peru and runs along the western shore to the Peruvian port of Puno, at the northern end. Desaguadero is noted for its lack of accommodation. At Yunguyo a side road to the right re-enters Bolivian territory and leads to Copacabana. (Hourly buses, taking 45 minutes, US$0.40.)

**Copacabana**, 158 km. from La Paz, is an attractive little town on Lake Titicaca. It has a heavily restored cathedral containing a famous 16th century miracle-working Dark Virgin of the Lake, also known as the Virgin of Candelaria, the patron saint of Bolivia. Candlelight procession on Good Friday. The cathedral itself is notable for its spacious atrium with four small chapels; the main chapel has one of the finest altars in Bolivia. An *hospicio* (serving now as an almshouse) with its two arcaded patios is worth a visit; ask permission before entering. There are 17th and 18th century paintings and statues in the sanctuary and monastery. Good food and drink at the hotels and in the market. Bank only opens Wednesday-Sunday (will change travellers' cheques); a few restaurants and shops give poor rates, so buy Bolivian money in Yunguyo (beware, much counterfeit money here) before crossing frontier, if coming from Peru. Major festival on 5-8 August makes town full, and dangerous. Vehicles are blessed in front of the church daily, especially on Sunday. There are good walks beside the lake for those unwilling to do penance on the hill, or to an Inca site, Horca del Inca, on the hill

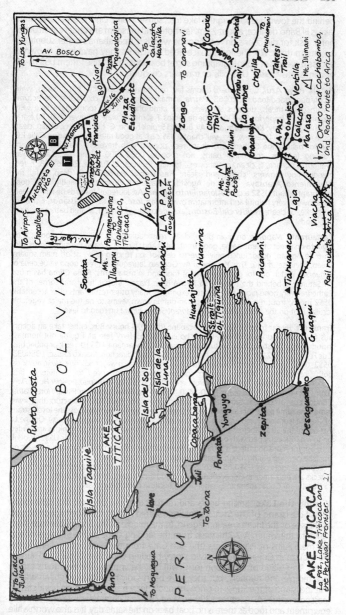

LAKE TITICACA
La Paz, Lake Titicaca and
the Peruvian Frontier.

behind the town overlooking the lake (rec. sunset walk). On the other side of the lake is El Baño del Inca, about 2 km. (an hotel and museum are under construction here). Ask for directions on reaching the woods. Copacabana's water supply can be intermittent. **NB** The local police need watching: they have been known to accuse travellers of "photographing secret buildings" and "fine" them US$10-20, or confiscate "false" US$ bills or travellers cheques.

**Hotels** *Playa Azul*, C, full board (rooms fair, half-board a possibility), hot showers, water supply poor, good food, T 320068; *Patria*, in main square, E, dirty, cold water; *Prefectural*, E with good meals, dubious showers, drab atmosphere, some rooms have lake view; *Alojamiento Imperio*, Calle Visconde de Lemos, F, some hot water (shower US$0.50 extra), will change money; *Kota Kahuaña*, Av. Busch 15, pink house, G, hot showers, cheap, clean, some rooms with lake view, rec., will change US$ cash at good rates. *Emperador*, Calle P.O. Murillo, behind the Cathedral, F, clean, rec., popular with travellers, washing done and washing facilities, communal baths, hot showers 0600-1300, highly rec; *Las Playas*, overlooking beach, F, clean, hot showers, laundry facilities; *El Turista*, Pando 378, F, rec., friendly, hot showers, cheap and clean; *Residencial Porteñila*, F, clean, safe, rec. *Alojamiento Aransaya*, Av. 6 de Agosto, F, basic but clean and friendly, with good restaurant, about US$2 a dish; *Alojamiento Aroma*, Av. Jauregui, towards beach, F, clean, hot showers, very helpful and informative owner; *San José*, next to *Ambassador*, E, 1 block from lake, G, clean; *Residencial Boston*, lakeside corner of plaza, F, shared bathroom, basic but good.

**Restaurants** *Napolés*, on main plaza, clean, reasonable prices, will change money; *6 de Agosto* on street of same name, good trout, salad and chips, US$2 and *Pensión Flores*, also on 6 de Agosto, good, lunch only; *Puerto del Sol*, on road to lake just off main square, cheap, filling set menu; *Tito Yupanqui* Av. Gonzalo Jauregui 123, rec., good value *cena* or *almuerzo*. Watch out for gringo pricing of food and in restaurants. *Peña Clima* has music on Saturdays, behind the market; *La Patria* is on Plaza Principal, left-hand corner of the Cathedral, very good *pique* dish, not too expensive. Many other restaurants offer acceptable US$2 meals; trout rec. The only vegetarian dish in town seems to be the maize vegetable tortillas (not on the menu) at *Snack Restaurant Super Turista* on road to lake.

**Transport** By car from La Paz to Copacabana (direct), 4 hours. Bus: either take an agency bus for US$5 and up (pick up at your hotel; US$0.65 ferry fare at Tiquina not normally included, e.g. Turisbus, US$13 return, or Diana Tours, Sagarnaga, US$10, rec.); or public bus: 2 de Febrero, T 377181, US$2.50, 5 hrs., 0800, 1500 each direction; Manko Kapac, T 350033, US$2, 0700 (arrive 0630, bus leaves when full) and 1315 each way; book one day in advance, both companies' offices are in plaza opposite entrance to cemetery. Bus, Copacabana-Yunguyo (for Peruvian frontier), hourly, US$0.40, from plaza below *Hotel Playa Azul* . Minibuses to Puno leave 1200-1430, US$3 from *Hotel Litoral* on Plaza, *Hotel Patria*, Cóndor bus (office near cathedral, will store luggage), or *Playa Azul* (Colectur); they leave same time same place for La Paz. To reach Copacabana (or Tiquina) you cross the lovely straits of Tiquina (coming from Peru, the ferry fare has to be paid in Peruvian currency). On the La Paz side of the Strait, there is a clean blue restaurant with excellent toilets. Vehicles are loaded on to a barge equipped with outboard motors. The official charge for a car is US$2, though they ask for more and there is a US$0.50 municipal car toll to enter Copacabana. Delays on the lake crossing during rough weather, when it can get very cold. Even when one has a bus ticket passengers pay US$0.65 each to cross on a separate boat and passports are checked (checks are also made in Copacabana, even if you aren't going to Peru). **N.B.** It is impossible to travel from Copacabana to Guaqui direct, because of border crossings.

**Visiting the Lake** Sailing boats and motor-boats can be hired in Copacabana to visit the **Island of the Sun**. It contains a sacred rock at its NW end, worshipped as the site of the Inca's creation legend. In the middle of the E shore are Inca steps down to the water. A 2-km. walk from the landing stage to the SE takes one to the main ruins of Pilko Caima (the Sun Gate from the ruins is now kept in the main plaza in Copacabana), a two-storey building with false domes and superb views. The Island of the Moon (or Coati) may be visited—the best ruins are an Inca temple and nunnery, but they have been sadly neglected. A cheap way to visit the Island of the Sun is to catch the public ferry from the Bolivian naval station (passport required); it leaves 1300 on Wed., Sat. and Sun. Worth taking camping equipment and food as there is no boat back on the same day. It is also worthwhile staying for the many beautiful walks through villages and Inca terraces, some still in use. Ask permission to camp at the *hacienda*, good spring water available opposite hydrofoil landing. Beware of constant harassment for photographs and of thieves. Boats (not tackle) are hired at reasonable rates for fishing. Dawns and sunsets are spectacular. At **Chúa**, on the lake, there is duck shooting, fishing, sailing and at **Huatajata** a yacht club—restaurant open to public, serves reasonable trout (highly rec.), and Crillon Tours International Hydroharbour and *Inca Utama Hotel* (*Hotel Chúa*, situated on lake between Huatajata and Tiquina, good). Bus La Paz—Huatajata/Tiquina, Transportes Titikaka, Av. Kollasuyo 16, daily from 0400, returning between 0700 and 1800.

In Huatajata there are several *alojamientos*, which only seem to come to life at weekends and in the high season. In the village contact Máximo Catari who has rooms for G p.p. and serves meals at *Inti Karka*, a 3-storey building on the waterfront (contact him also at Turismo de Aventura, Av. 16 de Julio 1639, P O Box 8412, La Paz). He can also arrange boats to the islands of Quebraya, Pariti, Kalahuta and Suriqui for about US$30. On Suriqui you can visit the museum/craft shops of the Limachi brothers and Paulineo Esteban, who helped in the construction, out of totora reeds, of Thor Heyerdahl's *Ra II*, which sailed from Morocco to Barbados in 1970. Heyerdahl's *Tigris* reed boat, and the balloon gondola for the Nazca (Peru) flight experiment (**see Peru chapter, Section 4** ), were also constructed by the craftsmen of Suriqui. Reed boats are still made on Suriqui, probably the last place where the art survives.

**Boats on Lake**  6 hours to Island of Sun and back, about US$35 for boat taking 8 (you can bargain), best ruins on S, good scenery on N side, but difficult to persuade boatmen to go there. As it is a 4-hour round trip to see all the temples, it may not be possible to do it all in a day. There is accommodation, bed and blankets, near the Inca steps and at Challa on the other side of the island, and some basic supplies from villagers. Ask for Juan Mamani Ramos in Challa. Similar rates for Island of the Moon. Motor boat trips from Copacabana to Suriqui may be arranged. (Sailing boats, which take five and cost less—about US$20, often suffer from lack of wind in the morning.) Rowing boat, US$6.50 an hour. Cheaper boats can be found by walking 15 km. along the lakeside outside Copacabana to Yampupata where fishermen cross in ½ hour, US$3, return. This is a lovely walk in itself, through unspoilt countryside. At the village of Sequañe ask for Señor Hilario Paye Quispe who will row you across and bring you back another day if you plan to stay on the Isa del Sol. Danger of sunburn on lake even if it does not feel hot. Warning: Several reports have been received of boat excursions giving less than value for money, and often giving free rides to the owner's friends and relatives encountered en route. Don't always take the cheapest possible offer, ask around and check what is included for your money.

Crillon Tours, Avenida Camacho 1223, run a hydrofoil service on Lake Titicaca with a bilingual guide. Leaving La Paz at 0600 (except Saturday), you get to Huatajata on Lake Titicaca for breakfast by 0800. The hydrofoil sets off at 0830, moves past groups of reed fishing boats, and stops in the Straits of Tiquina for a few minutes to watch the wooden ferry boats crossing. Only the Island of the Sun is visited to see the ruins. You arrive at Copacabana for sightseeing and a trout lunch, with local folk music. The short tour returns to La Paz from Copacabana; the longer one continues to Puno (Peru). Charge: US$160 from La Paz to Puno. Expensive but fascinating, not least for the magnificent views of the Cordillera on a clear day. Turismo Balsa's tour of the Lake, including Isla de Suriqui, has been recommended, except for the fact that the motor boat has no liferafts.

Tristan Jones, who crossed South America in his sailing cutter *Sea Dart* (see his book *The Incredible Voyage*, Futura Publications), spent over eight months cruising Lake Titicaca. He recommends visiting the islands of **Pariti**, where the weaving is very good indeed and, only a mile or so away, **Quebraya**, where there are pre-Inca *chulpas*, or tombs, stretching along the shore. "This was the ancient port for Tiahuanaco, when the lake fell back from that city. No-one lives there, and it is best always to go with an Aymará guide, for the locals are very jealous of the place." *An Insider's Guide to Bolivia* by Peter McFarren, gives a good historical background, including an interesting article about archaeological discoveries in Lake Titicaca, by Johann Reinhard (available in many bookshops and large hotels in La Paz).

"The only hotel on Lake Huanamarca, at Chúa, is now expensive, but the trout is good. "The Titicaca Indians' most interesting music, and quite rare, is at masses held for the dead."

## CROSSING THE PERUVIAN FRONTIER

We give below the journey by road (see Peruvian section 5 for other routes). A visa to Peru will cost US$5 in US currency (if you need one). Also, the Bolivian navy (assorted hovercraft and motor boats) may be seen at Tiquina. The road between La Paz and Tiquina is now motorway to El Alto, then surfaced.

No hotel at Tiquina, but ask for the Casa Verde, where you can stay for US$0.50 p.p. Two cheap eating places at Yunguyo.

Just as interesting as the water route is the bus journey to Puno, US$2, for 2-3 hour journey along the western side of the lake via Desaguadero at the border, the junction to Yunguyo (13 km. from Copacabana), Pomata, Juli and Ilave. Desaguadero-Puno takes 5 hours by taxi and 6 hours by bus. This is a colourful trip, with wonderful views of the lake against the snow-capped Cordillera. The La Paz-Desaguardero road is mostly good gravel with some fords (treacherous in the dark) and railway level crossings. The road on the Peruvian side is nearly all paved, and you really see the Indian life of the Altiplano. There are many checkpoints for motorists.

A colectivo from La Paz to Puno costs US$9-12 p.p. (8 hours). Colectivos can be caught at Desaguadero for Puno, US$2 for 2-3 hour journey. One problem with the Desaguadero route is that on Tuesday and Friday it is reported that cars are not allowed to cross because these days are set aside for "interchange of national produce". At the risk of another change it may be better (and certainly more scenic) to catch buses La Paz—Copacabana via Tiquina, Copacabana—Yunguyo (for Peruvian entry formalities) and Yunguyo-Puno (see page 234). This is possible in one day.

If you are leaving Copacabana for Peru, get exit stamp at Bolivian immigration office (open 0800-1900) on Yunguyo road. Be careful that dates stamped are correct on all documents. Generally, though, this is now a very straightforward border crossing, with customs and immigration posts at either side of the border; the buses/colectivos stop at each one, 4 in all (or you can walk, but it is over 1 km.). Make sure, however, if arranging a through ticket La Paz-Puno, that you get all the necessary stamps en route, and ascertain whether your journey involves a change of bus. Note the common complaint that through services La Paz-Puno (or vice versa) deteriorate once the border has been crossed, e.g. smaller buses are used, extra passengers taken on, drivers won't drop you where the company says they will.

It is also possible to enter/leave Bolivia via the east side of the lake. However, the Peruvians do not officially recognize the road as being a border crossing. (Officially, you must get your entry stamp in the Department of Puno, but as this is next to impossible on this route, you will run into difficulties later on.) The Bolivian frontier is at **Puerto Acosta** (there is an immigration office, beware extortionate demands by guards, but it is advisable to get an exit stamp in La Paz first, especially if you have not been staying at a recognized hotel—**see page 271**). One small *alojamiento* (G) but no restaurants. Bus La Paz (Cementerio district)—Puerto Acosta, US$2.50, Fri. 1130, Sat./Sun. 0630. The road to La Paz (fine during the dry season only) passes through splendid scenery while the area around Puerto Acosta is good walking country and the locals are friendly, but there have been reports of Sendero Luminoso activity in the area. Ask for directions to the thermal water swimming pool. The Acosta road northwards to Peru rapidly deteriorates and is only recommended in the dry season (approximately May to October). The only transport beyond Acosta is early on Saturday mornings when a couple of trucks go to the markets, some 25 km. from Puerto Acosta on the border (no formalities); the Peruvian and Bolivian markets are completely different.

**N.B.** Remember that if you wish to enter Peru from Bolivia you must have an onward ticket (or return ticket) out of Peru. A ticket outward from Peru can be purchased at Exprinter in La Paz, but you will have to pay in foreign currency rather than bolivianos.

## SOUTH FROM LA PAZ (2)

Flamingoes shimmering in the glare of salt-flats, geysers and volcanoes on the Chilean border, faded colonial glory in Sucre, Potosí and Cochabamba: the southwestern quarter of Bolivia is predominantly mountainous and stark. Around Oruro and Potosí, the poverty of the mines belies former wealth; around Cochabamba, the fertile foothills provide much of the country's grain and fruit.

*Oruro* is built on the slopes of a hill at an altitude of 3,704 metres. The population, mostly Indian, is 175,000. It is about 190 km. from La Paz, and is important as a railway centre and for its tin, silver, and tungsten. A 20,000 tons-a-year tin smelter has been built nearby at Vinto; open to visitors, but a permit has to be applied for, 24 hours in advance, in Oruro. There is good *pejerrey* fishing on a large nearby lake. Excellent daily market, near railway station. The zoo is not really worth a special visit. Rail travellers from Buenos Aires can, and from Antofagasta sometimes have to, alight at Oruro and continue to La Paz by bus. A severe water shortage puts showers at a premium. We are informed that in hotels water is only available in the mornings, owing to city ordinances.

**La Diablada** At carnival on the Saturday before Ash Wednesday, Oruro stages the Diablada ceremony in gratitude to Pachamama, the Earth Mother. Two figures, a bear and a condor, clear the way for a procession of masked dancers, led by two luxuriously costumed masqueraders representing Satan and Lucifer. Alternating with them in the lead are St. Michael the Archangel and China Supay, the Devil's wife, who plays the role of carnal temptress. Behind them come hundreds of dancers in ferocious diabolical costumes, leaping, shouting, and pirouetting. The parade ends in the crowded football stadium, where the masqueraders perform various mass and solo dances. These are followed by two masques: the first is a tragic re-enactment of the Conquest, in the second the golden-haired Archangel conquers the forces of evil in battle.

In the contest between good and evil, the result in favour of the good is pronounced by the Virgen del Socavón, the patroness of miners, and after the performance the dancers all enter her chapel, chant a hymn in Quechua and pray for pardon. The Diablada was traditionally performed by Indian miners, but three other guilds have taken up the custom.

The costume always features the heavy, gruesome mask modelled in plaster, with a toad or snake on top; huge glass eyes; triangular glass teeth; a horsehair wig; and pointed, vibrating ears. Tied around the neck is a large silk shawl embroidered with dragons or other figures, and the dancer also has a jewelled, fringed breastplate. Over his white shirt and tights he wears a sash trimmed with coins, and from it hang the four flaps of the native skirt, embroidered in gold and silver thread and loaded with precious stones. Special boots equipped with spurs complete the elaborate outfit. Satan and Lucifer wear scarlet cloaks, and carry a serpent twisted around one arm and a trident. The working-class Oruro district known as La Ranchería is particularly famous for the excellence of the costumes and masks made there. One of the most famous folklore groups is called Morenada. Carnival lasts 8 days with displays of dancing by day and night often superior to those given on the opening Saturday. There are two options for seating: municipal seats around the main plaza and on Av. Cívica, which cost US$9 for 3 days; Av. Cívica is a good spot because the street is wide and the dancers are unrestricted. The alternative is seating outside shops, also US$9, the streets are narrower so you are closer to the dancers, and to the water-bombers. To wander among the dancers you are officially supposed to purchase a photography ticket for US$15, but little checking seems to be done. Seats can be booked at the town hall. Take raincoats as protection against water pistols and *bombas de agua* (water-filled balloons). Latest reports suggest that the processions on Saturday before Ash Wednesday are fine, but degenerate thereafter as all the participants are drunk; also participants now have to be wealthy to afford to take part, so *campesinos* have been forced to the periphery (selling food, etc.). Beware of sharp practices and doubling of hotel prices during the period of carnival.

**Guide** *Carnival de Oruro.* Dance costumes and masks, Calle La Paz, 400 block.

**Hotels** *Repostero*, Sucre 370, T 50505, good by local standards with restaurant, but unfriendly, E with bath, hot water unreliable on upper floors, TV in some rooms; *Prefectural-Oruro*, Pagador y Galvarro, D, near station, bleak but quite comfortable, good restaurant; *Terminal*, above bus depot, T 53209/53127, D, modern, but with technical defects, hot water, night club, expensive restaurant; *Lipton*, Av. 6 de Agosto 625, E, with bath, TV and hot water (cheaper without bath and TV); *Residencial Turista*, opposite *Lipton*, F, basic but O.K. safe car park; *Residencial Ideal*, Bolívar 386, F, E with bath, clean, recent face-lift; *Osber*, Murguía y Washington, E, basic, dirty, run-down, no hot water and over-priced; *Hispanoamericano*, Galvarro y Aldana, opposite station, F, no hot water and no running water after 2200. *Alojamiento Central Oruro*, Potosí 5917, F, run-down, warm showers; *Alojamiento Ferrocarril*, Galvarro 6278, F, basic, no hot water, opp. railway station, nearby is *Alojamiento San Juan de Dios*, Galvarro 6338, "dirty, smelly, not cheap, avoid at all costs". *Alojamiento 15 de Octubre*, Av. 6 de Agosto 890, F, friendly and clean, breakfast and snacks served, rec.

**Restaurants** *Quick Lunch*, 6 de Octubre, good, big meals, cheap; *pizzería* at S. Galvarro 5865 has good *salteñas*; good *pizzería* opp. Post Office on Pres. Montes. *Le Grill*, Bolívar, near plaza, good, cheap. Vegetarian: *El Huerto*, Bolívar 359. *Pastelería La Polar*, C. Presidente Montes 5985, is good place to get warm; nameless restaurant at 6 de Agosto 1166, huge portions.

**Shopping** *Infol*, Ayacucho 426 for alpaca, high quality but not cheap nor a large selection and *Reguerín* on the junction with Mier; also sell devil masks. The municipal market has an interesting witchcraft section, said to be far better than the one in La Paz. A good handicraft shop is on Av. Cochabamba, opposite the market, although handicrafts are generally cheaper in Cochabamba.

**Museums** Worth a visit are Patiño legacies, e.g. the Sala de Conciertos (now a cinema). Museo Arqueológico Vivero Municipal, near the zoo on Calle Lizarraga (reached on foot, or Micro 'A Sud') has unique collections of stone llama heads and carnival masks. Guide available, US$0.75. Geology Museum at the university. Ask the tourist office whether they are open.

**Exchange** Banks not helpful. It is quite easy to change dollars (cash) on the street: good rates on Av. V. Galvarro, opposite train station, or at Ferretería Finkel, Calle Pagador 1491, near the market (large hardware store; owner, Don Ernesto, speaks English and is helpful and friendly). Cheques can be changed at pharmacy close to Ferretería Finkel.

**German Consulate** at Adolfo Mier.

**Sauna** Ayacucho y Galvarro, wet or dry, showers US$0.75. Duchas Oruro, 500 block of Av. 6 de Agosto (near bus terminal); Santa Bárbara, Pagador 6801.

**Laundry** Alemania, Aldana 280.

**Post Office** Presidente Montes 1456. **Telecommunications** Entel, Bolívar, 1 block E of plaza.

**Travel Agent** Jumbo Travel, 6 de Octubre, T 55005/55203, friendly and efficient, said to be able to book flights to Calama, Chile, although not clear from where.

**Tourist Office** Edificio Prefectural, Plaza 10 de Febrero (T 51764), open Mon.-Fri., 0900-1200, 1400-1800, has map of city, helpful. Also on Bolívar one block E. of plaza, Mon.-Fri., 0900-1200, 1400-1800, Sat. 0900-1200, more helpful than the main office.

**Trains** About 4 hours to **La Paz**, US$4 Pullman, US$3 special, and 5 to **Cochabamba** (Mon., Wed., Fri. 1150, also Mon., 0800) *ferrobus* US$3, Pullman US$1.60 special (13 hrs. in once weekly express, Mon. 0700); to **Potosí**, *ferrobus* once a week, express (1 a week), US$3.75 Pullman, US$2.25 special; to **Sucre**, same timetable, US$7 Pullman, US$5.50 special, *ferrobus* US$11.30. To **Villazón**, coming from La Paz, Mon. and Thurs., 2140, 19 hours, exhausting but exhilarating to hardy traveller, or Fri. 2310, US$13 Pullman, US$9 special. Ticket office opens at 0700, best to be there early. **Calama**, for Antofagasta (Chile), 30-36 hrs. very prone to delay. Wed. and Fri., 2000, US$15 one class only, tickets on sale only on day of departure, very crowded and dusty for first few stops. For more details see above under La Paz, **Railways to/from the Coast**.

**Buses** To/from **La Paz**, 3 hours, seven bus lines work the route, 8 departures daily by each one US$2; to **Potosí**, 8-10 cold and rough hours, US$4.50, two companies, both at 1900 daily; to **Cochabamba**, 5-6 hours, US$5, six lines, most leave 0800-1000 (one night bus 2000). To **Sucre**, best to go via Cochabamba if wet as the road to Potosí is so bad. Roads to **Río Mulato** and **Uyuni** are very bad, but some trucks work the route; train (8 hours) recommended. Bus agencies are all at the new terminal in the centre, on the corner of Buenos Aires and Aroma. Trucks to Potosí and Sucre leave from Av. Cochabamba near the Mercado Bolívar.

**Excursions** From Machacamarca, 24 km. S of Oruro, a branch line runs to Uncia (108 km.) and the ex-Patiño tin mines.

A taxi to Lake Uru Uru costs US$5-7.50 (agree price and waiting time in advance); or take Micro A to its terminus and then walk 1 hour along road, take Micro B for return trip, US$0.15 each way: flamingoes and other water-birds, highly recommended, but not at the height of the dry season (October) when wild life moves elsewhere. Boats may be hired only out of the rainy season.

There are hot springs at Obrajes, where there is the choice of private baths or swimming pool, both hot, and more springs at Capachos. Free facilities for clothes washing in the natural hot water. Wait at the bus stop at 6 de Octubre 1420 for the (intermittent) bus to both places, US$0.50 to Capachos. Taxis sometimes make the run. Take picnic lunch.

Visitors with a Land Rover, or similar, might explore the country W of Oruro towards the Chilean frontier. It's a day's drive to the western mountains following tracks rather than roads. There are no hotels in any of the towns, such as Escara or Sabaya, but lodging could be found by asking a school-teacher or local mayor. From Escara it is only 25 km. S to **Chipaya**, the main settlement of the most interesting Indians of the Altiplano. They speak a language closely related to the almost extinct Uru, their dress is distinctive and their conical houses unique. This is a very difficult trip without your own transport. Sometimes trucks leave from Plaza Walter Khon in Oruro for Chipaya; or the village may be reached by taking a bus to Sabaya or Turco, then a truck. Bring your own food; shelter for US$0.25 per head in adobe *alojamiento* . Bicycles may be hired in Chipaya to visit lake 2 hours away with great variety of bird life.

A one-day drive to the west is the **Parque Nacional Sajama**, the world's highest forest. The road is reported to be very bad. To climb **Sajama**, Bolivia's highest mountain (6,530 metres) take the Litoral La Paz-Arica bus and pay the full fare. Ask for the Sajama stop, 20 minutes past the village of that name, before Lagunas, and about 11 hrs. from La Paz. A cheaper way is to take a La Paz-Oruro bus as far as Patacamaya (1½ hrs. from La Paz), see below, then take a truck to Estación Tomarapi (dusty, but very interesting, US$2). Tomarapi is in the Parque Nacional Sajama; no fresh food is available in the Park, so take plenty from La Paz. If continuing into Chile (by truck—possible but hard) remember that no meat, dairy products, fruit or vegetables may be taken across the border. To return to La Paz, walk to Lagunas and take a truck or the Litoral bus. Crampons, ice axe and rope are needed for the climb, which is not technically difficult; the routes to base camp and beyond are fairly obvious. In Sajama village, Peter Brunnhart (El Gringo, in the first house you come to in town) has a book with descriptions of the various routes to the summit. Water is available, but beware of sulphurous streams. It can be very windy. Good bathing in hot springs 5 km. north of village, near to Sajama river.

*Patacamaya*, some 130 km. N of Oruro, 104 km. S of La Paz, has a Sunday market (no tourist items). Some cheap restaurants and accommodation e.g. *Los Angeles*, G, basic, no electricity can but candles provided.

About 100 km. S of Oruro is **Llallagua** (*Hotel Bustillo*, F; *Santa María, Hotel Llallagua*, F, the best). Nearby is the famous Siglo Veinte, the largest tin mine (ex-Patiño) in the country (now closed). There is an acute water shortage. Llallagua can be reached by bus from Oruro (Bustillo, 7 a day, US$1.65, Enta 0900, 1700 daily, US$1.45), but only trucks make the journey to Sucre (without going via Potosí), beautiful but uncomfortable. Also buses 1900 from La Paz.

A recommended driver is Freddy Barron M., Casilla 23, Oruro, T 55270, for excursions.

From Oruro a railway runs eastwards to Cochabamba (204 km.). It reaches a height of 4,140 metres at Cuesta Colorada before it begins to descend to the fertile basin in which Cochabamba lies. It is 394 km. from La Paz to Cochabamba by road, now paved to Oruro and from there paved except for 50 km. midway, where the going is very rough; about 8 hours by private car. A new highway is being built to Cochabamba, via Quillacollo. On the present road, a short cut from Caracollo to Colhuasi avoids Oruro and saves 65 km.

*Cochabamba*, Bolivia's third-largest city, founded in 1542, is set in a bowl of rolling hills and is an important agricultural centre. Population: 430,000; altitude 2,570 metres; excellent climate with average temperature of 18° C. It has fine buildings (though much of the modern building looks seedy), a University, an excellent archaeological museum, 25 de Mayo Norte 145, with a tiny but interesting collection of prehistoric pieces and Indian hieroglyphic scripts, and little-known collection of pre-Inca textiles (Mon.-Fri. 0900-1200, 1500-1800, Sat. 0900-1300, closed Sun. US$1.50 with guide), English speakers available. Many Spanish houses with overhanging eaves, and much for the tourist: a grand view from San Sebastián, a hill on the edge of the city (robberies reported, beware even of police); the Golf Club on Lake Alalay (you need a member to introduce you), and Los Portales, the Patiño mansion in the northern part of the city (take Micro G), set in beautiful grounds, completed after 10 years' effort in 1927 but never occupied; open Mon.-Fri. 1700-1800, Sat. 1000-1100, Sun. 1100-1200. Guided tours daily, starting at opening times, T 43137, useful library. It is also an educational centre for teachers and students, promoting literacy in the surrounding countryside. The Cathedral in the main plaza is pleasantly decorated; panels painted to look like marble. Just off the plaza is La Compañía, whose whitewashed interior is completely innocent of the usual riot of late Baroque decoration. The municipal market and the Cancha, a retail market (open every day, but best days Wednesday and Saturday), are also full of local colour, but the latter is a favourite haunt of thieves. Beware: street numbering can be chaotic; street names and numbers are written over each doorway, not on street corner signs.

An imposing monument overlooks the town from La Coronilla, part of the same hill as San Sebastián. It commemorates the heroic defence of Cochabamba by its womenfolk during the War of Independence. It has fine views and just below it is a charming little old bull ring, little used. The Palacio de Cultura, Av. Heroínas y 25 de Mayo, has a group of local museums under one roof and they sometimes show films (entrance free, but exhibits usually locked). Churches worth a visit include Santo Domingo (Santiváñez and Ayacucho) and Santa Teresa (Baptista and Ecuador); all opening times are erratic. The water is notoriously bad, especially in the rainy season.

**Festivals** *Fiestas* are frequent and fascinating. Carnival is celebrated 15 days before Lent. Rival groups (*cumparsas*) compete in music, dancing, and fancy dress, culminating in El Corso on the last Saturday of the Carnival. Beware the rains around and after Carnival, and water-throwing the day after, when you are likely to get drenched. *Mascaritas* balls also take place in the carnival season, when the young women wear long hooded satin masks.

Fiesta de la Virgen de Urkupiña, Quillacollo, see below; and 14 September, dancing.

**Hotels** *Gran Hotel Cochabamba*, Plaza Ubaldo Anze, T 43524/43300, beautifully set in the northern part of the city (2 blocks from Los Portales at La Recoleta), with garden, swimming pool (guests only) and tennis courts, good food, the most expensive, A. *Portales*, Av. Pando 1271, T 48507/48897, 5-star, swimming pool, a long way from centre, new. In the city: *Ambassador*, Calle España 349 (T 48777), private bath, hot water, telephone, modern, central and reasonable, A, good restaurant. *Capitol*, Colombia 418 y Mayo, T 24510, C, private bath, TV, clean and friendly but rather scruffy. *Residencial Escobar*, Uruguay y Nataniel Aguirre, T 29275, D with bath, but no toilet paper (hotel sells it at a price), hot shower, modern, mediocre; *Boston*, Calle 25 de Mayo 167, D, clean and friendly, restaurant, luggage deposit, mosquito net in most rooms, rec; *Hostal Doria*, Junín 765, T 45386, D with bath, good, clean; *Las Palmas*, Av. Salamanca 0617, D, spotless. *Gran Hotel Las Vegas*, D, bath, rec., Esteban Arce 352, behind Cathedral, T 29217/21029, central, friendly, but overpriced extras, e.g. laundry. *El Dorado*, 25 de Mayo 1034, T 21940, D, rec., clean, hot water; *Hostería Claudia*, Hamiraya 248 (between Colombia and Ecuador) E, with or without bathroom, garden, very friendly, safe car-park; *Colón*, in Plaza Colón, T 48101, D, hot water, breakfast included. *City Hotel*, Jordán 341, T 22903, near centre, F with shower but without breakfast, cheaper rooms on upper floors, clean, noisy but modern. Both *Alojamiento Oruro*, Junín S-0680, T 24107, F, and *Residencial Agustín López*, Agustín López 0859, T 27250, near bus station, F, clean, comfortable, hot water. *Residencial Pullman*, Av. Aroma L-0870, T 24073, F, hot showers. *Alojamiento Cochabamba*, Calle Nataniel Aguirre S-0385, T 25067, F, clean, rec.; *Florida*, 25 de Mayo 583, T 27787, F, clean and friendly, but noisy, laundry, safe deposit box, breakfast served, highly rec. (hot showers, shared bathrooms only); *Res. El Salvador*, 25 de Mayo 0420, T 27307, E with electric shower, clean, beware theft close to market but inconvenient for restaurants; *Residencial San Severino*, 25 de Mayo 621, hot showers and clothes washing facilities; *Res. Buenos Aires*, 25 de Mayo 291, F, clean communal baths; *Residencial Virgen de Copacabana*, Av. Arce y Aroma, nr. bus station, E, hot showers, spotless, friendly; *Residencial Elisa*, C. Agustín López, 0834, T 27846, E with bath; F without, breakfast and water for clothes washing extra, modern, clean, garden, 2 blocks from bus station, friendly, highly rec. *Casa de Huéspedes San Martín*, Antezana, between Jordán y Calama, pleasant. *Residencia Inca-Llacta*, Av. Arce S556, F, central, family atmosphere, "like a little oasis", rec. Many cheap and basic places to stay near the bus station, e.g. *Alojamiento Sucre*, F.

**Restaurants** *Las Tablitas*, Plaza 24 de Setiembre 0209, lunch or set dinner good value, otherwise expensive. *Suiza*, Av. Ballivián 820, T 45485, highly rec; *Langostinos*, nearby on same street, good seafood. *El Grill*, next to Los Portales, good, not expensive, you can eat in the garden. *China*, on Av. San Martín, good but dear. *Ming Ming*, on España, good Bolivian dishes, despite its name; *La Rosa Roja*, Plaza Colon, good. Grill specialities at *El Bruno*, corner of Antezana and Colombia; *Los Troncos*, Junín 0-0942, barbecued meats; *Gallo de Oro*, Calle Lanza Sur 0567, rec. *Palmiras*, Lanza, very good food; *Paso de Loro*, corner of Junín and Aroma, cheap and good; *Illampú*, Aroma 179, dinner US$1.20, cheap and tasty. Vegetarian restaurant opposite Jasmín on M. Rocha and Ayacucho, lunch US$1, rec. *Govinda*, between Plaza Colón and España, vegetarian, good value; another vegetarian restaurant is *Gopal*, Calle España, Galeria Olimpia, Indian-style lunch, US$1, and Italian in the evenings. *La Cantonata*, España y Mayor Rocha, Italian, highly rec.; many *confiterías* on España; many cheap places on 25 de Mayo and Bolívar *Cozzalini Pizzas*, Av. Heroínas, good; *Don Pollo*, top of the Prado next to the roundabout, good ceviche, US$1.50, friendly management. Many good and varied restaurants along the Prado, e.g. *El Jamaica*, local dishes. Excellent pastries and ice cream at the *Zurich Tea Room*, Av. San Martín Norte 143, closes 2000, *Salón Berna*, Av. San Martín Norte 209 y Colombia, Swiss pastry, ice creams inexpensive. Good ice-cream parlours on Av. Heroínas; *Cecy* (0452), good breakfasts but a little pricey, and next door, *Dumbo* (popular eating and meeting spot, also does cheap meals), among others. *El Caminante*, Arce S-0628, pleasant patio, excellent food including duck with salad and vegetables, US$3.

**Shopping** Main market is called San Antonio. Large market (La Cancha) near railway station (tourist items). *Fotorama* Cooperative for alpaca sweaters, stoles, rugs, etc. (expensive—run by Maryknoll Mission); there is also a branch at Av. de Heroínas, or *Amerindia* for good rugs and lengths of alpaca material, as well as ponchos and jumpers, T 49994 to visit offices and purchase items; or picturesque Indian market and nearby shops. *Artesanías Casa Fisher*, Calle Ramón Rivero 0.204, T 45625, good woollen goods. *Asarti*, Mayor Rocha 375, beautiful hand-made and machine-knitted sweaters, can make to order, expensive. For leather try *Confecciones Gamucuer*, Destacamento 317. Mercado Incallacta for fruit and vegetables excellent and very cheap, but on more expensive articles do not expect prices to drop very much when bargaining. Tourist items and all handicrafts are cheaper in La Paz. Try local hot drink, *api*, made from maize. Main markets Wed. and Sat.; beware pickpockets and thieves. **Cycle repairs** parts in market at Lanza 700 Sur. **Camera repairs** recommended at shop on General Achá, next door to *Cromos* and *Maxell* on Plaza 14 de Setiembre, reasonable prices rec. *Foto Broadway*, España y Colombia, for developing at reasonable prices, including slide transparencies. A very good **bookshop** is *Los Amigos del Libro*, Av. de Heroínas 311 y España, and Gral. Achá 110, stocks U.S. and English magazines as well as *South American Handbook*. Books cheaper than in La Paz. **Camping Equipment** available at shop on 25 de Mayo, just before plaza Colón; wide variety of goods, very helpful owner, speaks English and perhaps German.

**Local Transport** Micros and colectivos, US$0.10; *trufis* (vans), US$0.12; anything marked "San Antonio" goes to the market. Taxis: agree fare before getting in; about US$0.50 from anywhere to the Plaza; double after dark.

**Entertainment** Frequent concerts and plays at the elegant *Teatro Achá*; more popular stage productions (stand-up comedy, music and dance) at *Tra La La*, opp. Chilean consulate, or *Champagne*, Calle Ballivián. *Nostalgia* (discotheque, popular); *Pier Seven* (disco) Heroínas 464.

**Swimming** *El Paraíso*, halfway to Quillacollo (Km. 10), sauna and pool, US$0.50 entrance, accessible by bus or train. Tourist complex *El Carmen*, road to Quillacolla, US$2, popular, sauna, catch micro and sauna on Junín. Pool at Club Social, Calle Méjico (US$1.60), is open to the public as well as La Rivera on Simón López (Micro A) or Los Chorrillos, both US$1, crowded on Sunday (Micro G), or outside town there is *Posada de Los Cisnes* at Quillacollo, at Km. 13 on Cochabamba road (entrance US$1.60). Also at *Don Gerardo* at Km. 7, with restaurant. Pool, sauna, restaurant at Estancia El Rosedal at Tiquipaya, take bus number 12 from Antezana y Cabrera to end of line. Most are open only at weekends.

**Tennis** Club de Ténis de Cochabamba admits non-members for US$5 per day.

**Fishing** Excellent trout fishing in lake formed by the Corani dam, 48 km. N of Cochabamba.

**Exchange Houses** Exprint-Bol, Plaza 14 de Septiembre 252 (will change travellers' cheques into dollars at 2% commission); **American Ltda.**, Plaza 14 de Septiembre (poor rates). Universo, España 153, 1 block from plaza. Money changers congregate in Plaza Colón and one block away on Av. 25 de Mayo. Try also Los Amigos del Libro and Librería Juventud in main plaza. Warning of counterfeit bills from street dealers, check large denominations.

**Language Classes** Sra. Blanca de La Rosa Villareal, Av. Libertador Simón Bolívar 1108, esq. Oblitas, Casilla 2707, (T 44298) charges US$5 for a 45 minute lesson. Instituto de Lenguaje (Idelco), Plaza Busch, Bolívar 826, T 44868.

**Consulates W. Germany**, España 149; **USA**, Avenida Libertador Bolívar 1724, T 43216; **Brazil**, Potosí 1455 (opp. Patiño Museum), open 1400-1800; **Argentina**, Av. Pando 1329, visa applications 0900-1300; **Perú**, Av. Pando 1143.

**Addresses** At 25 de Mayo 25698, Telephone 21288, is the Centro Boliviano Norteamericano with a library of English-language books, open 0900-1200 and 1500-1900. Alliance Française, Santiváñez 187. Goethe Institute, Sucre, corner of Antezana.

**Immigration Office** next to Tourist Office, will extend tourist visas.

**Laundry** *Superclean*, corner of 16 de Julio and Jordán. US$0.65 per kg.; *Jet*, 16 de Julio, between Ecuador and Venezuela, US$0.70 per kg., and two others, similar prices, at Cabrera 485 and Av. Humboldt 313.

**Post Office** Av. Heroínas y Ayacucho, next to TAM office; Mon.-Sat. 0800-1900, Sun. 0800-1200. **Telecommunications** Entel, same location.

**Tourist Office** Calle General Achá and Plaza 14 de Septiembre, helpful and friendly, English and French spoken, free maps of the city but little other information to take away, only open in mornings. Kiosks at Jorge Wilstermann airport and near Entel building. A useful guidebook can be obtained from Los Amigos del Libro. City maps sold from kiosk outside post office. Recommended travel agency, Gitano Tours.

**Railway** Tickets available on day before travel (office opens 0600-1000, be there early). There are *ferrobuses* leaving for **La Paz** 3 times a week (not running July 1990), 8 hours; fares US$7 Pullman, US$6 special. Express train to **Oruro** 0700, 1 a week; *ferrobus* 4 a week, Tues., Fri., Sat. 0830, Sun. 1400, US$3 1st, US$1.60 2nd. Sit on left side for the best views.

**Air Service** Jorge Wilstermann airport. Airport bus is Micro B from Plaza 14 de Septiembre, taxis about US$2 (no set rates, so bargain). Daily by LAB to and from **La Paz** (½ hour), 15 kg. baggage allowance), book early for morning flights, and to **Santa Cruz** (½ hour). Three flights a week to **Sucre** and **Tarija**, also to **Trinidad** (connects with Riberalta flight). LAB in town at Ayacucho and Heroínas, open 0800; at airport LAB office opens 0500. TAM (Hamiraya 122, nr. Av. Heroínas) to La Paz; flights to **Riberalta** US$100, but infrequent; best to fly from La Paz or Santa Cruz, via Trinidad.

**Bus Services** Buses (overnight) and colectivos (day and night) to **Santa Cruz**, taking 10-12 hrs, US$6; the road goes via Villa Tunari, Puerto Villarroel, Buena Vista and Montero, a more northerly and lowland alternative to the mountain road via Epizana. The new route is through cocaine country so there are many checkpoints. To/from **La Paz** via Oruro (0800, 1000 and 1300 with Nobleza—offices on Calle Aroma, and about a dozen others, US$4-5, 8-11 hrs., over a terrifying road (but good surface for all but 1½ hours), you have to change buses in Oruro and get a new ticket at the same time on a different floor, luggage is automatically transferred to the new bus; or via Caracollo, by night or by day, 10-12 hours. The road to La Paz via Caracollo is paved all the way except for 50 kms. just after Caracollo. Bus to **Oruro**, US$5, 5-6 hrs. To **Potosí**, via Oruro. Daily to **Sucre**, by Flota Minera, Aroma 120, Flotas Bolívar, Unificada, Azul or Mopar—free drink and videos, rec., between 1800 and 1830, 12 hours, US$7, all but the first 2 hours are very bad; many other companies, most run night buses. To Sucre by day; take a bus or truck to Aiquile (bus every other day 1300), spend the night there, then take a truck to Sucre. There are 3 bus stations: along Av. Aroma, near Plaza San Sebastián, for long-distance bus offices; Av. 6 de Agosto y San Martín, near **La Coronilla** for local buses to **Tarata**, **Punata** and **Clisa**; Av. Oquendo (at the edge of Lake Alalay) to **Villa Tunari**, US$3.50; **Chimoré**, US$4.50; **Eterazama**, US$4.50; **Puerto Villarroel**, US$6; **Puerto San Francisco**, US$5; and other destinations—all leave 0800-1000 if sufficient passengers. Trucks to Oruro leave from Plaza San Sebastián. Trucks to Sucre leave from end of Av. San Martín (US$3.30). Trucks to Puerto Villarroel from Av. República, US$3.30.

**Excursions** To the N, in a high fault-block range of mountains, is Cerro Tunari, 5,180 metres. A road runs to within 300 metres of the top, usually sprinkled with a little snow. There are beautiful views of the Cochabamba valley from the mountain road which goes into the Parque Tunari from Cala Cala, ending at the lake which supplies drinking water; best in the afternoon, but no public transport.

Another somewhat difficult mountain road to the north, with little local traffic, climbs from Tiquipaya (take bus No. 12 from Cochabamba, US$0.15) to Chapisicca. Trucks leave Mon., and Thur., returning Tues. and Fri. with potatoes and wool for the Cochabamba market. Beautiful views on the ascent: good walks on the plateau to mountain lakes in lovely scenery.

**The Cochabamba basin**, dotted with several small townships, is the largest grain and fruit producing area in Bolivia. *Quillacollo* (20,000 people), a 20 minute bus ride from Av. 6 de Agosto y San Martín, just beyond the markets in Cochabamba (good Sunday market but no tourist items; the *campesinos* do not like being photographed). Fiesta de la Virgen de Urkupiña lasts 4 days with much dancing and religious ceremony (designed to make you rich), its date varies each year between June and August; very interesting, plenty of transport from Cochabamba. 2-3 km. beyond Quillacollo is a road to the beautiful Pairumani *hacienda*, centre of the Patiño agricultural foundation. The house may be visited (T 60082 to arrange visit, open Mon.-Fri. 1500-1600, Bus 7 or 38 from Cochabamba); the Patiño mausoleum may be visited if one is accompanied by a member of the family. Don't miss *Tarata*, a sleepy village with beautiful Plaza, nearby, and interesting church and convent on top of hill. Large procession on 3 May, day of Santa Cruz, with fireworks and brass band. Market day Thursday (bus also from Av. 6 de Agosto, US$0.50). *Punata*, an hour's bus ride from Cochabamba, has an interesting, lively market on Tuesday. Behind the main church, new vehicles are lined up to be blessed by the priest. The local speciality is *garapiña*, a mixture of *chicha* and icecream. Beyond Punata, at Villa Rivera, woven wall hangings are produced. Another 6 km. from Tarata is Huayculi, the population of which consists almost entirely of potters, who produce good ceramics for the Cochabamba market. Several houses may be visited to see the kilns and painting areas. Pick-up trucks sometimes run between Tarata and Arami, via Clisa and Punata, but no other public transport available. There is a large Sunday market at *Clisa*, accessible by bus from Av. 6 de Agosto. For those interested in *charangos* (of wood) a visit to Aiquile (6 hrs.) is recommended (by bus US$3.50; *Hotel Escudo*, F, basic). A railway runs from Cochabamba, through the Punata valley, as far as Aiquile. To the north is the Parque Tunari, which is partly forested, and Laguna Wara Wara at 4,000 metres surrounded by 4,500 metre mountains.

Ursula Kohlendorfer, from Gunskirchen, Austria, recommends a visit to *Tortoro*, a small village 120 km. from Cochabamba, set amid beautiful rocky landscape. Dinosaur tracks (fossilised?) can be seen by the stream just outisde the village. Ask at Santiago, the only shop, for the key to the Umjalanta cave, about 6 km. NW of Torotoro; a guide is necessary. Trucks go to Torotoro from Av. República y Pinta, near the market in Cochabamba, at 0600 daily, or a truck also goes from the market at Clisa at about 0800. Trucks return to Cochabamba every Monday and Friday, approx. 8 hrs. Take your own food as only drinks are sold at the shop. No accommodation, but ask the priest to find somewhere to sleep.

The *Inka-Rakay* ruins are near the village of Sipe-Sipe; the main attraction is the view from the site over the Cochabamba valley, as well as the mountains ringing the ruins. Take a bus to Quillacollo where the bus for Sipe-Sipe waits until there are enough passengers, shared *trufi* taxis also go, more frequently than the buses. *Trufi* No. 145 returns direct from Sipe-Sipe to Cochabamba. From Sipe-Sipe to the ruins there is either a 4 km. footpath, or a 12 km. road with almost no traffic, which, to walk, takes three to four hours. Either hitch or hire guides and Land Rover in Cochabamba. Several letters indicate that it might be less terrifying to walk but all admit that this is a beautiful trip. Start early for it is a full day. Leave the Square at Sipe Sipe going up the street past the church, then left at the top and then right when you come to the wider road. Follow this road to the ridge ahead. Just below the ridge, the road loses a little height to take a bend. There is an outcrop of rock and here look for a track leading away downhill. The Inka-Rakay ruins are about 200 metres below. **N.B.** Take food and plenty of water as there is none available and beware of theft on the footpath.

The 500-km. road via the mountains and Epizana to Santa Cruz (**page 264**) has been newly paved. Before the Siberia pass, 5 km. beyond Montepunco at Pocona

(Km. 119), the 23-km. road to **Inkallajta** (unpaved and very bad) turns off. The Inca ruins, on a flat spur of land at the mouth of a steep valley, are extensive and the temple is said to have been the largest roofed Inca building. To get there without your own transport a reader advises: "Take a micro to the checkpoint 10 km. from Cochabamba, take a truck to Km. 122, walk on towards Pocona or take a truck for 12 km. A large yellow sign indicates the trail. After approx. 10 km. the trail divides, take the downhill path and the ruins are a further 2 km. Take food and camping gear". At Km. 386 are the ruins of Samaipata, worth a stop (see page **269**). At **Epizana**, a lovely dilapidated colonial village, 13 km. beyond Montepunco (Km. 128), with poor hotels and service stations, a branch road, right—dusty, stony, and narrow in parts, but very scenic—goes 233 km. to Sucre, 7-8 hours drive. Totora, described as one of the loveliest sleepy, friendly colonial villages, is said to be better to stay in than Epizana, with two hotels and restaurants.

S of Oruro the railway from La Paz skirts Lake Poopó, over 90 km. long and 32 km. wide. From Río Mulato a branch line runs eastwards to Potosí (174 km.) and Sucre. The track reaches the height of 4,786 metres at Cóndor: one of the highest points on the world's railway lines.

**Potosí** (pop. 110,000), stands at 4,070 metres, the highest city of its size in the world. The climate is often bitterly cold and fireplaces are few; warm clothes essential. It was founded by the Spaniards on 10 April 1545, after they had discovered Indian mine workings at Cerro Rico, the hill at whose foot it stands.

Immense amounts of silver were once extracted from this hill. In Spain "éste es un Potosí" (it's a Potosí) is still used for anything superlatively rich. Early in the 17th century Potosí had a population of 113,380, but two centuries later, as its lodes began to deteriorate and silver had been found in Peru and Mexico, Potosí became little more than a ghost town. It was the demand for tin—a metal the Spaniards ignored—that lifted the city to comparative prosperity again. Silver, copper and lead are also mined. A new seam of silver has been discovered recently.

Large parts of Potosí are colonial, with twisting, narrow streets and an occasional great mansion with its coat of arms over the doorway. UNESCO has declared the city to be "Patrimonio de la Humanidad." Some of the best buildings are grouped round the Plaza 10 de Noviembre, the main square. The Convent of Santa Teresa (entry US$1.50, opening times vary, check at Tourist Office) has an interesting collection of colonial and religious art, but be prepared to listen to the obligatory guide explaining each and every item. The old Cabildo and the Royal Treasury—Las Cajas Reales—are both here, converted to other uses. The Cathedral (open only between 0900 and 1000 on Sundays) faces the square, and near-by is the Mint—the Casa Real de Moneda (founded 1572, rebuilt 1759)—one of the chief monuments of civil building in Hispanic America. The Moneda (entrance US$1, US$3.50 to take photos), has a museum in many sections. The main art gallery is in a splendid salon on the first floor: the salon better than the paintings. Elsewhere are coin dies and huge wooden presses which made the silver strip from which coins were cut. You are advised to wear warm clothes, as it is cold inside; a guided tour (essential) starts at 0900 and 1400. The smelting houses have carved altar pieces from Potosí's ruined churches. Open Mon.-Sat. 0900-1200 and 1400-1700. Among Potosí's baroque churches, typical of the Andean or "mestizo" architecture of the 18th century, are the Compañía (Jesuit) church, with an impressive bell-gable (1700), San Francisco with a fine organ (monastery closed to visitors, church can be visited in morning and evening, worthwhile for the views from the tower and roof, museum of ecclesiastical art, open 1400-1600, Mon.-Fri.), and San Lorenzo, with a rich portal (1728-1744); fine views from the tower. San Martín, with an uninviting exterior, is beautiful inside, but normally closed for fear of theft. Ask the German Redemptorist Fathers to show you around; their office is just to the left of their church. Other churches

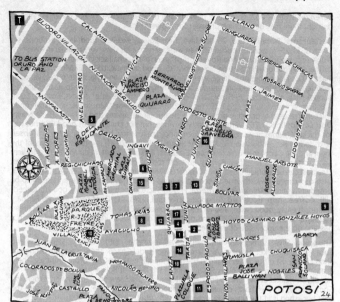

POTOSÍ 24

---

**Potosí: Key to Map**

1. Plaza 10 de Noviembre, 2. Plaza 6 de Agosto, 3. Plazuela Daniel Campos, 4. Cathedral, 5. Jerusalén, 6. San Lorenzo, 7. San Agustín, 8. La Compañia, 9. San Martín, 10. Convent of Santa Teresa, 11. Convent of San Francisco, 12. Casa Real de Moneda, 13. University Museum, 14. Alcaldía, 15. Central Market, 16. Handicrafts Market, 17. Tourist Office, 18. Post Office

to visit include Jerusalén, close to the *Hotel Centenario*, and San Agustín (only by prior arrangement with tourist office) on Bolívar, with crypts and catacombs. Tour starts at 1700, US$0.10 admission. From San Cristóbal, at Pacheco y Cañete, one gets a fine view over the whole city. The University has a museum with some good modern Bolivian painting (Mon.-Fri., 1000-1200, 1500-1700, entrance US$1).

**Festival** San Barolomé, end August, costumes for hire in artesanía market on Calle Sucre.

**Hotels** Best hotel is *Hostal Colonial*, Hoyos 8, C/D, a pretty colonial house (T 24265) near the main plaza, rec., has names and T numbers of guides, even if you're not staying there. *Turista*, Lanza 19 (T 22492), also LAB office, D, helpful, now remodelled, but no heating, and hot showers only in the morning, breakfast (US$1 only) highly rec. *Residencial Sumaj*, Gumiel 12, T 23336, F, small but warm rooms, double rooms on top floor good, with windows and views, mixed reports, good breakfast. *Hotel IV Centenario*, Plaza del Estudiante, T 22751, E, hot water all day, large rooms, comfortable, good restaurant, friendly, highly rec.; *Santa María*, Av. Serrudo 244, T 23255, D, clean, hot water; *Casa de Huéspedes*, San Agustín, 1st floor, opp. Hidalgo Tours, E with bath, clean, *Hotel Carlos V*, Linares 42, E, friendly, breakfast extra, rec.; *Alojamiento Ferrocarril*, Av. E. Villazón 159, F, basic, uncomfortable beds but clean (no hot water but hot showers available for US$0.55), friendly, close to the railway station. The best cheap lodgings (for which Potosí has a bad reputation) between Av. Oruro and Av. Serrudo, clean, but rarely with hot water; *Alojamiento Tumusla* (avoid ground floor—cold), near the bus station, F, grubby; *Hostal Oruro*, Oruro 292, F, shared shower, clean and basic; *Alojamiento La Paz*, Oruro 242, F p.p., hot shower US$0.50, clean, pleasant, washing facilities; *Residencial Copacabana*, Serrudo 319, T 27112, F, shared room, restaurant, dirty bathrooms, unfriendly, safe car park; *Villa Imperial*, dirty, noisy, same prices, good motorcycle parking, US$0.20 for hot shower. *Alojamiento San*

*Lorenzo*, Bustillos 967, G, close to market, very basic, no shower or hot water. In times of drought there may be rationing of water for showers etc.

**Restaurants** *Sumaj Orcko*, 25 de Mayo, near Bolívar, excellent food, large portions, set lunch US$1.25, reasonably priced Chilean wine, service a bit slow, very popular in evenings, highly rec., friendly; *Confitería Royal*, just off main plaza, small selection of good cakes and coffee; *El Aldabón*, Plaza 10 de Noviembre 35, good set meal, US$1; *El Mesón*, corner of Plaza 10 de Noviembre near Tarija, irregular opening, European-style, quite pricey, variously reported as excellent, and pretentious; *La Salteña*, Linares 20, rec, cheap, tasty *salteñas*, good service, also pizzas. *El Farol*, Tarija 28, coffee and "interesting" snacks; *Bolívar*, Sucre y Bolívar, 4 course lunch US$1.25, rec.; also on Sucre, pedestrian street, is *Cristal*, good chicken, reasonably priced. Cakes and ice creams along Linares and in Plaza 25 de Mayo. *Don Lucho*, Bolívar 765, large and tasty servings, but not cheap, meat good (but not rec. for chicken), *peñas* at weekends, check entrance fee for show before eating. *Peña Marisel*, next door is rec., shows on Fri. *The Sky Room* at Bolívar 701 has interesting views of the town and the Cerro, mediocre food. *Los Escudos*, Bolívar 853, set menu and á la Carte, very good, often rec. *Snack bar Bamby*, just off top of main square, good cheap lunches. Breakfast can be a difficult meal to find, but it is available in the Mercado Central, Calle Bolívar (also other meals): worthwhile to see if the hotel serves it as most restaurants seem to be closed at this time. *Alemana Confitería*, Hoyo y Sucre (opp. tourism kiosk), good (but check bill); *Coffee Shop*, Boulevard 20, good coffee and cakes and *Confitería Cherys*, Padilla y Linares, friendly, good cakes, also an unnamed place at Calle Mattos 30. To get fresh bread you have to be up at 0630-0700 and go to Bustillos between Ingavi and Oniste and up a passage on the upper side of the street.

**Shopping** Silver (sometimes containing nickel) and native cloth. Silver coins, jewellery and coca leaves in market between Av. Camacho and H. del Chaco. There is an interesting gift shop in the post office. Silver is sold in the main market near the Calle Oruro entrance. There is an informal swap market every Friday night at the Plaza, at Bolívar and Quijarro. There is a handicraft market at the junction of Calle Sucre and Plaza Saavedra (rec) but very expensive. Some Fridays the merchants organize music, food and drink (*ponche*), not to be missed. The best bookshop is at the University, open Mon.-Fri., 1000-1200, 1500-1700.

**Local Transport** Taxi within city limits US$0.30; approx US$0.50/km. for longer journeys. Buses US$0.10.

**Car Spares** VW spares are obtainable at Hauwa Ltd, but it takes several days to get parts from La Paz.

**Exchange** Ask at Tourist Office. Street changers around Oruro 430; also shops and restaurants around main plaza and on Bolívar between Sucre and Junín. Amex cheques may be changed at Hidalgo Tours, Junín y Bolívar (2% commission). Morales, Bertram y Schuett, Matos 19, and Distribuidora Cultural Sud, Bolívar 876, both change travellers cheques.

**Clinic** Clínica Británica, on Oruro near *Alojamiento La Paz*, clinics a.m. and p.m. English spoken, US$6.

**Sauna** Bath and showers in Calle Nogales. Sauna Florida, Plaza Chuquimina, near bus station, open Thurs. and Fri., US$1.50.

**Laundry** *Limpieza la Veloz*, Calle Quijarro, corner of Matos, Edificio Cademin, US$1.3 per kilo.

**Post Office** Lanza and Chuquisaca; unreliable for overseas mail.

**Police station** On Plaza 10 de Noviembre.

**Tourist Agents** Potosí Tours, corner of Padilla, on the Plaza, good tours of the city and mine (see below); Candelaria Tours, Bolívar 634, T 22458 and Tursul Ltda, Calle San Alberto, 24, T 21360. See also under **Excursions** below.

**Tourist Office** On 2nd Floor, Cámara de Minería, Calle Quijarro (T 25288). ½ block from main plaza, and booth on main plaza (both closed Sat. and Sun.); sells town maps (US$0.25), information booklet (US$2.50), helpful.

**Trains** To La Paz, *ferrobus*: book previous day only: once/twice a week, 0800, Tues., 10½ hrs., US$12 Pullman, US$8 special; express train once a week: Thurs., 2050, 13 hrs., US$5.75 Pullman, US$4 special (from La Paz, *ferrobus* Mon. 1910, express Thur. 1720). To Sucre, *ferrobus* two or three times a week, US$4.50 Pullman, US$3 special, *mixto*, Sat. 1400, 7 hrs., US$2.70. To Oruro, 8 hrs., *ferrobus* and express US$3.75 Pullman, US$2.25 special, with connection to Cochabamba.

To **Calama** for Antofagasta, take the bus to Uyuni daily between 1000 and 1400 from Villa Imperial, Toledo 216, off Av. Antofagasta where it crosses the railway, US$5, or there's a microbus on Wed. from about 50 metres from the station, US$6 (buy ticket night before or early same day and arrive in good time for the bus) and connect with the La Paz-Antofagasta train/bus route on Wed. or Fri. night. Alternatively, take the Tues. *ferrobus* to Oruro then book Pullman on train to Calama; fares can be paid in bolivianos. To Villazón, go to Uyuni and connect with La Paz-Villazón train there. Apparently there is a Sunday train as far as Tupiza, but little information at the station; it should take 18 hrs. but may be 24 hrs. late.

**Buses** Bus station out of town, on Av. Universitaria, below railway station and 20 minute walk (or *micros* L, I or L) from main Plaza; through buses from La Paz call here at the toll gate, as they are not allowed to enter city limits. To **Tarija**, 10 de Noviembre, Fri. and Sun. 0830, very poor buses; Tarija is reached by car or lorry leaving Plaza Minero (Bus "A"), full range of scenery. To **Villazón**, daily at 0800 1700 and 1900, 12 hrs., shop around for best price. To **Cochabamba**, 1800 daily, US$9. To **Sucre**, Soltrans, Quijarro 34, just off Plaza 10 de Noviembre, US$5, several daily, 5½ hrs., first at 0700; also Hidalgo (minibus), Bolívar y Junín, 0700, 1830, 4 hrs., US$5 incl. snack. **La Paz** (12 hrs., overnight only in either direction, US$9.50) leaves 1800 daily. **Oruro**, US$4.50, 8 hours. To **Uyuni**, Villa Imperial, Mon., Wed., Thur. at 1300. Trucks for **Tarabuco** leave from Plaza San Francisco. Heavy overbooking reported on buses, also, timetables change frequently; the trucks from the plaza are an alternative if you are in a hurry.

**Airport** under construction.

A suggested tour round the town is to walk down Quijarro from San Agustín on Bolívar as far as Oniste then return by Junín, looking at "the passage of the seven turns" on the way. There is a fine stone doorway (house of the Marqués de Otavi) in Junín between Matos and Bolívar. Calle Lanza 8 (now a school) was the house of José de Quiroz and of Antonio López de Quiroga. Along Millares between Chuquisaca and Nogales one sees on the right a sculpted stone doorway and on the left a doorway with two rampant lions in low relief on the lintel. Turning left up Nogales one comes to an old mansion in a little square. Turn left along La Paz and three blocks along there is another stone doorway with suns in relief. At the corner with Bolívar is the Casa del Balcón de la Horca. Turn left and one comes to the Casa de las Tres Portadas.

**Excursions** A 4½ hr. morning tour to the cooperative mines and ore-processing plant involves meeting miners and seeing them at work in conditions described as "like stepping back into the nineteenth century"; a contribution to the miners' cooperative is appreciated, take cigarettes and coca leaves as presents. If visiting the mines, wear old clothes and take a good torch and a handkerchief to filter the dusty air, visitors need to be reasonably fit; not recommended for claustrophobics or asthmatics. A longstanding guide is Eduardo Garnica Fajardo, Hernández 1035, Casilla 33, T 24708; he speaks English, French and some Hebrew. Another guide is Salustio Gallardo, Calle Betanzos 231, near Plaza Minero; also Braulio Mamani (T 23396/25786, and through Potosí Tours), to Mina Rosario; he speaks a little English. Juan Carlos González, Av. Japón 10, T 24074 or 26740/25591 (Agencia Hidalgo), takes small groups to private mines, Spanish spoken only. Marco Mamani, T 25375, Calle A. Pacheco 60, a little English spoken. More interesting than a visit to the State mine, which is now automated (visits daily at 0900, take microbus 100 from main square; rubber boots, lamp, helmet and jacket included in price). The price of tours to the mines is regulated at US$5 p.p. Some groups amount to 20-30 people, which is excessive for the small tunnels. It also seems that consideration for the miners is dwindling, leading to resentment.

A recommended Sunday trip is to Manquiri, a sanctuary in the mountains. Wait from 0730 at Garita de San Roque or at Plaza Uyuni for a truck. Another trip is to Caiza on the fork off the Tarija road at Ingeniero Cucho; for this you will need a tent, etc., as there is no hotel. Only one bus a day from Potosí: it should leave from Plaza del Minero at 1330 but is often late. Caiza is where cooperatives produce handicrafts in tin. Their Caiza outlet is the Belgian Catholic Agricultural School in the main square. Cheap *mantas* and other hand woven goods can be purchased at villages betweeen Challatapa and Potosí, on the road from Oruro along Lake Poopó. At Betanzos (1 hour on the Sucre road, well-paved for last 17 km.), the Feria de Papas is held within the first two weeks of May: folk dances, music and costumes, (buses from Plaza Uyuni, Potosí).

Some agencies offer trips to the great salt lakes, Laguna Colorada and Laguna Verdi, but we have received information that it would be better to organize a visit at Uyuni (see page **254**), as too much time is lost on the journey to and from Potosí; also, safety arrangements and equipment are often deficient, check first.

**Thermal Baths**  at lake below city. Laguna de Tarapaya, Miraflores truck or van from Plaza Chuquimina; above Tarapaya is the crater, which is reached by a track from 23 Km. point. When bathing take great care as the current is very strong; whirlpools can develop, which have claimed many lives. There are buses back from Tarapaya at 1400 and 1600. A good place to spend a lazy day resting. Also Chaqui (by truck or bus from Plaza Uyuni, tiring journey, but clean, pleasant baths), Tora and San Diego (on the main road to Sucre, it also has a restaurant). Alternatively there is a thermal pool 1 km. before the village on the other side of the river. It is best to get off bus at the bridge 400 metres on the Potosí side of the river and pool.

Hallam Murray writes: One of the most interesting and varied mountain walks I have experienced in Bolivia can be made from Potosí. It takes 8 hours at a gentle pace and covers about 24 km. (map Hoja 6435, serie H631, from Instituto Geográfico Militar is helpful but not essential). Take Av. Hoyos east out of Plaza Alonso Ibáñez and continue beyond the Iglesia San Martín. Follow the road or path south east for Laguna San Ildefonso (you climb the hill above the city). Ask directions if in doubt. This lake was built in 1767 to provide water for the city and is in a wonderful position. It has duck, and fish deep down in the clear water. Beyond, to the east, are some very inviting-looking, lumpy hills and mountains. Follow up the valley, passing herds of llama and old mine openings. It is probably best to start on the path to the south east of the lake (to right). This valley is full of fascinating plants, animals, and rock formations.

Continue beyond a second unnamed, and possibly dried-up lake and turn south to climb steeply to the adjoining valley, just beyond the peak of Cerro Masoni. The time from Plaza Alonso Ibáñez to the highest point between the two valleys is 4 hours. The views from this point are spectacular, with mountain peaks to the south towards Argentina. Closer at hand is moon-like scenery. This is an excellent spot for a picnic. Continue down and back to Potosí via the small lake which can be seen from the high point. Probably best to keep high to the left (south) of Lagunas San Sebastián and to approach Cerro Rico on its eastern flank. The walk back into Potosí is depressing and bleak, passing miners' houses, close to a heavily polluted stream and with the most extensively worked face of Cerro Rico to your left, but this is a side of Bolivia which should also be seen. Some feedback on this walk: "great, but beware of altitude effects, Cerro Masoni is at 4,920 metres above sea-level".

**_Sucre_**, (pop. 112,000) the official capital of Bolivia, is reached from Potosí (175 km.) by train (a grand trip) or by road (the best _dirt_ road in Bolivia). A branch road runs to it from Epizana on the old Cochabamba-Santa Cruz highway. The altitude is 2,790 metres, and the climate is mild (mean temperature 12°C, but sometimes 24°C in November-December and 7°C in June).

Sucre (originally Charcas) was founded in 1538. Long isolation has helped it to preserve its courtly charm; local law now requires all buildings to be painted original colonial white. Public buildings are impressive. Opening times are as reported but seem to be variable. Be prepared to get frustrated. Among these are the Casa de la Libertad (open 0900-1200 and 1400-1700, Sats., 0900-1200, US$0.50, US$1 to take photographs), where the country's Declaration of Independence was signed; the modern Corte Suprema de Justicia, the seat of Bolivia's judiciary, R. Moreno y Ravelo (entry free but must leave passport with guard, no photographs allowed); the modern Palacio de Gobierno; the beautiful 17th century Cathedral, open 0730-0915, and museum (US$0.25), open 1000-1200 and 1500-1700 (1000-1200, Sat.) (worth seeing are the Chapel of the famous jewel-encrusted Virgin of Guadalupe, 1601—closed in 1989, and the monstrance and other church jewels by appointment with the Padre Tesorero); the Consistorial building; the Teatro Gran Mariscal de Ayacucho and Colegio Junín. Sucre University was founded in 1624. Early 17th century wooden ceilings (_alfarjes_) with intricate patterns of Moorish origin are found in San Miguel (see below) and San Francisco (0700-0930 and 1600-1930).

Behind the town a road flanked by Stations of the Cross ascends an attractive hill, Cerro Churuquella, with large eucalyptus trees on its flank, to a statue of

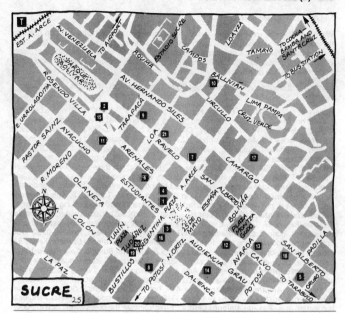

## Sucre: Key to map

*Public Buildings:* 1. Casa de la Libertad, 2. Corte Suprema de Justicia. *Churches:* 3. Cathedral, 4. San Miguel, 5. San Lázaro, 6. Santa Mónica, 7. San Francisco, 8. San Felipe Neri, 9. Santa Rita, 10. San Sebastián, 11. Santa Bárbara, 12. Santo Domingo, 13. Santa Clara. *Museums:* 14. Charcas, Anthropology & Modern Art, 15. Teatro Mariscal de Ayacucho. *Services:* 16. Post Office, 17. Entel —communications, 18. Tourist Office, 19. LAB, 20. *Hostal Sucre,* 21. Central Market.

Christ at the top. There is also a *mirador* in the square opposite La Recoleta, at the end of Calle Dalence. The cemetery is worth a visit, to see mausoleums of presidents and other famous people; take Calle Junín south to its end, 7-8 blocks from main plaza.

**Churches** **San Miguel,** recently restored (open 1800-2000), is very beautiful with carved and painted ceilings, pure-white walls and gold and silver altar. In the Baptistery there is a painting by Viti, the first great painter of the New World, who studied under Raphael. In the Sacristy are another of his paintings and some early sculpture. It was from San Miguel that Jesuit missionaries went south to convert Argentina, Uruguay and Paraguay. **San Felipe Neri,** church and monastery, attractive courtyard with cloisters. Roof gives view of city; open 1630-1700, US$0.50 entrance. Entrance requires a guide from Universidad de Turismo office, opposite the convent, at N. Ortiz 182. **Santa Mónica** (Arenales with Junín) is perhaps one of the finest gems of Spanish architecture in the Americas, note the main altar and pulpit in filigree (closed in 1987, but the ex-convent—now a school—can be visited). **San Francisco** in Calle Ravelo has altars coated in gold leaf; the bell is the one that summoned the people of Sucre to struggle for independence. **Capilla de la Rotonda** (Av. L. Cabrera, near the station), **Santa Rita, San Sebastián** and **Sta. Bárbara** (Plaza Pizarro). **Santo Domingo,** corner of Calvo and Bolívar (1545), open only Fridays and Sunday night. Next door at Calvo 212 is the **Santa Clara museum** with art gallery and silver collection (see below), and **Church of San Lázaro,** built in 1538 and regarded as the first cathedral of La Plata (Sucre). On the nave walls are six paintings attributed to Zurbarán; it has fine silverwork and alabaster in the Baptistery, open 0700-0745 Sat., and Sun. after church service at 1900. **La Merced** (Azurduy and Pérez) has gilded altar pieces.

**Warning** Police all wear uniform and carry I.D. cards with photographs. Insist on going to the police station, if possible with a witness, before showing passport or money to anyone without these credentials. Common targets are lone tourists who don't speak Spanish; places where scams frequently occur are Recoleta and Santa Clara. If in doubt call 110 radio patrol or the tourist office (see below).

**Festival** Independence celebrations, 24-26 May, most services, museums and restaurants closed.

**Hotels** Best hotel is *Hostal Cruz de Popayán*, Loa 881, T 25156/31706, C, rec., a beautiful colonial house with interior courtyard, no heating, good breakfast served in rooms; *Colonial*, Plaza 25 de Mayo, T 24709/254807, C, expensive but rec. for good breakfast; *Hostal Libertad*, Arce y San Alberto, 1st floor, T 23101/2, clean, spacious and comfortable rooms, friendly and efficient, highly rec.; near station, *Municipal*, Av. Venezuela, C (T 21074), rec., restaurant; *Hostal Sucre*, 3 stars, Bustillos 113, T 21411/31928, D, good, clean, rec.; *Hostal los Pinos*, Colón 502, T 24403/32212, clean, comfortable, hot showers, D. *Londres*, Av. H. Siles 949, T 24792, 3 blocks uphill from station, D with shower, restaurant, good ; and opposite, *Residencial Avenida*, No. 942, F, hot showers, breakfast, laundry, friendly and helpful; *Residencial Bolivia*, near plaza in Calle San Alberto, T 24346, E, with dangerous electric showers, hot water, noisy, breakfast included (clothes washing, cooking not allowed); *Residencial Oriental*, Calle San Alberto 9, E, clean, friendly but basic, hot water; *Residencial Charcas*, Ravelo 62, T 23972, E with or without bath, first floor very noisy, clean, helpful, opp. market, laundry, rec.; *Alojamiento El Turista*, Ravelo 118, F, clean, showers, 0700-1100 only, friendly, good meeting place for long-term travellers; *Alojamiento La Plata*, Ravelo 32, F, clean, central, opp. market, hot showers, rec.; *Residencial Bustillo*, Calle Ravelo 158, F, overpriced, clean and modern, hot water, shared showers, will store luggage at a price; *Alojamiento San Francisco*, esq. Av. Arce and Camargo, bath or shower, E with breakfast and bath, pleasant, meals available, recently redecorated and improved, safe motocycle parking, rec.; *Alojamiento Abaroa*, Loa 419, hot showers (electric), clean, good value; *Alojamiento Austria*, Av. Ostria Gutiérrez 33, E, hot showers, good value, restaurant, near bus station as well as *Alojamiento Central*, E, rec. (beware the buses which stop at 2000). Many cheap and basic places opp. central market.

**Restaurants** *Piso Cero*, Venezuela 241, good but expensive; *Las Vegas* on east side of Plaza (icecream, no breakfast, at lunchtime no drink without food, good evening meals); *Pizzería Napoletana*, on Plaza, excellent pizzas (evenings only) and good home-made ice cream; *Pecos Bill Pizza*, Bustillos, between plaza and *Hostal Sucre*, one of the few places open all day from about 1000, rec. The *Alliance Française*, Aniceto Arce 35, 1/2 block from main square, serves crêpes, ratatouille (rec.) Mon. to Fri. 1100-1300, 1600-2000, soft music etc—also occasional films and cultural events; good breakfast at *Leblon*, Aniceto Arce 99, opp. San Francisco church. *Las Tablitas*, Bustillo 198 esq. Colón, good lunches. *Mesón de don Enrique*, N. Ortiz, good; other places along Ortiz, near Plaza 25 de Mayo, are *Snack Paulista* (no. 14), no food but excellent fruit juices and milk shakes, and *Bibliocafé Sureña* (No. 30), good pasta, coffee and crêpes, "bohemian", with English and German magazines, closed Monday, and next door (No. 34-38), *Hawaii*, excellent set lunch, good food, not cheap but very pleasant; *Kultor-Café Berlin*, Avaroa 326, good food, German newspapers, peña every other Friday, closed Sunday (in same building as Instituto Cultural Boliviano Alemán—ICBA); and the *Humboldt Café*, Av. Junín 726, is also German run, with good German pastries. *Palace*, Plaza 25 de Mayo 38, good, reasonably priced; also on the plaza, *Confitería Palet*, good coffee and pastries, and *El Recreo*, Calvo 25, one block from the square, good lunches for US$1. *Los Bajos*, Loa 761, serves delicious sausages, daytime only. *Doña Máxima*, Junín 411, usually only cold food; *El Solar*, Bolívar 800, good but expensive and no prices written on menus (Sun. closed); *Snack Miriam*, España 67, good salteñas; *Snack Anni*, Avaroa y Bolivia, for the best empanadas. Foodstores in the new market, highly rec., serve clean cheap meals for US$1 until 1400. Good vegetarian food in Chinese restaurant opp. market. Good chicken and chips cafés on Camango between Arce and Loa. Typical of many Bolivian cities, not many restaurants open for breakfast, but there are many fruit juice and snack stalls in the market (No.21 on map). The local brewery produces an interesting sweetish porter or stout. *Café Hacheh*, Pastor Sainz 241, coffee bar and art gallery near university, interesting to visit. The local chocolate Toablada, is recommended.

**Shopping** Antique woven items must be sought. Permanent market along Av. Jaime Mendoza, for food and household goods. There is a wide selection in Calle Argentina, opposite Post Office, and *Coinca*, Loa 616, and *Candelaria* at Bolívar 634 (expensive).

*Artesanías Calcha*, Calle Hernando Siles 713, rec., very knowledgeable proprietor. *ASUR* project shop, San Alberto 413, T 32194, weavings from North Potosí and Tarabuco at very good prices, rec. Good selection in arcade at Junín 403. Doña Máxima can be found at the *Alojamiento Guadalupe*, Junín 411, opp. Central Market; she will take you to an Alladdin's Cave of superb weavings and textiles, upstairs 2 doors away; best to know what you're looking for, not especially cheap. *Charangos* from Tarabuco are obtainable in the main plaza. Prices for souvenir items tend to be much higher than in La Paz.

**Taxis** US$0.30 p.p. within city limits.

**Motor-cycle Mechanic** Sr Jaime Medina, Motorservi Honda, Calle René Calvo Arana, T 25484. Will service all makes of machine.

**Folklore** Centro Cultural Masis aims to promote traditional culture. It offers instruction in Quechua, traditional Bolivian music making and handicrafts; once or twice a week there are musical events and the snack bar holds exhibitions of textiles and photographs. Open 1530-2130. The director, Roberto Sahonero, who will give further details, is to be found at Bolívar 561 DS (T 23403, Casilla 463); he is usually at the centre Mon., Wed. and Fri., 1900.

**Museums** These include the University's anthropological, folkloric, and colonial collections at the **Charcas Museum** (Bolívar 700), and its presidential and modern-art galleries (open until 1800). The **Museo de Santa Clara** (Calle Calvo 212), displays paintings and musical instruments. The **Museo de la Recoleta** (Calle Pedro de Anzúrez, open in theory 0930-1130 and 1500-1730 US$0.50 for entrance to all collections) is at the Recoleta monastery, on a hill above the town, notable for the beauty of its cloisters and gardens; the carved wooden choirstalls in the chapel (upstairs) are especially fine. The **Glorieta mansion** (now very neglected), with the Princesa collection (leaflet available from tourist office), 5 km. outside the city bus E on the road to Potosí, has beautiful painted ceilings and Arabian gardens; worth a visit: "a delightful mixture of many styles", open Mon.-Fri. 0900-1200 and 1400-1800. It is in the military compound, passports must be surrendered at the gate, do not cross the river. **Museo de Historia Natural**, Calle San Alberto 156, opened in March 1990, "excellent" (open Tues.-Fri. 0830-1130/1400-1730).

**Exchange** **Banco del Estado**, no exchange facilities; **Banco Nacional**, cash only at a poor rate. **Banco Santa Cruz**, Calle España will change cash and travellers' cheques and give bolivianos on Visa card transactions. Travel agencies' rates are good and at **casa de cambio** on corner of Calvo y Plaza Monteagudo. **Ambar**, *casa de cambio*, San Alberto 7, T 31339, good rates, travellers cheques (US$ only) cashed at 1.5% commission. Most shops and hotels will change money. Street changers on Hernando Siles/Camargo between España and Junín.

**Cultural Institutes** The Goethe Institute shows films, has German newspapers and books to lend (1030-1230 and 1700-2000), runs English, Spanish and Quechua courses and its bar is a good meeting place. Instituto Cultural Boliviano Alemán (ICBA), Avaroa 326, offers courses in Spanish and Quechua and in various dance forms at reasonable prices (US$10 for 12 lessons, twice a week for 6 weeks), term dates variable. The ICBA also run a folk music *peña* on Fridays.

**Consulates** West German, Arenales 215 (T 21862). Spain, Pasaje Argandoña (T 21435); Italy, Defensa 33 (T 22650).

**Laundry** *Lavarap*, Bolívar 617, between Audiencia and Valence, quick, US$3 for 1 machine load.

**Hospital** Recommended, staffed by Japanese and locals. Dr. Gaston Delgadillo Lora, Colón 33, T 21692/21187, speaks English, French, German, rec.

**Saunas** San Roque and Acuario, Sat. and Sun. only, 1430-2000; Copacabana, just out of town (take taxi), Wed. to Sun., 1400-2000.

**Post Office** Argentina 50, between Estudiantes and Olañeta. **Telephone** Entel, España 271.

**Tourist Office** Calle Potosí 102 esq. San Alberto, T 25983, very helpful, map US$0.25. Check church and abbey opening hours. Sub-office at airport, helpful. Tourist information office opp. San Felipe Neri, at Nicolás Ortiz 182, is run by students studying tourism, who will show you around tourist sites for free (see above under **Churches**). All offices closed Sat. and Sun.

**Train Service** to Potosí, Oruro and La Paz usually twice a week overnight (book seats as far in advance as possible: to **Potosí**, US$4.50 Pullman, US$3 special—often no connection in the rainy season; to **Oruro**, US$7 first, US$5.50 second class, *ferrobus* US$11.30; to **La Paz** 20 hours (take food), US$10 Pullman, US$7.50 special. Station, behind Parque Bolívar, T

21114-21115, only open after 1500.

**Air Service** By LAB there is a Mon., Wed., Fri. La Paz-Sucre direct (US$25) air service, to La Paz via Cochabamba (US$16) on Tuesdays, Thursdays and Saturdays (US$48) and Santa Cruz daily. Puerto Suárez, 0900 Mondays, TAM. There are also LAB flights to Tarija (Mon., Wed. and Fri.) and Yacuiba, and F27 flights to Camiri (Tues., Thurs., Sat.). TAM fly on Wed. to La Paz, Santa Cruz and Puerto Suárez, and on Sundays to Santa Cruz. All flights heavily booked but some "stand by" available. Your best chance is to lie in wait at the airport; they know nothing in town. Airport 5 km. from town (T 24445). LAB office is at Bustillos 121-127 (T 21140), from where free bus for passengers leaves 1½ hrs. before flight. Taxi US$2; buses from main road (difficult to get on with luggage). *Trufi* No. 1. VW van goes from entrance to market, 1 block from main plaza, US$0.15. Beware of pickpockets at airport. Local airport taxes total US$3 (3 in all), pay before checking in.

**Bus** daily to/from **La Paz** via Cochabamba (18 hrs., US$11.50), very rough and roads liable to flooding during the rainy season, but worthwhile; via Potosí, US$17 (18 hrs.); to **Cochabamba** daily, 1800, 12½ hrs., US$7 (also by truck for about US$4, night trip caught at cement works 1½ km. off Cochabamba road—Micro A goes as far as turning); daily buses and *micros* to Potosí (0700, 1700 with Hidalgo, US$5, 4½ hrs., US$5 with Soltrans, Beni 97, corner of Bustillos, 0700, US$4.50, with Transtin, Tarapacá, between Arenales and Ayacucho). Trucks from the end of Bustillos, US$2.50-3.50, 6 hours, also *micros* leave from the bus terminus at about 0800, US$3.50, 5 hrs. Bus to **Santa Cruz**, via Cochabamba, Flota Unificada, highly rec. with video, Mon. and Thurs., 1700, 18 hrs., US$15, also Mopar (rec). Once a week to **Tarija** at 1030, Saturday, US$16, 18 hrs. To **Monteagudo**, Thurs. and Sun., 1500, US$5.30. **Oruro**, via Potosí or Cochabamba, none direct. To **Llallagua**, Wed. and Sat., 0700, US$8.20, 10 hours. (Take Micro A to bus station 3 km. from centre, taxi US$0.80, T 22029.)

**Excursion** *Tarabuco*, 3,295 metres, 64 km. by road and 78 km. by rail from Sucre, has a most colourful Indian market on Sundays, starting about 0930. Buses and trucks leave 0500-0900 from top of Calle Calvo, Sucre, 2 ½ hr. journey, US$1.50 (or taxi, US$40). Train (*ferrobus*) from Sucre, 0700, 2½ hrs., US$2, returning 1600, buy ticket at 0600 on day of departure (check in advance, track is liable to mudslides in rainy weather).

There is a direct bus to Cochabamba, US$9.50, 11 hrs. There are at least 2 budget hotels, including *Residencial Florida*, basic, dirty but friendly, lovely garden and display of butterflies and Bolivian bank-notes since 1911, G, restaurant not rec.; try *Bar California*, basic, or other restaurants. Festival with fair: Virgen de Rosario, 1st Sunday in October and 12 March. The Phujllay independence celebration in March, is very colourful and lively with even more costume and dance than the Rosario. Travel agencies organise special excursions and hotels fill up quickly. If you are hardy take a sleeping-bag and sleep in the only restaurant.

Although the market is popular with tourists, it is still worth a visit. Best bargains are to be had on weekdays, or before the bulk of tourists arrive, or late in the day. Our latest reports indicate that prices at the market are high, but that the real appeal is the Indians in their authentic dress. To see the weaving in progress, visits to Candelaria (two hours by truck from Tarabuco) or Macha (8 hours from Sucre), Pocata (one hour from Macha), or Ravelo will save you from hordes of other tourists (travel to Ravelo: by lorry or *micro*, mostly in the morning from departure point near airport, 3 hrs. one way; *micro*, US$1.30, check at shop at Hernando Siles 843 if it's running, it's supposed to leave at 0900, return 1600—lorries back to Sucre invariably full). Specially recommended is a trip to Potolo, where they weave red animals on a black or brown background. Trucks (Thurs. and Fri. in the dry season) go direct from near Sucre airport; in the wet, you can only get to Challanaca and you walk for 3 hours to get there—the prices will probably be lower in the wet season. It has even been suggested that it is cheaper to buy in Peru or from street vendors in Sucre—so check and compare. Swimming in the rainy season only at Cachimayo, Yotala and Ñujchu on the road to Potosí.

A main road runs SE from Sucre through Tarabuco, then at Padilla (2 hotels on plaza), a turn-off heads north 20 km. to *Villa Serrano*, where the musician Mauro Núñez lived. A music festival is held on 28-29 December. (The journey is beautiful through wild mountains.) At *Monteagudo* (about 350 km. from Sucre) there are direct buses to Santa Cruz, twice a week, US$8, 14 hrs. Several basic hotels: *Alojamiento los Naranjos* behind plaza, F, hot showers, *Alojamiento las Tablitas*, and *Alojamiento Oriental*, both on the main road. 460 km. from Sucre is *Camiri* (pop. 20,000), growing rapidly because of nearby oilfields—the oil refinery may be visited. Flota El Chaqueño runs from Sucre to Camiri twice a week in each direction, at least 20 hrs., US$16. From Camiri there is a bus to Santa Cruz which should be booked up well in advance as it is always crowded (terrifying road), office on Av. Busch next to *Gran Hotel Londres*, goes 4 times a week if enough passengers, 8 hrs., US$11; *camioneta* leaves from in front of the market when there are enough passengers, US$7.80, 7 hrs. (boring journey, dusty). As a garrison town it has some hotels (*Hotel Ortuño*, Calle Comercio, E; *Residencial Marieta*, Av. Petrolera 15, E; *Residencial Premier*, Av. Busch 60, E; *Residencial Familiar*, Calle Comercio, F; *Gran Hotel Londres*, Av. Busch 36, F), restaurants, bars (nothing is cheap) and also flights to La Paz and Santa Cruz, 180 km. There is a post office, but no parcels sent abroad. If you arrive by car: at Tránsito checkpoint pick up a slip of paper with instructions on how to reach Guardia where you collect permits to stay overnight. Next visit army post on Plaza de Armas to be checked there. Before leaving town visit Guardia again to collect a permit to proceed—all permits cost about US$0.50 each. Hotels will *not* accept car passengers without permit. S along a very bad road is ***Villa Montes***, more easily reached from Tarija (260 km., bus leaves Tues., Fri. and Sat. at 0700, US$11), famous for the highest temperatures in Bolivia; take mosquito repellant. Opposite the railway station 2 km. out of town is *Hotel El Rancho*, F, with bungalow-type accommodation; the food is expensive so eat in town. It is on the edge of the Gran Chaco and has a road and railway S to Yacuiba and Argentina and another dry-season road E to Paraguay which is O.K. for high clearance vehicles. We have received no recent reports about this latter route route which some maps show as a main road. *Hotel Pilcomayo*, F, dirty, communal bath, and *Hotel Demia*, F, clean and friendly. The bus trip via Tarabuco and Camiri to Argentina is very rough; poor road and little comfort. Two buses a week (Wed. and Sat. 0730) to Llallagua (**see page 239**).

**It is possible to drive from Camiri into Paraguay** direct in a truck or 4-wheel-drive, high clearance vehicle, carrying insect repellent, food and water for a week. No help can be relied on in case of a breakdown; a winch is advisable, especially after rain. There are some rivers to ford and although they are dry in the dry season they can be impassable if there is rain in the area. No buses go beyond Camiri on this road and Bernd Proissl (Wernau, Germany) adds "All travellers going through the Chaco are smuggling something". At Camiri, obtain a US$3 permit from the Guardia to go 64 km. (1½ hours) over a rough road to *Boyuibe*, the last town in Bolivia (*Hotel Guadalquivir*, or *Hotel Chaqueño* next door, both F, both serve meals); once there pay US$2 at Customs for an exit stamp. Passports must be stamped by commander of the army post south of the town. At Boyuibe fuel and water are available, and it is on the Yacuiba railway. A new line is being built West out of Boyuibe, then North, to Tarabuco, to link up with Cochabamba (it has reached Monteagudo).

¾ km. after the military checkpoint turn left past a large water tower. From then on just follow the most used road; accurate directions may be obtained from the army before leaving Boyuibe. It is 134 km. from Boyuibe to the Bolivian border post at Villazón (not to be confused with the other Villazón on the frontier with Argentina). At one point there is a disconcerting southward trend for several km.; for the first 70 km. a few estancias are seen, but nothing else except a total of 3 Bolivian customs posts. This section takes between 6 hrs. and up to 3 days if there are unseasonable storms. The officer at Villazón will give you your exit stamp. The army goes to Villazón once or twice a month; you can camp at Villazón, but no food is available, nor is there much water. The nine soldiers at each of the fly-infested lonely posts on either side of the border will vie for your company if you arrive at nightfall. Enormously appreciated by these poor fellows are small gifts of soft drinks, beer, cigarettes or canned fruit. They do six month stints here.

The Paraguayan post (passport check) is 3 km. from the Bolivian post. Camping is better here than at the Bolivian post because they have a shower and will let you use their kitchen. 13 km. from the Paraguayan border post is Fortín General Eugenio A. Garay. Here the commanding officer will give you entry stamps. The road is somewhat better from here on, sandy and bumpy but straight. There is a police check point at Mister Long, and another at an airforce base; both take time. It can take 9 hrs. to get to Mariscal Estigarribia, where there's a large military base and passports are cleared by the commandant. He is unavailable from 1300 to 1600, so be prepared for a wait. In this event, there's a nice German-run pension 100 yards away where you can get a meal and a room. Food is available in Mcal. Estigarribia.

One and a half hours from Mariscal is Filadelfia (340 km. from Fortín Garay). About 20 km. S of Filadelfia the road is asphalted all the way to Asunción. The birds along this road are incredible. (Much of this information was supplied by Tom Courtenay-Clack.)

The railway line S from Río Mulato goes through ***Uyuni*** (3,660 metres), the junction for the line to Chile. Warning: do not take photos between Uyuni and the border. Trains to La Paz (US$5.60 Pullman, US$3.75 special) and Oruro (3 express, 2 *trenes mixtos* a week to La Paz, plus an express and *ferrobus* to Oruro). Tickets for the train to Calama (coming from Oruro) can be bought on Fri. between 1700 and 1800. The road down from Oruro is sandy, and after rain very bad. Buses to Potosí, 1300, 12-18 hrs., microbus Thur. and Fri. 1300, US$5, 7 hrs., truck on Sunday from near Banco del Estado, US$4.50. Uyuni lies bitterly cold and unprotected on the plain at the edge of a vast salt lake, the Salar de Uyuni. Julián Quispe charges US$25 for 3 hour trip to the Salar. His green jeep holds 8 and is in front of the cathedral around 1000-1100. Bicycles may also be available for hire.

"When it still has water in it (up to 4 or possibly 6 inches), being in the middle of the Salar de Uyuni is like being an ant on a gigantic mirror. The blue sky merges into the blue water, the islands are perfectly reflected and since there is no horizon they appear suspended in space. Some areas may be dry, in which case the salt crust is as blinding-white and featureless as the most perfect snowfield (sunglasses essential)."—Stephen Saker, who endorses our warning on the **Ollagüe-Uyuni track (see below)**.

Uyuni's 20,000 inhabitants are mostly Indian. Its market is the only point of interest, best on Thurs. and Fri. (public showers). There is also supposed to be gasoline available at YPFB near cemetery.

**Hotels and Services** *Avenida*, F, renovated, clean, hot showers, bar. The patrón, Don Jesús Rosas, runs jeep excursions to the Salar (US$35). *Residencial Uyuni*, F, *Residencial Copacabana*, F, *Residencial Urkipiña*, F, all three on Av. Acre, basic and quite clean. *Restaurant Ferrocaril* not rec., better is *Restaurant 16 de Julio*, bland food rec. for delicate stomachs not up to the llama: "oatmeal soup, rice and potatoes, lightly seasoned with hot dog and cabbage". Banco del Estado will not change money. The pharmacy on the main street will change money, but it is very difficult to find out the current rate of exchange. Travellers' cheques cannot be changed anywhere, only US dollars cash. The Immigration Office on Calle Potosí also has a very helpful tourist office.

Motorists must be warned against a road from Río Mulato into Chile by way of Ollagüe. "Between Río Mulato and Uyuni it is deep soft sand and possible only for 4-wheel drive vehicles and trucks. Beyond there is the danger of getting lost on the many tracks leading over the deserted salt lakes, no gasoline between Uyuni and Calama (Chile), and little hope of help with a breakdown on the Bolivian side unless you don't mind waiting for perhaps a week. After rain the route is impassable. Where the road has been built up, *never* forsake it for the appealing soft salt beside it. The salt takes a man's weight but a vehicle breaks through the crust into unfathomable depths of plasticine mud below."—Andrew Parkin.

**Excursions** Dan Buck and Anne Meadows write: "*Laguna Colorada*, about 350-400 km. SW of Uyuni, 12 hours' straight driving over unmarked, rugged truck tracks, is featured in Tony Morrison's two books, *Land Above the Clouds* and *The Andes*. It is one of Bolivia's most spectacular and most isolated marvels. The rare James flamingos, along with the more common Chilean and Andean flamingos, breed and live in its red algae-coloured waters. The shores and shallows of the lake are crusted with gypsum and salt, a bizarre arctic-white counterpoint to the flaming red waters.

The standard rate for hiring a truck or jeep, Uyuni-Laguna Colorada 3 day round trip, is US$250-400, can be negotiated down to US$200. The Uyuni *Hotel Avenida* is a good contact for making arrangements. There is a welter of tracks, and even locals easily get lost. Truck rides can be arranged at the Sindicato de Chóferes in town, behind the church. A map, compass, and a guide are all useful, plus asking directions of every person one meets along the way—which won't be many. In our round trip we met no vehicles, only 4 *campesinos* on bicycles and a handful on foot. Going out we went Uyuni-Corpina-Quetena- Chica-east side Laguna Colorada; on the return we travelled west side Laguna Colorada-Alota-Uyuni. Beware: if approaching the lake from the east side, take the south shore of the lake to the *campamento*, it is longer but better than the north shore which is deep, treacherous volcanic ash and sand. A map of Laguna Colorada may be obtained from Instituto Geográfico Militar in Uyuni. Sr. Erasmo Ansa, Calle Loa between Uruguay and México, drives a truck to Laguna Colorada twice a week. He will leave you there and pick up after 2 or 3 days on his way back, US$25-50 depending on his load. 2-day excursions to Lagunas Colorado and Verde, with Sr. Otario Apala or Sr. Mario Alvarez, Barrio Obrero No. 13, Uyuni, for approx. US$300.

There is no dependable transport linking any of the towns and mining camps in the Uyuni-Laguna Colorada area. No one should travel in the area without cold-weather camping gear, sufficient food, etc. At Laguna Colorada, you must camp out of doors, but it may be possible to sleep inside adobe hut closest to lake, no facilities.

There is a truck on Saturdays which leaves Chiguana, a town on the Uyuni-Antofagasta railway, once the La Paz train arrives, going to **Laguna Verde**, 3 hrs., south of Laguna Colorada. There are also trucks which go to the Laguna Colorada and the Susana sulphur mine. A lorry back sometimes leaves on Friday afternoon, but this is by no means certain. There is transport from Uyuni with people taking petrol to the *campamento* at Laguna Colorada—ask at the mining offices at Uyuni. At Chiguana and Laguna Verde the army will normally provide a place to sleep (no bedding). You may also be able to sleep on a floor at the sulphur mine at Laguna Verde, or at the workers' quarters for the Sol de Mañana geothermal project, 45 km. from Laguna Colorada, although the latter is unreliable as there are not always workers there. Hot food can also be purchased although there is none at Laguna Colorada. Travel in this region is possible anytime between May and October, but there is no petrol, mechanical assistance or supplies S of Salinas de Garci Mendoza (270 km. from Oruro) or Uyuni (petrol in Salinas de Garci Mendoza is twice as expensive as in Uyuni). The army can be helpful for transport in the area if you persist.

The scenery between Laguna Colorada and Laguna Verde is spectacular (geysers, boiling mud pools, steaming streams, lakes with flamingoes, wind-eroded rocks). Lorries from the mines may give lifts from the border to Calama, and to San Pedro de Atacama in Chile, but food, warm clothing and a tent will be needed in case of being stuck overnight.

One can visit *Llica*, the capital of Daniel Campos Province, in 5 hours over the Salar by truck, or about 12 hours by boat, if there is enough water in the lake. There is a new, basic *Alojamiento Municipal* in town, F. Also Angel Quispe in the plaza has 3 beds. Food is "difficult". There is a teachers' training college but not much special to see. Two fiestas: July 26 and August 15. Good for llama and other wool handicrafts.

SW of Atocha, 2 hours by irregular bus or truck is San Vicente where Butch Cassidy and the Sundance Kid are said to be buried in an unmarked grave, following a gun battle with the police in 1908.

S of Uyuni, 200 km., is **Tupiza** (2,990 metres, 11,000 people), a centre of the silver, tin, lead, and bismuth mining industries (*Hotel Mitru*, F, private shower and bath; next to it is *Residencial Crillón*, F, very run down, with good motorcycle parking; much better for motorcyclists is *Res. Valle Hermoso*, Av. Pedro Arraya, T 589, F, hot showers, good, will let you park bikes in restaurant; also *Hotel Americano*, G, opposite railway station and, 2 blocks from the station, *Hotel Centro*, F, clean, friendly and quiet). Chajra Huasi, a palazzo-style, abandoned home of the Aramayo family, may be visited, across Río Tupiza. The statue in the main square of Tupiza is to the founding member of the Aramayo mining dynasty, pre-eminent in the late 19th, early 20th centuries, together with the Patiños and the Hoschilds. Chajra Huasi was expropriated by the government after the 1952 revolution. IGM office, for maps, is in the Municipal building. Three trains to border every week. *Ferrobus* to Oruro, Tuesday 0800, US$12, meals and drinks served on board, but expensive. Bad road from Potosí which goes on S to Villazón; often closed in rainy season because there is no bridge over the Río Suipacha. Bus to Villazón 3 hrs., US$2 (many daily).

Wendy Chilcott and Steve Newman (Sussex) write: "Follow the road to the left of the cathedral out of town between the cemetery and a barracks. Continue as road curves right until you reach a dry river bed. Follow this to the left towards the hills. After 200 m. take the right fork in the river bed. Here are some superb rock formations... huge pinnacles of rock and soil, only 4 inches thick—seem to defy gravity! The valley narrows rapidly but the path follows a stream bed for several hundred metres to a picturesque waterfall. Any further progress requires difficult scrambling but will eventually lead to the altiplano. " The whole walk takes 2 hours, worth it for the rock formations alone. Beautiful sunsets over the fertile Tupiza can be seen from the foot of a Christ statue on a hill behind the plaza.

From **Villazón** (pop. 13,000 ,good local market), on the border with Argentina, there is an improved road to Tarija, 965 km. by road from La Paz. The road linking Potosí with Villazón via Camargo is in poor condition and about 100 km. longer than the better road via Tupiza. For information on border crossing with Argentina **see Argentina Section 3**; US$1 usually charged for crossing; remember Argentina is 1 hour ahead (2 hours in summer) if making a connection. Little to see in Villazón (has two cinemas) and not at all welcoming; border area must not be photographed.

**Hotels at Villazón** *Residencia Martínez*, ½ block from bus station, well signed, F, hot water when town's supply is on; *Residencial El Cortijo*, clean, E, good value, hot water, restaurant; *Hotel Bolivia*, one block from border, F, hot showers. Restaurants opposite bus station and on first floor of covered market, for example *La Reposterion*, about US$1 a head.

**Argentine Consulate** in main plaza, open 1400-1700, Mon.-Fri.; not very helpful.

**Exchange** Money-changing at Cambio Porvenir or other *cambios* on main street, rates said to be good (cash only, also at shop by border that sells train tickets (see below); Banco del Estado does not change travellers' cheques. Out of hours try the Ciné Rex. Warning: do not show passport or money to men claiming to be plainclothes police.

**Buses** To **Potosí** at 1600 and 1700, 13-15 hrs., US$7 (unsurfaced road—terrible in the wet); to **Tupiza**, 0700 and 1500; to Tarija, Mon., Tues., Thur., Sun. at 1100, Wed. and Sat. at 0900 (US$6.50-7), 7 hours; trucks for Tarija from beside bus station. Watch out for overcharging by Panamericano bus company— the "direct" **La Paz** bus usually goes only as far as Potosí, and is very slow, but if you pay the La Paz fare you will be given another ticket in Potosí for the onward night bus (perhaps with another company), which works out cheaper. The Paz-Villazón takes 26 hrs., inc. change in Potosí, US$15 3/4 times a week. Bus station is near the main square, behind Ciné Teatro Libertador Bolívar; it is about 6 blocks from the border. Taxi to border, US$0.20 or hire porter, US$1, and walk across.

**Trains** To **La Paz** (very dusty and cold journey), 3/4 times a week, at 1450, arr. La Paz 1110 next day (US$12 Pullman, US$9 special). On Tues. and Sat. at 1530 a train leaves for La Paz with an expensive Pullman coach which has come right through from Tucumán (dep. Fri. 1500); arrival in La Paz scheduled for 0940 Sunday. Journey very crowded, especially 2nd class. Train stops at Tupiza for evening meal at 1900 (no cutlery or napkins provided), Atocha, Uyuni and Oruro, *tren mixto* twice a week to *Oruro*, Mon. and Thur. at 1500 (cold journey). The express from La Paz/Oruro connects with a bus to **Tarija** (in theory), tickets from railway station, about 1 km. out of town on main road. Tickets to La Paz can be bought (US$1 commission per ticket) at the first shop on the right next to the border.

At *Camargo*, on road from Potosí to Tarija, is an excellent restaurant, *Media Luz*. Guest rooms have been built for overnight stop.

*Tarija*, at 1,956 metres (pop. 73,000) was founded 4 July, 1574, in the rich valley of the Guadalquivir river. The road from Villazón, 183 km., is the shortest route from Argentina; there is also a road to Potosí via Camargo. The alternative route from Argentina via Bermejo (pop. 13,000, *casas de cambio* on main street, thorough customs searches), 216 km., is at a fairly low altitude and in a mild climate, but the views are rewarding; not recommended in the rainy season a month or so after. The road is in an appalling condition apart from 50 km. which are paved. Daily buses take 5 or 6 hours. Do not try to cycle. There is no railway. Tarija had a tumultuous struggle against Spain, declaring itself independent in 1807, and has a strong cultural heritage. Its own university was founded in 1946. There is a large archaeological collection; the entrance is at the corner of the building. Maize, vegetables, wheat, potatoes and splendid grapes thrive in the basin. Bolivia's best wines are produced here (no organized tours to *bodegas*, phone for appointment). Its people are markedly religious and strongly individualistic, and the Indian strain is less marked here than elsewhere in Bolivia. The modern Avenida Costanera gracefully flanks the curves of the river. The Casa Dorada is being reconstructed with a view to becoming the Casa de Cultura (interested visitors may be shown round by the restorer), note the figures in the roof. A good view can be had from Cerro San Juan; follow Calle D.Paz to the top of the rise where the buses gather, turn right on the cobbled street, then right through the gate and follow the Stations of the Cross to the top (it's about 4 blocks up from zoo).

The city is famous for its *niño* (child) processions: colourful and charming. During processions of San Roque in a 3-day festival from the first Sunday in September the richly dressed saint's statue is paraded through the streets; wearing lively colours, cloth turbans and cloth veils, the people dance before it as it goes, and women throw flowers from the balconies. Dogs are decorated with ribbons for the day. On the second Sunday in October the flower festival commemorates the Virgen del Rosario, and another takes place in Easter week.

**Hotels** *Prefectural*, T 2461/2, D with bath and pool, shabby, poor service (2 km. from city centre, upstream on road); *Hostal Carmen*, Ingavi 0-0784, T 3372/4342, E, shower, clean, good value; *Hostal Costanera*, Av. Las Américas, T 2851/4817, rec., reasonably-priced, modern facilities; *América*, Bolívar 257, hot showers, good, E, restaurant attached (good); opp. is *Residencial Bolívar*, E with bath, rec., clean, comfortable, hot water, breakfast US$1; *Residencial Londres*, N. Campo 1072, E, highly rec; *Residencial Miraflores*, Calle Sucre, F, clean and rec. *Terminal*, behind bus station, family-run, good lunches, suitable for a night's stop-over; *Residencial Ocho Hermanos*, near main plaza, F, clean, collective rooms only.

**Restaurants** *La Cabaña de Don Pepe*, Campos 138, has excellent steaks at reasonable prices; *El Rinconcito Andaluz* on the Plaza is cheap and the food reasonable. On La Madrid, *La Princesa* (excellent keperi—meat that is first boiled, then fried); for pizza and icecream on same street, unnamed parlour at the Agencia Kohlberg sign near Suipacha (opp. No. 268); *Café Puschkin*, Ingavi 0277; *Café Show*, Ingavi y Mariscal Sucre; *Snack Te Ve*, Sucre 622, just off plaza, expensive, small portions; *Al Solar*, vegetarian, US$1.50 set menu. Excellent food, cheap breakfast, in market, but get there before 1300. After, go to Calle Carrero. Try the local wines, e.g. the white Aranjuez, Arce, Colonial or Kohlberg, also local beer. **N.B.** Restaurants (and everything else in town) close in the middle of the day.

**Shopping** Craft goods in market and in co-operative shop in plaza; some cheap stuff, shoddy. Ceramics at *Frial Susy*, Sucre 776. Felt for hats at *La Nueva Italia*, Ingavi y Sucre; they will show you where to have your hat made up for US$3.50.

**Museum** Museo Universitario, Lema y Gral Trigo, interesting fossle display.

**Zoo** On Av. Costanera, (a tatty children's park, but worth the US$0.15 to see the condors.

**Exchange** Banco del Estado will change money. Try Comercial Salinas at Mcal. Sucre 758. Money changers on Bolívar at Daniel Campos, also at shops in the vicinity, between Colón and Suipacha. Better rates for australes than in Villazón.

**Consulates** West German Sucre 665, helpful. **Argentine** Corner of Ballivián and Bolívar, Mon.-Fri., 0800-1300.

**Post Office** Plaza Luis de Fuentes. **Telecommunications** Virginia Lema 843.

**Travel Agents** Internacional Tarija, Sucre 721, Tel.:4446/7, helpful.

**Tourist Office** General Trigo 662, very helpful, free map.

**Air Service** TAM and LAB to Cochabamba, La Paz (Mon., Wed., Fri.), Santa Cruz, Trinidad, Yacuiba, and Sucre (Tues). Flights are frequently cancelled and/or strike-bound. LAB office on Virginia Lema; TAM office between Sucre and Bolívar. Taxi to airport, US$1 p.p., or *micro* drops you 2 blocks away.

**Buses** Mon., Wed., Thurs. and Sat. on 935-km. route Potosí-Oruro-La Paz, leaving 1700 (26 hrs., US$16; check which company operates the best buses). To Potosí (386 km.), with 10 de Noviembre, takes 13 hrs. (US$12.50), cold. For Sucre, you must change buses in Potosí. To Villazón: EMTV, Tues., Thur., Sat., 0830, US$6.50, Veloz del Sud, 3/4 times a week, 1900, 6½ hrs., US$7; Cristal, 3 times a week, 0630; otherwise you need to take a local truck (US$5). Three to four times a week there is a combined bus/train service to Villazón and La Paz, US$22.75, leaves Tarija 0630, seat guaranteed on both services. Daily buses to Bermejo (1900-1930, 10 hrs., US$6, truck US$3.50) not recommended in rainy season; at Bermejo cross river by ferry to Agua Blanca, Argentina. To Villa Montes (see page 253), 12 hrs., Wed., 0730, US$11. Also to Yacuiba, 4 times a week at 2000 by Flota Tarija. The new bus station is in the outskirts on Avenida de Las Américas (30 mins. walk from centre, 7-8 mins. from airport). Cía. El Chapaco uses poor quality vehicles. Trucks to all destinations leave from Loma, near the market.

**Swimming** Municipal swimming bath down the hill from the Mercado Negro. Tomatito, bus from San Juan at 0800, a trip of 5 km., popular picnic area. For those with their own transport El Rincón de la Victoria, 18 km., or Tolomosita, 7 km., sandy beach on river bank, and Los Churros de Jurina with natural rock pools, 22 km., or the Ancón gorge. Sauna at Acuario, 15 de Abril 679. Also interesting walking tours.

---

## THE YUNGAS (3)

---

Lush forested slopes behind the mountains to the north of La Paz;

this is the main production area of citrus, bananas, coffee and coca leaves for the capital. It is also a favourite retreat for those escaping the Andean chill.

NE of La Paz a road runs to the Yungas. It circles cloudwards over La Cumbre pass at 4,725 metres; the highest point is reached in an hour; all around stand titanic snowcapped peaks and snowfields glinting in the sun. Then at Unduavi the paving ends; the road becomes "all-weather" (dangerous, especially in the rainy season, but it has been widened) and drops over 3,400 metres to the luxuriant green rain forest in 80 km. The little town of **Coroico** is perched on a hill at 1,525 metres; the scenery is beautiful. A visit to the old cemetery is recommended especially for camera buffs. The hillside is covered with orange and banana groves; delightful walks through paths down to the river where warm pools are ideal for bathing (and if you're not up to 2-3 hrs. walk each way, lifts are usually available in Coroico).

The roads to Coroico and to Coripata and Chulumani divide at Unduavi at a height of about 3,000 metres on the E side of La Cumbre. Here the well-surfaced road ends; the only petrol station is at Unduavi. There is no good place to eat at Unduavi, nor at Santa Rosa on the road to Coripata. From Coroico one can go by road into the Alto Beni beyond Caranavi; both Rurrenabaque and Trinidad can be reached by road. Note, if travelling by truck from La Paz to the Yungas via La Cumbre, the best views can be seen in May and June, when there is least chance of fog and rain on the heights. If you want to alight at La Cumbre, ensure you tell the driver beforehand for it is easy to miss in fog or cloud. It is very cold at La Cumbre and, further down, there are waterfalls at San Juan that baptise open vehicles—be prepared. For details of the La Cumbre—Coroico hike (Choro), **see page 229.**

**Festivals** There is a colourful four-day festival on 19-22 October. On 2 November, All Souls' Day, the local cemetery is festooned with black ribbons.

**Hotels** *Prefectural*, C, down the hill, below the convent, biggest in town with full board (E without food) but very run down, water 0700-1030 and 1400-1700, and food poor. *Sol y Luna*, uphill past cemetery, and Umopar (narcotics police) station, ½-hr. walk from town (ask for La Alemana, La Gringa, Victoria or Sigrid Fronius—all the same person!), F p.p. bed and breakfast, E full board, separate meals available, cooking facilities, also 2 small houses for rent, swimming pool, garden, highly rec. (also, Sigrid offers Shiatsu massage for US$7). *Lluvia de Oro* (good value, food rec., billiards downstairs, cheap), swimming pool, F, top floor rooms are best. *Hostal Kori*, swimming pool (open to all), good value, F, top floors rec., clean, good restaurant. *La Casa*, just down the hill from *Hostal Kori*, small, swimming pool, clean, with restaurant (below), rec. A camping site will be found by the small church on the hill overlooking the town—a stiff climb though; at the church take the left-hand path for another stiff climb to a waterfall (only worth it in the wet season). Coroico is an attractive place to wander around, especially towards evening. Hotels can be difficult at holiday weekends and as the area is a popular retreat for the rich from La Paz, prices are higher.

**Restaurants** *La Tasca*, only one menu and under new ownership, not as good as before; *La Casa* is German-run, good food and setting, excellent salads and fondue for dinner, wonderful views, rec.; *Kory*, good breakfast but very expensive; *El Rodeo*, Caranavi road, brilliant view, good food. The convent has been rec. for its chocolate biscuits, peanut butter and coffee liqueurs, and interesting cheap wine. Vegetarian dishes available from second to last stall on right in Mercado Municipal, highly rec. and remarked on as the only market stall where a man does the cooking.

**Horse Riding** Patricio and Danny (French), who live by the new hospital in Comunidad de Aparto, have 6 horses for hire, US$4.20/hr, US$8.60/3 hrs., for trekking in the mountains or just a few hours' riding; very friendly. Reservations in La Paz: Shuriya, Plaza Abaroa, Av. 20 de Octubre 2463, T 322041, 1100-1300, 1530-1930.

**Buses** from La Paz to Coroico (US$3) leave from Villa Fátima at 0830, on Tues., Thur., Fri. and Sat., returning from Coroico on Mon., Wed., Fri. and Sat. at 0700 and Sun. at 1300 and take 3-5 hours each way; sit on left hand side (book return to La Paz well in advance). Flota Yungueña (Av. de las Américas 354, Villa Fátima, La Paz) runs between La Paz, Coroico and other towns in the Yungas. Take Micros B,V,X,K, 131, 135, or 136, or *trufis* 2 or 9, which pass Pérez Velasco coming down from Plaza Mendoza, and get off at the service station, 20 metres before the booking office (it's 25 minutes from or to the suburb of Villa Fátima). Trucks to and from La Paz are more frequent (daily) and cheaper, US$2.20; they leave two blocks above the bus company. Pick-ups also take passengers, usually from outside the bus office, ask around. Trucks and pick-ups may drop you at Yolosa, the road junction 7 km. from Coroico; there is usually transport Yolosa-Coroico, US$0.50, or you can walk, uphill all the way, 2 hours. Transport can be a problem at holidays. Reconfirm onward bookings to and from Coroico as it is possible to get stuck for days at a time. The Flota Yungueña office is in the *Comedor Municipal*. In Coroico trucks leave from the market.

*Chulumani*, the capital of Sud Yungas, is the main regional centre. Citrus fruits are the main products from this area as well as some coffee. Along the road from Puente Villa to Coripata (*Hotel Florida*, F) you enter the main coca growing area of northern Bolivia and the countryside is quite different from that near Coroico, where coffee, as well as coca and fruits, is the main crop.

**Hotels** *Motel San Bartolomé* (T 358386), B, pleasant, some family rooms and cabins cheaper, superb jungle setting with faulous views of mountains, swimming pool, can be booked through the *Hotel Plaza*, La Paz, T 378311, Ext. 1221; and *Motel San Antonio*, C, with pleasant cabins and swimming pools (both Motels are out of town, a taxi ride or long walk away). *Hotel Bolívar*, cheap, clean and friendly. *La Hostería*, Junín, T 813255, D with or without bathroom, breakfast included, clean and friendly, with restaurant; *García*, on main square, E with, F without bath, basic, clean and cheap, rec.; *Residencial El Milagro*, F, good views; *Prefectural*, on outskirts, D, full board, with swimming pool (not always full).

*Hotel Tamapaya*, 95 Km. from La Paz, just outside Puente Villa, is in a beautiful setting, C with shower, good rooms, swimming pool, rec except for variable, expensive restaurant.

**Restaurants** Cheap food at *García* and at *Pensión Viviana*, Calle Lanza, for freshly-squeezed orange juice.

**Bus** La Paz-Chulumani, Flota Yungueña, 120 km., 6 hours, US$3.30. Minibus La Paz-Chulumani, 0830/1430 daily, and returns early afternoons daily, US$3.50, 3-4 hrs., more comfortable than the bus.

From below Coroico the road forks, the lower fork following the river NE to *Caranavi*, a very ugly town 164 km. from La Paz, at times along a picturesque gorge, towards the settled area of the Alto Beni . Market day is Saturday; lots of transport in late afternoon.

**Hotels** *Caranavi*, F, clean and friendly. *Prefectural*, F, not rec., but has a swimming pool. *Residencial Rosedal*, clean, friendly, cheap. **Restaurant** *Coroico*, opposite *Hotel Caranavi*, very good and cheap, highly rec.

**Bus** Yungueña buses leave La Paz for Caranavi at 0900 each day, US$5.20, or trucks from Villa Fátima at about 0830; the 164-km. journey takes 6-7 hours and trucks 12½ hours. Direct bus Coroico-Caranavi on Sundays, or you can take a truck, US$1.65. At Yolosa you may also be able to get transport to Caranavi. If you want to continue into the Beni Lowlands without going into Caranavi, wait at the checkpoint before the town where all transport has to stop and ask for a ride there.

Some 70 km. from Caranavi lies the gold mining town of **Guanay**, an interesting, friendly place at the junction of the Tipuani and Mapiri rivers. To stay, *Alojamiento Los Pinos*, opp. football pitch, G p.p., cold water, basic, clean, may arrange exchange of travellers' cheques (with commission—cash can be changed with shopkeepers or gold dealers). *Hotel Ritzy*, on main plaza, F, very clean, with mosquito nets. Camping is possible next to the football field. *Restaurant La Bamba*, opp. old *Panamericana Hotel* (apparently closed) good value, English spoken. Many other eating places on main street have fixed-price meals; one, with courtyard, monkey and parrot, serves excellent value breakfast of steak, eggs and tomato for US$0.75. Electricity is rationed—every 10 mins. or so. Other gold mining sites are Tipuani and Mapiri (canoe trips to Mapiri can be arranged, with overnight stay). Buses direct from La Paz, Yungueña and Estrella Azul, about US$8, also trucks, which make frequent stops and diversions.

Canoes go down the Río Beni from Guanay to Rurrenabaque (**see page 260**), 8-12 hrs., US$11-18 depending on how successfully you negotiate and availability of canoes. "Expreso" boats can also be hired, at a price, about US$450. The journey goes through gold mining settlements, then narrow, fertile river banks sown with peanuts.

**N.B.** The Yungas are a coca-growing region, so it is advisable not to wander too far off the beaten track.

## THE NORTHERN LOWLANDS (4)

From scrubby eastern lowlands to dense tropical jungle in the north, this is pioneer country: missionaries, rubber tappers and cocaine refiners. Improved roads to Rurrenabaque and Trinidad are opening up the area and wildlife expeditions are becoming increasingly popular.

**From Caranavi to the Beni Lowlands** From Caranavi, you can take a bus (once a week) to Sapecho (with a cocoa cooperative), where a bridge over the Río Beni has effectively cut off the old port for river access to the Lowlands, Puerto Linares. Trucks run from Caranavi to Sapecho and Rurrenabaque. Beyond Sapecho, the road passes through Palos Blancos 20 km. from the bridge (market day, Saturday; *Doña Luisa's* restaurant, good non-alcoholic *chicha*), from where a road has been opened to Yucumo, the centre of a large area of colonization. The road is passable only with 4 wheel drive, but there are occasional buses from Caranavi (13-15 hrs.). There are *hospedajes* (F) and restaurants in Yucumo. 550,000 ha. of jungle are under cultivation, rice, sugar, corn and fruit being planted. The Chimanes indians are trying to survive the influx of settlers from the altiplano. From Yucumo it is 50 km. to San Borja, a cattle-raising centre with hotels (F) and restaurants. It is also a cocaine district and in the centre are three identical, ugly cocaine mansions. From San Borja it is 7 hrs. by pick-up, US$12.50, to Trinidad (bus service expected to start in 1990); there are 5-6 river crossings and, in the wetlands, flamingoes, blue heron and a multitude of waterfowl.

At Yucumo, a second road branches NW to Rurrenabaque. The road from La Paz to Rurrenabaque has now been improved and Puerto Linares is no longer important as a harbour. What little accommodation there was has closed down, there are still a few shops but hardly any river traffic. It may still be possible to hire a boat, but very expensive and only likely in the wet season. Across the river is Santa Ana, originally an Indian village, more interesting than Puerto Linares, but again no services exist now.

*Rurrenabaque* is a small, picturesque jungle town, with San Buenaventura on its opposite bank. Plans to build a brewery are enforcing change. The main square was remodelled in 1989. You must register with the police on arrival.

**Hotels and Restaurants** *Santa Ana*, E with bath, less without, near main square, G p.p., clean, basic, cold water, good cake in kiosk; *Berlín*, near wharf, from G to F but all rooms dirty, insanitary, cold water, to be avoided.; *Porteño*, E with bath, less without, quite good; *Safari*, on outskirts, for tours, all rooms with bath, not open all year round. Best meals at *Club Social Rurrenabaque*, US$1.25; *Snack Horeb*, no sign, run by Jorge Pacheco, friendly, helpful, a good meeting place. Several restaurants offer fixed-price meals which are good value; several "shanty" type restaurants, 1½ blocks up from canoe dock, offer beef or chicken kebabs with rice, empanadas and chicha, all under US$1 an item. Try banana or papaya milk shakes from stop opp. *Hotel Berlín*.

**Transport** Bus to/from La Paz twice a week, Flota Yungueña and 16 de Noviembre, 20 hrs., US$18. TAM flies to Rurrenabaque from La Paz on Thur. (and back same day), US$18 each way, and LAB Sun. or Mon., US$23 each way. Trucks go to Riberalta, but boats are infrequent. Cargo boats once every 1-2 weeks, *Juan Pablo II*, rec. but food monotonous ("take ketchup to add or disguise flavour"), plenty of fresh fruit available at stops en route; the fastest and largest is the *Don Carlos* (Captain Fong), US$30 incl. meals, 5 days to Riberalta (take a hammock). In the rubber season, the *Don Carlos* stops at the *estancia* of the Fong Rocas family, where you can see the rubber process and the conditions of the indebted workers. There may also be boats to Santa Cruz (try radioing in advance to the Capitanía del Puerto at Rurrenabaque to find out about boats).

**Excursion** Agencia Fluvial, at floating restaurant to left of canoe dock runs a 4-day jungle tour on the Río Tuichi, US$10-20 p.p. per day (payable in dollars, travellers' cheques accepted at 2% commission). (Write to Tico Tudela, Agencia Fluvial, Rurrenabaque.) 3 nights are spent in the jungle, learning about plants, survival and the culinary specialities of the region (turtle eggs, wild pheasant, alligator tail, stingray, wild pig, duck, fish, fried bananas and "the sweetest grapefruit you'll ever taste"—Richard and Yvonne Ruming). You must take swimming costume, insect repellant to ward off sandflies and mosquitoes, and a camera. Prospective passengers are warned that the culinary delights are often achieved by the guides taking a pot-shot at any wildlife encountered en route. But the agency (Fluvial) is repeatedly rec. for their expert knowledge and well-organised trips.

Another route into Beni Department runs from Cochabamba NE for 200 km. to Todos Santos, on the Chaparé river, a tributary of the Mamoré (the previous narrow road has now been much improved and paved). To **Villa Tunari** by Chaparé bus at 1030 (no standing allowed, won't go if not enough passengers) from Av. Oquendo 985, Cochabamba, US$3.50, at least 5 hrs. (some Santa Cruz buses pass by, ask). Ask for the Piscinas Naturales for beautiful swimming. *Hotel Las Pozas*, 1 km. out of town, wonderful setting near Piscinas Naturales, own small pool, D with shared shower, excellent restaurant, excursions organized, but must be booked in Cochabamba in advance; *Hotel Las Palmas*, T 47554, D, also 1 km. out of town, clean, friendly, with pool and restaurant, rec.; *Hotel El Puente* Av. de la Integración, D, new; *Hotel Las Vegas*, basic but clean; *Pilunchi*, quiet and rundown, in centre, F; *La Querencia*, E, basic, insect repellent provided, and toads.

The Cochabamba—Santa Cruz lowland road goes through from Villa Tunari to **Puerto Villarroel** (*Hotel Hannover*, best, E, and some cheap *alojamientos*) from where cargo boats ply irregularly to Trinidad in about 4-10 days (see below). You can get information from the Capitanía del Puerto notice board. (There are very few stores in Villarroel. Sr. Arturo Linares at the Cede office organizes boat trips to the jungle—not cheap.) The Cochabamba-Villa Tunari run is highly recommended for scenery, and fishing at San Fernando.

From Cochabamba you can get a bus to Puerto San Francisco (US$5), Todos Santos or Puerto Villarroel. Bus Cochabamba—Puerto Villarroel US$5.30, from 0800 when full, 6 hrs., occasional searches and 5 checkpoints. As this is coca-growing territory the police advise: don't stray from the main road, don't talk to strangers and don't take other people's luggage. From Puerto Villarroel you can continue by road to Santa Cruz, or by boat down the Securé, Chaparé or Mamoré rivers to Guayaramerín, then by road to Riberalta and back up river to Santa Ana on the River Santa Elena, or Rurrenabaque, thence by road to Coroico and back to La Paz.

**Boat trip from Puerto Villarroel to Trinidad** Puerto Villarroel is the main port for the river transport to the north of Bolivia. The road network is being extended, but many roads can only be used in the dry season, so river transport is still an important means of communication. There are boats running between Puerto Villarroel, Trinidad and Guayaramerín on the Brazilian border, taking passengers. This trip is only for the hardy traveller. In the rainy season when the river is high it takes about 3 to 5 days to go from Puerto Villarroel to Trinidad, but in the dry season, i.e. between May or June and August-November, it may last 8 to 10 days (the river is lower, cleaner and there may be more animals to see on the shore). It is another 5 days to Guayaramerín. The launches do not provide berths; you just have to sleep on the cargo which, if you are lucky, may be sugar bags and the like. The fare to Trinidad is about US$15 for 3 days and nights, including meals (prices vary). The food is native, that is to say all kinds of fish, dishes like *massaca* (stewed yuca with cooking bananas, *charque* or dried meat, oil and salt) and turtle eggs. If you are fussy about food, don't make the trip because the kitchen is beyond description and the toilet facilities, too. Take your own drinking water, or water sterilizing tablets as the water served is taken from the river. The food served is very starchy and heavy because it is nearly always fried in oil, so supplement the diet with fruit and any other interesting food you can find beforehand (you can also take cigarettes and drink for the crew if you want). The trip is not as exciting as those in the real jungle; the countryside between Puerto Villarroel and Trinidad is more or less cultivated, with plantations of bananas and cattle ranches, some with 20-30,000 head. There is no jungle with orchids, alligators, etc., but one can see *petas*—small turtles basking in the sun, capibara, river dolphins, jumping fish, now and then monkeys playing on the beach, and many types of birds. At night, there are never-ending frog concerts. This trip could be described as quite relaxing if it was not for the poor food and the spartan accommodation.

Bathing in the river can be done without any harm.

If one does not know how to enjoy the "green symphony" as it is passing by, one should take a good book, as the trip might otherwise get very long!

A mosquito net is a "must", a hammock a good idea, and binoculars for watching the wildlife a useful extra.

***Trinidad***, the capital of the lowland Beni Department (237 metres), founded 1686, population 50,000, is reached by air from La Paz, Cochabamba, Riberalta or Santa Cruz, by road from Santa Cruz or by river from Puerto Villarroel. There are two ports, Almacén and Parador, check which one your boat is docking at. Parador is 3 km./1 hr. walk from town; cross the river by the main bridge by the market, walk down to the service station by the police checkpoint and take a truck, US$1.30. In the dry season, Oct.-Dec., boats do not reach Villarroel from the north. Food quite varied. The main mode of transport (even for taxis) is the motorbike.

**Hotels** *Ganadero*, Av. 6 de Agosto, Edificio Big Beni, T 21644/21727, B, rec., friendly, good restaurant, roof top pool, or opposite, *Monteverde*, T 22342/22738, C with or without a/c, all rooms have T.V. and mini-fridge, daily excursions organised to Balneario Topacare, rec. *El Bajío*, Av. Nicolás Suárez 622, T 21344/20203, C with bath and fan, breakfast extra, modern, swimming pool; *Mi Residencia*, Manuel Limpias 76, near plaza, T 21529/21376, C, friendly, clean; *Hostal Triny*, Calle Sucre, near Santa Cruz, D, good value, fan, clean, plenty of safe drinking water (a great rarity here); *Residencial Loreto*, Calle La Paz, E, clean. *Yacuma*, La Paz y Santa Cruz, upstairs rooms rec., clean, bargaining possible, E, restaurant, washing facilities, fan, unfriendly. Some cheaper alternatives on Calle 18 de Octubre. *Residencial Palermo*, E, Av. 6 de Agosto, T 20472, clean with hot water.

**Restaurants** *Moron*, Bolívar, almost opp. hospital, family run, excellent value fish dishes. *Dragón China*, Calama 700, good Chinese food; *Pacumutu*, Nicolás Suárez, for *plato común* and kebabs; *Snack Brasilia*, La Paz 662, serves a good dinner. *Carlitos*, on main square, rec. Sugar cane juice with lemon sold near the market—delicious. *Pescadería El Moro*, Bolívar and 25 Diciembre, excellent fish and another fish restaurant, out of town on the road to the airport, is *El Tiburón*, about US$2 for a main course. *La Casona*, on the main plaza, for good pizzas, set lunch US$1, closed Tuesdays; *La Estancia*, P.I. Muiva, excellent steaks. Ice cream and snacks at *Kivón* cafetería on main square, and cheap snacks also at *El Cabalino*, on 18 Noviembre. *Balneario Topacare* is a lakeside restaurant and bathing resort 10 minutes out of town; delicious local specialities, lunch or dinner, about US$5 a head, beautiful location, excellent bird spotting, favourite spot for locals at weekends, highly rec.

**Exchange** cash dollars at Farmacia de Tarno, Santa Cruz 470.

**Travel Agents** Tarope Tours, Av. 6 de Agosto 731, T 21468. Excursions to local *estancias* and down river to Amazonia, ask for Rosario.

**Transport** A road has been built to link La Paz with Trinidad (via San Ignacio, San Borja and Sapecho), and occasional colectivos and trucks use it (the latter attempt it all year, 24 hrs. if you're lucky, ask for El Bonchi at La Grigota hardware store); the road is of typical "penetration" standard, not for use during the rainy season, and gasoline is very difficult to come by. Take water, and a compass. Bus service to Cochabamba leaves 0700. Trinidad to Santa Cruz by road: 2 companies, Flota Puñata, US$13.50, and Trans Beni, US$12.50, each runs twice a week in the dry season, March-October; the route (Federal No. 9) is 612 km., via Casarabe (56 km.), Villa Banzer (68 km.), Santa María (208 km.), Ascención (250 km.), El Puente (312 km.), San Ramón (372 km.), San Julián (382 km.) and Montero (564 km.—all distances from Trinidad). From Casarabe to Villa Banzer is poor gravel, then it's dirt, tough going and impassable in the wet to San Julián, from where a good gravel surface goes to the Río Guapay and thereafter it is paved. A railway from Santa Cruz to Trinidad, via Montero and Colonia San Juan, has reached the confluence of the Ichilo and Grande rivers, 105 km. from Trinidad. The flight to La Paz is cheaper by TAM than by LAB (book early in either case). TAM to Cochabamba, US$22, plus US$1.20 tax, plus US$0.40 for each 1 kg. of baggage over 15 kg. A fleet of over 20 air taxis also provides local transport. LAB tend to cancel flights, especially during rainy season. Ask around at airport for private-hire air fare prices.

**Excursions**  Interesting for wildlife, as is the river trip (hire a motorbike or jeep to go to the river; good swimming on the opposite bank; boat hire US$5). 4 km. from town is the Laguna, with plenty of wildlife; the water is very warm, the bathing safe where the locals swim, near the café with the jetty (elsewhere there are stingrays and alligators). Motorbike taxi from Trinidad, US$1.

**San Ignacio de Moxos**, 90 km. W of Trinidad, is known as the folklore capital of the Beni Department. The traditions of the Jesuit missions are still maintained with big *fiestas*, especially during Holy Week and on 31 July, the town's patron saint's day. 60% of the population is Indian, speaking its own language. There are a few cheapish *residencias*, the best being *Don Joaquín*, on the main plaza, E, without bath, very clean, fan, family atmosphere. Electricity is supplied in town from 1900 to 2400. Several restaurants, including *El Sireri*, corner of the main square, good and cheap set lunches and delicious fruit juices, and *Don Chanta*, also rec. for tasty meat dishes; *Isireri*, good, but rather over priced (Hans and Veronica Liechti, Grenchen, Switzerland).

**Guayaramerín**  A primitive small town (pop. 12,500) and centre for gold prospectors, is on the bank of the Mamoré river, N of Trinidad, opposite the Brazilian town of Guajará-Mirim. Passage between the two towns is unrestricted, but if going from Brazil into Bolivia you need your passport stamped by the Bolivian consul in Guajará-Mirim before leaving Brazil, and by the Bolivian immigration office (closed 1100-1400). Similarly, if you are travelling into Brazil and not just visiting Guajará-Mirim, get your passport stamped when leaving Bolivia and entering Brazil (US citizens need visas to enter Brazil). Exchange money (cash and travellers' cheques 2-4% commission normally charged) in Bolivia, as this is very difficult in the State of Rondônia in Brazil. Boat trip, US$0.75, speed boat US$5 during day, more at night. If you don't want to stay, check the notice of boats leaving port on the Port Captain's board, prominently displayed near the immigration post on the river's bank. Boats up the Mamoré are fairly frequent—a three-day wait at the most.

**Hotels**  *San Carlos*, 6 de Agosto, a few blocks from launch dock, C for a suite, D for other rooms, some a/c, hot showers, clean, money exchange (dollars cash and travellers' cheques and cruzeiros), swimming pool, reasonable restaurant; *Santa Ana*, E, rec. *Litoral*, F, cold water only, friendly. *Central*, F, just off the Plaza, and *Mexo Plaza*, E, on the main Plaza.

**Restaurants**  Best is *La Puerta del Sol* for US$4-6 evening meals, or the old municipal market, two blocks west of the main square. *Snack Gino* at Av. 25 de Mayo 511 is also a possibility. At mid-day try the port area, where rapid short-order meals can be had for US$1-1.50.

**Buses to Riberalta**  2 hrs., US$4.75, 0800 and 1530 daily (first return bus at 0700). Also trucks available from the 1100 block of Gral. Federico Román.

**Air Transport**  Schedules for flights to Trinidad and to La Paz change daily; others to San Joaquín and Santa Ana. LAB and TAM offices at airport, 10 minute walk from town.

**Riberalta**  Only 175 metres above sea level, another expanding town (pop. 40,000) which, with the whole region, attained temporary importance during the natural-rubber boom of the late 19th century; the cattle industry is providing a new boost for the town. It is at the confluence of the Madre de Dios and Beni rivers, which together flow into the Mamoré a few km. N of Guayaramerín.

**Hotels**  *Noreste*, clean, friendly, *Cochabamba, Residencia, Santa Rita*, all F (without breakfast). *Residencias Julita*, F, small rooms, hot, no fan; *Comercial Lazo*, Calle N.G. Salvatierra (F, p.p., D with a/c, clean, basic; comfortable; washing facilities), *Colonial*, Plácido Méndez 1, F, dirty, cold showers, poor; *Residencial Los Reyes*, near airport, F, with fan, clean.

**Restaurants**  *Club Social Progresso*; *Club Social Riberalta*, better, on Maldonado; *Club Social Japonés*, Sucre opp. market, reasonable, about US$2.50 p.p.; *Restaurant Popular Cochabamba*, US$0.50. Restaurants on main square are mediocre; good meals in market, about US$1 for 2 courses; food stalls outside *Comercial Lazo*, tasty meals.

**Exchange**  Bazar La Paz on main Plaza buys dollars cash and travellers' cheques.

**Transport**  Flight, Riberalta-Cochabamba (US$100 TAM, US$105 LAB). LAB to La Paz, via Santa Cruz and Tarija (TAM to La Paz, US$65). Expect delays in the wet season. LAB office

Linares 31, TAM office is opposite LAB. Air taxi Riberalta-Cobija, US$400 in dollars. 2 bus companies (inc. Flota Yungueña) run to La Paz only after the wet season (ie after September); usually twice weekly, US$30, take plenty of food and drink (can take 36 hrs. to Rurrenabaque alone and no meals available until there), male passengers are required to dig bus out of the mud. A motorcycle can be hired for US$2 an hour (no licence or deposit required) for visits to jungle; taxi drivers can give you the address.

Boat trip from Riberalta to Puerto Rico via Río Aruña, from there to Conquista by road (US$4.10) and thence by Río Madre de Dios to Riberalta (US$5.25). There are long gaps between boats from Riberalta.

**N.B.** Food in the Beni tends to be expensive, but the steaks are good.

***Cobija***, capital of the lowland Department of Pando, N of La Paz, (pop. 7,000; 252 metres), only connections by air (e.g. TAM to Puerto Rico, Trinidad, La Paz, and LAB to Guayaramerín and Riberalta) and river transport. It is close to the Brazilian and Peruvian frontiers and the area has many Brazilian residents. Taxis charge US$12-15 for a day trip to Brasileia across the International Bridge. It is difficult to get more than a month-long entry stamp in your passport here; if needing longer, press for it.

**Hotel** *Prefectural*, Av. 9 de Febrero, central, F, cold showers, others more expensive.

---

## EASTERN BOLIVIA (5)

---

The vast and rapidly developing plains to the east of the Eastern Cordillera are Bolivia's richest area in natural resources. It probably has least to offer most visitors, but the remains of Jesuit missions east of Santa Cruz are worth a visit and the "Death Train" (Santa Cruz—Corumbá, Brazil) is a unique experience, dull, erratic but a most convenient land route.

***Santa Cruz*** de la Sierra (437 metres) is the only other city of note, capital of the Department of Santa Cruz, 552 km. by air from La Paz. Founded in 1561 by Spaniards who had come from Paraguay, Santa Cruz now has a population of 800,000, making it Bolivia's second city.

It is usually hot and windswept from May to August; when the cold *surazo* blows from the Argentine pampas during these months the temperature drops sharply; the rainy season is December-February. The Plaza 24 de Septiembre is the city's main square with the Cathedral (interesting hand-wrought colonial silver), the University and prefecture set around it. The Cathedral museum is open on Tuesdays and Thursdays (1000-1200, 1600-1800), and Sunday (1000-1200, 1800-2000). Worth seeing if only to wonder how such an isolated community maintained such high artistic standards (but entry is expensive). Pleasant residential areas are being developed on the outskirts of town. The water supply is very good, though typhoid and hepatitis are still a danger outside the city.

*Cruceños* are famous for their gaiety—their music, the *carnavalitos*, can be heard all over South America. Of the various festivals, the brightest is Carnival, celebrated for the 15 days before Lent: music in the streets, dancing, fancy dress and the coronation of a queen. Beware the following day when youths run wild with buckets and balloons filled with water—no one is exempt. The *mascaritas* balls also take place during the pre-Lent season at *Caballito Blanco*: girls wear satin masks covering their heads completely, thus ensuring anonymity!

Until recently Santa Cruz was fairly isolated, but new rail and road links in the 1950s ended this isolation and now there is an ever-increasing flow of immigrants from the highlands as well as Mennonites mostly from USA and Canada and Japanese settlers, such as the Okinawan colony 50 km. from Montero, to grow cotton, sugar, rice, coffee and other crops, which yield profusely. Cattle breeding and timber projects are also important. A trip out of Santa Cruz to see these newly-settled areas is interesting, especially towards the Río Grande or Yapacaní (beautiful birds and butterflies; the fish are highly recommended). About 7 km. E of town new Botanical Gardens are being developed. At the N edge of town (Barrio Equipetrol, towards airport) is a good, small zoo with a variety of tropical animals, birds and reptiles, take bus 8 or 16.

The exploitation of oil and gas in the Department of Santa Cruz has greatly contributed to the city's rapid development. There are several oil fields: at Caranda, 50 km. to the NW, at Colpa, 32 km. to the N and a large gas field at Río Grande, 40 km. to the SE. YPFB has an oil refinery at Santa Cruz.

**Warning**  The influence of drug-trafficking has made Santa Cruz an expensive and, according to many travellers, risky place. Always carry your passport with you as there are constant checks by Immigration. Failure to do so will result in extra hours at the police station. Watch out for the "planting" of drugs. If possible never be without a witness, always ask for the policeman's identity card (green, embossed with a coat of arms), take his name and number, and say you will take the matter to his superior. Try also to enlist the help of the military police. If troubled by the police, you may be able to get help from Radio Santa Cruz, Calle Marioflores y Güenda. Recent reports suggest that the city has made a big effort to improve its image, and the signs are that it is now a much safer place. However the complaints still out number the compliments nearly two to one, so caution is still advised!

**Hotels**  *Los Tajibos*, the biggest and most expensive, B/C, Av. San Martín in Barrio Equipetrol out of town, T 30022/51000, restaurant good but overpriced, swimming pool for residents only; *Cortez*, Av. Cristóbal de Mendoza 280, also out of town, on 2nd Anillo near the Cristo, T 31234, also has pool and good reputation, C, rec. for medium or long stays; *Las Palmas*, Av. Trompillo, near airport, T 30366/30533, new, friendly, rec.; *La Quinta*, 4-star, Barrio Urbari, T 42244, has individual chalets, good for families but out of town. In the centre of town is the *Gran Hotel Santa Cruz*, Pari 59, T 44811/48997, good with pool, B, much used by British visitors (with English managers), not really rec. for families; *Asturias*, Moldes 154, T 39611-14, with 2 pools, rec. for families C; all those mentioned above are air-conditioned. *Colonial*, Buenos Aires 57, T 33156, comfortable, rec., C; *Brasil*, Santa Bárbara 242, T 23530, D, breakfast, bath and friendly; *Alojamiento La Ramada*, Cañada 145, T 34-5541, D with bath, E without, clean, good, near bus station; *Roma*, 24 de Septiembre 530, T 38388/7, D, pleasant, good value, helpful, no restaurant; *Cataluña*, 10 km. N on Montero road, pool, basketball, grounds, D, very popular at weekends with Cruceños; *Viru-Viru* Junín 338, T 22687, D including breakfast, clean and pleasant, highly rec.; *Copacabana*, Junín 217, T 29924, D, with bath (E without), clean, friendly, cheap laundry service, rec.; *Bibosi*, Junín 218 (T 48887/51791), D-E, hot showers, breakfast extra, good; *Alojamiento Santa Bárbara*, Junín y Santa Bárbara 151, E, cold showers, helpful, clean, will store luggage, rec; *Alojamiento Oriente*, Junín 264, E, hot showers, rec; *Los Pozos*, opp. Mercado Los Pozos, F, hot shower, clean, safe; *Residencial Comercio*, Quijarro 439, also opp. market, F, clean, shared bathrooms, very friendly and helpful; *Res Ballivián*, Ballivián 71, F, clean, nice patio. *Residencial Bolívar*, Sucre 131, T 42500, E with breakfast, hot showers, some rooms with bath, nice courtyard with hammocks; *Residencial 26 de Enero*, Camiri 32, F, clean, with patio. For those taking buses, *Residencial Arze* at the back of the terminal, F, or *Querencia*, F, is about half a block north of the bus terminal and *Alojamiento San José*, Cañada 136, hot showers, clean, F, about 1½ blocks. For all hotels there is 3-tier pricing: locals, South Americans and others. All prices include taxes.

**Restaurants**  The best restaurants are the *Floresca*, Av. Velarde 136, which has a good discotheque upstairs; the **"85"** at Bolívar 85 is good with reasonable prices; *La Fonda de Ariel* (chicharrón on Sundays and pork), Av. Irala, and the *Ambassador*, Av. San Martín (all air-conditioned). *Victory* in Casco Viejo (old quarter), near Plaza, is expensive, but rec. for lunch and cakes. *Amadeo*, 21 de Mayo, just off Junín, Spanish, good value, rec. *Candilejas*, next to *Hotel Cortez*. *El Fogón*, Av. Viedma 436 and *La Buena Mesa*, 2nd Anillo near Cristo, both excellent for *parrillada* and *churrasquería*, and there are many other barbecue restaurants all around the 2nd Anillo; *Churrasquería El Palenque*, Av. El Trompillo y Santos Dumon, good; *Amadeus Pizzería*, Tercer Anillo 761, Barrio Equipetrol, T 45319, good; *Pizza Benetto*, René Moreno 165, highly rec. for "wicked" pizzas and cheap Argentinian wine; *El Mauricio Rancho*, Av. Ejército Nacional 505 for excellent steaks. Two quite good duck restaurants are located on Km. 2 (*Los Patos*) and Km. 8 on the road to Cochabamba. *El Surubí*, Av. Irala, serves only *surubí* (fish); *El Boliche*, Bení 222, serves good crêpes. Chinese restaurants include; *China Law*, Castedo Barba 127; *El Pato Pekín*, 24 de Septiembre, excellent, authentic Chinese; *Shanghai*, Av. 27 de Febrero 33, *Nueva China* on 24 de

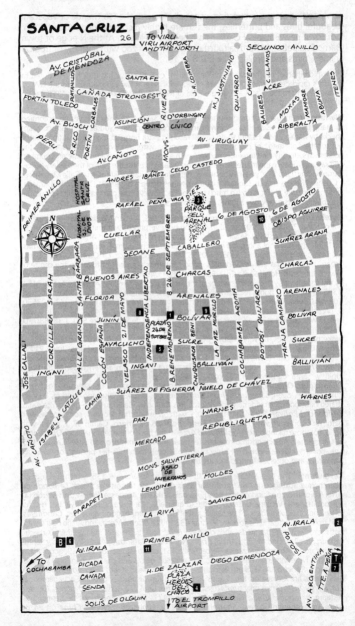

SANTA CRUZ
26

To VIRU
VIRU AIRPORT
AND THE NORTH

Av. CRISTÓBAL DE MENDOZA
SANTA FE
SEGUNDO ANILLO
PATANILLO
CAÑADA STRONGEST
J.R. COIMBRA
M.J. JUSTINIANO
QUIJARRO
CHIMPERO
C. LLANOS
ACRE
FORTIN TOLEDO
P. RICO
FORTIN CORRALES
ASUNCIÓN
RIVERO
D'ORBIGNY
CENTRO CIVICO
BAURES
MOXAS
MAMORE
ABUNA
ITENES
Av. BUSCH
PERU
Av. CAÑOTO
MOVS.
Av. URUGUAY
RIBERALTA
ANDRES IBÁÑEZ CELSO CASTEDO
Primer Anillo
HOSPITAL SANTA CRUZ
RAFAEL PEÑA VACA DIEZ
PARQUE EL ARENAL
6 DE AGOSTO
6 DE AGOSTO
OBISPO AGUIRRE
HOSPITAL S.J. DE DIOS
HOSPITAL S.J.DE DIOS
SANTA BARBARA
N
CUELLAR
SEOANE
CABALLERO
SUÁREZ ARANA
CHARCAS
BUENOS AIRES
CHARCAS
CHARCAS
CORDILLERA SARAH
VALLE GRANDE
FLORIDA
8 24 DE SEPTIEMBRE
ARENALES
ARENALES
ARENALES
JUNIN
8
1
BOLIVAR
9
BOLIVAR
COLÓN ESPAÑA
21 DE MAYO
PLAZA 24 DE SEPTBRE
BENE MORENO
BENI
LA PAZ MURILLO
AROMA
POTOSÍ QUIJARRO
TARJA CAMPERO
BOLIVAR
JOSE CALLAU
INGAVI
ISABELLA CATOLICA
AYACUCHO
VELASCO
INGAVI
5
SUCRE
CHUQUISACA
BALLIVIÁN
COCHABAMBA
SUCRE
BALLIVIÁN
CAMIRI
SUÁREZ DE FIGUEROA
ÑUELO DE CHÁVEZ
WARNES
Av. CAROTO
PARI
WARNES
REPUBLIQUETAS
MERCADO
MONS. SALVATIERRA
ASILO DE HUERFANOS
MOLDES
LEMOINE
SAAVEDRA
PARAPETI
LA RIVA
Av. IRALA
2
B 6
PRIMER ANILLO
POTOSÍ
Av. IRALA
11
PICADA
CAÑADA
SENDA
H. DE ZALAZAR
DIEGO DE MENDOZA
T
7
TO COCHABAMBA
PLAZA HEROES DEL CHACO
4
Av. ARGENTINA
TTE. A. PEÑA
SOLIS DE OLGUIN
TO EL TROMPILLO AIRPORT

Septiembre or the expensive *New Hong Kong* on Ballivián 137. *El Mandarín*, Av. Irala 673, and *Mandarín 2*, Av. Potosí 793, both excellent. Japanese *Kiku*, near Los Pozos market. Also good value is the *Bonanza*, Junín 177, across from the Post Office, clean. *El Dorado*, Libertad y Junín (main square), good; *Café España*, Junin y Colón España, good coffee, *salteñas* (a.m. only), snacks all day, cheap and cheerful; *Cochero's Bar*, Bolívar 165, good lunches; *Hannes*, Calle Campero, serves continental food, both English and German spoken. Outside the centre, *Chopp Rudi*, Av. Paraguay 739, and before that on same road, *La Corona Krone*, German and English is spoken in both and they serve good continental food. Many cheap restaurants near the bus terminal on the main avenida. Also on the extension of Calle 6 de Agosto behind Los Pozos market (daytime). Excellent *empanadas* are sold in the food section of Los Pozos market. The bakeries on Junín, Los Manzanos and España look scruffy but sell the local specialities: *empanadas de queso* (cheese pies), *cuñapés* (yuca buns), rice bread and *humitas* (maize pies); try the *Panadería Trieste*, 21 de Mayo 369, not the cheapest, but good breakfasts as well. *El Patio* and the *Palace* on the main square sell good cakes. *La Pascana* on the Plaza is a favourite of tourists and locals alike for meals, ice-cream and snacks, though service is slow. Ice-cream specialities at *Helados Alpine*, Junin 269, 2 blocks from main plaza, wide range of flavours, *Heladería Patty*, Quijarro 409, good and at *Kívón*, Ayacucho 267, highly rec.

**Books** *Los Amigos del Libro*, René Moreno 26, sells foreign language books (expensive) and *Newsweek*, and a useful guide *Con Usted La Señorial Santa Cruz de la Sierra* for US$0.25 (list of cheap boarding houses); *Cruz del Sur*, 21 de Mayo 62, sells *Time*. International magazines and newspapers often on sale in kiosks on main square.

**Shopping** Leather goods (Dorian, Florida 39, esq. Libertad, honest), baskets, hammocks. *Joyería Cosmos*, Handal Center, Loc. 13, Socabaya, corner of Av. Camacho y Av. Mcal Santa Cruz, for Bolivian and Inca designs in gold and silver, some colonial objects and pewter. Carvings and other objects made from beautiful *guayacán* and *jacarandá* wood (though reported these crack in drier climates). The *Los Pozos market* is new, clean, good for mid-day meals and worth going to in summer for its exotic fruits: *ambaiba* (looks like a glove and the fruit is sucked out of the "fingers"), *guaypurú* (like a cherry), *ocoro* (like a prickly mandarin), *achachayrú* (mandarin-like with hard skin), *pitón* (like sour grapes) as well as better-known tropical fruits. There are plenty of smuggled Brazilian goods on sale, exchanged for Bolivian coca. Beware of bag-snatching in the market. Another market (nothing for tourists, but also has a wide variety of fruit) is *Bazar Siete Calles*: walk down Vallegrande, past Ingavi.

**Taxis** About US$0.30 inside 1st Anillo, US$0.60 inside 2nd Anillo, fix fare in advance. Luggage extra.

**Entertainment** Discotheques: *El Mau-Mau*, open only during Carnival (a vast auditorium), *Reginne*, Av. Velarde, is the smartest new nightclub, entrance US$3, live music Mon., Wed., Fri. Another recommended night club is *El Cuerno Colonial* at España 162; on El Paso, *Tramps Bar* and *The New Orleans Bar* (both expensive). *Rincón Salteño*, nr. 2nd Anillo, Andean music Fridays and Saturdays 2200, friendly and homely atmosphere. *Tijuana Piano Bar Saloon* has offered a courtesy drink to bearers of the *South American Handbook* at Av. Velarde 230. They also co-own *Number One Disco*, Calle Boquerón 83. The bar at Hotel Los Tajibos usually has live music. There are numerous cinemas in town; see local press for details.

**Sports/Clubs** Tennis Club; Club Las Palmas, 2½ km. on road to Cochabamba, has 18-hole championship golf course and olympic-length pool; Club Hípico, riding club, nearby. Racquet Club, Barrio Ubari, racquet ball courts and saunas; Club de Caza y Pesca, Av. Argentina 317, T 35707, advice on fishing, hunting and safaris.

**Museums** Casa de la Cultura, on the plaza, with occasional exhibitions and also an archaeological display; has plays, recitals, concerts and folk dancing. **Museo de Historia Natural** in the university campus.

**Exchange** Bank of America, Velasco 19; **Banco do Brasil**, Libertad 156; **Banco Popular del Perú**, 24 de Septiembre 156; **Banco de la Nación Argentina**, Sucre 31; **Banco de Santa Cruz**, Junín (next to P.O.) will pay bolivianos on Visa card, no commission; also local banks. Open 0830-1130, 1430-1730. US$ can be telexed from anywhere in the world to **Banco Nacional de Bolivia**, who issues a cheque drawn on its own Brown Brothers, Harriman

---

## SANTA CRUZ: Key to map

1.Plaza 24 de Septiembre; 2. Plaza Ñuflo de Chávez; 3. Parque Arenal; 4. Plaza Héroes del Chaco; 5. Cathedral; 6. Bus Terminal; 7. Railway Station; 8. Post Office; 9. Municipal Tourist Office; 10. Mercado Los Pozos; 11. Instituto Boliviano de Turismo.

account in New York. This can be exchanged at one of two nearby *cambios*, paying 2% to the bank and 2% to the *cambio*. Use *casas de cambio* for money exchange, on 24 de Septiembre for example; in NW corner of Plaza 24 de Septiembre in entrance to a restaurant; **Ambar**, Arce y San Alberto; **Mendicambio** on main plaza will change travellers' cheques into dollars at 3% commission. **Magri Turismo**, Edificio Oriente, Of. 215, T 45663, 2 blocks from main plaza, the American Express agent doesn't change American Express travellers' cheques, but you may have to go there to have cheques certified before a *casa de cambio* will accept them. Money changers on Av. Libertad, and Plaza de Armas.

**Consulates** Brazil, 5. de Figueroa 127; **Argentina**, Banco de la Nación Argentina building main plaza, Sucre 31. **Uruguay**, Colón 58, Mon.-Fri. 0900-1100; **Paraguay**, Calle 4 Este, No. 14; **Peru**, La Paz 726; **British**, P.O. Box 3181, Centro Comercial Urbari, oficina 22 y 23, T 22250/36415. **Denmark**, Calle Arequipa 164, Casilla 4, T 2928, Mon.,-Fri., 0830-1200, 1430-1800.

**Health** Clínica Lourdes, René Moreno 362, T 25518. Dr. Pepe Arzabe, Quiroga Felix Romero 65, is reported to have specialised knowledge of regional illnesses.

**Post Office** Calle Junín 146. **Telecommunications** Entel, Warnes 83 (between Moreno y Chuquisaca), local and international calls, telex and fax.

**Tourist Agents** *Santa Cruz Tur* and *Orientur* are on the Plaza; *Exprinter* is at Libertad 149; *Magri Turismo*, address under **Exchange**, helpful, rec.; *Chovy Tours*, 21 de Mayo 309/317, T 24445, recommended; *Camba Tur*, Sucre 8; and *Turismo Balas*, Bolívar 16, recommended. Many agencies (there are over 100) are to be treated with caution since travel is not their primary business.

**Tourist Office** Independencia and Irala, 1st Anillo, and another branch on the corner of Bolívar and Murillos. Open Monday-Friday, business hours only, no city maps. Also kiosk at bus station.

**Air Service** LAB flies once or twice daily to La Paz and Cochabamba. LAB (once a week) and Líneas Aéreas Paraguayas (LAP—rec., once a week) fly Asunción-Santa Cruz. It is reported that up to US$40 can be saved by breaking your flight at Santa Cruz from Asunción and buying a La Paz ticket, rather than flying direct. Cruzeiro do Sul and LAB have 4 a week each to São Paulo and Rio de Janeiro (LAB, 2 to Rio). LAB and Aerolíneas Argentinas also fly to Salta (2 flights a week in all) and Buenos Aires (6 in all). There are also flights by LAB to Manaus, Caracas and Miami. LAB flies to some of the outlying towns in the Dept. of Santa Cruz and to Trinidad, Camiri, Sucre, Puerto Suárez (daily, US$112), book well in advance, San Ignacio de Velasco (Mon., Wed., Fri. but check with LAB), Tarija and Yacuiba. There is a weekly flight to Roboré and San Matías every Tues.—one can then enter Brazil via Cáceres, taxi US$2.40.

The international airport is at Viru-Viru, about 16 km. from the town. T 44411 or 33473, or Information on 181 (has Emigration/Immigration office, luggage lockers, duty free shop, and restaurant; no exchange facilities, but very helpful IBT Tourist Information Office speaks English and will change small amounts of money). The bus every 20 minutes to Viru-Viru leaves from the old Trompillo airport, or the bus terminal (US$1). Viru-Viru taxi, US$9 (beware of overcharging). TAM, office at Aeropuerto Trompillo, flies to Puerto Suárez (Tues., Fri., Sun.) fills up well in advance. Sucre (excess baggage over 15 Kg., US$1/Kg), and Yacuiba (daily). LAB office is at Chuquisaca y Suárez de Figueroa. On LAB internal services baggage allowance is 15 kg. (excess US$0.35 per kg.). Tax: internal US$2.75, international US$10. Often it is worth going out to the airport as neither LAB or TAM seems to be very aware of empty seats.

**Buses** Bus terminal on corner of Av. Cañuto and Av. Irala, T 338392. Most buses seem to run at night. Daily buses to **Cochabamba** (US$6, 9 hrs.) 0700 by Bolívar (sit on left for best views), 1000, or 1700 with connections to Sucre. Copacabana bus company rec. for its clean buses and punctuality, many other *flotas*, all leaving early morning or evening. Buses to Cochabamba now take the new, lowland route, via Montero, Buena Vista and Puerto Villarroel, which is no quicker than the old mountain route via Epizana. Some afternoon buses direct to **Sucre** US$12, 15-20 hrs, or via Cochabamba daily, US$15, 26 hrs. **Oruro** and **La Paz** US$14, 23 hrs.-Copacabana company to La Paz leaves 0830 and 1900, 13 hrs. to Cochabamba, 1 hr. change-over, then 7 hrs. to La Paz). For Sucre it is sometimes quicker and cheaper to fly, avoiding changing buses at Cochabamba, i.e. an extra 300 km. The only day time possibility for travel is by colectivo or truck to Cochabamba: either take Micro 17 to Km. 12 where there is a police checkpoint at which all the trucks stop, or go to the office of Transportes Peco in Av. Landívar, half a block west from the Cañuto statue, on Calle Ayacucho.

The fare after negotiation will only be marginally less than that for the bus, but at least you will get good views. Note that trucks to Cochabamba (if taking the old road) and Sucre traverse 3,000-metre plus mountains at night, so it's very cold: to Cochabamba 22 hrs., Sucre 32 hrs. Flota Chiquitana leaves for **San Ignacio** Mon., Wed. and Fri. (US$12), 18 hrs., more if raining. To **Camiri**, bus US$11, 8 hrs., *camioneta*, 7 hrs., US$7.80. 2 companies to **Trinidad**, Flota Puñata on Wed. and Sat. at 0600, US$13.50, and Trans Beni, same days at 1630, US$12.50; in the wet season, Nov.-Feb., the service may be cancelled. Lorries also leave for Trinidad from the Plaza behind the statue.

**Excursions** The new road route to Cochabamba passes through fertile lowland to the NW of Santa Cruz. It goes 37 km. N to **Montero** (pop. 30,000), where sugar and cotton are grown and processed, and on to Puerto Grether, high on the Río Ichilo, a tributary of the Mamoré. It then connects at Todos Santos with the 200-km. road to Cochabamba. A non-stop shuttle minibus service leaves from Santa Cruz bus station for Montero when full. From Santa Cruz buses and from Montero minibuses run to Buena Vista (*Pensión*); from there trucks run to El Terminal after which one can walk to the Surutú river, the eastern boundary of **Amboró National Park** (180,000 hectares)—walk to Cerro Amboró (guide required) recommended. There is a national park office in Buena Vista. The park is home to butterflies, humming birds, macaws, hoatzin and other native fauna (many of them endangered species). Beware of the insects—do not wear shorts or short-sleeved shirts; much wading is required to get around the park.

The country surrounding the city is flat and scenically uninteresting—except to the agriculturist. The sand-dunes (Las Lomas de Arena) 20 km. to the south are worth a visit; the scenery has been described as similar to deserts in a Walt Disney cartoon. You may be able to get there by taxi, but private transport is best. It may be possible to hitch at weekends, but a 4-wheel drive vehicle is normally required. Los Espejillos, where a mountain stream plunges over a waterfall and carves its way through limestone rocks down a beautiful green and forested valley is well worth the effort to get to—4-wheel drive, only in the dry season. Turn right at Km. 26 on the old Cochabamba road, cross the Piray river and drive some 12 km. up a forested valley. At a green field on the left (football goal posts) stop and walk a few hundred metres up to the stream. A favourite day trip is to the Yapacaní bridge where *surubí* from the river or *jochi* and *tatú* (armadillo) from the forest may be eaten in one of the riverside eating houses. The drive up to **Samaipata**, 120 km. along the old Cochabamba road, takes a full day—visit the Inca site, El Fuerte (entry US$1), near the town, an exhausting 3-hr. walk, but the drive up the Piray gorge and "over the top" makes a splendid trip. The ruins are some kilometres before Samaipata, coming from Santa Cruz; the side road to the left is signed to El Fuerte (take left fork when road appears to divide early on; cross river then uphill). In Samaipata is a good value, family hotel (try the local wine); a taxi from the town will go part of the way to the ruins. Take daily bus to Vallegrande which passes the site (2½-3 hrs.), or direct Sucre bus on old Cochabamba road.

South of Vallegrande is Pukara, from where a 4-5 km. walk will take you to the village of **Higuera**, where Che Guevara was killed. On 8 October each year, many people gather there to celebrate his memory; ask at the Universidad Gabriel René Moreno or Radio Santa Cruz about collective transport.

A recommended round trip taking about a week starts by arriving by train at San José de Chiquitos (with beautiful church that looks like a candle—see below). From there by truck to San Rafael (134 km.), San Miguel (169 km.) and then San Ignacio, and Concepción, all with interesting old churches. These Jesuit missions are also connected to Santa Cruz by bus, 4 times a week with Flota Chiquitana. LAB flies three times a week from Santa Cruz to San Ignacio. Buses also go from San Ignacio to Cáceres in Brazil every day, and there are *micros* from San Ignacio to San José three times a week at 1000 from the market. From **Concepción** there are daily tours to San Javier or Santa Cruz. Accommodation is limited, but best at **San Ignacio** (*Hotel Santa Cruz*; also luxury bungalows, US$55/d, or US$150 weekly for groups of over 6, contact Lucy Hartmann, Cochabamba, T 24258, and *Casa Suiza*, run by Señora Christina (speaks German) E, full board; visits arranged to *haciendas* with fishing and horse riding). Concepción is roughly 300 km. NE of Santa Cruz. Still reasonably wild though being opened up. Accommodation at *Grand Hotel Guarayas*, F; *Residencial 6 de Agosto*, shower, clean.

**Travel to Brazil** The Santa Cruz-Corumbá railway (take bus 4 from the centre to the station) is still rather primitive (and the time-table has been described as flexible, or pure fantasy) but has recently been improved; toilets are still dirty but there is an adequate dining car (food reasonable, coffee and cold drinks all twice normal prices). Trains stop at Quijarro near the frontier. From there travellers must go by taxi to Corumbá in Brazil; these meet the trains as they arrive and try to overcharge (fare should be about US$0.50 per seat; it's a further US$0.50

by bus from the border to Corumbá). The *ferrobus* train service is much faster and better, but also ends at Quijarro; it leaves Santa Cruz at 0800 Mon., Wed., Fri. 12-hr. trip, returning from Quijarro the following day at 1800 (meals served at seats). *Ferrobus* tickets are only available at the station (T 48488), and are sold out 1 week in advance; ticket office opens 0800-0830, but queuing starts at 0500 and touts try to pass on tickets (often forged) at double the proper price. Don't buy tickets for seats 2c and 2d, they don't exist. A Pullman train, with food but no a/c, leaves Santa Cruz on Tues. and Sat. at 1500, returning Wed. and Sun. 1100; a *rápido* leaves Santa Cruz Sat. and Thur. at 1330, returning Mon. and Fri. 1220 (scheduled journey time on each 19 hrs. but can take 3-5 days in wet weather). A *mixto* train runs from Quijarro on Wed., 1 2nd class coach only, 36 hrs. Fares: for ordinary trains Pullman, US$7.50 (comfortable, well sways a lot) first class US$6.50, second class US$4; *ferrobus*, Pullman, US$15, special, US$10. Check *all* times before setting out. Take a torch, whichever class you are travelling. It is a monotonous journey through jungle except for the frequent stops at trackside towns, where the train's arrival is the chief event in life. A rail flat-car can be hired to transport cars, US$185; you may have to wait several days for a flat-car, however. Only men are allowed to ride on the roof of the train. Food is available on the train or at frequent stops.

The ticket office at the station is not open before 0800 to Corumbá and Yacuiba (start queing at 0400-0500); purchase only the day before. The customs and emigration post at Quijarro closes very soon after the arrival of the *ferrobus*. You are advised to book as early as possible on all services to Corumbá, which are reported to be getting very crowded. Failing that you can try to buy a ticket on the platform 1/2 hr. before train departure. Foreign exchange generally little problem, but you are likely to be sold cruzeiros in largish denominations; also you will probably only be able to sell bolivianos in Bolivia, while a few dollars in cash have been known to make irritating border formalities less troublesome. However do beware of showing large quantities of money around. If there are heavy rains check that the line has not been washed out.

It is possible to go by road between Santa Cruz and the Brazilian border, but this is not recommended, especially in the rainy season. Take water, map, food and compass. The stretch between Santa Cruz and San José de Chiquitos has been washed away, so road traffic must go via Concepción and San Ignacio de Velasco (see above). After San José the road heads S from the railway at 7 de Mayo in a 128 km. detour until the railway is rejoined at Roboré (check compass because many tracks go to Paraguay). At Roboré the road narrows and deteriorates, being the worst stretch, to Corumbá. It is a 1,050 km. journey in all, without paving; in the wet allow 2 weeks.

Travellers who need a visa for Brazil are advised to obtain a visa before arriving in Santa Cruz. The Brazilian consulate in Santa Cruz normally takes 24 hrs. to process applications (if you apply at 0900, may be ready by 1200). Such travellers will be refused entry to Brazil unless they have a visa. Yellow-fever certificates are often asked for. All travellers, except Brazilian citizens, have to pay US$3 to the Bolivian Ministry of the Interior at the border; an official receipt is given.

On the railway, half way between Santa Cruz and Corumbá, is **San José de Chiquitos**, with huge Jesuit church. (*Hotel San Sebastián Silvestre*, F, basic, clean, good food, near railway station.)

**Puerto Suárez**  Beware thieves. *Hotel Sucre* on main plaza, F, barely adequate; *Hotel Banidi* (more comfortable and the most obvious), and *Residencial Puerto Suárez*, E, clean, fans and showers. *Hotel Bolivia*, D; *Hotel Beby*, Av. Bolívar 111, E, clean, welcoming. Beware the water, it is straight from the river. There are several G category hotels and cheap snack bars near the **Quijarro** train station, e.g. *Hotel Frontera*, mildly rec. as clean and OK and *Hotel Cochabamba*, 100 metres from the station, basic, clean and quiet. Most people prefer to go on to Corumbá where hotels are better.

The simplest way to Brazil is to fly La Paz-Puerto Suárez (twice a week with TAM, three times a week with LAB), then share a taxi to the border, US$6.50 (per car). Flights to Santa Cruz: LAB daily, TAM, Tues., Sat.; to Cochabamba, Wed. with LAB, via Santa Cruz. There is an airport immigration office where they will issue Bolivian exit/entry stamps.

A tip if travelling from Brazil to Bolivia is to arrive a week in advance, take a day trip from Corumbá to Puerto Suárez to purchase a train ticket at a travel agency (or book a flight), return to Brazil (to the Pantanal, say) and prepare yourself for the journey.

**Travel to Argentina**  To Salta by train takes 30 hrs. minimum and is a long and tiring trip via **Yacuiba** (11,000 people; many cheap hotels in town centre: *Hotel Monumental*, E, the best in town, and *Swins* is the only restaurant, rec. for its food and videos). First class and second class passengers must disembark at Yacuiba, taking taxi (US$0.50) to Pocitos on the border and walking across to Argentine side before boarding train for Salta. Tickets should be purchased from Incatur travel agents in Santa Cruz (beware of ticket touts). A more comfortable alternative is to take the *ferrobus* from Santa Cruz to Yacuiba (9-10 hour journey) and then to take a bus from Pocitos on the Argentine side of the border to Güemes (2 buses daily with connections to Salta and Buenos Aires). Train Santa Cruz—Salta with direct connection at Yacuiba, Wed. 1830, arr. Salta Fri. 1118, US$30 one way; in the other direction a night has to be spent in Yacuiba. Timetables show a *ferrobus* 4 times a week Santa Cruz—Yacuiba, 3 trains with restaurant car, 2 without (one of which provides the Salta connection). Such details must be verified on the spot. Trucks for Santa Cruz leave from Lourdes market, not advisable after rain. LAB flies to Santa Cruz and La Paz on Tues. and Sun., 1500 (supposedly); TAM also flies from here but has a much more flexible timetable.

---

## INFORMATION FOR VISITORS

**Documents**  According to the Bolivian Consulate in London, May 1991, a passport only is needed for citizens of the Western European (except France, Portugal, The Netherlands, Belgium and Luxembourg) and Scandinavian countries, and USA; all others need visas unless they have tourist cards, which can be obtained free from Consuls and travel agencies (check for changes at a Bolivian Consulate before arriving). They are good for 30 days and can be renewed, free, up to 90 days at the Ministerio del Interior in La Paz, Avenida Arce, Mon.-Fri. 0900-1830, Sat. 0900-1200 (this office may charge US$25, try elsewhere, e.g. in Cochabamba, or ask for 90 days on arrival). Extending tourist visas is time-consuming, and costs US$25; ensure that visas and passports are stamped with the same, correct date of entry or this can lead to "fines" later. Beware also of illegal charging on entry into, or exit from Bolivia. Business visitors (unless passing through as tourists) are required to obtain a Determined Object Visa quoting reference Tasa-03.03. D from a Bolivian consulate. This costs US$60. Hotels automatically register their guests with the immigration authorities but visitors staying as private guests should present their passports at the nearest immigration office.

Reports have been received of people impersonating Interpol men who want

---

# WILL YOU HELP US?

We do all we can to get our facts right in **The South American Handbook.** Each chapter is thoroughly revised each year, but the territory covers a vast area, and our eyes cannot be everywhere. A new highway or airport is built; a hotel, a restaurant, a cabaret dies; another, a good one, is born; a building we describe is pulled down, a street renamed. Names and addresses of good hotels and restaurants for "budget-minded" travellers are always very welcome. We would especially like to receive diagrams of walks, national parks and other interesting areas.

*Your information may be far more up-to-date than ours. If your letter reaches us early enough in the year it will be used in the next edition, but write whenever you want to, for all your letters are used sooner or later.*

Thank you very much indeed for your help.

**Trade & Travel Publications Limited**
6 Riverside Court, Lower Bristol Road, Bath BA2 3DZ. England

to see all your money—ask (politely) to see identification first and then only in front of friendly witnesses. Do not show money or passport to anyone not in police uniform. Genuine police and immigration staff are not above pretending that your documents are not in order, and demanding US$10 or so p.p. to "rectify" them. In such cases it is probably best to pay up with good grace.

**Airport** tax of US$12, foreigners must pay in dollars (only US$0.75-3 on internal flights, payable in bolivianos) is levied on leaving. Tax on airline tickets 12.3%. No tax if leaving overland, or if you stay in Bolivia less than 24 hours, although there have been reports of US$10 being charged overland.

### To Bolivia by Air

(1) *From Europe*: Either fly to Lima by Air France, etc., whence 11 flights a week to La Paz, or fly with Lufthansa from Frankfurt, with a change of aircraft in Lima; or via Rio de Janeiro, São Paulo or Buenos Aires. Tawa Tours, Sagárnaga 161, La Paz, T 329814, sells and confirms Aeroflot flights to Europe (probably the cheapest, but you need to reserve seat 3 weeks in advance in Bolivia). Another route is with Líneas Aéreas Paraguayas: Frankfurt-Brussels-(Madrid)-Asunción-Santa Cruz; on the outward journey you will have to stay for 1,3 or 5 nights in Asunción (first night may be paid for by LAP), but for the return there is an immediate connection.

(2) *From North America*: American from Miami to La Paz. Lloyd Aéreo Boliviano (LAB, no 1st class on international flights, but good service), daily from Miami via Caracas, Manaus and Santa Cruz, or Panama to La Paz. Otherwise, connections via Lima.

(3) *Within South America*: From Caracas twice weekly by LAB. From Lima, 11 a week by American, Aero Perú, LAB or Lufthansa. LAB excursion to Cuzco, once a week, US$148 return. From Arica, three times weekly each by LAB and LAN-Chile; this is a good route to Ecuador because from Arica AeroPerú flies to Guayaquil for US$140, Fri. and Sun., but this ticket is only available in Chile. From Santiago, 2 by LAB. From Buenos Aires, 4 flights by LAB and Aerolíneas Argentinas; to Salta, from Santa Cruz and Tarija with LAB with connections at Santa Cruz from La Paz and Cochabamba. LAB to Montevideo once a week, with a change of flight in Santa Cruz. From Asunción, one a week by LAB, 3 by American. From Rio and São Paulo, 4 a week by Cruzeiro do Sul and 1 a week by LAB (2 to Sáo Paulo only). *Note*: LAB international flights to and from points E of La Paz tend also to call at Santa Cruz or Cochabamba, or both.

**By Rail** From Argentina and Chile (**see page 226**).

**By Road** From Cuzco or Puno, several services. Peruvian and Bolivian roads partly paved. Also links with Argentina and Chile (see below).

**Motoring** (1) From Puno (Peru) via border stations at Desaguadero (for Guaqui and La Paz) or Yunguyo (for Copacabana, the straits of Tiquina, and La Paz). Peruvian customs at Desaguadero do not work after 1730 unless you are prepared to seek out the officials and pay them "overtime" (US$3 at weekends). Bolivian customs now operate to 1900 but immigration formalities can be completed at Copacabana if the border post is closed. Peruvian time is an hour behind Bolivian time.

(2) From Salta-Jujuy-La Quiaca (Argentina) to Potosí or Tarija. Roads ford many rivers in Bolivia and are impassable in wet weather (Argentine section, despite much work, is reported still to be bad). Bolivian border controls work mornings and 1400-1800 only. Argentina is one hour ahead of Bolivia, 2 in summer.

(3) Alternative routes lead from the Argentine province of Salta via Bermejo or Yacuiba into Tarija. Dry weather only.

(4) From Ollagüe (Chile) to Uyuni, very bad. A new dirt road has been built from Arica (Chile) via Tambo Quemado (being paved in 1991).

**Travel to Paraguay** Apart from the adventurous journey described on **page 253**, a cheap way of getting to Paraguay is to travel by bus to Salta or Orán (Argentina), then on to Asunción via Resistencia (Argentina).

**Duty-free Imports** 200 cigarettes, 50 cigars and 1 lb. tobacco; one opened bottle of alcoholic drink.

**Internal Air Services** are run by Lloyd Aéreo Boliviano (LAB) and TAM, the army airline, between the main towns. LAB offers a 28-day unlimited domestic flight ticket for US$119 for international travellers using LAB, which must be bought outside Bolivia (only one stopover per city is allowed, except for connecting flights; note that many flights radiate from La Paz or Cochabamba). To avoid paying the 12.3% tax on the air-pass, purchase it as an MCO outside the country, then exchange this for flight tickets later. You must enter Bolivia using LAB or on a foreign carrier with whom LAB may have a pooling arrangement. Also LAB is promoting limited stay tickets as well as the normal Apex type fares. Spouse fares (i.e. one goes free with one paying full fare) available on certain international flights. There are also reductions for special excursion flights. LAB will be glad to supply current information on request. Although LAB's services have been recommended, in out-of-the-way places TAM is more reliable than LAB, which will not go if there are insufficient passengers. Your seat priority on TAM is low, though. Insure your bags heavily as they tend to get left around.

**NB** If your internal flight is delayed keep your baggage with you and do not check it in until the flight is definitely announced. There have been robberies of prematurely checked-in baggage.

**Internal Roads** La Paz-Oruro, completely paved; Oruro-Challapata, paved first 30 km., then dirt (or mud in the wet season); La Paz-Tiquina: *autopista* to El Alto (toll US$0.25), then surfaced to Tiquina; La Paz-Cochabamba paved; Oruro-Cochabamba, all-weather; Cochabamba-Santa Cruz, mountain route paved, but in a very bad state, lowland route paved Cochabamba—Puerto Villarroel, Villa Yapacaní—Santa Cruz, with good gravel between; Cochabamba-Sucre and on to Potosí, S of paved road, paved for 127 km. to Totora, then dirt (bad in rainy season). Oruro-Potosí, dirt, very bad in rainy season. La Paz-Yungas, well-engineered and surfaced to Unduavi, but most roads in the Yungas offer "hair-raising driving". La Paz-Beni-Trinidad, mixed reports. Santa Cruz—Trinidad: paved from Santa Cruz to Puerto Banegas on Río Guapey, then gravel to San Julián, thereafter dirt (impassable in the wet) to Casarabe, whence poor gravel to Trinidad. Puerto Suárez-Arroyo Concepción open. Nearly all Bolivian road surfaces, even the paved sections, are bad, and after flooding or rough weather they are even worse. Even main roads may be closed in the rainy season.

**Buses** (interurban ones are called *flotas*, urban ones *micros*) ply on most of the roads. Reporting time is half an hour before the bus leaves, but you should always try to reserve a seat as far as possible in advance. In the wet season, bus travel is subject to long delays and detours at extra cost. On all journeys, take food and toilet wipes. They can be very dusty.

**Trucks** congregate at all town markets, with destinations chalked on the sides, they are not much less comfortable than buses or ordinary trains, but can be very dusty. They are normally about half the cost when there is competition. Otherwise they charge what they judge the market will bear and can therefore seem expensive.

**Motorists** (including motor-cyclists). A *carnet de passages* appears no longer to be required for those bringing a vehicle into Bolivia, but may be useful anyway. If hiring a car, the company can arrange a "blanket" driving permit for tourist purposes which is valid for several days and destinations. Tolls vary from US$0.50 to US$2.50 for journeys up to 100 km. You do need an International Driving

Permit (and, since a driving licence number is requested, also your national driving licence, or some ingenuity). Two authorisation certificates are required in La Paz: the first from the Automóvil Club Boliviano, corner of 6 de Agosto and Arce, and the second from the traffic police at the Comando Departamental, Organismo Operativo de Tránsito, corner of Mcal. Santa Cruz and Plaza San Francisco. For hints on high-altitude motoring, see **Introduction and Hints** at front of book.

**Petrol** (gasoline) 2 grades: 85 and 92 octane. Gas oil is slightly cheaper. Costs are higher in Guayaramerín, Riberalta and Puerto Suárez.

**Travel by Train** Trains are operated by Empresa Nacional de Ferrocarriles (ENFE). On *ferrobuses* and express trains, 1st and 2nd class are called Pullman and special (Especial) respectively. The "Pullman" services are reported to be quite comfortable. "Slow" trains have speeded up but they cannot take the curves and gradients at the same rate as the *ferrobuses*. Always check departure times in advance; timetables change too frequently for us to quote precise schedules.

**Walking** *Backpacking and Trekking in Peru and Bolivia*, 5th edition, published by Bradt Publications, describes 3-9 day hikes in the Cordillera Real within easy reach of La Paz. The local tourist office also produces a leaflet with sketch maps on walks available from La Paz. There are also some excellent guides available through local clubs.

**Camping** Chet and Jeri Wade, of Sacramento, California, tell us that one can camp almost anywhere in safety. Warm sleeping gear essential, even in the lowlands in the winter. Sleeping bags are also useful for getting some sleep on the buses or long distance trains, especially those crossing the Andes. Mosquito nets can be purchased in La Paz, but they are not cheap. Beware sandstorms S of Oruro. Camping gas is available in La Paz.

**Hotels** Throughout Bolivia the cheaper hotels impose their own curfews. In La Paz it tends to be midnight (check) but it can be as early as 2130 in Copacabana. These locking up times are strictly adhered to by hotel keepers. Clothes washing is generally not allowed. Accommodation at the cheaper end of the market costs about US$1.50 p.p. in a *posada*, US$2-3 in an *alojamiento* and US$3 upwards in a *residencial* (1991).

**Food and Drink** The normal international cuisine is found at most good hotels and restaurants. Some local dishes are interesting (see below). The 3 makes of local beer (Pilsener), lager-type, are recommendable; the local hot maize drink, *api* (with cloves, cinnamon, lemon and sugar), should be tried (usually US$0.12), as well as *singani*, distilled from grapes, good, cheap and bracing. *Chuflay* is pisco and 7 Up (or whatever carbonated drink is available). *Chicha* is a fermented maize drink, popular around Cochabamba. Bottled water cannot always be found, but is becoming more easily available, "sin" or "gas" (rain water is sometimes offered as alternative); the local tap water should not be drunk without first being sterilized. We do not recommend Bolivian market food except to the desperate and, of course, to those accustomed to South American food, but buy it only if it is cooked in front of you. Be very careful of salads; they may carry a multitude of amoebic life as well as vile green bacteria.

In the *pensiones* and cheaper restaurants a basic lunch (*almuerzo*—usually finished by 1300) and dinner (*cena*) are normally available. Lunch can also be obtained in many of the modern market buildings in the main towns.

*Salteñas* are meat stew pies, eaten regularly by Bolivians, mostly in the morning. Some are *muy picante* (very hot) with red chili peppers, but *medio picante* and *poco picante* ones can normally be obtained. For milk, try sachets of Leche Pil (plain, chocolate or strawberry-flavoured), at US$0.25 each.

**N.B.** Bolivian highland cooking is usually very tasty and often *picante*, which means highly spiced with chili peppers. Local specialities, which visitors should try, include *empanadas* (cheese pies) and *humitas* (maize pies); *pukacapas* are *picante* cheese pies. Recommended main dishes include *sajta de pollo*, hot spicy chicken with onion, fresh potatoes and *chuño* (dehydrated potatoes), *parrillada* (a Bolivian kind of mixed grill), *fricase* (juicy pork dish served with *chuño*), *silpancho* (fried breaded meat with eggs, rice and bananas), *saice*, a dish of minced meat with picante sauce, served with rice, potatoes, onions and tomatoes, and *ají de lengua*, ox-tongue with chilis, potatoes and *chuño* or *tunta* (another kind of dehydrated potato). The soups are also good, especially a *chairo* soup made of meat, vegetables, *chuño* and *ají* (hot pepper) to which the locals like to add *llajua* or *halpahuayca* (hot sauces always set on restaurant tables) to make it even more *picante*.

In the lowland Oriente region, the food usually comes with cooked banana and yuca; for example, *Pollo Broaster* is chicken with rice, chips, yuca and fried banana. The bread in this region is often sweet with cheese on top, and the rice bread is also unusual.

**Best Buys** Llama-and alpaca-wool knitted and woven items are at least as good as those from Peru. La Cancha market in Cochabamba is highly recommended but you *must* bargain. Ponchos, *mantas*, bags, *chullos* (bonnets). Gold and silverware. Musical instruments such as the *charango* (mandolin with armadillo-shell sound-box) and the *quena* (Inca flute), and other assorted wooden items.

**Security** Apart from the warnings given in the text, note that in some cities there is hostility to foreigners, mainly out of resentment to foreign involvement in anti-narcotics policies.

**Health** Whatever their ages, travellers arriving in La Paz by air (too quickly, that is, for a progressive adaptation to the altitude) should rest for half a day, taking very little food and drink. They will be up and doing the next morning. In Bolivia, do as the Bolivians do: above 3,000 metres, walk slowly, very slowly uphill. Never go out for the whole day without taking an outer garment: the temperature drops sharply at sunset. Inoculate against typhoid and paratyphoid (also have yellow fever inoculation and anti-malaria tablets if visiting the lowlands) and stock up on necessary medicines; they are dear in Bolivia. Visitors are being asked for yellow-fever vaccination certificates when visiting Santa Cruz or the Oriente. A yellow fever vaccination certificate, at least 10 days old, is officially required for leaving the country; LAB is very strict about this. We have also been asked to mention that hepatitis is very common. Chagas disease is endemic in the Yungas and other warmer parts of Bolivia. There is no known cure, so that adobe huts with thatched, or leaf-protected, roofs should be avoided as sleeping places because they play host to the *vinchuca* beetle which is the vector; half Bolivia's population has the disease, which leads to heart failure but shows few other immediate symptoms (see **Health Hints**, at the beginning of the book).

**Clothing** suitable for Great Britain, with a raincoat or light overcoat, should be worn by visitors to the Altiplano and the Puna, where it is particularly cold at night. The climate in the Eastern Lowlands is tropical. Oruro and Potosí are colder than La Paz; Cochabamba can be very warm. There is a prejudice against the wearing of shorts in town centres.

**The best time for a visit** is May to November, the dry season. May, June, and July are the coldest months.

**British Business Visitors** are strongly advised to consult "Hints to Exporters: Bolivia", which can be obtained from Dept. of Trade, Export Services Division, Sanctuary Blgs, 16-20 Great Smith Street, London SW1P 3DB. Similar publications for U.S. business visitors may be obtained from the Department of Commerce.

**Hours of Business** are normally 0900-1200 (sometimes 1130 in La Paz), and 1400-1800. Saturday is a half day. Opening and closing in the afternoon are several hours later in the provinces. Government offices are closed on Saturday. Banks 0900-1200, 1400-1630, but closed on Saturday.

**Public Holidays** 1 January, New Year's Day; Carnival Week, Monday, Shrove Tuesday, Ash Wednesday; Holy Week, Thursday, Friday and Saturday; 1 May, Labour Day; Corpus Christi (moveable); 16 July, La Paz Municipal Holiday; 5-7 August, Independence; 12 October, Columbus Day; 2 November, Day of the Dead; Christmas Day.

There are local holidays at Tarija, on 15 April; at Sucre on 25 May; at Cochabamba, 14 Sept.;

at Santa Cruz and Cobija 24 Sept.; at Potosí, 10 Nov.; at Beni, 18 Nov., and at Oruro, 22 Feb.

**Festivals** January (last week), La Paz, "Alacitas". 2 Feb., 25 Aug.: Virgin Copacabana. 3 May: Fiesta de la Invención de la Santa Cruz, various parts. In La Paz El Gran Poder, end May/early June, at the "Calvario". 23 June: San Juan, all Bolivia. 29 June: San Pedro y San Pablo, at Tiquina. 28 July: Fiesta de Santiago (St. James), Altiplano and lake region; Achocalla a convenient place to go to. 16 August: San Roque, patron saint of dogs, the animals are adorned with ribbons and other decorations. First weekend in October: San Francisco, dancing on the streets in Copacabana. 1 and 2 Nov.: All Saints and All Souls, any local cemetery. For other festivals on the Altiplano enquire at hotels or tourist office in La Paz. Remember that the cities are very quiet on national holidays, but colourful celebrations will be going on in the villages. Beware of water-filled balloons thrown during carnival in most cities—even the coldest. Unsuspecting tourists are favourite targets.

**Local time** 4 hours behind GMT.

**Currency** The unit of currency is the boliviano (Bs.), divided into 100 centavos. There are notes for 200, 100, 50, 20, 10, 5 and 2 bolivianos, and coins of 1 boliviano and 50, 20, 10, 5 and 2 centavos. The boliviano replaced the peso boliviano in 1986 at the rate of 1:1,000,000; bank notes and other paper denominated in pesos ceased being legal tender on 31 December, 1989. Change is often given in forms other than money: e.g. cigarette, sweet, or razor blade. It is almost impossible to buy dollars at points of exit when leaving or to change bolivianos in other countries. Inflation is low; there is no need to buy bolivianos in small amounts to avoid depreciation. The black market is more-or-less dead, since rates are no different on the street and in *casas de cambio*. *Cambios* in all the major cities will change travellers' cheques, and changing US$ cash presents no problems anywhere.

Credit cards are catching on rapidly in most cities, but usually in the more expensive places. It is possible to get cash against Visa and Mastercard in La Paz in some major banks (**see page 221**). Many shops displaying credit card signs do not, in fact, accept them.

**Cost of Living** Rents, appliances, and some clothing, and especially toilet goods and medicines, are high priced. With inflation now under control, Bolivia has become much more expensive for the traveller. La Paz, Cochamba and Santa Cruz, and indeed anywhere else touched by the drugs or gold trades are expensive. For basic hotel rates, see above; *almuerzos* cost from US$1-2; all other meals are dear.

**Electric Current** Varies considerably. Generally 110 volts, 50 cycles A.C. in La Paz, 220 volts 50 cycles A.C. elsewhere, but check before using any appliance. (You may even find 110 and 220 in the same room). US-type plugs can be used in most hotels.

**Post, Telegraph, and Telephone** Post offices use the post box (*casilla*) system. Items sent by post should therefore bear, not the street address, but the *casilla* number and town. Hours are Mon.-Sat. 0800-2000, Sun. 0800-1200. There is a national and international express post system; special counters and envelopes provided. Air-mail letters to and from Britain take between 5 and 10 days. Parcels to Europe by sea: US$3-5 per kg., good reports but may take up to 3 months to arrive.

Radio telephone services run by the Serval Company serve Cochabamba and other parts of the interior. There is now direct satellite communication with Bolivia. Direct calls possible from major cities to Europe, clear lines, delays minimal (station to station, US$7.20/3 mins.). No collect calls can be made. When making overseas calls, your passport is kept to ensure prompt payment. Reduced rates on Sunday. Phone calls within city limits are free for private calls; for public phones, coins/fichas are necessary.

**Media** In La Paz: morning papers—*Presencia*, daily (available in other main cities), about 75,000, the largest circulation, largely Catholic, with good coverage of world events; *Hoy* and *El Diario*. *Meridiano* (midday): *Ultima Hora*, and *Jornada* (evenings). In Cochabamba—*Los Tiempos*, *Extra*. In Oruro—*La Patria*, mornings (except Mondays). *El Mundo* and *Crónica Deber* are the Santa Cruz daily papers; *Deber* also appears in Trinidad. La Paz papers are on sale in other cities. The *Miami Herald* is sometimes available in La Paz. Also, there are about 85 radio stations, a commercial government T.V. station as well as a university T.V. service.

We are deeply grateful to Huw Clough for updating this chapter and to the following travellers for new information on Bolivia: Rob Allan and Bridgit Vale (Pietermaritzburg), Michael Auer

(Ottobrunn), Steven Avgort and Carol Seger (California), Sue Balcomb and Tom Hore, Tobias Banaschewski, Anne Heintel and Klaus Knobel (Marburg, Germany) Marlise Baumgarter and Niklaus Graber (Erlach, Switzerland), Kenneth Bell (Glasgow), Petra Bell and Hans-Georg Henle (Schwaigern, Germany), Matthew Bell (Market Lavington, Wiltshire), Hans and Lena Bengtsson (La Paz, Bolivia), Salik B. Biais (Montmorency), Inga Björk and Martin Hallén (Sveg, Sweden), Riemer De Boer (Netherlands) Astrid Bombosch (Heidelberg, Germany), Hildegard Börgel (Seevetal, Germany), Andreas Böttner and Annette Drinkuth (Otterstedt, Germany), Rochelle Rhea Brand (Portland, Oregon), Major C. J. Brightman (Salisbury), Gianmarco Broggini (Milan), Marion Büttner (Hamburg), Nelly and Steve Caplan (Winnipeg, Canada), Liora Carmona and Ofer Kastner (Kiryat Bialik, Israel), Paul Carter (Hamilton, New Zealand) and Vivienne Mitchell (Coleraine, N. Ireland), Alysia Cook and Phil Waterhouse (Twyford, Berks), Bryan Crawford (Invernesshire, Scotland), Andrea Cujnik (München, Germany), Alastair and Ann Cuthbert (Broome, W. Australia), Karen Dahl (Hamden, Conn), Bente Dalgaard (Copenhagen), Louise Dionne (St. John's, Newfoundland), Carolyn Dougall and Howard Johnson (Edinburgh), Nelle Driessen (Maastricht, Netherlands), Holger Eberhardt (Wesel, Germany), Barbara Egli (Volketswil, Switz.), Richard Everson and Jo Penty (West Wickham, Kent), Tim Farnworth (Market Harborough, Leicestershire), Farthing/Kohl (La Paz), Mrs. P.L. Fearon (London E6), Anthony Feeny (London EC1), Rüdiger Filbrich (Frankfurt/Main), Gregory William Frux (New York), May-Lill Garly and Palle Valentiner-Branth (Copenhagen), Eduardo Garnica Fajardo (Potosí), Yves Genier (Louay, Switzerland), Gerhard J. (Santiago), Theodor A. Gevert (São Paulo), Doris Goll (Gossau) and Andy Stocker (Buchrain, Switz.), Jacqueline Greig (Cuckfield, East Sussex), Pilou Grenié (Antibes), Eric Hamovitch (Montréal, Canada), Clare Hargreaves (London), Lucy Harper, Johanne Harvey and Niklaus Hutmacher (Gysenstein, Switzerland), Nell Henderson (Lima, Peru), Ian Henderson (London SW16), Ulrich Herbert (Stuttgart), Frank Hermann (Nauheim), Toni Hilton and Dr Prudencio Guzmán (Jupiter, Florida), Gert Jan Hof and Yvonne Evers (Huissen, Neth), Gabrielle Holmstrom and Bernut Wallner (Uppsala, Sweden), Ralf Hönsch and Martin Stark (Switzerland), Sarah A. Horniman (La Paz), Sabine Imhoff (Germany), Anne Toft Johnsen (Frederiksberg, Denmark), Karen Johnson (Coquitlan, B.C.), Martin Jung (Tübingen), A. P. Kirk (Middlesbrough), Klaus Koch (Rosenheim, Germany), Ursula Kohlendorfer (Gunskirchen, Austria), Andy Kuendig and Rosi Nueesch (Zuerich), Dr. Judith Kuriansky (New York), Christina Kuseffsky (Stockholm), Olivier Lair (Paris), Steve Larkworthy (Amersham), Henrik K. Larsen (V. Skerninge) and Mai Britt Noerskvu (Svendberg, Denmark), Peter Lawlor (Armidale, NSW), Hans Liechti and Veronica Araneda de Liechti (Grenchen, Switzerland), Judith Locher (Switzerland), Philipp Magura (Reutlingen, Germany), Markus Maier and Gitte Wiedmann (Zürich), Susan Marfield (Long Beach, California), Simon Mays Smith (Waldron, East Sussex), Tom Amies (Bucks) and Simon Davy (England), Julianne McCabe (California), Maggie Widow, Jean O'Leary and Bill Shaffer (San Anselmo, C.A.), Greg Merrell (Boston, Mass.) and Kevin Merrell (New York), Martin Merz (Hochfelden, Switzerland), Patrick Meyer (Ammerschwihr, France), Andy Millbank (Norwich), Alison Milner and Keith Doyle (Manchester), Kari Løvendahl Mogstad and Trond Eri (Norway), David Moodie (Adelaide, Australia), Matthias Müller (Berlin 31), Steve Newman and Wendy Chilcott (Horsham, West Sussex), Asbjørn Nielsen (Denmark) Vital Pajarola and Eva Grunder (Zurich), Jeff Perk (Carbondale, Illinois), Guido Pfister (Weisslingen, Switzerland), Thomas Pichler (Berlin 65), Paul Pichler (Weiz, Austria), Melanie and David Poley (England), John Pomfret (Woking, Surrey), Arthur Poyner (Chloe), Bernd Proissl (Wernau), Patricia Quintanilla (Cultural Attache, Bolivian Embassy, London) Johan Reinhard (La Paz), Wendy Richardson (London SW19), Hilda Riedler (Ismaning, Germany), Mrs. H. Rijkels-Redeleer (Den Haag), Bryan and Charmaine Roche (Cape Town), Ann Rodzai and Doug Hanaver (Ithaca, NY), Ms Alex Rossi (Norwich, Norfolk), Ken Sattell (Boulder, C.O.), Ronald Schaulin and Christina Brand (Reinach, Switz), Florian and Erdbeere Schulz (Berlin 27), Roland and Brigitte Schwarz-Aaschbacher (Rüderswil, Switz), Michael Scott-Watson (Roxburghshire, Scotland), Ulrich Sigel (Schorndorf, Germany), John A.M. Snow (Santa Cruz, Bolivia), Trevor and Lynn Stacey (Windhoek, Namibia), Kristin Stoltz (Trondheim, Norway), Martin Stucki (Daellikon, Switzerland), Benedikt Sudbrock and Corinna Jansma (Berlin), Guillermo Surraco and Siobhan Rhea de Surraco (Berkeley, C.A.), Fredi Suter (Goldau) and Claudia Räber (Oberkirch), L. Tapsall (Kensington, South Africa), Christoph Theis (Wiesloch, Germany), Åse Totland and Jarle Unneland (Ålesund, Norway), Ian Trontz (Brooklyn, NY), Jarle Unneland (Alesund, Norway), Pierre Vigna (Neuilly Sur Seine, France), Andreas Vogt (Mössingen, Germany), Peter and Miek Vullings (Panningen, Netherlands), Thomas Walbaum (Steinheim, Germany), Urs Wickli (Neu St. Johann, Switzerland), Stephanie Wharton (Camberley, Surrey), Ben Wiggersfeldt (Vildbjerg, Denmark), Jacqueline P M Williams (London SW1), Julie Williams (Muswellbrook, NSW), Manfred Wolfensberger (Uster, Switzerland), Manuela Wonisch (Kloten, Switzerland), Julian Woodhouse (London NW3), and Bart Zwart (Eindhoven, Netherlands).

# VARIG ARE NEVER FAR FROM BRAZIL.

Brazil is a country at the forefront of technological achievement. But it is also much more. There's a spirit about Brazil. A spirit of warmth and vitality. A spirit that's perfectly reflected in the friendly efficiency of its national airline.

VARIG is Brazil.

**VARIG**
*Brazilian Airlines*

# BRAZIL

## INTRODUCTION

BRAZIL, the fifth largest country in the world, has the eighth largest population. It is almost as large as the United States of America. Its 8,511,965 square km. is nearly half that of South America. For neighbours it has all the South American countries save Chile and Ecuador. Distances are enormous: 4,320 km. from north to south, 4,328 km. from east to west, a land frontier of 15,719 km. and an Atlantic coast line of 7,408 km. Its population of 150.4 million (1990) is half that of all South America, and one in every two is under 25 years of age.

Brazil's topography may be divided roughly into five main zones: the Amazon Basin; the River Plate Basin; the Guiana Highlands north of the Amazon; the Brazilian Highlands south of the Amazon; and the coastal strip. The two great river basins account for about three-fifths of Brazil's area.

The Amazon Basin, in northern and western Brazil, takes up more than a third of the whole country. This basin is plain, broadly based on the Andes and funnelling narrowly to the sea; most of the drained area has an elevation of less than 250 metres. The rainfall is heavy, for the winds from the north-east and south-east lose their moisture as they approach the Andes. Some few places receive from 3,750 to 5,000 mm. a year, though over most of the area it is no more than from 1,500 to 2,500 mm. Much of the basin suffers from annual floods. The region was covered by tropical forest, with little undergrowth except along the watercourses; it is now being rapidly cut down. The climate is hot and the humidity high throughout the year.

The River Plate Basin, in the southern part of Brazil, has a more varied surface and is less heavily forested than the Amazon Basin. The land is higher and the climate cooler.

Most of the remainder of Brazil's territory is highland. The Guiana Highlands, north of the Amazon, are partly forested, partly hot stony desert. Those that face the north-west winds get heavy rainfall, but the southern slopes are arid. The rainfall, which comes during the hot season, is about 1,250 mm. a year. The summers are hot and the winters cool.

The Brazilian Highlands lying SE of the Amazon and NE of the River Plate Basin form a tableland of from 300 to 900 metres high, but here and there, mostly in South-Eastern Brazil, mountain ranges rise from it. The highest peak in southern Brazil, the Pico da Bandeira, north-east of Rio de Janeiro, is 2,898 metres; the highest peak in all Brazil, the Pico da Neblina on the Venezuelan border, is 3,014 metres.

For the most part the Highlands cascade sharply to the sea. South of Salvador as far as Porto Alegre the coast rises steeply to a protective barrier, the Great Escarpment. In only two places is this Escarpment breached by deeply cut river beds—those of the Rio Doce and the Rio Paraíba; and only in a few places does the land rise in a single slope making for comparatively easy communication with the interior. Along most of its course, the Great Escarpment falls to the sea in parallel steps, each step separated by the trough of a valley.

The few rivers rising on the Escarpment which flow direct into the Atlantic do so precipitously and are not navigable. Most of the rivers flow deep into the interior. Those in southern Brazil rise almost within sight of the sea, but run westward through the vast interior to join the Paraná. In the central area the Escarpment rivers run away from the sea to join the São Francisco river, which flows northwards parallel to the coast for 2,900 km., to tumble over the Paulo Afonso Falls on its eastward course to the Atlantic.

The Great Escarpment denies to most of Brazil the natural valley outflows and lines of travel from the interior to the sea. Of its rivers the Amazon alone is directly navigable for a great distance inland.

**Climate** The average annual temperature increases steadily from south to north, but even on the Equator, in the Amazon Basin, the average temperature is not more than 27°C, and the highest recorded has been only 36°C. Six degrees more have been recorded in the dry north-eastern states. From the latitude of Recife south to Rio de Janeiro, the mean temperature is from 23° to 27°C along the coast, and from 18° to 21°C in the Highlands. From a few degrees south of Rio de Janeiro to the boundary with Uruguay the mean temperature is from 17° to 19°C. Humidity is relatively high in Brazil, particularly along the coast.

It is only in rare cases that the rainfall can be described as either excessive or deficient: few places get more than 2,000 mm.—the coast north of Belém, some

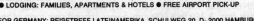

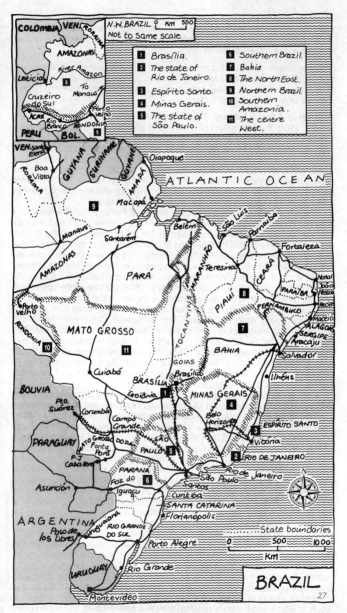

N.W. BRAZIL   0  KM  500
Not to same scale

1  Brasília.
2  The state of Rio de Janeiro.
3  Espírito Santo.
4  Minas Gerais.
5  The state of São Paulo.
6  Southern Brazil.
7  Bahia
8  The North East.
9  Northern Brazil.
10 Southern Amazonia.
11 The centre West.

ATLANTIC OCEAN

State boundaries

0      500      1000
Km

BRAZIL

of the Amazon Basin, and a small area of the Serra do Mar between Santos and São Paulo, where the downpour has been harnessed to generate electricity. The north-eastern droughts are caused not by lack of rainfall, but by irregular rainfall; the area is also subject to floods.

The rainy season in the South is from December to March; as this is also the holiday season in Brazil when hotels and flights tend to be booked solid, it seems a good time for tourists to stay away—unless, of course, they want to see the famous Carnival seven weeks before Easter.

**Political and Social History** The Portuguese, Pedro Alvares Cabral, landed in Brazil in 1500. The first system of government adopted by the Portuguese was a Capitânia, a kind of feudal principality—there were thirteen of them, but these were replaced in 1572 by a Viceroyalty. In the same year it was decided to divide the colony into two, north and south, with capitals at Salvador and Rio de Janeiro; it was not until 1763 that Rio became the sole capital. The Portuguese crown expected both a personal and a state revenue from its colony. This was raised partly by payment of a tenth of the produce from grants of land made to colonists, a fifth from mining production, and about forty other taxes.

Three hundred years under the paternal eye of Portugal had ill-prepared the colonists for independent existence, except for the experience of Dutch invasion (1624 in Salvador, and 1630-1654 in Recife). The colonists ejected the Dutch from Brazil with little help from Portugal, and Brazilians date the birth of their national sentiment from these events. In 1789 infiltration of European thought led to the first unsuccessful revolution against Portuguese rule, the Inconfidência in Minas Gerais, led by Tiradentes. When the troops of Napoleon caused the Portuguese Royal Family to sail in British ships to Brazil in 1808, the fate of the colony was decided: Brazil became the senior partner, as it were, in the Portuguese empire. King João VI returned to the mother country in 1821, leaving his son, the handsome young Pedro, as Regent. The Portuguese Parliament (the Cortes) mistrusted this arrangement, and called on Pedro to return, but the Brazilians asked him to stay. On 13 May 1822, he agreed to stay, and assumed the title of "Perpetual Defender and Protector of Brazil". On 7 September he declared Brazil's independence with the cry "Independence or Death" by the Rio Ipiranga; on 12 October he was proclaimed constitutional emperor of Brazil, and on 1 December he was crowned in Rio de Janeiro.

Dom Pedro the First had the misfortune to be faced by a secession movement in the north, to lose the Banda Oriental (today Uruguay) and to get somewhat involved in his marital relations. Finally, he abdicated as the result of a military revolt in 1831, leaving his five-year-old son, Dom Pedro the Second, in the hands of a regent, as ruler. On 23 July 1840, the lad, though only 15, was proclaimed of age and the regency discontinued. Dom Pedro the Second, a strong liberal at heart, promoted education, increased communications, developed agriculture, stamped on corruption and encouraged immigration from Europe. Under his rule the war with the dictator López of Paraguay ended in Brazilian victory. Finally, he declared that he would rather lose his crown than allow slavery to continue, and on 13 May 1888, it was finally abolished by his daughter, Princess Isabel, who was acting as Regent during his temporary absence.

There is little doubt that it was this measure that cost him his throne. Many plantation owners, who had been given no compensation, turned against the Emperor; they were supported by elements in the army and navy, who felt that the Emperor had not given due heed to their interests since the Paraguayan War. On 15 November 1889, the Republic was proclaimed and the Emperor sailed for Europe. Two years later he died in a second-rate hotel in Paris, after steadfastly refusing a pension from the conscience-stricken revolutionaries. At the time of the first centenary of independence in 1922 the imperial family was allowed to return to Brazil, and the body of Dom Pedro was brought back and buried in the cathedral at Petrópolis.

The history of the "Old Republic" (1889-1930), apart from the first ten years which saw several monarchist rebellions, was comparatively eventless, a time of expansion and increasing prosperity. Brazil declared war on Germany during both wars and Brazilian troops fought in the Italian campaign in 1944-45. In 1930 a revolution headed by Getúlio Vargas, Governor of Rio Grande do Sul, who was to become known as "the Father of the Poor" for the social measures he introduced, deposed President Wáshington Luís and Vargas assumed executive power first as provisional president and then as dictator. He was forced to resign in October 1945. In 1946 a liberal republic was restored and the following 18 years saw considerable economic development and social advance. There was, however, increasing government instability and corruption leading to growing military intervention in civil affairs; this culminated in the military movement of March 1964, which ruled until March 1985 with increasing liberalization and great economic success (up to 1980). In January 1985 a civilian, Tancredo Neves, representing a broad opposition to the military regime, was elected President by the electoral college introduced under the military's 1967 constitution. He was unable, because of illness, to take office: the vice-president elect, Sr. José Sarney, was sworn in as acting President in March 1985, and became President on Sr. Neves' death in April. A Constituent Assembly completely revised Brazil's constitution in 1987-88. A new constitution was approved in 1988 which opened the way for direct presidential elections to be held in November 1989. The elections were held in two rounds, the final result giving Fernando Collor de Melo, of the small Partido da Reconstrução Nacional, 53% of the vote, narrowly defeating his left-wing rival, Luis Inácio da Silva (Lula). President Collor took office on 15 March for a five-year term.

**Settlement and Economic History**    The first European settlement was at Salvador da Bahia, and the settlers came mainly from southern Portugal, with its feudal tradition of great estates. For the first few years Portugal, then much concerned with the Orient, paid little attention to Brazil. But about 1507 a second colony was settled at São Vicente, near Santos, and in 1537 a third at Olinda, near Recife. The settlers at São Vicente, who founded the first settlement in the highlands at São Paulo in 1534, were unlike those at Salvador and Recife: they came from the poorer and more energetic north of Portugal. All of them were attracted less by the prospect of earning their living by self-supporting labour than by opportunities of speculative profit. To do the work they impressed the primitive Tupi-Guarani Indians, many of whom died from European diseases (see *Red Gold*, by John Hemming). They cohabited freely with the Indians and, later, with slaves imported from Africa to run the huge estates.

Sugar cane had been introduced at São Vicente in 1532, but it was the wealthy settlers of the north-east who had the necessary capital to establish the crop and to buy African slaves to work it; the Indian, with his hunting-and-gathering culture, was a disappointment as a labourer. In the matter of sugar, Salvador and Recife had the advantages over São Vicente of being very much nearer home, and of having better ports and easier access to the interior. During the latter half of the 16th and the whole of the 17th centuries, the provinces of Bahia, Pernambuco, and Paraíba were the world's prime source of sugar.

The settlers at São Paulo, envious of the more fortunate north-east, sent out expeditions to explore the interior for gold, which had already been found in small quantities in their own streams. These hardy Bandeirantes pushed as far south as Colonia, opposite Buenos Aires, as far west as the Río Paraguay, and north into the area west of the sugar plantations of the north-east. In 1698 they struck gold in central Minas Gerais. More was found soon after in central Mato Grosso, and in 1725 in Goiás. Diamonds were discovered in 1729 north of the goldfields of Minas Gerais.

There was a great gold and diamond rush in which the sugar planters took part. Sugar by that time was on the decline: there was competition from the Caribbean; profits had fallen, and the Brazilians had made no attempt to lower costs by ploughing back profits: that was not in their tradition. The gold boom started early in the 18th century, lasted a hundred years, and then petered out. Minas Gerais was transformed from a wilderness into a well populated agricultural, pastoral, and mining region. It was as an outlet for this area that Rio de Janeiro was developed. Some of the wealth went to create the extraordinarily beautiful city of Ouro Preto, to-day a national monument of superb building, painting and sculpture, and the similarly attractive cities of São João del Rei, Mariana, Congonhas do Campo, Diamantina and others.

Brazil was ready for the next speculation, coffee, introduced about 1720 from French Guyane. Coffee planting began near Rio de Janeiro and at many places round the coast as far as the Amazon, but by 1825 it had mainly been concentrated in the Paraíba valley, west of the capital. From there it spread into São Paulo, where its cultivation attracted a large number of immigrants after 1850. About a third of the total production normally still comes from São Paulo state.

There have been many other typical Brazilian booms and recessions. The best known is the rubber boom in the Amazon valley; competition from SE Asia wiped it out after 1912. Sugar, coffee, and cocoa were alike the subject of booms. In each case Brazil was challenged by other sources of supply, where more intensive methods of production were applied.

This boom tradition still holds, but it is shifting from agriculture to industry: Brazilians today prefer to think of themselves as a rising industrial nation. Nevertheless, a great increase in production and export of manufactured goods has not prevented oases of prosperity being edged by deserts of poverty and wilderness.

**The People** At first the new colony grew slowly. From 1580 to 1640 the population was only about 50,000 apart from the million or so indigenous Indians. In 1700 there were some 750,000 civilized people in Brazil. Early in the 19th century Humboldt computed there were about 920,000 whites, 1,960,000 Africans, and 1,120,000 Indians and *mestiços*: after three centuries of occupation a total of only four millions, and over twice as many blacks as there were whites.

Modern immigration did not begin effectively until after 1850. Of the 4.6 million immigrants from Europe between 1884 and 1954, 32% were Italians, 30% Portuguese, 14% Spanish, 4% German, and the rest of various nationalities. Since 1954 immigrants have averaged 50,000 a year. There are some 1 million Japanese-descended Brazilians; they grow a fifth of the coffee, 30% of the cotton, all the tea, and are very active in market gardening.

Today the whites and near-whites are about 53% of the population, people of mixed race about 34%, and blacks 11%; the rest are either aboriginal Indians or Asians. There are large regional variations in the distribution of the races: the whites predominate greatly in the south, which received the largest flood of European immigrants, and decrease more or less progressively towards the north.

Most of the German immigrants settled in the three southern states: Santa Catarina, Rio Grande do Sul, and Paraná. The Germans (and the Italians and Poles and other Slavs who followed them) did not in the main go as wage earners on the big estates, but as cultivators of their own small farms. Here there is a settled agricultural population cultivating the soil intensively. It is only by such methods and by such an expansion that the wastes of the Sertão, given sufficient water, can be put to effective use. However, the Sertão has been relatively unaffected by European and Far Eastern immigration. Its inhabitants are people of mixed Portuguese and Indian origin (*mestiço*); most live off a primitive but ecologically effective method of cultivation known as "slash and burn", which involves cutting down and burning the forest for a small patch of ground which is cultivated for a few years and then allowed to return to forest.

The decision to found a new federal capital, Brasília, deep in the interior, was a symbolic act of faith in the future of the Sertão: a bold attempt to deflect population from the coastal regions to the under-developed central and western plateaux of the country.

Though there is no legal discrimination against black people, the economic and educational disparity—by default rather than intent of the Government—is such that successful Afro Brazilians are active almost exclusively in the worlds of sport, entertainment and the arts. By the way, don't refer to black people as "pretos" or "negros": describe them as "oscuros" or "gente de cor ".

The seven censuses of the present century show the growth of the population, from 17.3 million in 1900 to 119.0 million in 1980. Official estimates give the total popoulation at 148.9 million in 1985, compared with a total in 1990 of 150.4 million, estimated by external sources. In 1970, 56% of the population was urban; by 1990 this proportion had risen to 75%. Of the total labour force in 1988, 24% was occupied in agriculture, 15% in manufacturing, 12% in commerce, and 29.5% in services. The average life span has increased from 39 years in 1939 to 65 years today. The population grew 2.2% between 1981 and 1989. By region, population growth 1970-80 was: N, 5.0%; NE, 2.2%; S, 1.4%; and SE, 2.7%.

The population has historically been heavily concentrated in a comparatively small area—chiefly along the coastal strip where the original Portuguese settlers exploited the agricultural wealth, and further inland in the states of Minas Gerais and São Paulo where more recent development has followed the original search for gold, precious stones and slaves. Much of the interior of Pará, Amazonas, Goiás and the Mato Grossos has densities of one person per sq. km. or less. Brazil's attention is officially focused on these relatively underpopulated regions as a means of syphoning off some of the population excess in the urban centres—the industrialized South-East contains more than 50% of the total urban population and its two largest cities, São Paulo and Rio de Janeiro, both have over ten million people in their metropolitan and surrounding areas.

The urban population of Brazil increased at rates more than double the overall average rate, until the 1980s, and much of this growth has been concentrated in the larger cities—those over 100,000 (which numbered 95 in 1980). Internal migration is the major cause of these phenomenal growth rates, bringing to the cities problems of unemployment, housing shortage, and pressure on services which are already stretched to breaking point; shanty towns—or *favelas*, *mocambos*, *alagados*, according to the region—are an integral part of the urban landscape and a constant reminder of the poverty of some of the rural areas from which these people come. But while the North-East, because of its poverty, has lost many workers to the industries of the South-East, many rural workers from southern Brazil have moved north, drawn by the rapid development of Amazonia, creating unprecedented pressures on the environment.

The most recent official surveys indicate that 20% of the population is illiterate. Of the 13 million children between 7 and 14, 2 million have no school to go to. Of those who go to school, not all stay long enough to learn how to read and write. Adult literacy campaigns have, however, recently improved the picture.

**The Economy** Brazil is the world's tenth largest economy and eighth largest market economy. It has abundant and varied natural resources and a long-standing development record, the most striking features of which since 1945 have been state intervention and industrialization, particularly in the areas of energy, heavy industry, transport equipment and capital goods. The vast majority of consumer goods are now manufactured locally, as well as a wide range of capital goods. Since the 1970s there has been a rapid expansion of technology-based industries. Manufactures now account for 70% of total exports. Industry accounts for 38% of gdp and 25% of total employment.

Brazil remains a large farming country and is generally self-sufficient in food production. It is the world's largest producer and exporter of coffee. Since the mid-1970s soya and orange juice production have been developed, so that dominant positions in international markets in these products have been secured. Agriculture customarily produces about two-fifths of exports, 10% of gdp and 30% of total employment. However, the sector is backward in its use of techniques and yields are comparatively low. Mechanization is largely limited to southern areas. A concentrated land holding structure and a preference for export cash crops have generated structural problems which have prevented satisfaction of domestic demand for food.

The country is richly endowed with metals and other minerals. Brazil has up to a third of the world's total iron ore reserves, found mainly in Minas Gerais and certain parts of the Amazon basin, especially the Serra dos Carajás region (Pará). Brazil is also a significant exporter of manganese and gold and produces increasing amounts of tin and copper.

Energy sector development has aimed at substituting local for imported energy. Oil reserves are estimated at 2.1 bn barrels with substantial additions in recent years from the Campos basin off the coast of Rio de Janeiro state. Oil production has steadily risen to 0.6 m barrels a day, and this satisfies two-thirds of local requirements. Large investments have been made in hydroelectricity, alcohol and nuclear power. Hydroelectric plants produce 90% of electricity and several major schemes are in preparation. The Proálcool programme begun in 1974 aimed to substitute alcohol derived mainly from sugar cane for oil products, and 90% of the country's vehicles are powered by alcohol. However, the fall in oil prices in the 1980s rendered this programme uneconomic because of the massive subsidies to cane growers and official support fluctuates in line with the price of imported oil. A 620-Mw nuclear reactor at Angra dos Reis (Rio de Janeiro) came on stream in 1985, but financial restrictions have slowed nuclear power development.

High rates of inflation have been recorded in the 1980s and 1990s because of domestic and external factors. These included urbanization and food supply bottlenecks, energy consumption patterns heavily dependent on oil imports, public accounts disequilibrium, and generalized indexation covering wages, prices and financial instruments. A stabilization programme, known as the Cruzado plan, was introduced in February 1986, including a price freeze, introduction of a new currency, the cruzado, and partial dismantling of indexation. Inflation was sharply cut, but the generation of excess demand caused the plan to collapse by the end of the year and inflation soon rose again. In 1989 a new stabilization plan, dubbed the summer plan, was introduced when inflation rose to 1,000%. The new cruzado was created, worth 1,000 cruzados, but failure was inevitable considering the lack of political will to tackle the structural causes of inflation. It was left to the newly-elected Government in 1990 to introduce yet another currency, the cruzeiro, and sweeping economic reforms which effectively froze all savings and bank accounts, removed all subsidies and tax incentives and raised tax revenues. By keeping a very tight fiscal and monetary policy coupled with liberalization of foreign trade and the exchange rate, the Government hoped to eradicate inflation prior to easing liquidity and generating economic recovery. However, the Collor plan pushed the economy into deep recession while inflation remained intractable and informal indexation persisted in the absence of a reduction of the public sector deficit.

During the 1970s large-scale, high cost projects and current account deficits were financed by foreign borrowing, and Brazil accumulated the region's largest external debt, estimated at US$113bn at end-1988. From 1982 annual rescheduling agreements were concluded with creditors, with new money and, in 1983-85, IMF standby facilities. The World Bank and Inter-American Development Bank granted large loans for sectoral development. These arrangements did not, however, help to reduce the burden of interest payments and in February 1987 Brazil declared a moratorium on interest in order to preserve foreign exchange reserves and halt the net transfer of resources to creditors. The plan did not prosper and a year later reserves were even lower as lenders declined to extend credit and favourable terms were being awarded to other borrowers. In 1988 Brazil returned to the international financial community and negotiated a financing package from all creditors aimed at restoring its creditworthiness, but by 1989 it had moved back into arrears to preserve foreign reserves. The new administration was expected to negotiate a new debt package with all creditors in 1991.

**Government** The 1988 constitution provides for an executive president elected by direct popular vote, balanced by a bicameral legislature (72 seats in the Federal Senate, 487 seats in the Chamber of Deputies) and an independent judiciary. The vote has been extended to 16-year olds and illiterates. Presidential elections are held every 5 years, with a second round one month after the first if no candidate wins an outright majority. Congressional elections are held every four years, the deputies being chosen by proportional representation.

**Local Administration** Each State has a popularly-elected Governor who exercises the executive power, and a Legislative Assembly which legislates on all matters affecting provincial administration and provides for State expenses and needs by levying taxes. Each municipality has a similar structure, with a mayor (*prefeito*), also popularly elected, and a local council (*câmara de vereadores*).

**Railways**, of which there are about 30,500 km., were originally built to supply export markets and did not combine into a unified system. Brazil has two gauges, each of which makes up a complete system, so there is little transfer between them (some sections have been made mixed gauge). Three more gauges exist for the isolated Amapá Railway, the tourist—only São João del Rei line and the abandoned Perus-Pirapora line. About 2,450 km. have now been electrified. Many lines have been closed in recent years.

**Roads** Though the best paved highways are still heavily concentrated in the South-East, those serving the interior are now being improved to all-weather status and many are paved. Brazil has over 1.5 million kilometres of highways, of which in 1989 just over 130,000 km. were paved, and the recent road-building programmes have emphasized inter-regional connections and the opening up of the Centre, North and West of the country. Interurban bus services are frequent and good.

**Air Services** The first commercial flight in Brazil was in 1927. Because of the great distances and the comparative paucity of good highways and railways, aircraft have eased the traveller's lot more spectacularly in Brazil than in any other country. The larger cities are now linked with each other several times a day by air, and even the more remote points in the country can now be reached by light aircraft.

**Music and Dance** Perhaps because of its sheer size, Brazil has a vaster musical inventory than any other Latin American country, not only reflected in the immense regional spread of folk music but also in its successive waves of urban popular music. The Brazilian expresses him/herself through music and dance to an extraordinary degree and the music covers the whole spectrum from the utmost rural simplicity to the ultimate state-of-the-art commercial sophistication. The far north of the country is virtually in the Caribbean, while the extreme south shares its culture with the Rio de la Plata countries and it is here we will start. In Paraná, Santa Catarina and Rio Grande do Sul, the music is strictly European in origin, rhythm and instrumentation. Rio Grande do Sul shares Gaucho dances such as the Pericom and song styles such as the Milonga, Trova and Pajada with neighbouring Uruguay and Argentina. The Chula is a competitive dance for men to show off with (comparable to the Argentine Malambo), while the Pexinho is for men and women. The guitar and the accordion are the favourite instruments, also true for Santa Catarina and Paraná, where the names of the dances denote their European origins: Mazurcas, Valsas, Chotes, Polquinhas and Rancheiras. The Chimarrita is a song style that came straight from the Azores. If you are feeling sentimental, you sing a Toada, if energetic, you stamp your feet to a Fandango. Except for the Batuque de Rio Grande do Sul in Porto Alegre, closely related to the Candombe of nearby Montevideo, there is no African influence in the music of this region and none of that classic Brazilian syncopation.

Moving north into São Paulo, we enter an area rich in traditional folk dances and music, with the African admixture beginning to show up. At many religious festivals will be found the Congadas (European "Moors & Christians", but danced by blacks) and Moçambique (a stick dance for men), while the Samba de Lenço,

Fandango and Batuque are recreational dances for one or more couples. The instrumental accompaniment branches out into shakers (the *ganzá*), drums (*caixas* and *tambores*) and above all the guitar (*viola*). Try the great pilgrimage church at Aparecida do Norte on a Sunday. You might well see a group of religious dances. In the hinterland of Rio de Janeiro the Folias de Reis are out on the street from Christmas to Epiphany, singing from house to house, accompanying themselves on the *caixa* and *adufe* drums and the guitar, while in the old coastal towns of Parati and Angra dos Reis are to be found the Dança de Velhos (the old men), performed to the accordion. The Jongo is a dance of African origin for men and women, naturally with a drum accompaniment. And there is hardly need to mention Rio de Janeiro at carnival and its Samba Schools. Further north again, we come to the states of Espíritu Santo, Minas Gerais and Goiás. In colonial Ouro Preto, in Minas, you can hear the old Modinha sung to the Portuguese guitar as a serenade and be transported into the past. Espíritu Santo is home to the Ticumbi, a kind of Congada, danced to the guitar and shakers (*chocalhos*). Goias shares with Minas Gerais a very rich heritage of Portuguese derived religious folk song and dance, centred on Folias, Modas and Calangos.

Bahia is the heart of African Brazil and a very musical heart it is, born of the Yoruba religion that came with the slaves from what is now Nigeria. The resulting syncretic religion is known as Candomble in Bahia and the gods or "Orixás" are worshipped through song, dance and possession in the "Terreiros", directed by the priests (Pães-de-Santo) and priestesses (Mães-de-Santo). The mainly female adepts, dressed entirely in white, circle gracefully to the background chant of "Pontos" and the thunderous pounding of the *atabaques*, the tall drums. The two most revered priestesses are Mãe Olga de Alakêto and Mãe Menininha de Gantois. Similar syncretic African religions are found elsewhere in Brazil. Macumba in Rio, Xangô in the northeast and Umbanda all over. Another vital African element in Bahian folk music is the spectacualr dance-cum-martial arts form of Capoeira. Bodies whirl and cartwheel around each other to the sound of the *berimbau* (a one-stringed bow with resonator) and the accompanying chant. Related to the Capoeira is the stick dance Maculelê. Two of the best *berimbau* groups on record are Camafeu de Oxossí and the Cordão de Ouro. Bahia has a carnival almost as celebrated as that of Rio and here you can see the Afoxé, a serious religious dance, performed to drums alone.

North of Bahia is the Nordeste, with music that runs the whole gamut from black African to mediaeval Portuguese. In colonial times the church directed the peoples' musical energies into religious plays, songs and dances and a large number of these are still performed. The Bumba-Meu-Boi is a folk drama in the course of which a bull is killed and in due course brought back to life. Particularly popular in Piauí and Maranhão, its variants are found as far afield as Amazônia, where it is called the Boi-Bumbá and Paraná in the far south, where it is known as Boi-Mamão. Also popular along the coast from Ceará to Paraíba is a nautical drama of Portuguese origin called Marujada or Nau Catarineta, a version of Moors & Christians, accompanied by Portuguese guitar (*violão*), drums and the *ganzá* scraper. In Alagoas, Sergipe and Pernambuco we find the sword dance called Reisado, danced after Christmas, the Caboclinhos, who are dressed like Indians and dance with bows and arrows and the Guerreiros Alagoanos, a mixture of both. The last named are accompanied by the classical northeastern musical group called Terno de Pífanos, with the *pífano* vertical flute, accompanied by *maracas* and *ganzá*. The Banda de Pifanos de Caruaru in Pernambuco can be found on record. Recreational dance music in the Nordeste goes under the generic name of "Forró", said to be derived from the expression "For All", because the English companies operating at the turn of the century organized week-end dances for their workmen to which all comers were invited. Four very popular recreational folk dances of this region are the Ciranda (a round dance), the Coco, the Bate-Coxa (where the dancers bump bellies) and the Bambelô. Carnival in Recife, the largest city, is when and where to see the energetic and gymnastic Frevo, danced by young men with an umbrella in their hands, and the very stately and superbly costumed Maracatu dancers, with their queen and king. The Nordeste is equally rich in song styles, notably the Desafios, Emboladas, Cocos and Aboios. The Desafios are performed by so-called Repentistas or Violeiros, who accompany themselves on the Portuguese guitar and whose repertoire includes a large inventory of verse styles. They will sing about individual spectators, who then pay willingly for the compliment. The Emboladas and Cocos are similar, but faster and accompanied solely by tambourines, while the Aboios are haunting songs related to cattle and cattlemen. Repentistas and Emboladores can normally be found at work in markets throughout the region. The premier Repentista is Otacílio Batista do Pajeú, who sang to the Pope during the latter's visit to Brazil.

The music of the Nordeste has also been well propagated by more sophisticated groups that have based themselves on folk roots, such as the Quinteto Violado, Ariano Suassuna's Orchestra Armorial and Cussy de Almeida's Quinteto Armorial, not forgetting the veteran accordionist Luiz Gonzaga and the popular Alçeu Valença. As a result of the huge migration of *nordestinos* to the urban south, moreover, it is just as easy to hear this regional music in São Paulo as it is in Recife.

Finally to Pará and the Amazon in the far north, where the music has been heavily influenced from the Caribbean. The most popular musical genre here is the Carimbó, danced to a Merengue-type rhythm and played on drums, wind or brass (usually the clarinet) and strings, particularly the banjo. Notable performers are Pinduca ("O Rei do Carimbó"), Veriquete and Vieira. It is the last-named who thought up the term "Lambada" for his particular version of the Carimbó and the spectacular, thigh-entwining dance form introduced to the world in Paris by Karakos and Lorsac in 1988 had already been popular among young people at "Forrós" throughout the region for some years. The very traditional island of Marajó in the mouth of the Amazon has preserved versions of 18th. century dances, such as the Lundú and Chula.

The vast range of Brazilian regional folk music is only equalled by the chronological depth of its urban popular music, which surges like endless waves on a beach. For the origins we have to go back to Jesuit missions and Portuguese folk music, influenced and blended by African slaves, from which emerged the l9th century Lundús, Polcas and Maxixes that in turn gave way to the romantic and sentimental Choro song genre, (from *chorar*, to weep) , accompanied by guitar, flute and *cavaquinho* (small guitar), which became all the rage and indeed still has its adepts in Brazil today. Around the turn of the century the instrumentation turned to brass and Rio's urban Samba was born, a birth that was announced by the recording in 1917 of Donga's "Pelo Telefone". Names from this early period are Pixinguinha, Sinhô, Heitor dos Prazeres, Ary Barroso, Noel Rosa and of course Carmen Miranda, who took the Samba to Hollywood and the rest of the world. It also became intimately connected with the carnival in the form of Marcha Ranchos and Sambas de Enredo as the first samba schools were formed, of which Salgueiro, Mangueira, Partido Alto, Portela, Mocidade Independente and Beija-Flor are some of the most famous. With the Escolas de Samba came the Batucada or percussion groups playing the *pandeiro* (tambourine), *atabaque* and *tamborim* (drum), *agogô* (cowbell), *reco-reco*, *chocalho*, *afoxê* and *cuíca*. This is the real engine room of Samba. Listen to Lucio Perrone or Mocidade Independente de Padre Miguel. A new phase was ushered in with an invasion from Bahia and the Nordeste in the early 50's. From Bahia came Dorival Caymmi, who dropped his fishermens' songs in favour of the Samba, and Luiz Gonzaga, who brought his accordion, *zabumba* drum and *triangulo*, with which to play his Baiãos (his "Asa Branca" is a classic) and almost put the Samba itself into eclipse for several years. Almost, but not quite, for out of the ashes there soon arose Bossa Nova – white, middle class and silky smooth. Vinicius de Moraes and Tom Jobim were its heroes; 1958 to 1964 the years; Copacabana, Ipanema and Leblon the scene; "Samba de uma Nota Sí", "A Garota de Ipanema" and "Desafinado" the songs and Nara Leão, Baden Powell, Toquinho, João Gilberto, Luis Bonfá and Astrud Gilberto the main performers. Stan Getz, the American jazz saxophonist, helped export it to the world. What was now being called MPB (Música Popular Brasileira) then took off in several directions. Chico Buarque, Edu Lobo and Milton Nascimento were protest singers. Out of Bahia emerged "Tropicalismo" in the persons of Gilberto Gil, Caetano Veloso and his sister Maria Bethânia, Gal Costa, João Gilberto and "Som Livre". The words were important, but the rhythm was still there. Brazilian rock also now appeared, with such stars as Roberto Carlos, Elis Regina, Rita Lee, Beth Carvalho and Ney Mattogrosso. Recently the Bahianos have adopted Reggae. Still, Samba has survived, although now called "Pagôde" and amazingly, 40% of all Brazilian records sold are of Música Sertaneja, a highly commercialized pseudo-folk genre which is closer to American Country and Western than to most other Brazilian music. Listen to the "Duplas" of Tonico & Tinoco, Jaco e Jacozinho or Vieira & Vieirinha and you'll see. In the meantime a series of brilliant Brazilian instumentalists have become international names and often live abroad—Sergio Mendes, the guitaritst Sebastião Tapajos, flautist Hermêto Paschoal, saxophonist Paulo Moura, accordionist Sivuca, percussionists Airto Noreira and Nana Vasconcelos, singer Flora Purim and all-rounder Egberto Gismonti are but a few. On the top of a huge recording industry, we're now a long way from the grassroots and the haunting flute music of the forest Indians.

---

## BRASILIA (1)

---

The purpose-built capital of Brazil, with its second-half twentieth century design and its overflow communities.

**Brasília** On 21 April 1960, Rio de Janeiro ceased to be the Federal Capital of Brazil; as required by the Constitution, it was replaced by Brasília, 960 km. away in the unpopulated uplands of Goiás, in the heart of the undeveloped Sertão. The population of the Plano Piloto (the official name for central Brasília) is 411,000.

The new capital lies 1,150 metres above sea-level on undulating ground; the Federal District has an area of 5,814 square km. The climate, unlike that of the old capital, is mild and the humidity refreshingly low, but trying in dry weather. The noonday sun beats hard, but summer brings heavy rains and the air is usually cool by night.

The creation of an inland capital had been urged since the beginning of the last century, but it was finally brought into being after President Kubitschek came to power in 1956, when a competition for the best general plan was won by Professor Lúcio Costa, who laid out the city in the shape of a bent bow and arrow.

Along the curve of the bow are the residential areas made up of large six-storey apartment blocks, the "Super-Quadras". They lie on either side (E and W) of the "bow" (the Eixo Rodoviário) and are numbered according to their relation to the Eixo and their distance from the centre. Thus the 100s and 300s lie west of the Eixo and the 200s and 400s to the east; Quadras 302, 102, 202 and 402 are nearest the centre and 316, 116, 216 and 416 mark the end of the Plano Piloto. The numbering applies equally on either side of the centre, the two halves of the city being referred to as Asa Sul and Asa Norte (the north and south wings). Thus, for example, 116 Sul and 116 Norte are at the extreme opposite ends of the city. All Quadras are separated by feeder roads, along which are the local shops. There are also a number of schools, parks and cinemas in the spaces between the Quadras (especially in Asa Sul), though not as systematically as was originally envisaged. On the outer side of the 300s and extending the length of the city is the Avenida W3 and on the outer side of the 400s is the Avenida L2, both of these being similarly divided into north and south according to the part of the city they are in.

Asa Sul is almost complete and Asa Norte (which for years was looked down on) is growing very fast, with standards of architecture and urbanization that promise to make it more attractive than Asa Sul in the near future. The main shopping areas—with more cinemas, restaurants and so on, are situated on either side of the old bus station. Several parks—or at least green areas—are now in being. The private residential areas are W of the Super-Quadras, and on the other side of the lake.

At right angles to these residential areas is the "arrow", the 8-km. long, 250-metre wide Eixo Monumental. At the tip of the arrow, as it were, is the Praça dos Tres Poderes, with the Congress buildings, the Palácio do Planalto (the President's office), the Palácio da Justiça (Supreme Court) and the Panteão Tancredo Neves (a memorial to the president-elect who died in 1985 before taking office). The Cathedral and the Ministry buildings line the Esplanada dos Ministérios, W of the Praça. Where the bow and arrow intersect is the city bus terminal (Rodoviária), with the cultural and recreational centres and commercial and financial areas on either side. There is a sequence of zones westward along the shaft of the arrow; a hotel centre, a radio city, an area for fairs and circuses, a centre for sports, the Praça Municipal (with the municipal offices in the Palácio do Buriti and a great cross marking the spot on which the first mass was said in Brasília, on 3 May 1957), and, lastly (where the nock of the arrow would be) the combined new bus and railway station (Rodoferroviária) with the industrial area nearby. The most impressive buildings are all by Oscar Niemeyer, Brazil's leading architect.

The main north-south road (Eixo Rodoviário), in which fast-moving traffic is segregated, follows the curve of the bow; the radial road is along the line of the arrow—intersections are avoided by means of underpasses and cloverleaves. Motor and pedestrian traffic is segregated in the residential areas.

The Palácio da Alvorada, the President's residence, which is not open to visitors, is close to the lake. The 80-km. drive along the road round the lake to the dam is attractive. There are spectacular falls below the dam in the rainy season. Between the Praça dos Tres Poderes and the lake are sites for various recreations, including golf, fishing and yacht clubs, and an acoustic shell for shows in the open air. The airport is on the far side of the lake. Some 250 hectares between the lake and the northern residential area (Asa Norte) are reserved for the Universidade de Brasília, founded in 1962. South of the university area, the Avenida das Nações runs from the Palácio da Alvorada along the lake to join the road from the airport to the centre. Along it are found all the principal embassies. Also in this area is the attractive vice-presidential residence, the Palácio do Jaburu, again not open to visitors. This area is almost completed and very scenic.

**Sightseeing** A fine initial view of the city may be had from the television tower, which has a free observation platform at 75 metres up; also bar and souvenir shop; open 0800-2000, long queues Sat. and Sun. (the TV tower sways quite a bit). A general impression can be gained in a day by bus or taxi tour—don't try walking much unless fit and fairly impervious to heat (and even so not recommended for single females). This impression is best gained at weekends when the city is quieter, though then there are fewer buses to move you around (some say the city is "totally dead" at weekends). The city can also be seen at night by taking the Alvorada circular bus from the old Rodoviária. Bus maps are not available although buses are plentiful. It is worth telephoning addresses away from the centre to ask how to get there.

Congress is open to visitors Mon.-Fri. 0800-1200 and 1400-1700, guides free of charge (in English 1400-1600), and visitors may attend debates when Congress

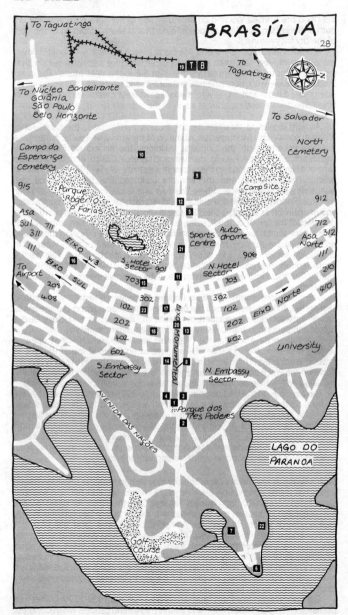

BRASÍLIA

28

To Taguatinga

To Taguatinga

To Núcleo Bandeirante
Goiânia
São Paulo
Belo Horizonte

To Salvador

North cemetery

Campo da
Esperança
Cemetery

915

Parque
Rogério
P Faria's

Camp Site

912

Asa
Sul

311

711

EIXO W3

EIXO SUL

S. Hotel
Sector 901

Sports
Centre

Auto-
drome

N. Hotel
Sector

906

703

712

Asa
Norte

312

111

210

410

111

To
Airport

208

408

102

302

EIXO Norte

302

102

202

202

402

Eixo Monumental

402

602

University

S. Embassy
Sector

N. Embassy
Sector

Parque dos
Tres Poderes

LAGO DO
PARANOA

Golf
Course

is in session. The Planalto may be visited; admission restricted to men in long-sleeved shirts and trousers and women in skirts, Fri., 0900-1100 and 1500-1700. The marvellous building of the Ministry of Foreign Affairs, the Itamarati, has modern paintings and furniture, beautiful water gardens and offers one of the most rewarding visits (guided visits at 1000 and 1600, free). Opposite the Itamarati is the Palácio de Justiça, the Supreme Court building, with artificial cascades between its concrete columns. Visiting (dress as for the Planalto), Mon., Wed., Fri., 1400-1900; Tues. and Thurs. 0800-1030. The Cathedral, on the Esplanada dos Ministérios, a most spectacular circular building in the shape of the crown of thorns (still under construction), is open 0900-1700; see also the Ceschiatti statues of the evangelists and the baptistery in the shape of a large pebble. The outdoor carrillon was a gift from the King of Spain. W of the TV tower on Avenida W3 Sul, at Quadra 702, is the Sanctuary of Dom Bosco, a square building constructed largely of blue glass. Other religious buildings worth seeing are the Fátima church (the Igrejinha) in the Asa Sul at Quadras 307-308, the Sanctuary of Our Lady of Fátima, the "orange caterpillar" on Av. W5 a little S of the Dom Bosco sanctuary, and the chapel (Ermida) of Dom Bosco, on the other side of the lake opposite the Alvorada, though the site is not well maintained. Some 15 km. out along the Belo Horizonte road is the small wooden house, known as "O Catetinho", in which President Kubitschek stayed in the late 1950s during his visits to the city when it was under construction; it is open to visitors and most interesting. A permanent memorial to Juscelino Kubitschek, the "Memorial JK", containing his tomb together with a lecture hall and exhibits, is worth visiting (open Mon.-Fri. 0900-1200, 1300-1800, Sat.-Sun. 0900-1900, entry US$0.50). The Brazilian Army headquarters, designed by Oscar Niemeyer, is interesting; the Monumental Parade Stand has unique and mysterious acoustic characteristics (the complex is north of the Eixo Monumental, between the "Memorial JK" and the Rodoferroviária). There are remarkable stained glass panels, each representing a state of the Federation, on the ground floor of the Caixa Econômica Federal.

Light industry alone is allowed in the city and its population was limited to 500,000; this has been exceeded and more people live in a number of shanty towns, with minimal services, located well away from the main city.

**Sculptures** Brasília is famous for its wealth of modern sculpture, Examples are: "Culture" (on the University campus), "The Meteorite" (above the Itamarati water-mirror), and "The Warriors" (in front of the Planalto)—all by Bruno Giorgi; "Justice" (in front of Palácio da Justiça), the four evangelists in front of the Cathedral and "The Water-Nymphs" (above the Alvorada water-mirror)—all by Alfredo Ceschiatti; "The Rite of Rhythms" (Alvorada gardens), by Maria Martins; and the beautiful "Mermaid" in front of the Navy Ministry on the Esplanada dos Ministérios. A statue of Juscelino Kubitschek is adjacent to the "Memorial JK".

**Ceremonies** The guard is changed ceremonially at the Palácio do Planalto on Tues., 0830 and 1730. The President attends if he is present.

**Local Holidays** Ash Wednesday; Maundy Thursday, half-day; 8 Dec. (Immaculate Conception); Christmas Eve.

**Hotels** Prices include breakfast, but 10% must be added. In the Southern Hotel Sector: *Nacional*, Lote 1, T 226-8180, L+, 4-star, pool service poor, reported not well maintained; *Carlton*, Quadra 5 bloco G, T 224-8819, A, 4-star, pool; *Bristol*, Quadra 4, bloco F, T 225-6170, A, 3-star, pool; *Riviera*, Quadra 3, bloco I, T 225-1880, B, 3-star; *Brasília Imperial*,

---

### Brasília: Key to map

1. Congress; 2. Palácio de Planalto; 3. Palácio da Justiça; 4. Itamarati; 5. Buriti; 6. Palácio da Alvorada; 7. Palácio do Planalto; 8. Ministries; 9. Army Ministry; 10. Observatory; 11. TV Tower; 12. Memorial JK; 13. National Theatre; 14. Cathedral; 15. Dom Bosco; 16. Igrejinha/Fátima; 17. Post Office, Telegraph and Postal Museum; 18. S. Banking Sector and Gold Museum; 19 Rodoferroviária; 20. Municipal Rodoviária; 21. Convention Centre and Tourist Office; 22. *Hotel Brasília Palace*; 23. Hospital.

Quadra 3, bloco E, T 225-7050, B, 2-star, deposit for room requested, good breakfast, motel-style; *Planalto*, Quadra 3, bloco A, T 225-6860, C, rooms in front noisy, city tours.

In the Northern Hotel Sector: *Eron Brasília*, Quadra 5, Lote A, T 226-2125, 5-star, L; *Aracoara*, Quadra 5, bloco C, T 225-1650, 4 star, A; *Casablanca*, Quadra 3, Lote A, T 226-0255, A, good, rooms on one side are noisy; *Diplomat*, Quadra 2, bloco L, T 225-2010, B, good; *El Pilar*, Quadra 3, bloco F, T 224-5915, B, friendly; *Byblos*, Quadra 3, bloco E, T 223-1570, C; *Aristus*, Quadra 2, bloco O, T 223-8675, good; and *Mirage*, Q2N, T 225-7150, fan, good, clean. Moderately-priced hotels can be found in the Northern Hotel Sector only. At weekends discounts can be obtained, worth bargaining.

The *Petrobrás Motel* at the Saída Sul is far from the centre but clean and cheaper (D) for motorists. Cheaper pensions available; enquire at airport information desk. *Cury's Solar* (Pousada), Neusa Batista Ribeiro, HIGS707, Bloco 1, Casa 15, T 243-6252, E-D, with hot shower, breakfast, laundry and kitchen facilities, rec. as good value (take bus 107 from Rodoviária). Teresa Tasso, SQN312-"K"-505, 70765 Brasília, T (061) 272-4243 or 347-4601, offers accommodation in an apartment in the Asa Sul at US$20 for the flat (2 rooms, kitchen, bath, laundry facilities), excellent value, Teresa gives city tours for US$40 and will collect you at the airport if you phone in advance (bus to flat from centre, 5 mins).

The hotels outside the city in Taguatinga (take 102 or 106 bus, EIXO) and Núcleo Bandeirante, though fairly basic, tend to be recommended for cheapness, but reported very difficult to get single rooms. Núcleo Bandeirante: *São Judas Tadeu*, E, noisy, clean but cockroaches, poor breakfast; *Hotel Rio de Janeiro*, E, O.K. for "young and hearty" but many mosquitoes; Taguatinga is pleasanter than the Núcleo, which is full of shanties; there are many cheap hotels and restaurants of a reasonable standard, for example, *Solar*, near Jumbo Supermarket, F, basic and clean. *Colorado*, Setor Hoteleira, Projeção B, T 561-3500, D, with bath, fridge, TV, good, in the centre; *Pousada Brasília*, next door, T 562-5055, E with bath and breakfast; *Globo*, CNB4, Lote 1, T 561-1716, E, without breakfast, friendly, basic. *Rodoviária*, E, without bath, more with, including breakfast, clean and friendly. Bus "Estrutural" from Brasília Rodoferroviária to Taguatinga Rodoviária where you change, without extra charge to 700 bus which passes, in order: *Camará*, QNE 16, F (hourly rentals also); *Palace*, CNB 11, E, clean, basic, hot water, communal shower; *Taguatinga*, by roundabout near clocktower, about 10 mins. from Rodoviária, F, hot showers, TV, back rooms are quieter, clothes-washing facilities, used by prostitutes. Bus 700 or 800 (marked "Eixo") goes from opp. Jumbo Supermarket in Taguatinga to old Rodoviária in Brasília. Very cheap accommodation in Formosa (see page 296).

**Camping** The city's main site is 2 km. out, by the Centro Esportivo, near the motor-racing track, with room for 3,100 campers. US$1.50 p.p., average charge, though apparently some travellers have stayed free. Take bus 109 (infrequent) from municipal Rodoviária. Agua Mineral Parque, 6 km. NW of city, direct buses only at weekend; US$1 p.p., mineral pool, showers. One site a few km. S on Belo Horizonte road, another out in the country about 70 km. E. Associação Brasileira de Camping (Edif. Márcia, 12th floor, Setor Comercial Sul, T 225-8768) has two sites: one at Km. 19 on the Belo Horizonte road and one 25 km. NE of Brasília at Sobradinho. Camping Clube do Brasil has site at Itiquira waterfall, 100 km. NE of the city, near Formosa; information from Edif. Maristela, room 1214, Setor Comercial Sul, T 223-6561. There is a Forestry Commission site 10 km. out of Brasília on the BR-041. There are signs to the sites. "Wild" camping is possible.

**Restaurants** There are new restaurants opening in Brasília every week. (The Southern Hotel Sector tends to have more; there are many cheap places on Av. W3 Sul. e.g. at Blocos 502 and 506.) At weekends few restaurants in central Brasília are open. The following are classified by their speciality:

International Cuisine: *Aeroporto*, terrace of international airport, very pleasant, food reported very good. Most of the big hotels' restaurants. *Restaurant Gaf*, Centro Gilberto Salomão, South Lake (very good, especially meat, but expensive).

For Brazilian food, there are several churrascarias (barbecues), for example *Churrascaria do Lago*, beside *Brasília Palace Hotel*; a number of Brazilian restaurants and some serving Northern Brazilian Amazonian food.

Seafood/Fish: *Panela de Barro*, Galeria Nova Ouvidor, Setor Comercial Sul; and others.

For European cuisine: Portuguese: *Cachopa*, Galeria Nova Ouvidor; Spanish: *O Espanhol*, Avenida W3 Sul, quadra 506; French: *Français*, 404 Sul; *Forty Five*, 203 Sul (overpriced); *La Chaumière*, 408 Sul. Italian/Pizzerias: *Kazebre 13*, Avenida W3 Sul, quadra 504; *Roma*, Avenida W3 Sul, quadras 501 and 511, good, quite cheap.

Chinese: *China*, 203 Sul; *New China*, 209 Sul (the best according to Chinese diplomats); *Fon Min*, 405 Sul; *Fon Pin*, 403 Sul; Japanese: *Nipon*, 314 Sul and 112 Sul. Also *El Hadji*, in *Hotel Torre Palace*, Setor Hoteleiro Norte, QD4, bloco A, 13, Arabic, very good.

Macrobiotic/Vegetarian: *Coisas da Terra*, Avenida W3 Norte, quadra 704; *Boa Terra*, Quadra 702, open for dinner.

Local: *Bom Demais*, Av. W3 Norte, Quadra 706, comfortable, inexpensive, serving fish, beef and rice, etc., live music at weekends (cover charge US$0.50). "For a good, cheap meal, eat at the crew's canteen at the airport, in a building to the right as you leave the main exit."

**Pubs**  There are two "English style" bars: *Gates Pub*, 403 Sul and *London Tavern*, 409 Sul. The *Grenada* bar near the *Hotel Nacional* (pedestrian area across road, 250 metres away) has good pavement atmosphere in early evening.

**Snack Bars**  (i.e. those serving *prato feito* or *comercial*, cheap set meals) can be found all over the city, especially on Avenida W3 and in the Setor Comercial Sul (e.g. *Max Burger*). Other good bets are the Conjunto Nacional and the Conjunto Venâncio, two shopping/office complexes on either side of the municipal bus station (Rodoviária), which itself provides the best coffee and *pásteis* in town (bottom departure level). For ice creams (especially tropical fruit flavours) try the two ice-cream parlours in 302 Norte or the *Marajoara* restaurant. Freshly made fruit juices in all bars; for Amazonian fruits try the bar at the eastern (i.e. Setor Bancário) end of the Galeria dos Estados.

**Shopping**  There are eight big shopping complexes, including the vast *Conjunto Nacional* on the north side of the Rodoviária, the *Conjunto Venâncio* on the south side, the *Centro Venâncio 2000* at the beginning of Avenida W3 Sul, *Park Shopping* and the *Carrefour* hypermarket just off the exit to Guará, 12 km. from centre. For fine jewellery, *H. Stern* has branches in the *Nacional* and *Carlton* Hotels and at the Conjunto Nacional and Park Shopping. The embassy sector is good for low-priced, high quality men's wear. For handicrafts try *Galeria dos Estados* (which runs underneath the *eixo* from Setor Comercial Sul to Setor Bancário Sul, 10 mins. walk from municipal Rodoviária, south along Eixo Rodoviário Sul) with shops selling handicrafts from all the Brazilian states; *Lampião*, 208 Sul; *Di Barro*, 302 Norte; *Zé Artesanato*, 215 Sul. For Amerindian handicrafts, *Artíndia* in the bus station and at the airport. Dried flowers (typical of the region) outside the Cathedral. There is a *feira hippy* at the base of the TV tower every Saturday, Sunday and holiday: leather goods, wood carvings, jewellery, bronzes. English books (good selection) at *Livraria Sodler* in Conjunto Nacional and at the airport.

**Car Hire**  Critical reports on Hertz cars hired at airport.

**Entertainment**  There are three auditoria of the Teatro Nacional, the Sala Villa-Lobos (1,300 seats), the Sala Martins Pena (450), and the Sala Padre José Maurício (120); the building is in the shape of an Aztec pyramid.

The Federal District authorities have two theatres, the Galpão and Galpãozinho, between Quadra 308 Sul and Av. W3 Sul. Concerts are given at the Escola Parque (Quadras 507-508 Sul), the Ginásio Presidente Médici (Eixo Monumental, near TV tower), the Escola de Música (Av. L2 Sul, Quadra 602) and the outdoor Concha Acústica (edge of lake near Brasília Palace Hotel). The Planetarium, on the Eixo next to the TV tower, gives shows Sat. and Sun. at 1600 and 1700.

There are 15 cinemas in the Plano Piloto; programmes are available daily by dialling 139 on the telephone, entrance is half price on Wed.

Information about entertainment etc. is available in two daily papers *Jornal de Brasília* and *Correio Brasiliense*. Any student card (provided it has a photograph) will get you into the cinema/theatre/concert hall for half price. Ask for "uma meia" at the box office.

**Nightclubs** in Conjunto Venâncio; in Centro Gilberto Salomão and in the main hotels.

**Museu Histórico de Brasília**  Praça dos Tres Poderes, really a hollow monument, with tablets inside; open Tues.-Fri. 0800-1200, 1300-1800.

**Museu de Ouro**  at the Banco Central exhibits old and new notes and coins and gold prospecting in Brazil; open Mon.-Fri. 1000-1600, Sat. 1400-1800.

**Museu Postal e Telegráfico da ECT**, Setor Comercial Sul, Ed. Apolo, Quadra 13, Block A. Very interesting, stamps, telegraphic equipment, etc. Entry, US$0.30. Closed Sun.-Mon.

**Museu da Imprensa Nacional**, Setor de Indústrias Gráficas, Quadra 6; bus 152 from municipal Rodoviária: admission free. Old printing and embossing equipment, etc.

**Exchange** Lloyds Bank, Avenida W3 Sul, quadra 506; First National Bank of Boston, Avenida W3 Sul, quadra 501; Citibank, Edifício Citibank, Setor Comercial Sul; Banco Francês e Brasileiro, Avenida W3 Sul, quadra 506; local banks. Open 0930-1630. Foreign currency (but not always Amex cheques) can be exchanged at these banks and at the branches of:

**Caixa Econômica Federal** at the airport; **Banco Regional de Brasília** and **Banco do Brasil**, Setor Bancário Sul. **American Express**, Kontik-Franstur, Setor Comercial Sul, Edifício Central, S/1007. **Diners Club** office, Av. W3 Norte 502. Use of international credit cards in Brasília tends to be difficult, though it should not be. Good exchange rates from hotels with "exchange-turismo" sign.

**Cultural Institutes** British Council: CRN 708/709 Bloco 3 Lotes 1 e 3, T 272-3060. Cultura Inglesa, SEPS 709/908 Conj. B. American Library: Casa Thomas Jefferson, Avenida W4 Sul, quadra 706, T 243-6588 and 243-6625. Institut-Cultural Goethe, Edifício Dom Bosco, Setor Comercial Sul, Bloco A, 114-118, Mon.-Fri., 0800-1700, 1600-2000.

**Embassies** British: SES, Quadra 801, Conjunto K, 70.408 Brasília, D.F. (with **British Commonwealth Chamber of Commerce**), or Avenida das Nações, Caixa Postal 070586, T 225-2710. **USA**: SES, Avenida das Nações 3, T 223-0120. **Australian**: Caixa Postal 11-1256, SHIS QI-09, Conj 16, Casa 1, T 248-5569 (in residential district, S of the lake). **Canadian**: SES, Avenida das Nações 16, T 223-7615. **Danish**, Av. das Nações 26, CP 07-0484, 70416, T 242-8188, open 0900-1200, 1400-1700. **German**: SES, Avenida das Nações 25, T 243-7466. **Netherlands**: SES, Av. das Nações 5, T 223-2025. **Swiss**: SES, Av. das Nações 41, T 244-5500; **Austrian**: SES, Av. das Nações 40, T 243-3111; **Swedish**: Av. des Nações 29, T 243-1444 (postal address: Caixa Postal 07-0419, 70.000 Brasília, D.F.).

**Immigration Office**, at end of W3 Sul.

**Poste Restante** Central Correio, 70001; SBN-Cj 03, BL-A, ED. SEDE DA ECT.

**Electric Current** 220 volts, 60 cycles.

**Tourist Offices** at the Centro de Convenções (Detur); small stand at Rodoferroviária, friendly but not very knowledgeable (open 24 hours, every day). Tourist office at the Air Terminal is on the international arrival side only, will book hotels, generally helpful; French and English spoken. Tours by bus (US$12-20), may be booked at the airport or *Hotel Nacional*: check that you will be taken back to the airport if you have a flight to catch. Touring Club do Brasil, on Eixo, has maps (members only).

**Tours** A good and cheap way of seeing Brasília is by taking bus rides from the municipal Rodoviária at the centre: the destinations are clearly marked. The circular bus route 106 goes right round the city's perimeter (you can also take buses 108 or 131). If you go around the lake by bus, you must change at the Paranoá dam to or from Paranoá Norte take bus 101, "Rodoviária", and to and from Sul, bus 100, bypassing the airport. Cheaper tours, from 1300-1700, from US$7 up, start from the downtown hotel area and municipal Rodoviária. All tour operators have their offices in the shopping arcade of the *Hotel Nacional*; Toscana has been recommended as cheap and good. Presmic Turismo, Galeria do Hotel Nacional, lojas 33/34, T 225-5515, offers full-, half-day and nighttime tours (0845, 1400 and 1930 respectively), from US$11.45 p.p. Kubitschek Turismo (Lucas Milhomens—speaks English), T 347-1494, rec. for city tour and information. Some tours have been criticised as too short, others that the guides speak poor English, and for nighttime tours, the flood lighting is inadequate on many buildings. Tour guides meet arriving air passengers at the airport, offering city tours, ending at a destination of your choice (3-4 hrs., English commentary, inexpensive but bargain)—a convenient way of getting to your hotel if you have heavy baggage.

**Roads** From Saída Sul (the southern end of the Eixo) the BR-040/050 goes to Cristalina where it divides; the BR-040 continues to Belo Horizonte and Rio de Janeiro, and the BR-050 to Uberlândia and São Paulo (both paved).

Also from Saída Sul, the BR-060 to Anápolis, Goiânia and Cuiabá; from Anápolis the BR-153 (Belém-Brasília) heads north to Belém (paved—for a description of this road, **see page 482)** and from Goiânia the BR-153 goes south through the interior of the states of São Paulo and Paraná (also paved).

From Saída Norte (the northern end of the Eixo) the BR-020 goes north to Formosa (1½ hrs by frequent buses from Brasília, 2 hotels, G, clean and friendly; cheap restaurants), Barreiras, and after Barreiras on the BR-242 (all paved) to Salvador and Fortaleza. The BR020 is in good condition for 120 km. At Alvorado do Norte (130 km.) there are cheap but very basic hotels. Posse (295 km.) is picturesque: **Hotels**: *Posse*, F; *Hoki Mundial*, F, friendly; *Rex*, E, all in Av. Padre Trajeiro. The road is slow with many potholes until Barreiras.

**Road distances**, in km.: Belém, 2,110; Campo Grande, 1,405; Corumbá, 1,834; Cuiabá,

1,127; Foz do Iguaçu, 1,415; Goiânia, 202; Manaus, 3,421; Porto Alegre, 2,021; Recife, 2,303; Rio, 1,204; Salvador, 1,529; São Paulo, 1,015.

**Buses** To **Rio**: 20 hours, 6 *comuns* (US$32) and 3 *leitos* (about US$64) daily. To **São Paulo**: 16 hours, 7 *comuns* (about US$20) and 2 *leitos* (about US$40) daily (Rápido Federal rec.). To **Belo Horizonte**: 12 hours, 9 *comuns* (US$19) and 2 *leitos* (US$38) daily (alight at Curvelo, 8½ hrs., US$11.20 for **Diamantina**). To **Belém**: 36 hours, at 0715, 1200, 1915, 2400 (US$55, Trans Brasília, buses poorly-maintained, but no alternative), *leito* (US$110) Tues., Wed. and Sat. To **Goiânia**: 2½ hours, every hour from 0600 to 2000 and at 2200 and 2400 (US$4.80). To **Cuiabá**, twice daily 1200 and 1945 (São Luiz), US$35, 20-24 hours, book journey in advance. To **Campo Grande**, US$37, 23 hours. To **Curitiba**: US$50, Tues., Thurs. and Sat. To **Porto Alegre**: 35 hours, every evening at 2100 (US$56). To **Natal**: every evening at 2000. To **Fortaleza**: 40 hours, every day at 0800 (US$64). To **Recife**: 40 hours. To **Salvador**: 27 hours, daily at 1200 and 2000 (US$40). To Anápolis, 2½ hours, US$4. Manaus via Porto Velho and Cuiabá involves several changes, taking up to 6 days (road is good as far as Porto Velho). Bus tickets for major companies are sold in a subsidiary office in Taguatinga, Centro Oeste, C8, Lotes 1 and 2, Loja 1; and at the city bus terminal. Left luggage, post office, telephone and telegram facilities available at new bus terminal (Rodoferroviária) beside the railway station, from which long-distance buses leave; bus 131 between Rodoviária, the terminal for city buses, and Rodoferroviária, US$0.40. The waiting room at the Rodoferroviária is very comfortable, but one is not permitted to sleep stretched out. There are showers (US$0.50). Both bus stations have large luggage lockers.

**Rail** In 1981 a metre-gauge rail link from Brasília to Campinas was opened; at Campinas one changes train for São Paulo. The train "O Bandeirante" leaves Brasília on Friday only at 2025 (but check in advance), arriving at Campinas at 1705 next day; there are several trains Campinas—São Paulo, but the most immediate connection (1827) will get you in at 2001 (or so the timetable says). Fare Brasília—São Paulo, 1st class US$23.20, sleeper US$39.20. A cheap and interesting way to the South; very slow, but it passes through some interesting country; sleeping cars are very good, book 10 days ahead. Cheap meals are served. The station is at the far end of the Eixo Monumental, past the TV tower.

**Air Services** Varig to Rio and São Paulo regular shuttle service (2½ hours in both cases); daily flights to other main cities; regional services to the interior of Goiás, São Paulo, Pará, etc. Vasp to Corumbá via Goiânia and Cuiabá, daily. Transbrasil offers reduced-fare night flights to Manaus at 0145 twice weekly. Bus 102 or 118 to airport, regular, US$0.65, ½ hour. Taxi is US$10 after bargaining, worth it. Left luggage facilities at airport (tokens for lockers, US$0.50). Airport tax US$1.25.

Of the seven *cidades satélites* that contain between them over half the Federal District's population, five are new and two (Brazlândia and Planaltina) are based on pre-existing settlements. **Planaltina**, 40 km. N of the Plano Piloto via Saída Norte, was originally a settlement on the colonial pack route from the mines of Goiás and Cuiabá to the coast. The old part of the town (50,000 inhabitants) still contains many colonial buildings. There are two good *churrascarias* on the main street and it is a good place for a rural Sunday lunch. 5 km. outside Planaltina is the Pedra Fundamental, the foundation stone laid by President Epitácio Pessoa in 1922 to mark the site originally chosen for the new capital.

Just before Planaltina, at Km. 30 on the road from Brasília, lies the point known as Aguas Emendadas: from the same point spring two streams that flow in opposite directions to form part of the two great river systems—the Amazon and the Plate. Permission from the biological institute in Brasília is now required to visit the site. Continuing along the same road (BR-020), at Km. 70 is the town of Formosa (*Hotel Mineiro*, E). Some 20 km. north of the town is the Itiquira waterfall (158 metres high). From the top are spectacular views and the pools at the bottom offer good bathing. It is crowded at weekends. There are four smaller falls in the area. Camping is possible. To get there take the road into the centre of Formosa and follow the signs or ask. It is not possible to get by bus to the Itiquira falls from Brasília in one day; the only bus from Formosa to Itiquira leaves at 1500 and returns the next morning.

In the other direction (S) take the Cristalina waterfall; take the BR-040 (Belo Horizonte road) and at Km. 104 take a left turn along a dirt road just after the highway police post. The waterfall is 11 km. along this road. The town of **Cristalina** is famous for its semi-precious stones, which can be bought cheaply in local shops.

Nearer Brasília, good bathing can be had at Água Mineral, two mineral pools 10 km. from the centre of the city. The newer pool is the better; turn right immediately after entering the main gate.

North West of Brasília, but only 15 minutes by car from the centre is the **Parque Nacional de Brasília** (about 28,000 hectares), founded in 1961 to conserve the flora and fauna of the

Federal Capital. For information, contact Delegacia Estadual do IBDF, Av. W-3 N, Q513, Edif. Imperador, rooms 301-320.

For information on the State of Goiás, which surrounds the Federal District, see page 480.

## STATE OF RIO DE JANEIRO (2)

The world-renowned Rio, with its beautiful location, carnival and much more besides (not all of it delightful), plus the hill and beach resorts nearby.

The State of Rio de Janeiro covers 43,305 sq. km. (the size of Denmark) and in 1985 had a population of 13.5 m., 88% of whom lived in metropolitan areas. The State is Brazil's second-largest industrial producer.

*Rio de Janeiro*, for 125 years the national capital, is on the south-western shore of Guanabara Bay, 24 km. long and from 3 to 16 km. wide. The setting is magnificent. The city sweeps twenty kilometres along a narrow alluvial strip between the mountains and the sea. The combination of a dark blue sea, studded with rocky islands, with the tumbling wooded mountains and expanses of bare grey rock which surround the city is very impressive. Brazilians say: God made the world in six days; the seventh he devoted to Rio (pronounced Heeoo by locals). God's work is now under threat from too many high-rise buildings and failure to maintain or clean the city adequately.

The best known of these rocky masses are the Pão de Açúcar (Sugar Loaf, 396 metres), the highest peak of a low chain of mountains on the fringe of the harbour, and the Corcovado (Hunchback), a jagged peak rising 710 metres behind the city. There are other peaks, including Tijuca (1,012 metres), the tallest point in the foreground, and 50 km. away rise the strangely shaped Serra dos Órgãos.

Rio has one of the healthiest climates in the tropics. Trade winds cool the air. June, July and August are the coolest months with temperatures ranging from 22°C (18° in a cold spell) to 32°C on a sunny day at noon. From December to March temperatures are high, from 32°C to 42°C. Sunstroke is uncommon, but humidity is high. It is important, especially for children, to guard against dehydration in summer by drinking as much liquid as possible. October to March is the rainy season, and the annual rainfall is about 1,120 mm. The population in 1985 was 5,650,000.

**History** The Portuguese navigator, Gonçalo Coelho, discovered Rio de Janeiro on 1 January, 1502, but it was first settled by the French, who, under the Huguenot Admiral Villegaignon, occupied Lage Island on 10 November, 1555, but later transferred to Sergipe Island (now Villegaignon), where they built the fort of Colligny. The fort has been demolished to make way for the Naval College (Escola Naval), and the island itself, since the narrow channel was filled up, has become a part of the mainland. In January 1567, Mem de Sá, third governor of Brazil, defeated the French in a sea battle and transferred the Portuguese settlement to the São Januário hill—the Esplanada do Castelo covers the site today. Though constantly attacked by Indians, the new city grew rapidly, and when King Sebastião divided Brazil into two provinces, Rio was chosen capital of the southern captaincies. Salvador became sole capital again in 1576, but Rio again became the southern capital in 1608 and the seat of a bishopric. There was a further French incursion in 1710-11.

Rio de Janeiro was by now becoming the leading city in Brazil. On 27 January 1763, it became the seat of the Viceroy. After independence, in 1834, it was declared capital of the Empire, and remained the capital for 125 years.

**Points of Interest** Two of the main streets are particularly impressive. The Avenida Rio Branco, nearly 2 km. long and 33 metres wide, is intersected by the

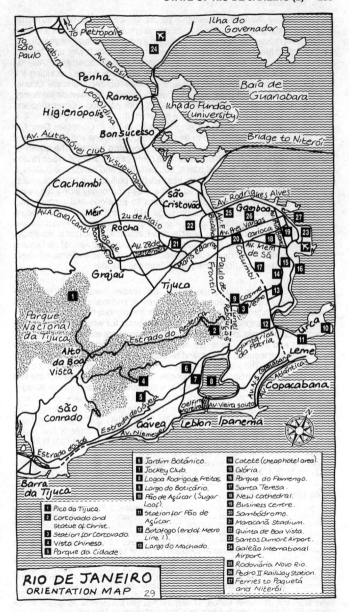

RIO DE JANEIRO
ORIENTATION MAP 29

1 Pico da Tijuca.
2 Corcovado and statue of Christ.
3 Station for Corcovado.
4 Vista Chinesa.
5 Parque da Cidade.
6 Jardim Botánico.
7 Jockey Club.
8 Lagoa Rodrigo de Freitas.
9 Largo do Boticário.
10 Pão de Açúcar (Sugar Loaf).
11 Station for Pão de Açúcar.
12 Botafogo (end of Metro Line 1).
13 Largo do Machado.
14 Catete (cheap hotel area).
15 Glória.
16 Parque do Flamengo.
17 Santa Teresa.
18 New cathedral.
19 Business centre.
20 Sambódromo.
21 Maracanã Stadium.
22 Quinta de Boa Vista.
23 Santos Dumont Airport.
24 Galeão International Airport.
25 Rodoviária, Novo Rio.
26 Pedro II Railway Station.
27 Ferries to Paquetá and Niterói.

city's main artery, the Avenida Presidente Vargas, 4½ km. long and over 90 metres wide, which starts at the waterfront, divides to embrace the famous Candelária church, then crosses the Avenida Rio Branco in a magnificent straight stretch past the Central do Brasil railway station, with its imposing clock tower, until finally it incorporates the palm-lined, canal-divided avenue formerly known as the Avenida Mangue. The Avenida Rio Branco is lined with ornate buildings, including the Brazilian Academy, National Art Museum, National Library, Municipal Council Chamber, and Municipal Theatre. The R. Ouvidor, crossing the Avenida Rio Branco half way along its length, contains the centre's principal shops. Other shopping streets are the RR. Gonçalves Dias, Sete de Setembro, Uruguaiana, Assembléia, and also the arcade running from Av. Rio Branco to the R. Gonçalves Dias. The most stylish shops, however, are to be found in Copacabana and in the various large shopping centres in the city (see under **Shopping** below). (The quality of souvenirs is higher in Copacabana than in the centre, and higher still in São Paulo.) The Av. Beira Mar, with its royal palms, bougainvilleas and handsome buildings, coasting the Botafogo and Flamengo beaches (too polluted for bathing), makes a splendid drive; its scenery is shared by the urban motorway along the beach over reclaimed land (the Aterro), which leads to Botafogo and through two tunnels to Copacabana, described on **page 319**. Some of the finest modern architecture is to be found along the Avenida Chile, such as the Petrobrás and National Housing Bank buildings, and the new Cathedral, dedicated in November 1976. There are many fine trees in the city. The photogenic Abricot de Macaco (Monkey's Apricot) has multi-coloured flowers, and large ball-shaped seeds hanging from the trunk, it originally came from the Guianas.

**Carnival**   Carnival in Rio is spectacular. On Shrove Tuesday and the three preceding days, the main avenues are colourfully lit, and many young people and children wear fancy dress. Special bandstands throughout the city are manned for public street-dancing (see *Daily Post/Brazil Herald* for where and when) and organized carnival groups, the *blocos carnavalescos*, are everywhere, dancing, drumming and singing. There are numerous samba schools in Rio. They are divided into four leagues, the first and second of which are allowed to parade in the Sambódromo. The second league (10 schools) parades on Saturday, the first league (16 schools) on Sunday and Monday. The order of appearance of the first league is determined by lottery, so there is no better day. Each school parades with 3,000-5,000 participants, divided into 40 groups and as many as 30 floats. Each school has 90 minutes to parade, and will lose points if it takes longer. The third and fourth leagues parade on Av. Rio Branco (less spectacular -has been described as a "mass of people walking up and down with three or four music groups"- but free). It may be possible to join a Samba school if you are in Rio for a long time, but costumes are expensive.

Each school chooses a theme, then composes a samba, and designs costumes and floats to fit it. All the schools are judged on each element, the best ones being

---

**Rio de Janeiro: Key to map**

1. Praça Mauá; 2. Praça da República and Campo de Santana; 3. Praça Duque de Caxias; 4. Praça Tiradentes; 5. Largo da Carioca; 6. Praça 15 de Novembro; 7. Passeio Público; 8. Parque do Flamengo; 9. Praça Mahatma Gandhi; 10. Praça do Expedicionário; 11. Aqueduto da Carioca (Arches, or *arcos*); 12. New Cathedral; 13. Monastery and church of São Bento; 14. Church of Candelária; 15. Church of Santa Cruz dos Militares; 16. Old Cathedral and Church of Carmo; 17. Monastery of Santo Antônio and Church of São Francisco da Penitência; 18. Church of Santa Luzia; 19. Church of São Francisco de Paula; 20. Itamarati Palace; 21. Paço Imperial; 22. National Archive; 23. Museu de Belas Artes; 24. Museu da Imagem e do Som; 25. Museu Histórico Nacional; 26. Instituto Histórico e Geográfico; 27 Museu de Arte Moderno; 28. Second World War Memorial; 29. National Library; 30. Tram terminus; 31. Ferry dock; 32. Riotur and Flumitur offices; 33. Central Post Office; 34. Teatro João Caetano; 35. Teatro Municipal; 36. Flower Market; 37. Mariano Procópio bus terminal (for greater Rio de Janeiro); 38. Menezes Cortes bus terminal (Castelo–a/c buses to Zona sul).

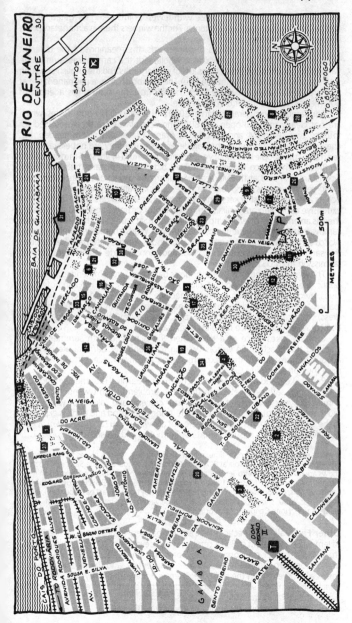

promoted to a higher league, those with fewest points being relegated, as in a football league. Competition is intense. For the winners there is a monetary prize, funded by the entrance fees.

To understand the traditions of the schools, the meanings of the different parts of the parade, and carnival as a whole, visit the carnival museum in the Sambódromo; although small, it has lots of photographs and the English-speaking staff are very informative (entrance free).The **Sambódromo**, a permanent site at R. Marquês de Sapucaí, Cidade Nova, not far from the centre, has a length of 600 metres, with seats for 60,000 people.

The Sambódromo parades start at 2030 and last about 12 hours. Gates (which are not clearly marked) open at 1800. The best places are those reserved for tourists, and sectors 4 and 11 (sectors 6 and 13 are not recommended, but cheaper). Seats are closer to the parade, but because they are not elevated you see mostly the people in front of you. Tickets (maximum 4) are sold through Banco do Brasil or the Banco Meridional in most big cities, and start at about US$30; tickets are also sold at the Maracanã Stadium box office, but touts outside will try to sell you places at double the price. Check availability, even if they say all tickets are sold. Tourist tickets range from US$138-240 to US$1,000 for the most expensive cabin and are available through Riotur or travel agencies. On Tuesday there is an amalgam of events including a huge float parade by the *grandes clubes carnavalescos*, and exhibitions by the previous year's champion samba groups, *blocos carnavalescos* and *frevo* and *rancho* groups. On the Saturday after carnival, the samba schools voted best on Sun. and Mon. parade in the Sambódromo (admission from US$20).

There are also innumerable fancy-dress balls (highly recommended); the main public one is at the Canecão (Sat. night) but there are scores more in hotels and clubs. Two that have been recommended are those at Clube Monte Líbano in Ipanema which have a different theme each night (you don't have to go in fancy dress), very crowded after midnight, and the Grande Gala Gay on Tues. (entry US$10). The Tourist Office has a list of all balls.

Carnival takes place at a time when Rio is packed with summer visitors enjoying the beaches. So visitors wishing to attend the Carnival are earnestly advised to make sure of their accommodation well in advance. Virtually all hotels raise their prices during Carnival.

Pickpockets and thieves are very active during Carnival (but the Sambódromo itself is quite safe—it's getting in that's the problem). Don't wander into dark corners on your own, don't brandish your camera, and take with you only as much money as you need for fares and refreshments (food and drink is expensive in the Sambódromo, glass and cans are not allowed if you take your own). It gets hot! Wear as little as possible (shorts or Bermudas and a T-shirt).

If you can't be there at Carnival time, rehearsals are held at various places from November onwards; e.g. the Portela *escola* at R. Arruda Câmara 81, Madureira, late Sat. nights. Samba shows are given at the Teatro Tereza Rachel, R. Siqueira Campos 143, Copacabana, on Mon. nights (not December), T 235-2119 (**see also page 314**); rec. Also, Beija Flor, one of the best samba schools, performs on Mon. nights at Urca (half-way up to Sugar Loaf Mountain), dinner available at 2000, show, US$10, starts 2200. Reservations required (on Fri. and Sat. at this venue is the "Noite Carioca" show, or a disco).

**Other Festivals** Less hectic than Carnival, but very atmospheric, is the festival of Iemanjá on the night of 31 December, when devotees of the spirit cults brought from Africa gather on **Copacabana, Ipanema and Leblon beaches**, singing and dancing around open fires and making offerings, and the elected Queen of the Sea is rowed along the seashore. There is a firework display on Copacabana beach at midnight, so the crowds tend to concentrate there, in front of the Copacabana Palace and Meridien hotels. At midnight small boats are launched as sacrifices to Iemanjá. Again, if you go, beware thieves.

The festival of São Sebastião, patron saint of Rio, is celebrated by an evening procession on 20 Jan., leaving Capuchinhos Church, Tijuca, and arriving at the cathedral of São Sebastião. The same evening an *umbanda* festival is celebrated at the Caboclo Monument in Santa Teresa.

## Museums and other Public Buildings

*All museums and the Jardim Botânico are closed over Carnival.*

The **Museu Nacional** in the Quinta da Boa Vista is said to be one of the most important museums in South America but is disappointing, and the park surrounding it is dangerous. The building was the principal palace of the Emperors of Brazil, but only the unfurnished Throne Room and ambassadorial reception room on the 2nd floor reflect past glories. In the entrance hall is the famous Bêndego meteorite, found in the State of Bahia in 1888; its original weight, before some of it was chipped, was 5,360 kg. Besides several foreign collections of note, the Museum contains collections of Brazilian Indian weapons, dresses, utensils, etc., and of minerals and of historical documents. There are also collections of birds, beasts, fishes, and butterflies. Open 1000-1645, closed Mon.; entrance US$0.50 (free Thursday). Buses: 472, 474, 475 from centre, Flamengo and Copacabana, 583 from Largo do Machado. Nearest metro São Cristóvão, but thieves operate by park entrance and in the park, taxi to the main door is safer. Some of the collections are open to qualified research students, but not to the general public.

**Museu de Fauna** also at Quinta da Boa Vista, contains a most interesting collection of Brazilian fauna. Open Tues.-Sun. 1200-1700.

The **Biblioteca Nacional** (National Library), at Avenida Rio Branco 219, was founded in 1810. Its first collection came from the Ajuda Palace in Lisbon, and today it houses over 2 million volumes and many rare manuscripts. The library is open Mon.-Fri. 1030-1830, and Sat. 1200-1800.

**Museu Nacional de Belas Artes** (National Museum of Fine Art) , at Avenida Rio Branco 199. There are about 800 original paintings and sculptures and some thousand direct reproductions. Exhibitions of works by contemporary Brazilian artists are often held here. Open Tues.-Fri. 1230-1800; Sat., Sun. and holidays 1500-1800; free.

Those interested in contemporary art will also visit the former Ministry of Education, designed by Le Corbusier, to see the great murals of Cândido Portinári, whose canvas, "Café", is in the Museum of Fine Art.

Opposite the Art Museum is the **Teatro Municipal**. Opera and orchestral performances are given here; the small museum that used to be below the theatre is now at R. São João Batista 103/105, Botafogo, normally open 1100-1700 Tues.-Sun, but reported closed since 1987.

The **Paço Imperial** (former Royal Palace on Praça Quinze de Novembro), a beautiful colonial building begun in 1743, has been restored. It has a gallery for tempory exhibitions and the occasional free concert.

The **Museu de Arte Moderna** (Museum of Modern Art), is a spectacular building at Avenida Infante D. Henrique 85, near the National War Memorial (**see page 306**). It suffered a disastrous fire in 1978; the collection is now being rebuilt, and several countries have donated works of art. There is also a non-commercial cinema. Entrance US$0.85, Tues.-Sat. 1200-1900 (open till 2200 on Thurs.), Sun., 1400-1900. Closed for repairs 1989, except for special exhibits.

The **Museu Histórico Nacional** on Praça Rui Barbosa (formerly Praça Marechal Âncora) contains a most interesting collection of historical treasures, colonial sculpture and furniture, maps, paintings, arms and armour, silver, and porcelain. The building was once the old War Arsenal of the Empire, part of which was built in 1762. Open Tues. to Fri., 1100-1700; Sat., Sun. and holidays 1400-1700; admission US$0.40. The building also houses the **Military Museum**.

**Museu Naval e Oceanográfico**, R. D. Manoel 15, daily 1200-1645. There is a particularly large collection of paintings and prints, besides the more usual display of weapons and figureheads.

The warship *Bauru* (ex-USS *McCann*) has been made into a floating museum, in the Glória Marina, opposite the war memorial on the Praia do Flamengo.

**Museu da Imagem e do Som**, also on Praça Rui Barbosa, has many photographs of Brazil and modern Brazilian paintings; also collections and recordings of Brazilian classical and popular music and a non-commercial cinema open Fri.-Sun. Closed for repairs.

The **Museu do Índio** (Museum of the Indian) is at R. das Palmeiras 55, Botafogo, T 286 0845, open Tues.-Fri., 1000-1800. Highly rec.; has handicrafts shop, which closes for lunch 1200-1400. It contains 12,000 objects from many Brazilian Indian groups.

The **Museu da Cidade** (Museum of the City) at Estrada Santa Marinha, Gávea, in the delightful Parque da Cidade (**see page 307**), contains a collection of Rio's historical objects. Open Mon.-Fri., 1300-1700; Sat.-Sun., 1100-1700. Buses from centre, 176, 178; from Copacabana, 591, 593 and 594.

The Fundação Raymundo Ottoni de Castro Maia, generally known as Chácara do Céu, R. Murtinho Nobre 93, has a wide range of art objects and particularly works of modern Brazilian painters. Take Santa Teresa tram to R. Dias de Barros, then follow signposts. Open Tues.-Sat. 1400-1700, Sun. 1300-1700, US$0.30. Castro Maia's former residence on the Estrada do Açude in the Tijuca Forest has same name and is also a museum, currently under restoration.

**Museo do Instituto Histórico e Geográfico,** Av. Augusto Severo 8 (10th floor), just off Av. Beira Mar, has a very interesting collection of Brazil's products and the artefacts of its peoples. Open Mon.-Fri. 1300-1700.

The **São Cristóvão Pavilion**, designed by Sérgio Bernardes, has the world's largest open floor space without columns or transverse walls, but is now closed to the public. It is in very poor condition. Sunday market is worth visiting for North Eastern food and hammocks. Bus 472 or 474 from Copacabana or centre.

The **National Observatory** (founded 1827) is on São Januário hill, R. Gen. Bruce 586, São Cristóvão. Visitors advised to call 248-1182 after 1700 to arrange a night viewing.

The **Casa de Rui Barbosa**, R. São Clemente 134, Botafogo, former home of the Brazilian jurist and statesman, containing his library and other possessions, is open Tue.-Fri. 1000-1615, Sats., Suns. and holidays 1400-1700. The large garden is also open to the public. Buses 106, 176, 178 from centre; 571 from Flamengo; 591 from Copacabana.

**Palácio do Itamarati**, the former Foreign Ministry, at Avenida Marechal Floriano 196, contains much interesting old furniture, tapestry and other objects of art. Now called Museu Histórico e Diplomático, open Tues.-Fri., 1200-1615 (doors close at 1700); free on Thurs.

**Museu da República**, in Palácio do Catete (R. do Catete 179), entrance in R. Silveira Martins, was the official residence of the President for 63 years when Rio was the Federal Capital. At R. do Catete 181 is the **Museu do Folclore Edison Carneiro**, good. Bus 571 from Copacabana, and close to Catete metro station.

**Guanabara Palácio**, once the residence of the Princess Isabel, daughter of Dom Pedro II, is now the office of the Governor of the State of Rio de Janeiro.

**Carmen Miranda Museu**, Tues.-Sun. 1100-1700, Flamengo park area in front of Rui Barbosa 560 (small display of the famous singer's gowns etc). **Museu de Imagens do Inconsciente**, Ramiro Magalhães 521, Engenho de Dentro, Mon.-Fri. 0800-1600. **Museu Villa-Lobos**, R. da Imprensa 16, Tues.-Sat. 1000-1600, with instruments, scores, books, recordings. **Capão do Bispo Estate**, Av. Suburbana 4616, Del Castilho, Mon.-Fri. 1400-1700 with archaeological exhibition.

**Planetarium**, Padre Leonel Franco 240, Gávea, Sat. and Sun. at 1600, 1700, 1830: inaugurated in 1970, sculpture of Earth and Moon by Mario Agostinelli. Free *choro* concert Fri. at 2100. Buses 176 and 178 from centre and Flamengo; 591 and 592 from Copacabana.

**Museu Aeroespacial**, Av. Marechal Fontenelle 2000, Campo dos Afonsos, Tues.-Fri. 0900-1600, early Brazilian civil and military aircraft.

**Carnival Museum**, Av. dos Desfiles, entrance by R. Frei Caneca, Tues.-Sun. 1100-1600.

**Museu Antônio Lago**, R. Andradas 96, centre, Mon.-Fri. 1400-1700. Reproduction of historical apothecary's shop.

**Amsterdam Sauer Museum**, Garcia d'Avila e Visconde de Pirajá, reproduction of a Brazilian mine and exhibition of gemstones. Open Mon.-Fri. 1000-1700.

## Churches and Religious Foundations

*Check opening hours before attempting to visit.*

The oldest foundation is the convent of the **Ordem Terceiro do Monte do Carmo**, built early in the 17th century on R. Primeiro de Março close to Praça 15 de Novembro, now used as a school. Its present church, the Carmo Church in R. Primeiro de Março, next to the old cathedral, was built in the 1770s and rebuilt between 1797 and 1826. It has strikingly beautiful portals by Mestre Valentim, the son of a Portuguese nobleman and a slave girl. He also created the main altar of fine moulded silver, the throne and its chair, and much else.

The second oldest convent is the seventeenth-century **Convento de Santo Antônio**, on a hill off the Largo da Carioca, built between 1608 and 1615. Its church has a marvellous sacristy adorned with blue tiles. St. Anthony is a particular object of devotion for women who want to find husbands, and many will be seen in the precincts.

The crypt contains the tomb of a Scottish soldier of fortune known as "Wild Jock of Skelater". He was in the service of the Portuguese Government during the Napoleonic War, and had the distinction of being appointed the first Commander-in-Chief of the Army in Brazil. The statue of St. Anthony was made a captain in the Portuguese army after his help had been sought to drive out the French in 1710, and his salary paid to the monastery. In 1810 he became a major, in 1814 a lieutenant-colonel, and he was granted the Grand Cross of the Order of Christ. He was retired without pay in 1914.

Separated from this church only by some iron railings is the charming church of **São Francisco da Penitência**, built in 1773. The carving and gilding of walls and altar are superb. In the ceiling over the nave is a fine panel painted by José de Oliveira. There is a museum attached to the church, open first and third Sun. of the month, 0700-1000.

The **Mosteiro** (monastery) **de São Bento** (1641); entrance at R. Dom Gerardo 68, contains much of what is best in the 17th and 18th century art of Brazil. "O Salvador", the masterpiece of Brazil's first painter, Frei Ricardo do Pilar, hangs in the sacristy. The carving in the church is particularly good. The Chapels of the Immaculate Conception and of the Most Holy Sacrament are masterpieces of colonial art. The organ is very interesting. The monastery is a few minutes' walk from Praça Mauá, turning left off Av. Rio Branco. Open 0730-1130, 1430-1830 (shorts not allowed). The intimate view of the harbour and its shipping from the grounds of the monastery (behind the church) is in itself worth climbing the hill on which it stands.

The **Old Cathedral** of São Sebastião, in the R. Primeiro de Março, was built between 1749 and 1770. In the crypt are the alleged remains of Pedro Alvares Cabral, the discoverer of Brazil (though it is only fair to note that Santarém, Portugal, also claims to be his last resting-place).

The **New Cathedral**, on Avenida República de Chile not far from the Largo da Carioca, dedicated in 1976, is a very exciting cone-shaped building. Its internal height is 68 metres, diameter 104 metres, external height 83 metres; capacity 5,000 seated, 20,000 standing. The most striking feature is four enormous stained-glass windows (60 metres high). It is still incomplete.

The Church of **São Francisco de Paula**, at the upper end of the R. do Ouvidor, was built in 1759. It contains some of Mestre Valentim's work—the carvings in the main chapel and the lovely Chapel of Our Lady of Victory. Some of the paintings, and probably the ceiling, are by Manuel da Cunha. The beautiful fountain at the back plays only at night.

The Church of **Nossa Senhora da Candelária** (1775-1810), on Praça Pio Dez, at the city end of Avenida Presidente Vargas, is well worth a visit to see its beautiful interior decorations and paintings. It is on the site of a chapel founded in 1610 by Antônio da Palma after he had survived a shipwreck, an event depicted by paintings inside the present dome.

In the R. de Santa Luzia, overwhelmed by tall office buildings, is the attractive little church of **Santa Luzia**. When built in 1752 it had only one tower; the other was added late in the 19th century. Feast day: 13 December, when devotees bathe their eyes with holy water, considered miraculous.

In the R. Primeiro de Março, at the corner of Ouvidor (near the Old Cathedral), is the church of **Santa Cruz dos Militares**, built 1780-1811. It is large, stately and beautiful.

The beautiful little church on the Glória hill, overlooking the Parque do Flamengo, is **Nossa Senhora da Glória**. It was the favourite church of the imperial family; Dom Pedro II was baptized here. Built in 1791, it contains some excellent examples of blue-faced Brazilian tiling. Its main altar, of wood, was carved by Mestre Valentim. The church, open 0900-1200 (only Sat.-Sun.) and 1300-1700 weekdays, is reached by bus 119 from the centre and 571 from Copacabana. The adjacent museum of religious art is open on application to the priest.

The church of **Nossa Senhora da Penha**, in the N suburb of Penha (early 20th century), is on a bare rock in which 365 steps are cut. This staircase is ascended by pilgrims on their knees during the festival month of October; there is a funicular for those unable to do this. Bus 497 from Copacabana, 340 and 346 from centre.

When the Morro do Castelo was levelled to build the Esplanada do Castelo, the old church of São Sebastião had to be demolished. Its successor, the Capuchin church of São

Sebastião in the R. Haddock Lobo, Tijuca, built in 1936, contains the tomb of Estácio de Sá, founder and first Governor of Rio de Janeiro.

Places where worship is conducted in English:
**Christ Church**, R. Real Grandeza 99, Botafogo (Church of England/American Episcopalian). The British School, for children of 5-16, is nearby.
**Chapel of Our Lady of Mercy,** R. Visconde de Caravelas 48, Botafogo (Roman Catholic, with primary school).
**Union Church** (Protestant undenominational) Services held at R. Parque da Lagoa de Marapendi, C.P.37154-CEP 22609 Barra da Tijuca.
**International Baptist Church**, R. Desembargador Alfredo Russel 146, Leblon.
**First Church of Christ Scientist**, Av. Marechal Câmara 271, room 301.
**Masonic Temple**, in the British School at R. da Matriz 76, Botafogo.
**Synagogues**, General Severiano 170, Botafogo; R. Barata Ribeiro, Copacabana.
**Swedish Church**, Igreja Escandinava, Av. Rui Barbosa 170, Bloco B 1, 5 And., T 551-6696, open 1300-2200, Sun. 1700-2100, will store luggage.
**British Cemetery**, R. da Gamboa 181, granted to the British community by Dom João, Regent of Portugal, in 1810. It is the oldest cemetery in Rio.

## Parks, Squares and Monuments

The city abounds in open spaces and squares, many of which have ornamental gardens and statuary.

On the Glória and Flamengo waterfront, with a view of the Pão de Açúcar and Corcovado, is the **Parque do Flamengo**, designed by Burle Marx, opened in 1965 during the 400th anniversary of the city's founding, and landscaped on 100 hectares reclaimed from the Bay. Behind the War Memorial (see below) is the public yacht marina.

In the park are many sports fields and a botanical garden; for children, there are a sailboat basin, a marionette theatre, a miniature village and a staffed nursery. There are night amusements, such as bandstands and areas set apart for dancing.

**The National War Memorial** to Brazil's dead in World War II (Monumento aos Mortos na Segunda Guerra) and the Museu de Arte Moderna (**see page 303**) are at the city end of the park, opposite Praça Paris. The Memorial takes the form of two slender columns supporting a slightly curved slab, representing two palms uplifted to heaven. In the crypt are the remains of the Brazilian soldiers killed in Italy in 1944-45. It is well worth a visit, but beach clothes and rubber-thonged sandals will get you ejected—and don't sit on the wall. The crypt and museum are open Tues.-Sun. 1000-1700.

Those who want to see what Rio was like early in the 19th century should go by bus to the **Largo do Boticário**, R. Cosme Velho 822, a charming small square in pure colonial style. Buses to Cosme Velho from all parts of the city. The square is close to the terminus for the Corcovado rack railway (**see page 320**).

(Jardim Botânico) **Botanical Gardens** founded 1808, closed Mon, open 0800-1800 in summer and 0830-1730 in winter (US$2); well worth a visit. The most striking features are the transverse avenues of 30-metre royal palms. There are over 7,000 varieties of plants, herbarium, aquarium, and library (some labels are unclear). The Gardens are 8 km. from the centre, 140 hectares in area; take any bus from the centre, e.g. 104, to Leblon, Gávea or São Conrado marked "via Jóquei". From Copacabana any bus whose number begins with 5 and ends with an even number, except 592.

Bird-watchers should visit the Botanical Gardens, preferably early in the morning. 140 species of birds have been recorded there. Flycatchers are very prominent (the social flycatcher, great and boat-billed kiskadees, cattle tyrant); also tanagers (the sayaca and palm tanagers, and the colourful green-headed tanager), and over 20 different kinds of hummingbird. Birds of prey include the roadside hawk, the laughing falcon and the American kestrel, and there are doves, cuckoos, parakeets, thrushes and woodpeckers, and occasional flocks of toucans. (John and George Newmark, Eastbourne.)

**Parque Laje**, near the Jardim Botânico at R. Jardim Botânico 414, almost jungle-like, has small grottoes, an old tower and lakes. (The Institute of Fine Arts is housed in the mansion.) Open daily, 0730-1730, admittance free.

**Quinta da Boa Vista**, formerly the Emperor's private park, contains the zoo (see below) and many specimen trees. The Palace now houses the National Museum (**see page 303**).

**Jardim Zoológico**, which contain Brazilian and imported wild animals, and a fine collection of birds (as well as many "visitors"—also good for bird-watchers), is in the Quinta de Boa Vista (admission US$1). Open 0800-1800 daily, except Mon. The gateway is a replica of Robert Adam's famous gateway to Syon House, near London. Near the Zoological Gardens is the Museu da Fauna which is small but excellent. Take bus 474 or 472 from Copacabana or Flamengo; bus 262 from Praça Mauá.

**Parque da Cidade**    A pleasant park a short walk beyond the Gávea bus terminus. It was previously the grounds of the home of the Guinle family, by whom it was presented to the City; the house itself is now the Museu da Cidade (**see page 304**). Admission to the park is free; open Tues.-Fri. 0730-1730, Sat., Sun. and holidays 1100-1700. The proximity of the Rocinha favela means that the park is not very safe. It is advisable to carry your passport (or copy) here because of frequent police checks.

**Jockey Club Racecourse**, at Praça Santos Dumont, Gávea, meetings on Mon. and Thurs. evenings and Sat. and Sun. 1400, entrance US$1-2, long trousers required, a table may be booked. Take any bus marked "via Jóquei". Betting is by totalizator only.

**Praça da República** and **Campo de Santana** is an extensive and picturesque public garden close to the Central Railway station. At Praça da República 197 lived Marshal Deodoro da Fonseca, who proclaimed Brazil a republic in 1889 (plaque). The Parque Júlio Furtado in the middle of the square is populated by playful agoutis (or gophers), best seen at dusk; there is also a little artificial grotto, with swans.

**Passeio Público** (turn right at S end of Avenida Rio Branco) is a garden planted by the artist Mestre Valentim, whose bust is near the old former gateway. Coin and stamp market on Sun., a.m.

**Praça Quinze de Novembro** contains the original royal palace (**see page 303**). Every Sat. 0900-1900, handicraft fair and flea market; nearby on waterfront is Sun. antiques market, 1000-1800.

**Praça Tiradentes**, old and shady, has a statue to D. Pedro I, first Emperor of Brazil. Shops in nearby streets specialize in selling goods for *umbanda* and *macumba*—African-type religion and magic respectively. Several theatres nearby.

**Praça Mahatma Gandhi**, at the end of Avenida Rio Branco, is flanked on one side by the cinema and amusement centre of the city, known as Cinelândia. The fountain (1789) by Mestre Valentim in the ornamental garden was moved here from Praça Quinze de Novembro in 1979.

**Parque do Catete** is a charming small park between the Palácio do Catete (Museum da República) and Praia do Flamengo; it has many birds and playful monkeys.

**Praça Paris**, built on reclaimed ground near the Largo da Glória, is much admired for the beauty of its formal gardens and illuminated fountains.

**Fountains**    The oldest, the Fonte da Glória (1789), has eight bronze spouts. Possibly the finest, although now sadly neglected, is at the back of the church of S. Francisco de Paula, at the inland end of the R. do Ouvidor. These, and nine other old fountains, are illuminated by night.

**Crime**    Rio has been getting worse, both for assaults and for pickpocketing, but the number of patrolling police has been steadily expanded in recent years. Precautions are advisable, especially on the famous beaches, where small boys work in gangs, some distracting your attention while others go through pockets and bags. It is best not to take any belongings to the beach. It is suggested to women that they do not visit the cinema alone. Venturing out alone at night is not advisable for anyone. After dark taxis do not stop to pick up passengers. Always carry some money (but never large amounts): robbers may be incensed and very aggressive if their victims have nothing at all. Do not wear jewellery or carry openly tourist goods such as a camera, maps or guide books to make yourself an obvious target (a reader advises carrying a local newspaper). Carry your belongings in a "day-pack", as the locals do (can be bought at any street corner—joggers' arm-bands have also been suggested; leg money belts have been recommended if larger sums of money have to be carried). Pickpockets and purse-snatchers operate at bus stops, bus turnstiles and among passengers while the bus is passing through a tunnel; also at street-corner newsagent stands. The centre of Rio can be dangerous at weekends, when most of the police force is patrolling the beaches. Among the more problematic areas at any time are Dois Irmãos, Santa Teresa, on Copacabana's Av. Atlântica and R. Belfort Roxo, on the train between the zoo and Maracaña stadium, Pão de Açúcar, Corcovado, Quinta da Boa Vista, Jardim Botânico/Jóquei Clube racecourse area, Princesa Isabel at the end of the Túnel Novo, the Rio Sul shopping centre bus stop and beyond Leblon out to Barra da Tijuca. To avoid swindling in bars, especially if sitting outside, pay as soon as you receive your order (although contrary to custom) and always ask for an itemized bill and check your change; alternatively, pay at the cash desk. Be especially careful after changing money in a public place; thieves often wait outside *câmbios*. Drivers, watch out for live snakes being thrown through open car windows: you jump out, the thief jumps in. The Tourist Police (Poltur) office is at R. Humberto de Campos 319, Leblon, but, if robbed, you must report the incident at the station in the district where the incident occured.

It should be added that Rio remains a beautiful and fascinating city. Whilst warnings should not be ignored, using your common sense should help towards a trouble-free visit.

**Hotels**  All hotels in the following list are air-conditioned. A 10% service charge is usually added to the bill and tax of 5% or 10% may be added (if not already included). Note that not all higher-class hotels include breakfast in their room rates. The following list begins with expensive hotels and then gives economy establishments, by area.

**Centre**  Well placed for transport, 30 min. from the beaches. Most offices and commerce are located here, but no night life, so not a secure area and not rec. for tourists: *Ambassador*, Senador Dantas, 25, T 297-7181, A; *Grande Hotel OK*, Senador Dantas, 24, T 292-4114, A; *Othon Aeroporto*, Av. Beira Mar, 280, T262-8922, A, somewhat run-down and expensive (3-star). Also 3-star is the *Luxor Hotel do Aeroporto* at Galeão Airport, T 398-5960, but prices in L range.

**Flamengo**  Residential area midway between centre and Copacabana: *Glória*, R. do Russel, 632, T205-7272, A+, stylish and elegant, highly rec.; *Novo Mundo*, Praia Flamengo, T 205-3355, A-A+, well rec. but noisy; *Flamengo Palace*, Praia Flamengo 6, T 205-1552, A, appears a bit old-fashioned.

**Copacabana**  The famous seaside residential and commercial area: many hotels on Av. Atlântica charge about 30% more for a room with a sea view, but some town-side upper rooms have equally fine views of the mountains. 5-star hotels: *Copacabana Palace*, Av. Atlântica 1702, T255-7070, L, British-owned, swimming pool, very good; *Meridien*, Av. Atlântica 1020, T275-9922, Air France hotel, world-renowned, L, but very expensive, pool, rooms quite small; *Rio Othon Palace*, Av. Atlântica 3264, T521-5522, L, pool, very good, as is *Rio Palace*, Av. Atlântica 4240, T521-3232, L and up, all rooms locked by central system at 0130. There are two excellent suites hotels: *Rio Atlantica*, Av. Atlântica 2964, T 255-6332, Fax 255-6410 with pool, 2 restaurants and other facilities (Swiss management); and *International Rio*, Av. Atlântica 1500, T 295-2323, Fax 542-5443, pool.

4-star hotels in Copacabana: there are 4 Othon hotels in this category, all in the A+ range (some rooms more): *Califórnia Othon*, Av. Atlântic 2616, T257-1900, good; *Savoy Othon*, Av. Copacabana 995, T 521-8282, very central, popular, commercial, quite noisy; *Olinda*, Av. Atlântica 2230, T257-1890, also good and the *Lancaster*, Av. Atlântica 1470, T541-1887. Next door to the *Lancaster* is *Ouro Verde*, Av. Atlântica 1456, T542-1887, excellent all round; 3 Luxor hotels: *Luxor Continental*, Gustavo Sampaio 320, T275-5252, *Luxor Copacabana*, Av. Atlântica 2554, T235-2245, *Luxor Regente*, Av. Atlântica 3716, T287-4212, all good hotels in the A+ -L ranges, well-placed. *Leme Palace*, Av. Atlântica 656, T275-8080, A+, also good, but poorer location, popular with tour groups. *Royalty Copacabana*, Toneleros 154, T 235-5699, 4 blocks from beach, a/c, swimming pool on 13th floor with view.

Copacabana 3-stars: *Castro Alves*, Av. Copacabana 552, T 255-8815, A, very comfortable and elegant, also commercial; *Apa*, República do Peru, 305, T255-8112, A; *Debret*, Av. Atlântica 3564, T521-3332, A, good; *Riviera*, Av. Atlântica 4122, T 247-6060, very good, excellent breakfast but other meals disappointing, well placed. *Plaza Copacabana*, Av. Princesa Isabel 263, T 275-7722, A, highly rec. as most hospitable. Copacabana 2-stars: *Praia Leme*, Av. Atlântica 866, T 275-3322, a pleasant, Austrian run, overlooking beach, English and German spoken; *Atlantis Copacabana*, Av. Bulhões de Carvalho 61, T 521-1142, B, a/c, TV, very good, close to Ipanema and Copacabana beaches. *Biarritz*, R. Aires Saldanha 54 T 521-6542, good, accepts American Express; *Toledo*, R. Domingos Ferreira 71, T 257-1990, good breakfast, single rooms are gloomy; *Santa Clara*, R. Décio Vilares 316, T 256-2650, D, rec., quiet.

**Ipanema/Leblon**  Outer seaside residential and commercial area: all the following are good, starting with the most luxurious, *Caesar Park*, Av. Vieira Souto 460, T 287-3122, L, pool; *Everest*, Prudente de Morais 1117, T287-8282, L, pool; *Marina Palace*, Av. Delfim Moreira 630, T 259-5212, L and *Marina Rio*, Av. Delfim Moreira 696, T239-8844, A+; and *Praia Ipanema*, Av. Vieira Souto 706, T239-9932. A+, pool; *Sol Ipanema*, Av. Vieira Souto

# Rio Atlantica Suite Hotel. A touch of Switzerland, right on Copacabana Beach.

*Setting new standards on Rio's hotel scene.*

■ Conveniently located in the heart of Copacabana, right on the Beach.

■ Minutes away from the city's financial/business center and shopping district makes the Rio Atlantica convenient for businessmen and tourists.

■ 18 floors with 228 suites and rooms, most featuring ocean view. Our suite accommodations are cost competitive with the standard rooms of hotels of the same category.

■ Round-the-clock security. Featuring in-room safety-deposit boxes and wet bars.

■ 2 restaurants serving the finest in Brazilian, international and Swiss cuisine ("Ao Ponto" and "Helvecia").

■ Ample facilities for business meetings and functions. 68-seat fully equipped auditorium.

■ Rooftop swimming pool, solarium, health club with saunas, exercise room and deck bar for the exclusive use of guests.

■ Drugstore/newsstand, boutiques, jewelry and gift shops.

■ Accommodations for handicapped available.

■ The newest and only hotel under Swiss management.

Management by

**CEM**
CASPAR E. MANZ
HOTELS & RESTAURANTS
SWITZERLAND

**rio atlantica**
SUITE HOTEL
Av. Atlântica, 2964 - Copacabana
22070 - Rio de Janeiro - RJ - Brazil
Tel: (021) 255-6332  Tlx: (21) 36 893
Fax: (021) 255-6410

For Reservations:  **SRS** STEIGENBERGER RESERVATION SERVICE  or directly with the hotel

320, T267-0095, A+; *Arpoador Inn*, Francisco Otaviano 177, T247-6090, A; *Vermont*, Visc. de Pirajá 254, T 521-0057, A, rec.; *Ipanema Inn*, Maria Quitéria 27, T 287-6092, good, swimming pool.

**São Conrado and further out**  Spectacular settings, but isolated and far from centre: the first three are luxury hotels with pools: *Sheraton*, Av. Niemeyer 121, T274-1122, L, *Nacional*, Av. Niemeyer 769, T322-1000, L, *Intercontinental*, Av. Litorânea 222, T322-2200, L+. *Atlântico Sul*, Av. Sernambetiba 18000 (Recreio), T437-8411, A.

**Economy Hotels** are found mainly in three districts of Rio: Flamengo/Botafogo (best), Lapa/ Fátima and Saúde/Mauá. Rates are for doubles, and include continental breakfast.

**Flamengo/Botafogo**  (Residential area between centre and Copacabana, with good bus and metro connections.) Walking from the centre, you will come across the hotels in this order: R. Cândido Mendes, off R. da Glória: *Monte Castelo*, No. 201 (T 222-1733), E (with bathroom), clean, central, safe deposit (not well guarded, get a receipt for your valuables). *Bahia*, Santo Amaro 42, E (without bath); clean; on same street, No. 75, *Opera*, E (a/c extra, cheaper without bath), also good, safe, near Glória metro (T 221-8759/242-3583). Across from here, on the hillside is Ladeira da Glória: *Turístico*, Ladeira da Glória 30, sold out Dec.-March, D, with bath, including breakfast, a/c, money and valuables can be left safely, good exchange rates, service may be lacking at busy times, tourist information provided; *Victória*, R. do Catete 172, D-E, with breakfast, bath and hot water, a/c, clean and friendly, also on R. do Catete: No. 233, *Rio Claro*, E, recently renovated, breakfast, shower, a/c, safe, rec.; No. 160, *Monte Blanco*, D, breakfast, bath, a/c, radio, refurbished, clean, friendly, but room theft has been reported (try for a room about 1200). To the left is R. Silveira Martins: No. 20, *Inglês*, D, reasonable breakfast. Walking down Praia de Flamengo you will come across the next streets: Ferreira Viana: *Regina*, No. 29, 2-star, C-D, a/c, bath, fridge, TV; No. 58, *Ferreira Viana* (E, with bath and breakfast, always heavily booked, valuables may be left safely). *Unico*, Buarque de Machado 54, T 205-9932, E, a/c, clean, friendly, rec. (nr. Largo do Machado metro). *Monterrey*, R. Artur Bernardes 39, E with bath, very good; at No. 29, *Rio Lisboa*, E with bath, a/c, cheaper rooms without bath, clean, safe, rec.—both hotels in this quiet street are family hotels. R. Paissandu: No. 34, *Venezuela*, E, with bathroom, very clean, but rooms small and breakfast poor; *Paysandu*, opposite *Venezuela*, E, very clean, comfortable and good value. Beyond Largo de Machado: R. Gago Coutinho: No. 22, *Serrano*, D, pleasant, helpful; and *Argentina*, Cruz Lima 30, C, rec.

**Lapa/Fátima**  Between Lapa and Praça Tiradentes is an inner residential area, less desirable than Flamengo. Parts of this area are deserted from 2200 on. Near Cinelândia metro station are a lot of cheap hotels, but many are hot-pillow establishments. In Lapa itself, near the Arches just beyond Passeio Público, is R. Joaquim Silva: No. 99, *Marajó*, D, with breakfast, varied rooms, clean; also *Love's House*, R. Joaquim Silva, E, ask for room with window, safe, respectable, good value. Passing under the Arches you come to Av. Mem de Sá (bus 127 from bus terminal): No. 85, *Mundo Novo*, E, clean, a/c. Turning towards Praça Tiradentes is R. Resende, No. 31, *Estadual*, D, good; No. 35, *Pouso Real*, D, good, but the area is dubious. *Marialva*, Gomes Freire 430 (nr. New Cathedral, convenient for Av. Rio Branco, buses etc.), 2 star, D with bath, a/c, breakfast in room, rec. Praça Tiradentes, *Rio Hotel*, clean, noisy rooms on Praça, quieter overlooking São Sebastião cathedral, D with breakfast (only served in rooms).

**Saúde/Mauá**  (Area between the railway station and the docks, a dubious part of town.) *Rio Grande*, R. Senador Pompeu 220, E, rec.; *Internacional*, R. Senador Pompeu 182, E, clean and friendly; *Dom Pedro II*, Senador Pompeu 226, F, quiet, friendly, rec. The very cheapest hotels in town are in this area, but it is not too safe at night.

In the traditional **Santa Teresa** district, R. Almirante Alexandrino 660, is the *Santa Teresa Hotel*, C, with swimming pool and full board. Also Dona Ana's hostel on the same street at No. 501, C, T 232-9603. Take the "Dois Irmãos" tram from Largo da Carioca.

There is a **Youth Hostel** on the tenth and eleventh floors of the *Casa do Estudante*, at Praça Ana Amélia 9 (R. Sta. Luzia), near Santa Luzia church, T 220-7123/7223, open all year, F—student card required—international youth hostel card is best, you can check in at any time of day, and can come in at any time of night, but after 0100 you must pay the lift man US$0.10. (Adverse opinion from some travellers—uncomfortable, showers not working.) Adverse reports of *Casa do Estudante Universitário*, Av. Rui Barbosa 762; said to be unsafe for property. Cheap food at canteens for those with international student cards. Other Youth Hostels at R. Almte. Alexandrino 2840, Santa Teresa (*Pousada do Garuda*, T 225-0393/236-1419), Santa Amaro 162, Glória, T 222-8576; R. Tan. Marones de Gusmão 85, Bairro Peixoto, CEP 22041, T 235-3317/237-5422; R. Pompeu Loureiro 99, T 236-0047; and R. Emílio Burla 41, Copacabana (T 236-6472), good, YHA card not necessary, but you pay a bit more without it, cleaner than the one at Sta. Luzia. Youth hostels are fully booked between Christmas and Carnival; if intending to stay at this time reserve well in advance. Remember that the "motels" in the suburbs and along the main highways are mainly for the use of very-short-stay couples.

The city is extremely noisy. An inside room is cheaper and much quieter. (If you are desperate and it is late, some smaller hotels and hostelries may let you sleep on the floor.)

**Apartments** are more expensive in Copacabana, Ipanema, Leblon, than in the centre or more northerly areas: for example, furnished apartments, accommodating up to 6, cost US$200 per month in Maracanã, about US$300 per month in Saúde, Cinelândia, Flamengo. Bookings for Copacabana at R. Barata Ribeiro 90, room 205, Copacabana, Av. N.S. da Copacabana 583, room 1007, T 235-3748, and at R. Barata Ribeiro 87/ 202, T 255-2016 or 237-1133. Also Rent Fiat Imobiliária Ltda, R. Barata Ribeiro 207 s/101—CEP: 22011, T 256-9986. *Hamburg Imobiliária*, Av. Copacabana 195, Loja 104, T 542-1446, Fax 275-9406, German run, specialize in flats, also offer tours at good rates. The *Praia Leme Hotel*, Av. Atlântica 866, has apartments, with maid and laundry service at Av. Princesa Isabel 7, close to the beach; in high season reservation is necessary. José Silva da Ferreira, R. Pompeu Loureiro 56A, Apto. 401, Copacabana (T 256-9957) lets good apartments; *Fantastic Rio* Hans Peter Corr, Avenida Atlântica 974, Suite 501 Copacabana 22010 Rio de Janeiro (T 541 8951, Fax 0055-21-237-4774), several apartments from US$60 upwards, 30% reduction for readers of *South American Handbook*, 30% reduction for people staying 4 weeks or more (U.K. representative Mr. B. Brown, 9 Turpins Green, Maidenhead, Berks, SL64QE, T 0628-30143, in Germany, Mrs L. Corr, T 0049-621-402721). Yvonne Reimann, Av. Atlântica 4.066, Apto. 605, T 227-0281, rents very safe apartments, well furnished and clean, a/c, maid service; Judith, T 257-8502 lets apartments near the beach; also Ruth Haeberlin, R. Hilario Gouveia 88, Apt. 702, T 236-4496, apartments for 1-3 people. *Rio Hotel Residencia*, Av. Sernambetiba 6250, Barra da Tijuca, offers one-bedroom suites (for 2) with sitting-room and kitchen and two -bedroom suites (for 4). *Rio Flat Service*, Almirante Guilhém 322, Leblon, reservations through SASS Ltda, Ataulfo de Paiva 566/305, T 274-9546, Telex: 30245. *New Rio Home Service*, Visconde de Pirajá 414, sala 522, Ipanema, T 521-2332, Fax 267-6090, Swedish-run, rec. Estate agents dealing in more expensive apartments include Tower Real Estate, R. Aníbal de Mendonça 157, Ipanema; Coroa Real, R. Buenos Aires 4 and Av. Copacabana 647, Loja 205/206; Lowndes and Sons S.A., Av. Presidente Vargas 290, 2° andar, T 253-5622. Appartur Imovéis Ltda, R Visconde de Pirajá 371, S/L 204, Ipanema RJ, T 287-5757/5797, TV, a/c, clean, quiet. For cheaper apartments, and rooms in private homes, try classified ads, e.g. *Balcão* (like *Exchange and Mart*), twice weekly, look for word "proprietário", *Rio Life*, or *Jornal do Brasil*, under section 100, subsection 101—Temporada. The word "conjugado" abbreviated to "conj" means a bedroom, usually with a bathroom but few cooking facilities, "vaga" a bed in a private home or in a shared room and "quarto" a room in a private house. Do check security arrangements in apartment buildings since robbery is common.

**Camping** Camping Clube do Brasil has beach site at Av. Sernambetiba 3200 (bus 233 from centre or 554 from Leblon, US$1.20—a long way from the centre), Barra da Tijuca, (half price for members). During January and February this site is often full and sometimes restricted to members of the Camping Clube do Brasil. Also at Recreio dos Bandeirantes, Estrada do Pontal 5900; *Ostral*, Av. Sernambetiba 18790; and *Novo Rio*, at 17.5 km. on Rio-Santos road. "Wild" camping possible on beaches further out; if trying it nearer centre, risk of thieves. If travelling by trailer, you can park at the Marina Glória car park, where there are showers and toilets, a small shop and snack bar. Pay the guards to look after your vehicle. Camping gear for sale at Montcamp, Teixeira de Melo 21, Ipanema, T 287-1143.

**Restaurants**: In Rio, avoid mussels! In early 1991, meals in 1st and 2nd class restaurants cost an average US$20 per head, without fancy sauces, etc. There are much cheaper places to eat as well. **Centre**: *Café do Teatro*, Rio Branco, Teatro Municipal, good food in grand manner. Shorts and scruffy gear not admitted; *Alba Mar* , fish, very good and reasonable, Praça Mal. Ancora 184-6; *A Cabaça Grande*, Casa das Peixadas, R. do Ouvidor 12, best for fish, closed Sun./holidays; *Rio Minho*, R. do Ouvidor 10, for seafood, expensive, old-fashioned, very good. *Spaghetti*, Av. Rio Branco 25, Italian, self-service, good salads, cheap; Vegetarian: *Superbom* Rio Branco 130, rec., lunch only. There are several Arab restaurants on Av. Senhor dos Passos, also open Sat. and Sun. *Taberna Carioca*, R. Carioca, reminiscent of a Basque bar, interesting dishes US$5, sufficient for 2. *La Table*, R. do Rosário, pancakes, good and cheap; *Luciano*, R. das Marrecas 44, all you can eat at buffet, and others on this street. Many lanchonetes for good, cheap meals in the business sector. Cheap eating places on Praça Tiradentes.

    **Santa Teresa**: *Bar do Arnaudo*, Alm. Alexandrino 316, B, rec. **Lapa**: *Semente*, R. Joaquim Silva 138, vegetarian. **Glória**: *Casa da Suiça* in same building as Swiss Consulate, R. Cândido Mendes 157, bar/restaurant, good atmosphere; several others on this street; *Hobby Lanches*, R. da Glória, near Metro, good, cheap; good Brazilian food in 1st floor cafeteria and adjoining restaurant (good views) at Santos Dumont airport, lunch only.

    **Flamengo and Catete**: there are a lot of eating places on R. do Catete: *Bar KTT*, US$2 for 2-course meal, excellent; No. 239, *Pastelaria Wong*, very cheap, good; No. 234B, *Amazônia*, downstairs, one-price counter service, upstairs for good, reasonably-priced evening meals, rec. *Restaurante e Pizzaria Guanabara*, No. 150, excellent value and selection; *Rio Galícia*, No. 265, very good pizza, good service; *Machado*, No. 286, good Italian food at reasonable prices; *No. 128*, no name, lunch only, communal tables, all you can eat for US$2, rec. *Restaurante Praia Bar*, Praia do Flamengo 144, elegant Italian, reasonable; *Lamas*, Marquês de Abrantes 18-A, excellent value, good food, go early; *Churrascaría Majórica*, many steak specialities, rec.; *Gaúcha*, R. das Laranjeiras 114, good. **Largo do Machado**: *Adega Real*, R. Gago Coutinho, very good. Plenty of pizza places.

    **Botafogo**: *La Mole*, Praia de Botafogo 228, good, cheap Italian food (other locations in Rio); *Neal's*, R. Sorocaba, US-style, burgers, chili, steaks, good value; *Manolo*, Bambina e M. de Olinda, very good value; *Natural*, R. 19 de Fevereiro 118.

    **Copacabana and Leme**: The main hotels, including particularly *Rio Palace*, the *Rio Atlântica Suite Hotel* and *Ouro Verde* (international food, highly rec.); *Churrascaria Marius*, at Leme end of Av. Atlântica, excellent but not cheap; *Churrascaria Palace*, R. Rodolfo Dantas 16-B, 22 different kinds of meat, very good (about US$20 p.p.); *Nino*, R. Domingos Ferreira 242-A, good but not cheap; *La Mole*, Av. N.S. de Copacabana, good service; *Suppentoft*, Av. Princesa Isabel 350, German, good for meals or just a beer. *Arataca*, Figueiredo de Magalhães 28, try *carne-de-sol* and *lagosta ao molho*; *A Marisquera*, Barata Ribeiro 232, good seafood; *Ponto d'Encontro* at 750, Portuguese, try baked *bacolhão*; *Rian*, Santa Clara 8 (international), excellent and reasonable, especially seafood; *Arosa* No. 110, lanchonette, very good and cheap. *Enotria*, R. Constante Ramos 115, Italian and 4 star. Cheap and good inclusive meal at *Frango na Brasa*, R. Constante Ramos 35; *Maxim*, Av. Atlântica 1850, good and reasonable, pleasant place and atmosphere; *La Tratoria*, Av. Atlântica (opp. *Hotel Excelsior*), Italian, good food and service; *Atlântico Terraço*, Av. Atlântico, good cooking.

    **Ipanema**: *Hotel Caesar Park*, rec. for Saturday *feijoada*, all you can eat; *Bardo Beto*, R. Farme de Amoedo 51 (T 267-4443) excellent food, big servings, good value; *Il Capo*, Visconde de Pirajá 276, T 267-8747, rec.; *Le Streghe*, R. Prudente Morais 129, *Satíricon*, Barão da Torre 192, Italian food and fish excellent. *Banana Café*, No. 368, colonial, library-style dining room, also rec.; *Porção* Barão de Torre 218, a very good *churrascaria*. Ipanema is quieter than Copacabana, many nice places round main square, Praça General Osório, such as *Romanos*. At corner of Prudente de Morais and Vicínius de Morais there are 4 restaurants: *Del Mare* particularly rec. *Vinícius*, R. Vinícius de Morais, a good place to meet young people. Health food at **Restaurante Natural**, R. Barão de Torre 171. *Delicats*, Av. Henrique Dumont 68, good Jewish deli.

    *Rive Gauche*, Av. Epitácio Pessoa 1484 (T 247-9993), French, excellent. **Leblon**: *Un, Deux, Trois*, R. Bartolomeu Mitre 123, very fashionable, restaurant, night club; *Antiquarius*, R. Aristides Espínola 19, restaurant-cum-antique shop, seafood and international cuisine. *Mediterráneo*, R. Prudente de Morais 1810, excellent fish, reasonable prices. In **São Conrado**, *El Pescador*, Praça São Conrado 20, Spanish-style fish restaurant, excellent value and variety of paellas. The *Sheraton* coffee shop has good *feijoada* on Sat. p.m.

Grill or barbecue houses (*churrascarias*) are relatively cheap, especially by European standards. There are many at São Conrado and Joá, on the road out to Barra da Tijuca (**see page 322**). Look for the "Churrascaria Rodízio", where you are served as much as you can eat. There are plentiful hamburger stands (literally "stands" as you stand and eat the hamburger) and lunch counters all over the city. *McDonalds* and *Big Bob's* (similar) can be found at about 20 locations each. *Galetos* are lunch counters specializing in chicken and grilled meat, very reasonable. In the "shopping centres" there is usually a variety of restaurants and snack bars grouped around a central plaza where you can shop around for a good meal. Most less-expensive restaurants in Rio have basically the same type of food (based on steak, fried potatoes and rice) and serve large portions; those with small appetites, and especially families with children, can ask for a spare plate, and split helpings. There are many juice bars in Rio with a wide selection. Most restaurants are closed on 24 and 25 December.

**Tea Rooms** For those who like their teas served English style, the sedate Belle Epoque 80-year-old *Confeitaria Colombo*, R. Gonçalves Dias 32 near Carioca metro station, is highly rec. for atmosphere, being the only one of its kind in Rio, with the original décor, open 0900-1800, no service charge so tip the excellent waiters. It has also a most attractive branch at Av. Copacabana 890. More modern but similar establishments in some of the main hotels, and at *Casarão*, Souza Lima 37A, Copacabana; *Traiteurs de France*, Av. Copacabana 386, delicious tarts and pastries, not expensive; *La Bonne Table*, Visc. de Pirajá 580 sala 407, Ipanema; and *Ponto de Encontro*, Barata Ribeiro 750B, Copacabana. *Café de la Paix*, Av. Atlântica, 1020; *Chá e Simpatia*, Av. Atlântica 4240; *Um Chorinho chamado Odeon*, Gávea Shopping Centre; *Bolo Inglês*, Cassino Atlântico Shopping Centre; *Concorde*, Av. Prudente de Morais 129. These establishments have become very fashionable.

**Shopping** A good jewellery shop is *Badofsky Brothers*, Av. Copacabana 680, Room 315, 3rd floor; English, German, French spoken. *Maximino Jeweler*, Av. Rio Branco 25, 11th floor, and other branches. *H. Stern*, jewellers, R. Garcia D'Avila 113, Ipanema; they also offer a tour, with head-phone commentary, of their lapidary and designing workshops, arranged through representatives at better hotels. *Gregory & Sheehan*, jewellers, R. da Alfândega 65, 1st & 2nd floors; *Corcovado Jóias*, Av. N.S. de Copacabana 209, Loja F; *Roditi* and *Amsterdam Sauer* offer free taxi rides to their workshops. For mineral specimens as against cut stones, try *Mineraux*, Av. Copacabana 195, Belgian owner. *Saara* is a multitude of little shops along R. Alfândega and R. Sen. dos Passos (between city centre and Campo Sant'ana) where clothes bargains can be found (especially jeans and bikinis). Good "hippy fair" at Ipanema (Praça General Osório on Suns.). **Shopping centres**: Rio Sul, at Botafogo end of Túnel Novo, Cassino (Copacabana), Norte Shopping (Meier), Plaza Shopping (Niteroi), Barra on Barra de Tijuca (**see page 322**). At São Conrado The Fashion Mall is smaller and more stylish.

**Cameras and Film Processing** *Dino's*, R. Buenos Aires 241; others in same street. Camera repair, Av. Rio Branco 151, 2nd floor, room 204. Kodachrome slide film difficult to get in Rio. For processing, Flash Studio, R. Viscondede Piraiá 156, expensive, and Lab Uruguaiana 143, for slide films; *One Houri Foto*, in the Rio Sul and Barra shopping centres, is rec.; also a laboratory at R. do Russel 344, Glória (1 hour for transparencies). Honório, R. Vinícius de Moraes 146-E, stocks lithium batteries. Nikon camera repairs, T Tanaka cia Ltda., Av. Franklin Roosevelt 39, of. 505, T 220-1127.

**Electronics repair** (radio, walkman, etc.), *Eletrônika Tekron*, R. Figueiredo Magalhes 870, Copacabana, T 235-4096, efficient, friendly.

**Bookshops** For international stock, *Livraria Kosmos*, R. do Rosário 155, good shop (in the centre and Av. Atlântica 1702, loja 5) and there are many others, e.g. *Livros Técnicos*, R. Miguel Couto 35, wide selection; *Nova Livraria Da Vinci*, Av. Rio Branco 185 loja 2/3, all types of foreign books; *Livrarias Siciliano*, Av. Rio Branco 156, loja 26, English, French and German books; also at N.S. de Copacabana 830 and other branches. *Unilivros*, Largo do Machado 29C, French and English bestsellers; *Livraria Nova Galeria de Arte*, Av. Copacabana 291D, international stock. *El Dorado*, Av. das Américas 4666, loja 207. Second-hand books also at *Livraria São José*, R. Carmo 61 (only a few in English); *Livraria Brasileira*, Av. Rio Branco 156, S/Loja 229 (some in English); under *Rio Hotel*, corner of R. da Carioca and Praça Tiradentes; *Livraria Antiquário*, Sete de Setembro 207 and in R. Pedro I, all in centre. Also on Av. Marechal Floriano, near Av. Rio Branco, especially at No. 63. On S side of Praça Tiradentes, *Casa dos Artistas* trades in second-hand paperbacks. Second-hand English books at the Anglican church, R. Real Grandeza 99, Botafogo.

**Markets** North-eastern market at Campo de São Cristóvão, with music and magic, on Sun. mornings. Saturday antiques market on waterfront, near Praça 15 de Novembro (1000-1800), and handicraft and flea market Sat. (0900-1900) in Praça 15; another in Largo da Carioca. Sunday stamp and coin market in Passeio Público, a.m. Sunday open-air handicrafts market at Praça General Osório, Ipanema. Markets on Wed. 0700-1300 on R. Domingos Ferreira and on Thur., same hours, on Praça do Lido, both Copacabana; also on Thur., good leather and jewellery market on 1 de Março in centre. Sunday market on R. da Glória, colourful, cheap fruit, vegetables and flowers. Excellent food and household-goods markets at various places in the city and suburbs (see newspapers for times and places).

**Buses** Good services to all parts, very crowded, not for the aged and infirm during rush hours. Hang on tight, drivers try to emulate Nelson Picquet and Ayrton Senna. Fare normally about US$0.10, watch your change. Bus stops are often not marked. Four private companies operate air-conditioned buses which can be flagged down practically anywhere: Real, Pegaso, Anatur and Carioca. They run from all points in Rio Sul (Barra, São Conrado, Leblon/Ipanema, Copacabana) to the city centre, Rodoviária and the airports. Fares about US$1 (US$2 to international airport).

**Trams** Try the remaining tram from Largo da Carioca (where there is a museum, open only Fri. 0830-1700) across the old aqueduct (Arcos) to Dois Irmãos or Paula Matos in Santa Teresa— historical and most interesting, and now refurbished, US$0.05. The trams are open sided, do not carry valuables.

**Taxis** The fare between Copacabana and the centre is US$7. There is a 40% surcharge between 2300 and 0600 and on Suns. and holidays. Taxis have red number plates with white digits (yellow for private cars, with black digits) and have meters. Smaller ones (mostly Volkswagen) are marked TAXI on windscreen or roof. Meters are often out-of-date because of inflation and drivers will consult updating sheets (make sure the updating sheet is not folded over and is an original in black and red, and not a photocopy—this is a well-known fiddle!); all the same, beware of overcharging, which is rife (**See also page 319** in Rodoviária section). Make sure meters are cleared and on tariff 1, except 2300-0600 on Sundays and in Dec. when 2 is permitted. If there is no meter, you *must* fix the fare before entering. Don't hesitate to argue if the route is too long or the fare too much. Radio Taxis (white with red and yellow stripe) are safer and not much more expensive, e.g. Cootramo, 270-1442, Coopertramo, 260-2022. Luxury cabs are allowed to charge higher rates. Inacro de Oliveira, T 225-4110, is a reliable taxi driver for excursions, only speaks Portuguese, rec.

**Underground Railway** Line 1 operates between Tijuca and Botafogo, via the railway station and Glória, with 19 km. in operation; it is being extended 1 km. at the Tijuca end and 7 km. at the other. It will go from Botafogo via Copacabana and on to Ipanema and Leblon (Jardim de Allah). Line 2, running past the Maracanã stadium northward to Irajá, will eventually run from Praça 15 de Novembro (Estação das barcas Rio-Niteroi), through the city centre, to Estácio. Line 1 operates 0600-2300, Line 2 0600-2000, but closed Sun and holidays. Fare US$0.15; integrated bus/metro tickets available (cheaper if bought in bulk). Substantial changes in bus operations are taking place because of the extended metro system; buses connecting with the metro have a blue-and-white symbol in the windscreen. The metro system is due for completion in 1993. If you speak Portuguese, apply to the Municipality and allow 10 days for arranging a sightseeing tour.

**Car Hire** For self-drive, try **Avis**, Rio International airport, less helpful than office at Praia do Flamengo 224 (205-5796); **Nobre**, Gustavo Sampaio 826 (275-5297) and Av. Princesa Isabel 350 (T 541-4646) Copacabana. **Telecar**, R. Figueiredo Magalhães 701 (257-2620). Many agencies on Av. Princesa Isabel, Copacabana. Credit card virtually essential. Recent reports suggest it is cheaper to hire outside Brasil, Budget rec. Remember service stations are closed in many places on Saturdays and Sundays; some agencies will supply gas to customers at the weekend.

**Car Repairs** Kyoso Team Mecânico Siquero Campos, at the entrance to the old tunnel, T 255-0506, a good mechanic who enjoys the challenge of an unusual car, highly rec.

**Night Clubs** Note that respectable night clubs permit entrance only to couples. Of most interest to the visitor will be shows featuring samba dancing, cheaper if you pay at the door. *Hotel Nacional* at São Conrado has the most lavish show in town. Other good samba shows at: *Oba-Oba*, Humaitá 110, e.g. US$20 without dinner, show considered one of the best in Rio, telephone to confirm price in advance. For the best Brazilian shows try *Canecão*, R. Venceslau Bras 215, T 295-3044, not expensive, where the best-known Carnival ball is now held. *Plataforma I*, R. Adalberto Ferreira 32, Leblon, getting better and better but beware of overcharging on drinks, arrive by 2000, show finishes 2300. Rio has its share of lively discotheques; among the best are; *Papagaio Disco Club*, Av. Borges de Medeiros 1426, Lagoa

(Fri.– gay and Sat. straight only); *Zoom* at São Conrado. 3 rec. bars in Flamengo area: *Tronbada*, R. M. de Abrantes 64, Spanish-style tapas, very popular; *Planalto Flamengo*, Largo de Machado end of R. do Catete, very friendly and crowded and, nearby, a bar at the corner of Paiçandu and Senador Vergueiro. *Scala*, Av. Afranio de Mello Franco, Leblon, large, 13¾ hr. show at 2300, lavish and loud, reasonably-priced drinks, entry US$11. Also in Ipanema on R. Vinicius de Morais 49-A, *Garota de Ipanema*, where the song "Girl from Ipanema" was written, excellent atmosphere, food reasonable. *Forró de Copacabana*, Av. N.S. de Copacabana 435, forró music upstairs on first floor, disco on second floor, very popular, cheap, safe for single women. On Fri., Sat. and Sun. nights, 2100-0200, there is dancing to live bands at *Circo Voador Domingueira* beneath Arcos da Lapa, in a circus tent, popular (other events during the week).

One of the centres of gay life is Cinelândia, in the centre; in this area extending up to the Viaduto is found the whole gamut of human life. The essentially local character of night life in this area seems to make it relatively safe. Another gay centre is Galeria Alaska, Av. N.S. de Copacabana 1241.

Another good place to see Brazilians at play, and at the same time for the English to feel some saudades (homesickness), is *Lord Jim Pub*, Paul Redfern 63 (Ipanema). Authentic pub atmosphere, afternoon tea, English food upstairs—steak-and-kidney pie, fish and chips. Phone in advance to check opening hours (usually closed Mon). *Porão* is a bar for the English speaking community, open Fri. 2100-0100, under the hall of Anglican/Episcopalian Christ Church, R. Real Grandeza 99, Botafogo.

There are also *gafieras*, restaurants or night clubs with live Brazilian music for dancing. The best (and most expensive) is *Carinhoso*, R. Visconde de Pirajá 22, Ipanema. Others, *Elite Club*, R. Frei Caneca 4, 1st floor, in the centre. *Asa Branca*, Av. Mem de Sá 17, Lapa, high class, expensive, live music daily. *Roda Viva*, beside the Sugar Loaf cable car station, entrance US$6, and *Cordão da Bola Preta* (pretty rough, but typical, only on Sat. evening), Av. Treze de Maio 13, 3rd. floor, beside the Municipal Theatre, centre; *Gafiera Estudiantina*, Praça Tiradentes Thurs., Fri., Sat., and one, enthusiastically rec., at Botafogo under the beach highway. Other bars which have music shows include: *Jazzmania*, Av. Rainha Elisabeth 769, T 227-2447, show at 2200; *Existe um Lugar*, Estrada das Furnas 3001; *Vogue*, R. Cupertino Durão 173, Leblon; *People*, Av. Bartolomeu Mitre 370, Leblon. In Barra de Tijuca there are a multitude of small night clubs, discotheques and gafieras, as well as some very luxurious motels for very-short-stay couples.

Many people look for Macumba religious ceremonies. Those offered on the night tours sold at hotels are not genuine, and a disappointment. You need a local contact to see the real ones, which are usually held in *favelas* and are none too safe for unaccompanied tourists.

**Theatres** There are about 20 theatres in Rio. The best known are: *Teatro Municipal*, Av. Rio Branco, for concerts, opera and ballet; *Tereza Rachel*, R. Siqueira Campos 143, Copacabana (has samba shows, much cheaper than night clubs); *Sala Cecília Meireles*, Largo da Lapa (often free classical concerts); *Teatro Villa-Lobos*, Av. Princesa Isabel, Copacabana; *Senac*, R. Pompeu Loureiro 45, Copacabana. Good value entertainment at "Seis e Meia" (1830) shows at various downtown theatres (e.g. *João Caetano* on Praça Tiradentes): 1½ hr. musical shows with top-name Brazilian artists—check local papers.

**Cinemas** A very few cut cheaper tickets to students, but not at weekends. Listings in *Jornal do Brasil* newspaper (best) and *O Globo*. Entrance is half price on Weds.

**Sports** Paissandu Athletic Club, Av. Afrânio de Melo Franco 330, Leblon—tennis, bowls, swimming, Scottish dancing, Tues., April-Oct., 2000-2230 non-members admitted. Leme tennis Club, R. Gustavo Sampaio 74—tennis. Rio de Janeiro Country Club, R. Prudente de Morais 1597, Ipanema—Tennis and swimming. Gávea Golf and Country Club, Estrada da Barra da Tijuca 2005—golf and polo. Itanhangá Golf Club, Jacarepaguá, visiting cards from Avenida Rio Branco 26, 16th floor. Clube Hípico Brasileiro, Av. Borges de Medeiros 2448, Jardim Botânico—riding; horse racing Sat., Sun., entrance US$1-2, long trousers required. Iate Clube do Rio de Janeiro, Av. Pasteur, Botafogo—yachting. Squash at R. Cândido Mendes 581, Glória, T 242-0642. Ice skating at Barra Shopping, Av. das Américas 466, Barra da Tijuca. Roller-skating at *Roxy-Roller*, opp. Clube de Regatas Flamengo on Av. Borges de Medeiros, Lagoa. Submariner, R. Ouvidor 130/608, T 252-9718, teaches water sports, hires equipment.

**Banks** Lloyds Bank, R. da Alfândega 33; Banco Internacional (Bank of America and Royal Bank of Canada), R. do Ouvidor 90; Banco Holandês Unido, R. do Ouvidor 101; Citibank, R. Assembléia 100; The First National Bank of Boston, Av. Rio Branco 110; Banco de Crédito Real de Minas Gerais, S.A., Av. Rio Branco 116; Banco Lar Brasileiro, R. do Ouvidor 98; and many others. Banks are open 1000 to 1630. Closed on Sat. Banco do Brasil at the International Airport is open 0800-2000 every day, Bolzano-Simonsen in Sector B is open to

2300. Banks use the legal tourist exchange rate.

**Exchange Houses** American Express, Av. Atlântica 2316, CEP 22-041, Copacabana; at Exprinter, Av. Rio Branco 132, cash and cheques (good rates also at their Av. N.S. de Copacabana branch); **Cambitur**, Av. Rio Branco 128, good rates, including Amex, Casa Piano, R. Visconde de Pirajá 365, Ipanema, also Praça da Paz, Ipanema, and Av. Rio Branco 88; **Turismo Portuguesa**, Av. Rio Branco 45; **Cualitour**, Av. Rio Branco 25B; **Behar Turismo**, Av. Rio Branco esq. Teófilo Ottoni-Visc. de Inhaúma, rec. for cheques; nearby **Casa São Jorge** changes Amex cheques at parallel rate; **Kontik**, Av. Presidente Vargas 309, Irmãos Capello, Av. Rio Branco 31A; **Sultur**, Av. Rio Branco 151C, Xanadu, R. do Rosário 171. In Copacabana (where parallel market rates are generally worse than in centre): **P. M.** (no travellers' cheques), Av. Copacabana 391-B and Av. Rio Branco 124-A; **Sala 309** (3rd floor), Ed. Monte Carmel, Av. N.S. de Copacabana 680, good rates; **Paladium Travel**, 3rd floor of Shopping Cassino Atlântico, Ipanema end of Av. Atlântica, Copacabana, Kraus, Praça Pio X 55, 2nd floor (German spoken), and Passamar, R. Siqueira Campos 7. (Try Atlântica Joias, R. Fernando Mendes 5). **N.B.** Many *câmbios* will give you the parallel rate for cash, but a worse rate for cheques; some will also change US$ cheques for US$ cash with a 4% commission. These transactions are not strictly legal, so you will have to look around for the *câmbios* that do them.

**Portuguese Language Courses** Instituto Brasil-Estados Unidos, Av. Copacabana 690, 5° andar, only for those with student visas; tourists will be referred to private teachers. Good English library at same address. Curso Feedback, branches in Botafogo, Centre, Copacabana and Ipanema (addresses in yellow pages): individual tuition from girl students about US$10/hr., rec. *Brasil Ativo* Rua Domingues De SÁ425/404 24.220 Niteroi-Rio de Janeiro, T 7112709.

**Cultural and Trade Institutions** The **British Council**, R. Elmano Cardim 10, Urca. T 295-7782. The **British School of Rio de Janeiro**, R. da Matriz 76. **Sociedade Brasileira de Cultura Inglesa**, Av. Graça Aranha 327, and in Copacabana, T 227-0147. **American Chamber of Commerce for Brazil**, Praça Pio Dez 15, 5th floor. **American Society and American Club**, Avenida Rio Branco 123, 21st floor. **USICA Reference Library**, U.S. Consulate General, Av. Presidente Wilson 147. The **American School of Rio de Janeiro**, Estrada da Gávea 132. **German Cultur-Institut** (Goethe), Av. Graça Aranha 416, 9th floor; open Mon.-Thur. 1200-1900, Wed.-Thur. 1000-1100. **Centro Cultural Banco do Brasil**, R. Primeiro de Março 66, free concerts and a good videothek. **Australian Trade Commission**, R. Voluntários da Pátria 45, 5°, Botafogo, T 286-7922; for visas etc. you must go to Brasília.

**Embassies and Consulates** Argentine Embassy, Praia de Botafogo 242; **Consul**, Praia de Botafogo 228, T 551-5198, very helpful over visas, 1130-1600; **Uruguayan Embassy**, R. Artur Bernardes 30; **Paraguayan Embassy**, Av. N.S. de Copacabana 427, room 303, 0900-1300, visas US$5; **Venezuelan Consulate**, Praia de Botafogo 242, 5th floor, open 0830-1300.

    **U.S. Consulate General**, Avenida Presidente Wilson, 147, T 292-7117.

    **British Consulate**, Praia do Flamengo 284, T 552-1422; **Irish Consulate**, Av. Princesa Isabel 323, 1205/9, Copacabana, T 275 0196, Fax 275-6299, Mon.-Fri. 1330-1600; **Swiss Consulate**, R. Cândido Mendes 157, 11° andar, Cx. Postal 744-7c-00, T 242-8035 (open 0900-1200, Mon.-Fri.); **West German Consulate-General**, R. Presidente Carlos de Campos 417, T 285-2333; **French Consulate**, Av. Pres. Antônio Carlos, 58, T 220-6022; **Austrian Consulate**, Av. Atlântica 3804, CEP 22070, T 227-0040/048/049; **Netherlands Consulate**, R. Sorocaba 570. T 246-4050. (Dutch newspapers here; also at KLM office on Av. Rio Branco.); **Swedish Consulate-General**, Praia do Flamengo 344, 9° andar, 22210, Rio de Janeiro, T 552-2422; **Danish Consulate**, Praia do Flamengo 284, Apt. 101, T 552-6149.

    **Israeli Embassy**, Av N.S. Copacabana 608-C, Copacabana, T 255 5432, Caixa Postal 12353; **S. Africa Consulate**, R. Voluntários da Pátria 45, 9th floor, Botafogo, T 266-6246.

**Policia Federal**, Av. Venezuela 2 (near Praça Mauá), for renewal of 90-day visa, US$4.

**Y.M.C.A.**, R. da Lapa, 40.

**Health** Vaccinations at Saude de Portos, Praça 15 de Novembro (international vaccination book and ID required). Policlínica, Av. Nilo Peçanha 38, rec. for diagnosis and investigation. Hospital Miguel Couto, Mário Ribeiro 117, Gávea, has a casualty ward (free), but no eye doctors T 274-2121; these can be found at Hospital Souza Aguiar, Praça da República III (casuality ward also free), T 296-4114. Dr. J.E. Kerr, R. Farme de Amoeda 75, Grupo 805, Ipanama, T 287-3808, English doctor, clinic open to 1100.
    Take note of local advice on water pollution; air pollution also occurs.

**Dentist** English-speaking, Amílcar Werneck de Carvalho Vianna, Av. Pres. Wilson 165, suite 811. Dr Djorup, Av Beira Mar. Mauro Suartz, Xavier da Silveira 45/808, T 521-7845/8897, speaks English and Hebrew, helpful.

**Laundromats** *Fénix*, R. do Catete 214, Loja 20; R. Marques de Abrantes, about No. 80 (Flamengo); Praça G. Osorio, Ipanema; *Lavlev Flamengo*, R.C. de Baepinédi 78, or R. das Laranjeiras 43, L28; Laundromat at 1216 Av. N.S. de Copacabana. In Rio Sul are self-service laundrettes such as *Lavlev*, about US$3-4 for a machine, including detergent and drying, 1 hr, also at R. Voluntário da Patria 248, Botafogo, Av. Prado Jnr 6313, Copacabana.

**Public Conveniences** There are very few in Rio de Janeiro, but many bars and restaurants (e.g. Macdonalds) offer facilities; just ask for the "banheiro" (banyairoo). Try the Castelo bus terminal in city centre. Also Praça Tiradentes, and 5th floor of R. da Assembleia 10 (same building as Riotur). Best conveniences are to be found in the Shopping Centres.

**Electric Current** 110-220 volts, 60 cycles, A.C.

**Post Office** Central Post Office, R. Primeiro de Março, CEP 20010, at corner of R. do Rosário. Overseas parcels may be sent from here. **Poste Restante** American Express, Av. Atlântica 2316, Copacabana (for customers), and all large post offices (letters held for a month, rec., US$0.10 per letter); Kontik Franstur will forward mail to their branches in Brazil without charge.

**Telephones** Buy *fichas* for calls from public phones (in acoustic shells) at chemists and news stands; they are hard to come by late at night. International calls at Av. Copacabana 462, 2nd floor, international airport, Praça Tiradentes (centre—where there is a special booth for overseas calls), Rodoviária, or R. Dias da Cruz 182-4, 24 hrs, 7 days a week, or at Santos Dumont airport, 1st floor (0530-2300). Collect calls, national and international, dial 107 (no charge).

**Cables** Embratel, Av. President Vargas 1012. Telegrams may be sent through any post office. Larger offices have telex.

**Travel Agents** *American Express Kontik Franstur*, Av. Atlântica 2316A; *Roxy*, Av. Winston Churchill 60, helpful, rec. (ask for Michael 0eary who speaks English); *Exprinter*, Av. Rio Branco, 128; *Manhattan Turismo Ltda*, R. da Assembléia 10, GR 3503, Centro, CEP 20-031, T 242-3779/3064, very helpful, cheap flights, English spoken; for cheap flights to Europe, *A.G.S. Viagem e Turismo Ltda*, R. Sta. Luzia 799, T 262-5867; *Brazilian Holidays*, R. Visconde de Pirajá 414, Suite 819/820, T 267-5749, Ipanema, English and German spoken, helpful regarding tickets and information; *Tour Brazil*, R. Farme de Amoeda 75/605, nr. Ipanema, T 521-4461, Fax 021-521-1056, very good English spoken; *Victor Hummel*, Av. Presidente Vargas 290/4, T 223-1262, Swiss-run, rec. T 231-1800. Also Swiss-run and highly rec., *South American Turismo Ltda*, Av. N. S. de Copacabana 788, 6th and 7th floors, T 255-2345; Marlin Tours, No. 605/1201, T 255-4433, Audrey speaks English. *Quality Travel*, Av. N.S. Copacabana 387, T 235-6888, Fax 236-6985, helpful with hotel bookings. Regular sightseeing tours operated by *Gray Line* (294-0393), *American Sightseeing* (236-3551), *Sul América* (257-4235), *Canbitur* (of Copacabana), *Passamar Turismo*, Av. Rio Branco 25 (233-8883, 233-4833, 253-1125; also at *Hotel Nacional*). *Adrianotour*, T 208-5103, for guided tours, reservations and commercial services (English, French, German and Spanish spoken). *Enasa*, for Amazon river travel, R. Uruguaiana 39 (Sala 1402); they try to sell tickets on first-class boats only.

For a good, private walking tour of Rio's cultural sights, contact Prof. Carlos Roquette, a professor of history, who charges US$20 p.p., T 322-4872, 24 hrs, write to R. Santa Clara 110/904, Copacabana, Rio de Janeiro, RJ 22041, English and French spoken.

**Tourist Information** There are several excellent information centres. Embratur, R. Mariz e Barros 13, near Praça da Bandeira, T 273-2212, gives information on the whole country. Riotur (for the city of Rio), R. da Assembléia 10, 7th floor (T 297-7117), sells a huge map of the city. Official Riotur information stands at Pão de Açúcar cablecar station (0800-2000); Marina da Glória, Flamengo; Rodoviária Novo Rio (the bus station—0600-2400; very friendly and helpful in finding accommodation). Riotur also has a multilingual telephone service operating 24 hours, T 580-8000. Flumitur (for the state of Rio de Janeiro) at Rio International Airport, helpful with hotel information and booking, can sometimes arrange discounts, and R. da Assembléia 10, 8th floor, very helpful. Touring Clube do Brasil, Pres. Antônio Carlos 130 and Av. Brasil 4294 (out of town) no English spoken.

   **N.B.** Tourist packs are sold for US$15 at the International Airport—these contain a map, restaurant list and a blank passport facsimile, which has no legal standing even though they may try to persuade you otherwise. Best guide to Rio, with excellent map, *Guia Quatro Rodas* *do Rio* in Portuguese and English, US$3 (the *Guia Quatro Rodas do Brasil*, published annually in Nov. also has a good Rio section). *Guia Rex* street guide, US$8. *Guia Schaeffer Rio de Janeiro* (US$3) is an excellent sheet. Also, *The Insider's Guide to Rio de Janeiro*, an annual guide book by Christopher Pickard, published by Streamline Ltda, Av. N.S. de Copacabana 605/1210 (distributed in UK and Europe by Roger Lascelles, 47 York Rd., Brentford, Middlesex, TW8 0OP, and in USA by Luso-Brazilian Books, 33 Nevins St., Brooklyn, New York 11217). Many hotels provide guests with the weekly *Itinerário* (*Rio This Month*); *Rio Life* is a free fortnightly magazine in English, it has information, articles and ads., T 580-8498.

**Maps** are available from Riotur information desks (US$1), Touring Clube do Brasil (US$0.40), newsstands (US$0.65), touring agencies and hotels; Geomapas tourist map is clear, US$1.20. Also maps free from H. Stern, the jeweller, at R. Visconde do Pirajá 490, Ipanema. Also from Paulini, R. Lélio Gama 75 (outside the entrance of the downtown tram station): topographical and other maps of Brazil and of South America. **Note** Tourist agencies do not normally provide lists of cheap accommodation for travellers; some initiative is required.

**Airports** Rio has two airports. The Santos Dumont airport on Guanabara Bay, right in the city, is used exclusively for Rio-São Paulo shuttle flights (US$153 return), air taxis and private planes. The shuttle services operate every half hour throughout the day from 0630 to 2230. Sit on right-hand side for views to São Paulo, other side coming back, book in advance for particular flights. The main airport (Galeão), on Governador Island, some 16 km. from the centre of Rio, is in two sections, international and domestic (including Vasp and Transbrasil's jet shuttle from Rio to São Paulo). Duty-free shops are well-stocked, but not especially cheap. The Real company runs an air-conditioned bus ( *frescão*) from Galeão to Santos Dumont Airport, via the city centre, every half-hour, unsafe at night as it goes through Flamengo park (for Flamengo/Catete hotel area, take this bus, then a taxi from Santos Dumont) and another goes to Copacabana (stopping at Av. Atlântica e Santa Clara) at approx. half-past every hour, with space for baggage, US$3 (also stops at Rodoviária). Difficulties reported in locating this bus in Copacabana for return to the airport. Air-conditioned taxis (Cootramo and Transcopass) have fixed rates (US$6 downtown, US$25 Copacabana), buy a ticket at the counter near the arrivals gate before getting into the car. The hire is for taxi, irrespective of number of passengers, and therefore the possibility of sharing with other passengers arises. Ordinary taxis also operate with the normal meter reading—make sure you are given the card which gives the number to phone if you are overcharged (about US$14 downtown, US$15 Copacabana). A good policy is to check at the Riotur counter before leaving, for folders, maps and advice; watch out for pirate taxis, whose drivers will want to charge up to US$50! Town bus No. 322 goes to Rio International airport, first one with direction Bananal. No bank or *câmbio* in departure hall of airport, and the 24-hour banks before passport control give worse rates than the lift attendants, etc. (if you can wait, on arrival, till you get into town, so much the better); Banco Bozano Simonsen, 1st floor, gives close to parallel rate. There is a wider choice of restaurants before passport control, but seats for flights are not allocated until after passport control. We have been told that X-ray machines at Galeão are not safe for film.

**Rail** Central do Brasil Railway to São Paulo is the only long-distance service: the "Santa Cruz" night train carries double-bedroom sleeping cars (US$20), a "poltrona-leito" (coach with leg rests), a diner and a bar-lounge, leaving 2300, arriving 0820— rec., book cabins 2 weeks ahead for weekend journeys, 3-5 days for weekdays in holiday times, provision of service is erratic, check! There are suburban trains to Nova Iguaçu, Nilópolis, Campo Grande and elsewhere. Buses marked "E. Ferro" go to the railway station.

**Buses** Bus fares to the following cities, with approximate journey times (book ahead if you can), are as follows:

|                  | distance km. | ordinary US$ | leito US$ | hours |
|------------------|-------------:|-------------:|----------:|------:|
| São Paulo        | 434          | 10.00        | 20.00     | 6     |
| Brasília         | 1,134        | 32.00        | 64.00     | 20    |
| Belo Horizonte   | 429          | 12.80        | 25.60     | 7     |
| Curitiba         | 839          | 20.00        | 49.00     | 12    |
| Florianópolis    | 1,154        | 26.00        | 52.00     | 20    |
| Foz do Iguaçu    | 1,500        | 29.00        | 58.00     | 23    |
| Porto Alegre     | 1,603        | 38.50        | 77.00     | 26    |
| Juiz de Fora     | 177          | 4.80         | —         | 4     |
| Vitória          | 519          | 12.80        | 25.60     | 8     |
| Salvador         | 1,690        | 40.00        | 80.00     | 28    |
| Recife           | 2,309        | 54.00        | 108.00    | 38    |

| Fortaleza | 2,861 | 72.00 | 90.00 | 48 |
| São Luís | 3,093 | 78.00 | — | 50 |
| Belém | 3,187 | 83.00 | — | 52 |

To **Campo Grande**, 21 hrs. with Andorinha, US$33. To **Santos**, 6 a day with Normandy, US$9.60, 7½ hrs., at 0800 and 2300 stopping at Parati, Ubatuba, Caraguatatuba and São Sebastião. The trip to Santos along the coast road can be done in one day, in either direction, but it needs an early start. To **Ouro Preto**, direct bus (Util) at 0830 and 2330 daily US$15, 8 hrs.

International: **Asunción**, 1,511 km. via Foz do Iguaçu, 30 hrs. (Pluma); **Buenos Aires** (Pluma), via Porto Alegre and Santa Fe, 44 hrs. (book 2 days in advance)also with Gral. Urquiza; **Montevideo**, only from São Paulo; **Santiago** de Chile, with Pluma or Gral. Urquiza, about 70 hours. The Buenos Aires and Montevideo services are fully booked a week in advance.

You are allowed to sleep at the bus station, if you don't lie down (no left luggage facilities). The main bus station (the Rodoviária, at Av. Rodrigues Alves, corner with Av. Francisco Bicalho, just past the docks, reached by buses 104 from the centre, 127 and 128 from Copacabana and 136, 456, 172 from Flamengo, or 170 from Largo do Machado and Flamengo, or taxi), has a Riotur information centre, very helpful. From Rodoviária, take bus 104 to Largo do Machado or to Catete for central location with buses and cheap hotels. The local bus teminal is just outside the Rodoviária: turn right as you leave and run the gauntlet of taxi drivers. The Real bus goes along the beach to São Conrado and will take luggage. **If you do need a taxi collect a ticket**, which ensures against overcharging, from the official at the head of the taxi queue. On no account give the ticket to the taxi driver.

**Hitch Hiking** To hitch to Belo Horizonte or Brasília, take a C-3 bus from Av. Presidente Antônio Carlos to the railway station, cross through the station to a bus station, and catch the Nova Iguaçu bus. Ask to be let off at the Belo Horizonte turn off. For the motorway entrance north and south take bus 392 or 393 from Praça São Francisco.

**Ferry Service** From the "barcas" at Praça 15 de Novembro, ferry boats and launches cross every 10 mins. to Niterói (20-30 mins., US$0.20); to Paquetá Island (70-90 mins., **see page 323** for fares). There are also hydrofoils ("aerobarcas") to Niterói every 10 mins. (about 10 mins., US$2.80). The Niterói ferry service is still being maintained, despite the competition from the 14 km. bridge linking the two sides of Guanabara Bay. (The approach to the bridge is on the elevated motorway from the centre, or via Av. Rio de Janeiro, in the Caju district; take the Av. Rodrigues Alves past the docks.) Bus 999 from the Passeio Público crosses the bridge.

## The Suburbs of Rio de Janeiro

*Copacabana*, built on a narrow strip of land—only a little over 4 square kilometres—between mountain and sea, has one of the highest population densities in the world: 62,000 per square kilometre, or 250,000 in all. Its celebrated curved beach backed by skyscraper apartments is an unforgettable "must" for visitors. On all Rio's beaches you should take a towel or mat to protect you against sandflies; in the water stay near groups of other swimmers; bathing is generally dangerous.

Copacabana began to develop when the Old Tunnel was built in 1891 and an electric tram service reached it. Week-end villas and bungalows sprang up; all have now gone. In the 1930s the Copacabana Palace Hotel was the only tall building; it is now one of the lowest on the beach. The opening of the New Tunnel in the 1940s led to an explosion of population which shows no sign of having spent its force. Buildings of less than 12 storeys are still being replaced by high flats and luxury hotels.

There is almost everything in this fabulous "city within a city". The shops, mostly in Avenida Copacabana and the R. Barata Ribeiro, are excellent; this is the area in which to watch, or participate in, the city's glamorous night life. A fort at the far end of the beach commands the entrance to Rio Bay and prevents a seashore connection with the Ipanema and Leblon beaches. However, parts of the military area are now being handed over to civilian use, the first being the Parque Garota de Ipanema at Arpoador, the fashionable Copacabana end of the Ipanema beach. Buses to and from the city centre are plentiful and cheap, about US$0.10. If you are going to the centre from Copacabana, look for "Castelo", "Praça 15", "E. Ferro" or "Praça Mauá" on the sign by the front door. "Aterro" means the expressway between Botafogo and downtown Rio (not open Sundays). From the centre to Copacabana is easier as all buses in that direction are clearly marked. Aterro bus does the journey in 15 minutes.

Beyond Copacabana are the beautiful seaside suburbs of Ipanema (a good place from which to watch the sunset) and Leblon; they are a little less built-up than Copacabana, and their beaches tend to be cleaner, though no less dangerous, than Copacabana's. Backing Ipanema and Leblon is the Lagoa Rodrigo de Freitas, a salt-water lagoon on which Rio's rowing and small-boat sailing clubs are active; too polluted for bathing. Beyond Leblon the coast is rocky; the Avenida Niemeyer skirts the cliffs on the journey past Vidigal, a small beach where the *Sheraton* is situated, to the outer seaside suburbs of São Conrado (beach polluted) and Barra da Tijuca (see next page). The flat topped Gávea rock can be climbed or scrambled up for magnificent views, but beware snakes. Buses from Botafogo Metro terminal to Ipanema: some take integrated Metro-Bus tickets, saving 25%; look for the blue signs on the windscreen. Many buses from Copacabana to Ipanema (buses 154 and 158 from Flamengo) and Leblon (buses 158, 434 and 488 from Flamengo, continuing to Barra da Tijuca).

**Santa Teresa**, a hilly inner suburb SW of the centre, well known as the coolest part of Rio, still has many colonial and 19th-century buildings, set in narrow, curving, tree-lined streets. See particularly the Convent (only the outside; the Carmelite nuns do not admit visitors), the Chácara do Céu Museum (**see page 304**), the Hotel Santa Teresa (the oldest house in the area), Vista Alegre, the R. Aprazível, and Largo de Guimarães. Santa Teresa is best visited on the traditional open-sided tram, described on **page 314.**

**Maracanã Stadium** is one of the largest sports centres in the world. The football ground has seating capacity for 200,000 spectators and most matches are played on Sun. about 1700 (entrance from US$0.50-*geral*-, to US$5 for a seat, good, safe, to US$12; matches are worth going to for the fireworks and samba bands of the spectators, even if you're not a football fan. N.B. agencies charge much more). Buses 433, 434 and 455 from Copacabana; 433 and 434 from Flamengo; from Leblon, 464 via Ipanema and Copacabana; 221 and 231 from Castelo; 249 and 269 from Praça Tiradentes; and 238 and 239 from Praça 15 de Novembro; from Praça Mauá, 241 or 262; also Metro from Botafogo and centre. Hotels can arrange visits to football matches: good idea Sundays when the metro is closed and buses very full. If you want the real football experience, take a bus three hours before the game, buy a ticket in the upper ring, people very friendly.

**Corcovado** (710 metres) is the hunch-backed peak surmounted by a 40-metre high statue of Christ the Redeemer completed in 1931, weighing, with its base, 1,200 tons. There is a superb view from the top (sometimes obscured by mist), to which there are a cog railway and a road; both car and train (30 mins. each way) put down their passengers behind the statue—there is a climb of 220 steps to the top, near which there is a café for light refreshments. To see the city by day and night ascend at 1500 or 1600 and descend on the last train; beware of thieves snatching through open windows. Mass is held on Sun. in a small chapel in the statue pedestal. The floodlighting was designed in 1931 by Marconi himself.

Take a Cosme Velho bus (422, 497, 498) to the **cog railway station at R. Cosme Velho 513**. Service every 10-20 minutes according to demand, journey time 10 minutes (cost: US$6 return; single tickets available). Minibuses also operate from the station, return trip (1 hour stop) US$3, tickets obtained from office. Also, a 206 bus does the very attractive run from Praça Tiradentes (or a 407 from Largo do Machado) to Silvestre (the railway has no stop here now). An active walk of one hour will bring one to the top, and the road is shady. (Best done in company; robberies are very common in this neighbourhood.) Coach trips tend to be rather brief. N.B. There is too much interference around the statue for

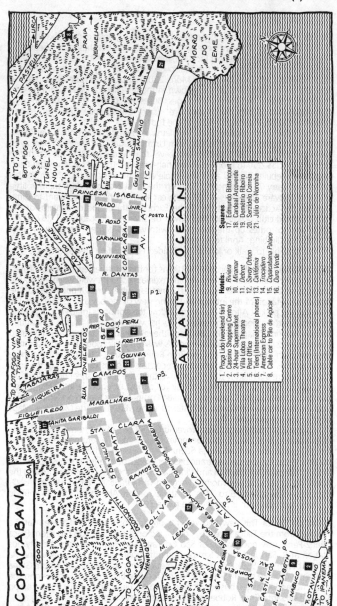

COPACABANA

500m

ATLANTIC OCEAN

**Hotels:**
1. Praça Lido (weekend fair)
2. Cassino Shopping Centre
3. 24-hour Supermarket
4. Villa Lobos Theatre
5. Post Office
6. Telerj (International phones)
7. American Express
8. Cable car to Pão de Açúcar
9. Riviera
10. Miramar
11. Debret
12. Savoy Othon
13. Califórnia
14. Trocadero
15. Copacabana Palace
16. Ouro Verde

**Squares**
17. Edmundo Bittencourt
18. Cardeal Arcoverde
19. Demétrio Ribeiro
20. Serzidelo Correia
21. Júlio de Noronha

taking video pictures.

**Pão de Açúcar** (Sugar Loaf, 396 metres) is a massive granite cone at the entrance to Guanabara Bay. The bird's eye view of the city and beaches is very beautiful. There is a restaurant (excellent location, mixed reports on food, closes 1900) and a playground for children on the Morro da Urca, half way up, where there are also shows at night (weekends and Mon., 2200). You can get refreshments at the top. On the small path that leads down in the direction of Morro Cara de Cão there are toucans and macaws in cages. Buses 107 or 442 (from the centre or Flamengo) and 511 or 500 "jardinière" (from Copacabana) take you to the cable-car station, Av. Pasteur 520, at the foot.

The cable car timetable: Praia Vermelha to Urca: first car goes up at 0800, and the last comes down at 2200. From Urca to Sugar Loaf the first connecting cable car goes up at 0815 and the last leaves the summit at 2200; the return trip costs US$5 (US$2.50 to Morro da Urca, half-way up). The old cableway has been completely rebuilt. Termini are now ample and efficient and the present Italian cable cars carry 75 passengers. Even on the most crowded days there is little queuing. Beware of thieves at the cable car starting point. If you want to climb the Pão de Açúcar, contact the Clube Excursionista de Rio de Janeiro, or the rock-climbing club, Andre Illa and Xavier de Silvera, Copacabana, T 237-5229. There are 35 routes up the mountain, with various degrees of difficulty (best months for climbing: April to August).

It is possible to walk or jog on the S side in the military area at the foot.

**Tijuca National Park**, open 0600-2100, is for those interested in taking a forest walk through mountain scenery. An approximately 2-3 hr. walk will bring you to the summit of the Pico da Tijuca (1,012 metres), which gives a good idea of the tropical vegetation of the interior and a fine view of the bay and its shipping. On entering the park at Alto de Boa Vista, follow the signposts (maps are displayed) to Bom Retiro, a good picnic place (1½ hrs walk), passing by the Cascatinha Taunay, Mayrink Chapel (built 1860) and the restaurant *A Floresta*. At Bom Retiro the road ends and there is another hour's walk up a fair footpath to the summit; take the path from the right of the Bom Retiro drinking fountain; not the more obvious steps from the left. The last part consists of steps carved out of the solid rock; take care of children at the summit as there are several sheer drops, invisible because of bushes. The route is shady for almost its entire length. The panels painted in the Mayrink Chapel by Cândido Portinari have been replaced by copies and the originals will probably be installed in the Museu de Arte Moderna. Maps of the Park are available.

Take a 221 from Praça 15 de Novembro, 233 or 234 bus from the Rodoviária (it is reported that the 233 bus becomes the 234 on the return journey) or 454 from Copacabana or from Praça Sáenz Pena, Tijuca (reached by metro) to Alto da Boa Vista, for the park entrance. Other places of interest not passed on the walk to the peak are the Paul and Virginia Grotto, the Vista do Almirante and the Mesa do Imperador (viewpoints). A good restaurant in Parque Floresta is *Os Esquilos*. Allow at least 5 to 6 hrs. for the excursion. Also, one of the Raymundo Castro Maia museums is nearby (**see page 304**).

**Barra da Tijuca** This new and very rapidly developing residential area can be reached from the Tijuca Forest by continuing on the 233 or 234 bus (from Praça Sáenz Pena, very good views of São Conrado and Barra), or from the city bus station at R. São José, from Santos Dumont airport, and from Copacabana via Leblon beach (bus 553). From Botafogo metro terminus, take bus 524; from Glória or Flamengo take bus 175 or 179. A comfortable bus, Pegasus, goes along the coast from the Castelo bus terminal to Barra da Tijuca and continues to Campo Grande or Santa Cruz. Robberies on the buses have been reported.

Barra da Tijuca is also one of the principal recreation areas of Rio, the prime attraction being its 20-km. sandy beach, with good waves for surfing; somewhat cleaner than Copacabana but fast becoming another "Costa del Sol". Bus 700 from Praça São Conrado (terminal of bus 553 from Copacabana) goes the full length of the beach to Recreio dos Bandeirantes. There are innumerable bars and restaurants, campsites (see page 312), motels and hotels. The facilities include Riocenter, a 600,000 sq.m. convention complex and the huge Barra Shopping and Carrefour shopping centres. The stylish Fashion Mall is opposite the golf club. Watch the hang-gliders jumping from the hilltops at weekends. View the beaches and hills from the air, Ultra Força Ltda, Av. Sernambetiba 8100, T 399-3114, 15 mins, US$50-60, negotiate. Live concerts on São Conrado beach during summer (Nov.-Feb.).

**The Autódromo** (motor racing track) is beyond Barra in the Jacarepaguá district. The Brazilian Grand Prix is held here or at Interlagos, São Paulo, alternately in January.

**Viewpoints**  Apart from the Pico da Tijuca, Corcovado and Pão de Açúcar, splendid views of different parts of Rio can be seen from the Vista Chinesa (420 metres), where from a Chinese-style pavilion one can see the inland lake (the Lagoa), Ipanema and Leblon; the Mesa do Imperador (Emperor's Table) and Vista do Almirante (Admiral's View) in the Tijuca Forest; and the Mirante de Dona Marta (340 metres) off the Corcovado road, with the same direction of view as the Corcovado, but as it is lower the details can be seen more clearly. There is as yet no public transport to any of these places.

*Paquetá Island* in Guanabara Bay can be visited by more or less two-hourly ferry services from Praça Quinze de Novembro, none between 1015 and 1330, last back at 2030 (fare US$0.40 by boat, 1 hr., US$4 by hydrofoil, 20 mins. journey, which more than doubles its price Sats., Suns. and holidays). Horse-drawn carriages hire (many have harnesses which cut into the horse's flesh); they do not stop at the interesting Parque Darke de Mattos. Tour by "trenzinho", a tractor pulling trailers, US$0.80, or on foot, quieter and free. Bicycles also can be hired. The island is noted for its gigantic pebble shaped rocks, butterflies and orchids. The house of José Bonifácio, the opponent of slavery, may be seen. Very crowded at weekends and public holidays, but usually very quiet during the week, though there can be aircraft noise. Reasonable food and drink prices.

Other boat trips, Aquatur (T 230-9273), Brazilian Marina Turismo, Camargo (T 275-0643), Passamar, Siqueira Campos 7 (T 236-4136), Greyline (T 274-7146), Soletur (Bay trips Sat. and Sun. only) and American Sightseeing, Av. N.S. Copacabana 605, Sala 1204 (T 236-3551). The last three offer a day cruise, including lunch, to Jaguanum Island (see page 330, under Itacuruçá) and a sundown cruise around Guanabara Bay, also deep-sea fishing expeditions and private charters.

Entering Rio from the W, an alternative to the BR-101 and Avenida Brasil, is to leave BR-101 on the road to Santa Cruz, continuing 6 km. to the fishing village of Sepetiba, quiet other than at weekends. Along the coast is Pedra de Guaratiba, from where you join Avenida das Américas, turning off right soon afterwards to Ponta do Picão and Guaratiba, a pretty seaside resort on a rocky, narrow, steep ledge between mountain and sea (good beaches and a playground for the rich). Another 2 km. along the main road is another (unmarked) right turn leading to a restaurant at the summit, with fantastic views, then down to Praia de Grumari, which is unspoilt except for 2 restaurants and a campsite (US$1 p.p.). It is then 30 km. to Copacabana, via Recreio dos Bandeirantes (Dieter Reinmuth).

## The State of Rio de Janeiro: East from Rio

*Niterói* (pop. 441,000) founded in 1573, the ex-capital of the State of Rio de Janeiro, is reached across the bay by bridge or ferries,

Of the frequent ferry boat and hydrofoil services (see page 319) from Praça 15 de Novembro, Rio, the slow, cheaper ferry gives the best views. There is a Flumitur tourist information booth to the right of the ferry-boat station. Nearby you can take the 33 bus (marked "via Froes") to the beaches of Icaraí, São Francisco and Jurujuba on the bay, a beautiful ride. Sit on the right-hand side. A few minutes' walk from where the bus route ends at Jurujuba are the attractive twin beaches of Adão and Eva, with lovely views of Rio across the bay. From Praça General Gomes Carneiro, near the ferry boats, take a 38 bus to Piratininga, Itaipu and Itacoatiara, fabulous ocean beaches and the best in the area, about 40 minutes' ride through picturesque countryside. The beaches inside the bay, though calm, are often overcrowded and polluted, but no more so than those opposite in Rio. The forts on this side of the bay include Santa Cruz (16th century, still a military establishment), Barão do Rio Branco (1633), Gragoatá and Nossa Senhora da Boa Viagem.

You should also visit the church of Boa Viagem (1633), built on an island connected to the mainland by a short causeway, a few minutes' walk from Icaraí beach. Nearby, on R. Tiradentes, is the Antônio Parreira Museum, opens 1300, dedicated to the eponymous artist. The Museu de Arqueologia de Itaipu is in the ruins of the 18th century Santa Teresa Convent, and also covers the archaeological site of Duna Grande on Itaipu beach.

The Rio-Niterói bridge (Ponte Costa e Silva) has a length of 14 km. Toll for cars, US$0.30. Motorway connection to centre of Rio. Bus 999 from the corner of Senador Dantas and Av. Beira Mar, Rio, crosses the bridge to Niterói and Icaraí (US$0.50); also 996 and 998 from the Jardim Botânico (all three go to the Rodoviária in Rio).

**Hotels** *Novotel Rio-Niterói*, Praia de Gragoatá, Telex 021-7252, A; *Samanguaia*, D; *Niterói Palace*, R. Andrade Neves 134, D-C; *Imperial*, D; Youth Hostel, *A.J. Solar dos Díos*, R. Santo Eduardo 63, T 709-0686.

**Clubs** Rio Cricket, bus 57 from ferry. Rio Sailing, bus 33 marked "via Froes".

**Electric Current** 110 volts, A.C., 60 cycles.

**Laundromat** *Lavlev*, R. Presidente Backer 138.

To the east of Niterói lie a series of salt-water lagoons, the Lagos Fluminenses. Two small lakes lie behind the beaches of Piratininga, Itacoatiara and Itaipu near Niterói, but they are polluted and ringed by mud. The next lakes are much larger, those of Maricá and Saquarema; though they are still muddy, the waters are relatively unpolluted, and wild life abounds in the scrub and bush around the lagoons. At the outlet to the lake of Saquarema (turn right off the main road at Bacaxá) is the holiday village of **Saquarema**. Of particular interest is the little white church of Nossa Senhora de Nazaré (1675) built atop a green promontory jutting into the ocean. Saquarema is the centre for surfing in Brazil, and the national championships are held here each year in May. Beware of strong currents, though.

The largest lake is that of **Araruama**, famous for its medicinal mud. It is so large that it seems more like a bay than a lagoon. The salinity is extremely high, the waters calm, and almost the entire lake is surrounded by sandy beaches, making it very popular with families looking for safe, unpolluted bathing. The major industry of the area is salt, and all around one can see the saltpans and the wind pumps used to carry the water into the pans. At the eastern end of the lake lies the village of **São Pedro de Aldeia**, which, in spite of intensive development, still retains much of its colonial charm, and has a lovely Jesuit church built in 1723.

**Hotels** in the lake district: Saquarema: *Sol e Mar*, B; *Katy Motel*, B; *Pousada do Holandés*, Av. Vilamar 377, at Itaúna beach, D, highly rec., many languages spoken by Dutch owner and his Brazilian wife (who runs the local day-care centre), good meals—follow the signs, or take a taxi (US$0.80), from Saquarema. Restaurant in Saquarema, *Tem Uma Né Chama* Teré, very good, in main square. Araruama: *Senzala*, on Iguabinha beach, 10 km. from Araruama, A with meals; *La Gondola*, on the lake beach, C, overpriced; *Parque Hotel*, A; *Lakes Hotel*, over the bus station, A; *Chalés do Coqueiral*, chalets on lake beach, A. São Pedro de Aldeia: *Solar de Iguaba*, C; *Vilabranca Village*, over 100 chalets, A with meals, and *Costa do Sol*, A, on Iguaba Grande beach, 14 km. from São Pedro. At Ponta Negra are *Pousada Colonial*, suites and bungalows in B range, breakfast included, T Rio, 451-6254 for reservations, and *Solar Tabauna*, T 748-1626, B, pool, both highly rec.

The ocean beaches beside these lagoons, except for the sheltered coves of Ponta Negra and Saquarema, are rough and lonely. The whole area is perfect for camping; there are campsites (including Camping Clube do Brasil) at Araruama (close to the *Parque Hotel*) and São Pedro de Aldeia. A very steep road connects the beaches of Itaipu and Itacoatiara with BR-106 (and on to Araruama) via the village of Itaipu-Açu, with beach and good camping. Most maps do not show a road beyond Itaipu-Açu; it is certainly too steep for buses.

An alternative to the route from Niterói to Araruama through the lagoons is via Manilla, Itaboraí and Rio Bonito, on the BR-101 and RJ-124; this is a fruit-growing region.

**Cabo Frio**, 156 km. from Rio, is a popular holiday and week-end haunt of Cariocas because of its cool weather, beaches, scenery, sailing and good under-water swimming (but mosquitoes are a problem). The ocean beach is much less frequented than the bay beach. The São Mateus fort nearby was built by the French; it is in a state of disrepair. If in the area, take a look at the huge church under construction at Arraial do Cabo nearby; it totally dominates the town (bus every 20 mins. from Cabo Frio). There are random car searches for drugs on the road to Buzios.

**Hotels**  A wide selection, from expensive down to *Colonial*, R. José Watzl Filho 96, D. *Jangada*, Granaola 220, near canal, D, very friendly, good breakfast, rec. *Nanaque*, 2 blocks from bus station, follow signs, 3 blocks from sea, E with bath and breakfast, clean, highly rec.; two similar nearby. Youth Hostel, both sexes, open all year to IYHF members (F p.p., more for non-members), on R. Kubitschek, 1 block from bus station, very friendly. 2 youth hostels in Arraial do Cabo, one at Escola Municipal Ione Nogueira (T 43-0369) and the other at R. Gen. Bruno Martins 9881 (T 262-6360).

**Camping**  Camping Clube do Brasil sites at Estrada dos Passageiros, near town; at Km. 135 on the Rio road, 4 km. outside town, in Palmeiras; and at Arraial do Cabo on Praia dos Anjos, crowded beach. 10 km. to S. Cambrás has a site at Estrada dos Passageiros. Also site at Cabo Yacht club.

**Buses**  Rodoviária is 2 km. from centre. Bus from Rio every ½ hr., 2½ hrs., US$6. To Búzios, from local bus terminus in town centre, every hour, US$0.80.

**Búzios**, NE of Cabo Frio, is an expensive resort built up in Portuguese colonial styles, with unmade roads so as to discourage fast drivers. It has 27 sandy coves, calm unpolluted waters (superb for windsurfing), beautiful scenery, plenty of good hotels and *pousadas* (mostly C upwards, e.g. *Casa D'elas Pousada*, and *Pousada do Sol*, Praia da Armação; *Pousada Casa de Pedra*, Trav. Lúcio A. Quintanilha 57, T (0246) 231499, D, TV, fridge, safe, in centre of town, rec.). Only the vicious mosquitoes come cheap). Best route from Rio (2 hrs. by car) is the paved road towards Macaé, with a paved turnoff to Búzios. Direct road from Cabo Frio (bus 45 mins.) is unpaved. Camping is allowed but dangerous. Tourist information office near bus station. Very crowded during Brazilian holiday season and extremely difficult to get hotel booking. Several good restaurants (try the *camarão tropical*) and popular bars. Tartaruga beach is not marked and not developed (take dirt road up small hill opp. *Pousada Baer Búzios*); there is a restaurant and snack bar in season.

Continuing to the north, one comes to the seaside resorts of Barra de São João, **Rio das Ostras** Hotel *Mirante do Poeta*, C, and others) and **Macaé** (Hotels: *Colonial*, C, friendly, comfortable; *Turismo* and *Panorama*, C; *Central*, R. Rui Barbosa, E, clean, nice, friendly, good breakfast, secure parking), all containing sheltered coves with good swimming and scuba diving. Macaé is also the supply centre for the offshore oil industry so there are usually several foreigners in town enjoying a beer.

From Rio and Niterói a first class highway, the BR-101, runs NE past Macaé to Campos (bus Rio-Macaé 2½-3 hrs., every ½ hr., Mil e Um or Rápido Macaense; bus Macaé-Campos, 1¾ hrs., US$2.40). At Km. 222 is the **Biological Reserve of Poço das Antas** (2 hrs. drive from Rio; it is not open to the general public, for details, Delegacia Estadual do IBDF, Av. Pres. Antônio Carlos 607-12°, CEP 20.000, Rio de Janeiro). Many animals (including the *mico-leão* marmoset—this is its only natural habitat) roam in the forest.

**Campos** (pop. 367,000) is a busy industrial city, some 276 km. (4½ hrs. by Mil e Um bus, hourly) from Rio de Janeiro (70 km. from Macaé). It stands 56 km. from the mouth of the Rio Paraíba, up which coffee planting originally spread to São Paulo state. Coffee is still grown near Campos, though the region is now one of the largest sugar-producing zones in Brazil. Important offshore oil discoveries have been made nearby. Town is quite interesting.

**Hotels** *Terraza Tourist*, Joaquím Tavora 22, D, 2-star; *Planície*, R. 13 de Maio 56, D; *Palace*, Av. 15 de Novembro 143, D. *Silva*, some way behind church on municipal square, E, breakfast, clean, safe parking.

Travelling N, as an alternative to BR-101 to Vitória, one can take a detour inland, going through São Fidélis, Cambiasca, Itoacara and on to **Santo Antônio de Pádua**, 130 km. from Campos, a pleasant town on the Rio Pomba. (*Hotel das Aguas*, a short walk from the centre, D, a resort hotel in a park with pool, health centre and bottling plant for the local mineral water which is used for treating cardiovascular illness; *Braga*, in town, E, clean, friendly, good food.) Take road No. 393 to Itaperuna, Bom Jesus do Itabapoana and into Espírito Santo, then road No. 484 to Guaçuí (*Grande Hotel Minas*, F, friendly, clean; *Restaurant Kontiki*, very good), one of the starting points for the Parque Nacional do Caparaó (**see page 348**). Then take the road 482 to Cachoeira do Itapemirim and the BR-101 (**see page 332**).

**Petrópolis** (population: 275,000) is a summer hill resort and industrial city at 840 metres, 68 km. N of Rio. It is reached by bus along a steep, scenic mountain toll road (US$1 weekdays, US$1.50 weekends). Until 1962 Petrópolis was the "summer capital" of Brazil; it was founded in 1843 as a summer refuge by Dom Pedro II. Now it combines manufacturing industry (particularly textiles, which may be bought cheaply) with floral beauty and hill scenery. The Imperial Palace (Museu Imperial), which seems to express very faithfully what we know of Dom Pedro II's character, is a modest but elegant building, fully furnished and equipped, containing the Crown Jewels and other imperial possessions. It is assiduously well-kept: one might think the imperial family had left the day before one's visit, rather than in 1889. Open Tues.-Sun., 1200-1730. Entry US$0.30. Well worth a visit is the Gothic-style Cathedral, completed in 1925, which contains the tombs of the Emperor and Empress (guide in English, US$0.20).

**Hotels** *Casa do Sol*, 4-star hotel 8 km. out on road to Rio, B; *Margaridas*, Monsenhor Bacelar 126, chalet-type hotel set in lovely gardens with swimming pool, charming proprietors, C; *Auto-Tour* (*Fazenda Inglesa*) at km. 51 on the Petrópolis by-pass, very chic, A, with meals; *Riverside Parque*, R. Hermogéneo Silva 522, C; *Casablanca Center*, General Osório 28, B; *Casablanca*, Sete de Setembro beside Imperial Palace, C, good atmosphere in older part, pool, very clean; *Casablanca Palace*, Primeiro de Março 123, C; *Gran Solar* (*Pousado do Carmo*), Benjamin Constant 288, C; *Dom Pedro*, D, on main square, pleasant; *Comércio*, opp. bus station, E, with breakfast; *Pensão Esther*, R. do Imperador, E, incl. breakfast.

**Camping** Associação Brasileira de Camping and YMCA, Araras district. Can reserve space through Rio YMCA, T 231-9860.

**Restaurants** *Churrascaria Majórica*, Av. do Imperador (ex 15 de Novembro) 754; *Dom Giovanni*, same street, less; *Cantina Italiana*, Paulo Barbosa 48, clean, pleasant; *Maloca*, Wáshington Luís 466; *Bauernstube*, João Pessoa 297.

**Attractions and Excursions** Museu Ferreira da Cunha, Fernandes Vieira 390 (old road to Rio) shows large collection of arms, open Sat. and Sun. (only to groups; need to arrange in advance) 0900-1700. Summer home of air pioneer Santos Dumont, showing early inventions. Palácio de Cristal in Praça da Confluência, former imperial ballroom and now exhibition centre. Orquidário Binot, R. Fernandes Vieira 390 (take bus to Vila Isabel; open Mon.-Sat., 0800-1100, 1300-1700), a huge collection of orchids from all over Brazil (plants may be purchased).

**Buses** leave from Rio every 15 mins. throughout the day (US$1.60), Sun. every hour, sit on the left hand side for best views. Return tickets are not available, so passengers must buy tickets for the return bus as soon as they arrive in Petrópolis. Journey 75 mins. each way. The ordinary buses leave from the Rodoviária in Rio; there is a new service of air-conditioned buses, hourly from 1100, from Av. Nilo Peçanha, US$2.40. There is a direct overnight bus from São Paulo.

***Teresópolis*** (pop. 115,000; 910 metres), near the Serra dos Órgãos, is 124 km. NE of Rio. It was the favourite summer residence of the Empress Teresa Cristina. See the Colina dos Mirantes hill, the Sloper and Iaci lakes, the Imbui and Amores waterfalls, and the Fonte Judith. Tourist information office some way from bus station (not very helpful). São Pedro festival on June 29 is celebrated with fireworks.

Martin Crossland writes: Leave the Rodoviária bus station in Rio on the 0800 bus or before (Viação Teresópolis) for the 1¾-hour ride and up into the mountains to Teresópolis (sit on right side of bus). Upon arrival at the bus station, buy another ticket right away for Petrópolis (Viação Teresópolis) for the 1200 bus in order to get a good seat, as the bus fills rapidly. This gives you 2¾ hours to wander around. If you feel up to a steep ½-hr. climb, try the Colina dos Mirantes for a sweeping view of the city and surroundings. For the less energetic, a taxi is not dear.

   The 90-minute drive from Teresópolis to Petrópolis is beautiful. (Sit on left side.) The views on either side are spectacular. Again, upon arrival in Petrópolis at 1330, buy your ticket to Rio (Facil or Unica). Take the 1715 bus "via Quitandinha", and you might catch the sunset over the mountains (in May, June, July, take the 1615 bus). This gives you time to visit most of the attractions listed in the city description.

**Hotels** *São Moritz*, Swiss-style, outside on the Nova Friburgo road, Km. 36, lowest rates, B, with meals; *Alpina*, Parque Imbui, on Petrópolis road, B; *Várzea Palace*, R. Sebastião Teixeira 41, E. *Florida*, Av. Lúcio Meira 467, E, with bargaining. Youth hostel: Retiro da Inglesa, 20 km. on road to Friburgo, Fazenda Boa Esperança (reservations, R. Papa Pio XII 50, Jardim Cascata 25963 Teresópolis).

**Camping** National Park, entrance to Teresópolis from Rio, full facilities; Quinta de Barra, km. 3 on Petrópolis road; Vale das Choupanas, km. 30 on Rio road.

**Restaurants** *Taberna Alpina*, Duque de Caxias 131; *Cantina Riviera*, Praça Baltazar de Silveira 112; *Bar Gota d'Água*, Praça Baltasar da Silveira 16 for trout or feijoada (small but rec.).

**Bus, Rio-Teresópolis** Buses leave every half-hour from Rodoviária. As return tickets are not issued, passengers should book for the return journey as soon as they arrive at Teresópolis. Time, 1¾ hrs. each way; fare US$2.40. From Teresópolis to Petrópolis, every 2 hrs. from 0900-2100, US$2.80.

About 30,000 hectares of the Serra dos Órgãos, so called because their strange shapes are said to recall organ-pipes, are now a **National Park**. The main attraction is the precipitous Dedo de Deus (God's Finger) Peak. There is also the rock formation Mulher de Pedra 12 km. out on the Nova Friburgo road, and the Von Martinó natural-history museum. The highest point is the Pedra Açu, 2,400 metres. A path leads up the 2,260-metre Pedra do Silo, 3-4 hours' climb. Entrance to park, US$0.25. IBDF (The National Forestry Institute, office in Teresópolis, Serra dos Órgãos, Casa 8, CEP 25.950) has some hostels, US$4.60 full board, or US$3.10 first night, US$1.50 thereafter, a bit rough. Camping, US$0.50. A good way to see the Park is to do the Rio-Teresópolis-Petrópolis-Rio circuit; a scenic day trip. The Rio-Teresópolis road, which passes right next to the Serra dos Órgãos, is a toll road (cars US$1, US$1.50 at weekends) from Km. 10.6.

***Nova Friburgo*** (pop. 143,000, 850 metres above sea-level), is a popular resort during summer months (around 30 hotels; restaurants), in a beautiful valley with excellent walking and riding possibilities. Founded by Swiss settlers from Fribourg, it can be reached by bus (US$4.80) from Rio (every hour) in 2 hrs. or by car in 1 hr. 45 min. Cable car from Praça dos Suspiros 650 metres up the Morro da Cruz, for view of rugged country. Road to Teresópolis paved.

**Hotels** *Bucsky*, T 22-5052, 5 km. out on Niterói road, B, with meals; *Sans-Souci*, T 22-7752, 1 km. out, B, with meals, D without; *Garlipp*, German-run, in chalets, B, with meals, at Muri, km. 70.5 from Rio, 10 km. from Nova Friburgo, T 42-1330. Under same ownership is *Fazenda São João*, C, T 42-1304, 11 km. from *Garlipp* up a side road (impassable in the wet), riding, swimming, sauna, tennis, hummingbirds and orchids; owner will meet guests in Nova

Friburgo or even in Rio. Also *Mury Garden*, T 42-1120, with swimming pool, B, with meals, reasonable, 10 km. away at Muri (Km. 70 on Niterói road). *Everest*, T 22-7350, behind Chess Club, E, comfortable, good breakfasts.

**Camping**  Camping Clube do Brasil has sites on Niterói road, at Cônego (7 km. out) and Muri (10 km. out). Cambrás site also at Cônego, and private site at Fazenda Sanandu, 20 km. out on same road.

## The State of Rio de Janeiro: West from Rio

*Volta Redonda* (pop. 219,000) stands on a broad bend of the Rio Paraíba at an altitude of 565 metres, 113 km. W of Rio along the railway to São Paulo. In 1942 it was a little village; today it has one of the largest steel works in Latin American. The mills are on the river bank and the town spreads up the surrounding wooded and gardened slopes.

**Hotels**  *Sider Palace*, R. 33 No. 10, C; *Embaixador*, Tr. L.A. Félix 36, 1-star, E; *Bela Vista*, Alto de Boa Vista, on a hill overlooking town, B.

Visitors who have a permit from the Companhia Siderúrgica Nacional, Av. Treze de Maio 13, Rio de Janeiro (apply ten days in advance), or locally from the *Bela Vista* hotel, are allowed to inspect the mills. Visits start at 0900, and last 2½-3 hrs. The town can be reached from Rio by buses or minibuses in 2½ hrs., US$2.40.

North of Volta Redonda is Miguel Pereira, set in the mountain region with an excellent climate; nearby is the Javari lake, a popular recreational spot. Two *Hotel-Fazendas* (both C) near Miguel Pereira are *Quindins* and *Javari*, both with restaurant, swimming pool, sports grounds, etc. In town is the *Rei dos Montanhas*, E, Swiss-chalet style, clean, chilly at night. Further north, and still in the mountains are the university centres of Vassouras and Valença; both are historical monuments. 35 km. from Valença is Conservatória, another colonial town. This region can also be reached via the Japeri turn-off on the BR-116 (a beautiful mountain drive). Some 30 km. W of Volta Redonda, in the town of Resende, is the Military Academy of Agulhas Negras. Grounds, with captured German guns of World War II, are open to the public. *Resende* can be reached by bus from Aparecida do Norte **(see page 372)**, several daily, US$2, or from Rio, frequent, 1¾ hrs., US$2.80, also from São Paulo and Volta Redonda.

**Hotels**  *Leme*, R. Dr. Cunha Ferreira, 100 m. from Rodoviária, clean, basic, F p.p.; *Dormitórios Amazônica*, Dr. Cunha Ferreira esq. Praça Oliveira Botelho. Shops across river before railway station.

In the same region, 175 km. from Rio, is the small town of *Penedo* (5 buses a day from Resende) which in the 1930s attracted Finnish settlers who brought the first saunas to Brazil. This popular weekend resort also provides horseback riding, and swimming in the Portinho river. Some 33 km. beyond Penedo (part of road unpaved) is the small village of *Visconde de Mauá*, which has cheap lodgings: enquire at *Vendinha da Serra* (run by John from Leeds), excellent natural food restaurant and store; *Pousada Beira Rio*, T 541801; *Pousada Vale das Hortênsias*, T 543030, both provide all meals, rec.; Youth Hostel, 5 km. along the road to Maringá. Fine scenery and walks, lots of holidaymakers, pleasant atmosphere; roads to 3 other small hill towns, Maringá (several E hotels), Marumbá and Mirantão, at about 1,700 metres. 6 km. up river from Maringá are the well-known Santa Clara falls. Buses to Visconde de Mauá from Resende, 1500 and 1630, 1½ hrs., US$2.40 (you reach Maringá before Visconde de Mauá). Further along the Dutra Highway (186 km. from Rio) is the small town of *Engenheiro Passos*, from which a road (BR-354) leads to São Lourenço and Caxambu in Minas Gerais **(see page 348)**, passing Agulhas Negras. One can climb Agulhas Negras from this side by taking the road from Registro pass (1,670 metres) to the Abrigo Rebouças refuge, which is manned all year round (take your own food, US$1 to stay), at 2,350 metres.

**Hotels**  Penedo: *Bertell*, B, with meals; *Pousada Penedo*, D, safe, clean, pool, rec., and

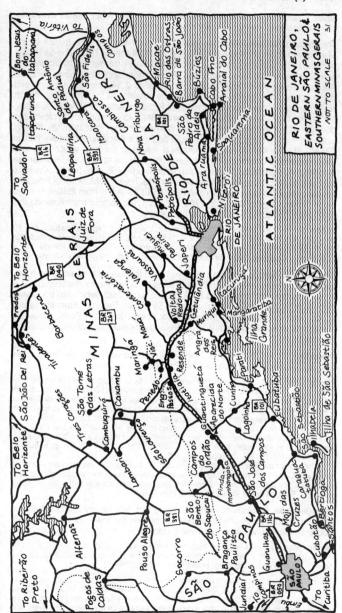

RIO DE JANEIRO, EASTERN SÃO PAULO & SOUTHERN MINAS GERAIS

NOT TO SCALE

others; 2 campsites. Engenheiro Passos: *Villa Forte*, B, with meals; *Pensão das Flores*, Visconde de Mauá, D, with meals. Nine campsites in the area.

The *Itatiaia National Park* (founded 1937), on the Serra de Itatiaia in the Mantiqueira chain of mountains, is a few km. N of the Via Dutra (Rio-São Paulo highway). The road to it is paved. The town of Itatiaia is surrounded by picturesque mountain peaks and lovely waterfalls. This is a good area for climbing (Pico das Agulhas Negras 2,787 metres, Pico da Prateleira 2,540 metres), trekking and birdwatching; information and maps can be obtained at the park office. Worth seeing are the curious rock formations of Pedra de Taruga and Pedra de Maçã, and the waterfall Véu de Noiva (many birds). Basic accommodation in cabins and dormitories is available in the park; you will need to book in season, say 30 days in advance, by writing to Administração do Parque Nacional de Itatiaia, Itatiaia 27540, RJ. The Administração operates a refuge in the park which acts as a starting point for climbs and treks: information on these from Clube Excursionista Brasileira, Av. Almirante Barroso 2, 8th floor, T 220-3695, Rio. Tres Picos wildlife trail near *Hotel Simon*; ask at hotel desk for info. There is a Museum of Flora and Fauna, closed Mondays. Entrance to Park, US$0.35. A bus from Itatiaia, marked *Hotel Simon*, goes to the Park, 1200, returns 1700; coming from Resende this may be caught at the crossroads before Itatiaia.

**Hotels** *Simon*, Km. 13 park road, A, with meals, lovely views; *Repouso Itatiaia*, Km. 10 park road, A, with meals; *Hotel do Ypé*, Km. 13 park road, B, with meals; *Fazenda da Serra*, Via Dutra Km. 151, B, with meals; *Jahu*, Via Dutra Km. 156, D, very friendly, clean, comfortable. **Camping Clube do Brasil** site is entered at Km. 148 on the Via Dutra.

**The new Rio-Santos highway**, and even more the parallel road along the coast, are making the forested and hilly coastal region SW of Rio more accessible. It is now complete right through to Bertioga (**see page 366**), which has good links both with Santos and (avoiding Santos) to São Paulo. There are direct Rio-Santos buses, and direct services from Rio to Angra dos Reis, Parati, Ubatuba, Caraguatatuba, and São Sebastião. Hotels and *pousadas* have sprung up all along the road.

*Itacuruçá*, 91 km. from Rio, is a delightful place to visit if you like fine scenery and peace and quiet, with islands off the coast.

**Hotels** On Ilha de Itacuruçá, is *Hotel Pierre*, reached by boat from Coroa Grande, north of Itacuruçá on the mainland, 5 mins. (boats also go from Itacuruçá); hotel has 27 rooms in price range L, restaurant, bars, sporting facilities. For bookings T Rio 521-1546 or 289-7546, or Saveiros Tours, 267-2792. The *Hotel Jaguanum*, Ilha de Jaguanum, Itacuruçá, has apartments and chalets with private bathrooms. There are beautiful walks around the island. Reservations for the hotel, which include the boat trip to and from the island (at 1000 and 1700), cost US$120-130 per day for two with all meals. The only extra is the bus, US$4.80 return, which picks you up at your hotel. Book by calling 235-2893 or 237-5119, in Rio, or enquire at Sepetiba Turismo, Av. N.S. de Copacabana 605, s. 202.

The sea is now reported to be too polluted for bathing, but you can walk along the railway to Castelo where the beach is cleaner. Ilha de Itacuruçá can also be reached from Muriqui, a popular beach resort 9 km from Itacuruça ; bathing also in the Véu de Noiva waterfall. The next beach along the coast is Praia Grande.

*Mangaratiba*, half-way from Rio to Angra dos Reis, has muddy beaches, but pleasant surroundings and better beaches outside the town, for example Ibicuí, São Brás, Praia Brava, Saco, Guiti and Cação.

**Hotels** *Moreira*, and *Mendoza* (both have same owner), E without breakfast (US$1.90 extra), without bath, good, clean; 2 others, more expensive. None is crowded because the town is not a tourist resort; Youth Hostel, Sítio Santo Antônio 12.

Daily ferry (Conerj) to Ilha Grande island (see below), at 0830 daily, 1½ hrs., highly rec.; return ferry Mon., Wed., Fri. at 1700, Wed. at 1600, other days at 1100. Fare US$0.75, US$1.50 weekends. Tues. and Thur. departures continue on to Angra dos Reis. Ferry departures and destinations can be checked at ferry station at Praça Quinze de Novembro, Rio. Buses from

Rio Rodoviária 7 a day, US$2.40.

**Angra dos Reis** (pop 70,000), said to have been founded in 1502, is 197 km. SW of Rio by road. A small port with an important fishing and shipbuilding industry, it has several small bays with good bathing within easy reach and is situated on an enormous bay full of islands. Boat trips around the bay are available, some with a stop for lunch on the island of Jipóia (5 hrs., US$7.50 p.p.; boats for hire US$10/hour). Of particular interest are the convent of Nossa Senhora do Carmo, built in 1593, the parish church (1626), the ruins of the Jacuecanga seminary (1797), and the Senhor do Bonfim church (1780).

**Hotels** *Frade*, road to Ubatuba, T 65-1212, A, the most expensive; *Palace*, Carvalho 275, C, and *Londres*, R. Pompéia 75, C; *Caribe*, D, central, and *Acrópolis*, R. de Conceição 255, T 65-1022, D, clothes washing facilities, rec. *Porto Rico*, E without breakfast, clean, quiet. At Km. 115 on BR-101 is *Hotel Porto Bracuhy*, B, with lots of facilities for watersports, nightly shows and dancing, restaurant, etc. (23 km. from Angra dos Reis). Youth Hostel at Km. 115 on Estrada Rio-Santos.

**Restaurants** For meat, *Adega dos Dragos*, good. *Taberna*, Raul Pompéia 33, good, popular, moderate prices; *Jacques*, R. de Comércio, good for seafood, also *Tropicalitá*, Largo do Convento do Carmo.

**Bus** Hourly from Rio's Rodoviária, Viação Eval, take the "via litoral" bus and sit on the left, US$4.80, 2½ hrs. Tourist information opposite the bus station.

The Hotéis do Frade group (*Frade do Retiro, Pousada Dom João* in Parati and *Hotel Portogalo*, 1½ hrs. from Rio on a cliff top) in conjunction with Aquatur owns a schooner, the *Frade-Mar*, which runs cruises off Angra dos Reis, exploring islands, snorkelling, diving, etc. Trips are Mon.-Wed., or Fri.-Sun.; bookings for cruises,and for Frade hotels: R. Joaquim Nabuco 161, Copacabana, 22080 Rio de Janeiro, T 267-7375, Telex: 31034, or Portuguese Tours Inc., 321 Rahway Av., Elizabeth, N.J. 07202, T 352-6112, Telex 138-203 or 178-051.

A road runs inland (about 18 km. beyond Angra), through Getulândia, to join the BR-116 either just S of Pirai or near Volta Redonda, through nice mountain scenery.

Two hours by ferry boat (Mon., Wed., Fri. at 1530, return 1015—so you have to stay 2 nights; for day trips, go from Mangaratiba) takes you on a most attractive trip through the bay to **Ilha Grande**, once an infamous pirate lair, and now occupied principally by fishermen and one of Brazil's larger prisons, with two good hotels, *Paraiso do Sol* (A, inclusive of meals, reservations, Rio, T 252-9158) and *Mar da Tranqüilidade* (B, reservations Rio, T 392-8475). Hotel reservations are necessary; alternatively you can camp on beaches; ask in the port at Angra dos Reis for a fishing boat going to Proveta, where you can stay in boat sheds or, if lucky, with a fisherman. It is a beautiful village, from which you can walk through tropical forest on a mountain to Praia do Aventureiro (a day's leisurely walk each way). Take mosquito precautions and register with police post in village of Abraão.

Beyond Angra dos Reis, the road continues 100 km. along the coast, past the nuclear-power plant at Itaorna, to **Parati** (pop. 23,300), a charming colonial town only recently accessible with the opening of the road. The centre has been declared a national historic monument in its entirety. It used to be a very important place, being the chief port for the export of gold in the 17th century. The churches were built separately for each race, Indian, black and white. There is a great deal of distinguished Portuguese colonial architecture in delightful settings. On the northern headland is a small fort, 15 mins.' walk, pleasant views. There is a festival of sacred music in September. The town centre is out of bounds for motor vehicles, in spring the roads are flooded, while the houses are above the water level. It is now very popular with tourists, and an expensive place to visit (changing dollars is difficult, travellers' cheques impossible). Local patchwork is for sale in the community centre on the waterfront, quilts for sale in gift shop in Santa Rita de Cassia church. Boat trips round the bay daily at 1200, returning 1700, US$10.50 p.p., beautiful trip; alternatively you can hire small boats by the hour. Take mosquito repellent.

**Hotels** *Pousada Pardieiro*, Ten. Francisco Antônio 74, T 71-1370, A, attractively housed in colonial building with lovely gardens, but always full at week-ends, does not take children. *Pousada Paratí*, R. do Comércio, T 71-1205, A, reasonable value; *Coixo*, Ten. Francisco Antônio 362, T 71-1460, central, B, pool, attractive patio, rec.; *Santa Rita*, R. Santa Rita 2, D, good, with bath and breakfast; other central *pousadas*: *do Ouro*, Dr. Pereira 145, A, *das Canoas* , R. Silveira 279, T 71-1133, rec., clean, swimming pool, a/c, and *Aconchego*, Domingos Gonçalves de Abreul, T 71-1598, both C; *Pescador*, Av. Beira-Rio, central, C; *Pouso Familiar*, R. J.V.Ramos 262, E, run by Belgian (Joseph Yserbyt) and his Brazilian wife (Lucia), near bus station, laundry facilities, English, French, German and Flemish spoken, T 0243-711475, rec.; *Hotel Solar dos Gerânios*, Praça da Matriz, D, clean, friendly, good breakfast; *Estalagem Colonial*, R. de Matriz 9, T 71-1626, D, clean, rec; *Pousada Patitiba*, E, without bath or breakfast, basic, hot; *Tia Palminas*, opposite Entel caravan, F, basic.

Good **restaurants**, *Paulinho*, a "sort of shed" on the waterside, good, cheap *churrascaria*; cheaper places away from older centre. e.g. *Ceu de Boca*, good; *Couto Marquese*, good, cheap, but small portions. Snack bars, *Maré Alta*, *Sem Nome* (expensive).

There is a small Camping Club site on the fine Pontal beach, very crowded in January and February, and also a private camping site and a site next to the police station after the bridge, US$2 p.p. Apart from camping, very little cheap accommodation.

**Tourist Information**, Praça Chafariz.

**Bus** 7 a day to **Rio** (4 hrs., US$10) and to **Angra dos Reis** (1½ hrs., every 2 hrs., US$2.50); three a day to **Ubatuba** (70 km.), **Taubaté** (170 km.) and **Guaratinguetá** (210 km.); four a day to **São Paulo** (0930, 2230, 5½ hrs., US$10, booked up quickly) and São Sebastião.

The coast road continues from Parati into the State of São Paulo. Another road, rough but scenic, climbs the Serra do Mar to Cunha and Guaratinguetá, also in São Paulo.

---

## ESPIRITO SANTO (3)

---

The coastal state, north of Rio de Janeiro which has a mountainous interior and a hot, damp seaboard. It is an important grower of coffee. In the north there are large forests containing hardwoods.

N of Campos (**see page 326**) is the State of Espírito Santo (pop. 2,429,000) with its capital at Vitória. The people are known as Capixabas, after a former Indian tribe. Just across the frontier between the states is the resort town of *Marataízes*, with fair hotels and good beaches.

**Hotels** *Praia*, Av. Atlântica 99, on beach, D; *Saveiros Palace*, Av. Miramar 119, on beach, D; *Dona Judith*, Av. Lacerda de Aguiar 353, D. **Camping** Municipal site on Praia do Siri, 10 km. from centre; *Xodó* private site, Av. Atlântica, 2 km. from centre.

The main road N passes *Cachoeira do Itapemirim*, a busy city on both banks of the fast-flowing Rio Itapemirim; many hotels of all classes.

Further north, 58 km. south of Vitória, is *Guarapari*, whose beaches attract many people seeking cures for rheumatism, neuritis and other complaints, from the radioactive monazitic sands. Bus from Vitória, 1 hr., US$1.25. (Both Marataízes and Guarapari are very crowded mid-Dec. to end Feb.)

**Hotels** *Porto do Sol*, Mediterranean style village on rocky point overlooking a calm beach, pool, sauna, etc., A, rec., T 261-0011, Telex: (27) 3178; *Coronado*, Av. Lourival de Almeida 312, B, T 261-1709; *Hostess*, R. Joaquim Silva Lima 701, B; *Atlântico*, Av. Edísio Cirne 332, T 261-1237 on beach, rec., D;

**Camping** Camping Clube do Brasil, Setiba beach, 9 km. from centre. Cambrás site off Vitória highway close to beach, 4 km. from centre. Private site near Cambrás site.

1 hour S of Guarapari, is Praia dos Castelhanos, near Anchieta (*Hotel Thanharu Praia*, good; *Restaurant Moacyr*, main courses US$2.75-4). Fishing/diving boat hire from Sr. Romildo, Peixaria do Onça (2 km. N of Anchieta) US$12 for 3 hrs., US$25 to Ilha dos Franceses. Also near Anchieta: is Praia Iriri, 30 km. from Guarapari, served by a regular bus; 2 beaches, beautiful setting, lodging in private houses is possible. Coquera has a bar and trees for

hammocks; 1 hour's walk S is a deserted beach, you must be self-sufficient, but shellfish and driftwood are plentiful.

There are coastal and inland road routes to *Vitória* (pop. 253,000) 509 km. from Rio de Janeiro, reached several times a day by plane (80 min.), and by bus (9 hrs.). Two bridges connect the island on which it stands with the mainland. The town is beautifully set, its entrance second only to Rio's, its beaches quite as attractive, but smaller, and the climate is less humid. On Avenida República is the huge Parque Moscoso, an oasis of quiet, with a lake, playground and tiny zoo. The Teatro Carlos Gomes, on Praça Costa Pereira, often presents plays, also jazz and folk festivals. The upper, older part of town, reached by steep streets and steps, is much less hectic than the lower harbour area which is beset by dreadful traffic problems. Vitória is a growing centre for the sport of sea fishing.

Its importance is due to its connection westwards with Minas Gerais by the Vitória-Minas railway, which transports for export millions of tons of iron ore and a large tonnage of coffee and timber. Ships drawing 11 metres and 240 metres in length can enter the port. A supplementary iron-ore port has been built at Ponta do Tubarão, near Vitória, to load ships up to 250,000 tons. These installations have led to some beach and air pollution at places near Vitória, such as Camburi (quite a pleasant beach, though, partly built up, palms, drink stands, fair surf).

See the fortified monastery of Nossa Senhora da Penha, on a high hill above the small settlement of Vila Velha. Most of the (unremarkable) structure, now in ruins, is of the 17th and 18th centuries; the views are superb. The Dutch attacked it in 1625 and 1640. Vila Velha has an excellent beach, but it is built up and noisy: take bus from Vitória marked Vilha Velha. A fine bridge has been built across the bay to Vila Velha; for bigger waves go to Barra do Jucu. Pleasant excursions in ferry-boats to Vila Velha.

**Warning** Robberies on the street are common.

**Hotels** *Senac Hotel* (Government-run hotel school), luxurious, swimming pool, restaurant, guests attended by student staff, on the ocean at R. Sete, 417 Ilha do Boi, B, T 227-3222; *Novotel*, Av. Adalberto Simão Nader 133, A, T 227-9422. *Helal*, Jerônimo Monteiro 935, B, T 222-2955; *São José*, Av. Princesa Isabel 300, C, T 223-7222; *Estoril*, Praça Pres. Roosevelt 532, D, a/c, some rooms overlook the port; *Vitória*, Cais de São Francisco 85, near Parque Moscoso, E with bath, excellent restaurant, changes money, good, clean; *Minister*, Av. Cleto Nunes, off Parque Moscoso, F; *Europa*, Sete de Setembro, corner of Praça Costa Pereira, F, clean, noisy but cheap, good value restaurant (nearby is a good value vegetarian restaurant and a money changer, ask at the hotel); *Avenida*, Av. Florentino Avidos 350(ish) (T 223-4317/ 0770), E with breakfast, friendly, clean. Hotels located in beach areas, Camburi to the N, Vila Velha to the S, both about 15 mins. from city centre. *Walter*, across from Rodoviária, adequate, but *Lisboa*, opp. Rodoviária, is not rec.

**Camping** Serra Verde and Dalla's, private sites with some facilities, about 30 km. N of the city on Manguinhos beach.

**Restaurants** *Mar e Terra* opp. Rodoviária, good food, live music at night; *Lavacar* and many others at Praia Camburi offer food and live music; *Lambahias* is a lively dancing place for the young, ½ km west of Bambini, buses each hour on the hour.

**Banks** Local banks. *Casa de Câmbio* at Vitur, Av. Getúlio Vargas, big ESCAL sign, next to *Bar Scandinave* (where moneychangers of a less trustworthy type can be found); **Plumatur**, Av. Governador Bley 465, Edif. Glória, Conj. 101, T 222-5955.

**Consulates** Danish, R. do Sol 141, Sala 210, T 222-4075, open 0900-1300, 1500-1900.

**Telecommunications** Embratel, Palácio do Café, Praça Costa Pereira 52. Tel.:30914.

**Tourist Information** Emcatur, Av. Getúlio Vargas (corner of Av. Jerônimo Monteiro), and at Rodoviária (bus. station, friendly, good free map). Plumatur, Av. Governador Bley (first floor), tourist information, coffee and parallel exchange rate.

**Buses** Rodoviária is 15 mins.' walk from centre. **Rio**, 8 hrs., US$12.80. To hitch to Rio, take Itapemirim bus to Aracatiba (26 km). 5 buses a day to **Campos**, US$3.90 (Itapemirim), one to Macaé, 2330. **Salvador**, 18 hrs., US$25; **Porto Seguro** direct 11 hrs. with lots of stops (Agua Blanca, dep. 0900), US$12.75, *Leito* direct leaves 2100, alternatively, take bus to

Eunápolis, then change buses which run every hour, US$1.60. To hitch to Salvador, take a bus to Sara, which is beyond Carapina; alight where the bus turns off to Sara. **Diamantina**, 5½ hrs., US$8. To **Ouro Preto**, 2215 only, Thurs., US$8.80; to **Belo Horizonte**, by bus, 8 hrs., US$9.60. Daily to **Porto Velho**, 61 hrs.

**Excursions**  Visit *Santa Leopoldina* or *Domingos Martins*, both around 45 km. from Vitória, less than an hour by bus (2 companies run to the former, approx. every 3 hrs.). Both villages preserve the architecture and customs of the first German and Swiss settlers who arrived in the 1840s. Domingos Martins (also known as Campinho) has a Casa de Cultura with some items of German settlement (Hotels *Campinho*, E, clean, breakfast, *Imperador*, 2 star, D). Santa Leopoldina has a most interesting museum (open Tues.-Sun., 0900-1100 and 1300-1800) covering the settlers' first years in the area, and a large number of fascinating constructions dating from the end of the last century showing Swiss and German influence.

To **Santa Teresa**, a charming hill town 2½ hours by bus from Vitória, US$2.80 (beautiful journey). 2 hotels, *Pierazzo*, E, *Glebo*, F, clean, and many restaurants. There is a unique hummingbird sanctuary—difficult to visit. Also the **Nova Lombardia National Biological Reserve**. Previous permission must be obtained to visit from Instituto Brasileiro de Desenvolvimento Florestal, Av. Mal. Mascarenhas de Moraes 2487, CP 762, CEP 29.000, Bento Ferreira.

75 km. N of Vitória is the town of Aracruz. A whole new town is being built beside the impressive Scandinavian/Brazilian cellulose plant, surrounded by vast new eucalyptus forests.

136 km. N of Vitória is **Linhares**, on Rio Doce, with good hotels, for example *Linhares*, C, best in town; *Grande*, E, pleasant, and others; *Restaurant Mocambo*, good and cheap. Mid-way between Linhares and Vitória, 5 km. off BR-101 between Fundão and Ibiraçu, is a Zen Buddhist monastery. 84 km. N of Linhares is São Mateus, a pleasant town with no decent hotels (*Grande*, E, tiny, bad rooms), 13 km. from good beaches (buses). The **Comboios Biological Reserve**, just S of Linhares, is designed to protect the species of marine turtles which frequent this coast (for information, contact IBDF at address above). Similarly the **Sooretama Biological Reserve**, also in the vicinity of Linhares; this protects tropical Atlantic rain forest and its fauna and birds.

The most attractive beaches in the State are around **Conceição da Barra**, 242 km. N of Vitória. Basic hotels *Cricaré*; *Nanuque*; and *Rio Mar*, E. Camping Clube do Brasil site with full facilities. An interesting excursion is to Itaúnas, 21 km. up the coast; the small town has been swamped by sand dunes, so it has been moved to the opposite river bank. There is now a fantastic landscape of huge dunes and deserted beaches. A few pousadas and a small campsite can be found. Bus from the *padaria* in Conceição da Barra at 0700, returns 1700.

---

## MINAS GERAIS (4)

A state with a number of fine colonial cities built during the gold rush in the 18th century, some splendid caves, the Rio São Francisco in the N, and several spas and hill resorts. The capital is Belo Horizonte, the country's first modern planned city, now a major industrial centre.

The inland State of Minas Gerais (pop. 15,239,000) somewhat larger than France, is mountainous in the S, rising to the 2,787-metre peak of Agulhas Negras in the Mantiqueira range, and in the E, where there is the Caparaó National Park containing the Pico da Bandeira (2,890 metres). From Belo Horizonte north are undulating grazing lands, the richest of which are in the extreme W: a broad wedge of country between Goiás in the N and São Paulo in the S, known as the Triângulo Mineiro. Most of the upland is also good grazing country. Being frost-free, Minas Gerais is again becoming one of the main producers of coffee.

Minas Gerais was once described as having a heart of gold and a breast of iron. Half the mineral production of Brazil comes from the State, including most of the iron ore. Diamonds and gold are still found. Its exports move through Rio

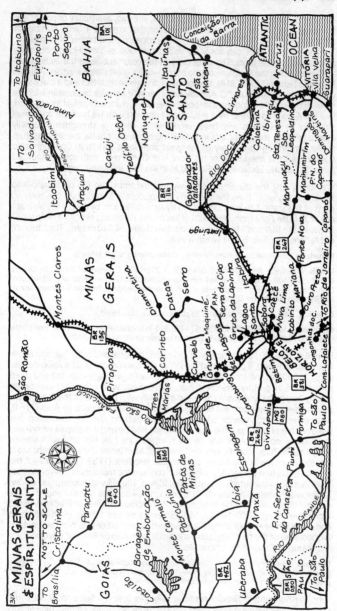

de Janeiro, Santos, Vitória and Angra dos Reis. The easy availability of power and the local agricultural and mineral production has created a large number of metal-working, textile, mineral water, food processing and timber industries.

The colonial cities can easily be visited from Rio or Belo Horizonte; many companies provide tours. The chief glory of the colonial cities is the architecture and, even more, the sculpture of one of the world's great creative artists, Antônio Francisco Lisboa (1738-1814), the son of a Portuguese architect and a black slave woman. He is known as "O Aleijadinho" (the little cripple) because in later life he developed a maiming disease (possibly leprosy) which compelled him to work in a kneeling (and ultimately a recumbent) position with his hammer and chisel strapped to his wrists. His finest work, which shows a strength not usually associated with the plastic arts in the 18th century, is probably the set of statues in the gardens and sanctuary of the great Bom Jesus church in Congonhas do Campo, but the main body of his work is in Ouro Preto, with some important pieces in Sabará, São João del Rei and Mariana (see following pages).

We survey first the places on, or easily reached from, the Rio de Janeiro-Belo Horizonte highway, then the colonial cities of central Minas, then the outlying parts of the State. 129 km. north of Rio by air and 155 km. by road is the pleasant city of *Juiz de Fora* (pop. 350,000). It lies on the Paraibuna river, in a deep valley between the Mar and Mantiqueira mountain chains, at 640 metres. The Museum of Mariano Procópio is well worth a visit.

**Industries** Steel-making, textiles, brewing, timber sawing, sugar refining.

**Hotels** *Ritz* (best), Barão do Rio Barras 2000, T 212-7300, C; *Imperial*, Batista de Oliveira 605, T 212-7400, D, simple, but well run. Many hotels on R. Getúlio Vargas of (our) category E. Boarding houses (F) in side streets, e.g. R. Marechal Deodoro, *Pensão Sulamericana* at No. 86, *Belo Horizonte* at No. 120.

**Camping** Camping Clube do Brasil site at Represa Dr. João Penido.

**Bus** Hourly from Rio 0600-2200, US$4.80, 3½ hrs. (spectacular trip), Belo Horizonte (many, US$8.80) and Petrópolis. Bus station outside town, Av. Brasil 3405.

From *Barbacena*, 103 km. on (with an important horse and cattle fair, and a rose festival in October), a paved road runs W to the colonial city of *São João del Rei* (pop. 75000), at the foot of the Serra do Lenheiro, with a fine bridge and three splendid 18th century churches: Pilar, the earliest, with rich altars and bright ceiling, and good *azulejos* in choir, and a sacristy with portraits of the Evangelists, new sacred art museum next door, entry US$0.10; São Francisco de Assis (1764), with exterior and interior sculptures by Aleijadinho (recent restoration has removed the plaster from the altars, revealing fine carving in sucupira wood) and the Carmo, on the other side of the river, designed by him and with interior sculptures by him, recently very well restored, all in white. Near São Francisco is the tourist office in the house of Bárbara Heliodora (1759-1819), one of the Inconfidentes (see page 342), which also contains the municipal museum, whose chief treasure is a reputed portrait of Aleijadinho. The railway museum (see below) is well worth seeing. Museu da Arte Sacra, small but well recommended. There are also the Museu de Arte Regional do Patrimônio Histórico, in Praça Severiano (open Tues.-Sun., 1300-1600, US$0.25), and a pewter factory (with exhibition and shop) run by an Englishman, John Somers. Tourist office also in old bus station. A good view of the town and surroundings is from Alto da Boa Vista, where there is a Statue of Christ (Senhor dos Montes).

**Festivals** The morning masses on Sundays and religious festivals at São Francisco (0915) and Mercês (1030)—behind and above Pilar— are accompanied by choir and orchestra who maintain a tradition of over 200 years of local composition.

John Parsons writes: *Tiradentes* (originally São José del Rei; pop. 8,500). The centre of this charming little town, 15 km. from São João, with its nine streets and eight churches, at the foot of the green Serra São José, hardly belongs to this century. The Santo Antônio church, first built in 1710, contains some of the finest gilded wood carvings in the country and a small but fine organ brought from Oporto in the 1790s. The reconstructed façade is said to follow a design by Aleijadinho. There is also a sun-dial by him. Also of unusual interest and charm are the Rosário church, with fine statuary and ornate gilded altars; this and Nossa Senhora das Mercês have interesting painted ceilings and the latter a notable statue of the Virgin.

At the bottom of the stone paved road which descends from Santo Antônio is the fine fountain (*chafariz*), installed in 1749. The water is brought by a stone aqueduct from springs in the forest at the foot of Serra São José, which offers fine walks including the lane beside the aqueduct. The museum, housed where Padre Toledo (another Inconfidente) once lived, is of particular interest and there are some good pieces of furniture exhibited. The simple pilgrimage church of Santíssima Trindade is also well worth seeing. Tourist Office in the Prefeitura, R. Resende Costa 71. See the artists' lithographic printing shop of Largo do Ó. There are attractive walks in the neighbourhood, and a 1½-hr. walk to the natural pools of Águas Santas.

**Barbacena Hotel** *Grogotó*, excellent, C; operated by Senac.

**São João del Rei Hotels** *Solar da Ponte*, A; *Novotel Porto Real*, Av. Eduardo Magalhães 254, T 371-1201, comfortable, B; *Lenheiro Palace*, Av. Pres. Tancredo Neves 257, T 371-3914, B/C, good; *Pousada do Sol*, C, 6km out on road to Tiradentes, T 371-1004; *do Espanhol*, R. Marechal Deodoro 131, C; cheap *pousadas* in same street; *Pousada Casarão*, opp. São Francisco church, C, converted mansion, Ribeiro Bastos 94, T 371-1224, swimming pool, delightful; *Colonial*, Manoel Anselmo 22, T 371-1792, D, clean and comfortable. *Pousada Ramón*, opp. bus station, F, good; *Brasil*, opposite railway station so back rooms much quieter, clean, friendly, cheap, E, rec., no breakfast (*Cafeteria Globo* in the same street, 2 blocks away, is good, though). *Hotel Porto Real* restaurant and *Restaurant Quinta do Ouro*, also good vegetarian restaurant, all rec. Good *Churrascaria* next to railway station.

**Buses** Rodoviária is 2 km. W of centre of São João. Direct buses to **Rio** leave 0800, 1600, 2330 Mon-Sat, 1600, 2215, 2350 Sun. and hols, 5 hrs., US$4, **São Paulo** 8 hrs, and **Belo Horizonte** 3½ hrs.

**Tiradentes Hotels** *Solar da Ponte*, Praça das Mercês (prop. John and Anna Maria Parsons) T 032-355-1255, atmosphere of country house, A, including breakfast and tea, only 12 rooms. Fresh flowers in rooms, bar, sauna, garden, swimming pool, light meals for residents only, for larger meals, the hotel recommends the local restaurants listed below. Also *Pousada Maria Barbosa*, *Antônio Teixeira*, Carvallio 134, T 355-1227, D, pool, very pleasant, *Hotel Wellerson*, T 355-1226, *Pousada Tiradentes*, E, *Hotel Ponto do Morro*, *Pousada de Laurit*, Direita 187, T 355-1268.

**Restaurants** Local food: *Quinta de Ouro*, rec.; *Churrascaria Ramón*, reasonable prices; *Estalagem*; *Padre Toledo*. Meat: *Thé*. Italian: *Donatelli*.

Recommended is the train trip between São João del Rei and Tiradentes (13 km.). The train has been in continuous operation since 1881, using the same locomotives and rolling stock, running on 76 cm. gauge track, all now lovingly restored and cared for. Maximum speed is 20 km. per hour. Price: US$1.20, one class only. Fri., Sat., Sun. and holiday steam train service to Tiradentes, 1000 and 1400, returning 1300 and 1700. Railway museum at the railway station in São João del Rei; open daily 0900-1200, 1330-1730; there are also a round house which has 16 vintage locomotives in superb condition, an engine shed and a steam-operated machine shop, still working.

From Belo Horizonte, the shortest road to São João del Rei is via Lagoa Dourada. Just past Lagoa Dourada is the turning (12 km.) for **Prados**, a small town 15 km. from Tiradentes known for its musical and handicrafts traditions. Near the turn is Entre Rios de Minas (*Hotel Camapuã*).

**Belo Horizonte**, the capital of Minas Gerais, is the third largest city in Brazil (pop. 2,300,000). It is situated over 800 metres above sea-level, surrounded by mountains, and enjoys an excellent climate (16°-30°C) except for the rainy season. It was founded 12 December 1897. Sights to be seen are the Praça da Assembléia, with three fine modern buildings: Legislative Assembly, church and Banco do Brasil; the Palácio da Liberdade, in Praça da Liberdade amid other fine *fin-de-siècle*-style public buildings (every Sun. morning and Thurs. evening an open-air craft market operates here—very good, also a flower market each Fri. from 1800 and an antique and occultism market each Sun.); the Palácio das Artes, Afonso Pena 1567, which is in the Parque Municipal and contains the Centro de Artesanato Mineiro (craft shop open 0900-1700, Tues.-Sun.); the Museu Mineiro, Av. João Pinheiro, 342 in old Senate building near centre (open Tues., Wed., Fri. 1230-1830, Thur. 1500-2100, Sat., Sun. 1000-1600); the Museu da Mineralogia Prof. Djalma Guimarães, R. da Bahia 1149, a Gothic building near the park, with interesting exhibits (open every day 0830-1730, entrance free); the Museu Histórico Abílio Barreto, R. Bernado Mascarenhas, in an old *fazenda* house which is the last reminder of Belo Horizonte's predecessor, the village of Arraial do Curral d'el Rey, built by João Leite da Silva Ortiz in the 18th century, with most interesting historical exhibits (open 1000-1700 Wed.-Mon, take bus 2902 from Av. Pena); the Museu do Telefone, Av. Afonso Pena 1180 (open Mon.-Fri., 0900-1800, Sun., 0900-1300); the railway station, with museum on 2nd floor showing a model railway and the railway headquarters in a mansion on the hill above the station, with locomotive and railway coach used by Dom Pedro II; the Parque Municipal (an oasis of green, right in the centre of the city, small amusement park and playground, not too safe at night). Museo Histórico Natural, in the Instituto Agronómico, R. Gustavo da Silveira 1035, T 461-7666, has a local geological and palaeontological display and good archaeological exhibits (take bus 3803A from Praça Rio Branco). An obelisk in Praça Sete de Setembro commemorates Independence, it is the centre for political protest.

Eight km. from the centre is the picturesque suburb of Pampulha, famous for its modern buildings and the artificial lake (many infestations, do not swim in it), many buildings designed by the renowned Brazilian architect Oscar Niemeyer (who later designed much of Brasília); in Pampulha the glass and marble Museu de Arte de Belo Horizonte may be visited (Av. Octacílio Negrão de Lima, open 0800-1800 daily, reported disappointing), as well as the Chapel of São Francisco (the interior of which was decorated by the Brazilian painter Cândido Portinári). There is a bus (not the 4403) from the city centre to the Jardim Zoológico (at the far end of the lake from the dam—small selection of birds with some rarities, animals well kept for the most part) that passes the chapel and also the Mineirão stadium about ¾ km. away (see below); bus 2004 goes from Av. Afonso Pena to the chapel.

In the southern zone of the city, on the Serra do Curral, the Parque de Mangabeiras has a good view of the city, forest trails, sports facilities and snack bars. The natural amphitheatre where the Pope spoke in 1982 is nearby; there is an iron monument marking the occasion (take bus 2001 from Afonso Pena between Av. Amazonas and R. Tamóios). In 1984, the Minascentro, a convention centre for exhibitions and congresses, was opened in the city centre. The huge Mineirão stadium is the second largest in Brazil after the Maracanã stadium in Rio. Belo Horizonte is one of the fastest growing of Brazil's main cities; atmospheric pollution has recently been reported.

The industrial area, about 10 km. from the centre, has now become the third largest industrial centre of Brazil, and apart from being the traditional centre of mining and agricultural industries (as well as diamond cutting and precious stones), it has steelworks and an automobile industry. The city has a good public transport system (red buses serve central and express routes, yellow circular routes, and blue diagonal routes), and taxis are plentiful, although hard to find at peak hours.

**Local Holidays**  Maundy Thursday; Corpus Christi; 15 August (Assumption); 8 December (Immaculate Conception).

**Electric Current** 120-220 A.C. 60 cycles.

**Hotels** (number of stars in brackets) *Othon Palace* (5), Av. Afonso Pena 1050, T 273-3844, L, deluxe, but in need of renovation according to latest reports; *Brasilton* (4), out of town at km. 3.65 on Rodovia Fernão Dias, Contagem, T 396-1100, L, very good restaurant, discount possible; *Real Palace* (4), R. Espírito Santo 904, T 273-3111, A+; *Internacional Plaza Palace* (3), R. Rio de Janeiro 109, T 201-2300, A, good but seedy part of town; *Boulevard Plaza* (3), Av. Getúlio Vargas 1640, Savassi district (chic), A+, T 223-9000, very nice; *Wembley Palace* (3), R. Espírito Santo 201, T 201-6966, A, excellent, central, clean, but poor rate for travellers' cheques; *Del Rey* (4), Praça Afonso Arinos 60, T 273-2211, A+; *Normandie* (3), R. Tamóios 212, T 201-6166, A, excellent grill; *Serrana Palace* (3), R. Goitacases 450, T 201-9955, A, pleasant restaurant but hotel rather run down, seedy area; *Estoril*, R. Carijós 454, T 201-9322, B with bath, comfortable, pleasant; *Ambassy* (3), R. Caetés 633, near bus station, T 201-0222, C, helpful, English spoken, clean, a/c, noisy, good restaurant; *Itatiaia* (2), Praça Rui Barbosa 187, T 212-3300, B, near railway station, central, clean, a/c, with bath and good breakfast; *Esplanada* (2), Av. Santos Dumont 304, T 273-5311. B (D without bath), clean, good restaurant, own garage; *Sul América Palace* (2), Av. Amazonas 50, T 201-1722, D, clean, friendly, TV and fridge in rooms, but reported to be run down; *Casa dos Municípios*, R. Rio Grande do Norte 1017, Funcionários (in Savassi, chic shopping area), T 226-5177, B, clean; *Continental* (2), Av. Paraná 241, T 201-7944, D, central, clean, friendly; *Vitória*, Curitiba 224, E without bath, good. Cheaper places are: *Maciel*, Av. Ol. Maciel 95, E, basic, clean; *Magnata*, R. Guarani 124, F, with breakfast, near bus station, cheap and clean, bath, good hot shower, safe dposit, rec.; *Madrid*, opposite Rodoviária, F, highly rec.; near bus station and in R. Curitiba many hotels are for very-short-stay couples. Within 10 mins. walk of Rodoviária, turn left along main road to R. Espírito Santo, No. 284, *Majestic*, E; No. 227, *São Salvador*, E; No. 237, *Magalhães*, F, basic, clean, friendly, cheap laundry service, good restaurant over the road. You may spend the night in the bus station only if you have an onward ticket (police check at midnight); area round bus station said to be dangerous. Youth hostel, *Pousadinha Mineira*, R. Januária 206, T 446-2911, 15 min. from Rodoviária, rec.

**Camping** Wild camping near Alto do Palácio, near river and waterfalls.

**Restaurants** *Tavares*, R. Santa Catarina 64 (local dishes), excellent value. Chinese: *Yun Ton*, R. Santa Catarina 946, rec.; Churrascarias: *Carretão Guaiba*, Av. do Contorno 8412; *Farrouilha*, Afonso Pena 3300; *Picanha na Tábua*, R. Curitiba, unprepossessing but highly rec.; *Chico Mineiro*, R. Alagoas, corner of Av. Brasil, local chicken specialities, good, closed Sun.; *Santa Felicidade*, R. Dr. Morais, good; *Arroz com Feijão*, typical food, Av. Contorno 6510, Av. Contorno 7438 and R. Antônio de Albuquerque 440, all friendly, reasonably-priced; *Pizzaiolo*, Av. Contorno 8495, good for pizzas. *Via Natural, No. 1*, Av. Afonso Pena 941, vegetarian, open till 2200 (except 2000 on Sun.); *Naturalmente*, Av. Andradas 367; *Superbom* (vegetarian), R. São Paulo, 971, 1100-1500, Mon. to Fri. *Mangueiras*, at Pampulha, next to Niemeyer chapel of São Francisco, very popular; *Dona Derna*, behind the Palácio de Liberdade, highly rec.; *Buona Távola*, R. Sta. Rita Durão 309, Funcionários, T227-6155, excellent Italian; *Alpino* (German), R. Tupinambás 173, good value and popular, corned beef and fresh boiled vegetables available, open-air; *Flor de Líbano*, opposite *Hotel Magalhães* at Espírito Santo 234, cheap and good. We are told that the splendid Minas typical dishes are more authentic— and more toothsome—outside Belo Horizonte.

**Tea rooms** *Era Una Vez Un Chalezinho*, R. Paraíba 1455; *Tia Clara*, R. Antônio de Albuquerque 617.

**Shopping** Mercado Central, Av. Aug. de Lima 744, large and clean, open every day, Saturday social centre. Market for fruit, vegetables, meat and other items at corner of R. Santa Catarina and Av. Amazonas (near Praça Raúl Soares). There are huge hypermarkets just outside the city on the highways to Rio and to São Paulo. Splendid delicatessen with foreign food and wines—and liquors—*Au Bon Gourmet*, R. Tupinambás 187. For gemstones, try *Manoel Bernardes*, R. Espírito Santo 835, very reasonable, ask for US saleswoman Manuela, who can arrange tours of workshops; *Gem Centre*, Av Alvares Cabral 45, good prices and selection, rec; *"Hippie fair"* Thurs. evenings and Sundays in Praça da Liberdade; Food and Antique fair, Praça da Independência, Sats., good home-made food; other fairs on Fri. and Sat. Belo is said to be very good for slide film, cheese and chocolate.

**Bookshop** *Daniel Vaitsman*, R. Espírito Santo 466, 17th floor, for English language books. Foreign language books at *Livraria Van Damme*, R. das Guajajaras 505, also good local and Portuguese selection (and said to change travellers' cheques); *Acaiaca*, R. Tamóios 72, good for dictionaries. Used foreign-language books at *Livraria Alfarrábio*, R. Tamóios 320.

**Car Hire** Nobre, Confins Airport and Av. Francisco Sales 1424, T 227-5700; and others.

**Nightlife** *Drosophila*, R. Ouro Preto, Bairro Preto, bar, dancing; *The Great Brasilien Disaster*, R. Tomé, Bairro Savass; funk, dancing; *Angelas Buffet*, R. Tomé, street café; *A Vida*, Av. Getúlio Vargas, bar, dancing.

**Exchange** Lloyds Bank, Av. João Pinheiro 580; Citibank, R. Espírito Santo 871; Banco do Brasil, R. Rio de Janeiro 750, Av. Amazonas 276; Banco Econômico, R. Bahia 360, 9th floor, and other local banks, 1000-1630. American Express, Kontik-Franstur, R. Espírito Santo 1204, T 273-1288. Exchange: H. Pichiommi, R. Espirito Santo and R. Guajanas. São Paulo Joios, Amazonas 105 offers a good rate; Nascente Turismo, Rio de Janeiro 1101, T 224-3334, ask for Luiz Carlos de Oliveira, changes money at a good rate.

**Consulates** British Vice-Consulate: Av. Afonso Pena 952, s. 500, Caixa Postal 576, T 222-6318; German, R. Carijós 244, T 222-3411; Austrian; R. José Américo Cancado Bahia 199, T 33 33 622. French, R. Prof Antônio Aleixo 843, 5th Floor, T335-5563; Italian, Praça Carlos Chagas 49, 2nd floor, T 335-5394; Netherlands, R. Alagoas 1460, 11th floor, T 221-0615; Denmark, R. Prof. Jerson Martins 166, T 441-4755. US: Serviço de Divulgação e Relações Culturais, Av. Alvares Cabral 1600, 3rd floor, T 335-3555.

**Places of Worship** Synagoga Beth Yacou, R. Pernambuco 326, T 2246013; Catholic Church, Av. Antônio Carlos 2747, T 442-7743, R. Bahia 1596, T 222-6059; Presbyterian Church, R. Ceará 1434, T 226-1844; Baptist Church, R. Joaquim de Fiqueredo 332, T 384-1322; Mormon Church, R. Levindo Lopes 214, T 233-7883; Adventist Church, R. Timbras 683, T 226-6144.

**Hospital** Mater Dei, R. Gonçalves Dias 2700, T 335-2200, has been rec; Alfredo Balena MedCentre, R. dos Otoni 927, a new private hospital. Dr Ricardo Queiroz Guimarães, Av. Brasil 1474, Funcionários, T 224-2020 for contact lenses and eye problems.

**Post Office** with poste restante, Av. Afonso Pena 1270. UPS, Salima T 222-9002.

**Tourist Information** Belotur (municipal information office), R. Tupis 149, 17th floor, T 222-5500; Turminas, Av. Augusto de Lima 785, T 201-0122/201-3875; Praça Sete de Setembro; at Rodoviária (particularly polyglot, reasonable free map of centre) ask for the Guia Turistico for events, opening times etc, railway station, airport (very helpful). Touring Clube do Brasil, Av. Afonso Pena 1913.

**Travel Agent** *Focus Tours*, R.Grão Mogol 502, in Sion district, T (031) 223-0358, telex (031) 3823 RAPT, run by Douglas and Nancy Trent, offer specialized tours all over Brazil and have a special interest in ecology and tours to the Pantanal. Tours in Minas to see a great variety of wildlife. Reliable information and a portion of their profits is used for conservation project in Brazil. *Mangabeira Turismo*, R. Goitcazes 71-8˚ andar, and *Unitour*, Av. Tupis 141, organize river trips on the São Francisco (see page 347).

**Buses** Rodoviária is by Praça Rio Branco at end of Av. Afonso Pena (left-luggage lockers, attended service 0700-2200). To Rio, 7 hrs., US$12.80 (ordinary), *leito*, US$25.60; to Brasília, 12 hrs., 9 a day incl. 2 *leitos*, only one leaves in daylight (0800), US$19, *leito* US$38. To São Paulo, 10 hrs., US$6; route passes the great Furnas reservoir. To Salvador US$35, 22 hrs., at 1800 and 1900 daily. For Porto Seguro take Gontijo bus to Nanuque, then Rio Doce bus to Eunápolis, then Espresso São Jorge to Porto Seguro, tickets may be booked through Belo, road poor in places, total time 22 hrs., US$28; to Recife, US$50; to Belém, US$76. To Cuiabá, Expresso São Luiz, 0800 and 2000 daily, 26 hrs., US$40; to Vitória, 8 hrs., US$9.60. To Campo Grande 2000, with Gontigo, a good route to Bolivia, avoiding São Paulo. For buses within Minas Gerais, see under destination.

**Airport** A new international airport near Lagoa Santa, at Confins, 39 km. from Belo Horizonte, has been opened. Taxi to centre, US$18; airport bus, either *executivo* from the exit, or comfortable normal bus from far end of car park every hour on the half-hour, US$1.50. From centre, catch bus at Terminal Turístico JK, R. Olegário Maciel and R. Guajajaras.

**Hitch-hiking** to Rio or Ouro Preto, take a bus marked "Shopping", to the shopping centre above Belo Horizonte on the Rio road.

**Excursions** Within easy motoring distance from Belo Horizonte are several of the 400 caves and grottoes for which Minas Gerais is famous. The best and most famous is the Gruta de Maquiné with 7 chambers, well lit, with guides, but hot—26˚C, 126 km. NW of Belo (well signposted and with restaurants nearby, bus at 0915, return at 1500, 2¼ hrs., US$3.20. In the nearby town of Cordisburgo is a museum to the writer Guimarães Rosa. The Gruta de Lapinha, almost as good, is only 51 km. N of the city (entrance to caves and small museum, US$0.30; bus at 0930, 1130 and others, via Pampulha, return 1230, 1600, 1¼hr., US$1.20

one way. Lapinha cave is closed Mon.

10 km. before Lapinha is the town of **Lagoa Santa**, a weekend resort for Belo Horizonte. The sandy beach on the lake (close to the town centre and bus station) is used for fishing, sun-bathing and boating (do not swim, the water is infected with schistosomiasis). Along the beach are bars and restaurants, with more in the nearby main square which also has two small hotels and an interesting modernistic church. The road to Belo Horizonte (half-hourly bus service, US$0.75) passes Belo Horizonte's new international airport. Bus Lagoa Santa-Lapinha every half hour.

To the NE of the city, a few km. off the BR-262, is the Serra de Piedade, a high peak giving spectacular views over the surrounding countryside. A popular excursion point but only accessible by car or special bus service. There are a small chapel and a *churrascaria*. From the peak can be seen the small town of **Caeté**, which has one or two interesting churches and the remains of an old ironworks near the railway station. Take the Conceição do Mato Dentro bus to Alto do Palácio; near there are waterfalls and campsites. Further from Belo, turn off the BR-262 (towards Vitória) at km. 73 and go via Barão de Cocais and Brumal to Caraçá (120 km.), where the monastery has been converted into a hotel (C), the site and region highly recommended. Reservations through Instituto São Vicente in Belo, T 031-441-5399. It is possible to stay in Santa Barbara, *Hotel Karaibe*, E; *Sta Inés*, E, 25 km. away on the road to Mariana and hitch-hike to Caraçá.
   From Belo Horizonte, excursions can be made to Nova Lima and the picturesque colonial cities described in the following pages. If short of time, Ouro Preto and Congonhas are the most outstanding. The road follows the Rio das Velhas in which, at points, one can see the *garimpeiros* waist-deep washing for gold.

**Nova Lima** (pop 47,000), about 27 km. SE of Belo by a good road, is set in eucalyptus forests. Its houses are grouped round the gold mine of Morro Velho, opened by a British firm in 1834 but sold to Brazilians in 1959, the deepest mine in the Americas. The shaft has followed a rich vein of gold down to 2,591 metres. There are interesting carvings by Aleijadinho, recovered from elsewhere, in the (modern) parish church.

   A paved road branching off the Belo Horizonte-Brasília highway leads (30 km., ½-hr.) to the colonial gold-mining (and steel-making) town of **Sabará** (pop. 74,000). Return by the old road over the mountain range of Serra do Curral for fine views. Sabará is strung along the narrow steep valleys of the Rio das Velhas and Rio Sabará. Its old churches and fountains, its rambling cobbled streets, its simple houses with their carved doors, and its museum of 18th century gold mining in the Intendência de Ouro (built 1732, open 1200-1700 Tues.-Fri.) are of great interest. The churches are so spread out that a taxi is advisable if you wish to see them all. Bus from Belo Horizonte, US$0.50, ½ hr., from separate part of Belo Rodoviária from main departure hall.

*Passeio a Sabará*, by Lúcia Machado de Almeida, with splendid illustrations by Guignard, is an excellent guide to the place. The main sights are the Prefeitura, in R. Pedro II, an old mansion, with oratory and main reception room (*salão nobre*) to be seen; the Imperial Theatre (1770, restored 1960) in the same street, for its fine interior; the Casa Azul, in the same street, for its portal; the Churches of Nossa Senhora do Carmo (1774), with doorway, pulpits and choirloft by Aleijadinho and paintings by Athayde; Nossa Senhora do Rosário dos Pretos (left unfinished at the time of the slaves' emancipation); São Francisco; Nossa Senhora da Conceição (1720) with much gilding, and paintings by 23 Chinese artists brought from Macau; and, last of all, Nossa Senhora do O, built in 1698 and showing unmistakable Chinese influence (paintings much in need of restoration), 2 km. from the centre of the town (take local bus marked "Esplanada"). Also the fountains of Kaquende (1757), and Rosário.

**Hotel**: *Pensão Bobagate*, above an art gallery, E, *Hotel de Ouro*, D-E, overlooking town, or ask for Senhor Sérgio at the Sports Centre, he may have accommodation. **Restaurants**: *O Quinto do Ouro*, close to the bus station; *314*, Comendador Viana 314, near main praça; *Imperial Restaurant/Pizzaria*, in R. Pedro II.

At 27 km. S along the Belo Horizonte-Rio de Janeiro highway a 68 km. road, the Rodovia dos Inconfidentes, branches off to Ouro Preto. On the way (48 km.) it passes Cachoeira do Campo, which was the centre of the regional mining administration in colonial times: now a sleepy, unspoilt village.

*Ouro Preto* (pop 61,400), the famous former capital of the State, was founded in 1711. There is a famous Escola de Minas (School of Mining), founded in 1876, in the fortress-like Palácio dos Governadores (1742), facing the main square (Praça Tiradentes); it has the interesting Museo de Mineralogia e das Pedras, a must, US$0.35, the only one open on Mondays (1200-1700), but closed Sundays. Opposite the Palace, next to Carmo Church, is the Museu da Inconfidência, a fine historical and art museum which has some drawings by Aleijadinho and the Sala Manoel da Costa Athaíde, in an annex; the building, begun in the eighteenth century, has been a prison and also the local chamber of commerce (open 1200-1730, entry, US$0.45). See the Casa das Contas, now also a museum (open 1230-1700), Sun 0800-1300. Another museum, the Casa Guignard, on R. Conde de Bobadela, displays the paintings of Alberto da Veiga Guignard, open Tues-Sat 0900-1700, Sun 1200-1700, free.

The city, built on rocky ground 1,000 metres above sea-level (cold and wet Oct.-Feb.) was declared a national monument in 1933. Its cobbled streets wind up and down steep hills crowned with 13 churches. Mansions, fountains, churches, vistas of terraced gardens, ruins, towers shining with coloured tiles, all blend together to maintain a delightful 18th century atmosphere.

Ouro Preto displays many superb baroque carvings, in wood and in soapstone, of the sculptor Aleijadinho. The church of São Francisco de Assis and the façade of the Carmo church are his work, and so are the two pulpits in the church of São Francisco, and much else.

In the **Praça de Independência** there is a statue of José Joaquim da Silva Xavier, known as Tiradentes, leader of the **Inconfidentes** (unsuccessful revolutionaries of 1789), and regarded in Brazil as the precursor of independence. Another Inconfidente, the poet Tomás Antônio Gonzaga (whose house at R. Cláudio Manoel 61 is close to São Francisco de Assis), was exiled to Africa. (Most Brazilians know his poem based on his forbidden love affair; visitors are shown the bridge and decorative fountain where the lovers held their trysts.) On 24 June of each year Ouro Preto again becomes, for that day only, the capital of the state of Minas Gerais.

**Churches** The following churches are all closed Mon., but are open at following times on other days: Santa Efigênia (1720, decorated with gold dust washed out of slaves' hair), Padre Faria, 0800-1200; Francisco de Assis, N.S. Conceição, 0800-1130, 1300-1700 (keep your ticket for admission to the museum); Senhor Bom Jesus, N.S. Carmo, 0800-1130, 1300-1700; N.S. Pilar (1733, heavily gilded work of Aleijadinho's father, Manuel Lisboa), Rosário, 1200-1700; das Mercês e Perdões, are open in afternoons only. The Antônio Dias parish church, Nossa Senhora da Conceição (1722), heavily gilded, contains Aleijadinho's tomb, and a museum devoted to him, Aleijadinho Paróquia, 0800-1130, 1300-1700. At least two days are needed to see them all; the tourist office on Praça Tiradentes (opens 0800, Portuguese only spoken) and the hotels offer a leaflet showing the opening times; also sells good map for US$0.80. Most of the churches now charge for admission, usually about US$0.45. Shorts may not be worn in churches.

The mid-18th century paintings by Mestre Athayde (1732-1827), to be seen in S. F. de Assis, Sta. Ifigênia and elsewhere, are of particular interest: the pigments were obtained from local iron ore and from forest fruits. They are also very fine artistically; he was a worthy colleague of Aleijadinho.

**N.B.** In most churches and museums, tourists' handbags and cameras are taken at the entrance and guarded in lockers.

Ouro Preto is famous for its Holy Week processions, which in fact begin on the Thursday before Palm Sunday and continue (but not every day) until Easter Sunday. The most famous is that commemorating Christ's removal from the Cross, late on Good Friday. This is very much a holiday period and many shops are shut—as indeed they are on winter weekends. Carnival is also memorable, with samba and happenings in the streets.

**Hotels** *Grande*, R. Sen. Rocha 164, T 551-1488, largest hotel in town and the only modern structure, designed by Oscar Niemeyer, A, not well kept; *Pouso Chico Rei*, a fascinating old house with Portuguese colonial furnishings, very small and utterly delightful, book in advance, R. Brig. Mosqueira 90, C, T 551-1274 (room No. 6 has been described as a "dream"); *Pousada do Mondego*, L, Largo de Coimbra 38, T 551-2040, beautifully kept colonial house, rec.; *Priskar*, R. Antonio Martins 98, T 551-2666, A, good facilities; *Luxor Pousada*, Praça Antônio

Dias 10, converted colonial mansion, no twin beds, friendly, clean, comfortable, T 551-2244, reservations in Rio, T 256-2680, A, restaurant good; *Hospedária Antiga*, R. Xavier da Veiga 3, T 551-2203, a restored colonial house, C, friendly, rec.; *Estrada Real*, 8 km. outside city, good but often fully-booked, T 551-2122; *Pousada e Galeria Panorama Barroco*, R. Conselheiro Quintiliano 722, fine views, T (031)551-3366, D (E p.p. without bath), with good breakfast, laundry facilties, book exchange, restored house with antique furniture, art gallery, music, videos, bulletin board for local events, reservations made, excursions organized, run by David and Lucia Peterkin (US/Brazilian), advice on serious climbing, exceptionally friendly and helpful, rec.; *Solar das Lajes*, R. Conselheiro Quintiliano 604 (T 551-3388), B with bath, a little way from centre, excellent view, being extended, friendly and well run; *Pilão*, Praça Tiradentes 51, on main square, T 551-3066, C, noisy; *Pousada dos Bandierantes*, R. das Mercês 167, T 551-1996, C, clean, beautiful views, rec.; *Colonial*, R. Camilo Veloso 26, B; T 551-3133; *Tófolo*, São José 76, near Contas fountain, B, sometimes overcharges, so pay in advance; *Pousada Ouro Preto*, Largo Musicista José dos Anjos Costa 72, T 551-3081, 4/5 rooms, E, clean, laundry facilities, hot showers, English spoken by owner, Gérson Luís Cotta (most helpful), rec.; at No. 26, same street, Rosana lets rooms, basic, clean, friendly, clothes washing, F; *Pensão* at R. Coronel Alves 2, T 551-2393, clean reasonable, friendly; *Conde*, R. Direita, D, old furniture, clean, rec.; *Miranda*, same street, E, shared shower; *N. S. Aparecida*, Praça Cesário Alvim 21, T 551-1091, E, better rooms good, cheaper rooms without bath, restaurant cheap. *Pousada Ciclo do Ouro* Felipe dos Santos 241, T 581-3201/2210, F, clean, laundry facilities, rec.;*Pousada São Francisco*, next to the church of that name, F, stunningly clean, highly rec.; *Pousada Tropicão*, São José, very basic but cheap. Try *pensões* in RR. Randolpho Bretas, Getúlio Vargas, Paraná. *Vermelha Dormitório*, Praça São Francisco de Assis 30, T 551-1138, quiet, shared shower, E. Also try *casas de família*, reasonably-priced, but more expensive if booked through tourist office. Difficult to get hotel rooms at weekends and holiday periods; a good idea to telephone ahead. A number of travellers have rec. staying in Mariana where hotels are cheaper; two buses an hour to Ouro Preto.

**Students** may be able to stay, during holidays and weekends, at the self-governing student hostels, known as *repúblicas*. Many are closed between Christmas and Carnival. Enquire at the city's tourist office.

**Camping** Camping Clube do Brasil, 2 km. N of city, is quite expensive but very nice. Do not camp beside the waterfall, Cachoeira dos Andorinhas, 1½ hrs. walk from city; there have been robberies there. Also a site reached by car up a very steep hill at the top end of town: about 5 km. Also at picnic site 4 km. west of Ouro Preto, and at Rio Acima nearby.

**Restaurants** *Calabouço*, good, Conde de Bobadela 132, with an antique shop; *Sobrenatural* on the same road, rec.; *Pasteleria Lampião*, good views at the back, US$2; *Chalet*, R. Camilo de Brito 214, warmly rec. *Chafariz*, R. São José 167, good local food; *Casa Grande* (watch your belongings) and *Forno de Barro*, both on Praça Tiradentes, good local dishes; *Casa do Ouvidor*, Conde de Bobadela 42, above De Bernardis jewellery shop (good), near main square, good. *Chelvo Verde*, R. Getúlio Vargas 250 (nr. Rosário church), good vegetarian and other dishes, pleasant, quite cheap; *Adega*, R. Teixeira Amaral, vegetarian smorgasbord, US$2.50. Cheap *lanchonetes* on opposite side of square to *Hotel Pilão*. Try the local *licor de jaboticaba*.

**Shopping** For precious stones, *Videmaju*, Praça Tiradentes 62 and R.C. Manoel 21, T 551-1551, the owner is a professor at the School of Mines. Buy soapstone carvings at roadside stalls and bus stops rather than in the cities; they are much cheaper. However, gems are not much cheaper from freelance sellers in the square than from the shops around the square, and in the shops themselves, the same quality of stone is offered at the same price—*Brasil Gemas* and *De Bernard* are recommended.

**Electric Current** 110 volts A.C.

**Exchange** Only very poor rates in town.

**Post Office** on R. Direita, opp. *Hotel Miranda*.

**Tourist Office** Praça Tiradentes 41, helpful, English spoken. Enquire here for details of accommodation in *casas de família*, *repúblicas* and other terms. Note, though, that foreigners are expected to want expensive hotels. It shows filmstrips at 0900, 1200 and 1600 on weekdays, 0930, 1030, 1300, 1500, 1600 at weekends and holidays. The tourist office at the bus station is helpful, map US$0.50. **Guides** Bandeira's *Guia de Ouro Preto* in Portuguese and English (US$3.50 with coloured map, US$1 with black and white one), normally available at Tourist Office. Also available is Lucia Machado de Almeida's *Passeio a Ouro Preto*, US$6 (in

Portuguese, English and French). A local guide for a day, Associação de Guias de Turismo, T 551-2655, is more expensive if obtained through Tourist Office. Ourotur runs a tour of Ouro Preto in a vintage-style bus, 0900 and 1430, from the bus station (T 551-2764).

**Transport** An early plane from Rio to Belo Horizonte and a bus (11 a day) gets to Ouro Preto by lunch (2 hrs.); bus fare, each way, US$1.25. Day trips are run; alternatively take bus from **Rio**, for example Util at 0830 and 2330 (US$15, 7½ hrs), return bus to Rio leaves at same times. There is a new bus station (Rodoviária) at Ouro Preto, above the town near the São Francisco de Paula church. Book your return journey to **Belo Horizonte** early if returning in the evening; buses get crowded. There are also buses to **Conselheiro Lafaiete** for connections to Belo Horizonte and Congonhas, and direct to **Congonhas** at 1400 and 1530, or to Rio via Barbacena and Juiz de Fora (direct bus to Rio is often fully booked 2-3 days, or weekends, in advance). Direct bus Ouro Preto to **Vitória** at 2100, US$8.80, 5½ hrs., (connection to Porto Seguro), daily. Direct bus to **São Paulo**, 1900, 11 hrs., US$20. Check that your bus ticket from Ouro Preto is in fact from Ouro Preto and not from Belo Horizonte. Two buses an hour to Mariana, if returning buses are full walk to the next village. Hitch-hiking to Mariana is said to be easy, start in Praça Tiradentes.

*Mariana* (pop. 34,000, 697 metres above sea level), another old mining city, founded 1696, much less hilly than Ouro Preto, is 12 km. E of Ouro Preto on a road which goes on to join the Rio-Salvador highway. See the beautiful old prison on Praça João Pinheiro (Cadeia, 1768, now the Prefeitura Municipal; the Carmo church (1784, steatite carvings, Athayde paintings, chinoiserie panelling), next to it is the fine São Francisco church (1762, granite painted to look like marble, pulpits designed by Aleijadinho, Athayde paintings and tomb, fine sacristy, one side-altar by Aleijadinho, entry, US$0.15) and the old Palácio dos Governadores connected with it; the Museu Arquidiocesano for its church furniture, gold and silver collection, Aleijadinho statues and ivory cross (R. Frei Durão 49, open 0900-1100 except Tues. and 1200-1700; entrance US$0.80, good guide book), Capela de Santo Antônio, wonderfully simple and the oldest. The Cathedral, Basílica de NS da Assunção, built 1711-1760, has been reopened, after repairs (entry US$0.15). Between the old prison and São Francisco is a stone monument to Justice, at which slaves used to be beaten. The house of the poet Afonso de Guimarães (buried behind the Igreja Santuaria), R. Direita 35, is open to visitors: photographs and letters (free). There are viewpoints at the churches of N.S. do Rosário (1752, with work by Athayde and showing Moorish influence) and São Pedro dos Clérigos (built in 1753). Some people still pan for gold in the river running through the town. Between Ouro Preto and Mariana is the Minas de Passagem gold mine, dating from 1719.

**Minas de Passagem** A guided tour visits the old mine workings, underground lake (take bathing suit) and the processing plant, entrance US$6 each, visiting hours 0900-1800, T Ouro Preto 551-1068, Mariana 557-1340/1255. Bus between Ouro Preto and Mariana, every 30 mins., all stop, US$0.25 to Ouro Preto, US$0.35 to Mariana; bus from Belo Horizonte (via Oruo Preto), US$1.60, 2¼ hrs. Taxi from Ouro Preto, US$6.40. There is a waterfall, Cachoeira Serrinha, where swimming is possible, ¾ hr walk from the bus stop to the mine. Monik Bernaerts, to whom we are indebted, gives the following directions: walk 100m in direction of Mariana, turn left, the road crosses a paved road, take the left fork, twice, after the second there is a yellow house on the left, where a trail starts, follow this across a paved road, turn left, a little further on there is a path to the right, which leads to the stream, walk up stream.

**Hotels** *Faisca*, R. Antônio Olinto 48, T 557-1206, E includes breakfast, spotless, excellent, friendly; *Müller*, Av. G. Vargas 34, T 557-1188, D, *Central*, R. Frei Durão 8, E, on attractive square, pleasant, quiet, clean but poor breakfast; *Providência*, R. Dom Silverio 233, T 557-1444, run by nuns, small rooms, D (electric shower), clean, quiet. The modern service station (posto) on the highway above the town offers good clean rooms at F, with hot showers.

**Restaurants** *Alvorada*, Praça Cláudio Manoel 42 *Tambaú*, Praça da Sé; *Papinha della Nonna*, D. Viçoso 27, Italian, rec. *Portão da Praça*, Praça Gomes Freire 108, excellent.

**Tourist Office** Praça Bandeirantes, helpful for a guide or pamphlet and good map. Get off bus at first stop in Mariana rather than continuing to Rodoviária. Tourist agency, Transcolta, Praça JK, T 557-2056; enquire also at Embratur, Praça Neves, T 557-1533.

*Congonhas do Campo* (pop. 35,000, altitude 866 metres) is a hill town with a good road through pleasant farming country connecting with Ouro Preto, and a paved 3½-km. road link with the Rio-Belo Horizonte highway. The town is dominated by the great pilgrimage church of Bom Jesus do Matozinho (1773), which opens at 0815; indeed there is little else of architectural interest. There is a wide view of the country from the church terrace, below which are six small chapels set in attractive sloping gardens, showing scenes with life-size Passion figures carved by Aleijadinho and his pupils in cedar wood. The church is mainly famous for its group of prophets sculpted by Aleijadinho, standing on the parapets of the terrace. These twelve great dramatic statues (thought of as Aleijadinho's masterpieces), carved in soapstone with dramatic sense of movement, constitute one of the finest works of art of their period in the world—not just in Latin America. Inside the church, as well as the Room of Miracles, there are paintings by Athayde and the heads of four sainted popes (Gregory, Jerome, Ambrose and Augustine) sculpted by Aleijadinho for the reliquaries on the high altar. (Buses run from opposite the Rodoviária to Bom Jesus, US$0.15.) Pleasant excursion to waterfall with park and swimming, at Cachoeira Santo Antônio.

Congonhas is also celebrated for its Holy Week processions, which have as their focus the Bom Jesus church. The most celebrated ceremonies are the meeting of Christ and the Virgin Mary on the Tuesday, and the dramatized Deposition from the Cross late on Good Friday. Pilgrimage season, first half of September, draws many thousands.

**Hotels** *Colonial*, opp. Bom Jesus, good and comfortable, breakfast extra, no showers/toilets in room, blankets only, D; *Santuário*, Praça da Basílica 76, with fascinating restaurant downstairs full of colonial handicrafts and good local food, right next to Bom Jesus, "a bit run down, but charming", friendly, E; *Freitas*, R. Marechal Floriano 69, E, basic. There are handicraft shops selling soapstone artefacts.

**Bus** From **Belo Horizonte**, 1½ hrs., US$1.20, 6 times a day, best to buy a return ticket. None direct from Rio; you have to change buses at Conselheiro Lafaiete (*Rhud's Hotel and Restaurant*, D; *Hotel Cupim*, on main Rio road, also B). To **Congonhas** from São João del Rei, take a São João-Belo Horizonte bus (5 a day) and alight at Murtinho, the crossing with the main Rio-Belo Horizonte highway (US$3.20); from there (it's an official bus stop) take a local bus (every ½ hr., US$0.80). Bus to **Ouro Preto**: either go via Belo Horizonte, or bus (every ½ hr.) to Murtinho or Conselheiro Lafaiete, quicker, US$0.50 (30 mins.), then to Ouro Preto, US$1.60 (4 a day), via Itabirito. Rodoviária is 1½ km. outside town.

Diamantina, the most remote of these cities, is reached from Belo Horizonte by paved road (289 km., 6 daily buses via Pássaro Verde, US$6.50, 5½ hrs.) but there is no scheduled air service. Take the road to Brasília almost as far as the turnoff for Curvelo (a lively town, *Hotel Sagarana*—5-star, very good; *Restaurant Denise* with sleeping accommodation, on main highway, very clean), then through the impressive rocky country of the Serra do Espinhaço. 30 km. N of Belo Horizonte on this road, is the *Hotel Fazenda* at Ipê Amarelo—horses to ride, etc. Further on, between Paraopeba and Caetanópolis, is the *Flora Eunice* (*Leite ao Pé de Vaca*) snackbar (good toilets) with small private botanic garden and zoo with contented animals, recommended. About 120 km. N of Belo Horizonte, 33,400 square km. of the Serra do Espinaço has been named as the **National Park of Serra do Cipó**, in view of its scenic beauty and rich variety of plant and animal life (IBDF office: Av. do Contorno 8121, CP 1304, CEP 30.000, Belo Horizonte).

*Diamantina* (pop. 37,000) centre of a once active diamond industry founded in 1729, has excellent colonial buildings. Its churches (difficult to get into, except for the modern Cathedral) are not so grand as those of Ouro Preto, but it is possibly the least spoilt of all the colonial mining cities, with carved overhanging roofs and brackets; try walking through the lower part of the town. This very friendly town is in the deep interior, 1,120 metres up amid barren mountains; it is the birthplace of the late President Juscelino Kubitschek, the founder of Brasília. His house has been converted into a museum.

After repeated thefts, the diamonds of the Diamond Museum, in the house of Padre Rolim, one of the Inconfidentes (see under Ouro Preto) have been removed to the Banco do Brasil. Diamonds are still sought; see traditional methods at Guinda, 7 km. away. *Passeio a Diamantina*, an excellent guide, is written by the author of *Passeio a Sabará*. The town's latest industry is the making of Portuguese Arraiolos-style tapestry carpets by hand, at a cooperative in the centre; it was started by a diplomat, Sr Flecha da Silva, who was perturbed by the amount of local unemployment, and it has become very successful. Also etchings on leather are made locally.

The house of Chica da Silva, an 18th-century slave who married a rich diamond contractor, is at Praça Lobo Mesquita 266 (not worth a visit, entry US$0.30); Chica has become a folk-heroine among Brazilian blacks.

**Hotels** *Tijuco*, Macau do Melo 211, T 931-1022, C, best, good food; *Grande*, R. da Quitanda 70, D, T 931-1520; *Dália*, Praça JK (Jota-Ka) 25, T931-1477, fairly good, E, opp. bus station. *J.K.*, E with breakfast, clean, friendly; *Pensão Comercial*, Praça M. Neves 30, F, basic. Other cheap hotels around the bus station. Wild camping near waterfall just outside town.

**Restaurants** *Bar-Restaurant Confiança*, R. da Quitanda 39, good. *Capistrana*, R. Campos Carvalho 36, near Cathedral square, rec. *Sarumba* bar, live music at weekends. *Serestas* (serenades) Fri. and Sat. nights; many young people in bars in Beco da Mota.

**Voltage** 110 A.C.

**Tourist Information** Dept. de Turismo in Casa de Cultura in Praça Antônio Eulálio 53, 3rd floor, pamphlets and a reliable map, also information about churches opening times.

**Buses** 6 a day to **Belo Horizonte**, via Curvelo, for connections to Brasília, with Pássaro Verde: 2½ hrs. to **Curvelo**, US$2.70, to **Belo Horizonte**, US$3.20. A slow but interesting trip to the north is possible by taking the bus to **Araçuaí**, 6 hr., then to **Itaobim**, 1½ hr., from where there are connections along the BR116 to **Bahia**.

**Excursion** Walk along the Caminho dos Escravos, the old paved road built by slaves between the mining area on Rio Jequitinhonha and Diamantina. A guide is essential (ask at the Casa de Cultura—cheap) and beware of snakes. Along the river bank to (12 km.) Biribiri, a pretty village with an abandoned textile factory. About half-way, swimming pools in the river; opposite them, on cliff face, animal paintings in red, age and origin unknown. Interesting plant life along river, and beautiful mountain views.

**Serro**, (pop. 17,000) 92 km. by paved road from Diamantina and reached by bus from there or from Belo Horizonte, is an unspoilt colonial town on the Rio Jequitinhonha with six fine baroque churches, a museum and many beautiful squares. It makes *queijo serrano*, one of Brazil's best cheeses, being in the centre of a prosperous cattle region. The most conspicuous church is Santa Rita, on a hill in the centre of town, reached by steps. On the main square, by the bottom of the steps, is the Carmo, arcaded, with original paintings on ceiling and in choir. The town has two large mansions: those of the Barão de Diamantina, now in ruins, and of the Barão do Serro across the river, beautifully restored and used as the town hall and Casa de Cultura; there are old mine entrances in the hillside behind the courtyard.

**Hotels** *Pousada Vila do Príncipe*, T 941-1485, D, very clean, in old mansion on main street, contains own museum, the artist Mestre Valentim said to have been born in slave quarters; other cheap hotels (e.g. *Dormitório*, R. Rio Branco, opp. Banco do Brasil, F). **Restaurants**: *Itacolomi*, Praça João Pinheiro 20, fair; good one on main square, also *Churrascaria Vila do Príncipe* nearby on main street.

Just by the Serro turnoff is the town of Datas, whose spacious church (1832) decorated in red and blue, contains striking wooden image of Christ with the crown of thorns.

**Tres Marias** Some 240 km. NW of Belo Horizonte is a lake five times as large as Rio de Janeiro bay, formed by the Tres Marias dam on the upper reaches of the São Francisco river. There is a motel, and **the power company, Cemig, runs a guest house** (book in advance through its head office at Belo Horizonte). At Barreiro Grande is the Clube Náutico Tres Marias, E, simple. There are plans to develop the Tres Marias area for tourism.

Almost the same distance SW of Belo is the even larger lake formed by the Furnas dam. It can be seen from the BR-381 road to São Paulo.

Also north of Belo Horizonte is **Pirapora**, terminus for boat journeys on the River São Francisco (**see also page 425**). The cutting down of trees, in part as fuel for the boats, and the low rainfall in recent years, has greatly reduced the flow. The Sobradinho lake, which was meant to save the river, is only one third full and it is feared that, in the long term, the production of energy will be reduced. The town itself is a tourist attraction because of the falls in the river which make for excellent fishing: catches weighing 73 kg. (160lb) have been reported. The sandy river beaches are used for swimming. The grotesque figureheads of the riverboats, carrancas, are made in the workshops of Lourdes Barroso, R. Abaeté 390. There are several hotels: *Canoeiras*, Av. Salmeron 3, T 741-1946, B, used by river-tour parties, *Pirapora Palace*, on Praça Melo Viana (7 blocks west and 1 block south of Rodoviária), T 741-1330, E, ask for room on garden, clean, friendly, safe, and *Hotel Rex*, R. Antônio Nascimento 357, F, small breakfast, not very good. Camping near the Praça on riverside. Restaurants: *Borretos* on the riverfront, and *Barrenko*, next door, better value. Watch the fishermen at work in their punt-like canoes.

The old river passenger service of the Companhia de Navegação do São Francisco (Franave) to Juazeiro has been discontinued, but it is still sometimes possible to arrange journeys down the river on cargo boats if you talk to the masters, in the port. If you can get on a cargo boat, the regular stops are at Januária (famous for Brazil's reputed best cachaça) and Bom Jesus da Lapa (a pilgrimage centre with a church built in a grotto inside a mountain, but a very poor town). Between Pirapora and Januária is the colonial town of São Francisco, with many attractive houses and a good handicraft market in the town hall; the boats do not always stop there. If you want to see the real Sertão, get off at Xique-Xique and take a bus to Utinga, Rui Barbosa and Itaberaba, then on to Salvador. Of the two remaining wood-burning stern-wheel boats, allegedly built for Mississippi services in the 1860s and imported from the USA in 1922 to work on the Amazon, one, the *Gaiola*, has been restored for tourist-agency use. A weekly trip (starting Sunday) is made downriver visiting various ports as far as São Francisco, organised by **Unitour or Mangebeira Turismo**, of Belo Horizonte, for about US$200 including return bus journey Belo-Pirapora (reportedly a jaunt for the wealthy).

If you can't get a boat, an adventurous journey to the Bahia coast is as follows: bus 0730 Pirpora-Montes Claros, next morning bus Montes Claros—Almenara (12 hrs.) then bus Almenara-Salto da Divisa (2½ hrs.), then after night in Salto at hotel facing bus station, take 0600 bus to Porto Seguro.

## Eastern Minas

Eastern Minas Gerais is not of great cultural or historical interest, but is a centre of semi-precious stone processing and crystal carving, and also contains the Serra do Caparaó, where are found several of Brazil's highest mountains. The two principal towns, Governador Valadares and Teófilo Otôni, are both on the BR-116 inland Rio-Salvador road, and both have good connections with Belo Horizonte. **Focus Tours (see Belo Horizonte, page 340)** offers nature tours in this area to see four rare monkey species, including the muriqui, and a number of other animals including tree sloths, maned wolves, and an incredible array of birds.

Douglas Trent writes:
**Governador Valadares**, (pop. 250,000) 324 km. from Belo Horizonte, 5½ hours by bus (US$8 normal, US$16 leito) and also by regional air service, is a modern planned city. The altitude is 170 metres. It is a centre of semi-precious stone mines and lapidation, as well as for the cut-crystal animals one finds in tourist shops all around Brazil.

**Hotels** *Governador Palace*, Av. Minas Gerais 550, B; *Real Minas*, Praça Serra Lima 607, C; *Panorama*, Mal. Floriano 914, T 21-7833, C; *São Salvador*, R. Prudente de Morais 915, D, clean.

**Restaurants** Main hotels; *JB*, R. Bárbara Heliodora 384, rec., huge servings; *Joazeiro*, R.

Pessanha 639; *Tabu*, good fish dishes.

**Hospital** São Lucas, R. Barão do Rio Branco 662, T 70-0121.

**Airport** is on the BR-381, 6 km. from the city centre with flights to Belo Horizonte and Ipatinga.

**Excursion** to the top of the Pico de Ibituruna, 960 metres.

*Teôfilo Otôni*, (335 metres, pop. 129,000), 138 km. from Governador Valadares, is a popular buying spot for dealers of crystals and semi-precious stones. The best prices in the state are found here (try K. Eluwar Ltda, R. Epamin 458—change money also).

**Hotels** *Nobre Palace*, Av. Francisco Sá 43; *Teôfilo Otôni*, BR-116 Norte km. 275, 5 km. from centre; *Lancaster*, R. Frei Gonzaga 142, D; *Metrópole*, Av. Francisco Sá 14, D; *Beira-Rio*, Av. Israel Pinheiro 671, E; *Presidente*, Av. Getúlio Vargas 183, F, clean, good breakfast, laundry facilities.

**Restaurant** *Amigo do Rei*, R. Benedito Valadares 161, T 521-4927.

**Bus** to Porto Seguro via Nanuque (*Hotel Minas*, at Rodoviária, F, adequate).

**Caparaó National Park**, 49 km. by paved road from Manhuaçu on the Belo Horizonte-Vitória road (BR-262), has the Pico da Bandeira (2,890m), Pico do Cruzeiro (2,861m) and the Pico do Cristal (2,798m). The park features rare Atlantic rainforest in its lower altitudes and Brazilian alpine on top. It is best to visit during the dry season (April-October). Camping is permitted within the park at two spots and it can be quite crowded in July and during Carnaval. (IBDF address under Serra do Cipó, **page 345 above**).

**Hotel** *Caparaó Parque*, near park entrance 15 mins. walk from the town of Caparaó, nice, C, T (032) 741-2559.

**How to get there** There are buses from Belo Horizonte, Ouro Preto or Vitória to **Manhumirim** (*Hotel São Luiz*, E, meal $1.10, good value, but *Cids Bar*, Travessa 16 do Março, has better food). From Manhumirim, take a bus direct to Caparaó, 0930, 1630 US$0.80, or to Presidente Soares (several, 7 km.), then hitch 11 km. to Caparaó. By car from the BR-262, go through the Manhumirim, Pres. Soares and Caparaó village, then 1 km. further to the hotel, which is 2 km. from the park entrance (small entry fee). Coming from Rio, leave BR-116 at Fervedouro and take BR-482 to Carangola. Just before this town branch N to Espera Feliz. About half way turn left again to Pres. Soares. From the park entrance it is 6 km. on a poorly-maintained road to the car park at the base of the waterfall. From the hotel jeeps (US$18 per jeep) run to the car park at 1,970 metres (2½ hrs.' walk), then it's a 3-4 hour walk to the summit of the Pico da Bandeira, marked by yellow arrows; plenty of camping possibilities all the way up, the highest being at Terreirão (2,370 m). It is very difficult to get to the Pico da Bandeira from Manhumirim and back in a day. This is good walking country. It may also be possible to visit local fazendas, for example Fazenda Modelo, 8 km. from Manhumirim.

## Southern and Western Minas

The spas of southern Minas Gerais are easily reached by road and in some cases by air from Rio de Janeiro and São Paulo. They are also popular holiday places with a great many hotels; the high season is from December through March.

*São Lourenço* (pop. 28,000) easily accessible from Rio de Janeiro (5-6 hrs. by bus) or São Paulo (6-7 hrs. by bus), stands at 850 metres above sea-level. There is a splendid park, tennis, boating, swimming, a flying field, and fishing from the Ilha dos Amores in a lake ringed by gardens and forests. Its rich mineral waters are used in the treatment of stomach, liver, kidney and intestinal complaints. There is an up-to-date hydro establishment for douches and for the famous carbo-gaseous baths, unique in South America. There is a grand ride through fine scenery to the Pico de Buqueré (1,500 metres).

*Caxambu* (pop. 20,000), N of São Lourenço, at 900 metres, is one of the more sophisticated of these resorts. Its waters are used for treating stomach, kidney and bladder diseases, and are said to restore fertility. They seemed to work for Princess Isabel, daughter of Dom Pedro II, who produced three sons after a visit. The little church of Santa Isabel da Hungária stands on a hill as a thank-offering. The mountains and forests around are very beautiful. View over the city from Morro Caxambu, 1,010 metres. Excellent hotels.

*Lambari* (pop. 14,400) ,a lesser-known resort, is 56 km. W of Caxambu by road at 900 metres. Efforts are under way to reopen the casino, closed in 1945. Hotels are not luxurious but fairly comfortable. The Parque das Águas has seven springs and a swimming pool. There are boat trips on the Lago Guanabara. Casino.

*Cambuquirá*, (pop. 11,000) a little N of Lambari by road at 946 metres, very popular, with friendly atmosphere and picnic sites close by.

*Poços de Caldas*, (1,180 metres; pop. 110,000) in western Minas, is reached by road or plane from São Paulo (272 km.), Rio (507 km.) or Belo Horizonte (510 km.). The city is sited on the crater of an extinct volcano in a mountainous area. Venetians from Murano settled here and established a crystal-glass industry. It is the best-known of the resorts, and is a traditional honeymoon centre. It has complete and up-to-date thermal establishments for the treatment of rheumatic, skin and intestinal diseases; you need a local doctor's certificate to use these facilities. Excursions include several lakes within a few km. of the city with boating and restaurants; the Véu das Noivas with its three waterfalls illuminated at night; the tall statue of Cristo Redentor at an altitude of 1,678 metres, which can be reached by cable car; nearby is an 80-metre granite rock, Pedra Batão. There are also the lovers' well, Fonte dos Amores, and the Japanese teahouse at the Recanto Japonês. A tourist train runs from Poços de Caldas to Aguas da Prata and back twice each Sunday (dep. 0900 and 1500, return 1130 and 1700, 1 hr. 15 mins. journey). Hippie fair every Sunday in Praça Pedro Sanches. Festivals include Carnival, São Benedito ending on 13 May, and recently established Festival de Música Popular Brasileira. Excellent climate. There is now a small industrial estate.

**Hotels** Some 80 hotels and pensions. *Palace*, Praça Pedro Sanches, T 731-3392, A, old fashioned but well run, with sulphur baths; *Continental*, Av. Francisco Salles 235, B; *Pousada Vale das Rosas*, Av. W. Brás 4500, T 721-4759, A; *Minas Gerais*, R. Pernambuco 615, T 721-8686, B.

**Restaurants** *Sem-Sem*, R. Assis Figueiredo 1080; *Cantina do Araújo*, R. Assis Figueiredo 1705.

**Buses** Rio, 8 hrs., US$9.50; São Paulo, 4½ hrs., US$5.50; both by Viação Cometa.

*Tres Corações*, also in southern Minas but not a spa, is the birthplace of Pelé, the legendary football star (statue). Hotels: *Italian Palace*, E; *Capri*, F; good food at *Cantina Calabresa*. Reached by daily buses from Rio, São Paulo and Belo Horizonte. Daily bus to (32 km.) *São Tomé das Letras*, beautiful hilltop village with frescoed 17th-century church and many caves in surrounding hills. Poçinhos de Rio Verde, a friendly hill resort, bus 1 hr; *Hotel Bosque das Fontes*, rec., at entrance to town, chalets, camp sites, restaurant, low cost steam and mineral baths; lake, horses and many trails.

Note that there are also mountain spa resorts (Serra Negra, Lindóia, Campos do Jordão) in São Paulo State (**see page 371**).

*Araxá*, (pop. 62,000) in the Minas Triangle, about 193 km. before Uberaba at 970 metres, is a quiet little place with thorium and radio-active waters and sulphur and mud baths. It can be reached from Rio (848 km.) or São Paulo (549 km.) Belo Horizonte (374 km.), by bus. Airport.

**Hotels** *Grande de Araxá*, luxury, 8 km. away, T 661-2011, A; *Colombo*, same location, T 661-3016, B; *Pinto*, Pres. O. Maciel 284, T 661-2551.

South of Araxá is the **Serra da Canastra National Park**, in which the Rio São Francisco rises. It is a cool region (temperatures in May and June average 18°C), best reached from Piumhi, on state road 050, 267 km. W of Belo Horizonte.

*Uberaba*, (pop. 245,000) also in the Minas Triangle, is on the Rio da Prata, 718 km. from São Paulo. It is an important rail and road junction, being on the direct highway between São Paulo and Brasília, and serves a large cattle raising district. At the beginning of May each year the Rural Society of the Minas Triangle holds a famous cattle and agricultural exhibition at Uberaba. Altitude, 700 metres. Hotels: *Palácio*; *Grande*. Bus from Belo Horizonte, US$9.50 (leito US$19), 7 hrs.

To the N of Uberaba is **Uberlândia** (pop. 312,000), founded in 1888; good communications by air and road (buses to Brasília, 6 hrs., US$8; to Belo Horizonte, 9 hrs., US$12, to São Paulo, US$12.80). *Hotel Nacional*, opposite Rodoviária, E, with view (cheaper without), shower and breakfast, clean.

---

## THE STATE OF SÃO PAULO (5)

**The state is the industrial heart of Brazil, with much agriculture too; the city is the financial centre. The metropolis does have much of cultural interest in the way of museums, and the famous Butantã Snake Farm. On the coast there are many fine beaches, although pollution is a problem; inland there are hill resorts.**

The State of São Paulo (pop. over 33,000,00), with an area of 247,898 square km., is larger than the states of New York and Pennsylvania together and about the same size as Great Britain and Northern Ireland. A narrow zone of wet tropical lowland along the coast rises in an unbroken slope to the ridge of the Great Escarpment—the Serra do Mar—at from 800 to 900 metres above sea level. The upland beyond the Great Escarpment is drained westwards by the tributaries of the Rio Paraná. The broad valleys of the uplands are surmounted by ranges of low mountains; one such range lies between the São Paulo basin and the hinterland of the state. West of the low mountains between the basin and the rest of the state lie the uplands of the Paraná Plateau, at about 600 metres above the sea. One of the soils in this area is the terra roxa, the red earth in which coffee flourishes. When dry it gives off a red dust which colours everything; when wet it is sticky and slippery. There is ample rainfall in São Paulo State; indeed, the highest rainfall in Brazil (3,810 mm.) is over a small area between Santos and São Paulo; at São Paulo itself it is no more than 1,194 mm. Temperatures on the plateau are about 5°C lower than on the coast, but it is only south of the latitude of Sorocaba that frosts occur and then not frequently. Temperatures are too low for coffee in the São Paulo basin itself, but the State produces, on average, about 7 million bags a year.

Between 1885 and the end of the century a boom in coffee and the arrival of large numbers of Europeans transformed the State out of all recognition. By the end of the 1930s there had arrived in São Paulo State a million Italians, half a million each of Portuguese and immigrants from the rest of Brazil, nearly 400,000 Spaniards and nearly 200,000 Japanese. Today the State produces 50% of the country's cotton, 62% of its sugar, a third of its coffee and over 50% of its fruit exports. It turns out 90% of Brazil's motor vehicles, 65% of its paper and cellulose, and 60% of its machinery and tools, being also responsible for 60% of the country's industrial consumption of electric energy. All this comes, in sum, to some 20% of Brazil's agricultural output and 65% (40% in São Paulo city alone) of its industrial production. São Paulo provides 33% of the total exports of Brazil and takes 40% of the total imports: nearly all pass through the port of Santos.

**São Paulo** (pop. 9,700,000) is 429 km. from Rio de Janeiro, and is connected with it by air, the Via Dutra highway, and the Central do Brasil railway. It was founded in 1554 by two Jesuit priests from São Vicente, Blessed José Anchieta and Padre Manuel Nóbrega, as a mission station. The original settlement, not yet effectively preserved, was at the Pátio do Colégio in the centre of the city, where a copy of Anchieta's original church has been built, using one of the surviving

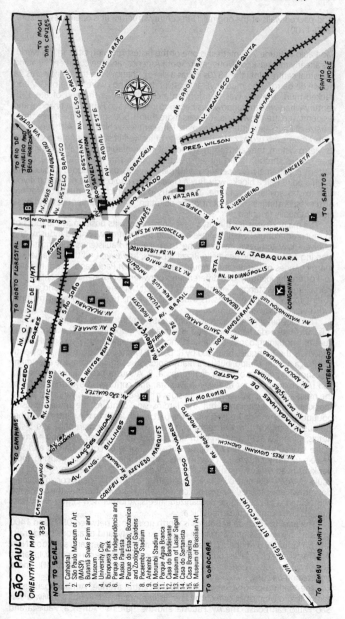

SÃO PAULO
ORIENTATION MAP
NOT TO SCALE
33 A

1. Cathedral
2. São Paulo Museum of Art (MASP)
3. Butantã Snake Farm and Museum
4. University City
5. Ibirapuera Park
6. Parque da Independência and Museu Paulista
7. Parque do Estado, Botanical and Zoological Gardens
8. Pacaembu Stadium
9. Anhembi
10. Morumbi Stadium
11. Parque Água Branca
12. Casa do Bandeirante
13. Museum of Lasar Segall
14. Casa do Sertanista
15. Casa Brasileira
16. Museum of Brasilian Art

mud-packed walls of the original 16th century structure (it is open Tues. to Sun., 1300-1700).

São Paulo (altitude 730 metres) is one of the fastest growing cities in the world. It is already the most populous city in South America, and the continent's leading industrial centre. Until the 1870s it was a sleepy, shabby little town known as "a cidade de barro" (the mud city), as most of its buildings were made of clay and packed mud. The city was transformed architecturally at the end of the 19th century when wealthy landowners began to invest in São Paulo as a financial and residential centre. Nowadays, it covers more than 1,500 square km.—three times the size of Paris—but little remains of its 19th century architecture. Although most of its citizens are proud of its skyscrapers, of its well-lit streets, and especially of its Metro system, they also mourn the loss of innumerable historical buildings and green areas through shortsighted planning policies in the 1980s. The traffic pattern is extremely exasperating: you may have to drive around 10 blocks to reach a point half a block away. Buy a *Guia de São Paulo* from a newstand if you plan to stay any length of time, it gives bus routes which are equally confusing. Also exasperating is the amount of air pollution: in dry weather eyes and nose are continually troubled.

The main reasons for the city's development lie in its position at the focus of so much agricultural wealth, while a strong tradition of work and industry and relatively low temperatures combine to make the Paulistanos the most hard working and energetic people in Brazil. Visitors, however, find the characteristic sharp changes of temperature troublesome and even Paulistanos seem to catch cold often. (Incidentally, one differentiates between Paulistas—inhabitants of the State—and Paulistanos— inhabitants of the city.) There is another and a most potent factor which explains its industrial growth: the availability of plentiful hydro-electric power.

The shopping, hotel and restaurant centre embraces the districts of Av. São Luís, the Praça da República, and R. Barão de Itapetininga. The commercial quarter, containing banks, offices and shops, is contained within a central district known as the Triângulo, bounded by R. Direita, Quinze de Novembro, São Bento and Praça Antônio Prado, but it is already rapidly spreading towards the apartment and shopping district of Praça da República. R. Augusta begins close to Avenida São Luis, extends as far as Avenida Paulista, and continues beyond into one of the most affluent areas, Jardins. Both sides of R. Augusta have a variety of shops, snackbars and restaurants, but the Jardins side contains the more exclusive boutiques and fashion houses, while the part which leads to the centre is a rather curious but colourful mix of seedy bars, saunas (mixed, or men only) and 5-star hotels. Cinemas are found on both sides as well as a number of shopping malls (close to Paulista). Avenida Paulista, once the home of coffee barons and São Paulo's wealthy citizens, is now Brazil's largest financial centre housing most banking head offices (most consulates as well), and the Museu de Arte de São Paulo (MASP—opened by Queen Elizabeth II in 1968). It is becoming a new downtown area, more dynamic, but considerably less colourful than the old centre with its maze of bustling pedestrianized streets. Another new centre is Av. Faria Lima, 8 km. from Praça da República.

The park in Praça da República is worth going into between 0800 and 1400 on Sun.: birds, trees and Brazilians in all their variety, and a famous handicrafts fair; on Saturday p.m. there is live music, and stalls sell sweets and salgados. Near the Praça is the city's tallest building, the Edifício Itália on the corner of Av. Ipiranga and Av. São Luís. There is a restaurant on top (pricey, but worth it), and a sightseeing balcony.

The Viaduto do Chá, which bridges the central avenue, Anhangabaú, leads to the Teatro Municipal, one of the few distinguished 19th-century survivals that São Paulo can boast. The Av. Paulista and the "jardins" América, Paulista and

Paulistano still contain some mansions of beauty and interest and are on the 702U Cidade Universitária bus route to the Butantã Institute or "snake farm". About 10 minutes' walk from the centre of the city is the old Mercado Municipal at R. Cantareira 306, covering an area of 27,000 square metres (open Mon.-Sat. 0400-1600); a new Mercado Municipal has been built in the outskirts. The Biblioteca Municipal, surrounded by a pleasant shady garden, is well worth visiting.

The Cathedral's foundations were laid over 40 years before its inauguration during the 1954 festivities commemorating the 4th centenary of the city. This massive building in neo-Gothic style, with a capacity for 8,000 worshippers, is in the heart of the city. Two central parks are Parque da Luz, Av. Tiradentes (110,000 square metres) and Siqueira Campos (Parque Trianon), Peixoto Gomilde 949 and Av. Paulista, open daily 0700-1830, a welcome green area in the busiest part of the city.

The large municipal stadium in the Pacaembu valley, a flourishing residential district, is well worth seeing. Built on Olympic lines in an area of 75,500 square metres, it holds nearly 70,000 spectators. Besides the flood-lit football ground and athletics field and basketball court, there are also a covered gymnasium, open-air and covered tennis courts, an illuminated 50-metre long swimming pool, a youth hostel, and a great hall for receptions and rallies. There is a larger stadium holding 100,000 people in Morumbi, one of the more elegant residential districts.

Typical of modern development are the huge Iguatemi, Ibirapuera and Morumbi shopping centres. They include luxurious cinemas, snack bars and most of the best shops in São Paulo. Parking in each for over 1,000 vehicles. On a rather humbler level are the big supermarkets of El Dorado (Av. Pamplona 1704) and Pão de Açúcar (Praça Roosevelt, near the *Hilton*); the latter is open 24 hrs. a day (except Sun.).

The palatial Jockey Club racecourse is in the Cidade Jardim area with easy access by bus (Butantã from República, among others). Race meetings are held on Mon., Wed. and Thur. at 1730 and Sat. and Sun. at 1500. The new town premises of the Jockey Club (R. Boa Vista) are well worth a visit.

**Ibirapuera** Take a Monções bus (675-C) from Ana Rosa metro station to Ibirapuera Park (designed by architect Oscar Niemeyer and landscape artist Max Burle) for the architecturally impressive new Legislative Assembly. There is also a planetarium equipped with the most up-to-date machinery (shows at 1600-1800 weekends and holidays, during the week for groups only, T 544-4606); a velodrome for cycle and motor-cycle racing; an all-aluminium covered stadium for indoor sports which seats 20,000 people. The Museu de Arte Contemporâneo, founded in 1963, has an important collection of Western and South American modern art. The collection is divided between the Bienal building, 3rd floor, in Parque Ibirapuera (entrance at back of building, open Tues.-Sun., 1200-1700, closed holidays, free) and a building at R. da Reitoria, 109, Cidade Universitária, open Weds.-Sun. 1000-1700, closed holidays, students free (it is hoped to unite the collection in a building under construction in the Cidade Universitária). Buses to Ibirapuera, 6414 (Gatusa) from Praça da Bandeira; to Cidade Universitária 702U or 7181 from Praça da República.

In this park, too, are the museums of Modern Art (Arte Moderna—MAM, Tues.-Fri. 1300-1900, Sat.-Sun. 1100-1900, Aeronáutica (showing the Santos Dumont plane; US$0.40 entrance, open Tues.-Sun. 1400-1700), and Folclore (same hours). There is also a unique display of nativity scenes and scenes of the life of Christ. (Concerts held at Christmas-time). At the entrance is a majestic monument to the Bandeirantes, or pioneers. All the Ibirapuera museums (except Aviation) are open Tues.-Sun., 1400-1700. (For other museums **see page 360.**)

**Anhembi** (Av. Assis Chateaubriand e R. Olava Fontoura, Santana) is the largest exhibition hall in the world. It was inaugurated in 1970 and all São Paulo's industrial fairs are held there. It has a meeting hall seating 3,500 people, three auditórios, 24 conference rooms (salas de reunião) and two restaurants. Parking space is provided for 3,500 cars. It may be reached by underground (short walk from Tietê station).

**Local Holidays** 25 Jan. (Foundation of City).

**Warning** Beware of assaults and pickpocketing in São Paulo. Thieves often use the mustard-on-the-back trick (see Introduction and Hints, **Security**).

**Hotels** Among the most luxurious are the *Maksoud Plaza*, Alameda Campinas 150, T

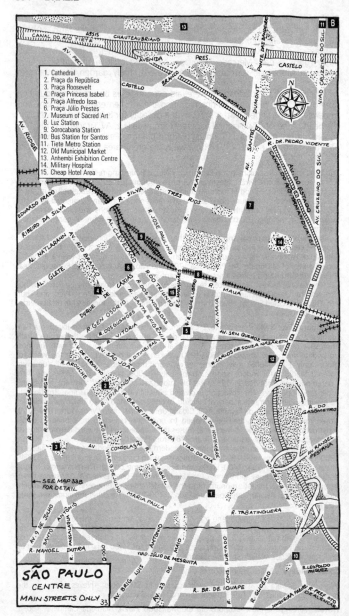

1. Cathedral
2. Praça da República
3. Praça Roosevelt
4. Praça Princesa Isabel
5. Praça Alfredo Issa
6. Praça Júlio Prestes
7. Museum of Sacred Art
8. Luz Station
9. Sorocabana Station
10. Bus Station for Santos
11. Tiete Metro Station
12. Old Municipal Market
13. Anhembi Exhibition Centre
14. Military Hospital
15. Cheap Hotel Area

SÃO PAULO
CENTRE
MAIN STREETS ONLY
33

251-2233; *Caesar Park*, R. Augusta 1508, T 285-6622; *Mofarrej Sheraton*, Alameda Santos 1437, T 284-5544 (rec); *Eldorado Boulevard*, Av. São Luís 234, T 256-8833 (excellent); *Hilton*, Av. Ipiranga 165, T 256-0033; *Holiday Inn Crowne Plaza*, R. Frei Caneca 1360, T 284-1144, Fax 251-3121, 5-star, central, small swimming pool, very comfortable; *Grand Hotel Cà d'Oro*, R. Augusta 129, T 256-8011; the *Brasilton*, R. Martins Fontes 330, T 258-5811, all in our price category L+ (corporate rates available) and with swimming pools, nightclubs and convention halls. The *Della Volpe Garden*, R. Frei Caneca 1199, T 285-5388, L, is rec.; *Grand Corona*, Basílio da Gama 101, T 259-8177, A, very fairly priced, and *Cambridge*, Av. Nove de Julho 216, T 239-0399, B (local standard class), have been rec. (although the last named's location is uninspiring).

There are many other good hotels, including in our L category, *Bristol*, R. Martins Fontes 277, T 258-0011; in our A+ category, *Samambaia*, R. Sete de Abril 422, T 231-1333 (discounts for cash and at weekeds); in our A category: *Excelsior*, Av. Ipiranga 770, T 222-7377; *Othon Palace*, R. Líbero Badaró 190, T 239-3277: *Jaraguá*, R. Major Quedinho 44, T 256-6633 and *Planalto*, Cásper Líbero 117 (Varig-Tropical chain), T 227-7311; and in our B category *Terminus*, Av. Ipiranga 741, T 222-2266, and *Solar Paulista*, R. Francisca Miquelina 343, T 257-2800.

A residential hotel, rec. for longer stays, is *Metropolitan Plaza*, Alameda Campinas 474, T 287-4855, L. A rec. "Apart-hotel" for longer stays is *Residencial Alameda Nothman* (Santa Cecília), Al. Nothman 682, T 222-6144. Apart-hotel *Del Rey*, R. Gen. Jardim 658, T 257-5288, US$50 a day, US$600 a month. *Residence Saint Peter*, R. Urussuí 271, T 282-0422; *Residence Saint James*, Al. Lorena 1160, T 280-8655, and 2 others. *Hores Belgrano*, R. Marquês de Paranaguá, 88, T 258-0255, B, central, English spoken, special rates for long stays, rooms with kitchenette. *Service-Flat Monterey*, Alameda Itu 265, Jardim Paulista, has been rec. for longer stays, at US$600/month; safe parking, comfortable accommodation.

*Banri*, R. Galvão Bueno 209, C, good, near metro station Liberdade (Japanese quarter). *Center Bela Vista*, 13 de Maio 198 (T 255-4042, C, near plenty of restaurants in an old Italian suburb (R. Santo Antônio/R. 13 de Maio, nr. Praça da Bandeira). There are scores of cheaper hotels, of which we append a selection: *Las Vegas*, R. Vitória 390 (corner Av. Rio Branco), D, excellent; *Continental*, same street, No. 223, D, clean, safe, highly rec. *Itauna*, D, Av. Rio Branco 280, well furnished, rec; *Lincoln* No. 47, E, excellent breakfast, friendly, safe, rec.; *Natal*, R. Guaianazes 41, D, modern, good rooms, rec.; *Paris*, R. João Adolfo 26, T 259-9395 (on other side of Anhangabaú metro station—down some steps and through a plazuela), D with shower, TV, clean, honest, highly rec.; *Joamar*, José de Barros, Centro, in the pedestrian area, D, hot showers, clean, safe, T.V., rec.; *Riviera*, Av. Barão de Limeira 117, T 221-8077, D, excellent value, highly rec. Also suggested: *S. Sebastião*, 7 de Abril 364 (T 257-4988/255-1594), D with bath, rec., cheap and clean; *Metro*, R. Vergueiro 1563, nr. Paraíso, T 549-8531, E without breakfast, quiet, convenient; *Cineasta*, Av. São João 613, 80 rooms, D, a/c; *Plaza*, Av. São João 407, 42 rooms, D; *Central*, Av. São João 288, E with shower, F without, clean, good if a little run down, central; many others in and around Av. São João. Very many of the cheap hotels are hot-pillow establishments.

Take the metro to Luz station and in the block behind the old Rodoviária, off Av. Rio Branco, there are scores of cheap hotels with prices ranging from category F to category C; try: R. Santa Ifigênia: *Trinidad*, No. 737, E, clean, friendly, good value; *Luanda*, No. 348, D, with breakfast, English-speaking owner, helpful, rec.; *Uai*, No. 66, C, clean and pleasant, rooms on street are good, rec. *Aliança*, R. Gral Osório 235, crnr. Sta. Ifigênia, E, nice; *Saturno*, Largo Osório 39, T 223-9561, F, hot water, soap and towel. R. dos Gusmões: *Galeão*, No. 394, E, clean, safe, helpful, hot showers; *Itaipu*, No. 467, D, good, clean. *Lisboa*, R. Cásper Líbero 390, E, basic, shared shower, safe; and *Lepanto*, No. 359, E, shower, TV, clean; *Lima*, Ipiranga 770, E, friendly, rec.; *Tatuí*, Praça Princeza Isabel 171 (on corner of Av. Duque de Caxias, 2 blocks from old bus station), F, clean with bath. N.B. the redlight district is in the blocks bounded by RR. Santa Ifigênia, dos Andradas, dos Gusmões and Av. Ipiranga, and is definitely not rec. for women travelling alone. *Comendadore*, Largo Santa Cecília, E, safe, quiet. *São José*, Alameda Barão de Piracicaba 221, E without breakfast, basic. *Casa do Politécnico*, R. Afonso Pena 272, cheap accommodation.   Accommodation of the youth-hostel type is available at the Pacaembu Stadium at a fee in (our) category E. A letter addressed to the Secretário de Esportes is required. The Youth Hostel (*Albergue da Juventude*) is in the Ibirapuera gymnasium, R. Manoel da Nóbrega e Estados Unidos, very cheap but you must first join the Brazilian YHA (15 de Novembro e Av. São João—office in centre) for about US$5 a year. International youth hostel at Parque Estadual do Jaguaré. Also Magdalena Tagkiaferro, Estrada Turística do Jaguará 651, km. 18, via Anhanguera, 05173 São Paulo (T 229-3787/3011).

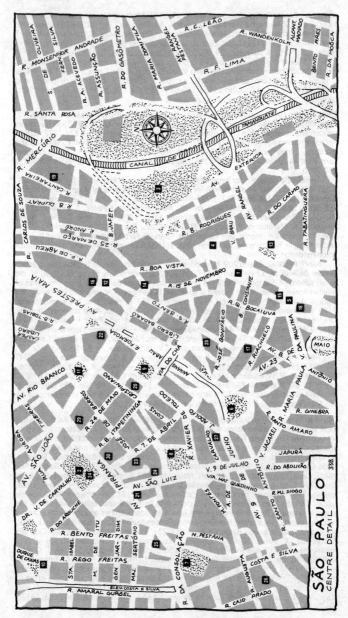

SÃO PAULO
CENTRE DETAIL
33B

**Electric Current** 110-220 volts A.C., 60 cycles.

**Camping** Cemucam, at Cobia (Rodovia Raposo Tavares, Km. 27). List of sites can be obtained from Camping Clube do Brasil, R. Minerva, 156—Perdizes (T 864-7133).

**Restaurants** Apart from the international cuisine in the first-class hotels listed above, here are only a few out of many:

**The best** (by all accounts): *Bassi*, R. 13 de Maio 334, T 34-2375, Bela Vista, for meat; *Don Curro*, R. Alves Guimarães 230, T 852-4712, Piaheiros, closed Mon., for seafood, especially paella; *Le Bistingo*, Al. Franca 580, T 289-3010; *Massimo*, Al. Santos 1826, T 284-0311, international cuisine; *Antiquarius*, Al. Lorena 1884, T 282-3015, Portuguese; *La Tambouille*, Av. 9 de Julho 5295, Itaim-Bibi, T 883-6276, French and Italian, closed Mon., reserve in advance.

**Portuguese** *Abril em Portugal*, R. Caio Prado 47, reasonable and good; *Bocage*, Al. Joaquim Eugênio de Lima 1377, excellent, about US$10 p.p. (on Sun. lunch only).

**Italian** *Cantina do Lellis*, R. Bela Cintra 1849, very reasonable, *salada Lellis* is a must, and fresh squid in batter; *Famiglia Mancini*, R. Avanhandava 81, Bela Vista, excellent, especially salads and cold dishes, always queues at the door; *Gigeto*, Avanhandava 63, good pasta, reasonable prices; *Trattoria del Sargento*, Al. Pamplona 1354, Jardim Paulista, good, popular; *Leonardo*, Al. Santos 1508, Bela Vista (opp. *Sheraton*), good; *Da Fiorella*, R. Bernardino de Campos 294, Brooklin (closed Mon. and Sun. p.m.), top quality vegetarian pasta, US$10 p.p.; *Don Cicillio*, Praça Tomás Morus 185, Perdizes, good homecooking in traditional surroundings; *Via Veneto*, Al. Barros 909, Sta. Cecília, good pasta and meat, very popular; *La Trattoria*, R. Antônio Bicudo 50, Pinheiros, closed Mon., midweek until 1900, Fri., Sat. till 0100, very good, reasonably priced food, *strozzapreti* a must, portions usually enough for 2; *La Farina*, Av. Ipiranga 924, for good cheap pasta, popular. Many Italian restaurants in Bela Vista/Bixiga area, especially R. 13 de Maio; good pizzerias are *Torre do Bixiga*, 13 de Maia, *Capuano*, R. Consarrão 416, *Margherita*, Al. Tietê 255.

**French** *L'Affliche*, R. Campos Bicudo 141, small, intimate, décor includes owner's collection of antique French posters (US$12 p.p.); *La Casserole*, Largo do Arouche 346, (centro), best known bistro in São Paulo, closed Mon. *Freddy*, Praça Dom Gastão Liberal Pinto 11; *Marcel*, Al. Lorena 1852, sensational soufflés.

**German** *Jucalemão*, R. Álvaro Rodrigues 320; *Bierhalle*, Av. Lavandisca 249, Indianópolis; *Arnold's Naschbar*, R. Pereira Leite 98, Sumarezinho, *Eisbein peruruca*, rec; *Bismarck* (excellent draught beer) and *Paprika* (very reasonable), on Av. Ibirapuera 3178 and 573 respectively.

**Swiss** *Chamonix*, Al. Lorena 1052, and *Le Jardin Suisse*, Al. Franca 1467, both in Jardim Paulista, expensive, very good.

**Russian** *Samovar*, R. Baronesa de Bela Vista 602, Aeroporto, good food, typical shows at weekends, closed Sun. **Hungarian** *Hungaria*, Al. Joaquim Eugênio de Lima 776, Jardins, very elegant, old world décor, good food, expensive; *Piroska*, Av. Jaú 310, cheap and good.

**Greek** *Zorba*, R. Henrique Monteiro 218.

**Arabic** *Almanara*, good and reasonable, Av. São João 1155 (Centro), Oscar Freire 523 (Cerqueiro César), R. Basilio da Gama 70 and Av. Vieira de Carvalho 109 (Consolação), *Mandalun*, Al. Itú 1564, Jardim Paulista, mainly Lebanese, high standard, not cheap; *Bambi*, Al. Santos 59, cheapish, good; *Rubayat*, Av. Vieira de Carvalho 116, Al. Santos 86 and Av. Faria 583, excellent meat, fixed price meals US$6.

**Oriental** (Japanese tends to be expensive) *Sino-Brasileiro*, R. Alberto Torres 39 (Perdizes); *Yamanga*, R. Tomás Gonzaga 66; *Iti Fuji*, Al. Jaú 487, typical Japanese, excellent; *Sushigen*, Av. Brig. Luis Antônio 2367, Lojas 13 and 14, very good *sushi* and *sashimi* but a bit overpriced; *Komazushi*, same street No. 2050, Loja 7, reasonably priced and good; *Shushi Kiyo*, R. 13 de Maio 950, Bela Vista, rec.; *Kokeche*, R. dos Estudantes 41 (Liberdade), good, reasonably-priced; *Korea House*, Galvão Bueno 43 (Liberdade). Many other Chinese and Japanese restaurants in Liberdade, the Japanese quarter, where there is a Japanese food

## São Paulo (Centre Detail): Key to map

1. Praça da Sé; 2. Praça da República; 3. Parque Dom Pedro II; 4. Pátio do Colégio and Museu Padre Anchieta; 5. Praça Dr. João Mendes; 6. Praça da Bandeira; 7. Praça Roosevelt and Church of Consolação; 8. Praça Dom José Gaspar and Municipal Biblioteca; 9. Praça Ramos Azevedo; 10. Largo do Arouche; 11. Largo Paiçandu; 12. Largo São Bento; 13. Praça Clovis Bevilaqua; 14. Praça Antônio Prado; 15. Cathedral; 16 São Bento; 17. São Francisco do Assis; 18. São Gonçalo; 19. Old Mercado Municipal; 20. Teatro Municipal; 21. Edifício Itália; 22. Central Post Office; 23 Embratel; 24. State Tourist Offices (2 locations). **Hotels:** 25. *Hilton*; 26. *Grand Cà d'Oro*; 27. *Cambridge*; 28. *Othon Palace*; 29. *Excelsior*; 30. *Samambaia*.

market in the square by the metro station.

**Indian** *Govinda*, R. Princesa Isabel 379, good, expensive.

**Vegetarian** Almost always the cheapest option in São Paulo. *Sattva*, R. da Consolação 3140; *O Arroz de Ouro*, Largo do Arouche 42-44 (shop as well, central); *Cheiro Verde*, Peixoto Gomilde 1413, Jardins, very good, more expensive than most; *Jasmin Casa de Chá*, vegetarian food and tea rooms, R. Haddock Lobo 932; *Intergrão*, Av. Rebouças 2036, macrobiotic; *Delícia Natural*, Av. Rio Branco 211 (4th floor), corner Av. Ipiranga, lunch only, good; *Sabor Natural*, same building, 1st floor, lunch only, good; *Folhas e Raizes*, Líbero Bádaro 370; *Saúde Sabor*, São Bento 500; *Vegetaliano*, D. Sampaio 155, Sto. Amaro, Italian vegetarian. "Vida Integral" newspaper (US$0.35) gives details of all health food restaurants and stores in São Paulo.

**General** *Terraço Itália*, on top of Edifício Itália (Ipiranga e São Luis), 41 floors up, good fixed price lunch, dancing with excellent band and superb view (must consume to be allowed to see the view), expensive, shorts and flip flops not allowed; *Mexilhão*, R. 13 de Maio 626, Bela Vista, very good seafood. *Paulista*, João Moura 527, Pinheiros, US$15-20 a head for top quality meat, popular; *Dinho's Place*, Al. Santos 45, Fri. excellent seafood buffet, otherwise good meat, pricey ; *Mate Amargo*, Av. Pompéia 1603, *churrascaria*, live music, rec.; *Rodeio*, R. Haddock Lobo 1468, excellent meat dishes; *Paddock*, Av. São Luís 258 and Av. Faria Lima 1541, traditional fare, excellent *feijoada*, US$20 p.p. or more; *Planeta*, R. Augusta, includes Brazilian dishes, rec.; *Um, Dois, Feijão e Arroz*, Praça de Sé 42 and R. Ipiranga 940, modest but very good traditional food; *Cantina Amigo Piolin*, R. Augusta 89, good and cheap; *Novo Olido*, Largo do Arouche 193, closed Sat., regional dishes from interior of São Paulo; *Bolinha*, Av. Cidade Jardim 53 for *feijoadas* (on Wed. and Sat.); *Oxalá*, Tr. Maria Antônia 72, just off Consolação, Bahian specialities at modest prices; *Bronx*, R. Haddock Lobo 1576, very reasonable traditional home cooking.

*McDonalds* and other fast food chains can be found all over the city as well as many other not quite so fast, but infinitely more interesting alternatives. *Frevinho Lanches*, R. Augusta 1563, famous for its *beirute* (speciality of São Paulo), as well as many other toasted sandwiches with pitta bread; *Baguette*, Consolação 2426, nr. Paulista, opp. Belas Artes cinema, good sandwiches, especially lively around midnight; *Absolute*, Al. Santos 843, best hamburgers in town; *Rock Dreams*, good hamburgers and sandwiches; delicious *pão de queijo* in *Lanchonete* of same name on Augusta (between Antônio de Queirez and Marquês de Paranagua—Centro). *Restaurante do MASP*, Av. Paulista 1578, in basement of museum, reasonably priced, often has live music.

**Bars** *Spazio Pirandello*, Augusta 311, Central, not expensive, good bar/restaurant, nice atmosphere, ideal bar for a chat over a few drinks; *Finnegan's*, Alameda Itú 1529 (esq. Consolação), Jardins, and Cristiano Viana 358 (esq. Artur de Azevedo), Pinheiros, rec., international clientéle; *Ritz*, Al. Franca 1088, Jardins, a bit overpriced but always lively, friendly, predominantly gay clientèle; *Riviera*, R. da Consolação 2450, opp. Belas Artes cinema, traditional haunt of students and "counter" revolutionaries since early 60s, noisy and a bit rough but kept under control by surly waiters. *Bar Brahma*, Av. Ipiranga 787 e São João, opened in 1940s, usually quiet in middle of downtown; *Café do Bixiga*, 13 de Maio 76 and lots of others in Brixiga/Bela Vista area with live music, e.g. *Café Piu Piu* and *Café Pedaço*, at 13 de Maio 134 and 140. Bixiga is traditionally known as the "Bohemian" area and bars here are usually cheaper than Jardins and Pinheiros areas. Jazz at *Opus 2004*, R. Pamplona 1187, Jardins, and *Sanza Jazz Bar*, R. Frei Caneca 304, Centro. *Café Paris*, Av. Waldemar Ferreira 55, nr. University, live Brazilian popular music most nights, US$1 cover charge for music, popular with students; also popular, *Bar Pourquoi Pas*, R. Caraibas 342, Pompéia, jazz, blues and rock.

**Shopping** All types of stores at **Shopping Center Iguatemi**, Av. Brig. Faria Lima, **Shopping Centre Ibirapuera**, Av. Ibirapuera (see page 353), and **Shopping Centre Morumbi**, also **El Dorado Shopping Centre** (corner of Av. Rebouças and Marginal Pinheiros). Souvenirs from *Mimosa*, Joaquim Nabuco 275, Brooklin Paulista; *Artindia*, R. Augusta 1371, loja 119 (Galeria Ouro Velho), T 283-2102; *Coisarada*, R. Tabapuã 390, Itaim Bibi (T 881-4810); *Casa dos Amazonas*, Av. São Luis 187, Galeria Metrópole, loja 14; *Ceará Meu Amor*, R. Pamplona 1551, Loja 7, good quality lace from the North East. *H. Stern*, jewellers, at Praça da República 242, R. Augusta 2340 and at Iguatemi, Ibirapuera and Morumbi shopping centres and at main hotels. Open air markets: **"Hippy" fair**, Praça da República, Sun. 0800-1400, very varied, many tourists, good selection of inexpensive fossils, Bahian food, lots of artists; **"Oriental" fair**, Praça de Liberdade Sun. p.m., good for Japanese snacks, plants and some handicrafts at Praça da Sé, Liberdade, Sun., very picturesque, with remedies on sale, tightrope walking, gypsy fortune tellers, etc. Below the Museu de Arte de São Paulo, an **antiques** market takes place on Sun., 0800-1700. There are **flea markets** Suns. in the main square of the Bexiga district (Praça Don Orione) and in Praça Benedito Calixto in Jardim América. São Paulo is relatively cheap for film and clothes (especially shoes). The **Ceasa flower market** should not be missed, Av. Doutor Gastão Vidigal 1946, Jaguaré, Tues. and Fri. 0700-1200. **Handicraft market** at Praça Campos de Bagatelle, Sun. 0800-1300.

**Bookshops** *Livraria Cultura*, Eva Herz e Cia., Av. Paulista 2073, Conjunto Nacional, new books in English; *Ilco*, Barão do Triúnfo 371, Brooklin Paulista, books in English. *Livraria Kosmos*, Praça Dom José Caspar 134, loja 30, international stock. *Livraria Alemã*, R. Laplace 159, Brooklin; *Librairie Française*, R. Barão de Itapetininga 275, 6th floor, wide selection. *Book Centre*, R. Gabus Mendes 29 loja 5, Consolação area books in English and German. *Duas Cidades*, R. Bento Freitas 158, nr. República, good selection of Brazilian and Spanish American literature. *Cinema Elétrico*, R. Augusta 973, Centro, and *Sola Cinemateca*, R. Fradique Coutinho 361, sell postcards and books on cinema and art.

**Camera Repairs** T. Tanaka Cia Ltd repair Nikon cameras, very helpful. Will give advice and addresses for other makes.

**Local Transport** Local buses (100 cruzeiros) are normally crowded and rather slow, but clean. Maps of the bus and metro system are available at depots, e.g. Anhangabaú. Taxis display cards of actual tariffs in the window, for "especial taxis", dearer but fewer hassles, T 223-1975 (Tele Taxi), call out charge US$1, calls not accepted from public phones.

**Metro** The metro, the first in Brazil, began operating in 1975. It has two main lines: north-south from Santana to Jabaquara; east-west from Corinthians Itaquera to Barra Funda, intersecting at Praça de Sé. A third line has opened on an experimental basis (from 1000-1500 daily) and is expected to be in full operation by Dec. 1991. It runs from Clínicas in the west, along Av. Paulista, to Ana Rosa in the south, joining the Jabaquera line at Paraíso and Ana Rosa. The East-West line (2) has been extended 14 km. from Barra Funda (the interchange with Fepasa and RFFSA railways and site of a future, third Rodoviária) to Itaquera. The system is clean, cheap and efficient; it operates from 0500-2400. Fare US$0.33, book of ten tickets US$2.85; backpacks are allowed. Combined bus and metro ticket are available, e.g. to Congonhas airport.

**Night Clubs** There are several first-class night-clubs serving excellent meals; they prefer couples to single people. Besides very good dance-bands, the majority have floor-shows in which internationally-famed artists perform. *A Baiúca*, Praça Roosevelt 256; *Tramp, Cotton Club* and *Stardust* at R. Franz Schubert 59, 159 and 1351 respectively, all quite expensive; *Plataforma 1*, Av. Paulista 424, dinner and folkloric show, very touristy but extremely popular; *Bar da Virada*, R. Simão Álvares 275, Pinheiros, very popular; *Mel*, R. Pamplona 1213 for lambada and Caribbean music; *Nightclub 150 (Maksoud Plaza)*, Al. Campinas 150, chic. *A Vila Samba* and *Barracão de Zino*, Av. Ibirapuera 2461 and 2384 respectively for samba.

**Discotheques** *London Tavern* (Hilton Hotel), Av. Ipiranga 165, closed Sun., expensive. Always new discos opening and closing in Jardins area: ask at *Ritz Bar*, Al. Franca for latest hot spots. The more established discos in this area are: *Up and Down*, R. Pamplona 1418, very popular, disco music; *Homo Sapiens*, R. Marquês de Itú 182, gay disco with floor show; *Nations*, R. Augusta, Jardins, between Al. Franca and Av. Paulista, very fashionable, up-to-the-minute music; *Aero Anta*, R. Miguel Isasa 404, Pinheiros, very popular, Brazilian rock, reggae, Afro-Bahian groups, live music from 2400-0200, disco till 0400, admission US$4 minimum. See *Illustrada* section of *Folha de São Paulo* for listings. Lambada discos may be found in R. Pamplona.

**Entertainment** The Teatro Municipal (magnificent interior recently restored) is used by visiting theatrical and operatic groups, as well as the City Ballet Company and the Municipal Symphony Orchestra who give regular performances. There are several first-class theatres: Aliança Francesa, Teatro Arena, Itália, Maria Della Costa, Paiol, Ruth Escobar among others. Free concerts at Teatro Popular do Sesi, Av. Paulista 313, at midday under MASP (Mon.-Sat.) and on weekends at the Memorial América Latina. See *Illustrada* section of *Folha de São Paulo* for listings of concerts, theatre and cinema. In cinemas entrance is usually half price on Wed.

**Golf Courses** About half an hour's drive from the centre there are two 18-hole golf courses, one at Santo Amaro, and another, the São Fernando Golf Club, Praça Dom Francisco Souza 54, in Santo Amaro, in beautiful surroundings. There is a sporting 9-hole course at São Francisco club, beyond the Butantã Institute.

**Sport** The most popular is association football. The most important matches are played at Morumbi and Pacaembu grounds. At Interlagos there is a first-class racing track (**see page**

364). There is yachting, sailing and rowing on the Santo Amaro reservoir. For nature trails, etc., Free Way, R. Leôncio de Carvalho 267, Paraíso, CEP 04.003 São Paulo, T 285-4767/283-5983.

**Culture and Education** There are three universities: the official university of São Paulo, the Pontifical Catholic University, and the Mackenzie University. The official University of São Paulo is now situated in the Cidade Universitária (buses from main bus station), outside the city beyond Pinheiros. There are a number of architecturally interesting buildings housing different faculties and the four museums of archaeology, ethnology, anthropology and mineralogy. (All keep different hours, but all are open Mon.-Thurs. 1400-1700.)

**Galleries and Museums** The **Museu de Arte de São Paulo** (founded by Assis Chateaubriand, Av. Paulista 1578, immediately above the 9 de Julho tunnel, nearest metro is Paraíso on the N-S line, or MASP-Trianon on the new line, or bus 805A from Praça da República) has a large group of French Impressionists, Florentine and Umbrian painters (including Botticelli and Raphael), several Hieronymus Bosch and Frans Post, sculptures by Rodin, a collection of 73 sculptures by Degas and paintings by Modigliani, Renoir, Toulouse-Lautrec, and some interesting work by Brazilian artists, including Portinári. Particularly interesting are the pictures of the North-East done by Dutch artists during the Dutch occupation (1630-54): the exotic tropical landscapes— even the Paulo Afonso falls!—have been made to look incredibly temperate. (Exhibitions vary, not all the artists above may be on view.) Temporary exhibitions are held in the basement. Entrance US$0.50, Tues.-Fri. 1300-1700, Sat.-Sun. 1400-1800. The **Museu de Arte Brasileira** is at R. Alagoas 903, Pacaembu, entrance free, Tues.-Fri. 1400-2200, Sat.-Sun. 1300-1800, houses collections of Brazilian artists such as Portinári, Anita Malfatti and Brecheret. Here also there are copies of Brazilian sculptures, including those of Aleijadinho. The **Museu de Arqueologia e Etnologia** is on the fourth and fifth floors of Bloco D in the students resident blocks (known as Crusp) in the main Arts Complex of the Universidade de São Paulo (USP), bus stop before the entrance to the Butantã Institute (**see page 363**). Every odd-numbered year the São Paulo Bienal at Ibirapuera has the most important show of modern art in Latin America, open from beginning of Sept. till Nov. For the other museums at Ibirapuera (including the Museum of Contemporary Art), **see page 353**, and for the Museu Paulista and Casa do Grito at Ipiranga, **see page 364.** In the Parque Modernista, R. Santa Cruz 325, Vila Mariana, is the first Modernist house, built by the Russian born architect Warchavchik; it was frequented by members of the modernist movement and now shows videos and photographs on the period (open Sat.-Sun., free).

There are two museums on Av. Tiradentes, near the Jardim da Luz; the **Museu de Arte Sacra** in the Convento da Luz, No 676 (open Tues.-Sun. 1300-1700, US$0.20) and the State Art Collection (**Pinacoteca do Estado**) at No. 141 (open Tues.-Sun. 1300-1900, free).

Not far from the Butantã Institute (**see page 363**) are the **Casa do Bandeirante** (being renovated) at Praça Monteiro Lobato, the reconstructed home of a pioneer of 400 years ago (Tues.-Fri. 1030-1700, Sat.-Sun. 0900-1700, free); and the **Casa do Sertanista**, a museum of Indian folklore and handicrafts mounted by the famous expert on the Indians, Orlando Villas Boas, at Av. Prof. Francisco Morato 2200, Caxingui, T 211-5341, open Tues.-Sun., 1030-1700, entrance free.

The **Casa Brasileira**, Av. Faria Lima 774, has been established as a museum of Brazilian furniture, Tues.-Sun., 1300-1700. **Museo Padre Anchieta**, Pátio do Colégio, is a restored mission house; inside are examples and relics of the Jesuit era, entrance US$0.50. The **Museu da Imagem e do Som** (MIS) is at Av. Europa 158, Tues.-Sun. 1400-2200, regular photographic exhibitions and archives of Brazilian cinema, video and music, which can be consulted by the public, nice café on ground floor. The **Museu de Lasar Segall**, at R. Alfonso Celso 362, Vila Mariana (near Santa Cruz metro station), shows the works of a German expressionist painter who emigrated to Brazil, with cinema and library, Tues.-Fri. 1430-1800, Sat. 1430-2000, Sun. 1430-1830. **Museu da Imigração Japonesa**, R. São Joaquim 381, Liberdade, Tues.-Sun. 1330-1730, excellent, nice roof garden, ask at desk for English translation of the exhibits. **Museo da Fundação Maria Luisa e Oscar Americano**, Av. Morumbi 3700, Morumbi, a private collection of Brazilian and Portuguese art and furniture, well-displayed, Tues.-Sun., 1000-1700. There is a **Museo da Discoteca e Biblioteca da Música** at R. Catão 611, 5th and 6th floors, open Mon.-Fri., 0900-1300 (take bus 819 P from Praça Princesa Isabel to Lapa district). **Museu do Telefone**, Martiniano de Carvalho 851, Paraíso, Tues.-Sun., 1400-1800, quite good, but you're not allowed to operate anything. **Museu CMTC dos Transportes Públicos**, Av. Cruzeiro do Sul 780, Tues.-Sun., 0900-1700. **Museu de Veterinária**, Cidade Universitária, Facultade de Veterinária, bloco 7, T 210-2122, ext. 475. **Museu do Papel** (Paper), R. Mauá 836, casa 25, Tues.-Fri. 1330-1700, Sat.-Sun. 1000-1400; **Museu do Relógio** (clocks and watches), rec. for enthusiasts, Av. Diógenes R. de Lima 2333, Pompéia; **Estação Ciência**, R. Guaicurus 1274, Lapa, Tues.-Wed. 1200-2200,

Thur. and Sun. 1000-2000.

The **Centro Cultural São Paulo**, R. Vergueiro 1000 (metro Vergueiro) has art and photographic exhibitions, a library, music and dance shows (often regional) and films; open daily until 2200. **Memorial da América Latina**, designed by Oscar Niemeyer, built in March 1989, at Av. Mário de Andrade 664, next to Barra Funda metro station, relief map of Central and South America under a glass floor in the section which houses a permanent exhibition of handicrafts from Mexico, Guatemala, Peru and Ecuador, library of photographs, books, magazines, newspapers and films shown on video, very impressive, restaurant, on weekends there are free concerts with Brazilian and Latin American musicians, programme available on request, entrance free (open Tues.-Fri. 0900-2100, Sat. 0900-1800, Sun. 1000-1800).

**Banks**  Opening hours vary from bank to bank, but most are open between 1000-1600, **Banco do Brasil**, R. 7 de Abril, near República. **Lloyds Bank**, R. Quinze de Novembro 143-165. (Open 1000-1630.) **Banco Internacional**, R. Quinze de Novembro 240. **Banco Holandês Unido**, R. Quinze de Novembro 150. **Citibank**, Av. Ipiranga 855, or Av. Paulista IIII (T 576-2211) will receive money from abroad (US\$20 charge, takes 5 days). **First National Bank of Boston**, R. Líbero Badaró 487. **Banco Lar Brasileiro** (Chase Manhattan owned), 131 R. Alvares Penteado, and other national banks. **Banco Mercantil de São Paulo**, Av. Paulista 1450, for cash advances on Access/Master Charge, but slow.

**Exchange**  Many *câmbios* near Praça da República. **American Express** (Kontik Franstur—address below) very helpful; **Exprinter**, Barão de Itapetininga 243, also deals in foreign currencies (cash only). **Boreal Turismo**, Praça da República, opp. Tourist Office, on Ipiranga. **Tourist Cambio**, R. Badaró (turn left off Viaduto do Chá); **Agency Faro**, Av. São Luis 157, for travellers' cheques; **Interpax**, Praça da República 177, loja 13, changes cheques at good rates. For parallel rates ask at tourist kiosks for details. **Thomas Cook assistance point**, R. Haddock Lobo-337, 2 Andar, 01414 S.P., T 259-3022. Most travel agents on Av. São Luis change travellers' cheques and cash at good rates.

**Trade and Cultural Institutions**  British Chamber of Commerce of São Paulo, R. Barão de Itapetininga 275, 7th floor; Caixa Postal 1621. T 255-0519. **Sociedade Brasileira de Cultura Inglesa**, Avenida Higienópolis 449. **American Chamber of Commerce for Brazil**, R. Formosa 367, 29th floor, T 222-6377. **American Library**, União Cultural Brasil-Estados Unidos, R. Coronel Oscar Porto 208, T 287-1022. **Goethe-Instituto**, R. Frei Caneca 1246 (open Mon.-Thurs. 1400-2030). **Instituto Hans Staden**, R. Cons. Crispiniano 53, 12th floor.

**Consulates**  **Argentine**, R. Araújo 216, 8th floor, T 256-8555 (open 0830-1300, very easy to get visa here); **Bolivian**, R. Quirino de Andrade 219, 3rd floor, (open 0900-1300), T 255-3555; **Chilean**, Av. Paulista 1009, T 284-2004; **Paraguayan**, Av. São Luiz 112, 10th floor, T 259-3579; **Uruguayan**, Al. Campinas 433, 7th floor, T 284-5988; **Venezuelan**, Itália 539, T 883-3000.

**American Consulate General**, R. Padre João Manuel 933, T 881-6511; **Canadian Consulate General**, Av. Paulista 854-5th floor, T 287-2122; **British Consulate General**, Av. Paulista 1938, 17th floor, Caixa Postal 846, T 287-7722; **Irish**, Av. Paulista 2006, 5th floor, 01310 São Paulo, T 287-6362; **Danish Consulate General**, Av. Indianópolis 381, T 571-6933, open 0900-1200, 1300-1630; **German**, Av. Brig Faria Lima 1383, 12th floor, T 814-6644; **Swiss Consulate-General**, Av. Paulista 1754, 4th floor, Caixa Postal 30588, T 289-1033; **Austrian Consulate-General**, R. Augusta 2516, 10th floor, T 282-6223; **French**, Av. Paulista 2073, T 287-9522; **Swedish Consulate-General**, R. Oscar Freire 379, 3rd floor, T 883-3322 (postal address: Caixa Postal 51626, 01499 São Paulo); **Dutch**, Av. Brigadeiro Faria Lima 1698, T 813-0522.

**Places of Worship**  St. Paul's Anglican (Episcopal) Church, R. Comendador Elias Zarzua 1231, Santo Amaro, T 246-0383. **Igreja Metodista**, Av Liberdade 659, T 278-5895. **Adventist**, R. Jaguá 88, T 279-8206. Presbyterian, R. Néstor Pestanha 106, T 255-6111. **Mormon Church**, Av. Prof. Francisco Morato 2430, T 570-2483. Synagogue Congregação Shalom, R. Comendador Elias Zarzur 568, Israelita Paulista, R. Antonio Carlos 553. **Templo Budista**, Av. do Cursino 753, T 63-4015. Lutheran church, Av. Rio Branco 34. Swedish Church, Igreja Evangelica Luterana Escandinava, R. Job Lane 1030, CEP 04639, T 011-247 88 29.

**Police** T 228-2276; Radio Patrol, T 190. Federal Police, Av. Prestes Maio 700, open 1000-1600 for visa extensions.

**Emergency and Ambulance**  T 192, no charge. **Fire** T 193.

**Physicians**  (English-speaking) Edwin Castello, José Maria Lisboa 861, s/104, T 287-9071; Ruy Silva, Conselheiro Brotero 1505, No. 64, T 67-2470; Wilson Frey, Barão de Jacegua 1103,

T 241-4474. Christel Schlúnder, R. Alvares de Azevedo 127, Sto. Amaro, T 247-5963, German speaking, and for children. Also Samaritans' Hospital, R. Conselheiro Brotero 1486. T 825-1122.

**Post Office** Correio Central, Praça do Correio, corner Av. São Joã and Prestes Máia, T 831-5222. Booth adjoining tourist office on Praça da República, weekdays only 1000-1200, 1300-1600, for letters and small packages only. **UPS** office, Brasinco, Alameda Jaú 1, 1725, 01420 São Paulo, T 852-8233, Fax 853-8563.

**International Telephone** R. 7 de Abril 295, near Praça da República.

**Telecommunications** Embratel, Av. São Luís 50, and Av. Ipiranga 344.

**Tourist Offices** Praça da República (very helpful), Praça da Sé and Liverdade metro entrances, Praça Dom José Gaspar (corner Av. São Luis), R. Augusta esq. Av. Paulista, R. Barão de Itapetinga, near Teatro Municipal; excellent free map at all these offices. Office at Guarulhos airport is helpful. For information on São Paulo State, Praça Antônio Prado 9, 6th floor, Av. São Luís 115. Very cheap tours (US$1 max.) leave tourist office at Praça da República every half hour Tues.-Sat. from 0900 to 1700 and Sun. 0900-1600; there are 8 different itineraries visiting Casa do Grito, Casa do Bandeirante, Pinacoteca do Estado, Butantã, among other places of cultural interest. Each tour lasts approximately 3 hours, tickets and full programme from tourist office in Praça da República, T 267-2122, ext. 627/640, Mon.-Fri., CMTC tours by metro on Sat.-Sun. from 0900-1000, 1400-1500 from Praça da Sé; information at Praça da Sé, T 229-3011. For weekly information on cultural activities, addresses and recommended bars, see *Veja São Paulo* of the weekly magazine *Veja*. Tourist offices have free magazines in Portuguese and English: *Where* and *São Paulo This Month*. Also recommended is Quatro Rodas guide to the City.

**Maps** of São Paulo in train timetables at news-stands (US$2.50), and in the monthly tourist guide published by the Prefeitura. Also obtainable from the tourist offices, the Rodoviária (upstairs), the better hotels, American Express and H. Stern, the jeweller. Map shops: **Mapolândia**, 7 de Abril 125, shop 40; **Metrópole Mapas**, Av. São Luís 153, Loja 1 (Galeria Metrópole). 2 private map producers: Geo Mapas, R. Libero Badaró 336, C.E.P. 01008, T 259-2166 (40% discount for volume purchases, excellent 1988 1:5,000,000 map of Brazil, town maps), and Editorial Abril, R. Geraldo Flaufino Gomez 61, Barrio Brooklin, C.E.P. 04575, T 545-8122.

**Travel Agents** *Wilson, Sons S.A.*, Av. São Luís 715; *Exprinter*, R. Barão de Itapetininga 243; *Receptur*, same street, 221; *Woehrle Turismo*, R. do Tesouro 47, cep 01013, T (011) 37-7594, USA T (011) 532-1105, helpful, German spoken; *Lema Turismo*, Av. Marquês de Itú 837, personalised excursions, Marta Schneider speaks 8 languages, including Hungarian; *Tunibra*, Praça da Liberdade 63, T 36-0101, helpful; *Itatiaia Publicidade e Turismo*, Cons. Crispiniano 69 (for hotel reservations especially); *Transatlântica Turismo*, R. Coronel Xavier de Toledo 98 (for local excursions); *AmEx* office in *Hotel Sheraton Mofarrej*, Al. Santos 1437, T 284-6622; *Kontik-Franstur* (American Express representative), R. Marconi 71. *Royal Turismo*, Manoel da Nóbrega off Av. Paulista, helpful to budget travellers; *Student Travel*, Estados Unidos 153, T 887 4242; *Audiotur* (ask for Janice Kawasake), Estados Unidos 627, T 887-3400, gives information about trains. Visits to coffee fazendas (May-June) and round trips into the surrounding country are organized by the travel agencies.

**Railways** São Paulo has four railway stations: **1) Estação da Luz**, T 227-3299, for RFFSA overnight service to Rio (the Santa Cruz, dep. 2300, 9 hrs., double cabins US$20, "poltrona-leito" car, diner and bar lounge); for broad gauge, long-distance trains to Campinas for Ribeirão Preto and for Brasília, changing at Campinas; US$39.20 sleeper (very good sleeping cars, book 10 days in advance), US$23.20 1st class, leaves on Sun. at 1000, reaching Campinas at 1143, and Brasília 0855 on Mon. (through tickets available); the track is bad, but the journey interesting; for express trains to São José do Rio Preto and Marília; to Baurú for Campo Grande and Corumbá—no through tickets from São Paulo to Campo Grande or Corumbá are sold; you must go by bus or train (0700) to Bauru (risking a day's wait there for train connections) from where Estrada de Ferro Noroeste do Brasil goes 3 times a week (but maybe cut to once) across Mato Grosso do Sul to Corumbá (34 hrs. from São Paulo), and on, after crossing frontier by road, from Quijarro (Bolivia) to Santa Cruz de la Sierra by the Estrada de Ferro Brasil-Bolívia (**see page 371**). Also from Luz, commuter services on former Santos a Jundiaí (ex São Paulo Railway). **2) Júlio Prestes station**, T 702-1400, for commuter services to southwest of the state (former Sorocabana); **3) Roosevelt**, T 292-5417, for commuters to Mogi das Cruzes (ex Central do Brasil) and eastern suburbs. Slower meter guage trains to Pres. Prudente. A new terminal, **Barra Funda**, has a metro station and handles Sorocabana and Santos a Jundiaí commuter services; all long distance trains into and out of Luz, except the Rio service, stop at Barra Funda; a new, weekend service "down the hill" to **Santos** dep. Barra Funda 0815, arr. Santos 1205, return—in the dark—1730 (superb scenery); also from Barra Funda 2 daily trains to **Presidente Prudente**, about 15 hrs.

**Roads** To take the picturesque new coast road to Rio, take the Via Anchieta to the Guarujá turn, before Guarujá take Bertioga turn and you're on the Santos-Rio highway. Motorists leaving the ring road for Curitiba and Iguaçu should follow Regis de Bittencourt signs. To hitch to Rio, take the metro to Ponte Pequeno, then a bus to Guarulhos, alighting where the bus turns off the Rio road for Guarulhos.

**Buses** To get to the new Rodoviária, take the metro to Tietê, very convenient. Left luggage US$0.80 per day per item. You can sleep in the bus station after 2200 when the guards have gone; tepid showers US$2.50. Bus to centre, US$0.40. Bus to **Rio**, 6 hrs., every 30 mins., US$10 (leito, 20), special section for this route in the Rodoviária; to **Curitiba**, 6 hrs., US$9 (leito, 18); to **Blumenau**, 9½ hrs., US$15; to **Porto Alegre**, 18 hrs., US$25 (leito, 48); **Rio Grande** 25 hrs., US$30 (leito 55); to **Belo Horizonte**, 10 hrs., US$16 (leito, 32); buy ticket and get on bus at Terminal Bresser, T 61.084-018; to **Ouro Preto**, daily, 11 hrs US$20. **Salvador**, 30 hrs., US$50 (leito, 100); to **Recife**, 40 hrs., US$67 (leito, 134); to **Fortaleza**, 48 hrs. US$67 (leito 146); to **Natal**, US$65, 55 hrs.; to **Cuiabá**, 24 hrs., US$36 (Andorinha at 1700, connects with Cuiabá-Porto Velho bus); to **Campo Grande** (Mato Grosso do Sul), 16 hrs., US$22; to **Porto Velho**, 60 hrs. (or more), US$75; to **Brasília**, 15 hrs., US$20 (leito, 40); to **Foz do Iguaçu**, 16 hrs., US$24 (leito, 50). To **Santos**, US$2.40 (there is a bus station for Santos and São Vicente at the southern end of the Metro line, at Jabaquara, buses from here leave every 5 minutes, taking about 50 minutes); **São Sebastião**, 4 hrs. US$6.40 (say "via Bertioga" if you want to go by the coast road, beautiful journey but few buses take this route—ferry from São Sebastião for Ilhabela); to **Parati, Angra dos Reis**, 2 daily, 8 hrs., US$10.

To **Montevideo**, via Porto Alegre, with TTL, departs 2200, 31 hrs. US$45 (leito 90—early booking recommended) cold a/c at night, plenty of meal stops, bus stops for border formalities, passengers disembark only to collect passport and tourist card on Uruguayan side. To **Buenos Aires** 36 hrs., US$70 (leito, 140); to **Santiago**, Pluma or Gral. Urquiza (both start from Rio), 56 hrs., US$110 (leito US$220); to **Asunción** (1,044 km.), 18 hours with Pluma or RYSA, US$28 (leito US$56).

**Air Services** There are air services to all parts of Brazil, Europe, North and South America from the new international airport at Guarulhos, also known as Cumbica, Av. Monteiro Lobato 1985, T 945-2111 (30 km. from the city); Money exchanges open 0800-2200 daily, post office, etc, 2 information booths. The local airport of Congonhas, 14 km. from the city centre, is used for the Rio-São Paulo shuttle, some flights to Vitória and private flights only. From Guarulhos there are airport taxis which charge US$32 on a ticket system. Metro bus service every 25 mins. to Guarulhos from Praça da República (NW side, corner of R. Arouche), US$7, very comfortable (in airport buy ticket at booth in Domestic Arrivals); cheap buses from Bresser and Jabaquara bus terminals to Guarulhos, without luggage space, usually crowded. Metro bus trip to the Rodoviária do Tietê and Congonhas airport, every 20-40 mins., approx. 1 hr. Inter-airport bus US$10. There are about four hundred flights per week to Rio de Janeiro (US153 return). All airline offices in triangle formed by Av. São Luís, Av. Ipiranga and R. da Consolação. Amex provides free transport for cardholders from airports to city centre.

**Air freight** Pan Am, at Carga Aérea Terminal, T531-4366/4052/9602, has a small package "sprint" service to the USA, max 30 kg., US$4.46/kg., but not for business purchases (for these you need an export broker)—open Mon.-Fri. 0900-1800. Varig will send anything, anywhere, for US$6.65/kg. (cheaper if paid in new cruzeiros), but involves more red tape, office next to Pan Am.

**The Butantã Snake Farm and Museum** Av. Dr. Vital Brasil 1500, Pinheiros, is the most popular tourist attraction. The snakes are milked for their poison six times a day but you may not witness this; the antidotes made from the venom have greatly reduced deaths from snakebite in Brazil. It also deals with spider and scorpion venom, has a small hospital and is a biomedical research institute. Open daily from 0900-1700 (except Mon.), entrance US$1.50. Informative museum (closed for renovation until Dec. 1991); details in English and Portuguese. From Praça da República take bus marked "Butantã" or "Cidade Universitária" (Nos. 701U or 7018) along Av. Paulista, and ask to be let out at Instituto Butantã.

**Parque da Independência**, in the suburb of Ipiranga, contains the famous Ipiranga Monument to commemorate the declaration of Brazilian independence; beneath the monument is the Imperial Chapel, with the tomb of the first emperor, Dom Pedro I, and Empress Leopoldina (open Tues.-Sun., 1300-1700). Take bus 4612 from Praça da República. The **Casa do Grito**, the little house in which Dom Pedro I spent the night before his famous cry of **Ipiranga**— **"Independence or Death"**—is preserved in the park (open Tues.-Sun. 0930-1700). The **Museu Paulista**, housed in a huge palace at the top of the park, has old maps, traditional furniture, collections of old coins and of religious art and rare documents, and a department of Indian ethnology. Behind the Museum is the Ipiranga Botanical Garden. Open Tues.-Sun. and holidays, 0930-1700. Take bus 478-P (Ipiranga-Pompéia for return) from Ana Rosa. There is a *son et lumière* show on Brazilian history in the park on Wed., Fri. and Sat. evenings at 2030.

**Parque do Estado** (Jardim Botânico), out at Água Funda (Av. Miguel Estefano 3687), has a vast garden esplanade surrounded by magnificent stone porches, with lakes and trees and places for picnics, and a very fine orchid farm worth seeing during the flowering season, November-December. Over 32,000 different kinds of orchids are cultivated. Open Tue.-Fri., 0900-1130, 1230-1700, Sat.-Sun. 0900-1600. The astronomical observatory nearby is open to the public Thurs. afternoons. Take metro to São Judas on Jabaquara line and bus from there.

**Zoological Gardens**   Av. Miguel Estefano 4241, near the Jardim Botânico, not more than half an hour's drive from the city centre. A very large variety of specimens can be seen in an almost natural setting of about 35 hectares of forest: a most interesting site. Open 0900-1700, admission US$0.45 (bus 4742, "Jardim Celeste", from São Judas). There is a wild-life park, Simba Safari, nearby, admission US$0.80 per pedestrian, US$2 p.p. with a car, open Tues.-Fri. 1000-1700, Sat.-Sun. 0900-1700.

**Aquarium**   The one formerly on Av. Pacaembu has closed, but the "Exotiquarium" on the bottom level of the Morumbi Shopping Centre claims to be the largest in South America, US$2; it has a pink river dolphin; open 1000-2200 (bus from Praça da República).

**Parque Água Branca** (Avenida Água Branca 455) has beautiful gardens with specimens of tropical plants, Brazilian birds and wild life. Pavilions house a well stocked aquarium, a zoo, and exhibitions of food produce.

In Tremembé, a little beyond Cantareira, half an hour from the down-town area, is the **Horto Florestal** (R. do Horto, in Parque Estadual da Cantareira, 7,900 ha.), containing examples of nearly every species of Brazilian woodland flora, 15 km. of natural trails, museum with exhibits of regional flora and fauna, view of São Paulo from Pedra Grande on the right of entrance to the park (admission US$0.80, daily, 0700-1730).

**Santo Amaro Dam**   (Old Lake), is 3 km. from the centre of Santo Amaro suburb. This is a popular boating resort with several sailing clubs and many attractive cottages along the shore. There is a bus (30 min.) from São Paulo to Santo Amaro.

**Interlagos** (Av. Interlagos, T 577-0522), which has a motor-racing circuit with 18 km. of track, is São Paulo's lake resort on the Santo Amaro dam. It can be reached from Santo Amaro by bus. Close to the track, where the Brazilian Grand Prix takes place every second year, usually in February, is the 32-km. long Guarapiranga artificial lake with good restaurants and several luxurious sailing and sports clubs (Av. Guarapiranga 575, open 0600-1700 daily). Camping Clube do Brasil site. Guarapiranga is less polluted than the other artificial lake, Billings, which also has restaurants.

*Pico de Jaraguá* (1,135 metres) the highest peak in the neighbourhood, gives good views of Greater São Paulo on a fine day. Lots of hang gliding here at weekends, many people go to watch. This peak is reached from Km. 18 on the Campinas highway (Via Anhanguera) by a good road through Taipas and Pirituba.

*Embu*, 28 km. from São Paulo, is a colonial town which has become a centre for artists and craftsmen. On Sunday afternoons there is a large and popular arts and crafts fair (0900-1800); not to be missed. Buses from close to the Largo de Pinheiros, São Paulo, or Santo Amaro bus.

## The Coast of the State of São Paulo

*Santos*, 63 km. SE of São Paulo and 5 km. from the open sea, is the most important Brazilian port. (Over 40% by value of all Brazilian imports and about half the total exports pass through it.) It is reached from Rio by ship (320 km.) in 12-15 hrs., and a direct highway between the two cities has been completed (**see** pages 330 and 367). A railway (no passenger service) and the Anchieta and Imigrantes highways run to São Paulo. A free-port zone for Paraguay, 1,930 km. by rail or road, has been established. A few km. outside the city there is an important industrial area round the steelworks, oil refinery and hydroelectric plant at Cubatão (known locally as the Valley of Death because of the pollution from chemical factories, among the worst in the world).

The plain upon which Santos, a city of 411,000 people, stands is an island which can be circumnavigated by small boats. The city has impressive modern buildings, wide, tree-lined avenues, and wealthy suburbs. The streets around Praça Mauá are very busy in the daytime, with plenty of cheap shops. In the centre, an interesting building is the Bolsa Oficial de Café, in R. 15 de Novembro. The night-life can best be seen in the Gonzaga area which has the large hotels. Although best known for its commerce, Santos is also a holiday resort, with magnificent beaches, all declared polluted at the end of 1990, and views. The port is approached by the winding Santos Channel; at its mouth is an old fort (1709). It is sometimes possible to visit naval ships, for details see the local press.

There are many monuments: one in Avenida Ana Costa to commemorate the brothers Andradas, who took a leading part in the movement for independence; one in the Praça Rui Barbosa to Bartolomeu de Gusmão, who has a claim to the world's first historically recorded airborne ascent in 1709; one in the Praça da República to Bras Cubas, who founded the city in 1534; and one in the Praça José Bonifácio to the soldiers of Santos who died in the Revolution of 1932. There are a disappointing municipal aquarium on Av. Bartolomeu de Gusmão (Ponta da Praia) and a Museu do Mar, R. República do Equador 81.

**Local Holidays** (in addition to national): 26 Jan. (Foundation of Santos); Good Friday; Corpus Christi.

**Hotels** *Parque Balneario*, complex at the centre of Gonzaga, Ana Costa 555, T (0132) 34-7211, Telex (13) 1241PBHS BR, A, with shopping centre; *Mendes Plaza*, Av. Floriano Peixoto 42, T (0132) 37-4243, Telex MHTX 13-3002, A; *Mendes Panorama*, R. Euclides da Cunha 15, T (0132) 37.2627, Telex MHTX 133003, B-C; *Atlântico*, Av. Pres. Wilson 1, T 37-8823, C, good value; *Gonzaga*, Av. Pres. Wilson 36, T 4-1411, D with bath; *Indaiá*, Av. Ana Costa 431, T 4-1134, C; *Transmontana*, R. Marechal Floriano Peixoto 202, rec.; *Maracanã Santos*, Pres. Wilson, 172, T 37-4030, beach front, C; *Avenida Palace*, Pres. Wilson 10, T 4-1166, beach front, C; *Santos*, Bartolomeu de Gusmão 16, C with bath; small, family-style hotels can be found in this area; many cheap hotels near the Orquidário Municipal, 1-2 blocks from the beach. *Vilazul*, Av. Sen Feijo, nr. Rodoviária, F, clean, a/c, breakfast.

**Restaurants** *Cibus*, Av Conselleiro Nébias, beach end, considered the best; *Hong Kong Palace*, Av. Conselheiro Nébias 288 (Chinese food); *Penhasco*, Ilha Porchat; first class *Pizzaria Zi Tereza*, Av. Ana Costa 451; *Churrascaria Tertúlia*, N0190, T (0132) 36-1461.

**Electric Current** 220 A.C. 60 cycles.

**Taxis** All taxis are supplied with meters. The fare is a fixed charge of US$0.40 plus US$0.15 per km. Taxi, Gonzaga to bus station, US$3.20.

**Banks** Banco Internacional, R. General Câmara 24; Banco Holandês Unido, Citibank, Banco do Brasil, all in the R. 15 de Novembro. The First National Bank of Boston, Praça Visc. de Mauá 14. Banks open: 1000-1630.

**Exchange Houses** Casa Faro, R. 15 de Novembro, 80 & 260; Casa Bancaria Branco, Praça de República 29 and Gonzaga, R Galeão Carvalhal 52/4.

**Consulates** British, R. Tuiuti 58, 2nd floor, Caixa Postal 204, 11010 Santos-SP, T 33-6111/34-6656. Danish, R. Frei Gaspar 22, 10th floor, 106, CP 726-11001, T 355-165, open 1000-1100, 1500-1700.

**All Saints Church** Praça Washington 92, José Menino. Services in English held every Sun.

**Telecommunications** Embratel, Largo Senador Vergueiro 1 and 2.

**Tourist Information** Praça dos Expedicionários 10, 10th floor; booths at Aquarium, Rodoviária, Casa do Café, Orquidário Municipal.

**Coastal Shipping** Irregular services to Brazilian ports by Companhia de Navegação Lóide Brasileiro. Consult their agents, R. General Câmara 22, 2nd floor, conjunto 34.

**Rail** The British-built Santos a Jundiaí up the hill to São Paulo is one of the railway wonders of the world; it passes through Cubatão and then, running on toothed tracks up the escarpment, interesting hill scenery. Passenger services were reintroduced at weekends in 1991 (schedule given under São Paulo). From Ana Costa station, a Fepasa (mixed) train may be taken to Embu Guaçu from where there is a bus to São Paulo.

**Air Services** From São Paulo; Santos has no airport.

**Bus Services** Buses start for most suburbs from Praça Mauá, in the centre of the city. There are buses to **São Paulo** (50 mins., US$2.40) at intervals of approximately 15 mins., from the Rodoviária near city centre. Enquire about being picked up or put down outside usual terminal points. Express cars also run to São Paulo at regular intervals. Fare, US$4.40 each way, per passenger. (The two highways between São Paulo and Santos are sometimes seriously crowded, especially at rush hours and weekends.) Buses for Santos are caught in São Paulo in the Jabaquara bus station, not the new Rodoviária. There are direct buses to **Rio** (Normandy company, 6 a day, 7½ hrs., US$9.60, leito at 2230, US$19.20); to Rio along the coast road is via São Sebastião, Caraguatatuba, Ubatuba and Parati.

**Excursions** To the coasts E of Santos (Guarujá, Bertioga, Ilhabela) and SW (Praia Grande—the beach was officially declared polluted at the end of 1990, Itanhaém). Short excursion along the Guarujá road to José Menino for the orchid gardens in the Praça Washington (flowering Oct.-Feb.). There is an open-air cage containing humming-birds of 20 different species and the park is also a sanctuary for other birds.

The *Ilha Porchat*, a small island reached by a bridge at the far end of Santos/São Vicente bay, has beautiful views over rocky precipices, of the high seas on one side and of the city and bay on the other. The Praias dos Milionários and São Vincente were officially declared polluted at the end of 1990. At the summit is a splendid night club, the *Top House Restaurante e Discoteca*. No entrance fee but there is a minimum charge of US$8.

To **Alto da Serra**, the summit of the forest-clad mountain range; magnificent views. The return journey can be done in under 2 hrs. by road.

**Monte Serrat** A funicular railway to the summit, where there is a semaphore station and look-out post which reports the arrival of all ships in Santos harbour, was not operating in 1991. There is also a quaint old church, dedicated to Nossa Senhora da Monte Serrat, said to have performed many miracles. The top can be reached on foot. Seven shrines have been built on the way up; annual pilgrimages are made by the local people. Fine views.

*Guarujá* (pop. 186,000).The route from Santos to the resort of Guarujá is along Av. Conselheiro Nébias to the seafront, continuing along the beach to the Guarujá ferry (every 10 min., free for pedestrians) at Ponta da Praia. On the other side proceed as far as Turtle Bay. During the season and weekends there is a long delay at the Ponta da Praia vehicle ferry; to avoid this take the ferry on foot and get the bus on the Guarujá side; motor boats also cross for US$0.10. There is a strong undertow on nearly all the Guarujá beaches; the Jequiti-Mar beach (officially called Praia de Pernambuco) is the safest. Perequê beach was officially declared polluted at the end of 1990. Golf club at Guarujá. (Trolleybus from Praça Mauá in Santos to the ferry, then buses.)

Turn left in centre of Guarujá and drive less than 1 km. to reach *Delphin Hotel* (L) and its restaurant *La Popote* at the beginning of the long beach of Praia da Enseada. Close by, at Av. Miguel Stefano 999, is *Casa Grande Hotel*, luxury, L, in colonial style, with clean beach. Facing sea is the luxurious *Ferraretto Hotel*, A+ (night club, swimming pool). Camping Clube do Brasil site at Praia do Perequê (where the best fish restaurants are), near municipal nursery. Good *churrascaria* opposite Rodoviária.

The Jequiti-Mar holiday complex, 8 km. beyond Guarujá on the road to Bertioga, is extremely attractive. There are private beaches (excellent swimming and boating) and very fine fishing grounds, and chalet accommodation, A or B, according to size and situation. There is an excellent restaurant and two night clubs; they are open each weekend and every night from December to March, in the holiday season. 2 km. further north is a beach where fishing boats land their catch—a number of good seafood restaurants line the seafront.

There are good sea-food restaurants on the road to *Bertioga*, an attractive place, where the fort of São João houses the João Ramalho museum (bus Guarujá-Bertioga, 1 hr., US$0.30). (Hotels: *Marazul*, Av. Tomé de Souza 825; *Indaiá Praia*, same street, No. 1079, both B; restaurants include *Zezé & Duarte*.) The coastal road beyond Bertioga is paved, and the new Rio-Santos highway, 1-2 km. inland, is completed, and provides a good link to São Sebastião. Going NE, the beaches are Praia de Bertioga. Praia São Lourenço, Praia Guaratuba and Praia Boracéia (campsite, meals served). 30 km. beyond Boracéia is the beach resort of Maresia (hotels, campsite), from where it is 21 km. to **São Sebastião** (two buses a day from Rio, 0830 and 2300, to Rio 0600 and 2330, heavily booked in advance; 4 a day from Santos, 3½ hrs.; buses from São Paulo (US$6.40) run inland via São José dos Campos, unless you ask for the service via Bertioga, only 2 a day), and **(free ferry) to Ilhabela** (4 hrs. by bus from Santos, 3 a day, US$4.80). There is a Museu de Arte Sacra in the chapel of São Gonçalo in the town centre. Tourist Office; Av. Dr Altino Arantes 174, friendly and helpful except regarding Ilhabela. The São Sebastião beaches of São Francisco and Praia do Centro were officially declared polluted at the end of 1990; foreigners can stay in the Camping Clube do Brasil grounds for US$3 a night. 6 km. S of São Sebastião is Camping do Barraquecaba Bar de Mar de Lucas, rec. (*Hotel Roma*, on the main square, excellent, E and upwards, very well rec.; *Recanto dos Pássaros*, Porto Grande, both C; *Arrastão*, B with most facilities; *São Paulo*, E with breakfast, clean, friendly.) Ilhabela tends to be more expensive in season, when it is cheaper to stay in São Sebastião.

Half-way between Bertioga and São Sebastião, on the Praia de Juqueí beach, is *Hotel Timão*, B, German-owned, with excellent fish meals.

**Ilha de São Sebastião** (Ilhabela). The island of São Sebastião, known popularly as Ilhabela, is now easily accessible by car or bus from Santos. A bus runs along the coastal strip facing the mainland. Cavendish, the English pirate, had his secret anchorage in one of the sheltered caves there. Last century it was used as a landing place for illegal slave-traffic.

The island is of volcanic origin, roughly about 390 sq. km. in area. Its highest peak, Morro do Papagaio, rises 1,300 metres above sea-level, with its bare peak often obscured by mist; the slopes are densely wooded. There are many beautiful waterfalls, easily accessible to the enterprising walker. Most of the flatter ground is given over to sugar-cane.

The only settled district lies on the coastal strip facing the mainland, the Atlantic side being practically uninhabited except by a few fisherfolk. The place abounds in tropical plants and flowers of the most extraordinary variety, and many fruits grow wild, whose juice mixed with cachaça and sugar makes as delicious a cocktail as can be imagined.

No alterations are allowed to the frontage of the main township, **Ilhabela**. Visitors abound during summer week-ends; motorists are warned to avoid those days as the car-carrying capacity of the ferry is very limited.

The energetic can climb over the hump of the island down towards the Atlantic, sometimes through dense tropical forest following the old slave trail, but for this 50-km. return journey a local guide is required. There is a rough road to the Atlantic side, but it is very difficult to drive. A visit to the terraced Toca waterfalls amid dense jungle close to the foot of the 970-metre Baepi peak will give you cool freshwater bathing (entry, US$0.50). In all shady places, especially away from the sea, there abounds a species of midge known locally as *borrachudos*. A locally sold repellant (Autum) keeps them off for some time, however. Those allergic to insect bites should remain on the inhabited coastal strip.

**Hotels** in Ilhabela: *Mercedes*, L, T 72-1071; *Ilhabela*, L, T 72-1083, Av Pedro Paulo de Morais 151, rec., good breakfast. Next door is *Itapemar*, T 72-1329, windsurfing equipment rented at US$3 an hour, A. *Petit Village*, Morro da Cruz 241, T 72-1393, B; *Solar dos Bandeirantes*, Bertini 165, T 72-1065, C and *Colonial*, Av. Brasil 1541, T 72-1033, B; *Pousada dos Hibíscos*, Av. P.P. de Morais 714, T 72-1375, B, good atmosphere, swimming pool, rec. There are several other less expensive pensions in D/E range. *Camping Porto Seguro*, accessible by two-hourly bus from Ilhabela.

**Restaurant** *Perequê*, Av. Princesa Isabel 337, reasonable. *Farol*, Av. Princesa Isabel 1634, Perequê, good, especially seafood, rec.

**Sightseeing**  Visit the old Feiticeira plantation, with underground dungeons. The road is along the coast, sometimes high above the sea, towards the south of the island. You can go by bus, taxi, or horse and buggy.

**Pedras do Sino** (Bell Rocks) These curious seashore boulders, when struck with a piece of iron or stone, emit a loud bell-like note. Another campsite nearby.

**Bathing** Bathing on the mainland side is not recommended because of oil, sandflies and jelly fish on the beaches and in the water. Praia dos Castelhanos, reached by a rough road over the island (no buses), is recommended.

**Transport** Passenger ferry every 2 hours; stops at Perequê and Ilhabela; separate car ferry runs through the night and serves Perequê only.

North of São Sebastião, on the Santos-Rio road, is São Francisco, a village with *Pontal Hotel* (not rec., expensive, noisy), good beaches. Further on is **Caraguatatuba**, with 17 good beaches to the NE and SW (several hotels, popular at weekends, good restaurants: Good camping site on beach and other sites. Direct buses to Caraguatatuba from Rio de Janeiro, São Paulo and Santos; direct buses from São Paulo do not use the coast road. Further E is **Lagoinha**, 34 km. W of Ubatuba, with chalets and sailing boats for hire. Exotic birdlife and virgin forest. *Maier's Mar Virado* is owned by Hans Maier, who speaks English and arranges hirings. Next is **Ubatuba**, with two Camping Clube do Brasil sites at Maranduba and Perequê-Açu beaches. In all, there are 72 beautiful beaches (Iperoig, Itaguá and Saco da Ribeira were officially declared polluted at the end of 1990), quite spread out, most with campsites (Grande, just S, and one 6 km. N of Ubatuba are rec.). There is also a yacht haven. The area gets very crowded at Carnival time as people from Rio come to escape the crowds in their city. Jewellery market on beach, Sats.

**Ubatuba hotels** *Tropicana*, Praia da Enseada, T 42-0461, B; *Xaréu*, J.H. da Costa 413, T 32-1525, central near beach, D, clean, quiet, friendly, rec.; *Solar das Aguas Cantantes*, Praia do Lázaro (11680 S.P., T 0124-42-0288), reached by local bus, swimming pool, restaurant, A; *Saveiros*, Praia do Lázaro (T 0124-42-0172), pool, restaurant, A+, run by a Rumanian, Lucian Strass, English spoken, who welcomes users of *South American Handbook*; *Mauricio*, Av. Abreu Sodre 607, nr. Praia do Perequê-Açu, has cheap rooms, friendly, clothes washing possible; *Manobra Chalés*, very helpful. **Youth Hostel** Cora Coralina, Rodovia Oswaldo Cruz, Km. 89, T 229-3787/229-3011, extension (ramal) 286 for details. Furnished flats and cottages may be rented from Lúcio Martins Rodrigues, R. Amaral Gurgel 158, Apto. 121—CEP.01221, Vila Buarque, São Paulo; T 853-8101, 532-0496, 577-6482, 221-1357. The flats are in the town centre, 400 m. from beach, the cottages 7½ km. from the centre with a natural swimming pool, each can sleep a maximum of 5 (bedroom for 2-3, 2 extra in living room), and has kitchen with cooker and fridge, bathroom and laundry facilities; rates payable in US or Canadian dollars, or any Western European currency.

The road from São Sebastião is paved, so a journey from São Paulo along the coast is possible, 5 buses daily. 25 km. S of Ubatuba at Baia Fortaleza is *Refugio de Corsário*, T 43-1126, D and up, a clean quiet hotel on the water front, sailing and swimming, a good place to relax. Ubatuba is 70 km. from Parati (see page 331), several buses daily, on the hour, from *Lanchonete Nice*, near Rodoviária. If driving from Ubatuba along the coast to Rio, one can stop for lunch at Porto Aquarius, where there is a cave and hotel in a beautiful setting (not cheap). Direct buses from Rio, São Paulo and Santos.

Straddling the border of São Paulo and Rio de Janeiro states is the **Parque Nacional Serra da Bocaina**, which rises from the coast to heights of over 1,900 metres, encompassing three strata of vegetation (IBDF office, Al. Tietê 637, Caixa Postal 7134, CEP 01.312, São Paulo).

In the opposite direction (SW) from Santos, it is 50 km. beside the Praia Grande to the town of **Itanhaém**, with its pretty colonial church and semi-ruined Convento da Conceição on a small hill. There are several good sea-food restaurants along the beach, and a Camping Clube do Brasil site nearby at Peruíbe beach, and many others which are cheaper. There are many attractive beaches here, and hot springs with medicinal mud (hotels *Maison Suisse*, *Príncipe*, *Glória*). The whole stretch of coast is completely built up with holiday developments. The beach of Itanhaém was officially declared polluted at the end of 1990. Frequent buses from Santos US$1.30, 1 hr.

Further south is the town of **Iguape**, founded in 1538. Typical Portuguese architecture, the small municipal museum is housed in a 16th century building. Buses from São Paulo, Santos, or Curitiba, changing at Registro (see below). It has a market, hotels and restaurants. (*Hotel Pousada Aguape*, R. Padre Homer,

E, good; *Hotel Rio Verde*, E, rec.). Camping Clube do Brasil site on beach. Opposite Iguape is the northern end of the Ilha Comprida with beautiful beaches stretching SW for 86 km. A continuous ferry service runs from Iguape (passengers free; cars at a small charge); buses run until 1900 from the ferry stop to the beaches and campsite Britânia (clean, friendly, drinkable tap water, tastes bad). The island is being developed as a resort; good restaurants, hotels, supermarket—fresh fish is excellent. At the southern end **Cananéia** is more commercialized than Iguape; it has 3 or 4 hotels (mostly D).

From Iguape it is possible to take a boat trip down the coast to Cananéia and Ariri. Tickets and information from Dept. Hidroviário do Estado, R. Major Moutinho 198, Iguape, T 41 1122. Boats leave Iguape on Mon., Thurs. (but check in advance), returning next day, or bus back from Cananéia. It is a beautiful trip, passing between the island and the mainland. The boat has a toilet, fresh water, and meals. In wet weather, the cabin gets crowded and uncomfortable. Ariri has no road connections; there is a hostel, F, run by the shipping line.

**Caves** Inland, W of the BR-116 are the caverns of the Vale do Ribeira; among the best known is the 8-km. Gruta da Tapagem, known as Caverna do Diabo (Devil's Cave—as huge "as a cathedral" with well-lit formations), 45 km. from Eldorado Paulista. The caves are open 0800-1100 and 1200-1700; bar and toilets. *Hotel Eldorado*, friendly, clean, with breakfast, E. Bus to Eldorado Paulista from Santos or São Paulo, US$4.10, 4-5 hrs., then hitch-hike on banana trucks or tourist buses (which run from both cities); most traffic on Sats. and Suns. From Curitiba, change buses at Jacupiranga for Eldorado Paulista. A suitable stopping place for visiting the caves area is **Registro** on BR-116, in the heart of the tea-growing region, populated mainly by Japanese Brazilians. (*Lito Palace Hotel*, D; *Hotel Continental*, F; *Hotel Brasília*, R. Brasília, round corner from Rodoviária, F, no breakfast, shower, clean, quiet; good *Churrascaria* next to bus station,). 43 km. from Caverna do Diabo is Caverna de Santana, 10 km. from the town of Iporanga; it has 5.6 km. of subterranean passages and three levels of galleries. (Iporanga is the most convenient town for visiting both sets of caves; it is 42 km. from Apiaí, which is 257 km. SW of São Paulo.)

## Towns in the State of São Paulo

About 13% of Brazil's population lives within 200 km. of São Paulo city, a circle which includes 88 municipalities. Four of them—the big ABCD towns— sharing a population of over a million, are Santo André, São Bernardo, São Caetano and Diadema; they have many of the largest industrial plants. There are some 70 cities in the State with populations of over 50,000 and São Paulo is linked with all of them by road, and several of them by railway. One important line, the broad-gauge Santos a Jundiaí, runs from Santos to São Paulo and across the low mountains which separate São Paulo city from the interior to its terminus at **Jundiaí** (pop. 315,000), 58 km. from São Paulo, which has textile factories and other industries. The district grows coffee and grain and there is an annual Grape Festival.

**Hotel** *Grande Hotel*, R. do Rosário 605, T 434-5355, with good restaurant.

A metre-gauge railway line now links Campinas and Brasília.

**Campinas** (pop. 850,000), 88 km. from São Paulo by the fine Via Anhanguera highway (many buses, US$2.50), is important as a clearing point for coffee, for its Agricultural Institute, and its rapidly growing industries. The Viracopos international airport is 11 km. from Campinas, which also has its own airport.

See fine cathedral, old market, colonial buildings, several museums (including Arte Contemporânea, Arquidiocesano, Carlos Gomes and, in the Bosque de Jequitibás, Histórico and Folclore), arts centre (noted symphony orchestra; the city is the birthplace of the noted 19th century Brazilian composer Carlos Gomes), and the modern university outside the city. Visits can be made to the Agricultural Institute to see all the aspects of coffee. A tourist train operates in Parque Taquaral.

**Hotels** *Royal Palm Plaza* Praça Rotatória 88, T 2-9085, L; *Vila Rica*, R. Donato Paschoal 100, T 31-5242, L; *Savoy*, R. Regente Feijó 1064, T 32-9444, A; *Opala Avenida*, Av. Campos Sales 161, T 8-4115, central, C. *Solar das Andorinhas*, a health farm with pool, sauna, horses, sports, etc. 18 km. outside city on the Mogi-Mirim road, L, with meals, T 39-4411. Many cheap hotels near Rodoviária, *Pensão Bandeirantes*, Av B. de Itapura, friendly, said to be the best of a bad bunch.

**Restaurants** *Bar Restaurante Barão*, Barão de Jaguará 1381 and *Churrascaria Gaúcha*, Av. Dr Campos Sales 515, excellent for Brazilian food. *Cenat*, R. Barão de Jaguara 1260, 2nd floor, closed Sat. (and Fri. for dinner).

**Shopping** H. Stern jewellers at Shopping Centre Iguatemi.

**Banks** Lloyds Bank, R. General Osório 859. The **First National Bank of Boston**, Av. Francisco Glicério 1275, and local banks. Open 1000-1630. Good rates at Valortec, T 311555; **Amex**, with Kontik Franstur, Av. Moraes Sales 711, 8th floor, T 317466.

**Community Church** Services in English at School of Language and Orientation, R. Eduardo Lane 270.

**Transport** Trains and buses to São Paulo, Ribeirão Preto, Araguari and Brasília, buses to Rio de Janeiro, 7 hrs., US$9.50. The metre-gauge Mogiana line, connecting with the broad-gauge Paulista at Campinas, serves the north-eastern part of the state. It goes through Ribeirão Preto to Uberlândia and Araguari in the Triângulo of Minas Gerais, a great area for fattening beasts which are trucked to the *frigoríficos* of São Paulo. No São Paulo-Ribeirão Preto tickets are sold, so you may have to wait a day at Campinas for a connection (or go by bus). From Araguari there is a line into the state of Goiás and to Brasília (train from Campinas daily except Sunday). 25 km. from Campinas, at Jaguariúna, is a railway preservation group with steam engines and wagons; hourly bus from Campinas US$0.80, or take the steam train itself from Campinas (station behind Carrefour, Anhumas, reached by town bus), Sat. and Sun., T 53-6067 for schedule. A light railway was due to open in Campinas in March 1991.

*Americana* (pop. 56,000), an interesting town, is 42 km. from Campinas. This area was settled by Confederate refugees from the south of the USA after the Civil War. Most of the original settlers soon returned to the States, but some stayed, and there still exist reminders of their occupation here. A visit to the cemetery reveals an unusual number of English surnames. (*Hotel Cacique*, R. Wáshington Luís 143, E.)

*Ribeirão Preto* (pop. 385,000), the centre of a rich coffee-growing district, also has a steel industry. The town is 402 km. from São Paulo by rail via Campinas or paved road (5 hrs. by bus); airport has TAM flights to São Paulo, Rio, Poços de Caldas. Altitude, 420 metres. It is a distribution centre for the interior of São Paulo State and certain districts in Minas Gerais and Goiás. Products: coffee, cotton, sugar, grain and rice.

**Hotels** *Stream Palace*, R. General Osório 850, T 636-0660, B, with TV; *Umuarama Recreio*, Praça dos Cafeeiros 140, T 637-3790, 6 km. from centre, very pleasant, pool, gardens, C; *Brasil*, R. General Osório 20, E; *Holiday Inn*, R. Alvares Cabral 1200, T 625-0186, A+-L.

All the southern part of the state and most of its western part are served by the metre-gauge Sorocabana railway. The main line runs from São Paulo through Sorocaba to Bauru, where it connects with the Noroeste, to Corumbá, 1,223 km. The line from a junction near Sorocaba extending (through connections with other lines) across the southern states to the border with Uruguay is for freight only.

*Sorocaba* (pop. 327,000), 110 km. west of São Paulo, is an important industrial centre. The altitude is 540 metres, and the climate temperate. It has textile mills; produces cement, fertilizers, footwear, hats, alcohol, wines; there are railway workshops, extensive orange groves and packing house installations. It is an important cotton centre. Other products are timber, sugar, cereals, coffee, and minerals. Communications with São Paulo are better by road than by rail; the Castello Branco highway passes nearby.

**Hotels** *Terminus*, Av. General Carneiro 474, T 32-6970, C; *Manchester*, R. 15 de Novembro 21, E, basic, friendly; *São Paulo*, cheap, TV extra, breakfast is all sweet.

There is a picturesque paved road along the Tietê valley from São Paulo to Bauru, via the colonial towns of Pirapora and Itu.

***Pirapora de Bom Jesus*** is a popular place of pilgrimage, in a most attractive setting on both sides of the river. ***Itu*** was founded by the Bandeirantes in the 17th century. The beautiful falls of Salto de Itu, 8 km. N, are flanked by a park and a textile mill.

**Itu Hotels**  *International*, R. Barão do Itaím 93, D; *Sabará*, Praça Padre Miguel 90, E.

**Camping**  *Casarão do Carmo*, km. 95 on the Jundiaí road; Itu, at km. 90 on the Cabreúva road.

***Bauru*** (pop. 220,000) was founded at the end of the last century. Its points of interest include the Horto Florestal, an experimental forestry station opened in 1928, the Vitória Regia amphitheatre in the Parque das Nações and the Tenrikyo temple, R. Newton Prado. It is used by Paulistanos as a weekend resort. Currency exchange is difficult.

**Hotels**  *Bekassin*, Av. Duque de Caxias 1717, T 24-3700, swimming pool, B; *Colonial*, Praça Rui Barbosa 248, T 22-3191, D; *Alvorada Palace*, R. Primeiro de Agosto 619, T 22-5900, C. Cheaper ones too, such as *Hotel Português* near bus station. Opp. railway station, *Lisboa*, E, clean, hot shower, restaurant, rec., very friendly; to right of railway station exit is *Cariani*, E, clean, good breakfast, rec. *Phenix*, near railway station, E.

**Restaurant**  *H 2 Churrascaria* Piauí 8-55; *Cantina Bello Nápoli*, 1° de Agosto 6-52, cheap. Homemade ice-cream at sorveteria near *Hotel Lisboa*.

**Rail**  to São Paulo, 4 a day (6½ to 7½ hrs., compared with Expresso da Prata bus to São Paulo, 5 hrs, US$8. Many timetable changes on this route, so check in advance. Trains to **Corumbá** via Campo Grande, scheduled to be reduced. There are no reliable connections between São Paulo-Bauru and Bauru-Corumbá or Campo Grande trains in either direction.

***Marília***, W of Bauru, is a pleasant clean town with a good hotel, *Sun Valley Park Hotel*, B, friendly. Texaco garage rec. for car repairs, top of hill, Japanese owner. Express trains run to São Paulo, 4 a day, 1 night train with sleeper.

***Ourinhos*** (pop. 100,000), founded in 1924 near the border with Paraná state, is surrounded by sugar cane plantations. It is a useful stop-over on the road from São Paulo to Foz do Iguaçu or Campo Grande (Hotels *Palace*, 5 stars; *Comercial*, R. Amornio Prado 38, E, friendly; a *dormitório* near the railway station; 6 restaurants, *Donna Maria*, rec.). It is on the railway which runs to Presidente Epitácio (**see page 400**) on the Paraná river. Further west is **Presidente Prudente**, another useful place to make bus connections for Campo Grande (US$14), Porto Alegre and São Paulo; also to Ribeirão Preto, US$12.50, 9 hrs. *Hotel Aruá*, A, single rooms poor but doubles said to be nice. *Hotel Alves* opp. bus station, E, clean, nice but noisy. Beware of assaults and pickpockets.

***Serra Negra*** (pop. 19,000) is a very pleasant spa town and summer holiday resort up in the mountains at 1,080 metres, 145 km. from São Paulo. Visitors tour the countryside in horse-drawn buggies. There are many first class hotels, a balneário and a small zoo.

**Hotels**  *Rádio Hotel*, T 92-3311, L, very nice indeed, and several others.

Near Serra Negra is the even better-known spa town of Lindóia, whose still waters are bottled and sent all over Brazil.

Another weekend resort, 70 km. north of São Paulo on the Dom Pedro I highway, is ***Atibaia***; nearby is the strangely-shaped Pedra Grande mountain summit. There are two campsites, Pedra Grande and Taba, which is near the *Hotel Village Eldorado* (with sports facilities, American-plan accommodation).

***Campos do Jordão*** (pop. 33,000), between Rio de Janeiro and São Paulo, is a mountain resort at 1,710 metres, in the Serra da Mantiqueira. It is prettily set in a long valley. The climate is cold and dry in winter and cool in summer, a great relief from the coastal heat and humidity. There are many hotels; but no airport, as yet.

The resort, about 190 km. from São Paulo, is reached by an 87 km. paved road from São José dos Campos, 100 km. from São Paulo, on the Presidente Dutra

(BR-116) highway. By car it takes about 3 hrs. from São Paulo, 6 to 7 from Rio de Janeiro.

**Places of Interest** Palácio Boa Vista, 4 km. from Abernéssia Centre, Governor's residence and museum, open Wed., Sat., Sun., 1000-1200, 1400-1700; Pedra do Baú (1,950 metres), to get there take a bus to São Bento do Sapucaí at 0800 or 1500, then walk to Paiol Grande and then on an unmarked path to the Pedra. Return buses from São Bento at 0915 and 1615. Near Paiol Grande is the small waterfall of Cachoeira dos Amores. Pico do Itapeva (2,030 metres) and Imbiri (1,950 metres) command a beautiful view of the Paraíba valley; see also Morro do Elefante (chairlift available); Gruta dos Crioulos; nature reserve at Horto Florestal (20 km.), signposted from chairlift station, very pretty —go in the morning to avoid crowds; lots of streams with bridges, waterfalls nearby. Campos do Jordão is a popular place for hikers; most of the roads leading off the main avenue lead to quiet areas with nice views, e.g. up Av. Dr. Antônio Nicola Padula, turn left 500 metres past Refugio na Serra for waterfalls and Pico do Itapeva. The villages of Emílio Ribas and São Cristóvão are connected by a railcar which runs frequently, US$0.15.

**Hotels** *Toriba*, Av. E Diederichsen, T 62-1566; *Vila Inglesa*, Sen. R. Simonsen, T 63-1955; *Refúgio Alpino*, T 63-1660, and others at Capivari. *Refugio na Serra*, Av. Dr. Antônio Nicola Padula 275, T 63-1330, C, comfortable, good breakfast, very helpful owners (some English spoken), rec.; Youth Hostel, R. Diogo de Carvalho 86, T 229-3787/3011, ramal 286; membership card and permission from Dr. Fernando at Tourist Office in the bus terminal required. Camping Clube do Brasil site in the Descansópolis district. Book accommodation in advance if going June/July.

**Restaurants** *Sole Mio* (on road to Horto Florestal), Italian, big portions; *Baden Baden*, German, good. Good cheese on sale at a shop just past sports centre on way out of town, also jams and chocolates; plenty of other chocolate shops. "Milbaho" mineral water is produced here.

Stalls on main square Thurs.-Sun. sell local produce. Exchange at Geneve Sweater shop, or Cadij Imóveis, "if they want to", check rates.

**Transport** Bus from **São Paulo**, US$4.80, 3 hrs.; from **Rio**, changing at São José dos Campos, US$8. No through rail service: railcars make round trips between Campos do Jordão and Santo Antônio do Pinhal, in season between 0800 and 0900 and at 1310, out of season (Oct.-Nov., March-April) at 1310 only, a bit bumpy, but beautiful views (sit on the right on the way there, left coming back): hills, valleys, tight corners. The train is very crowded even though you are assigned a seat; fare US$1.30 (buy ticket in advance, and get return immediately on arrival in San Antônio; watch your belongings on board). Whole trip takes about 3 hrs.: 1 hr. each way on train, 40 mins.-1 hr. in Santo Antônio (not much on offer there: a few snack bars, nice views, statue of Madonna and Child). There is a local railcar service within São José (very crowded but cheap). From Pindamonhangaba buses run to **São Paulo** and **Taubaté**; also to **Aparecida do Norte**, 1030, US$1.60. The short road down to "Pinda", starting from the paved road 24 km. SW of Campos do Jordão, is now paved (5 buses daily, 50 mins.). Railcar to **Pinda** leaves 1705 Mon.-Thurs. and weekends, from Pinda 0600 Tues.-Fri., 0930 weekends. A new road branching off the BR-116 near Caçapava provides a quicker drive from Rio, or São Paulo, than the route via São José dos Campos.

Nearer to Rio than the Pindamonhangaba turn, just off the BR-116, is ***Aparecida do Norte***, Brazil's chief place of pilgrimage and the seat of its patron saint, Nossa Senhora Aparecida. This small black image of the Virgin is said to have been taken by a fisherman from the nearby River Paraíba, and quickly acquired a miraculous reputation. It is now housed in a huge modern basilica in Romanesque style on top of a hill, with the clean white-walled, red-roofed town below.

For the route to the Paraná River, from São Paulo to Presidente Epitácio, **see page 400**.

## SOUTHERN BRAZIL (6)

This consists, from S to N, of the three states of Rio Grande do Sul, Santa Catarina and Paraná. Rio Grande do Sul is *gaúcho* (cowboy) country; it is also Brazil's chief wine producer. Throughout the south European settlement, especially from Germany, heavily influences

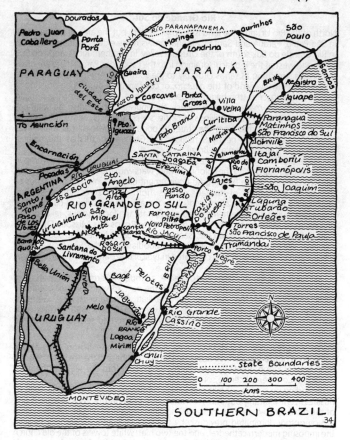

SOUTHERN BRAZIL

34

cultural and agricultural activity. The coast offers a variety of beaches and scenery while in the far west is one of Latin America's major natural attractions, the Iguaçu falls, and one of its largest manmade constructions, the Itaipu dam.

The conformation of the land is not unlike what it is further north; the Great Escarpment runs down the coastal area as far as Porto Alegre, receding from the coast in a wide curve between Paranaguá and Florianópolis. South of Tubarão to the borders of Uruguay the hills of southern Rio Grande do Sul, which never rise higher than 900 to 1,000 metres, are fringed along the coast by sand bars and lagoons.

## Rio Grande do Sul

North of the Rio Uruguai the land is deeply forested, but the area of prairie, small in São Paulo, Paraná and Santa Catarina, grows more extensive than the forest in Rio Grande do Sul, south of the Uruguai valley. In southern Rio Grande do Sul, south and west of the Rio Jacuí (draining into the Lagoa dos Patos) there are great grasslands stretching as far as Uruguay to the south and Argentina to the west. This is the distinctive land of the *gaúcho*, or cowboy (pronounced ga-oo-shoo in Brazil), of *bombachas* (the baggy trousers worn by the *gaúcho*), of the poncho and *ximarão* (or *mate* without sugar), the indispensable drink of southern cattlemen. There are many millions of cattle, sheep and pigs, and some 75% of all Brazilian wine comes from the state. Its population (who all call themselves *gaúchos*) now number nearly 9 million. Rio Grande do Sul has the highest proportion of literate people in Brazil.

There are three sharply contrasted types of colonization and land owning in Rio Grande do Sul. During the colonial period, wars with the Spaniards of Uruguay were frequent, and the Portuguese government brought into the grasslands of the south a number of military settlers from the Azores; these soldiers inter-married with the Brazilian herdfolk in the area. In the colonial period, also, the Jesuits built several settlements to acculturate the local Indians; relics of this process include the impressive ruins of the **Sete Povos das Missões Orientais** (São Borja, São Nicolau, São Luiz, São Lourenço, São Miguel, São João, Santo Ángelo). West from Porto Alegre, in the floodlands of the Rio Jacuí and its tributary, the Rio Taquari, rice is cultivated in typical Brazilian fashion: large estates with tenant workers.

At São Leopoldo, north of Porto Alegre, a group of Germans were settled in 1824 on their own small farms, and during the next 25 years over 20,000 more were brought into the area by the Brazilian Government. The Germans concentrated on rye, maize, and pigs. Between 1870 and 1890, settlers from northern Italy arrived, bringing viticulture with them, and settled north of the Germans at Alfredo Chaves and Caxias do Sul.

**Porto Alegre**, (pop. 1,275,000), capital of Rio Grande do Sul, lies at the confluence of five rivers which flow into the Rio Guaíba and thence into the great fresh-water lagoon, the Lagoa dos Patos, which runs into the sea. It is the most important commercial centre south of São Paulo.

Standing on a series of hills and valleys on the banks of the Guaíba, with its business centre jutting out into the water on a promontory, Porto Alegre is one of the most up-to-date cities in Brazil. The older residential part of the town is on a promontory dominated previously by the Palácio Piratini (Governor's Palace), the imposing modern cathedral, and the two high white towers of the old church of Nossa Senhora das Dores, but Governor and God have now been utterly dwarfed by the skyscraper of the Assembléia Legislativa. The streets in the centre are famous for their steep gradients. The climate is temperate through most of the year, though the temperature at the height of summer can often exceed 40°C. The surrounding suburbs are very pleasant. For instance, Ipanema, on the banks of the Guaíba, has a selection of bars and small restaurants; a popular rendezvous, with spectacular sunsets over the river.

Do not miss that section of the R. dos Andradas (R. da Praia) that is now permanently closed to traffic. It is the city's principal outdoor meeting place, the main shopping area, and by around 1600 it is full of people; at the peak hour of

---

**Porto Alegre: Key to map**

1. Parque Farroupilha; 2. Praça Senador Florência; 3. Praça 15 de Novembro; 4. Praça Mal. Deodoro; 5. Cathedral; 6. Prefeitura; 7. University; 8. São Pedro Theatre; 9. Palácio Piratini; 10. Mercado Público; 11. Alfândega; 12. Júlio de Castilhos Museum; 13. Post Office, Embratel; 14. Telephone Office; 15. Epatur Tourist Offices (x2); 16. Touring Club do Brasil; 17. *Hotel São Luiz*; 18. *Hotel Vitória*; 19. *Hotel Palácio*.

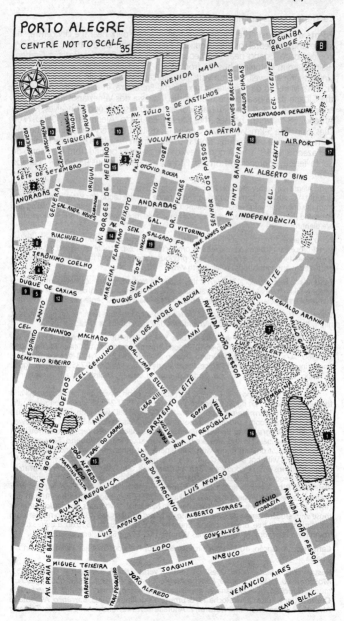

PORTO ALEGRE
CENTRE NOT TO SCALE 35

1900 the street is jammed for about 6 blocks.

**Points of Interest** The Parque Farroupilha, a fine park near the city centre; the interesting cathedral of the Anglican-Episcopal church of Brazil; the Jardim Zoológico do Estado near São Leopoldo (bus US$0.80), the Botanic Gardens (Bairro Jardim Botânico, bus 40 from Praça 15 de Novembro) and the Cidade Universitária are well worth a visit. The Mercado Público (said to be a replica of Lisbon's Mercado da Figueira) is next to the Prefeitura, in the centre of town. In the Cidade Baixa quarter are the colonial Travessa dos Venezianos (between RR. Lopo Gonçalves and Joaquim Nabuco) and the house of Lopo Gonçalves, R. João Alfredo 582, which houses the Museu do Porto Alegre, free, 0900-1700 Tues.-Sun. The 5-km. wide River Guaíba lends itself to every form of boating and there are several sailing clubs. Boat trips leave from Av. Maúa opp. the Ministério de Fazendo, US$3, 1 hr. A good view of the city may be had from the Morro de Santa Teresa, approached from Av. Padre Cacique (take bus 95 from R. Salgado Filho).

Porto Alegre is a fresh-water port for ocean-going vessels of up to 7,000 tons and 4.87 metres draught. Vessels must come up through Rio Grande and the Lagoa dos Patos, some 275 km. from the open sea. Large areas of reclaimed land have been used for residential building and to extend the port facilities and quays, now among the most up-to-date in Brazil. Mosquitoes are plentiful.

Porto Alegre's most important industries are food and farm products, textiles, metal-processing, chemicals and leather products. Chief exports are pinewood, rice, wheat, soya, meat, hides, wool, animal hair, semi-precious stones, wine and tobacco. A visit to Varig's installations and workshops is well worth while.

**Festivals** 2 February (local holiday) is the festival of Nossa Senhora dos Navegantes, whose image is taken by boat from the central quay in the port to the industrial district of Navegantes. Semana Farroupilha, celebrating gaúcho traditions, main day 20 September.

**Warning** The market area in Praça 15 de Novembro and the bus terminal are dangerous at night; thefts have been reported in Voluntários da Pátia and Praça Parcão.

**Hotels** *Plaza São Rafael*, Av. Alberto Bins 514, T 21-6100, L; *Conceição-Center*, Av. Senador Salgado Filho 201 (T 26-0610), good; *Alfred Executivo*, Av. Otávio Rocha 270, T 21-8966, A+; *Embaixador*, Jerônimo Coelho 354, T 28-2211, A+, 4-star, comfortable, unexciting restaurant; *Everest Palace*, R. Duque de Caxias 1357, T 24-7355 B; *Ritter*, Igo V. J. Veppo 55, T 21-8155, A, opp. Rodoviária, good service, English spoken, conveniently located.

*São Luiz*, Av. Farrapos 45, T 24-9522, c, spotless, good service, but near Rodoviária and the freeway and so a bit noisy; *Conceição II*, Garibáldi 165, T 24 3987, near Rodoviária, a/c, TV, fridge, OK, C; *Terminaltur*, opp. Rodoviária, T 27-1656, D with bath, a/c, TV, breakfast, heating, but small rooms and tiny bathrooms. *Coliseu*, Voluntários da Pátria, E with shower, clean; *Porto Alegre*, Pinto Bandeirantes 339, good, clean, quiet, rec, F; other hotels (in particular R. Garibáldi) in this area are used for very short stays. *Minuano*, Farrapos 31, E without breakfast or bath (more with bath), noisy but otherwise good, and *Elevado*, Av. Farrapos 63, E with hot shower, clean, very friendly, rec., both near bus station. *Savoy*, Av. Borges Medeiros 688, D, good value, *Santa Catarina*, R. Gen. Vitorino 240, D; *Praça Matriz*, Praça Mal Deodoro, E; *Palácio*, Av. Vigário José Inácio 644, D, central, clean, friendly, hot water, rec.; *Ritz*, André da Rocha 225, E, friendly, central, helpful, Spanish spoken; next door is *Finks*, same price range; *Uruguay*, Dr. Flores 371, E, very good; *Marechal*, R. Andrade Neves 123, E, basic, clean (not far from Mercado Municipal). Two *Casas dos Estudantes* (for those with student cards), at Av. João Pessoa 41, and R. Riachuelo 1355 (both not far from bus station), night free, breakfast and evening meal US$0.40, lunch US$0.60, if there's room. Youth hostel *Laçador*, R. Aurora Nunes Wagner 148, Morro Santa Tereza, T 287717.

**Camping** Do Cocão, 10 km. out on Viamão road; Praia do Guarujá, 16 km. out on Av. Gualba.

**Restaurants** Many good ones. General: *Everest Roof*, Duque de Caxias 1357; *Mosqueteiro*, Estádio Olímpico; *Rancho Alegre*, Cristóvão Colombo 2168, good "gaúcho" music; *Gauchão* at Rodoviária is good, with live entertainment nightly; *Churrascaria Quero-Quero*, Praça Otávio Rocha 47; *Grumete*, 24 de Outubro 905; *Barranco*, Av. Protásio Alves 1578. Vegetarian: *Ilha Natural*, R. Andrade Neves 42, lunches only. Chinese: *Tai Seng*

*Nhe*, Andradas 1097. **German**: *Printz*, Protásio Alves 3208; *Steinhaus*, Paulino Teixeira 415; *Floresta Negra*, 24 de Outubro 905. **Portuguese**: *Casa de Portugal*, João Pessoa 579; *Galo*, João Alfredo 904. **Italian**: *Copacabana*, Praça Garibaldi; *Cantina do Peppe*, Getúlio Vargas 273.

**Bars** (beer and sandwiches, music.) *Cia Sandwiches*, Getúlio Vargas 1430, sandwiches and music; *João de Barro*, R. da República 546, Cidade Baixa, food and music, including good jazz; *Julius*, José de Alencar 1348; *Sgt. Peppers*, Dona Laura 329.

**Electric Current** 110-120 A.C. 50 cycles.

**Bookshops** *Livraria Kosmos*, R. dos Andradas 1644 (international stock); *Livraria Lima*, Borges de Medeiros 539; *Livraria Globo*, Andradas 1416; airport bookshop. *Livres e Artes* bookstall in book market, Praça Senador Florêncio, new English books with front covers missing! Brasil-America Cultural Centre has free English library, next door used books are sold and exchanged.

**Shopping** *H. Stern* jewellers at Shopping Center Iguatemi and international airport. There is a street market (leather goods, basketware, etc.) in the streets around the central Post Office. Good leather goods sold on the streets. Sun. a.m. handicraft and bric-a-brac market (plus sideshows) Av. José Bonefacio (next to Parque Farroupilha). Very good food market.

**Entertainments** The old Hotel Majestic has become the **Casa de Cultura Mário Quintana**, at R. dos Andradas 736: this is a lively centre for the arts, with exhibitions, theatre etc. Plays by local and visiting companies at the theatres of São Pedro (opposite Government Palace) free noon and late afternoon concerts Sat., Sun., art gallery, café, and Leopoldina (Av. Independência). Modern cinemas. Centro de Tradição Gaúcha has *gaúcho* shows every Sat., starting at 2200.

**Sports** The Jockey Club at which races are held on Saturdays and Sundays; the Country Club (picturesque 18-hole golf course). British Club, Av. Carlos Gomes 534 (Montserrat).

**Swimming** from the beaches near or in the city is forbidden because of pollution. See "Beaches", below for out-of-town beaches.

**Museums** The **Museu Júlio de Castilhos**, Duque de Caxias 1231, has an interesting historical collection, and there is the **Museu do Trem** in the old railway station of São Leopoldo. **Museo de Arte do Rio Grande do Sul**, Praça Senador Florêncio (Praça da Alfândega), Tues.-Sun. 1000-1700, entry free, is interesting. **Varig airline museum**, open Wed. and Fri. 0900-1200.

**Exchange** on Av. Borges de Medeiros, good rate, cash only (e.g. **Agência Platina**, on corner with Andradas). Many câmbios in the centre will change travellers' cheques at parallel rates; e.g. **Platino Turismo**, **Dos Andrades e Av. Borges de Medeira** (only one to change travellers' cheques, Amex, but 6% less than cash), **Exprinter**, Sen. Salgado Filho 247 (best for cash); **Banco Econômico**, R. Uruguai 155, 8th floor, will change Amex cheques but below parallel rate; for other addresses consult tourist bureau brochure. **Lloyds Bank**, R. General Câmara 249 (open 1000-1630). **Banco do Brasil**, Uruguai 185, 10th floor, good rates for travellers cheques. **Citibank**, R. 7 de Setembro (open 1300-1700).

**Cultural Institutions** Sociedade Brasileira da Cultura Inglesa, Praça Mauricio Cardoso 49, Moinhos de Vento. **Instituto Goethe**, 24 de Outubro 122 (open Mon.-Fri., 0930-1230, 1430-2100). **Instituto Cultural Americano Brasileiro**, Mon.-Fri., 0800-2000 (Sats. 0800-1700).

**Consulates** U.S. Consulate, Genuino 421, corner of Mendeiros. **British Consulate** R. Itapeva 110, Sala 505, Edif. Montreal Bairro D'Areia, T 41-0720; **Austrian Consulate**, R. 7 de Setembro 1069, conj. 1714, Caixa Postal 1771, T 2460 77/85. **Argentine Consulate**, R. Prof. Annes Dias 112, 1° andar, T 24-6799/6810/6786. **Danish**, Av. Ipiranga 321, 5th floor, Bairro Menino Deus, CP 10105-90060, T 512-339966, open 0800-1200, 1400-1800.

**Dentist** Ursula Finkenwerder, R. Quintino Bocaiúva 655, Sala 301, Mon.-Fri. 0830-1130.

**Places of Worship** Sibra, R. Mariante 772.

**Telecommunications** Embratel, R. Siqueira de Campos 1245. T 41233.

**Post** For sending parcels abroad: R. Araújo Ribeiro 100; bring parcel unopened. **UPS** T 43-4972/42-4602 (Alvaro).

**Tourist Information** Epatur, Travessa do Carmo 84 (head office), helpful as is branch in Praça 15 de Novembro. Branch offices: Salgado Filho airport; interstate bus station, very helpful (free city maps); R. General Câmara 368; Av. Salgado Filho 366. CRTur (Companhia Riograndense de Turismo), R. dos Andradas 1137, 6th floor. Epatur maintains information booths at the frontier towns. A monthly booklet is available. City bus tour US$5, Regional tour US$15, Spanish or Portuguese only. **Touring Clube do Brasil**, Av. João Pessoa 623.

**Rail** The only long-distance passenger service from Porto Alegre is the line W to (386 km.) **Santa Maria** (pop. 197,000, *Hotel Itaimbé Palace*, A+, useful junction for road connections N to São Miguel mission ruins and Iguaçu, and S direct to Pelotas) and on to Cacequi, where the line branches for Uruguaiana (**see page 383**), for connections to Argentina, and for Santana do Livramento, for connections to Uruguay (by bus only, there are no longer passenger rail services in Uruguay). 3 days a week (Mon., Wed., Fri.) a standard train (no sleepers) leaves Porto Alegre at 0800 to Santa Maria, thence (after an overnight stop) 2 a week (Thur., Sat.) to Uruguaiana and 1 a week (Tues.) to Santana do Livramento. Return from the border towns may involve more than one night in Santa Maria. There is also a suburban service from Mercado station (Av. Mauá) north to Sapucaia do Sul, serving Esteio and Canoas. The suburban train service (faster than the bus) links the centre, Rodoviária and airport (10 mins.), 0500-2300.

**Buses** Bus to **Rio**, US$38.50 (*leito* 77), 26 hrs.; **São Paulo**, US$25 (*leito* 48), 18 hrs.; **Uruguaiana**, US$14, 8 hrs.; **Santa Maria**, 4¾ hrs., frequent service with Planalto; **Santana do Livramento**, 1230 and 2300, 8½ hrs., *leito* at 2330; to **Pelotas**, 8 daily, US$7, 3-4 hrs.; to **Gramado**, 8 daily, 2hrs.; to **Canela**, 5 daily, 2½ hrs.; to **Caxias do Sul**, almost hourly, 2 hrs., US$4.25, executivo service also. **Florianópolis**, US$8.80, 7 hrs. with Viação São Cristóvão (beware of overbooking and of stopping buses—e.g. Santo Anjo—on this route); **Curitiba**, US$16, 11 hrs.; **Blumenau**, US$13.50, 9 hrs.; **Rio Grande**, US$9.50, 8 per day, 0600 to 2000, 4½ hrs. **Foz do Iguaçu**, US$20, 15 hrs.; **Londrina**, 22 hrs. To **Cascavel** (Paraná) for connections to Campo Grande, Cuiabá and Porto Velho: daily except Sat. with Aguia Branca, 21 hrs., or Unesul, 19 hrs. To **Jaguarão** on Uruguayan border at 2400, 6 hrs., US$8.80.

Bus to **Montevideo**, with international buses TTL (daily 1730 and 2000) or Onda (daily 2200, not rec. as a/c is too cold and window blinds inadequate), 12 hrs., US$21; alternatively take bus to border town of Chuí at 0700 or 1200 daily, 7½ hrs., US$11, then Onda or Rutas del Sol to Montevideo (US$7-9, cheaper bought in Porto Alegre or Chuí than in Uruguay). Ouro e Prata operates a 2-3 times weekly service to Salto and Paysandú (Uruguay), via Santana do Livramento/Rivera. To **Asunción** with Unesul at 1900 daily via Foz do Iguaçu. Expresso Singer bus Porto Alegre-**Posadas** (Argentina) via Oberá, Alba Posse, Porto Mauá, departs 2100 on Tues., Thurs., and Sun. arriving following day at 1135. There are bus services to Buenos Aires 19 hrs. (depending on border) with Pluma, 1400 or 1500, 1900 and 2300, route is Uruguaiana, Paso de los Libres, Entre Ríos and Zárate, or 22 hrs. with General Urquiza company, Mon., Thurs. N.B. take your passport when purchasing international bus tickets.

The new and excellent bus terminal on Av. Mauá with Garibáldi has good facilities, including a post office and a long-distance telephone service until 2100. A regular bus runs from the Rodoviária to the airport, also the suburban train service (see above).

**Roads** Good roads radiate from Porto Alegre, and Highway BR-116 has a paved surface to Curitiba (746 km.). To the S it is paved (though some stretches are in poor condition), to Chuí on the Uruguayan frontier, 512 kms. In summer visibility can be very poor at night due to mist, unfenced cows are a further hazard. The new paved coastal road to Curitiba via Itajaí (BR-101), of which the first 100 km. is a four-lane highway, is much better than the BR-116 via Caxias and Lajes. The road to Uruguaiana is now entirely paved but bumpy.

**Air Services** There is a large modern international airport, Salgado Filho, 8 km. from the city, connected to the centre by train (see above). There are daily flights to Rio, São Paulo, Curitiba, Buenos Aires and Montevideo, and many other Brazilian cities. Vasp flies to Iguaçu and Brasília on Mon., Wed., Fri., and Sun. The airport is served by all Brazilian airlines, Pluna and Aerolíneas Argentinas.

**Excursion** Cervejaria Brahma, Av. Cristovão Colombo 545, offers tours of its brewery (but not Dec.-March).

**Beaches** The main beach resorts of the area are to the north of the city. The towns of *Tramandaí* (126 km.) and *Torres* (209 km.) are the most popular, with lots of luxury (and more reasonable) hotels and motels, bars, restaurants, and other standard requisites associated with seaside resorts. To celebrate independence in 1836, a cavalcade of horses reaches Torres on 16 September from Uruguay. To reach Florianópolis, take a bus from Torres to Araranguá and change. There is no lack of cheap accommodation, but hotels tend to be very full during the summer season. There are fully equipped campsites at both towns, and camping is also allowed on some beaches.

**Tramandaí Hotels** *São Jorge*, F. Amaral 19, T 661-1154, D, quiet, clean, bath, rec. Many more.

**Torres Hotels** *Dunas da Praia*, on beach, T 664-1011, A; *A Furninha*, R. Joaquim Porto 281, B, good service; *Farol*, R. José A. Pirasol 240, D to B with full board; *Grande Hotel Torres*, R. Júlio de Castilhos 124, C with bath, balcony and breakfast. *Salth*, Borges de Medeiros 209, T 664-1881, D with bath, friendly, clean; *Central*, same street No. 296, T 664-2580, D clean and friendly; Dec.-Feb. *São Domingo Youth Hostel* in a school building, F, Júlio de Castilhos 875, T 664-1865, clean. Other hotels, E-D, bath and breakfast are available.

**Restaurants** *Bom Gosto*, Rio Branco 242, churrascaria; *Sol Macrobiótico*, J. Castilhos 746, good cheap vegetarian with a cosy, personal atmosphere; *Casa de Peixe do Souza*, by the river, very good fish.

**Exchange** In Torres, **Banco do Brasil** and at Rodoviária.

Between the two towns are the resorts (heading south to north) of Atlântida (*Hotel Azul*), Capão da Canoa (*Hotel Kolman*, R. Sepé 1718, youth hostel *Riveira di Fiori*, Av. Venâncio Aires 711, T 265944, pool, rec., and others), Arroio Teixeira (Camping Clube do Brasil) and Arroio do Sal (*Hotel D'Itália*, Av. Assis Brasil 11, T 09, on beach, E, highly rec.; *Casa da Sogra*, good food).

**Roads** There is a paved road from Torres and Tramandaí (mostly prohibited to trucks) along the coast to Quintão, giving access to many beaches. A track continues to Mostardas, thence along the peninsula on the seaward side of the Lagoa dos Patos to São José do Norte, opposite Rio Grande. There is accommodation in Palmares do Sul (across the peninsula from Quintão) and Mostardas. South of Mostardas is Tavares on the **Lagoa do Peixe**, a national park, which is a resting place for migrating birds (details from R. Miguel Teixeira 126, Praia de Belas, Cidade Baixa, CEP 90,000 Porto Alegre). The road to the park is called the Estrada do Inferno. In Tavares, the red house on the praça is a hotel, no sign, rec.; several buses a week Tavares—São José do Norte (130 km.) and several daily to Porto Alegre.

Another popular beach area is south of Porto Alegre, around Cassino, near Rio Grande (**see page 382**). 40 km. to the south (towards Rio Grande) begins the Costa Doce of the Lagoa dos Patos; noted bathing points are Tapes, Barra do Ribeiro, Arambaré, São Lourenço do Sul (rec. camping site 1 km. out of town on lake shore) and Laranjal.

At **São Lourenço do Sul** is *Hotel Vilela*, R. Almirante Abreu 428, family hotel, clean, friendly. The town is a good place to stop to enjoy the lake, the beaches, fish restaurants and water sports.

**Inland** is the pleasant Serra Gaúcha, the most beautiful scenery being around the towns of **Gramado** and **Canela**, about 130 km. from Porto Alegre (chocolate factory between the two towns). There is a distinctly Bavarian flavour to many of the buildings. In spring and summer the flowers are a delight, and in winter there are frequently snow showers. This is excellent walking and climbing country among hills, woods, lakes and waterfalls. There are many excellent hotels at all prices in both towns, but it is difficult to get rooms in the summer. Local crafts include knitted woollens, leather, wickerwork, and chocolate. Gramado has two fine parks, Parque Knorr and Lago Negro, and Minimundo, a collection of miniature models. The town is decorated and, on Sat., about one week before 24 Dec. there is outdoor Christmas music; book hotels in good time as the town is crowded.

**Gramado Hotels** *Hortensias*, R. Bela Vista 83, T 286-1057, A; *Serrano*, Costa e Silva 1112, T 286-1332, A+; *Serra Azul*, R. Garibáldi 152, T 286-1082, A+; *Pequeno Bosque*, R. Piratina 486, B with bath, fridge, TV, good breakfast, located in wood close to Véu da Noiva waterfall; *Parque*, Leopoldo Rosenfeldt 818, T 286-1326, bungalows, good breakfast, friendly, maid will do laundry reasonably, C; *Ritta Höppner*, R. Pedro Candiago 305, T 054-286-1334, A in cabins, very good value, friendly, good breakfasts, German owners, cabins have TV, fridge, pool and miniature trains in grounds. *Luiz*, Senador Salgado Filho 432, T 286-1026, C, good breakfast, clean, among the cheapest; *Tia Hulda*, Av. Borges de Medeiros 1653, T 286-1813, friendly, C; *Dinda*, R. Augusto Zatti 160, T 286-1588, one of the cheapest, C; *Pousada Zermatt*, A. Acorsi e R. da Fé, T 286-2426, B, rec; try the *Planalto*, Borges de Medeiros 2001, T 286-1210, opp. Rodoviária, clean and friendly.

**Restaurants** *Saint Hubertus*, R. da Caixa d'Água; *Nápoli*, Av. Borges de Medeiros, good Italian. Coffee shop, *Tia Nilda*, Av. Pres. Costa e Silva. *Pyp* yoghurt factory, Av. S. Diniz 1030, has snack bar serving health food sandwiches and yoghurt. The local speciality is *café colonial*, a 5 o'clock meal of various dishes, including meats, rec. at *Café da Torre* (order one helping for 2 or more people, very filling). Visitors should also sample hot pinhões (pine nuts) and quentão (hot red wine, cachaça, ginger, cloves, sugar and cinnamon, often topped with gemada—beaten egg yolks and sugar).

**Tourist Office** Corner of Borges de Medeiros and Coronel Diniz, Gramado (3 blocks from Rodoviária, no English spoken), good maps and hotel lists.

**Canela Hotels** *Laje de Pedra*, Av. Pres Kennedy Km. 3, T 282-1530, L, but all amenities run down; *Vila Suzana Parque*, Theoboldo Fleck 15, T 282-2020, A+, chalets, heated pool attractive. *Bela Vista*, R. Oswaldo Aranha 160, T 282-1327, near Rodoviária, clean, good breakfasts, D. Cheap hotels: *Jubileu*, Oswaldo Aranha 223, F (acts as Youth hostel, T (054) 282-2133), reported unfriendly, and *Central*, Av. Júlio de Castilhos 146, E, clean, safe, rec.

**Camping** Camping Clube do Brasil, 6 km. from Canela, near waterfall in Parque do Caracol; excellent honey and chocolate for sale here. Sesi, camping or cabins, 2½ kms outside Canela, T (054) 282-1311/1697, clean, restaurant, rec.

**Wine merchant** in Canela, Joliment, Estrada de Morro, Calçado.

**Electric Current** 220 volts A.C.

**Bus** Several daily **Canela-Caxias** do Sul, 2 hrs., US$2.65. From **Florianópolis**, you have to go via Porto Alegre.

6 km. from Canela is the Parque Estadual do Caracol (bus marked "Caracol Circular" from outside Citral bus office at 0830, 1200 and 1700, US$0.35, 20 mins., return about ½ hour after departure time); a slippery path leads to the foot of the falls, which are 130 metres high (allow 1½ hrs. of daylight, it gets dark very quickly at the bottom in the forest). Good paths lead to smaller falls above Caracol; from the high point at Ferradura there is a good view into the canyon of the River Cai. Good views also from Moro Pelado, follow signs from behind the town (no bus, but nice walk through forest). 80 km. from São Francisco de Paula is the **Parque Nacional de Aparados da Serra**, where the major attraction is the 7.8-km. canyon, known locally as the Itaimbezinho, reported closed in Sept. 1990. Here, two waterfalls cascade 350 metres into a stone circle at the bottom. Tourist excursions, mostly at weekends, from São Francisco de Paula. At other times, take a bus to Cambara, get off at the cruce, from where it is 15 km. to the park—walk or hitch hike if you're lucky. There is a free campsite and a restaurant, which has a few rooms, in the park. From the restaurant one can walk to the canyon of Malacara. For experienced hikers (and with a guide) there is a difficult path to the bottom of Itaimbezinho, reported closed in Sept., 1990. One can then hike 20 km. to Praia Grande in Santa Catarina **(see page 384)**.

24 km. W of Gramado (99 km. from Porto Alegre, 30 km. from Caxias do Sul) is *Nova Petrópolis* (bus US$0.65), another city with strong German roots; there is a Parque do Imigrante, an open-air museum of German settlement. (Hotels include *Veraneio dos Pinheiros*, *Recanto Suíço*, 3 star, Petrópolis, *Veraneio Schoeller*, one-star.) N of Nova Petrópolis is Jammerthal, a valley in the Serra Gaúcha with German farms, many of whose inhabitants still speak German (go to Joanette and walk from there).

*Caxias do Sul* (pop. 267,000) 122 km. from Porto Alegre, is the centre of the Brazilian wine industry. The population is principally of Italian descent, and it is an expanding and modern city. Vines were first brought to the region in 1840 but not until the end of the century and Italian immigration did the industry develop. The church of São Pelegrino has paintings by Aldo Locatelli and 5 metre-high bronze doors sculptured by Augusto Murer. Good municipal museum at R. Visconde de Pelotas 586 (open Tues.-Sat., 0800-1200, 1400-1800), with displays of artefacts of the Italian immigration. The best time to visit is Jan.-Feb.

**Hotels** *Volpiano*, Ernesto Alves, 1462, A; *Cosmos*, 20 de Setembro 1563, A; *Alfred Palace*,

R. Sinimbu 2302, A+; *Itália*, Av. Júlio de Castilhos 3076, B; *Real*, R. Marquês de Herval 606, C; *Alfred*, R. Sinimbu 2266, A; *Bandeira*, same street, No. 2435, E with T.V. and bath; *Pérola*, corner Ernesto Alves and Marquês de Herval (No. 237), E, clean, good value; *Peccini*, R. Pinheiro Machado 1939, E, shared bath, good breakfast. *Samuara*, 10 km. out on RS-25 road, A+. Hotels fill up early p.m.

Good **restaurants**: *Fogo de Chão*, Os 18 do Forte 16, reasonably priced, live music (not touristy), "gaúcho"-style; also *Cantina Pão e Vino*, R. Ludovico Cavinato 1757, Bairro Santa Catarina, Caxias, good value; *Dom Rafael*, on main square, good value.

**Camping** Municipal campsite, 4 km. out on R. Cons. Dantas; Palermo, 5 km. out on BR-116 at km. 118; Belvedere Nova Sonda, 38 km. out in the district of Nova Pádua. At Garibáldi, near the dry ski slope.

**Exchange** Ask for Joel at Viagens e Turismo Galáxia, good rates.

**Tourist Office** Praça do Centro Administrativo; kiosk in Praça Rui Barbosa, also in Ed. Bonifa, Júlio de Castilho 1634, 2nd floor.

Caxias do Sul's festival of grapes is held in February-March. One should not miss the opportunity to visit the many *adegas* (but do not always expect free tasting), and the neighbouring towns of Farroupilha (*Hotels Don Francesco*, R. Dr. J. Rossler 88, 2 star; *Grande*, Júlio de Castilhos 1064) and Bento Gonçalves (hotels *Dall'Onder*, C, R. Erny Hugo Dreher 197, T (054) 252-3555; *Vinocap*, D, R. Barão do Rio Branco 245, T 252-1154/2566) and *Garibáldi*: hotels *Pietá*, João Pessoa 1728, T 262-1283, B; *Estação de Esqui*, B in cabins without breakfast; dry ski slope and toboggan slope—equipment hire, US$2 per hour. There is a "wine supermarket" on the road between Bento Gonçalves and Caxias; a selection of 40 wines at low prices. A good *adega*, with free tasting, is Cooperativa Viti Vinícola Emboaba Ltda, in Nova Milano (bus to Farroupilha, then change—day trip). Good tour and tasting (6 wines) at Adega Granja União, R. Os 18 de Forte 2346, US$0.25. That at Chateau La Cave (BR-116, Km. 143, Bairro São Ciro, bus from Sinimbu, US$0.15) is poor.

A restored steam train, Maria Fumaça, leaves Bento Gonçalves on Sun. at 0900 for Jaboticaba, 3½ hrs. with 2 stops for views; reserve in advance: Mal. Deodoro 70, T 252-1088.

On the road north, 112 km. from Porto Alegre, is **Osório**, a pleasant town near sea and lakes, with a good cheap hotel, *Big Hotel*, E.

*Rio Grande* (pop. 164,000) at the entrance to the Lagoa dos Patos, 274 km. S of Porto Alegre, was founded in 1737. The city lies on a low, sandy peninsula 16 km. from the Atlantic Ocean. To-day it is the distribution centre for the southern part of Rio Grande do Sul. Its cattle and meat industries are important.

During the latter half of the 19th century Rio Grande was an important centre, but today it is a rather poor town, notable for the charm of its old buildings. (Museu Oceanográfico, US$0.50, 0900, 1400-1700 daily, interesting, 2 km. from centre; bus 59 or walk along waterfront.) At Praça Tamandaré is a small zoo.

**Hotels** *Charrua*, R. Duque de Caxias 55, T 32-8033, rec. for good value, A; *Paris*, R. Marechal Floriano 112, T 32-8746, E, old, charming; *Novo Mundo*, nearby, F; *Europa*, R. Gen. Neto 165, main square,T 32-8133, C. Cheap hotels: *City, Iria*, both E (latter clean, friendly), on R. Luís Loréa; *Ritter*, Silva Paes 373.

**Restaurants** *Recanto Doce*, Silva Paes 370, cheap, friendly; *China Brasil*, R. Luís Loréa 389, good but not cheap; *Pescal*, Mal. Andréa 389, for fish, fairly expensive; *Angola*, Benjamin Constant 163 e Luís Loréa, very good and reasonable; *Caumo's*, Dr. Nascimento 389, good churrascaria; *Jensen*, Al. Abreu 650, near Rodoviária, good and cheap; *Bar Brejeiro*, Andrades 193, jazz upstairs.

**Exchange** Hotel Charrua for US$ notes.

**Cables** Embratel, R. Andrade Neves 94.

**Consulates** British, R. Francisco Marques 163, Caixa Postal 455, Centro, 96-200 Rio Grande, T 32-7788. Danish, R. Mal. Floriano 122, CP 92-96200, T 532-32-4422, open 0800-1200, 1330-1800.

**Tourist Office** R. Riachuelo, on the waterfront, behind the Cámera de Comércio and beneath the Hidroviária; good map and information.

**Transport** Frequent daily buses to and from Pelotas (56 km.), Bagé (280 km.), Santa Vitória (220 km.), and Porto Alegre (US$9.50, 4½ hrs.). To Itajaí, 14 hrs., US$20. Road to Uruguayan border at Chuí is paved, but the surface is poor (5 hrs. by bus, at 0700 and 1430, US$6.50).

**Boat Trip** By boat across mouth of Lagoa dos Patos, to pleasant village of São José do Norte, US$0.25, every hour from Porto Velho.

**Excursions** To *Cassino*, a popular seaside town on the Atlantic Ocean, 24 km., over a good road. The Cassino beaches are populous, but have no restaurants, hotels or facilities (note the statue of Yemanjá); those further N are mainly used in summer.

**Hotels** *Atlântico*, Av. Rio Grande, 387, C, clean, refurbished, special rates for students; *Marysol*, Av. Atlântica 900, C, near beach, friendly. Private campsite on Avenida 33, on the way out to Rio Grande. Camping Clube do Brasil site near town.

The breakwater (the Barra), 5 km. S of Cassino, no bus connection, through which all vessels entering and leaving Rio Grande must pass, is a tourist attraction. Barra-Rio Grande buses, from E side of Praça Ferreira pass the Superporto. Very good fishing. The coastline is low and straight, lacking the bays to the N of Porto Alegre; unfortunately the beach is used as a roadway. One attraction is railway flat-cars powered by sail, settle the price in advance; the railway was built for the construction of the breakwater.

*Pelotas* (pop. 278,000), on the BR-116, 56 km. N of Rio Grande, is the second largest city in the State of Rio Grande do Sul, on the left bank of the River São Gonçalo which connects the Lagoa dos Patos with the Lagoa Mirim. Its proximity to Rio Grande has hindered the development of its own port. Pelotas is prosperous, with an array of shops and pleasant parks. Like Rio Grande, it is rather damp.

Within a radius of 60 km., say an hour's drive, there are numerous excursions into the hilly countryside. Simple and clean accommodation and cheap, good and plentiful food can be found on the farms of settlers of German descent. 5 km. from Taím there is an ecological station with a small museum of regional animals; some accommodation for interested visitors.

**Hotels** *Estoril*, R. Gen. Osório 718, T 25-2411, a/c, reasonable, C; *Rex*, Praça Pedro Osório 205,T 22-1163, D, friendly, dowdy; *Grande*, Praça Pedro Osório 51, T 25-8139, old, some rooms with electric shower, F; *Germano*, next bus station, owner speaks some German, E.

**Camping** Municipal camp site on coast N of town, take bus Z3 from centre, superb site, fresh fish in village 2 km. away. 60 km. out at the Arco Iris waterfall, no facilities; *Cascata*, 25 km. out on the Cangussu road. Between Pelotas and Chuí, 1 km. S of junction with Rio Grande road, 1,200 metres from road at a working ranch, rec., clean, meals included.

**Restaurant** Tyrolean restaurant, opposite *Hotel Rex*, excellent, cheap. 29 km. out of town, on the road to Rio Grande, is an excellent restaurant owned by Tia Laura, who specializes in home cooking and *café colonial*.

**Exchange** Banco do Brazil will change travellers' cheques. Try Sr. Jesus Faria at 15 de Novembro 626 for good cash rate.

**Communications** Plane a day to Porto Alegre. Rodoviária is far out of town, with bus every 15 mins. to centre. Frequent daily buses to Porto Alegre, 244 km. (US$7, 3-4 hrs., paved road); Rio Grande, 90 min. (paved but in poor condition) buses stop at Praça 20 de Setembro; Jaguarão, on frontier with Río Branco, Uruguay (police post 3 km. before the bridge), paved; and inland to Bagé (*Hotel Medronha*, near bus station, E, without breakfast, clean) and other towns. The road to the Uruguayan frontier at Chuí (paved), has international bus service, but only a couple of daily buses Pelotas-Chiú Onda and TTL bus services (Montevideo-Porto Alegre) stop at the bus station for Montevideo (RR. Chile and Venezuela); tickets must be purchased from agency during day. Bus service to Buenos Aires via Uruguaiana. From Bagé, where there is a police post, the Uruguayan company Núñez runs buses 3 times a week to Melo, via Aceguá. Good direct road NW to Iguaçu via São Sepe (*Trevo Parque Hotel*, D, a/c, very friendly), Santa Maria (**see page 378**) and São Miguel mission ruins (see below).

The southern interior of the state is the region of the real gaúcho. Principal towns of this area include *Santana do Livramento* (pop. 70,000, bus and train, 3 a week, services to Porto Alegre) with its twin Uruguayan city of Rivera a great attraction of the latter being its casino. Rivera is  considered to have the better hotels and better exchange facilities. Duty free shopping.

**Hotels**: *Portal*, Av. Tamandaré 2076, B, T 242-2533, garage, clean, rec.; *Jandaia* B, R. Uruguai 1452 T 242-2288, rec; *Piranga*, cheap and clean, E; *Uruguaiana*, E, close to bus station.

In the extreme west are **Uruguaiana**, pop. 106,000, a cattle centre 772 km. from Porto Alegre (*Hotel Glória*, R. Domingos de Almeida 1951, A, good; *Progresso*, Flores da Cunha 1856, E, garage, friendly; *Palace*, Praça Rio Branco, E, without breakfast; *Fares Turis Hotel*, Pres. Vargas 2939, may let you leave your bags while you look around town) and its twin Argentine town of Paso de los Libres, also with a casino. A 1,400-metre bridge over the Rio Uruguai links the two cities; taxi or bus across about US$3. Buses connect the railway and bus stations, and centres of each city every half-hour; if you have to disembark for visa formalities, a following bus will pick you up without extra charge. Brazilian customs and immigration are at the end of the bridge, 5 blocks from the main praça, exchange and information in the same building. Exchange rates are better in the town than at the border. There are trains (twice a week) and bus services to Porto Alegre.

The west of Rio Grande do Sul also contains the Sete Povos das Missões Orientais (**see page 374**). The only considerable Jesuit remains in Brazilian territory (very dramatic) are at **São Miguel** (church, 1735-45, and small museum) some 50 km. from **Santo Ângelo**. (*Hotel Nova Esperança*, behind bus station, F, without breakfast; *Hotel Turis*, R Antônio Manoel 726, T (55) 312-4055, helpful, rec; *Maekli*, Av. Brasil 1000, E, rec.; other cheap central hotels near old railway station). At São Miguel there is a *son et lumière* show, weekdays at 2000, weekends at 1930, but ends too late to return to Santo Ângelo; in São Miguel village is *Hotel-Churrascaria Brillante*, E. East of Santo Ângelo is Passo Fundo, "the most *gaúcho* city in Rio Grande do Sul", so much so that the town's square boasts a statue of a maté gourd and bombilla— otherwise not much of interest; *Hotel dos Viajantes* opposite bus station, F. Planalto buses run from Uruguaiana via Barra do Quaraí/Bella Unión to Salto and Paysandú in Uruguay.

**Entering Uruguay** Those requiring a visa face problems: a medical exam is required before a visa can be issued, cost approximately US$20 and US$10 respectively. All buses, except those originating in Pelotas, stop at customs on both sides of the border; if coming from Pelotas, you must ask the bus to stop for exit formalities. You must have a Brazilian exit stamp to enter Uruguay. The Brazilian immigration office (and tourist caravan) is about 2½ km. from the border, on Av. Argentina; the bus from Porto Alegre stops here and the conductor hands over tourist cards to the officials. Make sure you get out to get your stamp, asking the driver to wait; or walk back from town at your leisure. The Brazilian border town, Chuí is much cheaper than its Uruguayan neighbour, so stock up with food and drink before crossing.

At Santana do Livramento all one need do is cross the main street, but the Uruguayan immigration is hard to find, in a side street. No customs formalities, but luggage is inspected on boarding bus for Montevideo, and there are checkpoints on the roads out of town. Bus to Montevideo, US$7-9. For motorists there are 3 customs offices in Santana do Livramento, about ½ hr. needed for formalities.

**Entering Brazil** from Uruguay, on the Uruguayan side, the bus will stop if asked, and wait while you get your exit stamp (with bus conductor's help); on the Brazilian side, the appropriate form is completed by the Rodoviária staff when you purchase your ticket into Brazil. The bus stops at Polícia Federal (Av. Argentina) and the conductor completes formalities while you sit on the bus. Buses run from Chuí to Pelotas (6-7 daily, US$6, 4 hours), Rio Grande (0700, 1400, 5 hrs., US$6.50) and Porto Alegre (1200, 2300, 7½ hrs., US$11); also from Chuí to Santa Vitória nearby, where there are a few hotels and rather quicker bus services to the main cities. N.B. Change all remaining Uruguayan pesos into cruzeiros before leaving Uruguay since not even black marketeers in Brazil want them. Also, if entering by car, fill up with petrol in Brazil, where fuel is much cheaper.

**Chuí hotels** *San Francisco*, Av. Colombia e R. Chile, E, shower, clean, restaurant; *Cairo*, Av. Uruguai, T 65-1109 opp. Atlantic petrol station), D, shower, breakfast, clean, TV lounge; on R. Chile, *Hospedagem Roberto* at No. 1631 and *Pensão* in private house at No. 767, F. *Atlantico*, Barra do Chuí, Km. 11; *Turismo* Av. Rio Branco 1078, T 63-1431, D. In Chuy (Uruguay), there is a *hospedaje* on Av. Brasil, opp. the Atlantic petrol station .

**Exchange** *Cambios* on Uruguayan side of Av. Brasil/ Av. Uruguay, between Calles L. Olivera and Gen. Artigas; best rates for AmEx travellers' cheques at **Val de Marne**.

**Post Offices** Av. Uruguay, between Colombia and Argentina (Chuí); Av. Brasil, 4 blocks from Gen. Artigas (Chuy).

**Telephones** in Brazil, corner of R. Chile and Av. Argentina; in Uruguay one block behind plaza, between Calles L. Olivera and Gen. Artigas.

**Tourist Information** On Av. Argentina (Chuí), 2½ km. from border; Uruguayan office in middle of Av. Brasil/Uruguay, at Av. Argentina/Calle Gen. Artigas junction.

## Santa Catarina

Further up the coast, in Santa Catarina (pop. 4,339,000), a group of Germans was settled at Lajes in 1822. In 1848 a new German-speaking settlement was founded at Blumenau. The Germans spread inland over the mountains from the port of São Francisco to Joinville. The Italians came later. Over northern Rio Grande do Sul and Santa Catarina the vast majority of people to-day can trace their origin to these immigrants.

In Santa Catarina, a state of small holdings, the farmer owns his land and cattle: the familiar European pattern of mixed farming worked by the family. Sixty per cent of the population is rural. There is coal in the S, and flourishing food processing and textile industries. Itajaí and São Francisco do Sul are the main ports, handling 90% of the trade. Except for the summer months of January and February, the beaches of Santa Catarina are pleasant and uncrowded.

Just across the border from Rio Grande do Sul (but not on the main highway—BR101) is **Praia Grande** (hotel, F, and churrascaria, just off praça, good and cheap; cheap hotel at bus station, F). Buses from Praia Grande go to **Araranguá**, on the BR101, 13 km. from which is the beautiful beach of Arroio do Silva (**Hotel Palace Scaini**, D-E, good food, clean, rec.). Some 75 km. N of Araranguá is the coalfield town of **Tubarão** (*Hotel Mossi*, in centre, E, excellent). Inland from the main road are the coalfields of Criciúma and Içara, all interesting, and the nearby beaches are good.

From Tubarão one can visit the Termas do Gravatal. (There is one first class hotel, and two others: *Petit Village*, F, a/c, mineral pool, good value, quiet, good food.) Also, buses go inland to Lauro Müller, then over the Serra do Rio do Rastro (beautiful views of the coast in clear weather). At Bom Jardim da Serra there is an apple festival every April. A dirt road continues to São Joaquim (**see page 387**), and over Pericó to Urubici (*Pensão Anderman*, E, clean, friendly, big meals). A new paved road is being built, as far as Santo Amaro da Imperatriz. There are direct buses from São Joaquim to Florianópolis.

J. P. Monnickendam, of Elstree, writes: About 60 km. inland from Tubarão is *Orleães*. It has one of the most interesting and least known museums in the area, which has an original water-powered workshop and sawmill, complete with waterwheel. It dates from the original settlers (late 19th century), and is still in working order. To get there one must get off the bus at the junction about 3 km. from the town.

386 km. NE of Porto Alegre, 15 km. from Tubarão, is the small fishing port of **Laguna** (pop. 50,000; *Hotel Laguna Tourist*, first class; *Hotel Itapirubá*, 4-star with beach and pool; *Turismar*, Av. Rio Grande do Sul 207, view over Mar Grosso beach, C, TV; several others, medium-priced, *Grande*, opp. post office, clean, E, without breakfast), in southern Santa Catarina. At Laguna is the Anita Garibáldi Museum, containing documents, furniture, and the personal effects of the Brazilian wife of the hero who fought in the 1840s for the independence of Rio Grande do Sul and later helped to unify Italy (US$0.05). Laguna's beach, 2 km. from the centre, is not very good, but 16 km. away (by ferry and road) are beaches and dunes at Cavo de Santa Marta. Also from Laguna, take a Lagunatur or Auto Viação São José bus to Farol (infrequent, US$0.70). You have to cross the mouth of the Lagoa Santo Antônio by ferry to get to Farol; look out for fishermen aided by dolphins (*botos*). Here is a fishing village with the alleged third oldest lighthouse in the world (Farol Santa Marta)—guided tours available (taxi, US$8.25, not including ferry toll). No hotels, but it is possible to bargain with fishermen for a bed. (Bus to/from Porto Alegre, 5½ hrs., with Santo Anjo Da Guarda; same company goes to Florianópolis, 2 hrs., but you can't buy a ticket before the bus arrives in Laguna—as soon as it comes in, follow the driver to ticket office.) Another 32

km. to the north of Laguna is the port of **Imbituba**, where there is a carbo-chemical plant, from which air pollution is very bad. Imbituba sends the coal mined in the area between Araranguá and Tubarão in coastal vessels to Rio de Janeiro, where it is railed to the steel mills at Volta Redonda for coking. The rail link between Imbituba and Tubarão is one of the busiest steam services in South America (freight only). There are good beaches (those near Garopaba and Araçatuba have been particularly recommended), and bus services to Porto Alegre.

The 124 km. N of Laguna is **Florianópolis** (founded in 1726, pop. 218,000) capital of the State, on the Ilha de Santa Catarina joined to the mainland by two bridges, one of which is Ponte Hercílio Luz, the longest steel suspension bridge in Brazil (closed to all traffic in 1983). The newer Colombo Machado Salles bridge has a pedestrian and cycle way beneath the roadway. It is a port of call for coastal shipping, 725 km. from Rio de Janeiro and 420 from Santos. The natural beauty of the island, beaches and bays make Florianópolis a popular tourist centre (only January and February are very crowded and expensive). The southern beaches are usually good for swimming, the east for surfing, be careful of the undertow. It seems a pity that the waterfront, scene of a traditional market, has been filled in and reclaimed and that the city is not in general better maintained. The cathedral on Praça 15 de Novembro has a life-size sculpture in wood of the flight into Egypt, originally from the Austrian Tyrol. Forts include the Santana (which houses a Museu de Armas de Policia Militar), São José da Ponta Grossa and Nossa Senhora da Conceição. There are three other museums, the Museu Histórico in the old Palácio Cruz e Souza, on Praça 15 de Novembre (1000-1800, Mon.-Fri., 1400-1800 Sat.-Sun.), the Museu de Antropologia at the Federal University (0900-1700 Mon.-Fri. 1300-1700 Sat.) and the Museu do Homem Sambaqui at the Colégio Catarinense, R. Esteves Júnior 159 (open 0800-1100, 1400-1700, Mon.-Sat.). There is a look-out point at Morro da Cruz (take Empresa Trindadense bus). Carnival is recommended as beautiful.

**Hotels** *Florianópolis Palace*, R. Artista Bittencourt and R. dos Ilhéus 26, T 22-9633, best, a/c, clean, TV, rec., but check bill, A+; *Royal*, Trav. João Pinto, T 22-2944, B, good; *Oscar Palace*, Av. Hercílio Luz 90, T 22-0099 C, watch the bill carefully; *Ivoram*, same street No. 66, T 22-5388, A, a discount in off season; *Veleiro*, R. Silva Jardim 234, T 23-6677, D with a/c and TV, rec., take Cidade Universitária bus.
    Within 10 minutes' walk of the Rodoviária: R. Felipe Schmidt, *Faial Palace*, No. 87, T 23-2766, A+, good restaurant; *Valerim*, No. 74, T 22-3280, central, B with bath, cheaper without (cheaper still off season), fridge, radio, T.V., stove, but not rec.; *Sumaré*, No. 53, D, good, clean, good value but check rooms for ventilation; *Querência Palace*, R. Jerônimo Coelho 1, T 22-2677, A, clean, good. On Conselheiro Mafra: *Felippe*, one block from 15 de Novembro at R. João Pinto 25, D, friendly, small rooms, 10% off to Youth Hostel members. *Dormitória Estrela*, R. Mafra, nr. R. Bento Gonçalves, very basic but cheap. *Pousada do Sol*, 7 km. from airport, T 222-2869, on the beach, pool, rec. On the mainland: *Oasis*, R. Gral. L. Bittencourt 201, D, with breakfast, clean, good (take bus 201 from here to bus terminal); *Bruggeman*, R. Santos Saraiva 300 T 44-2344, (bus 236 or 226 from Terminal Urbano do Aterro), C for motel-type rooms and 2-star accommodations; *Noblis* and *Continental* in the same road are cheaper. Cheap hotels around Rodoviária reckoned less good than those of similar price on the mainland, close to the bridge, take bus 236, ask the driver to stop at Saraiva. To rent a room, contact Levy Saboia, R. J. Colago 525, Jardím Santa Mônica, T 33-4684 (take a bus to Beira Mar Norte, alight at Santa Mônica supermarket); Apartment to let, Term Tur Joaquina, T 32-0059.

**Youth hostels** on the island: Ilha de Santa Catarina, R. Duarte Schutel 59 (T 22-3781); Barra da Lagoa (T 22-6746) and Fortaleza da Barra (T 32-0169), both on Estrada Geral da Barra da Lagoa; Praia do Campeche (T 22-6746) and Praia dos Ingleses (T 22-6746 also).

**Camping** Camping Clube do Brasil, São João do Rio Vermelho, near the lagoon, 21 km. out of town; also at Lagoa da Conceição, Praia da Armação, Praia dos Ingleses, Praia Canavieiras. "Wild" camping allowed at Ponta de Sambaqui. Beaches of Brava, Aranhas, Galheta, Mole, Campeche, Campanhas and Naufragados. 4 km. S of Florianópolis, camping site with bar at Praia do Sonho on the mainland, beautiful, deserted beach with an island fort nearby.

"Camping Gaz" cartridges from Riachuelo Supermercado, on R. Alvim with R. São Jorge.

**Restaurants** *Divina Comedia*, next to Cathedral, excellent food, friendly, run by American lady; *Manolo's*, R. Felipe Schmidt 71, near centre, good, but not cheap. *Lindacap*, R. Felipe Schmidt 178 on outskirts (closed Mon.), rec., good views. All the above give a good meal and beer for around US$7. *Pim-Pão*, R. Marechel Deodoro, good cheap breakfast, lunches; *Don Pepé Pizza*, Almirante Lamego, giant helpings; *Papparella*, R. Almirante 9, excellent pizzas; *Snack Bar Doll*, R. Vidal Ramos, open 0900-1900; *Rotisserie Acapulco*, R. dos Ilhéus 20, central, cafeteria-style, popular. Shrimp dishes are good everywhere. *Polly's*, Praça 15 de Novembro, good food and service, reasonable prices; *Macarronada Italiana*, Av. Beira Mar Norte 196, good. *Churrascaria Ataliba*, Rúa Jaú Guedes da Fonseca s/n, 2 km. from centre at Coqueiros, excellent rodízio, US$3.75. Vegetarian: *Sol da Terra*, R. N. Ramos 13, popular, *Vida*, R. Visconde Ouro Preto 62, *Neu Sol*, R. Vida Ramos 36 (all closed Sun.). *Padaria União*, R. Tenente Silveira, very good.

**Electric Current** 220 volts A.C.

**Car Hire** Auto Locadora Coelho, Felipe Schmidt 81, vehicles in good condition.

**Exchange** Banco do Brasil, R. dos Ilheus; Banco do Estado de São Paulo, Tenente Silveira 55; **Banco Estado de Santa Catarina**, Trajano 33. Turismo Holzmann, R. Conselheiro Mafra 53, parallel exchange rate in adjoining room. **Lovetur**, Av. Osmar Cunha 15, Ed. Ceisa and Centauru Turismo at same address. Money changers on R. Felipe Schmidt.

**Post Office** Praça 15 de Novembro 5, T 22-3188.

**Telecommunications** Telesc, Praça Pereira Oliveira 20, T 23-3700 (interstate and international telephones).

**Tourist Office** Head office: Portal Turístico de Florianópolis (Setur), at the mainland end of the bridge, 0800-2000 (Sat., Sun. 0800-1800); Praça 15 de Novembro, 0800-1800 (2200 in high season); at bus terminal, very helpful and multi-lingual (0700-2200, 0800-1800 Sat., Sun.), and airport, 0700-1800, (0800 Sat., Sun.); maps available, free.

**Transport** Daily flights to **Porto Alegre** and **São Paulo**. There is a new bus terminal with helpful tourist information at the east (island) end of the Ponte Colombo Machado Salles; the Terminal Urbano do Aterro for the island nearby, between the Rodoviária and the Mercado Municipal, which serves the northern beach towns, the east coast and most of the southern ones, and a further terminal at the junction of R. José da Costa and Av. Mauro Ramos which serves the other towns. All local bus destinations and schedules are clearly posted. Regular daily buses to **Porto Alegre** (US$8.80, 7 hrs.), **São Paulo**, US$18.50, **Rio**, US$26 ordinary, **Brasília**, 3 a week at 0300, US$36; **Curitiba** (US$8, 5 hrs.), **Blumenau** (US$4.80, 4 a day, 3 hrs.), **Joinville** (2½ hrs. direct, 3½ with stops) US$4.80 and other towns in the State. Also regular daily buses to Foz do Iguaçu (US$16.50, continuing to Asunción), to Campo Grande, 28 hrs., US$67, 1400 daily, to most other Brazilian cities and to Montevideo, US$45, by TTL. The coastal highway (BR-101) is preferred as an alternative to the congested inland BR-116; it runs close to Florianópolis but it is bad in places and has many lorries.

**Excursions** There are 42 beaches around the island almost all easily reached by public buses from the centre (buses of the Empresa Canavieras go from R. José da Costa, corner Av. Mauro Ramos to the northern towns and beaches, Empresa Ribeironense from next to the Rodoviária to the south-eastern ones, schedules from Tourist Office). The local buses (US$0.15) take you hourly to virtually every place on the island. To Lagoa da Conceição (Emflotur bus 403) for beaches, sand dunes, fishing, church of N.S. da Conceição (1730), boat rides on the lake (Ricardo, R. Man. S. de Oliveira 8, CEP 88062, T 320107, rents self-contained apartments, can arrange houses also, rec; restaurants: *Oliveira*, excellent seafood dishes; *Miguelão*, Praça Pio XII 5, poor value; *Leca*, try *rodízio de camarão*, prawns cooked in a dozen ways; *Caminho das Índias*, Av. das Rendeiras 69, warmly rec.); Tandem hang gliding, Lift Sul Vôo Livre, T 320543. Across the island at Barra da Lagoa is a pleasant fishing village and beach, with plenty of good restaurants, which can be reached by Emflotur bus 403 (US$0.15, every ½ hr. from Terminal Urbano, platform 5, *Hotel Camping Duvalerim*, F, on beach, rec. *Camping da Barra*, beautiful site, clean, helpful owner). Bus 401 goes to beach at Joaquina (surfing championships in January, *Hotel Cris*, T 32-0380, A, luxurious, rec). At Barra da Lagoa, *Cabanas da Barra*, R. Geral 23, D, good, German and English spoken. Hotel near Barra da Lagoa: *Gaivota* T 32-0177 (Familia Coelho), Praia do Moçambique, D, closed off season, excellent food; *Alburgue do Mar*, F, basic, friendly, good for lone travellers; *Pousada Ale-Pris*, F; *Dormitório Beira Rio*, G; *Mini-Hotel Caiçara*, good, clean, cheap; *Pousada Floripaz*, 2-bedroom apartments with kitchen, E per couple, restaurant and bar, T 323089, highly rec.

Mussels can be collected at the rocky headland, 1 km. further on there are clams, and, for the enthusiast, cannibal clams and sand urchins. Also visit the "city of honey bees" with a Museo da Apicultura, closes 1600 Sat., and the Church of Sto. Antônio Lisboa, take Trinidadense bus 331 or any bus going north, to the turn off, on the way to Sambaqui beach and fishing village. There is a pleasant fishing village at Ponta das Canas, walk 1 km. to Praia Brava for good surfing, and the beach at Canavieiras is good (*Hotel Moçambique*, C, in centre of village, noisy at weekends). In the north of the island, at Praia dos Ingleses (bus 602) is *Sol e Mar*, T 62-1271, C, excellent, friendly, rec. Other norther beaches: Jureré, Daniela and Forte (with fort and beautiful views). In the S of the island are Praia da Armação with, just inland, Lagoa do Peri (a protected area). Further south is Pantana do Sul, an unspoilt fishing village. *Pousada Sítio dos Tukanos*, E, Caixa Postal 5016, T 325084; take bus to Pantana do Sul, walk 6 km. or telephone and arrange to be picked up, German owner speaks English, warmly rec. Praia dos Naufragados and Farol beaches: take bus to Caieira da Barra do Sul and take 1-hr. walk through fine forests.

Excursions can be made on the mainland to the hot springs at Caldas da Imperatriz (41°C) and Águas Mornas (39°C); at the former are 2 spa hotels (*Caldas da Imperatriz*, C, meals and baths included, built in 1850 under the auspices of Empress Teresa Cristina, houses public baths; *Plaza Caldas da Imperatriz*, from B, with baths, swimming pools, very well appointed), at Águas Mornas, the *Palace Hotel* is on the site of the springs, A, baths open to public Mon.-Fri. a.m. only. Boat trips can be made from Florianópolis in the bay, T 22-1806, from US$4.50-6.80.

From Florianópolis a partly paved road runs SW inland via São Joaquim (see below) to **Lajes** (pop. 143,000) a convenient stopping place on BR-116 between Caxias do Sul and Curitiba. Despite the poor road, however, this journey is perhaps the most interesting in the State (3 buses a day do this journey in summer, 1 in winter, 5 hrs., via Alfredo Wagner, otherwise go via Blumenau). (*Grande Hotel*, good, but no heat; cheaper is *Presidente*, E; *Natal*, cheap, adequate; *Rodalar, Centauro*, clean, friendly, restaurant, both F, near bus station. Bus station is ½-hr. walk S.E. of centre. Voltage 220 A.C.)

**São Joaquim**, at 1,360 metres, the highest town in Southern Brazil, regularly has snowfalls in winter; very pleasant town with an excellent climate (Camping Clube do Brasil site). To the East of the town, in the Serra Geral is the **São Joaquim National Park** (33,500 hectares), with canyons containing sub-tropical vegetation, and araucaria forest at higher levels. The local IBDF office is at Av. Moura Ramos 187, Florianópolis (Caixa Postal 660, CEP 89.000). Hotels: *Nevada* (expensive meals) and *Maristela*, E (good breakfast) both on R. Manoel Joaquim Pinto, 213 and 220 respectively (5 mins'. walk from Rodoviária). Bus to Florianópolis 0830 and 2230, 7½ hrs., US$8. To Caxias do Sul, 4½ hrs., US$6. The bridge over the Rio Pelotas on the road to Cambará do Sul and Bom Jesús is closed, a new bridge is being built.

On the coast N of Florianópolis there are many resorts. They include **Porto Belo**, a fishing village of 12,000 people on the north side of a peninsula settled in 1750 by Azores islanders, with a calm beach and a number of hotels and restaurants (bus Florianópolis—Porto Belo with Praiana or Biguaçu, 8 daily, 3 on Sun.). West of Port Belo is Praia de Perequê (hotels *Tati*, F, T 69-4363, across from beach, and *Blumenauense*. F with bath and breakfast, on beach, T 69-4208). In Porto Belo itself is *Hotel Baleia Branca* (T 69-4011), with camping. Around the peninsula are wilder beaches reached by rough roads: Bombas (2 hotels), Bombinhas (*Pousada do Arvoredo*, T 69-4355, up on a hill), Mariscal, and, on the southern side, Cantinho (*Pousada Zimbros*, T 69-4225, C, less off season, on beach, sumptuous breakfast, restaurant, highly rec., spear fishing guide). Itapema (66 km., many hotels); **Camboriú** (86 km., once beautiful, now crowded and dirty, with 4 blocks of concrete jungle behind; a great many hotels, restaurants and campsites; buses from Florianópolis, Joinville and Blumenau) a few kms south, at Lojas Apple, there is a museum, zoo and aquarium; and Meia Praia, which is quieter and cleaner than Camboriú. Between Itajaí and Camboriú is the beautiful, deserted (and rough) beach of Praia Brava.

One hundred km. up the coast N of Florianópolis by the BR-101 paved road or by sea is the most important port in Santa Catarina: **Itajaí**, at the mouth of the Itajaí river. It is well served by vessels up to 5½ metres draught, and is the centre of a district largely colonized by Germans and Italians. Main exports: timber, starch, tapioca, sassafras oil, and tobacco. Population, 64,000. Airport. You can walk to Cabeçudas beach, which is quiet and small.

**Hotels** *Marambaia Cabeçudas*, at Cabeçudas beach, best, 6 km. out of town, A; *Grande*, R. Felipe Schmidt 44, good value, D; *Maringá*, N of town, friendly, cheap and clean, with Shell service station next door, providing good food, open all night. *Rex, Cacique*, both on R. Asseburg, cheap, near market. Rec. **Bar**, *Trudys*, on riverfront at end of main street, a good place in changing cash.

Resorts north of Itajaí include Piçarras, with sandy beaches interspersed with rocky headlands (ideal for fishing), and Barra Velha (*Hotel Mirante*, E, good, cheap restaurant, and 2 dearer hotels).

There is a 61 km. paved road to *Blumenau* (pop. 192,000), 47 km. up the Itajaí river. It is in a prosperous district settled mostly by Germans; see Museo da Família Colonial, German immigrant museum, Av. Duque de Caxias 78, open Mon.-Sat., 0830-1130, 1330-1730, US$0.10. German Evangelical Church. Places of interest include the houses, now museums (open 0800-1800) of Dr Bruno Otto Blumenau and of Fritz Müller (a collaborator of Darwin), who bought the Blumenau estate in 1897 and founded the town, which is a notable textile centre. A "traditional" Oktoberfest beer-festival was started in 1984 here, and was expected to become the second largest in the world after Munich's. Visitors report it is worth attending on weekday evenings but weekends are too crowded ("960,000 visitors in 1990"). It is repeated, but called a "summer festival", in the 3 weeks preceding Carnival ("5 visitors").

**Hotels** *Himmelblau Palace*, R. 7 de Setembro 1415, T 22-5800, A; *Blumenau Tourist Hotel*, 200 m. from bus station, D, helpful; *Garden Terrace*, R. Padre Jacobs 45, T 22-3544, A; *Grande Hotel*, Alameda Rio Branco 21, T 22-0366, A; *Glória*, R. 7 de Setembro 954, T 22-1988, B, German-run, excellent coffee shop (all aforementioned hotels have heating in rooms); *Plaza Hering*, 5-star, 7 de Setembro 818, T 22-1277, L, heating and a/c; *Central*, R. 7 de Setembro 1036, T 22-0570, basic, E with bath, F without, both without breakfast, clean, but not safe for luggage; *Herrmann*, central, Floriano Peixoto 213, T 22-4370, rec., E, shower, clean. *City*, R. Ângelo Dias 263, T 22-2205, E. Many cheap hotels do not include breakfast. Most hotels and restaurants very clean. Youth Hostel at R. Paraíba 66 (T 22-8420).

**Camping** Municipal campsite, 2 km. out on R. Pastor Osvaldo Hesse; Paraíso dos Poneis, 9 km. out on the Itajaí road, also Motel; Refúgio Alpino, 11 km. out on R. da Glória.

**Restaurants** Good German food at *Frohsinn*, Morro Aipim (panoramic view) and *Cavalinho Branco*, Av. Rio Branco 165, huge meals, but check the bill, international eating at *Moinho do Vale*, Paraguai 66. *Amigo*, Peixoto 213, huge cheap meals; *Caféhaus Glória*, in *Hotel Glória*, excellent coffee shop. On R. Alwin Schrader, *Biergarten*, with a "German" band on Sun. afternoon, and nearby *Bar Kriado*, with authentic Brazilian music, Mon.-Fri. only; dancing and good atmosphere at *Adega Espanhola*, R. 7 de Setembro; *Deutsches Eck*, same street No. 432, rec., esp. *carne pizzaiola*; *Gruta Azul*, Rodolfo Freygang, good, popular, not cheap. *Internacional*, Nereu Ramos 61, Chinese, very good, not particularly expensive; good Chinese food at R. 15 de Novembro 346, near Tourist office.

**Voltage** 220 A.C.

**Amenities** Teatro Carlos Gomes is also exhibition centre; public library open 0800-1800; German bookshops, Librerias Alemãs, at bus station and RR. 7 de Setembro and 15 de Novembro. Craft shop, Casa Meyer, 15 de Novembro 401.

**Exchange** At *Cambios/travel* agencies: *Vale do Hajaí Turismo e Cambio*, Av. Beira Rio 167, very helpful, German spoken; *International Turismo*, 1 block away. *President Turismo*, 7 de Setembro, 2nd floor; also *Turismo Holtzmann* nearby; *Ilhatur Turismo*, Rodolfo Freygang 5, 1st floor. *Tilotur Turismo*, Alameda Rio Branco e 15 de Novembro, 2nd floor; *Casa Rowder*, R. Curt Herring.

**International Telephones** Corner of Av. Brasil and República Argentina.

**Tourist Office** in town hall, R. 15 de Novembro 420, corner of R. Nereu Ramos, friendly, limited information; also kiosk on 15 de Novembro, good town map. Only Portuguese spoken.

**Bus** The Rodoviária for interurban travel is in the village of Fortaleza, US$0.10 by Rodoviária-7 de Setembro bus from the old bus station at Av. 7 de Setembro and Padre Jacobs (US$2.50 by taxi). Left luggage lockers at Rodoviária; tokens available in cafeteria on 2nd floor. Good bus connections in all directions from Blumenau. Blumenau to Caxias do Sul at 1930 only, arrives 0400, US$12; to Curitiba, 4 hrs., US$6.40.

**Excursions** By bus to Timbo and Pomerode (from riverside road opp. Prefeitura) past rice fields and wooden houses set in beautiful gardens. At **Pomerode**, 32 km., US$0.80 (*Hotel Central*, E, big lunches) there is an interesting zoo. Tourist office. The North German dialect of Plattdeutsch is still spoken here. The *Tortenparadies* serves excellent German cakes. Rex Bus goes to Iraguá from Pomerode; change for connection to Joinville, US$2.50. ½-day excursion to Gaspar to visit the cathedral set high above the river (Verdi Veli bus company from stop outside the huge supermarket on R. 7 de Setembro in the centre).

**To Iguaçu** As an alternative to a direct bus, daily from Florianópolis and Itajaí to Iguaçu via Blumenau, you can travel through rich and interesting farming country in Santa Catarina and Rio Grande do Sul, stopping at **Joaçaba**, a town of German immigrants (*Hotel Colonial*, at bus station, *Lotus*, across bridge, both F), Erexim (*Hotel Rex*, E, strong *gaúcho* influence), or **Iraí** Italian immigrant area, town with thermal springs (*Hotel São Luís*, E, with full board, town good for semi-precious stones), thence from any of these places to Pato Branco and Cascavel (**see page 396** for connections to Foz do Iguaçu).

**São Francisco do Sul** (pop. 23,000) 80 km. up the coast is the port for the town of Joinville, 45 km. inland at the head of the Cachoeira river. Most of the colonial architecture has been replaced by modern buildings. There are some excellent beaches nearby, such as Ubatuba, Enseada (hotels, pensions and 3 camp sites, Pascerella recommended) and Cápri. (At weekend trips to Ilha do Farol in port's supply boat.) Petrobrás oil refinery, but oil pollution has been reported, take mosquito repellant. (*Hotel Kontiki*, apartment "luxo", C, on Camacho 33, T 44-0232); *Hotel Avenida*, E with breakfast, clean, friendly; *Zibamba*, R. Fernandes Dias 27, central, C, good restaurant. The *Restaurante Franciscano*, on the Praia dos Coqueiros, is recommended, so are the *Metralhas* and *Flutuante* (good seafood.) Bus terminal is 1½ km. from centre. Direct bus (Penha) daily to Curitiba at 0730, US$4.80, 3½ hrs. Men are not allowed to wear shorts here.

**Joinville** (pop. 303,000) the state's largest city lies 2 km. from the main coastal highway, BR-101, by which Curitiba and Florianópolis are less than two hours away. To Guaratuba (**see page 395**) by bus, 1¼ hrs., US$1.60 (connections to Paranaguá).

See the Museu Nacional da Imigração e Colonização in the Palácio dos Príncipes, R. Rio Branco 229 (closed Mon.), which has a collection of objects from the original German settlement. The interesting Museo de Arte is in the old residence of Ottokar Doerfell, R. 15 de Novembro 1400 (open Tues.-Sun., 0900-1800). The Museu Arqueológico do Sambaqui has a collection dating back to 5000 BC (open Tues.-Fri., 0900-1200, Sat., Sun., and holidays, 0900-1200, 1400-1800; US$0.20). Museum of the sculptor Fritz Alt, R. Aubé (closed Mon.).

At Expoville, 4 km. from centre on BR-101 (continuation of 15 de Novembro) is an exhibition of Joinville's industry and an industrial museum. The industry does not, however, spoil the considerable charm of the city. There is an annual flower festival in the first fortnight of September.

**Hotels** *Tannehof*, Visconde de Taunay 340, T 22-2311, 4 stars, restaurant on 14th floor; *Anthurium Parque*, São José 226, T 22-6299, C, colonial style, good value, English spoken, friendly; **Novo Horizonte**, at bus station, basic, clean; **Konig**, 15 de Novembro 937, E; same street No. 811, **Mattles**, E, T 22-3582

**Camping** Camping Clube do Brasil, R. Saguaçu, Horto Florestal. Municipal site, same road, 1 km. from centre.

**Restaurants** *Pinheiro*, Rio Branco 299, is well worth a visit for excellent fish and shrimp dishes. For meat or German specialities, *Churrascaria Rex*, Bhunenan 3097, *Churrascaria Ataliba*, near Expoville, *Bierkeller*, 15 de Novembro 497. Vegetarian: *Cozinha Natural*, R. Marinho Lobo 38. The cheapest place to eat is the *Sociedade Ginástica*, R. Ginásticos—you don't have to be a member.

**Banks**  Banco do Brasil. Open 1000-1630.

**Tourist Office**  corner Praça Nereu Ramos with R. Príncipe; no information on cheap hotels. Good exchange rates

**Buses** To Blumenau, US$3.20, 2¼ hrs. The bus terminal is 2½ km. outside the town (regular bus service).

**Air Service**  Airport 5 km. from city. Daily flights to major cities.

**Excursions**  Four daily buses go to Ubatuba beach, a week-end resort (see above under São Francisco do Sul). The Sambaqui site of Rio Comprido can be reached by Gideon Bus, but there is not much to see. It is a pleasant trip to Jaraguá do Sul, European, hilly landscape.
   The festival of São João in June can be seen best in Santa Catarina at Campo Alegre, the first town on the road inland to Mafra. There are bonfires, a lot of (German) folk dancing, and large quantities of *quentão* (a hot drink made of red wine, cinnamon, ginger and *cachaça*) and *pinhões* (the nuts of the Paraná pine tree). It is a beautiful climb on the road from the BR-101 to Campo Alegre. The road continues through São Bento and Rio Negrinho to Mafra, from where a good road (the BR-116) goes to Curitiba.

## The State of Paraná

The Italians were first in Paraná, but apart from a few Germans most of the later settlers were of Slavonic origin—Poles, Russians, Ruthenians and Ukrainians. Paraná is now the leading producer of wheat, rye, potatoes and black beans, but its population, 8,308,000, no longer expands as quickly as it did, partly because of the displacement of rural workers following the uprooting of coffee plants in the more frost-prone areas and the turning of the land over to cattle. The recent boom crop, soya, also employs fewer workers throughout the year than coffee.

*Curitiba*, capital of Paraná state (pop. 1.5 million), is a modern city at 900 metres on the plateau of the Serra do Mar. It has won a well-deserved prize as one of the 3 cleanest cities in Latin America. The commercial centre is busy R. 15 de Novembro (old name: R. das Flores), which has a pedestrian area where there are Sat. morning painting sessions for children. Another pedestrian area is behind the cathedral, near Largo da Ordem, with sacred art museum, flower clock and old buildings, very beautiful in the evening when the old lamps are lit. Art market Sat. morning in Praça Rui Barbosa, and on Sun. morning in Praça Garibáldi (recommended), beside attractive Rosário church. The Civic Centre is at the end of Avenida Dr. Cândido de Abreu, 2 km. from the city centre: a monumental group of five buildings dominated by the Palácio Iguaçu, headquarters of the state and municipal governments. In a patio behind it is a relief map to scale of Paraná. The Bosque de João Paulo II behind the Civic Centre contains the Polish immigrants' museum: both are worth a visit. In contrast to the Civic Centre is the old municipal government building in French Art Nouveau style, now housing the Museu Paranaense in Praça Generoso Marques. Nearby, on Praça Tiradentes, is the Cathedral (1894). The most popular public park is the Passeio Público, in the heart of the city (closed Mondays); it has a good little zoo, a network of canals with boats, and a small aquarium. On the north east edge of the city is Parque do Barigui, take bus 450 "São Braz" from Praça Tiradentes. Near the shores of Lake Bacacheri on the northern edge of the city (R. Nicarágua 2453) is an unexpected Egyptian temple (the Brazilian centre of the Rosicrucians—visits can be arranged—take Santa Cândida bus to Estação Boa Vista, then walk). There are three modern theatres, the Guaíra for plays and revues (also has free events—get tickets early in the day), one for concerts and ballet, and the Teatro Paiol in the old arsenal. Many of the main streets have been widened and the city is being rapidly transformed.

**Local Holidays**  Ash Wednesday (half-day); Maundy Thursday (half-day); 8 September (Our Lady of Light).

**Hotels**  *Bourbon*, Cândido Lopes 202, T 224-8322, L, most luxurious in centre, newly restored; *Slaveiro Palace*, Sen. Alencar Guimarães 50, T 222-8722, central, A+; *Iguaça*

CURITIBA 36
(centre)
Not to Scale

1. Praça Tiradentes
2. Praça João Cândido
3. Praça Garibáldi and Flower Clock
4. Praça Generoso Marques and Museu Paranaense
5. Praça Santos Dumont
6. Praça Zacárias
7. Praça Carlos Gomes
8. Largo da Ordem
9. Cathedral
10. Rosário Church
11. Sacred Art Museum
12. Museum Guido Viário
13. Museum of Contemporary Art
14. Railway Museum
15. Post Office (X2)
16. Telephone Office
17. Tourist Kiosk
18. *Hotel Lancaster*
19. *Hotel Tourist Universo*
20. Cheaper hotels and wholesale market area
21. Short-distance bus terminal.

*Campestre*, on BR116, 8 km. from centre (road to São Paulo), T 262-5313, A, set in park, swimming pool, tennis, mini golf, horse riding. The following, in our category A+, are rec.: *Caravelle Palace*, R. Cruz Machado 282, T 223-4323, first class; *Lancaster*, R. Voluntários da Pátria 91, T 223-8953, tourist class; *Ouro Verde*, R. Dr. Murici 419, T 224-1633, standard class. *Mabu*, Praça Santos Andrade 830, T 222-7040, L; *Del Rey*, Ermelino de Leão 18, T 224-3033, A+, good restaurants. *Araucaria Palace*, Amintas de Barros 73, T 224-2822, B, good commercial hotel; *Curitiba Palace*, Ermelino de Leão 45, T 224-1222, B, central, very pleasant; *Tibagi*, Cândido Lopes 318, T 223-3141, B, central, new, business hotel. *Tourist Universo*, Praça Gen. Osório 63, B, T 223-5816, Sky TV, good restaurant, rec.; *Jaguarã*, opposite station, very clean, noisy, good breakfast, rec. (but not the buffet supper) B; *Climax*, R. Dr. Murici 411, T 224-3411, good value, popular, C; *Palace*, R. Barão do Rio Branco 58, E with bath, central, European atmosphere; *Regência*, R. Alfredo Bufrem 40, T 223-4557, D, with breakfast, excellent; *Cervantes*, same street No 66, T 222-9593, F, rec.

There are hotels in categories D downwards in the vicinity of the Rodoferroviária, but the cheaper ones are close to the wholesale market, which operates noisily throughout the night: *Nova Lisboa*, Av. 7 de Setembro 1948, E with breakfast, bargain for cheaper rates without breakfast, clean; *Condor*, No. 1866, D, a/c, TV, clean, breakfast, rec; *Itamarati*, Tibagi 950, 500 m. from Rodoferroviária, E, clean, with bath, fan, friendly; *Costa Brava*, R. Francisco Torres 386, T 262-7172, D, well rec.; *Império*, Av. Pres. Afonso Camargo 367, D with bath, E without, small and poor breakfast, take insect repellent; next door, *Maia*, D with bath, incl. breakfast, clean and quiet; *Wang*, same street, No. 549, no sign, F, safe, but run down; *Doral*, Mota 1144, T 222-1060, TV, frigobar in room, good breakfast, D; *Filadélfia*, Gen Carneiro 1094, T 264-5244, D, clean, good breakfast, private bath, 4 blocks from station through market; *Inca*, R. João Negrão, E, German spoken; *Ouro Preto*, Pedro Ivo, F, clean, quiet, sunny rear garden, rec.

*Casa dos Estudantes*, Parque Passeio Público, north side, F, with student card, 4 nights or more; *Casa de Estudantes Luterano Universitario*, R. Pr. Cavalcanti, T 223-8981, F, good. Youth hostels in Paraná state: Asociação Paranaense de Albergues de Juventude, Av. Padre, Agostinho 645, Curitiba PR, CEP 80.410; in the city, *Hans Staden*, R. Vol. da Pátria 475, 2nd floor, T 232-9012.

**Camping** Official site 7 km. N of city, on São Paulo road, US$1 a night. Camping Clube do Brasil, 14 km. out on same road.

**Restaurants** *Ile de France* (French), Praça 19 de Dezembro 538; *Schwarzwald*, Claudino dos Santos 63, beerhaus/ restaurant, in centre (German); *Matterhorn*, Mateus Leme 575, centre (Swiss). *A Sacristia*, R. João Manuel 197, restaurant, pizzeria, bar, very good; *Oriente*, R. Ebano Pereira 26 (1st floor), excellent, huge Arab lunch. On Av. das Torres, *OK*, at Uberaba, 7 km., churrascaria, and *Napolitana*, No. 2531, similar, both about US$10 p.p.; *Per Tutti*, same avenue; *Marumbi*, on road to Paranaguá. *Salão Italiano*, R. Padre G. Mayer 1095, Cristo Rei, T 262-0050, good Brazilian and Italian food. Local and Italian food and local red wine in nearby Santa Felicidade (10 km. out of town on road to Ponta Grossa), e.g. *Madalosso*, Av. Manoel Ribas 5875, Italian self-service, rec., and *Dom Antônio*, same street No. 6121, excellent. Sukiyaki at *Yuasa*, Av. Sete de Setembro, cheap and good, rec.

Vegetarian: *Transformação* (macrobiotic, shop also), Al. Augusto Stellfeld 781; *Vegetariano*, Carlos de Carvalho 127, 13 de Maio 222; *Verde Jante*, R. Pres. Faria 481, very good; *Super Vegetariano*, R. Pres. Faria 121, Cruz Machado 217, R. Dr. Murici 315, lunch and dinner Mon.-Fri., very good and cheap.

*Paláchio*, Barão Rio Branco, is all-night restaurant, good food and cheap; cheap food also near old railway station and a good meal in the bus station. Close to the Rodoferroviária is the market, where there are a couple of *lanchonetes*; also opp. the fruit market *Chammoróco*, good meat dishes. Students can eat at University canteen (student cards required). Hot sweet wine sold on the streets in winter helps keep out the cold. Rec. tea house: *Chez Arnold*, Av. Manoel Ribas 526, in the Mercês district. *Francis Drake*, Alameda Dr. Murricy 1111, a pub for pirates; *London Pub*, São Francisco 294, rec.

**Electric Current** 110 v. 60 cycles.

**Shopping** Curitiba is a good place to buy clothes and shoes. *H. Stern* jewellers at Mueller Shopping Centre.

**Local Transport** The city has a very efficient bus system; all bus stops have maps. Express buses on city routes are orange: for example, from centre (Praça Rui Barbosa) take Leste bus marked "Villa Oficinas" or "Centenário" for Rodoferroviária (combined bus and railway station).

**Museums** Museu Paranaense, Praça Generoso Marques (open Tues.-Fri. 1000-1800, other days 1300-1800, closed first Mon. of each month). **Museu David Carneiro**, on R. Comendador Araújo 531, Sat., 1400-1600. **Museo Guido Viário**, R. São Francisco 319, painter's house; **Museu de Arte Contemporânea**, R. D. Westphalen 16 (closed Sat., and Sun. morning). **Casa Andersen**, R. Mateus Leme 336, house of painter, open Mon.-Fri. **Museum Ferroviário**, Av. 7 de Setembro, in the old railway station, open Tues.-Fri., 1300-1800, Sat.-Sun., 0800-1200; **Museu do Expedicionário** (Second World War Museum), Praça do Expedicionário, open daily 0800-1800; **Museo do Automóvel**, Av Cândido Hartmann 2300 (Sat. 1400-1800, Sun. 1000-1200, 1400-1800), all worth a visit.

**Exchange** Banco Noroeste, 15 de Novembro 168, advances on Eurocard/Master Card. Best exchange rates at **Jade travel agency**, R. Quinze de Novembro 477 (cash only); **Triangle Turismo Travel**, Praça General Osório 213, cash and travellers' cheques; **Transoceania**, R. Mal Deodoro 500, good rate for cash or cheques; **Diplomata**, R. Presidente Faria 145 in the arcade.

**Cultural Institutes** Centro Cultural Brasil-Estados Unidos (Mon.-Fri., 0800-1200, 1400-2100); **Sociedade Brasileira de Cultura Inglesa** (British Council), R. General Carneiro 679 (Caixa Postal 505). **Instituto Goethe**, Rua Schaffenberg, nr. Military Museum, Mon.-Thur. 1500-1900, Library, Mon.-Tues. till 2130.

**Consulates** Austria, R. Marechal Floriano Peixoto 228, Edif. Banrisul, 17 andar, Caixa Postal 2473, T 22 46 795. **Germany**, Av. J. Gualberto 1237, T 252-4244; **Swiss**, Av. Mal. F. Peixoto, T 223-7553; **Uruguay**, R. Vol. da Pátria 475, 18th floor.

**Laundry** R. C. Laurindo 63, next to theatre, US$3 for 5 kg.

**Church** services held in German at the Evangelical Church.

**Post Office** Main post office is at Marechal Deodoro 298; post offices also at R. 15 de Novembro and R. Pres. Faria. **Telecommunications** Embratel, Galeria Minerva, R. 15 de Novembro. *UPS*, T 262-6180 (Waldomiro).

**Tourist Office** Av. Sete de Setembro 2077, CEP 80.050, Curitiba, maps and information in English. *Guía Turística de Curitiba e Paraná*, annual, US$4, on sale at all kiosks, has been rec. Paranatur has booths at Rodoferroviária, and at airport, helpful, English spoken, but no maps. Free weekly leaflet, *Bom Programa*, available shops, cinemas, paper stands etc.

**Transport** Rodoferroviária at end of Av. 7 de Setembro, very efficient (bus to centre US$0.10); short-distance bus services (up to 40 km.) begin at old bus station at R. João Negrão 340. Passenger trains to Paranaguá, see below.
  Frequent buses to São Paulo, including night bus at 2320 (6 hrs., US$6; leito 12) and **Rio de Janeiro** (11 hours, US$20, leito 40). To **Santos**, 3 a day (leito at 2300), 6½ hrs., US$11. Buses to **Foz do Iguaçu**, 6 buses a day, 10 hrs., US$11.50 (3 leito buses at night, US$21); to **Pelotas**, US$25, 18 hrs; to **Porto Alegre**, 10 hrs; to Londrina via Ponta Grossa, US$7, 8 hrs.; to Guaíra, 0700, 1915 and leito 1930 (12 hrs). Itajaí, 4 hrs., US$5.50; **Blumenau**, 4½ hrs., US$6.40. **Florianópolis**, 4½ hrs, US$8 (leito US$16). TTL runs to **Montevideo**, 26 hrs., US$36, 0300 departure (leito) US$72. If travelling by car to Porto Alegre or Montevideo, the inland road (BR-116) is preferable to the coastal highway (BR-101).

**Excursions** The beautiful Ouro Fino estate (34 km.) is open to the public every day except Mon., Dec.-March, and every second Sunday the rest of the year. The nearest bus stop is 16 km. away at Campo Largo, so car is the best way to get there. Advance permission needed, from R. Silva Jardim 167, Curitiba, T 232-7411, or phone Ouro Fino (041) 292-1913. Near Lapa (about 80 km. SW) is a free, secure campsite from which the Groto do Monge can be visited.
  20 km. from Curitiba (at Km. 119) on the road to Ponta Grossa on the Museu Histórico do Mate, an old water-driven mill where mate was prepared (free admission). On the same road is *Vila Velha*, now a national park, 97 km. from Curitiba: the sandstone rocks have been weathered into most fantastic shapes. There is a Camping Clube do Brasil site near Vila Velha, 85 km. from Curitiba. Alternatively, stay in Ponta Grossa (**see page 395,** last bus back, stops near Furnas at 1800). The park office is 300 metres from the highway and the park a further 1½ km. (entrance—also to Furnas, keep the ticket—US$0.60—opens at 0800). If taking a bus from Curitiba, make sure it's going to the Parque Nacional and not to the town 20 km. away. Transport from the Park to a swimming pool (free—costumes can be rented for US$1.20), 2 km. away. Princesa dos Campos

bus from Curitiba at 0730 and 0930, 1½ hrs., US$2 (return buses pass park entrance at 1500 and 1700). The Lagoa Dourada, surrounded by forests, is close by. Nearby are the Furnas, three water holes, the deepest of which has a lift (US$0.60—not always working) which descends almost to water level (the same level as Lagoa Dourada); entrance US$0.10. Bus from Vila Velha at 1310, 1610 and 1830, US$0.60, 4½ km. to turn-off to Furnas (another ¼y-hr. walk) and Lagoa Dourada (it's not worth walking from Vila Velha to Furnas because it's mostly uphill along the main road). From the turn-off buses to Curitiba pass 10 minutes before they pass Vila Velha. Allow all day if visiting all 3 sites (unless you hitch, or can time the buses well, it's a lot of walking). Since the afternoon buses which pass en route to Curitiba are often full, it may be advisable to go to Ponta Grossa and return to Curitiba from there.

Popular expeditions during the summer are by paved road or rail (4½ hrs.) to Paranaguá. The railway journey is the most **spectacular** in Brazil. There are numerous tunnels,with sudden views of deep gorges and high peaks and waterfalls as the train rumbles over dizzy bridges and viaducts. Near Banhado station (Km. 66) is the waterfall of Véu da Noiva; from the station at Km. 59, the mountain range of **Marumbi National Park** can be reached: see below. The ordinary train leaves Curitiba at 0800 Mon.-Fri., but there is no return from Paranaguá for passengers (in winter there is no weekday passenger service). On Sat. and Sun. the year round ordinary service is at 0700, arriving in Paranaguá at 1030 (US$2 one class, tickets on sale at 0600, except for Sun. train where on sale on Fri., no seat reservations—ticket office is closed on Sun.; sandwiches, chocolate and drinks for sale on board; the schedule may vary according to freight needs; do not trust printed schedules, ask at the station). Avoid the front coach and sit on the left hand side. A modern air-conditioned rail-car (the Litorina, called the automotriz) leaves at 0830 Sat. and Sun. only, arriving at 1120 (US$10 each way, reserved seats bookable 2 days in advance; latest reports suggest the service varies) with recorded commentary (in Portuguese, French, Spanish and English) and stops at the viewpoint at the Santuário da N.S. do Cadeado and at Morretes (only a few minutes). Sit on the left-hand side on journey from Curitiba (in the automotriz, the seats, not the car, are turned round, so you sit the same side in each direction). If Litorina is full, take bus to Paranaguá, US$2.10, then take Litorina back: return journeys start at 1530 (Litorina) and 1630 (ordinary train) so remember that in winter part of the ordinary train's journey is covered in the dark (also, on cloudy days there's little to see on the higher parts). The train is usually crowded on Saturdays and Sundays. Many travellers recommend returning by bus (1½ hrs., buy ticket immediately on arrival), if you do not want to stay 4½ hrs. A tour bus meets the train and offers a tour of town and return to Curitiba for US$5.

You can also visit **Antonina** (a port, not on main route) and **Morretes** (on main route), two sleepy colonial towns which can be reached by bus on the old Graciosa road, which is almost as scenic as the railway. Bus Paranaguá to Morretes at 1830, US$1, to Antonina, stopping en route at Morretes, 6 a day, (US$1.60). 12 buses daily Morretes-Curitiba US$1.60; 20 buses a day Curitiba-Antonina.

**Morretes hotel**: *Nhundiaquara*, in town centre, beautifully located, E and up, good restaurant; good restaurants in town (try "barreado", beef cooked for 24 hrs, especially good in the two restaurants on the river bank) and a river beach. 14 km. N of Morretes is the beautiful village of São João de Graciosa, 2 km. beyond which is the flower reserve of the Marumbi Park. The Graciosa road traverses the park for 12 km., with 6 rest stops with fire grills, shelters and camping. The park is very beautiful; you can also hike the original trail which follows the road and passes the rest-stops. Take food, water and plenty of insect repellent. The Marumbi Park can be entered at a gate 3-4 km. from the BR-116 Curitiba-São Paulo highway.

**Paranaguá** (pop. 95,000), and chief port of the state of Paraná and one of the main coffee-exporting ports, was founded in 1585, 268 km. south of Santos. It is on a lagoon 29 km. from the open sea and is approached via the Bay of Paranaguá, dotted with picturesque islands. The fort of Nossa Senhora dos Prazeres was built in 1767 on a nearby island; one hour's boat trip. The former Colêgio dos Jesuitas, a fine baroque building, has been converted into a Museu de Arqueológia e Artes Populares (Tues.-Sun. 1200-1700; entrance US$0.10). Other attractions are a 17th century fountain, the church of São Benedito, and the shrine of Nossa Senhora do Rocio, 2 km. from town. There are restaurants and craft shops near the waterfront. The part of town between the waterfront, railway station and new bus station has been declared a historic area. Paranaguá is a free port for Paraguay.

The paved 116-km. road to Curitiba is picturesque, but less so than the railway (see above), which offers one of the most beautiful trips in Brazil.

**Hotels** *Auana*, R. Correia de Freitas 110, T 422-0948, D, good value, rec. (but electric showers in the more expensive rooms). *Karibe*, F. Simas 86, T 422-1177, D-E, good value; *Litoral*, R. Correia de Freitas 66, E without breakfast, clean and comfortable; *Rio Mar*, on waterfront, E.

**Camping** Camping Clube do Brasil site at Praia de Leste, on the beach, 27 km. from Paranaguá.

**Restaurants** *Bobby's*, Faria Sobrinho 750, highly rec., esp. for seafood. *Danúbio Azul*, 15 de Novembro 91, good, not cheap, view of river, classical piano music; *Aquarius*, Av. Gabriel de Lara 40, good but not cheap seafood; there are cheap restaurants in the old market building; the *Yacht Club*, beyond *Danúbio Azul* is impressive and has a good bar.

**Exchange** Banco do Brasil, Largo C. Alcindino; *Câmbio*, R. Faría Sabrintio, for cash.

**Consulates** Danish, R. C. Correia Jr. 567, CP 101 83200, T 422 1666, open 0800-1200, 1400-1800.

**Tourist Information** kiosk outside railway station.

**Bus Station** All buses operated by Graciosa. To **Curitiba**, US$3, many, 1½ hrs. (only the 0745 in either direction and the 1545 to Curitiba take the old Graciosa road); direct to **Rio**, 15 hrs, US$32.

**Excursions** *Matinhos* is a Mediterranean-type resort, invaded by surfers in October for the Paraná surf competition; several cheap hotels, including *Bolamar* (F, basic, cheapest) and *Beira Mar*. 3 camp sites, but the municipal site is closed until November. Cruises on Paranaguá Bay by launch, daily from Cais do Mercado. Bus from Paranaguá at 1000, 1400 and 1615, US$0.80. 6 buses a day to Guaratuba, US$1. *Guaratuba* (which is less built up than Caiobá) has *Pensão Antonieta*, E, clean, dangerous showers, and other hotels; campsite. All Guaratuba buses pass *Caiobá* (*Hotel Caiobá*, D, cheapest). Caiobá to Guaratuba by ferry, free for pedestrians, US$1.25 for cars, 10 minutes, frequent departures.

To **Ilha do Mel**, take bus to Pontal do Sul (many daily, direct from/to Curitiba, 1hr., US$1.60); turn left out of the bus station and walk 25 metres to main road, turn right for 1½ km. and bear left along a sandy road for 2 km. to fishermen's houses from where a ferry runs (US$1.30). On the island, which is well-developed for tourism, there are bars, holiday homes, etc. Camping is possible on the more deserted beaches. At Praia dos Encantados, one can camp or rent a fisherman's house—ask for *Valentim's Bar*, or for Luchiano; *Estalagem Ancourado*, nr. the lighthouse, F, shared facilities, clean, friendly, meals cooked if required. Dona Ana and Dona Maria sell bread and cakes, and meals if you ask in advance. The beaches, caves, bays and hill walks are beautiful. 4 hrs.' walk from the village is an old Portuguese fort, possible to hitch a ride in a fishing boat back. If camping, watch out for the tide, watch possessions and beware of the *bicho de pé* which burrows into feet (remove with a needle and alcohol) and of the *borrachudos* (discourage with Autum repellent). In summer and at holiday times the island is very crowded.

About 117 km. from Curitiba the road inland (which passes Vila Velha— see page 393) reaches **Ponta Grossa** (pop. 223,000, 895 metres). It now calls itself the "World Capital of Soya" (as does Palmeira das Missões, in Rio Grande do Sul). Roads run north through Apucarana (Camping Clube site) and Londrina to São Paulo, and south to Rio Grande do Sul and the Uruguayan border.

**Hotels** *Vila Velha Palace*, R. Balduino Taques 123, T 24-2200, B; *Planalto Palace*, R. 7 de

Setembro 652, T 24-2122, plain and clean, D; *Scha Fransky*, R. Francisco Ribas 104, T 24-2511, D, very good breakfast; almost next door, same street No. 162, is *Central*, E, with fan and basin; *Luz*, F, basic, near railway station; *Casimiri*, next door, F, often full. *Esplanada*, in bus station (quiet, however), E with bath and breakfast, clean, safe. Try area around Praça Barão de Garaúna.

**Camping**  Camping Clube do Brasil, 26 km. out at the entrance to Vila Velha.

**Restaurants**  *Casa Verde*, near the *Central*, lunch only, rec.; there are cheap restaurants near the railway station.

**Buses**  Princesa dos Campos to **Curitiba**, 6 a day, 2 hrs., US$3.20; same company to **Iguaçu**, 4 daily, 11 hrs., US$12. To **Vila Velha** at 0700 and 0900 (return the same day is possible.)

In Alto Paraná in the extreme NW of the State, connections have traditionally been with São Paulo rather than with Curitiba. Large new centres of population have risen in a short time. In 1930 four Japanese and two Germans arrived in **Londrina** (pop. 346,000), developed by a British company. Today it is a city with skyscrapers, modern steel and glass cathedral, and wide streets (*Hotel Coroados*, Sen. Souza Naves 814, T 23-7690, D, standard; *Hotel dos Viajantes*, Av. São Paulo 78, F, clean, quiet, safe, friendly; *Hotel Triunfo*, R. Prof João Cândido 39, T 23-5054, F, clean, friendly; *Hotel Cravinho*, R. Minas Gerais 88, F, clean, friendly. Youth Hostel, R. Gomes Carneiro 315, centro Esportivo Moringão). **Maringá** (pop. 197,000, about a third Japanese) is 80 km. W of Londrina, founded in 1947. There is a small conical cathedral; Parque Ingá is shady, with a Japanese garden. Londrina and Maringá are good points for connections between the south (Porto Alegre), Foz do Iguaçu and Mato Grosso do Sul (Campo Grande). Bus from Londrina to Porto Alegre takes 22 hours; to Campo Grande 11 hours, via Presidente Prudente (**see page 371**). A number of bus services from Paraná state to Porto Alegre (Aguia Branca, Unesul) and to Campo Grande, Cuiabá and Porto Velho (Eucatur) commence at **Cascavel**, further S on the Curitiba-Iguaçu road (hotels: *Vila Paraguaya*, F, clean, simple; *Grand Prix*, Av. Brasil 5202, D, clean, good value).

## The Paraná River

In the extreme SW of the State, on the Argentine frontier, are the *Iguaçu Falls*, approached by a good paved road from Curitiba, through Guarapuava and Cascavel, with frequent bus services. There is an international airport about 14 km. from the Falls, and 32 km. from the Falls is the city of Foz do Iguaçu, with excellent road connections with Argentina and Paraguay.

For a detailed description of the Falls as a whole, and the Argentine side in particular, together with an account of road links between the Argentine and Brazilian sides, see the Argentine chapter, Section 8.

Ideally, one should first visit the Brazilian side to get some idea of the size and magnificence of the whole, and to take one's introductory photographs in the morning, and then cross to the Argentine side to see the details (quickest to get some australes on the Brazilian side), this can all be done in a day, starting at about 0700, but the brisk pace needed for a quick tour is very exhausting for the non-athletic in that heat. If one's time is very limited, then the Brazilian side, with its marvellous distant views, is the one to visit.

A 1½ km. paved walk runs part of the way down the cliff near the rim of the Falls, giving a stupendous view of the whole Argentine side (the greater part) of the falls. It ends up almost under the powerful Floriano Falls; a catwalk brought into use at the end of 1984 was closed again in 1989. Waterproof clothing can be hired although it is not absolutely necessary. An elevator (from 0800) hoists the visitor to the top of the Floriano Falls and to a path leading to Porto Canoa, if there is a queue it is easy and quick to walk up. A safari, Macuco, near the falls, costs US$18 for a guided tour, but it is better on the Argentine side. Helicopter flight over Falls—US$40 per head—lasts 4 minutes. (There is pressure for the helicopter rides to stop: the noise is seriously disturbing the wildlife, especially the birds.) There is a small but worthwhile museum 5 km. from the Falls (1 km. from park entrance is side road to museum, look for sign) and opposite it are some steps that lead down the steep slope to the river bank. Beautiful walk. It can be misty early in the morning at the Falls. Entry to the Brazilian side of the Falls is about US$1.50, payable at the National Park entrance. If possible, visit on a weekday when the walks are less crowded.

From Foz do Iguaçu, Dois Irmãos buses (from local bus station—*Terminal Urbana*—on Av. Juscelino Kubitschek, opp. Infantry Barracks, 1½ blocks from Rodoviária— interstate bus station) marked Cataratas run the 32 km. to the falls every 2 hours from 0800 to 2100, past airport to *Hotel das Cataratas*, takes 40 mins. At weekends, holidays and other high seasons, frequency increases to every hour. Buses return 0700-1900, about US$1 one way. The driver waits at the Park entrance while passengers purchase entry tickets. (The taxi fare is US$5.65, plus US$2.50 for each hour of waiting.) The tours of the Falls organized by the various hotels have been recommended in preference to taxi rides. At least 4 buses an hour from 0700 to 2100 (Transbalan, Viação Itaipu, Tres Fronteiras companies, about US$0.50) ply over the bridge between the *Terminal Urbana* and the bus station in Puerto Iguazú (combined tickets to Puerto Iguazú and the falls cost more than paying separately; when returning from Puerto Iguazú, ask to be let off in Foz).

Be sure to get a stamp on your passport if intending to stay in Brazil. There is an entry tax on the Brazilian side for car passengers only, not for bus passengers. If driving into Brazil insist on visiting customs. You must get entry papers for your car here or you'll have serious problems later.

There are Brazilian immigration offices on the Brazilian sides of the bridges into Paraguay and Argentina; if you are just visiting Ciudad del Este (formerly Ciudad Stroessner) or Puerto Iguazú and the Argentine side of the Falls and returning to Brazil the same day, no need to have your passport stamped. There are Brazilian customs patrols looking for undeclared goods on the roads past the frontier. Note that if entering or leaving a country and you have to visit customs and immigration, buses won't wait; take a taxi instead.

**Foz do Iguaçu** is a rapidly developing and improving town of about 200,000 people, with a wide range of accommodation and good communications by air and road with the main cities of southern Brazil, and with Asunción, Paraguay.

**Hotels**   On a height directly overlooking the Falls, 32 km. from Foz, is the **Hotel das Cataratas**, T 74 2666, Fax 74 1688, L+ (but 30% discount for holders of the Brazil Air Pass), an attractive colonial-style building with nice gardens and a swimming pool not without insects. Much wildlife can be seen in the grounds at night and early a.m. "Rates L". It is reported the money is exchanged only at the official rate, check before paying. Non-residents can have US$15 lunch here (midday and evening buffets, or else wait 45 minutes for *à-la-carte* dishes).

If you know which hotel you wish to stay in (and there are over 180), do not be put off by touts who say it no longer exists. Note also that touts quote room rates below what is actually charged; in high season (e.g. Christmas-New Year), you will not easily find a room under US$14 d.

Many out-of-town hotels on the Falls road state their address as km. from Foz. *Salvatti*, R. Rio Branco 577, T 74-2727, A, all a/c (with restaurant and cinema); *Internacional*, Almirante Baroso 345, T 73-4240, L, good; *Rafahin Palace*, Br 277-Km. 727, T 73-3434, bungalows to rent nearby; *Rafahin*, Mal. Deodoro 909, T 74-2635, B, good restaurant, pool, well spoken of. Rec.: *Foz Presidente*, R. Xavier da Silva 918, T 73-1361, B, shower, a/c, fair, restaurant, swimming pool, trips arranged to Falls, English spoken, convenient for buses. On road to Falls (Rodovia das Cataratas) are the *Bourbon*, all facilities, L (Km. 2.5), *Carimã*, A, (Km. 16), *Dom Pedro I*, A, (Km. 3, T 74-2011), *Panorama*, A, (Km. 12), *Belvedere*, A, (Km. 10.4), T 74-1344. *Colonial*, (Km. 16.5), T 74-1777, A+, near airport, swimming pool, fine location. *Continental Inn*, Av. Paraná 485, T 73-1329, good restaurant, a/c; *Lanville*, Jorge Schimmelpfeng 827, T 72-2211, B. On Av. Brasil: *Diplomata*, No. 678, T 74-3155, some a/c, D with shower, value for money, arranges taxi tours to Argentine side; *O Astro*, No 660, T 72-3584, D, clean, friendly, a/c; *City*, No. 938, T 74-2074, C, own bathroom, fan, hot water, clean; *Foz do Iguaçu*, No. 97, T 73-2511, B, good laundry and breakfast, will look after luggage, fair; *Bogari Palace*, No. 106, T 74-3922, A, excellent restaurant, swimming pool;

*Cisne*, No. 144A, T 74-2458, B, good breakfast, clean friendly, English spoken, fridge; *Imperial*, No. 168, T 74-2422, D with bath, clean. *Pietá*, R. Rebouças 84, T 0455-745581, C-D, pool, clean, friendly, good breakfast, car and guide, rec; *Luz*, Almte Barroso, T 73-1891, near rodoviária, D, clean, rec; *Turis*, R. Xavier da Silva 699, T 74-4955, D, fans, bathroom, noisy, excellent breakfast, organizes tours; *Solar*, same block as Rodoviária, entrance through shop, E, clean, rec.; *San Remo*, Kubitschek e Xavier da Silva 467, T 72-2956, E, a/c; *Goya*, Kubitschek 969, T 74-3955, E; *Bastos*, Castelo Branco 216, T 74-5839, E, a/c with bath, clean, secure, helpful, rec.; *Hospedaria Antunes*, Av. República Argentina, 288, F with coffee, fans, friendly, clean, quiet, rec; *Tarobá*, Tarobá 878, T 73-5437, quiet, clean, C with bath, a/c, rec.; *Riviera*, Mal. Deodoro 559 with Bartolomeu de Gusmão, E, clean, friendly; *Almeida II*, Mal Deodoro y Rui Barbosa, F, basic, rec. *Hospedaria*, R. Tarobá 501, Manuel Baiano, E, family atmosphere, breakfast in kitchen; *Trento*, Rebouças 665, T 74-5111, E, shared bath, clean, rec.; *Plaza*, Bartolomeu de Gusmão 376, T 74-2515, E, good, clean, rec.; *Senhor do Bonfim*, Almte Barroso 6, T (0455) 7-4540, E, clean, friendly; *Senhor do Bonfin II*, R. Naipi 960, E, clean, good; *Geny*, R. Tomé de Souza, E; *Hospedaria*, Floriano Peixoto 263, E with bath, F without, fridge, fan, clean, German spoken; *Hospedaria Janice*, Santos Dumont 1222, E, very friendly and helpful. Rec. accommodation: house of Gertrudis Roth, Rebouças 907, pleasant, 3 rooms, deals fixed up with restaurants, exchange dealers etc; Evelina Navarrete, R. Mar Floriano 1327, T 74-3817, clean, excellent breakfast, helpful, rec, English, French and Spanish spoken; Maria Schneider, Av. Jorge Schimmelpfeng 483, T 0455-742305, F, German spoken, country house atmosphere, rec. *IYHA* affiliated hostel, between immigration and the bridge, F. Be sure to leave hotels punctually, or you will be charged an extra day. Many hotels have a minibus service to the airport for guests for a small fee and also offer excursions to Falls.

**Camping** (pretty cold and humid in winter). By National Park entrance Camping Clube do Brasil, 17 km. from Foz, US$10 p.p. a night (half with International Camping Card), swimming pool, clean; park vehicle or put tent away from trees in winter in case of heavy rain storms, no restaurants, food there not very good, closes at 2300. Not permitted by hotel and Falls. Sleeping in car inside the park also prohibited. Avoid *Camping Internacional*, where several assaults have been reported, 5 km. from Foz centre.

**Electric Current** 110 volts a/c.

**Restaurants** Many open till midnight. *Rafahin* before the policia rodoviária post at Km. 533, with Paraguayan harp trio, good alcatra (meat), excellent buffet, but expensive, next to *Rafahin Palace Hotel* on Route 277, km. 727. *Santos Delavy*, Av. J. Kubitschek 393, Argentine owner, cheap and friendly; *Churrascaria Cabeça de Boi*, Av. Brasil 1325, large, live music, dinner US$5, also for coffee and pastries. *Cantina*, Av. Rodrigues 720, buffet, all you can eat, rec.; *Star Foz* R. Alm. Barroso 330, good steaks, outstanding value; *Clarks*, No. 896, excellent food, reasonable. A fruit shop and restaurant are next to the Atlantic gasoline station, 2 blocks from the bus station, and one block behind the bus station is an excellent churrascaria, *Espetão*. *Clark's*, Almte. Barroso 896, good, moderately-priced; *El Club Caxos*, Almte. Barosso 249, cheap; *Chapa*, behind the bus station, cheapest in town, excellent value; *Supermercado Maringo*, lunch counter US$2. Chicken meals with beer cost on average US$4 p.p.

   Beware of overcharging at *lanches* (small restaurants)—sometimes three times the posted price; have the right change available.

**N.B.** There are increased reports of night-time assaults at Foz, with thieves carrying knives or guns. Also, taxis are expensive and not worth the money for short distances in town.

**Entertainment** Discotheque *Whiskadão* with three different dance halls, Alm. Barroso 763, reasonable, lively at weekends. Fun fair, Centro de Diversões Imperial, on Av. Brasil.

**Consulates** **Argentina**, R. Don Pedro II, close to Paranatur, open 0800-1300; **Paraguay**, Bartolomeu de Gusmão 777.

**Health** Translation offered, doctor arranged by Edgar Leiminger, R. Mal. Deodoro 233, T (045) 574-5650, Spanish, English, German spoken.

**Post Office** Praça Getúlio Vargas 72, next to Tourist Office. *International phone* calls from the office on Rui Barbosa.

**Tourist Office** Paranatur, very helpful, Almirante Barroso 485. Kiosk on Av. Brasil, by Ponte de Amizade (helpful), will book hotels.

**Travel Agents and Currency Exchange** Beware of overcharging for tours by touts at the Rodoviária. *Transatlântica Turismo*, Av. Brasil 99, *Waterfall Travels*, Av. Brasil 267, Caixa

Postal 157 CEP 85 890, and others. *Dicks Tours* has been rec. for its all-day tour to the Brazilian side of the Falls, to Paraguay (Ciudad del Este) and to the Itaipú dam. *Wilson Engel*, T 741367 takes tours, up to 8 for US$30 for the Brazilian side, US$42 for the Argentine side, friendly, flexible. Recommended guides, Ruth Campo Silva, *STTC Turismo Ltda*, Av. Brasil 268, T 74-3122; *Chiderly Batismo Pequeno*, R. Almirante Barroso 505, Foz, T 74-3367, Very difficult to exchange on Sunday, but quite possible in Paraguay where US dollars can be obtained on credit cards. Banco do Brasil, Av. Brasil, good rates for travellers cheques; Banco Mercantil de São Paulo, Av. Brasil 1192, cash advances on Master Card/Eurocard; *Turismo Ortega*, Av. Brasil 1140, T 74-2256, also handles exchange; *Cambio Iguaçu*, Av. Brasil 268; *Casa Jerusalém*, Av. Brasil 1055, for cruzeiros, australes, guaraníes, good rates. *Frontur* on Av. Brasil accepts travellers' cheques, so does *Venson Turismo*, next to *Hotel Foz do Iguaçu*; many street changers nearby, good rates also at the airport.

**Excursions** From Foz, you can make an excursion to the 12,600-megawatt *Itaipú* dam, the largest single power station in the world, which Brazil and Paraguay have built nearby. The dam is 8 km. long. The power house 1½ km. Paraguay does not use all its quota of power so this is sold to Brazil, which powers all of Southern Brasil and much of Rio, São Paulo and Minas Gerais from Itaipú. Bus marked Canteira da Obra from Terminal Urbana goes every 40 minutes to the Public Relations office at the main entrance, visits free (but in groups only)—film in German, English or Portuguese and then the dam (stops for taking photos), ask in reception if you may see turbines. Tours (US$0.30) start at 0800, 0900, 1000, 1400, 1500, 1600; 0800, 0900, 1000, 1330 and 1430 on Sun., the first English tour starts at 0900. There are also an "executive" bus and agency tours but these are an unnecessary expense. If it's sunny, go in the morning as the sun is behind the dam in the afternoon and you will get poor photographs. You cannot go alone to the site as it is fenced in and guarded by its own security force. You can also visit the Paraguayan side, bus from Av. J. Kubitschek beside the military area to Ciudad del Este.

It is also possible to stay in Ciudad del Este visiting both sides of the falls without immigration stamps; documents must be carried at all times, however. Take the Foz do Iguaçu bus to interstate rodoviária or walk over the Ponte de Amizade (Friendship Bridge, Brazilian post open until 0200, pay US$2 in dollars, guaraníes or cruzeiros at the Paraguayan end) past Brazilian Customs and take Ponte-Cidade bus (US$0.10) to local bus station (10 mins. from Rodoviária) where buses go to the Falls or to Argentina. Taxi from Ciudad del Este to centre of Foz, US$10. It is not possible to change travellers cheques in Paraguay unless your passport is stamped.

**Airport** The Iguaçu international airport has daily flights from Río, São Paulo, Curitiba and Asunción, Paraguay, and good connections from other Brazilian cities. 3 flights a week to Buenos Aires. Taxis to town from the Brazilian airport 18 km from Foz, or about half-way between Foz and the Falls, are expensive (US$10, more at odd hours); Dois Irmãos town bus for US$0.15, first at 0530, does not permit large amounts of luggage (but backpacks OK). Varig/Cruzeiro office in Foz: Av. Brasil 821, T 74-3344; staff speak foreign languages; Vasp, T 74-2999.

**Buses** Rodoviária, Av. Brasil 99, behind *Hotel Foz do Iguaçu*, T 73-1525; has trustworthy baggage store; book departures as soon as possible. Foz is reached by many buses from **Curitiba** (9-11 hours, paved road, US$11.50, leito US$21), from Guaíra via Cascavel only (5 hrs., US$4.25), and from **São Paulo** (15 hours, about US$24 with Pluma, leito US$50). Foz-Florianópolis, daily, US$16.50, 16 hrs. Porto Alegre-Foz US$20, direct buses daily, 14 hrs. with Unisul, book in advance. To Campo Grande, 15 hrs. by Maringá company (3 hrs. to Cascavel, and 12 from there to Campo Grande); Nacional Expresso to Brasília direct, 26 hrs Saritur to **Belo Horizonte** at 2100, US$30, 24 hrs. There are direct buses from **Rio** (US$29 one way pullman bus), 22 hours (return to Rio daily at 0900 with Pluma direct, or 1400 with Maringá; leito to Rio, 1900, US$58, good for sleeping).

**Travel From Paraguay** By daily plane from Asunción to Foz do Iguaçu, or by paved road from Asunción (book in advance to take the 0730 bus from Asunción, arriving at 1300 at the Brazilian border and at the bus terminal at 1500) about US$5. (If you wish to return to Asunción the same day, get a small bus to the falls and return at 1730 to the bus station, to be back at 2400.) Several bus companies ply the route: Nuestra Señora, Rysa, Pluma etc., fare US$4-6 according to quality, about 5 hrs.

**Travel to Paraguay**, a visa costs US$15 for a 6-hr. service, US$10 with a 48 hr. wait. In addition, a tourist charge of US$5 is made at the border.

In the far NW of the state, also on the River Paraná, were the tremendous waterfalls known in Brazil as Sete Quedas (the Seven Falls), and in Spanish Latin America as the Salto de Guaíra;

they were drowned by the filling of the lake behind the Itaipu dam in 1982. Guaíra (about 130 km. N of Iguaçu by air or road) will not be flooded, but much of its agricultural land and its clay beds have been. **Presidente Epitácio** on the Paraná can be reached by bus from São Paulo, several daily, US$24 (passenger rail service discontinued). A luxury passenger vessel, the *Epitácio Pessoa*, sails twice monthly (weekly during holiday periods) on Wed. at 1700 downstream to **Guaíra**, 400 km. S, getting there at 1900 Thurs. evening. Return trips on Sat. at 1100, arrive at Pres. Epitácio at 2200 Sun. (Note: These schedules appear to be variable.) Cabins or cheaper accommodation available on lower decks. Bookings should be made in advance with: Comércio e Navegação Alto Paraná Ltda., Praça da República 177, Loja 15, São Paulo, T 259-8255, Telex: 011-32400. Passages can also be purchased (subject to space available) at the office by the port in Presidente Epitácio, and in Guaíra from Ernst Mann, Americatur, R. Alvorada 253. Alternatively it may be possible to obtain passage on a cargo boat.

The 4 km. from Guaíra to the lake can be walked or done by car (US$2.40 one way, return taxi up to US$10). Entrance to park US$0.30; small museum three blocks from Guaíra bus terminal, 0800-1100 and 1400-1700.

**Presidente Epitácio Hotel** *Itaverá*, Curitiba 622, E, including breakfast, good value, near station.

**Guaíra Lodging and Food** Near the bus station: *Palace Hotel*, Rui Barbosa 1190, T 42-1325, D; *Majestic*, opposite bus station, E with or without bath, with breakfast, good; also *Hotel Itaipu*, E with bath, hot showers, good food (restaurant closed Sun.); *Sete Quedas*, Otávio Tosta 385, E, with breakfast and sandwich lunch, not too clean; *Ichapena*, E, not very clean but very friendly; and others. **Camping** Municipal site at Bosque do Kartódromo. 2 km. out of town on the road from the bus station; ask at the Prefeitura for details. Basic facilities at each. **Restaurant** *O Chopão*, Otávio Tosta 69, pleasant.

**Buses** Guaíra-Campo Grande: buy a ticket (US$28) at the Guaíra bus terminal, take ferry to Ponta Porã, then bus to Mondo Novo, change bus there for Campo Grande; morning and night bus, 12 hrs. in all. There is a bus service between **Curitiba** and Guaíra, US$19, 10 hrs.; bus to **São Paulo**, US$24, 16 hrs.; Guaíra to **Presidente Epitácio**, US$2.80. The road is surfaced throughout. Also a bus from Londrina (US$11.50, 7½ hrs.) and Cascavel (connecting with bus from Iguaçu). The direct route **Iguaçu-Guaíra** is very bumpy, but interesting, takes 5 hrs. in the dry, but buses may be cancelled in the wet, US$8, or US$9.30 via Cascavel. There are also flights.

**Note** If entering Brazil from Paraguay in the Guaíra region, make sure to get passport stamped at the nearest available location (probably Foz do Iguaçu)—there is no passport control when coming off the boat from Salto Guaíra, Paraguay. There is an hourly passenger ferry service from Porto de Lanchas and Porto Guaíra to Paraguayan side, US$0.50, and hourly car ferry from Porto Guaíra. There is a time change when you cross the Paraná. The area is intensively patrolled for contraband and stolen cars, ensure that all documentation is in order.

---

## BAHIA (7)

Salvador, the capital of Bahia, is one of Brazil's most historic cities, with a wealth of colonial architecture. It is also dubbed "Africa in exile": the mixture of African and European finds its most powerful expression in Carnival. The state itself is a producer of cacao, sugar and oil. Its coast has many fine beaches, particularly in the south around Porto Seguro. Inland is the harsh Sertão, traversed by the Rio São Francisco.

Bahia is the southernmost of the nine states of the north-eastern bulge of Brazil. The other eight are Sergipe, Alagoas, Pernambuco, Paraíba, Rio Grande do Norte, Ceará, Piauí, and Maranhão. They cover 2.6 million square km. and contain a third of Brazil's people. The birthrate is the highest in Brazil, but so is the infant mortality rate. The average annual income from subsistence farming is deplorably low. Despite the misery, both regional and state loyalty remain ineradicable.

The nine states by no means form a homogeneous unity, but may be roughly

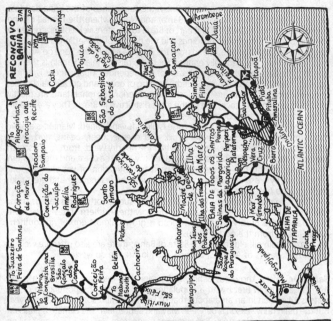

RECONCAVO - BAHIA - 37A

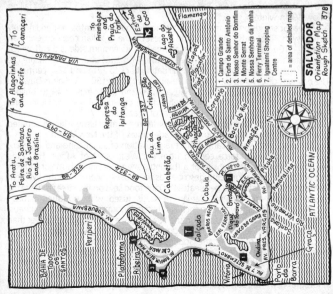

SALVADOR
Orientation Map
Rough Sketch 378

1. Campo Grande
2. Forte de Santo António
3. Nosso Senhor do Bomfim
4. Monte Serrat
5. Nossa Senhora da Penha
6. Ferry Terminal
7. Iguatemi Shopping Centre

□ = area of detailed map

divided into three contrasting parts. One is the sugar lands of the Zona da Mata along the coast between Salvador (Bahia) and Natal, where the rainfall can be depended upon. This was the first part of Brazil to be intensively colonized; hence the number of 16th century buildings and the density of old settlements are way above the national average. Inland from the Zona da Mata is the Zona do Agreste, with less rainfall, but generally enough for cattle raising. Inland again is the true interior, the Sertão, where rainfall cannot be depended upon; there is a little agriculture where water allows it but the herding of goats, and occasionally cattle, is more important. There are few blacks in the interior; the inhabitants are mostly of Portuguese-Indian stock, one of the most distinctive in Brazil. They are known as the *flagelados*, the scourged ones.

When there is rain, food in the zone is plentiful and varied. Manioc is a basic food; in addition, there are goat's milk and cheese, beef, beans, and sweet potatoes. But in the years of drought, when the hot dry winds from Africa scorch the earth, the effects can be tragic. Migration towards the coast and the southern towns begins, and the people are exposed to castigation of yet another sort: exploitation by grasping labour contractors. But at the first news that there is rain, the *flagelado* heads for home.

The main export crops of the north-east are sugar, cotton and cacao. Sugar and cotton have long been in decline, and now the southern states grow more than half of the Brazilian total. But cacao is grown almost entirely in southern Bahia, inland from the port of Ilhéus.

Brazil's main oilfields are in the State of Bahia; there are also offshore wells in the coastal waters of Alagoas, Sergipe and Rio Grande do Norte.

**Salvador** (often known as Bahia), is the capital of the state of Bahia. It is the fifth largest city in Brazil with a population of 2 million. The population of the state is 14 million in an area about that of France. It rains somewhat all the year but the main rainy season is between May and September. The climate is pleasant and the sun is never far away. Temperatures range from 25°C to 32°C, never falling below 19° in winter.

Salvador stands on the magnificent Bahia de Todos os Santos, a sparkling bay dotted with 38 islands. The bay is the largest on the Brazilian coast covering an area of 1,100 sq. kms. Rising above the bay on its eastern side is a cliff which dominates the landscape and, perched on top, 71 metres above sea level, are the older districts of Salvador with buildings dating back to 17th and 18th centuries. The bay was discovered by Amérigo Vespucci on 1 Nov 1501, All Saints Day. The first Governor General, Tomé de Sousa arrived on 23 March 1549 to build a fortified city to protect Portugal's interest from constant threats of Dutch and French invasion. Salvador was the capital of Brazil until 1763 at which stage it was the most important city in the Portuguese empire after Lisbon, ideally situated in a safe, sheltered harbour along the trade routes of the New World.

The city's first wealth came from the cultivation of sugar cane and tobacco, the plantations' workforce coming from the West coast of Africa. For three centuries Salvador was the site of a thriving slave trade and this major influx is responsible for Salvador being described as the most African city in the Western Hemisphere. The influence permeates the city: food sold on the street is the same as in Senegal and Nigeria, Bahian music is fused with pulsating African polyrhythms, men and women nonchalantly carry enormous loads on their heads, fishermen paddle dug out canoes in the bay, the pace of life is a little slower than elsewhere. The pulse of the city is *candomblé*, an Afro-Brazilian religion in which the African deities of Nature, the Goddess of the sea and the God of creation are worshipped. These deities (or *orixás*) are worshipped in temples (*terreiros*) which can be elaborate, decorated halls, or simply someone's front room with tiny altars to the *orixá*. *Candomblé* ceremonies may be seen by tourists—but not photographed—on Sundays and religious holidays. Contact the tourist office,

Bahiatursa, or see their twice monthly calendar of events.
Salvador today is a city of 15 forts, 166 Catholic churches, 1,000 *candomblé*

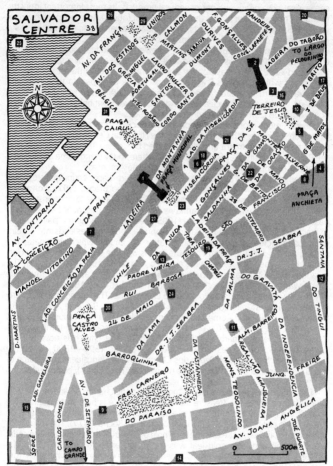

## Salvador: Key to Map

1. Lacerda Lift; 2. Gonçalves Funicular; 3. Cathedral; 4. Church of São Francisco; 5. Church of the Ordem Terceira de São Domingos; 6. Santa Casa da Misericórdia; 7. Conceição de Praia; 8. Church of the Ordem Terceira de São Francisco; 9. Church of São Bento; 10. Church of São Pedro dos Clérigos; 11. Church of Palma; 12. Church of Sant'Ana; 13. Nossa Senhora da Ajuda; 14. Convent of Lapa; 15. Convent of Santa Teresa/Museu de Arte Sacra; 16. Museu Afro-Brazileiro; 17. Museu da Cidade; 18. Museum of Santa Casa; 19. Casa de Rui Barbosa; 20. Casa das Sete Mortos; 21. Palácio Arquiepiscopal; 22. Solar do Saldanha; 23. Paço Municipal; 24. Solar de Berquó; 25. Fort of São Marcelo; 26. Customs House (Alfândega); 27. Palácio Rio Branco and Bahiatursa Tourist Office; 29. Central Post Office; 30. Post Office; 31. Mercado Modelo.

temples and a fascinating mixture of old and modern, rich and poor, African and European, religious and profane. It is still a major port exporting tropical fruit, cocoa, sisal, soya beans and petrochemical products. Its most important industry, though, is tourism; after Rio it is the second largest tourist attraction in the country, very popular with Brazilian tourists who see Bahia as an exotic destination.

The centre of the city is divided into two levels, the Upper city (or Cidade Alta) where the Historical Centre lies, and the Lower city (Cidade Baixa) which is the commercial and docks district. The two levels are connected by a series of steep hills called *ladeiras*. The easiest way to go from one level to the other is by the *Lacerda* lift which connects Praça Municipal (Tomé de Sousa) in the Upper city with Praça Cairu and the famous Mercado Modelo. There is also the Plano Inclinado Gonçalves, a funicular railway which leaves from behind the Cathedral going down to Comercio, the commercial district.

There is much more of interest on the Upper city. From Praça Municipal to the Carmo area 2 km. north along the cliff is the Historical Centre (Centro Histórico), now a national monument and also protected by Unesco. It was in this area that the Portuguese built their fortified city and where today stand some of the most important examples of colonial architecture in the Americas.

Dominating the Praça Municipal is the old Paço Municipal (Council Chamber—1660), while alongside is the Palácio Rio Branco (1918), once the Governor's Palace now the headquarters of Bahiatursa, the state tourist board. Leaving the square with its panoramic view of the bay, R. Misericôrdia goes north passing the Santa Casa Misericôrdia (1695—see the high altar and painted tiles) to Praça da Sé. This square with its mimosa and flamboyant trees leads into Terreiro de Jesus, a picturesque square named after the church which dominates the square. Built in 1692, the church of the Jesuits became the property of the Holy See in 1759 when the Jesuits were expelled from all Portuguese territories. The façade is one of the earliest examples of Baroque in Brazil, an architectural style which was to dominate the churches built in the 17th and 18th centuries. The whole church was built with Portuguese Lioz marble. The interior is particularly impressive, its vast vaulted ceiling and 12 side altars in Baroque and Rococco, framing the main altar completely leafed in gold. The tiles in blue, white and yellow in a tapestry pattern are also from Portugal. It houses the tomb of Mem de Sá and coloured marble and inlaid furniture. The church is now the city Cathedral and is open Tues. to Sun., 0800—1100 and 1500—1800. Across the square is the church of São Pedro dos Clérigos, while alongside is the church of the Ordem Terceira de São Domingos (Dominican Third Order), both rarely open to the public.

Facing Terreiro de Jesus is Praça Anchieta and the church of São Francisco. Its simple façade belies the treasure inside. The entrance is by a small door to the right of the main doors and leads to a sanctuary with a spectacular painting on the wooden ceiling, by local artist José Joaquim da Rocha (1777). The main body of the church is the most exuberant example of Baroque in the country. The cedar wood carving and later gold leaf was completed after 28 years in 1748. The cloisters of the monastery are surrounded by a series of blue and white tiles from Portugal. The church is open from 0800 to 1115 and 1400 to 1700. Next door (and with the same opening hours) is the church of the Ordem Terceira de São Francisco (Franciscan Third Order—1703) with its façade intricately carved in sandstone. Inside is a quite remarkable Chapter House with striking images of the Order's most celebrated saints.

Leading off the Terreiro de Jesus is R. Alfredo Brito, a charming, narrow cobbled street lined with fine colonial houses painted in different pastel shades. This street leads into the Largo do Pelourinho. Considered the finest complex of colonial architecture in Latin America, it was once the site of a pillory where slaves were publicly punished and ridiculed. It was also the site of the slave market. Nossa Senhora Do Rosario Dos Pretos church, the so-called Slave Church, dominates the square. It was built by former slaves, with what little financial resources they had, over a period of 100 years. The interior is much simpler than the Cathedral of São Francisco, with side altars in honour of black saints. The painted ceiling is also very impressive, the overall effect being one of tranquillity in contrast to the complexity of the other two churches. A small entrance fee is charged.

At the corner of Alfredo Brito and Largo do Pelourinho is a museum to the work of Jorge Amado (Casa da Cultura Jorge Amado), who lived in, and set many of his books, in this section of the city. His works have been published in 47 languages. A good way to get a feel of the city and its people is to read *Dona Flor and her two husbands*. The Carmo Hill is at the top of the street leading out of Largo do Pelourinho. The Carmo (Carmelite Third Order) church (1709) houses one of the sacred art treasures of the city, a sculpture of Christ made in 1730 by a slave who had no formal training, Francisco Xavier das Chagas, known as O Cabra. One of the features of the piece is the blood made from whale oil, ox blood, banana resin and 2000 rubies to represent the drops of blood. Opening hours are 0800 to 1200 and 1400 to 1730.

South of the Praça Municipal, in the direction of the mouth of the bay, is the more modern section of the city with many skyscrapers. R. Chile leads to Praça Castro Alves, with its monument to Castro Alves, who started the campaign which finally led to the Abolition of Slavery in 1888. Two streets lead out of this square, Avenida 7 de Setembro, a bustling street of shops and street vendors selling everything imaginable, and, parallel to it, R. Carlos Gomes. São Bento church (rebuilt after 1624, but with fine 17th century furniture) is on Av. 7 de Setembro. Both eventually come to Campo Grande (also known as Praça Dois de Julho). In the centre of the square is the monument to Bahian Independence, 2 July 1823. The British Club is just off the square on R. Banco dos Ingleses. Av. 7 de Setembro continues out of the square towards the Vitória area, indeed this stretch is known as Corredor da Vitória (Vitória Corridor). There are some fine homes along this street built during the last century as the city expanded in this direction. The Corredor da Vitória comes to Praça Vitória and continues down Ladeira da Barra (Barra Hill) to Porto da Barra. The best city beaches are in this area. Also in this district are the best bars, restaurants and nightlife. A little further along is the Forte de Santo Antônio, 1580, built on the spot where Amérigo Vespucci landed in 1501. It is right at the mouth of the bay where Bahia de Todos Os Santos and the South Atlantic Ocean meet.

The promenade leading away from the fort and its famous lighthouse is called Av. Oceânica, which goes along the coast to the new beach suburbs of Ondina, Amaralina and Pituba. The road is also called Avenida Presidente Vargas, but the numbering is different. Beyond Pituba are the best ocean beaches at Jaguaripe, Piatã and Itapoan (take any bus from Praça da Sé marked Aeroporto or Itapoan, about one hour, sit on right hand side for best views). En route the bus passes small fishing colonies at Amaralina and Pituba where *jangadas* can be seen. A *jangada* is a small raft peculiar to the northeastern region of Brazil used extensively as well as dug out canoes. Near Itapoan is the Lagoa do Abaeté, surrounded by brilliant, white sands. This is a deep, fresh water lake where local women traditionally come to wash their clothes and then lay them out to dry in the sun. The road leading up from the lake offers a panoramic view of the city in the distance, the coast, and the contrast of the white sands and fresh water less than a kilometre from the sea and its golden beaches. Near the lighthouse at Itapoan there are two campsites on the beach. A little beyond the campsites are the magnificent ocean beaches of Stella Maris and Flamengo, both quiet during the week but very busy at the weekends. Beware of strong undertow at these beaches.

See also the famous church of Nosso Senhor do Bomfim on the Itapagipe peninsula in the suburbs, whose construction began in 1745; it draws endless supplicants (particularly on Fri. and Sun.) offering favours to the image of the Crucified Lord set over the high altar; the number and variety of ex-voto offerings—often of parts of the body deemed to have been cured by divine intervention—is extraordinary. The processions over the water to the church on the third Sun. in January are particularly interesting.

Also on the Itapagipe peninsula is a colonial fort on Mont Serrat point, and at Ribeira the church of Nossa Senhora da Penha (1743). The beach here has many restaurants, but bathing from it is not recommended because of pollution (bus from Praça da Sé or Av. França).

**Local Holidays**  6 Jan. (Epiphany); Ash Wed. and Maundy Thurs., half-days; 2 July (Independence of Bahia); 30 Oct.; Christmas Eve, half-day. An important local holiday is the Festa do Nosso Senhor do Bomfim; it takes place on the second Sunday after Epiphany, but the colourful washing or *lavagem* of the Bomfim church takes place on the preceding Thurs. (usually mid-January). The Festa da Ribeira is on the following Mon. The most colourful festival of all is that of the fishermen of the Rio Vermelho district on 2 Feb.; gifts for Yemanjá, Goddess of the Sea, are taken out to sea in a procession of sailing boats to an accompaniment of *candomblé* instruments. The Holy Week processions among the old churches of the upper city are very colourful.

The **pre-Carnival festive season** begins towards the end of Nov. with São Nicodemo de Cachimbo (penultimate Sun. of Nov.), then comes Santa Bárbara (4 Dec.), then the Festa da Conceição da Praia, centred on the church of that name (open 0700-1130 normally) at the base of the Lacerda lift. (8 Dec. is the last night—not for those who don't like crowds!) The last week of Dec. is the Festa da Boa Viagem in the lower city; the beach will be packed all night on the 31st. On 1 January is the beautiful boat procession of Nosso Senhor dos Navegantes from Conceição da Praia to the church of Boa Viagem, on the beach of that name in the lower city. The leading boat, which carries the image of Christ and the archbishop, was built in 1892. You can follow in a sailing boat for about US$1; go early (0900) to dock by Mercado Modelo. A later festival is São Lázaro on the last Sun. in January.

**Folklore**  Carnival in Salvador is particularly lively, with nearly everyone in fancy dress and dancing in the streets. It runs from Thursday night to Wednesday morning. The carnival takes place in two areas, in the centre of the city, between Campo Grande and Praça Municipal (the more exciting) and by the Barra lighthouse (less crowded and safer). Basic grandstand seats at Campo Grande cost about US$15.

Visitors find carnival exciting and entertaining, but look out for the more violent elements and don't carry any valuables. For greater safety join an organised group, security guards hold ropes but there are no toilet facilities (Tietê VIPS, R Direita da Piedade next to Baita-Kão, US$60; Pike, R. da Aragã 9, T 245-0934, US$120). The *blocos* (samba groups) can be seen practising at any time from end-November; ask locals, Bene at *Zanzi-bar* or Bahiatursa for details. Many clubs have pre-carnival and Carnival dances; Baile das Atrizes has been recommended (always book tickets early). To make the most of carnival, arrive a week or two in advance and enjoy the festiies of the preceding week. In recent years the frenetic trio-electrico music has given way to the gentler African rhythms. The highlight of the Carnival are the Afoxés, Afro drumming groups who parade through the streets from mid-day to dawn. They can be seen practising from the end of November. For the Olodum drummers, see **Nightlife** below. Ilê Aiyê practices on Sat. from 2200-0400 in the Forte de Santo Antônio, Santo Antônio Além do Carmo, small admission fee.

The Bahianas—black women who dress in traditional 18th century costumes—are street vendors who sit behind their trays of delicacies, savoury and seasoned, made from the great variety of local fish, vegetables and fruits.

See Capoeira, a sport developed from the traditional foot-fighting technique introduced from Angola by African slaves. The music is by drum, tambourine and *berimbau*; there are several different kinds of the sport. If you want to attempt Capoeira, the best school is Mestre Bimba in Terreiro de Jesus, at R. Francisco Muniz Barreto 1. Classes are held in evenings (if you want to get the most out of it, knowledge of Portuguese is essential). There are two more schools in Forte de

Santo Antônio behind Pelourinho, but check addresses at tourist office. Exhibitions take place in the Largo do Pelourinho, very picturesque, in the upper city (cost: US$2). You can also see the experts practising outside the Mercado Modelo on most days and at Campo Grande and Forte de Santo Antônio on Sunday afternoons; they often expect a contribution. Negotiate a price before taking pictures or demands may be exorbitant. At the Casa da Cultura at Forte de Santo Antônio there is also free live music on Saturday night.

**Warning** Be very careful of your money and valuables at all times and in all districts. Avoid the more distant beaches out of season, when they are empty (e.g. Itapoan, Piatã, Placafor); on Sundays they are more crowded and safer. Conversely, the old city on Sundays is deserted and should therefore be avoided. At night, the historical centre (especially the Largo do Pelourinho), around and in the lifts, and buses are unsafe. On no account change money on the streets; this is a guaranteed way to be robbed. Leave valuables securely in your hotel (inc. wristwatch and cameras if possible), particularly at night. Parts of the centre to the NE of the Praça da Sé are run down and rather dubious, and one is warned not to walk down the Ladeira de Misericôrdia, which links the Belvedere, near the Lacerda lifts, with the lower city. Should a local join you at your table for a chat, leave at once if drugs are mentioned. The civil police are reported to be very sympathetic and helpful.

**Hotels** Those listed below are in the categories L, A+ and A. A 10% service charge is often added to the bill. Check which credit cards are accepted. All have swimming pools *Sofitel* (ex Quatro Rodas). R. da Passargada, Farol de Itapoan, T 249 9611, 5 star, A+, is a complete resort hotel 22 km. from city centre, extensive grounds, peaceful but plenty activities available e.g. golf, tennis, etc, shuttle bus to city centre. *Enseada das Lajes*, Av. Oceânica 511, Rio Vermelho, T 237 1027, L, family run, 9 rooms in what used to be a private house, antique furniture, excellent pieces of art, wonderful setting, 2 mins beach, member of Relais & Chateau association. *Bahia Othon Palace*, Av. Oceâanica 2456, Ondina, T 247 1044, 5 star, A+, nice rooms and views, excellent swimming pool, next to beach, average service; *Ondina Apart Hotel*, Av. Oceânica 2400, Ondina, T 203 8000, 5 star, A+, new, self-contained apts, on beach, highly rec.; *Hotel da Bahia* (Tropical), Praça 2 de Julho 2, Campo Grande, T 321 3699, 5 star, A+, refurbished well run hotel, owned by Varig, location noisy but convenient for city centre, daily courtesy bus to beach; *Meridien*, R. Fonte do Boi 216, Rio Vermelho, 5 star, A+, T 248 8011, well run, ocean views, no beach, nothing within walking distance so taxis must be used. *Grande Hotel da Barra*, Av. 7 de Setembro 3564, Barra, 4 star, A+, T 247 6011, excellent location on beach, small, friendly, ask for room with sea view; *Marazul*, Av. 7 de Setembro 3937, Barra, T 235 2110, 4 star, A+, on seafront; *San Marino*, Av. Oceânica 889 Barra, T 235 4363, 3 star, A, on ocean; *Ondina Praia*, Av. Oceânica 2275, Ondina, T 247 1033, 3 star, A, near beach; *Itapoan Praia*, Jardim Itapoan, Placafor, T 249 9988, 3 star, A, 20 km from centre near excellent beaches.

**Centre** (includes old city and main shopping area): *Palace*, R. Chile 20, T 243 1155, B, rec, much better value than *Chile* opp; *Bahia de Todos os Santos*, Av. Sete de Setembro 06 (Ladeira de São Bento), B, T 321 6344. *Paris*, R. Ruy Barbosa 13, T 321 3922, D, a/c rooms more expensive, shared showers, breakfast, restaurant in same building, rec; also *Pousada da Praça*, at No. 5, T 321 0642, D, breakfast, rooms with and without bath, clean, friendly, rec. *São Bento*, Largo de São Bento 2, T 243 7511, D, friendly, good cheap restaurant. Cheaper hotels on Av. 7 de Setembro: *São José*, No. 847, T 321 4928, E-D, safe, rec.; *Imperial*, No 751, Rosario, T 321 3389, D, a/c, breakfast, rec; *Madrid*, No 186, Mercês, T 321 9505, E; *Mercês*, No. 46, Mercês, T 321 0676, E; *Pousada Pampulha*, No 76, 1st floor, São Pedro, T 223 1240, E, breakfast, restaurant, laundry service. *Internacional*, R. da Faisca 88, T 241 5349, D, clean, convenient, good value. *Joana Angêlica* in street of same name, F, friendly, no breakfast.

It is not recommended that you stay in the hotels near Praça da Sé as this is a dangerous area at night. There are many hotels in this area and many travellers do stay there. The following have been rec: *Pelourinho*, R. Alfredo Brito 20, T 321 9022, C; Spanish is spoken in all of the following: *Solar São Francisco*, Cruzeiro de São Francisco, in front of São Francisco church, T 242 6015, F, breakfast available, English spoken; next door is *Colon*, T 321 1531, F; *Solara*, R. José Alencar 25, Largo do Pelourinho, T 321 0202, F, with shower, toilet, breakfast, clean, laundry facilities; *Jequié*, off Praça da Sé at Ciné Liceu, F, clean, no breakfast, some rooms better than others; *Vigo*, R. 3 de Maio 18, 2 blocks from Praça da Sé, E with bath and breakfast, fairly clean; *Ilheus*, Ladeira da Praça 4, 1st floor, T 243 2320, D-E, breakfast.

**Campo Grande/Vitória**. This is a much safer area, quieter and still central and convenient for museums: *Mater Café Teatro*, R. Marechal Floriano 5, Canela T 235 1958,

D with breakfast, clean (but poor locks on doors) with good café/restaurant next door called *Café dos Artistas*, Spanish spoken; *Anglo Americano*, Av. Sete de Setembro 1838, Vitória, T 247 7681, D with breakfast and bath, cheaper without bath (D), safe, discount if you pay in advance for 3 or more nights, clean, D, good gringo hotel in pleasant district, some rooms with bay view, rec; *Caramuru*, Av. Sete de Setembro 2125, Vitória, T 247 9951, D, breakfast, very friendly, clean, safe parking, rec; *Do Forte*, R. Forte de São Pedro 30, Campo Grande, T 321 6915, D, breakfast, bath; *Santiago* at No. 52, D, breakfast, bath, T 245 9293.

**Barra**   The best location to stay in: it is safe, has good beaches, is a short bus ride from the centre, has good restaurants in all price ranges and good nightlife. On Av. 7 de Setembro: *Barra Turismo*, No 3691, Porto da Barra, T 245 7433, B, breakfast, bath, a/c, TV, fridge, on beach, rec; *Solar da Barra*, No 2998, Ladeira da Barra, T 247 4917, C, some rooms with bay view; *Porto da Barra* No 3783, Porto da Barra, T 247 4939, C, friendly, clean, some rooms very small, on beach; *Pousada Malu*, No 3801, T 237 4461, D, small and friendly with breakfast, on beach. *Enseada Praia da Barra*, R. Barao de Itapoã 60, Porto da Barra, T 235 9213, C, a/c, or fan, good breakfast, clean, safe, friendly, money exchanged, laundry bills high otherwise good value, near beach; *Villa Romana*, R. Lemos Brito 14, T 247 6522, B, pool, restaurant, individual safes, rec; *Barra Praia*, Av. Alm. Marquês do Leão 172, Farol da Barra, T 235-0193, B, a/c, clean, one street from beach, rec; *Ritz*, R. Marqués de Caravelas 33, T 247 8459, D, a/c, bath, converted mansion, clean, friendly; *Seara Praia*, R. Belo Horizonte 148, Barra Avenida, T 235 0105, C, good breakfast; *Pousada Village Paulista*, R. Lord Cochrane 148, Barra, T 245 9099, D, fan, clean, English spoken, highly rec., excellent location; *Pousada da Carmen Simões*, R. 8 de Dezembro 326, E, safe, friendly, helpful.

**Atlantic Suburbs.** This is the modern suburban area built along the coast from Ondina to Itapoan stretching for 12 miles towards the airport. The best beaches in this area. *Ondina Plaza*, Av. Pres. Vargas. 3033, Ondina, T 245 8188, B, a/c, pool, good value, on beach, rec; *Amaralina*, Av. Amaralina 790, Amaralina, T 248 7822, C, a/c, near beach; *Pituba*, Av. Manoel Dias da Silva 1614, Pituba, T 248 5469, D, no breakfast; *Paulus*, Av. Otavio Mangabeira, Pituba, T 248 5722, B, a/c, pool; *Praia Dourada*, R. Dias Gomes 10, Placaford, T 249 9639, B-C, a/c, near excellent beach, rec; *Pituaçu Praia*, Jardim Iracema, Lote 27, Corsario. T 371 9622, B, a/c, 2 blocks from good beach; *Praia dos Coqueiros*, Av. Otavio Mangabeira 25, Placaford, T 249 9828, C, a/c, near excellent beach, rec; *Europa*, R. Genibaldo Figueiredo 53, Itapoan, T 249 9344, D, breakfast; *Grão de Areia*, Loteamento Jardim Piatâ, Quadra 25, Lote 23/24, Itapoan, T 249 4818, C, a/c, pool, near good beach; *Pousada Glória*, R. do Retiro 46, Itapoan, T 249 1503, E, with bath, no breakfast, near beach; *Pousada de Itapoan*, Av. D. Caymmi, V. dos Ex. Combatentes, Quadra 1, Lote 3, Itapoan, T 249 9634, D, breakfast, laundry, parking.

*Portal Da Cidade*, Av. Antonio Carlos Magalhães, 4230, next to bus station, T 321 0099, a/c, pool, B.

**Youth Hostels** are called Albergues de Juventude and most were opened in 1988-89. They cost E p.p. incl breakfast but cheaper if you have a YHA membership card. *Casa Grande*, R. Minas Gerais, 121, Pituba, T 248 0527; *CNEC do Salvador*, R. Bicuiba, Loteamento Patamares, near beach out of town; *Dois de Julho*, R. Areial de Cima 44, Largo 2 de Julho, Centro, T 243 9513; *Lagash*, R. Visc. de Itaboray 514, Amaralina, T 248 7399; *Senzala*, R. Florianopolis 134, Jardim Brasil, Barra, T 247 5678, good location; *Boca do Rio*, Av. D. Eugenio Sales 72, Lote 11, Boca do Rio, T 230 8371, near the popular Praia dos Artistas; *Solar*,. R. Macapá 461, Ondina, T 235 2235, good location for beach and city; *Costa do Sol*, R Arquimedes Gonçalves 226, T 241-4744, quiet; *Praia de Itapoan*, R. Boa Vista 5, T 249-1791.

**Pensionatos** are places to stay in shared rooms (up to 4 persons per room) e.g. *Pensionato No. 20*, Av. Cerqueira Lima; part or full board available. Houses or rooms can be rented for US$5-35 a day from Pierre Marbacher, R. Carlos Coqueijo 68A, Itapoan, T 249 5754 (Caixa Postal 7458, 41600 Salvador), he is Swiss, owns a beach bar at R. K and speaks English, French and German. At Carnival its a good idea to rent a flat; the tourist office has a list of real estate agents (e.g. José Mendez T 237 1394/6).

**Apart Hotels.** These are self-contained apartments with fully equipped kitchen and a/c, with all the facilities of a hotel, which can be rented by the day; standards are generally high. *Jardim Paraiso*, R. Contorno 7, Itapoan, T 249 3397, B, pool, near beach; *Bahia Flat*, Av. Pres. Vargas 235, Barra, T 247 4233, B, on beach, pool, sauna, rec; *Barra Apart Service*, R. Marques de Caravelas 237, Barra, T 247 5844, C; *Flat Jardim de Alã*, Av. Otavio Mangabeira 3471, Armação, T 371 5288, A, beautiful location by beach, pool, sauna, rec; *Manhattan Residence Service*, R. Maranhão 445 Pituba, T 248 9012, B, pool, gym, popular with businessmen; *Parthenon Farol da Barra Flat*, Av Oceânica 409, Barra, T 237 6722, B, pool, sauna, on beach, rec; *Pituba Apart Hotel*, R. Paraíba 250, Pituba, T 240 7077, A, pool, sauna.

**Camping** Near the lighthouse at Itapoan, take bus from Praça da Sé direct to Itapoan, or to Campo Grande or Barra, change there for Itapoan, about 1 hr., then ½ hr. walk; two campsites, one Camping Clube do Brasil, at US$6 p.p. per night (members half price), and a cheaper one opposite. Camping de Pituaçu, Av. Prof. Pinto de Aguiar, Jardim Pituaçu. Sea bathing is dangerous off shore near campsites.

**Bahian cuisine** is spiced and peppery. The main dish is *moqueca*, seafood cooked in a sauce made from coconut milk, tomatoes, red and green peppers, fresh coriander and *dendê* (oil made from the crushing of the fruit of the dendezeiro palm tree). It is traditionally cooked in a wok-like earthenware dish and served piping hot at the table. Served with *moqueca* is farofa (mandioc flour) and a hot pepper sauce which you add at your discretion, it's usually extremely hot so try a few drops before venturing further. The dendê palm oil is somewhat heavy and those with delicate stomachs are advised to try the *ensopado*, a sauce with the same ingredients as the *moqueca*, but without the palm oil.

Nearly every street corner has a Bahiana (see above under **Folklore**) selling a wide variety of local snacks, the most famous of which is the *acarajé*, a bean dumpling fried in palm oil. To this the Bahiana adds *vatapá*, a dried shrimp and coconut milk paté, fresh salad and hot sauce (pimenta). For those who prefer not to eat the palm oil, the *abará* is a good substitute. *Abará* is steamed, wrapped in banana leaves.

Three good Bahianas are *Chica*, at Ondina beach (beside **Saveiro Hotel**), *Gina* at Largo da Mariquita, Rio Vermelho and the one in front of *Tiffany's* restaurant on R. Barão de Sergy at Porto da Barra. The Bahians usually eat *acarajé* or *abará* with a chilled beer on the way home from work or the beach at sunset.

Another popular dish is *Xin-Xin de Galinha*, chicken on the bone cooked in dendê, with dried shrimp and squash.

**Restaurants Historial Centre**. *Cantina da Lua*, Terreiro De Jesus sq, open daily 1100-2300, music nightly, legendary; *Salada De Frutas*, Alfredo B rito 5, Mon-Sat 0830-1800, very good juices, snacks and light meals, clean, friendly, rec. *Ibiza Bar*, Alfredo Brito 11 (upstairs), open Mon.-Sat., 1100-2330, Sun. 1800-2330 good food, cheap. *Casa Azul*, Praça José Alencar. (Largo do Pelourinho) Mon.-Sat. 0900-1830, good juice bar with wide range of light snacks, clean, *Senac*, Praça José Alencar 8, state run catering school, a selection of 40 dishes including local ones, buffet, lunch 1130-1530, dinner 1830-2130, all you can eat for US$11, very popular, folkloric show in the evening at 2000. *Casa do Benin*, Praça José Alencar 29, Afro-Bahian restaurant, great surroundings, try the shrimp in the cashew nut sauce, closed Mon., open 1200-1600, 1900-2300, highly rec. *Bar Banzo*, Praça José Alencar 6 (upstairs) Mon.-Sat. 1100 to 2300, Sun. 1800 to 2300, cheap, good view of streetlife in Largo do Pelourinho below, friendly.

**Between Historical Centre and Barra** At Praça Da Sé, *Café Brasil*, good breakfast. *Bar Padrão*, R. José Gonçalves, near Praça Da Sé, rec. There are some good snack bars on Av. 7 de Setembro; *Kentefrio*, No. 379, the best, clean, counter service only, closed Sundays, rec; on same street, 600 block, *La Portuguesa*, good, cheap; *Casa D'Italia*, corner of Av. 7 and Visconde de São Lourenço, reasonable prices, good service; *Grao de Bico*, No. 737, very good vegetarian. *Frutos Da Terra*, R. Carlos Gomes, 21, vegetarian, good, fine view of bay and lower city. *Suave Sabor*, R. Cons. Lafaiete, vegetarian, US$2.50 for all you can eat. Another good vegetarian restaurant nearby is *Nutrebem*, Av. Joana Ângêlica 148. Also on same street is *Bela Napoli*, Italian, reasonable. *Casa Da Gamboa*, R. da Gamboa, beautifully located in old colonial house overlooking the bay, good reputation, open Mon. to Sat. 1200-1500 and 1900-2300, not cheap. An excellent Japanese restaurant is *Gan*, Praça A. Fernades 29, Garcia, intimate atmosphere, Tues.-Sun. 1900 till midnight, recommended. The best churrascaria in Salvador is *Baby Beef*, Av. A.C. Magalhães, Iguatemi, top class restaurant, excellent service, extremely popular, not expensive, highly recommended, open daily 1200-1500 and 1900-2300.

At the bottom of the Lacerda Lift is Praça Cairu and the famous *Mercado Modelo*: on the upper floor of the market are two very good restaurants, *Camafeu De Oxossi* and *Maria De São Pedro*, both specializing in Bahian dishes, great atmosphere, good view of the port, daily 1130 till 2000, Saturday lunchtime particularly busy. At the base of the Lift is *Cinquenta Saladas*, not only salads, very reasonable. On Av. Contorno, *Solar Do Unhão*, beautiful manor house on the edge of the bay, lunch and dinner with best folklore show in town, expensive.

**Barra Section** *Xangai*, Avenida 7 de Setembro, 1755 (Vitória) Chinese, reasonable; *Hotel Anglo Americano*, across the street, fair, cheap; also restaurant at *Hotel Bahia Do Sol*, No 2009, on first floor, good, reasonably priced; *Sandwich Bar*, R. Cesar Zama 60, great sandwiches, wide variety, open 1900 till 0200; *Tiffany's*, Barão do Sergy 156, 1900-2400, French, rec.; *Kasbah*, R. Barão do Sergy 67, Arab, rec, cheap, open 1200-1500 and

1900-2300, closed at weekends; three other good restaurants on same street are *Berro D'Agua*, No. 27 (upstairs, watch your head on stairway), good steaks, lively bar; *Alface e Cia*, wide range of salads and juices; *Cantina Roma* No 162, T 247-6973; *Unimat* supermarket, good cheap meals on 2nd floor.

Near the lighthouse at the mouth of the bay (Farol Da Barra area) there are a number of good fast food places: *Micheluccio*, Av. Oceânica 10, best pizza in town, always busy, friendly, rec; next door is *Baitakão*, good hamburger and sandwiches; *Speed Lanches*, nearby, good snack bar. *Mon Filet*, R. Afonso Celso, 152, good steaks, pastas, open 1830 till midnight; on same street, *Pastaxuta*, pizza, pasta, reasonable prices. The best Bahian restaurant in the area is *Frutos Do Mar*, R. Marques De Leão 415. A very good vegetarian restaurant is *Rama*, R. Lord Cochrane, great value.

Further along Av. Oceânica towards the Rio Vermelho district is *Sukiyaki*, No. 3562, an excellent Japanese restaurant, open 1200-1500, and 1900 till midnight, not cheap, rec. Also highly rec is *Extudo*, Largo Mesquita 4 T 237-4669, good varied menu, lively bar at night, attracts interesting clientele, open 1200 -1500 and 1900-0300, not expensive. *Marisco*, at Paciencia Beach nearby, good seafood, 1100-1500 and 1800-2100, good value. Next door is *Camburity*, good, wholesome regional food at a good price.

There is an interesting fish market at Largo Da Mariquita with a number of stalls serving food from noon until the small hours, recently built, clean, good atmosphere, popular with locals. A little further along a *MacDonald's* has recently opened at Amaralina and at Shopping Barra.

Further along Avenida Oceânica at Jardim Armação are three very good restaurants: *Yemanjá*, excellent Bahian seafood, open daily from 1130 till late, very typical, always busy, reasonably priced, good atmosphere, highly rec. Nearby is *Tamboril*, busy seafood restaurant, 1200 to 1600 and 1900 till midnight. *Deutsches Haus*, Av. Otávio Mangabeira 1221, good German cooking. The very best Bahian restaurant in the city is *Bargaço*, open daily midday till 1600 and 1900 till midnight, great selection of starters, oyster, lobster, fresh water shrimp, crab meat, etc, highly rec, expensive but worth it. *A Porteira* at Boca do Rio specialises in northeastern dishes including carne do sol (beef dried in the sun), 1200 to 1600 and 1800 to 2300, seafood dishes also served. A popular bar/restaurant is *Casquinha De Siri* at Piatã beach, daily from 0900 until last customer leaves, live music every night, cover charge US$2. The beaches from Patamares to Itapoan are lined by Barracas, thatched huts serving chilled drinks and freshly cooked seafood dishes, ideal for lunch and usually very cheap. At Itapoan the road goes left towards the airport along Av. Dorival Caymmi. *Restaurant Uaua*, Av. Dorival Caymmi 46 specialises in northeastern dishes, meat based, seafood also served, open Thurs. to Sunday. Friday and Saturday are very busy with *forro* dancing till 0400.

**Markets** The Mercado Modelo, at Praça Cairu, lower city, offers many tourist items such as wood carvings, silver-plated fruit, leather goods, local musical instruments. Lace items for sale are often not handmade (despite labels), are heavily marked up, and are much better bought at their place of origin (e.g. Ilha de Maré, Pontal da Barra and Marechal Deodoro, **see page 429**). Cosme e Damião, musical instrument sellers on 1st floor, has been rec., especially if you want to play the instruments. Bands and dancing, especially Sat. (but very much for money from tourists taking photographs), closed at 1200 Sun.; two restaurants on top floor, large balcony provides good view over harbour; restaurants on ground floor are cheaper. Photograph exhibition of the old market in basement. (Many items are often cheaper on the Praça da Sé in the nearby Cidade Alta.) Largest and most authentic market is the **Feira de São Joaquim**, 5 km. from Mercado Modelo along sea front: barkers, trucks, *burros*, horses, boats, people, mud, all very smelly, every day (Sun. till 1200 only), busiest on Sat. morning; interesting African-style pottery and basketwork; very cheap. (Car ferry terminal for Itaparica is nearby.) **Instituto Mauá** at Porto da Barra and the **Iguatemi Shopping Centre** sells good handicraft items, it is run by the government so prices are fixed and reasonable. Every Wed. from 1700-2100 there is a **handicrafts fair** in the 17th century fort of Santa Maria at the other end of Porto da Barra beach. On Sun. from 1700-2100, there is an open air market of handicrafts and Bahian food in **Porto da Barra**, a popular event among the local young people. Daily market of handicrafts in **Terreiro de Jesus** in the old city from 1000-1800. Also many shops in the **Pelourinho** area. Mosquito nets from *Casa dos Mosquiteros*, R. Pedro Sá 6F, Calçada, T 226 0715.

**Bookshops** *Livraria Brandão*, R. Ruy Barbosa 4-B, Centre (opp. *Hotel Paris*), T 243 5383, secondhand English, French, Spanish and German books. *Livraria Civilizaçao Brasileira*, Av. 7 de Setembro 912, Mercês, and in the Barra and Iguatemi shopping centres have some English books; also *Graúna*, Av. 7 de Setembro 1448, many English titles; *Livraria Planeta*, Carlos Gómez 44 e 7 de Setembro sells used English books. The bookshop at the airport has English books and magazines.

**Shopping** *H. Stern* jewellers at *Hotels Meridien*, *Othon* and *Bahia*, also at Barra and Iguatemi Shopping centres. Visit the stone-cutting workshops at *Breis* in the Largo do Carmo; best prices for cut stones and jewellery made to order in 24 hours with a genuine guarantee; *Simon Joalheiros*, Praça Anchieta, European designs. The Barra and Iguatemi shopping centres are big, modern and a/c with big department stores; few typical souvenirs, although soulless, can be practical. **Camera repair**: Pepe, R. da Ajuda, ed. Triunfo, first floor Centre.

**Local Transport** Taxi meters start at US$0.60 for the "flagdown" and US$0.15 per 100 metres. They charge US$15 per hour within city limits, and "agreed" rates outside. Taxi-drivers tend to overcharge, especially at night; the night-time charge should be 30% higher than daytime charges. Teletaxi (24-hr. service), 321-9988. Local buses US$0.30, air-conditioned *frescões* US$1. On buses and at the ticket-sellers' booths, watch your change and beware pickpockets. To get from the old city to the ocean beaches, take a "Barra" bus from Praça da Sé to the Barra point and walk to the nearer ones; the Aeroporto *frescão* (bus 2130) leaves Praça da Sé, passing Barra, Ondina, Rio Vermelho, Amaralina, Pituba, Costa Azul, Armação and Boca do Rio, before turning inland to the airport. A new bus service, the Jardineira, goes to Flamengo beach (30 km. from the city) following the coastal route. An open bus, it passes all the best beaches; sit on right hand side for best views. It leaves from the *Hotel da Bahia* at Campo Grande daily 0730-1930, every 40 mins. US$1.50.

**Car Rental** Avis, Av. Sete de Setembro 1796, T 237-0155, also at airport, T 249-2550; **Budget**, Av. Presidente Vargas 409, T 237-3396; **Hertz**, R. Baependi, T 245-2577, **Unidas**, Av. Sete de Setembro 4183, T 247-3224. If renting a car check whether credit card or cash is cheapest. National Car Rentals allow decision at the end of the rental.

**Hitching** out of Salvador, take a "Cidade Industrial" bus from the bus station at the port; it goes on to the highway.

**Nightlife** Tuesday evening in the Historical Centre is very busy. Many bars stay open until the small hours, most of them playing reggae music. *Bar Do Reggae*, R. João De Jesus 32, and *Bar Baro*, R. Alfredo Brito, are both very popular. *Bar Banzo* in the Largo do Pelourinho is also very lively. The main attraction is the rehearsal of the Olodum drummers; these are the most innovative of the carnival drumming groups and have attracted much attention after being featured on Paul Simon's 1990 album, *Rhythm of the Saints*. They rehearse in an open space known as the Quadra behind Teatro Antônio Miguel on R. João de Jesus from 1900-2300. They also rehearse on Sun. in Largo de Pelourinho from 1800-2300, but these rehearsals can be very crowded (at both, beware pickpockets). Note: Apart from Tues. the bars and restaurants in the Historical Centre close early for security reasons. It is recommended to come and go by taxi at night.

**Barra Section**: *Mordomia Drinks*, Ladeira Da Barra, enter through narrow entrance to open air bar with spectacular view of the bay, very popular; *Volupia*, Av. 7 De Setembro 510, Porto Da Barra, nightly, highly recommended, most "Bohemian" of the bars in the area, always full, interesting people, owners speak English, great music and famous passion fruit or mango daikiris; nearby is *Baixo Porto*, lively, open till 0400. *Bon Vivant*, R. Barão De Itapoã 2, closed Sundays, upstairs, quiet bar with good view of the bay, in front of Santa Maria fort; *Habeas Corpos*, R. Marques de Leão 172, famous street side bar, very popular; *Agua do Mar*, Av. Oceânica 639, open 24 hours a day, good snacks; *Barra Vento* across the street, popular open air bar on the beach front.

Further along the coast at Odina is the *Bahia Othon Palace Hotel* with a good disco called *Hippotamus*, busy at weekends, ination. In **Rio Vermelho** district are *Zouk Santana*, Largo da Santana, new disco bar, good sound system, nightly, go early; US$2 to enter, rec. *Bar Canoa* at the *Meridien Hotel* has live music every night, jazz, popular Brazilian music, cover charge US$6, 2100 till 0100. Dancing at *Carinhoso*, Av. Otavio Mangabeira, T 248-9575; *Champagne* at *Salvador Praia Hotel*, T 245-5033; *New Fred's*, Av. Visc. de Itaboraí 125, T 248-4399. *Intermezzo Bar* at Teatro Maria Bethania at Largo da Mariquita is a relaxed, friendly, open air bar; *Bual Amour* disco at Boca Do Rio, open Tues. to Sat. 2200-0400; *Sabor Da Terra*, near Boca Do Rio for the best lambada dancing in town (next door is a new disco called *Krypton*); *Concha Acústica*, Ladeira da Fonte. (behind Teatro Castro Alves, Campo Grande), concerts every weekend with best Brazilian musicians. rock, M.P.B. (popular Brazilian music), mainly during summer months, usually very cheap, open air, good venue. The barraca *Padang* at Stella Maris beach has beach dancing Fri. and Sat. nights in summer, attracts a surfing crowd, great location, good sound system; also popular at weekends.

**Theatres** Castro Alves, at Campo Grande (Largo Dois de Julho), frequent concerts; Teatro da Gamboa; Teatro Vila Velha; Senac; Instituto Cultural Brasil-Alemanha (ICBA): Teatro Santo Antônio, part of the Escola de Teatro da Universidade Federal da Bahia; Teatro de Arena.

**Cinema** Maria Bethania film theatre, Praça Colombo 4, Rio Vermelho, art and foreign films.

**Museums** The city has 27 museums. The **Museu de Arte Contemporânea**, converted from an old estate house and outbuildings off Av. Contorno, is only open for special exhibitions. The good restaurant(*Solar do Unhão*) is still there, and the buildings are worth seeing for themselves (take a taxi there as access is dangerous).

There is a remarkable **Museu de Arte Sacra** in the 17th century monastery and church of Santa Teresa, at the bottom of the steep Ladeira de Santa Teresa, at R. do Sodré 276. Many of the 400 carvings are from the Old World, but a number are local. Among the reliquaries of silver and gold is one of gilded wood by the great Brazilian sculptor Aleijadinho. Open Tues.-Sat. 0930-1130 and 1400-1730, US$0.40. Many of the treasures which used to be in an old mansion, the Casa de Calmon, Av. Joana Angélica 198, are here now. This important collection is well worth a visit. Opposite is **Tempostal**, a private museum of postcards, open Tues.-Sat., 1000-1130, 1400-1730, at R. do Sodré 276 (proprietor, Antônio Marcelino do Nascimento).

The **Carmo Church** has a museum with a collection of icons and colonial furniture; closed for renovation until 1992. Next door is the Third Order of the Carmo Church and Museum, open daily 0800-1200, 1400-1800; don't miss the carving of Christ by Francisco Xavier das Chagas (see above), entry US$0.10. **Museu Abelardo Rodrigues**, in the Solar Ferrão, Pelourinho (R. Gregório de Mattos 45, open Mon.-Fri. 1000-1200, 1400-1700, closed Tues., Sat.-Sun. 1100-1700), is another religious art museum, with objects from the 17th, 18th, and 19th centuries, mainly from Bahia, Pernambuco and Maranhão.

**Museu Costa Pinto**, Av. 7 de Setembro 2490, US$0.35 (1500-1900 except Tues., Sat. and Sun.) is a modern house with collections of crystal, porcelain, silver, furniture etc. It also has the only collection of *balangandás* (slave charms and jewellery), highly rec.

**Museu de Arte da Bahia**, Av. 7 de Setembro 2340, Vitória, Tues.-Sun. 1400-1800, poor.

**Museu Afro-Brasileiro**, in former Faculty of Medicine building, Terreiro de Jesus, open Mon.-Fri., 0900-1700, comparing African and Bahian Orixás (deities) celebrations, beautiful murals and carvings, highly rec. Medical and ethnographic museums in same complex.

**Casa do Benin**, below Igreja dos Pretos, shows African crafts, photos, video show on Benin and Angola, open Tues-Sat 1000-1800.

**Museu da Cidade**, Largo do Pelourinho (centre of old upper city), arts and crafts, old photographs, entrance free, Mon.-Sat. 0800-1200, 1330-1800. **Museu Hidrográfico**, Forte de Santo Antônio, free (Tues.-Sun. 1100-1700).

Thirty-six km. from the city is the **Museu do Recôncavo** (Museu do Vanderlei do Pinho, 0900-1200, 1400-1700) in the old Freguesia mill—1552 (closed for refurbishing), in which one can find artefacts and pictures of three centuries of the economic and social life of this region. The Casa Grande e Senzala (the home of the landowner and the combined dwelling and working area of the slaves) is still intact. It is a peaceful way to spend an afternoon, but difficult to get to by public transport, the museum is 7 km. from main highway. The **Museu Geológico do Estado** is at Av. 7 de Setembro 2195, Vitória, open Mon.-Fri. 1330-1830.

**N.B.** Many guides offer their services in museums, but their English is poor and their expectations of a tip high.

**Electric Current** 110-220 A.C., 60 cycles.

**Exchange** Do not be tempted to change money on the street (see above), especially in the Upper City (where rates are usually better). **Lloyds Bank**, R. Miguel Calmon 22; **Citibank**, Av. Estados Unidos; **Banco Holandês Unido**, Praça da Inglaterra; and national banks. **Banco Econômico**, Av. Oceânica 2400, Ondina (in *Ondina Apart Hotel* building). **Banco do Brasil**, R. Rio de Janeiro 750 (4th floor). **Banco Mercantil de São Paulo**, R. M. Calmon, near Mercado Modelo, and **Banco Nordeste**, close by, accept Master Charge cards, Banco Real, R. Ourivés (Visa). Also exchange shops, e.g. **American Express**, Kontik-Franstur, Praça da Inglaterra 2, 1st floor (Lower City); travel agency at **Estados Unidos 4** (in the arcade of Edifício Visconde de Cayru) changes travellers' cheques; **López e López**, R. Conselheiro Dantas 57, Edifício Paraguassu, Room 101. **Catedral Corretora de Câmbio**, R. Miguel Calmon 382-5°, in the Banco Francês e Brasileiro building; **funeral parlours** on Praça da Sé and Praça Anchieta give good rates. **Carlos**, Av. 7 de Setembro 1451, loja F, Campo Grande Sul, next to *Hotel Bahia*, T 245-3012/237-5331; **Asta**, R. Dantas 22/24, edifício Pradesco. *Hotel São José* gives good rates for travellers' cheques; the *Colón* gives good rates on Amex cheques. Good rates for cash (in small amounts) from manager of *Hotel Modelo*, at foot of Lacerda lift. Good rates also at Marquisa S.A. (Sr. Nelson), R. Visconde do Rosário 04, Edifício Senador Dantas, Conjunto 101-106 (corner R. Portugal).

**British Club**, Inglesa 20B, just off Campo Grande. **Cultura Ingelsa**, R. Plínio Moscoso 357,

Jardim Apipema. **Associação Cultural Brasil-Estados Unidos**, Av. 7 de Setembro 1883, opp. *Hotel Anglo Americano*, has a library and reading room with recent U.S. magazines, open to anyone, and at No. 1809 on the same avenue is the German **Goethe Institut**, also with library and reading room with recent papers.

**Consulates** British Vice-Consulate, Av. Estados Unidos 4, Salas 1109/1113, Ed. Visc. de Cairu, Caixa Postal 38, Comercio, T 243-9222, Mon.-Fri., 0800-1200, 1400-1730. **USA**, Av. Antonio Carlos Magalhães, Ed. Cidadella Center 1, Bala 410, Itaigara, T 358 9195/358 9166, Mon.-Fri., 0830-1130. **W**. Germany, R. Lucaia 281, Rio Vermelho, T 247 7106, Mon.-Fri. 0900-1200. **Austria**, R. Alm. Marqués do Leão 46, Apto 33, Barra, T 247 6013. **Belgium**, Centro Empresarial Iguatemi, Bloco B, Sala 809, Iguatemi, T 358 5431. **Denmark**, Av. Sete de Setembro 3959, Barra, T 247 9667, Mon.-Fri. 0900-1200, 1400-1700. **Spain**, R. Marechal Floriano 21, Canela, T 245 9055. **Finland**, C. Portinári 19, Barra, T 247 3312. **France**, Trav. Francisco Gonçalves 1, Sala 805, Comércio, T 241 0168, Mon.-Fri. 0900-1200, 1300-1700. **Holland**, R. Lauro Miller 8, Sala 503, Mon.-Fri. 0800-1130, 1400-1730. **Italy**, Av. Sete de Setembro 1238, Mercês, T 245 8564, Mon., Wed., Fri., 1500-1700. **Norway and Sweden**, R. Quintino de Carvalho 153, Apto. 601, Jardim Apipema, T 247 0528, Mon.-Fri. 0900-1200, 1400-1600. **Portugal**, Praça Piedade, Gabinete Português de Leitura, T 241-1633, Mon.-Fri. 0800-1400.

**Clinic** Barão de Loreto 21, Graça. Dr Argemiro Júnior speaks English and Spanish. First consultation US$40, second free. Dr Manoel Nogueira (from 1000-1200), Av. Joana Angálica 6, T 241-2377, English-speaking. Yellow fever vaccinations free at Delegação Federal de Saúde, R. Padre Feijó, Canela. Israeli travellers needing medical (or other) advice should contact Sr. Marcus (T 247-5769), who speaks Hebrew and is glad to help.

**Laundry** *Lavanderia Lavalimpo*, R. do Pilar 31, Comércio, Mon.-Sat. 0800-1800.

**Immigration** (for extensions of entry permits), Policia Federal, corner of RR. Polonia and Santos Dumont, Lower City. Show an outward ticket or sufficient funds for stay, visa extension US$7.

**Post Office** Main post office and poste restante is in Praça Inglaterra, in the Lower City, open Mon.-Sat. 0800-1800, Sun. 0800-1200. Other offices at Praça da Sé in Ed. Associaçao Bahiana de Imprensa on R. Guedes de Brito 1, T 240-6222; Rodoviária, Mon.-Sat. 0800-1800 (till 1200 on Sun.); Mercado Modelo; airport.

**Communications** Embratel, Av. Estados Unidos, near Mercado Modelo. Cia. Rádio Internacional do Brasil, R. Miguel Calmon 41. Telebahia has offices at Campo da Pôlvora, on R. Hugo Baltazar Silveira (open always), Barra and Iguatemi Shopping Centres, airport, Rodoviária and Mercado Modelo.

**Tourist Office** (with lists of hotels and pension stays in private homes) Bahiatursa, Palácio Rio Branco (former government palace, which may be viewed). R. Chile on Praça Municipal, open 0800-1830, English and German spoken. Visitors can obtain weekly list of events and itineraries (on foot or by car) planned by the city, well worth doing, but be warned that the itinerary goes through some very run down area of the city. Map, US$2, good; offices have noticeboard for messages. Also at bus station (good, English spoken), airport, helpful in finding hotels, in the Mercado Modelo, and other offices at Porto da Barra. Also details of travel throughout Sate of Bahia. Phone 131 any time for tourist information in English. **Maps** from Departmento de Geografia e Estatística, Av. Estados Unidos (opp. Banco do Brasil, lower city): also from newsstands; maps of Brazil US$1.50.

Bus tours are available from several companies: *L.R. Turismo, Itaparica Turismo* and *Alameda Turismo*: city tour (US$20 p.p.), Bahia by Night includes transport to Moenda restaurant, show and dinner (US$35 p.p.). All day boat trip on Bahia de Todos Os Santos from 0800-1700 including visit to Ilha das Frades, lunch on Itaparica (US$10 extra) US$35 p.p. *Tatu Tours*, Caixa Postal 1219, 40000 Salvador, BA., T 237 3161, Fax 237 7562, run by two Irishmen, specialise in Bahia, give private guided tours and can make any necessary travel, hotel and accommodation arrangements. They are represented in London by Travellers Tree, 116 Crawford St., London W1H 1AG, T 935 2291. *Submariner*, R. de Paciência 223, Rio Vermelho, T 237-4097, hire diving equipment, friendly.

**Buses** Bus station 5 km. from city but regular services to centre; bus RI or RII, "Centro-Rodoviária-Circular"; in centre, get on in lower city at foot of Lacerda lift; buses also to Campo Grande; journey can take up to 1 hr. especially in peak periods. Executive bus, quicker, from Praça da Sé runs to Iguatemi Shopping Centre from where there is a walkway to the bus station (take care in the dark, or a taxi, US$10). To **Recife**, US$20 (*leito*, 40), 13 hrs., 3 a day, 1800, 1930, 2100; plenty to **Rio** (28 hrs., US$25, *leito* 80, buy ticket 5 days in advance, 27 hrs. leaves at 1300, Itapemirin, good stops, clean toilets, rec.), São Paulo (30 hrs.), US$50, *leito* US$100, Belo Horizonte 22 hrs, 2 normal (US$35), 2 *leito* buses (US$70); to Fortaleza, 19 hrs., US$30 at 0900 and 2100 with Viação Brasilia; Ilhéus, 7 hrs., US$10, several; Valença, 10 a day, 5 hrs., US$7; Porto Seguro, 2000, 2100, 12 hrs., US$17 (*leito* 35); Maceió, US$17, 4 a day, 9-10 hrs, road bad in places, book early (only service, Empresa Bomfim at 2000); Belém US$50, 37 hrs. There are daily bus services to Brasília along the new (fully paved) road, BR-242, via Barreiras; buses leave at 1200 and 2000, 23 hrs. (US$40, *leito* 80). To Paulo Afonso, US$15, 10 hrs., leaving 0430, 2000, and 1910 on Sun., Wed. and Fri., partly paved road. (Travel agency Remundi, R. da Grécia 8, 1° andar, Cidade Baixa, T 242-5286, sells bus tickets.)

**Motorists** to Rio can do the trip on the BR-116 highway in 3 days, stopping at *Vitória da Conquista* (524 km. from Salvador), *Hotel Aliança*, D and *Hotel Livramento*, D, with restaurant; also Camping Clube do Brasil site at Km. 1,076 (bus to Salvador, 8 hrs., US$9.50; to Feira Santana; to Itaobim, 6 hrs., US$4.50; to Lençóis—change at Bominal—8 hrs.); Teôfilo Otôni, 946 km., or Governador Valadares, 1,055 km. (**see page 347**), and Leopoldina (1,402 km.). There are also various motels; two in the State of Bahia are at Vitória da Conquista; and at Feira de Santana; also between Feira and Salvador. Fairly good hotels are also available in Jequié (*Itajubá, Rex*, and motels), and basic ones in Milagres. Stopovers on the BR-101 coastal road can be made at Vitória and Itabuna (or Ilhéus), and there are many other towns on or near the coast.

**Rail** From Salvador there are only local train services.

**Air** Daily flights to Rio, São Paulo, Recife, Aracaju, Belém, Belo Horizonte, Brasília, Curitiba, Fortaleza, Foz do Iguaçu, Goiania, Ilheus, João Pessoa, Maceió, Manaus, Natal, Porto Alegre, São Luis, and Vitoria. Nordeste Regional Airlines, Av. Dom João VI 259, Brotas T 244 3355 has daily flights to Porto Seguro (US$100 one-way), Barreiras, Bom Jesus da Lapa, Guanambi, Paulo Afonso, Petrolina and Vitoria da Conquista in the interior of Bahia. Dois de Julho Airport is 32 km. from city centre. Buses from airport to Centre Aeroporto-Campo Grande US$0.35, at least 1 hr. Special *Executivo* bus Aeroporto-Praça da Sé along the coast road for hotels, US$1.30. Special taxi (buy ticket at airpot desk) US$20 night and weekends).

**Shipping** National coastal vessels.

**Excursions** From the lower city the train (Trem do Leste) leaves Calçada for a 40 min. journey through the bayside suburbs of Salvador—Lobato, Plataforma (canoes and motor boats for Ribeira on the Itapagipe peninsula), Escada (17th century church), Praia Grande, Periperi and Paripe (take bus for 17th century church at São Tomé de Paripe). The same trip can be made by bus, less picturesquely. From Ribeira a small boat goes 25 km. to *Ilha da Maré* between 0900 and 1100, connecting the island's villages of Itamoaba, Praia Grande and Santana (US$0.70); boat returns next day from Santana at 0400-0500. Santana is a centre for lace making, Praia Grande for basket-weaving. None of the villages has a hotel, but there are restaurants and bars and camping is possible.

There are ferries to Vera Cruz on the island of *Itaparica*, on the other side of the bay from the city. Passenger ferries (and smaller craft) from next to the Mercado Modelo every half-hour, 50-min journey. US$0.70, last boat returns at 1700, more expensive Sun, good juices at landing stage, the car ferry leaves hourly from São Joaquim (bus from in front of Lacerda lift to São Joaquim) to Bom Despacho, 45 min. journey. At Vera Cruz there are good beaches, swimming, horses and bikes for hire, but to other parts of the island one has to take a taxi. From Bom Despacho buses go to other parts of the island. The island has beaches most of which are dirty, but good one at Ponta de Areia (1 hr. walk from Itaparica town), and at *Club Mediterranee*, of which some very poor reports; it has adequate hotels (*Grande Hotel de Itaparica*, near sea, *Icaraí*, Itaparica, D, fair food, run by Fernando Mesquita, very friendly and obliging, and one at Gameleira), but poor family accommodation and inadequate car parking. At Aratuba (40 mins. by bus) is the highly rec. *Albergue da Juventude*, F for students—E, tranquil, clean and friendly with a shady garden, on the beach. Restaurants are expensive (although *Santa Bárbara* on the main square is good and inexpensive), but there are food shops and a self-service restaurant at the Paes Mendonça shopping centre in Gameleira. Camping is worthwhile. The church and fortress of São Lourenço are in Itaparica town. *Mar Grande*, which can be reached direct by ferry from Mercado Modelo (first one at 0630, last back at 1700, every half-hour, but hourly after 1600, 45 mins.), US$0.80, or by VW *Kombi* or launch from Itaparica (0630, 0900, 1400, 1700— may not leave until full), is very unspoilt, but beach very dirty. Houses can be rented. *Hotel Galeão Sacramento*, suites in four separate buildings, swimming pool and other sports facilities; *Pousada Arco Iris* , B, magnificent building and setting in mango orchard, overpriced hotel, good restaurant; next door is a campsite, same owners, filthy but shady, 1 block from beach and town centre; 2 other *pousadas*. Eat at *Philippe's Bar and Restaurant*, Largo de São Bento, good French and local food, local information in French and English, or at *O Pacífico*, Praça da Gamboa, local cuisine, rec., friendly and peaceful. There is a minibus service between Mar Grande and Itaparica. Bicycles for hire. At the southern tip of the island is Cacha Pregos (VW bus from Mar Grande, US$6.70); *Pousada Cacha Pregos*, next to supermarket, T 839-1594, D (bargain) with bath, fan, clean, no breakfast. Nice beaches across the bay, but you have to pay US$6.50 to get a boat across. From Bom Despacho on the island, trips can be made to the picturesque small colonial port of **Jaguaribe** and to Nazaré (see below), with its market (both on the mainland). Jaguaribe can be reached by boat from the Mercado Modelo, leaving Thursday and Saturday and returning Friday and Monday.

The Companhia de Navegação Bahiana provides excursions in the ship *Bahia de Todos os Santos*, from near the Mercado Modelo. An excursion along the city front (Tues., Thurs., Sat.), taking 3 hours, costs US$10; an all-day trip around the bay's islands, including a 3-hour stay at Itaparica, costs US$15 (Wed., Fri., Sun.). Small boats for trips round the bay may be hired privately at the fishing port (Porto dos Saveiros) at the W side of the Mercado Modelo. There is also an excursion to all parts of the city accessible by boat. For other excursions by boat contact agencies such as L. R. Turismo, Av. Sete de Setembro 3959; Grey Line, Av. Presidente Vargas 2456; Remundi, R. da Grécia, 8 (1st floor); Kontik, Praça da Inglaterra, 2. For cheaper excursions to the bay's islands, watch for notices in lunch bars and in bank windows in the lower city bank district, put up by employees looking for people to go on trips.

**Nazaré das Farinhas**, 60 km. inland from Itaparica, and reached over a bridge by bus from **Bom Despacho**, is an 18th-century town celebrated for its market, which specializes in the local ceramic figures, or *caxixis*. There is an especially large market in Holy Week, particularly on the Thursday and Good Friday. 12 km. from Nazaré (taxi US$4.50, also buses) is the village of Maragojipinha, which specializes in making the ceramic figures. Bus from Salvador, 1530, takes 5 hours.

**Feira de Santana** (pop. 355,000), 112 km. NW of Salvador on both the coastal BR-101 and the inland BR-116 roads to Rio, the centre of a great cattle breeding and trading area; its Monday market, known as Feira do Couro (leather fair), said to be the largest in Brazil, attracts great crowds to its colourful display of local products. The permanent Artesanato market in the centre has a bigger selection, including leather, than the Monday market. Bus every half hour from Salvador, 2 hrs., US$2.50. (Bus station has a wall of painted tiles made by Udo-Ceramista, whose workshop is Brotas, Av. Dom João VI 411, Salvador.)

**Hotels** *Luxor*, BR-116 Sul, Km. 437, T 221-5922, A; *Flecha Motel Feira*, D, about 20 km. away at Km. 171 BR-101; several cheap ones in Praça da Matriz and near the bus station, which is quite near the centre.

**The Recôncavo** The area around Salvador, known as the Recôncavo Baiano, was one of the chief centres of sugar and tobacco cultivation in the 16th century.

Leaving Salvador on the Feira road, at Km. 33 one forks left on the BR-324 to the **Museu de Recôncavo Vanderlei de Pinho (see page 412)**. Further W, round the bay, is São Francisco do Conde, 54 km. from Salvador, with a church and convent of 1636 and the ruins of Don Pedro II's agricultural school, said to be the first in Latin America.

At 60 km. from Salvador the BA-026 road branches off the BR-324 to Santo Amaro, Cachoeira and São Félix. Seventy-three km. from Salvador is **Santo Amaro da Purificação** (pop. 64,000) an old sugar centre sadly decaying, noted for its churches (often closed because of robberies), municipal palace (1769), fine main square, house of the poet and singer Caetano Veloso (his sister, the singer Maria Bethânia, is also from here), and ruined mansions including Araújo Pinto, former residence of the Barão de Cotegipe. Other attractions include the splendid beaches of the bay, the falls of Vitória and the grotto of Bom Jesus dos Pobres. Festivals in January and February (Santo Amaro and N.S. da Purificação) are interesting. Craftwork is sold on the town's main bridge. No good hotels or restaurants.

At 54 km. from Santo Amaro, and only 4 km. from the BR-101 coastal road, are the twin towns of **Cachoeira** (Bahia's "Ouro Preto"), and **São Félix**, on either side of the Rio Paraguassu below the Cachoeira dam. Cachoeira, recently declared a national monument, was twice capital of Bahia: once in 1624-5 during the Dutch invasion, and once in 1822-3 while Salvador was still held by the Portuguese. It was the birthplace of Ana Néri, known as "Mother of the Brazilians", who organized nursing services during the Paraguayan War (1865-70). There are beautiful views from above São Félix. Cachoeira's main buildings are the Casa da Câmara e Cadeia (1698-1712), the Santa Casa de Misericórdia (1734—the hospital, someone may let you see the church), the 16th-century Ajuda chapel (now containing a fine collection of vestments), and the Monastery of the Carmelites' Third Order, whose church has a heavily gilded interior. Other churches: Carmo (1548) and its Third Order (fine *azulejos* and gilding), the Matriz with 5-metres-high *azulejos*, and Nossa Senhora da Conceição da Monte. Beautiful lace cloths on church altars. All churches either restored or in the process of restoration. Ruined Jesuit seminary. Tourist office in the Casa de Ana Néri. Festivals: São João (24 June) "Carnival of the Interior" celebrations, well-attended by tourists, Boa Morte (early August), and a famous *candomblé* ceremony at the Fonte de Santa Bárbara on 4 December. Try the local dish, *maniçoba* (meat, manioc and peppers). Craftwork in ceramics and wood readily available. Buses from Salvador (Carnurujipe) every hour or so; Feira Santana 2 hrs US$1.40.

**Hotels** Cachoeira: *Pousada do Convento de Cachoeira* (run by Bahiatursa), T 724-1717, in newly restored 16th-century convent, C, good restaurant, *Pousada do Guerreiro*, 13 de Maio 40, T 724-1203, no restaurant; *Colombo*, basic, friendly, rec. *Santo Antônio* near the Rodoviária, E, basic, clean, safe, friendly, laundry facilities, rec.; *Youth Hostel*, Av. Parnamirim 417, T 268-4844/3390. **Restaurants**: *Cabana do Pai Thomaz*, excellent Bahian food, good value, also an hotel, F with private bath and breakfast; *Recanto de Oxum*, nearby, *Gruta Azul*, lunch only; *Do Nair*, R. 13 de Maio, delicious food and sometimes Seresta music. São Félix: *Xang-hai*, F, good, cheap food, warmly rec.

**Excursion** 6 km. from Cachoeira, on the higher ground of the Planalto Baiano, is the small town of Belém (turning 2½ km. on road to Santo Amaro). Church and seminary of Carmo. Healthy spot: people from Salvador have summer homes. We are told there is an 8 km. secret passage between the Carmo churches here and in Cachoeira, but have not seen it—reports welcome.

The tobacco centre of Cruz das Almas can also be visited, although transport is poor. The São João celebrations here (24 June) are not rec.: very dangerous games with fireworks are involved.

**Maragogipe**, (pop 41,000) a tobacco exporting port 22 km. SE of Cachoeira along a dirt road (BA-123), can also be reached by boat from Salvador. See the old houses and the church of São Bartolomeu, with its museum. The main festival is São Bartolomeu, in August. Good ceramic craftwork.

**Inland from Salvador** Motorists to Brasília can save a little time by taking the ferry to Itaparica, book in advance to avoid long queues, and then going across country to Itaberaba for the BR-242 highway. The journey can be broken at Itaberaba (*pousada*), Lençóis (see below), at Ibotirama on the River São Francisco; at Barreiras on the River Negro, where buses stop for 2-3 hrs. (*Hotel Vandelena*, D, full board); or at Alvorada do Norte (several poor-looking places), Sobradinho (*Hotel Alvimar*, D) or at Posse (Goiás). The road is paved from Salvador to Brasília, but it is reported full of potholes between Alvorado do Norte and Barreiras and poor between Salvador and Lençóis.

400 km. W of Salvador on the BR-242 to Brasília is **Lençóis** (pop. 6,000) a town which is a historical monument and a colonial gem, founded in 1844 because of diamonds in the region (there are still some *garimpeiros*). It is the headquarters of the new (1985) **Parque Nacional da Chapada Diamantina**. The Parque Nacional contains 1,500 square km. of mountainous country, with waterfalls (including the Cachoeira de Glass, 400 metres, the highest in Brazil), large caves (take care, and a strong torch, there are no signs and caves can be difficult to find without a guide), rivers with natural swimming pools and good walking tours. Roy Funch, the ex-director of the National Park, is an excellent guide and can be found

at his craft shop, Funkart, in the main square. There is also a Casa do Artesão, where children learn to fill bottles with patterns of coloured sand, a local speciality. There is a local liquor factory. 30 km. away is Morro de Pai Inácio with good views from the left-hand hill as you come up the gravel road, hard work scrambling down (bus from Lençóis at 0815, 30 mins., US$0.60); good *prato comercial* at the *churrascaria*. Paraíso bus from Salvador 0915 and 2030 (0900 and 2100 Sat.), US$10, Feira de Santana; buses also from Recife, Ibotirama, Barreiras or Brasília 16 hrs, US$18.

**Lodging and Food** *Pousada de Lençóis*, T (075) 3341102, B, with breakfast, swimming pool, rec.; Ze Carlos and Lia Vieira de Moraes have 2 excellent chalets in their huge garden at the entrance to the town, R. Gen. Viveiros 187, T (075) 334 1151, C, English spoken, good breakfast (he is a keen birdwatcher and an authority on the region, she makes excellent jams which are for sale). *Colonial*, T (075) 334-1114, D, *Tradição*, E with bath, breakfast, fridge, mosquito net, pleasant; *Pous Alegre*, R. Boa Vista 95, T (075) 334-1124, E with good regional breakfast, friendly, hot showers, good vegetarian restaurant; *Canto de Águas*, C, comfortable; *Pensão Diamantina*, R. Miguel Calmon, E, *Casa dos Nomadies*, simple and reasonable, F p.p.; 2 campsites, one 2 km. before Lençóis, one in the town centre (friendly, rec.). Restaurant: *Laredo*, good food.

## South from Salvador

271 km. from Salvador, on an asphalted road, is **Valença** (10 buses a day to Salvador, 5 hrs., US$7, and to Itabuna, Expresso São Jorge, 5 hrs., US$7, very slow, and Ilhéus), a small, attractive and bustling town at the mouth of the River Una (the quickest, cheapest way to get there is to take a ferry to Bom Despacho/Itaparica, from where it's 3 hrs. to Valença; the minor road shown on maps does not cross the estuary). Two old churches stand on rising ground above the town; the views from Nossa Senhora do Amparo are recommended. The town is in the middle of an area producing black pepper, cloves and *piaçava* (used in making brushes and mats). Other industries include the building and repair of fishing boats (*saveiros*). Tourist office opposite Rodoviária on other side of river, friendly. Valença and the beaches towards Ilhéus are being developed and are becoming less attractive to those wanting to get away from it all. The River Una enters an enormous region of mangrove swamps. The main attraction of Valença is the beaches on the mainland (Guabim, 14 km. N) and on the island of Tinharé. Avoid touts at the Rodoviária, they give misleading information and then offer an overpriced alternative.

**Hotels** *Rio Una*, T 741-1614, fairly chic, expensive, swimming pool; *Guabim*, Praça da Independência, T 741-1110, modest, D; good *Akuarius* restaurant; *Tourist Hotel*, Mal Floriano 167, F, good, friendly; *Cabana*, on road to Guabim, D, in high season, friendly, chaotic.

**Tinharé** is a large island (with good walking, beaches and camping, but no banks or exchange) separated from the mainland by the estuary of the River Una and mangrove swamps, so that it is hard to tell which is land and which is water. Boats (US$1.20) leave every day from Valença for Galeão (1½ hrs.) and also for Gamboa (1½ hrs.) and Morro de São Paulo (1½). The boat for the two last named leaves at 0800 and 1200 on weekdays, on Sun. at 0700, first returning from Morro de São Paulo at 0600 (fishing boats will go to Morro de São Paulo for US$3.20 p.p.). May be fewer boats in winter. Boats can be arranged in p.m., but not after dark. **Morro de São Paulo** is very popular in summer, situated on the headland at the northernmost tip of the island, lush with ferns, palms and birds of paradise, dominated by the lighthouse and the ruins of a Dutch colonial fort (1630). The village has a landing place on the sheltered landward side, dominated by the old gateway of the fortress. From the lighthouse a path leads to a ruined lookout with cannon, which has panoramic views. *Pousada Cio do Mar*, E with bath (D in season), fan, simple breakfast, lots of steps up to rooms; *Pousada Bora Bora*, F p.p., shared bath, OK; *Pousada da Tia Glória*, friendly, quiet; *Pousada Casa Rolã*, F with shared bath, has rooms for up to 4, near first beach; plenty of restaurants (*Gaúcho* good food, cheap; *Canto da Sereia*, excellent value, friendly; *Ilha de Saúde*, very good, esp. breakfast), bars, and small hotels and *albergues*, F (just ask by the fountain). The second beach is reported to be cooler at night, *Pousada*

*Una*, T (021) 61-2128, friendly but not perfectly secure. Camping is possible, but not too safe on the beach to the S of the village; washing at the public fountain. Fish can be bought from the fishermen in summer, or borrow a pole and catch your own at sunset. Secondhand books (English, German, and others) sold almost opp. *Pousada Bora Bora* nightly (when not raining), will trade 2 for 1 if he's in the mood. The place is expensive December-March, crowded at holiday times, but cheaper during the rest of the year. All roads are unmade, but beaches are good.

Galeão is another village in the island, but has no beach, only mangrove swamps. The church of São Francisco Xavier looks imposing on its hill. (Another island worth visiting is Boipeba.) It is sometimes possible to get a direct boat from Salvador, 2-3 times a week in summer, 6-7 hrs, ask for Sr. Cacu and the *Natureza* at the fishing port next to the Mercado Modelo.

On the coast, south toward Ilhéus, is the picturesque fishing village of **Itacaré**. It is a beautiful area with a protected beach with crystal-clear water to the right of town; across the river there are beaches with good surfing. It is becoming a popular weekend spot, especially for surfers.

**Hotels** *Pousada Litoral*, R. de Souza 81, 1 block from where buses stop, D, with bath, owner João Gavo, speaks English and can organize tours to out of the way beaches, hiring fishing boats, etc., rec. *Bela's Casa de Família*, nice rooms, F (next to *Hotel Santa Bárbara*); *Pousada Iemanjá*, near praça; *San Miguel*, 1 street from waterfront, nr. the cannon at N end of town, F, basic, uncomfortable; *Pousada da Paz*, nr. waterfront, S end of town. Camping site.

**Restaurant** *Marconi*, bar also, good, cheap, friendly.

**Buses** To Ilhéus (70 km.), 3-4 hrs., US$2.40; to **Salvador**, change at Ubaituba (3 hrs., US$1.60, several daily), 6 hrs. Ubaituba-Salvador, US$8, several daily.

**Ilhéus** (pop. 145,000), near the mouth of the Rio Cachoeira, 380 km. south of Salvador, serves a district which produces 65% of all Brazilian cocoa. Shipping lines call regularly. A bridge links the Pontal district (airport) to the mainland. The town is the scene of the famous novel by Jorge Amado, *Gabriela, Clove and Cinnamon*. The local beaches are splendid and the place is highly recommended for a short stay. Among the churches to visit: Nossa Senhora da Vitória, in Alto da Vitória, built in 17th century to celebrate a victory over the Dutch; São Jorge, in city centre; and the cathedral of São Sebastião on sea shore; Santana, in Rio de Engeho is one of the 3 oldest in Brazil. There is a cocoa museum near *Tio San Hotel*, open 1400-1800. Tourist office on Av. Soares Lopes, near cathedral.

**Local Festivals** include Festa de São Sebastião (17-20 January), Carnival, Festa de São Jorge (23 April), Foundation day, 28 June, and Festa do Cacau (October).

**Hotels** *Hotel Barravento* on Malhado beach, R. N.S. das Graças, T 231-3223, ask for the penthouse—usually no extra charge, B, including bath, breakfast and refrigerator; *Britânia*, T 231-1722, D, R. 28 de Junho 16, and at 29 the *San Marino*, T 231-3668, E, friendly, clean. *Pontal Praia*, T 231-3033, Praia do Pontal, B, swimming pool; *Ilhéus Praia*, Praça D. Eduardo (on beach), T 231-2533, B, pool, helpful, rec.; *Pousada G.G.*, Praça Cairu 18, E without breakfast (restaurant next door), clean, near beach. *Tio San*, R Antonio Levigne de Lemos, T 231-3668, *Pousada Cravo e Canela*, along beach F, clean, rec.; In R. Carneiro da Rocha are *Tropical*, No. 129, basic, and *Bahiano*, No. 94 (helpful, clean, friendly), each E, and two *dormitórios*. Plenty of cheap hotels near municipal bus station in centre.

**Restaurants** *Tokyo*, 2 de Julho, Japanese, very good, not cheap. At Pontal, *Cabana Cinco Estrellas*, excellent, cheap Bahian food. *O Velho Marinheiro*, on the waterfront, rec; *Come Ben*, nr. Praça Cairu, cheap and good; *Vesúvio*, Praça D. Eduardo, next to Cathedral, made famous by Amado's novel (see above), now Swiss-owned, very good but pricey; *Nogar*, Av. Bahia 377, close to the sea, good pizzas and pasta. Local drink, *coquinho*, coconut filled with cachaça, only for the strongest heads! Also try *suco de cacau* at juice stands. *Carlos Twity's* in Una, 40 kms S, for *shrimp muceca*, which Michael de Lapa opines "will knock your socks off".

**Buses** Station is some way from centre, but Itabuna-Olivença bus goes through centre of Ilhéus. Several daily to **Salvador**, 7 hrs., US$10 (*leito* US$20, Expresso São Jorge); 0620 bus goes via Itaparica, leaving passengers at Bom Despacho ferry station on the island—thence 50-minute ferry to Salvador. To **Itacaré**, early a.m. and 1530, 4 hrs., US$4; to **Eunápolis**, 7 hrs., US$4.80, this bus also leaves from the central bus terminal. Insist that taxi drivers have meters and price charts.

Buses run every 30 mins. to **Itabuna** (32 km.; pop. 167,000), the trading centre of the rich cocoa zone (also many lumber mills). Bus from Salvador, 6½ hrs., US$7.20. Of the hotels, the *Príncipe*, *Lord* and *Itabuna Palace* (Av. Cinquentenário 1061, B, restaurant) are probably the best (*Rincão Gaúcho*, E, small, friendly, overlooking river; opposite Rodoviária is *Dormitório Rodoviária*, F, basic; several motels on the outskirts). The paved BA-415 links Itabuna to Vitória da Conquista (275 km.) on the BR-116. Ceplac installations at Km. 8 on the Itabuna-Ilhéus road show the whole processing of cocoa. Tours of cocoa plantations can be arranged through the *Ilhéus Praia* hotel; Jorge Amado's novel *The Violent Lands* deals with life on the cocoa plantations.
    The beaches between Ilhéus and Olivença are good, e.g. Cururupe, and frequent buses run to Olivença. For the good beaches at Pontal, take "Barreira" bus and get off just past *Hotel Jardim Atlântico*. Hot baths (*balneário*) 18 km away, are reached by Viação São Jorge or Canavieiras buses. 115 km. S is Canavieras (pop. 30,000), a developing beach resort (*Pousada Maria*, C; *Mini-Hotel*, D; Camping at Praia de Atalaia).

About 400 km. south of Ilhéus on the coast is the old town of **Porto Seguro** (pop. 56,000), now developed for tourism; the airport has been enlarged to take jets, frequent buses from the new Rodoviária. Building is, however, subject to controls on height and materials, in keeping with traditional Bahian styles. (For the routes from Vitória see page 333 and from Belo Horizonte page 340). At Brazilian holiday times, all transport north or south should be booked well in advance.
    It was N of the site of Porto Seguro that Cabral first landed in 1500; a cross marks the supposed site of the first mass in Brazil on road between Porto Seguro and Santa Cruz Cabrália. A tourist village, Coroa Vermelha, has sprouted nearby, with souvenir shops selling Pataxó Indian items, beach bars, hotels and rental houses, all rather uncoordinated. From the roundabout at the entrance to Porto Seguro take a wide, steep, unmarked path uphill to the historical city (Cidade Histórica), three churches (N.S. da Misericórdia-1530, N.S. do Rosário-1534, and N.S. da Pena-1718), the former jail and the cross; a small, peaceful place with lovely gardens and panoramic views. 23 km. to the N of Porto Seguro is Santa Cruz Cabrália (simple accommodation -.e.g. *Pousada Xica da Silva* near bus stop, cheap, nice, good restaurant *Coqueiro Verde*—try *pitu*, a kind of crayfish); dugout ferry crosses the river, then a short walk to the beach at Santo André. Trips on the river can be made. Bicycles for hire at hardware shop, Dois de Julho 242, US$2 a day. In this area there are *borrachudos*, little flies that bite feet and ankles in the heat of the day; coconut oil keeps them off; at night mosquitoes can be a problem.

**Hotels** *Porto Seguro Praia*, 3 km. N of city on coast road, T 288-2321, B; *Cabanas do Tio João*, BR-367, Km. 64, 2 km. N of Porto Seguro, T 288-2315, a/c, pool, English and French spoken, rec.; *Phonécia*, Av. 22 de Abril 400, B, T 2882411; *Pousada Coqueiro Verde*, Rua "A" No. 01, T 288 2621, C, a/c, pool, sauna, rec.; *Pousada Albatroz*, Av. dos Navegantes 600, C, a/c, pool, rec., T 288 2394; *Vela Branca*, Cidade Histórica, T 288-2316, C, top of cliff, good; *Pousada Saveiros*, Av. Navegentes, D, good breakfast, will change travellers' cheques; *Estalagem Porto Seguro*, R. Mal. Deodoro 66, T 288 2095, old colonial house, C, a/c, fan, rec.; *Pousada Gaivota*, Av. dos Navegantes 333, T 288 2826, C, a/c, pool, sauna; *Pousada Chauá*, same Av. No. 800, C, a/c; *Pousada Solar da Praça*, Praça da Bandeira, C, bath, a/c, good seafront location; *Pousada Aquarius*, R. Pedro Alvares Cabral 176, D, bath, fan, English, French, Italian spoken, rec.; *Pousada Coral*, R. Assis Chateaubriand 74, T 288 2630, good breakfast, fan; *Chica da Silva*, Av. dos Navegantes 94, T 288 2280, D, friendly, family run; *Pousada Casa Azul*, 15 de Novembro 11, T 288-2180, C with bath, English spoken, good, swimming pool; *Pousada Coroa Vermelha*, Getúlio Vargas 12, T 288-2132, E, with bath, no breakfast, clean, good, friendly owners; a number of good, cheap *pousadas* on Av. Getúlio Vargas, most without breakfast; *Mar Azul* at No. 109, E with bath, clean, friendly; *Pousada Mar e Sol*, No. 223, E with bath in low season, discounts for monthly stays, clean, safe, filtered drinking water, very helpful manager (who teaches *Lambada*), highly rec.; *Pousada São Luiz*, E, rec. *Pousada do Cais*, Portugal 382, T 228-2121, C with bath, colonial house on sea-front, good; several others on same street; *Pousada Rio do Prado* (No. 236), rec., E with big breakfast; *Porto Brasília*, Praça Antonio Carlos Magalhães 234, E with breakfast, F without, clean, friendly; *Pousada Sapucaia*, E, clean, friendly; *Pousada Vera Cruz*, Av. 22 de Abril 100, T 288-2162, E with bath, good breakfast, clean. *Pousada Navegante*, near port, rec. *Pousada Raizes*, Praça dos Pataxós 196, T 288 2198, D with bath, fan, rec.; same square No. 278 is *Pousada Travessia*, T 288 2616, D with good breakfast. Some good, cheap *pousadas* on R. Mal. Deodoro at the port; *Pousada Sol Poente*, No. 40, T 288 2451, member of IYHA, US$5 p.p. in dormitory with card, US$7 without; *Carvalo Marino*, No. 100, E; *Estalagem da Yvonne*, No. 298, E with breakfast, D with a/c, T 288 2045; *Hospedaria do Pirata*, No. 249, E with good breakfast, bath, rec.; *Pousada de Sagres*, R. 15 de Novembro, T 288 2031, E with good breakfast, family run; *Pousada Sonho Meu*, same street No. 86, E with bath, breakfast, fan, good.

**Camping** *Camping dos Marajas*, Av. Getúlio Vargas, central, good facilities; *Camping do Sítio*, R. da Vala, mosquitoes can be a problem here.

**Restaurants** *Cruz de Malta*, R. Getúlio Vargas 358, good seafood; *Preto Velho*, on Praça da Bandeira, à la carte or self-service, good value; also good value is *Hall of Hunger*, R. Rui Barbosa 194, home cooking daily from 1200 to 2200, cheap; good breakfast at *Pau Brasil*, Praça dos Pataxós, and *Club dos Sem Casa*, R. Pedro Alvares Cabral 185, open 0800-2100, good, cheap lunches here also; *do Japonês*, Praça dos Pataxós 38, excellent value with varied menu, open 0800-2300, rec.; *Ponto do Encontro* on same square, No. 106, good simple food, friendly, owners rent rooms, open 0800-2400; *Sambuca*, on Praça dos Pataxós is good for pizzas; on same square is *Prima Dona*, No. 247, Italian, good. *Anti-Caro*, R. Assis Chateaubriand 26, good, rec., also antique shop, good atmosphere; *Casa da Esquina*, on same street, French, good, moderately priced. The best meat restaurant is *Churrascaria do Maça*, R. Mal. Deodoro 342, open 1500-2400, very good *picanha*, enough for 3 people, not expensive, rec.; *Les Agapornis*, Av. dos Navegantes 180, wide selection of crêpes and pizzas; *Tres Vintens*, Av. Portugal 1246, good imaginative seafood dishes, rec.; *Ninô*, 22 de Abril 100, good pizzas; *Grilhadaz*, same street, moderate prices; *New Jersey*, nearby, good, reasonable prices; *Vida Verde*, R. Dois de Julho 92, good vegetarian, open 1100-2100 except Sun., T 288 2766, rec.

**Entertainment** Porto Seguro is famous for the Lambada (see **Music and Dance**). The best place to see it is at *Boca da Barra* at Praia do Cruzeiro. Instructors are on hand from 1800-2000, then the locals take the floor until the small hours. No entry charge, not to be missed, nightly throughout the year. The strong local liqueur, *quarachaça*, a mixture of guaraná and cachaça, keeps the dancers going during the long hours; don't underestimate its strength. Another place to see Lambada is *Lambaporto*, busy only at weekends.

A good bar for live music is *Porto Prego* on R. Pedro Alvares Cabral, small cover charge. *Sotton Bar*, Praça de Bandeira, is lively. There are lots of bars and street cafés on Av. Portugal.

**Rentals Car** hire, Itapoan, Av. Portugal 1350, T 288-2710; **motorcycles**, Lupa Motos, Praça dos Pataxós, T 288-2868, expensive, heavy deposit required; **bicycles**, Oficina de Bicicleta, Av. Getúlio Vargas e R. São Pedro, about US$10 for 24 hrs.; also at Praça de Bandeira. **Diving equipment**, Portomar Ltda, R. Dois de Julho 178, also arranges diving and snorkelling trips to the coral reefs offshore, professional instructors.

**Exchange** Banks will not change money, but managers may privately. *Sergio Vanni*, Praça da Bandeira 100, 1st floor; good rates at *Agência do Descobrimento*, Av. Getúlio Vargas, lower rate for travellers' cheques, also arranges flight tickets and house rental. Rates are not as good in the big cities.

**Telephones** Telebahia service post, Praça dos Pataxós beside ferry terminal, open daily 0800-2000, cheap rates after 2000 so can be very busy at this time.

**Tourist Information** At the time of writing (April 1991), the local tourist board, Porturismo, was practically non-existent (booth on Praça dos Pataxós closed). Casa de Lenha, Praça Visconde de Porto Seguro, near port, has basic information.

**Buses** from Porto Seguro: F85MSalvador, daily, 12 hrs., *Leito*, 15 hrs, 4 a week, US$17 (*Leito* 35); **Vitória**, daily, 11 hrs, US$12.75; **Ilhéus** daily 0730, 5 hrs., US$10; **Eunápolis**, many on paved road, 1½ hrs., US$1.60. For **Rio** direct buses (São Geraldo), leaving at 1745, US$27, 18 hrs. For **Minas Gerais**, take a bus to Nanuque on the Bahia MG border, then change to Teôfilo Otôni. To **São Paulo** direct, 1045, 25 hrs. US$38; other services via Eunápolis or Itabuna (5 hrs., US$6.40). There is new Rodoviária on the road to Eunápolis, 2 km. from the centre.

**Air**  Nordeste daily from Rio, 1 stop, 3 hrs, also Rio Sul twice a week via Campos; Nordeste daily also to Salvador, São Paulo.

**Excursions**  Guided tours of the area with BPS, at the Shopping Centre, T 288-2373. Companhia do Mar (Cia do Mar, Praça dos Pataxós, T 288-2981) does daily trips by schooner to coral reefs off the coast. The most popular is to Recife de Fora, with good snorkelling; leaves daily 1000, returns 1700, about US$15. Other good trips to Coroa Vermelho and Coroa Alta, and south to Trancoso. For equipment hire, see above.

Across the Rio Buranhém S. from Porto Seguro (10 minutes, US$0.25, ferries take cars day time only, every ½-hr. day and night), and a further 5 km. (US$0.45 in bus), is the village of **Arraial da Ajuda**; about 15 mins. walk from the beach (better for camping than Porto Seguro). Pilgrimage in August to the shrine of Nossa Senhora da Ajuda (interesting room in church, full of ex-voto offerings—fine view from behind church). Ajuda has become very popular with tourists and there are many *pousadas*, bars and small shops. Parties almost every night, on the beach or in the *Broadway*; at the *Jaboba* bar the famous lambada is danced. Beach protected by coral reef. At Brazilian holiday times it is very crowded and, with the coastline up for sale, it may become overdeveloped in a few years. The beaches in this neighbourhood are splendid, for instance Pitinga, also protected by coral reef, Lagoa Azul and Mucugê. Porto Belo or Sta Cruz Cabrália buses go to the beaches frequently from the port.

**Hotels**  *Pousada Le Cottage* (across ferry from Porto Seguro, but before Ajuda, T 288-2181), French owner, Sr. Georges, D with bath, C in chalet; *Pousada Canto d'Alvorada*, on road to Ajuda, C in season, D out of season, Swiss run, 7 cabins, restaurant, washing facilities; *Thaina Plage*, D, highly rec., reserved in São Paulo T 011-533-5898, or in Paris T 43-26-31-41, and *Pousada Torrorão*, between village and beach, T 875-1260, D, restaurant, rec.; *Pousada das Brisas*, T 875-1033, B-C, clean, panoramic views, English, German, French and Spanish spoken; *Pousada Natur*, C and D, run by German environmentalist, clean, friendly, rec., English spoken T 288-2738; *Pousada Erva Doce*, T 875 1114, D, owners very friendly, good restaurant, well appointed chalets, highly rec.; *Pousada Caminho do Mar*, T 875 1099, English spoken, C/D depending on season, owners very informative and helpful, also highly rec.; *Pousada Girasol*, D with good breakfast, bath; *Pousada Tubarão*, beyond the church on the right, T 875 1086, D, good view of the coastline, cool, good restaurant; *Pousada Altomar*, next door, D without breakfast; *Pousada Tamarind*, on main square near church, E without breakfast, bath; *Pousada Nova Esperança*, nearby, E without breakfast, bath, rec.; *Pousada Tio Otto*, E without breakfast, alongside church; *Pousada Mangaba*, on way to the beach, bath, washing facilities, E without breakfast, friendly, rec.; *Pousada Maravilha*, Av. São João, D with good breakfast; *Pousada Miramar*, F without breakfast, cheapest accommodation in town, rec.

**Note**:  Above prices are high season prices unless otherwise stated, if staying for a long period they are negotiable; this is certainly true in the low season.

**Camping**  *Chão do Arraial*, 5 mins. from Mucugê beach, shady, good snack bar, also hire tents, rec. Also **Camping do Gordo**, on left shortly after leaving ferry, on beach but beach is not as good as Mucugê.

**Restaurants**  *São João*, near the church, is the best typical restaurant; *Asa Branca*, R. Santa Rita, very good *carne do sol de picanha*; *Manda Brasa*, on Broadway, good *prato feito*, cheap; *Le Gourmet*, R. São Joã, good international cuisine, specialise in French dishes, not cheap, rec.; *Mão na Massa*, an excellent Italian restaurant, behind the church, rec.; also recommended is *Varanda Grill*, good grilled fish, meat and chicken; *Erva Doce*, on way to the beach, good pizzas and lasagnes, rec.; *Tubarão*, behind the church has also been rec., regional and international dishes; *Café das Cores*, on way to the beach, good cakes and snacks, expresso coffee. Two good "barracas" on Pitinga beach are *Bar da Pitinga* and *Bar do Genésio*, fresh fried fish, shrimp etc.

**Phone**  Telebahia have a service post on the main square, open 0800 until 2200.

25 km. to the S of Porto Seguro and 15 km. from Ajuda is **Trancoso**, reached by bus, 5 a day (US$1.25, 50 mins., last returns at 1530, more buses and colectivos in summer), by colectivo, hitch-hiking or by walking along the beach; the road bridges are not safe, bus passengers alight and walk across. The village is simple

but also popular with tourists, beautiful beaches (some nude) and many Europeans have built or bought houses there. There are good restaurants around the main square. From the end of Praça São João there is a fine coastal panorama. Trancoso has a historic church. Colectivos run from Trancoso to Ajuda (US$1.90). Between Ajuda and Trancoso is the village of Rio da Barra. Caraíva with beautiful beaches, no electricity, can be reached by boat, 4 hrs. from Porto Seguro, 2 hrs. from Trancoso, or by bus via Eunápolis and Itabela.

**Trancoso Hotels** *Hotel de Praça*, B, bath, games room, good breakfast; *Pousada Calypso*, C, good apartments, comfortable, rooms at lower price also available, good library, German and English spoken, rec.; *Posada Canto Verde*, D with breakfast, bath, restaurant only in high season, rec.; *Caipim Santo*, to the left of main square, D with breakfast, the best restaurant in Trancoso, very friendly, bath, rec.; *Pousada do Bosque*, on the way to the beach, D, English, German and Spanish spoken, with breakfast, camping facilities also available, good value; *Pousada Sol da Manhã*, E, with breakfast; *Pousada Terra do Sol*, F without breakfast, good, rec. About 500 metres inland away from main square (known as the "quadrado") lies the newer part of Trancoso (known as the "invasão") with two good value *pousadas*, *Pousada Quarto Crescente*, English, German, Dutch and Spanish spoken, cooking facilities, washing also, D/E, very friendly and helpful owners, library, highly rec., about 15 mins. from beach. Another good *pousada* is *Luna Pousa*, further along on the left, E with breakfast, well ventilated, only 4 apts. There are many houses to rent, very good ones are rented by Clea who can be contacted at *Restaurant Abacaxi* on main square on right. You can leave a message for any one of the above mentioned *pousadas* by calling the Telebahia service post 867 1116, most people in town check there for messages on a daily basis. Like in Porto Seguro and Ajuda if you stay for a longer period you can nearly always negotiate a better price, this is certainly true in the low season.

**Restaurants** The best is *Caipim Santo*, natural cuisine, see above; *Urano*, just before the main square is also rec., good portions, usually enough for two; *Rama* has also been recommended; *Abacaxi* on main square does good breakfasts, light snacks and very good crêpes; *Galub Mahal* for Eastern dishes; good breakfast also at *Pé das Frutas*, *Maré Cheia* next door good simple dishes. Good ice cream at *Tão Vez*. Apart from restaurants which serve breakfast most others open at 1500 until 2200 or so.

South of Porto Seguro, reached by a paved access road from the BR-101 16 km. N of Itamaraju, is the **Parque Nacional de Monte Pascoal**, set up in 1961 to preserve the flora, fauna and birdlife of the coastal area in which Europeans made landfall in Brazil. The Pataxó Indian reservation is located at Corombau village, on the ocean shore of the park. Corombau can be reached by schooner from Porto Seguro. A small luxury resort has been built at Corombau. From Itamaraju (93 km. S of Eunápolis) the coastal towns of *Curumuxatiba* (*Pousada Guainamby*, R. Bela Vista, CEP 45983, German and Brazilian owned, small, clean, comfortable chalets, good views to long beach, good breakfast and fish and Italian meals, rec.) and Prado. Also reach from Itamaraju is the *Jacotoka* holiday village, which offers diving, surfing and riding in a tropical paradise. US$40-50 per day, reservations at 7 de Setembro 149, Porto Seguro, CEP 45820, T 288-2291, Fax 288-2540; it can also be reached by boat from Porto Seguro. Further south still is *Caravelas* (pop. 25,000) 130 km. S of Porto Seguro, developing resort (hotels on Praia do Grauçá, *Marina Porto Abrulhos*, C; *Pousada das Sereias*, D.; *Caravelense*, D.) buses to Teixeira de Freitas, Salvador and Nanuque.

John Raspey writes: The **Parque Nacional Marinho dos Abrolhos** is 70 km. E of Caravelas: 5 small islands (Redonda, Siriba, Guarita, Sueste, Santa Bárbara), and several coral reefs. The archipelago is administered by Ibama, the Brazilian Institute of Environmental Protection, and a navy detachment mans a lighthouse on Sta. Bárbara, which is the only island that may be visited. Permission from Parque Nacional Marinho dos Abrolhos, Praia do Kitombo s/n, Caravelas, Bahia 45900, T (073) 297-1111. The islands and surrounding reefs are home to birds, whales, fish and giant fire corals (also goats). Darwin visited them in 1830. A master authorized by the Navy to take tourists is Mestre Onofrio Frio in Alrobaça, Bahia, T (073) 293-2195.

**North from Salvador** The paved BA-099 coast road from near the airport is known as the Estrada do Coco (coconut road) and for 50 km. passes some beautiful beaches. The best known from south to north are Ipitanga (with its reefs), Buraquinho, Jauá, Arembepe, Guarajuba, Itacimirim, Castelo Garcia D'Avila (with its 16th century fort) and Forte. Buses serve most of these destinations.

Some 50 km. to the north of Salvador is the former fishing village of **Arembepe**, now a quiet resort. *Pousada da Fazenda* on the beach, thatched huts, good seafood, not cheap; *Pousada*, E; and restaurant *Mar Aberto*, T 824-1257, rec., food very good, English and French spoken; Verá's restaurant, try *pastel de banana*. There is an "alternative" village of palm huts, ½ hour walk along the beach, behind the sand dunes, café and swimming. Best beaches 2 km. N of town. Bus from Terminal Francés, Salvador, every 2 hours, 1½ hrs., US$1, last one back at 1700; or from Itapoan. Buses from Salvador run to Praia do Forte (75 km.), where there are Hotels *Club Maritime* (5-star, L, sports facilities, good meals), *Praia do Forte*, L, and a few *pousadas* (e.g. *Ouxi Mari*, clean, good breakfast, shower). There is also a fishing village, a ruin and turtles.

**Monte Santo**   About 270 km. N of Feira da Santana, and 38 km. W of Euclides da Cunha on the direct BR-116 road to Fortaleza, is the famous hill shrine of Monte Santo in the Sertão, reached by 3½ km. of steps cut into the rocks of the Serra do Picaraça (about 45 mins'. walk each way—set out early). This is the scene of pilgrimages and great religious devotion during Holy Week. The shrine was built by an Italian who had a vision of the cross on the mountain in 1765. One block north of the bottom of the stairs is the Museu do Sertão, with pictures from the 1897 Canudos rebellion. **Canudos** itself is 100 km. away at the junction of the BR-116 and BR-235 (direct buses from Salvador); religious rebels led by the visionary Antônio Conselheiro defeated three expeditions sent against them in 1897 before being overwhelmed. These events are the theme of two great books: *Os Sertões* (Revolt in the Backlands) by Euclides da Cunha, and *La Guerra del Fin del Mundo* (The War of the End of the World) by the Peruvian writer Mario Vargas Llosa. The Rio Vaza Barris, which runs through Canudos has been dammed, and the town has been moved to Nova Canudos by the dam. Part of the old town is still located 10 km. West.

**Hotels**   *Grapiuna*, Praça Monsenhor Berenguer 401 (T 275-1157), E-D, with bath (cheaper without downstairs), rec.; *Santa Cruz*, opp. Banco do Brasil, E, shared bath, basic but clean; pleasant bars. At Euclides da Cunha, on the BR-116 and 39 km. from Monte Santo, are *Hotel Lua*, simple and *Hotel Conselheiro*.

Part of the northern border of Bahia is the Rio São Francisco; on the opposite bank are Pernambuco and Alagoas. From Salvador, the BR-110 runs north to the river at Paulo Afonso; the road is paved for all but 71 km. between Cícero Dantas and Jeremoaba (turn W here on BR-235 to Canudos, 111 km.). 76 km. N of Jeremoaba is the **Parque Nacional de Paulo Afonso**. The Falls of **Paulo Afonso**, once one of the great falls of the world but now exploited for hydroelectric power, are 270 km. from the mouth of the São Francisco river, which drains a valley 3 times the size of Great Britain. There are 2,575 km. of river above the Falls to its source in Minas Gerais. Below the Falls is a deep, rock gorge through which the water rushes. The national park is an oasis of trees and the lake amid a desert of brown scrub and cactus. The best time to visit the Falls is in the rainy season (Jan.-Feb.); only then does much water pass over them, as almost all the flow now goes through the power plant. The best view is from the northern (Alagoas) bank. The Falls are in a security area; no admission for pedestrians, so you need to visit by car or taxi (US$4.50 an hour). Admission is from 0800 onwards, but it depends on the availability of guides, without whom one cannot enter; go to the tourist information office in the centre of the town and sign up for a tour of the hydroelectric plant, 2 hrs., US$5.75 per car.

There are the *Hotel Casande* (B), *Grand Hotel de Paulo Afonso* (B, a/c, TV, pool) and a guest house (apply for room in advance) at the Falls. The town of Paulo Afonso (pop. 86,000) is some distance from the Falls, reached by bus from Salvador, by paved road from Recife, bus, 7 hrs., US$8, or from Maceió (306 km.) via Palmeira dos Índios, partially paved. Hotels *Guadalajara* and *Paulo Afonso*, friendly, cheap; *Belvedere*, T 281-1814, D, a/c, swimming pool and *Palace*, T 281-1521, D with bath, a/c, swimming pool, "best value in town", next door to each other on R. André Falcão; *Hospedagem Lima*, very basic, F, near *Hotel Guadalajara*; *Hotel Dormitório*, F—all hotels within walking distance of bus terminal. Plenty of restaurants, e.g. *Kilanche*, next to Tourist Office. For information about Paulo Afonso and the *sertão*, ask the Italian fathers (Mario, Antonio and Riccardo) who are most helpful. Handicrafts (embroidery, fabrics) from Núcleo de Produção Artesanal, Av. Contorno s/n. It is possible, with plenty of time, to go upstream from Penedo (**see page 427**) to about Pão de Açúcar or Piranhas, but on to the Falls is complicated and involves non-connecting buses. **Piranhas**, (Alagoas), 80 km. from Paulo Afonso (road almost completely paved, buses difficult), is a charming town with good beaches on the Rio São Francisco; it has picturesque houses and an old railway station which is now a *Pousada* (3-4 rooms, F, restaurant) with a small museum (photographs of the severed head of Lampião, the Brazilian "Robin Hood").

**Travel on the River São Francisco (see page 347)**. The river is navigable above the Falls from above the twin towns (linked by a bridge) of **Juazeiro** (62,000 people), in Bahia, and **Petrolina** (74,000), in Pernambuco (buses from Salvador, 6 hrs., also from Recife, Fortaleza, Teresina) to Pirapora in Minas Gerais, linked by road to the Belo Horizonte-Brasília highway. Like Pirapora, Petrolina is famous for the production of *carrancas* (boat figureheads, mostly grotesque) of wood or ceramic. River transport has changed rapidly in the past few years; for information telephone Juazeiro (075) 811-2465. The BR-253 runs west from Canudos to Juazeiro, alternatively, from Salvador go to Feira de Santana, take the paved BR-324, then the BR-407, which continues through Petrolina to Picos in Piauí, (**see page 448**) junction for Fortaleza or Teresina. On the BR-324, 124 km. S of Juazeiro is Senhor do Bonfim, a busy market town with lots of life (also banks and post office).

John Hale writes: Juazeiro and Petrolina are thriving towns compared with many others on the upper São Francisco. Petrolina has its own airport and close to this is the small Museu do Sertão—relics of rural life in the North-East and the age of the "coronéis" and the bandit Lampião. *Hotel Newman*, Av. Souza Filho 444, T 961-0595, E; *Pousada da Carranca*, BR-122, km. 4, T 961-3421, D; *Espacial*, EF Leste Brasileiro km. 2, E; *Grande Rio*, R. Padre Praga, B; and *Restaurante Rancho Grande*. *Restaurante Panorâmico*, the only one on the river front, is good. Juazeiro is the poorer of the two cities. Hotels: *Grande Hotel*, R. Pititinga, T 811-2710, *Vitória*, T 811-2712, and *União* (rec.) and *Oliveira*, the last two in R. Conselheiro Saraiva. *Hotel Pousada de Juazeiro*, 6 km. S on BR-407, T 811-2820, C with bath, a/c, pool, restaurant, bar, pleasant. Unique restaurant known as the *Vaporzinho* is high and dry on the river front, a side-wheel paddle steamer (poor food), the *Saldanha Marinho*, built at Sabará in 1852. Market on Fri. and Sat.

Margy Levine and Jordan Young (Lexington, MA) write:
There are three new wineries in the area: one in Casa Nova (Bahia); Ouro Verde in Lagoa Grande (Pernambuco); and Fazenda Milano in Santa Maria da Boa Vista (Pernambuco), on the north shore of the Rio São Francisco. Fazenda Milano (24 km. from Lagoa Grande, towards Santa Maria da Boa Vista) was the first winery in the north-east, and makes wine from European grapes, with 150 hectares of vines. Owned by Forestier, a winemaker from the south, they make red, white and rosé, blended and varietals. You can visit the winery on Thursdays, if you call in advance on (081) 961-4669 or, in Recife, (081) 251-2200. Wine can be bought at US$3 for 3 bottles. When you get to the Fazenda Milano sign on the Lagoa Grande-Santa Maria road, turn south towards the river, and drive 8 km. on a dirt road to the gate.

---

## THE NORTH EAST (8)

---

The eight northeastern states are generally poor economically, but are neither poor historically (see Recife, Olinda, São Luis), nor culturally (e.g. "Forró" and other musical styles, many good museums, lacework, ceramics). There is a multitude of beaches: those in established resorts tend to be polluted, but you don't have to travel far for good ones, while off the beaten track are some which have hardly been discovered.

South of Cabo São Roque (Rio Grande do Norte) there is abundant rainfall, but in Pernambuco the zone of ample rain stretches only 80 km. inland, though it deepens southwards. São Luís in Maranhão also gets plenty of rain, but between eastern Maranhão and Pernambuco lies a triangle, with its apex deep inland, where the rainfall is sporadic, and occasionally non-existent for a year. Here the tropical forest gives way to the *caatinga*, or scrub forest bushes which shed their leaves during drought. In this area grow the palms that produce carnauba wax and babaçu nuts, and the tree that produces oiticica oil.

There was a brief period of colonization from northern Europe in the NE, when the Dutch West India Company, based at Recife, controlled some seven captaincies along the coast. They gained control in 1630, when Portugal was subject to Spain. After 1640, when Portugal freed itself, the colonists fought the Dutch and finally expelled them in 1654.

## Sergipe and Alagoas

247 km. N of Salvador, on BR-101, almost midway between the Sergipe-Bahia border is Estância, with pleasant hotels: *Turista*, E, and *Dom Bosco*, opposite, E, slightly cheaper, bath and breakfast, both pleasant.

*Aracaju* (pop. 360,000), capital of Sergipe (state pop 1,366,000), 327 km. N of Salvador, founded 1855, is a clean and lively town. It stands on the south bank of the Rio Sergipe, about 10 km. from its mouth, and can be reached from Maceió or Salvador by road. The city—unusually for Brazil—is laid out in the grid pattern. It has a beautiful park, clean streets (some in centre reserved to pedestrians); there is a handicraft centre, the Centro do Turismo, open 0900-1300, 1500-1900, in a restored colonial building on Praça Olímpio Campos, the cathedral square. A 16-km. road leads to the fine Atalaia beach: oil-drilling rigs offshore. There is an even better beach, Nova Atalaia, on Ilha de Santa Luzia across the river, reached by boat from the ferry station. On 8 December there are both Catholic (Nossa Senhora da Conceição) and Umbanda religious festivals.

**Hotels** *Parque dos Coqueiros*, L, Atalaia beach, T 243-1511, large pool, luxurious and attractive; *Brasília*, R. Laranjeiras 580, T 224-8022, D, good value, good breakfasts; *Serigy*, R. Santo Amaro 269 (T 222-1210), B, comfortable, no hot water in rooms; *Turista*, R. Divina Pastora 411, E, noisy, mosquitos, no hot water or breakfast, friendly; *Oasis*, R. São Cristóvão 466 in centre, T 224-2125, D with good breakfast, rec.; *Guanabara*, noisy, cold water in rooms, R. Florentino Menezes 161, E, good meals; *Amado*, R. Laranjeiras, F, fan, clothes washing facilities. Many cheap hotels in R. Santa Rosa. New *Youth Hostel*, T 231-9166, F, on road to Atalaia (take bus Os Campos, from Centre), no card needed, clean, friendly.

**Camping** Camping Clube do Brasil site at Atalaia beach.

**Tourist Information** Emsetur, Av. Barão de Maroim 593, maps of Aracaju, Laranjeiras, São Cristovão. *Artesanato* interesting: pottery figures and lace particularly. Fair in Praça Tobias Barreto every Sun.

*São Cristóvão* (pop. 37,000), SW of Aracaju on the road to Salvador, an unspoiled colonial town, was the old state capital of Sergipe, founded in 1590 by Cristóvão de Barros. Worth visiting are the Museu de Arte Sacra e Histórico de Sergipe, the Assembly building, the Provincial Palace and five churches including Misericórdia and Nossa Senhora da Vitória (all closed Mon.). Outdoor arts festival in 2nd half of October. Buses (São Pedro) from Aracaju, from old Rodoviária in centre, 30 mins.-1 hr. (No hotels, but families rent rooms near the bus station.)

15 km. from Aracaju is *Laranjeiras*, reached by São Pedro bus, from old Rodoviária in centre, 30 mins-1 hr. A small pleasant town, with a ruined church on a hill, it has two museums (Museu Afro-Brasileiro and Centro de Cultura João Ribeiro), and the Capela de Sant'Aninha with a wooden altar inlaid with gold. *Pousada Vale dos Outēiros*, D, rec.

70 km. west of Aracaju is *Itabaiana*, which has a famous gold market on Saturday.

The Rio São Francisco marks the boundary between Sergipe and Alagoas. The BR-101 between Aracaju and Maceió—the next port to the north—is paved, crossing the São Francisco by bridge between Propriá and Porto Real do Colégio.

**Penedo**, in Alagoas near the mouth of the River São Francisco, 451 km. from Salvador (US$14, 10 hrs., by daily bus at 0830; 115 km. from Maceió), is a charming town, with a nice waterfront park with stone walkways and walls. Old churches include Convento de São Francisco and N.S. dos Anjos. Long two-masted sailing vessels cruise on the river (they can be rented for US$3.75 per hour, regardless of the number of people, possibly stopping to swim or visit beaches on islands in the river). Frequent launches across the river to Neópolis, 25 mins., US$0.75. Also half-hourly car ferry (US$0.80; take care when driving on and off). Daily street market. Good hammocks. Buses from Maceió, US$3.20, 4 hrs. One bus to Aracaju daily, 0600.

**Hotels** *São Francisco*, Av. Floriano Peixoto, T 551-2273, C, rec. except for poor restaurant; *Pousada Colonial*, Praça 12 de Abril 21, T 551-2677, D with bath, good cheap restaurant, most rooms with view of Rio São Francisco; *Turista*, R. Siqueira Campos 148, T 551-2237, E with bath, rec., close to bus station; in same street *Majestic* and *Vitória*, both E; *Impérial*, Av. Floriano Peixoto, G, basic. Good **restaurant**, *Forte da Rocheira*, R. da Rocheira, good food, especially ensopada de jacaré (alligator stew).

**Tourist Office** in Casa de Aposentadoria, Praça Barão de Penedo, helpful.

**Maceió** (pop. 482,000), capital of Alagoas state (pop. 2,381,000), is about 287 km. NE of Aracaju by road, and 244 km. S of Recife. It is mainly a sugar port, although there are also tobacco exports and a major petrochemical plant. A lighthouse stands on an eminence built in a residential area of town (Farol), about one km. from the sea.

Two of the city's old buildings, the Government Palace and the church of Bom Jesus dos Mártires (covered in tiles), are particularly interesting, as is the recently restored Cathedral. The Associação Comercial has a museum, near the beach, in a beautiful, though deteriorating building. There is an enjoyable lagoon (Lagoa do Mundaú), 2 km. S at **Pontal da Barra**: excellent shrimp and fish at its small restaurants and handicraft stalls. It is a ten-minute taxi ride (US$2.50) from the town centre (or take "Ponta da Terra" bus) to Pajuçara beach, where there are a nightly craft market and several good hotels and restaurants. The beaches, some of the finest and most popular in Brazil, have in most cases a protecting coral reef a kilometre or so out, but it is said that underwater reef life is not plentiful, and visibility is poor. Good ones are Jatiúca, Cruz das Almas, Jacarecica all good for surfing, Guaxuma, Mirante, Garça Torta, Riacho Doce, all within 30 mins. taxi ride from town; buses to the last 4 from terminal, US$1.05, or local Mirante or Ipioca bus, US$0.10. Beaches fronting the old city and between Salgema terminal and the modern port area (Trapiche, Subra) are too polluted for swimming.

*Jangadas* take passengers to a natural pool 2 km. off Pajuçara beach (Piscina Natural de Pajuçara), at low tide you can stand on the sand and rock reef; on the days before or after the new or full moon, the tides are low and the bathing area is bigger (beware of sunburn). *Jangadas* cost US$3.45 per person per day (or about US$15 to have a *jangada* to yourself)— on Sundays or local holidays in the high season it is overcrowded, take mask or goggles (at weekends lots of *jangadas* anchor at the reef selling food and drink). From Maceió, a ferry crosses the lagoon to Coqueira Seca (30 mins., US$0.35), a small pretty fishing village.

Alagoas is one of the poorest and least developed states. Be prepared for delays, cancellations and changed opening times, Maceió, however, is a friendly city with a low crime rate and a Caribbean atmosphere.

**Local Holidays** 27 August (Nossa Senhora dos Prazeres); 16 Sept. (Freedom of Alagoas); 8 December (Nossa Senhora da Conceição); Christmas Eve; New Year's Eve, half-day.

**Hotels** It is better to stay on Praia Pajuçara than on Praias Avenida or Sobral: many hotels on Av. Dr Antônio Gouveia and R. Jangadeiros Alagoanos, Pajuçara. *Jatiúca*, Lagoa da Anta

220, T 231-2555, L, a/c, on the beach, swimming pool, heavily booked, good breakfasts, but small rooms with thin walls; *Pajuçara Othon*, R. Jangadeiros Alagoanos 1292, T 231-2200, A; *Verde Mar*, Av. Antônio Gouveia, 1, C with bath, a/c, hot water, TV, T 231-2669, very good; *Maceió Praia*, No. 3, T 231-6391, C, highly rec.; *Pousada Sete Coqueteiros*, No. 123, T 231-5877, C, rec. Good *pousadas* can be found in the Pajuçara beach district, not too expensive; e.g. *Buon Giorno*, Jangadeiros Alagoanos 1437, 1 block from beach, T 231-7577, D, a/c, fridge, clean, English-speaking owner, rec.; *Laguna Praia*, same street No. 1231, T 231-6180, clean, highly rec.; also *MarAzul*, E; *Pousada Rex*, E with bath, clean, friendly, honest, helpful, highly rec. (esp. the breakfast); *Pousada Amassina*, Jangadeiros Alagoanas, F, friendly; *Pousada Quinta Pruma*, No. 597, T 231-6065, E, clean, friendly; *Hotel do Mar*, Av. R. Kennedy 1447, T 231-3171, D, good. *Sol de Verão*, R. Eng. Mário do Gusmão, Ponta Verde, E with bath, F in small rooms without, clean, friendly; *Dos Corais*, R.H. Guimarães 80, one block from Ponta Verde beach, D, helpful. **Youth hostel** *Nossa Casa*, R. Prefeito Abdon Arroxelas 177, Ponta Verde, T 231-2246, F. *Hospedaria de Turismo Costa Azul*, Av. João Davino and Manoel Gonçalves Filho 280, T 231-6281, E, clean, hot shower, fan, English spoken, discounts over a week. 12 km. from the centre, on the beach, *Pousada Cavalo Marinho*, R. da Praia 55, Riacho Doce, facing the sea, T 235-1247, D-C, use of canoes and body boards included, hot showers, clean, German and English spoken, Swiss owner cooks dinner on request, highly rec. (nearby is *Lua Cheia*, good food and live music at night).

*Luxor*, Av. Duque de Caxias 2076, T 221-9191, first class, 4 star, L; *Atlântico* is further along, E-F; behind is *Praia Avenida*, Artur Jucá 1250, 2 star, C, clean, comfortable; *Sobral Praia*, Av. Assis Chateaubriand 8022 (Praia do Sobral), T 221-6665, B, shower, a/c, excellent restaurant, pool, reductions out of season; *Beiriz*, R. João Pessoa 290, T 221-1080, comfortable, A, pool; *Parque*, Praça Dom Pedro II 73, T 221-9099, D, a/c, good, central, comfortable; *Golf*, R. Prof. Domingos Moeda 38A (near the Cathedral), clean, F; *Pousada Sol e Mar*, Av. Rosa da Fonseca s/n, T 221-2615, E with bath, helpful owners, safe, rec. Cheap hotels (mostly without windows) in R. Barão de Ataláia, *Sany*, next to bus station, F with shower and fan, clean; *Reencontro*, next door, F. *Maceió*, R. Dr Pontes de Miranda 146, T 221-1883.

**Camping** There is a Camping Clube do Brasil site on Jacarecica beach, a 15-min. taxi drive from the town centre. Camping Pajuçara at Largo da Vitória 211, T 231-7561, clean, safe, food for sale, rec. Camping also possible on the Avenida beach, near the *Hotel Atlântico*.

**Electric Current** 220 volts A.C., 60 cycles.

**Restaurants** *Bem*, Praia de Cruz das Almas, good seafood and service; *Ao Lagostão*, Av. Duque de Caxias 1348, seafood, fixed price (expensive) menu; *Pizzeria Sorrisa*, Av. Alagoana e J. Pessoa Imperador, very cheap, good food, popular with Brazilians; *Bar das Ostras*, R. Cruzeiro do Sul 487, Vergel do Lago, expensive but good. Vegetarian: *O Natural*, R. Libertadora Alagoana (R. da Praia) 112; *Nativa*, Osvaldo Sarmento 56, good views; *O Dragão*, Antônio Gouveia 21, Pajuçara, Chinese; *Tempeiro Paulista*, Av. Antônio Gouveia 1103, typical food, good service, cheap. *Mello's Bar*, R. Epaminondas Gracindo 194 (continuation of Jangadeiros Alagoanas, at Pajuçara), excellent food and value; many food stalls (barracas) on Praia Pajuçara, e.g. *Sete Coqueiros* and *Pedra Virada* for shrimp. At Ponto da Barra, on the lagoon side of the city, *Alipio*, and many others. Good eating places on the road to Marechal Deodoro and at Praia do Francês. Local specialities include oysters, pitu, a crayfish (now becoming scarce), and sururu, a kind of cockle. Local icecream, Shups, has been rec.

**Entertainment** Teatro Deodoro, Praça Marechal Deodoro, in centre; Cinema São Luiz, R. do Comércio, in centre; *Arte 1* and *2*, Av. Antônio Gouveia 1113; Pajuçara and Iguatemi in shopping centre; the other cinemas tend to be fleapits. *Bar Chapéu de Couro*, José Carneiro 338, Ponto da Barra, is a popular music bar for young people. Many bars at end of Av. Roberto Kennedy by Parque de Sete Coqueiros, e.g. *Bar Lampião* (or *Tropical*), R. Kennedy 2585, food and *forró* every night.

**Museums** Instituto Histórico e Geográfico, R. João Pessoa 382, T 223-7797, good small collection of Indian and Afro-Brazilian artefacts. *Fundação Pierre Chalita*, Praça Floriano Peixoto 49, centre, T 223-4298, Alagoan painting and religious art. Both closed Sat. and Sun.

**Exchange** Banco do Brasil, etc. Open 1000 to 1600. *Aeroturismo*, R. Barão de Penedo 61 or *Pajuçara Turismo* on same road, which begins opposite Ferroviaria at Praça Valente de Lima (but not named on all maps). Good rates at *Luxor Hotel*.

**Telecommunications** Embratel, R. João Pessoa 57, Praça Dom Pedro II 84.

**Tourist Information** Ematur, Duque de Caxias 2014, Centro, T 221-8987; at Largo do

Livramento, on Av. Senador Mendonça. Also at airport and at Rodoviária. Helpful, has good maps.

**Buses** Rodoviária is 5 km. from centre, on a hill with good views and cool breezes. Luggage store. Take bus marked "Ouro Preto p/centro" or "Serraria Mercado" which has a circular route from centre to suburbs and bus terminal (taxi quicker—all local buses are very crowded, taxi to Pajuçara, US$3.45). Bus to **Recife**, 20 a day (but buses full), 4 hrs., US$4.80; to **Salvador**, 9-10 hrs., 4 a day (3 at night), US$17. **N.B.** If travelling to Salvador, or if booking through Bom Fim, check all details on your ticket; they are not reliable. Buses to most large cities including Belém, Fortaleza, Brasília, Belo Horizonte, Rio, São Paulo. To **Penedo**, several, 4 hrs, US$4.80.

**Airport** 20 km. from centre, taxi about US$13. Buses to airport from near *Hotel Beiriz*, R. João Pessoa 290 or in front of the Ferroviária, signed "Rio Largo"; alight at Tabuleiro dos Martins, then 7-8 min. walk to airport, bus fare US$0.40. Tourist flights over the city.

**Excursion** By launch or bus (22 km. South) past Praia do Francés to the attractive colonial town and former capital of Alagoas, **Marechal Deodoro**, with the fine old churches of São Francisco, Terceira Ordem (being restored) and Rosário. There is also the Museu de Arte Sacra, open Tues.-Sun., 0900-1700. The town is the birthplace of Marshal Deodoro da Fonseca, founder of the Republic; the modest house where he was born is on the R. Marechal Deodoro, close to the waterfront, open Tues.-Sun. The cleanliness of this little town is exemplary: on Mondays everyone is required by local law to sweep the streets. The trip by launch, leaving from Trapiche on the lagoon, is very pleasant indeed. Good local lacework. *Restaurant São Roque*, simple but good. A recommended excursion is to take Real Alagoas bus from in front of Ferroviária to Marechal Deodoro (every hour, US$0.75, 1 hr.) then after visiting the town spend some time (beware the *borrachudos* behind the beach) at beautiful **Praia do Francês**, the northern half of the beach is protected by a reef, the southern half is open to the surf where Quatro Rodas is to build a new hotel (restaurant and guest house *Tortuga*, rooms E, on beach; recommended restaurants *Panela Mágica*, *Avalon*, huge helpings, run by an Irishman ; try *agulhas fritas* on the beach); many existing hotels including *O Pescador* and *Pousada das Águas*, both D; *Pousada Yara*, E, clean, friendly; *Hotel do Francês*, D, further from the beach; *Agua Prai*, E, good, clean. Return to Maceió by bus (last one leaves 1800) or *kombi* van, 20 mins. Further out from Maceió is the beach of Barra de São Miguel, entirely protected by reef, with *Pousada da Barra*, good, new, and *Village Barra Hotel*, T 272-1207, B, pool, restaurant, excursions to other beaches. Rio Largo (35 km.) can be reached by train from the Ferroviária (not Sun.) along the lagoon Mundaú; it is quicker to return by bus.

There are many interesting stopping points along the coast between Maceió and Recife. At Paripueira, 40 mins. bus ride from Maceió (Rodoviária) is the *Paripueira Praia Hotel*, E, good value, very clean, friendly. Barra de Santo Antônio, 45 km. N, is a busy fishing village, with a palm fringed beach on a narrow peninsula, a canoe-ride away; accommodation can be found through local people, many beautiful beaches. *Peixada da Rita*, try prawns with coconut sauce, rec. Also Japaratinga (*Hotel Solmar*, F, 2 rooms, basic, good restaurant—bus from Maceió at 0515) and São José da Coroa Grande (*Hotel Lar Ana Luiza*, E, cheaper without breakfast; *The Pousada*, Av. Pedro Cavalcante 535, T 291-1112, F, rec.; a few families rent rooms); at low tide watch colourful fish in the rock pools on the reef. Along this coast, the protecting reef offshore prevents garbage and silt from being taken out to sea at high tide, so water is muddy and polluted. At.

## Pernambuco

About 244 km. N of Maceió and 835 km. N of Salvador is **Recife** (pop. 1,300,000), founded on reclaimed land by the Dutch prince Maurice of Nassau in 1627 after his troops had burnt Olinda, the original capital, is the capital of Pernambuco state (state population 7,106,000). It consists of three portions, all on islands: Recife proper, Santo Antônio, and Boa Vista. The three districts are connected by bridges across the rivers Capibaribe and Beberibe. Olinda, the old capital, is only 6 km. to the North (see page 436).

**Churches** The best of them are the churches of São Francisco de Assis (1612), on R. do Imperador; São Pedro dos Clérigos in São José district (1782, for its façade, its fine wood sculpture and a splendid *trompe l'oeil* ceiling), open Tues.-Fri. 0800-1130, 1400-1630, Sat. 0800-1200; Santo Antônio (1753), in Praça da Independência, rebuilt in 1864; Conceição dos Militares, in R. Nova (1708), grand ceiling and a large 18th century primitive mural of the battle of Guararapes (museum next door), open Mon.-Fri., 0700-1100, 1300-1600, Sat. 0700-1200; Nossa Senhora do Carmo, Praça do Carmo, (1675), open Mon.-Fri. 0800-1200, 1400-1800; Madre de Deus (1706), in the district of Recife, with a splendid high altar, and sacristy; the Pilar church (1680), R. do Pilar; the Espírito Santo (1642), the original church of the Jesuits, in Santo Antônio district; Santo Antônio do Convento de São Francisco (1606; beautiful Portuguese tiles), in the R. do Imperador; the Capela Dourada (Golden Chapel, 1697), in R. do Imperador (the finest sight of all, 0800-1130 and 1400-1700, Sat. 0800-1130: no flash photography; it is through the Museu Franciscano de Arte Sacra); S. José do Ribamar (19th century), in São José. There are many others. Most of them are closed to visitors on Sunday, because of services.

A few km. S of the city, a little beyond Boa Viagem and the airport, on Guararapes hill, is the historic church of Nossa Senhora das Prazeres, open daily 0800-1700. It was here, in 1648-9, that two Brazilian victories led to the end of the 30-year Dutch occupation of the North-East in 1654. The church was built by the Brazilian commander in 1656 to fulfil a vow. Boa Viagem's own fine church dates from 1707.

**Other Attractions** Forte do Brum (1626), is an army museum—open Tues.-Fri., 1300-1800, Sat.-Sun. 1400-1800. Forte das Cinco Pontas (with Museu da Cidade do Recife—cartographic history of the settlement of Recife—open Mon.-Fri. 1300-1800, Sat.-Sun. 1400-1800, free), built by the Dutch in 1630 and altered by the Portuguese in 1677. Visit the city markets in the São José and Santa Rita sections. Go fishing on *jangadas* at Boa Viagem with a fisherman. Visit sugar plantations in interior (though few tour agencies offer such trips).

Boa Viagem, now a southern suburb, is the finest residential and hotel quarter. The 8 km. promenade commands a striking view of the Atlantic, but the beach is crowded at weekends and not very clean. The main square has a good market Sats., with *forró* being danced. Good restaurants along sea shore. Bus from centre, take any marked "Boa Viagem"; from Nossa Senhora do Carmo, take buses marked "Piedade", "Candeias" or "Aeronautica"—they go parallel to the beach all the way to Praça Boa Viagem (at Av. Boa Viagem 500). Back to centre take buses marked "CDU" from the main road one block from the beach.

The artists' and intellectuals' quarter is based on the Pátio de São Pedro, the square round São Pedro dos Clérigos (see under **Churches**). Folk music and poetry shows in the square on Fri., Sat. and Sun. evenings and there are pleasant little restaurants, with good atmosphere, at Nos. 44, 46 and 47, and No. 20 *Caldeira de Cana e Petisqueira Banguê*. The square is an excellent shopping centre for typical North-East craftware (clay figurines are cheapest in Recife). Not far away is the **Praça do Sebo**, where the city's second-hand booksellers concentrate; this Mercado de Livros Usados is off the R. da Roda, behind the Edifício Santo Albino, near the corner of Av. Guararapes and R. Dantas Barreto.

The former municipal prison has now been made into a cultural centre, the **Casa da Cultura**, with many cells converted into art or souvenir shops and with

---

**Recife: Key to map**

1. Praça da República; 2. Praça da Independência; 3.Praça do Sebo; 4. Pátio de São Pedro and São Pedro dos Clérigos; 5. Capela Dourada; 6. Church of Santo Antônio; 7. Conceição dos Militares; 8. Nossa Senhora do Carmo; 9. Church of Madre de Deus; 10. Church of Pilar; 11. Church of Espírito Santo; 12. Santo Antônio do Convento de São Francisco; 13. São José do Ribamar; 14. Nossa Senhora do Rosário dos Pretos; 15. Matriz de Boa Vista; 16. Nossa Senhora do Livramento; 17. Forte do Brum; 18. Forte das Cinco Pontas/Museu da Cidade de Recife; 19. Teatro de Santa Isabel; 20. Teatro do Parque; 21. Teatro Apolo; 22. Palácio do Campo das Princesas (Governor's Palace); 23. New Municipality; 24. Casa da Cultura; 25. Diário de Pernambuco; 26. Museu do Trem and Central Metrô Station; 27. Banco do Brasil; 28. São José Market; 29. Post Office; 30. Telephone Office.

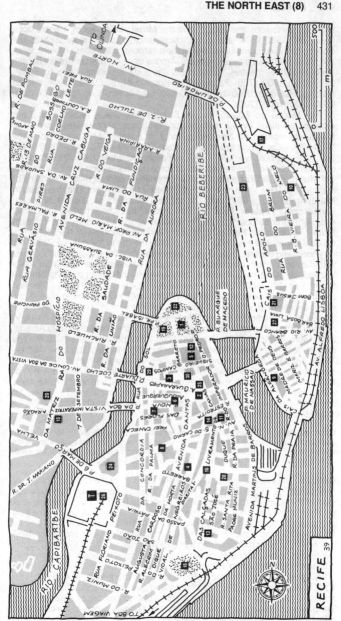

RECIFE 39

areas for exhibitions and shows, and the **Museu de Imagem e Som**, open Tues.-Sun., 1300-1900 (also public conveniences). Local dances such as the *ciranda*, *forró* and *bumba-meu-boi* are held as tourist attractions on Mon., Wed. and Fri. at 1700 (but may not happen). Among other cultural centres are Recife's three traditional theatres, Santa Isabel (Praça da República, open to visitors 0800-1200, 1400-1700), Parque (R. do Hospício 81, Boa Vista, newly restored and beautiful, open 0800-1200, 1400-1800) and Apolo (R. do Apolo 121, open 0800-1200, 1400-1700).

The **Museu do Estado**, Av. Rui Barbosa 960, Graças (closed Mon.), has excellent paintings by the 19th-century landscape painter, Teles Júnior. The **Museu do Homen do Nordeste**, Av. 17 de Agosto 2223 (open Tues.-Sun., 1100-1700), Casa Forte (open Tues., Wed., Fri. 1100-1700; Thurs. 0800-1700; Sat. Sun. and holidays 1300-1700) comprises the **Museu de Arte Popular**, containing ceramic figurines (including some by Mestre alino and Zé Caboclo); the **Museu do Açúcar**, which contains models of colonial mills, collections of antique sugar bowls and much else; the **Museu de Antropologia**, the **Nabuco Museum** (at No. 1865) and the modern museum of popular remedies, **Farmacopéia Popular**. Take the "Dois Irmãos" bus (check that it's the correct one, with "Rui Barbosa" posted in window, as there are two—one for each brother, we suppose) from in front of the Banorte building near the Post Office on Guararapes, half-hour ride 10 km. outside the city to the zoo (US$0.20, not very good) and **botanical gardens**; it passes the museum complex, and together with the zoo they make a pleasant day's outing. Also the **Museu do Trem**, Praça Visconde de Mauá, small but interesting, especially the Garrett steam locomotive (open Tues.-Fri., 1000-1200, 1300-1700, Sat.-Sun., 1400-1800). The first Brazilian printing press was installed in 1706 and Recife claims to publish the oldest daily newspaper in South America, *Diário de Pernambuco*, founded 1825. **Museu da Abolição (of Slavery)**, R. Benfica 150, Madalena, is worth a visit, in an early 19th-century tiled house, once owned by the abolitionist João Alfredo, open Mon.-Fri., 1000-1200 and 1400-1700 (but reported closed in 1990). You may like to visit **Cerámica Brennand**, a factory in the western suburbs at Várzea, 16 km. from the centre, on the Camaragibe road (take a taxi, or walk the 3 km. along R. Gastão Vidigal—past hotels *Costa Azul* and *Tropical*—from the end of the bus line along Av. Caxangá). They make ceramic tiles, and one of the brothers is a sculptor of idiosyncratic works on display, for those interested in the wilder shores of artistic endeavour. Entry is free, and it is very friendly. They also have a shop at Av. Conselheiro Aguiar 2966, loja 4, convenient for Boa Viagem.

**Local Holidays** 1 January (Universal Brotherhood). 24 June (São João). 16 July (Nossa Senhora do Carmo, patron saint of the city). São João, though cancelled by the Pope, is still celebrated with bonfires and fireworks on 24 June all over the State of Pernambuco—and, indeed, throughout Brazil. 8 December (Nossa Senhora da Conceição).

**Carnival** The carnival groups dance at the doors of all the churches they pass; they usually go to the Church of Nossa Senhora do Rosário dos Pretos, patron saint of the slaves, before proceeding in procession into the down-town areas. A small car at the head bears the figure of some animal; it is followed by the king and queen under a large, showy umbrella. The *bahianas*, who wear snowy-white embroidered skirts, dance in single file on either side of the king and queen. Next comes the *dama do passo* carrying a small doll, or *calunga*. After the *dama* comes the *tirador de loas*: he chants to the group which replies in chorus, and last comes a band of local percussion instruments.

Still flourishing is the dance performance of the *caboclinhos*. The groups wear traditional Indian garb: bright feathers round their waists and ankles, colourful cockades, bead and animal-teeth necklaces, a dazzle of medals on their red tunics. The dancers beat out the rhythm with bows and arrows; others of the group play primitive musical instruments, but the dance is the thing: spinning, leaping, and stooping with almost mathematical precision.

There is a *pre-carnavalesca* week, followed by the main days Sunday to Tuesday; on the Saturday the *bloco* "Galo da Madrugada" officially opens Carnival (wild and lively), see local press for routes and times. The groups taking part are *maracatu, caboclinhos, trocas, blocos, ursos, caboclos de lança, escolas de samba* and *frevo*. Usually they start from Av. Conde da Boa Vista and progress along R. do Hospício, R. da Imperatriz, Ponte da Boa Vista, Praça da Independência, R. 1° de Março and R. do Imperador. During Carnival (and on a smaller scale throughout the year) the Casa de Cultura has *frevo* demonstrations where visitors can learn some steps of this unique dance of Pernambuco (check local press for details of "Frevioca" truck and *frevo* orchestras during Carnival in the Pátio de São Pedro). The best place to see the groups is from the balconies of *Hotel do Parque*.

In the "Festivais Juninos", the June *festas* of São João and São Pedro, the *forró* is danced. This dance, now popular throughout the North-East, is believed to have originated when the British builders of the local railways held parties that were "for all".

**Hotels** (for Olinda hotels **see page 437**). In general, there is a shortage of good, mid-range hotels, plenty of multi-star hotels and plenty of flea-pits.
Hotels in the **centre** and away from the beach: in Casa Forte, NW of centre, is *Pousada Casa Forte*, Av. 17 de Aposto 735, T 268-0524, A, 3-star; in the centre (Santo Antônio), *Grande*, Av. Martins de Barros 593, T 224-9366, A, good service, friendly. *Recife Plaza*, Boa Viagem 50, B, overlooking the Rio Capibaribe, every comfort, fine restaurant.

In the cheaper categories: *Recife*, R. do Imperador 310, T 2240799, D with bath (cheaper without), central, pleasant; *Parque*, R. do Hospício 51, good value, F with cooked breakfast, safe, good bars and restaurants nearby; *Lido*, R. do Riachuelo 547, T 222-4660, E, good breakfast, hot water, friendly, rec.; *Pousada Paris*, R. do Riachuelo 630, Boa Vista, T 231-4627, E, good breakfast, fan, basic but pleasant. *América*, Praça Maciel Pinheiro 48, Boa Vista, 2-star, D with a/c (cheaper without), front rooms pleasanter, clean, quiet; *Palácio*, R. Henriques Dias 181, Boa Vista, D, T 221-0222, breakfast, quiet, friendly, mangoes in the patio. *Nassau*, Largo do Rosário 253, T 224-3977/3520, E, clean, hot showers, but a bit noisy (breakfast only, served on 7th floor, with a balcony overlooking the city). *Central*, Av. Manoel Barba 209, T 221-1472, D-E, clean, high ceilings, fridge, highly rec.

Hotels on or near the beach in **Boa Viagem**: *Recife Palace*, Av. Boa Viagem 4070, T 325-4044, L, 5-star; *Vila Rica*, No. 4308, T 326-5111, L, 4-star; *Internacional Othon Palace*, No 3722, T 326-7225, A, 4-star; *Savaroni*, No 3772, T 325-5077, A, 4-star; *Do Sol*, No. 987, T 326-7644, A, 4-star; *Jangadeiro*, No 3114, T 326-6777, A, 4-star; *Boa Viagem*, No. 5000, T 341-4144, A, 4-star, near beach; *Castelinho Praia*, No. 4520, T 326-1186, 3 stars, pool, bar, restaurant. Also in Boa Viagem, *Miramar*, R. dos Navegantes 363, T 326-7422, L, 5-star, near beach on R. Barão de Souza Leão, *Mar*, No. 451, T 341-5433, L, 5-star; *Casa Grande e Senzala*, Av. Conselheiro Aguiar 5000, T 341-0366, A, 3-star.

There are several cheaper hotels in Boa Viagem (check all prices carefully—beware of sudden price increases), *Marazul*, José Brandão 135, T 326-1900, D, comfortable, clean, friendly, pleasant, care with electric shower; *Aguamar Praia*, D, R dos Navegantes 492, a/c, TV, safe, helpful, good breakfast, highly rec; *Pousada das Flores*, R. Padre Leandro Carmelo 57, T 341-1989, D, German-owned, pleasant; *Pousada da Praia*, Alcides Carneiro Leal 66, D with bath, a/c (may be able to bargain lower rates for longer stays), mixed reports; *Solimar*, R. Solidômo Leite 180, D, near beach, bath, warm water, a/c, good location, friendly but pricey for what's offered; *Saveiro*, R. Conselheiro Aguiar 4670 (T 326-6073), no pool, mosquitoes, but new and clean, a/c, D; *Pousada Aconchego*, Félix de Brito 382 (T 326-2989) D with bath, a/c, pleasant, swimming pool, good meals, English-speaking owner; *Praia e Sol*, Av. Boa Viagem 5476, T 341-0674, a/c, helpful, reasonable prices; *200 Milhas*, No. 864, D, safe, highly rec.; *Praia Mar*, No. 1660, T 326-6905, D, small, clean, rec.; *Sea View*, R. dos Navegantes 101, E, Dutch-owned (Dutch, English, French spoken), small, very friendly, rec.; *Guest House Pousada*, Luis Marques Teixeira 155, E, a/c, secure, proprietor Ricardo Teixeira is a Sevagtur guide, helpful, highly rec., English and German spoken; *Pousada Casuarinas*, D, Antonio Pedro de Figuereido 151, T 325-4708, family-run, very friendly, fine garden, English spoken, warmly rec.; *Solar da Tia Cléo*, R. Joaquim Carneiro da Silva 48, T 326-3460/1090, no sign outside, E, fans, family atmosphere, fine garden, English spoken, clean, rec.

**Youth Hostel**: *Albergue 909*, R. dos Navegantes 909, E, cheaper for IYHA members, good breakfast and atmosphere. *Albergue Mandacaru*, R. Maria Carolina 75, E, T 326-1964; stores luggage, English and German spoken, good breakfast, rec.; *Maracatus do Recife*, R. Maria Carolina 185, T 326-1221, good breakfast, pool, clean, safe, friendly. For longer stays, rooms may be rented in the centre for about US$20 a month, make inquiries on the streets. For example, contact Dr. Bezerra dos Santos, R. Floriano Peixoto 85, Edif. Vieira da Cunha S/511, T 224-1098 (English-speaking dentist); Paulo Bezerra de Mello, DHL, R. do Riachueio 201, T 221-2000, rents an apartment for 3 at Boa Viagem, rec. Hotels near the bus station are not rec.; this area, especially Santa Rita, is dangerous at night.

During Carnival, private individuals rent rooms and houses in Recife and Olinda; Lins Turismo has listings as does the *Diário de Pernambuco*, or ask around the streets of Olinda. This accommodation is generally cheaper, safer and quieter than hotels, which inflate prices at Carnival.

**Electric Current** 220 volts A.C., 60 cycles.

**Restaurants** There are many good restaurants, at all prices, in the city, and along beach at Boa Viagem.

**City**: *Le Buffet*, R. do Hospício, good, helpful, friendly, English-speaking owner; *Fuji* (Japanese), R. do Hospício 354, economical, good tofu dishes; *Lisboa á Noite*, Hospício nr. Conde da Boa Vista, good, reasonable, open Sun. evenings (unlike many); *Leite* (lunches only), Praça Joaquim Nabuco 147/53 near Casa de Cultura, old and famous, good service, meal for US$4 (another branch in Boa Viagem, at Prof. José Brandão 409). *Galo de Ouro*, Gamboa do Carmo 83, rec., US$3 for main course; at No. 136, *Casa de Tia*, lunch only, must arrive by 1215, try *cosido*, a meat and vegetable stew, US$4, enough for 2, highly rec.; *Bar Esquina 17, Grande Hotel*, rec. *O Vegetal*, R. Cleto Campelo (2nd floor) behind Central Post Office, lunch only, less than US$3.50, highly rec., branches also at 1 de Março 25, 4th floor, and Av. Guararapes 210 (Santo Antônio), closed Sat.-Sun. *Casa dos Frios*, da Palma 57, loja 5, delicatessen/sandwich bar, salads, pastries etc., very good. Good baker *Nabuco* opposite park at R. do Sol and R. Concórdia.

**Boa Viagem**: Main hotels. *Churrasco*, Av. Boa Viagem 1700, rec.; *Maxime*, No. 21, is where the locals eat seafood; *Oficina da Massas*, No. 2232, Italian; good pizzas at *Pizza-Pazza*, Av. Cons. Aguiar 2348 and *Fiorentino*, R. Laete Lemos 60 (another branch at Av. Bernardo Vieira de Melo 4738, Candeias); *Canto da Barra*, same Av. No. 9150. 20 km. from centre at the far end of Candeias, the beach past the S end of Boa Viagem, very expensive, but excellent, live music (taxi from Boa Viagem US$4.30); *Ceia Regional*, R. Prof. Andrade Bezerra 1462 (by Centro de Convenções) rec. for regional dishes. *Shangai* (Chinese), Av. Domingos Ferreira 4719, excellent, plenty of food; *Futuba*, on a tiny side street towards beach from Av. Conselheiro Aguiar 1313, Japanese, good; *Chinés*, Herculano Bandeiro (just after bridge, on Boa Viagem side), good value; *Prá Vocês*, Av. Herculano Bandeira 115, Pinas (town end of Boa Viagem beach), good but pricey seafood; *Snack Bar Flamingo*, Av. Cons. Aguiar 542, good hamburgers and ice cream.

(For Olinda restaurants see under Olinda, **page 437**). Be careful of eating the local small crabs, known as *guaiamum*; they live in the mangrove swamps which take the drainage from Recife's shantytowns (*mocambos*).

**Bars** The following are suggested: *Depois do Escuro*, R. da Amizade 178, Graças, and the cafe/ice cream parlours *Fri-Sabor* and *Eskimo*, both close to Praça Boa Viagem. *O Beliscão*, Av. Boa Viagem, by Sea View Hotel, rec.; *Bar Sem Nome* at Jangada; *Mustang*, Av. Conde de Boa Vista, Boa Vista, also rec. for a beer and watching the "movimento". *Highlander*, English pub at Av. Domingo Ferreira 2222, Boa Viagem.

**Markets** Permanent craft market in **Casa da Cultura** (old prison). Mercado São José (1875) for local products and handicrafts. **Casa Amarela** for a truly typical market on Sats. Sun. evenings: **"hippy fair"** at Praça Boa Viagem, on the sea front, life-sized wooden statues of saints (a good meeting place is the *Bar Lapinha* in the middle of the square). New Sat. craft fair at **Sítio Trindade**, Casa Amarela: during the feast days of June 12-29, fireworks, music, dancing, local food. On April 23, here and in the Pátio de São Pedro, one can see the *xangô* dance.

**Bookshops** *Livraria Brandão*, R. da Matriz 22 (used English books and some French and German) and bookstalls on the R. do Infante Dom Henrique. *Livro 7*, a huge emporium with a very impressive stock, R. Sete de Setembro 329 and Guararapes airport. *Ao Livro Técnico*, R. Princesa Isabel, has thrillers in English and beginners' readers. A great local character, *Melquísidec Pastor de Nascimento*, second-hand bookseller, at R. Bispo Cardoso Aires, 215; also has a second-hand stall at Praça de Sebo (**see page 430**).

**Entertainment** The following have live regional music: *O Catedral da Seresta*, Bairro Torre;

*O Pirata*, Av. 16 de Agôsto, Bairro Casa Forte; *Maria Bonita*, Av. Domingo Ferreira, Boa Viagem. Also visit a typical North-Eastern "Forró" where local couples dance to typical music, very lively especially on Fridays and Saturdays. **Recife Ballet** shows in the Recife/Olinda Convention Centre, US$7.50, traditional carnival dances in full costume. **Discotheques** tend to be expensive and sophisticated.

**Exchange** Lloyds Bank, R. do Fogo 22; **Banco Internacional; Citibank**. Open 1000-1600. For good advice on exchange, ask at one of the consulates. **Amex office**, R da Concórdia 278. **Lins Câmbio**, R. da Palma corner with Guararapes, better rate than banks (but not as good as some others), but dollars cash only. Money changer hangs out at *Casa dos Frios* deli. next door. **Edifício Bancomércio**, 3rd floor, R. Matias de Alberquerque 223, takes cash and travellers' cheques. *Restaurante Leite*, Praça Joaquim Nabuco 147/53, good rates for travellers' cheques and cash. Good rates from Sr Manuel E. Cal Muinôs, R. Santa Rita 290; Monaco men's clothing store, Praça Joaquim Nabuco.

**Language Courses** Baynsches Institut, Av. Domingo Ferreira, Portuguese classes.

**British Council** Domingos Ferreira 4150, Boa Viagem, 0800-1500, library with current English newspapers.

**Consulates British**, Domingos Ferreira 222, sala 203, Boa Viagem, T 326 3733, open 0800-1130. **Danish**, Av. M. de Olinda 85, Ed. Alberto Fonseca 2°, CP 3450030, T 224-0997, open 0800-1200, 1400-1800. **Swedish**, R. do Moeda 63, 1st floor, 50.000 Recife, T 224-1622/1329/1772. **German**, Dantas Barreto 191, Edif. Santo Antônio, 4th floor. **U.S.**, Gonçalves Maia 163. T 221-1412.

**Laundrette** Av. Conselheiro Aguiar 1385, Boa Viagem. *Úosh*, Av. Domingo Ferreira.

**Church** Episcopalian, R. Carneiro Vilela 569.

**Post Office** including poste restante, Central Correios, 50001, Av. Guararapes 250 (or American Express, R. da Concórdia 278 for poste restante).

**Telecommunications** Embratel, Av. Agamenon Magalhães, 1114, Parque Amorim district, T 221-4149; also Praça da Independência. Telex, public booth, Av. Guararapes 250. **International Telephones** R. Diário de Pernambuco, 38; also at airport (first floor), noisy.

**Tourist Offices** Empetur (for the State of Pernambuco). Main office, Av. Conde Boa Vista and Alençar; Emetur (for Recife), Pátio de São Pedro, loja 10. At Carnival-time they have a full programme. Maps available: Empetur, US$0.33 (or from Tropical opposite); Empetur also publish walking tour schedules for Recife (one leaves Sun. 1500 from Santo Antônio church on Av. Dantas Barreto) and Olinda in several languages; also central map in monthly guide *Itinerário Pernambuco*. Offices at airport—24 hrs. (will book hotels, helpful, English spoken). Information trailer parked corner Av. Dantas Barreto and Av. Guararapes, 0800-1900.

Hours of opening of museums, art galleries, churches etc. are published in the daily newspaper *Diário de Pernambuco*.

**Rail** Recife is the centre of the Rede Ferroviária do Nordeste, with lines north to Paraíba and Natal (no passenger services), and a western route to Salgueiro. Commuter services, known as the **Metrô** but not underground, leave from the Central station; they have been extended to serve the new Rodoviária at São Lourenço da Mata (frequent trains, 0600-2300, US$0.10). If going to Boa Viagem from the Rodoviária, get off the Metrô at Joanna Bezerra and take a bus from there.

**Buses** A new Rodoviária, mainly for long-distance buses, has been built 12 km. outside the city at São Lourenço da Mata (it is called Terminal Integrado dos Passageiros, or TIP, pronounced "chippy"). There is a 30-minute rail connection to the central railway station, entrance through Museu do Trem (opp. Casa da Cultura) (US$0.10), 2 lines leave the city, take train marked Rodoviária, from Boa Viagem taxi US$15, bus US$0.40, 1 hr., from centre. The train to the centre is much quicker than the bus. Tickets for long and short distances may be bought from Lins Turismo (no commission) on Av. Guararapes, or in R. La Palma in São José, English spoken.

To **Salvador**, 13 hours, 3 a day (all at night) US$20 (*leito*, 40), 12 hrs. to **Fortaleza**, US$18, and 5 hrs. to Natal US$8. To **Goiana**, every ½ hr., US$1.50. To **Rio**, 50 hrs. (the road is severely pot-holed), US$54 (108 *leito*); to **São Paulo**, 40 hrs., US$67 (*leito*, 134); to **Belo Horizonte**, 36 hrs., US$60. To **Teresina** (Piauí), 19 hrs. (US$27), and further to **São Luís**, 26 hrs., US$38; to **Belém**, 34 hrs., US$48 (Boa Esperança bus rec.). To Paulo Afonso, US$8, 7 hrs. on completely paved road. To **Lençóis**, 20 hrs, US$24, bus continues to Brasília. Good roads N to João Pessoa, Natal and Fortaleza, W to Arcoverde and Caruaru (and ultimately

Belém), SW to Garanhuns and S to **Maceió**, US$4.80, 4 hrs. (Maceió can be reached either by the main road or by the coast road "via Litoral"); in all 20 buses daily. **Local Buses** The Prefeitura issues a guide to routes. Buses to the nearby destinations of Igaraçu and Itamaracá leave from Avenida Martins de Barros to Olinda, see below; those to beaches beyond Olinda from Av. Dantas behind the post office.

**Coastal Shipping** Lóide Brasileiro ships run frequently between Brazilian coastal ports. They have several up-to-date vessels, some de luxe.

**Air Services** The principal international and national airlines fly to Guararapes airport, 12 km. from the city. Direct flights from Europe with Air France from Paris and Air Portugal from Lisbon. Bus to airport, No. 52, US$0.40, 30 minutes from N.S. do Carmo. Tourist taxis at the airport are twice as expensive as ordinary red taxis picked up on the main road.

**Excursions** Any bus going south of Boa Viagem passes the Ilha do Amor; ask a fisherman to row you out to it and collect you at a set time, US$2. Walk across the island (10 mins.) to the Atlantic side for a fine, open, uncrowded beach (fish meals US$5). About 30 km. S of Recife, beyond Cabo, is the beautiful Gaibu beach, *Pousada Beto Qualhado*, cheap restaurants; Itapuama beach even more empty, both reached by bus from Cabo. **Cabo** (pop. 121,000), Pernambuco's main industrial city has interesting churches and forts and a Museu da Abolição, and at nearby Suape are many 17C. buildings and a Biological Reserve. **Porto de Galinhas**, further S still, is a beautiful beach, reached by bus from Recife US$1.50, via the town of Nossa Senhora do Ó, 2 hrs. (3 a day, but take 0930 since others don't allow enough time; last back at 1600, packed out). It has cool, clean water, and waves. *Solar Porto de Galinhas*, on beach, A-B, many facilities, beautiful place; *Porto do Sol*, A-B, very good restaurant, rec.; *pensão* of Dona Benedita in the street where the bus stops, very basic, clean; food at *Rang Bem* in same street.

**Biological Reserves** For information on Pernambuco's two reserves, contact IBDF, Av. 17 de Agosto 1057, Casa Forte, CEP 50.000, Recife. They are **Saltinho**, which preserves some of the last vestiges of Atlantic Forest in the North East, and **Serra Negra**, which has some of the last remaining forest at higher altitude in the interior.

*Olinda* (pop. 335,000), the old capital, founded in 1537 and named a "Patrimônio de Humandade" by Unesco in 1982, 6 km. to the north, is served by buses and taxis (US$4.50). This city, which has recently become very commercialized, contains many fine old colonial churches, monasteries and convents; tourist handout gives schedule of opening times (available in Casa da Cultura in Recife). Particularly interesting are the Prefeitura, once the palace of the viceroys; the monastery of São Bento, founded 1582, restored 1761, the site of Brazil's first law school and the first abolition of slavery, by the Benedictine monks (paintings, sculpture, furniture, open 0800-1100 and 1300-1700 daily) and the beautifully restored R. São Bento; the convent of Santa Tereza (1687), the monastery of São Francisco, 1585 (splendid woodcarving and paintings, superb gilded stucco, and azulejos, in Capela de São Roque, open daily 0800-1130, 1400-1630); the Igreja da Misericôrdia, built 1540, open daily 0700-1700, fine tiling and gold work, and Acadêmia Santa Gertrudes; the Cathedral (1537), the first church to be built in the city, of simple and severe construction; São João Batista dos Militares (1581), the only church not burnt by the Dutch; the Graças church (seminary) built 1582, no fixed visiting times; Nossa Senhora do Monte, built early 16C., likewise; the Carmo church (1588—under restoration), likewise, and the colonial public fountain, the Bica de São Pedro. There are some houses of the 17th century with latticed balconies, heavy doors and pink stucco walls, including a house in Moorish style at Praça João Alfredo 7, housing the *Mourisco* restaurant. There is a large colony of artists (as the superb grafitti at election times testify), and excellent examples of regional art, mainly woodcarving and terra-cotta figurines, may be bought in the Alto da Sé, the fine square on top of the hill by the Cathedral, or in the handicraft shops at the Mercado da Ribeira, R. Bernardo Vieira de Melo (Vieira de Melo gave the first recorded call for independence from Portugal, in Olinda in 1710.) There is a Museu de Arte Sacra in the beautiful former Palácio Episcopal (1696) at Alto da Sé 7, open Tues.-Fri., 0800-1200 and 1400-1800, Sat.-Sun. 1400-1800. At R. 13 de

Maio 123, in the old jail of the Inquisition, is the Museu de Arte Contemporânea; also the old slave market, where *capoeira* is practised on Suns, about 1800. A programme of restoration, partly financed by the Netherlands Government, has been undertaken in order to comply with the recently-conferred title of National Monument. The Museu Regional, R. do Amparo 128, is excellent.

**Hotels** At Casa Caiada, Av. José Augusto Moreira 2200 (T 431-2955), is *Quatro Rodas* (L), with swimming pool, excellent restaurant, tennis courts, gardens, very good. *Quatorze Bis*, Av. Beira Mar 1414, T 429-0409, C, friendly, helpful, clean, run by Dutchman. *Pousada dos Quatro Cantos*, R. Prudente de Morais 441, A-C, in a converted mansion, very good, highly rec. apart from alleged overcharging during Carnival, T 429-0220/1845; *Pousada São Francisco*, R. do Sol 127, T 429-2109/0386/1469, up to B, clean, comfortable, pool, rec.; *Albergue da Olinda*, R. do Sol 337, E, new, reasonable, clean, friendly, popular with gringos; *Pousadas do Mar* , E, Av. Beira Mar 497, Bairro Novo, T 429-2883, 16 rooms with bath, some a/c, very clean, cheaper for stay longer than 3 days. Also on Av. Beira Mar, *Hospedaria do Turista*, No. 989, D, excellent, T 429-1847; *Coqueiro Verde*, No. 1173, E, family atmosphere, excellent breakfast; *Marolinda* (No. 1615), 2 star, C, rec., rooms at front very noisy at weekends. *Flor da Manhã*, R. São Francisco 162, T 429-2266, D-E, clean, good food, beautiful views, friendly, safe, multilingual, rec.; Several **youth hostels**: *Portalinda*, Av. Beira Mar 295, Bairro Novo, T 429-3198; *Cheiro do Mar*, No. 95, very good small hostel with some double rooms; *Palanquim*, Prof. Cândido Pessoa 1833, Bairro Novo, T 222-1084.

At Carnival, the price of accommodation rises steeply. Houses or rooms may be rented at this time for 5-10 days. Ask also at the AmEx office in Recife about lodging.

**Camping** Olinda Camping, R. Bom Sucesso 262, Amparo, T 429-1365, US$5 p.p., space for 30 tents, 5 trailers, small huts for rent, quiet, well-shaded, town buses pass outside, rec.

**Restaurants** *L'Atelier*, R. Bernardo Vieira de Melo 91, Ribeira, small converted workshop with beautiful view, run by Swiss tapestry artists, excellent international food, local dishes with reservation (necessary) T429-3099, open Wed.-Sun. *Mourisco*, R. João Alfredo 7, calm and pleasant, discotheque attached; *Samburá*, Av. Beira Mar (no number—with terrace) rec. to try *caldeirada* and *pitu* (crayfish), also lobster in coconut sauce or daily fish dishes, very good; on Av. Beira Mar, *Ouriço*, local food good; *Gouiaba*, charcoal grill, facing sea, good value, rec; *Cantinho da Sé 305*, lively, good view of Recife; *Chin Lee*, excellent Chinese food; many others, mostly for fish. The traditional Olinda drinks, *Pau do Índio* (which contains 32 herbs) and *Retetel*, are both manufactured on the R. do Amparo.

**Entertainment** At Janga beach on Fri. and Sat., you can join in a *ciranda* at the bar-restaurant *Ciranda de Dona Duda*. For the less active, there is the *Casa da Seresta*, also in Janga on the beach side of the main road. On Praça do Carmo is *Cheiro do Povo*, a "Forró" dance hall.

Beginning at dusk, but best after 2100, the Alto da Sé becomes the scene of a lively street fair, with arts, crafts, makeshift bars and barbeque stands, and impromptu traditional music. Street urchins try to tell you the history of Olinda (for a price). The fair becomes even more animated at Carnival.

At Olinda's **carnival** thousands of people dance through the narrow streets of the old city to the sound of the Frevo, the brash energetic music which normally accompanies a lively dance performed with umbrellas. The local people decorate them with streamers and straw dolls, and form themselves into costumed groups to parade down the R. do Amparo; Pitombeira and Elefantes are the best known of these groups.

**Tourist Office** 13 de Maio 322, helpful and friendly, has a map with a recommended walking tour of the sights, opening times, as well as churches, museums and other places of interest, and houses to stay during Carnival. Beware of guides who offer a modest price and in the end charge an extra fee for the "tour".

**Transport from Recife** Take any bus marked "Rio Doce", No. 981 which has a circular route around the city and beaches, or No. 33 from Av. N.S. do Carmo, US$0.40 or "Jardin Atlântico" from beyond the central Post Office; from Boa Viagem, take bus marked "Piedade/Rio Doce" or "Casa Caiada/Piedade". From airport to Olinda by bus, take airport bus to Holliday (a Y-shaped building on Av. Conselheiro Aguiar, Boa Viagem), ask to be let off, and catch a "Rio Doce" or "Bairra de Jangada/Casa Caiada" bus to Praça do Carmo, Olinda. In all cases, alight in Praça do Carmo. Taxis between Olinda and Recife put their meters on to higher rates at the new Convention Centre (between the two cities), best to start a journey either way there.

**Beaches** The beaches close to Olinda are reported to be seriously polluted. Those further north from Olinda, beyond Casa Caiada, are beautiful, usually deserted, palm-fringed; at Janga, and Pau Amarelo. At many simple cafés you can eat *sururu* (clam stew in coconut sauce), *agulha frita* (fried needle-fish), *miúdo de galinha* (chicken giblets in gravy) and *casquinha de carangueijo* (seasoned crabmeat and *farinha de dendé* served in crabshells). Visit the Dutch fort on Pau Amarelo beach; small craft fair here on Sat. nights.

*Igarassu* (pop. 68,000), 32 km. N of Recife on the road to João Pessoa, has the first church built in Brazil (SS Cosme e Damião), the Livramento church nearby, and the convent of Santo Antônio with a small museum next door. The church of Sagrada Coração is said to have housed Brazil's first orphanage. Much of the town (founded in 1535) has been declared a National Monument; it is an attractive place, with a number of colonial houses and Brazil's first Masonic hall. Hotel: *Fazenda Praia da Gavoa*, Extrada do Ramalho, A; Camping Clube do Brasil has site nearby at Engenho Monjope, an old sugar estate, now a historical monument and interesting (it is 3 km. before Igarassu coming from Recife—bus US$0.50—alight at the "Camping" sign and walk 5-10 mins.). Igarassu buses leave from Av. Martins de Barro, Recife, 45 mins., US$0.55. N of Igarassu you pass through coconut plantations to Itapissuma, where there is a bridge to *Itamaracá* island, where, the locals say, Adam and Eve spent their holidays (so does everyone else on Sundays, now). It has the old Dutch Forte Orange; an interesting penal settlement with gift shops, built round the 1747 sugar estate buildings of Engenho São João, which still have much of the old machinery; charming villages and colonial churches, and fine, wide beaches. Buses from Recife (Av. Martins de Barros opp. *Grand Hotel*, US$0.75, very crowded) and Igarassu.

**Itamaracá Hotels** *Caravela*, T 544-1130, C with shower, good restaurant, on beach; *Pousada*, T 544-1152, C, pool etc., some minutes from beach; *Pousada Telhadão*, Av. Beira Mar 3, Quatro Cantos, D, clean, excellent restaurant, swimming pool, garden, warmly recommended; *Itamaracá Parque*, T 544-1030, B.

*Goiana*, on the Recife-João Pessoa road, founded 1570, is one of the most important towns for ceramics. Carmelite church and monastery, founded 1719, impressive but poorly restored; San Benedito, needs restoring; Matriz do Rosário, only open for 1800 mass, Soledade convent (1755); Amparo church with Sacred Art museum; Misericôrdia church (1723). The uniformity of many of the dwellings is due to their construction, for his workforce, by the owner of a now-defunct textile factory. *Hospedaria Durma Bem*, open weekends only; ask at Prefeitura at other times. Visit the workshop of Zé do Carmo, opposite the *Buraco da Giá* restaurant (excellent seafood; owner has tame crab which will offer you a drink), R. Padre Batalha 100. Just north of Goiana is a sugar-mill, Usina Nossa Senhora das Maravilhas, which can be visited during the week; ask for Dr Jairo.

At the Pernambuco-Paraíba border, a 27 km. dirt road to the fishing village of Pitimbu, with *jangadas*, lobster fishing, surf fishing, lobster-pot making. No tourist facilities but camping is possible; food from *Bar do Jangadeiro*. Bus from Goiana, US$0.50.

*Carpina*, 54 km. from Recife, 65,000 people, is well-known for its Carnival and for the traditional Epiphany festival early in January, and also for the carpets made in nearby village of Lagoa do Carro. There is a historical museum. Hotels (*Pousada das Acácias*, BR-408, B; *São João da Escócia*, Av. João Alfredo 136, D) and restaurants. *Tracunhaém* (pop. 10,600), is a peaceful town where fine ceramics are made; there are two interesting early 19C. churches. It is just N of Carpina, on to the road to Nazaré da Mata. Even the children are adept in working in clay.

*Caruaru* (pop. 191,000), 130 km. W of Recife by paved road (many buses, 2 hrs., US$3), has a big Fri. to Sun. market with a separate site across the river for leather goods, pottery and articles of straw, although it is disappointingly tourist-oriented now (smaller market on other days of the week). See the hand-painted textiles of Sr Valério Cristóvão, R. 13 de Maio 94, 1st floor; he is very helpful and his work depicts local history. The little clay figures (*figurinhas de barro*) originated by Mestre Vitalino, and very typical of the North-East, are a local speciality; many local potters live at Alto da Moura 6 km. away, where a house once owned by

Vitalino is open, but has no examples of his work. Bus, ½ hour, bumpy, US$0.30. Rodoviária is 4 km. from town. Bus to Maceió, 0700, 5 hrs., US$3.50. Bus to Fazenda Nova 1030, 1 hr., returns for Caruaru 1330.

**Hotels** *Do Sol*, T 721-3044, A (4-star) on hill outside town, good restaurant, pool; *Centenário*, 7 de Setembro 84, T 721-9011, D, clean, friendly, restaurant. Cheap *hospedarias* around central square, Praça Getúlio Vargas.

On the way to Caruaru is *Gravatá*, 60,000 people (*Hotel Fazenda Portal*, A, BR-232; *Grande da Serra*, BR-232, D; *Central*, Av. C.B. de Oliveira 301 (BR-232), D), known as the Switzerland of Pernambuco for its scenery and good hill climate.

During Easter Week each year various agencies run package tours to the little country town of *Fazenda Nova*, a few km. from Caruaru. Just outside the town is *Nova Jerusalém*, where from the Tuesday before to Easter Sunday, an annual passion play, suggested by Oberammergau's, is enacted. The site is one-third the size of the historic quarter of Jerusalem, with 12 permanent stages on which scenes of the Passion are presented; the audience moves from one to another as the story unfolds.

**Hotels in Fazenda Nova** *Grande*, best; *Mansão Verde*; *Fazenda Nova*.

**Camping** Close to site.

Good roads via Caruaru or Palmares run to the city of *Garanhuns* (pop. 100,000), 243 km. SW of Recife. It claims to be the best holiday resort in the North-East, partly because of its cool climate—it stands at 890 metres, and has an average temperature of 21°C—and partly because of its mineral waters and beautiful landscapes and parks.

**Hotels** *Grande Hotel Petrópolis*, Praça da Bandeira 129, T 761-0125. *Tavares Correia*, B, Av. Rui Barbosa 296, T 761-0900. **Camping**, *Camping Treze*, BR-432, km. 105.

*Arcoverde* (pop. 51,000), about 126 km. W of Caruaru, is a market town in the Sertão, market every Saturday, cool at night. Hotel: *Grande Majestic* (fair), D, with breakfast; *Dormitôrio O Barão*, F, clean.

*Triúnfo* (pop. 28,000), about 200 km. W of Arcoverde via Serra Talhada, is a delightful small town in Serra de Borborema, good climate, with great variety of crops, flowers and fruits. There are also a sugar mill that can be visited (Engenho Boa Esperança), waterfalls, sounding rocks, the convent of São Boaventura, and the Museu do Cangaça, showing the lives and relics of the traditional bandits of the Nordeste. Stay at *Hotel-Orphanage Lar St. Elizabeth*, run by German religious sisters, D, with private apartment and 3 excellent meals. Two buses daily to and from Recife (6½ hrs.); *Pousdada Baixa Serote*, E, superb breakfast, friendly, highly rec.

*Fernando de Noronha* is a small archipelago 345 km. off the NE coast. It was declared a Marine National Park in 1989. Only one island is inhabited. It used to be an independent dependency under military control but is now part of the state of Pernambuco administered from Recife. The islands were discovered 1503 and were for a time a pirate lair. In 1738 the Portuguese built the Forte dos Remédios, later used as a prison in this century; remains still exist as well as a semi-deserted village nearby. Sea landing is difficult but an airport has been built. Twice daily flights from Recife at 0800 and 1200 on 13 and 17 seater planes by Nordeste, T 341-3187, US$50 each way, 1 hr. 40 mins. Special permission is no longer required to visit the archipelago. This has led to an influx of tourists. Many locals are now dependent on tourism and it can be difficult to find fish as the fishermen are busy taking tourists on boat trips. Most food is brought from the mainland and prices are about double. Repellent is not available for the many mosquitoes. The island, which is dominated by a 321 metre peak, has many unspoilt beaches, interesting wildlife and fishing; scuba-diving and snorkelling are excellent. It is now prohibited to swim with the dolphins but they can be seen from the beach.

Only hotel, *Pousada Esmeralda*, can only be booked as part of a 7-day package tour from Recife, departures Sat. and Sun. through Mubatur in Recife T 341-4519, or Quadratur in Rio T 262-8011; cost is US$800 p.p. Holiday camp type cabins, a/c is only on from 2200 to 0600 so better to take room with fan. Food is only reasonable. Beware of similar packages at lower prices in other "pousadas" because they turn out to be rooms in family homes. Aeroporto Turismo in Recife offers such "deals". Independent travellers can go much cheaper as many local families rent out rooms with full board, US$15 p.p. per day. The best known is that of Suzanna and Rocha, rooms with fan and bathroom, but they never refuse a reservation and farm people out to other families with much inferior levels of accommodation. Vanilda across the street has been highly recommended. Boat trips and jeep tours around the island are available; also possible to hire a jeep or beach buggy. You can hitch everywhere as everyone stops. Scuba-diving is organised by Aguas Claras in the hotel grounds, but staff are regarded as unhelpful and unreliable. There is only one restaurant, called *Ilha Encantado*, near the hotel. Bars: *Bar da Vila* in the village of Remédios, only open in the daytime; *Bar Idade* on the Çonceição beach, daytime only with loud rock music; *Mirante Bar*, near the hotel, with spectacular view over Boldró beach, has loud music and at night is an open-air disco and the only nightlife on the island. Take sufficient new cruzeiros as dollars are heavily discounted. The time is one hour later than Brazilian Standard Time.

## Paraíba and Rio Grande do Norte

It is a bus ride of 2 hours through sugar plantations over a good road from Recife (126 km.) to **João Pessoa** (pop. 400,000), capital of the State of Paraíba (pop. 3,164,000), on the Paraíba River. Ocean-going ships load and unload at Cabedelo (pop. 21,600) 18 km. by road or rail. The old monasteries are worth seeing, and the 18th century church of São Francisco is a beauty (currently under restoration). Other tourist points include the Casa da Pólvora, an old gunpowder store which has become the city museum; the city parks; and trips on the Rio Paraíba. Airport for internal services. See the booklet *Relíquias da Paraíba*, by Padre Antônio Barbosa.

**Hotels** *Tropical* (ex-*Tambaú*), Av. Alm. Tamandaré 229, Tambaú, T 226-3660, A+, comfortable, good service, rec., though sometimes they pretend no standard rooms are available when they are; *Sol-Mar*, Rui Carneiro 500 e Tambaú, T 226-1350, C, pool, superb restaurant, highly rec.; *Gameleira*, Av. João Maurício 157, T 226-1576, opposite *Tropical*, E, good breakfast, rec., but noisy at night; *Costa Bela Praia*, Av. Négo 131, Tambaú, T 226 1570, C, rec., small; *Aurora*, Praça João Pessoa 51, central, T 221-2238, E with a/c and bath, clean, friendly; *Guarany*, R. Almeida Barreto 181 e 13 de Maio, T 241-2161, E (more with a/c and TV), clean, central, safe, friendly, rec. as good value, good breakfast; *Pedro Américo*, Praça Pedro Américo, 109, E, clean, central (no breakfast on Sun.); cheap hotels near the old bus station, e.g. *São Pedro*, R. Irineu Pinto 231, clean, basic, friendly, E. **Youth hostels**, on Av. das Trincheiras, at Palácio dos Esportes, T 221-7220/1, and *Cabo Branco*, Av. Pe-José Trigueiro 104, Praia de Cabo Branco, T 221-2903/226-6171; R. Bezerra Reis 82, T 226-5460/1988.

**Electric Current** 220 volts A.C, 60 cycles.

**Restaurants** Two good restaurants on Tambaú beach are *Adega do Alfredo* (Portuguese) and *Wan Li* (Chinese); *Pescador*, near Cabo Branco lighthouse; *Pavilhão do Chá*, pleasant, drinks, sandwiches, TV, open air, in centre.

**Exchange** Banco do Brasil, near Praça João Pessoa, 3rd floor, helpful.

**Telecommunications** Embratel, R. das Trincheiras 398.

**Tourist Information** PB Tur, Av. Getúlio Vargas 301, Centro João Pessoa; also bus terminal (helpful). Crafts at Casa do Artesão, R. Maciel Pinheiro near city bus station.

**Tourist Agencies** *Planetur*, Av. Miguel Couto 5, Loja 12, and *Hotel Tropical*. *Agência de*

*Viagens e Turismo Arnaldo von Sohsten*, R. Gama e Melo 100.

**Bus** Station is 10 mins. from centre; luggage store. To **Recife**, every 60 mins., US$2.50, 2 hrs. To **Natal**, every 2 hrs., US$4, 3 hrs.; to **Fortaleza**, 4 daily, 16 hrs., US$12.75. Warning: you will be refused permission to travel from João Pessoa Rodoviária wearing shorts, whether or not you arrived in shorts (Bermuda shorts are acceptable).

**Excursions** The principal beach and seaside resort is Tambaú, 7 km. from João Pessoa, take a taxi or bus (No. 510 "Tambaú" from outside Rodoviária, or "Lagoa" from city centre, alight at *Hotel Tropical*); excellent bathing; Mercado do Artesanato. The Centro Turístico Tambaú, Av. Almirante Tamandaré e R. Sen. Ruy Carneiro (in shopping mall) is helpful, with an informative book on all Paraíba and maps. North of Tambaú is Manaira beach, but the section near *Hotel Tropical/Tambaú* is too polluted for bathing. Cabo Branco club on Tambaú beach, open to visitors: good food, beautiful views. 14 km. south down the coast is the Cabo Branco lighthouse at Ponta do Seixas, the most easterly point of continental Brazil and South America; there is a panoramic view from the cliff top. The beaches below are palm-lined but oil-polluted. Take bus 507 "Cabo Branco" from outside Rodoviária, or "Lagoa" bus from centre and get out at last stop; hike up to the lighthouse. Not far from here is the José Américo de Almeida Museum in the former house of the novelist and sociologist. At Cabedelo are the impressive walls of the 17th-century fortress of Santa Catarina. If you take a Cabedelo bus and alight at Jacaré, about 12 km. from João Pessoa, there is an excellent beach with food stalls at weekends. In Jacaré, where the yachts tie up, is a bar run by an Englishman.

*Campina Grande* (pop. 280,000), the "Porta do Sertão", is 120 km. from João Pessoa (bus 2 hours), a rapidly growing centre for light industry and an outlet for goods from most of the North-East. There is a museum of modern art, and another of the cotton industry. Most genial climate. Near Campina Grande is Lagoa Seca, where the local craft is the making of figures in wood and sacking.

**Hotels** *Rique Palace Hotel* (excellent) is on the top floors of the tallest building in town, Venâncio Neiva 287, T 341-1433: the restaurant is on the 11th floor. Other hotels: *Ouro Branco*, João Lourenço Porto 20, C; *Barborema*, near old bus station, E, friendly. *Dormitório São Paulo*, also near bus station, F, cheap, clean. Many others near old bus station.

W of Campina Grande the main highway, still paved, leads on through *Patos* (*Hotel JK*, E) to Ipaumirim (Ceará). Here a left turn leads to the twin towns of *Crato* and *Juazeiro do Norte* (Ceará), oases of green in the dry Sertão. Mosquitoes can be a problem at night.

Juazeiro do Norte is a small pilgrimage town; it was the home of Padre Cícero, one of the unofficial saints of the North-East. A statue to him stands in the Logradouro do Horto, a park overlooking the town; either take the pilgrim trail up the hill or go by bus. **Hotels**: *Panorama*, C, good value; *Vieira*, corner of R. São Pedro and R. Santo Antônio, E, private bathroom and breakfast; and *Municipal*, E, rec.

Many beautiful fishing villages along the coast, often difficult to reach; one of the most popular is Baía Formosa in Rio Grande do Norte (daily bus from Natal, 2½ hrs.). No hotel; ask in town for accommodation in fishermen's houses, infinitely preferable to the overpriced accommodation at the *Miramar* bar.

*Natal* (pop. 510,000), capital of Rio Grande do Norte (pop. 2,244,000), on the estuary of the Rio Potengi, is about 180 km. to the north of João Pessoa. It is served by weekly coastal vessels and there is a railway S through the State of Paraíba to Recife and Maceió (only suburban passenger services). There is a large airport 13 km. from the city (taxi US$10). The old part of the city is called Cidade Alta. The main square, the Praça João Maria, oblong in shape, has a traditional cathedral at one end and a fine modern bank building at the other. The city is centred on the Av. Rio Branco. The church of Santo Antônio, R. Santo Antônio in the centre, dates from 1766, and has a fine, carved wooden altar. The Museu Câmara Cascudo, Av. Hermes de Fonseca 1398 (T 222-0923), has exhibits on archaeological digs, Umbanda rituals and the petroleum industry (open Tues.-Fri.,

0800-1100, 1400-1600, US$1.40). The Forte dos Reis Magos (16th-century) on the coast at Rocas is open Tues.-Sun. 0800-1700; between it and the city is a military installation, and the walk along the beach road is not very safe. Best to go in a tour, or by taxi; it is worth it for the views (entry US$1.40). The Casa da Música Popular Brasileira has dancing on Friday and Saturday night and Sunday from 1700, very popular. The Marine Research Institute at the Praia da Areia Preta can be visited; bus marked "Areia Preta" from Av. Rio Branco. Good local craftware Sats. at Mercado do Alecrim, along R. Quaresma near R. Gonçalves. At Mãe Luiza is a lighthouse with beautiful views of Natal and surrounding beaches (take city bus marked Mãe Luiza; get key from the house next door. Some 20 km. from Natal is the rocket base of Barreira do Inferno, near Eduardo Gomes, which can no longer be visited by foreigners. In mid-Oct. there is a country show, Festa do Boi, bus marked Parnamirim to the exhibition centre, it gives a good insight into rural life.

**Hotels** *Marsol Natal*, Via Costeira 1567, km. 7, Parque das Dunas, T 221-2619, 3-star, new; Via Costeira is a good place to stay, but hotels mostly in A-B range; e.g. *Barreira Roxa Praia*, T 222-1093, clean, helpful, good; *Imirá Plaza*, Costeira 4077, T 222-4105, on beach, pool, tennis, rec.; *Praia do Sol*, Av. Pres. Café Filho 750, Praia do Meio, T 222-6689, C, opp. beach, renovated, clean, quiet, a/c, TV, friendly, rec. *Natal*, Av. Mar Floriano Peixoto 104, E, clean, English spoken; *Fenícia*, Av. Rio Branco 586, D (more with a/c), with breakfast and shower, friendly, English spoken; *Bom Jesús*, No. 384, good value, popular; *Casa Grande*, R. Princesa Isabel 529, T 222-1513, E with a/c, F without bath, good breakfast, pleasant, excellent value; *Pousada O Caipira*, Manuel Maschado 354, E, clean, friendly, noisy at weekends, between beach and centre, take "Via-Tirol" bus; *Samburá*, R. Prof. Zuza 263, T 221-0611, C, rec.; *Beira Mar*, Av. Pres. Café Filho, Praia dos Artistas, T 222-4256, on the beach front, D, with breakfast, but no a/c, small, good value, popular; *Praia do Meio*, Av. Beira Mar, D, a/c, clean, friendly, good value; *Pousada Bejo Tropical*, R. Valentim de Almeida 10, F, T 221-5361, clean, helpful, warmly rec.; *Farol*, Av. Gouv. Silvio Pedrosa 174 (on beach), T 222-4661, D with a/c; *Le Bateau*, Praia de Areia Preta, D, on beach front, clean, helpful, good breakfast, English and French spoken. Also on beach, *Praia dos Artistas*, clean, helpful, good breakfast, rec; *Tirol*, Av. Alexandrino de Alencar 1330, T 221-3223, C, good but noisy. *Pousadas* at Ponta Negra and Genipabu beaches, e.g. *Caminho do Mar*, nr. Ponta Negra beach, clean, very friendly (Av. da Praia 3398, T 236-2079); *Ponta Negra*, E, pool, friendly, rec; *Pousada do Mar*, T 236-2509, D, pool; *Miramar* (Av. da Praia 3398, T 236-2079); *Bella Napoli*, *Pousada do Praia* offer some reductions for single people in double rooms. Cheap accommodation at *Casa de Estudantes*, near the Tourist Centre (separate facilities for men and women), "Via Tirol" bus from Rodoviária to centre passes here, very crowded in Suns. **Youth hostel**, *Meu Canto*, R. Dr. Manoel Dantas 424, Petrópolis, T 222-8351, highly rec.; *Lua Cheia*, Av. Estrela do Mar 2215, Conj. Algamar, Ponta Negra, T 236-2085.

**Camping** on the Praia do Forte beach, near the Forte dos Reis Magos, not rec. because unsafe. Camping Clube do Brasil site at Sítio do Jiqui, expensive. Vale das Cascatas, Ponta Negra beach, swimming pool, leisure facilities, US$4 p.p.

**Electric Current** 220 volts A.C., 60 cycles.

**Restaurants** *Casa de Mãe*, R. Pedro Afonso 153 (Petrópolis), regional food, rec.; R. Princesa Isabel No. 717-C has *Bom Demais*, cheap, good; same street, *Casa Grande*, good value; *Pietro's*, Av. Marechal Deodoro, opp. cathedral, cheap, good; *Raizes*, Av. Campos Sales, with C. Mossoró, good regional dishes; *Thin-San*, Av. Hermes da Fonseca 890, Tirol, Chinese, quite good, not expensive; *Chaplin*, Av. Pres. Café Filho 27 (Praia dos Artistas), very good seafood, expensive. Vegetarian (with shops): *Amai*, General Varela 624, and *A Microbiótica*, Princesa Isabel 524. Good, inexpensive lanchonetes on R. Judas Tadéu, just off Rio Branco. For snacks try the stalls on Praia do Meio, there are also various restaurants along the beach road nearby, where itinerant musicians play. Try the restaurants on the point that separates Praias dos Artistas and da Areia Preta (e.g. *Calamar*), for seafood.

**Telecommunications** Embratel, Av. Duque de Caxias 99. T 1230. International phone calls, Telern, 2 blocks behind cathedral.

**Exchange** Cash advances against Visa card at **Banco do Brasil** only, Av. Rio Branco 510. Natal is a very poor place to change money.

**Tourist Information** Centro de Turismo (a converted prison with handicraft shops) R. Aderbal de Figueiredo s/n, off R. General Cordeiro, Petrópolis; Rodoviária and Aeroporto Augusto Severo.

**Airport**  Augusto Severo, 15 km. from centre; flights to Belém, Brasília, Cuiabá, Fortaleza, Manaus, Recife, Rio, Salvador, São Paulo and other cities. Bus every half-hour from old bus station near centre US$0.55, taxi US$12.

**Bus**  (terminal, with luggage store, is about 6 km. out of town, bus "Cidade de Esperança Av. 9", "Areia Preta via Petrópolis" or "Via Tirol" to centre); to **Recife**, 5 hrs., US$8; to **Fortaleza**, 8 hrs., US$8 (*leito*—freezing—US$16); to **Maceio**, buses of Real Alagoas go either direct, or via Recifé, 4-6 hrs.; to **João Pessoa**, US$4, 3 hrs.

At Pirangi, 25 km. S, or 30 min. by bus from new Rodoviária, is the world's largest cashew-nut tree (*cajueiro*); branches springing from a single trunk cover an area of some 7,300 square metres. From Natal (Viação Campos), 5 times a day from 0630 to 1815, 3 on Sun., 0730, 0930, 1645; the snack bar by the tree has schedules of buses back to Natal. A number of good beaches and attractive villages may be found along this coast. North of Natal are extensive cashew plantations.

**Beaches**  Natal has excellent beaches (for example Ponta Negra, with many new hotels and restaurants, 20 mins. by bus from centre), pleasant and "quaint" atmosphere (not safe to wander alone on the dunes as there are robberies), some on the far side of the Potengi river, for example Redinha and Genipabu—where you can toboggan down the sand-dunes—reached by direct bus from old Rodoviária, last bus back from Genipabu at 1730 —N.B. muggings have been reported in Genipabu. (*Hotel Genipabu*, E, 2 km. from beach, marvellous views, isolated; *Mar-Azul*, E), few people are there from June-Oct. Praia do Meio, however, is reported as depressing and treeless. You can hire buggies to get to the beaches for US$20-30 a day, or by the hour, these are making the most popular beaches very noisy.

The state of Rio Grande do Norte (whose people are called "Potiguares" after an Indian tribe that now resides at Jacaré de São Domingos, municipality of Rio Tinto in neighbouring Paraíba state) has three main paved roads radiating from Natal: S to João Pessoa and Recife, SW to Caicó and W to Mossoró and Fortaleza. Between **Caicó** (*Hotel Guanabara*, rec., E) and **Mossoró** (pop. 158,000)—(*Hotel Termas*, B, comfortable, with a hot, mineral water pool system, each pool on a terrace, with temperatures ranging from 54°C at the top to 30°C at the bottom; *Hotel Grand*, E, *Hotel Pax* next to market; *Hotel Zenilândia*, E, highly rec.) there is a turning to **Patu** with its huge basilica on a hillside, with passable "hotels", rather primitive. From Mossoró you can visit the salt pans at Grossos on the coast, but get written permission from the administrative offices in Mossoró. Bus Mossoró-Aracati at 0800 with Emp. Nordeste, 2 hrs., US$1.85.

## Ceará and Piauí

From Mossoró the main road, BR304, enters Ceará and continues about 50 km. to **Aracati**, pop. 60,000 (*Hotel Litorânea*, E, clean, nr. Rodoviária: bus from Natal via Mossoró, 6 hrs., US$8; bus every two hours from Fortaleza 174 km., US$2.75).

From this town take a VW Combi-Bus to **Canoa Quebrada** (US$0.80, from corner of Gen Pompeu e Tableau João Paulo—taxi US$5), a fishing village on a sand dune, 10 km. from Aracati. There are now many *pousadas* (*Pousada Cultural*, E, basic, clean, friendly; *Pousada Ma Alice*, E, clean, safe, friendly; *Lua Morena*, E, chalets; 2 rooms behind *Sol de Manhã* café on mainstreet, clean, with shower, F, good breakfast in the café; *Tenda do Cumbe*, at end of road on cliff, thatched huts E, restaurant, warmly rec.; also on cliff above beach, *Pousada Ao Nascer do Sol*, E, clean, shower, friendly, hammocks for rent) and villagers will let you sling your hammock or put you up for about US$1.50 (Brendan is rec., but his food is expensive, European books exchanged; Sr Miguel rents good clean houses for US$7.50 a day); bars and restaurants for food, vegetarian food in *Espácio Cultural*, cheap seafood (don't drink the water); only a few places have running water. Nowhere to change money. The village is famous for its *labirinto* lacework and coloured sand sculpture, for sand-skiing on the dunes, for the sunsets, and for the beaches, though beware of jiggers (*bicho de pé*), best to wear shoes. Canoa Quebrada has been "discovered" and is becoming a major tourist attraction; basic tours (no food) from Fortaleza, 12 hrs., US$15.

87 km. from Fortaleza (too far for a day trip) is **Morro Branco** (4 km. from Beberibe—which is to 60 km. from Aracati, bus), with spectacular beach, craggy cliffs and beautiful views. *Jangadas* leave the beach at 0500, returning at 1400-1500; hotel-restaurants, E; *Cabana do Morro*, *Pousada do Morro*, E, clean, but mosquitoes, fan and shower, *Novo*, E, clean, noisy at weekends and *Recanto Praia*, E, clean, good breakfast, rec. (first two have swimming pool);

*Pousada Sereia*, E, on the beach, clean, good breakfast, friendly, highly rec.; *Rosalias's*, G, with use of kitchen, 50 metres from bus stop; or you can rent fishermen's houses; meals can also be arranged at beach-front bars (try *O Jangadeiro*). Double room for rent at *Bar São Francisco*, F, or 7-room house for rent. Beach buggies and taxi for hire, Marrambaia can be visited, some accommodation. São Benedito bus from Fortaleza, US$1.60; 2½ hrs., 4 a day. To get to Natal, take 0600 bus to Beberibe, then 0800 bus (only one) to Aracati, US$0.80, then on to Natal. Town is very crowded at holiday time. No money exchange available.

*Caponga* beach, further up the coast, is reached by direct bus from Fortaleza (2 a day) or by taking a bus from Fortaleza to Cascavel (80 mins., US$1.20) then a bus from Cascavel (20 mins., US$0.35); accommodation at *Caponga Praia*, on the beach front, simple cheap rooms and good meals, and at *Pousada Sereia*, very friendly, good, E. A ½-hour walk S along the deserted white-sand beach leads to a river mouth, offering a combination of fresh-and salt-water bathing. *Jangadas* set sail in the early morning (arrangements can be made to accompany fishermen on overnight trips); there is a fish market on the beach.

40 km. before Fortaleza, along the coast, is **Prainha**, a fishing village and weekend resort near the town of Aquiraz (bus terminal in Fortaleza opp. Escola Normal at 1430 and 1700, return 1530 and 1800). You can see *jangadas* coming in daily in the late afternoon. The beaches are clean and largely empty. *Prainha Solex Hotel*, R. Pericich Ribeiro 5, T 361-1000/01/02, ramal 156.7, D, pool, comfortable. Good fish restaurant, *O Leonção*, on same street. There are several small, cheap and good restaurants, where it is possible to see displays of the Carimbó, one of the north Brazilian dances.

**Fortaleza** (pop. 1,600,000), capital of the State of Ceará, is about 520 km. from Natal, NW along the coast (population of Ceará state 6,207,000). It is 1,600 km. by road from Belém and 885 km. from Recife. There are fair dirt roads throughout the State, and paved roads W to São Luís and SE to Recife; the federal highway S to Salvador (BR-116) is now largely paved but much is in poor condition.

A fine tourist centre in the old prison on the waterfront (Av. Senador Pompeu 350) includes the Museu de Arte e Cultura Popular (open Mon.-Fri., 0800-1200, 1400-1800, Sat. 0800-1200, most interesting), shops and restaurants. Other museums: Museu Histórico e Antropológico do Ceará, Av. Barão de Studart 410 (open Tues.-Fri., 0730-1230, 1430-1730, Sat.-Sun., 0800-1200, 1400-1800; take bus marked "Dom Luís"); in the next street, the Museu de Minerais, R. José Vilar 196 (open Mon.-Fri., 0700-1300), bus to centre, "Praia do Futuro" or "Serviluz". Museu das Secas, Pedro Pereira 683, 0800-1100, 1400-1700, collections of photographs and anti-drought equipment. Also visit Forte Nossa Senhora da Assunção, originally built by the Dutch. The mausoleum of President Castello Branco (1964-67), next to the state government building, may be visited. The new cathedral, in gothic style but built in concrete, stands opposite the Mercado Central, open 0600-1000; it has beautiful stained glass windows. At night the centre of town is dead, but by day it is very busy with vendors and crowds. Still, it is not over-agitated or dirty. Crime is reported to be on the increase in this previously safe city.

The local dance, "Forró", can be experienced at the *Clube dos Vaqueiros* out on the BR-116 road South, Wed. 2230; or at *Viva Maria*, Vieira e Estados Unidos, Sat. at 2200 (check by phone first).

**Local Holidays** 6 Jan. (Epiphany); Ash Wed.; 19 March (São José); Christmas Eve; New Year's Eve, half-day.

A festival takes place on the last Sunday in July, during which the traditional *jangada* (raft) races take place. On 15 August, the local Umbanda *terreiros* (churches) celebrate the Festival of Iemanjá on Praia do Futuro, taking over the entire beach from noon till dusk, when offerings are cast into the surf. Well worth attending (members of the public may "pegar um passo"— enter into an inspired religious trance—at the hands of a *pai-de-santo*). Beware of pick-pockets and purse-snatchers.

**Hotels** *Beira Mar*, on beach, T 224-9444, swimming pool, A+; *Novotel*, Av. Pres. Kennedy 2380, T 244-9122, A+; *Othon Palace*, 5-star, T 224-9177, beach front location; *Esplanada Praia*, Av. Presidente Kennedy 2000, T 224-8555, L; *Colonial*, 4-star, T 211-9644, A+, pleasant, with best grounds and biggest pool, laundry service, reported to be somewhat run down (10 mins. walk from Av. Kennedy). *Nordeste Palace*, R. Assunção 99 in centre, large rooms, friendly, good value; *Samburá Praia*, Av. Beira Mar 4530, T 224-8929, B, cheaper than most beach hotel, friendly; *Pousada Jardim*, run by Sr. Abelardo Bezerra at Ildefonso Albano 950, no sign outside (T 231-7991) in Aldeota district, by Iracema beach, B, very clean, friendly, nice garden, excursions arranged, many languages spoken, warmly rec.; another on same street, No. 644, E, clean and friendly (T 226-9206); *Pousada Vida da Praia*, José Vilar 252, T 244-6444, in same district, E, clean, safe, helpful, English spoken. *Ondas Verdes*, Av. Pres. Kennedy 934, T 226-0871, D, fan, TV, shower, clean, rec.; *Cabana Praia*, at R. João Lourenço 441 (T261-1399) and at Av. Rui Barbosa 555, T 261-4954, both C, small, friendly; *Passeio*, R. Dr. João Moreira 221, D with bath, fan, good breakfast, safe, storage, good value. *Caxambu*, General Bezerril 22 (T 231-0339), a/c, C with breakfast, and bath, clean, but poor food, central (opposite Cathedral, in market area). Note that the central area is deserted at night. *Amuarama*, T 227-4744, D, pool, sauna, by Rodoviária (6 km. from centre), entrance by service station. *Chevalier*, Av. Duque de Caxias 465, T 231-4611, E with bath and fan, pleasant; *Pousada Central*, Av. Dom Manuel, near Costa Barrios, T 252-5040, D, good value; *Lord*, Praça José de Alencar, T 231-6188, F and up, private bath, hot water, fan, large and clean but single rooms may be poor (restaurant not rec.). *Pousada da Praia*, Av. Mons. Tabosa 1315, Iracema, 2 blocks from beach, best rooms are the super-luxo on 2nd and 3rd floors, C, a/c, clean, friendly, also cheaper rooms, fan, valuables may be left in safe of English-speaking owner, rec., buses to centre stop at door; *Pousada Osvaldo Cruz*, R. Osvaldo Cruz, E, rec; *Pousada d'Antonietta*, Carlos Vasconcelos 660, T 224-3454, good breakfast, clean, quiet, 5 mins. from beach, buses to centre and other beaches nearby, E with bath; *Paraíso da Praia*, R. dos Pacajus 109, Iracema, small, on beach, helpful and friendly, good *trattoria* next door; *Apart-hotel, Aquidabá*, Av. Aquidabá 630, T 226-1405, at beginning of Praia Iracema, 20 mins.' walk from centre, F and up, with bath, pool and bar, clean, quiet; *Nossa Pousada*, Av. Abolição 2600, Meireles, E without bath, near beach, friendly, helpful. Inexpensive hotels along R. Senador Pompeu, e.g. No. 492, *Savoy*, E with breakfast (cheaper rooms without bath), basic, grubby but friendly; *Universo*, at No. 1152, F without breakfast, clean, friendly, may rent by the bed (i.e. single sex clients 3 to a room) smokers unwelcome, some rooms have mosquito nets; No.725, *Tio Patinho 2*, F, less good than *Tio Patinho 3*. *Jacanã*, R. 24 de Maio 845, E with breakfast; across street are *Tío Patinho 3* and *Dormitório Belo Horizonte*, noisy, both F. Try student houses on Av. Universitários, cheap or even free. **Youth Hostel**: R. Frei Mansueta 370, T 244-1254, IYHA card with photo necessary. *Albergue Praia de Iracema*, Av. Al. Barroso 998, T 252-3267, use of kitchen and laundry, clean, helpful, good location.

**Camping** Official site about 10 km south of city, 2 kms along a bumpy road off the highway, signposted, expensive US$3.50 p.p.

**Electric Current** 220 volts A.C., 60 cycles.

**Restaurants** Several good fish restaurants at far end of Av. Presidente Kennedy, where the boats come ashore between 1300 and 1500, for example, *Trapiche*, No. 3950 (seafood, expensive, but excellent except for wine list). At Praia de Iracema (Av. Kennedy 4616) are *Alfredo* (good fish) and, next door, *Peixada do Meio* (better). Italian are *La Trattoria*, Praia de Iracema between Tabajaras and Av. Kennedy, *Sandras*, Av. Perimetral, Praia do Futuro, lobster from US$7 upwards, has been specially rec. *Churrascaria Tourão*, Av. Mons. Tabosa, all you can eat for US$4.50. Good restaurant in Clube Náutico. A short taxi ride from Clube Náutico is *O Ozias*, R. Canuto de Aguiar 1449 (T 224-9067), good for seafood, but hard to find. Good Chinese: *HongKong*, Av. Pres. Kennedy 4544, Mucuripe. Vegetarian: *Alivita*, Barão do Rio Branco 1486, good, lunch only, US$1, Mon.-Fri.; *Céu da Boca*, R. Franklin Távora 136, lunch and 1800-2000 Mon.-Fri., good and inexpensive. *Kury*, R. Senador Pompeu 959, good food at reasonable prices; opp is a good Chinese restaurant. Another good place in centre is *Belas Artes*, Major Facundo 82, just up from Passeio Público. Cheap meals at railway station. Emcetur restaurant, *Xadrez*, in old prison, good atmosphere, open to 2400, reported safe to 2100. Good view of Fortaleza from *Restaurant Panorámico*, R. Mirante, in Mucuripe district, near the lighthouse. At *Pirata* club, Praia de Iracema, the "Forró" is danced. Mon.; many good bars along the beach cook local crabs and fish. *El Mirante*, on a hill with spectacular views has many lively bars and restaurants, accessible by car or taxi.

**Shopping** Fortaleza has an excellent selection of textiles at reasonable prices (among the cheapest in Brazil) and some handicrafts. Also good for clothes. The local specialities are lace (some hand-made) and embroidered textile goods; also hammocks (US$8-10—try Gerardo, Loja Cifa, Travessa Crato 28/32, in mall opp. Mercado central), fine alto-relievo wood carvings of North-East scenes, basket ware and clay figures (*bonecas de barro*). Bargaining is O.K. at the **Mercado Central** in the Praça da Sé, and the **Emcetur tourist market** in the old prison (more expensive). Every night (1800-2300), there are stalls along Av. Pres. Kennedy (the beach), lively but more expensive than the Mercado Central, where some stallholders will accept a better price if you're paying in dollars. The **Centro de Artesanato Lucila Távora** is decaying. Boutiques along Monsenhor Tabosa between Senador Almino and João Cordeiro. Cashew nuts at the Mercado Central are excellent.

**Car Hire**   Beach buggies rentable for US$30 a day plus small km. charge, from **Junna's Buggy**, Av. Abolição 2480, T 244-7872.

**Theatre**   Teatro José de Alencar, near railway station in centre, built 1810, building contains also newer theatre built 1910.

**Exchange**   Lloyds Bank, R. Barão do Rio Branco 862; **Banco do Nordeste**, Major Facundo 372, a/c, helpful, rec.; and other national banks; **Banorte** gives good rates. Open 0900-1630. Exchange at **Tropical Viagens**, R. Barão do Rio Branco 1233, English spoken, or at **Ari**, Sapataria Brasileira, R. Gen. Bezerril 259, or at the **Zely** shop in the old prison.

**Consulate**   Danish, Av. da Nações 26, CP 07-0484, 70416, T 242-8188, open 0900-1200, 1400-1700.

**Health**   R. Vincente Leite 631, English-speaking doctor.

**Post Office**   in centre. Parcels must be taken to Receita Federal office at Barão de Aracati 909, Aldeota (take "Dom Luiz" bus).

**Telephone**   International calls from Emcetur hut on Iracema beach and from Teleceará offices (R. João Moreira esq. R. Floriano Peixoto). **Telecommunications** Embratel, R. Castro e Silva 286/290.

**Tourist Information**   Emcetur, in ex-municipal prison, helpful, has maps. Open 0700-1800, Sun. 0700-1200. Also on Iracema beach.

**Tourist Agencies**   Hippopotamus Turismo, Prai de Iracema, tour to Jericuacuara rec. Advised that, in other cases, it is best to book beach trips through Emcetur.

**Rail**   South to Baturité (tourist train round trip Sun.).

**Air Service**   Direct flights to Belém, Recife, Rio and other cities in Brazil. Bus from airport to Praça José de Alencar.

**Bus Service**   New Rodoviária 6 km. from centre, bus from Av. Grl. Sampaio marked Aguanambi 1 or 2, US$0.25 (and others); no luggage store, only lockers. The Expresso de Luxo runs daily to **Recife** (12 hrs., US$8, leave at night), book early for weekend travel; also **Rio de Janeiro**, 48 hrs., US$72 (leito 144), **São Paulo**, 48 hrs., US$73 (leito 146), Crato, Parnaíba, and many other cities. To **Brasília**, Expresso Ipu-Brasília, same company to **Belo Horizonte**, 42 hrs. **Salvador**, 19 hrs., US$30; **Natal**, US$10, 8 hrs. (Nordeste has leito, an executivo at noon, and 5 semi-leitos which make only 3 stops); **Teresina**, US$11, 9 hrs. (at least); **São Luís**, US$19, 18 hrs., 4 a day; **Belém** US$25, 5 buses a day, 23 hrs. (2 companies, Exp. Timbira good). To Piripiri, for Parque Nacional de Sete Cidades, US$8, 9 hrs.
    To hitch to Teresina, take a bus W to the BR-222, the Teresina road.

**Beaches** are fine (take bus marked "P. Futuro" from Praça Castro Carreira, "Praia Circular" bus which does a circular route to Praia Futuro, or bus marked "Caça e Pesca", which passes all SE beaches on its route), and you can watch the boats coming in before sundown with their catch. The majority of high class hotels are on the beach from Praia de Iracema (which is the most popular beach, though now unsuitable for swimming; in the evenings everyone promenades along this beach). Other beaches not suitable for bathing are Diarios, Meireles, Volta da Jurema and Mucuripe all to the SE. Praia do Futuro is 8 km. to the SE (no shade). Iguape beach is recommended, but is at end of 90 min. bus ride—São Benedito bus marked "Iguape" from Praça F. de Melo (trips on jangadas for US$7). Northwest of the centre is Praia Barra do Ceará, 8 km., where the Ceará river flows into the sea. Praia de Icaraí 22 km. to the NW is under development. Beyond Icaraí, 12 km., is Combuco, a beautiful beach where one can swim safely and there are palm trees; Teto do Praia, cooking facilities, on beach, cheap (bus from Av. Tristão Gonçalves to Caucaia, then another bus).

Two hours NW of Fortaleza by bus is *Paracuru*, a small fishing port (fish readily available), pop. 30,000, which is being developed as Ceará's carnival city (restaurant Ronco do Mar, good fish dishes also *Balança do Mar* and a pizzaria; breakfast at Dona Luci's *sitio*, No. 25 in the market; *Boca do Poço* bar is scene of *forró* at weekends). It has some lovely deserted white sand beaches with good bathing, and the people are very friendly. Some 7 hours from Fortaleza is the sleepy fishing village of *Almofala*, served by many buses. There is electricity, but no hotels or restaurants, although locals rent hammock space and cook meals (usually US$2 p.p., food and lodging). Bathing is better elsewhere, but the area is surrounded by dunes and is excellent for hiking along the beach to nearby lobster-fishing communities. In Almofala, the church with much of the town was covered by shifting sands and remained covered for 50 years, reappearing in the 1940s.

Nestled in the dunes near the border with the state of Piauí is the tiny fishing community of *Jericuacuara* (known as Serrote by locals). It is becoming increasingly popular with travellers and Brazilians, crowded Jan. to March, despite the difficulty of getting there. There is no real road, so the trip is part of the adventure. Once there, the visitor is rewarded with towering sand dunes, deserted beaches with little shade, cactus-covered cliffs rising from the sea, and a chance to savour life in a sleepy, primitive fishing community, although it is becoming ever more geared to tourism. Pigs, chickens and donkeys roam the streets at will; there is no electricity and no running water (take your showers at the town pump). Fortunately, ice-cold beer is available in several tiny lantern-lit bars and there is "Forró" on Fri. and Sat. nights. *Hotel Papagaio*, D, is said to be the best. Many locals rent hammock space (US$1), hammocks, and cook food (about US$2 per day, room and board), and there are many *pousadas* (E): *O Alemão*, rec.; *Pousada Natur* with a restaurant belonging to a very helpful German; *São Francisco*, G, basic, but friendly; *Hotel Hippopotamus*, A, pool. There are several restaurants serving vegetarian and fish dishes (*Restaurante Central*, rec.). Fresh banana tart available most days at about 1300. Several shops sell basic provisions, so camping is possible. Horses can be hired to visit beautiful lagoons. Take the bus from Sobral or Fortaleza to Gijoca at 0800 or 2000 (8 hrs., US$4), then a jeep meets the bus: Jericuacuara from Gijoca costs about US$3 per person for the hour-and-a-half journey. Returning, the bus leaves Gijoca for Fortaleza at midnight and 0700. A direct journey from Fortaleza on a 2 or 3-day tour is possible in a VW Kombi, book through an hotel or T 244-5974, Maria do Carmo. You can also get there by boat "seasickness guaranteed", or bus from Camocim, *Hotel Lusitania*, F, (a little further west). Take a truck from Camocim to Guriú where hammock space can be found. The village musician sings his own songs in the bar. Walk 4 hrs., or take boat across the bay to Jericuacuara. Maceió beach is also reached from Camocim, take supplies, it is an unspoilt paradise.

The Serra de Maranguape with tropical growth and distant views back to the city is 30 km. inland from Fortaleza. The pilgrimage centre of Canindé may be visited, 108 km. SW of Fortaleza, 3-hour bus ride from Box 21 of the Rodoviária (Viação Nova Esperança). Large modern church on hill with carved baptistery doors, many ex-votos, interesting dry-land vegetation along route. (Hotels: *Plaza*, by basilica, food OK; *Santo Antônio*). Another inland town, *Baturité*, can be seen, 3 hrs. from Rodoviária (Box 45) by Redenção bus, mornings only, also a tourist train round trip Sundays.

The road to Sobral and Teresina, BR-222, is paved, but in poor condition. *Sobral* (pop. 112,000), the principal town in western Ceará and well-known for straw hats, has *Hotel Municipal*, E, meals available. At Tianguá, 311 km. from Fortaleza on the Teresina road, is *Serra Grande* hotel, all amenities, C, good.

The Ubajara cave in the **Ubajara National Park** is worth seeing; it is 18 km. off the road to Teresina, on a good paved road, 3 km. from Ubajara town. A cablecar used to descend the cliff to the cave entrance but has not been repaired since it broke down in 1985 and the visitors centre is closed. Ask for a guide at the park entrance (they leave at 0800 for the 6 km. round trip); a torch is necessary for the cave, which is an hour's walk down a rocky, wooded path (also take drinking water). The views of the *sertão* from the upper cablecar platform are superb. Here is the *Pousada Neblina*, E, near caves, with swimming pool, with breakfast and private shower, meals rec.; opposite is an unnamed hostel, G with bath, clean, friendly, rustic, restaurant, rec. In *Ubajara* town are *Hotel Gruta*, R. 31 de Dezembro 74, F, basic, good breakfast, and *Hotel Churrascaría Ubajara*, R. Juvêncio Pereira 370, E, clean and friendly, hot water, good breakfast, restaurant. Interesting Sunday morning market. Several buses a day to Fortaleza.

South of Sobral is the remote town of *Crateús* (pop. 68,000), paved road all the way to Fortaleza, with the *Crateús Palace Hotel*, very reasonable and clean, E, with breakfast. Good restaurant, *Churrascaria Pequena Cabana*, at back of hotel. Bus service from Crateús over very bad road to Teresina, every two days.

Between the states of Maranhão and Piauí runs the river Parnaíba. Near its mouth is the anchorage of Luís Correia, where ships unload for final delivery by tugs and lighters at **Parnaíba** (pop. 116,000) 15 km. up river, the collecting and distributing centre for the trade of Piauí: tropical products and cattle.

**Hotels** *Cívico*, Av. Gov. Chagas Rodrigues, T 322-2470, C with bath and a/c, good breakfast, friendly, rec.; *Rodoviária*, F and other basic hotels in the centre.

**Beaches** at Luís Correia, which with Parnaíba has radioactive sands (good hotel at Luís Correia, F). Some 15 km. from Parnaíba is Pedra do Sal: dark blue lagoons and palm trees. At Lagoa de Portinho there are bungalows, a bar and restaurant and it is possible to camp; canoes for hire.

**Teresina** (pop. 475,000) about 435 km. up the Parnaíba river, is the capital of the State of Piauí (pop 2,584,000), reputed to be the poorest in Brazil. There are paved road and rail connections (freight only) with the neighbouring state capitals. The city itself is reputed to be the hottest after Manaus (temperatures rise to 42°C). The Palácio de Karnak (the old governor's palace), just South of Praça Frei Serafim, can be visited, Mon.-Fri., 1530-1730; it contains lithographs of the Middle East in 1839 by David Roberts R.A. There is an interesting open market by the Praça Marechal Deodoro and the river is picturesque, with washing laid out to dry along its banks. The market is a good place to buy hammocks, but bargain hard. Every morning along the river bank there is the *troca-troca* where people buy, sell and swap, but it is no longer spontaneous; an under-cover complex (Mercado Central do Artesanato) has been built at R. Paissandu 1276 (Praça Dom Pedro II), open daily 0800-2200 (not weekends). Most of the year the river is low, leaving sandbanks known as *coroas* (crowns).

**Hotels** *Luxor Hotel do Piauí*, A, T 222-4911, and *Teresina Palace*, Paissandu 1219, T 222-2770; *Grande*, Firmino Pires 73, F, very friendly and clean; *Sambaíba*, R. Gabriel Ferreira 230-N, 2-star, T 223-6711, C, central, good; *São José*, João Cabral 340, T 223-2176, C, reasonable restaurant; *Fortaleza*, Felix Pacheco 1101, Prça. Saraiva, T 222-2984, F, fan, basic, rec.; many cheap hotels and *dormitórios* around Praça Saraiva. Many cheap ones in R. São Pedro: *Bom Clima*, No.890, E; *São Pedro*, No. 905, E; *Globo*, No. 861, E; and in R. Alvaro Mendes, *Glória*, at 823 (clean, best), and at 860, 906, all E.

**Restaurants** For fish dishes, *Pesqueirinho*, near the confluence of the rivers in Poti Velho district. Many eating places for all pockets in Praça Dom Pedro II (*Típico do Piauí*, good value).

**Shopping** Supermarket on Praça Marechal Deodoro 937, clean, good, fresh food. Local handicrafts include leather and clothes.

**Exchange** For parallel market try **Banorte Turismo**, Av. Pacheco and Barbosa. Larger hotels may be helpful (e.g. *Luxor do Piauí*).

**Laundry** *Tintoraria São Paulo*, Rui Barbosa 431, nr. *Luxor Hotel do Piauí*.

**Tourist Information** Piemtur, R. Alvaro Mendes 2003, Caixa Postal 36, information office at R. Magalhães Filho s/n (next to 55 N -English spoken); kiosks at Rodoviária and airport.

**Buses** The bus trip from **Fortaleza** is scenic and takes 9 hrs. (US$11, *leito* at 2100, arr. 0600, US$22). Another road, very bad, leads inland to Porto Franco and **Imperatriz** on the Belém-Brasília highway (**see page 451**); daily bus takes 26-40 hrs. for the trip to Imperatriz (US$14), depending on the state of the road; these buses are very crowded. There are direct buses to Belém, but avoid the non-express (*parador*) service. The road to São Luís is quite good, bar a few potholes. Another main road, runs SE to **Picos** (*Hotel Picos*, E, basic, but a/c); from there a good road runs via Salgueiro (many *pousadas*) to Recife (800 km.) and another to **Petrolina**, on the River São Francisco opposite the Bahian town of Juazeiro. Bus, one or two a day, 15 hrs., US$16. Buses from Petrolina/Juazeiro (**see page 425**) SE to Salvador. Bus to **Belém**, about 16 hrs., US$18. To São Luís, bus takes 7 hrs., US$8.

**Rail** Local services only, on a diesel service called the "metro".

**Air** Flights to Recife via Fortaleza, to Brasília and Salvador.

**Excursion** Some 190 km. NE of Teresina and 12 km. from Piracuruca is the interesting 20-sq. km. Parque Nacional de **Sete Cidades** with its strange eroded rock formations, just off the

Fortaleza-Teresina road. From the ground it looks like a medley of weird monuments. The inscriptions on some of the rocks have never been deciphered; one Austrian researcher in the 1920s suggested links with the Phoenicians, and the Argentine Professor Jacques de Mahieu, considers them to be Nordic runes left by the Vikings. There is plenty of birdlife. If hiking in the park, beware of rattlesnakes. IBDF guides drive round the park (2½ hrs.), you may be able to get around on their tractor, or else walk (takes all day, very hot, start early). Small booklet with sketch map (not really good enough for walking), entrance US$0.30. There are camping facilities (US$0.60) and two natural swimming pools, although several years of drought have lowered their water level drastically. Local food is limited and monotonous: bring a few delicacies, and especially fruit.

6 km. from the park entrance is the hotel *Fazenda Sete Cidades*, C, with private bathroom, swimming pool, good restaurant and free bicycle or horse transport (it is at Km. 63 on BR-222, T (086) 261-3642); also has a free pick-up to the park (and a most unpleasant zoo). In the park is a IBDF (Forestry Institute) hostel, G p.p., rooms with bath, pleasant, good restaurant, natural pool nearby, rec.

A free bus service leaves the Praça in **Piripiri** (in front of Telpisa office), 26 km. away, at 0700, passing *Hotel Fazenda Sete Cidades* at 0800, reaching the park 10 mins. later; return at 1630, or hitch-hike. Taxi from Piripiri, US$12, or from Piracuruca, US$15. Bus Teresina-Piripiri and return, throughout the day 2½ hrs., US$3.35. Bus São Luis-Piripiri, 1200, 1630, 2130, 10 hrs., US$10.40. Several daily buses Piripiri-Fortaleza, 9 hrs. US$8. Bus Piripiri-Ubajara (see above), marked "São Benedito", with Itapemirim, 2½ hrs.; US$3.20, first at 0700 (a beautiful trip, although one dirt stretch will get your belongings dusty unless protected by plastic). Hotels in Piripiri: *Dos Viajantes*, G, basic and clean; *Piripiri*, both near bus offices and behind the church. Exchange at the bank only.

In the south of the state is **Oeiras**, old capital of Piauí, where the state government is restoring some of the old buildings, such as the bishop's palace and the church of Nossa Senhora da Vitória.

## Maranhão

Maranhão state (pop. 4,978,000) is about the size of Italy; its land is flat and low-lying, with highlands to the S. The Atlantic coastline—a mass of sandbanks and creeks and sandy islands on one of which stands São Luís—is 480 km. long. A quarter of Maranhão is covered with *babaçu* palms, and by far the most important products are *babaçu* nuts and oil. Rice often takes second place, but well behind *babaçu*. There are salt pans along the coast. The huge Boa Esperança hydroelectric plant on the Parnaíba river now floods the State with energy, and some petroleum has been discovered. The main road from Teresina passes through the Maranhense town of Caxias, which has a good churrascaria, *Selva do Braz* (Av. Central 601), live music in the evening.

**São Luís** (pop. 560,000) the capital and port of Maranhão state, founded in 1612 by the French and named for St. Louis of France, is about 560 km. west of Fortaleza (1,080km. by road) and 400 km. SE of Belém (830 km. by road) in a region of heavy tropical rains, but the surrounding deep forest has been cut down to be replaced by *babaçu* palms. The city stands upon São Luis island between the bays of São Marcos and São José. The urban area extends to São Francisco island, connected with São Luís by three bridges. The old part, on very hilly ground with many steep streets, is still almost pure colonial (it has been restored with generally splendid results): the damp climate stimulated the use of ceramic tiles for exterior walls, and São Luís shows a greater variety of such tiles than anywhere else in Brazil, in Portuguese, French and Dutch styles. See the Palácio dos Leões (Governor's Palace—state rooms open Mon., Wed., Fri. 1500-1800, take passport, flip-flops, vest tops and shorts not allowed, beautiful floors of dark wood (*jacarandá*) and light (*cerejeira*), marvellous views from terrace) and the old slave market. The best colonial churches to see—some of them rebuilt and not improved by it—are the Cathedral and the churches of Carmo, São João, Rosário, and Santana. On Largo do Desterro is the church of São José do Desterro, finished in 1863, but with some much older parts. The restored Fortaleza de Santo

Antônio, built originally by the French in 1614, is on the bank of the River Anil at Ponta d'Areia. The Fonte do Ribeirão, Largo do Ribeirão, was begun in 1796. The Museu do Estado, in a fine early 19th century mansion (complete with slave quarters) at R. do Sol 302, US$0.35, is open Tues.-Fri., 1400-1800, Sat.-Sun., and holidays, 1500-1800. Also on the R. do Sol is the Teatro Artur Azevedo (1816). Visit the Fábrica Canhamo, a restored factory now housing an arts and crafts centre, near Praia Grande. The Centro da Creatividade Odylo Costa Filho, Praia Grande, is an arts centre with theatre, cinema, exhibitions, music, etc., with a bar and café, a good meeting place. Near the Travessa Ladeira there is live music at night. Museu de Artes Visuais, Av. Portugal 289, shows ceramics and post war art. The commercial quarter is still much as it was in the 17th century; best shopping area is R. de Santana near Praça João Lisboa.

**Festivals**  On 24 June (São João), the Bumba-Meu-Boi, see **Music and Dance**. For several days before the festival street bands parade, particularly in front of the São João and São Benedito churches. There are dances somewhere in the city almost every night in June. The São Benedito, at the Rosário church in August. Festival in October, with dancing, at Vila Palmeira suburb (take bus of same name).

**Hotels**  *Quatro Rodas*, 8 km. from centre on Calhau beach, T 227-0244, L, excellent, with all facilities; *Vila Rica*, 5-star, Praça D. Pedro II, T 232-3535, L, central, many amenities; *Pousada Colonial*, R. Afonso Pena, D-E, in beautiful restored, tiled house; *Lord*, E, R. Nazaré 258, T 222-5544 facing Praça Benedito Leite, comfortable, clean, rec., good breakfast; nearby is *Central*, Av. D. Pedro II 258, more expensive, but noisy at night with TV, C; also *Solar Imperador*, E, good value; *São Marcos*, D, Saúde 178, T 232-3763, restored colonial house, a/c, family-run, rec.; *Deodoro*, R. de Santaninha 535, CEP 65000, T 222-1196, Telex 098-2694, D, clean, friendly. More basic, but with excellent food, *Pousada Solar do Carmo*, Largo do Carmo, T 222-2455, D-E, pleasant, friendly, light and airy. Many cheap hotels in R. das Palmas, very central, and R. Formosa; *Novo Nazaré*, R. de Nazaré (extension of R. do Sol), F, central, fair facilities and breakfast, reckoned the best of the cheap hotels by one who has tried them all, although that distinction is now claimed for *Ribamar*, Praça João Lisboa; *Estrela* F, R. da Estrela 370, Centro (T 222-1083) clean, safe, rec; *Casa do Estudante*, R. do Passeio, 2 km. from centre. *Pousada da Praia*, R dos Magistrados 10, E, helpful owner, mosquitoes. At Ponta d'Areia: *Ponta d'Areia*, Av. dos Holandeses, Quadra 13 (T 227-2737), about 3 km. from centre, C, a/c, bath, hot water, TV, fridge, restaurant, pool; *Praia Mar*, T 227-4477, on the beach, A, 5-star, all amenities, opp. *São Francisco*, T 227-1155. **Youth hostel:** *O Cortiço*, R. 14 de Julho 93, central; *Albergue da Juventude*, R. 14 de Julho 88, T 222-6258, F, restaurant open for lunch to non-residents, rec.

**Restaurants**  *Solar do Ribeirão*, R. Ribeirão 141, T 222-3068, good buffet lunch and seafood, good value but not cheap, regional cuisine, closed Sat. p.m. and Sun.; *La Bohème*, on same street, very good food, live music, expensive, popular; *Candelabro*, R. do Egito, very expensive but excellent international cuisine; *Base de Edilson*, R. Vila Bessa, centre, shrimp only, excellent; *Hibiscus* Av. dos. Franceses, and *Tia Maria*, Av. Nina Rodrigues (Ponta d'Areia), seafood, rec.; *Base do Germano*, Av. Wenceslau Bras in Canto da Fabril district, excellent *caldeirada de camarão* (shrimp stew), about US$4 per head. *Ladeira*, massive portions, share. *Tia Dadi*, Praça Manuel Beckman, Beira Mar Centre, good regional dishes; *São Luís*, R. de Palma, meal US$3, rec.; *Kanto Lanches*, Nazaré y de Palma, cheap snacks, friendly. *Naturalista Alimentos*, R. do Sol 517, very good, natural foods shop and restaurants, open till 1900. Said to be more choice in new São Francisco district, just across bridge, e.g. *Oriental*, Av. Pres. Castelo Branco, good Chinese, and *Agapê*, good pizzas. Try the local soft drink called *Jesús* or *Jenève*.

**Exchange**  Travellers' cheques at Banco do Brasil; Agetur, R. do Sol 33.

**Consulates**  Danish, R. do Sol 141, Ed. Colonial, Sala 210, T 222-4075, open 0900-1300, 1500-1900.

**Health**  Clínica São Marcelo, R. do Passeio 546, English speaking doctor.

**Telecommunications**  Embratel, Avenida Dom Pedro II 190. T 2500.

**Portuguese Lessons**  Sra Amin Castro, T 227-1527. rec.

**Tourist Offices**  Av. dos Franceses, good information on walks in city. Taguatur, in *Hotel Central* building, good. Town maps from agencies. Funai shop at R. do Sol 371. Centro do Artesanato in main street of São Francisco suburb, over bridge from the city.

**Airport** Internal flights only. 15 km. from centre; buses ("São Cristovão") to city until midnight, US$0.35.

**Railway** Three trains a week on Carajás railway to Parauapebas, 13½ hrs., 890 km., leave São Luís 0800, Mon. Wed., Fri., return 0600, Tues., Thur., Sat. (crowded, take own food); for station take "Vila Nova" or "Anjo da Guarda" bus.

**Road** Bus station 12 km. from centre on airport road, "Alemanha" bus to centre. The Teresina-São Luís road is paved ("just about OK"), bus service, US$8, 7 hrs. Bus to **Piripiri**, US$10.40, 10 hrs.; Expresso de Luxo continues to Fortaleza. Bus to **Fortaleza**, US$19, four a day, 18 hrs. (road also paved). Also to **Recife**, US$38, 25 hrs.

**To Belém** Direct road via Santa Inês and Alto Bonito paved, in reasonable condition, with petrol stations not far apart (about 9 hrs. driving with stop for lunch). There is a bus service 13 hrs., US$17, three daily (no *leito*). There are occasional coastal ships of the Costeira line.

**Excursions** Calhau is a huge beach, 10 km. away, excellent *Churrascaria Pavan*; Ponta D'Areia is nearer to São Luís but more crowded. An hour's bus ride from São Luís is Raposa, a fishing village built on stilts; another fishing village is Ribamar, a half hour's bus ride from São Luís, from in front of the market.

To the East of the city, on the Atlantic Coast is the **Parque Nacional Lençóis Maranhenses**, 155,000 hectares of beaches, lakes and dunes, with very little vegetation and largely unstudied wildlife. For information, the IBDF office is at Av. Jaime Tavares 25, São Luis (Caixa Postal 276, CEP 65.000).

Some 22 km. away by boat is *Alcântara* (city population 4,000, municipality 20,000) the former state capital, on the mainland bay of São Marcos. Construction of the city began at the beginning of the seventeenth century and it is now a historical monument. There are many old churches (e.g. the ruined Matriz de São Matias) and colonial mansions (see the Casa, and Segunda Casa, do Imperador, also the old cotton barons' mansions with their blue, Portuguese tiled façades), the traditional pillory, the Pelourinho, in the Praça Gomes de Castro, also a small museum in the square (US$0.20) and the Forte de São Sebastião (1653) now in ruins. See also the Fonte de Mirititiva. Good beaches, good walking around the coast (can be muddy after rain), mosquitoes after dark. A rocket-launching site has been built nearby. Principal festival: Festa do Divino, at Pentecost (Whitsun).

**Transport** A boat service leaves São Luís daily at between 0700 and 0800, but check time at the dock the day before as departure depends on the tides. The journey takes 90 minutes, from close to the Governor's palace, for Alcântara, returning between 1300 and 1400, but check return time, US$1.60 plus US$0.35 each for boat to take you from ferry to Alcântara dock; sea can be very rough.

**Hotels** *Pousada do Pelourinho*, Praça Gomes de Castro, D, clean, friendly, good restaurant, communal bathroom; *Pousado do Imperador*, D, some rooms with bath; *Pousado do Mordomo Régio*, C, rooms with bath, TV, refrigerator, good restaurant. One can also stay cheaply in houses (e.g. Dona Maria, 3rd house on left on R. Neto Guterres, near harbour, US$1.50 for hammock space and 2 meals). Try bargaining for hammock space in private houses. Children who offer themselves as guides can help arrange accommodation in private houses, friendly but no great comfort; provide your own mineral water.

*Restaurante Tijupa* has very good home cooking but meals must be ordered in advance, owner Claudio is the best guide in town; *Bar do Lobato*, on the praça, is pleasant, with good, simple food, fried shrimps highly rec.

On the Eastern bank of the Rio Tocantins, at Maranhão's western border with Tocantins, is *Imperatriz*, a city serving a large cattle region. Go down Av. Getúlio Vargas and see the range of goods on offer. It is also in an area of violence over landholding; in 1986, a priest was shot in his church. To get to the ferry across the river, go along R. Luis Domingues, which runs parallel to Av. Getúlio Vargas. **Hotels**: *Poseidon*, R. Paraíba 740, T 721-4466, central, best, C, a/c, TV, swimming pool, rec.; *Anápolis*, BR-010, Km. 1345, T 721-2255, opp. Rodoviária, E, a/c, fridge, swimming pool, friendly; a lot of cheap hotels near Rodoviária. Restaurant *Bar Central* is OK. There is a good, expensive discotheque at Beira Rio, north of the ferry crossing, *Fly Back Disco Club*; it has two dance floors, one fast, one slow (for couples only). Telephone office on R. Rio Grande do Norte, a side street off Av. Getúlio Vargas, near *Hotel Poseidon*.

Lying on the Belém-Brasília highway, Imperatriz has bus connections with both cities; there is a slow, crowded bus service to Teresina. To get to Marabá on the Transamazônica, you can either take a Transbrasiliana bus direct, 7-10 hrs (starting on the Belém highway, the bus then turns west along a poorer road, passing finally through destroyed forest, new fazendas and unplanned settlements), or, a faster route, involving taking a ferry across the river in the early morning (0600-0700) to catch a pick-up on the other side, takes about 5 hours, but is more expensive.

## NORTHERN BRAZIL (9)

**Brazilian Amazonia, from the mouth of the great river to the Colombian and Peruvian borders. The cities of Belém, Santarém and Manaus are described, together with river travel between and excursions into the jungle. Also dealt with are the land and water routes to Venezuela.**

Northern Brazil consists of the states of Pará, Amazonas, Amapá and Roraima. The northern states of Rondônia and Acre are dealt with under Section 9, Southern Amazonia.

The area is drained by the Amazon, which in size, volume of water—12 times that of the Mississippi—and number of tributaries has no equal in the world. At the base of the Andes, far to the west, the Amazonian plain is 1,300 km. in width, but east of the confluences of the Madeira and Negro rivers with the Amazon, the highlands close in upon it until there is no more than 80 km. of floodplain between them. Towards the river's mouth—about 320 km. wide—the plain widens once more and extends along the coast south-eastwards into the state of Maranhão and northwards into the Guianas.

Brazilian Amazonia, much of it still covered with tropical forest, is 56% of the national area. Its jungle is the world's largest and densest rain forest, with more diverse plants and animals than any other jungle in the world. It has only 8% of Brazil's population, and most of this is concentrated around Belém (in Pará), and in Manaus, 1,600 km. up the river. The population is sparse because other areas are easier to develop; the rainfall is heavy, the humidity high and the climate hot; and the soil, as in all tropical forest, is poor.

Successive Governments have made strenuous efforts to develop Amazonia. Roads have been built parallel to the Amazon to the south (the Transamazônica), from Cuiabá (Mato Grosso) northwards to Santarém (Pará), and NE from Porto Velho through Humaitá to the river bank opposite Manaus. Agricultural settlements are being established along these roads, and great concern has been expressed at the wholesale destruction of the forest. The area is changing rapidly, especially under the impetus of major energy and mining projects for bauxite and iron ore now in progress. This is reflected in the burgeoning cities. Manaus now suffers from air pollution.

Anyone interested in the Amazonian development programme and its ecological, social, economic and political effects should read Richard Bourne's masterly *Assault on the Amazon* (London, Gollancz, 1978), *Dreams of Amazonia*, by Roger D.Stone (Penguin, 1986), or *Amazon* by Brian Kelly and Mark London (Harcourt Brace Jovanovich, New York, 1983).

### Along the Transamazônica

The Transamazônica, about 5,000 km. in length, represents the greater part of a direct road connection between Brazil's furthest E and furthest W points. It skirts the southern edge of the Amazonian plain, linking the following places: Estreito (junction with the Belém-Brasília highway, N of Araguaína, **see page 483**), Marabá (on the Tocantins river), Altamira (on the Xingu), São Luís do Tapajós, near Itaituba (on the Tapajós), Jacarèacanga, Humaitá (on the Madeira), Rio Branco, and Japim, in the far W of the State of Acre. The road was officially opened in December 1973; parts are paved and buses are running along virtually the whole length; they are operating between Marabá and Humaitá and there are also services from Santarém to the Belém-Brasília road and to Cuiabá along a very bad road; it is frequently impassable and closed in the rainy season (October onwards) and it is dangerous to stay in small villages en route.

From **Marabá** (pop. 200,000) (*Plaza*, Nova Marabá, by rodoviária, T 321-1661, D with a/c pleasant, helpful, some English spoken; *Pensão Nossa Senhora do Nazaré*, F, clean, near bus terminal; *Restaurant O Calmon* for fish) buses leave daily at 0430, 1200 and 1500 for Belém, for Santarém (34 hrs.) at 1730 and many daily for Imperatriz (7-10 hrs., US$8, there is also a pick-up to the bank of the Tocantins opp. Imperatriz, 5 hrs., but more expensive, US$10-12); buses can be caught going south at Toncantinópolis, opposite Porto Franco on the Belém-Brasília road. Also a bus can be taken to Araguaína, 12½ hrs., US$16; bus Marabá-Goiânia (change at Araguaína), US$40. Bus to Santa Inês (Maranhão, on Belém-Terisina road), 1700, 19 hrs., US$19. On these bus trips take plenty of food and drink—local supplies are expensive. With the filling of the Tucuruí dam the town (*Hotel Esplanada*, F,) has been moved; even so it suffers from flooding. The bridge across the Toncantins at Marabá is now open. Banco do Brasil will not cash travellers' cheques; parallel market in larger stores.

To visit the **Serra Pelada** gold mines, now worked by individuals on a very diminished scale, take a bus to Km. 6, change there to bus to Serra Pelada (0900, 1100, US$2.50, 3 hrs, last bus back 1700). (The mine was described on British Channel 4 television as "the largest swimming pool on Earth".) 11 km. before the town is a police post: search for weapons and alcohol (forbidden); second search at airport 2 km. from the mine. *Hotel Serra de Ouro*, E, all of wood, shower; good *Churrascaria* in main square near public TV set; juice bars and *DiscoTony* discotheque. No prior permission needed to visit the mines. The miners are usually friendly and like being photographed, but enquire about the conditions before going there.

From Marabá, or from São Luis or Belém, one can reach the Carajás iron mine (the largest mineral development in Brazil) by road or train (see under São Luis above, train can be caught at station 12 km. from Marabá, Mon. Wed., Fri. approx 2300; to São Luis Tues., Thurs., Sat. 0420). Plenty of Transbrasiliana buses daily Marabá-Carajás, 4-5 hrs, US$4.80; Military Police check for weapons and drugs at Curianópolis. Many unplanned towns along the road. To get into Carajás (checkpoint 35 km. from the project), you must have a permit, available from Companhia Vale Rio Doce (CVRD) in Marabá, São Luis, São Paulo or Rio (hotel bookings handled here too); apply in advance and have a good reason. There are flights from Brasília and São Luis by Varig and Vasp. Between Marabá and Belém, on the Tocantins river, is the Tucuruí hydroelectric scheme (which is causing much ecological damage), reached either by bus or by day and night riverboat from Belém. *Hotel Transamérica* best in Tucuruí; *Marajoara*, R. Lauro Sodré 685, T 787-1776, E, simple but OK. Floating bar (light meals), *Fluente*, 1½ km. N, take a taxi or motorboat, or walk, popular. To go to the dam, take bus "V Temp. I II" or " Vila Temporávia"; it is difficult to obtain a permit to visit the inside of the hydroelectric plant. From Marabá to Tucuruí, take Transbrasiliano bus, 3 a day, 8 hrs., US$8, road good to Itupiranga, deteriorates thereafter; also boat from Belém (32 hrs.).

The Transamazônica crosses the river Xingu at Altamira (pop. 47,000—*Hotel Globo*, D-E, good pizzeria opp.); the crossing is by ferry. The town is served by jets and boats from Belém, the airport is 8 km. from centre, no bus, exchange is difficult. Buses run from Tucuruí via Ripartimento. *Garimpeiros* sift the waters of the river bend to the east. No organised trips but a boat can be hired, US$20 per day, for a trip up the Xingu. Many animals. The area is an Assurine Indian reservation and it is not allowed to enter villages; buy food in Altamira.

**Rurópolis** (Presidente Medici) lies at the junction of the Transamazônica and the Santarém highway. Hotel run by Incra, "by all accounts, like the rest of the place: cracked, empty, dreaming of a future that never came" (Kevin Healey).

At **Itaituba** (the jumping-off place for the **Amazonia national park**; see Father Paul Zoderer, who may help to arrange a visit, at church on waterfront—nearest IBDF office, Av. Cons. Furtado 1303, Belém, CEP 66.000) the Transbrasiliana company has a bus station on the Rio Tapajós, near the ferry docks. Bus fare Itaituba-Marabá, US$25.

In **Humaitá** there are several basic hotels on the eastern edge of town; *Hotel Humaitá*, F, basic but friendly; *Aquarius Palace*, E with breakfast, is also the Expresos Humaitá bus stop; a similar hotel is the Andorinha bus stop. The Soltur bus station is in the centre. Lots of military activity in Humaitá.

There is very little traffic on the Transamazônica between Itaituba and Humaitá (1,028 km.); local drivers may give lifts. A ferry crosses the Rio Aripuanã at Vila do Carmo. The road is good for about 350 km. from Humaitá, then it deteriorates badly. It is hilly, narrow, and the jungle usually grows over the side of the road. Expresos Humaitá depart at 1500 daily. It takes 24 hours from Humaitá to Jacarèacanga, 597 km. (the town is 8 km. off the highway). One must stay overnight and catch the Transbrasiliana bus to Itaituba (24 hours, schedule erratic; the bus is replaced occasionally by a truck). There are two insanitary and expensive hotels in Jacarèacanga (try the gas station on the Transamazônica near the Jacarèacanga turn-off, they may have hammock space). Bus fare Humaitá-Jacarèacanga, US$25; Jacarèacanga-Itaituba, US$12; travel time depends on the weather conditions, the condition of the bus, and whether the driver decides to stop somewhere for the night.

## Up the Amazon River

The Amazon system is 6,577 km., long, of which 3,165 km. are in Brazilian territory. Ships of up to 4/5,000 tons regularly negotiate the Amazon for a distance of about 3,646 km. up to Iquitos, Peru. Regular passenger services as far as Manaus are operated by the State shipping line Enasa. Distances upstream from the river mouth to Manaus in nautical miles are:

| | | | |
|---|---|---|---|
| Belém | 80 | Santarém | 538 |
| Narrows (entrance) | 225 | Óbidos | 605 |
| Narrows (exit) | 330 | Parintins | 694 |
| Garupa | 334 | Itacoatiara | 824 |
| Prainha | 452 | Manaus | 930 |

**What to wear** Remember that some Enasa boats' restaurants do not permit shorts. Light cotton or poplin clothing for the day and, at night put on a sweater or coat, for it gets quite cold. From April to October, when the river is high, the mosquitoes at night can be repelled by Super Repelex spray or K13; protective clothing is advisable. Leather sandals fall apart in the wet, rubber ones are better, but proper shoes or boots are best for going ashore: there are many foot-attacking parasites in the jungle. (2 pairs of tennis shoes, so you always have a dry pair, is a good idea.) A hammock is essential on all but the most expensive boats; often too hot to lie down in cabin during day. Also take a hat and rain gear, such as a poncho with hood.

**Health** There is a danger of malaria in Amazonia, but no problems from mosquitoes on moving boats. Food may be cooked in river water; it is advisable to take your own food and water. On all classes of boat (except the most luxurious) sanitary standards are low and one is very likely to contract intestinal infections; take plenty of tablets (Colestase the locally available brand), toilet paper, soap, water sterilization tablets (none available in Belém) and some plain biscuits. A good idea also to take oranges, mineral water, tea bags, seasonings, sauces and jam. A yellow-fever inoculation is strongly advised; it is compulsory in some areas.

**N.B.** If going in the smaller boats, be prepared for mechanical breakdowns that prolong the journey. If you have the choice, remember that the small boats often keep close to the banks; the patient watcher can see plenty of wildlife.

Joanna Burrill and Henry Perks (of Hornsea, E. Yorkshire) have sent us the following information on river travel: Most boats have two decks and are divided into three classes: 1st class cabins (upper deck), which can be very hot and cramped; 1st class hammock space on upper deck, seems best as this is pleasanter during daytime; 2nd class hammock space on the lower deck, can be cramped because of cargo, and hot and noisy from the engine. Food is ample but monotonous. Fresh fruit is a welcome addition. Fresh coffee available; most boats have a bar of sorts. Plates and cutlery may not be provided. A strong fishing line and a variety of hooks can be an asset for supplementing one's diet; with some meat for bait, *piranhas* are the easiest fish to catch. Negotiate with the cook over cooking your fish. "The sight of you fishing will bring a small crowd of new friends, assistants, and lots of advice—some of it useful".

Light cotton hammocks" seem to be the best solution. Buy a wide one on which you can lie diagonally; lying straight along it leaves you hump-backed. Mosquito nets are not required when in motion as boats travel away from the banks and too fast for mosquitoes to settle, though repellant is a boon for night stops. Most boats begin their journeys in the evening, but stops en route come at any hour. If making connections en route it is easy to miss a boat in the night. On arrival at the final destination it is usually possible to negotiate with the captain to stay an extra night on the boat (perhaps more) for no extra charge. This can be useful if arriving in a town late.

**Exchange** facilities are sparse in Amazonia, outside Belém and Manaus. Bargaining with the masters of small boats may be greatly helped if one has some low-value dollar bills.

**Food in Amazonia** Inevitably fish dishes are very common, including many fish with Indian names, e.g. *pirarucu, tucunaré*, and *tambaqui*, which are worth trying. Also shrimp and crab dishes (more expensive). Specialities of Pará include duck, often served in a yellow soup made from the juice of the root of the manioc with a green vegetable (*jambo*); this dish is the famous *pato no tucupi*, highly rec. Also *tacaca* (shrimps served in *tucupi*), *vatapá* (shrimps served in a thick sauce, highly filling, simpler than the variety found in Salvador), *maniçoba* (a green vegetable mixed with cheaper cuts of meat). Avoid food from street vendors.

**Belém** (do Pará—population of city 1,120,000, of state 4,617,000), founded in 1616, 145 km. from the open sea and slightly S of the equator, is the great port of the Amazon. It is hot (mean temperature, 26°C), but frequent showers freshen the streets. There are some good squares and fine buildings. The largest square is the Praça da República; the main business and shopping area is along the wide Avenida Presidente Vargas leading to the river and the narrow streets which parallel it. The **Teatro da Paz**, one of the largest theatres in the country, is of neo-classical splendour, worth visiting, free concert and theatre performances are given (recently restored, open Mon.-Fri. 0800-1200, 1400-1800, tours cost US$0.40). There was much renovation of public places in 1985-87, but just as many old buildings are being replaced with ugly new ones.

Places to visit are the **Bosque Rodrigo Alves** (0900-1700 closed Mon.,) a public garden (which is really a preserved area of original flora), with a small animal collection, yellow bus marked "Souza" or "Cidade Nova"—any number—30 mins. from "Ver-o-Peso" market), and the **Museu Emílio Goeldi**. Both can be reached by bus from the Cathedral. The Museu Goeldi, Av. Magalhães Barata 376, takes up a city block and consists of the museum proper (with a fine collection of Marajó Indian pottery, an excellent exhibition of Mebengokre Indian lifestyle), a zoological garden (including manatees), and botanical exhibits including Victoria Régia lilies; open 0900-1200, 1400-1700, all day Mon, closed Fri. and Sun. pm. Entry US$0.80, additional charges for specialist areas, now renovated. The **Murucutu ruins**, an old Jesuit foundation, are reached by the Ceará bus from Praça República, through an unmarked door on the right of the Ceará bus station.

In the Belém market, known as **"Ver-o-Peso"** (see the weight) after the large scales on which the fish landed nearby were weighed, now has lots of gift shops with the charms on sale for the local African-derived religion, *umbanda*; the medicinal herb stalls are also interesting. In the old town, too, is the fort, which you can enter on request; the site also contains the *Círculo Militar* restaurant (entry US$0.75; drinks and *salgadinhos* served on the ramparts from 1800 to watch the sunset, restaurant is good). At the square on the waterfront below the fort the *açaí* berries are landed nightly at 2300, after picking in the jungle (*açaí* berries ground up with sugar and mixed with manioc are supposed to provide a balanced diet). Visit the **Cathedral** (1748) with several remarkable paintings, and directly opposite the 18th-century **Santo Aleixandre** church (now being restored) noted for its wood carving. The 17th-century **Mercês** church, near the market, is the oldest church in Belém; it forms part of an architectural group known as the Mercedário, the rest of which was heavily damaged by fire in 1978 and is being restored. The **Basilica of Nossa Senhora de Nazaré** (1909), built from rubber wealth, is an absolute must for its beautiful marble work and stained glass windows.

**Local Holidays** Maundy Thurs., half-day; 9 June, Corpus Christi; 15 August, accession of Pará to independent Brazil; Our Lady of Nazaré, second Sun. and fourth Mon. in October, known as Cirio. 30 Oct., half-day; 2 Nov., All Souls Day; 8 December, Immaculate Conception; Christmas Eve, half-day.

Cirio, the Festival of Candles in October, is a remarkable festival based on the legend of the Virgin of Nazaré, whose image is kept in her Basilica; it apparently was found on that site around 1700. To celebrate, on the second Sun. in October, a procession carries a copy of the Virgin's image from the Basilica to the cathedral. On the Mon., two weeks later, a further procession takes place, to return the image to its usual resting-place. There is a Cirio museum in the crypt of the Basilica, enter at the right side of the church; free. Exhibits from the celebrations of the past 100 years; enthusiastic guide. (All hotels are fully booked during Cirio.)

**Hotels** Expensive: *Hilton*, Av. Pres. Vargas 882, T 223-6500, L, swimming pool, sauna, restaurants; *Seltom*, 2 km. from airport, T 233-4222, A, swimming pool; *Novotel*, Av. Bernardo Sayão 4808, T 229-8011, L, with bath, a/c, TV, swimming pool, unprepossessing neighbourhood, far from centre (take Universidade bus); *Excelsior Grão Pará*, Av. Presidente Vargas 718, T 222-3255, B, fair breakfast, noisy a/c and internal rooms, reports vary, but good food, *Vitória Régia* restaurant, bars, swimming pool, sauna, Lusotur travel agency. Less expensive: *Vanja*, Av Benjamin Constant 1164, T 222-6688, B, good service, inexpensive rooftop restaurant, pool, rec.; *Regente*, Av. Gov. José Malcher 485, T 224-0755, 3-star, modest, comfortable, friendly, good breakfast; *Sagres*, Av. Gov. José Malcher 2927, opp. bus station, T 228-3999, air conditioning, good meals, swimming pool, English-speaking manager, B, reported run down; *Zoghbi*, R Padre Prudencio 220, T 241-1800, B, modern, rec.; *Verde Oliva*, Boaventura da Silva 1179 (T 224-7682), 10 mins. from centre, B, a/c, TV, good value, rec.; *Cambará*, 16 de Novembro 300, esq. Tamandaré, T 224-2422, B, a/c, good, mosquitoes; *Ver-o-Peso*, Castilhos Franco 214, T 224-2267, opposite Ver-o-Peso market, D, rooftop restaurant, TV and fridge in room, rec. *Central*, Av. Presidente Vargas 290 (T 222-3011), E without bath (D with bath and a/c), some rooms noisy, but friendly, clean, comfortable, good meals, a must for art-deco fans; *Vidonho*, same ownership, good, D-C with abundant breakfast, R. O. de Almeida, 476, T 225-1444, in a side street opp. *Novo Avenida*, Av. Presidente Vargas 404, T 223-8893, C, central, some rooms better than others, no backpackers, good breakfast; *Plaza*, Praça da Bandeira, T 224-2800, 2-star, D, a/c, bath, fridge, restaurant good value; across square is *Lis*, R. João Diogo 504 (old city), 1 star, D, with bath, a/ c, fridge, gloomy, short-stays accommodated, has good cheap restaurant, take care in this area, especially at night; *Vitória Régia*, Frutuoso Guimarães 260, E, with breakfast, noisy, clean, convenient for Enasa boats, owner changes money and cheques at good rates; next door but not so good is *Fortaleza*, Frutuoso Guimarães 276, D, with fan, safe; *Palácio das Musas* nearby, E, clean, friendly, built round a courtyard, large rooms; *Sete-Sete*, Trav. 1 de Março 677, E, comfortable, rec. Many cheap hotels close to waterfront, in old part of town.

**Camping** nearest at Mosqueiro, 86 km. away.

**Restaurants** All the major hotels have good but expensive restaurants. *Círculo Militar* rec. for Belém's best Brazilian food and situation in the grounds of the fort with view over river (good choice, try *filete na brasa*, expensive). *Churrascaria Sanambaia*, Quai Kennedy. *Casebre*, Av. Pres. Vargas 513, opp. Post Office, try *pato no tucupi*; (duck with kale) 1 serving US$4.50 is plenty for 2; *Trevu*, Pres. Vargas 396, good; *Marcilias*, Frutuoso Guimarães 329, good for fish; *Casa Portuguesa*, R. Manoel Barata 897, good, inexpensive; *Lá em Casa*, Av. Gov. José Malcher 247, try *menu paraense*, good cooking, expensive; *Miako*, Travessa 1 de Março 766, behind Praça de República (menu includes very good medium-priced oriental food); *Kyoto 294*, Trav. Dr. Morais 294, good Chinese; *Livorno*, Dr. Morais 314, good, mid-price; *Pizzaria Napolitano*, Praça Justo Chermont 12 (in particular pizzas and Italian dishes); *Cantina Italiana*, Benjamin Constant 1401, very good Italian food; *Churrascaria Tucuravi*, on the highway leading out of Belém, BR316, Km. 3. Vegetarian: *Nutribem*, R. Santo Antônio (off Av. Pres. Vargas) US$2 for as much as you can eat, lunch only; *Nectar*, Av. Gentil Bittencourt; *Boa Saúde*, Travessa P. Eutíquio 417, small, cosy and cheap; No. 248, pedestrian zone, good vegetarian, lunch only.

Specially rec. for tourists are also some very good snack-bars (mostly outdoors in Belém) where you can buy anything up to a full meal, much cheaper than restaurants: *Charlotte*, Av. Gentil Bittencourt 730, at Travessa Quintino Bocaiuva, for best *salgadinhos* in the city, also good desserts, very popular. A good bar next to *Hotel Central* , Pres. Vargas. *Só Delicias*, Nazaré 251, rec. for pastries, sweets, soft drinks. *La Crème*, snack bar on Praça Nazaré, sells exotic fruit ice creams, view of Basilica. *Sorveteria Cairu* in Umarizal has excellent ice creams, including 30 fruit flavours. *Casa dos Sucos*, Av. Presidente Vargas, Praça da República, serves 41 types of juice (including Amazonian fruits) and delicious chocolate cake (vegetarian restaurant upstairs). *Navegante*, R. Barata, *Tip-Top*, Trav. Pedro Catiquio and R. Pariquis (40 mins'. walk from harbour), excellent ice cream. *Bar do Parque*, next to Municipal Theatre, excellent place for meeting local people, the more flamboyant stroll here after 2100. There are also many street and market vendors, who, although they should be viewed with care, often sell delicious local food.

**Shops** in Av. Presidente Vargas; also try the Indian handicrafts shop at Praça Kennedy, set in a garden with Amazonian plants and animals. We have been told that Belém is an even better place than Fortaleza to buy hammocks, look in the street parallel to the river, 1 block inland from Ver-O-Peso.

**Entertainment**  *O Lapinha* discotheque/nightclub, good floor show, out of town, take taxi. *Rhinos*, Av. Nazaré 400, good discotheque, also *Pink Panther*, R. Aristedes Lobo 92. Lambada (see **Music and Dance**) originated in Pará.

**Exchange**  **Banco do Brasil**, Av. Presidente Vargas (near *Hotel Central*), good rates, and other Brazilian banks (open 0900-1630, but foreign exchange only until 1300). **Dias Lopes e Cia**, 5th floor R. Santo Antônio 316, also photo shop, 15 de Agosto on Av. Presidente Vargas, **Loja Morpho**, Presidente Vargas 362, **Orion Perfume Factory**, Trav. Frutuoso Guimarães, Sr. Milo, Travessa Campos Sales 28. *Central* (cash only), *Ver-o-Peso* and *Victória Régia Hotels*.

**Camera Repairs**  Neemias Texeira Lima, R. Manoel Barata 274, Sala 211, T 224-9941.

**Electric Current**  110 A.C., 60 cycles.

**Post Office**  Av. Presidente Vargas.

**Telecommunications**  Embratel, Travessa Quintino Bocaiúva 1186 (T 22-9099) or at the Post Office, Av. Presidente Vargas. For phone calls: Telepará, Av. Presidente Vargas.

**Consulates  Venezuelan:** 2 blocks from Trav. Benjamín Constant (new address unknown at time of going to press), open 0800-1300, T 222 6396. (Venezuelan visa takes 3 hrs., latest reports indicate that a yellow fever vaccination certificate is not required but best to check in advance—see also **Health** below, free for Danes, US$0.70 for Swedish, Swiss, W. German and Canadian citizens, US$2 for US citizens, all others US$10). **British**, R. Gaspar Viana 490, Caixa Postal 98, T 224-4822. **Swedish**, R. Santo Antônio 316, mailing address Caixa Postal 111, 66.000 Belém, T 222-4788, open 1600-1800; **Danish** (Consul Arne Hvidbo), R. Senador Barata 704, sala 1503, T 223-5888, (P.O. Box 826); **U.S.**, Av. Oswaldo Cruz 165. T 23-0800.

**Health**  A yellow fever certificate or inoculation was reported to be compulsory in mid 1990. Clínica de Medicina Preventativa, Av. Bras de Aguiar 410 (T 222-1434), will give injections, English spoken, open 0730-1200, 1430-1900 (Sat. 0800-1100). British consul has a list of English-speaking doctors.

**Tourist Office**  Municipal office, Detur, in airport and Rodoviária, good free map and guide. Hotel reservations made, including low-priced hotels. Paratur, Praça Kennedy on the waterfront, inside the handicraft shop; has a good map of Belém in many languages (but some references are incorrect). Town guidebook, US$2.75.

**Travel Agent**  *Ciatur*, Av. Presidente Vargas 645, T 224-1993, good half-day tour on water and in forest (US$13) and 32-hour trip to Marajó (US$200).

**Roads**  A good asphalted road leads E out of the city to the coast town of Salinópolis, some 223 km., at the extreme end of the eastern part of the Amazon Delta. Various paved roads branch off: 118 km. out of Belém one turns right on to the paved highway S to Brasília (2,120 km.). Straight on, the road leads to Bragança, the centre of an early, unsuccessful, attempt in the 1900s to transfer population to Amazonia. At Capanema (*Hotel São Luís*, F, good), on the road to Bragança, the road for São Luís, Teresina, Fortaleza and Recife branches right.

**Bus Services**  The Rodoviária is located at the end of Av. Gov. José Malcher 5 km. from centre, take Aeroclube, No. 20 bus, or Arsenal or Canudos buses, or taxi, US$5. It has a good snack bar and showers (US$0.10). There are four buses a day to **Brasília** (US$55), modern and comfortable, and also a *leito* bus— US$110, 36 hours. Belém-Imperatriz bus takes 10-12 hrs. (US$14). There are also direct buses from Belém to Marabá (16 hrs.), on the Transamazônica, via Porto Franco and Toncantinópolis, and then change to Santarém (Marabá-Santarém 34 hrs.). One direct bus Belém-Santarém once a week (US$36, more expensive than by boat and can take longer). To **Salvador** (US$50) and also to **Recife** (US$48), 1 daily, to each, 2000, 34 hrs. The trip to Recife can be broken at Teresina, Picos and Ouricuri, Pernambuco (*Hotel Independência*, T 933-1088, E, with bath). To São Luís, 3 a day, 13 hrs., US$17; to **Teresina**, US$18, frequent (but avoid Transbrasileira unless you want to stop everywhere); to **Fortaleza**, 1,595 km. 23 hrs., US$25, 4 daily; to **Rio**, US$83; to **Belo Horizonte**, US$76. If going to Campo Grande or Cuiabá, it may be better change in Goiânia than in Brasília.

**Hitch-hiking**  Going south, take bus to Capanema, 3½ hrs., US$3.20, walk ½ km. from Rodoviária to BR-316 where trucks stop at the gas station.

**Shipping Services**  Regular coastal services to Southern Brazil. Agency for international services, Agências Mundiais Ltda, Av. Pres. Vargas 121, T 224 4078.

Services to Manaus and Porto Velho by the **Government's Enasa boats** (office: Av. Presidente Vargas 41, T 223-3011 or 223-3572, Telex 2064, or R. Uruguaiana 39, sala 1402, T 222-9149 or 224-7267, Rio de Janeiro) whose schedules are published the 20th for the next month: they leave for Manaus at 2200 on the same day of the week in each month, normally Wed., but the day and frequency may change monthly, taking 5 days; they take cars and motorcycles (Sonave, Transnav, B. 15 de Novembre 226, T 222-9930/7025, and Jonasa are reportedly cheaper than Enasa; Envira also ship cars and have secure port facilities and showers.) You must show your passport when buying an Enasa ticket, at boat dock on Av. Castillo França (10-minute walk from centre). Ticket must be bought on Mon. for Wed. departure (but it is possible to buy on Wed. itself for an unofficial "fee"). Fare to Manaus, US$35, hammock space only, terribly crowded (least crowded are the couples' and single women's sections). Sanitary conditions are appalling; 3 meals a day are provided, but take your own food and drinking water (take your own cutlery to speed up the queuing). A hammock and rope are essential (easily bought for between US$5 and US$25, buy cotton ones); also useful is a light blanket. Arrive early (some say 8 hrs.) to ensure a good hammock space, chain belongings to a post in the hammock area (thieves abound) and don't drink from the drinking fountains on board: the small canteen sells mineral water, beer and soft drinks. Some advise sleeping outside, as it's cooler if the boat stops. For an inducement of say US$100, the captain may let you have a cabin. Enasa has a 10-day tourist service Belém-Santarém-Manaus-Santarém-Belém in new catamarans (*Pará, Amazonas*), leaving Belém every other Wed., Manaus every other Thurs., at 2000 with air-conditioned cabins, restaurant, swimming pool, bar, night club, with accommodation ranging from sharing in a 4-berth cabin, to internal double and external double cabins and special cabin. Also bookable through Soletur, R. Visconde de Pirajá 500, Suite 1708, 22410 Rio de Janeiro (T 239-7145, Telex 212 3858, 213 0237 SOLE BR); can include at extra cost a night in Manaus or Belém, or a week in Rio. Belém-Manaus (about US$70 less to Santarem in 4-berth and double cabins).

Non-Enasa fare to Manaus US$100 in covered hammock space (cabins US$200)—take food and water; look after your equipment, especially at night and in port. Ask guards at the dock gate for permission to look for a boat, there is no centralised information. Many boats will allow passengers to sleep on board free for 3 or 4 nights before sailing. Two companies that are recommended are Rodomar for destinations close to Belém (office near cathedral) and Fe em Deus, Av. Bernardo Sayão 3590 (take bus to Cremacão), recommended to Santarém *Fe em Deus IV*, 1st class hammock space, basic, crowded, take fruit, mineral water, books, 3 days, 4 nights). Also recommended to Santarém, *Cidade de Teresina IV* from quay 15, Trav. A. Montegro 192, T 522-2371, Benjamin Constant 1331, T 522-4521, cabin with fan, get a ticket if you pay in advance; Santo Agostinho company, Evani (nr. Fe em Deus) and *Terra Santa I*, also from Doca 15, Av. Bernardo Sayão, 3 meals included. Average fare for hammock space to Santarém, US$53, US$5-10 more for a cabin. Take a bus 514 from the city centre to the intersection 10 mins. beyond the Cata textile factory, and ask directions from there to the *posto comercial* area.

There is an **Enasa ferry to Macapá** about once a month, US$30 for hammock space, US$88 for cabin; check at docks; the Sonave vessel, *Idalino Oliveira*, sails approximately three times a month, departs Belém 0300 Weds., arrives Macapá 1000 Thurs., crowded, free chilled drinking water, good food and bar on board, passengers may embark at 2000 on night prior to sailing (tickets from Av. Castilhos 234), boat goes through the channels of Marajó Island; Representação do Governo do Território de Macapá ferry Belém-Macapá every 4 days or so, tickets from Av. Castilo França 234 (opp. Ver-o-peso), US$20 for hammock space, US$30 for cabin, 28 hrs. Enal, Av. Bernardo Sayão 1740, T 224-5210, sails Tues. and Sat., 36 hrs. Other non-regular sailings, *Príncipe do Mar* and *Príncipe do Mar II*, 2 days. Also *Barco Souza*, every Friday, return Tuesday (only 2 cabins), wait on board while cargo is loaded at Porto Santana; *São Francisco de Paula*, friendly, clean, food not too good, best to take some of your own. Weekly Enasa boat to Tucuruí on the Tocantins River at 1730 or later (with 5 stops, 32 hrs.; there are other boats to/from Tucuruí).

**Air Services** Bus "Perpétuo Socorro-Telégrafo" or "Icoaraci", every 15 mins. from Prefeitura to airport, US$1. Taxi to airport, US$9 (ordinary taxis cheaper than Coop. taxis, buy ticket in advance in Departures side of airport). Airport has a hotel booking service but operated by, and exclusive to, 5 of the more expensive hotels, discounts offered. Regular flights N to **Miami** once a week by Varig, S to **Brasília** and other Brazilian cities, and W to **Santarém** and **Manaus**, the latter with connection for **Leticia**, Colombia. To **Paramaribo**, twice, and **Cayenne** several times weekly. To **Oiapoque** on French Guyane frontier by Taba (R. O. de Almeida 408, T 223-8811). Travellers entering Brazil from Guyane may find it necessary to obtain a 60-day visa (takes two days) before airlines will confirm their tickets.

A suggested one-day sightseeing **tour**: "Go to the Ver-o-Peso market early in the morning when the boats are coming in and watch the unloading of the fish and the vendors in the market. Take a bus marked Souza at the market and ask the driver to drop you at the Bosque. Take the same bus back and get off at the Museu Goeldi in Av. Magalhães Barata. After visiting museum and gardens, walk down avenue to the Basílica (Nossa Senhora de Nazaré) and then on to the Praça da República. From the Edifício Manuel Pinto de Silva at this end of the Praça, you walk to the Teatro da Paz and along Av. Presidente Vargas. Before reaching the docks, turn left along, say, Av. Santo Antônio and Av. João Alfredo, through the shopping and commercial area (interesting narrow streets and open-fronted shops) to reach the harbour with its fishing boats and to the left the Prefeitura Municipal and Palácio do Governo. Beyond stand the Cathedral and the old fort and *Círculo Militar* restaurant. Depending on your progress, lunch can be taken by the Basílica (e.g. *Avenida* restaurant directly opposite), or on the terrace of Edifício Manuel Pinto, or, say, at *Hotel Central* on Av. Presidente Vargas.

**Excursions** Travel agents offer short and longer visits to the rivers and jungle. A return trip on the ferry from Ver-o-Peso to Icaoraci provides a good view of the river. The nearest beach is at **Outeiro** (35 km.) on an island near Icoaraci, about an hour by bus and ferry (the bus may be caught near the Maloca, an Indian-style hut near the docks which serves as a night-club). Further north is the island of **Mosqueiro** (86 km.) now accessible by toll bridge (US$0.20) and an excellent highway, with many beautiful sandy beaches and jungle inland.

Many hotels and weekend villas at the villages of Mosqueiro and Vila; rec. *Hotel Farol*, on Praia Farol, D, 1920s architecture in good repair, small restaurant, good views; *Hotel Murumbira*, on Praia Murumbira, C, pool, restaurant. Restaurants at Mosqueiro: in *Hotel Ilha Bela*, Av. 16 de Novembro 409, rec. for fish, at Praia Chapeu Virado; under same management is *Marésia*; *Pizzeria Napolitana*; *Sorveteria Delícia*, Av. 16 de Novembro, good local fruit ice creams, owner buys dollars. The traffic is heavy in July and at weekends, and hotels are full. Camping is easy. Buses Belém-Mosqueiro every hour from Rodoviária, US$1.20, 80 minutes.

**Marajó** Island is worth visiting for water buffalo hunting (use a camera, not a gun). It is becoming crowded at weekends. The island was the site of the precolumbian Marajoaras culture.

Boats leave Belém (near Porto do Sal, US$3, 5 hrs) most days for Ponta de Pedras (*Hotel Ponta de Pedras*, F, good meals). Bicycles for hire (US$1 per hr.) to explore beaches and the interior of the island. Fishing boats make the 8 hr. trip to Cachoeira do Arari (1 hotel, E,) where there is a Marajó museum. A 10 hr. boat trip from Ponta de Pedras goes to the Arari lake where there are two villages, Jenipapo (1 *pousada*, E,) built on stilts, "Forró" dancing at weekends, and Santa Cruz which is less primitive, but less interesting (a hammock and a mosquito net are essential). There are water buffalo on the lake. There is a direct boat service to Belém twice a week.

Trips to the island are arranged by the *Grão Pará Hotel* and travel agents in Belém. Alternatively, a light aircraft may be hired to see Marajó from the air e.g. from Kovacs, Av. Dr. Freitas, opposite the airfield of the Aero Clube do Pará.

At Soure, on the island, are *Hotel Soure* (walk straight on from Enasa dock, then take 3rd street on left), E p.p. full board, good excursions arranged; *Pousada Marajoara* and *Pousada Parque Floresta*, nearby, E, friendly and clean, good meals. *Pensão da Dona Maria*, G, 2nd Street 575 (*Bar Guarani*), simple rec. *Canecão*, Praça da Matriz, sandwiches, meals, rec. Changing money is only possible at very poor rates. Take plenty of insect repellent. There are fine beaches, Araruna (2 km.—take supplies and supplement with coconuts and crabs, beautiful walks along the shore), the Pesqueiro (bus from Praça da Matriz,1030, returns 1600, eat at *Maloca*, good, cheap, big, deserted beach, 13 km. away) and Caju-Una (15 km.).

**Salinópolis** (228 km.) about 4 hrs. by bus (US$4.50) on excellent highway, also worth a visit. Seaside resort with many small places where you can eat and drink at night by the waterfront, and fine sandy beach nearby (buses and cars drive on to the beach), a peaceful place mid-week. Best during holiday month of July. Atalaya, opposite Salinópolis, is pleasant, reached by taxi (US$8) or with a fisherman.

**Hotels** *Solar*, Av. Beira Mar s/n, D with bath, best in town, good restaurant; *Salinas*, on beach, E; *Jeanne d'Arc*, E with breakfast, reported poor value.

There are ferries and daily flights from Belém to **Macapá** (pop. 168,000) a town on the northern channel of the Amazon Delta, which used to be decrepit but is now improving, particularly along the riverfront. (The ferries often go to Porto Santana, 30 km. from Macapá, to which there are frequent buses, US$0.45, and shared taxis US$3.20 p.p., boats readily hired to visit river communities). Macapá is the capital of Amapá (agriculture, gold, manganese, coal, timber), one-quarter the size of France but with only 234,000 inhabitants. Each brick of the Fortaleza de São José do Macapá, built 1764, was brought from Portugal as ballast. Interesting market behind the Fortaleza. A handicraft complex has been built next to the Novotel. The riverfront has been pleasantly developed. There is a monument marking the equator halfway between Porto Santana and Macapá, known as Marco Zero, with nightclub underneath and more nearby.

The popular local beach is at Fazendinha (take bus of same name), extremely lively on Sundays.

**Hotels** *Novotel*, French-owned, on waterfront, T 222-1144, small, 4-star, A+, all rooms a/c, swimming pool, service and cleanliness strongly criticized as being far below acceptable standard; *Tropical*, Av. Antônio Coelho de Carvalho 1399, 20 mins. from centre, one star, T 231-3739, E with a/c (cheaper without), rec.; *Glória*, Leopoldo Machado 2085 (just round corner from *Tropical*, 20 mins. walk from centre), T 222-0984; *Santo Antônio*, Av. Coriolano Jucá 485, T 222-0226, near main square, E, very clean, fan, shower, good breakfast extra. *Meruno*, F, central, good value; *Amapaense Palace*, R. Tiradentes 109, T 222-3366, E-D, 2 star, a/c, cold showers, comfortable, clean (*lanchonete* in same building, poor). The following are 10-mins. walk from port and from Praça São José (where bus from Porto Santana stops): *Mata*, R. São José 2390, F with fan; *Mercúrio*, R. Cândido Mendes, 1300 block (no sign), F.

**Restaurants** *O Boscão*, Hamilton Silva 997, no sign, quite good; *Portenho*, Hamilton Silva 1390; *O Paulistano*, Av. Henrique Galúcio 412, a/c, good; *Pizza San Carlos*, Cândido Mendes 1199, good for lunch; *Lennon*, good pavement café, no meals, at R. Gen. Rondón esq. I.C.Nunes. Excellent ice cream sold in Macapá. e.g. *Sorveteria Amapaense*, nr. *Hotel Santo Antônio*, good, wide selection.

**Exchange** Banco do Brasil, near *Novotel*, or in *Novotel* itself, rates reported better than in Belém. Good rates also with gold merchants around Canal da Fortaleza.

**Transport** Ferries: Enal, R. Machado de Assis 59, Porto Santana, T 632-6141/6196, to Belém Wed. and Sun., Enasa depart by 10th of every month. Check departures at Porto São Benedito, Av. Bernardo Sayão 868, T 222-6025, **see page 458.** Four **flights** daily to Belém (including night flight), about 45 mins, with Cruzeiro do Sul (also to Santarém, Manaus daily) and Vasp. Taxi airport-town US$3.50, about 4 km.

Rubber was almost the only product of the Territory until the 1950s, when manganese was discovered 150 km. NW of Macapá. A standard-gauge railway, 196 km. long, the only one in Brazil, has been built from the mining camp to Porto Santana, from which there is an excellent road. Malaria is rampant in Amapá; the illiteracy rate is 85%; smuggling goes on in a big way. But the mining area—Icomiland, pop. 4,000—is a startling exception: swimming pools, football fields, bowling alleys, supermarkets, dance halls, movies, a healthy oasis in the wilderness.

IBDF office, R. Hamilton Silva 1570, Santa Rita, CEP 68.900, Macapá, has details on the **Cabo Orange National Park** in the extreme north of the Territory, and the **Lago Piratuba Biological Reserve**, neither accessible by road.

Sr João Batista de Oliveira Costa in Macapá is a good pilot who flies around the delta, particularly to the mouth of the Araquari river to see the *pororoca*, a tidal wave that travels upriver in the high tides of spring and autumn.

An unpaved road has been built from Macapá northward to the small town of **Oiapoque** (one government hotel, deteriorating, expensive and poor restaurant), on the coast near the French Guyane border; road completed halfway to Calçoene (government-owned hotel by bus stop E, expensive food in adjoining canteen; sleeping space advertised in a café on Oiapoque road, very cheap), via Amapá (*Tourist Hotel* and one other, E, clean, comfortable—one block from square towards docks, turn right, 2nd house on left). In the wet season, Jan.-May/June, buses and trucks only run on the sealed road; with luck it is possible to get to Calçoene, sometimes only Tartanga Grande. Amapá is better than Calçoene for travelling on. Macapá-Amapá bus, US$10.50, 6 hrs.; daily Estrela de Ouro bus Macapá-Calçoene from Praça Veiga Cabral (timetable varies), US$12.50, 7 hrs. (minimum), many delays, book at least 2 days in advance. 80 km. from Calçoene is Lourenço, the centre of the local gold rush. For the 216 km. from Calçoene to Oiapoque there is a bus scheduled for 0700, Mon., Wed., Fri. (US$8), but it often does not run (also an unscheduled government lorry, which does not run in the rainy season; you can hitch from Macapá, take a private lorry (little traffic), costing US$7 to 15, or hire a vehicle—for all means you will be overcharged. From Oiapoque a ferry goes to St. Georges (Fr. Guyane), US$2, 15 mins.—a bridge is being built; be sure to get exit and entry stamps on either side of the border: in Oiapoque the Federal Police station is 100 m. back from river near the church on the road to Calçoene, and in St. Georges visit the Gendarmerie Nationale (no customs). Prices in Oiapoque are about twice the rest of Brazil. It is impossible to get francs anywhere in St. Georges (try in Brazil). **Warning** Everyone must have a visa for entering French Guyane here, obtainable in Belém, but not Manaus. This is a most difficult border crossing for tourists: the authorities seem to believe that no-one other than Brazilians or Guyanais will want to make the attempt.

No regular sailings from Macapá to Oiapoque are made; try in Porto Santana where most boats are heading for illegal entry into Guyane (if you take one you'll have trouble explaining how you got in to the French authorities.) There are Taba flights twice daily from Macapá to Oiapoque continuing to Belém, unreliable service heavily overbooked in wet season, try stand-by at airport; Taba office in Oiapoque on the quay by the ferry, rarely open. Varig, Cruzeiro and Vasp have 4 flights a day between them to Belém. It is possible, but hard, to fly Amapá-Oiapoque. (Taxi into Oiapoque US$3, bus US$1.25.) If using Paris-Cayenne route as a cheap way to South America, it is recommended to fly Cayenne-Belém, compared with five days of discomfort and delays overland from Cayenne to Macapá (you have to fly Cayenne-St. Georges anyway.

## Belém to Manaus

A few hours up the broad river the region of the thousand islands is entered. The passage through this maze of islets is known as "The Narrows". The ship winds through 150 km. of lanes of yellow flood with equatorial forest within 20 or 30 metres on both sides. In the Furo Grande the vessel rounds a hairpin bend almost touching the trees, bow and stern.

After the Narrows, the first point of special interest is formed by the curious flat-topped hills, on one of which stands the little stucco town of Monte Alegre (airport), an oasis in mid-forest.

*Santarém* (pop. 250,000) 2-3 days upstream on the southern bank, stands at the confluence of the Tapajós River with the Amazon, just half-way between Belém and Manaus. It was founded in 1661, and is the third largest town on the Brazilian Amazon. The yellow Amazon water is mottled with greenish patches from the Tapajós; the meeting of the waters is said by some to be nearly as impressive as that of the Negro and Solimões near Manaus. There is now a road southwards to Cuiabá (Mato Grosso), meeting the Transamazônica at Rurópolis (**see page 453**). (The southward leg from the Transamazônica to Cuiabá begins about 90 km. W of this point, or 20 km. from Itaituba.) Timber, bauxite and gold discoveries have promoted very rapid growth of the city, which has become very expensive. It is the jumping off point for gold prospectors in the Mato Grosso territories to the South. It is reported that prospectors are exploited by high prices, and that lawlessness abounds in the goldfields. The unloading of the fish catch between 0500 and 0700 on the waterfront is an interesting scene. There are good beaches nearby on the river Tapajós.

**Hotels** *Santarém Palace*, close to city centre, Rui Barbosa 726, T 522-5285, good, C with bath and TV; *Tropical*, Av. Mendonça Furtado 4120, T 522-1533, B, de luxe, swimming pool seems to be unrestricted, friendly staff, good chef (but not "de luxe" cooking), meals for around US$5, excellent value; *San Rafael*, R. dos Bares 222 (T 232-8335/8488), B, pleasant, rec., English and German spoken; *City*, Trav. Francisco Correia 200, T 522-4719, D with bath, a/c, TV, radio, frigobar, good; *Central Plaza*, Praça Rodrigues dos Santos 877, D, with bath and fan, run-down, friendly, *São Luís*, Travessa Sr. Lemos 113, near market, D, reported dirty;

*Horizonte*, Travessa Lemos 737, E, clean; *Brasil*, Travessa dos Mártires, 30, E, including breakfast, good meals served, clean, good service, English spoken, owner plays chess; *Equatorial*, E, good value, friendly, but noisy.

**Restaurants** *Mascotinho* bar/pizzeria, on beach, popular, good view, US$5 for pizza for 2; *Storil*, Travessa Turiano Meira, 2 blocks from Rui Barbosa, good fish (dinner about US$4.25), live music, takes credit cards; *Ritz*, Praça do Pescador, good, US$3 lunch; *Lanchonete Luci*, Praça do Pescador, good juices and pastries; *Sombra do Jambeiro*, Trav. 15 de Novembro, Norwegian-owned bar and lanchonete, excellent meals.

**Banks** It is reported that hotels are unwilling to change dollars at the tourist rate, try **Farmácia Java** or travel agencies.

**Health** Dr Ihsan Youssef Simaan, T 522-3886/3982, speaks English and Spanish.

**Travel Agents** *Amazon Tours*, Trav. Turiano Meira 1084, T 091-522-2620, run by Steve Alexander (from Alaska), highly reasonable and recommended, has produced a useful guidebook on Santarém. He also has a property in the jungle for overnight tours, also highly recommended. *Gil Serique*, Caixa Postal 76, CEP 68100, T 522-5174, Telex 91-5489, English-speaking guide, rec. *Coruá-Una Turismo*, 15 de Novembro 185-C, CEP 68100 T 522-6303/7421 offers various tours, Pierre d'Arcy speaks French, rec.

**Airport** 15 km. from town. Internal flights only. Buses to centre or waterfront. From centre bus leaves in front of cinema in Ruy Barbosa every 80 mins from 0550 to 1910, or taxis (US$10 to waterfront); *Hotel Tropical* has a free bus for residents; you may be able to take this.

**River Services** Small launches leave for Manaus 2-5 days, most days, examples of fares to Manaus: US$90 1st class (upper deck cabin), US$45, 2nd class (upper deck hammock), US$35, 3rd class (lower deck). You may sleep on board (in hammock) days before departure. Enquire at the waterfront. Enasa, Thaiz Agripina Matos 1089; T 522-1138. For Manaus, *Moreira da Sibra III*; Luciatur; *Rio Nilo*, also rec.; and *Onze de Maio*, overcrowded, poor food, has bar; *Dejard Vieira*, Praça E. Ribeiro, T 533-1806, a reliable company. For Belém (average fare US$53), *Franz Rossy*, every second Thursday at 1200, 3-4 days; *Cidade de Teresina*, Wed. 1800, 2 nights, adequate. For Macapá (Porto Santana), 36-48 hrs., e.g. *São Francisco de Paula*, clean, efficient, friendly, good food, leaves Mons. at 1830. Boats, to Manaus or Belém, including Enasa, may leave from the waterfront in town, as well as from the "Cais do Porto" dock (where all boats arrive), about 4 km. from the centre; take bus marked "Circular" or "Circular Externo" (US$0.15), both of which go to Cais do Porto, and pass Rodoviária. Guards will allow you to enter the dock and look for boats, but you may have to wait several days for a cargo/passenger boat going in either direction. Along the river, closer to the centre, are numerous boats, usually leaving daily, for Itaituba (daily, 1800, arr. late next morning), Óbidos, Oriximiná, Alenquer or Monte Alegre. Do not buy tickets from touts.

**Buses** Rodoviária is on the outskirts, take "Rodagem" bus from the waterfront near the market, US$0.20. Santarém to Itaituba, 8 hrs. US$8.50; there connecting service east to **Marabá on the River Tocantins**, 28 hrs. (if lucky, can be 60 hours, or even 6 days), US$40, 1830 with Trans Brasiliana. Also to Imperatriz, 46 hrs., US$45, office on Av. Getúlio Vargas and at Rodoviária. (Beware of vehicles that offer a lift, which frequently turn out to be taxis.)

**Excursion** to Altar do Chão, a village set amid Amazonian vegetation on the river Tapajós, at the outlet of Lago Verde; hotel (D), comfortable; *Pousada* near the church, quiet, clean; luxury hotel to be built shortly; *Restaurant Mongote*, Praça 7 de Setembro, good fresh fish, huge portions; *Lago Verde*, try *calderada de tucunaré*; good swimming in the Tapajós from the beautiful, clean beach; bus from Mercado Municipal, Santarém, leaves 0500, 1100, 1600, 1½ hrs., returns 0630, 1230 and 1730 approx. (rugged, but fun). Boat tour from *Hotel Tropical* US$25. Also by 1000 bus to Porto Novo, 3 hrs. into jungle by a lake, bus returns 0330 next morning (you can sleep in it). Interesting wildlife on lake; canoe can be hired.

37 km. S from Santarém on a dirt road is *Belterra* (pop. about 8,000), where Henry Ford established one of his rubber plantations, in the highlands overlooking the Tapajós River. Ford built a well laid-out new town; the houses resemble the cottages of Michigan summer resorts. Many of the newer houses follow the white paint with green trim style. The town centre has a large central plaza that includes a band stand, the church of Santo Antônio (circa 1951), a Baptist church and a large educational and sports complex. There is a major hospital which at one time was staffed by physicians from North America and attracted people from Manaus and Belém. There has been little replacement of old trees: extraction has been the only activity. As a result, the rubber forest is in bad condition since the late 1940s. (*Hotel Seringueira*, E, with about 8 rooms and pleasant restaurant).

Fordlândia was the Ford Motor Company's first rubber plantation, founded in 1926, but it was never profitable; it is a friendly town since there are few visitors. *Hotel Zebu*, in old Vila Americana (turn right from dock, then left up the hill); one restaurant, two bars and three shops on town square. There is a little pebble beach north of the town.

Bus from Santarém to Belterra (from unmarked *Café Amazonas*, Travessa Moraes Sarmento between Rui Barbosa and São Sebastião), 1000 and 1230, Mon.-Sat., return 1300 and 1530, US$1.60, about 2 hrs.—note: one hour time difference between Santarém and Belterra so if you take the 1230 bus you'll miss the 1530 return bus). If driving, take Av. Santarém-Cuiabá out of town, which is paved for 8 km. At Km. 37 is a small Shell station; fork right and stop at the guardhouse; it's 15 km. into town, following the electricity cables. Boats from Santarém to Itaituba may stop at Fordlândia if you ask (leave Santarém 1800, arrive 0500-0600, US$10 for 1st class hammock space); ask the captain to stop for you on return journey, about 2300. Boats may stop for Belterra, but it's a walk of several km. from the river to town.

110 km. up-river from Santarém is **Óbidos** (pop. 45,000) a picturesque and clean city, located at the narrowest and deepest point on the river. For many kilometres little is seen except the wall of the great Amazonian forest. Small airport.

*Manaus*, the next city upstream, was at one time an isolated urban island in the jungle. It is the collecting-point for the produce of a vast area which includes parts of Peru, Bolivia and Colombia. There is superb swimming in the natural pools and under falls of clear water in the little streams which rush through the woods, but take locals' advice on swimming in the river; electric eels and various other kinds of unpleasant fish, apart from the notorious *piranhas*, abound and industrial pollution of the river is growing.

Until recently Manaus' only communications were by river and air, but now a road SW to Porto Velho, which is already connected with the main Brazilian road system, has been completed and partly paved. Another, not yet fully paved, has been built due N to Boa Vista, from where other roads already reach the Venezuelan and Guyanese frontiers.

Manaus (1.1 million people) is the capital of the State of Amazonas, the largest in Brazil (1.6 million square km), with a population of 2.1 million. Though 1,600 km. from the sea, it is only 32 metres above sea-level. The average temperature is 27°C. The city sprawls over a series of eroded and gently sloping hills divided by numerous creeks (*igarapés*). Dominating the centre is a Cathedral built in simple Jesuit style on a hillock; nothing distinguished inside or out. Nearby is the main shopping and business area, the tree-lined Avenida Eduardo Ribeiro; crossing it is Av. Sete de Setembro, bordered by ficus trees. The area between Av. Sete de Setembro and the rear of *Hotel Amazonas* is now reserved to pedestrians. There is a modern air-conditioned theatre. Manaus is building fast; 20-storey modern buildings are rising above the traditional flat, red-tiled roofs. It was the first city in South America to instal trams, but they have now been replaced by buses.

The main attractions are the **Botanic Gardens**, the well stocked public library, and the legendary Opera House, the **Teatro Amazonas**, completed in 1896 during the great rubber boom following 17 years of construction and rebuilt in 1929. It seats 685 people and was restored in 1974. A further restoration was started in 1987 and has now been completed; for information on programmes, T 233-0929/234-3525 (open Tues.-Sun., 0900-1500, guided tour US$2.50). Another interesting historic building is the **Mercado Adolfo Lisboa**, commonly known as the Mercado. It was built in 1902 as a miniature copy of the now demolished Parisian Les Halles. The wrought ironwork which forms much of the structure was imported from Europe and is supposed to have been designed by Eiffel. It was restored in 1978. There is a curious little church, the **Igreja do Pobre Diabo**, at corner of Avs. Borba and Ipixuna in the suburb of Cachoeirinha; it is only 4 metres wide by 5 metres long, and was built by a worker (the "poor devil" of the name); take Circular 7 Cachoeirinha bus from cathedral to Hospital Militar.

The remarkable **harbour installations**, completed in 1902, were designed

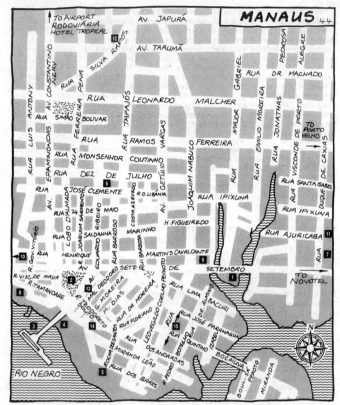

**MANAUS** 44

Key: 1. Palácio Rio Negro (Government Palace), 2. Cathedral, 3. Floating Harbour, 4. Alfândega (Customs House), 5. Mercado Municipal, 6. Opera House/Teatro Amazonas, 7. Museu do Índio, 8. Museu do Porto, 9. Museu do Homem do Norte, 10. Instituto Geográfico Histórico (off map), 11. Rubber factory, 12.Tourist Office, 13. Post Office, 14. *Hotel Amazonas*, 15. Cheap hotel area.

and built by a Scottish engineer to cope with the up to 14 metre annual rise and fall of the Rio Negro. The large passenger ship floating dock is connected to street level by a 150-metre long floating ramp, at the end of which, on the harbour wall, can be seen the high water mark for each year since it was built. When the water is high, the roadway floats on a series of large iron tanks measuring 2½ metres in diameter. The material to build the large yellow Alfândega (customs building) near the harbour was brought block by block from Scotland as ballast. Tourists can visit the docks 0730-2000 daily.

**Local Holidays** 6 Jan. (Epiphany); Ash Wed., half-day; Maundy Thurs.; 24 June (St. John); 14 July; 5 Sept.; 30 Oct.; 1 Nov., All Saints Day, half-day; Christmas Eve; New Year's Eve, half-day.

    **14 Jan.**: Anniversary of Praça 14 de Janeiro, commemorates the founding of the bairro; Samba Schools, street market, and fun fair. **Feb.**: Carnival, dates vary—5 days of Carnival, Amazonense culminating in the parade of the Samba Schools, Avenida Djalma Batista. **3rd**

**week in April**: Week of the Indians, Indian handicraft, talks, photographic exposition, various localities. **First fortnight of June**: Festival Marquesiano, three days of festival, regional and Afro-Brazilian dancing, Arabian, Russian and European folklore, held at the Campo da Amizade, São Raimundo; Festival Folclórico do Amazonas, **second fortnight**, Praça Francisco Pereira da Silva, Bola da Suframa. **Second fortnight of Aug**: this is reported to be second only to Carnival. Fair of the Amazonian Wood Furniture and Artefact Industry, SESI, Est. do Aleixo Km. 5. **10 Sept**: Travessia Almirante Tamandaré, swimming race across the Rio Negro (8500 metres) leaving from Praia da Ponta Negra; **also in Sept.**: Fair of the Amazonian Clothing Industry **second fortnight**, SESI, Est. do Aleixo Km. 5; Festival de Verão do Parque Dez, **second fortnight**, summer festival with music, fashion shows, beauty contests, local foods, etc., Centro Social Urbano do Parque Dez; Festival da Bondade, **last week**, stalls from neighbouring states and countries offering food, handicrafts, music and dancing, SESI, Est. do Aleixo Km. 5. **Nov.**: Festival Universitário de Cultura (entire month) with music, art and book exposition, organized by the students on the University Campus. **8 Dec.**: Procissão de Nossa Senhora da Conceicão, from the Igreja Matriz through the city centre and returning to Igreja Matriz for a solemn mass.

**N.B.** Manaus time is one hour behind Brazilian standard time (2 hrs behind during October-March when rest of Brazil is on summer time).

**Crime** is reported to be increasing. Take care of baggage and personal safety (see **Information for Visitors**).

**Hotels** Extremely crowded, especially in Jan.-Feb., when hotels often raise their prices steeply. Prices are high generally; we give high season prices, so reductions may be available at other times. Many hotels offer a special price for triple occupancy. 10% tax and service must be added to bills.

*Tropical*, Praia de Ponta Negra, T (92)238-5757, a lavish, 5 star Varig hotel 20 km. outside the city (taxi to centre, US$20), L+, very expensive, discount with a Varig air pass, *Restaurant Tarumã* open for dinner only, *churrascaria* by pool, open to non-residents on weekdays only (well-dressed non-residents may use pool on weekdays, take bus, US$3 for non-residents, from R. José Paranaguá in front of Petrobras building esq. Dr. Moreira 0830, 0930, 1130 to Hotel, 1200, 1400, 1500, 1800 to town, or take Ponta Negra bus, US$0.35, then walk to hotel). It is rarely full, except in Jan.-Feb. Parkland setting, pools when not being renovated, small zoo with animals in small cages, departure point for many river cruises, tennis. Do not exchange money here, official rate only; don't pay in dollars or with credit cards for same reason. Also away from centre, *Novotel*, Av. Mandii 4 in the Industrial Area, T 237-1211, L, 4 star, luxurious, pool, US$1.75 taxi ride from centre, reported markedly less good than *Tropical*; *Las Vegas*, Joaquim Nabuco 2235, D, restaurant, T 234- 0250; *Da Vinci*, R. Belo Horizonte 240, B, 3 km. from centre, pool, friendly service.

Central hotels: *Amazonas*, Praça Adalberto Vale, T 234-7679, 4 star, L, the ground floor is not rec., but rooms are reasonable, hot water, a/c, and it's the best of a poor lot for business travellers; opp. *Amazonas* is *Ana Cassia Palace*, expensive, R. dos Andradas 14, T 232-6201, A; A highly rec. Aparthotel is *St. Paul*, R. Ramos Fereira 1115, T (092) 233-3006, Fax 233-2471, best in town, A+, suites with bath, kitchen, living room, has pool, gym and sauna; its restaurant, *Le Point*, is excellent. *Lord*, Marcílio Dias 217/225,T 234-9741, L, some rooms a/c, expensive for what they offer, with good breakfast, good service; has a cheaper annex. *Premier*, Av. Eduardo Ribeiro 124, D some rooms with TV and fridge, friendly, good value; *São Rafael*, R. dos Barés 222, T 232-8488, B, clean, safe, helpful, tours arranged, close to waterfront and market. In Av. 7 de Setembro; *Palace* (593), T 234-5764, old refurbished building, a/c but cramped, C; *Monaco*, R. Silva Ramos 20, T232-5211, 3 star, A, rooms have good view, pleasant, rooftop restaurant/bar, but poor breakfast; *Nova Avenida*, Av. Pres. Vargas, D, helpful, rec.; *Janelas Verdes*, Leovegildo Coelho 216, T 233-1222, D, a/c, shower, TV, small, quiet (except Sun.), safe, T 233-1222; *Fortaleza*, R. dos Bares 238, E with fan, reasonable, rec; *Dez de Julho*, Dez de Julio 679, T 232 6280, D, a/c, clean, rec.

In R. G. Moreira: *Rio Mar*, (325, T 234-7409), incl. breakfast and bath C, poor service reported, central; *Central* (202), T 232-7887, C, some a/c, quiet, very good value; *Internacional* (168), B-C (2-stars), T 234-1315, a/c, friendly, central, coffee most of the day, good exchange rates; *Nacional* (59), T 233-0537, C with bath, fridge, a/c; *Rey Salomão* (No. 119, T 234-7374), E, clean, breakfast.

In Av. Joaquim Nabuco: *Doral* (687), E, T 232-4102, a/c, friendly, excellent breakfast, rec.; *Pensão Sulista* (347), T 234-5814, E with fan, no breakfast, laundry facilities; *Aurora* (130), E with bath, a/c, friendly, clean, noisy TV; *Artêrio*, No. 471, near corner with R. Lima Bacuri, E with a/c or fan, clean, large rooms with bath; *Bela Vista*, No. 278, E without bath *Manauara*, No. 129, E with bath, a/c, fridge, coffee all day, friendly, has TV; *Luz* and *Iguaçu*

T 232-9339, (Nos. 779 and 711 respectively) are better than most on this street: the former is singles only above a gym, clean, breakfast included at *Iguaçu*, both E. *Hospedaria Olinda*, R. L. Coelho y J. Paranaguá, F, clean, quiet; *Rio Branco*, R. dos Andradas 484, E, rec., avoid damp rooms on ground floor, clean, safe, laundry facilities, a/c, popular, friendly, clothes-washing facilities; *Dona Joana* No. 553, same street, T 233-7553, E, a/c, clean, good value, rec.; *Jangada*, F, same street, cooking allowed, rec.; other cheaper places in same area. *Nadie*, opp. Rodoviária, F.

*O Explorador* **Youth Hostel**, R. Silva Ramos 685 (central, T 234-6796, P.O. Box 2890), F p.p. not inc. bedding or beakfast, non-IYHA members welcome, popular, booked up 3 weeks ahead, tours arranged, Spanish, English, French and Italian spoken, rec.; **N.B.** Lori Kornblum suggests keeping your room key, in view of reports of staff allowing bogus police officers into guests' rooms. **N.B.** also, when taking a taxi from the airport, insist on being taken to the hotel of your choice, and not to the one which pays the driver commission.

**Camping** There are no campsites in or near Manaus; it is difficult to find a good, safe place to camp wild. It is possible to camp wild on the bank of the Rio Negro near the *Hotel Tropical*; through outskirts of city via Tarumã bathing waterfalls to Ponta Negra bathing beaches, 20 km. Good swimming. Bus daily (US$0.35). Camping Praia Dourada, showers, toilets, restaurant, boat hire, good swimming, busy at weekends.

**Electric Current** 110 volts A.C.; some hotels 220 volts A.C., 60 cycles.

**Restaurants** *Novotel* serves a rec. *feijoada completa* on Sat.; *La Barca*, R. Recife 684, wide variety of fish dishes, classy, popular, often has live music; *São Francisco*, Blvd. Rio Negro 195, 1/2 hr. walk from centre (or bus 705), in Educandos suburb, good fish, huge portion, US$5.50, highly rec.; *Panorama* next door, No. 199 (also good for fish, cheap). *Caçarola*, R. Maués 188, Cachoeirinha, T 233-3021, very good local fish dishes (take a taxi); Japanese at *Miako*, R. São Luís 230, also *Suzuran*, Blvd. Álvaro Maia 1683, Adrianópolis, good, closed Tues., taxi US$2; *Búfalo*, churrascaria, Joaquim Nabuco 628, all you can eat (of high quality) for US$13. *O Vegetariano*, R. Rui Barbosa 128, good, also take-away, open 1100-1430 Mon.-Fri.; another at Saldanho Marinho 429B; *Chapaty*, R. Costa Azevedo 105, vegetarian. *Mandarin*, Av. Eduardo Ribeiro 650, good Chinese, all you can eat, lunch US$5; *Maté Amargo*, R. Saldanha Marinho 603, good buffet, all you can eat; *Forasteiro*, R. Dr Moreira, No. 178, excellent fish dishes; *Mister Pizza*, R. José Paranaguá 104 (Praça da Polícia), good pizza and sandwiches, a/c, upstairs; *Fiorella*, R. Pará 640, good Italian; *Veneza*, Av. Getúlio Vargas 570, good Sat. *feijoada*; *Jangada Bar*, opp. *Hotel Amazonas*, good for snacks; good, but expensive snacks in *Hotel Amazonas* itself; *Alemã*, cafeteria, R. José Paranaguá/Praça da Polícia, good for juices, sandwiches, cakes; good *pratos* at Brasileiros department store, Av. 7 de Setembro. The floating retaurant in the harbour below the market building is rec. for best *tucunaré* fish. Many restaurants close on Sunday nights and Mondays. City authorities grade restaurants for cleanliness: look for A and B. Good juice bars along Av. Joaquim Nabuco, try *cupuacu*. **Lanchonete Pigalle** particularly rec.

The fishing catch is brought to the waterfront between 2300-0100, including the giant pirarucu. Good fruit and vegetable market by the port.

**Markets and Souvenirs** Go to the *Mercado Adolfo Lisboa* (see above) early in the morning when it is full of good quality regional produce, food and handicrafts (open daily 0500-1800). In Praçada Saudade, R. Ramos Fereira, there is a Sunday *Festa de Arte* from 1700; try prawns and calaloo dipped in *tacaca* sauce. In the Praça do Congresso, Av. E. Ribeiro, there is a very good Sun. craftmarket. See the two markets near the docks, best in the early morning. Indian handicrafts in the Museu do Indio, R. Duque de Caxias (nr. Av. 7 Setembro). The **Central Artesanato** Handicraft Centre (R. Recife s/n, nr. Detran) has local craft work. *Casa de Beija-Flor*—The House of the Hummingbird (R. Quintino Bocaiúva) good and centrally located. *Selva Amazônica*, Mercado Municipal, for wood carvings and bark fabric. For hammocks go to R.dos Andradas where there are many shops. In R. Duque de Caxias is a rubber factory open to the public.

**Bookshop** *Livraria Nacional*, stocks some French books, the *Livraria Brasília* has some English books.

**Car repairs** Mavel VW, highly recommended, English spoken.

**Entertainment** *Spectrum*, R. Lobo D'Almada 322. *Canoas*, Miranda Leão 167A, good live music, bar, expensive but rec. Cachoeirinha has a number of bars offering music and dancing, liveliest at weekends. *Superstar*, next to the terminal; *Orvalho da Noite*, R. Santalsabel 1000; *Nostalgia Clube*, R Ajuricaba 800; *Clube de Samba*, R Manicoré.

**Clubs** Ideal; Athletic Club of Rio Negro; Bosque (bathing pool, tennis courts).

**Cinema** The cinemas in Manaus are located in: R. José Clemente (opp. Teatro Amazonas); R. Joaquim Sarmento (corner R. 24 de Maio); Av. Eduardo Ribeiro (Manaus Shopping Centre); Av. Joaquim Nabuco (400m. north Av. 7 de Setembro); Av. Joaquim Nabuco (800m. north Av. 7 de Setembro); R. Jonathas Pedrosa (corner Av. 7 de Setembro). Most foreign films are shown with original soundtrack and Portuguese sub-titles. Afternoon performances are recommended as long queues often form for the evening performances.

**Museums Museu do Índio** (Indian Museum), kept by the Salesian missionaries, the museum's collection includes handicrafts, ceramics, clothing, utensils and ritual objects from the various Indian tribes of the upper Rio Negro, R. Duque de Caxias (nr. Av. 7 Setembro); open Mon.-Fri. 0800-1200 and 1400-1700, Sat. 0800-1200, T 234-1422, US$0.30; **Museu do Porto de Manaus** (Harbour Museum), kept by Portobras, the national harbour authority, holds various historical pieces, documents, letters, diaries and charts, R. Vivaldo Lima 61 (nr. Harbour); open Mon.-Sat. 0700-1100 and 1300-1700, Sun. 1200-1700, T 232-0096; **Museu Tiradentes**, kept by the Military Police, the museum holds selected historical pieces and old photographs, Praça da Policia; open Mon. 1400-1800, Tues.-Fri. 0800-1200 and 1400-1800, T 234-7422; **Museu de Minerais e Rochas** (Geological Museum) contains a large collection of minerals and rocks from the Amazon region, Est. do Aleixo 2150; Mon-Fri 0800-1200 and 1400-1800, T 236-1582; **Museu do Homem do Norte** (Anthropological Museum) reviews the way of life of the Amazonian population; social, cultural and economic aspects are displayed with photographs, models and selected pieces, Av. 7 de Setembro 1385 (nr. Av. J. Nabuco); open Mon-Fri 0800-1200 and 1300-1700, T 232-5373; **Instituto Geográfico e Histórico do Amazonas**, located in one of the older districts of central Manaus, houses a museum and library of over 10,000 books which thoroughly document Amazonian life through the ages, R. Bernardo Ramos 117 (nr. Prefeitura); open Mon.-Fri. 0800-1200, T 232-7077, US$0.20; **Museu de Ciências Naturais da Amazônia** (Natural Science Museum), newly inaugurated, has a pavilion with insects and fish of the region, Est. Belém s/n (difficult to get to, best take a taxi), Tues.-Sun. 0900-1700, T 244-2799.

**Jardim Botânico "Chico Mendes"** The botanical gardens, now renamed after the murdered Amazonian rubber tapper and trade union leader, contain a collection of plants from the Amazon region. Unfortunately the plants are not well named. Av. André Araujo s/n (Buses Aleixo, Coroado). Daily 0800-1200 and 1400-1700.

**Zoo** Run by CIGS, the Brazilian Army Unit specializing in jungle survival. About 300 Amazonian animals are kept in the Gardens, panthers, tapirs, monkeys, alligators and various species of birds (latest description of the conditions for the animals is "appalling"). Est. Ponta Negra 750. Bus 205 or 217 (marked "Ponta Negra"), US$0.35, every ½ hr from R. Tamandaré, opp. cathedral in centre, alight 400 metres past the 1st Jungle Infantry Barracks (a big white building). Open 0800-1700. Entrance for foreigners, US$0.75. Small zoo also at *Hotel Tropical*, see above. Instituto Nacional de Pesquisas Amazonas (INPA), Estrada de Aleixo, at km. 3, not far from the Natural Science Museum (any bus to Aleixo), has named trees and manatees (best seen Wed. and Fri. at 0830 when water is changed), caimans and giant otters; worth a visit and good for birdwatchers.

**Exchange Lloyds Bank**, R. Guilherme Moreira 147; **Banco do Brasil**, R. Marechal Deodoro (5th floor) and Airport (basement) changes dollars at tourist rate, efficient; many local banks. Open 0900-1600. Most offices shut afternoons. Foreign exchange operations 0900-1200 only, or close even as early as 1100. Reported that only Banco do Brasil and Lloyds will change US$ notes. It is possible to change US$ at the airport; open 24 hrs. a day. **Exchange** at the main hotels but not the *Tropical*, (see above), at Souvenirs de Manaus shop and at Luciatur, Av. Eduardo Ribeiro 365, Minitur and Selvatur (good rates); Sr Lima, R. Quintino Bocaiúva 189, Sala 34; try also bakery opp. *Hotel Rio Branco* for cheques, Francisco or Agostinho at 1st floor, Dr Moreira 105, in pedestrian shopping centre, and Sr. Ayoub, Av. 7 de Setembro 711. **Canto Turismo**, R. Rui Barbosa, good rates. It is not safe to change money on the streets.

**Consulates** Most open a.m. only. **Peruvian**, Conjunto Aristocratas, Chapada, R. A, Casa 19 (T 236-3666, open 0800-1400). **Colombian**, please note that apparently the Colombian consul (R. Dona Libânia 62, near opera house, T 234-5777) has been advising travellers from Manaus to Leticia that if they are only visiting Leticia they do not require a tourist card. Either get your Colombian tourist card before reaching Manaus or tell the consul you are travelling further into Colombia, which will probably then require proof of money and return ticket. **Venezuelan**, R. Recife 1620, T 236-0406 (bus Cachoeirinha Chapada, alight near Detran), 0800-1500; the Consul will give you a visa only if you have an air ticket into and out of Venezuela; 2 passport photos required. **Bolivian**, Av. Eduardo Ribeiro 520, Sala 1410, T

237-8686.

**British**, Eduardo Ribeiro 520, Sala 1202 T 234-1018. **United States**, R. Dr Machado 106 T 234 4546 (office hours) and 232 1611 (outside office hours), Mr. James R. Fish. Will supply letters of introduction for US citizens. **Germany**, R. Barrosa 355, 1st floor, room A, T 232-0890; **Spain**, Instalação 124, T 234-0465; **Dutch**, R. M.Leão 41, T 234-8719/223-6874; **Italy**, R. Belo Horizonte 240, T 234-8059; **Japanese**, R. Ferreira Pena 92, T 232-2000; **Danish**, R. M.Leão 45, T 233-6094; **Norway**, R. Terazina 256, T 234-7073; **Belgium**, 13 qd D conj Murici, T 236-1452; **Portugal**, R. Terezina 193, T 234-5777.

**Police** Take bus from *Hotel Amazonas* to Kissia Dom Pedro for Policia Federal post, people in shorts not admitted.

**Hospital** of tropical medicine, treatment free, some doctors speak a little English: take "Dom Pedro" bus from main terminal, about 20 min. ride. Dr Hank Koolen, T 234-5955, English-speaking, is sympathetic to sick gringos.

**Laundromat** Blvd Álvaro Maia 1570, Mon.-Sat. 0800-2200, coin operated, take mini bus ROTA 05 from Av. 5 de Setembro.

**Post Office** Main office including poste restante in Marechal Deodoro (for American Express, R. Saldanho Marinho 530). On the first floor is the philatelic counter where stamps are sold, avoiding the long queues downstairs. Staff don't speak English but are used to dealing with tourists. For airfreight and shipping, Alfândega, Av. Marones Santa Cruz (corner of M. Deodoro), Sala 106. For airfreight and seamail, Correio Internacional, R. Monsenhor Coutinho e Av. Eduardo Ribeiro, downstairs (bring your own packaging). **UPS** office, T (092) 232-9849 (Custódio).

**Telephone** TeleAmazon on R. Guilherme Moreira, opp. Banco do Brasil (most central); Av. Getúlio Vargas, about 7 blocks N of 7 de Setembro.

**Tourist Information** Emamtur, Praça 24 de Outubro, R. Tarumã 379 helpful, airport and floating harbour. Town map from *Hotel Amazonas* or from Amazon Explorers, *Hotel Lord*. *Guide Book of Manaus*, US$3, available from *Hotel Amazonas* and other places, in English, useful. *A Noticia*, newspaper, lists local entertainments and events. Tucumaré Turismo, R. Henrique Martins, T 234 5071, will give information and make reservations.

**Tours** There are many different kinds of tours: "luxurious", which are comfortable but "set up" for tourists; some aiming at seeing lots of animals, and others at seeing how the people in the jungle live. Be sure to ascertain in advance the exact itinerary of the tour, that the price includes everything (even drink and tips), that the guide is knowledgeable and he himself will accompany you, and that you do not want to kill anything rare. It is worth shopping around for the best service and bargaining may reduce prices. **N.B.** Guides must be officially registered with Embratur and must carry an identity card.

Bill Potter, resident in Manaus, writes: opposite Manaus, near the junction of the Rio Negro and the Rio Solimões, lies the Lago de Janauri, a small nature reserve. This is where all the day or half-day trippers are taken usually combined with a visit to the "meeting of the waters". Although many people express disappointment with this area because so little is seen and/or there are so many "tourist-trash" shops, for those with only a short time it is worth a visit. You will see some birds and with luck dolphins. In the shops and bars there are often captive parrots and snakes. The area is set up to receive large numbers of tourists, which may relieve pressure on other parts of the river. Boats for day trippers leave the harbour constantly throughout the day, but are best booked at one of the larger operators such as Amazon Explorers or Selvatour.

Those with more time can take the longer cruises and will see various ecological environments, but bear in mind that most tour operators will make a trip up the Rio Negro because it is easier to navigate, generally calmer and there are many fewer biting insects. There is also much less animal life in general, so to see any patience and luck are needed. To see virgin rainforest a 5 day trip by boat is needed. On the Rio Solimões there is more wildlife, but you are less likely to see anything because you'll be constantly fighting the mosquitos and sandflies.

Another alternative is to go up river to one of the jungle hotels. From the base, you can then take short trips into the forest or along the river channels.

Taking a transport boat from Manaus is not a substitute for a tour as they rarely get near to the banks and are only interested in getting from A to B as quickly as possible. The passengers see very little of the forest. An exception to this rule is the Enasa tourist service to Belém, where the boat tries to take a route more interesting for tourists.

*Amazon Explorers Manaus Ltda*, run by Manoel (Bebê) Barros, R. Quintino Bocaiúva

189, T 232-3052 his day's tour including "meeting of the waters", Lago do Janauari and rubber collecting and lunch has been highly recommended by most users; 32-hour trips, require a minimum of 4 people; other tours available. Boat *Amazon Explorer* available for hire at about US$230 per day. **Kurt Glück**, Quintino Bocaiúva 224, Caixa Postal 361, offers a more personal service; his shortest boat trips, which need to be booked as far in advance as possible, last five days in an open 5.5 metre canoe, and he explores many of the tributary rivers of the Amazon; maximum two persons. **Transamazonas Turismo**, Leonardo Malcher 734, T 232-1454/232-4326 (reservations through South American Turismo, Av. N.S. de Copacabana 788, T 255-2345, 22050 Rio de Janeiro), for parties of 10 or less offers a 3-days-plus stay at *Amazon Lodge*, a floating lodge on Lake Periquitão, 80 km. from Manaus, or *Amazon Village*, an hotel on dry land, about US$200 basic charge, inc. meals and transfers, + US$50 per night, recommended, book well in advance. **Windjammer Adventures Club**, owner and operator Hans Budig, multilingual, rec, Caixa Postal 541, AG.M. Coutinho 69000, T 234-6028/1580, USA T (212) 986-9191. *Ariaú Jungle Tower*, Rio Amazonas Turismo, at *Hotel Monaco*, R. Silva Ramos 41, T 234-7308, 35 km from Manaus on a side channel of the Rio Negro, 16 rooms and penthouse, 35-metre high observation tower and a 1-km walkway across a swamp, trips to Anavilhanas islands, US$250 basic fee inc meals and transfers, plus US$50 per night, generally good, but US$5 surcharge for non-residents. **Iaratur**, Guilherme Moreira 297, Room 21, 3rd floor, rugged trip, US$60 per day, rec.; **Iguana Tours**, R. Floriano Peixoto 210, S1 101, T 232-5305, US$60 per day, rec.; **Amazon Indian Tours**, R. dos Andrades, 335, basic cheap trips, US$100 for 5 days, rec. at the price. The better hotels also arrange tours (ask for Joe Sears in *Hotel Tropical*), and so do **Selvatur** (office in *Hotel Amazonas*, T 233-2900), Rio Negro trip, 0800-1300, with lunch at *Janaurylândia* floating hotel, returning at 1500. **Jungle Trips**, R.Guilherme Moreira 281, 3-day jungle trip, all included, irrespective of numbers. **Safari Ecológico**, Av. Marechal Câmara 160, Sala 621, Caixa Postal 3321, CEP 20.010, Rio de Janeiro, T (021) 240-6785, has been recommended for its 3 and 6 day/night ecological tours on the Amazon. (Manaus address: R. Lima Bacury 204, T 233-6910, bookings also through Carretour du Brésil, Paris; Brazil Nuts, Fairfield CT, USA; Jolivac, Montreal. All tours are accompanied by guide, scientific adviser and doctor; boat is equipped with full safety equipment; jungle walks, fishing, visits to cabocle settlements and boatyards, swimming, nighttime excursions.

There appears to be an endless supply of guides; the minimum cost for a tour in 1990 was US$40-50 p.p. per day, with some charging much more than that. Those listed below have been positively recommended by travellers: for trips on the Amazon and Rio Negro, **Moacir Fortes**, R. Miguel Ribas 1339, Santo Antônio, Manaus, T 232-7492 or through Amazonia Expeditions Ltd, Houston, T (713) 660-8115 (has his own 19-metre boat *Amazonia Expedition*), he speaks English and German. **Ernesto Carvalho**, Cx. Postal 2890, Manaus, contactable through *Hotel Rio Mar*, does a 3-day, 3 night trip 80 km. up the Solimões to the Lagoa do Janauaca, using local boats. Also **Gerry Hardy**, contact through *Hotel Rio Branco*, or T (092) 2376981, or **Paul Hardy**, R. Efigénio Sales, Cond. Jardim Vila Rica, Quadra B, Casa 6, 69060 Manaus, T 236 8734, English-speaking, 4 days US$150, min. 4 people, everything included extremely helpful, highly rec.; **Vincente Charles Juvencio**, P.O. Box 2552, T 232-4877, fluent English, trips highly rec. **FM Turismo** (director Pedro Neto), R. Saldanha Marinho 700, T 232-8811/233-9428, Telex 092-1348 FMUR, English spoken, specializing in special interest and professional groups, rec. **Manoel**, R.J. Pedrosa 313, T 232-2707, has his own agency and jungle lodge, US$40 p.p., per day, a few places in his own house, F with use of kitchen, rec; **Elmo de Morais López** and **Cássio Serra Vieira**, Amazon Tours, R. Henrique Martins 364, Centro, for 2-5 day tours, 2-4 people, sleeping in hammocks; **Gentil Metelo**, P.O. Box 2792, Manaus, T 236-5894/232-4876, has his own agency, 10-metre covered canoe, access to 14-metre, diesel-powered boat with crew, will arrange tours from 1 hour to 1 month, very knowledgeable, speaks Portuguese, English, French, Spanish and Italian; **Marco Valério Teixeira**, P.O. Box 2968, Manaus, T 234-1315/6, or contact through *Hotel Internacional*, offers a 3-day tour involving a one-day canoe journey beyond the Lago do Janauaca, one day in a camp, then the final day returning by bus (along BR-319) and ferry. **José Nunes** is a guide who speaks fluent English and has a combi for general transport (T 233-5102); **Cristóvão Amazonas Turismo**, Marechal Deodoro 89, Salas 605/1203, T 233-3231, experienced jungle guides, reasonably-priced tours for 1, 2 or more days, German, English, French, Italian, Spanish spoken, very helpful. **Miguel M. Barbará** (El Barón), Caixa Postal 1227, Manaus 69.000, operates the *XarR.* for tours on the Rio Negro, US$100-120 for 4; **Francisco Almeida**, *Aventura Turismo*, R. 10 de Julho 130, loja 2, P.O. Box 949, T 234-0197, also arranges tours on the Rio Negro; **Rubens Silva**, Eduardo Ribeiro 420, has been recommended for his 3-day trip up the Rio Branco for 2-5 people; **Carlos Francisco Viana**, Av. Epaminondas 751-9, US$60 p.p. for 3 days, all inclusive; **Francisco da Silva Karaja**, R. Dapaz 189A, T 238-5592, speaks English and French; **Luis Alberto Motta**, R.

Carla Tupinambá Nobre, Quadra 22, Casa 30, Conjunto Belvedere (take bus "Alvorada 2", alight at Panificadora Belvedere). Motorized canoes can be hired from behind Mercado Municipal, US$50 for 6-hr. trip, takes 8, with navigator/guide, goes to inaccessible places. Gemma McGrath advises, go to the docks by the meat market and ask for Capitão Julio, T 233 8741, or Capitão Pedro who arrange trips on demand, good food, they are knowledgeable about where to find wildlife, 3 days 2 nights US$50, "a mind-blowing experience".

For those prepared to spend around 10 days in the interior on a real expedition, contact **Carlos Colares**, Av. Atlântica 91, Raiz, 69.000 Manaus, T 092-237-1961, Telex 092-165 XPMNA, or P.O.Box 360, who conducts private excursions, with fishing, hunting and exploring in the more remote regions of the Rio Negro. Carlos Colares speaks good English. Similar tours arranged by **Sabrina Lima de Almeida**, R. Boa Esperança 6, T 237-7359, Portuguese speaking only, rec.

Generally, between April and September excursions are only by boat; in the period October-March the Victoria Regia lilies virtually disappear. Fishing is best between September and March (no flooding).

Bird-watchers can see many kinds of birds in and around the grounds of the *Hotel Tropical* (for instance: fly catchers—kingbirds and kiskadees, swallows, yellow-browed sparrows, aracaris—member of the toucan family, woodpeckers, woodcreepers, thrushes, anis, three species of tanager, two of parrots—the dusky and blue-headed). Sloths and monkeys may also be seen. Bird-lovers anxious to pursue their hobby on the Amazon River and its backwaters should contact Moacir Fortes, see above for address and further details (we are grateful to John and George Newmark of Eastbourne for this information).

The enterprising go to the Capitânia do Porto and find out what boats are making short trips; e.g., Manaus-Itacoatiara, US$10 first-class. For swimming, it is possible to travel to Ponta Negra beach (no shade) by Soltur buses for US$0.35, though beach virtually disappears beneath the water in April-August and is now polluted. Good swimming at Bolívar Falls; in the river Tarumã, where lunch is available, shade, it is crowded at weekends, and not too nice; take Tarumã bus from R. Tamandaré or R. Frei J. dos Inocentes, ½ hr., US$0.35 (very few on weekdays), getting off at the police checkpoint on the road to Itacoatiara.

About 15 km. from Manaus is the confluence of the Solimões (Amazon) and the Rio Negro, which is itself some 8 km. wide. Here you can see the meeting of the blue-black water of the Rio Negro with the yellow-brown Solimões flood; the two rivers run side by side for about 6 km. without their waters mingling. Tourist agencies run boat trips to this spot, or if travelling on a tight budget you can get up about 0330 in Manaus, take a "milk boat" such as the *Capitão Braga* (try to arrange the day before) at about 0400. It returns about 1300, passing through the confluence. Also the *Joanne d'Arc* leaves the dock area around 0730 and returns late afternoon, and the *Castelo II*, 0800 to 1500 to the confluence, US$3. Alternatively hire a motorized canoe from near the market for about US$10 per hr. (you'll need 3 or 4 hrs. to take in the experience properly). The simplest way is to take a taxi or No. 617 "Vila Buriti" bus to the Careiro ferry dock, and take the car ferry across. The ferry goes at 0700, returning 0900, 1200, returning 1500, and 1600, returning 2100 (approx.). You can also take small private launches across, 40 mins. journey, about US$10 per seat, ask for the engine to be shut off at the confluence, you should see dolphins especially in the early morning. A 2-km. walk along the Porto Velho road from the Careiro ferry terminal will lead to a point from which Victoria Regia water lilies can be seen in April-September in ponds, some way from the road. If you continue over the Capitari bridge, you reach unspoilt jungle. There are several small restaurants on the S bank in Careiro, where the road SW to Porto Velho and the South begins.

To **Manacapuru** to see a typical Amazon town, 84 km on AM-070 by bus, São Raimundo (30 mins.) at 0800 and 1000, there is a special bus which is quicker, ferry from São Raimundo (30 mins.) and 2-hr. bus ride (bus every hour, it is reported that a bridge is down and the trip takes much longer); buy bus ticket before you get on the ferry: don't wait till you arrive at the other side. A small market town on the Solimões W of Manaus, with three basic hotels, *Rio Branco*, clean, friendly, and *Il Maccarone* pizzeria, Av. Eduardo Ribeiro 1000, with its friendly Italian owner Mário. Another village one can visit is **Araçá**, a 3-hr bus ride from Rodoviária in the direction of Castanho; the journey includes a ferry crossing at the confluence of the Negro and Solimões (fare to Araçá US$0.70, bus leaves 0600 and 1100). The village is on the banks of the Rio Mamori; canoes can be hired for US$3-5 for a day (night trips also possible) and you may be able to sling your hammock in a private house. Plenty of wildlife close at hand. 3 buses a day return to Manaus. Helmut Zettl of Austria, recommends a trip from São Raimundo to Barcelos on the Rio Negro, in the boat *Emerson Madeiros*, 2 days, and a night an *Hotel Oasis*, where you can meet Tatunca Nara, a Brazilian von Daniken.

**Roads** To *Itacoatiara*, 285 km. E on the Amazon, with Brazil-nut and jute processing plants (bus service 8 a day, 4 hrs); now paved route AM-010, 266 km, through Rio Preto da Eva.

A mostly unpaved road in poor condition and closed in rainy season runs N from Manaus to Boa Vista (770 km.—see below). To hitch-hike from Manaus to Boa Vista, take a Tarumã bus to the customs building and hitch from there, or try at "posta 5", 2 km. beyond Rodoviária.

The Catire Highway (BR 319) from Manaus to Porto Velho (868 km.), which is supposedly paved with work continuing (in poor shape nonetheless throughout), sometimes closed March-May during the rainy season, and during the dry season for repairs (latest report, April 1991, said the road is impassable with no repair in sight). When the road is closed drivers have to ship a car down river on a barge. Bus, Manaus-Porto Velho, 0830 and 1400 with Eucatur, US$24, 24 hrs, more in rain, best to book in advance. Bus to Humaitá; 679 km., where the Catire Highway crosses the Transamazônica, twice a day, 18 hrs. (including 5 ferry crossings), US$15; three buses a day from Humaitá to Porto Velho (3 hrs. with one ferry crossing, paved stretch), 257 km., US$4.80. If driving this highway, the following information may be useful (but note that conditions change greatly according to season): the first ferry (Careiro da Várzea) is pretty disorganized; at Km. 40 there is a bridge and a floating grocery store; ferry at Km. 42; at the town of Careiro (second place of this name), about Km. 80, third ferry, there is a service station where you can camp, and the US priest here (Father Jim) welcomes English speakers at his church on the square. At Km. 245, Sentinela dos Pampas, there is a ferry across the Igapó-Açu, petrol and camping; between this ferry and Km. 325, Hevelândia (service station, branch road AM-464 84 km. SE to Madeira river opp. Manicoré) the road deteriorates, but improves a little to Piquiá, Km. 500, where there is a clean restaurant with showers and toilets (service station also at Jutaí, Km. 370). If there is no petrol at Km. 500, there is another station at Km. 570. As the road approaches the turnoff to Humaitá (Km. 672), it improves. Between Humaitá and Port Velho there is a service station at Km. 700.

Bus station is 5 km. out of town at the intersection of Av. Constantino Nery and R. Recife; take local bus from centre, US$0.35, marked "Aeroporto Internacional" or "Cidade Nova" (or taxi, US$6.40). Local buses to Praça 14 or airport leave from opposite *Hotel Amazonas* (take airport bus and alight just after Antártica factory) or take local bus to Ajuricaba.

**Air Services** International flights: Varig to Bogotá twice a week, Panama and Miami once each; LAB twice weekly to La Paz (via Santa Cruz), Caracas and Miami. Manaus-Iquitos, Cruzeiro do Sul, once or twice a week (Sat./Wed.), stopping at Tefé and Tabatinga for Leticia. To Georgetown, Guyana, Cruzeiro once a week stops at Boa Vista, otherwise to the Guyanas, connection must be made in Belém. Make reservations as early as possible, flights may be full. Do not rely on travel agency waiting lists; go to the airport 15 hrs. early and get on the airport waiting list.

Internal flights: There are frequent internal flights with Varig, Vasp and Transbrasil. The most frequent routes are Brasília-Rio, Brasília-São Paulo and the N.E. Coast milk run Santerém-Belém-Sao Luís-Teresina-Fortaleza-Recife. Transbrasil tends to be cheaper than the others. For flights to other Amazon towns call Taba (232-0149). Taba flights can be irregular and often reservations cannot be changed. Return reservations cannot be made with Taba when purchasing ticket. Vasp flies to Santarém, Altamira, Belém, São Luís, Teresina, Fortaleza, Recife, Brasília, São Paulo, Rio Branco, Porto Velho, Vilhena, Cuiabá and Campo Grande.

The taxi fare to or from the airport is US$20, but settle price before journey or obtain a ticket that fixes flat-rate fares, or take bus 608 or hourly bus 201 marked Aeroporto Internacional from R. Tamandaré near cathedral, US$0.35. Last bus at night to airport from R. Tamandaré at 2345; last from airport is 2330. (Taxi drivers often tell arrivals that no bus to town is available, be warned!) It is sometimes possible to use the more regular, faster service run by the *Tropical Hotel*; many tour agenices offer free transfers without obligation. Check all connections on arrival. N.B. Check in time is 2 hours in advance. Allow plenty of time at Manaus airport, formalities are very slow, and there are queues for everything. The restaurant serves good à la carte and buffet food through the day, "certainly much better food than you are going to get on your flight." It is possible to sleep on the airport observation deck if catching an early morning flight. Local flights leave from airport terminal 2: make sure in advance of your terminal.

**Shipping** For details of Enasa services, **see page 458.** We are advised that it is better to travel Manaus-Santarém and Santarém-Belém in local boats than to use the normal Enasa service, though to Belém the direct trip by M.V. *Benjamín* is acceptable. Enasa to Belém once a week at 1800, the day is normally Thur., but day and frequency may change every month, but in any one month it's the same day of the week (buy ticket in advance, Enasa office closes 1130 on Sat. very crowded, board early); 4 days, one class, hammock space only, US$35; insanitary, with inadequate number of life jackets; bar on board (foreigners 1st class only fare comparable with night flight). Take your own cutlery and utensils, they are unobtainable after the first meal; it is advisable also to take own food. The address of the Enasa line is R. Mal Deodoro 172, Ed. Galeria Central, 6th Floor, Suite 601, T 232-7084. Taxi from centre to docks, US$2. Occasional German vessels.

Fairly frequent (irregular) river boats to Tefé (3 days), and Benjamin Constant (see below). Boa Vista, 60 hrs to Carcaraí then 3½ hrs by bus. Porto Velho (US$140 in 2-berth cabin, US$60 2nd class, 7 days, 3 days downstream at high water, rec. boat, *Clívia*). Buy a hammock (*rede*—pronounced "hedgie", best in R. dos Andrades) if travelling 2nd or 3rd class, plenty of drinking water and plenty of books to read; often the boats only stop at night. Boats to Santarém almost every evening except Sun. (about 1800), from E end of dock, journey can be as little as 33 hrs.; prices vary, roughly US$35 lower deck, take earplugs to reduce engine noise, US$45 upper deck, US$90 cabin (Navio Motor Emerson); *Dejard Viera*, leaves Wed., 1800 37 hrs.; *Cidade de Natal*, well rec.; also rec. *Miranda Dias*, small, family-run, reasonable food and sanitary conditions; *Ayapua* (cold at night) including meals, leaves Manaus every Fri. 1830 (no guaranteed connection to Belém). Also rec. to Santarém, *Rio Nilo*, leaves Wed. 1800, clean, good food, 2 nights; also M.V. *Onze de Maio*, leaving each Tues. evening, its sister ship doing return at same time, good meals, top deck with chairs, tables. Shipping a car: Enasa (fortnightly) in cooperation with Transnav, Av. 7 de Setembro 1251, Room 612, T 234-1062/1570 (talk to Geraldo Brandão), ships cars to Belém for US$250, plus US$35 per passenger. Car's height must not exceed 3 m.; lock all valuables in car, set alarm, and check each day at least twice. 1 hr. customs at Belém (none in Manaus), cars and passengers disembark separately (pay staff for using wooden ramp if water is too low). Hammock space only, single men and women segregated, couples or couples with children not so; bring all food and drinking water, sanitary conditions disgusting. Also Sonave Cia, Entrada do Bombeamento 20, Compensa, Manaus, T 234-4803/4302, telex 092-2463 SOCN, rec., weekly to Belém, inc. meals (no variety), sleep in car or hammock; cheaper if you load the car on to an empty truck (trucks are shipped on pontoons, so you may get your car on one of these). Jonasa, which leaves from Compensa, is somewhat cheaper than Enasa and Sonave for shipping cars to Belém. The Capitânia do Porto, Av. Santa Cruz 265, Manaus, has a list of all shipping (you won't be allowed in wearing shorts). All boats, when berthed, display destination and time of sailing so you can check facilities and costs. Boats for Belém and international shipping leave from west end of the docks (entrance at Capitânia do Porto), all others from east end, where a new pier is being built. The shipping agencies are beside the market halls on left of BR316, 1 km. before the landing point, also the cargo harbour.

**N.B.** Be careful of food on the boats; may be cooked in river-water. You may need a visa to travel to Peru; consulate address above. Those arriving from Leticia should go to the police for their immigration entrance stamp, but you should get this in Tabatinga. Departures to the less important destinations are not always known at the Capitânia do Porto. Be careful of people who wander around boats after they've arrived at a port: they are almost certainly looking for something to steal.

**Passports** For those arriving by boat who have not already had their passports stamped, the immigration office is on the first of the floating docks next to the tourist office. Take the dock entrance opposite the cathedral, bear right, after 50 metres left, pass through a warehouse to a group of buildings on a T section.

**Tefé** (pop. 26,000) lies approximately halfway between Manaus and the Colombian border. The waterfront consists of a light sand beach; waterfront market Mon. a.m.; the nuns at the Franciscan convent sell handicrafts and embroidery; there are three small hotels and five pensions (*Anilce*, Praça Santa Teresa 294, E, clean, a/c, do not leave valuables in your room, very helpful; *Hotel Panorama*, rec., good restaurant), the restaurant *Au Bec d'Or* by the port, French/Amazonian cuisine. Airport with connection to Manaus. Recommended boat, *Captain Noones* (safe food, plenty of space, drinks on sale). Also *Jean Filho*, leaves Manaus 1800 Sat. (arrives Mon. p.m.), leaves Tefé Tues. 1900 (arrives Wed. p.m. or Thurs. a.m.). US$38 first class with good food, bottled water, 2nd class and small cabins available.

For jungle tours, contact Joaquim de Jesus López, R. Hermes Tupina No. 740, Barro Holaria, Tefé, not a professional guide, but he has been recommended for self-organized trips (cost for 4 for 1 week, US$200). No English spoken.

*Benjamin Constant* (pop. 15,000) on the frontier with Peru, with Colombian territory on the opposite bank of the river. Several hotels, including, *Benjamin Constant*, beside ferry, C, all a/c, some with hot water and TV, good restaurant, arranges tours, postal address Apartado Aéreo 219, Leticia, Colombia; *Mar Azur*, a/c, friendly; *Benjamín*, D, very basic. *Hotel São Jorge*, E, meal US$2, try bargaining, recommended; *Araponga*, C, run down; *Hotel Lanchonete PeR.na*, F, good food; *Márcia Maria*, E with bath, a/c, fridge, clean, friendly, rec. Eat at *Pensão Cecilia*, or *Bar-21 de Abril*, cheaper. Clothes shop on road reaching to port (left hand side) changes US$ cash. Boat services from Manaus, 7 days, or more; to Manaus, 4 days, or more. Boats from Manaus to Benjamin Constant normally go on to Tabatinga, and start from there when going to Manaus. Prices do vary, about US$50-60 for hammock space, US$100 for a cabin; try bargaining. Recommended vessels are *Almirante Monteiro*, *Dominique* and *Cidade de Teresina*, cleaner than most; *Clívia*, from Manaus every 2nd Sat., 6½ days, returns Wed., 3 days, good food, clean; *Itaúna* leaves Wed. or Sat. at 1900, 72 hrs. to Manaus, 3 meals included, take fresh water; *Comandante Soares*, but food is poor. The frigorífico *Conte Maciel* returns empty to Manaus every 10 days, comfortable, clean, good food. It is wise to bring food to supplement the rice, beans, chicken and salt fish, and sterilized water (some boats sell chilled beer or Coca Cola); mosquito spray is a must when you are in port, all year round.

Ferry (Recreio) to Leticia (Colombia) twice daily, US$2, 1½ hrs., ferry calls at **Tabatinga** (pop. 19,000), only 4 km. from Leticia. (*Hotel Miraflores*, E, clean, safe; *Halley*, F, reported dirty, *Residencial Aluguel Pajé*, F with bath, fan, clean; *Solimões*, run by the military—close to the airport—E with breakfast, other meals available if ordered in advance, excellent value, clean—some taxi drivers are unaware that this hotel accepts non-military guests, but there is a VW colectivo minibus from the barracks to town centre, harbour and Leticia; excellent *Tres Fronteiras* restaurant. Better accommodation is available in Leticia, there are no border formalities if you go no further into the country. Hammock (good) will cost US$12 in Tabatinga (try Rei de Redes on main road) or Benjamin Constant. It is difficult to change travellers' cheques in Tabatinga (try Casa Branca, Casa Verde or Casa Amarela on main road, or general manager of the main shopping centre), and far harder to purchase Peruvian intis than in Leticia. See under Manaus for flights Manaus-Tabatinga on route to Iquitos. Airport to Tabatinga by minibus, US$0.65. The Port Captain in Tabatinga is reported as very helpful and speaking good English. N.B. The port area of Tabatinga is called Marco. Mosquito net for hammock essential if sailing upstream from Tabatinga; much less so downstream.

**Entering Brazil from Colombia** Cross frontier between Leticia and Tabatinga. Boats to Manaus also depart from Benjamin Constant (see preceding paragraph and below). Brazilian exit/entry formalities at Marco (Tabatinga) are essential: walk through docks and follow road to its end, turn right at this T-junction for one block, white immigration building is opp. *Café dos Navegantes*, ten minutes' walk from docks, Mon.-Fri., 0800-1200, 1400-1800 (immigration also at airport, may not be open every day), proof of US$500 or exit ticket may be required. This is a frontier area: carry your passport at all times, but travel between Leticia and Tabatinga is very informal. Taxi to Leticia, US$6.50, colectivo US$0.35. Brazilian Consulate in Leticia, Calle 8, No. 8-71, Mon.-Fri., 1000-1600, requires two black-and-white passport photos and 36 hrs. for visa (best to get your visa beforehand); go there if you have entry problems coming from Peru into Brazil.

**Entering Brazil from Peru** Boats from Iquitos to the Brazilian border stop at Islandia, a mud-bank anchorage off Benjamin Constant (passengers are ferried by canoe between the two: Peruvian boats are not allowed to stop at Benjamin Constant). You must have a Peruvian exit stamp (obtained on the boat, or at Peruvian consulate in Leticia, or at Puerto Alegría practice seems to vary so check first in Iquitos), and you must get an entry stamp in Tabatinga (yellow fever certificate needed); without either you will be sent back to Peru. Don't wear shorts in the Brazilian immigration office. Take one of the ferries from Benjamin Constant to Tabatinga (1½-2 hrs., US$1.60, or hire a canoe, US$4.50), get off at first stop, walk 1 km. to the main road, police offices are on the right, the larger will stamp your passport. To get on to the ferry in Tabatinga it is necessary to walk the plank, narrow muddy and without a handrail. Tans flies Islandia to Iquitos, but there are no guarantees of flights.

**To Peru and Colombia** N.B. Exit stamps in Tabatinga are given at the airport, whether you are leaving by air or by boat (see above for office in town); you are permitted one week in transit; Tabatinga-Iquitos flights available on Wed. and Sun.; get your Brazilian exit stamp at the airport. Entering Colombia from Brazil, you must have a tourist card to obtain a stamp to go beyond Leticia, but there appears to be no problem in staying in Leticia without a stamp (but you cannot change travellers' cheques without a stamp); check these details on arrival. Colombian consulate on unnamed street opp. Restaurant *El Canto de las Peixadas*, open

0800-1400. Frequent sailings from Peruvian border jetties (Santa Rosa/Islandia) to Iquitos, US$15, 3 days. Peruvian tourist cards obtained from Puerto Alegría, 2 hours up river where boats stop for police checks (these formalities may change).

It is possible to get a launch from Manaus up the Rio Negro, *Rei Diocletian* leaves Thur. and Sat. for Barcelos, 30 hrs (Hotels *Oasis*, German spoken; *Macedo*). Boat to São Gabriel (see below) leaves Sat. 4½ days in rainy season, 8-9 in dry season (Nov.-Apr.), or wait at harbour for boats stopping for cargo or fuel. There are hardly any villages of more than a few houses; these places are important in terms of communications and food resources. It is vital to be self-sufficient in food and cash and to be able to speak Portuguese or have a Brazilian guide. Nova Airão, on the west bank of the Negro, is about two days upstream. It has a large boat-building centre at the south end, and a fish and vegetable market at the north end. Ice and bread can also be purchased here. The town has many similar houses of wood and corrugated-iron construction. It has a telephone (from which calls to Europe can be made—after a fashion). Airão is the starting point for the **Parque Nacional Jaú** (IBDF office in Manaus, BR-319, Km. 01, Distrito Industrial, Caixa Postal 185, CEP 69.000). Moura is about 5 days upstream from Manaus; it has about 120 people based around the military-run granite quarry. There are basic medical facilities and the military base has an airstrip (only usable September to December) and telecommunications. About a day further upstream is Carvoeira, almost opposite the mouth of the Rio Branco; although small, it has a vibrant festival in the first week of August. A great distance further upstream is São Gabriel da Cachoeira, from where you can continue to Venezuela (see Venezuela section). São Gabriel is near the **Pico de Neblina National Park** (Pico de Neblina is the highest mountain in Brazil, 3,014 metres, IBDF office in Manaus, see above); in São Gabriel, Tom Hanly, an Irish Salesian brother, is helpful, friendly and informative. The town has one hotel, cheap, clean, good food (ask for it), shops, 2 banks, no exchange, beautiful white beaches and, in the river, rapids for 112 km. Cargo boats ply to Cucuí at the Brazil/Colombia/Venezuela border (1 hotel, ask for Elias, no restaurants); with your embassy's assistance it may be possible to fly with the military (airport 8 km. from São Gabriel). From Cucuí daily boats to Guadalupe (Colombia), infrequent boats to Santa Lucía (Venezuela).

About two days up the Rio Branco is Santa Maria de Boiaçu, a village of about 30 families. There is a military airstrip which is in use in July and August, very basic medical facilities and an indirect radio link with Manaus. There are three small shops selling basic necessities (but they aren't often open), and several tiny, but lively churches. The Rio Branco is yellowish in colour, and less acidic than the Negro. Therefore, biting insects and their associated diseases are more prevalent outside the wet season. The river is better for fishing, though, and there is more wildlife to see. (We are grateful to Marianne Evans of Northampton, for much of this information).

River traffic on the Rio Branco connects Manaus with *Caracaraí*, a busy, but unattractive river port with modern installations. When the Manaus-Boa Vista road is washed out, this is the only route through to Venezuela. The *Rio Uaquiry* (captain Hernane Olivier Maximo) leaves early Tues. from Caracaraí, arriving in Manaus Thur. a.m. (returns Fri., arriving Caracaraí on Mon.), cabin US$50 with food, hammock space US$30 with food, arrive early to claim a good space, take water and extra food (in Manaus the boat ties up near the brick factory, not at the docks—ask at docks). There is a passenger boat once a fortnight, or you can ride on the barges which take trucks and their drivers (not recommended for single women). In the rainy season, Apr.-Sept., transport is quite easy to arrange (bargain for your fare, and sling your hammock under a truck); empty trucks offer cheaper fares for cars, talk to the drivers; it's an interesting journey, 96 hours upstream, 48 down, take water or purifying treatment. The river banks are closer, so there is more to see than on the Amazon and stops in the tiny riverside settlements are fascinating. Bus on from Caracaraí to Boa Vista costs US$4.80, 3 hrs.

**Hotels, Food, Services** *Márcia*, F, next to bus stop, a/c, breakfast, clean; *Roraima*, F, cold shower, basic; *3 Iramãos*, behind Rodoviária, E, clean, rec.; *Caracaraí*, down street from bus station, F, friendly but dirty; *Pizzeria Delícia*, good, English spoken; *Sorveteria Pizzaria Lidiany*, rec. Silas in the Drogaria on S side of town will change dollars.

**N.B.** The Perimetral Norte road marked on some maps from Caracaraí E to Macapá and W to the Colombian frontier does not yet exist; it runs only about 240 km. W and 125 km. E from Caracaraí, acting at present as a penetration road.

The road which connects Manaus and Boa Vista (BR-174 to Novo Paraíso, then the Perimetral, BR-210) is of rough dirt, except for the last 60 km. to Boa Vista, which are paved. It is often closed in the wet season owing to flooding; the best chance for bus travel is after September. For drivers on this route, some advise being defensive with regard to lorry drivers (who drive for too long, haul too much and drink); others say they are very helpful to anyone in difficulties. There are service stations with toilets, camping, etc., every 150-180 km., but all petrol is low octane; take a tow cable and spares. At Km. 100 is Presidente Figueiredo, with shops and a restaurant. About 100 km. further on is a service station at the entrance to the Uaimiri Atroari Indian Reserve, which straddles the road for about 120 km. Traffic may not stop in daytime except for emergencies or fuel; this part of the road is hilly, with virgin forest and jungle sounds. There is a police checkpoint and service station at the other end (Km. 325). At Km.359 there is a monument to mark the equator. At Km. 434 is the clean and pleasant *Restaurant Goaio*. The road junction 65 km. further on is a popular stopping place, with petrol, restaurant and showers. Beyond here, large tracts of forest have been destroyed for settlement, but already many homes have been abandoned. The road, built up with poor bridges, then enters a region of dense vegetation. 12 km. before Carcaraí, there is a ferry across the Rio Branco; continue then to Boa Vista. (If you do not want to go through the hassle of driving this route, you can try to have your vehicle taken by truck.)

Boa Vista has road connections with the Venezuelan frontier at Santa Elena de Uairen (237 km., a rough road, often closed and very slippery when wet, the only gasoline 110 km. south of Santa Elena) and Bomfim for the Guyanese border at Lethem.

**Boa Vista** (pop. 69,000), capital of the extreme northern State of Roraima (pop. 116,000), is 759 km. N of Manaus. Mount Roraima, after which the Territory is named, is possibly the original of Sir Arthur Conan Doyle's "Lost World". There is swimming in the Rio Branco, 15 mins., from the town centre (too polluted in Boa Vista) reachable by bus only when river is low. This town has a modern functional plan, which often necessitates long hot treks by the traveller from one function to another. It is an expensive place because of nearby goldmining; the influx of *garimpeiros* in the W of the state is threatening the existence of the Yanomami Indians, whose reserves have been violated. Industrial estate S of town. New government district is being built on the NW edge of town. Interesting modern cathedral; also a museum of local Indian culture (poorly kept). Taxi from airport should cost no more than US$10 (45 min. walk) and will assume you want *Hotel Tropical* unless you indicate otherwise.

**Hotels** Generally expensive and heavily booked. *Praia Palace*, A, on river, with beach, hard beds but service friendly, T (095) 224-4147 (good food in restaurant next door); *Eusébio's*, C-D, always full, book ahead, demand single if on your own, very good restaurant, swimming pool, free transport to bus station or airport, recommended; *Paraíso*, Getúlio Vargas e Araújo Filho, D with bath, popular with Guyanese shoppers (reportedly a centre for narcotics trading, very dirty, "arrogant and overpriced"); *Roraima*, Av. Cecília Brasil e Benjamin Constant, E-D with bath, not very good value; *Imperial*, E, Benjamin Constant, clean; *Colonial*, Ajuricaba 532, near Consolação church, D, a/c with bath and breakfast, clean; *Brasil* in R. Benjamin Constant 331 W near Drogafarma, E (do not confuse with sleazy *Hotel Brasa* in same street), also *Lua Nova*, No. 591, F without, E with a/c, English spoken, noisy, often full. *Casa Nova*, Av. Sebastião Diniz, D with a/c, E with fan. *Rodoviária*, at bus station about 1½ km. from town centre, F, communal rooms, clean, shower, clean, friendly, rec.; *Terraço*, Av. Cecília e Brasil 1141, F without bathroom, noisy, friendly; *Tres Nações*, Av. Ville Roy 1885, also close to bus station, E, some rooms a/c, others more basic, reported to be dirty; at No. 1906-24 Carlos Alberto Soares lets a room, F, warm shower, friendly, rec. There are also two missions who offer hospitality to those in need. If all else fails, sling your hammock in the trees around the Rodoviária.

**Camping** Rio Caviné, 3 km. N of town.

**Restaurants** *Senzala*, Av. Castelo Branco 1115, where the town's high society eats; *Casa Grande*, Av. Ville Roy, good; *Churrascaria Venezuela*, bus station; *Bigode*, on waterfront, fish, music at weekends; *Café Pigalle*, just off central square, next to *Eusébio's*, good food, drinks and atmosphere, open till all hours; *Góndola*, Benjamin Constant and Av. Amazonas, good; restaurant and bar in Parque Anana, near airport; *Vila Rica*, R. Ville Roy, near Rodoviária, good cheap lunch. Snacks at *Top Set*, Av. Jaime Brasil, *Catequeiro*, Araújo Filho with Benjamín Contant, rec. prato feito. Good prato feito at the restaurant by the petrol station opp. *Hotel Brasil*.

**Exchange** US$ and Guyanese notes can be changed in Boa Vista; try **Ramiro Silva**, Rimpex, Av. Jaime Brasil. Travellers' cheques in **Banco do Brasil**. There is no official exchange agency and the local rates for bolívares are low: the Banco do Brasil will not change bolívares. Best rate for dollars, **Casa Pedro José**, R. Araújo Filho 287, T 224 4277; try the chemist/drugstore on main square for dollar exchange or the Compra e Vende Ouro shop on Av. Araújo Filho, or the gold dealers in front of *Hotel Paraíso*.

**Health**  Yellow fever inoculations are free at a clinic near the hospital.

**Bus**  (See also Border Crossings below). To/from **Manaus**, by Eucatur, US$32, 18 hrs., leaves 0700, 1000, advisable to book because sometimes buses are fully booked days in advance, but go to bus station as extra buses may run, check times. Breakdowns are frequent and the road is poor (see above). Buses often run late, and the night bus has to wait up to 4 hrs. for the Rio Branco ferry. **Boa Vista-Caracaraí** US$4.80, 3 hrs. To **border**, see below. Rodoviária is on town outskirts, 3 km.; taxi to centre, US$4, bus US$0.35 (marked "13 de Setembro" to centre). Local bus terminal is on Av. Amazonas, just off central praça. Note that it is difficult to get taxi or bus to Rodoviária in time for early morning departures; as it's a 25 minute walk, book a taxi the previous evening.

**Hitch-hiking**  from Boa Vista to Manaus is fairly easy on the many trucks travelling to Manaus; try from the service station near the Rodoviária. You may have to change trucks at Caracaraí. At the ferry crossing over the Rio Branco there is usually a long queue of waiting hikers; try to arrange a lift on the ferry. Hitching to Santa Elena, Venezuela, is not easy; either wait at the bridge and police checkpoint on the road to the border, or try to find a Venezuelan driver on the square. Drivers often charge for hitches—maybe as much as a bus fare.

**Air Travel**  To and from Manaus; confirm flights before reaching Boa Vista as they are fully booked. Aircraft maintenance, baggage checking and handling are unreliable; Guyanese come to Boa Vista to buy goods unavailable in Guyana—make sure your luggage is not among the excess that has to be taken off the plane. No left luggage facilities at airport, and no public transport other than taxis.

**Border Crossing, Guyana**  Get exit stamp at police station in Lethem, Guyana, then take rowing-boat over border river Tacutu. No car ferry, but river can be forded in dry season. Once in Brazil, register at military camp at Bomfim (hotels: *Blessing*, F, and *Bomfim*) and get entry stamp (closed for lunch). Phone Bomfim 2290 (for one G$) for car to take you to Boa Vista (US$45), or if lucky, take a colectivo (US$15, 3 hrs.) or daily bus at 0800. The bus leaves Boa Vista for Bomfim at 1900 only (according to latest reports, schedules change), US$10, 3½ hrs.; luggage is checked at the Ministério da Fazenda checkpoint, before Bomfim, from where a jeep takes travellers to the Brazilian immigration post (US$1) and then walk the short distance to the river, 5 km. in all. To cross the river, yell "Boat" and a motor boat will come. It is very difficult to hitch between Boa Vista and Bomfim. From Bomfim to Boa Vista the road is acceptable (1 bus daily), but subject to washouts; bridge over Rio Branco. There is another border crossing at Laramonta from where it is a hard, but rewarding walk to the Guyanese town of Orinduik. A weekly jeep connects Laramonta with Boa Vista (US$25), also flights once a week, to Georgetown, often fully booked. A good rate for cruzeiros is reported in the Guyana border area. Cruzeiros can be changed into G$ in the shop at Brazilian immigration post; Bomfim is a much better place for exchange, but Boa Vista is best. If you need visa to enter Guyana, you must get it in Brasília or São Paulo; no consulate in Boa Vista.

**Border Crossing, Venezuela**  Everyone who crosses the border from Boa Vista, regardless of nationality, requires a visa (passport must be valid for 1 year). These can be obtained (allow 2-3 days, but recent reports suggest it can be much quicker) from the Venezuelan Consulate in Boa Vista, Av. Benjamín Constant 525E (T 095-224-2182, open Mon.-Fri. 0830-1300 but may close earlier—no shorts allowed); the only requirements are one passport photograph and an onward ticket (not an MCO). A "good character" reference from an employer is said to expedite matters. Health requirements are reported to have been relaxed: a malaria test certificate, yellow-fever vaccination certificate and certificate of medical checkup are no longer necessary, but be prepared for them anyway as reports vary. It is much simpler to get a visa for Venezuela in Belém (**see page 457**), or maybe even Rio (check in advance); if you have no alternative but the consulate in Boa Vista, you can ask for Embassy in Caracas to telex Boa Vista to prove that you are a bona fide tourist. Border officials may also insist on US$20 a day—however, regulations state that a visa is sufficient. Andorinha runs a daily bus between Santa Elena and Manaus, via Boa Vista, US$32.50. Buses leave the Rodoviária in Boa Vista for Santa Elena at 0800, if full there may be an extra bus at 0930, US$17 (stopping at all check points), take water, journey 6 hrs. Boa Vista-Ciudad Bolívar direct Thur. Border search is thorough (there are also road checks in Venezuela). Entry stamp can be obtained only in Santa Elena; border closes at 1700. Trucks leave for Venezuela from R. Benjamin Constant, drivers are not officially supposed to take passengers. For the price of the bus ticket you can pay for a lift in a truck and avoid an overnight stay. There are a bank and a basic hotel, *Pacaraima Palace*, on Brazilian side and you can camp. The road from the frontier is well-maintained and is being paved; it passes through some very scenic countryside.

---

## SOUTHERN AMAZONIA (10)

Rondônia and Acre, frontier areas, not just between Brazil and Peru and Bolivia, but also between the forest and colonization, between those who live off the forest and ranchers.

***Porto Velho*** (pop. 450,000), capital of the State of Rondônia with a population of 862,000 in 1985, but at least 1.2 million by the end of the decade. The city stands on a high bluff overlooking a curve of the River Madeira; at the top of the hill is the cathedral, built in 1950. The principal commercial street is Av. Sete de Setembro, which runs from the railway station and market hall to the upper level of the city, past the Rodoviária. Parks are under construction. Rondônia is the focus of experimental development in agriculture, with concomitant colonization of the area. At the same time, much of the state is being reserved for Indians and national forests. Porto Velho is expensive because of the local gold rush. About 20 km. from Porto Velho, the Samuel hydroelectric scheme is under construction, with a new town to house the workers. When it comes on stream in the 1990s, it will be insufficient to provide power for the states of Rondônia and Acre as was originally intended. The population has grown too rapidly. Malaria is common. With the growth in population, crime has increased in the city and outside.

The Madeira is one of the major tributaries of the Amazon. The four main rivers which form it are the Madre de Dios, rising a short distance from Cuzco (Peru); the Beni, coming from the southern Cordillera bordering Lake Titicaca; the Mamoré, rising near Sucre, Bolivia; and the Guaporé, coming out of Mato Grosso, in Brazil.

**Hotels** *Rondón Palace*, Av. Jorge Teixeira with Jacy Paraná, about 4 blocks to the left of bus station, T 223-3422, A, a/c, hot water, rec.; *Samaúma Palace*, R. Dom Pedro II, 1038, T 221-3737, B, nice rooms but said not too friendly (221-3159); *Vila Rica*, Av. Carlos Gomes 1616, T 221-2333, L, tower block, "flashy, flamboyant and mechanically efficient"; *Aliança*, 7 de Setembro 1160, C, a/c, rec. Hotels within sight of the Rodoviária: *Príncipe da Beira*, R. Getúlio Vargas 2287, D (221-6135); *Sampa*, F, also serves cheap meals. From Rodoviária, take bus No. 301 "Presidente Roosevelt" (outside *Hotel Pontes*), which goes to railway station at riverside, then along Av. 7 de Setembro, passing: *Guaporé Palace*, No. 927, E, a/c, restaurant; *Nunes*, No. 1195, F, probably best value among cheapest hotels; *Sonora*, No. 1103, E, clean, fan, clothes washing facilities; *Cuiabano*, in same street, F, friendly; *Rio*, Av. Joaquim Nabuco 2110, T 223-1430, F, basic, good breakfast, friendly, fairly good cheap meals; *Brasil*, Av. Pres. Kennedy, 15 mins. from Rodoviária, clean, cheap, breakfast. Hotels often full.

**Electric Current** 110 volts A.C., elsewhere in Rondônia 220 volts.

**Restaurants** At hotels; *Fiorella*, Joaquim Nabuco 2105, good pizza; *Caravela de Madeira*, R. Ariquemes 104, excellent fish, good atmosphere; *Remanso do Tucunaré*, Av. Brasília 1506, popular, cheap; *Carioca*, R. Prudente de Morais 2450, "a hole in the wall", pleasant service, very cheap.

**Shopping** Bookshop *Livraria de Rosa*, off Av. 7 de Setembro, near the port, a few English paperbacks; manageress speaks English. Indian handicrafts at *Casa do Índio*, R. Rui Barbosa 1407. Hammocks more expensive than in Manaus.

**Car hire** Silva Car, R. Almirante Barroso 1528, CEP 78.900, Porto Velho, T (069) 221-1423/6040, Telex (069) 1129 SLVL. US$30/day.

**Exchange** Banks; try *Hotel Vila Rica* (Carlos, the doorman, for cash), *Hotel Floresta* (cash), *Hotel Rio*, Varig/Cruzeiro office. Local radio news and papers publish exchange rates; try local businesses too. Difficult elsewhere in Rondônia.

**Laundry** *Lavanderia Marmoré*, Pinheiro Machado 1455b.

**Post Office and phones** Av. Pres. Dutra 3023 e Av. 7 de Setembro; to call collect use booths outside.

**Air Services** Airport 8 km. W of town, take bus marked Nacional, it stops at Policia Federal. Daily flights to Manaus, Brasília, Cuiabá, Rio Branco; once a week to Cruzeiro do Sul, via Rio Branco, Mon. Taba flies Mon., Wed. and Fri. about 1300 to Guajará Mirim.

**River Services** Manaus, 1st class, with passable food; 2nd class very crowded US$60. Journey takes 3-4 days when river high; as much as 7 days when low. The boat leaves on Thurs. and Sat. at 1800. 1st class means upper deck, with more hammock-hanging room, or, if lucky, one of two 2-person cabins (US$140). Advantages to 1st class: more room, better view, coffee with milk, meals served first. Food is safe to eat, though monotonous; water-purifying tablets or bottles of sterilized water strongly recommended. Carlos Cezar's boat leaves Wednesdays, transfer at Manicoré, trip including meals US$64, one class on deck. Shipping a car: São Matheus Ltda, Av. Terminal dos Milagros 400, Balsa, takes vehicles on pontoons, US$250 inc. passengers, meals, showers, toilets, cooking and sleeping in car permitted. Wait at the Capitânia do Porto in the centre of town for a possible passage on a cargo boat; these boats leave from Porto Bras, down river from Porto Velho. Porto Velho-Humaitá US$13.50 (boat *Dois de Junho*).

Six days a week a boat leaves at 1800 for Manaus from Manicoré, at the confluence of the Rivers Madeira and Manicoré, two nights and one day's journey, food included; boats from Porto Velho to Manicoré on Mon., Wed. and Sat. (1800, arr. 0200, but you can sleep on the boat), connecting with Manicoré-Manaus boats. **Manicoré** (about 10,000 people) is a pleasant town; the Praça de Bandeira is at the corner of Av. Getúlio Vargas and Av. Pedro Tinoco (one block to left of road that goes up from the dock). *Hotel Manicoré*, 4 blocks left from Praça on Av. Vargas, just before the big church; *Restaurant Tapuia*, 1 block from Praça in opp. direction to river on Av. Tinoco; slow but good restaurant at floating dock. Fruit market on Av. Vargas.

**Buses** New Rodoviária on outskirts of town, Av. Pres. Kennedy. Bus to **Manaus**, 1600, and 2000 normal (US$24), 1700 and 1800 (*leito* US$48), 24-26 hrs. (up to 4 days in the rainy season); to **Humaitá**, US$4.80; to **São Paulo**, change at Cuiabá, sixty-plus hrs., US$75; to Cuiabá, 23 hrs. US$28, take plenty of food and drink. Fast bus at 2030, Colibri, drug controls in operation. To Guajará-Mirim, see below. To Rio Branco, twice daily, 12 hrs., US$15. Daily bus with Eucatur from **Cascavel** (Paraná, connections for Foz do Iguaçu) via Maringá, Presidente Prudente, Campo Grande and Cuiabá to Porto Velho. To **Cáceres** for the Pantanal, Colibri, 18 hrs., US$19. To Vitória, daily, 61 hrs. Hitching difficult, try at the *posto* 2 km. out of town. For Manaus try at the ferry crossing just outside town (may be impossible in the rainy season).

**Roads** to Cuiabá (BR-364—Marechal Rondon Highway, 1,450 km., fully paved; **see page 493**); Rio Branco, 490 km., following Madeira-Mamoré railway, paved as far as the Acre border; to Humaitá (205 km.) on the Madeira river (fully paved), connecting with the Transamazônica Highway, and on to Manaus (877 km.), not completely paved and in poor condition. Road journeys are best done in the dry season, the second half of the year; the Manaus road (Catire Highway) is sometimes closed in the rainy season.

A result of the paving of BR-364 is the development of towns along it: Ariquemes (159 km. from Porto Velho, municipal pop. 200,000, buses hourly from 0600, 3-4 hrs., Banco do Brasil, some hotels, *Valerius Palace*, E; Nova Vida (200 km.), Jaru (257 km.), Ouro Preto d'Oeste (297 km. Harold Schmitz, Rancho Grande, CEP 78920 Ariquemes R.O. C.P. 361, organises rain forest trips, speaks English, German and Spanish, highly rec.). *Ji Paraná* (337 km., municipal pop. 200,000—bus to Porto Velho, US$11, 14 hrs.; to Cuiabá, 15 hrs. US$17.50, 35 *leito*; hotels *Horizonte*, E, rec. with reasonable restaurants, *Sol Nascente*, F with *churrascaria*, *Hotel Transcontinental*, B, rec.; trips to frontier towns possible, e.g. Nova Colina), Presidente Médici (373 km., 50,000 people), Cacoal (404 km., 200,000 people, Hotels *Cacoal Palace* (D) and *Amazonis*), Pimenta Bueno (440 km., pop. 50,000) and Vilhena on the Rondônia-Mato Grosso border (658 km. from Porto Velho, 710 km. from Cuiabá; *Diplomata Hotel*, D, near bus station; *Rodoviária*, F, rec.; *Gastão*, F). At Vilhena proof of yellow-fever inoculation required: if no proof, new shot. Two cities have grown without prior planning: Rolim de Moura, W of Pimenta Bueno, with a population of 110,000 and a *Transcontinental Hotel*, and Itarua do Oeste, 91 km. S of Porto Velho, at what used to be a bus waiting station (population about 5,000).

The **Pacaás Novos National Park**, 765,800 hectares, lies west of the BR-364; it is a transitional zone between open plain and Amazonian forest. Details from IBDF, Av. Gov. Jorge Teixeira, CEP 78.900, Porto Velho; also enquire here about the Jaru and Guaporé Biological Reserves in the State.

Porto Velho was the terminus of the Madeira-Mamoré railway of 367 km. (closed 1971),

Brazil's price to Bolivia for annexing the Acre territory during the rubber boom. It cost a life for every hundred sleepers, 6,208 in all, during construction. The line, built 1907-12, by-passed the 19 rapids of the Madeira and Mamoré rivers, and gave Bolivia an outlet of sorts to the Atlantic. It was supposed to go as far as Riberalta, on the Rio Beni, above that river's rapids, but stopped short at **Guajará Mirim** (pop. 41,000). 3 locomotives operate out of Porto Velho. The railway expert will enjoy the ancient steam locomotives in the railway station and on a siding 2 km. away. There are still two engines in working order, which run Sunday excursion trains as far as Santo Antônio, 7 km. away (US$0.15). Small railway museum at station has been moved so that the station can accommodate passengers on the newly restored line. The railway is now replaced by a fair road, partly paved, which uses its bridges (in poor condition); the 370-km. bus ride is far faster than the train was (8 buses a day from Rodoviário, 30 mins. walk from the town, US$19, takes 5½ hrs. or more depending on season—road, in poor condition south of Abunã, is often closed March-May). The Bolivian town of Guayaramerín is across the Mamoré river (speedboat service, US$1); it is connected by road to Riberalta, and there are air services to other Bolivian cities. An ancient stern wheeler plies on the Guaporé; 26-day, 1,250 km. trips (return) can be made on the Guaporé from Guajará Mirim to Vila Bela in Mato Grosso, fare includes food. 170 km. from Guajará Mirim, on the Guaporé river, is the Forte Príncipe da Beira, begun in 1777 as a defence of the border with Bolivia. The fort, which is being restored, can be reached from Costa Marques (20 km. by road), which can only be reached by air or by river.

If travelling by road between Porto Velho and Guajará Mirim, two possible stops are at Maluca dos Índios, from where you can visit villages of gold prospectors by the Madeira river; the other is from the railway bridge just before Vila Murtinho where you can see gold panners, and, walking a few hundred metres, the rapids on the Mamoré river.

**Guajará Mirim Hotels**  *Mini-Estrela*, Av. 15 de Novembro 460, C; *Fénix Palace*, Av. 15 de Novembro 459, E; *Hudson*, Av. Marechal Deodoro s/n, D, rec. *Alfa*, Av. Leopold de Mattos 239; *Mamoré*, F, clean, friendly; **Youth Hostel** Av. 15 de Novembro, Centro Deportivo Afonso Rodrigues, T 541-3732.

**Restaurant**  Best is *Oasis*, at Posto Nogueira service station, Av. 15 de Novembro 464.

**Museum  Museu Municipal** at the old railway station beside the ferry landing—small, with railway memorabilia and a few specimens of regional wildlife.

**Exchange  Banco do Brasil** (foreign exchange a.m. only). **Loja Nogueira**, Av. Pres. Dutra, esq. Leopold de Matos (cash only). There is no market in Brazil for bolivianos.

**Telephone** office: Av. B. Ménzies 751.

**Note**  If you need a visa to enter Brazil, apply to the Brazilian Consul at Guayaramerín (Bolivia), open 1100-1300, before crossing the Rio Mamoré into Brazil. If the Policia Federal are not on duty at the waterfront, you must get passport stamped at their office in town, address below. Similarly, before crossing into Bolivia you may need a visa (free) from the Bolivian consul in Guajará Mirim in Av. Lepoldo de Mattos, the same buildings as *Hotel Alfa*, Western Europeans can cross river and visit the Immigration Office; which closes at 1100 on Sat. You will need a Brazilian exit stamp from Policia Federal, Av. Antônio Correia da Costa 842.

From Abunã, 220 km. from Porto Velho (*Hotel Ferroviário*, E, including meals, however town is best avoided if at all possible) the road from Porto Velho continues W to **Rio Branco** (pop 45,000) the capital of the State of Acre, (pop. 385,000, 1985 figure). Hotels always crowded: *Pinheiro Palace*, Rui Barbosa 91, T 224-7191, C, , a/c, pool, friendly, rec; *Cuzco*, near airport, new; *Lux Palace*, R. Quintino Bocaiuva 397, T 224-7340, F, clean, friendly (20 mins from centre); *Inacio's*, C, overpriced, dirty, fair restaurant; *Rio Branco*, C, on park, nice but simple; *Amazonas*, *Fontes* (best of a bad bunch of budget hotels, F, not clean), *Fortaleza*, all on left bank. On right bank, *Sucessor*, F, showers, fan, clean, comfortable, friendly. **Youth Hostel**, Fronteira Verde, Trav. Natanael de Albuquerque, T 224-3997. Cheap meals at *Dos Colonos* near market. *Marayina*, for pizzas, sandwiches, cakes, ice cream, popular at night; *Casarão*, also popular; *Churrascaria Triângulo*, near airport, as much charcoal-grilled meat as you can eat, rec.; *Churrascaria Modelo*, R. Marechal Deodoro 360, less good. There is a park with a military post on one side; beyond is the Governor's palace and another park leading to the market on the bank of the Acre river. There is a bridge across the river, which is only navigable to Manaus in the wet season. The city has a cathedral, an airport and an agricultural research centre. Trips to see rubber tapping, or the religious colony at Colonia Cinco Mil, can be arranged by the travel agent in *Hotel Rio Branco*.

**Warning**  The road from Porto Velho to Rio Branco should be travelled with caution; the area is seriously affected by malaria. We have also received reports of lawlessness on the BR-364 after dark; to be safe, be in a city before nightfall.

At Rio Branco the Transamazônica Highway meets the road from Brasília and goes on to Cruzeiro do Sul and Japim; it is expected to reach the Peruvian frontier further W when completed; it is hoped that it will be continued by the Peruvians to Pucallpa. It is very difficult to get from Rio Branco to Cruzeiro do Sul by road because there is no bus service, and the occasional lorry goes mainly in the dry season; the road is frequently impassable. There is a plane (Cruzeiro do Sul) every Tues. and Thur. (originating in Manaus) and on Sat. and Sun. to Cruzeiro do Sul, US$60.

*Cruzeiro do Sul* (pop. 59,000) an isolated Amazonian town, is situated on the river Juruá; trips can be made on the river, for example to the village of Rodrigues Alves (2-3 hrs., return by boat or by road, 15 km.). In the jungle one can see rubber-tapping, and collecting the latex into "borrachas" which weigh up to 45 kg. Hotels: *Sandra's*, D; *Novo do Acre*, F, rec., a/c, clean; *Hospedaria Janecir*, F; *dos Viajantes*; *Flor de Maio*, F, facing river, clean, showers, full board available. Restaurant *O Laçador*, good food. Money changing is very difficult; none of the banks will change dollars. Try the airline staff (poor rates). From Cruzeiro do Sul to Pucallpa one can go either by air: Sasa, 50 mins.,—details from Blvd. Taumaturgo 25 (no phone), flies only when plane is full, it seats 5; undertake all formalities at Policia Federal before leaving. Alternatively one can go by boat when river is high (Nov.-Feb.): only for the hardy and well-equipped; journey takes about 10 days: 4 by boat to Tamburiaco, on rivers Juruá and Juruá-Mirim, then 2 days' walk through the jungle to the Peruvian border at Canta Gallo, then 3-4 more days by boat on the rivers Amonia and Abojao to Pucallpa. The regional airline Taba has a permit to fly to Eirunepé on the Juruá river from Manaus and Tabatinga; Eirunepé is a small town near Carauari, where Dutch missionaries live.

A road from Rio Branco (the BR-317), paved as far as Xapuri (the location of the Fundacão Chico Mendes in memory of the environmentalist and union organiser murdered in 1989), goes to Brasiléia (bus twice daily, 6 hrs., US$6.50, basic hotel, Federal Police give exit stamps), opposite the Bolivian town of Cobija on the Acre River, and finally to Assis Brasil where the Peruvian, Bolivian and Brazilian frontiers meet; across the Acre River are Iñapari (Peru) and Bolpebra (Bolivia). There is no public transport, and little else, beyond Brasiléia to Iñapari. In Assis Brasil, there is one small hotel (a dormitory, basic but clean, friendly), one snack bar, a bank which does not change US dollars (the hotel owner may be persuaded to oblige) and river transport only, which is dependent on the seasons.

**N.B. Rio Branco time is one hour behind Manaus time; this means two hours behind Brazilian Standard Time.**

---

# THE CENTRE-WEST (11)

A good area for seeing wildlife, in the vast, swampy Pantanal and in the less accessible Ilha do Bananal. Agriculture and colonization are encroaching on wildlife and Indian areas, but tourism is still relatively undeveloped. Corumbá, besides being one of the access routes to the Pantanal, is also the main land border crossing with Bolivia.

The so-called centre-west of Brazil is occupied by the states of Goiás, Mato Grosso and Mato Grosso do Sul (divided from Mato Grosso in 1977) . Goiás is one of Brazil's most rapidly developing agricultural areas, producing cattle, coffee, soya and rice. The Federal District of Brasília (**see page 290)** was subtracted in 1960 from the territory of Goiás, which has been further split to form the new State of Tocantins in the north.

*Goiânia* (pop. 925,000) 202 km. SW of Brasília, the second (after Belo Horizonte) of Brazil's planned state capitals, was founded in 1933 and succeeded Goiás Velho as capital of the State of Goiás (pop. 4,765,000) in 1937. Goiânia is a spacious city, with its main avenues excellently lit and ornamented with plants; tourists can enjoy the Parque Mutirama with its planetarium on the city's eastern side and the Horto Florestal, with good zoo and anthropological museum in the west; there are a racecourse and a motor racetrack. The Jaó Club on the edge of a reservoir provides for sun bathing and water skiing. Every Sunday morning there is a handicrafts fair in the city's central square, the Praça Cívica, where there is a small museum of local handicrafts, animals and Indian artefacts. From the Praça Cívica walk along Av. Goiás to see the painted walls of the Projeto Galería Aberto. Many city buses are also painted.

**Hotels** *Castro Park*, Av. Rep. do Líbano 1520, T 223-7766, A, new, warmly rec.; *Samambaia*, Av. Anhanguera 1157, T 261-1444; *Bandeirantes*, same street, No. 3278, T 224-0066; *Umuarama*, R. 4, No. 492, T 224-1555; *São Conrado*, R. 3, No. 652, T 224-2411; *Augustus*, Praça Antônio Lizita 702, T 224-1022 (all good D-C). Many cheap hotels e.g. *J. Alves*, opp. Rodoviária; *Santo Antônio*, Av. Anhanguera 6296, F. NW of the Rodoviária are the dormitórios, *Estrela Familiar*, F, basic, clean, friendly.

**Restaurants** Goiânia is much cheaper for eating and sleeping than Brasília. Restaurant at the Rodoviária for good food at very low prices, and plenty more eating places nearby.

**Bookshop** on R. 4 has some secondhand English books; will exchange.

**Exchange** National banks. Travel agents will exchange cash, poor rates for travellers' cheques.

**Immigration Office** R 235, Setor Universitária.

**Tourist Office** Goiastur, in the football stadium (Estádio Serra Dourada), very friendly: it's rather remote!

**Airport** Nearby, with daily flights to main cities.

**Roads and Buses** To Cuiabá (Mato Grosso) paved, 4 buses a day, US$18, 13 hrs.; continues to Porto Velho (Rondônia) and Rio Branco (Acre). At Iporã, 200 km. W of Goiânia on BR-158, one of the routes to Cuiabá, there is a good hotel; at Rio Verde, on the BR-060, another route, the *Hotel Vai Quem Quer*, D is a possible stop on the way, if desperate. To **Brasília** (about 17 a day, 2½ hrs., US$4.80) and **São Paulo** (bus services, US$30, 14 hrs.); **Campo Grande** 18 hrs. US$24. To Goiás Velho, 136 km.

**Anápolis**, 61 km. nearer Brasília, with a population of 161,000, is an important trading centre.

**Hotels** *Itamarati; Príncipe*. Many cheap ones around bus station, e.g. *Serra Dourada*, Av. Brasil 375, E, good value.

**Goiás Velho** (25,000 population), a picturesque old gold-mining town founded in 1727, was capital of the State of Goiás until 1937. There is a regular bus service between Goiânia and Goiás Velho. The city has seven baroque churches, the oldest being São Francisco de Paula (1761). *Borrachudos* (biting insects) are common in June and July.

**Museums** The Museu da Boa Morte in the colonial church of the same name has a small but interesting collection of old images, paintings, etc. The **Museu das Bandeiras** is in the old town hall and prison (Casa da Câmara e Cadeia), by the colonial fountain. The old **Government Palace**, with four rooms, is now open to the public, next to the red-brick Cathedral in the main square. A local tradition is the Fogaréu procession in Holy Week.

José Joaquim da Veiga Valle, who was born in Pirenópolis in 1806, was the "Aleijadinho" of Goiás. Many of his works are in the Boa Morte museum.

**Hotels** *Vila Boa*, T 371-1000, large, C, pool, views, reported closed for modernisation in 1990; *Minas Goiás*, F, clean, in R. Dr Americano do Brasil; *Araguía*, D, clean, rec.; *Itajuba*, E-F with breakfast, very clean.

**Restaurants** *Pito Aceso*, grills; *Hotel Vila Boa*; *Pedro's Bar*, good cold beef; *Dona Maninha*, R. Dom Cândido, regional food, good value; *Sobradinho*, simple good food. Try the local meat pie, *empadão goiano*.

**Shopping** Centro de Tradições Goianas, in *Hotel Vila Boa*.

**Excursion** Centro de Gemologia de Goiás, Quadra 2, Módulo 13, Daia, about 10 km. by bus from Anápolis, will show visitors how real and synthetic gem stones are distinguished; you can also buy stones. Cachoeira Grande, 7 km. from Goiás Velho on the Juçara road, has bathing place and snack bar.

**Pirenópolis**, another colonial town, is 128 km. from Goiânia, 220 km. from Brasília. There is a regular bus service between Anápolis and Pirenópolis (66 km.). **Hotels**: *Rex*, Praça da

Matriz, D, *Central*, F (for the desperate).

**Chapada dos Veadeiros**  This national park is about 200 km. N of Brasília, reached by paved road to Alto Paraíso de Goiás (buses from Brasília 1000 and 2200, US$4.80) and gravel road from there W towards Colinas. The park entrance is on a side turning from the Colinas road, just before the village of São Jorge. Bus from Alto Paraíso to São Jorge leaves 1600. The park's main attraction is a series of waterfalls on the Rio Negro, 7 km. from São Jorge by rough track; there are other falls about 2 km. from the park entrance. Camping is permitted; difficult to reach without a car, take food. There is an hotel, E, by the bus station in Alto Paraíso and a *dorimitório* (take a sleeping bag or hammock) in São Jorge. By jeep it is possible to cross from Alto Paraíso to the BR-242 Salvador-Brasília road, a very slow but beautiful journey of 150 kms.

**Caldas Novas** (pop. 12,500), 187 km. SE of Goiânia (many buses; best reached via Morrinhos on the BR-153 Goiânia-São Paulo highway) is a newly-developed thermal resort with good hotels and camp sites with hot swimming pools. Daily bus from Morrinhos, US$0.80, 1½ hrs. There are three groups of springs within this area: Caldas Novas, Fontes de Pirapetinga (7 km. from the town) and Rio Quente (25 km. from the town, bus from Caldas Novas; the *Pousada Hotel* -5 star—has lots of pools, entry US$20); water temperatures are 37-51°C.

**Hotels**  48 in all.  Very fashionable is *Hotel Turismo* (5-star, T 421-2244, L, full board, a/c) at Rio Quente, and, sharing some of its facilities, *Pousada do Rio Quente*, T 421-2255, 3-star, A+, full board, but not a/c. (The *Turismo* has a private airstrip; flights from Rio and São Paulo with agencies.) *Parque das Primaveras*, R. do Balneário, T 453-1355, A+, rec. by locals, cheaper than the Rio Quente places. *Tamburi*, R. Eça de Queirós, 10, T 453-1455, OK. *Serra Dourada*, Av. Correia Neto 574, T 453-1300, D, rec. *Goiás*, E with breakfast, rec.; *Imperial*, near Rodoviária, E, clean, friendly. Camping at Esplanada, and Camping Clube do Brasil site on the Ipameri road, 1 km. from the centre. Many other "Clubes e Campings": *Tropical*, US$1 p.p., 2 sites in town, can use both in 1 day, others mostly US$1.30 a day, all have snack bars.

**Restaurants**  *Hotel José*, cheap good food; *Caminho do Natural*, vegetarian, good, but expensive; *Berro d'Água* in Bairro do Turista rec.

Two other natural attractions in Goiás are the Cachoeira do Salto (160 km. from Brasília) and the thermal waters of the Lagoa de Aporé on the border with Mato Grosso. At Cristalina (120 km. from Brasília) there is a waterfall; also semi-precious stones for sale **(see page 297)**. The River Araguaia, forming the border between Goiás and the two Mato Grosso states, provides many sandy beaches and good fishing: 1,600 km. of the river are navigable by boat.

A dirt road connects Goiás Velho with Aragarças (on the Goiás side) and *Barra do Garças* (on the Mato Grosso side) on the River Araguaia (Barra can also be reached by a more southerly route from Goiânia). Barra has various hotels on Av. João Alberto, e.g. *Avenida*, clean, E; *churrascarias* near main bridge and on Av. João Alberto; pleasant river beach with bars and snacks; campsite on island in river; night-time entertainment by the port. A road to the north of Barra extends as far as São João do Araguaia; where this road crosses the Rio das Mortes is the town of *Xavantina* (*Hotel Xavantina*, F, basic; *Churrascaria Arca de Noé*, highly rec.). The road is paved as far as Serra Dourada (160 km. N of Barra). Anti-malaria precautions are recommended for the Rio Araguaia region. June-Oct. is said to be the best time to visit the region; low water allows camping on beaches and islands. Avoid July, when the fishermen and their families all come. Boats and guides can be hired in Aruanã, Britânia, Barra do Garças or Porto Luis Alves (*Pousada do Jaburu*, A including meals), guide Vandeir will arrange boat trips to see wildlife, take food and water. Interesting walks in surrounding jungle with Joel, ask at the hotel. There is good fishing for tucunaré in the Rio Cristalino. Beware of currents and do not swim where the bed is muddy or where sting rays are said to lurk. Piranhas are reported not to be a problem where there is a current and provided swimmers have no open wounds.

The BR-153, Brasília-Belém road, runs north through the heart of Goiás and Tocantins states. At Guaraí the road forks, one branch continuing west into Pará, then turning north to Marabá on the Transamazônica and onto Belém. The other branch goes to Araguaína, whereafter the BR-226 goes to Estreito in Maranhão, from where the BR-010 runs north through Imperatriz to Belém.

*Araguaína* (pop. 90,000) in the new state of Tocantins (pop. 1.1 million), is on the Brasília-Belém road (Brasília, 1,102 km.; Belém 842 km.; Imperatriz, 174 km.). Several hotels near Rodoviária including *Esplanada*, F p.p., may have to share a room, friendly, clean, fan, no breakfast, good; *Líder*, *São Jorge*, *do Norte* and *Goiás* (all F). Bus leaves Araguaína for Marabá 0700 and 1400. Ordinary bus to Goiânia takes 24 hours: try to get an express. If travelling to Belém or Brasília by bus, reservations are not normally accepted: be at the terminal 2 hrs. before scheduled departure as buses tend to leave early; as soon as bus pulls in, follow the driver to the ticket counter and ask if there are seats. Buses also to Santarém. Varig flights twice a week from Brasília.

Off the Brasília-Belém road are fast-developing frontier regions between the lower Araguaia and Xingu rivers. Kevin Healey writes: There is now a soaring concrete bridge spanning the Araguaia just south of Conceição do Araguaia, and the road connection to the Belém highway at Guaraí is now paved. (This is the only bridge across the Araguaia between Barra dos Garças and Marabá.)
    North and west of Conceição are many new townships and ranches. Places like Redenção and Xinguara are raw, dusty and not very salubrious for tourists. At Xinguara (pop. 20,000 already) is the *Hotel Rio Vermelho*, F, pretty grotty, pigsty outside windows, orange water in taps, bed legs in cans of paraffin to discourage ants and termites. To the west, Cumaru is a *garimpeiro* settlement, from where the local military governor keeps "law and order" over the gold mining centres near the Rio Fresco. Here, the miners and prospectors are already on the edge of the Gorotiré Indian Reserve and a road is poised to enter the Indian land. To the south is Campo Alegre (pop. 6,000), the centre of cow country, with a huge new slaughterhouse serving the corporate ranches around the region (e.g. the experimental ranch of Cristalino, owned by VW Brasil). This is a perfect place to see the destruction of the rainforest and the changing climate pattern.
    At *Conceição do Araguaia* the best hotel is the *Taruma Tropical* (E), each room a concrete cell, soft and squishy beds, ant parades along the walls, but clean and functioning bathrooms; a/c—when it works; the hotel is well-patronised by ranchers and absentee landowners from Brasília. The town has a frontier atmosphere, although mudhuts are being replaced by brick: cowboy hats, battered Chevrolet pick-ups, skinny mules and a red light district. Airport 17 km. SW. Conceição would be a useful base for visiting the Ilha do Bananal.

Douglas Trent, of Tropical Tours, Belo Horizonte (see page 340), writes: *Bananal* is the world's largest river island, located in the state of Tocantins on the northeastern border of Mato Grosso. The island is formed by a division in the south of the Rio Araguaia and is approximately 320 km. long. The entire island was originally a national park (called **Parque Nacional Araguaia**), which was then cut in half and later further reduced to its current size of 562,312 ha. (of an original 2 million). The island and park are subject to seasonal flooding and contain several permanent lakes. The island, and especially the park, form one of the more spectacular wildlife areas on the continent, in many ways similar to the Pantanal. The vegetation is a transition zone between the *cerrado* (woody savanna) and Amazon forests, with gallery forests along the many waterways. There are several marshlands throughout the island.
    The fauna is also transitional. More than 300 bird species are found here, including the hoatzin, hyacinthine macaw, harpy eagle and black-fronted piping guan. The giant anteater, maned wolf, bush dog, giant otter, jaguar, puma, marsh deer, pampas deer, American tapir, yellow anaconda and South American river turtle also occur here. The island is flooded most of the year, with the prime visiting (dry) season being from June to early October, when the beaches are exposed. Unfortunately, the infrastructure for tourism aside from fishing expeditions (the island is a premier spot for big fish) is very limited. Access to the park is through the small but pleasant town of *Santa Teresinha* (pop. 6,000) which is north of São Felix (see below), and is the gateway to the park. A charming hotel is the *Bananal*, Pça Tarcila Braga 106, CEP 78395 (Mato Grosso), B with full board. There is room only for 10; make your reservations well in advance. Reservations can be made by mail, allowing several months for the mail to get through, or through Focus Tours, T (031) 223-3811 Tlx. (031) 3823 RAPT BR.
    Permission to visit the park should be obtained in advance from Sr. Levi Vargas, Director of the Park, IBDF, R. 229, No. 95, Setor Universitário, 74.000 Goiânia. There is some simple accommodation for scientists at the park, which can sometimes be reserved at the address above or from IBDF, the National Parks department in Brasília. Bring your own food, and the severely underpaid but dedicated staff would appreciate any extra food or financial help, although it will not be solicited. A boat to the park can be lined up at the *Hotel Bananal*.

*São Félix do Araguaia* (pop. 15,000) is a larger town with more infrastructure for fishing. A very simple hotel with the best view in town is the *Mini Hotel Araguaia*, Av. Araguaia 344,

T (065) 522-1154, E with breakfast. They have a/c rooms, not rec., electricity is turned off at night and the closed-in room gets very hot. Another hotel, *Xavante*, is in the city centre. A good restaurant is the *Pizzaria Cantinho da Peixada* on Av. Araguaia, next to the Texaco station, overlooking the river. *Bar Paralelos* has live music. Many Carajás indians are found in town; a depot of their handicrafts is between the *Pizzaria* and *Mini Hotel* on Av. Araguaia.

Bananal can be visited from São Félix (with permission from Funai in the town) by crossing the river to the Carajá village of Santa Isabela de Morra and asking to see the chief, Aruiana, who can tell you the history of the tribe. The island can be crossed from São Félix to São Miguel de Araguaia by taking an 8-hour trip (departures twice a week) with Zico in his van (contact him at the *Bar Beira*). From São Miguel a 5-hour bus trip brings you to Porangatu (*Hotel Mauriti*, F, shower, restaurant) on the Belém-Brasília highway.

Access to both Santa Teresinha and São Félix is by Brasil Central/TAM flights, and to São Félix by bus from Barra do Garças, 17 hours, and from Marabá. The air service is unreliable and, as the planes hold just 15 passengers, it is common to get held over for a day or two. In Sta. Teresinha look out for a man in a yellowish taxi who kindly offers a free ride and then tries to collect outrageous sums from foreigners. There are legitimate taxis available—use them. Mosquito nets are highly recommended: high incidence of malaria.

It seems that from São Miguel de Araguaia you can head south on GO-164 for about 140 km; turn left to Peixe and cross the Rio Araguaia by ferry to Cocalinho. From here drive to the BR-158, crossing both the Rios Cristalino and das Mortes by more ferries (spectacular limestone caverns have been reported 20 km. before the Rio das Mortes ferry and 6 km. after the limestone quarry). At BR-158 turn left to Agua Boa (pop. 20,000, *Palace Hotel*, C; *Manga Rosa*, good churrascaria), then continue to Barra do Garças. If heading for the Pantanal, note that BR-070 from Barra to Cuiabá is in poor condition after the turn to Poxoréo; better to go to Rondonópolis, either for Cuiabá or Campo Grande.

In the far SW of Goiás is the **Emas National Park**, about 130 km. from Mineiros, a town just off the Brasília-Cuiabá road. Father Herbert Hermes (US) at the São José convent, Mineiros, can arrange permission to visit (necessary, or from IBDF address above), also Sr. José Roberto Carvalho at Prefeitura. A 3-day, 4-night visit to the Park costs about US$50. The park, of 1,300 sq. km., contains rolling prairies with numerous termite mounds, savanna-type woodland and forested rivers. Among the mammals encountered are armadillos, giant anteaters, marsh and pampas deer, the maned wolf and the rare giant otter. Birds include rheas, king vulture and crested screamers (seriema). It is reported that half the park was destroyed by fire in 1987.

To the west of Goiás are the states of Mato Grosso and Mato Grosso do Sul, with a combined area of 1,231,549 sq. km. and a population of only about 3.5 million, or under three persons to the square km. The two states are half covered with forest, with a large swampy area (220,000 sq. km) called the Pantanal (roughly west of a line between Campo Grande and Cuiabá, between which there is a direct road), partly flooded in the rainy season (**see page 490**). East of this line the pasture plains begin to appear. The Noroeste Railway and a road run across Mato Grosso do Sul through Campo Grande to Porto Esperança and Corumbá, both on the Rio Paraguay; much of the journey is across swamps, offering many sights of birds and other wildlife.

***Campo Grande*** (pop. 384,000) the capital of the State of Mato Grosso do Sul is a pleasant modern town. It was founded in 1899 and became state capital in 1979. Because of the *terra roxa* (red earth), it is called the "Cidade Morena". In the centre is a shady park and nearby the Casa do Artesanato (Av. Calógeras and Afonso Pena) has a good collection of Indian jewellery and arrows on sale. There is a market (Feira Livre) on Weds. and Sats. Mato Grosso do Sul (pop. 1,729,000) is a good region for buying cheap, good leather shoes.

**Museu Regional Dom Bosco (Regional Indian Museum)**, R. Barão do Rio Branco 1843 (open daily 0700-1100, 1300-1700, T 383-3994), has interesting exhibits and handicrafts of the Pantanal and Mato Grosso Indians. There is also a collection of animals, birds and butterflies (particularly good and well-preserved, if not well labelled) from the Pantanal, and a fossil collection.

**Hotels** *Jandaia*, R. Barão de Rio Branco 1271, T 384-4081, well located, best, A+. *Campo Grande*, R. 13 de Maio 2825, T 384-6061, a/c, luxury, A. *Concord*, Av. Calógeras 1624, T 384-3081, very good, swimming pool, a/c, A. *Fenícia*, Av. Calógeras 2262, T 383-2001, a/c,

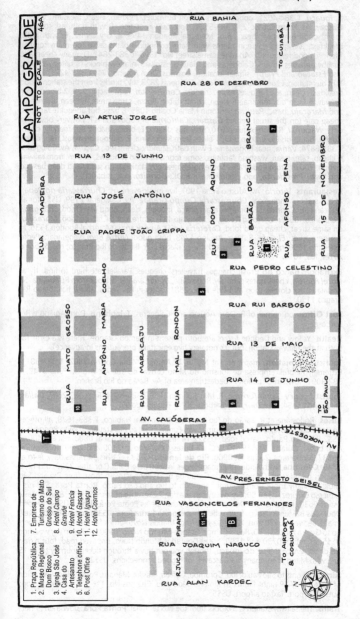

CAMPO GRANDE
NOT TO SCALE
46A

1. Praça República
2. Museo Regional Dom Bosco
3. Igreja São José
4. Casa do Artesanato
5. Telephone office
6. Post Office
7. Empresa de Turismo do Mato Grosso do Sul
8. Hotel Campo Grande
9. Hotel Fenícia
10. Hotel Gaspar
11. Hotel Iguaçu
12. Hotel Cosmos

RUA BAHIA
TO CUIABÁ
RUA 28 DE DEZEMBRO
RUA ARTUR JORGE
RUA 13 DE JUNHO
RUA JOSÉ ANTÔNIO
RUA PADRE JOÃO CRIPPA
RUA PEDRO CELESTINO
RUA RUI BARBOSO
RUA 13 DE MAIO
RUA 14 DE JUNHO
AV. CALÓGERAS
AV. NOROESTE
AV. PRES. ERNESTO GEISEL
RUA VASCONCELOS FERNANDES
RUA JOAQUIM NABUCO
RUA ALAN KARDEC
TO SÃO PAULO
TO AIRPORT & CORUMBÁ

RUA MADEIRA
RUA MATO GROSSO
RUA ANTÔNIO MARIA COELHO
RUA MARACAJU
RUA MAL. RONDON
RUA DOM AQUINO
RUA BARÃO DO RIO BRANCO
RUA AFONSO PENA
RUA 15 DE NOVEMBRO
RUA PIRAMA
R.JUCA

N

B. *Iguaçu*, T 384-4621, opposite bus station but quiet, modern, clean, pleasant, C, rec.; *Gaspar*, Av. Mato Grosso 2, T 383-5121, opp. railway station, D with bath, ask for quiet room, good breakfast, clean. *Rio*, Marechal Rondón 1499, in city centre, E, with bath, breakfast, a/c, good value in rooms with bath (communal baths serve too many rooms), friendly, good restaurant; *Anache*, same street No. 1396, T 383-2841, D; many cheap and shabby *pensões* on Avs. Calógeras and Mato Grosso within a few blocks of railway station; also *Estaçao* and *Priape*, similar location. *Cosmos*, Dom Aquino 771, T 383-4271, 1 block N of bus station, E, good value; *União*, E, Calógeras 2828, 1½ blocks from the station, good breakfast, clean, ask for quiet room, friendly; *Continental*, R. Maracaju 229, 2 blocks from railway, 5 from bus terminal, F, clean, comfortable; *Plaza*, same street, F, clean, unfriendly and *Maracaju*, basic; *Paulista*, António Maria Coelho 1085, F, basic but adequate facilities, cheap café (on the street behind *Gaspar*); *Califórnia* at Rodoviária is F, but very basic and dirty; *Nacional*, R. Dom Aquino 610, near bus station, E, basic, shabby but friendly, clean; *Rocha*, Barão do Rio Branco 343, 1 block from Rodoviária, E without breakfast, fan, clean, T 383-6874; *Vania*, near Rodoviária, F with bath, laundry, clean, rec.; *Caçula*, Av. Calógeras, F, cheap, safe, clean, washing facilities, some rooms have no windows, 300 m. from railway station, 700 m. from Rodoviária. Some hotels near bus station both seedy and dear, best go into town (*Presidente*, opp. Rodoviária, is F, OK; *Dormitório*, F, is basic).

**Restaurants** *Vitório*, Av. Afonso Pena 1907, live music evenings; *Churrascaria do Papai*, at bus station, huge meal; *Churrascaria Campo Grande*, Av. Calógeras 2199, US$3 for all you can eat; *Carinca*, SE corner of main *praça*, modern, clean, good plain food. *Shanghai*, Rio Branco 1037, rec.; *Hong Kong*, R. Maracaju 131, centre, good Chinese food; *Maracaju*, on same street, cheap good food; *Cafeteria Lojas Americanas*, Marechal Rondón 1336, in a supermarket; *El Café*, R. Dom Aquino 1248, both good. *Nutre Bem*, vegetarian, Pedro Celestino 1696, good. Plenty of good, cheap places in R. Barão de Rio Branco, e.g. *Sabor e Artes*, No. 1016.

**Exchange** Banco do Brasil changes travellers' cheques. Parallel rate hard to find, try at *Hotel Fenícia*, check notes carefully, Rodoviária, *Hotel Caranda*, 1 block from Rodoviária; Sr. Abdala in the clothes shop at 14 de Julho 2581; or try in Las Vegas billiard hall, Barao Rio Branco 1130.

**Post Office** on corner of R. Dom Aquino and Calógeras. **Telephone** Dom Aquino e Rui Barbosa.

**Health** Yellow and Dengue fevers are both present in Campo Grande. There is a clinic for both at the railway station, but it's not very hygienic (take precautions in advance).

**Tourist Information**, maps, etc. at MSTur, R. Antônio Maria Coelho 2802, T 382-3811. Extremely helpful. Empresa de Turismo do Mato Grosso do Sul, Av. Afonso Pena 314C, T 382-3091. Town information in pedestrian area of Av. Barão do Rio Branco.

**Tourist Agency** *Tainá Turismo*, R. Mal. Rondon 1636, T 384-6544, Telex 067-2607; *Dallas*, Rio Branco 1454. *Vax Tour*, Ruy Barbosa 3014, English spoken.

**Buses** Rodoviária at R. Barão do Rio Branco e R. Joaquim Nabuco, T 383-1678, all offices on 2nd floor; 2 long blocks' walk from town. Fun fair next to bus station. (Taxi to Rodoviária, US$2.80.) São Paulo, paved road, US$22 14 hrs. 9 buses daily, 1st at 0800, last at 2400, 3 *leito* buses. Cuiabá, US$18, 10 hrs., 12 buses daily, *leito* at 2100 and 2200. To Brasília, US$37 (Motta rec.), 23 hrs. at 0900. Rio de Janeiro, US$33, 21 hrs., 4 buses daily, *leito* at 1745. Corumbá, with Andorinha, many buses leaving before 0800 or after 2200, US$12, 6 hrs., on paved road. Campo Grande-Corumbá buses connect with those from Rio and São Paulo, similarly those from Corumbá through to Rio and São Paulo. Ponta Porã, 5½ hrs., Expresso Queiroz, US$6.50, 5 ordinary buses a day, 2 executive buses, US$9.75, 8 buses daily, 1st at 0630, last at 2130. Dourados, same schedule as Ponta Porã, 4 hrs., US$4. Beyond Dourados is Mundo Novo, from where buses go to Ponta Porã (0530) and to Porto Frajelli (many between 0420 and 1900, ½ hr.); from Mundo Novo ferries for cars and passengers go to Guaíra for US$0.30. Buses Campo Grande-**Mundo Novo**, 0900, 10 hrs. in dry weather, US$5.50, return 0730 and 1800; buses Dourados-Mundo Novo, unpaved road, four a day. No direct service to **Foz do Iguaçu**, though you can buy a through ticket; journey takes 15 hrs. with Maringá company via Cascavel, with good connections, US$24.50.

**Air** Daily flights to São Paulo, Rio, Corumbá, Cuiabá, Brasília, Manaus, Porto Velho. Reduction of 12% on VASP night flights to Rio and São Paulo. City bus No. 116, "V. Popular," stops outside airport. Taxi to airport, US$5.

**Trains** The railway station is 5 blocks from the bus terminal. **Ponta Porã**, slow train (9 hrs.)

Tues., Thur., Sat. at 1000 (lone females are advised to sit on left-hand side since, 1 hour before Ponta Porã, is a predominantly male factory town where you may get some unwanted attention). Ponta Porã to **Campo Grande** at 0720, Mon., Wed., Fri., US$6.50 1st class, US$3.50 2nd class on the train (this service is under threat—check). To **Corumbá**: train leaves Tues., Thur., Sat., 0820, Mon., Wed., Fri., 2100, 11 hrs, many timetable changes, the night service is due to be abandoned and the day service cut to once a week, so check in advance, meals served at seats, US$3. Fares US$15 1st class, US$10 2nd class, US$23 for a double sleeper (no advance ticket sales, office open 1 ½ hrs before train departs, a very tiring journey). Thefts and drugged food reported on this journey, especially in July when trains are very crowded. The only **trains to Bauru** are those which originate in Corumbá, leaving Campo Grande 1830, Mon., Wed. and Fri. (i.e. no local Campo Grande-Bauru train); check in advance if possible. First class fare to Bauru is US$9.

The Campo Grande—São Paulo journey can be broken at **Tres Lagoas** near the Paraná river and on the railway, and 10 hours by paved road to São Paulo (bus Campo Grande—Tres Lagoas, 6 hrs., US$12.75, dep. 0800, 1200 and 2230, an interesting journey). *Novo Hotel* near bus station, F. friendly.

The road from Campo Grande to the Paraguayan border passes through **Dourados** (*Hotel Alphonsus*, C, Av. Pres. Vargas 603). Good bus connections to Campo Grande, Ponta Porã and Mundo Novo (see under Campo Grande, Buses, above).

A road and railway run SW from Campo Grande to **Ponta Porã** (pop. 50,000) on the Paraguayan border opposite the town of Pedro Juan Caballero.

**Hotels** *Pousada do Bosque*, very nice motel type with a/c, restaurant and swimming pool, Av. Pres. Vargas, out of town, T 431-1181, C. *Barcelona*, R. Guia Lopes, maze-like building, pool, restaurant, a/c, D. *Internacional*, R. Internacional 1267, T 431-1243, D with a/c, E with bath or without, hot showers, clean, good breakfasts, rec.; *Francia*, E, opposite *Barcelona*, bath, clean, friendly, restaurant, US$3 for big meal. *Grande*, Av. Brasil 1181, E. *Dos Viajantes*, across park opp. railway station, F, very basic, clean.

**Restaurants** *Top Lanches*, beside *Hotel Barcelona*, cheap and friendly. *Chopão*, good food at reasonable prices. *Pepe's Lunch e Pizzeria*, good, fairly cheap; *Karina Lanches*, near Federal Police office, good, cheap; *Santa Antônia*, rec.

**Electric Current**  220 volts A.C.

**Exchange**  Banco do Brasil changes travellers' cheques. Several *cambios* on the Paraguayan side, but none deal in cheques. Many in the centre of town (but on Sun. change money in hotels or the gambling hall beneath Livraria Sulamérica).

The border post at Ponta Porã normally closes at 1700 (it is also closed on national holidays). The Federal Police office is in a new white building shared with an engineering supply company in the same block as the Expresso Queiroz Rodoviária, R. Mal. Floriano, open 0800. To reach Paraguayan control, follow the R. Guia Lopes 4 blocks into Paraguay. If crossing into Paraguay some nationalities require visa from Paraguayan consulate next door to *Hotel Internacional*, R. Internacional (check requirements carefully).

A new area of tourist interest in Mato Grosso do Sul is being established in the municipalities of **Bonito** (hotels: *Bonanza, Alvorado, Florestal*, all F; campsite at Ilha do Padre, 10 km. N of Bonito, very pleasant, no regular transport; restaurant, *Tapera*) and **Aquidauana** (several hotels around railway station, including *Fluminense*, F with fan and breakfast, a/c more expensive), where cave formations comparable to those found in the Lagoa Santa region of Minas Gerais are encountered. Two of the first to be opened are the **Lago a Azul and N.S. Aparecida** (Sérgio Gonzales in Prefeitura of Bonito controls entry), both 26 km. from Bonito (no buses) and some 260 km. from Campo Grande. Lago a Azul has a lake 150 metres long and 70 metres wide. It is best visited in Jan.-Feb., 0700-0900 for the light, but there are no organized visits as yet, so Brazilian holiday times are best. Bus Bonito-Campo Grande, US$6, 3 hrs, 0545 and 1600. Also possible by changing at Jardim. Daily bus between Bonito and Aquidauana, about 3 hrs. on dirt road. From Bonito there is a road to **Puerto Murtinho** where a boat crosses to Isla Margarita in Paraguay. Hotels *Eldorado*, F, friendly, clean, good food; *Beira Rio*, F, basic; *Caicaras*, F; *Americano*, F, 2 *lanchonetes, Churrascaria Gaspão*, Elia, taxi driver, will change money.

**Corumbá** (pop. 84,000) on the River Paraguai, with Bolivia on the opposite bank and beautiful views of the river, has millions of mosquitoes in Dec., Jan. and Feb., but is a pleasant place nevertheless. River boats ply occasionally between it and

Buenos Aires. The Forte Junqueira, the city's most historic building, which may be visited, was built in 1772. In the hills to the south is the world's greatest reserve of manganese, now beginning to be worked. From the Bolivian border town of Quijarro a 650-km. railway is open westwards to Santa Cruz de la Sierra, and there is a road of sorts. The Campo Grande-Corumbá road, via Aquidauana, crosses the Paraguai (now mostly paved, two service stations before the Rio Miranda bridge). The scenery between Campo Grande and Corumbá is most interesting, the road and railway follow different routes, but the train is more reliable than the bus (though slower). Corumbá is the best starting point for the southern part of the Pantanal, with boat and jeep trips and access to the major hotel/farms.

**Warning**  Police have very strict controls on drug-trafficking in Corumbá; there are many drug-runners, searches are very thorough.

**Climate**  Hot and humid (70%); cooler in June-July, very hot from Sept. to Jan.

**Hotels**  *Santa Mônica*, R. Antônio Maria Coelho 369, T 231-3001, a/c, B, good restaurant; *Alphahotel*, next door, F, clean, tours arranged. *Nacional*, R. América 936, A, good pool, T 231-6868; *Santa Rita*, Dom Aquino 860 (unsigned), T 231-5453, D, with bath, E without, bathrooms dirty otherwise clean but basic, noisy, good meals in restaurant, reported not safe for luggage; *La Siesta*, Dom Aquino 47, good, helpful, restaurant; *O Laçador*, R. América 482, T 231-6933, D without breakfast, rec; *Victoria Régia*, R. Ladário 271, F, clean, rec; *Moderna*, R. Delamaré 909, E, restaurant; *Schabib*, R. Frei Mariano 1153, F, basic but clean, owner friendly, multilingual and helpful; *Solar da Glória*, R. 13 de Junho 1297, T 231-3822, F, friendly; *Nova Horizonte* F, on steep street down to port, friendly and clean. *Esplanada*, opp. railway station, F, clean, cold shower, basic; *Côndor*, R. Delamaré, F, Modfull, next door, F; other small clean hotels: *Irure*, R. 13 de Junho 776, *Campus*, R. Antônio João 133, D-E, clean, good value; *Madrid*, R. Cuiabá 926, D, clean, *Lincoln*, R. 15 de Novembro, and *Pousada de Marieta*, América 243; *International*, in sight of Rodoviária, E, clean, friendly. **Youth Hostel** R. Antônio Maria, rec., the owner, Sr. Pontis, organizes jungle trips, cheaper for a group, negotiate price.

**Restaurants**  *Churrascaria Gaúcha*, R. Frei Mariano; *Tarantella* (Italian), R. Frei Mariano and América, large helpings, not cheap, but rec. *Barril de Ouro*, R. Frei Mariano; *Palácio das Pizzas*, at No. 468, friendly, good and cheap; *Peixaria de Lulu*, R. Antônio João, nr. centre, good fish; *El Dorado*, on waterfront, good for fish; *Churrascaria Rodeio*, 13 de Junho 760, very good, *Casa Mia*, R. Dom Aquino; good local food at corner of R. Delamaré and Antônio João, about US$6; on the waterfront you can eat good fish at *Portal do Pantanal* and *El Pacu*, run by a German, Hermann, and his Brazilian wife. Good beer in *Xaraes*, R. Gen. Rondon; Bolivian snacks in *'Sslato*, R. Dom Aquino.

**Shopping**  Arts and Crafts Centre, R. Dom Aquino Correa, in a converted prison.

**Exchange**  Banco do Brasil changes travellers' cheques from 1100 only. Casa Palestino, Frei Mariano, just below the Praça gives good rates. Many money changers at the border—cash only. Street traders in shopping street between R. Delamaré and Post Office.

**Tourist Office**  R. Delamaré 1557, T 231-6030, Portuguese only spoken, not very helpful.

**Shipping**  No regular passenger service to Asunción (see **Paraguay** chapter). It may be possible to get a boat to Porto Esperança and continue from there. Seek information at travel agents, *El Pacu* restaurant, or from small cargo boats at the waterfront. (See page 493, under Cáceres.)

**Air**  VASP daily to Campo Grande and on to São Paulo; VASP also daily to Cuiabá, Brasília, Goiânia, Belo Horizonte, and Rio de Janeiro. TAM, Tues., Sat., LAB, Mon., Wed., Sat., to Santa Cruz. Airline office at Pto. Suárez or 3 hrs. before flight at airport. Daily private flights to Santa Cruz, Bolivia, especially in rainy season—cheaper to travel overland to Asunción and fly from there.

**Trains and Buses**  The day train from Corumbá to Bauru, via Campo Grande and with very poor connections to **São Paulo**, leaves Mon., Wed. and Fri., at 0700, arriving in Campo Grande at 1830, and Bauru the next afternoon at 1600, US$27 (very crowded and tiring). To **Campo Grande** only, Tues., Thur., Sun. 1900, 11 hrs, double cabin US$23, single US$15, reclining seat US$10. All trains serve food. These times have been subject to frequent changes and are scheduled for reduction, check in advance (T station 231-2876). Tickets can only be

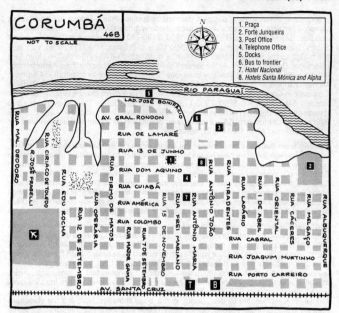

booked as far as Bauru (tickets can be bought from 1300 on previous day). Buses from Campo Grande to São Paulo are quicker, but dearer. The Corumbá-**São Paulo** bus journey takes at least 22 hrs. (US$28). As there is no fixed timetable the year round, confirm bus times in advance (T 231-3783); it is best to go Corumbá-**Campo Grande**, 6 hrs., US$12, many buses, then make a connection to all parts of Brazil. Two buses (Andorinha, rec.) to Rio daily 0800 and 2300, US$22, 28 hrs., with change Campo Grande, US$21. To **Cuiabá**, 18 hrs, US$24; to **Ponta Porã**, for Paraguay, daily, 12 hrs. Bus station is on R. Porto Carrero, next to the railway station and a few blocks from town centre (also for Andorinha buses; Viação Motta bus terminal is nearby). Taxis from both stations to centre are extortionate. Don't rely on getting a supply of cruzeiros in Bauru; exchange is difficult there. Stock up in Corumbá.

There are four train services to **Santa Cruz** in Bolivia, the *ferrobus*, *rápido*, *omnibus* and *mixto*; all leave from Quijarro, the Bolivian frontier station, not from Corumbá. The schedule of each appears to change frequently so check on arrival in Corumbá. There is a Bolivian railway office at Corumbá railway station for all details, tickets may be booked through Receptivo Pantanal agency. Tickets must be purchased in Quijarro on day of departure, go as early as possible (it may be best to stay in Quijarro to get a good place in the queue; 2 or 3 F hotels opp. station, basic). If the ticket office has "sold out", ask around on the platform as people buy up tickets and sell them for a few bolivianos more: the money-exchange women know all about it. Quijarro-Santa Cruz *ferrobus*, Tues., Thur., Sat. 1800, Pullman US$15, special US$10; *pullman* Quijarro-Santa Cruz Wed., Sun. 1100; *rápido*, Mon., Fri. 1220; *mixto* also leave twice a week; fares on last 3, Pullman US$7.50, first US$6.50, second US$4 (all converted from bolivianos). If immigration is closed, buy your train ticket before going there. It is worth buying a 1st class seat, which is much more comfortable on night trips than the 2nd class, but these are often mysteriously "sold out". 2nd class is on the baggage van floor, is crowded and there are no toilet or water facilities. A reader advises taking sticky tape to block up the cockroach holes. Stops at stations are brief; take your own water; journey time 19½ hrs (not rec.). Colectivo Corumbá-Quijarro, US$2.40, from in front of Dona Aparecida's store, *A Favorita*, R. Antônio Maria Coelho (Dona Aparecida changes money outside banking hours; bargaining recommended). Also taxis, US$12 per taxi; colectivo border—Quijarro US$1.50. The railway to Santa Cruz is liable to flood damage.

**Going to Bolivia** Immigration and emigration formalities are constantly changing so check procedure in advance. Have passport stamped by Brazilian Policia Federal at Corumbá bus station (open often at variance with published opening hours, 0600-1230, 1430-1630, Sat. and Sun. 0730-0830, 1100-1230, 1430-1630, 2130-2400). Brazilian exit stamp is valid for 5 days. Take bus from port end of R. Antônio Maria to Bolivian border (15 mins.), walk over the bridge to the Bolivian border post (white building), go through formalities, then take colectivo to Quijarro for train. At the border Bolivian police stamp passport free. At the frontier, it is not necessary to pay any money to anyone. Show ticket at border to return to Corumbá. Money changers at the border and in Quijarro offer same rates as in Corumbá. Bolivian Consulate in Corumbá: R. Antônio Maria Coelho 852 (colectivos may be caught nearby for frontier), Mon.-Fri., 0700-1100, 1500-1730, Sat. and Sun. closed. They tell everyone a visa is necessary, but this may not be true: check Bolivian section "Information for Visitors". Those who need a visa must pay US$5; a yellow fever vaccination certificate is required. Alternative to train: Bolivian LAB or TAM flights, see above.

**Coming from Bolivia**  If you arrive at the border when the Bolivian offices are closed (e.g. at night) and you therefore have no exit stamp, be prepared to be sent back for an exit stamp by Brazilian officials in Corumbá (the Bolivian border post opens at 0700). If you arrive in Brazil without a yellow fever vaccination certificate, you may have to go to R. 7 de Setembro, Corumbá, for an inoculation. When travelling from Quijarro, take a taxi (bargain fare) or walk to the Bolivian border, go through formalities (US$0.15), outside office take bus to Corumbá Rodoviária (US$0.10). Find a hotel then take a taxi or walk to railway station for Brazilian formalities (some buses go direct to the station): if you're in luck the office will be open.

**Pantanal**  This vast swampy area, located between Cuiabá, Campo Grande and the Bolivian frontier, is one of the world's great wildlife preserves, slowly being opened up to tourism. The flora and fauna are similar in many ways to those of the Amazon basin, though because of the more veldt-like open land, the wildlife can be viewed more easily than in the dense jungle growth. Principal life seen in this area are over 650 species of birds, in the main, waders and water fowl, storks (the *tuiuiu* or jabiru stork is almost 1.2 metres tall), herons, coots, ducks, as well as pheasants, quails and parrots. There are some 230 varieties of fish, from the giant *pintado*, weighing up to 80 kilos, to the voracious *piranha*. Fishing here is exceptionally good. Animal life is represented by deer, ocelot, puma, boar, anteaters, tapir, and the ubiquitous *capivara*, a species of giant aquatic guinea-pig. Probably the most impressive sight is the *jacaré* (Brazilian alligator). The extraordinary thing is that man and his domesticated cattle thrive together with the wildlife with seemingly little friction. Local farmers protect the area jealously. (Only one area is officially national park, the Biological Reserve of Cará-Cará in the municipality of Poconé, 135,000 hectares of land and water, only accessible by air or river. Permission to visit at Delegacia Estadual do IBDF, Av. Jaime Figueredo 550, CPA de Cuiabá, CEP 78.000, Cuiabá.) Hunting in any form is strictly forbidden. Fishing is allowed with a licence (enquire at travel agents); it is not encouraged in the breeding season Oct-Jan. The International Union for the Conservation of Nature is concerned at the amount of poaching, particularly of *jacaré* skins and *capivaras*. Recently, the Forestry Police have built control points on all major access roads to the Pantanal.

There are two distinct seasons. In the rainy season (Nov.-March, wettest in February), most of the land floods and flies abound, and cattle crowd on to the few islands remaining above water, while the wild animals have long since left the area, at this time an experienced guide and a 4-wheel drive vehicle are essential. The dry season (July to October) is the nesting and breeding season. The birds form vast nesting areas, with hundreds and thousands crowding the trees creating an almost unsupportable cacophony of sounds; the white sand river beaches are exposed and *jacarés* bask in the sun.

The Pantanal is not easy to visit. The best starting points are Cuiabá, Corumbá and Campo Grande, from where one finds public transport all around the perimeter, but none at all within. Hitching is not advised because of the amount of drug smuggling in the area. Litter is becoming a problem; don't contribute to it. Wild camping is possible if you have your own transport. Remember that the longer you stay the more likely you are to see rare wildlife. Wear long sleeves and long trousers and spray clothes as well as skin with insect repellant. In winter temperatures fall to 10°, warm clothing and covers or sleeping bag are needed at night.

There are several lodges with fair to good accommodation, some only approachable by air or river; most are relatively expensive. The best plan is to hire a car and check accommodation for yourself. Following is a list of those presently operating:

**From Campo Grande**: *Hotel dos Camalotes*, Porto Murtinho, 440 km. from Campo Grande; access by bus long, tedious, bumpy and dusty; best access by air taxi. 4-star luxury hotel on the shores of the Paraguai river, favoured by wealthy Paulistas, A, with full board. *Cabana do*

*Pescador*, 50 km. from Aquidauana on the Miranda river, access by bus to Aquidauana, and local bus to Bonito (**see page 487**), A, includes breakfast. *Pousada Agua Pek*, near Aquidauana, farmhouse hotel, horseriding, boat trips, trekking, full board, friendly and clean; *Pousada Caiman*, near Miranda, first class, full board, excursions, book in advance (Evidencia, Corumbá); *Fazenda Solabra*, T (067) 242-1162, 6 km. from Miranda, which is 209 km. from Corumbá, 198 from Campo Grande, is rec., A, including all meals; it is by the Rio Salobra (clear water) and Rio Miranda, with birds and animals easily seen. Take bus from Campo Grande to Miranda, and alight 50 m. from the bridge over Rio Miranda, turn left for 1,200 m to the *Fazenda*; by train, coming from Campo Grande, get out one stop after Miranda, 250 m. to the *Fazenda*. There is a good camp site 30 km. past Miranda. Alternatively, hire a car in Corumbá and drive to Miranda, but note that the dirt road is bad after rain (consequently not much traffic and more wildlife can be seen). Car with driver can be hired at Salobra for US$25.

To see the Pantanal cheaply, get off the bus from Campo Grande to Corumbá at the ferry across the Rio Paraguai (Porto Esperança). On the Corumbá side is a small hotel on the river bank, negotiate price. Walk down the road early a.m., or late p.m. (better on the Campo Grande side), or take a small boat from the hotel (maybe included in the price) to see a wide variety of animals and birds. Porto Esperança is on a spur line from the main Campo Grande-Corumbá railway, from Agente Inocêncio, but as rail services are being reduced, the option of going by train is limited. You can walk back along the track, but this is dangerous on the bridges, which have gaps between the sleepers.

**From Corumbá**: One day river trips available on river boats with a capacity of 80 passengers, US$20, transfers and hot fish meal inc. Tickets at travel agents. *Pousada do Pantanal*, 125 km. from Corumbá near the Campo Grande road at Fazenda Santa Clara (still a working cattle ranch), very comfortable, easy access by bus, reservations from all agencies in Corumbá; US$100 p.p. for groups of 4-6 for 3 days/2 nights, good food, with horseback, car and boat excursions, guides included, canoes, simple fishing gear, motor boats for rent (try bargaining in the off-season for reduced rates). *Fazenda Santa Blanca*, on the Rio Paraguai, 15 mins. by boat S of Porto Esperanza, B, full board, very clean and friendly, good kayak excursions, horseriding (US$5), information from R. 15 de Novembro 659, 79300 Corumbá, T 067-231-1460, or Flins Travel (Walter Zoss), R. do Acre 92, 6th floor, 602, CEP 20.081, Rio de Janeiro, T (021) 253-8588/0195, Telex 021 32971 ATDA or Safári Fotográfico, R. Frei Mariano 502, Corumbá, T 231-5797 Highly recommended is *Fazenda Leque*, Roberto Kassan (contact through R. América 262, Corumbá, T 231-1598): US$65 p.p. for 3 days, 6 per group, US$5-10 p.p. per day if you want to stay longer (1990 prices); take mosquito coils; unlimited use of horses and boats, on small lake behind the farm, good food; plenty of wildlife to be seen. *Ilha do Santo Antônio*, farm, rooms with bath, restaurant with good food, clean, boat, horse and trekking trips (reservations through Evidência or Melgatur); *Rancho no Paraíso* (Berenice), C, with food, 180 km from Corumbá in the middle of one of the most interesting sections of the Pantanal (Ñecolândia), very simple but clean, horse trekking, photo safaris, adventure programme (enquiries: Melgatur); *Pousada do Paraíso*, farmhouse now used as a hotel (booking as for *Santo Antônio*). The going rate for a 3-day photosafari by jeep is US$60 p.p. for 4-6 people (e.g. through Melgatour); also fishing trips for 4 days with Hotelboat for 8 (e.g. *Pérola do Pantanal* and *Pantanal Tours*, Corumbá—must be booked in advance). Hotels specialising in fishing, all reached from Corumbá by road: *Pesqueiro do Lontra*, A, including meals T (067) 383-4532, 180 km from Aquidauana on the Corumbá road. *Pesqueiro Tarumã* and *Pesqueiro Paraíso do Dourado* (contact Evidência Turismo). José Paraguaio, r. Manoel Cavassa 331, T (067) 231-1721, 3 day tours to *Fazenda São Joaquim*, US$60, rec.

**Travel Agents in Corumbá**: Evidência Turismo, R. Cuiabá 861, T 231-3840, Telex 67-7060, specializes in 1-day trips (English, French, Spanish spoken); **gatur**, Ladeira Cunha e Cruz 8, T 231-2523, Telex 67-7084, 2-8 day tours in N and S Pantanal, ecological trips, helpful (English and German spoken); **Receptivo Pantanal**, R. Frei Mariano 502, T 231-5795, helpful (1-day tour US$50, 3-day US$100, 4-day US$130; **Pantanal Tours**, R. Manoel Cavassa 61, T 231-4683, fishing trips by hotel boat; **Pérola do Pantanal Viagens e Turismo**, R.Manoel Cavassa 219, T 231-1460, good one-day river tour with *Lancha Pérola*. **Turismo Sandino**, R. Firmo de Matos, T 231-3345, rec. tours, good food; **Pantur**, R América 969, T 231-4343 helpful; **Crocodile Tours**, Nova Corumbá Q-18 C-14, 3 days US$60, meals good, Guides, Murilo Reis, R. Tiradentes 1127, rec.

Julie Williams (Muswellbrook, NSW) writes: On arival in Corumbá you will be met by private tour guides offering a tour on the spot. The tours are of 3-4 days, costing US$50-60 (includes all food, accommodation and transport). There is fierce competition between guides who provide similar services in the Ñecolândia region. Travel is in the back of a pick-up (good for seeing animals), up to a maximum of 6. Accommodation is in a hammock under palm thatch on a fazenda. Food is good. If you want flushing toilets, showers or luxury cabins, approach an agency. Guides provide bottled mineral water, but you must take a hat, sun screen and mosquito repellent. Gather a group together, shop around and "one of these tours could be the highlight of your travels". Guides who have been recommended include Jean, T 231-1510 and Bosco, T 231-1635, 3 days, 2 nights with 4-wheel-drive transport, US$65, Joaquin, Katu, or Murilo, ask in *Hotel Schabib*. Rey Tur, Manoel Cavassa 127, guide Ico, knows area well, rec.

Camping out is preferable to staying in *fazendas* because less driving (which scares animals) is involved, and you can see the wildlife at its greatest period of activity—dawn and dusk (protection against mosquitoes essential). In the wet season, access to the Pantanal from Corumbá is only by boat. Tues. boat Corumbá-Poconé, 36 hrs., US$12. Boats can be hired for US$35 a day. Cattle boats will take passengers on their round trips to farms in the Pantanal, 3 days, US$6.50 but take your own food—it is not possible to disembark. Ask at Bacia da Prata, 10 mins. out of Corumbá on the Ladário bus (the gatekeeper is unhelpful). Road trips from Corumbá into the Pantanal US$35 for 6 hours per vehicle.

**From Cuiabá**: Focus Tours of Belo Horizonte (**see page 340**) is specializing in tours in this part of the Pantanal. Ametur, Samariana and Confiança off day tours by car (US$40), along Transpantaneira to Fazenda Pixaim. *Hotel Fazenda Santa Rosa* reservations at the Samariana Turismo in Cuiabá, 250 km. from Cuiabá near Porto Jofre. A, with full board, no electricity, an old *fazenda*, under new management, mixed reports, pool stagnant, river trips not included and expensive, breakfast-eating parrot. Buses, every 1½ hrs. 0600-1900, run from Cuiabá to **Poconé** (a large town, 100 km., US$3) from where one can hire a car from *Hotel Skala*, E, in the main square or hitch (easy, but bumpy, especially in a truck) to Porto Jofre (just a gas station—many *jacarés* reported nearby), or hire a vehicle to get there, around US$150, the road from Poconé can be impassable if bridges are down, enquire before leaving (see under Cuiabá). Poconé also has *Pousada Pantaneira*, F, good restaurant, clean and simple, on Transpantaneira road, T 721-1220; to hitchhike to Pixaim or Porto Jofre, start at 0600 outside the hotel. *Hotel Joá*, G without bath, basic, acceptable; *3 Poderes Restaurant*, R. Beri, cheap good food. At Km. 30 on the Transpantaneira is *Hotel das Araras*, 10 rooms with bath, good food, home-made *cachaça* (hotel itself has no phone, but T 065-321 6754), rates L with full board (reservations at Samariana Cuiabá or Melgatur, Corumbá). Where the road crosses the Rio Pixaim is *Hotel Beira Rio*, 3 rooms with several beds in each, no electricity, good home-grown food (expansion is planned). *Fazenda Pixaim*, D, including food, has electricity, 170 km. from Cuiabá, halfway between Poconé and Porto Jofre; taxi US$27 from Poconé. Short river trips best at sunrise or sunset US$5 p.p. *Hotel-Fazenda Cabanas do Pantanal*, A, 142 km. from Cuiabá, 50 km. from Poconé by the rivers Pixaim and Cuiabá, on the northern edge of the Pantanal, 10 chalet bedrooms with bath, restaurant, boat trips (few in dry season), horse-riding, fishing, helpful proprietor and staff, everything except boat trips and bar drinks included in price (booking: Confiança, Cuiabá). Boats ply between Porto Cercado (near *Cabanas do Pantanal*) via Porto Jofre to Corumbá (48 hrs.) about once a week, e.g. *San Antônio* and *Elza*. Expeditours or Melgatur in Cuiabá can book a journey by car from Cuiabá to Porto Jofre, then hotelboat to Corumbá (or vice versa), 4 days.

Barão de Melgaço, 130 km. from Cuiabá (twice daily bus, US$4.80) on Rio Cuibá, is the starting point for the *Pousada Passargada*, programmes from 3 days up, full board, boat, car and trekking expeditions, transport from Barão de Melgaço. Owner speaks English, French and German, food excellent, highly rec., closed Dec. to Feb.; reservations in Barão de Melgaço on riverside, through Melgatur, Corumbá or Nature Safaris, Av. Mal. Rondon, Barão de Melgaço, or Av. N.S. de Copacabana 330, Rio de Janeiro, CEP 22020, T (021) 235-2840, Fax (021) 236-5285. Much cheaper, US$250, if booked direct with the owner, Maré Sigaud, Mato Grosso, CEP 786807, *Pousada Passargada*, Barão de Melgaço, *Pousada do Barão*, 6 chalets with bath, swimming pool, 1st class, boat and trekking expeditions (book through Melgatur). *Barão Tour Hotel*, in the town, apartments with a/c, restaurant, boat trips and excursions (T Cuiabá 322-1568, or Melgatur.)

**Travel Agents in Cuiabá** *Confiança*, Mariano 434, T 321-4142, very helpful travel agency, but tours to Pantanal are expensive. Also recommended *Expeditours*, Av. Gov. Ponce de Arruda 670, T 381-4959/5674, sightseeing, fishing trips for 4-5 days by boat; *Ametur*, R. Joaquim Murtinho 242, T 321-4948, very helpful, advice on Pantanal tours (also run their own tours, from 12 hours—US$30—to 5 days, not cheap); *Samariana*, R. Campo Grande 423, T 341-7947; *Melgatur*, Barão de Melgaço, Av. Augusto Leverger 38. All these agencies arrange trips to the Pantanal; for longer or special programmes, book in advance. Recommended guide, multilingual, **Andreas Hoeltgebaum**, he is usually at the airport; good guide and driver (own car), **Laércio Leite de Sá**, QDA28, Casa 21, T 381-1063.

Guides available at Cuiabá airport; **Vinícius de Albuquerque Maranhão** (through Geotur, R. Cel. Benedicto Leite 55-Porto Cuiabá, T (065) 824-2639) rec. A 2½-day tour with **Vinicius Maranhão** costs US$300 for everything except drinks; he has his own jeep, speaks excellent English and is very knowledgeable. **Cesar Magallon Arias**, "the Panamanian", R-065 C-04, Parque Cuiabá, 78000, T 361-2115, or contact through the *Aurea Palace Hotel*, knowledgeable, fluent English, small groups, approx. US$50 per day. **Joel Souza**, *Hotel Real Palace*, Praça Ipiranga 102, T 321-7703, 322-1268, good tours of Pantanal, but less reliable for services in town. Another guide is **Amilton Martins da Silva** (see below under **Youth Hostel**). Watch out for park rangers, who can be very helpful and friendly, after you have persuaded them you are not poachers or hunters. The research station 40 km. from the end of the Transpantaneira is for Brazilian scientists only.

Tours to N or S Pantanal arranged in Rio de Janeiro by *Pelajo Turismo*, Av. Rio Branco 52, 16th floor, T 296-4466 or 233-5085: from 4 to 8 days; also *Excursões Soletur*, and many others. In *São Paulo Evidência Turismo*, R. Dr. Costa Júnior 390, Perdizes, T 864-0400, Telex 11-82650. Most tours last 4 to 15 days, and are based at Corumbá. 20% discounts are offered in December, but this is the wet, and mosquito, season.

River trips from Cuiabá to Corumbá are very difficult since boats on the Cuiabá river are few and irregular. You can get to Corumbá by river from *Cáceres* (pop. 70,000), on the banks of the Rio Paraguai, 200 km. west of Cuiabá, very hot but clean and hospitable. There is a yacht club, with swimming pool, volley ball and children's playground. Annual cattle fair at the airport. Hotels: *Comodoro*, Praça Duque de Caxias; *Charme*, Col. José Dulce; *Ipanema*, R. Gen. Osório 540, good restaurant; *Fênix*, R. dos Operários 600, C-D, fridge, a/c, TV; *Santa Terezinha*, R. Tiradentes 485, F with fan, breakfast, not clean, friendly. Many other cheap hotels, e.g. *Hispano*, F, clean. *Hotel Barranquinho*, outside Cáceres, book in advance through Ametur, Cuiabá. Good restaurants: *Corimbá* on main square (fish specialities); *Bisteção*, on the waterfront; restaurant on stilts on opposite bank, good lunch US$4. Change money elsewhere: travellers' cheques take 10 days to change at the banks, Soteco by the main square changes cash at the official rate. For information on boat sailings, ask at the Capitânia dos Portos, on the corner of the main square at the waterfront. If possible phone in advance to Cáceres, Posto Arrunda, 221-1707 to find out which boats are going. Also Portobrás on the outskirts at the waterfront (T 221-1728), you may (with a lot of luck) be able to get passage on a boat; 3 days to Corumbá (8 the other way). These boats are officially not allowed to take passengers. You may have a better chance of getting a boat in Corumbá since there are more head offices and river traffic. In the dry season there are practically no boats to Corumbá. Bus Cuiabá-Cáceres, US$8, 10 a day (book in advance, very crowded), 3½ hrs. now that the road is paved, one stop in the jungle at a restaurant. At the waterfront you can hire a boat for a day trip (US$25).

From Cáceres to the Bolivian border: Get passport stamped by the Federal Police then take the 1600 bus to San Matías, Bolivia, where you must have your passport stamped (*Residencial Génova*, F, rec.; military flights on Fri. and Sun. to Santa Cruz via Roboré—book in advance).

**Cuiabá** (pop. 370,000, 1989) the capital of Mato Grosso state (pop. 1,660,000) on the Rio Cuiabá, an upper tributary of the River Paraguai, has an imposing government palace and other fine buildings round a green main square. Alt.: 165 metres. It is very hot; coolest months for a visit are June, July, and August, in the dry season. Good fishing in the Cuiabá and smaller Coxipó rivers (fish and vegetable market, picturesque, at the riverside); wildlife for photography, and the Aguas Quentes hot springs, 90 km. (*Hotel Aguas Quentes*) can be visited. The University of Mato Grosso has an attractive museum of Indian objects (closed Sat. and Sun.), and also has a small zoo.

**Hotels** *Jaguar*, Av. Getúlio Vargas 600, T 322-9044, A, overpriced; *Mato Grosso Palace*, Joaquim Murtinho 170 (T 322-9254), 4-star, A with bath and breakfast; *Aurea Palace*, Gen. Melo 63, T 322-3377, A, pleasant rooms, restaurant, swimming pool, good; *Fenícia*, Av. Getúlio Vargas 296, T 321-5122, C, with a/c, breakfast, shower, clean, central, good. *Real Palace*, Praça Ipiranga 103, D with shower, a/c, TV, good breakfast, helpful, good value; *Abudi Palace*, Coronel Escolástico 259, T 322-7399, good; *Bandeirantes*, Av. Coronel Escolástico 425, T 321-0920, D, a/c, out of centre; *Almanara*, Av. Coronel Escolástico 510, T 323-1244, D, opposite *Bandeirantes* and better. *Mato Grosso*, R. Comandante Costa 2522 (T 321-9121), 2-star, almost opposite the *Fenícia* and down a side street, small, clean, restaurant, good value, D-E. *Lagunas*, Av. Gen. Mello 166, E, small rooms, clean bathrooms, hot water; *Samara*, R. Joaquim Murtinho 150, central, E, hot shower, fan, basic but good, clean, friendly; *Dormitório Cézar*, *Brazil*, *San Francisco*, rec., near bus terminal, all F p.p.;

others in same area.

**Youth hostel** Albergue da Juventude, R. Cel. Otilis Moreira 445, T 319-1231; also contact Amilton Martins da Silva, Praça de República s/n, C.E.P. 78015, T 322-5363, or R. Duque de Caxias 19, Barrio Alvorada, C.E.P. 78070, T 319-1231, he also runs reasonably-priced tours to the Pantanal (only speaks Portuguese and a little Spanish, contact him through Turimat).

**Restaurants** *Regionalíssimo*, R. 13 de Junho nr Handicraft shop, regional food; *Beco do Candieiro*, R. Campo Grande 500; *Churrascaria Recanto do Bosque*, R. Cândido Mariano; *Bierhaus*, Isaac Póvoas 1200; *A Integral*, R. Antônio João s/n; *Hong Kong*, Av. Gen. Melo 639, Chinese; *Sachimi*, Av. Ipiranga 740, Japanese. On Av. C. P.A. are many good restaurants and small snack bars. The café at the corner of Mello and Valle has a bright atmosphere, but "toxic hamburgers".

**Electric Current** 110 volts A.C., 60 cycles.

**Entertainment** Cuiabá is quite lively at night; *Pino's Ball* bowling alley, on Av. C.P.A.

**Souvenirs** Handicrafts in wood, straw, netting, leather, skins, Pequi liquor, crystallized *caju* fruit, compressed *guaraná* fruit (for making the drink), Indian objects on sale at airport, bus station, and craft shops in centre, interesting.

**Money Exchange**, Ametur, R. Joaquim Murtinho.

**Car Hire** Unidas, Av. Isaac Póvoas 720, T 321-4646; **Nobre**, at airport, T 381-1651; **Localiza**, Av. Dom Bosco 963, T 321-0846; A VW Beetle costs about US$30 a day. (Beyond Poconé on the Transpantaneira, diesel and gasoline available in Porto Jofre, alcohol available in Pixaim.)

**Tourist Information** Turimat, state tourist authority (T 322-5363), Praça República, next to Post Office building. Good maps, friendly, helpful regarding hotels and car hire. Ramis Bucair, R. Pedro Celestino 280, is good for detailed maps of the region.

**Excursions** To *Chapada dos Guimarães*, 68 km. from Cuiabá (3 hotels and some apartments available *Hotel Turismo*, E, 1 block from Rodoviária, clean, good food, friendly, rec.; *Rio*, E, clean, good breakfast, rec.; *Sao João*, G, very basic). There is a festival last week in July, when accommodation is expensive and scarce. It is a pleasant ride into the mountains (Rubi bus from Cuiabá US$0.80—8 a day, or hire a taxi, US$20. Take insect repellent). See the 70-metre Véu de Noiva waterfall (12 km. from Chapada, get bus to drop you off after Buruti; there is a short route, or a longer route through forest to the falls, recommended, small restaurant), strange rock formations, canyons, and the beauty spots of Mutuca, Salgadeira (camp and waterfall), Rio Claro, Portão do Inferno viewpoint, and the falls of Cachoeirinhas (small restaurant)—all unspoilt. Chapada itself is a small village with the oldest church in the Mato Grosso, Nossa Senhora de Santana (1779), a huge spring-water public swimming pool, a good *churrascaria*, and restaurant (*Nivio's*, opp. church); it is still inhabited mainly by *garimpeiros* (diamond-seekers). Just outside the town is the official Geodesic Centre of South America, marked by a plaque on a plateau which offers panoramic views of the surrounding plains.

**Air Services** By air to Corumbá, São Paulo, Manaus, Campo Grande, Goiânia, Brasília, Rio de Janeiro, Belo Horizonte and Porto Velho.

**Buses and Roads** There is a paved road to Campo Grande (712 km.), on the Noroeste railway to São Paulo, and the 2,400 km. BR-364 road from Brasília to Porto Velho and Rio Branco passes through Cuiabá; it is paved all the way between Brasília, Cuiabá (1,127 km.) and is in good condition, but between Cuiabá and Porto Velho there are many pot holes. Service stations often provide free hot showers and the *prato comercial* is a cheap meal. The more direct road to Brasília through Barra do Garças and Goiás Velho (the BR-070) is paved also. Several paved feeder roads connect the BR-070 and BR-364. The Transpantaneira Highway, originally projected to connect Cuiabá with Corumbá, goes only as far as Porto Jofre on the Cuiabá River. Work has been suspended indefinitely because of difficulties, costs and ecological considerations.

Comfortable buses (toilets) to **Campo Grande**, 10 hrs., US$18, 12 buses daily, *leito* at 2000 and 2100. **Goiânia**, 14 hrs., US$18; direct to **Brasília**, São Luiz company, 24 hours, US$35. To **Porto Velho**, 10 buses a day, US$28 (Colibri said to be better than São Luiz). Spectacular scenery between Cuiabá and Porto Velho, road newly paved, 1,450 km., bus journey takes 21 hrs. (Andorinha 1700 bus São Paulo-Cuiabá connects with Porto Velho service). (Eventually a paved road from Brasília to Caracas is envisaged). To **São Paulo**, 24 hours, US$36, **Rio de Janeiro**, 32 hrs., US$50. Direct São Luiz bus to **Belo Horizonte**, 2000,

26 hrs., US$40; from Belo Horizonte bus passes through Ituiutaba (*Hotel São Luiz*, E, rec.), Nova São Simão (a new dam nearby), and Jataí. Now 4 buses daily (including one *leito*) to Manaus, via Porto Velho, around 80 hrs.

Hitch-hiking from Cuiabá to Manaus (2,294 km.) is possible—ask truck drivers for lifts at the roadside eating places. The road due N to Santarém (1,777 km.) has been completed and is paved to Colíder, where the paving diverts to Alta Floresta: daily bus at 2000. Yellow fever inoculations insisted on when travelling this route.

Rodoviária at Cuiabá is now on outskirts: bus link (No. 117) with centre costs US$0.15; bus terminal from corner of Murtinho and Vargas, behind church, off Praça República.

From **Rondonópolis** (pop. 101,000, many hotels, *Novotel*, A, try for a discount; *Dormitório Beija Flor*, near bus station, or *Sumaré*, clean but unfriendly, both E) about 215 km. SE of Cuiabá on the road to Goiânia, a paved road branches southwards to Campo Grande and thence to the western parts of the State of São Paulo.

**Buses from Rondonópolis** Brasília, US$19, 14½ hrs.; Goiânia, US$16, 11 hrs.; Campo Grande, US$8, 6½ hrs.; Presidente Epitácio, US$6.40; Presidente Prudente, US$9.50. Beware of overbooking on Viação Motta buses.

**Airport**, for internal flights.

**Indians** The Bororo tribe, on a reservation three hours by truck from Rondonópolis, have long been "civilized". It may be possible to visit the Xavantes at one of the Reservas Indígenas along the BR-158, N of Barra do Garças (**see page 482**). Funai is reluctant to permit travellers to visit Indian reservations on their own.

A journey along the Porto Velho road from Cuiabá (BR-364) demonstrates the amount of development along Brazil's "Far West" frontier, **see page 478**. A side road off the BR-364 goes to Vila Bela on the Guaporé River, which used to be the capital of Mato Grosso. It has a ruined church, cannon balls lying around, and is very interesting.

**N.B.** When travelling N of Cuiabá, yellow fever vaccination is obligatory; if you do not have a certificate, you will be (re)vaccinated.

---

## INFORMATION FOR VISITORS

**Documents** Consular visas are not required for stays of up to 90 days by tourists from Western European (except for French nationals) or South American (except Bolivia and Guyana) countries, Finland, Morocco, Bahamas, Barbados, Trinidad and Tobago, and the Philippines. For them, only the following documents are required at the port of disembarkation: valid passport (or *cédula de identidad* for nationals of Argentina, Chile, Paraguay and Uruguay); and a return or onward ticket, or adequate proof that you can purchase your return fare, subject to no remuneration being received in Brazil and no legally binding or contractual documents being signed. If coming from Bolivia, Colombia or Peru (or certain African countries), you must have valid yellow fever vaccination certficiate. Venezuelan passport holders can stay in Brazil for 60 days on filling in a form at the border. (Some consulates, e.g. Santiago, ask to see an onward ticket, persistence, adequate money and showing a credit card may overcome this). 90-day renewals are easily obtainable, but only within 15 days of the expiry of your 90-day permit, from Policia Federal, open till 1600: the procedure is, buy 3 DARF forms from a *papeleria* and take them back to a bank; pay US$2 tax; then go to Policia Federal who will stamp the extension in your passport after they have seen onward flight tickets, receipt from the bank for the tax, and proof of sufficient funds for your continued stay. Some points of entry refuse entry for longer than 30 days, renewals are then for the same period, insist if you want 90 days. For longer stays you must leave the country and return (immediately if you wish) to get a new 90-day permit. US, Canadian and French citizens and people of other nationalities, and those who cannot meet the requirements above, *must* get a visa before arrival, which may, if you ask, be granted for multiple entry. Do not lose the emigration permit they give you when you enter Brazil. Leaving the country without it, you may have to pay up to US$100 per person.

Officially, if you leave Brazil within the 90-day permission to stay and then re-enter the country, you should only be allowed to stay until the 90-day expires. Usual practice, though, is to give another 90-day permit, which may lead to charges of overstaying if you apply for an extension.

You must always carry identification when in Brazil; it is a good idea to take a photocopy of the first 5 pages of your passport, plus that with your Brazilian immigration stamp, and leave your passport in the hotel safe deposit. Always keep an independent record of your passport details. In Rio it is a good idea to register with your consulate to expedite document replacement if yours gets lost/stolen.

**Airport Tax** US$15 is charged for international flights and, for internal flights, US$0.50-US$1.50 depending on the class of airport. Tax is waived if you stay in Brazil less than 24 hrs.

**How to Get to Brazil: By Air** Brazil is connected with the principal cities of Europe by Air France, KLM, Scandinavian Airways, Lufthansa, Alitalia, Iberia, Swissair, Aerolíneas Argentinas, Varig and TAP. Varig flights from London to Rio (three times a week) take only 11½ hrs. British Airways flies three times weekly, non-stop London to Rio and on to São Paulo. Cheap carriers to Europe are Pluna and LAP (non-IATA) from Rio to Madrid. Varig fly to Salvador from Frankfurt, Rome and Paris.

Brazil is connected to the USA direct by Varig, Pan American, American Airlines, Aerolíneas Argentinas and Japan Airlines (Varig—4 times—and Japan Airlines twice a week, fly Tokyo-Los Angeles-Rio, and Pan Am, LA-Rio). The cheapest route is probably from Miami. Non-stop New York-Rio by Pan-Am or Varig is 9 hrs. 20 min. Lloyd Aéreo Boliviano (non-IATA) flies twice weekly between Miami and Manaus/Rio; book through Monark Turismo, Visconde de Pirajá 207, Ipanema, Rio (T 287-9746).

All South American capitals are connected by air services to Rio. Caracas, 3 weekly (Varig, Viasa); Bogotá, 3 weekly (Varig, Avianca); Lima, 6 weekly (AeroPerú, Varig); La Paz, weekly (Cruzeiro; also LAB to São Paulo); Quito/Guayaquil, once a week with Varig; Asunción, daily with Varig, also LAP, Iberia and Ladeco; Santiago, several daily (LAN-Chile—also daily from São Paulo, Ladeco, Varig and others); Montevideo, about 20 weekly (inc. Varig, Pluna); Buenos Aires, several daily; Paramaribo, once a week each by Cruzeiro do Sul and Air Guayne to Belém; Cayenne-Belém by Cruzeiro do Sul (twice a week), Air Guyane, Air France (three times a week) heavily booked. Iquitos, Peru, via Tabatinga (on the Brazilian border with Colombia, a few km. from Leticia) to Manaus by Cruzeiro on Wed and/or Sat. If buying a ticket to another country but with a stop over in Brazil, check whether two tickets are cheaper than one.

For many travellers flying to Rio de Janeiro from Europe via South Africa, there is little difference in air fares compared to the direct route. Varig and SAA have one flight each per week between Rio and Johannesburg, and Capetown. Varig has a weekly flight from Rio to Luanda and to Lagos. Airline tickets are expensive in Brazil, buy internal tickets with cruzeiros. External tickets must be paid for in dollars or proof shown that cruzeiros were bought at the official rate.

**N.B.** Regulations state that you cannot buy an air ticket in Brazil for use abroad unless you first have a ticket out of Brazil.

**By Sea** For shipping lines that carry passengers to Brazil, see **Introduction and Hints. N.B.** There is an 8% tax on international shipping-line tickets bought in Brazil.

**By Car** To drive in Brazil you need either a translation of your home driving licence, or an international licence. There are agreements between Brazil and all South American countries (but check in the case of Bolivia) whereby a car can be taken into Brazil (or a Brazilian car out of Brazil) for a period of 90 days without any special documents; an extension of up to 90 days is granted by the customs authorities on presentation of the paper received at the border, this must be retained; some reports suggest this may be done at most customs posts and at the Serviço de Controle Aduaneiro, Ministerio da Fazenda, Av. Pres. A. Carlos, Sala 1129, Rio.

This now applies to cars registered in other countries; the requirements are proof of ownership and/or registration in the home country and valid driving licence (international or from home country). It is better to cross the border into Brazil when it is officially open (from 1300 to 1800 Mon. to Fri.) because an official who knows all about the entry of cars is then present. The motorist should in any case insist on getting the correct paper "in accordance with Decree No. 53.313/63", or he might find it impossible to get the 90-day extension. You must specify which border station you intend to leave by, but application can be made to the Customs to change this. If you want to leave by ship the Touring Club in Rio (possibly also elsewhere, but this is less definite) will arrange it for about US$60; you can also arrange the paper yourself by taking your car away by ship, but it takes about two days and costs about US$15 in port and police charges; the Touring Club provides information on how to go about it. (Klaus Elgner, of Hannover, reports this can be done with a letter in Portuguese saying you wish to leave by ship plus passport number, vehicle number, entry forms data plus an *ordem de embarque* supplied and stamped by the shipping agent. These should be presented to the Customs.) Crossing by a land border is, in any case, easier and probably cheaper. In 1991 the cost of shipping car from Rio de Janeiro to Hamburg in a container was US$3,000 (Hamburg-Süd line), port handling charges extra.

Any foreigner with a passport can purchase a Brazilian car and travel outside Brazil if it is fully paid for or if permission is obtained from the financing body in Brazil. Foreigners do not need the CPF tax document (needed by Brazilians—you only have to say you are a tourist) to purchase a car, and the official purchase receipt is accepted as proof of ownership. Sunday papers carry car advertisements and there are second-hand car markets on Sun. mornings in most cities—but don't buy an alcohol-driven car if you propose to drive outside Brazil. It is essential to have an external intake filter fitted, or dust can rapidly destroy an engine. VW Combi vans are cheapest in Brazil where they are made, they are equivalent to the pre-1979 model in Europe. Be sure to travel with a car manual and good quality tools, a VW dealer will advise. There are VW garages throughout the continent, but parts (German or Latin American) are not always interchangeable. In the main, though, there should be no problems with large components (e.g. gears). If a lot of time is to be spent on dirt roads, the Ford Chevrolet pickup is more robust. A letter in Spanish from your consul explaining your aims and that you will return the vehicle to Brazil can make life much easier at borders and checkpoints. Brazilian cars may not meet safety regulations in N. America and Europe, but they can be easily resold in Brazil.

**Customs** Clothing and personal articles are free of import duty. Such articles as cameras, movie cameras, portable radios, tape-recorders, typewriters and binoculars are also admitted free if there is not more than one of each. Tourists may also bring in, duty-free, 2 litres of spirits, 2 litres of champagne, 3 litres of wine, 600 cigarettes, 25 cigars, 280 grams of perfume, and 700 grams of toilet water. Duty free goods may only be purchased in foreign currency.

**Air** Internal air services are highly developed. A monthly magazine, *Guia Aeronáutico*, gives all the timetables and fares. All four national airlines—Varig, Vasp, Cruzeiro and Transbrasil (said to be rather cheaper)—offer excellent service on their internal flights (although Varig has been criticised recently for overbooking, losing baggage, delays and giving poor information to passengers). Between 2200 and 0600, internal flights cost 30% less than daytime flights. On some flights couples can fly for the price of one-and-a-half. A 30% discount is offered on flights booked 25 days or more in advance.

Varig/Cruzeiro offer a 21-day Airpass, which costs US$440. The Airpass must be purchased outside Brazil by holders of an international flight ticket to Brazil, routes must start in either Rio or São Paulo, no journey may be repeated, it may not be used on the Rio-São Paulo shuttle. The airpass is limited to 5 coupons, to which a maximum of 4 may be added (purchased outside Brazil) at US$100 each. No sector may be repeated in the same direction; the itinerary may be changed in Brazil. Make sure you have two copies of the Airpass invoice when you arrive in Brazil; otherwise you will have to select all your flights when you book the first one. Remember that domestic airport tax has to be paid at each departure. Hotels in the Tropical and Othon chains, and others, offer discounts of 10% to Airpass travellers; check with Varig, who have good hotel reservation service. We have been told that it is advisable for users of the Airpasses to book all their intended flights in advance or on arrival in Brazil, as so many internal flights are full these days, especially around summer holiday and Carnival time. Converting the voucher can take some hours, do not plan an onward flight immediately, check at terminals that the air pass is still registered, faulty cancellations have been reported. Cost and restrictions on the Airpass are subject to change. An alternative is to buy an internal flight ticket which includes several stops.

The small feeder airlines have been formed into scheduled domestic airlines, and now operate Brazilian-built *Bandeirante* 16-seater prop-jets into virtually every city and town with any semblance of an airstrip. It has been reported that Cruzeiro do Sul and Varig may combine their flights, with consequent last minute changes in flight time and/or number. **N.B.** Internal flights often have many stops and are therefore quite slow. Foreigners are not allowed to travel on Brazilian air force flights. Most airports have left-luggage lockers (US$0.80 for 24 hours).

**Road Transport**   There is no lack of transport between the principal cities of Brazil; few are connected by railway, but almost all are by road. Ask for window seats (*janela*), or odd numbers if you want the view. Brazilian bus services have a top speed limit of 80 kph (buses are supposed to have governors fitted). They are extremely comfortable (many have reclining seats and toilets), stopping fairly frequently (every 4-5 hrs.) for snacks; the cleanliness of these *postos* has greatly improved, though generally less good in the poorer regions. Buses only stop at official stops. Take something to drink on buses in the North. The bus terminals are usually outside the city centres and offer fair facilities in the way of snack bars, lavatories, left-luggage stores, local bus services and information centres. *Leito* buses ply at night between the main centres, offering reclining seats with foot and leg rests, toilets, and sometimes in-board refreshments, at double the normal fare. For journeys over 100 km., most buses have chemical toilets. Air conditioning can make *leito* buses cold at night, so take a blanket or sweater (and plenty of toilet paper); on some services blankets are supplied; others have hostess service. Bus stations for interstate services and other long-distance routes are usually called *rodoviárias*. It is not easy to sell back unused bus tickets. Some bus companies have introduced a telex system enabling passengers to purchase return tickets at point of departure, rather than individual tickets for each leg. Buses usually arrive and depart in very good time; you cannot assume departure will be delayed. In the South East and South a *Horário de Ônibus* is available at *rodoviárias* (not available for North or North East). Many town buses have turnstiles which can be inconvenient if you are carrying a large pack. Urban buses normally serve local airports.

**Taxis**   Taxi meters are out of date. Drivers have a list of price alterations which should be consulted: make sure it's not a photocopy as that is a well-known minor swindle! Make sure the meter is cleared and shows tariff 1, except 2300-0600 and in Dec. when 2 is permitted. Check that the meter is working, if not, fix price in advance. The radio taxi service costs about 50% more but cheating is less likely. Taxis have a 40% surcharge on Sundays. If you are seriously cheated note the number of the taxi and insist on a signed bill, threatening to go to the police; it can work.

**Motoring**  Most main roads between principal cities are now paved. Some are narrow and therefore dangerous.

**Car Hire**  It is reported that car hire is more cheaply arranged outside Brazil. It is essential to have a credit card in order to hire in Brazil. Avis is found only in the major cities and have only a time-and-mileage tariff. National, i.e. Localiza, is represented in many places, often through licencees. Head office: Av. Bernardo Monteiro 1563, Belo Horizonte, T (031) 800-2360; connected with InterRent/Europcar in Europe, will accept credit cards from InterRent/Europcar and offers unlimited mileage if booked in advance from Europe on a fixed US$ rate.

**Note**  It is virtually impossible to buy premium grades of petrol/gasoline anywhere. With alcohol fuel you need about 50% more alcohol than regular gasoline. Larger cars have a small extra tank for "gasolina" to get the engine started; remember to keep this topped up. Fuel is only 85 octane (owing to high methanol content), so be prepared for bad consumption and poor performance and starting difficulties in non-Brazilian cars in winter. Diesel fuel is cheap and a diesel engine may provide fewer maintenance problems for the motoring tourist. Service stations are free to open when they like, but have mandatory opening hours of Mon.-Sat. 0600-2000. Very few open during Carnival week.

**Hitch-hiking**  Information on hitch-hiking (*carona* in Portuguese) suggests that it is difficult everywhere. Try at the highway-police check points on the main roads (but make sure your documents are in order) or at the service stations, or *postos*. Large increases in the price of gasoline and restrictions on its sale have diminished the amount of road traffic, especially pleasure traffic at weekends.

**Rail**  Trains are appreciably slower than buses. There is a sleeper service between Rio and São Paulo. There are services in the state of São Paulo and between Campinas and Brasília. There is a service between Porto Alegre and the Argentine and Uruguayan frontiers at Uruguaiana and Santana do Livramento. More and more services are being withdrawn; travellers are normally advised to go by air or road. Timekeeping is good on the whole.

**Hotels**  The best guide to hotels in Brazil is the *Guia do Brasil Quatro Rodas*, with good maps of regions and towns. Motels on the outskirts of cities are primarily used by very short-stay couples. The type known as *hotel familiar*, to be found in the interior—large meals, communal washing, hammocks for children—is much cheaper, but only for the enterprising. Usually hotel prices include breakfast; there is no reduction if you don't eat it. In the better hotels (our category D and upwards) the breakfast is well worth eating: rolls, ham, eggs, cheese, cakes, fruit. Normally the *apartamento* is a room with a bath; a *quarto* is a room without bath. The service stations (*postos*) and hostels (*dormitórios*) along the main roads provide excellent value in room and food, akin to truck-driver type accommodation in Europe, for those on a tight budget. The star rating system for hotels (five-star hotels are not price controlled) is not the standard used in North America or Europe. For information about Youth Hostels contact Contej, Esrado de Sá, R. Vinicius de Morales 120, Rio de Janeiro. Low-budget travellers with student cards (photograph needed) can use the Casa dos Estudantes network. **Warning**  Hotel safe-deposits are not always secure, if money, etc. is counted ask for a receipt: take a substantial part of your funds in travellers' cheques. Leave rooms in good time so frigobar bills can be checked; we have received reports of overcharging in otherwise good hotels.

Business visitors are strongly recommended to book accommodation in advance, and this can be easily done for Rio or São Paulo hotels with representation abroad. Varig has a good hotel reservation service, with discounts for its customers.

**N.B.** Taxi drivers will try to take you to the expensive hotels, who pay them commission for bringing in custom. Beware!

**Camping**    Members of the Camping Clube do Brasil or those with an international campers' card pay only half the rate of a non-member, which is US$10-15 p.p. The Club has 43 sites in 13 states and 80,000 members. For enquiries, Camping Clube do Brasil, Divisão de Campings, R. Senador Dantas 75—29° andar (T 262-7172), Rio de Janeiro. Private campsites charge about US$5 p.p. For those on a very low budget and in isolated areas where there is no camp site, service stations can be used as camping sites (Shell stations rec.); they have shower facilities, watchmen and food; truck drivers are a mine of information; some have dormitories. There are also various municipal sites; both types are mentioned in the text. Campsites often tend to be some distance from public transport routes and are better suited to those with their own transport. Never camp at the side of a road; wild camping is generally not possible.

Good camping equipment may be purchased in Brazil and there are several rental companies: Rentalcenter, Av. Brig. Luís Antônio 5088, São Paulo (T 852 0081 and 853 5147) and Av. Bernardino de Campos 661, Santos (T (0132) 41489); Camping Service, R. Tibiriçá 115, Brooklyn, São Paulo. For special jungle equipment, Selva SA, R. do Carmo 65-3° andar, Rio de Janeiro (T 242 9695); for equipping camping vans, Camp Car, R. Piauí 375, Todos os Santos, Rio de Janeiro. It may be difficult to get into some Camping Clube campsites during the high season (Jan.-Feb.). Camping gas cartridges are easy to buy in sizeable towns in the South e.g. in HM shops. *Guia de Camping* is produced by Artpress, R. Araçatuba 487, São Paulo 05058; it lists most sites and is available in bookshops in most cities. Quatro Rodas publishes a *Guia de Áreas de Camping* annually. Most sizeable towns have Laundromats with self service machines. *Lavanderias* do the washing for you but are very expensive.

**Food**    The food can be very good indeed. The most common dish is *bife (ou frango) com arroz e feijão*, steak (or chicken) with rice and the excellent Brazilian black beans. The most famous dish with beans is the *feijoada completa*: several meat ingredients (jerked beef, smoked sausage, smoked tongue, salt pork, along with spices, herbs and vegetables) are cooked with the beans. Manioc flour is sprinkled over it, and it is eaten with kale (*couve*) and slices of orange, and accompanied by glasses of *aguardente* (unmatured rum), usually known as *cachaça* (booze), though *pinga* (drop) is a politer term. Almost all restaurants serve the *feijoada completa* for Saturday lunch (that means up to about 1630). Bahia has some excellent fish dishes (**see note on page 409**); some restaurants in most of the big cities specialize in them. *Vatapá* is a good dish in the north; it contains shrimp or fish sauced with palm oil, or coconut milk. *Empadinhas de camarão* are worth trying; they are shrimp patties, with olives and heart of palm. A mixed grill, including excellent steak, served with roasted manioc flour (*farofa*; raw manioc flour is known as *farinha*) goes under the name of *churrasco* (it came originally from the cattlemen of Rio Grande do Sul), normally served in specialized restaurants known as *churrascarias* or *rodízios*; good places for large appetites. Minas Gerais has two splendid special dishes involving pork, black beans, *farofa* and kale; they are *tutu á mineira* and *feijão tropeiro*. A white hard cheese (*queijo prata*) or a slightly softer one (*queijo Minas*) is often served for dessert with bananas, or guava or quince paste. Meals are extremely large by European standards; if your appetites are small, you can order, say, one portion and one empty plate, and divide the portion. Unless you specify to the contrary many restaurants will lay a *coberto opcional*, olives, carrots, etc., costing US$0.50-0.75. **NB** The main meal is usually taken in the middle of the day; cheap restaurants tend not to be open in the evening. **Warning** Avoid mussels, marsh crabs and other shellfish caught near large cities: they are likely to have lived in a highly polluted environment. In a restaurant, always ask the price of a dish before ordering.

For vegetarians, there is a growing network of restaurants in the main cities. In smaller places where food may be monotonous try vegetarian for greater variety. We list several. Most also serve fish. Alternatives in smaller towns are the Arab and Chinese restaurants.

There is fruit all the year round, ranging from banana and orange to strawberries (*morango*), pineapple (*abacaxi*) and avocado pear (*abacate*). More specialized fruits include mango (*manga*), pawpaw (*mamão*), custard-apple (*fruta do conde*) and guava (*goiaba*). One is especially recommended to try the *manga de Uba*, a non-fibrous small mango. Also good are *mora* (a raspberry that looks like a strawberry), *jaboticaba*, a small black damson-like fruit, and *jaca* (jackfruit), a large yellow/green fruit.

The exotic flavours of Brazilian ice-creams should be experienced. Try *açaí*, *bacuri*, *biribá*, *buruti*, *cupuaçu* (not eveyone's favourite), *mari-mari*, *mucajá*, *murici*, *pajurá*, *pariri*, *patuá*, *piquiá*, *pupunha*, *sorva*, *tucumá*, *uxi* and others mentioned below under "drinks".

If travelling on a tight budget, remember to ask in restaurants for the *prato feito* or *sortido*, a money-saving, excellent value *table-d'hôte* meal. The *prato comercial* is similar but rather better and a bit more expensive. *Lanchonetes* are cheap eating places where you must pay before eating. *Salgados* (savoury pastries), *coxinha* (a pyramid of manioc filled with meat or fish and deep fried), *esfilha* (spicey hamburger inside an onion-bread envelope), *empadão* (a filling—e.g. chicken—in sauce in a pastry case), *empadas* and *empadinhas* (smaller fritters of the same type), are the usual fare. Hamburgers are referred to as "X" (pronounced "shees"—often spelt on menu-boards "cheese"), e.g. *X-Salada*. In Minas Gerais, *pão de queijo* is a hot roll made with cheese. A *bauru* is a toasted sandwich which, in Porto Alegre, is filled with steak, while further north has tomato, ham and cheese filling. *Cocada* is a coconut and sugar biscuit.

**Drinks** Imported drinks are expensive, but there are some fair local wines. Chilean and Portuguese wines are sometimes available at little more than the cost of local wines. The beers are good and there are plenty of local soft drinks. *Guaraná* is a very popular carbonated fruit drink. There is an excellent range of non-alcoholic fruit juices, known as *sucos: caju* (cashew), *pitanga*, *goiaba* (guava), *genipapo*, *graviola* (= *chirimoya*), *maracujá* (passion-fruit), *sapoti* and *tamarindo* are recommended. *Vitaminas* are thick, mixed fruit or vegetable drinks, often with milk. *Caldo de cana* is sugar-cane juice, sometimes mixed with ice. Remember that *água mineral*, available in many varieties at bars and restaurants is a cheap, safe thirst-quencher (cheaper still in supermarkets). Apart from the ubiquitous coffee, good tea is grown and sold. N.B. If you don't want sugar in your coffee or *suco*, you must ask when you order it.

Among the better wines are Château d'Argent, Château Duvalier, Almadén, Dreher, Preciosa and Bernard Taillan. The red Marjolet from Cabernet grapes, and the Moselle-type white Zahringer have been well spoken of. It has often been noticed that a new *adega* starts off well, but the quality gradually deteriorates with time. Greville Brut champagne-type is inexpensive and very drinkable. A white-wine *Sangria*, containing tropical fruits such as pineapple and papaya, is worth looking out for. The Brahma and Antárctica beers are really excellent, of the strong lager type, and are cheaper by the bottle than on draught. Buying bottled drinks in supermarkets, you may be asked for empties in return.

Some genuine Scotch whisky brands are bottled in Brazil; they are very popular because of the high price of Scotch imported in bottle; Teacher's is the most highly regarded brand. Locally made gin, vermouth and campari are very good. The local firewater, *aguardente* (known as *cachaça* or *pinga*), made from sugar-cane, is cheap and wholesome, but visitors should seek local advice on the best brands; São Francisco, Praianinha, Maria Fulô, "51" and Pitu are recommended makes. Mixed with fruit juices of various sorts, sugar and crushed ice, *cachaça* becomes the principal element in a *batida*, a delicious and powerful drink; the commonest is a lime batida or *batida de limão*; a variant of this is the *caipirinha*, a *cachaça* with several slices of lime in it, a caipiroska is made with vodka. *Cachaça* with Coca-Cola is a *cuba*, while rum with Coca-Cola is a *cuba libre*.

**Tipping** is usual, but less costly than in most other countries, except for porters. Hotels and restaurants, 10% of bill if no service charge but small tip if there is; taxi drivers, none; cloakroom attendants, small tip; cinema usherettes, none; hairdressers, 10-15%; porters, fixed charges but tips as well; airport porters, about US$0.50 per item.

**Best Buys** Jewellery (especially in Minas Gerais), costume jewellery, and articles made of gemstones, such as lamps; ornamented articles of jacaranda and other tropical hardwoods; clay figurines from the North-East; lace from Ceará; leatherwork; strange pottery from Amazonia; carvings in soapstone and in bone; tiles and other ceramic work, African-type pottery and basketwork from Bahia. Good general shops for those with little time to search are "Folclore" shops in Copacabana next to *Rio Othon Palace* and also in Ipanema. Many large hotel gift shops stock a good selection of handicrafts at reasonable prices. Brazilian cigars are excellent for those who like the mild flavours popular in Germany, the Netherlands and Switzerland.

Recommended purchases are musical instruments, e.g. guitars made of fine, exotic woods, other stringed, and percussion instruments. A shop worth visiting is Pro-Musica, Av. Copacabana 435, Lojas M e N, Posto 2, T 237-2688, Rio de Janeiro.

**Security** As pointed out in the chapters on Rio de Janeiro and Salvador, personal safety in Brazil has deteriorated of recent years, largely because of the economic recession of the early 1980s and crime is now reported to be increasing in the north east. The police are reported to be charging for documents reporting crimes if these are required quickly.

Apart from the obvious precautions of not wearing jewellery, do not travel alone (this applies especially to women), do not camp or sleep out in isolated places and if you are hitch-hiking, never accept a lift in a car with two people in it. Money belts are safer than bags for your valuables. One reader advises women to buy a cheap skirt and handbag locally to avoid looking like a gringo. If you are held up and robbed, it is worth asking for the fare back to where you are staying. It is not uncommon for thieves to oblige. Do not leave valuables in hotel rooms. If you cannot get a receipt for valuables in a hotel safe, seal the contents in a plastic bag and sign across the seal. Never trust anyone telling "sobstories" or offering "safe rooms", when looking for a hotel, always choose the room yourself. Overcharging is rife; Ted Stroll of San Francisco advises, "temper your legitimate exasperation at minor rip-offs: remember that economic privation has many Brazilians close to the edge, and that those with a sense of honour are probably as ashamed of exploiting you as you are angry at being exploited". The corollary is be generous to those who give you a good deal. Travellers are most vulnerable when carrying baggage, if possible take a taxi.

**Warning** Most houses and hotels outside the large cities have electric showers operated by water pressure, delivering a supply of tepid to warm water. Despite electrical earthing, these showers are potentially dangerous. Care must be exercised in their use. Do not touch the appliance with wet hands or when the water is turned on.

**Health** Vaccination against smallpox is no longer required for visitors, but vaccination is necessary against yellow fever if you are visiting Amazonia, or are coming from countries with Amazonian territories, e.g. Bolivia, Colombia, Ecuador, Peru. Poliomyelitis vaccination is required for children from 3 months to 6 years. It is strongly recommended to have a yellow fever inoculation before visiting northern Brazil since those without a certificate will be inoculated on entering any of the northern and centre-western states, probably in unsanitary conditions. If you are going to Amazonia, or to other low-lying forested areas, malaria prophylaxis is advised (this can be difficult to obtain in some areas) and water purification tablets are essential. Dengue fever is now endemic in Brazil, and Rio is one of the worst places: protect yourself against mosquitoes. Also, in the Amazon basin, sandflies abound; take a good repellent and get inoculations against hepatitis and typhoid. Be very careful about bathing in lakes or slow rivers anywhere in Brazil: harmful parasites abound (including the snails that carry schistosomiasis—this disease is rampant in Minas Gerais and most of central Brazil). South of the Amazon beware of *borrachudos*, small flies with a sharp bite that attack ankles and calves; coconut oil deters them. Water should not be drunk from taps unless there is a porcelain filter attached or unless you have water sterilizing tablets ("Hydrosteril" is a popular local brand); there is mineral water in plenty and excellent light beer, known as "chopp" (pronounced "shoppi"), and soft drinks. For those who have been in Brazil for a while, *água gelada* (chilled water) is usually safe to drink, being filtered water kept in a refrigerator in most hotels, restaurants and stores. Avoid ice in cheap hotels and restaurants; it is likely to be made from unfiltered water.

Yellow fever **(see page 495)** and some other vaccinations can be obtained from the Ministério da Saúde, R. Cais de Pharoux, Rio de Janeiro. Less common vaccinations can be obtained at Saúde de Portos, Praça 15 de Novembro, Rio de Janeiro. It is reported that shots of immunoglobulin against hepatitis are not screened against Aids, which is widespread. Local condoms are reported not to be reliable.

Tampons are available, but are expensive.

An excellent hospital, supported by the American and British colonies in São Paulo, is Hospital Samaritano, R. Conselheiro Brotero 1486, São Paulo (T 51-2154). If staying in Brazil for any length of time, it is recommended to take out Brazilian health insurance; Banco Econômico and Citibank are reported to provide good advice on this matter.

**Climate and Clothing** Conditions during the winter (May to September) are like those of a north European summer in Rio de Janeiro (including periods of rain and overcast skies), but more like a north European autumn in São Paulo and the southern states. Summer-weight woollens can be worn without discomfort in winter in Rio de Janeiro (temperatures vary at this season from 14°C to the high 20s), but further south something heavier is often required. It can get very cold in the far South. In São Paulo, which is in the Highlands, light-weight clothing is only required in the summer; the climate can be treacherous, however, with large temperature changes in a brief space of time. It can get surprisingly cold S and W of Rio, and on high ground anywhere in Brazil, at night; warm clothes are needed. The season of heavy rains is from November to March in Rio and São Paulo, January to April in the north, and from April to August around Recife.

Summer conditions all over the country are tropical, but temperatures of 40°C are comparatively rare. On the coast there is a high degree of humidity. The luminosity is also very high; sunglasses are advisable.

Casual clothing is quite cheap to buy; indeed we are advised that even fashionable clothing is cheap by London and Paris standards. In general, clothing requirements in Brazil are less formal than in the Hispanic countries. It is, however, advisable for men visiting restaurants to wear long trousers in Rio and Manaus (women in shorts are also likely to be refused entry), trousers and jackets or pullovers in São Paulo (also for cinemas). As a general rule, it is better not to wear shorts in official buildings, cinemas and inter-state buses. Trousers and long-sleeved shirts are advisable for visits to government offices and on flights.

**Best Time** for a visit is from April to June, and August to October, inclusive. Businessmen should avoid from mid-December to the end of February, when it is hot and people are on holiday. These are not good months for tourism either, because hotels, beaches and means of transport tend to be crowded. July should also be avoided: it is a school holiday month. The climax of the soccer season is in Nov. and Dec.

**British Visitors** are referred to "Hints to Exporters: Brazil", obtainable from Dept. of Trade, Export Services Division, Sanctuary Bldgs, 16-20 Great Smith Street, London SW1P 3DB.

**Hours of Business** are 0900-1800 Mon. to Fri. for most businesses, which close for lunch some time between 1130 and 1400. Shops are open on Sat. till 1230 or 1300. Government departments are open from 1100-1800 Mon. to Fri. Banks 1000-1500, but closed on Sat. The British and American embassies' hrs. are 0830-1245 and 1415-1700 Mon. to Fri. The consular section's hrs. are 0830-1230; 1330-1630 Mon. to Fri.

**National Holidays** are 1 January (New Year); 3 days up to and including Ash Wed. (Carnival); 21 April (Tiradentes); 1 May (Labour Day); Corpus Christi (June); 7 September (Independence Day); 12 October, Nossa Senhora Aparecida; 2 November (All Souls' Day); 15 November (Day of the Republic); and 25 December (Christmas). The local holidays in the main cities are given in the text. Four religious or traditional holidays (Good Fri. must be one; other usual days: 1 November, All Saints Day; 24 December, Christmas Eve) must be fixed by the municipalities.

Other holidays are usually celebrated on the Mon. prior to the date.

**Time** Brazilian Standard Time is 3 hrs. behind GMT; of the major cities, only the Amazon time zone, Manaus, Cuiabá, Campo Grande and Corumbá are different, with time 5 hrs. behind GMT. The State of Acre is 4 hours behind GMT. Clocks move forward one hour in summer for approximately 5 months, (usually between October and February or March) but times of change vary. This does not apply to Acre.

**Currency** The currency unit is the cruzeiro, which in March 1990 replaced the new cruzado, itself introduced in January 1989 to replace the cruzado. The new cruzado and the March 1990 cruzeiro are identical in value. At the time of going to press there were in circulation all sorts of notes dating from four currency revisions, some overstamped. Be very careful to check what you get. Old 5,000 and 10,000 cruzado notes, overstamped 5 and 10 new cruzados, are no longer legal tender. Any amount of foreign currency and "a reasonable sum" in cruzeiros can be taken in; residents may only take out the equivalent of US$4,000.

Money sent to Brazil is normally paid out only in Brazilian currency, so do not have more money sent to Brazil than you need for your stay in the country itself. In most large cities Citibank will hold US personal cheques for collection, paying the day's tourist dollar rate in cruzeiros with no charge. Banco do Brasil offers the same service with small charge. Tourists cannot change US$ travellers' cheques into US$ notes, nor can they obtain US$ travellers cheques on an American Express card.

From 1989, banks were permitted to exchange foreign currency at a new tourist rate, which was set close to the black, or parallel rate (which was illegal). In March 1990 the exchange rate was unified. By the end of May 1991, three rates were still being quoted; the trade rate (Cr 280:$1), the tourist rate (Cr309:$1) and the parallel rate (Cr314:$1). The Banco do Brasil in most major cities will change cash and travellers' cheques; also Lloyds Bank branches. For the latest rate, see **Economic Indicators** near end of book. If you keep the exchange slips, you may convert back into foreign currency one-third of what you changed into cruzeiros. This applies to the official markets only; there is no right of reconversion unless you have an official exchange slip. The parallel market "mercado paralelo" is so common that travellers use it without problems (as far as we have been told). It is to be found in travel agencies, exchange houses and among hotel staff. Loiterers outside hotels will direct you to money changers—they will expect a tip. It is also possible to change money on the street, but this is very dangerous, especially in the Upper City in Salvador, where conmen abound. Finding the parallel market where there are no exchange houses may involve a lot of walking; ask around in imported goods shops, chemists, souvenir shops or big hotels. The best rates are to be found in the tourist centres. If you want to use the parallel market, take plenty of US dollars in cash, and be prepared to haggle (note, however, that travellers' cheques are a safer way to carry your money, but also that rates for cheques are usually lower than for cash, make sure there are no additional charges before signing travellers' cheques). Wherever possible in the text, we quote prices converted from cruzeiros to dollars at the parallel rate; travellers should bear this, and subsequent fluctuations in both the exchange and inflation rates, in mind when working out budgets. Black market and official rates are quoted in the papers and on TV news programmes. While inflation is high, change only what you need for a few days at a time, except when travelling in remote areas. Look in the daily press for advance warning of hikes in transport or other prices as a result of inflation.

**Credit cards** are widely used; Diners Club, Master Card and American Express are useful. Visa-Elo is the Brazilian Visa but many places will not take overseas Visa. Master Charge/Access is accepted by Banco Econômico and Banco Real and some airline offices, overseas credit cards need authorisation from São Paolo, this can take up to 2 hrs, allow plenty of time if buying air tickets. In southern Brazil Mastercard, known as Credicard, and Eurocard are accepted, Banco Noroeste and

Banco Mercantil do São Paulo will make a cash advance in large cities. Banco do Brasil handles money forwarded on Visa card. Credit card transactions are charged at the tourist official rate. Cash advances on credit cards will only be paid in cruzeiros at the tourist rate, incurring a 1½% commission. Automatic cash dispensers are becoming common in Brazil: you need only a passport and address to open an account with a large Brazilian bank, and you can then draw cash from a machine as required.

**Cost of Living** There has been heavy inflation in Brazil for some years. In shops, prices of articles are often given by letter, to which a frequently-revised rate sheet applies. In 1990, early 1991, Brazil was not a cheap country for foreign visitors, but since this chapter was prepared at a time of continuing economic revision prices may have changed at the time of the book's use.

**Weights and Measures** The metric system is used by all.

**Postal charges** are high (we do not publish rates owing to the rapid changes caused by inflation). Air mail takes 4 to 6 days to or from Britain or the U.S.; surface mail takes some 4 weeks. "Caixa Postal" addresses should be used when possible. Leaflets on postal rates are not issued; ask at the post office. Some post offices will not accept picture postcards unless enclosed in an envelope. Postes restantes usually only hold letters for 30 days. Letters from abroad may be subject to random checks by Brazilian officials. You can buy charge collected stamps, Compraventa de Francamento (CF) for letters only, to be paid on delivery. The Post Office sells cardboard boxes for sending packages internally and abroad (they must be submitted open); pay by the kilo; you must fill in a list of contents; string, but not tape, provided. Postal services are reported to have deteriorated because of the theft of stamps for resale (franked and registered letters are more secure, but check that the amount franked is what you have paid, or the item will not arrive). Some post offices have installed posting machines, stamps are not needed. Aerogrammes are most reliable. It may be easier to avoid queues and obtain higher denomination stamps by buying at the philatelic desk at the main post office. Poste Restante for AmEx customers efficiently dealt with by the AmEx agents, Kontik-Franstur, with offices in most large towns. Courier services such as DHL and UPS (rec.) are useful, but note that they may not necessarily operate under those names.

**Telephone** The system has been greatly improved. There is a trunk-dialling system linking all parts: for the codes look up DDD in the telephone directory. There are telephone boxes at airports, post offices, railway stations, hotels, most bars, restaurants and cafés, and in the main cities there are telephone kiosks *for local calls only* in the shape of large orange shells, for which *fichas* can be bought from bars, cafés and newsvendors; in Rio they are known as *orelhões* (big ears). Phone calls are priced thus: normal rate 1200-1400, 1800-2000; twice normal rate 0800-1200, 1400-1800; 50% cheaper than normal 2000-2300, 75% cheaper 2300-0800. Phone calls abroad are US$5.20 per minute to Europe. Note that Brazil is now linked to North America, Japan and most of Europe by trunk dialling (DDI). Codes are listed in the telephone directories. AT and T offers a service to USA subscribers, for information call 1-800-874-4000. For collect calls from phone boxes (in Portuguese: "a cobrar"), dial 107 and ask for the *telefonista internacional*. No collect calls available to New Zealand, though to Australia is OK. It is useless trying to dial long-distance from hotels or orange *orelhões*, as a blocking device is installed on those lines. There are special blue *orelhões* for long-distance DDD calls; for these you need to buy *fichas interurbanas* from telephone company offices. Making phone calls abroad from hotels are very expensive.

**Fax service** operates in main post offices in major cities, charges are cheaper than telephone if messages are short and on one sheet of paper.

**Cables** Cable facilities are available at all post offices, and the main ones have public telex booths. Post offices are recognizable by the ECT (Empresa de Correios e Telégrafos) signs outside. There is a 40% tax added to the cost of all telegraphic and telephonic communications, which makes international service extremely dear. Local phone calls and telegrams, though, are quite cheap. Make sure that hotels equipped by telex facilities can send outgoing telexes; some are unable to do so, or only at certain times of day.

**Press** *Daily Post/Brasil Herald*, the only English-language daily in Brazil published in São Paulo, not Mons. The main **Rio** papers are *Jornal do Brasil*, *O Globo*, and *Jornal do Commércio*. **São Paulo** Morning: *O Estado de São Paulo*, *Folha de São Paulo*, *Gazeta Mercantil* and *Diário de São Paulo*. Evening: *A Gazeta*, *Diário do Noite*, *Ultima Hora*. A monthly publication, *Jornal de Turismo* (Largo do Machado 29, Rio), gives notes on tourism, hotel prices, timetables, etc.

There is a similar monthly magazine in English, *Rio Visitor* (R. Marquês de São Vicente 52, Loja 318, Gávea, Rio).

English-language radio broadcasts daily at 15290 kHz, 19m Short Wave (Rádio Bras, Caixa Postal 04/0340, DF-70 323 Brasília).

**Language** The language is Portuguese. Efforts to speak it are greatly appreciated and for the low-budget traveller, Portuguese is essential. If you cannot lay your tongue to "the language of the angels", apologize for not being able to speak Portuguese and try Spanish, but note that the differences in the spoken languages are very much greater than appears likely from the printed page and in remoter parts you may well not be understood, and you will certainly have difficulty in understanding the answers.

One important point of spelling is that words ending in "i" and "u" are accented on the last syllable, though (unlike Spanish) no accent is used there. This is especially important in place names: Parati, Iguaçu. Audioforum, 31 Kensington Church Street, London W8 4LL, T 071-266 2202 does cassette courses on Brazilian Portuguese (£149 and £161.25).

**Working in Brazil** Work-permit restrictions are making it harder to find work as an English language teacher than it used to be, though many people do it unofficially and leave Brazil every 90 days in order to re-enter as tourists. One's best bet would be in a small language school. Or advertise in the Press.

**Information** All Brazil's States, and most cities and towns have their own tourist information bureaux. They are not usually too helpful regarding information on very cheap hotels, tending to imagine that no foreign tourist should consider staying in anything of that kind. It is also difficult to get information on neighbouring states. *Quatro Rodas*, a motoring magazine, publishes an excellent series of guides in Portuguese and English at about US$5 each. Its *Guia do Brasil* is a type of Michelin Guide to hotels, restaurants (not the cheapest), sights, facilities and general information on hundreds of cities and towns in the country, including good street maps. The same company also publishes a camping guide and more specialized guides to Rio, São Paulo, Salvador and the South, with other cities and areas in preparation. These guides can be purchased at street newspaper vendors throughout the country. Quatro Rodas Guides may be bought in Europe from 33 rue de Miromesnil, 75008 Paris, T 42.66.31.18, Fax 42.66.13.99, or Distribuidora Jardim, Quinta Pau Varais, Azinhaga de Fetais, Camarate 2685, Lisbon, Portugal, T Lisbon 947-2542. In USA: Lincoln Building, 60 East 42nd St., Suite 3403, New York, NY 10165, T 557-5990/3, Fax 983-0972. Note that telephone yellow pages in most cities (but not Rio) contain good street maps which, together with the Quatro Rodas maps, are a great help for getting around. There is also the "Transbrasil Guide to Attractions and Services" with maps, in Portuguese, English and French. A new publication in 1990 is *Backcountry Brazil* by Alex Bradbury (Bradt Publications), with chapters on the Pantanal, the Amazon and the Nort East Coast, as well as practical tips.

Many of the more expensive hotels provide locally-produced tourist information magazines for their guests. Travel information can be very unreliable and it is wise to recheck details thoroughly.

We wish to offer our grateful thanks for updating the Brazilian chapter to Sylvia Brooks. We thank also Michael Wooller of Lloyds Bank Economics Department for additional information. Also to the following residents and travellers: Rob Allan and Bridgit Vale (Pietermaritzburg), Monique Ammann and Gorda Kinzel (Geneva), Lars Andersson (Halmstad, Sweden), Rick Ansell and Paulette Milego (Porto Alegre), Rick Ansell and Paulette Milego (Porto Alegre), Kate Ashley (Marlborough, Wilts), Frank Bakker and Nike Darley (Amsterdam), John Banhart (München, Germany), Marlise Baumgarter and Niklaus Graber (Erlach, Switzerland), Monique Belleau (Quebec), Erik Bernesson (Båstad, Sweden), Gordon Bethell (St. Leonards of Sea, East Sussex), Ortun Bettering (Rio de Janeiro), Salik B. Biais (Montmorency), Carsten Blomeyer (München, Germany), Riemer De Boer (Netherlands) Andreas Böttner and Annette Drinkuth (Otterstedt, Germany), Binka Le Breton (Muriaé, Minas Gerais), Gianmarco Broggini (Milan), Go Bruêns (Utrecht, Netherlands), Gootje Bruêns (Utrecht, Netherlands) and Mayke de Groot (Leiden), Elizabeth Buettner (Ann Arbor, M.I.) and Alexander Protopapas (Pasadena, California), Marion Büttner (Hamburg), Steve and Jeanette Campbell (Sucre, Bol.), Liora Carmona and Ofer Kastner (Kiryat Bialik, Israel), Max G. Chapman (Melbourne), M. Collins and D. Power (Altrincham, UK), Alysia Cook and Phil Waterhouse (Twyford, Berks), Bryan Crawford (Inverness), Rudy Cruysbergs and Karen Schulpzand (Dilbeek, Belgium), Andrea Cujnik (München, Germany), Alastair and Ann Cuthbert (Broome, W. Australia), Louise Dionne (St. John's, Newfoundland), Gerd Dörner (Eberstadt), Arthur S. Dover M.D. (Watsonville, C.A.), Henk van Dyk Holger Eberhardt (Wesel, Germany), Beate Echols and Michael Shub (Berkeley, CA), Dee, Coralle Edwards (New Zealand) and Joy Gregory (London

N1), Dr Brian Elce (London WC1), René Erhardt and Lorena Ibañez (Berlin and Caracas), Daniel Ezekiel (Vancouver, BC), Tim Farnworth (Market Harborough, Leicestershire), Morley Farwell (Lone Butte, BC), Anthony Feeny (London EC1), Susan and Mark Field (Welwyn Garden City), Rüdiger Filbrich (Frankfurt/Main), Arnon Friedman (Tel Aviv, Israel), May-Lill Garly and Palle Valentiner-Branth (Copenhagen), Walter Gebhardt (Erlangen), Theodor A. Gevert (São Paulo), Doris Goll (Gossau) and Andy Stocker (Buchrain, Switz.), Jacqueline Greig (Cuckfield, East Sussex), Pilou Grenié (Antibes), Miki Gvili (Tel Aviv, Israel), Kevin Healey (Melbourne, Australia), Ian Henderson (London SW16), Else Henningsen (Copenhagen), Ulrich Herbert (Stuttgart), Gert Jan Hof and Yvonne Evers (Huissen, Neth), Heidi Holck Jorgensen and Martin Riis (Silkeborg, Denmark), Ralf Hönsch and Martin Stark (Switzerland), Rolf Hönsch (Grüt) and Martin Stark (Salzbach, Switzerland), Roderick Hunter (Telemaco Barba, Pwaná), Sabine Imhoff (Germany), Magnus Jando and Anna Daun (Lund, Swe), Karen Johnson (British Columbia, Canada), Marij v. Kaathoven (Hertogenbosch, Netherlands), Wolfgang D. Kleine (Windhoek, Namibia), Ulrike Krauss (Edinburgh), Heike Krohn (Berlin 46), Daniel Küng (Wohlen, Switzerland), Gerald Lange (Dolldorf, Germany), Henrik K. Larsen (V. Skerninge) and Mai Britt Noerskvu (Svendberg, Denmark), Melchior Lengsfeld (Basel), Melinda, Louis and Aviva Lenoff (Santiago) Eliana S. and Prof. Jeff H. Lesser (Connecticut, U.S.A.), John Lewis (London NW2) for a particularly helpful contribution, Nick Louth (Amsterdam), Markus Maier and Gitte Wiedmann (Zürich), Rosi Marbach and Lorenz Meier (Birsfecden, Switzerland), Douglas Markham (Houston), Cherry Martin and Marcella Paolacci (Fortaleza, Brazil), Noel Maye (Queens, NY), Simon Mays-Smith (Waldron, East Sussex), Julianne McCabe, Maggie Widow, Jean O'Leary and Bill Shaffer (San Anselmo, C.A.), Gemma McGrath (London N8), Peter McPherson (Sale, Australia), Heidi and Peter Merdian (Weinstadt, Germany), Greg Merrell (Boston, Mass.) and Kevin Merrell (New York), Andy Millbank (Norwich), Alison Milner and Keith Doyle (Manchester), Bernard Milward (Salvador), Ben Morgan (London SW8), Catherine Morris-Adams (West Derby), Deirdre Mortell (Corrigaline, County Cork), Klaus Namer (Kempten, Germany), Lothar Nehrke (Dortmund), Pia Neuenschwander (Bremgarten, Switzerland), Steve Newman and Wendy Chilcott (Horsham, West Sussex), Asbjørn Nielsen (Denmark) Sean O'Flynn and Conor O'Sullivan of Tatu Tours, Salvador, Bahia, Noreen O'Flynn, Suzanne Olde and Dave Wendt (Amsterdam), Alice Owen and Ian Davie (Newton Abbot, Devon), Vital Pajarola and Eva Grunder (Zurich), Veronika Paul (San Carlos, CA, U.S.A.), Adrian Pennink (London W4), Mirco and Cristina Perot (Grüt, Switz), David and Lucia Peterkin (Ouro Preto, Brazil), Shauna Picard and Grant Findlay (Melbourne, Australia), Thomas Pichler (Berlin 65), Melanie and David Poley (England), John Pomfret (Woking, Surrey), Michal Porat (Kfar Monash, Israel), Arthur Poyner (Chiloe), Bernd Proissl (Wernau), Brigitte Ramseier and Remo Schenker (Gretzenbach, Switzerland), John Rashak (Whitehouse Station, NJ), John Raspey (Argentina), Hans Riess (Berlin), Toby Robinson (London SW2), Martin and Mary Roche (Co. Kildare, Ireland), Bryan and Charmaine Roche (Cape Town), Joseph J. Rodríguez, Winifred Hughes Rodríguez and Jo Ann Manderscheid (Snyder, New York), Henrik Rosen/c (São Carlos, SP, Brazil), Emerich Roth (Manaus), Nick Saunders and Sarah Jaggs (London W1), Ronald Schaulin and Christina Brand (Reinach, Switz), Thomas Schalk (Osnabrüch, Germany), Martin Schafer (Aarau, Switzerland), Lenhard Schnitzer (Hamburg 20), Dieter Schoop (Maceió), Dieter Schoop (Münchenstein, Switzerland), Florian and Erdbeere Schulz (Berlin 27), Michael Scott-Watson (Roxburghshire, Scotland), R.T. Shannon (Auckland, New Zealand), Ulrich Sigel (Schorndorf, Germany), Tony Silard (Washington, D.C.), B. Spiers and Diane Simpson (Christchurch, New Zealand), John Spraos (London NW11), Trevor and Lynn Stacey (Windhoek, Namibia), Paul Steele (São Paulo, Brazil), Hans and Ina Stoffregen (Celle, Germany), Eva Süsstrunk and Roland Ruprecht (Berne), Jerry Swallow (Almeda, CA), John J. Szehuish (USA), L. Tapsall (Kensington, South Africa), Birgitte Thale (Denmark), Martin Theander Christoph Theis (Wiesloch, Germany), Michael Turner (Burnham-On-Sea), Jarle Unneland (Alesund, Norway), Mark Van Den Boer (Tilberg, Netherlands), Levy Venanzius (Disla, Switzerland), Andreas Vogt (Mössingen, Germany), Béatrice Völkle (Gampelen, Switz.), Peter and Miek Vullings (Panningen, Netherlands), Thomas Walbaum (Steinheim, Germany), Joanna Watts and Shaun Pinchbeck (Bath), Allan Wearden (Blackburn, Lancs), Barbara Weidemann (München, Germany), Thorsten Weiland (Leichlingen, Germany), Dr Volker Weinmann (São Paulo, Brazil), Hans-Martin Werner (Freiburg-Ebnet, Germany), Gerhard Westerdorf (Rosenheim, Germany), Trish and Tony Wheeler (Southport, Queensland), Urs Wickli (Neu St. Johann, Switzerland), Ursula Widmer (Zurich), Prof. Clive Willis (Manchester, U.K.), Julie Williams (Muswellbrook, NSW), Maristela Winter (Denver, Colorado), Petra Witteler (Frankfurt, Germany), Manfred Wolfensberger (Uster, Switzerland), H.H. Worringen (Meerbusch, Germany), F Worthington (Leicester), Dario Zito (São Paulo, Brazil), Hod Zoiberman (Petach-Tikra, Israel) and Bart Zwart (Eindhoven, Netherlands).

# CHILE

## INTRODUCTION

CHILE, with an area of 756,626 square km., is smaller than all other South American republics save Ecuador, Paraguay, Uruguay and the Guianas. Its territory is a ribbon of land lying between the Andes and the Pacific, 4,329 km. long and, on average, no more than 180 km. wide. Of this width the Andes and a coastal range of highland take up from a third to a half. Chile contains within itself wide variations of soil and vast differences of climate; these are reflected, from area to area, in the density of population and the occupations of its almost 13 million people.

In the extreme north Chile has a frontier with Peru running ten km. north of the railway from the port of Arica to the Bolivian capital of La Paz. Its eastern frontier—with Bolivia in the far north and with Argentina for the rest of its length—is along the crest of the Andes, gradually diminishing in height from Santiago southwards to the southern seas, where the Strait of Magellan lies, giving access to the Atlantic. Chile's western and southern coastline is 4,500 km. long.

Down the whole length, between the Andes and the coastal range, there runs a valley depression, though it is less well defined in the north. North of Santiago transverse ranges join the two massifs and impede transport, but for 1,044 km. south of the capital the great longitudinal valley stretches as far as Puerto Montt. South of Puerto Montt the sea has broken through the coastal range and drowned the valley, and there is a bewildering assortment of archipelagos and channels.

From north to south the country falls into five sharply contrasted zones:
1. The first 1,250 km. from the Peruvian frontier to Copiapó is a rainless hot desert of brown hills and plains devoid of vegetation, with a few oases. Here lie the

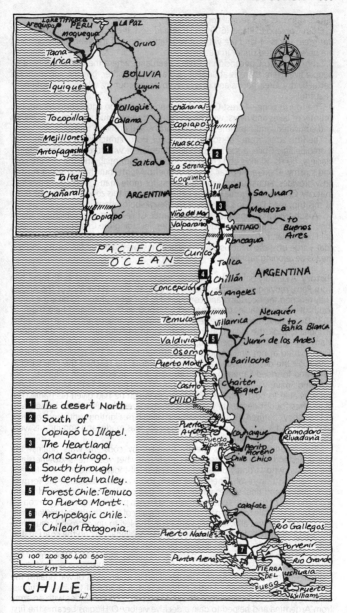

1. The desert North
2. South of Copiapó to Illapel.
3. The Heartland and Santiago.
4. South through the central valley.
5. Forest Chile: Temuco to Puerto Montt.
6. Archipelagic Chile.
7. Chilean Patagonia.

CHILE

nitrate deposits and several copper mines.

2. From Copiapó to Illapel (600 km.) is semi-desert; there is a slight winter rainfall, but great tracts of land are without vegetation most of the year. Valley bottoms are here cultivated under irrigation.

3. From Illapel to Concepción is Chile's heartland, where the vast majority of its people live. Here there is abundant rainfall in the winter, but the summers are perfectly dry. Great farms and vineyards cover the country, which is exceptionally beautiful.

4. The fourth zone—Forest Chile—between Concepción and Puerto Montt, is a country of lakes and rivers, with heavy rainfall through much of the year. Cleared and cultivated land alternates with mountains and primeval forests.

5. The fifth zone, from Puerto Montt to Cape Horn, stretches for 1,600 km. This is archipelagic Chile, a sparsely populated region of wild forests and mountains, glaciers, fjords, islands and channels. Rainfall is torrential, and the climate cold and stormy. There are no rail links S of Puerto Montt, but the Carretera Austral now provides almost unbroken road access for more than 1,000 kilometres S of that city. Chilean Patagonia is in the extreme south of this zone. To make the most of this trip, read Darwin's *Voyage of the Beagle* beforehand.

A subdivision of the fifth zone is Atlantic Chile—that part which lies along the Magellan Strait to the east of the Andes, including the Chilean part of Tierra del Fuego Island. There is a cluster of population here raising sheep and mining coal. Large offshore oilfields have now been discovered in the far South, and the area is developing rapidly.

**History** A century before the Spanish conquest the Incas moved south into Chile from Peru, moving across the desert from oasis to oasis at the foot of the Andes. They reached the heartland and conquered it, but were unable to take the forest south of the Río Maule; there the fierce Mapuches (Araucanians) held them. In 1537 Diego de Almagro, at the head of a hundred Spaniards and some thousands of Indians, took the Inca road from Peru south to Salta and across the Andes. Many of the Indians perished, but the heartland was reached; bitterly disappointed at not finding gold they returned to Peru. The next *conquistador*, who took the desert road, was Pedro de Valdivia; he reached the heartland in 1541 and founded Santiago on 12 February. Reinforced by fresh colonists from Peru and Spain, Valdivia widened his conquest and pushed S into Mapuche land, but was able to hold only the settlement to which he had given his name. The Mapuches fought desperately—they soon mastered the use of the horse—and in 1554 they captured Valdivia himself and killed him. Fighting continued for three centuries, and it was not until 1881 that peace was made, and immigrants were able to settle in the Mapuche lands.

The colonial period was greatly troubled by constant wars against the Mapuches and by internal dissensions, particularly between the landowners and the priests, who strongly objected to a system of Indian serfdom—the Indians were constantly in revolt. There have been, too, natural disasters in the form of earthquakes and tidal waves which have wiped out the cities again and again. From the end of the 16th century British and French pirates frequented the coasts. From the first, Chile formed part of the Viceroyalty of Peru; it was controlled from Lima, and trade was allowed only with Peru. This led to uncontrolled smuggling and by 1715 there were 40 French vessels trading illegally along the coast. It was not till 1778 that trading was allowed between Chile and Spain.

In 1810 a group of Chilean patriots, including Bernardo O'Higgins— the illegitimate son of a Sligo-born Viceroy of Peru, Ambrosio O'Higgins, and a Chilean mother—revolted against Spain. This revolt led to seven years of war against the occupying troops of Spain—Lord Cochrane being in charge of the insurrectionist navy—and in 1817 General José de San Martín crossed the Andes with an army from Argentina and helped to gain a decisive victory. O'Higgins became the first

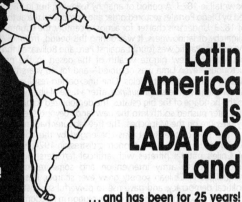

head of state: under him the first constitution of 1818 was drafted. But there was one thing which was dangerous to touch in Chile: the interests of the dominant landed aristocracy, and O'Higgins's liberal policies offended them, leading to his downfall in 1823. A period of anarchy followed, but in 1830 conservative forces led by Diego Portales restored order and introduced the authoritarian constitution of 1833. Under this charter, for almost a century, the country was ruled by a small oligarchy of landowners. It was during this period, from 1879 to 1883, that the War of the Pacific was fought against Peru and Bolivia; all three contestants were claiming the new nitrate wealth of the desert in the north. Chile emerged victorious—even Lima was occupied—and for 40 years thereafter it drew great wealth from the nitrate fields. One unexpected result of the war was that the Chilean land workers or *inquilinos*, after a taste of liberty, were unwilling to return to the bondage of the big estates; the demobilized soldiers migrated to the cities, and later pushed south into the new lands beyond the Bío-Bío recently opened by pressure on the Mapuches. The free labourer had made his appearance.

The rule of the Right was challenged by the liberal regime of President Alessandri in 1920. Acute economic distress in 1924, linked to the replacement of Chile's natural nitrates with artificial fertilizers more cheaply produced in Europe, led to army intervention and some reforms were achieved. The inequalities in Chilean society grew ever sharper, despite the maintenance of political democracy, and gave rise to powerful socialist and communist parties. President Eduardo Frei's policy of "revolution in freedom" (1964-70) was the first concerted attempt at overall radical reform, but it raised hopes it could not satisfy. In 1970 a marxist coalition assumed office under Dr. Salvador Allende; the frantic pace of change under his regime polarized the country into Left- and Right-wing camps. Gradually increasing social and economic chaos formed the background for Allende's deposition by the army and his death in September 1973. A military regime, led by Gen. Augusto Pinochet Ugarte, succeeded him. In its early years particularly, it suppressed internal opposition by methods which were widely condemned. Despite economic prosperity and efforts to make the regime more popular, President Pinochet's bid to be chosen for a further eight years in office after 1989 was rejected by the electorate in 1988.

A Christian Democrat, Patricio Aylwin Azócar, was elected President in 1989 and took office on 11 March 1990 in a peaceful transfer of power from military dictatorship to a constitutional, democratically-elected civilian government. The new Congress began work by suspending many laws passed by the military, prior to revising them. These included the anti-terrorist law, the death penalty, the budget, tax and labour legislation, curbs on freedom of expression and a plethora of laws decreed by the junta in its final months. In 1991 the National Commission for Truth and Reconciliation published a report with details of those whoe died or disappeared under the military regime, but mass human rights trials were not initiated.

**The People**　There is less racial diversity in Chile than in most Latin American countries. There are about 150,000 Mapuche Indians, 95% of whom live in the forest land around Temuco, between the Bío-Bío and Toltén rivers. A fifth is European; the rest is *mestizo*. There has been much less immigration than in Argentina and Brazil. The German, French, Italian and Swiss immigrants came mostly between 1846 and 1864 as small farmers in the forest zone S of the Bío-Bío. Between 1880 and 1900 gold-seeking Serbs and Croats settled in the far S, and the British took up sheep farming and commerce in the same region. The influence throughout Chile of the immigrants is out of proportion to their numbers: their signature on the land is seen, for instance, in the German appearance of Valdivia, Puerto Montt, Puerto Varas and Osorno.

The population (12,961,000 in 1989) is far from evenly distributed: Middle Chile (from Copiapó to Concepción), 18% of the country's area, contains 77% of the total population.

The Metropolitan Region of Santiago contains, on its own, about 39% of the whole population. The rate of population growth per annum—1.7%— is slightly under the average for Latin America.

The birth rate is highest in the cities, particularly of the forest zone. The death rate, 5.9%, is highest in the cities. Infant mortality is 22.8 per thousand live births; it is highest in the rural areas. There are 300 hospital beds per 100,000 population and 1,038 inhabitants per doctor. Life expectancy is 71. Of the total population, only 5.7% are illiterate.

Today, there is in process an intense urbanization of the populace. The cities are expanding, partly because so many people have left the land, and some 83% now live in the towns. Housing in the cities has not kept pace with the increased population; many Chileans live in slum areas called *callampas* (mushrooms) in the outskirts of Santiago and around the factories.

**The Economy** Chile is endowed with a diversified environment, allowing the production of all temperate and Mediterranean products. Agriculture, however, supplies only about 10% of gdp, employs 15% of the labour force and contributes about 15% of merchandise exports. Given the country's topography, only 7% of the land is devoted to crop production, while 16% is used for pasture. Traditional crops, such as cereals, pulse, potatoes and industrial crops (sugarbeet, sunflowerseed and rapeseed) account for about 37% of the value added of agriculture, and vegetables for about 25%. The area showing fastest growth is fresh fruit. Another area of expansion is forestry. Chile has over 9 m hectares of natural forest of which planted forests cover 1 m hectares, with more than 90% planted with insignis radiata pine, a species which in Chile grows faster than in other countries. Chile is the most important fishing nation in Latin America and the largest producer of fishmeal in the world. Industrial consumption absorbs about 93% of the fish catch; fresh fish and fish products contribute about 11% of merchandise exports.

The dominant sector of the economy is mining. Chile has been the world's largest producer of copper since 1982 and also produces molybdenum, iron ore, manganese, lead, gold, silver, zinc, sulphur and nitrates. Chile has a quarter of the world's known molybdenum ore reserves (3m tonnes), and is believed to have around 40% of the world's lithium reserves. Mineral ores, most of which is copper, account for half of total export revenue. Fluctuations in world prices for minerals therefore have a great impact on the balance of payments.

Chile is fortunate in possessing reserves of oil, natural gas and coal, and abundant hydroelectricity potential. About 60% of its energy requirements are met by oil and gas, 15% by coal, 24% by hydroelectricity and the balance by biomass. Almost all the country's hydrocarbon reserves are in the extreme south, on Tierra del Fuego, in the Strait of Magellan and the province of Magallanes. Oil reserves are estimated at 736 m barrels, 188 m of which are offshore.

Manufacturing has been particularly vulnerable to changes in economic policy: nationalization during the Allende administration in the early 1970s; recession brought about by anti-inflationary policies in the mid-1970s; increased foreign competition resulting from trade liberalization in the early 1980s, and greater exports together with import substitution in the mid-1980s. The contribution of manufacturing to total gdp fell from 25% in 1970 to 21% in 1989 although its share of exports rose. Activity is mostly food processing, metalworking, textiles and fish processing.

High rates of inflation were recorded in the first half of the 1970s, but were brought down from over 500% at the end of 1973 to less than 10% by end-1981, largely because of fiscal balance and an overvalued currency. Following the freeing of the exchange rate in 1982 inflation accelerated somewhat, but was successfully moderated by tight monetary control and a lower public sector borrowing requirement. Monetary policy was formulated to cope with high domestic indebtedness in the light of restrictive IMF programmes. IMF involvement was sought following a sharp fall in international commercial lending in 1982 and a decline in Chile's terms of trade. Chile has successfully negotiated several debt refinancing packages with commercial banks and with the Paris Club of creditor governments. In the second half of the 1980s, Chile's foreign debt declined as the Government introduced schemes whereby debt could be converted into equity in Chilean companies. By the 1990s, however, debt was rising again with higher disbursements from official creditors and voluntary new money from banks. Rising exports, on the other hand, meant that the debt; exports ratio was falling.

**Constitution and Government** After the deposition and death of President Salvador Allende on 11 September 1973, Chile was ruled by a military president, Gen. Augusto Pinochet Ugarte, and a 4-man-junta with absolute powers. The pre-1973 constitution was replaced, after a plebiscite, on 11 March 1981. Under this new constitution, which provides for an eight-year non-renewable term for the President of the Republic, a bicameral Congress and an independent judiciary and central bank, President Pinochet was to remain in office until the end of the decade. In 1988 a plebiscite was held to determine whether he should remain in office for a further 8 years. A large 'no' vote resulted in direct presidential and congressional elections in 1989. Patricio Aylwin (see above), the candidate of the Coalition of Parties for Democracy (CPD), won the presidential elections with 55.2% of the vote, while the CPD won 71 of the 120 seats in the Chamber of Deputies. The coalition won only 22 seats in the 47-seat Senate, its majority wiped out by nine seats held by Pinochet appointees, who could block constitutional reform. Gen Pinochet remained as Army Commander although other armed forces chiefs were replaced.

In 1974 Chile established thirteen regions to replace the old system of 25 provinces. The regions (now named) are subdivided into 51 new provinces.

**Communications** Chile's difficult topography—archipelagos, forests, mountains, deserts—makes communications other than by air a formidable problem. It would be much more serious if 90% of the Chilean population did not live in the compact central rectangle, with good roads and adequate railways, between La Serena and Puerto Montt. Only a short distance along one river—the estuary of the Bío-Bío—is navigable.

**Railways** There are 10,100 km. of line, of which most are state owned. Most of the privately owned 2,130 km. of line are in the desert north, where the northern terminal is Iquique. From the longitudinal Iquique-Puerto Montt trunk line branches run westwards to the ports and seaside resorts, and eastwards to mines and mountain resorts. The main gauge on the Valparaíso and southern lines is 5 ft. 6 in. (1.676 metres). Passenger services on N of Santiago have virtually ceased except for the international routes to La Paz.

Four international railways link Chile with its neighbours. There is a local line between Arica and Tacna, linking Chile with Peru. There are two railways to Bolivia: between Arica and La Paz (448 km.), and from Antofagasta via Calama to La Paz. Between Chile and Argentina there is only one line now in operation, between Antofagasta and Salta, in the Argentine north-west. There is no international service on this line. The Transandine Railway linking Santiago with Buenos Aires is disused on the Chilean side. The Ferrocarriles del Estado publish an annual *Guía Turística*, available in various languages from the larger stations.

**Roads** About one-half of the 88,000 km. of roads can be used the year round, though a large proportion of them are unimproved and only about 9,700 km. are first class. The region round the capital and the Central Valley are the best served.

The Pan-American (Longitudinal) Highway runs from Arica through Santiago to Puerto Montt and recently extended by the Carretera Austral to beyond Cochrane; from Llay-Llay a branch goes to Los Andes and over La Cumbre (Uspallata) pass to Argentina. Another main international road in the Lake District goes from Osorno across the Puyehue pass to Argentina. The Longitudinal Highway, vital to the Chilean economy, is paved throughout, but many sections are in a bad state.

Chile has an extensive system of protected natural areas, 7 million hectares in all. The areas, managed by Conaf (the Corporación Nacional Forestal), are divided into 30 national parks, 36 forest reserves and 10 natural monuments. Of the 76 areas, 46 have public access, and details of the majority are given in the text.

**Music and Dance** At the very heart of Chilean music is the Cueca, a courting dance for couples, both of whom make great play with a handkerchief waved aloft in the right hand. The man's knees are slightly bent and his body arches back. It is lively and vigorous, seen to best advantage when performed by a Huaso wearing spurs. Guitar and harp are the accompanying instruments, while handclapping and shouts of encouragement add to the atmosphere. The dance has a common origin with the Argentine Zamba and Peruvian Marinera via the early 19th century Zamacueca, in turn descended from the Spanish Fandango. For singing only is the Tonada, with its variants the Glosa, Parabienes, Romance, Villancico (Christmas carol) and Esquinazo (serenade) and the Canto a lo Poeta, which can be in the form of a Contrapunto or Controversia, a musical duel. Among the most celebrated groups are Los Huasos Quincheros, Silvia Infante with Los Condores and the Conjunto Millaray. Famous folk singers in this genre are the Parra Family from Chillán, Hector Pávez and Margot Loyola. In the north of the country the music is Amerindian and closely related to that of Bolivia. Groups called "Bailes" dance the Huayño, Taquirari, Cachimbo or Rueda at carnival and other festivities and precolombian rites like the Cauzulor and Talatur. Instruments are largely wind and percussion, including zampoñas (pan pipes), lichiguayos, pututos (conch shells) and clarines. There are some notable religious festivals that attract large crowds of pilgrims and include numerous groups of costumed dancers. The most outstanding of these festivals are those of the Virgen de La Tirana near Iquique, San Pedro de Atacama, the Virgen de la Candelaria of Copiapó and the Virgen de Andacollo.

In the south the Mapuche nation, the once greatly feared and admired "Araucanos", who kept the Spaniards and Republicans at bay for four hundred years—have their own songs, dance-songs and magic and collective dances, accompanied by wind instruments like the great long trutruca horn, the shorter pifilka and the kultrun drum. Further south still, the island of Chiloé, which remained in the hands of pro-Spanish loyalists after the rest of the country had become independent, has its own unique musical expression. Wakes and other religious social occasions include collective singing, while the recreational dances, all of Spanish origin, such as the Vals, Pavo, Pericona and Nave have a heavier and less syncopated beat than in central Chile. Accompanying instruments here are the rabel (fiddle), guitar and accordion.

## THE DESERT NORTH (1)

A desert zone with various oases: the main cities are Arica, Iquique, Antofagasta and Calama; the main points of interest the Andean landscapes of the Lauca National Park and San Pedro de Atacama (which also has remains of Atacameño culture), the Pacific coastline and mineral workings old and new.

The 1,250 km. between Arica and Copiapó are desert without vegetation, with little or no rain. The inhospitable shore is a pink cliff face rising to a height of from 600 to 900 metres. At the bottom of the cliff are built the towns, some of considerable size. The far from pacific Pacific often makes it difficult to load and unload ships. The nitrate fields exploited in this area lie in the depression between Pisagua and Taltal. Copper, too is mined in the Cordillera; there are two large mines, at Chuquicamata, near Calama, and at El Salvador, inland from Chañaral.

Life in the area is artificial. Water has to be piped for hundreds of km. to the cities and the nitrate fields from the Cordillera; all food and even all building materials have to be brought in from elsewhere. Only the small populations of the oases, such as Calama, are self-supporting.

There is some difference of climate between the coast and the interior. The coast is humid and cloudy; in the interior the skies are clear. The temperatures on

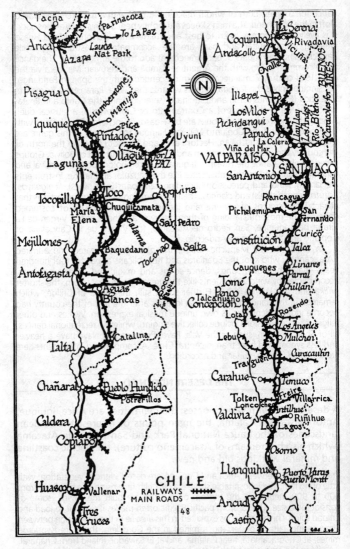

Tacna
Parinacota
To La Paz
Arica
Azapa
Lauca
Nat Park
Pisagua
Humberstone
Mamiña
Iquique
Pica
Pintados
Uyuni
Ollagüe por LA
PAZ
Lagunas
Tocopilla
Toco
Ayquina
María
Elena
Chuquicamata
San Pedro
Mejillones
Baquedano
Calama
Toconao
Salta
Antofagasta
Aguas
Blancas
Ocoma
Salta
Taltal
Catalina
Chañaral
Pueblo Hundido
Potrerillos
Caldera
Copiapó
Huasco
Vallenar
Tres
Cruces

Coquimbo
La Serena
Rivadavia
Andacollo
Vicuña
Ovalle
Illapel
Los Vilos
Pichidangui
Papudo
Viña del Mar
La Calera
VALPARAISO
SANTIAGO
San Antonio
Rancagua
Pichelemu
San
Fernando
Constitución
Curicó
Talca
Cauquenes
Linares
Tomé
Parral
Talcahuano
Penco
Chillán
Concepción
Lota
Rosendo
Lebu
Los Angeles
Mulchén
Traiguén
Curacautín
Carahue
Temuco
Villarrica
Tolten
Loncoche
Freire
Valdivia
Riñihue
Los Lagos
Osorno
Llanquihue
Puerto Varas
Puerto Montt
Ancud
Castro

Río Blanco
Los Andes
Laú Luy
Caracoles for BUENOS AIRES

**CHILE**
RAILWAYS ╫╫╫╫╫
MAIN ROADS ━━━━

48

the coast are fairly uniform; in the interior there is often a great difference in the temperature between day and night; the winter nights are often as cold as -10°C, with a cruel wind. Drivers must beware of high winds and blowing sand N of Copiapó.

Chile's most northerly city, 19 km. S of the Peruvian border, is **Arica**, with a population of 145,415, built at the foot of the Morro headland and fringed by sand dunes. The Andes can be clearly seen from the anchorage. The Morro, with a good view from the look-out park on top (an hour's walk along the road from town, ½ hr. by footpath from the south end of Colón, or 10 mins. by taxi), was the scene of a great victory by Chile over Peru on 7 June 1880.

There is no rain, winter or summer. The average, daytime winter temperature is 19°C, and the average summer temperature 24°C. It is frequented for sea-bathing by Bolivians as well as the locals. The attractive cathedral church, San Marcos, built in iron by Eiffel and fitted with bright coloured windows, is in the Plaza de Armas. It was brought to Arica from Ilo (Peru) in the 19th century, before Peru lost Arica to Chile, as an emergency measure after a tidal wave swept over Arica and destroyed all its churches. Eiffel also designed the customs house. A 63-km. railway connects the town with Tacna, in Peru, and another (448 km.) with La Paz, the capital of Bolivia; the old steam locomotive (made in Germany in 1924) once used on this line can be seen outside Arica station. In the station is a memorial to John Roberts Jones, builder of the Arica portion of the railway, and a small museum (key at booking office). It is this railway, over which today flow about half the legal imports and exports of Bolivia, that makes Arica important; it will become more important now that the international highway to Tambo Quemado, Bolivia, is completed for normal traffic. An oil pipeline runs from Bolivia. There are large fishmeal plants.

**The Free Zone** in the First Region now imposes customs duties on many articles, but vessels, aircraft and other transport still enter the Zone without payment of customs dues and other charges. Because of the free zone, overland travellers heading south are subject to baggage checks, the first at the bus terminal.

**Local Festival** Fiestas for the Virgen de las Peñas at the Santuario de Livircar in the Azapa Valley (see below) are held on the first Sunday in October and a lesser festival on 7-9 December (on 8 Dec. the festival moves to Arica). Take a bus from Av. Chacabuco y Vicuña Mackenna, then walk 12 km. from where it stops to the sanctuary. The December festival is not particularly outstanding but it takes place in a part of the valley not normally accessible.

**Hotels N.B.** In this area, *pensión* means restaurant, not hostel. *Hostería Arica* Av. Cdte. San Martín 599 (T 231201), best, A-A+ depending on season, accommodation is good value, good and reasonable restaurant, but all other services expensive (inc. breakfast, set lunch for US$6, free pisco sour on arrival) about 2 km. along shore, reached by frequent bus service along front (Nos. 7, 8), tennis court (free) hotel has lava beach (not safe for swimming), but there are two public beaches nearby, to left and right; *El Paso,* bungalow style, pleasant gardens, swimming pool, Av. Gral. Velásquez, 1109, T 231965, A with breakfast, good set meals US$6 inc wine; *Central,* 21 de Mayo 425 (T 252575), new, central, nicely decorated, B; *Res. Las Vegas 120,* Baquedano 120, T 231355, E p.p., clean, hot water, safe, central, English spoken, rec.; *Príncipe de Asturias,* Capitán Avalos 2041 (T 222289), B, new, motel-style; *Motel Azapa,* attractive grounds but several km. from beaches and centre: F. Sánchez 660, Azapa, T 222612, A, but cheaper cabins available, fair restaurant ½ km. away; *Diego de Almagro,* Sotomayor 490, T 232927, C, clean, rec, will store luggage; *Savona,* Yungay 380, T 232319, D, highly rec.; *Lynch,* Lynch 589, T 231581, C, cheaper without bath, clean, rec.; *Residencial Chungara,* Lynch 675 (T 231677), D with bath, clean, quiet; *Residencial Las Condes,* Vicuña Mackenna 628, T 251583, D, helpful, hot water, prices negotiable if staying a few days, rec.; *Residencial Puerta del Sol,* 21 de Mayo 480, D, 12 rooms, shared bath, meals available, clean, quiet, excellent service; *Residencial Blanquita,* Maipú 472, T 232064, D, clean, hot water; *San Marcos,* Sotomayor 376 (T 232149/232970), clean, helpful, C; *Residencial Ibáñez,* Sotomayor 580, E without bath, dark rooms; *Residencial Madrid,* Baquedano 685 (T 231479), E without bath, clean, good value but awful beds, theft from washing line reported; *Residencial Venecia,* Baquedano 739, T 252877, E, spotless, rec., hot water, small rooms; *Pensión Donoso,* Baquedano y Maipú, E, friendly, cheap, rec.; *Residencial Maipú,* Maipú 479, T 252157, E, basic, hot water, safe, old, good; *Residencial Leiva,* Av. Colón 347, T 232008, F without bath, clean, friendly, good value; *Residencial Velásquez,* Velásquez 669 (T 231989), D, basic, dirty, friendly; on same street *Res. Alondra,* No. 704, T 252482, F p.p. and *Res. Chillán,* No. 719, T 251677, E, safe, friendly, clean, good value. Sra. Leony Vidiella, Gonzálo Cerda 1030, close to bus station, E p.p. with breakfast, shared bath, cooking facilities, clean, safe, tepid water. In Jan.-Feb. the

PAN-AMERICAN HIGHWAY
NORTH: TO PERU
ALSO TO AIRPORT
LAUCA NATIONAL PARK
BOLIVIA

RIO SAN JOSÉ

1. San Marcos Church, 2. Municipality,
3. Eiffel Customs House, 4. Casino,
5. Taxis to Tacna, 6. Railway station for
La Paz, 7. Railway station for Tacna,
8. Harbour, 9. Tourist Office and
Post Office, 10. Entel (Telephones),
11. Bolivian Consul, 12. Peruvian Consul,
13. Market.

J.A. RIOS
M. BLANCO ENCALADA
CRAL VELASQUEZ
UNIVERSIDAD DE CHILE
AV SANTA MARIA
CEMENTERIO
INDEPENDENCIA
J. WAIDELLE
A. NGAMOS
LARCO HERRERA
SALVO
AV. B. VICUÑA MACKENNA
LASTARRIA
JUAN NOE
A. LATORRE
AV. ESMERALDA
CHACABUCO
O'HIGGINS
BAQUEDANO
P. LYNCH
MAIPU
GRAL VELASQUEZ
GRAL LAGOS
18 DE SEPTIEMBRE
PAN-AMERICAN HIGHWAY SOUTH TO AZAPA
ARTURO GALLO
SAN MARTIN
A. PRAT
COLON
P. MON
MAXIMO LIRA
BOLOGNESI
21 DE MAYO
M. BLANCO ENCALADA
SOTOMAYOR
7 DE JUNIO
SAN MARCOS
YUNGAY
EJERCITO
MORRO
FALDEOS EL MORRO
TO LA LISERA AND BEACHES SOUTH EL MORRO
CAMINO AL MORRO

**ARICA**

49

municipality supplies cheap basic accommodation, ask at the tourist office.

**Camping**   3 km. S of town, at Arenillas Negras; also at Villa Frontera, 15 km. N of Arica, and at the Vivero Municipal, 7 km. SE of town in the Valle de Azapa.

**Restaurants**   *Acuario*, Máximo Lira, Terminal Pesquero, good food and atmosphere, expensive; *El Rey de Mariscos*, Maipú y Colón, good seafood, pricey, rec.; plenty of seafood lunch places in the market; *El Arriero*, 21 de Mayo y Colón, good; *D'Aurelio*, Velásquez 615, good Italian, reasonable prices; *Pizzeriá 890*, 21 de Mayo 890, good pizzas; *Yuri*, Maipú 500, good food and service, cheap, rec.; *Bavaria*, Colón 613, good, with delicatessen and expresso coffee, repeatedly rec.; *Centro Español*, Bolognesi 317, pricey, good *almuerzo*. *Natura*, Bolognesi 367, good vegetarian, good value lunches; try also vegetarian lunches at *Naturista Snack Bar*, Maipú y Colón. *El Tambo*, in Poblado Artesanal, Hualles 2025, folk music and dancing. On Baquedano, good *chifa* in 600 block, fresh seafood, in Chinese Association building (built 1923), and *Americano* in 700 block for cakes and expresso coffee. *La Bomba*, Colón 357, at fire station, good value *almuerzo*; good cheese empanadas at Arturo Gallo 449. *Il Molino Vecchio*, 18 Septiembre y Lynch, excellent delicatessen and bread.

**Cafés**   *Café Stop*, 21 de Mayo 244, good coffee, rec.; *Schop*, 18 de Septiembre 240, good, cheap sandwiches; *Suceso Inn*, 18 de Septiembre 250, good coffee.

**Night-Clubs**   Casino, Gral. Velásquez 955, open all year, but not to everyone's taste. *Lido's*, Colón 341, opens 2200; *Sunset* discotheque, 3½ km. out of town in the Valle de Azapa, after 2300 weekends.

**Cinemas**   Colón, 7 de Junio 190; Rex, 21 de Mayo 570.

**Shopping**   *Feria Dominical*, Av. Costanera, Sun. a.m. only; *Poblado Artesanal*, Plaza Las Gredas, Hualles 2025 (take bus 2, 3 or 7): local 2, especially good for musical instruments; Mercado Central, Sotomayor, between Colón and Baquedano, mornings only. Fruit, vegetable and old clothes market at Terminal Agropecuario at edge of town; take bus marked "Terminal Agro". Arica is an important centre for cheapish electronic goods for Bolivian and Peruvian shoppers.

**Laundry**   *Lavandería Americana*, Lynch 651 and Lynch 260, reasonable, 48 hr service; *Lavandería La Moderna*, 18 de Septiembre 457, 24 hr service; *Lavandería Olimpia*, Lastarria 1235. All expensive, charge per item.

**Taxis**   Within city limit, US$0.25 p.p. on fixed distances.

**Car Hire**   Viva Rent a Car, 21 de Mayo 821, T 251121; Hertz, *Hotel El Paso*, Gral Velázquez 1109, T 252573, cheaper. American Rent A Car, Gral. Lagos 559, T 252234.

**Automóvil Club de Chile**   Chacabuco 460, T 237780.

**Car Service**   Shell, Panamericana Norte 3456; Esso, Av. Diego Portales 2462; Autocentro, Azola 2999, T 241241.

**Sports**   Golf, 18 hole course in Valle de Azapa, Panamericana Sur, turn right at Km. 7, open daily except Mon. Tennis: Club de Tenis Centenario, Av. España 2640, open daily.

**Bathing**   Olympic pool in Parque Centenario, Tues.-Sun., US$0.50; take No. 5A bus. Take No. 7 or 8 bus to beaches south of town, or walk along seaside promenade. For swimming La Lisera is better than El Laucho (very rocky), Playa Chinchorro rec. Playa Brava is popular for sunbathing but not swimming (dangerous currents). Strong currents also at Playa Las Michas which is popular with surfers. Playa Corazones, 15 km. to south (no buses, take taxi or hitch), rec. not for swimming but picnics and fishing.

**Museums**   At San Miguel, 13 km. from Arica in the Azapa Valley, is the **Museo Arqueológico** of the University of Tarapacá, the most important in northern Chile (see under Excursions). **Museo Antropológico**, University of Tarapacá Saucache Campus, Av. 18 de Septiembre 2222 (just beyond stadium), Mon.-Fri. 0900-1300, 1500-1900; **Museo Histórico Salitre**, Calle Sotomayor 415, voluntary contributions expected (closed August 1990). **Museo Histórico y de Armas**, on summit of the Morro, containing weapons and uniforms from the War of the Pacific.

**Exchange**   Many banks and money changers on 21 de Mayo and its junction with Colón. **Banco de Santiago** will exchange travellers' cheques for dollars cash, but at US$12 per transaction, daily limit US$500; no others will cash travellers' cheques. **Fincard** (Visa and Mastercard), 21 de Mayo 252, Mon.-Fri. 0900-1400, 1600-2100, Sat. 1000-1400, only pesos given, at varying rates. *Casas de Cambio*: **Marta Daguer**, 18 de Septiembre 330, good rates; **Cambio Fides**, Shopping Centre del Pacífico, Diego Portales 840, local 147; **Daniel Concha**, Chacabuco 300; **Tacora**, 21 de Mayo 171, good rates for cash; **Yanulaque**, 21 de Mayo 175, which stay open until 2000 but close all day Sun. Most large hotels also change cash. Rates for travellers' cheques are generally poor.

**Consulates** British Consul, the only one in Chile north of Valparaíso and Instituto Chileno—Británico de Cultura (library open Mon.-Fri. 0900-1200, 1600-2100), Baquedano 351, T 231098, Casilla 653. **Argentina**, M.Rodríguez 144, Depto. 41 (in a cul-de-sac, entrance at approx. A. Prat 550), T 231812, Mon-Fri. 0900-1300, Consul Sr Daniel Azzi Balbi, very helpful, onward ticket required, preferably out of Argentina, to obtain visa (US$15); **Bolivia**, 21 de Mayo 575, T 231030; **Denmark**, 21 de Mayo 399; **Peru**, San Martín 220, T 231020; **Germany**, 21 de Mayo 639, T 231551. Instituto Cultural Chileno Norteamericano, San Marcos 581. Instituto Chileno-Alemán de Cultura, 21 de Mayo 816.

**Post Office** Arturo Prat 305. To send parcels abroad, contents must be shown to Aduano (under main post office) between 1500 and 1700. Your parcel will be wrapped, cheaply, but take your own carton.

**Telephones** Entel-Chile, Baquedano 388, open 0900-2200. CTC, Colón 476 and at 21 de Mayo 211; VTR Telecommunications, 21 de Mayo 477, telex, fax, telegrams.

**Tourist Office** Sernatur, Calle Arturo Prat 305, 2nd floor; open Mon.-Fri. 0830-1300, 1430-1900. T 232101. Very helpful, English spoken, sells good map, US$3; Kiosk on 21 de Mayo between Colón and Baquedano, open Mon.-Fri., 0830-1300, 1500-1900.

**Travel Agencies** *Turismo Payachatas*, Prat 374, T 221687, rec.; *Jurasi*, Bolognesi 360 A, T 251696, will hold mail, helpful, good city tour for US$8.75, ½ day; *Kijo Tour*, Bolognesi 359, T 232245; *Huasquitur*, Sotomayor 470, helpful, English spoken, will cater for individual itineraries; and many others.

**Air Services** Airport at Chacalluta. Taxi to town US$13, shared taxi US$3 p.p. Airlines provide bus services to connect with arrivals and departures. Airline offices: LanChile, 7 de Junio 148, T 224738; Ladeco, 21 de Mayo 443, T 252021; Lloyd Aéreo Boliviano, P. Lynch 298, T 251919; AeroPerú, 7 de Junio 148, T 232852. Flights: to **La Paz**, LanChile (Mon., Tues., Fri.) and LAB (Tues., Thur., Sat.); to **Santiago**, Ladeco (Mon. direct, also daily via Iquique or Antofagasta) and LanChile (10 a week via Iquique or Antofagasta). To **Tacna**, **Lima** and **Guayaquil**, AeroPerú, reportedly difficult to obtain information about this service outside Arica but enquire at travel agencies in Arica. The duty free status of the city can make it a good place to book cheap flights to Miami, Caracas and other destinations.

**Rail** Direct ferrobus services to La Paz are operated by 2 companies, Payachatas and Coche Motor, leaving Arica Tues. and Sat. (both other days as well in Jan.-March) at 0930, 11 hrs., US$50 including meals, but not drinks. Book well in advance in Jan.-March, tickets from 21 de Mayo 51. Local trains run to the frontier towns of Visviri (Chile) and Charaña (Bolivia) every other Tues. (every Tues. in Jan.-March) at 2300, 9 hrs., US$12 1st class, US$7 2nd class, with connecting service to La Paz at 1000 Wed., arriving 1800 "with luck", US$18 pullman, US$12 special. Check details in advance. Charaña can also be reached by bus (Martínez, P. Montt 620) Tues. and Fri., 9 hrs., US$7. From Charaña there are train and bus connections to La Paz (see **International Railway** section under La Paz, Bolivia). On all journeys, take plenty of warm clothing; long delays, particularly at the frontier are common.

The line from Arica skirts the coast for 10 km. and passes into the Lluta Valley, whose vegetation is in striking contrast with the barrenness of the surrounding hills. From Kilometre 70 there is a sharp rise of 2,241 metres in 42 km. The line is racked for 48 km., but the rack is no longer used. At Puquíos station, Kilometre 112, the plateau is reached at 4,168 metres. The line continues through Coronel Alcerreca and Villa Industrial, before reaching its highest point at General Lagos (4,247 metres). In the distance can be seen the snowcapped heights of Tacora, Putre, Sajama, and their fellows. The frontier station of Visviri is at Kilometre 205, with a custom house. Beyond, the train enters Bolivia and the station of Charaña. In summer a tourist train runs from Arica to Coronel Alcerreca and back on Sundays, 0800, returning to Arica 2100.

To Tacna, Peru, by rail costs US$1.85, daily except Sun. 1200, 1700 and 1900, 1½ hrs. (exit stamp obtainable at station, but allow ½ hour for this—it is preferable to relying on the Town Hall); it is best to avoid Sats. because of crowds and delays at the border. Check times in advance, schedules change.

**Buses** Terminal at corner of Av. Portales and Santa María, T 241390, bus or colectivo No. 8 (US$0.10, or US$0.25), extensive baggage search prior to boarding. All long-distance buses are modern, clean and air-conditioned, but ask carefully what meals are included. To **Antofagasta**, Flecha Norte, US$11.50, 10-11 hrs., via Tocopilla, not a comfortable trip; other lines, some more expensive. Some services to destinations between Antofagasta and the capital involve a change in Antofagasta. To **Calama** and **Chuquicamata**, 10 hrs, US$11.50, several companies, all between 2000 and 2200, Tramaca rec. To **Iquique**, Zambrano, US$6, 4½ hrs. To **Santiago**, 28 hrs., a number of companies, e.g. Carmelita, Flecha Dorada, Ramos Cholele, Fénix and Flota Barrios, all US$35-42.50; also *salón cama* services, run by Fichtur, Flota Barrios, Fénix and others, US$50-60. Most serve meals and the more expensive, the more luxurious; student discounts available. To **La Serena**, 18 hrs., Fénix, US$32, and other companies. To **Viña del Mar** and **Valparaíso**, US$35; also *salón cama* service, Fénix, US$60, including poor meals.

**International Buses** To Arequipa, Peru, with Ormeño, 3 a day, US$12.50, supposedly 6 hrs. To La Paz, Bolivia Litoral, Chacabuco 454, service via border towns of Chungará (Chile) and Tambo Quemado (Bolivia) takes at the very least 20 hrs. (very cold at border—take blanket/sleeping bag, food, water and sense of humour), leaves on Mon. and Thurs., about 2400, US$23. US$ cash only can be exchanged with the Bolivian Immigration Officer at Tambo Quemado.

Colectivo taxis run to and from Tacna for about US$6 p.p. (telephone Arica 231376 or Tacna 2288) one way and take about an hour for the trip (drivers take care of all the paperwork—it's a fairly uncomplicated border crossing); depart from Chacabuco y Colón (Chilean colectivos are reported to be better than Peruvian ones). Bus costs US$2.10 and leaves from the bus station, as does Taxibus, 2 hourly, US$2. Money-changing at frontier, but reported better rates in Tacna.

Drivers are required at the Chile-Peru frontier to file a form, *Relaciones de Pasajeros* (7 copies, no carbons), giving details of passengers, obtained from a stationery store in Tacna, or at the border in a booth near Customs. You must also present the original registration document for your car from its country of registration. The first checkpoints outside Arica on the road to Santiago also require the *Relaciones de Pasajeros* from drivers. If you can't buy the form, details on a piece of paper will suffice or you can get them at service stations. The form is *not* required when travelling south of Antofagasta.

**N.B.** Remember that between October and March, Chilean time is 1 hr. later than Bolivian, 2 hrs. later than Peruvian time October to December (1 hr. vis-à-vis Peru the rest of the year).

**Excursions** To the Azapa valley by yellow colectivo from P. Lynch y Maipú. At Km. 13 is the Museo Arqueológico de San Miguel, part of the University of Tarapacá, containing Andean weaving, basketwork and ceramics (open Mon.-Fri. 1100-1800, Sat., Sun., and holidays 1300-1800, US$0.40, worth a visit). The museum shop sells woollen goods and specialist books and magazines. On the opposite side of the valley at San Lorenzo are the ruins of a *Pukará* (Inca fortress) dating from the 12th century.
   To the Lluta valley, N of Arica along Route 11: At Km. 14 and Km. 16 there are ancient images of llamas and humans on the hillside. The road continues through the Lauca National Park and on to Bolivia.

Before proceeding further, we offer the following advice on travelling off the beaten track in this region, kindly supplied by vulcanologist Dr. Lyndsey O'Callaghan. In all of the mountain areas of the North of Chile, it is important to note that weather and road conditions are very variable. The *carabineros* and military are very active trying to control the borders with Bolivia and Argentina, so they know about the conditions and are quite willing to tell, but only if asked.
   In many villages it is possible to rent a small unfurnished house, if you are planning to stay for a while. Ask for the schoolmaster (or mayor in larger villages). It may also be possible to stay in the small clinics (e.g. at Socaire or Chiu-Chiu).
   If you plan to stay in the mountains for any length of time, it is advisable to take small gifts for the locals: tea, sugar, coffee, salad oil, flour make very acceptable gifts. It is often possible to get people to bake bread etc. for you every day, but you need to supply flour, yeast and salt. If you are planning to do much cooking, then a good pressure cooker is indispensible (remember water boils at only 90 degrees at these altitudes). You may also get problems with kerosene stoves, petrol ones, though rather dangerous, are much more reliable.

Moreover, anyone travelling in this region should consult the *Turistel Norte* guide (see **Tourist Information** in Information for Visitors).

*Lauca National Park* A visit to the Parque Nacional Lauca, 149 km. E of Arica stretching to the frontier with Bolivia, is highly recommended. Situated at over 3,200 metres (beware of Soroche unless you are coming from Bolivia), the park includes numerous snowy volcanoes including 10 peaks of over 6,000 metres, two large lakes (Cotacotani and Chungará) and lava fields at Cotacotani. The wildlife includes a wide variety of waterfowl as well as vicuña, puma and vizcacha. The park is administered by Conaf (Corporación Nacional Forestal), Sotomayor 216, Arica, T 232856, closed weekends. During the rainy season (Jan. and Feb.) roads in the park may be impassable; check in advance with Conaf, from whom further information may be obtained. At the entrance to the park is *Putre*, a scenic village with a church dating from 1670. Putre is a good base for acclimatization. At *Parinacota*, 4,392 metres, at the foot of the Payachatas volcano, there is an interesting 17th century church—rebuilt 1789—with frescoes (local resident Lorenza de Calle knits alpaca sweaters, US$18-20; weavings of wildlife scenes also available). Lake Chungará, one of the highest lakes in the world at 4,600 metres, is a must for its views and its varied wildlife.

**Services** At Putre *Hostería Las Vicuñas*, 3 classes of room, bungalow-type, B, excellent; *Hostería San Martín*, E. At both hotels, groups of 15 or more get one person accommodated free; *Restaurant Oasis*, several rooms to let, cheap, good food. At **Chucuyo**, a village 30 km. E of Putre, there are two shops/restaurants, one of which has 2 rooms to let, a good place to stock up on food. There are two Conaf refuges in the park, but check in advance if they are open: At **Parincota** (4 beds; there is supposed to be oxygen for those suffering from soroche, but it is often not available) and at **Lake Chungará** (8 beds and floor space), both have cooking facilities, US$1.50 p.p., sleeping bag essential, take your own food, candles and matches.

**Transport** can be arranged with Turismo Payachatas, Huasquitur, or Jurasi (addresses above), US$18 p.p. with breakfast, lunch and oxygen, generally recommended although some find the minibuses cramped and dusty and you spend all day in the bus. Jurasi will drop you at Parinacota or Chungará and pick you up on their next tour. For 5 or more, the most economical proposition is to hire a vehicle; petrol is available in Putre, ask at the shop, take at least one spare fuel can.

The Arica-Bolivia road passes through the Park. Lorries leaving port of Arica early in the morning will often give lifts to the Park on their way to La Paz. Best place to wait is at the Poconchile control point 37 km. from Arica. From Parinocota you can hitch to Visviri on Tues. with lorries going to meet the train; catch the train to La Paz at Charaña. Hitching is good every second Sunday when trucks go to the international market at Visviri. Buses go daily from Arica to the gold mines in the park at 0600 and 1400. Flota Paco buses leave for Putre from Germán Riesco 2071, Arica (bus No. 7 from centre), on Mon., Tues., Thurs., Sat. at 0630 (leaving Putre following day at 1300), 4½ hrs., US$3. On Tues. at 0930 and Fri. at 2130 Martínez buses leave Arica (P. Montt 620) for Visviri on the Bolivian border (to connect with the La Paz train, see above); they pass Parinacota after 6-7 hrs., US$5 on Tues., US$8 on Fri.; buses return Wed. and Sat. at about 0800, passing Parinacota about 1400. Lake Chungará is on the road route to La Paz, it is a 1 hr. walk to the Chilean frontier post which opens at 0800 (closed 1200-1430) the Bolivian frontier post is much further. A long wait is likely, trucks pass infrequently, or you may be lucky and get on the Litoral bus which will charge full Arica-La Paz fare. The road from Arica to La Paz was being repaired in Dec. 1990.

South of Lauca is the beautiful **Reserva Nacional Las Vicuñas**, at 4,300 to 5,600 metres, which is suitable for "adventure tourism", to use Conaf's phrase. Be prepared for cold, skin burns from sun and wind, etc; there is no public transport. Administration is at *Guallatiri*, reached by turning off the Arica-La Paz road onto the A147 to Las Cuevas and Cerro Capitán. In the summer wet season, the road is only passable with four-wheel drive; take spare fuel. Open March-November. The same road leads into the **Monumento Natural Salar de Surire** (4,200 metres), which is open for the same months and for which the same conditions apply. Administration is in *Surire*, 7 hours from Arica. This can be reached by getting a ride in a borax truck; these run every day between July and Nov. from Zapahuira (a road junction between Bolivia and Arica). At Surire there is a Conaf *refugio* (may be closed).

**South from Arica** Several checkpoints on the Longitudinal south from Arica. It is illegal to take fruit S from Arica; there is a checkpoint for fruit at Cuya (Km. 105); 21 km. further on, to the right at Km. 131 are the Geoglifas de Chiza (sign-posted and easily accessible), a checkpoint for buses and lorries at Huara (Km. 234), and customs and fruit control at

Quillagua on Río Loa (Km. 430, where there is a museum of local Indian artefacts—key held by lady in telephone exchange). A sense of humour is required during fruit searches, especially on night buses. **N.B.** If driving S, en route to Quillagua there are some steep ascents and descents best tackled in daylight (at night, sea mist, *camanchaca*, can reduce visibility).

**Service stations** between the Peruvian border and Santiago can be found at: Arica, Cuya, Huara, Iquique, Pozo Almonte, Oficina Vitoria, Quillagua, Tocopilla, Oficina María Elena, Chuquicamata, Calama, Carmen Alto, Antofagasta, La Negra, Agua Verde, Taltal, Chañaral, Caldera, Copiapó, Vallenar, La Serena, Termas de Soco, Los Vilos, and then every 30 km. to capital.

Detours off the Pan-American Highway: to Tignamar (take a turning E about 20 km. S of Arica, 100 km. to the village) and Codpa (road E about 70 km. S of Arica), both interesting villages. The latter is an agricultural community in a deep gorge with interesting scenery. Codpa is 40 km. from the Pan-American Highway on a good dirt road.

At Km. 185 S of Arica on the Pan-American Highway there is an interesting British cemetery dating from 1876. 10 km. further S at Zapiga there is a cross-roads. One branch leads west for 41 km. to the run down nitrate exporting port of **Pisagua**. There is little left of this place, though some of the ruins of the nitrate port are still standing. There are a few quite good fish restaurants in the town and it makes a pleasant stop for a meal. Mass graves from the 1970s were recently discovered near here.

   However, the branch which leads east is much more interesting, though the road is not in very good condition, with deep sand and dust causing problems. After 67 km. there is the picturesque village of Camiña where there is a basic hostal. 45 km. further on is the Tranque de Caritaya, a dam which supplies water for the coastal towns set in splendid scenery with lots of wildlife and interesting botany (especially *llareta*). Travelling further east along mountain roads (not in very good condition) leads through magnificent volcanic scenery to **Isluga** (120 km. from Caritaya). This remote area, the **Parque Nacional Volcán Isluga**, contains some of the best scenery in northern Chile. Conaf wardens are at Enquelga in the Park. Isluga has a traditional, Andean walled church and bell tower. It is, in theory, possible to drive north from Isluga through the Salar de Surire (see above) via Guallatiri to the Parque Nacional del Lauca, and from there to Bolivia, or via Putre and Poconchile to Arica or Peru.

The best way to return to the Pan-American Highway, if going south, is via the road to the village of Cariquima (35 km. south of Isluga), and take the road via the thermal springs at Chuzmisa (100 km. from Cariquima). It is possible to stay in a basic hotel at Chuzmisa. The water here is bottled and sold throughout northern Chile. Chuzmisa lies about 3 km. down a side road, but it is signposted. From Chuzmisa a good dirt (last part paved) road leads to Huara on the Pan-American Highway (80 km.) passing on the left, at Km. 67, the Giant of the Atacama, reported to be the largest geolyph in the world (best viewed from a distance). The round trip from Zapiga to Huara is about 540 km., and fuel is not available between Cuya (80 km. N of Zapiga) and Huara.

Humberstone, at the junction of the Pan-American Highway and the road to Iquique, is a large nitrate ghost town. 2 km. beyond the junction to Humberstone is the Oficina Santa Laura, the earliest nitrate plant in Chile, through which you can walk.

*Iquique*, the capital of I Región (Tarapacá) and one of the main northern ports, is 304 km. by road south of Arica. The name of the town is derived from the Aymará word *ique-ique*, meaning place of "rest and tranquillity". It was founded in the 16th century on a rocky peninsula sheltered by the headlands of Punta Gruesa and Cavancha. The city was partly destroyed by earthquake in 1877. It has some old wooden houses with columns and balconies (especially along Baquedano), many of which were built by the "Nitrate barons" between 1880 and 1903, an outstanding square, Plaza Prat, with a clock tower and bell, and wide avenues bordered by trees. One, Av. Balmaceda, runs along the coast. The Museo Regional, Baquedano 951, open Mon.-Fri. 0900-1300, 1600-2100 and Sat., 1000-1300, contains an extensive display covering 6,000 years (entry US$0.40). At the seaward end of Calle Esmeralda is the old Aduana, scene of a battle between congressional supporters and troops of President Balmaceda in 1891. Next to it is a Naval Museum concentrating on the 1879 battle—see below (entry US$0.10, open Tues.-Sat. 0930-1230, 1430-1800, Sun. and holidays 1000-1300). The Palacio Astoreca on Calle O'Higgins 350 esq. Lynch, built in

1904 by a Spanish nitrate millionare, formerly the Intendencia and now a cultural centre, has fine pinewood architecture and exhibitions of shells (open Tues.-Fri. 1000-1300, 1600-2000, Sat. and Sun. 1000-1300, US$0.40). Population: 140,300. There are checkpoints on the road N to Arica, on the road S at Quillagua, and on the road inland (to Mamiña).

The harbour is well protected and ships tie up to load at modern docks. Sealions and pelicans can be seen from the harbour. To get closer to the sealions, ask at the shipyard if they'll let you cross the yard; you may get a guide, a helmet and even a boat. It was at Iquique that the *Esmeralda* and another wooden ship, under Captain Arturo Prat, resisted the attack of the Peruvian ironclad ship *Huáscar* on May 21, 1879, during the War of the Pacific (see page 585). The main exports are fishmeal, fish oil, canned fish and salt. At weekends there are cruises around the harbour from the passenger pier, US$0.50.

Iquique has a Free Zone (Zofri), at the north of town: it is worth a visit (much better value than Punta Arenas), goods from Hong Kong and Taiwan, reasonably priced cameras, electronics and cheap Ektachrome films are sold (open Mon. 1630-2100, Tues.-Fri. 1000-1300, 1630-2100, Sat. 1000-1400).

**Local holiday** During the ten days before 16 July there is a religious festival, "La fiesta de Tirana", at a village 70 km. E of Iquique (near Pica, see page 525). Over 100 groups dance night and day, starting on 12 July, before making their pilgrimage to the church of the Virgen del Carmen. All the dances take place in the main plaza in front of the church; no alcohol is served. Accommodation is impossible to find, other than in organized camp sites (take tent) which have basic toilets and showers.

**Hotels** *Hostería Cavancha*, Los Rides 250, T 21158, L, south of city, on water's edge; *Primeras Piedras*, street of same name, T 21358, 3 km. from city, A, good food, friendly; *Playa Brava*, Playa Brava 3115, T 22705, A with breakfast, good, new wing built; *Tamarugal*, Tarapacá 369, T 24365, central, clean and modern, A/B, good restaurant. *Camino del Mar*, Orella 340 (T 20465), restored building, clean, simple, C; *Arturo Prat*, Av. Aníbal Pinto 695, T 21414, facing Plaza Prat, A; *Barros Arana*, Barros Arana 1330 (T 24420), clean, modern, good value, C; *Inti-Llanka*, Obispo Labbe 825 (T 26383), B/C, good; *Durana*, San Martín 294 (T 28085), good, B; *Phoenix*, Aníbal Pinto 451 (T 21315) room with bathroom, breakfast, old but nice, C; *Plaza*, Plaza Prat, D (but bargain), clean, friendly; *España*, Tarapacá 465, near Plaza Condell, E, shared bath, friendly, warm water, dirty. *Res. Li Ming*, A. Arana 705, near Thompson (T 21912), E, and *Res. Nan-King*, Thompson 752 (T 23311), D, clean, good value; *Residencial Catedral*, Obispo Labbe 253, T 23395, C, clean, friendly, but breakfast expensive; *Residencial Marclaud*, Juan Martínez 753, E, rec., quiet, clean, motor-cycle parking (good cheap restaurant at the corner); *Res. José Luis*, San Martín 601, E, spacious, clean; *Res. Esmeralda*, Esmeralda 394, F, basic but clean; *Residencial Sol del Norte*, Juan Martínez, E, clean, airy rooms, courtyard, shared showers and toilets, laundry facilities, rec.; *Condell*, Thompson 684 esq. Vivar, nice, clean, quiet, D.

**Restaurants** *Club de la Unión*, reasonable lunch. Also, the *Sociedad Protectora de los Empleados de Tarapacá* (Plaza Prat) is open to tourists and has reasonable prices. *Centro Español*, on main square, excellent meals well served in cool, Moorish decorated 100-year-old rooms; attractive, but expensive. *Jugoslavenski Dom Club Social*, Plaza Prat, 5 course menu for US$4 in old-fashioned setting; *José Luis*, Serrano 476, good food, pleasant atmosphere, good value *almuerzo*; *Bavaria*, Wilson y Pinto, good but not cheap; *Rapa Nui*, Amunátegui 715, for good, cheap, local food. *Grecia*, Thomson 865, good, inexpensive; *La Estancia*, Amunátegui 765, good fish, inexpensive; *El Marino*, Esmeralda 392, good, "you eat what the family eats". Several good, inexpensive seafood restaurants (e.g. *Bucanero*) can be found on the second floor of the central market, Barros Arana with Latorre; also cafés opp. the bus station, on the wharf, sell good, cheap fish lunches. *Bahía*, on seafront, cheap, good fish; *Portofino*, Thompson 650. *Club de Yates* at the harbour serves very expensive meals. *El Rey del Pescado*, Bulnes y Juan Martínez, very nice local place with good and cheap seafood dishes, "menú de la casa" a bargain. *Chifa Fu-Wa*, Barros Arana 740, rec, Chinese.

**Cafés** *Salón de Té Chantilly*, Tarapacá 520; *Café Diana*, Vivar 836; *Pinina*, Ramírez y Tarapacá, juices, ice-cream; *Samoa Grill*, Bolívar 396, good coffee and snacks.

**Car hire** Hertz, Juan Martínez 2040, T 26316.

**Cinema** Ciné Tarapacá, Serrano 202, shows foreign films.

**Post Office** Correo Central, Bolívar 466. **Telecommunications** CTC, Serrano y Ramírez; Entel (international calls), Gorostiaga 287; Telegrams at TelexChile, Lynch y San Martín. **NB** Correos, Telex/Telefax and Entel all have offices in the Plaza de Servicios in the Free Zone.

**Exchange** National banks. **Fincard** (Visa and Mastercharge), Serrano 424, open Mon.-Fri. 0900-1400, 1600-2100, Sat. 1000-1400. Difficult to change travellers' cheques in town. Parallel market with best rates for cheques and cash at *casas de cambio* in the Free Zone.

**Tourist Information** Aníbal Pinto 436. T 21499; open Mon.-Fri. (closed 1300-1500), and at Sala La Peyrouse, Baquedano 919, open Mon.-Fri. 0930-1300, 1600-1900, Sat. 0930-1300. (Display of Aymará craftwork on second floor.) **Automóvil Club de Chile**, Serrano 154, T 22422.

**Travel Agencies** *Iquitour*, Tarapacá 465B, Casilla 669, T 22009, tours to Pintados, La Tirana, Humberstone, Pica, etc., 0900-1900, lunch included, US$20, a lot of time spent eating and bathing. *Flonatur*, Sgto. Aldea 786B.

**Fishing** Broadbill swordfish, striped marlin, yellowfin tuna, oceanic bonito, March till end of August. In the harbour there are hundreds of sea lions (for a closer look you can hire a boat for a few dollars).

**Bathing** Balneario Cavancha (good) and Huaiquique, reasonable, November-March. Restaurants at Cavancha. Piscina Godoy, fresh water swimming pool on Av. Costanera at Aníbal Pinto and Riquelme, open p.m., US$1.

**Buses** Terminal at N end of Patricio Lynch (not all buses leave from here); bus company offices are near the market on Sargento Aldea and B. Arana. To **Arica**, buses and colectivos, frequent, US$6, comfortable in spite of various checkpoints. To Antofagasta, frequent, US$12, a dusty, hot 8-hr. drive through the desert, relieved by the occasional oasis. To **Calama** and **Chuquicamata**, daily at 2100, 2130 and 2200, 8 hrs. to Calama. To Calama, US$9, Kennybus not rec. To **Tocopilla** along the coastal road, minibuses, several companies, 4 hrs., US$7; also buses to **Tocopilla** along Pan-American Highway. To La Serena, 10-11 hrs., US$22. To **Santiago**, 28 hrs., Carmelita are the cheapest, others (Ramos Cholele, Flota Barrios) charge US$30-35 (US$61 for Barrios *salón cama*).

**Airport** Diego Aracena international airport, 35 km. S at Chucumata. Taxi from outside *Hotel Prat*, Plaza Prat, US$3, T 26184. Airport bus to city centre, US$2. LanChile, Av. Aníbal Pinto 641, T 21118; Ladeco, Aníbal Pinto 444, T 24794 (Santiago-Iquique daily; to Calama, 1715, US$32, en route to Antofagasta and Santiago). To Antofagasta, Arica and Santiago daily by LanChile.

**Excursions** Hire a car and drive south along the Pacific coast to see sealions, *guano*, fishing settlements and old salt works, including the ghost town of Guanillos, complete with castle. Good roads run to the nitrate fields, which are 900 metres above sea level. From Pozo Almonte on the Pan-American Highway, an unpaved road runs NE to the hot mineral springs in the mountains at Termas de **Mamiña** (2,700 metres), where there is an interesting church (1632), a radiactive mud spring (Baño El Chino; open 0930-1300) and good accommodation for tourists (*Hotel Termas de Salitre*, C p.p., full board, thermal pool in each room, electricity till midnight, swimming pool open 0930-1300; *Termal La Coruña*, B, good, nice views; *Tamarugal*, C, thermal pool in each room; *Residencial Ipla*, D, cheapest, 2 others; *cabañas* to let and campsite). Electricity till 2230. The rainy season in Mamiña is mainly in January and is called *Invierno Boliviano* (Bolivian winter). Transport from Iquique: minibuses from B. Arana y Latorre, Mon.-Sat. 1600; from Mamiña, 0800; Sun. from Iquique 0930, from Mamiña 1800, US$3.

The Pan-American Highway continues South: 13 km. after the turn-off to Iquique is a detour to La Tirana (10 km.—see above) and fertile oasis of **Pica** (2,750 metres) a centre of Spanish settlement during the colonial period. The town is famous for its pleasant climate, its citrus groves and its two natural springs, the best of which is Cocha Resbaladero (open 0700-2000 all year, changing rooms, snack bar, beautiful rock-pool, entry US$0.70).

**Services** *Hotel San Andrés*, Balmaceda 197, E with large breakfast; *O'Higgins*, T 741322, E; *Residencial El Tambo*, P. Ibáñez 60, E, old fashioned, good restaurant; *Motel Resbaladero*, D full pension, good pool; also *cabañas* for rent. *Restaurant Palomar*, Balmaceda 74, excellent *almuerzo*.

**Transport** from Iquique: Santa Rosa, Latorre 973, daily bus from Iquique 1630, 2 hrs; from Pica 0700. Several companies (Flotatur, S. Aldea 790; Julia, B. Arana 965) operate minibuses but services vary. If travelling by car, a quicker route to Pica is by turning E off the Pan-American

Highway at Pintados, 43 km. S of Pozo Almonte.

La Tirana and Pintados fall within two of the three areas which make up the **Reserva Nacional Pampa del Tamarugal**, the third part is some 60 km north of Pozo Almonte, straddling the Pan-American Highway.

*Tocopilla* is 244 km. S of Iquique along the coastal road, offering fantastic views of the rugged coastline and tiny fishing communities (365 km. via the much better Pan-American Highway). The town is dominated by the port facilities used in the export of nitrate and iodine from two famous nitrate fields—María Elena (68 km.), and Pedro de Valdivia (85 km.). In the centre is the copper concentrate plant of Cía. Minera de Tocopilla. Population: 22,600. There is a sports stadium and two good beaches: Punta Blanca (10 km. south) and Caleta Covadonga. There is also fine deep sea fishing if you can find a boat and a guide.

**Hotels** *Chungará*, 21 de Mayo 1829, C, comfortable, clean, rec., no restaurant; *Vicuña*, 21 de Mayo 2096, C, modern, good restaurant; *Hostal Bolívar*, Bolívar 1332, T 811903, D, clean, friendly. *Hostal Central*, Aníbal Pinto 1241, E, friendly, clean; *Res. La Giralda*, 21 de Mayo 1134, F.

**Restaurants** *Club de la Unión*, Prat 1354, good *almuerzo*, cheap; *Kong Jong*, 21 de Mayo 1833, reasonable value, Chinese; *El Pirata*, 21 de Mayo 1999, *parrilladas*. Good seafood at the Muelle Pesquero opposite the old wooden clock tower.

**Automóvil Club de Chile** 21 de Mayo 1377, T 811059.

**Road Transport** To **Antofagasta** 8 a day, several companies, US$8; to **Iquique**, by bus and minibus along coastal road, 4 hrs, US$7, frequent. No direct services to **Santiago**, go via Antofagasta or take Tramaca or Flota Barrios to Vallenar or La Serena and change. Bus company offices are on 21 de Mayo. There are two paved roads out: a 185-km. coast road S to Antofagasta via Mejillones (see below) and the other E up the narrow valley 72 km. to the Pan-American Highway (with a short spur to María Elena and Pedro de Valdivia nitrate mines) and on to Chuquicamata. From Tocopilla to Chuquicamata is poor, particularly the eastern half which is eroded by the heavy lorries which use it (requires careful driving). A new coastal road runs N to Iquique.

The coast road Tocopilla-Antofagasta is paved all the way, but deteriorates after 78 km., there is no fuel. The route runs at the foot of 500-metre cliffs, behind which are mountains which are extensively mined for copper, often by *piquineros* (small groups of self-employed miners). There are larger mines, with the biggest concentration inland of Michilla (80 km. S). The treatment plants use the "tin can" process, hence the heaps of rusting cars and metal junk. Despite the unprepossessing appearance, this is a good place to stop for a meal.

A zig-zag road (very steep) winds up the cliffs to the mine at Mantos de la Luna about 35 km. S of Tocopilla. At the top there are rather dead-looking groves of giant cactus living off the sea mist which collects on the cliffs. Wildlife includes foxes (*zorros*).

The coast is rocky though there are good beaches at Poza Verde (70 km. S of Tocopilla) and Hornitos (104 km., town is dead except at week-ends). There is also the Tocopilla Yacht Club (45 km.) and Punta Blanca (25 km.), which have bars and restaurants.

The main interest is the ruins of Cobija, the coastal end of the silver trail from Potosí. This town was destroyed by an earthquake in 1877, and captured by the Chileans in the War of the Pacific two years later. Mud brick walls, the rubbish tip (right above the sea) and the wreckage of the port are all that is left of the town. There is an amazing ransacked cemetery about 1 km. from the ruins on the approach road. 15 km. further down the coast are the atmospheric ruins of Gatico.

*Mejillones*, 60 km. N of Antofagasta (140 km. S of Tocopilla), has a good natural harbour protected from westerly gales by high hills. Until 1948 it was a major terminal for the export of tin and other metals from Bolivia: remnants of that past include a number of fine buildings including the Capitanía del Puerto and the Edificio Municipal. Today the town, population 4,000, lives solely by fishing, coming alive after 1700 when the fishermen prepare to set sail. The sea is very cold because of the Humboldt current.

**Accommodation and Food** *Hostería Luz de Luna*, A. Goñigg 99, T 582, C, accommodation in summer only, restaurant; *Residencial Elisabeth*, Alte. Latorre 440, T 568, E, friendly, restaurant. Municipal campsite behind the fishing port. *Juanito Restaurant*, Las

THE DESERT NORTH (1)

Heras 241, excellent *almuerzo*; *Sion-Ji*, Andalican 641, Chinese, good value..

**Antofagasta** is 1,373 km. N of Santiago and 700 km. S of Arica. It is the capital of II Region (Antofagasta), and its population of 200,000 makes it the largest city in northern Chile. It exports the nitrates of the area and the copper of Chuquicamata. A huge anchor stands high in the mountains, and was used as a navigational aid by ships. The main historical interest lies in some ruins at the edge of town, and a Bolivian silver refinery dating from 1868 (Huanchaca, now a military zone—you may visit, but not take photos), but it is lively and attractive, with two universities of high standing, an elegant municipal theatre, quite good parks and public gardens, an interesting waterfront, a clock tower on the main plaza donated by the British community, and very expensive shops. The Edificio Ex Aduana, opposite the Museo Regional, originally the Bolivian customs office in Mejillones, was dismantled and moved here after the war of the Pacific. The modern sports stadium is close to the most popular beach, the Balneario Municipal, at the beginning of Av. Ejército (take bus No. 10). The climate is delightful (apart from the lack of rain); the temperature varies from 16°C in June/July to 24°C January/February, never falling below 10°C at night. The tap water is not potable.

**Local Holiday** 29 June, San Pedro, patron saint of the fishermen: the saint's image is taken out by launch to the breakwater to bless the first catch of the day. **Festivals** On the last weekend of October, the foreign communities put on a joint festival on the seafront, with national foods, dancing and music.

**Hotels** *Plaza*, Baquedano 461, T 222058, B, modern, noisy, clean, comfortable; *Antofagasta*, Balmaceda 2575, T 224710, run-down, garage, swimming pool, lovely view of port and city, A with breakfast (discount for Automóvil Club members, but still not very good value), beach; *Pieper*, Sucre 509, T 223433, C, clean, modern, warmly rec.; *Diego de Almagro*, Condell 2624, T 222840, B, good for the money but a bit tatty; *San Marcos*, Latorre 2946, C, modern, comfortable; *San Antonio*, Condell 2235, T 225086, C, clean, good but noisy from bus station; *Residencial La Riojanita*, Baquedano 464, E, good, use of kitchen permitted, hot water on demand, noisy; *Residencial Paola*, Prat 766, T 222208, E, noisy, friendly; *Res. Cobre*, Prat 749, T 225162, E, shared bath (D with bath), hot water, clean (acts as youth hostel, no cooking facilities); *Res. O'Higgins*, Sucre 773, E, big, old, dirty, no hot water. *Tatio*, Av. Grecia 1000, T 225707, B, modern building, out of old town on the beach, has buses converted into caravans, D, friendly, beautiful views, acts as youth hostel, no cooking facilities.

**Camping** South of the city on route to Cososo, Las Garumas, Km. 16, US$10 for tent, US$15 for cabins; hot water, showers and beach (reservations Av. Angamos 601, casilla 606). Rucamóvil, Km. 17, T 226734 and 7 *cabañas*, T 221988. All open year-round. Also La Rinconada, north of city, off road to Mejillones, between La Portada and Juan López.

**Restaurants** *Marina Club*, Av. Ejército 0809, good fish and seafood dishes and a view, expensive but worth it; *Tío Jacinto*, Uribe 922, friendly, good seafood; *El Arriero*, Condell 2632, meat dishes, pricey; *Bavaria*, J. S. Ossa 2428, excellent meat and German specialities, not cheap; *D'Alfredo*, Condell 2539, good Italian food. *Club de la Unión*, Prat 474 (quite good). Difficult to find any coffee, etc., before 0900. *Café Express* and *Café Caribe*, both at Prat 482, good coffee; ice cream at *Gattino*, Matta 2429 and *Fiori di Gelatto*, Latorre y Baquedano, highly rec.; *Chico Jaime* above the market, surrealistic decor, seafood, *almuerzo* US$2, mixed reports. Many eating places in the market. Good cheap lunches at *El Rincón de Don Quijote*, Maipú 642, and *Sociedad Protectora de Empleados*, San Martín 2544 (no sign), very popular with locals.

**Clubs** Club de Tenis Antofagasta, Av. Angamos 906, connected with Av. Brasil.

**Market** Municipal market, corner of Matta and Uribe.

**Car Rental** Rent-a-Car, Prat 810, T 225200; **Avis**, San Martín y Bolívar, T 221668 (small car US$250/week, inc. tax, insurance, free km.; Suzuki jeep suitable for Altiplano roads US$350/week); **Budget**, A. Prat y Balmaceda (pick-up, US$50/day); **Hertz**, Balmaceda 2646 (T 223549), offer city cars and jeeps (group D, Toyota Landcruiser) and do a special flat rate, with unlimited mileage, if you hire the car for over a week.

**Bookshop** *Multilibro*, Baquedano 522.

**Discotheques** *Popo's*, Av. Ejército (far end from town).

**Cinemas** Gran Vía, Av. Angamos; Nacional, Sucre 735; Colón, San Martín 2755; Teatro de la Barra, Condell 2495 (cine and live theatre).

**Museums** Museo Regional, in former Gobernación Marítima building, Balmaceda 2798, closed Mon.; **Museo Antropologicó**, Pasaje López, Prat 482 y Latorre, closed for repairs; **Museo Geológico** of the Universidad Católica del Norte, Av. Angamos 0610, inside the university campus, open Mon.-Fri.

**Exchange** Banks in main square will not buy or sell Argentine or Bolivian money, and only change dollars at poor rates and 5% commission. **Fincard** (Visa and Mastercard), Prat 461, oficina 401, 24 hrs a day, T 251775. Best rates at **Inter-Santiago**, Latorre 2528, Local 12. At weekends try **Licorería San Marcos**, Latorre 2428. **Licores Mitjans**, Baquedano y Latorre. **N.B.** There is no official opportunity to change currency S of Antofagasta until you reach La Serena.

**Swimming** Olympic pool at Condell y 21 de Mayo, US$1.20, open till 1800, best to go in a.m.

**Laundry** *La Ideal*, Baquedano 660, laundry and dry cleaning; *París*, Condell 2455, laundry and dry cleaning.

**Post Office** Washington 2613; **Telephones**, Entel Chile, Prat 649 and at Condell 2141.

**Travel Agent** *Tatio Travel*, Latorre 2579, T 225698/223192, Telex 225242 TATIO CL, English spoken, tours arranged for groups or individuals, highly rec. *Turismo Cristóbal* in *Hotel Antofagasta*, helpful. Alex Joseph Valenzuela Thompson, Edif. Vaticano, Prat 548, oficina 701, T 243322/242713, FAX 222718/222818, Aptdo Postal 55, offers to guide German speakers around the area.

**Tourist Office** at Baquedano 360 (one block from sea front), T 223004; Kiosk on Balmaceda in front of *Hotel Balmaceda* (both open Mon.-Fri. only); kiosk at airprot (open summer only). **Automóvil Club de Chile**, Condell 2330, T 225332.

**Customs Agent** Luis Piquimil Bravo, Prat 272, oficina 202, excellent, fast service, efficient.

**Roads** To Tocopilla, 187 km.; to Mejillones, 62 km.; to Pedro de Valdivia, 168 km.; to María Elena, 193 km.; to Taltal, 307 km.; to Calama, 196 km.; to Chuquicamata, 206 km. **N.B.** the Pan-American Highway between the N and S exits to Antofagasta; beware of flying stones from lorries. This route does avoid Antofagasta and the long climb out. Fuel at La Negra, then no more for 200 km. (Aguas Verdes) is not paved (22 km.) (Caracoles and La Negra respectively).

**Buses** The main bus terminal is at S end of town, Av. Argentina y Díaz Gana, but each company has its own office in town (some quite a distance from the centre). Some, like Tramaca, go only from their own terminal. Buses for **Mejillones** and **Tocopilla** operated by Fepstur, Kenny bus, Chile Bus and Carmelita depart from the Terminal Centro at Riquelme 513. Bus company offices as follows: Tramaca, Uribe 936; Flota Barrios, Condell 2764; Flecha Dorada, Latorre 2951; Géminis, Latorre 3055; Atahualpa, Uribe 936; Fénix Pullman Norte, San Martín 2717; Incatur, Maipú 554; Turis Norte, Sucre 625; Libac, Condell 2765. To **Santiago**, 20 hrs. (luxury double decker/sleeper coach, Flota Barrios, US$50 including drinks and meals, pullman US$24); 30% reduction on Inca, Tramaca, and Géminis buses for students, but ask after you have secured a seat; many companies: fares range from US$21, Carmelita, US$25, Ramos Cholele, Fénix, US$36, Geminis, US$43, Fichtur, book 2 days in advance. If all seats to the capital are booked, catch a bus to **La Serena** (8 hrs., US$15, or US$25 with lunch and supper, go by day to see the scenery) or Ovalle and travel to Santiago from there. To **Valparaíso**, US$17.50. To **Arica**, US$10 (Flecha Dorada), 13½ hrs., Tramaca, US$11.40. (It is forbidden to take fruit south from Antofagasta because of fruit-fly control.) To **Chuquicamata**, Flecha Dorada leaves at 0700, returns at 1900, as well as many others. To **Calama**, several companies, US$4 (Tramaca, 3 hrs.). To **San Pedro de Atacama**, no direct services—go via Calama. Direct to **Copiapó** on Thurs. and Sat. at 2230, US$10.50. Frequent buses to **Iquique**; US$12, 8 hrs., checkpoints near Iquique for foreigners.

**Bus to Argentina** Atahualpa, Sat., and Géminis, Wed., US$50; via Calama, immigration check at San Pedro de Atacama, then on to high Cordillera (very cold) and to San Antonio de los Cobres; change bus at Salta. There is nowhere to change Chilean pesos en route. (No service July-September.)

If hitching to Arica or Iquique try at the beer factory a few blocks N of the fish market on Av.

Pinto, or the lorry park a few blocks further N. If hitching S go to the police checkpoint/restaurant/gas station La Negra, about 15 km. S of the city.

**N.B.** There are no railway passenger services from Antofagasta. The famous journey to Bolivia starts from Calama (see below), and the line into Argentina carries no passengers.

**Air**  To Santiago, LanChile (Balmaceda 2584, T 226089) and Ladeco (Prat 242, T 222860) fly daily. Ladeco flies once a week to La Paz, Bolivia. Bus from *Hotel Antofagasta* to airport US$1, check at LanChile office for schedule. Taxi to airport US$7, but cheaper if ordered from hotel. Bus No. 20 to airport, every 2 hrs., from San Martín y Prat, US$0.50.

**Excursions**  There are two favourite spots for picnics: near the town of La Chimba, and the fantastic cliff formations, the symbol of the Second Region, at La Portada, 16 km. north, reached by taking bus No. 20 from Plaza de Armas by the Cathedral (every 2 hrs. from 0730, US$0.50), or any bus fro Mejillones from the Terminal Centro, asking the driver to drop you at the junction for La Portada. Last bus back leaves at 2030. Taxis charge US$10. Hitching is easy. From the junction it is 25m. to the beach (beware of dogs) where there is an excellent seafood restaurant and café. A number of bathing beaches are also within easy reach. Juan López 31 km. N of Antofagasta is a windsurfers' paradise. Buses at weekends in summer only. For those with their own transport, follow the road out of Juan López to the beautiful cove at Conchilla. Keep on the track to the end at Bolsico. The sea is alive with birds, including Humboldt penguins, especially opposite Isla Santa María.

215 km. NE of Antofagasta is the oasis town of **Calama**, population 100,365, at an altitude of 2,265 metres. The Cía. Sud Americana de Explosivos manufactures high explosives. The town is modern, expensive and has a developed commercial centre. 2 km. from the centre on Av. B.O'Higgins is the Parque El Loa (open 1000-1800 daily), which contains a reconstruction of a typical colonial village built around a reduced-scale reproduction of Chiu Chiu church. Nearby in the park is the Museo Arqueológico y Etnológico, with an exhibition of pre-hispanic cultural history (open Tues.-Fri. 1000-1330, 1430-1800, Sat.-Sun. 1100-1830). Calama is a useful point to stay for a day or two to get used to the altitude before going higher.

Travellers by car coming from the N can drive via Chuquicamata, although the road is quite poor on either side of that town, or, from the S, by a paved road (94 km.—police checkpoint at Baquedano, also meals available) leaving the Pan-American Highway 98 km. N of Antofagasta at Carmen Alto (petrol and food). This road passes interesting industrial archaeological sites at the abandoned nitrate mines (*oficinas*); look for the rubbish dumps of old bottles, shoes and other articles.

**Sierra Gorda** is the centre of a concentration of small copper and silver mines, 63 km. before Calama. If you are interested in minerals, ask in the café with the tree growing out of its centre to see the owner's collection of exotic copper minerals and fossils. Just after Sierra Gorda, there is a turning to the east along a good dirt road (which gradually deteriorates) leading to a network of tracks connecting old silver workings most of which closed at the end of last century. These are good places for collecting bottles etc., and are much less turned over than the nitrate oficinas. Water is available at the top of the pass on the main road NE of Sierra Gorda. There is a police checkpoint at Dupont, just before Calama.

**Hotels in Calama**  *Hostería Calama*, Latorre 1521, T 211511, A, comfortable, good food and service; *Alfa*, Sotomayor 2016, T 211565, A, reasonable; *Topotel*, Camino Aeropuerto 1392, T 212208, 274-67701 in Santiago, A+, first class, swimming pool, popular, bar and restaurant; *Lican Antai*, Ramírez 1937, T 212970, A+ with breakfast, good service and good restaurant, TV, phone, safe, travel agency, car hire, rec.; *Atenas*, Ramírez 1961, T 212666, C, clean; *Quitor*, Ramírez 2116, T 211716, A, good. *Casablanca* on Plaza, Sotomayor 2160, T 211722, B; *Genesis*, Granaderos 2143, D, near Tramaca and Géminis bus terminals, clean, rec.; *El Sol*, Sotomayor 2064, T 211722, D with bath, E without, clean, rec.; *El Loa*, Abaroa 1617, T 211963, D, English spoken; *Residencial Internacional*, Gral. Velázquez 1976, T 211553; hot water, D, friendly but noisy; *Residencial Casa de Huéspedes*, Sotomayor 2079, clean, shared hot shower, D; *Res. Splendid*, Ramírez 1960, T 212141, D with bath, cheaper without, clean, hot water, breakfast US$1; *Res. John Keny*, Ecuador 1991, T 211430, C, modern, clean, friendly, car park; *Prat*, Vivar 1970, E, cheap, cold water; *Res. Toño*, Vivar 1973, next to Kenny bus, F, shower, "a bit of a dive"; *Los Andes*, Vivar, 1920, G, basic, cold shower, friendly, stores luggage; *Capri*, Vivar, F, friendly but dirty, hot water, not rec.; *Residencial El Tatio*, P. L. Galo, 1987, T 212284, E, basic, friendly, noisy, clean, reasonable; *Luxor*, Vargas 1881, G p.p., clean, friendly.

**Restaurants** *Bavaria*, Sotomayor 2095, modern, clean, good coffee and delicatessen; *El Eden*, Abaroa y Antofagasta, cheap, good food; *Café Bavaria*, Parcela 76, good breakfasts; good eating at market. *Nueva Victoria*, Abaroa, serves early breakfast, good, cheap, other meals. *Club Yugoslavo*, Abaroa 1869 (Plaza de Armas), serves good lunches, US$2.50. *Mariscal JP*, Felix Hoyos 2127, 4 houses from Tramaca bus, good seafood. Good ice cream at *Fior di Gelalo*, Plaza de Armas.

**Car Hire** **Comercial Maipo S.A.**, Barrio Industrial, sitio 14, T 212204, take taxi—½ hr. out of town; Hertz, Latorre 1510 (T 211380); **Comercial Automotriz Miranda**, Granaderos 2625, T 211175, helpful. **American's**, Latorre 1512, T 211220, **Maxso**, Abaroa 1100, T 212194, jeep US$80/day. **Budget**, cheapest. A hired car, shared between several people, is an economic alternative for visiting the Atacama region, and is much cheaper than hiring one in San Pedro de Atacama.

**Cinemas** Central on Latorre and another on Ramírez, near plaza.

**Exchange** Rates are generally poor. Banks do not accept cheques, but hotels do. **Fincard** (Access and Visa), Latorre 1751, oficina 207, Mon.-Fri. 0900-1400, 1600-2000, Sat. 1100-1300. Try also **La Media Luna clothes store**, Ramírez 1992 (poor rates); **Copper Tour**, Sotomayor 2016, for travellers' cheques and cash, *Hostería Calama* (fair rates); Money changers selling Bolivian money for Chilean can be found outside the railway station (last chance before Oruro or La Paz). If arriving from La Paz by train on Sat. p.m. without pesos, you may find nowhere to obtain them, but try Tramaca or Morales Moralitos bus offices or *farmacias* (poor rates); better to get some before leaving Bolivia.

**Consul** The Bolivian Consulate (Vicuña Mackenna 2020) is open 0900-1230 and 1530-1830, Mon.-Fri., friendly, helpful.

**Laundry** Ramírez 2216; Ramírez 1867, English spoken (Mon.-Sat. 0900-2100); Sotomayor 1984, both expensive.

**Travel Agents** *Copper Tour* (address above); *Talikuna*, Gral. Velázquez 1948, T 212595; tours to Atacama region when enough people want to go, very long day's travel, better to go from San Pedro.

**Tourist Office** José La Torre and Mackenna, T 211314. Map of town, arranges car hire and tours to El Tatio geysers, Salar de Atacama, US$30 p.p., minimum 6 people. Open Mon.-Fri. 0900-1300, 1430-1900 Sat.-Sun. 0900-1300. **Automóvil Club de Chile**, Av. Ecuador 1901, T 212770.

**Buses** Daily bus services to **Santiago** (23 hrs., fares from US$27, Tramaca 4 a day, US$38.70, Géminis, to US$53.35 Flota Barrios *salón cama*), **Arica**—often involves a change in Antofagasta (Géminis, 2130 and Tramaca, 4 until 1730 daily, may be more in summer, US$11.50), **Iquique** (US$9) and **Ovalle**. Also to **San Pedro** daily, with Tramaca on Félix Hoyos y Granaderos (see below for fares and schedules), Morales bus continues to **Toconao** Tues., Thurs., Sat.; to **Chuquicamata** (see below). **Antofagasta**, 3 hrs., several companies, e.g. Tramaca, hourly on the half-hour till 2130, US$4 and Libac, US$2.50 (cheapest). Bus to **Salta**, Argentina, Wed., 24 hrs., US$48 with Géminis (Av. Granaderos), and Atahualpa, also once a week, both heavily booked in advance.

**Air** LanChile (Latorre 1499, T 211394) and Ladeco (Mackenna 2020, T 211355) flights to Antofagasta and Santiago leave daily. Taxi to town US$3 (courtesy vans from Hotels *Calama*, *Alfa* and *Lican Antai*).

**Rail** Antofagasta (Chile) and Bolivia Railway to Oruro (no longer to La Paz, apparently—1990) starts at Calama now. Bus leaves Antofagasta (Uribe 936) to connect with train leaving Calama on Thurs. at 2300 (check in advance), via Ollagüe (Fri. 0800) and Uyuni, arriving in Oruro Fri. 2300 (all times are "pure fantasy": the journey can take 36 hours). Note that before leaving you must visit (a) the Bolivian consulate for visa if needed, and (b) the railway station. It is advisable, but not necessary, to visit the railway office at Bolívar 255, Antofagasta, to make sure if there is a seat, but they can be purchased (with luck) at Calama. You must have your passport with you when buying ticket. Fare US$20. Although seats are assigned, the designated carriages may not arrive; there is a mad scramble to occupy several seats (to sleep on) and for luggage space. The journey is very cold, both during the day and at night (-15°C); there are reports of water freezing on the train. Sleeping bag and/or blanket essential. Restaurant car provides cheap refreshments, but better to take your own; food is also available at Ollagüe and Río Mulato (only for the conditioned). The journey is very crowded, very slow and uncomfortable, but the scenery is spectacularly beautiful. The highest point of the line is reached at Ascotán (3,960 metres) and the line then descends to 3,735 metres at Cebollar, where it skirts a great borax basin 39 km. long. From Ollagüe, a 77 km. branch line runs north to the copper mines of Collahuasi. Apparently there is no longer a change of trains at Ollagüe, near the frontier, but check in advance: if a change is necessary, your ticket is supposedly valid for both trains but ensure that it is stamped with a seat reservation for the second and be quick at the changeover, where there are scenes of considerable palaver with smugglers throwing their gear on and throwing others' off. For the 174 km. from Ollagüe to Uyuni the line maintains an almost uniform height of 3,660 metres.

Uyuni, the junction with the branch of 90 km. to Atocha, gives rail access, via Villazón on the Argentine border, to Buenos Aires, a route which is not interrupted by snowstorms. Río Mulato is the railway junction for Potosí, but it may be better to go to Oruro for transport to Potosí and Sucre, Cochabamba and La Paz as connections may be poor (details in Bolivian chapter). After crossing the Bolivian border you may need bolivianos to buy food on the train, so if you have no bolivianos make sure you have some small dollar notes for changing into bolivianos at the first stop in Bolivia. Money can be changed at Ollagüe (Chilean Customs) and Oruro. **Watch baggage** at Oruro; the thieves are notorious, even grabbing bags through open windows.

On certain days a freight train goes to Ollagüe with one or two passenger cars attached; no fixed schedule, ask at station, buy ticket a few hours before departure, US$2, not crowded. No passengers are allowed to cross the border on the train, so you have to walk 15 km. to the Bolivian station if there's no connecting train to persuade an engine driver to take you if an engine is going. Get on a freight train in Bolivia for Uyuni, US$10, again, no schedule. Take warm clothes, food, blankets and plenty of time. This is the only way to see the Salar de Uyuni by train in daylight.

**N.B.** Remember, if arriving from La Paz between October and March, then Chile is 1 hr. later than Bolivia.

**Excursion** As the road enters Calama (from Antofagasta), there is a turning to the left to Ojos de Opache (signposted). It passes through the market garden supplying Calama and ends at a petrifying spring, where objects put in the water become encrusted with dissolved minerals.

At **Chuquicamata**, a clean, modern town (population 20,000), 16 km. from Calama at 2,800 metres, is the world's largest open-cast copper mine (state-owned). It is an astoundingly large hole. All the processes can be seen; there are guided tours (in Spanish only), 3 hrs, US$1.50, with a film show, usually Mon.-Fri. at 1000 (but times and days of visits alter frequently so check details at tourist office in Calama). Tours leave from Puerta Una; register at the Public Relations Office nearby ½ hour beforehand (be in good time because space is limited), passport essential. No filming permitted; photographing the smelter plant not permitted. You must wear a long-sleeved garment (shorts and skirts not allowed) if you wish to see the industrial plants; children under 12 are not normally allowed to enter. Buy postcards before the tour as the office closes before the tour ends.

The tour office cafeteria nearby serves a good fixed menu lunch, US$2 for 4 courses. Guest house at east end of Plaza, nice, but book at Santiago or Antofagasta; overnight accommodation may be difficult. There is a country club with a golf course at Río Loa.

**Bus** Colectivo from Sotomayor y Abaroa in Calama to **Chuquicamata** tourist office for the tour, US$0.75, ½ hr., frequent. To **Arica** at 2200 (weekends at 2300), US$10, 9 hrs. To **Antofagasta**, ten a day, US$6. To **Iquique** at 2300. To Santiago at 1400, US$28, 24 hrs.

Within 40 km. of Calama there are several small towns and villages nestling in remote oases in the Andean massif. Just E is the village of **Chiu Chiu**, with a very interesting church, dating from 1611, and nearby a unique, perfectly circular, very deep lake. An ancient fortress and rock carvings are to be found in the Río Loa valley. This excursion is only possible by private or hired car. Due E of Chuquicamata, 37 km. on the way to Ayquina (**see page 534**), are the pre-Incaic ruins of **Lasana**, a national monument, with explanatory tablets (soft drinks and beer on sale). They are arguably the most impressive in Chile.

From Calama to Ollagüe you can go via Chiu-Chiu and Lasana, direct via Lasana, or direct via Conchi (take the turning signposted Lasana from the Calama-Chuquicamata road, then turn left/north). At **Conchi**, there is a spectacular view from the bridge over the Río Loa, but it is a military zone, so no photographs allowed. Access to the river is by side tracks, best at Santa Bárbara; interesting wildlife and flower meadows, trout fishing in season (permit from Gobernación in Calama).

Estación San Pedro (16 km. from Conchi) has quite an interesting old village and small gorge, away from the railway station. Possible to camp at the station (ask the station master). There is a *carabinero* checkpoint at Ascotán, the highest point of the road at 3,900 m. After Ascotán the road becomes worse, especially where it crosses the Salares de Ascotán and Ollagüe (ask at Ascotán or Ollagüe about the conditions, especially in December/January or August). There are many llama flocks along this road and flamingoes on the salars. **N.B.** The desert to the eastern side of the road is extensively covered by minefields.

5 km. before Ollagüe is the sulphur mining camp of Buenaventura. It is possible to camp here. If you want to go to the summit of Ollagüe volcano, ask for a lift on the mine truck to the mine at 5,800 m. (only 150 m. short of the summit). Amazing views of volcanoes and salt flats.

419 km. from Antofagasta, at 3,690 metres, on the dry floor of the Salar de Ollagüe near the Bolivian border, is **Ollagüe**, surrounded by a dozen volcanic peaks of over 5,000 metres. Population: 500. **N.B.** There is no petrol between Calama and Uyuni in Bolivia. If really short try buying from the *carabineros* at Ollagüe or Ascotán, the military at Conchi or the mining camp at Buenaventura. The only real answer is to take enough. A 77-km. spur railroad of metre gauge runs to the copper mines of Collahuasi, and from there a 13-km. aerial tram to the highest mine in the world: the Aucanquilcha, at 6,100 metres. Its sulphur is taken to Amincha, a town at the foot of the volcano, to be refined. The highest passenger station in this spur is Yuma, at 4,400 metres. Ollagüe can be reached by taking the Calama-Oruro train (see above) but, if you stop off, you will have to hitch back as the daily freight trains are not allowed to carry passengers. There is also a bus (Transportes Abaroa, Vivar 1962) on Tues. nights from Calama, heavily booked in advance. Bad unmade road from Ollagüe into Bolivia (**see Section 2, Bolivia, South from La Paz**).

At this altitude nights are cold, the days warm and sunny. Minimum temperature at Ollagüe is -20°C, and at the mine, -37°C. There are only 50 mm. of rain a year, and water is very scarce.

An interesting excursion can be made N from Ollagüe to the village of Coska with its traditional agriculture and herds of llamas and alpacas.

The main stock animals are llamas and alpacas, whose principal forage is the *ichu* bunch-grass covering the lower slopes. There is no timber. *Taqui*—dried llama dung— and *tola* scrub are used for cooking fires, but the main fuel is *yaretal*, a resinous moss growing in pillow-like masses in rocky outcrops from 3,500 to 5,000 metres high. Its calorific value is half that of bituminous coal. It apparently is an Ice Age relic, growing very slowly but now worked out in this area. Across the border in Bolivia there is plenty, which is used as fuel for the Laguna Verde sulphur mine. It is claimed, like mineral land, and broken up with dynamite into chunks for transport.

103 km. SE of Calama by a good road is **San Pedro de Atacama**. There is no fuel, food or water on the road. At the top of the pass half way to San Pedro is an unpaved turning to the left which leads through interesting desert scenery to the small, mud-brick village of Río Grande. Look out for vicuñas and guanacos on the pass. The paved road skirts the Cordillera de la Sal about 15 km. from San Pedro. Spectacular views of sunset over to the Western Cordilleras. The old unmade road, which crosses the new road several times traverses this range through the Valle de La Luna (see **Excursions** below), but is effectively blocked by sand dunes, allowing no passage to San Pedro. This road is partly paved with salt blocks. Along the road are various archaeological remains.

San Pedro de Atacama, at 2,436 metres, is a small town (pop. 1,600) more Spanish-Indian looking than is usual in Chile, well worth a visit. Both Diego de Almagro and Pedro de Valdivia stopped in this oasis (Valdivia's house on the main square may be visited by knocking at the brown door next to it and asking for the key). The impressive archaeological museum, now under the care of the Universidad Católica del Norte (Mon.-Fri., 0800-1200, 1500-1900-summer; Sat., and Sun., 1000-1200, 1400-1800, entry US$0.30), is a fascinating repository of artefacts, with an insight into hundreds of years of Atacameño culture, the collection of Father La Paige, a Belgian missionary who came to San Pedro in 1955. Labels on displays are good and there is a comprehensive booklet in Spanish. The anthropologist Héctor Garcés is a mine of information at the museum. Graham Greene tells us that "the striking feature of the museum is . . . the mummies of Indian women with their hair and dresses intact dating from before the Conquest, and a collection of paleolithic tools which puts the British Museum in the shade". (These mummies are not on display but are open to visitors on request.)

**Hotels** *Hostería San Pedro*, on Solcor, recently refurbished, B, rec., Australian joint proprietors Luis Hernández and Mrs. Bobbee Andrews have prepared a short guide to the area in English, German, French, Spanish and Japanese; the *hostería* has a swimming pool (US$1.40 for non-residents for a day), shop and a Copec petrol station, tents for hire, US$3 for 2 people, camping in grounds, US$0.75 p.p., 2 cabins with 6 and 3 beds, hot water, electricity 1800-2300, restaurant (good lunch US$8.75) and bar, "Llamaroo" supermarket, T 21-1511. *Residencial Chiloé*, Domingo Atienza, E, clean, good, hot water; *Residencial Solcor*, 2 blocks from plaza, G p.p., friendly, good meals; *Pukará*, D, Tocopilla 28, cold water, mixed reports; *Pensión Florida*, on Tocopilla, E, hot water intermittent, shared baths, safe, fleas, dirty; *Hostal-camping Takha-Takha*, on Tocopilla, E p.p. (F camping), hot water, good sanitary facilities, some tents for rent, friendly and clean, good restaurant, vegetarian food. *Residencial Juanita*, on the plaza, F, no hot water, friendly, restaurant; *Residencial Andacollo*, good, friendly; *Restaurant Porvenir*, on Toconao, F, only one room, rec. If arriving after "lights out" and there is nowhere to stay, ask the police if they will let you stay in their office.

**Restaurants** Mainly in hotels and residencials: *Andacollo*, best in town, rec.; *Porvenir*, cheap, good; try also *Juanita* and *Chiloé* for cheap lunches. Don't drink the tap water, it contains a high level of arsenic.

**Exchange** Best done elsewhere, no cheques, poor rates for cash. If stuck try Almacén El Chagüito, Tocopilla 28, or *Hostería San Pedro*.

**Car Hire** is almost impossible in San Pedro. Calama is much easier.

**Swimming Pool** Piscina Oasis, at Pozo Tres, 3 km. outside village, was drilled in the late 1950s as part of a mineral exploration project, open all year 0500-1730 daily (except Thurs). US$0.50 to swim, sometimes empty. Worth asking around before walking there. Camping US$0.55.

**Electricity** Only from 1 hour after sunset till 2300-2400, depending who is on duty, what film is on TV, or so they say. *Residenciales* supply candles, but better to buy them in Calama beforehand.

**Tours** Turismo Ochoa, opened by Héctor Ochoa, rec.; Sánchez and Nativa, both on Pedro de Valdivia. Tours can also be arranged from *Hostería San Pedro* (expensive); *Hostal Takha-Takha* (guide Zahel is rec.), *Residencial Chiloé* and *Pension Florida*. Sra María Luisa Baron, chief archaeologist of the area, arranges trips to the Salar and geysers. Contact her through *Residencial Chiloé*. Usual tour rates: to Salar de Atacama (best at sunset) US$14; to Valle de la Luna (best at sunset) US$9; to El Tatio (begin at 0400) US$15.

**Buses** From Calama there are Tramaca buses daily at 1100, extra buses Jan.-Feb., especially at weekends, 2 hrs., US$3.50 (US$6 return, if possible book in advance, especially for Sun. travel), returning from the plaza at 1800 (1845 Sat.-Sun. in Jan.-Feb.); the bus goes on to Pozo Tres before coming back to San Pedro at 1700. There are also buses run by Yusmar, leaving Calama daily at 0800, returning in the afternoon (US$3.50), and by Morales Moralitos, leaving Calama Mon.-Sat. 1600, returning at 0800.

**Excursions** The Valle de la Luna, with fantastic landscapes caused by the erosion of salt mountains, is traversed by a road 13 km. from San Pedro; the San Pedro-Calama bus does not pass through the valley but passes the old road which used to cross it (most bus drivers know where it is and will let you out—the sign is not visible if coming from Calama). From here it is a stiff 5-hr. walk back to San Pedro and can only be done in the middle of the day. Far better is to walk from San Pedro on the old road, 3 hrs. there, 3 hrs. back (don't expect a lift), aim to get there just before sunset. Take water, hat, camera and torch. There are no signs for the return to San Pedro, but the road is straight all the way. A suggested walk is to go 4 km. down the road to Calama; at a small sign turn left till you stand at the top of a deep valley. Climb down the dunes with care then explore the valley to the right. There are no cars or roads here, just giant crystals of gypsum. Walk back and leave the valley turning left where you climbed down; always keep Licancábur volcano ahead of you. In all 5½ strenuous hours; take water and protection against the sun. If you are in your own car (4-wheel drive essential to cope with sand dunes), make the detour on your way south (i.e. from Calama), as from N drifting sand makes uphill driving difficult.

The Pucará de Quitor, pre-Conquest hill fortification, restored in 1981, is a 3 km. walk N of San Pedro along the river bed. A further 4 km. up the river there are Inca ruins at Catarpe. Driving through the Valle de la Luna at sunset, with the Licancábur volcano, 5,916 metres, in the background, is a superb experience. The best places to see the sunset are at the Pucará de Quitor, or the football pitch (cancha). The archaeological site at Tulor, 9 km. from San Pedro, is a stone-age village; worth a visit on foot (you can sleep in two reconstructed huts), or take a tour, US$5 p.p.

An interesting route from San Pedro de Atacama to Calama is to go north on a maintained road which passes the Baños de Puritama (27 km., truck drivers leaving from behind the police station for the sulphur mine at 0500 may give you a lift and collect you on return), then to the geysers about 100 km. N of San Pedro at El Tatio. The geysers about 100 km. N of San Pedro, at an altitude of 4,500 metres, are at their best 0630-0830. There is no public transport, so if going in a hired car, make sure the engine is suitable for very high altitudes and is protected with antifreeze; 4-wheel drive is essential. If driving in the dark it is almost impossible to find your way: the sign for El Tatio is after the turn off coming from San Pedro de Atacama. Near El Tatio is a workers' camp which is empty apart from one guard, who will let you sleep in one of the huts in a bed. Give him a tip and take your own food. If you stay here, you can hike to surrounding volcanoes if adapted to altitude. Hitching to El Tatio is impossible; the police advise against it. Tours arranged by those mentioned above. Also ask the army outside San Pedro, who may give groups of 10-12 people a lift in a truck (US$3 p.p.); beware, it gets very cold in the truck. From Calama, trips for El Tatio leave at 0300, continuing to San Pedro and the Valle de la Luna, arriving back at 2000 (US$30 p.p.).

There are 3 alternative routes between El Tatio and Calama: direct, on an atrocious track, to Caspana, beautifully set among hills, with an interesting museum. Between Caspana and Toconce are pampas grass filled valleys with llama herds. It is proposed to make the area north of San Pedro, including El Tatio and Caspana, a national park.

N of El Tatio to Linzor; here you can turn W to Toconce, which has extensive prehispanic terraces set among interesting rock formations. If visiting Toconce, check in with the *carabineros* in the square. Then to Calama via Lasana and Chiu Chiu, or via **Ayquina**, in whose ancient church is enshrined the statue of the Virgin of Guadalupe. Her feast-day is 8 September, when pilgrims come from far and wide. There is a day-long group dancing to Indian rhythms on flute and drum. Towards sunset the Virgin is carried up a steep trail to a small thatched shrine, where the image and the people are blessed before the dancing is renewed at the shrine and all the way back to the village. The poor people of the hills gather stones and make toy houses all along the route: miniatures of the homes they hope to have some day.

With a detour, the thermal waters and ruins of Baños de Turi may be visited and, 35 km. north, Cupo, which has a *fiesta* on 19 March (San José). Between this village and Turi is a large, ruined prehispanic settlement at Paniri with extensive field systems, irrigation canals (including aqueducts) and a necropolis. Some of the fields are still in use. The area around Cupo is one of the best for seeing the Atacama giant cactus (*Notocereus atacamensis*). Flamingos can be seen on the mudflats. The Vegas de Turi is an important site for the llama and sheep herders, who believe it has curative properties. At several times in the year, herders from a wide area congregate with their flocks, especially in September.

The third alternative is to continue North from Linzor to Inacaliri and the Ojo de San Pedro saltflat. Follow the road along the Río San Pedro Valley and cross the Río Loa at Conchi. The Río San Pedro has been a route for herders and silver caravans for centuries and there are many sites of interest, although access is on foot. For details on Conchi, Lasana and Chiu Chiu, see page 531 above.

A well-surfaced road south of San Pedro runs through groves of acacia and pepper trees to Toconao (40 km.). There are many tracks leading to the wells (*pozos*) which supply the intricate irrigation system. Most have thermal water but bathing is not appreciated by the local farmers. The groves of trees are havens for wild life especially rheas (ñandu) and Atacama owls.

About 4 km. before you reach Toconao, there are some vehicle tracks heading east across the sand. They lead to a hidden valley 2 km. from the road where there is a small settlement called Zapar. Here are some well-preserved pre-hispanic ruins on the rocky cliffs above the cultivated valley. The sand is very soft and 4-wheel drive is essential. *Toconao*, with some 500 inhabitants is on the eastern shore of the lithium-salt lake Salar de Atacama. All houses are built of bricks of white volcanic stone, which gives to the village a very characteristic appearance totally different from San Pedro. Its colonial clock tower is modelled in the same volcanic stone by the local craftsman and it has an attractive oasis called Quebrada de Jérez. The quarry where the stone (*sillar*) is worked can be visited. Worth visiting also are the vineyards which produce a unique sweet wine, and the tree-filled gorges with their hidden fields and orchards. Hitch from San Pedro (most traffic at weekends). Tours arranged in San Pedro. Camping possible along river bank of Quebrada de Jérez.

Ask the *jefe de carabineros* in San Pedro or Toconao for a chance to go with police patrols to the Bolivian or Argentine border areas (paying your share of fuel).

From San Pedro de Atacama one can cross into Argentina over the pass of Laguna Sico (4,079 metres) to San Antonio de los Cobres. Travellers by car should make careful enquiries into road conditions (often impassible in rainy season, 1 Jan. to mid-March, and blocked by snow in winter); gasoline may be bought in Calama or at *Hostería San Pedro*. Passport control and customs clearance must be undertaken in San Pedro.

The first village reached is Toconao (see above; cars registered at the entrance to the village); the Atacama desert can be seen in the distance. The road heads south through the scenic villages of Camar (where handicrafts from cactus may be bought) and Socaire (which has domesticated llamas, knitwear for sale). 20 km. S of Socaire is the beautiful Laguna Miscantí where wildlife abounds, including 3 types of flamingo: Andean, Chilean (white and pink, no black) and James (small, with yellow legs). After Socaire the road goes on to the mine at Laco (one poor stretch below the mine), proceeding to Sico, which has replaced the higher, more northerly Huaytiquina pass (4,295 metres) to Catúa and San Antonio de los Cobres.

10 km. S of Toconao the old road branches E towards Huaytiquina. In a deep *quebrada* below Volcán Láscar is the small agricultural settlement of Talabre, with terracing and an ancient threshing floor. Above the *quebrada* is an isolated, stone-built cemetery. Large flocks of llamas graze where the stream crosses the road below Láscar. After a steep climb, you reach the Laguna Lejía (4,190 metres), where flamingoes abound. You then pass through the high plains of Huaytiquina (4,275 metres), where only a few herdsmen are found. This crossing is not open for road traffic to Catúa, the first Argentine settlement, after which the road crosses the railway, descends into the ghost-like town of Agua Castilla, and after 8 km. reaches San Antonio de los Cobres. It is a further 3½ hours by car to Salta.

60 km. further south from Toconao, on a road that branches initially W between Camar and Socaire, is the attractive village of *Peine*, which is the site of the offices of the lithium extraction company. There is also a pool filled by thermal springs where you can swim. Woollen goods and knitwear are made here. To the east of the village lies a group of beautifully coloured hills (colours best at sunset) with good views over the Salar de Atacama. It is worth asking if the offices' access road can be used to visit the Salar de Atacama's spectacular salt formations.

Other villages worth visiting include Tilomonte and Tilopozo, S and W of Peine. The road can be followed to Pan de Azúcar where it joins the road to Argentina via the Portezuelo de Socompa. It is possible to stay at Pan de Azúcar (hot showers and water). From Pan de Azúcar a good road leads back to San Pedro de Atacama along the western side of the Salar.

Pan de Azúcar is on the road which leads from the Pan-American Highway, 50 km. S of Antofagasta to Socompa on the Argentine border. The road passes the mining centre at La Escondida (owned by RTZ) and continues, after Pan de Azúcar, in bad condition to Monturaqui. This is the source of the green onyx which is much used for carving in northern Chile. Formalities for crossing into Argentina are completed at Socompa. The road carries on to San Antonio de los Cobres and Salta.

If coming into Chile by train on the Salta-Socompa line, cross into Chile immediately and ask about freight trains to Baquedano (you may have to wait days—the staff at the railway and customs offices are helpful, but officially the freight trains are not allowed to carry passengers). Trains may go only as far as Augusta Victoria, where there is a mining camp from which you can get a pick-up to Antofagasta, or to Baquedano if you want to go to Calama (bus from Baquedano police control point).

Some 175 km. **S of Antofagasta** there are ruined nitrate mines at Oficina Alemania and Oficina Flor de Chile (just off the Pan-American Highway). Mining tracks lead off to the E, but there are no real signs. A good one leads East from Aguas Verdes (fuel) to Plato de Sopa, a camp built into caves above a salt flat.

The next important port to the south is **Taltal**, 309 km. S of Antofagasta, connected with it by the Pan-American Highway and a poor but scenic road along the coast. A town of wooden buildings, many dating from the late 19th century when Taltal prospered as an important mineral port of 20,000, it is now a nitrate and copper ore centre with 8,275 people. There is an archaeological museum on Av. Prat. There is an airport, but few flights.

**Accommodation and Food** Hostería Taltal, Esmeralda 671, C, excellent restaurant, good value almuerzo; **Verdy**, Ramírez 345, D with bath, E without, clean, spacious, restaurant; **San Martín**, Martínez 297, E without bath, good almuerzo. Viña del Mar, Serrano 762, E. **Restaurant** Caverna, Martínez 247, good seafood.

**Buses** To Santiago 2 a day; to Antofagasta 6 a day.

**Chañaral**, a neglected looking town with wooden houses perched on the hillside is 100 km. S of Taltal and 400 km. S of Antofagasta by sea or Pan-American Highway. In the heyday it was the centre for the nearby copper mines of El Salado and Las Animas. Population, including Potrerillos and Caleta Barquito: 39,225. Tourist office on coastal road outside town, open summer only.

**Accommodation and Food** Hostería Chañaral Miller 268, T 80055, B, excellent restaurant; **Mini**, San Martín 28, C, restaurant; **Jiménez**, Merino Jarpa 551, E without bath, friendly, clean, rec., restaurant good value; **La Marina**, Merino Jarpa 562, F, basic. **Restaurants** in hotels; **Rincón Porteño**, next to Jiménez, good and inexpensive.

**Buses** Terminus Merino Jarpa 854. Frequent services to Antofagasta (US$10) and Santiago.

**Excursions** North of Chañaral is the **Parque Nacional Pan de Azúcar**, which consists of the Isla Pan de Azúcar on which Humboldt penguins and other sea-birds live, and some 43,700 hectares of coast whose vegetation, mainly cacti, is nourished by frequent sea mists (camanchaca). There are some fine beaches in the park (popular at weekends). Access by secondary road from Chañaral (22 km. to Caleta Pan de Azúcar), or more easily from the Pan-American Highway (45 km. N, then side road 20 km. W). After rain in some of the gullies there are tall purple lilies. Conaf office, Atacama 898, Copiapó, T 3404/2571; wardens in the park.

12 km. E of Chañaral is a paved road to the mine of El Salvador. This follows a valley which contains the outflow of the mine purification process. All along it there are people extracting metal ore from the water by building primitive settling tanks. Climb above El Salvador to Hostería Louis Murray, no booking possible, just turn up. Daily flights from Santiago to El Salvador.

**Copiapó**, 240 km. S of Chañaral, capital of III Región (Atacama), is situated 60 km. inland in a ribbon of farms and orchards about 150 km. long on the river Copiapó, the river generally regarded as the southern limit of the Atacama desert. It is an attractive mining centre with an important mining school, and a population of 70,000. There is a monument to Juan Godoy, a mule-driver, who, in 1832, discovered silver at Chañarcillo (see below). The plaza is interesting, with a wooden Cathedral dating from 1851. The best mineralogical museum in Chile is at Colipí y Rodríguez, 1 block from Plaza de Armas (east); Tues.-Fri. 1000-1300, 1600-2000, Sat. and Sun. 1000-1300, US$0.50. Many ores shown are found only in the Atacama desert. Also Museo Regional Atacama Copiapó, Atacama y Rancagua, entrance US$0.35, interesting. Open Tues.-Fri. 0930-1230, 1530-1900, Sat. 0930-1230, Sun. 1000-1300. The museum at the railway station is dull, but an early steam locomotive can be seen at the university on the northern highway.

**Hotels** San Francisco de Selva Los Carrera 525, A, modern; **Hostería Las Pircas**, Av. Kennedy s/n, T 213220, A, bungalows, pool, dining room, good apart from service, out of town; **Palace**, Atacama 741, C, patio, pleasant; **Derby**, Yerbas Buenas, 396, T 212447, C, clean.**Inglés**, Atacama 337, T 212797, C; **Residencial Rodríguez**, Rodríguez 528, T 212861, E, friendly, good comedor, rec.; **Residencial Rocío**, Yerbas Buenas 581, T 215360, F, good value, clean, rec.

**Restaurants** 5 km. from *Las Pircas*, *La Carreta*, on Carretera de Copayapu, ranch-style, very good meat and fish; *Bavaria Restaurant*, on main square, excellent but not cheap. *Chifa Hao Hua*, Colipi 340, good Chinese; *Pampas*, Maipú y Atacama, smart, pleasant.

**Car Hire** Av. Kennedy 310, T 2964.

**Exchange** Fincard (Visa and Access), Chacabuco 389, open Mon.-Fri. 0900-1400, 1630-1930, Sat. 1030-1300.

**Tourist Office** N side of Plaza de Armas, helpful.

**Airport** LanChile, O'Higgins 640, and Ladeco, daily to Santiago via La Serena, with connections to Antofagasta and Arica.

75 km. W of Copiapó is the port of *Caldera*, which has a pier of 230 metres; 1½ km. to the S there is a terminal for the loading of iron ore. There is a fruit inspection for all passing through Caldera going South; this applies to bus passengers, whose luggage is searched.

**Hotels** *Costanera*, Wheelwright 543, C takes credit cards, simple rooms, friendly; *Hostería Puerta del Sol*, Wheelwright 750, T 315205, B inc. tax, cabins with bath and kitchen, view over bay; *Portal del Inca*, Carvallo 945, T 315252, B inc. tax, shower, cabins with kitchen, English spoken, restaurant not bad, order breakfast on previous night; *Pucará*, Ossa Cerda 460, T 315258, C; *Los Andes*, Edwards 360, E. **Restaurant** *Miramar*, at pier, good seafood.

**Buses** Several a day to **Copiapó** and **Santiago**; to travel N, take a bus to Chañaral (Inca-bus US$1.60), then change.

*Bahía Inglesa*, 6 km. S of Caldera, 6 km. W of the Highway, is popular with Chileans for its white sandy beaches and unpolluted sea (can get crowded Jan.-Feb. and at weekends). The climate is warm and dry the year round. It was originally known as Puerto del Inglés after the arrival in 1687 of the English "corsario", Edward Davis. Accommodation at *Los Jardines de Bahía Inglesa*, Av. Copiapó, *cabañas*, D, T 315359, open all year; *Camping Bahía Inglesa*, Playa Las Machas, T (Copiapó) 3360. *El Coral* restaurant has some cabins (C, T 315331), Av. El Morro, overlooking sea, good seafood, groups welcome, open all year. *Britannia-English Pub*, Av. El Morro (Tom and Teresa Clough, P.O. Box 100, Bahía Inglesa, Caldera, III Región), traditional atmosphere, darts, dominoes, pints, etc., bar snacks, British and international beers, bed and breakfast planned. Buses almost hourly from Copiapó with connections from the north; taxis and colectivos US$1 from Caldera all year; frequent micro service Jan. and Feb. US$0.25.

**Excursions** 90 km. SE up the river valley from Copiapó is the Centro Metalúrgico Incaico, an Inca bronze foundry, connected by a paved road. Difficult by public transport: one bus a day from Copiapó (get off at Valle Hermoso), but bus returns immediately. No accommodation in nearby villages of Los Loros, Villa Hermoso, Las Juntas.

50 km. S of Copiapó on the Pan-American Highway is a signposted turning to Chañarcillo. This was one of the 19th century's richest silver mines, becoming the second largest in the Americas. The tips are being reworked and this has destroyed much of the ruins.

A road rises NE through the pass of San Francisco in the Andes to Tinogasta, in Argentina (suitable only for 4 wheel-drive vehicles, often closed by landslides). South of the pass rises the Ojos del Salado mountain, believed to be the third highest peak in the Americas; its height is now thought to be in the range of 6,875-6,887 metres. There is fumarolic activity 300 metres below the summit of Ojos del Salado, which makes it a contender with nearby Pissis, and Cotopaxi in Ecuador for the title of the world's highest active volcano.

---

## SOUTH OF COPIAPO TO ILLAPEL (2)

Yet more desert before the Heartland is reached. The main oases are the valleys of the Huasco and the Elqui. At the mouth of the latter is the neo-colonial resort city of La Serena. Nearby is one of the southern hemisphere's astronomical centres.

The second geographic zone, lying between the valleys of the Copiapó and the Aconcagua, contains the southern half of III Región (Atacama) and the whole of Región IV (Coquimbo) (population at 1982 census, 419,956; 1987, 459,400). The zone is about 600 km. long.

This is a transitional zone between the northern desert and the fruitful heartland. S of Copiapó the central valley is cut across by transverse spurs of mountain which link the Andes and the coastal *cordillera*. Between these spurs several rivers flow westwards. Southwards the desert gives way slowly to dry scrub and bush interspersed with sand dunes. This desert is of little interest except after rain. Then it is covered with a succession of flowers, insects and frogs, in one of the world's most beautiful wildlife events (graphically shown in Michael Andrews' *The Flight of the Condor*, episode 2, BBC TV). Rain, however, is rare: there is no rain in summer; in winter it is light and lasts only a short time. It is about 115 mm. at Copiapó and 500 m m. at Illapel. In the river valleys under irrigation, fruit, vines, and barley are grown, and some alfalfa for cattle. There are many goats.

*Vallenar* (airport), 144 km. S of Copiapó, is the chief town of the Huasco valley and the second city of III Región, with a population of 38,000. Near the municipal stadium is the Museo del Huasco, containing artefacts from the valley (Tues.-Fri. 1030-1230, 1530-1900; Sat.-Sun. 1000-1230).

The valley is an oasis of olive groves and vineyards. There are Pisco distilleries at Alto del Carmen and San Félix; a sweet wine known as Pajarete is also produced.

**Hotels** *Hostería Vallenar*, Ercilla 848, T 611847, A+, excellent, pool, Hertz car hire office, restaurant reputed to be among the best in Chile; *Real*, Prat 881, C; *Cecil*, Calle Prat 1059, T 611272, D with bath and hot water, clean, rec.; *Viña del Mar*, Serrano 611, E, clean, *comedor*, smoking disapproved of; several *residenciales* nearby. **Restaurants** *Bavaria*, Santiago y Serrano, good, not cheap; *El Fogón*, Ramírez 944, for meat dishes, *almuerzo* good value; *Shanghai*, Ramírez 1267, Chinese; cheap places along S end of Av. Brasil.

**Excursions** To *Huasco*, a pleasant town and interesting port 56 km. W at the mouth of the river. 1½ km S. of Huasco is a terminal for loading iron ore from the deposits at Algarrobal, 52 km. N of Vallenar. (*Hostería Huasco*, B, only place to stay; *Restaurant Escorial*, best; cheap seafood restaurants near port.) To *Freirina*, 36 km. from Vallenar, 21 km. from Huasco, easily reached by colectivos from either. Founded 1752, Freirina was the most important town in the valley, its prosperity based upon the nearby Capote goldmine and on later discoveries of copper. On the main plaza are the Municipalidad, (1870) and the Santa Roasa church. No accommodation. Up the rugged and spectacular Huasco valley to Alto del Carmen, 30 km., where the river divides; an unpaved road leads up the Carmen valley to San Félix (*Residencial San Félix*, G, basic); another runs up the Tránsito valley to El Tránsito (*Pensión Santa Anita*, G, basic). Buses from Verdaguer 658, Vallenar.

130 km. S of Vallenar there is a turning to the old mines at El Tofo. Some trees have a precarious hold on life as a result solely of fog. Follow the road to the sea for some spectacular scenery and wildlife.

*La Serena*, on the coast 187 km. S of Vallenar, 480 km. N of Santiago (108,000 people) is the capital of IV Región (Coquimbo). Built on a hillside 2 km. inland from Coquimbo Bay, it is one of the pleasantest towns in Chile, with many neo-colonial buildings and pretty gardens. Around the attractive Plaza de Armas are most of the official buildings, including the Post Office, the Cathedral (built in 1844 and featuring a carillon which plays every hour) and the Historical Museum (see below). There are 29 other churches, several of which have unusual towers. La Recova, the new market, at Cienfuegos y Cantournet, includes a large display of handicrafts and, upstairs, several good restaurants. A pleasant boulevard, Av. Francisco de Aguirre (known as the Alameda), runs from the centre to the coast, terminating at the Faro Monumental, a neo-colonial style mock-castle. A series of beaches stretch from here to Peñuelas, 6 km. south, linked by the Avenida del Mar. There are as yet only a few apartment blocks, hotels and restaurants along this part of the bay.

**History** La Serena was founded by Juan de Bohón, aide to Pedro de Valdivia, in 1544, destroyed by Diaguita Indians in 1546, rebuilt by Francisco de Aguirre in 1552, and sacked by the English pirate Sharpe in 1680. Legends of buried treasure at Guayacán Bay, frequented by Drake, persist. The present-day layout and architectural style has its origins in the "Plan Serena" drawn up in 1948 on the orders of Chilean president, Gabriel González Videla, a native of the city.

**Hotels** *Mediterráneo*, Cienfuegos 509, Casilla 212, T 215233, A+ including good breakfast, rec.; *Francisco de Aguirre*, Córdovez 210, T 222991, A, with breakfast, shower, good rooms, reasonable restaurant; *Berlín*, Córdovez 535, T 222927, C, clean, safe, efficient, rec.; *Londres*, Córdovez 566, T 211906, D, old-fashioned, restaurant; *Pucará*, Balmaceda 319, T 211966, B with bath and breakfast, good; *Alameda*, Av. de Aguirre 450, T 213052, D, run down, clean and comfortable; *Residencial Brasilia*, Brasil 555, T 212263, C, good, friendly; *Hostal Del Mar*, Cuatro Esquinas (near beach) C, also *cabañas*, clean, friendly. *Res. Chile*, Matta 561, T 211694, E, basic, clean, hot water a.m. only; *Residencial El Loa*, O'Higgins 362, D with shower, good inexpensive home cooking (US$2.50-3 per main meal), friendly; *Residencial Petit*, de la Barra 586, T 212536, D, hot water; *Res. Norte Verde*, Cienfuegos 672, T 213646, E, dirty, not rec.; *San Juan*, Balmaceda 827, E, good; unnamed *residencial* at Av. de Aguirre 411, G p.p. in dormitories, clean. Family *pensión* of Isabel Ahumada Rolle, Eduardo de la Barra 315, E. Private accommodation at Cienfuegos 324, G p.p., clean, friendly; Brasil 690, F p.p., clean, friendly; Los Carrera 680, F p.p., at Adolfo Ballas 1418, T 223735, F and Andrés Bello 945 both have kitchens and equipment, living rooms, etc. **Motel** *Les Mouettes*, Av. de Mar, T 214216, A, good; several more motels along the beach. The road from La Serena to Coquimbo is lined with accommodation, from hotels to *cabañas*, and restaurants.

**Campsite** Camping Peñuelas, Los Pescadores 795, T 313818. Maki Payi, 153 Vegas Norte, about 5 km. N of La Serena, near sea, friendly, rec., self-contained cabins available; US$5 per tent and US$9.50 p.p. for chalet. Hipocampo, 4 km. S on Av. del Mar (take bus for Coquimbo and get off at Colegio Adventistu, US$2.50 p.p. by Playa El Pescador), T 214276.

**Restaurants** *Club Social*, Córdovez 516 (first floor), unpretentious but excellent value. *Cirio's*, Francisco de Aguirre 431, T 213482, old-fashioned, honest, good lunch, US$5, rec.; *Rapsodia*, Arturo Prat 470, tea house with good cakes; *Domingo Domínguez*, Prat 572, good Italian, pricey but worth it; *Mesón Matías*, Balmaceda 1940, excellent Spanish, elegant, expensive but highly rec.; *La Mía Pizza*, O'Higgins 460, Italian, good value, inexpensive; *Mai Lai Fan*, Córdovez 740, good Chinese, reasonably priced; *La Serena*, O'Higgins 490, good meat and fish dishes, inexpensive lunches; *Maracuya*, Caracol Colonial, Balmaceda 460; for good, inexpensive lunches try the restaurants on the upper floor of the Recova market. Several good cafés: *Tito's*, O'Higgins y Córdovez, popular meeting place; *Café do Brasil*, Balmaceda 461, good coffee; *Café La Crêperie*, O'Higgins y de la Barra, crêpes, light meals, occasional live music; *Bocaccio*, Prat y Balmaceda, modern, smart, popular.

**Shopping** *La Recova* for handicrafts, though many items imported from Peru and Bolivia; *Cema-Chile*, Los Carrera 562; *Las Brisas* supermarket, Cienfuegos y Córdovez.

**Museums** **Historical museum** in the Casa Gabriel González Videla on the Plaza de Armas, including several rooms on the man's life. Open Tues.-Sat. 0900-1300, 1600-1900, Sun. 1000-1300, entry US$0.50; **Museo Arqueológico**, Córdovez y Cienfuegos, interesting collection of Diaguita and Molle Indian exhibits, especially of most attractively decorated pottery; open Tues.-Sat. 0900-1300, 1600-1900, Sun. 1000-1300, entrance, US$0.35. There is a **mineralogical museum** in the University of La Serena, Calle A. Muñoz between Benavente and Infante (for geologists, open Mon.-Fri. 0930-1230, free).

**Car Hire** Hertz, Francisco de Aguirre 0225, T 213955/212639, **Automóvil Club de Chile**, Eduardo de la Barra 435, T 211504, small car US$250/week (inc. tax, insurance, free km.) or US$870/month, pick-ups and jeeps US$300-350/week.

**Discotheques** *La Burbuja*, Balmaceda 677. *Cesare*, Av. del Mar.

**Exchange** Fincard (Visa and Mastercard), Balmaceda 391, Local 217, Mon.-Fri. 0900-1400, 1600-2030, Sat. 1000-1400. **Casas de Cambio**: Viajes Val, Prat 560 (open Sat. 1100-1400); Cambio Fides, Caracol Colonial (basement), Balmaceda 460 (open Sat. 1030-1330)—if closed try Petronio, the leather shop opposite. Note that La Serena is the last place to change travellers' cheques before Antofagasta.

**Telecommunications** Long distance calls from Córdovez 446 and La Recova market.

**Tourist Office** Main Sernatur office in Edificio de Servicios Públicos, 1st floor (next to the Post Office on the Plaza de Armas, open Mon.-Fri. 0830-1330, 1430-1830. Kiosks at bus terminal (summer only) and at Balmaceda y Prat (open Mon.-Sat. 1100-1400, 1600-1900), helpful.

**Travel Agents** *Ingservitur*, Los Lirios 300, Coquimbo, T 312943, varied programme of tours, depending on demand; *Gira Tour*, Balmaceda 370, Oficina 301; *Turismo Cristóbal*, Cordóvez 210.

**Transport** Bus terminal, El Santo y Amunátegui, in Coquimbo direction (about 8 blocks N of the centre). Buses daily to **Santiago**, several companies, 7 hrs, US$8.35-10; to **Arica**, US$20; to **Calama**, US$17, 16 hrs. To **Valparaíso**, 7 hrs., US$10; to **Antofagasta**, 13 hrs., several companies, US$15-18, and to **Iquique** 20 hrs, US$22. Bus to **Vicuña**, Transportes Via Elqui, Calle Peni y Benavente, 9 daily, 2 hrs, US$1.20; *colectivo* to Vicuña, Empresa Nevada del Sol de Elqui, Domeyko 550, T 21450, others from Av. Aguirre y Balmaceda; to **Coquimbo**, from Av. Aguirre y Cienfuegos, US$0.25, every few mins.

**Airport** LanChile (O'Higgins 365, T 215768) 5 times a week to Santiago and Copiapó.

**Excursion** La Serena is at the mouth of the Elqui river valley, where the Nobel Prize-winning poet Gabriela Mistral was born. She described the valley as "confined yet lofty, many-sided yet simple, rustic yet a mining area". The branches of the road up the valley all lead to fertile nooks, to shady vegetation, to dense groves, to gardens fed by the very sap of the hills". Of the *elquinos*, the people of the valley, she says that "even the most taciturn of them come out with witty and charming remarks". There are still a few descendants of the Diaguitas, the tribe that inhabited the valley at one time. The road up the valley is paved as far as Varillar, 24 km. beyond Vicuña, the capital of the valley. Except for Vicuña, most of the tiny towns have but a single street. There are mines, orchards, orange groves and vineyards in the valley, which is the main pisco-producing area of Chile, the climate and soil being ideally suited to the cultivation of grapes with a high sugar-content. Of the 9 Pisco distilleries in the valley, the largest is Capel in Vicuña. Huancara, a delicious liqueur introduced by the Jesuits, is also produced in the valley.

**Vicuña**, population 6,000, 66 km. E of La Serena, is a small, clean, friendly, picturesque town. On the W side of the plaza are the municipal chambers, built in 1826 and topped in 1905 by a prefabricated medieval-German-style tower—the Torre Bauer—imported by the German-born mayor of the time. Inside the chambers is a gallery of past local dignatories. The Museo Gabriela Mistral is at Calle Gabriela Mistral y Riquelme (open Tues.-Sat. 0900-1300, 1500-1700, Sun. 1000-1300, entry US$0.40). Tourist office at San Martín 293. There are good views from Cerro La Virgen, N of town. The Capel Pisco distillery is 1½ km. E of Vicuña, to the right of the main road; guided tours (in Spanish) are offered on Mon.-Fri. 0930-1130 and 1400-1800; no booking required.

**Hotels** *Hostería Vicuña*, Sgto. Aldea 101, T 411301, A, swimming pool, tennis court, excellent restaurant. On Gabriela Mistral: *Gran Hotel Jasna*, at No. 542, T 411266, D with bath (cheaper without), hot water, charming, clean, safe, restaurant; *Residencial Moderna*, at No. 718, E, full board available, no hot water, nothing modern about it, but quiet, clean, very nice; *Residencial Mistral*, at No. 180, F, basic, restaurant; unnamed residencial at No. 743, hot water, vineyard, restaurant.

**Camping** *Camping y Piscina Las Tinajas*, E end of Chacabuco, swimming pool, restaurant.

**Restaurants** Mainly on G. Mistral: *Club Social de Elqui*, at No. 435, good food, attractive patio, *almuerzo* US$3; *Estercita*, at No. 518, good seafood; *Mistral*, at No. 180, very good food, popular with locals, good value *almuerzo*; *Halley*, at No. 404, good meat dishes, pricey; *Yo Y Soledad*, Prat 364, inexpensive, good value.

**Buses** To **La Serena**, about 10 a day, most by Vía Elqui, first 0800, last 1930, 2 hrs., US$1.20, *colectivo* US$1.40; to **Santiago** via La Serena, Expreso Norte at 1145 and 2200; to **Pisco Elqui**, 4 a day, Vía Elqui and Frontera Elqui, 1 hr, US$1.40.

From Vicuña the road continues up the valley another 18 km. to Rivadavia where it divides: the main route (Route 41) winding through the mountains to the Argentine frontier at Agua Negra. The road over the pass, after years of closure, has been reopened, only between 1100-1700, some buses make the crossing; in winter it may be shut by snow. At Chapilca, 14 km. beyond Rivadavia, beautiful hand-woven rugs may be bought. The other branch of the road runs through Paihuano and Monte Grande (where the tomb of Gabriela Mistral is situated) to Pisco Elqui (*Hostería de Don Jaun*, E, fine views, excellent breakfasts; *Restaurant Elqui*, good, cheap, pleasant, not always open; *Las Vegas* campsite. One bus a day to La Serena).

Beyond Monte Grande, on the road to El Colorado, are several Ashram places, some of which welcome visitors (e.g. Rama Mission, 12 km. from Monte Grande); one can camp ("a firm belief in UFOs is a help"—Quentin Crewe). Bus from Vicuña plaza to Monte Grande

US$1.20, from Monte Grande you can walk or take a pick-up if one is running to a self-contained community where you can stay up to 4 days (take sleeping bag and food); ask for Gladys or Juanita. May be possible to go with transport to El Indio mine to get higher up the valley.

The La Serena district is one of the astronomical centres of the world, with three observatories: **El Tololo**, 89 km. SE of La Serena in the Elqui Valley, 51 km. S of Vicuña, which belongs to Aura, an association of US and Chilean universities. This possesses the largest telescope in the southern hemisphere, eight others and a radio telescope. It is open to visitors on the first Sun. of every month, 0900-1200, 1300-1600, only with permission: write or phone Aura, Calle Mariátegui 2438, Santiago, T 274-5884/496-568, or Casilla 603, La Serena, T 213-352 (the office is at Colina Los Pinos, on a hill behind the new University—personal applications can be made here for all three observatories). They will insist that you have private transport, but you can hitch (49 km. to the junction in the direction of Vicuña, then another 38 km.). Since only 8 cars are allowed in per day, hitching needs a lot of luck (note that you must have permission, even if you hitch).

**La Silla**, 150 km. NE of La Serena, which belongs to ESO (European Southern Laboratory), financed by 7 EC countries, comprising 12 telescopes. Open first Sat. of the month, 1430-1730, no permission required; for prior information (essential), Alonso de Córdoba 3107, Santiago, T 228-5006/698-8757, or write to Casilla 567, La Serena, T 213-832/213-320. From La Serena it is 114 km. to the turn-off, then another 36 km.
   **Las Campanas**, 156 km. NE of La Serena, 30 km. N of La Silla, belonging to the Carnegie Institute, has 4 telescopes and is altogether a smaller facility than the other two. It is open without permission every Sat. 1430-1730, T 213-032, or write to Casilla 601, La Serena. Go to the same junction as for La Silla, then 40 km. in a different direction. For La Silla and Las Campanas those without private transport can take the 1100 Pullman Fichtur bus towards Vallenar (2 hrs., US$3.25) and get out at the junction (desvío); hitch from there. It is possible to hire a car with driver to visit all three sites in one day for US$22.
   It is essential to apply well in advance to visit, especially during Chilean holiday periods. Three travel agents in La Serena, Ingservitur, Gira Tour and Turismo Cristóbal, receive tickets from the observatories and arrange tours, but these are often booked up well in advance. If you already have a visitor's permit, try these agencies to see if you can join their group transport.

*Coquimbo* (pop. 106,000), 12 km. S of La Serena and on the same bay, is a port of considerable importance, with one of the best harbours on the coast and major fish-processing plants. The city is strung along the N shore of a peninsula. Most of the commercial life is centred on 3 streets which run between the port and the steep hillside on which are perched many of the poorer houses. On the S shore of the peninsula lies the suburb of Guayacán, with an iron-ore loading port and a steel church designed by Eiffel. Nearby is La Herradura, 2½ km. from Coquimbo, which has the best beaches.

**Hotels**   Generally much cheaper than in La Serena. *Lig*, Aldunate 1577, D, comfortable, friendly, good value, near bus terminus; *Punta del Este*, Av. Videla 170, D, nice rooms; *Iberia*, Lastra 400 (facing Plaza de Armas), D, friendly, good value, rec.; *Prat*, Bilbao y Aldunate, C, comfortable, pleasant; *Claris*, Aldunate 669, E, old-fashioned, rambling hotel with bar and *comedor*, live music on Fri. and Sat., popular with sailors. Several hotels in La Herradura, including *Hotel La Herradura*, Av. Costanera 200, C.

**Camping**   Camping La Herradura, T 312084.

**Restaurants**   Lots of good fish restaurants including *Sal y Pimiento del Capitán Denny*, Melgarejo 879, one of the best, pleasant, old-fashioned; *La Picada*, Av. Costanera near statue of O'Higgins, excellent, pricey; *La Barca*, Ríos y Varela, modest but good; *La Bahía*, Pinto 1465, excellent, good value. Several good seafood restaurants (known as *pensiones*) at the municipal market, Melgarejo between Bilbao and Borgoño (*El Callejón* has been rec.); *Mai Lai Fan*, Av. Ossandón 1, excellent Chinese, rec.;*Tavola Calda*, Bilbao 451, good Italian, good value; *El Brasero*, Av. Alessandri, for meat lovers, pricey.

**Museum**   In 1981 heavy rain uncovered 39 ancient burials of humans and llamas which had been sacrificed. A small museum has been built in the Plaza Gabriela Mistral to exhibit these.

**Tourist Office**   Kiosk in Plaza de Armas (open summer only).

**Buses**   No bus terminal, buses leave from bus company offices around junction of Aldunate,

Videla and Matta. To La Serena, every few mins, US$0.25.

**Excursions** Good beaches to the S at Totoralillo (good swimming), Guanaqueros (35 km.) and Tongoy (48 km.).

***Tongoy***, an old fishing port and copper foundry, is a rapidly growing resort occupying the whole of a small peninsula: to the S the Playa Grande is 14 km. long; to the N the Playa Socos is 4 km. in length.

**Services** *Hotel Yachting Club*, best, C; *Panorámico* and *Samay*, overlooking fishing port, both E; *Plaza*, on main square, E; several basic *residenciales*. Wide range of restaurants—try the *marisquerías* near the fishing port, excellent value. Bus services from Coquimbo, Ruta Costera, to Guanaqueros, 45 mins, US$0.80; to Tongoy, 1 hr. US$1, frequency varies according to season and day (more on Sun.). Colectivos from Coquimbo, US$1.40 to Guanaqueros, US$1.70 to Tongoy. If motoring, watch the fuel gauge; the nearest service station is at Coquimbo.

From here to Santiago, the Pan-American Highway mainly follows the coastline, passing many beautiful coves, alternatively rocky and sandy, with good surf, but the water is very cold, as is the air. The last stretch before Santiago is through green valleys with rich blue clover and wild artichokes. Beware, the green caterpillars crossing the road in November sting!

From La Serena or Coquimbo, 51 km. SE by road, is the little town of ***Andacollo***. (colectivo, US$2.40; bus, US$1.70—last 20 km. of road very bad). Here, on 24 to 28 December, is held picturesque religious ceremony. The pilgrimage to the shrine of the miraculous Virgen del Rosario de Andacollo is the occasion for ritual dances dating from a pre-Spanish past. The church is huge. Alluvial gold washing and manganese and copper mining in the area. No hotel, but some *pensiones*; during the festival private houses rent beds and some let you pay for a shower. Colectivos run to the festival from Calle Benavente, near Colocolo, in La Serena, but "purists" walk (torch and good walking shoes essential). 2 villages are passed on the route, which starts on the paved highway, then goes along a railway track and lastly up a steep, dusty hill.

***Ovalle*** (population 66,000) is 86 km. S of Coquimbo in the valley of the Limarí river, inland from the sea. It is the centre of a fruit, sheep-rearing, and mining district. Market days are Mon., Wed., Fri. and Sat., till 1600; the market (*feria agrícola*) is by the railway on Benavente. The town is famous for its *talabarterías* (leather workshops) and for its products made of lapis lazuli which is mined locally (and is cheaper than in Santiago—try *Artesanía de Lapis Lazuli*, Libertad 472). The Paloma dam, at the confluence of the Grande and Huatulame rivers, SE of Ovalle, is one of the largest in Chile.

**Hotels** *Hotel de Turismo*, Plaza de Armas, T 620159, B, best in town, excellent restaurant; *American Hotel*, V. Mackenna 169, T 620722, D, friendly, helpful; on Libertad, *Buenos Aires*, No. 136, D, no locks on doors, O.K.; *Roxy*, No. 155, T 620080, D, constant hot water, clean, friendly, patio, *comedor*, highly rec.; *Francia*, No. 231, T 620828, D, pleasant, friendly, restaurant; *Venecia*, No. 261, T 620968, E; *Residencial Bristol*, Araucano 224, D, pleasant spacious building, restaurant. For cheaper accommodation try *Residencial Londres*, Independencia 60, or *Residencial Lolita*, Independencia 274. Several cheap *residenciales* in Calle Socas (short stay).

**Restaurants** *Club Social*, V. MacKenna 400 block, excellent fish dishes though pricey; *Club Social Arabe*, Arauco 255, spacious glass-domed premises, excellent Middle-Eastern food, good prices; *El Quijote*, Arauco 294, intimate atmosphere, good seafood, inexpensive; *Alamar*, Santiago 259, excellent seafood, good value; *El Bosco*, Benavente 88, good, cheap. Good value *almuerzos* at *Hotel de Turismo* and at *Casino La Bomba*, Aguirre 364, run by fire brigade. For drinks and snacks try *Café Caribe Express*, V. MacKenna 241; *Yum Yum*, V. MacKenna 21, good, cheap, lively; *D'Oscar Bar*, Plaza de Armas; *Pastelería Josti*, Libertad 427.

**Museum** *Museo Regional*, Calle Independencia, open Tues.-Sun. 1000-1600, has 3 rooms, information on petroglyphs and a good collection of Diaguita ceramics and other artefacts.

**Tourist Offices** Two kiosks on the Plaza de Armas.

**Buses** 2 a day to **Santiago**, at 0930 and 0030, 6½ hrs., US$7, Empresas LAN and Chispa.

To **La Serena**, 5 a day, 2 hrs, US$2.

**Excursions** The **Monumento Nacional Valle del Encanto**, about 22 km. from Ovalle, has Indian petroglyphs as well as dramatic boulders, its own microclimate, cacti and lizards. No local bus service; you must take long distance bus and ask to be dropped off—3 km. walk to the valley; may be necessary to hitch back. Camping facilities are being upgraded. The **Parque Nacional Fray Jorge** (40 km.) has interesting forest land, which contrasts with the otherwise barren surroundings (very poorly signposted). Open Sat., Sun. and public holidays only; visits closely controlled due to risk of fire. (Scientific groups may obtain permission to visit from The Director, Conaf, Cordóvez 281, La Serena, T 211124.) Round trip in taxi, US$30. 2 km. N of Ovalle along Monte Patria road is Balnearia Los Peñones, on a clean shallow river. NE is the **Monumento Nacional Pichasca**, which has archaeological remains and petrified tree trunks. Daily bus from Ovalle to Río Hurtado pass the turn off 42 km from the city.

*Termas de Socos*, 35 km. S of Ovalle, has fine thermal springs (entrance US$1.30), a good hotel (A, T Ovalle 1373, Casilla 323) and a campsite (about US$1.50 p.p.) nearby. Bus US$2.

About 165 km. S of Ovalle by road, and 59 km. by new paved road from Los Vilos, is *Illapel*, in the basin of the river Choapa (Hotel). Population: 25,600. Fruit, grains and cattle are raised in the valley.

*Los Vilos*, 280 km. S of Coquimbo, is a small seaside resort with frequent launches to the off-shore Isla de La Reina and a beautiful nearby beach (26 km. S) at *Pichidangui*. On the pier at Los Vilos are some old, British-manufactured railway engines; the pier is only used now for fishing from. Good fresh seafood is available near the harbour.

**Hotels in Los Vilos** *Cabañas Antulanquen*, A (negotiable during off season), good service, own porch, kitchenette, rec.; *Hostería Puquen*, good restaurant, clean, honest, C, good restaurant; *Hostería Arrayán*, clean, C; *Lord Willow*, Hostería 1444, overlooking beach and harbour, D with breakfast and bath, pleasant; *Bellavista*, Rengo 20, E, shared bath, hot water, clean. The *Panamerican Motel* is right on the highway, Km. 224, and is a convenient stopping place between La Serena and Viña del Mar or Santiago; it claims to be American style, which will surprise Americans, but is quite good. Campsite on Av. El Bosque. **In Pichidangui**: *Motel El Bosque*, rec.; *Motel Pichidangui*, Francis Drake s/n, B, swimming pool; various other hotels and *pensiones* in every price range. Restaurants tend to be pricey although there is a food shop. Only 1 bus daily Pichidangui-Santiago, but N-S buses on the Highway are in walking distance of the beach.

Just south of Pichidangui is Los Molles, a small town where many wealthy residents of Santiago have their summer homes. There are two small hotels, one down at the beach and the other on the cliff overlooking the beach. *Restaurant La Pirata Suiza*, excellent European-style cooking, run by a Swiss couple.

**See page 523** for list of service stations between Santiago and the Peruvian border.

---

## SANTIAGO AND THE HEARTLAND (3)

**The capital and its surroundings, from the Río Aconcagua to the Río Bío-Bío; within easy reach are Andean ski resorts, or Pacific beaches, such as the international resort of Viña del Mar. On the same stretch of coast is the port of Valparaíso.**

Nearly 70% of the people of Chile live in the comparatively small heartland. The rural density of population in the area is exceptional for Latin America: it is as high as 48 to the square km. in the Central Valley running S from Santiago to Concepción.

From a third to half of the width of the area is taken up by the Andes, which are formidably high in the northern sector; at the head of the river Aconcagua the peak of Aconcagua, the highest in the Americas, rises to 6,964 metres. S of Talca, and to the W of the main range, there is a series of active volcanoes; the region suffers from earthquakes. There is a mantle of snow on the mountains: at

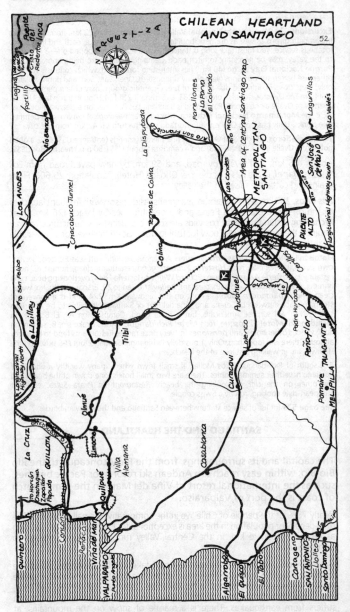

CHILEAN HEARTLAND AND SANTIAGO

52

Aconcagua it begins at 4,300 metres; at Curicó at 3,350; at Bío-Bío at 1,980. The lower slopes are covered with dense forests. Between the forest and the snowline there are alpine pastures which narrow towards the S; during the summer cattle are driven up to these pastures to graze.

The coastal range takes up another third of the width. It is lower here than in the northern desert, but the shoreline is still unbroken; it is only at Valparaíso, San Antonio and Talcahuano (the port for Concepción) that good harbourage is to be found. The coastal range is over 2,130 metres high in the N, but it falls gradually to about 600 metres near Concepción.

Between the coastal range and the Andes lies the Central Valley; most rivers cross it at right angles and cut their way to the sea through narrow canyons in the coastal range, but the Maule and the Bío-Bío have broad valleys along the whole of their courses. The valley of the Aconcagua is separated by a mountainous spur from the valley of the Mapocho, in which Santiago lies, but from Santiago to Concepción the Central Valley is continuous. The land here is extremely fruitful.

There is rain during the winter in the heartland, but the summers are dry. The rain increases to the S. On the coast at Viña del Mar it is 483 mm. a year; at Talcahuano it is 1,168 mm., but is somewhat less inland. Temperatures, on the other hand, are higher inland than on the coast. There is frost now and then in the Central Valley, but very little snow falls.

**Santiago**, founded by Pedro de Valdivia in 1541, is the fifth largest city in South America, with 4m people, and one of the most beautifully set of any, standing in a wide plain, 600 metres above the sea. The city is crossed from E to W by the Río Mapocho, which passes through an artificial stone channel, 40 metres wide, spanned by several bridges. Public gardens, laid out with admirable taste, are filled with flowers and kept in good order. The magnificent chain of the Andes, with its snow-capped heights, is in full view for much of the year, rain and smog permitting; there are peaks of 6,000 metres about 100 km. away. More than half the country's manufacturing is done here; it is essentially a modern capital, full of skyscrapers, bustle, noise, traffic and smog (tables for which are published in the daily papers, as are the numbers of car registration licence plates which are not allowed into the city each day).

The centre of the city lies between the Mapocho and the Avenida O'Higgins. From the Plaza Baquedano (Plaza Italia), in the E of the city's central area, the Mapocho flows to the NW and the Avenida O'Higgins runs to the SW. From Plaza Baquedano the Calle Merced runs due W to the Plaza de Armas, the heart of the city; it lies 5 blocks S of the Mapocho. On the eastern and southern sides of Plaza de Armas there are arcades with shops; on the northern side is the Post Office and the Municipalidad; and on the western side the Cathedral and the archbishop's palace. The Cathedral, much rebuilt, contains a recumbent statue in wood of St. Francis Xavier, and the chandelier which lit the first meetings of Congress after the liberation; it also houses an interesting museum of religious art and historical pieces. In the Palacio de la Real Audiencia on the Plaza de Armas is the Museo Histórico Nacional (see **Museums**, below). A block W of the Cathedral is the Congress building; the Congress, which held no sittings after 1973, has now been moved to Valparaíso to a purpose-built building. The original Congress building is at present the Ministry of Foreign Affairs. Nearby are the law courts. At Calle Merced 864, close to the Plaza de Armas, is the Casa Colorada, built in 1769, the home of the Governor in colonial days and then of Mateo de Toro, first President of Chile. It is now the Museum of the History of Santiago.

The Avenida O'Higgins (usually known as the Alameda) runs through the heart of the city for over 3 km. It is 100 metres wide, and ornamented with gardens and statuary: the most notable are the equestrian statues of Generals O'Higgins and San Martín; the statue of the Chilean historian Benjamín Vicuña Mackenna who, as mayor of Santiago, beautified Cerro Santa Lucía (see **Parks and Gardens** below); and the great monument in honour of the battle of Concepción in 1879.

From the Plaza Baquedano, where there is a statue of General Baquedano and the Tomb of the Unknown Soldier, the Alameda skirts, on the right, Cerro Santa Lucía, and on the left, the Catholic University. Beyond the hill the Alameda goes past the neo-classical National Library on the right, which also contains the national archives. Beyond, on the left, between Calle San Francisco and Calle Londres, is the oldest church in Santiago: the red-walled church and monastery of San Francisco. Inside is the small statue of the Virgin which Valdivia carried on his saddlebow when he rode from Peru to Chile. Beside the church is the Museo de Arte Colonial. On the left, a little further along, is the University of Chile; the Club de la Unión is almost opposite. The Teatro Municipal is on Calle Agustinas with Calle San Antonio 149, and nearby on Calle Nueva York is the Bolsa de Comercio.

N of Plaza de la Libertad, hemmed in by the skyscrapers of the Centro Cívico, is the **Palacio de la Moneda** (1805), containing historic relics, paintings and sculpture, and the elaborate "Salón Rojo" used for official receptions. Until 1990 at least, written permission was required to visit the Moneda, and that was difficult to obtain. The Moneda was damaged by air attacks during the military coup of 11 September 1973; repairs are now completed and the presidential offices have been restored. In front of the Palace is the statue of Arturo Alessandri Palma, who was President of the Republic for two terms.

The Alameda runs westwards to the Planetarium and, opposite it on the southern side, the Estación Central (or Alameda), the railway station for the S. On Avenida Matucana, running N from here, is the very popular Parque Quinta Normal. About seven blocks west of the Estación Central is the southern bus terminal.

Four blocks north of the Plaza de Armas is the interesting Mercado Central, at Puente 21 de Mayo. The building faces the Parque Valenzuela, on which is the Cal y Canto metro station, the northern terminus of Line 2, and, at its western end, the former Mapocho railway station. No trains run from the station, which is being converted into a cultural centre; exhibitions are already being held there. The centre is planned to include the prison which is beside it (currently in use) and will involve the demolition of both the prison and nearby Terminal del Norte bus station. Four blocks west of Mapocho station is the northern bus terminal. If you head east from Mapocho station, along the river, you pass through the Parque Forestal (see below), before coming back to Plaza Baquedano.

Between the Parque Forestal, Plaza Baquedano and the Alameda is the Lastarria neighbourhood (Universidad Católica metro). For those interested in antique furniture, objets d'art and old books, the area is worth a visit, especially the Plaza Mulato Gil de Castro (Cale José V. Lastarria 305). Occasional shows are put on in the square, on which are the Museo Arqueológico de Santiago in a restored house, a bookshop (*Librería Latinoamericana*), handicraft and antique shops, and art gallery, the Instituto de Arte Contemporáneo and the *Pergola de la Plaza* restaurant. Nearby, on Lastarria, are the Jardín Lastarria, a cul-de-sac of craft and antique shops (No.293), *Gutenberg, Lafourcade y Cía*, an antiquarian bookseller (No.307), the Ciné Biógrafo (No. 131) and, at the corner with Merced,

---

**Santiago Orientation: Key to map**

1. Plaza de Armas; 2. Cerro Santa Lucía; 3. Plaza de la Libertad; 4. Plaza de la Constitución; 5. Plaza Baquedano; 6. Parque Forestal; 31. Airport bus; 32. Parque O'Higgins; 33. Plaza Ercilla; 34. Parque Quinta Normal, and Museo del Ferrocarril; 35. Museo de Historica Natural; 36. Museo de la Aviación; 37. Cerro San Cristóbal; 38. Funicular; 39. Virgen; 40. Observatory of the Catholic University; 41 Teleférico; 42. Jardín Zoológico; 43. Museo de los Tajamares/Parque Balmaceda; 44. Providencia district; 45. Bellavista district; 46. Los Leones; 47. Former Mapocho station; 48. Market; 49. Sernatur; 50. Conaf; 51. Palacio Cousiño.

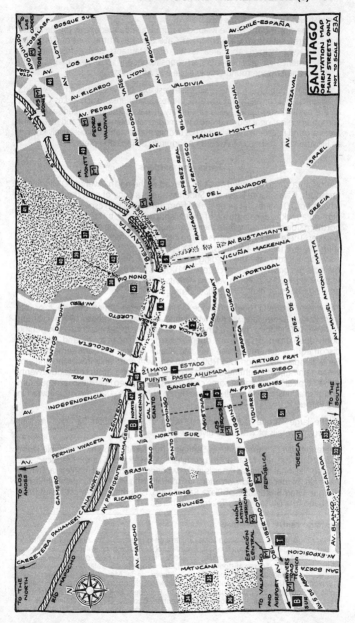

SANTIAGO
ORIENTATION MAP
MAIN STREETS ONLY
NOT TO SCALE 53A

the Instituto Chileno-Francés (see below).

On the north bank of the Mapocho from Plaza Baquedano is the Bellavista district, stretching from Calle Loreto to Calle Concha. At the foot of Cerro San Cristóbal (see below), this area is full of restaurants and cafés, theatres, entertainments, art galleries and craft shops (especially those selling lapis lazuli, a semi-precious stone found only in Chile and Afghanistan).

East of Plaza Baquedano, the main east-west axis of the city becomes Avenida Providencia which heads out towards the residential areas, such as Las Condes, at the eastern and upper levels of the city. It passes the new headquarters of Sernatur (the national tourist board), the modern shopping, office and restaurant areas around Pedro de Valdivia and Los Leones metro stations (collectively known as Providencia), to become Avenida Apoquindo at Tobalaba metro.

## Parks and Gardens

Cerro Santa Lucía, bounded by Calle Merced to the north, Avenida O'Higgins to the south, Calles Santa Lucía and Subercaseaux is a cone of rock rising steeply to a height of 70 metres. It can be scaled from the Caupolicán esplanade, on which, high on a rock, stands a statue of that Mapuche leader, but the ascent from the northern side of the hill, where there is an equestrian statue of Diego de Almagro, is easier. There are striking views of the city from the top (reached by a series of stairs), where there is a fortress, the Batería Hidalgo (the platform of which is its only colonial survival—the building is closed). Even on smoggy days, the view of the sunset is good; the Cerro closes at 2100. It is best to descend the eastern side, to see the small Plaza Pedro Valdivia with its waterfalls and statue of Valdivia. The area is famous, at night, for its gay community.

The great Parque O'Higgins (Parque O'Higgins metro station on Line 2, or bus from Parque Baquedano via Avs. Mackenna and Matta), is about 10 blocks south of Avenida O'Higgins. It has a small lake, playing fields, tennis courts, swimming pool (open from 5 Dec.), an open-air stage for local songs and dances, a discothèque, the racecourse of the Club Hípico, an amusement park, Fantasilandia, admission US$1.50 (open on weekends only in winter, and not when raining), kite-fighting contests on Sunday, and a group of about twenty good "typical" restaurants, some craft shops, the Museo del Huaso, an aquarium and a small insect and shellfish museum at El Pueblito. Cars are not allowed in the Parque.

In the large Parque Quinta Normal, north of the Estación Central, are four museums, details of which are given below.

There are several other parks in Santiago, but perhaps the most notable is the Parque Forestal, due N of Santa Lucía hill and immediately S of the Mapocho. The Museo Nacional de Bellas Artes is in the wooded grounds and is an extraordinary example of neo-classical architecture (details below). The Parque Balmaceda (Parque Gran Bretaña), E of Plaza Baquedano, is perhaps the most beautiful in Santiago (the Museo de los Tajamares is here).

---

## Santiago centre: Key to map

1. Plaza de Armas; 2. Cerro Santa Lucía; 3. Plaza de la Libertad; 4. Plaza de la Constitución; 5. Plaza Baquedano; 6. Parque Forestal; 7. Cathedral; 8. Archbishop's Palace; 9. San Francisco Church and Museo de Arte Colonial; 10. Santo Domingo; 11. Palacio de la Moneda; 12. Municipalidad; 13. Museo Histórico Nacional; 14. Congress; 15. Palacio de la Justicia; 16. Museo de la Santiago/Casa Colorada; 17. Museo de la Merced; 18. Museo de Arte Precolombino; 19. Museo de Bellas Artes; 20. Biblioteca Nacional; 21. Teatro Municipal; 22. Bolsa de Comercio; 23. Universidad de Chile; 24. Club de la Unión; 25. Plaza de Mulato Gil de Castro/Lastarria neighbourhood; 26. Argentine Embassy; 27. Post Offices; 28. CTC Telephone Office; 29. Entel Telephone Office; 30. Federación de Andinismo; 31. Airport bus.

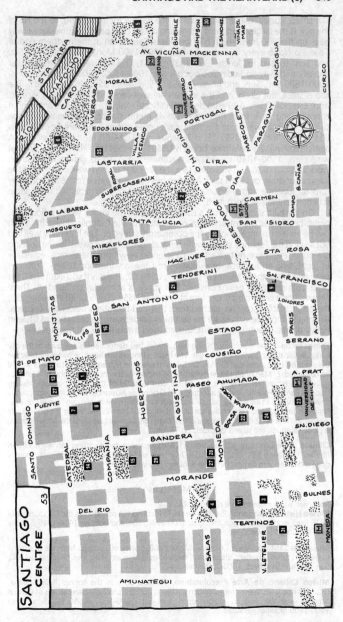

SANTIAGO
CENTRE
53

The sharp, conical hill of San Cristóbal, the Parque Metropolitano, to the NE of the city, is the largest and most interesting of the city's parks. A funicular railway goes up the 300-metre-high hill from Plaza Caupolicán at the northern end of Calle Pío Nono every few minutes from 1000-1900 Mon.-Fri., 0900-1930 Sat. and Sun. (closed for lunch 1330-1430); US$1, US$1.15 return. The funicular passes on its way up Jardín Zoológico (open 1000-1300, 1500-1800 weekdays, 1000-1800 Sat., Sun. and holidays, US$1.25 in week, US$1.40 weekends). The zoo is small, but clean, and the animals are well-cared for. A *teleférico* ascends from Estación Oasis, Av. Pedro de Valdivia Norte (only taxis go there, although it is not a long walk from Pedro de Valdivia metro station), via Tupahue to the summit, a short way from the funicular's upper station. The fare from Oasis is US$1.80 to the top, US$1.15 to Tupahue and US$1.80 return to Tupahue. A combined funicular/teleférico ticket is US$2. The *teleférico* runs 1000-1930 at weekends, 1500-1830 weekdays (in summer only), so to get to Tupahue on weekdays out of season you must take the funicular up and walk down from the summit (or drive, or take a taxi). An open bus operated by the *teleférico* company runs to Tupahue and the summit from the Pío Nono terminal with the same schedule as the *teleférico* itself.

On the hill's summit stands a colossal statue of the Virgin, which is floodlit at night; beside it is the astronomical observatory of the Catholic University which can be visited on application to the observatory's director. The hill is very well laid out around the Tupahue station, with terraces, gardens, and paths; in one building is a good, expensive restaurant with a splendid view from the terrace, especially at night, and an Enoteca, or exhibition of Chilean wines and tastery. (You can taste one of the three "wines of the day", US$0.30, and buy if you like.) The Casa de la Cultura has art exhibitions and free concerts at midday on Sundays. There are two good swimming pools: one at Tupahue, US$2.20 (US$2.70 at weekends); the other, Antilen, can be reached from the road that starts below the Enoteca. Also in the Tupahue vicinity are the Botanical Gardens, with a collection of Chilean native plants, beautifully laid out, guided tours available (recommended).

**Things to do** Ballet is popular. During the summer, free performances are given in the city parks, but seats are usually hard to get. The theatre (houses are listed below) is more active than in most Latin American capitals. Daily lists of events in *El Mercurio* and *La Epoca* should be consulted; *El Mercurio's Wikén* magazine on Friday has the most comprehensive listings.

During November there is a free art fair on the banks of the Mapocho River flowing through Parque Forestal, lasting a fortnight. In October or November there are a sumptuous flower show and an annual agricultural and industrial show (known as Fisa) in Parque Cerrillos. Religious festivals and ceremonies continue throughout Holy Week, when a priest ritually washes the feet of 12 men. The image of the Virgen del Carmen (patron of the Armed Forces) is carried through the streets by cadets on 16 July.

**Climate** In the central region the climate is Mediterranean: temperatures can reach 33°C in January, but fall to 13°C (3°C at night) in July. Days are usually hot, the nights cool. There is quite a difference in climate between Santiago and Valparaíso.

## Museums

Note, almost all museums are closed on Monday.

**Museo Histórico Nacional**, Plaza de Armas 951, covers the period from the Conquest until 1925 (well worthwhile); open Tues.-Sat. 1000-1730, Sun. and holidays 1000-1345 (Sunday free, but donation welcome).

**Museo de Santiago**, Casa Colorada, Merced 860, history of Santiago from the Conquest to modern times, excellent displays and models, guided tours; open Tues.-Sat., 1000-1800, Sun. and holidays (free), 1000-1300, free.

**Museo Chileno de Arte Precolombino**, Bandera 361, in the former Real Aduana, recommended, representative exhibition of objects from the precolombian cultures of Central America and the Andean region; open Tues.-Sat. 1000-1800 (US$0.35), Sun. (free) 1000-1400. Booklet, US$0.35.

**Museo Iglesia de la Merced**, MacIver 341, colonial religious art and archaeological collection from Easter Island; Tues.-Fri. 1000-1300, 1500-1800, Sat. 1000-1300.

**Museo de Arte Sagrado**, in the Cathedral, open Monday only, 1030-1300, 1530-1900, free.

**Museo de Arte Colonial**, Londres 4, beside Iglesia San Francisco, religious art, including one room with 54 paintings of the life of St Francis; in the cloisters is a room containing Gabriela Mistral's Nobel medal; also a collection of locks; Tues.-Sat. 1000-1800, Sun. 1000-1400, US$0.25.

**The Palacio de la Alhambra**, Compañía 1340 (with Amunátegui) is a national monument sponsored by the Society of Arts; it stages exhibitions of paintings as well as having a permanent display; open Mon.-Fri. 1100-1300, 1700-1900, T 80875.

**Biblioteca Nacional**, Moneda 650, temporary exhibitions of books, book illustrations, documents, posters, etc.

At Calle Dieciocho 438, some 5 blocks S of the Alameda, is the **Palacio Cousiño**, a large elaborate mansion amongst crumbling buildings and shanties; it contains some good oriental rugs and 19th-century European furniture. It is run by the Corporación Cultural as a museum; open Tues.-Sun. 1000-1300, free, but donations welcome. Visitors must be accompanied by a guide and wear cloth bootees to protect the floors.

**Museo Nacional de Historia Natural**, in the Parque Quinta Normal, has exhibitions on zoology, botany, mineralogy, anthropology, ethnography and archaeology; open Tues.-Fri. 1000-1230, 1400-1730, Sat.-Sun. 1100-1300, 1500-1700, US$0.35 (Sunday free). The **Museo Ferroviario** is also in the Quinta Normal; it has 13 steam engines built between 1884 and 1953 (open Tues.-Fri., 1000-1215, 1500-1700, Sat., Sun. and holidays, 1100-1315, 1500-1715). The **Museo Aeronáutico**, by the Parque Quinta Normal (Av. Portales 3530) is also worth a visit; Tues.-Sun. 1000-1800, free, T 90888. Also in the Quinta Normal is the **Museo Ciencia y Tecnología**, open same hours as **Ferroviario**. Nearby, at Av. O'Higgins 3349, is the excellent **Planetarium**, open Weds.-Fri. 1900, Sat.-Sun. 1700, 1900 and 2030, T 762624.

**Museo Arqueológico de Santiago**, in Plaza Mulato Gil de Castro, Lastarria 307, temporary exhibitions of Chilean archaeology, anthropology and precolombian art; open Tues.-Sat., 1100-1400, 1600-2000, Sun. 1100-1400, free.

In the Parque Forestal is the **Museo Nacional de Bellas Artes**, which has a large display of Chilean and foreign painting and sculpture, and contemporary art exhibitions are held several times a year (Tues.-Sat. 1000-1800, Sun. and holidays 1000-1330; free on Sunday). In the west wing of the building is the **Museo de Arte Popular Americano**, a collection of North and South American folk art (this wing is awaiting renovation, so only a small part of the exhibition is on display). Similarly, the **Museo de Arte Contemporáneo** is on limited view as it is normally housed in the west wing.

**Museo Tajamares del Mapocho**, Parque Balmaceda, Av. Providencia 222, an exhibition of the 17th and 18th century walls built to protect the city from flooding by the river, and of the subsequent canalization; Tues.-Sat. 1000-1800, Sun. 1000-1330.

**Museo Benjamín Vicuña Mackenna**, Av. V. Mackenna 94, recording the life and works of the 19th century Chilean historian and biographer; occasional exhibitions.

In Parque O'Higgins, at Pueblito: **Museo del Huaso**, a small, interesting collection of criollo clothing and tools; Tues.-Fri. 1000-1300, 1430-1715, Sat., Sun. and holidays 1000-1800, free; **Municipal Aquarium** at Local 9, Tues.-Fri. 1000-2000 (till 2100 Sat., Sun., holidays—small charge); **Museo de Insectos y Caracoles**, Local 12, a collection of indigenous items, same hours as the aquarium but open till 2200 at weekends and holidays.

**Museo de la Escuela Militar**, Los Militares 4500, Las Condes, with displays on O'Higgins, the Conquest, the Pacific War and a room devoted to the medals of Gen. Pinochet, Mon.-Fri. 0930-1230, 1500-1800, Sat. 0930-1430, Sun. 1430-1800, free.

**Museo de Artes Decorativas**, Casas Lo Matta, Av. Presidente Kennedy 9350, Vitacura, a new, beautiful museum containing Don Hernán Garcés Silva's bequest to the nation: antique silverplate from South America and Europe, 16th-18th century Spanish colonial and European furniture, 15th century Books of Hours, housed in an 18th century country mansion. Guided tours available; by bus, take Intercomunal No.4 from Mapocho station, or take a taxi; in either case ask to be let out at "Casas lo Matta".

The house of Pablo Neruda, the poet, **La Chascona**, is at F. Márquez de la Plata 0192, Bellavista, now restored after earthquake damage in 1985 and headquarters of the Fundación Pablo Neruda. For an appointment to visit the poet's library, art and photo collections, T 778741 (**see also page 542**).

**Hotels** Check if breakfast and 18% tax is included in the price quoted.

Hotels in the upper price brackets in the Providencia area are: *San Cristóbal Sheraton*, Av. Santa María 1742, T 745-528, FAX 223-6656, L, with all facilities, also *Sheraton Towers*, slightly cheaper; *Santa María*, Av. Santa María 2050, T 232-6614, A+; *Los Españoles*, Los Españoles 2539, T 232-1824, A+; all three north of the Río Mapocho. *Orly*, Pedro de Valdivia 27, close to Pedro de Valdivia metro station, T 232-8225, A+, but has smaller, cheaper rooms with less comfort, small, comfortable hotel but reported unreliable over reservations, has apartments for rent on Juana de Arco, just off Av. Pedro de Valdivia, 3 blocks S of Av. Providencia, good, US$70 a day (reductions may be possible). *Posada del Salvador*, Av. Eliodoro Yáñez 893, nearest metro Salvador, T 492-072, B with bath, friendly, English, French, German, Italian spoken.

Expensive hotels in the central area: *San Francisco Kempinski*, Alameda 816, T 392-832, FAX 397-826, Lufthansa affiliated, 5-star, L, good; *Holiday Inn Crowne Plaza*, Av. B. O'Higgins 136, T 333-552, FAX 336-015, L, all facilities, also good; also in L range, *Carrera*, Teatinos 180, T 698-2011, *El Conquistador*, Miguel Cruchaga 920, T 696-5599, and *Galerías*, San Antonio 65, T 384-011; *Tupahue*, San Antonio 477, T 383-810, A+. *City*, Compañía 1063, T 724-526, A, old-fashioned, clean, rec.; *Conde Ansúrez*, Av. República 25, T 698-3779, A, convenient for central station and southern bus terminal, clean, helpful, safe, luggage stored (100 metres from metro República); *Libertador*, Av. O'Higgins 853, T394-212, A, helpful, rec., will store luggage, good restaurant, bar, roof top pool; *Riviera*, 'Miraflores 106, B without breakfast; *Panamericano*, Teatinos 320 y Huérfanos, T 723-060, A, comfortable, serves popular business lunch between 1230 and 1530; on Huérfanos, *Don Tito*, No.578, T 391-987, A+, good, English spoken; *Santa Lucía*, No. 779, 4th floor, T 398-201, garage 2 blocks away, A, clean, comfortable, but run down; *; Gran Palace*, No. 1178, T 712-551, A, with shower, clean, noisy rooms facing street (others quiet), good restaurant. *Hostal del Parque*, Merced 294, just across from Parque Forestal, T 392-694, L, excellent; *Foresta*, Subercaseaux 353, T396-262, A+, and *Monte Carlo*, Subercaseaux 209, T 339-905, both at bottom of Santa Lucía, the latter rec., modern, restaurant, with heating, A-A+.

Mid-price hotels in the centre: *Apart-Hotel Agustinas*, Agustinas 1990, T 711-002, clean, quiet at back, B, rec., secure parking; *Du Maurier*, Moneda 1512, T 724-257, B, handy for catching early (0630) Aerobus Tour Express; *Residencia Alicia Adasme*, Moneda 2055, T 6960787, hot water, friendly, with breakfast, B; *Miraflores*, Riquelme 555, C, clean, good value; *Imperio*, O'Higgins 2879, near central station, T 97774, B with bath, good restaurant; *Vegas*, Londres 49, B, clean, TV/radio, decent-sized rooms, more with breakfast; *Hotel Turismo Japón*, Almte. Barroso 160, T 698-4500, B, helpful, clean, good breakfast, manager speaks English, rec.; *España*, Morandé 510, T696-6066, D without bath, hot water, clean, friendly; *Cervantes*, Morandé 631, C, overpriced, T 96-5318, ; *Residencial Tabita* (Tabita Gutiérrez), Principe de Gales 81 (cul-de-sac off Moneda 1452, T 715-700), C with breakfast, safe, central, temperamental hot showers upstairs, popular; *São Paulo*, San Antonio 357, T 398-031/2/3, C with bath, clean, good value. *Santa Victoria*, Vicuña MacKenna 435, T 345-753, C, quiet, small, safe, family run, rec.

Cheaper central hotels: *Residencial Londres*, Londres 54, T 382-215, near San Francisco Church, former mansion, Victorian furniture, some gloomy rooms, otherwise rec. repeatedly, D, more with bath (don't confuse with *Hotel Londres* opp., which is not rec.), breakfast US$0.65 extra; *París*, Calle París 813, nearby, D with bath, quiet, clean, also short-stay; *Residencial Opera*, París 898, E without bath, no hot water, basic, clean, friendly; *Residencial Mery*, Pasaje República 36, off 0-100 block of República (T 696-8883), big green building down an alley, D, hot showers, quiet, rec.; *Res. Alemana*, República 220 (no sign), T 712-388, nr. Metro República, D, hot water, clean, pleasant atmosphere, good cheap meals available, rec. *Res. Santo Domingo*, Santo Domingo 735, near MacIver, central, D with full board (or without, shared bath), good cheap lunches Mon.-Fri., but small, dirty rooms; *Indiana*, Rosas 1339, T714-251, convenient for buses to centre, only front rooms with bath, hot water, back rooms poor, basic, bed bugs, D; *Gran*, Morandé y San Pablo, E-D (with bath), simple but OK, short and long stay; *Nuevo Valparaíso*, Morandé 791, F without bath, noisy, E with bath, quieter, basic; *Souvenir*, Amunátegui 856, F, old, rambling place with chatty parrots.

Convenient accommodation for southern bus terminal and Estación Central: *Residencial Midi*, Av. Unión Americana 134, E, huge rooms with ancient furniture, laundry facilities; *Antiguo Palace*, San Alfonso 24, 2 blocks E of Central Station, 1 metro stop from southern bus station, E, good value, clean. Those on República (see above) are only 2-3 metro stops away. On F. Reich, 100-200 block, behind the bus terminal are *Roma* and *México*, both F p.p. Sra Isaura Tobar Urra, Federico Scott 130, N side of Alameda opp. bus terminal, E p.p. without breakfast, good meals available, hot water, clean, good. *Marconi*, O'Higgins 2532, E without bath, clean, cheap rooms on Avenida, very noisy, 15 mins. from bus terminal.

Around the northern bus terminal, *Caribe*, San Martín 821, E p.p., clean, basic, hot showers, convenient to centre and bus station, mainly short-stay. Many on Gen. MacKenna (e.g. *San Felipe*, at No. 1248, T 713816, F p.p., rec.), between the bus terminal and Cal y Canto Metro. **N.B.** Many hotels on Morandé, Gen. Mackenna, San Martín and San Pablo are convenient for northern bus terminal, but are in the red light district and are therefore cheap in both senses of the word.

As the above list shows there is little good accommodation under US$10 a night. Travellers can find comfortable guesthouse lodging through *Amigos de Todo el Mundo*, Av. Bulnes 285, dept. 201, PO Box 52861 Correo Central, T 726-525, Sr Arturo Navarrete, prices from US$6 with breakfast, other meals extra, monthly rates available, rec. *Casa Paxi*, Av. Llico 968, 1 block from Metro Departamental, E p.p. in home of rec. guide Pieter van Bunningen; Sra Marta, Amengual 035, Alameda Alt. 4.400, T 797592, lado Norte (metro Ecuador), E p.p., good family accommodation; Alicia Bravo, Artemio Gutiérrez 1328, T 556-6620, F p.p., helpful, friendly. *Casa del Estudiante Americano*, Huérfanos 1891, F p.p., good dormitory accommodation—acts as youth hostel out of season, must be in bed by 2200 and out by 1000 (Metro Los Héroes—7 blocks from centre over motorway).

For longer stay accommodation, read the classified ads in *El Mercurio*, flats, homes and family *pensiones* are listed by district. Furnished apartments in the centre cost between US$250 and US$320 a month, or in Providencia about US$420; if you want a phone you may have to provide an *aval*, or guarantor, to prove you will pay the bill, or else a huge deposit will be asked for. Estate agents handle apartments, but often charge 1/3 of the first month's rent as commission, while a month's rent in advance and 1 month's deposit are required. Rec. apartments are *Edificio San Rafael*, Miraflores 264, T 330-289, Fax 222-5629 US$30 a day double, minimum 3 days, US$275 a month, very central. Staying with a family is an economical and interesting option for a few months. A recommended estate agent is Sra. Carmen Martínez Jara, Av. 11 de Septiembre 2155, Ed. Panorámico, Torre B, oficina 502, T 251-7331/231-595. Providencia and Las Condes are residential districts, but the latter is some way from the centre; the area west of Plaza Baquedano, east of Cerro Santa Lucía and south of Parque Forestal is good and central; or you could try Bellavista, but not Calle Pío Nono where the nightlife goes on until 0300.

**Youth Hostel** information available from Av. Providencia 2594, oficina 421 (between metros Los Leones and Tobalaba), T 231-5649 (worth getting list of YH addresses around country as these change year by year—even in Santiago). Supplies student cards (no questions), US$8. Hostels in the capital, Grajales 2013, very popular, book in advance, T 726100, Almte. Latorre 447-449, T 698-8315, not rec., dirty, noisy and run down, and Sazie 2107, 1 block from the other two, rec., not usually fully booked, T 722-269; Metro República for all 3, G p.p.

**Camping** The campsite on San Cristóbal hill has been closed because of muggings. Alternatives are the Farellones road near the river; or S of Santiago near Puente Alto (take Av. J. Pedro Alessandri S to Las Vizcachas and La Obra where there is a small park on left side of road). At Km. 25 S of city on Panamericana, Esso garage offers only a vacant lot near highway. Club Camping Maki, and Casino Camping, both 70 km. from Santiago, **see page 563.** Rec. camping at Tenis Centrum Alemán, Parcela 68, Santa Ana de Chena, Camino Lonquén, run by Dieter and Myriam Mittelstaedt (take Panamericana Sur for 9 km., turn right at blue and white water tower, then 4.5 km. on road to Los Espejo, look for sign, then 4 km. on right; Flota del Talagante bus from Terminal Sur); foot, showers, small restaurant, US$1.50 p.p. per day. Standard camping gas cartridges can be bought at Unisport, Providencia 2503, or Santo Domingo 1079. Other equipment for camper-vans from Bertonati Hnos, Manuel Montt 2385. Caravans (US model Tioga) can be rented from Castanera Turismo, Av. Providencia 1072, local 14 D. Tent repairs: Juan Soto, Silva Vildosola 890, Paradero 1, Gran Avenida, San Miguel, Santiago, T 555-8329. Reinaldo Lippi, Toesca 2171, makes tents, sleeping bags, back packs, etc., and does repairs, most helpful. Camping goods from Club Andino and Federación de Andinismo (**see page 564 below**): expensive because these articles are imported. Cheaper boots from Edvobal, Paseo Las Palmas 2242, metro Los Leones, T 251 5488. Repair of camping stoves at Casa Italiana, Tarapacá 1120.

**Restaurants** In addition to those at the main hotels and those in Parque O'Higgins there are, in the centre of the city: *Da Carla*, MacIver 577, Italian food, very good, expensive; also Italian, *San Marco*, Huérfanos 618, serving seafood and vegetarian as well, not cheap (US$12 p.p. with drinks) but excellent; *Le Due Torri*, San Antonio 258, expensive, closed Sun.; *Les Assassins*, Merced 297, French, rec.; *La Omelette*, Agustinas near AmEx, clean and good, closes 2100. *Gran Parrillada la Brasileña*, San Diego 265, huge portions, rec.

Seafood: *Don Lucho, Rey del Pescado*, Banderas 848, good food but poor atmosphere; *Atelier*, Tenderini 171, rec., good, but expensive; *El 27 de Nueva York*, Nueva York 27, central, good; *Savory Tres*, Ahumada 327, good and reasonable, particularly seafood. Some of the best seafood restaurants are to be found in the Mercado Central (by Cal y Canto metro), or on the other side of the Mapocho from here.

For mainly local food in the centre: *Chez Henry*, on Plaza de Armas, excellent *empanadas, parrillada de mariscos* a speciality, dining room at back of butcher's shop has live music and dancing, a/c is cold (also does take away meals), also has a delicatessen at Alameda 847, which is highly rec.; also in Plaza de Armas, *Raison d'Or*, good *pastel de choclo*, pleasant place to have a drink and watch the world go by; on Phillips, the small street off the east side of the Plaza is *La Zanahora*, clean, good lunches. *Torres*, O'Higgins 1570, traditional bar/restaurant, good food, reasonable prices; *Fuente de Soda Orion*, O'Higgins y Manuel Rodríguez, cheap, good pizzas; *Silvestre*, Huérfanos 956, open 0800-2400, good buffet-style, US$3; *Mermoz*, Huérfanos 1048, good; *Bar Nacional No. 1*, Huérfanos 1151 and *Bar Nacional No. 2*, Bandera 317, good restaurants; *Guima*, Huérfanos y Teatinos, good, reasonable prices, good value *almuerzo*; *Café Dante*, Merced 801 y San Antonio, for *pastel de choclo*; *Bar Central*, San Pablo 1063, typical food, rec.; *Verdijo*, Morandé 526, good food, noisy, cheap and popular; *Bar-restaurant Inés de Suárez*, Morandé 558, cheap and good; *El Lugar de Don Quijote*, café, and *Parrilladas de Don Quijote*, restaurant, good, corner Morandé and Catedral; two doors away is *Congreso*, popular at lunchtime. *Los Adobes de Argomedo*, Argomedo 411 y Lira, hacienda-style, Chilean food and spectacular floor show including cueca dancing, salsa and folk, Mon.-Sat., only place in winter which has this type of entertainment on a Monday. There are many cheap places along Paseo Ahumada, between the Plaza de Armas and the Alameda.

Oriental in the centre: *Guo Fung*, Moneda 1549, rec.; *Yuet Wong Chan*, Agustinas 715, delicious food; *Chifa Kam Thu*, Santo Domingo 769 y 21 de Mayo, good value; *Pai Fu*, Santa Rosa 101 y París, good; all Chinese. *Izakaya Yoro*, Merced 456, good, cheap, Japanese.

In the Lastarria and Bellavista neighbourhoods: *La Pergola de la Plaza* in Plaza Mulato Gil de Castro, but better still, and close by, is *Quiche Lorraine* in the Instituto Chileno-Francés, Merced 298 y Lastarria, highly rec. for food, drink and ambience. *El Biógrafo*, Villavicencio 398, bohemian style, good cheeses, rec.; *Café Universitario*, Alameda 395 y Victoria Subercaseaux (near Sta. Lucía), good, cheap *almuerzos. Eladio*, Pío Nono, nr. foot of San Cristóbal funicular, good steaks, but expensive; also near the funicular station on Pío Nono are *La Puña* and *Los Ladrillos*, popular, lively; *Café del Cerro*, Ernesto Pinto Lagarrigue 192, T 778-308, with live music (check *El Mercurio* for programme), US$2 door charge, highly rec. *Zingarrella*, Pío Nono, Italian, good. Many cafés/bars/restaurants on Pío Nono.

Outside the centre, in Providencia: *La Pizza Nostra*, Providencia 1979, sells good Italian food as well as pizzas, real coffee, pricey; *da Renato*, Mardoqueo Fernández 138 (metro Los Leones), Italian, good; *El Parrón*, Providencia 1188, *parrilladas*, the local dice game of "dudo" is played in the bar; *Lomit's*, Providencia 1980, good; *Gatsby*, Providencia at Pedro de Valdivia, American food, as-much-as-you-can-eat buffet US$8, lunch/dinner US$10, snack bar open till 2400, tables outside in warm weather, good; *Aquí Está Coco*, La Concepción

236, good seafood, expensive; *del Centro Catalá*, Av. Suecia 428 near Lota, good, reasonably-priced. Recommended places on El Bosque Norte, Providencia: *München*, No. 204, German, *Angus*, No. 0111, international.

Many first-class restaurants out of the centre can be found in the Las Condes district, including grills, Chilean cuisine (often with music), French cuisine and Chinese. They tend to be more expensive than central restaurants. Good examples are *Canta Gallo*, Av. Las Condes 12345 (Las Condes bus passes it); *Seriatutix*, Av. Colón 5137, restaurant and disco, live music, café, great atmosphere; *Praga*, Vitacura 3917, Czech; *Mexicano*, Vitacura 2916, Mexican; *Martín Carrera*, Isidora Goyenechea 3471, good nouvelle cuisine.

Vegetarian restaurants: *El Rápido*, Banderas 347, excellent *empanadas*, fast service for busy people; *El Huerto*, Orrego Luco 56, rec., open daily, live music Fri. and Sat. evenings; *El Naturista*, Moneda 846, popular, rec., also has a branch in Providencia, Orrego Luco Sur 42; *El Vegetariano*, Huérfanos 827, Galería Victoria, expensive, mixed reports; *Eos*, Av. Francisco Bilbao 3008, Providencia (metro Tobalaba), excellent, "no smoking, no alcohol"; *Govinda*, MacIver 531.

**Cafés and Bars** Many bars (some serve snacks) on Pedro Valdivia, very popular. *Café Paula*, several branches, e.g. Estado at entrance to Galería España, excellent coffee and cake, good breakfast, also on San Antonio opp. the Teatro Municipal. *Café Colonia*, MacIver 133, rec.; *Café Santos*, Huérfanos 1011 y Ahumada, popular for "onces" (afternoon tea). Try *Café Haití* and *Café Caribe*, both on Paseo Ahumada and elsewhere in centre and Providencia, for delicious coffee. *Tip-Top Galetas* rec. for freshly baked biscuits, branches throughout the city, e.g. Merced 867. *Villa Real*, Pedro de Valdivia 079, rec.; *Salón de Té Tavelli*, Drugstore precinct, Providencia 2124, rec. *Café de la Dulcería Las Palmas*, Antonia López de Bello 190 (Bellavista), good pastries and lunches; *La Casona de San Ysidro*, Alameda 151, T 334-046, student-type café with Chilean folk music Fri. and Sat. night, rec.; *Bob Bon Oriental*, Merced 345, superb Turkish cakes. *Cafetería Berri*, Rosal 321, live music at weekends; *Rincón de las Brujas*, O'Higgins 564, good music.

*Geo Pub*, Encomenderos 83, owner Francisco Valle speaks English, pub and restaurant with travel films once a week in winter, music occasionally, popular with travellers, rec.; *Phone Box Pub*, Providencia 1670, T 496627, slightly more expensive; *Violin Pub*, Providencia 1684, good lunch; *Golden Bell Inn*, Ernando Aguirre 27, English pub atmosphere, popular with expatriates; *Cross Keys Pub*, Las Bellotas 270 local 5, opp. *La Mia Pappa*, near Los Leones metro, English, with darts, pints, etc., good value. Note that almost all hotel bars are closed Sun.

For snacks and excellent ice cream, try *Coppellia*, Av. Providencia 2211, *Bravissimo*, same avenida No. 1406, and *El Toldo Azul*, at No. 1936.

**Clubs** Ñuñoa (T 223 7846), with swimming pool, tennis courts and school; Polo y Equitación San Cristóbal; Chess Club, Alameda O'Higgins 898, Mon.-Sat. 1800, lively.

**Shopping** *El Almacén Campesino*, Purísima 289, Bellavista, handicrafts from all over Chile. Best bargains are handicraft articles, black pottery (best bought in Pomaire, 50 km. away, **see page 563**) and beautiful wrought copper and bronze. Good shops for local copper work are *Bozzo* at Ahumada 12 in the centre, and at Av. Providencia 2125. The gemstone lapis lazuli is best bought in the numerous outlets on Bellavista (shop around), but is cheaper around the market. *H. Stern* jewellery shops are located at the *San Cristóbal Sheraton* and *Carrera* hotels, and at the International Airport. *Cema-Chile* (Centro de Madres), Portugal 351 and at Universidad de Chile metro stop, *Artesanía Popular Chilena*, Av. Providencia 2322 (near Los Leones metro), and *Artesanía Chilena*, Estado 337, have a good selection of handicrafts, and so do *Cema-Chile* branches in the provinces. *Talleres Solidarios*, 1st floor Vicaría de la Solidaridad, on Plaza de Armas (next door to the Cathedral). *Pel y Pel*, Pedro de Valdivia 20, fur and leather articles, good. Antique stores in Plaza Mulato Gil de Castro and elsewhere on J.V. Lastarria (Merced end).

Beside and behind the Iglesia de los Dominicos, on Av. Nueva Apoquindo 9085, is *Los Graneros del Alba*, or *El Pueblo de Artesanía*, open daily except Mon., 1130-1900; all types of ware on sale, classes given in some shops. *Restaurant El Granero* is here. To get there, take a small, green Los Dominicos bus from Av. Providencia, or Apoquindo bus, as long as either is marked "Camino del Alba", or take an Apoquindo bus, similarly marked, from Metro Escuela Militar; get out at the children's playground at the junction of Apoquindo y Camino del Alba, at the foot of the hill leading up to the church, and walk up.

Mercado Central, between Puente y 21 de Mayo by the Río Mapocho (Cal y Canto metro) is excellent but quite expensive; there is a cheaper market on the opposite bank of the river. *Centro Artesanal Santa Lucía*, on Av. B. O'Higgins (Santa Lucía metro) has a wide variety of woollen goods, jewellery, wood, etc.; there are other craft markets in an alleyway, 1 block S of Av. B. O'Higgins between A. Prat and San Diego, and at Pío Nono y Av. Santa María, Bellavista. The shopping arcade at the Central Station is good value, likewise the street market outside. Many charity clothes shops around Bandera 600 block, good for winter clothes for travellers who need them. There is a good outside fruit market at Puente 815, by Frutería Martínez. There is an antique fair on Sun. (1000-1400) in the summer and a Fiesta de Quasimodo on the first Sunday after Easter at Lo Barnechea, 30 min. by bus from Santiago.

**Bookshops** Book prices tend to be high compared with Europe. *Librería Albers*, Merced 820, local 7 and Av. Tobalaba 032 (Spanish, English and German—good selection, cheaper than most); *Librería Altamira*, Huérfanos 669; *Feria Chilena del Libro*, Huérfanos nr. McIver, and in Drugstore precinct, Providencia 2124; *Librería Inglesa* (*Librería Kuatro*), Pedro de Valdivia 47, English books, sells *South American Handbook*. There are many bookshops in the Pedro de Valdivia area on Providencia. Second-hand English books from arcade at San Diego 121, 1½ blocks south of Alameda and *Librería El Patio*, Providencia 1652, nearest Metro stop Pedro de Valdivia; exchange for best deal. Also, from Henry at Metro station, Los Leones and *Books*, next to *Phone Box Pub*, in the courtyard at Providencia 1670 (the artist's shop in same precinct sells attractive cards). *Librairie Française*, books and newspapers, Calle del Estado 337. As well as the antiquarian bookshop mentioned above in the Lastarria district, there are other good antiquarian bookshops on Merced around the corner from Lastarria, e.g. *América del Sur Librería Editorial*, No. 306, *Libros Antiguos El Cid*, No. 344. Many stalls on Paseo Ahumada/Huérfanos sell foreign newspapers and journals.

**Camera Repairs** Harry Müller, Ahumada 312, oficina 402, rec.; speaks German and English. For Minolta and Canon repairs, Asatecnic, Nueva York 52, Of.302, rec. Many developers on Ahumada offer 24-hr service of varying quality.

**Buses and Taxis** There are three kinds of buses: the small fast kind called *liebres* (hares) which cost US$0.30-0.40 a ride; the regular buses at US$0.25, and the large buses marked Expreso, US$0.35. Taxi drivers are permitted to charge more at night, but in the day time check that the meter is set to day rates. Taxis are now abundant (black with yellow roofs), and not expensive, with a minimum charge of US$0.50 (50% surcharge on basic rate after 2230). At bus terminals, drivers will charge more—best to walk a block and flag down a cruising taxi. Large blue taxis do not have meters. There are also colectivo taxis to the suburbs, US$0.70. Visitors going outside the city should arrange the charge beforehand. The private taxi service which operates from the bottom level of *Hotel Carrera* has been rec. (same rates as city taxis).

**Underground Railway** The first line of the underground railway system (Metro) runs west-east between San Pablo and Escuela Militar, under the Alameda, and the second line runs north-south from Cal y Canto to Callejón Ovalle. The connecting station is Los Héroes. Line 3 is to be constructed between Buen Pastor and Vivaceta. The ticket for Line 1 costs 90 pesos; save queuing by buying a ten-ticket booklet (carnet), 800 pesos. The ticket for Line 2 costs 60 pesos (carnet 700 pesos). Tickets are not interchangeable. The trains are fast, quiet, and full. The first train is at 0630 (Mon.-Sat.), 0800 (Sun. and holidays), the last about 2245. Metrobus services connects with the underground railway at Lo Ovalle for southern Santiago and Escuela Militar for Vitacura, Las Condes and Apoquindo.

**Car Hire** Hertz, Avis and Budget available from airport. **Hertz** (Av. Costanera 1469, T 225-9328, and airport, T 601-9262) has a good network in Chile and cars are in good condition. **Avis** also at Eliodoro Yáñez 869, T 495-757. **Automóvil Club de Chile** car rental, Marchant Pereira 122, Providencia, T 274-4167/6261, discount for members and members of associated motoring organizations (rate for a Nissan Sunny, US$39/day with 150 km., or US$242/week, unlimited km., insurance US$6.35/day). A credit card is usually asked for when renting a vehicle. Tax of 16% is charged. If possible book a car in advance. Note that in the capital driving is restricted according to licence plate numbers; look for notices in the street.

**Theatres** Teatro Municipal, Agustinas y San Antonio, stages international opera, concerts by the Orquesta Filarmónica de Santiago, and the Ballet de Santiago, throughout the year; on Tues. at 2100 there are free operatic concerts in the Salón Claudio Arrau; tickets range from US$7 for the cheapest seats at the ballet to US$80 for the most expensive opera seats. Teatro Universidad de Chile, Plaza Baquedano, is the home of the Orquesta y Coro Sinfónica de Chile and the Ballet Nacional de Chile; prices from US$1.25-3.50 for concerts to US$1.25-13.50 for ballet.

There are a great number of theatres which stage plays in Spanish, either in the original language or translations, e.g. La Comedia, Merced 349, Abril, Huérfanos 786, Camilo

Henríquez, Amunátegui 31, Centro Arrayán, Las Condes 14891, El Galpón de los Leones, Av. Los Leones 238, El Conventillo, Bellavista 173. Four others, the Opera, Huérfanos, California, Irarrázaval 1546, Humoresque, San Ignacio 1249 and Picaresque, Recoleta 345, show mostly Folies Bergères-type revues. Outdoor rock concerts are held at the Estadio Nacional, Av. Unión Latino Americana (metro of same name), at the Teatro Teletón, Rosas 325 (excellent sound system), and elsewhere.

**Cinemas** "Ciné Arte" (quality foreign films) is very popular and a number of cinemas specialize in this type of film: El Biógrafo (Lastarria 181), Normandie (Av. B. O'Higgins 143), Cámara Chile (Miraflores 544), Espaciocal (Goyenechea y Vitacura), Tobalaba (Providencia 2563), Microciné del Barrio (López de Bello 083) and others, full details are given in the press. Other cinemas tend to show "sex, violence and war". Seats cost about US$1.25 with reductions on Wed. (elsewhere in the country the day varies).

**Night Clubs** Some of the restaurants and cafés which have shows are given above. Listings are given in *El Mercurio*, or *La Epoca*. *La Cucaracha*, Bombero Núñez 159 (Bellavista) is very popular, floorshow at 2330, US$3.50 cover charge, orchestras, dancing. Several tango clubs including *Club Troilo*, Cumming 795, cheap, unpretentious (tango classes 1800-2000, Fri. and Sun.). *El Tucano Salsateca*, P. de Valdivia 1783, 4th floor, Wed.-Sun. 2200-0600, US$2, fashionable. *Peña Nano Parra*, San Isidro 57, good folk club, cheap.

**Discotheques** *Gente*, Av. Apoquindo 4900, also *Baltas*, Av. Las Condes, both expensive, but good, US$10 p.p. Many more, mainly in the Providencia and Las Condes areas.

**Swimming Pools** Antilen (closed Mon.) and Tupahue, better, open daily 1000-1500 (Mon.-Fri., US$2, Sat.-Sun. US$3), both on Cerro San Cristóbal (check if they are open in winter, one usually is). In Parque O'Higgins, same prices. Olympic pool in Parque Araucano (nr. Arauco Shopping Centre, closest Metro E.Militar), open Tues.-Sat. 0900-1900 November-March.

**Running** The Hash House Harriers hold runs every other week; information through the British Embassy and Consulate.

**Tennis** Santiago Tennis Club; also, Club de Tenís Jaime Fillol, Rancho Melnichi. Par.4. See also Tenís Centrum Alemán, under **Camping** above.

**Bowling** Bowling Center, Av. Apoquindo 5012.

**Racecourses** Club Hípico, racing every Sun. and every other Wed. afternoon (at Viña del Mar, January-March); Hipódromo Chile every Sat. afternoon; pari-mutuel betting.

**Exchange** Banco Central de Chile, one block from Plaza Constitución, demands the minimum of formalities, although there is usually a commission charge for most transactions. **Banco O'Higgins**, Av. Agustinas, will change travellers' cheques into dollars with commission on transactions between US$100-1,000 (Mastercard or AmEx cheques). American Express, Agustinas 1360 (No. 1173 for travel information and mail collection), does not charge commission (no limit on changing cheques into dollars). **Citibank**, Ahumada 40 (no commission on its own travellers' cheques into dollars or any other currency). **Afex**, Moneda 1148 and P. de Valdivia 044, good rates. Banks, open from 0900 to 1400, but closed on Sat. Exchange houses are also closed on Sat.

Official daily exchange rates are published in *El Mercurio* and *La Epoca*. Parallel market rate can be obtained at corner of Agustinas and Ahumada and around the Moneda; agents on the street take you to exchange offices (bargain with them before going to the office, but it is safer to go to the office direct). Travellers' cheques attract a worse rate than cash on the street. Most exchange houses are on Agustinas and Huerfanos. **Financiera Ciga**, Agustinas 1287, Ugarte, Bundera 59-61, **Casa de Cambio Blancas**, opp. *Hotel Orly* on Pedro de Valdivia, and **Exprinter** are rec. for good rates, low commission, also **Inter**, Moneda 940, upstairs office at Ahumada 131 (oficina 103), **Cambios Andino**, Ahumada 1062 and **Teletour**, Bandera 191. **Sr. Fernando Sáez** (travel agent), M. Cousiño 150, Oficina 322, T 382885, for good exchange rates (and australes). **Casa de Cambio**, Calle Bombero A. Ossa 1010, Of. 214 (near Ahumada/Agustinas), open 0900-2200 (Mon.-Fri. only, but operates from travel agency next door on Sat a.m.). **General Holley 66**, Providencia, also gives good rates. Ideally, be introduced to someone who will change dollars at optimum rates. Mastercard and Visa at **Fincard**, Morandé 315, T 698-4260/2465-67/699-2632, offers its full range of services (even lost or stolen cards are replaced in a couple of days); open 24 hrs. Mastercard also at **Intercambio**, Edif. Santiago Center, Moneda 940, local 221, official rates for cash against the card.

**Language Courses** Centro de Aprendizaje Acelerado, Genova 2015, Depto. 21,

Providencia, T 494891, Spanish in groups or individually.

**Cultural and Trade Institutions** Instituto Chileno Británico de Cultura, Santa Lucía 124, 0930-1900, except 1330-1900 Mon., and 0930-1600 Fri., has English papers in library (also in Providencia, Dario Urzúa 1933, and Las Condes, Renato Sánchez 4369), runs language courses; **British Chamber of Commerce**, Bandera 227, Casilla 536, T 698-5266; **British Council**, Av. Eliodoro Yáñez 832, nr. Providencia, T 223-4622. The British community maintains the **British Commonwealth Society** (old people's home etc.), the interdenominational Santiago Community Church, at Av. Holanda 151 (Metro Tobalaba), Providencia, which holds services every Sunday at 1045. English Schools: The Grange, Redlands, Santiago College, Craighouse and The Brandford School, all coeducational.

Instituto Chileno Francés de Cultura, Merced 298, in a beautiful house (see also under **Restaurants** above); Instituto Chileno Alemán de Cultura, Goethe-Institut, Esmeralda 650; **German Chamber of Commerce**, Ahumada 131. Instituto Chileno de Cultura Hispánica, Providencia 927; Instituto Chileno Italiano de Cultura, Triana 843; Instituto Chileno Israeli de Cultura, Moneda 812, oficina 613; Instituto Chileno Japonés de Cultura, Providencia 2653, oficina 1902.

Instituto Chileno Norteamericano de Cultura, Moneda 1467, good for US periodicals, cheap films on Fri.; also runs language courses.

Instituto Cultural del Banco del Estado de Chile, Alameda 123, regular exhibitions of paintings, concerts, theatrical performances; Instituto Cultural de Providencia, Av. 11 de Septiembre 1995 (metro Los Leones), art exhibitions, concerts, theatre; Instituto Cultural Las Condes, Av. Apoquindo 6570, near beginning of Av. Las Condes, also with art exhibitions, concerts, lectures, etc. Academia Chilena de la Historia, Clasificador 1349, Correo Central, for information and help on archaeology.

**Embassies and Consulates** Argentine Embassy, Vicuña Mackenna 41 (T 222-8977), Australians need letter from their embassy to get visa here, open 0900-1400 (visa US$15, free for US citizens), if you need a visa for Argentina, get it here or in the consulates in Concepción, Puerto Montt of Punta Arenas, there are no facilities at the borders; Brazilian Embassy, McIver 255, 15th floor, T 398-867; Bolivian Embassy, Av. Santa María 2796 (T 232-8180, Metro Los Leones); Panamanian Embassy, Bustos 2199 (open 1000-1330); Paraguayan Consulate, Huérfanos 886, Oficina 514, T 394-640; Peruvian Embassy, Av. Providencia 2653, Oficina 808, T. 232-6275.

U.S. Embassy, Agustinas 1343 (reported to be relocating soon); U.S. Consulate, T 710133, Merced 230 (visa obtainable here); Canadian Embassy, Ahumada 11, T 696-2256 (prints a good information book). Australian Embassy, Gertrudis Echeñique 420, Las Condes, T 228-5065. New Zealand Embassy, Av. Isadora Goyenechea 3516, Las Condes (T 487071). South African Embassy, Av. 11 de Septiembre 2353, Edif. San Román, 16th floor. Thai Consulate, Suiza 1553, open 0900-1300.

British Embassy and Consulate, La Concepción 177, 4th floor, Providencia 1800 (metro Pedro de Valdivia), T 223-9166, Casilla 72-D, will hold letters (also reported to be planning to relocate); German Embassy, Agustinas 785 (T 693-5031/ 693-5035); Netherlands Consulate, Calle Las Violetas 2368, T 223-6825, open 0900-1200; French Embassy, Condell 65, T 225-1030; Norwegian Embassy, Av. Vespucio Norte 548, T 228-1024; Belgian Embassy, Av. Providencia 2653, depto. 1104, T 232-1071; Danish Embassy, Av. Santa María 0182, T 376056; Austrian Embassy, Av. Pedro de Valdivia 300, Barros Errázuriz, 3rd floor. Italian Embassy, Clemente Fabres 1050, T 223-2460. Spanish Consulate, Av. Providencia 329, 4th floor, T 40239; Swedish Embassy, 11 de Septiembre 2353, Torre San Ramón, 4 piso, Providencia, T 231-2733, Fax 232-4188; Swiss Embassy, Av. Providencia 2653, 16th floor, T 232-2693, open 1000-1200 (metro Tobalaba).

**Policia Internacional** for lost tourist cards, etc., Olivares 1229, 2nd floor, metro Los Héroes or La Moneda.

**Laundry** Very few wet-wash places in the centre: there is one at Monjitas 510 and another at Bandera 572, but there are plenty of dry-cleaners, e.g. Merced 494. Nearby, just S of Metro Universidad Católica there are several, including American Washer, Portugal 71, Torre 7, local 4, US$3, open 0900-2100 including Sun., can leave washing and collect it later; Maytag, Portugal 28, Torre 4, Local 4. Diagonal Paraguay 371, about US$0.65/kg., quick, rec., open till 1930 (closed Sun.) Wet wash laundries in Providencia include Marva, Carlos Antúnez 1823 (Metro Pedro de Valdivia), wash and dry US$8; Providencia 1039, full load, wet wash, US$5, 3 hrs. At the corner of Providencia and Dr. Luis Middleton there are several self-service dry cleaners (Metro Pedro de Valdivia, 11 de Septiembre exit).

**Synagogue** on Tarapacá, 3 blocks S of Alameda O'Higgins.

**Health**   Emergency hospital at Marcoleta 377 costs US$12. For a yellow fever vaccination Hospital San Salvador, Salvador 420, T 2256441. Arrive at correct time, Tues. 0900-1000, or you have to pay for a whole capsule (enough for 20!) Also Vaccinatoria Internacional, Hospital Luis Calvo, Mackenna, Antonio Varas 360. Clínica Central, San Isidro 231, T 222-1953, open 24 hrs, German spoken; Dr. Torres, Av. Providencia 2330, Depto 23, excellent, speaks English. Dentist: Antonio Yazigi, Vitacura 3082, Apto 33, T 487962, English spoken, rec. **Emergency Pharmacy**, Portugal 155 (T 382439).

**Post Office**   Agustinas 1137, Plaza de Armas, poste restante well organized (though only kept for 30 days), list of letters and parcels received in the hall of central Post Office; also has philatelic section, for stamp collectors. Another office at Moneda 1155. If sending a parcel, the contents must be checked at Post Office; parcel is then sealed for US$0.75.

**Cables and Telephones**   Compañía de Teléfonos de Chile, Moneda 1145. International phone calls also from: Entel, Huérfanos 1132, Mon.-Fri. 0830-2200, Sat. 0900-2030, Sun. 0900-1400, calls cheaper 1400-2200; Fax upstairs. Fax also available at CTC offices, e.g. Mall Panorámico, 11 de Septiembre, 3rd level (phone booths are on level 1) and Telexchile, Morandé 147. There are also phone offices at some metro stations, e.g. La Moneda and Pedro de Valdivia for local, long-distance and international calls. International telex service, Bandera 168. Local calls require 3 10-peso coins.

**Tourist Information**   Servicio Nacional de Turismo (Sernatur—the national tourist board), Av. Providencia 1550 (Casilla 14082), T 698-2151, Telex SERNA CL 240137, between metros Manuel Montt and Pedro de Valdivia, next to Providencia Municipal Library, open Mon.-Fri. 0900-1900. Sat. 0900-1300. English spoken and maps (road map US$1.50), brochures and posters are available. Information office also at the airport, open 0900-2100 daily. N.B. Many tourist offices outside Santiago are closed in winter, so stock up on information here.

   A recommended guide book is *Turistel*, published annually in three parts, *Norte*, *Centro*, and *Sur* (or in a combined edition), sponsored by the CTC telephone company, with information and a wealth of maps covering the whole country, in Spanish only. Each volume costs between US$6-10, depending where you buy it, but buying the whole set is better value; they can be found in CTC offices, bookshops, but best of all in the news stands in the centre of the city. There is also a *Turistel* camping guide. The publisher is Impresora y Comercial Publiguías S.A.

   Excellent road maps (US$1.75) and information may be obtained from the **Automóvil Club de Chile**, Vitacura 8620, T 212-5702/3/4/7/8 (Metro P. de Valdivia then bus to Vitacura, or a US$6 taxi ride from the centre), which also gives discounts to members of affiliated motoring organizations. Geophysical and topographical maps (not cheap) are available from **Instituto Geográfico Militar**, at their sales office, Alameda 240 (Universidad Católica metro) or main office Dieciocho 407 (opposite Palacio Cousiño, Toesca metro), closed in the holiday season. The Biblioteca Nacional, Moneda 650, has an excellent collection of maps which can be photocopied. **Conaf** (Corporación Nacional Forestal), Presidente Bulnes 259, oficina 206 (main office at No.285), T 696-0783/3801, has little written information for visitors to take away, but there are documents and maps about the national park system that can be consulted or photocopied. Walkers' maps are not available outside Santiago. Write to the Departamento de Estudios Vialidad Nacional, Morandé 59, oficina 344, Santiago, to see if their set of 14 maps of the country (scale 1:500,000—border areas 1:1,000,000) is available. Maps on sale from news kiosks: Esso road and town plans, Copec, Inupal and others.

**Travel Agencies**   *Wagons-Lits Cook* (Calle Agustinas 1058, Casilla 1534), *Turismo Cocha* (American Express representatives with mail service), Agustinas 1173 (check also AmEx bank at Agustinas 1360 for mail). *VMP Ltda*, Huérfanos 1160, Local 19, T and Fax 696-7829, for all services, German, English, French, Italian and Portuguese spoken. For local tours: *Tour Service*, Teatinos 333, 10th floor, T 6960415/727166; *Sportstours*, Teatinos 304, T 696-8832/698-3058, German-run, are helpful, 5 day trips to Antarctica (offices also at Hotels Carrera, and San Cristóbal); *Ace Turismo*, O'Higgins 949, T 6960391, city tour, $12 for ½ day. *Altue Expediciones*, Encomenderos 83, T 232-1103, for wilderness trips, rec. (above *Geo Pub*). Climbing and adventure tours in tenth region and elsewhere, *Antu Aventuras*, Casilla 24, Santiago, T 271-2767, Telex 440019, RECAL CZ. *Turismo Cabo de Hornos*, Agustinas 814, Of. 706, T 338480/1, for DAP flights (Punta Arenas-Puerto Williams) and Tierra del Fuego/Antártica tours. *All Travels*, Huérfanos 1160, local 10, T 696-4348, good for flight tickets, ask for Vivian Zuvanich de Selamé; *Eurotur*, Huérfanos 1160, local 13, for cheap air tickets to Europe; *MTK Tours*, Huérfanos 752, has been recommended for cheap flights, also **Beach Tours**, Huérfanos 1052, local 34, T 710-806/715-368. **Blanco**, Pedro Valdivia near Providencia, good for flight information and exchange. **Rapa-Nui**, Huérfanos 1160, specializes in trips to Easter Island. **Turismo Grace**, Victoria Subercaseaux 381, T

693-3740, good service.

**Airport** Arturo Merino Benítez (at Pudahuel), 26 km. from Santiago with a speed limit. Airport taxi, about US$15, fixed taxi fares on board by cab rank, but confirm fare before entering taxi. Pullman service by Aerobuses Tour Express to and from city centre, Moneda 1523, T 717380 (US$1.20) buses every ½hr., 0630-2100, ½-¾ hr. journey (service from airport after 2115 to meet incoming flights); plenty of luggage space; Metropuerto from Plazoleta Las Héroes, Metro Los Héroes, returns from airport to La Moneda, US$1, half-hourly service (0625-2115); Empresa Turismo Bar-C from your house or hotel to airport (or vice-versa), any time day or night, T 246-3600/1 for reservation (cheaper than taxi). Internal flights by LanChile and Ladeco operate from the International Airport. For schedules, see under individual towns. On arrival, get entry card from desk at entrance to arrivals hall before proceeding to immigration, otherwise you will be sent back. Bank and Afex *cambio* (better rates) outside customs hall; Sernatur office in same area will book accommodation. There are some shops, but they are very expensive, as are the bar and restaurant. Buy your wine etc. in town.

**Airline Offices** LanChile, sales office: Agustinas 640, Torre Interamericana, T 632-5505; reservations T 632-3211; Ladeco, Huérfanos 1157, T 698-1258 and Pedro de Valdivia 0210, T 251-7204; Aerolíneas Argentinas, Moneda 756; Viasa, Agustinas 1141, 6th floor; Varig, Miraflores, between Agustinas and Moneda; KLM, San Sebastián 2833, Piso 2, T 2330011; Aeroflot, Agustinas 640, Local 5; South African Airlines, Moneda 970, 17th floor, next to Lufthansa. LAP, Agustinas 1141, 2nd floor.

**Rail** International service to Buenos Aires suspended. No passenger trains to northern Chile nor to Valparaíso and Viña del Mar. All trains leave from Estación Central at Alameda O'Higgins 3322. Buses from northern bus terminal to Estación Central, Nos. 34 and 45, 10 mins., US$0.30, or take metro and change at Los Héroes. The line runs to Rancagua, San Fernando, Curicó, Talca, Linares, Parral and Chillán, thereafter services go to 1) **Concepción**, 2) **Temuco**, with a bus connection to **Valdivia**; no passenger services are operated S of Temuco, except in January and February to Puerto Montt via Osorno. Schedules change with the seasons, so you must check timetables before planning a journey. See under destinations for fares and notes on schedules. *Expreso* services do not have sleepers; some *rápidos* do (in summer *rápidos* are booked up a week in advance). *Dormitorio* carriages were built in Germany in 1930's, bunks lie parallel to rails, US-Pullman-style (washrooms at each end, one with shower-bath—visit early before the hot water has run out); an attendant for each car; bar car shows 3 films—no cost but you must purchase a drink ticket in advance. There is also a newer, *Gran Dormitorio* sleeping car (1984), with private toilet and shower, US$10 extra for 2, rec. For the *expresos* there are no reservations (get your ticket the morning of the day the train leaves and sit on the train as soon as you can get on; otherwise you'll stand for the whole journey). Free hot water supplied, so take own mug and coffee. Also a car-transporter service to Concepción and Temuco. Trains are still fairly cheap (though none too reliable), although 1st class is generally dearer than bus; meals are good though expensive. Check for family service, senior citizen and student discounts. Trains can be cold and draughty in the spring. Booking offices: for State Railways, Alameda O'Higgins 853 in Galería Hotel Libertador; T 301818/330746, Mon.-Fri. 0830-1900, Sat. 0900-1300; or Metro Esc. Militar, Galería Sur L-3, T 228-2983; central station, open till 2230, T 699-5718/699-1682; for Antofagasta-La Paz, Ahumada 11, Of. 602, T 698-5536. Left luggage office at Estación Central.

**Buses** There are frequent, and good, interurban buses to all parts of Chile. (**NB** Many leave early because of tight competition: arrive at bus station early.) Check if student rates available (even for non-students), or reductions for travelling same day as purchase of ticket; it is worth bargaining over prices, especially out of the summer season. Also take a look at the buses before buying the tickets (there are big differences in quality among bus companies); ask about the on-board services, many companies offer drinks for sale, or free, and luxury buses have meals and wine, colour videos, headphones. Reclining seats are common and there are also *salón cama* sleeper buses. Fares from/to the capital are given in the text. On Friday evening, when night departures are getting ready to go, the terminals are murder.

There are 4 bus terminals: 1) Terminal del Norte, Gral. Mackenna y Amunátegui, T 712-141, about 5 minutes' walk from Cal y Canto metro station (Line 2), due to be relocated in 1991/1992; from here buses leave for northern destinations, and some international services (see below). 2) Terminal de Buses Sur, Av. B. O'Higgins 3878, T 791-385, nearest metro Universidad Técnica/Universidad de Santiago (both names are used); buses from here go to southern destinations. 3) To Viña del Mar/Valparaíso, Bus and Pullman Tur-Bus have their own terminal on Al. B. O'Higgins 3712, next to Estación Central, metro Estación Central or Universidad de Santiago, Línea 1. A new terminal is reported at Los Héroes just off the Alameda, booking offices of about 10 companies. Varmontt buses, who run an expensive service to Puerto Montt, have their own terminal at Av. 21 de Septiembre 2212 (office on 2nd floor), metro Los Leones; many companies have offices away from the terminals, at which their buses call.

See the note under **Taxis** about not taking expensive taxis parked outside bus stations. Also, do not change money at the bus terminals; if coming from Argentina, try to get some pesos before you arrive.

**International Buses**    Long distance: to **Buenos Aires**, from southern and northern terminals, US$37-45, 22 hrs.; also to **Montevideo**, several companies, most involving a change in Mendoza, e.g. El Rápido, US$50, 28 hrs., meals included; **Caracas** (Tues. and Fri. 0900); **Lima** US$70, 51 hrs., it is cheaper to take a bus to Arica (US$35 and up), another to Tacna (US$1.75), thence bus to Lima. **Bogotá** (7 days); **São Paulo** and **Rio de Janeiro** (US$85 and US$90 respectively); Asunción (US$70); **Guayaquil** (US$85); and **Quito**. Tramaca, from northern terminal, runs a *combinación* service which links with the train from Calama to **Uyuni** and **Oruro** in Bolivia. Géminis, also from northern terminal, goes on Tues. to **Salta**, Argentina, changing in Calama, US$55. Short distance: there are frequent bus and *colectivo* taxi services from the Terminal del Norte over the Andes to **Mendoza**, 6 hrs., or so, about US$15 on either; taxis also go from the southern terminal, touts will approach you. All buses now go through the Cristo Redentor tunnel, and it is no longer possible to go to the Cristo Redentor statue from the Chilean side. TAS-Choapa, from northern terminal, has been rec.; Cata is not rec. Many *colectivos* for Mendoza go from the 800/900 blocks of Morandé, more expensive than the buses, but with shorter waiting time at customs: Chi-Ar taxi company, Morandé 890, rec., leaves at 0800 and charges US$16 for Santiago-Mendoza; Chile-Bus, Morandé 838, at 0830, US$15.50; Cordillera Nevada, Morandé 870, T 698-4716, or Local 61 at southern terminal, drive very fast. Have some small change available for tipping Argentine porters at the border.

**Shipping**    M/n *Evangelistas*: Puerto Montt-Puerto Chacabuco, Navimag, Miraflores 178, piso 12, T 696-3211, Telex 341234 NISA CK (or contact Turismo Cocha, Agustinas 1173, T 6983341, for 1st class; also Agentur, see below). Transmarchilay, Agustinas 715, oficina 403, T 335959, Telex 340334 MARCHI CK, for services between Chiloé and the mainland, ferry routes on the Carretera Austral and on Lake General Carrera. M/n *Skorpios*: luxury cruise out of Puerto Montt to Laguna San Rafael, Constantino Kochifas C., MacIver 484, 2˚ piso, Oficina 5, Santiago T 336-187, Telex 340592 NATUK CK, FAX 336-752. M/n *Quellón*: cruise out of Puerto Montt to Laguna San Rafael, early December to late March, Agentur, Huérfanos 757, oficina 601, T 337118, Telex 645387 AGENT CT. Enquire at Agentur for trips to Antarctica and for Empresa Marítima del Estado, Empremar. Navimag, Transmarchilay and Empremar also sail to the Laguna San Rafael in summer.

**Hitch-hiking** to Valparaíso, take Metro to Pajaritos and walk 5 minutes to W—no difficulty. Or, take bus "Renca Panamericana" from MacIver and Monjitas. To hitch south, take Metro to Estación Central, then Buses del Paine at Calle Borja as far as possible on the highway to the toll area, about US$1, 75 mins.

## Excursions from Santiago

On the NE outskirts in Las Condes is the Santuario de la Naturaleza Yerba Loca, administered by Conaf, open September to April (small entrance fee). Several small resort towns are easily reached by car from the capital. Peñalolén, 16 km., a beautiful view of the city if there's no smog (bus in front of Mapocho station at Av. Independencia and Balmaceda, some hiking possibilities); Colina (915 metres), an attractive, popular spa in the mountains 32 km. to the N (bus from Av. La Paz and Juárez, US$0.50 one way), *Hotel Termas de Colina*, E p.p., T 844-1408, thermal baths, US$3.70, swimming pool, US$2.70 (crowded at weekends), last return bus at 1900; San José de Maipo, some 80 km. to the SE (return journey by car: 3 hrs., buses every 15 mins. from N end of Parque O'Higgins, return fare US$1.75), particularly beautiful in spring; just beyond is the mountain town of Melocotón (*Millahue Hotel*, D p.p.). Just past Melocotón between San José de Maipo and El Volcán is San Alfonso, in the Callejón del Maipo (*Posada Los Ciervos*, from C with breakfast and shared bath to A with bath and full board, good; *Residencial España*, F p.p., clean, comfortable, restaurant, also others; Campsite at the Comunidad Cascada de las Animas, T 251-7506, also rents cabins—C for 4, hot water, cooking equipment etc.—sauna, horseriding). The walk to the Cascada de las Animas is pleasant; ask permission to cross the bridge at the campsite as private land is crossed. Buses at hourly or 2-hour intervals from Parque O'Higgins, Santiago. Beautiful mountain-river area, with vineyards. Three buses a day (US$2) run from Parque O'Higgins (same metro) to El Volcán in the Andes, 77 km. to the SE (1,400 metres); there are astounding views, but little else (the village was wiped away in a landslide). (Bus, 0800 Sat. and Sun., to Puente Alto.) From El Volcán the road runs 12 km. E and then N to the *Refugio Alemán Lo Valdés*, A-frame chalet accommodation, clean, cold water, no electricity, D p.p. with full board, good food, rec., a good place to stay for mountain excursions, open all year. A splendid region which deserves the journey required to get there. 12 km. away are hot natural baths, Baños Morales (*Hostería Club del Campo*, F p.p., full board E p.p.; excellent café in the village, serving homemade jam—it closes at Easter for the winter); open from October (bus leaves daily from Parque O'Higgins at 0730, arriving at Baños Morales 1100, US$2 each way; returns at 1800—buy return on arrival to ensure seat back; alternatively, hitch back to Santiago on quarry lorries). There is a mountain club hut in Baños Morales, friendly and helpful if you are planning to climb any of the nearby peaks. By Baños Morales is **El Morado National Park** with a glacier. Drinks can be obtained from Negro José nearby. The Lo Valdés area is popular at weekends and holiday times, but is otherwise deserted.

S of Santiago is the **Reserva Nacional Río Clarillo**, reached by Micro No. 32 to El Principal, 1 km. from the entrance. It is in the precordillera and can be visited at any time of year for its landscapes.

The small towns in the Aconcagua Valley to the N—San Felipe, Jahuel and Los Andes—are described in the section "To Buenos Aires across the Andes", page 565.

page 565.

The National Votive Temple of Maipú, of fine modern architecture and stained glass, 30 min. by car (or about 45 mins. by bus from corner of Calle Teatinos and Av. Bernardo O'Higgins) from Santiago, commemorates O'Higgins' battle; interesting (open daily 0800-2100, also daily mass at 1830, 1730 Sat., 1000-1400, 1600-2000 Sun. and religious holidays), and so is the attached Museo del Carmen of carriages, furniture, clothing and other colonial and later items, Sat. 1600-2000, Sun. and holidays, 1100-1400, 1600-2000.

**Campsites** Excellent facilities about 70 km. from Santiago at Laguna de Aculeo, called **Club Camping Maki**. Facilities include electricity, cold water, swimming pool, boat mooring, restaurant, US$2 p.p. daily, but only available to members of certain organizations. An alternative site is El Castaño camping (with casino), 1 km. away, on edge of lake, US$2 for 2 per night (beware of overcharging). Very friendly, café sells fruit, eggs, milk, bread and kerosene. Good fishing. No showers, water from handpump.

**Pottery** is best bought in **Pomaire**, a little town about 80 km. from Santiago towards the coast, where the artists can be observed at work. The area is rich in clay and the town is famous for its cider (*chicha de uva*, 3 strengths: *dulce, medio* and *fuerte*) and Chilean dishes; try *Restaurant San Antonio*, welcoming, semi-outdoor, good food and service. Pomaire may be reached by Melipilla bus from Calle San Borja, Santiago, bus station behind Estación Central metro station, every few minutes, US$0.85 each way, Rutabus 78 goes on the motorway, 1 hr., other buses via Talagante take 1 hr. 25 mins. (alight at side road to Pomaire, 2-3 km. from town, colectivos every 10-15 mins.); en route, delicious *pastel de choclo* can be obtained at Restaurant *Mi Ranchito*. Both Pomaire and Melipilla have been rebuilt after the 1985 earthquake, although the former is said to have lost some of its character.

**Vineyards** Another agreeable excursion is to the vineyard of Concha y Toro at Puente Alto, 40 km. south of Santiago. Tours of the *bodega*, and wine can be bought direct from vineyard. Pirque vineyard of Concha y Toro, entry free, tour at 1400, bus from San Francisco and Tarapacá, ¾ hour, US$0.50. The Undurraga vineyard at Santa Ana, south-west of Santiago, also permits visits on weekdays (tours given by the owner-manager, Pedro Undurraga). Take a Melipilla bus (but not Rutabus 78—see above) to the entrance.

**Horse-Breeding** A specially rec. excursion is to **Los Lingues**, a private *hacienda* 120 km. S of Santiago, where it is said the best horses in Chile are bred. Rosie Swale was lent two of them for her epic ride from Antofagasta to Cape Horn, described in *Back to Cape Horn* (Collins, London, 1986). Visits can be arranged to the C.17 house, a gift of the King of Spain, at Hacienda Los Lingues, Torre C. de Tajamar, Of. 205, Santiago, T 223-3518, Telex 340200 STORE CK. To 6060 LINGUE. A one-day tour costs US$35 p.p. including transport, rodeo and lunch; vacations (all inclusive) cost US$125 per day p.p. (the Hacienda is a member of the French Hotels et Relais de la Campagne).

**Skiing** There is an excellent ski centre at *Farellones*, 51 km. E of Santiago at 2,470 metres, and reached by car, bus, or truck in under 90 min.: *Motel Tupungato* (Candelaria Goyenechea 4750, Santiago, T 211-7341), Refugio Club Alemán Andino (D p.p., El Arrayán 2735, Santiago, T 232-4338, 1800-2000 May- June) and *Posada Farellones*. Most skiers stay in the two *refugios* belonging to Santiago's universities (full board C p.p.). High season: June to September/October, weather depending. An excellent network of five ski-lifts. There are excursions for a day from Santiago at US$15, including ski-lifts ticket; enquire Ski Club Chile, Goyenechea Candelaria 4750, Vitacura (north of Los Leones Golf Club), T 211-7341. In season, small buses leave from Av. Apoquindo (El Faro shopping centre), Sat. and Sun. between 0800 and 0900, but it is easy to hitch from the junction of Av. Las Condes/El Camino Farellones (petrol station in the middle): take a Las Condes bus from Calle Merced almost to the end of the line. Alternatively, go by ordinary bus which leaves at 0800, weekdays, from front of Omnium building, Av. Apoquindo (Escuela Militar metro), US$5 return (buy ticket day before, office open until 2000). Beautiful views for 30 km. across ten Andean peaks. Incredible sunsets. Large restaurants. No telephone, only communication is by radio. Five min. away by car (6 km.) is the village of La Parva with twelve lifts, 0900-1730 (*Condominio Nueva Parva*, good hotel and restaurant, reservations in Santiago: Roger de Flor 2911, T 231-3411, or T 220-8510), where the runs are a little easier. In summer, this is a good walking area. Lift ticket, US$12, and equipment rental, US$7-10 depending on quality. Two skiing areas close by, both of which are undergoing massive investment, are El Colorado (accommodation in *Edificios Los Ciervos* and *Monteblanco*, T Santiago 333564 or 393908, San Antonio 486, of. 151), with 3 triple chairlifts and a ski lodge, and Valle Nevado (owned by Spie Batignolles of France). Valle Nevado aims to be the largest ski resort in South America by 1992; its hotel is incredibly expensive (L+ and then some), but the resort is very highly regarded. Casa Valle Nevado, Gertrudis Echeñique 441, T 480-839/484-995, Fax 487-525. There are 8 runs, 2 chairlifts, 6 skilifts and many more are planned. Sunglasses are a must for skiers.

Other skiing and mountaineering clubs: **Club Andino de Chile**, Enrique Foster, 29, ski club (open 1900-2100 on Mon. and Fri.). **Federación de Andinismo de Chile**, Almirante Simpson 77 (T 232 4338), open daily; has a small museum (1100-1330, 1500-2000, free), sells equipment and guides to the mountains around Santiago (US$2.50) and the extreme south (e.g. Paine, US$4.35). Little other information available, apart from the addresses of all the mountaineering clubs in the country, it has a mountaineering school. Club Alemán Andino, Arrayán 2735, open Tues. and Fri., 1800-2000. Also try Skitotal, Apoquindo 4900, Oficina 32,33,43, T 246-0156, for one-day excursions.

**Portillo**, 145 km. from Santiago and 62 from Los Andes, is the greatest centre for skiing and winter sports in Chile. The weather is ideal, the snow conditions excellent, the runs many and varied; 12 lifts carry skiers up the slopes. The season is from June to September/October, weather depending. Cheap package can be arranged at the beginning and out of the season. On three sides the mountains soften into snow-clad fields and finally slope gently into the Laguna de Inca, 5½ km. long and 1½ km. wide; this lake, at an altitude of 2,835 metres, has no outlet, is frozen over in winter, and its depth is not known. Out of season this is another good area for walking, but get detailed maps before setting out.

Portillo is easily reached from Santiago by daily bus services (except in bad weather). In summer, ask the bus driver to stop, as it is not a routine call and on the way down you may have to hitch to the customs station with your baggage. In summer take a bus to Los Andes (US$2.25), then to Río Blanco (US$0.70), then hitch (see page 565). The train service from Santiago no longer operates.

**Hotels** *Hotel Portillo* (L), including a cinema, night club, swimming pool, sauna baths and medical service, on the shore of Laguna de Inca. Rates include meals, tax and service; accommodation ranges from lakefront suites to family apartments to bunk rooms without or with bath (much cheaper, from C up). A+ fabulous view, and parking charges even if you go for a meal; jacket and tie must be worn in the dining room. Self-service lunch, US$12 p.p. Lift charges are US$12 per day. Open all year. Reservations, Roger de Flor 2911, T 231-3411,

Telex 440372 PORTICZ, Santiago. Cheaper food available at *Restaurant Yuly* across the road, and *Restaurant Los Libertadores* at the customs station 1 km. away. *Hostería Alborada*, A+, including all meals, tax and service. During Ski Week (last in Sept.), about double normal rate, all included. Reservations, Agencia Tour Avión, Agustinas 1062, Santiago, T 72-6184, or Calle Navarro 264, San Felipe, T 101-R.

There are boats for fishing in the lake; but beware the afternoon winds, which often make the homeward pull 3 or 4 times as long as the outward pull. There are some gentle ski slopes for beginners near the hotel. The major skiing events are in August and September. Mules for stupendous expeditions to the Cristo, to the glacier at the head of the valley or of the Cerro Juncal, to the pass in the west side of the valley.

**Lagunillas** is a favourite ski-resort only 50 km. from Santiago, 2 hours by gravel road along the beautiful Maipo valley road to the Ojo de Agua area. Accommodation in the lodges of the Club Andino de Chile (bookings may be made at Ahumada 47, Santiago).Tow fee US$12; long T-bar and poma lifts; easy field.

**To Buenos Aires across the Andes** The Pan-American Highway runs north from Santiago to the rich Aconcagua Valley, the so-called Vale of Chile. The transandine route to Argentina branches east just after Llay-Llay.

**San Felipe**, the capital of Aconcagua Province, is 96 km. from Santiago and 128 km. from Valparaíso; it is an agricultural and mining centre with 42,000 inhabitants, 635 metres above sea level, with an agreeable climate. Part of the Inca highway has recently been discovered in the city; previously, no traces had been found further south than La Serena. A paved highway (13 km.) runs N from San Felipe to the old town of Putaendo.

**Hotel** *Hostería San Felipe*, Merced 204, T 510508, C.

**Termas de Jahuel** (hotel, T 511240, L), is high in the Cordillera (1,190 metres) 18 km. by road from San Felipe. The hill scenery includes a distant view of Aconcagua. Good roads in the neighbourhood.

**Curimón**, between San Felipe and Los Andes, has a historic church, with a small museum attached.

Sixteen km. SE of San Felipe is **Los Andes**, in a wealthy agricultural, fruit-farming and wine-producing area. There are monuments to José de San Martín and Bernardo O'Higgins in the Plaza de Armas, and a monument to the Clark brothers, who built the Transandine Railway (much of which is now either disused or pulled up). Good views from El Cerro de la Virgen. Trail starts at the municipal picnic ground on Independencia (easy to climb taking approx. 1 hr.). It is 77 km. to Santiago by road. See also under Valparaíso **Rail** for train service to the coast. Population: 30,500. Altitude: 730 metres.

**Hotels** *Continental*, Esmeralda 211, T 421013, C; *Plaza*, Esmeralda 367, T 421929, B, good but restaurant expensive. *Central*, Esmeralda 278 (1 block from bus station) T 421275, E, reasonable and very friendly (excellent bakery opposite, try the empanadas). *Valparaíso*, Sarmiento 160, F, clean; *Baños El Corazón*, at San Esteban, T 421371, with full board, A+, use of swimming pool but thermal baths extra; take bus San Esteban/El Cariño (US$0.50). *Restaurante Círculo Italiáno*, near bus station, rec. **Exchange**: Cambio Inter at *Plaza Hotel*, good rates, changes cheques.

Beyond Los Andes the Pan-American Highway passes into the Cordillera and winds along the Río Aconcagua for 34 km. until it reaches the village of *Río Blanco* (1,370 metres), set at the confluence of two rivers which go to form the Río Aconcagua: the Blanco and the Juncal. There is a fish hatchery with small botanical garden at the entrance of the Andina copper mine. *Hostería Luna*, 4 km. before Río Blanco on road from Los Andes, good value, clean, helpful, good food. *Hostería Guardia Vieja*, expensive but untidy, 8 km. beyond town. Possible to camp. Buses run daily from Los Andes; from Santiago, Bus Ahumada, at 1930 daily, direct, 2 hrs., US$2.

(Do not wait around at Los Andes for bus transport to Argentina as the local buses only go as far as Río Blanco; much better from Santiago. Hitch-hiking over Andes possible on trucks from Aduana building in Los Andes).

Beyond Caracoles (Customs post; long delays; no fruit can be taken across) the highway over La Cumbre (Uspallata) pass rises by steep grades to the Redentor tunnel. The tunnel is open from 0800 to 1800, Chilean time. Toll US$0.50. The top of the old pass, with the statue of Christ the Redeemer, at an altitude of 4,200 metres, is 8 km. beyond the tunnel and can be reached by a good, unpaved road only from Las Cuevas on the Argentine side (no access from Chilean side). However, if you leave your passport at the Chilean border post, you can walk further on to just before the tunnel into Argentina. Take the old road up to Cristo Redentor for superb views, and even better views from the hill on the left of the pass; start early in the morning because clouds often come up in the afternoon. Take food and windproof jacket and cap. The frontier is crossed at the foot of the statue, which is dwarfed by the scenery. The mountain views (including Aconcagua) are stupendous; as are the wild flowers in late January and early February. On the far side of the Andes the road descends 203 km. to Mendoza, where there are road and rail connections for Buenos Aires. The road from the tunnel to Mendoza is in fair condition, all of it paved.

**Valparaíso**, capital of V Región (Valparaíso), is the principal port and second-largest city (population 277,000) of Chile, and an important naval base. With the construction of a new congress building on Plaza O'Higgins, it is now the seat of the Chilean parliament. In 1991 the new congress and its surrounding plazas and approaches was not complete. The city is situated on the shores of a sweeping bay and on a crescent of hills behind. Seen from the ocean, it presents a majestic panorama: a great circle of hills is backed by the snow-capped peaks of the distant Cordillera. The climate is good, for the summer heat is tempered by fresh breezes and sunshine mitigates the unkindness of a short winter. (The mean annual temperature is 15°C, with -1°C and 31°C as the extremes.)

Founded in 1536, the city became in the nineteenth century the major centre of British naval and commercial activity on the Pacific coast of South America, before declining in importance with the opening of the Panama Canal in 1914. Little of its colonial past has survived the sequence of pirates, tempests, fires and earthquakes, although a remnant of the old colonial city can be found in the hollow known as El Puerto, grouped round the low-built stucco church of La Matriz. The last devastating earthquake was in 1906, and most of the principal buildings date from that time. Until recently, all buildings were low, as a precaution against earthquakes, but during the last few years modern multi-storey blocks have appeared. There was another serious earthquake in July 1971 and, most recently, in March 1985.

There are two completely different cities. The lower part, known as "El Plan", is the business centre, with fine office buildings on narrow streets strung along the edge of the bay. Above, covering the hills ("cerros"), is a fantastic agglomeration of tattered houses and shacks, scrambled in oriental confusion along the littered back streets. The lower and upper cities are connected by narrow winding roads, steep flights of steps and 16 *ascensores* or funicular railways dating from the period 1880-1914. The most unusual of these is Ascensor Polanco (entrance from Calle Simpson, off Av. Argentina a few blocks SE of the bus station), which is in two parts, the lower of which is a 160 metres vertical tunnel through the rock.

The heart of the city is the Plaza Sotomayor, dominated by the former Intendencia (Government House), now used as the Regional Naval Headquarters. Opposite is a fine statue to the "Heroes of Iquique." The passenger quay is one block away (handicraft shops on quay) and nearby is the railway station, from which passenger services run on the metropolitan line to Los Andes. The streets of El Puerto run on either side from Plaza Sotomayor. Calle Serrano runs NW for 7 blocks to the Plaza Echaurren, on which stands the old church of La Matriz. A block beyond rises the bold hill of Cerro Artillería, crowned by the huge Naval Academy and a park. To the W of the Cerro the Avenida Playa Ancha runs to a stadium, seating 20,000 people, and to Playa Ancha park. From the western base of the hill the Avenida Altamirano runs by the sea to Las Torpederas, a picturesque bathing beach. The Faro de Punta Angeles, on a promontory just beyond the Playa Ancha, was the first on the West Coast; you can get a permit to go up. On another high point on the other side of the city is the Mirador de O'Higgins, the spot where the Supreme Dictator exclaimed, on seeing Cochrane's liberating squadron: "On those four craft depends the destiny of America".

Leaving Plaza Sotomayor by the Calle Serrano and Plaza Echaurren, the Plaza Aduana is reached, where there is an *ascensor* for the Paseo Veintiuno de Mayo, a terrace on Cerro Artillería giving views of the bay and the hills. The New Year is celebrated by a firework display on the bay, which can be seen from this and the many other terraces on the surrounding hills (arrive early for a good place).

**Sightseeing** Launches run trips around harbour from Muelle Prat, 30 mins., US$0.65, to Playa Las Torpederas and to Viña del Mar; other boats for hire for fishing. **N.B.** Don't photograph naval ships or installations. The Camino Cintura is the only road which connects all the hills above Valparaíso; it affords constantly changing views, perhaps the best being from Plaza Bismark. No. 9 "Central Placeres" bus gives fine scenic drive over hills to the port; also bus "Mar Verde" (O) from Av. Argentina near the bus terminal to Plaza Aduana.

**Warning** Pickpockets operate in El Puerto around La Matriz.

**Hotels** *Prat*, Calle Condell 1443, T 253082, 220 beds, A, gloomy, restaurant; *Residencial Dinamarca*, Dinamarca 539 (from Plazuela Ecuador—just S of Condell y Bellavista—take any micro which includes "Cementerios" among its destinations: *residencial* is opp. cemetery entrance; or climb 10 minutes up Av. Ecuador), E, hot water, clean, excellent value, also short stay. Many cheap hotels on Cochrane and Blanco Encalada, S of Plaza Sotomayor, but very few are recommendable, one that is O.K. is *Residencial Lily*, Blanco Encalada 866, T 255995, 2 blocks from Plaza Sotomayor, E, clean, safe (despite no locks on doors). *Residencial Gemini*, Pedro Montt 2062, T 255537, E, good, clean, and *Gemini II*, Condell 1386, T 215544; *Reina Victoria*, Plaza Sotomayor 190, T 212203, D, with small breakfast, hot shower, clean and central but noisy. *Residencial Mi Casa*, opp. bus terminal, E, friendly, safe, cheap. *Sra Mónica*, Av. Argentina 322, Casa B, T 215673, 2 blocks from bus terminus, E, clean, friendly. *María Pizarro*, Chacabuco 2340, Casa No. 2, highly rec., E p.p. Many of the "cheap" hotels in the Chacabuco area are for short-term occupation only. Youth hostel office at Edwards 695, 3rd floor, will extend membership; nearest hostel in Viña del Mar.

**Restaurants** *Krill*, Errázuriz 210, across street from docks, rec. for seafood; *El Faro*, Errázuriz 342, good food, rec.; *Bar Inglés*, Cochrane 851 (entrance also on Blanco), good food and drink, traditional, rec., not cheap; *Café Riquet*, Plaza Anibal Pinto 1199, also traditional, comfortable, good coffee and breakfast, rec.; *Cinzano*, Plaza Anibal Pinto, old style bar/restaurant, good value; *Los Porteños*, Valdivia 169, near market, lunch only, very good; *Al Galeone D'Oro*, Independencia 1766, Italian, not cheap but good; *Hamburg*, O'Higgins 1274, German management, German beer, beware of overcharging. *Bote Salvavidas* on the harbour, good, at Muelle Prat; *Delmónico*, Prat (near Plaza Sotomayor), good, cheap lunches, popular; *La Rotunda*, Prat 669, good food; *Casino Social de Pescadores*, Altamirano 1480, good, cheap fish meals. Lots of cheap places for lunch between Plaza Sotomayor and Plaza Aduana, and round bus station.

**Bookshop** *Librería Universitaria*, Esmeralda 1132, good selection of regional history. *Librería Ivens*, Plaza Aníbal Pinto, specializing in up-to-date French and German newspapers; many others.

**Transport** Taxis are more expensive than Santiago: a short run under 1 km. costs US$1. Public transport good. Trolleybuses still run, also extensive bus routes. Fares within city limits US$0.20.

**Museums** Museo Municipal de Bellas Artes, with Chilean landscapes and seascapes and some modern paintings, housed in Palacio Baburizza, Paseo Yugoslavo, art nouveau palace overlooking harbour (free), open Tues.-Sun. 1000-1800; take *Ascensor El Peral* from Plaza Justicia, off Plaza Sotomayor. Museo del Mar Almirante Cochrane, housing collection of naval models built by local Naval Modelling Club, good views over port, Tues.-Sun. 1000-1800, free, take Ascensor Cordillera from Calle Serrano, off Plaza Sotomayor, to Cerro Cordillera; at the top, Plazuela Eleuterio Ramírez, take Calle Merlet to the left. Museo Naval, in the old Naval Academy on Cerro Artillería, Paseo 21 de Mayo, naval history 1810-1880, including exhibitions on Chile's two naval heroes, Lord Cochrane and Arturo Prat, Tues.-Sun. 1000-1800, US$0.35 (take Ascensor Artillería from Plaza Aduana). Museo de História Natural, in nineteenth-century Palacio Lyon, Condell 1546, good collection on Columbian cultures of Easter island and **Galeria Municipal de Arte**, in cellars of Palacio Lyon, both closed Mon.

**Exchange**   National banks. Open 0900 to 1400, but closed on Sat. Rate of exchange at **Banco de Santiago** (Prat 816) and **Banco de Crédito e Inversiones** (Cochrane 820) good. **Exprinter**, Prat 895 (the building with the clocktower at junction with Cochrane), good rates, no commission on travellers' cheques (open 0930-1400, 1600-1900); **Inter Cambios**, Errázuriz 627, near railway station, good rates; **Gema Tour**, Esmeralda 940. When *cambios* are closed, street changers operate outside Inter Cambios.

**Addresses**   British Consul, Blanco 725, oficina 26, T 256117, Casilla 82-V; YMCA (Asociación Cristiana de Jóvenes), Blanco 1117; YWCA (Asociación Cristiana Feminina), Blanco 967 Valparaíso Seamen's Institute, Blanco 394, Instituto Chileno-Norteamericano, Esmeralda 1069.

**Telecommunications**   VTR Telecommunications, Cochrane 825.

**Tourist Office**   in the Municipalidad building, Condell 1490, oficina 102, open Mon.-Fri. 0830-1400, 1530-1730. Kiosks at bus terminal (good map available), helpful, open 0900-1300, 1500-1900 (closed Thur., March-Nov.) and in Plaza Victoria, open weekends only Nov.-March. For day trips around Valparaíso and Viña del Mar, Turismo Continental T 6992807.

**Airlines**   LanChile, Esmeralda 1048, T 251441; Ladeco, Blanco 951, T 251001.

**Rail**   Valparaíso-Santiago 0730 Sat.; 1835 Sat. Sun. and holidays. Regular service on Merval, the Valparaíso metropolitan line, Valparaíso, Viña del Mar, Quilpue, Limache, Quillota, La Calera, Llay-Llay, San Felipe and Los Andes (and intermediate stations) to Viña del Mar every 15-30 mins, trains that run the entire route at 1800 daily, 1430 Mon.-Fri. (not holidays), 0805, 1200 and 1445, Sat., Sun. and holidays, fare Valparaíso-Los Andes US$1.50, 3 hrs. *El Porteño* tourist trains runs on Sun., 1 Jan.-28 Feb. and on most public holidays. There is talk of extending the line to the Argentine border as a "tourist resource".

**Buses**   Excellent and frequent bus service to **Viña del Mar** (25 min.) US$0.25 from Plaza Aduana, passing along Av. Errázuriz; colectivos to Viña US$0.40. To **Santiago**, 2 hrs., US$2 Tur Bus and Pullman Bus, others US$1.85 (returns to the capital heavily booked on Sun. p.m.); to **Concepción**, 11 hrs., US$12. **La Serena**, 8 hrs., US$10. To **Arica**, Fénix *salón cama* service, US$60. Terminal Rodoviario is on Pedro Montt 2800 block, corner of Rawson, 1 block from Av. Argentina; plenty of buses to/from Plaza Sotomayor (the bus terminal was due to be resited in 1991).

If driving from Santiago there are two tunnels, toll of US$2.25 paid at the first; several other tolls.

**Hitch-hiking**   to Santiago is easy from service station on Av. Argentina.

## Excursions from Valparaíso

About 25 minutes from Valparaíso, on the road to Santiago (Ruta 68) is the **Reserva Nacional Peñuelas**, surrounding the artificial Lago Peñuelas. Access is permitted for walking and fishing; administration at park entrance. Laguna Verde, a couple of hours' dusty walk over the hills (or a short road journey bus No. 3, marked "Laguna Verde" from Plaza Aduana) to the W of Valparaíso, is a picturesque bay for picnics. Camping site *Los Olivos*, good facilities, well run and friendly. Further S still is Quintay where there is camping; reached by turning left at Peñuelas on the main Santiago-Valparaíso road.

If driving from Valparaíso to the Argentine border, Route 62 runs through Viña del Mar, climbs out of the bay and goes through (16 km.) *Quilpue*, 1½ km. from El Retiro, a popular inland resort with medicinal springs. It crosses a range of hills and reaches the Aconcagua Valley at **Limache** , a sleepy market town, 40 km. from Valparaíso (population 22,511). Between Quilpue and Limache is Peñablanca, the town of the white windmills. 8 km. from Limache is Olmué, beyond which is **Parque Nacional La Campana**, an area of native woodland, including the Chilean palm (*kankán*), much varied birdlife, and the Cerro La Campana which Darwin climbed in 1836. Extensive views from the top, but a guide may be necessary because there are a number of ascents, some of which are very difficult. Route 62 joins Route 60 just before *Quillota*, an orchard centre (Balneario El Edén, 5 km out of town, good swimming), continuing to La Calera (88 km. from Valparaíso), where it joins the Pan-American Highway; turn SE and E for Llay-Llay, San Felipe, Los Andes and the pass over the mountains to Mendoza.

## Pleasure Resorts near Valparaíso

*Viña del Mar*, one of the foremost South American seaside resorts, is 9 km. from Valparaíso by one of the innumerable express buses, which run along a narrow belt between the shore and precipitous cliffs. Halfway, on the hill of Los Placeres, is the Universidad Técnica. The popular bathing resort of El Recreo is passed, then Caleta Abarca with its crowded beaches, floral clock and big *Hotel Miramar*. Beaches are often closed because of pollution.

At the entrance to Viña del Mar there is a steep bluff, worth climbing for the views over Viña from its *paseos*. Here also is Cerro Castillo, the summer palace of the Presidents of the Republic. Below, to the left, is the lagoon of the Marga Marga, crossed by a bridge which leads direct to the Casino, built in the 1930s and set in beautiful gardens, US$2.40 to enter, jacket and tie for men required (open all year). Population: 259,300 (1982).

One of the sights is the municipally owned Quinta Vergara, superb gardens with a double avenue of palms. The Palacio Vergara, in the gardens, houses the Museo de Bellas Artes and the Academia de Bellas Artes. Part of the grounds is a children's playground, and there is an outdoor auditorium where concerts and ballet are performed in the summer months, and an international song festival is held every February.

"The Song Festival is lively, with the emphasis more on the "shows" of the special guests, famous latino singers, and European and local rock bands than on the unknown contestants" (Glyn Fry and Trui Anseeuw). Schedules may be delayed to fit in with TV programming and standards of organization and performance (with some exceptions) have slipped of late. Take warm clothes if staying till the end. Tickets from the Municipalidad US$3-US$15, seats are numbered so no need to arrive till 2100. For the final evening touts sell tickets outside the Quinta Vergara.

The Teatro Municipal is on Plaza Vergara. Near the Valparaíso Sporting Club with its racecourse and playing fields are the Granadilla Golf Club and a large stadium. In the hills behind is a large artificial lake, the Laguna Sausalito, adjacent to Estadio Sausalito (home to Everton soccer team, among many other sporting events). It possesses an excellent tourist complex with swimming pools, boating, tennis courts, sandy beaches, water skiing, restaurants, etc. Entry US$2.50, children under 11, US$1.75; take colectivo No. 19 from Calle Viana.

**Festival** El Roto, 20 Jan., in homage to the working men and peasants of Chile.

**Hotels** Many in A+-A range, some with beach. *San Martín*, Av. San Martín 667, T 972548, A+ with breakfast; *Alborada del Mar*, San Martín 419, A, tastefully decorated; *José Francisco Vergara*, Calle Dr. von Schroeders 367, T 664022, A, has garden houses for up to 5; *Alejandra*, 2 Poniente 440, T 974404, with shower and breakfast, B (C in low season, breakfast included); *El Escorial*, two places: one at 5 Poniente 114, the other at 5 Poniente 441 (T 975266), C with breakfast, shared bath, clean, central. *Residencial Blanchait*, Valparaíso 82, T 974949, clean, C with breakfast, hot water, clean, good service; *Residencial Magallanes*, Arlegui 555, T 685-101, with breakfast, clean, friendly, run by a family, good meals, C. *Residencial France*, Montaña 743, E, clean, safe. There are a great many more places to stay.

**Motels** Several at Reñaca (6 km. from Viña del Mar).

**N.B.** It is cheaper to stay in Valparaíso and commute to the Viña beaches.

**Youth Hostel** Agua Santa 153, US$3 p.p. a night for YHA card holders, breakfast included, other meals available, no cooking facilities; family rooms available. Open Jan.-Feb.

**Camping** Camping Reñaca, Santa Luisa 401, US$3.50 per tent. Unofficial site in woods behind Quinta Vergara park. Camping gas and similar articles for sale at Valparaíso 464.

**Restaurants** At hotels; *Cap Ducal*, Av. Marina 51, expensive, rec. *Casino Chico*, Valparaíso 99, Chilean and international dishes; *Salón de China*, 4 Norte 201; *Han's Dragón*, Libertad y 8 Norte; *Machitún Ruca*, San Martín 529, excellent. *Casino Español*, Alvarez 580, good, reasonably priced, good value *almuerzo*; *Las Gaviotas*, 14 Norte 124, Chilean meat dishes, not expensive, live music. Many restaurants on Av. Valparaíso, try in the Galerías (arcades, e.g. *Café Big Ben). Oxford's,* Arlegui 228, snacks and drinks, English spoken, friendly, rec. Many smaller ones along the sea front. *Terminal Pesquero,* 1st floor, interesting.

*El Poncho,* Av. Borgoño 16180, Reñaca, good seafood and service; also at Reñaca, overlooking the sea, are *Anastassia,* Av. Borgoño 15000, excellent international menu, expensive; *Hotel Oceanic,* very good, expensive.

**Market** At intersection of Av. Sporting and river, open Wed. and Sat.

**Car Hire** Euro Rent-A-Car, in *Hotel O'Higgins,* clean cars, efficient.

**Discotheque** *Topsy Topsy,* Santa Luisa 501, Reñaca.

**Museums Museo de la Cultura del Mar;** in the Castillo Wulff, contains a collection on the life and work of the novelist and maritime historian, Salvador Reyes, Tues.-Sat. 1000-1300, 1430-1800, Sun. 1000-1400; **Museo de Bellas Artes,** Quinta Vergara, Tues.-Sun. 100-1400, 1500-1800; **Palacio Rioja,** Quillota 214, built at turn of century by a prominent local family and now used for official municipal receptions, ground floor preserved in its original state, open to visitors 1000-1400, 1500-1800, Tues.-Sun. **Museo Argueológico,** Calle 4 Norte 784, with objects from Easter Island and Mapuche silver, open Mon.-Fri. 1000-1800, Sat.-Sun. 1000-1400, entry US$0.20. An Easter Island statue stands onn the lawn between the railway and the beach just beyond Caleta Portales, at the border between Viña del Mar and Valparaíso. **Centro Cultural,** Libertad 250, holds regular exhibitions; **Instituto de Oceanografía,** in Montemar, Reñaca (bus No. 9).

**Cultural Associations Instituto Chileno-Británico,** 3 Norte 824, T 971061; **Instituto Chileno—Norteamericano de Cultura,** 3 Norte 532, T 662145; **Casa Italia** (cultural centre, consulate, restaurant), Alvarez 398; **Goethe Institut,** 3 Norte 599, T 976581; **Instituto Chileno-Francés,** Alvarez 314, T 685908.

**British Community** The community here maintains several schools, including: St. Margaret's and Mackay. There is also an Anglican church, with a resident English chaplain, postal address Casilla 561. Full details from British Consulate.

**Exchange** Many *casas de cambio* on Arlegui including **Afex,** 641 (open 0900-1400 Sat.); **Cambio Norte,** 610; **Cambio Andino,** 644; also in the tourist office. **Fincard** (Visa, Mastercard), Ecuador 259.

**Tourist Office** Av. Marina esq. Puente Libertad, T 883154. Arrangements may be made at the Tourist Office for renting private homes in the summer season. **Automóvil Club de Chile** 1 Norte 901, T 971815.

**Buses** to Santiago, US$2-3, 2 hrs., frequent, many companies (heavily booked in advance for travel on Sun. afternoons); to **La Serena,** 6 daily, 8 hrs., US$10, to **Antofagasta,** 20 hrs., US$20. Terminal at Av. Valparaíso and Quillota.

**Excursions** In the eastern suburbs, beyond El Salto, is the Jardín Botánico Nacional, a national park in the Parque del Salitre. Beyond Reñaca beach (6 km. N, very popular with young people) is Cochoa with its large sealion colony, 100 metres offshore.

**Resorts N of Valparaíso** There is a very fine drive N of Viña del Mar along the coast (many motels being built) through Las Salinas and Reñaca to Concón, then inland to Quintero. Las Salinas, beach between two towering crags, is very popular. *Concón,* on the south shore of a bay at the mouth of the Río Aconcagua, is 12 km. N of Reñaca (from Viña del Mar take bus 9 from Av. Libertad between 2 and 3 Norte). Main attractions: tennis, bathing, fishing, and riding. Main eyesore: an oil refinery (not visible from beach). Near the Concón beach there is a very interesting pelican colony. There is also a new inland road, much faster than the coast road, between Viña del Mar and Concón.

**Concón Hotels** *Playa Amarilla,* T 811915, and several motels. Good seafood *empanadas* at bars. *Vista al Mar,* Av. Borgoño 21270, T 812-221, good fish restaurant, US$7 per plate. *Don Chico,* Av. Borgoño 21410, good seafood; *Mirador Cochoa,* Av. Borgoño 17205, good, pricey.

**Campsite** Las Gaviotas. Camping Mantagua Playa.

**Horse riding** Horses for hire from Ernesto Farias Usario, Las Encinas 55, Las Romeras, Concón Alto (last bus stop on route 9 or 10 from Viña del Mar or Valparaíso), US$2/hour. Rides in forest or along sand dunes.

Another 16 km. to the N of Concón over the new bridge is the fishing village of *Quintero,* the naval aviation centre. On the N shore of the bay at Las Ventanas are a power station and copper processing plant. **Hotels** *Isla de Capri*, Av. 21 de Mayo 1299, T 930117, D, pleasant, clean; *Hotel Yachting Club*, Luis Acevedo 1736, T 930061, A. *Monaco*, D without breakfast, run down but interesting, good views. A number of *residenciales* at the resort.

*Horcón* (also known locally as Horcones), set back in a cove surrounded by cliffs, is a pleasant small village, mainly of wooden houses. On the beach hippies sell cheap and unusual jewellery and trinkets. Vegetation is tropical with many cacti on the cliff tops. Seafood lunches with the catch of the day, sold at any number of stalls on the seafront, are rec. The resort is best avoided in Jan.-Feb. when it is packed out. **Hotels** *Horcón*, E p.p., fair; *Aranciba* , E without bath, also *cabañas* D, restaurant; and *El Faro*, F p.p., basic, all on beach. **Camping** at entrance to village. **Restaurant** *El Ancla* rec.; *Reina Victoria*, cheap, good.

From Las Ventanas the road continues N past Maitencillo, where there are large numbers of chalets but no hotels, to the fashionable resort of *Zapallar* (33 km. N of Las Ventanas). There are several fine mansions along Av. Zapallar. Three km. S at Cachagua a colony of penguins may be viewed from the northern end of the beach. No cars are allowed on the Zapallar seafront. Excellent bathing, but water is cold. **Hotels** *César*, T 711313, A+, very nice but dear, good, reasonably-priced food in *Restaurant César* (different management), on seafront; hotels are relatively expensive for what is offered. *Papudo*, 10 km. further N, formerly connected with Santiago by rail, rivalled Viña del Mar as a fashionable resort in the 1920s but has long since declined. Hotels *Moderno*, D; *Di Peppino*, T 711482; many more.

**Buses** from Valparaíso and Viña del Mar: To Concón, bus 9 or 10 (from Av. Libertad between 2 and 3 Norte in Viña), US$0.30; to Quintero and Horcón, Sol del Pacífico, every 30 mins, US$0.35-US$0.50; to Zapallar and Papudo, Sol del Pacífico, 4 a day (2 before 0800, 2 after 1600), US$1.60.

**Resorts Near the Mouth of the Río Maipo** The Río Maipo flows into the sea near the port of *San Antonio*, 113 km. from Santiago and 112 km. south of Valparaíso. San Antonio (population 60,000) is connected with Santiago by railway (no passenger services) and a motorway between the two is due for completion in 1991. Its shipping shows a considerable growth, mostly at the expense of Valparaíso. The port exports copper brought by railway from the large mine at El Teniente, near Rancagua. San Antonio was badly damaged by the earthquake of March 1985. South of San Antonio are Llolleo (4 km.) at the mouth of the Maipo, a famous resort for those who suffer from heart diseases, and 7 km. further Rocas de Santo Domingo, the most attractive and exclusive resort in this area with 20 km. of beaches and a golf course; even in high season it is not very crowded.

**Hotels** At San Antonio: *Jockey Club*, 21 de Mayo 202, T 31302, C, best good views, restaurant; *Patria*, Pedro Montt 194, E; *Colonial*, Pedro Montt 196, E. At Llolleo: *Oriente*, Inmaculada Concepción 50, T 32188, D p.p.; *Residencial El Castillo*, Providencia 253, T 373821. At Santo Domingo: *Rocas de Santo Domingo*, La Ronda 130, T 31348, B.

**Transport** Buses from San Antonio: To **Valparaíso**, Pullman Bus, every 45 mins until 2000, US$2; to **Santiago**, Pullman Bus, every 20 mins, US$2. Rail: passenger train, supposedly daily, Santiago-San Antonio-Cartagena 15 Dec.—15 March only.

*Cartagena*, 8 km. N of San Antonio and the terminus of the railway is the biggest resort on this part of the coast. The administrative centre lies around the Plaza de Armas, situated on top of the hill. To the south is the picturesque Playa Chica, overlooked by many of the older hotels and restaurants; to the north is the Playa Larga. Between the two a promenade runs below the cliffs; high above hang old houses, some in disrepair but offering spectacular views. Cartagena is a very popular resort in summer, but out of season especially it is a good centre for visiting nearby resorts; there are many hotels and bus connections are good.

**Hotels** *Biarritz*, Playa Chica, T 32246, D; *La Bahía*, Playa Chica, T 31246, D; *Violeta*, Condell 140, D, swimming pool, good views; *El Estribo*, just off Plaza de Armas, F p.p. with breakfast, E p.p. full board, basic, cheap *comedor*.

North of Cartagena are several small resorts including Las Cruces, El Tabo and *El Quisco*, a small fishing port with 2 beautiful white beaches. *Algarrobo*, 29 km. N of Cartagena, is the largest of these and the most chic, with its large houses, yacht club, marina and pengiun island (no entry). In summer there are boat tours round the island from the jetty. On the road between El Tabo and El Quisco is the village of Isla Negra where the house of the Chilean poet Pablo Neruda is located. The beautifully-restored Museo-Casa Pablo Neruda is open Tues.-Fri. 1100-1300, 1500-1700, Sat.-Sun. 1100-1700 for guided tours, small groups only—book either at Museum 30 mins before opening or—safer—in advance by contacting the Fundación Neruda (see under Santiago Museums).

**Hotels** At Las Cruces, *Residencial La Posada*, E, good birdwatching. At El Tabo: *Hotel El Tabo*, T 33719, C, quite nice, and *Motel El Tabo*, next door (overfull in Jan.-Feb.). At El Quisco, *Hotel El Quisco*, Av. Isidora Dubournais 166, D p.p. with breakfast, clean; others on this avenue; *Motel Barlovento* Calle El Quisco 0520, T 81030, C; *Cabañas Pozo Azul*, Capricornio 234, SE of town, quiet, D; *residenciales* 100-200 m. from beach in E range. Excellent seafood restaurant *La Caleta* on beach. At Algarrobo, *Panamericano*, Alessandri, C; *Costa Sur*, Alessandri, C; *Uribe*, behind Costa Sur, D, pleasant, quiet; *Residencial San José*, Av. Principal 1598, F p.p., basic, no hot water; *Vera*, Alessandri 1521, T 81132, D with breakfast, good. At Isla Negra: Hosteria Santa Elena, C, beautiful building and location, restaurant, rec.

**Buses** between Algarrobo and Santiago, Pullman Bus, every 20 mins, 2 hrs, US$3, stopping in Cartagena and the resorts along the coast (but not San Antonio). Services between Algarrobo and San Antonio also by Empresa de Buses San Antonio (frequent, last bus around 2000) and Empresa Robles.

---

## THE CHILEAN PACIFIC ISLANDS (4)

Two national park possessions in the Pacific: Juan Fernández Islands, a little easier to reach now than in Robinson Crusoe's time, and the unique Easter Island.

*Juan Fernández Islands*, some 650 km. W of Valparaíso, were discovered by Fernández in 1574. They are now a national park administered by Conaf. One of them was the home (1704-09) of Alexander Selkirk (the original of Defoe's *Robinson Crusoe*), whose cave on the beach of Robinson Crusoe island is shown to visitors. The main island has 550 people housed in simple wood frame houses, who fish for *langosta de Juan Fernández* (a pincerless lobster) which they send to the mainland. The village of San Juan Bautista has a church, schools, post office, and wireless station. The official names of the three islands are: Robinson Crusoe (previously Más a Tierra), Alejandro Selkirk (previously Más Afuera) and Santa Clara (the smallest island).

The climate is mild, the vegetation rich, and there are plenty of wild goats—and some tourists, for the islands are now easily reached by air. There are no beaches to speak of. The boat service, about every three weeks from Valparaíso on the *Río Baker* and *Charles Darwin*, is for cargo and passengers, modest accommodation, 36-hour passage; Agentur, Huérfanos 757, oficina 601, T 337118, Santiago. Pesquera Chris, Cochrane 445 (near Plaza Sotomayor), Valparaíso, T 216800, 2 week trips to the island (5 days cruising, a week on the island), from US$200 return. No fishing or cargo boats will take passengers; the simplest way is to fly. There is an air taxi daily in summer (subject to demand) from Santiago (Los Cerrillos airport, US$490 round trip), by Taxpa, Nueva York 53; also from Valparaíso. The plane lands on an airstrip in the W of the island; passengers are taken by boat to San Juan Bautista (1½ hrs., US$2 one way). In summer, a boat goes once a month between Robinson Crusoe and Alejandro Selkirk if the *langosta* catch warrants it, so you can visit either for a few hours or a whole month.

The anvil-shaped peak, El Yunque, is the highest peak on Robinson Crusoe and it was upon this hill that Selkirk lit his signal fires. A tablet was set in the rock at the look-out point by British naval officers from HMS *Topaze* in 1868, to commemorate Selkirk's solitary stay on the island for 4 years and 4 months. Selkirk, a Scot, was put ashore from HMS *Cinque Ports* and was taken off by a privateer, the *Duke*. The look-out (Mirador de Selkirk) is the only easy pass between the north and south sides of the island. During the First World War, two British destroyers, HMS *Kent* and *Glasgow* sank a German cruiser, the *Dresden*, in the bay upon which the village is located. The ship (which was actually scuttled)

RAPA NUI
EASTER ISLAND
55

is still on the bottom; a monument on shore commemorates the event and, nearby, unexploded shells are embedded in the cliffs.

Each February, a yachting regatta visits the islands; it originates in Algarrobo, sails to Robinson Crusoe, thence to Talcahuano and Valparaíso. The bay is full of colourful and impressive craft, and prices in restaurants and shops double for the duration. (Thomas G. Lammers, Miami University, Department of Botany).

**Hotels** *Hostería Robinson Crusoe*, A (US$30-35 d, full board, plus 20% tax), about 1 hour walk from the village. *Daniel Defoe Hotel*, A+, at Aldea Daniel Defoe; *Hostería Villa Green*, good. Lodging with villagers is difficult. T Valparaíso 81573.

***Easter Island*** (Isla de Pascua, Rapa Nui) is just S of the Tropic of Capricorn and 3,790 km. W of Chile; its nearest neighbour is Pitcairn Island. It is triangular in shape, 24 km. across, with an extinct volcano at each corner. Its original inhabitants called the island Te Pito te Henua, the navel of the world. The population was stable at 4,000 until the 1850s, when Peruvian slavers, smallpox and emigration (encouraged by plantation-owners) to Tahiti reduced the numbers. Now it is about 2,500, of whom about a quarter are from the mainland, mostly living in the village of Hanga Roa. Just north of Hanga Roa, there is a reconstructed site with a temple, houses and a ramp leading into the sea. Further along, there is a mediocre museum (Mon. to Sat., 0900-1200, 1400-1700, Sun. 0900-1500). About half the island, of low round hills with groves of eucalyptus, is used for sheep and cattle, and nearly one-third constitutes a National Park. The islanders, of Polynesian origin, have preserved their indigenous songs and dances, and are extremely hospitable. Tourism has grown rapidly since the air service began in 1967. Paid work is now more common, but much carving is still done. The islanders have profited much from the visits of North Americans: a Canadian medical expedition left a mobile hospital on the island in 1966, and when a US missile-tracking station was abandoned in 1971, vehicles, mobile housing and an electricity generator were left behind. The unique features of the island are the 600 (or so) *moai*, huge stone figures up to 9 metres in height and broad in proportion. One of them, on Anakena beach, was restored to its (probably) original state with a plaque commemorating Thor Heyerdahl's visit in 1955. Heyerdahl's theories, as expressed in *Aku-Aku, The Art of Easter Island* (New York: Doubleday, 1975), are not as widely accepted as they used to be, and South American influence is now largely discounted (see below). Other *moai*, at Ahu Tepeu and Ahu Tahai, have since been re-erected. The rainy season is from February to the end of August; the tourist season from September to April. Useful information is contained in David Stanley's *South Pacific Handbook*, and there is a very thorough illustrated book by J. Douglas Porteous, *The Modernization of Easter Island* (1981), available from Department of Geography, University of Victoria, BC, Canada, US$6.

David Bulbeck, an anthropologist from Adelaide, writes: Far from being the passive recipient of external influences, Easter Island shows the extent of unique development possible for a people left wholly in isolation. It is believed to have been colonized from Polynesia about AD 800: its older altars (*ahu*) are similar to those of (French) Polynesia, and its older statues (*moai*) similar to those of the Marquesas Islands. The very precise stone fitting of some of the *ahu*, and the tall gaunt *moai* with elongated faces and ears for which Easter Island is best known were later developments whose local evolution can be traced through a comparison of the remains. Indigenous Polynesian society, for all its romantic idylls, was competitive, and it seems that the five clans which originally had their own lands demonstrated their strength by erecting these complex monuments. The *moai* were sculpted at the Rano Raraku quarry and transported on wooden rollers over more or less flat paths to their final locations; their red topknots were sculpted at and brought from the inland quarry of Puna Pau; and the rounded pebbles laid out checkerboard fashion at the *ahu* all came from the same beach at Vinapu. The sculptors and engineers were paid out of the surplus food produced by the sponsoring family: Rano Raraku's unfinished *moai* mark the end of the families ability to pay. Over several centuries from about AD 1400 this stone work slowed down and stopped, owing to the deforestation of the island caused by roller production, and damage to the soils through deforestation and heavy cropping. The birdman cult represented at Orongo is a later development after the islanders had lost their clan territoriality and were concentrated at Hanga Roa, but still needed a non-territorial way to simulate inter-clan rivalry.

**Things to See** The visitor should see the crater of the volcano Rano Kau with its reed-covered lakes; best for photographs in the afternoon. The adjacent ceremonial city of Orongo with its petroglyphs (entrance US$5, pamphlet in Spanish extra) is famous for the birdman cult and gives good views of Motu Nui, Motu Iti and Motu Kaokao, the so-called bird islets. The volcano Rano Raraku; the statues at Ahu Tahai; the beaches of Ovahe and Anakena (Thor Heyerdahl's landing place, also restored *moai*); and the *ahu* and *moai* at Vinapu, Akivi/Siete Moai, Pitikura, Vaihu and Tahai. Ahu Tongariki, once the largest platform, was badly damaged by a tidal wave in 1960. Cave paintings at Ana Kai Targata. Music at the 0830 Sun. mass is "enchanting". Museum near Tahai, US$0.40, disappointing, most objects are reproductions.

**Handicrafts** Wood carvings, stone moais, best bought from the craftsmen themselves, such as Antonio Tepano Tucki, Juan Acka, Hipolito Tucki and his son (who are knowledgeable about the old culture). The municipal market, east of Tahai, will give you a good view of what is available—no compunction to buy. There is a Cema-Chile store; the airport shop is expensive. Good pieces cost between US$30 and 150. Souvenirs at *Hotu Matuu's Favorite Shoppe* have been described as "top dollar and she will not bargain", but she does have the best T-shirts.

**Accommodation and Food** A comprehensive list of all accommodation available is displayed at the airport information desk. Note that room rates, especially in *residenciales* can be much cheaper out of season and if you do not take full board. *Hotel Hanga Roa*, Av. Pont (L) including all meals (120 beds), does not take credit cards, breakfast included, T 299; *Hotel Otai*, Te Pilo Te Henua, T 250, A+, comfortable, friendly, run by a family, rec.; *Hotel Victoria*, Av. Pont, T 272, A+, friendly, helpful owner Jorge Edmunds arranges tours; *Iorana Hotel*, on Ana Magara promontory (5 mins. from airport), T 312, 14 rooms, friendly, excellent food, convenient for visiting Ana Kai Targata caves; *Topo Ra'a*, Atamu Kekena, T 225, A+, 5 mins. from Hanga Roa, very good, helpful, excellent restaurant; *Easter Island Hotel*, Av. Policarpo Toro, Hanga Roa, A+, breakfast and dinner (excellent restaurant), good service, nice garden (T 294). Homes offering accommodation and tours (rates ranging from

US$18 to US$35, including meals): Yolanda Ika's (*Residencial Taire Ngo Oho*, T 259), A with breakfast, rec., modern; Krenia Tucki's *Residencial Kai Poo*, Av. Pont, A, small, clean, friendly with hot water; *Residencia Hanga Roa Reka*, T 276, A full board, good, friendly, camping US$5; María Georgina Hucke, of Tiki Tours, B with half board, rec.; *Residencial Pedro Atán* (A+, full board, T 329, Av. Policarpo Toro); Sophia Gomero and María Luisa Pakarati, *Res. El Tauke* (Clementina Riroroko Haoa), T 253, same rates as *Hanga Roa Reka*, excellent, airport transfers, tours arranged; *Res. Taheta One One*, T 257, same rates, ask here for cheap motorbike rental, US$8/day; *Res. Apina Nui*, Hetereki, T 292, A+ (C-B low season), good food, helpful; *Res. Holiday Inn* (Viviane Tepano), T 337, B p.p. with breakfast and one meal, excellent food, hot water, rec; *Inn at Tahai* (María Hey), A+ full board, rec.; Anita and Martín Pate's guesthouse, opp. hospital in Hanga Roa, C half board in high season, less low season, clean, good food; María Cecilia Cardinale, near Tahai Moai, D with breakfast, camping US$5; María Goretti, rooms D with breakfast, camping US$6; Sra. Inez Pateñarez, Calle Make Make, Hanga Roa, private house accommodation. Emilio and Milagrosa Paoa, A with full board, rec. accommodation and tours. Some families (such as Anakena and Raraku) and *Residencial Pedro Atán* will rent their gardens to travellers with a tent, US$7, with meal; the lack of natural water makes this uncomfortable. On arrival at the airport, visitors are met in force by guest-house keepers, drivers, horse-hirers, etc. Unless it is a particularly busy season there is no need to book in advance; mainland agencies make exorbitant booking charges.

*Kopa Kabana* restaurant, quite good; another opp. municipal market (which does not sell food). There are a couple of expensive supermarkets, cheapest is ECA on main street. Local produce which can be found free (but ask) includes wild guava fruit, fish, "hierba Luisa" tea, and wild chicken. Food, wine and beer expensive because of freight charges, but fruit and bread are cheap, and fish bought from the fishermen is good value. Average prices: coffee/tea US$0.35, meals about US$6, snacks US$0.80, beer/cola US$0.90 in most bars and restaurants. Bring all you can from the mainland (and remember that wine, whisky, watches, clothing—especially army surplus gear and tennis shoes—are good items for barter). Vegetarians will have no problems on the island. There are two discotheques in Hanga Roa. Both are popular, but drinks are expensive: a bottle of pisco costs US$5, canned beer US$1.20. *Porifico*, the original island disco, is open Thur. 2100-2400, Fri.-Sat. 2300-0300, entrance free, good entertainment. Beware of extras such as US$3 charge for hot water.

**Camping** Free in eucalyptus groves near the Ranger's house at Rano Raraku, and at Anakena. Officially, camping is not allowed anywhere else, but this is not apparently strictly enforced. Several habitable caves around the coast: e.g. between Anakena beach and Ovahe.

**Warning** The water on the island is not safe to drink; its high magnesium content may make you sick: drink only boiled or iodized water. Ask for the local herbal infusion which is a remedy for sickness. Bottled water costs US$2 for 1½ litres. Also, although the islanders are very nice about getting you a horse—they will get you *any* horse, so beware.

**Transport on Easter Island** There are no taxis and the only *colectivo* is often off the road. LanChile office in *Hotel Hanga Roa* provides tours of the island (including during stop-overs). A horse can be hired for US$10 a day or less, and is the best way to see the island as long as you are in good shape for riding. Another good way of getting around is by bicycle, but none is available for rent; buy or rent a robust one in Santiago (LanChile transports bikes free up to a limit of 20 kg.). After 4 days you can sell a bike on the island. Aku-Aku Tours arrange accommodation with islanders and excursions around the island, US$25 per person for full day, US$13-14 for half-day. Krenia Tucki of *Residencial Kai Poo* will also organize jeep tours, US$25 per day, as will Michel Fage. Some islanders, including Fernando and Marcelo León (Pai Tepano Rano, rec.) and Hugo Teave (good English, well-informed, polite) also provide tours. Charles Wilkins, Agencia de Viajes Mahinatur Ltda, T 20, English-born guide, rec., as is Victoriano Giralde, Kia-Koe Tours: provides transport for groups, arranges various activities and owns a local supermarket. Others may provide internal transport at a discount but be discreet, as an islander so doing is subjecting himself to social disapproval. The English of other tour guides is often poor. Good maps are available on the island. For instance that of Antoni Pujador Iti, 2nd edition 1988; Motu Iti "Ediciones del Pacifico Sur", Hernando de Aguirre 720, Depto. 63, Providencia, Santiago. Cheaper if bought outside Chile.

For **hiking**, allow at least a day to walk the length of the island, one way, taking in all the sites. It is 5 easy hours from Hanga Roa to Rano Raraku (camp at ranger station); 5 hrs. to Anakena (camp at ranger station, but ask first). You can hitch back to Hanga Roa, but there aren't many cars. Anyone wishing to spend time exploring the island would be well-advised to speak to Conaf first (T 236); they also give good advice on special interests (biology, archaeology, handicrafts, etc.).

**Vehicle Rental** If you are hiring a car, you should do the sites from south to north since travel agencies tend to start their tours in the north (also a high-clearance vehicle is better-suited to the roads than a normal vehicle). Jeep hire at **Sunoco service station**, Vaihu, T 325 or 239, on airport road, US$8/1 hr., US$16/4 hrs., US$30/8 hrs. **Hertz**, opp. airport, US$30/12 hrs. There is no insurance available, drive at your own risk (be careful at night, many vehicles drive without lights). Motorbikes may be rented for about US$30 a day including gasoline (Suzuki 125 rec. because of rough roads). Rentals from Av. Policarpo Toro, T 326.

**Bank** at Tahai, open 0900-1400 daily. Bank charges 10% commission per cheque. Prices are quoted in dollars, but bills can be paid in pesos; there is an island-wide conversion rate about mid-way between the mainland official and parallel rates. AmEx credit cards are accepted on the island, and while most places accept travellers' cheques, cash dollars are expected. Best rates of exchange at Sunoco service station. Kia-Koe Land Operator, *Hanga Roa Hotel*, changes AmEx cheques. **Post Office** 0900-1700.

**Tourist Office** Kia-Koe, at *Hanga Roa Hotel*, excellent range of excursions which include all the island's sites in 2½ days (to see it all you must start with the 1530/1600 tour on the day you arrive).

**Travel Agency** Mahinatur Ltda, will make your car reservations in advance.

**Medical** There are a 20-bed hospital, 2 resident doctors and 2 dentists on the island.

**Time Zone** Easter Island is always 2 hrs behind the Chilean mainland, summer and winter time.

**How to Get There** LanChile fly three times a week the year round, Sun., Wed., Fri. (1990), 5 hrs. Return to Santiago is Mon., Thur., Sat. (Mon., Wed. and Sat. out of season). LanChile's office on the island is at *Hotel Hanga Roa*, T 79, T 78 for reservations, reconfirm flights here—imperative; do not fly to Easter Island unless you have a confirmed flight out (planes are less crowded to Tahiti, to which LanChile's flights continue, than back to Santiago). For details of LanChile's air passes which include Easter Island and which must be purchased outside Chile, see **Information for Visitors**. It may be cheaper to buy a simple return with pesos exchanged on the parallel market. The fare in 1991 was US$812 return, but out of season it may be reduced; confirm and reconfirm all bookings as flights are heavily oversubscribed. Students studying in Chile eligible for 30% discount. If flying to, or from Tahiti, check if you can stay over till another flight or even if there is time for sightseeing before the flight continues—US$10 stop-over sightseeing tours can be arranged (in either case it won't be long enough to take it all in properly). Don't take pesos to Tahiti, they are worthless in French Polynesia. The airport runway has been improved. A US project to extend the airfield, to provide an emergency landing for space shuttles, has been completed.

**Airport tax** Flying from Santiago to Easter Island incurs the domestic tax of US$3.50; if flying to Tahiti without stopping on Easter Island you pay the international departure tax of US$12.50. The airport tax for international flights from Easter Island to Tahiti is US$5.

Dr. R. H. Webber writes: "It is possible to walk around the main part of the island in two days, either camping at Anakena or returning to Hanga Roa and setting out again the next day (but most correspondents agree that this is far too quick). From Hanga Roa, take the road going past the airport and continue northeast until you come to a right turn at a wireless station. Continue along the south coast, past many *ahus* to Rano Raraku (20 km.). The statues have been pushed over in some places, exposing the hollow chambers where human bones are still to be found.

"There are also many temple sites in the Hanga Nui area nearby; the road goes past "the trench of the long-ears" and an excursion can be made to Poike to see the open-mouthed statue that is particularly popular with local carvers. The jeep-track continues to Ovahe, passing many temple sites and conical houses. At Ovahe, there is a very attractive beach with pink sand and some rather recently carved faces and a cave.

"From Ovahe, one can return direct to Hanga Roa or continue to Anakena, site of King Hotu Matua's village. From Anakena the coastal path is variable in quality, but there are interesting remains and beautiful cliff scenery. At Hanga o Teo, there appears to be a large village complex, with several round houses, and further on there is a burial place, built like a long ramp with several ditches containing bones.

"From Hanga o Teo, one can venture inland to Aku Akivi, where there are several other sites and a cave at Tepahu. Near here there is a trail to Puna Pau; a track near the church leads to the top of the volcano.

"Rano Kau, south of Hanga Roa, is another important site to visit; one finds the curious Orongo ruins here. One final place not to be missed is Vinapu, where the *ahu* masonry work rivals that of the Incas."

A shorter walk is from Hanga Roa to Ahu Akivi, down to the South West coast, and back to Hanga Roa (8 km. one way).

**Recommended reading**, *Islas Oceánicas Chilenas*, edited by Juan Carlos Castillo (Ediciones Universidad Católica de Chile, 1987), contains much information on the natural history and geography of Juan Fernández and Easter Islands.

## SOUTH THROUGH THE CENTRAL VALLEY (5)

One of the world's most fruitful and beautiful countrysides, with the snowclad peaks of the Andes delimiting it to the E, the Central Valley contains most of Chile's population. It is a region of small towns, farms and vineyards, with several protected areas of natural beauty. To the south are the major city of Concepción, the port of Talcahuano and the main coal-mining area.

Road and railway run S through the Central Valley; the railway has been electrified from Santiago to just S of Temuco. Along the road from Santiago to Temuco there are several modern motels. From Santiago to San Fernando, the highway is dual carriageway, with two tolls of US$2.50 to pay.

*Rancagua*, the capital of VI Región (Libertador General Bernardo O'Higgins), 82 km. S of Santiago (1 hr. 10 mins bus, US$2.10), is an agricultural centre with a population of 167,000, where a battle was fought in 1814 by O'Higgins against the Royalists. Its Merced church is a national monument; it also has a historical museum. El Teniente, the largest underground copper mine in the world, is 67 km. to the E, at 2,750 metres; a permit to visit may be obtained in Santiago only (Huérfanos 1270). 28 km. E from Rancagua by road, are the thermal springs of Cauquenes.

**Festivals at Rancagua** The national rodeo championship is held there at the end of March. Festival del Poroto (Bean Festival), 1-5 Feb.

**Hotels** *Turismo Santiago*, Av. Brasil 1036, T 225060, C; *España*, San Martín 367, T 223963, D with bath, less without, central, hot water, pleasant, clean; *Rancagua*, San Martín 85 y Cáceres, T 232663, D with bath, quiet, clean, secure parking, rec. *Termas de Cauquenes*, T 297226, A, quiet, clean, expensive but excellent food (colectivo from Rancagua market, US$1.10). Many hotels do not accept guests before 2000, or may charge you double if you arrive in the afternoon. Some 50 km. south is *Hacienda Los Lingues*, see page 563.

**Exchange** Fincard (Visa, Mastercard), Astorga 485, Mon.-Fri. 0900-1400, 1530-1930, Sat. 1000-1300.

**Tourist Office** Germán Riesco 277, T 225777, helpful, English spoken. **Automóvil Club de Chile**, Ibieta 09, T 223575.

**Rail** Trains from Santiago, at least 4 a day, about 1 hr. 10 mins., US$2 *económico*, US$2.65 *superior*.

To the south west of Rancagua, in the valleys of rivers Cachapoal, Claro and Zamorano, the land is given over to fruit growing (including the estates of Viña Concha y Toro). Towns such as Doñihue, San Vicente de Tagua Tagua and Peumo have their roots in an Indian past which has been replaced by the *huaso* (cowboy) and agroindustry. West of Peumo is Lago Rapel, the largest artificial lake in the country (camping, water sports, etc. at Bahía Skorpios). The lake feeds the Rapel hydroelectric plant, best reached from Melipilla.

*San Fernando*, founded in 1742, capital of Colchagua Province, with 44,500 inhabitants, is 51 km. S of Rancagua. It stands in a broad and fertile valley at a height of 340 metres. A road (buses) run W to the seaside resort of Pichelemu (120 km., 86 paved), with beaches, camping and a great many hotels and *residenciales*. A road runs E towards the Cordillera and bifurcates: the northern branch runs to the Termas del Flaco, near the Argentine frontier (camping,

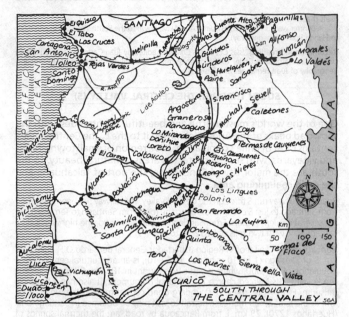

*cabañas* and hotels, but open only in summer); the southern branch goes to the resort of Sierra Bella Vista, a private *fundo* where many Santiago businessmen have holiday houses. Cowboy rodeos in October and November.

**Hotels** On Av. Manuel Rodríguez: *España*, No. 959, T 711098, C; *Marcano*, No. 968, T 712917, E; and *Imperio*, No. 770, T 712322.

*Curicó*, 60 km. S of San Fernando and 192 km. from Santiago, is in the heart of the wine country; population: 85,000. The surroundings are picturesque and the town's main Plaza de Armas is one of the finest in the country. In the plaza there are lovely fountains with sculptures of nymphs, black-necked swans and a monument to the Mapuche warrior, Lautaro, carved from the trunk of an ancient beech tree. The church of San Francisco, a national monument on the plaza, contains 17th century sculptures from Spain. At the junction of Carmen and Av. San Martín is the imposing Iglesia del Carmen. The Centro Cultural, Merced 437, is worth a visit; it has an art gallery, cinema, auditorium for concerts and an excellent cheap café. Overlooking the city, the surrounding countryside and with views to the distant Andean peaks is Cerro Condell (100 metres); it is an easy climb to the summit where there are a number of walks. The fine, broad and tree-lined Avenida Manso de Velasco leads to Parque Balmaceda, in which is a bust of the poet, Gabriela Mistral.

There is a toll (US$2.50) on the Longitudinal Highway south of Curicó. The city has a good road connection with Argentina, via Paso Vergara (Paso del Planchón, 92 km. from Curicó) to San Rafael (transport schedules from Turismo Bucalemu, Yungay 621). (We are grateful to Simon Watson Taylor for much new information on Curicó.)

**Hotels** *Luis Cruz Martines*, Prat 301 y Carmen, T 310552, B, breakfast extra, elegant, comfortable, good; *Comercio*, Yungay 730, T 311516, C, similar facilities and likewise rec.;

*Prat*, Peña 427, near Plaza de Armas, E., not all rooms have windows, but clean, hot water, heated lounge and good value; opp. is *Residencial Rahue*, No. 410, similar rates, meals extra, hot water, annex rooms have no ventilation, but otherwise acceptable; *Res. Central*, Av. Prat, 2 blocks from station, E, good value. On the outskirts of town, at Km. 190 on the Panamericana is *Hostería y Restaurante Agua Negra*.

**Restaurants** *El Fogón Chileno*, Yungay 802, excellent for meat and wines; *Villota*, Merced 487, popular, especially for lunch, very good value; *American Bar*, Yungay 647, coffee, pizzas, good sandwiches, pleasant atmosphere, open early a.m. to late p.m. inc. weekends, rec.; *Café-Bar Maxim*, Prat 617, light meals, good coffee, beer and wine. Many good, cheap restaurants in the streets around the Plaza de Armas.

**Exchange** Fincard, Carmen 498, for Visa and Mastercard.

**Laundry/Dry Cleaners** *Limpiabien*, Prat 454 (and other branches), quick, efficient.

**Tourist Office** Municipalidad building, 2nd floor, Plaza de Armas, helpful, has street map. **Automóvil Club de Chile**, Chacabuco 759, T 311156.

**Buses** To Santiago US$3. Companies have their own terminals for interprovincial destinations. Local buses, including to coastal towns, from rural bus terminal, O'Higgins y Prat, one block from railway station. Many southbound buses by-pass Curicó, but can be caught by waiting outside town.

**Rail** Station is at the end of Prat, 4 blocks west of Plaza de Armas. To/from Santiago, US$3 *económico*, US$3.65 *superior*.

**Excursions** A road runs W to Licantén, 26 km. from the popular sea beaches of Iloca. North of Iloca is another popular resort, *Llico*, reached either by a coastal route or by an inland road which branches off the road to Licantén. (*Hostería Llico*; *Residencial Miramar*, good seafood restaurant; *Pensión Chile*, F, clean, friendly. Buses: one a day from Curicó, two daily in summer). Just before Llico are Lago Vichuquen (hotels, camping at Bahía Mansa, and watersports) and **Laguna de Torca**, a natural sanctuary for wildlife (there are *miradores* for birdwatching, the administration is 4 km. away at Llico, open September-April). From Curicó you can also visit the **Siete Tazas National Park**, where a river flows through seven rock bowls, each with a pool emptying into the next by a small waterfall. The river then passes through a canyon, 15 metres deep but only 1½ metres wide, which ends abruptly in a cliff and a beautiful waterfall. Go to Molina, 26 km. S of Curicó, from where buses run to the Park, daily in Jan. and Feb., three times a week in March, and Oct.-Dec., once a week at other times. It may be possible to hitch there and back in a day, but you have to set out very early. The park is open October to March. Camping may be permitted at the park or 5 km. away at Parque Inglés (*Hospedaje* open summer only).

*Talca*, 56 km. S of Curicó (258 km. from Santiago) is the most important city between Santiago and Concepción and an important maufacturing centre; it is the capital of VII Región (Maule), and has a population of 300,000. It was founded in 1692, and destroyed by earthquake in 1742 and 1928; it has been completely rebuilt since 1928. Chilean independence was declared in Talca on 1 January 1818. The market is near the bus station, where there are also stalls selling cheap food. A 175 km. road runs E through the pass of Pehuenche (2,490 metres) to San Rafael (Argentina). Near the border is Lago Maule (2,130 metres). The road passes through some of the finest mountain scenery in Chile, but permission to visit this area must be obtained from the Vice Comandancia del Regimiento de Infantería No. 16, Calle 3 Oriente, Talca (T 38159). There is no transport, accommodation or food there. A visit to an old estate at Villa Cultural Huilquilleru is rec., 10 km. away.

**Hotels** *Plaza*, 1 Poniente 1141, T 231515, A, good commercial standard; *Claris*, 1 Sur 1026, T 232202, C; *Alcázar*, 2 Sur 1359 and 7 Oriente, E, breakfast and meals available, rec. as reasonable and clean. Also, *Cordillera*, 2 Sur 1360, T 233078, E p.p., near new bus terminal. *Don Otto's*, 4 Oriente y 1 Norte, best atmosphere in town.

**Museum** Museo O'Higginiano, 1 Norte 875 y 2 Oriente, entrance US$0.35, open Tues.-Sat. 0930-1300, 1500-2000, Sun. 1000-1300; interesting.

**Tourist Office** Edificio Intendencia (at the town hall), T 33669. **Automóvil Club de Chile**, 1 Poniente 1267, T 223-2774.

**Bus** Terminal, corner 12 Oriente and 2 Sur. To Chillán, frequent service, US$2; also frequent to Constitución, 2 hrs., US$1.20.

**Train** Station at 2 Sur y 11 Oriente. Most trains from the capital to Concepción, Chillán and Temuco stop here; fare from Santiago, US$3.65 *económico*, US$5 *superior*.

**Excursion** To *Vilches*, the starting point for the climb to the volcanoes Quizapu and Descabezado (3,850 metres) 2 buses a day, US$1.50, 2-2½ hrs., leave Talca 1300 and late p.m., leave Vilches 0700 and 1730. *Hostería Rancho Los Canales*, C p.p. bed and breakfast, use of kitchen, log cabins C between 4 people, hospitable, knowledgeable family (postal address: Casilla 876, Talca). 2 km beyond the town is the **Area de Protección Vilches**, with 20 km. of beautiful walks; visit the lakes Los Patos, La Encantada and El Toro, and the Piedras Tacitas, a stone construction supposedly made by the aboriginal inhabitants of the region. The administration is near the *Hotel Altos de Vilches*; there is a visitors' centre in the park (2 daily buses from Alto Vilches).

**Constitución**, 105 km. from Talca by rail (daily service), and also reached by paved road from San Javier, is the centre of a prosperous district producing grain and timber, but its main attraction is as a seaside resort. The beach, an easy walk from the town, is surrounded by very picturesque rocks. There are good views from Cerro Mutrún, at the mouth of the river (access from Calle O'Higgins). The scenery is attractive, despite nearby factory. There are plenty of hotels and *pensiones*, but accommodation is difficult from January to March, and bookings must be made well in advance.

**Hotels** *Hostería Constitución*, Echeverria 460, T 671450, A, best; *Residencial Bulnes*, Bulnes 673, E, hot water, clean. *Residencial Sebastián*, Freire 249, E, good.

There are two **Reservas Nacionales** south of Constitución, in the vicinity of Chanco: **Los Ruiles**, protecting woods and flowers (open October-March), daily buses from Constitución or Cauquenes, on the road to the coast from Parral), and **Federico Albert**, ½ km. from Chanco (bus), which covers a marginal zone of woods and encroaching sand (visitors' centre, 4 paths of 5 km., open October-March).

About half-way between Talca and Chillán is the road and rail junction of Parral, 342 km. S of Santiago, celebrated as the birthplace of the Nobel Prize-winning poet Pablo Neruda.

**Chillán**, 105 km. S of the road junction for Linares, was the birthplace of Bernardo O'Higgins. In Chillán Viejo (SW of the centre) there is a monument and park in his honour; it has a 60-metre long mural depicting his life (an impressive mosaic of various native stones), and a Centro Histórico y Cultural, with a gallery of contemporary paintings by regional artists (park is open 0900-1300, 1500-1900). (Chile's naval hero, Captain Arturo Prat, was born 50 km. from Chillán, at Ninhue.) It is an important agricultural centre, capital of Ñuble province, with a population of 134,000. When the city was destroyed by earthquake in 1833, the new city was built slightly to the N; that, too, was destroyed by earthquake in 1939 and there was a further earthquake in 1960. It is a pleasant city with a modern cathedral. The Mercado y Feria Municipal (covered and open markets) sells regional arts and crafts, and has many cheap, good restaurants, serving regional dishes; open daily, Sun. until 1300. Murals by David Alfaro Siqueiros, the great Mexican artist, in the library of Escuela México (Av. B. O'Higgins between Vega de Saldias and Gamero).

**Hotels** *Gran Hotel Isabel Riquelme*, Arauco 600, T 223664, A; *Rucamanqui*, Herminda Martín 590 (off Plaza de Armas), T 222927, B, clean, spartan; *Cordillera*, Arauco 619, on Plaza de Armas, T 225222, B, 3-star, small, all rooms with heating and bath, good; *Quinchamalí*, El Roble 634, T 223381, C, central, quiet, clean, hot water, heated lounge. On Libertad: *Libertador*, No. 85, T 223255, D, large rooms, clean, hot water; *Real*, No 219, T 221827, D, good; *Ruiz de Gamboa*, O'Higgins 497, T 221013, C with bath, D without, good value; these three are a few minutes' walk from the railway station and are much better than the closer hotels such as *Chillán*, Libertad 65, *Santiago*, next door, and *Bahía*, opp. station, reported clean but basic, E; *Claris*, 18 de Septiembre 357, T 221980, 2 blocks from plaza, friendly, E, good value, hot water; *Residencial Su Casa*, Cocharcas 555, T 223931, cheap, clean (owner is a dog- and rose-lover), parking.

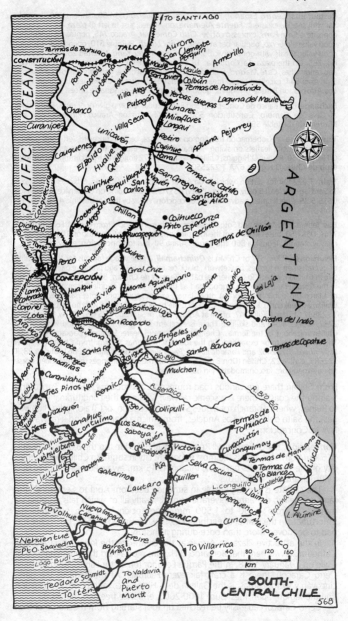

SOUTH-
CENTRAL CHILE

56B

**Restaurants** *Centro Español*, Plaza de Armas, *almuerzo* US$4.50, dinner US$8, separate bar with snacks, excellent. *Fuente Alemana*, on Arauco, just to left of plaza, for churrasco; opposite is *Café París*, expresso coffee. *Club Comercial*, Arauco 745, popular at lunchtime, good value *almuerzo*, popular bar at night; *Quick Lunch*, El Roble 610, open 0800-2400 for good value meals with good service. 2 good Chinese: *Jai Yang*, Libertad 250 and *Taipe* at No. 285. On the plaza: *La Copucha*, 18 de Septiembre y Constitución, inexpensive meals and sandwiches; *Café Madrid*, 5 de Abril 608, good for coffee, open weekends; *La Masc'a*, 5 de Abril 544, excellent cheap meals, *empanadas de queso*, drinks, rec. In Chillán Viejo, *Los Adobes*, on Parque O'Higgins, good food and service, reasonable prices.

**Exchange** Both Banco de Concepción and Banco Sudamericano give poor rates. Better rates at *Casa de Cambio*, Constitución 550, or *Café París* on Arauco. Fincard (Visa and Mastercard), El Roble 553.

**Tourist Office** In Gobernación building on main plaza, central courtyard, left-hand gallery; street map of city, leaflets on skiing, Termas de Chillán, etc. Another office reported at Av. O'Higgins 250, Parque O'Higgins, Chillán Viejo, T 223272 (long way from centre). **Automóvil Club de Chile**, O'Higgins 677, T 222550.

**Train** T 222424 for station, which is on Av. Brasil opp. Calle Libertad, 5 blocks from plaza. To **Santiago**, at least 5 daily, 5½ hrs., *Salón* US$7-7.35 depending on the service, *económico* US$5-5.35. Check times in advance. To **Concepción**, either by train or bus link, 4 a day, US$2, 2 hrs.

**Bus** Terminal at Maipon and Sgto. Aldea for local buses (4 blocks from centre). For **Santiago**, 7 hrs, US$7.50, buses leave from the interprovincial terminal at Constitución 10 y Brasil (opp. railway station). Tegualda 860 and Barrios Arana 90, bus to **Concepción**, every ½ hr.

**Excursions** 27 km. SW of Chillán is **Quinchamalí**, a little village famous for the originality of its craftsmen in textiles, basketwork, black ceramics, guitars and primitive paintings (all on sale in Chillán market). To the thermal baths, **Termas de Chillán**, 82 km. E, 1,850 metres up in the Cordillera, reached by a good road all the way. Season: middle December to the end of March (no public transport at other times, except tours from *Hotel Isabel Riquelme* in Chillán at weekends). Here the Ski Club de Chile has a tourist centre with hotel (L, full board, T 223887 Chillán, Casilla 247, office at Arauco 600, or Santiago T 251-5776, Av. Providencia 2237, locales 42-4) and ski-lifts. There is excellent ski-ing on the slopes and views of the Chillán volcano, E of the Termas. Cheaper than centres nearer Santiago; packages available. This ski resort is to be expanded. On the road to the Termas, 70 km. from Chillán are *Hotel Los Pirineos*, T 222462 and *Parador Jamón, Pan y Vino*, 18 de Septiembre 661, oficina 23, T 222682, Casilla 22, Chillán (Don Emilio Chamorro). The latter arranges recommended horse riding expeditions (accommodation in our R range).

From Chillán there are various road routes to Concepción: (1) SW to Penco and S along the coast—there is a scenic railway; (2) along the Longitudinal Highway to Bulnes, where a branch road goes SW to Concepción; or (3) along the Highway past the Salto del Laja to Los Angeles, from which a main road and a railway run NW to Concepción.

**Concepción**, the capital of VIII Región (Bío-Bío), 15 km. up the Bío-Bío river and 515 km. from Santiago, is the most important city in southern Chile and the third city of the Republic. Its port, Talcahuano, is 15 km. away. Population: 240,000 (with Talcahuano: 468,000).

The climate is very agreeable in summer, but from April to September the rains are heavy; the annual average rainfall, nearly all of which falls in those six months, is from 1,250 to 1,500 mm. Concepción has been outstandingly unfortunate in the matter of earthquakes; it was founded in 1550, but its site has had to be moved more than once during its history.

In the attractive Plaza de Armas at the centre are the Intendencia and the Cathedral. It was here that Bernardo O'Higgins proclaimed the independence of Chile on 1 January 1818. In the Parque Ecuador (on Victor Lamas, at the foot of Cerro Caracol), there is a craft fair every February. At the edge of the park, Lincoyán y Víctor Lamas, is the Galería de la Historia, covering both Concepción and the region, open Tues.-Sun. 1000-2000, entrance free (worth a visit).

Cerro Caracol can easily be reached on foot starting from the statue of Don

Juan Martínez de Rozas in the Parque Ecuador, arriving at the Mirador Chileno after 15 minutes. There are two other sets of steps up the hill. Chile's largest river, the Bío-Bío, and its valley running down to the sea lie below. On the far side of the river you see lagoons, the largest of which, San Pedro, is a water-sport centre. On the city side, among cypress trees, is the modern Barrio Universitario. A stroll through the grounds, which are beautifully kept with geese, ducks, swans, hummingbirds and a small enclosure with *pudu-pudu* (miniature deer) is rec.; the Casa del Arte here contains a fine allegorical mural, 35 by 6 metres, the *Presencia de América Latina*, by Jorge González Camerena (closed Monday). There is a golf club on the road to Coronel, La Posada, by the side of a picturesque lake.

There are striking massive rock formations along the banks of the Bío-Bío estuary. Concepción is linked with Talcahuano, on the bay, by railway (no passenger services) and 2 good roads, half-way along one of which is the Club Hípico's racetrack. Races are held on Sun. and holidays. A branch road leads to good beaches, including Penco with two good seafood restaurants. It passes through the Parque de Hualpén, which can be reached by bus in summer (US$1) and taxi all the year (US$10). In it, on a farm, is a small museum containing curious local and Mapuche Indian items. Nearby is the strikingly set beach of Desembocadura del Río. Two other beaches are Las Escaleras (a private club)—a flight of natural stairs down a sheer 53-metre sea cliff leads to it—and Ramuntcho, named after a novel by a visitor in 1875: Pierre Loti.

Concepción is one of Chile's industrial centres. It has plenty of the most important industrial raw material, water, and good port facilities at Talcahuano and other places in the bay. It is near the coalfields, has ample sources of hydroelectric power, good rail and road communications with the consuming centres further N, and plenty of room to expand.

**Hotels** *El Araucano*, Caupolicán 521, T 230606, A+; *Ritz*, Barros Arana 721, T 226696, B, reasonable; *Alborada*, Barros Arana 457, Casilla 176, T 228226, A+; *Tabancura*, Barros Arana 790, 8th floor, T 226927, B, clean, highly rec.; *Alonso de Ercilla*, Colo Colo 334, T 227984, B; *Residencial Antuco*, Barros Arana 741, flats 28-33 and *Residencial San Sebastián*, Barros Arana 741, flats 34-35, both C, both rec. *Res. Colo Colo*, Colo Colo 743, E, central, spartan, hot water, heated lounge, pleasant, welcoming, rec.; apart from this one, good budget accommodation is hard to find; *Residencial Central*, Rengo 672, D with breakfast, friendly, spacious; *Res. Metro*, Barros Arana 464, E, hot shower, but basic, rooms without windows; *Res. Concepción*, Freire 552, across from the market, run down; *Res. O'Higgins*, Av. O'Higgins 457, central, D, pricey, grubby, cold, poor breakfast; *Pablo Araya*, Salas 643-C, E.

**Restaurants** *El Rancho de Julio*, Barros Arana 337, Argentine parrillada, good value; *Piazza*, Barros Arana 327, good pizzas; *Rincón de Pancho*, Cervantes 469 (closed Sun.), excellent for meat, mainly, but also pasta and congrio, good service and ambience; *Tagore*, Lincoyán 660, grills, seafood and excellent vegetarian main dish, small, intimate, good service and value, open till late inc. Sun.; *Novillo Loco*, Portales 539, good food, efficient service. *Le Château* (French), Colo Colo 340, for seafood and meat, but overpriced and closed Sun. Oriental: *Yiet-Xiu*, Angol 515, good, cheap; *Ta-Tung*, Lincoyán 540, similar value and quality, Cantonese; *Chung Hwa*, Barros Arana 270. *Hotel Concepción* restaurant, Barros Arana 101, is good value; *Big Joe Saloon*, O'Higgins 808, just off plaza, popular at lunchtime, closed Sun. a.m. but open in p.m., good breakfasts, vegetarian meals, snacks and pizzas. *Saaya 1*, Barros Arana 899, excellent panadería/pastelería/rotisería, highly rec. Vegetarian: *Naturista*, Barros Arana 244, good fresh juices, soups and other dishes, live guitar music at lunchtime. Many *fuentes de soda* in centre; *Fuente Alemana*, Av. O'Higgins, rec.; those on the Plaza de Armas include *Café El Dom*, Caupolicán side, open Sun. 0900, *Café Haiti*, Plaza end of Caupolicán, also open Sun. a.m., and *Café Status*, on first floor, pleasant, reasonable lunches; *Royal Pub*, O'Higgins 796, not a pub but a rather posh snack bar serving fat sandwiches, all named after famous Britons, go to look at the menu if nothing else, try to puzzle out the relationship between the fillings and who they are named after (closed Sun. a.m., opens Sun. 1900); *Salón Inglés*, next door, is an English tea shop, "good for expats longing for a cuppa"; *Nuria Café Bar*, Barros Arana 736, serves very good breakfasts and lunches, good value; good sandwiches at *Entrepanes*, Caupolicán, between B.Arana and Freire. The market place, bounded by Freire, Caupolicán, Maipú and Rengo, has excellent seafood and the best pastel de choclo, also good for fruit, vegetables, cheese and sausages (closes 2000, 1400 on Sun.). (Thanks are due to Simon Watson Taylor for his extensive research for the improvement of this section.)

**Country Club**, Pedro de Valdivia, outside swimming pool, tennis.

**Car Hire** Hertz, Lord Cochrane 862, T 223121; **Budget**, Arana 541, T 225377.

**Museum** Museo de Concepción, near Barrio Universitario, Tues.-Sat. 1000-1300, 1400-1700, Sun. 1430-1730; entrance US$0.30; interesting on history of Mapuche nation. See above for Galería de la Historia.

**Exchange** Cambios Fides, Barros Arana 565, local 58, Galería Internal, lower ground floor below *Hotel Araucano*, best rates for travellers' cheques; **Fincard** (Visa, Mastercard), O'Higgins 402, open 24 hrs. **Banks** such as Banco Concepción charge high commission on travellers' cheques.

**Cultural Institutes** Aliance Française, Colo Colo y V. Lamas, library, concerts, films, cultural events; **Chilean-British Cultural Institute**, San Martín 531 (British newspapers, library); **Chilean-North American Institute**, Caupolicán 301 y San Martín, has library ; **Chileno-Italiano**, Barros Arana.

**British Consul** Dr. John F. Pomeroy, Castellón 317, T (041) 225655, Casilla 452.

**Post Office** and telex, O'Higgins y Colo Colo. There is a CTC **telephone** opposite, also at Barros Arana 673, local 2. Entel, Caupolicán 567, 2nd floor.

**Laundry** Many laundries and dry cleaners in the centre especially in Freire 900 block.

**Tourist Office** Aníbal Pinto 460 on plaza, T 223272. Will advise on the more expensive hotels and *residenciales*. **Automóvil Club de Chile**, San Martín 519, T 226554, for information and car hire (T 222070).

**Travel Agent** *Pawulska Tour*, A. Pinto 367, T 238720/225039, Fax 228337, arranges tours, flights, translation, interpretation, and welcomes travellers for a chat.

**Air** In the summer, flights daily to and from Santiago (in winter, only four a week) and connections to Temuco, Puerto Montt and Punta Arenas. The new jet airport is by the fast road from Talcahuano and Concepción. LanChile, Barros Arana 541, T 25014; Ladeco, Barros Arana 451, T 240025/228792.

**Rail** 3 regular daily trains to/from **Santiago**, 9 hrs.; in summer the service is increased: *salón* US$10-11 depending on service, *económico* US$8-9, sleeper from US$12 to US$33.35 for *departamento*. Connections by rail or road to **Chillán**; no regular, direct services to **Temuco** (a seasonal service runs once a day). Station at A. Prat with Barros Arana. Ticket office Galería Alessandri, local 6, T 225286, or T 226-925 for station.

**Buses** Long distance terminal on outskirts, on Av. Gen. Bonilla, next to athletics stadium; buses from Av. Maipú in centre. To and from **Santiago**, 8½ hrs., US$7 (cheapest is Sol del Pacífico, US$4, not very comfortable but OK); to **Loncoche**, 7 hrs., US$6.50; to **Puerto Montt** several companies, US$7.50-9, about 12 hrs., only one ½ hour stop so take food and drink with you; to **Pucón**, 8 hrs., US$7.35. Igi-Llaima, to **Temuco**, 5 hrs., US$4.25, and other companies. To **Los Angeles**, US$1.50. Best direct bus line to **Chillán** is Línea Azul, 2 hrs., US$2, at 0700. For a longer and more scenic route, take Costa Azul bus which follows old railway line, through Tomé, Coelemu and Ñipas on to Chillán (part dirt-track, takes 5½ hrs.). Frequent service to **Coronel** (US$0.45). For Arauco and Bío-Bío region (including **Cañete**) buses leave from railway station on Av. Prat. To **Contulmo**, 0745 and 1545, US$2.55. To **Lota**, from Carrera y Prat, every 15 mins., 1 hr., US$0.50 (ask tourist office for details of all services).

**Excursion** To the **Museo y Parque Hualpen**, a house built around 1885 (now a national monument) and its gardens, donated to the city by Pedro del Río Zañartu; it contains beautiful pieces from all over the world, 2 hr. visit, rec. (open Tues.-Sun. 0900-1230, 1400-1800, free). Take a city bus to Hualpencillo, ask driver to let you out then walk 40 mins. or hitch. You have to go along Av. Las Golondrinas to the Enap oil refinery, turn left, then right (it is signed). To *Lirquén*, 15 km., a small, old, pretty town of wooden houses with a good beach (walk along railway to reach it). Recommended. Plentiful cheap seafood for sale (try *Casa Blanca*, on Calle Manuel Rodríguez). At **Penco**, 12 km. from Concepción, near the beach, is *Casinoriente*, another good seafood place, and *Hotel La Terraza*, Penco 20, T 451422, D. Local buses from Av. Prat 484 take 20-30 mins., US$0.40. 16 km. further along is *Tomé*, 1½ hrs., US$0.70, another picturesque village; *Restaurante Piña*, main Plaza (owner speaks English); *Hotel Roxy*, Sotomayor 1077, T 378, D, and *Linares*, Serrano 875, T 538, E. An interesting cemetery,

Miguel Gulán Muñoz, is set on a cliff overlooking the ocean. *Dichato*, a 1-hr. bus ride (37 km.) away, is also worth visiting: it is a beautiful fishing village and has the oceanographic centre of the University of Concepción. In summer it is a busy holiday resort. *Hotel Chicki*, P. L. Ugalde 410, T 681004, D; *Montecarlo*, Ismael Valdés 685, E; *Restaurant Monte Carlo*, on beach, good. Private Museo del Mar, by Benjamín Ortega, interesting, free. Take a local bus to the tiny village of Cocholgüe.

Between Concepción and Lota (see below) are the Lagunas San Pedro Chica (swimming) and Grande (water sports), just across the Bío-Bío river. Nearer Lota are Playa Negra (small, few people, black sand) and Playa Blanca (bigger, bars, cafés, crowded, white sand, free campsite), both on the Bahía de Coronel (see below).

*Talcahuano*, on a peninsula jutting out to sea, has the best harbour in Chile. It is Chile's main naval station; its dry docks accommodate vessels of 30,000 tons. Population: 228,000. 1½ km. away the steel plant at Huachipato has its own wharf to unload the iron ore shipped from the N. "Base Naval" bus from main plaza in Concepción, going W on O'Higgins.

**Hotel** *Res. San Pedro*, Manuel Rodríguez 22, T 542145, D. **Restaurants** *Bentoteca*, on seafront, a row of four restaurants sharing one window facing the harbour, superb fish and seafood in each one, rec., reasonable prices. *El Alero de los Salvo*, Colón 3396; *La Aguada*, shellfish dishes; *Domingo Lara Lara*, Aníbal Pinto 450, seafood specialities, excellent.

The *Huáscar*, a relic of the War of the Pacific, is in the naval base. On 21 May 1879, at the beginning of the war, the Peruvian Navy's huge ironclad, the *Huáscar*, and a small one arrived at Iquique. Chile sent two small wooden ships under Captain Arturo Prat to challenge them. Prat fought with ferocity. When his broken vessel, the *Esmeralda*, was rammed by the *Huáscar* Prat called upon his men to follow him, boarded the enemy and continued fighting until he was killed. Chile later captured the *Huáscar* at the battle of Angamos, Mejillones, on 8 October 1879. The ship is open daily 1030-1630, but the schedules do change. Photography is permitted, but passports must be handed in at main gate.

A railway to Curanilahue links Concepción with the coal-producing districts to the south. It crosses the Bío-Bío by a 1,885-metre bridge, the longest of its kind in Chile. A new road bridge has been built. The town of *Coronel*, in the heart of the coal area, is 29 km. from Concepción. Coronel was the scene of a British naval defeat in 1914 (the *Good Hope* and *Monmouth* were sunk by the *Scharnhorst*—a monument was dedicated in November 1989), which was later avenged at the Falklands/Malvinas with the destruction of the German squadron. The coast is very picturesque, the country wooded.

**Buses** Buses to **Concepción** every hour. Bus to **Lota** US$0.25.

*Lota*, 8 km. S of Coronel, is a coal-mining centre with 52,000 inhabitants. To the west of the town, on a promontory, is the famous Parque de Lota (Cousiño Isidora), laid out with views of the sea by an English landscape architect in the last century. It contains many flower gardens, romantic paths, and peafowl and pheasants roaming freely. (Admission US$0.60, no picnicking; open 1000-1800 daily, till 2000 in summer.) The Cousiño mining company runs an excellent ceramic factory. The road is paved beyond Lota as far as the seaside resort of Laraquete (an hour's run by car from Concepción), where there are miles of golden sands, and on to Arauco, past the Celulosa Arauco wood-pulp plant.

**Hotels** In Lota: *Residencial Roma*, ½ block from main plaza, reasonable; *Residencial Central*, Cousiño 656, E. In Laraquete: *Laraquete*, on Gabriela Mistral, main street, E, friendly, small rooms, baths in poor repair. Several *residenciales* close to beach. In Arauco: *Hostería Arauco*, P. de Valdivia 80, T 551131, B. *Plaza*, Chacabuco 347, T 551265, E;

**Buses** to **Coronel** (20 min.), and **Concepción** (1½ hrs., US$0.50). Many southbound buses by-pass the centre: catch them from the carretera.

From Curanilahue, 96 km. from Concepción, a 32 km. road runs to Los Alamos, where a bus (26 km.) can be taken W to **Lebu**, a fishing port and coal washing centre with a population of 17,000 (*Hotels Central*, Pérez 183, T 511904, C and some cheaper rooms, clean, good; *Rocha*, Pérez 309, T 511939, E; *Res. Alcázar*,

Alcázar 144, F with breakfast, cold water, friendly). It lies at the mouth of the Río Lebu, and is the capital of Arauco province (buses S leave from Los Alces, next to train station). The lower river reach and the beach are popular with tourists in summer. The views from the hill behind the town are majestic.

13 km. S of Los Alamos, is *Cañete*, a small town on the site of Fort Tucapel where Pedro de Valdivia and 52 of his men were killed by Mapuche warriors in 1554. Museo Mapuche de Cañete, half-hour walk from town in direction of Contulmo. Open, Tues.-Sun. 1000-1230, 1400-1800. Entrance US$0.60. Interesting for its architecture, landscape, gardens with flowers cultivated by the Mapuches. Ask for Sr. Mauricio Rivera Osorio.

**Accommodation**  *Hotel Nahuelbuta*, Villagran 644, T 611251, main street near plaza, E, private parking; *Alonso de Ercilla*, opposite, No. 641, T 611974, E, clean; *Derby*, Nariñan 680, T 211621, E, central, clean, friendly, good restaurant; *Gajardo*, 7° de la Línea 817 (1 block from plaza), F, old fashioned, friendly, pleasant. Some shops rent rooms, E. Mormons in Calle Condell offer accommodation, free and friendly.

**Buses**  3 night buses to and from **Santiago**, 12 hrs. Buses to **Purén**, US$1.50; sit on right-hand side to get good views of Lago Lanalhue. To **Concepción**, 3 hrs., US$2.50.

From Lebu or Los Alamos you can go to Puerto Peleco on the highly picturesque Lago Lanalhue, 63 km. S of Lebu (buses S leave Los Alces, next to train station). 3½ km. S of Peleco, the road forks, the west branch running parallel to the coast (from this road, a dirt road goes along the south side of the lake to *Hostería Lanalhue*—16 km. from Peleco. A nice location—and continuing to Contulmo bus terminal, taxi US$14, negotiable). By taking the west branch of the road for about 25 km. and then asking the way to Contulmo, you can reach the south-eastern end of the lake after crossing a high ridge from which you can see both the ocean in the W and the snow-capped Andes to the E. In **Contulmo** *Hotel Contulmo* is highly recommended, D (Millaray 116, Eduardo Videla and family love to break out the wine and guitar with visitors); *Hotel Central*, Calle Millaray no sign, also D and very hospitable. Taxi from Contulmo to lake beach US$2; swimming good, but fishing not so. Bus Contulmo-Temuco, Thiele company, 3 a day, US$3, at least two a day to Concepción, US$2.55 (check times in advance).

Travelling S from Chillán on the Longitudinal Highway, the next major centre is **Los Angeles**, capital of Biobío province, a town of 106,000 inhabitants in a wine, fruit and timber district. Founded in 1739 as a fort, it is now a pleasant, expanding city, with a large Plaza de Armas; Colón is the main shopping street. There is a good daily market.

**Hotels**  *Gran Hotel Müso*, Valdivia 222 (Plaza de Armas), T 323163, B, good restaurant open to non-residents; *Mariscal Alcázar*, Lautaro 385 (Plaza de Armas), T 321275, A; *Mazzola*, Lautaro 579, T 321643, C. *Res. Winser*, Colo Colo 335, E; *Res. Santa María*, Caupolicán, next to bus station, D, hot shower, TV, breakfast extra. Private house at Caupolicán 651, E, basic but OK. Youth hostel: *Complejo Turístico Los Manantiales*, Caupolicán 332, camping and cabins, open 1 March to 31 December.

**Restaurants**  *El Arriero*, Colo Colo 235, T 322899, good *parrillas* and international dishes; *Julio's Pizzas*, Colón 452 and *Rancho de Julio*, Colón 720, excellent *parrilla*.

**British Cultural Institute**  Vicuña 648.

**Post Office**  on Plaza de Armas.

**Tourist Office**  Av. Caupolicán and Villagrán; also kiosk on Plaza de Armas. **Automóvil Club de Chile** Villagrán y Caupolicán, T 322149.

**Bus**  to **Santiago**, 9 hrs., US$7.50. To **Viña del Mar** and **Valparaíso** 10 hrs., US$8.25, 4 daily to **Concepción**, US$1.50, 2¼ hrs. Hourly buses to **Temuco**, US$2.30. To **Curacautín**, daily at 0600, 3 hrs., US$2.25.

**Excursion**  The *Salto del Laja* is a spectacular waterfall in which the Laja plunges 47 metres over the rocks. It costs a few pesos to enter the "parque" and walk up to the falls, or to walk on the hotel side. There is a good motel (the *Motel Salto del Laja*, B, address: Casilla 562, Los

Angeles) with fine restaurant, 2 swimming pools and chalet-type rooms on an island overlooking the falls. Also at or near the falls are *Camping Los Manantiales* and Motels *El Pinar* and *Los Coyuches*. It is 6 hrs. drive from Santiago (by bus, US$7.25). To see the falls, buy bus ticket (Bus Sur or Bio Tal) from Los Angeles (32 km., US$0.60, ½ hr.—fairly frequent buses back to Los Angeles) or Chillán (US$2).

A road runs to the **Parque Nacional Laguna de Laja** past the impressive rapids of the Laja river. A car can take about 3 hours to get to the lake, where there is stark volcanic scenery of scrub and lava, dominated by the Antuco volcano and the glacier-covered Sierra Velluda. Take a bus to Abanico (*Hostería del Bosque*, E, pool, restaurant), 20 km. past Antuco (US$1.35, 2 hrs., 5 a day but only 0845 in a.m., return 0715), then 4 km. to park entrance, passport retained by guards till you leave (details from Conaf in Los Angeles, José de Manzo 275, 0800-1300, 1430-1800 Mon.-Fri.). *Cabañas y Camping Lagunillas*, 50 m. from the river, 4 km. from the ski slopes, campsite US$1.65 p.p. or US$4.65 for 3 or more. Camping not permitted on lake shore. 21 km. from the lake is the *Refugio Chacay* offering food, drink and bed (B, T Los Angeles 222651); two other *refugios*: *Digeder*, E, and Universidad de Concepción, both on slopes of Volcán Antuco, for both T Concepción 221561, office O'Higgins 734. Following the road one reaches the Club de Esquí de los Andes with two ski-lifts, giving a combined run of 4 km. on the Antuco volcano (season, May-August). There is swimming in the Río Duqueco, ten minutes away by bus, US$0.80.

The road continues from Los Angeles to Santa Bárbara on the Bío-Bío river (*Restaurant Las Tortoras*, rec.) and then via Collipulli (campsite), Victoria, Púa and Lautaro to Temuco.

From Collipulli and Los Angeles paved roads run W to **Angol** (35,000 people), capital of the Province of Malleco (IX Région), founded by Valdivia in 1552, seven times destroyed by the Indians and rebuilt. Bus from Santiago US$6.50, Los Angeles, US$1.20, or Collipulli. Worth seeing are El Vergel experimental fruit-growing station, the Dillman S. Bullock regional museum with precolumbian Indian artefacts (open daily 0830-1300, 1500-1800, US$0.50, a 5 km. bus-ride from town) and the San Francisco church. 35 km. W is the **Parque Nacional Nahuelbuta**, in the coastal mountain range, reached by bus to Vegas Blancas, 0700 and 1600 Mon., Wed., Fri., 1½ hrs., US$1, 27 km. from Angol, then walk (or possibly hitch) 7 km. to park gate, and a further 7 km. to the campsite (US$0.70 to enter park, US$0.70 to camp—there are many free campsites on the way to the entrance). The park has many araucaria trees (monkey-puzzles) and viewpoints over both the sea and the Andean volcanoes. Rough maps are available at the park entrance for US$0.25. Roads run W to Los Sauces and Purén. Bus to Temuco, US$2.15.

**Hotels** *La Posada*, at El Vergel, T 712103, D p.p. full board, clean, friendly; *Millaray*, A+, Prat 420, T 711570, C; *Olimpia*, Lautaro 194, T 711517, C; *El Parrón*, O'Higgins 345, T 711370, E; *Residencial Olimpia*, Caupolicán 625, T 711162, D; *Residencial Prat*, Prat 499, T 711096, E, clean, spacious.

*Mulchén*, a small, old-fashioned town, 32 km. to the south of Los Angeles, has few cars, no concrete and is a glimpse of a world gone-by.

A small town which has hot springs nearby, **Curacautín**, is 56 km. SE of Victoria (on the Longitudinal Highway, Ruta 5) by paved road; bus from Los Angeles or Temuco.

**Curacautín Hotels** *Turismo*, Tarapacá 140, T 116, E, clean, good food, comfortable, best value; *Plaza*, Yungay 157, T 56, D; *Residencial Rojas*, Tarapacá 249, E without bath, good meals, rec.

The beautiful pine-surrounded Termas de Tolhuaca, with hot springs, are 35 km. to the NE of Curacautín by unpaved road, or 57 km. by unpaved road from just N of Victoria. (*Hotel Termas de Tolhuaca*, A with full board, use of baths, and horse riding included, good; *Residencial Roja*, E, hot water, food; camping near the river, good.) It is about 9 km. from the hotel to the **Parque Nacional Tolhuaca**, in which are the waterfalls of Malleco and Culiebra, and Lago Malleco; superb scenery and good views of volcanoes from Cerro Amarillo (the park is open Dec.-April). SE of Curacautín (32 km. by road) are the hot springs and mud baths of Río Blanco (hotel), at 1,046 metres on the slopes of the Sierra Nevada and near Lago Conguillo (bus to Conguillo National Park—see below—only at 1800). 18 km. E of Curacautín are the Termas de Manzanar (open all year), reached by bus from Temuco and Victoria (*Hotel Termas*, B, but also has simple rooms with bath but not luxurious; *Hostería Abarzua*, E, simple, friendly).

The nearby Lonquimay volcano has the Puelche ski-run, season May-November. The volcano begun erupting on Christmas Day 1988; the new crater is called Navidad. To see it, access is made from the village of Malalcahuello, 15 km. away and half-way between Curacautín and Lonquimay town. In Malalcahuello, the teacher at the school charges US$8.50 for the car to drive up to the volcano and collect you later; Sra. Naomi Saavedra at *Residencial Los Sauces* also arranges lifts (D full board, or F p.p. with use of kitchen, hot water, good value). You can also stay at a refuge in the **Reserva Nacional Malalcahuello-Nalcas** on the slopes of the volcano (D, hot showers, open ski-season only); this is 10 km. from the bus stop where the driver lets you off, 5 km. from the volcano. The bus to take is Erbuc, Temuco-Lonquimay, US$2 to Malalcahuello, 4 a day, 4 hrs., 5½ to Lonquimay town, US$2.80. There is accommodation in Lonquimay, but little transport to the volcano. The road Curacautín-Lonquimay town, 57 km., passes the Salto del Indio (Km. 14), before which is a turnoff to Laguna Blanca (25 km. away, take fishing gear, ask Sernatur about trucks), and Salto de la Princesa, just beyond Manzanar. The next village is Malalcahuello which, besides the services mentioned above, has a steam-powered carpenter's shop, with oxen hauling logs.

## THE LAKE DISTRICT (6)

**Yet more beautiful scenery: a variety of lakes, often with snow-capped volcanoes as a backdrop, stretch southwards to the salt water fjords which begin at Puerto Montt. There are a number of good bases for exploring (Valdivia has the added attraction of forts a river trip away) and many national parks. The section ends with the delightful island of Chiloé.**

South from the Bío-Bío river to the Gulf of Reloncaví the same land formation holds as for the rest of Chile to the N: the Andes to the E, the coastal range to the W, and in between the central valley. The Andes and the passes over them are less high here, and the snowline lower; the coastal range also loses altitude, and the central valley is not as continuous as from Santiago to Concepción. The climate is cooler; the summer is no longer dry, for rain falls during all the seasons, and more heavily than further N. The rain decreases as you go inland: some 2,500 mm. on the coast and 1,350 mm. inland. This is enough to maintain heavy forests, mostly beech, but there are large clearings and an active agriculture; irrigation is not necessary. The farms are mostly medium sized, and no longer the huge *haciendas* of the N. The characteristic thatched or red tiled houses of the rural N disappear; they are replaced by the shingle-roofed frame houses typical of a frontier land rich in timber. The farms raise livestock, fruit and food crops, and the timber industry is being encouraged.

About 20,000 Mapuches live in the area, more particularly around Temuco. There are possibly 150,000 more of mixed blood who speak the Indian tongue, though most of them are bilingual.

A Mapuche music festival (plus market) is normally held mid-February in Villarrica. Enquire at the Santiago or Temuco tourist office.

Between parallels 39° and 42° S is found one of the most picturesque lake regions in the world. There are some 12 great lakes of varying sizes, some set high on the Cordillera slopes, others in the central valley southwards from Temuco to Puerto Montt. Here, too, are imposing waterfalls and snowcapped volcanoes. Anglers revel in the abundance of fish, the equable climate, and the absence of

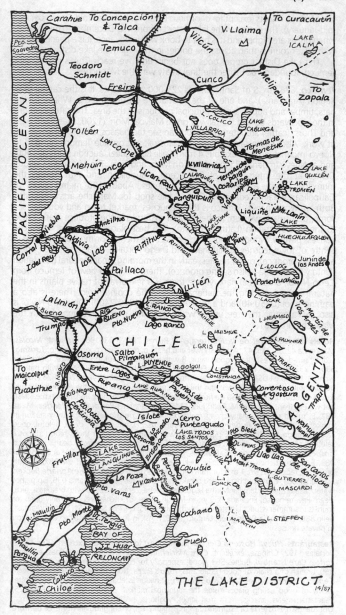

THE LAKE DISTRICT

14/57

troublesome insects (except for enormous horseflies between mid-December and mid-January). The season in the lake district is from mid-December to mid-March, when prices are higher and it is best to book well in advance. It is a peaceful area, with fewer tourists than across the border in the Argentine lake district.

The Lake District proper does not begin until we reach Chile's newest city, Temuco, founded 1881 after the final treaty with the Mapuches.

**Temuco**, 676 km. S of Santiago, has 225,000 inhabitants. It is the capital of IX Región (Araucanía), and one of the most active centres in the area. The cattle auctions in the stockyards behind the railway on A. Malvoa, Mon. (1200, sheep and pigs) and Thurs. (cattle) are interesting; you can see the *huasos*, or Chilean cowboys, at work. Also, cattle sales at Feria Agroaustral, just outside Temuco on road to Nuevo Imperial, on Fri. (take bus 4 from Calle Rodríguez), auction starts at 1400, and at Nuevo Imperial, 35 km. away, on Mon. and Tues. The Municipal Cultural Centre at the intersection of Balmaceda, Caupolicán and Prat houses the municipal library, a theatre, and art galleries. About 100 metres away, at Caupolicán y Balmaceda is the Cema-Chile shop for Mapuche arts and crafts. Both are worth a visit. Temuco is the Mapuches' market town and you may see some, particularly women, in their typical costumes in the produce market next to the railway station (Lautaro y Pinto). The best places to look for Mapuche textiles, pottery, woodcarving, jewellery etc. are the indoor municipal market in centre of town (corner of Aldunate and Diego Portales—it also sells fish, meat and dairy produce); or, for textiles, early in the morning, near the rural bus station (Pinto y Balmaceda—also selling produce). There is a grand view of Temuco from Cerro Ñielol, a national park, where there is a fine array of native plants in the natural state, including the national flower, the *copihue rojo*. There is also a bathing pool (US$0.40) and a restaurant (open 1200-2400). On Cerro Ñielol is also La Patagua, the tree under which the final peace was signed with the Mapuches in 1881.

**Hotels** *Nuevo Hotel de la Frontera*, A+, Bulnes 726, T 236190, excellent; *Nicolás*, Mackenna 420, T 235547, A with shower and heating, restaurant, poor all round; *Turismo*, slightly run-down restaurant, good value, B with bath, C without, good service, Claro Solar 636, T 232348, near main square; *Espelette*, Claro Solar 492, T 234255, B with bath, C without, breakfast US$1, excellent, clean, friendly; *Continental*, A. Varas 708, T 231166, B, popular with business travellers, and the bar is popular with locals in the evening, cheaper rooms without bath, rec.; *Casa de huéspedes Centenario*, Aldunate 864, D with breakfast, hot water, clean; *Oriente*, M. Rodríguez 1146, C, clean, rec.; *Residencial Méndez*, Matta 382, E, mixed reports. Many cheap *residenciales* and *pensiones* near railway station in market area, including *Rupangue*, Barros Arana 182, D, hot shower, clean, helpful, good value; *Omega*, Av. Pinto 91, E p.p., hot shower, clean, friendly but thefts reported, not a salubrious area; *Flor Acoca*, Lautaro 591, E, hot water, breakfast, clean. Unnamed *hospedaje* at Pedro Lagos 576, E, meals, good, friendly; another *hospedaje* at Claro Solar 483, E, clean, friendly; Sra. Veronica Kiekebusch, Av. Alemania 0649 (T 247287), D with breakfast, rec., buses No. 1 or 9 for train and rural bus stations; *Hospedaje Adriane Becker*, Estebáñez 881, E without bath, good breakfast, friendly, rec.; also Alemania 035, E p.p., hot water, pleasant; Casa familiar Mirtha Lagos de Concha, Zentano 525, D with breakfast, nice, clean. Private house, Encalada 959 y San Martín, E, use of kitchen, rec., but only open for tourists in summer (student hostel in winter); Bulnes 995, E; Claro Solar 151, E with breakfast; Bello 886, E; *Familia Rodríguez*, Lautaro 1149, F. Ask in Tourist Office for accommodation in private houses.

**Restaurants** *Nueva Hostería Clei*, Bulnes 902, next to LIT terminal, excellent; *Kim Long*, Portales 1192, Chinese, excellent; *Café Mariel*, in mall between Prat y Bulnes, excellent coffee; *Café Istanbul*, Bulnes 563, good, especially for coffee; also on Bulnes: *Dino's*, No. 360, branch of a chain of good restaurants; *Julio's Pizza*, No. 778, wide variety, not cheap; *Centro Español*, Bulnes 483. *Club Alemán*, Senador Estebáñez 772, away from centre. Plenty of good eating places inside the municipal market. *Rincón Naturista*, Prat 425, vegetarian meals, snacks, fresh fruit juices, yoghurts, health food shop, bookstore, rec. Outside town: *Hostería La Estancia* (dancing), highly rec., on Longitudinal Norte; *La Cumbre*

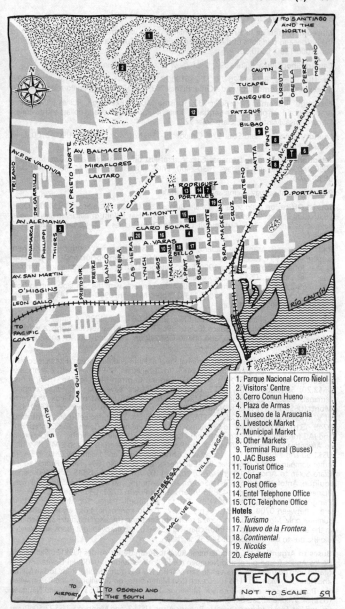

1. Parque Nacional Cerro Ñielol
2. Visitors' Centre
3. Cerro Conun Hueno
4. Plaza de Armas
5. Museo de la Araucania
6. Livestock Market
7. Municipal Market
8. Other Markets
9. Terminal Rural (Buses)
10. JAC Buses
11. Tourist Office
12. Conaf
13. Post Office
14. Entel Telephone Office
15. CTC Telephone Office
**Hotels**
16. *Turismo*
17. *Nuevo de la Frontera*
18. *Continental*
19. *Nicolás*
20. *Espelette*

TEMUCO
NOT TO SCALE  59

*del Cerro Ñielol* (dancing), on top of Cerro Ñielol.

**Museum** Museo de la Araucania, Alemania 084, a well-arranged collection devoted to the history and traditions of the Mapuche nation. Open Tues.-Sat. 0830-1300, 1500-1900; Sun. 1000-1300, US$0.50.

**Camera Shop** Ruka, Bulnes 394, helpful, owner speaks German.

**Car Hire** Hertz, Bulnes 726-733, T 236190/231226, US$45 a day. Budget, Montt 498, good value; Automóvil Club de Chile, Bulnes 763, T 231283; Puig, on Portales, cheap.

**Exchange** Turcamb, Claro Solar 733; Turismo Money Exchange, Bulnes 655, Galería Arauco, local 1, on plaza; Inter-Santiago, Bulnes 443, local 2. All deal in dollars and australes. Fincard (Visa, Mastercard), Claro Solar 922.

**Laundry** *Lavajet*, Claro Solar 574; Caupolicán 110, Nos. 4 and 5, open 0900-2100 daily; Portales 1185, expensive.

**Telephones** Centro de Llamadas CTC, A. Prat just off Claro Solar and plaza, Mon.-Sat. 0800-2400, Sun. and holidays 1030-2400. Entel, Bulnes 307, casi M. Rodríguez, daily 0830-2200.

**Post Office** at railway station and Prat y Portales.

**Tourist Office** on main square, at Calle Bulnes 586, esquina Clara Solar, T 234293. Open 0830-2030, all week in summer, Mon.-Fri. in winter. Has full list of places to stay. Also at Balmaceda and Av. Prat. Automóvil Club de Chile, Bulnes 763. Conaf, Bilbao 931, T 234420.

**Rail** Station at B. Arana and Lautaro, T 226925. Passenger services south of Temuco were suspended in 1991, except for a service in Jan. and Feb. To Concepción once a day, but not all year. To Santiago: once a day, 1900 (from Santiago at 2015), with an extra train in summer, fares: *económico* US$7, *superior/salón* US$10-11 (depending on service), sleeper US$16.65-23.35, compartment US$51.50. A bus connects with the Santiago train to/from Valdivia. Ticket office at Bulnes 590, T 233522, open Mon.-Fri. 0900-1300, 1430-1800, Sun. 0900-1300 as well as at station.

**Air** Airport 6 km. from the city. LanChile, Bulnes 667, T 211339, 4 times a week to Concepción and Santiago. Ladeco (Bulnes 396, T 236739) has several flights a week to Valdivia, Osorno and Santiago; also one to Concepción. Varig and Pan Am agent at Salfa vehicle showroom, Mackenna y Bello.

**Bus** to neighbouring towns from Terminal Rural at Pinto and Balmaceda. Flota Erbuc (also at Miraflores y Bulnes, and Balmaceda 1415), to Curacautín, US$1.35, 7 daily, 2¾ hrs; also to Lonquimay, 4 daily, 5½ hrs., US$2.80, Laguna Captren Mon. and Fri. 1645, 4 hrs., US$2.20; Santiago, 2100, US$5. Long-distance buses leave from individual company terminals. Buses Cruz del Sur from V.Mackenna 671, 3 a day to Castro, 10 a day to Puerto Montt (US$5.25, 5½ hrs.), to Valdivia US$2; to Osorno US$3.30. Other buses in 600 block of V. Mackenna (nr. Claro Solar): ETTA, Longitudinal Sur, Thiele (for Lebu and Contulmo, 0745, 1310, 1600, 3½ hrs. to Contulmo, US$3, change here for Cañete and Concepción), and JAC for Santiago. JAC's main terminal is at Mackenna y Bello for all other services except to Argentina (see below): Villarrica and Pucón many between 0705 and 2045, 1½ hrs., US$1.50 and 2 hrs., US$1.75 respectively, Coñaripe, 3 hrs., and Lican Ray (2 hrs.). Several other companies on Claro Solar, 500-600 blocks, e.g. LIT at No. 694. Fénix, Pedro Lagos y Claro Solar, to Arica (2200 and 2245, arrives 1400 2 days later, US$45 or US$60 *cama*), Iquique, Antofagasta (US$35), La Serena and Santiago, also Pucón and Valdivia. Power, Bulnes 174 and Balmaceda 1438 to Villarrica and Pucón 0730 (US$1 and US$1.35), and Panguipulli at 0730, 2 hrs., US$1.65. Also to Panguipulli, Pangui Sur, Miraflores 871, 10 a day between 0700 and 1915, 3 hrs., US$2, also to Loncoche, Los Lagos, Mehuin in summer only. Most companies have a service to Santiago (try also Unión del Sur, Bonanza in the arcade at Balmaceda y Pinto), charging US$6-10, usually overnight (book in advance). Bío Bío bus to Concepción (US$4.25), six daily.

**Buses to Argentina** JAC from Terminal Rural to Junín de los Andes (US$12), San Martín de los Andes (same price) and Neuquén (US$20), Wed. and Fri. 0400; Igi Llaima and San Martín both go three times a week to San Martín; Nar Bus from Terminal Rural to San Martín and Neuquén, Mon.-Fri., US$16.50 each (San Martín buses go via Villarrica and Pucón when the Tromen Pass is open); Ruta Sur, Miraflores 1151, to Zapala (US$12.50) and Neuquén (US$18), Wed. and Sat. 0400; La Unión del Sud, Miraflores 1285, same destinations Wed., Fri. and Sat. Fénix (address above) to Buenos Aires, US$52, and Mendoza, US$22.50. Buses on the Zapala route go via the Pino Hachado pass, not Icalma.

**Excursions** A road and railway run W to (55 km.) Carahue. About 30 km. further, at the mouth of the navigable River Imperial, is **Puerto Saavedra**, where there is a stretch of beach with black volcanic sand. It comprises 3 distinct towns: the first administrative; the second, 2 km. away, the fishing port with one poor *residencial*; the third, a further 2 km., the tourist area with many *hosterías* in E-F category. It is reached from Carahue by car (1 hr.), or by bus from Temuco Terminal Rural (Nar Bus, 0730, 0800, 0930, 2½ hrs., US$1.20).

From Puerto Saavedra there are interesting excursions to Nehuentue, on the other side of the river, or to Lagos Budi and Trovolhue, both well worth seeing. Trovolhue is reached by a specially chartered launch which takes 4 hrs. to go up the Moncul River. Puerto Domínguez, on Lago Budi, a picturesque little place famous for its good fishing, is reached by dirt road from Carahue (40 km.). From Puerto Saavedra beach or fishing port, walk 1 hr. to Balsa Budi from where a raft goes to Isla Huapi. A further 3 hrs.' walking leads to a ferry for Puerto Domínguez.

"Another pleasant trip through Mapuche country is to take a minibus from the Central Market to the country town of Chol-Chol, 30 km. to the north-west. There are daily buses (Huincabus from Terminal Rural, 1 hr., 4 times between 1100 and 1430, US$0.60, or García/Gangas from same terminal at 1000), laden with corn, vegetables, charcoal, animals, as well as the locals. The trip traverses rolling countryside with panoramic views. On a clear day it is possible to see five volcanoes. Nearer Chol-Chol, the traditional round houses made of thatch (*rucas*) can be seen. There is not much to see in Chol-Chol itself, but it does have a delicious wild west flavour somehow. " (Ian H. Dally, Iglesia Anglicana de Chile). For an overnight stay and information, contact Sra. Lauriza Norváez, Calle Luzcano (s/n), who prepares meals, and is very helpful. You can continue from Chol-Chol to Imperial and Puerto Saavedra, but bus connections few and slow (stay overnight in Puerto Saavedra).

The 3,050-metre Llaima volcano has at its foot one of the prettiest skiing resorts in Chile: *Llaima*, at 1,500 metres, 80 km. E of Temuco. It stands in the middle of two large **national parks**, **Los Paraguas** (named for the umbrella-like araucaria pine trees—best visited August-October according to Conaf) and **Conguillio** (open 20 Nov.-13 March). The latter, too, is full of araucaria forests and contains the Laguna Conguillio and the snow-covered Sierra Nevada. It is one of Chile's most popular parks, but is deserted outside the Jan./Feb. season. The best way to get to the park is to drive yourself, preferably in a high-clearance vehicle and with clear instructions on which roads shown on maps are suitable and exist. There are three routes, on all of which there is public transport, via Curacautín, via Melipeuco or via Cherquenco. Take a bus from Temuco to Curacautín (see page 587) then a bus at 1830, Mon. and Fri. towards the park, 1 hr., US$1, or hitch, to Conaf hut (you can camp nearby). It is then 10 km. to Laguna Captren situated in araucaria forest, where you pay a park entrance fee of US$0.50; campsite (US$4 including firewood but no other facilities), good hiking. 6 km. further on is Laguna Conguillio (take the Sendero de los Carpinteros), with a visitor's centre, campsites (US$6 per site, hot water, showers, firewood; *cabañas*, summer only, US$20, sleep 6, no sheets or blankets, gas stove) and café/shop,

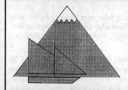

from where you can hike into the Sierra Nevada. At Laguna Verde in the Park is a free campsite without facilities. 15 km. beyond Laguna Conguillio, mostly across deserted lava fields, is the other entrance to the park, and then it is 13 km. though farmland to the village of Melipeuco (*Hotel Central*, E, good; *Hosteria Hue-Telén*, Pedro Aguirre Cerda 1, C, good; Nar Bus from Temuco Terminal Rural to Melipeuco, 5 daily, 0900-1830, 3 hrs., US$1.30, last back to Temuco at 1630). Transport can be arranged from Melipeuco into the park, but in summer buses from Temuco go, via Melipeuco, right through the park (3 a week). The third alternative is to go to Cherquenco (road paved to Vilcún, the road very poor for the last 40 km., high clearance essential. Daily buses Temuco-Cherquenco). It is then a 2-3 day hike around Volcán Llaima to Laguna Conguillio, dusty, but beautiful views of Laguna Quepe, then on to the Laguna Captren *guardería*.

For details of these excursions visit the Corporación Nacional Forestal, IX Región, Caupolicán y Bulnes, Temuco. For best touring, hire a 4-wheel drive vehicle in Temuco.

The way from Temuco to Villarrica follows the paved Longitudinal Highway as far as Freire (24 km.), then (also paved) runs 63 km. SE. A road to Villarrica from the S runs substantially parallel with the old railway line from Loncoche. Wooded Lago Villarrica, 21 km. long and about 7 km. wide, is the most beautiful in the region, with snow-capped Villarrica volcano (2,840 metres) in the background.

*Villarrica*, pleasantly set at the extreme SW corner of the lake, was founded in 1552 but destroyed by the Indians in 1602; the present town (24,000 population) dates from 1882.

**Festival**  Festival Cultural Mapuche in second week of February.

**Hotels**  *Yachting Club*, Gen. San Martín 802, T 411191, pleasant atmosphere, terraced gardens, swimming pool, restaurant, boating and fishing, rec., A, but cheaper rooms in motel annex; *Hotel El Ciervo*, Gen. Koerner 241, T 411215, A, German-run, beautiful location, also rec.; *Hostería Kiel*, Gen. Koerner 153, T 411631, B, lakeside, clean, friendly; *Hotel y Cabañas El Parque*, 3 km. out of Villarrica on Pucón road, T 411120, Casilla 65 (or T Temuco 235872), lakeside with beach, tennis courts, B without breakfast, good restaurant set meals, highly rec.; *Hostería de la Colina*, J.A. Ríos 1177, overlooking town, T 411503, Casilla 382, run by N. Americans, C with breakfast, large gardens, restaurant, rec.; *Hostería Rayhuen*, Pedro Montt 668, T 411571, D with breakfast (B in summer), clean, rec.; *Hostería Bilbao*, Henríquez 43, T 411186, C; *Gerónimo de Alderete*, Gerónimo de Alderete 709, T 411370, C. *Residencial Puchi*, Valdivia 678, T 411392, E, hot water, good restaurant; *Casa San Jorge*, Calle Catedral, E, is a Scouts' hostel, good value dormitory accommodation. *Residencial Victoria*, Muñoz 530, E, p.p., clean; *Hospedaje Dalila Balboa*, San Martín 734, E, clean, cheap; unnamed *hospedaje* at Vicente Reyes 854, near JAC terminal, F p.p., good breakfast, good value; *Hospedaje Las Cabañitas*, Henríquez 398, E, good value, clean, restaurant, owner also has *cabañas* near lake, C. Youth hostel, *Residencial San Francisco*, Julio Zegers 646, F p.p. in shared rooms. Also, rooms in private homes, e.g. Calle Francisco Bilbao 969, run by Tom Funk, E; at No. 537 (Eliana Castillo), F p.p., clean, friendly; at No. 827 and also V. Letelier 702, E p.p., (open throughout the year).

**Camping**  2 sites just outside town on Pucón road, *Los Castaños* and *du Lac*. Many more on S side of Lake Villarrica, see under Pucón (below). Also 25 km. south of Villarrica (1 hour, US$1 bus), at Lican-Ray on Lago Calafquén (see below). Bus leaves from near tourist office. Summer houses available in Dec.-Feb.

**Restaurant**  *Club Social*, P. de Valdivia 640, good; *El Rey de Mariscos*, Letelier 1030, good seafood; *Rapa Nui*, V. Reyes 678, good and cheap; *Yandally*, Camilo Henríquez 401. *Panaderías*, at Gral. de Aldunate 632 and 635; *Café 2001*, Henríquez 379, coffee and ice-cream, good.

**Exchange**  Banco de Osorno will change travellers' cheques; Casa de Cambio, Letelier 570; also Carlos Huerta, Anfión Muñoz 417, for cheques and cash (dollars and australes—rec. that only men deal with him). Rates are generally poor.

**Laundry**  *Lavandería y Lavaseco Villarrica*, Andrés Bello 348, T 411449.

**Post Office**  Anfión Muñoz esq. General Basilia Urrutia, open 0830-1230, 1400-1800 (Mon.-Fri.), 0830-1230 (Sat.). Telex service also available. Entel, Reyes 721.

**Tourist Office** Valdivia 1070; information and maps (open all day all week in summer).

**Travel Agency** *National Travel*, O'Higgins, climbing tours inc. equipment from US$20.

**Buses** To Santiago, US$10. To Pucón, in summer every 30 mins, ½ hr journey., US$0.60; to Valdivia (JAC, Reyes 616), US$2.50, 3 a day, 3-5 hrs.; daily service to Panguipulli at 0700, US$2, scenic ride. To Coñaripe and Liquiñe at 1600 Mon.-Sat., 1000 Sun. Temuco, JAC, US$1.50. To Loncoche (road and railway junction), US$1.15. N.B. JAC has 2 terminals: long distance at Reyes y Montt, local on Reyes between Henríquez y Muñoz. To Argentina at 0615 on Tues., Thurs. and Sat. with Empresa San Martín (Av. A. Muñoz 417) and at 0730 on Mon., Wed. and Fri. with Igi-Llaima, US$12, but passes can be blocked for four months by snow. If Tromen Pass is closed, buses go via Panguipulli instead of Pucón.

*Pucón*, a most attractive little town on the south-eastern shore of Lago Villarrica, can be reached by bus from Villarrica (26 km.) or Temuco, not by water. Pucón has a good climate and first-class accommodation. The black sand beach is very popular for swimming and watersports on the lake (prices given below). The season is from 15 December to 15 March, when the town is extremely crowded and very expensive. Off season it is very pleasant but many places are closed. There is a pleasant walk to La Península for fine views of the lake and volcano, pony rides, golf, etc. (private land, you must get permission first). Launch excursion from the landing stage at La Poza at end of O'Higgins at 1500 and 1900, US$4 for 2 hours. There is a large handicraft centre where you can see spinning and weaving in progress. The town is scheduled for major development, with plans to build on La Península and around La Poza, the yacht harbour. A Centro de Ski is under construction so that Pucón may become a winter sports centre. Some predict that by the mid-1990s Pucón will be a second Viña del Mar.

**Pucón Hotels** In summer, December to February, add 20% to hotel prices; at this time rooms may be hard to find—plenty of alternatives (usually cheaper) in Villarrica. State owned *Gran Pucón*, Holzapfel 190, T 441001 (9-hole golf course), open mid December to April, L, disappointing, sauna and squash open to non-residents off season for entrance fee; *Interlaken*, A+, Caupolicán on lakeside 10 minutes from town, T 441276, Swiss run, chalets, rec., will exchange travellers' cheques (only open December to February); *Antumalal*, luxury class, 30 metres above the shore, 2 km. from Pucón, T 441011, very small (18 rooms), picturesque chalet-type, with magnificent views of the lake (take lunch on terrace), expensive and excellent, A+, with meals (open year round; good beach, and good fishing up the river. *La Posada*, Valdivia 191, T 441088, open Dec.-Feb., C with bath, cheaper without, full board available; *Hostería Suiza*, O'Higgins 112, T 441945, C, clean, has a small café which is cheap and serves excellent empanadas; *Turista*, O'Higgins 136, T 441153, C (D low season), with bath, friendly, clean; *Gudenschwager*, Pedro de Valdivia 12, T 441156, classic Bavarian type, C (B with bath), views over lake, volcano and mountains, attentive staff, comfortable, excellent restaurant, rec. (open in summer only). *Araucarias*, Caupolicán 243, T 441286, A, clean, comfortable but not luxurious; *Saint John*, hostería and campsite, 2 km. on Villarrica road, open Dec.-March, rooms D p.p., camping US$7.50-11 for 5, full board available, Casilla 154, T 441165/90; *Residencial Lincoyán*, Av. Lincoyán, T 441144, D with bath, cheaper without, clean and comfortable; *Hostería Viena*, summer only, cabins for 6 only, clean and pleasant; *Hostería El Principito*, Av. Gral. Urrutia and Fresia, T 441200, C, with bath, good breakfast, very friendly, rec.; *Salzburg*, O'Higgins 311, T 441907, E with bath and breakfast (summer only), rec., German spoken, some rooms with view over volcano (possible to borrow crampons). *Hospedaje El Fogón*, O'Higgins 472, T 441267, E, good value, good breakfast, next to JAC buses; *Hostería Milla Rahue*, Av. O'Higgins 460, T 441904, D, clean, good inexpensive restaurant, convenient for JAC. Familia Acuña, Palguín 233 (ask at *peluquería* next door), good, E without breakfast, hot water, use of kitchen and washing facilities. Juan Torres, Lincoyán 445, T 441248, good, clean, cooking facilities (log fires in winter), very friendly, E including breakfast, use of kitchen, home-made marmalade, information on climbing Villarrica and the Huerquehue National Park; *Hospedaje Sonia*, Lincoyán 485, T 441269, E, warm showers, use of kitchen, has a notebook listing all the good places to stay in Chile, friendly, rec.; *Casa de Familia*, Don Juan, Lincoyán 815, cooking facilities (information on climbing Villarrica); *El Refugio*, Lincoyán 348, E with breakfast, good; Sra. Lucía Sandoval, Lincoyán 565, E, good; next door is Sra Lucila Oliva, (Pasaje Chile 225), E, use of kitchen, highly rec.; family at Perú 720 has accommodation E, use of kitchen, will help organize excursions to Volcán Villarrica and Huerquehue National Park; also Roberto y Alicia Abreque, Perú 170, E, clean, rec., has information on excursions; *Don Pepe*, Urrutia 592, E inc. breakfast, good, restaurant is quite cheap; many other families have rooms—look for the signs or ask in bars/restaurants, e.g. next to garage opp. *Gran Hotel Pucón*.

**Camping** Next to lake, 20 mins. walk from town, US$7 for two. There are several campsites between Villarrica and Pucón: *Acapulco, Playa Linda* (Villarrica), *Suyay, Lorena*, 10 km. from Villarrica (also rents *cabañas*); *Huimpalay*, 12 km. from Villarrica; *Millaray*, 7 km. S of Pucón; *Trancura* and *Saltos del Molco; Albergue Juvenil*, US$1 p.p./night, tent provided, sleeping bags required, 2 km. out of town. In fact, there are so many establishments along the lake's southern shore that you cannot get to the water's edge unless staying in one. On the road to Tromen Pass, *Cabañas El Dorado*, US$18 for 2, good site, poorly maintained. Cheaper sites en route to Caburga.

**Restaurants** *Pizzería Che Thomas*, Palguín 465, good value, small place run by Jorge; *El Fogón*, O'Higgins, next to JAC office, good meat (*hospedaje* behind); *Il Ristorante*, O'Higgins 323, Italian, fresh pasta, rec., moderate prices; *El Refugio*, Lincoyán 348, *Le Demago*, Lincoyán 361 (plus *Pub Naf-Naf*); *Carnes Orlando*, bar/restaurant/butcher's shop, Ansorena near Urrutia; *Pastelería Suiza*, next to *Hostería Suiza* on O'Higgins; *Café Brasil*, Fresia, good, especially pancakes. *Holzapfel Backerei*, Clemente Holzapfel 524, German cafe/restaurant, rec.

**Exchange** Good rates at the big **supermarket** on O'Higgins (also changes cheques). **Banco del Estado** de Chile, O'Higgins casi Lincoyán.

**Car Hire** Hertz, Fresia 220, US$65 for cheapest car (inc. tax, insurance, and 200 km. free); same prices per day at *Gran Hotel*. **Bicycle Hire** Taller de Pollo, Palguín, US$5/day.

**Watersports** Water-skiing, sailing, windsurfing at the beach by *Gran Hotel* and La Poza beach end of O'Higgins (more expensive than hotel, not rec.); hotel rates: waterskiing US$10 for 15 mins., Laser sailing US$5/hour, US$25/day, sailboards about the same, rowing boats US$1.50/hr.

**Laundry** on Colo-Colo, good.

**Telephone** International service at O'Higgins 170.

**Travel Agents** On O'Higgins: **Nieve y Sol** (esq. Lincoyán, also at *Grán Hotel Pucón*), **Altue**, No. 371, **Nacional Travel Club**, No. 323, and **Expediciones Chonos** (Sr Ricardo Vázquez). All arrange trips to thermal baths, trekking to volcanoes, whitewater rafting, etc. and are exceedingly good value. (Altue prices, 1990: rafting, US$12 for 1½-2 hrs., 3 trips a day; climbing Villarrica, US$32, 12 hrs., equipment provided; mountain bike tours to glaciers, waterfalls, etc, US$22, all day. **Sergio Catalán**, T 441269 (office) or 441142, Gerónimo Alderete 192, tours, excursions and taxi service all year round. **Sharpa**, Ansorena 355, T 441070, for climbing expeditions and hire of equipment. Taxi excursions from O'Higgins y Ansorena.

**Tourist Office** Av. Caupolicán and Av. Brasil, very helpful, ask here about all types of accommodation; Cema-Chile shop at same location. If closed, Municipal at O'Higgins and Palguín will provide information and sells fishing licences (US$1/month).

**Bus** JAC terminal: O'Higgins 478 for **Villarrica, Temuco** (US$1.75, about 20 a day) and **Valdivia** (0630, 1545, 1845, US$2.50), better to change in Valdivia than in Temuco for **Puerto Montt**, JAC to **Santiago**, US$10 from O'Higgins 480. At Palguín 383, agency for Servi-Tur, Tur-Bus—sleeper bus US$20 to the capital, Inter Sur, Fénix, Power and Igi-Llaima. LIT, for Temuco and Santiago, O'Higgins y Palguín. Cordillera, Av. Miguel Ansorena (nr. O'Higgins, next to minimarket) for **Paillaco** and **Lago Caburgua**—see below. Colectivos to **Villarrica** from O'Higgins y Palguín. **Buses to Argentina**: Buses from Temuco to Junín pass through Pucón, fares are the same as from Temuco.

Pucón and Villarrica are celebrated fishing centres, for the lake and the very beautiful Lincura, Trancura and Toltén rivers. The fishing is now reported to be even better further S, in Lago Ranco (**see page 602**) for example. Local tourist office will supply details on licences and open seasons etc.

**Excursions** from Pucón may be made to the active **Villarrica** volcano in the Villarrica National Park 8 km. S of the town (entry US$0.75). Following a number of deaths in recent years, restrictions on access to the park have been imposed: entry is usually only permitted to tour groups with a qualified guide, charge US$25-30 including transport to park entrance and hire of equipment; at the park entrance equipment is checked; entry is refused if the weather is poor. Do not under any circumstances attempt this climb alone. There is a refuge without beds 4 km. inside the Park, insecure and in desperate need of renovation. Campsite with drinking water, toilets, below refuge. The volcano can be climbed up and down in 8-9 hrs. (go in summer when days are longer), good boots, iceaxe and crampons, and sun block essential—beware of sulphur fumes at the top. Guides, see above under Travel Agents. Also Alvaro Martínez, Cristóbal Colón 430; Juan Carlos, at Lucila's *pensión*, or his pool room on main street; Joaquín, who lives in Calle Brasil, contact him at Sonia's residencial (he used to be a rescue worker, very experienced). Many others, all with equipment; beware charlatans, ask at the tourist office. Crampons, ice axe, sunglasses can be rented for US$3.60/day from the Taller de Pollo bicycle shop on Calle Palguín, Pucón, near fire station—a cloth mask moistened with lemon juice helps to filter the sulphur fumes at the summit.

To Lago Colico to the N and volcanic Lago Caburgua, very pretty, to the NE, both in wild settings (row-boats may be hired, US$1.50 per hour). Lago Caburgua is unusual for its beautiful white sand beach whereas other beaches are black sand of volcanic origin (campsite, T 236989, expensive in season, US$2.50 car, US$6.50 tent, but cheap out of season, US$2.50 for tent). Visit also the Ojos de Caburgua, beautiful pools fed from underground. Cordillera bus departs 1230, returns 1400, 2nd bus (in summer only) leaves 1700 and returns next morning (US$1 single), but there are colectivos or you can try hitching. No shops, so take own food. Three more beautiful lakes are Verde, Chico and Toro in the **Huerquehue National Park**, W of Lago Caburgua; there is a well-signed track to them from the car park at Lago Tinquilco (it is more-or-less straight uphill, 2 hrs.—sign says 5 km., but worth it). In Huerquehue there are 20 lakes in all and they keep changing. For Huerquehue, take Cordillera bus to Paillaco, beyond Caburgua, 1½ hrs., US$1, from where it's 7 km. (3 uphill, 3 down, 1 along Lago Tinquilco) to park entrance, where there is a campsite. 2 km. before the Huerquehue Park entrance, the Bratt family (German spoken) take in guests and let people camp for US$1.50; they also rent rowing boats on the lake. Park open officially only Jan.-March, but you can get in at other times. Warden very helpful; people in park rent horses and boats. Take your own food. To protect against horse flies, do not wear dark clothes.

Outside the Huerquehue Park are the Huife thermal baths (T 441222, PO Box 18, Pucón), US$3.20, including use of one pool, "very upmarket, but pleasant". Termas de Quimaico can be reached from the road to Huife: new, less ostentatious than Huife, camping allowed, 2 cabins and *hostería* (*centro turístico* under construction). To the thermal baths of San Luis, N of the road to Argentina, 25 km. from Pucón, small hotel, ½ hr. walk to Lago del León and Palguín, S of the same road (*Hotel*—address, Casilla 1D, Pucón—D full board, F in small huts with bath, German-speaking owner, cool swimming pool, baths US$1.75, lots of hikeable waterfalls in the area, e.g. Salto El León, entry US$0.30, slippery walkways). A new complex is being built at Palguín, which is 36 km. from Pucón. Here is the entrance to the Quetrupillán section of the Villarrica National Park (high clearance vehicle necessary, horses best), free camping in the park, *refugio* at first campsite. Ask rangers for the route to the other entrance.

Two excursions from Pucón close to Lago Villarrica: 2-km. walk along the beach to the mouth of the Río Pucón, with views of the volcanoes Villarrica, Quetrupillán and Lanín. To Quelhue, across the Río Pucón: walk 7 km. or take a taxi (US$1.35) to the ferry stage ferry across the river, the first stage is river-powered, the second a rowing boat, both free but tip the boatman (ferry operates 0800-1300, 1400-1800 Mon.-Fri., 0800-1200, 1400-1800 Sat.). La Reducción de Quelhue is supposed to be a Mapuche village, but no traditional dress, language or customs are used, and the children ask for money. The walking is pleasant, though, towards the N shore of the lake, towards Caburgua, or up into the hills through farms and agricultural land, with views of the three volcanoes and, higher up, of the lake. You cannot go too far up into the hills without meeting gates by a bridge.

There is a road from Pucón to the Argentine town of Junín de los Andes. The route is past the volcanoes of Villarrica and Quetrupillán and round Lago Quellelhue, a gem set between mountains at 1,196 metres above sea level. On the border, to the S, is the graceful cone of Lanín volcano (3,747 metres), and beyond the border is Lago Tromen, much visited by Argentine tourists. Conaf campsite 5 km. from border, on a good dirt road by Lago Tromen, no amenities. The Argentine road from the border to Junín de los Andes goes on to San Martín de los Andes, and via Lago Hermoso and Villa Angostura (a beautiful drive) to Bariloche. There is a more direct road from San Martín de los Andes to Bariloche but it is not so interesting (see under Argentina, **The Route to Chile from Bariloche** in Section 9).

About 25 km. S of Villarrica and 125 km SE of Temuco is *Lican-Ray*, with 2 good beaches, on Lago Calafquén, full of islands and good for fishing. Boats can be hired from the beach (US$1.50 an hour). The resort is very crowded in season. Several buses daily in summer from Villarrica (JAC—7 a day, 3 on Sun.— and García, Reyes y Henríquez) and, in Jan.-Feb., there are frequent direct buses from Santiago and Temuco. 4 km. away to the E is the river of lava formed when the Villarrica volcano erupted in 1971. Buses Mon.-Sat. at 0730 from Lican-Ray to Panguipulli.

**Hotels** (most closed out of season) *Bellavista*, Cacique Punulef 240; *Refugio*, A, Canadian-owned, on Playa Grande, open all year, has a Travellers' Exchange Library for English-language books, all donations of paperbacks (in reasonable condition) welcome, please send to Jack D. Feka, Casilla 299, Temuco—for information contact the hotel. *Cabinas Los Pinos*, 3 blocks from lake, E, nice; *Río Negro*, Gerónimo 776, E; Hugo Linolilli 235, F; several motels (e.g. at *Cabañas El Eden*, Huenuman 105, C for a chalet for 6 with hot water; *El Conquistador*, Cacique Millaqueo s/n), *hosterías*, and camping sites (e.g. *Camping Las Gaviotas*, 3 km. E). *Café Ñaños*, Gral. Urrutia 105, very good, reasonable prices, helpful owner.

A road, 14 km., runs SE from Lican-Ray to **Coñaripe**, at the eastern end of Lago Calafquén. At first sight, the village is dusty and nondescript, but its setting, with a black sand beach surrounded by mountains, is very beautiful. There is a good walk from the left-hand side of the beach back through the fields to Coñaripe. This is a popular Chilean tourist spot; *Hotel Antulafquen*, E p.p., homely; *Hospedaje House*, F p.p. with breakfast; cheap campsites near private houses; buses to Panguipulli, 3 a day, US$1. A road around the lake's southern shore leads to Lago Panguipulli (see below).

The Longitudinal Highway (Ruta 5) runs from Loncoche (81 km. S of Temuco, good place for hitching) through Lanco to Paillaco and Osorno. At San José de la Mariquina, a road branches off Ruta 5 to Valdivia, 42 km. from the Highway (bus Lanco-Valdivia, Chile Nuevo, US$0.85, 4 a day, fewer at weekends). The road from Valdivia to Ruta 5 going S is not in very good condition; the Highway is rejoined by Paillaco.

*Panguipulli*, on the W bank of the lake of the same name, is in a beautiful setting, with roses planted in all the streets (the name is Mapuche for "hill of lions"). It is reached by paved road from Lanco, with buses from Santiago, Temuco and Valdivia; there are also road connections to Lake Calafquén and Villarrica. Excursions can be made to Lagos Panguipulli, Calafquén, Neltume and Pirehueico, and south to the northern tip of Lago Riñihue at El Desagüe (*Hostería Riñimapu*, T 388, B, excellent). There is a new 30-km. road around the lake to Choshuenco, a beautiful coastline, wooded, with cliffs and sandy beaches. Buses leave daily for Choshuenco at 1530 and 1630 along the North bank of the lake, 2 hrs, US$1.50, but it is not possible to return from Choshuenco on same day. (Bus returns from Choshuenco at 0645 and 0700.) Choshuenco volcano is at the SE end; on it Club Andino de Valdivia has ski-slopes and a *refugio*. For fishermen, daily excursions on Lago Panguipulli are recommended. The waterfalls of Huilo-Huilo are most impressive; the river channels its way through volcanic rock before thundering 100 metres down into a natural basin. They can be reached by the Choshuenco bus, get off beyond Choshuenco about 1 km. from Neltume and walk 200 metres to the falls, or at *Alojamiento Huilo Huilo*, where the road crosses the Huilo Huilo river. From here it is a 1½ hr. walk the following day to the falls. Alternatively, walk from Choshuenco along Puerto Fuy road for 3½ hrs. and turn right at sign to the falls. It's 22 km. from Choshuenco to Puerto Fuy, an interesting 5-hour walk. Another road S from Choshuenco goes to the turn off for the Club Andino *refugio* on Volcán Choshuenco and to Enco, at the eastern end of Lago Riñihue (**see page** 602). A scenic road runs through rainforest around the Choshuenco volcano from Puerto Fuy to the river Pillanleufú, Los Llolles and Puerto Llifén on Lago Ranco (see below); in 1989 this road was reported closed to the public, enquire at the lumber mill at Neltume (Sr. Thomas Morefield), 5 km. from Neltume, 3 km. from Puerto Fuy.

A boat crosses Lago Pirehueico Tues., Thurs., Sat. at 1700, US$3, 2-3 hrs. from the Argentine side to Puerto Fuy; bus daily from Puerto Fuy to Panguipulli at 0600, 3 hrs., US$2, except Sun. when it runs from 1700 from Neltume, 7 km. from Puerto Fuy. Ferry returns to Pirehueico at 0900: a beautiful boat trip. *$8 pp very basic*

**Hotels** At **Panguipulli**: *Central*, clean, hot water, D, ~~not very~~ friendly, good breakfast; *Residencial La Bomba*, E; *Hostería Quetropillán*, Etchegaray 381, T 348, C, comfortable, food; also, private house opposite, E, clean, good breakfast; Sra. Pozas, Pedro de Valdivia 251 (D, clean, clothes washing extra). *Las Brisas* restaurant, has rooms to let, E; *Restaurante* *Valparaíso*, rec.; *Café Central*, Martínez de Rosas 880; few places to eat in Panguipulli. At *several incl. Café Real* **Liquiñe**: *Hostería Termas de Liquiñe*, B p.p.; private houses, E. At **Choshuenco**: *Hotel Choshuenco*, E, good meals; various *hosterías*, including *Hostería Rayen Trai* (former yacht club), María Alvarado—s/n, good food, rec.; Sra. Elena Arrigada, Padre Vernave 198, E, rec.; free camping. At **Pirehueico and Puerto Fuy**: beds available in private houses, F p.p. At **Neltume**, *Pensión Neltume*, F, meals.

**Campsite** Chollinco, on Lago Ranco, 8 km. from Futrono. Municipal campsite at Panguipulli 3 km. outside town, US$3 with all facilities, rec; free camping on lakeside at Panguipulli possible. Also, at Los Molinos; and at Choshuenco on the lake shore (food shops in the village), and Puerto Fuy on the beach (take your own food, none available to buy).

**Tourist Office** in plaza next to police station.

**NB** No foreign exchange facilities.

**Bus** to **Santiago** daily at 1845, US$9; 14 daily (Sun. only 4) buses (several lines) from/to **Valdivia**, 2 hrs., US$1.50 and 9 daily to **Temuco** (e.g. Power at 1800, 2 hrs., US$1.65, or Pangui Sur, 10 a day, US$2, 3 hrs.) To **Calafquén, 3 daily at 1200, 1545 and 1600**. To **Choshuenco** 1530, US$2, return 0630. To **Coñaripe** (with connections for Lican Ray and Villarica), 4 a day, 1½ hrs., US$1.40 from depot in Calle Freire, 100 metres uphill from **Hostería Quetropillán**.

There is a road from Panguipulli to Coñaripe, on Lago Calafquén, which offers superb views of the lake and of Villarrica volcano, whether you are travelling on foot or by bus. Some buses continue to Lican Ray. It is not possible to travel by bus from Villarrica to Choshuenco on a Sunday; you have to stay overnight in Coñaripe, then take a bus to Panguipulli and make a connection there.

*Valdivia*, a pleasant city standing where two rivers join to form the Río Valdivia, is 18 km. from the port of Corral and the Pacific Ocean. It is the capital of Valdivia Province and has a population of 140,000. It is 820 km. by rail or road (about 16 hrs.) from Santiago.

The city is set in a rich agricultural area receiving some 2,300 mm. of rain a year; it was founded by Pedro de Valdivia in 1552. Lord Cochrane's greatest victory for Chilean independence was at Valdivia, when he took the forts at Corral, Amargos and San Carlos (the Niebla fort surrendered—see below). From 1850 to 1860 a comparatively small number of German colonists settled in the area; their imprint in terms of architecture and agricultural methods, order, education, social life and custom is still strong. In particular they created numerous industries, most of them on Isla Teja (5 by 2 km.) facing the city. The Universidad Austral de Chile was founded in Valdivia in 1954. On the tree-lined, shady Plaza de la República, a new cathedral is under construction. Avenida Prat (or Costanera) runs around the bend in the river, from the bus station to the bridge to Isla Teja, the boat dock and the riverside market, which is fascinating.

**Festival** Semana Valdiviana, 12-18 Feb.

**Hotels** *Pedro de Valdivia*, Carampangue 190, T 212931, A with bath, good; *Naguilán*, Gen. Lagos 1927, T 212851/52/53, A, clean, quiet; *Palace*, Chacabuco 308 y Henríquez, T 213319, B, good, comfortable; *Raitúe*, Gral. Lagos 1382, T 21503, C with bath; *Villa del Río*, A with bath, Av. España 1025, T 216292, restaurant expensive (try salmon in almond sauce), rents apartments with kitchen; *Melillanca*, rec. but pricey, A, Av. Alemania 675, T 212509. *Villa Paulina*, Yerbas Buenas 389, T 216372/212445, B, hot showers, clean, pool, parking, highly rec. On Picarte, *Hostal Montserrat* (No. 849), C with breakfast, clean, comfortable; the Salvation Army (US$1.50); *Residencial Anilebu*, No. 875 (nr. bus station) and *Residencial Germania*, No. 873, T 212405, clean but no heat in small rooms, C with breakfast; cheaper hotels in same street include No. 915, F p.p., (summer only), Nos. 979 and

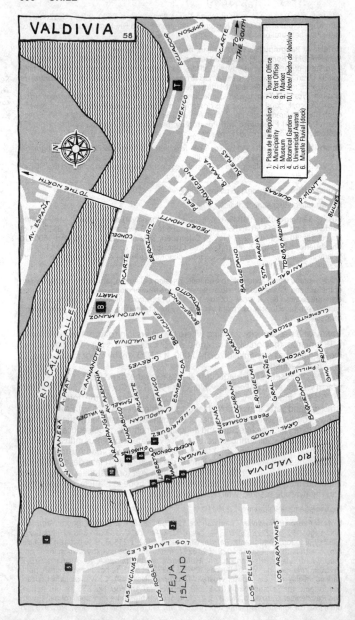

VALDIVIA    58

1. Plaza de la Republica
2. Municipality
3. Museum
4. Botanical Gardens
5. Universidad Austral
6. Muelle Fluvial (dock)

7. Tourist Office
8. Post Office
9. Market
10. Hotel Pedro de Valdivia

1005 (no hot water); No. 953, opposite bus terminal, E with breakfast, good value, clean, heated lounge. *Hospedaje Turismo*, Gral. Lagos 874, T 215946, old German house, pleasant family atmosphere, rec. *Unión*, Prat 514, T 213819, E, central; *Hostal Centro Torreón*, P. Rosales 783, E with breakfast, shared bath, old German villa, nice atmosphere, car parking; *Hospedaje* at Arauco 905, E, clean, friendly. Student *pensiones* include Arauco 852. The house at Aníbal Pinto 1335 (T 3880) is friendly and cheap; *pensión* of Sra. Armida Navarrete Uribe, Calle A.R. Phillippi 878, D/E, full board if desired, hot water, good value; *Residencial Calle-Calle*, Múnoz 597, nr. bus station, E, clean, good value; *Hospedaje* de Señora A. de Prussing, opp. bus terminal, A. Muñoz 345, E p.p. with breakfast, clean, friendly; Sra. Segovia, A. Muñoz 353, opp. bus station, D, breakfast, hot water, rec.; *Ana María Vera*, Beauchef 684, F, clean, friendly, cooking facilities, highly rec.; and Sra. Paredes, García Reyes 244, E with breakfast, hot water, rec. For houses offering lodgings in D-E range in summer, leave bus station and turn right into Calle Anwandter (e.g. No. 624, E p.p., with breakfast, comfortable, friendly), or left into Av. Picarte. Casa de Orielle Hermosilla, Carlos Anwandter 400, F p.p., very good.

**Campsite** Quillín, between Ranco and Valdivia. Also in Parque Saval, Valdivia. White gas impossible to find, other than in pharmacies/chemists.

**Restaurants** *Centro Español*, Calle Henríquez, good, lunch US$3.50; *Club de la Unión*, on Plaza, serves a large lunch US$3 p.p.; *Sociedad Protectora E.E. de Comercio*, Independencia y Libertad, near Plaza, good seafood and cheap; *El Conquistador*, on plaza at O'Higgins, on 1st floor, good food, reasonable prices, live music at weekends; *Dino*, good, Plaza de la República (Maipú y P. Rosales); *Palace*, Arauco y P. Rosales, popular, good atmosphere, reasonable prices; *Delicias*, Camila Henríquez 372, T 213566, rec. for meals and cakes (open Sun. a.m.); *Selecta*, Av. Ramón Picarte 1093, clean, good fish and meat; *Café Haussmann*, O'Higgins 394 (good tea and cakes); *Bomba Bar*, Caupolicán 594; *Phoenix Haus*, Av. Viel s/n, on Isla Teja; restaurant on house boat in the dock, good seafood; several restaurants on the Costanera facing the boat dock, have good food and good atmosphere. *Cafetería* at Chacabuco 423 has simple, cheap food; *Entrelagos*, Pérez Rosales 622, ice cream and chocolates. Bakery: *La Baguette*, Libertad 110, Picarte 813 and Caupolicán 435, French-style cakes, brown bread. Health food shop and restaurant; *La Vie Claire*, Caupolicán 435A (next to *La Baguette*), good light meals, juices, yoghurts, muesli, etc, rec.

**Clubs** Chilean-North American Institute, Calle Beauchef; Santa Elvira Golf Club (9 holes); tennis, sailing, motor, and rowing clubs like Phoenix on Teja Island; also Club Español.

**Museum** Museo Austral, run by University on Isla Teja, free in off-season, US$0.70 in summer, cartography, archaeology, history of German settlement (including cemetery), local Indian crafts, etc. Open Tues.-Fri., 1000-1300, 1500-1800. Also on the island, near the library in the University, a **botanic garden** and **arboretum** with trees from all over the world. "Lago de los Lotos" in Parque Saval on the island—has beautiful November blooms.

**Car Hire** Hertz, Picarte 624, T 215252; **Turismo Méndez**, Gral Lagos 1249, T 3205.

**Exchange** Banco del Estado at Arauca y Camilo Henríquez (huge commission on traveller's cheques), also **Banco Osorno**, P. Rosales 585, and **Banco Concepción**, Picarte 370, will change cash and cheques, but slightly better rates at Turismo Cochrane, Caupolicán 544, rec. for changing pesos to australes and for travellers' cheques. Fincard (Visa, Mastercard), Galería Los Castellanos, oficina 18, Mon.-Fri. 0900-1400, 1500-1930, Sat. 0900-1330.

**Tourist Office** Calle Arturo Prat 555, by dock. Good map of region and local rivers. Helpful kiosk in bus station next to the news stand. **Automóvil Club de Chile**, Caupolicán 475, T 212378, also for car hire. **Conaf**, Ismael Váldez 431.

**Rail** Station at Ecuador 2000, off Av. Picarte, T 233522; information and booking office at Arauco 220, T 213574. No passenger services; only bus connection with Santiago trains from Temuco.

**Bus** Terminal is at Muñoz and Arturo Prat, by the river. To **Santiago**: several companies, 13 hrs., most services overnight, US$10-14; Pullman daily to and from central and southern towns. Half-hourly buses to **Osorno**, 1 hr. 40 mins., several companies, US$2. To **Lanco**, US$2. Thrice daily to **Llifén**, US$2.50. 15 buses daily to **Panguipulli**, US$2. Many daily to **Puerto Montt**, US$2.50, 3 hrs. To **Puerto Varas**, ETC bus, 3 hrs., US$2.35. To **Frutillar**, on Pullman Sur Temuco-Puerto Montt bus, US$2.75, 3 hrs. To **Villarrica**, by Bus JAC, a day, 3-5 hrs., US$2.50. For **Pucón** change at Villarrica, to Bus JAC. To **Bariloche** via Osorno (10 hrs.) with Bus Norte and Tas Choapa, 5 a week. Twice daily to **Riñihue**, Mon.-Sat., 1630 and

1830, Sun. 1945 and 2015.

**Air** LanChile (Camilo Henríquez 379, local 9, T 213042) and Ladeco (Caupolicán 579, local 18, T 213392) to Santiago every day except Saturday.

**Excursions** The district has a lovely countryside of woods, beaches, lakes and rivers. The various rivers are navigable and there are pleasant journeys to Futa, Putabla, and San Antonio, behind Isla Teja and through the Tornagaleanes, the Isla del Rey (these journeys can only be made in a rented motor boat). Among the waterways are countless little islands, cool and green.

At the mouth of the Río Valdivia are remains of the fortifications built by the Spanish to defend the entry to Valdivia. There are two centres for visiting the area, **Niebla** on the north bank and **Corral** on the south. In all there are the ruins of 17 forts but the principal ones to see are the Fuerte de la Pura y Limpia Concepción de Monfort de Lemus, a substantial earthwork fort on a promontory W of Niebla; opposite it, in Corral, the Castillo de San Sebastián with a battery of 24 guns and a view upriver to Volcán Llaima in the distance; Castillo San Luis de Alba in Amargos, 20 minutes' walk along the coast from Corral; and, in midstream, the Castillo de San Pedro de Alcántara in Isla Mancera. This last has the most standing buildings; all are national monuments. Niebla is also a bathing resort with seafood restaurants and accommodation (*Hospedaje Papi*, F, clean, cooking facilities, meals, friendly, camping, rec.; *Hosterías Riechers*, D, and *Santa Clara*, E); information and telephone office by the fort. Further round the coast is Los Molinos, a seaside resort on the ocean. The fishing port of Corral has several restaurants (e.g. *Español* opp. the dock, good seafood), and an unnamed *residencial* on Calle Arica, E. 4 km. along the coast from Corral is San Carlos, with its *Hostería los Alamos* (E), a delightful hideout for those seeking a quiet life. The coastal walks are splendid. Isla Mancera is a pleasant place to stopover on the boat trips, but it has no restaurants and gets crowded when an excursion boat arrives.

The tourist boats (*Neptuno* or *Calle-Calle*) to Isla Mancera and Corral, including a guided half-day tour (US$11.50 with meals—cheaper without) leave the Muelle Fluvial, Valdivia (behind the tourist office on Av. Prat 555), times vary, details from the Tourist Office. Cheaper boats to Corral leave 5 times a day, from 0800, from Muelle Fluvial, Valdivia and return between 0800 and 1900, 1½-hour journey; only twice a day in winter; they usually go out via Niebla (ferry dock is 20 mins. walk from the fort, near the Copec station) and call at Isla Mancera (if you want to stop en route, you must first pay full fare, US$0.70 then US$0.50 for each "leg"; some boats make a 1¼-hr. stopover on Isla Mancera en route back to Valdivia). The river trip is beautiful, but you can also take a bus to Niebla from Calle Yungay (river end), Valdivia, roughly twice an hour between 0715 and 1945, 20 mins., US$0.45 (bus continues to Los Molinos, US$0.55, students US$0.10), then cross to Corral by boat (US$0.50) and return to Valdivia by river. Colectivo Valdivia-Niebla, US$0.50. There are occasional buses from Valdivia to Corral.

**Mehuin**, on the coast, 2 hrs. bus ride north from Valdivia through San José de La Mariquina; post office, good sea bathing and several hotels: *Hostería Millalafquen*, T 279, *Hotels Mehuin* and *Playa*. Queule, 6 km. from Mehuin, has two simple *residenciales*. Good beach but bathing dangerous at high tide because of undercurrents; safer to bathe in the river near ferry.

A road runs E from Valdivia along the River Calle Calle to Los Lagos (61 km.- 2 buses a day from Valdivia in summer), and on to the beautiful **Lago Riñihue** (39 km.). The road around the southern edge of the lake from Riñihue to Enco is now closed (except in summer only), so Choshuenco at the SE end of Lago Panguipulli can only be reached by road from Panguipulli or Puerto Fuy. Riñihue, a beautiful but very small and isolated village, is worth a visit. Campsite by the lake; *Restaurant del Lago* has rooms, E (no meals).

Access from the Longitudinal Highway to lovely, island-starred **Lago Ranco** and, beyond it, to **Lago Maihue** is made from Los Lagos, or from a point 18 km. S of Los Lagos, 11 km. N of Paillaco. These two roads join to meet the road around the lake some 5 km. W of Futrono at the northern shore. The road curves round the north of Lago Ranco to **Llifén**, a picturesque place on the eastern shore. From Llifén, a visit can be paid to Lago Maihue (Cordillera Sur bus Valdivia-Llifén twice daily, once Sun.).

**Hotels** *Hostería Chollinco*, 3 km. out of town on the road towards Lago Maihue, A, overpriced, poor food, limited electricity, swimming pool; *Hostería Lican*, C; *Hostería La Cascada*, Torremolinos 357, A+; *Huequecura*, Casa 4, A+, including meals and fishing services. 4 campsites in the vicinity.

On the south side of Lake Ranco is Lago Ranco, an ugly town (several small hotels and *residenciales*, houses to let in summer, campsites—bus from Osorno, see below) and Riñinahue (*hostería*, A); the road is terrible (lots of mud and animals, including oxcarts), but is worth taking to see an older lifestyle, the beautiful lake, waterfalls and sunsets on the distant volcanoes (if walking, beware the numerous guard dogs in the area). There is excellent fishing on the S shore of the lake. On the western shore is Puerto Nuevo (hotel of same name, A+, very good, watersports, fishing on the Río Bueno). Roads from Puerto Nuevo and Lago Ranco run W to La Unión (*Hotel Unión*, Letelier 497, T 2695, D), which is bypassed by the Longitudal Highway.

Río Bueno is at the crossroads of the Lago Ranco-La Unión road and the Highway (Ruta 5). Some 42 km. S of this point is Osorno, another centre for exploring the Lakes.

***Osorno***, 911 km. from Santiago and 105 km. N of Puerto Montt (103,000 people) was founded in 1558. It was destroyed shortly after its foundation, and was later settled by German immigrants, whose descendants are still of great importance in the area. The city has some old wooden buildings mixed in with the new (e.g. on Calle Mackenna). On the large Plaza de Armas stands the modern, concrete cathedral, with many arches, repeated in the tower, itself an open, latticed arch with a cross superimposed. Behind the new railway station is the Fuerte Reina Luisa, constructed 1793, restored 1977, with only the river front walls and end turrets standing. The old railway station, down the line from the new, is almost derelict, but its forecourt is used by some buses and shops.

**Hotels**  *Waeger*, Cochrane 816, T 233721, P.O. Box 802, Fax 237080, A+, 4-star, restaurant, comfortable, rec. *Del Prado*, Cochrane 1162, T 235020, swimming pool, garden, good meals, well-located, charming, A+; *Villa Eduviges*, Eduviges 856, T 235023, C; *Inter-Lagos*, Cochrane 515, T 234695, A; *Gran* (good restaurant), main square, O'Higgins 615, T 232171, B, with bath; *Tirol*, Bulnes 630, T 233593, B, with bath; *Residencial Hein*, Cochrane 843, T 234116, D, breakfast US$1.80, pleasant; *Residencial Riga*, Antahuer 1058, T 232945, C, highly rec. but heavily booked in season. *Residencial Schulz*, Freire 530, D with breakfast, hot water, other meals extra. *San Fernando*, Bulnes 836, E; *Hospedaje Eliano del Río Cortés*, Bulnes 876, E. *Residencial* at Amunátegui 520, run by Sra. Gallardo, near bus terminal, good, D; *Residencial Ortega* (strongly rec.) Colón 602, nr. Errazúriz, 1 block from bus terminal, toilet facilities limited, E; others near bus terminal: at A. Pinto 1758, E inc. breakfast and hot water, T 238024; *Los Carrera 1387*, 50 m. from bus terminal, E, basic, friendly, excellent meals; *Residencias/Restaurantes La Paloma* (Errázuriz 1599), *Richmond*, (Lastarria 500 block) and *Ver-Mar* (Errázuriz y Lastarria, T 234429), are fairly basic. *Germania*, Rodríguez 741, E, no hot water, cooking facilities. Youth hostel: *Residencial Stop*, Freire 810, F p.p. in shared rooms, or contact Secretaria Provincial de la Juventud, Bilbao 850. Private houses at Germán Hube, pasaje 1, casa 22, población Villa Dama, E, hot water, clean, use of kitchen, rec.; Lynch 1306 (1 block from bus station, use of kitchen).

**Restaurants**  *Bahía*, Ramírez 1076, rec. for quality and economy; *Peter's Kneipe*, M.Rodríguez 1030, excellent German restaurant; *Café Dino*, on the plaza, restaurant upstairs, bar/cafeteria downstairs, good. *Luca's Pizzas*, Cochrane 551, pizzas, pastas, burgers, etc., fair. Good restaurant in the bus station. Try chicha (cider) or local pisco sour.

**Shop**  *Reinares and Thone*, Ramírez 1100, for good fishing gear.

**Museum**  Museo Histórico Municipal, Matta 809. Entrance in Casa de Cultura, free; Mon.-Fri. 1000-1200, 1500-1830, Sat. 1100-1300, 1600-1800: old photos, archaeology and anthropology, history, black and white reproductions of old masters.

**Garage**  Automotriz Salfa Sur SA, Fco. Bilbao 857; Automotriz Amthauer, Amthauer 1250. **Car Hire**, Hertz, Bilbao 857, T 235402.

**Laundry**  Av. Arturo Prat 678 (allow at least a day).

**Exchange**  Fincard for Visa and Mastercard, Mackenna 877, Mon.-Fri. 0900-1400, 1530-1900, Sat. 0930-1330. For parallel rates try **Cambio Tur**, Mackenna 1010, T 4846; Frontera Ltda., Ramírez 949, local 5 (Galery Catedral).

**Post Office**  O'Higgins 645, also Telex. **Phone Office** Ramírez at central plaza and Juan

Mackenna y Cochrane.

**Tourist Office** Provincial government office, on Plaza de Armas, O'Higgins s/n, 1st floor, left.
**Automóvil Club de Chile**, Bulnes 463, T 232269, information and car hire.

**Club Andino** Juan Mackenna esq. Manuel Bulnes, 3rd floor.

**Buses** Most leave from the bus terminal 1 block from municipal market at Errázuriz 1400.
Left luggage at terminal open 0730-2030. Bus from centre, US$0.30. Frequent buses to
**Santiago**, US$11, 16 hrs. Cruz del Sur to Santiago US$18 pullman, US$36 *cama*, to **Puerto
Montt** US$1.65, to **Castro** US$4.65, to **Concepción**, US$7.65, to **Temuco**, US$3.35, to
**Punta Arenas**, US$27. Other services to Punta Arenas: Sur, Mon. and Sat., Turisbus, Mon.
and Thurs., Eurobus and Bus Norte. Varmontt buses every ½ hr. (from about 0700 to 2200)
to **Alto Frutillar** (US$1.25), **Llanquihue**, **Puerto Varas** and **Puerto Montt** (US$2). To
**Puerto Octay**, US$1.50, Vía Octay company 6 daily between 0815-1930 (return 0800-1930)
Mon.-Sat., Sun. 5 between 0800 and 2000 (4 return buses). Buses to **Valdivia**, every half
hour, 1½-2½ hrs. journey depending on company (e.g. Trans Norte, Etta, Cruz del Sur),
US$2 and up. To **Lago Ranco**, Buses Ruta 5, 6 a day from 0810, 2 hrs., US$1.50. To **Entre
Lagos, Puyehue** and **Aguas Calientes**, Buses Puyehue from the municipal market; to Entre
Lagos, 4 a day, 0915-1500, return 1600, 1800, 1900, 1 hr., US$1; Puyehue and Aguas
Calientes, 0915, 1130, 1530, return 1230 and 1730 (1600 also on Sat., in theory), 2 hrs.,
US$1.35 (US$2.35 return). Local bus to **Anticura** (Chilean customs post) leaves at 1620, 3
hrs., 22 km. from border.

**Rail** Station at Juan Mackenna 600, T 232992. No passenger services, except Jan. and Feb.
to/from Santiago and Puerto Montt.

**Air** LanChile, Manuel Antonio Matta 844, T 236688, Ladeco, Mackenna 975, T 236102.
Ladeco operates flights Osorno-Santiago Mon., Wed., Fri., Sun. LanChile Mon.-Fri.

**To Argentina via the Puyehue Pass**. The Argentine town of Bariloche can be reached by
Route 215 through the Puyehue pass (paved most of the way). Although less scenic than the
ferry journey across Lake Todos Los Santos and Laguna Verde (**see page 613**) this crossing is
cheaper, more reliable and still a beautiful trip. Buses Cruz del Sur, Sun. 1215, US$16.65, to
Bariloche; Turismo Lanín, also to Bariloche, Tues., Wed., Fri., Sun. 1000, US$20; Tas Choapa
daily to Bariloche, 1120, and to Mendoza, US$21.65, to Buenos Aires, US$52, Montevideo,
US$62, Rio de Janeiro, US$88. Buy tickets for international buses from the bus terminal, not
through an agency.

**Excursions** Route 215 runs E past the Pilmaiquen waterfall (35 km.) to Entre
Lagos, Lago Puyehue and the thermal waters at **Termas de Puyehue** (US$3.50
p.p. for bathing, 0900-2000); 2 hrs. by car, 2½ by bus (schedule under Osorno
**Buses**). The bus does not stop at the lake (unless you want to get off at *Gran
Hotel Termas de Puyehue* and clamber down), but turns off Route 215 and goes
4 km. further to Aguas Calientes The main road continues to Anticura *Hostería
y Cabañas Anticura*; *Camping Catrue*) and the Puyehue pass.

*Aguas Calientes* has the headquarters of the **Puyehue National Park**, an open
air swimming pool with hot thermal water beside the Río Chanleufú, open
0830-1900, US$1.35, children US$0.85 and a very hot indoor pool, open
Mon.-Fri. 0830-1230, 1400-1800, Sat., Sun. and holidays 0830-2030, US$2.15,
children US$1.50-1.65. There is a Conaf campsite with private sites (US$10 per
site), cabin type accommodation (at top of our C range, T 236988, take food if
you want to cook) and a café. A private house, to the right just before the bridge,
offers beds at F p.p., or full board, D, highly rec. In the Puyehue National Park is
surviving temperate rain-forest. Three marked paths can be followed: Los Rápidos,
1 km. to falls on the Río Chanleufú (the trail starts at the entrance to the outdoor
pool, if you don't want to swim, just say you're going to Los Rápidos); El Recodo,
a continuation of Los Rápidos up the river bank; El Pionero, 1,800 metres up to a
viewpoint (good for the exercise before you bathe). The trees are lovely: listen
to the birds and watch for kingfishers by the river.

The road from Aguas Calientes continues 18 km. to **Antillanca** through a
lovely region of small lakes and fairytale forests. (*Hotel Antillanca*, T
235114/232297, A without food, at foot of Volcán Casablanca, 4 km. from crater,

$50 per double / 10% dis 3 nights or more
5% menores al motorizajos

excellent hotel/restaurant/café, with pool, sauna and small ski resort, 2 ski lifts.) The views from Antillanca are breathtaking, with the snow-clad cones of Osorno, Puntiagudo, and Puyehue forming a semicircle. The tree-line on Antillanca is one of the few in the world made up of deciduous trees (southern beech). It is possible to hike from Antillanca to Volcán Casablanca for even better views of the surrounding volcanoes and lakes; no path, information from Club Andino in Osorno. No public transport from Aguas Calientes to Antillanca, try hitching—always difficult, but it is not a hard walk.

**Hotels at Lago Puyehue**  *Gran Hotel Termas de Puyehue* has a hot-springs swimming pool (T Osorno 232157), large and well kept, A p.p. (cheaper May to mid-Dec.), main meals and breakfast expensive, generally overpriced, in beautiful scenery, heavily booked Jan.-Feb. (Telex 273146, SOTERCL; accommodation also in private house nearby, E p.p. full board). In **Entre Lagos**, *Pub del Campo*, highly rec. restaurant, reasonable prices, owner is of Swiss descent; *Villa Veneto*, Gral. Lagos 602, T 203, D; *Hostería Entre Lagos*, Ramírez 65, lake view, T 647225, D. *Hospedaje Millarey*, E p.p. with breakfast, excellent, clean, friendly; *Restaurant Jardín del Turista*, very good. On the S lakeshore are: *Chalet Suisse*, Ruta 215, Km. 55 (Casilla 910, Osorno, T Puyehue 647208, Osorno 064-234073), *hostería*, restaurant with excellent food; a few km. beyond, *hospedaje y cabañas* at Almacén Valenciana; *alojamiento* at Shell station after Km. 60, before *Motel Ñilque*, T 232356, or (0647) 218, cabins, A+, half-price May-October, fishing trips, watersports, car hire. *Hostería Isla Fresia*, located on own island, T 236951, Casilla 49, Entre Lagos, B, transport provided.

**Camping**  *El Manzano*, Route 215, Km. 58; *Camping No Me Olvides*, Km. 60; *Playa Los Copihues*, Km. 60 (hot showers, good), all on S shore of Lake Puyehue; *Camping Playa Puyehue*, Km. 75. Wild camping allowed at Aguas Calientes fortunately, the Conaf site is very expensive (see above); ask the rangers.

A further excursion can be made to the S shore of Lago Rupanco (65 km.) taking the road to Puerto Octay and turning E after 33 km. This lake is very beautiful and much less developed than most of its neighbours. At the western end of the lake is *Hostería y Cabañas El Paraíso*, T 236239; at the eastern end is *Hotel Bahía Escocia*, run by Ian and Alice Hamilton (Casilla 1099, T 0647-254, Telex 273002 BOOTH CL), beautiful setting, most hospitable, hot water, good meals, warmly rec.; tennis, boating, walking. Access by car only, 40 km. of dirt road. Bus from Osorno, Piedras Negras at either *Minimarket El Capricho*, Mackenna y Colón, or from Estacíon Viejo (old railway station), leaves 1645, 1545 on Sat., returns from Piedras Negras midway along the southern shore at 0700.

Drive or take bus (US$0.60, frequent) N of Osorno to Río Bueno, celebrated for its scenery, to La Unión, and to **Trumao**, a river port on the Río Bueno, whence a launch may be taken to La Barra on the coast; leaves Wed. and Sat. only at 0900, 5 hrs., US$6; returns Sun. at 0900.

The sea beaches at Maicolpue (60 km. from Osorno—*Hostería Müller*, on the beach, E, clean, good service, rec., campsite) and Pucatrihue (*Hostería Incalcar*, summer only) are worth a visit in the summer (daily bus service).

From Osorno it is 106 km. S to Puerto Montt, including 25 km. along the shore of *Lago Llanquihue*. Across the great blue sheet of water can be seen two snowcapped volcanoes: the perfect cone of Osorno (2,680 metres) and the shattered cone of Calbuco, and, when the air is clear, the distant Tronador (3,554 metres). Lago Llanquihue covers over 540 square km. and is the third largest natural lake in South America. There is a road, 187 km. long, around it.

At the northern tip of the lake is **Puerto Octay**, just 56 km. SE of Osorno. Founded by German settlers in 1851, it is a small town in a lovely setting (buses daily). Tourist office open Mon.-Fri. 1000-1200, 1500-1700 (Jan. and Feb. daily 0900-2100). 5 km. away is the Peninsula of Centinela with lodging, camping, a launch dock, bathing beaches, water sports. From the headland are fine views of the volcanoes Osorno, Calbuco, Puntiagudo and the Cordillera de los Andes; a very popular spot in good weather. 7 km. E of Puerto Octay is Playa Maitén, "highly recommended, nice beach, marvellous view to the Volcán Osorno, no tourists". Further on is Las Cascadas, surrounded by picturesque agricultural land, old houses and German cemeteries. The small settlement at Las Cascadas also has vacation houses. For a circuit by car from Osorno, follow the road from Puerto

Octay along the lakeside, with the Osorno volcano on your left, to Ensenada, a short distance up the road (20 mins.) is Petrohué with its beautiful falls, and the Osorno volcano again in the background, and Lago Todos los Santos; continue to Puerto Varas, then along the W side of the lake to Octay and back. Note that the road round the north and east sides of the lake is poor, necessitating speeds of 20-30 kph at best in places. *Café Kali* on main square at Octay, Amunátegui, is recommended.

**Hotels Puerto Octay** *Haase*, Pedro Montt 344, T213, very pleasant, B (rooms with and without bath), US$70 for rooms, breakfast and supper for family of 6; *Posada Gubernatis*, Calle Santiago s/n, lakeside, clean, comfortable, C. *Hospedaje Raquel Mardorf*, Germán Wulf 712, F p.p.; *Hospedaje La Naranja*, Independencia 561, F p.p.; *hospedaje* at Pedro Montt 712, upstairs next to church, E, clean, quiet, hot water at certain times, same owners have *Restaurant La Cabaña* at No. 713 (T 202), which is good. **Centinela** (3 km. S): *Hotel Centinela*, Casa 114, Península de Centinela, T 22 (Pto. Octay), D (rooms with or without bath), meals US$6 with wine, nice setting, friendly staff; *Hostería La Baja*, Península de Centinela. **Las Cascadas** *Centro de Recreación Las Cascadas*, T 235377; *Hostería Irma*, on lake, 2 km. past Las Cascadas, F, run by 3 Marías, good food, very pleasant. Several farms on the road around this side of the lake offer accommodation, look for signs.

**Camping** *Centro de Recreación Las Cascadas* and Villa Las Cascadas picnic area (free); at Playa Maitén, rec.; Centinela municipal site, US$4 per group.

**Buses** To **Osorno** 7 a day; to **Frutillar**, twice daily Jan.-March, Mon., Wed., and Fri. April-Dec; to **Las Cascadas** Mon.-Fri. 1700, return next day 0600.

About half-way down the west side of the lake is *Frutillar*, in fact two towns: Alto Frutillar, with a railway station, just off the main highway, and Bajo Frutillar on the lakeside, 4 km. away. It is 5 minutes by colectivo between the two towns, US$0.25.

Bajo Frutillar is possibly the most attractive town on the lake. A beautifully kept town, it offers a highly-regarded classical music festival in late January to early February (accommodation must be booked well in advance). The Museo Colonial Alemán, including watermill, a model of a German colonial house, a blacksmith's shop, and a *campanario* (circular barn with agricultural and dairy machinery and carriages inside), gardens and handicraft shop, is well worth a visit. Open 1000-1200, 1500-1800, closed Tues., US$0.40 (maintained by the Universidad Austral de Chile).

**Accommodation and Food** *Hotel Frutillar*, Av. Philippi 1000, on stilts above lake, T 277, A, best, good restaurant and bar, Andina del Sud travel agency in reception; *Casona del 32*, B with bath and breakfast, comfortable old house, central heating, English and German spoken, T 369, Caupolicán 28, P.O. Box 101; *Hospedaje Costa Azul*, Philippi 1175, T 388, C-D, mainly for families, good breakfasts; also on Philippi: *Hospedaje Vivaldi*, No. 851-5, T 382, Sra. Edith Klesse, D p.p., quiet, comfortable, excellent breakfast and lodging, also family accommodation, rec.; *Winkler*, No. 1155, T 388, C; *Las Rocas*, No. 1227, T 397, D with breakfast; *Hospedaje Trayen* at No. 1285, T 205, E, excellent breakfast, clean; *Hospedaje Kaisersseehaus* (Viola Luisa Herbach Fuchslocher), No. 1333 (Casilla 13, T 387), F p.p., hot water, good food (extra), very comfortable and welcoming, English, German, Spanish spoken, highly rec. Many more in the lower town. *Frutillar Alto*, Calle Principal 168, E, clean.

**Camping** *Playa Maqui*, 7 km. N of Frutillar, T 9123, fancy, expensive; *Los Ciruelillos*, nr. Frutillar, T 9123, most services.

**Restaurants** The *Club Alemán*, Av. Philippi 747, has a good restaurant; there is a Bar Restaurant upstairs at the Fire Station, opp. *Hotel Frutillar*. *Bierstube*, A. Varas, open 1600-2400. Many German-style cafés and tea- rooms on Calle Philippi (the lakefront, e.g. *Salón de Te Frutillar*, No. 775). *Der Volkladen*, O'Higgins y Philippi, natural products, chocolates and cakes, natural cosmetics. *Café Hermosa*, good breakfast (view of lake and Volcán Osorno). Budget travellers should eat at *Bar/Restaurant Colonial*, Winkler 353, Alto Frutillar, US$3.35 for excellent 3-course meal, "country" cooking.

**Services and Transport** Toilet, showers and changing cabins for beach on O'Higgins. Cama-Chile shop, Philippi y O'Higgins. Tourist Office on lakeside opp. *Club Alemán*, helpful; Viajes Frutillar in Alto Frutillar (Richter y Alissandre) run tours. Bus every half hr. from Varmontt terminal on San Francisco, Puerto Varas to Alto Frutillar, US$0.65. Varmontt bus from Puerto Varas continues to Osorno, 1¼ hrs., US$1.25. All buses leave from Alto Frutillar; 3 times a week to Puerto Octay from Opec station.

**Puerto Varas**, a beauty spot of about 23,300 inhabitants, is on the shore of Lago Llanquihue, with standard roses grown along the streets. It is 1,008 km. from Santiago and only 20 by paved road from Puerto Montt. Parque Philippi, on top of hill, is a pleasant place to visit; walk up to *Hotel Cabañas del Lago* on Klenner, cross the railway and the gate is on the right. The views are a bit restricted by trees and the metal cross at the top is unattractive (so is the electric clock which chimes the quarter-hours in town). Casino charges US$2.65 entry, including first drink.

**Hotels** *Puerto Varas*, Klenner 351 (*Gran Hotel Turismo*), T 2524, A, luxury class with casino, a huge, ugly place; *Cabañas del Lago*, Klenner 195, T 2291, cabins, A, adequate; *Bellavista*, V. Pérez Rosales 60, T 20211, A, cheerful, rec., no restaurant, but breakfast service, overlooking lake; *Hospedaje Loreley*, Maipo 911, T 2226, C, rec., homely, quiet, good restaurant; under construction, *Los Alerces*, in medium price range; *Licarayén*, San José 114, T 2305, small, A with bath, highly rec., book in season; *Residencial Hellwig*, San Pedro 210, E, rooms and bathrooms clean and neat, water usually tepid, not welcoming; *Asturias*, Del Salvador 322, T 2446, A, friendly, discounts for cash, fine restaurant; *Hostería La Sirena*, Santa Rosa 710, C-D incl. breakfast, comfortable, good restaurant, on hill overlooking the town. Also cheap *residenciales* opposite bus station and in Plaza de Armas.

*Motel Ayenteno*, V. Pérez Rosales 950, clean, comfortable cabins, friendly, T 2270; *Motel Altué*, Av. V. Pérez Rosales 01679, T 2294, B, incl. breakfast; *Motel Sacho*, San José 581, T 2227, C. Residencial at Salvador 423, D, run by a German lady, rec., as is María Schilling Rosas' *hospedaje* at La Quebrada 752; *Carmen Bittner*, Martínez 564, E p.p. with excellent breakfast, German spoken, rec.; *Hospedaje Walker*, Martínez 576, F p.p. with breakfast, clean, quiet; Sra. Elly. A. Prat 151, E with breakfast; *hospedaje* at Santa Rosa y Mirador, E with breakfast. Familia Niklitschek-Pozas, Calle Imperial 8 (opp. *Motel Trauco*), highly rec.

**Camping** On S shore of Lago Llanquihue starting at Puerto Varas: Km. 10, Playa Hermosa (T Puerto Varas 8283, Puerto Montt 252223), fancy, expensive; Km. 11, Playa Niklitschek, full facilities; Km. 20, Playa Venado; Km. 49, Conaf site at Puerto Oscuro, beneath road to volcano, very good.

**Restaurants** *Club Alemán*, San José 413, best, dinner, expensive; *Mercado*, next to market, excellent food, good service, not cheap but good value; *Café Asturias*, San Francisco 302, good empanadas and other food (same management as hotel of same name); *Ibis*, Pérez Rosales, next to *Motel Ayentemo*, rec.; *Central*, San José 319, good coffee, cakes, pies and breakfast, opens early. *Domino*, Del Salvador 450, good, cheap; *Costa Azul*, Av. Pérez Rosales 01071, 2 km. from town towards Puerto Chico, in wooden building (expensive motel restaurants just beyond it aren't worth visiting). *El Molino*, an excellent coffee house in an old water mill, on road to Ensenada 22 km. from Pto. Varas.

**Car Hire** Llancahue, Del Salvador, English spoken, helpful.

**Fishing** The area around Puerto Varas is popular for fishing. A licence costs US$2.50 a year, obtainable from the Municipal offices.

**Exchange** Turismo Los Lagos, Del Salvador 257 (Galería Real, local 11), open daily 0830-1330, 1500-2100, Sunday 0930-1330. Better rate of exchange for travellers' cheques obtained in Puerto Montt.

**Phone Office** Salvador y Santa Rosa.

**Travel Agents** *Andina del Sur* (Del Salvador 243, T 2511) offers trips from US$25 to Lago Todos los Santos, Peulla, Cerro Tronador and return, plus other excursions, good. Also *Turismo Nieve* (on San Bernardo, rec.), *Turismo Puerto Varas*, *Turismo Casoria Alemana*, *Turismo Llancahue*, *ACE Turismo* and *Varastur* (San Francisco 272).

**Tourist Office** Del Salvador 328, 0900-2100 in summer, helpful, will find cheap accommodation; also art gallery.

**Buses** To **Santiago**: Igi-Llaima (office San Francisco 516) leaves from Salvador at 1830, arrives 1130 (US$11.50). To **Puerto Montt** every ½ hr. from Varmontt station (San Francisco 600 block), 30 mins., US$0.65; same company, same frequency to Frutillar and Osorno.

To **Bariloche**, Andina del Sud's Puerto Montt-Bariloche service passes through Puerto

Varas and can be caught here, details under Puerto Montt **To Argentina**. You can hitch, or take a local bus (cheaper, 1130 from **Res. Hellwig**) to Petrohué en route to Bariloche, but you must spend the night there before catching the ferry. It is not possible to go by private car from Puerto Varas direct to Bariloche, as the ferry on the Argentine side does not take cars; one must go via Osorno.

**Excursions** Buses from Puerto Montt run every day on the southern side of the lake between Puerto Varas and (50 km.) Ensenada, in the south-eastern corner of the lake, continuing to Ralún, Cochamó and Río Puelo (see below and **Excursions** from Puerto Montt). In summer, buses go daily from Puerto Montt and Puerto Varas in the morning to Ensenada, Laguna Verde, Petrohué Falls and Lago Todos Los Santos, US$5, good value. The drive around the lake is very picturesque. On the northern road are Puerto Octay and Centinela (**see above**).

Puerto Varas is within easy reach of many famous beauty spots—Desagüe, Totoral, Frutillar, Los Bajos, Puerto Octay (direct bus only from Osorno), Puerto Chico, Puerto Fonck, La Poza, Isla Loreley, Volcán Calbuco, La Fábrica, Puerto Rosales, Playa Venado, Ralún and Río Pescado. The Falls (Salto) of Petrohué should not be missed. The whole countryside with its primeval forest, deep blue rivers and snowcapped volcanoes is very beautiful; interest is added by the timber-frame buildings with shingle roofs—even the churches.

La Poza is a little lake to the S of the main lake and reached through narrow channels overhung with vegetation; a concealed channel leads to yet another lake, the Laguna Encantada. The motor-boats that tour Lago Llanquihue stop at Isla Loreley, very beautiful and well worth a visit.

It is only 16 km. by a scenic paved road from **Ensenada**, a lovely spot at the eastern end of Lago Llanquihue to Lago Todos los Santos, a long irregularly shaped sheet of water, the most beautiful of all the lakes in southern Chile. The ports of **Petrohué** at its western and **Peulla** at its eastern ends are connected by boat, costing US$8; it leaves Petrohué at 1030, Peulla at 1500 (not Sun. 2½ hrs.—most seating indoors, no cars carried). This is the only public service on the lake and it connects solely with the Andina del Sud tour bus (see under Puerto Montt). If you prefer to go walking, ask for the park guard, Hernán, who organizes expeditions from Petrohué in the summer months. Peulla is a good starting point for hikes in the mountains. Trout and salmon fishing at Petrohué are excellent. The waters are emerald green. There is a shop in Petrohué; bread is sold by Sra. Marci González every morning, ask at the post office. The Salto de Petrohué (entrance, US$0.35) is 4 km. from Petrohué, 10 km. from Ensenada (a much nicer walk from Petrohué). At the other end of the lake, the Cascadas Los Novios, signposted above the *Hotel Peulla*, are a steep walk, but are stunning once you reach them; don't forget to turn round to see the views. The falls, Lago Todos Los Santos and the surrounding areas to the borders with the Puyehue National Park and Argentina fall within the **Parque Nacional Vicente Pérez Rosales**.

Petrohué and Peulla are infested by *tavanos* (local horseflies) in Jan. and Feb. Cover up as much as possible with light-coloured clothes.

**Hotels** At **Ensenada**: *Hotel Ensenada*, T 2888, A with bath, olde-worlde (closed in winter) good view of lake and Osorno Volcano; *Cabañas Brisas del Lago*, D, chalets for 6 on beach, good restaurant next door but one, highly rec. for self-catering, but bring your own food; *Hostería Los Pumas*, 3 hrs. up the hill only, in season only, C; *Ruedas Viejas*, T 312, C for room, or in cabin, about 1 km. from Ensenada, fairly basic, hot water, has popular restaurant, good value; opp. is *Moteles Hostería*, D with breakfast, clean, comfortable; about 2 km. from town is *Pucará*, C, also with good restaurant (the steaks are rec.); opp. is *Hospedaje Opazo*, E with breakfast, no hot water, friendly; *Hospedaje Arena*, on same road as *Ruedas Viejas* but nearer police station, C with breakfast, rec.; *hospedaje* above Toqui grocery, E p.p., use of kitchen, beach in the back yard, rec. Ensenada has little more than the hotels, restaurants (*Canta Rana* rec. for bread and kuchen) and a few pricey shops; bring your own provisions. At **Petrohué**: *Hostería Petrohué*, B, with bath, D b and b, comfortable; the only other place to stay is *Familia Küscher* on other side of river, E p.p.

with breakfast, meals available for US$3.50, cold water, electricity only 3 hrs. in p.m., dirty, noisy, poor value, camping possible; Refugio above being repaired. *Fundo El Salto*, near Salto de Petrohué, D p.p. very friendly, fishing trips also arranged, Casilla 471, Puerto Varas. At **Peulla**, on the opposite shore: *Hotel Peulla*, A+ (cheaper out of season), beautiful setting by the lake and mountains, restaurant and bar, poor beds, cold in winter, often full of tour groups (tiny shop at back of hotel); *Residencial Palomita*, 50 metres W of Hotel, E p.p. half board, family-run, simple, comfortable but not spacious, separate shower, this is the only accommodation, advertised as such, apart from the Hotel, but *Restaurant Rabinito*, C half-board, has one small double room, clean, hot shower, lunch available, reasonable food, and accommodation is also available with local residents: Elma Hernández Maldonado, E p.p. with breakfast, clean; Roberto Téllez, F p.p. half board; Silvia Belasci and others. You can also stay at the Conaf guard's house (Jorge), F p.p., but lock all bags. Homemade marmalade, dulce de leche available from Mrs. Gisela Schwitzgaeble, Ruiz Moreno 938. Otherwise food hard to find in Peulla, so take your own.

**Camping** At Peulla, opp. Conaf office, US$1.50; at Petrohué, a National Parks Environment Centre for the Parque Nacional Vicente Pérez Rosales with display and slide show (camping US$4 p.p.), near *Hotel Petrohué*; an unofficial one by lake shore 1 km. beyond *Hotel Ensenada* at Playa Larga, basic.

**Bus** Bohle bus Puerto Montt-Petrohué US$5, 1230, via Ensenada and Puerto Varas with stops for views and lunch, rec.; a bus returns from Petrohué at 1700. There are day return bus and boat tours to Peulla from Puerto Montt, with possibility of continuing to Bariloche. If planning to go to Bariloche in stages, book through to Bariloche in Petrohué, not Peulla because onward connections from Peulla may be full and the accommodation is not so good there. Note also that it is difficult to hitch from Ensenada to Petrohué and that the local bus leaving Ensenada at 1230 misses the boat to Peulla. Fare Petrohué-Bariloche US$87, Andino del Sud, same as from Puerto Montt.

A good hike from Ensenada goes to Laguna Verde, with a beautiful circular trail behind the lake (take first fork to the right behind the information board), and then down the road to a campsite at Puerto Oscuro on Lago Llanquihue. The site is quiet and secluded, a good spot for a picnic. It is about a 45 minute hike from *Hotel Ensenada*.

A paved road runs 31 km. SE from Ensenada along the wooded lower Petrohué valley to **Ralún**, on the salt-water Estuario de Reloncaví. Here is the *Hotel Ralún*, at S end of the village, a magnificent timber building to a fine modern design by Cristián de Groote, with a choice of rooms or cabins, warmly rec., A+ (25% more in summer than rest of year) plus US$35 p.p. full board (cabins rented at US$80 a night). Telex 240048 Santiago; address Casilla 678, Puerto Montt. *Restaurant El Refugio*, 1 km. N of *Ralún*, rents rooms; also *Navarrito*, restaurant and lodging; *Posada Campesino*, simple room; *El Encuentro*, village shop and post office, with telex, all F p.p. Bus from Ensenada, US$0.70, daily 1015; more easily reached by bus from Puerto Montt. (Buses Bohle, 5 a day from 1000-1930, 4 on Sat., return 0700-1830, US$1.85).

In 5 hours you can hike from Ralún to Lago Cayutúe, then a further 3 to the town of Cayutúe. At the 5-6 houses in Ralún before you cross the big bridge you can buy bread, honey and cheese. Follow the main road to the first turning on left which goes up a valley. The dirt road ends at a farm, ask directions to a track which is 100 metres to the right. Continue to another farm, where the track goes right, round a fence. Good views of the valley behind you from the top of the pass; descend to Lago Cayutúe, set between two mountain ranges with forest around it. Good camping and swimming at the lake (Aad Bol, Poelijk, Neth., and Trish Clements, Faulconbridge, Australia).

Lago Todos los Santos has no roads round it; the shores are deeply wooded and several small islands rise from its surface. A boat trip to Isla Margarita on the lake costs US$3.50, ½ hr. each way, with ½ hr. on the island where there is a beautiful crater lake (leaves Petrohué 1500, run by Andino del Sud). Private launches can be hired for other trips, for instance to Cayutué (about US$30) on a southern arm of the lake.

In the waters of the lake are reflected the slopes of **Volcán Osorno**. Only experienced climbers should attempt to climb right to the top, ice climbing equipment required: there are many deep crevasses, the weather can change suddenly, never go alone, and set off early in the morning; there is a shelter for hikers. Antu Tours organize a one-day hike to the summit for a reasonable fee (rec.). They can be contacted through their postal address: Casilla 24, 29 Santiago

29; T 2712767, Telex 440019 RECAL CZ.

The Club Andino Osorno (address under Osorno) has three shelters (US$3 p.p.) at La Picada (84 km. from Osorno, turn off at Puerto Kloker—29 km. SE of Puerto Octay), on the ski slopes on the Osorno volcano at 950 metres; *Las Pumas* on the Volcán Osorno at 900 m., with plenty of beds at US$2 p.p. and cooking facilities, very friendly guards (apply at the Oficina de Turismo de Osorno). At 1,200 metres is **Refugio Teski Club**, E, 4 hrs. walk from *Hotel Ensenada* (where you should check if the *refugio* has food), bleak site above the tree line; not open all year (usual ski season is June to September). *La Burbuja* ski centre, with 2 *refugios*, open all year, is reached by a 19 km. road which turns off the road around Lago Llanquihue at Puerto Oscuro, just N of Ensenada. If you wish to climb Volcán Osorno, ask first at Las Pumas or Refugio Teski for advice. To reach Volcán Osorno, take bus to Ensenada from Puerto Varas then walk 12 km. to Las Pumas. A ski resort is under construction on Volcán Osorno.

Beyond the hilly shores to the E are several graceful snow-capped mountains, with the mighty Tronador in the distance. To the N is the sharp point of Cerro Puntiagudo (2,278 metres), and at the north-eastern end Cerro Techado (1,720 metres) rises cliff-like out of the water.

***Puerto Montt***, capital of X Región (Los Lagos), 1,080 km. from Santiago, is the terminus of the railway. The first German colonists arrived in 1852; they have remained to this day a small but influential percentage of the 112,000 inhabitants. The houses are mostly faced with unpainted shingles; here and there stand structures in the Alpine manner, all high pitched roofs and quaint balconies. The little fishing port of Angelmó, 2 km. from the centre of town, is noted for its seafood restaurants and handicrafts. It has become a tourist centre and the market area there is being refurbished. Costanera bus along D. Portales costs US$0.25, but it's an easy stroll past the handicraft stalls which line the road between the ferry terminal and Angelmó (woollen items from Chiloé are cheaper in Ancud and Castro, but there's greater choice in Angelmó).

The port is much used by fishing boats and coasting vessels, and it is here that passengers embark for Puerto Chacabuco, Aisén, and for the long haul S to Punta Arenas. A paved road runs 55 km. SW to Pargua, where there is a ferry service to Chiloé.

**Hotels** Check Tourist Office. *Vicente Pérez Rosales*, Antonio Varas 447, T 252571, Telex 270056, A+, with bath and breakfast, some rooms noisy, excellent restaurant, seafood and tourist information, rec. *Rayson*, Benavente 480, A, new, helpful; *Le Mirage*, Rancagua 350, T 255125, B, quite good but cheaply built, T 255125; *Colina*, Tacna 81, T 253502, A with bath, expensive, clean, some rooms with sea view, breakfast extra, restaurant, bar, car hire; *Burg*, Pedro Montt y Portales, T 253813, modern, central heating, centrally located, good, A, interesting traditional food in restaurant; *Montt*, Av. Varas and Quillota, T 253651, C with bath, C without, clean, friendly, good value (good restaurant); *Hostal Panorama*, San Felipe 192, T 254094, C, steep climb up steps to get there, some rooms with bath, some with view, under new management in early 1991, good restaurant; *Millahue*, B, T 253829, Copiapó 64, good food; *Residencial Urmeneta*, Urmeneta 290, T 253262, D with bath, E without, clean, comfortable, good breakfast, rec.; *Residencial La Nave*, Ancud y Varas, D, clean, pleasant, good inexpensive restaurant; *Miramar*, Andrés Bello 972, T 254618, C, breakfast US$1, hot water, across Av. Diego Portales from museum and bus terminal; *Hospedaje Alemán*, Egaña y Copiapó, E with breakfast, good, clean, safe, German spoken; *Residencial Amy*, Illapel 149, E without bath, central, friendly; *Residencial Embassy*, Calle Valdivia 130, D, clean, breakfast US$1 extra, will store luggage, few bathrooms and some rooms lack windows, but otherwise good; *Residencial Talquino*, Pérez Rosales 114-116, T 253331, near bus terminal, D, hot water, clean; *Residencial Calipso*, Urmeneta 127, T 254554, E, shared bath, hot water, breakfast extra, clean (acts as youth hostel); *Residencial El Turista*, Varas esq. Ancud 91, D with and without bath, with breakfast, clean, comfortable, rec. *Residencial Sur*, San Felipe 183, D (poor breakfast extra), basic, clean; *Residencia Punta Arenas*, J. J. Mira 964, E with breakfast, hot water, basic but clean. Many private homes give you a bed for US$5 p.p. up, look for signs in windows, particularly rec. is *Casa Haraldo Steffen*, Serrano 286 (T 253823), E, with breakfast, excellent, homemade bread and jam; *Uncle Renato*, Guillermo Gallardo 621, US$2 with own sleeping bag, very basic, popular, packed in summer: *casa de familia*, G. Gallardo 552, T 253334, E with breakfast, D with bath, cooking facilities, clean, comfortable, pleasant. There are also several inexpensive

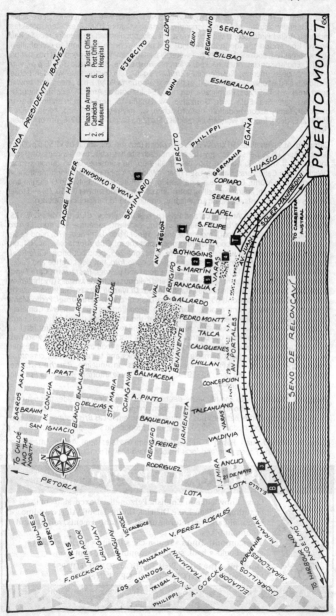

PUERTO MONTT

1. Plaza de Armas
2. Cathedral
3. Museum
4. Tourist Office
5. Post Office
6. Hospital

SERRANO
BUIN
REGIMIENTO
BILBAO
ESMERALDA

LOS LEONES

EJERCITO

BUIN

PHILIPPI

EJERCITO

GERMANIA
COPIAPO
SERENA
ILLAPEL
S.FELIPE
QUILLOTA
B.O'HIGGINS
S. MARTIN
RANCAGUA
G. GALLARDO
PEDRO MONTT
TALCA
CAUQUENES
CHILLAN
CONCEPCION

EGAÑA
HUASCO

AV. JUAN J. SOLER MANFREDINI

TO CARRETERA AUSTRAL

AVDA. PRESIDENTE IBAÑEZ
AVDA. B. O'HIGGINS
PADRE HARTER
SEMINARIO
AV. X REGION

VIAL
RENGIFO
LAMUNATEGUI
ALCADE
L.ROSS

A. VARAS
A. VARAS
AV. PORTALES

BENAVENTE
BALMACEDA
A. PINTO

A. PRAT
M. CONCHA
BLANCO ENCALADA
STA MARIA
OCHAGAVIA
DELICIAS

BARROS ARANA
BRAHM
SAN IGNACIO

N
PETORCA

TO CHILOÉ
AND THE
NORTH

BAQUEDANO
RENGIFO
FREIRE
URMENETA
RODRIGUEZ

VALDIVIA
ANCUD
J.J.MIRA
21 DE MAYO
LOTA
LOTA
ELILLO

TALCAHUANO

SEÑO DE RELONCAVI

BULNES
URRIOLA
IRIS
MIRADOR
URUGUAY
PARAGUAY
F.OELCKERS
VERGEL
CALBUCO

V. PEREZ ROSALES

MANZANAL
LOS GUINDOS
TRIGAL
PHILIPPI
A. GOECKE
E.VIVAR
TRAUMANN

PORVENIR
CHORILLOS
ECUADOR
ILLOS
MIRAFLORES
MIRAMAR

TO HARBOUR AND
ANGELMO

hostels in Calle Huasco, e.g. at No. 16, E, with breakfast (hot water), but much better is No. 126, E, friendly; also No. 143, G p.p., friendly, pleasant; J. J. Mira 1002, E, excellent, breakfast included; Aníbal Pinto 328, D with breakfast, friendly, popular, can do laundry, rec.; Sr. Raúl Arroyo, Concepción 136 (go to the "inland" end of Concepción, turn right to end of alley), D, with breakfast, cooking facilities, hot water, Navimag agency, meets people at bus station, helpful, English spoken, often packed, cramped; *Hospedaje*, Balmaceda 300, E p.p., with breakfast, clean, friendly; *Residencial Familiar*, Egaña 538, picturesque wooden house, friendly, breakfast only; Urmaneta 894, 2nd floor (*Peluquería Poly*), E p.p., clean, hot shower, good breakfast, T 257203; Balmaceda, esq. Vial 754, Ida Soto de Arcas, F, very friendly, good breakfast, safe; *Sra. Egla J. de González*, Av. España 15, next to train station, E with breakfast, family accommodation, use of kitchen, warmly rec.; Sra Kimico, Porvenir 52, T 252312, E, clean, friendly, wonderful breakfast; Sra Mina Barrio, Trigal 309, E, use of kitchen, clean.

**Camping** At Chinquihue, 10 km. W of Puerto Montt (bus service), about US$1.50 p.p. Open October-April US$8 per site, for any size of tent. Each site has table, two benches, barbecue and plenty of shade. Toilets and showers. Small shop, no kerosene. Good camping shop, "Winkler", on Calle Varas, will buy used gear. "Wild" camping possible along the front. 4 km. E of Puerto Montt, Copec have a network of 18 "Rutacentas" between Quillagua and Puerto Montt, which, apart from selling petrol and oil, have good shower (US$0.25) and toilet facilities and restaurants. Camping Los Alamos, on the road to Panitao and Calbuco.

**Restaurants** *Embassy*, Ancud 106 and Pelluco, seafood, pricey; *Club de Yates*, Av. J.S. Manfredini, on waterfront beyond railway station, excellent, expensive seafood; *Centro Español*, on Quillota (2nd floor), moderate prices; *Super Yoco*, Urmeneta 478, good value; *Kiel*, Capilla 298, excellent food and atmosphere, not cheap; *Club Alemán*, Varas 264, old fashioned, good food and wine; *La Petit Café*, Rancagua 245, good but pricey; *Café Real*, Rancagua 137, good for *empanadas, pichangas, congrio frito*, hot dogs, coffee and cakes; *Café Central*, Rancagua 117, good atmosphere, food and pastries. *Restaurant Café Dino*, Varas 550, excellent restaurant upstairs, snacks and delicious pastas downstairs (try the lemon juice). *La Llave*, by the sea, in railway station, good. *Di Napoli Pizzas*, Guillerno Gallardo 119; *Patts Pizza*, Pedro Montt 65, excellent, clean, good service; *Café Amsel*, Pedro Montt y Portales, good variety and quality; *Plato's*, Av. Diego Portales 1014, Galería Comercial España, cheap, good. Excellent and cheap food at the central bus depot (all credit cards accepted). Restaurants in market at Angelmó, and on the road there, highly rec. for fish (not so good for hygiene but food can be trusted, ask prices first as there is no menu). *Asturias*, between craft market and harbour, friendliest in town, same food as in market but cleaner. Try *picoroco al vapor*, a giant barnacle whose flesh looks and tastes like crab; *curanto*, a regional dish (seafood, chicken, sausages and potatoes). In Angelmó, *Rancho Patache*, Pasaje Martí, on corner, 2nd floor, T 252974, very good, simple, informal. Bakery: *La Estrella*, Gallardo 174, self-service, good.

**Shopping** Woollen goods and Mapuche-designed rugs. Cheaper at roadside stalls between port and Angelmó (see above) than at tourist shops in town (cheaper still on Chiloé, but less choice). New craft market between bus terminal and Empremar. *Las Brisas* supermarket opp. bus station, very good, open 0900-2200 daily; local produce on sale opp. bus terminal.

**Museum** Museo Juan Pablo II at Avenida Diego Portales opp. Ancud, interesting: memorabilia of the Pope's visit, and local history. Open Mon.-Fri. 1000-1300, 1500-1900;

Sat., Sun. 1100-1900.

**Car Hire** Hertz, Urmeneta 1036, T 55000/52122; **Automóvil Club de Chile**, Cauquenes 75, T 252968, and several at airport. Others are **Avis**, Benavente 878; **Budget**, San Martín 200; **Dollar** (Rosse Turismo), Varas 447; **Sport**, Benavente 531, 4th floor; **First**, Varas 437; **Famas**, best value and very reliable.

**Exchange** Impossible on Sun. You are advised to change money here if visiting Chiloé as reports indicate that is difficult outside Castro and that rates are poor. **Banco Chile** (cash only poor rates). Waiting time in banks can be 3 hours; commission charges vary widely. Good rates at **Galería Cristal**, A. Varas 595, **El Libertador**, Urmeneta 529-A, local 3, and **Turismo Latinoamericano**, Urmeneta 351. **Fincard** (Access and Visa), A. Varas 575, open Mon.-Fri. 0845-1400, 1530-1900, Sat. 0930-1300. *Hotel Pérez Rosales* will change money at parallel market rate. **La Moneda de Oro** at the bus terminal will exchange Latin American currencies (Mon.-Sat. 0930-1230, 1530-1900). Obtain australes for Argentina before leaving Chile.

**Consulates** Argentine, Cauquenes 94, 2nd floor, T 253996; **German**, Chorrillos 1582, Tues.-Thur. 0930-1230, T253001; **Spanish**, Rancagua 113, T252557; **Dutch**, Seminario 350, T 253428.

**Laundry** Opposite Banco O'Higgins on Pedro Montt; *Center* at Varas 700, one at San Martín 232, and *Unic* at Chillán 149. Laundry prices generally high (US$7 for 3 kg.).

**Post Office** Rancagua 120, open 0830-1900 (Mon.-Fri.), 0830-1200 (Sat.).

**Telephone Office** on Pedro Montt between Urmeneta and A. Varas, and at Chillán 98.

**Tourist Office** Sernatur, Quillota 120; often has leaflets on Chiloé—stock up as information difficult to obtain on the island. The headquarters of Sernatur is at Edificio Intendencia Regional, Av. Décima Región 480, (3rd floor), Casilla 297, T 256999, Telex 270008. Open 0830-1300, 1430-1730 Mon.-Fri. Also on Plaza de Armas a kiosk run by a schoolteacher with Sernatur assistance in high season, open till 1800 on Sat., good. Town maps available. Telefónica del Sur and Sernatur operate a phone information service (INTTUR), dial 142 (cost is the same as a local call). Dial 149 for chemist/pharmacy information, 148 for the weather, 143 for the news, etc. The service operates throughout the tenth region. Sernatur in Puerto Montt has a reciprocal arrangement on information with Bariloche, Argentina.

**Travel Agents** **Empresa Andina del Sud**, very close to central tourist kiosk, Varas 437 (Casilla 15-D, T 253253/254692/357797) sells a daily tour at 0830 (not Sun.) to Puerto Varas, Parque Nacional V.Pérez Rosales, Petrohué, Lago Todos los Santos, Peulla and back (without meals, US$13, with meals US$21, with overnight at *Hotel Peulla*, US$23), and to other local sights. **Varastur**, Varas 595, runs tours to Petrohué (US$1 with lunch), Puyehue, Frutillar, or Ancud (US$13.30). **Trauco Tours**, Egaña 82 (nr. railway station), T and Fax (65) 258555, open 0900-1800 every day, for all information, equipment hire and sale, book swap, specialist tours arranged, English-owned and run.

**Rail** Station at San Felipe 50, T 254908. Apart from Jan. and Feb. there at no passenger services to Puerto Montt, only bus connection with pullman to Temuco. 1991 summer service due to start on 15 Dec., once a day, 22 hrs., bench seats only. Ticket office opens 0830-1130, 1300-1700.

**Bus Service** Bus station on sea front, at Av. Diego Portales and Av. Lota, has telephones, restaurants, *casa de cambio* (left luggage, US$0.20 per item for 24 hrs.). To **Puerto Varas** (US$0.45), **Llanquihue** (US$0.65), **Frutillar** (US$1) and **Osorno** (US$2) every 30 min. between 0750-2050 (2120 Sun.), 1½ hrs. with Varmontt, either from main terminal or own terminal at Copiapó y Varas. To **Santiago**, express 15 hrs., average fare US$17, US$24 *cama* (most buses stop ½ hr. for dinner); Varmontt are the most expensive, double-decker bus (US$82 including bed, cocktails, cold dinner, breakfast). Bus service to **Punta Arenas**, Bus Norte, Turibus, Fernández Sur and Ghisoni, between once and three times a week, US$46-55 depending on company, departing either 0800 or 1100 (bus goes through Argentina, but you don't need australes because the bus company purchases meals, etc., and you pay the driver's assistant), 38 hrs. Many buses daily to **Temuco** US$4.65-7, to **Valdivia**, US$3-4; **Concepción**, US$7.50-9. For services to **Chiloé, see page 616.**

**To Argentina** Via Lago Todos Los Santos: this route to Bariloche, involving ferries across Lake Todos Las Santos and Laguna Verde is very beatiful, though the mountains are often obscured by rain and heavy cloud. Bus/ferry service by Andino del Sud from Puerto Montt daily (also from Puerto Varas), US$87; fare does not include lunch in Peulla (*Hotel Peulla* is expensive—for alternatives **see page 609**). Other services to Bariloche: Bus Norte via Puyehue (daily 0900, or night bus, change in Osorno); Tas-Choapa, three times a week direct 0930, three times via Lago Todos los Santos 0900; Lanín, via Osorno, 2 times weekly 0800, no toilets, plenty of stops; Cruz Sur, Sun. 1030; Río de la Plata, 3 times a week, 0800, average fare US$15 (see also routes to Argentina given below). Lanín also goes to Neuquén, as does Igi Llaima (also to Zapala).

Hitch-hiking is difficult and may take as long as four days between Puerto Montt and Bariloche. When driving north out of Puerto Montt (or out of Puerto Varas, Frutillar, etc.), look for signs to "Ruta 5".

**Air Service**    Ladeco run 5 flights a week to Coyhaique or Balmaceda; LanChile 6, fare 1991 US$64; at least 3 daily flights to Santiago first normally at 1100, last 1845, US$121. LanChile flies daily to Punta Arenas, Ladeco 5 times a week, US$141. In January, February and March you may well be told that the plane to Punta Arenas is booked up; however, cancellations may be available from the airport. Aerosur, Serena 149, T 252513, run twice daily service to Chaitén, Mon.-Sat., 1115, 1415, and to Palena and Futaleufú Tues. and Fri., US$46 (return US$91). Flights to Argentina, TAN to Bariloche, Tues., Wed., Thur., Fri., 1/2 hr, US$40; El Tepual airport is 16 km. from town, bus to bus terminal, ETC, US$0.85, 20 mins. LanChile bus to centre of town, US$0.70 (check with LanChile for schedule; check with other airlines for buses for their flights). LanChile, San Martín 200, T253141 and Ladeco offices at Benevente 350, T 253002. Don Carlos, Quillota 139, T 253219, flies to Chaitén, 1115 and 1515 Mon.-Fri., Sat. 1115 (fares under Chaitén), and runs regular charters for 5 passengers to Bariloche, US$515, Chaitén, US$364 and Coyhaique, US$955.

**Shipping Offices in Puerto Montt:**    Navimag (Naviera Magallanes S.A.), Terminal Transbordadores Angelmó, T 253318/253754, Telex 370055 NAMAG CK. Empremar, Av. Diego Portales 1450, Tel. 252548, Telex 370001 EMAR CK. Constantino Kochifas C., Angelmó 1660 y Miraflores (Castilla 588), T 252952, Telex 370161 NATUK CL. Transmarchilay Ltda., A. Varas 215, T 254654, telex 370043 Marchi CK.

**Stop Press**    June 1991: It is reported that Empremar Sur has been declared bankrupt and that all its services out of, and south of, Puerto Montt have ceased; if this is so, all ferry services south of Puerto Montt will be affected and travellers should check arrangements in advance.

**Shipping Service**    Taxi from centre to ferry terminal, US$1.35. The service of the roll-on/roll-off vehicle ferry m/n *Tierra del Fuego* of Navimag to Puerto Natales was withdrawn in May 1991. At the time of going to press it was not known if another vessel would operate on this route. We retain a description in case one does: The dramatic 1,460 km. journey first goes through Seno Reloncaví and Canal Moraleda. From Bahía Anna Pink along the coast and then across the Golfo de Peñas to Bahía Tarn it is a 12-17 hrs. sea crossing, usually rough. The journey continues through Canal Messier, Angostura Inglesa, Paso del Indio and Canal Kirke (one of the narrowest routes for large shipping). The only regular stop is made off Puerto Edén (1 hr. south of the Angostura Inglesa), where the local Alacalufe Indians come out to sell their shellfish. In Puerto Edén there are 3 shops, all stocking pasta and lemon mayonnaise, not much else; there is one off-licence, one café, but no hotel or camping facility, nor running water. It is, though, the drop-off point for exploring Isla Wellington, which is largely untouched, with stunning mountains. Take all food; maps (not very accurate) are available in Santiago.

The roll on/roll off vehicle ferry m/n *Evangelistas* of Navimag, runs twice weekly to Puerto Chacabuco (80 km. to the west of Coyhaique), Wed. and Sat., returning from Puerto Chacabuco on the following day. From end-December to mid, or end-March the schedule changes to include a Sunday-Tuesday trip from Puerto Chacabuco to Laguna San Rafael, so Pto. Montt to Pto. Chacabuco is Wed. and Sat., but return to Pto. Montt is Tues. and Thurs. The cruise to Puerto Chacabuco lasts about 24 hrs. First class accommodation include 2 cabins with bath (US$80-210 depending on which cabin and number of occupants); tourist class, 14 bunks (about US$56, food extra); and third class, 400 reclining seats (US$30, type "B", US$33, type "A"). Fare to Laguna San Rafael US$106, reclining seat, or US$167 in tourist bunk, US$170-450 in cabin. First class reservations must be made in advance at the Santiago offices(**see page 562**). There are canteens and bars on board.

The m/n *Calbuco* of Empremar (Empresa Marítima del Estado) leaves Puerto Montt every Tuesday for Puerto Chacabuco. Arrives on Fridays at 0800, and returns to Puerto Montt on Sundays at 0900. From late December through early March she sails from Puerto Chacabuco on Thursdays at 2000, stays Saturdays 0900 to 1900 at Laguna San Rafael, calls again at Puerto Chacabuco on Sundays at 0800 and returns to Puerto Montt on Tuesdays at 0800. She is a simple ship with only 4 berths in 2 cabins plus 36 seats in tourist class and 53 seats in 3rd class. The fare from Puerto Montt to Puerto Chacabuco is US$30 first class, US$19 tourist class; to Laguna San Rafael US$105 first class, US$65 tourist class (food on board poor, advisable to supplement with own provisions). Sailing dates are published in *El Mercurio* newspaper.

Between August and May, the m/n *Quellón* of Empremar leaves Puerto Montt on Saturdays at 1130, calling at Melinka, Puerto Aguirre, Pto. Chacabuco (with a shore excursion to Coyhaique), Laguna San Rafael, returning to Puerto Montt via Río Cisnes, Puyuguapi, Castro, arriving back on Fridays at 0800. This journey is sold on a round-trip basis only by Empremar's agent in Santiago (address under **Shipping Offices**) and Puerto Montt. There are three classes of cabin and three pricing seasons; fares range from US$540-771 (April-May) to US$617-881 (Dec., Jan. Feb.). It has been reported that the ship has tiny cabins, many without washbasin, insufficient toilet and shower facilities, small public room and bar, but we must add that we have received a number of satisfactory comments.

Empremar also run a service on the *Río Cisnes* from Puerto Montt to Laguna San Rafael every Friday at 1600 between September and April. Primarily for motorists, the route is: Pto. Montt-Chaitén by boat; Chaitén-Río Cisnes overland; Río Cisnes-Laguna San Rafael-Pto. Chacabuco by sea; Chacabuco-Coyhaique-Río Cisnes overland; Río Cisnes-Quellón (Chiloe) by sea, then overland (plus ferry) to Puerto Montt. The ship has one vehicle taking 8 passengers. Fares include transport of your vehicle, bar and lodging in Puyuguapi: low season US$357-554 (Sept.-Nov., March-April), US$408-633 (Dec.-Feb.). The boat claims to lower lifeboats at the glacier but does not appear to.

The m/n *Skorpios 1* and *2* of Constantino Kochifas C. leave Pto. Montt on Saturdays at 1100 for a luxury cruise with stops at Puerto Aguirre, Melinka, Laguna San Rafael, Quitralco, Castro (each ship has a slightly different itinerary) and returns to Puerto Montt on Fridays at 0800. The fare varies according to season, type of cabin and number of occupants: a double ranges from US$420 (low) to US$600 (high) on *Skorpios 1* and from US$700 (low) to US$1,000 (high) on *Skorpios 2*, which is the more comfortable of the two. It has been reported that there is little room to sit indoors if it is raining on *Skorpios 1*, but generally service is excellent, the food superb and at the glacier, you chip your ice off the face for your whisky.

Transmarchilay Ltda. runs a ferry service from Chonchi to Chaitén in summer (2 Jan.-15 March, see under Chonchi); the rest of the year it runs Pargua-Chaitén and back, Thur. p.m. and Mon. a.m. returning Mon. and Fri. both p.m., 9 hrs., US$4.65 p.p. Its vessel *El Colono* sails Chonchi-Puerto Chacabuco in summer (see under Chonchi) and the rest of the year from Pargua Tues. and Fri., 27 hrs., fares under Puerto Chacabuco. For sailing dates, their timetable should be consulted. Ticket availability better at the ports than at head office.

See also under Chaitén for passenger services on Terminales Marítimos Chilenos.

**Excursions** The wooded island of Tenglo, close to Puerto Montt and reached by launch, is a favourite place for picnics. Magnificent view from the summit. The island is famous for its *curantos*, a local dish. Chinquihue, W of Angelmó, has many seafood restaurants, with oysters as a speciality. East of Puerto Montt, Chamiza, up the River Coihuin, has fine fishing. There is a bathing beach (polluted) at Pelluco, 4 km from Puerto Montt (several good restaurants). Isla Guar may be visited by boat from Angelmó harbour (1600, 2 hrs.); boat returns from other end of island at 0730. The north shore is rocky. Accommodation, if lucky, at the church; best to camp.

The (cargo) launch trip from Angelmó jetty up the Reloncaví estuary (8 hrs.) is very beautiful, fjords, sealions, dolphins, local colour, and rec. The estuary is the northernmost of Chile's glacial inlets. At **Cochamó**, towards the northern end of the estuary, there is the *Hotel Cochamó*, basic but clean, E, friendly, good meals, rec., and a large number of *pensiones* (just ask), e.g. *Mercado Particular Sabin*, E p.p., Calle Catedral 20 (Sra. Suni, next to *Hotel*), Sra. Flora Barrientos offers floorspace in her bar/restaurant/drugstore, same street No. 16, E; also *Restaurant Copihue* and *Residencial Gato Blanco*, both E; cheapest accommodation in same street, No. 2, by the pier (floor space only). Cochamó itself is pretty but limited; a side trip is to the Termas de Sotomó, but this requires an affinity for mud. Cochamó can be reached from Puerto Montt by road via Ralún (**see page 609**) (Buses Bohle's 1300 and 1700 services from Puerto Montt to Ralún continue to Cochamó Mon.-Fri.; also Buses Río Frío.) or by boat to Río Puelo (a small settlement 3 km. from Puelo) and then by bus at 0700 daily. At Río Puelo rowing boats and a barge for cars cross the river; on the other bank buses go to Puerto Montt at

0700 and 1700. At Puelo, lodging is available with families—try Roberto and Olivia Telles, simple, clean, no bath/shower, meals on request, beverages inc. beer and wine can be bought a few houses away. This is a most peaceful place. It is 5-6 hours from Angelmó to Río Puelo (advisable to take warm clothes, food and seasickness pills if windy). Among the boats that go is *Rosita Carmen*, Captain Juan Carlos; book a seat and ascertain departure time 2-3 days in advance. Information is available from a booth in the harbour at Angelmó.

There is a beautiful 2-day hike from Cochamó through forests to Cayutúe, a quiet, peaceful village (see the Bradts' book, *Backpacking in Chile and Argentina*, for route); the settlement is on Lake Todos los Santos and occasional boats go to Petrohué—US$30 to hire one (**see page 608**); you can camp by the lake.

The Río Maullin, which rises in Lago Llanquihue, has some interesting waterfalls and good fishing (salmon). The little fishing village of **Maullin**, founded in 1602 (*Motel El Pangal*, 5 km. away, T 244, B), at the mouth of the Río Maullin, is worth a visit. **Calbuco**, centre of the fishing industry, with good scenery is on an island linked to the mainland by a causeway. It can be visited direct by boat or by road. Puerto Montt is a good centre for excursions to the lakes via Puerto Varas. From Puerto Montt to Puerto Varas by the old (dirt) road is a short but beautiful journey.

## Chiloé

The Isla de **Chiloé** is 250 km. long, 50 km. wide, 9,613 sq. km., and has a population of 116,000. There are two main towns, Ancud and Castro (airport), and many fishing villages. Seaweed is harvested for export to Japan. Typical of the island are substantial wooden houses (*palafitos*) built on stilts over the water. The hillsides in summer are a patchwork quilt of wheat fields and dark green plots of potatoes. Inland are impenetrable forests. There has recently been appreciable development, and power and water shortages and poor sanitation are now things of the past. Though the weather is often cold and foggy, the island is extremely beautiful when the sun is out. Sweaters and woollen caps are good purchases. Music is popular, with many players in the waterfront cafés in Castro. The local sailing sloops, *lanchas*, are fast being replaced by diesels, very few can be seen now. Chiloé was settled by the Spanish in the sixteenth century and became a centre for missionary activity: the island is dotted with seventeenth and eighteenth century Jesuit churches. The islanders of Chiloé were the last supporters of the Spanish Crown. When Chile rebelled the last of the Spanish Governors fled to the island and, in despair, offered it to Britain. Canning, the British Foreign Secretary, turned the offer down. The island finally surrendered to the patriots in 1826, the last remaining Spanish possession in South America.

**Transport to Chiloé** From Puerto Montt buses run 15 times a day (US$1.50) to **Pargua** (55 km., 1 hr.) on the Straits of Chacao. (At Pargua, *Hotel La Ruta*, on A. Prat. At **Chacao**, *Pensión Chiloé*, E; *Hospedaje Angelino*, E.) There are two ferry terminals in Pargua, one in town, one down a dusty road from town; check which when you get there. Most buses go right through to Ancud and Castro (e.g. Trans Chiloé at 0810, 1220 and 1820, Varmontt at 0800, 1230 and 1830, Bus Norte at 1115, but the company with most services is Cruz del Sur, 10 a day to Ancud and Castro, 5 to Chonchi and Quellón. Fares from Puerto Montt: Ancud, US$2 (Trans Chiloé US$1.65), Castro US$4.15 (Trans Chiloé US$4), Chonchi, US$4, Quellón, US$5.15. Note that there are direct bus services from Osorno, Valdivia, Temuco and Los Angeles to Chiloé. Buses drive on to ferry across the Chacao Strait to Chiloé (passengers can get on or out of the bus). Transmarchilay run frequent ferries (two vessels in summer) and Cruz del Sur runs ferries for its buses; the buses have priority, but cars are also taken. There are 24 trips a day to Chiloé by the ferry (US$0.50); cars US$4 one way (20 mins. crossing). The Tourist Office in Ancud have a number of brochures of different circuits on Chiloé which are very useful (e.g. Circuito Histórico Cultural, Circuito Mitológico, Excursión al Sur de Chiloé), all are free.

***Ancud*** is 27 km. from the Straits of Chacao. The port is dominated by the Fuerte San Antonio, built by the Spanish in 1770. Near the Plaza de Armas is the Museo

Regional, with an interesting collection on the early history of Chiloé as well as the small sailing ship *Ancud* which, in 1843, sailed to the Straits of Magellan to claim the Peninsula for Chile. The tourist office is on the Plaza de Armas at Libertad 665.

**Hotels** *Quintanilla*, Libertad 751, rec., A, with bathroom and breakfast, open in summer only; *Hostería Ancud*, San Antonio 30, T 2340/2350, Telex 275002, A+ with bath and hot water, very comfortable, friendly and helpful, but meals overpriced; *Polo Sur*, Av. Costanera 630, T 2200, B with bath, hot water, good seafood restaurant, not cheap; *Hostería Ahui*, Av. Costanera 906, B with bath and breakfast, modern, clean, good views, T 2415; *Lydia*, Chacabuco 630, T 2990, C with bath and restaurant, overpriced; *Montserrat*, Baquedano 417, T 2957, B with bath, hot water, breakfast; *Cabañas Las Golondrinas*, end of Baquedano, T 2453, B with bath, hot water and kitchenette; *Moteles Huaihuén*, A. Pinto 1070, T 2554, B; *Hospedaje Santander*, Sargento Aldea 69, F, clean, rec.; *Residencial Montenegro*, Blanco Encalada 531, T 2239, F p.p., fair, no hot water; *Residencial* on Aníbal Pinto 515, good, F p.p. *Hospedaje Miranda*, Anibal Pinto 505, cheap, friendly, hot water; *Residencial Weschler*, Cochrane 480, T 2318, D, clean, friendly, comfortable, view of bay; *Hospedaje Bellavista*, Bellavista 449, E, with sleeping bag on floor much cheaper, no hot water; Edmundo Haase Pérez, Ramírez 299, F p.p. with breakfast, clean, basic, good value; also Ramírez 396, T 489, Sra. Edith Hualibota, F p.p., nice; Elverrez 442, F p.p. with breakfast, cold water; Pudeto 357, E, fair, next to watch shop; Elena Bergmann at Aníbal Pinto 382 (5 rooms in private house), clean, friendly, F p.p.; Irma Miguel, Pudeto 331, F p.p., clean, homely; Sra. Lucía, San Martín 705, F; Familia Reuter-Miranda, Errázuriz 350, T 2261, F p.p. with breakfast, clean, spacious, hot showers, rec. In summer, the school on Calle Chacabuco is open for lodging, US$1.30 p.p.

**Camping** Camping Playa Larga Huicha, 9 km. N of Ancud, E per site, bath, hot water, electricity.

**Restaurants** Seafoods, especially king crabs (very cheap), almejos and cheese in market area. *Balai*, Pudeto 119, seafood, meat, sandwiches; *Carmen*, Pudeto 145, Chilean cooking, pasteles; *Coral*, Pudeto 346, good, not cheap; *Jardín*, same street No.263, good local food, not cheap; *Macaval*, Chacabuco 691; *El Trauco*, Blanco y Prat, seafood; *Lydia*, café-restaurant, Pudeto 254, Chilean and international; *El Cangrejo*, Dieciocho 155, seafood highly rec.

**Travel Agent** *Turismo Ancud*, Pudeto 219, Galería Yurie, T 2235, Telex 297700 ANCD CL.

**Bus** Ancud-Castro, US$1.50; frequent buses daily on both routes, 1½ hrs. No direct Sunday bus from Ancud to Dalcahue, need to stay in Castro. To **Puerto Montt**, Cruz del Sur 11 times between 0710 and 2000, office on Chacabuco nr. Pudeto, Varmontt 3 a day from *Hotel Polo Sur*, Trans Chiloé also 3. Local buses leave from terminal at Pto. Montt 538.

**Shipping** Transmarchilay has offices in Ancud, Libertad 669 (T 2317/2279, Telex 375007 MARCHI CK.).

Walk from Ancud along the beach towards Faro Corona (34 km. to Punta Corona), good views, interesting birdlife, dolphins can be seen, but the beach is not suitable for swimming. A side road from the Ancud-Castro highway leads to Chepu on the west coast, famed for its river and sea fishing.

***Castro*** Capital of the Province and a very friendly town, 88 km. from Ancud (NB if driving between the two, watch out for humps and hollows in the road). There is a tremendous variety of styles in housing, including houses on stilts (*palafitos*) above the water, on the northern side of town and by the bridge over the Río Gamboa. Cheap woollen articles (hats, sweaters, gloves) can be found at Feria, or Mercado Municipal de Artesanía on the waterfront; they are the best value in X Región, especially if you bargain. *Palafito* restaurants have been put up behind the market. The large cathedral (1906), strikingly decorated in lilac and orange, with excellent wooden interior on the Plaza de Armas, was built by Italian architect, Eduardo Provosoli. The Museo Municipal on the second floor of the Cultural Centre, Serrano 320, contains history, folklore, handicrafts and mythology of Chiloé. The Museo de Arte Moderno is near the Río Gamboa (open 1000-2000). Very good views of the city from Mirador La Virgen on Millantuy hill above the cemetery. Tourist kiosk in main square only open in summer. Conaf at

Gobernación, 3rd floor, Plaza de Armas. S of Castro at Quilquico there is a wooden church dating from 1767.

**Hotels** *Hostería Castro*, Chacabuco 202, T 2301, B with bath and breakfast, hot water, good restaurant, interesting building (in summer coach and boat trips are organized to other places on the island); *Unicornio Azul*, Pedro Montt 228, T 2359, A+ in summer, good but expensive for what is offered; *Cabañas Centro Turístico Nercón*, 5 km. S, rooms with bath, hot water, heating, restaurant, tennis court; *Gran Alerce*, O'Higgins nr. Mistral, B with bath and TV, excellent rooms and breakfast; *Hilton*, Ramírez 385, D, good value, friendly, restaurant; *Residencial Mirasol*, San Martín 815, good, E, next to bus station, noisy; *Hospedaje Guillermo*, San Martín 700, F p.p. clean, cheap; *Hospedaje Angie*, San Martín 747, F p.p., small rooms, cooking facilities, clean, pretty; also near bus terminal, *Hospedaje Chiloé*, San Martín, 800 block, E, breakfast, clean, rec. *La Bomba*, Esmeralda 270, T 2300, E, without bath, cheaper on 3rd floor, clean, good value, hot water, 3 course menu (US$4). *Quinta Niklitschek*, Panamericana Norte 331 (3 km. north), better inside than out, C; *Residencial Lidia*, Blanco Encalada 276, T 2331, F p.p., clean, cold shower, good; *Res. Inés de Banen*, Blanco Encalada 266, F p.p., OK, breakfast US$1; *Costa Azul*, F p.p., Lillo 67, T 2440, friendly, hot water, bed bugs, but restaurant poor value; *Res. El Gringo*, Av. Lillo 51, F p.p., O.K.; *Plaza*, Blanco Encalada 38, T 5109, C with bath, D without, rec. on 3rd floor, breakfast included, 2 fair *comedores*, good seafood, not cheap; *Moteles Auquilda*, Km. 2, Panamericana Norte, T 2458, C. *Residencial Estrella*, O'Higgins 657, F p.p., with breakfast; *Hospedaje Turístico*, O'Higgins 831, E, good breakfast, pleasant; *Hospedaje* at Las Delicias 287, E, hot shower, nice family and place; Serrano 488, above TV shop, E with breakfast,rec.; Esmeralda 233, with bath; Adriana Gutiérrez, Freire 758-9, E, breakfast, clean, good value; also good, Freire 497; Maruja Vera, O'Higgins 841; Chacabuco 449 (no hot water); La Torre 212, F p.p., friendly, clean, good breakfast with homemade bread. Esmeralda 153, F with breakfast; Sotomayor, 442, F, rec.; Gamboa 588, F, cooking facilities; San Martín 879 (Sra. Judith Mancia), F. Basic accommodation in Jan. and Feb. in the Gimnasio Fisical, Calle Ramírez, G with breakfast, clean.

**Camping** Camping Pudú, Ruta 5, 10 km. N of Castro, cabins, showers with hot water, sites with light, water, children's games.

**Restaurants** *Palafito* restaurants near the Feria Campesina offer good food and good value. *Lidia*, Blanco Encalada 276, good, friendly (café, *pastelería*, restaurant and *residencial*—see above); *Gipsy*, O'Higgins 548, very good; *Sacho*, Thompson 213, good food, not too dear, clean; *Miga's*, Blanco Encalada 74, for *empanadas*; *Stop Inn Café*, Banco del Estado building, 2nd floor, Plaza de Armas, good coffee; *Chilo's*, San Martín 444, rec., good lunches. *Octavio*, Lillo 67, T 2440, seafood incl. *curantos*. *Maucari*, Lillo 93, good seafood, not expensive. In the market, try *milcaos*, fried potato cakes with meat stuffing; also *licor de oro*, like Galliano.

**Shopping** See above for market. Cema-Chile outlet on Esmeralda, opp. *Hotel La Bomba*. *Libros Chiloé*, Serrano y Blanco, books in Spanish on Chiloé.

**Exchange** Banco del Estado de Chile on main square accepts travellers' cheques (at a poor rate). Better rates at Chacabuco 286.

**Post Office** On O'Higgins, W side of square; **phone office** O'Higgins y Ramírez, 3 blocks N of square.

**Doctor** Muñoz de Las Carreras, near police station, surgery 1700-2000 on weekdays, rec.

**Tours** Varmontt, Plaza de Armas, day trips around the island, Jan. and Feb. only. **Ladeco** agency on Serrano, opp. *Hostería Castro*. LanChile agency, Thompson 245.

**Buses** The Municipal Terminal is on San Martín, 600 block, before Sgto. Aldea. From here, Trans Chiloé to Ancud and Puerto Montt 3 a day, 3½ hrs, US$4; Bus Norte to Ancud, Puerto Montt, Osorno and Santiago (1815), Wed. to Puerto Montt and Punta Arenas, and daily to Puerto Montt at 0830 with connection to Bariloche; Bus Sur, Mon., Sat. 0630 to Punta Arenas; also Ghisoni and Varmontt. Local buses: Arroyo to Cucao Tues., Thur. 1130, Sun. 0900, return 1400, Sat. 1500, US$2, no advance sales, fight for a seat; to Chonchi and Huillinco, Mon., Wed., Fri. 1130, 1630; Cárdenas to Dalcahue; buses to Puqueldón and Queilén.

Cruz del Sur buses (T2389) and buses for Achao leave from the terminal behind San Francisco cathedral: Cruz del Sur to Ancud and Puerto Montt 11 a day (0700-1930—last bus to ferry at 1830), also to Osorno, Valdivia, Temuco, Concepción, Santiago (1545 Pullman, 1600 *cana*); 5 a day to Chonchi and Quellón (0700-1845). At least 4 buses daily to Achao (0700-1700) via Dalcahue and Curaco de Vélez. Turibus for Concepción and Santiago next to *La Bomba*; Trans Chiloé on square; Varmontt, Balmaceda 289, T 2776, next to *Hotel Plaza*.

**Dalcahue** 21 km. N of Castro, the wooden church dates from 1858, on older foundations. Market on Sundays, from 0700 to 1300 at this picturesque village (better value in Castro or Puerto Montt). Good choice early on, but better bargains in late morning. Tourist kiosk in season. Bus from Castro, 40 mins., US$0.75. Colectivos also available. (*Pensión Montaña*, M. Rodríguez 9, E, basic; *Pensión San Martín*, San Martín 1, T 2207, E, better; *Pensión Niemun*, Freire, F, clean, pleasant, restaurant; many private houses offer accommodation. *Restaurant La Dalca*, Freire 502, good food and service, rec.). Further N still, on the east coast is Quemchi, with *Gran Hotel Alerce*, O'Higgins y Gabriela Mistral, A with bath, heating, sauna and restaurant. Tenaún, 40 km. E of Dalcahue, is an interesting fishing village with a good 18th-century church.

**Achao**, on the Island of Quinchao, (ferry from Dalcahue, every hour, US$3 return); is a quiet, pretty fishing village with a wooden church, built in 1730, which inspires most of the other churches in the area.

**Services** *Hospedaje Sao Paulo*, Serrano 52, E, reasonable, hot water; *Hotel Delicia*, Serrano y Delicias, E, clean, friendly, small restaurant; good *pensión* at Riquilme 5, F; *Casa de Familia*, Zañarte 19; *Restaurant Central*, Delicias, simple, cheap, good; *Restaurant La Nave*, on waterfront, delicious salmon, rec.; *Cocinería Insular*, E, friendly, rec. excellent breakfast; *Restaurant Mar y Velas*, on waterfront, rec. **Tourist Office**, Serrano y Progreso (Dec.-March only).

**Chonchi**, 25 km. S of Castro (bus US$0.75, paved road), is a picturesque fishing village with rambling shingled houses painted in many colours and a lively wharf for fishing (wooden church built 1754, remodelled in neo-classical style 1859). There is another eighteenth-century church at Villipulli, 3 km. north. Visit Opdech (Oficina Promotora del Desarrollo Chilote), on waterfront, which has a weaving cooperative. *Posada Antiguo Chalet*, Irarrazával, T 221, winter B, summer A, charming, beautiful location, very good; *Hospedaje Chonchi*, O'Higgins 379, T 288, D, full board available, very nice; *Pensión Turismo*, Andrade y Alvarez, E with breakfast. Rooms available in *Hostería* next to *Provisiones Magallanes*, F p.p. in shared room, or floor space, use of kitchen; at *Almacén la Patagonia* at Cerda, 178, E, use of kitchen; and Cerda 160. *Restaurant La Parada*, on left half way down hill from centre to quay, very good value. *Remi*, on waterfront, good food, cheap *almuerzo*, rec. **Exchange**, Nicolás Alvarez, Centenario 429, cash only.

A visit to the island of **Lemuy** is rec.; 90 sq. km., quiet, with good walking through undulating pastures and woodland. Daily ferry service from Chonchi; terminal 4 km. from Chonchi, then, once across, 8 km. (no bus) to the main town, Puqueldón which offers basic accommodation, clean, E, good food, in Calle J. M. Carrera. *Restaurant Lemuy* (G p.p., basic, clean, good food) is next to the municipal offices and *Café Amancay* opposite (bus from Castro). Good walks to Lincay, 5 kms., or Lincura, one-day expedition.

**Queilén**, 46 km. SE of Chonchi, is a pretty fishing village with a long beach and wooden pier. Buses from Castro, 1¾ hrs, US$1.50. (*Residencial Segovia*; *Pensión Chiloé*; *Restaurant Melinka*, good.)

In summer only (2 Jan.-15 March), the Transmarchilay ferry *Pincoya* sails from Chonchi to Chaitén on the mainland, Tues., Wed., Thurs. at 0800, 6 hrs. crossing, US$26.50 per car, US$4 p.p. Transmarchilay's *El Colono* sails Chonchi-Puerto Chacabuco Wed. and Fri., 1400, again in summer only, 22 hrs., US$52.50 per car, reclining seats US$22. From 15 March to 29 Dec. ferries go only from Pargua to Chaitén and Puerto Chacabuco. Transmarchilay office, Av. Costanera s/n, T 319. Enquire first, either in Santiago, Puerto Montt or Chonchi.

**Cucao**, a village 40 km. west of Chonchi and one of two settlements on the West coast of Chiloé, can be reached by road. There is an immense 15 km. beach with thundering Pacific surf and dangerous undercurrents. Nearby is the **Chiloé National Park** (opened in 1984), with reception centre, small museum, helpful staff, guest bungalow available for visiting scientists (apply to Conaf, through your Embassy, stating environmental interests). The forests in the park are vast, but there is a series of signposted walks. There is a 15 km. walk from Cucao to Cole Cole (*refugio*) in the national park, a good hike with great views. The next *refugio* is at Anay, 9 km. further along the coast and there are 2 others (access difficult). Many houses rent horses for US$1/hour, US$5/day. Camping, US$2.50 at entrance, free firewood, no car access, 15 min. walk from bridge in village (wild camp here in camper van). Accommodation in Cucao, E, with full board or *demi-pension* at *Provisiones Pacífico* (friendly), Sra. Boreuel or with Sra Luz Vera, next to school (rec.); one shop. For buses from Castro see above; hitching is very difficult. Taxis can be rented for about US$20; for a bit more Alfredo Alvarez will drive out from Castro, wait for several hours and take you back. Half way between Castro and Cucao is Huillinco, a little town on a large lake, a charming place to stop on the way to the ocean (one *hostal*, F p.p. with good food, or stay at the Post Office).

*Quellón* Southernmost port on Chiloé; 92 km. from Castro, fishing boats built at wharf, pleasant beaches (*Hotel Playa*, P. Montt 245, T 278, D, good, clean, hot water, restaurant; same street, No. 217, *Hostería Quellón*, T 250, D, basic; *Residencial Estrella del Mar*, A Gómez García 18, G p.p., very basic; *Pensión Vera*, A. Gómez García, casi P.Montt, E, good, clean; *Residencial El Tráfico*, on waterfront, F p.p., restaurant. *La Pincoya*, La Paz 64, T 285, E; *Restaurant Las Brisas*, Miramar 25, cheap, accommodation F p.p. *Restaurant Rucantú* on waterfront, good food, good value.) Daily service from Castro to Quellón, US$2, 2 hrs.

## ARCHIPELAGIC CHILE  From Puerto Montt to Cape Horn (7)

A wet and windy region of mountains, channels and islands: to get an idea of the magnificent sea-scapes, take a boat to the glacier at Laguna San Rafael; or of the equally impressive landscape, take the Carretera Austral either north or south from Coyhaique, the main town.

South of Puerto Montt lies a third of Chile, but its land and its climate are such that it has been put to little human use: less than 3% of the country's population lives here. There is no real dry season. On the offshore islands and the western side of the Andes it is frequently wet and windy, particularly south of the Río Baker. North of that river, the summers are drier than the winters, but to the south, summers are windier and marginally wetter. Impenetrable forest covers much of the land, although in many parts there is stark evidence of the felling of trees which began in the nineteenth century. Wood is used for construction, fencing and fuel; in this last respect it is in such demand in population centres like Coyhaique that it costs as much as petrol in winter.

It is only the northern part, as far south as Coyhaique, and the far S that are inhabited. S of Chiloé, for 1,100 km., there is a maze of islands—the tops of submerged mountains—separated by tortuous fjord-like channels, a veritable topographical hysteria. It is fortunate for shipping that this maze has a more or less connected route through it: down the channel between Chiloé and the mainland, about 290 km. of open sea beyond the southern tip of Chiloé and then down the Moraleda, Mesier, Inocentes and Smyth channels into the Straits of Magellan. In some places along this route the tide levels change by 12 metres. In one particular place two sharp-cut walls, 900 metres high, enclose the constricted channel which leads to Puerto Natales; here the waters are deeper than the cliffs are high and slack water lasts for 30 mins. only. The Smyth Channel enters the Straits of Magellan at Cape Thamar. January and February are probably the best months for a trip to this region.

With the opening of the **Carretera Austral Presidente Pinochet** (Southern Highway) in 1988, the Pan-American Highway has been extended a further 1,013 km. through southern Chile to Cochrane. The highway is divided into three major sections: Puerto Montt-Chaitén (242 km.) with three ferry crossings; Chaitén-Coyhaique (435 km.), and Coyhaique-Cochrane (336 km.). By early 1990, the road had been extended some 40 km. beyond Cochrane; the eventual goal is Puerto Yungay, a further 85-km. to the south west.

Although the section from Puerto Montt to the border between Los Lagos, X Región, and XI Región Aisén del General Carlos Ibáñez del Campo, does not strictly belong to Archipelagic Chile, we deal with the Carretera Austral as a single entity.

**Puerto Montt to Chaitén** Before setting out on this section, it is imperative to check when the three ferries are running, normally only from December to March, and to make a reservation for each if travelling by car. Book passage in Puerto Montt, rather than Santiago, at the Transmarchilay office, Antonio Varas 215, T 254654.

The road (Ruta 7) heads east out of Puerto Montt, through Pelluco, the city's black sand beach, and after an initial rough stretch follows the shore of the Seno Reloncaví to the first ferry across the Reloncaví estuary at Las Arenas. Allow 1 ½ hours to get there. The last part of this section passes the southern end of the **Parque Nacional Alerce Andino** which contains tall trees (alerces), some over a thousand years old (the oldest is estimated at 4,200 years old), and waterfalls. Park wardens are at the northern end of the park, at Correntoso (35 km. east of Puerto Montt) and Lago Chapo (46 km.); there are buses from Puerto Montt; also campsites.

**Ferry** Las Arenas-Puelche: ½-hr. crossing, US$4.65 for a car, at 0745, 0945, 1445, 1845 and 2045. Roll-on roll-off type.

61 km. from Puelche is *Río Negro*, also called Hornopiren after the volcano above it. Electricity 1900-0100. Buses Fierro run daily from Puerto Montt. Río Negro is at the head of a fjord at the mouth of which is Isla Llancahué, good for hiking in the forests amid beautiful scenery. *Hotel Termas de Llancahué* charges C p.p. full board (excellent food), hot spring at the hotel. To get there, broadcast a message on Radio Reloncaví in Puerto Montt (US$0.50) asking to be picked up at Río Negro at a specified time. The hotel will send an open boat for you; the one-hour crossing affords views of dolphins and fur seals. Efforts are under way to preserve areas of ancient emerald araucaria and alerce forest around Volcán Hornopiren, coordinated by Ancient Forest International and Codeff, the Chilean Sierra Club.

**Hotels** at Río Negro: *cabañas* at Copec service station, *Perlas del Reloncaví*, clean, pleasant, good restaurant (may not have fuel); the cabins are usually taken before the rooms in the two other hotels, the *Holiday Country*, on the road to Pichanco, D p.p., hot shower, restaurant, and the *Hornopiren*, at the water's edge, next to the sawmill.

There are no buses S from Río Negro. By car, leave Río Negro at 0600 to drive the 35 km. for the 0800 ferry at Pichanco (there is little opportunity to camp at Pichanco and just one small stand offering food and drinks). The ferry takes 2½ hrs. to cross the length of the Fiordo Comau to Leptepu. There is one other sailing at 1500 (fare is US$11.50 per car; reverse on to the ferry to cope with the steep slope from the dock at Leptepu). Soon after the ferry sets out it passes a narrow channel to the left; in here the German light cruiser *Dresden* hid from the British fleet in 1915. The crew was protected by the local German community. After disembarking from the morning ferry at Leptepu, try to get away quickly to Fiordo Largo, the next ferry, 10 km. away. This boat has about half the capacity of the previous one so if you miss it you will have to wait 2 hours for its return. It runs every two hours between 0800 and 2000, ¾-hour crossing Fiordo Reñihue to Caleta Gonzalo, US$4 per car (reverse on).

After Caleta Gonzalo there is a steep climb on a coarse gravel surface to Laguna Blanca. Caleta Santa Bárbara, a black sand beach with nice camping and swimming, is at Km. 44. It is a further 12 km. to Chaitén.

**Chaitén to Coyhaique** The port of *Chaitén* has grown in importance because of the military camp and the new road. The town is quite well-laid out, but is a typical transit place, either full or empty, depending on the movements of the ferries from Pargua or Chonchi. Fuel is available in Chaitén.

**Hotels and services** *Hotel Continental*, Juan Todesco 18, T 202, D, no heating nor private bath, but good meals, very helpful and friendly, rec.; *Restaurant/Hotel Mi Casa*, Av. Norte, T 285—on a hill—rec., D with bath, water heaters in rooms, or F in youth hostel, negotiable, the owners prefer you to eat in their restaurant; *Hostería Schilling*, B, Av. B. O'Higgins 243, T 295, on waterfront, with bath and heating (hot water is turned on or off on the intuition of the landlady, check your shower before entering), no restaurant; *Hotel/Restaurant Cordillera*, Todesco y O'Higgins, D. *Residencial Astoria*, Av. O'Higgins 442, T 263, E with breakfast, shared bath, clean, bar downstairs; *Pensión* at Juan Todesco 205, E (F for floor space), hot water and meals extra, free use of kitchen; large youth hostel, E, sleep on floor; free campsite 4 km. N, with hot showers and close to sea. *Café-restaurante Flamengo*, Av.

O'Higgins 218, T 314, excellent, popular with travellers; *Restaurante Mahurori*, Independencia 141. Shopping and most facilities. Phone office in supermarket next to *Hostería Schilling*.

**Transport** Transmarchilay ferry from Pargua, 15 March-29 Dec. Sun. late p.m., returning Mon. late p.m., and Thur. returning Fri. From 2 Jan. to 15 March the ferry runs between Chaitén and Chonchi on Chiloé, Mon. 1700, Tues. and Wed. 1500, from Chaitén, 6 hrs., US$4 p.p., US$26.50 per car. Check in advance for exact times; office is two doors from *Hostería Schilling* at Av. O'Higgins 243, T 272. There is also a ferry to Puerto Montt for trucks, Ro-Ro *Mercedes*, Terminales Marítimos Chilenos, which will also take passengers but with no shelter, standing only, unless someone lets you get in their vehicle, 3 times a week (Mon., Wed. and Fri. from Puerto Montt), 12 hrs, US$8. Office is in a hardware store (*ferretería*) on Juan Todesco.

Flights Puerto Montt-Chaitén-Puerto Montt with Don Carlos, Juan Todesco 42, T 275, 1220 and 1600, Mon.-Fri., 1220 on Sat., US$28 (US$53 return); Aerosur, twice daily to Puerto Montt Mon.-Sat., US$28 (US$46 return).

Artetur runs microbuses between Chaitén and Coyhaique, twice a week (US$20) 12-14 hrs. The service depends very much on demand and in winter especially may not run all the way (i.e. only to La Junta). On the full service, the bus stops overnight in La Junta in winter but only briefly in summer. Other stops on request, but it is easier to go right through than pick up a bus on route. Hitching the whole route takes about a week, but you must be prepared for a day's wait if you find yourself out of luck.

There is superb salmon fishing in the rivers, and the local people are very friendly. 25 km. S of Chaitén is Amarillo (accommodation in village bar, E, breakfast US$1); 5 km. from the village are thermal baths (2 wooden sheds with very hot pool inside, US$1.50 p.p.), camping possible and one cabin for hire with woodstove and bath, sleeps 4, B (accommodation is being extended). From the thermal baths it is possible to hike along the old trail to Futaleufú, 4-7 days, not for the inexperienced, be prepared for wet feet all the way. The trail follows the River Michinmawida (passing the volcano of the same name) to Lake Espolón. A sporadic ferry crosses the lake taking cargo only to Futaleufú. Campsite at this end of the lake also has bungalows (see below).

At Puerto Cárdenas 46 km. S of Chaitén, on the northern tip of beautiful Lago Yelcho (out of 10 houses and a police post, there are 2 places to stay, inc. *Residencial Yelcho*, full board available); beautiful setting. Free campsite 3 km. after the river crossing, ask the owners in a little white house near the lake. An elderly, free ferry crosses the Río Yelcho at Puerto Cárdenas (all day till 1800 in winter, 2000 in summer, stops 1230-1330 for lunch). A bridge is under construction. At Km. 60, on the western side of Lago Yelcho is a free Conaf campsite (limited facilities) from which it is a 2 hour walk to the glacier which can be clearly seen from Puente Ventisquero on the road. At **Villa Santa Lucía**, 31 km. from Puerto Cárdenas, a road branches east to Argentina. Santa Lucía has 30 houses, a military camp, one small shop, bread from a private house, and accommodation on main street at No.7 (Sra. Rosalía Cuevas de Ruiz, basic, meals available), No. 13, breakfast US$1, and No. 16, not bad, all F p.p., none has hot water.

The road to the border is single track, gravel, passable in a regular car, but best with a good, strong vehicle; the scenery is beautiful. Accommodation can be found at La Cabaña, Puerto Piedra (Camping y Cabañas, T 280) and Puerto Ramírez (*Hostería Río Malito*—Sr. Soto—nearby, rooms, camping, fishing), whence there are two roads to the Argentine border at **Futaleufú** and **Palena** (several *pensiones*, Expreso Yelcho bus from Chaitén twice a week). 6 km. before Futaleufú, turn left to Lago Espolón for campsite and cabins, E per bed, US$3.75 for a motorhome; gorgeous lake, warm enough for a quick dip (take care with the current), superb rainbow trout fishing, ask for the Valebote family's motorboat. Aníbal, who owns the campsite, sells meat, bread, beer and soft drinks and will barbecue lamb. The area around Espolón and Futaleufú has a microclimate, 30°C in the day in summer, 5° at night.

**Hotels and transport Futaleufú** Res. *Carahue*, O'Higgins 322, D; *Hotel Continental*, Balmaceda 597, E p.p., basic, hot water, clean, rec., cheap restaurant. A microbus runs from Chaitén to Futaleufú on Tuesday, at least. At the small grey store, Kitty, at the school corner on Balmaceda, ask about bus Futaleufú to the border, Tues. and Fri. 1300 approx., US$1.25, ½ hr. From the border (new bridge over the Río Grande), bus to Esquel, US$3, 2 hrs. Esquel is the starting point for several Argentine national parks.

Coming from Argentina, allow 1½ hrs. for formalities; continue from Futaleufú to Puerto Ramírez, but don't go into Ramírez, take the unsigned right turn to Chaitén (left goes to Palena). **N.B.** Only transit visas are issued at border points, so you must either leave within 10 days or renew your entry stamp at an immigration office.    is signed

Between Villa Santa Lucía and La Junta are two, free, water-driven ferries (0800-2200 in summer, 0800-1900 winter). **La Junta** (where the buses stop) is at the confluence of Río Rosselot and Río Palena, 151 km. from Chaitén, 270 km. from Coyhaique. It is a drab, expensive village, but the fishing is good and the walks to Lake Rosselot beautiful. 3 *hosterías*, *Residencial Copihue*, Antonio Varas 611, D p.p., few rooms but nice, shared bath, hot water, good meals; another one at Antonio Varas 33, E, breakfast US$1.50, use of kitchen. Fuel is available at La Junta.

**Puerto Puyuguapi** (also spelt Puyuhuapi), about half way, at the end of the Puyuguapi Canal, is an intriguing town founded by Germans in 1935. There is a famous carpet factory in the village. 18 km. southwest of the village, accessible only by jeep and boat, there are several springs with 50°C water filling two pools near the beach (rent a boat for a group, for US$15 p.p., baths cost US$4.75 p.p., children under 11 half price, take food and drink). The *Hostería Termas*, T 2741515, has accommodation in our B range p.p. **Parque Nacional Queulat** nearby is, according to legend, the place where the rich town of Césares once was. The Ventisquero (glacier) Colgado can be seen in the park, about 25 km. S of Pto. Puyuguapi, very beautiful, camping possible; also the Salto del Cóndor waterfall. The Portezuelo Queulat is the highest pass on the Carretera.

**Accommodation and services** *Residencial Alemana*, Av. Otto Uebel 450, C, a large wooden house on the right-hand side of the road which leads from the quayside through the village, 150 metres before the police post, owned by Sra. Ursula Flack Kroschewski, very good board and lodging; *Hostería Ludwig*, on the road south, D, excellent, often full; *Hospedaje Tita*, D, basic; *pensión* of Sra. Leontina Fuentes, Llantureo y Circunvalación, E, clean, hot water, good breakfast for US$1; 300 metres south at Sur Rolando, stay at Sra. Sophía's house; *pensión* at Tureo 18, F p.p. There is a dirty campsite by the sea behind the general store. The store is behind the service station, which sells fuel until 2100. There are 2 bars. Transport out of Puyuguapi is very scarce; bus office of Artetur on Suray.

At **Puerto Cisnes** along the Seno Ventisquero (33 km. from the main road), you can buy food and find accommodation (*Posada Gaucho*, D p.p. with breakfast, dinner available, welcoming, hot water, *pensión* at Carlos Condell y Dr. Steffen, D p.p., with breakfast, hot shower, friendly; also a youth hostel and campsite). There are buses Wed. and Sun. at 1100 to Coyhaique with Litoral, 5½ hrs, US$8, Mansur on Tues., US$8, and with Pudú Mon. and Fri. at 0830.

The Río Cisnes is rec. for rafting or canoeing; 160 km. of grand scenery, with modest rapids except for the horrendous drop at Piedra del Gato; there is a 150 metre cliff at Torre Bright Bank. Good camping in the forest. At Cisne Medio (no hotel, restaurant or telephone), there is **a road to La Tapera** and to the Argentine border. A few km. N of Cisne Medio provisions and lodging can be found at Villa Amengual. 10 km. S of here is the **Reserva Nacional Lago Las Torres**, a wonderful lake with good fishing and a small Conaf campsite (free).

Villa Mañihuales, 20 km. S of El Tocqui copper mine, is connected by bus with Coyhaique (Trans. Mañihuales, one a day except Sun., US$2). There are at least 3 *pensiones*, inc. *Pensión Bienvenido*, E, clean, friendly, and restaurant *Villa Mañihuales*, F p.p., friendly, breakfast US$0.75 (both right-hand side of road going S at south end). After Mañihuales the road forks west to Puerto Aisén, east to Coyhaique. At Villa Ortega on the Coyhaique branch, the *Restaurant Farolito* takes guests, E, rec.

XI Región (Aisén) lies between Chiloé and Magallanes. Its original inhabitants were Tehuelches (Tzónecas, or Patagones), who lived on the pampa hunting guanacos, ñandúes (rheas) and huemules (a large indigenous deer, now almost extinct), and Alacalufes (Kaweshour, or Canoeros), who were coast dwellers living off the sea. The arrival of the Spaniards, who called the region Trapananda, led to little more than exploration of the coast by navigators and missionaries. Inland exploration in the nineteenth century was greatly helped by Fitzroy's cartographical surveys; George Charles Muster, Enrique Simpson Baeza and Juan Steffen led the main expeditions, travelling up the rivers. Colonization followed the first commercial enterprises (timber extraction, cattle farming) on an east-west axis, from Argentina or the sea, with Puerto Aisén-Coyhaique becoming the most important route.

**Puerto Aisén** used to be the region's major port, but it has been replaced by Puerto Chacabuco, 15 km. to the west. They say it rains 370 days a year in Puerto Aisén (pop. 13,050), quite an attractive town at the meeting of the rivers Aisén and Palos. There are few vestiges of the port left, just some boats high and dry on the river bank when the tide is out and the foundations of buildings by the river, now overgrown with fuschias and buttercups. To see any maritime activity you have to walk a little way out of town to Puerto Aguas Muertas where the fishing boats come in. There is a good walk to Laguna Los Palos, 2 hours. Folklore festival in 2nd week of November. A new bridge over the Aisén and paved road lead to **Puerto Chacabuco**; a regular bus service runs between the two. The harbour is a short way from the town and is a dreary place to hang around waiting for the ferry, especially on a wet evening (a new passenger waiting area is being built). Services given below are in Puerto Aisén unless stated otherwise.

**Accommodation** hard to find, most is taken up by fishing companies in both ports. In Puerto Aisén: *Motel Imperio y Gastronomía Carrera*, Cochrane 465, T 332551, B with breakfast, new and smart; *Hotel Aisén*, Chacabuco 130, T 332672, B; *Residencia de lo Nene*, Av. Serrano Montaner 57, T 332725, E, clean, full board available; *Roxy*, hotel and restaurant, Aldea 972, T 332704, E; *Plaza*, O'Higgins 237, T 332784, E without breakfast; *Residencial Marina*, Aldea 382, F p.p., clean, only cold water; *El Fogón*, Aldea 355, both with *comedor*; unnamed *pensión* at Aldea 1026, F p.p. with sleeping bag; *Café-Restaurant Yaney Ruca*, Aldea 369, E, clean, friendly. No campsite but free camping easy.
    In Puerto Chacabuco: *Parque Turístico Loberías de Aisén*, J. M. Carrera, T 115, B; *Hotel Moraleda*, O'Higgins, T 332784, E.

**Exchange** on Plaza de Armas will only change cash, not travellers' cheques.

**Post Office** on other side of bridge from Plaza de Armas; **telephone office** on south side of Plaza de Armas, next to *Café Rucuray*, which posts boat information.

**Tourist Office** in Municipalidad, Arturo Prat y Sgto. Aldea, 1 Dec. to end-Feb. only; helpful.

**Bus** to **Puerto Chacabuco**, Las Cascadas on Montaner Serrano, to left of Sgto Aldea (main street) walking away from Plaza de Armas, 6 a day between 0800-1730, 30 mins, US$0.60, return 0830-1800; colectivo US$1.35 p.p.
    Las Cascadas to **Coyhaique**, 3-4 a day between 0830-1900 (Sun. and holidays between 0845 and 1930), US$1.35; Transaustral, Sgto. Aldea next to No.348, 3 a day; Don Carlos taxi-bus, 5 a day, US$2.50. When a ferry is in, buses to/from Coyhaique go to Puerto Chacabuco, US$2, details at bus offices.

**Shipping Offices** Empremar, Teniente Merino 728, T 332725, or Agemar, Teniente Merino 909, T 332726, Puerto Aisén; Navimag, Sargento Aldea 398, T 332699, Puerto Aisén; Transmarchilay, Av. O'Higgins s/n, T 144, Puerto Chacabuco. It is best to make reservations in these companies' offices in Puerto Montt, Coyhaique or Santiago (or, for Transmarchilay, in Chaitén, Ancud or Chonchi). For trips to Laguna San Rafael, see below; out of season, they are impossible to arrange.

**Ferry Services** Transmarchilay's *Colono* runs from Puerto Chacabuco via the Canal Moraleda to Chonchi on Chiloé on Mon., and Thur. at 1500 and takes 22 hours (seats US$15, without a seat US$12, car US$52.50); meals are available. This service operates 2 Jan. to 15 March only, and in this season the ship also makes an excursion to Laguna San Rafael each Saturday at 2100, returning Mon. 0800 (fares, including food, from US$106-280, ranging from economy class to cabin). For the rest of the year the *Colono* goes to Pargua, 27 hours, about 3 times a week, seats US$18 in economy, US$27 stern, US$36 bow, cabins from US$125-180 p.p. Navimag's *Evangelistas* sails each Thur. and Sun. from Puerto Chacabuco to Puerto Montt, taking about 24 hours (fares under Puerto Montt, the *pionero* seats are quite spacious and comfortable and there is a cafeteria selling burgers, sandwiches, soft drinks, beer, hot beverages, etc.); it too diverts from its schedule in summer to run a trip to Laguna San Rafael

These maps are for interest only
and are not of political significance

# KEY TO
# MAP SECTIONS

CARIBBEAN SEA

**④**

FOR GALAPAGOS ISLANDS
SEE PAGE 2

The Grenadines
Los Roques (Ven.)
I. de Margarita
GRENADA
St George's
⑤
65°
65°

La Tortuga
La Asunción
Carúpano
Güiria
Tobago
TRINIDAD
AND
TOBAGO
400 miles
600 km.
100   200   300
200       400
1:16M

acas
Cumaná
Pto la Cruz
Barcelona
Caripito
Pen. de Paria
G. de
Paria
Port of
Spain
Trinidad
San Fernando
Zarara
Anaco
Maturín
El Tigre
Tucupita
Barrancas
Boca
Grande
10°

Cd Bolívar
Orinoco
Cd Guayana
Upata
Mabaruma

NEZUELA
Cd Piar
La Paragua
Emb. de
Guri
Charity
Suddie
V. en Hoop
Georgetown
New Amsterdam
Nieuw Amsterdam

El Dorado
Salto
del Angel
Bartica
Linden
Paramaribo
Nieuw
Nickerie
Totness
Marienburg
Sinnamary
I. du Diable
/ Devil's I.

La Gran
Sabana
Roraima
2810
Kaieteur
Fall
Apoera   Witagron
Albina
Kourou
Cayenne

San Marguida
Sta Elena
SURINAME
Blommesteinmeer
FRENCH
GUIANA
Oiapoque

Orinoco
Bonfim
GUYANA
Julianatop
1280
Serra Tumucumaque
Calçoene
Amapá
AMAPÁ

Boa Vista
Lethem
Sa do Navio
Equator
Macapá
Pto Santana

ucuara
RORAIMA
Caracaraí
Barcelos
Negro
Carvoeiro
Oriximiná
Obidos
Amazonas
Monte
Alegre
Gurupá
Xingu

Tefé
Manacapuru
Manaus
Careiro
Parintins
Itacoatiara
Santarém
Altamira
S. Félix

AZONAS
Coari
Codajás
Purus
Borba
Itaituba
Tapajós
Aveiro
5°

V
Coari
S
Madeira
Novo
Aripuanã
Pimenta

Canutama
Manicoré
Aripuanã
Jacareacanga
Iriri

Lábrea
Humaitá
Prainha
Serra do Cachimbo
Xingu

Madeira
Porto Velho
Aripuanã
Teles Pires
Cachimbo
S. Félix

Abunã
Guajará-Mirim
Rondônia
Serra do
Pareci
BRAZIL
10°
Sa dos Caiab
Formosa
São Félix

Manore
RONDÔNIA
Guaporé
60°

⑦

Tropic of Capricorn

1:16M

| | | | | | | |
|---|---|---|---|---|---|---|
| 0 | | 100 | 200 | 300 | 400 miles | |
| 0 | 200 | 400 | 600 km. | | | |

**ALAGOAS** Maceió
Propriá Arapiraca Penedo
**SERGIPE** Aracaju
Sen. do Bonfim Serrinha Estância
Lagarto
Jacobina R. de Jacuípe Alagoinhas
Feira de S. Cachoeira **Salvador** (Bahia)
Castro Alves Nazaré
Itabuna B. de T. os Santos
R. de Contas Valença
**BAHIA** Iaçu Jequié Ilhéus
Caetité Vitória da Conquista Itabuna Itapetinga
Chapada Diamantina
Ibotirama Canavieiras
Barra Salinas Belmonte
Bom Jesus da Lapa Pôrto Seguro
Barreiras São Francisco
Montes Claros Januária Aracuaí
Espinhaço Teófilo Otoni Nanuque Caravelas
Diamantina Itambacuri
Corinto Curvelo Gov. Valadares Olhanaraju
Pirapora Diamantina São Mateus
Paracatu Pinheiro Itabira Caratinga Linhares
Patos de Minas Fabriciano Colatina **ESPÍRITO**
Araxá Divinópolis Manhuaçu Caraçica **SANTO**
**Belo Horizonte** Ponte Nova Vitória
**GOIÁS** Brasília Formosa Pará de Minas Mar de Espanha Vila Velha
Catalão Lafaiete Barbacena Cachoeiro de Itapemirim
Franca Passos São João del Rei Juiz de Fora São João da Barra
Uberaba Pouso Alegre Itaperuna Campos
Ribeirão Prêto Lavras Nova Friburgo
São João Alfenas Volta Redonda Petrópolis Macaé
Fernandópolis Uberlândia Poços de Caldas Barra Mansa Nova Iguaçu Magé
Ituiutaba Caldas Novas São Carlos Campinas Niterói
Ceres Jaraguá Barretos Limeira **Rio de Janeiro**
Anápolis Pirenópolis São José do R. Prêto Piracicaba Sorocaba
Rio Verde de Goiás **Goiânia** Catanduva Jaú São José dos Campos
Iporá Boiandira Araçatuba Bauru Santo André São Paulo Santos
Jataí Iturama **São Paulo** São Vicente
Aruanã Fernandópolis Marília Itapetininga Itanhaém
**MATO** Pres. Vargas Panorama Assis Botucatu Itararé Iguape
**GROSSO** Mirassol Pres. Epitácio Ourinhos Apucarana Itapeva Paranaguá
Mineiros Pres. Prudente Londrina Jacarezinho Castro
**Cuiabá** Pres. Venceslau Maringá C. Mourão Guarapuava **PARANÁ** Ponta Grossa
Planalto de Mato Grosso Paranavaí Goio-Erê **Curitiba**
Fátima du Sul Campo Grande Umuarama Cascavel Matra
Rondonópolis Dourados Ponta Porã Foz do Iguaçu Guaíra Guarapuava
**MATO GROSSO DO SUL** Três Lagoas Toledo Palmas
São Félix do Coxim Paranaíba Guairá Cataratas do Iguaçu

Sa Forma Sa Caiabis Diamantino
Pto. Artur
São Félix do Araguaia Ilha do Bananal
Aragarças
São Miguel

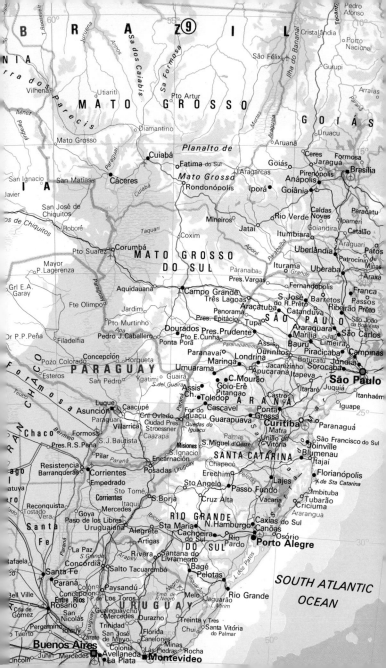

São Paulo
Sorocaba
Itapetininga
Itapeva
Itararé
Jaguariaíva
Itapeva
Iguape
Paranaguá
São Francisco do Sul
Joinville
Blumenau
Ilha de Sta Catarina
Florianópolis
Tubarão
Criciúma
Araranguá
PONTA
GROSSA
Castro
P A R A N Á
C. Mourão
Ch. Toledo
Cascavel
Foz do Iguaçu
Pato-Erê
Pitanga
Guarapuava
União da Vitória
Lajes
Vacaria
Caxias do Sul
Canoas
Porto Alegre
S A N T A   C A T A R I N A
Palmas
Chapecó
Erechim
Passo Fundo
N. Hamburgo
Pelotas
Assis
Pres.
For. do
Santa Cruz do Sul
Cataratas do
Iguaçu
São Miguel do Oeste
Sto Ângelo
Cruz Alta
Santa Maria
R I O   G R A N D E
D O   S U L
Cachoeira
Cacequi
Bagé
Rio Grande
Santa Vitória
do Palmar
Lagoa dos Patos
P A R A G U A Y
San Pedro
Esteros
Asunción
Luque
Paraguarí
Villarrica
Coronel Oviedo
Caazapá
Encarnación
Ciudad Pres.
Stroessner
Posadas
Pilar
Formosa
S. J. Bautista
Pres. R.S. Peña
Ytororó
Misiones
S. Ignacio
Ciudad del Guairá
Salto del Guairá
Caacupé
Santa Catalina
Yatimí Guairá
Caaguazú
C H A C O
G R A N   C H A C O
Resistencia
Barranqueras
Corrientes
Goya
Reconquista
Tostado
Esteros del
Iberá
Sto Tomé
S. Borja
Uruguaiana
Santana do Livramento
Alegrete
Rivera
Artigas
Salto
Tacuarembó
Durazno
U R U G U A Y
Treinta y Tres
Melo
Rocha
Punta del Este
Maldonado
Minas
Montevideo
Florida
Canelones
San José
de Mayo
Mercedes
Trinidad
Colonia
La Plata
Avellaneda
Buenos Aires
Río de la Plata
Chascomús
Dolores
Gral Guido
Gral
Madariaga
Va Gesell
Mar del Plata
Miramar
Necochea
Tres Arroyos
Bahía Blanca
Cnl
Pringles
Coronel
Dorrego
Balcarce
Tandil
Azul
Las Flores
Ayacucho
General
Lavalle
Chivilcoy
Chacabuco
Lincoln
Junín
Pergamino
San Nicolás
Rosario
Santa Fe
Paraná
Concepción del Uruguay
Gualeguaychú
Gualeguay
Concordia
Colón
Paysandú
Mercedes
Villaguay
C. del Eje
Cruz del Eje
S. Francisco
Alta Gracia
Villa María
Río Cuarto
Bell Ville
Cda. de Gómez
Venado Tuerto
Rufino
Laboulaye
La Paz
Santiago del Estero
S. Miguel de
Tucumán
Catamarca
La Rioja
Córdoba
Mercedes
V. Dolores
San Luis
V. Huidobro
Gral Alvear
San Rafael
Mendoza
San Juan
S. Agustín
Chilecito
Tinogasta
Londres
Belén
Andalgalá
Aimogasta
Cafayate
Salta
S. Salvador de Jujuy
Metán
S. Pedro
S. de Juárez
Salinas Grandes
Catamarca
Santiago
del Estero
A R G E N T I N A
L A   P A M P A
Sta Rosa
Telén
Gral Acha
Utracán
Macachín
Catriló
Trenque Lauquen
Pehuajó
Carhué
Guaminí
Olavarría
S A N   L U I S
M E N D O Z A
S A N   J U A N
Antofagasta
Taltal
Chañaral
Caldera
Copiapó
Vallenar
Huasco
La Serena
Coquimbo
Ovalle
Illapel
Los Vilos
Quintero
Viña del Mar
Valparaíso
San Antonio
Quillota
Rancagua
San Fernando
Curicó
Talca
Constitución
Linares
Parral
Chillán
Cauquenes
Tomé
Talcahuano
Concepción
Coronel
Lota
Los Ángeles
Santiago
S. Felipe
Los Andes
Jáchal
Valle Fértil
Puna de
Atacama
Antofalla
Salar de
Antofalla
Ojos del Salado 6880
Pissis 6779
Bonete 6872
S. de Aizana
S. de la Puna
Tuparro 6700
Juncalito
Pastos Grandes
S O U T H

10

⑪

## ON THE SAME SCALE

1:16M

| 0 | 100 | 200 | 300 | 400 miles |
|---|-----|-----|-----|-----------|
| 0 | 200 | 400 | 600 km. | |

ATLANTIC OCEAN

FALKLAND ISLANDS
ISLAS MALVINAS

Jason Is
West Falkland
Ps puerto
Weddell
East Falkland
C. Dolphin
Stanley
Beauchene Is
Fanfar

South Georgia
C. Alexandra        Grytviken
Shag Rocks          C. Disappointment

La
Osorno
Pto Varas
Puerto Montt
Ancud
I. de Chiloé  Castro °Achao
Paso Limay
Lmhue Huapi
S Carlos de
Bariloche
El Bolsón
Ñorquinco
Esquel
Maquinchao
Valcheta
Viedma
C. Carmen de Patagones
Golfo
San Matías
Pto Piramides
Punta Delgada
Pto Madryn
Rawson
Pto Lobos
Golfo
Pmb. F.
ameghino
Camarones
C. Dos Bahías

C H U B U T
Castre
Las Plumas
Trelew
Gaimán
L.C. Huapi
L. Musters
Sarmiento

I.  Achao
°Quellón
Chonos
Archipiélago
de los
Chonos

Melimoyu
2400
Pen.
de Taitao
G. de Penas
Campana
Hanover
Esmeralda
Madre de Dios
I. Wellington
Arch. de la
Reina Adelaida
Desolación
Santa Inés

Coihaique
Balmaceda
Pto Aisén
L. San Valentin
L.Gral Carrera
Cochrane
O'Higgins
Lautaro
2380
Vedma
Pto Natales
Pen.
Muñoz
Cerro
Gamero
Pen.
de Brunswick
Punta Arenas
Porvenir

Magallanes
L.C. Huapi
Buenos Aires
Perito
Moreno
Colonia
Las Heras
Deseado
Gobernador Gregores
S. Julián
Sta Cruz
Bahía Grande
Río Gallegos
Río
Turbio

C. Tres Puntas
Deseado
Pta Médanosa

Comodoro Rivadavia
Golfo
San Jorge
Caleta
Olivia

S A N T A   C R U Z

Río Grande
Tierra del
Fuego
Isla Grande
de Tierra
del Fuego
Ushuaia
Navarino
Sts Is Wollaston
C. de Hornos
Hoste
Londonderry
I. de los Estados
San
San Diego

Str. de Magallanes
Beagle

ATLANTIC

OCEAN

40°
45°
50°
55°

⑫

**TRINIDAD** 1:4M

Toco
Arima
Princes Town
Port of Spain
Guayaguayare
San Fernando
Bonasse
Gulf of Paria

**TOBAGO** 1:4M

Charlotteville
Plymouth
Scarborough

**JAMAICA** 1:4M

Montego Bay
Falmouth
St. Ann's Bay
Annotto Bay
Port Antonio
Brown's Town
Spanish Town
**Kingston**
Port Morant
Blue Mtn. Pk. 2256m
May Pen
Mandeville
Mt. Denham 996m
Black River
Savanna la Mar
Portland Point
Portland

ATLANTIC OCEAN

Leeward Islands

Virgin Is.
Anguilla
St. Martin
St. Croix
St. Kitts
Nevis
Barbuda
Montserrat
Guadeloupe
Point-à-Pitre
**ANTIGUA**
**DOMINICA**
Roseau
Martinique
Fort-de-France
Windward Islands
Castries
**ST. LUCIA**
**ST. VINCENT**
Kingstown
**GRENADA**
St. Georges
**BARBADOS**
Bridgetown
Tobago
**TRINIDAD AND TOBAGO**
San Fernando

LESSER ANTILLES

San Juan
Ponce
**PUERTO RICO**
Mayagüez
Mona Passage

CARIBBEAN SEA

NETHERLAND ANTILLES
Aruba
Curaçao
Bonaire
Willemstad
Pto. Fijo
G. de Venezuela
Coro
Tucacas
Cabimas
**Maracaibo**
La Tortuga
La Guaira
**Caracas**
Barcelona
Asunción of Spain
Cumaná
Carúpano
I. Margarita

Pta Gallinas
Uribia
Riohacha
Santa Marta
**Barranquilla**
Cartagena
VENEZUELA

THE BAHAMAS

Eleuthera I.
Cat I.
Andros Is.
Nassau
Long I.
Acklins I.
Caicos Is.
Turks Is.
Gt. Inagua I.
Crooked I.
Straits of Florida

GREATER ANTILLES

Hispaniola
Santiago
Cap-Haïtien
Gonaïves
**HAITI**
Port au Prince
Les Cayes
**DOMINICAN REPUBLIC**
Santiago
La Romana
Santo Domingo
Azua
Windward Passage

**La Habana**
Matanzas
Santa Clara
Sagua la Grande
Cienfuegos
Sancti Spíritus
Camagüey
Holguín
Bayamo
Santiago de Cuba
Turquino 2005m
C. Cruz
Guantánamo
I. de la Juventud (I. de Pinos)
Pinar del Río

JAMAICA
Montego Bay
Spanish Town
**Kingston**
Savanna la Mar

1:16M

400 miles
600 km.

0   100   200   300   400

Cayman Is.

HONDURAS
L. de Caratasca
C. Gracias a Dios
Puerto Cabezas
Prinzapolca
NICARAGUA
Bluefields
COSTA

# Rio Atlantica Suite Hotel.
## A touch of Switzerland, right on Copacabana Beach.

*Setting new standards on Rio's hotel scene.*

- Conveniently located in the heart of Copacabana, right on the Beach.
- Minutes away from the city's financial/business center and shopping district makes the Rio Atlantica convenient for businessmen and tourists.
- 18 floors with 228 suites and rooms, most featuring ocean view. Our suite accommodations are cost competitive with the standard rooms of hotels of the same category.
- Round-the-clock security. Featuring in-room safety-deposit boxes and wet bars.
- 2 restaurants serving the finest in Brazilian, international and Swiss cuisine ("Ao Ponto" and "Helvecia").

- Ample facilities for business meetings and functions. 68-seat fully equipped auditorium.
- Rooftop swimming pool, solarium, health club with saunas, exercise room and deck bar for the exclusive use of guests.
- Drugstore/newsstand, boutiques, jewelry and gift shops.
- Accommodations for handicapped available.
- The newest and only hotel under Swiss management.

(Sunday 2000, returning Tuesday), US$106 for a seat, cabins from US$167 sharing to US$270 double with bath (US$450 single).

The paved road from Puerto Aisén to Coyhaique passes through the **Parque Nacional Río Simpson**, with beautiful waterfalls and good views of the river. There is a campsite near the turning to Santuario San Sebastián.

*Coyhaique* (population, 40,000), the administrative and commercial centre of the region, is located in a large green valley surrounded by mountains. The town provides a good base for hiking and skiing excursions in the area and has a good Museo Regional de la Patagonia Central in the Liceo San Felipe Benicio on the pentagonal square (in term time, if the museum is closed, ask the secretaría for the key; in holidays it should be open, US$0.35, small but interesting with photos of early settlers, history, paleontology, fauna and archaeology). When entering Coyhaique from the airport, look left from the bridge over the Río Simpson for the Piedra del Indio, a rock outcrop which looks like a face in profile. Petrol is available in Coyhaique, several stations.

**Hotels**  In summer rooms are in very short supply; the tourist office has a full list of all types of accommodation, but look out for notices in windows since any place with less than 6 beds does not have to register with the authorities (several on Baquedano and Almte. Simpson).
   *Don Hotel*, José de Moraleda 440, T 221643, B; *Los Ñires*, Baquedano 315, T 222261, A with breakfast, pleasant; *Residencial Puerto Varas*, Serrano 168, T 221212, E without bath, check which of the bathrooms has hot water, restaurant and bar, basic, tatty; *Residencial Navidad*, Baquedano 198, F p.p. without bath or breakfast (which is US$1.25 extra), comedor; *Hospedaje* at Baquedano 20, T 222520, Patricio y Gedra Guzmán, room in family home (also 3 comfortable flats), F p.p., use of kitchen, breakfast with homemade bread, tent sites with bathroom and laundry facilities down by the river, English spoken, most hospitable; *Residencial Carrera*, 12 de Octubre 520, F p.p. without breakfast; *Residencial* at Cochrane 532 (no sign), F, quite nice except for bathroom; *Res. La Pastora*, Prat 553, D, no hot water, meals available. *Hospedaje* Hermina Mansilla, 21 de Mayo 60, E with breakfast; *Pensión América*, 21 de Mayo 233, F p.p., dirty, basic, not rec. Other *hospedajes* and family accommodation (usually about US$5): Ignacio Serrano, T 222287, Manuel Torres de la Cruz, good breakfast, cheap, rec.; Ignacio Serrano 91, Sra. Berly Pizarro Lara, T 211522, C full board, English spoken, rec.; Colón 203, E p.p., pleasant, use of kitchen, Sr. Fidel Pinilla arranges tours; Colón 495, E p.p. without breakfast (more with), hot water, clean; Ignacio Serrano 391, T 221408, D with breakfast, not as good; Carrera 33-A, rec.; *Hospedaje* with restaurant at Baquedano 444, another at No. 102, also Freire 554. Youth hostel in summer at one of the schools (it changes each year), F p.p. with sleeping bag.

**Camping**  At Baquedano 20, see above; about 3 km. north, up a steep bumpy road off the Chaitén road, rec. on road to Puerto Aisén at Km. 32, confluence of Ríos Correntoso and Simpson; and at Km. 37, in Reserva Nacional Río Simpson.

**Restaurants**  *Loberías de Chacabuco*, Barroso 553, good seafood; *Mi Pub*, Prat y Dussen, pizzas and sandwiches; *Estancia*, José Carrera y Moraleda, also rents rooms (F p.p., hot water) and allows use of kitchen; *Café Oriente*, Calle 21 de Mayo y Condell, good bakery, tea; *Café Kalu*, A. Prat 402, serves good set meals, hamburgers. *Café Ricer*, Calle Horn, good; *Los Colonos* in an arcade on Horn; *Cafetería Alemana*, Condell 119, nice, excellent cakes and coffee; *Café L'Express*, in mall at Condell 140; *Pollo Listo* (fast food) F. Bilbao 234 and *Todo Pollo*, 21 de Mayo 552.

**Shopping**  *Feria de Artesanía* on the square; *Cema-Chile* on square, between Montt and Barroso. Large well-stocked supermarkets: *Brautigam*, Horn, Prat y Bilbao (closed Sun.), *Central*, Magallanes y Bilbao, open daily till 2230; 2 small ones on Prat, Nos. 480 and 533, open Sun. Dehydrated camping food available. Food, especially fruit and vegetables, is more expensive than in Santiago.

**Car Hire**  Automóvil Club de Chile, Bilbao 583, T 221847, rents Suzuki jeeps, about US$25/day, plus fuel. Hertz, Moraleda 420, T 223456.

**Taxis**  US$5 to airport (US$1.65 if sharing); fares in town US$1.35. To Puerto Ibáñez US$60, to Puerto Chacabuco US$40, to Puerto Aisén US$34. 50% extra after 2100. Colectivos congregate at Prat y Bilbao, average fare US$0.35.

**Laundry**  Bilbao y Magallanes.

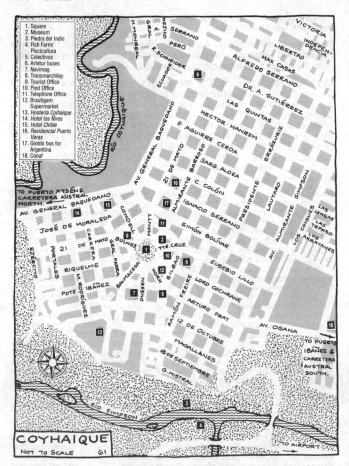

1. Square
2. Museum
3. Piedra del Indio
4. Fish Farm/
   Piscicultura
5. Colectivos
6. Artetur buses
7. Navimag
8. Transmarchilay
9. Tourist Office
10. Post Office
11. Telephone Office
12. Brautigam
    Supermarket
13. *Hostería Coihaique*
14. *Hotel los Ñires*
15. *Hotel Chile*
16. *Residencial Puerto
    Varas*
17. Giobbi bus for
    Argentina
18. Conaf

COYHAIQUE
NOT TO SCALE                G1

**Post Office** Cochrane 202, open Mon.-Fri. 0830-1230, 1430-1800, Sat. 0830-1200.

**Telephone office** at Barroso 626, open till 2200, opens on Sun. about 0900. **Telex**, 21 de Mayo 472.

**Exchange** Prat 340, oficina 208, T 223342, and **Turismo Prado**, 21 de Mayo 417, T 221271, both will change travellers' cheques. For australes, dollars and cheques go to **Lavaseco** on Gral. Parra. **Fincard** (Visa and Mastercard), A. Prat 340, local 1, T 223202, Mon.-Fri. 0900-1400, 1530-1900, Sat. 0930-1330.

**Travel Agents** *Turismo Prado*, address above; *Expediciones Coyhaique*, Bolívar 94, T 222300, FAX 222500. Both offer tours of local lakes (US$20) and other sights (e.g. US$56 to Ventisquero Colgante), arrange Laguna San Rafael trips, etc.; Prado does historical tours, while Expediciones does fishing trips and excursions down the Río Baker. *Fiordo Queulat*, 21 de Mayo 466, oficina 311, T 221331, Fax 222500, trips to Queulat glacier, adventure and nature tourism, fishing, etc.

**Tourist Office** Cochrane 320. **Conaf** office, Ogana 1060. Maps (photocopies of 1:50,000 IGM maps) from Dirección de Vialidad on the square.

**Shipping** Transmarchilay, 21 de Mayo 417, T 221971, Telex 377003 MARCHI CK. Navimag, Dussen 340, T 223306.

**Buses** Terminal at Lautaro y Magallanes; most buses leave from here, but not all. To/from *Puerto Montt*, Moraida Hermanos, via Bariloche, all year. To **Puerto Aisén**, US$2, Transaustral, 5 a day, 4 on Sun., La Cascada, 3-4 daily, and Don Carlos taxi-bus US$2.50, 4-6 a day, the route is extended to Puerto Chacabuco, US$2.50, if there's a boat in. **Puerto Cisnes** Pudú Sun. and Thur., Mansur, Wed., Litoral Tues. and Sat. at 1100, US$8. There are daily buses to **Mañihuales** (not Sun.), Trans Mañihuales, US$2 and to **Balmaceda**, Libertad (at Simpson y Magallanes), US$1.35. Empresa del Norte at the terminal runs a round trip service to Villa Simpson (US$0.85), Villa Frei (US$1), Seis Lagunas, Lago Atravesado (all US$1.15), Coyhaique, Mon., Wed., Fri. 0730 and 1730, 2 hours there and back.

In summer Pudú runs twice a week to **Puerto Ibáñez** on Lago Carrera, the Chilean section of Lago Buenos Aires (US$4.50), to connect with *El Pilchero* ferry, see below; Transaustral also connects with *El Pilchero*, Mon. and Fri. 1630, US$5. In winter, colectivos connect with *El Pilchero*, leaving Mon. 1730 (stay overnight in Pto. Ibáñez) and Sat. 0700, from Calle Prat, beside *Res. La Pastora/*Farmacia Regional, No. 553, 3 hrs., US$6.65.

Buses on the **Carretera Austral**: north, with Artetur, Baquedano 1347, T 223368, Tues. 0800, Sat. 0700, US$20, may be an extra services in summer, in winter may go only as far as La Junta, South, also with Aerobus, T 221172, to **Cochrane** (in minibus), Mon. 1200, Wed., Fri., 0900, 7½ hrs. lunch stop at Río Tranquilo (returns Tues., Thur., Sun. 0900). Pudú, at terminal, T 221008, to Cochrane on Mon. and Thur. in small bus, 1100, 7 hrs., and Tues. and Sat. at 0900 in a standard bus taking 12 hrs. because it stops in all the settlements on the way; each Pudúbus returns following day at 1100 (small) and 0900 (large); all services charge US$17.50.

**Travel to Argentina** To Comodoro Rivadavia Empresa, Giobbi, Bolívar y Barroso, T 222067, Tues., Thurs., Sat. 0800, US$27, 12-13 hrs. via Coyhaique Alto, Río Mayo and Sarmiento. Other routes are via Balmaceda or Puerto Ibáñez, but there is no through transport. Alternatively, the routes south of Lago General Carrera, via Chile Chico (public transport—see below), or through Villa Chacabuco and Paso Roballos, north of Cochrane (no public transport, road passable in summer, but often flooded in spring, if hitching allow a week). Beware, many border posts closed at weekends. If looking for transport to Argentina it is worth going to the local Radio Santa María, Bilbao y Ignacio Serrano, and leave a message to be broadcast.

**Air** Airport, Teniente Vidal, about 5 km. from town including a steep climb up and down to the Río Simpson bridge. LanChile flies daily from Santiago (not Sun.), with stops in Concepción and Puerto Montt; Ladeco flies daily via Puerto Montt, Valdivia and Los Angeles or Osorno. Ladeco and LanChile office at Gral. Parra 215, T 221188. Air taxi to visit glaciers, US$400 (five passengers), also to southern archipelagic region. Transporte Aéreo "Don Carlos", Subteniente Cruz 63, T 222981 to Chile Chico (Tues., Thur., Sat.), US$21, and Cochrane (Mon., Wed., Fri., US$31.50, 45 mins., rec. only for those who like flying, with strong stomachs, or in a hurry).

**Excursions** Excellent views of the Río Simpson valley from the hill, 4 hrs. walk north of town, at **Reserva Forestal Coyhaique**. South to the lakes Elizalde (good salmon fishing), Atravesado, Frío, Castor and Pollux. Skiing at El Fraile in winter (it's rather a bleak place out of the ski season). Reserva Forestal Mañihuales, 76 km. from Coyhaique, was largely destroyed by forest fires in the 1940s, but the views are good. **Monumento Natural Dos Lagunas**, lakes Toro and Bonito, 21 km. on the Coyhaique Alto road, is worth a visit.

The Carretera Austral continues south of Coyhaique. At Km. 35 is El Blanco, a hamlet with *pensión* at *Restaurant El Blanco* (or *El Nuevo*—F, breakfast US$0.75). At Km. 41 a branch road E leads to **Balmaceda** on the Argentine frontier (no accommodation, daily bus to Coyhaique, 0730, US$1.35, Ladeco flights from Santiago via Temuco and Puerto Montt—taxi from airport to Coyhaique, 1 hr., US$6, minibus US$4.50). Further south on the Carretera Austral at Km. 106 a branch road south leads to **Puerto Ibáñez**, on Lago Carrera. There are three *residenciales*: Ibáñez, Bertrán Dixon 01 (clean, warm, hot water) and, next door, *Mónica*, good meals (both E p.p.), and *Hostería Bajada Río Ibáñez*, D. Petrol/gasoline available at Luis A. Bolados 461 (house with 5 laburnum trees outside); it's sold in 5-litre containers. 6 km. away are some grand waterfalls on the Río Ibáñez.

To reach **Chile Chico** (population 2,200), a quiet, friendly but dusty town on the southern shore of Lago Carrera, one can either go by boat from Puerto Ibáñez or go through Argentina. The region prides itself in having the best climate in Southern Chile with some 300 days of sunshine; much fruit is grown as a result. Rainfall is very low but strong winds are common. Annual festival at end-January. The lake itself, a beautiful azure blue, covers 2,240 sq. km.; the Chilean end is predominantly Alpine and the Argentine end (Lago Buenos Aires, 881 sq. km.) dry pampa.

**Hotels**  at Chile Chico: *Aguas Azules*, Rodríguez 252, T 320, D full board (E without), rec. *Residenciales Frontera*, O'Higgins 332, T 314, F p.p., good food, clean rooms, rec., except for bathrooms; new *residencial* in Sector Las Chacras, E p.p. with breakfast. Private house, Blest Gana 240, basic but nice, F p.p.; turquoise house at O'Higgins 332, F p.p., clean, rec.; also O'Higgins 43, E p.p., good meals. Youth hostel at Blest Gana 320, from Jan. to end Feb. (just an empty house, no electricity or furniture, US$0.80 p.p., ask next door). *Casa Quinta/No me Olvides* (María Sánchez de Campaña), E p.p. just by Puerto Márquez on road to Argentine border, clean, cooking facilities, warm, no hot water, honey, eggs, fruit for sale, rec. Free campsite at Bahía Jarra, 15 km. east. **Restaurants** Apart from *residenciales*: *Cafetería Elizabeth y Loly* on Plaza serves coffee and delicious homemade cakes; will prepare meals if asked (expensive), also has rooms at D; *La Cabañita*, typical, cheap; *Rapa Nui*, cheap and good. Supermarket on B. O'Higgins, buy wine here. It is very difficult to change dollars (*Café Elizabeth y Loly* changes dollars at bank rate in small amounts); change australes in shops and cafés on main street (very poor rates). Ask at the Municipalidad or at the tourist office on O'Higgins for help in arranging tours.

Regular service by Transmarchilay car ferry, *El Pilchero*, across the lake, leaves Puerto Ibañez for Chile Chico 0800 Tues. and 1100 Sat. (check all times on arrival—2½ hrs, each way: US$2 p.p., US$26 for car; offices in Santiago, Puerto Montt, Chaitén, Chonchi, Ancud, Puerto Chacabuco or Coyhaique). The Sat. boat from Puerto Ibañez goes only to Chile Chico, returning on Sun. at 1600 (1400 in winter); the Tues. service continues from Chile Chico to Fachinal, Cristal, Mallín Grande, Puerto Sánchez and Río Tranquilo, arriving back in Puerto Ibáñez on Wed. This schedule operates 2 Jan.-15 March (when extra service may be put on). From 15 March to end Dec. only the Tues. service runs regularly, the Sat. one goes according to demand. Buses and jeeps meet the ferry in Puerto Ibáñez for Coyhaique. Number of passengers limited to 70; locals given preference, no reservations possible. Jeeps run from Chile Chico to Los Antiguos, the Argentine border, US$1.70; from here connections can be made to Perito Moreno. (90 days entry given for Argentina crossing at Chile Chico, but only 10 days on the rough road between Puerto Ibáñez and Perito Moreno.)

Chile Chico is connected by road along the S shore of the lake only as far as Fachinal (50 km.—people will let you stay for free, take sleeping bag). From here there is a trail to Mallín Grande, 18 km., takes all day; we have no direct proof of this trail, only report (however, a road is being built between these two points). Mallín Grande is a ferry jetty and little else, although people will put you up for free if you have a sleeping bag. A road runs to *Puerto Guadal* (shops, post office; *Hostería Huemules*, D with breakfast, good views; Sr. Félix Elías, no sign, near port in big, old brown building, E p.p., hot water, meals available, rec; also at Quemel "Sade" Guerrero—1st shop you see from jetty, No. 382 on corner of Los Pinos. *Restaurant La Frontera*, Los Lirios y Los Pinos). Pudú has a bus service between Guadal and Mallín Grande on Tues. and Wed., US$2 each way, the only traffic otherwise is on Tues. when the ferry calls. The road continues from Guadal to El Maitén on the Carretera Austral. If you wish to take *El Pilchero* to see Lago General Carrera from the water and then connect with the Pudú bus service (or Aerobus at Río Tranquilo, see below) for Cochrane or Coyhaique, an overnight stop in Mallín Grande or Río Tranquilo may be necessary and careful checking of schedules in advance will be essential.

The country to the S and W of Chile Chico provides good walking for the mountaineer. The weird rock formations and dry brush-scrub give a "wild west" feel to the country. The northern and higher peak of Cerro Pico del Sur (2,168 m.) can be climbed by the agile from Los Cipres (beware of dogs in farmyard). You will need a long summer's day and the 1:50,000 map. Follow the trace trail until it peters out, then navigate by compass or sense of direction until the volcano-like summit appears. After breaching the cliff ramparts at an obvious point, there is some scrambling and a 10-foot pitch to the summit: indescribable views of the Lake and Andes. (Brian Spearing)

The Carretera Austral branches off the Coyhaique-Puerto Ibañez road 97 km. S of Coyhaique. It goes through Villa Cerro Castillo (small supermarket, basic *residencial* on main street), named after the fabulous nearby mountain, which looks like a fairytale castle, with pinnacles jutting out of thick snow. This and other peaks in the northern wall of the Río Ibáñez valley, are in the **Reserva Nacional Cerro Castillo** (*guardería* on the Senda Ibáñez, opposite Laguna Chinguay, open Nov.-March). The Carretera climbs out of the valley, passing the aptly-named Laguna Verde and the Portezuelo Cofré. It descends to the boggy Manso valley, with a good campsite at the bridge over the river, watch out for mosquitoes, then goes on to Bahía Murta (the village, just off the Carretera on the northern tip of the central "arm" of Lago General Carrera, has *Res. Patagonia*; *Res. y restaurante Lago Gen. Carrera*, welcoming; free camping by lake, good view of Cerro Castillo). The road follows the lake's western shore; the colour of the water is an unbelievable blue-green, reflecting the mountains that surround it and the clouds above. At Río Tranquilo, where the buses stop for lunch at *Residencial Los Pinos* (F p.p., basic, also a *hospedaje* nearby on the Carretera Austral), fuel is available at the ECA store from a large drum (no sign). The Carretera continues to skirt the lake to its southwestern tip at El Maitén (turn off for Guadal). It then becomes steeper and more bendy (in winter this stretch, all the way to Cochrane, is icy and dangerous).

Just past Puerto Bertrand, a good place for fishing, is a sign to the Nacimiento del Río Baker, with the most abundant water of any Chilean river. Note how the colours of the rivers and lakes change in this region. The road climbs up to high moorland, passing the confluence of the Ríos Neff and Baker, before winding into Cochrane. The scenery is splendid all the way; in the main the road is rough but not treacherous. Watch out for cattle on the road and take blind corners slowly.

**Cochrane** (1,500 people) sits in a hollow a little distance west of Lago Cochrane. It is a simple place, sunny in summer, good for walking and fishing. Northeast of the town is the **Reserva Nacional Tamango**, administered by Conaf in two sectors (Tamango, 9 km. by dirt track, and Húngaro, 4 km., which reaches down to Lago Cochrane). In the Húngaro sector are a few remaining huemules (deer—two radio-tagged); there are also guanaco in the pampa part, foxes, lots of birds including woodpeckers and hummingbirds and lenga forest. It is inaccessible in the four winter months. Ask in the Conaf office on the square about visiting because some access is through private land and tourist facilities are still in the planning stage. The views from the reserve are superb, over the town, the nearby lakes and to the Campo de Hielo Norte to the west.

**Accommodation, food and services** *Hostería Wellmann*, Las Golondrinas 36, T 171, C, hot water, comfortable, warm, good meals, rec.; *Residencial Austral Sur*, Sra. Sonia Salazar, A. Prat s/n, T 150, E with full board, hot water, very nice; *Residencial Rubio*, Teniente Merino 04, T 173, Sra. Elva Rubio, also very nice, D full board, E bed only, breakfast US$1.65, lunch and dinner US$3.25 each; *Hospedaje Cinco Hermanos*, Húngaro y Steffen, G p.p., E p.p., with full board, free camping if you eat at *hospedaje*; *La Tranquera* restaurant and residencial, Av. San Valentín 651, at entrance to town, F p.p., hot water, friendly, poor food. In summer it is best to book rooms in advance. Restaurants: *La Sota de Oro*, Tte. Merino; *Café Lematin*, Merino y Maitén; *El Viajero*, Maitén.

Pudú bus office is in *Bottillería Quiaco*, Tte Merino daily bus leaves 0915, arrives in Coyhaique 2030, US$15); Don Carlos office is in *Residencial Austral Sur*. Petrol is available, if it hasn't run out, at the Empresa Comercial Agrícola (ECA) until a filling station has been completed. Horses can be hired for excursions in the surrounding countryside, ask around, e.g. at *Hostería Wellmann*.

The Carretera is being constructed further south of Cochrane with a view to reaching Puerto Yungay. En route, it will bypass Tortel, a village built on a hill above the sea. It has no streets, no proper plan, only wooden walkways ("no hay ni una bicicleta"). It trades in wood with Punta Arenas and fishes for shellfish (such as *centolla* and *loco*). Access is either by Don Carlos plane, or by horse, several days journey from Cochrane.

Some 150 nautical miles south of Puerto Aisén is the *Laguna San Rafael* glacier, 30 metres above sea level, and 45 km. in length. It calves small icebergs, carried out to sea by wind and tide. The thick vegetation on the shores, with snowy peaks above, is typical of Aisén. The glacier is one of a group of four that flow in all directions from Monte San Valentín. This icefield is part of the **Parque Nacional Laguna San Rafael** (1.35m. hectares), regulated by Conaf. The only way there is by plane or by boat: Air Taxi from Coyhaique (Don Carlos), US$100 each if party of 5; some pilots in Puerto Aisén will fly to the glacier for about US$85, but many are unwilling to land on the rough airstrip. The glacier is best seen from the sea: there are 9 official cruises: Empremar's *Calbuco*, *Río Cisnes* and *Quellón* (see under Puerto Chacabuco and Puerto Montt); *Skorpios I* and *II* (under Puerto Montt); Navimag's *Evangelistas* and Transmarchilay's *Colono* (see under Pto. Chacabuco); *Mar del Sur*, 21 de Mayo 417, 2nd floor, T 221271, Coyhaique, or Matias Cousiño 82, oficina 1106, Santiago, T 6985100/6984784, Fax 698589, fares from US$280 to US$360 p.p., or US$2,542 + tax to charter; *Odisea*, a motorized sailing boat, from 7 Nov.-29 April, US$680 for cruise (flight with Ladeco Santiago-Coyhaique extra), T 330883 Santiago (*Hotel Crowne Plaza*), or Sgto. Aldea 679, Puerto Aisén, T 332879. Local fishing boats from Chacabuco/Puerto Aisén take about 18-20 hrs. each way, charging the same as the tourist boats. Ask for Jorge Prado at the port (he takes a minimum of 7, more expensive than others); Andino Royas, Cochrane 129; Justiniano Aravena, Dr. Steffen 703; Rodrigo Azúcar, Agemar office, T 716; or Sr. Ocuña, ask at the port. These unauthorized boats may not have adequate facilities.

The *Calbuco* of Empremar, a government supply ship, leaves Chacabuco on Thurs. at 2000, returning from the Laguna on Sat. at 1800, arriving Chacabuco on Sun. at 0800, two lifeboats make the trip to the glacier (bring food as you may be left at the glacier for 3 hours). Operates to San Rafael only between December and March, book in advance in Aisén in Jan./Feb. season (all year round the *Calbuco* runs from Puerto Montt to Puerto Chacabuco). Fares given under Puerto Montt **Shipping**. (On the return journey you can continue to any of stops back to, and including Puerto Montt, 48 hrs.) Rooms can be hired for US$1.50 p.p. at the old hotel administered by Conaf (bring a week's supply of food: unless lucky enough to hitch back on another boat, you'll have to wait for the *Calbuco*; also bring anti-mosquito cream and candles—no electricity. Water can be scarce and the hot shower only works when water is plentiful, 2 very cold waterfalls nearby if necessary—take biodegradable soap). At the glacier there is a small ranger station. The rangers are willing to row you out to the glacier in calm weather, a 3-hr. trip. Robert af Sandeberg (Lidingö, Sweden) describes this journey as follows:

"The trip in the rowboat is an awesome venture. At first it is fairly warm and easy to row. Gradually it gets colder when the wind sweeps over the icy glacier (be sure to bring warm clothes—a thick sweater, and waterproof jacket are rec.—Ed.). It gets harder to row as small icebergs hinder the boat. Frequently somebody has to jump onto an icefloe and push the boat through. The glacier itself has a deep blue colour, shimmering and reflecting the light; the same goes for the icebergs, which are an unreal, translucent blue. The glacier is very noisy; there are frequent cracking and banging sounds, resembling a mixture of gun shots and thunder. When a hunk of ice breaks loose, a huge swell is created and the icebergs start rocking in the water. Then great care and effort has to be taken to avoid the boat being crushed by the shifting icebergs; this is a very real danger."

In the national park are puma, pudu pudu (minature deer), foxes, dolphins, occasional sealions and sea otters, and many species of bird. Walking trails are limited (about 10 km. in all) but a lookout platform has been constructed, with fine views of the glacier.

**N.B.** If you plan to go to Laguna San Rafael by boat, check first with the Gobernación Marítima in Puerto Aisén that the boat is licensed for the trip.

---

## CHILEAN PATAGONIA (8)

The glacial regions of southern Patagonia and Chilean Tierra del Fuego. Punta Arenas and Puerto Natales are the two main towns, the latter being the gateway to the Torres del Paine and Balmaceda national parks. In summer, a region for hiking, boats trips and the southernmost crossing to Argentina.

Magallanes (XII Región), which includes the Chilean part of Tierra del Fuego, has

17.5% of Chile's total area, but it is inhabited by under 1% of Chile's population. In summer rains are frequent. In winter snow covers the country, except those parts near the sea. The country is then more or less impassable, except on horseback. Strong, cold, piercing winds blow, particularly during the spring, when they reach a velocity of 70 to 80 km. an hour. During the winter they do not blow all that hard, and from May to August a strong wind is almost exceptional. The dry winds parch the ground and prevent the growth of crops, which can only be cultivated in sheltered spots.

Until the discovery of oil—Tierra del Fuego and N of Magellan Strait produce all Chilean oil—the most important industry was the breeding of sheep. At one time there was a large British colony there; it has been diminishing steadily of late. Coal has been discovered on the Chilean side of the frontier, at Pecket, but the mine is considered uneconomic; miners still cross into Argentina to work at Río Turbio.

**Punta Arenas**, the most southerly city in Chile, and capital of XII Región, 2,140 km. S of Santiago, is on the Straits of Magellan at almost equal distance from the Pacific and Atlantic oceans, 1,432 nautical miles from Valparaíso, and 1,394 from Buenos Aires. The population is about 113,500. Most of the smaller and older buildings are of wood, but the city has expanded rapidly, and practically all new building is of brick or concrete. All the main roads are paved and the country roads are of gravel; when driving in Patagonia, some form of windscreen protection is absolutely essential. Punta Arenas is a busy little city somewhat neater looking than the average Chilean town. The Plaza de Armas is also Plaza Muñoz Gamero, with a statue of Magellan with 4 Fuegian Indians at his feet. The cemetery, at Av. Bulnes 929, is even more fantastic than the one at Castro (Chiloé), with a statue of Indiecito, the little Indian, and many memorials to pioneer families and victims of shipping disasters (open 0800-1800 daily). Walk up Calle Fagnano to the Mirador Cerro La Cruz for a view over the city.

Punta Arenas is the centre of the sheep farming industry in that part of the world and exports wool, skins, and frozen meat. Besides the export of oil and gas, there is the regular carriage of crude between the Strait oil terminals and the refineries in central Chile. Good roads connect the city with (240 km.) Puerto Natales in Ultima Esperanza and Río Gallegos in Argentina. Punta Arenas has certain free-port facilities; the Zona Franca is 3½ km. N of the centre (shops open 1000-1200, 1500-2000 Mon.-Sat.). (The restaurant is open at lunch time on Sundays.)

There is an excellent modern museum in the Colegio Salesiano, "Mayorino Borgatello" dealing with the Indians, animal and bird life of the region, and other interesting aspects of life in Patagonia and Tierra del Fuego, at Av. Bulnes 374, entrance next to church. Open Tues.-Sat. 1100-1600, Sun. 1100-1300, hours seem to change frequently (entry US$0.70). Museum of regional history, Braun Menéndez, Calle Magallanes 949, off Plaza de Armas, located in a mansion built by one of the early millionaires, is well worth visiting. Part is set out as room-by-room regional history, the rest of the house is furnished and visitors are taken round in groups by a guide. Closed Mon., otherwise open 1100-1600, till 1300 on Sun. (entry US$0.50). The Instituto de la Patagonia, Av. España y Los Flamencos (opp. the University), open Mon.-Fri. 0900-1200, 1500-1700, has an open air museum. The British School on Waldo Seguel, and St. James' Church next door, are wooden, in colonial style. N.B. Calle Pedro Montt runs East-West, while Calle Jorge Montt runs North-South.

**Hotels** *Cabo de Hornos*, Plaza Muñoz Gamero 1025, T 222134, A+, excellent, rec.; *Los Navegantes*, José Menéndez 647 (Casilla 230, T 224677), A+, excellent restaurant, slightly cheaper than *Cabo de Hornos*; *Savoy*, same street, No. 1073, T 225851, B, pleasant rooms but some lack windows, good place to eat; *Mercurio*, Fagnano 595, T 223430, A with breakfast, bath, TV and phone, good restaurant and service, rec.; *Cóndor de Plata*, Av. Colón 556 (T 227987/224301), A, very good; *Hostal de la Patagonia*, O'Higgins 478, T 223521,

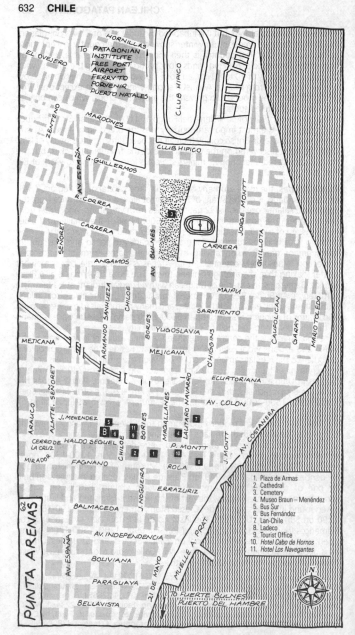

1. Plaza de Armas
2. Cathedral
3. Cemetery
4. Museo Braun – Menéndez
5. Bus Sur
6. Bus Fernández
7. Lan-Chile
8. Ladeco
9. Tourist Office
10. Hotel Cabo de Hornos
11. Hotel Los Navegantes

B with bath, excellent; *Turismo Plaza*, José Nogueira 1116 2nd floor, T 221300, C (cheaper without bath), pleasant; better value is *Residencial París*, J. Nogueira 1116, T 223112, 4th floor, C, rec., heating, though some rooms are without windows. *Monte Carlo*, Av. Colón 605, T 223448, D with bath, E without, with breakfast, clean, rec.; *Ritz*, Pedro Montt 1102, T 224422, D, fine; *Residencial Villegas*, Boliviana 238, E with meals, dirty; *Residencial Central*, Balmaceda 545, C with breakfast; *Chalet Capital*, Armando Sanhuesa 974 (Casilla 213, Mirtha Mansilla Giner), D, good, comfortable, welcoming; *Residencial Roca*, Calle Roca 1038, T 223803, E, no locks on doors, clean; unnamed *residencial* at Armando Sanheuso 933, E, good value, clean; *Casa Deportista*, O'Higgins y Errazúriz, T 222587, E p.p. with breakfast, cheap meals, cooking facilities, several bunks to a room, noisy; *Residencial Internacional*, Arauco 1514 (esq. Boliviana, T 223677), F p.p., highly rec., hot water, large meals, use of kitchen, popular. Private house, Sra. Carolina Ramírez, at Paraguaya 150, E, nice and friendly, breakfast included, safe motorcycle parking, meals; Sra. Lenka, José Miguel Carrera 1270, F with breakfast, heating, clean, use of kitchen, rec.; Nena's, Boliviana 366, friendly, E with breakfast, highly rec. but won't take everyone; Mireya Cárdenas, Boliviana 375, E with breakfast, use of kitchen, good meals, rec.; also Boliviana 238, rec., E, a bit noisy; Boliviana 533, F p.p., with breakfast. Youth hostel-style accommodation at Calle Bella Vista 577, F p.p., kitchen, hot showers, clean; Sra. Inés Ojeda de Alvorado, Av. España 1291 y Balmaceda, E, heaters, shared bath with hot water, pleasant. In summer accommodation may be available at a private school at Lautaro Navarro 842, T 223467, E, clean, safe, cooking facilities, garden, rec. Accommodation available in many private houses, usually F p.p.,—ask at tourist office. **Camping** in Reserva Forestal Magallanes, 8 km. from Punta Arenas (check with Tourist Office for directions).

**Restaurants** Main hotels. *El Mercado*, Mejicana 617, T 227415, open 24 hrs., reasonably-priced lunch, expensive dinner; *Club de la Unión*, Plaza Muñoz Gamero 716, accepts non-members for meals, and is reported to be very good. *Centro Español*, Plaza Muñoz Gamero 771, above Teatro Cervantes, very good food, good prices; *Garage*, Pedro Montt 988, good decor but expensive. Seafood at *Sotitos*, O'Higgins 1138, good service and cuisine, expensive; also good on O'Higgins, *El Fogón* (parrillada) and *Beagle*, good value. *Lucerna*, Bories 624, T 222792, local food, reasonably priced, good; *Dino's Pizza*, Bories, cheap, good, big pizzas; *Café Garogha*, Bories 817, open Sun. p.m., pleasant but busy at night. *Asturias*, Navarro 967, T 223763, good food and atmosphere; *La Cabaña del Cangrejo*, Menéndez 608, great seafood; *Golden Dragon*, Colón 529, good Chinese, inexpensive; *Café Monaco*, Bories y Menéndez, cheap snacks and drinks. Cheap fish meals available at stalls near the fishing cooperative near the docks. The bakeries on Calle O'Higgins are well worth a visit, with excellent rye bread sold on Mons. and Thurs. Try Polar beer. Lobster has become more expensive because of a law banning fishing them with nets, allowing only lobster pots.

**Shopping** For leather goods and sheepskin try Balmaceda 459 or the Zona Franca. Camera film is cheaper in the Zona Franca. Good warm second-hand clothing at *Doberti*, Zona Franca, Local 237. *Fénix Libros*, Lautaro Navarro 1125, good selection of books on regional history.

**Sport** 9-hole golf course 5 km. from town on road to Fuerte Bulnes.

**Car Hire** Hertz, Lautaro Navarro 1064, T 222013; **Avis**, nearby on same street. **Autómovil Club**, O'Higgins 931, T 221888, **Budget** is opposite; **Avips**, Mejicana 730, US$40 for 1 day, with 250 km., tax extra; Turismo Pehoé, 21 de Mayo 1464, T 224223/224506; **Turismo Cabo de Hornos**, Plaza Muñoz Gamero 1039, T 222599.

**Exchange** National banks. Open 0900 to 1400 but closed on Sat.; but the **Casa de Cambio Andino**, Roca 886, Office 25 is open until 1900 on Fri. **Fincard** (Mastercard and Visa), Pedro Montt between 21 de Mayo and Navarro. Argentine australes can be bought at *casas de cambio*. Good rates at **Cambio Gasic**, Lautaro Navarro 549, T 222396, **La Hermandad**, same street No. 1099, T 223991, **Cambio Taurus**, 21 de Mayo 1502, and at **Bus Sur** office on Menéndez 565, T 224864 and Lautaro Navarro 1001, T 225656 (accepts travellers' cheques). **Kiosco Redondito**, Mejicano 613, T 227369. If banks and *cambios* are closed, exchange is available at *Hotel Los Navegantes*, José Menéndez 647, or *Hotel Cabo de Hornos* (worse rates than *cambio* in same building).

**Consulates British Vice-Consul** Mr Roderick Matheson, Sarmiento 780, Casilla 327, helpful and friendly. **Argentine Consulate** Av. 21 de Mayo 1878, open 1000-1400. Visas take 24 hrs., US$15. **German**, Independencia 865 (T 223781), **Danish**, Bories 911 (T 221850), **Dutch**, 21 de Mayo 1243 (T 224275), **Swedish**, Errazúriz 891 (T 224107), **French**, Colón 399 (T 224482), Italian, Balmaceda 357 (T 223518), **Norwegian**, Mejicana 916 (T

222156).

**British School** founded 1904, co-educational.

**Laundry** *Lavasol*, self-service, O'Higgins 969, Mon.-Fri. 0900-2200, weekend 1000-2000, US$3.35 per machine, wash and dry; *Lavaseco Josseau*, Pinto 766.

**Dentist** Dr. Hugo Vera Carcamo, España 1518, T 227510, rec.

**Post Office** Carlos Bories y J.Menéndez, open 0830-1230, 1400-1830 (Mon.-Fri.), 0830-1230 (Sat.), closed on Sundays.

**Telex** Bories 911. Fax and Telex, VTR, Bories 801, T 225600. **Telephones** Nogueira 1116, Plaza de Armas, 0800-2200, international and local, and Lautaro Navarro between Pedro Montt and J. Menéndez, both open Mon.-Fri. 0830-2200 and 0900-2200 weekends. For international calls at any hour *Hotel Cabo de Hornos*, credit cards accepted, open to non-residents.

**Tourist Office** Sernatur, Waldo Seguel 689, Casilla 106-D, T 224435, at the corner with Plaza Muñoz Gamero, 0830-1230, 1430-1830. Helpful, English spoken. Kiosk on Colón between Bories and Magallanes (ask for Juanita Cofré, who has room to let at Boliviana 533, F with breakfast, and is helpful on travel on supply boats and planes to Antarctica). Turistel Guide available from kiosk belonging to *Café Garogha* at Bories 831. **Conaf**, J.Menédez, between Montt and Quilota.

**Travel Agents** *Skartour* and *Cabo de Hornos Tur*, Plaza Muñoz Gamero 1013 and 1039. *Ventistur* in lobby of *Hotel Las Navegantes*, T 223795, competent, run by Sr. Ernesto Fernández de Cabo, helpful and excellent for arranging tours to Patagonia. *Turismo Aventour*, J. Nogueira 1255, T 224926, English spoken, helpful, organizes trips from Punta Arenas to Puerto Williams by plane, with 2-3 days visiting glaciers around Tierra del Fuego by boat (US$500-600). *Austral Adventure Services* (Lautaro Navarro 975, T 228159, Telex 380090 AASPA CK) arranges tours and adventure expeditions in the region (they also provide information on boat trips to glaciers and the southern Patagonian icecaps). And others.

**Shipping** Navimag, office at Independencia 840, T 226600 and 222593, Telex 380060-NAVIN CK; see under Puerto Montt about cancellation of Puerto Montt—Punta Arenas, or Puerto Natales service. Government supply ships are recommended for the young and hardy, but take sleeping bag and extra food, and travel pills. Empremar's *El Navarino* to Puerto Edén, Chacabuco and Valparaíso sometimes sells passenger tickets. Ask at Tourist Office for details or enquire at Empresa Marítima del Estado (Empremar), Lautaro Navarro 1338, T 223015/225238. For transport on navy supply ships to Puerto Williams, enquire at Tercera Zona Naval, Calle Lautaro Navarro 1150, or ask the captain direct. All tickets on ships must be booked in advance Jan.-Feb..

**Ferries** Regular services between Punta Arenas and Puerto Porvenir (Tierra del Fuego) in *Melinka*, leaving Tres Puentes (5 km. from Punta Arenas) at 0900 Wed. Fri. Sat. (1000 Sun.), depending on tides, US$4 p.p., US$2 per bike, US$25 per vehicle. Reservations essential especially in summer, obtainable from Agencia Broom, Roca 924. Timetable subject to change: check in advance. It returns from Porvenir (Sampaio 302) same day at 1400 (1700 Sun.) 2¾ hrs. each way. Bus to ferry at either end is US$0.25, take "Tres Puentes" bus to within 250 m. of ferry at Punta Arenas, or take colectivo No. 14 or 15 (US$1.50) all the way.

**Air Services** LanChile and Ladeco run daily flights to **Puerto Montt**, US$141 (sit on right for views) and **Santiago** (night flight at 0330, bus from office at 0200, flight costs US$100). LanChile, Lautaro Navarro 999, T 227079; Ladeco, Roca 924/Lautaro Navarro 1061, T224927/226100. Aerovías DAP, Carrero Pinto 1022, T 223958, fly to **Porvenir** daily (US$15), and to **Puerto Williams** Wed. and Sat. (US$60 single), plus other irregular flights, with a Twin-Otter aircraft. (Heavily booked so make sure you have your return reservation confirmed.) Aerovías DAP fly from Punta Arenas to **Port Stanley** on the Falkland Islands/Islas Malvinas if demand is sufficient. Military (FACh) flights approx. twice a month to Puerto Montt; information and tickets from airforce base at the airport, T 213559; need to book well in advance. Reserve passages in advance in January and February. Bus from airport, US$1.50; colectivos run from Colón y Magallanes. LanChile, DAP and Ladeco have their own bus services from town. The airport restaurant is good.

**Bus Service** To **Río Gallegos**, daily, 4 companies (at least 2 a day except 1 on Sun. and Mon.—e.g. El Pingüino, Lautaro Navarro 549, T 222396/228448 (one bus daily), and Viajes Vera, 21 de Mayo y Boliviana (Thurs. 0900, Sun. 1000), English spoken, helpful, book in advance. All leave before 1300, US$15, officially 5 hrs., but can take up to 8, depending on customs, 15 mins. on Chilean side, up to 3 hrs. on Argentine side, including ½ hr. lunch at km. 160. All customs formalities now undertaken at the border, but ask before departure if this has changed. To **Río Grande**, Hector Pacheco at Lautaro Navarro y Mejicana, Mon. and Thur. 0700 via Punta Delgada, return Tues. and Fri. 0700, 12 hrs., US$25, heavily booked. Apparently a Punta Arenas—**Ushuaia** bus service began in Jan. 1991, weekly on Sun. **Puerto Natales**, 4 hrs. 0900, 1800 with Fernández, Chiloé 930 (rec., coffee served, Victoria Sur, Colón 798) and Buses Sur, José Menéndez 565, twice a day, US$6.20. Several companies run a service through Argentina to **Puerto Montt** and **Santiago** (most do not run in winter): including Bus Norte, Ghisoni, Fernández, Turibus, Bus Sur. Fare to Puerto Montt US$46-55, to Santiago US$65. Trans Chiloé, Bus Sur, and others also run to **Castro**, Chiloé via Puerto Montt.

**Skiing** Cerro Mirador, only 9 km. west from Punta Arenas, one of the few places in the world where one can ski with a sea view. Transtur buses 0900 and 1400 from in front of *Hotel Cabo de Hornos*, US$3, return. Daily lift-ticket, US$4.50; equipment rental, US$6 per adult. Mid-way lodge with food, drink and equipment. Season June to September/ November, weather depending. Contact the Club Andino (on the hill, not far from Las Minas Reserve) about crosscountry skiing facilities. Also skiing at Tres Morros.

**Excursions** Within easy reach are Puerto Hambre and Fuerte Bulnes, a reconstructed, old fort, a 56-km. trip (see below for tours). At Río Penitente is Morro Negro, a large rock outcrop. The trip can be done in a day. 7½ km. west of town is the **Reserva Forestal Magallanes** (follow Independencia right through town and up the hill). In the reserve is the Mirador de la Garganta del Río Las Minas, with views over Punta Arenas and Tierra del Fuego. There is a botanical trail (US$0.30); there are sandcliffs which one can descend with care to the Río Las Minas valley (good camping facilities), but beware of boggy ground, and thence back to Punta Arenas. Another reserve on the Brunswick Peninsula is **Laguna Parrillar**, 53 km. from Punta Arenas, protecting the lake and the vegetation around it (no public transport, open Oct.-April). A small penguin colony at Otway Sound, 60 km. N of Punta Arenas, can be visited; the attentions of some tourists, chasing the birds or trampling over the hatcheries, have led to a decline in the number of penguins (in windy weather the birds go underground so there is nothing to see).

The most interesting excursions are to the Ultima Esperanza region (see below under Puerto Natales) and so to the Torres del Paine National Park. Ventistur offer excursions from Fri. night to Sat. night; Turismo Pehoé, 21 de Mayo 1464, goes to Paine for US$200; Cabo de Hornos Tur organize tours with station wagons. Sr. Mateo Quesada, Chiloé 1375, T 222662, offers local tours in his car, up to 4 passengers.

The fjords and glaciers of Tierra del Fuego (70 km. by schooner) are exceptionally beautiful. Once a fortnight there is a 22-hr. 320-km. round trip to the fjord d'Agostino, 30 km. long, where many glaciers come down to the sea. A three-day tour to Puerto Natales, the glacier, Balmaceda and Torres del Paine can be arranged from Punta Arenas with meals and accommodation included. Empresa Buses Fernández, Calle Chiloé 930, runs this excursion and also afternoon excursions to Club Andino and the Fuerte Bulnes (US$15), and to the penguin hatchery on Otway Sound (US$15). They also run a 3-day, Puerto Natales/Cueva Milodón/Paine trip for US$110 with food and lodging (at *Hotel Eberhard*, Puerto Natales); the trip is quite flexible and variations in itinerary or duration can be accommodated. *Peña Trovador*, Pedro Montt 919, runs tours to Fuerte Bulnes (Tues. Thur. Sat. Sun. at 1430, US$3), and to the penguin colonies at Otway Sound (Mon. Wed. Fri. at 1430, US$4). Turismo Balmar, Magallanes 619 and Aiketour, Menéndez 750, Oficina 6 (T 226916), also go to the penguin colonies. Taxis to Fuerte Bulnes or Otway Sound, US$30 for 4 people.

***Antarctica*** Punta Arenas has become the number one starting point for visits to Antarctica. The following possibilities exist: Turismo Cabo de Hornos, Plaza Muñoz Gamero (Casilla 62-D), Punta Arenas, T 222599, Telex 280342 HORNO CL, now offers in March and October six-day packages, which include three nights accommodation at the *Hotel Estrella Polar* at the Teniente Rodolfo Marsh base on King George Island in the South Shetlands. Air transport is by Chilean Air Force (FACh) C-130 Hercules aircraft. Cost US$2,500. Lindblad Travel, P.O. Box 912, Westport CT 06881, USA, T (203) 226-8531, has made cruises to Antarctica with the luxury chartered Chinese ship m/v *Yao Hua* of 10,151 grt. Fare range US$2,490-15,325 for land/cruise arrangement. Telex 643443 LIND UR.

Society Expeditions Cruises, 723 Broadway East, Seattle WA 98102, T (206) 324-9400, (800) 426-7794, Telex (910) 444-1381, using the luxury small cruise ships *World Discoverer* of 3,153 grt and *Society Explorer* of 2,367 grt (formerly *Lindblad Explorer*), have made cruises to Antarctica, fare range US$4,750-17,775. In addition, the *World Discoverer* has made an Antarctica Circumnavigation from Ushuaia, Argentina to Wellington, New Zealand. Fare range US$8,900-23,900.

Adventure Network International, 200-1676 Duranleau St., Vancouver, BC, Canada V6H 3S5, T (604) 683-8033, Telex 0636-700-749 MBX CA leads climbing and skiing expeditions to Antartica. Local contacts: Calle Jorge Montt 747, T 225370, Punta Arenas, may be able to secure a seat on a flight for US$600, return same day; Hugh MacLeay, Casilla 0124, Punta Arenas, T 212566, Telex 380076 LANAS CK; Javier Lopetegui, Portales 780, San Bernardo, Santiago, T 028593081. *Hotel Cabo de Hornos* arranges trips to Antarctica in October. Depending on the number of travellers, the price ranges from US$800 to US$2,200 for a 2-day visit.

In 1991, South Pacific Expeditions (address unknown) began tourist cruises to the Antarctic region aboard the naval vessel *Aquiles*, US$1000 for 12 days, US$500 p.p. group rates, lectures may be by scientists. These budget cruises sell out quickly, but are much better than those on the other naval ships such as *Yelcho*, or *Janqueo*, which charge US$80 per day with food, cramped accommodation, often long walks across icy decks to the toilet, etc., trip lasts 20 days. The only way to secure passage on these ships is to ask at the port; the navy will deny all knowledge of taking passengers.

Note that any voyage by sea to Antarctica will involve 2 days crossing the Magellan Straits and Drake Passage before you see anything (then 2 days returning). When you arrive, good weather cannot be guaranteed; storms may keep you in a sheltered harbour, fog obliterates the views, and it snows. Be prepared for this and for seasickness, take warm gear, waterproof outerwear and boots and, when the weather is fine and you go ashore, respect the environment. (We are grateful to Dana Denniston, Lexington, KY, for much of this information.) Anybody booking any of these tours through an agency should check precisely what is offered and what may be omitted if the weather is bad. Reports vary on facilities.

**Puerto Natales** (17,000 people) is 247 km. N of Punta Arenas and close to the Argentine border at Río Turbio. It stands on the Ultima Esperanza gulf amid spectacular scenery, and is the jumping-off place for the magnificent Balmaceda and Paine national parks.

**Hotels** *Eberhard*, Pedro Montt 25, T 411208, A, excellent views, good; *Juan Ladrilleros*, Pedro Montt 161, modern, A with bath and breakfast, good restaurant, clean, T 411652; *Natalino*, Eberhard 371, T 411968, clean and very friendly, C, breakfast included (tours to Milodón Cave arranged); *Palace*, Ladrilleros 105, T 411134, A, good food; *Austral*, Valdivia 955, T 411593, clean, friendly, good food, run by Eduardo Scott, E, without bath, D with bath and breakfast, hot water. *Residencial Temuco*, Ramírez 202, T 411120, friendly, reasonable, good food, F p.p.; opp., next to *zapatería* at Bulnes 810, is Elba Edita Solo Pérez, T 411026, E p.p., breakfast US$0.50, homemade bread and jam, clean, hot water, laundry, use of kitchen, will store luggage; *Residencial La Busca*, Valdivia 845 (no sign outside), E, run down, cheap food available; *Res. Termas de Puyehue*, O'Higgins 484, E including breakfast, clean, use of kitchen, laundry facilities, highly rec.; *Pensión Magallanes* on Calle Magallanes (no sign), F p.p., hot water, many mountaineering parties stay here, the owner's son runs day excursions to Lake Grey. *Residencial Grey*, Bulnes 90, T 411542, E incl. breakfast, hot water, some rooms with heating, very friendly, clean, good but expensive dinners; *Residencial Bulnes*, Calle Bulnes 407, T 411307 (no sign), beside police station, good, E p.p., stores luggage; *Casa de Familia Dickson*, Bulnes 307, T 411218, F p.p., good breakfast, other meals available to order, rec.; *Casa de familia*, Bulnes 317, T 411061, F p.p., clean, good breakfast, helpful, rec.; *Garahue*, Bulnes 370, E, breakfast and hot water, nice; *Casa de familia Elsa Millán*, Philippi 405, F p.p., breakfast US$1, homemade bread, hot water, warm, friendly, cooking facilities, rec.; similar at O'Higgins 70, 431 and 484 (rec.), at Baras Arana 155, and Perito 443; *Casa de familia* at Galvarino 846, F p.p. with breakfast, rec.; Sra. Nelly, Uvaldo Segero (opp. hospital), F p.p., friendly, clean, use of kitchen; *Pensión Ritz*, Carrera Pinto 443, F p.p. with breakfast, E p.p. full pension, friendly; private house at Magallanes 1, F p.p. with breakfast, friendly, cheap meals; Sra Bruna Mardones, Pasaje Don Basco 41 (off Philippi), E with breakfast, clean, friendly, meals on request; Ana y Ernesto, Baras Arana 175, small and cosy. Sra Elsa, Philippi 427, F with breakfast, repeatedly rec.; Sra. Teresa Ruiz, Esmeraldas 463, E with breakfast, good value, cheap meals extra, quiet, friendly, rec.

Hotels in the countryside and around include: *Hostería Llanura de Diana*, Km. 220 Road 9 Sector Río Tranquilo, T 222350, on road to Punta Arenas (hidden from the road), A, highly rec.; *Posada de Cisne de Cuello Negro,* a former guest house for meat buyers at the *frigorífico,* A, friendly, clean, reasonable, all rooms with bath, excellent cooking, 5 km. from Puerto Natales at Km. 257 Road 9 Sector Puerto Bories; *Patagonia Inn,* A, Km. 257 Road 9 Sector Dos Lagunas, T 222599, 23 km. from Puerto Natales, open only from November to March; *Hostería El Pionero,* Cerro Castillo, Km. 315 Ruta 9, B with basin but not bath, country house ambience.

**Restaurants** *Nikol's,* Barros Arana 160, seafood and salmon very good; *Socorro* is also rec. for seafood, reasonably priced, as is *Don Alvarito,* Blanco Encalada 915; *El Marítimo,* Pedro Montt 214, good seafood and salmon, good views; *Mari Loli,* Baquedano 615, excellent food, good value, vegetarian dishes. *La Ultima Esperanza,* Eberhard 354, rec. for salmon, seafood; *La Costanera,* Bories y Ladrilleros, good food, superb views; *Café La Tranquera,* Bulnes 579, good coffee, meals, snacks. *Melissa,* Encalada, good crêpes and cakes; *Centro Español,* Magallanes 247, reasonable restaurant. *Club de Pesca y Caza Río Serrano,* Eberhard 261, excellent food, take away lunches, moderate prices; cheap meals at *Club Deportivo Natales,* Eberhard 332.

**Car Hire** Andes Patagónicos, Blanco Encalada 226, US$85 per day inc. insurance and 350 km. free; others US$80 a day, or US$85 with driver. Best to have international driving licence here; national licence may restrict insurance cover. Hire agents can arrange permission to drive into Argentina (cheaper than renting a car in Argentina).

**Fishing** Tackle for hire at Andes Patagónicos, Blanco Encalada 226, T 411594, US$3.50/day for rod, reel and spinners; if you prefer fishing with floats, hooks, split shot, etc., take your own. Other companies up to 5 times as expensive (but see **Camping** under Torres del Paine).

**Exchange** Travellers' cheques can be changed only into pesos, at 1% commission. *Casas de cambio* on Blanco Encalada 226 (Andes Patagónicos) and 266 where australes can be changed. Cambio Stop, Baquedano 380, good for cash (also arranges tours). Another two at Bulnes 683 and 1087 (good rates); others on Prat.

**Museum** Museo De Agostini, Tierra del Fuego fauna.

**Laundry** at *Tienda Milodón,* on Bulnes.

**Telephones** Blanco Encalada y Bernardo Philippi.

**Travel Agents** *Turismo Paine,* Calle Eberhard. *Urbina Tours,* Eberhard 554, T 411965, Telex 298200 CL (contact either here or at Tourist Office in Punta Arenas, tours to Paine National Park, Milodón Cave, etc. in 11-seater Toyota; also tours tailored to individual requirements (2 weeks notice required). *Lago Grey,* Bulnes 622, not very helpful. *Adventur,* Eberhard y Montt, reported not very reliable.

**Tourist Office** in kiosk on waterfront, Av. Pedro Montt y Phillipi, helpful; maps for US$1 from Eberhard 547, reasonable, closed on Sun. **Conaf,** Encalada, between O'Higgins and Chorillos.

**Buses** to Punta Arenas, 6 times daily, 4 hrs. US$6.20. Bus Fernández, Eberhard 555 (0900 and 1830), Bus Sur, Baquedano 224 (booking office—buses depart from Turismo Urbina, Eberhard 554, T 411965) and Victoria Sur also on Baquedano. Book in advance. To **Coyhaique** via Calafate, Urbina Tours, 4 days, US$120 (Nov.-March).

To **Argentina**: Thrice weekly to Río Gallegos (Argentina): Alvaro Gómez, Baquedano 244, Wed. and Fri. 0730, Sun. 1030, met at border by San Caferino bus, US$10.70; hourly to Río Turbio (Argentina), US$1.50, 2 hrs. (depending on Customs—change bus at border). 1000 bus to Río Turbio arrives in time for 1300 El Pingüino bus to Río Gallegos. To **Calafate,** in summer Bus Sur goes Mon.-Thurs. at 0830 for US$36, 7 hrs.; Luís Díaz, Patricio Lynch 170, T 411050, US$20 (trips also to Torres del Paine, Punta Arenas, camping equipment for hire); Empresa Gómez runs a minibus direct to Calafate, Argentina, for US$36, Mon., Wed. and Fri. (Nov.-March). Several other companies run minibuses to Calafate for about US$25 p.p.: Scott Turs, at *Hotel Austral* (no schedule); Urbina Tours, Mon. and Fri. in summer; Adventur, summer only; Turismo Lago Grey, Mon. and Fri. in summer, US$28, including 2 hours at the Moreno Glacier. The cheapest route is to take El Pingüino bus from Río Turbio to La Esperanza and wait there (no more than an hour) for a Río Gallegos bus to Calafate, US$14.

If driving, note that there is no petrol between Puerto Natales and Calafate.

**Shipping** (See page 614 on services from Puerto Montt). Navimag office: Independencia 840 Punta Arenas, T 222593, 226600, Telex 380060 NAVIN CK, and Pedro Montt 380, Terminal Marítimo, T 411287/411642, Puerto Natales (direct telex with Punta Arenas office, which is better).

**Excursions** A recommended walk is up to Cerro Dorotea which dominates the town, with superb views of the whole Ultima Esperanza Sound. Take Río Turbio bus and alight at jeep track for summit. 25 km. NW of Puerto Natales the **Monumento Natural Cueva Milodón** can be visited. It now contains a plastic model of the prehistoric ground-sloth whose bones were found there in 1895. (Free camping once entrance fee has been paid.) Fernández bus is cheapest, going on Fri. and returning Sun., mid-Nov. to mid-March only; at other times, take a taxi (US$15 return). Both Adventur and Fernández tour buses to Torres del Paine stop at the cave. A cutter, the *21 de Mayo*, sails from the pier to **Balmaceda National Park** 2-3 times a week, if enough passengers book, US$25, expensive lunch extra, US$6 (all travel agents handle the trip). *21 de Mayo* is operated by Juan C. Alvarez, Ladrilleros 171, T 411-176; max 50 passengers. The boat has life jackets and modern communications and navigation equipment. A ketch, the *Compass Rose*, also sails to Balmaceda Glacier and may hoist sails on the return if the wind is suitable. A long trip to view glaciers and the rugged mountains at the S end of the Patagonian ice cap. The Balmaceda Glacier hangs almost 100 metres up a cliff, its meltwaters forming waterfalls into the sea; the boats tie up at a small jetty nearby and a 10-minute walk leads to the Sarmiento Glacier which enters a small lake, partially covered by blocks of floating ice from the glacier. On the trip one may see dolphins, sea-lions (in season), black-neck swans, and the quaint steamer ducks.

145 km. NW of Puerto Natales is the ***Torres del Paine*** National Park, covering 1,630 sq. km., a "must" for its wildlife and spectacular scenery. Along the (gravel) road it is common to spot the Andean condor and herds of *guanaco*. The Torres and Cuernos del Paine are oddly shaped peaks, surrounded by glaciers, which fall straight down to the valleys, now covered with beautiful lakes at 50 to 200 metres above sea level. The glaciers Grey, Dickson and Zapata are three of the main ones branching off the huge mass forming the Patagonian icecap.

There are about 250 km. of well marked hiking trails and nine National Park shelters; take food, a tent, sleeping bag, sleeping mat and cooking gear. Allow a week to ten days to see the park properly. The area is very popular in summer and the *refugios* often crowded, and in poor condition.

The park is administered by the forestry department (Conaf) with a centre at the southern tip of Lake Pehoé and seven guardhouses located throughout the park. There the friendly wardens (*guardaparques*) give advice and one should register with them before setting out for a hike.

The scenery in the Park is superb. Walking along the trails one is constantly rewarded by changing views of fantastic peaks, ice-fields, vividly coloured lakes of turquoise, ultramarine and grey and quiet green valleys. Wild life abounds: one can expect to see *guanaco*, hares, foxes, condors, black-neck swans and many other birds. Apparently the park has a micro-climate especially favourable to plants and wild life. The Park is open all year round, although snow may prevent access in the winter: best time is December-March.

The most popular hike starts from either the administration building at the south end of Lake Pehoé or the Park entrance, and takes seven days going from *refugio* to *refugio* past the spectacular Grey Glacier and round the back of the Cuernos and Torres del Paine. It is arduous, the longest lap being 30 km., but not too steep; the chief hazard is the wind. Footbridges are occasionally washed away, but in Feb. 1991 all were in place on the circular route; Operation Raleigh rebuilt many sections in 1990.) To walk from the administration just to Grey Glacier takes at least 4½ hours to the *refugio* at the N end of Lake Pehoé (no firewood nearby), then a further 6-10 hours to Grey Glacier (where there is a *refugio*) and back. Ask at the park administration about a boat trip to Laguna Grey glacier, at least 8 people required, US$14 inc. sandwiches, cake, coffee and pisco, a stunning trip.

Another recommended walk is to Ventisquero (glacier) del Francés, 2 hrs. from Pehoé to the Río Francés, 5 hrs. on to Campamento Británico (the path is hard to find, and involves crossing the hazardous Río Francés at the snout of the glacier). Also recommended is the walk to Lake Pingo (plenty of wildlife, icebergs in the lake), with *refugios* half way and at the Lake.

The walk to the Torres Base is recommended: from the Park entrance it is 2 hrs. to the *refugio* and campsite at Laguna Amarga, then 1½ hrs. to an *estancia* where you can camp.

From here it's 3½ hrs. to the lake, a well-marked path, but the last ½ hr. is up the morraine; it's well worth humping camping gear up and spending the night.

Descriptions of several walks in the Torres del Paine area are found in *Backpacking in Chile and Argentina* (Bradt Publications).

*Refugios* are free (except for Refugio Lago Toro, see below), but an entrance fee to the Park (US$5) is charged. Most of the *refugios* have cooking areas, so take your own food (beware of mice!) as it is expensive to buy and limited in the Park. The areas around the *refugios* are becoming badly littered: please take your rubbish away. In most cases a tent is preferable to the *refugios* and is essential if doing a complete circuit. Also essential are protective clothing against wind and rain and strong footwear. Maps (US$2), are obtainable at Conaf offices in Punta Arenas or Puerto Natales and at the Park administration centre, the latest map, Feb. 1991, has been recommended as accurate. Maps can also be bought from *Hotel Austral*, Puerto Natales, or try at the tourist kiosk (not Sernatur) in Punta Arenas. The Visitor Information Centre, an old *estancia*, has a good slide show on Sat. and Sun. at 1900; guards will store luggage and arrange transport back to Puerto Natales. Wardens know how many people are on each route so you can find out which *refugios* are likely to be full. Horses may be rented from Brigitta Buhofer (nr. *Posada Río Serano*) for US$18, 6 hrs. with guide; horses for beginners and experienced riders available.

**Accommodation** *Posada Río Serrano*, B, some rooms with bath, some with shared facilities, breakfast extra ½ km. from park administration, with expensive restaurant and a shop. (Reservations advisable: Serco Ltda., Casilla 19-D, Punta Arenas, T 223395). *Hostería Pehoé*, A, 60 rooms, private facilities, 5 km. S of Pehoé guardhouse, 11 km. W of park administration, on an island with spectacular view across the Lake to Paine Grande and Cuernos del Paine, runs a boat up to Grey Glacier (but you may have to arrange your own transport to the boat from the hotel), good meals, welcoming. (Reservations: Turismo Pehoé, 21 de Mayo 1464, T 224223 in Punta Arenas or Nataniel 31, office 68, T 718709, Telex 240875 PEHOE CL in Santiago). *Refugio Lago Toro*, near administration centre, US$3 p.p., sleeping bag essential, cooking facilities, in good condition, good meeting place (open summer only).

**Camping** Pehoé (32 lots, hot shower US$4.65 p.p.) and Camping Río Serrano (25 lots) are operated by Serco Ltda., Camping Laguna Azul (10 lots) and Laguna Amarga (15 lots) by Conaf (all except Pehoé US$3.50). Camping and lighting fires are permitted outside official campsites (e.g. at Lago Grey), but only where indicated by park wardens. You can camp outside *refugios*, but firewood is hard to find in their vicinity. Equipment hire in Puerto Natales from travel agencies and others, e.g. Luis Díaz, Patricio Lynch 101, T 411050, *Cambio Stop* on Baquedano, *Andes Patagónicos*, Blanco Encalada 226 (check tents are waterproofed from this agency). Average charges, per day: tent US$3-5, sleeping bag US$3-5, mat US$1.50, raincoat US$0.60, also cooking gear. Paraffin is available at Galvarino 745, Puerto Natales, but not in hardware stores.

**Transport** Bus Sur (address above) runs a daily service to Paine National Park between December and March (till Easter Sunday, depart 0630-0830 Sun.—returns 1100, US$6), 3½ hrs. dusty. Out of season they go twice weekly if there are 5 or more passengers (US$13.50). The bus is often full, but some seats are reserved for passengers from 28 de Noviembre, so you could hitch there. Urbina Tours and Adventur (addresses above) also run buses to the park most days between December and March, depending on demand, US$7-10. **N.B.** All these services are liable to be suspended without notice. It is a good idea to organize your return date in advance to coincide with other returning groups to keep return costs down.

To go from Torres del Paine to Calafate (Argentina) either return to Pto. Natales and go to Río Turbio for bus to La Esperanza, or hitch from the park to Cerro Castillo (106 km. S of the administration), the Chilean border point, cross to Paso Cancha de Carreras (Argentina) and try to link with the Río Turbio-La Esperanza-Río Gallegos bus schedule, or hitch. (Note that it is easier to visit this region on a circuit Ushuaia-Torres del Paine-Calafate than vice versa.)

**Tours** For all-in trips from Punta Arenas **see page 635**. Eduardo Scott, who speaks English and is very knowledgeable, can be contacted at his hotel, *Austral*, Valdivia 955, Puerto Natales (T 411593), he organizes tours of the Park in a 6-seater bus (about US$60 per day—increasingly mixed reports). Also José Torres of Sastrería Arbiter in Calle Bulnes 731 (T 411637). Enap weekend tours in summer cost US$45 including accommodation and meals. Taxi costs US$80 per day, run by Sergio Zaley (Arturo Prat 260), but may be cheaper if you catch him when he's going to the Park anyway. A minibus can be hired for about US$50 at

Puerto Natales, to take a party of up to 8 to a *refugio* in the Paine National Park. After mid-March there is no public transport and trucks are irregular.

Hiring a pick-up from Budget in Punta Arenas is an economical proposition for a group (up to 9 people): US$415 for 4 days. If driving yourself there, the first 61 km. from Pto. Natales to Cerro Castillo is poor with too much gravel, the next 60 km. to the entrance better, then in the Park, the roads are narrow, bendy with blind corners, use your horn a lot; it takes about 3½ hrs. from Pto. Natales to the administration. Petrol may not be available in the park.

***Tierra del Fuego*** is the island off the extreme south of South America. It is surrounded by the Magellan Strait to the north, the Atlantic Ocean to the east, the Beagle Channel to the south—which separates it from the southern islands—and by the Whiteside, Gabriel, Magdalena and Cockburn channels etc. which divide it from the islands situated to the west. The western side belongs to Chile and the eastern to Argentina. It produces most of Chile's oil.

In Chilean Tierra del Fuego the only town is ***Porvenir***, with a population of 4,500, several hundred from Yugoslavia. There is a small museum, the Fernando Cordero Rusque, Samuel Valdirieso 402, mainly Indian culture.

**Porvenir Hotels** *Los Flamencos*, Teniente Merino, T 580049, best, A; *Rosas*, O'Higgins 296, T 580088, C with bath, hot water, heating, restaurant and bar, rec.; *Residencial Cameron* (ask at bar called *Somos o no Somos*), E, for shared room, "friendly folk", good meals, sleep on dining-room floor for US$1; *Central*, Phillippi 298, T 580077, C, hot water; *España*, Soto Salas 698, E, good restaurant; *Residencial* at Santos Mardones 366, E (D with full board), clean, friendly, heaters in rooms, hot water, good; *Res. Colón*, Damián Riobó 198, T 580108, D p.p.; many good *pensiones*, D, with full board. *Yugoslav Club* does wholesome and reasonable lunch (about US$5), also *Restaurante Puerto Montt* for seafood. Many lobster fishing camps where fishermen will prepare lobster on the spot.

Other hotels on Chilean Tierra del Fuego: *Hostería de la Frontera*, on the Chilean side of the border, at San Sebastián, E in the annex which is 1 km. away from the more expensive main building. At Cerro Sombrero, 46 km. S of Primera Angostura: *Hotel Tuculmen*, E, rec.; *Pensión del Señor Alarcón*, G, good, friendly.

**Exchange** at *Estrella del Sur* shop, Calle Santos Mardones.

**Buses on Tierra del Fuego** Two a week between Porvenir and Río Grande (Argentina), Wed. and Sat. 1400, Transportes Senkovic, Carlos Bories 295, US$12.50 (buy ticket early on the day of travel). Bus from Rio Grande arrives 1300, ferry to Punta Arenas leaves 1400; from terminal to ferry, taxi US$1, bus (if running) US$1, ferry US$2; trip takes 7-8 hrs. depending on border crossing. Beware: taxis are not allowed to cross the border. If you go to the police station and ask for a ride to the border on a truck, you can save the fare to Río Grande. Hitch-hiking elsewhere is difficult as there is so little traffic. Argentine time one hour ahead of Chilean time. N.B. If crossing from Argentina, Chile does not allow entry of fruit, vegetables, dairy produce or meat. All stocks will be confiscated.

Bus from Calle Manuel Señor, Porvenir, Mon. and Fri., 1700, US$10, to Cameron, from where a road runs SE to Estancia Vicuña. Before Vicuña is a scenic fishing-ground; beyond Vicuña a horse trail leads across the Darwin Range to Yendegaia. From there you can either retrace your steps, or cross the unmanned border to Ushuaia (get permission from the Argentine consul in Punta Arenas first).

***Puerto Williams*** is a Chilean naval base on Isla Navarino, S of the Beagle Channel, the most southerly place in the world with a permanent population (about 1,500-1,800. Position 54° 55' 41" South, 67° 37' 58" West). It's a small, friendly, remote place. The island is totally unspoilt and beautiful, with a chain of rugged snowy peaks, magnificent woods and many animals, including beaver. The *Hotel Patagonia*, on the edge of Lauta bay, T 223571, with attractive locally-made furniture and soft furnishings, roaring log fire in lounge, is now owned by the Navy (but run by Ladeco), L in summer, much less in winter, meals US$16 (monthly rates available); 2 km. out of town, splendid walks. Hotel can arrange car trips to the beaver dams, cascades, and other sights (the Ubika Village, 2 km. east of town, the place where the last descendants of the Yamana people live; the local *media luna* where rodeos are held). *Residencial Onashaga* (run by Señor Ortiz—everyone knows him), E plus meals, which are good, pleasant, helpful, full board available; bakery next to *Café Beagle*, E, full board; you can also stay at private houses. Ask where you can eat king crab (*centolla*) pizza. *Restaurant Beagle* on coast, excellent. There is a supermarket. You can camp near the *Hostería*: collect drinking water from the kitchen, bring food from Punta Arenas as it is expensive on the island, but you can buy gasoline for stoves at the *Hostería*. Aeropetrol will charter a plane, if a sufficiently numerous party is raised, to Cape Horn. Near Puerto Williams there is a *centolla* canning factory which is well worth a visit (closed Feb.-March).

**Museum** Excellent **Martín Gusinde** museum in Puerto Williams, full of information about vanished Indian tribes, local wildlife, and voyages including Charles Darwin and Fitzroy of the *Beagle*. Open 1000-1300, 1500-1800 (Tues.-Fri.); 1500-1800 (Sat.-Sun.), Monday closed. Admission free.

**Offices** Post Office, telephone, telex, Aerovías DAP, LanChile, Ladeco in the centre of town (maps available). Tourist Office (closed in winter) near the museum. Ask at the yacht club on the off chance of hitching a ride on a private yacht. Captain Ben Garrett offers adventure sailing in his schooner *Victory*, from special trips to Ushuaia to cruises in the canals (US$1,400 a day charter), Cape Horn, glaciers (US$175 p.p. per day, 6 min.), Antarctica in Dec. and Jan. (US$1,950 per day, 10 passengers). Write to Cruise "Victory" Correo Puerto Williams.

**Transport to Tierra del Fuego** For ferry services from Punta Arenas, **see page 634.** There are two ferries running across the Primera Angostura (First Narrows), 170 km. NE of Punta Arenas, between Punta Delgada (*Hotel El Faro*, E; *Hosteria Tehuelche*, 17 km. from port, D with restaurant) and Punta Espora, schedule varying with the tides. Reservations at the ferry. Price US$1 p.p. and US$12 per car, one way. There is no ferry between Ushuaia and Puerto Williams, but see under Ushuaia (Argentina) for possibilities of boat crossings (e.g. on the *Barracuda*). By air from Punta Arenas—weather and bookings permitting, Aerovías DAP (Ignacio Carrera Pinto 1022, T 223958 Punta Arenas and Oficina Foretic, T 80089, Porvenir) fly twice daily to Porvenir, but not Sat., US$15 to Porvenir, and Wed. and Sat. to Puerto Williams, US$60 single; cheaper are Cabo de Hornos (TACH), Montt 687, T 223335 (Señoret 408, Porvenir), also twice daily to Porvenir, Mon. and Fri. to Puerto Williams. Heavily booked so make sure you have your return reservation confirmed. The flight to Puerto Williams is beautiful, with superb views of Tierra del Fuego, the Cordillera Darwin, the Beagle Channel, and the islands stretching S to Cape Horn. Also army flights available (they are cheaper). Boat Punta Arenas-Puerto Williams: *Ñandú* or Ultragas leaves on a fixed schedule every 10 days, about 2400, arrives 1700 each way, reclining chairs, no food, US$45 one way. Enquire at the office, Independencia 865, next to service station.

---

## INFORMATION FOR VISITORS

**Travel Documents** Passport and tourist card only are required for entry by all foreigners except citizens of France, New Zealand, Mexico, Guyana, Haiti, Suriname, Kuwait, African countries and the Communist countries, who require visas. National identity cards are sufficient for entry by citizens of Argentina, Brazil, Paraguay, and Uruguay. The tourist card is valid for 90 days and is renewable for 90 more; it is available from Chilean consulates, immigration office at the Ollagüe land frontier, as well as at Arica, airline offices and most aircraft bound for Chile; it will be surrendered on departure. If you wish to stay longer than 180 days (as a tourist), it is easier to make a day-trip to Argentina and return with a new tourist card, rather than to apply for a visa, which involves a great deal of paperwork. An onward ticket is officially required but is seldom asked for. On arrival you will be asked where you are staying in Chile. Visa is required for French passport holders, US$5.25; valid for no more than 90 days, strictly one entry only. This can create problems if you wish to travel overland to or from Tierra del Fuego since the Argentine-Chilean border is crossed more than once, requiring multiple entry. A student card is very useful for obtaining discounts on buses, etc. Student cards can be obtained from Providencia 2594, Local 421 and cost US$8, photo required (no questions asked).

All foreigners who wish to work in Chile must obtain visas. Smallpox vaccination and health certificates no longer required.

**Airport Taxes** 3,700 pesos, or US$12.50 for international flights; US$5 for domestic flights. There is a tourist tax on single air fares of 2%, and 1% on return fares beginning or ending in Chile; also a sales tax of 5% on all transport within Chile. **N.B.** Foreigners can only pay for air tickets in US dollars, not Chilean pesos.

**How to get there by Air From Europe**: Air France from Paris (3 per week), Iberia and LanChile from Madrid (2 each), KLM (2), Lufthansa (2), Alitalia (1) and Aeroflot (1), via Luxembourg fly to Santiago. Some flights go via Rio/São Paulo, Montevideo and Buenos Aires; others via New York, Lima and/or other points in northern S. America. Also, Varig, Aerolíneas Argentinas, Viasa and Avianca offer services between Europe and Santiago, with connections via Rio, Buenos Aires, Caracas and Bogotá respectively.

**From North America**: American Airlines fly at least twice a day from Miami, once direct, once via Buenos Aires, and three times a week via Lima (this flight originates in New York). LanChile has 5 flights per week from New York and Miami and 1 non-stop from Miami alone. Also from Miami, Ladeco flies both non-stop and either via Bogotá and Guayaquil or Bogotá and Arica; Pan Am 7 per week. Also from Miami fly Viasa, Ecuatoriana and LAB with connections in Caracas, Guayaquil or La Paz. From Los Angeles there are flights with LanChile and Ecuatoriana (neither non-stop). From other US cities, connect with LanChile flights in Miami, New York or Los Angeles. CP Air have 2 flights per week from Toronto, with which connections are made from Montreal and Vancouver. LanChile flies once or twice a week, depending on season, between Tahiti (making connections from Japan, Australia and New Zealand) and Santiago; they stop over at Easter Island. For excursion fares between Australia/New Zealand and Chile, the stopovers at Easter Island now carry a surcharge of about US$125.

**Within South America**: from Buenos Aires (about 40 per week) by LanChile, Ladeco, Ecuatoriana, Aerolíneas Argentinas, Aeroperú, Avianca, CP Air, Air France, Iberia, KLM, Alitalia, Swissair or Pan Am; from Mendoza by Aerolíneas Argentinas or Ladeco twice a week each. From Montevideo (6 per week) by LanChile, Pluna, KLM; from Asunción (5 times a week) by LAP and Ladeco; from Rio/São Paulo, non-stop by LanChile, Ladeco, Varig, Lufthansa or by several other European airlines via Buenos Aires; from La Paz (3 per week) by Lloyd Aéreo Boliviano (LAB); from Caracas, LanChile, Viasa and Avianca (none non-stop); from Lima (12 per week) by Aeroperú, American Airlines and LanChile; from Bogotá (6 per week) by Avianca and Ladeco; from Ecuador, Ecuatoriana from Quito via Guayaquil, Ladeco non-stop from Guayaquil.

To Arica, from La Paz (8 per week) by LAB and LanChile.

**From Neighbouring Countries** by land. There are railways from La Paz (Bolivia) to Calama for Antofagasta, and to Arica. All passenger services have been suspended on the lines between Chile and Argentina. Roads connect Santiago with Mendoza, and Osorno and Puerto Montt with Bariloche, in Argentina. Less good road connections N and S of Santiago are described in the main text. The roads connecting N Chile with Bolivia are poor.

**Customs** Allowed in free of duty: 500 cigarettes, 100 cigars, 500 grams of tobacco, 3 bottles of liquor, camera, and all articles of personal use. Fruit, vegetables, meat, flowers and milk products may not be imported. It has been reported that bringing a video recorder into Chile involves a great deal of paperwork.

**Internal Air Services** LanChile and the private airline Ladeco both fly between Santiago and Arica, Iquique, Antofagasta, Calama, Copiapó, La Serena, Concepción, Temuco, Los Angeles, Osorno, Puerto Montt, Coyhaique and Punta Arenas. In addition, LanChile flies to El Salvador, and Ladeco to Valdivia and Balmaceda. Try and sit on the left flying S, on the right flying N to get the best views of the Andes. LanChile and Ladeco usually have a bus service from airport to town, check at the desk on arrival.

Small airlines which operate on a regional basis are given in the text.

LanChile offers a 21-day "Visit Chile" ticket; 5 prices: US$250, valid for Santiago and northern Chile, or Santiago and southern Chile; US$450 for all mainland Chile; Pacific 1, US$812, Santiago-Easter Island-Santiago; Pacific 2,

US$1000, valid for a trip to Easter Island and either northern Chile, or southern Chile; Pacific 3, US$1,200 for all mainland Chile and Eastern Island. It must be purchased abroad in conjunction with an international ticket and reservations made well ahead since many flights are fully booked in advance. **N.B.** The ticket cannot be changed, though reservations can, so it is worth including as many destinations as possible. It is also possible for the route Santiago – Antofagasta – Arica – Santiago to take a coupon ticket which allows greater flexibility. Ladeco offers a "matrimonial" ticket with discount to wives travelling with husbands.

**Surface Transport**  Buses are frequent and on the whole good. Apart from holiday times, there is little problem getting a seat on a long-distance bus; most have toilets, serve drinks (sometimes free) and sandwiches. Stops are infrequent. Prices are highest between Dec.-March. Since there is lots of competition between bus companies, fares may be bargained lower. Students generally get discounts.

  **Trains** in Chile are moderately priced, and not so slow as in other Andean countries, but dining car food is expensive. There are no passengers services N of Santiago and S of the capital passengers are only carried as far as Temuco, except Jan.-Feb. when services continue to Puerto Montt. There is a railway information office at O'Higgins 853 (at end of arcade), Santiago, for all lines except the Antofagasta-Bolivia (Ahumada 11, Oficina 602, T 698-5536). English spoken.

  **Shipping** information is given in the text under Santiago and all the relevant southern ports. Local newspapers are useful for all transport schedules.

**Taxis** have meters, but agree beforehand on fare for long journey out of centre or special excursions. A 50% surcharge is applied after 2100 and Sun. Taxi drivers rarely know the location of any streets away from the centre. There is no need to tip unless some extra service, like the carrying of luggage, is given.

**Motoring in Chile**  Car drivers require a *Relaciones de pasajeros* document, available at borders, and must present the original registration document of their vehicle, as must motor cyclists. The Carta Caminera from the Dirección de Vialidad is the most detailed road map (series of twenty-six) but is only available at Vialidad, Marsende and Alameda, Santiago. Reasonable road maps may also be obtained from the Automóvil Club de Chile, Av. Vitacura 8620, Santiago; or other regional offices. Members of foreign motoring organizations may join the Automóvil Club de Chile, and obtain discounts at hotels. Town maps from the Automóvil Club and Copec service stations. The *Turistel* Guides are very useful for roads and town plans, but note that not all distances are exact and that the description "ripio" (gravel) usually requires high clearance; "buen ripio" should be OK for ordinary cars. Hydrographic maps from Instituto Hidrográfico, Malgarejo 59, Valparaíso. Gasoline costs US$1.80 a gallon; it becomes more expensive the further north and further south you go. Diesel fuel is only available along the Longitudinal Highway. Spare car parts available from many shops on Calle Diez de Julio, Santiago. Yamaha motorcycle spares are sometimes available.

  Car drivers should have all their papers in order and to hand since there are frequent checks, but fewer in the south. When driving in the south (on the Carretera Austral particularly), and in the desert north, always top up your fuel tank and carry spare petrol/gasoline. Tyres need to be hard-wearing (avoid steel belt); it is recommended to carry more than one spare.

**Car Hire**  Many agencies, both local and international, operate in Chile. Vehicles may be rented by the day, the week or the month, with or without unlimited mileage. Rates do not normally include insurance (about US$6.50/day) or 13% VAT. A small car, with unlimited mileage costs about US$300 a week, a pick-up US$500. Note that the Automóvil Club de Chile has a car hire agency (with discounts for members or affiliates) and that the office may not be at the same place as the Club's regional delegation.

**Hitch-hiking** is easy and safe, but in some regions traffic is sparse.

**Walking** Serious walkers are advised to get *Backpacking in Chile and Argentina*, edited by Clare Hargreaves (Bradt Publications) 1989 edition. Also recommended: *Chile and Easter Island: A Travel Survival Kit*, by Alan Samagalski (Lonely Planet).

**Skiing** Bradt Publications' *South America Ski Guide*, to be published in late 1991, gives thorough coverage of all Chile's ski areas.

**Andean Project** For those interested in the Andean region of Chile, the Directors of the Andean project will be very pleased to give information. Contact Mrs Pat Vincent, Los Españoles 2420, Dpto. 24, Providencia, Santiago.

**Hotels** On hotel bills service charges are usually 10%, and taxes on bills are 18%. Whether or not the 18% is added to bills in hotel restaurants that are signed and charged to the hotel bill depends on the policy of the establishment. When booking in make certain whether meals are included in the price or only breakfast or nothing at all, and don't rely on the posted sheet in the bedroom for any prices. Small *residenciales* are often good value. If you are looking for a motel, ask for a *motel turístico*; most motels are short stay.

**Youth Hostels** There are youth hostels throughout Chile; average cost about US$2.50-3 p.p. Hostels are open only from Jan. to the end of February and a Chilean membership card is necessary (US$3.50). They are usually crowded and noisy, with only floor space available. An additional stamp costing US$4 enables one to use the card in Argentina, Uruguay and Brazil. This can be obtained from the Asociación Chilena de Albergues Turísticos Juveniles, Providencia 2594, oficina 420-421, Providencia, Santiago, T 231-5649; together with a useful guidebook of all Youth Hostels in Chile, *Guía Turística de los Albergues Juveniles*. If you carry an IYHF card you can stay in summer in makeshift hostels in many Chilean towns, usually in the main schools.

**Camping** is easy but no longer cheap at official sites. A common practice is to charge US$10 for up to 5 people, with no reductions for less than 5. "Camping Gaz International" stoves are recommended, since green replaceable cylinders are available in Santiago. Copec run a network of 33 "Rutacentros" along Ruta 5 which have showers, cafeterias and offer free camping. Free camping is also available at many filling stations.

**Local Dishes** A very typical Chilean dish is *cazuela de ave*, a nutritious stew containing large pieces of chicken, potatoes, rice, and maybe onions, and green peppers; best if served on the second day. Another popular Chilean dish is *empanadas de horno*, which are turnovers filled with a mixture of raisins, olives, meat, onions and peppers chopped up together. *Pastel de choclo* is a casserole of meat and onions with olives, topped with a maize-meal mash, baked in an earthenware bowl. *Prieta* is a blood sausage stuffed with cabbage leaves. The popular *empanada frita*, a fried meat pasty, is delicious. A normal *parrillada* is a giant mixed grill served from a charcoal brazier. The *pichanga* is similar but smaller and without the brazier.

What gives Chilean food its personality is the seafood. The delicious conger eel is a national dish, and *caldillo de congrio* (a soup served with a massive piece of conger, onions and potato balls) is excellent. *Paila Chonchi* is a kind of bouillabaisse, but has more flavour, more body, more ingredients. *Parrillada de mariscos* is a dish of grilled mixed seafood, brought to the table piping hot on a charcoal brazier. Other excellent local fish are the *cojinoa*, the *albacora* (swordfish) and the *corvina*. An appetizing starter is the shellfish *loco* (known to Australians as abalone), and in the S one should try the *centolla* (king crab). *Cochayuyo* is seaweed, bound into bundles, described as "hard, leathery thongs". Avocado pears, or *paltas*, are excellent, and play an important role in recipes. The *erizo*, or sea-urchin, is also commonly eaten. Make sure whether vegetables are included in the price for the main dish; menus often don't make this clear. Always best, if being economical, to stick to fixed-price *table d'hôte* meals or try the local markets. A *barros jarpa* is a grilled cheese and ham sandwich and a *barras luco* is a grilled cheese and beef sandwich. *Luche* is a black cake, like "flakey bread pudding". *Sopaipillas* are cakes made of a mixture which includes pumpkin, served in syrup (traditionally made in wet weather). *Ice cream* is very good; *lúcuma* and *chirimoya* are highly recommended flavours.

Lunch is about 1300 and dinner not before 2030. *Onces* (Elevenses) is tea taken at 1700 often accompanied by a couple of fried eggs. The cocktail hour starts at 1900. Waiters are known as *garzón*—never as *mozo*. Good, cheap meals can usually be found in Centros Españoles or Casinos de Bomberos. By law restaurants have to serve a cheaper set meal at lunchtime; it is called *colación* and may not be included on the menu.

It seems impossible to get real coffee unless you go to expresso bars and specify *café-café, expresso*. If you ask just for *café*, you get soluble coffee. The soluble tea should be avoided. If you order "*café*, or *té, con leche*", it will come with all milk; to have just a little milk in either, you must specify that. After a meal, instead of coffee, try an *agüita*—hot water in which herbs such as mint, or aromatics such as lemon peel, have been steeped. There is a wide variety, available in sachets, and they are very refreshing.

**Drinks** Imported whisky and other spirits are still cheap, but are increasing relatively in price. The local wines are very good; the best are from the central areas. Among the good *bodegas* are Cousiño Macul, Santa Carolina, Undurraga, Concha y Toro, Tocornal, San Pedro and Santa Helena. Santa Elena (no H) is less good. The bottled wines are graded, in increasing excellence, as *gran vino, vino especial* and *vino reservado*. Champagne-style wines are also cheap and acceptable. A small deposit, US$0.30, is charged on most wine bottles. Beer is quite good and cheap; the draught lager known as Schop is good; also try Cristal Pilsener or Royal Guard. Malta, a brown ale, is recommended for those wanting a British-type beer.

Good gin is made in Chile. Reasonably good brandy, *anís* and crème de menthe are all bottled in Chile. *Vaina* is worth trying, and so is the traditional Christmas drink, *cola de mono*, a mixture of *aguardiente*, coffee, milk and vanilla served very cold. *Pisco* is worth sampling, especially as a "Pisco Sour" or with grapefruit or lemon juice. *Manzanilla* is a local liqueur, made from *licor de oro* (like Galliano); *crema de cacao*, especially Mitjans, has been recommended. *Chicha* is any form of alcoholic drink made from fruit; *chicha cocida* is 3-day-old fermented grape juice boiled to reduce its volume and then bottled with a tablespoonful of honey. Cider (*chicha de manzana*) is popular in the South. *Chicha fresca* is plain apple juice.

**Tipping** Standard is 10% in hotels and restaurants and 20% in bars and soda fountains. Railway and airport porters: US$0.10 a piece of luggage. Make a deal with dock porters. Cloakroom attendants and cinema usherettes: US$0.05. Hairdressers: 10% of bill. Taxi-drivers are not tipped.

**Shopping** There is an excellent variety of handicrafts: woodwork, pottery, copperware, leatherwork, Indian woven goods including rugs and ponchos in the South. Good quality at the Cema-Chile shops (Av. Portugal 351, Santiago, and main provincial cities). VAT is 18%.

**Health** Tap water is fairly safe to drink in the main cities but bottled water is safer away from the larger centres. Hotels and restaurants are usually clean. Inoculation against hepatitis and typhoid is a wise precaution. Travellers should not eat salads, strawberries or ground-growing food; hepatitis and typhoid are all too common as the result of the use of untreated sewage for fertilizer (check what extra precautions against typhoid are necessary e.g. 3-pill preventative treatment, available locally.)

**Clothing**  Warm sunny days and cool nights are usual during most of the year except in the far S where the climate is like that of Scotland. Ordinary European medium-weight clothing can be worn during the winter (June to mid-September). Light clothing is best for summer (December to March), but men do not wear white tropical suits.

**Seasons**  The best time for a visit to Santiago is between October and April when fine weather is almost assured, but business visits can be made any time during the year. During the holiday season, between January and March, it is sometimes difficult to make appointments.

**Hours of Business**  Banks: 0900-1400, but closed on Sat. Government offices: 1000-1230 (the public is admitted for a few hrs. only). Business houses: 0830-1230, 1400-1800 (Mon. to Fri.). Shops (Santiago): 1030-1930, but 0930-1330 Sat. British business visitors are advised to obtain "Hints for Exporters: Chile" from the Department of Trade, Sanctuary Bldgs, 16-20 Great Smith Street, London SW1P 3DB.

**Public Holidays**  1 Jan., New Year's Day; Holy Week (2 days); 1 May, Labour Day; 21 May, Navy Day; 15 Aug., Assumption; 18, 19 Sept., Independence Days; 12 Oct., Discovery of America; 1 Nov., All Saints Day; 8 Dec., Immaculate Conception; 25 Dec., Christmas Day.

**Time**  GMT minus 4 hrs.; minus 3 hrs. in summer. Clocks change from mid-September or October to early March.

## Currency and Exchange

The unit is the peso, its sign is $. Notes are for 500, 1,000, 5,000 and 10,000 pesos and coins for 1, 5, 10, 50 and 100 pesos. There is a shortage of change so keep a supply of small denomination coins.

Travellers' cheques are widely accepted at reasonable rates if exchanging them for cash, they must be changed before 1200 in banks, but this limitation does not apply in exchange shops (*cambios*) and hotels, which give better rates than banks (rates tend to worsen after the banks close and at weekends). Travellers can buy pesos on the parallel (black) market, which is tolerated, at slightly better rates. *El Economista* quotes rates, and you can get fairly close to the *paralelo* nowadays in *cambios* and hotels (rates tend to fall around Christmas and the New Year). Rates are usually better in Santiago than elsewhere in the country. Changing travellers' cheques can be time-consuming and has become difficult in most towns apart from Arica, Antofagasta, Santiago and Puerto Montt. Traveller's cheques can be changed into dollars, but check if a commission is charged as this practice seems to vary. Foreigners may no longer exchange pesos for dollars when leaving the country. Diners' Club, Visa and Mastercharge are common in Chile (Bancard, the local card, is affliated to the last two—offices, called Fincard, can be found in most cities and will give cash against the cards), but American Express is less useful (use in American Express banks does not incur commission).

**Living Conditions and Cost**  Shops throughout Chile are well stocked and there is a seasonal supply of all the usual fruits and vegetables. Milk in pasteurized, evaporated, or dried form is obtainable. Chilean tinned food is dear. Food is reasonable, but food prices vary tremendously. Santiago tends to be more expensive for food and accommodation than other parts of Chile.

In 1990-1991, cheap accommodation in Santiago was normally about US$7 p.p. while north and south of the capital rates were about US$5-6 p.p. Breakfast in hotels, if not included in price, was about US$1.80 (instant coffee, roll with ham or cheese, and jam). In almost every town, private houses offer *alojamiento* (bed, breakfast and often use of kitchen) for about US$3.50-4.25 p.p. (bargaining may be possible). Southern Chile can be expensive between December 15 and March 15.

The **metric** system is obligatory but the quintal of 46 kilos (101.4 lb) is used.

**Electric Current**  220 volts A.C., 50 cycles

**Posts**  Airmail takes 3-4 days from the UK. Seamail takes 8-12 weeks. There is a daily airmail service to Europe with connections to the UK. Poste restante only holds mail for 30 days; then returns to sender. Lista de Correo in Santiago, Central Post Office, is good and efficiently organized. On no account send anything of value through the postal service, letters are frequently opened, or go astray, both entering and leaving the country. Astonishing how throughout Chile one post office official will charge rates different from the next, and they are all "right".

**Telephones** International telephone and telegraph communications are operated by Entel, CTC (Compañía de Teléfonos de Chile), and Telefónica del Sur, who have offices throughout the country; their rates are slightly different. Calls may be made collect, but with difficulty to some places (e.g. West Germany). Cheap rates on international calls at Entel are all day Sat., Sun. and holidays to all destinations except Japan, Australia and E Asia (0700-1859), Mon.-Fri. 1900-0659 to North and South America, 1400-0459 to Europe, Africa and W Asia and 0700-1859 Japan, Australia and E Asia. 3 minute call to Europe costs US$10.35 (US$7.25 cheap rate); to Australia US$14 (US$7.25 cheap rate, Entel); cheap rate to N and S America US$6, but US$5 to Argentina and Uruguay. Entel should be the cheapest for international calls since CTC routes its calls through Entel. Phone abroad from a private line is cheaper after 1800.

New telephone boxes, accepting coins, can be used to make local, long-distance and overseas calls, for making collect calls and receiving calls. Local calls from a public booth cost 50 pesos in any combination of coins (even 100 peso coin with change given), or *fichas* bought from kiosks.

Fax is operated by Entel and VTR, who have offices throughout the country. VTR also operate telex services. Amex Card holders can often use telex facilities at Amex offices free of charge.

**Media** Santiago daily papers *El Mercurio, La Nación, La Epoca* (liberal/left), *La Segunda, La Tercera* and *La Quarta. Las Ultimas Noticias. El Cóndor,* weekly in German.

Weekly magazines; *Hoy, Qué Pasa; Análisis, Ercilla* and *Panorama Económico* are best economic journals. Monthly: *Rutas* (official organ, Automobile Association).

**Sports** Sernatur will give all the necessary information about sport. **Skiing** Season from June to September/October, weather depending. For information write to: La Federación de Ski de Chile, Casilla 9902, Santiago. Horse racing is also popular and meetings are held every Sunday and on certain feast days at Viña del Mar, Santiago and Concepción throughout the year; horseback riding is also popular. Santiago and Valparaíso residents fish at the mountain resort of Río Blanco, and some of the world's best fishing is in the Lake District. The licence required can be got from the local police or such angling associations as the Asociación de Pesca y Caza, which gives information on local conditions. Other popular sports are football and basket ball. Viña del Mar has a cricket ground; on Saturdays there are polo matches at Santiago.

**Language** The local pronunciation of Spanish, very quick and lilting, with final syllables cut off, can present difficulties to the foreigner. See also Argentine **Information for Visitors**.

**Tourist Information** The national secretariat of tourism, Sernatur, has offices throughout the country (addresses are given in the text). City offices provide town maps, leaflets and much useful information. In addition, a much-used series of guide books is that called *Turistel,* details of which are given under Santiago. These books give far greater detail than we can provide.

Our warmest thanks are due to Charlie Nurse, who visited Chile in 1990, for updating this chapter. We are grateful to the following travellers: Ace and Laurie (Salem, O.R., U.S.A.), Rob Allan and Bridgit Vale (Pietermaritzburg), John Allen (London SW14), Michael Auer (Ottobrunn), Frank Bakker and Nike Darley (Amsterdam), Sue Balcomb and Tom Hore, Daria Barnes and Felipe Rodriguez (New Zealand), Marlise Baumgarter and Niklaus Graber (Erlach, Switzerland), Maarten Beeris (San Pedro de Atacama, Chile), Matthew Bell (Market Lavington, Wiltshire), Petra Bell and Hans-Georg Henle (Schwaigern, Germany), Erik Bernesson (Båstad, Sweden), Ortun Bettering (Rio de Janeiro), Salik B. Biais (Montmorency), Inga Björk and Martin Hallén (Sveg, Sweden), Dieter Blessing and Gertrud van Ackern (München), Riemer De Boer (Netherlands) Astrid Bombosch (Heidelberg, Germany), Jan Boogman (Uzwil) and Josef Kaufman (Knutwil, Switzerland), Hildegard Börgel (Seevetal, Germany), Binka Le Breton (Muriaé, Minas Gerais), Major C. J. Brightman (Salisbury), David Brigden (U.K.), Elizabeth Buettner (Ann Arbor, M.I.) and Alexander Protopapas (Pasadena, California), Susan A. Bullock (Spring City, TN), Jeff and Sue Burgess (Sydney, Australia), Marion Büttner (Hamburg), Steve and Jeanette Campbell (Sucre, Bol.), Nelly and Steve Caplan (Winnipeg, Canada), Liora Carmona and Ofer Kastner (Kiryat Bialik, Israel), Paul Carter (Hamilton, New Zealand) and Vivienne Mitchell (Coleraine, N. Ireland), Max G. Chapman (Melbourne), Tim Cobb (Dorking) and Caroline Wren (Conisbrough), Dr. Simon Collier (Colchester), Alysia Cook and Phil Waterhouse (Twyford, Berks), Bryan Crawford (Inverness), Bryan Crawford (Invernesshire, Scotland), Andrea Cujnik (München, Germany), Helen Cullen (Basingstoke) Bente Dalgaard (Copenhagen), Dana Denniston (Lexington, KY), James Derry (Courtenay, BC), Gordon Dickson (Fareham, Hants), Carmen Diéguez (Miami, U.S.A.), Louise Dionne (St. John's,

Newfoundland), Carolyn Dougall and Howard Johnson (Edinburgh), Anna Economides (Santiago), Barbara Egger (Caracas), Barbara Egli (Volketswil, Switz.), Richard Everson and Jo Penty (West Wickham, Kent), Daniel Ezekiel (Vancouver, BC), Tim Farnworth (Market Harborough, Leicestershire), Rüdiger Filbrich (Frankfurt/Main), R. Flohr (Köln), Harry Floyd (London W8), John Foss (Durango, C.O.), Patricia Fromm (Giessen, Germany), Glyn Fry and Trui Anseeuw (Hyde, Cheshire), Ricardo García García (Madrid), May-Lill Garly and Palle Valentiner-Branth (Copenhagen), Walter Gebhardt (Erlangen), Yves Genier (Louay, Switzerland), Gerhard J. (Santiago), Carsten Gerrens (Hamburg), Theodor A. Gevert (São Paulo), Jacqueline Greig (Cuckfield, East Sussex), Pilou Grenié (Antibes), Luis Guzmán Molina (Chillán), Patricio Guzmán Molina (Cohaique, Chile), Eric Hamovitch (Montréal, Canada), Mark Hancock and Veronica Egan (Ross-on-Wye, Herefordshire) for much useful information, Johanne Harvey and Niklaus Hutmacher (Gysenstein, Switzerland), Martin Hautkappe (München, Germany), Kevin Healey (Melbourne, Australia), Carolyn Helmke (Berkeley, California), Ulrich Herbert (Stuttgart), Rian Hermens (the Netherlands), Bettina Herweck (Darmstadt, Germany), Fritz Heskusius (Leiden, Netherlands), Gaby and Otto Heuer-Oeschger (Lenzburg, Switzerland), Toni Hilton and Dr Prudencio Guzmán (Jupiter, Florida), Gert Jan Hof and Yvonne Evers (Huissen, Neth), Gabrielle Holmstrom and Bernut Wallner (Uppsala, Sweden), Ralf Hönsch and Martin Stark (Switzerland), Sarah A. Horniman (La Paz), Eric Horne (Rye, U.S.A.), David Hutchinson and Susan Maddox (London W8), Primrose Hutton (Bulli, NSW), Barry Isaac (Miami Beach, Florida), Floris Italianer and Victorine van Pelt (Bussum, Neths.) John Kirby (Eastbourne, New Zealand), Andy Kuendig and Rosi Nueesch (Zuerich), Dr. Judith Kuriansky (New York), Christina Kuseffsky (Stockholm), Gerald Lange (Dolldorf, Germany), Herbert Levi (Buenos Aires), John Lewis (London NW2), Reni Lindauer and Hugo Wey (São Paulo), Judith Locher (Switzerland), Hans and Christine Lomosse (Ludvika, Sweden), Neil A. Macdougall (Toronto).

Philipp Magura (Reutlingen, Germany) for a most helpful contribution, Markus Maier and Gitte Wiedmann (Zürich), Susan Marfield (Long Beach, California), Douglas Markham (Houston), Simon Mays Smith (Waldron, East Sussex), Tom Amies (Bucks) and Simon Davy (England), Julianne McCabe, Maggie Widow, Jean O'Leary and Bill Shaffer (San Anselmo, C.A.), Peter McPherson (Sale, Australia), Selena Merrett (London N7), Martin Merz (Hochfelden, Switzerland), Patrick Meyer (Ammerschwihr, France), Bernard Milward (Salvador), Kari Løvendahl Mogstad and Trond Eri (Norway), Toby Molins (Santiago), Catherine Morris-Adams (West Derby), Deirdre Mortell (Corrigaline, County Cork), Hilary Murray (Dublin 4), Steve Newman and Wendy Chilcott (Horsham, West Sussex), Nikolaus Nolden (Berlin), Vital Pajarola and Eva Grunder (Zurich), Jeff Perk (Carbondale, Illinois), Guido Pfister (Weisslingen, Switzerland), Piero, John Pomfret (Woking, Surrey), Arthur Poyner (Chiloe), Bernd Proissl (Wernau), Brigitte Ramseier and Remo Schenker (Gretzenbach, Switzerland), John Rashak (Whitehouse Station, NJ), Jamie Rein (Boston, Mass), Wendy Richardson (London SW19), Hans Riess (Berlin), Bryan and Charmaine Roche (Cape Town), Joseph J. Rodríguez, Winifred Hughes Rodríguez and Jo Ann Manderscheid (Snyder, New York), Ann Rodzai and Doug Hanaver (Ithaca, NY), Tal Rosenthal (Kibbutz Bet-Haemek, Israel), Marius Ross (Santiago), Ms Alex Rossi (Norwich, Norfolk), Robin Russ (Longwood, FL), Ken Sattell (Boulder, C.O.), Nick Saunders and Sarah Jaggs (London W1), Ronald Schaulin and Christina Brand (Reinach, Switz), Lesley Schaffer (Los Angeles), Bettina Schmeiduch and family (Böblingen, Germany), Dieter Schoop (Münchenstein, Switzerland), Roland and Brigitte Schwarz-Aaschbacher (Rüderswil, Switz), Michael Scott-Watson (Roxburghshire, Scotland), Trevor and Lynn Stacey (Windhoek, Namibia), John Stonestreet (Cambridge, UK), Guillermo Surraco and Siobhan Rhea de Surraco (Berkeley, C.A.), Eva Süsstrunk and Roland Ruprecht (Berne), Fredi Suter (Goldau) and Claudia Räber (Oberkirch), Martin Theander Christoph Theis (Wiesloch, Germany), Roger Thornton and Paul Gadd (London N5), Åse Totland and Jarle Unneland (Ålesund, Norway), Ian Trontz (Brooklyn, NY), Adrian Turner and Caroline Caulfield-Giles (Trauco Tours, Puerto Montt) Michael Turner (Burnham-On-Sea), Jarle Unneland (Alesund, Norway), Dirk Vandersypen (Managua), Mark Van Den Boer (Tilberg, Netherlands), Pierre Vigna (Neuilly Sur Seine, France), Andreas Vogt (Mössingen, Germany), Béatrice Völkle (Gampelen, Switz.), Simon Watson Taylor (London W14) for a wealth of thoroughly-researched material, Joanna Watts and Shaun Pinchbeck (Bath), Dr Volker Weinmann (São Paulo, Brazil), Urs Wickli (Neu St. Johann, Switzerland), Ben Wiggersfeldt (Vildbjerg, Denmark), David Williams (London N1), Basil Wishart (Lerwick, Shetland Isles), Manfred Wolfensberger (Uster, Switzerland), Manuela Wonisch (Kloten, Switzerland), Meg Worley (Knoxville, Tennessee) and Peter Grover (Montreal, Canada), Helmut Zettl (Ebergassing, Austria), and Hod Zoiberman (Petach-Tikra, Israel).

# COLOMBIA

## INTRODUCTION

COLOMBIA, with 1,138,618 square km., is the fourth largest country in South America. It has coast lines upon both the Caribbean (1,600 km.) and the Pacific (1,306 km.). Nearly 55% of the area is almost uninhabited lowland with only 4% of the population; the other 96% are concentrated in the remaining 45%, living for the most part in narrow valleys or isolated intermont basins, or in the broad Caribbean lowlands. The population is infinitely varied, ranging from white, Indian, and black to mixtures of all three.

The 620,000 square km. of almost uninhabited land in Colombia lie E of the Eastern Cordillera. Near the foot of the Cordillera the plains are used for cattle ranching, but beyond is jungle. Islands of settlement in it are connected with the rest of the country by air and river, for there are no railways and very few roads: communication is by launch and canoe on the rivers.

In the populous western 45% of the country four ranges of the Andes run from S to N. Between the ranges run deep longitudinal valleys. Of the 14 main groups of population in the country, no less than 11 are in the mountain basins or in the longitudinal valleys; the other three are in the lowlands of the Caribbean.

The first 320 km. along the Pacific coast N from the frontier with Ecuador to the port of Buenaventura is a wide, marshy, and sparsely inhabited coastal lowland. Along the coast N of Buenaventura runs the Serranía de Baudó. E of this range the forested lowlands narrow into a low trough of land; E of the trough again rise the slopes of the Western Cordillera. The trough (the Department of the Chocó) is drained southwards into the Pacific by the Río San Juan, navigable for 200 km., and northwards into the Caribbean by the Río Atrato, navigable for 550 km.; there are vague plans to link the two rivers by canal. The climate is hot and torrential rain falls daily. The inhabitants are mostly black.

From the borders of Ecuador two ranges of mountain, the Western Cordillera and the Central Cordillera, run N for 800 km. to the Caribbean lowlands. Five peaks in the Western Cordillera are over 4,000 metres but none reaches the snowline. The Central Cordillera, 50-65 km. wide, is much higher; six of its peaks, snow clad, rise above 5,000 metres and its highest, the volcano cone of Huila, is 5,439 metres. There is hardly any level land, but there are narrow ribbons of soil along some of the rivers.

Between the two ranges, as they emerge from Ecuador, lies a valley filled in the S to a height of 2,500 metres by ash from the volcanoes. Not far from the frontier there is a cluster of self-subsisting Indians around Pasto. Further N between these two ranges lies the Cauca valley; in its northern 190 km., roughly from Popayán N past Cali to Cartago, there is an important agricultural region based on a deep bed of black alluvial soil which yields as many as five crops a year. This valley, which is at a height of about 1,000 metres and up to 50 km. wide, is drained northwards by the Cauca river. Cali is the business centre of the valley, and a road and railway run from Cali over a low pass of less than 1,500 metres in the Western Cordillera to Buenaventura. Sugar cane was the great crop of this valley in colonial times, but has now been varied with tobacco, soya, cotton, pineapple, and every other kind of tropical fruit. There is still some cattle raising. Coffee is grown on the Cordillera slopes above 600 metres. A "Tennessee Valley" scheme of development to drain the swamps, control floods, irrigate parched areas, improve farming, and produce electric power has been applied in the Cauca Valley since 1956.

At Cartago the two Cordilleras close in and the Cauca valley becomes a deep gorge which runs all the way to the Caribbean flatlands. In the Cordillera Central, at an altitude of 1,540 metres, is the second largest city and industrial centre in Colombia: Medellín. Much of the coffee and 75% of the gold comes from this area. N of Medellín the Cordillera Central splits into three ranges, separated by streams flowing into the Caribbean.

Near Latitude 2°N, or about 320 km. N of the Ecuadorean border, the Eastern Cordillera, the longest of all, rises and swings N and then NE towards Venezuela. About Latitude 7°N it bifurcates; one branch becomes the western rim of the Maracaibo basin and the other runs E into Venezuela, to the S of the Maracaibo basin.

Between this Eastern Cordillera and the Central Cordillera runs the 1,600 km. long Magdalena river, with the Caribbean port of Barranquilla at its mouth. There are more intermont basins in the Eastern Cordillera than in the others. Some of its peaks rise above the snow line. In the Sierra Nevada del Cocuy (just before the Cordillera bifurcates) there is a group of snowy peaks, all over 5,200 metres; the highest, Ritacuba Blanca, reaches 5,493 metres. The basins are mostly high, at an altitude of from 2,500 to 2,750 metres. In the Lower Magdalena region the river banks are comparatively deserted, though there are a few clearings made by the descendants of black slaves who settled along the Magdalena after their emancipation. There are oilfields in the valley, particularly at Barrancabermeja.

In a high basin of the Eastern Cordillera, 160 km. E of the Magdalena river, the Spaniards in 1538 founded the city of Bogotá, now the national capital. The great rural activity of this group is the growing of food: cattle, wheat, barley, maize and potatoes.

Roads run N from Bogotá to the basins of Chiquinquirá and Sogamoso, over 160 km. away. Both are in the Department of Boyacá, with Tunja, on a mountain between the two, as capital. Both basins, like that of Bogotá, produce food, and there are emerald mines at Muzo, near Chiquinquirá.

There are other basins in the N of the Eastern Cordillera: in the Departments of Santander and Norte de Santander at Bucaramanga and Cúcuta, and a small one at Ocaña. Movement into these basins by Europeans and *mestizos* did not take place until the 19th century, when chinchona bark (for quinine) rose into high demand. By 1885 this trade was dead, but by that time coffee was beginning to be planted. In Bucaramanga coffee is now the main crop, but it has been diversified by cacao, cotton and tobacco, all grown below the altitude suitable

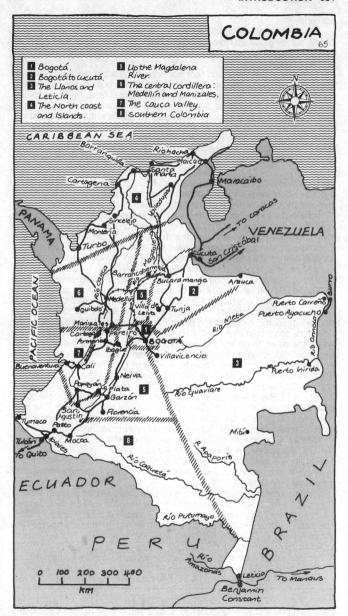

# COLOMBIA
65

1. Bogotá.
2. Bogotá to Cúcuta.
3. The Llanos and Leticia.
4. The North coast and Islands.
5. Up the Magdalena River.
6. The central Cordillera: Medellín and Manizales.
7. The Cauca valley.
8. Southern Colombia

CARIBBEAN SEA

PANAMA

PACIFIC OCEAN

VENEZUELA

Barranquilla
Riohacha
Maicao
Santa Marta
Cartagena
Maracaibo
Valledupar
Sincelejo
Montería
Turbo
Quibdó
Medellín
Río Cauca
Barrancabermeja
Bucaramanga
Cúcuta
San Cristóbal
TO CARACAS
Arauca
Puerto Carreño
Puerto Ayacucho
Villa de Leiva
Tunja
Río Meta
Río Orinoco
Manizales
Cartago
Pereira
Armenia
Ibagué
BOGOTÁ
Villavicencio
Puerto Inírida
Buenaventura
Cali
Neiva
Popayán
La Plata
Garzón
Río Guaviare
San Agustín
Florencia
Mitú
Tumaco
Pasto
Mocoa
Ipiales
R. Apaporis
Tulcán
TO QUITO
Río Caquetá
Río Magdalena

ECUADOR

PERU

BRAZIL

Río Putumayo
Río Amazonas
Leticia
TO MANAUS
Benjamin Constant

0  100  200  300  400
km

for coffee.

There is one more mountain group in Colombia, the Sierra Nevada de Santa Marta, standing isolated from the other ranges on the shores of the Caribbean. This is the highest range of all: its snow-capped peaks rise to 5,800 metres within 50 km. of the coast.

To the W of this Sierra, and N of where the Central and Western Cordilleras come to an end, lies a great lowland which has three groups of population on its Caribbean shores; at Cartagena, Barranquilla and Santa Marta. The rivers draining this lowland (the Magdalena, Sinú, Cauca, San Jorge and César) run so slowly that much of the area is a tissue of swamps and lagoons with very little land that can be cultivated. Indeed the whole area E of the channel of the Magdalena is under water at most times of the year. When the floods come, large areas of the land W of the Magdalena—the plains of Bolívar—are covered too, but during the dry season from October to March great herds of cattle are grazed there.

**History** Before the coming of the Spaniards the country was occupied by Indians, most of whom were primitive hunters or nomad agriculturists, but one part of the country, the high basins of the Eastern Cordillera, was densely occupied by Chibcha Indians who had become sedentary farmers. Their staple foods were maize and the potato, and they had no domestic animal save the dog; the use they could make of the land was therefore limited. Other cultures present in Colombia in the precolumbian era were the Tairona, Quimbaya, Sinú and Calima. Exhibits of their and the Chibcha (Muisca) Indians' gold-work can be seen at the Gold Museum in Bogotá. (**see page 666**)

The Spaniards sailed along the northern coast as far as Panama as early as 1500. The first permanent settlement was by Rodrigo de Bastidas at Santa Marta in 1525. Cartagena was founded in 1533. In 1536, Gonzalo Jiménez de Quesada (who wrote a full account of his adventures) pushed up the Magdalena river to discover its source; mounting the Eastern Cordillera in 1536, he discovered the Chibchas, conquered them, and founded Santa Fe de Bogotá in 1538. In the meantime other Spanish forces were approaching the same region: Pizarro's lieutenant, Sebastián de Benalcázar, had pushed down the Cauca valley from Ecuador and founded Pasto, Popayán and Cali in 1536. Nicolás de Federmann, acting on behalf of the Welser financiers of Germany, who had been granted a colonial concession by Charles V, approached from Venezuela. Benalcázar reached Bogotá in 1538 and Federmann got there in 1539. As in Peru, the initial period of settlement was one of strife between contending *conquistadores*. The royal Audiencia de Santa Fe set up in 1550 gave the area a legislative, judicial and administrative entity. In 1564 this was followed by a **presidency of the kingdom of Nueva Granada** controlling the whole country and Panama, except Benalcázar's province of Popayán. The Presidency was replaced in 1718 by a viceroyalty at Bogotá which controlled the provinces now known as Venezuela as well; it was independent of the Viceroyalty of Peru, to which this vast area had previously been subject.

The movement towards independence from Spain was set going in 1794 by a translation into Spanish by the *criollo* Antonio Nariño of the French Declaration of the Rights of Man. The movement was given point and force when, in 1808, Napoleon replaced Ferdinand VII of Spain with his own brother Joseph. The New World refused to recognize this: there were several revolts in Nueva Granada, culminating in a revolt at Bogotá and the setting up of a *junta* on 20 July 1810. Other local juntas were established: Cartagena bound itself to a *junta* set up at Tunja. Late in 1812 the young Bolívar, driven out of Venezuela, landed at Cartagena. In a brilliant campaign in 1813 he pushed up the Magdalena to Ocaña, and from there to Cúcuta, and obtained permission from the *junta* at Tunja to advance into Venezuela. In 90 days he marched the 1,200 km. to Caracas over mountain country, fighting six battles, but he was unable to hold Caracas and withdrew to Cartagena in 1814.

Napoleon fell in 1815, and the Spanish Government immediately set about reconquering, with some success, Venezuela and New Granada. General Pablo Morillo took Cartagena after a bitter siege of 106 days (Bolívar had withdrawn to Jamaica) and was later "pacifying" Bogotá with a "Reign of Terror" by May 1816.

Bolívar had by now assembled an army of Llaneros, fortified by a British legion recruited from ex-servicemen of the Peninsular wars, in Venezuela at Angostura, or Ciudad Bolívar as it is called today. In the face of incredible difficulties he made a forced march across the Andes in 1819. After joining up with Santander's Nueva Granada army, he defeated the royalists at the battle of the Swamps of Vargas in July and again at Boyacá on 7 August. He entered Bogotá three days later.

Bolívar reported his success to the revolutionary congress sitting at Angostura, and that body, on 17 December 1819, proclaimed the Republic of Gran Colombia, embracing in one these present republics of Venezuela, Colombia, and Ecuador. A general congress was held at Cúcuta on 1 January 1821, and here it was that two opposing views which were to sow such dissension in Colombia first became apparent. Bolívar and Nariño were for centralization; Santander, a realist, for a federation of sovereign states. Bolívar succeeded in enforcing his view for the time being, but Gran Colombia was not to last long; Venezuela broke away in 1829 and Ecuador in 1830. The remaining provinces were named Nueva Granada; it was not till 1863 that the name Colombia was restored.

Almost from its inception the new country became the scene of strife between the centralizing pro-clerical Conservatives and the federalizing anti-clerical Liberals. The Conservative president Tomás Cipriano de Mosquera (1845) encouraged education, began building roads, adopted the metric system, and put steamers on the Magdalena. The Liberals were dominant from 1849 for the next 30 years of insurrections and civil wars. In 1885 the Conservatives imposed a highly centralized constitution which has not been modified in this respect to this day. A Liberal revolt in 1899 turned into a civil war, "the War of the Thousand Days". The Liberals were finally defeated in 1902 after 100,000 people had died. It was in 1903 that Panama declared its independence from Colombia, following U.S. pressure.

After 40 years of comparative peace, the strife between Conservatives and Liberals was re-ignited in a little-publicized but dreadfully bloody civil war known as *La Violencia* from 1948 to 1957 (some 300,000 people were killed); but this was ended by a unique political truce. It was decided by plebiscite in 1957 that the two political parties would support a single presidential candidate, divide all political offices equally between them, and thus maintain political stability for sixteen years. In 1978 the agreement was ended, though some elements of the coalition (representation of the main opposition party in the Cabinet, for instance) were allowed to continue until 1986. Sr. Belisario Betancur, the Conservative president from 1982-86, offered a general amnesty to guerrilla movements in an attempt to end violence in the country. Following an initial general acceptance of the offer, only one of the four main guerrilla groups, the FARC, upheld the truce in 1985-7. In May 1986, when the Liberal candidate, Sr. Virgilio Barco, won the presidential elections, FARC's newly-formed political party, the Unión Patriótica, won 10 seats in congress; the Liberal party took the majority. Right-wing groups, unwilling to accept the Unión Patriótica, began a campaign of murder against UP's elected representatives. By the begining of 1990, 1,040 party members had been killed since the UP was formed in 1985. This, together with continuing left-wing, and drugs-related, violence, provoked civil instability into the 1990s. During the campaign for the 1990 presidential and congressional elections violence brought the assassination of the Liberal Party and the UP presidential candidates, Luis Carlos Galán and Bernardo Jaramillo. President Barco pledged to crack down on the drugs barons and an international effort was launched to bring them to justice, but opposition to extradition of suspects to the USA stymied progress.

In the March 1990 parliamentary elections, the Liberal Party won 60% of the seats, against 37% for the Conservatives. Presidential elections were held on 27 May, 1990. The Liberal Party candidate and eventual winner was César Gaviria Trujillo, a former Finance Minister and Interior Minister, who won a clear majority in the March primaries after taking up the candidacy of the murdered Luis Carlos Galán. Gaviria appointed a coalition government made up of Liberals from rival factions, Conservatives and the M-19 leader. A plebiscite held concurrently with the presidential elections showed clear support for reform of the 1886 constitution. In December 1990, therefore, a 73-member Constituent Assembly was elected, in which no single party won a majority, to reform the constitution by 5 July 1991. There was broad agrement that the electoral system, Congress and the judiciary needed modernizing and democratizing. As a result, general elections were expected to be held in October 1991, although not due until 1994. In June 1991, peace talks begain in Caracas with the FARC and the ELN with the aim of arranging a ceasefire while simultaneously secret surrender terms were being negotiated with Pablo Escobar, the alleged leader of the narco-terrorists. In 1990, traffickers were offered immunity from extradition and reduced prison sentences if they surrendered to the authorities.

**The People of Colombia** The regions vary greatly in their racial make-up: Antioquia and Caldas are largely of European descent, Pasto is Indian, the Cauca Valley and the rural area near the Caribbean are African or *mulatto*. No colour bar is legally recognized but it does exist in certain centres. Colombia has 19 cities with over 100,000 people. Total estimated population in 1990 was 32,978,000, with an annual growth rate of 2.1%.

About 67% live in the cities, with 32% of the work force engaged in agriculture, pastoral and forest pursuits, hunting and fishing. The birth and death rates vary greatly from one area to the other, but in general infant mortality is high (37 per 1,000 live births; the mortality rate is 7.4 per 1,000). The birth rate (1983-88) was 27.9. Hospitals and clinics are few in relation to the population. About 66% of the doctors are in the departmental capitals, which contain 12% of the population, though all doctors now have to spend a year in the country before they can get their final diploma. Deplorable *barrios clandestinos* (shanty-towns) have sprung up around Cali, Barranquilla, Cartagena and Buenaventura.

**The Economy** Agriculture is the most important sector of the economy, contributing about 19% of gdp and employing 29% of the labour force. It is also the largest earner of foreign exchange, with over 57% of total legal exports. The traditional crops are coffee, flowers, sugar cane, bananas, rice, maize and cotton. Colombia is the leading producer of mild Arabica coffee and second to Brazil in world production. Output has declined since 1984 as the Government has encouraged diversification, but coffee remains the dominant export item with up to 50% of total revenues, depending on world prices.

Manufacturing contributes 20% of gdp, with agricultural-related activities such as food processing, drink and tobacco accounting for 35% of the sector's value added. Textiles and clothing are also important, and provide an outlet for home-grown cotton. Heavy corporate indebtedness in the first half of the 1980s affected the growth of manufacturing and led to a decline in employment to only 15% of the total labour force. In the second half of the decade, however, strong growth was shown by chemicals, textiles and clothing, transport equipment, cement, metalworking and paper and unemployment fell.

Although contributing only 6.4% of gdp, mining, mainly oil and coal, was the most dynamic sector of the economy in the 1980s, with growth rates of over 20% a year. With the exception of a few major projects, mining is concentrated in the hands of small scale producers with little technology or organization. Much of their output remains outside the formal economy. Colombia is, however, the largest producer of gold and platinum in Latin America, and these two metals, together with emeralds, have traditionally dominated the mining sector. Mining of precious metals, including silver, is primarily in the Departments of Antioquia and El Chocó; huge gold deposits have also been discovered on the borders of the Departments of Cauca and Valle, while others have been found in the Guairía, Vaupés and Guaviare regions near the Brazilian border. In 1984, Colombia became self-sufficient in energy. Rising production of hydrocarbons moved the oil trade into surplus for the first time in ten years and by 1988 oil imports had virtually ceased. Development of energy sources has been given high priority to satisfy domestic requirements and to diversify exports. Most of the oil production comes from the Magdalena basin, but these are older fields which are running down. The discovery of the Caño Limón field near Arauca has raised output to around 400,000 barrels a day. As well as oil and gas, Colombia has the largest coal reserves in Latin America, which partial surveys have put at 16.5 bn tonnes. The largest deposits are in the Cerrejón region, where a huge project has been set up to mine and export steam coal from a new port at Bahía de Portete. Hydroelectricity now accounts for 70% of installed generating capacity. It has an advantage over thermal power because 75% of the nation's hydroelectric potential is in the central zone, where 80% of the population live. Total potential is said to be 100,000 MW, of which only about 5% is harnessed.

Current account surpluses in the late 1970s during the coffee price boom were turned into large deficits in the first half of the 1980s, reaching over US$3bn in 1982 and 1983, because of lower export receipts and rapidly rising imports. However, Colombia was able to avoid having to reschedule its foreign debts, and took steps to adjust its external accounts. The devaluation of the peso was speeded up, reinforced by import restrictions and export incentives. The fiscal accounts were also turned around and the public sector deficit was reduced from 7.5% of gdp in 1984 to 2.0% in 1986 while economic growth remained positive throughout the 1980s. The World Bank and the IMF endorsed the Colombian economic strategy and commercial banks continued to lend to the country to refinance loans falling due.

**Constitution and Government** Senators and Representatives are elected by popular vote. The Senate has 112 members, and the Chamber of Representatives has 199. The President, who appoints his 13 ministers, is elected by direct vote for a term of four years, but cannot succeed himself in the next term. Every citizen over 18 can vote. Reform of the 1886 Constitution was undertaken by a Constituent Assembly in 1991 (see above, **History**).

Administratively the country is divided into 22 Departments, 5 Intendencias, 5 Comisarias, and the Special District of Bogotá.

Liberty of speech and the freedom of the press are in theory absolute but in practice more limited. The language of the country is Spanish. Its religion is Roman Catholicism. There is complete freedom for all other creeds not contravening Christian morals or the law.

**Education** The literacy rate is 82%. Education is free, and since 1927 theoretically compulsory, but many children, especially in rural areas, do not attend. There are high standards of secondary and university education, when it is available.

**Communications** A major problem still facing the country is that of surface transport. Its three Cordilleras, separated by valleys often no more than 1,500 metres above sea-level, make internal communications extremely difficult. The 3,700 km. of narrow-gauge railways and the 38,200 km. of roads have eastern and western systems, with inter-communicating laterals (see maps and text). Only about 10% of the road system is paved. Given these difficulties it is natural that Colombia, which ran the first airline in South America, has taken ardently to the air.

**Music and Dance** No South American country has a greater variety of music than Colombia, strategically placed where the Andes meet the Caribbean. The four major musical areas are (a) the mountain heartland, (b) the Pacific coast, (c) the Caribbean coast and (d) the Llanos or eastern plains. The heartland covers the Andean highlands and intervening valleys of the Cauca and Magdalena and includes the country's three largest cities, Bogota, Cali and Medellín. It is relatively gentle and sentimental music, accompanied largely by string instruments, with an occasional flute and a *chucho* or *carángano* shaker to lay down the rhythm. The preferred instrument of the highlands and by extension Colombia's national instrument, is the *tiple*, a small 12-stringed guitar, most of which are manufactured at Chiquinquirá in Boyacá. The national dance is the Bambuco, whose lilting sounds are said to have inspired Colombian troops at the Battle of Ayacucho in 1824. It is to be found throughout the country's heartland for dancing, singing and instrumentalizing and has long transcended its folk origins. The choreography is complex, including many figures, such as la Invitación, los Ochos, Los Codos, Los Coqueteos, La Perseguida and La Arrodilla. Other related dances are the Torbellino, where the woman whirls like a top, the more stately Guabina, the Pasillo, Bunde, Sanjuanero and the picaresque Rajaleña. Particularly celebrated melodies are the "Guabina Chiquinquireña" and the "Bunde Tolimense". The following fiestas, among others, provide a good opportunity of seeing the music and dance:- La Fiesta del Campesino, ubiquitous on the first Sunday in June, the Fiesta del Bambuco in Neilva and Festival Folklórico Colombiano in Ibagué later in the month, the Fiesta Nacional de la Guabina y el Tiple, held in Velez in early August, the Desfile de Silleteros in Medellín in the same month and Las Fiestas de Pubenza in Popayán just after the New Year, where the Conjuntos de Chirimía process through the streets.

On Colombia's tropical Pacific coast (and extending down into Esmeraldas, Ecuador) is to be found some of the most African sounding black music in all South America. The Currulao and its variants, the Berejú and Patacoré, are extremely energetic recreational dances and the vocals are typically African-style call-and-response. This is the home of the *marimba* and the music is very percussion driven, including the upright *cununo* drum plus *bombos* and *redoblantes*. Wakes are important in this region and at these the Bundes, Arrullos and Alabaos are sung. Best known is the "Bunde de San Antonio". The Jota Chocoana is a fine example of a Spanish dance taken by black people and tuned into a satirical weapon against their masters. The regional fiestas are the Festival Folklórico del Litoral at Buenaventura in July and San Francisco de Asís at Quibdó on 4 August. Quibdó also features a "Fiesta de los Indios" at Easter.

The music of Colombia's Caribbean lowlands became popular for dancing throughout Latin America more than 30 years ago under the name of "Música Tropical" and has much more recently become an integral part of the Salsa repertory. It can be very roughly divided into "Cumbia" and "Vallenato". The Cumbia is a heavily black influenced dance form for several couples, the men forming an outer circle and the women an inner one. The men hold aloft a bottle of rum and the women a bundle of slim candles called "espermas". The dance probably originated in what is now Panama, moved east into Cartagena, where it is now centred and quite recently further east to Barranquilla and Santa Marta. The most celebrated Cumbias are those of Ciénaga, Mompós, Sampués, San Jacinto and Sincelejo. The instrumental accompaniment consists of *gaitas* or *flautas de caña de millo*, backed by drums. The *gaitas* ("male" and "female") are vertical cactus flutes with beeswax heads, while the *cañas de millo* are smaller transverse flutes. The most famous conjuntos are the Gaiteros de San Jacinto, the Cumbia Soledeña and the Indios Selectos. Variants of the Cumbia are the Porro, Gaita, Puya, Bullerengue and Mapalé, these last two being much faster and more energetic. Lately Cumbia has also become very much part of the Vallenato repertoire and is therefore often played on the accordion. Vallenato music comes from Valledupar in the Department of Cesar and is of relatively recent origin. It is built around one instrument, the accordion, albeit backed by *guacharaco* rasps and *caja* drums. The most popular rhythms are the Paseo and the Merengue, the latter having arrived from the Dominican Republic, where it is the national dance. Perhaps the first virtuoso accordionist was the legendary "Francisco El Hombre", playing around the turn of the century. Today's best known names are those of Rafael Escalona, Alejandro Durán and Calixto Ochoa. In April the Festival de la Leyenda Vallenata is held in Valledupar and attended by thousands. Barranquilla is the scene of South America's second most celebrated Carnival, after that of Rio de Janeiro, with innumerable traditional masked groups, such as the Congos, Toros, Diablos and Caimanes. The Garabato is a dance in which death is defeated. Barranquilla's carnival is less commercialized and more traditional than that of Rio and should be a "must" for anyone with the opportunity to attend. Other important festivals in the region are the Corralejas de Sincelejo with its bullfights in January, La Candelaria in Cartagena on 2 February, the Festival de la Cumbia in El Banco in June, Fiesta del Caiman in Ciénaga in January and Festival del Porro in San Pelayo (Córdoba). To complete the music of the Caribbean region, the Colombian islands of San Andrés and Providencia, off the coast of Nicaragua, have a fascinating mix of mainland Colombian and Jamaican island music, with the Calypso naturally a prominent feature.

The fourth musical region is that of the great eastern plains, the so-called Llanos Orientales between the Arauca and Guaviare rivers, a region where there is really no musical frontier between the two republics of Colombia and Venezuela. Here the Joropo reigns supreme as a dance, with its close relatives the Galerón, the slower and more romantic Pasaje and the breathlessly fast Corrido and Zumba que Zumba. These are dances for couples, with a lot of heel tapping, the arms hanging down loosely to the sides. Arnulfo Briceño and Pentagrama Llanera are the big names and the harp is the only instrument that matters, although normally backed by *cuatro*, guitar, *tiple* and *maracas*. Where to see and hear it all is at the Festival Nacional del Joropo at Villavicencio in December.

---

## BOGOTA (1)

---

**The capital, with its wealth of museums and historic buildings, and nearby towns for a weekend excursion out of the city, including the cathedral in a salt mine at Zipaquirá.**

***Bogotá***, capital of the Republic and a city of 4.8 million people, is on a plateau at 2,650 metres. The average temperature is 14°C (58°F). It is built on sloping land, and covers 210 square km. The central part of the city is full of character and contrasts: colonial buildings stand side-by-side with the most modern architecture. For the most part the houses are low, with eaves projecting over the streets; they are rarely brightly painted. The traffic is very heavy.

Visitors should not be too active for the first 24 hrs. Some people get dizzy at Bogotá's altitude. Be careful with food and alcoholic drinks for the first day also.

There is a very good view of the city from the top of Monserrate, the lower of the two peaks rising sharply to the E. It is reached by a funicular railway and a cable car. The new convent at the top is a popular shrine. At the summit, near the church, a chairlift (US$0.20) and a platform give a bird's-eye view of the red-roofed city and of the plains beyond stretching to the rim of the Sabana. Also at the top are a Wild West-style train for children, several restaurants and snack bar (good *tamales*, US$1), and the Calle del Candelero, a reconstruction of a Bogotá street of 1887. Behind the church are popular picnic grounds. The fare up to Monserrate is US$1.60 adult return (US$0.80 child), four trips per hour. The funicular works only on Sun. and holidays (expect to have to queue for an hour if you want to go up before about 1400, and for coming down); the cable car operates 0900-1800 weekdays, 0600-1800 on Sun.

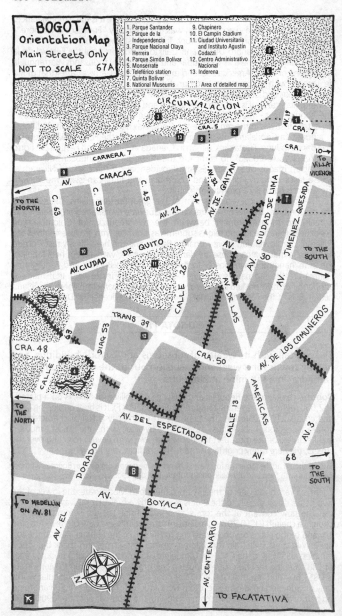

BOGOTA
Orientation Map
Main Streets Only
NOT TO SCALE 67A

1. Parque Santander
2. Parque de la Independencia
3. Parque Nacional Olaya Herrera
4. Parque Simón Bolívar
5. Monserrate
6. Teleférico station
7. Quinta Bolívar
8. National Museums
9. Chapinero
10. El Campín Stadium
11. Ciudad Universitaria and Instituto Agustín Codazzi
12. Centro Administrativo Nacional
13. Inderena

⋯⋯ Area of detailed map

CIRCUNVALACION

CRA. 5
CRA. 7
CRA.
AV. 19

10 →
TO VILLAVICENCIO

CARRERA. 7

AV. CARACAS

C. 63
C. 53
C. 45
C. 34

AV. J.E. GAITAN
AV. 22

TO THE NORTH

DE QUITO
AV. CIUDAD

CIUDAD DE LIMA
JIMENEZ QUESADA

CALLE 26

AV. DE LAS
AV. 30

TO THE SOUTH

TRANS 39
DIAG 53

CRA. 50
AV. DE LOS COMUNEROS

CRA. 48
CALLE

TO THE NORTH

AMERICAS
CALLE 13
AV. 3

AV. DEL ESPECTADOR
AV. 68

TO THE SOUTH

DORADO
AV. EL

AV. BOYACA

TO MEDELLIN ON AV. 81

AV. CENTENARIO

TO FACATATIVA

The neighbourhood can be dangerous though there is a police station nearby. At weekends, especially Sundays which is a local day of pilgrimage, there are so many people that it is usually safe to walk (or shuffle) up and down Monserrate. However during the week, muggings are frequent even in daylight. Take a bus or taxi to the foot of the hill Mon.-Fri., and never be tempted to walk down from the top. Taxi to foot, allowing 1 hour at the top, US$5.30.

At the foot of Monserrate is the Quinta de Bolívar, a fine colonial mansion, with splendid gardens and lawns. There are several cannons captured at the battle of Boyacá. The house, once Bolívar's home, is now a museum showing some of his personal possessions and paintings of events in his career. (Open 1000-1700, Tues.-Sun.; its address is Calle 20, No. 3-23 Este; charge US$0.50.)

The Plaza Bolívar, with a statue of the Liberator at its centre, is at the heart of the city; around the Plaza are the narrow streets and massive mansions of the old quarter (known as the Barrio La Candelaria), with their barred windows, carved doorways, brown-tiled roofs and sheltering eaves. The district is popular as a residential area and has an artists' community. Most of the mansions and best colonial buildings are in this district: the Palace of San Carlos, the house of the Marqués de San Jorge (housing an archaeological museum), the Municipal Palace, the Capitol, and the churches of San Ignacio, Santa Clara, San Agustín, and the Cathedral.

The Calles (abbreviated "Cll.", or "C") run at right angles across the Carreras ("Cra." or "K"). It is easy enough to find a place once the address system, which is used throughout Colombia, is understood. The address Calle 13, No. 12-45 would be the building on Calle 13 between Carreras 12 and 13 at 45 paces from Carrera 12; however transversals and diagonals (numbers with letters appended) can complicate the system. The Avenidas, broad and important streets, may be either Calles (like 19) or Carreras (like 14). Av. Jiménez de Quesada, one of Bogotá's most important streets, owes its lack of straightness to having been built over a river-bed. Carrera 7, one of the main shopping streets, is now closed to motor traffic on Sundays and holidays.

The street map of Bogotá on **page 660** is marked with numerals showing the places of most interest for visitors. Each place will be described under the numeral for it in the map.

1. The Plaza Bolívar, heart of the city, coeval with the city's foundation. On the eastern side is the Palacio Arzobispal, with splendid bronze doors. To one side of it is the colonial Plazuela de Rufino Cuervo. Here is the house of Manuela Sáenz, the mistress of Bolívar. On the other side is the house in which Antonio Nariño printed in 1794 his translation of "The Rights of Man" which triggered off the movement for independence.

See the Casa del Florero or Museo 20 de Julio in a colonial house on the corner of Plaza Bolívar with Calle 11. It houses the famous flower vase that featured in the 1810 revolution and shows collections of the Independence War period, including documents and engravings. Entry fee US$0.40, open Tues.-Sat., 0915-1830. On the northern side of the Plaza is the Corte Suprema de Justicia, wrecked in a guerrilla attack in 1985. A new Corte Suprema de Justicia is under construction.
2. The Cathedral, rebuilt in 1807 in classical style. Notable choir loft of carved walnut and wrought silver on altar of Chapel of El Topo. Several treasures and relics; small paintings attributed to Ribera; banner brought by Jiménez de Quesada to Bogotá, in sacristy, which has also portraits of past Archbishops. There is a monument to Jiménez inside the Cathedral. In one of the chapels is buried Gregorio Vásquez Arce y Ceballos (1638-1711), by far the best painter in colonial Colombia. Many of his paintings are in the Cathedral.
3. The beautiful Chapel of El Sagrario, built end of the 17th century. Several paintings by Gregorio Vásquez Arce.
4. Alcaldía Mayor de Bogotá.
5. The Capitolio Nacional, an imposing building with fine colonnades (1847-1925). Congress sits here.
6. The church of Santa Clara, another colonial church, is now a religious museum and concert hall.
7. San Ignacio, Jesuit church built in 1605. Emeralds from the Muzo mines in Boyacá were

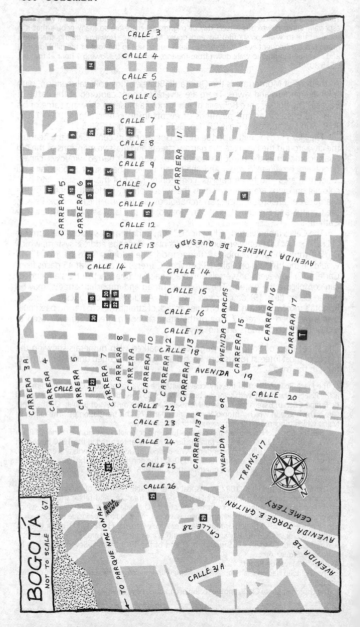

BOGOTÁ
NOT TO SCALE
67

used in the monstrance. Paintings by Gregorio Vásquez Arce.

8. The Palacio de San Carlos, where Bolívar lived. He is said to have planted the huge walnut tree in the courtyard. On 25 September, 1828, there was an attempt on his life. His mistress, Manuela, thrust him out of the window and he was able to hide for two hours under the stone arches of the bridge across the Río San Agustín. Santander, suspected of complicity, was arrested and banished. Now the president's official residence, with a huge banquet hall used for state affairs. The guard is changed—full-dress uniform—every day at 1700.

The Museo de Arte Colonial, across from the Palacio de San Carlos (Carrera 6, No. 9-77) is one of the finest colonial buildings in Colombia. It belonged originally to the Society of Jesus, and was once the seat of the oldest University in Colombia and of the National Library. It has a splendid collection of colonial art and paintings by Gregorio Vásquez Arce, all kinds of utensils, and 2 charming patios. Open Tues. to Sat. 0930-1830; Sun. and holidays, 1000-1700. Entry fee US$0.40 for adults; students US$0.20.

9. Church of María del Carmen, with excellent stained glass and walls in bands of red and white.

10.**Teatro Colón**, Calle 10, No. 5-32 (operas, lectures, ballets, plays, concerts, etc.), late 19th century with lavish decorations. Seating for 1,200, and very ornate.

11. The Casa de la Moneda (Mint), built in 1720, is at Calle 11, No. 4-93. Open Mon.-Sat. 0900-2100, Sun. and holidays, 0900-1800. In the same street, No. 4-16, is the Banco de la República's Biblioteca de Luis Angel Arango formerly one of the best endowed and arranged in South America, though showing signs of decline, with 3 reading rooms, research rooms, an art gallery and a splendid concert hall. There are exhibitions and regular concerts (free on Monday evenings, US$0.75 on Sunday morning, and full-price on Wednesday, student tickets at US$0.75). The architecture is impressive and the lavatories are recommended.

12. Palacio de Nariño (1906), the presidential palace. Spectacular interior, fine collection of modern Colombian paintings. Free tours Sat. morning with guide, 0930 in Spanish, 1000 in English, though not on a regular basis (enquire). It is not open to the public any other time.

13. Church of San Agustín, strongly ornamented (1637). Fine paintings by Gregorio Vásquez Arce and the Image of Jesus which was proclaimed Generalísimo of the army in 1812.

14. Santa Bárbara church (mid-16th century), one of the most interesting colonial churches. Paintings by Gregorio Vásquez Arce.

15. Church of San Juan de Dios, well worth a visit.

16. Parque Mártires (Park of the Martyrs) with monument, on the site of the Plaza in which the Spanish shot many patriots during the struggle for independence.

17. Palacio de Comunicaciones (postal and telegraph), built on the site of the old colonial church of Santo Domingo.

18. The Banco de la República, next to Parque Santander. Next to the Bank is the wonderful Museo del Oro (see page 666). In Parque Santander there is a bronze statue of Santander, who helped Bolívar to free Colombia and was later its President.

19. Gobernación de Cundinamarca, almost as imposing as the Capitolio. Corinthian style.

20. San Francisco church (mid-16th century), with notable paintings of famous Franciscans, choir stalls, and a famous high altar (1622). Remarkable ceiling is in Spanish-Moorish (mudéjar) style.

21. Church of La Veracruz, first built five years after the founding of Bogotá, rebuilt in 1731, and again in 1904. In 1910 it became the Panteón Nacional e Iglesia de la República. José de Caldas, the famous scientist, was buried along with many other victims of the "Reign of Terror" under the church. Fashionable weddings.

22. La Tercera Orden, an old colonial church famous for its carved woodwork, altars, and confessionals.

23. Las Nieves, old colonial church, has been demolished and replaced by an ugly modern church.

24. Planetarium, Museo de Historia Natural and Museo de Arte Moderno, in Parque de la Independencia. Two daily showings of best foreign modern painters, US$0.30. (see also page 665)

25. *Tequendama Hotel.* Nearby (on Carrera 7 and Calle 26) are the church and monastery of San Diego, a picturesque old building recently restored. The Franciscan monastery with fine Mudéjar ceiling was built in 1560 and the church in 1607 as its chapel. It is now used as a crafts shop by Artesanías de Colombia. SE of the *Tequendama Hotel* is the Biblioteca Nacional, with entrance on Calle 24.

---

**Bogotá: Key to map (For Nos 1-25), see text above**
26. Museo de Arqueología; 27. Museo de Arte y Tradiciones Populares; 28. Colegio Mayor de Nuestra Señora del Rosario; 29. Corporación Nacional de Turismo; 30. Airmail office/Avianca.

**Warning** The old part around Plaza Bolívar and from Calle 28, extending to the centre and South (i.e. declining Calle numbers) is less dangerous than it was, with increased police patrolling. The central area is less safe at weekends after 1900. Mugging, however, may occur in other parts of the city. Around Carrera 16, Calle 16 is unsafe at night and taxi drivers may refuse to let tourists out in this area. Carrera 13 (Avenida Caracas) y Carrera 10 is reported unsafe (1990) at any time. Any "officials" in uniform asking to register your money are almost certainly thieves.

Under state-of-siege legislation police may shoot and kill a suspect during any narcotics operation and it will be automatically classified as self-defence. A large number of would-be drug traffickers have been killed in this way.

The Judicial Unit for Tourism (Tourist police) offers 24-hour service for tourists at Carrera 7, No. 27-42, T 283-4930. If you are robbed of documents, contact police at Calle 46 y Carrera 14, of valuables, police at Calle 40, No. 8-09.

**Hotels** Book hotels in advance whenever possible. Tax of 15% may be additional to the bill. The following expensive hotels are recommended: *Bogotá Royal*, Av. 100, No. 8A-01, T 2183261, L, said to be one of the best in South America; *Tequendama*, Cra. 10, No. 26-21, T 2861111, A+, restaurant serves excellent *ajiaco*, but poor report of service and value in 1991; *Charleston*, Cra. 13, No 85-46, T 2180590, L; *El Belvedere*, Tr. 18, No. 100-16, T 2577700, A; *Los Urapanes*, Cra. 13, No. 83-19, A, very pleasant, smart, but friendly, smaller hotel; *Continental*, Av. Jiménez, No. 4-16, T 2425901, C; *Nueva Granada*, Av. Jiménez, No. 4-77, T 2816121, B. Other luxury and 5-3 star hotels: *Hilton*, Cra. 7, No. 32-16, T 2329898, A+, a little outdated, but good restaurant, swimming pool and gym, check accounting carefully; *La Fontana*, Diagonal 127A, No. 21-10, T 2747868, L; *Bogotá Plaza*, Calle 100, No. 18A-30, T 2364940, L; *Bacatá*, Calle 19, No. 5-20, T 2432210, A; *Dann*, Calle 19, No. 5-72, T 2840100, A; *El Presidente*, Calle 23, No. 9-45, T 2435020, B.

*Nuechatel*, Calle 90, No. 7A-66, A, old-fashioned, safe district, good restaurant but poor plumbing; *Las Terrazas*, Calle 54, No. 3-12, C, 2-star, T 2555777, very clean, "rustic charm", nice view of city; *Apartamentos 82*, Carrera 14, No. 81-34, C, good service, pleasant safe part of the city, rec.; *Monserrat*, Av. Caracas, 18-08, D, rec., clean, impeccable service; *Regina*, Carrera 5, No. 15-16, D, with private bath, TV, phone, friendly, good; *Bogotá Internacional*, Carrera 7A, No. 21-20, T 343898, D, very central, comfortable, clean, restaurant and bar, highly rec.; *La Hostería de la Candelaria*, Calle 9, No. 3-11, T 286-1479/242-1727, Aptdo. Aéreo 15978, D, highly rec. for comfort, atmosphere and service (good for longer stays).

On Calle 14 near Carrera 4 are: *Dann Colonial*, No. 4-21, C; opposite is *Santa Fe*, No. 4-48, hot shower, good service, E, quiet, clean, friendly, safe, warmly rec.; *Hotel la Candelaria*, Carrera 4, No. 14-87, E with bath, heating, good value; also rec., *Residencia Aragón*, Carrera 3, No. 14-13, clean and safe, F, friendly and honest, no hot water, warmly rec. (cheap taxi to airport can be arranged).

*San Diego*, Carrera 13 y Calle 24, D, T 2842100, friendly, clean, large rooms, good value, accepts credit cards but not Amex travellers' cheques; *Del Duc*, Calle 23, No. 9-38, T 2340080, D, friendly, clean, good French restaurant; *Avenida 19*, Avenida (Calle) 19, No. 5-92, D, with shower, good price considering its central location, clean, very helpful service; *Hostal Residencias Moreno*, Transversal 33 No. 95-28, T 257-9127, D inc. two meals, two house taxi drivers, nearby frequent bus service to town centre, very friendly, safe for left luggage, quiet, comfortable, hot water, highly rec.

*Regis*, Calle 18, No. 6-09 (also known as *Residencias María*), E (C with shower), sometimes hot water, old-fashioned, run down but safe, clean, safe parking for car or motorcycle; *Hollywood*, Calle 18, No. 8-68, E, clean but small rooms with bath; *El Turista*, Av. Jiménez, between Cras. 4 and 5, E with bath, hot water, safe, small establishment, rec.; opp is *Zaratoga*, E with bath, quite nice; *Internacional*, Av. Jiménez, nr. *Nueva Granada*, E, hot water, safe, friendly; *Panamericana*, Calle 15, No. 12-70, T 2421802, E, good, with bath, helpful; *María Luisa*, Calle 14, between Calles 15 and 16, hot water, very reasonable and food is good; *Residencia Dorantes*, Calle 13, No. 5-07, very clean, E (cheaper without bath), hot water, reasonable, safe, rec.; *Residencias Ambala*, Carrera 5, No. 13-46, T 2412376, E, cheap, clean, friendly and central.

*Fiesta Avenida*, Carrera 14, No. 47-28, T 2853407, F, rec; *Residencias Avenida Fénix*, Carrera 16 between Calles 15 and 11, G, with bath, friendly, family atmosphere, clean; *Residencias Panamá No. 2*, Carrera 16, No. 16-88, T 241-04-05, F, friendly, clean, safe, hot shower (unsafe area). *Rey*, Calle 20 y Carrera 5, F, simple, safe, very central, rec; *Residencias Americana*, Calle 13 and Carrera 16, clean, G, safe, but only cold water; *Camelia*, Calle 16, No. 15-20, F, clean, safe, limited hot water, good value, T 243-4131; *Asturias*, next door (No. 15-36), T 242-0931, F, same standard but no hot water; *Residencia Bucamaranga*, Calle

15, No. 16-68, G with bath, cold water, basic; *Residencia La Escalinata*, Calle 15 near Carrera 10, F, hot water, rec.; many other cheap hotels in this area, which is dangerous especially for women alone.

We are informed that from Calle 12 southwards, Carrera 13 westwards is not salubrious: visitors are therefore advised to pick hotels in streets NE of Calle 12, with higher numbers. There are certainly many hotels between Calles 13 and 17 and Carreras 15 and 17, many of which are cheap, some of which are clean. Private vehicles should be parked in lockable, guarded parqueaderos.

**Youth Hostel Association** Alcom, Apartado Aéreo 3220, Carrera 7, No. 6-10, T 280-3041/280-3202, Fax 280-3460; IYHA member, has a full list of 18 hostels around the country. In the capital there is a hostel in La Candelaria at Carrera 6, No. 10-32, 7th Floor, T 2821787, with 80 beds. In Cundinamarca Department there is a hostel at *Centro Vacacional La Esperanza*, 79 km. from Bogotá and two on the road to Melgar (see **Excursions South-West**).

**Restaurants** 10% value-added tax is now charged. *Refugio Alpino*, Calle 23, No. 7-49, is an excellent international restaurant; *Casa San Isidro*, on Monserrate, good, not cheap; *El Café de Rosita*, Carrera 3, No. 8-65, connected with *Hostería de la Candelaria*, breakfast, lunch, bar and tapas, concerts Thurs. and Fri., rec.; *Casa Vieja*, Av. Jiménez 3-73, traditional Bogotá food, live music, atmosphere better than the food; *El Zaguán de Las Aguas*, Calle 19, No. 5-62, local dishes, atmosphere and national dancing in evening, but expensive and poor cooking and drinks (beer and soft drinks not available) very expensive; *Donde Canta la Rana*, Carrera 24-C, No. 20-10 Sur, a few km. from centre, is refreshingly local and unspoilt, open 1400-1900. *Tierra Colombiana*, Carrera 10, No. 27-27, good, expensive food, evening floor show. *Doña Bárbara*, Calle 82, corner of Carrera 11, dinner costs US$4-7, excellent latino jazz played.

*Na Zdorovia*, Cra 14, No. 80-71, Russian, very good; *Viva Villa*, Calle 82, No. 12-70, Mexican, good food, rec; *Cafetería Romana*, Av. Jiménez, between Carrera 6 and 7, all meals, very clean, indifferent pasta, but excellent, expensive breakfast menu, well rec., as are its sister restaurants *Sorrento* (round the corner from *Romano*) and *Salerno*, Carrera 7, No. 19-43, good value. For excellent, inexpensive Arab food, *Ramses*, Carrera 7, No. 18-64, but service very slow. *La Fragata*, Calle 15, No. 9-30 and Calle 77, No. 15-36, expensive but excellent for sea food.

*Punta Roja*, Carrera 7 y Calle 24, good 3-course meal for US$2; *Pollo Suiza*, Cra. 6 y Av. Jiménez, good set lunch for US$1.10. Of the many places selling burgers, *Bl Burger*, Av. 19 y Cra. 4, has been rec. as the best value. *Dominó*, a chain of good, fairly cheap, typical food restaurants, at Calle 19 with Cra. 3, Cra. 11 with Calle 71; another chain is *Crepes y Waffeles*, good value; good cheap local food at *Regia*, Calle Pallau (next to Gold Museum); *Empanadas La 19*, Avenida 19, No. 8-56, good, cheap meals and snacks; *El Ranchito China*, Carrera 4 between Calle 15 and 16, cheap and open late; *Delphi*, opposite Teatro Gaitán, Carrera 7 No. 22-66, rec. for cheap meals. *Freddy*, Carrera 15, No. 16-55, good, budget, popular. A cheap two-course meal can be had in the cafetería of the Ley and Tía supermarkets. For the traveller on a budget, *bandeja* (the local *plato del día* can cost US$1.50-2 for a 2-course meal at the right places).

*El Vegetariano*, Calle 22, No. 8-89, set meals for US$1, rec. (the restaurant on 3rd floor with only a small sign); there are other branches at Calle 18, No. 5-74, Calle 14, No. 5-00, and Carrera 8, No. 21-39, self-service, not as good as the others, but open on Sun., none is open in the evening; *El Trópico*, Carrera 8, No. 17-72, vegetarian restaurant, good food (especially the fruit cake) and whole wheat loaves for US$1.20 (4-course meal, US$3); *El Vegetariano Fleber*, Calle 17, No. 10-49, good; *Vegetariano de Sol*, Calle 63, No. 10-62 with Yoga Institute in Plaza de Lordes. *Jugos Cali*, Carrera 11, No. 64-60, mostly juices, with pastries. 4 rec. vegetarian restaurants, all with the same owner, are: *El Champiñón*, Transversal 20, No. 122-05 (T 213-2278), near Unicentro, *Samovares*, Carrera 11, No. 69-89 (T 249-4549—lunch only, fixed menu, US$6, nice atmosphere), Carrera 11, No. 67-63 (T 249-6515) and Av. Caracas No. 32-64 (T 285-6095). *El Integral Natural*, Carrera 11, No. 95-10, health food shop with a few tables at street level, restaurant downstairs, fixed menu US$1.50; *Los Vegetarianos*, Calle 41, No. 8-65 (good); *Acuarius*, Carrera 16, No. 43-30, good vegetarian food, rec. Vegetarian food, excellent, at Calle 74, No. 12-30 and at Carrera 8, No. 11-19, near Plaza Bolívar.

On Sunday nights it is difficult to find anywhere open; try Calle 22 (the entertainment district).

All along Carrera 15 in El Chicó are shops, bars and restaurants, many of which have tables out on the pavement. *Tony Roma's*, Carrera 15 esq. Calle 77 and Calle 93, No. 13-85, good quality food and excellent service. *Café Libre*, Carrera 15, near Universidad Católica, bar with live music, also serves lunches; *Café Oma*, Carrera 15, Calle 89/90, good food and coffee, nice atmosphere, open till 0100; *Café Omo Lago*, Carrera 15, No. 82-60. *Chicanos*, Carrera 11, No. 78-70, good value and quality (about US$15-20 for 2), excellent juices and cocktails; *Shamua*, Calle 85, No. 11-69, good cocktails, small selection of well prepared food, US style. Many small, popular bars and cafés around Calle 82, Carreras 12, 13, 14, frequented by young people, not cheap.

**Tea Rooms** (Pastelerías) *Benalcázar*, near Plaza de las Nieves on Carrera 8, No. 20-25, excellent pastries; *La Suiza*, Calle 25, No. 9-41, excellent pastries; *Panadería Florida*, Carrera 7, No. 20-82, also has good pastries;. *Fábrica del Pan*, Av. Jiménez at Carrera 8, good for breakfasts, teas, snacks, reasonably priced. A chain of *Cyranos* throughout the city offers good pastries.

**Shopping** 10% value-added tax on all purchases. *Artesanías de Colombia* (state-owned), Almacén San Diego, in the old San Diego church, Cra. 10, No. 26-50, Almacén Las Aguas, next to the Iglesia de las Aguas, Carrera 3A, No. 18-60, has good selection of folk art and crafts, at fair prices. There is a shop in the **Museo de Artes y Tradiciones Populares**, which is recommended. See *H. Stern's* jewellery stores at the International Airport, *Hilton Hotel* and *Tequendama Hotel*. A street market on Avenida Jiménez and Carrera 14 (Avenida Caracas) sells cheaper *ruanas*, blankets, leatherware, etc. Permanent crafts markets at Calle 100, Carrera 15 and Carrera 7 opp. *Hotel Tequendama*. There is another market, at Christmastime only, which is good for handicrafts, at Carrera 10, Calle 10. Another seasonal market is held at Carrera 7 and Calle 72. Mercado de Pulgas (fleamarket) on Cra. 3, from Calle 19, north, on Sunday afternoons and holidays. It is a popular place and bar at the north end sells cheap beer and has a reggae band playing all afternoon (on no account wander around here other than on Sunday).

High-quality leather goods on Calle 18, between Carreras 4 and 7, also at *Todo en Cuero*, Calle 19, No. 6-56, next to the Museo de Oro Calle 16 Carrera 64, and Carrera 10, between Calles 13 and 19. Shopping centre at Chapinero, Carrera 13, Calles 55-60, specializes in men's shoes and leather. Women's shoes are found on Calle 18 between Carrera 7 and 9. Boutiques are to be found in El Chicó on Carrera 15, Calles 76-100. *Galería Cano*, Edificio Bavaria, Carrera 7, Bogotá Hilton, Unicentro, Loc. 218, Airport, sells gold and gold-plated replicas of some of the jewellery on display in the Gold Museum. *Mitus* (in *Hotel Tequendama*) also sells reproduction jewellery from its own workshop, and Indian pottery. For hammocks, try Pasaje Rivas, Carrera 10, No. 10-54, big choice, good quality, bargain prices. Primitive paintings are often on show in the *Galería El Callejón*, Calle 16, No. 6-34, as well as old maps and prints. *Galería Alfred Wild*, Calle 82, No. 13-28, has excellent but pricey drawings and paintings. *Banco de Fotografías Movifoto*, Calle 15, No. 4-66, has a very large selection of postcards from all over Colombia. There are several antique shops around Calle 66 and Carrera 11; check yellow pages for precise addresses.

The pavements and cafés along Av. Jiménez, below Carrera 7, Parque de los Periodistas, and Calle 16 and Carrera 3, are used on weekdays by emerald dealers. Great care is needed in buying: bargains are to be had, but synthetics and forgeries abound. (Beware of stones that seem too perfect or have a bluish colouring.) Also jewellery shops in the basement of *Hotel Tequendama*, and on Calles 12 and 13, between Carreras 7 and 9. Modern textiles and knitwear can be bought at low prices at *Unicentro*, a large shopping centre on Carrera 15 at Calle 127A (take "Unicentro" bus from centre, going N on Cra. 10—takes about 1 hr.). *Cafam*, Av. 68 with Calle 72, is said to be cheaper than Unicentro. *Centro Granahorrar*, Av. Chile (Calle 72) between Carreras 10 and 11 is another good shopping centre; also *Metropolis*, Calle 68 y Carrera 68 (with *Exito* supermarket opposite), and *Boulevard Niza*, Av. Suba, Calle 11-127. *Técnica*, Carrera 7A, No. 16-13 (first floor) will put gold lettering on leather goods quickly and cheaply.

Heavy duty plastic for covering rucksacks, etc., is available at several shops around Calle 16 and Av. Caracas; some have heat sealing machines to make bags to size.

**Bookshops** *Librería Buchholz*, Carrera 7, No. 27-68 (opp. *Hotel Tequendama*), also at Calle 59, No. 13-13 (Chapinero); useful advice in a number of languages, low prices. *Librería Aldina*, Carrera 7, Calle 70-80, most helpful on books and Bogotá alike, excellent stock of English-language books, open 0930-1930, Sat. 0930-1700. *Librería Nacional*, Carrera 7, No. 17-51 (has small selection of English bestsellers). *Librería Francesa*, Calle 65, No. 9-07. *OMA* Cra 15, Calle 75, good art and literature books. *Librería Lerner*, Av. Jiménez, No. 4-35 (no English books). *Ateneo*, Calle 82, No. 13-19, in the north of the city, good selection of Colombian titles, knowledgeable staff; *Librería Tercer Mundo, Carrera 7, No. 16-91, knowledgeable; Librería Cultural Colombiana*, Calle 72, No. 16-15; *Casa de Libro*, Calle 18 between Cras. 7 and 6. Books in Colombia are generally expensive. Book Exchange Stalls,

Calle 19, between Carreras 7 and 10.

**Photography** *Foto Japón*, branches all over the city, have been rec. for developing, US$10 for a roll of 36, with free film.

**Taxis** have meters (although newer ones are reported not to have them); insist that they are used. Starting charge, US$0.35, plus US$0.07 for every 90 metres, minimum charge US$0.85. Additional charge of US$0.35 after 2000 and on public holidays and Sun. (a list of legal charges should be posted in the taxi).

Tan and green tourist taxis can be rented by the hour or the day through the *Tequendama Hotel*, most of the drivers speak English and are very helpful. Taxis are relatively cheap, so it is worthwhile taking one if you are carrying valuables, or at night. Taxi tours with Jaime Carvajal (Spanish spoken only), T 203-1063.

**Travel in Bogotá** Bus stops in centre by red and yellow "Paradero" boards; otherwise flag buses down. Bus fares are US$0.10, *busetas* charge US$0.15. Green buses with letters TSS (i.e. unsubsidized) cost US$0.12. There are some "super-executive" routes with plush seats and videos, at US$0.30-0.50 (if traffic is heavy you might see the whole film). Fares are a bit higher at night and on holidays. Urban buses are not good for sightseeing because you will be standing as likely as not. A metro is planned.

**Car Rental** Dollar Rent-a-Car, airport and Cra. 13, 82-28; **Hertz**, at airport, and at Carrera 10, No. 26-35; **National**, Carrera 7, No. 33-27; **Hernando Zuluaga & Cía**, Carrera 7, No. 20-80; **Aquilautos Ltda.**, Carrera 7, No. 34-81. **Avis**, Calle 79, 53-70, Cra 10, 27-79 and at airport.

**Night Life** Monserrate Room at the *Tequendama*; *Unicorn*, Calle 94, No. 7-75, expensive and spectacular; Many popular bars and dancing places on Carrera 5 with Calle 25, entrance between US$2-3, relatively safe area. Try *El Viejo Almacén*, Cra. 5 y Calle 13-14, run by an aged Argentine lady who plays 78 tango records and sells reasonably priced beer and aguardiente (on Fri. and Sat. only).

**Theatre** Many of the theatres are in the Candelaria area. Teatro Colón details on **page 661.** The following are the equivalent of the British fringe theatre: La Candelaria, Calle 12, No. 2-59; Sala Seki Sano, Calle 12, No. 2-65; Teatro Libre, Calle 13, No. 2-44; Teatro Popular de Bogotá, Calle 5, No. 14-71.

**Cinema** Cinemateca Distrital, Carrera 7 No. 22-79; good films, US$0.85. Also on Carrera 7: Teatro Municipal, No. 22-53; Metro, No. 21-78; Tisquesa, No. 27-29; Av. Chile shopping centre cinema, Calle 71, between Carreras 11 and 13 (usually prize-winning films). Ciné Club Latino, Auditorio Comfenalco, Cra. 4, No. 19-85, US$0.75. The Museo de Arte Moderno shows different films every day, all day. Foreign films old and new are shown on weekend mornings at 1030 in commercial cinemas and there are many small screening rooms which run the occasional feature. Consult *El Espectador* or *La Prensa*, and handbills all over town for what is on; frequent programme changes. Admission, US$0.70.

**Sports** Bull fighting on Sats. and Suns. during the season, and every 2-3 weeks fro the rest of the year, at the municipally owned Plaza de Santamaría, near Parque Independencia. In season, the bulls weigh over 335 kg.; out of season they are "comparatively small and unprofessional". (Local bullfight museum at bullring, door No. 6.) Boxing matches are held here too. Horse races at Hipódromo los Andes, on Autopista Norte, races at 1400 (entrance US$1 and US$0.35), and at the Hipódromo del Techo, in the SW, on Sats., Suns. and public holidays. Nearby is the Municipal Stadium, which can hold 50,000 spectators. Football matches are played here.

**Football** Tickets for matches at El Camplin stadium can be bought in advance at *Cigarrería Bucana*, Calle 18, No. 5-92. It is not normally necessary to book in advance, except for the local Santa Fe-Millionarios derby. Take a cushion; matches Sun. at 1545, Weds. at 2000.

**Museums** (all closed on Mondays) The **Museo Nacional**, on Carrera 7, No. 28-66, the Panóptico, an old prison converted into a museum (to the NE of the map), founded by Santander in 1823. Its top floor houses a fine art section, comprising national paintings and sculptures. Open Tues.-Sat. 0930-1830, Sun. 1000-1700, US$0.55. Many of its pre-conquest exhibits have been transferred to the **Museo Arqueológico**, see No. 7-43, see below. See map: 8 for **Museo de Arte Colonial**, under 1 for **Museo 20 de Julio** and 11 for the Banco de la República's Luis Angel Arango library (US$0.20, half price for students.

The **Museo de Arte Moderno**, Calle 24, No. 6-55, entry US$0.28, half price for students (open Tues.-Sun. 0900-1900), good café. If you want to photograph in the museum you must obtain permission from the office. The **Planetarium** and **Museo de Historia Natural**, Calle

26 with Carrera 7, open Tues.-Fri. 0900-1800, Sat., Sun., and holidays, 1000-1800 (see map, no. 24).

The **Museo Mercedes de Pérez**, formerly the Hacienda de El Chicó, a fine example of colonial architecture, is at Carrera 7, No. 94-17. It contains a world-wide collection of mostly 18th century porcelain, furniture, paintings, etc. Open Tues.-Sun., 0930-1230, 1430-1700.

The **Museo de Arte y Tradiciones Populares** is at Carrera 8, No. 7-21 in an old monastery and exhibits local arts and crafts. It has a shop, selling handicrafts at higher prices than Artesanías de Colombia, and a reasonably-priced bar and restaurant (dishes typical of different regions of Colombia served in colonial setting, usually with regional traditional music). Open 0900-1730, Tues.-Sat., Sun. and holidays 1000-1400. The shop is not open on Sun. and holidays. Entry fee US$0.25.

**Museo Siglo XIX**, Carrera 8, No. 7-91, founded by the Banco Cafetero, has a collection of 19th-century painting, clothes and furniture. Open Mon.-Fri., 0900-1800, Sat., 1300-1700. US$0.28.

The **Museo Arqueológico** (belonging to the Banco Popular) is a fine and extensive collection of precolumbian pottery, assembled in the restored mansion of the Marqués de San Jorge, Carrera 6, No. 7-43. The house itself is a beautiful example of 17th century Spanish colonial architecture. US$0.60 entry. Open: 1000-1700, Tues. to Fri.; 1000-1300, Sat.-Sun. There is a restaurant.

**Museo de Desarrollo Urbano (Urban Development)**, Calle 10 No. 4-21 (open Tues.-Sat., 0900-1800, Sun. and holidays, 1000-1800), interesting maps and photos of the development of Bogotá in an attractive colonial house near the Palacio San Carlos.

**Museo Militar**, Calle 10, No. 4-92, history of Colombian armed forces and good collection of weapons.

**Quinta de Bolívar** (Simon Bolívar museum), Calle 20, No. 3-23 Este, open Tues.-Sun., 1000-1700, his residence in Bogotá with documents, period rooms, nice garden.

**Casa-Museo Jorge Eliécer Gaitán**, Calle 42, No.15-52, is former residence of the populist leader whose assassination in April 1948 triggered the infamous "Bogotazo", at the outset of La Violencia.

**Instituto Nacional de Investigaciones Geológico-Mineras** has a library and pleasant museum at Diagonal 53, No. 34-53. Entrance US$0.10.

**Museo de los Niños**, Carrera 48, No. 63-97, natural sciences explained for children, created by Sra. Ximena Rosas with funding from industry.

**Museo del Oro** (the Gold Museum), is in splendid premises at the Parque de Santander (corner of Calle 16 and Carrera 6-A, see No. 18 on map). This collection is a "must", for it is unique. No less than 30,000 pieces of precolumbian gold work are shown. Open: Tues. to Sat., 0900-1600; Sun. and holidays, 0900-1200. (People in shorts not allowed). Charge, US$0.75 (US$0.10 on Sat., US$0.35 for children). Do not miss seeing the collections kept in a huge strong-room on the top floor. Several film shows a day; at 1200 and 1530 they are in English. Arrange a free tour in English, in advance, at the office on the 2nd floor.

The ancient gold objects discovered in Colombia were not made by the primitive technique of simple hammering alone, but show the use of virtually every technique known to modern goldsmiths.

The **Universidad Nacional** (about 13,000 students) is off the map, to the NW. The fine buildings are coated with political graffiti, and foreigners are not usually welcome on the campus. The oldest centres of learning are in the old centre: oldest of all is the Colegio Nacional de San Bartolomé (C 10, No. 6-57), in the same block as the Chapel of El Sagrario (3 on map), founded 1573. The second oldest, founded on December 18, 1653, is the Colegio Mayor de Nuestra Señora del Rosario (C 14, No. 6-25); its beautiful colonial building is well worth a look (you can buy a good cheap lunch at the cafeteria; it is not far from the Gold Museum).

**Banks** Banco de la República, the only bank permitted to exchange travellers' cheques in denominations of less than US$50 (up to 1500 Mon.-Thurs., to 1630 Fri., no commission charged), will give cash on American Express card, but not Visa, which is accepted at most other banks; leave plenty of time. You may need your passport rather than the DAS approved photocopy. **Banco Anglo Colombiano**, Carrera 8, No. 15-60, and eleven local agencies. **Banco Royal de Colombia**, Av. Jiménez with Carrera 8, will change cheques for US$50 but charges commission. Banks' commission is up to 5% on travellers' cheques. Open 0900-1500 Mon. to Thurs. and 0900-1530 on Fri. Closed on Sat.; also closed at 1200 on last working day of month.

**Exchange** American Express, Tierra Mar Aire Ltda, edif. Bavaria Torre B, Local 126, Carrera 10, No. 27-91, T 283-2955, Telex 41424 BOGCL. **International Money Exchange**, Carrera

7, No. 32-29, open till 1600 on Sats., check all transactions carefully; exchange at Av. 19, No. 15-35. **Exprinter** on Av. Jiménez and Carrera 6. Inside you can only get pesos and no travellers' cheques are exchanged, but the black market operates on the pavement outside, or try the kiosk right there, Peruvian and Ecuadorean currencies available (rates generally little different from official rates). Check the rate first, though, and if using it, be extremely careful. Normally, the best rates you will get are at the Banco de la República.

**Cultural Institutions** British Council, Calle 87, No. 12-79, T 236-25-42/257-96-32 has a good library and British newspapers. **Anglo-Colombian School**, Transversal 30, No. 152-38; postal address: Apartado Aéreo 52969, Bogotá 2. **English School**, Calle 170, No. 31-98 (T 254-1318 or 254-8874), Apartado Aéreo 51284, Bogotá. **American School**, Colegio Nueva Granada, Carrera 2E, No. 70-20, T 212-35-11. **Centro Colombo Americano**, Calle 109A, No. 17-10, T 2144960, Spanish courses, rec.

**Language Courses** Universidad Javeriana, Carrera 10, No. 65-48, T 2123009, recommended for full Spanish language and cultural courses; short, one-month courses in June, July and August, US$130.

**Embassies and Consulates** Venezuelan Consulate, Avenida 13, No. 103-16, T 256-3015, hrs. of business 0900-1230, 1300-1500, visas cost US$10, but allow 3 days (if they don't merely send you to Cúcuta; it is hard to persuade them to give visas to overland travellers). Ecuadorian Consulate, Calle 100, No. 14-63, T 257-9947 (hard to reach by phone); Brazilian Embassy, Calle 93, No. 14-20, T 218-0800; Peruvian Embassy, Calle 94, No. A7-A26, T 257-2726. Bolivian Embassy, Calle 78, No. 9-57, T 2118962. Panamanian Consulate, Calle 87, No. 11A-64, T 236-7531; Mon.-Fri., 0900-1300 (take "Usaquén" bus going north from centre, US$0.15). Costa Rican Consulate, Carrera 15, No. 80-87, Mon.-Fri. 0900-1300, T 236-1098. Guatemalan Consulate, Transversal 29A, Calle 139A, No. 41, T 2745365, Mon.-Fri., 0900-1200, visa takes 48 hrs., US$10 (cash only), one photo, one airline ticket (does not have to be return), tourist visa free for Canadians; takes 48 hours. Mexican Consulate, Calle 99, No. 12-08, Mon.-Fri., 0900-1300.

U.S. Embassy, Calle 38, No. 8-61 (mailing address: Apartado Aéreo 3831, Bogotá 1, D.E.), T 285-1300/1688. Canadian Embassy, Calle 76, No. 11-52; T 217-5555, open 0800-1630 (mailing address: Apartado Aéreo 53531, Bogotá 2, D.E.).

British Embassy, Calle 98, No. 9-03, 4th floor, T 218-5111, postal address: Apartado Aéreo 4508. German Embassy, Carrera 4, No. 72-36, 6th floor, T 212-0511. French Embassy, Avenida 39, No. 7-94. French Consulate, Carrera 7, No. 38-99, T 285-4311. Belgian Embassy, C.26, No.4A-45, piso 7, T 282-8881/2. Finnish Embassy, Calle 72 No 8-56, 7th floor, T 212-6111. Norwegian Consulate, Carrera 13, No. 50-78, Oficina 506, T 235-5419. Swedish Embassy, Calle 72 No. 5-83, T 255-3777. Danish Embassy, Calle 37, No. 7-43, 9°, Bogotá 2, T 232-6753/93. Swiss Embassy, Carrera 9, No. 74-08, oficina 1101, T 255-3945, open Mon.-Fri. 0900-1200. Italian Consulate, Calle 70, No. 10-25 (Aptdo. Aéreo 50901), T 235-4300. Israeli Embassy, Edificio Caxdac, Calle 35, No. 7-25, piso 14, T 2877783/808/962.

**DAS** Immigration office, Carrera 28, No. 17A-00, open 0730-1530, T 277-9211; Dirección de Extranjería (for renewing entry permits), Calle 100, about 2 blocks from Ecuadorean Consulate.

**Laundry** La Solución No. 2, Carrera 5, 21-84, 0800-1200, 1400-1900, US$0.75 for 1 kg. Piccadilly, Calle 63, No. 7-10; Burbujas, Edificio Procoil, Avenida 19, No. 3A-37, open Mon.-Sat. 0730-1930, Us$3.65 per machine load for wash, dry and iron, 24-hr service. Panorama, Carrera 7, Calle 67. Drycleaners: Lavaseco, Av. Jiménez, No. 4-30.

**Sauna** Los Andes, Carrera 4, No. 16-29, good service, US$3.20, open daily 1000-2200. Sauna San Diego, Carrera 7 near Calle 25, turkish bath and sauna US$2.50 to enter, US$2.50 massage, rec.

**Health** Cruz Roja Nacional, Avenida 68, No. 66-31, T 250-661/231-9027/231-9008, open 0830-1800. Centro Médico La Salud, Carrera 10, No. 21-36, 2nd floor, T 243-13-81/282-40-21. Clínica Bogotá, Carrera 17, No. 12-65 (not a safe area to walk in), discourages travellers from having gamma-globulin shots for hepatitis. Walter Röthlisberger y Cía Ltda., Calle 25A, No. 13A-28, T 2836200, imports medicines, including Vivotif for typhoid and gamma globulin, and stores them correctly; trade prices. The US Embassy will advise on doctors, dentists, etc. Profamilia, Calle 34, No. 14-46, for contraceptives. For health information, T 15; emergency medical service (TAS), T 277-6666. Clínica Marly and Clínica del Country are well-equipped private hospitals. Dr. Arturo Corchuelo at Calle 89, No. 12-21, T 2188710, recommended for orthopaedic problems.

**Postal Services** Main airmail office and foreign *poste restante* in basement of Edificio Avianca, Carrera 7, No. 16-36, open 0700-2200 Mon. to Sat. closed Sun., and holidays (0830-1200, 1530-1700, Mon. to Fri. for *poste restante*, letters kept for only a month). At weekend the Post Office only franks letters; stamps for postcards are not sold. Pharmacies and newsagents in Bogotá have an airmail collection. Parcel post, Calle 13 and Carrera 8, US$1.50 to US$4 per kilo to overseas destinations.

**International Telephone Calls** from several Telecom offices in centre of Bogotá (e.g. Carrera 13 y Calle 17; Calle 23, No. 13-49); all close within half an hour of 2000.

**Travel Agents** recommended: *Lands of Colombia*, Carrera 16, No. 72A-16, friendly (helpful, English-spoken). *Tierra Mar Aire*, Cra. 10, No. 27-91, is Amex agent; does city tours from *Hotel Tequendama* (T 286-1111). Similar tours of the City (4 hrs.) can be arranged from *Hotel Nueva Granada*, much better value than tours to Zipaquirá (each costs about US$14). *Viajes Don Quijote*, Carrera 10 No. 27-51, also organizes tours of the city, 3½ hrs. by day, and 4 hours by night in a country-type bus (*chiva*) with musicians on the back seat. *Expedición Colombia*, Edificio KLM, piso 9, Calle 26, No. 4A-45, T 284-8284/8456, runs tours to the Llanos by private, chartered plane.

**Tourist Offices** Corporación Nacional de Turismo (CNT), Calle 28, No. 13A-15, T 281-4341, Edificio Centro de Comercio Internacional (the name at the top of the building is Banco Cafetero), Mon.-Fri., 0830-1230, 1400-1700, and Sat. 0900-1200, take passport; they will tell you which parts of the country are unsafe, good maps of major cities available; at Eldorado Airport and new bus terminal (both helpful, will book hotel rooms). Municipal tourist office, *Alcadía* offices on Plaza Bolívar (Carrera 8, No. 10-65, 1st floor, S side of Plaza), and Carrera 35, No. 26-18 (Edif. Lotería de Bogotá). The Coordinadora de Turismo de Bogotá (Carrera 13, No. 27-95) has daily tours of the city with interpreters. For information on 24-hr. chemists (pharmacies), events, attractions, etc., T 282-0000.

   **Inderena, the National Parks Office**, is on Diagonal 34, No. 5-84, T 2851172, for information and permission to visit the parks (very helpful), some permissions may take a day or two. Good maps of Bogotá and road maps of Colombia can be purchased in the drugstore nearest the main road in the *Hotel Tequendama* arcade. Hiking **maps** from Instituto Geográfico, Agustín Codazzi, Carrera 30 y Calle 45, US$0.75 each (topographical details are generally accurate, but trails and minor roads less so). Esso road maps from service stations, US$0.40.

**Thefts** Most hotels charge US$0.10 a night for insurance against theft. If you have something stolen go to the Corporación Nacional del Turismo for help and collect the insurance; this will probably take a few days of strenuous effort, but it has been known to work.

**Airport** The airport at El Dorado has the world's second largest landing field. "Tourist Guide" policemen have white armbands. The taxi fare from airport to city is usually about US$4 (30% more at night and early a.m.). There are colectivos (US$0.50 plus luggage p.p.) from airport to centre; also buses, US$0.10 (not easy with bulky luggage). In the city centre buses and colectivos can be picked up on Avenida 19, anywhere between Carreras 3 and 10 at which they turn right for the airport; colectivos can also be taken from the corner of Av. Jiménez de Quesada and Avenida 14 (Avenida Caracas); buses marked "Aeropuerto" or "Universitaria Dorado"; colectivos marked "Aeropuerto". Make sure you get a registered taxi, where a policeman notes the numbers and gives you a paper stating fares, found at left (from inside) side of main terminal or Avianca terminal (drivers try to overcharge all the same). Unofficial taxis not advisable. Watch belongings outside airport, especially at night. Airport shops are beautiful, and there is a restaurant. Free Colombian coffee inside the customs area, between gates 2 and 3. Many snack bars and restaurants on first floor. Hotel reservations can be made at the airport but their hotel rates are often out of date. The cheapest is in our Category D. Exchange rates are marginally lower than in the city, but pesos cannot be changed back into dollars at the airport without receipts. Airport bank does not change travellers' cheques, and charges commission. N.B. If flying from Colombia to Mexico and you do not need an exit ticket from Mexico, you may have difficulty persuading Avianca staff otherwise. Allow 1½ hrs. for checking in and security.

   For internal flights, which serve all parts of the country, **see page 753**. For domestic shuttle flights to Medellín/Montería, Cali/Pasto, and Barranquilla, go to Puente Aéreo terminal, 1 km. before main terminal on Av. El Dorado. Avianca international flights also use this terminal (usually Miami and New York). It is more comfortable but there is not as much duty-free shopping (there is a 100 pesos tax payable at this terminal). You have to cross eight busy lanes of traffic to get a bus into town, and negotiate two drainage ditches. As a rule, all flights are overbooked, so book well in advance. The Avianca office is at Carrera 7, No.

16-36, T 266-97-00. Satena, Avenida 19, 13A-18, T 283-55-57/282-55-57, military airline, not best for comfort and delays. SAM, Carrera 10, No. 27-91, T 266-9600/283-3313. Many international airline offices are closed on Sat. and Sun. **See page 752** for procedure to obtain refunds on unused tickets.

**Rail** Although there are 3,700 km. of railways (metre gauge) in Colombia, the only long-distance route carrying passengers from Bogotá to **Santa Marta**, called the "Tayrona", which runs once a week (Mon. 0800), only between 1 December and 31 March. For the rest of the year you must go to **La Dorada** to take the "Expreso del Sol" train to Santa Marta, and that only goes twice a week (Tues. and Fri. 1400). Luggage is checked into locked compartments, so you need to have light clothing available before journey starts. Sit on right to avoid afternoon sun. Note that the entire rail network is in poor condition and trains are subject to delay. Station is at Calle 13 and Carrera 20. "Germania" bus goes from railway station to the city centre. Special excursions on steam trains go to **Zipaquirá** and **Nemocón**, Sun. and holidays 0900 (details under Nemocón **page 672**).

**Buses** There is a long-distance bus terminal on Av. Boyacá between El Dorado (Av. 26) and Av. Centenario (Calle 13). There is also access from Carrera 68. To get to the terminal take bus marked "Terminal" from "Terminal Transportes" bus stop at corner of Av. Jiménez de Quesada and Cra. 15, or colectivo taxi from Av. 13 y Av. Caracas, US$0.35 (this is the only method in the evening, no buses). To get into town take Route No. 1 or No. 3 at the terminal and get off at Carrera 13 esq. Calle 13, closest to the centre (from this junction "Germania" bus goes to the centre). A *buseta* (US$0.05) runs from Carrera 68 to the terminal and back. Taxi US$2.50 (plus US$0.15 at night—police give price slip; avoid the unofficial taxis, normally touting for particular hotels), or take colectivo from beside Ruta 3 bus stop, US$0.30. The terminal is well-organized, comfortable and safe; free self-service luggage trolleys are provided. There are shops and restaurants. There are showers at the terminal (between Nos. 3 and 4), US$0.40, soap and towel provided. If possible, buy tickets at the ticket office before travelling to avoid overcharging. Companies are grouped according to routes. **Fares and journey times are given under destinations below**. Note that if you wish to avoid the Quindío pass on journeys west and south, it is best to fly to Armenia or Pereira, about 25 mins. flight. Velotax busetas are slightly quicker and more expensive than ordinary buses, as are colectivos, which go to several long-distance destinations.

**Bus to Venezuela** It is better not to buy a through ticket to Caracas with Exp. Berlinas as this does not guarantee a seat and is only valid for 2 Venezuelan companies; moreover no refunds are given in Cúcuta. Sometimes the border with Venezuela is closed because of illegal immigration; in this case, tickets can be refunded in Bogotá. Ideally, if you have time make the journey to Cúcuta in two stages to enjoy the scenery to the full. Bus connections from San Antonio de Táchira in Venezuela to Caracas are good.

## Excursions from Bogotá

If you have a car, drive round the Av. Circunvalación for splendid views. The salt mines of Zipaquirá are described on **page 671**. Other excursions are to the beautiful artificial lake of Muña, formed by a dam; to **Sopó**, in the Sabana (63 km.), where they venerate an image of the Saviour which has appeared in an eroded stone; the paintings of angels in the church are very strange and worth seeing (ask at the Casa Cural for entry to church—give a tip); in Sopó a restaurant (previously *Nicolás*) serves good local dishes. Nearby are the Alpina yoghurt factory (no free samples) with another restaurant, *La Embarrada*, opposite, which specializes in cooking meat in clay dishes on coals; Parque Puerto de Sopó (with artificial lake) at km. 32.5 on Autopista Norte, and an amusement park a few km. N. For the Falls of Tequendama, **see below**. For Tunja (2 hrs. over first-class road), and Guatavita Nueva, **see page 673**. Bogotanos like to warm up at weekends: popular destinations are Melgar (**see below**) and Girardot (**page 716**). About half-way to Girardot, near Fusagasugá (**see below**) is *Hotel Miramonti*, C, Italian-run family place, very quiet. To the east of Bogotá is *Choachí*, an attractive village set in a valley, where there are hot springs (good food at *El Colonial*, 1½ blocks from main square). Flota Macarena bus, Av. 17, No. 23-96, T 277-3900, several a day. A turnoff from the Choachí road brings one to the Santuario de San Francisco, with better views of Bogotá than one can get from Monserrate.

**Hiking**  "Salsipuedes" is a hiking group based in Bogotá, hiking 15-40 km. every Saturday on trails in Cundinamarca; a very friendly group which welcomes visitors. Contact Alfonso Gamboa, Diagonal 123, No. 50-30, Bogotá, T 2839980 office, 2536228 home.

Longer excursions are taken in four main directions, which are dealt with in the following pages. They are to the south-west (Fusagasugá, Melgar), the north-west (Facatativá, Guaduas, Villeta), the north (Chía, Zipaquirá) and the north-east (along the Cúcuta road). A fifth direction, east to the Llanos, will be dealt with separately.

**South-West**:  The Simón Bolívar Highway runs from Bogotá to Girardot (**see page 716**); this 132-km. stretch is extremely picturesque, running down the mountains within 5 km. of the Salto de Tequendama (take the exit marked to El Colegio).

At the *Salto de Tequendama*, the water of the Río Bogotá or Funza falls 132 metres over the lip of the Sabana; the water is dirty with sewage but the falls are still a spectacular sight though the smell can be most unpleasant. The site is 31 km. from Bogotá in an amphitheatre of forest-clad hill sloping to the edge of a rock-walled gorge. There is a good bus service from Bogotá.

After the Tequendama Falls turning is *Fusagasugá* which lies in a rich wooded valley famous for its fruits. A few kilometres beyond is the *Hotel Catama*. Fusagasugá is noted for its good climate and Sunday market. Population: 22,460, with an admixture of the wealthier families from Bogotá during the summer. A visit should be paid to the Jardín Luxemburgo for its splendid orchids, best flowering Nov.-Feb. but it is a long walk out of town; the Jardín Clarisa for orchids, and that at the Casa de la Cultura are pleasant. There are bathing spots on the Sumapaz river. Altitude: 1,740 metres. From Bogotá, Autos Fusa (Carrera 22, No. 14-27) and Cootransfusa (Carrera 14, Calle 10), US$1.

**Hotels**  *La Scala*, F, rec.; *Castillo*, E, rec. There are many luxury hotels on the road to Melgar.

From Fusagasugá, a bumpy 1½ hr. bus ride will take you to **San Bernardo**, a pretty little town. The cemetery has a macabre attraction; looking through a window near the central "altar" you see mummified figures, including a woman and child, assembled in the dimly lit cellar.

From Boquerón, beyond Fusagasugá, a side road goes about 10 km. to *Pandi* where there is a park with ancient stones. Nearby, on the road to Incononzu, is a famous natural bridge in a spectacular and very deep gorge through which runs the Sumapaz river.

*Melgar*, near Girardot, is a popular weekending place for Bogotanos who like a little warmth. There are lots of hotels in the area most of which have swimming pools; it is best to try whichever you like the look of and move on to another if it is full; the *Esmeralda, Plaza Crillón* (D) and *Nuevo Guadaira* have been recommended; there are also camping sites and the state-subsidized Cafam vacation centre, best visited in mid-week. Toll at 14 km. S of Fusagasugá, US$0.50, and 20 km. S of Bogotá, US$0.40.

Between Bogotá and Melgar are 2 youth hostels: *Centro Vacacional Los Guaduales* at Chinauta (Km. 68), and *Parador Camping El Laurel* at Silvania. Details from Alcom; see under Bogotá.

**North-West**:  The Sabana de Bogotá is dotted with white farms and groves of eucalyptus. The road passes through two small towns, Fontibón and Madrid. *Fontibón*, 10 km. from Bogotá, has a good colonial church, and about 3 km. outside the town are stones with Indian pictographs; nearby, on the road from the old Techo airport to Bogotá, there are replicas of San Agustín statues.

*Facatativá*, a town of 22,460 people, is 40 km. from Bogotá. Some 3 km. from Facatativá, on the road to the W, is the Piedras de Tunja, a natural rock amphitheatre of enormous stones; it has numerous Indian pictographs and has now been established as a park with an artificial lake. A road goes SW from Facatativá through Tocaima to Girardot. From **Tocaima**, a small, attractive holiday town (several hotels; *Bella Vista*, D, clean, friendly, good simple food, swimming pool, no hot water), a road runs through beautiful mountain country, via La Mesa, to Mosquera on the road between Madrid and Fontibón. This is a good alternative to the Simón Bolívar highway from Girardot to Bogotá.

71 km. from Facatativá is **Villeta** (9,700 inhabitants), which has become a popular weekend resort for the Bogotanos. Not far away are the waterfalls of Quebrada Cune. Hotels: *Pacífico* and *Mediterráneo* (both have swimming pools and are expensive); less expensive is the *Colonial Plaza*, Carrera 4, No. 6-07 (corner of main square), good restaurant, with swimmimg pool, pleasant. On road to Bogotá is *Balneario El Descanso*, F, swimming pool, safe parking. Near the centre is *Llamarade* restaurant, good value; many good ice cream parlours around the square. The road continues to Honda (see page 714).

Midway between Villeta and Honda is **Guaduas**; in the main square is a statue of the liberator Policarpa Sala Varrieta. Also in the main square is a delightful colonial hotel. Public swimming pool in town. There is a Sunday market. Best local dish is *quesillos*. Bus to Honda, US$1.20, 1 hr. The surrounding countryside is beautiful, including waterfalls at Versalles (10 km.). Hotel: *Tacuara*, swimming pool, riding, *cabañas*, B; *Cacique*, 1 km. outside village, and *Real Agrada*, in resort area.

**North**: An interesting trip from Bogotá can be made to the salt mine of Zipaquirá and to the large centre of population around Chiquinquirá. Bogotá is left by an *autopista*, a northern extension of Avenida Caracas and Carrera 13. The *autopista* ends after 24 km. at an intersection where a road leads off left at a right-angle for Chía and Zipaquirá. Taking this road you soon come to a fork which takes you left to Chía and right to Zipaquirá. At the beginning of the road to Zipaquirá is the *Restaurant Arrieros*, where *antioqueño* food is served by waiters in the appropriate dress and *antioqueño* music is sometimes played.

**Chía** has a graceful colonial bridge and a typical Sunday market (bus from Av. Caracas, Bogotá US$0.25). Near Chía is Terijo, whose metalworks is famous. On the way there you pass through Fonqueta, where tapestries are made. Walk, or take a bus to La Barbanera church on a hill overlooking the Sabana de Bogotá. Good restaurant just outside Chía, *Andrés Carne de Res*.

From Chía (via Cájica, 22,000 pop., pleasant town with good shopping) to **Zipaquirá** (40,850 people), centre of a rich cattle farming district, and famous for its rock salt mine, which has enough salt to last the world 100 years, though it has been exploited for centuries. The church in the attractive central Plaza is also worth a visit for its stonework (despite its external appearance, it has a modern interior).

The immense black galleries of salt gleaming under electric lights are most impressive and a little eerie. A road has been opened into the galleries but because of damage cars are no longer allowed to drive in. You can walk its whole length in 15 mins. An underground cathedral dedicated in 1954 to Nuestra Señora del Rosario (patron saint of miners) is about 4 mins. on foot from the entrance and very impressive. The roof is 23 metres above the floor and the main altar table is a block of salt weighing 18 tons. It took ten years to complete. To photograph the interior you need a strong flash *and* a fast film. Entry is on a hill, which is a 20 mins. walk from the Plaza (adults US$0.90, children US$0.45, open Tues.-Sat. 1000-1200; 1300-1615, Sun. 1000-1600, but check: we have been told in late 1990 that the cathedral is open only on Sundays and holidays) Many buses from Avenida Caracas, Bogotá, US$0.30 each way, 1¼ hours. The Zipaquirá bus station is 15 minutes' walk from the mines and cathedral. Tours are also arranged by some of the Bogotá hotels and cost about US$15. Zipaquirá can also be reached from Tunja (see page 673), by taking a Bogotá-bound bus and getting off at Alcaro for connection to Zipaquirá, US$2. Leave plenty of time for the return journey as it can be difficult to stop Bogotá-Tunja buses at Alcaro.

The *Hostería del Libertador*, near the mine, good food, but no longer a hotel. *Hotel Colonial*, E, without bath, clean and friendly. Restaurants on main square, *El Mesón del Zipa*, good, cheap food, US$1.50-2.00; *Los Pijaos*, pleasant.

Not far from Zipaquirá, at **Nemocón**, there are salt mines and a church, but the mines are sometimes closed to visitors, following accidents. A side (dirt) road connects with the Bogotá-Cúcuta highway.

A steam-hauled *tren turístico* on Sundays and holidays at 0900 from the main station in Bogotá, calling at a halt at Calle 100 and Carrera 15 at 0927, going to Zipaquirá and Nemocón: 2 hrs. 20 mins. to Zipaquirá, 2 hrs. 45 mins. to Nemocón, where the train is met by the town band. At Nemocón there is time to have lunch and look around before train returns, leaving at 1510 (1540 from Zipaquirá), back in Bogotá at 1800. Tickets (US$6 return) in Bogotá from Tierra Mar Aire travel agency. You are advised to book in advance. Restaurant in Nemocón, *El Colonial*, 100 metres from the station.

**Ubaté** is 48 km. by road to the N. On Sunday, the market in the big plaza has nothing of interest for the tourist. It is the cheese-making centre of the Sabana; the church is being refurbished. Here a branch road runs E to Lenguazaque (6,125 people). Close by, at Chirbaneque, is a worked-out emerald mine in lovely scenery. A spur from this road branches left to Guachetá, 21 km. from Ubaté, and slightly larger than Lenguazaque. Nearby is the Laguna de Fúquene (Devil's Lake) hotel, about 4,850 hectares of water with four cultivated islands.

**Chiquinquirá**, 50,000 people, 134 km. by road from Bogotá, is on the W bank of the Suárez river at 2,550 metres. It is a busy commercial centre and the focus of a large coffee and cattle region. In December thousands of pilgrims honour a painting of the Virgin whose fading colours were restored by the prayers of a woman. In 1816, when the town had enjoyed six years of independence and was besieged by the Royalists, this painting was carried through the streets by Dominican priests from the famous monastery, to rally the people. The town fell, all the same.

**Hotels** *Moyba*, Carrera 9, No. 17-53, facing square, F, with bath (cheaper without); *Residencias San Martín*, Carrera 9, No. 19-84, F, basic; *Residencias Viajero*, G, opposite Banco de Colombia, good, cheap meals. Many others.

**Restaurant** *El Escorial*, good but expensive.

In the shops of Chiquinquirá are displayed the toys made by local Indians: some ceramics painted in gay colours and others white and porous as they come from the kiln; tops and teetotums and other little things carved from tagua nuts; orange-wood balls to catch on a stick; the most durable tambourines in the world; shining, brightly coloured gourds; diminutive nine-stringed guitars on which children try the first measures of the *bambuca*; many scapularies; but better than anything else, the little pottery horses from Ráquira, or, by the same Indian craftsmen, little birds that whistle, hens with their chicks, and enchanting little couples dancing to an orchestra of guitars and mandolins.

**Bus** from Chiquinquirá to **Villa de Leiva** takes 1¾ hr., US$1.70 **(see page 674)**. Bus to **Tunja**, 3 hrs., US$3.25; to **Zipaquirá**, US$2.75; to **Bogotá**, 2½ hrs., US$3 (last returns at 1730); all from bus station.

**Excursion** A road runs 105 km. SW to **Muzo**, on the banks of the Río Carare, 600 metres above sea-level. Population: 5,000. Sixteen km. away a famous open-cast emerald mine has been worked since 1567, and long before that by the Muzo tribe of Indians. In 1989 it was reported that police permission is needed to visit the mine, and it has become a dangerous area.

There are roads from Chiquinquirá to Tunja, the capital of the Department, and to Barbosa. Both are on the Bogotá-Cúcuta highway and are described below. On the Tunja road a short branch right at Tinjacá leads to **Ráquira**, where Indians make the pottery described above (sold in about 10 shops on the main street, including branch of Artesanías de Colombia). There's nowhere to stay, not much to eat. Avoid the *Carlos Andrés* restaurant on the main plaza. At weekends it is possible to eat at the Museo de Arte y Tradiciones Populares. There are reports of a hotel with restaurant being built on the plaza. Market day Sunday. 30 minutes' walk along a very rough road is a beautiful 16th-century monastery, the Convento de la Candelaria, with anonymous 17th-century paintings of the life of St. Francis; they sell honey to finance the monastery (visiting times 1400-1700). *Parador La Candelaria*, C, adjoining monastery, picturesque, good food. Also nearby are some waterfalls. The old colonial town of Villa de Leiva is also on this road. Ráquira is best reached from Tunja although there are direct buses from Bogotá (Rápido El Carmen, 0545, 0715, US$2.50, 6 hrs., returning

1300) on an appalling road. Last bus to Tunja 1330. If stuck after 1330, walk 5 km. to Tres Esquinas on Villa de Leiva-Chiquinquirá road (70 km.), where buses pass between 1530-1630, mostly going E. There is a direct bus to and from Villa de Leiva daily.

---

## BOGOTA TO CUCUTA (2)

The main road route from Bogotá to Venezuela has some spectacular stretches. It passes through, or near, several colonial towns and gives access to the Sierra Nevada del Cocuy, excellent climbing and hiking country.

A 618-km. road runs NE from Bogotá to Cúcuta, near the Venezuelan border, through Tunja, Moniquirá, Barbosa, Socorro, San Gil, Bucaramanga and Pamplona. It runs through some beautiful scenery, and is good most of the way. Toll points 10 km. N of Bogotá, US$0.40, and at La Cara, S of Tunja, US$0.40. The railway via Tunja to Duitama and Sogamoso is now for freight only. The road out of Bogotá is the *autopista* to near Chía (**see page 671**), then follow Tunja signs.

At Sesquilé you can take a minor road to the right, to Guatavita Nueva.

*Guatavita Nueva* This modern town, 75 km. from Bogotá, was built in colonial style when the old town of Guatavita was submerged by a hydroelectric reservoir. Although the blend of old and new is fascinating, Guatavita Nueva has failed as a social experiment. All the country folk have left and it is now a week-end haunt for Bogotanos and tourists. (During the week the town is empty.) Cathedral, artisan workshops, museum, and small bull-ring for apprentices to practise Sun. afternoons. Sun. market best in morning, before Bogotanos get there. Bus from Bogotá (Flota Valle de Tenza, Carrera 25, No. 15-72, recommended; Flota Aguila, Carrera 15 No. 14-59), US$1.25, 2-3 hrs., departures 0730, 0800 and 0930; last return bus at 1730. You can walk (or ride, US$7 per horse) from the town to the Laguna de Guatavita (also called Lago de Amor by locals), where the legend of El Dorado originated, but it is a long (2-3 hr.) walk. It is easier to approach the lake from a point on the Sesquilé-Guatavita Nueva road (the bus driver will let you off at the right place) where there is a sign offering "Alpina Yoghurt" and a kiosk. It is a 2 hr. walk along a dirt track from the main road to the lakeside. This track can be driven to the lakeside (in the dry season, in a good car); turn right near the barn with the red door, and right again opposite small lake. Beside the lake are houses of rich Bogotanos.

There are no hotels in Guatavita Nueva, although rooms are sometimes to be found.

The basis of the El Dorado (Gilded Man) story is established fact. It was the custom of the Chibcha king to be coated annually with resin, on which gold dust was stuck, and then to be taken out on the lake on a ceremonial raft. He then plunged into the lake and emerged with the resin and gold dust washed off. The lake was also the repository (as with the *cenotes* in Yucatán, Mexico) of precious objects thrown in as offerings; there have been several attempts to drain it (the first, by the Spaniards in colonial times, was the origin of the sharp cut in the surrounding hills) and many items have been recovered over the years. The factual basis of the El Dorado story was confirmed by the discovery of a miniature raft with ceremonial figures on it, made from gold wire, which is now one of the most prized treasures of the Museo de Oro in Bogotá. Part of the raft is missing; the story is that the gold from it is now reposing in one of the finder's teeth! (Read John Hemming's *The Search for El Dorado* on the subject.)

Beyond Chocontá (15,300 inhabitants), 88 km. from Bogotá, the route is across the western slopes of the Eastern Cordillera to Tunja, 137 km. from Bogotá.

*Tunja*, 180,000 inhabitants, capital of Boyacá Department, stands at 2,820 metres in an arid mountainous area. The climate is cold; mean temperature, 12°C.

One of the oldest cities in Colombia, it was refounded as a Spanish city by Gonzalo Suárez Rendón in 1539. It was then the seat of the Zipa, one of the two Chibcha kings. The old city has been compared with Toledo, but the modern city is far less attractive. Of the many colonial buildings the most remarkable is the church of Santo Domingo, a masterpiece begun in 1594; the interior is covered with wood most richly carved. Another is the Santa Clara chapel (1580), now the hospital of San Rafael, with some fine wood carving. In Parque Bosque de la República is the adobe wall against which three martyrs of the Independence were shot in 1816. Market open every day (good for *ruanas* and blankets). Friday is main market day.

The house of Don Juan de Vargas has been restored as a museum of colonial Tunja (0800-1200, 1300-1800). The Casa del Fundador Suárez Rendón, Plaza Bolívar, dates from 1540-43 and is one of the few extant mansions of a Spanish *conquistador* in Colombia; open as a museum (except Mon. and Tues.); see the unique series of plateresque paintings on the ceilings. The church of Santa Bárbara is full of colonial woodwork, and in the nearby parish house are some notable religious objects, including silk embroidery from the 18th century. Some houses still have colonial portals. There are some fine colonial buildings on Plaza Bolívar opposite the Cathedral. Also impressive is the church of San Ignacio.

The city formed an independent Junta in 1811, and Bolívar fought under its aegis during the campaign of the Magdalena in 1812. Six years later he fought the decisive battle of Boyacá, nearby (see below). For the Piedras de Tunja see under Facatativá **page 670**.

**Hotels** *Hostería San Carlos*, colonial style, good restaurant, highly rec.; *Pensión Suárez Rendón*, Plaza Bolívar (good food, F, friendly but basic); *Res. Lord*, Calle 19, No. 10-64, F, small rooms but hot water, clean, friendly, rec.; *San Francisco*, Carrera 9, No. 18-90, on Plaza Bolívar, near cathedral, E, clean, friendly, check bill; *Don Camilo* on Plaza Bolívar, F, clean and friendly; *Príncipe*, F with limited hot water, small rooms but clean, near bus station, 5 mins. from Plaza Bolívar, rec.; *Americano*, on Carrera 9 near Plaza Bolívar, F, good. *Conquistador* on the corner of Plaza Bolívar, F, has hot water, is safe and clean, but many rooms don't have outside windows. Area around bus station said not to be safe at night.

**Restaurants** *San Ricardo*, Calle 19, No. 8-38, good; *Surtipan*, Calle 20, No. 12-58, good cakes and coffee; *Estar de Hunzahúa*, Calle 20, No. 11-20 (2nd floor), good food and value, rec.; *Bodegón de los Frayles,* beside the church of San Ignacio, one block from the Plaza Bolívar, rec. as friendly with good food.

**Bank** Banco de la República, Carrera 11, No. 18-12.

**Tourist Office** In Casa del Fundador, Plaza Bolívar, helpful but not always accurate.

**Bus** Station is a steep 500 m. from city centre; from Bogotá 2½-4½ hrs., US$3, Duitama, Cotrans, and others.

**Excursions from Tunja** The battle of Boyacá was fought about 16 km. south of Tunja, on the road to Bogotá. On the bridge at Boyacá is a large monument to Bolívar. Bolívar took Tunja on 6 August 1819, and next day his troops, fortified by a British Legion, the only professional soldiers among them, fought the Spaniards on the banks of the swollen Río Boyacá. With the loss of only 13 killed and 53 wounded they captured 1,600 men and 39 officers. Only 50 men escaped, and when these told their tale in Bogotá the Viceroy Samao fled in such haste that he left behind him half a million pesos of the royal funds. There is now a huge modern restaurant overlooking the site.

On a hillside outside Tunja is the carved rock throne of the Chibcha king, the Zipa; ask for directions from the Tourist Office.

At **Paipa**, between Tunja and Duitama, there are municipal thermal baths, US$0.75, 30 mins. bus ride from Tunja, US$1, then 30-min. walk from plaza (taxi from plaza US$0.55, from hotel US$0.75—taxi drivers are likely to take you to a hotel of their recommendation, not yours). *Hotel Sochagota*, overlooking the lake, has a swimming pool fed by hot springs, C, cabins for hire, with 2 bedrooms, bathroom, log fires and private hot spring pools. Among the many other places to stay are *Panorama* (C, meals US$2.50, huge swimming pool, Turkish bath, sauna), *La Casona*, F, *Casablanca*, D and *cabañas*, hotels and *residencias* ranging from our D range to F p.p. There are 7 restaurants: it's a popular centre for Colombians, but travellers reported in 1990 that generally the water was not clean and the area was noisy and crowded.

*Villa de Leiva*, an extremely pretty place, is reached by a branch road, left, at Arcabuco. (Toll at Arcabuco, US$0.40.) The drive affords some beautiful views and, at Km. 20 from Villa de Leiva, there is a left turn for the **Iguaque National Park** (3 km.) run by Inderena, which is the site of interesting oak woods, flora, fauna and several lakes. There is a tourist centre with accommodation for 60 and a restaurant. There are guided paths and a marked trail to Lake Iguaque, a walk of 2½ hours. Getting there can be difficult; most likely day for a lift is Saturday, market day, be prepared to walk. (Camping is allowed, free and safe.) The town dates back, like Tunja, to the early days of Spanish rule, but unlike Tunja, it has been declared a national monument so will not be modernised. The first president of Nueva Granada (**see page 652**), Miguel Venero de Leiva, lived in the town. There are two colonial houses which are worth a visit: the house in which Antonio Nariño lived (Carrera 9, No. 10-39, open Tues.-Sun. 0900-1230, 1400-1800)—he translated the *Rights of Man* into Spanish—and the building in which the first Convention of the United Provinces of New Granada was held. Also worth a visit is the restored birthplace of the independence hero Antonio Ricuarte. A palaeontological museum has been opened 15 mins. walk N of the town on Carrera 9. The shops in the plaza have an excellent selection of Colombian handicrafts, while the Saturday market, not yet geared to the tourist trade, still offers many bargains. On the Plaza Mayor is the Casa-Museo Luis Alberto Acuña, housing fascinating examples of Acuña's work (recommended, entry US$0.70, extra to take photographs). The Monasterio de las Carmelitas has one of the best museums of religious art in Colombia, open Sat. and Sun. 1400-1700.

The mountains around Villa de Leiva abound in fossils. 5 km. along the road to Chiquinquirá can be seen the complete fossil of a dinosaur now housed in a room, entry US$0.30, there are road signs to it, ask for *El Fósil* (open 0800-1200, 1300-1600, Thur. only 1300-1600); the children sell fossils and rough emeralds. 2 km. from El Fósil along this road is the turning for (1 km.) the archaeological site known as El Infiernito, where there are several huge carved stones believed to be giant phalli and a solar calendar (0900-1200, 1400-1700, closed Mon., admission US$0.50). 3 km. after the Infiernito turning is the Monastery of Ecce-Homo (founded 1620), which is worth a visit; note the fossils on the floor at the entrance. There is a bus from Villa de Leiva at 0930 each morning, going to Santa Sofía, US$0.50, it's half an hour to the crossing, then a 2 km. walk to the monastery. The road goes through the desert of La Candelaria, a beautiful, highly-eroded countryside. Note the rectangular cromlech with 24 menhirs. The town tends to be full of visitors at weekends and bank holidays and is generally expensive.

**N.B.** It is better not to visit Villa de Leiva on Mondays or Tuesdays as almost everything is closed. Also there are few services in Villa de Leiva, buy fuel etc. in Tunja. The houses are closed Monday-Friday out of season, but the trip is worth while just for the views. In any event, the town and surrounding hills are excellent for long, peaceful walks.

**Hotels** *El Molino la Mesopotamia*, Calle del Silencio, which used to be a colonial mill, very good, C, meals US$4, breakfast US$3, including all meals (US$12.50), 10% rebate for booking 10 days ahead (closed during the first weeks of January), swimming pool, home cooking, excellent food, beautiful gardens. *Mesón de la Plaza Mayor*, Calle 79, No. 10-11, C (B full board), beautifully restored *hospedaría*, owner, Mauricio Ordóñez, speaks English, helpful; *Los Llanitos*, 5 min. walk from main plaza, D, quiet, hot water, very friendly, good food; *El Marqués de San Jorge*, D, pleasant, on Calle 14, No. 9-20; *Hospedaje El Mesón de Los Virreyes*, Carrera 9, No. 14-51, D, with bath, good restaurant; *Cabaña Jequeneque*, opposite *La Mesopotamia*, D, with breakfast, open only at week-ends but rec. Unnamed *residencia* on Plaza Bolívar (the only one), F, hot water, pretty. Accommodation with Señora Carmen Castaneda, Calle 14, No. 7-51, 4 rooms, all giving onto a flower-filled patio, E, clean, friendly; also Familia Fitata, Calle 12, No. 7-35, E (F in week), breakfast extra, friendly, clean, safe. *Hostería La Roca*, Calle 13, No. 9-54, E-D, clean and pleasant, with rooms overlooking main square and reasonable breakfast, noisy at night because of bar music. The telephone connection from Bogotá is poor and most hotels have reservation numbers in Bogotá. Booking essential during holidays, and advisable at weekends (try bargaining Mon.-Thurs.). **Camping** at Los Olivares near village of Sáchica, 4 km. from Villa de Leiva (no services). Also Indirena's *Vivero*, 15 mins. walk N of plaza on road to Arcabuco (just before palaeontological museum), nice place with bathroom, warm shower, ask for Juan.

**Restaurants**  Several on the main square, in, and opposite, the bus station. *La Parrilla*, Carrera 9, No. 9-17 and *Los Kioskos*, Carrera 9, No. 11-52; *Nueva Granada*, Carrera 9, No. 13-69, good value, friendly, owner Jorge Rodríguez, plays classical music; *El Parrilón de los Caciques*, W side of town on Carrera 9, No. 9-05, warmly rec., good value. *Los Balcones*, just off plaza, cheap, early breakfasts; *Freilon*, recently opened nearby; *El Estar de la Villa*, Calle 13, No. 8-89, good.

**Post Office**  in Telecom building, Calle 13, No. 8-26.

**Transport**  Buses to Leiva from Tunja, 1 hr. 5 mins., US$1 with Flota Reina or Valle de Tenza company. (From Bogotá to Villa de Leiva, via Tunja, takes 4 hrs., US$3.50.) Colectivo taxis leave the bus station in Tunja for **Villa de Leiva** every hour and return from the main square. Leiva bus station in 8th block of Carrera 9. It is recommended to book the return journey on arrival. If driving from Tunja, watch out for rockfalls. Another way of getting to Villa de Leiva is via Sáchica, either directly from Tunja or, coming from Bogotá, turning left (W) at the Boyacá monument, via Samacá.

From Tunja there are two possible routes to Cúcuta; the main road, almost entirely paved, goes via Bucaramanga, but the other via Duitama and Málaga, rejoining the main road at Pamplona, is also interesting, though there are few filling stations N of Duitama. In **Duitama** there is the interesting tourist complex Punta Larga, close to a furniture manufacturer. (*Isobel*, Carrera 18, No. 18-60, clean, quiet, F; many others nearby). About 3 km. from Duitama, on the road to Belencito, there is another hotel, also in an old *hacienda*, the *Hostería San Luis de Ucuenga*. Bus Duitama to Bucaramanga at 0900, 9 hrs., US$9; to Málaga at 0800, sit on right side for best views, 6 hrs. At Duitama turn right for **Sogamoso**, where a good museum of archaeology has been opened on the site of the centre of the precolumbian city. This was an important Chibcha settlement; destroyed by the Spaniards, but it has been reconstructed on site. Their arts of mummification, statuary, and gold working are shown in the museum (closed Mon.). It is possible to camp in the museum grounds if you ask permission. A museum of religious art is open on the road from Duitama to Sogamoso (most valuable exhibits were stolen in 1981). *Hotel Hacienda Suescún*, E, nearby in old *hacienda*, excellent service (but food not too good); many hotels near bus station e.g. *Hostal Aranjuez*, G, basic, safe, very helpful, *Residencia Embajador*, F, clean, friendly, rec.; *Santa Marta*, F, not rec. (Bus Bogotá-Sogamoso US$4, 4 hrs.) E of Sogamoso the churches of Mongua (a pleasant colonial town, 20 km.) and Topaga are worth a visit, and so is the mountain-ringed **Lago de Tota** (3,015 metres above sea level), south of Sogamoso. The *Refugio el Pozo Azul*, on the lakeside, is a private club run by Gary Clements and his Colombian wife, who will extend membership to readers of *The South American Handbook*; an excellent place to stay, in D price range, also has cabins for up to 7 people, US$40. Good food, fresh trout caught in the lake, suitable for children, very friendly atmosphere. Boats and fishing tackle for hire; good walking in pastoral surroundings, and bird-watching country; recommended to book in advance, postal address: Apartado Aéreo 032, Sogamoso, Boyacá (or through Gladys García, Representative, Calle 80, No. 12-37, Bogotá, T 255-8682). Also on the lake is *Las Rocas Lindas*, D with bath and hot water, US$2.50 for each extra person, 2 cabins for 7 (US$30), one for 8 at Playa Blanca across the lake (US$40), boats for hire, dining room, bar, fireplaces, recommended. The owner, Sr. Mauricio Moreno Arenas, is very friendly. **Aquitania**, a cold, expensive town on the lake, is a centre of onion growing, with a nice camp ground called Playa Blanca nearby, with services and cafeteria. It is reached by bus from Sogamoso, US$0.75, 1 hr.; bus from Bogotá (Rápido Duitama), via Tunja and Sogamoso, goes round the lake to Aquitania, passing Cuitiva, Tota and the *Rocas Lindas* and *Pozo Azul* hotels (3 hr. wait in Aquitania). In Aquitania, *Residencia Venecia*, Calle 8, No. 144, F, with restaurant *Lucho* below, reasonable.

Just before the descent to the Lago de Tota, a road branches left, leading in 4 hours to **Yopal**, capital of the Intendencia de Casanare in the Llanos. (Pop. 10,000.) The road passes through *páramo* and virgin cloud forest. A fine waterfall can be reached in one hour's walk from the DAS checkpoint just above Pajarito. The best *residencias* in Yopal are usually full; direct buses from Sogamoso. **N.B.** Casanare and Arauca beyond are centres of guerrilla activity.

NE of Duitama, on the road to Málaga, is the turning at Belén for Paz de Río, where Colombia's national steelworks is sited; visitors can see over it. The road goes N to **Soatá** (*Residencias Colonial*, excellent, good restaurant; *Hotel Turístico*, E, swimming pool) and then descends to the very dry, spectacular valley of the Río Chicomocha.

By the bridge over the river at **Capitanejo** is the turning to the very attractive **Sierra Nevada del Cocuy** in the Eastern Cordillera. In Capitanejo are two hotels where the bus stops: *Residencia El Córdobes* and *Villa Del Mar*, both G, and 2 more on the *parque* on block below bus stop, all are basic. The Sierra extends in a half circle for 30 km., offering peaks of rare beauty, lakes and waterfalls. The flora is particularly interesting. Everyone wears ponchos, rides horses and is very friendly. The area is good for trekking and probably the best range in Colombia for rock climbers. The most beautiful peaks are Cocuy (5,100 m.), Ritacuba Negra (5,200 m.), Ritacuba Blanca (5,200 m.) and El Castillo (5,400 m.). The main towns are **Cocuy**, on one side of the Sierra (tourist office on Carrera 3, No. 8-06, *Residencia Cocuy*, F, cold water, meals, laundry); and **Guicán**, on the other side, a friendly place. There are 2 rival hotels, *Brisas del Nevado*, G, and *Las Montañas*, G, basic, but pleasant, laundry facilities, overlooks main plaza, thin walls (guests leaving for the 0400 bus will wake you). At *Las Montañas*, Teresa Cristancho or Jorge Ibáñez can arrange a stay in cabins at 3600 metres (US$5.50, 9 beds, well furnished, open fires, electrically-heated showers); or camping (US$1.25), horse rental (US$4.55/day) and guide service (same price) with Dionisio and Berthilda López at the last house before the Nevado on Ritacuba Blanca, highly rec. From here it is 3 strenuous hours' walk to the snowline on Ritacuba Blanca. This would also be the best base for the 2-3 day walk round the N end of the Sierra and into Ratoncito valley, which is surrounded by snow-capped mountains. A milk truck ("el lechero") leaves Guicán at about 0600 for La Cruz, 1 hr. walk below the cabins, arriving 1100, getting back to Guicán around 1230, a rough but interesting ride. Both towns are 1-1½ hrs. drive by jeep from the mountains, so it is recommended to stay higher up (jeep hire about US$14.75 from José Riaño or Orlando Corea in Guicán).

Above Cocuy, accommodation is available at Estadero Don Pastor and, probably, Hacienda La Esperanza. Horses can be hired at both places. La Esperanza is the base for climbing to the Laguna Grande de la Sierra (3-4 hours), a large sheet of glacier-fed water surrounded by 5 snow-capped peaks, and also for the 2-day walk to the Laguna de la Plaza on the E side of the Sierra, reached through awesome, rugged scenery. Permission to camp can easily be obtained from the friendly people. It takes 1 to 2 days to walk between the two towns; maps available in Cocuy and at La Esperanza. It takes 8-10 days to trek from one end to the other through a central rift, but equipment (crampons, ice pick, rope etc.) is necessary. The perpendicular rock mountains overlooking the Llanos are for professionals only. The best weather is from December to April.

**Transport** Paz de Río bus Bogotá-Cocuy (from Av. 6, Cra. 15), 13 hrs., US$10; Paz de Río or Libertadores Capitanejo-Cocuy at 0400 and 1200, US$1.85, to **Guicán**, 3-4 hrs., US$2.30. From Guicán buses leave at 0400, 1600 and 1800 for **Capitanejo, Duitama** (US$5.15), **Paipa** (9 hrs., US$5.55) and points north. For points north, or to get to this area from the north, change at Capitanejo.

The area around **Málaga** is very picturesque: pretty red-tiled villages, horsemen in ponchos and cowboy hats, and mountains (some covered in flowering trees). The roads are twisty but spectacular. In Málaga there are several hotels (including *Príncipe*, near main square, F, shared bathroom, clean, friendly, good meals, strongly rec.) and restaurants, e.g. *La Riviera*, Carrera 8, No. 13-61, good food. Good bus services to Duitama (6 hrs.), Bucaramanga and Pamplona. The road from Málaga to Bucaramanga is another spectacular trip through the mountains, but the road is not good and is very tortuous.

The main road from Tunja goes on to **Barbosa** (*Hotel Príncipe*, clean rooms with private bath; youth hostel at *Parador Turístico Barbosa*; *El Palacio del Pollo*, good, simple roadside restaurant), 64 km. NW in the Department of Santander.

A road runs NW from Barbosa to the Magdalena at Puerto Olaya, opposite Puerto Berrío. Eighteen km. from Barbosa is **Vélez**, a charming little town where horses and mules are raised. (*Hotel Galés*, G.)

The road (toll at Santana, US$0.40) goes NE for 84 km. to **Socorro** (pop. 23,500), with steep streets and single storey houses set among graceful palms. It has a singularly large and odd stone church. The local museum, La Casa de la Cultura, is worth seeing, as is the market which is open every day.

At Socorro, in 1781, began the revolt of the peasant *comuneros*: not a movement for independence but a protest against poverty. It was led at first by a woman, Manuela Beltrán, and then, when other towns joined, by Juan Francisco Berbeo. They marched as far as the salt town of Zipaquirá, N of Bogotá; rebel terms were accepted by the Spaniards, and sworn to by the Bishop of Bogotá, but when they had returned home troops were sent from Cartagena and there were savage reprisals. Another woman from Socorro, Antonia Santos, led guerrillas fighting for independence and was captured and executed by the Spaniards in 1819; her statue is in the main square. The Casa de Cultura museum (opening hours vary according to season) has disappointingly little information on these local heroines, but is still worth a visit.

**Hotels** *Tamacara*, swimming pool, B-C; *Venezia*, F, with shower, has dining room, nice old rooms, good value (single women beware peeping toms); *Sucre*. **Restaurant** *Panadería Imperial*, Calle 14 y Cra. 13, very good, simple; avoid the local hamburger joint.

From Socorro, a road leads N and W to Barrancabermeja. 21 km. along is **Barichara**, a beautiful colonial town at 1,336 metres, population 8,400, founded in 1714 and designated as a national monument to preserve its character. There are many places of historical interest, the most important being the house of the former president Aquiles Parra (the woman next door has the key). An interesting excursion is to Guane, a town 9 km. away by road, or 1½ hrs. walk by trail, where there is an archaeological museum in the priest's house, large collection of coins and a mummified woman (admission, US$0.25).

**Hotels** *Corata*, Carrera 7, No. 4-02, F, with private bath, restaurant and lovely cathedral views. *Posada Real*, Carrera 7, No 4-78, F; *Santa Barbara*, Calle 5, No. 9-12, T 7163, D, old colonial house refurbished in 1989 owned by two British Council scholars Mario and Nubia de Gallegos; quiet, clean showers in rooms, all meals available. You can make reservations in Bogotá, at Carrera 16A, No. 79-61, T 6103425. **Restaurant** *La Corsona*, Calle 6, Carreras 5-6, cheap, good food, friendly.

Another 20 km. N of Barichara is **Zapatoca** a sleepy town which at one time controlled the traffic between highland Santander and the Magdalena. Local products include juicy sweets (*cocadas*) and *pauche*, a balsa type wood painted and carved into many forms. There is also a small "rather goofy" museum. The road continues to Barrancabermeja, see page 712.

About 21 km. beyond Socorro, NE on the main road to Bucaramanga, is **San Gil**, a friendly colonial town with a good climate, which has the tourist attraction of El Gallineral, a riverside spot whose beautiful trees are covered with moss-like tillandsia. Good view from La Gruta, the shrine overlooking the town (look for the cross). The town has become a truck stop on the Bogotá-Bucaramanga road, and accommodation facing the main road is noisy.

**Hotels** *San Gil*, Calle 11, F, showers, clean, friendly; *Alcantuz*, Calle 11, No. 10-15, E, clean, free coffee, good location, pleasant but noisy facing street; *Residencias Royal*, Calle 10 y Carrera 10, F with bath but no a/c; *Residencias Guananta*, Calle 11 (same block as *Hotel Bogotá* and *Colombia*), F, small, clean, hard beds, noisy in daytime; *Residencia Abril*, Cra. 10, Calle 8, E, secure parking, refrigerators in rooms (contents overpriced), relatively quiet; *Residencias Señorial*, Calle 10, Cra. 8, E, pleasant and quiet.

**Restaurants** Just outside Pinchote on the road from Socorro to San Gil is the *Mesón del Cuchicote*, which specializes in dishes from the Santander region. A good restaurant in San Gil is *Herberduc*, US$2-5; *Central*, Calle 10, No. 10-70, good and cheap; *Antojos*, Carrera 9, No. 11-19, good juices; also good and cheap is *Santandereano*; *La Palma*, across from *Residencias Abril*, rec.; *Bambi*, Cra. 10—at night it is a discotheque; *Dusi's King*, on plaza, fast food.

**Transport** Bus to Bogotá, US$6; to Bucaramanga, US$1.90, 2½ hrs; to **Barichara** from Calle 12, US$0.75, 1 hr. You can fly to Bogotá and Málaga.

A road runs E from San Gil to Onzaga (bus), through Mogotes and San Joaquín, dropping from high mountain ridges to tropical valleys. From Onzaga it is 20 km. to Soatá (**see page 676**); no regular public transport, if walking make sure you take the right road. 1 hour east of San Gil is Charalá, which has a beautiful plaza with a statue of José Antonio Golán, leader of the 1781 Comunero revolt. Also an interesting church and Casa de la Cultura; very attractive lush scenery.

About 24 km. beyond San Gil, a little off the road, is the picturesque village of Aratoca, with a colonial church. Ten km. further on, the descent from the heights along the side of a steep cliff into the dry canyon, with spectacular rock colours, of the Río Chicamocha is one of the most dramatic experiences of the trip to Cúcuta, but, if driving, this is a demanding and dangerous stretch.

**Bucaramanga**, 420 km. from Bogotá, is the capital of Santander Department. It stands at 1,018 metres on an uneven plateau sharply delimited by eroded slopes to the N and W, hills to the east and a ravine to the S. The city was founded in 1622 but was little more than a village until the latter half of the 19th century. The metropolitan area has a population of 700,000, which has expanded rapidly because of the success of coffee, tobacco and staple crops. The Parque Santander is the heart of the modern city, while the Parque García Rovira is the centre of the colonial area. Just off Parque García Rovira is the Casa de Cultura. Casa Perú de la Croix, Calle 37, No. 11-18, is a beautiful colonial mansion (closed, temporarily it is hoped, since 1989). There is a pleasant park where the market next to the bus station used to be. The city's great problem is space for expansion. Erosion in the lower, western side topples buildings over the edge after heavy rain. The fingers of erosion, deeply ravined between, are spectacular. The Club Campestre is one of the most beautifully set in Latin America. There is an amusement park, Parque El Lago, in the suburb of Lagos I, SW of the city on the way to Floridablanca. On the way out of the city NE (towards Pamplona) is the Parque Morrorico, well-maintained with a great view. There is a sculptured Saviour overlooking the park, a point of pilgrimage on Good Friday.

Average maximum temperature is 30°C; average minimum, 19.4°C. Rainfall is about 760 mm., and humidity is high (68% to 90%).

The annual international piano festival is held here in mid-September in the Auditorio Luis A. Calvo at the Universidad Industrial de Santander, one of the finest concert halls in Colombia.

**Hotels** *Chicamocha*, luxury, Calle 34, No. 31-24, A, a/c, clean; *Bucarica*, spacious, on main plaza, C, private bathroom, telephone, exceptionally good value, good restaurant and snack bar; *Ruitoque*, nr. plaza, D, nice, colour TV; *Zulima*, Calle 36, Carrera 22, E, with bath, no hot water, also has an annex on Calle 31; *Balmoral*, uphill from centre, Calle 35, Carrera 21, E, with bath; *El Pilar*, Calle 34, Carrera 25, E (bargain), clean, hot water, quiet, highly rec.; good service and food; *El Edén*, Calle 31, No. 19-25, one block from bus station, E, clean, safe; *Tamana*, Carrera 18, No. 30-31, E with bath, F without, clean, friendly, rec. A few blocks uphill from the bus terminal are several *residencias*; Residencias Tonchala, Calle 56, No. 21-23, F, with bath, good; *Nutibara*, Calle 55, No. 21-42, F, T. 78860, shower, fan, rec.; *Amparo*, Calle 31, Carrera 20, E, with bathroom, good; Hostal Doral, Calle 32, No. 21-65, G, family business, clean, safe, several nice tiny rooms; *Morgan*, Calle 35 y Carrera 19, E-F, 2 blocks from bus station, central, old and new wings, O.K. Wide variety of hotels on Calle 31, between Carreras 18-21. Accommodation at the *Club Campestre*, E, is good, but you must have an introduction; try the mayor's office or Chamber of Commerce. **Note**: Since Bucaramanga is the site for numerous national conventions, it is sometimes hard to find a room.

**Camping** Half-an-hour drive S of Bucaramanga, on left of dual carriageway, with swimming pool and waterside restaurant.

**Restaurants** *Di Marco*, Calle 48, Carrera 29 esquina, excellent meat; *La Casa de Spagheti*, Calle 33, Cra. 32, cheap and good; *La Tranquera*, Carrera 33, Calle 40, good Baby Beef, US$6; *Fujiyama*, Calle 38, No. 33-34, Chinese; pizzas at: Piz Pan Pum, Carrera 33, No. 31-107 (next to Cinema Rivera), *Zirus*, Calle 56, No. 30-88, friendly, owner speaks a little English; *Super Pizza*, Centro Comercial Cabecera (pizza by the slice, hamburgers, etc.). good snack bars including *Mucho Pinchos* (Calle 54, No. 31-07), *Pollo Lee*, Carrera 33, No. 30A-27, Korean run, good chicken in sauce.

Vegetarian: *Genesis*, Calle 35 y Carrera 25, good; *El Toronjil*, vegetarian at Carrera 33,

No. 52-123, a bit dear; *Govinda*, Indian vegetarian, Cra. 20, Calle 35/36, excellent lunch US$2.50. *Berna*, Calle 35, No. 18-30, best pastries in town. Try the *hormigas*(large black ants), a local delicacy mainly eaten during Holy Week. Service in Bucaramanga's many restaurants is slow, so be warned.

**Shopping** Camping equipment, *Acampemos*, Calle 48, No. 26-30, last place in Colombia to get camping gas cartridges before Venezuela. Handicrafts in Girón (expensive—see below) and typical clothing upstairs in the food market, Calle 34 y Carreras 15-16. Similar articles (*ruanas*, hats) in San Andresito. *Fería de artesanías* in first 2 weeks of September, usually near the Puerta del Sol.

**Discotheques** On road to Girón are *El Pulpo* and *Capricornio*; *Ulisses 2000*, Av. Quebrada Seca y Carrera 28, gay. Many on Carrera 33, try *Silver Rose*.

**Transport** Most taxis do not have meters but the fare within the city is US$0.70 (US$0.75 at night); beware of overcharging from bus terminals. Buses charge US$0.10.

**Museums** *Museo de Arte Moderno*, Calle 37, Cra. 26, US$0.20. Also **Casa de Bolívar**, Calle 37, No. 12-15, an interesting museum (0900-1200, 1400-1700, free, closed Sat. and Sun.).

**Banks** *Banco Anglo Colombiano*, Calle 36, No. 20-04, and agency on Carrera 15. *Banco de la República*, Carrera 19, No. 34-93, is the only bank authorized to cash travellers' cheques. Long queues (cheques and passports have to be photocopied) Many other banks. Open Mon.-Fri. 0800-1130, 1400-1600, and last working day of month, 0800-1030. Closed Sats.

**Tourist Office** On main plaza in *Hotel Bucarica* building, Calle 35, No. 18-70A, friendly and knowledgeable, T 338461 (closed 1200-1400). City maps for sale.

**Airport** Palonegro, on three flattened hilltops on other side of ravine S of city. Spectacular views on take-off and landing. 3 Avianca flights to *Bogotá*, regularly overbooked; also to *Cúcuta*. Flights to *Medellín* are better value and less hassle than going by bus. Taxi, US$3-4; colectivo, US$1. Buses are scarce despite the fact that some bus boards say "Aeropuerto" (direction "Girón/Lebrija" from Diagonal 15).

**Roads** To the Magdalena at Barrancabermeja, 174 km.; to Cúcuta, 198 km.; to Bogotá, 420 km.; to Medellín, 1,010 km.; to Santa Marta, 550 km., all paved.

**Buses** Bus terminals are mostly around Diagonal 15, S of the centre, until the new terminal on the Girón road has been completed. To **Bogotá**, 8-11 hrs., US$9 (Pullman) with Berlinas del Fonce, Carrera 18, No. 31-06 (this journey is uncomfortable, there are no relief stops, and it starts off hot and ends cold in the mountains, come prepared), Copetran, Calle 55, No. 17B-57, recommended for advance bus reservations, has 3 classes of bus to Bogotá including Pullman, 10 hrs, US$10; Expreso Brasilia, Calle 31, Cra. 18-19, T 422-152, runs to Bogotá but they sell tickets only half an hour before departure. **Tunja**, 9 hrs., US$5.10; **Barranquilla**, 9 hrs. (US$11.50 first class with Copetran); to **Pamplona**, Copetran, 3 a day, US$2.85 (pullman), US$2.30 (*corriente*); **Cúcuta**, 6 hrs., US$4.25 (Pullman), Berlinas buses often arrive full from Bogotá, Copetran also US$4.50 and colectivo US$6. The trip to Cúcuta is spectacular in the region of Berlín (see below). **Santa Marta**, 9 hrs., maybe more according to season, US$15 with Copetran; **Barrancabermeja**, 3 hrs., US$1.90, a scenic ride with one rest stop permitted; this road is paved. Hourly buses to **San Gil**, US$1.90. To **Berlín**, US$1. Other companies with local services to nearby villages on back roads, e.g. the colourful folk-art buses of Flota Cáchira (Calle 32, Cra. 33-34) which go North and East.

**Excursions** The suburb of *Floridablanca*, 8 km. SW, has the famous El Paragüitas gardens (also known as the Jardín Botánico), belonging to the national tobacco agency, reputed locally as "a replica of the Garden of Eden"; look for the alligators round the lake. You can get a free pass (two needed if you want to visit both a.m. and p.m.) to the gardens from the Tourist Office in town. The gardens have been recently reconstructed and open at weekends (1000-1130 and 1500-1630 only). It's a 2-hour walk from Bucaramanga to Floridablanca, but not very interesting; there are plenty of buses. Take the Cotandra bus (US$0.25) from Carrera 22, Bucaramanga, either Florida Villabel which goes by El Paragüitas, or Florida Autopista (continuation of Carrera 33) which goes direct to the square in Florida and you have to walk about a km. Toll on road to Floridablanca, US$0.20. *Rincón Santanera* restaurant, Cra. 8, No.4-41, good local food.

Lebrija (pop. 20,400), 17 km. to the W, is in an attractive plain. Rionegro (pop. 36,750) is a coffee town 20 km. to the N with, close by, the Laguna de Gálago and waterfalls. *Girón*(pop. 27,500) a tobacco centre 9 km. SW of Bucaramanga on the Río de Oro, is a quiet and attractive colonial town, filled with Bumangueses at weekends, with a beautiful church. The buildings are well preserved and the town unspoilt by modernization. By the river are *tejo* courts and popular open air restaurants with *cumbia* and *salsa* bands; in the square at weekends, sweets and *raspados* (crushed ice delights) are sold. (Hotels: *San Juan de Girón*, B, outside town on road from Bucaramanga, swimming pool, restaurant uninspired; *Río de Oro*, in centre, F, but make sure you get a lock for the door. Restaurant: *Mansión del Fraile* on the square, in a beautiful colonial house, good food—Bolívar slept here on one occasion, ask to see the bed; *La Casona*, Calle 28, No. 27-47, friendly, rec., try their "fritanga gironesa". It seems no food is available after 1900.) Take the bus from Carrera 15 or 22 in Bucaramanga, US$1.45. In **Piedecuesta**, 18 km. SE of Bucaramanga (bus from Carrera 22, US$0.35, 45 mins.), you can see cigars being hand-made, furniture carving and jute weaving—cheap, hand-decorated *fique* rugs can be bought. There are frequent buses to all these places; a taxi costs US$5. Corpus Christi processions in these towns in June are interesting. They are all dormitory towns for the city, so there is plenty of public transport.

Another excursion is to **California**, about 60 km. NE of Bucaramanga, where there are gold mines that tourists can visit.

The road (bad and narrow) runs E to Berlín, and then NE (a very scenic run over the Eastern Cordillera) to Pamplona, about 130 km. from Bucaramanga.

**Berlín** has been recommended to the hardy camper as challenging and rewarding. The village lies in a valley at 3,100 metres, the peaks surrounding it rise to 4,350 metres and the temperature is constantly around 10°C, although on the infrequent sunny days it may seem much warmer. The scenery is awesome. The inhabitants are tolerant of visitors; ask a farmer for permission to camp in his field. There is a tourist complex with cabins and there are several basic eating places. It has been recommended as an ideal place to appreciate the grandeur of the Eastern Cordillera and the hardiness of the people who live on the *páramo*.

**Pamplona**, Department of Santander del Norte, lies amid mountains at 2,200 metres. Population, 40,000. The town is definitely worth seeing. Founded in 1548, it became important as a mining town but is now better known as a university city. Few modern buildings have as yet broken its colonial harmony. Cathedral in the spacious central plaza. The earthquake of 1875 played havoc with the monasteries and some of the churches: there is now a hotel on the site of the former San Agustín monastery, but it may still be possible to visit the ex-monasteries of San Francisco and Santo Domingo. The Iglesia del Humilladero, adjoining the cemetery, is very picturesque and allows a fine view of the city. Museum of religious art at Calle 5 y Carrera 5. See the Casa Colonial archaeological museum, Calle 6, No. 2-56, open Tues-Sat., 0900-1200, 1400-1800; Sun., 0900-1200. The town's Easter celebrations are famous throughout Colombia.

**Hotels** *Cariongo*, Carrera 5, Calle 9, D, very good, excellent restaurant (locked parking available); *Residencia Doran*, Carrera 6, No. 7-21, E with bath (F without), large rooms, good meals, US$1.50; *Imperial*, Cra. 5, on main plaza, F (cheaper without carpet), large sparse rooms, noisy; *Orsua*, on main square, F, clean, friendly, cheap, good food also available; *Lincoln*, on the Plaza, F, simple, but good beds, private bath and hot water; *Llanos*, Calle 9 y Carrera 7, G, shared bath, cold water, motorcycle parking, rec. Hotel accommodation may be hard to find at weekends, when Venezuelans visit the town.

**Restaurants** *El Maribel*, Calle 5, No. 4-17, cheap lunch; *La Casona*, Calle 6, No. 6-57, limited but good menu; *Fuente de Sifón*, on main square, student-run, good music. *El Rincón Paisa*, also on main plaza, good; *Portal Alemán*, Calle 7 y Cra. 6, good meals, especially breakfasts; *Angelitas*, Calle 7 y Cra. 7, best coffee in town; *Piero's Pizza*, Calle 9 y Cra. 5, good pizza.

**Shopping** Pamplona is a good place to buy *ruanas*. Good indoor market.

**Exchange** Banks do not change dollars or travellers' cheques in Pamplona, but try the store at Calle 6, No. 4-37, where "Don Dolar" will change cash and travellers' cheques; also Cochabamba store on Carrera 6, one block from the square.

**Tourist Office** Calle 5 y Carrera 6, on main plaza.

**Buses** To Bogotá, US$11.50, 13-16 hrs.; to Cúcuta, US$1.65, 2½ hrs; to Bucaramanga, US$2.85, 4 hrs, great views; to Málaga from main plaza, 5 a day from 0800, 6 hrs., US$3.10, beautiful but very hard journey (continues to Capitanejo); to Tunja, US$9, 12 hours (leaving at 0600). To Berlin, US$1.75.

It is a run of 72 km. from Pamplona through sparsely populated country, descending to an altitude of only 215 metres, to **Cúcuta**, capital of the Department of Santander del Norte, and only 16 km. from the Venezuelan frontier, which was founded 1734, destroyed by earthquake 1875, and then rebuilt, elegantly, with the streets shaded by trees, and they are needed for it is hot: the mean temperature is 29˚C. Population: 600,000. Coffee is the great crop in the area, followed by tobacco. There are also large herds of cattle.

Cúcuta, because it is the gateway of entry from Venezuela, was a focal point in the history of Colombia during the wars for independence. Bolívar captured it after his lightning Magdalena campaign in 1813. The Bolívar Column stands where he addressed his troops on 28 February, 1813. At El Rosario de Cúcuta, a small town of 8,000 inhabitants 14½ km. from Cúcuta on the road to the frontier, the First Congress of Gran Colombia opened on 6 May, 1821. It was at this Congress that the plan to unite Venezuela, Ecuador, and Colombia was ratified; Bolívar was made President, and Santander (who was against the plan) Vice-President. (Santander was born at a *hacienda* near El Rosario which is now being developed as a tourist centre.) The international bridge between Colombia and Venezuela is a few km. from El Rosario; just beyond it is San Antonio del Táchira, the first Venezuelan town, and 55 km. on is San Cristóbal.

**Hotels** *Tonchalá*, Calle 10, Av. 0, B, good restaurant, swimming pool, air conditioning, airline booking office in hall; *Tundaya*, Av 7 y Calle 8, 1-star, E, clean, safe, very good restaurant, breakfast US$10; *Lord*, Av. 7 between Calles 9 and 10, E, nice rooms, good restaurant and service, safe; *Casa Blanca*, Av. 6, No. 14-55, D, good, reasonable meals, rec.; *Aurora*, Calle 11 No. 3-52, F, central, friendly, good cheap restaurant; *Residencia Los Rosales*, near bus station, Calle 2, 8-39, fan and private bath, good; F; *Imperial*, Av. 7, No. 6-28, F with bath, clean, secure, highly rec.; *Residencia Mary*at bus station, E, with bath (cheaper per person in triple room), good. *Amaruc*, Av. 5, No. 9-37, E, with fan, private bath, no hot water; *Residencias Nohra*, Calle 7, No. 7-52, G, common bathroom, quiet; Private *Residencia Leo*, Av. 6A, No. 0-24 N, Barrio La Merced, T 41984, F, run by family Mogollón de Soto, private bath, clothes washing, free coffee all day, rec. **Youth Hostel** at El Rosario de Cúcuta in *Hotel El Saman*, with bar, restaurant, disco and pools. Details from Alcom in Bogotá.

**Restaurants** *"M"*, also called *Chez Esteban*, on road to Venezuela, very good; *Bahía*, just off main square, pleasant; other good restaurants at reasonable prices are *El Pollo Especial*, *Cantón*(Chinese) and *Las Acacias*, Avenida 5, rec.

**Shopping** A good range of leather goods at possibly the best prices anywhere in Colombia. Cuchitril, Av. 3 No. 9-89, has a selection of the better Colombian craft work.

**Exchange** A good rate of exchange for pesos is to be had in Cúcuta, at the airport, or on the border. There are money changers on the street all round the main square and many shops advertise the purchase and sale of bolívares. The price is usually better than at the Banco de la República, Diagonal Santander, Avs. 3E y 4E. Change pesos into bolívares in Cúcuta or San Antonio—difficult to change them further into Venezuela. AmEx and Citicorp travellers' cheques can be exchanged only in Banco de la República.

**Tourist Office** Calle 10, No. 0-30, helpful, has maps, etc. At airport. Other maps obtainable from Instituto Geográfico, Banco de la República building, in the main plaza.

**DAS Office** Avenida Primera, No. 28-55, open 0800-1200 and 1400-2000 daily. Bus ride from town centre to Barrio San Rafael. Taxi from border US$1 (shared), will wait for formalities, then US$0.80 to bus terminal. Women should **not** visit this office alone. There is also an office at the airport which will deal with land travellers.

**Airports** At Cúcuta for Colombian services (to **Bogotá**, at least twice a day with Avianca; cheaper with Satena). Airport 10 minutes by taxi, US$1.70. To **Barranquilla** and **Cartagena**, 1 flight per day (it is cheaper to buy tickets in Colombia than in advance in Venezuela). Also at San Antonio, Venezuela (30 minutes) for Venezuelan domestic lines. At latter, be sure all baggage is sealed after customs inspection and the paper seals signed and stamped.

**Note** Cúcuta is a great centre for smuggling. Be careful.

**Transport** To **San Cristóbal** colectivo, US$2; bus, US$1 (Bolivariano); to **San Antonio** taxi

US$6; bus US$0.30. Bus to **Bogotá**, hourly, 17-24 hrs., US$15, Berlinas del Fonce 1400, 2 stops, including 15 mins. with free refreshments in Bucaramanga (US$2 extra for *cochecama*), or Bolivariano, 20 hrs., often delayed at check points. There are frequent buses, even during the night. To **Bucaramanga**, US$4.25, 6 hrs, with Berlinas del Fonce Pullman, several departures daily; from there a connection to Barranquilla can be made. To **Tunja**, US$9. The road is bad for the first part of the journey. Bus station: Avenida 7 and Calle O (a really rough area). Taxi from bus station to town centre, US$2.

**Warning** All travellers report that the bus station is overrun with thieves and conmen. You must take great care, there is little or no police protection. Watch out for dubious money changers, ticket sellers and security officers claiming to be from the tourist office. These "officials" ask travellers to declare, for "insurance purposes", the amount of money they are carrying. The money is placed in plastic envelopes and returned for you to secrete about your person. Should the bus be robbed later, you are told, the company will reimburse you. In fact, you will have lost part of your money before you even board the bus. Resist this larceny as strongly as possible. Don't put your valuables in bus company "safety boxes"; you'll get out half what you put in (Berlinas del Fonce is the most trustworthy company). Make sure tickets are for buses that exist; tickets do not need to be "stamped for validity". For San Cristóbal, only pay the driver of the vehicle, not at the offices upstairs in the bus station. If you have the time, check where your bus will be leaving from before you travel rather than wandering around with your belongings, looking lost. If you are told, even by officials, that it is dangerous to go to your chosen destination, double check. We are told (late 1990) that you can get good information in the money change shops upstairs in the bus station. If the worst happens, the victimised should report the theft to the DAS office, who may be able to help to recover what has been stolen (but see above).

There are good roads to Caracas (933 km. direct or 1,046 km. via Mérida), and to Maracaibo (571 km.). Bus to Caracas, 14 hrs., Expreso Occidente, two daily, US$13; taxi colectivo US$15.75.

**From Venezuela to Colombia** It is cheaper to fly Caracas-San Antonio, take a taxi to Cúcuta (US$6), then take an internal Colombian flight, than to fly direct from Caracas to Colombia. It will, of course, take longer. The airport transfer at San Antonio is well organized, with taxi drivers calling at necessary immigration offices, and at exchange places, the trip taking 25 mins. You do not have to buy your Colombian ticket in Cúcuta, you can make a reservation and purchase a ticket in a travel agency in Venezuela some days in advance (check exchange rates to see whether it is better to pay in Venezuela or Colombia). With a computer (*localizador*) reference number, you can avoid queues.

If arriving by bus, make sure bus stops at border for Venezuelan exit formalities. If you need one, obtain your Colombian tourist card at the border, and entrance stamp from the DAS in Cúcuta (see above). It is essential to obtain entry stamps (passport and/or tourist card) at the border. You will otherwise have problems with police checks, banks and leaving the country. You can also be fined. Border checks in Cúcuta are very strict. Air travellers can undertake all Colombian formalities at Cúcuta airport.

**From Colombia to Venezuela** All visitors need a visa and tourist card to enter Venezuela. There is a Venezuelan Consulate at Cúcuta (Av. O, Calle 8—open 0800-1300, Mon.-Fri.) which supplies these—same applies at Venezuelan Embassy in Bogotá (may send you to Cúcuta for visas, etc.). You must also provide one photograph for a visa; evidence of onward transportation out of Venezuela, often with a date, is officially required (but often not asked for in Cúcuta—it is necessary in Bogotá), and proof of funds is sometimes requested. In 1990 applicants had to pay from US$2 to US$10 into the Banco Comercial Antioqueño on Avenida 6 (open until 1130 only), then take the receipt back to the Consulate. The process is pretty chaotic, be pushy and start early in the day. You are strongly advised to obtain visa and card from the Venezuelan embassy in your own country, if you know in advance when you will be arriving at the frontier. (Just to visit San Antonio de Táchira in Venezuela, no documents are required.) As there are no Colombian exit/entrance formalities at the international border bridge, it is necessary to obtain a DAS exit stamp before leaving the country from the offices in Cúcuta (see above). If you do not, you will be turned back by Venezuelan customs officials, and the next time you enter Colombia, you will be subject to a fine of US$7.50.

Entering or leaving Colombia by car, you must have your passport stamped at the DAS in town and the car papers stamped at the Customs (Aduana) office on the road to the airport—watch hard for the small sign. At the Customs Office is a restaurant serving excellent, large meals for US$2. Venezuelan car documentation is checked at the border post in San Antonio.

7 km. from Cúcuta is Zulia (Petróleo *buseta*), worth a visit if waiting for a Venezuelan tourist card.

The Andes chain N of Cúcuta is the branch which sweeps north to the Guajira Peninsula after the bifurcation of the Eastern Cordillera near Cúcuta: the other branch crosses into Venezuela. This western branch is the Sierra de Perijá y Motilones, in which live the Motilones Indians, the only Indians in Colombia who have refused to accept absorption into the larger nation. Little is known of them; they have killed many of the missionaries sent to convert them, and the anthropologists sent to study them.

## THE LLANOS AND LETICIA (3)

The extensive cattle lands from the Cordillera Central to the Orinoco are a good place to get away from it all—in the dry season. Leticia is Colombia's foothold on the Amazon.

A spectacular 110-km. road (due for improvement) runs SE from Bogotá to **Villavicencio**, capital of Meta Department in the Llanos at the foot of the eastern slopes of the Eastern Cordillera. Population: 300,000. Rice is now grown near Villavicencio and milled there for transport to Bogotá. Altitude: 498 metres. The town fills up at weekends. It is also full of military police owing to guerrilla activity to the SE.

**Hotels** *Villavicencio*, in town, D, suites available, a/c, hot water, very comfortable, good restaurant, tell them if you don't want extras—TV, telephone, newspaper—and you won't be charged; *Inambú*, E plus extras, Calle 37A, No. 29-49, central; *Savoy*, Carrera 31, No. 41-01, E, with shower and air conditioning, clean and friendly; *Residencias Medina*, Calle 39D, 28-27, F, common shower, fair, washing facilities; *Residencias Don Juan*, Carrera 28, No. 37-21 (Mercado de San Isidro), attractive family house, E, with bath and fan, sauna, safe, rec. *Residencias Myriam* (off main square), F, fairly clean, check roof for leaks.

**Restaurants** Some on main square: others, some with swimming pools, on the road to Puerto López.

**Tourist Office** on main square (Plaza Santander), helpful.

**Airport** Flights to **Miraflores** and **Mitú** for those who want to see "uncommercialized" jungle. To **Puerto Carreño**: Urraca, a freight service with some seats, 0630, Mon., Wed., Fri., arrive early to get a seat, 1½ hrs. Taxi to town, US$2; bus US$0.30.

**Buses** La Macarena and Bolivariano run from Bogotá about every half-hour, US$2.75, 4 hrs.; alternatively there are colectivos (e.g. Velotax, US$3.50, or Autollanos who run every hour, US$5.25). Be prepared to queue for tickets back to Bogotá.

Villavicencio is a good centre for visiting the Llanos and jungles stretching 800 km. E as far as Puerto Carreño, on the Orinoco, with Venezuela across the river. Cattle raising is the great industry on the plains, sparsely inhabited by *mestizos*, not Indians. The cattle town of San Martín to the south of Villavicencio may be visited by bus, 1½ hrs., US$1.20 each way.

A good asphalt road has been built E from Villavicencio to **Puerto López** on the Meta river, a port of call for large river boats. Hotels: *Tío Pepe*, D, with swimming pool; *Marichal*, E, fans but no a/c, swimming pool; two good *residencias*: *Doña Empera*, F, friendly, but a bit run down, and *Popular*, F, cheaper, friendly, every bed with mosquito net. Good food at *Restaurante Yamiba*. The road E (unpaved and poor, but reported to be about to be improved) continues through horse and cattle country for another 150 km. to Puerto Gaitán, where there are hotels and restaurants (*Hotel Mi Llanura*, opposite the church between the two squares, F, clean, friendly, mosquito nets). There are several buses a day from Puerto López to Puerto Gaitán, 3 hrs., US$2.50. Good views from the bridge across the Río Manacacías and great sunsets. The road goes on a further 150 km. through San Pedro to Arimena where the road branches: one road goes N to the Río Meta at El Porvenir, where a ferry (dry season only) takes you across the river to the Orocue tourist centre, E, swimming pool, excursions. The main road, now degenerated to a rough track impassable in the wet season, continues E for more than 500 km. down the Río Meta to its junction with the Orinoco at **Puerto Carreño** (population about 5,000). In the dry season (Nov. to Feb.) there is a weekly bus down this road (Tuesday).

**Services and Entry/Exit Formalities** Two banks (one of which changes travellers' cheques); shopkeepers will exchange Venezuelan bolívares. The DAS office and Venezuelan Consulate are on the Plaza Bolívar. Passports are checked at the waterfront, then you must go to the DAS office and insist on having your passport stamped on entry. You may encounter problems over documents; the military are active in the area and frequently demand permits and proof of how much money you have, and carry out spot checks. There is a Satena office.

**Puerto Carreño hotels** *Residencias Mami*, F, next to Satena office; *Hotel Samanare*, Av. Orinoco No. 1-67, F p.p. more expensive with fan, clean, meals US$3; *Residencias La Vorágine*, F, friendly, clean, safe, good; the *residencia* on the waterfront doubles as a brothel.

**N.B.** The rainy season is April/May to September when it is humid, flooded and accessible only by air.

For boats to Puerto López, be prepared to wait 4-5 days; check with Ulises, a bar owner on the river front by the moorings (he gives free coffee to those prepared to help with his son's English lessons). In the dry season, a bus runs on Thursday to Puerto López from Puerto Carreño at 0500, taking 2 days, night spent at La Primavera, US$25 (Flota La Macarena).

**Air Services** To Villavicencio and Bogotá with Satena on Wed. and Sat., about US$53 to Bogotá, 2 hrs. 50 mins.

**To Venezuela** Launches take about 25 minutes to cross to Burro, stopping at Puerto Páez, from which Caracas can be reached by road. *Por puesto* service is available to Puerto Ayacucho. Both Puerto Páez and Puerto Ayacucho are connected to Caracas by air. It is possible to cross from Puerto Ayacucho to *Casuarito* in Colombia by ferry across the Orinoco. Duty free shops, modest restaurants few or no formalities. Casuarito appears to have no road connection with the rest of Colombia.

For fishing excursions from Puerto Carreño, contact Jairo Zorro, owner of the *Samanare Hotel* (15% discount to *South American Handbook* owners, refer to "Klaus El Alemán, amigo de Juancho"). He will arrange trips up the Ríos Meta, Vita, Tomo or De Agua, depending on time available. The rate for a canoe with guide is about US$50; count on US$20-30 a day for fuel; to hire fishing gear costs US$5 a day (bring your own). Equipment can be bought in Puerto Carreño or Puerto Ayacucho. The trips are rough, sleeping in hammocks on the river bank (lots of mosquitoes), but great adventure with unforgettable sunsets, alligators, *babillas* (small alligators) and jaguars. (Klaus Brandl, Buenos Aires.)

The road S from Villavicencio is surfaced as far as San Martín. It runs on to **Granada** (*Hotel Yali; Tío Pepe Motel*, very clean) and from there deteriorates rapidly. **Vistahermosa** (Macarena bus from Bogotá, 0845, US$5, 9 hrs.), situated near the break-point between the Llanos and the jungle, lies further S along this road (*Residencias Royal* is cheap and comfortable; *Pampa Llanura*, opposite the Flota La Macarena office, G, very clean and friendly; *Lilian's* restaurant). It is normally a good place from which to visit the Sierra de la Macarena, a Tertiary outcrop 150 km. long by 35 km. broad. Its vegetation is so remarkable that the Sierra has been designated a national park exclusively for scientific study, although latest reports suggest that the flora are rapidly being destroyed by colonization, with much marijuana and coca being planted, and the area has in any case been occupied by guerrillas since about 1982. The road from Vistahermosa to the Sierra de la Macarena is very muddy in the wet season (March-Nov.). From a small place called Puerto Lucas (colectivo from Vistahermosa) you can hire horses and guide for the three hour ride to the escarpment. For more than a quick visit you will need to camp. For the energetic, a worthwhile trip is to the Sardinata or Cañones falls. Both can be reached from Maracaibo, which is a day's walk from Vistahermosa. If you wish to visit the Sierra de la Macarena, seek advice on conditions in advance.

To the SE of Villavicencio, along the river Vaupés, and near the border with Brazil, is **Mitú**, which can be reached by air from Villavicencio and Bogotá (Satena). On arrival in the town you must fill in an entry card at the police station. Several anthropological studies are being carried out in the Mitú area and trips can be made from the town to Indian villages. The cost of a trip down river to visit an Indian village where you stay overnight is approximately US$10, plus the cost of the fuel, at US$1.60 a gallon, used by the boat. Take your own food. Recommended guides in 1989: Hilario Gondura, his son José Ignacio, Jacinto Ortis, Orlando Morena. Good local buys are baskets and bark paintings.

**Hotels** *La Vorágine*, E, shower, fan, clean, owned by Sr. León who will help you to arrange trips; *JM*, F, friendly, helpful, morning coffee, next to Satena office. Plenty of **restaurants** around, recommended: *Restaurant de la Selva*, a meeting place of the pilots who fly into Mitú.

A gold mine, the Taraira mine, has been worked since 1986 near the Brazil border. Make friends with the pilots if you wish to visit.

Plenty of reserve gasoline should be carried when travelling by car in the Llanos, as there are few service stations. Take food with you, unless you can live by gun and rod. Everybody lets you hang up your hammock or pitch your tent, but mosquito nets are a must. "Roads" are only tracks left by previous vehicles but easy from late December till early April and the very devil during the rest of the year. More information on the Llanos can be obtained from the office of the Gobernación del Departamento de Meta, Calle 34 and Carrera 14, Bogotá.

*Leticia*, 3,200 km. up the Amazon on the frontiers with Peru and Brazil, a fast-growing community of 70,000, is a clean modern town. It is rapidly merging into one town with neighbouring Marco in Brazil. There is a modern, well equipped hospital. The best time to visit the area is in July or August, the early months of the dry season. At weekends, accommodation may be difficult to find. Tourist services are better than in Tabatinga or Benjamin Constant (Brazil).

**Hotels** *Parador Ticuna*, B, has 19 apartments (all with bathrooms which have hot—usually—and cold running water, and a/c, when working) which can each sleep up to 6. The hotel has a swimming pool (uncleaned), bar and restaurant, and is a little run down. The owners of the *Ticuna* also operate the *Jungle Lodge*, on Monkey Island, 2 hrs' boat ride from Leticia (see below). They also operate the *Colonial*, 16 double rooms and one triple, all with airconditioning or fans, power and water unpredictable, swimming pool, cafeteria, noisy, unhelpful staff, B, US$6 per additional person, not including tax and insurance (not rec. at present). *Anaconda*, C, overpriced, hot water; there is a restaurant (beware overcharging) which serves meals for about US$6, swimming pool; *Residencias Marina*, Carrera 9 No. 9-29 (T 27201/9), D/E, TV, some a/c, cold water, good breakfast and meals at attached restaurant, clean; *Residencias Ferrando*, Carrera 9 No. 8-80, E, well equipped but electricity only at night, clean, rec.; *Residencia Leticia*, Calle 8, No. 11-93, F, very friendly (not possible to sling hammock), good value, laundry facilities, clean, use of kitchen, warmly rec.; *Residencia Familiar*, Calle 8, cheap, F, friendly, laundry facilities; *Primavera*, Calle 8 between Cras. 9 and 10, F with bath and fan. (*Parador Ticuna* and *Hotel Colonial* boil water.)

**Restaurant** *Tres Fronteras* (across from *Hotel Colonial*), good. Several small sidewalk restaurants downtown with set meals at around US$1. Restaurant opposite *Residencia Leticia* serves good lunches and dinners, and *Señora Mercedes*, 3 doors from *Residencia Leticia*, serves good, cheap meals until 1930. *Heladería Bucaros* offers empanadas, sandwiches, juices, etc. Cheap food (fried banana and meat, also fish and pineapples) is sold at the market near the harbour. Also cheap fruit for sale.

**Museum** Recently set up by **Banco de la República**, covers local ethnography and archaeology. A beautiful building with a terrace overlooking the Amazon. Small Amazonian **zoo** (huge anacondas) and **botanical garden** on road to airport.

Leticia is a good place to buy typical products of Amazon Indians, but the growth of Leticia, Tabatinga, Marco and Benjamin Constant has imposed an artificiality on the immediately surrounding Amazon territory.

**Exchange** The *cambio* next to the *Anaconda Hotel* has good exchange rates for dollars, cruzeiros or intis. The street money changers and *cambios*, of which there are plenty, give a better rate of exchange than the banks, which charge a 15% levy on travellers' cheques, except Banco de la República on American Express. Travellers' cheques cannot be changed at weekends, and are hard to change at other times.

**Brazilian Consulate** very efficient and helpful; 2 black and white photos needed for visa (photographer nearby).

**Tourist Office** Calle 10, No. 9-86. **DAS** office, Carrera 8 (between Calles 9 and 10), near Brazilian consulate. Make sure you get an entry stamp here before going to the airport for flights into Colombia. If you need a visa, but not a tourist card, to visit Colombia, don't be bullied into purchasing one of the latter.

**Excursions** If you choose to go on an organized tour, do not accept the first price and check that the supplies and equipment are sufficient for the time you will be away. It is cheaper and better to find yourself a local guide, but make sure he has a good reputation and fix a definite price before you set out. You can hire a dug-out for about US$3 a day. Motorboats cost much more (e.g. US$54, 8 hrs, for 10 people). *Turamazonas*, *Parador Ticuna*, Apto. Aereo 074, T 7241, offers a wide range of tours including day visit to Yagua and Ticuna Indians, jungle walk and stop at **Monkey Island** (rec.); provisions and bedding for overnight safaris are supplied by the agency, whose staff are all expert, at Monkey Island. You can stay at the *Jungle Lodge*, though visitors in 1989 found it little used and run down. There are not many monkeys on Monkey Island now, those left are semi-tame. Turamazonas has US representation at 855A, U.S. 19S, Tarpon Springs, FL 33581, T (813) 934-9713. The Inderena office, Centro de Visitantes Yewae, Leticia, will plan a trip for you and put you in touch with guides. (Rec. as reliable in 1989: Fernando Martínez, Jugaluis Valencia, Gervite Rodríguez, Angel Mejía, Miguel Mejía.) You can also stay at their centre in the **Parque Nacional Amacayacu** US$8 for full board. Other reputable tour companies are *Amaturs* (in lobby of *Hotel Anaconda*) and *Kapax*. The following tours are available: to Benjamin Constant to see a rubber plantation, 8 hrs.; to Monkey Island to see Ticuna and Yagua Indians, overnight trip, with full board. Turamazonas offers tours up the river to visit Indian communities, 3 days (price depends on number of people in group), recommended. Recommended tours from Leticia to Puerto Nariño are run by *Punto Amazónico*, Carrera 24, No. 53-18, 2° piso, Bogotá, T 249-3618 (guides Fernando and José), including fishing, visits to Indians, alligator watching for 4-5 days, about US$375 including flights and hotel accommodation. Many independent guides can be found on the river front; for one day excursions to Yagua Indians (gifts of food and provisions much appreciated), Victoria Regia waterlilies, Monkey Island and more (check that those recommended by posher hotels do not overcharge). A recommended guide is Luis Daniel González, Carrera 8, No. 9-93 (he can either be found at the airport, or contacted through *Hotel Anaconda*; he runs a variety of tours, is knowledgeable and speaks Spanish, Portuguese and English; a one-day tour, inc. meal and fuel costs US$110). Another recommended is Daniel Martínez, speaks good English and is knowledgeable about the jungle and the Indians. Make sure the guides bring rubber boots as it can be quite muddy. Cheap guides do not have the experience or first aid equipment of the main tour companies, and there have been many instances of boats breaking down and guides getting drunk and abandoning their clients. If you choose to go on a night excursion to look for cayman make sure the boat has powerful halogen lights.

When going upstream remember that the slower and dirtier the boat, the more mosquitoes you will meet. (You can swim in the Amazon and its tributaries, but do not dive; this disturbs the fish. Also do not swim at sunrise or sunset when the fish are more active, nor when the water is shallow in the dry season, nor if you have a wound, however slight, which might open up and bleed.)

**Transport** Avianca flies to Leticia (Tabatinga airport if Leticia's is closed) from Bogotá, Mon., Wed., Fri., Sun.; Leticia to **Bogotá**, departs 1450, arrives 1635, continues to **Cali**; Satena has flights to/from Bogotá on Thur. and Sat. It is possible with some persuasion to return to Bogotá by freight plane, but you have to sit with the cargo, often refrigerated fish. Check with Satena crew, who stay in the *Hotel Colonial*, if there is a seat available, or at the airport. (From Bogotá by freight plane, you have to be at the halls of the cargo companies—all at the same place—at 0400, and ask which company is flying. If you want to try this, be prepared for a long wait, particularly returning from Leticia to Bogotá, and look as little like a tourist as possible.) Líneas Aero Caribe cargo flights twice a week; flight time 3½-4 hrs. Cruzeiro do Sul flies Manaus-Tabatinga (for Leticia)-Iquitos and back on Sat.; Taba operates three flights weekly Manaus-Tabatinga-Manaus. It is also possible to get a seat on a Petrobrás plane to **Manaus**. This leaves every Friday, and can be arranged with the crew, who stay at the *Anaconda Hotel*. A letter of recommendation helps. Taxi to airport, US$1.90. Expect to be searched before leaving Leticia airport, and on arrival in Bogotá from Leticia. If arriving in Leticia by plane with a view to leaving for Brazil or Peru, get your exit stamp at the airport while you are there.

The cheapest way to get to Leticia is by bus to **Puerto Asís**, and then by boat (**see page 748**). There are twice-daily ferries between Leticia, Tabatinga and Benjamin Constant, Brazil (US$5, 1½-2 hrs., US$15 in private launch); if leaving Brazil by this route, disembark at Tabatinga and obtain exit stamp from office which is 1 km. from dock: turn right one block at main street, office is on the left. There is a Colombian Consular Office near the border on the road from Tabatinga, where Colombian tourist visas are issued on presentation of 2 passport photographs. Most boats down to **Manaus** take passengers—all leave from Benjamin Constant, perhaps Tabatinga—none from Leticia. Departure times are uncertain, and the boats tend to be overcrowded. The trip takes at least 4½ days; there is a better selection of provisions in Leticia, but purchases are much cheaper in Benjamin Constant. Boats to **Peru** from Tabatinga wharf La Ronda sail daily at 1800 and take passengers and cargo. For boats travelling on the Brazilian and Peruvian Amazon (to Manaus and Iquitos), see under the relevant sections of the Brazil and Peru chapters. Remember to get your passport stamped by the DAS office near the church, just off main square in Leticia before you leave the area; there are no customs formalities for everyday travel between Leticia and Tabatinga in Brazil, taxis cost US$5.65 from a rank (or US$7.55 if you want to stop to change money, immigration, etc. en route to harbour), or US$0.70 as colectivos (N.B. colectivos increase their charges after 1800); bus, US$0.20; 24-hour transit stamps can be obtained at the DAS office for one-night stays in Leticia, although it appears that these are not necessary if you are not going beyond Leticia—best to check, though. If you are going further into Brazil from Colombia, check the details under Brazil, Benjamín Constant/Tabatinga.

**N.B.** Robert Smith and Geoffrey Dempsey tell us that if entering Colombia at Leticia, from Brazil en route to Peru, you should try to get your tourist card before Manaus because the Colombian consul there will tell you that a card is not needed just for passing through Leticia. This is not true: you must have a card. If you do have to see the consul in Manaus tell him you are going further into Colombia—you may have to show an onward ticket, or money—this may get you a card.

It is reported that for travellers interested in Amazonian wild life the Putumayo is more accessible than Leticia; it is best reached from Pasto (see page 748).

---

## THE NORTH COAST AND THE ISLANDS (4)

Caribbean Colombia, very different in spirit from the highlands: the coast stretches from the Darién Gap, through banana plantations, swamplands and palm plantations to the arid Guajira. The main resorts are Cartagena, which is also steeped in colonial history, and Santa Marta, near which is the Tairona national park with precolombian remains and the unique Sierra Nevada de Santa Marta coastal range.

The climate is much the same for the whole area: the heat is great—ranging from 26° to 36°C, and there is a difference of only 2° between the hottest and coolest month. From November to March the heat is moderated by trade winds.

Character, like climate, seems to change in Colombia with the altitude. The *costeños* (the people of the coast) are gayer and more light-hearted than the more sober people of the highlands. (The contrast is sharply drawn in the great modern Colombian novel, *Cien años de soledad*, by Gabriel García Márquez.) The coastal people talk very fast, slurring their words and dropping the final s's.

**N.B.** In this region hotel prices are subject to high and low season variations: high season is 15 December-30 April, and 15 June-31 August.

*Barranquilla*, with one million people, is Colombia's fourth city. It lies on the western bank of the Río Magdalena, about 18 km. from its mouth, which has been deepened and the silted sandbars cleared so that it is now a seaport (though less busy than Cartagena or Santa Marta) as well as a river port. Those who know the people say they are the most friendly in Colombia.

Barranquilla is a modern industrial city with a dirty central area near the river, and a good residential area in the north-west, beyond Calle 53. The principal boulevard is Paseo Bolívar; there is a handsome church, San Nicolás, formerly the Cathedral, in Plaza San Nicolás, the central square, and before it stands a small statue of Columbus. The new Catedral Metropolitana is at Carrera 45, No. 53-120, opposite Plaza de la Paz. This was visited by the Pope in 1986. There is an impressive statue of Christ inside by the Colombian sculptor, Arenas Betancourt. The commercial and shopping districts are round the Paseo Bolívar, a few blocks N of the old Cathedral, and in Calle Murillo. The colourful and vivid market is between Paseo Bolívar and the river, the so-called Zona Negra on a side channel of the Magdalena. Good parks in the northern areas; the favourite one is Parque Tomás Suri Salcedo on Calle 72. Stretching back into the north-western heights overlooking the city are the modern suburbs of El Prado, Altos del Prado,

Golf and Ciudad Jardín, with the German-run *El Prado Hotel*. There are five stadia in the city, a big covered coliseum for sports, two for football and the others cater for basketball and baseball. The metropolitan stadium is on Av. Murillo, outside the city.

**Festivals**  Carnival, lasting four days, parades, floats, street dancing and beauty contests.

**Hotels**  *El Prado*, the social centre, swimming pool and tennis courts, B, good restaurant, sauna, some distance from the centre (Carrera 54, No. 70-10, T 340001;) in same district, *Royal*, Carrera 54, No. 68-124, T 357800, B, good service, with swimming pool, modern; *Davega*, Calle 72 y Carrera 44, T 359020, D (incl tax), good value, rec.; *Villa Venecia*, Calle 61, No. 46-41, T 414107, D, clean, TV, a little noisy but rec.; *Cadebia*, Calle 75, No. 41-79, T 456144, D; *El Golf*, Barrio El Golf, Cra. 59b, No. 81-158, D; *Dann*, Cra. 51b, No. 19-246, opened in 1989. *Zhivago*, Plaza Bolívar, very good, E, without bath; *Horizonte*, Calle 45 y Carrera 44, F with bath, clean, quiet, fan, rec.; *Embajador*, Calle 34 (Paseo Bolívar), No. 40-66, F with bath and phone, very good. **Note**: hotel prices may be much higher during Carnival. Watch for thieves in downtown hotels.

**Restaurants**  *La Puerta de Oro*, Calle 35, No. 41-100, central, a/c, good for meals (inc. breakfast); *Jardines de Confucio*, Cra. 54, No.75-44, good Chinese food, nice atmosphere; various Lebanese with belly-dancers; several Chinese and *pizzerias*.

**Market**  San Andrecito, or "Tourist Market", Vía 40, is where smuggled goods are sold at very competitive prices; a good place to buy film. Picturesque and reasonably safe. Any taxi driver will take you there.

**Bookshop**  *Librería Nacional*, Carrera 53, English, French and German books. Maps from Instituto Agustín Codazzi, Calle 36, No. 45-101.

**Local Transport**  Taxis within the town cost US$1.40.

**Entertainments**  Teatro Amira de la Rosa. **Night Life** *La Cabaña* at *Hotel El Prado*. Famous disco *Agua Sala* at beach.

**Museum**  Small **archaeological** collection, Calle 68 No. 53-45 (Mon.-Fri. 0900-1200, 1400-1700), with big physical relief map on front lawn. Also, Museo Romántico, Cra. 54, No. 59-199, history of Barranquilla.

**Zoo**  There is a well-maintained zoo with some animals not often seen in zoos, but many are in small cages, Calle 74, Cra. 50 (bus "Boston/Boston" or "Caldes/Recreo"), entrance US$0.60, students US$0.30, 0830-1200, 1400-1800. All the trees are labelled.

**Exchange**  Banco Royal de Colombia; Banco Anglo Colombiano, Calle 34, No. 44-43, with agency on Calle 72; **Banco Internacional de Colombia**. Open: Mon.-Thurs, 0800-1130, 1400-1600; Fri. 0900-1130, 1400-1630; last working day of month 0800-1130. *Casa de cambio* El Cacique, Calle 34, No. 43-108, T 326392, reliable. **American Express** agency at Tierra Mar Aire, downtown.

**Consulates**  Venezuelan Consulate, Calle 70, No. 53-74 (Centro Financiero El Prado, 4° piso), T 580048/582832, 0800-1500 (take "Caldas/Recreo" or "Boston/Boston" bus), visa issued same day, but you must be there by 0915 with photo and US$10 cash (less for some nationalities; onward ticket may not be requested. **US Consulate**, Centro Comercial Mayorista, Calle 77, No. 68-15, opposite zoo (Apartado Aéreo 51565), T 45-70-88 or 45-71-81 (visas obtainable only in Bogotá). **British Consulate**, Cra. 44, No. 45-57, T 326936; **W. German Consulate**, Calle 80, near Vía 40 (ask for Herr Schnabel). **Danish Consulate**, Carrera 45, No. 34, Edificio Libertad, T 414235. **Dutch Consulate**, Carrera 42H, No. 85-33, T 341282; **Spanish Consulate**, Calle 51, No. 37-64, T 313694.

**Police**  (for declarations of theft, etc.), Policia F2, Calle 47 y Carrera 43.

**Tourist Information**  at main hotels and at Calle 72, No. 57-43, of. 401, T 45-44-58 or 33-66-58. CNT is at Carrera 54, No 75-45, T 454458. A recommended taxi-driver/guide to the city is Henry Robinson, T 35-37-14; he speaks English. Locals will show you beautiful beaches off road to Cartagena.

**Airport**  Ernesto Cortissoz airport is 10 km. from the city; there is plenty of transport of all types. City bus from airport to town, US$0.10 (US$0.15 on Sunday). Taxi to town, US$4.50 (taxis do not have meters, fix fare in advance). Special bus from outside the airport, US$2.50 (to town, take only buses marked "centro"); the bus to the airport (marked Malambo) leaves from Carrera 44 up Calle 32 to Carrera 38, then up Calle 30 to Airport. Taxi to Cartagena,

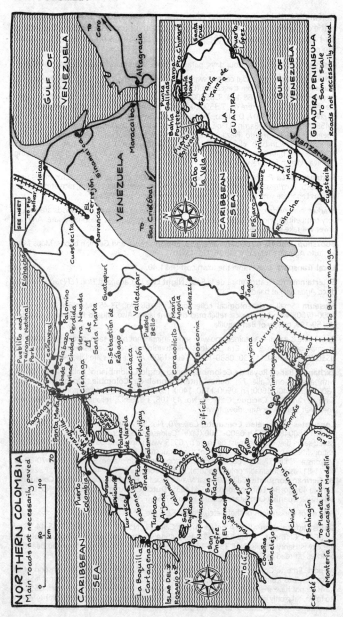

NORTHERN COLOMBIA
Main roads not necessarily paved

GUAJIRA PENINSULA
To some scale
roads not necessarily paved.

US$40. Avianca to Aruba as well as Colombian destinations; Lacsa to Caracas, Panama and San José, and connections to Mexico City, other Central American capitals and Los Angeles.

**Buses** Most bus companies operate from Calle 34 and Carrera 45 (Brasilia and Copetran at Calle 45 y Carrera 35). To **Santa Marta**, US$1.80, Pullman (or US$1.60 in non-a/c, Coolibertador), about 2 hrs., also direct to Santa Marta's famous Rodadero beach; to **Montería**, US$9.25, 8 hrs.; to **Medellín** by Pullman, US$16, 16hrs.; to **Bucaramanga**, US$11.50 with Copetran, a/c, first class, departures at 1130 most days, arriving 2030; to **Bogotá**, 20-24 hrs., US$20 direct; to **Caucasia**, US$9, 11 hrs. To **Maicao** US$6.50, 5 hrs. (with Brasilia, every ½ hour from 0100-1200); to **Cartagena**, 3 grades of bus, 3 hrs. (US$2.25 with Transportes Cartagena, US$2.75 with Expreso Brasilia, by Brasilia Van Tours mini-bus, US$2, from their downtown offices as well as the bus terminals), 2 hrs. by colectivo, US$2.50.

**Warnings** When leaving by air for the USA, you may be searched by drug squad police; they are very civil, but acquisitive—check your belongings afterwards. Tourist Police can be very rough when searching foreigners. Beware also of people claiming to be ships' officers who say they can arrange a passage if you pay in advance; buy a passage only in a recognized shipping office or agency. If shipping a car into Barranquilla allow 2 days to complete all paperwork to retrieve your car from the port.

**Roads** Regular buses from Paseo Bolívar and the church at Calle 33 and Carrera 41 to the attractive bathing resort of **Puerto Colombia**, 19 km. (US$0.50, ½ hr.). Beach clean and sandy, water a bit muddy. S along the Magdalena to the little town of Palmar de Varela. On this road, 5 km. from the city, is the old colonial town of **Soledad**, with 16,000 inhabitants. The cathedral and the old narrow streets round it are worth seeing.

Barranquilla-Cartagena, a good paved road but driving is violent, and cyclists have reported muggings. From Baranoa a branch road runs to Usicurí (72 km. from Barranquilla), known for its medicinal waters and for the grave of the popular Colombian poet, Julio Flores. The main road goes on via Sabanalarga (50 km. from Barranquilla) to Cartagena. From Sabanalarga an all-weather road continues to Puerto Giraldo, a port on the Río Magdalena linked by ferry with the small town of Salmina (ferry 0500 to 1800). A spectacular new bridge over the Río Magdalena gives a fine view of Barranquilla and the river. An all-weather road leads to Fundación, on the Atlántico Railway, and a junction point with the road from Santa Marta to Bucaramanga and Bogotá, which is now paved throughout, though surface somewhat uneven.

**Cartagena**, old and steeped in history, is one of the most interesting towns in South America. Its population is 564,000. An arm of the river, 145 km. long, canalized in 1650 by Spain—the Canal del Dique—from Calamar to Cartagena allows free access for ships from the up-river ports.

What interests the visitor is a comparatively small part of Cartagena, the old walled city almost completely surrounded by the Caribbean sea on the W, the waters of the Bay of Cartagena on the S, and lakes and lagoons to the N and E. Cartagena was one of the storage points for merchandise sent out from Spain and for treasure collected from the Americas to be sent back to Spain. A series of forts protecting the approaches from the sea, and the formidable walls built around the city, made it almost impregnable.

Cartagena was founded by Pedro de Heredia on 13 January, 1533. There were then two approaches to it, Bocagrande, at the northern end of Tierra Bomba island—this was a direct entry from the Caribbean—and Boca Chica. Bocagrande was blocked after Admiral Vernon's attack in 1741, and thereafter the only approach was by the narrow channel of Boca Chica from the S. Boca Chica leads into the great bay of Cartagena, 15 km. long and 5 km. wide. The old walled city lies at the head of it.

Entering Boca Chica by sea, the island of Tierra Bomba is to the left. At the tip of a spit of land is the fortress of San Fernando (entrance fee, US$0.60; guide, US$1.50 for one to five people); boat trips to it (1 hr.) are worth while. Opposite it, right on the tip of Barú island, is the Fuerte San José. The two forts were once linked by heavy chains to prevent surprise attacks by pirates. North of Barú island stretches Manga island, much larger and now an important suburb. At its northern end a bridge, Puente Román, connects it with the old city. This approach was defended by three forts: San Sebastián del Pastellillo built between 1558 and

1567 (the Club de Pesca has it now) at the north-western tip of Manga Island; the fortress of San Lorenzo near the city itself; and the very powerful Castillo San Felipe de Barajas inland on a height to the E of the city. Yet another fort, La Tenaza, protected the walled city from a direct attack from the open sea. The huge encircling walls were started in 1634 and finished by 1735. They were on average 12 metres high and 17 metres thick, with 6 gates. They contained, besides barracks, a water reservoir.

In spite of its daunting outer forts and encircling walls Cartagena was challenged again and again by enemies. Sir Francis Drake, with 1,300 men, broke in successfully in 1586, leading to a major reconstruction of the ramparts we see today. Neverhteless the Frenchmen Baron de Pointis and Ducasse, with 10,000 men, beat down the defences and sacked the city in 1697. But the strongest attack of all, by Sir Edward Vernon with 27,000 men and 3,000 pieces of artillery, failed in 1741 after besieging the city for 56 days; it was defended by the one-eyed, one-armed and one-legged hero Blas de Lezo, whose statue is at the entrance to the San Felipe fortress.

Cartagena declared its independence from Spain in 1811. A year later Bolívar used the city as a jumping-off point for his Magdalena campaign. After a heroic resistance, Cartagena was retaken by the royalists under Pablo Morillo in 1815. The patriots finally freed it in 1821.

The old walled city was in two sections, inner and outer. Much of the wall between the two was razed a few years ago. Nearly all the houses are of one or two storeys. The houses in El Centro were occupied by the high officials and nobility. San Diego (the northern end of the inner town) was where the middle classes lived: the clerks, merchants, priests and military. The artisan classes lived in the one-storey houses of Getsemaní in the outer city.

The streets are narrow and rarely straight. Each block has a different name, a source of confusion, but don't worry: the thing to do is to wander aimlessly, savouring the street scenes, and allow the great sights to catch you by surprise. Our map is marked with numerals for the places of outstanding interest. The most attractive streets have been given a star (*). Most of the "great houses" can be visited.

The numbers stand for the following places:

1. The Puente Román, the bridge which leads from the island of Manga into the Getsemaní district. Visitors should on no account miss seeing the *casas bajas* or low houses of Getsemaní, but be careful; it is not a very safe neighbourhood.

2. The chapel of San Roque (early 17th century), near the hospital of Espíritu Santo.

3. The church of Santísima Trinidad, built 1643 but not consecrated till 1839. The plaza in which it stands is most interesting. North of the church, at number 10, lived Pedro Romero, the man who set the revolution of 1811 going by coming out into the street shouting "Long Live Liberty".

4. The monastery and church of San Francisco. The church was built in 1590 after the pirate Martín Côte had destroyed an earlier church built in 1559. The first Inquisitors lodged at the monastery. From its courtyard a crowd surged into the streets claiming independence from Spain on the morning of 11 November, 1811. The Iglesia de la Tercera Orden is now the Teatro Colón.

Immediately to the N is Plaza de la Independencia, with the landscaped Parque del Centenario just off it. At right angles to the Plaza runs the Paseo de los Mártires, flanked by the busts of nine patriots executed in the square on 24 February 1816 by the royalist Morillo when he retook the city. At its western end is a tall clock tower. Passing through the tower's arches (the main entrance to the inner walled city) we get to

5. The Plaza de los Coches. Around almost all the plazas of Cartagena arcades offer refuge from the tropical sun. On the W side of this plaza is the famous Portal de los Dulces, a favourite meeting place.

6. Plaza de la Aduana, with a statue of Columbus and the Palacio Municipal.

7. Church of San Pedro Claver and Monastery, built by Jesuits in 1603 and later dedicated to San Pedro Claver, a monk in the monastery, who was canonized 235 years after his death in 1654. He was called the Slave of the Slaves (El Apostol de los negros): he used to beg from door to door for money to give to the black slaves brought to the city. His body is in a glass coffin on the high altar, and his cell and the balcony from which he sighted slave ships are shown to visitors. Entry, US$0.50. Guides charge US$1.

8. Plaza de Bolívar (the old Plaza Inquisición), very pleasant, and with a statue of Bolívar. On its W side is

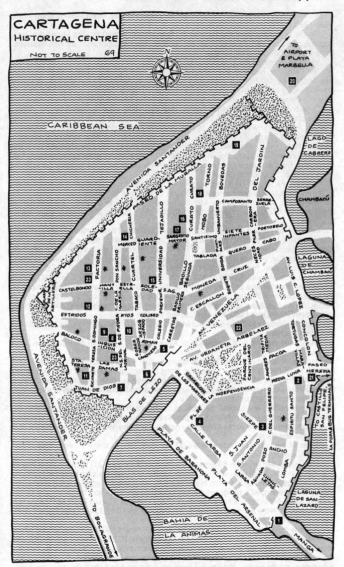

**CARTAGENA**
HISTORICAL CENTRE
NOT TO SCALE 69

CARIBBEAN SEA

9. The Palacio de la Inquisición, established in 1610, but the building dates from 1706. The stone entrance with its coats of arms and well preserved and ornate wooden door is very notable. Indeed the whole building, with its overhanging balconies, cloisters and patios, is a fine example of colonial baroque. There is a very pleasant historical museum at the Palacio,

and a library. Entry charge US$0.55; good historical books on sale. Open Mon-Fri, 0800-1130, 1400-1730.

On the opposite side of the Plaza to the Palacio de la Inquisición, the Museo del Oro y Arqueológico has been installed in an old building. Gold and pottery, very well displayed. Entrance free, but closed on Sunday.

In the NE corner of Plaza de Bolívar is

10. The Cathedral, begun in 1575 and partially destroyed by Francis Drake. Reconstruction was finished by 1612. Great alterations were made between 1912 and 1923. A severe exterior, with a fine doorway, and a simply decorated interior. See the guilded 18th century altar, the Carrara marble pulpit, and the elegant arcades which sustain the central nave.

11. **Church and convent of Santa Teresa, founded 1609, now occupied by the police.**

12. The church and monastery of Santo Domingo, built 1570 to 1579 and now a seminary. The old monastery was replaced by the present one in the 17th century. Inside, a miracle-making image of Christ, carved towards the end of the 16th century, is set on a baroque 19th century altar. Most interesting neighbourhood, very little changed since the 16th century. In Calle Santo Domingo, No. 33-29, is one of the great patrician houses of Cartagena, the Casa de los Condes de Pestagua, now the Colegio del Sagrado Corazón de Jesús. North of Santo Domingo, at

13. Calle de la Factoria 36-57 is the magnificent Casa del Marqués de Valdehoyos, now owned by the tourist authority and containing a Tourist Office; open to visitors.

14. The church and convent of La Merced, founded 1618. The convent—a prison during Morillo's reign of terror—is now occupied by the Law Courts and its church is the Teatro Municipal.

15. The monastery of San Agustín (1580), now the Universidad de Cartagena. From its chapel, now occupied by a printing press, the pirate Baron de Pointis stole a 500-pound silver sepulchre. It was returned by the King of France but the citizens melted it down to pay their troops during the siege by Morillo in 1815. Adjoining the university is the Edificio Ganem, which offers a good, free view of the city from the 9th floor.

16. The church of Santo Toribio de Mongrovejo. Building began in 1729. In 1741, during Admiral Vernon's siege, a cannon ball fell into the church during Mass and lodged in one of the central columns; the ball is now in a recess in the W wall. The font of Carrara marble in the Sacristy is a masterpiece. There is a beautiful carved ceiling (*mudéjar* style) above the main altar. Opens for Mass at 0600 and 1800, closed at other times.

17. Casa del Consulado (Calle Sargento Mayor) was one of the great houses but has now become a teachers' college.

18. Church and monastery of Santa Clara de Assisi, built 1617-21, now the Hospital de Santa Clara.

19. Plaza de las Bóvedas. The walls of Las Bóvedas, built 1799, are some 12 metres high and from 15 to 18 metres thick. Cars can drive along the rampart, from which there is a grand view of the harbour. At the base of the wall are 23 dungeons, now containing tourist shops. Both a lighted underground passage and a drawbridge lead from Las Bóvedas to the fortress of La Tenaza on the sea shore.

20. Casa de Núñez, just outside the walls of La Tenaza in El Cabrero district opposite the Ermita de El Cabrero and 5 minutes from the old bullring; here lived Rafael Núñez, president (four times) and poet (he wrote Colombia's national anthem). His grandiose marble tomb is in the adjoining church.

Three of the sights of Cartagena are off our map. One of them is the Fortress of San Fernando, already mentioned.

The Castillo San Felipe de Barajas, across the Puente Heredia (21) from the outer walled city, stands on the hill of San Lázaro, 41 metres above sea-level. Building began in 1639 and it was finished by 1657. Under the huge structure are tunnels lined with living rooms and offices. Some are open and lighted; visitors pass through these and on to the top of the fortress. Baron de Pointis, the French pirate, stormed and took it in 1697, but Admiral Vernon failed to reach it in the abortive attack of 1741. Entrance fee US$2.35 (US$1 for Colombians). Guide US$1.50 for one to five people.

A lovely road leads to the summit of La Popa hill, nearly 150 metres high, from which there is a fine view of the harbour and the city (entry US$0.85). Here are the church and monastery of Santa Cruz and restored ruins of convent dating from 1608. In the church is the beautiful little image of the Virgin of La Candelaria, reputed a deliverer from plague and a protector against pirates. Her day is 2 February. For nine days before the feast thousands of people go up the hill by car, on foot, or on horseback. On the day itself people carry lighted candles as they go up the hill. The name was bestowed on the hill because of an imagined likeness to a ship's poop. It is dangerous to walk up on your own; either take a guided tour, or take a public bus to Teatro Miramar at the foot of the hill (US$0.50), then bargain for a taxi up, about US$2.50 (or US$5 from centre of town). The Tourist Office recommends a guided tour from an agency opposite the *Hotel Playa* in Bocagrande, for US$5.50, which also takes in San Felipe and San Pedro Claver. You can tour the old town and Bocagrande in a *chiva*, a brightly coloured wooden seated bus with a live band in the back.

**Festivals**  The other great feast, apart from Candlemas, is on 11-14 November to celebrate the independence of Cartagena. Men and women in masks and fancy dress roam the streets, dancing to the sound of *maracas* and drums. There are beauty contests and battles of flowers and general gaiety. This festival tends to be wild and can be dangerous. **Caribbean Music Festival** for 5 days in March, groups from all over the Caribbean region and beyond perform salsa, reggae, etc.; loud and fun. There is a **film festival** at the end of April.

**Warnings**  Carry your passport (or, safer, a DAS-approved photocopy of it) at all times. Failure to present it on police request can result in imprisonment and fines. Regarding sea passages, see warning under Barranquilla (**page 691**). In addition, if offered a job on a ship to the USA, Central America, San Andrés or wherever, it is almost certainly a "con". Should you nevertheless believe it is genuine, insist on full documentation at the Seamen's Union office and do not make any arrangements on the street.

Beware also of self-appointed tourist guides who charge very highly for their services, and can turn nasty if thwarted. Bus travellers are met by people offering to recommend a hotel; their services are not necessary and may lead to "coincidental" theft later. Expert pickpockets reported in crowded areas in town and on the beaches. Quiet Sunday mornings require special care, cameras a particular target. Generally, the central areas are reported safe and friendly.

**Hotels**  On Bocagrande beach, 10 mins by bus from city: *Cartagena-Hilton*, El Laguito, A+, T 50666 (Apto. Aéreo 1774); *Capilla del Mar*, A+, Calle 8, Carrera 1, T 51140, excellent French restaurant, swimming pool on top floor, be careful of their travel desk and check any reservations they make for you, no connection with restaurant of same name ½ km. away; *Las Velas*, Calle Las Velas, No. 1-60, T 80000, C, opposite *Caribe Casino*, warm water all day, showers, good restaurant; *Hotel del Caribe*, Cra. 1, No. 1-114, T 50155, B, all rooms a/c, older half nicer, administration could be better, nice grounds, swimming pool in the (expensive) restaurant, pancakes rec.; *India Catalina*, Carrera 2, No. 7-115, T 55392, C, very good, with a/c, safe, clean (acts as youth hostel); *Residencias Internacional*, Av. San Martín 4110, T 50-675, D, with bath and a/c, clean, safe, friendly; opposite at No. 5-86 is *Flamingo*, C (D in low season), T 50301, with bath and a/c, clean, helpful, pleasant, eat on the terrace, highly rec.; *Succar*, Carrera 2, No. 6-40, D, clean, helpful. *Playa*, Av. 2a, No. 4-87, T 50552, D, all rooms with private bathroom, a/c, very clean, open air bar, restaurant (breakfast, US$1), swimming pool, noisy disco next door, *Leonela*, Carrera 3a, 7-142, D, quiet, comfortable; *Residencia Punta Canda*, Calle 7 between Cras 2 and 3, E, reasonable and everything works. On Carrera 3, there are plenty of small, pleasant *residencias*, for instance Carrera 3, No. 5-29, D in season, clean and friendly. Apartments may be rented from Apartments Intercontinental, Diagonal 1 y Calle 1, e.g. US$40 a day for 6, on Bocagrande next to *Hilton*.

In town: *Del Lago*, Calle 34, No. 11-15, T 44192, D, no hot water, phone, no singles, reasonable; *Montecarlo*, between Av. Urdaneta Arbelaez and Av. Venezuela, T 45013, D, good value, big neon sign on the roof, good reliable laundry next door. *Hostal Santo Domingo*, Calle Santo Domingo, No. 33-46, E, basic but clean and quiet, well located, rec.; *Veracruz*, Calle San Agustín, opp. San Agustín church, D (more with a/c), clean, safe, with or without a/c, helpful but noisy from disco on ground floor; *Bucarica*, San Agustín 6-08, F, quite popular with travellers, but rooms vary a lot and acts as brothel; *Residencial Pacoa*, Calle Pacoa, F, noisy, uncomfortable but friendly; *Magdalena*, same street, F with bath, cold water, fan, clean but small rooms; *Roma*, Tripita Media, E, with bath, basic; *Lina*, San Andrés y Tripita, F, clean with restaurant; *Monterrey*, Camellón de los Mártires (opposite the clocktower), F, clean, safe, friendly, central; *Real*, Calle Espíritu Santo 29-70, E with shower, basic, mice, laundry service, not very safe area; *Residencias Familiar*, Calle Espíritu Santo 29-197, T 648374, F, family owned, safe, friendly, rec., not to be confused with *Hotel Familiar*, Calle del Guerrero, No. 29-66, near Media Luna, F, clean, friendly, use of kitchen, rec.; *Tropicana*, Plaza Independencia, F, run down but friendly, helpful and clean; *Carisma*, Cuartel y Soledad, F, clean, safe, but unfriendly, not rec. *Residencias Venecia*, Calle del Guerrero No. 29-108, F, friendly, rec. some rooms with fan, clean and secure; *Doral*, Media Luna, nice, friendly, No. 10-46, fan, large rooms, E, safe courtyard where you can park cycles/motorbikes, good cheap restaurant; *El Refugio*, Calle Media Luna, No. 10-35, F, friendly, good beds; *Hostal Valle*, Calle Media Luna, No. 10-15, F, very friendly, hot water, some rooms with private bath, free coffee, discounts for long stay, helpful owners, the Guzmane. *Media Luna*, Media Luna y Centenario, F without bath, clean, good value; *San*

*Felipe*, Media Luna 943, with rooms in F range, and good cheap meals; many cheap hotels on Calle Media Luna are brothels; area not advisable for women on their own. On the road to the airport are several hotels and *pensiones*, particularly at Marbella beach, e.g. *Bellavista*, Av. Santander, E, clean, nice patio, English-speaking owner, Enrique Sedó, secure, note that the CNT maps shows the *Bellavista* closer to the airport than it really is.

**N.B.** Hotel prices tend to go up by as much as 25 per cent in December each year (i.e. increase Bocagrande hotels by a letter in our range at this time; in town nothing is below E); hotels tend to be heavily booked right through to March. Either book well in advance yourself, or avoid the city at this time. For hotel insurance, add 5%, plus US$0.05 p.p. per day.

**Camping** In a secure walled garden at *Hotel Bellavista*, Av. Santander, on the beach, US$2.50 p.p.; camper vans also welcome (price in E range). People camp on the beach, but may be troubled by thieves—and the police.

**Restaurants** *Nautilus*, facing the statue of La India Catalina, seafood; another *Nautilus*(same menu and service) on road to airport in Marbella; yet another *Nautilus*, Carrera 3, Bocagrande, good but expensive; *Capilla del Mar*, rec., sea food dinner for 2, US$20-30; all-you-can-eat buffet on Tues. (shrimp) and Fri. (seafood) for US$15. Also in Bocagrande, Av. San Martín, *Fontana di Trevi*, Italian, rec.; *Palacio de las Frutas*, Av. San Martín y Calle 6, good *comida corrida* for US$1.10; *La Fonda Antioqueña*, Cra. 2, No. 6-161, traditional Colombian, nice atmosphere; *La Piragua*, Carrera 2, an open-air bar with live music, dancing, pleasant.

Away from Bocagrande: *La Langosta*, Av. Venezuela, just outside old city walls, good food, reasonable prices; *Nuevo Mundo*, Calle 30, No. 8B-62 serves typical menu, cheap, good sized servings. Many restaurants around Plaza Independencia have meals for about US$2. Restaurants in Calle San Andrés cost about US$1.30, with plenty to eat. Several Chinese restaurants in the old city, e.g. *WingWah*, Calle Ayos, good food, rec. Vegetarian restaurant and health food shop, *Santísimo*, lunch under US$1. *Panadería La Mejor*, Av. Arbeláez, good for breakfast, fine wholemeal bread, coffee, yoghurt; *Panificadora la Española*, Calle 8, No. 7-61, fresh bread and pastries.

At cafés try the *patacón*, a biscuit made of green banana, mashed and baked; also in Parque del Centenario in early morning. At restaurants ask for *sancocho* a local soup of the day of vegetables and fish or meat. Also try *obleas* for a snack, biscuits with jam, cream cheese, or caramel fudge.

**Market** There is a new market out of town, which is disappointing; bus from Av. Urdaneta Arbeláez. The fish market is in the SE suburbs of the old city.

**Shopping** A good selection of *artesanías* on Plaza Bolívar, but in general (except for leather goods) shopping is much better in Bogotá. Woollen *blusas* are good value, US$8-12; try the *Tropicano* in Pierino Gallo building in Bocagrande. Also in this building are reputable jewellery shops. *H. Stern* has a jewellery shop in the Pierino Gallo shopping centre and at the *Hilton Hotel*. Suntan oils and lotions can vary in price as much as 100%—shop around. Comercial Centro Getsemaní, Calle Larga between San Juan and Plaza de la Independencia, a large new shopping centre has many establishments. *Magali París*, Av. Venezuela y Calle del Boquete, is an a/c supermarket, with cafeteria (pizza, good café con leche), good for escaping the heat when exploring old Cartagena. Good badges for backpacks from the shops along the wall of the old prison.

**Gambling** Casino Turístico, Av. San Martín and Casino de Caribe at Pierino Gallo shopping centre, Bocagrande.

**Car Rental** National and Hertz at airport; Avis at *Hilton Hotel*.

**Local Transport** Within the city large buses (with no glass in windows) cost US$0.05, short-wheelbase type (with glass windows), US$0.10. **Taxis** from Bocagrande to the centre should be less than US$1; to the airport US$2.20; centre to airport US$2 (more at night). Try to fix price for journey before committing yourself. A horse-drawn carriage can be hired for US$9, opposite *Hotel El Dorado*, Av. San Martín, in Bocagrande, to ride into town at night (romantic but rather short ride).

**Sport** Fishing; yachting. Windsurf rental, Bocagrande, US$6.50 per hour. Also bullfights and cockfights. The former take place mainly in January and February in the new Plaza de Toros on Av. Pedro de Heredia away from the centre; the latter throughout the year on Sat., Sun. and holidays. On Sat. and Mon. at 1500 cockfighting takes place at the Gallerita Popular de la Quinta and on Sun. at 1600 at Club Gallístico Pedro Rhenals in El Bosque.

**Art Gallery and Museum** Contemporary Latin American paintings, **Banco Ganadero**,

Plaza de la Aduana. Nearby is the **Museo de Arte Moderno** (open Mon.-Fri., 0900-1200, 1500-1800, Sat., 1000-1200), opposite the San Pedro Claver church.

**Exchange** Banco Anglo Colombiano. **Banco Royal** changes American Express travellers' cheques up to a maximum of US$300, with US$10 commission. **Banco de la República**, on Plaza Bolívar, changes American Express and Thomas Cook cheques, with commission, fingerprints and photo taken. There are many *cambios*; the only ones we've heard of changing travellers' cheques are *Caja de Cambio Caldas*, Av. San Martín, No. 4-118, Bocagrande, and on the corner of Plaza de los Coches, downtown. Be sure to count the pesos yourself before handing over your dollars. Never change money on the street, they are nearly all crooks and will short-change you. **American Express** (Tierra Mar Aire), Bocagrande, Carrera 4, Calle 8, is a travel agency only. Travellers' cheques can be changed Sat. a.m. (arrive early) at **Joyería Mora**, Román 5-39, in the old city.

**Anglican Church** Calle Ricuarte, services in English can be arranged.

**Post Office** beside Avianca office between Avs. Venezuela and Urdaneta Arbeláez.

**Venezuelan Consulate** Carrera 12, No. 557 Bocagrande, no visa issued without onward ticket, two photos required, minimum wait 24 hrs., do not wear shorts! Better try elsewhere. **DAS** just beyond Castillo San Felípe, behind the church (ask), very helpful. **Canadian Honorary Consul** (for emergencies only), Calle de la Inquisición con Santo Domingo, esq., No. 33-08, Apto. 201. **Danish Consulate**, Edif. Banco de Bogotá, Oficina 601, T 643669.

**Tourist Office** Carrera 3, No. 36-57 (Plaza Bolívar, T 43400); also at Casa del Marqués de Valdehoyos, Calle de la Factoría (T 47015/9). Also at the airport, but you will only be given information on the more expensive hotels. Town plan for US$0.20. Recommended guide, Fernando Vargas Osorio, Calle de Magdalena, No. 7-52.

**Shipping** There are modern wharves. It is possible to ship a car from Cartagena to Panama. Interoceánica, Centro Carrera 4a, No. 31-14, T 45976/ 44047; cargo ships. Comar agency for Lykes Line, formalities take 3 days; Lykes sails to New Orleans, taking passengers (more expensive than flying). Cargo ships are not allowed to take passengers to San Andrés; some may risk it, charging about US$25. You have to ask the captain; ships leave from Embarcadero San Andrés, opp. Plaza de la Aduana. There are boats leaving most days for points south along the coast and up the river Sinú to Montería, and the Atrato as far as Quibdó. For the trip to Quibdó **see page 730**. See also under **Warning**, above.

**Airport** Crespo, 1½ km. from the city, reached by local buses from Blas de Lezo, SW corner of inner wall. Bus from airport to Plaza San Francisco US$0.10. Taxi to Bocagrande US$3, to town US$2, less if you share. Commuter flights to Barranquilla. Tourist information desk gives list of taxi prices. Good self-service restaurant. No exchange facilities. SAM and Avianca offices both near the post office. From December to March all flights are overbooked—even reconfirming and turning up 2 hours early doesn't guarantee a seat; don't book a seat on the last plane of the day.

**Buses** All long-distance buses leave from Calle 32, with Av. Pedro Heredia, near foot of San Felipe fortress (any bus marked "E-Villa" goes to the old city and Parque Centenario). Pullman bus from Cartagena to **Medellín** 665 km., US$11 (1st class). Several buses a day, but book early (2 days in advance at holiday times), takes 13-16 hrs. The road is now paved throughout, but in poor condition with 4-5 checkpoints. To **Santa Marta**, US$4.75 (with Brasilia, Calle 32, No. 20D-55), 4 hrs., also cheaper lines, US$3.50. To **Barranquilla** US$2.25 with Transportes Cartagena, 3 hrs., or US$2.75 with Expreso Brasilia pullman or La Costeña, US$2.60, 3 hrs. To/from **Bogotá** via Barranquilla and Bucaramanga with Expreso Brasilia pullman, four a day, US$23, may take 21-28 hrs., depending on number of check-points. To **Magangué** on the Magdalena US$4, 4 hours with Brasilia. To **Valledupar** with Expreso Brasilia, pullman US$8.50 (with a ½ hour stop in Barranquilla), for Sierra Nevada and Pueblo Bello. To **Riohacha**, US$7.50. Bus to **Maicao** on Venezuelan frontier US$4.75 (with Expreso Auto Pullman, Expreso Brasilia at 2000, or Unitrasco, Av. Pedro Heredia), 12 hrs.; the road is in good condition, except for 30 km.

**Beaches** Take bus from Plaza de la Independencia to Bocagrande, which has good beaches (although dirty and often crowded). The Boca Chica beach is also dirty, and the boat service there unreliable. Boats leave from Plaza de la Independencia; the round trip can take up to 2 hrs. each way. *Ferry Dancing*, US$2 about half the price of luxury boats, carries dancing passengers; the much faster launches cost US$3.50. For about US$1.50 you can take a tour round the fort of San Fernando in a dugout canoe. There are boats from the city; the last return trip is at 1230. Swimming is good. Boats taking in Boca Chica and San Fernando are

US$5 return without lunch or US$10.50 with lunch (children under 12, half price); Alcatraz run a daily trip from the Muelle Turístico leaving at about 1000, returning at 1530 (very good juice stands along the wharf which also sell *patacones con queso*, fried plantain with a slice of cheese). There is a daily cruise to **Islas del Rosario**, US$14.50 including lunch (possible to bargain in low season), with Alcatraz, leaving 0630, returning 1630. The boat may stop at the San Fernando fortress (entrance US$0.60) and Playa Blanca on the mainland for 1 hr. (bargain with boatman to leave you for a day, camp on the beach, and continue the cruise next day—Playa Blanca is crowded a.m., but peaceful after the tour boats have left). There are several restaurants on the beach, the best *La Sirena* run by Carmen (La Española), good food, reasonably priced. You can also reach Playa Blanca by taking the bus to Puerto Caballo, crossing the Canal de Dique and thence by truck to the beach; interesting trip, cost about US$2. At the Islas del Rosario is an aquarium in the sea, worth visiting, entrance US$1 not included in the boat fare. There are cheaper boats to the islands, shop around. Marbella beach, just N of Las Bóvedas (the locals' beach, and therefore quieter than Bocagrande) is good for swimming, though subject at times to dangerous currents.

**Excursions from Cartagena** To the little fishing village of **La Boquilla**, E of Cartagena, about 20 mins. past the airport. One small hotel, *Los Morros* (E, clean, good food) and campsite. On Sat. and Sun. nights people dance the local dances. Go there by taxi, US$3 (there is a reasonable bus service, and Carlos drives a green Dodge regularly to the bus terminal, US$0.50); can be dangerous for pedestrians and cyclists. Visit the mangrove swamps nearby to see the birds. To **Turbaco**, 24 km. SE by road (Botanical Garden, 1½ km. before village on the left, student guides, worth a visit for ½-day excursion. To **San Jacinto**, 1½ hrs. (73 km.) by road S of Cartagena, good place for local craft work, e.g. hammocks.

Ninety-six km. S of Cartagena along the coast is **Coveñas**, the terminal of the 420-km. crude oil pipeline from the Barco oilfields to the N of Cúcuta, on the Venezuelan frontier (*Hotel y Motel Fragata*, on the beach, reported overpriced, fleas). 20 mins away, E, is **Tolú** village (*Residencias Manuelito*, F, and *Residencias El Turista*, very friendly, has own generator, F; *Residencias La Cabaña*, at western end of beach road, F, no running water, friendly; many fish stalls along the beach) whose beaches are not as nice as those at Coveñas, which are unsigned—ask to be let off the bus. A good trip from Tolú is 3 hrs. to Múcura island in the Islas de San Bernardo. Good for camping but take your own supplies. W of Coveñas are beautiful beaches at Porvenir, no food available, afternoon buses infrequent. Coveñas is 40 minutes from

**Sincelejo**, capital of Sucre Department, a cattle centre 193 km. S of Cartagena on the main road to Medellín (pop. 109,000). It is well known for the dangerous bull-ring game, likened to the San Fermín festivities in Pamplona, Spain, in which bulls and men chase each other. Also at Eastertime there is the "Fiesta del Burro" where they dress up donkeys and prizes go to the best and the funniest. A big party for three days. The town is hot and dusty and power cuts are a factor of life.

**Hotels** *Majestic*, Carrera 20, No. 21-25, E; same range are *Palace*, Calle 19, No. 21-39, and *Marcella*, Calle 21, 23-59; *Finzenu*, Carrera 20 and Calle 22, D, with a/c and some good basic eating; *Sincelejo*, Plaza Santander, F with shower, clean, friendly, fair restaurant. *Panorama*, Carrera 25, 23-108, E, with air-conditioning.

Near Sincelejo is the finca of José Gonzalo Rodríguez Gacha, the notorious "drug baron" where he was caught and killed by the security forces in December 1989.

127 km. S of Sincelejo is **Planeta Rica**, 60 km. beyond which there is a camping site in the grounds of the *Parador Chaubacú* (US$4 per tent); next door is the *Mesón del Gitano*. Eleven km. further on is **Caucasia**, which makes a good stopping point if you want to break the journey from Cartagena to Medellín. *Auto Hotel*, best, quiet, heavily booked; *Hotel Playa Mar*, F, good food, friendly, noisy; *Hostería Horizontes*, D, calm, spacious, two swimming pools, good restaurant. *Residencias San Francisco*, Carrera 49 y Calle 45, E, with bath, good value. Chinese restaurant, 3 doors up, good cheap food. A nice place to visit, Jardín Botánico, entrance fee US$0.25. About half way between Caucasia and Medellín is **Valdivia** with a spectacular bridge over the Cauca. The road continues to Yarumal (see page 726).

**Montería**, capital of Córdoba Department, on the E bank of the river Sinú, can be reached from Cartagena by air, by river boat, or from the main highway to Medellín. (Bus from Cartagena—dual carriageway almost completed, US$5.25, 5 hrs., with Brasilia, has own terminal in Montería.) It is the centre of a cattle and agricultural area turning out tobacco, cacao, cotton and sugar. Present population is 144,000. Compared with other Caribbean cities there is little to attract the tourist except for the one fine church, picturesque street life and the extremely friendly people. Average temperature: 28°C. Road to Planeta Rica (airport).

**Hotels** *Sinú*, Carrera 3, Calle 32, C, a/c and swimming pool, watch out for short changing in the restaurant; *Alcázar*, Carrera 2, No. 32-17, F, comfortable and friendly, restaurant not always open; *Embajador*, F, fan, OK; lots of cheap dives in the neighbourhood; *Residencias Imperial*, Carrera 2, F.

**Warning** There is a high risk of kidnapping in rural areas of Sucre and Córdoba departments; tourists are advised not to stray from the beaten track.

On the Gulf of Urabá is the port of *Turbo*, now a centre of banana cultivation, which is booming. It is a rough frontier community; not too law-abiding, tourists are advised to be very careful. Turbo may be reached from Cartagena and from Medellín (6 buses a day, a gruelling 13-16 hrs., US$7.50; 4-wheel drive to Montería, 5 hrs., US$6, rough dirt track between Turbo and Valencia, several army checkpoints). **Hotels**: *Playa Mar*, D, the best; *Sausa*, D, running water in early morning only, helpful owners, pleasant dining room; *Residencia Sandra*, F, good; *Residencia Turbo*, *Residencia Marcela*, both F and best value; good rooms are hard to find, most hotels are brothels; in Playa district: *Miramar*, *Rotitom*, both D. No banks are open for exchange of travellers' cheques on Monday or Tuesday, either don't arrive then, or have dollars in cash with you.

186 km. S of Turbo, on the road to Antioquia (**see page 726**), is Dabeiba (*Residencia Diana*, on main street, F, simple, clean, very helpful, free morning coffee).

To visit the **Los Katíos National Park (see below)**, go first to the Inderena office in Turbo, where all information is available (recommended trip). A description of routes by boat and overland from Colombia to Panama will be found below; note that if going from Colombia to Panama via Turbo you should get an exit stamp from a DAS office. The nearest we have heard of is at Apartadó, 30 km. from Turbo (40 mins. in colectivo, US$0.80, closed Sat. and Sun.), although Cristóbal Gil, at *Hotel Playa Mar*, Turbo, is reported to give exit stamps. If leaving Colombia, check the facts in Cartagena (or any other place with a DAS office); if arriving from Panama, you can either go to the police in Turbo for a letter stating your arrival date, then go to DAS in Montería or Cartagena, or just go straight there and explain yourself in full. We have also been informed that the immigration office at the Panamanian port of Puerto Obaldía can be extremely obstructive. Think twice about taking a trip in a small boat between Panama and Colombia other than the regular boats shown below: the majority are contraband, even arms runners and if stopped, you will be in trouble. (Even if not stopped you will have difficulty obtaining a DAS entry stamp because the captain of the boat must state officially that he is carrying passengers into Colombia.) If taking a reputable cargo boat be sure to arrange with the captain the price and destination before departure. Boats may also be stopped outside Turbo for medical checks: yellow fever inoculations will be given (free) to all without a certificate. Spend your surplus pesos in Colombia, they are impossible to change at fair rates in Panama.

## From Colombia to Panama

The simplest way is to fly from Barranquilla, Bogotá, Cali, Cartagena, Medellín or San Andrés. There are also various routes involving sea and land crossings around or through the *Darién Gap*, which still lacks a road connection linking the Panamanian Isthmus and South America. Descriptions of these routes are given in the *Mexico and Central American Handbook* (although in the direction Panama-Colombia), and a more detailed account is given in *Backpacking in Mexico and Central America* (Bradt Publications—new edition in preparation in 1991). While maps of the region are available, there is no substitute for seeking informed local advice. In all cases, it is essential to be able to speak Spanish.

One route is from Bahía Solano (see page 730) or Jurado in Chocó Department (Jurado can be reached by plane from Turbo). Canoes go from both towns to Jaqué, 50 km. N of the Colombian border, from where you can fly to La Palma, capital of Darién in Panama (one *pensión* F, cooking and laundry facilities, English spoken). Launches and dugouts go from La Palma to Puerto Lardo on the Río Sabanas, from where it is a 2-hour walk (or hitch on a truck) to Santa Fe on the Panamá-Yaviza road. (Bus Santa Fe-Panamá 6-8 hrs.; flight with Parsa, T Panamá 26-3883/3808, La Palma—Panama City 3 times a week).

On the Caribbean side, the starting point is Turbo on the Gulf of Urabá. From Turbo boats sail to Acandí (at 0800), Zapzurro (in Colombia) and Puerto Obaldía (Panama) also at 0800, 5 hrs, US$26, from where boats go to Colón, planes to Panama City (daily except Sun.).

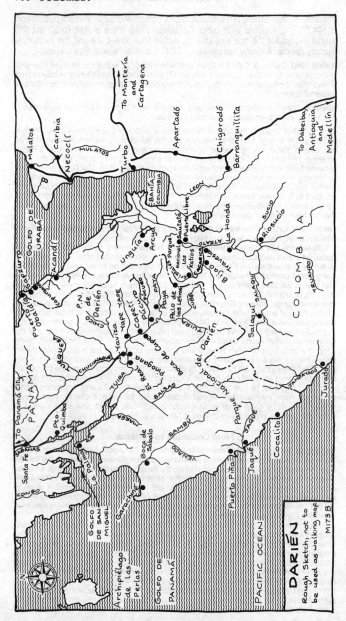

**DARIÉN**

Rough Sketch, not to
be used as walking map

M173B

*Residencial Cande* in Pto. Obaldía is E, good with meals at US$1.50. If your papers are not in order on arrival in Puerto Obaldía you will be sent back to Colombia. There is an overland route from Puerto Obaldía which involves a 4-hour walk to the foot of the Darién range (guide essential, US$10), crossing the hills to the Río Tuquesa (3 hrs.) and following the river downstream with a great many crossings and one night camping out, to Maranganti (immigration post). From here a dugout can be taken to B. Vigía; walk to the next village, Villa Calleta, where two US missionaries, Doug and Ernie, work (take care with directions on this stretch). From Villa Calleta you walk along the Río Chucucanaque to join the Yaviza-Panama City road near La Pinita. Note that locals on this route are very wary of foreigners (much illegal immigration). We are grateful to Jamie Butler of Petersfield, Hants., for this information.

Two alternative routes from Turbo cross the Gap to Paya, from where there is a well-trodden route to Yaviza: Paya-Pucuro, 5-6 hrs. on foot; Pucuro-Boca de Cupe, by dugout, US$15-30; Boca de Cupe-Pinogana, also by dugout, US$15 p.p., plus a walk, 2 hrs. in all; Pinogana-Yaviza, walk and ferries/dugouts. From Yaviza (one hotel, *Three Américas*, E, basic) buses can be caught to Panama City, US$15, 10-14 hrs., road subject to wash-outs.

The first route to Paya: motorboat Turbo-Travesía/Puerto América through the Bahía de Colombia, the Great Atrato Swamp and down the Río Atrato, with much birdlife to be seen (US$6-10 if scheduled, US$130 to hire a boat); then another boat to Bijao (3 hrs., US$30). From Bijao you have to get by boat to Cristales in the Los Katios National Park; the Inderena rangers may take you for US$30. At Cristales there is an Inderena hut; 7 hrs. through the Park on foot is Palo de los Letras, the frontier stone, from where it is 4-6 hrs. to Paya.

The Katios National Park (**Warning**: entry by motorized vehicle is prohibited), extending in Colombia to the Panamanian border, can be visited with mules from the Inderena headquarters in Sautatá (rangers may offer free accommodation, very friendly). In the park is the Tilupo waterfall, 125 metres high; the water cascades down a series of rock staircases, surrounded by orchids and fantastic plants. Also in the park are the Alto de la Guillermina, a mountain behind which is a strange forest of palms called "mil pesos", and the Ciénagas de Tumaradó, with red monkeys, waterfowl and alligators.

The second route to Paya: take a boat from Turbo across the Gulf of Urabá into the Río Tarena to Unguía (accommodation, restaurants). From here it is 3-4 hours to the frontier, then 3 hours to the Río Paya. You then hike down the Paya river through dense jungle to Paya itself (about 12 hours). Do not attempt the Unguía-Paya route without a guide.

Dr Richard Dawood, author of *Travellers' Health: How to Stay Healthy Abroad*, and photographer Anthony Dawton, crossed the Darien Gap at the end of the wet season (November). We are pleased to include Dr Dawood's health recommendations for such a journey: **Heat** Acclimatization to a hot climate usually takes around 3 weeks. It is more difficult in humid climates than in dry ones, since sweat cannot evaporate easily, and when high humidity persists through the night as well, the body has no respite. (In desert conditions, where the temperature falls at night, adaptation is much easier.) Requirements for salt and water increase dramatically under such conditions. We had to drink 12 litres per day to keep pace with our own fluid loss on some parts of the trip.

We were travelling under extreme conditions, but it is important to remember that the human thirst sensation is not an accurate guide to true fluid requirements. In hot countries it is always essential to drink beyond the point of thirst quenching, and to drink sufficient water to ensure that the urine is consistently pale in colour.

Salt losses also need to be replaced. Deficiency of salt, water, or both, is referred to as heat exhaustion; lethargy, fatigue, and headache are typical features, eventually leading to coma and death. Prevention is the best approach, and we used the pre-salted water regime pioneered by Colonel Jim Adam and followed by the British Army; salt is added to all fluids, one quarter of a level teaspoon (approx 1 gram) per pint—to produce a solution that is just below the taste threshold. Salt tablets, however, are poorly absorbed, irritate the stomach and may cause vomiting; plenty of pre-salted fluid should be the rule for anyone spending much time outdoors in the tropics.

**Sun** Overcast conditions in the tropics can be misleading. The sun's rays can be fierce, and it is important to make sure that all exposed skin is constantly protected with a high factor sun screen—preferably waterproof for humid conditions. This was especially important while we were travelling by canoe. A hat was also essential.

**Food and Water** Diarrhoea can be annoying enough in a luxurious holiday resort with comfortable sanitary facilities. The inconvenience under jungle conditions would have been more than trivial, however, with the added problem of coping with further fluid loss and dehydration.

Much caution was therefore needed with food hygiene. We carried our own supplies, which we prepared carefully ourselves: rather uninspiring camping fare, such as canned tuna fish, sardines, pasta, dried soup, biscuits and dried fruit. In the villages, oranges, bananas and coconuts were available. The freshly baked bread was safe, and so would have been the rice.

We purified our water with 2 per cent tincture of iodine carried in a small plastic dropping bottle, 4 drops to each litre—more when the water is very turbid—wait 20 minutes before drinking. This method is safe and effective, and is the only suitable technique for such conditions. (Another suggestion from Peter Ovenden is a water purifying pump based on a ceramic filter. There are several on the market, Peter used a Katadyn. It takes about a minute to purify a litre of water – Ed.) It is also worth travelling with a suitable antidiarrhoeal medication such as Arret.

**Malaria** Drug resistant malaria is present in the Darien area, and antimalarial medication is essential. We took Paludrine, two tablets daily, and chloroquine, two tablets weekly. Free advice on antimalarial medication for all destinations is available from the Malaria Reference Laboratory, T (071) 636 8636 in the UK. An insect repellent is also essential, and so are precautions to avoid insect bites.

**Insects** Beside malaria and yellow fever, other insect-borne diseases such as dengue fever and leishmaniasis may pose a risk. The old fashioned mosquito net is ideal if you have to sleep outdoors, or in a room that is not mosquito-proof. Mosquito nets for hammocks are widely available in Latin America. An insecticide spray is valuable for clearing your room of flying insects before you go to sleep, and mosquito coils that burn through the night giving off an insecticidal vapour, are also valuable.

**Ticks** It is said that ticks should be removed by holding a lighted cigarette close to them, and we had an opportunity to put this old remedy to the test. We duly unwrapped a pack of American duty-frees that we had preserved carefully in plastic just for such a purpose, as our Indian guides looked on in amazement, incredulous that we should use these prized items for such a lowly purpose. The British Army expedition to Darien in 1972 carried 60,000 cigarettes among its supplies, and one wonders if they were for this purpose! The cigarette method didn't work, but caused much amusement. (Further discussion with the experts indicates that the currently favoured method is to ease the tick's head gently away from the skin with tweezers.)

**Vaccinations** A yellow fever vaccination certificate is required from all travellers arriving from infected areas, and vaccination is advised for personal protection.

Immunization against hepatitis A (with gammaglobulin) and typhoid are strongly advised.

Attacks by dogs are relatively common: the new rabies vaccine is safe and effective, and carrying a machete for the extra purpose of discouraging animals is advised.

In addition, all travellers should be protected against tetanus, diptheria and polio.

You can get some food along the way, but take enough for at least 5 days. Do take, though, a torch/flashlight, and a bottle of rum for the ranger at Cristales. It is highly recommended to travel in the dry season only, when there is no mud and fewer mosquitoes. If you have time, bargains can be found.

Taking a motorcycle through Darién is not an endeavour to be undertaken lightly, and cannot be recommended. Ed Culberson (who, in 1986 after two unsuccessful attempts, was the first to accomplish the feat) writes: "Dry season passage is comparatively easy on foot and even with a bicycle. But it simply cannot be done with a standard sized motorcycle unless helped by Indians at a heavy cost in dollars...It is a very strenuous, dangerous adventure, often underestimated by motorcyclists, some who have come to untimely ends in the jungle".

**San Andrés** and **Providencia**, two small and attractive, but very expensive, islands in the Caribbean Sea, have belonged to Colombia since 1822. They are 400 km. SW of Jamaica, 180 km. E of Nicaragua, and 480 km. N of the Colombian coast. Henry Morgan had his headquarters at San Andrés. A road circles the island, of coral, some 11 km. long rising to 104 metres. The original inhabitants, mostly black, speak some English, but the population has swollen with unrestricted immigration from Colombia. The population in 1988 was put at 35,000, but it could now be about 65,000. Main products: coconuts and vegetable oil. Main problem, deteriorating water and electricity supplies (in most hotels the water is salty—a desalination plant was installed in 1987). Places to see: the beautiful Keys, like Johnny Key with a white beach and parties all day Sunday (US$1.90 return, you can go in one boat and return in another), and the so-called Aquarium (US$2 return), off a Key where, using a mask and wearing sandals as protection against sea-urchins, you can see colourful fish. Boats to these places all leave a.m.; none

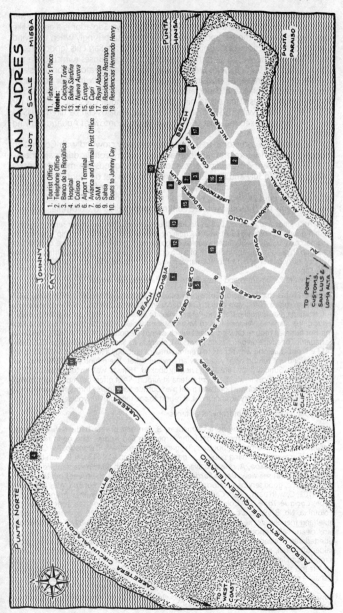

SAN ANDRES
NOT TO SCALE

1. Tourist Office
2. Telephone Office
3. Banco de la República
4. Hospital
5. Coliseo
6. Airport Terminal
7. Avianca and Airmail Post Office
8. SAM
9. Sahsa
10. Boats to Johnny Cay
11. Fisherman's Place

**Hotels:**
12. Cacique Toné
13. Bahía Sardina
14. Nueva Aurora
15. Europa
16. Capri
17. Royal Abacoa
18. Residencia Restrepo
19. Residencias Hernando Henry

p.m. Snorkelling equipment can be hired on San Andrés for US$4-5, but it is better and cheaper on the shore than on the island. The Hoyo Soplador is a geyser-like hole through which the sea spouts into the air most surprisingly when the wind is in the right direction. Less spoilt parts of the island are San Luis (good beach), Sound Bay and the west side (but no beaches this side). Buses (which circle the island all day) US$0.25. Bicycles are a popular way of getting around on the island and are easy to hire, e.g. opposite *El Dorado Hotel*—usually in poor condition, choose your own bike and check all parts thoroughly (US$1.10 per hour, US$6 per day); motorbikes also easy to hire, US$3.60 per hour. Cars can be hired for US$15 for 2 hours, with US$6 for every extra hour. Pedalos can be hired at US$4 per hour. Diving trips to reef cost US$50 with Pedro Montoya at Aquarium diving shop.

The islands are a customs-free zone; they are very crowded with Colombian shoppers looking for foreign-made bargains. Although alcoholic drinks are cheap, essential goods are extremely costly, and electronic goods are more expensive than in the UK. In July and August, it is very difficult to get on flights into and out of San Andrés; book in advance if possible. Checking in for flights can be difficult because of queues of shoppers with their goods. There is a customs tax of 15% on some items purchased if you are continuing to mainland Colombia.

Only cruise ships and tours go to San Andrés; there are no other passenger services by sea. To ship a vehicle costs US$900 with bargaining (officially US$1,300). To ship a vehicle to Panama costs US$400-450. Interoceánica cargo ships, T 6624-6625. Beware of offers of tickets on ships to/from San Andrés, or of a job on a ship, these are con tricks. Officially, ships may not carry passengers to the mainland; if you want to leave by sea, speak only to the ship's captain.

There are Panamanian and Costa Rican consulates on San Andrés.

**Airport** Flights to most major Colombian cities: to Bogotá and Medellín with Aces, SAM (you can arrange a 72-hr. stop-over in Cartagena) and Avianca (dearer); SAM and Avianca fly to Cartagena, Barranquilla, Cali and Pereira. Also to Guatemala City, San José (both daily), Tegucigalpa, Panama. Avianca flies to Miami twice a week. Note that Panama, Costa Rica and Honduras all require onward tickets which cannot be bought on San Andrés, can be in Cartagena. For advice on purchasing tickets to Colombia via San Andrés, **see page 752**. Care: SAM will not issue one way tickets to Central America. You buy a return, and SAM office on the mainland will refund once you show an onward ticket. The refund (less 15%) may not be immediate. Sunday flights are always heavily booked. 15 mins. walk to town (taxi US$2.50 p.p.). All airline offices in town, except Satena at airport. SAM offers hotel packages as well as the airfare, but booking a hotel and meal plan outside San Andrés through a travel agent is not always a satisfactory arrangement. It is best to see the hotel for yourself.

Carry your passport (or photocopy) at all times.

**Hotels** *Nueva Aurora*, Av. de las Américas, B, fan and private bath; *Bahía Marina*, Carretera San Luis, B, swimming pool, the largest on San Andrés, and good restaurant; *Decameron*, Av. Colombia, B, pool, a/c, TV, good restaurant, rec.; *El Dorado*, Av. Colombia, No. 1A-25 (casino, swimming pool), C; *Abacoa*, Av. Colombia, T 4133/4, B, with bath and a/c; also *Royal Abacoa*, A, on same avenue at No. 2-41, with good restaurant; *Isleño*, Av. La Playa, C, great sea view; *Bahía Sardina*, Av. Colombia, across the street from the beach, a/c, TV, fridge, good service, comfortable, clean, no swimming pool; *Europa*, Av. 20 de Julio, No. 1-101, C, with bath, clean; *Capri*, Av. Costa Rica, No. 1A-110, B, with bath and a/c, good value; *Cacique Toné*, Av. Colombia, Cra. 5, A, deluxe, a/c, pool, on sea-front; *Tiuna*, Av. Colombia, No. 3-59, A, a/c, swimming pool; *Verde Mar*, Avenida 20 de Julio, D, T 5525, quiet and friendly, a/c, new, rec.; *Las Antillas*, Av. 20 de Julio, No. 1A-81, D with bath and fan, clean, safe, good water (inc. for drinking), good value; *Mediterráneo*, Av. Los Libertadores, D, clean, friendly; *Residencias Hernando Henry*, C, restaurant, fan, clean, good value, often full, on road from airport. *Residencia Restrepo*, Av. 8, "gringo hotel", near airport—turn left to beach, then left, second left at fish restaurant and it's a hundred metres on left (no sign—you pass a good food shop on the way, breakfast, juices, snacks), noisy ("share a room with a Boeing 727"—till midnight), F or G for a hammock in the porch, clean, some rooms with bath, breakfast US$0.50, other meals US$1.50, good place for buying/selling unwanted return halves of air tickets to/from Central America or the Colombian mainland. Campsite at South End said to be dirty and mosquito-ridden.

**Restaurants** *Popular*, on Av. Bogotá, good square meal for US$4. *Bahía*, good food; *Fonda Antioqueña Nos. 1 and 2*, on Av. Colombia near the main beach, and Av. Colombia at Av. Nicaragua, best value for fish; excellent fruit juices at *Jugolandia*, Calle 20 de Julio; *Jugosito*, Av. Colombia, 1½ blocks from tourist office towards centre, cheap meals; *Fisherman's Place*, in the fishing cooperative at N end of main beach, very good, simple. Good ice cream next to *Hotel Gran Internacional*. *The Barboat*, a floating bar, off the beach between the Centro Comercial Dann and Club Naútico, English and German spoken, waterskiing and windsurfing rental, also instruction available, water taxi to the Keys. Fish meals for US$2.50 can be bought at San Luis beach.

**Taxis** round the island, US$8; to airport, US$3; in town, US$0.60; *colectivo* to airport, US$0.50.

**Exchange** Banco de la República (Mon.-Fri., 0800-1100 and 1400-1500; Sat. morning only) will exchange dollars and travellers' cheques; **Banco Cafetero** will advance pesos on a Visa card. **Aerodisco** shop at airport will change dollars cash anytime at rates slightly worse than banks, or try the **Photo Shop** on Av. Costa Rica. (Rates are lower than in Bogotá.) Many shops will change US$ cash; it is impossible to change travellers' cheques at weekends. (Airport employees will exchange US$ cash at a poor rate.)

**Tourist Information**, Avenida Colombia No. 5-117, in front of *Hotel Isleño*, English spoken, maps.

**Providencia**, commonly called Old Providence, 80 km. back to the NNE from San Andrés, is 7 km. long and is more mountainous than San Andrés, rising to 610 metres. There are waterfalls, and the land drops steeply into the sea in places. It is also an expensive island. The 3 main beaches are Manchinal Bay, the largest, most attractive and least developed, South West Bay and Freshwater Bay, all in the South West. Most of the accommodation is at Playa Agua Dulce (Freshwater): *Cabañas El Recreo* (Captain Brian's), E, p.p.; *Cabañas El Paraíso*, *Cabañas Aguadulce* and *Hotel Royal Queen*; *Ma Elma's* rec. for cheap food and *Morgan's Bar* for fish meals and a good breakfast for US$2; at Santa Isabela on the N end of the island, *Flaming Trees Hotel*, E, clean, restaurant, good value, but a long way from the beach; at Smooth Water Bay, *Dutch Inn* (C full board) and several houses take in guests. Camping is possible at Freshwater Bay. Truck drivers who provide transport on the island may be able to advise on accommodation. The sea food is good, water and fresh milk are generally a problem. Horse riding is available, and boat trips can be made to neighbouring islands such as Santa Catalina (an old pirate lair), and to the NE, Crab Key (beautiful swimming and snorkelling), day trip from 1000 to 1500, about US$7 p.p. Superb views can be had by climbing from Bottom House or Smooth Water to the peak. Day tours are arranged by the Providencia office in San Andrés, costing US$35 inclusive. SAM fly from San Andrés, US$30, 25 mins., up to 5 times a day, bookable only in San Andrés. (Return flight has to be confirmed at airport. Tourist office at airport.) Boat trips from San Andrés take 8 hours, but are not regular.

**Santa Marta**, capital of Magdalena Department (pop. 350,000), the third Caribbean port, is 96 km. E of Barranquilla, at the mouth of the Río Manzanares. It is best reached from Barranquilla by the paved road along the coast, which passes salt pans and skirts an extensive and most interesting lagoon, the Ciénaga de Santa Marta, in which all types of water birds, plants and animals may be seen. (There has been an ecological disaster there, as a result of cutting off the egress to the sea to build the coast road.) There is a paved road S to Bucaramanga (**see page 679**) and Bogotá.

Santa Marta lies on a deep bay with high shelving cliffs. The climate ranges seasonally from hot and trying to hot but pleasant in February and March; occasionally one can see snow-clad peaks of the Sierra Nevada to the E, less than 50 km. away and 5,800 metres high.

Its sandy beaches stretch from the Simón Bolívar airport to Punta Aguja across the Rodadero de Gaira and the little fishing villages of Villa Concha, surrounded by meadows and shady trees, and Taganga (see below). A jutting rock—the Punta de Betín—rises from the sea in front of the city and is topped by a lighthouse. Rugged Isla del Moro, 3 km. off Santa Marta, completes the panorama. Playa El Rodadero is the most fashionable and tourist-oriented part of Santa Marta, though it lies some distance W of the city (local bus service, taxi, US$1.80) It is extremely dangerous to wander off the beaten track at Rodadero: correspondents have been robbed at gunpoint. Many of the buses coming from Barranquilla and Cartagena stop at Rodadero on the way to Santa Marta. There is also a dirty, unsafe beach with a seaside promenade close to the centre of town.

Santa Marta was the first town founded (1525) by the *conquistadores* in Colombia. Founder: Rodrigo de Bastidas. Most of the famous sea-dogs—the brothers Côte, Drake and Hawkins—sacked the city in spite of the two forts built on a small island at the entrance to the bay. It was here that Simón Bolívar, his dream of Gran Colombia shattered, came to die. Almost penniless he was given hospitality at the *hacienda* of San Pedro Alejandrino, 5 km. to the SE. He died on 17 December 1830, at the age of 47, and was buried in the Cathedral, but his body was taken to the Pantheon at Caracas 12 years later. The simple room in which he died and his few belongings can be seen today (admission, US$0.10, open Tues.-Sat. 1330-2000): take the "Mamatoca" bus from the waterfront (Carrera 1C) to the *hacienda*, US$0.20.

**Warning** The north end of town, beyond the railway station, is very dangerous and travellers are advised not to go there alone. We have received reports of tourists being robbed at gunpoint of everything including their clothes in daylight. If you arrive by bus, beware taxi drivers who take you to a hotel of their choice, not yours (no doubt for a commission). Also beware of "jungle tours" sold by street touts in Santa Marta and avoid the trail to Pueblito.

**Hotels** In town: *Residencia Park Hotel*, Carrera 1C, No. 18-63, on sea front, D with shower, reasonable; *Tairona*, Carrera 1, No. 11-41, T 32408, D, with fan, bath, clean and safe; *Dos Virreyes*, Calle 12, No. 1-34, near waterfront, can be bargained to E, only 5 rooms, with fan and shower, friendly, rec.; *Miramar*, Calle 10C, No. 1C-59, F with bath (cheaper rooms without), "gringo hotel", safe for parking motorbikes, restaurant, very friendly, safe, 2 blocks from railway station and beach (not to be confused with *Hotel Residencias Miramar*, Carrera 1C, No. 18-23), will guard your luggage, rec.; several others nearby, e.g. *Res. Marinas*, Calle 10, No. 1C-83, F, clean, friendly, fan, bath; *Hotel Residencias Yarimar*, Carrera 1A, No. 26-37, E, clean, fan, noisy; *Yuldama*, Cra. 1, No. 12-19, C, T 32889, clean a/c, reasonable food; **Youth Hostel** *Hotel Nabusimake*, details from Alcom in Bogotá.

At Rodadero Bay: *Tamacá*, best, Carrera 2, No. 11A-98, C, good service, fine pool; *Irotama*, L, km. 14, between airport and Rodadero Bay, has bungalows; *Residencias Edma*, Carrera 3, No. 5-188, Rodadero, D, a/c, clean, cafeteria, welcoming; *La Sierra*, Carrera 1, No. 9-47, B, disorganised, not currently rec., though relatively inexpensive restaurant; *Residencial Bastidas*, Cra. 2, F, shower, friendly, laundry facilities; *Valladolid*, E, Carrera 2, good value, large clean rooms, helpful, rec.; *Santa Mar*, at Km. 8, D. In season, it is difficult to find a single room for less than US$4. Apartments: *Patuca*, on beach, US$40 for 8. Bungalows for 8 for rent from Isidro Ramos, casa 5, Manzana G, Rodadero del Mar, Santa Marta.

**Motels** *El Rodadero*, Calle 11, No. 1-29, D, swimming pool, English-speaking manageress (Marino Salcedo), very helpful; and others.

**Restaurants** *Vegetariano*, Calle 12, No. 6-18, good breakfast; a good vegetarian restaurant is at Calle 10 y Cra. 6, reasonable prices. *Yarimar*, Carrera 1A, No. 26-37, next to hotel of same name, good seafood; opp. is *La Terraza Marina*, also rec. for seafood. *El Platanal*, Calle 13, No. 1-33, good cheap food, good service. *La Gran Muralla*, Carrera 5, No. 23-77 and *Oriental*, Calle 22, No. 3-43, both good Chinese. *Toy San*, Calle 22, Chinese, good, big portions. *Bermuz*, Calle 14, No. 4-08, good, cheap;

At Rodadero there are a number of good restaurants, some pricey, some good value; there are also very good juice kiosks along the seafront.

**Museum** Casa de la Aduana, Calle 14 y Carrera 2, displays an excellent archaeological collection, including a large number of precolombian gold artefacts. Open Tues.-Sat., 0800-1200, 1400-1800, Sun. 0800-1200, during the tourist season, Mon.-Fri., 0800-1200, 1400-1800, the rest of the year; entry free.

**Exchange** Change money at the **Banco de la República**, on Carrera 5, No. 17-04; open 0800-1100 and 1400-1530. **Amex** office Tierra del Mar, Calle 15, No. 2-60. *Casas de cambio* in 3rd block of Calle 14, many others on this street. In Rodadero, Apto. 201, Carrera 1, No. 9-23.

**Tourist Office** in the former Convent of Santo Domingo, Carrera 2, No. 16-44. There is also an office at Rodadero, Calle 10, No. 3-10. **Inderena** office, Carrera 1C, No. 22-77, and at the Quinta de San Pedro Alejandrino. **DAS Office** Corner of Calle 26 y Carrera 9.

**Train** "Expreso del Sol" leaves on Mondays and Thursdays at 0700 for **La Dorada**; 24 hrs.

(US$10), long delays possible. One class only; meals at US$1.50 each, quite good. From La Dorada, one can also take a bus to **Bogotá (see page 714)**. The "Tayrona" runs to **Bogotá** once a week (Wed.) between 1 December and 31 March only. The "Nutibara" runs once a week to and from **Medellín** during the same months (on the same day of the week); connects with the "Tayrona" at Grecia.

**Buses** Terminal is at Calle 24 and Carrera 8 (take a taxi or walk to Calle 22, then take "Playa" bus to centre, passing waterfront—Carrera 1C). To/from **Bogotá**, 22 hrs., US$20, 4 a day; coming from the capital check that if the bus is continuing to Barranquilla, you will be dropped in Santa Marta, not short of it. The Copetran bus to **Bucaramanga** takes about 9 hrs. (US$15). Journey time will be affected by the number of police checks. There is a good meal stop at Los Límites. From Bucaramanga the buses take 8 hrs. to Bogotá (11 minimum by 2nd class). Buses to **Barranquilla**, 2 hrs. (US$1.60-1.80); to **Cartagena**, 4 hrs. (US$3.50, or US$4.75, Brasilia). To **Riohacha** US$2.85, 3 hrs.; Pullman to **Maicao**, US$4.50, these non-airconditioned. buses stop at the Venezuelan border on the way to **Maracaibo** for exit and entry stamps, usually better organized than at Cúcuta. There are three buses a day (Brasilia) direct to **Rodadero Beach** from Barranquilla, taking 2 hrs. and costing US$1.50. They return to Barranquilla at 1300, 1530 and 1730. Fastest service to Barranquilla and Cartagena reported to be Transportes la Costeña.

**Airport** Simón Bolívar, 20 km. from city; bus, US$0.20, taxi from Santa Marta, US$7, from Rodadero, US$2.40. During the tourist season, get to the airport early. Note, planes are full, book well ahead.

**Port** It can take up to 4 working days to get a car out of the port, but it is usually well guarded and it is unlikely that anything will be stolen. (See also under **Motorcycles** in **Information for Visitors**.)

**Sightseeing Tours** in air-conditioned jeeps run by Airline travel agency at centre. Launches leave Rodadero beach every hour for the Aquarium, modest, not as good as the one at Islas del Rosario near Cartagena, US$3 return (includes admission). From the Aquarium, one can walk (10 mins.) to the Playa Blanca (White Beach) where one can swim in less crowded conditions than elsewhere—food available at the beach. Small Indian figures are sculptured at José Pertuz, Calle 38, Carrera 17. They cut stone with traditional instruments and will chisel animals etc. to order. They are sold on Rodadero beach.

**Excursions** Close to Santa Marta (bus US$0.10, 30 mins. taxi US$2, 10 mins.) is the fishing village and beach of **Taganga**, with hotel *La Ballena Azul*, D, most attractive, friendly, comfortable, clean, restaurant, also run boat tours to secluded beaches, ask Mauricio about tours, horses for hire (postal address: Aptdo Aéreo 799, Santa Marta, Telex 38886 CCSMT CO). One can stay with Joselito Guerra on the beach, G for hammock space, secure for luggage, or rent houses on beach (not secure). Restaurants expensive, but a good one is *Tibisay*, seafood. Swimming good, especially on Playa Grande, 25 mins'. walk round coast, but thieving is common there. Taganga is quiet during week, but trippers from Santa Marta pour in on Sun. On the E shore of the Ciénaga de Santa Marta, is **Ciénaga**, a town of 75,000 people. Cotton, bananas, tobacco and cacao are grown in the area. Hotels in Ciénaga: *Tobiexe; Naval.* (Granturismo tours to Ciénaga are not recommended; much too fast). South of Ciénaga, just before Fundación, is **Aracataca**, birthplace of Gabriel García Márquez, fictionalised as Macondo in some of his stories (notably *Cien años de soledad*). His home, called a museum, may be seen in the backyard of La Familia Iriarte Ahumada—just ask for directions. As a museum, it is disappointing. There are *residencias* (G), but it is better to stay in Fundación. Best hotel is *Carolí*, Carrera 8, No. 5-30, Fundación, F (E with a/c); others all in this price range. Do not walk between Aracataca and Fundación at night, otherwise it is safe. Bus Fundación-Aracataca, US$0.15; Fundación-Ciénaga, US$0.75; Fundación-Barranquilla, US$3.50. Banana growing in the area has now been replaced almost entirely by African palm plantations.

To go to the **Ciudad Perdida**, discovered in 1975, permission is required from Inderena, Carerra 1a, No. 22-77, Santa Marta, T 36355; it is not always given because the area is dangerous. The site covers 400 hectares, at 1,100 metres altitude, near the Río Buritaca; comparisons have been made with Machu Picchu.

Ciudad Perdida was founded between 500 and 700 AD and was surely the most important centre of the Tairona culture. It stands on the steep slopes of Cerro Corea, which lies in the northern part of the Sierra Nevada de Santa Marta. It consists of a complex system of buildings, paved footpaths, flights of steps and perimetrical walls, which link a series of terraces and platforms, on which were built cult centres, residences and warehouses.

You can reach Ciudad Perdida by helicopter from Santa Marta in about 20 minutes, by arrangement. Ask at Helicol, at the airport, or at Corporación Nacional de Turismo, Carrera 2a, No. 16-44 (T 35773). Price: about US$290 there and back with a 3 hour stay.

More adventurous trekkers can reach Ciudad Perdida in a six/eight days' excursion, leaving about 0700 from Santa Marta market, at the corner of Carrera 11 and Calle 11.

Toyota jeeps go up to La Tagua (about 3 hours), where it is possible to rent mules and pay local guides (but see below). You can go on alone, but route finding is difficult. You need to take hammock, plenty of protection against mosquitoes, sleeping bag, warm clothing for the night, torch, plastic bags to keep everything dry, and strong, quick drying footwear. Check conditions, especially information on river crossings, and ensure you have adequate food before you start. The first day's walking is about 7 hours, through fine wild scenery. The first night will be spent in a hammock in a typical farmhouse. They are very hospitable, but you need to take your own food. The second day will bring you up to the heights of Alto de Mira where, after 8 hours' walking, you will stay the night in a hammock in a typical "bohío", where a group of archaeologists is still working. With their permission, you may be able to stop for a day to visit the excavations. The third day will bring you down to the Buritaca river and then, through impressive scenery, up to the steps which bring you to the archaeological site of Ciudad Perdida. The visit to the town will take you the fourth day; there is nowhere to stay as yet. The return to Santa Marta will take you three days.

Archaeologists and army guards will ask you for your permit. Don't forget that Ciudad Perdida is a National Park: it is strictly forbidden to damage trees and collect flowers or insects.

One week trips organized by the tourist office in Santa Marta cost US$200, but can be bargained much lower: price includes mules, guide and food, 3 days' hike there, 1 day at site, 3 days back. Hotels in Santa Marta or Taganga may charge up to US$400 p.p. Recommended guides: Frankie (ask at the tourist office about him), Joselito (see above under Taganga) and his cousin Pacho. Also Jairo García, who lives at the *Residencia Miramar*, in Santa Marta, rec; cost US$120 for 6 days (1989). *Hotel Miramar* is reported as arranging the 6 day trip for US$100 with Carlos as guide (1990). Care: there are many unscrupulous guides about, checking with the Tourist Office is recommended.

Jim Lindsay of the Australian Embassy in Caracas recommends a circuitous route to the site, which can be arranged through *Hotel La Ballena Azul* (above). It costs about US$250 p.p. for the 6-day round trip, all inclusive. Its advantage is that it avoids all settlements, especially in the drug-growing lower valleys and Kogui villages which may not welcome foreigners. He also recommends Juan Mayr's book, *The Sierra Nevada of Santa Marta*( Mayr y Cabal, Apartado Aéreo 5000, Bogotá) which deals beautifully with the Ciudad Perdida.

The **Tairona** national park, 35 km. E of Santa Marta in the Riohacha direction, wild woodland on the coast, is beautiful and unspoilt. Take a Maicao or Riohacha bus to the park entrance (US$0.70), then walk or hitch 5 km. to beach at Cañaveral (a safe place to visit). Alternatively, there is a tour bus at 1000 from *Park Inn* in Santa Marta, direct to Cañaveral, return at 1500, US$3 (not long enough). Bathing not recommended as there is heavy pounding surf and the tides are treacherous. The place is not without thieves, but a most attractive spot for camping; the beach is less crowded and cleaner than Rodadero. (There are splendid and deserted sandy beaches, to which you have to walk, about 5 km. E of Cañaveral, but take care, the park borders drug growing areas and can be dangerous.) Relics of ancient Tairona culture abound. A taxi to Cañaveral and back from Santa Marta costs US$14. A guided tour round the Pueblito archaeological site is free, every Sat. or as arranged, under escort of a park guard (a full tour from *Hotel Irotama*, including transport and guide, costs US$55). Many camping and hammock places on the path from the Park to Pueblito. Camping in the Park at Cañaveral costs US$3 per site. The camp at Cañaveral has facilities but there is only one restaurant with a tiny store, so take all supplies. There are plenty of mosquitoes, but a very attractive site. Beware of falling coconuts! Two good camping sites at Arrecifes, the first US$2 for tent, US$1.10 for hammock space, US$2 to hire hammock, US$2.85 for hut, fresh water shower and toilets, the second cheaper, but no electricity or showers, one good restaurant (but not cheap), a basic shop and guardroom for gear, soft drinks available (e.g. from Alberto), beautiful beach nearby (sea dangerous). Avoid, if possible, camping at Finca Martínez—dirty, narcotics centre; Finca Bermúdez (on the road to Pueblito) has better camping, for US$1 p.p., though latest reports are that both these fincas are abandoned. Walking in the park, it is 1 hour from the entrance to Cañaveral, then another hour to Arrecifes; follow the beach for ¼ hour to Rancho Viejo from where a clear path leads S to Pueblito (1½ hrs.). On the way to Pueblito, there is a huge mango tree, useful in season since there is little fruit in the park. At the site there are Indians; do not photograph them. From Pueblito you can either return to Cañaveral, or continue for 2 hours to Calabazo on the Santa Marta-Riohacha road. It is advisable to inform park guards when walking in the park; also wear hiking boots and beware of bloodsucking insects. You will see monkeys, iguanas and maybe snakes. In the wet, the paths are very slippery.

You need to obtain permission from Inderena to camp in the park if you are not staying in Cañaveral, but this is normally forthcoming if you specify where you intend to stay. Hotels in Santa Marta will help to arrange your trip to Tairona.

**Riohacha**, capital of Guajira Department, 160 km. E of Santa Marta, is a port of 75,000 people at the mouth of the Río César: low white houses, sandy streets, no trees or hills. It was founded in 1545 by Nicolás Federmann, and in early years its pearling industry was large enough to tempt Drake to sack it (1596). Pearling almost ceased during the 18th century and the town was all but abandoned. (It is best to travel from Riohacha in a luxury bus, early a.m. as these buses are less likely to be stopped and searched for contraband.)

**Hotels** *Gimaura*, (state-owned), on beach, D, including breakfast, they allow camping (free) in their grounds, with outside shower; *Los Delfines*, E, clean, friendly, one block from sea and central plaza, two from Venezuelan consulate. *Hostal Ota*, opposite the bus station, E, fan, clean, friendly, expensive food; *Residencia Yatoonia* (or *Yalcarón*), Carrera 7, No. 11-26, T 73-487, F, private bath, clean, safe, helpful, half way between beach and bus station. *International*, Carrera 7, No. 12A-35, F, friendly, patio, safe, free iced water, rec.

Many small **restaurants** along sea-front. *Tizones*, opp. *Los Delfines*, Carrera 2 y Carrera 10, rec. for food and juices (takes Visa and Diners Club); *Golosinas*, café near the beach, good food, friendly service. All accommodation and food is expensive (no hotel or *pensión* costs less than US$5). You can sling your hammock for free at the police station. There are an airport, a cinema, a tourist office on the beach front and a bank, which changes dollars cash, but not if you're in your beachwear. The best place for buying mantas and other local items is *La Casa de la Manta Guajira*, Carrera 6, No. 9-35, be prepared to bargain. At the weekend, Riohacha fills up, and bars and music spring up all over the place. The sea is clean, despite the red silt stirred up by the waves.

**Venezuelan Consulate** Calle 7, No. 3-75 (hours 0900-1300, and closed from 1500 Fri. to 0900 Mon.). With two passport photographs and an exit ticket most can get a visa on the same day, but be prepared for an interview with the consul himself; visas cost US$10 for all but Danish citizens (free), US, West German and Swiss (US$0.70).

**Tourist Office** Carrera 7, No. 1-38. **DAS Office** (immigration) Calle 1 y Carrera 6, T 72407.

Going south from Riohacha on an alternative road to Maicao and the Venezuelan frontier, you come to Cuestecita (*Hotel Turismo*; *Restaurant La Fogata*), where you can turn southwest to **Barrancas**. Here a large coal mine (one of the largest in the world—El Cerrejón) came into operation in 1986. A good dirt road and an industrial railway (no passengers) have been built between the mine and the new Puerto Bolívar in the Bahía Portete, many millions of tons of coal are being exported annually. Visitors are apparently welcome, but it would probably be best to make arrangements first at the El Cerrejón main office in Barranquilla.

Continuing on this road, which takes you either round the Sierra Nevada to Barranquilla and Santa Marta via Fundación (see above) or south to Bucaramanga, you come to **Valledupar**, capital of César Department, said to be an unfriendly town, population 202,000. Valledupar claims to be the home of the *vallenato* music, in which the accordion features prominently. Each year there is a *vallenato* festival from 29 April to 1 May.

**Hotels** *Vajamar*, C, Carrera 7, Calle 17, pool, expensive food; *Sicarare*, two-star, Carrera 9, No. 16-04, D; cheaper 2-star hotel is *Kurakata*, Calle 19C, No. 7-96; *Residencia El Triunfo*, Carrera 7, No. 19-31, F with bath, fan, clean, good, but slightly dubious part of town; next door is *Hotel/Restaurant Nutibara*, excellent cheap meals and breakfast, excellent fruit juices; several other hotels in this street.

**Transport** Bus from Santa Marta, 8½ hrs., from **Cartagena**, US$8.50 (with Expreso Brasilia); to **Bucaramanga**, 8 hrs US$12. You can fly to **Bogotá**.

**The Sierra Nevada**, covering a triangular area of 16,000 sq. km., rises abruptly from the sea, or from lowlands which nowhere reach over 300 metres above sea-level. "Indeed, the north slope is one of the most striking anywhere, lifting from the Caribbean to 5,800-metre snow peaks in about 45 km., a gradient comparable with the south face of the Himalaya, and unequalled along the world's coasts. The interior is made up of some eight E-W ranges with their intervening valleys. The lower parts of these interior valleys are flanked by forests—the homes of primitive Indians as well as of pumas, jaguars, and a variety of snakes and birds—but for the most part the Sierra is almost lunar in its sterile grandeur, bleak *páramos* leading to naked crag and scree and glacier, where only an occasional questing condor moves. In the rocky heart of the area are a large number of small, beautiful lakes, many in cirques."—Frank F. Cunningham, in an excellent illustrated article on exploring the Sierra in *The Geographical Magazine*. The rainy season in these mountains ends November; January is best month for a visit.

It is necessary to obtain a safe-conduct pass from the Casa Indígena (45 minutes out of town) and the police in Valledupar before visiting the Sierra Nevada, if you are going further than San Sebastián. From Valledupar the best route is along the Guatepurí valley. Jeeps and buses run from Valledupar, Carrera 7A, Calle 18, Nos. 37-55, to Pueblo Bello, 2 hrs. US$1.50. In Pueblo Bello (*Hotel El Encanto*, F, good meals US$1, friendly; *El Hogar de Mamí*, E, very clean; *El Hogar de Mercedes*, F), enquire for jeeps to **San Sebastián de Rábago**, the central village of one of the four tribes of Indians living in the Sierra, the Arhuacos (jeep owners Quico and Gudar Neader are the only ones who go frequently, US$20 per vehicle, or US$3 per seat, 2-2½ hrs.). It is set in beautiful surroundings and is the epitome of an Indian village; the jeep driver may be able to arrange for you to stay on a farm; Doña Inés recommended, F, clean, friendly, good food. Also recommended is Ñoco, a mestizo who has lived in the valley for 30 years; he has floor space and rents mules for trips in the Sierra (US$7 per mule and per guide, per day). Ñoco himself may act as guide if he is free (he runs a grocery store); he is very knowledgeable. Camping is also permitted in the valley.

Before hiking in the Sierra, visitors must pay a "tourist tax" to the Arhuaco chief in San Sebastián (at the police HQ); this ranges from US$7 to US$15, depending on what you want to do. (Do not leave litter or disrespect the Indians' sacred grounds.) **The Indians of the Sierra** distrust strangers (stay on paths; do not stray on to private land) and do not take kindly to being photographed, especially without permission. However they like to be given sea-shells which can be ground into powder and mixed with coca leaves and such a gift may improve their reaction to strangers and cameras. Those interested in the Arhuaco culture should seek out Celso Domingo, a dentist in Pueblo Bello, himself an Arhuaco. **N.B.** The Sierra Nevada is a marijuana-growing area—take care.

A recommended guide to the Sierra Nevada is Mauricio Guevera (T Bogotá 213-7002), who organizes treks (but not all year). You need to be fit for his 12-day hikes through the villages, valleys alive with butterflies, flowers and waterfalls, and to the lakes and the snowfields and summit of Pico Colón at 5,750 metres (Jim Lindsay, Australian Embassy, Caracas). It is also possible to hike on the coastal side of the Sierra, but it is absolutely essential to take a guide through the marijuana districts. Recommended is Juancho, at *Restaurant Pilón de Gaira*, at Rodadero, Santa Marta, or at the village of Bonda, half an hour from Santa Marta by taxi. Juancho is an ethnologist (formerly of Medellín) who has lived with Kogui Indians for 13 years, owns a farm and speaks the different dialects. You need to be fit for his treks too. US$130 p.p. for a week, maximum 6 people, minimum 4. Trekking tours to the Nevada de Santa Marta can also be arranged in Santa Marta, check with the Tourist Office.

From Valledupar on to Codazzi is asphalted, but not beyond until the road joins the paved Bucaramanga-Santa Marta highway. There is a possible overnight stay at Curumaní (*Hotel Himalaya*), or at Aguachica, just off the road.

Beyond Riohacha to the E is the arid and sparsely inhabited **Guajira Peninsula**. The Indians here live primitively, collecting dividivi, tending goats, and fishing. They are Guajiros, and of special interest are the coloured robes worn by the women. To visit a small part of the Peninsula you can take a bus from Riohacha (they leave twice a day from the Indian market) to Manaure for US$1.50. It is an uncomfortable 3-hr. drive through fields of cactus but offers fine views of flamingoes and other brightly coloured birds. **Manaure**, which is known for its salt flats, has a *residencia* (*Hotel Flamingo*, G). From Manaure there are *busetas* to **Uribia** (one basic *residencia*, no running water, but fresh water is a problem throughout the Guajira) and thence to Maicao. In Uribia you can buy handicrafts intended for local, not tourist, use by asking around. You can get *busetas* from Uribia to Puerto Bolívar (from where the coal is exported) and from there transport to Cabo de Vela, near the northern tip of Colombia, where the lagoons shelter vast flocks of flamingoes, herons and sandpipers. There are fine beaches and, in Cabo de Vela, a basic but friendly, Indian-run hotel, *El Mesón* (rooms, hammock veranda, showers, good meals—excellent fried fish), or sling a hammock at *El Caracol* (US$1.50 p.p.) where there is an expensive restaurant (better value next door at *La Tropicana* if you order food in advance). Sunsets in the Guajira are magnificent. There is a paved road from Riohacha to Maicao near the frontier. The Caribbean coastal highway, now paved, runs direct from Santa Marta along the coast to Riohacha, and the Riohacha-Maicao road (also paved) has been greatly improved. Now that there are no flights from Barranquilla to Maracaibo, taxi or bus to Maicao, and colectivo to Maracaibo is the most practical route.

**N.B.** The Guajira peninsular is not a place to travel alone, parties of 3 or more are recommended. Also remember it is hot, with little cover and very little water.

*Maicao* is full of Venezuelan contraband, and is still at the centre of the narcotics trade. Its streets are unmade and it has a considerable reputation for lawlessness; most commercial premises close before 1600 and after 1700 the streets are highly unsafe. If at all possible travellers should avoid Maicao and the road services that go there, which are liable to ambush.

Entering Venezuela, everyone needs a visa; a transit visa will only suffice if you have a confirmed ticket to a third country within 3 days. The Venezuelan Consul in Maicao is reluctant to grant visas, given the area's reputation: much better to get a visa in Barranquilla or Riohacha; with all the right papers, border crossing is easy. Entering Colombia, immigration is at the border. If you enter by *por puesto*, make sure the driver stops at the Colombian entry post. If not you will have to return later to complete formalities.

**Hotels in Maicao** *Maicao Juan Hotel*, C, the only safe one; *Residencia Gallo*, E, private bath and pool; *Hotel Hilda*, C, reasonable; *El Parador*.
    If stuck in Maicao, seek out Francisco Agudelo at ARA, Carrera 9, No. 13-16, T 8133, who can make arrangements with Guajira Tours, Riohacha, and help with transport, money changing, etc.

**Buses** (basic): to Riohacha, US$1.10; **Santa Marta**, US$4.50; **Maracaibo**, US$3.25 (Expreso Maicao, 0400-1800); **Barranquilla**, US$6.50. **Cartagena**, US$4.75-7.50. There are bus services along the Caribbean coastal highway, and also **flights** Barranquilla-Maicao (Aces). Colectivo, Maicao-Maracaibo, US$4.50 p.p., or infrequent microbus, US$2.75.

## UP THE MAGDALENA RIVER (5)

The old waterway from the Caribbean, now superseded by road and air, leads from Barranquilla to the limit of navigation at Girardot. The route passes snow-capped volcanoes and *tierra caliente* weekend resorts before climbing to the river's upper reaches near the remarkable archaeological site of San Agustín.

Passenger travel by the lofty paddle boats on the river has now come to an end, though the adventurous traveller may still find an occasional passage by cargo paddle boat. But in general the only way of getting from one place to the other along the river is by motor launch (*chalupa*), and this is more expensive. Insect repellants should be taken, for mosquitoes are a nuisance. Guerilla activity has been reported in the Magdalena valley away from the river and the main roads.

The Magdalena is wide but shallow and difficult to navigate because of surface eddies, and there are little whirlpools over submerged rocks. Away to the NE, in the morning, one can see the high snow-capped peaks of the Sierra Nevada de Santa Marta.
    At Tenerife Bolívar had his first victory in the Magdalena campaign. At Zambrano (pop. 4,000), a cattle centre 96 km. beyond Calamar, there are tobacco plantations. There is a road W to the N-S Cartagena-Medellín road, and a trail E to the oil fields at El Difícil. Near Pinto the river divides: the eastern branch, silted and difficult, leads to **Mompós**, an old town of 20,000 people: cattle farming and tobacco, and the scene of another victory for Bolívar: "At Mompós", he said, "my glory was born." Mompós was founded in 1537 and, thanks to its comparative isolation, preserves its colonial character more completely than any other town in Colombia. Old buildings are the Casa de Gobierno, once a home of the Jesuits, and the Colegio de Pinillos. There are 7 churches and the Easter celebrations are said to be among the best in Colombia. The town is well known in Colombia for handworked gold jewellery. Airport. Malaria is endemic in the surrounding countryside.

**Mompós Hotels** *Residencias Unión*, Calle 18, No. 3-43, F, with bath and fan; *Hostal Doña Manuela*, Calle Real del Medío, 17-41, D, a converted colonial house, quiet and peaceful but run down; with cockroaches, nearby *Residencias Aurora*, F, shower, fan, nice and friendly; also *Residencias Solmar*, Calle Carrera 18-22, near main square, F, clean, friendly, basic; *Residencia Leyla*, overlooking main sqaure and the river, G, basic but acceptable.

**Restaurant** *La Brasa*, facing river.

**Transport** Bus from **Cartagena** with Unitransco and Brasilia daily, 4 hrs., US$4, but you can only book as far as **Magangué**. From Magangué you have to take a launch either direct to Mompós, 2 hrs., US$12.60, or to **Bodega** and thence by jeep or taxi, 1½ hrs, US$2. You can also reach Mompós in 2 hrs. by *chalupa* from **El Banco** to the SE (buses to Santa Marta, Barranquilla etc.). Plenty of willing hands to carry your luggage to and from the launch, jeep and bus—for an outrageous fee! From Magangué, buses also go to **Barranquilla** and **Sincelejo**. There is a Mon. to Fri. air service (Aces) from Barranquilla to Mompós. It is also possible to reach Mompós from Barranquilla by *chalupa* changing at Plato, but we do not have good information on the time needed or the price.

Most vessels go by the western arm of the loop to **Magangué** (pop. 40,800), the port for the savannas of Bolívar. To El Banco the charge is US$3, by *chalupa* 2¼ hrs. A road runs W to join the N-S Cartagena-Medellín highway. 5 hotels inc. *Mardena*; 10 *residenciales*, cheapest *Londres*, *Brasil* or *Hotel Medellín*, all G p.p.

Beyond Magangué, the Río San Jorge, 379 km. long, 240 km. of it navigable, comes in from the Western Cordillera. Later the Río Cauca, 1,020 km. long, comes in from the far S. Its Caribbean end is navigable for 370 km., and it is navigable again for a distance of 245 km. in the Cauca Valley above the gorge.

At **El Banco** (*Residencias Las Delicias*, Calle 9 near jeep terminal, F, basic; *Residencia Ocaña*, cheaper, G p.p., basic, clean, noisy; about a dozen others), 420 km. from Barranquilla (airport, one flight each weekday US$27), the river loops join. This is an old, dirty and beautiful town of 10,250 people. Along the river front are massive stone stairways. The Cordilleras are in the distance, a blue range on either side of the valley. Pink herons and blue macaws much in evidence. There are many sandy islands in the river to complicate navigation. A difficult trail leads N of El Banco to the small town of Chimichagua (pop. 5,000), on the shores of the large lake of Zapatosa. Continuing upriver are the small towns of Gamarra (pop. 3,700) and Puerto Wilches (5,600). Daily buses from El Banco to Bucaramanga, US$7, Cúcuta and Valledupar. *Chalupa* service El Banco-Barrancabermeja with Cootransfluviales, 0800, 7 hrs., US$10.

Some 30 km. above Puerto Wilches is **Barrancabermeja** (usually referred to as Barranca), so called because of the reddish-brown oil-stained cliffs on which it stands. With a population of 66,400, the town is an important oil centre; it is a warm, humid place with an interesting indoor market, but the oil refinery is prominent. *Chalupa* to Puerto Boyacá, 0845, 6 hrs., US$10. In 1989, this city was reported to be "incredibly violent"; we have had no reports of appreciable improvement.

**Hotels** *Residencias Ferroviario*, G with bath, opp. railway station, friendly. *Santa Fe*, in town, G, clean and friendly; many more around the train station and in town. A shop at Calle 19, Avs. 18 y 19 sells good bread and muesli. *Iris*, just up road from port, F, clean, friendly.

**Rail** 4 to 6 trains a week to **Santa Marta**, 2 to **Bogotá**, daily to **Medellín**, according to the timetable in 1991, but check carefully. Time to Medellín, 12 hours but "not too exhausting".

**Puerto Berrío** (airport; 12,750 inhabitants) is on the W bank 100 km. above Barrancabermeja and 756 km. from Barranquilla. It is the river port for Medellín and the rich Antioquia Department. A railway from Medellín runs down the slopes of the Cordillera Central and over a low pass to Puerto Berrío, where it connects with the Bogotá-Santa Marta line. Bus to Barbosa, 10 hrs., US$4.50.

**Hotels at Puerto Berrío** *Hotel Magdalena*, pleasant, on a hilltop near river, E; *Residencias El Ganadero*, F, with bath, clean, modern, with ceiling fans. Many other hotels, *residencias* and *apartamentos*. **Restaurants**: *Tabrona*; *La Buena Mesa*, good big meals; *Heladeria Joi*, good ice cream and sundaes.

**Rail** To Santa Marta, Bogotá and Medellín, check days and times at *Grecia* station, 4 km.

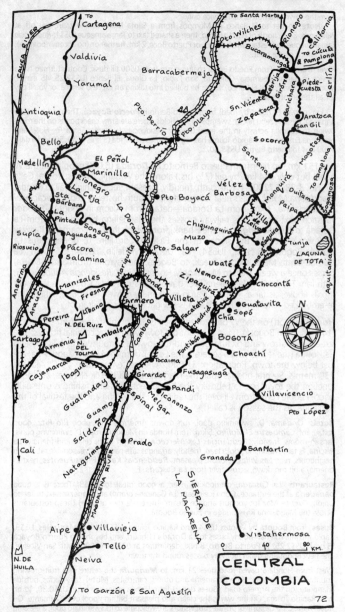

CENTRAL
COLOMBIA

72

from the town and hotels, taxi service only.

**Note**: to get to El Banco or Mompós from a Santa Marta-bound train, get off at Palestnios, 8 hrs. north of Puerto Berrío, then a shared taxi to Tamalameque (US$1; *Residencia Tamalameque* and restaurant, F, basic), or Puerto Boca, 2 km. further on (no accommodation), then take a motor boat.

**River Transport** From Puerto Boca, *chalupas* run from 0500 till dusk; Cootrafturmag has a service to Barrancabermeja, Gamarra, San Pablo, La Gloria, El Banco (US$2.25, 45 mins.), Mompós (changing at El Banco). Don't be bullied into taking an *expreso* service, or you'll pay for all the empty seats.

75 km. upriver (5 hours by road) from Puerto Berrío is **Puerto Boyacá**. The road is mostly unpaved, passing zebu *fincas*, swamps and oil fields. There are army checkpoints on the road, owing to guerrilla activity in the area. (Hotels: *Residencias Lusitania*; *Santa Fe*; *Hotel* and *Heladería Embajador*.) Rápido Tolima has regular buses to Honda (3 hrs., US$1.50) and a daily 1100 bus to Puerto Berrío, US$3.50.

It is 151 km. up river from Puerto Berrío to **La Dorada** (6,000 people) on the W bank, but only 134 km. by rail (7½ hrs.) along the W bank. (Hotels: *Rosita*, Calle 17, No. 3-28, T 72301, F, with bath, friendly, pleasant, rec.; on highway to Honda, *Magdalena Motel*; others near railway station; youth hostel at *Centro Vacacional La Magdalena*, 3 km. from La Dorada—details from Alcom in Bogotá—*Parador Turistico* next door). This railway crosses the Magdalena by a bridge from La Dorada to **Puerto Salgar**, on the E bank, from which the Cundinamarca Railway (198 km.) goes up the slopes of the Eastern Cordillera to Bogotá. Bus La Dorada-Bogotá, 5 hrs., US$4, La Dorada-Medellín, US$4.25. Train La Dorada-Santa Marta twice a week; to Bogotá, the Tayrona (from Santa Marta) passes once a week, Dec. to March only. Hotels: *Salgar*; *Residencia Antioquia*, G, with fan. The Lower Magdalena river navigation stops at La Dorada as there are rapids above, as far as Honda. Cargo is taken by railway to Honda, where it is re-embarked. The Upper Magdalena is navigable as far as Girardot.

*Honda* (airport) on the W bank of the river, is 32 km. upstream from La Dorada (149 km. from Bogotá). It is a pleasant old town with many colonial houses. The streets are narrow and picturesque, and the town is surrounded by hills. El Salto de Honda (the rapids which separate the Lower from the Upper Magdalena) are just below the town. Population: 31,600. Average temperature: 29°C. Altitude 230 metres. Several bridges span the Magdalena and the Guali rivers, at whose junction the town lies. In February the Magdalena rises and fishing is unusually good. People come from all over the region for the fishing and the festival of the Subienda, as the season is called.

**Hotels** *Ondama*, D, swimming pool, run down; *América*, with pool; *Río Ritz*, good restaurant; *Campestre El Molino*, 5 km. from Honda on Mariquita road, D, swimming pools, fans in rooms, friendly; *Residencias Las Mercedes*, E, with bath, clean and friendly; *La Piscina*, E, fan, swimming pool, clean, friendly, arranges safe parking at reasonable rates with neighbours, rec.; *Las Villas*, F, clean, pleasant; *Residencias Katty*, F; *Los Puentes*, next to cinema, a bit run down, across river from *La Cascada*, F.

**Restaurants** *La Cascada*, overlooking river, a good meal for US$3. There is a good *panadería* at the entrance. Good ice cream (La Campiña brand) at *heladería* next to Teatro Unión; *Fuente Mar* for yoghurt and ice cream. There is a row of good cheap restaurants across the Magdalena River bridge in Puerto Bogotá.

**Buses** from Bogotá by Velotax US$4, and Rápido Tolima, US$3, 4 hrs. **Manizales**, US$3. Rápido Tolima run half-hourly buses to **La Dorada** (1 hour), and beyond, to **Puerto Boyacá** (3 hrs.), US$2.25. To **Puerto Berrío**, 8 hrs., departures at 0300 and 0800 with San Vicente. The new Bogotá-Medellín highway passes round the town.

West from Honda a paved road goes 21 km. to **Mariquita** the centre of a fruit-growing country (13,000 people; *Hotel Bocaneme* and others; campsites; **Motel** *Las Acacias*, outside Mariquita, on the Armero road.) Buses depart from Honda every half hour, US$0.30, ½ hr. with Rápido Tolima. On the way is the clean and pleasant bathing pool of El Diamante. On again is the Club Deportivo: private, but visitors are welcome to its swimming pool, a blessing in this climate. There is another, El Virrey, in Mariquita. The town has several old houses and buildings: a mint, the viceroy's house, the parish church. Here José Celestino Mutis lived for 8 years during his famous Botanic Expedition towards the end of the 18th century (when he and his helpers accumulated a herbarium of 20,000 plants, a vast library, and a rich collection of botanical plates and paintings of native fauna). The collection was sent to Madrid, where it remains. Mariquita was founded in 1551, and it was here that the founder of Bogotá, Jiménez de Quesada, died in 1579. From Mariquita a road runs W up the slopes of the Central Cordillera to Manizales.

**Fresno**, in the heart of a big coffee growing area, is 30 km. from Mariquita. The road to Honda is appalling. Bus to Manizales (83 km.) US$2.80 (Rápido Tolima).

From Mariquita the road turns S to (32 km.) Armero, which used to be a cotton growing centre. This town and surrounding villages were devastated by the eruption of the Nevado del Ruiz volcano (**see page 731**) in November 1985. (Armero can be reached by colectivo from Honda; no lodging in Armero, nearest at Lérida, 12 km. S, a "really nasty village"—Hotels *Central*, F, cheapest, not too clean, unfriendly, *Colonial*, *Tundama*, F p.p.—,Mariquita or possibly Guayabal; no drinks available in Armero, either, only icecream and flowers; there are lots of mosquitoes, though). A branch road runs 35 km. W to **Líbano**, 29,700 inhabitants. (Hotels: *Cumanday*; *Rex*.) Coffee is the great crop here, with potatoes in the uplands. Away to the W looms the peak of Nevado del Ruiz, which before its eruption was the second highest in the Cordillera Central. Bus from Líbano to Ibagué, US$2.25, 4 hrs.

From Armero a branch road runs down to the Magdalena past Gambao to **Ambalema** (Hotels: *Barcelona*; *Nariño*). At Gambao the river is crossed for the road to Bogotá. The main road from Armero goes direct for 88 km. to Ibagué.

**Ibagué**, capital of Tolima Department, is a large city (350,000 inhabitants), lying at the foot of the Quindío mountains at 1,250 metres. It is cooler here (22°C) than in the valley. Parts of the town are old: the Colegio de San Simón is worth seeing, and so is the market. The Parque Centenario is very pleasant. The city specializes in two things; hand-made leather goods (there are many good, cheap shoe shops) and a local drink called *mistela*. There is an excellent Conservatory of Music.

The National Folklore Festival is held during the third week of June. The Departments of Tolima and Huila commemorate St. John (24 June) and Sts. Peter and Paul (29 June) with bullfights, fireworks, and music.

**Hotels** There are many hotels of reasonable quality which are quite comfortable. *Ambala*, Calle 11, No. 2-60, C, not good value, slow service, no hot water; *Bram*, E, Calle 17 and Carrera 4, convenient, clean, secure, and insect-free; *Acapulco*, near bus station, E, hot water, shower, clean and pleasant, but noisy; *Ambeima*, Carrera 3 No. 13-32, E; *Raad*, E, next door; both good. *Residencia Puracé*, opposite Tolima bus station, E; *Montserrat*, Calle 18, Carrera 1 y 2, G p.p., clean, quiet.

**Restaurants** *Toy Wan*, Carrera 4, Chinese. 24 hr. restaurants include *Punto Rojo*, in the shopping precinct on Carrera 3, and *Punto Fácil*, Calle 15 y Carrera 3. Vegetarian, *Govinda*, Carrera 2 y Calle 13.

**Tourist Office** Carrera 3, between Calles 10 and 11; helpful; closed Sat. and Sun. The Instituto Giográfico Agustin Codazzi has an office at Calle 14A, No 3-14, 3rd Floor, for maps.

Just outside, on the Armenia road, a dirt road leads to the slopes of the **Nevado del Tolima**. Gerhard Drekonja of Vienna writes: For climbing the Nevado del Tolima (5,215 metres) take in Ibagué at 0600 the *mixto* train to Juntas and El Silencio (2 hrs.). From there half-an-hour walk to the primitive but fabulous thermal waters (90°C) of El Rancho (simple sleeping accommodation and food available). The climb starts from El Rancho. It takes 8 to 10 hours to the top; equipment (crampons and pica) indispensable. The final climb has to be done at sunrise because clouds and mist invariably rise around 0800. From the top a breathtaking view across the other snowcapped mountains of the Cordillera Central. For information contact Cruz Roja Colombiana in Ibagué, Zona Industrial

El Papayo, near the east entrance to the city, T 646014, who can put you in touch with a climbing group, Asociación Tolimense de Montañistas y Escaladores. Nevado del Tolima is the southernmost "nevado" in the **Parque Nacional Natural Los Nevados** which extends up to Nevado del Ruiz overlooking Manizales (see under Manizales and Pereira). A local mountain guide with some Himalayan experience and well rec. is Manolo Barrios, Barrio La Francia, Casa 23, Ibagué, T 646726.

There is a road to Girardot, 79 km. E on the Magdalena, going on to Bogotá which is 224 km. by road from Ibagué. On this road is the village of **Gualanday**, with **Hotel Rozal**, F, clean, friendly, safe for motorcyclists and 4 good roadside restaurants (*Dona Eva's* also has accommodation). **Espinal**, pop.: 80,000, is an important agro-industrial town, but of little interest to the tourist. *Bucaros*, in centre of town, F, private bath, clean, with restaurant. Also a 2-star hotel is being built outside the town. Restaurant *Parador Rokoko*, on the main street is costly but has decent meals; *El Maestro*, behind Mobil station on W side of main street, cheap and good. Bus to Ibagué, 1 hr., US$0.75, just flag one down; bus to Neiva, US$2. Toll between Ibagué and Espinal, US$0.50; between Espinal and Girardot, US$0.40. W of Ibagué the road runs over the 3,350-metre high Quindío Pass to Armenia, 105 km. from Ibagué across the Cordillera Central. The bus trip to Pereira takes 4 hrs. and costs US$2.55. To Cali, on Flota Magdalena pullman, 7 hrs., US$5.75; ordinary buses US$4; Velotax US$5. To Bogotá, 4½ hrs., US$3.75 with Velotax, US$3.50 by bus. Bus to Popayán, US$6.75.

Between Ibagué and Armenia, on the E side of the Quindío Pass, is **Cajamarca**, a friendly town in a beautiful setting; *Residencia Central*, G; *Nevado*, expensive, somewhat noisy; both on same street, friendly and clean. Interesting market on Sunday.

**Girardot** (airport) is on the Upper Magdalena. Altitude, 326 metres; population, 70,000. The climate is hot and there are heavy rains. Here the navigation of the Upper Magdalena ends, although in dry weather boats cannot get this far; walk across the fine steel bridge to see merchandise being loaded and unloaded—coffee and hides are the main items, although shipments of the former have declined considerably. Launch rides on the river can be taken, starting from underneath the bridge. A 1-hour trip to Isla del Sol is rec. (US$4). Large cattle fairs are held on 5-10 June and 5-10 December. There is a two-storey market, at its best in early morning but nevertheless good all day, and another good market on Sun. mornings. Bogotanos come down here at weekends to warm up.

**Hotels** *El Peñón*, on site of former *hacienda* just outside town, fashionable bungalow complex, casino, huge pool, lake, B per bungalow. *Bachué*, Carrera 8, No. 18-04, C, modern large cooled pool, excellent, rooms a/c with bath and TV, restaurant; *Rincón*, on main street, Calle 19, No. 10-68, F, balcony, fan; *Los Angeles*, on main plaza, D, clean, friendly, rec.: *Waldorf*, on market square, F, clean, showers; *Residencias La Paz*, Carrera 1 E, No. 11-3. Opp. new bus terminal, *Maroti*, F, and *El Cid*, F with fan; *El Dorado*, G, shared bath, basic.

**Restaurants** *Laresa*, Carrera 8a, US$2-3 for a meal; *Club 60*, across the bridge, US$3-8. There is a good food market.

**Banks** Only the **Banco de la República** will change travellers' cheques in Girardot.

**Roads** To Bogotá, 132 km., bus costs US$3, about 3½ hrs.; bus to **Neiva**, US$2.55, 3½ hrs.; to **Ibagué**, 78 km. To Fusagasugá, US$1.65.

Another centre of population in the Magdalena Valley lies upstream from Girardot, with Neiva as its capital. Coffee and tobacco are grown on the slopes here, and cattle are raised in the valley.

The road, and its short branches E and W, runs through a number of small towns of under 25,000 people. One of these, 35 km. from Girardot, is **Guamo**, with 21,000 inhabitants. Just before Guamo is a marked turn off to La Chamba, where internationally famous pottery is made and sold. The pottery is fired in the afternoon; lots of mosquitoes here. Eight km. beyond Guamo is **Saldaña**, where there are irrigation works that have made 15,000 hectares available for rice, sesame and cotton.

**Hotel at Guamo** *Lemayá*, modern, swimming pool, best in region. At El Espinal, before the road to La Chamba is *Hotel Yuma*, new. At **Saldaña**, *Hotel Saldaña*, not too good.

A pretty spot is the reservoir located near **Prado**, Tolima. Turn off the Ibagué-Neiva road at Saldaña for 25 km.; it is well signposted. There is a dirt road for the last 12 km. past

Purificación, where you cross the Magdalena. Buses can be caught in Bogotá, Ibagué and all intermediate towns. A pleasant government hotel is at the lake (D, B for cabin for 6-10, free camping on the shoreline, water-skiing US$2.50, short trip with a boat). The pretty part of the lake is hidden from the end of the road and must be seen from a boat. Official boat trips to the islands are about 3 times cheaper than those of "sharks" operating here; the official mooring-point is down the slope at the end of the road. Swimming is good and the water is warm, but wading is not advisable because of the presence of the fresh-water stingray. Cheap hotels are available in Prado, 4 km. from the lake. There are restaurants of questionable quality in town. Excellent food can be obtained at the end of the road in the boat-dock area, but sanitation leaves something to be desired.

A little beyond the 50 kilometre stone from Neiva you can turn to the left, cross a fence, and see the Piedra Pintada de Aipe, a stone not in fact painted but carved by precolumbian Indians with designs akin to the shapes of some of the gold pieces in the Museo del Oro at Bogotá.

**Neiva**, capital of Huila Department, has a population of 150,000. It was first founded in 1539, when Benalcázar came across the Cordillera Central from Popayán in quest of El Dorado. It was soon after destroyed by the Indians and re-founded in 1612. It is now a pleasant, modern city. There are rich coffee plantations around Neiva, for here the valley bottom is high enough to be in the coffee zone. The cathedral was destroyed by earthquake in 1967. There is a large and colourful market every day. Tourist information is given at the cultural centre with museum and gallery on the main square. Altitude: 470 metres; very hot.

**Fiesta** from 18 to 28 June, when the Bambuco Queen is elected, with folklore, dances and feasting.

**Hotels** *Hostería Matamundo*, in old *hacienda* 3 km. from centre, on road to Garzón and San Agustín, C, a/c, swimming pool, good meals, US$2.50-7, but slow and poor service, disco (does not accept Visa card; will not put extra beds in room for children); *Tumbaragua*, Calle 5A, No. 5-40, C, no swimming pool or hot water but nevertheless rec.; *Americano*, Carrera 5, No. 8-65, D, clean, swimming pool; *Plaza*, Calle 7, No. 4-62, D, swimming pool, fan, pleasant but food expensive and not reliable; *Central*, Cra. 3, No. 7-82, E, meals US$1 each, near market, good value. *Res. San Agustín*, near bus station, F, basic, clean; nearby, *Gloria*, G, adequate; *Res. Nena*, across from back of Coomotor terminal, F, clean, quiet, friendly. Several cheap hotels are to be found off the square where the bus companies are centred. Many small boys meet the buses and suggest accommodation.

**Restaurants** *Hostería Los Cerros*, Calle 11, No. 32-39; *El Caimo*, Calle 8, No. 7A-22; *Los Gauchos*, Carrera 15, No. 5-12; *Neiva Viejo*, Calle 9, No. 6-49.

**Exchange** Banco de la República, Carrera 5, No. 5-73, including AmEx cheques.

**Airport** La Marguita, 1½ km. from city. Aires and Satena fly from **Bogotá** (Aires to Bogotá daily; to **Cali**; to **Medellín**, either direct or via **Ibagué**. Satena flies to **Leguizamo**, via Florencia daily. Taxi to bus terminal about US$0.85 (overcharging probable).

**Bus** No central bus station. To **Bogotá** (331 km., paved road), 5½ hrs., US$5. Regular bus service with Autobuses Unidos del Sur (Carrera 2, No. 5-32), Cootranshuila (0600) and Coomotor to **San Agustín**, US$5, 5½ hrs. (US$4.50 by colectivo). To **Garzón**, US$3; to **Pitalito**, US$4.35. To **La Plata**, for Tierradentro. To **Espinal**, 3 hrs., US$2, good road except for stretch between Nataguima and Aipe. To **Pasto**, US$9; to **Popayán**, US$7.75, ordinary bus at 0330, 1000, 1930, to **Florencia**, US$6.50. Long-distance buses leave from Carrera 2, Calles 5 and 6.

**Warning** At the bus stations, both off and on buses, in Neiva, Garzón and especially Pitalito, theft is rife.

**Excursions** To Rivera, a ½ hr. drive S, with thermal springs and swimming pools to cool off; to the Tacacoa desert to the N, past Tello and Villavieja, where there is a museum showing prehistoric finds in the area; to the Betania dam project with boat trips on the lake formed by the dam, from the village of Yaguará.

Beyond Neiva lie the plains of Huila Department, arid, but still capable of supporting cattle, and dominated by the snow-capped Nevado del Huila to the NW. The road runs S from Neiva, past (92 km.) **Garzón**, a pleasant cathedral town set in mountains with roads W across the Cordillera to Popayán and SE to

Florencia, capital of the Intendencia of Caquetá (**see page 722**), and is paved past Pitalito to San Agustín. *Pitalito* (72,000 people), has little to offer the tourist. See map of area, **page 745**.

**Hotels at Garzón**: *Damasco*, D, colonial building, rec., good meals for US$3; *Cecil*, near bus station, E, with private bath. The *Abeyma*, a state hotel, is rec., D; it is possible to camp in the grounds, US$1. *Residencias Pigoanza*, on main square, E, rec. 32 km. before Garzón, at El Gigante, is *Posada*, E, swimming pool, hot shower, restaurant (breakfast overpriced); good views between El Gigante and Garzón. At **Pitalito** there is a *Hotel de Turismo*. There are 2 hotels with swimming pools: the *Calamó*, C, hot water, and the *Timanco*, a 3-star hotel; *Residencia Pitalito*, F, without shower, reasonable, Calle 5 round corner from police station; *La Laroyano*, on main street, cheap, adequate; *Residencial El Globo*, main street, F, clean, basic. *Grand Hotel*, F, bath, good food. *Restaurant Cando* rec.; also *Napolitano*, good, cheap.

**Transport** If you hitch you'll find it fairly easy to Garzón; slower on to San Agustín, but plenty of buses and colectivos (US$1). Buses in Pitalito go from Calle 3a; Taxis Verdes from the main square (US$9 to Bogotá). Bus to Mocoa (in the Putumayo), US$7, 7 hrs., also jeeps from market square, 2 in a.m. Aires fly from Bogotá to Pitalito, via Neiva, on Thur. and Sun. at 1600, 1¾ hrs, US$35, returning to Bogotá Thur. 1650, Sun. 1430, but the plane only goes if there are enough passengers (confirm tickets 24 hrs. in advance).

South of Pitalito is the **Cueva de los Guácharos** National Park; take a bus to Palestrina, US$1, 1 hour, and then walk for 6 hours along an eroded, muddy path. Between December and June swarms of oilbirds (*guácharos*) may be seen; they are nocturnal, with a unique radar-location system. The reserve also contains many of the unusual and spectacular cocks-of-the-rock. The rangers are particularly friendly, providing tours and basic accommodation; permission to visit the park must be obtained from the Inderena offices in Pitalito, Neiva or Bogotá.

The way to the remarkable Tierradentro underground burials in man-made caves painted with geometrical patterns is given on **page 742**; they can be reached by Popayán bus from San Agustín, Pitalito or Garzón, with a change at La Plata, or at the Cruce San Andrés de Pisimbalá.

*San Agustín* (altitude 1,700 m.) is 27 km. from Pitalito (all paved). Here, in the Valley of the Statues, are some hundreds of large rough-hewn stone figures of men, animals and gods, dating from roughly 3300 B.C. to just before the Spanish conquest. Nothing is known of the culture which produced them, though traces of small circular bamboo straw-thatched houses have been found. Various sculptures found here are exhibited in the National Museum at Bogotá, and there are some life-sized copies of San Agustín originals along the highway from Bogotá to the superseded Techo airport, near Fontibón. There are about 20 sites; information can be obtained from the tourist office, Calle 5, No. 15-47, T 73019, open 0830-1230, 1330-1730, Mon.-Fri., 0900-1200, 1300-1700, Sat. and Sun., Sr Joaquín Emilio García is most helpful in all matters, he speaks English, French, Italian and a little German. Free maps to the area can only be obtained here or in Bogotá. It is recommended that visitors arriving in San Agustín should go initially to the tourist office which has a list of all hotels, their prices and quality, and a price list for guides, taxi rides and horse hire.

The nearest sites are the Parque Arqueológico and the Bosque de las Estatuas (open 0800-1600 daily, entrance to both costs US$1, half price for students, tickets valid for 2 days), both about 2½ km. from San Agustín town, 1½ km. from the *Hotel Yalconia*, and less than 1 km. from the *Hotel Osoguaico*. The statues in the Parque are *in situ*, though some have been set up on end and fenced in with wire; those in the Bosque (a little wood) have been moved and rearranged, and linked by gravel footpaths. Of particular interest are the carved rocks in and around the stream at the Fuente de Lavapatas in the Parque, where the water runs through the carved channels (visitors should not miss the Cerro de Lavapatas, above the Fuente, which has an extensive view, closes at 1600); refreshment stands at "Fuente" and on the way up to Lavapatas. There is a museum in the Parque which contains pottery and Indian artefacts (entry included on Parque ticket, closes at 1700). You can get a very good idea of the Parque, the Bosque and the museum in the course of three hours walking. The whole site leaves an unforgettable impression, from the strength and strangeness of the statues, and the great beauty of the rolling green landscape. The further sites are a very long walk away: use of a jeep or a horse appears advisable.

Rainy season April-June/July, but it rains somewhat during most of the year, hence the beautiful green landscape; the driest months are Nov.-March. The days are warm but sweaters are needed in the evenings; average temperature 18°C.

The *fiesta* of Santa María del Carmen is held in mid-July (not on a fixed date) in San Agustín. Two festivals in June are San Juan (24th) with horse races and dances, and San Pedro (29th) with horse races, dances, fancy dress, competitions and other events. In the last week of October, the Casa de Cultura celebrates La Semana Cultural Integrada, with many folklore events from all parts of the country. There are cockfights in San Agustín on Sundays at 2030.

**Warning** Beware of "guides" and touts who approach you in the street. Have nothing to do with anyone offering drugs, precolumbian objects, gold, emeralds or other precious minerals for sale; drugs will lead to problems with the authorities, other items will be fakes.

**Hotels** *Yalconia*, outside town, B full board, some rooms with hot water, very pleasant, swimming pool, T (980) 373001/3730013 (camping allowed next door, sheltered tents available). Between San Agustín and the Parque Arqueológico is the *Osoguaico*, friendly, warm water, very clean, restaurant, E, laundry, swimming pool, camping site, US$1 p.p. *Central*, Calle 3, No. 10-32, near bus offices, E, with bath (F, in the 3 rooms without bath, or G if you want a room just to dump your luggage in during day's visit), good meals at US$1.50, it is possible to do laundry here (but keep an eye on your clothes), clean and friendly, secure motorcycle parking, will hire horses, English and French spoken. *Colonial*, Calle 3, No. 10-54, F, shower, clean, pleasant, good restaurant, monkeys and parrots in the garden, rec.; *Residencias Náñez*, Calle 5a with Carrera 16, F, singles may have to share room, hot water (usually), friendly and clean; guests may use the kitchen; also the owners have horses for rent (US$5 for 5 hrs., check them first) and will act as guides to the archaeological sites. *Mi Terruño*, Calle 4, No. 15-85, 5 rooms, F, colonial house, some rooms with bath, hot water, friendly, morning coffee, rec., owner Carlos Arturo Muñoz also has 3 cabins, *Los Andaqui*, for rent. *Residencias Luis Tello*, Calle 4a, No. 15-33, run by a teacher, hot water, pleasant and friendly, good value, G; also *Residencias Cosmopólita*, Cra. 16, No. 4-91, clean, safe, friendly, E, rec. *Residencias Eduardo Motta*, Calle 4, No. 15-71, has five rooms, friendly, clean, hot water, F, hard beds, but with morning coffee, quiet, rec; similar establishment run by Luis who runs the post office, F; *Residencia Familiar*, Calle 3, No. 11-14, one block down from Coomotor-Autobuses Unidos del Sur office, 7 rooms, hot water extra, laundry, friendly, G p.p., book meals in advance or eat next door at the *Colonial*, horses for hire; *Residencias La Gaitana*, Calle 6A, No. 14-47, F with bath, warm water, clean, nice terrace. Small boys (and thieves **beware**) will meet you off the bus with offers of such accommodation; they are also remarkably competent guides in many languages. There is accommodation in private houses for about US$2 p.p., which is often preferable (ask, for example, for Sra. Elena Rojas de Llanos, "La Gorda", near the church, whose house is clean, safe, but no hot water). Ask at Tourist Office about cabins for rent for about US$4, with hot showers and cooking facilities. Accommodation at the farm of Constantino Ortiz is rec., 3½ km. from town, bordering on the Parque Arqueológico, 4 rooms, meals and horses available, peaceful, inexpensive, good cooking, plenty of morning coffee, also has camping; reservations at Calle 5, 1113 in town.

**Camping** *El Camping* and *Camping Ullumbe* both provide tents or charge per site, both good. Next to *Yalconia* is Rafael Gómez's campsite, clean, pleasant, toilets, lights, laundry service, horse hire (see below).

**Restaurants** *Brahama*, Calle 5, No. 15-11, vegetarian meals and comida including soup and drink (also meat dishes), good fruit salads, rec. (has horses and jeeps for rent); *Superpollo*, Diagonal a la Iglesia, US$2 for half chicken, good; *El Paraíso*, Calle 3 and Carrera 11, good; *Acuario*, Calle 3, very good, but expensive; *La Martina/Las Negras*, very good local food, only Sat. p.m., all day Sun. and Mon.; *Los Idolos*, good also; *La Negra*, Carrera 12, No. 3-40, good tamales; *Surahbi*, new, rec. for vegetarian food and meat dishes, meal for US$1.10; *Nayn*, Cra. 11 y Calle 3, across from bus offices, good comida; *Palacio de Jugos*, Carrera 13, No.3-32, excellent fruit juices; also at *Heladería de Turista*, Calle 3, No. 10-20, friendly, excellent fruit juices with at least a half glass refill on request; next to *Osoguaico* is *Mulales*, very good; opp. *Yalconia*, *Villadolly*, local and international food, rec. Tap water is not safe to drink.

**Shopping**  Film is available in several shops. Leather goods are beautiful and priced reasonably. Many local shops make boots to your own design for about US$27.50 (double-check the price beforehand); *Calzado Líder* is highly recommended, or *Artesanías El Viajero*, Calle 3 no. 11-33. Recommended handicraft shop is *Intillay*, Calle 5, No. 14-28 (wood and stone sculptures, weavings, jewellery). Don't buy artefacts on the street; if they are not fakes, their sale is illegal. Market day in San Agustín is Monday.

**Exchange**  Travellers are warned to change travellers' cheques before arriving in San Agustín; the **Tourist Office** and the small shop opp. police station will exchange cash only, at a poor rate; the **Banco de Colombia** will not change money but does give cash on Visa cards; 0800-1300 Mon. to Fri., 0800-1000 Sat.

**Transport**  San Agustín may be reached directly from Bogotá by taxi (Taxis Verdes have one service a day, leaving at 0300, US$11, 10-12 hrs. will pick you up at your hotel in Bogotá—ticket must be bought one day in advance—from San Agustín, Calle 3, No. 11-57, 0500) or by bus (Coomotor, from new bus terminal, 4 a day, US$10, 12 hours; from San Agustín, Calle 3, No. 10-71). Alternatively there are frequent services from Bogotá to Neiva (approx. hourly, US$7, 6 hrs.) as well as some to Pitalito (Taxi Verde costs US$9, leaving Bogotá at 0730 and 1030). From Neiva there are 6 buses a day to San Agustín, inc. Coomotor and Cotranshuila, taking 6 hrs. and costing US$5; to Neiva the 1000 Autobusco bus arrives in time for 1630 flight to Bogotá. The journey from Pitalito takes 11½ hrs., costs US$1 by jeep. To **Popayán** and **Cali**, Coomotor daily via Pitalito, Garzón and La Plata, US$9 to Popayán, US$10.60 to Cali. The bus stops at La Plata (for Tierradentro), 5 hrs; Rápido Tolima (Calle 3, No. 10-53) goes to Medellín at 2100, 15 hrs., US$15, also to La Plata at 1600, US$4.20, 6 hrs., and another company at 1700, US$5.15; buses to **Garzón** at 1230, 1430 and 1730, from where more buses go to La Plata for Tierradentro. **See also page 740.**

A new 135-km. direct route has been opened between **Popayán** and **San Agustín** (via Isnos, Coconuco and the Puracé National Park); it is very scenic, but unpaved, with one stretch of 20 km. single track, suitable only for jeeps and trucks. There are also frequent bus services, daily, with Cootranshuila at 0700 and 1030 (office on Calle 3, No. 10-58), slow, 6 hrs., US$6; also Sotracauca (Calle 3, No. 10-53) at 0600, continuing to Cali (US$10) and Coomotor on this route to Cali at 1700, 9 hrs. It may be advisable to book seats the day before. (For information ask in the tourist office.)

There is good riding in the neighbourhood. The rate for hiring horses works out at between US$1.50-2 per hour; US$8.50 for a full day. (Check the horses carefully before you hire them—they do not all, for instance, have shoes.) You must pay for the guide's horse, plus usual tip equivalent to the cost of one horse for the trip you have made. Good horses are hired out by Sra. Luz Angélica de Martínez, Calle 7, No. 14-16. For horses without guides there is a place on the road to the Archaeological Park by the football pitch. The Horse Hirers' Assocation is at C.5 No. 15-47, T 373080/373019. There are 3 types of guide: *Baquianos* (white identity cards), permitted only to accompany visitors to sites reached on horseback; *Alquiladores*, who own horses, but may not explain the statues or enter the Archaeological Park; and qualified, *Guiatur* guides (orange cards) who are fully trained, may explain all the sites, and charge US$6 to explain the Archaeological Park, US$12 for full day's guidance. Always ask to see a guide's identity badge; if you have any problems, ask at the Tourist Office or seek a tourist police officer. Highly recommended are Fabio Harvey Burbano (Spanish only) and Lucio Marino Bravo (English spoken), both orange card holders; good *baquianos* are Juan Arcos and Joel Muñoz, speaks little English but is very considerate and helpful; Jorge Palacios, who has a handicrafts shop opposite *Hotel Yalconia*, has also been recommended as a horseback guide. Lucas Peña at *Hotel Central* will act as guide on treks in the area; he also provides information on money exchange, etc. "Jerry" Luis Alfredo Salazar, Cra. 12 No. 2-78, speaks English, French and a little German, good guide, but check horses and the value of his tour carefully; Lucás Garzón, Calle 3, No. 11-55, has also been recommended for information, horses, etc. Another recommended guide for the longer excursions (4 days, Puerto Quinchana-Valencia and return) is Sr. Segundo Arsenio Guzmán (see below). You will need warm clothing and waterproofs. The services of Edgard José Chávez are not rec. (attempted rape reported), nor are those of Carlos Chávez, Carlos Gómez, Segundo Gómez, Eliás Paniquita, Alvaro Cerquera and Jaime Armel Guerrero (on CNT advice).

Alternatively, jeeps may be hired and about 8 people can fit in one! Prices vary according to the number of sites to be visited. The *Hotel Central* offers a one-day excursion by jeep to Alto de los Idolos, Alto de las Piedras, and the 2 waterfalls. When hiring a jeep, be clear about what you are to be shown before setting out, don't be rushed, don't let the driver pick up people *en route*, and don't let the driver charge more than the tourist-office-approved rate. To be safe, book through the Tourist Office which runs its own, popular tour in a brightly-painted *chiva*, daily at 0900, book the day before. US$6.50 p.p. (15% discount for students) to the narrows, Obando, El Palmar, Alto de los Idolos (entry not included), Isnos (lunch US$1.20), Alto de las Piedras, Saltos de Bordones and Mortiño.

The area offers excellent opportunities for hiking, although some trails to remote sites are not well marked. Two sites easily reached on foot are El Tablón (5 sculptures) and La Chaquira (figures carved on rocks and good view of Río Magdalena). At the site of La Pelota, two painted statues were found in 1984 (well worth a visit, a 3-hr return trip, 6 hrs. if you include El Tablón and La Chaquira, 15 km. in all). The latest archaeological discovery (1986) in the area is a series of at least 30 stones carved with animals and other designs in high relief; they are on the right bank of the Río Magdalena, near the Estrecho (narrows) to which jeeps run. This trip is especially recommended. The leaflets given out by the Tourist Office disagree about distances to the sites. For accurate route information, seek advice from Joaquín Emilio García at the office. Probably best for several people to organize their trips together; prospective horseriders and jeep passengers tend to congregate at the health-food restaurant near the Tourist Office.

The best books on the subject are *Exploraciones Arqueológicas en San Agustín*, by Luis Duque Gómez (Bogotá, 1966, 500 pages) or *San Agustín, Reseña Arqueológica*, by the same author (1963, 112 pages); a leaflet in English is obtainable from tourist offices. The Colombian Institute of Archaeology has published a booklet (English/ Spanish), at US$1.80, on San Agustín and Tierradentro (**see page 742**), available at museums in San Agustín and San Andrés (also available at the Tourist Office, free).

The visitor with time to spare should visit Alto de los Idolos, or about 10 km. by horse or on foot. Inexperienced riders should be warned that the path is very steep in places. On foot it is a lovely (if strenuous) walk via Puente de la Chaquira, but 27 km. by road via San José de **Isnos** village (which is 5 km. from Alto de los Idolos), and to which a bus can be taken, US$1, 0500 on Sat. return bus at 1100, 1300, or catch a bus from the *cruce* on the Pitalito road or hitch, well signposted (the site is open until 1600, entry US$1). Here on a hill overlooking San Agustín are more and different statues known as *vigilantes*, each guarding a burial mound (one is an unusual rat totem). The few excavated have disclosed large stone sarcophagi, some covered by stone slabs bearing a sculpted likeness of the inmate. Alto de las Piedras, 6 km. from Isnos, has a few interesting tombs and monoliths, including the famous "Doble Yo". The Director of the Parque (Sr. Alvaro León Monsalve) can arrange transport and guide to outlying sites. Only less remarkable than the statues are the orchids growing nearby. There is the *Parador de los Idolos* (3 rooms), ½ km. from Alto de los Idolos, new, D. From San Agustín the Bordones waterfalls can be visited; best with a car; there is a 13-room *Parador* right by the falls, E, clean and pleasant (reservations at San Agustín Tourist Office).

From Isnos many of the sites can be visited by road. As you come S into Isnos from Popayán, turn left just after the bridge (sign Salto de Bordones). 6 km. on right is Alto de las Piedras, and 8 km. further is Bordones village. Turn left at end of Bordones and there is (½ km.) parking for the falls. Coming S through Isnos, turn right off main street to Alto de los Idolos (5 km.). From Isnos it is about 20 km. to San Agustín; after 7 km. turn left (½ km.) to Salto del Mortiño, 300-metre falls.

Market day is Sat. in Isnos (*Hospedaje Nueva*, F)—bus at 0500 from San Agustín.

It is possible to walk from San Agustín to the Lago Magdalena, involving a bus ride or 6-hour walk the first day, 7-hour walk the second, and 8-10 hours walking on the third, either to the lake and back to the second *refugio*, or on to Valencia. Good bases for this excursion are *Residencias El Paraíso*, at Puerto Quinchana, 30 km. away on the road to the source of the Río Magdalena, 2 km. from the Cementerio Indígena de Quinchana, owned by Sr. Arsenio Guzmán, F, friendly, peaceful, restaurant; *Residencias El Páramo* at Juntas on same road, beautiful countryside, owner Alvaro Palechor, F, clean, safe, friendly, restaurant.

## Caquetá

Lying to the E of the Cordillera Oriental is the Intendencia of Caquetá, reached by air, or by road from Neiva or Garzón. This region, although still sparsely populated, is an area of intensive settlement as people move down from the highlands to turn the area into a livestock region. The natural forest cover around Florencia, the capital of the Intendencia, has been cleared and for well-established, undulating pasturelands, dotted with tall palms—the fruits of which are a delicacy for grazing cattle. To the SE, beyond the cleared lands, lie little-touched expanses of tropical forest inhabited by indigenous tribes and wide varieties of Amazonian flora and fauna.

The road Neiva-Florencia is 260 km.: possible in one day, but it is recommended that travellers should try to complete the last 100 km. over the mountains into Florencia by daylight. From the Garzón-San Agustín road, the only route for vehicles into Caquetá branches off at Altamira. Here the surfaced road ends and becomes a single-track dirt road, originally engineered in 1932 during the Leticia dispute between Colombia and Peru. The climb up over the mountains passes through a region of small farms (some of their cultivated fields appear to be on almost vertical valley sides), through sugar-cane cultivation and up into cloud at the higher points of the route. Soon after the summit, and on a clear day, there are extensive views out over Caquetá and then the road winds down through substantial forests—ablaze with the colours of tropical flowers in the dry season (Jan.-March) and into the lowlands. The lower section of the road into the lowlands is prone to frequent landslides (or *derrumbes*) because of weak geological structures.

The roads in Caquetá run from Florencia along the foothills of the Cordillera; eventually a road is planned to run from Puerto Asís through Florencia to Villavicencio, skirting the foothills of the eastern Andes. Other routes are difficult and seasonal (although tracks, or *trochas*, are laid out as part of the settlement scheme) and the main lines of communication into the lowlands are by boat along the rivers Caquetá and Guayas and their tributaries.

**Florencia** (pop. 78,000) is the capital of the region and the centre for settlement in Caquetá, originally established in 1908. The square contains sculptures, fountains, a large forest tree (*saba*) and flower beds. When the road to Garzón is obstructed by landslides, petrol supplies are limited. Overnight, cars are best left in the care of the fire-station (US$0.20 a night).

**Fiesta** The local Saint's day is on 16 July, when there is a candlelight procession in the evening around the town.

**Hotels** located around the central square are reputed to be the more salubrious. **Cafés, Restaurants** Plenty, but prices tend to be high because much food is trucked in. Vegetarian restaurant on main street for good patacones.

**Bank** Cash cheques at the **Banco de la República**.

**Buses** There are regular services from Neiva (US$6.50, 7 hrs.), Garzón and Altamira to **Florencia** (bus Altamira to Florencia, US$3.15) and frequent services as far as Puerto Rico and Belén. Bus to **Bogotá** costs US$19.50.

**Air Services** To Puerto Asís, with Satena, on Mon., Wed., Fri., daily to **Neiva** (Satena and Aires) and to **Leguizamo, San Vicente del Caguán** and **Solano**, with Satena. Several planes a day to **Bogotá**.

**Excursions** From Florencia down the Orteguaza river: take a morning bus to Puerto Lara or a bus to San Antonio (US$3.25) where there is a cheap hotel; you can visit Indian villages.

From Florencia the road runs northeastwards as far as Puerto Rico: it is paved for 34 km. to La Montañita and then unsurfaced, passing through El Paujil (2,750 pop.), where the *residencias* are unnamed and are situated alongside the road into the town. A dry-weather road runs from here for 21 km. towards Cartagena before giving way to a mule track. Then, on the Puerto Rico road, comes El Doncello (5,500) a very pleasant town, overlooked by the church which has a brightly painted steeple. The *Residencias Americanas* is highly recommended, F. Popular Sun. market. Next comes Esmeralda, a small settlement located on a ford that is too deep for cars, although trucks and buses may cross, and there is a wooden suspension bridge over the river for which the toll is US$0.20. The hotel there provides a very plain but excellently cooked breakfast.

**Puerto Rico** (4,950) is at the end of the road—which is interrupted by the River Guayas. It is possible to cross the river by ferry (US$0.08) and travel by bus as far as San Vicente where a mule-track goes over the Cordillera to Algeciras in Huila Department. Puerto Rico is a river port; ferries travel downstream to Río Negro (1½ hrs.) and Cartagena (4½ hrs.). Houses built down by the river are raised on stilts above possible flood levels. River boats are made and repaired by the riverside. **Hotels** and *residencias* are full on Sat. nights—book a room early in the day. *El Gran Hotel*, despite its name, provides basic amenities. *Hotel Almacén* is the only place in Puerto Rico serving fresh fruit juices.

The road southwest from Florencia to San José is unsurfaced. At Morelia there is a poor branch road S to the River Pescado, where a ferry will take you across the river to the town of Valparaíso (1,175). *Hotel Ceilán* is cheap and friendly; there is also the *Hotel Turista*. From Valparaíso mule tracks go further into the lowlands. If travelling to Valparaíso by car, make sure it is left well away from the river when catching the ferry as, during times of flood, the river may rise rapidly overnight. Morelia to Belén de los Andes is an unsurfaced road, passing through some very interesting scenery, and crossing very clean, fast-flowing rivers by metal bridges. For some reason prices are higher in **Belén** (2,235) than in other towns in Caquetá.

Hotels fill up very quickly, and mosquito nets are not always provided, although they are needed. In the area are a group of co-operative farms, and an oil palm plantation. From Belén an unsurfaced road runs to Albania (1,075) a small frontier settlement with only one hotel. A semi-surfaced road runs from here towards the new areas of settlement.

Anyone wanting to look at wildlife in Caquetá must travel beyond the settlement area. Toucans, monkeys, macaws etc. are kept as pets, but there is little wild-life. Boats and canoes are easily hired, but horses and mules are more difficult, especially in the dry season when they are needed to transport the harvest.

## THE CENTRAL CORDILLERA: MEDELLIN AND MANIZALES (6)

Medellín and Manizales are both busy, industrial centres yet, for all the commerce and coffee, the surrounding countryside is green, mountainous and pleasant. From the Cordillera Central to the Pacific stretches Chocó Department, thickly wooded, mountainous and undeveloped, but rewarding to explore.

The Central Cordillera lies W of the Magdalena River. In it are two of the most important cities in Colombia: Medellín, the third largest city in the country, and Manizales. Manizales can be reached by a road (309 km.) passing through Facatativá and Honda; or through Girardot to Ibagué, then over the high crest of the Quindío pass via Armenia. (For the road from Manizales to Medellín, **see page 729**.) Medellín can be reached from Bogotá by road three ways: the highway opened in 1982 (**see page 726**); the old direct road (478 km.) with a 207-km. unpaved stretch from La Dorada to La Unión; and the third via Manizales.

The town of Antioquia was founded in 1541, but the Spaniards, eager for gold, were not interested in the hinterland, which was then very sparsely inhabited by nomadic Indians who made very poor agricultural labourers. But during the 17th century a new wave of settlers came to Colombia from Spain; many of them were Jewish refugees who were deliberately seeking isolation, and found it in the little valley of the Río Aburrá, where they founded the city of Medellín in 1616. They were farmers with their families rather than *conquistadores*: they had an extraordinarily high birth rate; they intermarried very little with either Indian or black; and they divided the land into small farms which they worked themselves. Their exports were small: a little gold and silver from their streams. They lived on the food they themselves produced: maize, beans, sugar-cane, bananas, fruit.

In the early 19th century the settlement began to expand and to push out in all directions, particularly to the S. The settlers followed the forested slopes on the western side of the Central Cordillera and occupied all the cultivable land. Manizales, 120 km. S, was founded in 1848. In the second half of the century new lands were occupied further S.

It was coffee that brought stability to this expansion, but they were slow to adopt it. Coffee appeared in the Magdalena Valley about 1865, but none was being exported from Antioquia before the end of the century. It was the 1914-18 war that suddenly gave a fillip to the industry: within 20 years the Departments of Antioquia and Caldas were producing half the coffee of Colombia, and they are by far the most important producers today. The industrialization of Medellín followed the coffee boom. There has been little immigration since the original settlement, but the natural growth in population has been extraordinary.

**Medellín**, capital of Antioquia Department, is a city of 1.6 million people, at an altitude of 1,487 metres. It could hardly be less advantageously placed, for it faces forbidding mountain barriers in nearly all directions. Its climate alone, that of an English summer day (21°C), is in its favour, despite a certain amount of smog. Yet Medellín is one of the main industrial cities of Colombia, and seethes with energy. The first looms arrived in 1902. Today the city produces more than 80% of the textile output of the country, and textiles account for only half its industrial activity. A metro is planned for the city. Excellent views from Cerro Salvador (statue on top), SE of city, and from Cerro Nutibara, S of city, where there are an outdoor stage for open air concerts, sculpture park, miniature village, souvenir shops and restaurants.

Medellín is a well-laid-out industrial city. There are four universities, together with other higher educational institutions. The old colonial buildings have nearly all disappeared, but there are still some 17th century churches left: the old Cathedral on Parque Berrío and the churches of San Benito, La Veracruz, and San José. The new Cathedral of Villanueva (Catedral Metropolitana), built between 1868 and 1931, one of the largest brick buildings in the world, is on Parque Bolívar, an attractive place. Below the statue of Bolívar in the park are inscribed the words of the conquered Indian leader Choquehuanca to his visitors: "With the centuries, your glory will grow as the shadows grow when the sun sets". Three churches of the 18th century survive: San Ignacio, in Plaza San Ignacio, San Juan de Dios, and San Antonio. The city's commercial centre, Villanueva, is interesting for its blend of old and modern architecture, including many skyscrapers. There is a fine sculpture, Monumento a la Vida, next to the Edificio Seguros Suramericana on Calle 50, where exhibitions of work by leading South American artists are held on the ground floor. The cattle auctions on Tues. and Thurs., held in specially built cattle yards on the outskirts, are interesting. There is a zoo, **Zoológico Santa Fe**, in the southern section of the city (Carrera 52, No. 20-63), mainly of South American animals and birds; reached by the Guayabal bus (US$0.07; admission US$0.80). In the zoo grounds is the Museo Santa Fe (closed Mon. and Tues.), costing an extra US$0.20 to enter. Christmas illuminations are very good, in Parque Bolívar and Cerro Nutibara.

Travellers should take the same safety precautions as they would in any large city, particularly at night, but remember that Medellín has been the centre of narcotics, and anti-narcotics operations. It is, nevertheless, a friendly place. You are advised to check conditions before going.

**Hotels** *Intercontinental*, Variante Las Palmas, T 266-0680, the best, some distance from the centre, A, excellent; *Amaru*, Carrera 50A, No. 53-45, T 511-21-25, A, central, quiet, good, expensive restaurant with excellent service; *Ambassador*, Carrera 50, No. 54-50, T 511-53-11, C, in connection with *Veracruz*, Carrera 50, No. 54-18, T 511-55-11, B, with bath, swimming pool, very good, restaurant on 11th floor gives fine view over city; *El Balcón*, near *Intercontinental*, in Transversal Superior, T 246-00-82, A, beautiful view of the city, good meals, US$6 p.p.; *Nutibara* (casino and swimming pool), Calle 52A, No. 50-46, T 511-51-11, A; *Residencias Nutibara*, an annex facing hotel of same name, slightly cheaper with all the same facilities; *Europa Normandie*, Calle 53, No. 49-100 (T 241-9920), C, restaurant, cafetería, sauna, disco, central, fair; *Horizonte*, Carrera 47 No. 49A-24, T 511-61-88, C, good and popular restaurant; *Eupacla*, Carrera 50, No. 53-16, T 231-18-44, C, central, noisy, mosquitoes, but helpful staff; *Comercial*, Calle 48, No. 53-94, E, friendly, clean, hot water available in some rooms, the best of which are on the top floor, doors barred to all but residents after 1800, meals US$2; *Holiday*, Carrera 45, No. 50-25, E, with bath, clean, 5 mins. walk from centre; *Linton*, Cra. 45, No. 47-74, F with bath and hot water, very clean, good value, safe parking nearby US$0.50 per night, central. *Residencias Doris*, Carrera 45, No. 46-23, F, family run, clean sheets every day, locked night and day, good value, rec.; *Samaritano*, Carrera 45, No. 45-25, E, clean and friendly, but noisy; *Casa Blanca*, Carrera 45, No. 46-09, E, safe but noisy; *Romania*, Av. Echeverri, Calle 58, No. 50-46, F with bath, clean, a bit noisy. Many *residencias* on Carreras 54 and 55, but this is not a safe area; a safer area for accommodation is around Carrera 43. Calle 45 is said to be an unsafe street.

**Restaurants** *Hato Viejo*, opp. *Intercontinental Hotel*, good local cuisine (another branch on Carrera Junín); *La Sombrilla*, *La Yerra* and *Los Cristales* are all on the same road, good. *Asados La 80*, Cra. 81, No.30-7, very good, large steaks for about US$3. In El Poblado *Frutos del Mar*, Carrera 43B, No. 11-51, good seafood; *La Crèperie*, opposite (No. 11-88), French; on Av. Poblado (Av. 43A): *Piemonte* (No. 5A-170); *La Bella Epoca*, Calle 4 Sur, No. 43A-9, very good and expensive, on road to Envigado; *Aguacatala* , Carrera 43A, No. 7 Sur-130, and *La Posada de la Montaña*, Carrera 43-B, No.16-22, both outside off road to Envigado, good, Colombian food. Vegetarian: *Govinda*, Calle 51 No. 52-17. There are several round-the-clock cafés in the vicinity of Cra. Junín between Maturín and Amador which serve cheap meals. Two good self-service restaurants are *La Estancia*, Carrera 49, No. 54-15, on Plaza Bolívar, and *Contenalco*, Calle la Playa, between Av. Oriental and El Palo, clean, cheap, very busy in rush hours. Many good, cheap restaurants on Carrera 49, e.g. *Versalles*, on pedestrian precinct between Av. La Playa and Plaza Bolívar. Excellent pastries at *Salón de Té Astor*, Carrera 49, No. 53-39. Many cheap cafés near bus station.

**Shopping**   Silver seems cheaper than in Bogotá. Poor selection of handicraft shops in the city, but there are *artesanía* shops on the top of Cerro Nutibara and there is a small handicrafts market at Calle 52 near Cra. 46 with many hippy stalls. **Mercado San Alejo**, Parque Bolívar, open on the first Saturday of every month except January, and before Christmas it is there Sat. and Sun. (handicrafts on sale at good prices). Many of the textile mills have discount clothing departments attached where good bargains can be had; ask at your hotel. *La Piel*, at Calle 53, No. 49-131, has an excellent selection of leather goods at very reasonable prices (the selection and price of leather goods in Medellín is better than Bogotá). *Supermarket Exito* (Cra. 66, No. 49-01, Calle 10, No. 43E-135, Poblado) is reasonable for cheap leather bags. There are several shopping centres.

**Bookshop**   *Librería Continental*, Junín No. 52-11, sells foreign-language books.

**Photography**   For developing, Almacenes Duperly (several branches, e.g. Calle 52, No. 46-28), good quality at US$8 for 36 print, 136 film with copies, and US$2 for a new Fuji 100 ASA-136 (after developing).

**Taxis**   Pay what is on the meter plus US$0.90. From airport, about US$2.70.

**Discotheques**   in central hotels, and in El Poblado district. Many discos and popular dance halls on Calle 50, between Carreras 65 and 75, and Carrera 70, between Calles 36 and 44, also in Envigado, near Plaza Envigado. For a dark, underground and lively young place, try *Selva* (from San Diego roundabout, turn into the street right of Cra. 43A, which nearly runs parallel, and then turn left at the second or third crossroad).

**Music**   Monthly concerts by the Antioquia Symphony Orchestra. Band concerts in the Parque Bolívar every Sun. at 1130. Open air concerts, on Sundays, of Colombian music on Cerro Nutibara.

**Museums**   Museo Etnográfico Miguel Angel Builes, Carrera 81, No. 52B-120, has an extensive collection of artefacts housed in beautiful new building. The **Museo de la Madre Laura**, Carrera 92, No. 33B-21, has a good collection of indigenous costumes and crafts from Colombia, Ecuador and Guatemala. **Museo El Castillo**, Calle 9 Sur, No. 32-260, formerly a landowner's home, has interesting objects and beautiful grounds; entry US$1.20; take bus to Loma de los Balsos, El Poblado (US$0.07), then walk 1 km. up the hill until you see the road lined with pine trees to the right. Open 1300-1700, closed Sun. The **Museo de Antioquia**, Carrera 53 y Calle 52, opp. main post office, shows contemporary pictures and sculptures, including works by Fernando Botero, Colombia's leading contemporary artist (now living in U.S.A.), US$0.50. **Museo de Arte Moderno**, Carrera 64B, No. 51-64, small collection, open Tues.-Fri., 0900-1300, 1500-1800. **Casa Museo Maestro Pedro Nel Gómez**, Carrera 51B, No. 85-24, T 2332633, house of the contemporary painter and sculptor. **Museo Antropológico** at University of Antioquia, Calle 67, No. 53-108 (new campus). **Museo Filatélico**, on 4th floor of Banco de la República building. Most museums are closed on Mondays.

**Botanical Gardens**   Joaquín Antonio Uribe gardens, Carrera 52, No. 73-298, near the new campus of the University of Antioquia, which include an aviary and an orchid garden, are open daily, 0900-1730, US$0.40 entrance, well worth a visit (some of the plants are named); there is a restaurant, pleasant but not cheap. There is also a zoo (**see page 724**); take Marinilla bus from centre. Also visit El Ranchito, an orchid farm between the towns of Itagüí and La Estrella (entry US$0.50; April to June is the best time to visit).

**Bullfights**   at the bull-ring of La Macarena, Calle 44 and Carrera 63, in February.

**Exchange**   Banco de la República, Calle 50 (opp. Parque Berrío), changes travellers' cheques, but your photo will be taken; has other branches; **Banco Anglo Colombiano**, Calle 50 (Bolívar), No. 51-06; agency on Calle 45, No. 55-65 and two others; and various other Colombian banks. Open: Mon.-Thurs. 0800-1130, 1400-1600; Fri. 0900-1130, 1400-1630; last working day of month 0830-1100. Main hotels will cash travellers' cheques for residents when banks are closed.

**British Consulate**  Calle 9, No. 43-893, T 246-3114. **Danish Consulate**, Calle 51, No. 42-61, T 239-7696. Addresses of others in the phone book. **N.B.** the **Venezuelan** consul will not issue visas.

**Post Office**  Main airmail office in Avianca building, Carrera 52, Calle 51A, Mon.-Sat., 0700-2200.

**Telecommunications**  Pasaje Junín and on corner of Calle 49 and Carrera 50.

**Travel Agents**  *Tierra Mar Aire* (American Express agents), Calle 52, No. 43-124, T 511-4183, helpful. *Viajes Marco Polo*, Calle 48, No. 65-94, T 230-5944, recommended; also *Terra Nova*, Calle 5A, No. 39-107, T 266-5000, who run an excursion by train to Cisneros, 3 hrs. journey, with 3-4 hours for a picnic and swim (US$5.20).

**Tourist Office**  Calle 57 No. 45-129, T 254-08-00, in bus station (some English spoken, helpful), and in airport (will book hotel rooms), and Turantioquia, Carrera 48, No. 58-11, T 254-3864, has good maps, good information on Antioquia and owns 5 good hotels in the Department. For a cheap tour of the city take any "Circular" bus, for US$0.06.

**DAS**  T 341-5900, also at Calle 19, No. 80A-40 in Belén la Nubia section, T 34-1451; **Tourist Police** at airport, T 287-2053; police T 112; general information T 113.

**Airport**  A new airport, José María Córdoba, 38 km. from Medellín and 13 km. from Rionegro, has been opened (1985); *Presto* restaurant. Taxi to town US$7, colectivo US$3, *buseta* to centre, via bus terminal, US$2, frequent service, about 1 hr. journey, sit on right going to town (catch bus in town by *Hotel Nutibara*). To Rionegro, bus US$0.15, taxi US$8.50. By air to **Bogotá**, 45 mins. with Avianca, on shuttle flight, every ½ hour between 0730 and 1630. Daily flight to **Panama** with SAM or Copa, but you will have to buy a return unless you have another exit ticket out of Panama.

**Rail**  Apart from a daily train to **Barrancabermeja** (scheduled at 0700 but check in advance) and the Medellín-Santa Marta train, called the "Nutibara", in December to March, there are no regular passenger services from or to Medellín. The "Nutibara" connects with the **Bogotá-Santa Marta** "Tayrona" at Grecia (Puerto Berrío). For the tourist train from and to Cisneros, see above under Travel Agents.

**Buses**  The new bus terminal for all long-distance buses is about 3 km. NW of the town centre, with shops, cafeterias, left luggage (US$0.30 per day) and other facilities. Quite safe. Bus service to city centre, US$0.15, buses to station from Calle 50, marked: "Terminal de Transporte". To/from **Bogotá**, 9-12 hrs. US$13, every 40 minutes or so, with 5 companies, to **La Dorada**, US$4.25. To **San Agustín**, Rápidos Tolima, 0600, US$15. Frequent buses for **Cali**, Flota Magdalena US$8, 10-13 hrs. Frequent buses to **Manizales**, 6 hrs. US$6.50 1st class, 4.50 2nd, by Empresa Arauca. To **Cartagena**, Brasilia, 17-20 hrs., or 14 hrs., by Pullman bus, Us$11; road paved throughout but poor. To **Barranquilla**, US$16 by Pullman, 16 hrs. To **Cartago**, 8 hrs., Flota Magdalena, US$5. To Pereira, 8 hrs., US$6.25 by Flota Occidental Pullman. To Sincelejo, 9½ hrs. To Popayán, US$13.25, 16 hrs. To Turbo US$7.50.

**Roads**  The new **Medellín-Bogotá highway** has been completed, but beware of landslides in wet weather. The road is totally paved but there are potholes, waterfalls and detours between Medellín and Honda. There are many campgrounds along the route, for example 130 km. and 150 km. from Medellín. On the way from Honda to Medellín is *Doradel* with a large zoo called Hacienda Nápoles and several hotels, e.g. *La Colina*, C, pool, rec. 10 km. beyond Doradel, a dirt road to the left (badly signposted) leads to *La Danta* where there is a cave with *guácharos* (oilbirds). Village boys will lead you there for a tip, take torches. At *Marinilla* 40 km. from Medellín, there is a reservoir in picturesque surroundings, swimming possible, accommodation nearby.

A paved road, 665 km. long, goes N to Cartagena, and another S to Manizales, which provides an alternative route to Bogotá. There are two other important roads: one, 383 km. NW through Antioquia to Turbo, on the Gulf of Urabá; and another, 478 km. SE from Medellín through Sonsón and La Dorada and on to Bogotá. The latter is paved as far as Rionegro, but from Rionegro to Sonsón is in a bad state of repair. The scenery compensates for this to some extent. Also attractive is the road to Quibdó through coffee, tobacco and pineapple plantations.

**Excursions**  A run N along the Cartagena road to (132 km.) *Yarumal* in a cool mountain climate (61,250 people, friendly town with fine views from Paroquia La Merced; many hosterías; *Residencias Horizontes*, E, hot showers, clean, quiet, welcoming; next door is *Cafetería La Estancia*, excellent; *Restaurante La Nena*), or NW (many hotels and resort areas, crowded weekends) to (80 km.) *Antioquia* (13,275 people) will give a good idea of the very beautiful countryside, excellent walking. Antioquia lies just W of the Cauca river; it was founded as a gold mining town by the Spaniards in 1541, the first in the area, and still retains its colonial atmosphere, with interesting Christmas/New Year fiestas. Until 1826 it was the capital of the Department. The fine old Cathedral is worth seeing, as is the church of Santa Bárbara. There are two small museums close to the church. There is an interesting wooden bridge, 300 metres long, 3 km. downstream from the steel bridge which the buses use—ask for directions or take a taxi. Hotels: *Mariscal Robledo*, D, 37 rooms, swimming pool, good; *Hostería Real*, 2 km. from town, C full board, good food, pool; *Del Río*, also outside, *San Pedro* in resort area, or you can stay en famille with Marta Merizalde de Roldán, Cra. 11, No. 9-39, very friendly and informative, pretty garden. There is good food in the main square US$1 for a full meal. Bus from Medellín US$1.50 (Flota Urbara or Transporte Sierra), 2½ hrs. The road goes on to Turbo (daily bus at 0900), on the Gulf of Urabá (**see page 699**).

Another interesting excursion from Medellín is along the Sonsón road SE to (39 km.) the town of *Rionegro*, in (a delightful valley of gardens and orchards. Here was born one of Bolívar's generals, José María Córdoba, the hero of the battle of Ayacucho. Medellín's new airport has been built 13 km. away. The Casa de Convención (where the 1863 Convention took place) is now an archive museum, entry US$0.20. The cathedral, with its gold and silver altar, deserves a visit. A museum of religious artefacts is behind the altar (entry US$0.20) and you can climb up behind the Virgin donated by Philip II to look down into the cathedral. There are processions in Easter Week. Many interesting pottery and ceramics factories in Rionegro area, hardly mechanized, as well as leather working; these welcome visitors and explain the processes. A day trip can cost US$15, but the Medellín-Rionegro *rápido* taxi service is very cheap. Bus to Rionegro, from Calle 44, No. 44-43, US$0.75, one hr.; bus back to Medellín from plaza every ½ hr. Prices of leather goods are high. 10 km. from Rionegro (15 minutes by colectivo, leave when full from plaza, US$0.50; buses every 2 hrs., US$0.15) is **Carmen de Viboral**, well-known for its pottery; there are several factories just N of the market place.

**Rionegro Hotels**  *Rionegro*, E, friendly, dark rooms, cold water; *Gutier*, central, D with restaurant; *Oasis*, Carrera 50, No. 46-23, D, with restaurant, bar, laundry, TV in rooms. *Residencias Onassis*, F with bath, good value; *Residencias David*, same price, both near market.

Beyond Rionegro to the east is **El Peñol**, a precipitous, bullet-shaped rock which towers above the surrounding hills and lakes. It has been eroded smooth, but a spiral staircase has been built into a crack which extends from the base to the summit. Entrance to rock, US$0.30. A snack bar has been built at the summit, and the views are very fine (meals available only in holiday seasons). Cabins can be rented at the foot of the rock for about US$28 per day (sleep six, everything except food provided), T Medellín 234-6966, Santamaría y Cía; architects, Calle 81A, No.51-79. Bus to the rock and to the pretty town of Guatapé with Cía. Fco. López, US$1.20. Bus back to Medellín is harder to catch; best take a colectivo to town of Peñol and bus from there. From Rionegro, take a colectivo to Marinilla (US$0.25, leaves from near market), then wait for the San Rafael bus which passes El Peñol (US$1.20); from Marinilla you can also take a colectivo to the new town of Nuevo Peñol (US$0.70), then another to El Peñol (US$0.50)—in all about 2 hrs., either route.

On the road to El Retiro is Fizebad, an old estate house, restored with original furniture and artefacts, and a display of flowering orchids; entry US$1.75. In El Retiro itself is a small colonial church and an even older chapel which is seldom open: ask for the caretaker. On the road to La Ceja, have lunch in *Parador Tequendamita*, in a beautiful setting by a waterfall. The route is through splendid scenery, and one can see typical Antioquian life and costume. (To Fizebad by bus, catch a La Ceja or El Retiro bus).

**La Ceja**, also on the Sonsón road, is well worth a visit. Transportes La Ceja cover the route; the journey takes 1¾ hrs. For the energetic, any one of the surrounding hills affords an excellent view of the area. *Hotel Primavera* and one other, both delightful, have rooms (F). Youth hostel at *Centro Vacacional La Montaña*, details from Alcom in Bogotá. At **Sonsón**, there are the *Tahami* (F, very good value) and *Imperio* (F) hotels. Ask for the Casa de los Abuelos, an old house with a printing press, which produces a weekly newspaper, and many other historical objects.

At **Bello**, 6½km. N of Medellín (pop. 153,000), is the hut in which Marcos Fidel Suárez, President 1918-1922, was born. It is completely covered in with glass for its preservation.

    A good trip is by car to **Hatillo**, 32 km. along a road which parallels the railway to Puerto Berrío, and then another 80 km. along a new road to Caldas. There are many restaurants along this road.

To the SW of Medellín, the towns in the coffee-growing district (Fredonia, Jericó, Jardín, Venecia) are worth visiting; all have basic inns. The scenery is beautiful.

At **Envigado**, 10 km. S of Medellín, craftsmen have for generations turned out the traditional *antioqueño* pouch called *carriel*, carried by the men. Now used for money, its original use was for coffee samples.

55 km. S of Medellín is **Santa Bárbara**, at 1,857 metres on a green hill top, with stunning views in every direction of coffee, banana and sugar plantations, orange-tiled roofs and folds of hills. *Hotel Palomares* on main square, F, clean, well-maintained; restaurants and cafés also on square, as is the large church. Bus to Medellín, US$1. 140 km. S of Medellín is **Supia**, a pleasant little town with new hotel, *Mis Ninietas*, near plaza, no sign, F with bath, clean and good. Supia is 13 km. N of Riosucio (**see page 729**).

**Manizales** is dominated by its enormous (still unfinished) concrete Cathedral and the Nevado del Ruiz volcano, which erupted so catastrophically in November 1985. The city was founded in 1848 by settlers from the Department of Antioquia; it has a population of 450,000 and is the capital of the small Department of Caldas, which originally (until 1965) contained what are now the new Departments of Quindío and Risaralda. The old Department, now known as Viejo Caldas, produces about 30% of all Colombian coffee and picturesque coffee farms abound.

Manizales, at 2,153 metres above sea level, rides its mountain saddle uncompromisingly, the houses falling away sharply from the centre of the city into the adjacent valleys. The climate is extremely humid—average temperature is 17°C, and the annual rainfall is 3,560 mm.—and frequently the city is covered in cloud. The best months of the year are from mid-December through to early March, and early in January the Fair and Coffee Festival is held, with bullfights, beauty parades and folk dancing. The city looks down on the small town of Villa María, "the village of flowers", although with the rapid expansion of Manizales, Villa María is now almost a suburb.

The architecture is predominantly modern with high-rise office and apartment blocks, although traditional architectural styles are still seen in the suburbs and the older sections of the city. The departmental government building, the Gobernación, opposite the Cathedral in the Parque Bolívar, is an imposing example of neo-colonial architecture; the bull-ring built 25 years ago is an impressive copy of the traditional Moorish style. The suburbs stretch away North (with best shopping around Calle 59) and South of the city centre and are reached by a four-lane highway lined with flowers—marguerites—which grow to enormous proportions (as also the geraniums) because of the damp and the altitude. Chipre, a recreational park, provides a good view of the city (well-visited on Sundays); El Tanque, near Chipre, is another vantage point.

**Hotels** N.B. in January, during the fiesta, hotel prices are grossly inflated. *Las Colinas*, Carrera 22, Calle 20 (T 29400), three-star, two bars, good restaurant, very comfortable, C; *Europa*, Av. Centenario, No. 25-98 (T 22253), near the bull-ring, restaurant for breakfast only, comfortable and clean, D; *Rokasol*, Calle 21, No. 19-16, near bus station so noisy, hot water, clean, all rooms have bathrooms, E, good restaurant, set meal US$2; *Villa Kempis*, on road to Pereira, about 2 km. past bull-ring, old religious retreat house, beautiful view over the valley, very quiet, hot water a.m. only, restaurant and bar, good food at moderate prices, T 32961/30187, D; *Tama Internacional*, Calle 23, No. 22-43, next to Cathedral, E, with bath, meals US$1, clean and cheap, but noisy. Cheaper: *Residencias Margarita*, Calle 17 between Carreras 22 and 23, F, quiet, good, safe, private parking opposite US$0.75 per night; *Residencias Nueva York*, Calle 18 between Cras. 22 and 23, extremely clean, hot water, clothes-washing facilities, some bar noise in front but rec., F: *Residencias Caldas*, Carrera 19, No. 22-45, near bus station, F, US$1 surcharge on holidays, hot water, quiet, good; *Cosmos*, opp. bus terminal, F, clean but overpriced, hot water with luck.

*Hotel Termales Arbeláez*, 25 km., from Manizales on the road to the Nevado El Ruiz, D, hot swimming pool, private bathrooms, restaurant.

**Restaurants** *Las Redes*, Carrera 23, No. 75-97, predominantly sea food, good but pricey; *Vitiani*, Carrera 23, No. 25-32, Italian and European food, quite smart, food and wine fairly expensive, has good trout and excellent crab-claws (muellas de cangrejo); *La Suiza*, Carrera 23, No. 26-57, good fruit juices and cakes; *Caballo Loco*, Calle 21, No. 23-40, expensive pizzas; *El Ruiz*, Carrera 19, No. 22-25, filling 3-course meal.

**Teatro de los Fundadores** is a modern cinema-theatre auditorium. Interesting wood-carved mural by local artist, Fernando Botero, who also has murals in the entrance hall of the Club Manizales and *Hotel Las Colinas*. Events held here and at other locations during Theatre Festival in first two weeks of September.

**Museums Bellas Artes**, anthropology museum with interesting selection of findings from Indian tombs (and a marvellous view of the Nevado El Ruiz), open in the afternoon (erratically) after 1400. **Banco de la República**, Carrera 23, No. 23-06, gold and anthropology museum open during banking hours, classical music every afternoon in the Bank. **Universidad de Caldas**, natural history museum open every day from 0800 to 1200 and 1400 to 1800 (take a "Fátima" bus to the University). **La Galería del Arte**, Av. Santander at Calle 55, exhibitions of work by local artists, pictures can be bought.

**Bank** Banco Anglo Colombiano, Carrera 22, No. 17-10, and other banks. Open 0800-1130, 1400-1600, Mon. to Thurs., 0900-1130, 1400-1630 Fri. only. Last working day of the month 0830-1130.

**Tourist Office** Parque Bolívar, opposite Cathedral, well-organized. **DAS Office** Carrera 23 y Calle 24.

**Airport** Manizales has a small airport, La Nubia, and the regional airline Aces provides an efficient and punctual service to Bogotá, Medellín, and Cali.

**Buses** New terminal with good restaurant, Calle 19 between Carreras 15 and 17. Buses to **Medellín**: Autolegal via Neira and Aguadas, 6 hrs., US$4.50; Empresa Arauca via Anserma, 10 hrs., 1st class, US$6.50 ordinary, US$4.50; colectivo to Medellín, US$8.55. Both routes offer impressive scenery, but the shorter route is largely unpaved between Aranzazu and La Pintada. Bus to **Bogotá**, 8-10 hrs. by Expreso Bolivariano Pullman, US$7, 9 hrs.; 7½ hrs. by Flota El Ruiz *buseta*, US$8.50—beautiful scenery. To **Honda**, US$3 (Expreso Bolivariano). Cali by bus Expreso Palmira, 5½ hrs., US$4.50 ordinary; Pullman 6 hrs., US$6. To **Cartago**, 4 hrs., every 20 mins., US$1.25; Pereira, Expreso Palmira, Expreso Trejos, hourly, 1¼ hrs., excellent road, beautiful scenery, US$1 ordinary. Armenia, Expreso Palmira, 3 hrs., US$2. **N.B.** Unlike in other places, town buses stop only at bus stops.

**Excursion** To see the full process of coffee growing, apply to the Comité Departmental de Cafeteros de Caldas, Carrera 22, No. 18-21, T 41706; recommended.

**Parque de los Nevados** national park includes **El Ruiz, Santa Isabel, El Cisne** and **Tolima**—all snow-capped peaks. Contact Inderena (National Conservation Institute) for details. To climb El Nevado del Ruiz, see Pereira, and under Ibagué for El Nevado de Tolima. We should be grateful for more information about Santa Isabel and El Cisne. Also La Laguna del Otún, where there is trout fishing by permission of Inderena. To reach park take Bogotá road, then branch road leads to (22 km.) viewpoint for Nevado del Ruiz. La Esperanza is the point to leave the main road for excursions towards the volcano.

**Roads** To Medellín direct, 265 km. via the winding mountain road through the picturesque towns of Salamina (*Residencia Puerto Nuevo*, F, opp. bus office, clean, good meals), Pácora and Aguadas, all perched on mountain ridges, to La Pintada (*Hostería Los Farallones*, C, nice pool, meals fair), but further if we go West across the Cauca river via Arauca, Anserma, *Riosucio* (a delightful old town with fine mountain views all round and a large colonial church next to the Arauca bus terminal; many restaurants, bars and shops); and then on to La Pintada. Manizales-Honda-Bogotá: all paved but in poor condition. The road climbs to 3,000 metres, with most superb scenery and little traffic. First accommodation is in Padua, then Fresno (cheap hotels), Mariquita and Honda. (See page 714).

## Chocó

*Quibdó*, the capital of Chocó Department, is a small, very friendly jungle town (pop. 41,000). There is a good museum at the Escuela Normal. Sunday market is attended by many Indians, some painted, who arrive by canoe. Boats can be hired for river trips; try Ruffo at the sawmill, US$20 an hour.

**Accommodation and Food** *Hotel Citará*, D; *Dora Ley*, F with bath, cheaper without, both with fan, rooms vary greatly in quality, meals available; *Pacífico*, E, good, with bath, its restaurant, *Club Náutico*, on 2nd floor has good food and views; several *residencias* including *Del Río*, E, and *Darién*; Carrera 4, G with bath and fan, only *residencia* with space to park motorcycle. Restaurant *El Paisa* rec.; *Chopán* bakery, good pastries and coffee.

**Transport** Quibdó can be reached (1) by bus from Medellín, US$6.75, 11 hrs.; (2) from Buenaventura by boat up the Río San Juan to Istmina and on by road (**see page 736**); (3) by plane from both Medellín and Cali and (4), much the best, by the **Río Atrato**: small speedboats go to and from Riosucio (not the Riosucio between Medellín and Manizales), US$40 p.p., large cargo boats go from Quibdó to Riosucio, Turbo and Cartagena (one week, US$35 p.p. inc. meals, warm clothes and blankets necessary at night, wash in river water, stops allow enough time to disembark and look around).

A road is planned from Quibdó to the Pacific Coast at **Bahía Solano**, good for skin-diving. This region has dense tropical rainforests which descend the mountain slopes to the sea. Several footpaths offer great natural beauty as the untouched forests begin at the beaches, or just beyond the villages. There are a number of lovely bays and beaches in the area, which is popular with Colombian tourists but is, as yet, relatively undiscovered by foreigners. The local population is mostly black, very friendly and honest. From Bahía Solano an 18 km. road runs to El Valle (transport US$1.25 p.p., allow several hours to find a car then an hour for the journey). From El Valle you can reach the natural park of **Ensenada de Utría**, US$5.35 round trip by boat. Alternatively you can walk; this takes 3 hrs. and, when you reach the bay, you have to wait either for a boat to take you to the Inderena office, or for low tide to walk across (1¼ hrs., through impressive tree roots). The whole walk can be wet and swampy as Chocó is one of the rainiest places on Earth (dry season end Dec.-March). Until *cabañas* are completed, staying overnight at Ensenada de Utría is not permitted, although, if you arrive very late, they may not send you back. Between October and November and at Easter-time, whales approach the shore. (We are grateful to Eckhart Harm of Tornesch, Germany, for much new information on Chocó.)

**Accommodation and Food** *Cabañas El Almendral*, 40 mins. by decrepit taxi from Bahía Solano, rec. for its setting on the Pacific, for river trips and accommodation, E p.p., book through Aces which runs the airlink. At Bahía Solano: *Hotel Balboa*, E; *Bahía*, F; ask for Estrella, who works in the tourist office at the airport, she has a private *hostal*, G p.p., and permits camping in her garden at US$0.90 p.p. (she is known in the village). 2 Youth hostels at Bahía Solano, details from Alcom in Bogotá. Camping space available at the *cabañas* in El Valle, US$0.90 per tent, but rain can be heavy. Eating is better in the *cabaña* zone in El Valle than in the village itself.

**Transport** Bahía Solano can be reached by air from Bogotá, Cali, Medellín or Quibdó (Satena, Aces); one way from Medellín US$35, from Quibdó US$16.50. If flights are full in high season (from Christmas to February), it is often possible to get a seat in Quibdó, which can be reached by land. Boats from Buenaventura to Bahía Solano, about US$20; **see page 699** for boats to Panama—these take passengers.

---

## THE CAUCA VALLEY (7)

Modern and colonial cities line the fertile but narrow Cauca valley, whose focus is Cali, the country's southern industrial centre. From here the Pacific port of Buenaventura is reached. The Pan-American Highway climbs out of the valley to Popayán, a richly historic city which gives access to the *páramo* of the Cordillera Central and the burial caves of Tierradentro—excellent walking country.

From Manizales a road runs S to Pereira (fine scenery) and then to Cartago, at the northern end of the rich Cauca Valley, which stretches S for about 240 km. but is little more than 30 km. wide. The road goes S up this valley to Cali and Popayán, at the southern limit of the valley proper. There it mounts the high plateau between the Western and Central Cordilleras and goes through to Ecuador. From Cali a railway (no passengers) and a road run W to the Pacific port of Buenaventura. The Valley is one of the richest in Colombia. From Cartago S the Río Cauca is navigable by barges up to Cali.

*Pereira*, capital of Risaralda Department, 56 km. SW of Manizales, stands overshadowed by green mountains, at an altitude of 1,476 metres, above the Cauca Valley. Population, 450,000; a centre for coffee and cattle. It is a pleasant modern city, founded in 1863, with an undistinguished cathedral and four parks: the best is the Parque del Lago, with an artificial lake; a fountain is illuminated several times a week. (Good Christmas illuminations, too.) There is a lively market. Outside it is a zoo (bus from town centre to zoo, US$0.06.)

**Hotels** *Meliá Pereira*, Carrera 13, No. 15-73 (T 50-770/53-970, Apartado Aéreo 4050), 5-star, A (taxes not included), restaurant, bars, swimming pool; *Gran*, Calle 19, No. 9-19, C, restaurant, bar, travel agency, etc.; *Res. Metropolitana*, Cra. 7 No. 17-21, E, hot water, TV, friendly, some noise; *Royal*, Calle 16, No. 7-56, F, with bath and hot water, clean, highly rec.; *Residencia Edén No. 1*, Calle 15, Carrera 10, near market, F, clean, friendly. Plenty of *residencias* in Calle 19, e.g. *Savoy*, F with bath. Youth hostel, *Centro Vacacional Viejo Caldas*, 10 mins. by car from Pereira, details from Alcom in Bogotá.

**Restaurants** *La Ricura*, Carrera 8, No. 22-21, very good meal, US$1.50; *El Manolo*, Calle 20, No. 8-22, which has good meals for over US$4 near the market; vegetarian restaurant *Naturista No. 2*, Calle 19, No. 5-73, good. *Pequeña Italia*, Fiducentro, Carrera 12, Calle 19, run by Mike Homyak, expat American, Italian and international good; *El Mirador*, on a hill overlooking the town (ask Tourist Office for directions), good food and views.

**Banks** Banco Anglo Colombiano, Carrera 9, No. 17-48. Banco Internacional. Open 0800-1130, 1400-1600, Mon.-Thurs., 0900-1130, 1400-1630, Fri. Last working day of month, 0800-1030.

**Transport** Matecaña airport is 5 km. to the S (bus, US$0.05). SAM and Avianca flights to and from Bogotá, Cartagena, Cúcuta, Medellín and San Andrés.

New bus terminal, clean, with shops, outside city centre. Bus to Armenia, 1 hr., US$1, a beautiful trip; to Cali, US$3.50, 4½-5 hrs.; Manizales, US$1, 1½ hrs.; to/from Bogotá, US$6.50, 7 hrs., rough journey, not recommended for motorbikes (bus route is via Girardot, Ibagué and Armenia).

**Excursion** 15 km. away, at Santa Rosa de Cabal, a poor 11-km. road branches off to Los Termales, where waters from a hot spring cascade down a mountain into a swimming pool, (unpleasant at weekends). There are also cold showers fed from a natural spring. The hotel (B) is overpriced and food in the restaurant is disappointing. Bus Pereira-Santa Rosa, US$0.20; then bargain for a jeep ride, US$4, to the springs. Package tours from Santa Rosa to Los Termales, including meals and one night's lodging, are available, but an afternoon excursion is the best value.

From Pereira, a 2-day excursion to the **Ucumari Park** is recommended. This is one of the few places where the Andean spectacled bear survives (but you won't see one). Above 4,000 metres in the park are spectacular *frailejón* plants. Hikes can be made to the Nevado del Ruiz (5,399 metres). Park guards run an excellent *refugio* (La Pastora, US$2 bunk bed, good meals, US$1.20, hot shower, very good). Take a bus from Pereira (Transportes Florida, Calle 12, No. 8-82) at 0900 and 1440, to El Cedral (1½ hrs.—return at 1130 and 1630), then walk 2 hours to the *refugio* through lush forest. Reservations for the *refugio* must be made in advance at El Lago, piso 12, Calle 25 between Carreras 7 and 8. We have no clear information on whether **Nevado del Ruiz** is safe to climb after the 1985 eruption which, apart from ejecting millions of cubic metres of dust, devastated the town of Armero to the east, killing over 25,000 people. Approximately 10% of the ice core melted, a major cause of landslides and mudflows.

**Armenia**, capital of Quindío Department, is in the heart of the Quindío coffee district; population 350,000; altitude 1,838 metres; mean temperature 19°C. This modern city, founded in 1889, is the seat of Quindío University. The Bogotá-Armenia-Cali road is fully paved, but slow through the mountains; fog at night, reckless drivers and stray animals make the Quindío Pass (3,350 metres) a hazard at night. A newer, more direct road from Armenia to Cali, joining the Panamericana S of Zarzal, has heavier traffic than the old road.

**Hotels** *Palatino*, Calle 21 at Cra. 14, E-D, central, comfortable; *Izcay*, Calle 22 with Cra. 14, D; *Residencial El Viajero*, opp. bus station, but 15 blocks from the centre of town, E; *Pensión Nueva York*, Carrera 19, No. 23-52, basic but clean and cheap, G; *Moderno Aristi*, Calle 18, Carrera 20, E, with bath, hot water, clean.

**Restaurants** *Frisby*, Carrera 16, No. 20-22, good pizza or fried chicken. Vegetarian: *Manjar*, Calle 18, No. 15-52 and *Rincón*, Carrera 16, No. 18-28, closed Sun.

**Archaeological Museum** Calle 21, No. 16-37; closed Sun.

**Airport** El Edén, 13 km. from city. Fog often makes air services unreliable.

**Transport** To Neiva, Flota Magdalena, 0100, 0400, 2230, US$4.75. To Ibagué, US$2. To/from Bogotá: Velotax bus, US$6, hourly, 9 hrs.; Velotax colectivo, US$8, 7 hrs. Daily **train** at 0630 to **Cali**.

Before the road drops into the Cauca Valley, between Armenia and Buga is *Sevilla*; *Hotel Estelar Sevilla*, good, B/C; *Residencias Soratama*, Cra. 49, No. 51-48, F, secure parking; others similar. 30 minutes' bus-ride from Armenia is Montenegro, a coffee centre (ask at FNC office on Plaza Bolívar about visits to *fincas* in the district); Plaza Bolívar is heavily wooded.

*Cartago*, 64,830 people, about 17 km. SW of Pereira, is on a small tributary of the Cauca river before it takes to the gorge separating the two *cordilleras*. Coffee, tobacco and cattle are the main products. Founded in 1540, it still has some colonial buildings, particularly the very fine Casa de los Virreyes. Visit the cathedral, with the cross apart from the main building.

**Hotels** Around Plaza Bolívar: *El Gregorio*, Carrera 5 y Calle 10, D, swimming pool, a/c; *Central*, Carrera 6, No. 11-51, G, basic; *Residencias El Dorado*, Carrera 6, No. 11-16, G. *Río Pul*, Carrera 2, No. 2-146, F, fan and bath, clean, rec. Many others in area around bus terminals (Carrera 9) and railway station (Carrera 9 y Calle 6); those in the same block as Flota Magdalena office are better value than the others.

**Restaurants** *Mullipán*, Carrera 6 y Calle 12, good cheap meriendas; *El Portal*, Carrera 6 y Calle 11, good churrascos.

**Post Office** on Plaza Bolívar.

**Cinema** Roblero, Calle 11 between Carreras 5 and 6 (opp. *Hotel El Gregorio*).

**Transport** Local **train** service to **Cali** via Zarzal, Tuluá (vegetarian restaurant *Vivamejor*, Carrera 26, No. 31-64, good), Buga, Palmira: *tren ordinario* at 0450 and 1405, US$2; *ferrobus* at 0625 and 1635, US$3 (crowded); 4-6 hrs., occasional derailments; on weekends and holidays, El Expreso Caleño at 1245. **Bus** to Cali, US$3.50, 3½ hrs.

About 27 km. S of Cartago is *La Victoria* (the Pan-American Highway bypasses it to the east), a pleasant, small colonial town with a shady plaza. There is a *Hotel Turista* (F, family atmosphere, clean and friendly, will change US$ cash), one block from the plaza, and several restaurants. La Victoria is in the centre of a scenic area where cattle are raised, and cotton, sorghum, maize and soya are grown. You can cross the Río Cauca by turning right off the road going to the south (good fishing Jan., Feb. and July) and 10 km. (paved road) further on is *La Unión* at the foot of the mountains on the west side of the valley. La Unión is a small agricultural town, a centre for grape production. *Residencia Los Arrizos*, and *Residencia El Cacique*. The countryside around offers good walks. Just south of La Unión is Rondanillo, a small town in the hot Cauca Valley, with a museum of paintings by the Colombian artist, Omar Rayo. A road runs E to the main highway at Zarzal.

About 50 km. S of Cartago is Zarzal, and 71 km. S again is *Buga*, an old colonial city of 75,220 people and a centre for cattle, rice, cotton, tobacco and sugar cane. Founded in 1650, and its modern Cathedral contains the image of the Miraculous Christ of Buga to which pilgrimages are made. N of Buga, at Uribe (50 km.), is the junction of the road S from Medellín with the one from Bogotá and Venezuela. Bus to Cali, US$1.50. Toll 22 km. S of Buga, US$0.40.

**Hotels** *Guadalajara* (swimming pool), D, rec., cabins for family groups, excellent restaurant and self-service cafeteria; *La Casona*, E, good; *residencias* around Cathedral usually good value. *Res. Palermo*, Calle 9, No. 9-82, G with bath, clean.

**Excursion** If you take the road from Buga to Buenaventura you come to the man-made Lago Calima. Taking the southern route round the lake, 42 km. from Buga is the *Hotel del Lago Calima* (D) set in very pleasant surroundings on the edge. There is no swimming pool, but some brave people swim in the lake, which is cold at about 16°C, and a kilometre deep. Closer to Buga on this road, before the Río Cauca, is the Laguna de Sonso Reserve, which is good for birdwatching.

47 km. from Buga is *Palmira*, in the Department of Valle; population, 163,000. Good tobacco, coffee, sugar, rice and grain are grown, and there is a College of

Tropical Agriculture. The Pan-American Highway runs direct to Popayán via Pradera, but the road through Cali is preferable. The best road S is from Palmira through Candelaria and Puerto Tejada, avoiding Cali, to Popayán; paved, straight, not much traffic. (Taxi connection with Cali, 29 km. south, US$5.55; bus US$0.45, Transportes Palmira, terminal on Calle 30, near Cra. 33)

**Hotels** *Residencias Belalcázar*, Calle 30, No. 31-29, F, with bath, G without, clean, friendly, good value; many other cheap places. **Restaurants** *Paradero los Parrales*, good breakfast, good service, clean loos.

At La Manuelita, 5 km. N of Palmira, is a famous sugar estate. Beyond La Manuelita any of 3 roads running E will reach, in 12 km., the fine restored colonial *hacienda* of El Paraíso, where the poet Jorge Isaacs (author of *La María*, a Colombian classic) lived and wrote. Entry US$0.50; there is a café. To visit the *hacienda*, take a bus from Palmira, corner of Cra. 25 and Calle 26, at 1230 (another in a.m.), which passes the *hacienda* ½-an-hour later (US$0.55); returns about 1515. 9 km. from El Paraíso is a sugar cane museum in the Hacienda Piedechinche (open 0930-1600, closed Mon.; admission, US$0.20), 42 km. from Cali, take a bus to Palmira, then taxi, or take bus from Cali to Amaime, a small place on the road to Cartago, US$0.60, then wait for bus to Santa Elena, which passes the turn off to the Hacienda. You can walk from Amaime: take the turning marked "El Paraíso" and walk for one hour to the turn off to the Hacienda (marked "Museo de Caño"), then it's another ½ an hour. There is no public transport connection between the two *haciendas*. Tours of this and Hacienda El Paraíso arranged by Comercializadora Turística Ltda, Carrera 4, No. 8-39, local 101, Cali (US$10, including transport, entrance fee, guided tour and lunch).

*Cali*, capital of Valle Department (1.6 million people), is the third largest city in Colombia, set in an exceptionally rich agricultural area producing sugar, cotton, rice, coffee and cattle. Altitude: 1,030 metres; average temperature: 25°C, hot and humid at mid-day but a strong breeze which blows up about 1600 makes the evenings cool and pleasant. It was founded in 1536, and until 1900 was a leisurely colonial town. Then the railway came, and Cali is now a rapidly expanding industrial complex serving the whole of southern Colombia. South of Carrera 10 are many one- and a few two-storey houses, tiled and wide-eaved. Through the city runs the Río Cali, a tributary of the Cauca, with grass and exotic trees on its banks. On one overlooking mountain, from which the best views are obtained, there is a statue of Christ visible for 50 km. and there are three large crosses on another mountain. The statue of Benalcázar, the city's founder, is worth a look, beautiful views of the city. It is also worth while going up the skyscraper Torre de Cali for a view of the city, but you have to buy an expensive meal as well. Two nearby *haciendas*, El Paraíso (see above under Palmira) and Cañas Gordas, have important historical associations.

The church and monastery of San Francisco are Cali's best buildings. Inside, the church has been renovated, but the 18th century monastery has a splendidly proportioned domed belltower. The 18th century church of San Antonio on the Colina de San Antonio is worth seeing and there are fine views. Cali's oldest church, La Merced (Calle 7, between Carreras 3 and 4), has been well restored by the Banco Popular. The adjoining convent houses two museums: Museo de Arte Colonial (which includes the church) and the Museo Arqueológico with precolumbian pottery (US$1, but well worth it). More Indian pottery can be seen in the Sociedad de Mejoras Públicas, across the street from La Merced; this collection belongs to the Universidad del Valle. Another church worth seeing is La Ermita, on the river between Calles 12 and 13. The orchid garden along the Río Aguacatal, near the centre, is well worth seeing.

The city's centre is the Plaza de Caicedo, with a statue of one of the independence leaders, Joaquín Caicedo y Cuero. Facing the square are the Cathedral, the Palacio Nacional and large office buildings. Across the river, which is 2 blocks from the Plaza de Caicedo, is the Centro Administrativo Municipal (CAM) and the main post office.

Although a centre of both guerrilla and counter-insurgency activity and drug and anti-drug operations, the atmosphere in Cali is quite relaxed. However, carry your passport (or photocopy—DAS approved) at all times and be prepared for police checks.

**Fair** Held during December; bullfights, masquerade balls, sporting contests. National Art Festival in June (painting, sculpture, theatre, music, etc.). Also in June Feria Artesanal at Parque Panamericano, Calle 5, handicrafts and excellent leather goods.

**Hotels** *Intercontinental*, Av. Colombia, No. 2-72, recently extended, tennis and pool, rec., *Los Farallones* restaurant with shows, good barbecues and buffets, A (weekend discounts); *Americana*, for businessmen, B, a/c, Carrera 4, No. 8-73; *Dann*, opposite *Intercontinental*, A, (with weekend discounts), service could be improved, but good; *Don Jaime*, Av. 6, No. 15N-25, B, good, restaurant rec.; *Menéndez*, Av. Colombia, No. 9-80, D, all rooms have own bath, good, reasonably priced meals available, nice old colonial building, popular with Colombians; *del Puente*, Calle 5, No. 4-36, D, with bath, clean, will store luggage, rec.; *Aristi*, Carrera 9, No. 10-04, 3-star, C, but weekend discounts, rec., large and old by Cali standards, turkish baths, rooftop pool, restaurant; *New York*, Calle 12, No. 3-62, D, clean, hot water, basic, near bus station and market; *Los Angeles*, Carrera 6, No. 13-109, E, good; *La Merced*, Calle 7, No. 1-65, D, swimming pool, pleasant young staff are very helpful, restaurant expensive, English spoken, rec.; *Hotel Residencias Stein*, Av. 4N, No. 3-33, B, full board, C, bed only, friendly, very good, quiet, excellent food, dinner for non-residents US$5, French, German and English spoken, Swiss-run, swimming pool; *Residencial Paseo Bolívar*, Av. 3 Norte, No. 13N-51 (T 68-50-67) and *Paseo Bolívar II*, Av. 3N, No. 13N-43 (T 68-28-63), both F, cold water, clean, safe (cheaper rates for long stay); *Bremen*, Carrera 6, No. 12-61, T 761998, some rooms with bath, F; *del Río*, Carrera 2 N, No.24-82. G p.p.; *Centralia*, Calle 31 near bus terminal, F, clean, safe; *Amoblador las Américas*, Calle 25, 2N-31, E with bath, F without, cold water, clean, safe; *Granada*, Calle 15 Norte, No. 4-44 (T 621477), F or E, but you are not given keys to rooms and your belongings are not safe, two *amobladores* next to it. It is possible to rent a furnished apartment in Cali for about US$45 per month.

**Restaurants** Cali is a good place for eating (but restaurants close early, and many close on Sun.): *Don Carlos*, Carrera 1, No. 7-53, excellent seafood, elegant and expensive; *Hostería Madrid*, Calle 9, No. 4-50, European specialities, good service, above-average price; *Restaurante Suizo*, Carrera 30 y Diagonal 29, Swiss, excellent fondue bourguignonne, pleasant atmosphere, reasonably priced; *El Quijote*, Carrera 4, No. 1-64, atmospheric, European dishes, expensive; *Simonetta*, Diagonal 27, No. 27-117, pleasant, reasonable, Italian dishes; *Dominique*, Av. 6N, No. 15N-25, good Italian food and service, reasonable; *La Terraza*, Calle 16, No. 6N-14, elegant, music and dance, nice atmosphere; *El Cortijo Andaluz*, Carrera 38 and Calle 53, atmospheric (converted residence), Spanish food; *Los Girasoles*, Av. 6N, Calle 35, steaks, other meat grills, good atmosphere; *Los Gauchos del Sur*, Calle 5 about Carrera 60, Argentine-style grilled meat, dancing, excellent food, very reasonable; *China*, Av. 6N, No. 24-52, excellent food and service, pleasant atmosphere, large servings for reasonable price; *Shanghai*, Av. 8N, No. 17-33, Chinese, excellent food in utilitarian setting, takeaway, very reasonable; *El Rancho*, S end of Av. 6, near municipal building, good local food, draught beer, pricey, closed Sun.; *Los Panchos*, Carretera a Meléndez with Autopista Sur, very good Colombian food, a favourite of Caleños; *Gloria*, Carrera 6, Calle 14, good and cheap; *Mauna Loa*, Centro Comercial del Norte, seafood a speciality, reasonably priced, Lebanese food too; *Mac Club*, Centro Comercial Imbanaco (Calle 5a and Carrera 39), hamburgers and hotdogs, excellent, cheap, good hamburgers also at *Primos*, near Calle 5, Carrera 34; *La Calima*, Carrera 3, No. 12-06, good meal US$1.30, always open; At least 10 eating places in the bus station, *Doble Vía* is the best.

Vegetarian: *Raices*, Calle 18N, No. 16-25, open Mon.-Sat. lunch and dinner, good; *Govindas*, Calle 14, No. 4-49.

You can find lots of European-style side-walk places along Av. 6 at good prices. Cheaper are the *fuentes de soda*, mostly with Colombian-style cooking, a decent meal for US$3-4. There are also *Masserna* on Carrera 7 between Calles 10 and 11 and *La Sultana*, Calle 10, on the corner with *Hotel Aristi*. Try their buñuelos (cheesy fritters) and the pandebono (cheesy buns) next door at *Montecarlo*. Cafés and ice-cream parlours abound near the university, across the river from the main part of town.

**Shopping** *Platería Ramírez*, Carrera 11b, No. 18-64, for gold, silver, brass, jewellery, table settings, etc. *Artesanías de Colombia*, Calle 12, No. 1-20 and for larger purchases Av. 6 N, No. 23-45. For boots and shoes *Chaparro* (Botas Texanas), Av. 6, No. 14N-14, T 651007, good, owner Edgar speaks a little English. Best shopping district: Av. 6N, from Río Cali to Calle 30 Norte.

**Bookshop** *Librería Nacional*, on main square, has a café. Bookstalls on the sidewalk on

Cra. 10 near Calle 10.

**Taxis** Black taxis are the most reliable; ensure that meters are used. Prices, posted in the window, start at US$0.11. On holidays an extra charge is made.

**Nightclubs** Locally known as "Grills". The ones along the Av. Roosevelt and along Calle 5a are safest and best known.

**Entertainments** Teatro Experimental, Calle 7, No. 8-63, T 781249; films Wed. nights at Centro Colombo-Americano (see below).

**Sports** Within its Villa Olímpica in San Fernando, Cali has three stadia: the Pascual Guerrero Stadium, holding 50,000 people, the Olympic Stadium, holding 7,000 people and the Piscinas Olímpicas, 3,000. Another stadium holding 18,000, the Monumental de Cali, is 10 minutes from the city on the road to Meléndez. Outside the city also is the new, first-class bull-ring.

**Museums** Museo de Arte Moderno La Tertulia, Av. Colombia, No. 5-105 Oeste (10 mins. from centre) has an exciting exhibition of S. American art, open Tues.-Sat. 0900-1300, 1500-1900, Sun. and holidays, 1500-1900. **Museo de Historia Natural**, Cra 2 Oeste, No. 7-18, pre-Colombian exhibits as well as biological specimens from the area, similar opening hours. Two other museums are mentioned in the introduction above.

**Parks and Zoos** Lovely walks and parklands stretch along both sides of the Río Cali. There is a zoo on the South bank some distance from the centre, entrance US$0.50. There is an orchid garden, Orchideorama, Av. 2N, No. 48-10, T 643256.

**Exchange** Banco Anglo Colombiano, Calle 11, No. 4-48 (Plaza de Caicedo), and agencies on Avenida Roosevelt and Av. 6; **Banco Internacional**; **Banco Royal de Colombia**, Calle 3; **Banco Francés e Italiano**; **Banco Colombo Americano** and other national banks. Open: Mon.-Thurs., 0800-1130, 1400-1600; Fri., 0900-1130, 1400-1630. Last working day of month, 0800-1130. Closed Sats. Money can be changed at Almacén Stella, Carrera 8, No. 9-64 (by *Hotel Aristi*) open 0800-1200, 1400-1800, or at travel agents.

**Consulates** Swiss: Carrera 5, No. 8-50. US Consul from Bogotá visits monthly at the centro Colombo-Americano, Calle 13N, No. 8-45, T 67-35-39. **British**, Ed. Garcés, Calle 11, No. 1-07, No. 409, T 783-2752. **Danish**, Av. 4 N, No. 4-46, T 614-368.

**Post Office** Adpostal for national service, Calle 10, No. 6-25; Avianca for international service, Calle 12N, No. 2a-27. **Telecom** Calle 10, No. 6-25.

**Tourist Office** Corporación Nacional de Turismo, Calle 12N, No. 3-28 (T 686972); regional office, Carrera 3, No. 8-39 (closed Sat. and Sun.). Maps, posters and general information. **DAS** office, Av. 3N, No. 50N-20 (T 643809). Also co-operative for shopping. There is a Thomas Cook office at Wagons-Lits, Cra. 4 No. 8-20. Good street map from municipal building just N of river at Calle 11.

**Rail** passenger services to **Cartago** (4 a day, 5 at weekends, US$3, 4 hrs.) and **Armenia**, 5 hrs. 15 mins., once a day; both trains go to Palmira and Buga.

**Buses** New bus terminal (connected by tunnel to railway station) is at Calle 30N, No. 2A-29, 25 mins. walk from the centre (leave terminal by the taxi stands, take first right, go under railway and follow river to centre). Hotel information available; good food at terminal. *Casa de cambio*, cash only. Showers on second level (US$0.40). There are plenty of local buses between the bus station and the centre, which charge US$0.06. Taxi from centre to bus station, US$2. Buses to **Popayán**, US$3, 2½-3 hrs., also colectivos. To **Pasto**, US$8, 9 hrs.; to **Ipiales** (direct), US$10, 12 hrs. or by Bolivariano Pullman, US$8, departures at 0400 and 0615 and 0800; Coomotor have a direct service to **San Agustín** via Popayán, Coconuco and Isnos, US$10.60, and a service at 0900 to San Agustín via La Plata (much slower than the new road via Isnos); Sotracauca also run Cali-Popayán-Coconuco-Isnos at 0500, 9 hrs., US$10. To **Cartago**, 3½ hrs., US$3.50; to **Ibagué**, US$6, 7 hrs.; to **Buenaventura**, US$3.15, 4 hrs.; to **Manizales**, US$4.50, 5 hrs.; to **Medellín**, US$8, 11-15 hrs.; to **Bogotá**, 10-15 hrs., by Magdalena (rec.) and Palmira, US$10 (sit on left hand side of the bus). *Busetas* (Velotax and others) charge about 50% over bus prices but save time; taxi-colectivos about 2½ times bus prices and save even more.

**Airport** Palmaseca, 20 km. from city, has *casa de cambio*. International standard, with good *Hotel Aeropuerto Palmaseca*. Frequent services to Bogotá, Medellín, Pereira, Ipiales, Cartagena, Barranquilla, San Andrés, Leticia (Mon., Wed., Fri.). Minibus from airport to bus terminal (2nd floor), every 10 minutes, approx. 30 mins., US$0.75. Colectivo to city about US$1; taxi, US$6. Direct flights (Avianca) to Panama; also to Miami and New York.

145 km. by road from Cali (4 hrs.) over a pass in the Western Cordillera is **Buenaventura**, Colombia's only important port on the Pacific. It was founded in 1540, but not on its present site. It stands on the island of Cascajal, 16 km. inside the Bay of Buenaventura. Beaches such as La Bocana, Juanchaco and Ladrilleros (many small hostels and restaurants) may be reached by motor launch, but they are not very safe. Trips to beaches cost between US$10-40 for 10-person launch (rate per launch, not per person).

Buenaventura is 560 km. by sea from Panamá, 708 km. by road from Bogotá. Population, 122,500, mostly black. Mean temperature, 27°C. It rains nearly every day, particularly at night; the average annual rainfall is 7,400 mm. (relative humidity 88%). There are still problems with malaria. The port handles 80% of Colombia's coffee exports, and 60% of the nation's total exports, including sugar and frozen shrimp.

The commercial centre is now entirely paved and has some impressive buildings, but the rest of the town is poor, with steep unpaved streets lined with wooden shacks. It is more expensive than Cali and it is difficult to eat cheaply or well. Festive atmosphere every night. S of the town a swampy coast stretches as far as Tumaco **(see page 747)**; to the N lies the deeply jungled Chocó Department, where the most important gold and platinum mines are found.

**Hotels** *Estación*, B, good restaurant; on Carrera 3 with Calle 3, *Del Mar*, C, restaurant, TV, phone in rooms, and *Balmoral*, E with bath. Several F and G hotels on Carrera 5, e.g. *Comfort*, a/c; *Colombia*, fan, *Felipe II*, a/c, D with bath, restaurant. *Bahía*, Calle 3, F, clean, friendly. *Gran*, E with bath; *Continental*, Carrera 5, No. 4-05, E with bath; opposite is *Europa*, F without bath.

**Camping** With the permission of the commandant, it is safe to camp in the police compound at the docks while awaiting your ship.

**Restaurants** *Los Balcones*, Calle 2 y Carrera 3, very good, but expensive. Self-service restaurant on main plaza, clean, modern, open 24 hrs. *La Sombrita de Miguel*, on road to El Piñal, good seafood, reasonable prices. Chinese restaurant in street leading NE from telephone building. Good seafood at Pueblo Nuevo market, but not very cheap.

**Exchange** Do not change money in Buenaventura, but in Cali.

**Tourist Office** Calle 1, No. 1-26, Mon.-Fri., 0800-1200, 1400-1800. Cámara de Comercio nearby is also helpful; has plan of city.

**Transport Air Services** Local airport only; flights to Cali.

The toll **road** to Cali is fully paved; the toll is about US$0.40 for cars and US$0.10 for motorcycles. The ordinary road is not paved. (Both give beautiful views of mountains and jungle, and from the old road you can reach the **Parque Nacional Farallones**. To reach the park, take the dirt road S from the plaza in Queremal, at 1,460 metres, about 1 hr. from Cali, 3½ hrs. from Buenaventura.) There are plenty of buses to Cali, US$3.15 each way, 3 hrs. Colectivos run at half-hourly intervals to Cali, US$4.75 p.p.

Grace Osakoda from Hawaii tells us that you can get from Buenaventura to Quibdó **(see page 729)** on the Río San Juan, but that boats are scarce out of Buenaventura (lumber boats from El Piñal only go about a day and a half upstream, and port authorities are strict about allowing passengers on cargo boats). One way is to take a bus from Pueblo Nuevo, Buenaventura, to San Isidro on the Río Calima (28 km., 6 hrs., terrible road), then a motorized dugout (*panga*) to Palestina on the Río San Juan. From there take a dugout going upstream; they rarely go as far as Istmina, which is connected by road and bus to Quibdó. Try to get as far as Dipurdú (no hotels, but friendly locals who offer sleeping space, shops with tinned goods), from where daily boats go to Istmina.

Shannan Shiell, from Glasgow, recommends a visit to the island of **Gorgona** which is about 150 km. down the coast from Buenaventura. Until a few years ago, it was Colombia's high security prison (a sort of Alcatraz), convicts were dissuaded from escaping by the poisonous snakes on the island and the sharks patrolling the 30 km. to the mainland. However, now it is a nature reserve, controlled by Inderena. All visitors, research students, scientists and tourists must obtain a (free) pass to go there. Facilities on the island are run by Inderena employees. It is virtually unspoilt with deserted sandy beaches and an abundance of birds (pelicans, cormorants, geese, herons) that use the island as a migration stop-over. There are paths to follow to see monkeys, iguanas, and a wealth of flora and fauna. Collect your own coconuts. You can stay in cabins on the island (US$5) and there is a restaurant with (naturally) a mainly fish menu. You can take your own food but all non-biodegradable items must be taken off the island.

To get there, apply for a pass at the office of Inderena in Buenaventura (their offices elsewhere in Colombia will advise you). There is a fair amount of paperwork, but persevere. Boats leave every 2/3 days in the evening from the El Piñal dock in Buenaventura. The trip, US$23 return, takes up to 10 hours depending on conditions. You can book a bunkbed in advance. You may be able to make arrangements in **Guapi** on the mainland to make the 1 hour boat trip free to Gorgona Island, and Guapi can be visited from Gorgona with Inderena staff going to the market.

Local basket-weaving is on sale, as are musical instruments such as the guaza (a hollow tube filled with seeds) and the marimba (about US$15). The only passable place to stay in Guapi is the *Hotel El Río* run by Pedro Arroyo, who speaks a little English, and his brother Camilo. The only way out of Guapi is by boat or by plane to Cali, US$36.

The paved Pan-American Highway (142 km.) runs S through the Cauca Valley from Cali to Popayán. (Toll, US$0.40.) It takes 2½-3 hrs. by bus through splendid scenery. At first we pass through a land of rich pastures interspersed with sugar-cane plantations. To left and right are the mountain walls of the two Cordilleras. The valley narrows and we begin to climb, with occasional glimpses E of the Nevado del Huila (5,750 metres).

**Warning**  All of rural Valle Department off the main roads is unsafe because of guerrilla activity. Similarly, Cauca Department E of the Highway is not recommended for tourists.

**Popayán** is in the valley of the Pubenza, at 1,760 metres, in a peaceful landscape of palm, bamboo, and the sharp-leaved agave. (Pop. 250,000.) The early settlers after setting up their sugar estates in the hot, damp Cauca valley, retreated to Popayán to live, for the city is high enough to give it a delightful climate. To N, S, and E the broken green plain is bounded by mountains. To the SE rises the snowcapped cone of the volcano Puracé (3,960 metres).

Popayán was founded by Benalcázar, Francisco Pizarro's lieutenant, in 1536. After the conquest of the Pijao Indians, Popayán became the regional seat of government, subject until 1717 to the Audiencia of Quito, and later to the Audiencia of Bogotá. It is now the capital of the Department of Cauca. The equestrian statue of Benalcázar on the Morro de Tulcán overlooks the city; it is worth climbing this hill, which is the site of a pre-Columbian pyramid, or even better the one with the three crosses on top, for the views. The streets of two-storey buildings are in rococo Andalusian style, with beautiful old monasteries and cloisters of pure Spanish classic architecture. Look for the Puerto Chiquito, a colonial bridge constructed in 1713 (Calle 6, Cra 2). it is said that Simón Bolívar marched over this bridge.

In March 1983, an earthquake devastated the city. Following restoration work, Popayán has come fully back to life and has managed to retain its colonial character. The Cathedral (Calle 5, Cra. 6) and the following churches are now open again: San Agustín (Calle 7, Cra. 6), Santo Domingo (Calle 4, Cra. 5, used by the Universidad del Cauca), La Ermita (Calle 5, Cra. 2), La Encarnación (Calle 5, Cra. 5), San Francisco (Calle 4, Cra. 9), El Carmen (Calle 4, Cra. 3). The town centre has been fully restored. Walk to Belén chapel, which is also open (Calle 4 y Cra. 0), seeing the statues en route, and then continue to El Cerro de las Tres Cruces if you have the energy, but best not to go alone (there are plenty of guides offering their services). Popayán was the home of the poet Guillermo Valencia; it has given no fewer than eleven presidents to the Republic.

The scientist Francisco José de Caldas was born here in 1771; it was he who discovered how to determine altitude by variation in the boiling point of water, and it was to him that Mutis (of the famous *Expedición Botánica*) entrusted the directorship of the newly founded Observatory at Bogotá. He was a passionate partisan of independence, and was executed in 1815 during Morillo's "Reign of Terror".

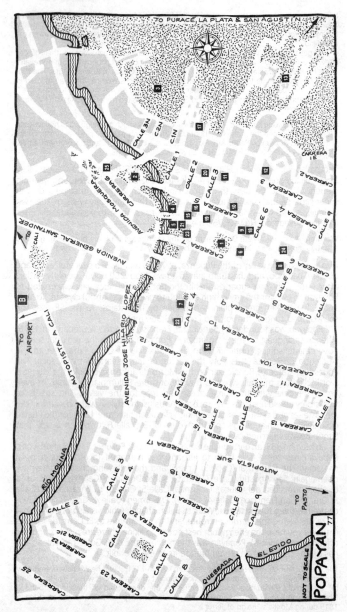

POPAYÁN

TO PURACÉ, LA PLATA & SAN AGUSTÍN

NOT TO SCALE

At weekends you will find people playing "sapo", see under **Sports** in **Information for Visitors**. A good place is along the La Plata road near Belén Church. During the week, the open markets are interesting—Bolívar market, Calle 1N, Cra. 5 is best in the early morning—local foods such as *pipián*, *tamales* and *empanadas*.

**Festivals** Easter processions, every night of Holy Week until Good Friday, are spectacular; the city is very crowded. The childrens' processions in the following week are easier to see. The children assume all the rôles of the official processions to the delight of parents and onlookers. As at Pasto (but less violent), there are the Día de los Negros on 5 Jan. and Día de los Blancos on 6 Jan.; drenching with water is not very common, but don't walk under windows when you see people on the first floor.

**Hotels** *Monasterio*, Calle 4, No. 10-50, in what was the monastery of San Francisco, lovely grounds, swimming pool, C, very good, T (939) 22191-6 with shower, pool open to non-residents, US$1.20. *Los Balcones*, Calle 3, No. 6-80, D, hot water, Spanish-style restaurant for breakfast and lunch (often closed), good, will change travellers' cheques; *Camino Real*, Calle 5, No. 5-59, T 21546/21254, P.O.Box 248, C, good service, excellent restaurant (try their 6 course dinner US$7), friendly, rec.; *Viajero*, Calle 8, No. 4-45, F, with bath, hot water, quiet, helpful, modern, highly rec; *El Príncipe*, Calle 8, No. 4-35, F with shower and hot water, rec; *Hostal Santo Domingo*, Calle 4, No. 5-14 (T 21676), D, with bath, friendly, good value, in recently restored colonial building; *Casa Grande*, Cra. 6, No. 7-11, T 35604/35908, E, family run, hot water, convenient, will store luggage, highly rec.; *Pakandé*, Cra. 6, No. 7-75, T 23846, F, clean, good beds, hot shower, rec.; *La Casona del Virrey*, Calle 4, No. 5-78, E, hot water, big rooms with bath, friendly, nice colonial house, warmly rec; *Casa Suiza*, Calle 4, No. 7-79, E, pleasant, hot water, clean but cockroaches; *Ermita*, near Capilla Ermita, E, private bath, TV, good breakfast, accepts Visa, rec.; *Residencias El Castillo*, Carrera 4 esq. Calle 1, D, bath and hot water, clean, very friendly, cafeteria and bar; there are many on Carrera 5 e.g. *Residencias Bolívar*, Cra. 5, No. 7-11, F, clean, pleasant, good restaurant, parking across street; nearby *Residencia Panamá*, G, good, hot water, good food, rec, doors close at 2200; *Residencias Cataluña*, Cra. 5, No. 8-27, F, clean, quiet, friendly; *Casa Familiar*, Cra. 5, No. 2-41, F, clean, good breakfast for US$1, hot water, family-run, no sign, highly rec. *Residencias San Agustín*, Cra. 6, No. 1N-15, behind the old bridge, clean, good beds, washing facilities; *Hospedaje Granada*, Cra. 6 near park, G, good value rooms and *comida corrida*; *Residencia San Diego*, just around the corner (turn right off Carrera 6), F, no hot water, but clean and safe, noisy from disco next door; *Plaza Bolívar*, Carrera 6N-12, F with bath, hot water, clean, safe, good value; many others in this area (around Parque Bolívar and market), but many are basic and/or brothels and the vicinity is dark.

**Restaurants** *Delicias Naturales*, Calle 6A, No. 18-21, good, cheap, vegetarian; *Café El Alamo*, Calle 3, No. 5-65, nice colonial atmosphere and good coffee; *El Pasaje*, Calle 3, Carrera 2, good, reasonably priced typical food; good value pizzas at *Don Sebastián*, Calle 3, No. 2-54, and *Nuevo Italiano*, Calle 4, No. 8-83, who also cater for vegetarians. For good lunches (US$1); *Punto Aparte*, Carrera 9, No. 6N-09; *Heladería Dinaro*, Carrera 5 y Calle 4, very nice, good breakfasts; *Pollo Pío Pío*, Calle 6, No. 8-11, good, friendly, open till 0300. On the continuation of Cra. 6 across the bridge from centre there are many cafeterias, bars and discos (good café: *Pitufos*, cheap, large menu). *La Brasa*, Calle 6, Cra. 6, has a set lunch and evening meal for US$1.20. *La Fontana*, Calle 6, between Carreras 7 y 8, excellent bakery with café serving meals and sandwiches.

**Bars** For music try *El Muro*, Calle 7, Cra. 6, or *Anarkos*, Calle 6, Cra. 5 for salsa. *El Trapiche 2* and *Maxim's* on the road out to Cali are the best nightclubs.

**Taxis** No meters; normal price within city is US$0.50, or US$0.60 at night.

**Museums** Now open (but not on Mondays): **Museo Negret**, Calle 5, No. 10-23, US$0.40, with works, photographs and furniture of Negret. **Museo Guillermo Valencia**, Cra. 6 y Calle

---

## Popayán: Key to map

1. Plaza Mayor/Parque Caldas; 2. Parque Mosquera; 3. Morro de Tulcán and Statue of Benalcázar; 4. Puente Chiquito; 5. Puente del Humilladero; 6. Cathedral; 7. San Francisco; 8. San Agustín; 9. La Encarnación; 10. Santo Domingo; 11. El Carmen; 12. La Ermita; 13. Belén; 14. Museo Negret; 15. Museo Guillermo Valencia; 16. Casa Mosquera; 17. Museo de Historia Natural; 18. Colegio Mayor de Cauca; 19. Tourist Office; 20. Telecom; 21. Banco de la República; 22. *Hotel Monasterio*; 23. *Hotel Los Balcones*; 24. *Hotel Casa Grande*; 25. Cheap hotel and Mercado Bolívar area.

3, birthplace of the poet; **Casa Museo Martínez**, Calle 3 out of town; **Museo Casa Mosquera**, Calle 3, No. 5-14; **Museo de Historia Natural**, Cra. 2, No. 1A-25. Small collection in **Banco de la República**. All others damaged and closed.

**Cinemas** Teatro Popayán, Calle 4, Carrera 8/9, best; Teatro Anarkos, Carrera 5, Calles 6/7. Teatro Bolívar, Calle 7, Cra. 3, shows black and white classics.

**Exchange** Banco de la República, Carrera 6, No. 2-78, is the only one that changes foreign currency and travellers' cheques, but will not give dollars change if changing a portion of a large bill. (Open 0800-1130; 1400-1600, Mon.-Thur., until 1630 on Fri.) However, the *Hotel Monasterio* will accept travellers' cheques when you pay your bill and will give you change in pesos. There is also **Salvador Duque** at Diana shop on the main plaza, near the cathedral. For US$ notes, change them with **Don Carlos Castrillón**, owner of *Hotel Los Balcones*, Calle 3, No. 6.80, for the best rate.

**Post Office** Carrera 7, No. 5-77. **Telephone Office** Telecom, Carrera 4 y Calle 3.

**Tourist Office** Carrera 6, No. 3-69, between Puente del Humilladero and Plaza Mayor (T 22251), has good maps of the city, prices of all hotels and pensions, and bus schedules and prices. Ask for Sra. Haydée Gasca de Varela about accommodation. They are very friendly and helpful, giving information on places of interest, will tell you where horses may be hired for exploring, and will store your luggage. In addition to normal hours, they are open Suns. until 1200. Ask at the Tourist Office about which areas of the city are unsafe. They also offer coffee, and sell local crafts; telephone and mail service. The Tourist Office and the Colegio Mayor de Cauca have details on art exhibitions and concerts. Try also the Casa de la Cultura, Calle 5, No. 4-33, for information on cultural events.

**Buses** Popayán has a new bus terminal, next to the airport, 15 mins. walk from the centre (Ruta 2-Centro bus, terminal to centre, US$0.10, or taxi, US$0.50). Luggage can be stored safely (receipt given); there is a charge to use the toilets, and a US$0.07 departure tax. From the bus station, turn left to statue of Bolívar, then take second right to Parque Bolívar; here are the market and cheap hotels. To/from Bogotá, US$15, 16 hrs. To Cali, US$3, 2½-3 hrs., or Velotax microbus, US$4.25, colectivos leave from the main plaza (US$3.50); to **Pasto**, with Coop de Nariño, Carrera 6, No. 2-16, 1130, Cootranar (cheapest, but not too reliable), Flota Magdalena, Exp. Bolivariano and Supertaxis del Sur, US$5, 5-8 hrs., spectacular scenery (sit on right); to **Medellín**, US$13.25, 16 hrs.; to **Ipiales**, something runs every hour but many buses arrive full from Cali, book in advance; Supertaxis at 1230, US$6, or bus, up to US$8.65 (Transportes Ipiales at 0700, Bolivariano at 0530 or 0900, the best), 7½-10 hrs. To **San Agustín** (confusing routes and schedules), La Gaitana, 11 hrs., at 0900 and 2000, Coomotor, 13 hrs., US$9 each once a day. Cootranshuila buses run over the new road via Isnos to San Agustín from bus terminal, twice a day (one at 1300), US$6, 6 hrs or more depending on the weather; also Sotracauca at 0900. Sit on the left side for the best views. To **Tierradentro** (Cruce de Pisimbalá), with Sotracauca, 5 a day between 0500 and 1500 (T 26-46), US$3, 4-6 hrs.; and goes to La Plata. Best to take the 0500 or 1000 bus, as the 1300 and 1500 will land you at the Cruce when it's dark, leaving you with a long unlit walk. Flota Magdalena to **La Plata**, US$3.75, 5 hrs., also Unidos del Sur (not via Tierradentro). To **Puracé**, US$1, 2 hrs. (Pullman is slightly more, Sotracauca at 0600, La Gaitana 0700, Coomotor later in a.m.) To **Silvia** (see below), daily Coomotorista *buseta* at 0800 (US$1.30) or: take Expreso Palmira bus to Piendamó on Cali road, every ½ hour, US$0.60; from there, colectivo to Silvia, US$0.70. On market day (Tuesdays) buses leave directly to Silvia at 1100.

**Air Services** Airport is 20 mins. walk from the centre. Service to Bogotá with Aires, usually daily at 0925. Daily flight to Ipiales with Intercontinental, 20 mins. flight at 0745 (office on main plaza). Avianca office for airmail, Carrera 7, No. 5-77.

**Excursions** A favourite is the drive northeast to Silvia, at 2,521 metres, one way through Totoró (partly paved) and the other through Piendamó (paved) two beautiful routes. In Piendamó there is *Hotel Central* behind the former railway station (E, clean, quiet, but has seen better days).

*Silvia* lies in a high valley. It is no longer an Indian town; the Indian market on Tues. mornings seems to be full of Otavalo Indians from Ecuador and their goods—more expensive than in Otavalo. The market is at its best between 0600 and 0830. Not much to buy, but very colourful. Guambiano Indian farms can be reached by local bus: ask for the "paradero de los Guambianos". A typical Indian settlement, La Campana, is ½ hour on the bus; 1½ hours' walk downhill back to Silvia. The Indians wear their typical blue and fuchsia costumes, and are very friendly and communicative. It is not safe to park cars in the street at night in Silvia, and guerrilla activity has been reported in the area. Horse hire from Sr. Marco A. Mosquiro, under US$1 per hour. On market days you can take a bus to Totoró (on the Popayán-Tierradentro road), departs 1200, US$0.50, and then a bus from Totoró to Tierradentro, US$1.25.

**Hotels** *Casa Turística*, E, helpful, good food; *Cali*, an old house, with good craft shop, E, including food, a little primitive, but very pleasant. *Ambeina*, F (3 beds per room), clean, friendly, efficient, rec., good meals; *Residencias La Villa*, about 200 metres up main road, G, basic but friendly, negotiate your price; *Cali*, F, good meals but poor plumbing. *La Parrilla*, F, water supply erratic, basic, restaurant has reasonable, cheap food. *Taberna El Buho*, friendly, with live music Sats. p.m.

For those who like to go off the beaten track, Sr. Camilo Arroyo (address: Carrera 3, No. 4-65, Popayán) arranges trips towards the coast, W of Popayán, for birdwatching or gold-panning (his family has a *finca* on the coast). He charges about US$50 a day p.p., depending on the length of the trip, size of the party, etc. His trips into the mountains are reported as less interesting—obtain full details before embarking on one.

**Road to Neiva** (page 717) from Popayán across the Central Cordillera, which is paved from Puerto Seco to Neiva, has interesting sights off it (best seen from left-hand side of the bus). Drive 37 km. along it (or take 0400, 0900 or 1100 bus, US$1) to the small town of *Puracé*, which has several old buildings. *Residencias Cubina*, F, clean, safe, friendly, cold showers, secure parking, no restaurant in the town but two stores will prepare meals on request. Drive to the Escuela and walk 5 mins. to see Chorrera de las Monjas waterfalls. About 11 km. E of Puracé towards Neiva a road branches S from the main road; 1 km. along this road is another fork at El Cruce de la Mina (bus 0530, US$0.50), the right branch leads to the Puracé sulphur mines (3,000 metres) 5 km. away; 1 km. along this road is a left fork to Pilimbalá, signed "Piscinas" (1½ km.) where are the Puracé National Park office, 5 warm sulphur baths in stone pools (which can be smelt a km. away), and a path leading to Puracé volcano. The Park is open all the week, but reduced service on Mondays. The volcano is steep; loose ash makes footholds difficult. It takes up to 5 hours to get to the top (4,646 metres). Close to the main road (which continues to La Plata), and more easily reached from El Cruce de la Mina are Laguna San Rafael (10 km. from Pilimbilá), the Cascada de Bedón (15 km), the Cueva de los Guácharos (26 km.), and the Termales de San Juan (17 km., but only 700 metres from the main road; cafeteria; entry US$0.10; 2 hrs. by bus from Popayán). 112 hot sulphur springs combine with icy mountain creeks to produce spectacular arrays of multi-coloured mosses, algae and lichens—a must if you are in the area. Buses on the Popayán-La Plata route go near Pilimbalá and will drop you near any of these places (fare from Popayán about US$1.50). The Tourist Office in Popayán will supply full information. The Park's fauna include the spectacled bear and mountain tapir. The only accommodation in the Park is at the thermal baths of Pilimbalá—cabins with up to six beds, D per cabin, up to 4 persons E, make reservations at Popayán Tourist Office (very cold, blankets and wood for the fire provided—rooms for 2 in the cellar can be hired at F rates); power goes off at 2200, but candles are provided. Camping costs US$3 p.p. and there are an expensive, but good restaurant/bar and a picnic area.

**N.B.** There has been some guerrilla activity in the areas traversed by this road.

Take warm clothes (and a sleeping bag) if climbing the volcano or visiting the baths (take towels); the nights are cold and blankets in the mountain cabins are thin. The weather is best, especially for climbing the volcano, in July and August, or between December and March. The highest point on the road is Quebrada Honda, at 3,340 metres above sea level.

*Coconuco*, at 2,734 metres, has beautiful landscapes. Turn to the right off the Popayán-Neiva road after 21 km. (16 km. short of Puracé); then 7 km. along is Coconuco (*Hotel de Turismo*; *Casa Familiar*, G, basic). There are good, clean and hot thermal baths near the village (entry US$0.35, camping US$1.50; *chiva* from Popayán may take you part of the way up if you ask. There is a track from town which is quicker than the road). Drive on 12 km. to the impressive scenery of the Paletará highland, where you can traverse vast areas of primeval forest; a bus to the village of Paletará takes 1 hour and costs US$0.40. Bus from Coconuco to Popayán, US$1, 1 hr, 1600 and 1700. The direct 130-km. road from Popayán to San Agustin (**see page 720**) through Coconuco was opened in March 1985.

The Tierradentro Archaeological Park, (see below), can be reached from Popayán, or San Agustín via *La Plata* (20,000 people), 147 km. from Popayán, 210 km. from San Agustín. Direct bus service with Coomotor from La Plata to Bogotá, 10 hrs., at 0900 and 2100.

**Hotels** *Berlin*, by church on square, 4 blocks from the bus office, E with bath, F without, friendly, but unappealing toilets and bugs in the beds; next door is *Residencias Tunubalá*, F, OK, friendly; *Brooklyn*, clean, F, and *Norteño*, in the same price range; *Pensión Murucuju*, basic place to sleep and eat; *Residencias Nariño*, F, *Viajero*, opp. Sotracauca office, G, basic but convenient; *La Familia*, F, dirty, unfriendly.

**Restaurants** *Es Aquí*, good meals for US$2; *Noche y Luna*, just off main square, very good. There is a café in the house where Bolívar stayed in 1829. *Patolandia*, good, cheap fruit juices. There is a cinema (2030).

From La Plata drive 35 km. NW to Guadualejo where one road goes N to Belalcázar (12 km.—a dusty drive). Another road continues NW to *Inzá* (17 km.); hotels *Inzá* and *Ambalá*. Nine km. before Inzá is the Cruce de Pisimbalá, sometimes known as the Cruce de San Andrés, where a road turns off to San Andrés de *Pisimbalá* (4 km.), the village at the far end of the Tierradentro Park.

At Pisimbalá there is a unique and beautiful colonial church with a thatched roof; for the key ask behind the church. Some few km. before reaching Pisimbalá you pass the Tierradentro Museum of indigenous culture, hours: 0700-1100 and 1300-1700, entrance US$0.40, camping is not allowed. Make sure you see both parts of the museum.

At the archway directly opposite the museum or at Pisimbalá village you can hire horses (US$2 an hr. or less, but make sure they are in good condition)—or you can walk—for visiting the *Tierradentro* man-made burial caves painted with geometric patterns. There are four cave sites—Segovia, El Duende, Alto de San Andrés and El Aguacate. The main caves are now lighted, but probably as well to have your own torch. If you don't have one, try to borrow one from the park administration office. Entry US$1.10. The surrounding scenery is splendid. It is very crowded at Easter-time.

For people on a one-day visit: go to Segovia, which has over 20 tombs, 5 of which are lit (these 5 are not opened until 0800-0900). Nos. 9, 10 and 12 are best decorated; Nos. 8 and 28 are also impressive. The site is a 20 min. walk uphill from the administration building. El Duende (two of the four tombs are very good), is 15 mins. beyond Segovia. El Aguacate is a 2 hrs. hike one way, and one can return via El Alto de San Andrés (Nos. 1 and 5 tombs the best—the guards at Segovia and El Alto are very helpful). Take water with you.

At El Tablón in the Parque there are 8 stone statues. There are several more in the new plaza at Inzá. A beautiful area for walking. From behind El Tablón, you can walk back to the museum via El Duende and Segovia in 2½ hrs. The surroundings have spectacular natural beauty; see small Indian villages in the mountains, e.g. Santa Rosa, 2 hours' hard walk beyond El Duende (get exact directions before setting out).

The Páez Indians in the Tierradentro region can be seen on market days at Inzá (Sat.), Pisimbalá (Wed.), and Belalcázar (Sat.); all start at 0600. The second floor of the museum at Pisimbalá is dedicated to their work: not to be missed. Take bus (US$0.50) from Tierradentro to Inzá market, on Sat. (buses leave from 0200); best to go into Pisimbalá and out again to be sure of getting a seat. On Saturdays there is plenty of transport going to and from Inzá on the Tierradentro road.

**Hotels at Tierradentro** A short way up from the museum, state-owned *Albergue de San Andrés*, E, good, restaurant and swimming pool (also available to non-residents, US$0.80). Houses on either side of the Albergue offer accommodation, F, meals for US$1.50; green house next to museum, 2 rooms available, G, clean, friendly, rec.; *Residencia Turista*, in the village, basic, clean, F p.p., insufficient bedding; *Hospedaje El Viajero*, Sra. Marta de Angel, F, friendly, meals US$1.20 excellent; between Pisimbalá and museum, *hospedaje* of Sra Pola Angel de Velasco; *Hospedaje Lucerna*, next to museum, clean and friendly, F, showers, quiet, free coffee and fresh orange juice on request, highly rec., will let you camp for US$0.50. Other cheap accommodation in village: *Residencial Pisimbalá*, "opposite the museum and up a bit", F, good, clean, set meal; *Residencias El Viajero* (Marta Veláquez), F, meals US$1, clean, friendly, rec. *Residencia El Bosque*, F, cold showers, cheap meals, friendly dueña collects coins, rec.; *Residencias Murujuy*, F (breakfast, US$0.65, lunch and dinner, US$1); *Residencias Las Veraneras*, F p.p. 2 houses, 300 metres from Archaeological Park, rent rooms for US$2 p.p., clean, run by friendly young couple, restaurant, attractive garden and murals painted by locals. *El Gauchito* in Pisimbalá village, F, clean, pleasant, family atmosphere, meals available, rec.; camping.

**Restaurants** *Pisimbalá*, good food, cheap, rec.; good fruit juices at the *Fuente de Soda y Artesanía* store. The house of Nelli Parra de Jovar, opposite the museum with the long antenna, is rec. for abundance; you must book meals in advance. She can also give up to date information on accommodation. At Dalia's home, *Su Repuesto*, almost opp. *Hosp. Lucerna*, good meals for US$1.25, again best to arrange in advance.

**Transport** The road from Popayán to Tierradentro is difficult and narrow, but this is compensated by the beautiful scenery. In late 1990 three buses a week ran from Pisimbalá to **Popayán**, Mon., Wed., Fri., 0800, but on other days they went from Gruce (schedule from Popayán to Pisimbalá unknown). Sotracauca buses from Popayán, US$3, 4-6 hrs. to **Cruce Pisimbalá**; take one of two morning buses as the two afternoon ones land you at the Cruce after dark. Walk (about 2 km.) from there to the museum. The village is another 20 mins. walk from the museum. Bus Cruce Pisimbalá-Popayán, 0600 (unreliable), 0800 and 1300, 5 hrs. If you want to go to **Silvia**, take this bus and change to a colectivo (US$1) at Totoró. There are buses on market day, or trucks (US$1). Buses from Tierradentro to **La Plata** leave at 0900 and 1500 (unreliable) from the Cruce, US$2, 3 hrs.; if you cannot get a direct Cruce-La Plata bus, take one going to Belalcázar (US$1), alight at Guadualejo from where there is a more frequent service to La Plata; or one can hitch. On Fri. only, a bus leaves from Pisimbalá village for La Plata at 0400. Similarly, on Fri. only, a bus from La Plata to Pisimbalá goes at 1200, otherwise the only La Plata-Tierradentro bus (Sotracauca) leaves daily at 0500 for Inzá; alight at Cruce (2½ hrs.). Private jeep hire La Plata-Tierradentro, US$27.50, or less if you agree to pick up other passengers. The road follows the spectacularly beautiful Páez valley. Buses from La Plata to Neiva and Bogotá.

From San Agustín, take Coomotor at 0600 to **La Plata**, 5 hrs., US$3.50, or La Gaitana at 0530 or 1600. Next morning, take the 0500 Sotracauca bus from La Plata to Cruce de Pisimbalá, arrives 0800 (continues to Inzá and Popayán). Alternatively, on arrival in La Plata, take a pick-up to Guadualejo (US$1), then hitch, or try to get a bus going past Tierradentro (about 3 per day). Buses from La Plata to San Agustín at 0700, 0900 and 1500, and to Popayán at 0500 (Sotracauca).

Another site of archaeological interest is *La Argentina*, best reached from La Plata (some direct buses), 8 km. off the La Plata-Popayán road. Gillian Handyside writes; It is set in beautiful surroundings but is largely ignored by the archaeological authorities and the tourist board. The Museo Arqueológico de la Platavieja contains statues and ceramics as interesting as those found at San Agustín. Ask for Sr. Carlos Hernández, who runs the museum almost singlehanded and is extremely knowledgeable about the archaeological aspects of the area. (He also keeps bees, and sells honey.) The Universities of Los Andes, Cauca and Pittsburg run an archaeological project at La Argentina during the dry season: contact Carlos Hernández for details.

---

## SOUTHERN COLOMBIA (8)

---

# From Popayán to Ecuador, including the mangrove swamps of the Pacific coast and the Amazonian-type lowlands of the Río Putumayo.

The Pan-American Highway continues S from Popayán to Pasto. The entire road is now paved, but very poor between Popayán and El Bordo. After El Bordo (*Hotel*

*Patia,* E, fan, cold water, rec.; *Residencias Confort,* on main road, F, simple but recommended) the road improves, taking a new route and the 294-km. drive takes 5 hrs. The express bus takes 7 hrs. in ordinary conditions, though landslides often block the road. 93 km. S of Popayán is a tourist complex including hotel, swimming pool and campsite.

If one has time, the old route via La Unión and Mercaderes can be done by bus; enquire at Popayán or Pasto bus terminals. There are three basic hotels at La Unión.

143 km. S of Popayán is **Mercaderes**, a small town with a pleasant climate. Hotels (F) are good and the *Restaurante Tropical* is recommended. 30 km. before Pasto is Chachagui, where the *Hotel Imperio de los Incas* is recommended, E with bath, friendly, swimming pool, 2 km. from Pasto airport. Toll N of Pasto US$0.30.

**Pasto,** capital of the Department of Nariño, stands upon a high plateau (2,534 metres) in the SW, 88 km. from Ecuador, with a population of 370,000. The city, which retains some of its colonial character, was founded in the early days of the conquest. Today it is a centre for the agricultural and cattle industries of the region, which exports little. Pasto varnish (*barniz*) is mixed locally, to embellish the strikingly colourful local wooden bowls. A visit to the church of Cristo Rey (Calle 20 y Carrera 24) near the centre is recommended. Also La Merced, Calle 18, is worth seeing for its rich decoration and gold ornaments. From the church of Santiago (Carrera 23 y Calle 13) there is a good view over the city to the mountains, San Felipe (Calle 12 y Carrera 27) has green tiled domes. The interior courtyard of the municipal building on the main square (corner of Calle 19 and Carrera 24) has 2 tiers of colonnaded balconies. The Banco de la República, Calle 19, No. 21-27, has a small, free museum, library and auditorium.

During the new year's *fiesta* there is a Día de los Negros on 5 Jan. and a Día de los Blancos next day. On "black day" people dump their hands in black grease and smear each other's faces. On "white day" they throw talc or flour at each other. Local people wear their oldest clothes. Things can get quite violent. On 28 December and 5 Feb., there is also a Fiesta de las Aguas when anything that moves—only tourists because locals know better—gets drenched with water from balconies and even from fire engines' hoses. In Pasto and Ipiales (**see page 749**), on 31 December, is the Concurso de Años Viejos, when huge dolls are burnt; they represent the old year and sometimes lampoon local people. On Suns. a game of paddle ball is played on the edge of the town (bus marked San Lorenzo) similar to that played in Ibarra, Ecuador.

During the wars of independence, Pasto was a stronghold of the Royalists and the last town to fall into the hands of the patriots after a long and bitter struggle. Then the people of Nariño Department wanted to join Ecuador when that country split off from Gran Colombia in 1830, but were prevented by Colombian troops.

**Hotels** *Morasurco,* Avenida de los Estudiantes, B, rec., reasonable restaurant; *Zorocán,* Calle 18, No. 22-33, C, bath, TV, a/c, indifferent restaurant; *Sindagua,* Calle 20, No. 21B-16, D, rec.; *Cuellar's,* Carrera 23, No. 15-50, D, roomy, well-furnished, new, some noise from bowling centre underneath, but rec.; *El Duque,* Carrera 20 between Calles 17 and 18, E, including TV and shower, comfortable, rec.; *Mayasquer,* Av. de las Américas, 16-66, E, with bath, clean, friendly, restaurant; next door at No. 16-40 is *Juanambú,* E, friendly, clean, safe, F for rooms without bath, rec. *Isa,* Calle 18, No. 22-33, E with bath, clean, helpful, safe, 100 metres from bus station; *Residencias Colón,* Carrera 22, No. 19-61, F, clean, friendly, hot water; *Mallorca,* Calle 18, 21a-45, F, pleasant, hot water a.m.; *Nueva York,* Carrera 19 bis, 18-20, F, clean rooms, dirty toilets, hot shower, friendly, near Magdalena bus company, the only place in the town where you can put a motorcycle inside; *María Belén,* Calle 13, No. 19-15, clean, safe, quiet, friendly, hot water; *Cartagena* , near bus station, cheap, adequate, and others in F price range; *Manhattan,* Calle 18, 21B-14, F, clean, pleasant, hot water old-fashioned, big rooms, rec.; *Embajador,* Calle 19, No. 25-57, F, quiet, private bath, patio where you can park motorbikes; *Residencia Indi Chaya,* Calle 16, No. 18-23 (corner of Cra. 19 and Calle 16), T 4476, F, good value, clean, good beds, carpets, hot water, safe; *Residencias Galeras,* Calle 17, nr. bus station, F, hot water, communal bath, clean, safe; *Residencia Santa Isabel,* Calle 19, No. 20-39, F, clean, close to bus station. *Viena,* clean, Carrera 19B, No. 18-36, G, cheap and near bus station.

**Restaurants** *El Chalet Suizo,* Calle 20, 41-80 (T 4419), high class food; *La Esquina del*

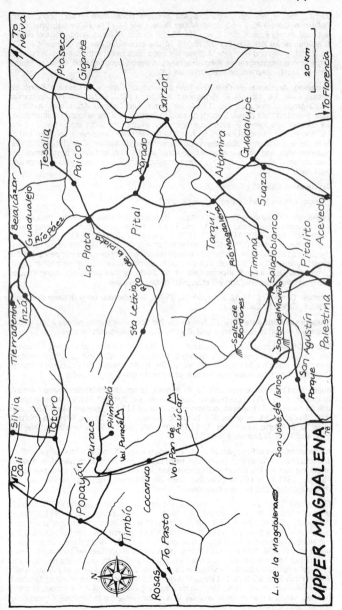

*Barril*, Calle 19, No. 28-12, good; *Viena*, opposite *Hotel Nueva York*, good, cheap; *Pollorrico*, Carrera 25, 17-50, good. *Mister Pollo*, Calle 17 y Cra. 26, central, good, clean fast food. *Punto Rojo*, Calle 17, No. 21B-38, self service, 24 hours, good choice of dishes; *El Mundo de los Pasteles*, Cra. 22, No. 18-34, cheap *comidas*; *Rancho Grande*, Calle 17, No. 22-03, cheap and open late. A cheap but good place to eat is the self-service cafeteria at the Amorel shopping centre. *Riko Riko*, near bus station, good fast food; similar *La Espiga* close by. Most restaurants on main street are OK.

**Shopping** *Artesanías de Colombia* have a branch on Carrera 25. *Casa del Barniz de Pasto*, Calle 13, No. 24-9, *Artesanías Nariño*, Calle 26, No. 18-91; *Artesanías Mopa-Mopa*, Carrera 25, No. 13-14, for *barniz*. See *Colegio Artesanías*, run by a government institute (Sena), 5 km. N on road to Popayán. Visitors welcome. Leather goods are cheaper here than in Bogotá, Ecuador or Peru. Most of the shops are on Calles 17 and 18. Also try the municipal market for handicrafts. *Mercado Campesino*, southern end of Calle 16, esq. Carrera 7. *Supermercado Confamiliar de Nariño*, Calle 16b, No. 30-53, recommended, and, more convenient, *Ley* on Calle 18, next to Avianca postal office. On main square (Calle 19 y Cra. 25) is a new shopping centre with many types of shops and restaurants.

**Drycleaners** Calle 18 y Carrera 27.

**Cinema** Carrera 25 and Calles 17 and 18, good.

**Exchange** For changing travellers' cheques, **Banco de la República** on the main square. **Banco Anglo Colombiano**, Calle 17, No. 21-32, and at Amorel, and other national banks. Open Mon.-Thur., 0800-1130, 1400-1600; Fri., 0900-1130, 1400-1630; closed Sat. Last working day of month, 0800-1100. If going to Tumaco, this is the last place where travellers' cheques can be cashed. A *cambio* off the main square will change sucres into pesos, but the Banco de la República will not, though it does change Amex cheques without charging commission. **Optica San Francisco**, Calle 19, No. 24-86, by the main square, changes sucres into pesos and vice versa, and will change US dollars into either.

**Airmail** Carrera 23, 18-42 and Calle 18, 25-86. **Telephones** Long distance calls from Telecom, Calle 17 y Carrera 23.

**Ecuadorean Consulate** Calle 17, No. 26-55, 2nd floor. Four photos needed if you require a visa (but this office is not very knowledgeable about requirements for visas).

**Tourist Office** Just off the main square, Calle 18, No. 25-25, friendly and helpful, but closed Sat.-Sun. It will advise on money changing. **Maps** of Colombia and cities from Instituto Geográfico Agustín Codazzi, Calle 18, No. 23-36, 1st floor (Banco del Occidente building). The **DAS** office in town will give exit stamps if you are going on to Ecuador.

**Buses** Most buses leave from Calle 18. **To Bogotá**, 23 hrs., US$19.50 (Bolivariano Pullman). To **Ipiales**, 2 hrs., US$2, Cooperativo Supertaxis del Sur; by bus, US$1.50, sit on left hand side for the views. To **Popayán**, ordinary buses take 10-12 hrs.; expresses take 5-8 hrs., cost US$5. To **Cali**, US$8, expresses, 8½-10 hrs. To **Tumaco**, 11 hrs. by bus, 10 hrs. by minibus, US$6.50. To **Puerto Asís**, 11 hrs., US$4.75 with Trans Ipiales or Bolivariano (both Calle 18), 0500 and 1100. To **Mocoa**, 8 hrs, US$4.

**Air Services** Daily to **Popayán**, 20 mins., and **Bogotá**, US$55; to **Cali** with Avianca at 0800, and to **Ipiales** by Avianca on Fri. Aerotal, Pasto to Cali, daily at 0800; to **Medellín**. Avianca to **Leticia** via Cali. The airport is at Cano, 40 km. from Pasto; by colectivo (beautiful drive), 45 mins. US$1.90 or US$11.35 by taxi. There are no currency exchange facilities, but the shop will change US$ bills at a poor rate.

**Excursions** There are some gold mines in the area. The volcano, Galeras (4,276 metres), overlooks Pasto to the W. Quiescent since 1934, it began erupting again in 1989. Check at the tourist office on whether it is safe to climb on the mountain and whether you need a permit. A highway traversing all kinds of altitudes and climates has been built round it; the trip along it takes half a day. A rough road goes to the summit where there is an army post guarding a TV relay station. A taxi (arrange previous day, if possible) will take you to about 200 metres from the top; there is a fine view and the soldiers are glad to see people. If you can't get a taxi, take a bus to the village of San Vicente, then hitch as far up as you can, which will probably leave a 3-hour, but pleasant walk to the top. On it lies the village of *Sandoná* where Panama hats are made; they can be seen lying in the streets in the process of being finished. Sandoná market day is Saturday. (It is a worthwhile trip to Sandoná, 4 buses daily, the last back to Pasto is at 1700.)

## Tumaco Region

The 250-km. road W from Pasto to Tumaco is paved for 20 km. beyond Túquerres, but is then unsurfaced and subject to landslides—check in Pasto. The region is very different from highland Colombia, with two-storey Caribbean-style wooden houses and a predominantly black population. Small farms are mixed with cattle ranches, rice farms and oil-palm plantations. Cocoa is grown. The coastal area around Tumaco is mangrove swamp, with many rivers and inlets on which lie hundreds of villages and settlements; negotiate with boatmen for a visit to the swamps or the beautiful, newly- developed island tourist resort of **Boca Grande**, US$7.50 minimum, the trip takes 30 mins.; ask for Señor Felipe Bustamante, Calle Comercial, Apto. 224, T 465, who rents canoes and cabins, has a good seafood restaurant and owns *Hotel Los Manglares* on the island, where water and electricity supplies are irregular.

**Tumaco** has a population of about 100,000; the unemployment rate is very high, the living conditions are poor, and the services and roads in the town are not good. It is in one of the world's rainiest areas; the yearly average temperature is in the 25-35°C range. The movement of the tides governs most of the activities in the area, especially transport. A natural arch on the main beach, N of the town and port, is reputed to be the hiding place of Henry Morgan's treasure. Swimming is not recommended from the town's beaches, which are polluted; stalls provide refreshment on the beach. Swimming is safe, however, at El Morro beach, north of the town, only on the incoming tide (the outgoing tide uncovers poisonous rays). Hotels are well subscribed and of varying quality: it is advisable to get a bed early in the day. The northern part of the town is built on stilts out over the sea. Visit it during the daylight as it is reported to be dangerous at night, and not just because you could fall through the holes in the wooden pavements into the sea. The area is also noted archaeologically for the finds associated with the Tumaco culture. The town has problems with water and electricity supplies. There is one cinema. There are no money exchange facilities (except in some shops that will buy dollars and sucres at a poor rate; change money in Cali or Pasto).

**Hotels** *Villa del Mar*, D, Calle Sucre, modern, clean, with shower, toilet and fan, no hot water, good café below; *Claudia*, Calle Mosquera, E, with restaurant; *Residencias Don Pepe*, near water-front and *canoa* dock, friendly but basic; *Porvenir*, G, far from luxurious, most of the family friendly. Children meet arriving buses to offer accommodation; most cheap places are in Calle Comercial, many houses and restaurants without signs take guests—nearly all have mosquito nets. Try opp. Trans Ipiales, under Cootranor sign, or 2 doors from Trans Ipiales (Barbería Nueva), both F. **Food**: The main culinary attraction of the town is the fish, in the market and restaurants, fresh from the Pacific. A number of good restaurants on the main streets, Calles Mosquera and Comercial. **N.B.** Be very careful of food and water because there are many parasites.

**Transport** Tumaco to **Pasto**, 11 hrs. (10 hrs. by minibus), US$6.50, with Supertaxis del Sur or Trans Ipiales (better), 4 a day, very rough but interesting ride. An alternative is to catch a bus from Ipiales to Espino (US$0.60, colectivo, US$0.90) and there change buses for Tumaco (US$4, 7½ hrs., rough ride). There are no hotels in Espino. There are daily **flights** to and from **Cali** with Aces and on Wed., Fri. and Sun. with Satena, 1 hr. Flights also to **Pasto**.

**To Ecuador** It is possible to travel to Ecuador by water, but only by motorized canoe. Part of the trip is by river, which is very beautiful, and part on the open sea, which can be very rough; a plastic sheet to cover your belongings is essential. Take suncream. Daily service at 0800 to San Lorenzo, 7 hrs. (but can take 14) US$6.50, Coop. de Transportes, tickets from Calle Comercial (protective plastic sheeting provided). Señor Pepello, who lives in the centre of Tumaco, owns two canoes: he leaves on Wed. and Sat. at 0700 for San Lorenzo and Limones in Ecuador—book in advance. Also enquire for Señor Lucho, or ask around the water-front at 0600. DAS stamp for leaving Colombia should be obtained from the **DAS** office in Tumaco, Calle Sucre, No. 6-13, office open on weekdays only. Visas for Ecuador (if required) should be obtained in Cali or Pasto. Entry stamps for Ecuador must be obtained in the coastal towns.

120 km. from Tumaco is Junín where you can turn north, and in 57 km. come to the interesting town of **Barbacoas**, a former Spanish gold-producing centre which still retains the remains of an extensive water-front, a promenade and steps coming down through the town to the river. Gold is still panned from the rivers by part-time prospector-farmers. *Hotel Telembi*, F, basic, friendly; *Residencial*, F, poor, unfriendly. Restaurant *Telembi* on the river front, good food. Problems with water and electricity supplies. River trips on the supply boats are possible, about US$6.75 for 8 hrs. Bus to Pasto, US$6, rough trip. The road to Barbacoas is limited to one-way traffic in places— enquire at the chain barring the road at Junín and the operator will telephone down the line to see if the route is clear for you to pass.

## The *Putumayo*

One hour E of Pasto, on the road to Mocoa (capital of the Intendencia of Putumayo) is **Laguna La Cocha**, the largest lake in S Colombia (sometimes called Lago Guámez). By the lake is the Swiss-run *Chalet Guámez*, D, well recommended, particularly for the cuisine, cabins sleeping up to six can be hired, US$23; free van-camping allowed. Rafael Narváez has cheap, basic rooms to let. The chalet will arrange a US$22 jeep trip to Sibundoy, further along the road. Boats may be hired for US$2.20 per hour. La Cocha may be reached by taking a bus to El Encano and walking the remaining 5 km. Or walk 20 mins. from the bus stop to the fishing village of El Encano, where you can enjoy trout at very low prices at one of the many small restaurants, and from here take a *lancha* to the chalet for US$2-3. There is also a government hotel nearby, *Sindamanoy*, C, chalet style, good views, inviting restaurant with good but expensive food, free van-, and tent camping allowed with manager's permission. From the hotel you can take a 10-minute boat trip to the Isla de la Chorota nature reserve; interesting trees, but little wildlife. Taxi from Pasto, US$11.

The road from Pasto to the Putumayo deteriorates rapidly after El Encano. It is dangerous between Sibundoy and El Pepino and care should be taken, but there is a magnificent view out over the Putumayo by a large statue of the Virgin, just before the final descent.

**Sibundoy**  There is a beautiful church on the main plaza, completed in 1968. About a quarter of the valley is now reserved for Sibundoy Indian occupation. Market Sunday. Best handicraft shop is Fudak, Calle 16 No. 16-73, a cooperative run by the Kamza Indians. Also Marcelino Chindoy, Carrera 18, 18-66, who travels a lot around Colombia and can normally be found at handicrafts fairs in Bogotá. Roasted guinea-pig (*cuy*) may be eaten in the restaurant here. Bus from Pasto (3 hrs., US$2.25), passing through Colón (*residencias*) and Santiago.

**Hotels and Restaurants**  *Hotel Turista*, F, clean; *Oriente*, F, pleasant, with restaurant, best value in town; better meals at *Hotel Sibundoy*, also F; *Restaurant Viajero*, just off main street. You can camp in the hills, where there are lovely walks and you can see all kinds of flora and fauna.

**Mocoa**, the administrative capital of the Intendencia of Putumayo, is small (21,000 people), with a number of hotels (*Viajero*, D; *Central*, off main plaza, F, very clean and friendly) and *residencias*, e.g. *Residencia Colonial*, Carrera 6, No. 8-10, G, spartan but safe. The town has a very modern square, new offices and modern developments. Sugar-cane is grown in the area. The road to Puerto Asís is good, passing through a recently cleared area supporting cattle ranching. 8-12 hrs. by bus from Pasto, US$4; bus to Pitalito, 7 hrs., US$7, also jeeps. Bus from Sibundoy, US$2, 5 a day, continuing to Puerto Asís; a few police checks, a bit hair-raising in places, but stunning scenery between Sibundoy and Mocoa ("some of the best in Colombia").

**Puerto Asís** is the main town and port of the Putumayo. River traffic is busy. All boats that leave for Leticia (with connections to Manaus) are cargo boats, and only sail when they have cargo. Those carrying gasoline (and most do) are forbidden to take passengers. Only one company, Navenal, normally takes passengers, and it can be weeks between their sailings. One can also try the army for a passage. Fares are about US$100; at least 8-10 days; it is best to see the Jefe de la Marina, or the Oficina de Transporte Fluvial, about a passage. Another possibility is to take a *canoa* to Leguizamo (see below), and try for a passage there. By boat to Leguizamo takes 2-3 days, US$4.50, food US$2.50 per day. For those interested in flora and fauna it is necessary to travel down river, beyond new areas of settlement. Boats will not go unless the rivers are high; sometimes, they get stuck halfway.

There are regular flights to and from Puerto Asís three times a week by Satena to Bogotá, via Florencia. Flights to Florencia are on Mon., Wed. and Fri. at 1000 with Sarpa, who also fly to Leguízamo. Occasional flights to Leticia.

**N.B.** Puerto Asís is a marketing centre for cocaine.

**Hotels** *Residencias Nevado*, Carrera 20, close to the airport, well kept and comfortable, air-conditioning optional, F, without board. *Residencias Liz*, Calle 11, F, with bath, very friendly; *Residencia Volga*, Calle 10, No. 23-73, F, basic, safe; *Residencias Patiño*, G, rec.; *Residencias Gigante*, Calle 10, 24-25, F, clean. There are plenty of cheap hotels in the port, but it is hard to find a room late in the day.

**Buses** may be taken to **Pasto** (a 10 hr. journey, at 0500, 0600 and 0900 daily, on mostly mountainous roads, US$4.50, be prepared for military checks). Bus **Sibundoy**-Puerto Asís, US$3.25. Five buses a day to **San Miguel**, 4 hrs., near the Ecuadorean border (US$3) where the Sun. market provides a meeting place, and where *canoas* may be hired to visit villages 2-4 hrs. away on the river.

*San Miguel* There are several very basic hotels, e.g. *Mirador*, F, safe and *Residencias Olga* which has 6 single rooms. Accommodation away from the river is non-existent, except in Orita, W of Puerto Asís, a small town on the oilfield. You can cross to Ecuador from here, get your exit stamp from the DAS office in Puerto Asís or Mocoa. The boat trip up the San Miguel river via Puerto Colón to La Punta takes 1/2 hour and costs US$1.50. There is a bus to Lago Agrio (US$0.60).

*Leguízamo*, downstream from Puerto Asís, can also be reached by air from Florencia, with Satena, daily, flight originates in Neiva. A national park (**Parque Nacional de Paya**) has been established between Puerto Asís and Leguízamo, but so far in name only. There are boats to Leticia and to Peru, but transport on all boats carrying gasoline is forbidden. For information go to Naval at the port, Transporte Fluvial Estrella del Sur (Carrera 27, off Calle 10) or Transporte Fluvial Amazonas (Carrera 20, 14-59—English spoken). Hotels: *Leguízamo*, *Madrago*, *Marlene*, *Viajero*, *San Pablo* and *Caucaya*, all G, basic. *Caucaya* is reported comfortable with very nice owners. Further downstream are El Encanto and the nearby village of *San Rafael*, which is a good place to see the Huitoto Indians, a four day trip by launch, the most important of the many tribes which live along the Putumayo river. At San Rafael there is a mission at which it is possible to stay.

It is possible to carry on down the Putumayo which now forms the boundary between Colombia and Peru, then crosses into Brazil, becoming the Río Iça to join the Amazon at Santo Antônio. Leticia is 300 km. upstream on the Amazon towards Peru. From El Encanto to Leticia is about 10 days, but getting a passage beyond the Brazilian border is problematical. The border town is *Tarapacá* (airport). There is a basic *Residencial*, plenty of spiders and mosquitoes. It can be quite cold at night.

We are informed that travellers interested in Amazonian plants, birds and animals will find Putumayo more accessible, with more abundant wild life, than Leticia. Restaurant food in the Putumayo region is often uninspiring; take some canned goods for variety. There is a road of a sort from Mocoa to Puerto Limón, on the Río Caquetá (see Caquetá section, **page 721**).

## South to Ecuador

Passing through deep valleys and a spectacular gorge, buses on the paved Pan-American Highway cover the 84 km. from Pasto to Ipiales in 1½-2 hours (toll US$0.40). The road crosses the spectacular gorge of the Guaitara River near El Pedregal, 40 km. from Pasto. A detour via Túquerres (part unpaved) and its plain takes over an hour more; it reaches 3,050 metres at Túquerres, dropping to 2,440 at Guachucal, and rising again to 2,740 metres at *Ipiales*, "the city of the three volcanoes", with about 30,000 people; famous for its colourful Friday morning Indian market. The Catedral Bodas de Plata is worth visiting.

If you have time, a visit to the nearby Sanctuary of the Virgin of *Las Lajas* is definitely recommended. On days set apart for religion, dazzlingly clean Indians come down from the hills in their traditional bright colours. Seen from afar the Sanctuary is a magnificent architectural conception, set on a bridge over the canyon: close to, it is very heavily ornamented. The altar is set into the rock face of the canyon which forms one end of the sanctuary. There are great pilgrimages to it from Colombia and Ecuador (very crowded at Easter) and the Church must be second only to Lourdes in the number of miracles claimed for it. The Church recognizes one only. Colectivo from Carrera 6 y Calle 4, Ipiales, US$0.30 p.p., taxi, US$5 return (it's about a 1½-hour walk, 7 km.); 3 basic hotels and a small number of restaurants at Las Lajas. Try local guinea pig and boiled potatoes for lunch.

**Hotels** *Mayasquer*, 3 km. on road to frontier, D, modern, nice restaurant, very good, swings for children, discothèque, T (9304) 2643; *Central*, Carrera 6a, 14-48, E, pleasant, clean; *Nueva York*, Calle 13, No. 4-11, near main square, G, run down, friendly; *Colombia*, Calle 13, No. 7-50, F, hot water, mice but otherwise quite clean, parking for motorbikes; opp. at No. 7-59 is *Valparaíso*, F, hot water; *Korpawasi*, Carrera 6, No. 10-47, E, good food, plenty of blankets; *India Catalina*, Carrera 5a, No. 14-88, G, new, hot shower, good value, 2 blocks from main plaza; *Oasis*, Cra. 6, No. 11-34, 1 block from main plaza, G, shower, ask for hot water, clean, helpful; *Belmonte*, Carrera 4, No. 12-111 (near Transportes Ipiales), F, very clean, hot water, rec., but crowded; *Residencia Tequendama*, Carrera 5, No. 14-08, F, family atmosphere, very basic; *San Andrés*, Carrera 5, No. 14-75, F, clean, TV, hot water; same street, No. 14-25, *Residencias Santa Fe*, F. Young travellers can expect to be questioned and searched by police soon after checking in to a hotel.

**Camping** Possible above the bus parking lot, or free behind last Esso station outside town on road north.

**Restaurants** *Don Lucho*, Carrera 5, No. 14-13 (*antioqueño*); *Greenhouse*, Carrera 6, No. 16-73, good, reasonable prices. Plenty of cheap restaurants. Meals in Almacenes Ley cost US$1. Many good bakeries on Carrera 6, or *Panadería Galaxia*, Calle 15, No. 7-89, for a good cheap breakfast.

**Cinemas** 2 on Calle Principal on road to Las Lajas.

**Museum** Small, set up by Banco de la República.

**Exchange** It is possible to cash travellers' cheques only at the **Banco de la República**, a few blocks from the main square (closed 1100-1400); you will have to show two different pieces of identification and may have to recite passport number from memory. *Casa de Cambio* at Carrera 6, No. 14-09. There are money changers in the street and on the border, but they may take advantage of you if the banks are closed. Better rates are to be had in Quito. There is an agency of **Banco Anglo Colombiano**, Carrera 6, 3 blocks from main square.

**Frontier** Ipiales is 2 km. from the Rumichaca bridge across the Carchi river into Ecuador. The frontier post stands beside a natural bridge, on a new, concrete bridge, where the customs and passport examination takes place from 0800 to 1800.

You obtain your Colombian exit stamp from the DAS at the frontier post. You have to get your entry stamp and tourist card for Ecuador at the frontier; if the border office is closed, you must go to the police station just before Tulcán. This applies at weekends, closed 1200-1400; taxis on the fast road to the border do not pass the police station. There is an Ecuadorean consulate at the Rumichaca bridge, open weekdays. Ecuadorean officials do not usually give more than 30 days for visiting the country, but extensions are easy to obtain, from Amazonas 2639, Quito and the Migración offices in provincial capitals. Motorists have their *carnets* stamped at the border (very efficient). You may be required by Ecuadorean customs to show that you have enough money for your stay in the country. There can be long queues crossing into Ecuador.

Colombian customs have the same basic requirement of US$20 a day (US$10 for students), though you are not always required to show that you have this amount. Entering Colombia, tourist cards are issued at the frontier, and there is no need, if driving your own vehicle, to go through Tulcán: take the road signed Rumichaca. If entering Colombia by car, the vehicle is supposed to be fumigated against diseases that affect coffee trees, at the ICA office at the border; the certificate must be presented in El Pedregal, a village 40 km. beyond Ipiales on the road to Pasto. (This fumigation process is not always carried out.) There is a duty-free shop about ½ km. from the border. There are frequent police checks on the buses going to Popayán and neighbouring areas.

**Transport** From Ipiales to **Tulcán**: colectivo 6 blocks from main park (waits till all seats are full), US$0.25 to the frontier (buses to Ipiales arrive at the main park—they may take you closer to the colectivo point if you ask). Colectivo from frontier to **Tulcán** US$0.75 after bargaining (ask the fare at the tourist office at the border); to go to bus terminal, take blue bus from central plaza, US$0.05. Taxi to border, US$2 after bargaining; from border to Tulcán, US$2. From Ipiales airport to the border by taxi, about US$5.50; to centre of Ipiales US$3.25.

From Tulcán's modern bus terminal, which is some distance from the town centre, buses go to Quito throughout the day; a beautiful five-hour Andean trip.

Bus to **Popayán**, Expreso Bolivariano, US$7, 7½ hrs., hourly departures, 0430-2030; Transportes de Ipiales, US$7 (neither on main square, best to take taxi from border), Super Taxis and Cootranar *busetas*, US$6, beautiful trip. Bus to Cali, US$8-10, 12 hrs. To **Pasto** with minibus from main square, US$2 (frequent police checks); Flota Bolivariano buses every hr., US$1.50, 1¼ hrs. Buses to **Bogotá** leave every other hour between 0500 and 0830, US$20 (note, if coming from Bogotá, there is an hour's stop in Cali; bus leaves from a different level from which it arrived).

San Luis airport is 6½ km. out of town. "Intercontinental" flights to/from Bogotá daily. TAME (of Ecuador) has flights to Quito from Tulcán. Mon.-Fri. at 1245.

---

## INFORMATION FOR VISITORS

**Documents** A passport is always necessary; an onward ticket is officially necessary, but is not always asked for at land borders. Nationals of the following countries do not need visas or tourist cards: Argentina, Austria, Barbados, Belgium, Brazil, Costa Rica, Denmark, Ecuador, West Germany, Finland, Holland, Ireland, Italy, Japan, Liechtenstein, Luxemburg, Netherlands Antilles, Norway, Peru, Portugal, St. Vincent and the Grenadines, South Korea, Spain, Sweden, Switzerland, Trinidad and Tobago, UK, Uruguay. You are given 90 days permission to stay on entry. An extension (*salvoconducto*) for a further 30 days can be applied for at the DAS office in any major city. Application must be made within 3 weeks of the expiry of the first 90 days and two weeks are needed for authorization from the Ministerio de Relaciones Exteriores in Bogotá. The 30-day extension runs from the day authorization is received by the DAS office (so if you apply on the last of your 90 days you could get 45 days more). Leaving the country and re-entering to get a new permit is not always allowed. Citizens of those countries not listed above need a visa or tourist card (free). Normal validity for either is 90 days; extensions must be applied for at the Ministerio de Relaciones Exteriores in Bogotá. Whether you need a tourist card or visa depends on your nationality, so check at a Colombian consulate in advance. Tourist cards are issued by CNT offices (in New York, or Caracas, for instance), or by Colombian airlines or authorized foreign carriers. Visas are issued only by Colombian consulates. A visa is required by U.S. and Israeli citizens (for example), who must be prepared to show 1 photograph, an onward or return ticket, as well as a passport (allow 48 hours). Alternatively, in the USA only, Avianca issues tourist cards (transit visas), valid for 15 days, costing US$10—these cards are renewable only by leaving the country. In Miami insist at the Consulate, as they will assume that you can work it all out through the airline. U.S. citizens who arrive in Colombia by air from a third country without a visa must get a tourist card on the plane, otherwise they will be fined. Citizens of Asian, African, Middle Eastern and socialist countries (including Cuba), must apply at least 4 weeks in advance for a visa. You may find that your onward ticket, which you must show before you can obtain a visa, is stamped "non-refundable". If you do not receive an entry card when flying in, the information desk will issue one, and restamp your passport for free. Visitors are sometimes asked to prove that they have US$20 for each day of their stay (US$10 for students). Note that to leave Colombia you must normally get an exit stamp from the DAS (security police). They often do not have offices at the small frontier towns, so try to get your stamp in a main city, and save time.

**N.B.** It is highly recommended that you have your passport photocopied, and witnessed by the DAS (about US$0.20). A notary can also do this. This is a valid substitute (although some travellers report difficulties with this variant), and your passport can then be put into safe-keeping. Also, photocopy your travellers' cheques and any other essential documents. For more information, check with DAS or your consulate.

**Airport Taxes** There is an airport exit tax of US$15, from which only travellers staying less than 24 hours are exempt. When you arrive, ensure that all necessary documentation bears a stamp for your date of arrival; without it you will have to pay double the exit tax on leaving (with the correct stamp, you will only be charged half the exit tax if you have been in the country less than 30 days). Visitors staying more than 60 days have to pay an extra US$10 tax, which can only be avoided by bona-fide tourists who can produce the card given them on entry. There is a 15% tax on all international air tickets bought in Colombia for flights out of the country (7.5% on international return flights). It is not possible to avoid the purchase tax by buying tickets outside the country, as the charge is included automatically. Do not buy tickets for domestic flights to or from San Andrés island outside Colombia; they are much more expensive. When getting an onward ticket from Avianca for entry into Colombia, reserve a seat only and ask for confirmation in writing, otherwise you will pay twice as much as if purchasing the ticket inside Colombia.

**Travel by Air** British Airways has a twice weekly service from London to Bogotá, via Caracas. Airlines with services from continental Europe are Air France, Iberia, and Lufthansa. Avianca, the Colombian national airline, flies from Frankfurt via Paris, Madrid and Caracas.

Frequent services to and from the U.S. by Avianca and American, the latter from Miami only, daily to Bogotá and Cali, 4 a week to Barranquilla. The cheapest flight from Miami to Bogotá is via Panama with a couple of hours' stopover with Air Panama. Another cheap route is Miami-San Andrés, then take a domestic flight to your Colombian destination. You can save up to US$50 this way going from Miami to Bogotá. Other flights from Miami: Avianca to Cartagena, Barranquilla, Pereira, Medellín, Cali, and San Andrés; Ladeco to Bogotá.

**From Neighbouring Republics** Lacsa flies from San José to San Andrés and Barranquilla. To Mexico City with Avianca and Varig from Bogotá. Sahsa flies to San Andrés from Honduras and Panama, 4 times a week. SAM flies from Bogotá and San Andrés, to San José, and Guatemala City daily. Fares between Central America and Colombia are cheaper with a change in San Andrés, rather than direct.

If flying from Guatemala to Colombia with SAM, via San José and San Andrés, you have to purchase a round-trip ticket, refundable only in Guatemala. To get around this (if you are not going back to Guatemala) you will have to try to arrange a ticket swap with a traveller going in the other direction on San Andrés. There is, however, no difficulty in exchanging a round-trip ticket for a San Andrés-Colombian ticket with the airline, but you have to pay extra. Lacsa, Copa, Air Panama, Avianca, SAM and others fly from Panama to Colombia; do not be persuaded by SAM desk at Panama airport to buy an onward ticket out of Colombia—this may not be needed—if you fail, SAM in Bogotá will give refunds: first you must go to the DAS, Extranjería section, show your passport and ticket and obtain a permit for a refund; then go to the SAM office. **Colombia-Panama** with Copa: one may not enter, or obtain a visa for, Panama without a return or onward ticket, so you must buy a return ticket and then sell half in Panama once you have purchased a flight ticket out of Panama, or purchase a Panama-San José ticket and get your money back, less the tax. Obtaining refunds is time consuming and you will not get your money in dollars outside Panama. **Motorcycles** may only be sent cargo; remove oil, petrol, battery and anything breakable. In Panama, cargo companies are: Copa to Barranquilla (T-Panama-384290), Girag (T 645685/384326) to Medellín and other cities, Translatin (T 384001) to Bogotá and Cali, Lac (T 384439) also Cali. Retreiving your motorcycle may take up to 2 days, but paperwork costs as little as US$10. The cheapest way to fly to Quito is to fly to Ipiales (Intercontinental from Bogotá), cross the border by road and take another 'plane at Tulcán. Avianca, Iberia, Lufthansa, Air France, Aeroperú, Viasa, Ladeco and Ecuatoriana go S from Colombia. Avianca and Viasa fly

Bogotá-Caracas.

For a cheap means of flying from Venezuela to Colombia, **see page 683.**

**Customs**  Duty-free admission is granted for portable typewriters, radios, binoculars, personal and cine cameras, but all must show use; 200 cigarettes or 50 cigars or 250 grams of tobacco or up to 250 grams of manufactured tobacco in any form, 2 bottles of liquor or wine per person.

**Internal Air Services** are flown principally by Avianca, SAM, Aces, Aires, Satena and Intercontinental. They serve the whole country, the larger towns and cities receiving flights usually daily, the smaller places perhaps only once a week. Avianca offers a round ticket (*Conozca a Colombia*) giving unlimited domestic travel for 30 days on Avianca or SAM; conditions are that it allows up to ten stops, it must be bought outside Colombia in conjunction with an international air ticket, children up to 12 pay 50%, infants are free, the Air Pass is non-refundable unless the whole has been unused, one may not pass through each city more than once (except for transfers), and a proposed itinerary (not firm) must be submitted when buying the ticket (Leticia and San Andrés may be included). There are three prices: US$325, available all year, not open to Colombians or residents abroad, may be used in conjunction with any transatlantic carrier; US$224, available all year, open to Colombians legally resident abroad, passengers must fly Avianca transatlantic; the third pass, US$190, is available for 8 days use only, and cannot be used in June, July, August or December, open to Colombians legally resident abroad, Avianca must be the transatlantic carrier. For single flights, the army airline Satena tends to be cheaper than Avianca. Avianca's domestic shuttle flights (Puente Aéreo) go from Bogotá to Medellín/Montería, Cali/Pasto and Barranquilla; for example to Medellín every ½ hour between 0730-1630. But it is best to book a ticket as for an ordinary flight: just turning up will involve a long wait. Stand-by tickets are available to Barranquilla, Cali, Medellín; known as PET, *pasajero en turno*. Domestic airports are good, though the tourist facilities tend to close early on weekdays, and all Sundays. In-flight service and airline services on the ground tend to be poor.

**Buses**  Travel in Colombia is far from dull. The buses are generally fairly comfortable. Air-conditioned buses are often very cold (so take a sweater), or very hot (because the a/c has broken down, and the windows cannot be opened). The curtains may be down to keep the bus cool and/or to allow passengers to watch the video (so not much good for sightseeing); if you are not keen on crime thrillers, or Rambo, take a walkman, or insist on finding a bus without a video, or one where it is broken—there usually is one! The luggage compartment is normally locked, but it is wise to keep an eye on your bags. Breakdowns are many. In all parts, police checks on buses are frequent. Note that meal stops can be few and far between, and short; bring your own food. Be prepared for climatic changes on longer routes. A full colectivo, such as a "Taxi Verde", costs only twice as much per person as a bus seat. The excellent minibus (*buseta*) services of Velotax have been recommended. If you entrust your luggage to the bus companies' luggage rooms, remember to load it on to the bus yourself; it will not be done automatically. There are few interdepartmental bus services on holidays. Always take your passport (or DAS-approved photocopy) with you: identity checks on buses are frequent.

**Taxis**  Whenever possible, take a taxi with a meter, and ensure that it is switched on, otherwise you will be overcharged. All taxis are obliged to display the additional legal tariffs that may be charged after 2000, on Sundays and fiestas. If a taxi has a meter, do not haggle the price; if it does not (and most taxis on the N coast do not), fix a price beforehand. Don't take a taxi which is old; look for "Servicio Público" on the side. Women do not travel alone in taxis at night. If the taxi "breaks down", take your luggage out if you are asked to push, or let the driver push; it may be a trick to separate you from your luggage.

**Motoring** Roads are given in the text. Motor fuel: "premium" 95 octane (only in large cities), about US$0.70 per US gallon; "corriente" 84 octane, US$0.55 per US gallon. Diesel prices are similar. Roads are not always signposted. If driving yourself, avoid night journeys; vehicles may be unlighted and it can be dangerous. The roads are often in poor condition, lorry- and bus-drivers tend to be reckless, and stray animals are often encountered. Police checks are frequent, keep your documents handy. There are frequent tolls, Us$0.50-1; motorcycles don't have to pay. In town, try to leave your car in an attended car park (*parqueadero*), especially at night. If you are planning to sleep in your car, it is better to stop in a *parqueadero*; you will be charged a little extra. In many guarded carparks, only the driver is allowed in; passengers must get out at the entrance.

National driving licences may be used by foreigners in Colombia, but must be accompanied by an official translation if in a language other than Spanish. International drivers licences are also accepted. To bring a car into Colombia, you must also have a valid, third-party insurance policy, documents proving ownership of the vehicle, and a tourist card/transit visa. These are normally valid for 90 days and must be applied for at the Colombian consulate in the country which you will be leaving for Colombia. Details of length of stay and car specifications will be sent to Bogotá and customs at the border, where the document should await your arrival. Carry driving documents with you at all times.

**Car hire** is very expensive in Colombia. Even if you are paying in cash, a credit card may be asked for as proof of identity (Visa, Mastercard, American Express), in addition to passport and driver's licence. Main international car rental companies are represented at principal airports but may be closed Saturday p.m. and Sundays.

**Motorcycles** can be brought in by sea. In 1990 one correspondent shipped two Yamaha XT500 bikes from Hamburg to Santa Marta with Grancolombiana (Agenty Gebrüder Specht, Hamburg) for US$225 each. The cost was by cubic metre, so they were knocked down to use as little space as possible. It took 3 days to clear customs at a cost of US$50 but only passports and shipping documents required. (Bringing a bike in by land only takes a few minutes). One year's stay permission granted, and INTRA issued national driving license against international driver's licence. Spare parts, tyres, etc. readily available in Colombia for Yamaha XT and Honda XL models (although supplies are less good for models over 500 c.c.), so Colombia is a suitable country for rebuilding a bike on a long trip. It took another correspondant 2 days to clear a bike coming from Panama at the airport in Medellín. A *carnet de passage* is sometimes, but not always, required. Parking at night can be a problem, but some hotels listed have patios or their own lock up garages nearby. Otherwise use *parqueadores* (see **motoring** above).

**Hitch-hiking** (*autostop*) seems to be quite easy in Colombia, especially if you can enlist the co-operation of the highway police checkpoints outside each town. Truck-drivers are often very friendly, but be careful of private cars with more than one person inside, especially if you are travelling on your own; they may be unmarked taxis. There have been many reports of muggings of cyclists in the Caribbean coastal area.

**Climbing** For information ask at the Centro Naciónal de Montaña, Transversal 10, No. 106-35, Bogotá, T 2140884. Maps can be obtained at the Instituto Geográfico (see under Bogotá, Tourist Offices). If you have a guide or are invited on a mountain tour, make certain costs/charges are clear before you start. For specific area details, see under Sierra Nevada del Cocuy, Valledupar, Ibagué, Manizales and Pereira.

**Hotels** There is a tourist tax of 5% on rooms and an insurance charge, but no service charge, and tipping is at discretion: 10% is generous. The more expensive hotels and restaurants also add on 10% VAT (IVA). Food is not expensive. A good lunch costs about US$5-6. A restaurant meal that business people might give to prospective customers would cost from US$6 to US$12 p.p. In many hotels outside the main cities you can only stay (very cheaply) at *en pension* rates and no allowance is made for missing a meal. The Colombian tourist office has lists of authorized prices for all hotels which are usually at least a year out of date. If you are overcharged the tourist office will arrange a refund. Most hotels in Colombia charge US$1 to US$6 for extra beds for children, up to a maximum (usually) of 4 beds per room. On the Caribbean coast and San Andrés and Providencia, high season is 15 December-30 April, 15 June-31 August. Although most hotels, except the very cheapest, offer private WC and shower as a matter of course, hot water often comes only in the more expensive hotels or in colder zones. Wash basin plugs are universally in short supply. Prices are normally displayed, if not, bargain.

**Camping** Sites are given in the text. Colombian Tourist Office has a list of official sites, but they are seldom signposted on main roads, so can be hard to find. Permission to camp with tent, camper van or car is readily granted by landowners in less populated areas. Those in camper vans may camp by the roadside, but it is neither particularly safe, nor easy to find a secluded spot. Vehicles may camp at truck drivers' restaurants.

Colombia is one of the few countries which sell "white gas" for camping stoves etc., so stock up here.

**Food** Colombia's food is very regional; it is quite difficult to buy in Medellín, say, a dish you particularly liked in Bogotá. Restaurants in smaller towns often close on Sundays, and early on weekday evenings: if stuck, you will probably find something to eat near the bus station.

*Locro de choclos* is a potato and maize soup so rich and nourishing that, with salad and coffee, it would make a meal in itself. Colombia has its own variant of the inevitable *arroz con pollo* (chicken and rice) which is excellent. For a change *pollo en salsa de mostaza* (chicken in mustard sauce) is recommended. *Ajiaco de pollo* is a delicious chicken, maize, manioc, cabbage and potato stew served with cream and capers, and lumps of avocado; it is a Bogotá speciality; another Bogotá speciality is *sobrebarriga* (belly of beef). *Bandeja antioqueña* costs US$3 in most places and consists of meat grilled and served with rice, beans, potato, manioc and a green salad; the simpler *carne asada* may be had for as little as US$2. *Mazamorra*, boiled maize in milk, is a typical *antioqueño* sweet, and so is *salpicón*, a tropical fruit salad. *Lechona* (sucking pig and herbs) is a speciality of Ibagué. Cartagena's rice with coconut can be compared with rice *a la valenciana*. In Nariño, guinea pig (*cuy*, *curí* or *conejillo de Indias*) is typical. *Tamales* are meat pies made by folding a maize dough round chopped pork mixed with potato, peas, onions, eggs and olives seasoned with garlic, cloves and paprika, and steaming the whole in banana leaves (which you don't eat); the best are from Tolima. A baked dish of squash, beaten eggs and seafood covered with sauce is known as the *souffle de calabaza*. *Magras* is a typical Colombian dish of eggs and chicken baked together and served with a tomato sauce. *Sancocho* is a filling combination of all the tuberous vegetables, including the tropical cassava and yam, with chopped fresh fish or any kind of meat, possibly chicken. From stalls in the capital and the countryside, try *mazorcas* (roast maize cobs) or *arepas* (fried maize cakes). On the Caribbean coast, eat an egg *empanada*, which consists of two layers of corn (maize) dough that open like an oyster-shell, fried with eggs in the middle, and try the *patacón*, a cake of mashed and baked plantain (green banana). *Huevos pericos*, eggs scrambled with onions and tomatoes, are a popular, cheap and nourishing snack for the impecunious—available almost anywhere. *Pandebono*, cheese-flavoured bread is delicious. A good local sweet is the *canastas de coco*: pastry containing coconut custard flavoured with wine and surmounted by meringue. *Arequipe* is very similar to fudge, and popular (it is called *manjarblanco* in other parts of South America). *Almojábanas*, a kind of sour-milk bread roll, are delicious if fresh: "one day old and they are a disaster". There is, indeed, quite an assortment of little fruit pasties and preserves. Then there are the usual fruits: bananas, oranges, mangoes, avocado pears, and (at least in the tropical zones) *chirimoyas, papayas*, and the delicious *pitahaya*, taken either as an appetizer or dessert and, for the wise, in moderation, because even a little of it has a laxative effect. Other fruits such as the *guayaba* (guava), *guanábana* (soursop), *maracuyá* (passion fruit), *lulo* (*naranjilla*), *mora* (blackberry) and *curuba* make delicious juices, sometimes with milk added to make a *sorbete*—but be careful of milk in Colombia, and *sorbetes* are best left alone. Fruit yoghurts are nourishing and cheap (try *Alpina* brand; *crema* style is best). *Tinto*, the national small cup of black coffee, is taken ritually at all hours. Colombian coffee is always mild. (Coffee with milk is called *café perico*; *café con leche* is a mug of milk with coffee added.) *Agua de panela* is a common beverage (hot water with unrefined sugar), also made with limes, milk, or cheese.

**Drink** Many acceptable brands of beer are produced. The local rum is good and cheap; ask for *ron*, not *aguardiente*, because in Colombia the latter word is used for a popular drink containing aniseed (*aguardiente anisado*). Try *canelazo*—cold or hot rum with water, sugar, lime and cinnamon. Local table wines include Santo Tomás; none are very good. General food and wine tips: wine is normally about US$3.50-4.50 in restaurants for an acceptable bottle of Chilean or Argentine; European wines are very expensive.

**Warning** Great care should be exercised when buying imported spirits in shops. It has been reported that bottles bearing well-known labels have often been "recycled" and contain a cheap and poor imitation of the original contents. This can be dangerous to the health, and travellers are warned to stick to beer and rum. Also note that ice is usually not made from potable water.

**Tipping** Hotels and restaurants 10%. Porters, cloakroom attendants, hairdressers and barbers, US$0.05-0.25. Taxi-drivers are not tipped.

**Best Buys** Emeralds in Bogotá; handworked silver (excellent); Indian pottery and textiles. The state-run Artesanías de Colombia for craft work (see under Bogotá). In Antioquia buy the handbag—*carriel antioqueño*— traditionally made from otter skin, but nowadays from calf skin and plastic trimmed at that. At Cartagena crude rubber is moulded into little dyed figurines: odd but attractive. Clothing and shoes are cheap in Medellín. The Colombian *ruana* (poncho) is attractive and warm in any cool climate, and comes in a wide variety of colours; it may, however, be cheaper in Ecuador. Silver and gold work is cheaper than in Peru. Good duty-free shop at Bogotá airport. Leatherwork is generally good and not expensive especially in southern Colombia.

**Security** Most travellers confirm that the vast majority of Colombians are honest and very hospitable. Sadly, reports of crime, sometimes violent, are still received. In addition to the general advice given in of the **Introduction and Hints** section, the following local conditions should be noted. The warning against accepting cigarettes, chewing gum, sweets or any other type of food from fellow bus-passengers cannot be emphasized too strongly. This crime is particularly common between Popayán and San Agustín, and Bogotá and Ipiales. We have received a number of reports confirming this practice. That said, the southern area from Popayán to the Ecuadorian border is generally safer, and freer from thieves, than points further north.

Colombia is part of a major drug-smuggling route. Police and customs activities have greatly intensified and smugglers increasingly try to use innocent carriers. Travellers are warned against carrying packages for other people without checking the contents. Penalties run up to 12 years in none too comfortable jails, and the police sometimes behave very roughly towards those they choose for a spot check at airports; complaints have been made in this connection to the Colombian authorities. (Indeed taking suspicious boxes, packages or gift-wrapped presents of your own through customs could give problems.) All young travellers are suspect, so be very polite if approached by policemen. If your hotel room is raided by police looking for drugs, try, if possible, to get a witness to prevent drugs being planted on you. Colombians who offer you drugs may well be setting you up for the police, who are very active on the north coast and San Andrés island, and other tourist resorts.

Since 1989, much publicity has been given to the attempts by the authorities to tackle the "drug barons". Generally travellers have not been affected and simple robbery is a much greater problem. When travelling by bus, try to get a window seat on the side where your luggage is stowed, so you can check what luggage is taken from the bus. Many bus companies give luggage tags (like airlines). Try to avoid having your luggage put on top; you won't be allowed to jump out of the bus at every stop to check it's still there. In town buses, do not open windows so wide that belongings can be snatched; beware of pickpockets by the doors. Small *busetas* are marginally safer than buses because there is only one door for escape. Travelling by car, always keep an eye on your petrol cap, windscreen wipers and hub caps. Thieves tend to be particularly active in and around bus and railway stations. It is socially acceptable for women to keep banknotes in their bras.

Avoid money changers on the street who offer over-favourable rates of exchange. They often short-change you or run off with your money, pretending that the police are coming. Beware of counterfeit dollars and pesos.

If someone accosts you on the street, saying he's a plain-clothes policeman or drugs officer, and asks you to go to his office, offer to go with him to the nearest policeman (the tourist police where possible) or police station, or to your hotel if it's dark. He may well be a "confidence man" (if he doesn't ask to see your passport, he almost certainly is). These conmen usually work in pairs. The best advice at all times is to take care, and above all to use your common sense.

Also be prepared for frequent bus stopping and searches which are conducted in a rather haphazard and capricious manner. Travellers in private cars are also stopped often, but not necessarily searched. Some roads are more heavily policed than others, and you can expect to be stopped several times when travelling to or from the Caribbean coast and when coming from Ecuador into Colombia. There is some guerrilla activity in Colombia: the departments near Venezuela have been mentioned, also the Pasto, Tierradentro and San Agustín areas; the Magdalena Valley in Santander and the Turbo/Urabá region. Police and army checks are common in this respect also. All luggage is searched leaving Leticia airport and most tourists are checked arriving in Cartagena from the airport. It has been reported that the police charge 10% of the value of stolen articles for making out a declaration for insurance claims.

**Health**  Emergency medical treatment is given in hospitals: if injured in a bus accident, for example, you will be covered by insurance and treatment will be free. Bogotá has well-organized sanitary services, and the water may be safely drunk. Take sterilizer with you, or boil the water, or use the excellent mineral waters, when travelling outside the capital. Choose your food and eating places with care everywhere. Fruit drinks made with milk should be avoided. Hepatitis is common; have a gamma-globulin injection before your trip. Falmonox is recommended locally for amoebas. Mosquito nets are useful in the coastal swampy regions. There is some risk of malaria and yellow fever in the coastal areas and the eastern *llanos*/jungle regions; prophylaxis is advised. The local insect repellant, Black Flag, is not reliable. Tampons are readily available.

**Climate and Clothing**  Climate is entirely a matter of altitude: there are no seasons to speak of, though some periods are wetter than others. Tropical clothing is necessary in the hot and humid climate of the coastal fringe and the eastern *llanos*. In Bogotá medium-weight clothing is needed for the cool evening and night. Medellín requires light clothing; Cali lighter still; Manizales very similar to Bogotá. A dual-purpose raincoat and overcoat is useful in the uplands. Higher up in the mountains it can be very cold; woollen clothing is necessary.

The **best time for a visit** is December, January and February: the driest months. But pleasure—it happens sometimes—is in conflict with duty, because most business people are then on holiday. There is heavy rain in many places from June to September.

**Hours of Business** Mon. to Fri., commercial firms work from 0800 to mid-day and from 1400 to 1730 or 1800. Certain firms in the warmer towns such as Cali start at 0700 and finish earlier. Government offices follow the same hours on the whole as the commercial firms, but generally prefer to do business with the public in the afternoon only. Embassy hours for the public are from 0900 to noon and from 1400 to 1700 (Mon. to Fri.). Bank hours in Bogotá are 0900 to 1500 Mon. to Thurs., 0900 to 1530 on Fri. except the last Fri. in the month when they close at 1200; banks in Medellín, Cali, Barranquilla, Bucaramanga, Cartagena, Pasto, Pereira and Manizales open from 0800 to 1130 and 1400 to 1600 on Mon. to Thur.; on Fri. they are open until 1630 but shut at 1130 on the last Fri. in the month; banks in Popayán, Cúcuta, Neiva, Tunja, Ibagué and Santa Marta open from 0800 to 1130 and 1400 to 1530 on Mon. to Fri. and 0800 to 1100 on Sat. and the last day of the month. Shopping hours are 0900 to 1230 and 1430 to 1830, including Sat.

**British Business Travellers** should consult "Hints to Exporters: Colombia", from Room CO7, Export Services Branch, Department of Trade, Sanctuary Bldgs, 16-20 Great Smith Street, London SW1P 3DB. Similar U.S. publications may be obtained from the Department of Commerce, Washington, D.C. Also, *Colombian News Letter*, published monthly by the Colombian American Association Inc., 150 Nassau Street, New York, N.Y. 10038.

**Public Holidays** are on the following days: 1 January: Circumcision of our Lord; 6 January: Epiphany*; 19 March: St Joseph*; Maundy Thursday; Good Friday; 1 May: Labour Day; Ascension Day*; Corpus Christi*; Sacred Heart*; 29 June: SS. Peter and Paul*; 20 July: Independence Day; 7 August: Battle of Boyacá; 15 August: Assumption*; 12 October: Discovery of America*; 1 November: All Saints' day*; 11 November: Independence of Cartagena*; 8 December: Immaculate Conception; 25 December: Christmas Day. When those marked with an asterisk do not fall on a Monday, or when they fall on a Sunday, they will be moved to the following Monday.

**Time Zone** Colombia is 5 hours behind GMT.

**Currency** The monetary unit is the peso, divided into 100 centavos. There are coins of 50 centavos (rare) and of 1, 2, 5, 10, 20 and 50 pesos; there are notes of 50, 100, 200, 500, 1,000, 2,000 and 5,000 pesos. Large notes of over 1,000 pesos are often impossible to spend on small purchases as change is in short supply, especially in small cities, and in the morning. There is now a limit of 500 on both the import and export of pesos. Travellers' cheques are becoming a little easier to change in Colombia. Owing to the quantity of counterfeit American Express travellers' cheques in circulation, travellers may experience difficulty in cashing these cheques, but the procedure is always slow, involving finger printing and photographs. It is also very difficult, according to our correspondents, to get reimbursement for lost American Express travellers cheques. The best advice we can give is to take Thomas Cook's or a US bank's dollar traveller cheques in small denominations. Sterling travellers' cheques are practically impossible to change in Colombia. The few, legitimate *casas de cambio* give rates slightly worse than the banks, but are much quicker. Also in circulation are counterfeit US dollar bills in denominations of US$50 and US$100; US$20 bills are therefore more readily accepted. It is generally dangerous to change money on the streets, and you are likely to be given counterfeit pesos. The safest way to obtain black market rates is at the border in a neighbouring country.

As it is unwise to carry large quantities of cash, **credit cards** are widely used, especially Diners' Club and Visa; Master Charge is less common, while American Express is only accepted in high-priced establishments in Bogotá. Many banks (e.g. Banco Cafetero) advance pesos against Visa, and Banco de Occidente and Banco Industrial de Colombia give cash advances against Mastercard, though there is talk of a possible government charge.

**Weights and Measures** are metric, and weights should always be quoted in kilograms. Litres are used for liquid measures but US gallons are standard for the petroleum industry. Linear measures are usually metric, but the inch is quite commonly used by engineers and the yard on golf courses. For land measurement the hectare and cubic metre are officially employed but the traditional measures *vara* (80 centimetres) and *fanegada* (1,000 square *varas*) are still in common use. As in many other countries food etc. is often sold in *libras* (pounds), which are equivalent to ½ kilo.

**Electric Current** 120 volts AC., is general for Colombia. Transformer must be 110-150 volt A.C., with flat-prong plugs (all of same size). Be careful with electrically heated showers.

**Mail** There are separate post offices for surface mail and airmail. Send all letters by airmail, for surface mail is very unreliable. Avianca controls all airmail services and has offices in provincial cities. Correspondence with U.K. is reported to be good. It costs US$0.25 to send a letter or postcard to the U.S., and US$0.27 to Europe; a 1 kg. package to Europe costs US$13 by air (Avianca). Note that the AmEx agent, Tierra Mar Aire, does not accept mail to be held for AmEx customers.

**Telecommunications** Empresa Nacional de Telecomunicaciones has offices in all main cities.

**Telephone** systems have been automated; the larger towns are interconnected. Inter-city calls must be made from Telecom offices unless you have access to a private phone. Long-distance pay 'phones are located outside most Telecom offices, also at bus stations and airports. They take 20 peso coins. 1 peso coins for ordinary 'phones may be bought in 20 peso packets from Banco de la República. From the larger towns it is possible to telephone to Canada, the U.S.A., the U.K., and to several of the Latin American republics. International phone charges are high (about US$6 a minute to USA, US$8 to Europe, US$12 to Australia) but there is a 20% discount on Sun., a deposit is required before the call is made which can vary between US$18 and US$36 (try bargaining the deposit down), US$1 is charged if no reply, for person-to-person add an extra minute's charge to Canada, 2 minutes' to UK; all extra minutes' conversation costs ⅓ more. *Collect*, or reversed-charge, telephone calls can be made from El Dorado airport (enquire) but otherwise are only possible from private telephones; make sure the operator understands what is involved or you may be billed in any case. It is also possible that the operator, once you have got through to him/her, may not call you back. The surest way of contacting home, assuming the facilities are available either end, is to Fax your hotel phone number to home, and ask them to call you.

**Press** Bogotá: *El Tiempo, El Espectador* (both Liberal); *La República* (Conservative), *El Siglo* (extreme Conservative). Medellín: *El Mundo, El Colombiano*; Cali: *El País, Occidente, El Pueblo*, all major cities have daily papers. Magazines are partisan, best is probably *La Semana*. U.S. and European papers can be bought at Drugstore Internacional, Carrera 10, No. 26-71, just north of *Tequendama Hotel* in Bogotá.

**Sport** The game of *tejo* is still played in Cundinamarca, Boyacá and Tolima. In Pasto and Popayán it is played under the name of *sapo* (toad). This is the Spanish *juego de la rana*, in which a small quoit has to be thrown from an improbable distance into a metal frog's mouth. There are bullrings at Bogotá, Cali, Manizales, Medellín, Sincelejo and Cerete. Polo is played at Medellín and Bogotá. Most of the larger towns have stadia. Association football is the most popular game. American baseball is played at Cartagena and Barranquilla. Cockfights, cycling, boxing and basketball are also popular.

Fishing is particularly good at Girardot, Santa Marta, and Barranquilla; marlin is fished off Barranquilla. There is good trout fishing, in season, in the lakes in the Bogotá area, particularly at Lake Tota, in the mountains.

**Tourist Information** The Corporación Nacional de Turismo (CNT), with its headquarters at Bogotá, has branches in every departmental capital and other places of interest. They should be visited as early as possible not only for information on accommodation and transport, but also for details on areas which are dangerous to visit. CNT also has offices in New York: 140 East 57th St., T 688-0151; Caracas: P.B. 5 Av. Urdaneta Ibarras a Pelota, T 561-3592/5805; Madrid: Calle Princesa No. 17 Tercero Izquierda, T 248-5090/5690; and Paris: 9, Boulevard de la Madeleine, 75001 Paris, T 260-3565. For details on National Parks, go to the Inderena Office in Bogotá (address on **page 668**). For birdwatchers, *A Guide to the Birds of Colombia*, by Steven Hilty and William Brown, is recommended.

The Automobile Club in Bogotá has offices on Avenida Caracas, No. 46-64 (T 2451534 and 2452684). Branches are at Manizales, Medellín, Cali, Barranquilla and Cartagena. It supplies Esso, Texaco and Mobil maps: good, but not quite up-to-date; a full set of Hojas de Ruta costs US$2.50. The Texaco map has plans of the major cities. Even the Shell series lacks detail. Maps of Colombia are obtainable at the Instituto Geográfico Militar, Agustín Codazzi, Carrera 30 y Calle 45, open 0800-1530, Bogotá, or from their office in Pasto. Drivers' route maps are available from the CNT. Buchholz and Central bookshops have a few country and Bogotá maps. Editorial Colina publish a series of books with colour photographs on different parts of Colombia (Cartegena, Antioquia, San Agustín) which have been recommended. Some of the photographs can be obtained as postcards.

This section has been updated by Peter Pollard to whom we are most grateful. Thanks are also due to Joaquín Emilio García (CNT, San Agustín) and to the following residents and travellers: Ralph Arnold (Vegreville, Canada), Arno Michael Auer (Ottobrunn), Claudia Beinhardt (Deisenhofen), Allen Belkin and Debra Riklan (Yonkers, NY), Erik Bernesson (Båstad, Sweden), Salik B. Biais (Montmorency), Andreas Böttner and Annette Drinkuth (Otterstedt, Germany), Pamela Caunt and Bob Brass (London N1), Max G. Chapman (Melbourne), Trina Cholewick (Montréal, Canada), Andrew Clarke (Bucaramanga, Colombia), Dr. Tony Daniels (Coton, Salop), Brett Dawson and Ivanka Lupenec (Toronto), Hans van Dijk (Hilversum), Gavin Dispain (Adelaide), Gerd Dörner (Eberstadt), Diane E. Floyd (Sale, Wiltshire), Monika Friedhoff and Ignaz Utz (Frankfurt and Biel, Switz), Dámaso Gallastegi (Bergara, Spain), Joaquín Emilio García (CNT, San Agustín) for important updating material, Yves Genier (Louay, Switzerland), Theodor A. Gevert (São Paulo), Kenrick Ghosh (Bogotá), David Ginsberg (Huntington Station, NY), Peter Glatte and Simone Wolschinkski (Walhorn, Belgium), Doris Goll (Gossau) and Andy Stocker (Buchrain, Switz.), Andrew Grassie and Sara Gilbert (Lewes), David Graves (Brooklyn, N.Y.), Kurt Gyger and Regula Geser (Mollis, Switzerland), Ulrich Harlan (Berlin), Eckhart Harm (Tornesch, Germany), Daniela Heblik (Hüttenberg, Germany), Gert Jan Hof and Yvonne Evers (Huissen, Neth), Cathy and Chris Holman (Sale, Cheshire), Rolf Hönsch (Grüt) and Martin Stark (Salzbach, Switzerland), Sabine Imhoff (Germany), Paul James and Deborah Scattergood (Walsall), Marian Janssen (Rosmalen, Netherlands), Nicola Keirren (Melba, Australia), Anke Kessler (Berlin), Stuart and Wendy Knill (Kidderminster, Worcs), Daniel Küng (Wohlen, Switzerland), Mathias Lassen (Weiberstadt, Germany), Ileike Liebers (Berlin), Judith Locher (Switzerland), Markus Maier and Gitte Wiedmann (Zürich), Douglas Markham (Houston), Anders Mattsson (Lund, Sweden), Patrick Meyer (Ammerschwihr, France), George Migeod (Worthing), Alison Milner and Keith Doyle (Manchester), Dr. A. L. Minter (Sandwich, Kent), Catherine Morris-Adams (West Derby), Matthias Müller (Berlin 31), Monica Napper (Eastbourne, UK), Lars Nelson and Gerd Schütze (Iserlohn and Neuss, Germany), Asbjørn Nielsen (Denmark) Fiorenzo Peloso (Landquart, Switzerland), Shauna Picard and Grant Findlay (Melbourne, Australia), David F. Pinder (Sale, Cheshire), Josef Rama Souto (Recklinhausen, Germany), Jamie Rein (Boston, Mass), Bryan and Charmaine Roche (Cape Town), Peter Roth (London NW6), Dä Roz Us Kölle Piero Scaruffi (Redwood City, CA, U.S.A.), John Shearer and Stephanie Toohey (NSW, Australia), Irene Strassel and Thomas Vogt (Switzerland), Fredi Suter (Goldau) and Claudia Räber (Oberkirch), Christoph Theis (Wiesloch, Germany), Alan P.M. Thompson (Sevenoaks, Kent), Åse Totland and Jarle Unneland (Ålesund, Norway), Michael Turner (Burnham-On-Sea), Dirk Vandersypen (Managua), Béatrice Völkle (Gampelen, Switz.), H.M. Wams (Amsterdam), Thorsten Weiland (Leichlingen, Germany), Urs Wickli (Neu St. Johann, Switzerland), Manuela Wonisch (Kloten, Switzerland), Meg Worley (Knoxville, Tennessee) and Peter Grover (Montreal, Canada).

## WILL YOU HELP US?

We do all we can to get our facts right in **The South American Handbook.** Each chapter is thoroughly revised each year, but the territory covered is vast, and our eyes cannot be everywhere.

*Your information may be far more up-to-date than ours. If your letter reaches us early enough in the year it will be used in the next edition, but write whenever you want to, for all your letters will be used.*

Thank you very much indeed for you help.

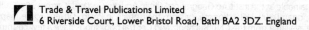 Trade & Travel Publications Limited
6 Riverside Court, Lower Bristol Road, Bath BA2 3DZ. England

# ECUADOR

## INTRODUCTION

ECUADOR is bounded by Colombia to the north, Peru to the east and south and the Pacific Ocean to the west. Its area is about 283,520 square km., which makes it the second smallest republic in South America.

The Andes, running from the Colombian border in the north to the borders of Peru in the south, form a mountainous backbone to the country. There are two main ranges, the Eastern Cordillera and the Western Cordillera, separated by a 400-km. long trough, the Central Valley, whose rims are from 40 to 65 km. apart. The rims are joined together, like the two sides of a ladder, by hilly rungs, and between each pair of rungs lies an intermont basin with a dense cluster of population. These basins, which vary in altitude between 1,800 and 3,000 metres, are drained by rivers which cut through the rims to run either west to the Pacific or east to join the Amazon. The whole mountain area is known as the Sierra.

Both rims of the Central Valley are lined with the cones of more than thirty volcanoes. Several of them have long been extinct, for example, Chimborazo, the highest (6,310 metres), Cayambe (5,790 metres), standing directly on the equator, Illiniza (5,263 metres) and Altar (5,319 metres). At least eight, however, are still active; Cotopaxi (5,897 metres), which had several violent eruptions in the nineteenth century; Tungurahua (5,016 metres), which had a major eruption early this century; Antisana (5,704 metres), which showed signs of activity in the 1960s; Pichincha (4,794 metres), which erupted in 1981, and Sangay (5,230 metres) one of the world's most active volcanoes, continuously emitting fumes and ash. Nowadays all the main peaks except for Altar and Sangay, which are less accessible, are climbed fairly regularly.

East of the Eastern Cordillera the forest-clad mountains fall sharply to the plains—the Oriente—through which meander the tributaries of the Amazon. This eastern lowland region makes up 36% of Ecuador's total territory, but is only

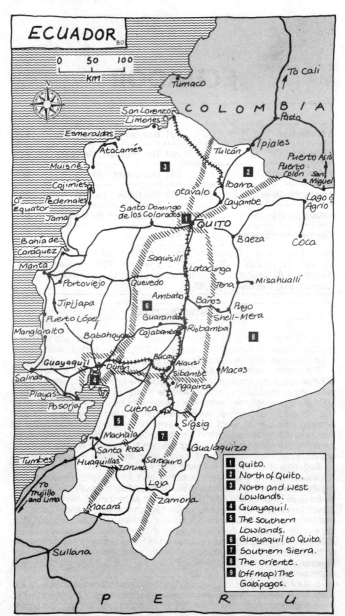

1 Quito.
2 North of Quito.
3 North and West Lowlands.
4 Guayaquil.
5 The Southern Lowlands.
6 Guayaquil to Quito.
7 Southern Sierra.
8 The Oriente.
9 (Off map) The Galápagos.

sparsely populated by native Indians and agricultural colonists from the highlands. In total, the region has only 5% of the national population, but colonization is now proceeding rapidly in the wake of an oil boom. There are substantial oil reserves in the northern Oriente near the Colombian border, and exports began in 1972.

Between the Western Cordillera and the Pacific lies the Costa, 685 km. from north to south and some 100 km. wide. It is from this area that Ecuador draws the majority of its agricultural products for export. Guayaquil, the main city of this region, is 464 km. from the capital, Quito, which lies high in a northern intermont basin.

**The Sierra** There are altogether ten intermont basins strung along the Sierra from north to south. There is little variation by day or by season in the temperature in any particular basin: temperature depends on altitude. The basins lie at an elevation of between 2,100 and 2,750 metres, and the range of shade temperature is from 6°C to 10°C in the morning to 19°C to 23°C in the afternoon. Temperatures can get considerably higher in the lower basins. There is one rainy season, from November to May, when the average fall in Quito is 1,270 mm; the skies are mostly cloudy or overcast at this time and there are frequent rainfalls during the afternoons and nights. Over half the area is now grassy *páramo* on which cattle and sheep are raised and subsistence crops grown. What crops are grown is determined by altitude, but the hardiest of them, the potato, cannot thrive above 3,800 metres or so. The intermont basins produce livestock, poultry, wheat, barley, oats, maize, quinoa, fruit and vegetables, some of which find their way down to the coastal plain.

Some 47% of the people of Ecuador live in the central trough of the Andes, and the majority are pure Indians. Most of the land is held in large private estates worked by the Indians, but some of it is held by Indian communities. With the limited application of an agrarian-reform programme, the *huasipungo* system whereby Indians were virtual slaves on the big highland *haciendas* is now disappearing, and co-operatives are proliferating. Though many Indian communities live at subsistence level and remain isolated from national centres, others have developed good markets for products using traditional skills in embroidery, pottery, jewellery, knitting, weaving, and carving.

**The Costa** Most of the Costa region is lowland at an altitude of less than 300 metres, apart from a belt of hilly land which runs west from Guayaquil to the coast and trends northwards. In the extreme north there are two rainy seasons, as in Colombia, and a typical tropical rain forest. But the two rainy seasons soon merge into one, running from December to June. Further south, the later the rains begin, the sooner they end: at Guayaquil the rains normally fall between January and April. The forests thin out too in the more southerly lowlands, and give way to thorn and savanna. The Santa Elena Peninsula and the south-western coast near Peru have little or no rainfall.

The main agricultural exports come from a small area of lowland to the SE and N of Guayaquil. It lies between the coastal hills and the Andes; rains are heavy, the temperature and the humidity high: ideal conditions for the growth of tropical crops. One part of this Guayas lowland is subject to floods from the four rivers which traverse it: bananas, normally accounting for half the exports of the lowland, are grown here, as well as rice. Cacao too is farmed on the natural levees of this flood plain, but the main crop comes from the alluvial fans at the foot of the mountains rising out of the plain. High on these same alluvial fans excellent coffee is also grown; cacao, bananas, coffee and sugar, whether processed or unprocessed, are about 30% of the exports by value. Cotton is developing. A major new activity is shrimp farming, which has greatly altered the coastal landscape in some areas and harmed mangroves. Nevertheless, the industry is a major employer and foreign exchange earner. Add to this that the Guayas lowland is a great cattle-fattening area in the dry season, and its importance in the national economy becomes obvious. A good network of paved roads now links Guayaquil with the major zones of agricultural production, and the once thriving river-ports have now declined. Along the northern coast, the main areas of population are at Esmeraldas, along the highways inland, in the irrigated lands of northern Manabí, and near Manta, Montecristi, and Jipijapa.

Two areas of the coastlands have experienced spectacular rises in population and agricultural production: El Oro Province in the extreme south, centred on the town of Machala, and the Quevedo-Santo Domingo zone along the Andean fringe to the north of Guayaquil. In both areas, highland settlers have mixed with coastal entrepreneurs to produce a particularly progressive agriculture. Irrigation in El Oro has produced a thriving zone of very intensive banana plantations. In the Quevedo-Santo Domingo area, large areas of forest have been cleared; bananas used to be the main crop, but are now being replaced by African palm. Further north, in Esmeraldas Province, there still remain large areas of land which could be cleared and developed for farming, although the fertility of this zone is reputedly much lower than that of the Quevedo, Guayaquil and Machala areas.

**History**  The Incas of Peru, with their capital at Cuzco, began to conquer the Sierra of Ecuador, already densely populated, towards the middle of the 15th century. A road was built between Cuzco and Quito, and the empire was ruled after the death of the Inca Huayna Capac by his two sons, Huáscar at Cuzco and Atahualpa at Quito. Pizarro's main Peruvian expedition took place in 1532, when there was civil war between the two brothers. Atahualpa, who had won the war, was put to death by Pizarro in 1533, and the Inca empire was over.

Pizarro claimed the northern kingdom of Quito, and his lieutenants Sebastián de Benalcázar and Diego de Almagro took the city in 1534. Pizarro founded Lima in 1535 as capital of the whole region, and four years later replaced Benalcázar at Quito by Gonzalo, his brother. Gonzalo later set out on the exploration of the Oriente. He moved down the Napo river, and sent Francisco de Orellana to prospect. Orellana did not return: he drifted down the river finally to reach the mouth of the Amazon: the first white man to cross the continent in this way.

Quito became an *audiencia* under the Viceroy of Peru. For 280 years Ecuador more or less peacefully absorbed the new ways brought by the conqueror. Gonzalo had already introduced pigs and cattle; wheat was now added. The Indians were Christianized, colonial laws and customs and ideas introduced. The marriage of the arts of Spain to those of the Incas led to a remarkable efflorescence of painting, sculpting and building at Quito. In the 18th century black slave labour was brought in to work the plantations near the coast.

There was an abortive attempt at independence in the strongly garrisoned capital in 1809, but it was not until 1822 that Sucre, moving north from Guayaquil, defeated the Spanish at Pichincha and occupied Quito. Soon afterwards Bolívar arrived, and Ecuador was induced to join the Venezuelan and Colombian confederation, the Gran Colombia of Bolívar's dream. On 26 and 27 July, 1822, Bolívar met San Martín, fresh from liberating Lima, at Guayaquil. What happened at that mysterious encounter is not known, but San Martín left it silently for a self-imposed exile in France. Venezuela separated itself from Gran Colombia in 1829, and Ecuador decided on complete independence in August, 1830, under the presidency of Juan Flores.

Ecuador's 19th century history was a continuous struggle between pro-Church conservatives and anti-Church (but none the less devotedly Catholic) liberals. There were also long periods of military rule from 1895, when the liberal General Eloy Alfaro took power. During the late 1940s and the 1950s there was a prolonged period of prosperity (through bananas, largely) and constitutional rule, but the more typical pattern of alternating civilian and military governments was resumed in the 1960s and 1970s. Apart from the liberal-conservative struggles, there has been long-lasting rivalry between Quito and the Sierra on one hand and Guayaquil and the Costa on the other.

The country's eastern jungle territory has been reduced from that of the old Audiencia of Quito by gradual Peruvian infiltration, which means that the country's official claim to be a "país amazónico" has little relation to present reality. This process reached an acute phase in 1941 when war broke out with Peru; the war was ended with the Rio de Janeiro Protocol of 1942 which allotted most of the disputed territory to Peru. Ecuador has denounced the Protocol, and the country's official policy remains the recovery of all the territories of the Audiencia of Quito. Border skirmishes occur at times although there has been no serious incident since 1981.

The first presidential and congressional election under the 1978 constitution took place on 29 April, 1979. Prior to then there had been military rule for seven years, attended by growing oil-based prosperity, until 10 August 1979 when President Jaime Roldós Aguilera was inaugurated for a five-year term. His policy was to follow a programme of gradual reform. In May 1981, President Roldós was killed in an air crash and was succeeded by the vice-president, Osvaldo Hurtado Larrea. In 1984 President Hurtado handed power over to his elected successor and political opponent, the conservative León Febres Cordero, the first time in 23 years that such a transfer of power had occurred. President Febres Cordero's free market orientation was rejected by voters in the 1988 presidential and congressional elections. Rodrigo Borja Cevallos, leader of the centre left Izquierda Democrática, was inaugurated as president on 10 August 1988. Presidential and congressional elections are due in 1992.

**Population** About 50% of Ecuador's 10,490,000 (1989) people are Indians, 40% *mestizo*, 8.5% European; the remainder are black or Asian. Roughly 48% live in the Costa region west of the Andes, and 47% in the Andean Sierra. Migration is occurring from the rural zones of both the coast and the highlands to the towns and cities, particularly Guayaquil and Quito, and agricultural colonization by highlanders is occurring in parts of the coastal lowlands and the Oriente. The population growth rate, 1980-88, was 2.9%; birth rate, 1987, 35.4. The mortality rate per 1,000 inhabitants is 7.6, while infant mortality per 1,000 live births is 69.6. About 69% of the inhabitants over 15 years of age are literate. 54% of the population is urban (living in a cantonal or provincial capital—urban growth rate 1981-88, 4.7%), and 46% is rural. National average population density is 39 per square kilometre, the highest in South America. Average income per head has risen fast in recent years like that of other oil-exporting countries, but the distribution has not improved and a few citizens are spectacularly wealthy.

**The Economy** In the early 1970s, Ecuador underwent a transformation from an essentially agricultural economy to a predominantly petroleum economy. From 1972 when substantial domestic oil output began, economic growth has largely followed the fortunes of the oil market, except in 1983, when freak weather conditions resulted in large crop losses. Agriculture's contribution (including fishing) to gdp has dwindled from over 22% in 1972 to about 16% although it still employs over a third of the labour force. The major export crops of bananas, coffee and cocoa are grown on the coast. Ecuador is the world's largest exporter of bananas. Production is being promoted with increased plantings of high-yielding varieties and provision of technical assistance and quality control. Coffee is the most extensive of Ecuador's cash crops, accounting for over 20% of total agricultural land, but it is also the lowest yielding crop. Cocoa production has been increased by a rehabilitation programme after the 1983 floods, but although yields have trebled, output of 498 kg per hectare is still well below Brazil's 914 kg/ha.

Fishing is a growing industry, offering lucrative export potential. As well as tuna, sardines and white fish, shrimp farming is booming along the coast and has provided export earnings and much-needed jobs for agricultural workers. Mining has been relatively unimportant historically, but the discovery of about 700 tonnes of gold reserves around Nambija (Zamora) in the southeast created intense interest in precious metals and over 12,000 independent miners rushed to prospect there.

Although Ecuador's share of total world oil production is small (0.65%), foreign exchange earnings from oil exports are crucial to the economy. The main producing area is in the northern Oriente, and a 495-km. trans-Andean pipeline carries the oil to Esmeraldas on the coast, where it is refined and/or exported. There are also reserves of natural gas, mainly in the Gulf of Guayaquil, but these have not yet been fully developed. Hydroelectric potential is estimated at 90,000 MW, but generating capacity in the mid-1980s was only 2,000 MW. New projects on the Paute, Pastaza and Coca rivers could raise capacity to 12,000 MW by the end of the century.

Ecuador's foreign debt rose sharply in the 1970s when oil exports began and in the 1980s it joined other debtor nations in refinancing its external obligations. Adherence to free market economic policies in IMF programmes brought international approval and by 1985 Ecuador was widely acclaimed as a model debtor with sufficient creditworthiness to return to the voluntary market for loans. However, in 1986 oil prices crashed, cutting Ecuador's oil receipts by half, followed in 1987 by an earthquake which destroyed part of the trans-Andean pipeline and damaged other oil installations, causing a cessation of oil exports. It was clear that huge amounts of finance would be necessary for reconstruction of economic infrastructure and villages which had been destroyed. The effects on public finances were considerable, resulting in a higher rate of inflation. Subsequent loss of confidence in the Government's economic management resulted in a massive demand for dollars and a heavy devaluation of the sucre. Arrears on debt payments to all creditors built up and it was only in 1989 that the Government felt able to regularize some payments and begin negotiations with both official and private creditors. Progress was not sustained, however, and in 1990 Ecuador again fell out of compliance with its IMF programme and broke off discussions with commercial banks.

**Government** There are 20 provinces, including the Galápagos Islands. Provinces are divided into cantons and parishes for administration.

Under the 1978 constitution, the vote was extended to include all literate citizens over the age of 18. The president and vice-president are elected for a four-year term. The president may not stand for re-election. The legislative branch consists of a single Chamber of Representatives of 71 members, of which 59 are provincial representatives elected for a two-year term and 12 are national representatives elected for a four-year term.

**Music and Dance** Culturally, ethnically and geographically, Ecuador is very much two countries—the Andean highlands with their centre at Quito and the Pacific lowlands behind Guayaquíl. In spite of this, the music is relatively homogeneous and it is the Andean music that would be regarded as "typically Ecuadorian". The principal highland rhythms are the Sanjuanito, Cachullapi, Albaza, Yumbo and Danzante, danced by Indian and Mestizo alike. These may be played by brass bands, guitar trios or groups of wind instruments, but it is the *rondador*, a small panpipe, that provides the classic Ecuadorian sound, although of late the Peruvian *quena* has been making heavy inroads via *pan-Andean* groups and has become a threat to the local instrument. The coastal region has its own song form, the Amorfino, but the most genuinely "national" song and dance genres, both of European origin, are the Pasillo (shared with Colombia) in waltz time and the Pasacalle, similar to the Spanish Pasodoble. Of Ecuador's three best loved songs, "El Chulla Quiteño", "Romántico Quito" and "Vasija de Barro", the first two are both Pasacalles. Even the Ecuadorian mestizo music has a melancholy quality to it not found in Peruvian "Música Criolla", perhaps due to Quito being in the mountains, while Lima is on the coast. Music of the highland Indian communities is, as elsewhere in the region, related to religious feasts and ceremonies and geared to wind instruments such as the *rondador*, the *pinkullo* and *pifano* flutes and the great long *guarumo* horn with its mournful note. The guitar is also usually present and brass bands with well worn instruments can be found in even the smallest villages. Among the most outstanding traditional fiestas are the Pase del Niño in Cuenca, the Mama Negra of Latacunga, carnival in Guaranda, the Yamor in Otavalo, plus Corpus Cristi and the Feast of Saint John all over the highlands. Among the best known musical groups who have recorded are Los Embajadores (whose "Tormentos" is superb) and the Duo Benítez-Valencia for guitar-accompanied vocal harmony, Ñanda-Mañachi and the Conjunto Peguche (both from Otavalo) for highland Indian music and Jatari and Huayanay for pan-Andean music.

There is one totally different cultural area, that of the black inhabitants of the Province of Esmeraldas and the highland valley of the Río Chota. The former is a southerly extension of the Colombian Pacific coast negro culture, centred round the marimba xylophone as an instrument. The musical genres are also shared with black Colombians, including the Bunde, Bambuco, Caderona, Torbellino and Currulao dances and this music is some of the most African sounding in the whole of South America. The Chota Valley is an inverted oasis of desert in the Andes and here the black people dance the Bomba. It is also home to the unique Bandas de Mocha, whose primitive instruments include leaves that are doubled over and blown through.

---

## QUITO (1)

*Quito* (2,850 metres), with a population of 1,234,000, is within 25 km. of the equator, but it stands high enough to make its climate much like that of spring in England, the days warm or hot and the nights cool. Because of the height, visitors may initially feel some discomfort and should slow their pace for the first 24 hours. Mean temperature, 13°C, rainfall, 1,473 mm.; rainy season: Sept. to May with the heaviest rainfall in April, though heavy storms in July are not unknown. The day length (sunrise to sunset) is constant throughout the year.

Few cities have a setting to match that of Quito, the second highest capital in Latin America (La Paz, the administrative capital of Bolivia, is the highest). The city is set in a hollow at the foot of the volcano Pichincha (4,794 metres). It was an Inca city, refounded by Sebastián de Benalcázar, Pizarro's lieutenant, in 1534. The city's charm lies in its colonial centre, where cobbled streets are steep and narrow, dipping to deep ravines. Through this section hurries the Machángara river, nowadays too polluted to wash clothes in. Westwards the valley is closed by Cerro Panecillo; from its top, 183 metres above the city level, there is a (restaurant, closed 1990) fine view of the city below and the encircling cones of volcanoes and other mountains. There is a new statue on the hill to the Virgen de las Américas; Mass is held in the base on Sundays. There is a good view from the observation platform up the statue.

**Warning** On no account should you walk up the series of steps and paths to the Virgin which begin on García Moreno (where it meets Ambato) as assaults are very common: take a taxi up and leave your valuables behind.

The heart of the city is Plaza Independencia, dominated by a somewhat grim Cathedral (open 0800-1000, 1400-1600) with grey stone porticos and green tile cupolas. On its outer walls are plaques listing the names of the founding fathers of Quito, and inside are the tomb of Sucre (tucked away in a corner) and a famous Descent from the Cross by the Indian painter Caspicara. Beside the Cathedral, round the corner, is El Sagrario, originally built as the Cathedral chapel, now being restored. Facing the Cathedral is the old Archbishop's Palace, which has been renovated and now houses shops. On the northeast side is the new concrete Municipal Palace which fits in quite well, despite its material. The low colonial

Palacio de Gobierno, on the northwest side of the Plaza, is silhouetted against the great flank of Pichincha (open 0900-1200, 1500-1800, free but you can only see the patio); on the first floor is a gigantic mosaic mural of Orellana discovering the Amazon, and the President's offices are on the second floor. Portraits of all the presidents are hung in the yellow room. The balconies looking over the main square are from the Tuilleries in Paris; a gift of the French government shortly after the French Revolution.

The best way to see old Quito is to walk its narrow streets. Wander down the Calle Morales, main street of La Ronda district (traditionally called Calle Ronda and now a notorious area for pickpockets and bag slashers), one of the oldest streets in the city, past Plaza Santo Domingo to Carrera Guayaquil, the main shopping street, and on to shady Parque Alameda, which has the oldest astronomical observatory in South America (open Sat. 0900-1200). There are also a splendid monument to Simón Bolívar, various lakes, and in the NW corner a spiral lookout tower with a good view. The traditional colonial area is being preserved, with the buildings painted white and blue, but other parts of the city are being radically altered as a result of road improvements.

From Plaza Independencia two main streets, Carrera Venezuela and Calle García Moreno, lead straight towards the Panecillo to the wide Av. 24 de Mayo, at the top of which is a new concrete building where the Indians are supposed to do their trading since the street markets were officially abolished in 1981. Street trading still takes place, however, and there are daily street markets from Sucre down to 24 de Mayo and from San Francisco church west up past Cuenca.

Plaza San Francisco (or Bolívar) is west of Plaza Independencia; on the north-western side of this plaza is the great church and monastery of the patron saint of Quito, San Francisco, the earliest religious foundation in South America (1535), see below. Plaza Santo Domingo (or Sucre), to the south-east of Plaza San Francisco, has to the SE the church and monastery of Santo Domingo, with its rich wood-carvings and a remarkable Chapel of the Rosary to the right of the main altar. In the centre of the square is a statue to Sucre, pointing to the slopes of Pichincha where he won his battle against the Royalists. The modern University City is on the NW side of the city, on the lower slopes of Pichincha by the Avenida de las Américas.

There are altogether 86 churches in Quito. The fine Jesuit church of **La Compañía**, in Calle García Moreno, one block from Plaza Independencia (open 0930-1100, 1600-1800) has the most ornate and richly sculptured façade and interior. See its coloured columns, its ten side altars and high altar plated with gold, and the gilded balconies. Several of its most precious treasures, including a painting of the Virgen Dolorosa framed in emeralds and gold, are kept in the vaults of the Banco Central del Ecuador and appear only at special festivals. Not far away to the north is the church of **La Merced**. In the monastery of La Merced is Quito's oldest clock, built in 1817 in London. Fine cloisters entered through door to left of altar. La Merced church contains many splendidly elaborate styles; note the statue of Neptune on the main patio fountain.

The church of **San Francisco** (open 0600-1100, 1500-1800), Quito's largest is said to be the first religious building constructed in South America by the Spanish and is rich in art

---

## Quito New City: key to map

1. Parque Andrade; 2. Plaza Rocafuerte; 3. Plaza Mantilla; 4. Plaza Paul Rivet; 5. Iglesia Sta. Clara de San Millán; 6. Iglesia El Girón; 7. Iglesia Santa Teresa; 8. Iglesia El Belén; 9. Ministry of Public Works; 10. Ministry of External Relations; 11. Universidad Católica (museums); 12. Ministry of Finance; 13. Cultural Library; 14. Casa de la Cultura; 15. Nuevo Hospital Militar; 16. Colegio Militar; 17. Palacio de Justicia; 18. Palacio Legislativo; 19. Instituto Panamericano Geografía e Historia; 20. Instituto Geográfico Militar (IGM); 21. Ministry of Public Health; 22. Maternity Hospital; 23. Colegio Mejía (museum); 24. Consejo Provincial de Pichincha; 25. Astronomical Observatory; 26. Banco Central (museums); 27. CETUR (Tourist Office); 28. Ecuadorian Tours (Amex); 29. Turismundial; 30. TAME; 31. SAETA and Red Cross; 32. Banco Holandés Unido and Dutch Consulate; 33. Lloyds Bank; 34. Casa de cambio "Rodrigo Paz"; 35. United States Embassy; 36. Hotel Colón; 37. Alameda Real; 38. Tambo Real; 39. Residencia Los Alpes; 40. Hotel Embassy; 41. Inca Imperial; 42. Coral Internacional; 43. Libri Mundi.

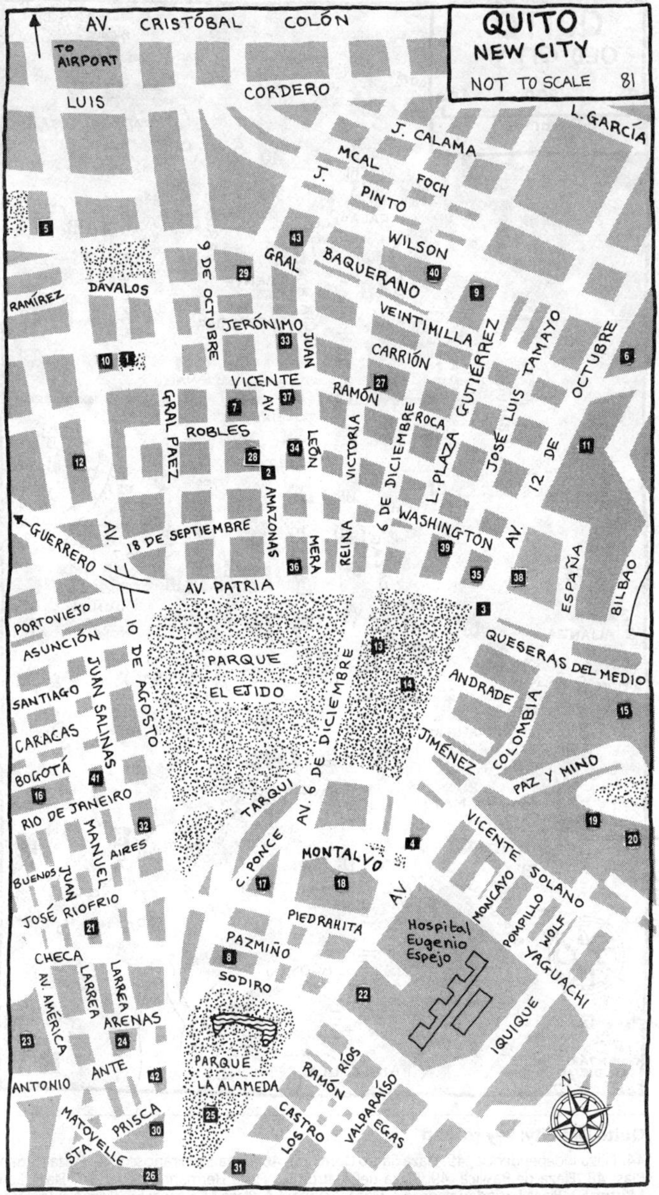

QUITO
NEW CITY
NOT TO SCALE 81
TO AIRPORT
AV. CRISTÓBAL COLÓN
LUIS CORDERO
L. GARCÍA
J. CALAMA
MCAL FOCH
J. PINTO
WILSON
GRAL BAQUERANO
VEINTIMILLA
CARRIÓN
RAMÓN ROCA
9 DE OCTUBRE
JERÓNIMO
VICENTE
ROBLES
DÁVALOS
RAMÍREZ
GRAL PAEZ
AV. AMAZONAS
JUAN LEÓN MERA
REINA VICTORIA
6 DE DICIEMBRE
L. PLAZA GUTIÉRREZ
JOSÉ LUIS TAMAYO
AV. 12 DE OCTUBRE
WASHINGTON
AV. 18 DE SEPTIEMBRE
GUERRERO
AV. PATRIA
ESPAÑA
BILBAO
QUESERAS DEL MEDIO
ANDRADE
COLOMBIA
JIMÉNEZ
PAZ Y MINO
PARQUE EL EJIDO
PORTOVIEJO
ASUNCIÓN
10 DE AGOSTO
JUAN SALINAS
SANTIAGO
CARACAS
BOGOTÁ
RIO DE JANEIRO
MANUEL
BUENOS AIRES
JUAN
JOSÉ RIOFRIO
CHECA
AV. AMÉRICA
LARREA
LARREA
ARENAS
ANTE
ANTONIO
MATOVELLE
STA PRISCA
TARQUI
AV. 6 DE DICIEMBRE
C. PONCE
MONTALVO
AV
PIEDRAHITA
PAZMIÑO
SODIRO
PARQUE LA ALAMEDA
RAMÓN RÍOS
LOS CASTRO
VALPARAÍSO
EGAS
Hospital Eugenio Espejo
VICENTE SOLANO
MONCAYO
POMPILLO
WOLF
YAGUACHI
IQUIQUE
N
1 2 3 4 5 6 7 8 9 10 11 12 13 14 15 16 17 18 19 20 21 22 23 24 25 26 27 28 29 30 31 32 33 34 35 36 37 38 39 40 41 42 43

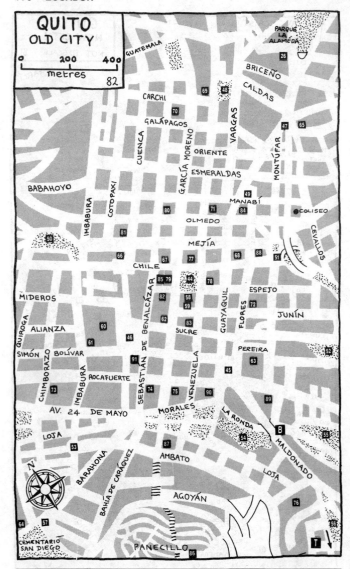

## Quito Old City: key to map

44. Plaza Independencia; 45. Plaza Santo Domingo; 46. Plaza San Francisco; 47. Plaza de San Blas; 48. Plaza de Basílica; 49. Plaza del Teatro; 50. Plaza Hermano Miguel; 51. Plaza San Martín; 52. Plaza Lucinda Toledo; 53. Plaza Victoria; 54. Plaza M. Sáenz; 55. Plaza Santa Rosa;

treasures. The two towers were felled by an earthquake in 1868 and rebuilt. A modest statue of the founder, Fray Jodoco Ricke, the Flemish Franciscan who sowed the first wheat in Ecuador, stands at the foot of the stairs to the church portal. See the fine wood-carvings in the choir, a magnificent high altar of gold and an exquisite carved ceiling. There are some paintings in the aisles by Miguel de Santiago, the colonial *mestizo* painter. His paintings of the life of Saint Francis decorate the monastery of San Francisco close by. Adjoining San Francisco is the **Cantuña Chapel** with sculptures.

Many of the heroes of Ecuador's struggle for independence are buried in the monastery of **San Agustín** (Flores and Mejía), which has beautiful cloisters on 3 sides where the first act of independence from Spain was signed on 10 August, 1809. The church of **El Carmen Moderno** has a fine collection of Quito ceramics. In the recently restored monastery of **San Diego** are some unique paintings with figures dressed in fabrics sewn to the canvas -a curious instance of our present-day "collage". Ring the bell to the right of the church door to get in, entrance US$0.75, 0900-1200, 1500-1700, all visitors are shown around by a guide. Also **La Concepción**, Mejía and García Moreno; **San Blas**, Guayaquil and 10 de Agosto. The **Basílica of Guápulo** (1693), perched on the edge of a ravine SE of the city, is well worth seeing for its many paintings, gilded altars, stone carvings of indigenous animals and the marvellously carved pulpit. In 1990 it was open but the interior was full of scaffolding for repairs. Take bus 21 (Guápulo-Dos Puentes) from Plaza de Santo Domingo, or walk down the steep stairway near *Hotel Quito*. Notice also the curious new "French Gothic" basilica under construction (since 1926) on a hill in the centre of the town. (You go up Carrera Venezuela to see it, puffing all the way, but it's worth while to see the local sculptors and stonecutters at work, if you can get friendly with the administrator.)

**Note**  A number of churches were temporarily closed after the 1987 earthquake and were still being restored in 1991. There are fears for the survival of La Compañía, El Sagrario and El Carmen Bajo, where the threat of subsidence from long term structural faults was compounded by earthquake damage.

**Houses**  The house of Sucre is at Venezuela 573, a beautiful restored house, open daily, entry free. The house of Benalcázar is on Olmeda with Benalcázar, a colonial house with a courtyard and some religious statues on view to the public. The house of Camilo Egas, a recent Ecuadorean artist, on Venezuela, has been restored by the Banco Central; it has different exhibitions during the year, entrance US$0.75.

Modern Quito extends northwards into a wide plain; it has broad avenues, fine private residences, parks, embassies and villas. Av. Amazonas, from Av. Patria to about Av. Colón, and the adjoining streets comprise Quito's modern tourist and business area: travel agencies, airlines, hotels and *residenciales*, exchange houses, moderate to expensive restaurants—several with sidewalk cafés, arts and crafts stores and stalls, jewellery stores, book stores, car rental agencies, and pastry shops are all clustered in this neighbourhood. Av. Amazonas has British-style double-decker buses running along it and on to the airport, it is also open to private cars. On Sun. La Alameda and El Ejido parks are filled with local families.

**Museums**  Quito prides itself on its art. Check museum opening times in advance. The **Casa de la Cultura Ecuatoriana**, a large circular building at the east side of Parque El Ejido, has good collection of Indian costumes, a picture gallery, the Museo de Arte Moderno, the Natural History Museum previously in the Eloy Alfaro military college, an exhibition of Ecuadorean books, and a unique and impressive museum of musical instruments. (Normal opening hours: 0900-1800, Tues.-Sat., 1000-1400, Sun. There is a good collection of Ecuadorean sculptures and painting at the **Museum of Colonial Art**, on the corner of Cuenca and Mejía. The **Museo de San Francisco** has a fine collection of religious art, open 0900-1130, 1500-1730,

56. Plaza La Recoleta; 57. Plaza San Diego; 58. Cathedral; 59. El Sagrario chapel; 60. San Francisco church, monastery and museum; 61. Catuña chapel; 62. Iglesia de la Compañía; 63. Iglesia de Santo Domingo (museum); 64. Iglesia San Diego (convent and museum); 65. Iglesia de San Blas; 66. Basílica de la Merced; 67. Iglesia de la Concepción; 68. Iglesia de San Agustín (and museum); 69. The Basílica; 70. Iglesia San Juan; 71. Iglesia de Carmen Bajo; 72. Iglesia de Santa Catalina; 73. Iglesia San Roque; 74. Convent of Carmen Alto; 75. Hospital Chapel of San Juan de Dios; 76. Iglesia San Sebastián; 77. Archbishop's Palace; 78. Municipal Palace, including Tourist office; 79. Government Palace; 80. Instituto Ecuatoriano de Cultura Hispánica (Casa de Benalcázar); 81. Museum of Colonial Art; 82. Municipal Museum of Art and History; 83. Casa de Sucre (museum); 84. Teatro Sucre; 85. General Post Office; 86. Panecillo lookout.
Hotels: 87. *Gran Casino*; 88. *Viena International*; 89. *Grand*; 90. *Caspicara*; 91. *Sucre*.

entrance US$0.35, while the **Museo de Santo Domingo** has a further collection open Mon.-Fri., 0800-1100, 1500-1700, but not of quite the same quality. Similar collection in **Museo de San Agustín**, Chile y Guayaquil, open Mon.-Sat. 0830-1230, 1430-1800, interesting exhibition of restoration work (closed for reconstruction in 1990). The **Museo Jijón y Caamaño**, now housed in the Catholic University library building, has a private collection of archaeological objects, historical documents, portraits, uniforms, etc., very well displayed. Open 0900-1200, 1500-1800. Admission: US$0.30. There is also a Shuar ethnographic museum at the university. There are two first class museums in the Banco Central (Av. 10 de Agosto), the **Archaeological Museum** on the fifth floor (open Tues.-Sun. 0930-1500) with beautiful precolumbian ceramics and gold and a video film on Ecuadorean culture and the different Indian tribes, and the **Museo Colonial y de Arte Religioso** on the 6th (open Tues.-Fri. 0900-1700). There are guided tours in English, French and German—Entrance fee is US$1 for foreigners, US$0.35 for Ecuadoreans, US$0.20 for students, but free on Sunday. There is a fine museum in Bella Vista north east of Quito, **Museo Guayasamín**: as well as the eponymous artist's works there is a precolumbian and colonial collection, highly rec.; open Mon.-Fri. 0900-1230 and 1500-1830, Sat. 0900-1230, free admission. Works of art may be purchased and also modern jewellery made by the artist's daughter, ask to see the whole collection as only a small portion is displayed in the shop. The museum is near the Channel 8 TV station, take Batán-Colmena bus no. 3 marked Bella Vista. Other museums: **Municipal Museum of Art and History**, Espejo 1147, near main plaza, was the old municipal offices, free; underneath is the cell where the revolutionaries of 1809 were executed (waxwork), well worth a visit, but not for the claustrophobic; **Museum of Ethnology**, Departamento de Letras, Ciudad Universitaria, Tues. to Fri. 0900-1230, Wed. and Fri. 1500-1700, Tues. and Thurs. 1500-1830; **Museo Histórico Casa de Sucre**, the beautiful house of Sucre on the corner of Venezuela and Sucre, see the skull with the bullet hole, open 0830-1230, 1330-1600, Tues.-Fri., 0900-1300, Sat. **Museo de Artesanía**, 12 de Octubre y Madrid. **The Museo-Biblioteca Aureliano Polit** at the former Jesuit seminary beyond the airport has a unique collection of antique maps of Ecuador. Open Mon. to Fri. 0900-1200 and 1500-1800. Take the Condado minibus from the Plaza San Martín in Av. Pichincha. **Cima de los Libertadores**, museum at the site of the 1822 Battle of Pichincha, splendid view (open 0900-1200, 1500-1800). The Tourist Office recommends taking a taxi there as the suburbs are dangerous, but you can take a bus to the south of the city and walk up. **Vivarium** Fundación Herpetológica Gustavo Orces, Av. Shyris 1130 y Av. Portugal, impressive number of South American and other snakes, reptiles and amphibians, entrance US$1, open Tues.-Sun., 0900-1300, 1400-1800.

**Note** Quito has become a tourist centre and unfortunately, theft is on the increase, especially in parts of the old city. **N.B.** also: throughout Ecuador, you must carry your passport (or a copy) at all times.

**Festivals** A New Year fiesta, the Inocentes, from 28 Dec. to 6 Jan., fills the streets with people; much bitter satire on the politicians on 31 Dec., very entertaining and good-humoured (New Year's Day itself is very quiet, everything is shut). Another festival, Fundación, for week ending 5 Dec., celebrates foundation of city. Hotels allowed to charge extra. Everything except a few restaurants shut on 6 Dec. Bullfights, and music in streets. On 11 Dec., there is a children's day festival. Throughout the whole Christmas period Quito is crowded, hotels are full and the streets are packed with vendors and shoppers.

Carnival at Shrovetide is celebrated, as elsewhere in the Andes, by throwing plastic bags of water at passers-by (especially tourists), so you need a raincoat and umbrella at that season. The Good Friday processions are most impressive. Fancy-dress parades for Hallowe'en, celebrated last Sat. in October, along Av. Amazonas.

**Hotels** Note that major hotels change their prices daily in line with the devaluation of the sucre. In these establishments foreigners are expected to pay in dollars. The newest and best in the **New City** is *Oro Verde*, 12 de Octubre y Cordero, L, Swiss-run, cold atmosphere, pool, casino, restaurants. *Quito*, high up on González Suárez, with nice pool, A+, good view, rooms in need of refurbishment in 1991, often room on weekdays as business travellers prefer the more central *Colón Internacional*, Amazonas y Patria, P.O. Box 3103, T 560-666, Fax 563-903, A+, excellent food, good discotheque, shopping arcade, casino and many useful services, non-residents should dress neatly for best service. *Alameda Real*, Amazonas y Roca, L, can be booked through KLM airline, all rooms are suites and many have kitchenettes, good breakfast buffet US$3, rec. *Tambo Real*, 12 de Octubre y Patria opp. US Embassy, B, rec., pleasant service, good rooms, T.V., ideal for business visitors, casino, restaurant slow and extras can mount up, bar drinks expensive; *Chalet Suisse*, Calama 312 y Reina Victoria, A, rather overpriced, only 12 safes, check availability, restaurant; *Residencia Los Alpes*, Tamayo

233 y Washington, B, behind US Embassy, popular with Americans, "alpine" interior, clean, friendly, comfortable, water pressure poor on third floor, comfortable dining rooms, food variable, rec.; *Floresta*, Isabel La Católica 1005 y Salazar, B, bath, T.V., phone, parking, restaurant, safe and very quiet, rec.; *Hostería Los Andes*, Muros 146 y González Suárez behind British Embassy, D, spotlessly clean, hot water, cable TV in lounge, most speak fluent English, French, Spanish, manager holds PhD in anthropology, brother works as guide, rec.; *Hotel Real*, Av. 6 de Diciembre, in front of Parque El Ejido, E, bath, central, clean, but noisy; *Dan*, Av. 10 de Agosto 2482, E, a/c, private bathrooms, noisy rooms on Avenida, good food, services and laundry, rec. *Ambassador*, 9 de Octubre 1046 y Colón, C with bath, renovated, clean, friendly, rec; *Monte Carlo*, Portoviejo y 10 de Agosto, E, clean, disorganized, laundry facilities; *Residencial Portoviejo*, Portoviejo y Americas, T 235-399, highly rec., F, Chilean owner, laundry service, scary electric showers; *9 de Octubre*, 9 de Octubre 1047 y Colón, T 552-424, E, shower, hot water 4 hrs. a.m., 4 hrs. eve., friendly, noisy, quick laundry service, safe deposit; *Res. Dapsilia*, 9 de Octubre 650 nr. Dávalos, T 550-529, F, good, hot showers, not enough toilets, parking, meals, luggage and bicycle store, highly rec.; *Residencial Italia*, Av. 9 de Octubre 237, G, shared bath, some rooms without windows, basic, rather cold at night, family-run, rec.; *Residencial Cumbres*, Baquedano 148 y Av. 6 de Diciembre, D, inc. breakfast, no credit cards, good value, clean, helpful, large breakfast; *Royal Inn*, 6 de Diciembre 2751, E, comfortable, helpful owner; *Versailles*, Versalles 1442 y Marchena, E, nice, clean, car park, restaurant; *Pensión Loty's*, Marchena y Americas, T 522-531, E, bath, garden, nice furnishings, immaculate, friendly; *El Taxo*, Foch 909 y Cordero, F p.p., hostal-type, large family house, friendly, helpful, open fire, constant hot water, kitchen facilities, good meeting place; *Residencial Los Angeles*, Luis Cordero y 6 de Diciembre, F, popular with Peace Corps, often full. *Pickett*, Pres. Wilson near J.L. Mera, E, reliable hot water; *Embassy*, Pres. Wilson 441 y 6 de Diciembre, T 561-990, C inc. tax, highly rec., clean, well furnished, showers, parking, good French and Ecuadorean restaurant; *6 de Diciembre*, Av. 6 de Diciembre 1230, D, private bath, quiet, comfortable large rooms, clean, constant hot water, some English spoken, luggage stored, disco and restaurant downstairs. *Posada del Maple*, Juan Rodríguez 148 y 6 de Diciembre, D with bath, E without, friendly, gringo hotel, cooking facilities, T 544-507, 237-375; *Residencial Santa Clara*, Gustavo Darquea Terán 1578, F, just off 10 de Agosto, clean, laundry service, quiet, comfortable, luggage store security poor, water problems, some English spoken; *Residencial Carrión*, Carrión 1250 y 10 de Agosto, E, 20 rooms with bath, restaurant, bar, garden, good value; *Majestic*, Mercadillo 366 y Versalles, E, well-furnished, bar, cafeteria, restaurant, clean, quiet and friendly; *Residencial St. James*, Versalles 1075 y Carrión, E, clean, friendly, rec.; *Plaza Indoamérica*, Pérez Guerrero 477 y Versalles, E, clean. Further north are *República*, Av. República y Azuay, E, clean, reasonable; *Zumay*, Av. 10 de Agosto y Mariana de Jesús, E, clean, hot showers, no water after midnight, laundry service, will store luggage; and *Res. Román*, Av. Tomás de Berlanga 531, near airport, T 248-289, parking.

In between the new and old cities are: *Coral Internacional*, Manuel Larrea 164, E, spacious, popular with families, clean, cafeteria, open 0730-2200; *Inca Imperial*, Bogotá 219, D with bath, cold water, Inca style with lavish decor, safe to leave luggage, restaurant variable, busy lunchtimes, quieter in evenings, laundry service expensive, car park; *Hostal El Ejido*, Juan Larrea 535 y Riofrío, E, clean, hot water, overpriced; *Residencial Portoviejo*, Portoviejo y Av. América, G, shared bath, safe, friendly, clean, free luggage store, rec.; *Residencial Dorado*,

18 de Septiembre 805, F, intermittent water, basic, higher standard, dearer wing across the street; *Residencial Marsella*, Los Ríos 2035, T 515-884, G p.p., clean, hot water 0700-1130, good rooftop terrace with views over Parque La Alameda, top floor rooms rec., luggage store US$1/bag, laundry facilities, good breakfasts, convenient location; *Atahualpa*, Manuel Larrea y Riofrío, G, convenient location, basic, no hot water, clean, safe, friendly. *Oriente*, Yaguachi 824 y Llona (nr. Instituto Geográfico Militar), T 546157, F, with bath and kitchen, safe, family-run, discounts for longer stays. *Casa Patty*, Tola Alta, Iquique 2-33 y Manosalvas, T 510-407, son of Pensión Patty in Baños, large rooms, G, new beds, hot showers, kitchen, terrace, laundry facilities, clean, friendly, helpful, safe for left luggage, highly rec.

In the **Old City**: *Real Audiencia*, Bolívar 220, D, past its prime but good value, spacious, well furnished rooms, front rooms a bit noisy, TV, laundry service, baggage stored, highly rec., restaurant, bar on top floor good for sunset drink; *Benalcázar*, Plaza San Francisco, friendly, safe, laundry facilities, rec.; *Sucre*, Plaza San Francisco, G, friendly, helpful, water tepid, laundry facilities, free luggage store, roof top views; *Quitumbe*, Espejo 815 y Flores, F, clean, secure, rec. but not enough bathrooms, street-facing rooms noisy; *Gran Casino*, Garcia Moreno 330 y Ambato, T 516-368, G-F, famous gringo hangout, rooms and beds have seen better days, dirty and noisy but a popular meeting place, sauna and steam bath US$1.10 good, bring own towel, cheap laundry service and cheap restaurant, no menus, prices arbitrary, theft from rooms and safes reported, you either love it or hate it; round the corner, same owner, better quality is *Gran Casino Internacional*, 24 de Mayo y Bahía, E, clean, luggage store, good restaurant, own travel agency which sells trips to the Galápagos, unreliable, reported cancellations without refunds, and Oriente (see under Travel Agencies); *Viena Internacional*, Flores y Chile, D, English spoken, clean, large rooms, quiet, hot water in mornings, phone, laundry, good meals, safe, opposite is *Viena*, F, T 213-132, hot water, friendly, but clothes sometimes stolen from line and luggage storage, popular with travellers; *San Agustín*, Flores 626 y Chile, E with bath, clean, hot water, rooms expensive, restaurant variable; *Canarias*, Flores 856, E, rec.; *Catedral Internacional*, E, Mejía 638 y Cuenca, hot shower, good rooms; *Huasi Continental*, Flores y Sucre, F, hot water, quiet, clean, friendly, good value; *Montúfar*, Sucre 162, F, with bath, modern, hot water, clean, safe, highly rec.; *Hogar*, Montúfar 208, F, parking, luggage store; *Rumiñahui*, Montúfar 449 y Junín, E with bath, hot water, safe, laundry facilities, good value; *Italia*, Junín y Flores, G, new, clean, basic, hot showers, safe, quiet, thin mattresses, friendly, family-run; *Félix*, Guayaquil 451, F, very old, ramshackle house, hot water; *Yumba Imperial*, Guayaquil near Plaza Santo Domingo, F, clean, safe, friendly, quiet, laundry facilities, top rooms overlook old city, rec.; *Santo Domingo*, Plaza Santo Domingo, G, clean, hot water, noisy; *Venezia*, Rocafuerte y Venezuela, G, clean, water tepid, often full.

In the vicinity of the Terminal Terrestre: *Grand*, Rocafuerte 1001 (T210-192/519-756), E-F with or without bath, clean, safe, friendly, free bag storage, same-day laundry attached, restaurant, highly rec.; *Caspicara*, Rocafuerte, corner of Plaza, Santo Domingo, not a safe area at night, G, clean, big rooms, hot water, good value, noisy, particularly at weekends (a brothel?), friendly, but watch your belongings, unsafe to leave baggage; *Juana de Arco*, Rocafuerte 1311 y Maldonado, E, only back rooms with shower, front rooms cheaper but noisier, good restaurant next door. Many cheap hotels on Calle Morales, e.g. *Cumandá*, No. 449, T 516-984, E, comfortable, showers, T.V., laundry, restaurant, garage, excellent service, rec., clean, safe, noisy from proximity to bus station but quieter at the back; *Los Shyris*, Calle Morales (La Ronda) 691, F with shared bath, hot water, safe, laundry, restaurant downstairs;

*Pensión Ramírez*, No. 781. On Maldonado: *Colonial*, No. 3035, E, hot water (most of the time), poor mattresses, safe although not a safe area at night, quiet, laundry, cheaper annex; *Amazonas*, No. 915, F, safe, cold water, restaurant (often closed); *Indoamericano*, No. 3022, F, tepid water in a.m., well furnished, clean, washing facilities; *Ingatur*, No 3226, F, hot water, clean, washing facilities, safe; opposite is *Capitalino*, G, pleasant, hot water; *Guayaquil No.1*, No. 3248, F, hot water, will store luggage for small fee, safe, basic. Many also on Loja in the red light district.

If you need to fly out early, *Aeropuerto*, D, is opposite the terminal, some rooms with kitchen, bath, safe, rec.

If you prefer not to stay in a hotel, Sra. Rosa Jácome has an apartment in the centre, T 503-180 (evenings), one double with bath and two single rooms, F p.p., use of kitchen and phone, will arrange outings, friendly and helpful, meets most incoming flights at airport in her taxi (an historic monument in itself); *Denmark House*, Ulloa 1710 y Cuero y Caicedo, T237-195, G p.p., cooking facilities, good information; *La Casa Felix Eliza*, Isabel La Católica 1559 near Cólon and 12 de Octubre, T 233-602, E, central, hot water, kitchen and laundry facilities, cheerful, highly rec.; *La Casona Albergue*, Andalucía 213 near La Católica University, T 230-129/544-036, E, Chilean-run, comfortable, kitchen and storage facilities, inc. breakfast, rec.

For longer stays with room, kitchen, TV, laundry service etc., the following have been recommended: *Apartamentos Reina Victoria*, Reina Victoria y Veintimilla 724, friendly, clean, central, one room with kitchen US$100/month, three rooms with kitchen US$115/month, with T.V., phone, T 521-336; *Apartotel Mariscal*, Robles 958 y Paez, US$17/night, 20% less a month. Apartments for rent are advertised in *El Comercio*, though it is difficult to rent for under 6 months.

**Note** Those travelling by car may have difficulty parking in the centre of Quito and are therefore advised to choose the less central hotels.

**Restaurants** There are few restaurants in the Old City, although these tend to be cheaper, with more local and fast food types, than in the New City, where more foreign styles can be found. It is difficult to find places to eat in the Old City in the evenings, especially after 2200. As well as hamburger places, fast food in Quito is usually chicken, spit roasted. Many restaurants throughout the city close on Sun. **N.B.** Prices listed are often inaccurate. Restaurants with stickers indicating acceptance of credit cards do not necessarily do so. Check first. The following list is by type; all restaurants are in the New City unless otherwise stated.

**International** The *Oro Verde* has a superb restaurant, US$20-25 p.p., and *Café Quito*, where lunch buffet is about US$5 and breakfast buffet is US$4. Excellent food at *Hotel Colón Internacional*, spectacular Sun. buffet, all you can eat, rec.; buffet breakfast in the restaurant, cheaper in snack bar, excellent pastry shop too. In the *Hotel Quito*, *Techo del Mundo* restaurant and *Cayambe* coffee shop are good, buffet breakfast excellent value; *Rincón La Ronda*, Belo Horizonte 400 y Almagro, excellent food but expensive, often has folklórico shows in evenings. *Excalibur*, Calama 380, expensive; in the north of the city is *La Vista Real*, Sun. buffet US$4 p.p.; *Palladino*, 10 de Agosto 850 y Patria, continental cuisine, expensive but good view over old and new town.

**Ecuadorean and General** In the Old City: *Viena*, Chile y Flores; *El Criollo*, Flores 825, service criticized, clean, tasty, specialities; *Inti*, Mariana de Jesus y Hungría, typical, good service; *Monaco*, García Moreno y 24 de Mayo, cheap; *Punto Verde*, Wilson 433 y 6 de Diciembre, open 1100-2000, clean, good service; *Cafeteriá Galeriá Libri Mundi*, opp. and owned by Libri Mundi bookshop, good art exhibits in lovingly restored building, garden, quiet, good coffee; *Rincón del Amazonas*, Ramírez Dávalos 152, great *parrilladas*, moderately cheap, good food, friendly, beware of overcharging; *Famacebiche*, Av. Naciones Unidas in shopping centre, Manabí-style cooking; *Gran Plaza*, Espejo y Guayaquil, huge meals for US$1.50, tasty, good value, rec.; *Los Olivos*, near Santo Domingo church, Ecuadorean, clean, good service, economical; *Café Madrillón*, Chile 1270 y Benalcázar, rec.; *Cafetería Dominó*, Venezuela y Mejía, cheap lunches, snacks, juices especially naranjilla, good for breakfast and coffee; cheap meals in the market behind the shoe shops on Flores y Olmedo, 1130-1400. In the New City: *Mamá Clorinda*, Reina Victoria y Calama, Ecuadorean, cheap; *Cafetería Matrioshka*, Pinto 376 y Juan León Mera, good food and value; *La Choza*, 12 de Octubre y Cordero, typical Ecuadorean food; *Terraza del Tártaro*, Veintimilla 1106 y Amazonas (no sign), top of building, good views, good steaks, good value, pleasant atmosphere; *El Padrino*, Bossano y 6 de Diciembre, clean, good Ecuadorean food, cheap; *El Peñón*, 10 de Agosto, popular with locals, mixed reports (avoid chicken). *Super Papa*, 6 de Diciembre 1329 y Roca, delicious stuffed baked potatoes, some vegetarian, sandwiches and salads, excellent cakes, takeaway service, inexpensive, highly rec., popular for notices and advertisements, open Mon.-Fri., 0830-2030, Sat., 0830-1630.

**French**  Usually very smart, used by businessmen on expense accounts. *Rincón de Francia*, Roca 779 y 9 de Octubre, highly rec., reservation essential; *Le Bistrot*, González Suárez 139, T 523-649, best gourmet food in town, expensive, smart, live music at 2100, closed Sun.; a sister restaurant is *Amadeus Restaurant and Pub*, Coruña 1398 y Orellana, T 230-831 and 566-404, very good French cuisine and concerts, usually 2300 Fri., rather formal, dresses and ties; *Fondue Bar*, Juan Rodríguez 175, fondues and French, reasonable prices, closed Sun., Mon. *La Marmite*, Mariano Aguilera 287, good food; *La Peche Mignon*, Belo Horizonte 338 y 6 de Diciembre, expensive but good; *Rincón de Borgoña*, Eloy Alfaro 2407, run by former waiters of *Rincón de Francia*, excellent; *Chantilly*, Roca 736 y Amazonas, restaurant and bakery, good and reasonably priced; *La Fite*, La Niña 559 y J.L. Mera, good; *La Crêperie*, Calama 362, good but not cheap; *La Belle Epoque*, Whimper 925 y 6 de Diciembre, expensive but very good food and service. *Chalet Suisse*, Calama 312 y Reina Victoria, good steaks and some Swiss dishes, expensive but very good; **German** *El Ciervo*, Dávalos 270 y Páez, good food but slow service, highly rec. by a German traveller, German newspapers available; *Taverna Bavaria*, Cordero y Juan León Mera, good food, friendly atmosphere but not cheap, German, French and English spoken, tours to mountains, Oriente and Galápagos arranged. *Der Rhein*, 6 de Diciembre 3467 y Bélgica, German owner, very clean, good service, excellent food but expensive. *Viena* (Austrian) Av. Amazonas opp. C.C.I. shopping centre.

**Middle-eastern**  *Scherezade*, Calama 329, T 520-117, Arabian food, some vegetarian dishes, excellent salad bar, reasonably priced.

**Spanish**  *Mesón de San Isidro*, Amazonas y Juan de Azcaray near bull ring in north of city, considered by some the best restaurant in Quito; *La Rana Verde*, Juan León Mera near Veintimilla, good tapas and more, reasonably priced; *Costa Vasca*, 18 de Septiembre 553, entre Páez y 9 de Octubre, good food and atmosphere; *El Hobo*, Amazonas 3837, steaks and paella, English spoken. In the Old City, *Las Cuevas de Luis Candela*, Benálcazar y Chile and Orellana y Coruña, not cheap, closed Sun. *El Limonar*, Juan Rodríguez 228 y Reina Victoria, good food, excellent value; *La Vieja Castilla*, La Pinta 435 y Amazonas, very good, expensive, but highly rec.; *La Paella Valenciana*, República y Almagro, huge portions, seafood, good service, good value; *La Puerta de Alcalá*, Lizardo García 664 y J.L. Mera, delicious *tapas*, very good and cheap.

**Italian**  *La Gritta*, Santa María 246, entre La Rábida y Reina Victoria, smart, home made pasta, very good, food and wine expensive for Ecuador; *Trattoria del Veneziano*, Roca 562 y J.L. Mera, good, but wine expensive; *La Bettola*, Cordero 11-87 y J.L. Mera, T 239-396, rec.; *Taberna Piemonte*, Av. Eloy Alfaro, above stadium, excellent, expensive; *La Trattoria de Renato*, San Javier y Orellana, nice atmosphere, expensive, *Vecchia Roma*, Roca 618 y J.L. Mera, good food and atmosphere; *Via Margutta*, Salazar 1093 y 12 de Octubre, expensive, pretentious; *Michele*, Páez 259 y J. Washington, very good; *Marina Yate*, Calama 369 y J.L. Mera, good, medium price. **Pizza** *El Hornero*, Amazonas 854 y Veintimilla, excellent pizzas cooked over wood, highly rec., but not enough waiters; *Roy's Cervecería y Pizzería*, Amazonas nr. Orellana, and in Centro Comercial Naciones Unidas, good; *Farina Pizzería*, Carrión, entre J.L. Mera y Av. Amazonas, very good, fast service, popular with locals; *Pizza Nostra*, Amazonas 252 y Washington, not cheap. *Master Pizza*, Amazonas between Robles and Roca, good; *Exxus Pizzas*, Los Shyris near Parque La Carolina, good pizzas with large-screen video.

**Latin American and US**  *Churrasqueria El Toro Partido*, Amazonas y Veintimilla, cold buffet and meat at US$2 for as much as you can eat, good; *La Guarida del Coyote*, Carrión 619 y Amazonas, and at Jápon 542 y Naciones Unidas, good Mexican food, pleasant atmosphere; *El Coyote de Eduardo*, Calle El Universo 645 y Los Shyris, T 432-580, Mexican, very popular; *Bom Bocado Paratí*, Pinto y Amazonas (opposite Varig office), small restaurant with best Brazilian dishes in town; *Churruscaría Tropeiro*, Veintimilla 564 y 6 de Diciembre, Brazilian-style, good salad bar; *Tex Mex*, Reina Victoria 225 y 18 de Septiembre, closed Sun., good food, lively; *Rincón Ecuatoriano Chileno*, 6 de Diciembre y Oriano, delicious, rec. *Rincón Cubano*, Amazonas 993 y Veintimilla, Cuban, rec. *Hyatt*, Juan León Mera y Bruna, southern US menu, very select; *Adam's Rib*, Juan León Mera, American ribs, good atmosphere, small portions, expensive, poor service, jazz concerts from 2200 on Fri. *Bentley's*, J.L. Mera y Robles, expensive.

**Steak**  *Casa de mi Abuela*, J.L. Mera  1649, steak and salad, rec.; *Columbus* steak house, Colón 1262 y Amazonas, good value, popular, open Sun. *Papy Zuko's*, Colombia y Luis Sodiro (near Parque La Alameda), excellent steaks, modern restaurant with video, good value;

*El Toro House*, Washington 885 y Páez, all the meat you can eat, great salads; *Gong*, Juan León Mera, nice atmosphere, good peppersteak; *Martín Fierro*, Inglaterra 1309 y República, good quality, friendly service. **Seafood** *Moby Dick*, Amazonas 272; *Pedro El Marino*, Lizardo García 559 y Reina Victoria, rec. for lunch; *La Jaiba*, Reina Victoria y Colón; *Los Redes de Mariscos*, Amazonas 845 y Veintimilla, excellent food, lovely atmosphere, wines expensive, highly rec. (closed Sun. p.m.); under same management but more upmarket, *Mare Nostrum*, Foch 172 y Tamayo, good seafood, cold rooms; *El Cebiche*, J.L. Mera 1232 y Calama, and on Amazonas, delicious seafood, best ceviche in town.

**Oriental** *Pekin*, Bello Horizonte 197; *Chifa Gran Pino*, Colón y Juan León Mera, good; *La Casa China*, 12 de Octubre y Cordero, excellent, moderately priced; *Kontiki*, Whimper 1094 y Diego de Almagro, Polynesian, amazing cocktails, very good; *Chifa Mayflower*, 6 de Diciembre y Robles, good Chinese food; *Chifa El Chino*, Bolívar y Guayaquil in Old City, good cheap lunch. *Chifa Palacio*, José Calama 434 y Amazonas, good food, reasonably priced, but slow service; *Arriane*, on Colón y Reina Victoria, great Korean food.

**Vegetarian** *La Champignon*, Robles 549, gourmet, highly rec.; *La Cabaña*, Cordero 1489 y Amazonas, friendly, excellent food, but expensive; *El Márquez*, Veintimilla 315 y Plaza, good; *Herbal Centro Vegetariano*, Colón 1485, good lunches; *Girasól*, Oriente 581 y Vargas, cheap. The British Council does a good vegetarian lunch.

**Pastry Shops/Bakeries** The *Pastelería* in the *Hotel Colón* building is excellent; *Casa de Pan*, Rocafuerte y García Moreno, described as best bakery in Old City; *La Cosecha*, main bakery on Los Shyris near Villarosel across from Parque Carolina, several other outlets for homemade breads, doughnuts, oatmeal cookies; *El Cyrano*, Portugal y Shyris, wholemeal bread, pastries, highly rec., French owner also runs excellent ice cream shop *Corfu* next door. *El Túnel*, Amazonas 1036 y Pinto; *Tip Top*, *Panadería Sevila*, Edificio Torre Reina, Almagro y Luis Cordero, delicious cakes and breads, try the sweets, Mon.-Fri. 0630-1930, Sat. closes midday; *Pastelería Sevilla*, 9 de Octubre y Ramírez Dávalos, fairly good breakfast; *El Bocadillo*, just off Amazonas, very good cappuchino and expresso coffee; *Haripan*, Wilson y 6 de Diciembre, good breads and pastries; *Las Cerezas* fruit bar, García Moreno 1355 y Olmedo, nice patio, friendly, good juices and fruit salads; *Su Café*, Flores 5-46, small coffee shop, rec. for breakfast; *Té House*, Reina Victoria y Calama, excellent home made pastry; *Heladería Zanzibar*, on Guayaquil, near Plaza Santo Domingo and on Benalcázar 860, excellent ice cream; *Baguette*, Amazonas 2525 y Mariana de Jesús, sells good pasteurized cheeses; good cheeses and meats at *Delicatessen Español* next to Libri Mundi, Juan León Mera y Veintimilla; *Panadería Nap*, Colón, just N of Amazonas, good, wide selection, several branches; *Pastelería Frederica*, 10 de Agosto 679, rec. for very fresh cachos. *Top Cream*, Naciones Unidas, nr. Amazonas, and on 6 de Diciembre, for high-quality ice cream, milkshakes; *La Frutería*, Colón 958, serves the "best fruit salad in Ecuador".

**Bars** In New City: *Rumors*, Juan León Mera at Veintimilla, popular with Peace Corps, good atmosphere, not cheap; *El Pub*, opp. *Hotel Quito*, reported in decline with change of management, English menu, including fish and chips. *Reina Victoria*, on Reina Victoria 530 y Roca, darts, both places meeting points for British and US expats; *Don Charlos*, Olmedo 407 y Fermín Cevallos, good music, serves hot Wayusi (like Schnaps), dancing, fun; *No Hay Problema*, small bar on Av. Calama near *Chalet Swiss*, popular, Mexican food, good choice of drinks, international music; *El Pobre Diablo*, Santa María, near *La Gritta* restaurant, new, popular, trendy; *Black Forest Bar and Café*, 12 de Octubre y Muros, wide screen T.V., disco room, well-stocked bar, also book exchange. In Old City, Teatro Bolívar has a good wine bar.

**Bookshops** The *South American Explorers Club* (see below) has the best selection of guidebooks in English and maps covering Ecuador and the rest of South America. *Libri Mundi*, Juan León Mera 851 y Veintimilla open Mon.-Sat., 0800-1800, and at the *Hotel Colón Internacional*, open Mon.-Fri., 0800-1800, Sat.-Sun., 1700-2000, Spanish, English (some second-hand available), French, some Italian books, records, Ecuadorean maps when in stock (cheaper at other bookshops), has a notice-board of what's on in Quito; very highly recommended. *Librería Universitaria*, García Moreno 739; *Libro Express*, Amazonas y Veintimilla; *Su Librería*, books in English and German, García Moreno 1172 y Mejía; *Librería Científica*, Av. Colón y Juan León Mera; *Librería Cima*, Av. 10 de Agosto 285 y Sta. Prisca, good selection in Spanish; *Pomaire*, Av. Amazonas 863 (Spanish mainly). *Ediciones Abya-Yala*, 12 de Octubre 14-36 (T 562-633). The United States Information Service has an excellent library. *Biblioteca Luz*, Vargas 218 y Esmeraldas, runs a book exchange (mainly Spanish) charge US$1. Bookshop at Centro Comercial Popular, Flores 739 y Olmedo, T 212-550, sells half price books and magazines, some French and English books. Foreign newspapers at newsstand in *Hotel Colón* which also has a comfortable reading room open to non-residents.

**Shopping** Articles typical of Ecuador can be bought in the main shopping districts centred on Avenidas Amazonas and Guayaquil. There are carved figures, plates and other items of local woods, balsa wood boxes, silver of all types, Indian textiles, buttons, toys and other things fashioned from tagua nuts, hand-painted tiles, hand-woven rugs and a variety of antiques dating back to colonial days. Panama hats are a good buy; *Eljuri*, Chile 1062. Indian garments (for Indians rather than tourists) can be seen and bought on the north end of the Plaza Sucre and along the nearest stretch of the nearby Calle General Flores. *Ocepa*, at Carrión 1336 y Versalles, good selection, government-run, also Jorge Washington 252 y Amazonas, near *Hotel Colón*, Amazonas 2222 and *La Granja*, and in Old City on Espejo y Venezuela; branches also in Guayaquil and Cuenca. Near *Hotel Quito* at Av. Colón 260 is *Folklore*, the store of the late Olga Fisch, a most attractive array of handicrafts and rugs, but distinctly expensive, as accords with the designer's international reputation; also at *Hotel Colón* and *Hotel Quito*.

*Productos Andinos*, an artisans' co-operative, Urbina 111 y Cordero, good quality, reasonably priced, recommended. After it in quality is *Artes*, Av. 6 de Diciembre 1118 y Veintimilla. *La Bodega Exportadora*, Juan León Mera 614 y Carrión, is recommended for antiques and handicrafts, and so is *Renacimiento*, Carrión y Mera. *Galería Latina*, next to Libri Mundi at J.L.Mera 823 y Veintimilla, has fine selection of handicrafts from Ecuador, Peru and Bolivia; *Centro Artesanal*, Juan León Mera 804, *El Aborigen*, Washington 536 y J.L. Mera and *Ecuafolklore*, Robles 609 entre Amazonas y J.L. Mera, have all been recommended. *Coosas*, Juan León Mera 838, the factory outlet for Peter Mussfeldt's attractive animal designs (bags, clothes etc.). Goldwork from *Antigüedades el Chordeleg*, 6 de Diciembre y Cordero. *Artesanías El Jaguar*, Juan León Mera 234 and 18 de Septiembre, behind *Hotel Colón*, souvenirs especially from the Oriente, the owner, Gladis Escobar, paints balsawood birds in colours of your choosing (not cheap). Ceramics made by Shirma Guayasamín at *Tierra y Fuego*, 6 de Diciembre y Veintimilla. *Handicrafts Otavalo*, Calle Sucre 255 and García Moreno, good selection, but expensive. *Aurorita*, Calle Flores 646 y Mejía, T 620-313, nice, traditional and cheap place to buy folk instruments.

*Mercado Ipiales*, on Chile from Imbabura uphill, is where you are most likely to find your stolen camera for sale. The other market is on 24 de Mayo and Loja from Benalcázar onwards. On Av. Amazonas, NE of *Hotel Colón*, are a number of street stalls run by Otavalo Indians, who are tough but friendly bargainers. Bargaining is customary in small shops and at street stalls. Recommended shops include *Hamiltons*, for jewellery, *El Huaquero*, Juan León Mero, good jewellery, not cheap, and *Bonita Fashions* where you can have a leather jacket made to order in 48 hours. Leather goods at *Chimborazo*, Amazonas (next to Espinal shopping centre) and *Aramis*, Amazonas 1234; *Su Kartera*, Sucre 351 y García Moreno, T 512-160, with a branch on Veintimilla 1185 between 9 de Octubre y Amazonas, manufacturers of bags, briefcases, shoes, belts etc.; *Camari*, Marchena 260, is a direct sale shop run by an artisan organisation. See *H. Stern's* jewellery stores at the airport, *Hotel Colón* and *Hotel Quito*. Recommended watchmaker, Sr. Torres, *Relojería Patek Phillippe*, Mejía 329. *La Guaragua*, Washington 614, sells *artesanías* and antiques, excellent selection, reasonable prices; *Joe Brenner* sells folk art and handicrafts at reasonable prices at Galería Sul, Pontevedra 698 y Salazar near *Hotel Quito*, recommended for quality and price. *El Scarabejo Azul*, Portugal 948 y Shyris, near southern end of La Carolina, Indian handicrafts and works by modern craftsmen using indigenous materials. Rainproof ponchos at shops along Flores between Espejo and Bolívar. *Casa de los Regalos*, Calle Mañosca 456, for souvenirs and antiquities. "Typical" articles tend to be cheaper outside Quito.

*Supermaxi* supermarkets offer 10% discount on purchases if you buy a Supermaxi card; this is available at the main counter. There are Supermaxi stores at the Centro Comercial Iñaquito and at the Multicentro shopping complex on Av. 6 de Diciembre y La Nina, about two blocks N of Colón, open 0830-1230, 1530-1900. Multicentro on Amazonas on the way to the airport; buy masks and snorkels for the Galápagos here. *El Feria* supermarket on Calle Bolívar between Venezuela and G.Morena sells good wines and Swiss, German and Dutch cheeses. Cheap food at Frigorífico Los Andes, Calle Guayaquil. *Casa Americana*, on Venezuela, inexpensive department store. Macrobiotic food at *Vitalcentro Microbiótico*, Carrión 376 y 6 de Diciembre. *La Frutería* market at corner of 12 de Octubre y Colón sells *La Cosecha* bread and high quality fruit and vegetables, some imported food and international newspapers for less than hotels.

"*Bluet Camping Gas*" is reported to be easily obtainable: try *Importadora Vega* opp. Banco Central, or *Deportes Cotopaxi*, 6 de Diciembre y Baquedano, or *Globo*, 10 de Agosto, sometimes have it in stock but it's expensive. For primus stoves and parts, *Almacenes Jácome*, Chile 955 (nr. Guayaquil). For hiking boots, *Calzado Beltrán*, Cuenca 562. For mosquito nets, hunting and climbing gear: *Capitán Peña*, Flores 200 y Bolívar.

Excellent art supply shops **S. Bandra**, Juan Rodríguez 159 between Av. Almagro and 6 de Diciembre, T 238-572.

**Camera Repairs and Equipment** *Foto Gómez*, Olmedo 827; *Gustavo Gómez*, Asunción 130 y 10 de Agosto, Ed. Molina, 1st floor; *El Globo*, 10 de Agosto in departmental store, sells Fuji slides and print film, stored properly, refrigerated; *Japon Color Express*, Amazonas 507, slide film, Fuji RD 100-36, US$7, 1 hr lab. *Maxi Color*, Amazonas 1700 y Orellana, one hour processing service, English spoken; *Kodak*, Orellana 476 y 6 de Diciembre, also at 10 de Agosto 4150 y Atahualpa; *Fujicolor*, Roca y Gutiérrez; *Kis Color*, Amazonas 1238 y Calama, helpful with repairs, will develop and print 36 exposure film for US$7, better quality for 24-hr printing from 1 hr service, passport photos in 3 mins. Several places for cheap processing on Plaza Santo Domingo. *Interfoto*, Juan León Mera 1567, and *Foto Estudio Gran*, Simón Bolívar 140 y Plaza Santo Domingo for repairs and parts. Film is reportedly cheaper than in neighbouring countries but only ASA100 and 200 available. The Kodak processing laboratory has been criticised as dirty and careless; a recommended processing lab is that of Ron Jones, Domingo de Brieva 641 y Diguja (Grande Centeno), take bus to Av. América, get off at TV channel 4, walk up hill, he develops Fuji and Kodak, slides/prints, B/W or colour, helpful and informative.

**Local Transport** Standard fare on local buses and *busetas* is US$0.07, slightly more after 1900 and at weekends. The British style double-decker bus running along Av. Amazonas to the airport costs US$0.10. Other buses are allowed along Av. Amazonas only before 0830. All tickets are bought on the bus; correct fare is sometimes expected. Standard **taxi** tariff in the city is US$0.60 to US$2 and not more than double by night; no increase for extra passengers; by the hour, US$4 up. Although the taxis now have meters and are required by law to use them, drivers sometimes say they are out of order. Insist on the meter being used, it is always cheaper! If they have no meter, it is imperative to fix fare beforehand. After dark meters do not apply: negotiate fare first. Taxis are not required to use meters from the airport. A negotiated fare of US$2-2.50 to the new town and US$3 to the old town is reasonable but they will often try to charge up to US$10. If arriving on an international flight walk back to domestic arrivals where they charge less, or walk out of the airport to Av. Américas and hail a taxi which will use a meter, or catch a bus. For trips outside Quito taxi tariffs should be agreed beforehand: usually US$30-32 a day. Outside main hotels cooperative taxi drivers have a list of agreed excursion prices which compare favourably with tourist excursion prices; most drivers are knowledgeable and speak some English.

**Car Rentals** All the main car rental companies (Hertz, International Avis, Ecuacar, Budget, Dollar and Carros Diligentes) are at the airport, with some having small offices in the city. **Ecuacar** has been particularly recommended, helpful staff, a week's hire of a small car with 1,400 "free" kms. cost US$215 in 1991. **Expo Auto**, Av. América 1116 y Bolivia (Plaza Indoamérica), rec., helpful, cars in good condition, own repair shop. It is impossible to rent a car without an international credit card. You may pay cash, which is cheaper, but they want the card for security. **Land Rover** specialists at Calle Inglaterra 533, Talleres Atlas. Also Luis Alfredo Palacios, Iturralde and Av. de la Prensa, T 234341 and Expo, Av.América 1116 y Bolivia. 24-hour filling station where Baeza road enters Quito.

**Night Clubs** *Licorne*, at *Hotel Colón Internacional*; discos at *JK*, Amazonas 541, *Mamma Rosa*, Amazonas 553, *Tobujas*, Amazonas y María, *La Diligencia*, 9 de Octubre 158, *Luis XVI*, Cordero 994 y Foch, rec.; *Castaway*, mainly for couples, Colón y Amazonas; *Gato Son*, Carvajal y Aldama, salsa, popular, bohemian atmosphere; *Salsa Bar*, Carrión y Reina Victoria, salsa disco. *Salsoteca*, Salazar, but relocating in 1990, good salsa disco, friendly; *Candela*, J.L. Mera, salsa; *Seriboo*, Veintimilla y 12 de Octubre, salsa and rock, rec., Thurs.-Sun.; *Club 330*, Whimper y Coruña, "only for the cool". *Tulsa*, República 471 next to Ciné República, is a dance hall frequented by US expatriates (country and western and some salsa).

Local folk music is popular and the entertainment is known as a *peña*. Places include *Lira Quiteña*, Amazonas y Orellana; *Rincón Sentimental* and *Pan y Canto*, both at Veintimilla y 6 de Diciembre; *Rincón Andino* on Veintimilla, small but entertaining; *Peña del Castillo*, Calama 270 y Reina Victoria; *Billy Cutter*, Cordero 1952; *Guayusas Bar*, Juan León Mera 555, good music, reasonable prices, rec., but small, T 553-274; *Peña del Chino*, and *Ñucanchi Llacta*, both at Rodríguez y Almagro; *Las Jarras* and *Inti Illimani*, both at Baquedano y Reina Victoria. Most places do not come alive until 2230.

**Theatre** Teatro Sucre, Calle Flores with Guayaquil, the most elegant (box office down side-street, Montúfar, and is unmarked—brown door). Weekly concerts during the rainy season, but buy tickets in advance. Symphony concerts are free. Ecuadorean folk ballet

'Jacchigua' presented every Wed. 2200, entertaining, colourful and loud. Advance tickets from Metropolitan Touring. Teatro Prometeo adjoining the Casa de la Cultura Ecuatoriana, 6 de Diciembre y Tarqui. Agora, open-air theatre of Casa de la Cultura (12 de Octubre y Patria) stages many concerts. Also, plays at the Patio de Comedia, 18 de Septiembre, between Amazonas and 9 de Octubre. Good music at Teatro Equitorial Experimental; check posters in Plaza Teatro for details. Centro Cultural Afro-Ecuatoriano (CCA), Calle José Luis Tamayo 985 y Lizardo Garúa, Casilla 352, Sucursal 12 de Octubre, T 522318, sometimes has cultural events and published material (useful contact for those interested in the black community). Many cultural events, usually free of charge; see the listings section of *El Comercio* for details.

**Cinema** The *Colón* (10 de Agosto y Colón), *República* (Av. República) and *Universitario* (Av. América y A. Pérez Guerrero, Plaza Indoamérica, Universidad Central) usually have the best films, the former often has documentaries with Latin American themes. There are many others, especially in the Old City, mostly showing violent films; usually there is a standard entry charge (US$1 or less)—stay as long as you like.

**Sport** A local game, *pelota de guante* (stone ball), is played, Saturday afternoon and Sunday, at Estadio Mejía. Football is played Sat. afternoons (1200 or 1400) and Sun. mornings (maybe as early as 0800) at Estadio Atahualpa (6 de Diciembre y Naciones Unidas, any northbound bus on 6 de Diciembre marked "Estadio" goes there), and basketball in the Coliseo. The first week of December is the main bullfighting season. Tickets are on sale at 1500 the day before the bullfight; an above-average ticket costs US$2.70 but you may have to buy from touts. Cockfighting in a very old Pollodrome, Calle Pedro Calixto y Chile, Sat., Sun., Mon., 1400-1900, US$0.25 plus bet. There is a cold spring-water swimming pool on Maldonado beyond the Ministry of Defence building (US$0.10), hot shower (US$0.10); a public heated pool is in Miraflores, at the end of Calle Universitaria, you must take swimming cap, towel and soap to be admitted, open Tues.-Sun., 0900-1600, US$0.75; another public pool at Batan Alto, on Cochapata, near 6 de Diciembre and Villaroel. Rugby is played at Colegio Militar on Sun. 1000. Inquire at *El Pub*.

**Climbing** Nuevos Horizontes Club, Venezuela 659, T 215135, on Pasaje Amador near Plaza Independencia, meets evenings (1900 or 2000), will advise on **climbing Chimborazo and Cotopaxi**, including purchase or hire of crampons, ice axes etc., but does not hire them (best to have with you). Non-members may go on the club's trips if these are not fully-booked. Padre José Ribas of Colegio San Gabriel is helpful. **Sr. Enrique Veloz** of Riobamba arranges trips to Chimborazo (**see page 828**), but he does not guide all climbs himself because of overdemand and many of the guides to whom he subcontracts have been reported as inexperienced and do not know how to react when something goes wrong. This has had fatal results. Useful climbing equipment stores (and sources of information) are Equipo Cotopaxi, 6 de Diciembre y Patria, Altamontaña, Av. Universitaria 664 y Armero, T 520-592, equipment rentals, rec., Campo Abierto, 6 de Diciembre y Roca (closed weekends), and Sierra Nevada, 6 de Diciembre 1329 y Roca, T 232149 or home 261873. Usual charge for hiring equipment is US$1-2 per item per day, plus US$60 deposit in cash or cheques; stores may buy your used equipment. Freddy Ramírez, who runs Sierra Nevada, highly rec. as a mountain guide. Freddy and his brother Milton speak English and French and also do jungle tours. He has a 4-wheel drive Toyota jeep for rent. Other clubs for climbers: Sadday, Manabí, near Plaza Independencia; the Club de Andinismo of the Universidad Católica in Quito meets every Tuesday at 1930 and welcomes visitors. Those needing a professional climbing guide can try Alan Cathey (T 230-847) who is fluent in English, Spanish and German and can also arrange ice climbing trips. Marco Cruz, guide for Sierra and Selva, can be contacted through Metropolitan Touring. He is reported to be the best, but also the most expensive. Camilo Andrade, Pres. Wilson 643-apto. 135, T 520-263 (speaks 7 languages), recommended for climbing expeditions, trekking equipment rental; he has a Land Rover for transportation. Hugo Torres, Adventure Travels, Juan León Mera 741 y Veintimilla, T 322-331, Fax 569-741, P.O. Box 16-190 CEQ, Quito, very experienced, English speaking, 4-wheel drive vehicle. Nelson de la Torre, La Cumbre 189, Sector 32, Quito, T 242704, is a climbing guide and can organize climbing and trekking tours; he is fluent in English. The agencies offer climbs up the Illinizas (2 days, US$125), Cotopaxi (3 days, US$230), Tungurahua (4 days, US$260). For trekking/climbing trips inexpensively arranged in Europe contact Val Pitkenthly, Flat 1, 44 Elsworth Road, London NW3 3BU, T 071-722 3080, rec. For climbing the volcanoes, proper equipment and good guidance are essential. Mountain rescue facilities are inadequate, it can take many hours to start a rescue operation and lack of equipment severely hinders success.

**Exchange** Lloyds Bank, Av. Carrión y Amazonas, with Torres de Colón, Jipijapa and San Agustín agencies, quick service, rec.; **Citibank**, Reina Victoria y Patria (own cheques only); **Banco Holandés Unido**, 10 de Agosto 911; **Bank of America**, Patria y Amazonas gives

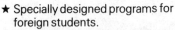

cash only on its own Visa cards; **Filanbank**, 10 de Agosto, opposite Archaeological Museum, provides cash against all Visa cards with no commission; **Banco Internacional**, opposite Bank of America, notes only; **Banco de Pichincha**, Amazonas y Colón branch, good exchange rates for cash; **Banco Guayaquil**, Colón y Reina Victoria, arranges US$ cash advances on Visa without commission or limit and change US$ travellers' cheques into dollars cash with no commission; **Banco Popular**, Amazonas 648, good service; **Banco del Pacífico**, Amazonas 720, 1st floor, slow service, cash advance on Mastercard only in sucres. **Banco Consolidado**, Guayaquil y Olmedo, good rate for cash but does not accept cheques. **Banco de los Andes** very slow for cash advances against Eurocard or Unicard. Good rates at **Banco de la Producción**, Amazonas, opp. Ecuadorian Tours. Open 0900-1330. Closed Sat. Master Card, Amazonas y Veintimilla, in Banco Pacífico building. Bank open Sat. and Sun. in departure lounge at airport. The **American Express** representative is **Ecuadorian Tours**, Amazonas 339, T 560-488. AmEx cheques available at Lloyds Bank, Amazonas branch. Ecuacambio, Av. de la República 192 y Almagro, Thomas Cook agents.

**Exchange Houses** **Casa Paz**, Venezuela 659, and Av. Amazonas 370, T 563-900, will change travellers' cheques into US$ cash up to US$300 for US$0.50 commission, plus all major currencies, slightly better rates for holders of international student cards, open 0900-1300, 1500-1800, Mon.-Fri. **Jaramillo Arteaga**, Mejía 401 y Venezuela, and Colón y Amazonas, will change cheques into US$ cash, no limit, commission charged, photostat of passport required for first transaction, thereafter receipt will suffice, good rates. **Multicambio**, Venezuela 689 and Roca 720, T 567-344, open Mon.-Fri., 0830-1330, 1430-1730, no commission charged, good rates, no queues. The airport *cambio* and the *Hotel Colón* are the only places you can change money on Saturdays and Sundays (*Hotel Colón*, Sat. 0900-1800, Sun. 0900-1200, quick service, no commission). If you have trouble cashing American Express or Thomas Cook's travellers' cheques, try the **Banco Popular**. You are advised not to buy Peruvian intis until you get to the border; you will get a much better rate in Peru.

**Language Courses** at the *Universidad Católica*, Av. 12 de Octubre 1076 y Carrión, *Instituto de Lenguas y Lingüística*, T 529-240: 6-week Spanish courses, US$120, large classes; courses in Quechua. They will provide student cards, valid for reductions in Peru. Quito has become the major centre in South America for language schools catering for foreigners. We received favourable reports in 1990 on the following: *Edinburgh Linguistic Center*, Calle Jorge Drom 945 y Av. G. Villarroel, T 446877, Fax 564012, P.O. Box 17-21-0405; *Academia Español Los Andes*, Pérez Guerrero 441 y Versalles, T 565-856, Casilla 676-A; *Centro Ecuatoriano de Español*, Leonidas Plaza 1133 y Cordero, T 531-141, Casilla 737-A; *Academia Español "One to One"*, Amazonas 1001 and Wilson, T 239-030, Casilla 209-A; *Escuela Israel*, Olmedo 552 y Flores; *Academia Equinoccio*, Ed. M.M. Jaramillo Artega, room 913, Gran Colombia 242, T 517-718, Casilla 2782; *Ecuador Spanish School*, Patria 840 y 10 de Agosto, 2nd floor. *New World Spanish School*, Av. Amazonas 662 y R. Dávalos, 5, P.O. Box 10502, Suc. 4, Quito.

Schools usually offer courses of 7 hours or 4 hours tuition per day, either in groups or on a one-to-one basis. Several correspondents have suggested that 4 hours a day is normally sufficient. Charges range between US$1.50 and US$5 per hour for one to one classes, but beware of extras which may not be mentioned in the initial quote. Schools can arrange accommodation with families for about US$60 a week full board. For an individual tutor, Ramiro Pesantez professionally tutors Spanish, T 565-628, US$2/hr., rec.

**British Council** Amazonas 1615 y Orellana, T 232-421, Fax 565-720, postal address: Casilla 1197. In a different building on Amazonas 1534, there is a library, open Mon.-Fri., 0800-1245, 1500-1915, which stocks back copies of British newspapers and a good café with cheap bacon and eggs.

**Embassies Colombian Consulate**, Av. Amazonas 353, insists on a ticket to leave Colombia before issuing a visa. **Peruvian** and **Brazilian Consulates** both in Edificio España, Av. Colón y Av. Amazonas. **Venezuelan Consulate**, Coruña 1733 y Belo Horizonte, visa US$10, takes 3 working days.

**U.S.A.**, Av. Patria y 12 de Octubre, T 562-890. (The US embassy does not hold mail for US citizens.)

**U.K.**, Av. González Suárez 111 (opposite *Hotel Quito*), letters to Casilla 314, T 560-309/669/670/671. The Consulate is in a separate building a few doors away. **Germany**, Av. Patria y 9 de Octubre, Edificio Eteco, 6th floor, T 232-660. **Austria**, Av. Patria y Amazonas, Edificio Cofiec, 11th floor, T 545-336. **Denmark**, Av. República del Salvador 733 y Portugal, Edif. Gabriela 3, T 458-585/786, 437-163, open 0900-1700; **Sweden**, Ed. Las Cámeras, 2nd floor, Av. República y Amazonas, Apartado 420-A, T 454-872/452-010 (a.m. only). **France** Diego de Almagro y Pradera, Edificio Kingmann, 2nd floor, T 569-883 for consulate, embassy at Plaza 107 y Patria, will hold letters for French citizens; Alliance Française at Eloy Alfaro 1900. **Switzerland**, Catalina Herrera 120Y Av. Amazonas, Edificio Xerox, 2nd floor. **Canadian Honorary Consul**, Ed Banco Popular, 6 de Diciembre y República. **Honorary Dutch Consul**, 10 de Agosto y Buenos Aires 136, 4th floor of Banco Holandés Unido (a.m. only), T 567-606, P.O. Box 6294 CCI. **Honorary Irish Consul**, T 235-713 (a.m. only). **Israeli Embassy**, Av. Eloy Alfaro 969 y Amazonas, P.O. Box 2138, T 565-509/510-2. **Belgium**, Juan León Mera 863 y Wilson, T 545-340 and 545-348.

**Immigration Office** Independencia y Amazonas 877. For visa extensions, Av. Amazonas 2639, open 0800-1200 and 1500-1800; take bus 15 or double-decker bus along Amazonas; go early and be prepared to wait; service more reliable a.m. in Extranjería, Robles y Páez, Mon.-Thurs., 0830-1230, for visas other than tourist.

**Police** Criminal Investigations, Calle Montúfar y Olmedo. To report a robbery you must make a *denuncia* within 48 hrs. of the attack on official paper. If over 48 hrs., you will need a lawyer.

**Medical** The British embassy has telephone numbers of English-speaking doctors; other embassies provide similar information. Hospital Voz Andes, next to Voz Andes radio station, Villalengua 263 (T 241-540), emergency room, quick, efficient, rec., fee US$4, some English spoken (American-run), has out-patient dept., reached by No. 1 bus to Iñaquito; the new American hospital, the Metropolitano, Av. Mariana de Jesús, T 431-520 to the N of the New City, has also been rec. Catch a bus along 10 de Agosto or Av. América and walk up. Or taxi, about US$0.60. Very professional, not cheap, gamma globulin costs about US$12. A rec. paediatrician is Dr Luis Caicedo. Credit cards accepted. Among health centres recommended are Centro Médico Alemania (Dr Klier speaks German), Eloy Alfaro y Alemania. Clínica Pichincha, Veintimilla 1259, amoebic dysentry tests, results within hours, US$2.50; Clínica Americana Adventista (some English spoken) 10 de Agosto 3366, 24 hrs., US$5. Clínica San Francisco, 6 de Diciembre y Colón, 24 hrs, x-rays. For amoebic dysentery tests, Análisis Médicos Automatizados, Alpallana 477 y Whymper, Ramírez Dávalos 202, T 545-945; Centro Médico Martha Roldós, Plaza Teatro, Hepatitis B injections for US$0.30, but buy own syringe, needle and phial from *Fybeca* chemist (see below). Dr Rosenthal, La Rábida 160, German spoken. Dr Vargas Uvidia, Colombia 248, T 513-152, speaks English and French; Dr Pancho, República 754 y Eloy Alfaro, T 553-206, speaks German. **Dentist**: Dra Rosa Oleas, Amazonas 258 y Washington (T 524-859); Dr Fausto Vallejo, Madrid 744 (1 block from end of No. 2 Camal/Colón bus line), rec., very reasonable; Dr Roberto Mena, Tamayo 1255 y Colón, speaks English and German. **Optician**: Optica Luz, Amazonas y Veintimilla, professional helpful, good value for repairs, eye tests and new glasses. All-night **chemist**, *Farmacia Alaska*, Venezuela 407 y Rocafuerte (T 210-973); *Droguería Doral*, on Amazonas, is a well-stocked, inexpensive pharmacy/chemist; also *Fybeca* on Guayaquil in the Old City (sells typhoid/paratyphoid pills—Vivatif, Swiss). For injections and prescriptions, Rumipampa 1744 y Vasco de Contreras, opp. Coliseo de Colegio San Gabriel (old city), T 457-772.

**Public Baths** Montúfar 534 (Old City), no sign, 0730-1930, cheap, good.

**Laundromat** *Lavanderías Modernas*, can take 2 days, Av. 6 de Diciembre 24-00 y Orellana (US$0.37 per 450 grams). *Lavyseca*, Cordero y Tamayo, laundry and dry cleaning, US$0.30/kg., takes 24 hrs. *Lavandería América*, Venezuela 264 (48 hours service); *Lava Duplex*, Reina Victoria y Carrión. Lavandería on C. Colón y 10 de Agosto. A laundromat in the Multicentro on the third floor charges about US$0.60 per load. Dry-cleaning,

*Martinizing*, Av. Colón y Mera in Centro Comercial Americana, 1 hr. service, from Av. América go up Av. La Gasca, take first right.

**Places of Worship** Joint Anglican/Lutheran service is held (in English) at the Advent Lutheran Church, Isabel la Católica 1419, Sun., 0900. Synagogue at 18 de Setiembre y Versalles.

**Charity** The Centro del Muchacho Trabajador, or Working Boys' Centre, run by the Christ of the Andes Mission, is a charitable organization which welcomes visitors who wish to see the progress it is making in improving the conditions of the shoe-shine boys. It is located on one side of the Plaza San Martín coming down the Calle Chile from the Plaza de la Independencia. Handicrafts made by the boys are on sale at Caperucita Roja in the Palacio Arzobispal, Calle Venezuela with Chile, shop 12 and at some *artesanías*.

**Post Office** The main post office is at Eloy Alfaro between 9 de Octubre and 10 de Agosto. Philatelic bureau on 7th floor. Post office in old city is at Benalcázar 769 y Chile (this is the only post office open on Sat. mornings). Post Office also in Ecuatoriana building at Reina Victoria y Av. Colón. *Post Restante*, at the post offices at Benalcázar and at Eloy Alfaro: all *post restante* letters are sent to Benalcázar 769 unless marked "Correo Central, Eloy Alfaro". Do not have letters sent to you care of American Express, unreliable. For parcels service and letters to Europe via Lufthansa **see page 875**. Philatelic service, 3 de Octubre 354 y Eloy Alfaro, 7th floor.

**Telecommunications** International and interprovincial calls are only possible from the Ietel offices at Av. Colón y 6 de Diciembre, open 0900-2100. Fax service and one-minute international phone calls (Europe US$8/minute) so that you can be called back if necessary, available through Intimexpo, Amazonas 877 y Wilson, Edificio Visecom, Oficina 306, T 568-617, Fax 568-664 (Mon-Fri 0830-1800). Ietel does not have a fax service. Collect calls are not possible from Ecuador.

**South American Explorers Club** Toledo 1254 y Luís Cordero, T 566-076, Mon.-Fri. 0930-1700, is a non-profit organization staffed by volunteers which provides a wide range of information on South America through its resource centre, library and quarterly journal as well as selling guidebooks, maps and equipment, both new and used. Annual membership

US$25. Non-members are welcome but asked to limit their visits. Write to Apartado 21-431, Eloy Alfaro, Quito. Official representatives in UK: Bradt Publications, 41 Nortoft Rd., Chalfont St. Peter, Bucks, SL9 0LA, T 02407-3478.

**Tourist Office** Corporación Ecuatoriana de Turismo (Cetur) at Reina Victoria 514 y Roca (T 239-044) and the new Palacio Municipal, Plaza Independencia, open Mon. to Fri., 0800-1630 (T 514-044); provide maps and other information. Cetur also has a kiosk on the corner of Amazonas and Carrión. Some staff speak English.

**Maps** Instituto Geográfico Militar on top of the hill at the eastern end of El Ejido park, on corner of Patria. Opposite the entrance to the Casa de Cultura on 12 de Octubre, running SE up the hill is a small street, Jiménez, which becomes Paz y Miño, follow this up and round to the IGM on the right. You have to exchange your passport for a visitor's pass. Map and air photo indexes are all laid out for inspection. The map sales room (helpful and efficient) is open 0800-1600, Mon.-Fri. They sell the best maps, covering most areas of Ecuador, about US$1.50 each. Buy your maps here, they are rarely available outside Quito.

**Tourist Agencies** *Ecuadorian Tours* (American Express agent), Av. Amazonas 339, T 560-488 (Poste Restante can be sent for clients, Aptdo. 2605, Quito) but is reported unreliable; *Metropolitan Touring*, helpful for information for non-customers, Amazonas 235, T 524-400; also downtown and at *Hotel Quito*; general agents for Galapagos Cruises and Transturi; runs tours to the Galápagos, also arranges climbing, trekking expeditions led by world-known climbers, as well as tours of Quito, generally rec., *Transturi*, part of Metropolitan Touring, operate a cruise ship, the *Flotel Francisco de Orellana*, in 4-5 day trips from Coca along the jungle rivers. *Turismundia*, friendly, Av. Amazonas 657 (reservations to Galápagos). *Seitur*, for the Galápagos and elsewhere, Pinto 525 y Amazonas, helpful, fluent English. *Yanasacha*, Av. República 189 with Diego del Almagro, T 528-964, arranges trips to the Galápagos and Oriente as well as mountaineering expeditions. *Viajes Americanos*, Amazonas y 18 de Septiembre, Edif. Alamo, T 546-586, IATA member, some English spoken, highly rec., including to Galápagos. *Samoa Tours*, Ramírez Dávalos 151 y Amazonas, T 239-892/524-135, very friendly, trips to Galápagos have been rec.; *Coltur Travel*, Páez 370 y Robles, T 545-777, Casilla 2771; *Sierra Nevada*, 6 de Diciembre 1329 y Roca, helpful, provides information and sells tours to Galápagos and Oriente, also specializes in climbing; *Napo Tour*, Patria y 10 de Agosto (7th floor) has been rec. as efficient and cheap, it is better value to book Napo's *Anaconda Hotel* (near Misahuallí) in Quito than to book in Misahuallí (it is also cheaper to make your own way there than to go with Napo Tour). *Sangay Touring* (operated by *Hotel Sangay* in Baños) can be contacted in Quito for trips to the Oriente, T 432-066. *Alpa Tours*, Amazonas 631 y Carrión, rec., very helpful, good for cheap flights to Bolivia or Chile. *Etnotur*, Juan Léon Mera y L. García, helpful, English and German spoken, jungle (rec.), mountain and Galápagos tours. *Latin Tour*, office at airport, organizes various trips around the country in a jeep, English speaking and very friendly staff, frequently rec. *Pablo Prado*, Rumibamba 730 y Av. de la República, T 446-954/542-142, for tours in 4-wheel drive vehicle, especially for photographers. *Horizontes Ecuatorianos*, Pinto 560 y Amazonas, T 230-463, Fax 502-399, P.O. Box 850-A, Quito, arranges a variety of specialized tours and Galapagos tours, 12-passenger van and driver for hire, English spoken, friendly and helpful. The *Hotel Gran Casino Internacional* sells tours to the Galápagos (although many complaints and unfavourable reports received, others are fully satisfied) and sometimes sells cheap airfares to Galápagos with TAME. Icelandair, Av. Diego de Almagro 1822 y Alpallana, T 561-820 for tickets to Europe via Iceland, student discounts.

*Galasam Cía. Ltda.*, Pinto 523 y Av. Amazonas, and Amazonas 1316 y Cordero, T 561-470, Fax 567-662, operates Economic Galápagos Tours as well as Condor Tours, Uniclán, Yanasacha, Sol Mar Tours and their tours can be purchased in Switzerland: Artou, 8 rue de Rive 1204, Geneva; France: Delta Voyages, 11 Rue Edouard Jacques, Paris 75014; Italy: Nouvelles Frontières, Vicolo del Divino Amore 180, 00186 Rome; Peru: Top Tours, A. Miró Quesada 247, Of. 704, Lima and El Punto, Av. Nicolás de Piérola 742, Lima 1; USA, Latin American Student Travel, 43 Millstone Road, Randallstown, MD 21133, T (301) 922 2409; Canada, Galapagos Tour, 745 Gerrard Street East, Toronto, M4M 1Y5 T (416) 469 8211, exclusive representatives, prices are the same as in Ecuador. For other agencies organizing tours to the Galápagos, see page 865.

**Airport** Mariscal Sucre Airport. Taxi (yellow) to centre US$2.50 (beware of black taxis which charge at least double). From airport catch bus 16 to go to Plaza Santo Domingo. The No. 1 Iñaquito and Aeropuerto buses go to the airport, look for a sign "*Aeropuerto*" on the windscreen; also No. 43, Marím-Carcelén. Double decker buses run all the way along Av. Amazonas to the airport. Beware of self-styled porters: men or boys who will grab your luggage in the hope of receiving a tip. There are no facilities for long-term left luggage at the airport, but there are at *Hotel Aeropuerto*, just outside the terminal, US$2 per day. Watch out for thefts by security officials when searching your bags; it has been reported that while you walk through the metal detector they remove money from your hand baggage. There are three duty-free shops in the international departure lounge; they sell few appliances and no film.

A monthly booklet, *Transport Junior*, supplement to *Revista Transport*, 150 sucres, gives details of all international and national flights, and phone numbers of all airlines in Quito and Guayaquil.

**Internal Flights** There are about 14 flights a day to and from **Guayaquil**, book in advance for daytime flights, US$17.35 (TAME, Saeta, SAN) and 2 to **Cuenca** (US$18.10). There are daily flights to **Esmeraldas** (US$12.20), **Manta** (US$16.70), **Tulcán** (US$9.80), **Loja** (except Sun., US$21.45), **Lago Agrio** (US$11.35) and **Coca** (US$12.70), and the **Galápagos**; daily flights to **Portoviejo** (US$16.70) and 2 a week to **Macas** (US$13); TAME, Reina Victoria y Colón (T 524-023) another TAME office is at Av. 10 de Agosto 239; SAN/Saeta office at Colón y 6 de Diciembre. Prices are payable in US$ or sucres and are increased every six months, all airlines charge the same. Cancellations are frequent.

The Icaro flying school will organize trips in a light plane along "Avenue of the Volcanos", 4-5 people.

**Buses** Most main roads are paved, so interurban buses are fast and tend to be reliable. The Terminal Terrestre, at Maldonado and Cumandá (near Plaza Santo Domingo), handles all long-distance bus services and is really the only place to get information on schedules. From Terminal Terrestre to Av.Amazonas area take red and white or blue and white bus "Colón-2-Camal". Take No. 10 bus marked "*terminal terrestre*" from city, No. 1 Bartolo-Miraflores from Plaza Santo Domingo, or a taxi (US$1.50). Most buses marked "*terminal terrestre*" do not go right to the bus station but stop 300-500 metres away, which is awkward if you have luggage. There are company booking offices but staff shout destinations of buses leaving; you can pay them and get on board. To **Santo Domingo de los Colorados**, 2½ hrs., US$1; to **Quevedo via Santo Domingo**, US$2, 4 hrs.; **Esmeraldas**, US$2.50, 6 hrs. by Trans Esmeraldas, sit on right side; Trans Ibarra much quicker, or by Aerotaxi minibus, 5½ hrs., 8 a day (for which you need a reservation), US$2.10, 12 passengers. Buses to **Otavalo**, every 20 mins, 1¾—2½ hrs., US$1, 9 a day (Transportes Otavalo goes into Otavalo; Transportes Andina by-passes the centre). Some buses pass *Hotel Colón* and will pick up passengers there. To **Ibarra**, 2-2½ hrs., US$1.25 or US$2 by minibus (Taxis Lagos de Ibarra), to **Tulcán**, 4 hrs. (Velotaxi, Espejo), US$2, every ½ hr. Buses to **Guayaquil**, 8 hrs., US$2.75 with Trans Ecuador or Aerotaxi, ½ hourly between 0100-2400. Ambato, US$1, 2 hrs.; **Cuenca**, 10 hrs., US$3.75 (Turismo Flota, Imbabura), minibus, 8 hrs., US$4.50; to **Latacunga**, 1½ hrs. (Velotaxi, Espejo), US$0.75; to **Riobamba**, 3½ hrs., US$1.50 (Transportes Chimborazo, 6 hrs., US$1.40). To **Baños** 3 hrs., US$1.30 (Trans. Baños. ½ hourly). To **Huaquillas**, 12 hrs., US$4; to **Machala**, US$4, 11-12 hrs. (Also minibuses.) For buses out of Quito it is often advisable to reserve the day before as they may leave early if they are full. To **Oriente**: **Lago Agrio**, US$4, 9½ hrs.; **Coca** (Trans-Baños), US$5, 0700 and 1400 daily, 10 hrs. **Puyo**, US$2, 7 hrs (US$2.50, 9 hrs. via Baeza); **Tena**, US$2.50, 6½ hrs. (US$3, 8 hrs. via Ambato). Panamericana, Maldonado 3077, runs an "international" bus to **Bogotá**, but this involves many changes and greater expense; it is better to take a bus to the border and change. There are now no direct through buses to **Peru** so take a bus to Huaquillas via Machala, cross the border and catch one of the Peruvian long-distance buses from Tumbes on to Piura, Trujillo and Lima, complete trip about 36 hrs. The alternative route for crossing the Peruvian border via Loja and Macará takes much longer than the Machala route. Tepsa has an office at Pinto 539 y Amazonas but avoid buying Peruvian bus tickets here as they will be half the price in Peru; tickets also sold for other S.American destinations.

Drivers should note that there is now a ring road around Quito, and a by-pass to the S, the Carretera de Amaguaña.

**Railway** station is two km. S of centre, along continuation of Calle Maldonado, reached by buses along that street (e.g. No. 1 or Colón-Camal, No. 2). The ticket office at the station is frequently closed. Severe rains and flooding destroyed much of the track in 1983 but repairs have been made and the route Quito-Durán (Guayaquil) may reopen end-1991, check. Trains to **Riobamba** provide spectacular views along the "Avenue of the Volcanoes". Conflicting reports about services: there is usually a daily *autoferro* (bus mounted on train chassis) at 1500, 5 hrs., tickets on sale one hour before departure, but you miss the best views owing to cloud and nightfall. Buy tickets in advance. Services are liable to alteration, cancellation or delay especially in the rainy season: enquire in advance; train information T 266-144. Metropolitan Touring does 2-day tour: down to Riobamba by train on Tues. or Sat., overnight

Riobamba, back by bus.

**Cruz Loma and Rucu Pichincha** Cruz Loma is the low southern one of the two antenna-topped peaks overlooking Quito from the west (to the N is a peak with loads of antennae, known as Antennae Hill). On a clear day you can see about 50 km. down the central valley and to the east. In 1991 an armed man was assaulting, raping and robbing hikers; you are warned not to walk in this area without checking safety first, ask at South American Explorers Club. Do not try to walk up from Av. 24 de Mayo in central Quito as this is extremely dangerous (frequent attacks reported—on no account go alone): if walking go up Av. La Grasca to Highway Occidental—then take the track which begins at the "Boom" gate just past the eucalyptus forest (beware of dogs—take a stick). To save time and energy take a taxi or bus, e.g. No. 14, to Toctiuco, to the upper reaches of the city and start from there (allow at least 3 hrs to reach the summit). There are roads up to both peaks, but traffic is sparse. Try hitching early in the morning, but remember that it is difficult to hitch back after about 1730 and you will have to walk in the dark. The road to the northern hill is better for hitching; it leads to the radio station at the top of the hill; take bus no. 5 from Calle Gabriel García Moreno. No water is available so be sure to carry adequate supplies, especially if going on to Rucu Pichincha. **Rucu Pichincha** (4,700 metres) cannot be seen from Quito, but can be climbed either via Cruz Loma or via its neighbour. The path to its foot runs due west over and around hummocks on the rolling, grass-covered *páramo*. The climb up to the peak is not technical, but it is rocky and requires a bit of endurance. About half an hour beyond Rucu Pichincha, is a second peak, Paso de Muerte. From Cruz Loma to Rucu Pichincha peak takes about 4 hrs and the return about 2. Take rainproof and cold-weather gear just in case. (*Note*: please pick up your flotsam; the area is rubbish-strewn enough as it is.)

**Guagua Pichincha** A recommended route for climbing Guagua Pichincha volcano is to take a bus to Lloa, from where a 4-wheel-drive track goes to a *refugio*, with beds and cooking facilities maintained by Defensa Civil, at the crater rim (if walking allow 6 hrs). The descent into the crater is scree and sand, and very steep; use of a rope is not strictly necessary but advisable (not for the novice): following the route is difficult despite the occasional route markers and it is easy to get lost when clouds move in. There are fumaroles and thermal springs at the bottom, not enough to cook eggs in, and the ground sometimes shakes under you. Allow 2 hrs for the descent and another hour to reach the thermal springs.

**Excursions** 23 km. N of Quito is the **Mitad del Mundo** Equatorial Line Monument at an altitude of 2,483 metres near San Antonio, also known as Mitad del Mundo. The exact equatorial line here was determined by Charles Mane de la Condamine and his French expedition in 1735. The monument forms the focal point of a park and leisure area built as a typical colonial town, with restaurants, gift shops, international pavillions (mostly no them) etc., and has a museum inside (open Tues.-Fri., 0900-1500, Sat.-Sun., 1000-1600). Admission to the monument and the museum US$0.75. The museum is run by the Central Bank; a lift takes you to the top, then you walk down with the museum laid out all around with different Indian cultures every few steps. There is a Planetarium with hourly 30-min. shows and an interesting model of old Quito, about 30-foot square, with artificial day and night, very pretty, unsignposted, which took seven years to build. A paved road runs from Quito to the Monument, which you can reach by a "Mitad del Mundo" bus (US$0.20, over 1 hr.) from the Parque Hermano Miguel, bus fills instantly; beware of pickpockets on the bus. Two minutes' walk before the Monument is the restaurant *Equinoccio*, good food, not cheap, live music. Available at the restaurant are "certificates" recording the traveller's visit to the Equator. Other restaurants are now being opened. An excursion to Mitad del Mundo by taxi with 1 hr wait is about US$8.50.

A few km. beyond the Monument is the **Pululagua** crater, well worth visiting, and there is now a paved road. Trucks will take you from the Mitad del Mundo bus stop, round trip US$2. Continue on the road past the Monument towards Calacalí. After a few km. (1 hr walk) the road bears left and begins to climb steeply; the paved road to the right leads to the rim of the volcano and a view of the farms on the crater floor. Buses to Calacalí (infrequent) will drop you at the fork, from where it is a ½ hr walk. Plenty of traffic at weekends for hitching a lift. There is a rough track down from the rim to the crater, to give an impression of the rich vegetation and warm micro-climate inside the crater. Also in the vicinity of the Monument, 3 km. from San Antonio beyond the Solar Museum, is the ruined Inca fortress of Rumicucho. Restoration poor, but situation magnificent (investigations under the auspices of the Museum of the Central Bank, entry US$0.15). Start early if you want to visit all these in one day.

Before San Antonio, on the road to Calacalí, is the village of Pomasqui, near where was a tree in which Jesus Christ appeared to perform various miracles, El Señor del Arbol, now enshrined in its own building. In the church nearby is a series of charming paintings depicting the miracles (mostly involving horrendous road accidents); well worth a visit. You may have to find the caretaker to unlock the church (we are grateful to Hilary Bradt for this information).

For the naturalist, the best place in Ecuador to see the cock-of-the-rock (which sounds like pigs) is in the protected woodland near the village of **Mindo** to the west of Pichincha volcano, 90 km over bad roads to the NW of Quito. There are lots of other birds too, the climate is mild and the scenery beautiful; said to be the best accessible Pacific slope montane cloud forest at 1,400-1,600 metres. Mindo has a clean *pensión* in the square (G) and two restaurants, *Julio's*, the best, English speaking, very friendly, wonderful *papas fritas*. The reserve has a hut 4 km. from the village beside a river, where visitors can stay, D, but take food and sleeping gear, no facilities. There are trails from the hut, looked after by a local ecology group which has an office in the main street of Mindo. Quito contact for the hut is *Familia Montalvo*, Manoso 1011, Casa 7, T 455-344. Guides cost US$4 for 3 hr walk to the *refugio* or US$18 p.p. with three meals for a day trek, run by Milton Narváez and Hugolineo Omate. Walks include one to a 100-metre waterfall deep in the forest. From the village there is a good walk starting above the yellow *hacienda*, a forest road ends in a beautiful trail through undisturbed forest. Ask for Don Pedro Peñafiel in the village who will act as a guide. Bus San Pedrito leaves *Terminal Terrestre*, Quito, Wed., Sat., 0600, 3-5 hrs, buy tickets in advance, or 0600, 1100 and 1500 to Los Bancos 25 km. to the W, get off at Mindo junction and walk 8 km.

The Equator line also crosses the Inter-American Highway 8 km. south of Cayambe, where there are a concrete globe beside the road and a mark on the road itself. Midday by the sun, incidentally, is between 1200 and 1230. Take Cayambe bus (2 hrs, US$0.80) and ask for Mitad del Mundo.

The **Parque Pasochoa**, 45 mins by car from Quito, is a subtropical natural park set in mountain forest, run by the Fundación Natura, Av. América 5653 y Voz Andes, T 447-343/4, 459-013, who provide further information, a map of suggested walks and guided tours. Entrance US$1. Camping is permitted in the park (US$20 for 2 nights); take all your own equipment, food and water as there are no shops and take your rubbish away with you. From Quito buses run from the centre of Villaflora district to Amaguana (ask the driver to let you off at the "Ejido de Amaguana"); from there follow the signs for the Bosque Natural Pasachoa, about 7 km. walk, not much traffic for hitching. By car, take the highway *Los Chillos* to between Sangolqui and Amaguana. You will see a soccer field on the right, take next left onto cobblestone road, turn right at the church and at every following intersection, about 8 km.

According to the vulcanologists, the best hot springs in Ecuador are the Baños de **Papallacta**, 80 km. E from Quito, 1 km. from the road to Lago Agrio. There are 4 thermal swimming pools and one cold pool fed by a river, open 0600-1800. You can camp in the pastures up towards the baths. There are showers, toilets and changing rooms. The restaurant is open daily. The farm next door sells milk and cheese. Buses from Quito: take a bus to Lago Agrio or Baeza (drivers charge full fare), or take a local bus from the Partida de Tumbaco, on 6 de Diciembre just north of Av. República to Pifo, from where it is a 1½ hr walk to Papallacta (hitching easy at weekends). You can also stay in the village at *Quiteñita*, G, clean and friendly, also shop and *cafeteria*. In the valley of Chillos (SE, 1 hr by car) are the thermal pools of Alangasí and El Tingo. A few km. from El Tingo is La Merced, which has thermal baths. Camping is allowed in the vicinity. Further on from La Merced is Ilaló, a semi-private swimming club, admission US$2 but clean, fewer mosquitoes and people.

Another interesting trip is to **Sangolquí** about 20 minutes away by bus. There is a busy Sun. market (and a lesser one on Thurs.) and few tourists, and there are thermal baths nearby (pop. 18,000). Take Coop. Marco Polo bus from Terminal La Marín, S of Plaza San Martín. At Laguna Mica, at 4,000m., near Hacienda Pinantura close to Píntag, condors can quite often be seen.

Day tours via Cotopaxi to Indian fairs at Pujilí and at Saquisilí (**see page 836**), about 93 km. each way, or to Cotopaxi itself.

## NORTH OF QUITO (2)

The landscape from Quito to the Colombian border is mountainous, with views of the Cotacachi, Imbabura and glacier-covered Cayambe peaks, interspersed with lakes. Otavalan Indians predominate, the men striking in their short, white trousers, blue ponchos, and long braided hair; their Saturday market is a major tourist attraction.

A railway (no passengers) and the Pan-American Highway run north-east from Quito to Otavalo (121 km.) and Ibarra (145 km.). At Ibarra, the railway and Highway separate. The railway goes north-west to the Pacific port of San Lorenzo, a very spectacular trip, passenger services only from Ibarra: the highway runs north for another 108 km. to Tulcán and on to Ipiales in Colombia. The Pan-American Highway is now paved for the whole stretch Quito-Tulcán.

**Calderón**, 30 km. N of Quito, is the place where miniature figurines are made of bread; you can see them being made (not on Sun.), and prices are much lower than in Quito. Especially attractive is the Nativity collection. Prices range from about US$0.10 to US$4 (excellent value). See the Indian cemetery on 1-2 November, when the graves are decorated with flowers, drinks and food for the dead. Corpus Christi processions are very colourful. Many buses from Quito (corner of Colón and 10 de Agosto). Take food as restaurants are reported to be poor.

The road for the north traverses the Indian area around Calderón, descends the spectacular Guayllabamba gorge and climbs out again to the fertile oasis of Guayllabamba village, noted for huge avocados and chirimoyas. Further north the road runs through dry, dusty land before irrigated land is reached again at **Cayambe** (pop. 14,168); *Pensión Cayambe*, G, clean, friendly, stores luggage, dominated by the snow-capped volcano of the same name. This area of rich dairy farms produces a fine range of European-style cheeses. Try the local *bizcochos con queso*. Cayambe is the Agrarian Reform Institute's showplace; its only major project. The monastery of the Salesian fathers in Cayambe has a superb library on indigenous cultures.

Between Guayllabamba and Cayambe, before entering Tabacundo, a narrow dirt road (signed Tolas de Cochasqui) to the left leads to Tocachi and further on to the Estancia **Cochasqui** national archaeological site; the whole area is covered with hills of pyramid shapes and ramps built between 900 and 1500 AD by Indians of the Caras or Caranquis tribe. Festivals with dancing at the equinoxes and solstices. Note the spectacular wind-eroded rocks. Students offer free, 20-min. guided tours which are recommended. A more interesting hike to the site is to take the next turn-off from the Pan-American Highway signposted to Cochasqui. Walk up through the village and follow the road into a small canyon and over a bridge. There are short cuts via trails, but ask locally. The only bus to pass the turn off to Cochasqui is Transportes Lagos' Quito-Otavalo route via Cayambe; ask driver to let you out at the sign; from there it's an 8 km. walk (if you arrive at the sign between 0900-0930, you should get a lift from the site workers). Taxi from Cayambe US$8 round trip.

Rob Rachowiecki writes that about 1 km. before Cayambe is an unmarked cobbled road heading right for 26 km. to the Ruales-Oleas-Berge refuge at about 4,800 metres, opened in 1981. It costs US$2.50 p.p. a night and provides beds (bring sleeping bag, it is very cold), but no equipment. It is named after three Ecuadorean climbers killed by an avalanche in 1974 while pioneering a new route up the Cayambe volcano from the west. This has now become the standard route, using the refuge as a base. The climb is heavily crevassed, especially near the summit, and is more difficult and dangerous than either Chimborazo or Cotopaxi. Cayambe (5,790 metres) is Ecuador's third highest peak and the highest point in the world which lies directly on the Equator. You can take a *camioneta* from Cayambe to Piemonte (at about 3,500 metres) or a taxi for US$4. From Piemonte to the *refugio* it is a 3-4 hr. walk, sometimes longer if heavily laden, the wind can be very strong but it is a beautiful walk. It is difficult to get transport back to Cayambe. A milk truck runs from Cayambe to the *hacienda* at 0630, returning between 1700-1900.

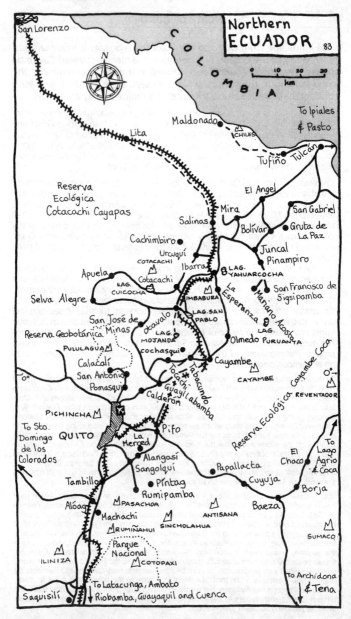

The road forks north of Cayambe: to the right a cobbled road, the very scenic *carretera vieja*, runs through Olmedo, Zuleta and Esperanza, to Ibarra; to the left, the main paved road crosses a *páramo* and suddenly descends into the land of the Otavalo Indians, a lively and prosperous group who have been making commercial woollens for over fifty years. The men are recognizable by their white, bell-bottomed, mid-calf-length trousers (whitened by using a special reed in washing), long braided hair and blue ponchos. Although some work on *haciendas* between San Pablo and Ibarra, most of the scattered homes in the fields belong to Indians.

An alternative route from Quito to Otavalo is via San Antonio (Inca ruins of Rumicucho) and San José de Minas. The road curves through the dry but impressive landscape down to the Río Pita, then climbs again, passing some picturesque oasis villages. After Minas the road is in a very bad condition and a jeep is necessary for the next climb (beautiful views; at both junctions on this stretch, take the left fork) and then descent to join the Otavalo-Selva Alegre road about 15 km. from Otavalo. The journey takes about 3 hours altogether and is rough but magnificent.

***Otavalo*** (population 18,000) is at 2,530 metres in beautiful countryside which is worth exploring for 2 or 3 days. In the Plaza Bolívar is a statue of Rumiñahui, a local leader who successfully resisted the Incas; Otavalans argue that they are the only pure Ecuadorean Indians. The town is notable for its colourful Indian fair on Sat. The fair is a "must" for tourists. There are 3 markets in different places: (a) textiles and *artesaniás*, 0600-1330 in Plaza de Ponchos; (b) livestock, 0530-1000, outside town in the Barrio San Juan at Cotocachi turnoff; (c) produce, 0700-1300, in Plaza 23 de Mayo. The market is rated highly for woollen goods, though it is now rather highly organized and touristy and prices are not low; very little of the traditional weaving is now to be seen and many of the ponchos are made of orlon (these are easily recognizable). The earlier you get there the better; prices tend to be higher after 1100 when the organized trips from the *Hotels Quito* and *Colón* arrive. Bargaining is essential, but difficult. All the same, Otavalo is the best place in Ecuador to buy a man's woollen poncho or jerseys. Your chances of being allowed to photograph Indians will improve if you buy something first, then ask politely. Watch out for pickpockets and bag slashers in the market. (Goods sold in the market can also be bought in local shops, sometimes cheaper and with less bargaining. There are also a couple of leather shops.) There are also markets on Sun. and Wed. That on Sun. is not as busy as on Sat., but you still need to be early or wait until the tour groups have left to get a good bargain.

The Otavalo Indian weavers come from the villages of Peguche (also jerseys), Ilumán, Carabuela and Quinchuqui, close to Otavalo. They are very friendly but do not expect to pay less than in Otavalo. At Ilumán there are also several hat makers, fascinating to watch, get your hat made here if you have a large head. For a tour contact Rafael Perugachi, Calle Sucre 12-16; or Zulaytour, Sucre y Colón. Otavalo textile shops include *Tejidos y Artesanías Atahualpa*, Bolívar 1015, and *Coop. Indígena de Tejidos Peguche*, Bolívar 910. **Note**: If planning a spending spree, bring plenty of cash; Otavalo can be as expensive as Quito, and the exchange rate is very unfavourable, even in the bank. Banks are open until 1330 on Sat. The Intipungo Touring Office will change money at a reasonable rate.

We have received many reports of stealing from Otavalo hotel rooms and cars; ensure that your door is always locked, even if your absence is very brief and never leave anything in your car or taxi, even if it is being watched for you. Thieves work in teams, be vigilant.

**Hotels** May be full on Fri. nights, before fair, when prices go up. It is often cheaper (and more pleasant) to stay in Ibarra and catch an early bus for the market. Water is not always available in Otavalo. **Yamor Continental**, at northeast end of town, D, comfortable, some small cabins, lovely building, swimming pool, restaurant; **Otavalo**, Roca y Montalvo, E-D, hot water, cheaper rooms without bath or outside window, clean, fine old building with attractive patio, car park motorbike, rec., the new part across the street is clean but noisy, Indian music on Fri. nights, nice restaurant, set menu with infrequent changes (homemade ice cream in the *Golden Eagle* coffee shop but pizzas are not rec.); *Residencial El Rocío*, Morales, F, clean, safe, friendly, the owner, Sr. Cobos offers expeditions to surrounding villages in his truck, 0830 departure, highly rec; *Riviera y Sucre*, Moreno y Roca, G p.p. shared bath, hot water, laundry facilities, cafeteria, good breakfasts, table tennis, book exchange, safe, English, French and Dutch spoken by the Belgian owner, who is an expert on the area, highly rec. 15 mins walk from market; *Residencial El Indio*, Sucre 12-14, F, also has suites with sitting room and balcony, F for 3 people, rec., hot water, clean, restaurant, reports of theft from rooms. *Pensión Los Andes*, Roca y Montalvo, G, grimy (see under Museums below). *Inti Nan*, J. Montalvo 602 y Sucre, F, shared bath, new, nice clean rooms, small, friendly, cafeteria; *Pensión Los Angeles*, Colón 4-10, G, friendly, very cheap, intermittent hot water; *Mahual Huasi*, G, clean, small rooms, close to market area; *Los Pendoneros*, Av. Abdón Calderón y Bolívar, G, clean, safe, hot showers, some rooms can be noisy, near bus terminal; *Residencial Centenario*, Pasaje Saona y Jaramillo, F, clean, good parking; *Isabelita*, Roca 1107 y Quiroga, G, F during fiesta, quiet, hot water, laundry facilities, very clean, helpful, parking space, rec. *Pensión Otavalo*, G p.p., basic, noisy from disco behind, showers, laundry facilities, friendly; opp. is *Colón*, F; *Residencia Santa Marta*, F, on Calle Colón, pretty courtyard, some large rooms, ask for hot water, clean, not enough toilets or bathrooms, safe, popular; opp. is *Colón*, F; *Residencia Santa Ana*, Colón, big clean rooms, hot water, nice garden, good breakfasts. *La Herradura*, Bolívar 10-05, T 920-304, G, hot water, rec. House rental from *El Sandwich Viajero*, Sucre 10-02, weekly or monthly.

**Restaurants** *El Triunfo*, Moreno y Jaramillo, good breakfast early, English spoken. *Oraibi*, pleasant courtyard, good breakfast, inexpensive, good service, vegetarian dinner choices; *Ajadero Crystal*, Bolívar, clean, noisy jukebox. *Tuparima*, Bolívar y Calderón, friendly atmosphere, open fire, local and vegetarian dishes, "cheapest beer in Ecuador", rec; *Ali Mikuy*, on corner of Plaza de Ponchos, vegetarian food, juices, beer, good banana bread but mixed reports about service, cleanliness and dairy products, avoid the soyaburgers; *Guacamayo*, Sucre y Colón, open weekends, clean, good food, pricey, lovely garden for lazy afternoons, popular; *Jatun Pacha*, Morales 410 y Jaramillo, vegetarian, open all day, good wholemeal and spiced bread and lovely jams, inexpensive; *Mama Rosita*, Sucre, 1 block from plaza, prepares vegetarian meals if you order them in a.m. *Parenthese Pizza*, Morales y Sucre, shut Tues., good pizzas, vegetarian choice, sandwiches, disinfected salads, news bulletin board; *Crhys del Burger*, Bolívar 8-19, good for breakfast and light lunch; *La Familia Sucre*, Mercado Centenario 13-06, at the Plaza de Ponchos, good for breakfast; *Heladería Zanzibar*, good ice cream; *Hard Rock Café*, next to Plaza de Ponchos, good music, nice atmosphere; *Chifa China*, Colón 4-17, excellent and cheap; *Casa de Corea*, opposite *Hotel Otavalo*, Oriental food, good and cheap; *Chifa Tien An Men*, near Moreno and Bolívar, reasonable, generous portions, tasty food, inexpensive; *Copacabana*, Montalvo y Bolívar, basic, reasonable, set meal about US$1; *Cafetería Shanandoa*, Salinas y Jaramillo, good pies, milk shakes and ice cream, expensive but good, popular and friendly, rec. for breakfast; *Tapiz Café*, Sucre 12-03, good, friendly, breakfast highly rec; *Snack El Sandwich Viajero*, Sucre 10-02, friendly owners; *Centro Latino*, Sucre y Calderón, good fried chicken and grills; *Royal*, on main plaza, clean (even the toilets), meal with cola about US$1.40.

**Entertainment** *Peña Amauta* Modesto Jaramillo y Salinas, the best, good local bands, friendly and welcoming, mainly foreigners, US$0.60 entrance fee; *Peña de los Chaskis*, Jaramillo y Salinas; *Peña Yamor*, Atahualpa y Olmedo, a bit out of town but often has large shows with 6-8 bands for about US$1.50. Try the *guayusa*, a drink of *puro de caña* heated with *panela* and lemon, "makes even the worst dancer into Fred Astaire"; *Peña Tucano*, Morales 5-10 y Sucre, nice place, good music, friendly; *Peña Tuparina*, same owners as restaurant, Morales y 31 de Octubre, rec. Peñas normally only on Fri and Sat from 2200. 2 cinemas; *Apolo*, on Bolivia. There is also a cockpit (*gallera*), at 31 de Octubre y Montalvo, fights Sat. and Sun. 1500-1900, US$0.50. On the Panamericana, Yanuyacu has three swimming pools, volleyball courts and is full of Otavaleños on Sun.

**Games and Festivals** Near the market, a ball game is played in the afternoons. It is similar to the game in Ibarra described below except that the ball is about the size of a table-tennis ball, made of leather, and hit with the hands, not a bat. From 24 to 29 June, at the Fiesta de San Juan, there is not much action in the street but there are bullfights in the plaza and regattas on the beautiful Lago de San Pablo, 4 km. away (bus to Espejo, US$0.20). There is the *Fiesta del Yamor* from 3 to 14 September, when local dishes are cooked roulette played and bands in the plaza, as well as bull fights. Tourists are advised to take care as Indians drink heavily on these occasions and may not be as friendly when intoxicated.

**Museums** Instituto Otavaleño de Antropología, exhibition, on Panamericana Norte; Museo Arqueológico César Vásquez Fuller, at *Pensión Los Andes*, Roca y Montalvo (free

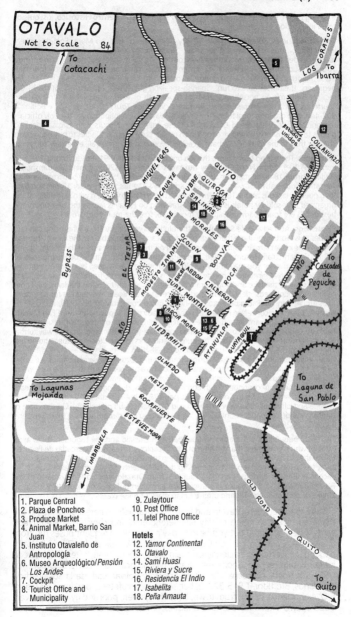

OTAVALO
Not to scale
84

To Cotacachi
To Ibarra
LOS CORAZOS
Bypass
QUITO
MIGUEL EGAS
RICAURTE
DE OCTUBRE
QUIROGA
SALINAS
MORALES
BOLIVAR
EL TETAR
MODESTO JARAMILLO
COLON
AV. ABDON CALDERON
JUAN MONTALVO
ROCA
SUCRE
RÍO
PIEDRAHITA
GARCIA MORENO
ATAHUALPA
GUAYAQUIL
OLMEDO
MEJIA
ROCAFUERTE
ESTEVES MORA
TO IMBABUELA
Estados Unidos
COLLAHUAZO
MANGANGAN
RÍO
To Cascadas de Peguche
To Laguna de San Pablo
OLD ROAD TO QUITO
To Quito
To Lagunas Mojanda

1. Parque Central
2. Plaza de Ponchos
3. Produce Market
4. Animal Market, Barrio San Juan
5. Instituto Otavaleño de Antropología
6. Museo Arqueológico/*Pensión Los Andes*
7. Cockpit
8. Tourist Office and Municipality
9. Zulaytour
10. Post Office
11. Ietel Phone Office

**Hotels**
12. *Yamor Continental*
13. *Otavalo*
14. *Sami Huasi*
15. *Riviera y Sucre*
16. *Residencia El Indio*
17. *Isabelita*
18. *Peña Amauta*

if staying there); **Museo Jaramillo**, Bolívar, off Parque Central. **Centro Histórico**, just outside town in direction of Cotacachi.

**Tourist Agencies** *Zulaytour*, Sucre 1014 y Colón, run by Rodrigo Mora, English spoken, information, map of town, slide show, horse-riding, tours, good value, repeatedly recommended (N.B. there is another Zulaytour, on the same street but not rec.); *Intipungo Touring*, Sucre 11-06, T 920-391, run adventure tours, climbing expeditions, local tours and horse riding US$20/day, e.g. to Lago Cuicocha, 5-hr or 2-3 tours available, not rec. for beginners, horses 'like to run', Spanish-speaking guide, rec.; *Intiexpress*, Sucre 11-06, rec. for 5-hr trek on horseback, good for those with or without experience, friendly and courteous staff, well-trained horses, beautiful ride; *Inca Tours*, Calderón 402 y Bolívar, T 902-446, also organize local tours. The original Zulaytour and Intipungo are the only officially recognized tour operators in Otavalo. All these agencies run tours with English-speaking guides to artisans' homes and villages, which usually provide opportunities to buy handicrafts cheaper than in the market. We have received favourable reports on all, especially Zulaytour.

**Transport** There is no bus station, though one is planned for 1991. Bus to **Ibarra**, every 15 mins, US$0.15, ½ hr From **Quito** by taxi takes 1½ hrs (US$20); by minibus (Transportes Andinas) from 18 de Septiembre and Av. Guerrero, 1½ hrs, US$1.75; by bus from Terminal Terrestre (Cooperativa Otavalo, Coop Las Lagos) 1¾-2½ hrs, US$1, every 15 mins on Sat., long queues, last bus about 1800. The Tourist Office in Quito will help with reservations; the organized tour sold by hotels is expensive. Travelling on Friday is rec. as the best prices and best goods are found early on Saturday morning before the tourist bus arrives.

**Excursions** At the Lago de San Pablo is the Club de Tiro, Caza y Pesca where one can rent canoes. It is worth walking either to or back from Lago de San Pablo for the views, the walk back via the outlet stream from the lake (staying on the right hand side of the gorge), taking 2-3 hrs, is particularly recommended. The path is rather indistinct at the beginning so keep down by the river or you may find yourself rock climbing. Quite steep but lovely views. The 13-roomed *Hotel Chicapán*, E, on the lakeshore is recommended; from the restaurant there is a fine view of the lake and Imbabura mountain. *Cabaña del Lago*, on the lakeside, E, has cabins with bunk beds, clean, good food, service crticized. Boats and pedalos for hire, pony rides etc. Also in San Pablo del Lago (half-hourly buses from Otavalo, US$0.10, taxi US$1) is *Hostería Cusín* in a converted *hacienda*, C, book in advance, popular (run by an Englishman, Nick Millhouse). Pleasant setting. Horses for hire. There are also other restaurants. From San Pablo del Lago it is possible to climb the Imbabura volcano, 4,900 m and almost always under cloud—allow at least 6 hrs to reach the summit and 4 hrs for the descent. Easier, and no less impressive, is the nearby Cerro Hearmi Imbabura, 3845 m.

It is also possible to hike much further south to the Lagunas Mojanda, impressive crater lake 17 km. from Otavalo and also accessible by car on a bad cobbled road (take a tent, warm sleeping bag, and food, no accommodation). From Laguna Grande de Mojanda (also called Caricocha) the route continues south about 5 km. before dividing: the left-hand path leads to Tocachi, the right-hand to Cochasqui (see page 791): both are about 20 km. from Laguna Grande and offer beautiful views of Quito and Cotopaxi (cloud permitting). On the shore of Laguna Grande is a basic mountain hut from which you can climb Fuya Fuya (4,259 m.) and Yanaurco (4,289 m.).

There is a network of old roads and trails between Otavalo and the Lago San Pablo area, none of which takes more than an hour or two to explore. To reach the Cascadas de Peguche follow the old railway track through the woods in the direction of Ibarra until the track drops away to the left and a dirt path continues up the hill towards the waterfall—allow 1-1½ hrs each way. Beware of dogs, they bite. Four km. from Otavalo are cold ferrous baths at the Fuente de Salud, said to be very curative (John Streather) but opening hours very irregular. Zulaytour and Intipungo Touring offer tours to many of these places.

Off the road between Otavalo and Ibarra is **Cotacachi**, where leather goods are made and sold, although quality has deteriorated and choice is limited; credit cards widely accepted but you have to pay a premium. Frequent buses run from Otavalo, A. Calderón y 31 de Octubre. (Hotels: *El Mesón de las Flores*, D, bath, parking, converted ex-hacienda off main plaza, good meals, often live music at lunch, highly rec.; *La Choza* restaurant, typical local dish, *carne colorado*, for US$1.50; *Hostal Cuicocha*, Av. 10 de Agosto y Bolívar, Edif. de la Sociedad de Artesanos, 3rd floor, T 915-327, E, bar, restaurant, cafetería, parking; *La Mirage*, E-D, ex-hacienda ½ km. from town, beautiful garden, pool and gymnasium, very good rooms with fireplace and antiques, lovely restaurant but food nothing

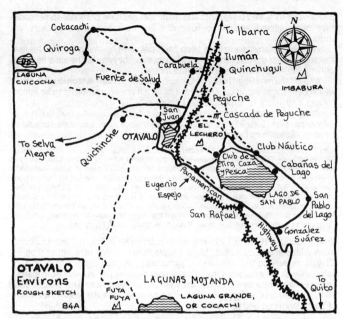

special, expensive, good excursions, rec; and others.) A few km. from Cotacachi (turn off at Quiroga), at an altitude of 3,070 metres lies Laguna **Cuicocha**, which has been developed for tourism (entrance US$0.15 to the nature reserve). This is a crater lake with two islands, although these are closed to the public for biological studies. The Ministry of Agriculture also maintains a research station/visitors' centre on the lake shore, open 0800-1600 every day. The restaurant on the lake shore, *Muelle*, has a dining room overlooking the lake, clean, moderate prices. Nearby is *El Mirador* with food, friendly service, excellent view (return transport to Otavalo provided for US$5.50). Motor boats can be hired for groups of five or more. There is a path around the lake, which takes at least 6 hrs. (best to go anticlockwise), and provides spectacular views of Cotacachi, Imbabura and, occasionally, glacier-covered Cayambe peaks (best views in early morning). Hilary Bradt adds: Although it's perfectly possible—and exciting—to walk round the lake, the path does not follow the rim all the way because of deep ravines. The second half (if you walk anticlockwise) is very difficult and many people lose the path and end up floundering through thick scratchy vegetation on the steep hillsides. Best to go to the halfway look out point, then return the same way by the service road. This will take two to three hours, depending on how often you stop to admire the view or the orchids that grow in profusion near the trail.

The slopes of Cerro Cotacachi, N from the lake, are a nature reserve. From Otavalo or Ibarra take Cotacachi bus (US$0.10), and try to get a truck or colectivo to Laguna Cuicocha from Cotacachi, US$1.60, one way; they await the buses from Otavalo. Alternatively, hire a *camioneta* in Otavalo for Laguna Cuicocha, about US$5.50 for five people. A taxi costs US$2 one way from Cotacachi. The 3-hr walk back to Cotacachi is beautiful; after 1 km. on the road from the park entrance, turn left (at the first bend) onto the old road. You can also walk from Otavalo. Detailed maps of the Otavalo-Ibarra region are available from the IGM

# 798 ECUADOR

in Quito but they are 20 years old and many features have changed; some roads have been altered and some footpaths are now impassable because of undergrowth.

**Warning** Many people have been badly poisoned by eating the blue berries which grow near the lake. They are *not* blueberries; they render the eater helpless within 2 hrs, requiring at least a stomach pump.

Also off the main road between Otavalo and Ibarra is **San Antonio de Ibarra**, well known for its wood carvings, most of which are now reported to be either "cheap and nasty or expensive and tasteless". For the exceptions, visit the workshop of Moreo Santacruz, and the exhibition of Osvaldo Garrido in the Palacio de Arte. Luís Potosí's gallery on the main square has some beautiful carvings. (Buses from Ibarra, 13 km., ten mins.)

John Streather recommends a visit to **Apuela**, in the lush tropical valley of the Zona del Intag (*Pensión Apuela*, G, grim; small restaurant) for the thermal baths of Nungulví nearby (1 hr walk—cleaned daily). Apuela buses from Otavalo on a new dirt road (4 a day, crowded, passengers often sick) pass Nungulví, where the swimming pool is emptied for cleaning on Tues. and Fri. Before Apuela, the *Hacienda La Florida* offers full board for US$30 p.p. per day and a wide range of nature walks in primary subtropical rainforest and excursions. Essential to book in advance. Casilla 18, Otavalo, Imbabura, Ecuador (or Latitudo 0°, T 440672, Quito). About 2 hrs drive (bumpy track) from Ibarra are the clean, hot mineral swimming pools of Chachimbiro in the parish of Tumbariro. Buses from Ibarra 5 a day (2½ hrs).

**Ibarra**, founded 1606, at 2,225 metres, population 80,000, is a pleasant colonial town with some good hotels. Many people prefer to stay here rather than in Otavalo, remarking that the town is picturesque, in good condition, clean and safe, while all the excursions from Otavalo can be done just as easily from Ibarra. Local festival, Fiesta de los Lagos, last weekend of September, Thurs.-Sun.; also 16 July, Virgen del Carmen. Some interesting paintings are to be seen in the church of Santo Domingo and its museum.

**Hotels** The better class hotels tend to be fully booked during Holy Week and at weekends. *Hostería San Agustín*, 1 km. south of the bus station on Quito road, D, beautiful location, clean, friendly, good service, hot water, good food; 1 km. further south is *Hostería Chorlavi*, set in a converted hacienda, D, US$2.50 for extra bed, also cabins, excellent *parrillada* and folk music and crafts on Sun, discotheque at weekends, good value restaurant, pool open to non-residents US$0.30; *Ajavi*, between town and bus station, C, pool and very good restaurant; *El Dorado*, Oviedo y Sucre, D, clean, good restaurant; *Nuevo Colonial*, E, clean, restaurant, parking; two *Residencial Madrids*, at Olmedo 857 y Oviedo, E, clean, comfortable, good views from upper rooms; and at Moncayo y Sánchez, E, clean; *Residencial Imperio*, Olmedo 8-62 y Oviedo (T 952-929), F with bath, hot water, TV, a bargain; *Hotel Imbabura*, Oviedo 9-33 y Narváez, G, cheap, will store luggage, splendid showers, big rooms, basic, take padlock,2 owner has considerable local knowledge, friendly; *Residencial Imbabura*, Flores y Narváez, G, hot showers, old and basic, pretty garden, rec.; *Residencial Familiar*, Moncayo 726 y Olmedo, E, clean and good; *Los Alpes*, E, Velasco 732 y Bolívar, clean with private bath; *Pensión San Lorenzo*, Olmedo 1056, G, no hot water, clean; *Residencial Astoria*, G, Velasco 809, safe, can store luggage, friendly, basic, not very clean, upper rooms have beautiful view, large terrace, laundry facilities; *Residencial Colón*, Narváez 5257 y Velasco, G (more with bath), hot water, pleasant, clean, friendly, laundry facilities, will change money, convenient for train. *Residencial El Príncipe*, Sánchez y Cifuentes 882, G, basic but clean, restaurant. Several others, F and G, along Bolívar, Moncayo and Olmedo.

**Restaurants** *Hostería Chorlavi* restaurant rec. (but it is crowded with tour buses on Sat. lunchtime), likewise *Hotel Ajavi*. *El Chagra*, Olmedo 7-48, rec., reasonable prices; *Marisquería Las Redes*, Oviedo 638 y Sucre, seafood, food poisoning reported, accept US$ at top rate. Good breakfast and excellent bread at *Café Pushkin*, Olmedo 7-75 and at *Mejor Pan*, Olmedo 7-52. *El Caribe*, Flores 757, chicken and local food, excellent three-course set meal for US$0.60. *Imperio*, Calle Olmedo, good Chinese food; *Chifa Muy Buena*, Olmedo 723, does a good *Chaulafan*, "muy buena"; *El Dorado*, Oviedo y Sucre, seafood, good, expensive, snacks; *Portón de Sevilla*, Oviedo 764, seafood; *Caldera del Diablo*, G. Moreno 443, expensive but good value; *Koco Rico*, Olmedo 724, and *Asadero a las Doradas*, Oviedo 720, both chicken; *Luchino's*, Sucre y G. Moreno, pizzas, hamburgers, good for snacks; *Pizzería El Horno*, Moncayo 6-30, good pizza and lasagna; *Panificadora Danés*, Cifuentes

8-44 y Sánchez, good bread and *conchas*; *La Estancia*, García Moreno 7-66, very good grill but not cheap. *Los Helados*, Calle 27, near main plaza, for good ice cream; also *Heladería La Nevada*, Velasco 837 and *Crema Jugetoña*, Colón 721 y Bolívar, good coffee, ice-cream and fruit salads. Local specialities are sweets made from walnuts, blackberries (*arrope de mora*) and other fruits, and nougat (*nogada*).

**Exchange** Banco Continental, Cifuentes y Moncayo, and **Banco Central** change travellers' cheques. *Las Redes* restaurant, *Residencial Colón* and Farmacia Sudamericana, Olmedo 864 y Moncayo will change US$ notes. **Policambios**, Olmedo 7-82, esquina Oviedo. Disagro, Av. Guerrero 6-66, buys Colombian pesos and US$ at good rates, no commission.

**Immigration** Olmedo y L.F.Villamar (T 951-712), very quick for extensions.

**Tourist Office** Cetur is at Liboreo Madera 452.

**Things to Do** Museo Fray Pedro (open 0900-1200, 1500-1800, US$0.15, closed Sun.), Santo Domingo church, religious art, also has a zoo. Balneario Primavera, Sánchez y Cifuentes 323, pool, sauna, turkish bath. *Peña Pedregal*, near football stadium; Casa Cultural, near Terminal Terrestre, Piano bar, *El Encuentro*, Olmedo 953. Ibarra is very quiet, even on Sat. nights the locals go to Otavalo for the peñas and bars. A unique form of paddle ball is played on Sat. and Sun. near the railway station, also on way from bus station to centre, on left, just before the built-up area. The players have huge spiked paddles for striking the 2 lb. ball. On weekdays they play a similar game with a lighter ball.

**Bus** Bus station (Terminal Terrestre) is 1 km. S of town, reached by bus No. 2 from centre to **Quito** 2-3 hrs, US$1, about 50 departures a day. Colectivo taxis for about US$2, taxis US$16. To **Yahuarcocha**, US$1. To **Tulcán**, US$1, 2½ hrs. To **Otavalo**, ½ hr starting at 0500, leave two blocks down from the railway station and call at the Terminal Terrestre later. Buses from **Cotacachi** and **Quiroga** also start here.

**Excursions** Alexander Tkany, of Karlsruhe, recommends a visit to Guachara, NW of Ibarra, reached by bus from Ibarra railway station (US$0.10), or by train from Ibarra to Carchi and then bus. Tourists unknown, people friendly, mountains beautiful and hitch-hiking very possible. A pretty village to visit close to Ibarra, 10 km. directly south on the road to Olmedo, is **La Esperanza**, in beautiful surroundings with an Inca road which goes to Cayambe. Accommodation: *Casa Aída*, F, basic, Aída speaks some English and cooks good vegetarian food. (Bus from Ibarra passes *Aída*.) Eugenio makes leather bags and clothes cheaply to measure; e.g. US$60 for trousers; good quality, rec. One particular lady does extremely fine embroidery; ask in village for her house. You can climb Cuilche volcano in 2 hours from La Esperanza for beautiful views; from the top you can walk down to Laguna de San Pablo, 3 hrs. You can also climb Imbabura volcano more easily than from Lago San Pablo; allow 8 hrs round trip.

At edge of **Lago Yahuarcocha** are *Parador El Conquistador*, 8 rooms, D, large restaurant, rec., run by Cetur, and *Hotel del Lago*, no accommodation, only refreshments.
   It is possible to walk to Lago Yahuarcocha (4 km.) in about 1½ hrs. Follow Calle 27 to the end of town, cross the river and walk to the right at the first junction. At the end of this road, behind 2 low buildings on the left, there is a small path going steeply uphill. There are beautiful views of Ibarra and then from the top of the hill over the lake surrounded by mountains and the village of the same name. Yahuarcocha, "bloody lake" in Quechua, named because legend says that the water turned red when the Incas threw in the bodies of the defeated Otavalo Indians. There are frequent buses back to Ibarra from the village. The beauty of the lake has been disfigured by the building of a motor-racing circuit round its shores.

Laguna Puruanta, 45 km. SE of Ibarra on Río Pisque, can be visited by bus to Pinampiro (US$0.40, 1 hr), then walk to San Francisco de Sigsipamba (15 km.) and on trails from there to the Laguna. Return to Ibarra via Mariano de Acosta to complete 2-day excursion.

A 193 km. railway runs from Ibarra to the port of San Lorenzo (**see page 812**), N of Esmeraldas. An *autocarro* runs Mon., Wed., Fri. (check the day before), taking from 9 to 12 hrs (US$1.10). The train is very crowded. On alternate days it only goes as far as Lita (see below) arriving 1100-1500, less crowded. Thieves are very active at the station and on the train; take as little luggage as possible, but you will need food and drink (aggressive beggars, dressed in banana leaves and coconut-shell masks, are reported to stop the train demanding money—ignore them). You must queue up at 0500 for the tickets, office opens at 0600, and push like mad. Even when you get your seat numbers you have to fight to get on the *autocarro* to secure them—sheer mayhem. Sit on the right side of the train: the track is on the left side of the valley down to San Lorenzo. The ride on top of the train is spectacular but sometimes prohibited; watch out for low branches, tunnels, electricity wires and rain, which makes the roof slippery and dangerous, there is nothing to hang on to. The track is in very poor condition and lengthy delays and derailments are common. Warm clothes are recommended in case you are delayed overnight somewhere.

Leaving Ibarra, the train descends past Salinas into the narrow gorge of the Río Mira (called Chota upstream) inhabited by blacks growing fruit and sugar cane, who sell fruit at the station (the train stops for 15 mins for breakfast). After three hours the valley widens near Collapi (730 metres) and the land becomes better watered and has been more recently colonized. Lita (460 metres) is reached after five hours and a stop is made for refreshment—all foreigners' passports are checked at Lita. 1 km. uphill from the station is a *residencia*, G, adequate, clean, no hot water. Two basic restaurants. Lights out at 2200. Botanists researching in the tropical forests on the hills around Lita say each hill top has more different species of plant than the whole of Canada. Through the lowlands cultivated land becomes commoner until we reach San Lorenzo.

North of Ibarra the Pan-American Highway goes past Lago Yahuarcocha, and descends to cross the Chota valley. The Highway divides in the valley, and you can go to Tulcán either via El Angel over a long stretch of *páramo* or, like most of the heavy vehicles, further east over eroded hill sides via San Gabriel (see below). On the El Angel road at the village of Chota and on the San Gabriel road at El Juncal, the highway descends to a mere 1,520 metres; in the tropical Chota valley you can buy excellent fruit from the local blacks, descendants of slaves brought from Africa in the 17th century by Jesuits to farm their estates. The El Angel route is still heavy going; the San Gabriel route is a good paved road but is subject to landslides, when the traveller is taken over poorly marked or unmarked dirt roads.

About 20 mins to the west, off the El Angel road, is the town of **Mira** (pop. 5,000; bus from Ibarra, US$0.55, 1 hour; from Tulcán, 1600, 1½ hrs, US$1). Some of the finest quality woollens come from this part of the country; there are two women in Mira who produce them for export and a cooperative which sells in the town at export prices. There are two carnivals held each year, on 2 February, and 18 August, with fireworks and free flowing Tardón, the local *aguardiente*. There is a clean *residencia* (Mira, G, basic but good beds), but very few restaurants; the best is the *Bar Latino*. Stretches of virgin rain and cloud forest along the Río Mira are accessible to the adventurous.

John Streather writes: **San Gabriel** (pop. 13,000) is a good place from which to visit the **Gruta de la Paz**, about 10 km. to the south, on the way to Bolívar. (Buses from Ibarra, Mira—US$0.50, 1hr— and Tulcán; *Residencial Montúfar*, G, basic.) (If you are driving, the road branches off the Panamericana at the village of La Paz. The sign says 7 km. to "Grutas", but it is more like 4 km., on a cobblestone road which leads down into mosquito country, but with beautiful views and at least two thundering waterfalls.) There is a huge hotel, but it only opens sporadically and unpredictably—mainly for religious conferences. Buy tickets (US$0.20) for the hot showers and warm swimming pool from the convent before going down to the grotto, near which are the showers and the pool, which is only open from Thur. to Sun. inclusive. There is a restaurant of sorts on the bridge above the grotto. There is very little traffic on the road so plan to walk both ways. There is a weekly excursion to the Gruta de la Paz from Tulcán.

**Tulcán** is a chilly town of 33,000 people at an altitude of 2,960 metres, the centre of a rich farming area. It is not particularly interesting for the tourist except for the famous cemetery, where the topiarist's art reaches its apogee; bushes are trimmed into fantastic figures of animals, plants, geometrical shapes etc. Camera essential (take bus from terminal). Ecuador's unique form of paddleball is played every afternoon by the south side of the cemetery.

The migration office is situated at the border at Rumichaca, so all exit formalities are carried out there. The office and the border are open 0600-2100 with skeleton staff at lunch-time (if not closed till 1400). Visas and tourist cards to enter Colombia can be obtained at the Colombian Consulate, Bolívar 54-076 y Junín (Mon.-Fri. 0830-1200, 1400-1600—better to get visas in Quito). See the Colombia Information for Visitors section, **Documents**, for which nationalities need which. Two photos for a visa and an onward ticket or MCO for visa or tourist card are needed. Colombian entry stamp is given at the border. Because of the high volume of local traffic, border crossing is fairly relaxed. Coming from Colombia into Ecuador, entrance stamp is given at the border. If entering Ecuador by car, fumigation costs US$1.50 and *carnet de passages* (essential) must be stamped at the border. When leaving Ecuador by car, some travellers have not needed to go into Tulcán, whereas others have had to return to the town for customs formalities. Immigration office is at the border. A new 4-km. highway leads from Tulcán to the border. The old road descends tortuously for 6½ km. through the mountains to the Río Carchi, on the border, which is crossed by the natural bridge of Rumichaca (*Parador de Rumichaca*, D, pool, restaurant, casino, discotheque) and a new concrete bridge. Ipiales is 1½ km. beyond the bridge. *Colectivos* Tulcán-border US$0.75 every few mins and border to Ipiales US$0.20. Taxi to border US$1.50, to Ipiales US$4. Airport between Tulcán and border, Mon.-Fri. TAME flight to Quito at 1245 (usually fully booked) there is a TAME office in Tulcán in the basement of *Hotel Azteca*, Bolívar y García Morena.

**Hotels** *Azteca*, E, the best in town, soap, towels, TV, restaurant, but noisy from the discotheque downstairs; *Frailejón*, Sucre y Rocafuerte (T 980-129/981-149), E with bath, hot water, T/V, good but expensive restaurant; *Quito*, Ayacucho 450, G, clean, central; *Pensión Minerva*, G, 10 de Agosto y Bolívar, clean but cold; annex in centre, F, overpriced; *Residencial Carchi*, G, Sucre 576 y Pichincha, friendly, no hot water; *Residencial Oasis*, F, 10 de Agosto 395 y Sucre, private showers; *El Paso*, F, Sucre y Pichincha, communal shower sometimes has hot water. *Res. Ecuador*, opp. bus station, F, hot water, clean but poor bathrooms; *Avenida*, also opp. bus station, G, no hot water, not good. If all are full (which they tend to be at weekends), try police station.

**Restaurants** *Avenida*, Bolívar y Ecuador, opp. bus station; *Terminal*, in bus station, reasonable. Many along Sucre: *Restaurant El Paso*, Chinese, good; and other *chifas*. *Parrilladas*, Roberto Sierran y Bolívar, good typical food, near cemetery; *Max Pan* for good breakfasts. Good cheeseburgers at *Café de la Rueda* just off main square.

**Camping** Possible at the sports field next to the cemetery.

**Transport** Bus, if you can get one, is cheaper, US$0.15. Bus to **Quito** 4 hrs, US$2, every ½ hr with Velotaxi or Espejo; to **Ibarra**, 2½ hrs, US$1. **Otavalo**, US$1.40, 3 hrs (make sure bus is going to Otavalo; if not get out on the Highway at the turn off), or take bus to Ibarra and then collective taxi. To **Guayaquil**, 20 a day, 11 hrs, US$5. Plenty of colectivos also. Bus terminal is long uphill walk from centre; best to take taxi or little blue bus.

**Exchange** The many money changers on both sides of the border will exchange cash. It is reportedly difficult to change travellers' cheques, but try *Casa Paz cambio*, on Ayacucho in front of *Hotel Quito*, or **Carlos Burbano**, Bolívar y Junín. For those arriving in Ecuador, change only what you need to get to Quito, where the rate is better. **Banco de los Andes**, Sucre y Junín, is the only bank which will undertake foreign currency transactions (cash only).

**Excursions** Weekly minibus trips with Cooperativa 11 de Abril, US$2 return, from opp. *Hotel Carchi*, to Gruta de la Paz (see above) at 0800 on Sats., and to Aguas Hediondas at 0800 on Suns. (leaves only if enough passengers). There are 3 daily buses from opp. Colegio Tulcán, near the cemetery, 0600, 0630, 0900, to Maldonado, passing Tufiño, 1 hr. From Tufiño walk 2 km. to turnoff for Aguas Hediondas, then 6 km. to springs themselves. You can probably hitch back to Tufiño. (Taxi Tulcán-Aguas Hediondas, US$6, including one hour wait.) John Streather tells us that Aguas Hediondas (stinking waters) is a pool of boiling sulphurous mineral waters in a wild, impressive, lonely valley. An ice-cold stream of melted snow water passes nearby—you need to direct it into the pool to make it cool enough to enter! These waters are said to cure spots, rheumatism, etc. If you take your passport you can walk from Tufiño over the border to the various hot, warm and cold mineral baths, with a restaurant (friendly and cheap) about 2 km. away in Colombia (the public baths are free but not very clean, the private ones are clean and cost only US$0.20). You can spend the morning at these baths and return to Ecuador for the 1400 bus back to Tulcán, so long as the passport is shown at the border (a rope over the village street). There are five pools at Tufiño—the top, hot, one is good for liver and kidneys, the one below the restaurant for the nerves and rheumatism. The cold pool is some distance from the four others which are all close together. The landscape and the plants on the way up to Aguas Hediondas are really marvellous.

Another, longer but rewarding, trip from Tulcán is to go down to the hot jungle riverside town of Maldonado—same bus as for Tufiño—small *pensiones*, good swimming. The road to Maldonado passes the foot of the trail to the Chiles volcano. On the way up you see many Frailejón plants (related to the Puya Raimondii of Peru and found also in Venezuela).

## THE PACIFIC LOWLANDS (3)

The region's fertile banana lands, shrimp farms and oil refineries provide the bulk of the country's exports. Dirty, noisy, bustling towns on mosquito-infested estuaries are interspersed with charming fishing villages. Beaches range from overcrowded to deserted, but interest in the latter is growing rapidly. The Machalilla National Park protects an important area of primary dry tropical forest, precolumbian archaeological sites, coral reef and wildlife.

From Quito, a scenic bus trip can be taken to (129 km. US$1.05, 2½ hrs) **Santo Domingo de los Colorados**, in the W lowlands (pop. 66,661). There is a small daily market and a large Sun. market, but very few Indians now come to the town so both it and the market itself are unexciting and scruffy. You would do better to hire a taxi and go to their villages to see the Colorados (about US$15 for 2 hrs). Very few of them now wear the traditional hair dress. They are generally not keen on dressing up for gringos to photograph and you will probably be charged about US$4. Santo Domingo, now the hub of roads radiating to Quito, Guayaquil (by bus 5 hrs), Esmeraldas (bus, 4 hrs—the road is very bad N of Rosa Zárate) and Manta, once had the boom town air of the American west a century ago, but is now dusty, noisy, and decaying. Shops in the town are open Tues.-Sun., and banks Tues.-Sat. There is a cinema.

Carnival water throwing is particularly vigorous in Santo Domingo.

**Hotels** Out of town: *Zaracay*, C, 2 km. out of town on the road to Quito, restaurant, casino, noisy disco, gardens and a swimming pool, good rooms and service, best available, advisable to book (T 750-023), especially at weekend. Nearby is *Hotel del Toachi*, just W of *Zaracay*, E, best in this range, good showers, swimming pool. On the same road, 20 km. from Santo Domingo, is *Tinalandia*, a bit run down but pleasant and small, run by Doña Tina (of Russian origin), chalets (musty smell) with bathrooms, A+ inc. meals, with its own golf course overlooking the Toachi valley, and excellent food. The hotel attracts golf playing executives or diplomats from Quito and keen birdwatchers. Many species of birds, flowers and butterflies in the woods behind (open to non-residents for US$3 a day). Poorly signposted, take small road between Km. 16 and 17 from Santo Domingo on the right (for cheaper accommodation near *Tinalandia*, *Florida* in Alluriquín, 7 km. away on main road, F, with swimming pool).
    In town: (no hotels will take credit cards) *Caleta*, Ibarra 137, E, good restaurant, private bath, good; *Colorado*, 29 de Mayo y Quevedo, F, a bit noisy; two *Hostales Turistas*, *No. 1* at 3 de Julio y Latacunga and *No. 2* at Ambato y 29 de Mayo, both F with bath (hot water); *No. 2* basic, noisy, no windows; *Hostal San José*, G, Latacunga y 3 de Julio, run down and dirty; *Pensión Don Pepe*, Calle Quito, F, clean, friendly, quiet. *Amambay*, quite good, water on demand; *Residencial Madrid*, G, Av. 3 de Julio 438, good and clean but used as a brothel and many rooms without windows.

**Restaurants** *Parrilladas Argentinas*, Chilenas, on Quevedo road Km. 5, for good barbecues. *Mocambo*, Tulcán y Machala, good; *La Fuente*, Ibarra y 3 de Julio, good; *Rico Pollo*, Quito y Río Pove, for chicken; two *chifas*, *Nuevo Hongkong* and *Nueva China*, on the Parque Zaracay; *Corea*, 3 de Julio y San Miguel. Several snackbars and pizzerias. *Juan El Marino*, 1.5 km. from Monument Square on road to Quevedo, reasonably priced, huge portions.

**Exchange** Banco Internacional, Esmeraldas y Quito.

**Immigration** Camilo Ponce (police station), T 750-225.

A busy paved highway connects Santo Domingo de los Colorados with Esmeraldas to the North (see page 808). On this road is Quinindé (Rosa Zárate), where *Residencial Paraíso* is clean and quite good, water 24 hrs a day. A good, paved road runs W via El Carmen and Chone to the popular seaside resort of Bahía de Caráquez, 340 km. from Quito (see page 807). 13 km. beyond Santo Domingo is the excellent *La Hacienda*, C, 20 rooms, restaurant, swimming pool, small zoo. The twisty road before Chone winds through an area of strange conical hills topped by tall palm trees. Further on it passes villages and towns with wooden houses on stilts and bicycle rickshaws. Another highway goes S to **Quevedo** (78,000 people) 1½ hrs by bus. (At Km. 47 from Santo Domingo is *Río Palenque*, B p.p. inc. 3 meals, a biological field station, good bird watching, T 561-646 or 232-468 in Quito for information and reservations.) Set in fertile banana lands and often flooded in the rainy season, Quevedo is known as the Chinatown of Ecuador, with a fair-sized Chinese colony. It is a dusty, noisy, crowded town which has grown exceptionally rapidly over the last 25 years.

**Hotels** None offers a quiet night. *Olímpico*, Bolívar y 19a, D, good restaurant, near stadium; *Ejecutivo Internacional*, E, 7 de Octubre y Calle Cuarta, modern, large rooms, a/c, private bath, good value, clean, the least noisy; *Guayaquil* opposite is a brothel, basic, G, prices vary for different rooms. *El Cóndor*, E with a/c, F without; *El Turista*, F; *Continental*, F, basic; *Charito*, Bolívar 720, F. All are on, or near Av. 7 de Octubre and the plaza.

**Restaurants** *Hotel Olímpico*, best. Most others along 7 de Octubre: *Rincón Caleño* (Colombian), 1103; *Chifa 51* (Chinese, disappointing), 928; other *chifas* at 806, 809 and 707; *Tungurahua* (local food), 711. Snackbar, *Quevedo City*, Bolívar y 4a.

**Roads and Buses** Quevedo is an important route centre. The old highway from Latacunga in the highlands to Quevedo carries very little traffic; it is extremely twisty in parts and in poor condition but it is the most beautiful of the routes connecting the highlands with Portoviejo, Manta and the coast. (Bus, Quevedo-Latacunga, Cotopaxi line, 6 hrs, US$1.50. Bus (*chiva*), Quevedo- Portoviejo, from 7 de Octubre and Calle 8, 5 hrs, US$1.40, uncomfortable, watch your possessions.) On this road is the *Selva Negra* hotel, basic accommodation, but excellent food.

Quevedo is connected with Guayaquil by two paved highways (bus, 3 hrs, US$1.25), one through Balzar and Daule, one through Babahoyo (41,000 people). Bahía de Caráquez can be reached via Velasco Ibarra, Pichincha, Rocafuerte and Calceta. The roads give a good idea of tropical Ecuador, with its exotic birdlife and jungle and plantations of cacao, sugar, bananas, oranges, tropical fruits and rice. To Quito, 4 hrs, US$1.80.

**The Coast** Popular beach resorts of the Pacific lowlands can be reached along a paved highway (toll) from Guayaquil. The road divides at Gómez Rendón (Progreso), 63 km. One branch leads to Villamil, normally known as **Playas**, the nearest seaside resort to Guayaquil (2 hrs by frequent bus—US$1). Look out for the bottle shaped Ceiba trees between Guayaquil and Progreso, where the landscape changes and 2-5 metre cacti are prominent. Playas' old charm as a fishing village has gone, although every day single-sailed balsa rafts can still be seen among the motor launches returning laden with fish. These rafts are unique, highly ingenious and very simple. The beach shelves gently, and is 200-400 metres wide. As a resort, it is still neat, clean and small, unlike Salinas, with mostly small hotels and seafood restaurants along the beach, filled by Ecuadoreans at weekends. As an alternative to the main beach take the unsurfaced road going north which leads to a long sandy beach backed by salt flats and giant cactus. Ecuadoreans flock to the sea from January to April and traffic is very heavy along the coastal roads. Anyone who goes to the beach in May-December will have it largely to himself, except on Sundays.

**Hotels** *Residencial Cattan*, sea view, D with good food, E without; *Miraglia*, F, run down but clean, sea view, showers, fresh drinking water, parking for motorcycles; *Playas*, E, beach hotel with seawater showers and plain rooms without fans or a/c, good restaurant; *Rey David*, E, sea view; *Acapulco*, F, clean, friendly, restaurant, sea view; *El Galeón*, E, beside the church, friendly, clean, mosquito nets or netting over the windows, water all day, cheap restaurant with excellent seafood attached; *Turístico*, F, just off square, clean, mosquito nets; *Hostería La Gaviota*, 500 metres out on Posorja road, D, colour TV, a/c, but rooms shabby with cockroaches, friendly, good clean restaurant. *Residencial California*, and *Restaurant Jalisco* nearby, good cheap food. *Hostería Costa Verde*, cheap, clean, F. Camping at S end of beach. Casino. There are a lot of little fish restaurants along the beach but not all are open during the week.

There is a water shortage all along the coast; drinking water has to be brought by tanker from Guayaquil and no hotel can guarantee water in the rooms at all times. There are showers on the beach.

An interesting place to visit, a walk or short drive from Playas, is the little village of El Morro. There is a picturesque wooden church and a large rock formation known as El Muerto. Beyond Playas lies **Posorja**, at the mouth of the Guayas estuary, home to a large commercial fishing fleet and fish processing plants. The ocean front is rubbish-strewn and muddy. Posorja and other coastal towns are receiving a population influx because of the economic boom caused by shrimp farming. Local people catch young shrimp in the sea and estuaries and sell them to large commercial ponds where they are grown to market size. From Esmeraldas to Machala, the ocean front is being transformed by shrimp farming. Native mangrove swamps are being destroyed rapidly; heavy construction equipment can be seen everywhere.

West of Gómez Rendón (Progreso) the road to Salinas runs through a vast area of arid thorn-scrub land whose inhabitants look very Indian and produce little besides charcoal. At **Santa Elena** the road forks. To the left, south, we pass a petroleum refinery and enter the busy port and regional market centre of **La Libertad** (Hotel Villa María, G, very run down, on Malecón, as are Lido and Seven Seas, both G, mediocre; Samarina, E, Cetur-run, some bungalows, swimming pool, restaurant, coffee shop, bar, with views of oil refinery and tankers; Hotel Turis Palm, Av. 9 de Octubre, F, fan, bath—G without, older place and a bit run down, next door and similar is Reina del Pacífico). Buses every hour to Manglaralto (US$0.75), Puerto López and Jipijapa from near market. Bus to Guayaquil US$1.25.

A few km. further on, surrounded by miles of salt flats, is **Salinas**, the self-styled best resort in Ecuador (population, 21,000, buses from Guayaquil, US$1, at the new Terminal Terrestre about 2½ hrs; return journey, go to La Libertad by bus or colectivo and take bus from terminal there). The beaches are not good and the town is becoming increasingly more developed, expensive, crowded and ugly; it is very quiet outside the holiday season (Dec.-Easter and July-Sept.). The best time for swimming is Dec.-May. The flat-topped hill at Punta Santa Elena dominates the landscape. Good deep-sea fishing and water-skiing. Pesca Tours, on the seafront, rents boats for US$250; four lines from the boat, you may keep any dorado you catch but Pesca Tours keeps the marlin. Car racing at the Autódromo.

**Hotels** Salinas, D, modern, off Malecón, restaurant reported good; **Miramar**, with casino, B, with bath and telephone. **Samarina**, C, or B bungalow with 6 beds, acceptable; **Cantábrico**, D, lines of hammocks outside, 4-course set meal; **Yulee**, D, with own bath (but try bargaining), clean, excellent food, friendly, well placed for beaches; **Residencial Rachel**, 2 blocks from beach, E, mosquito nets inadequate. 5 km. before Salinas, at Santa Rosa, is **Hotel Don Mincho**, on main road, D, bath, pool, clean, friendly.

**Restaurants** Saavedra rec. for large portions of well cooked fish for about US$1.50. Mar y Tierra, close to Hotel Miramar, expensive but excellent seafood, especially lobster; also near the **Miramar** is Flipper, cheap, simple, clean and friendly. Discothèque, El Caracol. Night club, **Che Papusa** (near town hall), normally known after its owner as **Donde el Roy**.

**Exchange** It is not possible to change travellers cheques' in Salinas. Not all banks change cash; you can change cash at the supermarket and the Hotel Salinas but the rate is bad.

**Cables** Ietel public telex booth at Radio Internacional.

At Baños San Vicente, about 7 km. E of La Libertad, just off the main road to Guayaquil, Cetur has opened a large tourist complex, where for US$0.30 admission you have use of the whole facility, including swimming pools, thermal baths and a mud hole to cure assorted ailments. There is still more construction work to be done; a hotel is planned when finance is available.

**Punta Carnero** is on the S shore of the Santa Elena peninsula, 8 km. S of La Libertad. Magnificent 15-km. beach with wild surf and heavy undertow, virtually empty during the week (Hotels: Punta Carnero, A, restaurant, swimming pool; Hostería del Mar, D, T 775-370 or Guayaquil T 324-006, opened 1991, restaurant, swimming pool, family suites to let on weekly basis). A few kms. to the E of Punta Carnero, along the coast, lies **Anconcito**, a picturesque fishing port at the foot of steep cliffs; pelicans and frigate birds gather round the colourful boats when the catch is brought in. Nowhere in town to stay; further on is Ancón, centre of the declining local oilfield.

The northward fork of the road at Santa Elena leads along the coast (past Ballenita, pleasant beach, surfing with two good ceviche restaurants, cottages can be rented) as far north as Puerto de Cayo. All this coastal road is now paved, much of it in good condition. A number of attractive fishing villages along this stretch of coast contain the modern bungalows of Guayaquileños. Almost all the villages have good beaches, and there is particularly good swimming near the attractive fishing villages of Palmar and Ayangue (only hotel is *Hostal Un Millón de Amigos*, clean, friendly, good food, rec.; village very crowded at weekends), but respect the ocean, there can be a fierce undertow at times making it dangerous: check locally. Many kinds of cactus are found in this area because of the dry climate (fewer than five days of rain a year). A typical dish from this region is *sopa de bola de verde*, made from several kinds of vegetable: green *plátano* is crushed, kneaded and formed into balls filled with green peas and diced carrots.

At **Valdivia**, a small port, is the site of the supposed Japanese-Jomón culture contact, via fishermen, about 3000 B.C. Little for the visitor to see; the little museum is closed; most artefacts discovered at the site are in museums in Quito and Guayaquil.

**Manglaralto**, the main centre of the region north of Santa Elena, is reached by bus from Guayaquil (change at La Libertad) as well as by numerous trucks.

**Hotels** *Alegre Calamar*, N end of town, F, big, airy rooms, shared bath, mosquito nets, clean, good seafood restaurant; *Corona del Mar* restaurant has rooms, near main plaza, F with bath, not very clean; *Habitaciones* next to post office, F, bath, and a bungalow for rent. Sra. de Arcos' house next to post office. It is a nice place to stay and bathe, with a good, quiet, clean beach, but little shelter. Good surf. Take plenty of sun tan lotion. *Comedor Familiar* has meals weekends only; also *Comedor Florencia*, moderately cheap and friendly.

**Bus** to La Libertad, US$0.75; to Jipijapa, US$1.55.

3 km. N, at Montañita beach (nice, but some sandflies), reported best surfing in Ecuador, cottages to let (Gabriela rents tents; *Rincón de Amigos*, G, dormitory or cabins, Irish-owned, on waterfront, friendly, good food.), 1 hr, US$0.70, by bus or truck from La Libertad or Santa Elena.

North of Manglaralto the rainfall increases and the paved road continues through lush tropical scenery via Puerto Rico and Salango to Puerto López, set in an impressive bay with hills on either side. Near Puerto Rico is *Alandaluz*, an ecological/tourist centre, F p.p. or E p.p. with full board, bamboo houses or camping, health food restaurant, bar, bakery, organic gardens, beach, highly rec., good base for exploring nearby villages and Machalilla National Park. Take Transp. Manglaralto bus on Libertad-Jipijapa route and ask to get off in Puerto Rico. Write to *Alandaluz*, Casilla 66c, Agencia 15, Quito or T 604-173 in Puerto López or T 450-992 in Quito. A visit to the archaeological dig at the fishing village of **Salango**, 5 km. south of Puerto López, is recommended. Some beautiful artefacts have been found, all of which are housed in a very interesting museum close to the beach. There are two new restaurants in the village. The main attraction in **Puerto López** is the arrival of the fishermen at 0800 and again at 1630. The whole town seems to assemble on the (dirty) beach to greet the hordes of small boats and buy the fish. It seems to be easy to go out with the fishermen in their boats. Next to the sports field is a small museum with information on the nearby **Parque Nacional Machalilla**. The Park extends over 35,000 has., including Isla de la Plata and Isla Salango offshore, and is concerned with preserving marine ecosystems as well as the dry tropical forest and archaeological sites on shore. Excellent for bird watching, also several species of mammals and reptiles. Rec. guide, Johnson Morante Coronel, who can be contacted through the National Park office located just off the main road in Puerto López, T 604-145. About 5 km. N of Puerto López on the road to Machalilla there is a dirt road to the right marked to Agua Blanca. Here 5 km. from the main road, in the National Park, amid hot, arid scrub, is a fine, small archaeological museum containing some fascinating ceramics from the Manteña civilization found at the Agua Blanca site. Camping at Agua Blanca and further along the track at San Sebastián.

Offshore is Isla de la Plata, interesting for the similarities with the wildlife of the Galapagos, which can be reached by small boat; plenty of seabirds, including the Galápagos albatros, frigates and three different boobies, can be seen, and there is also precolumbian pottery. Contact the Machalilla National Park office for hiring a boat. A day trip for 8-9 people costs US$70. Take precautions against the sun.

**Lodging and food** *Residencial El Pacífico*, also called *Beip*, F, on sea front, clean, basic, but insecure; *Residencial Soroya*, one street W, a dump, G; *Restaurant Viña del Mar* rents rooms next door, F, friendly but no running water, dirty bathrooms downstairs, good, cheap food. *Carmita* on the Malecón, seafood, highly rec. for quality and freshness. Another restaurant on sea front, next to *Carmita*, serves good *ceviche* and cold beer; *Acapulco* restaurant on main street, video shows nightly at 1930. Try the local avocado *licuados*, rec.

**Buses** 1½ hrs, US$1, hourly to Jipijapa. To **La Libertad**, 1 hr US$1; to **Manglaralto**, 1 hr, US$1, to **Portoviejo**, 1 hr on good road, 68 km.

Further north of Puerto López is Puerto de Cayo (one hotel, E, several restaurants, nice beaches).

A new dirt road has been made from Manglaralto to the main Guayaquil-Manta road. This road climbs into the humid hills of S Manabí, then descends to the dry savanna scrub around **Jipijapa** (27,500 inhabitants), an important centre for the region's farmers, trading cotton, fruit and kapok (from the fat-trunked ceiba tree). (*Pensión Mejía*, E, 2 blocks from plaza, cockroaches, basic, noisy. Bus from Manglaralto, 2½ hrs, US$1.75.) Thirty-two km. across dusty hills is **Montecristi** (8,190 people), below an imposing hill, high enough to be watered by low cloud which gives the region its only source of drinking water. The town is also famous for its Panama hats which, along with cane-work products, are much cheaper than in Quito.

Soon after, we reach **Manta** (100,000 people), the main commercial centre of western Ecuador, a noisy, busy, and dirty town with a few steep streets and a fine wooden church. By all accounts it has not much to recommend it, but a stroll up and down the sea wall (taking care against pickpockets) on a Friday or Saturday evening, or sitting at a bar on a cool evening along the sea wall is a pleasant way to pass the time. The area around is denuded and poor, with many shanty towns. With its twin town, Tarqui, reached by a road bridge, it has the largest population W of Guayaquil. The Tarqui beaches are reported to be better than those at Manta, which are filthy and smelly and not safe. Fishing boats are built on the beach. The Banco Central museum, Calle 9 y Av. 4, has interesting specimens of the Huancavilca-Manteña culture (AD 800-1550); open during banking hours, curator speaks English and French. Sites can be visited from Bahía de Caráquez. All streets have been given numbers; those above 100 are in Tarqui. Most offices, shops and the bus station are in Manta.

**Hotels** Wider selection of hotels in Tarqui. *Las Gaviotas*, Malecón y Calle 106, E, on beach, dirty, a/c, poor restaurant, tennis; *Manta Imperial*, D, Calles Playa y Murciélago, on beach, a/c, poorly maintained, not up to standard in either accommodation or restaurant, pool, private parking, disco and dancing; *Las Rocas*, Calle 101 y Av. 105, D, a/c, private parking, restaurant poor; *Panorama Inn*, Calle 103 y Av. 105, E, a/c, bath, TV, rec., swimming pool and restaurant. Also on Tarqui beach, *Residencial Eugenia*, Malecón y Calle 105, F, safe, comfortable, hot water, laundry facilities, clean; *Miami*, Malecón y Calle 107, F, private bath, good; *Playita Mía*, Malecón y Calle 103, G, restaurant, shared bath, very basic. *Residencial Capri*, near bus station, G, good value. *Americano*, Av. 106 y Calle 105, E; *El Inca*, Calle 105 y Malecón, T 610-440, E, bath, T.V., phone, fan or a/c, large rooms, older hotel, good and reasonably priced restaurant, friendly and helpful, rec.

**Restaurants** Cheap restaurants by Tarqui market, Av. 108 y Calle 102; and on the nearby beach. *El Ceibo*, in the centre, is rec. *El Boulevard* on Tarqui beach near the Plaza Tarqui, good fish and seafood, reasonably priced; *La Cascada*, Av. 105 y Calle 103, cafeteria with swimming pool; *Georgie*, Calle 16 y Av. 7, good fish, cheap. *Pelicán*, Malecón y Calle 105; *La Tebanda*, Playa y Murciélago, on beach, good food, chairs for children; *Parrilladas Ponce de León*, opp. entrance to the ship terminal, large, delicious and inexpensive servings of sausage, beef and chicken, rec.; *La Tortuga*, on seafront, food good but service poor; *Santa Ana*, 2 blocks inland from Malecón, good cheap meals.

**Post Office** above Banco de Pichincha; **Telephone** Ietel on road to the beach.

**Tourist Office** Cetur, Edificio Emapa. **Travel Agents** Ecuadorian Tours, at Av. 2 y Calle 13; Metropolitan Touring at Av. 3 y Calle 12.

**Immigration** Av. 4 de Noviembre y J-1 (police station).

**Exchange** Casa de Cambio Zanchi, Banco de Pichincha and Banco del Pacífico change travellers' cheques. Filanbanco accepts Visa.

**Air Service** Eloy Alfaro airport nearby. Every day by TAME to Quito, every day except Sun. to Guayaquil.

**Buses** To **Quito**, 8 hrs, US$3.70; **Guayaquil**, 4 hrs, US$2; **Esmeraldas**, 8 hrs, US$3; **Santo Domingo**, 6 hrs, US$2.10; **Portoviejo**, ½ hr, US$0.30; **Jipijapa**, 45 mins., US$0.50; **Bahía de Caráquez**, 3 hrs, US$1. All from bus station.

24 km. inland from Montecristi is **Portoviejo** (156,250 inhabitants), a major commercial centre with connections by road with Quito (bus, 7 hrs with Reina del Camino, US$2.75) and Guayaquil. Bus station out of town, taxi US$0.40.

**Hotels** *Ejecutivo*, B, very good, very expensive, extra charge for the guard, but unfriendly, does not accept Visa despite sign outside. *París*, off main plaza, E; *Residencial Maroles*, 2 Av./Calle 1, F, friendly, noisy. *Cristal*, Calle Ricaurte 106, F, beware of peeping Toms, clean, cold water, not good for women; *San Marcos*, Olmedo y 9 de Octubre; The restaurant *Chifa China* on the plaza has a clean, cheap hotel upstairs. Other restaurants: *Mariano*, Morales y Sucre, good food; good Chinese restaurant at bus terminal; *El Palatino*, off main square, good coffee and cheap local specialities. *Peña Gol Bar* for post 2100 drinking. Two cinemas.

From Portoviejo a road goes E to Quevedo (147 km). At Calderón, branch NE for Calceta, Chone (36,000 people) and on to Santo Domingo de los Colorados. From Calceta and Chone paved roads run 50 km. past the Chone estuary with its shrimp farming and knots of bamboo houses on stilts, to *Bahía de Caráquez* (18,000 people), a tranquil town in a pleasant setting on the seaward southern end of an inlet. The river front is attractively laid out, but there are water shortages except in the hotels with their own supply. Smart new homes fringe the seaward side. The town is a centre of banana and other agricultural exports as well as shrimp farming and is increasingly popular as a beach resort. On Isla de los Pájaros in the bay are many seabirds (boats, one a.m., one p.m., the best time, 2 hrs to Isla de los Pájaros and Isla Fragatas, US$5 p.p., min. 2 pers., falling to US$2.50 max. 20 pers.; hire a launch, US$5 per hour); launches can also be hired to visit mangrove islands. Ask for Sr. Colorado at the place where ferries leave for San Vicente.

**Hotels** *La Piedra*, Malecón, C, pool, restaurant, laundry, modern, good service, access to beach, lovely views; *Herradura*, Bolívar y Malecón (beach), D, good restaurant, good service, very pretty, rec.; *Americano*, Ascazubi y Morales, D with a/c and bath; *Manabí*, nearby, G, clean and friendly; *Hostal Querencia*, on main road at entrance to town, E, clean, friendly; *Victoria*, Calle Montúfar 807, G, basic, friendly; *Residencial San José*, Calle Ascazubi 110, G, basic, unfriendly, tries to overcharge foreigners; *Residencial Vera*, Ante y Bolívar, F, noisy, own water; *Palma*, Bolívar y Arenas, G, clean; overpriced restaurant below; *Residencial Tamarindos*, G, clean, friendly. On the road to San Agustín, 7 km. beyond Bahía is *Hostería Quinta*, C, motel-style, a/c, refrigerator, T.V., warm showers, pool, tennis, restaurant, guarded, clean, rec.

**Restaurants** *Brisas del Mar*, Bolívar y Malecón, good fish, cheap; *Los Helecheros*, cafetería, good and clean, Bolívar y Malecón; *Chifa China*, cheap, good, Bolívar y Ascazubi. *Los Mellizos*, near hospital, excellent fish, very cheap; *El Galería*, Bolívar, expensive; *Miramar*, Malecón, overpriced; good *comedor* next to *Hotel Vera*.

**Exchange** Only at Banco Industrial, Malecón (very poor rate), or try the manageress at Banco Central (be nice to the security guards).

**Tour Agency** *Guacamayo*, T 690-629, excursions to mangroves, beaches, caves, bird watching, etc.

**Bus** companies include Coactur, Reina del Camino and Ruta Ecuatoriana: from Bahía de Caráquez to **Quito**, 8 hrs, US$3.20, **Esmeraldas**, 8 hrs, US$3, and **Portoviejo**, 2 hrs. To **Guayaquil**, 5½ hrs, US$2.80; to **Manta**, 3 hrs, US$1.

**Airport** at San Vicente (see below): Air Transportes Bahía flies twice a day to **Guayaquil**, with connections to **Pedernales**.

From Bahía de Caráquez to the highlands there are two main roads. The first one is via Chone and El Carmen to Santo Domingo. The second one is via Calceta and Rocafuerte to Pichincha, Velasco Ibarra and on to Quevedo. Alternatively you can go from Calceta on an unpaved dry weather road directly to Pichincha, 4-wheel drive rec., two rivers without bridges, not deep, very scenic.

35 km. S of Bahía de Caráquez is San Clemente, a beautiful beach with *cabañas* and houses for rent and some hotels (*Eden*, D, with bath; *Aza*, 150 metres from the beach, 800 metres

N of San Clemente, E with bath, clean, good seafood, rec.). Some Portoviejo-Guayaquil buses pass San Clemente. 3 km. S of San Clemente is San Jacinto, with **Hotel San Jacinto**, E, on the beach.

Those interested in exploring the coast further north can take the ferry (every 5 mins, US$0.13, also car ferry) from Bahía de Caráquez to **San Vicente**, on the far side of the Río Chone, a thriving market, nice beaches (*Hotel Vacaciones*, D, restaurant, TV in rooms; *Centro Vacacional "Life"*, Dávila y García Moreno, D, full board; *Hotel San Vicente*, on main road, G, shared bath, basic, mosquito nets; about 3 km. from San Vicente are *Cabañas La Playa*, US$20 for beach chalet sleeping 5, good food in restaurant; other *cabañas* on beach), and on by bus, truck or car north along the beach to Canoa, thence inland, cutting across Cabo Pasado through the more humid pasture-lands to the small market centre of **Jama** (small *pensión*).

From there the road runs parallel to the beach past coconut groves, inland across some low hills and across the Equator to **Pedernales**, another small market town on the coast, nice beaches around, lots of shells, bus from San Vicente (4 daily), 6 hrs, US$3; several houses where you can stay (*Hotel Turismo*, F, basic, clean, helpful; *Cabañas Cañaverales*, F; *Playas*, near airport, under renovation in 1991, cheapest rooms F, price depends on bath, a/c, TV, friendly, clean; *Residencial Comedor El Gitano*, F, meals, friendly) and 2 or 3 eating places. A rough new road has been finished between Pedernales and El Carmen (thence to Sto. Domingo and Quito)—the two towns are expected to become booming tourist resorts—and on to Cojimíes (enquire if passable in rainy season).

Buses, two a day, take 7 hrs from San Vicente (US$3.50), 45 mins. from Pedernales (truck US$0.50, colectivo US$1.10) to **Cojimíes**: *Residenciales España*, G, shabby, no water; *Mi Descanso* and *Cojimíes*—all look the same; *Hotel Coco Solo* is 14 km. before Cojimíes, D, overpriced, nice but no services and no choice in restaurant. Flower-decorated house on same street will serve meals at any hour; other houses serve food; one restaurant, *El Caracol*, good but expensive. Cojimíes was a major pre-conquest centre; little of this is noticeable now, although many artefacts are still dug up, it is being continually eroded by the sea and has been moved about three times in as many decades. A boat leaves at high tide every Sat. for Esmeraldas, stopping at Chamanga (US$4, 7 hrs) and one from Esmeraldas on Sat. as well. There is a boat to Manta on Wed. and a direct canoe to Muisné (US$4) at 0600, 2 hrs. The entry into Cojimíes and Muisné is treacherous and many boats have been thrown into the shallows by swell.

North of Cojimíes is a rich banana-growing region. **Muisné**, an island reached by road from Esmeraldas (bus US$1, 3 hrs, and a canoe over to the island, US$0.10), is the centre and main outlet of this area; through it some 50,000 stems of bananas a month are exported via Esmeraldas. On the Río Sucio, inland from Muisné and Cojimíes, is an isolated group of Cayapa Indians, some of whom visit the towns on Sun. Women should avoid *Residencial Narcisita*, we have been warned of sexual attacks by the owner; *Galápagos*, on far side of town from docks, closest to beach, safe, E with bath, F without, modern, clean, washing facilities, rec; *Sarita*, F, clean, private bathroom; *Mi Residencial*, G, basic; *Pensión Reina*, G, basic; you can also rent small huts on the beach, G p.p., few if any have electricity or water, beautiful setting; *Cabañas Ipanema*, 200 m. from beach, F, bath, clean, safe, friendly, rec. There are several simple seafood *comedores*, try fish in coconut sauce or local shrimp. Also *Delicias del Mar*, Australian-run, good food, good service; *Mario's Bar*, open late(ish). *Delfín*, in palm hut on beach, good food, nice people, rooms to let planned, rec. No meals after 1900. The beaches 10-15 mins walk from town, are large at low tide but practically disappear at high tide. There is a lot of litter and wood lying around and hordes of mosquitoes, but also wildlife: turtles, sea snakes, crabs and birds. In the wet season there are boats between Muisné and Cojimíes, mostly early a.m., US$3, 2 hrs buy ticket at bus stop, take water proofs. Cargo boats ply between Muisné and Manta. A new road has been built between Muisné and Bolívar inland, behind the beaches; easier but less scenic. Be careful on the beaches; we have received reports of rape and violent attacks. If staying in huts on the beach beware thieves who may remove the roof to enter.

**Esmeraldas** (117,000 people) is reported dirty and overpriced. The electricity and water supplies are still inadequate, water shortage often last weeks. The main street is closed to traffic from 1930 to 2130 nightly. Gold mines nearby, tobacco and cacao grown inland, cattle ranching along the coast, timber exported, and an oil pipeline from the Oriente to an ocean terminal at nearby Balao; an oil refinery has been built nearby. A new road bridge over the river at San Mateo upstream from Esmeraldas gives a direct road link to the General Rivadeneira airport. Las Palmas, just N of Esmeraldas, is being developed as a resort: several hotels have been built and restaurants opened. There is a broad sandy beach but it is reported as unsafe (theft) and filthy. White people have been advised to avoid the shanty-town on the Malecón. The atmosphere is certainly not pleasant for women travelling alone. Even the water is muddy as it is close to a naval harbour and people use the beach as a speedway. Buses to Las Palmas (US$0.05, taxi US$1) leave regularly from the main square in Esmeraldas.

Mosquitoes and malaria are a serious problem throughout the province of Esmeraldas in the rainy season. All the beaches have mosquitoes that come out in hordes at night and bite through clothing. Take plenty of insect repellant because the Detán sold locally does not work well. Most *residencias* provide mosquito nets (*toldos* or *mosquiteros*); don't stay anywhere that does not. Best to visit in dry season, June-December. Use lots of sun tan lotion or cover up, even when it's cloudy or you are used to the sun.

**Hotels**  Best in Esmeraldas are *Apart Hotel*, Av. Libertad 407 y Ramón Tello, D, excellent, good restaurant, and *Roma*, E, Olmeda y Piedrahita, with its *Restaurant Tres Carabelas*; *La Pradera*, 7½ km. S on Atacames road, D, a/c, swimming pool, tennis courts, restaurant, and *Europeo*, D, between Esmeraldas and Las Palmas, no a/c, but the restaurant is very good, German-owned but under Chilean management. *Galeón*, Piedrahita y Olmedo, E, bath, a/c; *Corea*, Mañizares y Bolívar, F, rec., private shower, ask for water; fan; *Americano*, Sucre y Piedrahita, F with fan and bath, dirty, smelly, thin walls, noisy; *Diana*, Mañizares y Sucre, good, private showers, safe, F. *Hostal Domínguez*, G, on Sucre near Plaza Central, noisy, hot water, open all night; *Valparaíso I*, Libertad y Pichincha, G, very basic but good value, cheap restaurant. *Turismo*, Bolívar 843, G, basic, with bath and fan, clean and friendly. Other cheaper hotels include *Bolívar*, F and cheaper still, *Central*, F, and *Asia*, F, 100 metres round the corner from the bus station, both are basic but clean. Generally, hotels in the town centre are not up to much and you are rec. to stay in the outskirts. Some hotels are not keen to take single travellers.

Las Palmas offers the best hotels along Av. Kennedy: *Cayapas*, D, a/c, showers and hot water in all rooms, overpriced, good restaurant; *Hotel del Mar*, E-D, on sea front, modern, mixed quality and size of rooms but all a/c and mosquito proofed, restaurant closed at 1400, not cheap, good breakfast. *Colonial*, Platat y L. Tello, D; *Chimborazo*, G, cheap and noisy.

**Restaurants**  In Esmeraldas: *Chifa Restaurante Asiático*, Mañizares y Bolívar, Chinese, excellent; *Pelican*, Malecón, very good, popular, vegetarian dishes, expensive but worth it. *La Marimba Internacional*, Libertad y Lavallén, has been rec.; *Daruma*, Olmedo y Mejía, is Japanese and local. *Café Congenita*, near *Hotel Americano*, for iced tea, milk shakes; other soda fountains at Olmedo y Piedrahita. In Las Palmas, *Atenas Tiffani*; Kennedy 707, good food but expensive; *Bayardo*, on the Malecón, good food, lively host, cheaper than *Tiffani*. *Artrang*, main plaza, good food, good value; *Las Redes*, main plaza, good fish, cheap; *Budapest*, Cañizares 214 y Bolívar, Hungarian-run, clean, pleasant. *Balcón del Pacífico*, Bolívar y 10 de Agosto, nice atmosphere, good view overlooking city, cheap drinks. There are numerous typical restaurants and bars by the beach selling ceviches, fried fish and patacones, etc.

Throughout Esmeraldas province a cheap meal is the *comida típica*, fish, rice, boiled *plátano*, sometimes beans (*minestre*), called *tapao*. There is also *cocado*, fish, crabs or shrimp cooked in coconut cream served with rice and *plátano*. There is a soup made of shellfish and coconut milk which is very good. *Cocada* is a sweet made of brown sugar and grated coconut; *conserva* is a paste of guava, banana and brown sugar, wrapped in banana leaves.

**Shopping**  There is a Cayapa basket market across from the Post Office, behind the vegetables. Also three doors down, Tolita artefacts and basketry. **Exchange** at bank until 1200; at Botica Koch, Sucre y 9 de Octubre, good rates.

**Entertainment**  In Esmeraldas, *El Portón* peña and discotheque, Colón y Piedrahita; *El Guadal de Ña Mencha*, 6 de Diciembre y Quito, peña upstairs, marimba school at weekends; good *Bar Asia* on Bolívar by main Parque. *Los Cuervos*, discotheque. In Las Palmas, *El Náutico* and *Déjà Vue* on the Malecón, a/c, discotheques. Cockfights, Eloy Alfaro y 9 de Octubre, weekends.

**Music**  Esmeraldas has been called "the capital of rhythm". The people prefer the livelier sound of Caribbean *salsa* to the *cumbia* heard in the sierra, and have retained the African-influenced marimba, usually accompanied by a bombero, who plays a deep-pitched bass drum suspended from the ceiling, and a long conga drum. Where there is a marimba school you will also find dancers, and the women who are too old to dance play percussion and chant songs handed down the generations, many with Colombian references, but the best marimba can only be seen in the backwoods of the province on Sundays and holidays as that in Esmeraldas is only for tourists.

**Cinema**  Ciné Bolívar, Bolívar y 9 de Octubre, is the best, with a/c and upholstered seating. Three other cinemas offer more basic accommodation with bats and rats.

**Immigration**  Av. Olmedo y Rocafuerte, T 720-256.

**Tourist Information**  The tourist office (Cetur) is in the Edificio de la Alcaldía, Bolívar 517 y 9 de Octubre, 2nd floor, half a block from the main square, singularly unhelpful.

**Buses**  Terminal Terrestre planned for 1991. To **Quito**, US$2.50, 8 hrs, 30 a day, good paved road, Trans-Esmeraldas, Av. Piedrahita 200 (deafening music, sullen service), or by Occidental; by Aerotaxi (small bus), 5 hrs, 12 passengers, reserved seats, office on main square. To **Santo Domingo**, US$1.40, 4 hrs; to **Ambato**, 5 times a day with Coop. Sudamericana, 8 hrs, US$2.50; to **Guayaquil**, hourly, US$5, 7 hrs; to **Portoviejo** and **Manta**, US$2, to **Quevedo**, 6 hrs. To **La Tola** (road good to Río Verde), many daily, US$1.60, 5 hrs; to **Muisné**, 28 daily with La Costeñita, US$1, 3½ hrs; to **Súa** (road reasonable), Same and Atacames every half hour from 0630 to 2030, 1-1½ hrs.

**Boats**  to Limones and San Lorenzo: service irregular; ask at Port Captain's office at Las Palmas. Combined boat/bus service leaves for San Lorenzo at 1330.

**Airport**  General Rivadeneira on the road to La Tola; several buses to La Tola and Borbón, not necessary to go into Esmeraldas if you want to go on to San Lorenzo or other places. Daily flights to Quito with TAME, ½ hr.; taxi to centre, 30 km, about US$1.75 (Esmeraldas), no buses, US$7 to Atacames, US$8 to Súa, US$12 to Same.

***Atacames***, a beach resort 25 km. S of Esmeraldas, is still attractive, and the palm trees on the beach (washed away in 1983) are growing again. Atacames is famous for its black coral. Most accommodation has salt water in the bathrooms; fresh water is not always available and not very good. *Hotel Jennifer*, E, cold shower, fan, clean; *Hotel Tahiti*, with shower, E, reductions for longer stays, friendly, theft from rooms reported, serves breakfasts, good restaurant, try the prawns, but check your bill carefully, also has nice cabins, F; *San Baye*, just past *Tahiti* at the end of the beach, F, good and cheap; *Atacames*, at the beach, E, with bath; *Hostería Los Bohíos*, C, prices cheaper (F) in low season (June, July, August); for a bungalow, bathrooms with salt water but there are fresh water showers too, safe, clean; *Hostería Cayapas*, beach huts, F, cooking and barbecue; *Casa Blanca*, Urbanización Iñaquito, cabins for 6, with bathroom, kitchen, F p.p., on beach; *Vasco*, nearby, one block from beach, E, a/c, ask for water to be turned on, friendly, beautiful garden; *San Sebastián* and *Marbella*, beach huts for 5, both F; *Residencial Sol de Oriente*, F, clean, near beach. *Castel Nuovo*, 3 km. N on road to Esmeraldas, C with bath and fan, swimming pool, on beach, rec.; *La Pradera*, 4 km. along Esmeraldas road, pool, restaurant, good value. *Edén*, cabins in F range, good location on beach, rec. Tents or beach bungalows can be hired at under US$1 a night; no facilities but can arrange with hotels. *Lumbaye* bungalows are rec., cheaper off-season. Beach bungalows with showers at *Cabañas Costa del Sol*, F, good water supply, good breakfast and seafood; *Cabañas Arco Iris*, D, shower, fridge, clean, rec., charming, N end of beach, T Quito 525-544 for reservations or in Atacames T 731-069, English, Spanish, German and French spoken; *Cabañas South Pacific*, F, clean, American owner, fresh water showers. Rats are common in all these beach huts, and insect repellant is essential.

Restaurants on beach are reasonable, mostly seafood; try *Comedor Pelicanos*, fresh fish, chicken, ceviche, occasionally music, rec.; also *Cafetería Pelícanos*, best, includes vegetarian dishes and salads; *El Tiburón*, on beach, good seafood, cheap; *Comedor Popular*, good Italian and criollo cooking, order special requests in advance. 2 discotheques on beach. *Cocada*, a sweet made from different nuts, brown sugar, cocoa, etc., is sold in the main plaza. **Warning**: It is reported that there have been many assaults on campers and beach strollers. Walkers along the beach from Atacames to Súa regularly get assaulted at knife point where there is a small tunnel, gangs seem to work daily. The sea can be very dangerous, there is a powerful undertow and many people have been drowned.

***Súa***, another beach resort a little S of Atacames, is quiet, friendly, with a beautiful bay with pelicans and frigate birds, but the sandy beach is very dirty, crowded and not rec. Robbers at S end of beach near fishing village. *Pensión Palmar*, G, cabins; *Residencial Quito*, G; *Mar y Sol*, G, washing facilities poor. The hotels along the seafront vary little in standard but quite significantly in price. *Hotel Súa*, French-run, clean, friendly, good French restaurant; *Motel Chagra Ramos*, on beach, F, clean, fan on request, good restaurant. Insect repellant is essential along this coast. Beyond Súa is Playa de **Same**, quiet, with a beautiful, long, clean, grey sandy beach lined with palms, safe for swimming and good birdwatching in the lagoon behind the beach; *Club Casablanca*, A+, restaurant, tennis courts, swimming pool, luxurious (reservations Wagons-Lits Turismo, Ed. Galicia, Diego de Almagro 1822 y Alpallana, Quito, T 554-933/4/7, Telex 22763 VALEJO ED); *Hostería Rampiral*, E p.p., new, clean; places for rental of *cabañas*, *Centro Turístico Manila*, D per cabin, 8 cabins for 4 people, great restaurant, good *caipirinhas* (reservations Wagons-Lits Turismo); *La Terraza*, F p.p., 5 cabins for 3-4, good Spanish-run restaurant (reservations *Restaurante La Bettola*, Quito, T 239-396); *Cabañas Isla del Sol*, F p.p., 12 cabins for 4-6, bath, clean, spacious, cold shower, electric light, comfortable, safe, good restaurant, rec., stoney beach front, cabins are close together and road traffic is very audible, reservations T 731-151, Atacames, or telegram to Casilla 358, Esmeraldas; *Complejo Turístico Las Canoas*, F p.p., 21 cabins, 2-6 people, primitive but comfortable, cold shower, electric light, more cabins on sea front, away from road, reasonable restaurant (Reservations Wagons-Lits Turismo); *El Acantilado*, 14 rooms for 2-3 people, 30 cabins up to 5 people, T 235-034 in Quito, cooking facilities, on hill by the sea, S of Same, no palm trees. All cabins about US$5-6 p.p. with water and electricity; booking advisable at holiday times and weekends. Bus from Súa to Same, La Costeñita, 15 mins, 18 km., US$0.10, make sure it drops you at Same and not at *La Casablanca*, buses pass every 30-60 mins, look out for sign for *Cabañas Isla del Sol*. **Tonchigüe**, a quiet little fishing village, 1 hr S from Esmeraldas beyond Súa, is also lovely during the rainy season (Dec.-May). Bus Atacarmes-Tonchigüe, US$0.40.

There are no good beaches for swimming north of Esmeraldas. Río Verde, where the paved road ends, has a dirty beach and one hotel, *Paz y Bueno*, F, basic (N side of river). It was the setting for Morriz Thompson's book on Peace Corps life, *Living Poor*. Beyond Río Verde is **Rocafuerte**, recommended as having the best seafood in the province, including oysters and lobsters. At **La Tola**, where one catches the boat for Limones and San Lorenzo, the shoreline changes from sandy beaches to mangrove swamp. The wildlife is varied and spectacular, especially the birds. La Tola is 3½ hrs (US$1.50) from Esmeraldas, by bus, three daily a.m., dusty, uncomfortable, buses often get stuck. Four boats go daily from La Tola to San Lorenzo via Limones, 2 hrs, US$1.50 (beware overcrowding); seem to connect with boats from Esmeraldas. Try to avoid staying overnight in La Tola; take a raincoat.

Mangrove coastlands stretch north into Colombia, and have only two towns of note in Ecuador: Limones and San Lorenzo.

**Limones**, the main commercial centre, largely a saw-mill town, is the focus of traffic down-river from much of northern Esmeraldas Province where bananas from the Río Santiago are sent to Esmeraldas for export. The Cayapa Indians live up the Río Cayapas and can sometimes be seen in Limones, especially during the crowded weekend market (uninteresting), but they are more frequently seen at Borbón.

Limones has two good shops selling the very attractive Cayapa basketry; selection includes some items from Colombia. The first is opposite *Restaurant El Bongó* and the second by the dock opposite Banco de Fomento.

Two hotels, both execrable. Limones is "the mosquito and rat capital of Ecuador". A hired launch (6 pers. US$1.40 p.p., 1½ hrs) provides a fascinating trip through mangrove islands and passing hundreds of hunting pelicans. Information on boat journeys from the Capitanía del Puerto, Las Palmas, reached by bus No. 1 from the main square in Esmeraldas. From Limones you can also get a canoe or boat to Borbón. Better to stay at San Lorenzo.

**Borbón** (*Residencial Capri*, F, with marimba dance hall next door; *Panama City*, G, modern, friendly, clean, mosquito nets, rec.), with population almost entirely black, is on the Río Cayapa past mangrove swamps. Buses to/from Esmeraldas, US$1.40, 4 hrs, 0600-1700, hourly; to Limones and San Lorenzo at 0730 and 1100. Upstream are Cayapa Indian villages. From Borbón hire a motor launch or go as a passenger on launches running daily around 1100-1200 to the mouth of the Río Onzole, Santa María (board and lodging with Sra. Pastora at missionary station, F, mosquito nets, or at the *Residencial*, G, basic, will prepare food but fix price beforehand, owner offers 5 hr jungle trips to visit Cayapa villages), Zapallo Grande and on to San Miguel; Borbón to San Miguel, US$5 p.p., 3 hrs. At the confluence of the Cayapas and Onzole rivers, there is a fine lodge built by a Hungarian (for advance bookings write to Stephan Tarjany, Casilla 187, Esmeraldas), C with full board, good value, clean, warm showers. Jungle walk with guide and small canoes at no extra charge. Water skiing available, US$12/hr. Steve organizes special tours to visit remote areas and a trip to the Ecological Reserve, US$50 p.p. per day inc. transport and food. Zapallo Grande is a friendly village with many gardens, where the American missionary Dr Meisenheimer has established a hospital, pharmacy, church and school. You will see the Cayapa Indians passing in their canoes and in their open long houses on the shore. San Miguel has a church and a few houses, beautifully situated on a hill at the confluence of two rivers. You can sleep in the rangers' hut, F, basic. It is possible to make excursions into the jungle, US$12-18 per boat, 2-3 people, ask for an official guide, e.g. Don Cristóbal. From there you go back 5 hrs downstream to La Tola where you can pick up the bus from Esmeraldas or go on to Limones and San Lorenzo.

**San Lorenzo** is relatively more attractive than Limones. There is a beach nearby at San Pedro (no facilities), reached by boat, Sat. and Sun. at 0800 and 1400. The best places to see *marimba* are two schools, one Esmeraldeña and one Colombiana. The latter practice on Calle 24 de Mayo between *Residencial Pailón* and *Residencial Ibarra*; you can't miss the sound. The former practice Wed. and Sat. nights, are more disciplined, better musicians and dance more. They have toured the continent and are led by a woman called Lydia who can make marimbas to order. *Marimba* can be seen during the local fiesta on 30 Sept. San Lorenzo is an expensive town, with a poor water supply. There is a cinevideo, half a block from *Residencia Ecuador*. When arriving in San Lorenzo, expect to be hassled by children wanting a tip to show you to a hotel or restaurant. Robbery is common but the police often recover part of your stolen property.

**Hotels** *Wilma*, F, basic, ask for rooms 15 or 16, they are newer and bigger; **Residencial Margaritas**, F, friendly, clean, good showers, Imbabura y Ortiz; **Carondelet**, main square, F, some rooms with view, others with bath, others like boxes, mosquito nets, friendly, reliable, owner sells guests railway tickets so you do not have to queue early in the morning; *Jhonny*, Ayora y 24 de Mayo, renovated, good, cheap; *Ecuador*, Alfaro y 10 de Agosto, F with bath and a/c, cheaper without, clean, quiet, good value, restaurant OK, basic, laundry facilities, mosquito net not provided; **Residencial Vilmar**, Imbabura y Mariano, G, near the station. **San Lorenzo**, Alfaro y 10 de Agosto, G, rec. for meals, but not so good to stay; **Residencial Ibarra**, Coronel y 24 de Mayo, possibly the best, G, some rooms with fan, clean, friendly. **Restaurants** *El Fogón*, Garces, near railway station, excellent camarones. **Chifa Pack Choy**, E. Alfaro y Imbabura, good, Chinese. *Rumory's* marimba and discotheque at Imbabura y 10 de Agosto. Insect repellant is a "must" in San Lorenzo. Be sure to check your bedding for scorpions.

**Train** The *autocarro* (motor rail-coach) leaves Tues., Thurs., Sat., from the station 10 mins from town centre, tickets on sale from 0545. The train journey gives an excellent transect of Ecuador (**see page 799**). To **Ibarra**, US$1.10, up to 12 hrs, departing at 0600. The train can get very crowded and angry passengers unable to board have been known to beat up the driver! Because of heavy rains, roadworks and landslides, delays and derailments are frequent. Best view is from the roof but beware of bats in the tunnels and of water bombs during the trip. If you are not allowed on the roof do not put your bags up there, theft reported. Two meal stops at Lita and Carchi, military control at Lita, the Colombian border is not far away, passport checks. Be careful when taking photos in Lita.

**Boats** Dugouts, with motors, to **La Tola** (every ½hr., 0730-1400, 2 hrs, US$1.50) and **Borbón** (3 hrs, US$2), via Limones, US$1. Boats leave daily at 0730 and 1400 (stops at Tambilla and Limones en route), bus from there to Esmeraldas, through ticket US$2.75. Beautiful journey but dusty bus trip. Launch to **Esmeraldas** at 0500 and 0730; plane to Quito at 0930, tickets at airport at 0800.

From San Lorenzo there are boats to **Tumaco** in Colombia on Tues., Thurs., Sat., 1000, 4½ hrs, US$7, but gringos are not normally welcome as passengers because contraband is being carried. When arriving in San Lorenzo from Tumaco, the customs office run by navy personnel is in the harbour, but you have to get your passport stamped at the immigration office in Ibarra or Esmeraldas because the immigration police in the *Hotel Imperial* office do not handle passports. Problems may arise if you delay more than a day or two before getting an entry stamp, as the immigration police in Ibarra are less easy-going.

Nancy Alexander, of Chicago, writes that about 75% of the population of Limones, Borbón and San Lorenzo has come from Colombia in the last fifty years. The people are mostly black and many are illegal immigrants. Smuggling between Limones and Tumaco in Colombia is big business (hammocks, manufactured goods, drugs) and there are occasional drug searches along the N coastal road.

---

# GUAYAQUIL (4)

---

**Guayaquil**, the chief seaport and commercial city, founded in 1537 by Francisco de Orellana, stands on the west bank of the Guayas river, some 56 km. from its outflow into the Gulf of Guayaquil. Its population of 1,699,000 makes it the largest city in the Republic. The climate is at its best from May to December with little or no rain and cool nights, though the sky is overcast more often than not. The heat and humidity during the rainy season, January to April, are oppressive. The Puerto Marítimo, opened in 1979, handles about 90% of the country's imports and 50% of its exports.

The city is dotted with small parks and pleasant gardens. A waterfront drive, known as the Malecón, runs along the shore of the Guayas river. Here are the splendid Palacio Municipal and the severe Government Palace. From the landing pier of the Yacht Club the drive is known as the Paseo de las Colonias. The main street, Avenida 9 de Octubre, runs due west from a central pier; there are 11 piers in all, 6 to the north of 9 de Octubre, 4 to the south. About half-way along it is the Plaza Centenario, the main square of the city, where stands the large liberation monument set up in 1920. On Calle Pedro Carbo, between Vélez and 9 de Octubre, the restored interior of the colonial church of San Francisco is beautiful. At La Rotonda, on the waterfront near the beginning of Av. 9 de Octubre, is a statue commemorating the famous and very mysterious meeting of Bolívar and San Martín in 1822. The dazzling white cemetery, with massive, ornate tombs of the wealthy, north of the city at the foot of a hill, is worth seeing, but best to go on Sundays when there are plenty of people about. The snow-capped peak of Chimborazo can sometimes be glimpsed from Guayaquil.

The city is bustling and prosperous, and much cleaner than it used to be. The locals are much livelier and more open than the people of Quito. There are clubs for golf, tennis, yachting, and a race track set in delightful surroundings some 5 km. outside the city: there are a football stadium and an enclosed coliseum for boxing, basketball, etc. The pleasant suburb of Urdesa, NW of the city, contains some of the best restaurants and places of entertainment.

One of the oldest and most interesting districts is Las Peñas, at the foot of Cerro Santa Ana, by the river. Here is the city's first church, Santo Domingo (1548). Nearby is an open-air theatre, the Bogotá. Then, up the hill, there is a flat space where two cannon point riverward, a memento of the days when pirates sailed up the Guayas to attack the city. Here begins a curving, narrow colonial street, Numa Pompilio Llona. Paved with huge stone slabs, and lined with many fine houses which used to be an artist's colony, it is picturesque but somewhat neglected. To reach Las Peñas, turn left at end of Av. 9 de Octubre and carry on along the Malecón, to its end. It is a picturesque but still poor area; even the locals say it is unsafe and you are advised not to walk up the adjacent streets on Cerro Santa Ana.

The pride of Guayaquil is the enormous River Guayas bridge linking the city with Durán, the rail terminal on the east bank of the Guayas River. About half an hour is saved in comparison with the ferry journey, which costs US$0.06 and leaves every 15 min. from Muelle 5. From Durán, paved highways fan out to Babahoyo, Milagro, Riobamba (pass 4,120 metres high on the way), Cuenca and Machala.

**Warnings** Guayaquil has many thieves and pickpockets, especially outside the hotel entrances and on the waterfront, often working in pairs, and the area south of Calle Ayacucho is generally unsafe. Except in the best hotels, there is a chronic water shortage. Dengue fever has been reported.

**Local Holidays** 9 and 12 October. 24 and 25 July, Bolívar's birthday, and Foundation of the City; Carnival is in the days before Lent: watch out for malicious throwing of water balloons, mud, ink, paint etc.; women are prime targets. In contrast New Year's Eve is lots of fun, there is a large exhibition of tableaux, featuring *Años Viejos*, along the Malecón, children begging for alms for their life-size *viejos*, families with cars taking their *viejos* for rides through the centre of town, and a vast conflagration at midnight when all these figures are set on fire and explode.

**Museums** The Museo Municipal is housed in the Biblioteca Municipal, at Sucre with Pedro Carbo (near the *Hotel Continental*) where there are paintings, gold and archaeological

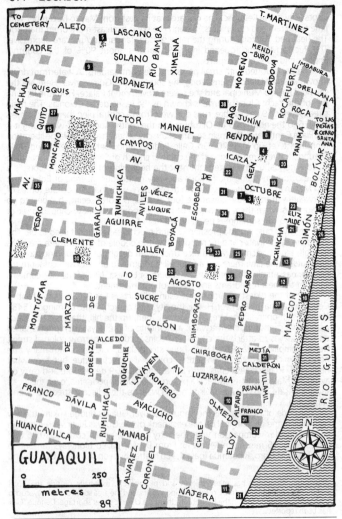

GUAYAQUIL

0 _____ 250

metres

89

**Guayaquil: Key to Map**

1. Parque Centenario; 2. Parque Bolívar; 3. Parque Rocafuerte; 4. Parque Pedro Carbo; 5. Parque de la Madre; 6. Cathedral; 7. Iglesia San Francisco; 8. Basílica de la Merced; 9. Iglesia San Agustín; 10. Iglesia San Alejo; 12 Palacio Municipal; 13. Palacio de Gobernación and Immigration; 14. Supreme Court; 15. Casa de la Cultura; 16. Biblioteca Municipal and Musuem; 17. La Rotunda and Bolívar/San Martín monument; 18. Clock Tower; 19. Banco Central; 20. Lloyds Bank; 21. Bank of America; 22. TAME; 23. Ecuatoriana; 24. Tourist Office; 25. Post Office/letel; 26. Yacht Club; 27. Red Cross; 28. Librería Científica; 29. Unicentro Shopping Mall; 30. Central Market; 31. Other Markets; Hotels: 32. *Gran Guayaquil*; 33. *Unihotel/Plaza*; 34. *Palace*; 35. *Alexanders*; 36. *Continental*; 37. *Italia*; 38. *Residencial Pauker*.

collections, a section on the history of Guayaquil and also a good newspaper library. The museum (which contains Shuar heads) is open Wed.-Fri. 0900-1200 and 1500-1800; Sat. 1000-1500, Sun. 1000-1300. Entrance US$0.15 for Ecuadoreans and US$0.40 for foreigners (free on Sat., but passport must be left at desk). The Central Bank's **anthropological museum** is at José de Anteparra 900 and 9 de Octubre, open Mon.-Fri. 1000-1800, Sat. and Sun. 1000-1300. There is an impressive collection of prehistoric gold items at the museum of the **Casa de la Cultura**, together with an archaeological museum, Av. 9 de Octubre 1200 and Moncayo, open Mon.-Fri. 0900-1200 and 1500-1830, Sat. 0900-1600. There is a **small zoo**, open Sun., at the Colegio Nacional.

**Hotels** Hotel prices, which are higher than in Quito, are set by the Tourist Board and should be posted inside hotel. Rooms are much in demand in better hotels, the cheap ones being pretty basic, and singles seem very hard to find. All tend to be heavily booked, particularly in the week before July 24, the *fiesta*. Usually you have to pay the room rate in advance and if paying by credit card you have to sign a blank slip which they fill in when you depart.

The best hotel is probably *Oro Verde*, 9 de Octubre y García Moreno, L, restaurants, bar, disco, pool, also good are *Unihotel*, Clemente Ballén 406 y Chile, L, good restaurant; *Gran Hotel Guayaquil*, Boyacá 1600 y 10 de Agosto, L, good restaurants, swimming pool, sauna, etc.; *Continental*, Chile y 10 de Agosto, T 329270, Fax 325454, L (a KLM Golden Tulip hotel), rec.; *Apartamentos Boulevard*, 9 de Octubre 432, A, rec.; *Rizzo*, Clemente Ballén 319 y Chile, T 325-210, B, T.V., bath, a/c, friendly, safe, central on Parque Bolívar, room service, *Café Jambelí* downstairs; *Palace*, Chile 214 y Luque, A, completely refurbished (1990), best value for business travellers, good restaurant, travel agency, fax and telex services; *Plaza*, Chile 414 y Clemente Ballén, T 324195, B-C, unfriendly, some cheaper rooms, international newspapers, nice restaurant with expensive buffet; *Doral*, Aguirre y Chile, B, a bit run down; *Alexanders*, Luque 1107 y Pedro Moncayo, C, very comfortable but unfriendly, no water at night, noisy and restaurant poor; *Majestic*, 9 de Octubre y Boyacá, E with bath, not all rooms have hot water; *Residencial Cervera*, E, Gral. Córdoba 1036, a/c, clean, some rooms with bath; *Residencial Metropolitana*, V.M. Rendón 120 y Panamá, E-F, large rooms, poor beds, laundry facilities, a/c, no hot water, clean, safe for luggage; *Los Andes*, Garaycoa y Aguirre, D, noisy, T.V., large, some windowless rooms, disco; *Residencial Embajador*, Chimborazo 1106, F, clean but shower rarely works; *Pensión Pauker*, Baquerizo Moreno 902, F, English spoken, rooms on street side noisy, mixed reports, run down, noisy, dirty, beware cockroaches; *San Juan*, Vélez y Boyacá, E, own bathroom, no a/c, acceptable but most rooms without windows; *Vélez*, Vélez y Quito, F, with bath, hot water, TV, fan, clean; *Sanders*, Pedro Moncayo 1100 y Luque, E-D, with bath, phone and fan (D a/c, these rooms overpriced), central; *Victoria*, Moncayo y Colón, F, shower, clean but noisy; *Santa María*, E, Villamil 102, central, adequate, restaurant; *Ecuador*, Pedro Moncayo 1125, F, rooms dark but clean, best on first floor; *Orchidea Internacional*, Centro Comercial at Villamil 210, F, good, clean, TV, a/c, hot water; *Libertador*, Parque Centenario, G with bath, no glass in windows, good value, friendly; *Colonial*, Rumichaca y Urdaneta, F, bath, clean, safe, rec.; *Hotel USA*, Rumichaca y Quisquis, F, basic but bright, clean, good value; *Ecuatoriana*, Sucre y Rumichaca, F, cockroaches, used by short-stay couples, some rooms with no window; *Delicia*, Clemente Ballén 1105, G, clean, fair, try to get room away from street. Sra Greta Portugal at Imbabura 214 y Rocafuerte, Aptdo 4-2, lets rooms at price category D, rec. Total tax of 20% on all hotel rates.

**Restaurants** Centre: *El Fortín* restaurant in the *Hotel Continental* won the Gran Collar Gastronómico Internacional competition worldwide and has excellent food (but poor service); the cheaper *La Canoa* has local food. *1822* restaurant at the *Gran Hotel Guayaquil*, expensive, but pleasant surroundings, high quality cuisine with good daily outdoor barbecue at pool-side. Good dining at *Le Gourmet* and *La Fondue* in *Hotel Oro Verde*, also good value lunch and dinner buffets (US$7) and salad buffet (US$1.50) its coffee shop, *El Patio*, has nice and reasonably priced platos típicos. *The Steak House*, García Moreno 811, opposite *Hotel Oro Verde*, pleasant atmosphere, good food and service. Good food at other hotels. *El Parque*, top floor of Unicentro, highly rec. (US$12-15 p.p.), buffet lunch (US$3 for as much as you can eat), overlooks Parque Bolívar. Well-known and expensive *Caracol Azul*, 9 de Octubre 1918 y Los Ríos, wonderful seafood and meats (US$12-15 p.p.). For good ice cream and cheap lunches, *Crema*, Chimborazo y 9 de Octubre.

Also on 9 de Octubre: *San Remo*, No.737, varied menu, Italian and Ecuadorean, well prepared; *La Rotonda*, No.432, 1st floor of casino, good large portions, not cheap; *Pizzería Italia*, No.706, expensive; *Bavaria*, No.1313, German run, good meat; also on this street, lots of US-style snack bars, quite expensive, and the usual fast food at *Burgerking* and *Kentucky Fried Chicken*. Also central: *Don Vito*, Carchi 803 y 9 de Octubre, disco and bar, closed Sun; *El Pirata*, riverboat on waterfront at Victor Manuel Rendón, good food, reasonable prices, "good place to watch the river life go by"; *Anderson*, 810 y Hurtado, good, French, closed Sun.; *Pique y Pase*, Alejo Lascano 16-17 y Carchi, typical; *Café Jambelí*, Parque Bolívar at *Rizzo Hotel*, 1950s mod decor, very good coastal dishes, seafood, popular with expatriates; *Pizzalandia*, Carchi y 1° de Mayo, good pizza. Local food at *Clérico*, Junín 213 y Panamá; *Muelle 5*, Malecón opp. Roca, expensive; *El Camino*, Pedro Ycaza y Córdova, economical, best at lunchtime, owned by English-speaking Jaime Mendoza. Many good *chifas*, including *Himalayas*, Sucre y Chile, cheap, good food; *Gran Chifa*, Pedro Carbo 1018, ornate, reasonable prices. Best ice cream at *Il Gelato Italiano*, 9 de Octubre y Carchi, also in Urdesa. *Submarine* sandwich shop, 9 de Octubre y Chile, excellent; *Galleta Pecosa*, 10 de Agosto y Boyaco, cakes and cookies.

Restaurants outside the centre are mostly in Urdesa and Kennedy suburbs. Urdesa: *Juan Salvador Gaviota*, Boloña 603 y Décima, good seafood, closed Sun.; *Il Fiorentino*, Datiles y V.E. Estrada, international, closed Mon. *Trattoria Da Migliorini*, La Primera 604 y Las Monjas, opposite letel, very good Italian food, service excellent; *Costa Brava*, Catalan food, Las Monjas 303 y Cuarta; many others of all kinds along V.E.Estrada. Kennedy: several on Francisco Boloña and Av. Kennedy. Tax on restaurant bills 20%.

**Shopping** Guayaquil has four shopping centres, the Policentro, the Unicentro, the Centro Comercial Urdesa and the Albán Borja shopping centre. To buy handicrafts, the best places are Madaleine Hollander's shop in the *Oro Verde*, (expensive), and *Manos* (offshoot of *La Bodega* in Quito) at the *Grand Hotel Guayaquil* and also in Urdesa, e.g. *Coosas* on V.E. Estrada, same quality as in Quito. Every day except Sun., Otavalan Indians sell their handicrafts under the arcades along Calle Chile between 9 de Octubre and Vélez. Beware of newly manufactured "Inca relics" and "Jívaro shrunken heads" sold in souvenir shops. *Artesanías del Ecuador*, 9 de Octubre 104 y Malecón, are good and reliable, and so are *Ocepa*, V.M.Rendón 405 y Córdova. The prices here differ little from those in the towns where the goods are made. Good shops include *Inca Folklore* in the Edificio Gran Pasaje, Av. 9 de Octubre 424, *Arte Folklore Otavalo*, 9 de Octubre 102 y Malecón; *Artesanías Cuenca*, Vélez 110; and *Artesanías Mariel*, Vélez y Chile. There is an *H. Stern* jewellers shop at the airport. Stands in street near Post Office, and a small market in Calle Chile, between 9 de Octubre and Vélez, next to San Francisco church, open daily. Camera repairs at Calle Aguire 714, 2nd floor. Another camera shop is at Luque and Chimborazo, but reports that stolen cameras are sold as new.

Everyone in Guayaquil, rich, poor and in-between, does their shopping at the Bahía, or black market, located along Pichincha, S of Colón and along Olmedo. A wide selection of shoes, appliances, TVs, radios and houseware can be found along Pichincha. Clothing is along Pedro Carbo and Olmedo. There is a food market ("bahía") in a covered area on Huancavelica near Pichincha, behind the Cepe gasoline station. Watch your valuables; however the area is generally safe, lots of police. Most name-brand goods will probably be counterfeit. Camping gas at Casa Maspons, corner of Ballén 517 y Boyacá.

**Books** *Librería Científica*, Luque 223 y Chile, good for field guides to the flora and fauna of South America and the Galápagos. *Librería Selecta*, Aguirre 717. *Librería Cervantes*, Aguirre 606A. *Su Librería* at Chimborazo 416. Book Exchange at *Nuevos Horizontes*, 6 de Marzo 924.

**Local Transport** Buses and colectivos about US$0.06 (most visitors dare not try them, but they are not lethal although once on it is difficult to get off). The *busetas*, or minibuses, are cheap and safe to ride. Ruta 15 will take you from the centre to Urdesa, 13 to Policentro, 14 to Albán Borja. *Buseta* passengers and drivers have been occasionally robbed by armed thieves, but generally in the poorer areas of the city. For more roomy travel the *Servicio especial* buses marked with blue and white diagonal stripes are clean and convenient. To get off at your stop, yell *pare*. Taxis: short runs, US$0.50; to Policentro or Urdesa, US$0.08; to the airport US$1, city centre to Terminal Terrestre, US$1; by the hr US$1.50. To Durán, across bridge, US$4.50; also ferry. Taxis are notorious for overcharging; check on fare before entering.

**Car Hire** Hertz, Avis, Budget, Dollar, Ecuacar (has been particularly rec.) at airport, town centre offices and main hotels, prices around US$30 a day, inc. insurance and tax, for a small car. Dollar offers competitive prices but the cars are often reported in poor condition.

**Entertainment** Discos and bars in the good hotels. Also *El Corsario*, Los Ríos y Piedrahita; *Buccaneer* and *Flashdance* in centre; *Cuartito Azul*, Luque y Garaycoa; *Zebras*, Los Ríos y 9 de Octubre. There is a *peña* (folklore show) at *Rincón Folklórico*, Malecón 208 y J.Montalvo. Casinos at *Oro Verde*, *Unihotel* and *Boulevard* hotels. See *El Universo* for cinemas and other entertainments. Cinemas cost US$0.70, one double bill.

**Horse-Racing** Hipódromos Buijo and Río Verde in Salinas. Parimutuel betting. Amazingly low standard.

**Exchange** **Lloyds Bank**, Pichincha 108-110 and Merado and Urdesa agencies, advances money on Visa card. **Banco Holandés Unido**, P. Ycaza 454 y Baquerizo Moreno, T 312-900; **Citibank**, Av. 9 de Octubre, Citicorp cheques only; **Bank of America**, Elizalde 100. Open 0900-1330. Closed Sat. US$ cash on Visa, no commission; **Banco del Pacífico**, Pichincha y Fco. P. Ycaza, recommended, advances money on Master Card and changes Thomas Cook travellers cheques into dollars cash for small commission (San Francisco 300 building, 9th floor, next to Plaza San Francisco, enter either from Pedro Carbo or Gen. Córdova). **Banco Popular**, Pedro Carbo y 9 de Octubre, changes Amex travellers' cheques into cash dollars, commission 1%. **Filanbanco**, 9 de Octubre between Pichincha and P. Carbo, advances on Visa, good rates, no commission.

There are several *Casas de Cambio* on Av. 9 de Octubre, also many on Av. Pichincha, between Aguirre and 9 de Octubre. All the *cambios* in the centre will exchange Amex travellers' cheques, though the banks generally offer better rates. **Cambiosa**, 9 de Octubre 113 y Malecón, rec.; also **Cambitur**, near *Pensión Pauker*. Most open 0900-1900, shut on Saturday. **Wander Cambios** at airport open 7 days a week (poorer rates than in town).

**Consulates** **Peru**, Av. 9 de Octubre 411, 6th floor, T 512-738. 0900-1330. **Bolivia**, P. Ycaza 302 of. 601, T 304-260. **Uruguay**, V. M. Rendón 1006, T 513-461. **Brazil**, Ciudadela Nueva Kennedy, Calle 9 Este A 208 y LAB, T 393-875; **Argentina**, Aguirre 104. **Venezuela**, Chile 329, T 528-563; **Colombia**, Aguirre 116 y Pichincha, 6th floor, T 526-008. **Austria**, Av. 9 de Octubre 1310, T 392-307. **Netherlands**, Av. 9 de Octubre 2309, 5th floor. T 366-410. **Switzerland**, 9 de Octubre 2105. **Italy**, 9 de Octubre y Baquerizo Moreno. **Germany**, 9 de Octubre 109; **Denmark**, General Córdoba 604 y Mendi Buro, 3rd floor, of. 304, T 308-020, open 0900-1200. **France**, Pedro Carbo 613, entre Luque y Aguirre, 5th floor. **Canada**, Ed. Torres de la Merced, 4th floor, office 11, Córdova 800 y Rendón (T 313-747/303-580). **USA**, 9 de Octubre 1571 y García Moreno, T 323-570.

**Telecommunications and post** Instituto Ecuatoriano de Telecomunicaciones (Ietel). Telephone company and post office share same block, Pedro Carbo y Aguirre. Public telex booth. Many kiosks in arcades all round it, each with the flag and name of a different country, plenty of stationery.

**Medical** Dr. Angel Serrano Sáenz, Av. Boyacá 821, T 301-373, English speaking. Dr. Alfonso E. León Guin, Centro de Especialidades, Av. Boyacá 1320 y Luque, T 528-179/517-793; open 1100-1300 and 1400-1900 and Sat., also English speaking. The main hospital used by the foreign community is the Clínica Kennedy, T 396-963. It also contains the consulting rooms of almost every kind of doctor.

**Places of Worship** Episcopalian Church of USA; Lutheran Church; Anglican Church, Luis Urdaneta y Malecón del Salado, Urdesa.

**Immigration** Av. Pichincha y Aguirre (Gobernación), T 514-925/516-789, for visa extensions.

**Tourist Bureau** Cetur, Malecón 2321 y Av. Olmedo, first floor; T 518-926, 526-241. Friendly but seem poorly informed, Spanish speaking only, open 0900-1600, Mon.-Fri. Map of Ecuador. A Policía de Turismo man can be hired for a guided tour of Guayaquil. Cost will be about US$4 per hr for taxi (2 hrs will do) and US$3 to the Policía de Turismo.

**Travel Agents** Reportedly, none is open at weekends. *Galasam Cía Ltda.*, Edificio Gran Pasaje, sala 1107, Av. 9 de Octubre 424, T 306-289; their Galápagos programme is called Economic Galápagos Tours; see Galápagos section (**page 861**) for details. *Metropolitan Touring*, Pichincha 415 y Aguirre. *Machiavello Tours*, 9 de Octubre y Anteparra (rec.). *Galápagos Cruises*, Los Ríos 0-80, T 390-893. *Gordon Tours*, 9 de Octubre 2009, rec. *Ecuadorian Tours*, 9 de Octubre 1900 at corner of Esmeraldas, is agent for American Express, T 397-111. *Orbitur*, Aguirre 100, T 325-777, tours to the Galapagos, friendly and helpful.

**Rail** Service to Quito suspended in 1983 but scheduled to recommence end-1991. Travellers arriving in Durán and ferrying to Guayaquil land on the Malecón Bolívar about 10 blocks N of the Palacio de Gobernación. The first ferry is at 0600, the last at 2130 but buses run later. Bus 17 goes to Durán. Taxi to Durán from Guayaquil early is US$2.50. Accommodation in Durán, *Pensión La Paz*, near station, F; *Durán*, G, with bath, good, clean, ask for fan, one block from station, next door is *Los Angeles*, similar. From **Durán to Alausí**, services are subject to alteration: there is a daily train leaving at about 0630, 12 hrs, US$0.75. Tickets on sale from 0530. It is important to check details in advance. The train stops for some hours to change engines at Bucay, leaving there about 6 hrs after departure from Durán; you can take a bus to Bucay, 2 hrs, and catch the train there. Some days the train goes only to Bucay, not through to Alausí. It is difficult to do a round trip Guayaquil-Alausí in one day, a bus Alausí-Riobamba, Riobamba-Guayaquil gets you back to Guayaquil at about 0100 the next day, not a rec. time of arrival.

**Bus Services** The new bus station (Terminal Terrestre) is near the airport, just off the road to the Guayas bridge (no left luggage depot, but well-organized). **Town buses** 2, 66, 69, 70, 71 and 76 from new bus station to centre, US$0.06, taxis not metred (to city centre US$1). Several companies to **Quito**, US$2.75, 8 hrs. To **Cuenca**, US$2.85, 5 hrs; **Riobamba** 5 hrs, US$2.15. **Santo Domingo de los Colorados**, 4¾ hrs, US$2. **Manta** 5 hrs, US$2; **Esmeraldas** 7 hrs, US$5; to **Portoviejo**, 3½ hrs, US$2, and to **Bahía de Caráquez**, 5½ hrs, US$2.80. **Machala** (for Peru) 3½ hrs, US$2, frequent, or by minibus 2½ hrs, leave at 20 minute intervals between 0600 and 1900, 10 kg. baggage limit. For the **Peruvian border**, to **Huaquillas**, avoiding Machala, US$2.50, 5 hrs; via Machala, 6 hrs. To **Ambato**, US$2.50, 6½ hrs. To **Alausí**, 4 hrs, US$2. Regular and frequent buses to **Playas** (2¼ hrs, US$0.90) and to **Salinas** (2½ hrs, US$1). Colectivos are not rec. for journeys to the Sierra, they drive too fast and are dangerous. **Trucks** carry freight and passengers, slower, bumpy, cheaper than buses, and you see better. Inquire at Sucre 1104.

**Simón Bolívar Airport**, near the centre. US$0.12 for bus (sometimes allow backpacks on board), No. 2 from Malecón, No. 3 from Centro Cívico, No. 69 from Plaza Victoria. If going straight on to another city, get bus directly to bus station, which is close by. US$1 for taxi from centre or from airport, but if you are arriving in Guayaquil and need a taxi from the airport, walk ½ block from the terminal out to Av. Las Américas, where taxis and *camionetas* wait for passengers. The fare will be about half of what you will be charged for the same trip by one of the drivers who belong to the airport taxi cooperative. Cetur advises that visitors should not pay more than US$2.50 for taxis from the airport to town. There are several car hire firms at the airport; an information desk; Cetur office; a *cambio*.

**Air Services** About 14 flights daily to **Quito**, US$17.35 (TAME, Saeta, SAN; ensure seats are confirmed, not standby). Sit on the right side for the best views. There are flights to **Cuenca** (Mon.-Fri. US$14), **Manta** (1-2 a day, US$13.35), **Loja** (1 a day, US$13), **Machala** (US$10.85) and **Ambato** (3 a week, US$18.20). Daily to **Galápagos** (see page 861). Commuter flights are also available on small 5 or 7 seater planes with Cedta and Lansa from the Avioneta terminal on the city side of the international terminal; weekday flights to the Peruvian frontier, to **Bahía de Caráquez** and **Pedernales**. TAME, 9 de Octubre, Edif. Gran Pasaje (T 305-800); SAN, Vélez 296 y Chile; Saeta, Escobedo 1114 y 9 de Octubre (T 303-024). Flights to **Lima**: Aero Perú (9 de Octubre). Andes Airlines will ship vehicles to Panama. When passing through Guayaquil by air, do not put valuables into backpacks checked into the hold, things go missing.

**Excursions** To Playas, Salinas and the Santa Elena peninsula (see page 804). Cerro Blanco is a wildlife area set aside as a privately-held reserve by Cemento Nacional on the road going west towards Salinas, a sign saying Urbanización Puerto Azul. Here there is a huge cement works and the park area lies behind it. To get in, get permission from Eduardo Aspiazu, head of Fundación Natura in Guayaquil, T 394-850/394-878. Camping is possible with permission. A road circles the area with many tracks dodging in and out. Be careful not to get lost. It's mostly a dry forest area with scrub and kapok on the southern flanks. The area contains an amazing amount of wildlife despite being so close to the largest city in Ecuador. You can see puma, jaguar, tayra (badger), howler monkeys, ocelot, coatis (little raccoons), peccaries, and it is excellent for birdwatching: owls, grey hawk, crane hawk, snail kite, etc. Lakes near the bottom of the area are home to a variety of waterfowl. Peace corps volunteer, Eric Horstman, is working on a trail and interpretation centre.

---

## THE SOUTHERN LOWLANDS (5)

Thriving banana plantations and shrimp farms are the economic mainstay of the coastal area bordering the Gulf of Guayaquil, with rice, sugar, coffee and cacao also grown. The Guayas lowlands are subject to flooding, humidity is high and biting insects are fierce. Large areas of mangroves characterize the coast leading south to Huaquillas, the main border crossing to Peru.

On the southern shore of the Gulf of Guayaquil is **Puerto Bolívar** (Hotels: *Pacífico* restaurant and *Jambelí*, both basic, G), built above a mangrove swamp and backed by jungle. Approximately one million tonnes a year of banana exports pass through this port. It serves (6½ km.) *Machala*, a growing agricultural town of 158,800 with an annual banana fair in September. The area is an unattractive (mosquitoes) but prosperous irrigated banana zone. It is also a centre for pond shrimp production. From Machala paved roads run inland to Pasaje (26 km.; *Hotel Pasaje*, F with bath), and Arenillas (76 km.), and NE from **Puerto Bolívar** via Pasaje and Girón to Cuenca. An all-weather road runs SE through Arenillas to Loja (161 km.).

Buses run every 10 min. from Puerto Bolívar to Machala (20 mins journey), and taxis are available. The airport is about 1 km. from town centre, beside local prison. Cedta flies from Guayaquil to Santa Rosa (Hotels: *Santa Rosa*, F, good, one block from main plaza; also *Residencia Santa Rosa*, Av. Colón, on corner with Hotel, G, dirty and noisy, other cheap *residencias* on Av. Colón), which is closer to the Peruvian border than Machala.

**Machala Hotels** *Encalada*, Tarqui y 9 de Octubre, D, T 920-681, restaurant, bar, cafetería, disco; *Rizzo*, Guayas y Bolívar, D, T 921-511, a/c, T.V., suites available, slightly worn luxury, pool, casino, cafetería, restaurant, rec. for breakfast as well as dinner; *El Oro*, Sucre y Juan Montalvo, D, T 922-408, refurbished, good, excellent but very expensive restaurant; *Perla del Pacífico*, Sucre 603 y Páez, D, T 920-915, T.V., a/c, no hot water; *Inés*, Montalvo y Pasaje, E, T 922-301, good restaurant; *Gran Hotel Machala*, Juan Montalvo y Rocafuerte, F, dirty and noisy, no fan, T 920-530; *Residencial El Oro*, 9 de Mayo y Bolívar, G, basic but OK; *Las Cuevas de los Tayos*, F, clean, parking, rec.; *Residencial Internacional*, Guayas y Sucre, F, clean, friendly, fan, rec; *Hotel Ecuatoriano*, 9 de Octubre y Colón, F, unfriendly, overpriced, bath, a/c. A mosquito net may be needed for sleeping.

**Restaurants** *Cafetería San Francisco*, Sucre block 6, good filling breakfast; *Café Jambelí*, coastal dishes and seafood, rec.; *Pepe's Parrillada*, Av. 9 de Octubre y 9 de Mayo, specializes in kebabs and steaks, bife better than lomo; *Parrillada Sabor Latina*, Sucre y Guayas, steaks and grills; *Pío Pío Rico Pollo*, Av. Guayas, chicken; *Norberto's*, near town centre, very good; *Chifa China* and *La Peña*, both 9 de Octubre y Guayas; two branches of *Kingburger* offer good hamburgers, clean; *La Fogata*, near telephone office, for good chicken. In **Puerto Bolívar**, *El Acuario* offers excellent value in seafood dishes (on main street which runs back from the pier). A good spot for a beer and toasted sandwich or ceviche is the *Miramar* bar at the pierhead.

**Cinemas** There are several, of which *El Tauro* is the best, a/c, cushioned seats, good sound. The *Teatro Municipal* has wooden benches and rats, US$0.32 a seat.

**Sport** A development just outside Machala on the Pasaje road has two large outdoor swimming pools. The Machala tennis club has three clay and two concrete courts, a swimming pool and a club house. It is situated on the left-hand side of the Santa Rosa road just after the roundabout where the Pasaje road branches off, about 5 km. from Machala. Cockfighting takes place every Saturday afternoon at the cockpit on Calle 9 de Octubre.

**Exchange** Banco del Pacífico, Rocafuerte y Tarqui, changes travellers' cheques and notes; the *casas de cambio* do not change cheques.

**Peruvian Consulate** At the NW corner of Colón y Bolívar, 2nd floor.

**Post Office** Bolívar y Montalvo; telephone and cable office, **Ietel**, 9 de Octubre near stadium.

**Travel Agent** *Ecuadorian Tours*, Bolívar y Guayas.

**Tourist Office** Cetur, Tarqui y Primera Constituyente; maps are in the basement.

**Buses** The bus companies Occidental, Panamericana, Ecuatoriano Pullman and Rutas Orenses (the best safety record) have depots in the town with direct services to **Quito** (12 hrs, US$4.50), **Guayaquil** (3½ hrs, US$2), **Esmeraldas** (11 hrs, US$3.70), **Loja** (7 hrs, US$2.75). Hourly service to **Cuenca** by Empresas Pullman Sucre, Sucre block 7, US$2.70, 3½ hrs, "exciting ride guaranteed" along a winding road. Also Transportes Azuay, Juan Montalvo 1508 y Boyacá.

**Excursions** From the old pier on the Puerto Bolívar waterfront motorized canoes go to the tourist beach at Jambelí, on the far side of the mangrove islands which shelter Puerto Bolívar from the Pacific. The beach is long and safe but there is no shade. Canoes cost US$12 return (arrange return time with boatman) or there is a regular boat service (US$1 p.p.), 1000 and 1300 returning 1500 and 1700 on weekdays, more frequent at weekends. A trip to the quieter beach at La Bravita can be arranged, but there are no facilities and again no shade, so take drinks, etc. If arranging a trip to the beach at Costa Rica (2 hrs) be sure to carry passport as a military post has to be passed. This beach is pleasant but the waves and currents can be dangerous. The trip through mangrove channels is interesting, especially for bird watchers. All the above locations suffer from ferocious mosquitoes after about 1630 and it is better not to stray off the sand at any time as the driftwood is infested with biting insects. The gold mines at Zaruma can be visited. Frequent buses to Zaruma, Transportes TAC, Colón y Rocafuerte.

**Crossing the Border into Peru** The normal route overland to Peru is via Machala. Buses run 8 times a day (US$0.50, 1¾ hrs) to **Huaquillas**, the Ecuadorean border town, something of a shopping arcade for Peruvians (all shops close about 1730), described by one traveller as a " seedy one-horse banana town full of touts with black briefcases". Travellers who haven't obtained their Peruvian tourist cards in Guayaquil or Quito can get them at the border.

**Hotels at Huaquillas** *Parador Turístico* Huaquillas, E, at N of town, Cetur-operated, swimming pool, restaurant and bar; *Residencial Huaquillas*, Córdovez y 9 de Octubre, G, basic, clean; *Residencial San Martín*, opp. Customs on main street, G, dirty, noisy, mosquito nets, convenient; *Internacional*, G p.p., bath, mosquito net, cockroaches, dirty, noisy; *Guayaquil*, opposite Customs, F, clean, mosquito nets, noisy, rec; *Mini*, Av. República, G, mosquito net, dirty, reasonable restaurant downstairs.

**Restaurants** Best at *Parador Turístico*; also *Rapa Nui*, on ground floor of *Residencial Mini*, and *Sinqi*, Av. de la República, good, expensive. Expect bananas with everything here. There appear to be no set meals.

Complete Ecuadorean formalities at customs and immigration, Av. de la República y Portovelo, in Huaquillas, then walk along the main street and across the bridge. At the bridge, the police check passports. The Peruvian immigration and customs post is about 60 m. past the bridge; from here colectivos and buses run to Tumbes, US$0.70 (taxi to Tumbes, waiting at border for formalities, US$5). The border is officially open 0800-1800, but long lunches are common (Ecuadorean lunch 1200-1400) and the Peruvians like to go home early. It is often best to cross just after lunch when the officers are still sleepy and do not pay you much attention but before 1700. Peruvian time is one hour earlier than Ecuadorean in Jan., Feb. and March. From Tumbes (or from the border), fast long-distance buses run to Lima. If you want to go to Tumbes airport ask to be let out at the turn off, leaving you a 500 m. walk, otherwise *colectivos* try to take you into town and then all the way out again.

Border practices tend to vary, so check to make sure what the authorities require. For example, Australians need a consular visa (US$12, available in Machala) from Peru's consular office near the main plaza, but much quicker in Guayaquil or Quito.

**Warning** Officially, a ticket out of Peru is necessary for entry into the country. Although rarely asked for, some agencies reportedly still sell cheap tickets for non-existent runs out of Peru. (Tepsa sells tickets in Quito at twice the price they are in Peru.) If you are required to show a ticket, you can buy a Miscellaneous Charges Order, valid one year, minimum US$150, but remember there is a 10% tax on all tickets bought in Ecuador. (We have been told that one traveller's MCO was not accepted by Peruvian officials as an exit ticket.) Peruvian customs and police have asked for bribes at this crossing.

The Peruvian inti has been greatly devalued recently, so verify the rate with travellers leaving Peru (new sol due in circulation, July 1991). Avoid changing near either of the immigration posts; in general the rates at the border are very poor, the best rate is usually for cash dollars. Be sure to count your change carefully; the money changers (recognizable by their black briefcases) are positively dishonest, and clever, particularly with pocket calculators. Travellers leaving Peru should get rid of their intis inside Peru, and buy sucres on the Ecuadorean side. At Huaquillas, better rates are obtained in the town (though not at the bus terminus) than in the vicinity of the border post when buying sucres, though it is difficult to change travellers' cheques.

Coming from Peru into Ecuador; take a bus to Tumbes and a colectivo from there. Some travellers crossing border from Peru to Ecuador at Huaquillas report being required by the Ecuadorean authorities to show an exit ticket (a bus ticket will do) but this is now less common. At opening time, the Ecuadorean National Anthem is played and then people and livestock cross over with a minimum of border formalities.

**Buses** There are a few direct buses from Huaquillas to **Quito** each day, 12 hrs, US$4; most go via Quevedo, but if you get a slower one via **Riobamba** and **Ambato** you may see all the great volcanoes. To **Guayaquil** about 5 hrs, including several stops at military check points, US$2.50. If in a hurry to reach Quito or Guayaquil, it may be advisable to change buses in Machala. Ecuatoriano and Panamericana have a reciprocal arrangement regarding tickets across borders and onwards, but there are few through bus services between Ecuador and Peru. (Direct bus at 1500 from Huaquillas to Piura, US$5, 6 hrs, and Trujillo.) To **Cuenca** several daily, 4 hrs, US$3.10. To **Loja**, 4 daily, 7 hrs, US$2.50. The road is completely paved going up the coast towards Guayaquil and then turning inland at El Triunfo. The road Huaquillas-Machala-Girón-Cuenca has been reconstructed and is the fastest route to Cuenca. Direct buses Huaquillas-Cuenca infrequent, quicker to change buses in Machala.

An alternative point for crossing Peruvian border is Macará in Loja Province (**see page 849**).

## FROM GUAYAQUIL TO QUITO (6)

A spectacular railway rises from the fertile Guayas valley up to the Sierra passing through some of the loveliest mountain scenery in Ecuador. Colourful Indian markets and historic colonial towns nestle among the cones of volcanoes over 5,000 metres high.

**Note to Motorists** There is a 3¼-km. bridge from Guayaquil across the river to Durán. A good paved road from there (summit at 4,120 metres) connects with the Andean Highway at Cajabamba, near Riobamba (**see page 823**).

The floods in 1983 closed the Guayaquil-Quito railway for through traffic. Contracts for repair work were awarded in 1985 but it will be several years until normal service can be resumed. The Riobamba-Quito service (223 km.) is in operation. Service on the Alausí-Guayaquil (142 km.) section was resumed in 1987 (**see page 817**). The lowland section is in very poor condition. We have retained the description of the full journey in the hope that the complete service will be restored at end-1991 as planned.

The 464-km. railway line (1.067 metre gauge), which was opened in 1908, passes through 87 km. of delta lands and then, in 80 km., climbs to 3,238 metres. At the summit, at Urbina, 3,609 metres is reached; it then rises and falls before debouching on to the Quito plateau at 2,857 metres. The line is a most interesting piece of railway engineering, with a maximum gradient of 5.5 per cent. Its greatest achievements, the Alausí loop and the Devil's Nose double zigzag (including a V switchback), are between Sibambe and Alausí, on the reopened section.

Leaving the river the train strikes out across the broad, fertile Guayas valley. It rolls through fields of sugar cane, or rice, past split cane houses built on high stilts, past sugar mills with their owners' fine homes. Everywhere there are waterways, with thousands of water-birds.

The first station is *Yaguachi*. On 15 and 16 August more than 15,000 visitors pour into this little town to attend the feast day celebrations at the church of San Jacinto, who is honoured in the region for having put an end to many epidemics.

The first stop of importance is *Milagro*, a large but uninteresting town of 77,000 people (*Hotel Viker*, F, no food, communal washing facilities; *Hotel Marta*, F; *Hotel Azuay*, G, near station, dirty, unfriendly, fan, bath; *Restaurant Topo-Gigio*, nearby, good, cheap food). (Bus to Guayaquil US$0.30.) Women swarm about the train selling pineapples which are particularly sweet and juicy. About 87 km. from Durán the train stops at *Bucay*, at the base of the Andes (*Pensión Turismo*, G, clean, basic; market Sunday), where a steam engine is attached. Buses run parallel to the train between Bucay and Guayaquil, but take only 2 as opposed to 4 hrs. You can sit on the roof but you will get covered in soot after a few hours.

The landscape spreads before you in every shade of green; row on row of coffee and cacao trees, with occasional groves of mango and breadfruit trees, banana plantations, fields of sugar cane, tobacco, and pineapple. The train follows the gorge of the Río Chanchán until it reaches **Huigra**. By road Bucay to Huigra is still rough going. After leaving Huigra the train crosses and recrosses the Río Chanchán, and then creeps along a narrow ledge between the mountain and the canyon. Here begins the most exciting part of the trip. The first mountain town reached is Chanchán, where the gorge is so narrow that the train has to pass through a series of tunnels and bridges in its zigzag course. Next is **Sibambe** (no hotels, ask in the village for a room or bring camping gear, do not stay at station, if stuck, walk 1 hr to PanAmerican Highway), the junction for trains to Cuenca. A train leaves Sibambe at 0500 for Cuenca (service resumed), arrives at 1100, returns 1400. There is also a daily *autocarro* for tourists to Cuenca run by Metropolitan Touring. Shortly after leaving Sibambe the Quito train starts climbing the famous Nariz del Diablo (Devil's Nose), a perpendicular ridge rising in the gorge of the Chanchán to a height of 305 metres. This almost insurmountable engineering obstacle was finally conquered when a series of switchbacks was built on a 5.5 per cent grade. The air is chilly and stimulating.

Next comes **Alausí**, an old and colourful village (Sunday market), in the mountains on the Pan-American Highway, popular with Guayaquileños (in 1991 the end of the railway line from Durán, but expected to reopen through to Quito at end-year): daily train at 0900, tickets on sale from 0700): *Residencia Tequendama*, G-F, clean, friendly, hot water, dangerous electric shower, rec.; *Hotel Europa*, opposite, F, safe parking in courtyard. *Hotel Panamericano*, G, clean, food poor; *Hotel Gampala*, F, basic, clean, tries to overcharge, breakfast available, check restaurant bill carefully; unnamed hostal, Calle Eloy Alfaro 149, behind station, G, a bit noisy, more or less clean, friendly. Restaurants: *Paradero Chumpisti, Salón Oriental*. The restaurant scene is grim. By road Alausí is best reached from Riobamba, bus 2 hrs; the Cuenca and Guayaquil road links are less good. Bus Alausí-Quito at 0400 and 0800, 5½ hrs, US$1.75, often have to change in Riobamba; to Cuenca, 4 hrs, a fight to get a seat; to Ambato hourly, 3 hrs, US$1, from main street. Coop Patria has a small office where you can buy bus tickets to Guayaquil, Cuenca or Riobamba. Other cooperatives have no office, but their buses pass through town, some at the highway and some go to the main plaza.

You can walk 15 km. on the railway track to **Chunchi**, a friendly village with a Sunday market. One unnamed *pensión* just off main square, ask for directions, also a filthy *hospedaje* near the station. Buses from the square, several daily, to Riobamba.

An Inca trail to Ingapirca (see page 846) can be followed: it starts at **Achupallas**, 25 km. from Alausí. A truck leaves Alausí almost every day, between 0900-1200 from outside *Residencia Tequendama*, US$0.40 to Achupallas. Take food and drink with you, there is nothing along the way. The path is wide to begin with but disappears after 4-5 hrs walking.

**N.B.** There were no trains in 1991 on the following section. After crossing the 120 metre long Shucos bridge, the train pulls into Palmira, on the crest of the first range of the Andes crossed by the railway. The train has climbed nearly 3,350 metres in less than 160 km. Precipitous mountain slopes covered with temperate-climate crops such as wheat and alfalfa gradually change to a bleak, desolate *páramo* (moor) where nothing grows except stiff clumps of grass. Now and then the drab landscape is brightened by the red poncho of an Indian shepherd watching his sheep, although pine reforestation projects are beginning to change the view. One by one the great snow-capped volcanoes appear: Chimborazo, Carihuairazo, Altar, Tungurahua, and the burning head of Sangay. They seem very close because of the clear air.

**Guamote** is another point on the Pan-American Highway, five hours by car from the capital. There is an interesting market on Thursdays and some good half day walks in the area. There is a *pensión*, F, near the railway station and also some places to eat nearby. There have been reports of finds of Inca pottery and gold in the area. The train skirts the shores of Laguna Colta, before reaching the fertile Cajabamba valley. The lake and surroundings are very beautiful and just a short bus trip from Riobamba. At the edge of the village along the main road is a small chapel, La Balbanera, dating from 1534, making it the oldest church in Ecuador, although it has been restored several times because of earthquakes. *Restaurant La Balbanera*, next to the church, good food with local dishes. A road is being built to Macas (see page 858). Sit at the front of the bus as the road descends steeply to Cajabamba for a splendid view of the volcanoes.

**Cajabamba** is a small, rather poor town. In 1534 the original Riobamba was founded on this site, but in 1797 a disastrous earthquake caused a large section of the hill on the north side of the town to collapse in a great landslide, which can still be seen. It killed several thousand of the original inhabitants of Riobamba and the town was moved almost twenty kilometres north-east to its present site.

The new Riobamba has prospered, but Cajabamba has stagnated. Colourful, Colta Indian market on Sun., small but uncommercialized and interesting (easily reached by bus from Riobamba, 25 mins, US$0.10). There are few restaurants and only one hotel out of town on the Panamericana towards Cuenca.

Cajabamba is connected to Riobamba and Quito by a good paved highway and there is another paved highway from Cajabamba to Bucay and Guayaquil. A fairly good dirt road leaves the Pan-American Highway soon after Cajabamba, to the west; it is one of the oldest of the coast-Sierra routes and links Cajabamba with Guaranda and Babahoyo.

**Riobamba** (2,750 metres) is the capital of Chimborazo Province. It has 148,000 inhabitants, is built on a large flat site and has broad streets and many ageing but impressive buildings in need of repair. Altogether, it seems a quiet, dignified place, with the nickname "Sultan of the Andes". Riobamba has many good churches and public buildings, and magnificent views of three of the great volcanic peaks, Chimborazo, Altar and Tungurahua. Four blocks NE of the railway station, along Calle Juan de la Valle, the Parque 21 de Abril affords an unobstructed view of Riobamba and environs; the park also has a colourful tile tableau of the history of Ecuador and is especially fine at sunset. San Antonio de Padua church near Parque 21 de April tells bible stories in the windows.

Riobamba has a new market building, but only a small part of the activity at the Saturday market takes place there. Buying and selling go on all over town. The "tourist" market in the small plaza south of the Convento de la Concepción museum is a good place to buy local handicrafts—*ikat* shawls (*macanas*), embroidered and finely woven belts (*fajas*), blankets, embroidered dresses and shirts, Otavalan weavings and sweaters, *shigras*. Indian women come to the plaza each week with sacks full of bead and coin necklaces, old belts and dresses, blanket pins (*tupus*), and much more. Since Indian-style clothing is also sold here, the plaza is full of colourful Indians from different parts of Chimborazo province, each group wearing its distinctive costume. Two blocks east, there is a huge produce market in another plaza, also pottery, baskets, hats. All the streets in this area are filled with traders. There are also 2 markets on Weds.: Mercado La Condamine and Mercado San Alfonso. A variety of *pelota* games can be seen on Sunday afternoons. On Saturdays at 2100 there are cockfights on the corner of Tarqui with Guayaquil, entrance US$0.25. Open-air restaurants do a flourishing business in that Andean delicacy, roast *cuy* (guinea-pig). Hotel prices rising during independence *fiestas* around 20 April, and rooms are difficult to obtain during the November basketball tournament. There are three cinemas.

The Convento de la Concepción, Orozco y España, entrance at España y Argentinos, has been carefully restored by the Banco Central and now functions as a religious art museum with gold artefacts as part of the exhibition, open Tues.-Fri. 0900-1200 and 1500-1800, Sun. 0900-1200. Admission: US$0.60 for Ecuadoreans, US$1 for others. The guides are friendly and knowledgeable (tip expected). The priceless Custodia de Riobamba Antigua is the museum's greatest treasure, one of the richest of its kind in South America. Well worth a visit.

**Hotels** In January, schools from the coast bring children here on vacation and many hotels are full. *El Galpón*, A/B, Argentinos y Zambrano, pool, sauna, in decline, dirty, food costly and poor (pleasant location on hill overlooking city); next to it is *Chimborazo Internacional*, D, attentive service, spacious rooms with fridge and cold drinks, fully carpeted, noisy discotheque, restaurant with good food at reasonable prices; *Hosteria La Andaluza*, 10 km. from Riobamba at the foot of Chimborazo, with views of Tungurahua and Altar, B, good walking, friendly, good restaurant; *Hostería El Troje*, 4½ km.on road to Chambo, D, pleasant, tourist centre, restaurant; *Liribamba*, Pichincha y Primera Constituyente, E, only serves breakfast, rec.; *Humboldt*, Av. Daniel León Borja 3548, E without breakfast, clean, with bath; *Segovia*, Primera Constituyente 2228, E, friendly, thefts reported, hot water mornings only, rooftop view of the volcanoes, restaurant expensive. *Los Shiris*, 10 de Agosto y Rocafuerte, E, with private bathroom, overpriced, cramped, clean, nicely furnished, friendly, noise from nearby disco, restaurant good; *Imperial*, Rocafuerte 22-15 y 10 de Agosto, F, art deco style, a good quality hotel, hot water, private or shared bathroom, laundry facilities, can store luggage, friendly and comfortable, but loud music from bar on Fri. and Sat. nights. *Whymper*, Av. Miguel Angel León 23-10 y Primera Constituyente, T 964-575 (named after the noises emitted by budget travellers when informed of the price), E, private bath, hot water, large beds, spacious rooms, cafeteria serves breakfast any time; *Zeus*, Borja 4139, E

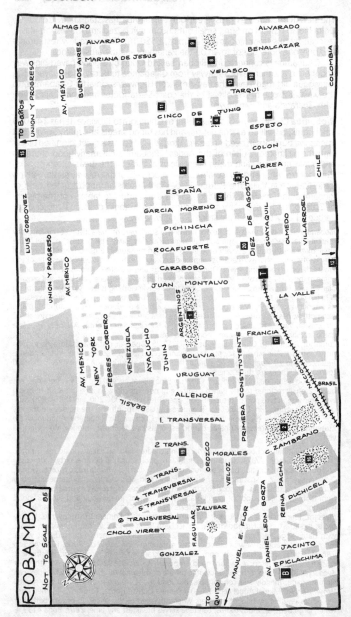

RIOBAMBA
Not To Scale 85

with bath, clean, friendly, good restaurant, English spoken; *El Altar*, Km. 2 on Ambato road, F, no hot water, food poor; *Americano*, F, overpriced, noisy, dirty, above restaurant of same name on Borja near station; *Colonial*, G, clean, usually hot water, hard beds; *Venecia*, Dávalos 2221 y 10 de Agosto, G, hot water; *Metro*, Borja y Lavalle, F with or without bath, a pleasant, central, traditional hotel, large rooms, good beds; *Residencial Camba Huasi*, 10 de Agosto 2824, G, laundry facilities, clean, dormitory beds, hot water, spacious, friendly, owner is a mountaineer and organizes trips to Chimborazo, safe parking in courtyard; *Hotel Las Retamas*, E, opp. bus station, takes credit cards (no Amex), warm water at times, noisy, slow service in restaurant, not rec.; *Bolívar*, Calle Carabobo, G, hot water, no Frankenstein switch; *Residencial Rocío*, Brasil 2168, F, bath, hot water, clean, friendly, safe, quiet; *Residencias Villa Ester*, Unidad Nacional y Lavalle, F, hot shower, basic; *Puruhua*, F, near bus station at Eplicachima 2076 y Borja, friendly, fairly clean, but noisy; nearby is *Monterrey*, Rey Cacha y Eplicachima, F with or without bath, clean, good.

**Restaurants** None of high quality. *Chuquiragua*, 2 km. out on Quito road, typical restaurant; *Steak House*, Magdalena Dávalos y Veloz, good food; *El Rodeo*, 10 de Agosto y García Moreno, a bistro, not cheap but good; *Cabaña Montecarlo*, García Moreno 2041, good food, friendly service, popular with tourists; *León Rojo*, Primera Constituyente 2625, German-run, very clean, good food, not cheap; *Hilton*, Av. Borja, good steaks; *Candilejas*, 10 de Agosto, good, clean, cheap lunches; *Chifa Joy Sing*, Guayaquil near station, cheap, excellent; *Chifa Pale Hua*, García Moreno y 10 de Agosto, vegetarian dishes, good value; *Chifa China*, León Borja opp. *Hotel Puruhua*, good, cheap; *Chifa Internacional*, Veloz y Dávalos, Chinese food, good; *Chifa Chung Wah*, 10 de Agosto 2558, good food; *Café Paola*, Olmedo y 10 de Agosto, empanadas, service and quality poor; *Valentín*, 10 de Agosto, "average pizzas but liveliest bar in town"; *Pato Juan*, España y 10 de Agosto, snack bar, pleasant. Many other snackbars along 10 de Agosto, of which *Pollo Gus*, simple chicken and chips, but cheap and tasty. *La Chosita*, near bus station, for snacks, clean and cheery; *Gran Pan*, Moreno y Constituyente, good coffee and biscuits.

**Entertainment** *Peña*-restaurants *Media Estocada*, Borja y Duchicela, and *Parrillada Gaucha*, Unidad Nacional. *Peñas* at *Taquí Huasi*, Orozco y 4a Transversal, and *La Casa Vieja*, Orozco y Tarqui. Disco, Thurs.-Sun, at *Zero*, Km. 1½ on road to Cajabamba.

**Note** In Riobamba jail is a British citizen, Jimmy, who welcomes visitors and may even show you around, Tues. and Thurs. morning visits only. You must hand in your passport at the gate and your bags will be searched. Cigarettes and chocolate appreciated.

**Exchange** Banco Internacional, 10 de Agosto y García Moreno.

**Immigration** España y Guayaquil.

**Post Office** Primera Constituyente between García Moreno and España (second floor).

**Tourist Office** Cetur, Calle Tarqui 2248 y Primera Constituyente (very helpful). Open Tues.-Sat. 0800-1200, 1430-1700. Addresses for hirers of climbing equipment. Souvenir shops on 10 de Agosto between Carabobo and Rocafuerte.

**Transport** All trains to Guayaquil were suspended in 1983 after heavy rains destroyed much of the track but should be resumed end-1991. A daily train runs to **Quito**, 0500, 5 hrs, US$0.65, check details and buy tickets in advance. For **Guayaquil**, take the 0430 or 0530 bus for Cuenca, which arrives in Alausí after 1½ hrs in time to catch the 0900 train (you may have to pay fare to Cuenca to be sure of a seat). A tourist train runs to **Quito** on Sun. and Wed. a.m. (details from Metropolitan Tours or other travel agencies). **Buses** to **Quito**, US$1.40-1.50, 3½-6 hrs, about every 30 mins; to **Guaranda**, US$0.80, 2 hrs, beautiful views; to Ambato, US$0.40, 1 hr; to **Cuenca**, 6 a day via Alausí, 5½ hrs, US$3. This road is paved but landslides are a constant hazard and the road is often under repair. A popular route to Cuenca, entirely on paved roads, is via El Triunfo, on the Guayaquil bus US$2 to **El Triunfo**, where you change buses, then US$2.50 to Cuenca; mostly good roads and scenery. For a day trip to **Ingapirca (see page 846)**, take 0530 bus to Cuenca, getting off at El Tambo at about 1000. Bus back to Riobamba passes through El Tambo at about 1600 (last one about

---

**Riobamba: Key to map**

1. Parque 21 de Abril; 2. Parque Guayaquil; 3. Parque Sucre; 4. Parque Maldonado; 5.La Concepción; 6. La Merced; 7 Santa Bárbara; 8. San Francisco; 9. La Basílica; 10. Mercado Concepción; 11. Mercado San Alfonso; 12. Mercado La Condamine (off map); Tourist Office; 14. Post Office; 15. Bus to Baños and the Oriente; 16. Estadio; 17. Plaza de Toros; 18. Gallera (cockfights); 19. *Hotels Galpón* and *Chimborazo*; 20. *Residencial Cambi Huasi*.

1930). Bus to **Santo Domingo**, US$2, 5 hrs; to **Baños**, US$0.50, 1 hr; to **Puyo**, US$1.10, 3½ hrs direct. There are 2 buses (US$3.50, 8-10 hrs) to **Huaquillas** every evening (1915 and 2100) with Patria, which avoid Guayaquil; book the day before, arrive early and be prepared to fight for your seat. Bus to **Guayaquil**, about 35 a day, US$2.15, 4½ hrs; the trip is really spectacular for the first two hours. There are pirate buses which charge more than the regular lines and do not sell tickets in the bus station, first come first served, they can be useful when all the others are full up. There is a well-run Terminal Terrestre on Eplicachima y Av. D. L. Borja for buses to Quito, Guayaquil, Ambato, etc., but buses to Baños and the Oriente leave from the Terminal Oriental, Espejo y Córdovez. Taxi across town from one terminal to the other, US$1.

**Excursions** to **Guano**, an attractive hemp-working and carpet-making town of 6,000 inhabitants 10 km. to the north, with prehistoric monoliths on a nearby hilltop; there are frequent buses or taxi, US$2, but nowhere to eat. You can have rugs made to your own design. Although there have been reports of declining quality you can still see enormous rugs on sale, rather expensive. Sun. market. After Guano you can take the bus on to Santa Teresita from where it is a 20 min walk downhill to Balneario Las Elenas: 3 pools, 1 tepid, 2 cool. Superb view of Altar and Tungurahua as you walk through pasture land.

**Climbing** To climb Chimborazo contact Enrique Veloz Coronado, mountain guide and technical adviser of the Asociación de Andinismo de Chimborazo, Chile 33-21 y Francia, Riobamba (T 960-916). He will provide all the necessary equipment; you must agree on a fee with him for the trip you want to make (**see page 828**). He is best reached after 1500 and is very helpful even if you don't need his services as a guide. Also recommended is Marcelo Puruncajas, Espejo 24, who rents equipment and is a cheap guide. For Sangay, take a taxi to Alao and hire guides or carriers of food, tents, etc. there; remember you have to pay for and organize the food for your porters separately, otherwise you have to pay them a lot more. Make sure the fee covers the return journey as well. Also Expediciones Andinas (Marco Cruz), Argentinos 3860 y Zambrano, T 964-915 (office), 962-845 (house), recommended (he is a certified guide of the German Alpine Club).

To the crater of **Altar**. Travel to Penipe by bus (bargain for the price) from Baños or Riobamba/Ambato, then to Candelaria by truck, or bus which passes between 1200 and 1400. Walk out of the village, cross the bridge and go up about 2 km. to the park station (a green building with a National Park sign), where you pay your entrance fee. You can stay there overnight, although it is not a *refugio*, beds, warm water, shower, cooking facilities and friendly keeper. It is not always open, ask in Riobamba beforehand at the Ministry of Tourism or the Sangay National Park office, Primera Constituyente y Pichincha, Ministry of Agriculture. In Penipe ask for Ernesto Haro, who will take you to the station in his jeep (US$3 one way) and pick you up from there at a pre-arranged time. The track to the Altares leads on up a steep hill past the Hacienda Releche, but it is best to ask someone to point out the faint track which branches to the left about 30-40 minutes after the Hacienda and leads up a hill to a ridge where it joins a clear track. This goes south first and then turns east up the valley of the River Collanes. It is about 8 hrs to the crater which is surrounded by magnificent snow-capped peaks. It is possible to camp in the crater, but better still, about 20 mins before you turn into the broad U-shaped valley leading up to the crater there is a good-sized cave, the floor of which is lined with dry runs; there is a fire ring at the entrance. Guides to Altar can be hired for about US$3.50 a day, and horses are US$3.50 each a day. Because of damage done to the track by mudslides the route is hazardous and you would be unwise to do it alone. Consult the National Park Office about conditions, they are in radio contact with the Guardería at Candelaria.

From Riobamba to Quito the road is paved. Between Riobamba and Cevallos the railway reaches its highest point at Urbina (3,609 metres). At the pass, there are fine views in the dry season (June is probably the first safe month) of Chimborazo and its smaller sister mountain, Carihuairazo. Then the railway and the Pan-American Highway wind down towards the Ambato basin. Between Riobamba and Ambato is Mocha, where guinea-pigs (*cuy*) are raised for the table; you can sample roast *cuy* at stalls by the roadside. The valley's patchwork of fields gives an impression of greater fertility and prosperity than the Riobamba zone. The houses seem larger and better built, and almost universally, a small crucifix crowns the roof, where figurines of domestic animals are also found. Large areas of apple orchards and onion fields are passed before Ambato is finally reached.

**Ambato** (population 140,000) was almost completely destroyed in the great 1949 earthquake and is not a very attractive city, coming alive only during festivals and market days. The modern cathedral faces the attractive Parque Montalvo, where there is a statue of the writer Juan Montalvo (1833-1889) who is buried in a memorial in a neighbouring street. His house (Bolívar y Montalvo) is open to the public; entrance free (T 821-024). In the Colegio Nacional Bolívar, at Sucre y Lalama, there is an interesting museum of stuffed birds and other animals and items of local historical interest, rec. (US$0.05, closed Sat. and Sun. and school holidays). The Quinta de Mera, an old mansion in gardens in Atocha suburb, open 0900-1200, 1400-1800, can be reached by bus from Espejo y 12 de Novembre. Out along the River Ambato (a pleasant walk) is the prosperous suburb of Miraflores. Ambato has a famous festival in February, the *Fiesta de frutas y flores*, during which it is impossible to get a hotel room unless you book ahead; similarly in Riobamba, Baños and Latacunga. The town has the unique distinction of prohibiting water-throwing at carnival, making it safe for tourists at this time! It is an important centre for the manufacture of rugs and has some excellent tourist shops in the centre, look for colourful and good-quality cloth shoulder bags. Leather clothes can be specially made quite cheaply. On a clear day Tungurahua and Chimborazo can be seen from the city.

The main market is held on Mon., and smaller markets on Wed. and Fri.; they are interesting, but have few items for the tourist. Most of the action takes place in the streets although there are also two market buildings.

**Hotels** *Ambato*, Guayaquil y Rocafuerte, C, best, clean, restaurant, casino, squash, highly rec.; *Florida*, Av. Miraflores 1131, D, pleasant, clean, set meal good at US$3; *Villa Hilda*, C, overpriced, in Av. Miraflores, German spoken, laundry, restaurant good, limited menu but lots to eat, big garden. Buses from the centre stop outside the *Florida*. *La Lira*, Montalvo y Cevallos, E, good, cheaper for long stay; *Cumandá*, 12 de Noviembre 2494, F with bath, clean, safe, basic, water supply erratic in this area; *Carrillo*, F, Av. de las Américas, clean, basic water supply, sometimes used as a brothel, near bus station, restaurant; *Residencial Americano*, Plaza 12 de Noviembre, G, basic, hot water; *Surtrek*, Los Syris y Cordero, F, owner speaks German and English, is an experienced guide and organises mountain and jungle tours, bicycles also for hire. *Ejecutivo*, 12 de Noviembre 1230 y Espejo, T 820-370, E, bath, hot water, parking; *Vivero*, Mera 504 y Cevallos, E, shower, good. There are a lot of cheap *pensiones* and hotels on Calle Juan León Mera; *Residencial Laurita* has been rec.

**Restaurants** *Cabaña del Negro*, Av. Miraflores 263, good seafood; *El Alamo*, Swiss-owned, excellent meals, now three restaurants, one at Sucre 660, *El Alamo Júnior*, self-service, for snacks, and the *Gran Alamo*, round the corner at Montalvo 520. *La Borgoña*, 13 de Abril y Mera, French; *Chambord*, Quito y Rocafuerte, international; *El Pollo Loco*, Lalama y Sucre, chicken, likewise *Pollo Rico*, Alfaro 521; local cooking at *Rincón Criollo*, Eguez y Bolívar. Seafood at *Monarca*, Bolívar y Eguez (best), *Las Sauces*, Mera y Bolívar, and *El Tiburón No. 2*, Primera Imprenta y 5 de Junio. Oriental at *Chifa Casa China*, Espejo, in front of *La Unión*; *Chifa Nueva Hongkong*, Bolívar y Martínez, and *Chifa Internacional*, 12 de Noviembre y Aillón; also along Cevallos (e.g. *Chifa Jao Fua* at No. 540, popular). Grills: *La Brasa*, Montalvo y Olmedo, *El Gaucho*, Bolívar y Castillo, and *El Faraón*, Bolívar y Lalama. Many good cafeterias and snackbars. *Mama Miche*, Centro Comercial, open 24 hrs. For rockbottom prices with rather dubious hygiene, try the markets. *Happy Chicken*, next to *Hotel Vivero* for clean, cheap, fast food.

There is a *peña* on Fri. and Sat., *Peña del Tungurahua*, in block 2 of the Centro Comercial.

**Exchange** Only Citibank travellers' cheques can be changed at **Citibank**, Calle Sucre; **Banco de Guayaquil** gives cash advance on Visa; **Banco del Pacífico** changes notes only, gives cash advance on Mastercard, 3% commission. **Cambiaria Pichincha**, Darquea y Sevilla, accepts travellers' cheques; **Cambiato**, Bolívar 686, changes Visa cheques, cash, European and Latin American currencies, no commission; money exchange at *Café Español*, Montalvo 607, Mon.-Sat., 0900-1800.

**Immigration** Av. Fermín Cevallos y Juan León Mera, T 820-000.

**Tourist Office** Cetur is next to the *Hotel Ambato* on the 900 block of Calle Guayaquil. Open 0830-1230, 1430-1830, Mon.-Fri.

**Travel Agents** *Metropolitan Touring*, Bolívar 471; *Coltur*, Cevallos 536; *Ecuadorian Tours* (American Express) Bolívar 678. *Surtrek*, Av. de los Shyris y Luis Cordero, T 821-353, P.O. Box 865, Ambato, is a climbing agency operated by Gerhard Schutz, arranges guided climbs of most major peaks, rents and sells equipment, manufactures good quality backpacks to order, speaks German, Spanish, English, rec.

**Buses** To **Quito**, 2 hrs, US$1. To **Guayaquil**, 6½ hrs, US$2.50. To **Cuenca**, US$4, 7 hrs, to get to Cuenca in daylight take a morning Guayaquil bus to El Triunfo and pick up a Guayaquil—Cuenca bus, or take a bus to Biblián and change there. (There can be some discomfort from descent to under 200 metres and subsequent climb up to 2,600, and you may have a long wait at El Triunfo; this route is 2 hrs slower than the direct one.) To **Baños**, paved road, lovely scenery, 45 mins., US$0.40. To **Latacunga**, ¾ hr., US$0.50. To **Santo Domingo de los Colorados**, 4 hrs, US$1.60; to **Tena**, US$2.20, 6 hrs. To **Puyo**, US$1.10, 3 hrs. To **Esmeraldas**, US$2.50, 8 hours. Main bus station is 2 km. N from centre, near the railway station; town buses go there from Plaza Cevallos in the city centre.

Ambato is connected by the excellent paved Pan-American Highway south to Riobamba and north to Latacunga and Quito. To the west, a narrow, winding road (now paved) leads up the valley of the Ambato river, over a high area of desert called the Grande Arenal, past Carihuairazo and Chimborazo, and down through the Chimbo valley to Guaranda. This spectacular journey takes about three hours.

This route can be walked, and is worthwhile for the valley, the páramo crossing and the hot springs along the way. From Ambato, pass the *Plaza de Toros* on your left and follow the winding road down to the *estación de bombeo*, where a road branches off to the left. You are now on the old road to Guaranda, alongside Río Ambato, which you follow all the way. From here it is 3 hrs walk or 1 hr by frequent bus or truck to the turn off for Pasa. Here the interesting part of the hike starts as the river winds through the narrow valley. After 4 hrs you reach the village of Llagua, the last houses and camping place before entering the *páramo* with its scarce vegetation and rough climate. About 3 hrs from the village you see a big church-like building on the opposite bank, cross the river here and go back along the small channel for about 15 mins until you see the hot pools, surrounded by big rocks; the cold river is close by. Continuing on the old road you reach the new road in 2½ hrs, at the foot of Chimborazo where frequent buses pass for Ambato or Guaranda. If you do the trip on a Thurs. you may catch a pickup early in the morning to the market in Llagua, thus enabling you to do the trip in one day.

**Excursions** To Salasaca (see below); to Picaihua by frequent bus to see the local work from *cabuya* fibre, and to Pinllo to see the leather work.

*Chimborazo*, 6,310 metres: there are two routes up the mountain:
1) The South West face: there are no direct buses so take a taxi (US$25 for one day, US$30 return next day or later, US$15 one way; rec. driver is Segundo López, Taxi 89, found at taxi stand in Mercado Santa Rosa, Av. Guayaquil y Rocafuerte, Riobamba) from Riobamba to the Edward Whymper refuge, which takes 1½ hrs., 47 km., or a bus to San Juan village and hitch from there. The road ends at 4,800 metres, where there is a new refuge (guarded, mattresses on the floor, cooking facilities, running water, toilet, bring food and light, very cold at night), or you can walk up to the Edward Whymper refuge at 5,000 metres which is at the foot of the Thielman glacier. There should be two keepers at this refuge, which provides water and a bed (sleeps about 20, also very cold at night, can get crowded at weekends). Both refuges are now managed by Alta Montana and a US$0.75 fee is charged for a day visit. Overnight stays are US$5 but card carrying members of a club pay half price. Take padlock for the small lockers under the bunks. Beware of thieves if you leave anything in the refuge or even in your car at 4,800 metres. From the refuge to the summit the climb is 8-9 hrs and the descent about 4 hrs. There are three routes depending on your experience and ability. Recommended to start at 2400 or 0100. There is a road from San Juan to Pogyos round Carihuairazo, making a round trip by jeep, Riobamba-Chimborazo-Ambato, possible.
2) The North West face, or Pogyos route: Take the Guaranda bus from Ambato along the new paved road or a truck along the spectacular old road (50 km.) to the valley of Pogyos. At Pogyos (4,000 metres) there is a house with a metal roof where you can hire mules for US$4 each to carry your luggage. (Beware of pilfering from your bags on ascent.) Walk about 3 hrs to the Fabián Zurita refuge (4,900 metres) which is uninhabitable. From the refuge to the summit is an 8-hr climb and 3-4 hr descent. Advisable to start at 0100. Take tents and water (obtainable at Pogyos, containers in Ambato). (We are grateful to Enrique Veloz Coronado—**see page 780**—for much of this information.)
Dr Sverre Aarseth writes that in order to climb this mountain it is essential to have at least one week's acclimatization above 3,000 metres. The best season is December and June-September. Sr. Héctor Vásquez at Colegio National Bolívar, Ambato, has helped many

expeditions with travel arrangements and information; he is a top-grade mountaineer. The original Whymper route is harder than the Pogyos route, but it is more accessible and there are more climbers in case of difficulty; the afternoon descent is particularly hazardous owing to stones rolling from the scree (the upper part is quite straightforward with two or three on a rope). Previous parties will most likely have left marker flags; these are often needed for descent in a cloud. Very soft snow between first and second summit but usually there will be a good path from previous parties (otherwise snow shoes might be needed). The ascent to the summit is very steep and partly exposed (falling could be fatal). No one without mountaineering experience should attempt the climb, and rope, ice-axe and crampons must be used. Carihuairazo (5,020 metres) is a spur of Chimborazo.

The Fiesta de las Nieves is celebrated at the 4,800 m. shelter on the second or third Sun. in December—music and dancing, rather touristy, no folkloric roots, but at least buses from Riobamba go to the mountain.

**Guaranda** (14,000 inhabitants) is the capital of Bolívar Province. It is a beautiful, clean, quiet town which, because it is built on seven hills, proudly calls itself "the Rome of Ecuador". Carnival is very enjoyable. Market day is Sat. The daily *paseo* in the main square is from about 1800 to 2100 exactly. Guaranda is connected by a new paved road to Ambato (several buses) and Babahoyo, and a poor, narrow road to Riobamba. It is the main centre for the wheat and maize-growing Chimbo valley, but has long stagnated since newer, faster routes replaced the old Guayaquil-Quito road through Babahoyo and Guaranda. A water-powered grist mill on the river welcomes visitors.

**Hotels** *La Colina*, high up on Av. Guayaquil, C, rooms bright and attractive, terraces give good view of town and surrounding mountains, restful, friendly, good value, restaurant mediocre; *Cochabamba*, García Moreno y 7 de Mayo, E with bath, nice rooms, good service, best in town; *Pensión Ecuador*, opposite, F; *Residencial Bolívar*, Sucre y Rocafuerte, F, very good, hot showers; *Matiaví*, Av. Eliza Mariño, F, clean, next to bus station; *Residencial Acapulco*, 10 de Agosto y 9 de Abril, G, basic.

**Restaurants** *Rumipampa*, Parque Simón Bolívar, best in town, try churrasco; *La Choza*, 10 de Agosto between Sucre and Pichincha, good tacos. *Hotel Cochabamba*, variable, limited selection, not cheap; *Guaranda* soda bar on G. Moreno y Pichincha.

**Buses** Bus station on road to Ambato. To **Ambato**, US$1.20, 3¼ hrs; **Riobamba**, US$0.70, 2½ hrs; **Guayaquil**, US$1.75, 3½ hrs; **Quito**, several a day US$1.75 or take bus to Ambato and change. Taxi to **Riobamba** 1½ hrs, US$11.50.

**Excursion** North of Guaranda, 1½ hrs by taxi along poor roads, is Salinas (de la Sierra), pop. 5,000, noted for its cheeses and sweaters, which are also sold in Quito. No buses except maybe on Sat.; hitching is difficult.

To the east of Ambato, an important road leads to Salasaca, Pelileo, and Baños and then on along the Pastaza valley to Mera, Shell Mera, Puyo and Tena in the Oriente (**see page 857**). It is paved to Puyo.

**Salasaca** is a small modernized village 14 km. (½ hr.) from Ambato, at the centre of the Salasaca Indian zone. The Salasacas wear distinctive black ponchos with black trousers and broad white hats; this is said to reflect perpetual mourning for the death of their Inca, Atahualpa. Most of them are farmers, but they are best known for weaving *tapices*, strips of cloth with remarkable bird and animal shapes in the centre. A co-operative has fixed the prices on the *tapices* it sells in its store near the church. Throughout the village the prices are the same, and no cheaper than in Quito. If you have the time you can order one to be specially made; this takes four to six weeks, but is well worth the wait. You can watch the Indians weaving in the main workshop opposite the church.

**Pelileo**, 5 km. beyond Salasaca, is a lively little market town which has been almost completely rebuilt on a new site since the 1949 earthquake. In all, Pelileo has been destroyed by four earthquakes during its 400-year history. The new town springs to life on Saturday, the main market day. The ruins of Pelileo Viejo can be seen about 2 km. east of the present site on the north side of the road to Baños. *Fiesta* on 22 July. Regular buses from Baños, 15 min.

From Pelileo, the road gradually descends to Las Juntas, the meeting point of the Patate and Chambo rivers to form the Pastaza river, and where the road from Riobamba comes in. It then continues along the lower slopes of the volcano Tungurahua to Baños (25 km. from Pelileo). The road gives good views of the Pastaza gorge and the volcano.

**Baños** (1,800 metres) is a holiday resort with a supposedly miraculous Virgin and hot springs; very busy at weekends and increasingly touristy. The central Basilica attracts many pilgrims; the paintings of miracles performed by Nuestra Señora de Santa Agua are worth seeing. There is a *fiesta* in her honour in October with processions, bands, fireworks, sporting events and a lot of general gaiety. The Basilica de Baños has a museum (stuffed birds, Nuestra Señora's clothing). There is another civic *fiesta* on 15 December to celebrate the town's anniversary when each *barrio* hires a *saka* band and there are many processions. The following day there is a parade in which spectators are outnumbered by participants. There is a zoo off the road to Puyo on the left, about 1 km. from town, run by the Church authorities, US$0.20 entrance, cages far too small and excessive loudspeaker noise. The Pastaza river rushes past Baños to the Agoyán falls 10 km. further down the valley, nearly dry now because of the construction of a hydroelectric dam. The whole area between Pelileo and Baños has a relaxing sub-tropical climate (the rainy season is usually from May to October, especially July and August). It is here that Ecuador's best *aguardiente* is made. Street vendors sell *canelazo*, a sweet drink of *aguardiente*, lime, water and cinnamon, also jawsticking toffee (*tafi*, also known as *melcocha de caña* or *alfeñique*) made in ropes in shop doorways, and painted balsa-wood birds (see *El Chaguamango* shop by Basílica). Two sets of thermal baths are in the town: the main set is by the waterfall close to the *Hotel Sangay*; the Santa Clara baths are about ½ km. further W, up against the mountain, and the third, the Salado, which is pleasanter (but very busy so go early), is 1½ km. out of town on the Ambato road (entrance to each, US$0.75). The baths open at 0430, go early, fewer people, water cleaner and hotter. There are regular buses every 30 mins between the Salado baths and the Agoyán Falls, passing by the centre of town. All the baths can be very crowded and the water not very hot. **Interesting side trips** are possible from the main Pelileo-Baños highway across the main valley, north to Patate, or up the Chambo valley to Penipe and Riobamba, or take taxi to Puente Vendas, 2 hrs, US$2.20, beautiful ride.

**Note**  Baños is a good meeting place to form a group to visit the Oriente, more interesting than Misahuallí, if you have to wait a few days.

**Hotels**  *Sangay*, C inc. tax, with bath, beautifully situated close to waterfall, restaurant (rec.), sauna, whirlpool, steam bath and pool all open to non-residents, tennis and squash courts, accommodation in chalets reported better but more expensive, than in rooms, rec. Also a few rooms in basement, F, but sometimes no warm water. Information and some equipment for expeditions to the jungle and volcanoes may be provided by the hotel. *Villa Gertrudis*, Montalvo 2975, good situation on edge of town, with lovely garden, D, demi-pensión, reserve in advance, rec.; *Cabañas Bascún*, on edge of town (nr. El Salado hot springs), D, quite comfortable, pool, sauna (US$1.50 to non-residents), tennis, restaurant; *Paraíso (Humboldt)*, Ambato y Haflants, D with board or F without food, bath, dirty, not all rooms have running water and electricity, beautiful view from front rooms; *Palace*, opposite *Sangay* (even closer to waterfall), old-fashioned, a little dark and musty, but nice garden and pool at the back, friendly, good value, restaurant, breakfast US$1, dinner US$3. *Residencial Magdalena*, Oriente y Alfaro, E with bath, clean, warm water, rec.; *Hostal Los Helechos*,

---

**Baños: Key to map**

1. Basilica and Museum; 2. Virgen baths; 3. Banco del Pacífico; 4. Tourist Office; 5. Post Office and telephones; 6. Market. **Hotels:** 7. *Sangay*; 8. *Cabañas Bascun*; 9. *Flor de Oriente*; 10. *Magdalena*; 11. *Patty*; 12. *Teresita* and *Americano*. **Restaurants:** 13. *Monica's*; 14. *Regina's*; 15. *El Paisano*; 16. *Rincón de Suecia.* **INSET** 17. El Salado baths; 18. Zoo; 19. Agoyán Falls; 20. La Cruz; 21. San Martín (shrine and bridge); 22. Inés María Falls.

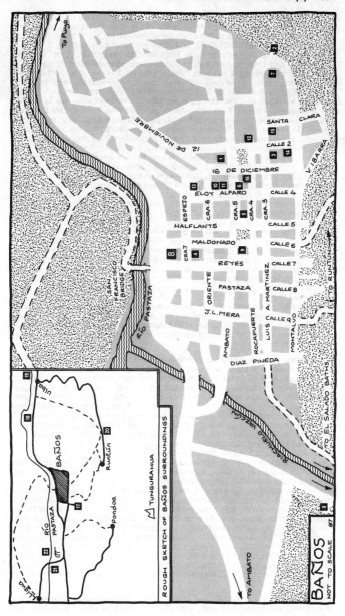

To Puyo

12 DE NOVIEMBRE

SANTA CLARA

Calle 2

16 DE DICIEMBRE

ELOY ALFARO

ESPEJO

CRA 6

CRA 5

CRA 4

CRA 3

Calle 4

HALFLANTS

MALDONADO

CRA 7

Calle 5

Calle 6

REYES

PASTAZA

J. ORIENTE

Calle 7

Calle 8

J.L.MERA

Calle 9

AMBATO

ROCAFUERTE

LUIS A. MARTINEZ

MONTALVO

DIAZ PINEDA

SAN FRANCISCO Bridge

RÍO PASTAZA

VIBARRA

To RUNTÚN

To EL SALADO BATHS

RIACHUELO VÁZCÚN

To AMBATO

**BAÑOS**
NOT TO SCALE

To Ulba

Runtún

RÍO PASTAZA

BAÑOS

Pondoa

To Lligua

ROUGH SKETCH OF BAÑOS SURROUNDINGS

⛰ TUNGURAHUA

E, on Parque Central, close to Post Office and Ietel, restaurant, noisy but rec.; *Timara*, near plaza on Calle T. Haflants (ask for *Tienda de Mariposas*—butterfly shop), G, hot showers, clean, laundry facilities, use of good kitchen, good breakfast, rec, owner's English-speaking son takes tours to Oriente (US$20/day, US$30/day for longer trips), good food, plenty of water, avoid visits to zoos; *Pensión Patty*, Eloy Alfaro 556, near market, G, rec., clean, but check sheets have been changed, basement rooms poor, otherwise good facilities, use of kitchen, laundry, comfortable and quiet, family-run, the helpful owner is a mountaineer and can offer good, free advice, sell maps and hire equipment; *Residencial Los Pinos*, Rocafuerte y Maldonado, F, clean, friendly, ask for front room with view, preferably on second floor; *Casa Nahuazo*, via al Salado, T 740-315, E p.p. inc breakfast, bath, hot water, run by ex-Peace Corps; *Residencial Baños*, F, Ambato y Alfaro, good, washing facilities; *Café Cultura*, T 740-419, has 3 rooms, F, clean, run by friendly Danish family, library, Danish breakfast for under US$1, rec., see below; *Residencial Teresita*, Parque de la Basílica, G, cooking facilities, hot water, prices vary; *Alborado*, on the plaza opposite *Teresita*, F with shower, modern, clean, friendly, rooms have balconies overlooking the square; *Americano*, G, 12 de Noviembre y Martínez, basic but friendly, cooking facilities available, thin walls. *Flor de Oriente*, Ambato y Maldonado, E, accepts credit cards, very good, three rooms have balconies, can be noisy at weekends, clean, electric showers, *Su Café* downstairs, rec. There are two *Residenciales Las Delicias*, *1*, on the Parque Central, F, front rooms have lovely view, but are noisy, friendly; *Las Delicias 2*, Ambato y Haflants, is newer, both reported dirty; *Residencial de Mary*, T. Haflants 656, G, very clean, hot water, small rooms, private Spanish lessons from English/German speaking daughter, US$2; *Residencial Olguita*, overlooking plaza, G, basic, O.K.; *Agoyán*, F, opposite Basilica, clean, good, ask for front room overlooking square; *Anita*, Rocafuerte y 16 de Diciembre, F, behind the market, clean, friendly, quiet, use of kitchen, parking for motorcycles; *Lina*, opp., F with bath, G without, friendly, clean, rec., parking for motorcycles; *El Santuario* above Banco del Pacífico, F with bath, hot water on request, good value; *Chile*, in nearest square to bus station, clean, comfortable, private bath; *Santa Clara*, 12 de Noviembre y Montalvo, G, clean, hot water, use of kitchen possible, washing facilities, some rooms without windows, noisy, nice garden, good for motorcycles, rec.; *Pensión Guayaquil*, on Parque de la Basílica, F, old and picturesque, good food, more or less clean, laundry facilities, but no private baths; *El Castillo*, Martínez y Santa Clara, G or F with meals, some rooms with bath, near waterfall, quiet, clean, hot water, restaurant; *Charvic*, near Terminal Terrestre, F, clean, rec. Several near corner Ambato with Alfaro. Houses for rent on a weekly basis: the owners of *El Paisano* restaurant have three houses, US$24 for the most expensive. Camping is not recommended on the mountainsides as several people have frozen to death.

**Restaurants**   Many close by 2130. *El Marqués No. 1*, on Montalvo, just beyond Hotels *Sangay* and *Palace*, in old house, closes early, good steaks for US$2, quiet and friendly. *El Marqués No. 2*, 16 de Diciembre y Rocafuerte, indifferent, expensive international food; *Monica's*, Alfaro y Espejo, popular gringo meeting place, good, but be careful with overcharging, very slow service; *Donde Marcelo*, Ambato nr. 16 de Diciembre, good, inexpensive, friendly gringo bar; *Le Petit Restaurant*, Eloy Alfaro 2-46 y Montalvo, Belgian-owned, excellent French cuisine, slow service but good value; next door Haflants y Montalvo, Christian and Gaby Albers Wetzl bake and sell fresh sourdough bread (and rent horses rec., *residencial* planned for 1991); *Chifa Oriental*, Ambato 669 y Alfaro, fair food, low prices, friendly; *Chifa Come Bien*, nr. main square, friendly, cheap; *Hostal Los Helechos*, good food, wide selection, slow service; *Salón Latino*, Parque de la Basílica, good seafood, clean, slow but worth waiting; *Mercedes Cafetería* round the corner from *Patty*, good breakfast of muesli and pancakes, reasonable prices; *Café Alemán*, German-run, friendly, good breakfasts, good food; *Central Chifa*, on main street, very good, cheap *jugos*, pastas and meat, huge portions; *Café Cultura*, opp. *Palace*, Danish-run, excellent vegetarian snacks and cakes, clean and smart; *El Paisano*, rec., Martínez y Santa Clara, on road to *Sangay* hotel, vegetarian, but meat also served, also good for breakfast, with yoghurt; *Rincón de Suecia*, opposite *Acapulco*, pizzas, good, Swedish and English spoken; *Reginas*, 12 de Noviembre y Montalvo, is a German café, good breakfasts, good cakes, good meeting place, very popular, excellent Irish coffee; *La Fuente*, on main street, good set meal; *Lucerno*, also on main street, check prices on menu and on bill; *Edén*, nr. bus terminal, good food, large breakfasts, cheap, slow service; *Cafetería Chushi*, on Maldonado opp. bus station, good breakfast and snacks, fast service, has guidebooks for consultation and book exchange (small fee); *Pan de Casa*, next to market, good breakfasts, hot bread, rec.; *Pan Rico*, Parque Central, cheap breakfasts, hot bread.

**Entertainment**   Cockfighting, Coliseo, Sun. from 1800. *Peñas La Burbuja* (Pasaje interior de la ciudadela) and *Agoyán* (near main baths), Fri. and Sat. *La Salsateca*, 1 block from main plaza, open all week. *Hard Rock Café*, Eloy Alfaro near market, beer, cheap drinks, "good old rock, favourite gringo hangout".

**Bank**  Banco del Pacífico, Carrera 3 y Calle 2, changes US$ travellers' cheques and currency, but only from 0900-1330.

**Spanish Classes**  given by Norwegian Jörgen Grönneberg, Corinca, 16 de Diciembre y Martínez, 5th floor, rec. Also offers guided tours by car of volcanoes and local sites. José M. Eras, Montalvo 5-26 y Santa Clara, T 740-232, English speaking retired teacher, less than US$2/hr; Elizabeth Barrionuevo, T. Haflants 6-54, T 740-314, German speaking, same price.

**Book Exchange**  J.Urquizo (local artist), 12 de Noviembre y Ambato and at *Chifa Oriental*.

**Camping Equipment**  from Vatoxi Maldonado 651 y Oriente, T 740-051, also makes backpack covers and repairs luggage.

**Laundry**  Clothes can be washed at the municipal washhouse next to the main baths for US$1.20 a bundle.

**Tourist Information Office**  on Parque Central (Haflants y Ambato) open Tues.-Sat., 0800-1200, 1400-1800; another near bus terminal, friendly, helpful. Good maps, town map US$0.50, hiking maps US$0.30, but distances and times reported incorrect. These are private tourist agencies and organize excursions to the jungle and volcanoes. They have equipment to rent and buy used equpment from travellers.

**Buses**  To Quito, via Ambato, US$1.30, 3½-5 hrs.; to Ambato, ¾ hr, US$0.40; to Riobamba, 1 hr, US$0.50; to Latacunga, 1½-2½ hrs, US$0.60; to Puyo, 2 hrs, US$0.80 (road has been reopened after 1987 earthquake damage); pack your luggage in plastic, it all goes on top of the bus and the road passes under a spectacular waterfall; for Macas, change at Puyo, 0830, US$1.30, 6 hrs, magnificent scenery, sit on right; to Tena, 5½ hrs, US$1.80 by bus (more leg room) with Coop. Riobamba, or US$2 by *buseta*, only three direct buses Baños-Tena, but frequent passing buses from Riobamba and Ambato (or change at Puyo); seat reservations rec. (but buses don't always leave); to Misahuallí, change at Tena, buses leave every 20 mins., US$0.30, 1 hr; or at the Río Napo crossing, see page 855. The bus station is on the Ambato-Puyo road a short way from the centre, and is the scene of vigorous volleyball games most afternoons.

From Baños it is possible to climb **Tungurahua** (5,016 metres—part of Sangay National Park); follow road opposite police control on Ambato side of town, then first mule track to right of store and follow the path to Pondoa; do not follow the road up to the baths. If you are driving to Pondoa, take the main Ambato road and turn off to the left about 1 km. from the town centre. The road runs parallel to the main road for several km. before turning east into the mountains. Park the car at the shop in Pondoa. The walk from the shop to the beginning of the trail takes 30 mins. *Pensión Patty* in Baños arranges equipment, guides (reported disappointing, min. US$32 a day for two climbers and US$16 for each extra one), and jeeps to Pondoa Tues., Thurs., Sat. 0830, US$1 p.p. (return 1600-1700 next day); *Pensión Santa Clara* also has guides; there is also an occasional bus from Baños to Pondoa, and a milk truck leaves at 0800 daily from *Pensión Patty*. It returns from Pondoa at 1400. It takes 2-5 hrs walking from the park entrance to reach the Santos Ocaña *refugio* (3,800 metres—US$1, purchase ticket either at the shop in Pondoa, where sketch map of route can be obtained, or at the refuge) situated 3-4 hrs below the snowline, then about 4 hours from the *refugio* to the summit early next morning (about 0330). Leave summit about 0930 as clouds come down later in the day: allow 2 hours for descent to *refugio* and leave *refugio* by 1400 in order to get back to Baños on same day. Take a sleeping bag and food; there are cooking facilities at the *refugio*, but no eating utensils and rarely any lighting, no heating and it can be cold. For a guide and pack animals enquire at Baños tourist office or Pondoa shop; guide and mule for 1 pack US$5, for 2 packs, US$7. Horses can be hired for US$0.90 an hour (see Julio Albán, Segundo Sánchez or Víctor Barriga near the Plaza Central or through tourist office). A tiring but rewarding climb; requires little experience and, depending on season, crampons for the summit (check in Baños beforehand). Best season is December to March.

There are many interesting walks in the Baños area. You can cross the Pastaza by the San Francisco suspension bridge across the main road from the bus station. Short hikes include the Bella Vista cross overlooking Baños, a steep climb from Calle Maldonado, 45 mins-1 hr, take drinks; Illuchi village, a steep 1¾ hr climb with marvellous views over the valley and Tungurahua; San Martín shrine, ¾ hr, which overlooks deep rocky canyon with the Pastaza River thundering below; beyond the shrine is a path to the Iñes María waterfall, round trip 2 hrs; along the old road to Ambato to Lligua, a flowery little village straddling the Lligua River at its junction with the Pastaza; to Runtún, a village of a dozen mud dwellings, two sporting a billiard table, from which there is a splendid view of Tungurahua (6 hrs round trip). Cold drinks sold at the billiard hall, no food. There are two paths from Baños to Runtún, one from south end of Calle 9, the other from Calle 6.

20 km. from Baños on the Puyo road are the Río Verde falls; a bus goes from the Baños terminal, ¾ hr, US$0.12. Cross river and take path to right of last house on right, take immediate left fork, trail down to suspension bridge with view of falls reported blocked half way in 1990.

Guides in Baños: apart from Carlos at *Pensión Patty*, there is Sebastián Moya, who can be found at Tsantse Tours (*Pensión Patty*—T 740-202). He is a Shuar Indian who will lead tours anywhere (careful planning needed to minimize travelling time), food not included. You may have to wait some weeks for him to be free. Also contactable through *Pensión Patty* is mountain guide Carlos Alvarez, who takes climbs in both the Sangay and Cotopaxi National Parks. Marco Bermeo Velástegui of Cruceros Fluviales Misahuallí (T 740-599) organizes tours to the Oriente (very mixed reports). Geovanny Romo, small agency on Maldonado opp. bus station, jungle tours, experienced, US$25 p.p. per day for trips originating in Coca; also arranges horseback tours from Baños. Christian, a German, also has good horses for rent, rec. He keeps about 14 horses in different areas to cater for different excursions, from 1-7 days; a popular trek starts from Runtún with transport from Baños, US$9. English, Spanish, German spoken, contact Christian at Calle T. Haflants 1-31 y Juan Montalvo, T 740-609.

We have received some critical reports of tours out of Baños, especially of Ayahuasca Tours and its guide Efrain Zabala. Beware also of a guide called Ernesto or El Jefe.

Horses to hire on the square in front of the Post Office, US$0.75 per hour, without guide, for trekking in the mountains.

North from Ambato the railway and Pan-American Highway (many buses) pass through **Salcedo**, good Thurs. and Sun. markets; *Hostal Las Piedras*, G, on Parque; *Residencial Las Vegas*, Bolívar y Paredes, F, hot water, private showers; *Restaurant Ritz*, Bolívar y Sucre, chicken) to Latacunga, the capital of Cotopaxi Province.

**Latacunga**, with 45,000 inhabitants, is a place where the abundance of light grey lava rock has been artfully employed. Cotopaxi is much in evidence, though it is 29 km. away. Provided they are not hidden in the clouds, which unfortunately is all too often (try the early morning), as many as nine volcanic cones can be seen from Latacunga. The central plaza, Parque Vicente León, is a colourful and beautifully maintained botanical garden, where some shrubs are sculpted into various shapes (e.g., figures and flowers). Locked at night. There are several other gardens in the town including Parque San Francisco and Lago Flores. The colonial character of the town has been well preserved.

Just off the Parque Vicente León is the Pasaje Catedral, a colonial building converted into an arcade of shops, offices, and a small art gallery that features a 17th-century aerial view painting of Latacunga (open Tues.-Sat. 0830 to 1800). Casa Cultural, the Museo Etnográfico (closed Sun. and Mon.). There is a Sat. market (also, but smaller, on Tues. and Thurs.) on the Plaza de San Sebastián; goods for sale include *shigras* (fine woven, colourful straw bags) and homespun wool and cotton yarn. Tourist Office at Quito 73-12.

**Festival**  The Fiesta de Nuestra Señora de la Merced (22-24 Sept.) is celebrated with dancing in the streets. Some of the masks and costumes used are on display in the Casa Cultural. Mama Negra festival, colourful costumes, headdresses and masks, in November.

**Hotels**  *Cotopaxi*, on main square, E, with bathroom, good, safe for luggage, not very clean, building activity, friendly, parking, hot water after 0700, rec., ask for view over plaza (these rooms noisy at weekends); *Estambul*, Belisario Quevedo 7340 y Salcedo, F, clean, quiet, public parking at rear, rec., trips to Cotopaxi National Park; *Latacunga*, on main Quito road, E with bath, TV, and phone, cheaper rooms without on second floor but they have no hot water, friendly, restaurant rarely open at weekends. *Jacqueline*, Antonio Vela 78-33, G, friendly, basic, hot water, clean. Also *Costa Azul*, G, unfriendly, good meals; this and the *Residencial Los Andes* (F) are along the Ambato road. Accommodation is not abundant. 10 km. from Latacunga, on Ambato road at Rumipamba, is *Hostería Rumipamba de las Rosas*, D, hot showers, clean, guarded, nice garden inc. small zoo, swimming pool, tennis, table tennis, lake, restaurant, highly rec.

**Restaurants**  *Los Copihues*, Quito 70-83, nice waiters, popular meeting place; *La Carreta*,

Quito 150, good 4-course lunch; *Cyrano*, 2 de Mayo 7674, chicken, good breakfast US$1; *El Mashca*, Calle Valencia, good, large portions, open until 2200; *Chifa Tokio*, Guayaquil 45-58, moderate prices, good value; *Chifa Yut Wah*, Quinchero y Ordóñez 6973, good, cheap; nearby on same street, *Chifa Formosa*, cheap, good value; *Salón Coseñita*, Echeverría 1143, good cheap meals; *El Estudiante*, Antonio Vela 78, lunch US$0.50. *La Borgoña*, Valencia between Quijano and Ordóñez, good value, friendly; *Pollo Dorado*, 5 de Junio y Vela, good value, US$1.30; milkshakes and real coffee recommended at *Pingüino*, Quito y Salcedo; *Los Alpes*, opposite the *Cotopaxi*, good, cheap. *Happy Pizza*, Parque San Francisco, Calle Ramírez Fita, T 800-721, open 1100-1400, 1600-2200, good coffee and pizza; *Pollos Gus*, cheap roast chicken, on Ambato road. Ice cream store off main square, Salcedo y Quito. *Pingüino*, Quito 73-100, one block from Plaza. Difficult to eat after 1900 and difficult to find breakfast before 0800-0900. Try the local dish, *chugchucarro*, fried meat with corn, bananas, popcorn and porkskin.

**Exchange** Banco de Pichincha on Plaza, cash only 0900-1300, poor rate; **Banco Popular** opp. changes cash and traveller's cheques; **Cambio Centro**, Guayaquil 43-19; **Cambiaria Corrales**, Av. Amazonas 76-45.

**Post Office** on Belisario Quevedo, near *Hotel Estambul*.

**Buses** to **Quevedo** from Calle 5 de Junio 53-28, in front of *Costa Azul*, 4½ hrs, US$1.60; to **Quito** from *mercado central*, every 15 mins, 2 hrs, US$0.75; to **Ambato**, ¾ hr., US$0.40; to **Guayaquil**, US$2.50, 6 hrs. To **Saquisilí** from Calle Mechor de Benari des 78-35 next to *mercado central*. Day trips to **Cotopaxi** (see page 837) can be arranged with a taxi for about US$22. Day-trip by taxi to **Zumbahua, Quilatoa**, return to Latacunga is US$30.

If driving, it is possible to do a round trip, Latacunga – Pujilí – Zumbahua – Quilotoa crater – Chugchilán – Sigchos – Toacazo – Saquisilí – Latacunga, 200 km.

A fine paved road leads west to *Pujilí* (beautiful church but closed most of the time; good Sun. market; also, but smaller, poorer, on Wed.; beware local illicit liquor and pickpockets, 15 km. away (bus, US$0.18) and then on over the Western Cordillera to Zumbahua, Macuchi and Quevedo.

   *Zumbahua*, a cluster of 40 houses by an old *hacienda*, 1 km. from main road, 65 km. from Pujilí, has a fine Sat. morning market (a local market for produce and animals, not tourist items, but rated as one of the most interesting and colourful in Ecuador and not to be missed) with llamas on view (two basic *residenciales* on the main plaza, both G, no water, no light, dirty; only restaurant is on main road outside village. Local people reported not to want to rent rooms to foreigners, best to arrive by 1500, check situation, allowing time to get bus out at 1730 if you do not get a room). Take windcheater, can be windy and dusty. Buses US$0.60 from Latacunga depart every two hours from 0400 from Pan-American Highway outside the town, but the best for continuing to Quilotoa, 0630, leaves opp. *Residencial Costa Azul* (cross 5 de Mayo bridge from the old town towards Quevedo, buses line up just past traffic lights) 2 hrs, beautiful ride. Bus drivers on the Latacunga-Quevedo line often do not want to take tourists to Zumbahua as they want to fill up the bus with people going to Quevedo, for whom seats are reserved i.e. you have to stand for Zumbahua. Return buses from Quevedo every two hours until 1900. Car hire has been rec. Many interesting crafts are practised by the Indians in the neighbouring valley of Tigua: skin paintings, hand-carved wooden masks, baskets.

   Zumbahua is the point to turn off for a visit to *Quilotoa*, a volcanic crater filled by a beautiful emerald lake, to which there is a steep path from rim. From the rim of the crater several snowcapped volcanoes can be seen in the distance. It is reached by a dusty road which runs north from Zumbahua (turn right and over the bridge at the fork in the road, there are no road signs and the crater can only be recognized when you are on top of it) to Quilotoa and on to Chugchilán (this last stretch is the worst). At the crater itself, expect to be besieged by persistent beggars and Indians trying to sell pictures. Take a stick against dogs on the road. Also be prepared for sudden changes in the weather. It is possible to stay in a simple hut owned by Sr. Jorge Lataconga at the crater, G, he also sells water, soft drinks and bread and will take you on a day trek round the lake if you wish. The walk to Quilotoa is 9-10 km., or about 2-3 hrs hike from Zumbahua; take water as that from the lake is quite sulphurous and water is generally hard to find. A daily bus, Transp. Vivero, takes teachers to schools in Zumbahua and Quilapungo, leaving at 0600 arriving 0815 in Quilapungo (0750 in Zumbahua), from where it is less than 1 hr walk to the crater. Alternatively, you can get a bus on Saturdays, US$0.15, but it will only go part of the way, leaving you with a ½ hr walk to the crater. Trucks go up after the Saquisilí market on Thurs. p.m. During the wet season, the best views are in the early morning so those with a tent may wish to camp. Alternatively, hitch a truck (which is easy on market day); you will be dropped close to the volcano; trucks back from Zumbahua leave about midday on market day, and a bus goes to Latacunga at 1300. Vehicles bound for Chugchilán drop the traveller 5 mins from the lagoon, those for Ponce on the Ponce turnoff, still about a 40-min. walk north. Hitching a return trip should not be left till late in the afternoon.

The Sat. trip to Zumbahua market and the Quilotoa crater is one of the best excursions in Ecuador, despite the poor accommodation in Zumbahua (see above). Macuchi, on the main road to Quevedo some way beyond Zumbahua, is a mining centre for gold and various non-ferrous metals. The mines were developed in the 1930s by an American company, and now they are almost abandoned.

It is 20 km. from Quilotoa crater to **Chugchilán**, a very poor village in one of the most scenic areas of Ecuador, a beautiful but tiring walk along the edge of a canyon. Water is available from small streams, but take a purifier. If you continue from Chugchilán through Sigchos (Sun. market, basic *pensión* and a few restaurants; regular buses 3 hrs to Latacunga) to Toacazo, take care if driving as there is deep shifting sand in places on the way, keep to the track. From Toacazo the road is paved to Saquisilí.

About 45 min. by bus north-west of Latacunga is the small but very important market town of **Saquisilí**. Its Thurs. (0700-1100) market is famous throughout Ecuador for the way in which all eight of its plazas and most of its streets become jam-packed with people, the great majority of them local Indians with red ponchos and narrow-brimmed felt hats. The best time to visit the market is between 0900 and 1000 (0700-0800 for the animal market); be sure to bargain, prices may be inflated. Rated the best market in Ecuador by a traveller who has visited them all, but less good for textiles than Otavalo. Saquisilí has colourful Corpus Christi processions.

Dan Buck and Anne Meadows write: Tightly woven decorated baskets plentiful but expensive, though somewhat cheaper than in Quito. Bargain hard, there is a lot of competition for your custom. Livestock market hectic and worth a visit. Some animal buyers set up small corrals in which they collect their purchases. Trucks brimming with oranges and yellow and red bananas; reed mats, fans, and baskets; beef, pork and mutton parts piled on tables; Indian women hunkered down beside bundles of onions, radishes, and herbs, and little pyramids of tomatoes, mandarin oranges, potatoes, okra, and avocados; *cabuya* and *maguey* ropes and cords laid out like dead snakes; and a food kiosk every five feet offering everything from full *almuerzos* to *tortillas de papa*.

**Accommodation** *Pensión Chavela*, main plaza, G, basic, friendly, good views, billiards and gambling hall downstairs, noisy; *Salón Pichincha*, Bolívar y Pichincha, G, good restaurant-bar below, excellent for pre-market breakfast, cheap set menu, friendly, not very clean, secure motor cycle parking. Some basic restaurants can be found in the same district (at the entrance to the village).

**Transport** The Saquisilí and Cotopaxi bus companies have frequent services between Latacunga and Saquisilí (US$0.10, ½ hr) and several buses a day run to Saquisilí from Quito (catch them in Quito bus terminal, US$0.65, 1½-2 hrs). Alternatively you can catch an Ambato bus from Latacunga, ask the driver to let you off at the junction for Saquisilí and get a passing pick-up truck (US$0.25) from there. The *Hotel Quito* and the *Hotel Colón* in Quito both organize efficient but expensive taxis for a 2-hr visit to Saquisilí market on Thurs. Bus tours cost about US$20 p.p., taxis can be found for US$35, with 2 hr wait at market.

North of Latacunga, the railway and the Pan-American Highway cross one another at Lasso, a small village with a milk bottling plant and two recommended cafés serving dairy products. Just north of Lasso, east of the highway, is the San Agustín hill, thought to be a prehistoric pyramid.

The area around San Agustín is owned by the Plaza family, which has two large *haciendas* and breeds bulls for the bull-fights in Quito in December. One of the two *haciendas* is actually at the base of the San Agustín hill and includes some converted Inca buildings.

About 2 km. off the road from Latacunga to Quito, near Lasso, is the *Hostería La Ciénega*, a good restaurant also operating as a small hotel (C) in an old *hacienda* with outstanding gardens, an avenue of massive, old eucalyptus trees to the hacienda and a small private chapel; accommodation is very good, service in the restaurant very slow, but it is also a good place for lunch or a drink after visiting Saquisilí market (reserve accommodation in advance at weekends); horse-riding US$1.50 per hour. It used to belong to the Lasso family when their land spread from Quito to Ambato (T Quito 549-126). Take the bus from Quito to Ambato and get off 2 km. south of Lasso.

A little beyond San Agustín, a poor road leads off towards the Cotopaxi volcano, at the Parque Nacional de Cotopaxi sign. National Park authorities are breeding a fine llama herd on the lower slopes. Just north of Cotopaxi are the peaks of Sincholahua (4,893 metres), Rumiñahui (4,712 metres) and Pasochoa (4,225 metres).

*Cotopaxi* (6,005 metres). Rob Rachowiecki writes: There are two entrances to the Cotopaxi National Park: the first is near a sign for the NASA satellite tracking station, from where one can walk (no vehicle access) the 3 km. to the NASA station (army-run now, can be visited with preauthorization from Instituto Geográfico Militar, 4th floor, oficina Clirsen, in Quito) and then continue for over 30 km. more along a signposted dirt road, past two campsites, through the National Park gates, past Lake Limpio Pungo, past the old Armada Nacional refuge and on to the parking lot (4,600 metres) where the road ends. From here it is 30 mins to 1 hr to the José Ribas refuge (4,800 metres, beware of altitude sickness). The second entrance, about 6 km. further south, is marked by a small Parque Nacional de Cotopaxi sign. It is about 28 km. from here to the refuge. Nearly 1 km. from the highway, turn right at a T junction and a few hundred metres later turn sharp left. Beyond this the road is either signed or you take the main fork; it is shorter and easier to follow than the first route which you join just before the Park gates.

The ascent from the refuge takes 6-11 hrs, start climbing at 0100 as the snow deteriorates in the sun. Equipment and experience are required. Climb the sandy slope above the hut and head up leftwards on to the glacier. The route then goes roughly to the right of Yanasacha and on to the summit. Allow 2-4 hrs for the descent.

Dr. Sverre Aarseth writes that the best season is December-April; strong winds and clouds in August-December but still possible for experienced mountaineers. The route is more difficult to find on Cotopaxi than on Chimborazo (**see page 828**); it is advisable to seek information from Quito climbing clubs (Nuevos Horizontes is the best). The snow and ice section is more heavily crevassed than Chimborazo and is also steeper; however it is less climbing time.

Visitors to the Parque Nacional de Cotopaxi must register when entering the park. The park gates are open 0700-1800 with lunch 1200-1400. The refuge (US$3.50 a night) has a kitchen, water, and 30 beds but only 8 mattresses. Bring sleeping bag and mat, also padlock for your excess luggage when you climb. Check climbing conditions with the guardian of the refuge. There are many campsites in the Park (a good spot is Laguna Limpiopungo, but it is very cold). If you have no car, the best bus to take from Quito is the Latacunga bus and get off at Lasso. Do not take an express bus as you have to get off before Latacunga. A truck from Lasso to the parking lot costs US$30 for 4 people, one-way, no bargaining. If you do not arrange a truck for the return you can sometimes get a cheaper ride down in a truck which has just dropped off another party. Trucks are available from Latacunga for about US$25 round trip—ask at the *Hotel Estambul*.

At Cotopaxi the road and railway begin to dip into the Quito basin. In a valley below the bleak *páramo* lies the town of **Machachi**, famous for its mineral water springs and very cold swimming pool (US$0.35). The water, "Agua Güitig", is bottled in a plant 4 km. from the town and sold throughout the country. Machachi produces a very good cheese. Cockfights on Sun. *Pensión El Tiempo*, F, clean; *Restaurante Moderno*, round corner, very good; *Mejía*, G, dirty, noisy, no door lock, no water. Bus to Quito, 1½ hrs., US$0.35. Taxi to Cotopaxi, US$16 per car.

Machachi is a good starting point for climbing **Illiniza**. Illiniza Norte can be climbed without technical equipment but a few exposed, rocky sections require utmost caution, allow 2-4 hrs. for the ascent; for Illiniza Sur (4 hr ice climb) experience of ice climbing is essential. Alternatively, traverse the lower slope, passing below the steep ice gully, take the next, gentler slope up and meander across several other slopes to the summit. There are still some steep, technical sections on this route and full climbing gear and experience are absolutely necessary. There is a *refugio* below the saddle between the two. Very small shelter, take all camping gear except tent. A pick-up truck along the deteriorating road to the 'Virgen' is about US$9, from there 4 hrs walk to the refuge. Take everything you need inc. candles. Cheaper to get a bus from Machachi to El Chaupi, 10 km. S and about 7 km. from the Panamericana. From El Chaupi it is a 5-hr walk to the refuge, beautiful view of peaks.

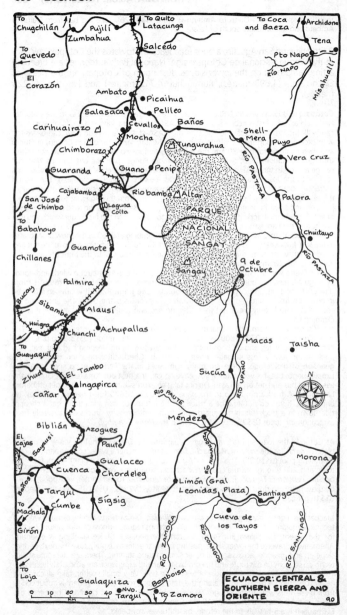

ECUADOR: CENTRAL &
SOUTHERN SIERRA AND
ORIENTE

90

## THE SOUTHERN SIERRA (7)

The colonial city of Cuenca, built on the site of an older, indigenous settlement, is the focal point of the southern sierra. A pleasant climate and magnificent mountain scenery make it ideal walking country, while undisturbed páramo and cloud forest are home to many birds and other wildlife.

The Pan-American Highway and railway S of Sibambe to Cuenca run through mountainous country and high above the valleys of the west-bound rivers. The countryside is poor, dry, chilly and wind-swept, and the Indians small, withdrawn and wrapped-up. Near Gun and Cañar, more Indians, dressed in black, are seen. At Gun an all-weather road runs to Cochancay in the coastal lowlands, from where there are paved roads to Guayaquil and Machala. Towards Cuenca the road loses height and the land is more intensively farmed. There are excellent roads linking Quito-Guayaquil and Guayaquil-Cuenca, which meet at El Triunfo on the coastal plain. Some transport goes this way rather than using the direct road, although there the scenery is magnificent; there are often detours which lead to deep ravines and precipitous peaks. The main road south divides at Cajabamba into two equally respectable-looking paved roads to Cuenca and Guayaquil.

**Cañar**, 80 km. N of Cuenca (36 km. N of Azogues), is famous for its double weaving and is a good area for walking; it is close to the Inca ruin of Ingapirca (**see page 846**). Market on Sun. (*Residencia Mónica*, main square, G, only hotel, often full, may try to overcharge, 10 rooms, clean, hot water, laundry facilities, owner offers tour service to Ingapirca; *Flamingo Restaurant*, Bolívar 106, dirty; restaurants close about 1830.) Bus every 30 mins to the Terminal Terrestre in Cuenca, US$0.60, 2 hrs; also to Quito and El Tambo.

**Azogues** (14,452) is 31 km. N of Cuenca (1 hr by bus) and a centre of the panama hat industry, though good quality hats for sale only at the large Sat. morning market (*Hotel Charles*, F, in centre, friendly; *Residencial Tropical*, G, showers sometimes electrocute guests). The market is colourful and beautifully situated on the hill from the Panamericana to the church, lovely view. Both Azogues and nearby Biblián have attractive churches overlooking the towns from neighbouring hillsides.

**Cuenca** (2,530 metres), with 250,000 people, was founded by the Spaniards in 1557 on the site of the indigenous settlement of Tomebamba. Although it is the third largest city in Ecuador it has retained a small town feel. The climate is spring-like, but the nights are chilly. The city has preserved its colonial air, with many of its old buildings constructed of the marble quarried nearby. On the central square, Parque Calderón, are the old cathedral and a fine new cathedral, started in 1885 (containing a famous crowned image of the Virgin), the work of the German architect Padre Johannes Baptista Stiehle, who also designed many other buildings in the Cuenca area. Modern stained glass, a beautiful altar and an exceptional play of light and shade inside the cathedral make it worth a visit.

**Museums**   The **Banco Central "Pumapungo"** museum (open Mon. 1300-1600, Tues.-Fri. 0900-1600, Sat. 0900-1200, free), Calle Larga y Huayna Capac, on the edge of town is at the Tomebamba site where excavations are continuing. It contains all the pottery, bones, statues etc. found at the site. Go on to the roof for a good view of the site, the river and of Cuenca. It is often shut if the exhibition is being changed. Padre Crespi (died June 1982) used these artefacts to support his theory that the Phoenicians reached Cuenca via the Amazon. About 300 metres from the Pumapungo site, at Larga 287, there are excavations at the Todos Los Santos site, which reveal traces of Inca and Cañari (pre-Inca) civilizations (open Mon.-Fri., 0800-1600). The **Instituto Azuayo de Folklore**, Cordero 722 y Sucre, 3rd floor (open Mon.-Fri. 0800-1200, 1400-1800) has an exhibition of popular art. **Museo del Monasterio de la Concepción**, Hermano Miguel 633 between Pres. Córdova and Juan Jaramillo, well-displayed collection of religious and folk art, extensive collection of lithographs by Guayasamín housed in a cloistered convent founded 1599. Open Tues.-Fri. 0900-1630, Sat. 0900-1230. There is a **modern art museum** at Calles Sucre y Talbot, on the Plaza San Sebastián, and a small museum, art gallery and bookshop in the **Casa de la Cultura**, Luis Cordero y Sucre (second floor). Look out for the wall of niches in the courtyard, each niche contains a statue of a saint. A lovely, restored colonial house is the Casa Azul on Gran Colombia y Pedro Aguirre, housing some small shops, restaurant and a little museum, cultural visits also arranged. The **Casa de los Canónigos**, Calle Luis Cordero 888 opp. Parque Calderón, houses the **Galería del Portal**, T 833-492, original Latin American works of art for exhibition and sale.

The churches which deserve a visit are the old Cathedral, which has a fine organ, La Concepción (see above), San Blas, San Francisco, Santo Cenáculo, and Santo Domingo. Many churches are open at irregular hours only and for services, because of increasing problems with theft.

There is a colourful daily market in Plaza Rotary where pottery, clothes, guinea pigs and local produce, especially baskets, are sold. Be careful of pickpockets in the market. If you are robbed, however, contact the police, their efficiency has been praised by one traveller who had most of his money returned to him after paying them a small fee.

**Festivals** On Christmas Eve morning there is an outstanding parade: Pasada del Niño Viajero, probably the largest and finest Christmas parade in all Ecuador. Children and adults from all the *barrios* and surrounding villages decorate donkeys, horses, cars and trucks with symbols of abundance: strings of dollar bills, bottles of Cinzano, strings of lemons and peppers, bunches of bananas, whole roasted chickens with banknotes in their beaks, toys etc. Little children in colourful Indian costumes or dressed up as Biblical figures ride through the streets accompanied by Indian musicians. The parade starts between 1000 and 1100 and ends in the Plaza de Armas, which is a good place to watch it, 2-3 hours later. Travellers in Cuenca over New Year's Eve report that the festivities include the parading and burning of effigies (some political, some fictional) which symbolize the old year; there is also much water throwing and tourists are a prime target. The festivities seem to go on all through January. The burning of straw puppets (*el hombre viejo*) takes place at the moment of the New Year throughout Ecuador. There are also festivals on 10-13 April (Foundation of Cuenca) and 3 November (Independence, but these do not usually involve processions). There are also festivities involving the throwing of buckets of water at Carnival time before Lent and around Easter, and tourists in Cuenca and throughout southern Ecuador can expect to be thoroughly soaked. Visitors are welcome at the water plant, with its gardens. Septenario, a religious festival in June, lasts a week. On Parque Calderón a castle is burnt like a firework every night after a mass.

**Warning** There is a man who asks female travellers to write letters for him to non-existent friends, and then invites them out. Also reports that he claims to be a businessman planning to travel abroad, who asks women to answer questions and then go with him to meet his "sister", or a "woman friend", by way of thanks. He is a known rapist and dangerous, but seems to have close relations with the police. Avoid him.

---

### Cuenca: Key to map

1. Plaza Calderón; 2. Plaza de San Sebastián; 3. Plaza María Auxiliadora; 4. Plaza Rotary and Market; 5. Parque Luis Cordero; 6. Parque de la Madre; 7. New Cathedral; 8. Old Cathedral; 9. San Blas; 10. Santo Domingo; 11. San Francisco; 12. Museo del Monasterio de la Concepción; 13. Museo del Banco Central; 14. Ruinas de Todos Santos; 15.Museo de Arte Moderno; 16. Casa de la Cultura; 17. University; 18. Immigration; 19. Post Office; 20. Ietel; 21. Tourist Office; 22. Bus to El Cajas; 23. Stadium. **Hotels** 24. *El Dorado*; 25. *Presidente*; 26. *El Conquistador*; 27. *Crespo*; 28. *Milán*; 29. *Alli-Tiana*.

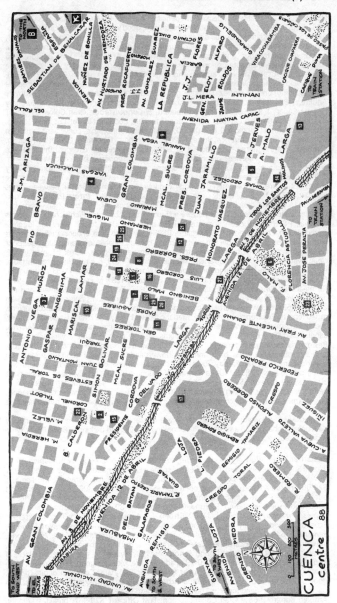

CUENCA
centre  88

**Hotels** Hotels are relatively expensive in Cuenca. *El Dorado*, Gran Colombia y Luis Cordero, T 831-390, B, night club, the best in town, restaurant, good view; *La Laguna*, Ordoñez Lasso, run by Swiss Hotels International, on lake in outskirts of town, A, T 831-200, pleasant rooms, but service not equivalent to cost, quick laundry, small pool which is in shade most of p.m. restaurant "pretentious and expensive"; *Hostería El Molino*, D, Km. 8.5 on road Azogues-Cuenca, pleasant position between road and river, Spanish run, typical Ecuadorean dishes, pool, rustic style, rec., advisable to book; *Crespo*, Calle Larga 793, T 827857, B, friendly and comfortable, lovely rooms, with good restaurant overlooking river, very clean, a lovely building; *Crespo Annex*, D, not as good, Cordero 422 y Larga; *Alli-Tiana*, Córdova y Aguirre, T 831-844, E, clean, hot water unreliable; *Hurtado de Mendoza*, Sangurima y Huayna Capac, T 831-909, E, good, restaurant; *El Conquistador*, Gran Colombia 665, T 831-788, E, without breakfast, sauna, good, friendly, good restaurant but slow service; *Presidente*, Gran Colombia, T 831-066, D, good value, comfortable, convenient, good 9th floor restaurant; *Tours Cuenca*, Borrero 1069, large rooms, TV, central, D with bath, clean; *Catedral*, Padre Aguirre 8-17 y Sucre, T 823-204, E, overpriced but cheaper rates for Peace Corps and other service organizations, spacious, modern, but not very warm. English-speaking manager, safe, laundry service, good food; *Gran Hotel*, Torres 9-70 y Bolívar, T 831-934, E, clean, hot water, laundry service, good restaurant, beautiful patio, some rooms not secure, can be entered through window; *Tomebamba*, Bolívar, between Torres and Tarqui, T 831-589, E, quiet, clean, hot water, good breakfast. *Internacional*, Benigno Malo 1015 y Gran Colombia, T 831-348, D, vaulted ceilings, a/c, TV, comfortable beds, hot water at all hours, pleasant but expensive restaurant, good bar, rec.; *Pichincha*, Gral. Torres y Bolívar, T 823-868, F, clean, spacious, helpful, hot water, clean towels every day, luggage stored; *Milán*, Pres. Córdova 989 y Aguirre, T 835-351, E with bath, cheaper without, rooms with balconies, good view over market, friendly, helpful, reliable for storing luggage, poor breakfast, warmly rec., often full, best to reserve; *Residencial Niza*, Mariscal Lamar 4/51, F, clean, water not too hot; *Residencial Atenas*, Cordero 1189, F, bath, clean, comfortable, helpful, but not safe for left-luggage; *Residencial Norte*, Mariano Cueva 11-63 y Sangurima, G, clean, hot showers; *Residencial Sánchez*, G, Muñoz 428 y Mariano Cueva, T 831-519, set meal rec.; *Emperador*, F-E, Gran Colombia 10-77, T 825-469, rather smelly and run down, tiny rooms with no windows, no water at night, front rooms noisy; *Siberia*, F, Gran Colombia 531, hot water, bargain for room rates, laundry facilities, central and convenient, mixed reports; *Residencial Colombia*, Mariano Cueva 11-61, T 827-851, G, clean but noisy, overlooking market, hot showers. In the vicinity of the bus terminal are: *Residencial Tito*, Sangurima 149, T 829-734, F, safe but rooms are very dark, restaurant very good value; *Residencial España*, Sangurima 117, T 824-723, E, with bath and TV, F without bath, friendly, laundry facilities, hot water, but communal showers and toilets messy, good restaurant, safe parking for motor cycles; *Samay*, Tomás Ordóñez y Sangurima, E with bath, cheaper without, clean, can be noisy, T 831-119; *La Ramada*, Sangurima 551, F, friendly, clean and pleasant but noisy; *El Galeón*, Sangurima 240, T 831-827, E, clean, large, modern rooms, own bathroom, hot water, parking; *El Salvador*, Av. España, F, with bath, hot water, clean, friendly; *Los Alamos*, F, modern, communal hot shower, clean, Av. España, opposite main bus terminal.

Furnished two-bedroom apartments are available; *El Jardín*, Av. Pumapungo y Viracochabamba, US$38 a week plus tax, cooking facilities and parking, T 804-103, or write to address above, Casilla 298.

**Restaurants Foreign styles** *El Jardín*, Presidente Córdova 7-23, lovely, superb food, (closed Sun.), expensive; *Rancho Chileno*, España y Elia Liut, good steak and seafood, slow service, pricey; *Claro de Luna*, Benigno Malo 5-96 between Juan Jaramillo and Larga, T 821-067, restaurant and cocktail bar, open Mon.-Sat., 1100-1500, 1800-2300, excellent food but be prepared to wait for it; *Tupahue*, 12 de Abril 1107 (near Vergel church), also Chilean, good food, expensive. **Italian** *La Tuna*, Gran Colombia 8-80, opp. *Dorado*, pizzas and trout, popular; *Pizzería*, Calle Colombia 8-80. **Criollo** *Los Capulíes*, Córdova y Borrero, excellent Ecuadorian food, friendly, lovely setting, reasonable prices; *Balcón Quiteño (Nos 1 and 2)*, Sangurima 649 near market, popular, quick service; *La Carreta*, Córdova 7-54, good, inexpensive, variety of local dishes; *Café El Carmen*, Sucre y Malo, corner of cathedral square, excellent local food and juices, good atmosphere, friendly service, good meeting place; *El Pedregal Azteca*, Gran Colombia 10-29 y Padre Aguirre, Mexican, good; *El Escorpión*, Malo y Largo, cheap, very good, rec.; *Los Sauces*, Unidad Nacional y Gran Colombia, original dishes, good sauces, medium priced; *Parrillada Argentina*, above, barbecued fish and meat, top prices; *Nutibara*, Sangurima y Luis Cordero, inexpensive, limited menu; *D'Bernardo*, Antonio Borrero 9-68 y Gran Colombia, opp. Post Office, T 829-967, breakfast, dinner, excellent food and coffee, open daily 0800-2300; *El Bucanero*, Sangurima 617, set meals, clean, small helpings; *El Túnel*, Gral. Torres 8-60, T 823-109, reasonably priced, quick service, romantic atmosphere, good; *La Cantina y Fonda*, Borrero y Córdova, refurbished mansion, delicious local food, professional service, good value. **Vegetarian** *El Bosque*, Luis Cordero 12-07 y Sangurima; *El Paraíso*, Ordóñez 1023; *Primavera*, Borrero 5-29, whole food shop, also at Mariano Cueva 9-58; good one at Gran Colombia y Tomás Ordóñez. **Seafood** *El Cangrejo*, Av. 12 de Abril (just beyond El Vergel church, near hospital), for lunch; *Marisquería La Mona* Huayna Capac, delicious, cheap, huge helpings; *El Acuario*, Huayna Capac 138; *El Calamar*, Pizarro 148 y España. **Oriental** *Chifa Pack How*, Presidente Córdova 9-89 y Aguirre, rec; *Chifa China*, Hermano Miguel 9-40, good food, fair prices. **Snackbars, bakeries, etc** *Los Pibes*, Gran Colombia y Cordero, good pizzas, moderately priced; *Trattoría Césare*, Cordero y Larga, clean; *Pity's*, Gran Colombia 2087, hamburgers, rec.; almost next door, *Pollos Gus*, Gran Colombia y Unidad. *Pis Pis*, chicken restaurant at bus station, excellent chicken and chips; *Picadilly*, bar with snacks, Pres. Borrero entre Sucre y Córdoba, nice. *Heladería Holanda*, Benigno Malo 9-45 y Colombia, Dutch-Swiss, superb ice cream, sandwiches, sweets, excellent breakfasts, real coffee, open Sun. until 1900, popular meeting place, rec.; *Helados Honey*, Mariscal Lamar 4-15, clean, cheap, rec. milkshakes; *Capuchino*, Bolívar y Aguirre, good real coffee and liqueur coffees; *Monte Bianco*, Bolívar near San Blas church, good cakes, ice cream; *Café Austria*, Bolívar 1262 and Tarqui, good cakes, pies, sandwiches and coffee, Austrian run, rec.; *Top Cream*, Gran Colombia, ice cream; *Mi Pan*, Pres. Córdova 824 between Cordero y Malo, opens 0730, excellent bread, cakes, tarts, doughnuts, good breakfast; *Dulce Día*, Av. España near Terminal Terrestre, good doughnuts. There is a good supermarket at Luis Cordero y Córdova, one block from Plaza Calderón. *El Suspiro*, Hermano Miguel 681, opp. Tourist Office, sells wonderful, locally-made chocolates and milk-based sweets, sometimes serves coffee, open Mon.-Sat. 0900-1200, 1400-1830.

**Bars** *Picadilly Pub*, Borrero 7-30 y Pres. Córdova, up market, clean, relaxing; *La Barra*, Pres. Córdova, local brew.

**Shopping** Many craftware shops along Gran Colombia, in *El Dorado* hotel (good quality), and on Benigno Malo. These include *Ocepa*, *Productos Andinos*, *Artesanías Atahualpa*, *Arte Artesanías*, *El Tucán*, *Arte del Pacífico* and *Artesanías Paucartambo*. *Artesanías Antigüedades* at Borrero y Córdova has some lovely textiles, jewellery and antiques. *Bazaar Susanita*, Benigno Malo 1092, for good woollen sweaters at reasonable prices. Good souvenirs are carvings, leather, basketwork, painted wood, onyx, woven stuffs (cheapest in Ecuador), embroidered shirts, etc. On Bolívar, between Mariano Cueva and A. Miguel, are two shops side-by-side which sell excellent sweaters. For leather goods try *Cuero y Turismo*, Cordero 11-53. There are several good leather shops in the arcade off Bolívar between Benigno Malo and Luis Cordero, quality and price comparable with Cotacachi. *Artesa*, Presidente Córdova 6-96 y Borrero, with several branches around the city, sells modern Ecuadorean ceramics at good prices. Expensive shops on Borrero, behind old cathedral. *Joyería Turismo*, owned by Leonardo Crespo, at Gran Colombia 9-31, has been recommended; he will let wholesale buyers tour his factory. Jewellery prices are reported as high: shop around. High quality Panama hats are made by *Homero Ortega*, Vega Muñoz 9-33, T 823-429, and at Hermano Miguel 6-78, who exports all over the world; panama hats also at Tarqui 6-93 y Córdova and on Benigno Malo. Check the quality very carefully as some tend to unravel and shops are unwilling to replace or refund. Interesting market behind new cathedral. A Centro Comercial has opened in the industrial park, with interesting shops. Camping Gaz is available at several locations and there is a big camping equipment shop 1½ blocks from Parque Calderón.

**Photography** Foto Ortiz, Bolívar 569 y Hermano Miguel. Wide range of film. Good same day developing.

**Entertainment** Discos at Hotels *Conquistador* and *Alli-Tiana*, and *Las Galaxias*, Núñez de Bonilla 239. *Peñas* at *Hotel la Laguna*, outside town and *La Pantera Rosa*, near airport. Many cinemas.

**Exchange** **Citibank**, Gran Colombia 749 (charges commission, no cheques); **Banco la Previsora** rec. for fast and uncomplicated service; **Filanbanco** reportedly won't change Visa cheques despite being Visa agents. **Banco del Pacífico** advance money on Mastercard, 3% commission. **Cambidex**, Luis Cordero 9-77 are helpful, good rates. **Cambistral** in City Hall on Sucre 664 y Malo changes Latin American and European currencies, travellers' cheques as well as cash; **Cambiosur**, Borrero 8-20 y Sucre; good rates for cheques and cash, no commission, rec. **Cambiazuay**, Calle Antonio Borrero y Cortázar 838, cash and travellers' cheques. **Microcambios**, Hermano Miguel 8-84 y Bolívar, 2nd floor, T 834-137, owner speaks some English. Generally the rates are very variable.

**British Honorary Consul** Sr. Teodoro Jerves, Av. España y Chapetones, T 831-996. **Alliance Française**, Tadeo Torres 1-92, open Mon.-Fri., 0830-1230, 1430-1830.

**Post Office** on corner of Calles Gran Colombia and Borrero. **Ietel** on Benigno Malo between Córdova and Sucre.

**Immigration** Bolívar y Luis Cordero (Gobernación), T 824-020.

**Laundry Service** *La Química*, Borrero 34 y Sucre, excellent next day service.

**Tourist Office** Cetur, Miguel 686 y Córdova, open Mon.-Fri. only, 0800-1200, 1430-1600 (1800 in July-Sept.) helpful. Maps of Cuenca US$0.20. Map of the city also available from major hotels. Local maps are not very accurate.

**Travel Agents** *Yroo Tours*, Larga y Malo, English spoken, recommended; *Santa Ana Tours*, Presidente Córdova y Borrero (T 832-340) run day tours, to El Cajas US$24 p.p., by train to San Pedro, bus to Ingapirca and return. Also *Metropolitan Touring* and *Ecuadorian Tours*, both at Sucre y Malo. A recommended guide for the Cuenca area is **Vicente López Cárdenas**, T 823-790, well-informed on local flora and culture, Spanish speaking only. *Inti-Raymi*, Calle Sucre 6-87, very helpful, rec. Also rec. is **Juan Rodríguez**, Calle Juan Iñiguez 2-47, Casilla 725, Cuenca, T 810-527, English speaking, for El Cajas, Zorocucho, Ingapirca, all the major peaks, Ingapirca-Achupallas hike. **Juan Carrasco**, Bolívar 5-40 T 831-976 rec. as mountain guide, Spanish and English speaking, has climbed in the USA, Peru and all the major peaks in Ecuador, rec. for hikes of one or more days, rock climbing, mountaineering.

**Taxis** US$0.40 for short journey; US$0.50 to airport; US$3 per hr. Local buses US$0.05.

**Buses** The Terminal Terrestre is on Av. España, a 20-min. walk northwest of the city centre, or take a minibus, US$0.05. To **Riobamba** 5½-6 hrs, US$3, scenic. **Ambato**, US$4, 7½ hrs (travel during day because scenery is magnificent, the road, not all paved, goes from 2,600 metres to under 200 and up again); **Baños**, from 12 de Noviembre, Turismo Baños; **Quito**, 9½-10½ hrs, US$3.75. To **Loja**, 5 hrs with San Luis, US$2.85; **Machala**, 4 hrs, US$2.70; to **Guayaquil**, 5 hrs, US$2.85 (road now entirely paved)—shop around for most comfortable bus. Turismo Oriental (4 daily, better buses) and Coop. Sucúa (3 daily) go to **Sucúa** (10 hrs) and **Macas** (11 hrs), US$2.50, day bus rec. for spectacular scenery, left side best overall although right side good for last part with views of approach to tropical lowlands. To **Huaquillas**, 4-6 hrs., US$3.10, at 2100—sit on left (the bus sometimes stops for 2 hrs in Machala, it is often better to get a local bus from there to Huaquillas). The evening bus arrives in Huaquillas at 0300, but passengers sleep on the bus till daylight. Be prepared for frequent police checks on the way. To **Azogues**, US$0.25, leaves when full. To **Saraguro** US$2, 6 hrs. To **Macas**, 8-11 hrs, US$3.50. Buses to **Gualaquiza**, 10 hrs.

**Trains** The train service to **Sibambe**, leaving daily except Sun. at 1400, 5-8 hrs, US$0.80, has been restored. There is also a special tourist *autoferro* to Sibambe run by Metropolitan Touring, daily service. Check beforehand as all services are liable to alteration. To get to the station, take bus marked Gapal on Gran Colombia to its last stop, US$0.05.

**Air Service** The airport is 5 mins walk from the Terminal Terrestre. Local buses run along the road outside. Quito (twice daily, US$18.10) and Guayaquil (US$14 Mon.-Fri.) with TAME (office at airport) and SAN, office on Bolívar and Cueva. Information given at TAME office on Av. Benigno Malo is reported unreliable, double check.

**Excursions** There are sulphur baths at Baños, with a beautiful church in a delightful landscape, 5 km. S of Cuenca. Two separate warm baths, of which the lower one is better (US$0.80 for private bathroom, US$0.40 for swimming pool), the upper one is rather dirty (US$0.40). There are *Residenciales Baños* and *Rincón de Baños*, both F with bath, on the main road, and the *Hostería Durán*, C, rec., with restaurant, pool and amenities, at the baths. Buses 0600-2330 from Cuenca (from Cueva y Lama), US$0.10, taxis US$1.80, or walk 1½ hrs.

About 40 km. NE of Cuenca in the beautiful Paute Valley is the *Hostería Uzhupud*, A, deluxe, good rooms (those at back have best views), swimming pool, very good food, sports fields, small zoo, gardens, lots of orchids, used by the Cuenca wealthy, highly rec., Casilla 1268, Uzhupud, Paute, T Cuenca 821-853 (taxi from Cuenca US$5-7, bargain hard); also *Residencial Cutilcay*, G.

E to **Gualaceo** (Sun. market, picturesque, not catering to tourists), 45 mins by bus every ½ hr, on a recently-paved road, US$0.25 (leave from corner of Terminal Terrestre) pretty town in beautiful landscape, with charming plaza and fine new church with splendid modern glass; woollen goods sold on main street near bus station, embroidered goods sold from private home above general store on main square; hotels: *Parador Turístico*, C, T 828-661 in Cuenca, away from village, chalets, rooms, new, nice, swimming pool, restaurant; *Hostería Rivera*, E; *Gran Hotel Gualaceo*, F; *Residencial Gualaceo*, F; and *Español*, basic, G; restaurant *Manabí* on main road to Cuenca, *Café Alemán*, just off main square, good cheap lunches and nice cakes. Good shoes made locally; splendid bargains. To **Chordeleg** by colectivo (plenty), or by local bus, US$0.10 from Gualaceo market square, every ½ hr (direct bus from Cuenca, 1 hr, US$0.30), a village famous for its crafts in wood, silver and gold filigree (very little precolumbian design) and pottery, also panama hats, although it is very touristy nowadays and quality has fallen. Watch out for fake jewellery. Joyería El Brillante has been found to sell gold-plated silver for solid gold. Joyería Puerto del Sol, on Juan B. Cobos y Eloy Alfaro, has been recommended. There are some good shops selling beautiful ceramics. The church is interesting with some lovely modern stained glass. Try *Restaurante El Turista*. Chordeleg has a small Museo de Comunidad of fascinating local textiles, ceramics and straw work, some of which are on sale at reasonable prices. The walk between the two towns is a good uphill one from Gualaceo to Chordeleg, and a pleasant hour downhill in the other direction. With your own vehicle (4WD advisable), you can drive back to Cuenca through San Juan and San Bartolomé (2 small mines after this village welcome visitors).

Ingemar Tholin of Västerås, Sweden, recommends taking a bus (US$0.50, 1½ hrs) from Cuenca to Sígsig (S of Gualaceo, 83 km. from Cuenca, *residencial*, G, *Restaurante Turista* only fair), and from there another to Chiquïnda, 0900, 2½ hrs, buy tickets night before (stay overnight with Sr. Fausto, the teacher). A trail from Chiquïnda goes to Aguacate (4-5 hrs walking), a village of 70 people. After about 3 hrs the trail divides by a small school on the left. Take the left fork. Sr. Jorge Guillermo Vásquez has a *hospedaje*, G, very basic but friendly, coffee and popcorn for breakfast, horses can be hired for trekking to caves. There are shops, electricity at night only, and good *fiestas* at Christmas and New Year, and carnival in February (very popular). From Aguacate either walk 4 hrs or hire a horse to continue SE to Río Negro, a friendly village, from where daily buses or trucks at 1300 and 1600 go to Gualaquiza (1-2 hrs on dirt road, US$0.35—**see page 860)**. A road is being built between Sígsig and Gualaquiza, along a beautiful and unspoilt route; the trail can be hiked by the intrepid but is not yet passable by wheeled vehicles; take a minimum of luggage. Gualaquiza is rather dirty and the men bother female travellers. Buses to Cuenca, 2200 are often full, try going to Loja 2200, 9 hrs, instead.

NW of Cuenca, **El Cajas** is a 28,000 hectare national recreation area with over 260 lakes, 2½ hr bus trip (one daily, except Thurs., between 0600 and 0630 from the San Sebastián church esquina Simón Bolívar y Coronel Talbot, bus back between 1400 and 1600, US$1, arrive early as the bus can get very full, hitchhiking difficult, little traffic). Ideal but strenuous walking, 3,500-4,400 metres altitude, and the climate is rough. It is best to arrive in the early morning since it can get very cloudy, wet and cool, after about 1300. The páramo vegetation (chuquiragua, lupin) is beautiful and contains interesting wildlife (Andes gull, black frogs, humming birds, even condors); on a clear morning the views are superb, even to Chimborazo, some 300 km. away. There is a refuge, G p.p., with four bunks and cooking facilities in the park which you can book at the Ministry of Agriculture in Cuenca, but this is not essential and just as easy at the Park. Take food, candles, sleeping bags and warm clothes. Local maps are not always exact, better to get the IGM map in Quito. The park is easy to miss; avoid being carried 8 km. further to the village itself, ask for *Refugio Toreadora*, which is in front of the Laguna Toreadora at 3,800 metres. A trail around the lake takes 2-4 hrs depending on your acclimatization to altitude. Camping possible but you need good equipment, sleeping bag, warm clothing and waterproofs as it can get very wet; it is not possible to hire equipment in Cuenca. Take also food, water, stove and gas (no firewood available). There are organized tours to the lakes from Cuenca, but these tend to be expensive, up to US$34. Alternatively, hire a private truck, US$16 with driver. A rec. 2-day walk is to take the bus to about 15 kms. past the park refugio into the Río Miguir valley. Follow the footpath up the valley containing Laguna Sunincocha and a chain of subsidiary lakes. Continue to Cuicocha and down the Río Chico Soldados valley. Hitch back to Cuenca on the Soldados road, but on Wed. night or Thurs. a.m. to catch traffic going to Cuenca market; no buses. Take a tent, store etc., it can be cold, compass useful if cloudy (often), parts of the walk are over 4,000 metres.

Closer to Cuenca (than El Cajas) is the **Bosque de Mazán**, with cloud forest vegetation on the lower slopes becoming paramo in the higher places. Here you can see a lot of birds, including mountain toucans, humming birds and condors. The area is protected by a local nature conservation group, with some European workers. Postcards are sold in *Heladería Holanda* to raise funds. For walks and guided tours contact Amigos de Mazán Tierra Viva, Gran Colombia 5-20, Casilla 1891, Cuenca, T 824-621. There is also a contact in the UK for the Río Mazán Project, T Norwich (0633) 611-953, 610-993.

To the **Laguna de Zorocucho**: catch the bus at the Plaza Santo Domingo to Sayausi (US$0.05) and walk from there; about 2 hrs from Sayausi take a dirt road to the left and walk a further 20 minutes. There is good trout fishing in the lake and the river.

A beautiful hour-long bus trip on the Machala road from Cuenca takes one to the town of Girón, whose beauty is spoiled only by a modern concrete church. From there trucks take passengers up a winding road to the hamlets of San Gregorio and Chumblín. Friendly inhabitants will act as guides to three lakes high in the *páramo* where excellent trout-fishing is to be had. Take camping gear.

Ecuador's most important Inca ruin, **Ingapirca**, (3,160 metres) can be visited from Cuenca. Ingapirca is commonly known as a fortress complex although this is contradicted by archæologists. The central structure is an *usnu* platform probably used as a solar observatory. It is faced in fine Inca masonry, and it is interesting to note that the length is exactly three times the diameter of the semicircular ends. This may have been connected with worship of the sun in its morning, midday and afternoon positions. (John Hemming). Ten mins walk away is the "face of the Inca", an immense natural formation in the rock looking over the landscape. There is a good museum (open Tues.-Sat. 0900-1700), which sells a good guide book (US$0.80), and will look after belongings.

You can take an organized excursion (US$5.20, depending on numbers), a taxi for the 5-hr. round trip from Cuenca bus terminal (US$35), or take any Guayaquil, Quito or Cañar bus. On the first two, ask to be let out at Tambo (2 hrs., US$0.50), 7 km. past Cañar (and 16 km., 3 hrs walk from the site, hitching reported possible), thence take a bus, colectivo, or truck to Ingapirca (US$0.15-0.30). Coop Cañar runs hourly buses Cañar-Tambo from 0600, US$0.50. There is a daily 0600 bus from Cañar direct to Ingapirca. Last colectivos leave Ingapirca at 1800 for Tambo. *Hospedaje* at Tambo on main street, near service station, no sign, red and white house, F, good value, hot water, opp. *Rancho Grande* restaurant. *Restaurant El Turista*, good and cheap food. There is also a route from 2 km. before Cañar at a very bad side road to the right, 14 km. from Ingapirca. A third route is to go to San Pedro by bus or train, where there is a municipal *hospedería* where travellers can stay free of charge (although difficulties have been reported in obtaining the key); a 3 km. dirt road leads to the ruins. On Fri. there is an Indian market at Ingapirca. There is a good co-operative craft shop next to the church. Camping at the site is possible. There is no hotel at Ingapirca, but there are 2 basic restaurants at the entrance, and a third, *Inti Huasi* (good), in the village; the *refugio* has benches, table and fireplace but no beds or electricity, water is intermittent. Ask at the museum for a key (if one is available) and for permission to stay overnight, included in museum fee of US$2 (you may have to surrender your passport at 0900 only).

**Warning** Be careful of overcharging by truck drivers.

There is a 2 day hike to Ingapirca from Achupallas (**see page 822**—take Coop. Chunchi or Coop. Patria bus from Riobamba to La Moya, then truck to Achupallas or a direct truck from Alausí). It is a spectacular walk through valleys and on vestiges of an Inca trail; the locals are very friendly; take a fishing rod if you have one—the route is described in Rob Rachowiecki's *Climbing and Hiking in Ecuador*. The IGM map (Juncal sheet, 1:50,000) is very useful. The name Ingapirca does not appear on the Cañar 1:50,000 sheet and you may have to ask directions near the end.

From Cuenca, the Pan-American Highway runs S to La Y, about 20 km. away near the village of Cumbe. Here the road divides into two: one continuing the Pan-American to Loja (beautiful views on both sides) and the other, which is faster (or less slow), running to Pasaje and Machala. (One traveller reports that on a night trip on this route, the bus driver stopped before beginning the descent, made a collection from the passengers and having made the sign of the Cross, apparently tossed the money over the edge of the cliff.) Santa Isabela and Pasaje (pop. 27,000), the main towns along the route, have little to recommend them. Most buses travel NW to El Troncal and then S down the coast road to reach Machala and Huaquillas for the Peruvian border (**see page 820**).

The Pan-American Highway climbs S from La Y and rises eventually to the 3,500 metre Tinajillas pass. The road descends sharply into the warm upper Jubones valley past cane fields and rises again near the small town of Oña (no hotels, seek help from the priest). (From there it weaves through highland *páramo* pastures and then descends towards Saraguro. Here we meet Indians once more, the most southerly Andean group in Ecuador, dressed all in black. They wear very broad flat-brimmed hard felt hats: the men are notable for their black shorts (sometimes covered by a whitish kind of divided apron) and a particular kind of double bag, the *alforja*, and the women for their pleated black skirts, necklaces of coloured beads and silver *topos*, ornate pins fastening their shawls. They have entered the money economy with vigour: many now take cattle across the mountains east to the tropical pastures above the Amazonian jungle.

The (partly gravel) road runs through **Saraguro** (picturesque Sun. Indian market—the Indians wear black, the men with a long plait of hair), over the mountain and then makes a long, very tortuous, descent towards Loja. The direct Cuenca-Loja road is under reconstruction and when the widening and paving are completed it will be one of the most beautiful and breathtaking in Ecuador without the discomfort offered by the longer, alternative route via Arenillas. Bus to Cuenca with Coop. Viajeros, 4 daily, US$1.50.

In Saraguro, two pensions, *Nueva York* over the *farmacia* on Calle Loja, F, friendly, family-run, freezing shower, and the other run by Sra. Rosa Armijos, unsigned, opp. church to S, Calle Loja No. 03-5, G, clean, cold water, laundry facilities. Restaurant: *Salón Cristal*, behind the church. The restaurants are poor, but cheap food in the market. It is a very cold town.

*Loja* (2,225 metres, 160,000 inhabitants), lies near the Oriente. There are crude but original paintings on the patio walls of many of the old houses. There are two universities, with a well-known law school. Some of the Universidad Nacional buildings have good murals. The cathedral and San Martín church have painted interiors. Museum on main square, by bank, 0900-1500. The town, encircled by hills and pleasant countryside, can be reached by air from Quito or Guayaquil to La Toma and then 35 km. by paved road. There is a market on Sat., Sun. and Mon., attended by many Saraguro Indians. Souvenir and craft shops on 10 de Agosto between Kennedy and 18 de Noviembre. The fiesta de la Virgen is held on the second weekend of September; it is very difficult to find a room and all prices rise.

**Hotels** *Ramses*, Colón 14-31 y Bolívar, T 960-868/961-402, D, bath, phone, TV, fairly good restaurant; opp. is *Libertador*, Colón 14-30 y Bolívar, T 962-119, Casilla 412, D, bath, TV, suites available, restaurant *La Castellana*, parking; *Vilcabamba*, on river/sewer, D, clean; *Residencial La Rivera*, Universitaria y 10 de Agosto, E, good; *Hostal Quinara*, opp. *La Rivera*, E, also good; *Saraguro Internacional*, Universitaria 724, E, hot water, TV, restaurant open Mon.-Fri.; *Ejecutivo Sudamérica*, Universitaria 1076 y Azuay, F, good, also "video club"; *Metropolitano*, 18 de Noviembre y Colón, F with bath and TV, hot water, clean; *París*, 10 de Agosto 1637,clean with electric hot showers, F, bargain for good rate, near food market, rec.; *Hostal Carrión*, Colón 1630 y 18 de Noviembre, T 961-127, G, basic, clean, safe; *Primavera*, Colón 1644, G, clean, cold shower; *Miraflores*, 10 de Agosto 1656, G, can bargain, clean; *Londres*, Sucre 741 y 10 de Agosto, F, constant hot water, clean, a bit dingy, laundry facilities, unfriendly, reports of theft from locked rooms; *Acapulco*, Sucre 747 y 10 de Agosto, T 960-651, G, clean, no hot water, private bathroom, safe for leaving luggage. Basic *residenciales* in G range for instance on Rocafuerte; also *Alborada*, Sucre 1279 y Lourdes, F with shower, clean; *San Andrés*, Miguel Río Frío, G, friendly, more or less clean, very cheap.

**Restaurants** *José Antonio*, Sucre between Colón and Eguiguren, excellent *cebiche* and seafood, enthusiastic chef, highly rec. *La Cascada*, Sucre y Lourdes, very good food; *Suizo Lojano*, Guerrero y Eguiguren, international; *Palace*, Eguiguren y Sucre, local food; *Trece*, Universitaria y Colón, also Eguiguren 1468, good. Other criollo places are *Cordillera*, 10 de Agosto 1419; *La Choza*, Sucre y Riofrío. *La Tullpa*, 18 de Noviembre, opp. Parque Bolívar, cheap, good *churrasco*; *Delfín Dorado*, Imbabura y Sucre, excellent fish dishes and some steaks, inexpensive, friendly; *La Casona*, 18 de Noviembre near Imbabura (the better of 2 branches), near Cuenca bus terminal, good, rec. Chicken at *Rico Pico*, 18 de Noviembre y Colón. Seafood at *Pescadería Pacífica*, Bolívar 931; and *Doscientas Millas*, Bolívar y Eguiguren (evenings only). Vegetarian: *Acuarius*, Mercadillo 15-45, Sucre y 18 de Noviembre, 2nd floor. *Chifa 85* on main plaza, clean, friendly, good quality food, including Chinese dishes.

Chinese also at *Chifa Feliz*, Eguiguren y 18 de Noviembre. Good *Unicornio* piano bar on main square. Good snacks, pastries and yoghurt at *Pastelería Persa* (2 locations—one at Rocafuerte 14-58). *Helados de Paila*, Av. Kennedy, nr. market, good icecream and snacks; *Topoli*, Riofrío y Bolívar, best yoghurt in town, good for breakfast; *Top Cream Ice Cream*, Kennedy y Colón, best ice cream in town.

**Shopping** *Cer-Art Ceramics*, precolumbian designs on mostly high-gloss ceramics, produced at the Universidad Técnica with workshop and retail shop.

**Exchange** Filanbanco, Calle Bernardo Valdivieso 740, changes cheques, other banks do not. No *casas de cambio*; good rate for US$ in gift shop in front of *Hotel Acapulco* (El Universo agent changes money at weekends at poor rate).

**Tourist Office** Cetur is at José A. Eguiguren 17-27 y Av. Kennedy, T 962-964, open Mon.-Fri., 0800-1200, 1400-1800.

**Flights** TAME office on Eguiguren with main plaza, closes at 1600, reserve seat in Cuenca if you want to leave from Loja the next day, or get an open ticket at the airport and push and shout to get on the plane. Daily flight to Guayaquil and Quito (same flight) except Sun. Colectivos depart Loja 0530 to La Tola airport, US$2, can arrange for hotel pick up. Colectivos found outside TAME, most are reliable.

**Buses** Most buses leave from a small terminal on Guerrero y 10 de Agosto, others leave from small offices in same area. To **Cuenca**, 6 hrs, 7 a day, US$2.65 with San Luis (18 de Noviembre e Imbabura), sit on right hand side; **Machala**, 10 a day, 7 hrs, US$2.75. Cooperativa Loja (10 de Agosto y Cuarto Centenario) runs many buses in all directions, including Quito, 4 a day, US$5 (Trans. Santa to Quito, 12 hrs, US$5), and Guayaquil, 5 a day, 11 hrs, US$4.40, and two nightly buses to Huaquillas at 2030 and 2230; **Macará**, 4 daily, 7 hrs, US$1.50. To **Saraguro**, 6 daily, 2½ hrs. To **Zamora**, Transp. Chinchipe.

**Excursions** The entrance to the **Podocarpus National Park**, spectacular walking country, lush tropical cloud forest and good for bird-watching, is about 15 km. south of Loja on the Vilcabamba road. Permits from the Ministerio de Agricultura office, on Riofrío just off Bolívar, 2nd floor, in Loja who provide a somewhat adequate map. Park guardian Miguel Angel is very knowledgeable and helpful. Additional information from conservation group, Arco Iris, P.O. Box 860, Loja, or contact member Rodrigo Tapia, T 960-895. Take a Vilcabamba bus, park entrance is 20 mins from Loja, then 6 km. hike to guard station. Direct transport by taxi only., US$10 round trip, can arrange later pick up from guard station. Camping possible.

*Vilcabamba* (1,520 metres) is a 1½ hr bus ride. Sur Oriente, Calle Azuay and Av. Kennedy, hourly (US$0.50) from Loja. People here were reputed to live to over 100 as often as not; recent research has eroded this belief, but it's still a very pleasant and healthy valley, wonderful for a few days relaxation, with an agreeable climate, 17°C min., 26°C max. *Hostelería Vilcabamba*, E, excellent, comfortable, pool, jacuzzi, bar, good Ecuadorean restaurant, massage, fitness instruction, run by Cortez family, who also run the attractive *Parador Turístico*, E, with restaurant and bar; *Hotel Valle Sagrado*, G, on main plaza, basic but clean, friendly, hot showers rarely work; there are 4 restaurants on the plaza, including *Cabañita*. *Madre Tierra*, cabins, E p.p. full board, reductions for a long stay, health food (home made, home grown), horses to rent (about US$15 per day for 2 horses, food and gear), mud treatment, private sun bathing, steam baths, herbal cures, beautiful setting about 2 km. before village, English and French spoken; the Mendoza family make travellers very welcome. Write in advance to Jaime Mendoza, P.O. Box 354, Loja, Ecuador. At the upper end of the Vilcabamba Valley, 4 km. from the village, are the highly rec. *Cabañas Río Yambala*, F, beautiful views in all directions, kitchen facilities if required, shopping done for you, or meals provided, hot showers, laundry service, clean, helpful and very friendly, horses for rent with or without guide, trekking arranged with tents, sleeping bags, food etc. provided, take *camioneta* from Sra. Carpio's shop (where you can also check availability of cabins), one block down from main square of Vilcabamba. Horses can also be hired from Roger Toledo, opp. Post Office, US$4 per day, he will organize 3-day trips into the mountains. Craig Money (Gregorio) runs a popular book swapping library.

The scenic road to Zamora (40 km.) is narrow but in good condition. You can carry on from there into the Oriente.

There are two routes from Loja to Machala, one of which goes through Piñas and is rather bumpy with hairpin bends but has the better views, the other is paved and generally quicker (depending on the driver). Machala can be avoided, however, if you take a Machala bus to the Huaquillas crossroads, called La Avanzada, and there catch another one straight to Huaquillas, the border town.

There is also a road into the Oriente, at Zaruma (on this road), where there are interesting carved wooden houses. The old Portovelo gold mines at Zaruma are worth a visit.

An alternative, more scenic route to Peru is, however, available from Loja via **Macará**, a dusty town on the border, in a rice-growing area, with road connections to Sullana near the Peruvian coast. (Population 8,000; altitude 600 metres.)

**Hotels** *Paradero Turístico*, E, best, pool, restaurant may not be open, not far from centre; *Residencial Paraíso*, F, without bath, Veintimilla 553, new and clean, laundry facilities; *Guayaquil*, F, with shower, not rec., fleas, large cell-like rooms; *Internacional*, G, by Loja bus office and *Amazonas*, Rengel 418, G, friendly, clean, basic, on same street. Restaurants *Colonial Macará*, Rengel y Bolívar (helpful, but food not too good), and *Macará*, opposite, a cafeteria; *Soda Bar Manolo* for breakfast.

Leaving Loja on the main paved highway going westward, the airport at **La Toma** is reached after 35 km. (If flying to or from La Toma, stay at Catamayo, nearby, *Hotel El Turista*, Av. Isidro Ayora, G, shared bath, basic, friendly, *Restaurant China* opp., good, cheap; *Hotel San Marcos*, on plaza; taxi to airport US$1). On arrival at La Toma airport by air, colectivo taxis will be waiting to take you to Loja, 45 mins., US$2, they fill up quickly so choose a driver, give him your luggage claim ticket and he will collect your checked luggage. At La Toma (where you can catch the Loja-Macará bus), the Pan-American Highway divides into two branches, one, the faster, via Velacruz and Catacocha (Loja-Catacocha paved, Catacocha-Macaná good gravel) (1 hotel, G, over-priced, very basic, no running water, and a *Residencial 'Turistas'*; *Restaurante Sidoney*, good, cheap), and the other going to Macará via Cariamanga. The road is unpaved but fair, offering lovely views. The bank at Macará does not change money, so change sucres through the *ambulantes* to give you enough intis to last you until you reach Sullana (Peru). You can change money at the market in the town centre, fair rates for US$, poor rates for Intis (a new sol was due to be introduced in July 1991). A Peruvian tourist card can be obtained from the Peruvian Hon. Consul in Macará, if he is available, or at the border if not already obtained in Quito or Guayaquil. There is a 2½ km. walk or taxi ride (US$1, up to US$2 in a pick-up from Macará market—less if more passengers; coming from Peru, drivers will overcharge, particularly if you are too tired to walk) to the international bridge over the Río Macará. Border crossing formalities (0800-1800) can last about 1 hr. Peruvian officials may ask to see an onward ticket out of Peru. A colectivo (US$2.20, 3-4 hrs) is then taken from La Tina on the Peruvian side to Sullana from where it is ½ hr to Piura, a better place to spend the night. No hotels, and only food stalls, in La Tina. Buses leave Sullana from Av. Buenos Aires in early a.m.; if none running, there are plenty of *camionetas* to the border. There are many military checkpoints along the route but these are not usually a problem. Coop Loja buses every 2 hrs from 0600-1500 from Macará to Loja (6 to 8 hrs, US$1.50), Unión Cariamanga at 0400 and 1000 (half the road is paved and half in poor condition), so the whole journey can be done in a day if you arrive at the border at noon. The Loja-border journey takes only 3½ hrs by car. There is less likelihood of bureaucratic hassle or of drug-pushing at Macará than at Huaquillas, but since not many travellers go by this route, be prepared for extensive, but generally good-natured searches by bored officials. Also, officials are not above acquiring things, or asking for a bribe if you do something unusual, such as crossing the border after 1800 and returning the next day to get your passport stamped. If you are asked to pay, ask for a receipt and note the official's name and number in full view of him.

---

## THE ORIENTE (8)

East of the Andes the hills fall away to tropical lowlands, sparsely populated with Indian settlements along the tributaries of the Amazon. Agricultural colonists have cleared parts of the forest for cattle rearing, while even more isolated areas are major oil producers, leading to the gradual encroachment of towns into the jungle.

Ecuador's eastern tropical lowlands can now be reached by four different road routes, from Quito, Ambato, Cuenca or Loja. These roads are narrow and tortuous and subject to landslides in the rainy season, but all have regular, if poor bus services and all can be attempted in a jeep or in an ordinary car with good ground clearance. Their construction has led to considerable colonization by highlanders in the lowland areas. Several of the towns and villages on the roads can be reached by air services from Quito, Cuenca and Guayaquil, and places further into the immense Amazonian forests are generally accessible by river canoe or small aircraft. The country is particularly beautiful, and some of the disadvantages of other parts of Amazonia, such as the inadvisability of swimming in the rivers, are here absent. Anti-malaria tablets are recommended, however, and be sure to take a mosquito net and an effective repellent. A yellow fever vaccination is recommended for travel into the Oriente.

Travel agencies (e.g. Metropolitan Tours of Quito, *La Selva*—see under Coca) do trips to the Oriente or to the Napo River, with meals, flights, lectures included. Going by bus and/or boat you can do a round trip much more cheaply, but you should allow a week. The Oriente also has an unpredictable air service provided by army planes; passengers pay insurance, US$1-2; apart from that, fares are low and the flights save a lot of time. Frequent military checks; always have your passport handy. You may be required to register at Shell-Mera, Coca, Misahuallí, Puerto Napo and Lago Agrio.

**The Route from Quito** From Quito, through Pifo, to Baeza, the road is paved to the top of the pass, near where it worsens. A new road was built in 1987, following the earthquake which destroyed the old road to Coca. It crosses the Eastern Cordillera at an altitude of 4,064 metres at a pass just north of the extinct volcano **Antisana** (5,704 metres, which, according to Cliff Cordy, gets vast quantities of snow, has huge glaciers and is the hardest peak in Ecuador to climb), and then descends via the small villages of Papallacta (**see page 790**), and Cuyuja to the old mission settlements of Baeza and Borja. The trip between the pass and Baeza has beautiful views of Antisana, high waterfalls, tropical mountain jungle, *páramo* and a lake contained by a glacial moraine almost on the equator.

**Baeza** is a small town in the beautiful setting of the Quijos pass, recommended for long scenic walks (beware trucks passing) with many waterfalls (the town is about 2 km. off the main road—get off Lago Agrio bus at the police checkpoint and walk up the hill; Tena bus goes through the town). The old Spanish cobblestone trail can be found if you go past the hospital and cemetery; the path goes up over the hill (a beautiful walk). Because of the climate, *ceja de montaña*, orchids and bromeliads abound. Trout in the rivers. (See the books of Padre Porras Garcés, Centro de Investigaciones Arqueológicas, Pontífica Universidad Católica del Ecuador, Quito on archaeological remains in the area). The old settlement, however, is dying as people have moved to a new town 1 km. down the road towards Tena. Most of the restaurants are in the new town.

**Hotels** *Oro Negro*, G, residencial and restaurant, at Tena/Lago Agrio junction, rooms with bath and cold water. *Nogal de Jumandi*, G, basic wooden house on road to Tena, clean, no private bath, friendly, helpful, food available.

**Restaurants** *Gina*, not rec. and *Lupita*, good, opposite each other on Calle Chimborazo. *Guanya*, good *meriendas*, excellent breakfasts US$1, friendly, TV, frequented by local teachers. Everything closed by 2030.

At Baeza the road divides: one branch heads S to Tena, with a newly constructed branch road going directly via Loreto to Coca (7 hrs). The other goes NE to Lago Agrio, following the Quijos river past the villages of Borja, a few km. from Baeza (small hotel on roadside; *residencial* on corner of plaza, clean, cold shower, meals provided; basic restaurant *Costa Azul*) and El Chaco (hotel and eating places all reported as dirty) to the slopes of the still active volcano Reventador, 3,485 metres. (At the village of Reventador there is a *pensión, de los Andes*, G, basic, clean, and a restaurant.) The road winds along the north side of the river, past the impressive 145-metre San Rafael falls (to see them, get off bus at Inecel sign about 2½ hrs from Baeza, walk down side road, and then down a steep path, for 45 mins to a bridge; ask people working there to let you pass, then it's a further 15 mins walk—camping possible, but take all equipment and food). The road then crosses the watershed between the Coca and Aguarico rivers. A ferry operates 0600-1800 across the Aguarico river until the bridge is rebuilt. The road runs along the north bank of the river to the developing oil towns of Santa Cecilia and Lago Agrio.

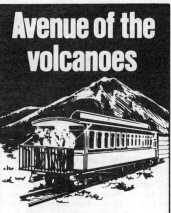
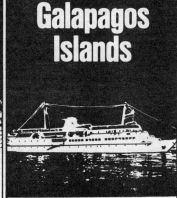

*Lago Agrio* is growing rapidly and has about 30,000 inhabitants: it is still a rough place but the infrastructure is improving; excursions into the jungle can be made. Virtually everything in the town is along the main road, Av. Quito. Electricity is turned off 0100-0600.

**Hotels** *El Cofán*, C, inc. taxes, a/c, best, but overpriced, no hot water, TV, fridge, clean, restaurant mediocre, very expensive, food poisoning reported; *La Mexicana*, F, reasonable, mosquito nets; *Willigram*, F with own bath, doors unlockable, noisy, above bar; *Putumayo*, F, shared bathroom; *San Carlos*, F, clean, safe, a/c, G p.p. with fan; *Machala 2*, F, clean, safe, friendly, restaurant, insufficient bathroom facilities; *Residencial Sayonara*, F with bath, good, sometimes water shortages; *Hilton*, *Oro Negro*, *Chifa China* (restaurant) and *Chimborazo*, all G with shared bathrooms, also *Ecuador*, on main street, beds clean, rooms damp. *Comercial Calvopeña* is the best place to buy groceries and supplies. *Mi Cochita* beside *El Cofán*, cheap, good chicken.

**Exchange** Several *casas de cambio* on Av. Quito, good rates for notes.

**Transport** Daily TAME flight to **Quito** at 1100, book 1-2 days in advance. **Buses to Quito** (US$4, 9½ hrs), **Baeza** (US$2.10, 6 hrs), **Coca** (US$1.10, 3 hrs) and **Tena** (US$3.20, 9 hrs).

From Lago Agrio it is possible to take a bus to Chiritza and then a 2 hour boat ride to San Pablo de Kantesiya, a small village on stilts with one hut where visitors can stay. There are buses north to La Punta (US$0.40, 1¼ hrs.), make sure you get an exit stamp from Migración in Lago Agrio, Quito 111—police station, T 125), where you hand in your Tourist Card to the military and get a boat across the Río San Miguel to the village of San Miguel in Colombia (La Punta-San Miguel, 1 hr., US$2) and from there you can catch a jeep or bus (5 hrs.) to Puerto Asís and on to Hormiga (1 hr., hotels and restaurants), then bus to Mocoa (D.A.S. office and border formalities) and Pasto. For permission to go downriver on the Aguarico (as opposed to an exit stamp) go to the Brigada (military post) rather than Migración because the store owner there will give you permission to go anywhere as long as you buy something from his shop.

At Lago Agrio, a temporary ferry crosses the Aguarico River (bridge washed away), then the road heads south to **Coca** (officially named Puerto Francisco de Orellana—pop. 16,000), a river port at the junction of the Coca and Napo rivers; the route via Loreto also involves a ferry crossing a few km. before Coca. The place is described as a typical oil town, dirty, noisy, with heavy drinking. All foreigners going beyond town into the jungle have to register with the police. The bank will not change travellers' cheques, do it before you arrive. Food and supplies are reportedly less expensive in Coca than in other parts of the Oriente. At Carnival, water and petroleum throwing is the sport. There is usually no electricity after midnight.

**Hotels** *Oasis*, near the bridge at the end of town, G p.p., clean, comfortable, hot water and fans, rec.; *Auca*, E with shower, F without, comfortable, dirty, electricity in p.m., big garden with monkeys roaming free, poor food but crowded, manager speaks English, good meeting place to make up tour party; *Florida*, on main road from airport, G with fan, good; *Residencial Rosita*, G, noisy, cold water, unsafe, not rec. *Tungurahua*, F, favourite with oil workers, rooms OK, but dirty toilets and showers and 3 basic *residenciales*: *Turingia*, *Lojalita* (F) and *Camba Huasi*.

**Restaurant** *Los Cedros*, down by river, 2 blocks from Capitanería, good fish, *patacones*, *yuca*, fairly expensive; *Doña Erma*'s set meal is cheap and filling; *Venecia*, good food, away from main market area; *Mama Carmen*, good for early breakfast; *El Buho*, good food, jungle specialities, capibara etc., reasonably priced; *King Burger*, cheap, good chicken and chips, friendly, ask for Braulio Llori Pugachi, a recommended, good value jungle guide.

**Tours** Coca is now the most logical place from which to arrange tours into the jungle. Many of the guides who previously operated in Misahuallí have moved to Coca. All guides out of Coca charge about US$25-35 p.p. per day, but you may have to bargain down to this. You are strongly advised to check what precisely is being offered, and that the price includes equipment such as rubber boots, tents, mosquito nets, cooking equipment and food, and transport. Trips which do not go beyond the Río Napo itself are not worth taking since you will see nothing. The South American Explorers Club in Quito can provide updated information about jungle tours, recommended guides and how to arrange your trip. Among the guides who have moved from Misahuallí are Carlos Lastra, who has been recommended as knowledgeable, cheerful and a good cook (he does not speak English), Wymper Torres (*Hotel Anca*), and Wilson Vasco (also good, but no English spoken, can be contacted in Baños, Misahuallí at *Hotel Jennifer* or Coca at Tagaeri Crucero Fluvial, his three brothers, Daniel, Jonas and Walter also offer tours, rec., no litter, no killing of animals, no intrusion of Indians' privacy). Canoes and guides for jungle trips can be hired from Fernando Silva, who lives at the end of the riverside lane next to the bridge. Kevin Johnsrude warns "Insist that there be no hunting or dynamite fishing or the only animals you will see will be in your soup!" More expensive is Fluvial Tours (minimum 4 people). Pedro Grefa offers 5-day jungle tours on the Río Tiputini: take the 1200 Ranchero bus of Coop. de Coca from Coca to the bridge over the Río Tiputini (2½ hrs, US$0.50); his is the small, wooden house at left side of bridge. (Shell has a camp here, drinks only available.) Allow a day for the trip to be organized, ask for fruit and vegetables to be included in the provisions, take a torch and insect repellent, and ask Pedro (or his nephew Carlos—also rec. as leader) not to throw litter away in the jungle.

Transturi of Quito (Orellana 1810 y 10 de Agosto, T 544-963) do trips from Coca into the jungle on a floating hotel, *Flotel Orellana*, US$200 (3 days) per person in double cabin, US$375 (4 days) or US$465 (5 days) including Quito-Coca air fare and all meals, guides, etc. and visits to Limón Cocha, Monkey Island, *Hacienda Primavera*, and Pompeya Catholic mission. *Hacienda Primavera* is 2 hours downstream from Coca and is open to those not on Transturi's tours. There are clean, basic rooms available (F p.p.), or you can camp (US$0.50). Meals cost US$2.50, breakfast US$1.50, bring bread. There is a generator but candles are used for after-generator hours. Excursions are not cheap (e.g. US$13 to Monkey Island, US$30 to Monkey Island and Pompeya, US$45 to the above and Limón Cocha, divide prices by number of people (1-10) and add 10% service) and there is not much wildlife to see apart from birds, but it is supposed to be possible to hire canoes from the *hacienda* to visit other places along the Napo. The *Flotel Orellana* stops here for a visit. It has been reported that independent travellers to *Primavera* have experienced overcharging and dishonesty on transport back to Quito, and to/from Coca, and difficulties in arranging independent activities.

La Selva, a jungle centre 3 hrs down the Napo from Coca, has been frequently recommended for the quality of its accommodation and food, and its interesting excursions into the jungle; 4-night packages from Quito including all transport, lodging, and food, not cheap, but worth it. Book at *La Selva*, 6 de Diciembre 2816 y James Orton, P.O. Box 635/Suc. 12 de Octubre, Quito, T 550-995/554-686, Telex 2-2653 JOLEZ ED, Fax 563-814 or through most travel agencies in Quito.

**Transport** Bus to Quito (twice daily), 9 hrs, US$5, take food and drink as stops are often only 10 mins; to **Lago Agrio**, 3 hrs, US$1.10; to **Tena**, 2 daily, 8 hrs, US$2.50; to **Misahuallí**, 14 hrs; to **Baeza**, 9 hrs, US$3.25.

**Flights to Quito** with TAME, reserve at least one day in advance, best to arrange soon after arrival, Mon.-Sat. There are military flights to **Tena** and **Shell-Mera** from Coca on Mon., Wed. and Fri. Petroecuador oil company also flies Quito-Coca and sometimes takes travellers on board the small planes. **NB** Do not walk or ride from the airport to town up the side street which leads to *Hotel Auca*, the police make thorough, and acquisitive searches of arriving passengers here.

For **passenger boats** out of Coca, ask at the military post in the marina. There are no regular passenger boats to Misahuallí now that a road has been completed from Coca to the Baeza-Tena road. Canoes only go if there are 8 or more passengers, taking about 14 hours, if it is not reached before nightfall, the party will camp beside the river. For a price, of course, the willing traveller can hire his own canoe with owner and outboard motor to take him anywhere along the Napo. (To Misahuallí the charge is about US$120. Take a cushion and waterproofs for self and luggage.)

Canoes (irregular service, best to hire your own) pass Coca carrying passengers and cargo down-river to Limón Cocha (where *Flotel Orellana* has a lodge, closed to guests other than their own tour parties), the Capuchin mission at Pompeya with a school and museum of Napo culture, and Nueva Rocafuerte. Local tours can be hired from Limón Cocha and also canoes to return to Coca. Halfway between Coca and Nueva Rocafuerte is Pañacocha (*Pensión*, G, friendly, but watch out for jiggers in the mattresses), near which are the magnificent lagoons of Pañacocha and Pihuallicocha on the Panayacu River.

In **Nueva Rocafuerte**, the missionaries and Sra. Jesús let rooms; there are no restaurants. There is a Monday boat from Coca to Nueva Rocafuerte but you must get a military permit to enter the area. The officer has to write exactly the area you wish to visit and you have to leave your passport. The boat takes 24 hrs at least (hammocks provided) US$5.50. You can stay overnight at Pañacocha. It is possible to hire boat and guide in Nueva Rocafuerte, but it would be wise not to add tourism to the pressures to which the Waorani Indians are already subjected (e.g. oil exploration on their land). Some guides also kill animals found en route. There is a cargo boat back on Mon. but it doesn't always run and you may have to wait until Fri. To Coca it is a 2½-day ferry ride (US$9) with an overnight stop at Sinchichieta and a meal stop at Pañacocha. It is possible to cross from Nueva Rocafuerte into Peru but it is not a recommended route because of dangers associated with drugs trafficking and border disputes. Officially you get an exit stamp from Migración in Puyo and a Peruvian entry stamp in Iquitos but it is not an easy crossing and rarely done.

Roads from both Baeza and Coca go South to Archidona, a village (*Residencial Carolina*, F; *Residencial Regina*, pleasant and friendly) centred around its mission and an extraordinary church and luxuriant square, and **Tena**, 10 km. further S, the capital of Napo Province. Both settlements have good views of Sumaco, an extinct volcano to the north (3,807 metres), and both have a large lowland Quechua Indian population living in the vicinity, many of whom are panning for gold in the rivers. These Indians are unlike the Indian groups further into the Oriente forests. "They are Quijos, of Chibcha stock, and their old territory extended in pre-conquest times from Puerto Napo up the Quijos pass to Papallacta and from there down to Coca. Their forthright character, bravery and their inherent honesty have not changed since the days when they held the Spaniards back from their efforts to find "El Dorado'." (Jay Louthian, Florida). From Tena or Archidona, a visit can be made to the famous Jumandí caves by the Río Latas, 10 km. N. of Archidona (taxi, or bus from Archidona, ½ hr). It is necessary to go with a guide; take good boots and a strong torch. It is very muddy (sometimes full of water) so it can be useful to take spare clothes. The side ducts of the caves are extremely narrow and claustrophobic. There are several colonies of the vampire bat (*Desmodus rotundus*) in the caves. Before going, make full enquiries about routes and conditions.

**Hotels** *Hostal Villa Belén*, on Baeza road, N of town, E, new, friendly, clean, cold shower, quiet, restaurant planned, rec.; *Mol*, E, with bath, clean, restaurant closed, garage, rec.; *Hotel Sheraton*, E, bit noisy but fairly well equipped; *Tena*, G, noisy at night, due to restaurant below; *Amazonas*, F, clean, near main square; *Jumandy*, G, clean, friendly, breakfast from 0600; *Enmita*, G, near bus station, reasonable restaurant; *Res. Hilton*, F, good and clean; *Danubio*, next door, F, clean, friendly; *Res. Alemania*, F, good and fairly clean, E with own bath. *Hostal Baños*, near bus station, G, very basic, clean, interesting wildlife after dark, frogs hop into bed with you; *Res. Alexander*, F, 2 rooms with bathroom, near bus station. A modern resort-style hotel is *Auca*, E, on the river out of town, 1½ km. on road to Archidona, Cetur-run, restaurant and bar, nice grounds, discotheque, casino, swimming in river, electricity and water unreliable.

**Restaurants** In Tena, *Don Quiño*, good, reasonable; *Niagara*, *Oriental*, reported as hostile to gringos; *Tena*; *Chifa China*, good, cheap, open late. Throughout the Oriente there are small, set-menu restaurants, about US$1.

**Buses** Quito (via Baeza), 5 daily (Coop. Baños, and 1 each Amazonas and Pelileo), US$2.50, 5 hrs, book in advance; **Baeza**, US$1, 3 hrs; **Ambato** (via Baños), 10 a day (several companies), US$2.20, 6 hrs; **Riobamba** (via Puyo and Baños), 5 daily. **Archidona** every 20 mins, US$0.08, 15 mins; **Misahuallí** every 20 mins, US$0.35, 1 hr (via Puerto Napo, US$0.08, 15 mins) to **Coca**, 6 a day, 2 companies; **Jumandy** at 1800 to Lago Agrio; **Puyo**, US$1, 3 hrs. To **Ahuano** 0600 and 1100, return 0800, 1400.

**Flights** to Shell-Mera with the Air Force, Mon., Wed., Fri., at about 1100, 20 seats, rec.

**Excursions** To Amaroncachi in the jungle, trips, organized by Patricia Corral de Uribe and her husband, Calle Tarqui 321, Tena, T 886-372. To the Comunidad Capirona, 1 hr. by bus then 3 on foot from Tena, run by FOIN, Federación de Organizaciones Indígenas de Nago; information from Sr. Tarquino Tapuy, Calle Augusto Rueda, Casilla Postal 217, Tena. Fees per day from US$30-40 p.p. depending on number in party.

From Tena the main highway (unpaved) runs southward to Puyo. The whole area is a large-scale producer of sugar cane, yuca and *naranjillas* (an orange fruit related to the tomato, used for making a delightfully refreshing fruit drink). Puerto Napo, a few km. south of Tena, has a bridge across the Napo river (2 hotels near the bridge). Here is the turn-off for Misahuallí; if travelling N from Puyo, avoid going into Tena by getting off the bus here.

On the north bank, a road leads eastwards to **Misahuallí**, about 17 km. downstream, a small port (pop. 1,000) at the junction of the Napo and Misahuallí rivers. From the **Napo bridge** you can get a ride in a truck, US$0.50, or colectivos. At the *Hacienda Popoyal*, half way between Puerto Napo and Misahuallí, the owners welcome travellers. Misahuallí used to provide one of the best opportunities to visit the jungle, being one of the easiest places to get to, as it is only 7-8 hrs from Quito and 5 hrs from Baños. However, there is not a great deal of wildlife around Misahuallí, although butterflies and birds are plentiful, and for animals you are advised to go further into the jungle to Coca (which is overtaking Misahuallí as a tour centre) or to take an excursion lasting several days; the one to three-day trips have been described as disappointing. Oil exploration in the area is also diminishing chances of seeing wildlife. There is a fine, sandy beach on the Río Misahuallí, but don't camp on it; the river can rise suddenly and unexpectedly. A nice walk is along the Río Latas, where there are some small waterfalls. You walk through dense vegetation for about 1½ hrs, often through water to get to the largest fall and pass quite a few pools where you can swim. To get there catch the bus towards the Napo bridge and ask to be set down by the river, which you follow upstream.

**Hotels** In the F price range (or G where stated): *El Paisano*, F/G, good meeting place, clean, washing facilities, hammocks, nice garden, rec., eight rooms behind restaurant, good breakfast, try the banana pancakes; *Fifty*, on main square, G p.p., communal baths, good, friendly, vegetarian restaurant; *Milca Isca*, on main square, friendly, clean, cheap, good restaurant, English spoken; *Sacha*, owned by Héctor Fiallos, basic, bamboo walls, noisy, at point where rivers meet, dirty, apes in the garden, path to hotel floods when rains heavy, buy souvenirs of the Oriente here, cheaper than in Baños or Quito; *El Albergue Español*, owned by Dr. José Ramón Edesa and Cristina Olsen (same ownership as *El Popoyal*—see above), F p.p. meals US$1.50, new, all rooms with bath, family rooms sleep six, highly rec., information of tours, horse-riding planned; *Balcón del Napo*, G, basic, central, meals available, clean, friendly, noisy from disco at weekends, safe motorcycle parking; *Amazonas*, on riverbank nr. square, clean, friendly, basic, 2 rooms with bath, reasonable; *Etsa*, G with or without bath, very simple, owner is guide Carlos Cordero. Douglas Clarke now provides basic accommodation in bamboo huts with bunk beds behind the restaurant, showers available. Beware of thieves poking hooks through the floor.

**Restaurants** The best is *El Albergue Español*, highly rec.; Douglas Clarke's *Restaurant Dayuna* is reasonably good and cheap, as is *El Paisano*, mostly good vegetarian food (but meat should be treated with caution), poor service, popular meeting place for gringos, hence its nickname *Restaurant Paleface*. *Jenifer*, cheap, good restaurant on plaza.

**Hotels Down River** *Anaconda*, B, on Anaconda Island in the Río Napo, about 1 hr by canoe, US$1.20 downstream from Puerto Misahuallí, reservations required; consists of three bungalows of bamboo and thatch, with space for about 48 guests, no electric lights, but flush toilets and cold showers, with water available most of the time. Own zoo with animals in small, unsatisfactory cages. Watch out for thieving monkeys. The meals are good. Canoe and hiking trips arranged, US$50 for 4 days, meals and guides inc., guides only speak Spanish. Opposite, on the river bank at *Ahuano*, is *Casa del Suizo* (Swiss, Ecuadorean-owned), C p.p. full board (but little scope for vegetarians), cheaper with shared bath, highly rec. for hospitality, and location, electricity till 2200, animal sanctuary, trips arranged (for further information contact Gulliano Bonello, Koescherruetistr. 143, 8052 Zurich, Switzerland, T 01-302-37-27). No public canoes from Misahuallí on Sun. p.m., only private hire, US$30, but there are buses Tena-Ahuano, 2 hrs, US$1.50, ask to be dropped at ferry point. 8 km. downstream from Misahuallí is *Aliñahui Cabins*, 25 mins by boat but also reached by road on the southern bank of the Río Napo, 25 km. from the bridge in Puerto Napo. Seven cabins with 2 bedrooms and bathroom, A-B full board, Cuban-German owners speak English. Reservations in Quito, Margarita Schenkel, Av. Eloy Alfaro 28-54 y Portugal, T 448-439, P.O. Box 5150, CCI, Quito. 4 km. away is Jatun Sacha (quechua meaning "big forest") a biological station of about 180 hectares of land, 80% of which is primary forest. It is an area set aside by its founders Alejandro Suárez, David Neill and Michael McColm for biological field research. So far, 345 bird species and 78 frog types have been identified in the area. Good views, excursions, walking and riding. Sleeping facilities for 20 in open air cabins is provided along with cooking facilities (bring own food and sleeping bag). Equipment for collecting and drying plant specimens is available. Fee is US$5/day. Reservations can be made by writing Casilla 2177, Quito, Ecuador. *Hotel Jaguar*, 1½ hrs downstream from Misahuallí, congenial atmosphere, C p.p., with full board, vegetarians catered for, good value, reservations (not always needed) from Quito, Ramírez Dávalos 653, T 239-400, a full tour (3 days) including transport from Quito, all meals and good excursions into the jungle costs US$170 p.p. (US$70 from Misahuallí) with an extra charge of US$32 for each additional day. Avoid paying in US$ as they give you a very bad rate (independent canoe journey there costs US$30, except by public canoe at 1100).

There are many guides available to take parties into the jungle for trips of 1 to 10 days, seeing river and jungle flora and fauna, the Cuyabeno National Park and other jungle locations, all involving canoeing and varying amounts of hiking. Guides are now licenced, travellers should ask to see a guide's licence. Note that guides are moving to Coca, where it may be easier to get a tour party together; another good place to collect a group is Baños, rather than Misahuallí itself. The going rate is between US$20 and US$35 p.p. per day, depending on season and length of trip. This should include food and rubber boots, which are absolutely essential (but see below). Overnight tours are recommended only for the hardy. Héctor Fiallos, of Fluvial River Tours (information in Quito T 239-044), arranges one-day outings, and it is possible to make 3- and 4-day tours. A 6-day tour takes in the Cuyabeno National Park (special permit needed and may be difficult to get) and the Aguarico River. A 10-day tour goes down the Napo to Nuevo Rocafuerte and up the Aguarico to the Cuyabeno National Park. Reports have reached us, however, that Héctor is less conscientious than he used to be and does not accompany his parties, leaving them in the care of less experienced guides: Domingo, Enrique (knows the jungle well but the tour is rather routine) and Bolívar have been recommended but not others. There are also other tour operators using Hector's name. We have received very mixed reports of trips arranged by Cruceros Fluviales Primavera (also based in Baños). Julio Los Angeles will arrange anything you wish to do; 4-day tour on Río Tiputini to see animals is the minimum time (you can see very little in a shorter time); a 6-day tour includes floating downriver on balsa rafts made by Julio, highly recommended by those who like peace and quiet and offering the opportunity of sighting wildlife undisturbed by motor launches. Luis Alberto García, Emerald Forest Expeditions, P.O. Box 247, Tena, with office in Misahuallí, leads trips from Misahuallí (US$28 p.p./day) and from Coca, inc. transport, food and group gear, speaks English and is very knowledgeable, though lacks a bit of conservation awareness. Adonis Muñoz of Caiman Tours has also been warmly recommended as good English-speaking guide (and cook). He was born in Limón Cocha and studied biology in the U.S.A. Douglas Clarke (speaks English), who runs the *Restaurant Dayuna*, and his sister, Billy, arrange trips with other guides. Their one-and two-day walks are recommended. Also trips to Coca, to smaller rivers and lagoons, Limón Cocha, and longer ones into the jungle of up to ten days, similar to those organized by Héctor Fiallos but reportedly slightly more expensive. At *Hotel Balcón del Napo* contact Galo, who does 7-day jungle tours, or Carlos Sevilla, whose tours are up to 18 days, both are well recommended. (Carlos Sevilla can also be contacted via his sister in Quito, T 241-981). Another tour operator is Walter Vasco, of Experiencia en Selva y Río, who has 2 or 3 canoes for fairly inexpensive trips. Luis Duarte has been recommended as very knowledgeable, but unless you insist otherwise, you will dine on products of his hunting: cayman, monkey, piranha fish and turtle eggs! He too can be contacted at the *Balcón del Napo*. Other good guides: Jaime Recalde and Eugenio Martínez, good meals, contact them at *Balcón del Napo*, interesting on fauna and flora; Domingo Andy of Ñuca Sacha agency, quiet but interesting, tour to Pañacocha slow but good; Elías Arteaga, office on main square, good meal at his house afterwards; Fernando Alomia, maximum 4 people, lives at *Residencial La Posada* on corner of square by road leading to the river; Sócrates Nevárez, runs 1-10 day tours including trips further down Río Napo, well-organized; Carlos Herbert Licuy Licuy, locally born, good on history, legends and culture of the area.

Some tours have been criticized for too much walking for too few rewards, so make sure your guide knows enough to make your effort worthwhile; an inexperienced guide can mean a boring, or even distressing, walk. Remember that, however good your guide is, organization may be bad, resulting in delays. If short of time, think twice about taking a tour. Consider also the harmful effects of visiting Indian villages. Some guides visit zoos of hotels where animals are kept in unsatisfactory conditions; make sure beforehand that zoos are not on the itinerary. Travellers into the Oriente must have their passports stamped at the naval office, which is clearly marked at the canoe embarkation point. Note the letter on the wall from the First Congress of the Waorani denouncing the invasion of tourists. Many guides visit their villages without prior arrangement or payment. Fees for chartering a canoe are open to bargaining; fares on excursions are fixed. Every canoe pilot is supposed to have his passenger list checked before going downstream but this is not always done. For your own safety ensure that the authorities have a record. Essential items for a trip of any length are rubber boots (or, if you prefer, two pairs of suitable light shoes—keep one pair dry), sleeping bags, rain jackets, trousers, not shorts, binoculars, insect repellant, sun tan lotions, mosquito net, water-purifying tablets, sticking plasters. The cautious might also take a tent, stove, extra food and playing cards. Wrap everything in plastic bags.

**Transport** Buses from Quito via Baños and Tena, about 8 hrs, several daily; also from Quito via Baeza and Tena, about 7 hrs.

Owing to the completion of the road to Coca, there are no regular boat services to Coca, Limón Cocha and Nueva Rocafuerte; canoes ply this route but only when there are 8 passengers or more (out of season this may be once or twice a week, 9 hrs. to Coca, 9-14 back). When canoes are running get your ticket at the Armada del Ecuador office, where you register the day before. During and after heavy rainfall there are obviously no services, nor are there any services during a long dry period. You can rent a boat to Coca, US$130 up to 20 people, leaves only a.m. Take something to sit on.

**Puyo** is the most important centre in the whole Oriente and the junction for road travel into the southern Oriente and for traffic taking the **route to/from Ambato** via Baños (**see page 830**). The pioneer fringe has now left Puyo far behind, and its wooden buildings are giving way to concrete and cement. The electricity supply is turned off promptly at midnight. There is a cinema, Coliseo, the Ñucaloma discotheque, and a cock-pit (cockfights Sun. 1400). Immigration office in Gobernación handles visa extensions.

The road from Puyo to Baños has been reconstructed. It is a dramatic journey with superb views of the Pastaza valley and a plethora of waterfalls. From Baños to Ambato is paved. **Shell-Mera** (a few km. W of Puyo, 50 km. from Baños, 1½ hrs, *Hotel Esmeraldita, Residencial Azuay*) has an army checkpoint where foreigners must register if coming from Ambato, and an airfield.

**Hotels** *Hostería Turingia*, Orellana y Villamil, E, small huts with bath, in tropical garden, comfortable but noisy, restaurant quite expensive but good; *Hostería Safari*, on road to Puerto Napo outside town, E, quiet, peaceful; *El Araucano*, Celso Marín 576, T 885-227, F p.p. with bath, G, without, Chilean owned, family atmosphere, clean, hot water, newly furbished, video club, bread and cake shop, restaurant; *Europa*, F, with bath, good value and good restaurant, also newer *Europa Internacional*, E (bright, pleasant, good restaurant), and *California*, F, slightly cheaper, noisy, all on Calle 9 de Octubre; *Grenada*, Calle 27 de Febrero y Orellana, G, dirty; *Pensión Susanita*, 9 de Octubre y Orellana, E, cafeteria, rec. Some other *pensiones* F or G.

**Restaurants** *Hostería Turingia*, set meals, poor service; *Europa* (next to *Hostal*) 9 de Octubre y Marín, good; *Rincón Ambateño*, on river front, follow 29 de Julio, restaurant and pool complex; *Delicia* (local), *Ejecutivo*, *Viña del Mar* and *El Delfín* (both seafood), all on Marín; *Chifa China*, 9 de Octubre y 24 de Mayo, clean. *Mistral*, Atahualpa y 9 de Octubre, good for breakfast; *Pan Selecto*, Marín y 9 de Octubre, good, fresh bread. *El Chileno*, fuente de soda run by owner of *El Araucano*, rec.

**Buses** to Baños, US$0.80, 2 hrs; **Ambato**, US$1.10, 3 hrs; **Quito**, US$2, 7 hrs; **Tena**, US$1, 3½ hrs (fight for a seat, rough road). Riobamba, US$1.10, 3½ hrs Most buses leave from the new Terminal Terrestre on the outskirts of town (10-15 mins. walk). Those for Macas leave from small station near new market at far end of Atahualpa, past Amazonas (sign says Transportes Amazónicas), leaves daily 0500, 0900 and occasionally in p.m.

**Flights** Air Force to Tena; Macas via Taisha, good views. Shell-Mera can also be reached by military flight from Quito, ½ hr; also flights to Macas. Military flights from Shell-Mera to Montalvo and Tiputini.

Betsy Wagenhauser writes: "The first leg of the Puyo-Macas bus (US$1, 3 hrs) goes as far as Chuitayo, a small settlement at the junction of the Upshin and Pastaza rivers. There is no bridge, so travellers cross on a home-made catamaran of two dugouts strapped together (US$0.25, US$3.50 for a car) powered by outboard motors. When the river is low this is no problem, but during the rainy season, it could be treacherous. The current is swift, and debris swept down from upriver could cause the "ferry" to overturn. Another crossing option is a heavy cable stretching the width of the river connected to high platforms on either shore. Attached to the cable is a cage-like contraption, large enough to hold 2. You climb the platform, enter the cage, then release the catch. The cage swings along the cable, high over the river, to the other side. Definitely an interesting ride!

On the opposite shore, a bus arrives to carry passengers the rest of the way to Macas (US$1, 3 hrs). It stops often at small settlements, mostly inhabited by Shuar descendents. The ride is slow and rough, the road hard packed dirt, full of potholes. The jungle which borders this road is beautiful."

**Macas,** the capital of Santiago-Morona province, situated high above the broad Río Upano valley, is developing rapidly thanks to nearby oil deposits. At about 1,000 metres, the climate is not too hot and the nights are even cool. Its environs are very beautiful and the surrounding hills give excellent views of the volcano **Sangay**, 5,230 metres, within the Sangay National Park, entrance US$10, reached by bus to village of 9 de Octubre, Wed. and Sun. 1600, then walk. You can cross the River Upano (footbridge) and take bus (½ hr.) to the Salesian Sevilla-Don Bosco mission. Good swimming. The whole settlement area has been developed for beef production. In Taisha, a village E of Macas, the *Casa Morocho* rents a few basic rooms, G; on the road to the mission there is a small stream in which you can swim or wash clothes. It is possible to visit the jungle from Macas and there are agencies specializing in tours to villages inc. flight, US$30-50 p.p. However, it is advisable to contact the Shuar Federation (see below) before taking a tour and verify what is involved before signing any contract. Malaria precautions essential.

**Macas Hotels** *Peñon del Oriente*, most modern, F, rec, clean, secure, hot water (electric showers, but not problematic), good views from roof; *Orquídea*, 9 de Octubre y Sucre, F, with bath, quiet, clean and bright, ebds comfortable, roof restaurant mostly closed; *Peñón del Oriente*, Domingo y Amazonas, F p.p., clean, good, firm beds, electric showers; *Hostería del Valle*, 5 km. out on Sucúa road, self-contained cabins, F. Others are all G: *Mayflower*, one tiny bathroom but clean rooms, *Residencial Macas*, clean and friendly; *Hotels Splendit* (run down), *Amazonas*, *Residenciales Emperatriz* and *Elvira* (over liquid gas store); *Pensión Turismo*, basic.

**Restaurants** *Chifa Pagoda China*, Amazonas 15-05, delicious, generous portions, good value, rec.; *Chifa Perla Oriental*, *Mesón Dorado* and bus station restaurant, all on 10 de Agosto. *Rincón del Miguel*, Soasti y 10 de Agosto, Chifa menu, wide variety, rec.; *Eros Café*, Amazonas y Tarqui, good for snacks, breakfast, friendly owners.

**Cinema** next to letel, 24 de Mayo y Sucre, weekends only.

**Transport** Flight to Quito, TAME, two a week, sit on left for best views of Sangay. Bus to **Cuenca**, 11 hrs, US$3.50, Transportes Sucúa, 1700, miserable dinner stop in Limón; hourly to **Sucúa**, 1 hr, no regular service on Thurs. Two bus companies Macas-Puyo: Coop. San Francisco continues to **Ambato** and **Quito**, 0300 and 1230, US$2 to **Puyo**, 6 hrs; Coop. Macas almost hourly from 0600-1500. No buses **Macas-Guamote**.

**Sucúa** 23 km. from Macas is of particular interest as the centre of the now-civilized branch of the ex-head-hunting Shuar (Jívaro) Indians; their crafts can be seen and bought but it is tactless to ask them about head-hunting and shrinking. You can contact the Shuar Federation at Domingo Comin 17-38 (Calle Tarqui 809) for information about visiting traditional villages, though they tend to be somewhat resistant to tourists.

**Hotels** *Oriente*, clean, but run down, restaurant; *Rincón Oriental*, clean and friendly, good set meals, F; *Cuenca*, G, small rooms, basic, clean but toilets filthy; *Hostal Alborada*, F, clean, cheap, good restaurant. Bar/restaurant *Sangay*, opp. **Rincón Oriental**.
     There are an interesting bookshop and (ten minutes walk from the town centre) a small museum and zoo in the Centro de Formación.

Nearby is the Río Upano, 1½ hrs walk, with plenty of Morpho butterflies; also the Río Namangoza, 15 mins walk, with rapids, good swimming, but be careful after rain.

From Sucúa, the road heads south (2 hrs) to (Santiago de) Méndez (*Pensión Miranda*, *Residencia Medina*, both G, basic). Here a newly constructed road goes east into the jungle (9 hrs) to the village of Morona, located on the Morona river just at the (disputed) Peruvian border (no accommodation, camping possible). No border crossing is permitted. At this time the area is newly opened and not set up for tourists, no accommodation available. However, it is virtually unexploited, and the wildlife and primary forest abundant. With the opening of the road, colonists and exploitation will shortly follow, but until then, for the more adventurous, an attempt to arrange a jungle excursion from Morona could prove to be an incredible experience.
     Along the Méndez-Morona road is the junction of the Zamora-Coangos rivers. East of the confluence, at the village of Santiago, a canoe can be hired (about US$30) to a point from where you can walk in 2½ hours to the Cueva de Los Tayos, a huge cave, 85 metres in depth. The trail is obscure, and a guide is necessary; Mario Cruz, in conjunction with Metropolitan Touring in Quito, organizes treks from the capital.

2 hrs, 50 km. S of Méndez is **Limón**, official name General Leónidas Plaza (*Res. Limón*, G, clean, modern, basic; *Res. Paraíso*, G, basic; *Restaurante Rico Pollo Turco*). Buses, all from Calle Quito, go to Cuenca, Macas and Gualaquiza. It is some distance N of the turn-off for the **route to Cuenca**. From Limón, the road to Cuenca (132 km.) passes through Gualaceo and El Descanso; it is a longer route (Macas-Cuenca) than from Quito, but just as spectacular. From Limón the road rises steeply with many breathtaking turns and the vegetation changes frequently, partly through cloud forest and then, at 4,000 metres, through the

páramo, before dropping very fast down to the valley of Gualaceo. There is a police checkpoint on the Limón-Gualaceo road where foreigners have to register. Nowhere to stay along the road.

A round trip by car Cuenca-Gualaceo-Limón-Sucúa-Macas-Mera and onwards to Quito is possible now a bridge across the Pastaza River has been completed. Quicker access to Quito will be given by the construction of a road between Macas and Riobamba; it has reached 9 de Octubre, N of Macas, and from the mountains is being built out of Guamote (**see page 822**). If travelling by public transport on this route enquire at the bus stations in Macas or Puyo about the condition of the roads.

From Limón, it is 3-4 hrs to Gualaquiza on the route from Loja to the Oriente.

**From Loja** The road to the Oriente (**see page 847**) crosses a low pass and descends rapidly to **Zamora**, an old mission settlement about 65 km. away at the confluence of the Rivers Zamora and Bombuscara. The road is beautiful as it wanders from *páramo* down to high jungle, crossing mountain ranges of spectacular cloud forest, weaving high above narrow gorges as it runs alongside the Zamora river. The area has scarcely been affected by tourism yet. For the mission at Guadelupe, take a La Paz bus, which goes up the Yacuambi valley. The town itself is not very interesting, being a midway point for miners and gold prospectors heading further into the Oriente. The best month is November, but except for April-June when it rains almost constantly other months are comfortable. There are two entrances to the **Podocarpus National Park** here (see above under Loja). The lower altitude of the Zamora side of the Park makes wet weather less threatening but waterproof hiking boots are essential. Permission to enter the Park from the Ministry of Agriculture, US$2 entrance, is essential. MAG office at town entrance, open Mon.-Fri., 0900-1800. At weekends pay at the Park headquarters Bombuscara refuge, taxi US$1.50 to the entrance, 1 km. walk to refuge. Camping possible near refuge. Park guardians can suggest walks. Incredible bird life, mountain tanagers flock around refuge.

Another park entrance is 2 hrs. by bus to the south. From the Zamora bus terminal, you can take a 'ranchero', or wooden, open-sided bus to Romerillos, which is a collection of a few houses and a MAG office. Bus departs Zamora 0630 and 1415, return to Zamora at 0815 and 1600. This area is definitely off the beaten track but for the virgin cloud forest and amazing quantity of flora and fauna, it is unmatched. A 3 to 5 day hike is possible into this part of the park, but permission is not only needed from the MAG office in Zamora but from the mining company. MAG will get the permission for you after filling out a few papers. T 900-141 and let them know you are interested in entering the area. Ing. Luis Cuenca is in charge of the Podocarpus Park, and Luis Tambo is helpful as well. This area contains one of the last major habitats for the spectacled bear and many birds, such as the mountain toucan, Andean cock-of-the-rock, umbrella bird, green jay, etc. Most food supplies can be obtained in Zamora (but expensive), though all camping gear must be carried, as well as fuel for stoves. There are no gas stations in Zamora.

**Hotels** *Maguma*, E, best; *Res. Venecia*, G, shared bathroom; *Zamora*, F, clean; *Amazonas*, F. *Seyma*, F, one block from main plaza on 24 de Mayo, clean, friendly, rec.. **Restaurants** in *Hotel Maguma* (best), *GranRitz*, good, and *Comedor Don Pepe*. *Esmeraldas* in market area opp. bus terminal, good, rec.

**Buses** All leave from Terminal Terrestre. To *Loja*, 4 a day, 2½ hrs; to *Cuenca*, 1 daily via Loja, over 10 hrs; to *Yantzaza* and *La Paz*, 6 a day.

*Nambija* is a gold mining town outside Zamora, a frontier town with its own, limited, law and order. It is not entirely safe to visit, gold miners can be suspicious and trigger happy.

From Zamora, the road follows the Zamora river to *Gualaquiza*, a pioneer town off the tourist track. It is surrounded by densely forested mountains, in which are interesting side trips. Very little can be purchased here so take your own supplies (and don't forget your antimalarials). If you intend to explore the area, bring tent and sleeping bag. Among the excursions are: caves near Nuevo Tarqui, the Salesian mission at Bomboisa; Tutusa Gorge (3 hrs walk, 2 hrs by boat, take a guide, e.g. Sr. José Castillo); Aguacate, 6 hrs walk, near which are precolumbian ruins, presumably Inca (food and bed at Sr. Jorge Guillermo Vázquez); and Yumaza, 40 mins walk, for more precolumbian ruins, possibly Inca (2 sites). The valley produces large quantities of *naranjillas* and some sugar cane, maize, bananas and yuca.

**Hotels** *Turismo*, G, good value, restaurant; *Residenciales Estambul* and *Amazonas*, both G, basic. *Restaurante Gualaquiza* is best of a mediocre lot.

**Buses** to **Cuenca** (0700, 2000 and 2100), 6 hrs; **Loja** (0300 and 2200); **Macas** (1800), 10 hrs.

## GALAPAGOS ISLANDS (9)

Lying on the Equator, 970 km. west of the Ecuadorean coast, the Galápagos consist of 6 main islands (San Cristóbal, Santa Cruz, Isabela, Floreana, Santiago and Fernandina—the last two uninhabited); 12 smaller islands (Baltra, with an airport, and the uninhabited islands of Santa Fe, Pinzón, Española, Rábida, Daphne, Seymour, Genovesa, Marchena, Pinta, Darwin and Wolf) and over 40 small islets. The islands have a total population of nearly 10,000 and because of immigration the annual growth rate is about 12%. The largest island, Isabela (formerly Albemarle), is 120 km. long and forms half the total land area of the archipelago. Its notorious convict colony was closed in 1958; some 650 people live there now, mostly in and around Puerto Villamil, on the S coast. San Cristóbal (Chatham) has a population of 2,321 with the capital of the archipelago, Puerto

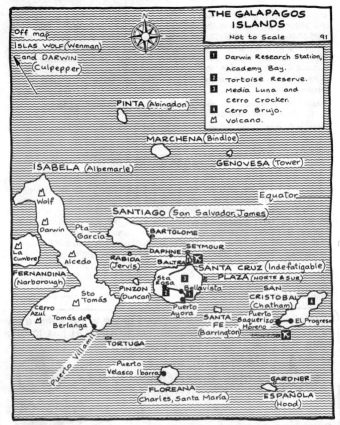

THE GALAPAGOS ISLANDS

Not to Scale 91

1 Darwin Research Station, Academy Bay.
2 Tortoise Reserve.
3 Media Luna and Cerro Crocker.
4 Cerro Brujo.
🌋 Volcano.

Off map
ISLAS WOLF (Wenman)
and DARWIN (Culpepper)

PINTA (Abingdon)

MARCHENA (Bindloe)

ISABELA (Albemarle)

GENOVESA (Tower)

Equator

Wolf

SANTIAGO (San Salvador, James)

Darwin     Pta Garcia

BARTOLOME

DAPHNE     SEYMOUR

La Cumbre     Alcedo

RABIDA (Jervis)     BALTRA

SANTA CRUZ (Indefatigable)

FERNANDINA (Narborough)

Sta Rosa     PLAZA (NORTE & SUR)

PINZON (Duncan)

Bellavista

SAN CRISTOBAL (Chatham)

Cerro Azul

Sto Tomás

Puerto Ayora

Tomás de Berlanga

SANTA FE (Barrington)

Puerto Baquerizo Moreno

El Progreso

TORTUGA

Puerto Velasco Ibarra

GARDNER

FLOREANA (Charles, Santa María)

ESPAÑOLA (Hood)

Baquerizo Moreno. Santa Cruz (Indefatigable) has 3,154, with Puerto Ayora, the main tourist centre; and Floreana (Charles) fewer than 50. The group is quite widely scattered; by boat, Puerto Baquerizo Moreno and Puerto Ayora are 6 hours apart.

The islands are the peaks of gigantic volcanoes, composed almost exclusively of basalt. Most of them rise from 2,000 to 3,000 metres above the seabed. Eruptions have taken place in historical times on Fernandina, Isabela, Pinta, Marchena, Santiago and Floreana. The most active today are Fernandina, Isabela, Pinta and Marchena, and fumarolic activity may be seen intermittently on each of these islands. There have been recent eruptions on Volcán, Sierra Negra, Isabela and Fernandina.

The Galápagos have almost certainly never been connected with the continent. Gradually, over many hundreds of thousands of years, animals and plants from over the sea developed there and as time went by they adapted themselves to Galápagos conditions and came to differ more and more from their continental ancestors. Thus many of them are unique: a quarter of the species of shore fish, half of the plants and almost all the reptiles are found nowhere else. In many cases different forms have evolved on the different islands. Charles Darwin recognized this speciation within the archipelago when he visited the Galápagos on the *Beagle* in 1835 and his observations played a substantial part in his formulation of the theory of evolution. Since no large land mammals reached the islands, reptiles were dominant just as they had been all over the world in the very distant past. Another of the extraordinary features of the islands is the tameness of the animals. The islands were uninhabited when they were discovered in 1535 and the animals still have little instinctive fear of man.

The most spectacular species to be seen by the visitor are the giant tortoise (species still survive in 6 or 7 of the islands, but mostly on Isabela); marine iguana (the only seagoing lizard in the world and found throughout most of the archipelago; it eats seaweed); land iguana (on Fernandina, Santa Cruz, Santa Fe, Isabela, Seymour and Plaza); Galápagos albatross (which nests only on the island of Española, it leaves in December and returns in late March-early April); Galápagos hawk, red-footed, blue-footed and masked boobies, red-billed tropic-bird, frigate birds, dusky lava gulls, mockingbirds, 13 species of Darwin's finches (all endemic and the classic examples of speciation quoted by Darwin); Galápagos sea-lion (common in many areas) and the Galápagos fur-seal (on the more remote and rocky coasts). Santiago and Plaza islands are particularly interesting for students of these species.

There is a National Park Tax which every visitor has to pay on arrival; in 1991 it was US$40, payable only in sucres, US$ cash or travellers cheques. The number of tourists to the island is controlled by the authorities to protect the environment but critics claim that the ecology is seriously threatened by current levels. Limits have been increased from 12,000 in 1974 to 60,000 in 1990, but tourism infrastructure remains fairly basic.

Alban Johnson and Luci Montesinos Aguilar write: The most-visited islands (and main attractions) are Plaza Sur (many birds flying close to the cliff top), Santa Fe (land and sea iguanas, sea-lions), Seymour Norte (magnificent frigate birds, blue-footed boobies), Rábida (sea-lions, flamingoes, pelican rookery), and Santiago (James Bay for fur seals; Sullivan Bay and Bartolomé Island for fantastic lava fields and maybe a few penguins). On a tour of these islands it may be possible to go also to Punto García on Isabela to see flightless cormorants (it takes at least a full day to climb up one of the volcanoes to see the tortoises). Daphne Island with very rich birdlife may be visited by each boat only once a month (a permit is required).

More distant islands are Española (blue-footed boobies, masked boobies, waved albatross, brightly-coloured marine iguanas), Genovesa (red-footed boobies, frigate birds and many others) and Fernandina (penguins and many other birds). Floreana, San Cristóbal and Baltra have little wildlife, and on Santa Cruz it is worth visiting the Darwin Station, Tortoise Reserve and Tortuga Bay. All the other islands are closed to tourists.

Tours generally leave from Puerto Ayora, but can finish at Baltra for the airport. Take some chocolate and biscuits with you; you will certainly miss them if you don't. Boat operators tend to underestimate the amount of drinking (mineral) water (they may not supply any, see below) and overestimate the amount of Coca Cola that foreigners drink. Food can be good if they catch fish, poor if not.

In 1959, the centenary of the publication of Darwin's *Origin of Species*, the Government of Ecuador and the International Charles Darwin Foundation established, with the support of Unesco, the Charles Darwin Research Station at Academy Bay 1½ km. from Puerto Ayora, Santa Cruz, the most central of the Galápagos islands, open Mon.-Fri. 0700-1300, 1400-1600, Sat. 0700-1300. A visit to the station is a good introduction to the islands as it provides a lot of information. Collections of several of the rare races of giant tortoise are maintained on the station as breeding nuclei, together with a tortoise-rearing house incorporating incubators and pens for the young. The Darwin Foundation staff will help bona fide students of the fauna to plan an itinerary, if they stay some time and hire a boat. Avoid visiting in July and especially August (high season).

**Travel to the Islands** There are 2 airports, one at Baltra, across a narrow strait from Santa Cruz, the other at Puerto Baquerizo Moreno, on San Cristóbal. The two islands are 96 km. apart with regular boat services only twice a week. When booking make sure your flight goes to the island of your choice. There are flights with SAN to Puerto Baquerizo Moreno (San Cristóbal) from Guayaquil and connecting flights from Quito (on Mon., Wed. and Sat.). The round trip in 1991 cost US$330 from Guayaquil, and US$374 from Quito (though there are no direct flights from Quito and it is cheaper to book separate flights from Quito to Guayaquil and Guayaquil to Galápagos). One-way tickets are available and it is now possible to buy an open-ended ticket (valid one year). SAN will change dates for return to mainland. SAN offers 25% discount to holders of International Student Identity Cards; they require a photocopy. Go to the office in Av. Cristóbal Colón y 6 de Diciembre. TAME flies daily, except Sunday, to Baltra, and also offers 25% reductions on flights originating in Quito to holders of International Student Identity Cards (details from office at Edificio Pichincha, 6th floor,

Amazonas y Colón, Quito, two photocopies of ID required; American Express, Av. Amazonas, Quito, sells student cards for US$10); return to Guayaquil is permitted. You can not get a discount on tickets bought on the islands. Beware of "temporary" fare increases, e.g. in December; buy your ticket in November. Tour operators still buy up blocks of seats in advance and they always try to sell you one of their excursions. For this reason, if time is limited, it is probably advisable to go for a package tour. If you cannot get a flight within a week, try going to the airport to get a seat on stand-by. If you are using Ecuatoriana for an international flight to Ecuador you can buy a ticket Quito-Baltra-Quito cheaper if bought outside the country. Saeta has excellent 30-day excursion packages Miami—Quito/Guayaquil—Galápagos (SAN to San Cristóbal)—Guayaquil/Quito-Miami (US$584 June 1990), usually cheapest deal, but you land in a more difficult place for arranging tours, rec. if you have 10 days available.

The Air Force flights, known as *logísticos*, are handled at the Departamento de Operaciones of the Air Force at the Ministry of Defence, Av. Maldonado y la Exposición, Quito. To enter the office, leave identification, but not your passport. Latest reports (1990) indicate that foreigners are not often allowed on these flights. Foreigners need the special authorization of the general commander of the Air Force, but this is not usually granted, even to those with the support of their embassy and letters of introduction from a recognized educational/research institution where they work or study. (Note: UK Embassy charges £25 for a letter.) For those who do succeed, a Lockheed C-130 Hercules departs Quito for Guayaquil, San Cristóbal and Baltra at 0700 on Sat., be there at 0500. The flights are not reliable and flying for two hours in a cargo aircraft with no windows and no facilities is not much fun.

There are now many travel agencies operating tours of the Galápagos Islands. Their quality and price varies considerably so shop around. Prices are no longer significantly cheaper in the low season (Feb.-May, Sept.-Nov.) but ask if an agency has 1-3 spaces to fill on a cruise; you can sometimes get them at 20% discount.

We have received persistent reports that tour operators, whether contacted on the mainland or the Galápagos, are unreliable in sticking to their agreed programme, and that some of the guides deviate from the scheduled route, wasting time in port and leaving out some islands. This is sometimes because not all passengers are on the same length of tours and boats come into port to change passengers. Avoid tours where you sail all day and stay at *pensiones* and eat at restaurants; you can not go so far and you waste valuable time eating and sleeping on land. Insist on a written itinerary or contract prior to departure as any effort not to provide this probably indicates problems later (written contracts seem to be ignored, none-the-less). The South American Explorers Club (Quito: Toledo 1254 y Cordero, T 566-076–Apartado 21-431, Quito; Lima: Av. Rep. de Portugal 146, Breña, T 314-480–Casilla 3714, Lima 100; USA: P.O. Box 18327, Denver, CO 80218, T 303-320 0388) has produced a useful, brief guide to the Galápagos which includes a specimen contract for itinerary and living conditions. Ensure that not more than a half-day is spent on either Santa Cruz or San Cristóbal for restocking of provisions. Count your money regularly and don't leave your beach gear unattended if other boats are in the vicinity when you are ashore. If you have problems afterwards, take your contract to the Capitanía (port captain).

In Guayaquil, **Galasam** (Economic Galapagos Tours), Av. 9 de Octubre 424, Edificio Gran Pasaje, 11° piso (T 306-289/313-724, Telex 42680 GALASA ED, Fax 313-351) sell flights as well as their own tours and can sell air tickets for their tours at a discount by using the free market. If you book the SAN flight to San Cristóbal with them, they throw in the Ingala boat

trip to Santa Cruz free. In Quito, Galasam is at Pinto 523 y Av. Amazonas, T 550-094 and at Amazonas 1316 y Cordero, T 561-470, Fax 567-662. Heavy demand for Galasam tours has led to reports of unfriendliness. The Galasam 8-day tours departs Mon., Tues., Wed. and Sat., depending on the boat, prices range from about US$500 to US$700. In 1991 they were operating with three 16-passenger boats in superior tourist class: *Dorado, Cruz del Sur* and *Estrella del Mar,* one fairly spartan 8-passenger boat in tourist class: *Yolita,* and three boats in economy class: *Darwin, Albatros* and *Jesús del Gran Poder;* the last two will be refitted for 1992 to take 12 passengers and will be equipped for diving. In 1992 another superior tourist class boat: *Islas Plazas,* will be incorporated. The more luxurious boats have specially trained bilingual guides. Galasam say the guides on the smaller boats are English-speaking, but their knowledge of English may be very limited. It has also been alleged that their boats sometimes travel in convoy, that prices on board are exorbitant and they only provide beer and coke (coke ran out after 2 days—take plenty of drinking water).

Metropolitan Touring, Av. Amazonas 239, Casilla 2542, Quito (represented in the USA by Adventure Associates, 5925 Maple, Suite 116, Dallas, Texas 75235), T 524-400 offers 7-night cruises on the M.V. *Santa Cruz* (90 passengers), about US$250 a day, said to be the best boat, very professional service, with multilingual guides. They also have five yachts for private charters. Macchiavello Tours of Guayaquil (Anteparra 809 y 9 de Octubre, T 392-892) is ordering two new boats from Italy.

Other recommended agencies with tours to/in the Galápagos are: Galápagos Cruises, Los Ríos 0-80, Guayaquil, T 390-893, Telex 3610 ETICAG; Coltur, Robles y Páez 370, Quito, T 545-777, Telex 2302, with an office in Puerto Ayora; Nuevo Mundo, Av. Amazonas 2468, Quito T 552-617, Telex 2484; Castro Turismo, Vélez 205, Guayaquil, T 512-174; Famitur, Veintimilla 928 y Amazonas, Quito, T 529-742; Samoa Tours, Victoria 907 y Wilson, Quito, T 551-597; Ceviar, 9 de Octubre, Guayaquil. The *Hotel Gran Casino* in Quito, Av. 24 de Mayo y Bahía, arranges 8-day tours, unreliable, and refunds are difficult to obtain if they cancel. Kayaking trips in the Islands are organized by Northern Lights Expeditions, 5220 NE 180th, Seattle, WA 98155, USA.

There are cargo ships making the trip, but dates are irregular, the chances of a passage slim and some interesting but remote ports are missed. Check with the naval port authorities on the Malecón in Guayaquil, or with the boats themselves several days prior to departure. *Iguana* leaves on the 7th of each month, *Congal* on the 17th and *Piquero* on the 27th. None is reported to be reliable. We have received reports of a ban on passengers travelling on cargo ships, but it may still be worth trying. T401-004 for agent for *Piquero,* who can tell you where to reach the Captain. Fare to the islands US$100, tour round the islands US$100, return US$100.

From Britain, inclusive tours can be booked through Twickers World, 22 Church Street, Twickenham, TW1 3NW, or through the Coltur representative in London, Cecilia Irivalo, T 071-221 0968. David Horwell, naturalist and author of *Galápagos, the Enchanted Isles,* London, Dryad Press, 1988 (£7.95), arranges tailor-made tours to Ecuador and the Galápagos islands. For further details write to him at Galapagos Adventure Tours, 29 Palace View, Bromley, Kent, BR1 3EJ, England.

From the airport on Baltra, one takes a combination of bus (US$1), ferry (US$0.45) and bus (US$1.50) to Puerto Ayora, Santa Cruz. The whole process takes at least 3 hours. Airport buses leave Puerto Ayora (Pyky supermarket) at 0800 and 0830 for Baltra (best buy ticket night before—not possible for Sat. bus though). TAME office in Puerto Ayora closes Sat p.m. and Sun. Hotel may make prior arrangements.

**Travel between the Islands**  There are official (Ingala) sailings on Tues. and Sat. from Santa Cruz at 1200 to San Cristóbal (US$10.50), returning at 1200 on Mon. and Wed. The old and slow *Estrella del Mar* runs once a week Isabella-Santa Cruz, schedule varies. The Ingala office in Puerto Ayora is next to the hospital on the road inland from the waterfront. Get your name on the list here as early as possible on the day before sailing, buy ticket for San Cristóbal on day of departure between 0800 and 1000 and be at the quay at 1100. We have received reports that it is well nigh impossible to get your name on the list as residents have priority, then Ecuadorians and lastly foreigners. The Ingala office in Puerto Baquerizo Moreno is up the hill on the road leading inland, on the edge of town.

The best centre from which to visit the Islands is *Puerto Ayora,* Santa Cruz. Here you can hire boats (lists available from National Park Service) and a two-week sojourn will allow you to see most of the Islands. If you only have a short time, the northern islands are the more scenic with the more interesting wildlife. Reservations are strongly recommended for June-August and December-April. For cheaper tours it is generally recommended that you form a group of six to ten people once you reach the Islands, talk to people about the boats they may have used and then talk to the boat owners (known as *dueño*), not the captains, about what you wish to do. Bargain over the route and the price, and get a firm commitment from the owner on dates and itinerary, leave a deposit "to buy food" and get a receipt; however, prices have risen sharply and boat owners have made several attempts to form a cartel so that it is now difficult to find a small boat taking six to eight people for less than US$45-50 p.p. per day for a full load, often excluding food, drinks and US$2 harbour exit tax (small boats are essentially for travellers who do not mind a lack of privacy and facilities). Some boats travel by night (check if they have radar) which allows much more time for visiting the islands. If travelling to the more distant islands, night sailing should be standard, and should not incur extra expense. Try to make sure you have a full itinerary for the last day—otherwise the boat may bring you back at around 1500. Larger, more comfortable boats can cost twice as much, especially if they have bilingual guides. Each boat has to be accompanied by a Park-trained guide, either a naturalist (who will be English-speaking, more knowledgeable and therefore more expensive), or an auxiliary; this is arranged by the boat owner. Most boats operate 4-8 day cruises, it appears that only the 50-berth *Isabela*, owned by Etica, can be booked for longer—up to 3 weeks. The *San Juan* is recommended for its speed, which allows you to see as much in 7 days as some do in 10; it is also one of the cheaper boats. Also recommended is the *Golondrina*; decent boat, friendly crew, knowledgeable guide and excellent food. *Evangelina* is a better boat, good guide, excellent food, cheaper. The *Aida María*, which sails at night, is highly rec; contact the owner at the Aida María pharmacy in Puerto Ayora, his son is the captain, good cook and crew. Coltur (see above) has been recommended for visits to North Seymour and Caleta Tortuga Negra on the north coast of Santa Cruz. Their representatives can arrange tours on the *Pirata* (Augusto and Georgina Cruz), which has been recommended for its friendly and helpful staff and good cooking; Georgina Cruz is English.The *Angelito* has been highly recommended, partly because the captain navigates by night so that you have more time on the islands by day. Others recommended in this category are *Española* (8 passengers), *Sulidae*, also 10 passengers, *Lobo del Mar* (10 passengers), *Dorado* (15 passengers), *Daphne* and *San Antonio* (8). The trimaran *Wind Shadow* (slow if there's no wind), owned and sailed by Richard Núñez, costs US$320 per day (maximum capacity 4); Sr. Núñez is knowledgeable and speaks English. It must be stressed, however, that a boat is only as good as its crew and when the staff change, so will these recommendations. Check that the small boats can carry enough food and supplies for the length of journey so you do not waste a day restocking. Many boats require you to provide your own drinking water: check this when you make arrangements. It may be possible to travel on a fishing-boat, though this will be to a predetermined destination—try the Ingala office and the Capitanía del Puerto for information, though the latter may not be very helpful as fishing boats are not supposed to take passengers. Priority on fishing boats tends to go to Ecuadoreans. It may also be possible to travel on supply ships—ask the crew.

**Note**: If not booking a cruise in advance, it can take several days to arrange a tour, so allow yourself plenty of time (up to a week in high season). If you do get stuck, the Tourist Office in Puerto Ayora offers one-day tours (US$36 p.p. with lunch; departure 0600-0800) to Seymour Norte, Plaza Sur or Santa Fe. These smaller islands have a good sample of animal species (although fewer in numbers) and, together with sightseeing on Santa Cruz, can be a worthwhile experience for the tourist with only limited time, although you arrive at the hottest time of day when the animals are having a *siesta*. There is excellent swimming with the sealions at Santa Fe. Never miss the chance to do a bit of snorkelling, but enquire carefully about the likelihood of sharks (*tiburones*—not all are dangerous).

Byron Rueda offers day trips for 10 in his dinghy *Santa Fe* to Santa Fe and to the Plaza islands (US$18). His office is on the Ninfa dock and he also represents other boats (open 0800-1800). Isabela Tours, Av. Darwin, opp. *Sol y Mar*, can arrange day tours to other islands and transport to San Cristóbal and Isabela with their yacht, *Judy II*, helpful guide, Alex, if you can find him at the office. Glass bottomed boat trips, 4-8 hrs, can be taken from the inner harbour, Puerto Ayora, friendly owner, speaks English and Spanish, is knowledgeable about marine life and has masks and snorkels for snorkelling from his boat.

**The Cost of Living** in the Galápagos is high, particularly in the peak season (December, July and August). Most food has to be imported although certain meats, fish, vegetables and fruit are available locally in the Puerto Ayora market. Bottled drinks are expensive.

**Hotels at Puerto Ayora** Hotel space is limited (more are being built) and reservations are strongly rec. in high season. *Galápagos*, A+ (local class 1), bungalows with private bathroom, the only hotel with hot water, ocean-view, laundry service, generator, restaurant with fixed menu, price and time, fruit and meat from hotel farm, near Darwin Research centre, reservations can be made through Ecuadorean travel agencies, day excursions can be made from hotel in Pedro and Sally García's own dinghy for 10, the *Fernandina*. *Delfín*, on far side of Academy Bay, with lovely beach, D (1), meals extra, well rec., accessible only by boat, write to Mrs Sievers. *Residencial Angermeyer*: about 20 beds, F, cooking facilities, small rooms, no fan, running water often problematic, described as very simple, and idiosyncratic; Mrs Angermeyer keeps the place spotlessly clean and is a mine of information, for guests, on good and bad boats. There is a peña next door. *Sol y Mar*, 20 beds (double, triples and quadruples) in cabins; D (1), without meals; B, with 3 meals; 10% discount for stays of 2 weeks or more; reservations can be made by writing to the owner (Sr. Jimmy Pérez), or Macchiavello Tours, Casilla 318, Guayaquil. *Fernandina*, T Galapagos 122 or Quito 538-686, family run, friendly, helpful staff, good meals, electric shower heaters; *Flamingo*, G, shower, fan, decent, clean; *Los Amigos*, Av. Darwin next to TAME office, G p.p. without bath, run by Sra. Rosa Rosera, cool, airy rooms, very pleasant, laundry facilities. *Castro*, D (2), with private bath, owned by Sr. Miguel Castro, he arranges 7-day inclusive tours, including Friday TAME flight, rec. He is an authority on wildlife and his tour includes one or two nights away visiting the islands of Plazas and Santiago, and a day-trip to Santa Fe, with visits to the tortoise reserve and the Darwin Institute. *Colón*, 22 beds (doubles) in third class rooms; F (3), without food; D, including 3 meals. Write to Sra. Piedad Moya. *Elizabeth*, F with bath (3), reasonable, now remodelled, has running water; *Las Ninfas*, D, very close to harbour, basic, cold showers, good restaurant, has its own boat at reasonable price for day trips and Fernando Jiménez is helpful with arrangements; *Lobo de Mar*, E (2) with bath, 30 beds, modern, clean, can do laundry on roof, noisy on occasions; *Gloria*, F, 12 beds, simple, you can cook your own food over a wood fire, mosquito repellant needed; *Darwin*, E, with bath, clean, restaurant (order meals in advance), rec. but don't leave valuables in your room; *Las Palmeras*, B, private bath, cafeteria, laundry facilities, pleasant, clean; *Salinas*, opposite, also E, 20 beds. *Santa Cruz*, F (3).

**Restaurants at Puerto Ayora** Expect slow service and shortages of items such as flour which will reduce menu availability. *Rincón del Mar*, near the plaza, best, good food, reasonable prices; *Don Enriques*, main road, local dishes; *Los Gemelos*, near the school, good breakfast, home made yoghurt and marmalade, good value; *La Garrapata*, open air, on road to research station, popular meeting place for travellers, pizzas, hamburgers, cakes, morning and evening but no Sun.; *Las Peñas*, very good value restaurant, big helpings, good service, opp. *Pirata*; *El Booby*, faces the volleyball court on the seafront, across the street from the iguana statue, family run, no speciality, pleasant, reasonable prices, crowded at night; *El Pescador*, Av. Darwin on corner just past the Chinese restaurants, excellent value, set meals, good fish; *Rincón del Alma*, good food but rather expensive, no prices on menu; *Fausto's*, between Gloria and Angermeyer hotels, good pizzas, friendly owner speaks English, exchanges paperback books and changes cheques; *Four Lanterns*, facing Pelican Bay, good, Italian/vegetarian, reasonable (dinner US$1.50); *Pastry Shop* (in front of hospital) for snacks and drinks; *Ninfa Dock Bar/Restaurant*, on dock, excellent grilled lobster, changes money, meeting place; nearby is *Pasty Pan* for bread and cakes (not open Sun.) *La Terraza*, main street, bar and restaurant; *Chifa Asia* on main street, decent; *Viña del Mar*, on main street, basic, O.K. *Henri's Snack Bar*, main street, German run, good meeting place, good breakfasts, good *rosti*, pastries, snorkel equipment for rent; *Snack Bar Popeyes*, in the plaza, Chilean run, *empanadas* and the best fruit juices in town; *Carmen's* pastry shop rec., good coffee and sweets; *Fragata Bar*, good, on road to research station, as is *Galaps Pizzería*. *Pelikano*, good value breakfast, early morning meeting place and *Pastik-Shock* cafeterias. *Banana Bar*, near Angermeyer hotel, serves delicious banana flambée. Restaurants serve lobster dinners at US$5; *merienda* costs between US$1.50-2.

**Entertainment** Three discos (*La Terraza, Five Fingers* and *Disco Light*) and one *peña-disco* (*Peter Cheese*) in Puerto Ayora.

**Hints** For boat charters and camping trips most basic foodstuffs generally can be purchased in the islands (e.g. Pyky supermarket in Puerto Ayora), although occasionally there are shortages. However, no special items (dehydrated or freezedried foods) are available other than a few common ones such as oatmeal and dried soups. Fresh milk available in Puerto Ayora from Christine Aldaze, 0930, on main road (24 hrs notice appreciated). There is a shortage of drinking water on Santa Cruz; some travellers have warned against drinking water, but mineral water is expensive and often unavailable. Take your own water bottle with you: there is a purification plant at the *pizzería* next to the *Hotel Gloria* and you can buy water there. Electricity is off between midnight and 0600 and INECEL cuts power to a different section of town from 1900-2200 every night. Most hotels have a portable generator.

Medicines, sun lotions, mosquito coils, film, and other useful items are either not available or cost a lot more than on the mainland. It may be advisable to take sea-sickness tablets; the waters south of Santa Cruz are particularly choppy. Take plenty of film with you; the birds are so tame that you will use far more than you expected; a telephoto lens is not essential, but if you have one, bring it. Snorkelling equipment is particularly useful as much of the sea-life is only visible under water. Masks and snorkels can be bought in Quito from *Captain Peña*, on the corner of Plaza Santo Domingo and Flores, prices from US$5-11, models adequate for the Galapagos. Most of the cheaper boats do not provide equipment. It is possible to sell them afterwards either on the islands or try the *Gran Casino* travel agency in Quito. Masks and snorkels can be rented from *Henri's Snackbar*, US$1.25 a day. There is a souvenir shop next to *Angermeyer's* hotel, Galápagos Souvenirs, and a camera repair place next to the cemetery near the Darwin Station (bad reports, unreliable, overcharges, best avoided). *Artesanías Bambú*, near *Hotel Galápagos*, sells local handicrafts, printed T-shirts, etc.

There is a cinema at Puerto Ayora—each evening at 2015. Information and retrieval of lost property from Radio Santa Cruz, next to Catholic Church. Short-stay camping permitted at the Caseta in the highlands.

There is a hospital in Puerto Ayora; consultations are free, medicines reasonably-priced, but they can not perform operations.

Take care not to drop litter, there is already too much scattered around the island, which is highly undesirable in a National Park and is a safety and health hazard for wildlife.

**Warning**: Valuables should be watched.

**Exchange** It is advisable to take plenty of cash; there are few facilities for cashing cheques in Puerto Ayora, and rates are about 5% less than for cash. Some boats accept US$ while others only accept sucres; take plenty of sucres, you can always sell them to other travellers. The *Hotel Sol y Mar* and *Ninfa* restaurant will change notes and cheques, but at a poor rate. There is a bank at Puerto Ayora but it will not change money at all and will not accept credit cards. Several shops change US$ notes. Good rates for cheques and cash at *Fausto's Pizzeria*.

The **Post Office** seldom has stamps available.

**Immigration** The police will extend visas with a little persuasion for those who overstay their visa or tourist card; but such extensions are reportedly not valid.

**British Consul** David Balfour, c/o Etica, Barrio Estrada, Puerto Ayora.

**Tourist Office** Cetur, near the pier, open Mon.-Fri. 0800-1200, 1500-1800, T 328-312, 324-471. Information also available at the boat owners' cooperative office nearby.

**Excursions on Santa Cruz** From Puerto Ayora buses leave the main square frequently from 0800 to 2100 for Santa Rosa, Bellavista and Baltra (fare for all destinations US$1). There are also trucks (cheaper). On roads to the main sites hitching is easy but expect to pay a small fee. Walk to Tortuga Bay on marked path for excellent sunsets and nice beach. A new, shorter track, 2 km. long (1½ hours) has been opened: turn at *Hotel Elizabeth* off main road, then left at *Hotel Santa Cruz*. Take drinking water.

Hike to the higher parts of the island called Media Luna, Puntudo and Mt. Crocker. Trail starts at Bellavista, 7 km. from Puerto Ayora. Round trip from Bellavista is 4 to 8 hrs, depending upon distance hiked, 10-18 km. (permit and guide not required).

There are two natural tunnels (lava tubes) 1 km. from Bellavista (on private land, US$0.70 to enter, torch provided—it takes about ½ hr to walk through the tunnels).

Hike to the Chato Tortoise Reserve; trail starts at Santa Rosa, 22 km. from Puerto Ayora. Horses can be hired at Santa Rosa, US$6 each, guide optional US$6.50 extra. Round trip takes one day. The Puerto Ayora-Bellavista bus stops at the turnoff for the track for the reserve (US$0.95). It's a hot walk; take food and drink. From Santa Rosa, distance to different sites within the reserve is 6-8 km. (permit and guide not required).

Two sinkholes, Los Gemelos, straddle the road to Baltra, beyond Santa Rosa; if you are lucky, take a *camioneta* all the way, otherwise to Santa Rosa, then walk (4-5 mins). A good place to see the Galápagos hawk and barn owl.

Visit the giant Galápagos tortoises in pens at the Darwin Station, a short distance from Puerto Ayora. Small tortoises in rearing pens may be observed. The Station has a museum (explaining the geology and natural history of the islands) and a library. There are also public lectures (details from Cetur office near the pier). Movies are shown on Sundays, one about the Galapagos and one for fun, free.

***Puerto Baquerizo Moreno***, on San Cristóbal island to the E, is the capital of the archipelago, with a new airport with flights Mon., Wed. and Sat. by SAN. The island is being developed as a second tourist centre. Three Ingala boats a week to Puerto Ayora (US$10.50); fishing boats also take passengers (US$7 to Puerto

Ayora). Be warned that it can take several days to find room on a boat to Puerto Ayora or Santa Cruz.

**Hotels** *Grand Hotel Cristóbal*, owned by SAN, opp. a white beach to E of town, A with bath (not inc. tax), good restaurant; *Mar Azul*, on road from airport, D with bath, hot showers, clean, rec., restaurant; *Residencial Northía*, E with bath; *Cabanas Don Jorge*, close to beach, F p.p., clean, friendly, "not luxurious"; *Res. Miramar*, F, good value, clean restaurant, expensive; *Pensión Gloria*, pleasant family, but leaky roofs, new rooms are being added; *Res. Flamingo*, F, basic, clean, friendly; *Hotel San Francisco*, E, good, clean, friendly. *Delfín*, G, basic but cheap.

**Restaurants** *Rosita*, best in town; *Chatham*, good; *Laurita*, fair; *La Terraza*, on beach; *Fragata*, on road to airport. *Cafeteriá Tagu*, cheap.

There is a hospital but if you need an operation you have to go yourself to the pharmacy to buy everything they need.

**Excursions** Bus (shuttle) to El Progreso, then short walk to El Junco lake, tortoises may be seen on the way. From El Progreso (eating places), a trail crosses the high lands to Cerro Brujo and Hobbs Bay; also to Stephens Bay, past lakes. 2 buses go to the crater lake in the middle of the island, and may continue to the other side. A three-hour hike to Galapaguera in the NE allows you to see tortoises in the wild. Boats go to Punta Pitt in the far N where you can see all three boobies. SAN organizes a day trip (ask at *Grand Hotel*) to Point Lobo, reported as disappointing, and another to Española; the latter is often cancelled because the sea is too rough for their small boats. Both Española and Hood are within day trip reach.

*Isabela Island* There are three hotels: *Alexandra*, E, nice site on the beach; *Loja*, E, on the road to the highland, fairly clean, sometimes water shortages, patio, friendly staff, cheap and very good restaurant; *El Rincón del Bucanero*, on the beach, more expensive. There are a few *comedores* but food is seldom available unless you order in advance. Isabela is not highly developed for tourism but if you have a few days to spare it is worthwhile spending time there. Good walks in the highlands and beautiful beaches. Tours to the volcanoes can be made with two guides, compare prices. A 3-5 day trip can be arranged in Puerto Ayora at Darwin 606, US$45/day, 10 people required. The climb up the volcanoes takes 3 days, one for the ascent, one at the top and one to come down.

**The Galápagos Climate** can be divided into a hot season (January to April), when there is a possibility of heavy showers, and the cool or *garúa* season (May to December), when the days generally are more cloudy and there is often rain or drizzle. Daytime clothing should be lightweight. (Clothing generally, even on "luxury cruises" should be casual and comfortable.) At night, however, particularly at sea and at higher altitudes, temperatures fall below 15°C and warm clothing is required. Boots and shoes soon wear out on the lava terrain. A good supply of sun block and skin cream to prevent windburn and chapped lips is essential. A hat is also recommended. Apart from Tortuga Bay, there are no beaches on Santa Cruz, but several on San Cristóbal.

**Information** The *Galápagos Guide* by Alan White and Bruce White Epler, with photographs by Charles Gilbert, is published in several languages; it can be bought in Guayaquil in Librería Científica and the airport, Libri Mundi (US$5) in Quito, or at the Charles Darwin station. *Galápagos, the Enchanted Isles*, by David Horwell **(see page 866)**. Highly rec. is *Galápagos: a Natural History Guide* by Michael H. Jackson (US$20 from Libri Mundi, Quito), used by all the guides. A must for birdwatchers is *Field Guide to the Birds of the Galápagos* (US$20). A map of the Galápagos, drawn by Kevin Healey and illustrated by Hilary Bradt, is published by Bradt Enterprises (who also sell a range of books on subjects related to the islands—41 Nortoft Road, Chalfont St. Peter, Bucks SL9 0LA, England, T 02407-3478, Fax 734-509262). The National Park now publishes a good guide in English and Spanish, with plans of all the places where visitors are allowed to land: *Guide to the Visitor Sites of Parque Nacional Galápagos*, by Alan and Tui Moore, US$3.30. National Park Office, Puerto Ayora, Santa Cruz, Mon.-Fri. 0800-1200, 1400-1800, Sat. 0800-1000. For more information write to the Director of the Charles Darwin Research Station or the Superintendent of the Galápagos National Park Service, Isla Santa Cruz, Galápagos (correspondence in English.)

---

# INFORMATION FOR VISITORS

---

**Documents** Passport (valid for at least six months required on arrival at Quito airport), and a tourist card valid for 90 days (tourists are now allowed only 90 days in any 365-day period, i.e. you can not leave in December and return in January, you have to wait twelve months for another 90-day entitlement) obtainable on arrival. You are required to say how many days you intend to stay and the card will be stamped accordingly; most travellers are given 15 or 30-day stamps irrespective of their requests (at Huaquillas, Macará and Tulcán), and travellers arriving by air may be given a stamp valid for only 10 days (transit pass) unless they request otherwise. It is therefore better to overestimate as you can be fined on leaving the country for staying too long. An extension can be routinely obtained at the Department of Immigration in Quito or Guayaquil, or at the Gobernación offices of several provincial capitals (addresses in the text); make sure the extension is given an official stamp. Evidence of sufficient funds (see below) is sometimes required. A visa is required for French nationals (US$10), New Zealanders (US$7) and for business people and students who stay longer than 90 days (3 photos required), application to be made in home country, and they must get an exit permit with both tax and police clearance. It costs US$17 for renewing a visa after its expiry date.

The procedure for obtaining a student visa involves taking a letter from the school at which you will be studying to the Ecuadorean consulate, a letter from your bank and a ticket out of Ecuador (or South America), plus a fee of US$30 in cash (only dollars, wherever paid): it is illegal to study on a tourist visa.. There are many other essential procedures, for which at least 6 passport photos will be required (4 face, 2 profile). Holders of student visas do not have to pay the Cuoto de Compensación Militar on leaving, although business visa holders do. Verify all details at the Consulate before departure.

Tourists crossing from Colombia or Peru may be asked for evidence that they possess US$20 p.p. for each day they propose to spend in Ecuador. Theoretically you must have an onward ticket out of Ecuador, but this is almost never enforced if you are travelling overland. However, travellers arriving from Miami with Ecuatoriana have been refused entry without a ticket and an MCO may not be sufficient.

For a car or motorcycle a *carnet de passage* (*libreta de pasaje*, known locally as a *tríptico*) issued in the country which issued the tax plates is required; failing that a bond equal to the value of the car will be demanded and you will waste a week with paper work. If bringing in a motorcycle by air it can take over a week to get it out of customs, even with a *carnet de passage*. You need a customs agent, who can be found around the main customs building near the airport, fix the price in advance (about US$30 for two motorcycles in 1990). Best to accompany the agent all the time and a letter from the Club Automóvil del Ecuador can be helpful. Shipping in a vehicle through Guayaquil is also hazardous; you will be charged by customs for every day the car is left there and will need assistance from an agent. Spare cash may be needed for oiling the wheels. A police or customs agent will accompany you to the border if you do not have the right papers, and you will have to pay him about US$10 a day plus his accommodation and food. If you need boxes/cartons to send bicycles home, Global Transportes, Veintimilla 878 y Av., Amazonas, 3rd floor, might be able to help you (German-run).

**Warning**  Always carry your passport with you, or a photocopy with the immigration visa date, except when travelling in the Oriente or border areas when the real thing is required.

**Air Taxes**  There is a 10% tax on international air tickets for flights originating in Ecuador, regardless of where bought, and 12% on domestic tickets, and a tax of US$25, payable only in dollars, on all passengers departing on international flights.

**How to Get There By Air**  Air France flies weekly from Paris to Quito. Iberia flies from Madrid to Quito via San Juan, Puerto Rico, and Bogotá, twice weekly. KLM flies weekly from Amsterdam to Guayaquil via Curaçao and Quito. Lufthansa flies from Frankfurt twice weekly via Bogotá. Viasa flies from Caracas with connecting flights to several European destinations.

There are flights from New York with Ecuatoriana, the national company, which also flies from Chicago, Miami and Los Angeles. Saeta also flies from Miami, rec., its slogan is that every passenger flies first class.

Ecuatoriana flies from the following Latin American destinations: Buenos Aires (Quito and Guayaquil—also Aerolíneas Argentinas, Guayaquil only), Bogotá, (also Avianca, Iberia and Lufthansa to Quito; Aerolíneas Argentinas and Ladeco to Guayaquil), Caracas, Lima (Quito and Guayaquil), Mexico City, Panama, Santiago de Chile (Quito and Guayaquil—also Ladeco from the latter). AeroPerú has an overnight flight from Miami to Guayaquil; the plane goes on to Buenos Aires via Lima and Santiago. From Brazil weekly Varig flights to Guayaquil and Quito from Rio and São Paulo. There are no direct flights from Paraguay, Bolivia, or Uruguay. Varig/Ecuatoriana/Lacsa (using Varig aircraft) fly from San José, Costa Rica. Connections with other Central American capitals in Panama City. Avianca flight Panama City—Quito via Bogotá pays for overnight accommodation in *Hotel Bacatá*, Bogotá and transport to/from airport. For all international connecting flights into/out of Ecuador, consult the monthly *Transport Junior* booklet, 150 sucres.

**Customs** Personal effects, a litre of spirits and a reasonable amount of perfume are admitted free of duty. No foreign cigarettes are allowed to be brought into Ecuador.

**Internal Air Travel** The local airlines Saeta, SAN and TAME operate internal flights between the main cities. TAME and SAN fly to the Galápagos; both have received favourable reports on reliability and baggage control. Also local airline Cedta operating Santa Rosa, near Machala-Guayaquil. Ecuavia operates charter flights. There are air taxis (Cessnas or Bonanzas) to anywhere you want to go to, also helicopters. On internal flights passengers may have to disembark at intermediate stops and check in, even though they have booked all the way to the final destination of the plane. Seats are not assigned on internal flights.

**Railway Travel** The railways are not too comfortable or reliable. The total track length is 1,043 km., but the system is not yet completely restored following the 1983 floods. The Quito-Riobamba, Guayaquil-Alausí, Sibambe-Cuenca and Ibarra-San Lorenzo stretches are in operation for passengers.

**Road Travel** Bus travel has improved greatly and is generally more convenient, and cheaper, than in other Andean countries. Since most buses are small they fill up and leave at frequent intervals. Half the 17,700 km. of road are open the year round. The length of paved highway is developing rapidly, including Quito-Guayaquil, Quito-Riobamba, Quito-Tulcán, Guayaquil-Cuenca, Guayaquil-Riobamba, Riobamba-Baños and the lowland (Costa) road Huaquillas-Machala-Guayaquil-Babahoyo-Santo Domingo-Esmeraldas. When touring by car, beware the bus drivers, who often drive very fast and rather recklessly (passengers also please note).

**Car Rental** Cars are available at US$25-35 per day, but there is a minimum three-day rental period. Impossible to hire with unlimited mileage, but on extended rentals you may receive a limited amount free (e.g. 500-1,000 km., with US$0.10 and up per additional km.). Insurance is US$5, and tax is 6 per cent on the total transaction. Four-wheel drive vehicles cost US$50-70 a day, less for longer hire, plus 1,500 km. free mileage. Some car hire firms do not have adequate insurance policies and you will have to pay heavily in the event of an accident. Be sure to check the car's condition, not forgetting things like wheelnuts. Also make sure it has good ground clearance. Beware of large potholes and crevices in any road. Always carry your passport and driving licence; there are police checks on all the roads leading out of main towns and you can be in serious trouble if you are unable to present your documents. The lack of road signs can be a nuisance. Gasoline costs US$0.50 per US gallon for 80 octane and US$0.60 for 92 octane (only in the main cities). Gasoline shortages are common, so fill up where you can. Diesel costs US$0.42 per gallon.

The Instituto Geográfico Militar, on top of the hill at the E end of El Ejido Park, Quito (**see page 787**), produces a 1:1,000,000 map of Ecuador which is quite good, but large. A comprehensive road map (1989 edition) is also available as well as various other maps, US$0.50-$0.80 apiece. There are also road maps issued as a small booklet (US$2) with 26 partial maps published by Nelson Gómez, Editorial Camino.

**Hitch-hiking** on the main roads is reported to be easy in the north, but nearly impossible south of Riobamba, and it can be very cold in the mountains in the back of a truck (when hitching, it is common to pay a small sum). In the arid S the unpaved roads are dusty; use a wet cotton handkerchief to filter the air you breathe. Whether hitching or driving always take plenty of drinking water.

**Walking** Walkers are advised to get *Climbing and Hiking in Ecuador* (see next para.).

**Climbing** can be arranged through climbing clubs in Quito and other cities, or those associated with universities. Recommended guides to climbing: *Climbing and Hiking in Ecuador*, by Rob Rachowiecki and Betsy Wagenhauser (published by Bradt Enterprises) and *The Fool's Mountaineering for Ecuador and Peru* (from the South American Explorers' Club in Quito or Lima, US$3.50). Edward Whymper's, *Travels among the Great Andes of the Equator* (published by Gibbs M. Smith, Salt Lake City) is available from Libri Mundi. The quality of hired equipment needs scrutiny (see Quito section).

**Accommodation** outside the main towns; almost standard prices are charged of US$1.50-2 p.p. (without bath) in a *pensión, residencial*, or hotel (where this is the minimum charge). One can bargain at cheaper *pensiones* and *residenciales*. Outside the provincial capitals and the resorts of Salinas and Playas, there are few higher-class hotels. Service of 10% and tax of 10% are added to 1st and 2nd class hotel and restaurant bills. The cheaper hotels charge at most 5%, generally. Hotel owners tend to try and let their less attractive rooms first, but they are not insulted if you ask for a bigger room, better beds or a quieter area. The difference is often marked.

**Camping** White gas, like US Coleman fuel, is not available. Campers should be sure that their stove will either burn Camping Gaz, a compressed gas which comes in a non-refillable cylinder, kerosene, or regular car gas/petrol. For stoves, kerosene is known as "kerex" and is available in outdoor markets in towns and cities outside Quito. Pure alcohol fuel is sold in hardware stores. **See also page 778.**

**Food** Well worth trying are *humitas tamales* made of sweet maize), *llapingachos* (fried mashed potatoes with cheese), and *locro* (a soup of stewed potatoes and cheese topped with an avocado), served, with a beer, at bars. Local food is usually unspiced, though you may add *ají* (red pepper) sauce to make it (very) hot. *Tamales de moracho* (not unlike Venezuelan *hallaca*) and *empanadas de moracho* are delicious (same insides, breadcrust outside); *fanesca*, a kind of fish soup with beans, meat, and more, sold in Easter Week, is filling and rich. A typical food (but a matter of taste) is roast *cuy* (guinea pig). Hamburger meat is not always safe in Ecuador. *Cacho*, a croissant-like pastry, is cheap and filling. If economizing ask for the set meal in restaurants, *almuerzo* at lunchtime, *merienda* in the evening—very cheap; it costs between US$1 and US$2. *Ceviche*, marinated fish or shrimp is usually served with popcorn and roasted maize, delicious when safe. There are interesting *encocada* (coconut) dishes on the coast. The fruits are magnificent:

try *mamei colorado*, a fruit of the avocado family. A good sweet is *quimbolito*, a sweet sponge pudding made with maize flour. *Ponche* is a drink of hot milk, egg and cinnamon, a bit like unsweetened egg custard. Chocolate lovers can try the *Superior* and *Rico* bars, good quality, excellent value.

**Drink** The local wines, often made from bananas, are safe but sickly, and cannot be recommended. Argentine and Chilean wines are cheaper than European or US ones. The best fruit drinks are *naranjilla*, *taxo* and *mora* (blackberries), but note that fruit juices are often made with unboiled water. Main beers available are Pilsener and Club. International drinks, when they can be had, are costly. Good *pisco*, *aguardiente* (Cristal is recommended), *paico* and *trago de caña*. The usual soft drinks, known as *colas*, are available. Instant coffee or liquid concentrate is common, so ask for *café puro* if you want real coffee.

**Tipping** Hotels and restaurants, 10% usually in the bill (in cheaper restaurants, tipping is uncommon—but obviously welcome!). Taxi, nil. Airport and railway porters, US$0.08-0.20, according to number of suitcases; cloakroom attendants, US$0.04, hairdressers, 20%.

**Security** Although Ecuador is generally one of the safer countries in the region, there have been reports of increased problems as a side effect of the drug situation in Colombia: police searches are now more frequent. If your luggage is searched, make sure that you are present during the search: women travelling alone, especially in Otavalo, should beware of police officers who ask to look at their passport and then insist on taking them to police station. Theft is becoming more common, although not on the scale of, say, Peru, and thieves work in gangs, particularly in old Quito, Guayaquil and along the beaches.

**Health** Amoebic dysentery is a danger. Visitors should drink mineral water (Güitig or Manantial), avoid uncooked vegetables or salads, and be inoculated against typhoid. Hepatitis (jaundice) is a very real risk and should be inoculated against with gamma globulin; see "Health Information" in front of book. Travellers in the Oriente and the Costa are advised to take anti-malaria tablets; chloroquinine and Fansidar (Falcidar) are both available in chemists/pharmacies without prescription. Mosquito netting is also useful, a good mosquito repellant essential (not a local one—they don't work). Also recommended is an anti-itch cream in the Oriente. Yellow-fever vaccination is recommended for travel into the Oriente. Cholera vaccination is not available. There are excellent hospitals both in Quito and Guayaquil. Climbers are warned to undergo a period of acclimatization before attempting to scale the volcanoes.

It has been reported that the free rabies vaccine given out in Ecuador is made from mouse brain and is said to be dangerous, if not fatal. Human diploid vaccine (the correct type) can be ordered from USA through the US Embassy, but it is expensive. You are recommended to get a rabies vaccination at home, in which case a booster-type injection is all that is needed if you are bitten (note that the initial vaccine is very costly).

**Women** Tampons are difficult to obtain, particularly outside major cities and very pricey when stocked.

**Children** Agua Linda is a good and safe bottled water for young children. Luggis are the best disposable nappies/diapers, other makes are useless.

**Clothing** Spring clothing for Quito (mornings and evenings are cold). In Guayaquil tropical or light-weight clothes. Laundering is excellent, but dry cleaning expensive.

The **best time for a visit** is from June to October, during the dry season, though September can sometimes be wet. The coastal area is extremely hot and wet from December to May.

**Information** for business travellers is given (1) in "Hints to Exporters: Ecuador", available from Department of Trade, Sanctuary Buildings, 16-20 Gt. Smith Street, London SW1P 3DB; (2) the Ecuadorean-American Association, Inc. (55 Liberty St., New York, NY 10005) issues monthly bulletins and a free sample copy may be requested. Telephone directories in Ecuador have "green pages" giving useful tourist information, sometimes in English. Business travellers may wish to consult the *Ecuadorean News Digest*, published by the Ecuadorean American Association, 150 Nassau St., New York, NY 10038.

**Public Holidays** New Year's Day; 6 January; Monday and Tuesday before Lent (Carnival); Holy Thursday; Good Friday; Holy Saturday; 1 May-Labour Day; 24 May-Battle of Pichincha; 24 July-Birthday of Bolívar; 10 August-Independence of Quito, Opening of Congress, 9 October-Independence of Guayaquil, 12 October-Discovery of America; 1 November-All Saints' Day; 2 November-All Souls' Day; 3 November-Independence of Cuenca; 6 December-Foundation of Quito; Christmas Day. At carnival, water throwing is increasing and becoming violent; tourists are good targets for buckets of water. In Baños they mix it with flour and/or ink; in Cuenca it is usually in balloons, *bombas*, but goes on from 1 Jan to end of Carnival; in Ambato water throwing is banned during Carnival but spraying shaving foam and throwing confetti is not. After 3 or 4 days you may run out of clothes.

**Local Time** is 5 hrs behind GMT (Galápagos, 6 hrs behind.)

**Currency** The sucre, divided into 100 centavos, is the unit of currency. Bank notes of the Banco Central de Ecuador are for 5, 10, 20, 50, 100, 500, 1,000 and 5,000 sucres; there are nickel coins of 50 sucres, 10 sucres, 5 sucres, one sucre, 50, 20 and 10 centavos (although centavos have dropped out of regular use now). The one sucre coin is also sometimes called an *ayora*.

There is no restriction on the amount of foreign money or sucres you can take into or out of Ecuador. It is said to be easier to cash Bank Americard cheques than American Express cheques. It is very easy to change US$ cheques into US$ notes at the *cambios*; the commission varies so it is worth shopping around and *cambios* sometimes run out of US$ notes; you can try to bargain for a better rate than shown on the blackboard. Many *cambios* ask to see the receipt for travellers' cheques purchased abroad. US$100 notes may be difficult to change, many banks regard them with suspicion. Ecuador is the best place in South America to have money sent to. All major **credit cards** are widely accepted in banks and cambios, but note that although many hotels and restaurants have signs indicating acceptance of credit cards, this is often not the case; always check first. Note that difficulties have been reported with Amex cards, an alternative credit card may be more useful. It is quite difficult to change US$, whether cheques or bills, outside the main towns, especially in the Oriente.

**Weights and Measures** The metric system is generally used in foreign trade and must be used in legal documents. English measures are understood in the hardware and textile trades. Spanish measures are often used in the retail trade.

**Electric Current** 110 volts, 60 cycles, A.C. throughout Ecuador.

**Posts** Many post offices away from Quito may not know the foreign rates (10g air-mail to the Americas US$0.20, Europe about US$0.35) and give incorrect ones. For a small extra charge you can certify your letters and parcels; ask for "con certificado" when you buy stamps, so that they are stamped separately (US$0.12 extra). The only post office (probably in all Ecuador) which deals in International Reply Coupons is in Quito, at Eloy Alfaro y 9 de Octubre (new city). For sending parcels: up to 20 kg. maximum dimensions permitted is 70 X 30 X 30 cms. Take contents and packaging (unpacked) to the Correo Marítimo Aduana, Dávalos y Ulloa (next to the Santa Clara Market) (Mon.-Fri. 0800-1600) for customs inspection. Parcels can also be sent from the post office at Reina Victoria y Colón. The Post Office at the airport is more helpful and the smaller quantity of packages being handled should mean less chance of them going astray. Rates vary according to weight and destination. There is no surface mail service. Packages under 2 kg. can be sent "certificado" (US$2 per kg. to USA, US$15 up to 5 kg., US$27 up to 10 kg. to Europe) from the post offices at Benalcázar 769 and at Eloy Alfaro. Transpak (also called STAIR), Amazonas y Veintimilla, will ship out packages for about US$4 per kg. to USA, minimum charge about US$50. Letters for Europe bearing the correct postage can be dropped off at the Lufthansa office, 6 de Diciembre 955 y 18 de Setiembre, to be sent in the next international bag; by 1200 Mon. for Tues. flight, or by 1200 Fri. for Sat. flight. Packages coming in to Ecuador should be less than 2 kg. and of no stated value to avoid hefty import duty.

**N.B.** The postal service is reported to be highly unreliable, with frequent thefts and losses. Some correspondents report that parcels and letters sent "certificado" are more vulnerable to theft and that packages should be marked as "used clothing" and the value declared as

US$0.00. Even if not certifying your mail, watch to see that the stamps are franked (then they, at least, cannot be stolen). For cardboard boxes and large, strong, plastic-lined envelopes, try Japon Color Film Lab on Amazonas, Quito.

**Telecommunications** All the principal towns have long-distance telephone facilities.

Telephone call to Europe is US$17 for first 3 min and US$5 per min thereafter (there is no signal to indicate that your time is up). For international operator dial 116, normally only 5-20 minute wait for call to UK. There is an acute shortage of lines, expect long waits from outlying areas. All collect calls were suspended in February 1990. A charge is made for person-to-person calls even when the person is not there. Telegrams, ordinary US$4.30 first 7 words and US$0.57 per word thereafter, nightletter US$0.20 per word. There are public telex booths in the best hotels in Quito and Guayaquil (US$13.50 for 3 mins), and at Cuenca.

**Newspapers** The main newspapers are *El Comercio, Hoy, Tiempo,* and *Ultimas Noticias,* in Quito; *Expreso, El Telégrafo, El Universo* (with good international news), *La Prensa, La Razón* and *Extra* (an afternoon paper), in Guayaquil; *El Mercurio,* in Cuenca; *La Opinión del Sur,* in Loja; and *El Espectador,* in Riobamba. Newspapers cost more outside their town of publication, up to double the price in the Oriente.

**Sport** The Sierra country is excellent for riding, and good horses can be hired. Quito, Guayaquil and Riobamba have polo clubs. There are golf clubs at Guayaquil and Quito and on the Santa Elena Peninsula. There is excellent big-game fishing for bonito and marlin off Playas, Salinas and Manta. Bull fighting is rarely seen at Guayaquil, but there is a well-known bullfight festival on Dec. 6 at Quito. A favourite sport is cock fighting; every town has its pits, but association football is fast taking over as the national sport. Baseball, volleyball and basket-ball are also popular. There is Sunday horse-racing at Guayaquil.

**Wild Life** includes the jaguar, puma, tapir, several kinds of monkey, the armadillo, ant-bear, squirrel, porcupine, peccary, various kinds of deer, and many rodents, including the guinea pig. There are also tortoises, lizards and iguanas. Among the birds are condors, falcons, kites, macaws, owls, flamingoes, parrots, ibises, cranes, and storks. Unhappily, every type of insect is found in the coastal towns and the Oriente. The Galápagos Islands have their own selection of nearly tame wildlife.

**National Parks** All foreigners have to pay to enter each national park, the charge for the Galápagos is now US$40. There is no separate National Parks office, Parks fall under the Ministry of Agriculture (MAG). The MAG in Quito can provide some tourist information but it is best to contact the MAG office in the city nearest the Park you wish to visit, e.g. the Cuenca MAG office for El Cajas, Loja for Podocarpus, etc. **Fundación Natura,** Av. América 5653 y Voz Andes, Quito, T 447-343/4, 459-013, is a private charitable organization concerned with nature reserves. They have some limited tourist information, notably on Pasachoa, which they manage; there is a resource library and knowledgeable staff who can give technical information on parks and reserves.

**Indigenous Tribes** The Quechua, Shuar and Scoya Indians in Pastaza welcome tourists in a controlled way, in order to sell their beautiful products; some work as guides. Contact the Organización de Indígenos de Pastaza (OPIP) in Puyo, T 885-461, they can also give you a list of indigenous museums and artesan workshops. CONFENIAE, the confederation of Amazon Indians is another good contact at Km. 5 outside Puyo, T 885-343, or at their office in Quito, Av. 6 de Diciembre 159 y Pazmino, T 543-973. Care is required when visiting the Oriente and taking tours to Waorani villages without prior arrangement, the Waorani are at great risk from the tourist invasion and do not appreciate being treated as a spectacle.

We are most grateful to Sarah Cameron for updating this chapter. We should also particularly like to thank Betsy Wagenhauser and Soairse McClory of the South American Explorers Club, Quito, for the information they provided; Hallam, Carole and Quinton Murray for help on Cuenca and the Pacific coast; and David Horwell for material on the Galápagos; also the following residents and travellers: Christian and Gaby Albers-Wetzl (Baños, Ecuador), John Allen (London SW14), Ralph Arnold (Vegreville, Canada), Arno Michael Auer (Ottobrunn), Steven Avgort and Carol Seger (California), Hubert Baierl (Neusaess, Germany), Frank Bakker and Nike Darley (Amsterdam), Jamie Banford, Marlise Baumgarter and Niklaus Graber (Erlach, Switzerland), Claudia Beinhardt (Deisenhofen), Allen Belkin and Debra Riklan (Yonkers, NY), Petra Bell and Hans-Georg Henle (Schwaigern, Germany), Ortun Bettering (Rio de Janeiro), Riemer De Boer (Netherlands) Andreas Böttner and Annette Drinkuth (Otterstedt, Germany), Klaus Brandl (Rio de Janeiro, Brazil), David Brigden (U.K.), Jean Brown (Galapagos, Ecuador), Nelly and Steve Caplan (Winnipeg, Canada), Lydia Carter (Canada) and Urs Hafeli (Switzerland), Paul Carter (Hamilton, New Zealand) and Vivienne Mitchell (Coleraine, N.

Ireland), Christine (Baños, Ecuador), Tim Cobb (Dorking) and Caroline Wren (Conisbrough), Alysia Cook and Phil Waterhouse (Twyford, Berks), Andrew Craig (Arlington, East Sussex), Geert Crompholt (Belgium) Alastair and Ann Cuthbert (Broome, W. Australia), Stewart Dallos (Fremantle, W. Australia), E. Dalla Vecchia (Malo, Italy), Dr. L. Delgado (Teddington, Middlesex), Hans van Dijk (Hilversum), Gavin Dispain (Adelaide), Carolyn Dougall and Howard Johnson (Edinburgh), Jacquie Dowie (North Adelaide), Nelle Driessen (Maastricht, Netherlands), Barbara Egli (Volketswil, Switz.), Kirsten Eichhorn (München, Germany), Richard Everson and Jo Penty (West Wickham, Kent), Rüdiger Filbrich (Frankfurt/Main), Diane E. Floyd (Sale, Wiltshire), Derek Gatherer (Glasgow), Paul Geerits (Gent, Belgium), Yves Genier (Louay, Switzerland), Col. and Mrs. Richard George (Macon, GA), Theodor A. Gevert (São Paulo), Michael Gilliland (Eire) and David Weaver (U.K.), Steve Gilman (Norcross Georgia), Peter Glatte and Simone Wolschinkski (Walhorn, Belgium), Doris Goll (Gossau) and Andy Stocker (Buchrain, Switz.), Michael S. Gonin (Canberra), Andrew Grassie and Sara Gilbert (Lewes), David Graves (Brooklyn, N.Y.), Thomas Gray (Houston), Pilou Grenié (Antibes), Michael Günther (Albstadt, Germany), Kurt Gyger and Regula Geser (Mollis, Switzerland), Sandy Hain (Palo Alto, CA), Eric Hamovitch (Montréal, Canada), Mark Hancock and Veronica Egan (Ross-on-Wye, Herefordshire) for much useful new material, Clare Hargreaves (London), Ulrich Harlan (Berlin), Johanne Harvey and Niklaus Hutmacher (Gysenstein, Switzerland), Martin Hautkappe (München, Germany), Mike and Sallypahn Hawkins (Bangkok), Peter Hazdra (Vienna), Daniela Heblik (Hüttenberg, Germany), Ian Henderson (London SW16), Ulrich Herbert (Stuttgart), Jorn Herner (Denmark), Gert Jan Hof and Yvonne Evers (Huissen, Neth), Cathy and Chris Holman (Sale, Cheshire), Sabine Imhoff (Germany), Brigitte Juetz (Oberrieden, Switzerland), A. P. Kirk (Middlesbrough), Dr. Eberhard Klinge (Quito), Ursula Kohlendorfer (Gunskirchen, Austria), Tom Krasner (Miami Beach, Florida), Andy Kuendig and Rosi Nueesch (Zuerich), Andreas Kühn (Germany), Christina Kusoffsky (Stockholm, Sweden), Olivier Lair (Paris), Henrik K. Larsen (V. Skerninge) and Mai Britt Noerskvu (Svendberg, Denmark), Peter Lawlor (Armidale, NSW), John Lewis (London NW2), Ileike Liebers (Berlin), Waltraud Linke (Berlin 12), Judith Locher (Switzerland), Hans and Cristine Lomosse (Ludvika, Sweden), Markus Maier and Gitte Wiedmann (Zürich), Daniel J. Marinello (Cotati, C.A.), Susan Marfield (Long Beach, California), Julianne McCabe, Maggie Widow, Jean O'Leary and Bill Shaffer (San Anselmo, C.A.), T. W. Meeson (London W4), Mariann Metzer and Andrea Stark (Germany), Patrick Meyer (Ammerschwihr, France), Alison Milner and Keith Doyle (Manchester), Kari Lvendahl Mogstad and Trond Eri (Norway), David Moodie (Adelaide), Matthias Müller (Berlin 31), Monica Napper (Eastbourne, UK), Lars Nelson and Gerd Schütze (Iserlohn and Neuss, Germany), Steve Newman and Wendy Chilcott (Horsham, West Sussex), Helmut Niedertscheider (Moerfelden, Germany), Asbjørn Nielsen (Denmark) Peter Opdemom (Rheurdt), Vital Pajarola and Eva Grunder (Zurich), Tim Pearson (Fort Collins, Colorado), Fiorenzo Peloso (Landquart, Switzerland), Rik Pennartz (Guayaquil, Ecuador), Shauna Picard and Grant Findlay (Melbourne, Australia), Thomas Pichler (Berlin 65), David F. Pinder (Sale, Cheshire), Dave Polei (UK), John Pomfret (Woking, Surrey), Suzanne Popp (Ragensburg, Germany), Anna Price (London N10), Sarah Price (Great Britain), J.R. Wright (Switzerland), R. de Boer (Holland) and Fiona McNeaney (England), Maria and Harvey Reeder (Northridge, CA, U.S.A.), Jamie Rein (Boston, Mass), Wendy Richardson (London SW19), Carol Sue Richardson (San Francisco), Hilda Riedler (Ismaning, Germany), Bryan and Charmaine Roche (Cape Town), Ann Rodzai and Doug Hanaver (Ithaca, NY), Alex Rossi (Norwich, Norfolk), Dä Roz Us Kölle Alison Sanders and Errol Robathan (Tonbridge, Kent), Nick Saunders and Sarah Jaggs (London W1), Isabel Saxer (Schlieren, Switzerland), Thomas Schalk (Osnabrüch, Germany), Martin Schafer (Aarau, Switzerland), Jelle Scharringa and Linda Schrijver (Utrecht, Netherlands), Thomas Schalk (Osnabrück, Germany), Bianca Schmid (Wien, Austria), D. Schöttler (Lennestadt), Sonja Schubert (Landshut, Germany), Florian Schulz (Berlin), Roland and Brigitte Schwarz-Aaschbacher (Rüderswil, Switz), Michael Scott-Watson (Roxburghshire, Scotland), Martina Seefeld (Schwäbisch Gmünd), Diana Seiler (Berlin), John Shearer and Stephanie Toohey (NSW, Australia), James Siever (Wiesbaden, Germany), M. Skol (Fort Lauderdale, Florida), Maria Anna Stadler (München, Germany), Barbara Stettler (Bolligen, Switzerland), Rue Swabey (Chobham, Surrey), Christoph Theis (Wiesloch, Germany), Åse Totland and Jarle Unneland (Ålesund, Norway), Ian Trontz (Brooklyn, NY), Dirk Vandersypen (Managua), Mark Van Den Boer (Tilberg, Netherlands), E.A.N. Vauderkuip-Zilvold (Cuenca), Levy Venanzius (Disla, Switzerland), Ric Verwer (Santa Barbara, C.A.), Béatrice Völkle (Gampelen, Switz.), H.M. Wams (Amsterdam), Joanna Watts and Shaun Pinchbeck (Bath), Manuela Wonisch (Kloten, Switzerland), Peter Woods and Wendy Thompson (Christchurch, New Zealand), S. Wyatt (Vilcabamba), Helmut Zettl (Ebergassing, Austria), Carlos Zorrilla (Otavalo), and Bart Zwart (Eindhoven, Netherlands).

# PARAGUAY

## INTRODUCTION

PARAGUAY is entirely landlocked, encircled by Argentina, Bolivia and Brazil. Its total land area is put at 406,752 square km., cleft into two quite distinct parts by the great Río Paraguay. It has over 4.0 million people (roughly 41% living in towns). It has not as yet fully developed its potential, partly because it was deeply involved in two out of the three major wars staged in Latin America since independence.

To the W of the Río Paraguay is the Chaco (246,950 square km., nearly 61% of the country's area), a sparsely inhabited tract of flat and infertile country. E of the river is Paraguay proper (159,800 square km.), a rich land in which almost all the population is concentrated. Paraguay proper is itself divided into two contrasting areas by a high cliffed formation which runs almost due N from the Río Alto Paraná, W of Encarnación, to the Brazilian border. E of this cliff lies the Paraná plateau; W of it, as far as the Río Paraguay, lie gently rolling hills and flat plains.

Paraguay's southern boundary with Argentina from the confluence of the Río Paraguay to that of the Río Iguazú is the Alto Paraná. From the Iguazú falls, the Lago Itaipú and the Alto Paraná form the eastern border with Brazil; from Guaíra falls (now flooded) the northern boundary with Brazil runs north-westwards across the land mass to the confluence of the Apa and Paraguay rivers. From Resistencia as far N as Asunción the Río Paraguay is the western boundary with Argentina. From Asunción as far N as the confluence with the Apa, the river divides Paraguay into two. For some distance N of the entry of the Apa, the Río Paraguay is the Chaco's eastern boundary with Brazil. The S border of the Chaco with Argentina is along the Río Pilcomayo; its W and N borders are with Bolivia.

**The Paraná Plateau**, ranging from 300 to 600 metres in height, has comparatively heavy falls of rain and was originally forest. Across the plateau, much of which is in Argentina and Brazil, runs the Río Paraná. West of the high cliff which forms the western edge of the plateau lies a fertile plain stretching to the Río Paraguay. This plain is diversified by rolling, wooded hills. Most of Paraguay's population is concentrated in these hilly lands, stretching SE from Asunción to Encarnación.

Much of the flat plain is flooded once a year; it is wet savanna, treeless, but

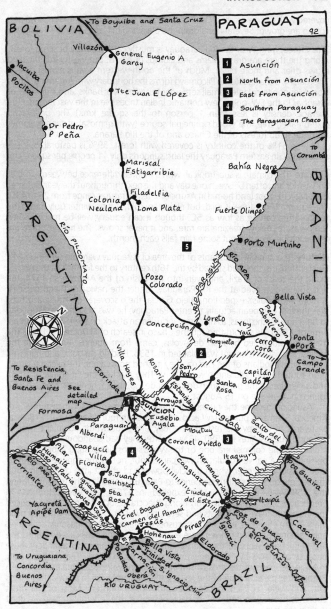

BOLIVIA — To Boyuibe and Santa Cruz — PARAGUAY
92

Villazón
General Eugenio A Garay

| | |
|---|---|
| **1** | Asunción |
| **2** | North from Asunción |
| **3** | East from Asunción |
| **4** | Southern Paraguay |
| **5** | The Paraguayan Chaco |

Yacuiba
Pocitos
Tte Juan E López
Dr Pedro P Peña
To Corumbá
Mariscal Estigarribia
Bahía Negra
Filadelfia
Colonia Neuland
Loma Plata
Fuerte Olimpo
ARGENTINA
Río Pilcomayo
BRAZIL
**5**
Porto Murtinho
Río APA
Pozo Colorado
Río PARAGUAY
Bella Vista
Concepción
Loreto
Pedro Juan Caballero
Yby Yaú
Horqueta
Cerro Corá
Ponta Porã
To Campo Grande
Villa Hayes
**2**
Rosario
San Pedro
capitán Badó
To Resistencia, Santa Fe and Buenos Aires
Clorinda
see detailed map
San Estanislao
Santa Rosa
Arroyos
ASUNCIÓN
**1**
Eusebio Ayala
Curuguaty
Formosa
Paraguarí
Mbutuy
Salto del Guairá
Alberdi
Caapucú
Villa Florida
Coronel Oviedo
**3**
Pilar
Humaitá
Paso de Patria
S.Juan Bautista
Caaguazú
Hernandarias
Itaquyry
To Guairá
Río PARANÁ
Corrientes
S Ignacio Guazú
Sta Rosa
Caazapá
Ciudad del Este
Itaipú
Yacyretá-Apipé Dam
Ayolas
San Cosme
Cnel Bogado
Carmen del Paraná
Jesús
Pirapó
Foz do Iguaçu
Río Iguazú
ARGENTINA
Hohenau
Bella Vista
Cascavel
To Uruguaiana, Concordia, Buenos Aires
Posadas
Encarnación
Trinidad
S.Ignacio Miní
Eldorado
Obera
RÍO URUGUAY
BRAZIL

covered with coarse grasses. On this plain, rice, sugar, tobacco, grains, soya and cotton are grown. Several rivers drain the plain and hill lands into the Paraguay.

**The Chaco**, lying W of the Río Paraguay is mostly cattle country or scrub forest. Along the there are grassy plains and clumps of palms, but westwards the land grows drier and more bleak. Much of the north-western area is almost desert. The marshy, unnavigable Río Pilcomayo forms the boundary with Argentina. Apart from Mennonite colonies, small settlements on the river banks, and a number of *estancias* in the SW, only a few nomadic Indian tribes live in the vast region. (The average density is less than 1 person to the square km..) The *quebracho* (axe-breaker) tree, the world's principal source (with mimosa) of tannin, comes from the scrub forests of the Chaco and of the Río Paraná.

Some 51% of the country is covered with forest, 39% is pastoral, 5.4% is agricultural. In eastern Paraguay the land supports only 11 people per square km.

**Climate** The climate is sub-tropical, with a marked difference between summer and winter and often between one day and the next throughout the year. Summer (Jan.-March) is hot (and humid in Asunción). Temperatures range from 25 to 43C. The autumn (April-June) is mild, but nights are cold. During winter (July-Sept.) the temperature can be as low as 5C, though it can equally well be much higher. Temperatures below freezing are rare, and it never snows. The heaviest rains are from October to April, but some rain falls each month.

**History** The original inhabitants of the area of Paraguay were the semi-nomadic Guaraní Indians; they had spread by the 16th century to the foothills of the Andes, along the coast of Brazil, and even into the basin of the Amazon. In 1524, the first Spaniards arrived at the Río Paraguay, under the navigator Diego de Solís. A member of Solís's expedition, Alejo García, the discoverer of the Iguazú falls, was the first European actually to enter Paraguay; he was also the first European to fight against the Incas, as his career included an attack on them with a Guaraní army of 2,000. He set out through the Chaco in search of El Dorado in 1525. The main expedition, led by Juan de Ayolas, came from Buenos Aires, where the earliest Spanish settlement was planted in 1536. Finding no gold, and harassed by the hostile Indians of the Pampa, they pushed north along the river, seeking a short route to the gold and silver of Peru. They reached the Guaraníes in 1537 and a member of the party, Juan de Salazar de Espinosa, is generally credited with founding Asunción on 15 August.

Asunción became the nucleus of Spanish settlement in southeastern South America. Spaniards pushed NW across the Chaco to found Santa Cruz, in Bolivia, eastwards to occupy the rest of Paraguay, and southwards down the river to re-found Buenos Aires in 1580, 43 years after they had abandoned it.

During the colonial era one of the world's most interesting experiments in dealing with a native population was carried out, not by the conquerors, but by their missionaries, over whom the civil power had at first little control. In 1609 the Society of Jesus sent missionaries to Paraguay to civilize the Indians. During the 158 years until they were expelled in 1767, the Jesuits formed 30 "reductions", or settlements, run along theocratic-socialist lines. They induced the Indians to leave the forests and settle in townships, where they helped build magnificent churches, employing unsuspected native skills in masonry, sculpture, and painting. Selected natives were even given a sound classical education. The first reductions were further north, but they were forced to abandon these because of attacks by the *bandeirantes* of São Paulo, Brazil. They settled finally in Misiones; parts of the area of settlement are now in Argentina and southern Brazil. After the expulsion of the Jesuits, the reductions fell to pieces: the Indians left, and were reduced to peonage under other masters. Most of the great churches have fallen into ruin, or been destroyed; the few that remain are dealt with in the text.

Paraguay got its independence from Spain, without bloodshed, on 14 May, 1811. Gaspar Rodríguez de Francia, known as "El Supremo", took power in 1814 and held it until 1840. His policy of complete isolation was a response to the landlocking of Paraguay by the *porteños* of Buenos Aires who wished to annex it: no one might leave the country, no one might enter it, and external trade was not permitted, but Paraguay achieved a high level of self-sufficiency. Rodríguez de Francia was followed as president by Carlos Antonio López, who ruled until his death in 1862. He reversed Rodríguez de Francia's policy of isolation and in 1854 began the building of the Central Paraguayan Railway from Asunción to Encarnación. He was followed by his son, Mariscal Francisco Solano López, who saw himself as the Napoleon of South America and is today the most venerated of Paraguay's heroes. His Irish mistress Madame Eliza Lynch, who encouraged him in his ambitions, is also held in high esteem. In 1865 he became involved in the war of the Triple Alliance against Brazil, Argentina and Uruguay. His motive was that Uruguay, with whom Paraguay had a treaty of reciprocal help, had been occupied by Brazil and Argentina and forced to oppose Paraguay. The war was disastrous for the Paraguayans, who held out against overwhelming odds until Mariscal López was killed at Cerro Corá in 1870, when the war ended. Out of a population of 800,000, only 194,000 were left alive after the war, and of these only 14,000 were male (only 2,100 of whom were over 20); out of 400,000 females at the beginning of the war, 180,000 survived. Paraguay was occupied for eight years during which time it was deprived of all its gold reserves, many national treasures and 156,415 square km. of territory. (Brazil took 62,325 square km., Argentina 94,090 square km.; previously Paraguayan were the Iguazú falls and the town of Posadas, once called San José del Paraguay.) (For further reading on the origin and aftermath of the War of the Triple Alliance, see *Paraguay: un destino geopolítico*, by Dra Julia Velilla Laconich de Aréllaga; *Genocídio Americano: a Guerra do Paraguai*, by Júlio José Chiavenalto; *Women on Horseback*, by William E. Barrett.) After 1870 a certain number of European immigrants arrived; their descendants are still influential in the social life of Paraguay. Various religious communities were among them; the Mennonites, mostly of German descent, who are largely responsible for the development of the Chaco, are the most notable.

The country's history since the "National Epic" of 1865-1870 has been the story of a recovery from disaster, but this process received a severe setback in the wars with Bolivia which broke out intermittently between 1929 and 1935 over the Chaco. The Paraguayans, fighting with their customary courage and tenacity, triumphed, and were given a large area of the Chaco in the final settlement. Bolivia was given an outlet, of little use, to the Río Paraguay.

After the Chaco War, Paraguay endured several years of political dictatorship, followed by disorder. This period was ended by the seizure of power in 1954 by General Alfredo Stroessner, soon appointed President. Thereafter he gained the support of the Colorado Party (founded in 1888), which was an integral part of his regime. He held power through repeated reelection until he was deposed in 1989 (surpassing El Supremo's 26-year tenure by 9 years) by General Andrés Rodríguez. On 1 May 1989, Gen. Rodríguez, also of the Colorado Party, won a presidential election unopposed, and he promised to hand over the presidency to an elected successor in 1993. The apparent commitment to greater democracy permitted opponents, who had previously boycotted, or been banned from elections, to gain an unprecedented number of seats in the legislative elections of the same date.

**The People of Paraguay** Because Spanish influence is smaller than elsewhere, the people of Paraguay today are bilingual, speaking both Spanish and Guaraní. Outside Asunción, most people speak Guaraní by preference. There is a Guaraní theatre, it is taught in private schools, and books and periodicals are published in that tongue, which has official status as the second national language. There are about 39,000 Indians left: two-thirds of them are in the Chaco, and one-third in the southern part of Paraguay proper.

Population: 4.28 m (1990 estimate). Annual growth: 3.2%; urban growth: 3.9%. Life expectancy at birth: 67 years. Infant mortality: 42 per thousand. Some 44% live in towns. 43% work on the land, 12% in industry. 25% of all Paraguayans live abroad.

**The Economy** Paraguay is essentially an agricultural country; farming employs 43% of the labour force, and accounts for 30% of gdp. Agricultural exports earn over 93% of Paraguay's foreign exchange with normally about 70% coming from cotton and soya. Cattle raising and meat exports used to be the principal agricultural activities, but their importance has declined as a result of uncompetitive pricing policies and import restrictions in potential markets. Fluctuations in the value of exports characterize the performance of Paraguay's main commodities, since they are so subject to the weather and world prices. Other major products are timber, tobacco, tung and other industrial oilseeds, essential oils (mainly petit grain) and *quebracho*. Self-sufficiency in wheat has been achieved since 1985, and the country now grows most of its basic food requirements.

Industry has traditionally been dependent upon agriculture: for instance, cotton ginning, sugar milling, textiles, meat packing, timber processing and extraction of *quebracho*, industrial and essential oils. The country industrialized fast in the 1970s and early 1980s, and manufacturing now accounts for 17% of gdp. On the back of hydroelectric development, Paraguay has its own cement industry and a steel plant opened in 1986. Both these, shipbuilding and the distillation of alcohol for fuel and other purposes, are state-owned. 12% of the workforce are employed in manufacturing, 7% in construction.

The massive hydroelectric scheme undertaken by Brazil and Paraguay at Itaipú on the Río Paraná is reported to be the largest of its kind in the world. Both the total cost, of about US$15.3bn, and the final capacity, of 12.6m kilowatts, are to be shared equally between the two countries. Paraguay's share substantially exceeds domestic requirements and the surplus energy is being sold to Brazil now that a high-tension line to São Paulo is in place. Paraguay is cooperating with Argentina on the construction of the Yacyretá-Apipé plant, also on the Paraná, with capacity of 2.7m kilowatts. A third Argentine-Paraguayan hydroelectric project, Corpus, has been postponed until the turn of the century at the earliest. Paraguay has its own hydroelectric facility at Acaray.

Until 1983, Paraguay managed to offset its current account and trade deficits with capital inflows for Itaipú. Since the completion of civil works, the overall balance of payments has fallen into deficit, with a consequent drain on international reserves. In 1986, the situation was exacerbated by the World Bank and the Inter-American Development Bank refusing to disburse loans until a more realistic exchange rate was adopted.

When General Stroessner was ousted at the beginning of 1989, the new administration moved quickly to introduce economic reforms, including freeing the exchange rate and lifting many controls. This had the effect of dramatically improving registered foreign trade flows; previously about half of all exports and imports were contraband. Dwindling reserves led to restructuring of Paraguay's debt to Brazil, its major creditor, and bilateral deals were expected with others, to spread out maturities on the estimated US$2.6 bn foreign debt.

**Government** There was a new Constitution in 1967. Executive power rests with the President, elected for five years. There is a two-chamber Congress (Senate 36 seats, Chamber of Deputies 72). Voting is secret and obligatory for all citizens over 18. Uniquely in Latin America, the Constitution permits the immediate reelection of the President.

**Communications** The only practicable water route is by the Paraná to the Plata estuary, and Buenos Aires is 1,450 km. from Asunción. So difficult is the river that communication with Buenos Aires was mainly by road before the railway to Asunción was opened in 1913. Most freight is now moved to Buenos Aires, or to Santos or Paranaguá in Brazil, by good paved roads, though river barges still ply along the Paraná. For major roads, **see page 890.**

There are only about 440 km. of railways: the standard-gauge, 370 km. public railway from Asunción to Encarnación, the 64 km. from San Salvador (on Asunción-Encarnación line) to Abaí and some small switching operations on former industrial lines.

**N.B.** After the fall of President Stroessner, it was understood that all references to his name throughout the country would be removed. Ciudad Presidente Stroessner has been officially renamed Ciudad del Este; the airport, too, has been given a new title, Silvio Pettirossi (named after a pioneer of flying in Paraguay).

**Music and Dance** The music of Paraguay is a curiosity. Although this is the only South American country the majority of whose population still speak the original native tongue, the music is totally European in origin. The 17th and 18th century Jesuits found the Guaraní people to be highly musical and when their missions were established, the natives were immediately and totally indoctrinated into European music, of which they became fine performers, albeit not composers or innovators. A good example is Cristóbal Pirioby (1764-94), who changed his name to José Antonio Ortiz and moved to Buenos Aires to perform. At his death he left a large collection of musical instruments and sheet music of works by Haydn, Boccherini, etc. After the disastrous War of the Triple Alliance there was an abandonment of things national and even the national anthem was composed by a Uruguayan. Although black slaves were introduced to the country, they became quickly absorbed and there is no trace of black influence in the music. Neither is there any Guaraní element, nor infusion from Brazil or Argentina. Virtually the only popular instuments are the guitar and harp and it is the latter in particular that has come to be the hallmark of all that is musically Paraguayan, with the assistance of such brilliant performers as Félix Pérez Cardoso and Digno García. Paraguayan songs are notably languid and extemely sentimental and the present repertoire is not "traditional", but of 20th century origin and by known composers. Of the three principal musical genres, two are slow and for singing, while one is lively and purely for dancing. The two singing genres are the Canción Paraguaya (or Purajhéi) and the Guarania, the former being a slow polka, of which the earliest and most famous example is "Campamento Cerro León" about the War of the Triple Alliance. The Guarania was developed by José Asunción Flores as recently as the 1920s and includes most of the country's best loved and oft-repeated songs, such as "India", "Mi Dicha Lejana" and "Recuerdos de Ypacaraí". Equally celebrated and far more vigorous is that favourite of harp virtuosos, the wordless but onomatopeic "Pájaro Campana".

For dancing there are the lively Polca Paraguaya and Polca Galopada, first mentioned in print in 1858. It has similarities with the Argentine "Gato" for instance and is not a true polka nor a gallop, the names of these popular European dances having been attached to an existing Paraguayan dance of unknown name. The Polca is a dance for couples, whilst the even livelier Galopa is usually danced by groups of women, the so-called "Galoperas", who swing round barefoot, balancing a bottle or jar on their heads. This in turn has developed into the "Danza de la Botella" or bottle dance, a more recent variant for virtuoso individual performance. Other less well known dances are the Valseadas (a local variant of the waltz), the Chopi or Santa Fé (for three couples), the Taguato, Golondrina, Palomita and Solito, the last named a kind of "musical chairs".

Paraguayan music first came to the attention of the outside world soon after the second world war and a number of artists such as Luis Alberto del Paraná and Los Paraguayos have achieved world fame. At the other end of the spectrum the four barefoot old men of the Banda Peteke Peteke from Guajayvity near Yaguarón play their own traditional music on two *mimby* flutes and two little drums, a small idiosyncratic island in an ocean of harp music.

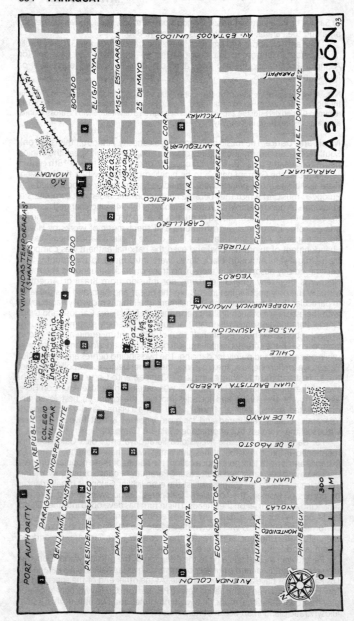

ASUNCIÓN

## ASUNCION (1)

*Asunción*, the capital and largest city in Paraguay, is built on the shores of a bay cutting into the eastern bank of the Río Paraguay, almost opposite its confluence with the Pilcomayo. Its population is around 1 million. The city, built on a low hill crowned by the large modern church of La Encarnación, is laid out in the colonial Spanish rectangular manner; many avenues are lined with beautiful trees, including orange, rubber and jacaranda. The central plazas of the city are drenched in colour during July-August with the prolific pink bloom of the *lapacho* trees, which grow everywhere. The oldest part is down by the water's edge, but none of the public buildings is earlier than the last half of the 19th century. Dwelling houses are in a variety of styles; new villas in every kind of taste have replaced the traditional one-storey Spanish-Moorish type of house, except in the poorer quarters.

You see most public buildings by following Calle El Paraguayo Independiente from the Aduana (Customs House). The first is the Palacio de Gobierno, built during the Triple Alliance War in the style of the Louvre (easy to walk around and take photographs now). In Plaza Constitución stands the Congreso Nacional (debates can be attended during the session from April to December, on Thursdays and sometimes Fridays), with the Cathedral at the corner of the square. Two blocks SW, along Calle Chile, is Plaza de los Héroes, with the Pantéon Nacional de los Héroes based on Les Invalides in Paris, begun during the Triple Alliance War and finished in 1937. It now contains the tombs of Carlos Antonio López, Mariscal Francisco Solano López, an unknown child-soldier, Mariscal Estigarribia, the victor of the Chaco War in the 1930s and other national heroes. The national cemetery, which resembles a miniature city, with tombs in various architectural styles, is on Av. Mariscal López, 3 km. from the centre.

The best of several parks are Parque Carlos Antonio López, set high and, if you can find a gap in the trees, with a grand view (doctor and sports supervisor in attendance); Parque Caballero; and Parque Gaspar Rodríguez de Francia. The Botanical Gardens are 6 km. out, on Av. Artigas with Primer Presidente at Trinidad, quickly reached by bus (Nos. 2, 6, 23, and 40, US$0.15, about 35 mins; outward they can be caught on Luis A. Herrera, or Nos. 24, 35 or 44B from Oliva or Cerro Corá). They lie along the Paraguay river, on the former estate of the López family, and have an enormous range of plants (poorly maintained), an eighteen-hole golf course, and a little zoo, which has inspired some unfavourable comments and protests. Entrance fee US$0.10, or US$0.60 for 2 persons and a car. The Gardens temporarily housed the Maca Indians when they were moved from their reservation across the river; they were moved again in 1985 to very poor conditions to the north of the Gardens (take bus 42 or 44, entrance US$0.15, guide US$0.80, the Indians expect you to photograph them, Us$0.25). The López residence is in the Gardens; a typical Paraguayan country house with verandahs, which has become a natural history museum and library. The beautiful white church of Santísima Trinidad (on Santísimo Sacramento, parallel to Av. Artigas), where Carlos Antonio López was originally buried, dating from 1856 with paintings inside, is well worth a visit.

---

### Asunción: Key to Map

1. Palacio de Gobierno; 2. Congreso Nacional; 3. Customs; 4. Cathedral; 5. Encarnación Church; 6. San Roque Church; 7. Pantéon Nacional de los Héroes; 8. Casa de la Independencia Museum; 9. Nacional Archive and Museo de Bellas Artes; 10. Railway station; 11. Tourist Office; 12. Post Office; 13. Centro Paraguayo del Diagnóstico; 14. British Embassy; 15. Lloyds Bank; 16. Citibank; 17. Finamérica; 18. American Express; 19. Deutsche Bank; 20. Casas de cambio; 21. Compañía Marítima; 22. Police Station; 23. *Hotel Chaco*; 24. *Hotel Guaraní*; 25. *Hotel Husa*; 26. *Hotel Plaza*; 27. *Hotel Presidente*; 28. *Hotel Lord*; 29. LAP.

**N.B.** Plaza de la Independencia is often referred to as Plaza Constitución, it should also be noted that Plaza de los Héroes is called Plaza Independencia on some sources. Av. España originally extended as far out as Av. San Martín, but the section between Av. Kubitschek and Av. Santísimo Sacramento was renamed Av. Generalísimo Franco (not to be confused with Presidente Franco) and the remaining section between Av. SS. Sacramento and Av. San Martín was renamed Av. General Genes. Many people still use the name Av. España for the whole of its original length, ignoring the renamings.

**Hotels** The hotel bill does not usually contain a service charge. It pays to tip when you arrive as well as when you go, say US$1 to the table waiter at both ends of a week's visit. Many hotels have electric showers.

**Outside Asunción:** 12 km. from town, at Itá Enramada, on its own beach on the Río Paraguay is *Hotel del Yacht y Golf Club Paraguay*, L, 3 restaurants, super luxury, with pool, gym, golf, tennis, airport transfers, etc.; many extras free. The *Hotel y Casino Itá Enramada*, 7 km. S of Asunción, A/B, with breakfast (rec.), free bus link with town, 7-hectare park, swimming pools, sauna, tennis, mini-golf, water-skiing on river, reservations through KLM, or Hugen Int, Fort Lauderdale, Fla (T 1-800-327-8571), fishing nearby, "Honeymooners get 20% off", T 33041/9.

**In Asunción:** *Excelsior*, L/A, Chile 980 between Manduvirá and Piribebuy, telex 5192, T 95632/5, best, new 175-room tower, another under construction, conference facilities, etc.; *Chaco*, Caballero y Mariscal Estigarribia, A with breakfast, parking one block away (but no garden), rooftop swimming pool, good restaurant, T 92066/9 (Fax 444223); *Cecilia*, rec., Estados Unidos 341, T 210033/034, A, very smart, good restaurant; *Guaraní*, Oliva e Independencia Nacional, T 91131/139, efficient, courteous, clean, A, good value, reasonable restaurant with good buffet; *Internacional*, Ayolas 520, T 94113, A, rec.; *Husa* (a Brazilian chain hotel), 15 de Agosto 420 y Estrella, B, 1st class, all rooms a/c, TV, swimming pool, restaurant, rec. cafeteria, bars, laundry service; *Presidente*, Azara 128, B, with breakfast and a/c, *Oliver's* restaurant rec., live music, entire hotel remodelled; *Gran Armele*, Av. Colón, B, with breakfast, a/c, T.V., clean, rec.; *Gran del Paraguay*, Residente y Padre Pucheu, B-C, in a park out of town, with swimming pool and a night club on Fridays, was the palace in which López lived, full of character; the recommended restaurant with floral murals, was the private theatre of Eliza Lynch; an air-conditioned annex has been built in the gardens, breakfast. *Touring 25*, 25 de Mayo 1091, C, small, modern, includes breakfast. *Paraná*, Caballero y 25 de Mayo, D with breakfast, central, secure, discounts negotiable, short-stays catered for too; *Sahara*, Oliva 920 nr. Montevideo, C with breakfast, a/c, good, small pool, interesting garden; *Gran Renacimiento*, Chile 388 y Estrella, central, B, a/c, friendly service, but poor value; *Señorial*, colonial style (Mcal. López 475 y Perú), C, with breakfast, a/c, swimming pool, parking, good restaurant, strongly rec.; *Azara*, Azara 850 (T 49754), E with bath and a/c, less with fan, recommended by Auto Club and travellers, most rooms face a shady patio and pool

*Residencial Ideal*, Azara 1549, E without breakfast, clean, quiet, very friendly; opposite is *Daniel*, F with bath, fan and breakfast; *Española*, Herrera y Yegros, D with bath, laundry, with meals, friendly, small rooms; *Ambassador*, Montevideo 111, F, with bath, very old, run down but friendly; *Lord*, Tacuary 576, E with bath (electric showers), meagre breakfast, Korean owner, going downhill and noisy; *Hispania*, Cerro Corá 265, F, Korean-run, watch bill carefully, friendly, recently refurbished, front rooms noisy; *Oro*, Caballero 521, E, friendly, rec; *Lago Ypoa*, Azara 1161, small, rec., F, used by Peace Corps volunteers; *Oasis*, Azara 736, E without bath or breakfast, friendly, Korean owned, pleasant, safe; *Ñandutí*, Presidente Franco 551, D with bath and breakfast, clean, comfortable, friendly; *Cardel*, Ygurey 1145 esq. Av. Dr. Eusebio Ayala, modern, clean, quiet, D, near Pettirossi market, excellent breakfast; *Casa Menonita*, República de Colombia 1050, E, friendly, German spoken, plain food (bus stop here for Filadelfia). Specially for German-speaking travellers: *Castillo*, Cruz del Chaco 959, D, German-owned, clean and friendly, T 605356.

*Ipiranga*, Av. México 489 with Cerro Corá, Korean-run, E, with bath, OK; *Miami*, México 449, T 444950, D with breakfast, clean; *Rosa*, 25 de Mayo 350, F with bath, clean, rec. although used for short stay, good book exchange; *Margarita*, Paraguarí y Azara, F without bath and breakfast, more with bath, clean, noisy, basic. *Residencial Milagros*, Nuestra Señora 1053, E with breakfast and bath, business travellers from neighbouring countries, good food opposite at *Bar Chaconi*; *Residencial Itapúa*, Calle Fulgencio R. Moreno 943, quiet, comfortable, decent breakfasts, lunch available. Two hotels at the railway station, one is *Plaza*, simple but acceptable, E, the other is not good. *India*, General Díaz near Av. Montevideo, F, clean and pleasant. *Residencial Familiar*, Eligio Ayala 843 near railway station, E, without breakfast, friendly, clean, will do washing. *Hospedaje El Sol*, Lapacho 185 (2 mins from bus station), Korean-run, E, good, but rooms very small; Family *pensiones* are expensive, in the D range.

**Camping**  The pleasant site at the Botanical Gardens now charges a fee, US$1.20 per car plus US$0.30 per person, US$0.60 p.p. plus tent, cold showers and 220v electricity, busy at weekends. If camping, take plenty of insect repellant and beware large (but harmless) toads. You can camp at rear of *Restaurant Westfalia*, T 31772, owner speaks English, French, German, very knowledgable, US$1 per night for car, cold showers, noisy, animals. Take Av. Moreno, towards Ciudad del Este, turn right after going under two bridges into General Santos. *Rest. Westfalia* is 3 km. on, 5 km. from Asunción.

**Restaurants**  Most closed Sunday. Average price of a good meal in quality restaurants, US$9-15. *La Preferida*, Estados Unidos and 25 de Mayo 1005 T 91126, rec. (part of *Hotel Cecilia*); *Talleyrand*, French, reported best in town, Estigarribia 932, T 41163; *La Pergola del Bolsi*, Estrella 389, good, wide choice of wines, good for breakfast; under same ownership and posher, *La Pergola Jardín*, Perú 240, very good food and service (US$12-13). *Le Grand Café*, Oliva 476, French-owned, good value set lunch. You can get a fantastic view of the city from the *Panorámico*, 14 de Mayo 150, 13th floor, expensive, but good; *Munich*, Eligio Ayala 163, good German food, excellent value; *Hostería del Caballito Blanco*, Alberdi 631, Austrian-run, good food and service; *San Marcos*, Alberdi y Oliva, friendly, good for snacks in Café, restaurant attached; *Di Trevi*, Palma 573, excellent; *San Roque*, Eligio Ayala esq. Tacuary, traditional, rec.; *Arche Noah*, Tacuary y 25 de Mayo, quite expensive but good; *Germania*, Cerro Corá 180, rec., reasonable prices; *Bayern-Stuben*, Av. Sucre 2689, excellent German (Bavarian); *Westfalia*, Bavarian style, see above under **Camping**.

*La Piccola Góndola* , Av. Mcal López y Juan de Motta, is very good for Italian (and other) food, so is *Buon Appetito*, 25 de Mayo near Av. Mcal. López y Juan Motta.*Da Vinci*, Estrella 695, rec.; *Pizzería Vecchio*, San Martín 535 y Bertoni, T 601053, good; *Antica Trattoria Alpina*, Sucre 1645 y San Martín, T 601254, English and Italian spoken.

*El Encuentro*, Azara 548, entre México y Paraguari, good food, value and service. Good cheap lunches (try puchero) at *Copetín El Oro*, Benjamín Constant 473, behind central post office.

*Asunción*, Estrella y 14 de Mayo (opp. Deutsche Bank), bar and restaurant very good, service a bit slow; Plenty of good, cheap places on Colón, 4D of Estrella. *Bistro*, part of *Hotel Husa* at 15 de Agosto y Estrella, good and reasonable; *Lucho*, Estados Unidos 564, good local food, cheap. *Rincón Chileno*, Estados Unidos 314, friendly, excellent empanadas; *Tío Toms*, quiche and pizza, Av Perú y Estigarribia; *El Molino*, España 382 near Brasil, good service and food (particularly steaks). *American Fried Chicken*, on Plaza de los Héroes (open Sunday). For good roast chicken try *Nick's Restaurant*, Azara 348 near Iturbe (open Sunday).

There are many good oriental restaurants including: *Celestial*, Herrera 919, highly rec.; *Sinorama*, Av. Próceres de Mayo 265; *Corea*, Perú y Francia, excellent; *Hoy*, Alberdi 642; *Hiroshima*, authentic Japanese , on Chóferes del Chaco; and others. Plenty of Korean places around Perú y Francia.

Vegetarian restaurants: *Dharma Shala*, Díaz 929, good; *Restaurant 2000*, Colón, good vegetarian food, Brazilian run; *Krunch*, Estrella 716, vegetarian lunches; *Wagner*, Presidente Franco 828, excellent bread and sweet shop; good icecreams next door. Various ice cream parlours and fast food outlets are to be found in Av. Brasilia, near Av. España e.g. *Heladería París*, Brasilia y Siria, is very popular; also rec. are *Heladerios 4D* and *Sugar*. *Bar Victoria*, corner of Chile and Oliva, has good food. For drinks and tea, *Salón de Té San Marco*, Alberdi y Oliva, rec.

Paraguayan harp music, bottle dancing, good food and service at *Jardín de la Cerveza*, Av. República Argentina y Castillo, US$10, strongly rec. (but sometimes they ask extra money for the music), and *Yguazú*, Chóferes del Chaco 1334 (San Lorenzo) US$30 for two, good meat, both some distance from centre. Good Paraguayan harp/guitar group at *Churrasquería Sajón*, Av. Carlos A. López, bus 26 from centre. More central are: *La Curva*, Av. Próceres de Mayo 212, cheap beer and reasonable food, several typical groups play 2100 to 0300 and *Yaci Morotí* bar on Humaitá, near Chile, at weekends.

**Shopping**  Calle Colón, starting at the port, is lined with good tourist shops, and so are Calles Pettirossi, Palma and Estrella. *Boutique Irene*, Montevideo 463, also rec. for leather goods. Calle Franco for handmade furniture. For wooden articles and carvings go to *Artes de Madera* at Ayolas 222; *Artesanía Raity* at Pai Pérez 778, woodcraft, prints and paintings, rec.; *Casa Vera* at Estigarribia 470 for Paraguayan leatherwork, cheap and very good. Other recommended shops, *Artesanía Kuarajhy*, Pte Franco 663; *Casa Overall*, Mcal. Estigarribia 397, nr. Plaza Uruguaya, good selection; *Victoria*, *Arte Artesanía*, Iturbe y Ayala, interesting selection of wood carvings, ceramics etc. rec. Check the quality of all handicrafts carefully, lower prices usually mean lower quality. A small but excellent fruit and vegetable market is to be found at San José behind the España supermarket. The markets are worth a visit, especially the Pettirossi (food and ordinary clothes). There is a daily market on Av. Dr. G.R. de Francia, and a Saturday one on Plaza de la Independencia, where the nuns from Villeta sell their hand-made clothing for children. Supermarkets are usually well stocked, especially with imported liquor. Outside Asunción, visit Luque (musical instruments and jewellery—**see page 892)** and Itauguá (lace) – **see page 895.** By Latin American standards, prices of electronic goods in the Korean-run shops are very low. Cameras can be bought cheaply in Paraguay; the selection of all types of consumer goods is better in Ciudad del Este, and there are good prices in Pedro Juan Caballero.

**Bookshops** *Librería Internacional*, Estrella 723 y Juan O'Leary and Palma 595 y 15 de Agosto, good for maps; also *"Books"* at Mcal. López 3971, at Villa Morra shopping centre, also carries English stock (at 3-4 times UK prices); magazine/newspaper kiosk *El Lector* on Plaza Uruguaya and 25 de Mayo has a selection of foreign material; *Colonial*, General Díaz 380, good new and second hand, English speaking proprietor, rec;. *Librería Alemana*, Av. Luis A. de Herrera 292, warmly rec. for German books and publications.

**Taxis** Minimum fare in Asunción is US$0.50 plus US$0.10 for every 100 metres. The average journey costs about US$2. (Check if there is an extra charge for luggage, and that the meter has not been speeded up). Hire by the hour; about US$4. Tip 10%.

**Trams (Streetcars)** One line, the No 5, still runs through the centre, along Calles Palma (one way) and Estrella (the other).

**City Buses** The system is extensive, running from 0600-2400; buses stop at signs before every street corner. Journeys within city, US$0.25, including from the centre to the new bus terminal, e.g. No 8 (not much fun with bulky luggage). Keep your ticket for inspection until you leave bus.

**Night Clubs and Discotheques** *Musak*, Bertoni y José Ocampos; *Caracol Club*, Gral. Santos y Porvenir; *Playboys*, 14 de Mayo y Oliva; *Tabasco Club*, 1 de Marzo y Felicidad; *La Salsa*, Papa Juan XXIII y Oddone (Latin American Disco). There are floor shows in several hotels, e.g. *Hotel del Yacht* (*Scruples*) and *Hotel Casino Itá Enramada* (open every day in summer, Saturdays in winter).

**Municipal Theatre**, Pte. Franco, nr. Alberdi, has an extensive winter programme of concerts and ballets (entry US$4). *Teatro Arlequín*, Gral. de Gaulle y Quesado, and *Teatro El Lector*, Av. San Martín y Austria have productions most of the year. Concerts are given at the Teatro de las Américas, J. Bergés 297. **Cinema** programmes are given in the press; some offer 3 films at one price (US$2.50).

**Museums** Museo Nacional de Bellas Artes, Iturbe y Mcal. Estigarribia, Mon.-Fri. 0700-1100, 1500-1900, recently renovated with a good collection of Spanish paintings; also an interesting selection of 20th Century Paraguayan art. In the Botanical Gardens are the **Museo de Historia Natural** and the **Museo Indigenista**, both open Mon.-Sat. 0730-1130, 1300-1700, Sun. 0600-1200, 1300-1700, neither in good condition. In the **Casa de la Independencia** (14 de Mayo y Presidente Franco) is an interesting historical collection; this was where the 1811 anti-colonial revolution was plotted; entry free. **Panteón Nacional de los Héroes**, esq. Palma y Chile, open every day. **Museo Historico Militar** in the Antiguo Colegio Militar, originally a Jesuit chapel built in 1588, open daily 0700-1430, 1500-1800, an interesting record of the country's turbulent past, well displayed in a renovated building. **Museo Dr. Andrés Barbero**, 200 block of España (near Estados Unidos), open Mon.-Fri., 0800-1100, anthropological, free, with a good collection of tools and weapons etc. of the various Guaraní cultures. *Centro de Artes Visuales*, at Isla de Francia, access via Av. Gral. Genes, bus 30 or 44A from the centre, Tues.-Sat. 0900-1200, 1600-2000; in this complex there are displays of popular religious art, mainly painted wooden figures, and a room full of eerie ritual masks; also exhibitions of contemporary Paraguayan art including some striking murals, highly recommended. Most museums are small and basic, mainly because of lack of interest and funding in the Stroessner years. Things are gradually improving.

**Exchange** Banks that give dollars charge 2-3% commission. **Lloyds Bank**, Palma y O'Leary (and six agencies in Greater Asunción) will give US dollars; **Finamérica** (ex-Bank of America), Oliva esq. Chile; **Citibank**, Estrella y Chile (will change Citibank travellers' cheques into dollars cash); **Banco Corporación** (ex-Chase), V.E. Haedo e Independencia Nacional; **Banco General** (ex-Boston), Chile y Haedo (will give US dollars); **Bank of Commerce and Industry**, Caballero esq. Haedo (will give US dollars); **Interbank**, 14 de Mayo 339; **Deutsche Bank**, Estrella y 14 de Mayo (charges 2% commission on money sent from W. Germany – very fast service, 2 days – paid by cheque which can be cashed into dollars at Cambio Guaraní for 3%

commission); *Banco Sudameris* (ex-Francés e Italiano), Oliva e Independencia Nacional. *Banco Holandés Unido*, Independencia Nacional y V.E. Haedo. Also Argentine, Brazilian and local banks. *Banco Unión* branch at Estrella y Alberdi (and throughout the country) will give quick cash advances in guaraníes on Visa or Mastercard in about 15 minutes, English spoken, friendly, only between 0800-1100.

Several *casas de cambio* on Palma (open Mon.-Fri. 0730-1200, 1500-1830, Sat., 0730-1200; rates for neighbouring countries' currencies usually good, except bolivianos), Deutsche Marks can be changed at good rates, and all rates are better than at the various frontiers. Be careful to count money received from street exchange-sellers (Palma and surrounding area – their rates are less good when banks and *cambios* are closed). *Casas de cambio* do not like changing sterling travellers' cheques, the only ones that will do it are *Cambio Paraná* on Palma and *Casa de Cambio La Moneda*, 25 de Mayo 127, good rates. Some only change one type of dollar travellers' cheque. Some ask for proof of purchase before changing. *Cambio Guaraní*, Palma 449, between 14 de Mayo and Alberdi, T 90032/6, is good, will change dollar cheques into dollars cash, but charges 2% commission for this. German spoken at *Cambios Menno Tour*, Azara 532. *Cambios Yguazú* (Palma) is OK (Thomas Cook, but can't replace your lost or stolen cheques). See **Currency** section in Information for Visitors.

**Embassies and Consulates** Brazilian Consulate, in Banco do Brasil building on main square (open 0800-1200, Mon.-Fri.), Nuestra Señora de la Asunción y Oliva (may charge US$10 for visa), T 448084; **Argentine Consulate**, corner of España and Perú, T 212320, open 0700-1100, visas processed in 1-2 hours, photograph needed. **Chile**, Guido Spano 1740, T 660344; **Bolivian Consulate**, Eligio Ayala 2002, T 22662; **Peruvian Consulate**, Av. Mcal. López 648, T 200949; **Uruguay**, Av. Brasil y Siria, T 25022 (visas processed immediately if exit ticket from Uruguay, overland travel to Uruguay and onward country visas can be shown); **Mexico**, Edif. Ytá Ybate, esq. Cerro Corá y Juan O'Leary, T 444421. **Ecuador**, Herrera y Yegros, T 446150; **Venezuela** O'Leary y Haedo, T 444243.

**US Embassy and Consulate**, Av. Mcal. López esq. Kubitschek, T 201041; **South Africa**, Banco Sudameris, piso 4, esq. Cerro Corá e Independencia Nacional.

**Great Britain**, Presidente Franco 706, esquina O'Leary, 4th floor (Casilla 404), T 449146; **Switzerland**, O'Leary 409 esq. Estrella, T 48022; **Spain**, Calle 25 de Mayo 175, esq. Yegros T 90686/7; **Danish Consulate**, Nuestra Señora de la Asunción 766, T 90617; **Swedish Consulate**, Bogado 1039-47, T 205561/9; **Dutch Consulate**, Franco y 15 de Agosto; **Austrian Consulate**, Av. Ayala y B. de las Casas, T 25567. **W German**, Av. Venezuela 241; **France**, Av. España 676, T 23111; **Israel**, Ed Líder, piso 3, O'Leary y Gen. Díaz.

**Cultural Institutions** The US-Paraguay Cultural Centre has a good library at España 352 (open Mon.-Fri. 0900-2000, Sat. 0900-1200, also has snack bar); **Peace Corps**, address from US embassy. **Instituto Anglo-Paraguayo**, España 457, where you can acquire much useful information and read English newspapers. **Goethe Institut** behind Goethe school, J. de Salazán 310, small library (being expanded 1990) with a few newspapers, open 1600-2000. **Centro Cultural Paraguayo-Japonés**, J. Correa y A. Velasquez, **Alianza Francesa**, Mcal. Estigarribia 1039, T 210382, snack bar. All these institutes have special events, film shows, etc., details in *Fin de Semana*, a publication available at the tourist office, hotels and elsewhere.

**General Post Office** Alberdi, Benjamín Constant y El Paraguayo Independiente. T 48891, 0700-2000, but closed for lunch. Also Fax service and philatelic museum, open 0700-1800, Mon.-Fri.; 0700-1200, Sat. Post boxes throughout the city carry address of the nearest place one can purchase stamps. Register all important mail; you must go to main PO for this. *Poste Restante* charges about US$0.10 per item collected. There are sub-offices at the railway station and at the docks. Postage stamps tend to be large—take care when writing postcards!

**Telephone** Antelco, corner Nuestra Señora de la Asunción and E. Ayala, nr. Cathedral, for international calls; also Manuel Domínguez y Gral. Bruguez, both 24 hrs.

**Places of Worship** Anglican Church: St Andrew, on España with Uruguay; Synagogue at Gen. Díaz 657.

**Police**, T 46105.

**Laundry** *Lavamático*, Yegros 808 y Fulgencio Moreno. *Lava Pronto*, Azara 850, T 45147, good, quick service. *Lavafácil*, México y Moreno, good, cheap, fast. *Lavarap* at Hernandarias 636, one block from Colón and General Díaz, no siesta, open Sun. and holidays, T 447478.

**Photographic** Repairs: Panatronic, Benjamín Constant 516. Rodolfo Loewen, Camera Service, Blas Garay y Morelo, T 23807. Slide film costs US$3, print film US$2.50 (35 mm.).

Good place for buying cameras, *Casa Fanny*, Mcal. Estigarribia 144.

**Travel Agencies**  (all very helpful) *Inter-Express* (Amex), Yegros 690; *Maral* on 25 de Julio y Caballero; *Continental*, Benjamín Constant 777. *American Tours*, Independencia Nacional, under *Hotel Guaraní*, both German and English spoken. *Grupo Cataldi*, Estrella 876, T 90458, can occasionally pick up at airport; real estate agents (German run) with good contact in hotels and apartment accommodation. *Menno Tour*, Azara 532, is also staffed by Germans and will book buses to Foz etc.

**Tourist Office**  Palma 468. Desk in hall of Dirección Nacional de Turismo, open 0800-2000, T 445306, 449521, 447865. Helpful, free map, also one available for sale in bookshops.

**Airport**  Silvio Pettirossi, 15 km. NE of centre. There is a desk where you can book a taxi to your hotel, US$5. Bus 18A to the centre (Calle Oliva-Cerro Corá), from centre e.g. at Azara y Antequera, US$1.14, stops every 15 minutes just outside the airport perimeter at the road fork, 300 metres from the main entrance. Ask to be set down at road fork. (Do not walk on the grass outside the airport or the police will fine you). Bus 18A to the bus terminal. Buses only recommended outside rush-hours, with light luggage. Líneas Aéreas Paraguayas (LAP) has its own colectivo, which collects from hotels, US$3.10 p.p., as does TAM. Enquire at airline offices. LAP office at Oliva 467.

A new airport terminal has been built (duty free facilities, small *casa de cambio* – turn left as you leave customs and immigration, but rates poorer than in centre – handicraft shop and restaurant), 1 km. from the old building. There is a helpful tourist office on the ground floor at the airport; they will book Varig flights to Foz do Iguaçu, as well as arranging transport into town (minibus arrives and leaves from Iberia Office), finding accommodation and changing money at poor rates.

**Rail**  Presidente Carlos Antonio López Railway to **Encarnación** (370 km.) journey time 26 hours (scheduled 15½) and **Buenos Aires** (1,477 km.) about 44 hours, Tues. 1755 (better to take bus to Encarnación and catch train in Posadas). A wood-burning steam locomotive, pulls the train to Encarnación (first 12 hrs. in the dark), US$2.50, 1st class (rec.—no sleeper), US$1.90 2nd class; tickets on sale 2 hrs. before departure. Only 2nd class coaches cross the international bridge to Posadas, when passengers for Buenos Aires transfer. Good hot food can be ordered for US$1.50, drinks US$0.30. In dry weather dust, and in wet weather rain, gets into 2nd-class carriages. Track liable to flooding. (Trains may be cancelled on public holidays, such as Christmas. Check day, time and if the train is running.) See under Excursions for a trip to see the woodburning locomotives. At the station is a steam engine called *Sapucai*, built in 1861. The platform is too short for trains, which block Calle Bogado when loading.

**River Boats**  To **Concepción** (26 hrs.) with Flota Mercantil del Estado (FME), Estrella 672-682 (tickets from here only). Weekly (every Tues., 0800—returns Wed. 1600, but check times, sailings vary with the seasons), US$14 1st class, US$10 2nd class (4 beds to a cabin, men and women not segregated, comfortable, but 2nd class food is not recommended – take food with you), US$7 3rd class (wooden benches on upper deck, some hammocks can be rented, but better bring your own and mosquito repellant). Restaurant on board; said to be good. Boats are modern, elegant and comfortable. Other boat lines work this route, but they are less comfortable, although cheaper, with no regular sailings (e.g. *Guaraní*, which sails to Concepción every Sun., returns Wed., US$6.50 p.p.); enquire at the small boat dock to the right of the main dock; you will have to take your own food, water, toilet paper, warm clothes for the night (or mattress and blanket), mosquito repellent.

When conditions permit FME sails to **Corumbá, Brazil**, on Friday at 0800, arriving Tuesday 1200; 2nd class costs US$37, 3rd class US$27. When the boat does not go to Corumbá, it stops at Bahía Negra, close to the frontier. Check details beforehand. **See also page 894.**

Ferry to **Puerto Pilcomayo** (Argentina) about every 20 minutes (US$0.50, 5 mins) from Itá Enramada (Paraguayan immigration), take bus 9 from Asunción (Argentine immigration closed at weekends for tourists). Boats south to **Pilar** and Argentina are few and irregular. Compañía Marítima Paraguaya SA, Presidente Franco 199 esq. 15 de Agosto, for all shipping enquiries.

**Roads**  There is a 20 km. road NW across the Río Paraguay at Remanso to Villa Hayes and on through the Chaco (Route 9) to Filadelfia and Bolivia, 805 km. (an account of a direct journey from Bolivia by this road will be found on **page 902**). Route 8 is now paved N from Coronel Oviedo, 100 km. to San Estanislao (see also under **Coronel Oviedo, page 896**), where it becomes successives Routes 3 and 5 (being paved for about 100 km.) and runs 305 km. N and then NE, to Pedro Juan Caballero on the Brazilian frontier. Also paved are the long-distance Route 1 to Encarnación (372 km.), and Route 2 to Coronel Oviedo, which leads

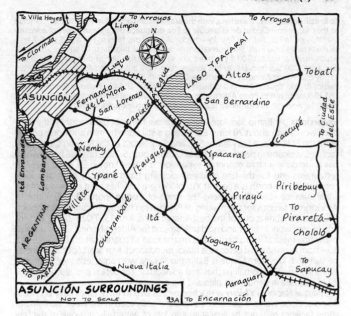

**ASUNCIÓN SURROUNDINGS**
NOT TO SCALE                                    93A

to Route 7 to Ciudad del Este and the Iguazú falls (362 km.). A round trip Asunción-Ciudad del Este-Encarnación-Asunción is easily done. The roads are described in the text.

**Buses** All buses leave from the bus terminal, out of town at República Argentina esq. Fernando de la Mora. Take local bus numbers (*Línea*) 8, 10, 25, 31, 38, on Oliva, Haedo, or Cerro Corá in the centre for Terminal Nuevo; from the terminal to the city, get off the bus at the corner of General Díaz and Chile. Taxi from down town, rec. if you have luggage, US$2 p.p. or US$4 per taxi. Buses take 1 hr., taxis 20 minutes from the centre to the terminal. The terminal has tourist information desk (reported unfriendly), restaurant (quite good), café, shops, and lots of noisy televisions. Hotels nearby: turn left from front of terminal, 2 mins' walk. Many bus companies still maintain ticket offices around Plaza Uruguaya. Bus times and fares within Paraguay are given under destinations.

**To Uruguay** COIT runs to **Montevideo**, 0800, Sat. and Wed., 20 hrs., US$48. Brújula runs Tues. and Fri., with a third service in summer, US$45; another company, Lysa, is cheaper (the route is Encarnación, Posadas, Paso de los Libres, Uruguaiana, Bella Unión, Salto, Paysandú—the only customs formalities are at Bella Unión; passport checks here and at Encarnación).

**To Argentina** There is a road N from Asunción (passing the Botanical Gardens on Primer Presidente) to a concrete arch span bridge (Puente Remanso – US$1 toll) which leads to the border at Puerto Falcón (about 40 km.) and then to **Clorinda** in Argentina. The border is open 24 hours a day; last bus from Falcón to the centre of Asunción at 1830. The colectivo fare from Asunción to the border (at Falcón) is US$0.80; from Falcón to Clorinda costs US$0.25. It is cheaper to take the local bus to Clorinda, and then continue on Argentine services than to book through.

Buses Asunción-**Buenos Aires** (21 hrs.) daily with , Nuestra Señora de la Asunción (1330), Chevallier Paraguaya Godoy, via Rosario and Santa Fe, also with Brújula and La Internacional, each 6 times a week (average fare US$42). To **Resistencia** (US$13) and **Formosa**, 2 a day, Brújula and La Internacional; Brújula once a week and Cacorba (3 times) to Córdoba. To **Posadas**, Singer 3 a week at midnight, or go to **Encarnación** (frequent service) and cross the river to Argentina.

**To Brazil** Nuestra Señora and Rysa, with the Brazilian companies Pluma and Unesul, continue to their Asunción—Ciudad del Este route to **Foz do Iguaçu** (Paraguayan buses all advertise that they go to Foz, but very few do—check); all luxury bus fares to Foz are US$5, 5-7 hrs., six direct buses a day in all. Seat reservations recommended; take the 0100 bus (easy to sleep), which arrives at Foz at 0700 if you want to visit the Brazilian side of the Iguaçu falls in one day; take 1200 bus from falls to bus station, then 1430 bus back to Asunción – remember to buy cruzeiros in Asunción. To **Curitiba**, US$24 with Pluma, buses daily, 15½ hrs.; to **São Paulo**, Rápido Yguazú, Pluma and Brújula, US$24 (*leito*, US$48). Pluma to Rio de Janeiro, US$30. Unesul run to Porto Alegre 4 times a week; Nacional Expresso to Brasília 3 times a week. Services also to **Blumenau** (Catarinense) and **Florianópolis** (Pluma).

**Excursions** At Barrio San José Obrero (follow the river bank north) is the local brick works with about 20 kilns. Everything is still done by man and horse power. From the FME dock a ferry leaves Sat. and Sun. across to the Rowing Club, many facilities, welcoming people. To **Villeta** (27 km., pop. 5,232), on the E bank, which has undergone a rapid economic expansion; it is well known for good river-fish restaurants and for the fine children's clothing hand-made by nuns at a local convent. A little north is a park at Ytororó where trenches used in the war of the Triple Alliance can still be seen. The town of **Luque** (pop. 24,917), close to Asunción, is famous for the making of Paraguayan harps, difficult to find though (Guitares Sanabria is one of the best-known firms, Km. 13, T 023-2291), and for fine filigree work in silver and gold (ask around for Alberto Núñez). There are also many fine musical instrument shops on the road to Luque; get off the bus – No. 30 – from Asunción just before the major roundabout. Mariscal López' house may be visited. 8 km. from Luque is Balneario Yukyry, with an artesian well, springs, swimming pools, football pitches and a snackbar; for details and reservations, T 23731 (closed in winter, but pleasant trip anyway).

Parque Nacional **Ybicuy** is reached by bus two to three times daily US$1.85, 4 hours. Good walks, a beautiful camp site (hardly used in the week, no lighting, some facilities may not be available) and lots of waterfalls; it is one of the few areas of protected forest in the country. At the entrance is a well-set out park and museum as well as the reconstructed remains of the country's first iron foundry (La Rosada). The only shops (apart from a small one at the entrance selling drinks, eggs, etc..) are at Ybicuy, 30 km. away (*Hotel Pytu'u Renda*, E/F, good food, clean, cooking facilities, friendly; *Pensión Santa Rosa* and *San Juan*, both F). Bus from Ybicuy at 0430 and 1120, returning 0700 and 1345, goes as far as camp site, 2 km. beyond the museum. Crowded on Sundays but deserted the rest of the week.

The most popular trip is east to Itauguá, and San Bernardino and Aregua on Lago Ypacaraí (**see page 895**).

A short steam train trip to Aregua leaving Asunción station, one hopes, at 1215 daily except Sun., takes 1 hr., US$0.30. The engine burns exotic tropical hardwoods; Ian and Carol Martin of Falmouth, tell us that this is the only train they know of where passengers lower the windows to sample the aromatic smoke (but watch out for cinders). Bus for return trip via Itauguá (last bus from Aregua to Asunción 2100). It may be possible to take a boat from Aregua to San Bernardino and then return: a good outing. For a longer look at the countryside, take a tour for US$30 from any travel agent (pick-up at your hotel – about US$60 with private taxi drivers) to drive the "Circuito Central" also called "Circuito de Oro": Asunción – San Lorenzo – Itá – Yaguarón – Paraguarí – Chololó – Piraretá – Piribebuy – Caacupé – San Bernardino – Ypacaraí – Itauguá – Aregua – Capiatá – Asunción. Some 200 km. on paved roads, 7 hrs. Lions, at Alberdi 454, 1, T 90-278, run a full service of trips. Alternatively, from San Lorenzo, take Route 1 towards Encarnación and at Km. 28 (LP Petrol station) turn right to Guarambaré, a sleepy town in the sugar area with many Peace Corps trainees. From May to November bullock carts and trucks take the cane to the factory, 1 km. past the electricity sub-station. After your visit continue to Guarambaré (bus Asunción-Guarambaré, 45 mins, US$0.15, every 10 mins from terminal). Take the second dirt road on the right after the Plaza and for about 10 km. continue through typical farmlands and citrus orchards. The road then continues through Ypané, Nemby and back to Asunción via Lambaré. In Lambaré, near the *Itá Enramada Hotel*, is Lambaré hill with very good views.

A 3-hour colectivo ride from Asunción is Sapucay, 88 km. away, where the main workshops for the wood-burning steam locomotives are located. There are cheap *hospedajes* in Sapucay; either stay there, or take the Asunción-Encarnación train which passes through Tues. at 2115.

## NORTH FROM ASUNCION (2)

**The Paraguay river dominates this section, still a main trade route between Brazil and Argentina.**

A boat trip up the Paraguay to Concepción, about 312 km. N of Asunción, is one of the easiest ways of seeing more of the country. The winding river is 400 metres wide, with a lot of traffic, for in the absence of a direct road between Concepción and Asunción (though there are roads via the Chaco and by Coronel Oviedo) this is the main trade route for the products of northern Paraguay: cattle, hides, *yerba mate*, tobacco, timber and *quebracho*. For passenger sailings, see under Asunción, **River Boats**.

**Concepción** (pop. 35,000), a free port for Brazil, lies on the E bank. This pleasant, friendly, quiet and picturesque town is the trade centre of the N, doing a considerable business with Brazil. There is a library, municipal theatre and "higgledy piggledy" museum, all under one roof, and a market, to which farmers bring their goods in oxcarts. A new bridge across the Río Paraguay is now open.

**Hotels** *Victoria*, Franco y Caballero, D, good, breakfast; cheap and clean, private bath with hot water, rec.; on same street, *Center*, F with bath and breakfast; *Concepción*, Don Bosco 311, E with bath, no breakfast. *Francés*, Presidente Franco 1016, D with bath and a/c, E bath and fan, cheaper without bath, no breakfast, restaurant, recently renovated, clean and friendly. *Paraguay*, F, restaurant excellent, good food at low prices. Also F, *Boquerón*, Iturbe y Franco, quiet area;. *Cosmos* (clean, fan, breakfast included) and *Bar Estrella del Norte* (near port), both F, basic but possible.

**Restaurants** The restaurants of *Hotels Victoria* and particularly *Francés* are good. Also, *Tedacar*, on Franco, pleasant with seating in the garden behind; *Candilejas*, Mcal. Estigarribia 744, good food and music (Fri. and Sat.).

**Exchange** Bancopar, Garay y Franco, open a.m.

**Communications** The bus station is on the outskirts, 8 blocks up Gral. E.A. Garay. There is an urban microbus (Línea 1) which shuttles between terminal and the port. Arriving in town by bus, get out in town centre, don't wait for bus station. There is a bus from Concepción to **Horqueta**, 50 km. to the E (1 hr., US$0.55), a cattle and lumbering town of 10,000 people. There is a dry-season road – frequently closed – from Concepción W across the Chaco, to **Pozo Colorado** on the Transchaco highway, 146 kms. Efforts are being made to improve the road, parts are now paved but it can take 3 days in the rain to drive. Bird life is spectacular. The Concepción-Pozo Colorado bus normally takes 2 hours, US$2.75, but it is difficult to get onward connections. Bus companies from **Asunción**: San Jorge, Lambaré and Nuestra Señora de Asunción, 8-11 hrs., fare about US$8, Concepción-Asunción via Coronel Oviedo, several buses each day, bad road, rains often delay departures, via Pozo Colorado theoretically takes 6½ hours, several daily, US$6.50, road impassable with heavy rains. Bus to **Pedro Juan Caballero**, 4-6 hrs., several, US$5, good paved road.

**Air Service** Asunción-Concepción flights are operated by LATN, Aeronorte and TAM (which tends to be cheapest). TAM to Asunción daily at 0800, 40 mins., US$22, book as early as possible (only 25 seats), free colectivo from TAM office on main street to airport. On Fridays TAM flies from Asunción and Concepción to Vallemí, Fuerte Olimpo and Bahía Negra, all three villages to N of Concepción on the Río Paraguay. Air services to these places are irregular because runways are sometimes flooded or muddy. There is no direct air connection between Concepción and Pedro Juan Caballero.

**Shipping** To **Asunción**, Weds. 0800 and Sat., depending on the season and water levels: check, US$14 1st class, US$10 2nd class (no segregation, no locks on doors), US$7 3rd class, 19 hrs., Agencia Marítima Ramón Velázquez, Nanawa 547, near dock for information on other sailings

You can enter Brazil, as long as you have a Paraguayan exit stamp, by taking a boat from Asunción or Concepción to Isla Margarita, where you can get a ferry to Porto Murtinho, Brazil.

(You cannot get a Brazilian entry stamp there: for that you must go to Cáceres, Corumbá or Campo Grande.) You can take boats to the small communities on the river, but there are few places to stay.

When it is not possible to go by boat to Corumbá, Brazil (i.e. when the river is in flood), FME sails from Asunción to **Bahía Negra**, from where it returns 1 hr. after arrival. Bahía Negra has neither hotel nor bank, but the policeman is very helpful, although he will require you to obtain all entry and exit stamps. Sra. Ferreira will change money, at a poor rate. It is possible to hire a small boat to Porto Coimbra (Sr. Ferreira or Sr. Silva), about US$80, and from there go by boat to Porto Esperança, from where you can catch a train to Corumbá (US$1). Entry at Porto Esperança requires a yellow fever certificate and much red tape because the official, Sr. Sanitário, is not used to the unexpected. Since local river traffic is sparse, this trip is recommended only for the adventurous and patient. You can fly from Bahía Negra to Asunción.

There is a 215 km. road (Route 5—first 112 km. unpaved but moderate, last 100 km. paved) from Concepción, eastwards to the Brazilian border. The road is very scenic. 60 km. along the road from **Yby Yaú** (junction with road to Coronel Oviedo, fuel, restaurants) to Pedro Juan Caballero is a short road to the **National Park of Cerro Corá**, which is the site of Mariscal Francisco Solano López' death, with a monument to him and other national heroes; the site is constantly guarded. It has hills and cliffs (some with petroglyphs), camping facilities, swimming and hiking trails. Administration office is at Km. 180 on Ruta 5, 5 km. past the main entrance towards Pedro Juan Caballero.

The border town of **Pedro Juan Caballero** (pop: 37,331), is opposite Ponta Porã, Brazil, which has a road and railway to São Paulo and the Atlantic coast. The two towns are divided only by a road (Rua Internacional) and the locals come and go as they please. To cross into Brazil officially, first obtain a Paraguayan exit stamp (the office was last reported at Calle Curupayty 552), then report to Brazilian federal police in Ponta Porã. If you need a Brazilian visa go first to the Brazilian consul, open 0800-1200 at Francia 830 near Alberdi in P.J. Caballero. If you are entering Paraguay, ensure you obtain a tourist card at the Paraguayan border (without it you will have to pay US$3 on leaving the country). From P.J. Caballero there are daily flights to Asunción, US$24 (they may be suspended after heavy rain, at which time buses may not run to Asunción either, though colectivos, which cost about 25% more than buses, may run when buses do not). Much cheaper here than Asunción for most purchases. A good shopping street is Mcal. López, cheap liquor and electronics. It has been reported that some caves have recently been discovered nearby and may be visited.

**Hotels** *Peralta* (F) on the same street as the TAM offices. *Eiruzú*, C, with breakfast, clean, modern, rec., swimming pool, good restaurant; *La Siesta*, A/B, modern, luxury, good restaurant, close to border with Ponta Porã; *Corina*, very clean with breakfast, D, Central, T 2960, rec.; *Guavira*, F, no breakfast, clean and comfortable; *La Negra*, F, clean.

**Restaurants** Try the hotels, or the Brazilian side. However *Parrillada El Galpón*, Mcal. López 892, is rec.

**Exchange** Bancopar, Banco del Paraná for exchange. At least 6 *casas de cambio*. For travellers' cheques you can go to the *casas de cambio*, or to *Hotel Eiruzú*, one block behind the *casas de cambio* (also deal in the European currencies). You may have to show receipt for purchase of travellers' cheques (if you don't have it, try *Cambio Amambay*, near *Hotel Eiruzú*). There are many street changers.

**Buses** Several to **Concepción** US$5, 4-6 hrs. To **Asunción**, direct, 8-9 hrs., US$10 (US$24 deluxe sleeper) and slower buses, 11-12 hrs. (indirect), e.g. Cometa del Amambay at 0900 and 1700, US$8.

## EAST FROM ASUNCION (3)

Small towns with interesting local crafts, leading to jungle on the Brazilian border and the major attractions of Ciudad del Este, the Itaipú dam and the nearby Iguazú Falls.

**Route Two** The Mariscal Estigarribia Highway leaves Asunción past typical markets, reached by bus from Asunción (including Nos. 12, 27 and 29). At Km. 12 is **San Lorenzo** (pop. 74,359), an industrial town with the National School of Agriculture (Universidad de Agronomía) – it has an extensive insect collection;

also excellent Centro de Promoción de Artesanía Indígena, Bogado 584, open Tues.—Sat, 0830-1200, 1400-1800, basket work, ceramics and other handicrafts for sale at very reasonable prices (non-profit-making organization run by Catholic Relief Services), and small but interesting Museo Aqueológico, near cathedral, free, good Indian section. Recently opened is the Museo Guido Boggiani, Bogado 888, Tues.—Sat. 1000-1200, 1500-1800, a collection built up by the Italian anthropologist who researched the tribes of the northern Chaco at the turn of the 19th/20th Century; well worth a visit. Here is the Balneario El Tigre, with swimming pool and shady trees. (*Hotel San Lorenzo*, Gral. Caballero y Cerro Corá, T 2261, F with breakfast, excellent).

At Km. 20 is *Capiatá*, founded in 1640, where there is a fine cathedral with remarkable 17th century sculpture made by Indians under the tutelage of the Jesuit Fathers. A left turn here (sign-posted) goes to Lago Ypacaraí via an inexpensive toll road, 7 km.

Km. 30, *Itauguá* (pop. 5,369), founded in 1728, is where the famous *ñandutí*, or spiderweb lace, is made. The blocks of uniform dwellings in the broad plaza, with their reddish tile roofs projecting over the sidewalk and their lines of pillars, are very close to the descriptions we have of Guaraní Jesuit settlements. The church and the market (closed Sunday) are worth seeing, and the town looks most attractive with the *ñandutí* work spread or hanging outside the houses; you can buy the most beautiful hammocks, tablecloths, shirts, hats and dresses locally made. There is a 3-day festival in mid-July, including processions and the crowning of Señorita Ñandutí. Accommodation poor (there is only one *pensión*, F), but Itauguá is only 45 mins by bus from Asunción, US$0.60.

At Km. 40 a branch road, 8 km. long, leads off to **San Bernardino**, on Lago Ypacaraí, by bus from Asunción (Route 2, 56 km., 1 hr., US$0.90) or by rail to Ypacaraí and thence by microbus. The lake is 24 km. by 5. There are facilities for swimming and water sports, with a sandy beach, but the water is dirty; frequent cruises from the pier during the tourist season, Dec.-Feb., when it is crowded.

**Hotels** *Casino San Bernardino*, B, swimming pool, a/c, by the lake 3 km. from town, T 301; *Del Lago*, lakeside in town, C/D, T 201; *Acuario*, also lakeside, 2 km. from town centre, B, T 371; *Santa Rita*, lakeside, D, pretty garden, German owners, good restaurant, T 258. It is possible to find rooms in private houses.

**Camping** At Km. 43 is Casa Grande Camping Club with all facilities. For information, Corfín Paraguaya, Ayolas 437 y Estrella, T 92360/1, Asunción, or direct, T (0511) 649. It is possible to camp right on the lake but there are many mosquitoes, inadequate sanitary facilities and not much safety for your personal belongings.

*Aregua*, a pretty town on the slopes above the lake, 20 km. from San Bernardino, is also a resort, with interesting ceramics cooperative, a church and convent. An increasing number of houses are being built around the lake. You can stay at the *Hospedaje Restaurant Ozli*, E, reasonable, restaurant mediocre.

**Restaurants** La Rotunda, on the waterfront; Las Palmeras.

At Km. 54 is **Caacupé** (pop. 9,105), a popular resort and religious centre. Its sights include the beautiful Basilica of Our Lady of the Miracles, whose day is 8 December. The old church has been demolished, but a small replica has been built about 5 blocks away. The very beautiful new basilica, with copper roof, stained glass and polychrome stone esplanade, was consecrated by the Pope in 1988. There is an interesting market next to it, where one can buy pottery, etc., and swimming pools in the streams nearby. Parque Anka, outside town on the Asunción road, has a swimming pool, tennis courts, ponies, a Disneyland, camp site and good restaurants.

Thousands of people from Paraguay, Brazil and Argentina flock to the shrine. Besides fireworks and candle-lit processions, pilgrims watch the agile gyrations of Paraguayan bottle-dancers; they weave in intricate measures whilst balancing bottles pyramided on their heads. The top bottle carries a spray of flowers and the more expert dancers never let drop a single petal.

**Hotels** *El Uruguayo*, F, with good restaurant, friendly service; *San Blas I*, F.

**Camping** Club de Camping Melli, all facilities, Km. 53, close to Caacupé, T (0511) 313.

**Excursions** Poor roads lead to several interesting churches. One is at Tobati, a tobacco centre, with local pottery and woodwork, 16 km. to the N. At Km. 64 beyond Caacupé a paved road runs 13 km. SE to *Piribebuy* (pop: 5,902, *Pensión Santa Rosa*, F, basic; *Restaurant Rincón Viejo*, reasonable), founded in 1640 and noted for its strong local drink, *caña*. In the central plaza is the church (1640), with fine sculptures, high altar and pulpit. There is also an interesting Military History museum. Near the town are the attractive small falls of Piraretá. The road goes on to Chololó, (Hotel: *Parador Chololó*, rec.) and good views from a hill, and you can visit the Chololó falls (motel); it reaches Route 1 at Paraguarí, 28 km. from Piribebuy.

At Km. 132, but off the main road (buses drop passengers at El Cruce – a roundabout), is **Coronel Oviedo**, an important road junction (pop. 21,782).

**Hotels** *Hospedaje Juancito*, O'Leary y Carmelo Peralta, F with bath, mosquito net, nice garden, rec.; *Hotel Ramírez*, E, clean and good; *El Rey*, on main road 2 km. S of town centre, E, clean, modern, breakfast included, rec.; *San Pedro*, 100 m. from *El Rey*, E, rec.; *Pensión Ñanda* Roga, F, without breakfast, basic but friendly; on main road to the West, *Hotel Alemán*, rec.,

South, Route 8 is paved for 42 km. to Villarrica and continues S (unpaved) through Caazapá to Coronel Bogado on Route 1, 264 km. from Coronel Oviedo. 27 km. along Route 8, a side road runs to Yataíty where a local cooperative sells ponchos, fine weaving and embroidery. At the end of November there is a *feria artesanal* with folk music and dancing, exhibitions etc. There are German agricultural communities nearby.

*Villarrica*, 173 km. by road or rail from Asunción and 219 from Encarnación, with 21,203 people, is delightfully set on a hill rich with orange trees. It has a fine cathedral. The museum behind the church has a foreign coin collection; please contribute. Products of the region are tobacco, cotton, sugar, *yerba mate*, hides, meat and wine produced by German settlers (interesting locally made pineapple wine). Horse-drawn taxis.

**Hotels** *Ybytyruzu*, on main street E p.p. with breakfast, new, better than most; *Guaíra*, F, near bus terminal, shower, fan, noisy; *Pensión el Toro*, Mcal. López 521, F; *Hospedaje La Guairana*, next door (537), F, with restaurant; *Asunción*, Thompson y Aquideban, a/c, fan; *Hospedaje El Porvenir*, Thompson 144, F, basic; *Plaza*, Mcal. López, F, clean, friendly.

**Restaurants** *Mesón Universitario*, González 623, in part of a colonial pavilion, open all day; *París*, C.A. López 100, good food; *Refugio*, Gral. Díaz 578, reasonable prices; *El Tirol*, C.A. López 205, German owned, set lunch, "possibly the only cheesecake in Paraguay"; *El Palacio de las Empanadas*, Gral Díaz 533; *Los Amigos*, Melgarejo 828, good food, sidewalk eating at night; *Capri*, San Roque y Gral. Díaz, local food, inexpensive; *Miami Bar*, La Plaza de Municipalidad, good food, rec.; *La Tranquera*, 3 km. from centre, by train station; *Angelo's* on main square, decent.

**Bus** to Coronel Oviedo US$1.50; to Asunción, US$3 (Empresa Guaireña); also direct service to Ciudad del Este, 4 daily.

There are three German colonies near Villarrica. 7 km. north is a turn off to the east, then 20 km. to Colonia Independencia, *Hotel Tilinski*, D, peaceful, German spoken, swimming pool (filled with river water), no meals; *Che Valle Mi*, Sr. Jacob Esslinger, Correo Melgarejo, T 05418-241, rec.; next door is *Ulli y Klaus* restaurant, also rec.; also a good restaurant, with German chalet style accommodation, *Hotel Restaurant Panorama*, set on top of a hill on the road 12 km. from Colonia Independencia. Makes a good stop, especially for German-speaking travellers, who can also visit the German cooperative farms. There is camping nearby at Melgarejo with full facilities. Direct bus to Asunción, three daily (US$1.60, 4 hrs.), as well as to Villarrica.

East from Coronel Oviedo, the paved Route 7, runs 195 km. through cultivated areas and woods and across the Caaguazú hills to the spectacular 500-metre single span "Friendship Bridge" across the Paraná (to Brazil) at *Ciudad del Este* (formerly Ciudad Presidente Stroessner), where there is a grass-strip airport. This was the fastest growing city in the country (83,000 inhabitants) until the completion of the civil works of the Itaipú hydroelectric project, for which it is the centre of operations. Ciudad del Este has been described as the biggest late-night shopping centre in Latin America, but it is mainly directed towards Brazilian and Argentine visitors who find bargain prices for electrical goods, watches, perfumes etc. Prices are decidedly high for N. American and European visitors. Also watch the exchange rates if you're a short-term visitor from Argentina or Brazil; hotels and restaurants tend to be dearer than elsewhere in Paraguay. The leather market is well worth a visit, be sure to bargain. The nearby towns of Hernandarias (pop: 32,000; *Hotel El León*, E, clean, quiet) and Puerto Presidente Franco (pop: about 24,000; *Hotel Rosa*, D, with bath, clean) have also had a tremendous increase in population and activity.

**Hotels** (incl. breakfast) *Hotel de la Tour* at Paraná Country Club, 5 km. from centre, superb, A, Swiss-owned, excellent restaurant (US$12-16 p.p.), swimming pool, gardens, beautiful view; *Catedral*, Av. C. A. López 840, C, a/c, with swimming pool, restaurant; *Executive*, Av. Adrián Jara y Curupayty, T 8981/8982, B (incl. breakfast – restaurant rec.); *Floresta*, Av. Teniente Cabello y C.A. López, B, T 8255/8197; *Santo Domingo*, Emiliano R. Fernández y Miranda, T 2505, C, superb. *Mi Abuela*, Adrián Jara 128, rec., E, including breakfast, good value, shared shower, fan, not very clean; *Puerta del Sol*, Boquerón 111, D with bath, a/c, clean, just off main street; *Viena*, next door, above restaurant, E with breakfast, clean, German family. *Tripolis*, Av. San Blas 331, E, a/c, friendly, clean; *Munich*, E.A. Fernández y Cap. Miranda, rec.; *El Cid*, Camino Recalde, 1 block N of Ruta 7, E, breakfast, bath, fan. Other cheap ones near market.

**Restaurants** *Tripolis* for good moderately-priced meal. *Tai Fu*, Chinese, very good value, on 8th floor above *Casa Mona Lisa*, López y Rodríguez, good views. *Coreio*, Av. San Blas 125, T 60448, good Korean food, meal about US$5; *Osaka*, Calle Jara and, 100 metres away, *New Tokio*, Jara 202, both very good, authentic Japanese meal for US$3; *Dolíbar*, clean and fair value. Cheaper ones in market.

**Exchange** Banco Holandés Unido; Lloyds Bank agency; local banks (open Mon.-Fri. 0730-1100). Dollars can be changed into cruzeiros in town, but exchange may be better and easier in Foz do Iguaçu; note that money changers do not operate at the Brazilian end of the Friendship Bridge. Cheques generally not accepted.

**International Phone** Antelco, near centre on road to bus terminal.

**Communications** The road links with the Brazilian road system at Foz do Iguaçu across the bridge, from where another 32-km. road leads to the Iguazú falls. Passengers disembark on each side of the bridge. The international bus then goes to the inter-city depot, behind Av. Brasil, at the edge of Foz do Iguaçu. Crossing from Paraguay to Brazil other than on the international bus, you just pass through Paraguayan customs etc., walk across, visit Brazilian immigration, then take a bus to the city terminal (*terminal urbana*), US$0.05, just outside Foz, opposite a military training camp. From Brazil, pedestrians seem to walk across the bridge on the north side, this allows those returning from Paraguay carrying TVs and such bulky purchases an easier passage on the south side. The walk takes 10-15 minutes. There is a local bus from Calle San Blas, Ciudad del Este to Foz, every 15 mins., 0600-2000, which drops you off at Brazilian immigration; keep your ticket and continue to Foz free on the next bus. Remember to put your watch forward 1 hr. From the *terminal urbana*, buses run to the Falls; if only visiting the Brazilian side of the Falls, immigration procedure on the Paraguayan and Brazilian sides of the Friendship Bridge is minimal, even for those normally requiring a visa to visit Brazil. If in doubt, though, obtain all necessary exit and entrance stamps. If entering Paraguay, sit next to the bus exit so you can alight to visit Brazilian immigration for your exit stamp. Travellers report this crossing is very busy at weekends and not all buses stop at immigration. Paraguayan taxis cross freely to Brazil from Ciudad del Este, but bargain hard. You can pay in either currency.

Direct journeys to Argentina may be made by launch from Puerto Presidente Franco to Puerto Iguazú, US$0.50, about every 2 hours.

Many buses (US$8) and colectivos (up to US$10) run to and from Asunción, 3-7 hrs. Nuestra Señora and Rysa reported to run the best buses; also Sirena del Paraná and others. Bus to Encarnación, along fully paved road, 4 hrs., US$4.

The *Monday* falls, 10 km. from Ciudad del Este, are worth visiting by taxi. There is good fishing below the falls.

The huge **Itaipú** hydroelectric project is close to Ciudad del Este, and well worth a visit. Take a bus from Terminal Urbano to the Visitors' Centre, open 0730-1200, 1330-1700, Sun. and holidays 0800-1200, 1330-1630. Free conducted tours of the project include a film show half an hour before bus tour, starting at 0900, 1030, 1430, 1530 Mon.-Sat.; on Sundays and holidays they are at 0830, 0930, 1030, 1400, and 1500 (check times in advance). Take passport. If you don't like guided trips but still wish to visit the project call the Centro de Recepción de Visitas at the site (T8682), or apply to head office in Asunción (T 207161).

From Hernandarias, boat trips on Lago Itaipú go to Puerto Guaraní where there is a museum.

A paved road runs north from Coronel Oviedo. At 56 km. is Mbutuy (good *parador*, restaurant, petrol station) where a dirt road (Route 10) goes NE to Salto del Guaira, named for the waterfalls now under the Itaipú lake. Here there is a 900 hectare wildlife reserve. There is now a ferry to Brazil. There are daily buses from Asunción (14 hrs.). A wide, dry-weather road runs N from Hernandarias, via Itaquyry to the Coronel Oviedo – Salto del Guaira road at Cruce Guaraní.

36 km. north of Mbutuy is San Estanislao, museum, hotel, (E). North of San Estanislao, the road is paved to Lima and Santa Rosa (107 km. from San Estanislao), where there is petrol, *pensión* and restaurants. Here a dirt road runs SW to Nueva Germania (27 km.), a Mennonite colony, and further to San Pedro and Puerto Antequera on the Río Paraguay (88 km.). A further 23 km. N of Santa Rosa, a dirt road runs NE through jungle to Capitán Badó (120 km.) in the Cordillera Amambay which forms the frontier with Brazil. Another road follows the frontier north to P.J. Caballero (100 km.). 50 km. beyond the turn off to Capitán Badó is Yby Yaú, see page 894.

---

## SOUTHERN PARAGUAY (4)

**An attractive area of fertile landscapes, but especially notable for the Jesuit settlements with many fine churches now being restored or completed to the original plans.**

**Route One** runs through some of the old mission towns to Encarnación, 370 km. away, on the Alto Paraná.

Km. 37, *Itá* (pop. 9,310), an old town turning out rustic pottery (by Rosa Britez as you enter village). Km. 48, *Yaguarón*, founded in 1539, was the centre of the Franciscan missions in colonial times. It is set on a river at the foot of a hill in an orange-growing district, and has a famous church, begun by the Franciscans in 1640 and finished in 1720, reconstructed in 1885 and being renovated in 1990. (Open 0700-1100, 1400-1900.) The tints, made by the Indians from local plants, are still bright on the woodcarvings. Stations of the Cross behind the village lead to a good view of the surroundings. Most of Paraguay's petit-grain comes from the area. (For the by-road to Caacupé see page 895.) Buses every 15 mins or so from Asunción (US$0.75). (*Hotel Silva, Bar Elsi*, both F.)

"The corridor, or outside walk under a projecting roof supported by pillars, is a typical feature of Paraguayan churches. Generally it runs all the way round the church, forming an entrance portico in front. An excellent example is the church at Yaguarón. It is the prototype of the mission sanctuaries of the early 18th century, when the structure was built with a sturdy wooden skeleton and the walls – simple screens of adobe or brick – had no function of support. The belfry is a modest little wooden tower somewhat apart from the church; in the missions it also served as a *mangrullo*, or watch tower." - Paul Dony.

**Museum** Museo Doctor Francia, 700 metres from church, with relics of Paraguay's first dictator, "El Supremo". Open Tues., Thurs., Sat. 1500-1700; Sun. and holidays 0930-1130; 1500-1700.

Km. 63, **Paraguari**, founded 1775, the N entrance to the mission area, is on the railway (5,724 people), set among hills with many streams. Its church, though cruder, is reminiscent of that at Yaguarón. It has a curious bell tower.

**Hotel** *Hospedaje Bonanza*, F, friendly owners, basic.

24 km. north of Route 1 from Eusebio Ayala (pop: 5,316) is the **Vapor Cué National Park** with peaceful swimming and fishing in the river in the middle of fertile cattle country. It contains the remains of seven steamships sunk during the War of the Triple Alliance. Several boilers and one ship have been reconstructed. Camping is permitted, public transport runs to within 4 km. of the site. Transport can be hired in the village.

At Carapeguá Km. 84, there is a turn off Route 1 to Ybycuy; 18 km. away is one of the more accessible National Parks **(see page 892).**

Just before Km. 141 where the Tebicuary river is crossed by bridge (toll) is Caapucú (*Hotel Misiones*, F; bus from Asunción, US$1.25). At Km. 161 is **Villa Florida**, an ideal holiday resort for sailing, fishing and relaxing, with several hotels (*Nacional de Turismo, Las Mercedes*, 7 km. NE, good restaurant) and 2 *paradores*, camping near the river (good fishing); also at **Centú Cué**, 5 km. away, on the banks of the Tebicuary river, there are hotels (*Parador Centú Cué*, D full board, pleasant, peaceful; *Dorado*, D) and camping facilities, for reservations at either, T Asunción 206570 or directly to Centú Cué 083219. At San Miguel (Km. 178), all types of woollen articles are on sale (blankets, shawls, ponchos, hammocks, etc.). The small, peaceful town of **San Juan Bautista**, about half-way between Asunción and Encarnación, is worth a stop (pop. 6,872, *Waldorf Hotel*).

**San Ignacio Guazú**, Km. 226, is a delightful town which was the centre of an evangelical programme. Several typical Hispano-Guaraní buildings survive, pavillions and colonnades. An excellent museum, originally the Jesuits' art workshop, displays fine religious images and a reredos framing the Niño Jesus Alcalde. (Hotels: *Arapizandú*, F with restaurant; *El Puente*, F.) 12 km. to the NE along a cobbled road is Santa María, with another fine museum with some 60 Guaraní sculptures amongst the exhibits. The church has a lovely altar-piece of the Virgin and Child (if closed ask at the museum). Good local *artesanía* shop; simple *pensión*/restaurant on the plaza. You can get to Santa María by colectivo from San Ignacio.

From San Ignacio Guazú a road, Route 4, 156 km., runs W to **Pilar** (pop. 13,135), 306 km. S of Asunción, opposite the confluence of the Paraguay and the Bermejo, coming in from the Argentine Chaco. The road continues south west to the extreme SW tip of Paraguay, near Humaitá, the site of a heroic siege during the War of the Triple Alliance. Flights from Pilar to Asunción and Resistencia, Argentina, on Mon. and Thurs. by LAP. There are occasional boats to Argentina and Asunción.

At Santa Rosa (Km. 248), the church and adjacent oratorio have a beautiful Annunciation group and frescoes of the flight of the Holy Family's house from Nazareth to Loreto in Italy (poorly restored; ask for the priest to open it up). One local hotel: *Avenida*, F, on the outskirts. A road at Km. 262 leads 52 km. SW to Ayolas, associated with the Yacyretá hydroelectric scheme (*Hotel Nacional de Turismo*, D with shower, poor breakfast, otherwise OK; *El Dorado*, E, with good restaurant). Between the main road and Ayolas is Santiago, another important Jesuit centre founded in 1669 with a fine church, carved wooden doors and reredos depicting St. Francis Xavier and St. Philip. Also a fine wooden carving of Santiago slaying the Saracens. This is carried round the town on 25 July, the Saint's feast day. Coronel Bogado (pop. 5,180), Km. 319, is the southern limit of the mission area.

Turn off Route 1 just before Coronel Bogado for **San Cosmé y Damián** (343 km. from Asuncion). This is a remarkable place founded as a Jesuit mission in 1632, but moved to the present site in 1760, only 7 years before the Jesuits were expelled from the Spanish colonies. Hence the great church and ancillary buildings were never completed, though many of the wood carvings were saved. Now a huge completion project is under way following the original plans. Part of the nave is already roofed and is open for mass. Access to the site is possible during working hours, ask for the curator. Nearby is a neat new town where some of the Yacyretá dam workforce live. Route One reaches the Alto Paraná at Carmen del Paraná, Km. 331, 40 km. W of Encarnación, the terminus of the railway from Asunción. **Encarnación** (pop. 60,000), a busy port on the Alto Paraná, is connected by a bridge to the Argentine town of Posadas; the bridge was completed in 1990 and there is a bus across every 15 minutes (bicycles are not allowed to cross, but officials may give cyclists a lift). The town is a centre for the construction of the Yacyretá-Apipé dam to be shared by Paraguay and Argentina. Encarnación exports the products of a rich area: timber, soya, *mate*, tobacco, cotton, and hides; it is fast losing its traditional and very rural appearance. (Travellers should be prepared for cold weather, despite the latitude). The upper part of the town is not especially interesting, although prices here are lower than downtown near the river. The lower, older part of the colonial town will be flooded when the Yacyretá dam is completed. The cost of living is higher in Encarnación than in most other parts of Paraguay, but at present tourist goods and electrical equipment are much lower priced than in Posadas. The road parallel to the Alto Paraná to Ciudad del Este is now paved.

**Hotels** *Novohotel Encarnación*, A, first class, Route 1, km. 2, T 071-5120/24; *Repka*, Arquitecto Pereira 43, pretty garden, private baths, very good home cooking, E, bed and breakfast; *Cristal*, Estigarribia 1157, D, restaurant, good value; *Viena*, Calle Capitán P.J. Caballero 568 (T 071-3486), nr. bus station, beside Antelco, D with bath and small breakfast, German-run, good food, garage; *Paraná*, Estigarribia 1414, D, without breakfast, satisfactory; *Central*, Mcal. López 542, E, includes private bath and breakfast, German spoken; *Viera*, a/c, good location, E (F with fan), Estigarribia and 25 de Mayo, private bath; *Hospedaje Liz*, Estigarribia 1767, F with shower, fan, hot water, clean, good patio; *Hotel Liz*, same owner as *Hospedaje*, Av. Independencia 1746, F, new, rec.; *Suizo*, Mcal. Estigarribia 562, 3 blocks S of bus terminal, F without bath, E with, breakfast, clean; others near railway station, should be avoided even by the desperate. *Hospedaje*, Capitán P.J. Caballero 560, E, good value; *Pensión Vila Alegre*, Antequera 951, F, very basic but the people are pleasant and the food excellent.

**Restaurants** *Rubi*, Chinese, Mcal. Estigarribia 519, good; *Parrillada las Delicias*, Estigarribia 1694, good steaks, comfortable, Chilean wines; *Cuarajhy*, Estigarribia y Pereira, terrace seating, good food, open 24 hours; *Ñasaindy*, Estigarribia 900, for snacks; *Karanday*, Gral. Caballero, good grill. Good restaurants by the bus station, *Itapúa*, López y Cabañas.

**Taxis** Horsedrawn (about US$0.25), but prices tend to be high if drivers suspect you don't know the distance you want to travel. Some motor driven ones for those in a hurry. Horse-drawn taxi from railway station US$1.25 (compared with US$3.75 by car).

**Exchange** Lloyds Bank, agency at Villarrica y Mariscal Estigarribia, open Mon.-Fri. 0845-1215; **Banco Unión**, Estigarribia 1404, will change travellers' cheques (with purchase receipt). Many money-changers at the Paraguayan side but will only change notes. *Casas de cambio* for travellers' cheques on Mariscal Estagarribia.

**International Phone** Antelco, Capitán P.J. Caballero y Mcal. López, 0700-2200, unfriendly.

**Tourist Office** Oficina de Cultura, Municipalidad building, Kreusser y Estigarribia, helpful; street map of city.

**Consulates** Argentina, at Cabañas y Mallorquín. Germany at Memmel 631.

**Transport** Train to Asunción, 17 (can take 24) hours, US$2.50, 1st class (no sleepers), US$1.90, 2nd class, Wed. at 1530 (2nd class carriages commence journey at Posadas at 1230).
  The bus terminal is at Estigarribia y Memmel; good cheap snacks at terminal. To/from **Asunción**, Alborada, Flecha de Oro, Rysa, Nuestra Señora de la Asunción, all except last named at least 4 a day, 6 hrs., US$8.50; colectivo with Halcones. Bus to **Trinidad**, US$0.40, 30 mins, every hour. Bus to **Ciudad del Este** US$4, several daily, 4 hrs. Buses also to **Villarrica**. The new San Roque road bridge connects Encarnación with **Posadas**, with colectivos from terminal crossing every 15 minutes 0600-2400, US$1, 30 mins. (when you get off at immigration each end, keep ticket and catch next bus).

On arrival, remember to obtain your tourist card which costs US$3, payable in dollars, australes or guaraníes. Argentinians staying less than 24 hours do not need tourist cards.

From Encarnación a paved road (Route 6) goes NE to Ciudad del Este. At Km. 21, just beyond Capitán Miranda, is *Hotel Tirol*, C/B, with 40 double rooms, chalets, 2 swimming pools, terraces, comfortable, but used as a stopover for Argentine coach tours. A further 7 km. towards Ciudad del Este is ***Trinidad*** where there is a great Jesuit church, once utterly in ruins but restoration is proceeding and a museum is being set up. The church was founded in 1706 by Padre Juan de Anaya; the architect was Juan Bautista Prímoli. For information, or tours of the ruins, contact Sr. Augusto Servián Goana, the curator who lives close by. A US$3 booklet by Clement MacWaspy is available at the site. A visit to the church and museum is recommended (hours of opening 0730-1130, 1330-1730), also for the surrounding countryside. Near the ruined church at Trinidad is a small modern church; it contains a large carved wooden statue of the Deity, so hollowed at the back that a priest in hiding could simulate the resounding voice of the Eternal Father to impress the Indians of the mission. Many buses go from Encarnación to and through Trinidad (a taxi tour from Encarnación costs about US$30). You can stay at the Centro Social, food and shower available, take sleeping gear; camp behind the souvenir stall.

Ten Km. NW of Trinidad is Jesús, where another group of Jesuits finally settled in 1763. In the five years before they were expelled they commenced a massive construction programme including church, sacristy, *residencia* and a baptisty, on one side of which is a square tower. There is a fine front façade with three great arched portals showing an unexpected oriental influence. Beautiful views in all directions. Irregular buses go from Encarnación (1½ hours) and Trinidad. Enquire locally.

From Trinidad the road goes through or near a number of German colonies including Hohenan (Km. 36), Obligado, Bella Visa (Km. 42) and, at Km. 67, a cobbled side road leads to Pirapó, a Japanese settlement. This is a prosperous agricultural area, attractive countryside and facilities for travellers en route. Eventually Route 6 meets Route 2 close to Ciudad del Este.

## THE PARAGUAYAN CHACO (5)

A remarkable area of low marshlands and estates developed by German-speaking Mennonites and other religious groups. Birdlife is spectacular.

The Paraguayan Chaco covers 24 million hectares, but under 100,000 people live there. A single road, the Transchaco Highway, runs in a straight line north-west to the Bolivian border 20 km. beyond Nueva Asunción, at General A. Garay. It is paved more or less to Mariscal Estigarribia and a dirt road thereafter, very difficult to negotiate after rain. The elevation rises very gradually from 50 metres opposite Asunción to 450 metres on the Bolivian border.

The Chaco is divisible into 3 terrains. The first, the Low Chaco, leaving Asunción, is open palm forest and marshes, much of which is permanently beneath shallow water. The lack of slope and the impermeable clay hardpan mean the water hardly moves. The palm forest is used for cattle ranching of the most extensive type, some *estancias* lying several hundred km. down tracks off the highway. The cattle are very mixed – English Herefords, Indian Brahmins, and Brazilian. Most *estancias* are chronically overstocked and overgrazed; calving rates are very low. Remote *estancias* have their own airfields, and all are equipped with 2-way radios.

The Middle Chaco, around the capital, Filadelfia, has been settled by Mennonites, latterday Baptists chiefly of German extraction who arrived in Paraguay from 1930 onwards. They set up three distinct colonies: Menno (from Canada and Mexico, but originally from Russia); Fernheim (the first group directly from Russia) and Neuland (the last group to arrive, also from Russia, after 1945). The Mennonites speak "plattdeutsch" – a cross between Dutch and German, and normal "hochdeutsch"; very few speak Spanish. Altogether there are 118 villages with a population of about 10,000 Mennonites, 10,000 Indians and a very small number of other immigrants. The natural cover is scrubland with a mixture of hardwoods, and more cactus further north. The bottle-tree with a pear-shaped, water-conserving, trunk, and the *quebracho* (axe-breaker), used for tannin, are native.

The Mennonites, who run their own banks, schools, hospitals and a cooperative agricultural system, are the only organized community in the Chaco. They are mainly crop-farmers (though they also run dairy cattle and make cheese and butter) and grow grapefruit, lemons, groundnuts, sorghum and cotton.

From Filadelfia an alternative route goes north and into the north-west Chaco where most of the remaining jaguars are found. This road is very rough, but the main highway remains negotiable by car although it narrows. In the western sector scattered military outposts are the only human presence. The whole area is under military jurisdiction; the visitor may find a letter of authorization or military introduction useful.

The north-western part, the High Chaco, is a low thorn forest, an impenetrable barricade of hard spikes and spiny branches resistant to fire, heat and drought. Occasional tracks lead off the highway for a short distance. Towards Bolivia cactus becomes more concentrated. There are a few *estancias* further south, where the brush is bulldozed into hedges and the trees left for shade. In summer it is very hot. The animal life – wild hog, puma, jaguar, tapir – congregates around the water-holes at night. The whole area is a national park.

The primeval character of the Chaco is reflected in the 1975 discovery of a kind of wild hog, formerly thought extinct since the Pleistocene era, now listed as Wagner's peccary. When camping out fires should be kept up to deter the local fauna; the greatest danger is from several species of poisonous snakes. Grass round the tent should be cut. The highway is a smuggling route from Bolivia, so it is unwise to stop for anyone in the night. In the High Chaco there is almost no traffic.

The Chaco's Indian population is nomadic and Guaraní-speaking, and sets up little brushwood and mud villages wherever there is a plentiful food-supply. The Indians eat everything, bird and mammal, and even the poisonous snakes. The great delicacy is armadillo. Anthropologists have found the Indians' social structures, marriage and death rites as inscrutable as the surrounding countryside. They are friendly and peaceful, and periodically work on the *estancias*.

No expedition should be without supplies of water, food and fuel. Although there are service stations in the Middle and Low Chaco self-sufficiency is advised. Ill-equipped expeditions have had to be rescued by the army or have come to grief. In winter temperatures are warm and comfortable by day, cooler by night. In summer heat and mosquitoes make it very unpleasant (pyrethrum coils – *espirales* – are available throughout the region). The Low Chaco is one of the foremost bird habitats in the world, and although bird-life may be enjoyed from the road it is still comparatively unknown and rarely visited. Until recently entry into the Chaco was by plane only. The rapid development of the Highway will surely open it up before long; land purchases, especially by foreigners, and oil exploration are on the increase.

To reach the Transchaco, you leave Asunción by the route across the Río Paraguay to Villa Hayes. At Km. 270 is Pozo Colorado (turning for Concepción, **see page 893**). Then after a further 80 km., one starts seeing the Mennonites' neat little homes with painted wooden shutters, surrounded by flowering plants and orchards. A good place to eat on the Transchaco is at Km. 415, called Cruce Loma Plata; fuel also available. The centres are Filadelfia and Loma Plata, clean modern agricultural communities with wide unpaved streets. *Filadelfia*, 472 km. from Asunción, is the largest centre in the Chaco. The Unger Museum at Filadelfia (US$0.90) gives a good idea what this industrious people had to go through to make this rich area what it is today (ask at the Information Office, two doors left of *Hotel Florida*, for opening times). Some Indian tribes live nearby, but have been "civilized", seemingly to their disadvantage.

**Hotel** *Florida*, in Filadelfia, new wing with a/c and private bath, C, very comfortable, old section, fans and shared bath, F (uncomfortable, beetles), sells excellent German cakes. **Restaurants**: *La Estrella* recommended for good ice cream and *asados*; another good restaurant *La Girasol*, opposite; *Remi*, on same street, pizzas and good ice cream. Plenty of good ice cream parlours (you need them in the heat), but no bars. 2 km. south-east is the Parque Trébol, a charming public park, with facilities where one can camp. Lots of frog noise at night, however.

**Buses** The Mennonite bus company, Chaco Boreal, leaves from the colonies for Asunción daily, US$7; in Asunción, Chaco Boreal leaves from Comité Central Menonita at 1800 daily. Nasa leaves Filadelfia for Asunción at 1900, make reservations early (in Asunción, office is at Colombia 1050, T 26059, dep. 1400, stopping at main bus terminal at 1430, and 2200, US$11); the bus from Asunción stops at all 3 communities and ends at Neuland There is a travel agency, the Reiseburo, close to *Hotel Florida*.

Nearby is **Loma Plata** (*Hotel Loma Plata*, E/F, with restaurant, can be booked from the Mennonite centre in Asunción). Good hotel in the village of Neu Hallestadt, Neuland, is

*Boquerón*, E with breakfast. Ask around in Filadelfia for people to drive you round the Mennonite communities (US$0.15 per km.).

**To Bolivia** From Filadelfia to the Bolivian border 20 km. beyond General Eugenio A. Garay is 304 km. Best to fill up with fuel at Filadelfia; well-stocked supermarkets in Filadelfia and Loma Plata. There are sparse facilities (cafés, fuel) until Mariscal Estigarribia (*Hotel Alemán*, E with breakfast, friendly). You can change money at the supermarket *Chaparral*, and local German priests may offer you a bed. Thereafter only military outposts or *estancias* may offer food, fuel and perhaps a bed for the night. At Km. 662 a Centro Urbano Rural is under construction, with motel and service station, at Estancia La Patria. 95 km. bryond La Patria there is an airbase (at Nueva Asunción) where you can get water, but you may have to show your papers and be registered. Trucks travel all the way to Bolivia, three a week at the last count. They stop at the Esso Station on the Hindenbergallee in Filadelfia. You can try to hitch. Frequent Army identity checks are inevitable. It is important to have photographs on documents which are a good likeness to the bearer. Backpackers need expect no special difficulties. Take plenty of food and water since even the smallest amount of rain can cause delays. You can camp 13 km. short of General Garay at Fortín Mt. Long. If possible, do not give up your passport to the *guardia* if staying overnight, you may have to wait to have it returned the following day. For the continuation of this route, see under **Boyuibe** in **Bolivia, Section 2**.

Some maps show another route to Bolivia, going west from Mariscal Estigarribia to Fortín Infante Rivarola on the border, then through Ibibobo to Villa Montes. We have received no reports on this or other routes through the Chaco to Bolivia and Argentina.

---

## INFORMATION FOR VISITORS

**Documents** A passport is required. Visitors are registered on arrival by the immigration authorities and get their documents back immediately. For a stay of up to 90 days, visitors are issued tourist cards, on arrival by air or land; they cost US$3 (payable in dollars or guaraníes – cheaper). This procedure applies to those who do not require visas. Citizens of the following countries do NOT need a visa (January 1990): USA, Canada, UK, Germany, Austria, Belgium, Spain, Italy, Holland, Denmark, Norway, Sweden, Switzerland, Israel, Japan, Argentina, Uruguay, Brazil, Chile, Ecuador, Colombia, El Salvador, Guatemala. All others must apply for a visa, which is free, presenting a valid passport and photograph. If you do not complete formalities you can be turned back at the border, or have trouble when leaving Paraguay.

**Airport Tax** is US$5, payable in US$ or guaraníes (tends to be cheaper).

**Flights from Europe** Iberia has one weekly flight to Asunción from Madrid, via Rio and São Paulo. Líneas Aéreas Paraguayas (LAP – now a member of IATA) has a twice-weekly service from Frankfurt, via Brussels and/or Madrid (once a week with a refuelling stop in Dakar, Senegal). From other points in Europe, slow connections can be made via Rio or São Paulo (Varig or LAP). Routes from Europe via Brazil offer greater ticketing flexibility than other options.

**From North America** American operates three times a week New York-Miami-Lima-La Paz-Asunción. LAP also operates flights from Miami to Asunción. Alternatively from New York, connections every day via Rio, but Varig's connecting flights are slow. From California, connections via Lima or Miami.

**Within South America** From Montevideo (once a week) by Líneas Aéreas Paraguayas (LAP) or Pluna; from Buenos Aires by Aerolíneas Argentinas (from Aeroparque domestic airport via Corrientes, or direct from Ezeiza), or LAP (from Ezeiza international airport); from Santiago (6 a week) by Ladeco (Chile) and LAP; from Lima (5 a week) by LAP or American; from La Paz (three a week) by American or once a week with LAB via Cochabamba and Santa Cruz (Bolivia), LAP also flies from Santa Cruz once a week; from Rio, São Paulo and Iguazú Falls (daily) by Varig; from São Paulo and Rio de Janeiro thrice weekly by LAP; from Río and São

Paulo, without stop at Iguazú, two Ladeco (Chile) and one Iberia flight per week.

**By Sea from Europe** for freight, the only regular all-water direct service is Europe-Paraguay Line from Grangemouth, Rotterdam, Bremen, Hamburg, Antwerp and Bilbao, owned by Hamburg Süd Eggert & Amsinck, Ost-Weststrasse 59, Hamburg 11, and van Nievelt, Goudriaan & Co, BV, Veerhaven 2, 3016 CJ Rotterdam. Agent: Belserve/Belgian Maritime Services, Antwerp (T 03-232 25 44).

**By Land/River from Argentina** The international rail route from Buenos Aires to Posadas is given on **page 890.** There is a paved road from Buenos Aires via Santa Fe to Clorinda and then on new paved roads via the borders at Puerto Pilcomayo and the new Remanso Castillo suspension bridge to Asunción: 1,370 km., about 23 hrs.; also via Posadas to Encarnación across the new San Roque bridge. Good bus services on these routes. After the border at Puerto Falcón, before the Remanso Castillo bridge, a road forks to the Paraguayan Chaco (paved part of the way) and on to Bolivia. Boat services on the Río Paraná between Buenos Aires and Asunción are irregular, depending on the level of the river.

**To/From Brazil** The headwaters of both the Paraguay and the Alto Paraná are in Brazil. There are unscheduled boat services from Asunción northward along the Paraguay river to Porto Esperança, Brazil (from which there is a railway to São Paulo), and scheduled services to Corumbá (1,220 km. – **see page 890)**, which is connected by road, rail and air with Bolivian and Brazilian cities. The normal means of surface communications are by road between Foz do Iguaçu and Ciudad del Este, and between Pedro Juan Caballero and Ponta Porã. Frontier with Brazil is officially closed at weekends but it is worth checking as sometimes passports will be stamped on Sunday.

**International Bus Services** See under Asunción, **page 891.**

**Customs** "Reasonable quantities" of tobacco products, alcoholic drinks and perfume are admitted free of duty.

**Travel in Paraguay: By Air** There are scheduled services to most parts of the country by Líneas Aéreas de Transporte Nacional (LATN) and to Concepción, Vallemí, Bahía Negra and Fuerte Olimpo by Transportes Aéreos Militares (TAM). Planes can be chartered.

**By Rail** Passenger services are very slow. There are police on all passenger trains; make sure you are carrying your documents.

**By Road** Buses ply on the main roads. For motorists, there are sufficient service stations in Paraguay, except in the Chaco area. Motorists should beware stray cattle on the road at night. Diesel fuel is US$0.25 per litre in Paraguay; gasoline users should use only *super* (Shell Spark Aider Super is recommended), US$0.45 per litre (which is 93 octane; regular gas, *alconafta*, contains 10-15% alcohol at US$0.40 per litre). It is highly recommended that drivers in Paraguay (and neighbouring countries) use diesel-powered vehicles as almost all the locals do: not only is diesel usually cheaper than gasoline, but a diesel engine will not stop in water, has no ignition/carburettor problems, and will not encounter the corrosive effects of alcohol in the fuel. Motor fuel and oil are sold in Paraguay by the litre. The documents needed in Paraguay for private cars are international car registration and driver's licence. **Warning**: beware of traffic police claiming that an International Driving Licence is not valid, or some other vague charge, and then demanding an "on-the-spot fine" of US$5 (at the very least). For entry into Brazil the only document necessary is the title to the car (or other proof of ownership). Touring y Automóvil Club Paraguayo has an adequate road map but, we are told, not updated since 1985. It is essential to drive at walking pace through military areas and stop completely if a flag ceremony is in progress.

**Car Hire** Average rates are US$27 a day for a 2-door vehicle to US$52 for a

4-door with a/c, 100 km. free (prices National/Europcar, Dec. 1990). Weekly and free kilometres available. Hertz offers unlimited mileage for reasonable rates, free delivery to airport, minimum rental 3 days, but no insurance whatsoever. You will be responsible for any accident, damage or theft.

**Motor Repairs** A recommended mechanic is Lauro C. Noldin, Dr. Moleón Andreu 493 y 4ta Proyectada, Barrio Santa Librada, Asunción, T 33933; he repairs Land Rover, Range Rover, Jaguar and all makes of British, European, American and Japanese cars, diesel and petrol engines, motorcycles, power generators for motor homes. Bosch Garage Office, Chispa SA, Carios y José Rivera, Asunción, T 553315/7. Recommended garage, especially for Volkswagen repairs: Rodolfo Stecher, Av. Fernando de la Mora 920, Asunción. Caravan and camper repairs at Metalúrgica Anahí SRL (Sr. Julio Schmidt), República de Colombia 261, Km. 7, Fernando de la Mora, Asunción, T 503335. For diesel service, MBT service garage at Av. Eusebio Ayala y Lapacho Km. 4, T Asunción 553318. Land Rover body repairs at Taller San José of José Escobar at Battilana, casi Santo Domingo, T 203311. A recommended Land Rover parts source is Repuestos Agromotor at Herrera 604, Asunción. Good mechanics at Premetal Alemán, near crossing Eusebio Ayala with Rep. Argentina (T 64131). Spares are available in Paraguay for all makes of car (European, North American, Asian); also available are most makes of tyre.

**Food and Drink** Typical local foods include *chipas* (yuca bread flavoured with egg and cheese), *chipa soo* (maize bread with meat filling) and *sopa paraguaya* (a kind of dumpling of ground maize and cheese). *Soyo* is a soup of different meats and vegetables, delicious; *albóndiga* a soup of meat balls; *bori bori* another type of soup with diced meat, vegetables, and small balls of maize mixed with cheese. *Palmitos* (palm hearts) should not be missed; the beef is excellent in better class restaurants (best cuts are *lomo* and *lomito*). Paraguayan *chorizos* (sausages) are good. *Parrillada completa* is recommended. *Surubí*, a Paraná river fish, is prepared in many different ways, and is delicious. Sugar-cane juice, greatly beloved, is known as *mosto*. Fruit is magnificent. Very typical of Paraguay is *tereré* (cold *mate* with digestive herbs) for warm days and hot *mate* to warm you up on cold days. The national wine is not recommended (better is imported from Chile), but the local lager beer is acceptable and the cane-sugar spirit, *caña* is good (the best is "Aristocrat"; ask for "Ari").

**Tipping** Hotels, restaurants, 10%. Railway and airport porters US$0.15 a suitcase. Taxis, 10%. Porters at docks US$0.40 a suitcase. Cinema usherettes are not tipped.

**What to Buy** The famous *ñandutí* lace, made exclusively by the women of Itauguá (**see page 895**). The local jewellery is also attractive. Handmade *ahopoi* (fine cloth) is suitable for shirts and blouses, and there are cotton thread belts in all colours. The best place to buy these items is Villarrica. Tourists are often attracted by the leather articles, the pottery and small wooden articles made from Paraguayan woods. See also "Shopping", under Asunción (**page 887**). Imported goods, especially cameras and film, are cheaper in Paraguay than in most other Latin American countries (although prices in the UK, for instance, are cheaper).

**Security** The proverbial "official-looking" letter is useful. Searches for "communist" literature may still be made at land borders. Since President Stroessner was deposed the political atmosphere is more relaxed and political discussion more open. Avoid provocation however, e.g. taking pictures of "military" installations. Apparently, hitch-hiking is still illegal, although possible in rural areas. Generally, travellers find Paraguay safer than the neighbouring countries, but check prices and change.

**Health** Tuberculosis, typhoid, dysentery, and hepatitis are endemic. Hookworm is the most common disease in the country, and there is much venereal disease, goitre and leprosy. Visitors should be inoculated against tetanus, typhoid, and paratyphoid. Be very careful over salad and tap water. Local mosquito repellant, *Repel*, and pyrethrum coils are effective. Dengue fever (**see Health Information**) has recently been reported. Medical fees and medicine costs are high. The Centro Paraguayo del Diagnóstico, Gral. Díaz 975 y Colón, Asunción, is recommended as inexpensive, foreign languages spoken. Clínica Integral de Mujer, Mcal. Estigarribia 1085 y Brasil, Asunción, T 94722, has been recommended as a good gynaecological clinic. Dentists can be found either at the centre, or at Odontología 3, Mcal. Estigarribia 1414 y Pai Pérez, T 200175, Asunción.

**Business Visitors** Foreign business is transacted in Asunción, Ciudad del Este and Pedro Juan Caballero (with retail outlets particularly in the last two). From May to October is the best time for a visit. British business travellers are advised to get a copy of "Hints to Exporters: Paraguay", obtainable from the Department of Trade, Sanctuary Buildings, 16-20 Gt Smith Street, London SW1P 3DB.

**Clothing** In summer, January to March, tropical clothing, sunglasses and an umbrella are needed. The best time to visit is from May to September, when the heat is not too oppressive.

**Business Hours** Paraguayans are up early and many shops, offices and businesses open between 0630 and 0700. *Siesta* (generally observed during the hot season) is from 1200 to 1500. Commercial office hours are from 0730 to 1100 or 1130, and 1430 or 1500 to 1730 or 1900. Banks: from 0730 to 1100, closed on Saturday and Sunday. Government offices are open 0630 to 1130 in summer, 0730 to noon, in winter, open on Sat.

**Official Holidays** 1 Jan; 3 Feb; 1 March; Maundy Thursday, Good Friday; 1, 14, 15, May; Corpus Christi, 12 June; 15, 25, Aug.; 29 Sep.; 12 Oct.; 1 Nov.; 8, 25 Dec.

**Time Zone** 3-4 hours behind GMT (clocks go on 1 hour in local summer time).

**Currency** The Guaraní (plural Guaraníes) is the unit of currency, symbolized by the letter G (crossed). There are bank notes for 100, 500, 1,000, 5,000 and 10,000 guaraníes and coins for 1, 5, 10 and 50 guaraníes. It is possible to buy US dollar bills in Asunción (**see page 888**), and rates for all foreign currencies, except bolivianos, are reasonable. Get rid of all your guaraníes before leaving Paraguay; there is no market for them elsewhere (except in some *cambios* in Buenos Aires or Montevideo). *Casas de cambio* will cash travellers' cheques for US dollars in Asunción for a 1% commission; they sometimes want to see customers' records of purchase before accepting travellers' cheques. Visitors are advised to check on the situation on changing travellers' cheques in advance. Visa and Mastercharge cash advances are a possibility in Asunción. Street dealers operate from early in the morning until late at night, even at weekends or public holidays. In Asunción their rates are marginally better than the *casas de cambio* during business hours only, but they are not recommended at Ciudad del Este.

Visa and Mastercharge credit cards are widely accepted even for small purchases. Foreign-issued Visa cards may not always be accepted though a phone call will often resolve the problem; Visa is displayed as Unioncard. Credit card transactions are subject to a 10% tax.

**Cost of Living** is generally cheap. Hotels in our G range are rare although there are many good ones in our F-E ranges, with breakfast, private shower and toilet.

**Weights and Measures** The metric system is used except by carpenters, who use inches.

**Electricity** Nominally 220 volts AC and 50 cycles, but power surges and voltage drops are frequent. European round pin plugs are used.

**Postal and Telegraph Services** Postal services are cheap and efficient. A normal airmail letter to Europe costs US$0.25 and a registered air letter US$0.35. Register important mail if you want it delivered. Parcels may be sent from main post office on El Paraguayo Independiente, Asunción. Rates: up to 5 kg, US$4 by surface, US$10 by air; 15-20 kg, US$10 by surface, US$35 by air. Packages under 2 kg should be handed in at the small packages window, not "encomiendas". Customs inspection of open parcel required.

The telephone service (few telephone boxes) links the main towns, and there is a telephone service with most countries, operated by Antelco. Collect calls are difficult, charge US$0.30 extra. A phone call to Europe, Australia, and South Africa costs US$2.50 a minute; USA, Canada, US$2 a minute; Spain, US$1.50 a minute. Fax to Europe US$3 per page from Asunción Post Office, more in other towns, to receive 3 pages US$1.20. A telex message to Britain is US$5 (1 minute). There is a US$2.50 tax charged by the Post Office for all telexes sent or received in Paraguay.

**Newspapers** *El Diario; Hoy, La Tarde, Ultima Hora, El Diario Noticias* and *El Pueblo* are published daily in Asunción. English-language papers from Argentina and Brazil are available the following day at corner of Estrella and Chile.

**Sports** Football is very popular. Tennis and horse-racing are popular. There are two rowing and swimming clubs of some 2,000 members, and a motor-boat club with 150 members, in Asunción. Swimming in the Río Paraguay is not recommended: beware stinging starfish where there is mud on the islands and beaches. Golf is played in the Botanical Garden, and there is a Paraguayan Aviation Club. There are two boxing rings. Fishing, basketball and rugby football are popular.

**Tourist Information** The Dirección Nacional de Turismo has an office at Palma 468 in Asunción. Information about weather and roads from Touring y Automóvil Club Paraguayo (TACP) at 25 de Mayo y Brasil (who also produce a road map), and the office of the traffic police in Asunción. The best map is available from Instituto Geográfico Militar, Av. Artigas (on the way to the zoo), price US$4.50, take passport. Small national maps, made by the Army, can be bought from the TACP, at bookshops and bus terminals. The USAID office has a good booklet on Paraguay. Other books: *Así es el Paraguay* (with maps and very useful information) and *Paraguay, Land of Lace and Legend* (reprinted 1983, available from bookshops and Anglo-Paraguayan and US-Paraguay cultural institutes in Asunción); also *Green Hill, Far Away*, by Peter Upton.

We are most grateful to Peter Pollard for doing the updating and to the following travellers: Simon Watson Taylor for much detailed information, Rob Allan and Bridgit Vale (Pietermaritzburg), Rick Ansell and Paulette Milego (Porto Alegre), Frank Bakker and Nike Darley (Amsterdam), Petra Bell and Hans-Georg Henle (Schwaigern, Germany), Gordon Bethell (St. Leonards of Sea, East Sussex), Go Bruëns (Utrecht, Netherlands), Bryan Crawford (Inverness), Kirsten Eichhorn (München, Germany), Tim Farnworth (Market Harborough, Leicestershire), Rüdiger Filbrich (Frankfurt/Main), Glyn Fry and Trui Anseeuw (Hyde, Cheshire), Theodor A. Gevert (São Paulo), Doris Goll (Gossau) and Andy Stocker (Buchrain, Switz.), Michael S. Gonin (Canberra), Loukas Grafakos (Papagou, Greece), Pilou Grenié (Antibes), Eric Hamovitch (Montréal, Canada), Lucy Harper, Gert Jan Hof and Yvonne Evers (Huissen, Neth), Ralf Hönsch and Martin Stark (Switzerland), Sabine Imhoff (Germany), Karen Johnson (British Columbia, Canada), Anne Toft Johnsen (Frederiksberg, Denmark), Wolfgang D. Kleine (Windhoek, Namibia), Melinda, Louis and Aviva Lenoff (Santiago) Herbert Levi (Buenos Aires), John Lewis (London NW2), Karl Liebhardt (Asunción), Hans Liechti and Veronica Araneda de Liechti (Grenchen, Switzerland), James Maas (Panama), Markus Maier and Gitte Wiedmann (Zürich), Simon Mays Smith (Waldron, East Sussex), Tom Amies (Bucks) and Simon Davy (England), Andy Millbank (Norwich), Bernard Milward (Salvador), Karen Müller (Port Elizabeth, South Africa) and Annika Henrysson (Karlskoga, Sweden), Steve Newman and Wendy Chilcott (Horsham, West Sussex), Asbjørn Nielsen (Denmark) Veronika Paul (San Carlos, CA, U.S.A.), Guido Pfister (Weisslingen, Switzerland), Thomas Pichler (Berlin 65), Melanie and David Poley (England), Arthur Poyner (Chiloe), Bernd Proissl (Wernau), John Raspey (Argentina), Florian and Erdbeere Schulz (Berlin 27), Ulrich Sigel (Schorndorf, Germany), Christoph Theis (Wiesloch, Germany), Roger Thornton and Paul Gadd (London N5), Jarle Unneland (Alesund, Norway), Andreas Vogt (Mössingen, Germany), Peter and Miek Vullings (Panningen, Netherlands), Thomas Walbaum (Steinheim, Germany), Dr Volker Weinmann (São Paulo, Brazil), Manfred Wolfensberger (Uster, Switzerland), Julian Woodhouse (London NW3), and Bart Zwart (Eindhoven, Netherlands).

# PERU

**Maps** Country, 909; Lima, 920; Lima Orientation, 941; Lima to Callejón de Huaylas, 946; Trujillo and environs, 961; Northern Peru, 966; Cajamarca and environs, 970; Chiclayo and environs, 980; Southern Peru, 997; Arequipa, 1005; Puno, 1013; Cuzco, 1021; Urubamba Valley, 1035; Huancayo, 1047; Oroya-Pucallpa, 1057; Iquitos, 1065.

## INTRODUCTION

PERU, the third largest South American country, with an area of 1,285,216 sq. km. (over twice the size of France) presents formidable difficulties to human habitation. The whole of its western seaboard with the Pacific is desert on which rain seldom falls. From this coastal shelf the Andes rise steeply to a high Sierra which is studded with massive groups of soaring mountains and gouged with deep canyons. The highland slopes more gradually eastwards; the mountains in its eastern zone are deeply forested and ravined. Eastward from these mountains lie the vast jungle lands of the Amazon basin.

The coastal region, a narrow ribbon of desert 2,250 km. long, takes up 11% of the country and holds 44% of the population. When irrigated, the river valleys are extremely fertile. Almost 600,000 hectares are watered today, creating 40 oases which grow cotton throughout the country, sugar-cane and rice in the N, and grapes, fruit and olives in the S. Petroleum comes from the N and Amazonia. The coastal zone is the economic heart of Peru; it consumes most of the imports and supplies half of the exports. Climate is determined by cold sea-water adjoining deserts: prevailing inshore winds pick up so little moisture over the cold Peruvian current that only for five months, from June to October, does it condense. The resultant blanket of cloud and sea-mist extends from the S to about 200 km. N of Lima. This *garúa* dampens isolated coastal zones of vegetation (called *lomas*) and they are grazed by livestock driven down from the mountains. The Peruvian coastal current teems with fish, and Peru has had the largest catch in the world; however, in recent years, the *anchoveta* shoals have moved southward into Chilean waters. At intervals during December-April a current of warm water, known as "El Niño", is blown S from the equator over the cold offshore waters

PERU 94

COLOMBIA

ECUADOR

BRAZIL

BOLIVIA

CHILE

PACIFIC OCEAN

Guayaquil — To Quito
Machala
Cuenca
Tumbes
Loja
Macará
Río Tumbes
Sullana
Piura
Río Piura
Jaén
Chachapoyas — 3
Iquitos — Río Amazonas — Leticia
Río Marañón
Moyobamba
Yurimaguas
Río Huallaga
Río Ucayali
Cajamarca
Chiclayo
Pacasmayo
Pucallpa — 8
Trujillo
Chimbote
Corás
Huaraz — Tingo María
Cruzeiro do Sul
Huánuco
Cerro de Pasco
La Merced
Pativilca
La Oroya — 7
Brasiléia
Iñapari
Callao
LIMA — 1
Huancayo
Puerto Maldonado — 6
Huancavelica — Ayacucho — Machu Picchu
Pisco — Andahuaylas — Cuzco
Ica — Abancay — Sicuani
Nazca — 4 — 5
Juliaca — Lake Titicaca
Chala — Puno — Copacabana
Arequipa — Juli
Matarani — Moquegua — LA PAZ
Mollendo — Ilo
Tacna
Arica
To Santiago

1 Lima.
2 North West from Lima.
3 The Northern Oases
4 South East from Lima.
5 Arequipa — Puno-Cuzco-Machu Picchu.
6 The South Eastern Jungle.
7 Inland from Lima.
8 Cerro de Pasco to Iquitos.

and the surface temperature rises, the fish migrate, and evaporation is so great that the desert is deluged with rain which creates havoc (most recently in 1983).

In the Sierra, at an average altitude of 3,000 metres, which covers 26% of the country, live about 50% of the people, an excessive density on such poor land. This high-level land of gentle slopes is surrounded by towering groups and ranges of high peaks. Ten are over 6,000 metres; the highest, Huascarán, is 6,768 metres. There are many volcanoes in the S. The continental divide is the western rim of mountains looking down on the Pacific. Rivers which rise in these mountains and flow towards the Amazon cut through the cold surface of the plateau in canyons, sometimes 1,500 metres deep, in which the climate is tropical. Pastoral farming is possible on about 13 million hectares of the plateau; the deep valley basins contain the best land for arable farming.

The plateau, mountains and canyons are inhabited mostly by Indians. There are 5,000 Indian communities but few densely populated settlements. Their literacy rate is the lowest of any comparable group in South America and their diet is 40% below acceptable levels. Nearly 99% of the rural population and 60% of the town dwellers have no running water or drainage. About two million Indians speak no Spanish, their main tongue being Quechua, the language of the Incas; they are largely outside the money economy.

A mostly Indian labour force of over 80,000 is engaged in mining, and mineral exports from the Sierra represent half of total exports. Minerals are extracted as far up as 5,200 metres. Some of the sheep-farming areas are at altitudes ranging up to 4,250 metres.

The wide areas of high and wind-swept Altiplano in S Peru are near the limit of agriculture—though some potatoes and cereals (*quinoa* and *cañihua*) are grown—but the Indians use it for grazing llamas, alpacas and sheep; it cannot support cattle. The pastoral Indians of the area live off their flocks; they weave their clothes from the wools, eat the meat, use the dried dung for fuel and the llamas for transport. They are, in short, almost entirely self-supporting.

The **Montaña**, or **Selva**, the forested eastern half of the Andes and the land beyond covered with tropical forest and jungle, is 62% of the country's area but holds only about 5% of the population. Its inhabitants are crowded on the river banks in the cultivable land—a tiny part of the area. The few roads (given in the text) have to cope with dense forest, deep valleys, and sharp eastern slopes ranging from 2,150 metres in the N to 5,800 metres E of Lake Titicaca. Rivers are the main highways, though navigation is hazardous and the draught of the vessels shallow. The area's potential is enormous: immense reserves of timber, excellent land for the production of rubber, jute, rice, tropical fruits and coffee and the breeding of cattle. Few of these products come out by road to the W; most of them converge by river on Iquitos, which is 11,250 km. from Callao via the Panama Canal and the Amazon but only 1,010 km. as the condor flies.

Oilfields have been discovered southwards from the Ecuadorean border and estimates indicate that about 80% of Peru's oil reserves are in the jungle area. The Nor Peruano oil pipeline links the Amazon area with the coast.

**Climate** The climate of the highlands is varied: the W side is dry, but the northern and eastern parts get very heavy rains from October to April, and are heavily forested up to a limit of 3,350 metres: the grasslands are between the forest line and the snowline, which rises from 5,000 metres in the latitude of Lima to 5,800 metres in the S. Most of the Sierra is covered with grasses and shrubs, with Puna vegetation (bunch grass mixed with low, hairy-leaved plants) from N of Huaraz to the S.

**Pre-Conquest History** Three major obstacles restrict our knowledge of ancient Peru. First, the very terrain of the country is a challenge to present, let alone, past inhabitants. The Andes are the most seismically active mountain range on Earth; devastating earthquakes and landslides have damaged or destroyed whole cities. The tropical lowlands have defied exploration; remains of the past may still be hidden in the undergrowth. Flashfloods unleashed by the El Niño current sweep down the north coast at unpredictable intervals, driving away the fish and washing away the adobe houses and irrigation canals. Fortunately the coastal desert from Chan Chán south to Paracas has revealed an "American Egypt" for archaeologists, although this has meant a bias towards the coastal region and a reliance on the contents of tombs for information.

Secondly, the lack of the written word has deprived us of any firsthand record of the everyday lives of the earliest settlers. The Spanish chroniclers based their accounts on the Incas' own version of the past, but this was inevitably coloured with propaganda, myth and folklore.

The third problem is looting, virtually a national industry, incited by demand from the international antiquities market. Gangs of *huaqueros* plunder sites too numerous to be policed or protected by archaeologists (the recent spectacular discovery of the grave of a Moche nobleman at Sipán in the northern desert was only made in the wake of the looters' efforts).

In spite of these handicaps, Peru has revealed one of the richest precolumbian histories in the Americas, of highly advanced societies that prevailed against awesome odds.

The Incas told the Spaniards that before they established their Tawantinsuyo empire, the land was overrun by primitives constantly at war with one another.

There were, in fact, many other civilized cultures dating back as far as 2000 B.C. The most accomplished of these were the Chavín-Sechín (c.900-200 B.C.), the Paracas-Nazca (c.200 B.C.-500 A.D.), the Huari-Tiwanaku (c.750 B.C.-1000 A.D.), and the Moche-Chimú (200 B.C.-1400 A.D.).

It is generally accepted that the earliest settlers in Peru were related to people who had crossed the Bering Straits from Asia and drifted through the Americas from about 20,000 B.C. Theories of early migrations from across the Pacific and Atlantic have been rife since Thor Heyerdahl's raft expeditions in 1947 and 1969-70. More recent studies of people living in the jungle near Chachapoyas (**see page 973**), have produced claims of Viking descendancy.

Human remains found in a cave in Lauricocha, near Huánuco, have a radiocarbon date of c.7500 B.C., but the earliest signs of a village settlement in Peru, were found on the central coast at Pampa, dating from 2,500 B.C. Between these two dates it is thought that people lived nomadically in small groups, mainly hunting and gathering but also cultivating some plants seasonally. Domestication of llamas, alpacas and guinea pigs also began at this time, particularly important for the highland people around the Titicaca basin.

The abundant wealth of marine life produced by the Humboldt Current, especially along the north coast, boosted population growth and settlement in this area. Around 2,000 B.C. climatic change dried up the *lomas* ("fog meadows"), and drove sea shoals into deeper water. People turned more to farming and began to spread inland along river valleys.

As sophisticated water irrigation and canal systems were developed, farming productivity increased and communities had more time to devote to building and producing ceramics and textiles. The development of pottery also led to trade and cultural links with other communities. Distribution of land and water to the farmers was probably organized by a corporate authority, and this may have led to the later "Mit'at" labour system developed by the Incas.

The earliest buildings constructed by organized group labour were *huacas*, adobe platform mounds, centres of some cult or sacred power dating from the second milennium B.C. onwards. Huaca Florida was the largest example of this period, near the Río Rimac, later replaced by Huaca Garagay as a major centre for the area. Many similar centres spread along the northern coast, most notably Aspero and Piedra Parada.

During this period, however, much more advanced architecture was being built at Kotosh, in the central Andes near to Huánuco. Japanese archaeological excavations there in the 1960s revealed a temple with ornamental niches and friezes. Some of the earliest pottery was also found here, showing signs of influence from southern Ecuador and the tropical lowlands, adding weight to theories of Andean culture originating in the Amazon. Radiocarbon dates of some Kotosh remains are as early as 1850 B.C.

For the next thousand years or so up to c.900 B.C., communities grew and spread inland from the northern coast and south along the northern highlands. Farmers still lived in simple adobe or rough stone houses but built increasingly large and complex ceremonial centres, such as at Las Haldas in the Casma Valley. As farming became more productive and pottery more advanced, commerce grew and states began to develop throughout central and north-central Peru, with the associated signs of social structure and hierarchies.

Around 900 B.C. a new era was marked by the rise of two important centres; Chavín de Huántar in the central Andes and Sechín Alto, inland from Casma on the north coast.

The chief importance of Chavín de Huántar was not so much in its highly advanced architecture as in the influence of its cult coupled with the artistic style of its ceramics and other artefacts. The founders of Chavín may have originated in the tropical lowlands as some of its carved monoliths show representations of monkeys and felines.

Objects with Chavín traits have been found all along the coast from Piura to the Lurin valley south of Lima, and its cult ideology spread to temples around the same area. Richard L. Burger of Yale University has argued that the extent of Chavín influence has been exaggerated. Many sites on the coast already had their own cult practices and the Chavín idols may have been simply added alongside. There is evidence of an El Niño flood that devastated the north coast around 500 B.C. Local cults fell from grace as social order was disrupted and the Chavín cult was snatched up as a timely new alternative.

The Chavín cult was paralleled by the great advancements made in this period in textile production and in some of the earliest examples of metallurgy. The origins of metallurgy have been attributed to some gold, silver and copper ornaments found in graves in Chongoyape, near Chiclayo, which show Chavín-style features. But earlier evidence has been discovered in the Andahuaylas region, dating from 1,800-900 B.C. The religious symbolism of gold and other precious metals and stones is thought to have been an inspiration behind some of the beautiful artefacts found in the central Andean area. The emergence of social hierarchies also created a demand for luxury goods as status symbols.

The cultural brilliance of Chavín de Huántar was complemented by its contemporary, Sechín. This huge granite-faced complex near Casma, 370 kms. north of Lima, was described by J.C. Tello as the biggest structure of its kind in the Andes. According to Michael Moseley of Harvard University, Chavín and Sechín may have combined forces, with Sechín as the military power that spread the cultural word of Chavín, but their influence did not reach far to the south where the Paracas and Tiwanaku cultures held sway.

The Chavín hegemony broke up around 500 B.C., soon after which the Nazca culture began to bloom in southern Peru. This period, up to about 500 A.D., was a time of great social and cultural development. Sizable towns of 5-10,000 inhabitants grew on the southern coast, populated by artisans, merchants, government administrators and religious officials.

Nazca origins are traced back to about the second century B.C., to the Paracas Cavernas and Necropolis, on the coast in the national park near Pisco. The extreme dryness of the desert here has preserved remarkably the textiles and ceramics in the mummies' tombs excavated. The technical quality and stylistic variety in weaving and pottery rank them amongst the world's best, and many of the finest examples can be seen in the museums of Lima.

The famous Nazca Lines are a feature of the region. Straight lines, abstract designs and outlines of animals are scratched in the the dark desert surface forming a lighter contrast that can be seen clearly from the air. There are many theories of how and why the lines were made but no definitive explanation has yet been able to establish their place in Peruvian history. There are similarities between the style of some of the line patterns and that of the pottery and textiles of the same period. It is clear from the sheer scale of the lines and the quality of the work that, whatever their purpose, they were very important to the Nazca culture.

In contrast to the quantity and quality of the Nazca artefacts found, relatively few major buildings belonging to this period have been uncovered in the southern desert. Dos Palmas is a complex of rooms and courtyards in the Pisco Valley and Cahuachi in the Nazca Valley is a large area including adobe platforms, a pyramid and a "wooden Stonehenge" cluster of preserved tree trunks. As most of the archaeological evidence of the Nazca culture came from their desert cemeteries, little is known about the lives and social organization of the people. Alpaca hair found in Nazca textiles, however, indicates that there must have been strong trade links with highland people.

Nazca's contemporaries on the north coast were the militaristic Moche who, from about 100-800 A.D. built up an empire whose traces stretch from Piura in the north to Casma, beyond Chimbote, in the south. The Moche built their capital, Chan Chán, in the middle of the desert, outside present day Trujillo. The huge pyramid temples of the Huaca del Sol and Huaca de la Luna, overlook the biggest adobe city in the world. Moche roads and system of way stations are thought to have been an early inspiration for the Inca network. The Moche increased the coastal population with intensive irrigation projects. Skilful engineering works were carried out, such as the La Cumbre canal, still in use today, and the Ascope aqueduct, both on the Chicama river.

The Moche's greatest achievement, however, was its artistic genius. Exquisite ornaments in gold, silver and precious stones were made by its craftsmen. Moche pottery progressed through five stylistic periods, most notable for the stunningly lifelike portrait vases. A wide variety of everyday scenes were created in naturalistic ceramics, telling us more about Moche life than is known about other earlier cultures, and perhaps used by them as "visual aids" to compensate for the lack of a written language.

A spectacular discovery of a Moche royal tomb at Sipán was made in February 1987 by Walter Alva, director of the Bruning Archaeological Museum, Lambayeque. Reports of the excavation in the National Geographic magazine (Oct.'88 and June '90), talk of the richest unlooted tomb in the New World.

The cause of the collapse of the Moche empire around 600-700 A.D. is unknown, but it may have been started by one of the periodic El Niño flash floods and finished by the encroaching forces of the Huari empire.

The decline of the Moche signalled a general tipping of the balance of power in Peru from the north coast to the southern sierra. The ascendant Huari-Tiwanaku movement, from c.600-1,000 A.D., combined the religious cult of the Tiwanaku site in the Titicaca basin, with the military dynamism of the Huari, based in the central highlands. The two cultures developed independently but, as had occurred with the Chavín-Sechín association, they are generally thought to have merged compatibly.

Up until their own demise around 1440 A.D., the Huari-Tiwanaku had spread their empire and influence across much of southern Peru, northern Bolivia and Argentina. They made considerable gains in art and technology, building roads, terraces and irrigation canals across the country. The Huari-Tiwanaku ran their empire with efficient labour and administrative systems that were later adopted and refined by the Incas. Labour tribute for state projects had been practised by the Moche and was further developed now. But the empire could not contain regional kingdoms who began to fight for land and power. As control broke down, rivalry and coalitions emerged, and the system collapsed. With the country once again fragmented, the scene was set for the rise of the Incas.

The origins of the Inca dynasty are shrouded in mythology and shaky evidence. The best known story reported by the Spanish chroniclers talks about Manco Capac and his sister rising out of Lake Titicaca, created by the Sun as divine founders of a chosen race. This was in approximately A.D. 1,200. Over the next three hundred years the small tribe grew to supremacy as leaders of the largest empire ever known in the Americas, the four territories of Tawantinsuyo, united by Cuzco as the umbilicus of the Universe (the four quarters of Tawantinsuyo, all radiating out from Cuzco, were 1—Chinchaysuyo, north and northwest, 2—Cuntisuyo, south and west, 3—Collasuyo, south and east, 4—Antisuyo, east.

At its peak, just before the Spanish Conquest, the Inca Empire stretched from the Río Maule in central Chile, north to the present Ecuador-Colombia border, containing most of Ecuador, Peru, western Bolivia, northern Chile and northwest Argentina. The area was roughly equivalent to France, Belgium, Holland, Luxembourg, Italy and Switzerland combined, 980,000 square km. For a brief description of **Inca Society**, see under Cuzco.

The first Inca ruler, Manco Capac, moved to the fertile Cuzco region, and established Cuzco as his capital. Successive generations of rulers were fully occupied with local conquests of rivals, such as the Colla and Lupaca to the south, and the Chanca to the northwest. At the end of Inca Viracocha's reign the hated Chanca were finally defeated, largely thanks to the heroism of one of his sons, Pachacuti Inca Yupanqui, who was subsequently crowned as the new ruler.

From the start of Pachacuti's own reign in 1438, imperial expansion grew in earnest. With the help of his son and heir, Topa Inca, territory was conquered from the Titicaca basin south into Chile, and all the north and central coast down to the Lurin Valley. The Incas also subjugated the Chimú, a highly sophisticated rival empire who had re-occupied the abandoned Moche capital at Chan Chan. Typical of the Inca method of government, some of the Chimú skills were assimilated into their own political and administrative system, and some Chimú nobles were even given positions in Cuzco.

Perhaps the pivotal event in Inca history came in 1532 with the death of the ruler, Huayna Capac. Civil war broke out in the confusion over his rightful successor. One of his legitimate sons, Huascar, ruled the southern part of the empire from Cuzco. Atahuallpa, Huascar's half-brother, governed Quito, the capital of Chinchaysuyo. In the midst of the ensuing battle Francisco Pizarro arrived in Tumbes with 179 men. When Atahuallpa got wind of their presence there was some belief that Pizarro and his *conquistadores* on horseback were Viracocha and his demi-gods predicted in Inca legend. In need of allies against Huascar, Atahuallpa agreed to meet the Spaniards at Cajamarca.

**Conquest and after** Francisco Pizarro's only chance against the formidable imperial army he encountered at Cajamarca was a bold stroke. He drew Atahuallpa into an ambush, slaughtered his guards, promised him liberty if a certain room were filled with treasure, and finally killed him after receiving news that another Inca army was on its way to free him. Pushing on to Cuzco, he was at first hailed as the executioner of a traitor: Atahuallpa had killed Huascar after the battle of Huancavelica two years previously. Panic followed when the *conquistadores* set about sacking the city, and they fought off with difficulty an attempt by Manco Inca to recapture Cuzco in 1538. (For the whole period of the Conquest John Hemming's *The Conquest of the Incas* is invaluable; he himself refers us to Ann Kendall's *Everyday Life of the Incas*, Batsford, London, 1978.)

Peruvian history after the arrival of the Spaniards was not just a matter of *conquistadores* versus Incas. The vast majority of the huge empire remained unaware of the conquest for many years. The Chimú and the Chachapoyas cultures were powerful enemies of the Incas. The Chimú developed a highly sophisticated culture and a powerful empire stretching for 560 km. along the coast from Paramonga south to Casma. Their history was well-recorded by the Spanish chroniclers and continued through the Conquest possibly up to about 1600. The Kuelap/Chachapoyas people were not so much an empire as a loose-knit "confederation of ethnic groups with no recognized capital" (Morgan Davis "Chachapoyas: The Cloud People", Ontario, 1988). But the culture did develop into an advanced society with great skill in roads and monument building. Their fortress at Kuelap was known as the most impregnable in Tawantinsuyo. It remained intact against Inca attack and Manco Inca even tried, unsuccessfully, to gain refuge here against the Spaniards.

In 1535, wishing to secure his communications with Spain, Pizarro founded Lima, near the ocean, as his capital. The same year Almagro set out to conquer Chile. Unsuccessful, he returned to Peru, quarrelled with Pizarro, and in 1538 fought a pitched battle with Pizarro's men at the Salt Pits, near Cuzco. He was defeated and put to death. Pizarro, who had not been at the battle, was assassinated in his palace in Lima by Almagro's son three years later. For the next 27 years each succeeding representative of the Kingdom of Spain sought to subdue the Inca successor state of Vilcabamba, N of Cuzco, and to unify the fierce Spanish factions. Francisco de Toledo (appointed 1568) solved both problems during his 14 years in office: Vilcabamba was crushed in 1572 and the last reigning Inca, Túpac Amaru, put to death. For the next 200 years the Viceroys closely followed Toledo's system, if not his methods. The Major Government—the Viceroy, the High Court (*Audiencia*), and *corregidores* (administrators)—ruled through the Minor Government—Indian chiefs put in charge of large groups of natives: a rough approximation to the original Inca system.

The Indians rose in 1780, under the leadership of an Inca noble who called himself Túpac Amaru II. He and many of his lieutenants were captured and put to death under torture at Cuzco. Another Indian leader in revolt suffered the same fate in 1814, but this last flare-up had the sympathy of many of the locally-born Spanish, who resented their status, inferior to the Spaniards born in Spain, the refusal to give them any but the lowest offices, the high taxation imposed by the home government, and the severe restrictions upon trade with any country but Spain. Help came to them from the outside world: José de San Martín's Argentine troops, convoyed from Chile under the protection of Lord Cochrane's squadron, landed in southern Peru on 7 September 1820. San Martín proclaimed Peruvian independence at Lima on 28 July 1821, though most of the country was still in the hands of the Viceroy, La Serna. Bolívar, who had already freed Venezuela and Colombia, sent Sucre to Ecuador where, on 24 May 1822, he gained a victory over La Serna at Pichincha. San Martín, after a meeting with Bolívar at Guayaquil, left for Argentina and a self-imposed exile in France, while Bolívar and Sucre completed the conquest of Peru by defeating La Serna at the battle of Junín (6 August 1824) and the decisive battle of Ayacucho (9 December 1824). For over a year there was a last stand in the Real Felipe fortress at Callao by the Spanish troops under General Rodil before they capitulated on 22 January 1826. Bolívar was invited to stay in Peru, but left for Colombia in 1826.

Important subsequent events were a temporary confederation between Peru and Bolivia in the 1830s; the Peruvian-Spanish War (1866); and the War of the Pacific (1879-1883), in which Peru and Bolivia were defeated by Chile and Peru lost its southernmost territory. A long-standing legacy of this was the Tacna-Arica dispute, which was not settled until 1929 (see under Tacna).

A reformist military Junta took over control of the country in October 1968. Under its first leader, Gen. Juan Velasco Alvarado, the Junta instituted a series of measures to raise the personal status and standard of living of the workers and the rural Indians, by land reform, worker participation in industrial management and ownership, and nationalization of basic industries, exhibiting an ideology perhaps best described as "military socialism". In view of his failing health Gen. Velasco was replaced in 1975 by Gen. Francisco Morales Bermúdez and policy (because of a mounting economic crisis and the consequent need to seek financial aid from abroad) swung to the Right. Presidential and congressional elections were held on 18 May 1980, and Sr. Fernando Belaúnde Terry was elected President for the second time. His term was marked by growing economic problems and the growth of the Maoist guerrilla movement Sendero Luminoso (Shining Path). Initially conceived in the University of Ayacucho, the movement now gets most of its support from highland Indians and migrants to urban shanty towns. Its main target is Lima-based authority and its aim is the overthrow of the whole system of government. The activities of Sendero Luminoso and another guerrilla group, Túpac Amaru, frequently disrupt transport and electricity supplies.

The April 1985 elections were won by the APRA party leader Alán García Pérez, who took office as President on 28 July 1985. During his populist, left-wing presidency disastrous economic policies caused increasing poverty and civil instability. In presidential elections held over two rounds in April and June 1990, Sr. Alberto Fujimori of the Cambio 90 movement defeated the novelist Mario Vargas Llosa, who belonged to the Fredemo (Democratic Front) coalition. Both candidates were entering national politics for the first time and the victor did not have an established political network behind him. He failed to win a majority in either the senate, where Cambio 90 won a sixth of the seats, or the lower house, where it gained a third. Fredemo, held a third of each house, and Apra a third of the senate and a quarter of the lower house.

**Population** 21.8m. (1989 estimate), growing at an annual rate of 2.6%. Just under 70% of the population is urban, and the urban growth rate in 1981-88 was 3.5%. Birth rate, 33.5 per 1,000 (1989); death rate 8.7 per 1,000 (1989). Infant mortality per 1,000 live births in 1989 was 83.3. The literacy rate is 87%.

**The Economy** Revitalization of agriculture, which accounts for 11% of gdp and 35% of employment, is a government priority, particularly in the Sierra to restore the self-sufficiency in food production of Inca times. The Costa (which occupies 11% of the land area) has traditionally been the dominant economic region, with excellent crops of cotton, rice, sugar and fruit where the coastal desert is irrigated. Coffee is the main export crop, earning US$155m in 1989, 4.4% of total exports. However, cultivation of coca has been the leading cash crop unofficially for several years and the Government is seeking ways of encouraging crop substitution.

Although employing only 2% of the workforce, mining contributes 10% of gdp and the six major minerals and metals (copper, iron, silver, gold, lead and zinc) account for over 40% of total export value. Copper and iron deposits are found on the southern coast, but the principal mining area for all minerals is the Sierra. Variable world prices, strikes, rising costs and an uncompetitive exchange rate in the late 1980s contributed to considerable losses for mining companies, and to reduced real output. The Fujimori Government policy is to revive private small scale mining and reincorporate the industry's 40% idle capacity, increasing production by US$400m over five years.

Peruvian oil accounts for 50% of domestic energy consumption. Production fell from 180,000 b/d in 1986 to 118,000 b/d at end 1990; most of it comes from the northeastern jungle, although some is produced on and off the northwestern coast. No major new reserves have been found since 1976 and proven oil reserves were down to 350m barrels at end-1989 from 835m in 1981. Local funds for investment fell in the 1980s, hence the need for foreign companies to invest in exploration, but in 1985 the García Government rescinded the operating contracts of three major foreign firms, adversely affecting investment prospects, despite subsequent new agreements. The Fujimori Government's policy of encouraging foreign investment aims at developing the vast Camisea gas and condensates field in the southeast jungle, where reserves are seven times Peru's proven crude oil reserves.

Manufacturing contributes 23% of gdp, employing 10% of the workforce. After high growth rates in the early 1970s, industry slumped to operating at 40% of its total capacity as purchasing power was reduced, and the cost of energy, raw materials and trade credit rose faster than inflation. A consumer-led recovery in 1986 led to most of manufacturing and the construction industry working at full capacity, but the boom was followed by a severe slump in 1988-1990.

Fishing suffered a dramatic decline in 1983 as the Niño current forced out of Peruvian waters the main catch, anchovy, whose stocks were already seriously depleted by overfishing in the 1970s. From being the world's leading fishmeal exporter, Peru was pushed into second place, behind Chile, with an annual average of 970,000 tonnes in 1985-89. However, in 1990 Peru regained its historical predominance with exports of 1,135,000 tonnes (Chile, 1,075,000 tonnes) because of rising demand for special quality fishmeal, particularly from salmon and shrimp farmers worldwide, improving technology and modernization helped by the abolition of the State monopoly which encouraged private investment.

Growing fiscal deficits in the 1980s led to increasing delays in payments of principal and interest on the foreign debt, estimated at US$22 bn. in 1990. As arrears accumulated to both multilateral agencies and commercial banks, the IMF declared Peru ineligible for further credits in 1986. On taking office, President García limited public debt service payments to 10% of foreign exchange earnings in order to maintain reserves to promote development. The need to import food, the low level of exports and the fall in disbursements of foreign capital in fact caused international reserves to fall. By 1987 the country was bankrupt after the free spending policies at the beginning of the administration and inflation soared as the Government resorted to printing money.

President Fujimori inherited an economy devastated by financial mismanagement and isolationist policies, with Peruvians suffering critical poverty, high infant mortality, malnutrition and appalling housing conditions. His Government had to deal with inflation, terrorism and drug trafficking, compounded in 1991 by a cholera epidemic which affected hundreds of thousands of people, cut food exports and sharply curtailed tourism revenues. An economic austerity package introduced in August 1990, raising fuel prices by 3,000% and staple foodstuffs by 500%, was the first stage of sweeping economic reform. Monetary and fiscal control was accompanied by liberalization of the financial system, foreign investment rules, capital controls and foreign trade; the tax code, ports and customs and labour laws were reformed and monopolies eliminated. Negotiations were begun with creditors to reinstate Peru in the international financial community, although arrears in payments to the IMF, the IDB and the World Bank had to be cleared before new loans could be made.

**Government** Legislation is vested in a Congress composed of a Senate (60 seats) and a Chamber of Deputies (180 seats). Men and women over 18 are eligible to vote; registration and voting is compulsory until the age of 60. The President, to whom is entrusted the Executive Power, is elected for five years and may not be re-elected until after one presidential term has passed. A new Constitution was approved in July 1979. In 1987 Congress approved a change in the administration of the country and a system of 13 Regions replaced the previous 25 Departments (divided into 150 Provinces, subdivided into 1,321 Districts).

**Education** is free and compulsory for both sexes between 6 and 14. There are public and private secondary schools and private elementary schools. There are 32 State and private universities, and two Catholic universities. A new educational system is being implemented as too many children cannot complete secondary school.

**Communications** Several roads and two railways run up the slopes of the Andes to reach the Sierra. These railways, once British owned, run from Lima in the centre and the ports of

Matarani and Mollendo in the S. There are in all 2,740 km. of railway. There are three main paved roads: the Pan-American Highway runs N-S through the coastal desert and sends a spur NE into the Sierra to Arequipa, with a partially paved continuation to Puno on Lake Titicaca which then skirts the lake to Desaguadero, on the Bolivian frontier, a total of 3,418 km.; the Central Highway from Lima to Huancayo, which continues (mostly paved) to Pucallpa in the Amazon basin; and the direct road from Lima N to Huaraz. Both roads and railways are given in the text and shown on sketch maps.

**Music and Dance**  Peru is the Andean heartland. Its musicians, together with those of Bolivia, have appeared on the streets of cities all over Europe and North America. However, the costumes they wear, the instruments they play, notably the *quena* and *charango*, are not typical of Peru as a whole, only of the Cuzco region. Peruvian music divides at a very basic level into that of the highlands ("Andina") and that of the coast ("Criolla").

The highlands are immensely rich in terms of music and dance, with over 200 dances recorded. Every village has its fiestas and every fiesta has its communal and religious dances. Those of Paucartambo and Coylloriti in the Cuzco region moreover attract innumerable groups of dancers from far and wide. The highlands themselves can be very roughly subdivided into some half dozen major musical regions, of which perhaps the most characteristic are Ancash and the North, the Mantaro Valley, Cuzco, Puno and the Altiplano, Ayacucho and Parinacochas. There is one recreational dance and musical genre, the Huayno, that is found throughout the whole of the Sierra, and has become ever more popular and commercialized to the point where it is in danger of swamping and indeed replacing the other more regional dances. Nevertheless, still very popular among Indians and/or Mestizos are the Marinera, Carnaval, Pasacalle, Chuscada (from Ancash), Huaylas, Santiago and Chonguinada (all from the Mantaro) and Huayllacha (from Parinacochas). For singing only are the mestizo Muliza, popular in the Central Region, and the soulful lament of the Yaravi, originally Indian, but taken up and developed early in the 19th century by the poet and hero of independence Mariano Melgar, from Arequipa. The Peruvian Altiplano shares a common musical culture with that of Bolivia and dances such as the Auqui-Auqui and Sicuris, or Diabladas, can be found on either side of the border. The highland instrumentation varies from region to region, although the harp and violin are ubiquitous. In the Mantaro area the harp is backed by brass and wind instruments, notably the clarinet, in Cuzco it is the *charango* and *quena* and on the Altiplano the *sicu* panpipes. Two of the most spectacular dances to be seen are the Baile de las Tijeras ("scissor dance") from the Ayacucho/Huancavelica area, for men only and the pounding, stamping Huaylas for both sexes. Huaylas competitions are held annually in Lima and should not be missed. Indeed, owing to the overwhelming migration of peasants into the barrios of Lima, most types of Andean music and dance can be seen in the capital, notably on Sundays at the so-called "Coliseos", which exist for that purpose. Were a Hall of Fame to be established, it would have to include the Ancashino singers La Pastorcita Huaracina and El Jilguero del Huascarán, the *charango* player Jaime Guardia, the guitar virtuoso Raul García from Ayacucho and the Lira Paucina trio from Parinacochas. However, what the young urban immigrant from the Sierra is now listening to and, above all, dancing to is "Chicha", a hybrid of Huayno music and the Colombian Cumbia rhythm, played by such groups as Los Shapis.

The "Música Criolla" from the coast could not be more different from that of the Sierra. Here the roots are Spanish and African. The immensely popular Valsesito is a syncopated waltz that would certainly be looked at askance in Vienna and the Polca has also suffered an attractive sea change, but reigning over all is the Marinera, Peru's national dance, a splendidly rhythmic and graceful courting encounter and a close cousin of Chile's and Bolivia's Cueca and the Argentine Zamba, all of them descended from the Zamacueca. The Marinera has its "Limeña" and "Norteña" versions and a more syncopated relative, the Tondero, found in the northern coastal regions, is said to have been influenced by slaves brought from Madagascar. All these dances are accompanied by guitars and frequently the *cajón*, a resonant wooden box on which the player sits, pounding it with his hands. Some of the great names of "Música Criolla" are the singer/composers Chabuca Granda and Alicia Maguiña, the female singer Jesús Vásquez and the groups Los Morochucos and Hermanos Zañartu.

Also on the coast is to be found the music of the small black community, the "Música Negroide" or "Afro-Peruano", which had virtually died out when it was resuscitated in the '50s, but has since gone from strength to strength. It has all the qualities to be found in black music from the Caribbean—a powerful, charismatic beat, rhythmic and lively dancing, and strong percussion provided by the *cajón* and the *quijada de burro*, a donkey's jaw with the teeth loosened. Some of the classic dances in the black repertoire are the Festejo, Son del Diablo, Toro Mata, Landó and Alcatraz. In the last named one of the partners dances behind the other with a candle, trying to set light to a piece of paper tucked into the rear of the other partner's waist. Nicomedes and Victoria Santa Cruz have been largely responsible for popularizing this black music and Peru Negro is another excellent professional group.

Finally, in the Peruvian Amazon region around Iquitos, local variants of the Huayno and Marinera are danced together with the Changanacui, to the accompaniment of flute and drum.

---

## LIMA (1)

---

Under the almost year-round fog, Lima's shady colonial suburbs are fringed by the *pueblos jóvenes* which sprawl over the dustry hills overlooking the flat city. It has a great many historic monuments and its food, drink and nightlife are the best in the country. Although not the most relaxing of South America's capitals, it is a good place to start before exploring the rest of the country.

*Lima*, capital of Peru, was the chief city of Spanish South America from its founding in 1535 until the independence of the South American republics in the early 19th century. It is built on both sides of the Río Rímac, lying at the foot of the Cerro San Cristóbal. From among the traditional buildings which still survive soar many tall skyscrapers which have changed the old skyline out of recognition. The city, which is now very dirty and seriously affected by smog for much of the year, is surrounded by "Pueblos Jóvenes," or shanty settlements of squatters who have migrated from the Sierra; much self-help building is in progress. ("Villa El Salvador, a few miles south-west of Lima, may be the world's biggest "squatters' camp" with 350,000 people building up a self-governing community since 1971. They pay no taxes to the government but when a school is built the government will pay for the roof—Paul Francescutti, Ontario, Canada). There are still signs of damage after the disastrous 1970 earthquakes nearby, especially in the Rímac section of the city. Many of the hotels and larger business houses have moved to the plush seaside suburbs of Miraflores and San Isidro.

Half of the town-dwellers of Peru now live in Lima. The metropolitan area contains six to seven million people, nearly one third of the country's total population, and two-thirds of its industries.

In the older part the way the streets are named may confuse the visitor. Several blocks, with their own names, make up a long street, a *jirón* (often abbreviated to Jr.). The visitor is greatly helped by the corner signs which bear both the name of the *jirón* and the name of the block. The new and old names of streets are used interchangeably: remember that Colmena is also Nicolás de Piérola, Wilson is Inca Garcilaso de la Vega, and Carabaya is also Augusto N. Wiese. The city's

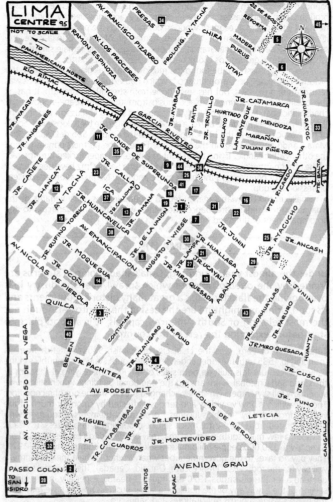

1. Plaza de Armas, 2. Plaza Grau, 3. Plaza San Martín, 4. Parque Universitario, 5. Alameda de Los Descalzos and Convento de Los Deacalzos, 6. Paseo de Aguas, 7. Cathedral, 8. La Merced, 9. Santo Domingo, 10. San Pedro, 11. Santuario de Santa Roaa and Museo Etnográfico de la Selva, 12. Las Nazarenas, 13. San Agustín, 14 Jesus María, 15. San Marcelo, 16. San Francisco, 17. Palacio de Gobierno, 18. Municipalidad, 19. Club Unión, 20. Congress, 21. Palacio Torre Tagle, 22. Casa Pilatos/Casa de Cultura, 23. Casa de la Riva, 24. Casa de Oquendo, 25. Casa de Las Trece Monedas, 26. Casa Aliaga, 27. Casa de la Rada, 28. Museo de Arte, 29. Museo del Tribunal de la Santa Inquisición, 30. Museo Banco Central de la Reserva, 31. Museo Peruano de Ciencias de la Salud, 32. Museo de Arte Italiano, 33. Museo Taurino/Plaza de Acho, 34. Museo Virreynal/Quinta de Presa, 35. Museo Berckemeyer, 36. Puente de Piedra, 37. Teatro Municipal and Teatro AAA, 38. Teatro Segura, 39. Panteón de los Próceres and old Universidad de San Marcos, 40. Foptur Tourist Office, 41. Correo Central, 42. American Express, Lima Tours, 43. Mercado Central, 44. Polvos Azules, 45. Cerro San Cristóbal.

urban motorway is often called "El Zanjón" (the ditch).

Only 12° S of the equator, one would expect a tropical climate, but from June to at least October the skies are grey; it feels chilly, clothes take ages to dry, and a damp *garúa*, or Scotch mist, is common. The rest of the year is mild and pleasant with temperatures ranging from 10° to 27°C (15° to 30°C in summer)

**History** The Universidad de San Marcos was founded in 1551, and a printing press in 1595: among the earliest of their kind in South America. Lima's first theatre opened in 1563. The Inquisition was introduced in 1569 and was not abolished until 1820. For some time the Viceroyalty of Peru embraced Colombia, Ecuador, Bolivia, Chile and Argentina. The city's wealth attracted many freebooters and in 1670 a protecting wall 11 km. long, which was demolished in 1869, was built round it. Lima's power was at its height during the 17th century and the early 18th, until the earthquake of 1746 destroyed all but 20 houses and killed 4,000 inhabitants. There were few cities in the Old World that could rival its wealth and luxury. It was only comparatively recently, with the coming of industry, that Lima began to change into what it is today.

**Sightseeing** The heart of the city, at least in plan, is still what it was in colonial days. A single block S of the Río Rímac lies the Plaza de Armas; the Desamparados Station of the Central Railway is quite near. Most of what the tourist wants to see is in this area. The newer parts of the city are based on Plaza San Martín, S of Jirón de la Unión, with a statue of San Martín in the centre. One and a quarter km. W is the Plaza Dos de Mayo. About 1 km. due S of this again is the circular Plaza Bolognesi, from which many great *avenidas* radiate.

The Jirón de La Unión, the main shopping street, runs to the Plaza de Armas; it has been converted into a pedestrian precinct (street theatre, street vendors, etc., in the evening). Later the pedestrian area will be extended to cover the southern half of Jirón de la Unión, from Plaza San Martín to Plaza Grau. In the two northernmost blocks of Jr. Unión, known as Calle Belén, several shops sell souvenirs and curios: the nearer the shops are to the best hotels the dearer the souvenirs are. Around the great Plaza de Armas stand the Palacio de Gobierno, the Cathedral (**see page 922**), the Archbishop's Palace, the Municipalidad and the Club Unión. The Correo Central (Post Office) is opposite the visitors' entrance to Government Palace. Running along two sides are arcades with shops: Portal de Escribanos and Portal de Botoneros. In the centre is a bronze fountain dating from 1650.

The **Palacio de Gobierno** (Government Palace) was built from 1921 to 1938, the site of and with some of the characteristics of Pizarro's palace. Visitors' entrance is on Jirón de la Unión. Guided tours at 1230, but you must present your documentation on previous day (Mon.-Thur. only). Under state-of-siege regulations it is difficult to get in at other times. The ceremonial changing of the guard behind the gates of the palace is worth watching, most days 0800 and 1245-1300 (check with the Tourist Office).

The **Municipalidad de Lima**, built 1945, has a picture gallery (open 0800-1500 Mon.,-Fri., free).

Near San Pedro, at Jirón Ucayali 363, is the **Palacio Torre Tagle**, the city's best surviving specimen of secular colonial architecture: a Sevillian mansion built in 1735. Now occupied by the Foreign Ministry, but visitors are allowed to enter courtyards to inspect fine wood-carving in balconies, wrought iron work, and a 16th-century coach complete with commode. During working hours Mon.-Fri,. visitors may enter the patio only.

A short taxi ride across the Río Rímac takes you to the Convento de Los Descalzos (**see page 923**) and the Quinta de Presa (incorrectly reputed to be the house of La Perricholi), now the Museo Virreynal(**see page 924**), closed at present for repairs.

La Perricholi—real name Micaela Villegas—was a beauty, wit, actress, and mistress of Viceroy Amat (1761-1776). Legend says he installed her in this mansion, but the house the Viceroy built for her was torn down last century. She has inspired plays, an opera (by Offenbach) and many books, the best known of which is Thornton Wilder's *The Bridge of San Luis Rey*.

The Puente de Piedra, behind the Palacio de Gobierno is a Roman-style stone bridge built 1610. Hundreds of thousands of egg whites were used to strengthen its mortar.

Other historic mansions worth visiting are the **Casa Pilatos**, opposite the San Francisco church at Jirón Ancash 390, now the Casa de Cultura, open 0830-1645, Mon.-Fri.; **Casa de la Riva** at Jirón Ica 426, T 28-2643, open 1000-1700 daily, the German Institute is on the second floor; **Casa de Oquendo** at Conde de Superunda 298, which stages art exhibitions; **Casa Negreiros** (a restaurant), at Jirón Azángaro 532; and **Casa de las Trece Monedas** (also a restaurant), at Jirón Ancash 536. The **Casa Aliaga**, at Unión 224, is still occupied by the Aliaga family and has recently been opened to the public; Vista Tours has exclusive rights to include the house in its tours (T 27-6624, or any travel agent). The house contains what is said to be the oldest ceiling in Lima and is furnished entirely in the colonial style. Don Jerónimo de Aliaga was one of the 13 commanders to arrive with Francisco Pizarro, and all 13 were given land around the main square to build their own houses when Lima was founded in 1535. The house of the author Ricardo Palma is open to the public, Mon.-Fri. 1000-1230, 1600-1900 (a.m. only Sat.), small entrance fee, Gral. Suárez 189, Miraflores—a 19th-century middle-class residence.

Other old mansions worth seeing: **Museo Berckemeyer** (art and bullfighting), Jr. Lima 341, a typical 17th-century *limeño* house—one of the few left; T 270025 for an appointment to visit, Mon.-Fri., 0830-1300. **Casa Barbieri**, Jr. Callao, near Jr. Rufino Torrico—a fine old 18th-century town house in the Sevillian style; ring bell in entrance hall for permission to look at the patios. **Casa Museo Prado**, Jr. Cuzco 448, visitable when Sr. Prado is in residence, a beautifully maintained house with early 19th-century front and, apparently, a 17th-century patio. **AAA Theatre** (Amateur Artists' Association), Jr. Ica 323, is in a lovely 18th-century house. **Casa de la Rada**, Jr. Ucayali, opposite Palacio Torre Tagle—an extremely fine mid-18th-century town house in the French manner; patio and first reception room open occasionally to the public (now belongs to a bank).

## Churches

The **Cathedral** (open to visitors 0930-1200, 1400-1700 every day) is on the Plaza de Armas. See the splendidly carved stalls (mid-17th century); the silver-covered altars surrounded by fine woodwork; mosaic-covered walls bearing the coats of arms of Lima and Pizarro and an allegory of Pizarro's commanders, the "Thirteen Men of Isla del Gallo"; in a small chapel, the first on the right of the entrance, are remains in a glass coffin originally said to be those of Pizarro, but later research indicates that his remains lie in the crypt. Museo de Arte Religioso in the cathedral, guided visits, ask to see picture restoration room, all-inclusive entrance ticket, US$0.90. The Archbishop's Palace was rebuilt in 1924, with a superb wooden balcony.

Four notable churches are quite near the Plaza de Armas: **La Merced** (open 0700-1230, 1600-2000 every day) and its monastery (open 0800-1200 and 1500-1730 daily) are in Plazuela de la Merced, Jirón de la Unión, two blocks from the Plaza de Armas. The first mass in Lima was said on this site. Very fine restored colonial façade, and attractive cloister. See the choir stalls and the vestry's panelled ceiling. At independence the Virgin of La Merced was made a Marshal of the Peruvian army. **Santo Domingo**, built 1549, is in Jirón Camaná (first block). In an urn in one of the altars are the remains of Santa Rosa de Lima (1586-1617), the first saint of the New World: 30 August is her day. Pope Clement presented, 1669, the alabaster statue of the Saint in front of the altar (entrance, US2.75, students US$1.25, open 0700-1300, 1600-2000 daily; monastery and tombs open 0930-1230, 1530-1730 Mon.-Sat.; Sun. and holidays a.m. only). The main hall has some interesting relics. **San Francisco**, open 1000-1300 and 1500-1730, in first block of Jirón Lampa, corner of Ancash, is a baroque church with Arabic influences, finished 1674, under reconstruction (but a great deal has been done). See carved "Sillería Coral" (1622), gold monstrance set with jewels made in Cuzco (1671), and José de Rivera's paintings (1672). The monastery is famous for Sevillian tilework and panelled ceilings in the cloisters (1620). Catacombs under church and part of monastery, well worth seeing; entry charge is US$2, by guided tour only, Spanish and English, last groups start at 1245 and 1745 daily. **San Pedro** (open 0700-1300, 1740-2030 every day), 3rd block of Jirón Ucayali, finished by Jesuits in 1638, has marvellous altars with Moorish-style balconies, rich gilded wood carvings in choir and vestry, and tiled throughout. Several Viceroys buried here; the bell called La Abuelita, first rung in 1590, sounded the Declaration of Independence in 1821.

**Santuario de Santa Rosa** (Av. Tacna, 1st block), small but graceful church. A pilgrimage centre; here are preserved the hermitage built by Santa Rosa herself, the house in which she was born, a section of the house in which she attended to the sick, her well, and other relics. Open 0930-1245 and 1530-1830 daily; entrance to grounds free.

**Las Nazarenas Church** (Av. Tacna, 4th block, open 0700-1130 and 1630-2000 daily), built around an image of Christ Crucified painted by a liberated slave in 1655. This, the most venerated image in Lima, and an oil copy of El Señor de los Milagros (Lord of Miracles), encased in a gold frame, are carried on a silver litter—the whole weighing nearly a ton—through the streets on 18, 19, and 28 October and again on 1 November (All Saints' Day).

**San Agustín** (Jirón Ica, 251), W of the Plaza de Armas, is a much changed old church, but its façade (1720) is a splendid example of churrigueresque architecture. There are carved choir stalls and effigies, and a sculpture of Death, said to have frightened its maker into an early grave. Open 0830-1200, 1530-1730 daily, ring for entry. Since being damaged in the last earthquake the church has been sensitively restored, but the sculpture of Death is in storage.

Fine 18th century carving also in gilt altars of **Jesús María** (Jirón Moquegua, 1st block), and in **Magdalena Vieja** (1557, but reconstructed in 1931), with altar pieces, of gilded and carved wood, particularly fine; it should be seen during visit to the Museum of Archaeology, Plaza Bolívar (in Pueblo Libre). Another church worth seeing for its two beautiful colonial doors is **San Marcelo**, at Av. de la Emancipación, 4th block.

The **Convento de Los Descalzos** on the Alameda de Los Descalzos in Rímac contains over 300 paintings of the Cuzco, Quito and Lima schools which line the four main cloisters and two ornate chapels. The chapel of El Carmen was constructed in 1730 and is notable for its baroque gold leaf altar. The museum shows the life of the Franciscan friars during colonial and early republican periods; the cellar, infirmary, pharmacy and a typical cell have all been restored. The library has not yet been incorporated into the tour. The convent is open Mon.-Sat. 0930-1300, 1400-1730, entrance US$1. Guided tour only, 45 mins. in Spanish, but worth it.

The church of **Santo Tomás** is now a school (Gran Unidad Escolar "Mercedes Cabello de Carbonera", on corner of Junín and Andahuaylas); it is said to have the only circular cloister in the world apart from St. Peter's in Rome, and a fine 17th-century Italian-designed baroque library. The headmistress is glad to show people round.

*Note: Churches are open between 1830 and 2100 unless otherwise stated.*

## Museums

**Museo Nacional de Historia**, Plaza Bolívar, Pueblo Libre, in a mansion built by Viceroy Pezuela and occupied by San Martín (1821-1822) and Bolívar (1823-1826). Exhibits: colonial and early republican paintings, manuscripts, portraits, uniforms, etc. Paintings mainly of historical episodes. 0900-1730, except Sat. Admission US$0.50. Bus 12 from corner of Tacna and Emancipación, minibus 2 from Rufino Torrico, bus 21, 42, 48 from Parque Universitario.

**Museo de Oro** (Museo Miguel Mujica Gallo—Gold Museum), is in 7th block of Prolongación Av. Primavera (Av. de Molina 1110), Monterrico, several km. from centre (T 352919); bus 76 from Av. Alfonso Ugarte, or bus 2 from Plaza San Martín to Miraflores (corner of Avenida Arequipa and Angamos), then change to colectivo 112 which passes the door (call out "bajo en el museo"); alternatively, take any of the buses (such as 55) going up Angamos, they go past the side road to the museum—bus 59b goes from Parque Unversitario to Angamos (get out after the bridge under Panamericana Sur), orange bus marked "Monterrico/Covina" from Plaza 2 de Mayo; by taxi, with 2½ hrs. at the museum, US$10 (US$3 without wait, 45 mins. from centre, 30 mins. from Miraflores). It is still privately owned. An underground museum contains items which have been exhibited in the world's leading museums. The collection includes precolumbian metals (99% pre-Inca), weavings, mummies and a remarkable arms collection. Well worth seeing, despite being poorly displayed and explained; catalogue costs US$9. Open daily (incl. Sun. and holidays) 1200-1900. Admission: US$5, students (with card) half price. No photography allowed. Good copies of ancient pottery are on sale and there are high quality craft shops in the garden.

**Museo de Arte**, Paseo Colón 125, in the Palacio de la Exposición, built in 1868 in Parque de la Exposición. More than 7,000 exhibits, giving a chronological history of Peruvian cultures and art from the 2,000-year-old Paracas civilization up to today. Excellent examples of 17th and 18th century Cuzco paintings, a beautiful display of carved furniture, heavy silver and jewelled stirrups, also precolumbian pottery. During the autumn and winter seasons, starting in April, there are guided tours, lectures and films every Friday evening (see also under **Cinemas** below). Several good, English-speaking guides. 0900-1630 Tues.-Sun. Admission US$2. Recommended guide: José Luis Vilches, who speaks English and French, and is most helpful and informative. English books for sale and exchange in the bookshop.

**Museo del Tribunal de la Santa Inquisición**, Plaza Bolívar, Calle Junín 548, near corner of Av. Abancay. The main hall, with splendidly carved mahogany ceiling, remains untouched. Court of Inquisition held here 1569-1820; until 1930 used by the Senate. In the basement there is an accurate re-creation *in situ* of the tortures. A description in English is available at the desk. Students offer to show you round for a tip; good explanations in English. Mon.-Fri. 0900-1900, Sat. 0900-1630.

**Museo Nacional de Antropología y Arqueología**, Plaza Bolívar (San Martín with Antonio Pola), not in the centre but in Pueblo Libre (T 63-5070), a museum for exhibition and study of art and history of aboriginal races of Peru. Most interesting textiles from Paracas and ceramics of Chimú, Nazca, Mochica and Pachacámac cultures, and various Inca curiosities and works of art. See the Raimondi stella and the Tello obelisk from Chavín, and the marvellous Mochica pottery, and a reconstruction of one of the galleries at Chavín. An impressive model of Machu-Picchu in the Sala Inca. Easily the most interesting museum in Peru. Open Mon.-Sun., 1000-1830. Admission US$4 (students half price), plus US$1 to take photographs with flash. Students guide you around for no charge, but give a tip. Guide book in English US$4.50; gift shop next door. Bus 12 from corner of Tacna and Emancipación, Bus 41M from Cuzco and Emancipacíon, Minibus 2 from Rufino Torrico, also bus 21, 24, 41 or 42 from Parque Universitario. Direction "Avenida Brasil", alight at General Vivanco.

There is also an archaeological museum at Puruchuco (**see page 944**), and at the excavated mound of Santa Catalina, Parque Fernando Carozi in La Victoria (an insalubrious district); minibus 1 or 46 from Plaza 2 de Mayo.

**Museo de la Nación**, Javier Prado Este 2465, San Borja, anthropological and archaeological exhibits from pre-Inca and Inca times, with a section on costume and weaving, rec. Open Tues.-Fri. 0900-2100, Sat., Sun., and holidays 1000-1900, entry US$3, guides are available. Take bus or colectivo from the centre or Miraflores to Javier Prado, then bus 13, 12 or colectivo to the museum (block 24).

**Museo Banco Central de Reserva**, Av. Ucayali and Lampa (one block from San Pedro Church, on same side as Torre Tagle Palace). Large collection of pottery from Vicus or Piura culture (AD 500-600) and gold objects from Lambayeque, as well as 19th and 20th century paintings. Both modern and ancient exhibitions highly recommended. (Don't be put off by the sombre bank exterior!) Tues.-Sat. 1000-1700, Sun. 1000-1300. Photography prohibited.

**Museo Etnográfico de la Selva**, Av. Tacna 120 (4 blocks NW of Plaza de Armas), houses cultural and household objects from Madre de Dios (under reconstruction 1990).

**Museo Nacional de la Cultura Peruana**, Av. Alfonso Ugarte 650, showing pots and popular art, and costumes worn by Indians in various parts of Peru, includes exhibition of *mate burilado* (carved gourds); open 1000-1700, Mon.-Fri., 0900-1700, Sat. Admission US$0.20 (students half price); US$0.70 to take photographs.

**Museo Arqueológico Rafael Larco Herrera**, Av. Bolívar 1515, Pueblo Libre, is the Chiclín pottery museum brought from Trujillo. The greatest number of exhibits stem from the Mochica period (AD 400-800). The Cupisnique period, dating back to 1000 BC, and the Nazca, Chimú, and Inca periods are also well represented. There is an erotica section in a separate building. This is a museum for the pottery specialist; it is more like a warehouse than a museum with few explanations, but the general visitor will enjoy the excellent collection of precolumbian weaving, including a sample of two-ply yarns with 398 threads to the inch. Also several mummified weavers buried with their looms and a small display of gold pieces. Admission US$3 (US$1.50 student-card holders), open Mon.-Sat., 0900-1300, 1500-1800, Sun. and holidays, 0900-1300. Photography not permitted. Bus 23 from Avenida Abancay, or minibus 37 from Av. Nicolás de Piérola (Colmena) or taxi (US$2).

**Museo Virreynal** (Quinta de Presa), is a fine 18th century mansion. Exhibits: colonial portraits, furniture, dresses, candelabra, and so on; one of the Viceroy's carriages is shown. Closed since 1986 for repairs.

**Museo Histórico Militar** (Real Felipe Fortress, Callao), has interesting military relics: a cannon brought by Pizarro, a cannon used in the War of Independence, the flag that flew during the last Spanish stand in the fortress, portraits of General Rodil and of Lord Cochrane, and the remains of the small Bleriot plane in which the Peruvian pilot, Jorge Chávez, made the first crossing of the Alps from Switzerland to Italy: he was killed when the plane crashed at Domodossola on 23 Sept. 1910. Open 0900-1200 and 1500-1700, Tues., Wed., Thurs.; 1400-1730, Sat., Sun. Entrance free. Closed April-August. Bus No. 63 from Post Office in Jirón Lima. The **Museo Miguel Grau**, Calle Lezcano 170 (near Basílica La Merced, just off Jr. Unión), is the house of Admiral Grau and has mementoes of the War of the Pacific. **Museo Morro de Arica**, Cailloma 125, Tues.-Fri., 1130-1900, gives the Peruvian view of the famous battle. **Museo Naval** (Av. Jorge Chávez, off Plaza Grau, Callao), open 0900-1230, 1500-1730 on Mon., Wed., Fri. and Sat. Admission free.

**Museo Hospital Dos de Mayo** open 0900-1800 daily, admission US$1.25.

**Museo Peruano de Ciencias de la Salud**, Jr. Junín 270 (just off Plaza de Armas), houses a collection of ceramics and mummies, showing precolumbian lifestyle; divided into five sections: *micuy* (Quechua for food), *hampi* (medicine), *onccoy* (disease), *hampini* (healing) and *causay* (life). Minibus Nos. 35 or 42 from Miró Quesada. Open: Wed.-Sat., 1000-1600, very interesting indeed. Admission, US$2. A guide is available in Spanish; signs in English and

Spanish.

**Pinacoteca Municipal** (Municipal Building, Plaza de Armas), contains a large collection of paintings by Peruvian artists. The best of the painters is Ignacio Merino (1817-1876). Rooms and furnishings very ornate. Open: Mon.-Fri., 0900-1300.

**Museo de Arte Italiano** (Paseo de la República, 2nd block), is in a building, Italian renaissance style, given by the Italian colony to Peru on the centenary of its independence. Open Tues.-Sun., 0900-1900, but 0900-2000 on Fri., US$1. Large collection of Italian works of art, but most of the paintings are reproductions, including lithographs and etchings. Now also houses Institute of Contemporary Art, which has many exhibitions.

**Museo de Historia Natural Javier Prado** (Av. Arenales 1250) belongs to Universidad de San Marcos. Exhibits: Peruvian flora, birds, mammals, butterflies, insects, minerals and shells. Prize exhibit is a sun fish (more plaster than fish)—only two other examples known, one in Japan and another in New Zealand. Open Mon.-Fri. 0900-1530, Sat. 0900-1300; admission US$0.25. Bus No. 54A or minibuses 13 and 73 from Av. Tacna.

**Philatelic Museum** (Central Post Office, off Plaza de Armas). Open 0800-1330, 1400-1600, Mon.-Fri., 0800-1330, Sat., 0900-1200, Sun. Incomplete collection of Peruvian stamps and information on the Inca postal system. There is a stamp exchange in front of the museum every Sat. and Sun., 0900-1300. You can buy stamps here as well (shop hours: Mon.-Fri., 0800-1200, 1400-1500).

**Museo Taurino** (Hualgayoc 332, Plaza de Acho Bull Ring, Rímac). Apart from matadors' relics, contains good collections of paintings and engravings— some of the latter by Goya. Open 0900-1300, 1500-1800. Closed Sat., Sun. and holidays in the afternoons. Admission US$0.20.

**Contemporary Folk Art Museum**, Saco Olivero 163, between Arenales and 3rd block of Arequipa, recommended. Shop in museum grounds. Open Tues.-Fri., 1430-1900; Sat. 0830-1200.

**Museo Arqueológico Amano** (Calle Retiro 160, Miraflores). A very fine private collection of artefacts from the Chancay, Chimú and Nazca periods owned by Mr. Yoshitaro Amano—one of the most complete exhibits of Chancay weaving. Particularly interesting for pottery and precolumbian textiles, all superbly displayed and lit. Open Mon.-Fri. Guided tours 1400, 1500, 1600, 1700. T 412909, at least one day in advance, for an appointment; try to get a small group (under 10) first. Admission free (photography prohibited). Bus No. 73 or Santa Cruz minibus (no. 13) from Av. Tacna, get out at Av. Angamos. Calle Retiro is unmarked: it is the street on your right as you stand with your back to the Pacific on the 11th block of Angamos.

**Colección Pedro de Osma** (Av. Pedro de Osma 421, Barranco). A private collection of colonial art of the Cuzco, Ayacucho and Arequipa schools. T 670019 for an appointment. No. 54A bus from Av. Tacna. (Apparently this museum is now closed.)

**Museo Numismático**, Banco Wiese, 2nd floor, Cuzco 245, T 275060 ext. 553, open Mon.-Fri., 0900-1300, free admission. Peruvian coins from the colonial era to the present day.

**Museum of Mineral Specimens** at Krystal S.A., León Velarde 537, Lince, Lima 14 (T 710713, 711379).

**Museo Miniatura de la Plaza de Armas del Siglo XIX** in the house of Dr. César Revoredo, Salaverry 3052, is a private small scale reproduction of the Plaza de Armas in the last century. Dr. Revoredo also has a fine collection of prints by Rancho Fierro, the 19th century *costumbrista* watercolour artist.

**Casa Galería de Esculturas de Sra. Marina Núñez del Prado**, Antero Aspillaga 300, Olivar de San Isidro, another private collection, of fine sculpture; phone for an appointment on Weds., or Sats. Two more private collections that occasionally open to visitors on application by telephone are: the collection of precolumbian artefacts belonging to Sra. Elsa Cohen, Esquina Larraburre Unánue 392 (Bus 54A, or minibus 13 from Tacna), and, at Parque Hernán Velarde 199, the collection of rural handicrafts (pottery, engraved gourds, etc.) belonging to Sra. E. Luza (bus 13, Tacna with Emancipación, or bus 2 from corner of Plaza San Martín).

Galería Wari 69, Cailloma 630, exhibits the tapestries of the Sulca family of Ayacucho; traditional designs and techniques are used in their beautiful work.

For those interested in modern Peruvian art, a gallery has been opened at Independencia

812, Miraflores, T 451058, by Gaston Garreaud, who speaks English and French and will kindly guide you if you make an appointment. Admission free.

*Note  Some museums are only open between 0900 and 1300 from Jan. to March, and some close altogether in January. Many are closed at weekends and on Monday. When electricity supplies are cut, many museums close.*

## Parks and Gardens

Lima and its suburbs have many parks and gardens. **Alameda de los Descalzos**, at the foot of the Cerro San Cristóbal, was laid out as early as 1610; it is a walk shaded by ancient trees and fenced by a wrought-iron grille. It was once a haunt of Lima's aristocracy. The marble statues, each representing a month of the year, and the marble seats date from 1856. Nearby is another walk, the **Paseo de Aguas**, created by the Viceroy Amat in the 18th century to please his mistress, La Perrichola. The great arch with cascades was rebuilt in 1938. This walk is in extremely poor condition.

**Campo de Marte** (Plaza Jorge Chávez and Av. Salaverry), a large open park, reportedly full of thieves and drug-pushers now. In the centre is a huge monument to the Peruvian soldier. The National Symphony Orchestra plays in the auditorium on the W side during the summer.

**Parque Universitario**, where the old San Carlos Jesuit church was turned into a Panteón de los Próceres **(Pantheon of the Heroes)** on the 100th anniversary of the Battle of Ayacucho. A graceful 18th century church with a circle of famous tombs under the rotunda. General Miller, the Englishman who fought in the wars of independence, and whose memoirs contain an excellent picture of the time, is buried here, and so is Admiral Guise, of Gloucestershire, who was killed at Guayaquil. Also the poet and composer who wrote the Peruvian national anthem. Next to the church is the former building of Universidad de San Marcos, which has now been restored and is used for meetings and conferences. Worthy of a visit are the beautiful patio and the small archaeological museum. In the centre is the clock tower presented by the German colony on the centenary of Peruvian independence. On the far corner of the park is the tall Ministerio de la Educación building.

Between Paseo Colón and Av. 28 de Julio is **Parque de La Exposición**, a quiet place shaded by trees; several of the main avenues border it. It was opened for the 1868 International Exhibition. The great Palacio de la Exposición, facing Paseo Colón, is now the Museo de Arte. South of the Parque de La Exposición is the **Parque Japonés**, which has a small admission fee.

**Parque de la Reserva** (Av. Arequipa, 6th block). In the middle is a statue of Sucre; of the other two statues, one is of Tangüis, who selected the famous cotton. By the park is the Edificio El Pacífico-Washington (British and Israeli embassies).

**Parque las Leyendas,** between Lima and Callao, is arranged to represent the three regions of Peru: the coast, the mountainous Sierra, and the tropical jungles of the Montaña, with appropriate houses, animals and plants, children's playground. Elephants and lions have been introduced so the zoo is no longer purely Peruvian (not recommended at weekends, too crowded). The Park is open 0900-1700 (closed Mon.), entrance US$0.35. There is a handicrafts fair (Feria Artesanal) at the entrance to the park; particularly good insect specimens can be bought here. Buses from Paseo de la República, in front of *Sheraton*, 23 and 57 from Plaza dos de Mayo; also minibus 75 from Jirón Azángaro goes direct to the park.

**Note**  You are recommended to consult the general **Security** section in the **Information for Visitors** and see also under **Buses** and Miraflores beaches below. Many visitors base themselves in San Isidro, Miraflores or Barranco (see **suburbs** below), rather than in the historic centre.

**Festivals**  18 January, Founding of Lima. The whole of February is Carnival, with plenty of water-throwing, especially on Sundays; if you don't want to get wet, stay in your room. If you don't mind (and it's quite refreshing), enjoy it and carry your own water balloon (some "jokers" mix paint, oil, etc. with the water, so watch out). 28 July, Independence, with music and fireworks in Plaza de Armas on evening before; last week of August, Cañete; October, month of Our Lord of the Miracles with impressive processions (see *El Comercio* for dates and routes); November (every other year), Pacific International Fair.

**Hotels**  Prices very negotiable outside peak July-August holiday season. Business travellers should ask for business rates. There is a 10% tax on hotel rooms, and a service charge of 13% is usually added (neither is included in prices below). In cheaper hotels water may be scarce in the middle of the day. The more expensive hotels charge in dollars according to the parallel rate of exchange at midnight.

Accommodation in **Miraflores**: *Miraflores César*, La Paz y Diez Canseco, (T 441212), L, luxury, very nice but expensive; *El Pardo*, Av. Pardo 420 y Independencia, (T470283, Fax 442171), A, a/c, satellite TV, fax and telex service, good restaurant; *María Angola*, Av. La Paz 610, (T 441280), A, rec; *Ariosto*, Av. La Paz 769 (Tel:441416, Telex: 21195), B, rec.; *El Condado* (close to *César*), L, deluxe. *José Antonio*, 28 de Julio 398, T 456870, A, clean, friendly, good restaurant, rec.; *Hostal Residencial Esperanza*, Esperanza 350, T 442411/444909, Fax 440834, B, with bath, TV, phone, pleasant; *Suites Larco*, Apart Hotel, San Martín 481, of. 202 (corner of 7th block Av. Larco), T 461461/461970, B for 3-room suite with kitchen, TV, phone, cleaning, guarded property; *Pensión Lucerna*, Calle Las Dalias 276 (corner Av. Larco), B with breakfast, friendly, clean, T 457321, rec.; *Grand Hotel Miraflores*, Av. 28 de Julio 151, very pleasant, T 479641.

*Residencial 28 de Julio*, 28 de Julio 531, T 470636/473891, C, with breakfast, parking, café and bar, phone and bathroom with each room, secure, reliable and pleasant staff, rec.; *Hostal El Ejecutivo*, Av. 28 de Julio 245, T 476310, C, including bath and breakfast, payment in dollars, overpriced but clean, tariff negotiable for long stay, safe, luggage can be left; *Pensión Alemana*, Arequipa 4074, T 456999, C, comfortable, clean, excellent breakfast (triple rooms available), book in advance, laundry service extra;, Arequipa 4074, T 456999, C, comfortable, clean, excellent breakfast (triple rooms available), book in advance, laundry service extra; *Hostal La Alameda*, Av. José Pardo 930, D with limited breakfast, friendly, front-facing rooms noisy, safe, clean, rec.; *Hostal Residencial Torreblanca*, Av. José Pardo 1453, T 479998/473363, C, including breakfast and tax, (pricing a bit haphazard), quiet, safe, laundry, restaurant and bar, friendly, clean and cosy rooms, helpful, rec.; *Ovalo*, Av. José Pardo, Plaza Morales Barros, T 465549, C, quiet, good, breakfast served; *Colonial Inn*, Cmdte. Espinar 310, T 466666, C, room service, TV, parking; *Hostal El Patio*, Diez Canseco 342, T 442107 (next to *Miraflores César*), C with reductions for long stays, clean, comfortable, friendly, English and French spoken; *Hostal La Castellana*, Grimaldo del Solar 222 (3 blocks E of Larco, between Schell and Benavides), T 443530, 444662, C (D off season), with bath, pleasant, good value, nice garden, safe, cafeteria, laundry, English spoken; *Hostal Señorial*, José González 567 (T 459724/457306), C, 60 rooms all with bath, including tax and breakfast, rec., clean, friendly, well-appointed, garden; *Hostal Palace*, Av. Miraflores 1088, C, very clean, comfortable, friendly; *Winnie's Bed and Breakfast*, La Calera de Monterrico, M-13, Lima 34 (close to Miraflores), T 455864, C, run by Winnie Reyes de Espinosa of VIP Travel Service, warmly rec. *Hostal Huaychulo*, Av. Dos de Mayo 494, T 451195, C, safe, helpful, excellent (German owner-manager, speaks English too); *Pensión José Luis*, Fco. de Paula, Ugarriza 727, San Antonio district, T 441015, D, use of kitchen, laundry facilities, very friendly English-speaking owner; *Hostal Catalina*, Toribio Polo 248 (½ block W of Av. Ejercito blocks 7/8), D negotiable, friendly, English spoken, bath, good transport connections, T 410192/424037; *Hostal Andalucia*, Jr. Tacna 472 (altura cuadra 44 Av. Arequipa), T 452707, D, very friendly and helpful, quiet, convenient.

Sra Emilia, Porta 264, T 473953, D with breakfast, friendly, clean and safe. *Pensión San Antonio*, Paseo de la República 5809, T 475830, E, shared bathroom, clean, comfortable, friendly, helpful, ask for hot water; *Imperial Inn*, Av. Bolognesi, E, clean, but noisy and run-down; *Pensión Yolanda Escobar*, Domingo Elias 230 T 457565, E, clean, facilities for preparing own breakfast, dueña speaks fluent English, rec. Visitors with vehicles are recommended to stay in Miraflores, since parking is difficult in the centre.

Accommodation at **San Isidro**, *Country Club*, Los Eucaliptos, T 404060, A; *Hostal San*

*Isidro Inn*, Av. Pezet 1761, just off Salaverry; *Hostal Limatambo*, Av. Aramburú 1025, B, T 419615, 24-hour snack bar, won the "América-86" award for good service and quality; *Residencial Beech*, Los Libertadores 165, T 40-5595, C, with bath, including breakfast, very helpful staff, garden, noisy, but rec.; *Garden*, Rivera Navarrete 450, T 421771, rec., A, good, large beds, shower, small restaurant; *Hostal Santa Mónica*, Av. Pezet 1419, D, T 419280, rec.; *Hostal El Golf Inn*, Av. A. Miro Quesada, round corner from Cuban Embassy, D with bath, E without, swimming pool, safe, friendly, hard beds; *Residencial Los Petirrojos*, Petirrojos 230, Corpac (Sra. Miri), D, T 416044, clean, spacious, breakfast included; *Hostal El Olivar*, Raymundo Morales de la Torre 385, T 417745, C with bath, friendly, garden, nice restaurant; *Hostal Firenze*, Chinchón (2 blocks from Las Camelias), T 227382, D, clean, family-run, hot water, English and Italian spoken, highly rec.; *Sans Souci*, Av. Arequipa 2670, T 226035, towards Miraflores, B with bath, clean, gloomy, noisy; *Hostal Antarki*, Chacarilla 250, clean, quiet, helpful, E.

In **Santa Beatriz**, between San Isidro and Centre, *Hostal Mont Blanc*, Jr. Emilio Fernández 640, T 247762/737762, D (negotiable) with bath, comfortable, clean, quiet area, safe, good service, café, bar, highly rec., 15 mins' walk or 5 mins' by minibus to centre, owner arranges excursions.

In **Barranco**, *Armendariz*, Av. Armendariz (between Miraflores and Barranco), E, on convenient 2 bus line, rec.

In **Magdalena del Mar**, *Los Cóndores*, Domingo Ponte 874, Magdalena Mar, C with bath, cheaper rooms available, safe, warm water, clean, free transport from airport, tour guide (Alfredo) operates from here. Also in Magdalena del Mar, *De Klomp*, Jr. Libertad 1439, T 612153, owned by a Dutch/Peruvian couple, cosy, clean, good, dormitory rooms at G p.p., bus stop for all directions round the corner. In **Lince** is *Hostal Ambassador*, Julio C. Tello 650, clean, safe, hot water, E, changes money for guests, highly rec.

In **central Lima**: Rec. in the upper price brackets: *Lima Sheraton*, Paseo de la República 170, T 333320, Fax 336344, L, *La Pascana*, coffee shop good; *Grand Bolívar*, Unión 958, Plaza San Martín, T 276400, Telex 25201 PECP, L (may be negotiable to C out of season), palatial old building, good ambience, helpful, excellent restaurant, have a pisco on the terrace overlooking plaza, highly rec; *Crillón* Colmena 589, T 283290, Telex 25274PE, A+, good food and service in *Skyroom*; *Plaza*, Nicolás de Pierola 850, T 286270, B, good restaurant, safe for luggage (cheaper in low season); *Gran Maury*, Ucayali 201, C/D, good bath, breakfast, helpful staff; *Savoy*, Cailloma 224, T 283520, B.

*Hostal Los Virreyes*, Jirón Cañete 826, C, comfortable, clean, hot water, central position, a bit noisy, rec.; *Hostal Renacimiento*, Parque Hernán Velarde 52, D, cheaper at the back, in a quiet cul-de-sac 2 blocks from central bus station, 10 mins walk from centre, not all rooms with bath but clean, helpful, T 318461/ 324821; *Pensión* at Hernán Velarde 72, run by Pablo W.See, T 246352, C, very good, 5 mins. by bus from centre. *La Casona*, Moquegua 289 (nr Jr. Cailloma and No. 56 bus route from airport), clean, secure, friendly; *Hostal San Martín*, Av. Nicolás de Piérola 882, 2nd floor, Plaza San Martín, T 285377, rec., good value, C inc. taxes, a/c, with bath, breakfast served in room, helpful, money changing facilities, Japanese run, good restaurant, good service; *Hostal Eiffel*, Jr. Washington 949, T 240188/249181, C, expensive but breakfast inc., very clean, hot water, safe; *Granada*, on Huancavelica 323, T 279033, D without breakfast, clean, safe, hot water, English spoken, friendly; *Grand Castle*, Av. Carlos Zavala Loayza 218, opp. Ormeño bus station, D, including breakfast (poor), hot water, comfortable, good service, Japanese restaurant, rec.; *Hostal El Tambo*, Av. Bolognesi 373, D, including breakfast, laundry, dry cleaners and supermarket all nearby. *Residencial Francia*, Samuel Velarde 185, Av. Ejército, T 617054, D including taxes and breakfast, bath, hot water, laundry facilities, swimming pool, gardens, very friendly and helpful, 20 min. bus ride from centre; *Hostal Wilson*, Jr. Chancay, E, a bit run down but friendly and safe for luggage deposit. *Hostal Belén*, Belén 1049, just off San Martín, Italian spoken, F, very popular, basic breakfast extra, hot water, friendly, music groups practising.

*Asociación de Amistad Peruano Europea*, Jirón Camaná 280, 7th floor, F, dormitory (16 beds), one shower, clean, friendly, laundry facilities, will store luggage. *Hostal Niza*, N. de Piérola 206, F (triples available), breakfast, friendly, central, clean but not so the toilets, basic, noisy; *Hostal San Sebastián*, Ica 712, T 23-2740, run by Nellie de Viana, E (F p.p. in dormitory), clean, friendly, English spoken, popular gringo place, safe to leave luggage, bit noisy on street corner, rooms on top floor mixed reports, restaurant, book exchange and laundry facilities (runs cheap taxi service to airport); *Hostal España*, Jr. Azángaro 105, E-F (cheaper in dormitory) in a restored house in old Lima, hot water 0600-2300, family run, English spoken, secure (also for motorcycles), can leave luggage, vegetarian café on roof terrace. *Residencial Roma*, Ica 326, E, hot water in mornings, safe to leave luggage, quiet, basic but clean, highly rec., often full, (next door are a good pastry shop and Roma Tours, a small travel agency); motorcycle parking; *Pensión Ibarra*, Av. Tacna 359, Apt. 162, 15th and 16th floors, no sign, E, including breakfast (less if staying several days), clean, friendly, very helpful owner, full board available;*Hostal Tauro*, Av. Tacna, F, clean, rec., 20 metres from airport colectivo terminal; *Hostal Samaniego*, Av. Emancipación 184, Apto. 801, near Plaza San Martín, G, rec., 15 spaces available (4 per room), hot water, friendly, safe, will store luggage for foreigners; *Casa de Hospedaje*, Pasaje Acisclo Villarán 365, no sign, central, E, F without breakfast, clean, homely, good; *Familia Rodríguez*, Av. N. de Piérola 730, 2nd floor, T 236465, F with breakfast, clean, friendly, will store luggage, dormitory accommodation with only one bathroom.

*La Granja Azul*, in B range, Carretera Central (turn off between Km. 13 and 14 of Carretera Central, buses from Parque Universitario every 15 minutes; last bus back leaves 2000 but a minibus leaves the hotel for Lima at 2200), restaurant specializing in exotic cocktails and chicken dishes, dancing every night, rec.

If arriving by air, especially at night, you can try the tourist office at the airport (beyond passport control) if you want to arrange a hotel room, but they are not always helpful. **Hotel reservations** for Lima and elsewhere in Peru can be made through Centro de Reservaciones, Av. Panamericana 6251, San Antonio/Miraflores, T 466-895.

**Youth Hostel** *Albergue Juvenil Internacional*, Av. Casimiro Ulloa 328, Miraflores, T 465-488, F, basic cafeteria, travel information, cooking and laundry facilities, double rooms and dormitories, swimming pool often empty, "spacious, clean and safe", rec. Open to non-members of the Youth Hostel Association, ten minutes walk from the beach. Transhotel bus between airport and Plaza San Martín passes, so does Ikaros bus (Av. Benavides stop), so does No. 2 from Av. Tacna to Miraflores, 30 mins. to centre; taxi to centre, US$6. **Albergue Juvenil Karima**, Chancay, F p.p. in dormitory, inc. breakfast, clean, friendly.

**Camping** Under no circumstances camp on or near beach at Miraflores, theft and worse is rife in these areas. Propane gas in heavy iron gas bottles available from Delta-Gas, Av. Benavides 5425, Lima. Camping gas (in small blue bottles) available from Trekking and Backpacking Club Peruano (address below) and from Técnica Import, Dávalos Lisson 323, nr. Washington, 0900-1300 and 1400-1700. Oechsle sell butane gas cartridges. N.B. Airlines do not allow the carriage of gas bottles.

**Baths** Baños Pizarro, Unión 284, steam rooms, US$3, cold showers only, café and swimming pool. Windsor Turkish Baths, on Miguel Dasso, San Isidro, separate facilities for men and women, steam, sauna, cold pool and whirlpool, US$4.

**Restaurants** Check all restaurant prices before ordering, especially if you have visited the city before; prices have soared in 1990/91 in upper and middle class establishments. A cheap *menú* (set lunch) still costs about US$2, but a meal in a moderate restaurant will cost US$15 (March 1991 prices).

In **Miraflores** we recommend the following: *Dom Beta*, José Gálvez 667, for seafood (mixed reports in 1991); *Rosa Náutica*, built on old British-type pier (Espignon No. 4) in Lima bay, near Miraflores, not to be missed, delightful opulence, finest cuisine (US$30 p.p.), sunset rec.; *El Jíbaro II*, Av. Elmer Faucett 1718, Bellavista, rec. for seafood; *Vivaldi*, Ricardo Palma 258, US$5-7 p.p., also for drinks and snacks, nice atmosphere; steaks at *La Tranquera*, Av. Pardo 285; *El Dorado* (Chinese), Av. Arequipa 2450, good food, expensive; *La Costa Verde* on Barranquito beach, excellent food and wine, pecan pie highly rec. but expensive, Amex accepted. *Rincón Gaucho* on Parque Salazar, T 474778, and *El Gaucho*, not far away on Av. Larco, two of the best steak-houses in Peru, both serve superb steaks imported from

Argentina; *Haiti*, Av. Benavides 160, good food, cheap, rec. *Pardo's*, Av. José Pardo 498, good and large portions of chicken. *Salad House*, Av. Grau 164, 42 different salads, very good, open (except Mon.), 1230-1530, 1930-2300. Typical Peruvian restaurants can be found at the end of Avenida Brasil.

Vegetarian restaurants are *Bircher Berner*, Av. Schell 598, good value, *Govinda*, Schell 630, *Productos JJGC*, Manuel Bonilla 178 (off Larco, opp. Cine Pacífico), nondescript storefront, but excellent food (try crema de choclo).

Try also *Carlín*, Av. La Paz 644, excellent, expensive, seafood specialities, good coffee; several good restaurants (and good shopping) in El Suche shopping mall, in this area is *La Crèperie*, La Paz 635, delicious filled pancakes; *Manolo*, Larco 608, good food, meals US$2, popular, rec.; *The Brenchley Arms*, Atahualpa 174, T 459680, English pub serving English food, English speaking, informal and relaxed, tourist information. *Café Suisse*, Av. Larco 111, on main square, for cakes, coffee, European-style food and delicatessen. At same address is *La Tiendecita Blanca*, tea rooms/delicatessen, good cakes, sandwiches, coffee. Good ice cream at *Heladería Italiana*, Angamos Oeste 408 (really excellent); *Pastelería Sueca*, Av. Larco 759, good hamburgers, pastries and salads. *Liverpool*, Ricardo Palma 250, good food, Beatles music and décor. Excellent and large pancakes at *Palachinke*, Av. Schell 120, but not cheap.

In **San Isidro** these restaurants are rec.: *Aquarium* (at the *Country Club Hotel*); *Los Condes de San Isidro* (Av. Paz Soldán 290—an 18th-century mansion—T 222557) excellent; *Valentino's*, Calle M. Bañón 215 (near Camino Real and Av. Javier Prado), excellent food and service; *Don Adolfo*, Manuel Bañon 295, excellent food, helpful, friendly; *Micasa*, Augusto Tamayo 150 (Japanese); *Manos Morenas*, Conquistadores 887 (open 1200-1530, 1800-2400), criolla specialities, rich and tasty, big portions, criolla breakfast Sat.-Sun. 0830-1100, busy; and on same street *Cebichelandia* (another branch on Benavides in Miraflores) for excellent fish lunches. *Steak House*, Las Camelias 870, open 1200-2400, serves Argentine steak (about US$20 for 3 courses).

In **Barranco**, *El Otro Sitio*, Sucre 317, excellent Creole Buffet US$4-5, live music; *El Buen Gusto*, Av. Grau 323, good atmosphere and service, good selection of meat dishes, rec; *El Puente*, below Puente de los Suspiros; *Karamaduke*; *La Casa de Florentino*.

In **Magdalena**, *José Antonio* (Peruvian food, music after 2200), Monteagudo 210 B, strongly rec.

In **Monterrico**, near the Gold Museum, *Pabellón de la Caza*, Alonso de Molina 1100, expensive, but very good food and service, "sumptuous gastronomic treat". Also *Puerto Fiel*, Av. Primavera 1666, 3 blocks from Gold Museum, rec., seafood.

In **central Lima:** *L'Eau Vive*, Ucayali 370, across from the Torre Tagle Palace, run by nuns, open Mon.-Sat., 1245-1430, 2030-2230, fixed-price US$4 lunch menu (+ taxes and couvert), Peruvian-style in interior dining room, or à la carte in either of dining rooms that open on to patio, excellent, profits go to the poor. *Las Trece Monedas*, in an old colonial mansion off Av. Abancay (Ancash 536), excellent, local food, insist on an itemized bill; *Domino*, in an arcade off Unión, near San Martín, excellent breakfast, Swiss-owned, medium-priced, rec. *Parrilladas San Martín*, Plaza San Martín (opposite *Bolívar*), rec. (especially the anticuchos and sauces), US$5-8; *1900*, Belén 1030, very good, US$15 for dinner, drinks and salads in patio, live music from 1930. *Lukyi*, Callao 300, good Chinese, reasonable; *Wah Shing Chifa*, Ica almost opp. *Hostal San Sebastián* good and cheap; *Mario's*, N. de Piérola y Tacna, Argentine, cheap, relaxing; Cheaper restaurants include: *El Pan Nuestro*, Ica 129, 2 blocks from *Res. Roma*, breakfast US$1, lunch US$2, good food; *Bar Cordano*, Ancash y Carabaya, 1 block N of Plaza de Armas, 1920s décor, good, popular, rec; *Lucky Star*, N. de Piérola 733 (3 blocks from Plaza San Martín), 1000-2400, good restaurant/snack bar with Peruvian food. *Las 4 Estaciones*, Ica y Jr. Unión, pizzeria, good juices; *Pizzería Americana*, N. de Piérola (nearly opposite *Crillon Hotel*) is rec., though expensive; *El Barroco*, Jr. Cañete 349, good and reasonable. Also try Rímac district, over Puente de Piedra, for cheaper food, e.g. the chicken restaurants on Av. Trujillo. There are several inexpensive restaurants on Av. Venezuela, and good snack-bars on Unión, particularly *Las Vegas*, western-style, good, cheap. There are good cheap fish restaurants near Parque Universitario. On Jirón Ancash and Av. Abancay (near Buena Muerte church) there are restaurants serving good lunches. The church of San Francisco (Jr. Laupe) has beautiful garden restaurant, good food at reasonable prices.

Vegetarian restaurants at Carabaya 744 or Camaná 337, where a meal costs US$1.05, excellent; *Govinda*, Av. Callao 480 y Tacna, good value lunch and at Av. Arenales 674, Jesus María; *El Meson*, Moquegua 204, menú US$1.20, good; *Casa Naturista*, Abancay 839, cheap but not too good; *Avigail*, Av. Bolivia y Paseo de la República, expensive; *Centro Aplicación Naturista Sebastián Kneipp*, Jr. Loreto 379, Rímac, highly rec.; *Comedor Vegetariano Nuevo Mundo*, Camillo Carrillo 159, Jesús María, cheap, acceptable; *Natur*, Moquegua 132, rec., some English spoken.

A good coffee bar for snacks and sandwiches is *Googies* in Plaza San Martín; also *Tivoli* bar, Nicolás de Piérola 820; *Sandwich Tacna*, Tacna 327, popular and crowded at lunchtime. *Munich Cakehouse*, Cailloma 329 and Ica. Cake shop at Camaná 284 (1 block from Plaza de Armas) has been rec; good coffee at *Café de Paso*, Carabobo y Cuzco (stand-up coffee shop). Good bread rolls at corner of Moquegua and Unión. *Pastelería Lobatón*, Jr. Unión 672, good churros.

**N.B.** Most restaurants now have 20% added to the bill: 15% for tip and 5% for taxes (although this can vary according to the restaurant; some show no extra charges at all).

**Shopping** Silver and gold handicrafts of all kinds; Indian hand-spun and hand-woven textiles; manufactured textiles in Indian designs; llama and alpaca wool products such as ponchos, rugs, hats, blankets, slippers, coats, sweaters, etc.; *arpilleras*, appliqué pictures of Peruvian life (originated in Chile with political designs), made with great skill and originality by women in the shanty towns; fine leather products mostly hand made. The *mate burilado*, or engraved gourd found in every tourist shop, is cheap and a genuine expression of folk art (cheaper in villages near Huancayo). For handicrafts produced by cooperatives, with benefits going directly to the producers, contact the non-profit organization *Minka*, Barcelona 115, Lince, PO Box 14-0359, T 222132, open Mon.-Fri. 0900-1600 (nr. Clínica Lozada, Av. Javier Prado y Salaverry). There is an exhibition room displaying the whole range of Peruvian handicrafts and the regions in which they originate. Minka also provides information and addresses about producer groups throughout Peru; it will arrange for purchases made outside Lima to be transported to the capital and posted abroad. For further information contact Norma Velásquez.

*Silvania Prints*, Colmena 714 (near *Hotel Bolívar*), Conquistadores 905 (San Isidro) and in lobby of *Miraflores César Hotel*, sell modern silk-screen prints on Pima cotton with precolumbian designs. *Plaza México*, jewellery in precolumbian designs. On Av. Nicolás de Piérola vendors sell oil paintings of Andean scenes, bargains abound. One of the best selections of folk art, but not the cheapest, will be found at the *Artesanías del Perú* shops in Lima. *Cerámica Los Reyes*, Av. Nicolás de Piérola. Ground floor of *Hotel Bolívar* for all metal, pottery, woollen and handicraft items, reasonably priced, credit cards accepted. *Artesanía Huamanqaqa*, Belén 1041 between Hotels *Sheraton* and *Bolívar*, the best store for high-quality weaving (but very expensive), specializes in Indian weaving from San Pedro de Cajas. Next door is a permanent exhibition with a century-old loom. Also try the 24 stores in *Restaurant 1900*, Belén 1030, very good arpilleras. *EPPA* (*Empresa Peruana de Promoción Artesana*) government store for Peruvian handicrafts in San Isidro (Av. Orrantia 610). *Antisuyo*, Jr. Tacna 460, Miraflores, an Indian cooperative run by an Englishwoman, sells high-quality handicrafts from all regions, reasonable prices, T 472557. *Art-Andina*, Belén 1045, good selection of Indian weaving and rugs at very reasonable prices. Precolumbian textiles can be bought from the *Casa de Antigüedades*, Av. de Emancipación 253. On Unión is *Casa Mas*, with a wonderful display of gold and silver handicrafts, and antiques. In Miraflores, lovely shopping arcade *El Suche*, at La Paz 646, but high prices in the woollen goods, ceramics and leather shops. Antiques available in Miraflores on Calle La Paz. Vicuña is unobtainable for the time being in Peru and Bolivia alike. See *H. Stern's* jewellery stores at Hotels *Miraflores César*, *Bolívar* and *Sheraton*, and at the International Airport. (Note: It is better to buy pullovers in the Sierra. However, although Lima is more expensive, it is often impossible to find the same quality of goods elsewhere.) Alpaca cloth for suits, coats, etc. (mixed with 40% sheep's wool) can be bought cheaply from factories: Cirsa, Av. Argentina 2400, microbus 93, 70 or 84 from Plaza Castilla; *Lanificio*, Nicolas Arriola 3090, San Luis, T 320859, better quality in their Arequipa factory (**see page 1007**) (gives 10% discount to foreigners attached to their embassies). Alpaca wool for knitting or weaving from *Alpaca* III, Av. Larco 859, Miraflores. Made-to-measure cotton shirts in 24 hrs. from Sr. Hurtado, "Sir", Jr. Carabaya 1108. A good tailor is Navarro Hermanos, in Belén, below the Tourist Office. There are bargains in clothing made from high quality Pima cotton. Records: *Discos del Mundo*, Unión 779, allows you to listen, in sound-proof booth, before you buy.

**Markets** Parque Diagonal/Kennedy, Miraflores (by *Restaurant Haiti*): jewellery, sandals made to measure, paintings and other handicrafts, Dec.-June, Wed. to Mon., in winter Sat. and Sun. only; **Feria Artesanal**, Av. de la Marina 790 and Av. Sucre westwards, in Pueblo Libre (take bus 2, 7, 10, or 48 on Av. Abancay, but watch your possessions, as thieves are numerous): extensive market selling woollen goods, leatherwork, bric-a-brac and Peruvian goods and souvenirs; sidestreets off **Lampa**: hardware; sidestreets off **Av. Colmena**: books; **Parque Universitario**: bargains; **Plaza San Martín**, behind *Hotel Bolívar*: ambulantes (money-changers). **Polvos Azules**, behind Central Post Office, 1 block from Plaza de Armas: sells just about anything (including stolen cameras), small handicraft section (ask directions), beware pickpockets. There is an interesting **flower market** with enormous arrangements near Plaza George Washington, on the way to the Gold Museum. Good **Indian** market on Avenida de la Marina, San Miguel, bus No. 10 from Miraflores.

**Bookshops** Fair selection of foreign-language books at *Librería Delta*, N. de Piérola 689, Todos shopping area, Galax commercial centre (Todos and Galax are the largest stores), Miraflores and Jorge Chávez airport. *ABC Bookstores* also sell foreign-language books. *Librería Studium*, Plaza Francia 1164 (also on N. de Piérola), sells history/travel books in English. *Studium* and *Librería de la Universidad de San Marcos* give student discounts. Tourist books in English, French and German also available from *Librería Ayra*, Jirón Unión 560, rec., will supply works in Quechua. *Librería Internacional*, Jirón Unión (corner of Plaza San Martín) has a wide selection of books on South America in all languages. Good English selection at *Epoca*, on Belén in the centre and on José Pardo in Miraflores, T 457430/450282. Bookshop on the plaza in Barranco has good selection, with a gallery and coffee shop. The *Book Exchange* at Ocoña 211a (near Plaza San Martín), open 1400-1900, is best place in centre for foreign-language books; will exchange them (mainly science-fiction, detective and porn) if bought there; also offers money transfer and postal service! *Librería El Pacífico* in Miraflores has the best selection of English books in Lima. Rare books, many shops on Av. Azángaro. French bookshop, *Plaisir de France*, Colmena 958. International newspapers, from newstands, Block 6, Av. N. de Piérola.

Secondhand books (mostly in English) from dark blue/green both on Plaza San Martin, esquina N de Piérola, and along Tacna, between Moquegua y Arequipa.

**Film** Agfa distributor at Av. Tomás Marsano 390; for cheap film try at the black market at Feria Polvos Azules, at Puente de Piedra. Foto Mare, Belén 1047. Many developers using Kodak equipment offer same-day service; all at similar prices. Many on Jr. Unión and Plaza San Martín; also Av. Larco, Miraflores. Fujicolor offer a free film with developing. Quality tends to be poor, although Profot, Av. Juan de la Fuente 760, San Antonio, Miraflores, 0900-1300, 1400-1700, is rec. for both slide and print developing. **Camera Repairs** Casa Hindú, Jr. Unión, between Plazas de Armas and San Martín, repairs Olympus cameras. Camera House, Larco 1150, Office 39, 2nd floor, Miraflores, Mon-Fri 1530-1900, ask for Clemente Higa, who is often there later in pm. Frankitec, Sr. Max Bürkli, Jr. Lampa 1115-104, Lima 1, T 284 331, repairs all cameras (Swiss technician).

**Pharmacy** Botica Inglés, Jirón Cailloma 336, sells Dr. Scholl foot supplies for those contemplating or recovering from the Inca Trail. Deza, Conquistadores, San Isidro (1 block from Ovalo Gutiérrez), modern, like a US drugstore, open 24 hrs. Tampons reported only available in Miraflores.

**Local Buses** Standard fares in Lima: buses and minibuses, US$0.20, sometimes half price with student card, not very reliable. The main routes, such as from Plaza San Martín down Av. Arequipa to Miraflores and on to San Isidro, are also served by colectivos, US$0.15, which continue late at night after many buses stop. The centre, between Tacna, Abancay and Nicolás de Piérola is now free of buses.

**Taxis** No taxis use meters, you must bargain the price beforehand and don't give in to demands for payment in dollars, unless you get a bargain! Also, insist on being taken to the destination of your choice, not the drivers', from about US$0.50 for short journeys up to US$2.50 from the centre to the suburbs (within the city US$1.25 on average). After 2400 and on holidays, 35%-50% surcharge. Be careful of black "pirate" taxis; they usually charge 50% more. Paco, T 616394, is dependable for phone hiring, similarly Willy, T 527456, speaks some English.

Drivers don't expect tips; give them small change from the fare. If hiring a taxi for over 1 hour agree on price per hour beforehand. To Callao, La Punta, San Miguel, Magdalena, Miraflores (should be US$1.50), Barranco, Chorrillos, by agreement, basis US$5 per hour. Rec., knowledgeable driver, Hugo Casanova Morella, T 857708 (he lives in La Victoria), for city tours, travel to airport, etc.

**Car Rental** Cars can be hired from **Hertz Rent-a-Car**, Ocoña 262 (beside *Hotel Bolívar*), T 289477; **Budget Rent A Car**, Airport, T 528706 and Miraflores; **Graf Automóviles Seleccionados**, S.A. (Avis), Av. Petit Thouars 915, Miraflores, T 233486; **Turamérica**, Ocoña 164 (beside *Hotel Bolívar*), T 276413, or Nicolás de Piérola 590 (opp. *Hotel Crillón*), T 278970. The condition of vehicles is usually very poor. Beware of deep street potholes. Make sure that your car is in a locked garage at night. Russian-made four-wheel drive Niva vehicles are often rented; they are up to the conditions of Andean driving, but Lada saloon cars are not. Note that it can be much cheaper to rent a car in a town in the Sierra for a few days than to drive all the way from Lima.

**Motor Parts** International Motors S.A. in Lima is the only Land Rover agent in Peru. Some BMW parts seem to arrive in Lima.

**Folklore** Every Sunday at the Coliseo Cerrado, Av. Alfonso Ugarte. AAA Theatre (see under **historic mansions** above), Ica 323, has folklore evening every Tues., 2015, admission US$3. Also at the Teatro Municipal, Jirón Ica (tickets US$0.60-3.60), Tues. 2000. Cooperativa Santa Elisa, Cailloma 824 (3rd floor) has a folk group every Wed., 2000. The Museo de Arte has seasons of Peruvian folklore on Weds., at 2000, US$1.20 entrance. Many peñas have opened in recent years; these are generally cheap, tavern-like places with Peruvian music, much dancing and audience participation, *Hatuchay Peña*, Trujillo 228 (across the bridge past the Post Office), Fri., Sat., 2100, entrance US$3, inexpensive, crowded, good, but best to phone for taxi late at night; *La Peña de Pocho Ugarte* in Miraflores; *Las Brisas de Lago Titicaca*, just off Plaza Bolognesi, rec.; *Peña El Ayllu*, Jr. Moquegua 247, open every night, entrance free, rec. *La Palizada*, Av. del Ejército 800, Miraflores; *Las Guitarras*, in Miraflores and *Wifala* on Calle Cailloma have been rec. Many others in Barranco around Plaza Grau and Puente de los Suspiros, e.g. *1900* above a bookshop on Plaza Grau and *Los Balcones* on Av. Grau; *La Estación de Barranco*, at Pedro de Osma 112, good, family atmosphere, varied shows, and *Latinoamericano* on same street; *Nosferatu* next to Puente de los Suspiros.

**Bars** (with music) *Charlie's Peppermint Bar*, Av. Corpac, *Percy's Candlelight Room*, Todos shopping centre, San Isidro. *Satchmo Jazz Bar*, Av. La Paz 538, Miraflores, good; *Studio One*, 2-3 blocks from Parque Kennedy, Miraflores, gay. *La Taverna*, Barranco, live folkloric or western music; *Juancito's Bodega Bar*, Barranco, rec. for local colour.

**Discotheques** *Las Rocas* in San Isidro is good and not expensive. *Keops* disco, San Isidro, is very popular with young Limeños. Good nightlife in Miraflores near Parque Diagonal and Av. Larco, with discos, video-pubs and pizzerías. Recommended in Miraflores, *Video Club*, just off Av. Diagonal; *La Miel*, min. consumption US$5.50 (pay as you go, don't wait for a big bill), and *Arizona*, US$4 (not very authentic, but good enough for a night out). *Unicorno del Mar* at Herradura beach in summer. *La Caverna*, Aviación 2514, San Borja. *La Maquina del Sabor*, Chorillos, South of Barranco, on cliff-top overlooking sea, popular on Sundays with the teenage crowd, admission US$0.50 and drinks cheap, live salsa and lively clientele, casual dress.

**Theatre** Most professional plays are put on at the Teatro Segura, Teatro Municipal (Jirón Ica, 300 block—also orchestral and ballet performances); Teatro Arequipa and Sala Alzedo; Teatro Marsano, Av. Petit Thouars, Miraflores. Others are produced by amateur and university groups. Teatro Cabaña in the Parque de la Exposición puts on a strong programme of progressive theatre, especially for Institutos shows, local and cheap, take student card. AAA Theatre Workshop, Jirón Ica 323. See the newspapers for announcement; the Sunday edition of *El Comercio* publishes all cinema and theatre details.

**Cinemas** Tickets cost about US$3 in Lima. Good films can be seen cheaply at the Cooperativa Santa Elisa, Cailloma 824, Thurs., Fri., Sat., and Sun. each week, Tel: 322641. Museo de Arte, Paseo Colón 125, has good international films, ask for monthly programme, rec.; Alianza Francesa (every Tues.), Av. Garcilaso de la Vega 1550, as well as at the British and North American-Peruvian Culture Associations (usually Thurs.) Ciné Pacífico Miraflores, in central Miraflores, most films in English with Spanish subtitles; Romeo y Julieta, by Parque Kennedy, Miraflores, usually has good films. Ciné Clubs are cheaper, but films are usually older (often no bad thing!) and the screen small; e.g. Raimondi, Alejandro Tirado 274, Lima; El Cinematografo, Pérez Roca 196, Barranco; Club Melies, Av. Bolívar 635, Pueblo Libre. Check in *El Comercio* under "C" (Cultural), for programmes.

**Sports** There are two bullfight seasons, one in October-November and a short one in March. They are held in the afternoons on Sun. and holidays. Tickets at 2nd block of Calle Huancavelica, or at the Plaza de Acho bullring early on the day of the *corrida*. Famous *toreros* practise in the Lima ring, the oldest in the Americas, and fighting bulls are of Spanish stock. Cockfights are frequently organized and advertised: the Plaza de Gallos at Calle Sandía 150, near Parque Universitario, is recommended. Horse racing, Hipódromo Monterrico, on Tues. and Thurs. evenings (1900) and Sat. and Sun. (1300) in summer, and in winter on Tues. evening and Sat. and Sun. afternoons. Colectivos on race days leave from the Plaza San Martín, fare US$0.20. The popular stand is not recommended. Tourists may enter the members' stand on production of their passports. For Paso horses, which move in four-step amble, extravagantly paddling their forelegs, National Paso Association, Miraflores, T 476331. The Lima, Inca, Granja Azul and La Planicie golf clubs and the Country Club de Villa all have 18-hole courses. The Santa Rosa, Cruz de Hueso and Huampani golf clubs have 9-hole courses. (Contact Gerard Astruck of Sudex S.A., T 28-6054, for particulars.) Polo and tennis are also played. Boxing or all-in wrestling (Sat. night) at the Coliseo Nacional.

Association football matches and various athletic events take place at the National Stadium, seating 45,000, in the centre of the city on ground given by the British community on the 100th anniversary of Peru's Declaration of Independence.

**Lima Cricket and Football Club**, Justo Vigil 200, Magdalena del Mar, T 610080/614030; anyone with a Commonwealth, US and possibly other foreign passport can become a temporary member (for a small fee)—ask the staff to phone a committee member. The club has extensive sports facilities, as well as football, rugby (training at 1700 on Thurs., May-October) and cricket, squash, swimming, snooker, etc. (Rugby players and cricketers are always welcome). Also cheap restaurant, pub and friendly place to meet people.

**Exchange** Banco de la Nación (e.g. Av. Abancay 491). **Citibank**, Las Begonias 580, San Isidro, charges 3% on its own travellers' cheques, open 0830-1245 in summer. **Bank of America**, Augusto Tamayo 120, San Isidro, will change Bank of America travellers' cheques into local currency, 1.5% commission. **Interbanc** at Jirón Ica y Jirón Unión changes cash and travellers' cheques. Peruvian banks: Open: Jan. 1 to March 31—0830 to 1130; April 1 to Dec.31—0915 to 1200. Closed Sat. except Banco de la Nación at Rufino Torrico 830 (opposite *Hotel Crillón*), which is open Sat. 0900-1200 (for changing dollar bills only) and also open in the afternoons 1600-1830; small and crowded, it can be quicker elsewhere. **Banco de Crédito**, cash given on Visa cards, no commission, good rates and low commission on Thomas Cook travellers' cheques at Av. Lampa 4aa (Centro) and Larco y Schell branch, Miraflores. **Visa**, Banco de Crédito (Jr. Lampa), 0900-1200, 1630-1830. **Mastercard**, Banco Continental, Seminario 320, 6th floor, San Isidro. Always check your money in the presence of the cashier, particularly bundles of pre-counted notes. Lost Thomas Cook cheques only replaced in Santiago de Chile or Quito.

Banks and *casas de cambio* frequently change their policies over foreign exchange transactions, so ask beforehand about where is best to go. In early 1991 the street rate was only about 1% better than that offered in banks, exchange houses and hotels. Banks and *casas de cambio* were changing travellers' cheques into dollars as well as intis; commission between 3-5%. *Casas de cambio* are the recommended places to change, around Av. Ocoña and a few in Miraflores; they are safe, and good value but you must bargain hard (e.g. *Cambio* at Av. N. de Piérola 805 which charges 4% commission). The **gold dealers** on Pasaje Los Pinos, Miraflores, give good street rates. Many money changers at corner of Plaza San Martín and Jirón Unión, and in the streets behind *Hotel Bolívar*, identified by their calculators and hiss of "dollars", change money at the parallel rate; some change other South American currencies (beware, many forgeries in circulation, street changers also short change you, often a hassle). Double-check amounts shown on calculators.

**British Schools** Markham College, for boys, is one of only four Headmasters' Conference Schools outside the Commonwealth. Colegio San Andrés, for boys, run by the Free Church of Scotland. Colegio San Silvestre, a school for girls at Miraflores, is represented in the Association of Headmistresses. Colegio Peruano-Británico, San Isidro, co-educational. In La Molina, Colegio Newton offers the international baccalaureate. **American Schools** Colegio Franklin Roosevelt, the American School of Lima, Monterrico, co-educational: Villa María, La Planicie (for girls); María Alvarado, Lima (girls).

**Cultural Institutions** Peruvian-British Cultural Association, Av. Arequipa 3495, San Isidro, with reading room and British newspapers (bus 1, 2, 54A). For other offices, library and film shows, Jirón Camaná 787, T 277927, classes only; theatre, Av. Benavides 620, Miraflores, T 454326. **British Council**, Alberto Lynch 110, San Isidro 27, T 704-350. **Teatro Británico** (amateur productions of plays in English), Calle Bella Vista, Miraflores. **Instituto Cultural Peruano y Norteamericano**, Cuzco 446, in centre, with library; branch at Av. Arequipa 4798, Miraflores. Language tuition, US$80 for 4 weeks, Mon.-Fri., 2 hrs a day. **American Chamber of Commerce**, Juan de Arona, San Isidro. **The American Society of Peru**, Av. Angamos 1155, Miraflores. Tel: 414545. **Goethe-Institut**, Jr. Nazca 722, Jesus María, Lima 11, Mon.-Fri., 1100-2000, library, theatre, German papers, tea and cakes. **Alliance Française**, Avenida Garcilaso de la Vega 1550, also in Miraflores.

**Spanish Classes** Centro de Idiomas de Lima, P.O. Box 772, Lima 100 (Av. Manuel Olguín 215, Monterrico, T 35 0601/5970), 4 grades of tuition, US$8-10/hour, classes suited to students travelling schedules, accommodation with families can be arranged (room with bath, about US$150 a month). Euroidiomas, Juan Fanning 520, Miraflores 4, 6 and 8 week residential courses (US$480, 890, 1200). Centro de Idiomas de la Católica, Camaná 956, in centre, T 239383/310052. See also Instituto Cultural Peruano y Norteamericano above.

**Embassies/Consulates** Argentine Consulate, Pablo Bermúdez 143, 2nd floor, Jesús

María, T 245984/28172, open 0800-1300.**Bolivian Consulate**, Los Castaños 235, San Isidro, T 228231 (0830-1330). **Brazilian Consulate**, Cmdte. Espinar 181, Miraflores, T 462635. **Chilean Consulate**, Javier Prado Oeste 790, San Isidro, T 407965. **Ecuadorean Consulate**, Las Palmeras 356, San Isidro, T 228138. **Colombian Consulate**, Natalio Sánchez 125, 4th floor, T 12074, Mon.-Fri. 0900-1230. **Venezuelan Consulate**, Av. Salaverry 3005, San Isidro, T 415948.

**U.S. Embassy, Av. Inca Garcilaso de la Vega 1400, Lima, T 338000; Consulate:** Grimaldo del Solar 346, Miraflores, T 443621/443921. (NB if registering your passport, you have to leave a photograph). **Canadian Embassy**, Av. Libertad 132, Miraflores, T 444015. **Australian Consulate**, contact Canadian Embassy. **New Zealand Embassy**, Av. Salaverry 3006, San Isidro (Casilla 5587), T 621890, open 0800-1600 Mon-Thurs., 0800-1300 Fri (no direct bus there). **South African Consulate**, contact Swiss Embassy.

**British Embassy and Consulate**, Edificio Pacífico-Washington, Plaza Washington, corner of Av. Arequipa (5th block) and Natalio Sánchez 125, 11th floor (Casilla de Correo 854), T 334738. In case of emergency, the embassy duty officer can be contacted through his bleeper service, T 320982/320053, extension (anexo) 216.(Yellow bus No. 2 passes the Embassy.). **Irish Consulate**, Carlos Povias Osores 410, San Isidro, T 230808. **Austrian Embassy**, Av. Central 64, 5th floor, San Isidro, T 428851. **West German Embassy**, Av. Arequipa 4210, Miraflores, T 459997. **French Consulate**, Arequipa 3415, San Isidro, T 704968. **Belgian Consulate**, Angamos 380, Miraflores, T 463335. **Swiss Embassy**, Av. Salaverry 3240, San Isidro, Lima 27, T 624090. **Swedish Embassy**, Las Agatas 189, La Victoria, T 406700/722425. **Norwegian Consulate**, Canaval Moreyra 595, T 404048. **Finnish Embassy**, Los Eucaliptos 291, San Isidro, T 703750. **Danish Consulate General**, Bernardo Monteagudo 201, San Isidro, T 621090, open 0900-1700. **Netherlands Consulate**, Av. Principal 190, San Borja, T 728635/721548, open Mon-Fri 0900-1200. **Italian Embassy**, Av. G. Escobedo 298, Jesús María. **Israeli Embassy**, Natalio Sánchez 125, 6° piso, Santa Beatriz, Aptdo 738, T 334431.

**N.B.** During the summer, most embassies only open in the morning.

**Useful Addresses Tourist Police**, Salaverry 1158, Jesus María, T 714579, friendly, helpful, English and some German spoken; rec. to visit them when you have had property stolen. **Dirección General de Migraciones**, Paseo de la República 585, open 0900-1300; if passport stolen can provide new entry stamps, also for visa extensions, given same day if you insist, otherwise next day. **Intej**, Av. San Martín 240, Barranco, can extend student cards, T 774105. **PSNC**: Nicolás de Piérola 1002-06, Plaza San Martín. T 283250. **YMCA**, Av. Bolívar 635, Pueblo Libre, membership required. **Biblioteca Nacional**, Av. Abancay (cuadra 4) y Miró Quesada.

**Doctor** Dr. Manfred Zapff-Dammert (German), Av. Monte Grande 109, of. 208, Chacarilla del Estanque, Lima-33, Monterrico, T 361532 (office), 350292 (private), highly recommended. Dr. Alejandro Bussalleu Rivera, Instituto Médico Lince, León Velarde 221, Lince, T 712238, speaks English, good for stomach problems. Malaria pills from Dr. León on 3rd floor of Ministerio de Salud, Av. Salaverry.

**Hospitals** Anglo-American Hospital, Av. Salazar, 3rd block, San Isidro. T 403570 (rec. for injections; stock gamma globulin). Hospital de Niñas, Av. Brasil, vaccination centre at the side. Anti-rabies centre, Chacra Ríos.

**Dentists** Ana María Torres, Octavio Espinoza 443, San Isidro, T 229638; Ramón Castillo

Mercado, Alfredo Salazar 583, San Isidro, T 297083.

**Laundry** *Continental*, Callao 422, same-day and next-day laundry and dry-cleaning, good, but expensive. *Miraflores*, Tarapacá 199 and *Inclán*, Miraflores; insist on an itemized receipt. *Autoservicio*, Porta 198, Miraflores, fast, US$1.20 per machine. *Burbujitas*, Porta 293, Miraflores, 4 kg. wash and dry for US$1. Av. Petit Thouars 3139, Miraflores, US$2 wash and dry. *Lava Velox*, Atahualpa 175, Miraflores, US$2 a load, good. *Lava Center*, Víctor Maurtúa 140, San Isidro, T 403600, US$0.50 per kg. Good dry cleaning, but not cheap, at *Forty Minutes*, Jirón Lampa 1180 in centre.

**Non-catholic places of worship** The Union Church of Lima (Interdenominational), Av. Angamos 1155, Miraflores, Worship Service Sun. 1030, T 41-1472. Trinity Lutheran Church of Peru, Las Magnolias 495, Urb. Jardín, San Isidro. Church of the Good Shepherd, Av. Santa Cruz 491, Miraflores (Anglican) T 45-7908, Sun. 0800 Holy Communion, 1000 morning service. International Baptist Church of Lima, Coronel Inclán 799, Miraflores, T 75-7179, Worship Service Sun. 1000. Christian Science Society, 1285 Mayta Capac (near Av. Salaverry), Jesús María. English Benedictine Monastery, Jirón Olivares de la Paz, Las Flores (57M minibus from Plaza de Acho); Sunday Mass 0900, weekdays 1900. **Catholic Mass in English**, La Iglesia de Santa Maria Reina, Ovalo Gutiérrez, Av. Santa Cruz, Miraflores, T 24-7269, Sun. 0930.

**Post Offices** Central office is on Jirón Junín, west of the Plaza de Armas, hours: Mon.-Sat., 0800-1915, Sun., 0800-1200. On Av. Nicolás de Piérola, opp. *Hotel Crillón*. *Poste restante*, Camaná 195 (letters held for 2 months). Also on Av. Petit Thouars in Miraflores (1 block from intersection of Angamos and Arequipa), open 6 days a week. Express letters can only be sent from the Post Office at the airport. Be careful with the rates charged at this Post Office, they sometimes try to charge more than in the city. For parcels **see page 1082, Mail**.

**Telecommunications** International **phone** calls, fax and telex from Entel offices in Edificio Sudamérica on Plaza San Martín, and at Diez Canseco y Schell, Miraflores. For more details, see **Telephones in Information for Visitors**.

**Air Freight** Emery, in Callao, T 52-3643: to USA US$50 plus US$3 per kg.

**Tourist Offices** The Fondo de Promoción Turística (Foptur), Unión (Belén) 1066, T 323559 (open Mon.-Fri., 0900-1800, Sat., 0900-1200), highly recommended, many languages spoken, knowledgeable and helpful to budget-minded travellers, sells maps and has free brochures, Cuzco, Puno, Iquitos, etc. Head Office, Andrés Reyes 320, San Isidro, T 700781, Telex 21363 PE FOPTUR. Enturperú, which administers the State Tourist Hotel chain, is at Av. Javier Prado-Oeste 1358, San Isidro (a 15-min. taxi ride from the centre), open Mon.-Fri., 1000-1900, Sat., 0900-1300 (T 721928/T 228227/228094, telex. 20394; P.O. Box 4475), very helpful; rooms in the *hoteles de turistas* may be booked in advance. There are two tourist offices at the airport, which have lists of hotels and will ring to reserve rooms for travellers, or will book taxis—check whether prices are on the free or official rate; will also change money, very helpful staff. Ask for the helpful, free, *Peru Guide* published in English by American Express.

The Ministerio de Industria y Turismo, Calle 1 Oeste, Corpac, Lima 27, is very helpful regarding complaints and problems connected with travel agencies and touring.

**Maps** A good map of the whole country is available from street sellers in N. de Piérola and Plaza San Martín (published by Lima 2000, US$3.50). The Instituto Geográfico Militar (Av. Aramburu 1190, Surquillo, Lima 34), sells a standard map of Peru (1:2,200,000), US$1.15, department maps, US$0.85 and a 4-sheet map of Peru, 1: 1,000,000, US$8.70, good value, but only available as separate sheets at Av. Aramburu, black-and-white aerial photos available; passport may be required; they are open 0900-1600, Mon.-Fri.; Av. Aramburu open for map sales Mon.-Fri., 0800-1230, 1400-1530. Maps of N and S border areas are not sold. If you submit a letter to the IGM, giving your credentials and adequate reasons, plus a photocopy of your passport, you may be able to obtain maps of the border regions. No accurate maps of the jungle regions have yet been prepared. The Instituto Nacional de Planificación, Avenida República de Chile, also sells a large atlas of Peru, US$25. Petroperú maps for town centres recommended.

**South American Explorers' Club** Av. Rep. de Portugal 146 (Breña—in the 13th block of Alfonso Ugarte), T 31-4480, is a non-profit, educational organisation which functions primarily as an information network for Peru and South America. Membership is US$25 a year, which includes subscription to its quarterly journal, *The South American Explorer*, and numerous member services such as access to files of travel information, equipment storage, personal mail service, trip planning, etc. Open 0930-1700 Mon. to Fri.; non-members are welcome, but asked to limit their visits, staff very helpful. The clubhouse is attractive and friendly; it is not necessary to "explore" to feel at home here. They will sell used equipment on consignment (donations of used equipment, unused medicines etc., are welcome). Their map of the Inca Trail is good (US$4), and they sell an excellent map of the Cordillera Huayhuash. Other useful dyeline trekking maps include the Llanganuco-Santa Cruz trek in the Cordillera Blanca, and the Cordillera Vilcanota (Auzangate). There is a good library and they sell travel books and guides (at a discount to members), and some excellent handicrafts. For further information, and the most recent views on where and how to travel safely, write to: Casilla 3714, Lima 100, Peru; PO Box 18327, Denver, CO USA (T (303) 320-0388); or Apartado 21-431, Eloy Alfaro, Quito, Ecuador (T 566-076). (Also see the Bradts' *Backpacking* book, listed in "Information for Visitors"; all Bradt publications are on sale at the Club.)

**Trekking and Backpacking** Percy Tapiá, Casilla 3074, Lima 100, leads treks for groups on the Inca Trail, Cordillera Vilcabamba and Cordillera Blanca. Club Andino Peruano, Amatistas 263, La Victoria, Lima 13, also helpful; meetings on Thur., 1930-2130. Instituto Nacional de Recreación, Educación Física y Deportes (Inred), have an Andean specialist, César Morales Arnao, at the Estudio Nacional, Tribuna Sur, 3rd floor, T 329177. Trekking and Backpacking Club Peruano, Jr. Huáscar 1152, Jesus María, Lima 11 (T 22515), also at Huaraz; free information on Peru and South America, storage and gas cylinders available. Issues a magazine, *El Trekkero*, write for information. Open Mon.-Fri., 1730-1900, phone first at weekends.

**The Peruvian Touring and Automobile Club** Av. César Vallejo 699 (Casilla 2219), Lince, Lima (T 403270), offers help to tourists and particularly to members of the leading motoring associations. Good maps available of whole country; regional routes and the S. American sections of the Pan-American Highway available (US$2.10).

**Tourist and Archaeological Information** Best guide to archaeological sites is *Manual de Arqueología Peruana*, by Federico Kaufmann-Doig, on sale from stalls and most bookshops, published in Spanish, US$8; an abridged version, *El Perú Arqueológico*, US$2, covering pre-Inca remains, is also available. For serious students of Peruvian archaeology, Federico Kaufmann-Doig is the country's foremost expert and author of *Arqueología Peruana*. He can

be contacted in Lima, T 236675/499103. Recent excavations claim to have discovered Peru's Lost City Paititi near Puerto Maldonado. Those interested should contact Señor Fernando Bueno, director of the Saviours of the Treasure of Paititi Society, in Cuzco, T 221492, or Lima T 468552. Professional archaeologists should contact the Instituto Nacional de Cultura, Casilla 5247, Lima, or Centro de Investigación y Restauración de Bienes Monumentales del Instituto Nacional de Cultura, Jirón Ancash 769, Lima.

*Cut Stones and Crossroads: A Journey in Peru*, by Ronald Wright (Penguin Travel Library) is an excellent, modern travel book. Booklet *Lima, City of Treasures and Traditions* by Frances E. Parodi (published by the American Woman's Literary Club, Lima). *Guía "Inca" de Lima Metropolitana* is invaluable for finding less well known, but interesting, parts of Lima, as is the *Guía de Transportes de Lima Metropolitana* (US$1.75) for getting to them. For those interested in architecture, *Itinerarios de Lima*, by Héctor Velarde (in Spanish and English), and *Guía Reparaz del Perú*, by Gonzalo Reparaz Ruiz (Spanish, English and French) are very useful. Also useful is *Guide to Lima* by J. E. Maguiña and *The City of Kings: A Guide to Lima*, by Carolyn Walton (available from major bookshops). Spanish and English news in the lobby of the *Sheraton Hotel. Lima Times* publishes a monthly *Peru Guide* and sells some other travel books.

**Travel Agents** There are many, around Plaza San Martín and Av. Nicolás Piérola (Colmena). *Lima Tours*, Belén 1040, just off Plaza San Martín, American Express agent, slow for money changing, publishes a tourist guide (T 276624). *Creditio S. A.*, Schell 319, Oficina 706, Miraflores (T 444200/444727), efficient, helpful, English spoken; *Spazio Tours*, Juan Fanning 179, Miraflores, T 476451, or PO Box 18-5497, Lima, very helpful, highly rec.; *Explorandes*, Av. Bolognesi 159, Miraflores, rec.; *Key Tours* (Jorge Gonti Angeles), Av. Nicolás de Piérola 677, Of. 9, T 284311 rec. for swift and efficient arranging of tours throughout Peru and to La Paz. *Aventours*, Av. La Paz 442, Miraflores, Lima 18, T 441067, trekking, rafting, wildlife tours and more (office in Cuzco, Av. Pardo 505, T 237307). *Inca Express S.A.*, Av. Benavides 474, of. 104, Miraflores, T 442066/462754 friendly, helpful, efficient, rec.; *Lazer*, Calle Camara 780, Miraflores, helpful, well-informed, cheap flights arranged. *Majestic Tours*, Centro Comercial Centro Lima, Blvd 196-M (near *Sheraton*), will arrange virtually any itinerary, rec. *Tour Peruana S.A.*, Miguel Dasso 138, San Isidro, T 220751/221639, ask for Sigiario Carrizales, good for flight arrangements; *Nouvelles Frontières*, N. de Piérola 520, for cheap flights to Europe. *Victor Travel*, Moquegua 157, of. 202, T 279044/286674, rec. The Visa Tours tour of Lima has been rec. as pleasant and safe, T 276624. Julio E. Figueroa Cubas, Fco. Sarmiento de Gamboa 289, Urb. La Colonial, Callao, T 514748, private guide, rec. particularly for non-Spanish speakers, Lima tours, US$5 per hour; also Alfredo Hiromoto, T 312-709 (home), or 441-799 (*Hotel Diplomat*). A good archaeological tour guide is Rolando Peceros, T 276720. To contact the Lima Association of Guides, T 245131. **N.B.** A commission is charged for booking tickets, 20% usual, 50% complained of, ask before booking.

**Airport** The Jorge Chávez airport is 16 km. from the centre of Lima. For security reasons, people are not allowed into the airport unless they have a flight to catch. Luggage is checked several times, so arrive 3 hrs. before your departure (1½ hrs. for domestic flights). Taxi, about US$6 to centre, US$8 to Miraflores (negotiate price before leaving, hang on to your bag if surrounded by taxi touts—if you walk 100 metres outside the airport gate you can probably bargain a much cheaper price from taxis not working the airport route—but not recommended at night). Airport bus to centre (and also colectivos; look for big brown sign)

leaves from right-hand end of building as you step out of the door. Municipal blue bus 35 (US$0.20) and colectivo (outside the Air France office), to and from Plaza Dos de Mayo in the day-time, US$0.50 p.p. and per item of luggage. Minibus every 20 mins., US$0.75, from Calle Serrano, opposite Iberia office. Also, 15 and 35 from the Plaza Dos de Mayo leave for the airport; service about every 30 mins. No. 56 from airport enters Lima along Av. Emancipación. There is a cheap colectivo service from corner of Av. Tacna with Colmena (N. de Piérola) 733, from 0400 to 2000, colectivos wait until they have 5 passengers, US$0.50 p.p., and US$0.25 for luggage. Buses go from Trans Hotel, Camaná 828 (T 275697, 289812), supposedly 24-hour service, will also collect passengers from hotels (fares vary according to how much luggage you have and where you are going, but may be as high as US$28—1991—if they pick you up from a hotel away from the centre and from airport to town at night). Passengers report being let down by this service. Also from Miraflores (Avenida Ricardo Palma 280), every 20 min., US$2 p.p. (buses will collect travellers from private houses, US$3.20), T 469872. If using this service, book well in advance at Trans Hotel. At airport, T 518011; after leaving Arrivals turn right and go to desk at the end of the hall. The big hotels also have their own buses at the airport, and charge about the same. There is a duty-free shop but no duty-free cigarettes. Only official Corpac porters are allowed in the customs area. Money exchange is reported as good here, but avoid getting left with intis at the airport when leaving; changing them back into dollars at Banco de la Nación can take a lot of time, and you need to show the official exchange slips. Car rental booths in airport may buy intis. Left luggage costs US$2 per day, US$0.40 per hour per item. Foptur office at airport open daily 0830-1430, 2100-0200 (T 524416) in international area, 0600-1830 (T 333664) in national area. The Prohotel agent at the airport is very helpful with hotel bookings of all classes; there is a second hotel booking agency. Taxi drivers also tout for hotel business, offering discounts—don't let yourself be bullied. Safe to stay all night in 24-hour expresso-snack bar. There is a cheap airport workers' canteen "comedor de los trabajadores" also open to the public, just beyond the perimeter fence to the right of the main terminal.

Be prepared for extensive searches; have your money ready counted, the notes bundled together and the amount written on the outside. Also be prepared for extra charges for documents on arrival.

**Internal Air Services** To Andahuaylas, Arequipa, Ayacucho, Bellavista, Cajamarca, Chiclayo, Chimbote, Cuzco, Huánuco, Iquitos, Juanjui, Juliaca, Moyobamba, Piura, Pucallpa, Puerto Maldonado, Rioja, Tacna, Talara, Tarapoto, Tingo María, Trujillo, Tumbes and Yurimaguas. Details are given in text, under names of destinations, but note that tourist prices are double those for Peruvians—see **Information for Visitors**.

**Air Lines** Most international airlines have moved out to San Isidro and Miraflores. Faucett (Garcilaso de la Vega 865, Lima centre, T 338180; office in Miraflores Av. Diagonal 592, T 462031), Aeroperú (Plaza San Martín; more helpful than offices at airport, T 317627, or Av. Pardo 601, Miraflores, T 478333; 24-hr. reconfirmation service T 478333). Office hours are 0900-1800, Mon.-Sat.

**Rail** Central Railway of Peru maintains passenger and freight service to La Oroya (with an extension N to Cerro de Pasco) and SE to Huancayo (with an extension to Huancavelica): Desamparados station, behind Palacio de Gobierno. (For description of line **see page 1045**). Train to **La Oroya** and **Huancayo** departs 0740 daily April to October, arriving La Oroya 1300 and Huancayo 1600 (schedules published in *El Comercio*), service is cut to Mon., Wed., Sat. November-March. Check schedules in advance, train often suspended. The train from **La Oroya to Cerro de Pasco** also runs daily, but one cannot buy a through ticket from Lima. The Cerro de Pasco train leaves La Oroya at 1400, and should connect with the train from Lima, but the latter is rarely on time. If not wishing to go beyond La Oroya, colectivo back to Lima costs US$6 p.p., approximately, 5 hrs., you can make a day trip of it, being back by 2000. You can also return by bus, 7½ hrs. The return from Huancayo is at 0700, arriving Lima 1603. Single, 1st class, US$12, 2nd class, US$8; good cheap breakfast and lunch served. 1st class and buffet seats can be reserved for US$0.50—take a torch for the long, dark tunnels; ticket office opens 0830-1200, 1300-1600 Mon.-Fri., 0700-1100 Sat.; tickets can only be bought one day in advance in Lima; in the high season, tickets are often sold out for 1st class by 1200. Sit on the left; remember that the train changes direction at San Bartolomé, so you will be sitting on the right to begin with. Guard your possessions very carefully against pickpockets at the station (heavy police presence on the train). Only ticket holders are allowed on the platform. The station is closed on Sundays.

**Bus Companies** Coastal buses are usually good although liable to delays. Buses in the Sierra, in view of the road surfaces, often break down. The services of the Ormeño group, Zavalo Loayza 177, T 27-5679/28-8453, are generally recommended throughout Peru; Cruz del Sur are also generally well thought of. Tepsa, Paseo de la República 129, opp. *Sheraton* (T 731233) run N and S on the coast and to Pucallpa and Arequipa; they use older, more run-down buses than some other companies, but we are told they still tend to drive too fast for safety. Expreso Continental (Ormeño) to Trujillo, Piura and Tumbes, rec.; Chinchay-Suyo, rec. (northwards), Apurímac 391 and Av. Grau 525; also going north, Perú Express, Pacífico El Norte (to Chimbote), Atahualpa, Jr. Sandía 266, T 275838/287255 (to Cajamarca, Celendín, etc.), good; Sudamericano buses (Av. Nicolás de Piérola 1117) to Tumbes are variable and its service to Nazca is unreliable; Roggero are unreliable and slow. Along the South coast route, Ormeño, reliable, also to Arequipa and Cuzco (terminal at Calle Oyazaca, best go there by taxi, especially at night); Cruz del Sur, Paseo de la República corner with Almirante Grau (also go to Santiago). To **Cuzco**: via Arequipa, Cruz del Sur; via Nazca and Puquío, Ormeño, El Cóndor. To **Huancayo**, Compresa Cáceres, Av. 28 de Julio 2195, and Comité 22 colectivo, Av. Ayacucho 997, T 289082. To **Huánuco**: León de Huánuco, Av. José Gálvez 1734 (also to Pucallpa not rec., buses in bad condition); Nor Oriente, Luna Pizarro 365. Arrellano, for Huánuco and Tingo Maria, to be avoided because terminal is in dangerous La Victoria district. Expreso Intersa, Av. Nicolás de Piérola, 1631; El Trome, Montevideo 949. Colectivos leave for all parts of Peru from Parque Universitario. For prices of routes and more details, see under individual cities in pages following.

**International Buses** Tepsa runs a twice weekly service to **Santiago**, Chile (3 days, 3,500 km.) leaving Lima on Thurs. and Sun. at 1645, also Pul Bus Norte; Ormeño to Santiago, 2½ days, 3 meals included, and to Buenos Aires, inc. 3 meals, rec. El Rápido, Av. Carlos Zavala Loayza 177, T 283181, weekly to **Mendoza** and **Buenos Aires**, fare includes meals and one night in a hotel, takes 4 days. Connecting twice weekly services to **Guayaquil** and **Quito** (although there are no through buses; you can buy through tickets but they are very expensive and give no priority), leaving Lima on Wed. and Sun. at 0845. The trip takes 2½ days; often long frontier delays. If going to **Brazil**, make sure the bus company does not go via Santiago. There are direct buses from Arica (on Chilean border) to Brazil, saving time and money.

The international trips are much cheaper if one is prepared to take buses to frontier posts only, walk across frontiers, and buy tickets as one goes along (going to Ecuador, it is also possible that a Huaquillas—Quito bus booked in Lima will not exist). To enter Peru, a ticket out of the country may be required. If you have to buy a bus ticket, be warned: they are not transferable or refundable.

**Warning** The area around the bus terminals is very unsafe; thefts and assaults are more common in this neighbourhood than elsewhere in the city. You are strongly advised to consider taking a taxi to and from your bus. Make sure your luggage is well guarded and put on the right bus. It is also important not to assume that buses leave from the place where you bought the tickets.

In the weeks either side of July 28/29 (Independence), and of the Christmas/New Year holiday, it is practically impossible to get train or bus tickets out of Lima.

**Suburbs of Lima** The Avenida Arequipa connects the centre of Lima with Miraflores. Parallel to this is the Via Expresso, a 6-lane highway carrying fast traffic to the suburbs. San Isidro, Puerto Libre, Miraflores and parts of Lince have some good examples of Art Deco and Estilo Barca residential architecture. At *San Isidro* is El Olivar, an old olive grove turned into a delightful park (best visited in daylight). Beyond this is the Lima Golf Club where the Country Club is found, primarily a hotel, which incorporates the Real Club with swimming pools, tennis courts, etc. This is an 8 km. taxi ride from the centre of Lima. There are many good hotels and restaurants in San Isidro; **see main Lima lists, hotels page 927 and restaurants 930.** Between San Isidro and Miraflores is the Pan de Azúcar, or Huallamarca, a restored adobe pyramid of the Maranga culture, of about AD

---

**Lima Orienation: Key to map**

Circled Numbers 1. Pueblo Libre; 2. San Isidro; 3. Miraflores; 4. Barranca.
Squre Numbers 1. Plaza de Armas; 2. Plaza Grau; 3. Parque de Las Leyendas; 4. Campo de Marte; 5. Parque Central, Miraflores; 6. El Olivar; 7. Lima Golf Club; 8. Museos Nacionales de Historia and de Antropología y Arqueología; 9. Museo Arqueológico Rafael Larco Herrera; 10. Museo Amano; 11. Colección Pedro de Osma; 12. Huallamarca; 13. Universidad de San Marcos; 14. Instituto Geográfico Militar; 15. South American Explorers Club (see inset); 16. Plaza Dos de Mayo; 17. Plaza Bolognesi; 18. Parque Japonés; 19. Parque de la Reserva; 20. Museo de Cultura Peruana.
Miraflores 1. L'Ovalo; 2. Parque Central; 3. Parque Kennedy; 4. Plaza Bolognesi.

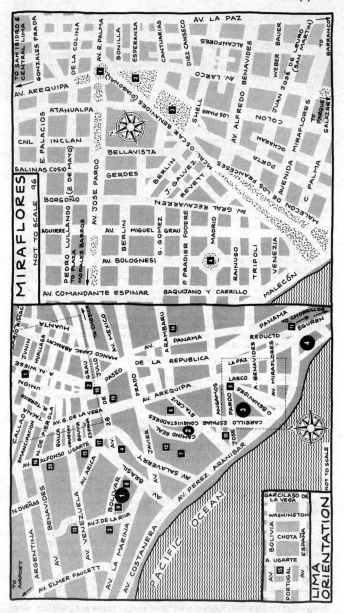

MIRAFLORES    96    NOT TO SCALE

AV. LA PAZ

TO SAN ISIDRO & CENTRAL LIMA

GONZALES PRADA

AV. AREQUIPA

DE LA COLINA

AV. R. PALMA

BONILLA

ESPERANZA

CANTUARIAS

DIEZ CANSECO

ALCANFORES

WEBER

BAUER

DE LEURO (SAN MARTIN)

TO BARRANCO

ATAHUALPA

AV. LARCO

JUAN JOSÉ

COLON

AV. ALFREDO BENAVIDES

MIRAFLORES

TO PARQUE SALAZAR

CNL INCLAN

E. PALACIOS

SALINAS COSIO

BELLAVISTA

SHELL

LOS PINOS

MCAL. OSCAR BENAVIDES (DIAGONAL)

OCHARAN

PORTA

C. PALMA

GERDES

BERLIN

J. GALVEZ

REVETT

MALECON DE LOS FRANCESES

AV. PALMA

BORGOÑO (2 DE MAYO)

AV. JOSÉ PARDO

AGUIRRE

PEDRO LULLANDO

TO PLAZA MORALES BARROS

AV. BERLIN

MIGUEL

G. GOMEZ

GRAU

AV. GRAL. RECAVARREN

P. PRADIER FODERE

MADRID

RAINUSO

TRIPOLI

VENEZIA

AV. BOLOGNESI

P. PRADIER

AV. COMANDANTE ESPINAR

BAQUIJANO Y CARRILLO

MALECÓN

---

RIO RIMAC

PUENTE

HUANTA

MANCO CAPAC

ARAMBARU

PANAMA

PANAMA

REDUCTO

TO CHORRILLOS

EGUREN

JUNIN

HUALLAGA

ABANCAY

AV. MEXICO

AV. DE LA REPUBLICA

LA PAZ

A. BENAVIDES

AV. MIRAFLORES

J. N. WIESE

UNION

GRAU

JULIO

PASEO

PRADO

LARCO

O. BENAVIDES

PARDO

CALLAO

TACNA

AV. G. DE LA VEGA

DE PIEROLA

R. TORRICO

AV. AREQUIPA

STA. CRUZ

ANGAMOS

JOSE PARDO

EMANCIPACION

QUILCA

URUGUAY

BOLIVIA

ESPAÑA

CAMINO REAL

CARRILLO ESPINAR CONQUISTADORES

N. DE PIEROLA

AV. ALFONSO UGARTE

AV. ARICA

AV. JAVIER

AV. SALAVERRY

N. DUEÑAS

AV. BENAVIDES

AV. VENEZUELA

AV. A. J. DE LA RIVA

BOLIVAR

BRASIL

AV. PEREZ ARANIBAR

AV. LA MARINA

AV. COSTANERA

PACIFIC OCEAN

ARGENTINA

TO AIRPORT

AV. ELMER FAUCETT

GARCILASO DE LA VEGA

WASHINGTON

CHOTA

AV. BOLIVIA

A. UGARTE

PORTUGAL

ESPAÑA

LIMA ORIENTATION

NOT TO SCALE

100-500 (Calle Nicolás de Rivera 201, small museum, open daily, 0900-1700, bus 1 from Av. Tacna, or minibus 13 or 73 to Choquechaca, then walk).

The road reaches the sea at *Miraflores*, the largest, most important suburb of Lima, with well stocked shops and many first class hotels and restaurants (see main Lima lists: hotels **page 926,** Youth Hostel, **page 929** and restaurants, **page 929)**. There is a handsome park in the middle of the shopping centre and at the end of Avenida Mariscal Benavides, which is commonly called Av. Diagonal, you can get the best view of the whole Lima coastline from Chorrillos to La Punta. The Mariscal Necochea clifftop park overlooks the Waikiki Club, a favourite with Lima surfers. Near Parque Kennedy is the artists' and craftsmens's quarter of L'Ovolo. Calle San Ramón, opp. Parque Kennedy off Av. Diagonal, is closed to traffic and lined with many pizzerias. On no account camp on Miraflores beach; it is extremely dangerous as well as pebbled and dust-blown because of cliff erosion. (In fact beware of thieves on any of the beaches near Miraflores, especially during school holidays.) You can see sealions at close quarters, but the fishing seabirds are not as numerous as they were.

**Buses to Miraflores** No. 2 from Plaza de Armas or Plaza San Martín, Nos. 2 and 53 from Emancipación and Tacna; others from Tacna and Huancavelica (US$0.20); buses to Miraflores run down Tacna, Garcilaso de la Vega and Arequipa. Taxi-colectivos recommended, Quilca and Garcilaso de la Vega, 2 blocks from Plaza San Martín US$0.25.

The road passes through *Barranco* (not to be confused with Barranca, 200 km. N of Lima), with an attractive plaza and nearby the interesting *bajada*, a steep path down to the beach, where many of Lima's artists live and exhibit their work; many old houses are under restoration. (Take bus No. 2 to Miraflores and Barranco beaches from Plaza San Martín, for US$0.25.) The next development on the coast is at *Chorrillos*, a fashionable resort (*Café Suizo* overlooking beach) with a cliff promenade, and boating. At Hacienda La Villa, an old Spanish *hacienda* worth visiting, there is occasionally open air dancing to *salsa* music. Near Chorrillos is the Playa de los Pescadores with seafood stalls, Playa Agua Dulce (a clean beach), and the Club Regatas de Lima. Beyond Chorrillos is *La Herradura*, another bathing resort with several restaurants. The private Club Unicornio is open to tourists. A beach road runs round the entire bay; the main access to it is either at the end of the Paseo de la República in Barranco or by the Bajada de Balta, which is at the end of Av. Diagonal in Miraflores.

Avenida Costanera passes through a run down seaside resort, *Magdalena del Mar*, served by a separate road and bus route from Lima. A little inland, along this route, is *Pueblo Libre*, where the Museo de Antropología y Arqueología, the Museo Arqueológico Rafael Larco Herrera and the Museo Nacional de Historia are found (see under Museums, **page 923,** as well as the old church of Magdalena Vieja (1557), which was unfortunately heavily damaged in the 1974 earthquake.

**N.B**. Bathing is not recommended at any of the beaches around Lima; the water is dangerous and contaminated (the municipality bans swimming at most beaches for this reason).

*Callao* Passengers coming to Peru by sea usually land at Callao (now contiguous with Lima). It handles 75% of the nation's imports and some 25% of its exports.

Callao's maritime terminal or inner harbour covers 100 hectares, and the largest vessels go alongside. Population, 545,000. San Lorenzo island, a naval station, protects the roadstead from the S; inland stretches the Rímac valley. It is a commercial place with no architectural beauty. Lima is reached by road (20 mins. by car or bus, US$0.20). Passengers are expected to be on board half-an-hour before the vessel's departure. (Some have been attacked and robbed just outside the dock gates.) There are some interesting shops in the area between Calle Constitución and Av. Sáenz Peña, and a market between Sáenz Peña and Buenos Aires. "The Club", the oldest English club on the W coast, is at Pasaje Ronald, Calle Constitución, Callao; there is an English cemetery.

**History** Drake and others raided Callao in the 16th century. An earthquake wiped it out in 1746. On 5 November 1820, Lord Cochrane boarded and captured, after a bloody fight in which he was wounded, the Spanish frigate *Esmeralda*. The Real Felipe fortress (1774), last stronghold of the Royalists in S. America, withstood a siege of a year and finally surrendered after terrible sufferings in 1826. It is still a military post, and tourists are allowed to visit it. The Museo Histórico Militar **(see page 924)** is in the old barracks. The railway to Lima, opened 17 May 1851, was one of the first in S. America.

**Leading Restaurant** *El Chalaquito,* Calle Constitución. A number of good fish restaurants can be found on Av. Sáenz Peña. There are a number of reliable bars in the Pasaje Ríos and Calle Constitucíon.

**Taxis** In Callao use taxis recommended by U.S. Embassy or port authorities—for safety's sake. About US$15 for 3 hrs.

**Consulates** British Vice-Consulate, Sáenz Peña 154. P.S.N.C., Calle Independencia 150 (Casilla 368), T 299040. Danish Vice-Consulate, Constitutción 328, Casilla 352, T 293690, open 0830-1700.

**Cables** Pasaje Ronald y Constitución 258. Sáenz Peña 160; T 29-0117 (Public Telex booth).

**Tourist Office** Foptur, Terminal Marítimo-Guardia Chalaca s/n, T 299210.

The Naval College is at *La Punta*, just beyond Callao, served by municipal buses and colectivos through Callao from Lima. La Punta is on a spit of land stretching out to sea; once a fashionable beach, but the water is cool. A new yacht club has been built on the N side. The walk along the seafront between Callao and La Punta has its charms.

The road from Callao to Lima is lined by factories. Shipyards, far from sea, load the fishing vessels they build on huge lorries and launch them into the ocean at Callao. The Universidad de San Marcos (founded May 12 1551) has now been transferred to a new University City, near the Naval Hospital.

On Avenida Marina between Lima and Callao, a turn-off opposite the entrance to the Feria del Pacífico grounds leads to the Parque Las Leyendas **(see page 926)**.

There are bathing, tennis, and a yacht club at *Ancón*, 30 km. NW of Lima, reached by a double-lane asphalted highway. Colectivo from Plaza 2 de Mayo in Lima, US$0.60, returns 1 block from Ancón Cathedral. It is the only real seaside resort in Peru, but no hotels apart from *Restaurant Cinco Luches*, which has rooms, E. Beaches are very small. Crowded Jan.-March holidays, good for fish (recommended restaurant, *Los 5 Tenedores* on the Corniche). On the way to Ancón is the pleasant Santa Rosa beach (entrance fee). Beyond Ancón is a Chancay cemetery, from which has come much Chancay weaving and pottery (as seen in the Museo Amano). There are also Inca ruins at Maranga and Chuquitanta, near Lima; unfortunately the latter cannot be visited at present.

**Excursions** *Pachacámac* is in the Lurín valley, 31 km. from Lima. When the Spaniards arrived, Pachacámac was the largest city on the coast. The ruins encircle the top of a low hill, the crest of which was crowned with a Temple of the Sun, a large pyramid built in 1350 of sun-baked bricks. (There are also a reconstructed Temple of the Virgins and the ancient temple of the Creator God.) Hernando Pizarro, brother of Francisco, came to Pachacámac in 1533; he destroyed images, killed the priests and looted the temples. The setting is marvellous, but the restoration has been criticized and vandals have been at work. Bus or colectivo from Lima, caught from Av. Montevideo, near Petro Perú station in 800 block. The buses (US$0.30, 1 hr.) and colectivos (US$0.60) go by way of Miraflores and Chorrillos, but tell the driver you are going to the *ruinas* or he will land you in Pachacámac town further on. A bus marked Lurin-Pachacámac leaves from behind Parque Universitario, Calle Montevideo, Lima, US$0.40. Taxi, 3 hr. trip, US$40. Closed Mon. and 1 May, open 0900 to 1700. Entrance US$4.

Pucusana, 50 km. from Lima, Silencio, Santa María and Cerro Azul, 90 km., are fishing villages with beaches that are much cleaner than those near Lima. Robbery is common on the beaches and you are advised to sit on your clothes and other possessions. Do not leave anything unattended when swimming.

Also to the South, up the Omas valley beyond Coalla are the Inca adobe structures at Los Gentiles (on the right, well before Omas) and, nearer Omas, Pueblo Viejo, Yampa and Viracocha. Take a colectivo from Plaza Santa Catalina, Jr. Puno (2 blocks from Av. Abancay), Lima to Mala, then hitch, or taxi, via Asia to the sites.

A second excursion is to Chosica, 40 km. up the Rímac valley. In the residential district of

**Chaclacayo**, just before Chosica, are the *Huampani Hotel*, C, modern, attractive, good meals, swimming pool (US$0.40), run by the Government's hotel chain, and *Residencial La Casa de los Olivos*, at Los Ficus 373 y Los Olivos, with restaurant and ten rooms. An excellent chicken meal at the *Granja Azul* (take bus 88M or 204 from Parque Universitario) and there are several other places on the road from Lima to Chosica. The *Hotel El Pueblo* has swimming pool, horse riding, tennis, a beautiful garden, entrance, US$3, used heavily for conventions. Try restaurant and campground of *Puerto del Sol*, owned by Sr. Italo de Neqzi Herreros. A delightful place for dinner and dancing is the restaurant *Fiesta*, at Km. 6 on the Central Highway. At Km. 33 is *El Bosque* Country Club (anyone may enter on payment of US$85), private lake, 4 swimming pools, tennis and ball courts, riding stables, bull ring, etc. Colectivos for Chosica leave from just W of Parque Universitario, near the Ministry of Education building. Buses, 204, 1M.

On the way to Chosica a diversion may be made at Km. 4½ to **Puruchuco**, to see the reconstructed palace of a pre-Inca Huacho noble; with small museum (ceramics, textiles, etc., from the lower Rímac or Lima valley) and a selection of indigenous plants and animals, open 0900-1700, Tues.-Sun. (closed 1 May and 28 July). Entrance US$1; Chosica bus or colectivo from Parque Universitario. One km. from Puruchuco are Huaquerones and Catalina Huaca sites now being restored. Nearby, at Chivateros, is a quarry said to date from 10,000 BC. The large adobe pre-Inca city of **Cajamarquilla** may also be visited, for which the turnoff (left, at Huachipa) is about 6 km. on from the Puruchuco turn. The site is difficult to find—you can't see it from the road—but look for a sign "Zona Arqueológica" in the middle of a brick yard. Keep on driving through the yard, and you will find Cajamarquilla at the end of an ill-kept dirt road. Open every day, 0900-1700. Beyond the Huachipa turn-off for Cajamarquilla, along the main road, there are precolumbian ruins at San Juan de Pariache and Huaicán-Tambo, 13½ and 16½ km. respectively from Lima.

**Chosica** (40 km.), the real starting place for the mountains, is at 860 metres, and is a popular winter resort because it is above the cloudbank covering Lima from May to October. One train a day and frequent buses and minibuses. Beyond the town looms a precipitous range of hills almost overhanging the streets. Up picturesque Santa Eulalia valley off the Rímac valley are the Central Fruit Culture Nurseries. There is some dramatic scenery on the road up the valley, fairly good as far as the hydroelectric station at Callahuanca, but the road is afterwards quite nasty in places, narrow and rocky. Population: 31,200.

**Hotels** *Residencial Chosica*, D; *Residencial San Jorge*, Av. Lima Sur 401, with hot water, rec., restaurant and bar.

**Bus** from Lima, No. 204, from 18th block of Calle Ayacucho (US$0.60); also 1M. Colectivos leave from near Education Ministry, just W of Parque Universitario and from Calle Montevideo around the corner from the Ormeño building in the centre.

Beyond Chosica, near the Santa Eulalia river (80 km. from Lima), is **Marcahuasi**, a table mountain about 3 km. by 3 km. at 4,200 metres, near the village of San Pedro de Casta (accommodation in a cold shelter only, less than US$1). The *meseta* has been investigated by Daniel Ruzo: there are 3 lakes, a "monumento a la humanidad" (40 metres high), and other mysterious lines, gigantic figures, sculptures, astrological signs and megaliths which display non-American symbolism. Ruzo describes this pre-Incaic culture in his book, *La Culture Masma*, Extrait de l'Ethnographie, Paris, 1956. Others say that the formations are not man-made, but the result of wind erosion. Trail starts behind the village of San Pedro bending to the left—about 2 hours to the *meseta* (guides about US$3 a day, advisable in misty weather). Bus to San Pedro de Casta US$2; bus to Lima US$2.50. Take food as no-one lives on the *meseta*, although there is a hut which provides good basic shelter; nights are cold. Srta. Paquita Castillo, T Lima 275251, arranges group tours.

Beyond Casta is San Juan de Iris, a tiny village, outside of which impressive ruins have been discovered (bus or truck from *Restaurant 41* in Chosica at 0900 if you're lucky, 7 hrs.).

There are the ancient (from 1500 BC) ruins of a small town on the hill of San Pedro de Casta, a fortress on the hills of Loma de los Papas (daily bus from Chosica at 0800), the ruins of Tambo Inca, and an ancient cemetery to the South.

The Central Highway to La Oroya (**see page 1045**) opens up possibilities of excursions by car with attractive stopping places like Matucana (1 hr.), San Mateo and Río Blanco (2 hrs.). The trip to La Oroya takes over 5 hrs., and crosses the Andean divide at 4,843 metres. An excursion may be made to Infiernillo ("Little Hell") Canyon, beyond Matucana, which is well worth seeing. The Lima-Chosica-Santa Eulalia-Huanza-Casapalca trip is the most impressive in the environs of Lima, and can be done in one day.

To the North, up the Chillón valley is Cantamarca. "Beyond Cantamarca one comes (writes John Streather) to the beautiful Abra de la Viuda pass, where one passes through the Bosque de Piedras (rocks in extraordinary shapes and sizes) and the Junín pampa to Cerro de Pasco."

## NORTH-WEST FROM LIMA (2)

A region of geographic and cultural contrasts. From the relentless grey coastal desert to the jewelled lakes and mountains of the Callejón de Huaylas. From smelly fishing ports like Chimbote, to the delicate artistry of pre-Inca ruins at Chavín de Huantar and others still being explored deep in the Andes.

**From Lima to Chimbote** Between Lima and Pativilca there is a narrow belt of coastal land deposited at the mouths of the rivers, but from Pativilca to the mouth of the Río Santa, N of Chimbote, the Andes come down to the sea. Between Lima and Pativilca cotton and sugar-cane are grown, though the yield of sugar is less than it is further N where the sunshine is not interrupted by cloud. Cotton is harvested from April to September by Indian migrants from the basins of Jauja and Huancayo. Much irrigated land grows vegetables and crops to supply Lima and Callao. Cattle are driven down from the Highlands to graze the *lomas* on the mountain sides when the mists come between June and October.

The Pan-American Highway parallels the coast all the way to the far N, and feeder roads branch from it up the various valleys. Just N of Ancón, the Pasamayo sand dune, stretching for 20 km., comes right down to the seashore. The old road which snakes along the base beside the sea is spectacular, but is now closed except to commercial traffic. The new toll road (US$0.85), which goes right over the top, is much safer and you get spectacular views over the nearby coast and valleys. **Chancay**, on the coast (no bathing, sea both dangerous and heavily polluted), suffers from severe water shortages, but there is a fresh water source on the beach; *Hostal Villa de Arnedo*, D, clean and friendly, pool and restaurant, rec.; *Hostal Chancay*, F, safe, friendly, can wash clothes; *Restaurant Rebeca*, good.

Just inland from Chancay is Huaral, which gives access to the Chancay Valley, up which are the extraordinary, little visited ruins of **Chiprac**, **Rupac** and **Añay**. Take a bus from Lima (from Plaza de Acho, by the buillring—beware of thieves) to Huaral, then take the Juan Batista bus, Tues. and Fri., to Huascoy, US$2, 2 km. beyond San Juan, itself up beyond Acos: "a hair-raising, breath-taking, bone shaking ride, up to 3,500 metres above sea level", one traveller writes. "Chiprac is a 2½ hour climb from here. Ask for the Salvador family, who have accommodation and Carlos is a guide for the ruins, rec." A guide is not strictly necessary; it is a good day's walk there and back with time to take photographs and eat. Rupac is best reached from La Florida; its ruins are the best preserved of the group, though less extensive than Chiprac. In San Juan, a man called Chavelo will act as a guide to Rupac, which can be reached via the pretty and deserted town of Pampas—also a day there and back. All the ruins have complete roofs, which is unique in Peru. Huascoy celebrates the Fiesta de San Cristóbal in the week before Independence, 28 July, with a procession, masses, dancing, fireworks and football matches. For Añay, go to Huaral as for the other ruins, then get transport to Huayopampa (basic accommodation) or La Perla whence the visit to the ruins can easily be made; get a guide to show you up from either village.

Turn right 5 km. along road to Sayán (see below) where there is a national reserve, Loma de Lachay, which has thousands of snail shells, locust-trees and much bird life. Or continue north, dual carriageway to Km. 101, to the small port of **Huacho**, 132 km. from Lima. It is the outlet for cotton and sugar grown in the rich Huaura valley. There is a cemetery near Huacho where mummies may be found. There are cotton-seed oil and other factories. Port and sea are sometimes alive with monstrous jellyfish. Pop.: 35,900.

**Hotels** *El Pacífico*, F, safe, dirty, water problems, inadequate clothes-washing facilities;

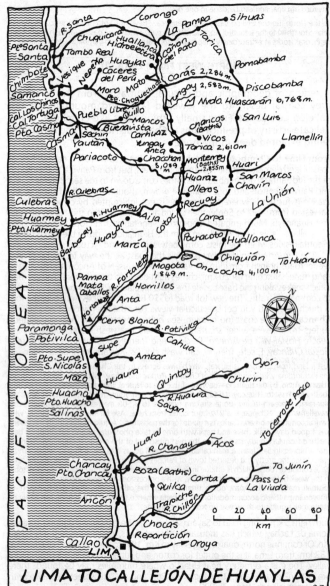

## LIMA TO CALLEJÓN DE HUAYLAS

97

*Italia; Grace; Hostal Maury*, E, basic but friendly. Camping is possible at El Paraíso beach.

The journey inland from Huacho, up the Huaura valley, is splendid (Lima to Huacho by bus: Transportes América S.A., Av. Colonial 129, Lima). Beyond Sayán are terrific rock formations, then the road passes through subtropical vegetation around **Churín**, which is visited for its hot, sulphurous springs; near here, at Chinchín, is *Albergue San Camilo*, C, excellent. From Chinchín, there are buses to nearby villages, such as Huancahuasi, where one can buy woven goods, see interesting churches, and spot *vicuña* in lovely surroundings. There are coal mines. Above 4,000 metres is a chain of lakes which reflect the Cordillera Raura (up to 5,800 metres). Road ends at Raura mine. Buses from Lima go to Churín, Oyón (between Churín and Raura) and Huamahuanca; Espadín y Hnos. at Ormeño terminal, US$6.

About 25 km. beyond Huacho is Medio Mundo, with a lake between the village and the sea. It is a good camping spot, with tents for rent; bring food and water. The turnoff is outside the village on the Pan-American Highway, to the left, look for the sign, "Albufera de Medio Mundo". It is hot and busy in summer.

Just across the river is **Huaura**, where the balcony is still preserved from which San Martín declared the country's independence from Spain. Try *guinda*, the local cherry brandy. We pass from the wide valley of Mazo through the irrigated valley of San Felipe. There is more desert and then the cotton-fields of San Nicolás lead to **Supe**, a small busy port shipping fishmeal, cotton, sugar and minerals (*Hostal Supe*, G; better is *Hostal Grau*, basic, G, clean, safe, comfortable, laundry, good value, next to which is a good restaurant: *El Norteño*). At Aspero, near Supe, is one of the earliest prehistoric sites in Peru (see History section, **page 914**). At **Barranca** the beach is long, not too dirty, though windy. Buses stop opposite the service station (*la grifa*) at the end of town. The straggling town of **Pativilca**, at Km. 203, has a small museum (bus from Lima US$4.80, 2½ hrs.—*Restaurant Cornejo*, good and cheap); a well-paved road turns off for the Callejón de Huaylas and Huaraz (**see page 952**). The road is paved to Conococha (4,080 m.) then in very poor condition to Catac and on to Chavín. 4 km. beyond the turn-off, beside the Highway, are the well preserved ruins of the Chimú temple of **Paramonga**. Set on high ground (view of the ocean), the fortress-like mound is reinforced by 8 quadrangular walls rising in tiers to the top of the hill (admission US$1.20, well worth visiting, taxi from Paramonga and return after waiting, US$4.50, otherwise hitch from Barranca). Not far from the fortress, the Great Wall (La Muralla) stretches across the Andes. Paramonga is a small port, 3 km. off the Pan-American Highway, 4 km. from the ruins and 200 km. from Lima, shipping sugar.

**Hotel** There is no hotel at Paramonga. There are several in Barranca: *Hotel Chavín*, F with bath, warm water, clean, good value, rec, front rooms are noisy, also restaurant on first floor for lunch and dinner (try *arroz con conchas*), breakfast bar and café opens onto street by main entrance; *Pacífico*, F with bath, clean, good value; *Hotel Casanova*, on main street, F with bath, clean, friendly, safe motorcycle parking; *Colón*, Jr. Gálvez 407, G, friendly, basic; *Jefferson*, Lima 946, F, clean, friendly; many others on main street, and plenty of bars and restaurants. As bus companies have their offices there, buses will stop there rather than at Pativilca or Paramonga. No buses run to the ruins, only to the port.

**Exchange** Banco de la Nación, Barranca, accepts travellers' cheques, although at poor rates.

**Bus** from **Lima to Paramonga**, Compañía Fortaleza or Empresa América recommended. From Lima to **Barranca**, 3 hrs. US$3, Empresa América, very comfortable. 1st class from terminal on outskirts; Compañía Fortaleza and Comité Cinco (2nd class) go to Barranca and Paramonga from Parque Universitario in Lima. Daily 0900, US$2.75 to Barranca, US$3 to Paramonga. Buses cover the 7-8 km. from Barranca to Paramonga. Bus from Barranca to **Casma** US$1.20; Ancash bus to **Huaraz**, 4 hrs., US$3.75. Truck, Pativilca-Huaraz, 5-6 hrs., US$2; many buses, first at 1030.

Between Paramonga and Chimbote (225 km.) the mountains come down to the sea. The road passes by a few very small protected harbours in tiny rock-encircled bays—Puerto **Huarmey** (small *Hotel de Turistas*, D, clean and good service, but noisy, being on Pan-American Highway at Huarmey town, not port), Puerto Casma, and Vesique. Tepsa bus Lima-Huarmey, US$4, US$8.50 by colectivo, from

Parque Universitario. From Casma a road runs through the **Callán pass** (4,224 metres) to Huaraz. A difficult but beautiful trip. Not all buses take this route, so check before leaving. From Casma to the pass (apart from the paved first 30 km.), the road is appalling (many land-slides), but once the Cordillera Negra has been crossed, the road is better (gravel, wide) with spectacular views. About 40 km. before Casma, at Km. 330, is *Restaurant San Miguel*, poor food and dirty, beware of stale pies, used by Tepsa as meal stop.

**Casma** The town was largely destroyed by the 1970 earthquake, but has since been rebuilt. A good new food market, but not much else to recommend.

**Hotels** *Hostal El Farol*, E, ask for cheaper rate in low season, good, with bathroom (no hot water), breakfast and dinner available (and sandwiches and coffee), pleasant garden setting; *Hostal Central*, on plaza, G p.p., dirty, cold, basic, but helpful; *Indoamericano*, F with bath, hot water, clean, good; *Chifa Tío Sam*, good, off plaza.

**Bus** From Parque Universitario, **Lima**, colectivo to Casma, US$8.80. Bus (Tepsa) from Lima 1800, to Lima leaves 1100 daily US$4.25; also Chinchay-Suyo, on main street, and Turismo Chimbote (main road opp. road on which *Hostal El Farol* is located), 4 a day, (truck, US$3). Bus to **Huaraz**, Chinchay-Suyo, 2300, daily and Moreno, 0700, 10 hrs., US$4.10. It is well worth making this trip in daylight to get the view of the Cordillera Blanca. Bus to **Trujillo**, Tepsa and Chinchay-Suyo, 4 a day, US$3.20, 3 hrs. Most buses pass Casma in the morning. At other times, take a bus to Chimbote (Empresa Casma S A), hourly, US$0.50.

**Excursions** From Casma, take a truck going to San Rafael and ask for Castillo (departures all day from the garage opposite Huaraz bus stop). After alighting, walk 2 km. uphill to a cemetery with pottery on the ground, and a Chimú castle of 4 concentric rings, with 3 towers in the middle, the Castillo de Chanquillo. Further on is a large wall with 13 towers on a ridge. Take water with you. The trucks return all day up to about 1600. There are several other sites around Casma: Sechín Alto, Pallka, Tokán, Mojeque, La Cantina, Tokachi and Huanchay.

**Sechín** At Km. 370 on Pan-American Highway, shortly before reaching Casma from Lima, watch for a large concrete sign to Sechín on the right. Follow the road indicated for about 2 km. until you reach the ruins (about one hour's walk). Three sides of the large stone temple have been excavated and restored. You cannot see the adobe buildings inside the stone walls, which belong to an earlier period. They were later covered up and used as a base for a second storey which unfortunately has been completely destroyed. Some experts think the temple and surroundings were buried on purpose. Others believe it was engulfed by natural disaster. The latter theory is supported by finds of human skeletons. Tombs have been found in front and at the same level as the temple. A wall of a large adobe building under excavation can be seen and runs round the sides and back of the temple. The site is open to tourists, 0900-1700 (US$3.40, children half price); ticket also valid for Pañamarca (**see page 949**), and there is an attractive, shady picnic garden. The Max Uhle Museum opened in 1984 by the ruins: interesting display of Sechín artefacts, entry US$0.25 and US$0.10 for cameras. It is quite easy to walk to the ruins from Casma. One must walk about 3 km. S to a well posted sign showing a left turn, then simply follow the road for 2 km. to the ruins. (Frequent colectivos from in front of market in Casma, US$0.30 p.p., or taxi US$0.50 p.p., but leave early in the morning; no buses.) 2 km. further along there are two pyramids of the late Chavín period, but these have not yet been excavated.

Sechín is one of the most important ruins on the Peruvian coast. It consists of a large square temple completely faced with carved stone monoliths—probably over 500 of them—which depict gruesome battle scenes: men being eviscerated, heads with blood gushing from eyes or mouths, dismembered legs, arms, torsos, ears, eyes and vertebrae. The style is unique in Peru for its naturalistic vigour. Within the stone temple is an earlier, pre-ceramic mud temple with painted walls. The temples are pre-Chavín, about 1500 BC. (John Hemming)

**Chimbote**, 420 km. from Lima, is one of Peru's few natural harbours, ample in area and depth of water. Rapidly growing population of 185,000; a new port has been built to serve the national steel industry: iron ore from Marcona field is shipped from the port of San Juan, 547 km. S of Lima; anthracite comes by railway from the hinterland, and power comes from the hydroelectric station in the Cañón del Pato, 129 km. inland. The steel industry creates heavy pollution; also Chimbote is Peru's largest fishing port; fishmeal is exported and the smell of the fishmeal plants is very strong. Bathing is forbidden on the beach near the hotel. Flocks of brown pelicans and masked boobies may be seen from the beach. Shanty towns have burgeoned around. Small airport, but no commercial flights. Public swimming pool at Vivero Forestal.

**Hotels** *Turistas*, State Tourist Hotel (D, with bath, meals US$3.50, uninspiring), Chimbote's cleanest snack bar, there are some cheaper but noisier rooms at the back, must ask, safe parking; *Presidente* (3 star), E, with bath, clean, friendly, hot showers, safe parking, poor snack bar, rec.; *Carabelle*, F, round corner from *Presidente*, hot water doesn't work, but good value; *Rivera*, E, good, clean, hot water, restaurant on top floor with good view but poor food; *El Santa*, E, with bath, clean and good; *Venus*, F, near Roggero and Moreno bus stations, useful if you arrive at 0200; in same district *Augusto*, Aguirre 265, F, with shower and toilet, overpriced, clean, front rooms noisy, water intermittent as everywhere in town, *Huáscar*, G p.p. very basic, clean rooms, filthy toilets, and *San Felipe*, F; *Felic*, Av. José Pardo, 552, F, noisy.

**Restaurants** *Pollo Gordo*, Prado y Aguirre, good chicken and cold beer; *San Remo*, Pardo y Villavicencio, seafood, good and cheap, good pisco sours; *Buenos Aires*, Aguirre near beach, popular lunch place; *Marisquito*, Bolognesi near Palacios, good local food, disco at night; *Franco* and *Venecia*, same block, good seafood. You can eat well and cheaply (US$0.50) in the market.

**Tourist Office** Av. Bolognesi 465.

**Buses** To Lima, best is Turismo Chimbote on Pardo, US$6.50, 6-7 hrs. The Santa valley road via Huallanca to the Callejón de Huaylas and beyond has been rebuilt, but is still hair-raising (scenery is superb). Bus leaves Chimbote for **Huaraz** daily at 0700 and 2000, via Caraz and Cañón del Pato, US$6.35, sit on left: Transportes Moreno, José Galvez (across bridge towards Trujillo), book the previous day, 8 hrs. (12 hrs. in rainy season). Road is unsurfaced to **Caraz** (bus to Caraz, US$5.25, 6 hrs., daily); bus to **Huallanca**, US$4.70. Bus Chimbote—Huaraz via Casma at 0700 and 1900; colectivo to **Casma**, 0700 and 0830 daily, US$1.70. Buses run Chimbote to **Trujillo**, US$1.25 (Empresa El Aguila, José Gálvez 317, hourly from 0600-2000), Tepsa at 1600; Colectivo to **Trujillo**, US$2.50, 2 hrs.

**Warning** Thefts are common around the Moreno bus station.

About 25 km. S of Chimbote a paved road leads E to the Nepeña valley, where a sculpted precolumbian tomb and the temple of Cerro Blanco may be found; also ruins at *Pañamarca* (pre-Mochica temple), 10 km. from the crossroads. Pañamarca is a town from the Mochica culture, where buildings and animal sculpture remains can be seen. 20 km. from Pañamarca is the site of Paredones with the "Puerta del Sol", and a stone carving, the "monolito de siete huacas".

From Chimbote a road branches off to the NE and, joining another road from Santa, goes up the Santa valley following the route, including tunnels, of the old Santa Corporation Railway. This used to run as far as **Huallanca**, 140 km. up the valley, but the track was largely destroyed by the 1970 earthquake. At Huallanca is an impressive hydroelectric plant, built into a mountain, which can not be visited. *Hotel Huascarán*, good, friendly; everything closes early. At the top of the valley the road goes through the very narrow and spectacular **Cañón del Pato** (where the road is closed to private vehicles because of fears of guerrilla attacks on the hydroelectric plant, but buses still ply) before reaching the Callejón de Huaylas and going on S to Caraz and Huaraz. From Caraz to Santa (200 km. unpaved) can be driven, in normal times, in 5 hours. The road up the Santa Valley is not recommended for cyclists owing to its poor condition.

Daniel Morgan, of Wellington, N.Z, writes: "At its mouth, the Santa Valley is fertile, being well-irrigated from the river. Further up it becomes barren. There is only rock, scree slides, exposed shale strata at angles up to the vertical (a must for geologists). The colours are fantastic: greys, blues, purples, oranges, reds, browns. The beauty is accentuated by the bright sun throwing jet black shadows, highlighting, contrasting, hiding.

"After Huallanca, the road clings to the side of a cliff as water thunders below and rock faces climb vertically on each side. Again light and shadow interplay, creating a fantastic vista like abstract art. Beyond the dam the valley flattens out. The walls are no longer vertical and you come back to Planet Earth. It is a hot, dusty, bumpy, and awesome trip."

*Caraz*, is now almost totally restored after the 1970 earthquake, and is reported a good centre for walking; splendid views of Huandoy and Huascarán. Information on mountaineering obtainable from the director of the Huascarán National Park in Huaraz, or the Tourist Office in Yungay. Excellent views of the northern *cordilleras* in July and August; in other months, mountains are often shrouded in cloud. One has to cross a river by cable (20 mins.) and go to Pueblo Libre to climb Tunaspampa. Caraz has a milder climate than Huaraz and is more suited to day excursions but it is difficult to change money there. There is a zoo, SE of town; take food for the animals.

**Hotels** *El Cafetal*, friendly, clean, hot water; *Hostal Carás*, Calle Sucre, F, dirty, hot showers; *Chavín*, just off Plaza, F with bath, new, clean, good value (but no views), said to be "best of a poor bunch"; *Hostal Suizo Peruano*. San Martín 1133, G with bath (cheaper without) clean and friendly. *Ramírez*, above Moreno terminal, G p.p., dirty, basic, helpful; *Morovi*, just outside town on Yungay road, F, clean, friendly, helpful, with bath and hot water; *Herrera*, F.

**Restaurants** *Jeny*, on plaza, good food and prices; *La Capullana*, excellent local dishes; *Juventud*, rec.; *La Punta Grande*, on corner of turn-off to Lago Parón, inexpensive local meals. Also, *Esmeralda*, Av. Alfonso Ugarte, cheap, good local food, friendly; *Djurjuri*, good food and atmosphere; *Chifa Lorena*, Jr. Sucre 1021, cheap local and Chinese food; unnamed restaurant at Sucre 1003, good, English spoken. About 1 km. S of Caraz, open-air *Restaurant Palmira*, serves excellent trout, reasonably priced (open 1200-1800); follow the sign for trout off the main road and go through German-owned carnation farm.

**Buses** Bus to **Lima** 14 hrs., direct 1500, via Huaraz (to which the 67-km. road is now paved) 0600. Also frequent buses to and from **Huaraz**, US$1.45 (last at 1900), 2 hrs., to Yungay, US$0.25. Bus to **Chimbote**, daily, 1000, 2200, 7 hrs., through the Santa Valley, US$5.25; Transportes Expreso Moreno, Jr. Daniel Villar 407, T 2014, through the Cañon del Pato, sit on right for views, US$2.50, 0930, 7 hrs; to Chimbote via Huaraz and Casma (US$3.60) at 0600 and 1800, with one hour stop in Huaraz, continuing at 0900 and 2100 respectively. Chinchay-Suyo to **Trujillo** at 1730, stops for dinner at Huaraz, US$10.

From Caraz a narrow, rough road branches E to Lago Parón, nestling right under the snow-capped peak of Huandoy; the water level has been lowered, and the lake is to be used for the Cañon del Pato hydroelectric scheme. Latest reports indicate that some of the lake's beauty has been lost, but that the gorge leading to it remains spectacular. For the best views you have to climb up unstable moraine. Taxi from **Caraz**, or from Huaraz, US$20 return, will wait all day at the lake, pick-up US$3 approx., bargain hard; Nevado Huáscaran Tours from Huaraz runs full day tour inc. 30-40 mins. at lake. One can stay at a lodge by the lake, US$1.60 p.p. (unguarded, and therefore may not be possible, at weekends), or at the houses 1-2 km. before the lake, US$1.20 p.p.

For hikes in the Cordillera Negra, a truck leaves from Caraz market at 1000 to Huata (dirty hotel, F; 2,700 metres) from where one can climb to the Quebrada de Cochacocha (3,500 metres) at the top of which is the Inca ruin of Cantu, and on to the Inca lookout, Torreón Andino (5,006 metres; also reached from Rocracallán, US$1.20 by truck from Caraz). Take water, food and tent with you. 6 km. down a track off the Caraz-Huata road are the Inca ruins of Chonta. Alternatively, Prof. Bernardino Aguilar Prieto (former teacher), San Martín 1143 (T 2161—rooms to let, G), close to *Hotel La Suiza Peruana*, Caraz, can advise in evenings on 2-3-day hikes in the Torreón Andino area. One can visit his apiary and sample the honey (sold at his town house) as well as camp for free at his farm, La Fronda (run down), 7 km. from Caraz, rooms G but you must bring bedding/food/candles etc., cheapest from Caraz, US$0.20. N of Caraz are hot springs at Shangol. The ruins of Pashash Cabana and Huandoval are reached from Chuquicara, about halfway along the Santa Valley road.

See below for access from Caraz to the Llanganuco—Santa Cruz hike; see also **page 957** for notes on walking in this area.

John Streather writes: "A spectacular circuit may be made to Chavín (**page 956**) from Caraz (or Huaraz). Take a Morenos Hnos. bus to Tres Cruces or Yuracmarca on the other side of the Cañón del Pato. A detour from Yuracmarca is along a frightening road to Corongo (0530 bus from Caraz, Empresa Callejón de Huaylas from the main square once a week), but only go in summer, or else you may be stuck for months. Eat at the baker's shop on the square; the baker is very helpful with information about ruins in the area. From Tres Cruces (basic friendly restaurant, but no accommodation) one can take daytime lorries to Pomabamba, passing pre-Inca *chullpas*, Yanac, Tarica (see page 952), the mining town of Pasacancha (hotel and restaurant) and the Callejón de Conchucos. The road continues through cold, wild mountains and valleys to Andaymayo and Palo Seco to Pomabamba, "city of the cedars"—where I saw not one cedar tree."

**Pomabamba** is worth a visit on several counts. There are very hot natural springs there, the furthest are the hottest and the best. The lady of the house also sells delicious orange-blossom honey from her own garden; however, fresh vegetables may be in short supply. Various hotels; the best is in a nameless house on the hill going down to the bridge over which lie the hot springs and the path to Yaino. *Hostal Pomabamba*, on main square, F, basic, safe for luggage; *Altamayo*, plaza, basic; *San Martín de Porras*, off the smaller plaza, basic. The restaurant on the corner of the main square is friendly and good (cold though); *Canela*, rec. There is a small museum opposite which the people in the courtyard offices will open free on request. Victor Escudero, who speaks English, runs One Pyramid Travel, Huaraz 209, T 721283; he specializes in archaeological tours, including some little known, unspoilt places, rec. Several good walks into the Cordillera Blanca start from nearby: via Palo Seco or Laurel to the Lagunas Safuna, from which one can go on, if hardy, to Mt. Alpamayo ("the most beautiful mountain in the world") and down to Santa Cruz and Caraz—several days' hard walking. Up to the quite large and extensive, though sadly dilapidated, ruins of **Yaino**, on top of a very steep mountain and visible from the main square of Pomabamba—though still a good 4½-5 hours walk away. Ask directions in the village and on the way too. If in doubt, veer left after about two hours of going fairly straight uphill. The ruins, when one reaches them, are certainly worth the effort. The walls are beautifully built and there are two very large buildings, a square one and a circular one. The site commands far and majestic views of the many peaks of the Cordillera. Again, the hardy could continue their walk (several days) to the two lakes of Llanganuco and so to Yungay in the Callejón de Huaylas, or down to Santa Cruz and Caraz on the other side. The walk to Yaino and back to Pomabamba can be done in a day if one starts early. Take a good lunch, and lots of juicy fruit—one gets very dehydrated climbing and perspiring in the thin dry air. It's also very cold high up if the sun goes in, so go with warm, waterproof clothing.

Cóndor de Chavín and Peruano Andino buses run S to Chavín and on to Lima, all at night. Buses to and from Lima via Chimbote are Empresa Marino (Ayacucho 1140, Lima), leaving Lima at 0800, Sun. and Wed., and Pomabamba at 0600 on the same days, 20 hrs.

The main road goes on to **Yungay**, which was completely buried by the 1970 earthquake—a hideous tragedy in which 20,000 people lost their lives. The survivors are housed just north of the old town, which is now recovering, with houses and a concrete market (Thurs. and Sun.). A new church is being built. The site now has a few monuments and a field of rose bushes.

**Bed and Board** A hotel without a signboard is on the left of the Carhuaz road (F); *El Señor Blanco's Hotel* (past maternity hospital), G, breakfast and dinner US$1.40, hot water, rec., mixed reports on security, and women need to beware of Sr. Blanco's overfriendly attitude; *Hostal Gledel*, Av. Arias Graziani (owned by Sra. Gamboa, who is hospitable and a good cook), F, clean, good, nice courtyard, rec.; *Hostal Yungay*, on plaza, F, clean; *Alojamiento Acuña*, F, clean, meals available. There is also private accommodation. Good food and drink can be found in the new market, and there is a good restaurant run by the local co-operative; also *Comedor Yungay* (good) and *El Portal* (fair). Provisions for trekking (e.g. tinned fruit, bread, vegetables, eggs, drink sachets, pasta, etc.) can be bought in Yungay.

Tourist Office on the plaza (rarely open); opposite is *Café El Palmero*, which offers simple accommodation. F. Moreno bus, Fitzcarrald 109, to Huaraz, US$0.75. There are several trucks which leave from the café for Lake Llanganuco (provided there are at least 10 passengers, US$2.50 single or return). A return allows only about an hour at the lake. Times of departure always change, so check at the Tourist Office. A tourist minibus to the lake leaves at 0800 on Sat., 2 hrs.

For trekkers, one of the finest walks (trees, flowers, birds, midges) is over the path by Huascarán and Lake Llanganuco (2 lakes: Orkoncocha and Chinancocha) from Yungay to Piscobamba (Yungay to Lake Llanganuco, trucks on Mon., Wed., Fri., at 0400, US$3, and Sun. from Huaraz, no trucks will go unless there are enough passengers, and departure is often delayed; trucks to Llanganuco continue on the new road to the Portachuelo Pass at 4,750 metres, beautiful views of Huascarán; return to Yungay at 1000). It is a 5-6 day hike over a well-travelled route, but don't try it unless you are properly equipped. After 3-4 days you reach Llumpa on the Chavín-Piscobamba road (basic accommodation, unfriendly people), from here there are 2 buses per week to Piscobamba, and 2 per week to Chavín. After Llumpa, the trek to Piscobamba becomes rather boring and tiring. There are 2 buses per week between Piscobamba, Pomabamba (see page 951) and Huaraz. Advice and registration for mountain hut at Llanganuco from National Park office. N.B. If making an excursion to photograph Huascarán and Huandoy, note that they are usually hidden by cloud after midday.

Deservedly the most popular walk in the Cordillera Blanca is from Llanganuco through the Portachuelo Pass to Colcabamba, and then through the Punta Unión (4,750 metres) to Cashapampa, Santa Cruz and Caraz. This hike takes 3-5 days and is well-signed. Guides useful, US$5-8 a day, will catch trout for you. Entrance to the National Park costs US$1.20 a day for foreigners to stay overnight (for a one-day visit US$0.60—overnight fee for Peruvians US$0.20). Some of the route is on Inca roads (**see pages 1070-1071**). The mountain flowers and humming birds at these altitudes are magnificent. The road to the lake (full of trout) continues up to the tongue of the glacier of Cerro Chopicalqui (not suitable for cars, 4,830 metres)—insect repellant needed; take food, warm clothes, tent, sleeping bag and a stove. The early morning trucks from Yungay on a new road running from Llanganuco over the Portachuelo Pass go to Vaquería, the first settlement after the pass; get off the truck at the tin shacks on the left after Vaquería; from there the trail descends on S side of stream to Colcabamba (3 hrs.), or crosses a stream below thatched farmhouse to join Colcabamba-Punta Unión trail above Colcabamba. At Yanamá, on the eastern side of the Cordillera Blanca (beyond Colcabamba—and not on the trail), there is lodging and food; a day's hike to the ruins above the town affords superb views (truck Yungay-Yanamá, US$3.25—ask at plaza in Yungay). At Colcabamba, the Calonge family welcome travellers with good meals and basic accommodation (G), and small shop, but very little on offer. Cashapampa, the first village at the bottom of the Santa Cruz valley, is at the end of the path and where the dirt road begins; it has basic accommodation; meals at the house of Sra. Zenaida Pajuelo. Above Santa Cruz (the next village, very basic accommodation—dirty and for midgets!) are hot springs at Huancarhuás, which are being "developed". Footpath Santa Cruz to Caraz.

**Transport** Bus Yungay—Colcabamba (or 150 m. above it), Wed. a.m., perhaps daily in season, US$2.10, or pick-up from square if 8 passengers, US$2.60 p.p. About 4½ hrs. to top of Postachuelo Pass (cold, have sweater accessible); the road is not for the faint-hearted, but great views. Trucks Colcabamba-Yungay most mornings except Sun., US$2.40 p.p., 4-6 hrs; best to get on in Colcabamba, they don't like stopping en route. From Caraz, colectivos go to Lake Llanganuco, US$2.40, or taxi US$20-25; pick-ups to Cashapampa at 0900-1100, US$0.90 p.p., bus Cashapampa-Caraz at 0500, US$1.20; pick-up Santa Cruz-Caraz on Sat. at 1500 or 1900.

After Yungay, the main road goes to Mancos at the foot of Huascarán (*Hotel Mancos*, F, lovely setting, but bathroom dirty, water rationing) and on to **Carhuaz** (daily bus service to Huaraz, and to Huallanca via the Cañón del Pato), with fair hotels (*Perú*, F, good restaurant; and *Gran Hotel*, E, pleasant, no hot water; *Hospedaje La Merced*, F, excellent, clean, friendly, hot water, rec.; *Casa de Pocha*, c/o Familia Figueroa, ½ mile out of town at foot of Nevado Hualcan, T 111, hot water (solar heated), sauna, home-produced food, horses for hire, opened July 1990. *Restaurant Palma*, good value) and very good walking in the neighbourhood; precolumbian baths at Vicus and La Merced, ruins at Cuntuyoc, Hualcan, Huacoy, Torojirca, Tuyo and Huamanvilca. Carhuaz has a *mestizo* festival on October 24, followed eight days later by an Indian festival. Before Huaraz the road goes to Marcará (bus to Huaraz, US$0.50), where there is a branch road 3 km. to **Chancos**, another thermal resort (*Hotel Chancos* closed but you can camp in the neighbourhood, 2 restaurants, minibus from Huaraz). Further up the Huandoy valley is Vicos, set in superb surroundings with views of Nevados Tocllaraju and Ranrapalca. From Vicos, one can walk through the Quebrada Honda to Chacas (*Hostal Pilar*); a road has been built to Chacas. From Chacas you can get transport to San Luis (**see page 1071**). The main road goes on to **Tarica** (*Hostal Sterling*, G, no hot water, food, friendly).

The valley's focus is **Huaraz** (population 80,000), capital of the Department of Ancash, at 3,028 metres, 398 km. from Lima. The city was half destroyed in the earthquake of May 1970. The Plaza de Armas has been rebuilt, except for the Cathedral, which is being resited elsewhere. The setting, with the peaks of Huascarán, Huandoy, and San Cristóbal in the background, is tremendous. Good panoramic views are to be had from the *mirador* at the cross (visible from Huaraz) one hour's walk from the town (turn left past the cemetery and head uphill through a small forest). Huaraz is becoming a very lively place, popular with young gringos and Peruvians alike. Market day is Thursday.

**Festival** Patron saints' day, 3 May, parades, dancing, music and fireworks; much drinking and overcharging. Prices shoot up at time of Independence celebrations, end-July. Semana del Andinismo end of May, international climbing and skiing week.

**Hotels**  *Termas de Monterrey*, 7 km. N (½ hr. in bus from Luzuriaga, near the bridge, US$0.25 but none after 2000, taxi US$2-3), run by State Tourist Hotel chain, rec. for walking, swimming in warm springs, D (accepts American Express), with bath, good meals US$3, swimming pool. Rock climbing behind hotel, but don't be too vigorous at the start; it's over 2,750 metres up. *El Patio*, near *Hotel Termas*, E incl. breakfast, friendly, no restaurant, nicely laid out, rec. *La Casa de Campo Yacarini*, Urbanización El Bosque-Palmira (3 km. from town), D-F, new house with garden, clean friendly and safe, sauna and hot baths, good family cooking, multilingual owner, highly rec. In town, *Hotel de Turistas*, Av. Centenario (T 2696), C, large rooms, clean, restaurant poor; *Marañón*, E, new, clean, near market, hot water limited; *El Tumi I*, San Martín 1122, E, with bath, good restaurant, fairly good; *Tumi II*, beside *Tumi I*, F with bath, good value; *Hostal Huandoy-Cusco*, F (triple rooms available), communal bathrooms, good; *Hostal Andino* (*Chalet Suisse*) C, Jr. Pedro Cochachín 357 (some way from centre), best hotel, clean, meals served (fondue expensive), safe parking, Swiss run, rec., beautiful view of Huascarán, climbing and hiking gear for hire; *Hostal Colomba*, Calle Francisco de Zela 210, bungalow, rooms D, plus 21%, family-run (German), garden, friendly, safe car parking, English spoken; *Cataluña*, Av. Raymondi 622, T 72117, F with bath, less without, cheaper accommodation in dormitory, restaurant, somewhat expensive, clean, safe, noisy, tepid water; *Hostal Colonia*, Malecón Sur Río Quillcay, F with bath, restaurant, patio, views of mountains, friendly, owner is a member of Guides Association and can advise on trekking and climbing, will store luggage. *Raymondi*, Av. Raymondi 820, F, central, bath, hot water (a.m. only in ground floor shower), comfortable, unfriendly, charges for left luggage, with café serving good breakfast; *Yanett*, Av. Centenario 106, E, friendly, hot water, clean, large rooms, rec., restaurant for breakfast; *Edward's Inn*, Av. Bolognesi 121, T 722692, E-F, clean, hot shower, laundry, friendly, food available, highly rec., popular, Edward speaks English and knows a lot about trekking and rents gear; under same ownership, *Alojamiento de Quintana*, Juan de la Cruz Romero 593, F, hot shower, laundry facilities, clean, hard beds, popular with trekkers. *Hostal Premier*, Av. Luzuriaga 651-53, T 721954, E with bath (cheaper without), not very hot showers, clean, modern, English spoken by owners' son, helpful, informative, rec.; *Landauro*, on Plaza de Armas, F, cheap, not particularly clean, basic, friendly, good breakfast place downstairs;. Behind, between Sucre and Morales, is the *Casa de Guías*, F, rooms for up to 6 people, with rec. restaurant, muesli, yoghurt and pizzas, guided tours organized; it houses the guide association of Huaraz, provides climbing and trekking information, and is a good meeting place for climbers, and there is a notice board for messages. *Hostal Colonial*, Av. Fitzcarald 368, F, owner is Swiss-trained mountain guide, will arrange treks, hot showers; *Hostal Continental*, 20 de Julio y Luzuriaga, G, clean, hot water, friendly, cafeteria, rec.; *Hostal Los Andes*, Av. Tarapacá 316, G p.p. low season, hot water, clean, friendly, with laundry, attractive but noisy, hard beds and prices shoot up in the peak season; *Albergue El Tambo*, Confraternidad Internacional—Interior—122 B, F, clean, clothes washing, 3 rooms with 12 beds, and cooking facilities, nice people; *Alpamayo*, same street No. 126, F with bath, G without, clean, quiet, rents camping eqpt., laundry (or do it yourself), rec. *Pensión Maguiña*, Av. Tarapacá 643, opposite Rodríguez bus terminal, noisy a.m., F, hot water, rooms single to 4-bed, clothes-washing facilities, breakfast available, rucksack store, clean, English and French spoken, helpful in arranging trekking and equipment hire, rec.; *Hostal Alfredo*, Jr. Victor Vélez (go N on Al. Fitzcarrald, cross bridge and take 2nd on right, 10 metres on right), F with shower, good; *Alojamiento Galaxia* (de Inés Herrera) Jr. Romero 638, limited hot water F, friendly, laundry facilities, rec.; *Hostal Oscar*, Morales, F with bath, hot water, cheap breakfast, rec.; *Familia Estella*, Jirón Nueva Granada 519, F, hot water very intermittent, friendly, safe, rec.; *Casa de Señora López* (ask near Estadio just off Avenida Bolognesi at Santa river end), F, luke-warm showers, safe, washing facilities for clothes, patio, very friendly, rec. *Familia Sánchez* Jr. Carás 849, G, clean, basic, warm water, helpful, cheap breakfast; *Alojamiento San Martín de Porras*, Las Américas, T 721061, F, clean, friendly, rec.; *Alojamiento Líder*, Fitzcarrald 233, G, hot showers, friendly, safe, rec. *Albergue Juvenil Los Capulíes*, Jr. Los Capulíes 160, Centenario—Huaraz (15 mins., walk from the centre—information from the owner's bodega at San Martín 618), F, clean, friendly, showers, cooking and washing facilities, rec. *Alojamiento Copa*, Jr. S. Bolívar 615, F, good, hot water, washing facilities, clean, the owner, Señora Alicia Jaimes is "incredibly sweet and helpful", and her son, Walter Melgarejo is a well-known guide. There are usually people waiting at the bus terminals offering cheap accommodation in their own homes. One rec. private house is at Señora Gamara's, Calle Valenzuela 837, G, friendly, clean, hot water, meals, laundry service.

**Hot Public Showers** on Av. Raymondi 904, US$0.20.

**Restaurants** Restaurant and bar at *Ebony 86*, Plaza de Armas, friendly, clean. *Tabariz*, Av. Centenario y Av. Raymondi, good food. On 28 de Julio is *Oja-Yo*, Chinese, good. *La Familia* at Luzuriaga 431, popular with gringos, vegetarian dishes, impersonal; *Leñador*, Luzuriaga 979, good coffee, snacks, German books. *Rivioli*, Av. Guzmán Barrón 244, good and cheap. *Francos Parrilladas*, Luzuriaga 410, good grills; *Pepe's Place*, Raymondi 622 (upstairs from *Hostal Cataluña*), expensive but good; *Tic-Toc*, Raymondi 639, good breakfasts; *Ticino*, Luzuriaga 651, pizzas and pastas; *La Posada*, Luzuriaga, good pizzas and lasagne, nice atmosphere, expensive; *Pizzería Mamma Mía*, Luzuriaga 808, excellent and cheap. *Créperie Patrick*, Luzuriaga 424 y Raymondi, excellent crêpes, fish, quiche, spaghetti and good wine; *Ebenezer*, opposite *Mamma Mía*, good local food, clean and cheap. *Las Puyas*, Morales 535, good cheap meals and breakfasts, popular with gringos; *Pío Pío*, Av. Centenario 329, rec.; *Amadeus*, next to Plaza, good breakfast and reputed best coffee in town. *Tasco bar*, Lucar y Torre, popular with climbers. *Sandy*, Av. Centenario y Raymondi, good, cheap, popular, rec; *Paccha'k Pub*, Centenario 290, folklore shows, local and international food, travel information. *Tejas*, Calle Francisco (parallel to Centenario), rec. for *cuy* (guinea-pig).

**Entertainment** There are discotheques at *Tabariz, Bodega*. *Peña El Rizzo*, Luzuriaga 455, shows Thurs., Fri., Sat.; *Imantata*, Luzuriaga 424, disco and folk music; *Tambo*, José de la Mar, folk music daily, rec, knock on door to get in.

**Museum** **Museo Regional de Ancash**, Instituto Nacional de Cultura, containing stone monoliths and *huacos* from the Recuay culture has been set up in the *Casa de Cultura*, well labelled and laid out. Open 1000-1700, Tues.-Sun., US$0.60, pay to take photographs.

**Camping** Several shops of the trekking agencies sell camping gaz cartridges. Bodega Santillana, Centenario 417, good for all supplies. Andean Sport Tours, Av. Luzuriaga 571, T 721612, German-owned, rents or sells camping equipment, incl. camping gaz cartridges; treks, climbing, donkeys for hire, US$2 a day, guides, US$5, tents, US$1.50 a day. Tent hire for five days about US$15. All prices standard, but not cheap, throughout town; US$100, or airline ticket, deposit usually demanded. All require payment in advance and will only give 50% of your money back if you return gear early.

**Shopping** Daily market (1600-2000) in covered sidewalks of Luzuriaga for local sweaters, hats, gloves, etc., wall hangings; good value.

**Car Hire** Empresa de Transporte Turismo Huascarán, Av. Raymondi 870, T 310099; vehicles not up to much.

**Exchange** Banco Internacional changes travellers' cheques; also behind Banco de la Nación on Plaza de Armas, open till 1800. Quite good rates from travel agents. Street changers on Luzuriaga.

**Laundry** *Fitzcarrel*, Fitzcarrald, close to bridge; *Lavandería El Amigo*, Bolívar y Sucre.

**Tourist Office** Foptur, Av. Luzuriaga 459 on main Plaza beside post office, T 721031, for Chavín tour and treks; ask there for Miguel Chiri Valle, English speaking, maps available, good for backpacking in the Cordillera Blanca. Also Pombamba 415, 1st floor, and ground floor of Palacio Municipal, Plaza de Armas. **Trekking & Backpacking Club**, San Martín 995 (Casilla 112), issues magazine *El Trekkero*, maps and library at office, also hires equipment and organizes tours. Better maps of the area are available in Lima. However, the Instituto de Geología y Minería (Av. Guzmán Barrón 582, open a.m. only) sells useful maps for hikers; *Hostal Andino* also sells IGM maps.

**Travel Agencies** *Explorandes*, 28 de Julio y Luzuriaga, adventure travel, good. *Pablo Tours*, Luzuriaga 501 and *Chavín Tours*, Av. Luzuriaga 502, organize trips to Chavín (US$7.50, all day), Llanganuco and the Huascarán park, the latter is more expensive. *Azul Tours*, Av. Luzuriaga 658, helpful, friendly staff, hires good quality trekking equipment, rec. *Montrek*, Luzuriaga 640, good for rafting on Santa river, US$15 (in dollars), including transport to/from Huaraz, 2-hour raft trip. Marco Ugarte, Unasam, Av. Centenario s/n, offers tours to Chavín (US$8.50 for day) and treks (US$35 per day, inclusive), he is a professor of English, and his services have been recommended. With companies apart from those rec. above, beware overcharging and unreliability. In the main, US$5-10 tours to sites other than Chavín are too short; private arrangements with taxis are preferable.

**Climbing and Trekking** Huaraz, which is the climbing centre of Peru, particularly between

May and October, is the headquarters of the Huascarán National Park (entrance US$1 per day). The office is on Av. Centenario 912 (Prolongación Av. Raymondi—5th block), behind the Ministry of Agriculture building, open 0700-1415, helpful staff. For organized treks, contact Percy Tapiá, Casilla 3074, Lima 100: prices range from US$26 (16-20 people), to US$40 (under 8 people) daily. One should also contact Andes Adventures, Jr. Simón Bolívar 925, Casilla Postal 925, T 721646, Telex 46502 PE CP, Huaraz, run by a Belgian, efficient, Spanish, English, French, German and Dutch spoken, reasonably-priced; also Eudes Morales Flores (speaks fluent English) at Pyramid Adventures, Casilla 25, office: Av. Luzuriaga No. 530, Huaraz, T 721864, rec. On the second floor of the *Hotel Residencial Cataluña*, Av. Raymondi, T 72117, José Valle Espinosa, "Pepe", hires out equipment (pricey), organizes treks and pack animals, sells dried food, and is generally helpful and informative. Carlos Rodríguez, *Tasco Bar de Lucho*, PO box 111, Huaraz, for climbing and trekking in the Cordillera Blanca. For general information about climbing and trekking, see *Casa de Guías* (in **Hotel** section).

**Buses, Lima** Ormeño (address in Lima section, book 12 hrs. in advance); Transportes Rodríguez, 3 a day, leaves from office at Roosevelt 354, Lima (timekeeping and maintenance criticized), and Tarapacá 622, Huaraz; Expreso Ancash, 4 a day (rec.), Av. Carlos Zavala 177, Lima, and Raymondi 845, Huaraz; Arellano-Intersa, Colmena 1635, Lima, and Raymondi 408, Huaraz; El Trome, Montevideo 1049, Lima, and Raymondi 422, Huaraz (not rec.); Empresa Huaraz, Leticia 655 (T 275260), Lima, and Raymondi 601, Huaraz, not rec; Empresa Callejón de Huaylas, Leticia 626 (leaves at 0730); Co-op. de Transportes Huaraz Ltda, Prolongación Leticia 1059, Lima, and Raymondi 680, Huaraz (neither too good). Transportes Tadeo, Arenillas 139, Act. Cda. 4, Av. Zarumilla, San Martín de Porras, Lima (an extremely dangerous area of Lima) and Raymondi 450, Huaraz. Return from Huaraz to Lima mostly in evenings, 8-10 hrs., average price US$7.50. Taxi to Lima, US$100 for 5.

**Other Buses** To Casma (150 km.) 6¼ hrs. Empresa Moreno, Raymondi, 8th block, 0900, US$4.10. Bus to Chimbote (Moreno, Av. Fitzcarrald 309) at 0800, 2000, US$6.35, 9½ hrs. via Cañón del Pato, overcrowded, often delayed, day travel advised for both safety and views, sit on the right for best and scariest views; via Casma 0900 and 2030. Bus to Marcará, US$0.60. Colectivos take visitors to see the Cordillera, and there is also a trip to the Chavín site, Huari and Huascarán. To Trujillo, US$9.50, only with Chinchay Suyo (Gamarra 736) departs 2030 and 2200, 10 hrs. via Pativilca. Truck to Pativilca on coast, 5 hrs., US$3.20, or buses Intersa (old, poor service) and El Trome. To Barranca, Ancash, US$3.60, 4 hrs. Bus to Caraz, US$1.45, 2 hrs. (Ormeño) colectivo frequent; to Yungay US$1.20 hourly. Buses Huaraz-Carhuaz-Yungay-Caraz run every ½ hr.

**N.B.** You are advised to take buses which arrive in Huaraz in daylight given the growth of terrorism in the area.

**Excursions** About 8 km. into mountains is ***Willcawain*** archaeological site (entrance, US$1), the ruins of a Tiahuanaco-style temple, dating from about AD 1000. The site is now signposted; walk down Av. Centenario and take the signed right turn 1 km. out of town, 2½ hrs. uphill walk; for better views on return, take right fork when passing the school, the main road is reached after 2 km. Beware of dogs along the way. Alternatively, take a colectivo towards Yungay or Monterrey, get out 2 stops past the *Hotel de Turistas*, turn right and then left at a house for "pirotécnicas" (fireworks). Bring torch. There are more ruins at the end of the track, which goes on 27 km. to Laguna Llaca, but taxis reluctant to go there because track is very poor. Excursion by taxi to the Parque Nacional de ***Huascarán*** costs about US$15; in the park, puya plants, which flower only once at the end of a hundred-year lifetime, usually May-August, reach heights of 10 metres; they grow in the Quebrada Pachacoto valley, some 57 km. S of Huaraz and 26 km. E of the road; there is no sign for the Park: the turning is 3 km. before Catac and the signpost is marked Huanzala. Carpa can be reached on foot, by truck, or by San Cristóbal bus from Catac (continuing to La Unión). You can see the Park cheaply by getting the early Huaraz-Lima bus to Pachacoto crossing, then hitch a ride on the road through the Park. Chavín Tours and others (all much the same) to the Huascarán Park include a visit to the glacier on the Quebrada Pachacota and to ice caves; take gloves and food, rec., 7½ hrs., US$6.50 p.p. in low season (negotiate), more in high (you also have to pay park entrance fee of US$0.60). Punta Callán, on the Cordillera Negra between Huaraz and Casma, may be reached (3 hrs.) by truck from the football stadium; spectacular views of the Cordillera Blanca. Hitch, or walk virtually straight down, 2-3 hrs. Inca ruins of Jongopampa are 32 km. from Huaraz. Take a colectivo to San Miguel de Aco, then walk the final 6 km. Other ruins include Canray Grande, Llasha, Pallasca, and Quequepampa. Hot springs and sauna at Chancos (see page 952); minibuses and trucks go there. Also hot springs at Monterrey with 2 clean swimming pools and baths, see under Hotels (*Termas de Monterrey*), open to non-residents.

S of Huaraz, off the main road, is **Recuay**, a provincial capital (*Hotel Santa*, G, clean, friendly, basic) where unusual pottery is sold. There are a museum and the Pueblo Viejo de Catac ruins here. Many buses run from Recuay to Huaraz and Catac (for Chavín).

**Chavín** The Chavín de Huantar ruins, of a fortress temple built about 600 BC, are about 3½-7 hrs. drive (depending on the bus, 109 km., avoid back seats) from Huaraz, reached by a rough and rocky spectacular road branching E from the main Huaraz-Catac road. Unesco has proposed that the site be designated a worldwide cultural heritage. Entry US$1, students US$0.50, camera permit US$0.75. The 1970 earthquake destroyed many of the underground structures and now only the first few levels can be toured, but work is now in progress to excavate and light the tunnels closed by the earthquake as well as other temple mounds so far unexplored. Open 0800-1600, 1000-1600, Sun. and holidays. The main attraction is the marvellous carved stone heads and designs in relief of symbolic "gourd" figures. The carvings are in excellent condition, though many of the best sculptures are in Huaraz and Lima. The famous Lanzón dagger-shaped stone monolith of 800 BC is found inside the temple tunnel. **N.B.** Entrances to the temple buildings are locked: you must either hire a guide at the gate or get a child from the caretaker's house to open them for you. Sr. Chiri, Foptur, can arrange permission to enter. You cannot rely on the chambers being lit; if they are not, ask for the guard—but anyway take a torch.

John Streather writes: There is only one carved head *in situ* on the walls of Chavín now. The best things are the finely drawn stone reliefs of condors, pumas and priest warriors— by far the finest work in stone of any Peruvian, or indeed any Andean, culture of any period. The lines are outstanding for their fluidity, sinuousness, complexity and precision. Nothing like them seems to have existed either before or after them: the earlier Sechín art is clearly a fount of inspiration, but is very clumsy when compared with the delicate exactitude of the Chavín. In many ways it resembles early Chinese art more than anything Andean—in its spirit and manner, though not in its symbolism, which is entirely Andean and American.

There are hot sulphur baths about 2 km. S of Chavín (US$0.15 for a bath, reported filthy; camping possible here). Beware of thieves in Chavín village; children try to sell fossils and stonework, or swap them for ballpens. Electricity 1800-0600.

**Hotels** *Gantu*, F (not rec.) and *Inca*, F, bathrooms filthy, basic but friendly; also *Monte Carlo*, main plaza, F, fairly clean, warm at night; *Monterrey*, F; *Casa de Alojamiento Geminis*, Jr. Túpac Yupanqui, F, fork left after bridge just past ruins, basic (no bath or shower, toilet in outhouse), but clean and friendly, all meals extra; *Albergue de Turistas*, D, with bath, modern, clean, breakfast expensive, beautiful setting, 1 km. from the town on road to Huari; *Alojamiento Chavín Turist Shelter*, 17 de Enero-Norte 831, F, basic, clean and friendly.

**Restaurants** Good one 1½ blocks from ruins, on road to them. *La Ramade*; *Chavín Turístico*, cheap and friendly; *Montecarlo*, very slow, indifferent food; *Comedor de Cooperativa de Chavín*, behind church, good but difficult to get in, closed between mealtimes. All eating places appear to close after 1830. (Better hotels in Huari, 44 km. further on.) Nowhere to change money in or near Chavín.

**Bus to Chavín** Huascarán from Huaraz, 1000 daily, returns 1000, US$2.40 (tickets available from the *Comedor El Sol*). A magnificent 6-hr. scenic journey, if frightening at times, passing through the mountains and along the Río Mosna gorge; spectacular views of the Yanamarey peaks and of many snow-fed waterfalls, road surface very poor. Trucks US$1.50, 7 hrs., but very cold. Several from Catac, early a.m. and late p.m. Chavín Tours, Pablo Tours and Corazón de Jesús (tours, generally preferable to public transport, about US$7.50) make daytime excursions to Chavín and other places of interest; collection from hotels at 0900. Taxi, Huaraz-Chavín, US$20, 3-4 hrs. return. Direct bus Chavín to Lima, 13 hrs. Peru-Andino, Av. Grau 525, Lima, Tues. at 1400, Sat. at 1300 to Huaraz, returning Mon. and Thurs. The Lima-Chavín bus goes on to Pomabamba or Huari. From Barranca, every second day by truck, US$2.50, 17 hrs., trip is very bumpy and cold.

**Hiking** For the active, there is the possibility of a 4-day walk from Olleros, reached by bus or truck from the *frigorífico* in Huaraz (US$0.35). The Olleros village carpenter, on the square, has a room where one can stay. Enquire at National Park Office about necessary equipment for walk. A good map of the route is available from the Instituto Geográfico Militar in Lima, or the Trekking and Backpacking Club in Huaraz, line maps from Don Pepe at *Hotel Cataluña*, Huaraz (ask directions from anyone you meet along the way). The first day you go half-way along the meadows to the first, nameless Quebrada; on the second, you climb the first pass and sleep in the next valley; on the third, you pass Punta Yanashallash and camp in the valley somewhere after it, but before Jato; on the last day you reach Chavín. The area is isolated, so be sure to take good camping equipment, extra food and plenty of warm clothing. A longer walk may also be made to the Laguna Verdecocha, a glacier lake; this is recommended for experienced climbers only. On the first day of the walk, one reaches the Quebrada Quilloc: the second day, the Quebrada Otuto and the Punta Yanashallash (altitude: 4,680 metres); several Inca remains may be seen en route. On the third day, the trail dips and rises like a roller coaster, passing through the Río Shongo valley (spectacular views of the Huachecsa gorge), finally reaching Chavín. A two-day walk from Huaraz to the Laguna de Churup (4,250 metres) a beautiful blue lake in a crater beneath a mountain peak beyond the small village of Pitec is possible; a guide is necessary for the inexperienced (ask for Victor, US$6 per day), or a very good map to find the Laguna. A pick-up is supposed to go half-way there, but it is hard to find. It is 18 km. from Huaraz, of which the first 15 km. are easy, in the valleys (locals will advise on the route)—follow Av. Raymondi E out of Huaraz. Just before Pitec, turn right at a fork, and in Pitec, turn left, just before a mountain stream. From here it is very hard going, initially with no path, then occasional trail markers—the general direction is NE towards the snow-covered peak. The hike can be done in a day, with an early start; take sun cream and food.

There is a spectacular 2-day walk from Huari (contination of Lima-Chavín bus, above) to Chacas via Laguna Purhuay, as described by John Myerscough, from Derbyshire. "The route is clearly shown on the Instituto Geográfico Militar map, Huari is sheet 19. The walking is very easy, over a 4,500 m. pass and through two of the best valleys I've ever been in. Plenty of streams and lots of good places for camping. Amazing rock strata". **Accommodation** in **Huari** *El Dorado*, G, clean and comfortable, sunny patio, cold showers only. Also the *Paraíso* and *Ideal*. Restaurant *Los Angeles*, just off main plaza, popular. Also small fruit and veg. market and well-stocked chemist. In **Chacas**, the only hotel is *El Pilar*, G, with restaurant, very clean, comfortable, hot showers and laundry facilities. Other cheap *alojamientos* around plaza, plenty of shops and a small market. Early morning buses to Carhuaz.

**Warning** The Callejón de Huaylas has, in the past 2 years, been the target of many military/terrorist confrontations. The Cordillera Huayhuash, due to its remoteness, has been infiltrated by terrorist groups. Treks and climbs to this area have virtually ceased, and may even be prevented by the authorities. In the Cordillera Blanca, however, climbing and trekking is still possible, but the visitor should be aware that conditions could change overnight. Check with guides, agencies, locals before going into an area. It is a good idea to hire a Quechua-speaking *arriero* or porter to accompany you on long treks. Don't hike alone. Avoid staying overnight in remote villages, and *do not*, under any circumstances, involve yourself with the politics or in any political demonstration or military confrontation. If you can't leave the area immediately, remain silent and unobtrusive. Tourists in the Callejón de Huaylas have encountered hostility from local people and dogs (a stick is most useful— otherwise, throw stones).

**Advice to Climbers**: The height of the Cordillera Blanca and the Callejón de Huaylas ranges and their location in the tropics create conditions different from the Alps or even the Himalayas. Fierce sun makes the mountain snow porous and the glaciers move more rapidly. The British Embassy advises climbers to take at least six days for acclimatization, to move in groups of four or more, reporting to Club Andino or the office of the guide before departing, giving date at which search should begin, and leaving telephone number of Embassy with money. Rescue operations are very limited and there are only eight guides with training (by the Swiss). Insurance is essential, since a guide costs US$40-50 a day and a search US$2,000-2,500 (by helicopter, US$10,000).

Robert and Ana Cook (formerly of Lima) write of the *Callejón de Huaylas*: The heavy rainy season lasts from Jan. to Mar., while the dry season is from May to Sept. The mean daily temperature is determined by the altitude and hardly varies throughout the year. For instance, at 3,000 metres (the altitude of Huaraz) the mean temperature is 14°C.

Apart from the range of Andes running along the Chile-Argentina border, the highest mountains in South America are along the Callejón and perfectly visible from many spots. From the city of Huaraz alone, one can see over 23 snow-crested peaks of over 5,000 metres, of which the most notable is Huascarán (6,768 metres), the highest mountain in Peru. Although the snowline now stands at the 5,000 metres level, it was not long ago (geologically speaking) that snow and ice covered the Callejón at 3,000 metres. Despite its receding snowline, the Cordillera Blanca still contains the largest concentration of glaciers found in the world's tropical zone. From the retreating glaciers come the beauty and the plague of the Callejón. The turquoise-coloured lakes which form in the terminal moraines are the jewels of the Andes and visitors should hike up to at least one during their stay. At the same time these *cochas* (glacial lakes) have caused much death and destruction when a dyke has broken, sending tons of water hurtling down the canyons wiping out everything in their path. Now government engineers combat this problem by monitoring water flows and dyke stability.

Hilary Bradt writes: The Cordillera Blanca offers the most popular backpacking and trekking in Peru, with a network of trails used by the local people and some less well defined mountaineers' routes. Most circuits can be hiked in five days. Although the trails are easily followed, they are rugged and the passes very high—between 4,000 and nearly 5,000 metres—so backpackers wishing to go it alone should be fit and properly acclimatized to the altitude, and carry all necessary equipment. Essential items are a tent, warm sleeping bag, stove, and protection against wind and rain (climatic conditions are quite unreliable here and you cannot rule out rain and hail storms even in the dry season). Trekking demands less stamina since equipment is carried by donkeys. There are various trekking companies in Huaraz.

The South American Explorers' Club publishes a good map with additional notes on the popular Llanganuco to Santa Cruz loop, and the Instituto Geográfico Militar has mapped the area with its 1:100,000 topographical series. These are more useful to the mountaineer than hiker, however, since the trails marked are confusing and inaccurate. Recommended guides through the Cordillera Huayhuash are Catalino Rojas and Cerillio Zambrano, both from the village of Llamac; also Alejandro Kayupe in Chiquián. "Jefe", who sells maps and key chains in Chiquián, is to be avoided.

Apart from the book by Hilary Bradt (see "Information for Visitors"), the only useful guide to the area currently in print is *Peruvian Andes* by Philipe Beaud (which costs US$24), available through Cordee in the UK, some shops in Huaraz and The South American Explorers Club.

Probably the best way to see the Santa Valley and the Callejón de Huaylas, which contain some of the most spectacular scenery in Peru, is to take the paved road which branches off the coast road into the mountains just N of Pativilca (**see page 947**), 187 km. from Lima. (About 15 km after the turn off is *Restaurant El Viajero*, Panamericana Norte, km 185, good.) This route also gives a more spectacular view of the Cordillera Blanca. In 120 km. it climbs to Lake Conococha (delicious trout available in Conococha village), at 4,100 metres, where the Río Santa rises. After crossing the high level surface it descends gradually for 87 km. to Huaraz, and goes on to the Callejón de Huaylas, where it runs between the towering Cordillera Negra, snowless and rising to 4,600 metres, and the snow-covered Cordillera Blanca, whose highest point is the 6,768 metres high Huascarán. Farms appear at about 4,000 metres, but most of the farming is around Huaraz. The inhabitants grow potatoes and barley at the higher and maize and alfalfa at the lower altitudes. The valley has many picturesque villages and small towns, with narrow cobblestone streets and odd-angled house roofs. (At weekends and holidays beware of reckless Lima drivers on the roads.)

The alternative routes to the Callejón de Huaylas are via the Callán pass from Casma to Huaraz (**see page 948**), and via the Cañón del Pato (**page 950**).

There are two spectacular transandine routes from Huaraz to La Unión (and on to Huánuco for Cerro de Pasco, La Oroya, etc.; **see page 1056**). The first is by twice weekly direct bus or bus leaving Huaraz at 1100 (Señor Huascarán) to Conococha and from there another bus, via Chiquián to La Unión. At **Chiquián** (*Hostal San Miguel*, clean, simple) one can walk into the Callejón de Huayhuash. There are two poor bus services Lima-Chiquián: Landano, Ayacucho 1040, Lima, Mon., Wed., Sat. at 1100, returning to Lima Mon., Wed., Fri., 1100; Tubsa, Leticia 633, Lima, Mon., Wed., Fri., 1900 to Chiquián, and in both directions Tues., Thurs., Sat., 1400 (bus Huaraz-Chiquián from Av. Tarapaca 133, at 1130; then Chiquián-La Unión with Tubsa, Mon., Wed., Fri. at midnight). Or one can take a truck from the crossroads at Lake Conococha (a very cold place). The second is to take a Comité 5 bus to Catac (US$1.10, 1 hr., frequent service from 0630); ask to be set down at garage on the edge of Catac. Take a taxi or walk the 5 km. to Pachocoto (2 cafés with accommodation if stranded). If you cannot get a truck Pachocoto-La Unión (9 hrs., US$3.60), wait for a truck from Lima going to the mines at Huansalá (take warm clothes). The road passes through the Huascarán National Park and ascends to a high section with most rewarding views of gigantic geological features. From Huansalá, bus, truck or walk to Huallanca (8 km.) and take transport on to La Unión "through an entertaining gorge by a demanding gravel road" (Friedrich Dürsch). There are occasional trucks Huaraz-La Unión. Bus Huaraz-Huallanca, 3½ hrs., US$3.35

## THE NORTHERN OASES (3)

An area of great and diverse interest: elegant Spanish cities (Trujillo, Cajamarca, Chiclayo, Piura), vast ruins of highly-skilled pre-Inca cultures (Chan-Chan, Kuelap—in a region set for major tourist development—Sipán, Tucumé), local customs and on the coast, deep-sea fishing, surfing, or simply watching the "caballitos de totora" reed rafts at Huanchaco. And in between the oases, all the way up to Ecuador, the desert rolls on, sweeping grey dunes and dusty cliffs.

N of the mouth of the Río Santa the Andes recede, leaving a coastal desert belt of from 8 to 16 km. wide containing the three great oases of Northern Peru—the areas of Trujillo, Chiclayo and Piura.

N of Chimbote we cross the valleys of Chao and Virú, coming after 137 km. to the first great oasis of northern Peru, Trujillo. In the valley there is an abrupt line between desert and greenery; cultivation requires irrigation ditches which take their water from far up in the mountains. The area's port is **Salaverry**, exporting sugar and minerals, importing consumer goods and machinery. There is an 8 km. road to Trujillo.

The Quiruvilca copper mines are 120 km. inland by road from Salaverry. The concentrating plant at Shorey is connected with the mines by a 3 km. aerial cableway, and with its coal mine by a further 8 km. The ore is then taken by a 40 km. cableway to Samne, whence it is sent by road to Salaverry.

**Trujillo**, capital of the Department of La Libertad, disputes the title of second city of Peru with Arequipa. Population 750,000. The traveller entering Trujillo is delighted with its surrounding greenness against a backcloth of brown Andean foothills and peaks. Founded by Pizarro, 1536 (and named after his native town in Spain), it has moved with the times, but still retains many old churches, graceful colonial balconies and windows overhanging its modern pavements, of homes built during the reigns of the viceroys. Besides the Cathedral it has 10 colonial churches as well as convents and monasteries. Its Universidad de La Libertad, second only to that of San Marcos at Lima, was founded in 1824.

Near the Plaza de Armas is the spacious 18th century house in which General Iturregui lived when he proclaimed the city's freedom from Spain in 1820. It is now the exclusive Club Central and Chamber of Commerce, at Pizarro 688 (may be visited in mornings). Two other beautiful colonial mansions on the Plaza have been taken over by the Banco Central and Banco Hipotecario, which maintain as museums the parts they do not need as offices (they may be visited a.m.). Certain other mansions, still in private hands, may occasionally be visited with the help of Trujillo Tours; they include the magnificent Orbegoso house at Pizarro 316 and the one at Junín 682; also the Casa de los Condes de Aranda, Bolívar y Gamarra; the Casa del Mariscal de Orbegoso in the 5th block of Calle Orbegoso; Casa del Mayorazgo; Casa Ganoza Chopitea, 4th block of Independencia (which has a private museum that can be seen when Sr. Ganoza is in residence); Casa Madalengo, Pizarro y Gamarra; Casa Baanante, in Grau near Almagro.

The focal point is the spacious Plaza de Armas, with a sculptured group to the heroes of the Liberation (note the short legs on the statue, reportedly the result of the Church's plea that it should not be taller than the Cathedral). Fronting it is the Cathedral, with the old palace of the Archbishop next door; the *Hotel Trujillo*; the building in colonial style of the Sociedad de Beneficencia Pública de Trujillo; and the Municipalidad. Many churches were damaged in the 1970 earthquake. One of the best, La Merced at Pizarro 550, with picturesque moulded figures below the dome, is being restored, but part of the dome has collapsed because of building work next door. El Carmen church and monastery, has been described as the "most valuable jewel of colonial art in Trujillo". Other old churches include La Compañía, near Plaza de Armas; San Francisco on 3rd block of Gamarra; Belén on 6th block of Almagro; Santa Clara on 4th block of Junín; San Agustín on 6th block of Mariscal Orbegoso; Santa Ana on 2nd block of same street; Santo Domingo on 4th block of Bolognesi. There are also two markets, one on Gamarra and the Mercado Mayorista on Calle Roca. The city's water supply is generally poor.

**Museo de Arqueología**, normally open 0800-1400 in Jan.-March and 0800-1200, 1500-1800 the rest of the year, Pizarro 349 (entrance, US$0.60), recommended; it has an interesting collection of pottery. Another place to visit in Trujillo is the basement of the **Cassinelli** garage on the fork of the Pan-American and Huanchaco roads; it contains a superb private collection of Mochica and Chimú pottery. Be sure to ask for a demonstration of the whistling *huacos*; entry, US$0.85, open 0830-1130, 1530-1630. Sr. Cassinelli has plans to construct a larger museum. The University has a Zoological Museum, San Martín 368, corner with Bolognesi (0745-1300, 1500-1900); interesting displays of Peruvian animals, entrance free.

**Fiestas** Second half of September or first half of October transport and hotels booked. Other busy periods are around Mothers' Day (in March/April) and the last week of January. The Nacional Marinera contest is held each September (dancing by all ages, public participation and viewing welcomed).

**Warnings** As with all Peruvian cities, Trujillo is troubled by theft—beware of robbers working in pairs, especially beyond the inner ring road, Av. España, towards the hill and in the Sánchez Carrión district at night.

**Hotels** *Turistas*, Plaza de Armas, C with bath (cheaper without, or if paying in intis), accepts American Express, full of character, rooms on street are noisy, meals US$4, excellent buffet lunch on Sun.; Tour Peruvian S.A. travel agency in foyer for local trips. *Los Jardines*, 4 km. from centre, bungalows in garden, buses to town, D; *Opt Gar* (5th block Grau), C, with bath, good, friendly, rec., excellent restaurant (try sea food) and snack bar; *Los Escudos*, Orbegoso 676, T 243523, E, with bath very little hot water, small garden, rec, try the delicious puddings next door at 674; *Continental*, Gamarra, opp. market, E, clean, good, safe, occasional hot water, restaurant disappointing, overpriced; *Hostal Monterrey*, Av. Los Incas 256, T 241673, open 24 hrs., F, friendly, comfortable, but not very clean (close to Tepsa, good for late arrivals); 3 blocks down is *Hostal Rayers*, G with bath, hot water, friendly but dirty; *Primavera*, Nicolás de Piérola 872, E, noisy on the street side, modern and cool; *San Martín*, in 7th block of San Martín, F, with bath, good value, clean but some rooms damp, has more than 100 rooms, no restaurant. *Hostal Americano*, Pizarro 792, is a vast, old building, G, rooms without bath are noisy and very basic (back on to cinema, "listen to the film you saw the night before"), most rooms without window (Nos. 134 and 137 have windows, balconies and good views) basic, comfortable, "almost never has any water", 3rd floor is best for water, many gringos, possible to put motorbike inside, rec.; *Vogi*, on Ayacucho, E with bath, clean, highly rec. *Hostal Salaverry*, Independencia y Salaverry, F, friendly, public parking two blocks away; *Estmar*, César Vallejo 134, G without bath, cold water, basic. *Hostal Lima*, Ayacucho 718, popular with gringos, F without bath, baths terrible; similar standard is *Hostal Central*,

---

**Trujillo: Key to map**

1. Plaza de Armas; 2. Cathedral; 3. La Merced; 4. La Compañía; 5. San Francisco; 6. Santa Clara; 7. Santo Domingo; 8. Casa Iturrégui; 9. Casa de los Condes de Aranda; 10. Casa del Mariscal Obregoso; 11. Casa del Mayorazgo; 12. Casa Ganoza Chopitea; 13. Casa Madalengo; 14. Museo Casinelli; 15. Museo Arqueológico; 16. Museo Zoológico; 17. Post Office; 18. Foptur, Tourist Office; 19. Immigration; 20. Central Market; 21. Tepsa Office; 22. Tepsa buses; 23. Buses Díaz; 24. *Hotel Turistas*; 25. *Hotel Continental*; 267. *Hostal Americano*.

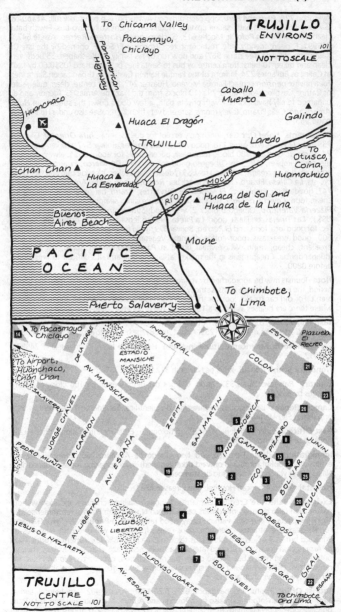

TRUJILLO ENVIRONS

NOT TO SCALE

101

To Chicama Valley
Pacasmayo, Chiclay

Panamerican Highway

Huanchaco

chan chan

Huaca El Dragón

TRUJILLO

Huaca La Esmeralda

Buenos Aires Beach

PACIFIC OCEAN

Puerto Salaverry

Caballo Muerto

Galindo

Laredo

To Otusco, Coina, Huamachuco

RÍO MOCHE

Huaca del Sol and Huaca de la Luna

Moche

To Chimbote, Lima

N

TRUJILLO CENTRE NOT TO SCALE 101

To Pacasmayo Chiclayo

To Airport, Huanchaco, Chan Chan

ESTADIO MANSICHE

AV. MANSICHE

DE LA TORRE

INDUSTRIAL

ESTETE

COLON

Plazuela El Recreo

SALAVERRY

JORGE CHAVEZ

D. A. CARRION

ZEPITA

AV. ESPAÑA

SAN MARTIN

INDEPENDENCIA

GAMARRA

FCO. PIZARRO

BOLIVAR

JUNIN

AYACUCHO

GRAU

PEDRO MUÑIZ

AV. LIBERTAD

CLUB LIBERTAD

JESUS DE NAZARETH

AV. ESPAÑA

ALFONSO UGARTE

BOLOGNESI

DIEGO DE ALMAGRO

ORBEGOSO

To Chimbote and Lima

ESPAÑA

Ayacucho 728; *Paris* and *Perú*, opp each other on Ayacucho, G p.p., usually full; *Acapulco*, Gamarra 681, G with bath, sauna upstairs. Hotel next to Chinchay Suyo bus, F with bath, clean; *Hostal Marco Polo*, Jr. Moche 613, G, clean, quiet. *Hostería Recreo*, Astete 647, T 246991, F, clean, friendly, safe, restaurant, rec.; *Hostería El Sol*, E, opened by the late Dr. Kaufmann of Coina (**see page 967**) and now run by his family, castle-shaped, 55 beds, very clean and quiet, 10 mins. from centre by bus to Santa Inés or Huanchaco (US$0.60 by taxi), at Calle Los Brillantes 224, in front of the Parque Ramón Castilla, in Urbanización Santa Inés. For a private *pensión* contact Familia Moreno, Huáscar 247, F, near centre, clean, quiet, safe, or Catrina Castillo, Pedro Muñiz 792 (10 blocks from the Plaza de Armas) G, friendly and an unnamed family have rooms, F with private bath, a few doors down the street from *Hotel Americano*, Calle Pizarro, lovely rooms, safe and very friendly, rec. See also under Huanchaco, page 965.

**Restaurants** *Hotel Opt Gar*, lunch only except for guests, rec.; *Chifa Oriental*, Gamarra 735, rec.; *El Pesquero*, Junín 118, good fish; *Pollos Bolívar*, Bolívar 577, chicken and salad. *24 Horas*, Jr. Gamarra 700 block, reasonably priced meals for about US$1, always open, as the name implies; *ABC*, on Orbegoso,good for chicken; *De Marco*, Pizarro 725, good, especially the ice creams, set menu for US$1, desserts and cakes, it's cycle club and welcomes cyclists. *La Calesa*, Pizarro 716, good snack bar; *Romano*, good. **Hotel Americano**, at Pizarro 747, good menu, highly rec.; *El Mesón de Cervantes*, Pizarro, bar-restaurant, polite, good cheap food; *Ceviche del Rey*, Av. Mansiche opposite clinic, seafood, open only until 1800. *Pizzería Valentino*, Orbegoso block 2, very good; *Subterráneo*, Plaza Murillo, set lunch US$1. *Las Tinajas*, on Plaza, good. *La Pileta* ,next to Tepsa bus office, Astete 472, strongly rec. for good local food, and *El Recreo*, Bolívar 879, good for breakfast. *La Miel*, Jirón Bolívar 600, good breakfasts, poor coffee, friendly. Vegetarian restaurant: *El Sol*, Pizarro 660, excellent, cheap, filling. Wholewheat bread at *Panadería Chalet Suizo*, Av. España e Independencia. Cheap meals in the market at Grau y Gamarra. It's difficult to find a meal before 0800.

**Note** Tourists may be approached by vendors selling *huacos* and necklaces from the Chimú period; the export of these items is strictly illegal if they are genuine, but they almost certainly aren't. For **old car freaks**, look for the funeral director's premises, just off the main square, where there are hearses as old as a 1924 Ford; the proprietor is happy to show you around.

**Taxis** Town trip, US$0.45. Chan Chán, Huanchaco, US$1.30. Taxi driver Jorge Enrique Guevara Castillo, Av. del Ejército 1259, Altos 1, rec. By the hour, in town, US$3, outside US$4.

**Peruvian-North American Cultural Institute** Húsares de Junín y Venezuela, T 245832, 232512.

**Honorary British Consul** Jesús de Nazareth 312, T (044) 235548.

**Laundry** *Rapilavo*, Grau 337, good, charges per item; laundry in 100 block of Pizarro charges by weight.

**Camera Repairs** Laboratorios de Investigación Científica, San Martín 745, over Fuji shop opp. *Hotel San Martín*, good.

**Post Office** Corner of Independencia and Bolognesi. Entel for international phone calls: Calle de la Puerta Aranda 680.

**Immigration** Edificio Demarco, 3rd floor, Diego de Almagro 225. Gives 90-day visa extensions (proof of funds and onward ticket required). Involves taking forms to Banco de la Nación, and waiting for papers to be stamped.

**Hospital** Anglo-American Hospital, good, reasonable fees.

**Exchange** Banco de Crédito, Gamarra, changes travellers' cheques and cash without commission (also cheques into dollars cash). Banco NorPerú on Pizarro, recommended for changing cheques and cash with no delay, good rates. Banco Popular del Perú, Gamarra, for cheques (a protracted operation, poor rates). Interbanc will give cash advances on Eurocard but at 3-4% commission, plus telex to Lima and 18% tax. América Tours, Plaza de Armas, cash dollars only at good rates; Ghia Tours, near Plaza, changes travellers' cheques outside banking hours, but double check the rates offered; casa de cambio on Plaza, fair rates. Street changers around the market and Bolívar 600 offer good rates (although they can change hourly); shop around.

**Tourist Office** Foptur, Independencia 628, T 24-1936; Pizarro 402, very helpful, and at airport. Maps and information also from Touring and Automobile Club, and from Gira Tours on Calle Independencia; maps from Librería Ayacucho, Ayacucho 570. Tourist Police have an

THE NORTHERN OASES (3)  963

office at Pizarro 422 on the corner of Plaza de Armas; they wear white uniforms and are extremely helpful; will even help lone travellers to visit Chan Chán safely.

**Travel Agents**  Sra. Carmen Melly, *Trujillo Tours*, Gamarra 440 (T 233-069), recommended for knowledgeable guides (Napoleon speaks good English and Italian) and efficient service. *San Valentín Tours*, Orbegoso 585 (T 232-812), ask for Sr. Jorge Sánchez, good local tours, very reasonable.

**Guides**  Pedro Puerta, an English speaking expert on Chan Chá and former college librarian, who has an office at Km. 560 on the Panamericana Norte, 2½ km. from the Plaza de Armas, offers interesting tours to Chan Chan, Huaca El Dragón, and Huaca La Esmeralda. He charges US$3 per hour for a 6-7 hr. tour, not including taxi hire and lunch for him and the taxi driver. He also sells prints of Chan Chan reliefs and Mochica pottery motifs, beautiful but expensive. He gives a slideshow at 2000 nightly at the *Hostal Americano*, free but you may be expected to buy one of his prints. Sr. Puerta is not an official guide, but is experienced and rec. The tourist office has a list of official guides (favourable reports received). Other experienced guides are Oscar, Trujillo Tours, and Gustava Prada Marga, Miguel Grau 169, Villa del Mar, US$10 for 5 hrs, plus US$16 for taxi. All other guides should be treated with suspicion.

**Air Transport**  Faucett, Pizarro 532, T 232232/232771, and AeroPerú, Junín 537, daily flights from Lima, 1 hr., Faucett from Tumbes. AeroPerú fly to Cajamarca (Mon., Fri., low season), 25 mins. Tarapoto and Juanjui (Tues. and Sat.). Faucett and AeroPerú to Iquitos, change at Tarapoto. Flights by Faucett to Cajamarca, Chiclayo, Chachapoyas and points N and to a multitude of small jungle towns. Taxi to airport, US$3; or take bus to Chan Chan and get out at airport turn-off.

**Buses**  To Lima, 551 km., by bus, 8-10 hrs. US$9 with Tepsa (3 a day—station in Trujillo, Av. Almagro, between Avs. España and Grau, tickets Astete 482), Peru Express, Chinchay-Suyo (5 a day, González Prada 337/Bolívar 702, insist on ticket before you board or you may get charged extra for luggage), Expreso Continental (part of Ormeño), Av. del Ejército, or Roggero; mostly at night. To Lima, Roggero departs at 0930, Chinchay-Suyo at 1000 and Panamericana at 1100, 2200 and 2330. Try to book your bus to Lima a day in advance: they fill up quickly. Buses to Lima quite frequent but difficult to go north as buses booked for days; try Emtrafesa (Av. Miraflores with España) N to **Pacasmayo** (US$1.20, 2½ hrs.), **Chiclayo** (US$5, 3 hrs.), Piura, Tumbes. To **Huaraz** (US$9.50, 10 hrs., depart 2030, daily (Jirón Bolívar 720, book ahead). To get to Huaraz by day without spending the night in malodorous Chimbote you will have to find transport to get you to Chimbote before the Moreno bus leaves at 0700. Bus to **Chimbote** US$1.25, 2 hrs., Empresa Cajamarca, Av. España 2023-27, Empresa El Aguila, Av. Nicaragua 220, hourly (book in advance in high season). Empresa Chinchay-Suyo leaves 1300; Chinchay-Suyo and Tepsa have buses to **Casma**, 3 hrs., US$2.50, and to **Tarapoto**, departing at 1200 daily. Empresa San Pedro, Av. Moche, 3rd block, every 2 hrs.; colectivo to Chimbote, 2 hrs., US$2.50. Colectivo to **Cajamarca** US$8, 1100, 6½ hrs., office at Ayacucho 896, reserve day in advance, at least 3 passengers required; Empresa Expreso Cajamarca, 0500 and 2200, US$3.75, colectivo with Díaz bus, Av. N. de Piérola 1059, US$9.50, El Cóndor buses (Pizarro 789) at night, 6-9 hrs., US$7.20 (also Etucsa block 20 of Av. España, 2200, rec.); Vulcano, Mansiche 299, T 235847 (also to Chiclayo, Chepen and Pacasmayo), to Cajamarca in daylight, take Chiclayo bus to La Cruz, turn-off for Cajamarca, and wait there for a colectivo to Cajamarca, US$4.50, 8 hrs. Chinchay-Suyo and Tepsa have buses to **Casma**, 3 hrs., US$3.20 and to **Tarapoto**, departing at 1200 daily. Colectivo to **Piura**, 1000 daily, US$15; bus to Piura (Tepsa, 2000, Chinchay-Suyo 1300 and at night), US$8, 6½-9 hrs. Tepsa to **Tumbes**, daily at 1930, US$12 and up, Expreso Moderno and Sudamericano (Jr. Montevideo 618), 12 hrs. Bus to **Sullana**, Sudamericano, Tepsa and also Chinchay-Suyo only overnight, 8 hrs. The road is paved till just after Sullana, then poor till within 50 km. of Tumbes. To **Tayabamba** (for ruins, **see page 967**) with Emp. Huancapata (Sucre, no number) Sundays only, dep. 1800, arrives Tuesday 1200, 40 hrs, US$5, very rough road. Bus returns Wednesdays only at 0800.

**Excursions from Trujillo**  About five km. to the crumbling ruins of **Chan Chán**, imperial city of the Chimú domains and largest adobe city in the world. The ruins consist of nine great compounds built by Chimú kings. The nine-metre high perimeter walls surrounded sacred enclosures with usually only one narrow entrance. Inside, serried rows of storerooms contained the agricultural wealth of the kingdom, which stretched 1,000 km. along the coast from near Guayaquil to Paramonga. Most of the compounds contain a huge walk-in well which tapped the ground water, raised to a high level by irrigation higher up the valley. Each compound also included a platform mound which was the burial place of the king, with his women and his treasure, presumably maintained as a memorial. The Incas almost certainly copied this system and transported it to Cuzco where the last Incas continued building huge enclosures. Chan Chán was taken by the Incas about AD 1450 but not looted; the Spaniards, however, despoiled its burial mounds of all the gold and silver statuettes and ornaments buried with the Chimú nobles. The dilapidated city walls enclose an area of 28 square km. containing the remains of palaces, temples, workshops, streets, houses, gardens and a canal. What is left of the adobe walls bears well-preserved moulded decorations and painted designs have been found on pottery unearthed from the debris of a city ravaged by floods, earthquakes, and treasure seekers. Heavy rain and flooding in 1983 damaged much of the ruins and although they are still standing, many of the interesting mouldings are closed to visitors. The Ciudadela of Tschudi has been reconstructed (15 min. walk from the road), open 0830 to 1600 (but it may be covered up if rain is expected).

A ticket which covers the entrance fees for Chan Chán, the Huaca El Dragón and the Huaca La Esmeralda (for 2 days,) costs US$4. A guide costs US$3.20 for one hour. Minibuses leave from José Gálvez 394, corner of Los Incas, near market, or corner of España and Orbegoso/Mansiche every 15 minutes, or from Salaverry, US$0.25, last one returns about 1200; Trujillo-Huanchaco bus, US$0.15 to Chan Chán entrance; these buses are worked by teams of pickpockets; taxi, US$1.55, rec.

**Warning** If you walk to the ruins from the main road, keep to the path. Do not go to Chan Chán alone or in couples; it is preferable to go with a guide. Guides are available at the ticket office. It has been rec. to arrive at 0900 as there are more guides and tourists around. White shirted, armed police are in evidence. Sgto. José Soto Ríos, T 251489, is a good guide, speaks English. Do not walk on Buenos Aires beach near Chan Chán as there is serious danger of robbery, and being attacked by dogs.

The restored temple, Huaca El Dragón, dating from the Mochica empire of between 800 and 100 BC, is also known as Huaca Arco Iris (rainbow), after the shape of friezes which decorate it. It is on the W side of the Pan-American Highway in the district of La Esperanza; taxi costs US$1.25; open 0800-1700.
    The Caballo Muerto ruins, about 11 km. inland up the Moche valley, are now forbidden to visitors, and the sculptures have been re-buried to protect them from robbers.

The poorly restored Huaca La Esmeralda is at Mansiche, between Trujillo and Chan Chan, behind the church. Buses from Pasaje Agustín, between Obregoso and Gamarra, 2 blocks from Plaza (not a friendly district).

A few km. south of Trujillo are the huge Moche pyramids, the Huaca del Sol and the Huaca de la Luna (open all the time, entry free), taxi about US$6 return, (ask around all the drivers for best rate) alternatively bus or colectivo marked Salaverry, El Alto or La Compiña, US$0.25 from corner of Zela near Mercado Mayorista, get out at Bodega El Sol on the right hand side of the road; opposite is a huge Sprite sign. Here starts a path to Moche, about an hour's interesting walk through farmland; it is inadvisable to walk unless in a large group. The pyramids consist of millions of adobe bricks and are the largest precolumbian structures in South America (the interior passageways of the Huaca de la Luna are not open to visitors; the site is under the control of the tourist police). An interesting feature of the site is the innumerable number of ancient pottery shards lying around on the ground. It is best to visit in the morning as the wind whips up sand in the afternoon.

The fishing village of **Huanchaco** is worth visiting to see the narrow pointed fishing rafts, known as *caballitos*, made of tortora reeds and used in many places along the Peruvian coast. Unlike those used on Lake Titicaca, these are flat, not hollow, and ride the breakers rather like surfboards (you can rent one on the beach). These craft are depicted on ancient Mochica and Chimú pottery. The village, now developed with the beach houses of the wealthy of Trujillo, is overlooked by a huge church from the belfry of which are superb views. Children sell precolumbian *objets d'art* and beads; do not eat fish in the hut-like restaurants as they aren't hygienic. Bus to Huanchaco (marked with a "B"), US$0.15, from corner of Av. España and Av. Mansiche (regular ringroad bus, every 10 mins.), or, after 1830, Pasaje Agustín, Trujillo, 2 blocks from Plaza about one an hour; taxi US$5. Fiestas throughout January and February.

**N.B.** The strength of the sun is deceptive; a cold wind off the sea reduces the temperature, but you can still be badly sunburned.

**Hotels** *Hostal Sol y Mar*, Jirón Ficus 570, E, with bath and balcony (some rooms without), kitchen facilities, friendly owner, garden, rec.; *Hostal Bracamonte*, Los Olivos 503, F, comfortable, good, chalets with private bath, or converted caravans, pool, own water supply, emergency generator, rents bicycles, secure, bar nearby, good pies and cakes (beware of monkey when eating lemon meringue pie, he's very fast), English spoken, highly rec.; *Hostal Huanchaco*, Larco 287 on Plaza, also F with hot shower, clean and friendly, swimming pool, cafeteria with home-made cakes and other good meals, video, pool table, highly rec.; *Hostal Las Palmeras*, Calle Las Palmeras, G-F, 6 rooms, hot water in bathrooms, cooking facilities, clean, American owner has extensive folk-art collection; *Hostal Chávez*, Calle D, Saavedra 400, G, clean, friendly; *Caballitos de Totora*, F, swimming pool, friendly, nice garden, but rooms not too clean, the owners are to open a vegetarian restaurant and hold cultural events at the hotel; cheap accommodation at the house of Señora Consuelo. Accommodation, inc. food, with families, easy to find, US$2-3 a day.

**Restaurants** Good fish restaurants on the sea front *La Casita de la Playa*, owned by Walter (an American), meals for US$1.25, highly rec; others on seafront tend to overcharge; *Violetta*, a private house near the plaza (good meals provided) and Familia Flores, popular; *El Tramboyo*, near the pier, good, helpful, friendly. *Lucho del Mar*, excellent sea food; *Piccolo*, 5 blocks from plaza, cheap, friendly, sometimes live folk music; *Colonial Club*, main square, run by Belgians, fish, chicken or meat, good, but not cheap. Try picarones, people come from Trujillo at weekends especially to eat them.

About 20 mins from Trujillo by bus, 15 by taxi (US$0.35 and US$3 respectively) is Las Delicias, with a clean beach and good surf. *Hostal Zlang* here is recommended, small, clean, F, quiet, shared baths, breakfast in *Bar-Café* attached, other meals available from other members of the family, owner very knowledgeable and his son offers tours of Chan Chán. Good restaurant serving traditional food around the corner (US$1.50-2.50).

A visit may be made from Trujillo to one of the sugar estates, say the Hacienda Cartavio, in the Chicama valley (43 km.). At Laredo (bus from Trujillo, near central market, 7 km.), a sugar refinery can be visited—the tour is free; apply to public relations office in administration building; there are also interesting ruins at Galindo, near Laredo. One of the biggest sugar estates in the world, also in the Chicama valley, is the Casa Grande cooperative. It covers over 6,000 hectares and employs 4,000 members. Visits (guided) are only possible before 1200;

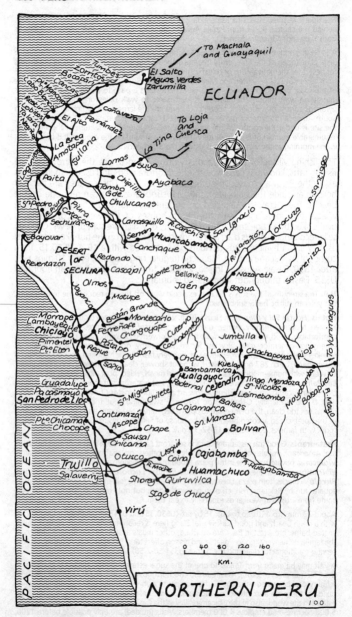

NORTHERN PERU

US$0.75 by bus. The Chiclín museum, once famous for items from Chan Chán, now contains interesting collection of colonial religious paintings and statuary. Ruins in the Chicama valley: Huaca Prieta and Chiquitoy; colectivos from Av. España, change at Cartavio.

132 km. E from Trujillo is the village of *Coina*, at 1,500 metres in the Sierra Alto Chicama, where the late Dr. Kaufmann, from Germany, opened a hospital for Indians and built the *Hostería El Sol*, with glorious views, E, for full board, F, bed only. Walking. English, French and German spoken. Information from the *Hostería El Sol*, at Calle Los Brillantes 224, Santa Inés, Trujillo (T 231933). Mail can be forwarded to Apartado 775, Trujillo.

To the NE of Trujillo is Cajamarca, which can be reached either from Trujillo or from Pacasmayo (paved throughout). The old road from Trujillo is terrible and (for cyclists especially) lonely, taking 12-15 hours (as opposed to 8 hrs. via Pacasmayo), but it is more interesting, passing over the bare puna before dropping to the Huamachuco valley. Off it lies *Otusco*, an attractive Andean town with an imposing but unfinished church and narrow cobbled streets. In Agallpampa there is one, unsigned *hostal* ("less than basic, no light, bath, toilet or water, and tries to overcharge"). Further on, at the mining town of Shorey, a road branches off to *Santiago de Chuco*, birthplace of the poet César Vallejo, where there is the annual festival of Santiago El Mayor in the second half of July. The main procession is on 25 July, when the image is carried through the streets. Close to Yancabamba is *Hostería El Viajero* and in Quiruvilca there is one hotel. The road runs on to the colonial town of *Huamachuco*, 181 km. from Trujillo, which has a huge main plaza and a controversial modern cathedral. There is a colourful Sunday market. A 2-hr. walk (take the track which goes off to the right just after crossing the bridge on the road to Trujillo) takes you to the extensive ruins of hilltop pre-Inca fortifications, Marcahuamachuco (car US$5 p.p.). Nearby, beyond the local radio station, 1 hr's walk, are the pre-Inca ruins of Viracochabamba.

**Huamachuco Hotels** *Hostal San Francisco*, Sánchez Carrión 380, F, clean, hot shower; *La Libertad*, G, not rec., rooms and bathrooms filthy; *Fernando*, G, Bolívar 361, good value, clean; also *Sucre*, G and *Hostal Huamachuco*, G. Rec. restaurants: *Caribe*, quite good, and *El Sol* (both on main square), *El Cairo*, Sánchez Carrión 754, good food and service, rec. and *Danubio*. Good snacks at *Salón Venecia*, Carrión near main plaza.

**Buses** Transportes Quiroz **from Trujillo**, (T 247011) US$5, 12 hrs., at 1530, 1700, 1800, take warm clothing; Antisuyo **to Trujillo** three daily, US$4, 10 hrs. There are also colectivos from Trujillo. Buses to **Cajamarca**, US$1.80; to **Casa Grande**, US$1. Direct bus to Lima, 24 hrs.

From Huamachuco buses (Empresa Huancapata which start in Trujillo) run to *Tayabamba* (important ruins nearby), on the far bank of the Marañón, passing through the old gold-mining centres of Pataz province, such as Parcoy and Buldibuyo. This journey takes a good 18 hours in "normal" conditions. Not far, but a time-consuming journey on mule-back, from Pataz itself (a friendly gold-mining town, about 100 km. from Huamachuco) are the unique circular ruins of El Gran *Pajatén* (pre-Inca); ask at Tourist Office in Cajamarca for details. A national park, Río Abiseo, incorporating Gran Pajatén, four other sites—La Playa, Las Papayas, Los Pinchudos and Cerro Central—and the surrounding cloud forest, is scheduled to open for visitors in 1991; until then you need a permit (hard to get) from the Instituto Nacional de Cultura in Lima. Also worth seeing in the Huamachuco area are Laguna Sausacocha (with Inca ruins, similar to those of Vilcashuamán, near Ayacucho, nearby) and *haciendas* Yanasara and Cochabamba, deep down in the valley of the river Chusgón, about 2-3 hrs. by truck east of the town. Yanasara, noted for its fighting bulls, is still in the hands of its long-term owner, Francisco Pinillos Montoya, a well-known local character. There is a guest house at Cochabamba, which used to be the Andean retreat of the owners of the Laredo sugar plantation, near Trujillo. The climate, at about 2,300 metres, is mild.

There is a 2-day walk from Bolívar in the NE to Huamachuco, parts of which follow an Inca trail used by Túpac Yupanqui (**see also page 1070**). One walks from Bolívar to Bambamarca, then down the stone steps leading to the Calemar trail, which crosses the River Marañón. At Pallar, there are trucks to Huamachuco. Be sure to take food, water, a small kerosene cooker and a compass; this is an arduous trip and not recommended for beginners.

From Huamachuco the road runs on 48 km. through impressive eucalyptus groves to *Cajabamba*, which lies in the high part of the sugar-producing and once malaria-infested Condebamba valley. It has an attractive Plaza de Armas. Several buses daily to Huamachuco; Quiroz, Antisuyo, about 3 hrs., US$2.20, also trucks and lorries. Two direct buses a day from Trujillo, 12 hrs. To Cajamarca, via San Marcos (below) with Empresa Díaz (unreliable) and Empresa Atahuallpa, 0500, US$3.

The best hotel is the *Flores* (F, with toilet, friendly, clean) on the Plaza de Armas; *Hostal Bolívar*, F, including fleas but without bath; also *Ramal*, F, friendly; *Restaurant Gloriabamba* good.

Cajabamba can also be reached in a strenuous but marvellous 3-4 day hike from Coina (see above). The first day's walk brings you to Hacienda Santa Rosa where you stay overnight. Then you cross the mountains at about 4,000 metres, coming through Arequeda to Cajabamba. The ruins at Huacamochal may be seen en route; the scenery is spectacular. It is advisable to hire a guide, and a donkey to carry the luggage. A map of the route is available from the Post Office in Coina.

The road continues from Cajabamba through **San Marcos** (3 hotels; *Nuevo*, G p.p. with bath, water shortages, but clean and quiet), important for its Sunday cattle market, to Cajamarca. Bus to Cajamarca (124 km.), Atahuallpa and Empresa Díaz leaving early in the morning, takes 6 hrs., US$3.60.

**Pacasmayo**, port for the next oasis northward, is 100 km. N. of Trujillo on the Pan-American Highway running N to Chiclayo (bus, 2 hrs., US$1). Population: 12,300.

**Hotels** *Ferrocarril*, F, on seafront, quiet and clean, no hot water (ask for water anyway); *Panamericano*, Leoncio Prado 18, F, with private cold shower, good value, friendly, clean, safe, reasonable restaurant downstairs; *San Francisco*, opp. *Panamericano*, F, basic, OK. Several cheap restaurants on the main street.

Pacasmayo is the best starting point for visiting Cajamarca (buses with Empresa Díaz, US$8.50). The new paved 180 km. road to it branches off the Pan-American Highway soon after it crosses the Río Jequetepeque. The river valley has terraced rice fields and mimosas may often be seen in bloom, brightening the otherwise dusty landscape. A few km. to N on other side of Río Jequetepeque are the ruins of Pacatnamú comparable in size to Chan-Chán—pyramids, cemetery and living quarters of nobles and fishermen, possibly built in Chavín period. Evidence also of Moche tribes. Micro bus to Guadalupe, 10 km. from ruins, and taxi possible from there (Ortiz family, Unión 6, T 3166), US$20. Where the Pan-American Highway crosses the Jequetepeque are the well-signed ruins of Fartan (separate from those of Pacatnamú, but probably of the same period). At the mining town of **Chilete**, a worthwhile diversion is to take the road N to San Pablo; 21 km. from Chilete are the stone monoliths of the Kuntur Huasi culture, which resemble those of San Agustín in Colombia. There are occasional buses from Chilete to the site, 1½ hrs., then 20 mins.' walk (no signs; you must ask locals), then a long wait for transport back, best to hitch. In Chilete, hotels *Amazonas* and *San Pedro*, G, filthy bathrooms, rooms hard to find on Tues. because of Wed. market; restaurant *Montecarlo* serves cheap *cuy* and other dishes. Truck to Chilete from the police control 1 km. from main plaza in Cajamarca, US$1. On the road to Cajamarca is Yonán, where there are petroglyphs.

An alternative route from Trujillo to Cajamarca, via Contumazá, passes through the cane fields and rice plantations of the Chicama valley before branching off to climb over the watershed of the Jequetepeque. From Contumazá, an attractive little town, trucks can be taken to Cajamarca, via Chilete.

**Cajamarca** (pop. 70,000, 2,750 metres), is a beautiful old colonial town and most important town in the northern mountain area. Here Pizarro ambushed and captured Atahuallpa, the Inca emperor. The Cuarto de Rescate (not the actual ransom chamber but in fact the room where Atahuallpa was held prisoner—closed on Tues. and after 1200 on Sat. and Sun.) can be seen (US$2, ticket also valid for nearby Belén church and nearby museums); a red line purporting to be the height of Atahuallpa's hand was only recently painted in. (The room was closed to the public for centuries, and used by the nuns of Belén hospital). The chamber also has two interesting murals. The Plaza where Atahuallpa was ambushed and the stone altar set high on Santa Apollonia hill where he is said to have reviewed his subjects are also shown (small entrance fee). There is a road to the top, or you can walk up from Calle 2 de Mayo, using the steep stairway. The Plaza das Armas has a 350-year old fountain, topiary and gardens (but little peace from the beggars and shoeshine boys). The Cathedral (San Francisco, seventeenth century, with catacombs) and Belén churches (handicrafts for sale in the cloisters) are well worth seeing; so are San Pedro (Gálvez and Junín), San José (C. M. Iglesias and Angamos), La Recoleta (Maestro and Casanova) and Capilla de La Dolorosa, close to San Francisco. Many belfries were left half-finished in protest against a Spanish tax levied on the completion of a church. The Cathedral, which took 350 years to build, was completed in 1960; it still has no belfry. Next to the Belén church (closed on Tues.) is a hospital (1774) for men and women. The women's hospital is an interesting musuem, one section with well-displayed archaeological finds, pots and textiles, and the other showing modern arts and crafts.

Points of interest include the Bishop's Palace, next to the Cathedral, and many old colonial houses with garden patios, and 104 elaborate carved doorways: see palace of the Condes de Uceda, now occupied by the Banco de Crédito on Jr. Apurímac 719; the house of Toribio Casanova, Jr. José Gálvez 938; the house of the Silva Santiesteban family, Jr. Junín 1123; and the houses of the Guerrero and Castañeda families. The Education Faculty of the University has a museum on Jirón Arequipa with objects of the pre-Inca Cajamarca culture, not seen in Lima; the attendant knows much about Cajamarca and the surrounding area. Open 0800-1200, 1500-1700, in winter, and 0800-1200 in summer, US$0.20 (guided tour). The University maintains an experimental arboretum and agricultural station. The Museo de Arte Colonial, at the Convento de San Francisco, is also worth a visit.

The town is a favourite among Peruvians for holidays, and has an interesting market with some crafts, especially noted for cotton and wool saddlebags (*alforjas*). Bargains of hand-tooled leather goods can be bought from the prisoners at the jail beyond the white arch on Calle Lima (7 blocks from Plaza de Armas). All museums are closed on Tuesdays (shops take a long lunch) but open at weekends. The rainy season is Dec.-April.

**Festivals** Plenty. Corpus Christi is a favourite. The pre-Lent Carnival is spectacular but includes much throwing of water, oil and paint, which can develop into fights between local youths and gringos. 28/29 July, Independence: *fiesta*, with bullfight and agricultural fair; prices shoot up. In Porcón, 16 km. to the NW, Palm Sunday processions are remarkable.

**Warning** Beware of pickpockets in the Plaza de Armas and in cinemas.

**Hotels** *Turistas* (60 rooms) in the Plaza de Armas, D, with private bath, helpful, laundry service, 2 restaurants, bar, ask to see room before booking. *Continental*, off Plaza, very clean, hot water, D, rec.; *Laguna Seca*, at Baños del Inca, C, in pleasant surroundings, clean, private hot thermal baths in rooms, swimming pool with thermal water, a bit dilapidated, horses for hire, food average. *Sucre*, Amalia Puga 815, near Plaza de Armas, G, with toilet and wash basin in each room, water a.m. only, good value, sometimes noisy, not very safe, poor restaurant upstairs; *Casa Blanca*, Plaza de Armas, E, room service, clean, safe, nice building and garden, good; *Gran Hostal Plaza*, Plaza de Armas 631, F, old building with handmade wood furnishings, mainly large rooms with many beds, private bath and balcony (G without bath), hot water but poor water supply, pleasant, rec. (especially room 4) with new annex (dirty but is open at 0200 when bus arrives); *San Francisco*, Jr. Belén 570, F, "a bit dirty, but friendly"; *Amazonas*, Jirón Amazonas 528, modern, F, clean, no hot water, friendly. *Jusovi*, Amazonas 637, F, comfortable, all rooms with private baths but hot water only in communal bathroom, safe, rec. Also on Amazonas (No. 1078), near Plaza, is *Hostal San Lorenzo*, E, hot water, clean. *Becerra*, Jr. Arequipa 195 (unsigned), F, intermittent tepid water, rec.; *Hostal Cajamarca*, E, in colonial house at Dos de Mayo 311, clean, hot water, rec. as the

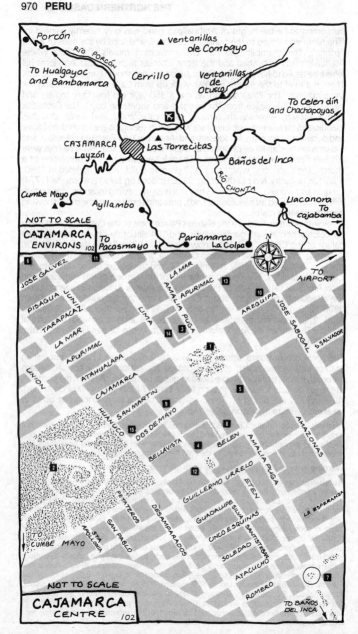

Porcón

RÍO PORCÓN

To Hualgayoc
and Bambamarca

Cerrillo

▲ Ventanillas
de Combayo

Ventanillas
de Otusco

To Celendín
and Chachapoyas

CAJAMARCA
Layzón ▲

Las Torrecitas

Cumbe Mayo ▲

Ayllambo

▲ Baños del Inca

RÍO CHONTA

Llacanora
To
cajabamba

NOT TO SCALE

**CAJAMARCA
ENVIRONS** 102

To
Pacasmayo

Pariamarca
La Colpa

N

TO
AIRPORT

JOSÉ GALVEZ

PISAGUA   JUNIN

TARAPACAZ

LA MAR

APURIMAC

ATAHUALPA

UNION

LIMA

LA MAR

AMALIA PUGA

APURIMAC

CAJAMARCA

SAN MARTIN

HUANUCO

DOS DE MAYO

PETATEROS

SAN PABLO

APOLONIA

STA.
APOLONIA

DESAMPARADOS

BELLAVISTA

BELEN

AREQUIPA

JOSÉ SABOGAL

S. SALVADOR

AMAZONAS

GUILLERMO URRELO

ETEN

GUADALUPE

CINCO ESQUINAS

SILVA SANTISTEBAN

SOLEDAD

AYACUCHO

ROMERO

LA ESPERANZA

AMALIA PUGA

TO
CUMBE MAYO

NOT TO SCALE

**CAJAMARCA
CENTRE** 102

TO BAÑOS
DEL INCA

best hotel, food excellent, good local guitarists, musicians welcome. The owners also run *Albergue San Vicente*, outside the town, in an old hacienda. *Hostal Prado*, Calle Lamar, G without bath, rec. Try to get a room in the sun, no heating for the cold nights. *Hotel Amalia Puga*, Amalia Puga 1118, G, no sign on door, friendly.

**Restaurants** *El Sitio*, Jr. Dos de Mayo 311, in *Hostal Cajamarca*, local specialities, friendly, informal, rec., peña in the evening. *Salas*, on Plaza, fast service, not expensive, good local food, best tamales in town; *El Zarco*, Plaza de Armas at Arequipa 170, very highly rec., much frequented by local residents, inexpensive, try the sopa fuchifú, humitas de maíz, also has short chifa menu; *El Real Plaza*, Jr. 2 de Mayo 569, good food, excellent hot chocolate; *La Namorina*, on edge of town on road to Baños del Inca, opposite Ché service station, renowned for its speciality, cuy frito (fried guinea-pig); *La Taverna*, Plaza de Armas, good variety, but food cold as in most places, reasonable prices, *Super Pollo* on Plaza, rec. for its jugo especial (made from algarrobina); *Capri*, Jirón Lima, good ice cream; excellent ice cream shop at Amalia Puga, near Plaza de Armas, try *pecanas* flavour. *Cajamarqueña*, Amazonas 770, very good, not cheap, tables in garden of colonial building; *Petit Café*, Calle Silva Santiesteban 365, nr. Belén church, good, sometimes live music at night, tasty juices, run by German and Peruvian couple. For early breakfasts go to the market.

**Tea Rooms** *Café Florida* on Plaza de Armas.

**Food Specialities** *Queso mantecoso* (full-cream cheese); *manjar blanco* (sweet); *humitas* (ground maize with cheese); *cuy frito*; eucalyptus honey (sold in the market on Calle Amazonas; said to be a cure for rheumatism). Try the flaky pastries filled with apple or *manjar blanco* from the street sellers. The area is renowed for its dairy produce; many shops sell cheese, *manjar blanco,* butter, honey, etc, or go to La Cajamarquiña factory and shop on Amazonas.

**Shopping** Handicrafts are cheap, and good leather items at the prison, but bargain hard. Items can be made to order.

**Exchange** Banco Nor Perú, corner of Lima and Tarapacá, exchanges dollars with commission. Some of the hotels, restaurants and shops, e.g. *Hotel Casa Blanca, Rest. Cajamarqueña,* may help out with travellers' cheques if you're patronizing them. **Street changers** on Arequipa just off Plaza de Armas.

**Addresses** Post Office, Jr. Lima 406; Entel Perú, Jr. San Martín 363; Telephone office for international calls, on Plaza de Armas; Hospital, Av. Mario Urteaga; Guardia Civil, Plaza Amalia Puga.

**Tourist Information** Foptur, Santisteban 144, T 92-2228, helpful good maps (open 0830-1300, 1430-1700). Ask here for car hire.

**Travel Agents** *Cajamarca Tours*, Dos de Mayo 323, guides do not speak English, despite what they claim. A group of local guides have formed *Cumbemayo Tours* (Amalia Puga 669 T 922938, or 2nd floor *Hostal Plaza*), with tours to Ventanillas de Otusco (US$5 p.p.) Cumbe Mayo (US$7.50 p.p.), Kuelap and Gran Vilaya (US$30 p.p. a day, 7 day tour) and *Inca Atahuallpa Tours* (Jr Junín 1288, Aptdo 224, T 922495, or Jr. Amalia Puga 695); they do good economical trips, e.g. to Cumbe Mayo itself (US$5 p.p.), the pottery workshop at Ayllambo, 3½ km. out, and the Palm Sunday celebrations at Porcón. *Aventuras Cajamarca*, enquire at *Hotel Casa Blanca*, trips to Kuelap, Jorge Caballero, rec. Several travel agenices around the Plaza de Armas offer trips to local sites (see below) and further afield (eg Kuelap).

**Air Service** AeroPerú flights to Lima via Trujillo on Tues., Thurs., Sat. mornings. Cheaper to pay for each stage separately. **Warning**: Delays at Cajamarca are all too frequent.

**Buses** Daily buses and colectivos to **Lima** (bus, US$13), **Trujillo** (7-8 hrs., US$9.50 with Empresa Díaz); **Chiclayo** (US$7, 6-7 hrs. by Empresa Díaz, Ayacucho 758 y Amazonas, 1400 and 2100, with El Cumbe, Av. Atahuallpa, near El Che filling station (grifo) about 1½ km. from centre, 0700, 1100 and 1500, with Atahuallpa—best and cheapest—at 1430, Comité de Autos 2, and Chinchay-Suyo). Tepsa leaves for Trujillo and Lima at 1400 and 1700, 17 hrs; Empresa Díaz for Trujillo at 2000, for Chimbote, for Lima at 1800 (1730 from Tourist Hotel, "Presidential service" non-stop) and for **Celendín** at 1200 4½ hrs, US$3.20. No day time

---

**Cajamarca: Key to map**

1. Plaza de Armas; 2. Santa Apollonia hill; 3. Cathedral; 4. Belén church and hospital; 5. San Francisco Convent and Museo de Arte Colonial; 6. San Pedro; 7. La Recoleta; 8. Cuatro del Rescate; 9. Casa Silva Santiesteban; 10. Museum of Education Faculty; 11. Post Office; 12. Foptur, Tourist Office; 13. Central Market; 14. *Hotel de Turistas*; 15. *Hostal Cajamarca*.

buses to Trujillo, only colectivos, ask at tourist office. Empresa Expreso Cajamarca, Amazonas 807, US$3.75, Comité de Autos 12 and 40 also go to Trujillo. Atahuallpa to Lima, 15 hrs., US$13, overnight, rec.; to Celendín daily at 1200, sit on right for best scenery (also to Cajabamba, Chota, Cutervo). Also daily to and from **Cajabamba** (Empresa Díaz, who also go to Bambamarca, or Atahuallpa at 1000), US$3, 6 hrs. (milk trucks will also take passengers to Cajabamba).

**Excursions**  To Ayllambo, 1½ hr. walk, 3½ km., from Av. Independencia, a village which specializes in ceramics. You can visit the *Escuela/Taller* where children learn pottery, open Mon.-Fri. 0730-1200, 1300-1700, Sat. 0730-1230. 6 km. away, easily reached by bus, are the warm sulphurous thermal springs known as Los Baños del Inca, where there are baths of different temperatures ("Take one with the temperature you like—this may not be the one they point you to") clean water early morning (US$0.10, excellent). Atahuallpa tried the effect of these waters on a festering war wound. Nearby can also be seen La Collpa, a *hacienda* which is now a cooperative farm of the Ministry of Agriculture with bulls for breeding and a lake and gardens. At 1400 the campesinos can be seen handmilking the cows, some of which come when called by name. There is a minibus service from the main square, US$0.15.

The surrounding countryside is splendid. Look out for the local building method called Tapial, made of compressed adobe alternating with layers of stones or wood. Other excursions include Llacanora, a typical Andean village in beautiful scenery and Ventanillas de Otusco, part of an old pre-Inca cemetery (minibus from town, US$0.15), with a gallery of secondary burial niches (US$2.20 entry for foreigners, but can be photographed from road with ease). A good walk, 10 km., is from Baños del Inca on Celendín road to Ventanillas de Otusco (start from the bridge and take the path along the left side of the brook), through beautiful countryside. The walk takes little more than an hour. A new road continues to Ventanillas de Combayo, some 20 km. past the burial niches of Otusco; these are more numerous and more spectacular, being located in a rather isolated, mountainous area, and are distributed over the face of a steep 200-metre-high hillside. A one-day round trip can be made, taking a bus from Av. Arequipa to Ventanillas de Otusco (½ hr.) or colectivos leaving hourly from Revilla 170, US$0.15, walk to Baños del Inca (1½ hrs, 6 km.); walk to Llanacora (1 hr., 7 km); then a further hour to La Collpa.

Cumbe Mayo, mountain village, rec. (20 km. SW of Cajamarca but no bus service; it is dangerous to go alone, take a guided tour, prices vary up to US$5; taxi US$15). A milk truck goes daily to Cumbe Mayo leaving at 0400. Ask Sr. Segundo Malca, Jr. Pisagua 482; small charge, dress warmly. On Sunday a minibus goes to Cumbe Mayo at 0600 returning at 1600. Leaves from Calle Revilla 170. An aqueduct can be followed for several km., very remarkable; also, be sure to take a strong torch; alternatively you can walk and ask local passers-by the way. The trail starts from the hill of Santa Apollonia (Silla del Inca), and goes to Cumbe Mayo straight through the village and up the hill; at the top of the mountain, leave the trail and take the road to the right to the canal. The walk takes 3 hours, but is not difficult and you do not need hiking boots. The Indians use the trail to bring their goods to market. On the way to Cumbe Mayo is the Layzón ceremonial centre, the same period as Huacaloma. Other Inca ruins in the area include Tantarica, Torrecitas, and San Pedro de Pacopampa.

North of Cajamarca is Hualgayoc (**see page 984**). Trip with fantastic scenery. There is excellent trout served in restaurant on the way there; easy to find as it is the only place for a long way. Order on your way there to eat on the way back.

South of Cajamarca, through Santa Catalina and Trinidad, are the Inca and pre-Inca ruins of Tantarica, near Cholol.

Cajamarca is the starting point for the northern route to Iquitos. From Cajamarca there are several buses daily to *Celendín* (Empresa Díaz leaves at 1200, 4½-5 hrs., 112 km., US$3.20), where there are several hotels off the main plaza (*Amazonas*, G with toilet, clean, friendly, helpful, rec.; *Hostal Celendín*, F, with bath, check room is clean before booking, good restaurant; *José Galves*, G, basic, dirty toilets, humid rooms, but plenty of character; *Restaurant Jalisco* on Plaza de Armas, simple, not cheap, also *Salazar* and *Buen Amigo*, Calle 2 de Mayo, next to *José Galves*, or eat at market; cinema and cock fighting Sunday night in the local arena). Festival July 16 (Virgen del Carmen). There is also an interesting local market on Sunday where you can buy cheap sandals and saddlebags. The town has electricity from 1800 to 0100. The road follows a winding course through the northern Andes, crossing the wide and deep canyon of the Río Marañón at Balsas after 55 km. (2½ hrs.). The road climbs steeply with superb views of the mountains and the valleys below. The fauna and flora are spectacular as the journey alternates between high in the mountains and low in the rain forest. After rain, landslides can be quite a problem. There are some interesting Inca ruins on the road between Celendín and Leimebamba (146 km.).

Bus to Chachapoyas from Jr. Salaverry 595 (private house) Sun. 1900, 12-14 hrs., US$7 (11 hrs. to Tingo, US$6); on other days you must try your luck to find a truck to Chachapoyas, US$6.40, 14-16 hrs., take food on all journeys, bad roads and uncomfortable buses. Don't take a *buseta* or *camioneta* from Celendín to Chachapoyas. They charge up to US$15 and you'll be "dead on arrival." All transport is difficult in the rainy season. Ask at the police checkpoint what transport is going.

*Leimebamba* is a pleasant town with 2 hotels, the better of which is *Escobedo*, G, friendly owner has lots of local information, toilets, cold shower; 3 restaurants, including *Oasis*, just off Plaza de Armas, and *El Caribe* on the Plaza. Trucks park in main square, leave 0300-0600 for Celendín and Chachapoyas; buses run daily to Celendín; daily bus Leimebamba—Chachapoyas 0500, returning after lunch, also pick-ups in p.m. from Chachapoyas. Of the ruins in the area **La Congona**, a Sachupoyan site, is 2½ hrs. walk away, take the trail at the end of the street with the hotels and climb up (next to police station). The trail levels out and follows round the mountain, then down into a little valley. La Congona, a system of 3 hills can be seen: aim for the right-hand (easterly) conical hill with a visible small cliff. The trail, now a small track, reaches a gate. Go through the gate and continue until the trail divides. Straight ahead goes to a farmer's hut (he can give directions to the ruins), but the correct route is to the right winding up above the hut. Rather than following this path round the side of the hill, leave it when it levels out (after 10-15 mins.) and head straight up the hill to a dense mass of ferns. With a bit of hunting you should find a trail through the ferns. Follow this for 10 mins., which leads to a road. Turn left on the road and continue round, above a field of maize. At the top of this field is another gate beside the road (which has narrowed to a path). Go through the gate and climb straight up the hill to a trail winding over the crest of the hill next to the cliff, above which are the ruins. Once on the trail at the crest of the hill, you have to climb the adjoining, higher hill which rises above the cliff. There is no trail here: head straight up for 15-20 mins. as best you can, some sections are near vertical. At the very top the ruins are clustered in a small area, impossible to see until you are right above them. They are covered in brambles and thick undergrowth, so a machete would be very useful. The views are stupendous and the ruins worth the effort. This is the best preserved of 3 sites, with 30 decorated round stone houses (some with evidence of 3 storeys) and a watch tower. The other hills have been levelled. It is worth following the trail along the crest beyond these hills, and then to the left, down through rain forest (muddy), eventually to join the main trail. (A good day's walk—Haydn Washington, Australia; supplementary information from Monica Napper, Eastbourne.)

The road on to Chachapoyas is poor (dry weather only), but the scenery is magnificent. Food and warm clothing are necessary; usually only chicken and rice is available in the villages. Gasoline may be available in Leimebamba but cannot be relied on. If you want to go through to Iquitos, better to fly.

*Chachapoyas*, population 50,000, altitude 2,400 m., is the capital of the Department of Amazonas and has been called the friendliest town in Peru. If you have any problems contact the Guardia Civil (green uniforms), very friendly and more helpful than P.I.P. (Amazonas), in the town and countryside. Archaeological and anthropological information can be sought from the local anthropologist, Carlos Torres Mas, who is the head of the Instituto Nacional de Cultura, in the 1200 block of Libertad, also advises about walks in the area (will store luggage). Those interested in the abundant archaeological sites in the area should read Gene Savoy's *Antisuyo* (British edition: *Vilcabamba*). There is also a Tourist Office on Calle Amazonas, a few blocks from the Plaza de Armas, the director, Don Segundo Pastor, and Cortés Domínguez Bobadillo are helpful, luggage can be stored here (there is a small but good museum in the same building).

**Hotels** *El Dorado*, Ayacucho 1062, F, hot water, clean, helpful, rec.; *Johumaji*, Jr. Ayacucho 711 (T 138), F, with bath, cheaper without, some rooms have hot water, safe for luggage; *El Danubio*, Junín 572, F, clean, hot water, safe for luggage, rec., son of owner works for P.I.P.; *Casa Blanca*, F; *Hostal Kuelap*, Jr. Chincha Alta 631, G with bath, cheaper without, hot water extra (electric showers); *Continental*, Jr. Ortiz Arreta 441, G. The *Hacienda Santa Isabel* is a beautiful lodge on the outskirts, connected to a chain of lodges throughout the jungle, built by U.S. engineer Charles Motley (those interested in *Los Tambos Chachapoyanos* should contact Sr. Carlos Torres Mas, above). A new tourist hotel is planned at Laguna Pomacocha, 3 hrs. by bus from Chachapoyas.

**Restaurants** *Chacha*, on Plaza de Armas, clean, good for bistec apanado, friendly; *Oh Qué Bueno*, limited menu; good pastries also at *Patisserie*, Jr. 2 de Mayo 558; *Kuelap*, same street as *Johumaji*, good, large portions, friendly, rec.; *Chifa El Turista*, Amazonas 575 near post office, is reasonable, friendly and helpful; *Café Bar Mary*, 2 blocks SE of Plaza de Armas, clean, good, cheap; *Monte Carlo*, opp. market entrance, cheap, friendly; *Mio Mio*, near Post Office, good value chicken restaurant; good fruit juices at stall 67 in the market; *Los Michitos*, Jr. de la Merced 604.

For leatherwork, Zapatería "El Cairo": a pair of boots costs US$27.

**Buses** To **Chiclayo** 3 times per week (Olano, US$15, 1000, 1100, on Sat., none on Sun.) via Bagua and Jaén (18-25 hrs.). Delays of one day or more are possible because of bad road conditions. Trucks more frequent to Bagua (see below). Daily service with Atahuallpa to *Cajamarca*, 19-23 hrs. Several buses a week, 12-14 hrs., US$7, to **Celendín** 230 km. (not for those without a head for heights), trucks run, 16 hrs., US$6.40. You can alight in Tingo, for Kuelap. Some trucks will take passengers to Moyobamba or Bagua, or Tingo in afternoon; remember most trucks do shortish runs and be prepared to change trucks frequently. *Bagua* (no hotels reported) is a good place to reach by truck (US$3.60 from Chachapoyas) as Cruz de Chalpón runs an overnight bus service (US$7.20) from there to Chiclayo. There are two Baguas, Grande and Chica, with about 20 km. between them; each sells half the available bus tickets. Bagua Chica has the better eating places.

**Air Service** A new airport has been built; AeroPerú, office on main square (open 0800-0900, if closed go directly to airport), fly Lima-Chiclayo-Chachapoyas on Mon., US$50 (plane returns immediately to Chiclayo, about 0900), frequent delays and protestations that flight is fully booked (it usually is—very hard to get a seat). *Camioneta* from AeroPerú office to airport 0700 (20 mins.), or truck from Plaza de Armas up to 2 hrs. before flights leave, US$0.25. Also Wed. flights to Rioja and weekly to Selva. Aeronorte fly to Chiclayo Fri. once, perhaps twice a month. Flights are not reliable and are often cancelled.

**Guide** Martín Antonio Oliva, Jr. Amazaonas 557 (or *Bar Chacha*), Chachapoyas, acts as a guide to most of the sites described below.

**Excursions** Huancas, which produces unique pottery, can be reached by a 2-hour walk on the airport road; also Inca and pre-Inca ruins.

Bernard Van Den Dool from Holland recommends a trip 2 hrs. NW of Chachapoyas (by bus on a dangerous road, also colectivos) to Lamud. One cheap hotel on the main plaza. Near Lamud are several ruins: Trita and Pueblos de los Muertos, Luya, the latter with intact tombs built into an impressive cliff face, also known as Solmol or Carajúa. Hard to find, essential to ask for local guide.

40 km. from Chachapoyas are the pre-Inca ruins of *Monte Peruvia* (known locally as Purunllacta), hundreds of white stone houses with staircases, temples and palaces (2 hrs. from Lamud). "8 km. from Monte Peruvia is Puente de Conica, where you can see precolumbian burial figures in niches on the cliffside, known as the Purumachus de Aispachaca" (John Streather).

The road is now open via Chachapoyas to *Mendoza*, a hair-raising five-hour journey from Chachapoyas by *camioneta*, daily at 1000, US$1.20 (return 0200, sometimes 0700). Mendoza is the starting point for an ethnologically interesting area in the Guayabamba Valley where there is a high incidence of very fair people. Some maintain that these people are descendants of Vikings who reached South America (Kaufmann Doig, Dr Jacques de Mahieu of Buenos Aires), others that they are a local group (called by Morgan Davis the Cloud People), while they themselves say they are descended from Conquistadores (which is unlikely since the Spanish chronicler Garcilaso de la Vega describes them resisting the Incas before the conquest). The region is in the *selva*, very remote, and can be reached on foot from Mendoza or Limabamba (2 hrs. by *camioneta* from Mendoza), but a road is under construction. Seek all advice locally (we are grateful to Helmut Zettl of Ebergassing, Austria, for this information). Helmut Zettl mentions another white-skinned tribe in Chirimoto, a very basic settlement near Leimebamba. Ask for Padre Juan Castelli, an Englishman living there for 40 years. No transport available, 2 hrs. hard walk through jungle.

"Two hours by truck on the road to Mendoza is Molinopampa, which marks the starting point of an adventurous five-day hike to Rioja. Only experienced hikers should attempt this journey, which is very difficult. Food supplies for the whole journey should be purchased at Chachapoyas and a guide, absolutely essential, hired at Molinopampa. The steep trail leads through waist-high unbridged rivers, over the cold, high Sierra and then for three days one follows the muddy trail down to the dense and humid jungle. We were accompanied by exotic butterflies, and never a quiet moment with the chattering of birds and monkeys. The whole magic of the jungle—trees, birds, animals and insects—can be seen untouched in their natural surroundings." (Katrina Farrar and Andy Thornton).

*Tingo* (1,800 metres), 37 km. from Chachapoyas, is reached by driving S up the Utcubamba valley from Chachapoyas; several pick-ups, at 0630-0700 from Chachapoyas, but be in Tingo by 1500 to ensure you get one to Chachapoyas, US$1.20, 1½ hrs. in dry, up to 3½ hrs in wet (trucks infrequent from Celendín US$6.40—leave at 0300, 12 hrs., driver collects you from hotel); buses Tingo—Leimebamba and Cachapoyas daily (from Leimebamba in a.m., returning p.m.). There is a new *hostal* over the bridge on left as you enter from Celendín, with water, clean, basic bathrooms, good meals and a cheap *pensión*, at the entrance to the village painted blue and white, F, mouldy, good restaurant; *Restaurant Viajero* on main road has rooms, G, good breakfast, clean, reasonable prices, and can arrange horses, to go to Kuelap; *Hotalito Tingo*, G, friendly, basic, rec.; no electricity in Tingo. Sunday market. If you have luggage, best to leave it in one of two cafés (reliable).

A 3-4 hr. steep walk uphill (take waterproof, food and drink, and start early a.m.), leads to **Kuelap** (3,000 metres), a spectacular pre-Inca walled city. Its massive stone walls are as formidable as those of any precolumbian city. Some reconstruction has taken place, mostly of small houses and walls, but the majority of the main walls on both levels are original, as is the cone-shaped dungeon. There are a number of defensive walls and passageways, many houses, but virtually no carvings of any type. An interesting feature is that all the buildings are circular. Entrance fee is US$3 (the ruins are locked; the proprietor, Gabriel Portachero, has the keys and accompanies visitors, he's very informative and friendly). Kuelap is very remote: you are advised not to try to visit the site from the coast unless you have a week to spare: the roads are bad and the public transport spasmodic. The new road from Tingo to Kuelap is very circuitous (1½ hrs. by car from Tingo). A truck may be hired in Chachapoyas for the day; also donkeys can be hired for US$1 per day. If walking from Tingo, follow the path upstream on the right-hand side of the river and take the path to the right before the bridge, after ½ an hour there is a sign to Kuelap, the track is steep. In the rainy season it is advisable to wear boots; at other times it is hot and dry. After 2 hours the track passes a stream; purify this water if you need to drink it. After another hour you reach a cluster of houses. Red arrows mark the path. Soon the walls of Kuelap become visible at the top of the hill. The last house to the right of the track offers accommodation (bed US$0.20, good meals, friendly, helpful); a bit further on the left is an area of flat land outside the Project Kuelap office. At the archaeologists' research station you can hire cot and bedding for US$1 a night and leave luggage safely. There is also a camping area.

The whole area is full of largely unexplored remains; some of them have been studied by the Swiss archaeologists Henri and Paula Reichlen (who surveyed 39 sites in 1948—see *Récherches archaeologiques dans les Andes du haut Utcubamba*, in *Journal des Américanistes*, which includes an accurate map), and the American archaeologist Gene Savoy (who went further than the Reichlens-see his book *Antisuyo*); Kaufmann Doig refers to them as the "12 Cities of the Condors"; his map showing their location is in his *Arqueología Peruana*. See also the booklet on Kuelap, available at the Tourist Office in Chachapoyas, very informative.

Mark Babington and Morgan Davis write: Kuelap, discovered in 1843, was the last outpost of a lost white race, known variously as the Sachupoyans or the Chachas, who were in retreat from the advancing Inca around the years 1450-1470. Up till now Kuelap and La Congona were the only Sachupoyan ruins to have been explored in any detail whatsoever. The fact is that Kuelap was the final refuge of the Sachupoyans in a region which must have supported at least one million people before the arrival of the Inca. The known area inhabited by the Sachupoyans extends north from Leimebamba to Chachapoyas, and west as far as the Marañón.

"In 1977 a team of three Americans explored the area between the Marañón and Utcubamba Rivers; they were the first to do so. They left an account of their journey in the

American magazine *Outside*. Inspired by their account the two of us decided to retrace their steps. This is surely a region which overwhelms even Machu-Picchu in grandeur and mystery. It contains no less than five lost, and uncharted cities; the most impressive of which is Pueblo Alto, near the village of Pueblo Nuevo (25 km. from Kuelap). It was discovered some 60 years ago by the father of a local farmer, Juan Tuesta, with whom we stayed. By far the majority of these cities, fortresses and villages were never discovered by the Spaniard; in fact many had already returned to the jungle by the time the Spaniard arrived in 1532. The sites are situated in the tropical rain forest, and on the upper slopes of the *puna*. Furthermore many of them are to be found on or near the trails which today still provide the only medium of transport in this heavily populated and agricultural region. On a recent map of the area, with which we were provided in Chachapoyas, no less than 38 sites can be counted; but Ojilcho and Pueblo Alto, for example, are not charted on this new 1977 map in spite of their enormous dimensions. If all this sounds a bit exaggerated and inaccessible, we must add that the local farmers are conversant with the ruins, whether charted or not. It is among these people that one must look for information, provision and hospitality and, most important of all, guides and mules. The area, though well populated, provides virtually no facilities for the traveller. One should be cognizant of the difficulties ahead before attempting this journey, though this is not to say the trip is beyond the ability of most. Hiking gear is essential: sleeping bags, tents and canned goods (and a machete—Ed.). Small gifts are also much appreciated by the local people in return for their hospitality. (Take money in small notes as villagers do not have change for larger.) Water is no problem, unless it is the rainy season (Feb.-May). Travelling at this time is not advised as the mountain passes are shin-deep in mud.

Oscar Arce Cáceres based at "El Chillo" 4½ km. outside Tingo, who owns a farm and knows the area very well, will help the traveller. The trek into this area, like the walk up to Kuelap, starts from Tingo; the way is all mule track. In Magdalena (a 15-minute walk from Tingo), Abram Torres will be happy to provide one with his services as guide, and his mule, for the first leg of the journey as far as Choctamal, about 4 hours away.

**Levanto** is 2 hrs by new road (*camioneta* at 0600-0700, no scheduled return) or 6 hrs. walk from Chachapoyas by the road, or 3½ hrs by mule track, ask in Chachapoyas market if anyone returning to Levanto will guide you for a small fee (it is also possible to walk from Tingo—see below). Levanto was the first Spanish capital of the area and the Spaniards built directly on top of the previous Sachupoyan structures. Although, not many years later, the capital was moved to Chachapoyas, Levanto still retained its importance, at least for a while, as it had been one of the seven great cities of the Sachupoyans as described by Cieza de León and Garcilaso de la Vega. The Kuelap East-West Highway starts at Levanto and links with the Inca military highway at Jalca Grande. Nowadays Levanto is a small, unspoilt, and very beautiful colonial village set on flat ground overlooking the massive canyon of the Utcubamba river. Kuelap can, on a clear day, be seen on the other side of the rift. Levanto is a good centre for exploring the many ruins around, being the centre of a network of ancient ruins, fortified redoubts, residential areas and many others.

Very close to Levanto are the ruins of **Yalape**, recently cleared under the supervision of Sr César Torres Rojas, a resident of Levanto. Yalape seems to have been a massive residential complex extending over many hectares and including many well-preserved examples of typical Sachupoyan architecture and masonry with quite elaborate and beautiful friezes. Its scale, like that of Kuelap, can be only described as titanic. In fact the whole area is covered in ruins, almost every prominent hilltop in the immediate vicinity has at least a watchtower of some sort.

To walk from Tingo to Levanto, head up to Magdalena, then down to the bridge at Cundechaca (½ hr); walk for 1 hr. on the main road to Teya until the end of the valley and the bend in the road from E to S; here look for the path which leads down into a small gorge, crosses the river and passes the little farm which is visible from the main road. From there it's a steep, 3-hr walk on the well-defined Inca road on a ridge between two gorges into Levanto. (You can add 2½ hrs to this walk by starting at Kuelap—possible in a day.) As yet there is no official accommodation as such in Levanto, although plans are being made to build a small *alojamiento*. However, small groups of travellers are very welcome and beds and bedding are provided in the mayor's office and village meeting hall. Sr Torres Mas, in Chachapoyas, will put the traveller in touch with César Torres Rojas, in Levanto, with regard to all the above. César is entertaining and very friendly, as well as being the official guardian and archaeological supervisor of Levanto. There is one small shop and bar in the village (selling coffee and Pepsi, but little food). Using Levanto as a staging point, many beautiful and interesting walks can be done in the area. Taxi from Cachapoyas to Levanto and back, including driver waiting while you look around, US$25.

About 65 km. SW of Chachapoyas, the largest ruined complex yet discovered in South America, **Gran Vilaya**, was found in 1985 by Gene Savoy. There are 80 inter-connected city-type layouts, comprising some 24,000 structures. It faces the Río Marañón at 2,850 metres.

Another Sachupoyan site is **Cerro Olán**, reached by colectivo to San Pedro (near Tingo), then a ½-hr. walk; here are the remains of towers which some archaeologists claim had roofs like mediaeval European castles.

From Chachapoyas the next stretch of the road is 2-3 hrs. through more of the beautiful river canyon (pick-up truck leaves about 0830, or when full) to a small crossroads, **Pedro Ruiz**, where you continue on to Yurimaguas or return to the coast. Plenty of trucks in Pedro Ruiz go to the Selva and to Chiclayo (via Bagua not Celendín). There is basic accommodation (*Hostal Marginal* with good, cheap restaurant, and one other, both F), but advisable to stay the night if you arrive late as most trucks to Rioja leave at 0500-0700. Pedro Ruiz to Rioja is about 14 hrs., US$8, on an appalling piece of road; in the rainy season, this and the continuation to Moyobamba and Tarapoto can be very bad.

An hour before Rioja on this road is the new town of Nueva Catamarca (a few thousand inhabitants, *Hotels Puerto Rico*, on main road, and *Perú*, off to the right towards Rioja). There is a large market for local produce. Hourly colectivo to Rioja, US$1, 45 mins; colectivo to Chachapoyas US$12, 11-12 hrs.

From **Rioja** (an attractive, friendly town, 3 hotels, *Hostal San Martín*, Gran 540, *San Ramón*, Jr. Faustino Maldonado 840 and *Carranza*, Jr. Huallanga, all basic, and *Restaurante Los Olivos* rec.) there is a road to Naranjillo and Aguas Verdes, with a 5-hr. walk to Venceremos, a pleasant way to see the jungle in good weather (don't attempt otherwise). An excursion can made to the Cueva de los Huácharos, unexplored caves, take a torch; by truck to La Unión (45 mins.), walk 40 mins. to Palestina then 50 mins. more to the caves, ask locals for directions.

A road with plenty of transport (about ½ hr.) runs to **Moyobamba**, capital of San Martín district (ruins of Pueblo de los Muertos nearby) (915 metres, 14,000 people). Tourists must register with the P.I.P; tourist office on plaza. Moyobamba is a pleasant town, in an attractive valley. It was hit by an eathquake in April 1991. Mosquito nets can be bought cheaply.

**Hotels** *Turistas*, D with breakfast, 1 km. from centre, fine situation, pool, good restaurant; *Hostal Inca*, E with bath, new, clean, good but noisy; *Hostal Cobos*, F with bath, good; *Hostal Country Club*, F, clean, comfortable, friendly, nice garden, rec.; *Hostal Los Andes*, F, clean; *Monterrey* and *Mesía*, both basic and cheap. **Restaurants** *El Sol del Norte*, good and cheap; several others.

**Exchange** Viajes Turismo Río Mayo, Jr. San Martin 401.

**Flights** AeroPerú flights from Lima to Chiclayo stop at Rioja (Wed. and Sun.).

**Excursions** Puerto Tahuiso is the town's harbour, where locals sell their produce at weekends. From Morro de Calzada, there is a good view of the area; truck to Calzada, 30 mins., then walk up, 20 mins. Baños Termales (4 km. from Moyobamba on Rioja road), worth a visit. The more adventurous can hike to the Jera waterfalls in the jungle near Moyobamba. Take a truck in the direction of Tarapoto; alight at the restaurant at Km. 218. Take a good path through a well-populated valley (cross 2 bridges), then along the river, through dense jungle, with 3 more river crossings (no bridges—dangerous). A local guide is necessary to find the falls. Information is available from the Instituto Nacional de Cultura, Jr. Benavides, 3rd block. Guides: Emigdio Soto, an expert on trips to native communities in the Alto Mayo area, contact him at the Projecto Especial Alto Mayo; Orlando Peigot Daza, for jungle trips (no English), at Yurayacu village. There have been guerrilla and drug activities in this region; take good care.

The road is paved for a short way out of Moyobamba, then deteriorates to

*Tarapoto* (colectivo from Moyobamba, 3½ hrs., US$9, truck, 5 hrs., US$6), is a busy town with several hotels. Good local market 1½ blocks from Plaza de Armas on Av. Raimondi. The journey from Rioja to Tarapoto costs about US$6.80 and it is best to carry food because of endless delays and road problems. A through bus service (Chinchaysuyo) runs to Chiclayo, via Moyobamba, Rioja, Bagua and Olmos; and same company runs to Trujillo, US$16, at least 36 hrs. Rioja, Moyobamba and Tarapoto are growing centres of population, with much small-scale forest clearance beside the road after Balsapata. The road is heavily used by trucks, with fuel and meals available. When/if the road is improved, the area will surely boom. Until then, food and accommodation will remain expensive.

**Hotels**  *Turistas* (D, with bath, excellent meals US$3.50) 1 km. out of town, non-residents can use the swimming pool for US$1; *Tarapoto*, E with fan, clean; *Las Palmeras*, just off Plaza, F; *San José*, 4 blocks from Plaza, clean and friendly, restaurant; *Juan Alfonso*, F, with shower, noisy, Jr. Pedro de Urzúa. *Hostal Residencial Grau*, Plaza de Armas, G, communal, cheap (in both senses of the word), shower. *Edinson*, Av. Raimondi, 1 block from Plaza de Armas, E with bath (less without), cold water, clean and comfortable; *Hostal Americano*, F, fan and private bath with each room. *El Sereno*, E with shower, clean. Plenty of others.

**Restaurants**  *Río de Janeiro*, *Sadel*, *Tiveli*, *Chalet Venecia*, *La Pascana* and *Achín* good; *Heladería Tip Top* and *Cream Rica* for ices. *Las Terrazas*, good, rec. Many others. Coconut water is recommended as coconuts abundant. Jirón Gregorio Delgado 268 sells excellent liquor at US$0.50 a glass (uvachado and siete raíces).

**Exchange**  Banco de Crédito, Maynas 134, efficient, no commission on travellers' cheques.

**Tourist Office**  Foptur, Gregorio Delgado 240, T 2753.

**Air Transport**  US$1.75 per taxi airport to town (no bus service, but no problem to walk). Flights by Faucett and AeroPerú to Lima (50 mins.), Iquitos, Juanjui and Yurimaguas, but book in advance, particularly in rainy season. Those visiting Tarapoto and Iquitos would be advised to visit Tarapoto first, as aircraft leaving Iquitos tend to overfly Tarapoto; possible to be stuck there for days. AeroPerú flies to Tarapoto from Lima, Iquitos, Chiclayo, Trujillo, Juanjui and Yurimaguas. Faucett has similar routes, and daily flights to and from Trujillo and Chiclayo. Many smaller airlines operate flights to Yurimaguas e.g. Aerotaxi Ibérico: turn up at airport at 0700-0800, wait for it to open, wait for people to turn up, wait for a list for your destination to be drawn up and you should get away later in the morning, 50 min. flight.
   **Excursions**  La Mina de Sal, salt mine outside the city; Laguna Sauce, 3 hrs. by truck; Laguna Venecia.

Between Tarapoto and Moyobamba a road leads off to *Lamas* (colectivo from Tarapoto, US$1.45, 35 km.), where there is a picturesque Indian community completely unspoilt by tourism; also a small museum, with exhibits on local Indian community (Lamistas), ask at the café opposite if museum shut, and a new restaurant en route, *El Mirador*, recently opened by Tom, an American, and his Peruvian wife. Market in the early morning. Interesting journey also from Tarapoto to Tingo María (see page 1059), not advisable in the rainy season. From Tarapoto to Yurimaguas (136 km.—see page 1060), the road can be very bad in the wet season, taking at least 13 hrs. for trucks (at 0800 or earlier, US$9), also colectivos, US$12. There is also a daily bus (10 hrs.). Truck/pick-up leaves for Yurimaguas (usually 0800-0900, and in p.m.) from Jorge Chávez 175, down Av. Raimondi 2 blocks, then left 5 blocks along Av. Pedro de Uruaz (pick-ups from this street to other destinations). About 14 km. from Tarapoto on this road are the 50-metre falls of Ahuashiyacu, which can be visited by tour from Tarapoto (US$18 incl. lunch) or by hiring motorcycle from Grand Prix, corner Shopajo and Raimondi, US$3.50 an hour. A restaurant nearby serves reasonable food and has 2 rooms to rent (G p.p., basic but OK). The road continues for 10 km. through lush vegetation to a small village (with restaurant). Once the plains are reached, the road improves and there is more habitation. 55 km. from Tarapoto is the village of El Pongo (2 restaurants, electricity, no hotel). At km. 40, 96 km. from Tarapoto (US$7.25, 7 hrs.) there is a bridge over the Shanusi river and the small village of Shanusi. It is possible to leave your truck here and take a boat ride down the river, meeting the Huallaga at Yurimaguas. There is no accommodation at Shanusi, take a hammock, and no electricity. Canoe leaves daily at about 0600 for Yurimaguas, US$2.20, 4½ hrs., plenty of birdlife and river traffic to be seen. From Yurimaguas on the Huallaga River, launches ply to Iquitos.

## Pacific Coast North of Trujillo

When Spanish conquistadores first encountered the broad, north Peruvian coastal valley oases, they marvelled at the creativity and sophistication of these desert farmers and fishermen. Early 16th century accounts describe enormous precolumbian settlements and sacred places, now impressive monumental ruins.

Today the rural population has its centre at Chiclayo, the bustling city and capital of the department of Lambayeque, a melting pot of ancient and modern traditions and tastes. Recent archaeological discoveries nearby have attracted tourists and scientists to northern Peru.

Ruins of a splendid past are not the only treasures Lambayeque offers. Today's rural peasantry are also inheritors of many of the customs and technologies of their Moche forebears, who were master craftsmen in many fields. Artisan markets, primitive ocean going vessels, folk curing sessions and colourful religious "fiestas" enliven any visitor's stay. In addition, the north sports Peru's finest beaches for bathing and surfing, blessed with a balmy, rainfree climate the year round.

Sandwiched between the Pacific Ocean and the Andes, Lambayeque is one of Peru's principal agricultural areas, and its chief producer of rice and sugar cane. Even so, archaeological studies indicate that prehispanic people here cultivated some 25% more land than farmers today. The extensive irrigation canals and reservoirs of north Peru constitute one of the major technological achievements of ancient America. Disused aqueducts and ridged fields can easily be explored.

N from Trujillo are three ports serving the Chiclayo area. The more southerly is **Puerto Etén**, a quaint port 24 km. by road from Chiclayo; in the adjacent roadstead, Villa de Etén; Panama hats are local industry; festival of the Divine Child of the Miracle, 2-17 June. **Pimentel**, N of Etén, is larger, a favourite summer bathing place, with a broad sandy beach (very crowded on Sundays). The surfing between Pimentel and the Bayovar Peninsula is excellent, reached from Chiclayo (14½ km.) by road branching off from the Pan-American Highway. Sea-going reed boats (*caballitos de totora*) are used by fishermen and may be seen here and at nearby **Santa Rosa**, whose fishermen use two groups of totora reed boats (*caballitos*) and *bolicheros* (pastel-painted boats which line the shore after the day's fishing)—a pleasant, 1-hr walk from Pimentel. Small hotel, *Perú*, restaurant *Bello Horizonte*. The seafood is superb: two specialities are *tortilla de rayo* (manta ray) and *chingurito*, a ceviche of little strips of dried guitar fish (chewy, but good). The 3 ports may be visited on a pleasant ½ day trip. A blue bus leaves Chiclayo market place every ½ hr. for Pimentel and Santa Rosa. Colectivos run frequently from Pimentel to Santa Rosa, and on to Etén and back to Chiclayo (10 mins. from Santa Rosa, 15 mins. from Pimentel). To avoid paying excess luggage charges for weight above 15 kg, buy ticket in advance, and catch bus outside terminal (no scales!).

**Chiclayo** was founded in the 1560s as a rural Indian village by Spanish priests. It now has a population of over 260,000 and has long since outgrown other towns of the Lambayeque Department, of which it is the capital. A major commercial hub, Chiclayo also boasts distinctive cuisine and musical tradition (*Marinera*, *Tondero* and afro-indian rhythms), and an unparalleled archaeological and ethnographic heritage (see **Excursions**). A walking tour in the centre reveals the mixture of creole, Spanish and Indian architecture along curving, narrow streets, once precolumbian canals now filled and paved with cobble stones.

On the Plaza de Armas is the 19th century neoclassical cathedral, designed by the English architect Andrew Townsend, whose descendants can still be identified among the town's principals. The Palacio Municipal (Municipal Palace) and private Club Unión line Calle Balta, the major avenue. Continue five blocks north on Balta to the Mercado Modelo, one of northern Peru's liveliest and largest

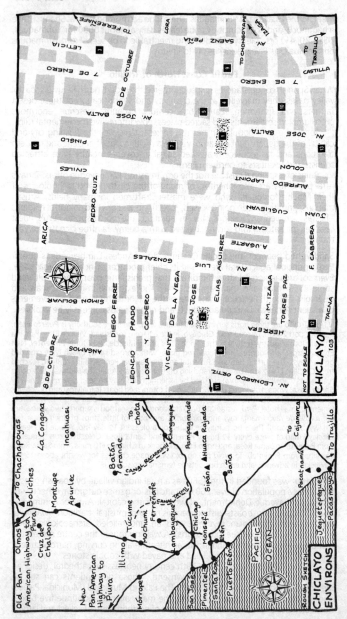

CHICLAYO
103

CHICLAYO ENVIRONS
ROUGH SKETCH

daily markets. Don't miss the colourful fruits (including enormous 2lb/900 gram avocados), handicrafts stalls (see "*Monsefú*") and the well-organized section (off Calle Arica) of ritual paraphernalia used by traditional curers and diviners (*curanderos*). James Vreeland, an American anthropologist living in Chiclayo, considers the Chiclayo *mercado de brujos* (witch doctors' market) to be one of the most comprehensive in South America, filled with herbal medicines, folk charms, curing potions, and exotic objects used by *curanderos* and *brujos* to cure all manner of real and imagined illnesses. (Note: As in all markets, don't let your enthusiasm cloud your common sense; take good care of your belongings.)

**Hotels** *Turistas*, Villareal 115, T 234911, D, with bath, E, without, meals included, helpful, but service can be wanting, some distance from business centre, but there is much traffic noise, swimming pool, safe car park; *Garza*, Bolognesi 756, nr. Balta, T 228172, with bath, hot water, takes credit cards, convenient, excellent bar and restaurant, *El Cazador*, highly rec, swimming pool, car park, tourist office in lobby provides maps, information in English, Land Rovers, jeeps and minibuses for hire; *Sipán*, Virgilio Dall'Orso 150, T 242408, with bath, hot water, takes credit cards, good restaurant downstairs; *Obby*, Francisco Cabrera 102, T 231074, Fax 51-074-229282, E-D, good value, English spoken, rec; *Costa de Oro*, Balta 399, E, central, poor, but good restaurant *Ebony* downstairs; *Inca*, L. González 622, T 233814/237652, E with bath, clean and good, safe parking; *Paraíso*, Pedro Ruiz 1064, T 228161, near market, good value, E; *Oriental*, Arica 825, T 226308, nr. market, good Chinese-style food downstairs; *Sol Radiante*, Izaga 392, T 237858, central, small, comfortable, no restaurant, but friendly owner will provide breakfast; *Royal*, San José 787, T 233421, F, cheaper without bath, old, clean, poor beds, smelly toilets, basic, restaurant downstairs is good value; *Miami Beach*, Tte. Pinglo 169, T 227116, popular, but fading; *Hostal San Ramón*, Héroes Civiles 169, T 233931, F, friendly, clean, comfortable, restaurant, car park, possible to get motorcycle in entrance; *Europa*, Elías Aguirre 466, T 235672, F with or without bath, good value, clean, friendly, restaurant, some hot water; *Lido*, on same street, F with bath, clean. Several cheap hotels on Calle Balta, near bus offices. Some hotels prohibit clothes-washing in rooms because of the high cost of water.

**Restaurants** *Fiesta*, Av. Salaverry 1820 in Ocho de Octubre suburb, T 228441, local specialities, first class, very expensive; *Le París*, M.M. Izaga 716, T 235485, excellent, international and creole food, not cheap. First-class and very reasonable food (usually good breakfast) at *Roma*, Balta 512, T 238601, popular with locals; *Bristol* on Balta, good and cheap, with a *comedor municipal* next door to *Ebony*, also *El Tauro*, reasonable prices, and *Cruz de Chalpón* (good breakfasts) on same street; *Imperial*, and others on Balta, choose according to outward cleanliness; *Che Claudio*, Bolognesi 334, T 237426, parrillada with reasonable empanadas and house wine; *Snack Bar Elías*, Aguirre 830, just off Central Plaza, small, efficient, quite clean, good apple pie, lomo sandwiches and sweets at reasonable prices; *Chifa Cantonés*, Juan Cuglievan 470, wide variety of traditional chifa/Chinese food, dining room on 2nd floor; *Fuente de Oro*, Cabrera 1213, and *Las Tinajas*, Elías Aguirre 957, excellent seafood at reasonable prices: *Men-Wha*, Pedro Ruiz 1059, delicious, large helpings, Chinese.

**Local Food and Drink** Ceviche and *chingurito* (see above); *cabrito*, spiced stew of kid goat; arroz con pato, paella-like duck casserole; humitas, tamale-like fritters of green corn; *King Kong*, baked pastry layered with candied fruit and milk caramel; *chicha*, fermented maize drink with delicious fruit variations.

**Folklore** *Los Hermanos Balcázar*, Lora y Cordero 1150, T 227922; *El Embrujo*, Vicente de la Vega, T 233984.

**Exchange** Change travellers' cheques at **Banco del Norte Continorte** and **Banco de Crédito**. Be prepared to wait. The **travel agency** next to *Hotel Royal* will change cash or cheques at reasonable rates out of banking hours. Beware of counterfeit bills, especially among street changers on 6th block of Balta and on Plaza de Armas.

**Post Office** on Aguirre, 6 blocks from Plaza.

**Doctor** Juan Aita, Clínica Chiclayo, Av. Santa Victoria, T 239024, rec. as good general medical practitioner, José Gálvez Jaime, eye specialist, English spoken, Elías Aguirre 811, T 238234.

---

**Chiclayo and environs: Key to map**
1. Plaza de Armas; 2. Plaza Elías Aguirre; 3. Parque Obrero; 4. Cathedral; 5. Palacio Municipal; 6. Mercado Modelo; 7. Mercado Central; 8. Post Office; 9. Entel; 10. Indiana Tours; 11. *Hotel Turistas* (off map); 12. *Hotel Obby*; 13. *Hotel Costa de Oro*; 14. *Hotel Inca*.

**Tourist Office** Foptur, San José 867, oficina 201, helpful. Touring y Automóvil Club de Perú, Huancavelica 280, of. 406.

**Travel Agent** *Indiana Tours*, M.M. Izaga 774, T 51-74-242287, Fax 51-74-240833, highly rec. for trips to Sipán, Thor Heyerdahl's Kon Tiki museum in Túcume, Brüning Museum in Lambayeque and a variety of other daily and extended excursions with 4WD vehicles; very knowledgeable about the archaeology and ethnology of the region.

**Air Service** José Abelado Quiñones Gonzáles airport 1 km. from town. Daily Faucett (pm), office, Balta 600, T 237312; and Aeroperú (pm), office, Elías Aguirre 380, T 237151; jet flights from Lima, US$126 round trip ticket; flights to Rioja (Faucett, Tues. and Sun.), 1100; Aeroperú, Wed., 1145 (40 min.), Tarapoto (Faucett, Mon. and Tues., 1100; Aeroperú, Tues. and Sat., 1455 (40 min.).

**Buses and Colectivos** To Lima, Chiclayo Express, Mcal. Nieto 199, T 223071, or Nor Pacífico, Balta 809, T 231671, 2100, US$15 (most companies leave from 1600 onwards). To Trujillo, Empresa Emtrafesa on Av. Balta 110, T 234291, 6 blocks from plaza, leaves hourly from 0530 until 1430, then 6 between 1500 and 2000, US$5, 3 hrs. Bus to Piura, US$5, 3½ hrs., about 20 a day. *Micros* to Lambayeque leave from 200 block of San José, US$0.50, frequent. Direct bus to Cajamarca, Empresa Díaz, 1200 (old buses, frequent breakdowns) and El Cumbe, Av. Quiñones (much better), US$7, several daily. To Chachapoyas, D. Olano company (Vicente de la Vega 101, T 236310), US$15, 1300, except Sun., 18-25 hrs. depending on breakdowns; goes via Olmos and Jaén (see below), thereafter road is appalling to Pedro Ruiz, then O.K. to Chachapoyas. To Tarapoto, Chinchay-Suyo runs via Olmos, Bagua, Rioja (US$15) and Moyobamba. Bus to Huancabamba leaves Tues. and Fri., 1500, arrives 0530 next day, US$10 (Civa and Tepsa office, Balta 114b)—very rough ride, impossible to sleep. Tepsa to Tumbes, 0100 daily, US$10, 9½ hrs.; also Continental (Ormeño), Roggero (1930), Olano (rec.), and others (Nor Pacífico not rec.), all night buses US$7, 12 hrs., some continue to Aguas Verdes, on the border. To Sullana, Expreso Sudamericano, Pedro Ruiz 960, 0630, US$2.50 or Empresa Chiclayo, Leonardo Ortiz 10, 0730 and 1530, US$2.50. Trucks going in all directions leave from Calle Pedro Ruiz 948 and from the market.

**Local Festivals** Some of the towns mentioned here are described in **Excursions** below: 6 January, Reyes Magos in Mórrope, Illimo and other towns, a recreation of a medieval pageant in which precolumbian deities become the Wise Men; 4 February, Túcume devil dances; Holy Week, traditional Easter celebrations and processions in many villages; 27-31 July, Fexticum in Monsefú, traditional foods, drink, handicrafts, music and dance; 5 August, pilgrimage from the mountain shrine of Chalpón to Motupe, 90 km. N of Chiclayo, the cross is brought down from a cave and carried in procession through the village; 24 September, Virgen de los Mercedes in Incahuasi, 12 hrs. by truck E of Chiclayo (Indians still sing in the ancient Mochica language in this post-harvest festival); Christmas and New Year, processions and children dancers (*pastorcitos* and *seranitas*) in many villages, e.g. Ferreñafe, Mochumi, Mórrope.

**Excursions** A short distance from Chiclayo rises the imposing twin pyramid complex of **Sipán**, where excavations have brought to light a cache of funerary objects considered to rank among the finest examples of precolumbian art. Peruvian archaeologist Walter Alva, leader of the dig, continues to probe the immense mound that has revealed no less than five royal tombs filled with 2,000-year-old offerings worked in precious metals, stone, pottery and textiles of the Moche culture. In the most extravagant Moche tomb discovered, El Señor de Sipán, a priest was found clad in gold (ear ornaments, breast plate, etc.), with turquoise and other valuables. The find is currently being studied in West Germany and is due back at the Brüning Museum in Lambayeque in 1992. In another tomb were found a priest, sacrificed, llama and a dog, together with copper decorations. The excavations till 1990 were being sponsored by the National Geographic Magazine. You can wander around the previously excavated areas to get an idea of the construction of the pyramids. For a good view, climb the large pyramid across from the Sipán excavation. Nearby is the Pampagrande site (25 km. from Sipán), a Mochica city C.450 AD. To Sipán, colectivos leave from 7 de Enero 1552, US$0.25.

The colonial town of Ferreñafe, NE of Chiclayo, is worth a visit, as are the traditional Indian towns of Mórrope, on the Pan-American Highway N of Chiclayo, where pottery and textiles are made, Monsefú, SW, also for handicrafts, and Etén (see above). 51 km. S are the ruins of the town of Saña, destroyed by floods in 1726; 5 colonial churches can be seen.

A minor road runs to **Chongoyape** (bus from Chiclayo, US$1, 1½ hrs., leaves from Leticia 3rd block, just off Balta on N. of Plaza de Armas; hotel, F, near Plaza de Armas, without restaurant; *Restaurant Cascada*, main street, limited menu), a quaint old town 60 km. to the E (3 km. west are the Chavín petroglyphs of Cerro Mulato). Nearby are the vast Taymi precolumbian and modern irrigation systems. Also near Chongoyape are the aqueduct of Racarrumi, the hill fort of Mal Paso and the ruins of Maguín. **Batán Grande**, a site 50 km. from Chiclayo consisting of nearly fifty adobe pyramids where many precolumbian gold artefacts, notably the 915-gram Tumi, were found, is reached by a branch turning left off the Chongoyape road after Tumán, about 30 km. from Chiclayo (colectivos, US$1.20, from Pedro Ruiz—12th block—and Juan Cuglievan, go first to the museum in Lambayeque and get an "order" from the director, Dr Walter Alva, before visiting, then to the sugar cane cooperative (in which the ruins are set) from where you must get permission to visit the site, Mon.-Fri. only; directions hard to come by at the cooperative, seek sound advice before you go). The road goes to **Chota**, an attractive town with a fine Sunday market (several hotels, F, *Plaza* the best, clean; *Continental*, poor; *Hostal Elisabeth*, on plaza, cheap rooms with balcony, dirty bathrooms. *Restaurant San Juan*, good) where weavings are cheaper than in Cajamarca: cheap, friendly shops at 27 de Noviembre 144 and 246. Daily bus to Chiclayo a.m., 12-14 hrs.; bus to Cajamarca Wed., Fri., 9-10 hrs., return Tues. and Thurs. Occasionally buses, and many trucks, run on to **Bambamarca** (*Hotel Bolívar*, best; *Hotel Velásquez*, G, *Hotel Perú* has bugs; *Restaurant Pollos a la Brasa*, very good) which has an attractive Sunday morning market (truck from Chota US$1; Empresa Díaz to Cajamarca daily at 0600, 9 hrs., frequent stops, US$4, on Sun, there is a 2 hr. stop in Bambamarca for the market, some days also with Peregrino). Two buses a day pass through Chongoyape to Chota, 8 hrs., US$5. From there it goes on to **Hualgayoc** (a beautifully situated, quaint old mining town) and Cajamarca; a very interesting and beautiful journey, but few buses. The stretch from Bambamarca, about 90 km., to Cajamarca is exhilarating; the road climbs to about 4,000 metres through the Andean highlands with beautiful scenery of a *puna* landscape, nearly uninhabited, no fuel supply; it takes about 6 hrs. in a 4-wheel drive car. The whole trip between Chongoyape and Cajamarca takes about 2 days in a car, the road is particularly bad between Chongoyape and Chota, max. speed 25 kph. The Chiclayo—Chota bus passes through Cochabamba (no hotels, not a friendly place, police searches for drugs), 34 km. from Chota, from where you can hitch in a truck to **Cutervo**, a town of 6,000 people at 2,800 metres in green meadows. Cattle and vegetables are raised here. Hotels: *San Juan* on plaza, cheap but has bugs; nicer one by Ciné San Juan, several more. Restaurants: *Salón Azul*, very good; *Central*, very dirty. A very friendly town which tourists rarely visit—don't be surprised if the local radio station wants an interview. Many trucks to Cutervo, Tues.-Sat., return Mon.-Fri., bus from Chiclayo Sat., returns Sun. 2000. Local market Thurs. and Sun.

Ten km. to the N of Chiclayo is **Lambayeque**, population 20,700, worth a visit. The narrow streets are lined by adobe houses, many retaining their distinctive wooden balconies and wrought iron grill-work over the windows. The town has an old church and 3 early Spanish colonial chapels open on religious feast days. Its most interesting feature is the well-known, recommended Brüning Archaeological Museum, located in an impressive modern building. It specializes in Mochica, Lambayeque, Chimú and Vicus cultures, has a fine collection of Sipán and Lambayeque gold. The magnificent treasure from the tomb of a Moche warrior priest, found at Sipán in 1987, has also been displayed here (see above), open 0830-1245 and 1500-1730 on weekdays, 0900-1300, Sat., Sun. and holidays. Admission, US$0.75. Try the famous Alfajor King-Kong (a sweet).

The old Pan-American Highway to Piura (which skirts the Eastern edge of the Sechura desert) passes two major precolumbian sites, within easy reach of Chiclayo. About 45 km. north of Chiclayo lies the archaeological site of **Túcume**, ruins of a vast city built over a thousand years ago. A short climb to a hillside "mirador" offers the visitor an unparalleled panoramic vista of 26 major pyramids, platform mounds, walled citadels and residential compounds flanking a ceremonial centre and ancient cemeteries. Excavations in the heart of this fascinating site, led by Norwegian explorer-archaeologist, Thor Heyerdahl of *Kon-Tiki* fame, are quickly challenging many conventional views of ancient

Peruvian culture.

Some suspect that it will prove to be a civilization centre greater than Chan Chán. There is also evidence that the people of Túcume were intrepid seafarers. A 10-year excavation project led by Thor Heyerdahl is under way. Colectivos go from Chiclayo, Pedro Ruiz y Luis González, or Manuel Prado 425 y L. González; ½ walk from the town to the ruins. Alternatively, contact Indiana Tours (see above, **Travel Agent**). At Apurlec, 60 km. N, is stone wall surrounding hill and pyramids dating from Tiahuanaco period, as well as irrigation canals and reservoirs; the system was enlarged during Mochica, Chimú and Inca occupation of the site. To get there from Chiclayo, take bus from Pedro Ruiz or Alfonso Ugarte 1315 (bus continues to Motupe).

On the old Pan-American Highway 885 km. from Lima is *Olmos*, a tranquil place—*Hospedaje San Martín*, G, very dirty, bargain hard; *Hotel Remanso*, in restored farmstead, E including breakfast, bath, restaurant, English spoken, friendly, tour and recreation centre in the making (Feb., 91). During the last week of June the Festival de Limón is celebrated here. After Olmos, a poor road (being improved) runs eastwards over the Porculla Pass (2,150 metres); at Km. 257 is a restaurant, but there are better ones at Jaén and Bagua Chica. A road branching from Chamaya, N of Hualgayoc, leads to the towns of Jaén and Bellavista. N of Chamaya, travelling via Aramongo and Oracuza, one finds a symmetrical hill of niche tombs.

   *Jaén* (population: 3,600), an old settlement, has recently been revived as a rice-growing centre. The annual festival of the patron saint, Nuestro Señor de Huamantanga, is on 14 September. Hotels at Jaén: *Danubio*; *Hostal Lima*, not rec. A road has been built N from Jaén to San Ignacio (114 km.), near the frontier of Ecuador. It crosses the valley of the Chinchipe, renowned for its lost Inca gold. San Ignacio has a *fiesta* on 31 August. Another branch road from Jaén has been built SE to Chachapoyas, 263 km. from Olmos (**see page 973**), and has now been completed another 359 km. to Yurimaguas, on the Río Huallaga (**see page 1060**). A road also goes to Aramongo (280 km.), on the Marañón; it has been extended to Nazareth. From Nazareth two roads branch: one to Oracuza, via Puente Huabico and Puerto Delfus, and the other to *Sarameriza*, the most westerly point on the Marañon with a regular boat connection to Iquitos—it is 1 hr. downstream from Puerto Delfus. To reach Sarameriza, take a bus to Bagua (**see page 974**) from Chachapoyas or Chiclayo, US$8.50, 12-15 hrs., from where pick-ups run twice daily to Imasa. Get out at Campamento Mesones Muro, 15 mins. before Imasa (US$4, 7 hrs.), where you must register with the police (this can take time). For 150 km. from Mesones Muro to Sarameriza, you must wait for a pick-up (one should be along in 3-6 days) and then be prepared for a 2-3 day journey because of poor roads and missing bridges. The m/n *Fernández* makes the journey from Sarameriza to Iquitos every second week: downstream, 4 days, only a few cabins, so take a hammock; upstream, 6 days. If you can't wait for the boat, it is possible with local help to make a raft and sail downstream, camping at night, until the *Fernández* catches you up (Peter Legaard Nielsen and Niels Pedersen, Copenhagen).

At Lambayeque the new Pan-American Highway branches off the old road and drives 190 km. straight across the desert to Piura. There are a few restaurants along its length (e.g. one at the junction in the middle where you can sleep, another midway between Mórrope and Piura, "no hotels, no priest"). There is also a coast road, narrow and scenic, between Lambayeque and Sechura via Bayovar.

A large area of shifting sands—the Sechura Desert—separates the oasis of Chiclayo from that of Piura. Water for irrigation comes from the Chira and Piura rivers, and from the Olmos and Tinajones irrigation projects which bring water from the Amazon watershed by means of tunnels (one over 16 km. long) through the Andes to the Pacific coast. They will eventually water some 400,000 hectares of desert land. The northern river—the Chira—has usually a superabundance of water: along its irrigated banks large crops of Tangüis cotton are grown. A dam has now been built at Poechos on the Chira river, to divert water to the Piura valley. In its upper course the Piura—whose flow is far less dependable—is mostly used to grow subsistence food crops, but around Piura, when there is enough water, the hardy long-staple Pima cotton is planted. In 1983 the Niño current brought heavy rains and turned the Sechura desert into an inland sea. Damage to crops, roads, bridges and buildings was estimated at around US$1bn.

*Piura*, an oasis in the parched desert, is a proud and historic city, 264 km. from

Chiclayo. Population, 1,125,800. Founded in 1532, three years before Lima, by the *conquistadores* left behind by Pizarro (whose statue is in the Parque Pizarro). There are two well kept parks, Cortés and Pizarro, and public gardens. Old buildings are kept in repair and new buildings blend with the Spanish style of the old city. Three bridges cross the Río Piura, the oldest from Calle Huancavelica, for pedestrians, the second oldest from Calle Sánchez Cerro, and the newest from Calle Bolognesi, used by most traffic. Its special dish is the delicious *natillas*, made mostly of goats milk and molasses; its local drink is *pipa fría*, chilled coconut juice drunk from the nut with a straw. The winter climate, May-September, is very pleasant although nights can be cold and the wind piercing; December to March is very hot.

A few blocks from the Plaza de Armas, where the cathedral stands (gold covered altar, paintings by Ignacio Merino), is the San Francisco church, where the city's independence from Spain was declared on 4 January 1821, nearly 8 months before Lima. The colonial church of Las Mercedes has ornately carved balconies, three-tiered archway, hand-hewn supports and massive furnishings. San Sebastián, on Tacna y Moquegua, is also worth seeing. Birthplace of Admiral Miguel Grau, hero of the War of the Pacific with Chile, whose house Casa Museo Grau, on Jirón Tacna opposite the Centro Cívico, has been opened as a museum; it contains a model of the *Huáscar*, the largest Peruvian warship in the War of the Pacific, which was built in Britain. Interesting local craftwork is sold at the Mercado Modelo. Museo Complejo Cultural, with archaeological and art sections, is open on Huánuco, between Loreto and Sullana, 1 block from bus station.

Cotton has been grown mainly on medium-sized properties, which have changed hands frequently in recent years and which now form communal or co-operative farms, sponsored by the agrarian reform programme. Worth seeing as an example of a fine old plantation is the former Hacienda Sojo, in the lower Chira valley, which was the centre of the properties of the Checa family.

**Hotels** *Turistas*, D, excellent, friendly and efficient, good food, home made papaya jam for breakfast, the city's social centre, swimming pool being added, facing Plaza de Armas, highly rec. *Cristina*, Jr. Loreto between Plaza Grau and Jr. Ica, one block from Plaza, E, pleasant; *Hostal Esmeraldas*, opp. colectivo stop on Loreto, good rooms, E; *San Jorge*, F with bath, clean and good value, Jr. Loreto, 3 blocks from Plaza Grau, rec.; *La Terraza*, Av Loreto, 2 blocks from Grau monument, F with bath, G without, hot water, clean, fan or a/c, small rooms; *Hispaniola* on Ica, F, is similar; *Hostal Ica*, Ica, G, very cheap; *Continental*, Jr Junín 924, F without bath, clean; *California*, same street, same category, clean, pleasant; *Bolognesi*, E, with private bath, near Roggero bus terminal, good. On Pan-American Highway are *El Sol*, Sánchez Cerro 411, E, bath, snack bar, will change travellers' cheques at official rate; *Vicus*, D, with bath, quiet, restaurant poor. *Oriental*, F without bath, E with, clean but very noisy, with TV in reception, Jr. Callao. Over the river in Castillo, *Tacna*, G p.p., modern, and *Atenas*, G p.p., dirty, bargain for cheap price. *Amanta*, Apurímac y Cuzco, F, clean. It is extremely difficult to find a room in the last week of July because of Independence festivities. The city suffers from water shortages and there are reports that no hotel has hot water.

**Restaurants** *Ganso Azul*, a group of steak houses just out of town, rec. (but not a safe area at night). *Carburmer*, in Centro Comercial, very good but not cheap. *Las Tradiciones*, Ayacucho 579, reasonable prices, good service; opposite, *La Cabaña* serves pizzas and other good food, not cheap; *Ferny's*, next to *Hotel San Jorge*, good food, clean, on Loreto; *Café Concierto*, Cuzco 933, pleasant, popular, not cheap; *Las Redes*, Apurímac between Tacna y Libertad, pizzas, good atmosphere; *Brasil*, Huancavelica y Junín, good for breakfast and lunch, US$2; *Snack Bar*, Callao 536, good fruit juices. Good little cheap restaurants on Jirón Junín: *Chalán del Norte* at 722, *Bianca* at 732, *El Capri* at 715. *La Huerta*, Libertad 801 on corner of Plaza de Armas, sells 19 fresh juices, quesillo con miel (cream cheese and honey) and natillas.

**Shopping** Fuji film readily available. Good delicatessens around main square, selling local sweets; *natilla* factory on Sánchez Cerro, Miraflores, 4 blocks from bridge, sells *natilla* and *algorrobina* fruit drink. Market on Sánchez Cero, good for fruit.

**Exchange** Banco de Crédito recommended, changes travellers' cheques, open 0900 but exchange from 1000. Banco Continental, Plaza de Armas, changes travellers' cheques with commission.

**Honorary British Consul** Casilla 193, T (074) 323532.

**Post Office** on Plaza de Armas, very helpful.

**Tourist Offices** Foptur, Ayacucho 377, Plaza de Armas, next to Municipalidad, T 333720, has city maps and lots of information; and at airport. Touring y Automóvil Club del Perú, Sánchez Cerro 1237 (pink-walled building on right hand side entering Piura on Panamericana), good maps of Peru for US$1.25.

**Air** AeroPerú daily jet flights to and from Lima. Taxi to airport, US$1.50.

**Buses** Tepsa, Roggero and other buses leave daily to **Lima**, 17 hrs, average fare US$15, coming from Tumbes. To **Trujillo**, 6 hrs., buses run day (not a.m.) and night, US$8 (Chinchay-Suyo on Calle Libertad 1117-27, leaves at 2200 and 2400, also at 1300 to Chiclayo-Trujillo-Chimbote- Huaraz). To Trujillo in daylight, take through Chinchay-Suyo bus, or 0800 Empresa Chiclayo bus to **Chiclayo** (US$5, 3 hrs.) then change to Empresa Emtrafesa. To **Tumbes**, 6 hrs, US$7.20 (El Dorado, Sánchez Cerro, 4 a day, Compañía Petrolera, same location, 2130, continues to Aguas Verdes, or Empresa Chiclayo), with Tepsa, leaving at 1200 (coming from Lima, no reservations), or Sudamericana at 0400 (cheaper), colectivo US$12.50; to **Chiclayo**, US$4.20, 3½ hrs., leave 1400; colectivo to Chiclayo US$6. To **La Tina** for Ecuadorean frontier, take an early bus to Sullana (start at 0630, every 20 mins), then a truck, no buses. **N.B.** To the north of Piura, buses are subject to military checks.

**Excursions** 12 km. to the SW of Piura is the village of **Catacaos** (colectivos leave from Plaza Pizarro, US$0.50, bus US$0.35) famous for its *chicha* (maize beer, be careful, quality not always reliable), *picanterías* (local restaurants, some with music, *La Casa de Tales*, rec.), tooled leather, gold and silver filigree jewellery, wooden articles, straw hats (pricey) and splendid celebrations in Holy Week. Also from Piura, one can visit **Sechura**, a coastal town with a fine 17th-century cathedral (splendid west front-under renovation for a long time, normally closed to the public) and the *Hospedaje de Dios* (usually full of workmen from the oil terminal at Bayovar—forbidden to visitors). One can visit the coastal villages (no accommodation in any of them) of San Pedro (with a huge lagoon, edible crabs, flamingoes—if you're lucky, a superb beach and a fierce sun—best visited in the week, no facilities whatsoever; take bus or colectivo to the right fork past Vice, about 10 km. from Sechura then hitch); Yacila, a picturesque fishing village with a few fish restaurants, church on the beach (reached also by *camioneta* for Paita; Los Cangrejos beach nearby, where you can rent an apartment from Sr. Belcázar, but little food available, motel open in summer, no facilities in winter), La Tortuga, Parachique, Matacaballo (which has the best beach of these four places); Chullachay (the nearest beach to Sechura), Los Puertos and Angostura. Balsa reed-boats are common on the coast.

**Chulucanas**, 50 km. SE of Piura and 10 km. off the Pan-American Highway, is the centre of the lemon and orange growing area. *Hotel Ica*, Ica 636, F; *Restaurant Cajamarquino*, Ayacucho 530, good. **Canchaque** (*Hostal Don Félix*, central square, F, just tolerable; otherwise simple clean accommodation for about US$2 on right hand side of church), is a delightfully-situated small centre for coffee, sugar-cane and fruit production. Foreigners have to register here at the Policía de República. The difficult and tiring road, impossible for ordinary vehicles in the wet season, continues over a pass in the Andes of more than 3,000 metres to **Huancabamba** (*Hotel El Dorado*, F, good, clean, informative owner, with restaurant, on the main square; also a couple of others on the Plaza). Local specialities: *rompope*, a rich and strong drink made of egg, spices and *cañazo* (sugar-cane spirit); roast *cuy* (guinea-pig); and local cheeses. This very pretty town in a wonderful setting has three claims to fame. First, the predominance of European features, due to the fact that it was an important Spanish settlement in colonial times. Second, it is called "the walking town, *la ciudad que camina*", as it is built on irregularly slipping strata which cause much subsidence. Evidence for this includes the fall of the bridge over the Río Huancabamba some years ago. Third, and by far the most remarkable element, it is the base for reaching Las Guaringas, a series of lakes at about 4,000 metres. Around here live the most famous witchdoctors of Peru, to whom sick people flock from all over the country and abroad. Buses to the lakes at 0400 from main square.

Horses to the lakes can be hired, US$5; village of San Antonio below Lago Carmen, village of Salalá below Lago Shumbe (*Hotel San José*, G, very basic, take own food). Ignacio León, who owns a *bodega* opposite *El Dorado* runs an early pick-up service to outlying villages and takes trips at negotiable prices.

A bus from Piura to Canchaque and Huancabamba leaves daily at 0900 and 1000, at least 10 hrs. (and returns from Huancabamba 0700 and 1000), US$12, from the Civa office, Av.

Ramón Castilla 155 (buy ticket early on day before travelling). Truck US$11.50. If driving, take the Pan-American Highway south of Piura for 66 km. where there is a signpost to Huancabamba. Canchaque is 78 km. along this same road, at first paved, then dirt, and then there are 69 km. more of steep and winding road to Huancabamba.

By lorry from Piura, or bus from Sullana, is **Ayabaca**. John Streather writes: In the Andean summer—roughly the end of May till mid-September—it is worth making the long trip by lorry or bus (about 0600 from Piura market square, enquire the day, or days, before) to Ayabaca, whence many trips can be made to surrounding ruins, caves, petroglyphs and lakes. Mules are usually essential as are guides; mules about US$5 per day, guides the same. The man to contact in Ayabaca is Sr. Celso Acuña Calle, Jr. Cáceres 161. Buy food and medicine in Piura (enough for the guides too) before leaving, as it is in short supply in Ayabaca. The little town is near the Ecuadorean border in a lovely situation, but is unfortunately a centre of cocaine smuggling. Therefore be sure to carry passport and visa on all trips (in a waterproof bag) and, of course, stop whenever asked to by police. In summer one can usually get a lift to the village of Yanchalá where most trips begin. It is a long muleback journey from there to the petroglyphs of Samanga (booklet purchasable at Piura Catholic University), and another long muleback ride to the Inca fortress town of Aypate—large but very overgrown. Other places of interest are: the pre-Inca cemetery of Hualcuy, Inca ruins and good view from Cerro Granadillo; pre-Inca ruins of Potrero de los Chaves; mummies in the pre-Inca cave cemetery of Potrero de los Jiménez at Cerro Pajonal; 4 or 5 days by mule to the Cuatro Lagunas Sagradas—all different colours. Near Chicuate is the Ciudad Encantada which still awaits explorers or indeed any visitors at all, as it is in a very isolated region, beyond Laguna Shimbe, and the few locals are frightened to visit it. It is said to be a ruined Inca town. There are at least three hotels in Ayabaca; the best, nameless, is in the first street parallel to the square and directly behind the Banco de la Nación (which will almost certainly refuse to change money). Various restaurants too: the *Trébol* is probably the best of a mediocre bunch. A torch is essential for trips outside Ayabaca, as there is no electric light in the region. No one should attempt to journey outside Ayabaca without a guide: there is danger from drug smugglers as well as of getting lost in the trackless bush. The way to the lost Inca city of Chicuate is particularly dangerous: lightning in the pass that gives access, and thick fog descending over the 100 metres of narrow road that lead between two lakes. Easier to reach from Chulucanas (see above) is Frías, where there is a pre-Inca cemetery and more caves can be reached if you have enough time (few locals know of them), rough road, no facilities, beautiful countryside.

The port for the area is **Paita** (no public transport), 50 km. from Piura (colectivos and buses near Plaza Grau, US$1.80), which exports cotton, cotton seed, wool and flax. Population 51,500. Built on a small beach, flanked on three sides by a towering, sandy bluff, it is connected with Piura and Sullana by paved highways. Several colonial buildings survive, but they are in poor condition. The Paita-Piura road is now good, buses hourly from Parque Cortés, Piura, 45 mins. (get tickets from office on Av. Sullana, facing the park, US$1.80). Fishing, fishmeal and whaling (at Tierra Colorada, 6½ km. S of Paita) are prosperous industries.

**Hotels** Best is *Las Brisas*, Av. Ugarte, E with bath but scant, cold water, safe; *El Mundo*, 300 block of Bolívar, not bad but short-stay; *Miramar*, opp. Credicoop Paita, an old wooden mansion on seafront, looks expensive, but is filthy; *Ceci*, above pharmacy, F; *Pacífico* and others, none recommendable. Most are full anyway.

**Restaurants** *El Mundo*, Jr. Junín, quite good; much better is the restaurant on 2nd floor of Club Liberal building, Jorge Chávez 161, T 2141, good fish, seafood and crêpes, good value; others on Plaza de Armas.

**Exchange** Credicoop Paita, Jr. Junín 380 for dollars cash; helpful guard.

On a bluff looming over Paita is a small colonial fortress built to repel pirates. 25 km up the coast is **Colán**, a summer resort, reached by driving down a large, sandy bluff (no public transport); near the base is a striking and lonely church over 300 years old (it's in very poor condition). There is a good beach, but Colán is rather derelict since the agrarian reform; it used to be the favourite resort of the estate-owners.

Bolívar's mistress, Manuela Sáenz, lived the last 24 years of her life in Paita, supporting herself until her death in 1856 by weaving and embroidering and making candy after refusing the fortune left her by her husband. The house may be visited if you ask the people living in it, but there's not much to see.

**Sullana** (population 151,000), 39 km. N of Piura, is built on a bluff over the fertile

Chira valley. It has a long market on the main avenue; a busy, modern place.
**Warning** Robberies of travellers are common.

**Hotels** *Hostal y Restaurant San Miguel*, Calle J. Farfán 204, opposite bus companies, E
(G in shared rooms), helpful, good showers, staff will spray rooms against mosquitoes; *Chifa
Cantón*, next door, serves good food cheaply, but smaller portions than in *San Miguel*;
*Hostal Aypate*, Av. José de Lama, E, comfortable, showers; *Hostal Príncipe*, Espinal 588,
G, clean and friendly; *Buenos Aires*, G p.p., Av. Buenos Aires, 15 mins. from city centre,
friendly but bathrooms dirty; *Res. Wilson*, Tamaraya 378, G p.p. large rooms, dirty facilities,
friendly. *Hostal La Siesta*, Av. Panamericana 400-04 (T 2264), at entrance to town (direction
Talara), D, 3-star, hot water, swimming pool, café, laundry.

**Exchange** On main street, near Bata shoe shop, usual touts, *cambio* upstairs changes
travellers' cheques, but wait till after 1100 for today's rate.

**Bus** to Tumbes, US$2.75. **Piura**, 45 mins., US$1.20 bus, US$1.60 colectivo (if you have
time, it is worth continuing to Piura rather than staying in Sullana); **Chiclayo**, Tepsa, 4 hrs.
also with Sudamericano or Empresa Chiclayo, US$4. **Trujillo**, 8 hrs., Sudamericano (US$4),
Ormeño (US$3.50), plenty, but nights only and better to book 1 day ahead. To **Lima** with
Sudamericano, Tepsa (*presidencial*, US$16, 1820, ordinary, US$10.20, 1830, 16-17 hrs.),
Panamericana, US$8, Roggero. Colectivos to Paita, Colán and Esmeralda leave from the main
road parallel to the market; buses to Máncora and Talara (Empresa EPPO) from market area.

**To Ecuador** At Sullana the Pan-American Highway bifurcates. To the E it crosses
the Peru-Ecuador frontier at La Tina and continues via Macará to Loja and Cuenca;
the road is paved to Las Lomas (75 km.), but thereafter is poor, though
marvellously scenic. Many trucks and other vehicles leave at 0600 from Av. Buenos
Aires in Sullana to the border at La Tina, US$6 p.p., 4 hrs, return from border to
Sullana 1030 or when full; taxis also go, US$8 per seat, 3-4 hours. There are many
army checkpoints en route. Unaccompanied women are advised to take the better
route (see below). No accommodation at La Tina (in El Suyo, 14 km. from La Tina,
are 2 small hotels). At the border the officials may try to get extra payments from
those entering Peru, stand your ground if possible—the Peruvian can be found
at the nearby *cevichería* if not at his desk—walk over the bridge, pick-ups run
from the border to Macará. A bus leaves the Ecuadorean side at 1300 for Loja,
so you can go from Sullana to Loja in one day.

    **The better route** is the W road which passes through Talara and Tumbes,
crossing the border at Huaquillas and on via Machala to Guayaquil; it is asphalted
and has excellent bus services. All but a section of this road between Talara and
Los Organos (20 km.) has been rebuilt since the heavy floods in January 1983.

The main centre of the coastal oil area is *Talara* (135 km. from Piura, 1,177 km.
from Lima), in a desert oasis, which has a State-owned 60,000 barrel-a-day oil
refinery and a fertilizer plant. Water is piped 40 km. from the Chira River. The city
is a triumph over formidable natural difficulties, but was badly damaged in the
1983 floods and has many shanty districts. Population 44,500. La Peña beach, 2
km. from Talara, is still unspoilt.

**Hotels** Problems with water supply in all cases: *Pacífico*, A, most luxurious, swimming pool,
restaurant, bar, parking, pay in dollars; *Residencial Grau*, Av. Grau 77, near main square, E,
clean, friendly, possible to park one motor bike, owner changes dollars; *Royal*, wooden
building far from centre, G, run down; *Hostal Talara*, E, clean and comfortable. If in trouble
finding a bed, enquire at the police station.

**Restaurants** Many cheap ones on main square.

**Transport** Airport with daily flights to Lima by AeroPerú (not Sat.).

Paved highways connect the town with the Negritos, Lagunitos, La Brea and other oilfields.
Of historical interest are the old tarpits at La Brea, 21 km. inland from Punta Pariñas, S
of Talara, and near the foot of the Amotape mountains. Here the Spaniards boiled the tar to
get pitch for caulking their ships. Buses run to *Máncora* (wayside fish restaurants superb,
including lobster; *César*, rec.), a small attractive resort with good beaches, water warm
enough for bathing, surfing (best No.v-March). *Punta Ballena*, E p.p., full board, clean,
friendly, rec.; *Bamboe*, next to Tepsa on main street, basic, cheap (pay in advance), clean, G;

3 km. S, *Las Pocitas*, 9 rooms, attractive, friendly, fishing and harpooning trips, balsa rafts, food excellent US$9 for main meal, cheaper for full board (C). Punta Sal about 20 km. to the north has *Punta de Sal Club Hotel*, B p.p. full board, attractive, good beach, rec., watersports, pool, comfortable, relaxing (in Llma T 425961). Aqua Explorer arranges undersea activities, fishing, sailing and horseriding. Camping is reported to be safe along the beach between Talara and Tumbes, Punta Negra, rec. Bus Máncora-Tumbes, 2 hrs., US$2.50.

N of Talara, 51 km., is the small port of **Cabo Blanco**, famous for its excellent sea-fishing; scenery spoilt by numerous oil installations. Camping permitted free of charge at Cabo Blanco, by the Fishing Club Lodge, overlooking the sea (at least in the off-season June-December). Fishing Club, B, clean, attractive, rec., restaurant, pool, watersports, likely to be full in New Year period. Hemingway wrote *The Old Man and the Sea* here.

**Tumbes**, about 141 km. N of Talara, and 265 km. N of Piura, is the most northerly of Peruvian towns; it is a garrison town with 34,000 inhabitants (do not photograph the military or their installations—they will destroy your film and probably detain you). There is a long promenade, the Malecón Benavides, beside the high banks of the Río Tumbes. There are some old houses in Calle Grau, and a colonial public library in the Plaza de Armas with a small museum. The cathedral is 17th century but restored in 1985. There is a sports stadium; cockfights in the Coliseo de Gallos, Av. Mcal. Castilla, 9th block, Sun. at 1500, special fights 28 July and 8 Dec. The main products are bananas and rice. The water supply is not good.

**Hotels** *Turistas*, C, clean, restaurant, good food and service, parking, has nice garden, provides some tourist information; *Roma*, Plaza de Armas, basic, simple, few services, E; *Amazonas*, E, Av. Tumbes 333 (old name Tnte. Vásquez), clean, friendly, showers; *Córdova*, J. R. Abad Puell 777, F, with bath, no hot water, safe, clean, friendly, safe for motorcycle parking; *Hostal Estoril*, 2 blocks from main square, F, good, friendly; *Lourdes*, one block from main square, E with bath, clean, friendly, rec.; *Italia*, Grau 733, E, cold showers, friendly, good; *Florián*, E, near El Dorado bus company, clean, fan, private bath, rec.; opposite is *Hostal Elica*, F with bath, clean, good; *Hostal Tumbes*, Grau 614, F with bath, cold water, clean. *Hostal Patty*, Huáscar 513, G, clean, water for 2 hrs. in a.m. Many other cheap hotels. Hotels are often fully booked by early afternoon, so try to arrive early, and at holiday times it can be very difficult to find a vacant room.

**Restaurants** *Pez Espada*, good for fish, as is *Curich* in the Plaza de Armas. *Europa*, off main square, is rec., particularly for omelettes. *El Quarique*, Huáscar 319, small, friendly, shell decoration; *Samoa*, Av. Bolívar 235, nr. plaza, good, big portions; *El Brujo*, 7 de Enero 320, good value; *Chifa D'Koko*, Piura y F. Navarete, rec; *Mini Chifa*, Av. Tumbes (Tte. Vásquez), good local and chifa dishes. There are other inexpensive restaurants on the Plaza de Armas and near the markets. *Heladería La Suprema*, Paseo Libertadores, good ice cream, sweets and cold drinks. Try bolas de plátano, soup with banana balls, meat, olives and raisins, and sudado, a local stew.

**Exchange** Only in Banco de Crédito, opp. Banco Popular which is in a new building on the edge of the main square, poor rates. Bad rates at the airport. Money changers on the street (on Bolívar, left of the Cathedral) give a much better rate than banks or *cambios*, but don't accept the first offer you are given. None changes travellers' cheques.

**Post Office** San Martín 240; Entel **Telephone** office, San Martín 242.

**Tourist office** Foptur, Edificio Majestad, Alfonso Ugarte y Mayor Bodero, T 5054, helpful. Further information from Ricardo Pérez Saavedra, Pueblo Nuevo, Casilla 204, archaeologist, author, works for the Instituto Nacional de Cultura (ask to see his collection of figurines); Carlos Sáenz, Urb. Fonavi 4-16, T 523412, coordinator of Fundación Peruana para la Conservación de la Naturaleza (details on national parks); Luis Alvarez Saldariaga, Tarata 132, a fisherman who organizes trips on the Río Tumbes (US$20—also contact him through Doris Guerra at Foptur).

**Buses** Daily to and from **Lima**, 1,330 km. by Sudamericano, 1600, 1900, US$20 (overbooked, often subject to long delays); Expreso Continental (Ormeño group), new buses, 1130, 1600, 1800, 22 hrs., also Tepsa (often full, leaves 1100, 1800, 1900), 26 hrs., comfortable, rec.; for other companies, ask around (e.g. Roggero, not rec.); cheaper ones usually leave 1600-2100, dearer ones 1200-1400. All buses to Lima are very slow because of repeated police checks—no chance of sleep overnight. On the bus to Lima try to get a seat on the right hand side in order to have a good view of the coast. One can get tickets to anywhere between Tumbes and Lima with little difficulty, although buses are often booked well in advance; Piura is a good place for connections. To **Sullana**, poor road, except for first 50 km. from Tumbes, US$2.75. To **Talara**, 176 km., US$2.50 with El Dorado (colectivo US$7). To **Piura**, 276 km., US$7.20 with Tepsa, Empresa Chiclayo, 6 hrs. Colectivo, US$11. To **Chiclayo**, 548 km., US$10 (Tepsa). To **Trujillo**, 758 km., 5 a day, 12 hrs. from US$12. Look out for dolphins in the sea along this route. To **Chimbote**, 15 hrs., US$12.50 with Sudamericano, 16 hrs. Most buses leave p.m. from Av. Tumbes (formerly Tnte. Vásquez). Frequent buses to Aguas Verdes, 23 km., from market at 0600 onwards, colectivo, US$1.20, 20 minutes. Bus to Machala (Ecuador), US$5. Colectivo to Huaquillas (Ecuador), US$0.80. Hitching slow.

**N.B.** Travellers who hold a Tumbes-Huaquillas-Guayaquil ticket with Panamericana Internacional (bought outside Peru as an onward ticket) should note that Panamericana does not have an office in Tumbes. However, this ticket can be used for a colectivo (but not a taxi) to the border, caught at corner of Piura and Bolívar; if colectivo is full, you will be transferred to another company. Connection with bus at the border.

**Air** AeroPerú and Faucett, Lima to and from Tumbes daily (Faucett may be cheaper). Essential to reconfirm flights 24 hrs. before departure. Taxi to airport, US$1.50; taxis meet flights to take passengers to border, US$1.80, 2 mins.

**Excursions** Río Tumbes is navigable by small boat to the mouth of the river, an interesting 2 hr. trip with fantastic birdlife and mangrove swamps.

This is the only part of the Peruvian coast where the sea is warm all year. Two good beaches near Tumbes: one at Caleta La Cruz 16 km. SW, where Pizarro landed in 1532. The original Cruz de Conquista was taken to Lima. Easy to get to with regular colectivos (US$0.80 each way); *Motel*, E. **Zorritos**, 35 km. S of Tumbes, heavily damaged by the 1983 flooding but with a good beach (the water is not oily), *Hotel de Turistas*, E (reported closed for renovation), also *Punta Sal Chica*, 2 stars; the better of the 2 restaurants is *Arriba Perú*. Camping recommended. The first South American oil well was sunk here in 1863. Just north of Tumbes is **Puerto Pizarro**, a small fishing beach at the southern limit of the mangrove swamps. Take a boat across the lagoon to reach a good clean sandy beach (about 10 minutes journey, bargain hard). Festival of St Peter and St Paul, 29-30 June; colectivo No. 6 from Tumbes (US$0.50). *Puerto Pizarro Motel*, D, no hot water, restaurant dear and slow but food good, swimming pool, which is usually empty, watersports; *Restaurant Venecia*, seafood cheap, beware shellfish which may cause stomach upsets. Plenty of fishing and swimming; ideal for windsurfing and water-skiing but few facilities. The mangrove swamps are full of pelicans and a few tame ones beg for fish on the beaches. Three islands, Isla Hueso de Ballena, Isla del Amor, Isla de los Pájaros may be visited by boat, bargain hard, good for swimming and picnics, take food and water. Remains of Cabeza de Vaca abode cult centre of the Tumpis Indians can be found at Corrales, 5 km. S of Tumbes. They were heavily damaged by 1983 rains; Museo de Sitio nearby. **Bosque Nacional de Tumbes** (75,000 ha.) wildlife includes monkeys, nutria and crocodiles; **Parque Nacional Cerros de Amotape** (91,000 ha.) is a dry tropical forest with jaguars and anteaters, a guide essential. Mosquito repellant is a must for Tumbes area.

**To Ecuador** Small buses and colectivos (some marked "Puente Internacional") leave about every 20 min. and take 30 min. to get to **Aguas Verdes** on the Peruvian side of the international bridge (the Peruvian departure office opens at 0800, is closed 1200-1400 and after 1800; try not to arrive within 1/2 hour of the border closing). On the way most of them pass by the airport. By taxi it costs about US$5, colectivo fare is US$2 and bus fare US$1.25. If entering, they may refuse to accept a return ticket from another country as proof of intended exit from Peru; this is an invitation to bribery, be courteous but firm. Colectivos do not wait at customs. Some bus companies from Chiclayo and beyond go to the border. At Aguas Verdes a walkway leads to Peruvian Immigration; beware of dishonest money changers lingering outside. Get your exit stamp and proceed across the bridge into Huaquillas; 100 metres up is the Ecuadorean Immigration on the left. Change money with the men near the end of the bridge (they have briefcases on their laps and sit under umbrellas). They are not entirely scrupulous, so it helps to have your own calculator—bargaining essential. With a pass from the authorities at the border you can spend the day in Huaquillas, the Ecuadorean border town, as long as you are back by 1800. There is nothing much to see there, but Peruvians hunt for bargains. It is a thoroughly unscrupulous border, with chaotic opening hours. Tepsa leave from the border for Lima daily at 1000, 22-5 hrs., US$25; Tepsa to Tumbes at 1300 and later. A bus leaves Huaquillas at 1500 for Piura and Trujillo (US$8, 6 hrs. to Piura). Entering Peru, it may be easier to take a colectivo to Tumbes and then a bus south, rather than get on a bus from the border to a southern destination. These buses are usually full of shoppers and their goods and involve long stops at checkpoints.

When driving into Peru vehicle fumigation is not required, but there is "one outfit who will attempt to fumigate your vehicle with water and charge US$10 for their services." Beware of officials claiming that you need a *carnet* to obtain your 90-day transit permit; this is not so (but check before arriving at the border that rules have not changed).

**Warnings** Porters on either side of the border charge exorbitant prices: don't be bullied. Beware sharp practices by money changers. The money changers on the Ecuadorean side give a better rate than the banks in Tumbes (but not at the airport on the Ecuadorean side); always try to check the rate beforehand. For Intis it is better to change dollars, as poor rates for sucres. If you are going to change cheques into Ecuadorean sucres in Huaquillas, make sure you cross the border in the morning because the bank is closed after lunch. Do not change money on the minibus to Aguas Verdes, their rates are very poor. Relations between Peru and Ecuador are not good: Ecuadorean Customs tends to confiscate guidebooks and maps of Peru because they show as Peru's certain areas claimed by Ecuador.

Checks for goods smuggled into Peru are carried out, especially at Tepsa bus station as well as at Aguas Verdes. Checks are thorough, both of luggage and body. Checks also intermittently on road to Piura.

**N.B.** In Jan., Feb. and March, Peru is one hour ahead of Ecuador, but dates of time-change are different each year.

## SOUTH-EAST FROM LIMA (4)

**The mysterious Nazca lines, the precious Paracas bird reserve and Peru's wine and pisco-producing oases in and around Ica punctuate the desert south of the capital. The Pan-American Highway carries on down to Chile, with a dramatic branch inland, climbing to Arequipa.**

The group of oases south from Lima grow Pima cotton, sugar-cane and vegetables for Lima and Callao, but the more southerly valleys specialize in vines—Ica in particular is well known for this and its port, Pisco, has given its name to the well-known brandy sold all along the coast. The Pan-American Highway runs S from Lima through all the places now to be described to Tacna and Chile, it is 4 lane to Km. 116 and there are extensive repairs and new building as far as Km. 135. There are battery chicken houses all along the beach. At Km. 200 the *garúa* lifts.

The first 60 km. from Lima are dotted with a series of seaside resort towns and clubs, including **Santa María**, 40 km. from Lima, beautiful *Santa María Hotel*, A, meals included. At nearby **San Bartolo** is the *Posada del Mirador*, Malecón San Martín 105, T 290388, C in bungalows or A full board. **Pucusana**, is a charming fishing village (*Hotel Bahía*, good seafood). Excellent panoramas from the cliffs above the village. Hire a boat for an hour (fix price beforehand and stick to it); don't go in the direction of the only, smelly factory, but to the rocks where you can see seabirds close at hand. 14 km. S of Pucusana is **Chilca**, ½ hr. by colectivo from the market place, a small beach resort. Not much to see, but a long, deserted beach with camping possibilities. You can walk along the beach from Chilca to Salinas (5 km.), which has mineral baths. There are a few restaurants and *pensiones*. In summer (Dec.-Feb.), these places fill up with holidaymakers from Lima. At Mala, 24 km. S of Pucusana, is a hotel on the old Panamericana.

**Cañete** (hotels and restaurants; a rec. restaurant is *Cevichería Muelle 56*, Bolognesi 156), about 150 km. S of Lima, on the Río Cañete, is a prosperous market centre amid desert scenery. There is a road (no buses) to Huancayo (**see page 1046**).

At Cerro Azul, 13 km. N of Cañete, is a unique Inca sea fort known as **Huarco**, now much damaged. *La Malla* is an excellent fish restaurant.

35 km. N of Pisco, near Chincha Baja, is **Tambo de Mora**, with nearby archaeological sites at Huaca de Tambo de Mora, La Centinela, Chinchaycama and Huaca Alvarado. Chincha

itself is a fishing village where the negro/criollo culture is still alive. Their famous festival, Verano Negro, is at the end of February. On old *hacienda*, San José, is just outside Chincha (need your own transport); it operates as a hotel, with pool, restaurant, garden, small church, colonial crafts, C full board, book through Foptur. In Chincha Alta, a fast-growing town, is *Hostal La Rueda*, near plaza, F, breakfast extra, hot showers, swimming pool, lounge; several other good ones.

*Pisco*, population 82,250, the largest port between Callao and Matarani, 237 km. S of Lima, serves a large agricultural hinterland. The town is divided into two: Pisco Pueblo, colonial-style homes with patios and gardens; and Pisco Puerto, which has been replaced as a port by the deep-water Puerto General San Martín, beyond Paracas. In Pisco Pueblo, half a block W of the quiet Plaza de Armas, with its equestrian statue of San Martín, is the Club Social Pisco, the H.Q. of San Martín after he had landed at Paracas Bay. There is an old Jesuit church hiding behind the new one. You can book for trips to the Ballestas Islands (see below) at agencies around the main square, or through a hotel. Pisco is an alternative airport when landing is not possible at Lima. A 364 km. road has been built to Ayacucho, with a branch to Huancavelica (see Tambo Colorado, next page).

**Hotels** *Hostal Belén*, Plaza Belén, E, clean, comfortable, electric showers. *Embassy*, E with bath, clean, noisy, security reported suspect, nice bar on roof, has disco in Jr. Comercio just off Plaza de Armas, good, cheap trips to Ballestas Islands; *Hostal San Jorge*, Juan Osores 267, E, hot water, friendly, very clean, rec., arranges excursions; *Cesar*, 2 de Mayo, F; *Colonial*, clean, quiet, no private baths but good value. *Hostal Angamos*, Pedemonte 134, tiny rooms but good beds, clean, friendly, F, economical with water and light. Mosquitoes are a problem at night in the summer. The town is full at weekends with visitors from Lima. At Pisco Puerto, *Portofino*, F, basic, friendly, clean, in slum area on sea front, good seafood, arranges day excursion to Paracas, but avoid the nearby peña which is poor and can be dangerous. *Albergue Juvenil* (Youth Hostel) Jr. José Balta 639, Pisco Playa, T 2492, G, clean, friendly, kitchen and washing facilities.

**Restaurants** *As de Oros*, on the Plaza de Armas, good restaurant, reasonable prices, closed Mons.; *Las Vegas*, on Plaza, very popular; *Roberto's*, always busy, near Plaza, rec. for seafood; *Candelabra*, next to *Hotel Embassy*, quite expensive; *Bill More* near *Hotel Embassy*, good, cheap seafood, also at restaurant of *Hotel Portofino*; *Dan Piave*, on Plaza, excellent pisco sours, but lone women should beware of the owner; *La Fontana*, Lima 355, good food and pisco sours. *Piccolo-Bar*, near Plaza, good breakfast and coffee; *El Norteño*, off Plaza de Armas, good, cheap, clean; *Lucho y Mary*, Calle Independencia, friendly, excellent fish dishes and cheap, US$3.50 for two; a number of restaurants around M. de Mancera 160. Seafood restaurants along shore between Pisco and San Andrés, and in San Andrés (buses from Plaza Belén, near *Hotel Perú*) there are *La Estrellita*, rec., *Olimpia* (Grecia 200), and *Mendoza*, for fish and local dishes, all rec. Good fried chicken place opposite Ormeño: save your foreign cigarette packets for their mural! *Mendoza 2*, in Pisco Puerto, excellent simple fish restaurant.

**Exchange** Banco de Crédito on Plaza de Armas gives good rates, but only for Amex and cash.

**Tourist Office** on Plaza, next to **Hotel Pisco**; poor information.

**Transport** Bus to Lima, Ormeño (500m. from main plaza), US$3.50, recommended, 4 departures, 4 hrs., San Martín, Callao 136, 4 a day, rec.; Roggero, US$3.50, twice a day. To **Ayacucho**, US$12.50 with Ormeño, 12 hrs., 1730, often delayed, wear warm clothes as the road reaches 4,600 metres near Castrovirreyna and is very cold at night; Oropesa (Calle Comercial) to **Huancavelica**, US$11, 0800 daily, 13 hrs., very tiring, many stops; colectivo to Ica US$1.20, bus to **Ica**, US$1, 2 hrs. (Ormeño, Roggero). To **Arequipa** direct 1220 with Ormeño, arrive 0300, US$17. To **Nazca** by bus, US$3.50, Roggero, 1430 (3-4 hrs.), Ormeño, 5 daily, US$3.50, rec. (3½-4 hrs.), colectivos reported to be more reliable. Reservations can be made here at Nazca Tours for flights over the Nazca lines for US$50 p.p.

Fifteen km. down the coast from Pisco Puerto is the bay of *Paracas*, sheltered by the Paracas peninsula. (The name means "sandstorm"—they can last for 3 days.) The peninsula is a National Park (entrance US$3 for 2 days, no less), ask permission to camp, no water (don't camp alone, robberies are common); it is one of the best marine reserves, with the highest concentration of marine birds, in the world.

There are archaeological and natural history museums about 90 mins'. walk from the residential area along an isolated stretch of beach (no bus—take water and sun hat), but contents reported less interesting than the Ica museum. A monument on the sands marks the spot where San Martín set foot in Peru. The area has been developed as a resort: a beautiful bay, good sands, bathing (some pollution from local fishing industry, and beware of jellyfish) and fishing and excursions by boat to offshore islands. The Paracas necropolis, the burial place of a civilization which flourished here between 700 and 300 BC, has been buried by shifting sands and archaeologists can no longer visit it. About 17 km. from the museum is the precolumbian Candelabra traced in the hillside, at least 50 metres long, best seen from the sea, but still impressive from the land. Hitch along paved road which leads to Punta Pejerrey, get off at left fork and you will see a trail (1½ hrs. walk to Candelabra). La Mina, a small beach 2 km. from Lagunilla, and Punta El Arquillo are also worth visiting.

On the southern side of the peninsula there is a colony of sealions, with many species of birds (such as cormorants, gannets, gulls, terns, pelicans). On the northern side, in the bay, there are flamingoes (in June and July mainly)—only reached on foot from Paracas. Condors may be seen from the (bad) road between Paracas and Laguna Grande. Trips to the **Ballestas Islands** for US$7 upwards (including bus transfer) can be arranged at the agencies on the main plaza in Pisco, or (dearer) with the main hotels in Pisco and Paracas (e.g. US$17 from *Hotel Paracas*, 3½ hrs. in safe boat, minimum 8 passengers, take warm clothing). Blue Sea Tours, Calle Chosica 320, Pisco, has been recommended as giving the longest tours, with least disturbance of the wild life, US$7 p.p. Negotiate for a good price, someone there speaks Dutch. Also Ballesta Isla Tours on Comercio 100 may sell the trip more cheaply, incuding guide, rec. The trip to the islands, which are now a national reserve, takes about 5 hrs. all together, and is highly recommended (although some boats do not have life jackets, and are very crowded). You will see thousands of inquisitive sealions, guano birds, pelicans (the book *Las Aves del Departamento de Lima* by Maria Koepcke is useful); the boat returns past the Candelabra to the bay of Paracas where flocks of flamingoes and pelicans can be seen.

Taxi from Pisco to Paracas (return) US$8, but more if arranged by a hotel. Colectivo, one way, US$0.80 or less if you change at San Andrés. Small buses leave frequently from the market place in Pisco to Paracas (US$0.30, US$0.50 with stop at J. C. Tello museum—entry US$0.20; last bus from museum at 1630). A yellow bus for Enapu workers leaves Pisco main square 2300 for Paracas National Park; it may give you a lift. Good walking in Paracas peninsula, details available from Park Office or ask for "Hoja 28-K" map at Instituto Geográfico Militar in Lima (it is not safe to walk if alone). The Mirador de los Lobos is a cliff overlooking sealion beaches, 20 minutes by car from *Hotel Paracas*—no public transport and the road peters out after a while (make sure your car is in good repair), crossing salty sand flats and mountains. To see the park properly you need a vehicle; try hitching with a tour group.

**Hotels** *Paracas*, A, check your bill carefully, good hotel, bungalows on beach (T Pisco 2220 or Lima 464865) good food, not cheap, good buffet lunch on Sun., US$6 low season, US$9 high, fine grounds facing the bay, is a good centre for excursions to the Peninsula and flights over Nazca; it has tennis courts and an open-air swimming pool (US$2 for non-residents); it also houses the Masson ceramics collection (worth seeing). *Hostal Santa Elena*, 100 m. from the beach in the Paracas National Park, C, reservations in Lima T 718222; very clean, with restaurant "the cook is legendary". Safe beach for swimming (no manta rays or *pastelillos*—dangerous fish with sharp dorsal fin which hide in sand), local trips organized, highly rec. *Hostería Paracas*, C, clean, safe, pool, very good restaurant; *El Mirador*, E, at entrance to Paracas, no hot water, good service, boat trips arranged (US$10-12 p.p. 0800-1200), meals available. Camping is possible on the beach near the *Hotel Paracas*.

**Restaurants** Excellent fried fish at open-sided restaurants by the fishing boats, e.g. *Rancho de la Tía Fela*, in Lagunilla, where one can sleep for free on the floor.

Up the Pisco valley, 48 km. from Pisco on the road to Huaytará and Ayacucho, is **Tambo Colorado**, one of the best-preserved pre-Inca ruins in coastal Peru (entrance US$0.60); apparently a palace with ancillary buildings; the wall paintings have survived from Inca times. Buses from Pisco, 0800, Oropesa US$0.80 (3 hrs.). Alight 20 mins. after stop at Humay; the road passes right through the site. Return by bus to Pisco in afternoon; for bus or truck back to Pisco wait at the caretaker's house (he will show you his small collection of items found on the site), as the area is dangerous. Taxi from Pisco US$30. From Humay, go to Hacienda Montesarpe, and 500 metres above the hacienda is the line of holes known as "La avenida misteriosa de las picaduras de viruelas" (the mysterious avenue of smallpox spots) which stretches along the Andes for many kilometres (its purpose is still unknown).

**Huaytará**, on the Pisco-Ayacucho road, contains Inca ruins and baths, and the whole side of the church is a perfectly preserved Inca wall with niches and trapezoidal doorways.

From Pisco the Pan-American Highway runs 93 km. S to **Ica**, on the Río Ica, population 147,000. The image of El Señor de Lurén in a fine church in Parque Lurén draws pilgrims from all Peru to the twice-yearly festivals in March and October (15-21), when there are all-night processions. The San Jerónimo church at Cajamarca 262 has a fine mural behind the altar. Ica is famous for its tejas, a local sweet of manjarblanco (sold behind Lurén church); it is also Peru's chief wine centre and has a harvest festival in March. The Bodega El Carmel (on the right-hand side when arriving from Lima) can be visited; it is a pisco distillery and has an ancient grape press made from a huge tree trunk. The Vista Alegre wine and pisco distillery can be also be visited (Spanish essential) and its shop is recommended. Local bus drops you at the entrance, or 10-15 mins. walk on the other side of the river. 10 km. outside Ica, in the district of Subtanjalla, is José Carrasco González, Bodega El Catador, a shop selling home-made wines and pisco, and traditional handicrafts associated with winemaking. In the evening it is a restaurant-bar with dancing and music; best time to visit is during harvest, late Feb. to early April, wine and pisco tasting is usually possible. Open daily 0800-1800, take a bus from 2nd block of Moquegua, every half hour, US$0.10. Cachina, a very young white wine "with a strong yeasty taste", is drunk about two weeks after the grape harvest.

The waters of the Choclacocha and Orococha lakes from the eastern side of the Andes are tunnelled into the Ica valley and irrigate 30,000 hectares of land. The lakes are at 4,570 metres. The tunnel is over 9 km. long.

**Hotels** Las Dunas, A plus 13% tax and service, about 20% cheaper on weekdays, highly rec., in a complete resort with restaurant, swimming pool, horseriding and other activities, own airstrip for flights over Nazca, 50 mins.; Lima offices: Ricardo Rivera Navarrete 889, Oficina 208, San Isidro, Casilla 4410, Lima 100, T 424180; Turistas, large and modern, with swimming pool, C, with private bath, restaurant; Colón, Plaza de Armas, E, with bath, F without, basic, dirty, old, noisy, restaurant; Siesta II, Independencia, E, clean, ask for quieter back room, rec.; Lima, Lima 262, basic but quiet, F; Confort, Lamar 251, 4 blocks from square, E, clean, possible to park motorcycle; Presidente, E, with bath, clean, good, possible to park motorcycle here, too; Royal, and Ica (basic, noisy), both friendly, clean, F or G, and on 100 block of Calle Independencia; Europa, Independencia 258, G p.p., clean and friendly; Hostal Viña, diagonally across from Entel, G, shower, safe, helpful. Several good hotels on Castrovirreyna, Las Brisas, D and Silmar, D. El Carmelo, on the Pan-American Highway S of turn-off for Las Dunas, swimming pool. Hotels are fully booked during the harvest festival and prices rise greatly.

**Restaurants** Several on Lima, e.g. at Hotel Sol de Ica; on Plaza is Santa Anita; Siesta, Independencia 160; Macondo, Jr. Bolívar 300, fish good, rec. El Fogón, Municipalidad 276, good and cheap. Good one at Ormeño bus terminal. El Eden, Casa Naturista, vegetarian at Bolívar 387, menú US$0.75. Pastelería La Spiga, Lima 243, rec.

**Warning** Beware of thieves, for instance in the market, even in daylight.

**Museo Regional** Bus 17 from Plaza de Armas, open 0745-1900, Mon.- Sat.: Sun. 0900-1300 (US$0.50). Houses mummies, ceramics, textiles and trepanned skulls from Paracas, Nazca and Inca cultures; a good, well-displayed collection of Inca counting strings (quipus) and clothes made of feathers. Good and informative displays with maps of all sites in the Department. Behind the building there is a scale model of the Nazca lines with an observation tower, a useful orientation before visiting the lines. The attendant paints copies of motifs from the ceramics and textiles in the original pigments (US$1), and sells his own good maps of Nazca for US$1.65.

The museum on the Plaza de Armas, run by Dr. Javier Cabrera, has a collection of several thousand engraved stones. Open Mon.-Sat. 0930-1230 and 1730-2000 and sometimes open Sun. If visiting in a group T 234363. We are informed that some of these stones are fakes: people have talked to the craftsmen concerned. If authentic, the stones suggest the existence of a technologically-advanced people contemporary with the dinosaurs, but the archaeological establishment seems very reluctant to study them. If interested, contact Ms. Sophia Afford, Le Petit Canadeau, Le Plan du Castellet, Le Beausset, 83330, France, T 94 987241, a geologist who has written several articles on the subject. (There are so many stones that its is impossible to believe they are all fakes. Most are in a recognisably pre-Inca style, but, for instance, kangaroo and a giraffe in the style of a modern children's story book, strain the visitor's credulity. However, Dr Cabrera is an interesting character, worth a visit. Ed.)

**Exchange** Banco de Crédito will change travellers' cheques after 1000.

**Tourist Office** Av. Grau 148, T 235247, very helpful and courteous. Touring y Automóvil Club del Perú, Manzanilla 523.

**Buses** To Lima, Ormeño (Lambayeque 180) and Tepsa, US$6, 5 hrs.; Roggero 4 a day; colectivo to Lima, US$10.15. Several buses daily in the evening to Nazca, US$2.10, 2-3 hrs. Colectivo to Nazca, US$3.15; to Pisco, US$1.20; bus to Pisco, US$1 (Ormeño or Roggero). Bus to Arequipa, US$16 with Ormeño (a very popular route at weekends). Ormeño go to Cuzco Wed. and Fri., leaving 1700, 30 hrs., US$27. To Abancay with El Cóndor de Aymaráes at 1600, US$19, 20 hrs. (take blankets). Several departures to Tacna, e.g. 1700, arrive 0900.

5 km. from Ica, round a lake and amid impressive sand dunes, is the attractive oasis and summer resort of *Huacachina*, with natural mineral water. The *Hotel Mossone* (4 hours' drive from Lima), D, full board, is at the eastern end of the lake. Another good hotel is the *Salvatierra*; both are great places to relax. Sleeping in the open is pleasant here, and swimming in the lake is beautiful, but watch out for soft sand (and, as elsewhere, watch your belongings). Local bus from the square in Ica to Huacachina, US$0.40, 10-15 mins.

The southern oases, S of Ica to the Chilean frontier, produce enough to support themselves, but little more. The highlands grow increasingly arid and the coast more rugged. There are only thin ribbons of cultivable lands along valley bottoms, and most of these can be irrigated only in their upper reaches. However, there are a few exceptions: the cotton plantations between Ica and Nazca, the orange-growing centre at Palpa, the large and well-watered oasis with Arequipa at its centre, and the smaller oasis of the river Moquegua further S. In several places the Highway is not protected against drifting sand and calls for cautious driving.

*Nazca*, 141 km. S of Ica by the Pan-American Highway, is a town of 30,000 people set in a green valley amid a perimeter of mountains, 444 km. from Lima. Its altitude of 619 metres puts Nazca just above any fog which may drift in from the sea: the sun blazes the year round by day and the nights are crisp. **Warning** Beware of thieves if you arrive early in the morning off a bus.

The Nazcas had a highly developed civilization which reached its peak about AD 800. Their decorated ceramics, wood carvings and adornments of gold are on display in many of Lima's museums. The Nazca municipality's own museum, on the main plaza, has a small but fine collection (entry, US$0.25, open Mon.-Sat. 0900-1300, 1500-1800). The valley about 35 km. S of Nazca is full of ruins, temples, and cemeteries; the last-named are quite difficult to find, but taxis do excursions for about US$30 per car. The trip should be made by all who have time: mummies, bones, pottery shards and scraps of textiles may be seen lying in the desert sun, although the best pieces have of course been taken by grave robbers and archaeologists. At the edge of the town is the reservoir of Bisambra, whose water was taken by the Nazcas through underground aqueducts—many still in use—to water the land.

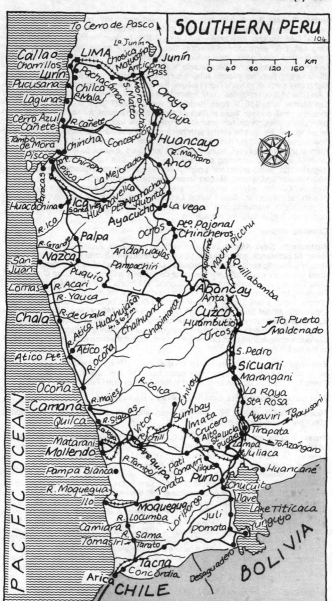

SOUTHERN PERU

104

**Hotels** *Turistas*, B, with bath (less without), clean, rooms with private patio, hot water, peaceful, rec., good meals, safe car park, swimming pool (US$1.20 for non-guests), rec. *Hostal Don Agucho*, Paredones y San Carlos (T 209), E, clean, friendly, rec.; *Nazca*, Calle Lima 438, F-G, warm showers (electric—beware), friendly, parties in courtyard at night, luggage store, helpful (only hotel with good information on tours, they also run cheap tours), safe motocycle parking, rec; *Montecarlo*, Jr. Callao, E with hot water (ask for it), F without, all rooms with bath, noisy rooms at front, bungalows at back D, small swimming pool, offers flights over the Lines plus one night's lodging but not all year round, mixed reports; *Konfort*, Calle Lima 587, G, small, clean, safe, intermittent water (as elsewhere), indifferent manager; *San Martín*, Arica 116, G, basic, electric showers; *Hostal El Sol*, E, basic but friendly, hot showers, small, on Jirón Tacna at Plaza de Armas; *Internacional*, Av. Maria Reiche, E, with bath, clean, quiet, cheap, hot water (if they ask for 10% tourist tax, they won't insist if you refuse to pay), rec. but be careful with belongings. *Hostal Alegría*, Jirón Lima 166, T 62, near bus station, F without bath, clean, basic, hot water, friendly and helpful, manager (Efraín Alegría) speaks English, rec, tours, flights and bus tickets to Arequipa arranged, reductions for IYHA members, swimming pool, washing facilities, safe luggage desposit, restaurant (flight inc. tax, taxi to airport and 1 night in hostal US$50); *Posada Guadalupe*, San Martín 480. Hostales opp. airport, *Maison Suisse*, rundown, food expensive, owned by Aeroíca, *Nido del Cóndor*, only for Aerocóndor passengers, but *Hostal Alegría* will get you a free pass to use the pool at *Maison Suisse*. *La Borda*, nr. airstrip, B, old hacienda, surrounded by cottonfields, swimming pool, excellent restaurant, quiet, helpful, rec., but about 5 km. from town, English-speaking manageress.

**Camping** *Wasipunko*, Panamericana Sur, Km 450.

**Restaurants** *Selva Alegre*, Lima, unfriendly service; *Oasis*, Arica 213, quite good and cheap; *La Esperanza*, good set lunch, Lima 594; *La Pascana*, Morzesky y Lima, rec.; *Cañada*, Lima 160, friendly, good seafood, reasonable; *Los Angeles*, half-block from Plaza de Armas, good, cheap, try sopa criolla, and chocolate cake, similar is *Concordia*. *Chifa Orlando*, on Lima, not original Chinese but cheap and good, 1¼ blocks from *Hostal Nazca* (direction Roggero); *La Taberna*, Jr. Lima 326, excellent seafood, bar, live music, friendly, popular with gringos, worth a look just for the graffiti; also *El Dorado*, Lima, near *Hotel Nazca*, good sopa criolla; *Mister Tiburón II*, Jr. Callao 195, next to *Hotel Montecarlo*, clean, good food. *Fuente de Soda*, near cinema, good *almuerzo*; the restaurant next to *Hostal Nazca* is cheap and good; at Cruz del Sur bus terminal, gringo restaurant, changes dollars, expensive food. Seafood is cheaper than beef. Do not drink the water, but the pisco sours are recommended as the best in Peru.

**Exchange** Difficult to change travellers' cheques, impossible at weekends; bring cash. **Banco de la Nación** exchanges at poor rate: better from **Chinese-owned paint shop** opposite Banco del Crédito. Cash can be changed in the square by *Hotel Turistas*, bargain hard.

**Post and telephone office** Lima 816; **police** Av. Los Incas, T 36.

**Tourist Office** Bolognesi 397. They will organize local tours for you and they sell books about the lines, but often closed.

**Buses** To Lima, about US$8, 8 hrs., Tepsa 1600, Ormeño, opp. *Turistas* and *Montecarlo* hotels about 8 a day, cheaper (best to take a morning bus, 0900, to arrive in daylight). Colectivo to Lima, Comité 3, Montevideo 581, US$13. To Arequipa, Ormeño, 7 a day (recommended as seats can be reserved, but dearer, and buses coming from Lima may be delayed); Sudamericano also OK (2030, 0300), all companies take about 12 hrs, US$7.20-10, delays possible out of Nazca because of drifting sand across the road; hold ups reported on this route, travel in daylight if possible—buses that leave round 0300, 0330 do most of the journey in daylight. Book ticket on previous day. Watch out for bus companies charging the full fare from Lima to Arequipa. Ormeño to Pisco, leaves at 0900, 1130, 1400, US$3.50, 3 hrs, rec.; Roggero to Pisco, US$3.50. Colectivo to Ica, US$3.15. Bus to Ica, US$2.10, 3-4 hrs. Ormeño, 0900, 1830, Tepsa, 2200, Roggero, 2030. Colectivo to Marcona, US$3. Bus to Tacna, US$14.50; Ormeño leaves at 1730, 2000 and 2300. Lima-Nazca-Cuzco takes 40 hours (can take 70 hrs.); the route is done by Ormeño twice a week, also Hidalgo. Cruz del Sur, Ormeño, Nazca-Cuzco, US$19, 30 hrs.; El Cóndor de Aymaráes to Abancay, Tues., Thurs., Sat., Sun., 21 hrs., from there take bus or colectivo to Cuzco. **N.B.** The Nazca-Cuzco route, through the Department of Ayacucho, is not safe at present.

**Excursions** The Fernández family, who run the *Hotel Nazca*, also have details of the Asociación de Guías de Turismo, a group of six guides trained by the Peruvian Ministry of Tourism. They offer three 2-hr. tours to the *mirador* on the pampa, cemetery at Chauchilla and nearby Inca ruins (e.g. the Estanquería—astronomical sighting posts) and aqueducts (US$6 each tour), rec. Also available is a tour to the pyramids of Cahuachi (17 km. W of Nazca on a very bad road), US$10 p.p. Tours only run if 4 people are more. Profesor Josué Lancho, Callao 771, T 327, offers tours in his car and gives lectures. Mario Raúl Etchebarne, T 85, is a well-informed guide with a car; also Juan Tohalino Vera, Jirón Lima 438, T Nazca 85, an official guide, rec. Recommended taxi-guides are Armando Denegri, office on Plaza de Armas by Aeroíca office, and José Barahona Calle, Jr. Bolognesi 282. All guides must be approved by the Ministry of Tourism: ask to see an identity card.

**Nazca Lines**  About 22 km. N of Nazca, along the Pan-American Highway, are the famous Nazca Lines. Cut into the stony desert are large numbers of lines, not only parallels and geometrical figures, but also some forming the shape of a dog, an enormous monkey, birds (one with a wing span of over 100 metres), a spider and a tree. The lines can best be appreciated from the air; it is now forbidden to walk or drive on them. The German expert, Dr Maria Reiche, who has studied the lines (mostly from a step ladder!) for over 40 years, lives in the *Hotel de Turistas*; she maintains that they represent some sort of vast astronomical pre-Inca calendar.

The lines are thought to have been etched on the Pampa Colorada sands by three different groups: the Paracas people 900-200 BC, Nazcas 200 BC-AD 600 and the settlers from Ayacucho at about AD 630.  Dr Reiche occasionally presents the free lecture given in the hotel every evening, when she is well enough. If not, her sister Dr. Renate Reiche delivers it for her. In 1976 she had a platform called the mirador put up at her own expense, from which three of the huge designs can be seen—the Hands, the Lizard and the Tree. Her book, *Mystery on the Desert*, is on sale for US$10 at the hotel, or it may be obtained for US$10 from Dr. R. Reiche Grosse, Kohlgarten 7, 8726 Hohenpeisserberg, W. Germany. Another good book is *Pathways to the Gods: the mystery of the Nazca Lines*, by Tony Morrison (Michael Russell, 1978), obtainable in Lima. Another theory is that the ancient Nazcas flew in hot-air balloons; this is based on the fact that the lines are best seen from the air, that there are burn (launching?) pits in many of the figures, and that there are pieces of ancient local pottery and tapestry showing balloonists, and local legends of flying men (which would be supported by the engraved designs on stones in Ica—**see page 996**) if these are proved authentic. See *Nazca, the flight of Condor 1*, by Jim Woodman, Murray, 1980 (Pocket Books, N.Y. 1977.) Georg A. von Breunig (1980) discounts both the above theories, claiming that the lines are the tracks of running contests. He bases his argument on the asymetrical surface level at curves in the designs and on the triangular fields which accord with human running characteristics, and with a number of runners starting from a straight line, then becoming an extended string of contestants. A similar theory was proposed by the English astronomer Alan Sawyer. Other theories are that the Nazca designs represent weaving patterns and yarns (Henri Stirlin) and that the plain is a map demonstrating the Tiahuanaco Empire (Zsoltan Zelko). *The Nazca Lines—a new perspective on their origin and meaning* (Editorial Los Pinos, Lima 18), by Dr Johan Reinhard, brings together ethnographic, historical and archaeological data on the lines, including current use of straight lines in Bolivia. Taxi-guides to the mirador, 0800-1200, cost US$5 p.p., or you can hitch, but there is not always much traffic. Ormeño bus leaves for the lines at 0900 (US$0.75); hitch back, but have patience. Go by an early bus as the site gets very hot. Better still, take a taxi and arrive at 0745 before the buses.

Small planes take 3-6 passengers to see the Nazca Lines; reservations can be made at the airport for flights with Aerocóndor: small planes, 3 passengers, good view (office opposite *Hotel de Turistas*, or can be booked at *Hotel Nazca*), or Aero Montecarlo (from hotel of that name; new planes and experienced pilots, and good). Aeroíca in Jirón Lima and at the airport, also fly over the lines. Price for flight US$50 (government-set price), but it may be possible to negotiate a lower price, US$25 upwards at quiet times, plus US$2 airport tax. Travellers' cheques accepted. Sra. Fernández from *Hotel Nazca* can arrange flights by joining single travellers into group parties. Flights should last from 30 to 45 minutes, but are sometimes cut to 20, and are bumpy with many tight turns—many people are airsick. Aerocóndor in Lima (T 425663, or at the *Sheraton Hotel*, T 333320) and Aeroíca (T 418614/418608) both offer flights over the lines from Lima in a one-day tour (lunch in Nazca) for US$260 p.p.; or flights from Ica for US$110 p.p. The best time to fly is early in the morning, or 1500-1600 (in October at least) to benefit from the horizontal light. (Taxi to airport, US$1.35, bus, US$0.10). The air companies (especially Aerocóndor) overbook early flights, then keep you waiting until later in the day when the light has deteriorated; criticisms received in 1991 of Aeroíca and Aerocóndor's level of helpfulness. For photographs, be careful you do not find yourself in a middle seat (small planes are best—a roll of 36 should allow 2-3 shots per figure).

Nanaska Tours does a tour of the Nazca lines on land, operated by Sr. Carlos Santa Cruz and Sr. Josué S. Lancho (both students of ancient culture), recommended.

**Nazca to Cuzco** (see warning under **Buses** above.) A very rough 470 km. road (can be driven in private car in 18 hrs.' driving time) cuts off through Puquío and NE to Abancay (**page 1053**) on the Ayacucho-Cuzco road. Many buses from Lima to Cuzco take this route, which is now being paved; it is mostly narrow with a very bad 25-km. stretch between km.187 and 212 from Abancay, but offers wild scenery; the journey may be broken at **Puquío** (159 km. from Nazca, *Hotel Los Andes*, F, with garage, "grim"; *Hostal Espinosa*, F, basic), although the town has little to recommend it and is freezing cold at night. Further on is Chalhuanca (*Hostal Zegarra*, dirty and cold, and *Hostal Porvenir*). From Puquío to Abancay is very hard for private cars: after the ascent from Puquío you reach the pampa and lakes where you can see flamingoes. About 160 km. from Abancay, you descend to the Pachachaca valley, which is followed to Abancay.

From a point 40 km. beyond Nazca along the Pan-American Highway a branch road (39 km.) runs to the ports of San Juan and San Nicolás, built to ship iron ore from the Marcona field, 29 km. inland, and Acarí, 53 km. E again, where a copper deposit is also being worked. San Juan, 553 km. S of Lima, has a beautiful deep-water bay.

After Nazca the Highway returns to the coast at Lomas (*Hotel Machora* with only 3 rooms and *Restaurant Melchorita*; *Capricho de Verano* and passes by Chala, Atico (*Alojamiento*, G, good and clean) and Ocoña, to Camaná (392 km. from Nazca).

**Chala**, 173 km. from Nazca, is a fishing village with beaches where condors may be seen. Good fresh fish available in the morning and possibilities of fishing with the local fishermen. Electricity all day. Between Chala and Camaná a missing bridge causes traffic delays on the highway.

**Hotel** *Grau*. One **restaurant** at N edge of town.

**Excursion** 10 km. N of Chala there are the large precolumbian ruins of Puerto Inca on the coast. Go 6 km. N on the Pan-American; at Km. 603 take the unpaved road on left. Follow this for 2 km., then take right fork another 2 km. to sea (bay with cliffs). Graf Rudolf of Geneva tells us that, on their discovery in the 1950s, the ruins were misunderstood and thus neglected. It is now recognised that this was the port for Cuzco. A French archaeologist runs a small hotel and restaurant on the beach, while studying the ruins. His wife, Mitzi Perales, will pick up guests from Chala, telephone messages can be left for her a day in advance at the Chala ENTEL phone office. Their hotel is basic, F, full board, excellent food, beautiful beach. The site is in excellent condition: the drying and store houses can be seen, on the right side of the bay is a cemetery, on the hill a temple of reincarnation, and the Inca road from the coast to Cuzco is clearly visible. The road was 240 km. long, with a staging post every 7 km. so that, with a change of runner at every post, messages could be sent in 24 hrs.

**Camaná** is a picturesque little town, 222 km. from Chala, with a good food market and pleasant beaches 5 km. away at La Punta (hourly buses from Camaná); good bathing but little shade. Rice is the principal crop.

**Hotels** *Camaná*, 9 de Septiembre, 1 block from plaza, E with bath and hot shower; *Plaza* on the plaza; *Central*, F, just off main square, not rec.; *Lider*, Av. Lima 268 (Pan-American Highway), E with bath, clean, good restaurant, safe motorcycle parking, rec.; *Villa Mar*, F, basic.

**Restaurant** *Chifa Hong Kong*, Plaza de Armas, good. The fresh-water shrimps are delicious.

Camaná sends its products to the small port of Quilca, S on the Río Quilca, in colonial times the unloading point for goods imported via Arequipa to Potosí (now in Bolivia). Now a seedy harbour. The village of Quilca is further along, perched on a cliff overlooking the Siguas river.

The Pan-American Highway swings inland from Camaná and runs along the top of a plateau with strange crescent-shaped dunes (**see page 1003**). The sudden descents into the canyons of the Siguas and Víctor rivers are interesting. Before Repartición a branch to the left leads to Aplao and the valley of the Río Majes.

From there continue past Coropuna, the highest mountain in southern Peru, to Andagua, a village lying at the head of the valley of the volcanoes (bus from Arequipa, Sun., Wed., Fri., 1530, with Empresa Delgado; basic accommodation at the mayor's house in Andagua). The Arequipa-Andagua bus goes on to Orcopampa, from which the thermal springs of Huancarama can be visited. A mining lorry leaves Orcopampa for Cailloma on the 12th and the last day of each month; this enables one to make a round trip from Arequipa.

At Repartición, 134 km. from Camaná, the Highway bifurcates: one branch runs through Arequipa into the highlands (near Arequipa is a new 39 km. toll road, US$0.25, Camaná-Arequipa, 172 km.); the other leads S to the Chilean border. From this latter road a branch leads off from La Joya W to Mollendo and Matarani.

**Mollendo**, 14,650 people, has now been replaced as a port by **Matarani**, 14½ km. to the NW. Port workers still live mostly in Mollendo, where the main customs agencies are. Three beautiful sandy beaches stretch down the coast, small beach nearest town is safest for swimming (swimming pool on the beach open Jan.-March). Mollendo now depends partly upon the summer attraction of the beaches and partly upon the 15,000 hectares of irrigated land in the nearby Tambo valley. On the coast, a few km. SE by road, is the summer resort of Mejía.

**Mollendo Hotels** *Salerno*, 30 rooms, all with bath, excellent seafood. *Aller*, Arequipa 681, E; *Hostal Cabaña*, Comercio 240, F, clean, good; *Royal*, Tacna 155, basic, clean; *Moderno*, Tacna 179, F; *Verana*, Arequipa 337, cheap.

**Restaurants** *Sea Room*, Pasaje San Francisco, overlooking the Pacific; *Venezia*, Comercio 188.

**Consulate** Danish Vice-Consulate, Calle Arequipa 164, T 2928, open 0830-1200/1430-1800.

**Bus** to Arequipa (Empresa Agarón), 2 hrs., US$2.45 twice daily; colectivo to Arequipa, US$3.55. To Tacna, 3 hrs., US$4.

The Pan-American Highway runs S from La Joya through Moquegua to Tacna and Arica (Chile). **Moquegua** (200 km. from Arequipa), population 10,460, described as "calm and clean", is a small town of winding cobblestone streets at 1,370 metres in the narrow valley of the Moquegua river. The plaza has llama-shaped hedges. The roofs are built with sugar-cane thatch and clay. Most of the valley below the city grows grapes and the upper part grows avocados (*paltas*), wheat, maize, potatoes, some cotton, and fruits. Climate: subtropical. Interesting cacti at Torata, nearby.

**Hotels** *Turistas* (1 km. from town), swimming pool, D, clean, friendly, hot water, restaurant fair, telephone calls expensive; *Limoñeros*, E, old house, basic rooms, showers, pretty garden, swimming pool (usually empty); *Hostal Comercio*, one block from Plaza, G, safe and friendly. **Restaurant** *La Sirena*, rec. for seafood and chicken dishes.

**Buses** Moquegua-Ilo, US$1.20, leaves at 1100. Returns from Ilo at 1700. **Moquegua-Tacna**, 0500, 3 hrs., US$1.50; **Moquegua-Puno**, San Martín, daily, about 10 hrs., US$8.

Moquegua's exports—avocados and wine—go by an excellent 96-km. road to the port of **Ilo** (population 95,000: *Hotel Turistas*, D, with or without bath, restaurant).

There are three Ilos: Ilo Viejo, in ruins after the earthquake of 1868; Ilo Nuevo, the present town, dirty, with a fishmeal factory, oil tanks, and dusty and sometimes cobbled streets and "half-door" saloons; and the spick and span village built by the Southern Peru Copper Corporation (hospital, cinema, playgrounds, etc.) for its engineers and their families.

The Southern Peru Copper Corporation is exploiting its copper property at Toquepala, at an altitude of 3,050 metres, and is developing its property at Cuajone nearby (good view of valley, which is full of cacti). All exports are through Ilo, along the 183-km. railway and road from Toquepala. The SPCC smelter is on the coast, 18 km. from the port of Ilo. Some 70 km. S of Moquegua a sign points to the Minas de Toquepala (64 km. by a good road); bus service from Tacna. **Toquepala** village, in a hollow, has a guest house (swimming pool), a church, club house and an American school, and is a pleasant place; however, it is a private mining community, and permission from the management must be obtained in advance to visit the village. A nearby cave contains paintings believed to date from 8000 BC, but it is very hard to find. Helio Courier planes reach it from Moquegua (12 min.) and Ilo (26 min.). Taxis from Ilo. In the desert between Moquegua and Tacna, John Streather tells us that engraved stones dating from 10,000 BC have been discovered.

**Tacna**, at 550 metres, backed by the snow-capped peak of Tacora, is 156 km. S of Moquegua by Pan-American Highway, 42 km. from the Chilean frontier, and 64 km. from the international port of Arica, to which there is a railway. Above the city, on the heights, is the Campo de la Alianza, scene of a battle between Peru and Chile in 1880. Tacna is 1,292 km. from Lima by road, 987 by air.

Tacna was in Chilean hands from 1880 to 1929, when its people voted by plebiscite to return to Peru. There are good schools, housing estates, a stadium to seat 10,000 people, an airport suitable for jet planes, many military posts and one of the best hospitals in Peru. Population: 46,250.

Around the city the desert is gradually being irrigated. The local economy includes olive groves, vineyards and fishing. The waters of Laguna Aricota, 80 km. N, are now being tapped for further irrigation and hydroelectric power for industry. The cathedral, designed by Eiffel, faces the main square, Plaza de Armas, which contains huge bronze statues of Admiral Grau and Colonel Bolognesi. The interior is austere but the round stained glass windows, each with a different motif, accentuate the fine, clean lines. The bronze fountain is said to be the duplicate of the one in the Place de la Concorde (Paris) and was also designed by Eiffel. The Parque Locomotiva (near city centre) has a British-built locomotive, which was used in the War of the Pacific. There is a very good railway museum at the station (0900-1500, US$0.10); the museum in the Casa de la Cultura has precolumbian pottery and war relics (very good, free, 1500-1800). Casino.

**Hotels**  *Turistas*, Av. Bolognesi, gardens, small swimming pool, tennis court, safe car park, D, with bath, meals expensive, but good breakfast for US$2, large rooms, clean, can make telephone bookings for other Tourist Hotels; *Central*, C with bath, near Plaza; *Holiday Suite*, with swimming pool and safe car park, 10 minutes' walk from centre, follow Av. Bolognesi to the University, from where it's one block to the left; *Don Quijote*, Leguía 940, E with shower, secure, clean, pleasant, near Chasquitur office for colectivos to Arica; *Lima*, on main square, E, with bath, bar, good restaurant, friendly, stores luggage; *Hostal Junín*, Junín, F, old house, hot water, good beds, clean. *Lido*, Calle San Martín 876, near Plaza, good, F; *El Dorado Hospedaje*, Calderón de la Barca 476, F. Accommodation is hard to find in the centre, especially at Christmas-time, because of Chileans on shopping sprees.

**Restaurant**  *Sur Perú*, Ayacucho 80, rec. *Los Tenedores*, San Martín 888, good, clean, expensive; *Hostal Lido*, San Martín 876 A, good value; *Pizzeria Italiana*, Libertad ½ block from San Martin, good; *El Sameño*, Arias Aráguez, near Ormeño bus terminal, good value fish restaurant. *El Pacífico*, Olga Grohaman 739, grills, chicken, seafood, good and cheap; *Helados Piamonte*, 1 block from *Hotel Turistas*, good ice cream.

**Tourist Office**  Foptur, San Martín 405, T 71-5352 (good map); Av. Bolognesi 2088 and Complejo Fronterizo Santa Rosa. Touring y Automóvil Club del Perú, Av. 2 de Mayo 55.

**Air**  Faucett daily jet flights to Lima, many cancellations; AeroPerú on Mon., Wed., and Sat. Taxi to town US$1.80 approx., but beware overcharging. No transport direct to border; cheapest way is taxi to town first, then take colectivo.

**Buses**  Smart new bus station in operation on Hipólito Unanue, to N of city. Some companies, inc. Tepsa and Ormeño still use their own terminals. Tacna-**Arequipa**, US$4.80, Ormeño, about 5 hrs., 6 a day, from Aráguez 698 y Grohaman. Berrios, Olga Grohaman 775, to Arequipa very slow, 5-6 police stops en route; better companies are harassed less, e.g. Ormeño. Colectivo to Arequipa, US$15, 6 hrs., leave from plaza, opposite church. Expreso Tacna, San Martín 201, T 2642, will collect from hotel. Several to Lima, tickets can be purchased several days before departure and buses fill up quickly; many passport checks; Tepsa (Leguía 981), noisy buses, at 1700, Ormeño 5 a day, average fare US$25; all take 21-23 hrs. Bus to Ilave, US$8, about 16 hours; Gironda (the best), Río Blanco and Ponce companies, all leave about 1700. Plenty of minibuses on from Ilave to Puno. To Nazca, US$14.50 (may be easier, and cheaper, to go via Arequipa). Bus Moquegua-Tacna, US$1.50, 3 hrs, Ormeño 7 a day, Sur Peruano. To Arica, see below.

The road E to Bolivia—via Tarata (where Inca terraces are still in use) and Challapalca to Ilave, where it connects with the Puno-La Paz highway—is gravel, not too bad in the dry season, though difficult in the rains.

**N.B.** Soon after buses leave Tacna, passengers' passports and luggage are checked, whether you have been out of the country or not. Train to Arica, 0700, 0800 and 1400, US$0.40, customs at station, you must purchase a ticket after getting your exit stamp (Chilean Consulate next to the station in Tacna.) Delays are common; this colourful journey takes 1½ hrs. Buses to Arica, e.g. Empresa Adsublata rec. (US$1.80). Plenty of colectivos to Arica, which will deliver you to a hotel (2 hrs., US$3 p.p., drivers present all documents to officials), Empresa Chasqui and Chiletur, which stop at both Peruvian and Chilean immigration; they leave from terminal area on Calle Coronel Mendoza. If going direct from the Tacna bus terminal, take a colectivo to this point, not to immigration, because you won't get a colectivo to Arica there. Despite what the Prefectura says, colectivos will take you across at weekends as well as during the week. Peruvian formalities are quick, Chilean ones take an hour, no fruit or vegetables are allowed into Chile. Coming into Peru from Chile, you can only change pesos into Peruvian currency with street money changers in Tacna (Banco de la Nación will not); the street rate is bad. Money changers line Av. Bolognesi, also at one end of new bus terminal "rates not too bad". Better when leaving Peru to change remaining Peruvian money to dollars at Banco de la Nación in Tacna and then buy pesos with dollars. Border closes at 2200, and Peruvian immigration is shut on public holidays. Entering Peru here, travellers are rarely asked for a return or onward ticket.

For those travelling by car between Peru and Chile, ask the taxi drivers at the rank beside the Tourist Hotel for details of border formalities, and buy *relaciones de pasajeros* (official forms) from a bookshop or from booth close to Customs; you will need eight (8) copies.

## AREQUIPA–PUNO–CUZCO–MACHU PICCHU (5)

All these places share great local pride and major tourist popularity: colonial architecture in Arequipa and Cuzco, the latter underpinned by massive Inca masonry; the tranquility of Lake Titicaca and the bustling folklore of Puno; the majesty of Machu Picchu, best viewed in the context of the once densely-populated heart of the Inca empire. All are set in the southern cordilleras of the Peruvian Andes, with smoking volcanoes, deep canyons, bleak altiplano and terraced valleys.

The Southern Railway no longer carries passengers between Mollendo and Arequipa, but there is a well-paved road from Mollendo to Arequipa via Matarani, about 130 km.

The **ash-grey sand dunes** near La Joya, on the Pan-American Highway and almost half way from the coast to Arequipa, are unique in appearance and formation. All are crescent shaped and of varying sizes, from 6 to 30 metres across and from 2 to 5 metres high, with the points of the crescent on the leeward side. The sand is slowly blown up the convex side, drifts down into the concave side, and the dunes move about 15 metres a year.

*Arequipa*, with about 850,000 people, 1,030 km. from Lima by road, stands at 2,380 metres in a beautiful valley at the foot of El Misti volcano, a snow-capped, perfect cone, 5,822 metres high, guarded on either side by the mountains Chachani (6,096 metres), and Pichu-Pichu (5,669 metres). The city has fine Spanish buildings and many old and interesting churches built of *sillar*, a pearly white volcanic material almost exclusively used in the construction of Arequipa. It was re-founded on August 15, 1540, by an emissary of Pizarro, but it had been an Inca city. It is the main commercial centre for the south, and its people resent the general tendency to believe that everything is run from Lima; business travellers should know this. The climate is delightful, with a mean temperature before sundown of 23°C, and after sundown of 14½°C. The sun shines on 360 days of the year. Annual rainfall is less than 150 mm.

Because of the danger of earthquakes the churches are low, the houses have one storey only, patios are small with no galleries. Roofs are flat and windows are small, disguised by superimposed lintels or heavy grilles. In recent years, higher buildings with large windows have been constructed.

**Points of Interest** The twin-towered **Cathedral** on the Plaza de Armas, founded 1612, largely rebuilt 19th century, remarkable for having its façade along the whole length of the church; **La Compañía** church, whose main façade (1698) and side portal (1654) are striking examples of the florid Andean *mestizo* style: see the **Capilla Real** (Royal Chapel) to the left of the sanctuary, and its San Ignacio chapel with a beautiful polychrome cupola (admission, US$0.10, open 0900-1130, 1500-1730, recommended); **Puente Bolívar**, designed by Eiffel. Arequipa has several fine seignorial houses with large carved tympanums over the entrances. The **Gibbs-Ricketts house** (now offices, open to public 1700-2000), with its fine portal and puma-head waterspouts, and the **Casa del Moral**, or Williams house (Banco Industrial, with museum) are good examples, as is the **Casa Govaneche**, Merced 201, now an office of the Central Bank (ask the guards who will let you view the courtyard and fine period rooms). One of the oldest districts is **San Lázaro**, a collection of tiny climbing streets and houses quite close to the *Hotel de Turistas* at Selva Alegre. Behind the cathedral there is a very attractive alley with more handicraft shops. Churches are usually open 0700-0900 and 1800-2000. The churches of **San Francisco, San Agustín, La Merced** and **Santo Domingo** are all well worth seeing. Opposite San Francisco is a handicraft centre, housed in a beautiful former prison. Next door is the **municipal museum** with much war memorabilia, open 0900-1730, interesting, US$0.25. The **archaeological museum** at the Universidad de San Agustín has a good collection of ceramics and mummies (it is being restored and a donation is expected for entry); apply to Dr. E. Linares, the Director. La Recoleta, a Franciscan monastery on the other side of the river, is well worth visiting, with museums; open 0900-1300, 1500-1700, entry US$0.60 (guide is not recommended). It contains several cloisters, a religious art museum, an Amazon museum and a library with many rarities. The church itself is open only 0700-800, 1900-2000.

By far the most interesting visit is to **Santa Catalina Convent**, opened in 1970 after centuries of mystery, the most remarkable sight in Arequipa; excellently refurbished, very beautiful, period furniture, kitchen utensils, and paintings. It is a miniature walled colonial town of over two hectares in the middle of the city; about 450 nuns used to live there in total seclusion, except for their women servants. The few remaining nuns have retreated to one section of the convent, allowing visitors to see a maze of cobbled streets, flower-decked cloisters and buttressed houses. These have been finely restored and painted in traditional white, browns and blues. Open 0900-1700, but entrance till 1600, admission US$3, daily, including Sun.; the tour they offer you at the entrance is worthwhile. The many pictures of the Arequipa and Cuzco schools are worth seeing. There is a small café, which sells cakes made by the nuns.

The flowered **Plaza de Armas** is faced on three sides by colonial arcaded buildings, and on the fourth by the Cathedral. The central **San Camilo market** (between Perú, San Camilo, Piérola and Alto de la Luna) is also worth visiting. At **Selva Alegre** there is a shady park in front of the *Hotel de Turistas*, which is within easy walking distance of all the famous churches and main plaza. Arequipa is said to have the best-preserved colonial architecture in Peru, apart from Cuzco. A cheap tour of the city can be made in a Vallecito bus, 1½ hrs. for US$0.30; a circular tour going down Calles Jerusalén and San Juan de Dios.

**Festivals** Interesting Holy Week ceremonies, culminating in the burning of an effigy of Judas on Easter Sunday and the reading of his "will", containing criticisms of the city authorities. Another festival at end-April and beginning-May fills the hotels. On 14 August, eve of the city's anniversary, there is a splendid firework display in the Plaza de Armas and a decorated float parade. On Sundays at about 1030 there is a civic and military parade on the Plaza de Armas.

**Warning** Thieves are very active in Arequipa. Beware particularly in market area, especially after dark, and in Calle San Juan de Dios between Plaza and bus offices; keep baggage secured in restaurants. Women travelling without men can expect much harassment here. However, the police have been complimented as friendly, courteous and efficient.

**Hotels** *Turistas*, Selva Alegre, C, with bath (less without bath), unsafe area, swimming pool (cold), gardens, good meals, pub-style bar, cocktail lounge, tennis court, Wendy house for children; *Portal*, C, Plaza de Armas, excellent, wonderful views, expensive but food and service disappointing, roof top swimming pool. *Posada del Puente*, Av. Bolognesi 101, T 21-74-44, D, good, restaurant, rec.; *Maison Plaza*, Plaza de Armas, D, with breakfast,

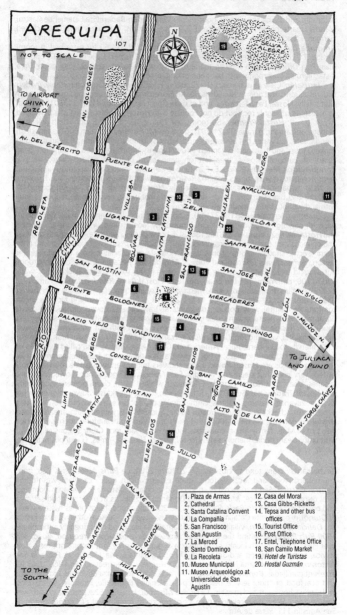

AREQUIPA
107

NOT TO SCALE

1. Plaza de Armas
2. Cathedral
3. Santa Catalina Convent
4. La Compañía
5. San Francisco
6. San Agustín
7. La Merced
8. Santo Domingo
9. La Recoleta
10. Museo Municipal
11. Museo Arqueológico at Universidad de San Agustín
12. Casa del Moral
13. Casa Gibbs-Ricketts
14. Tepsa and other bus offices
15. Tourist Office
16. Post Office
17. Entel, Telephone Office
18. San Camilo Market
19. *Hotel de Turistas*
20. *Hostal Guzmán*

bathroom and TV, clean, friendly, good value; *Villa Baden Baden* (Sra Bluemel de Castro), Manuel Ugarteche 401, Selva Alegre (T 222416), 6 rooms, D (F p.p.), breakfast included, German, French, English spoken, very informative about city's environs and climbing, rec.; *Arequipa Inn*, Rivero 412, modern hotel, D, with bath (US$4.60 for extra bed in room), garage, T 226077, slow service, owner unsympathetic; *Crismar*, Calle Moral 107, opposite main Post Office, D, with shower, modern, noisy, smelly toilets, central, food good; *Viza*, 3-star, Perú 202, all rooms with bath and phone, reports please.

*Jerusalén*, Calle Jerusalén 601 (T 222502/3), E, will change dollars, comfortable, modern with restaurant; next door at No. 605 is *Hostal Florentina*, F, hot water, good but washrooms a bit smelly; *Hostal Las Mercedes*, end of Calle Consuelo, P.O. Box 417 (T 213601), E, clean, safe, restaurant, highly rec. (but do not confuse with *Hostal La Merced*, in Calle La Merced, which is not); *Hostal Premier*, 50 rooms, Av. Quiroz 100, 2-star, E with bath, will store luggage, restaurant, garage (T 221-791); *Casa de Mi Abuela*, Jerusalén 606, E, very clean, friendly, safe, hot water, but beware electric showers, laundry, self-catering if desired, English spoken, tours and transport organized in own agency, which has good information, small library of European books, breakfast on patio or in beautiful garden, highly rec.; *El Conquistador*, Mercaderes 409, E, T 212916, clean, safe, lovely colonial atmosphere, credit cards accepted, owner speaks English; *Residencia Niza*, Calle Siglo Veinte 122, E (rooms, cabins and apartments), meals served, friendly; *Hostal Tumi de Oro*, San Agustín 311A, Cercado, 2½ blocks from Plaza de Armas, F p.p., hot water, breakfast on request, rooms with and without bath, laundry facilities, rec.

*Guzmán*, Jerusalén 408 (T 227142), F, hot water irregular, friendly, small café, laundry, patio for parking motocycle, very helpful, but dingy rooms, run down and thefts reported; and *Hostal Núñez*, Jerusalén 528 (T 218648), F, hot water, laundry, safe, clean, both crowded and opinions vary. *Excelsior*, Mercaderes 106, T 215241, F, clean, 6 rooms with private bath, warm electric shower, central, some rooms noisy, laundry facilities, safe for luggage and person, owner speaks German and English; *Mirador* (on Plaza de Armas), clean bedrooms but sagging beds, F, good, secure for luggage, friendly, some English spoken, hot water 0900-1700, bathrooms not too clean, but rec.; *Hostal Parra Residencial*, Av. Parra 97, T 223787, 5 mins. from station, clean, friendly, laundry facilities, F (some rooms with shower, US$1 more), rec.; *Le Foyer*, Ugarte 114, T 214658, F, hot water, washing facilities, clean, comfortable, central, very popular, discounts at travel agents downstairs; *Hostal Santa Catalina*, E or F, near Convent, clean, hot water, friendly, light bulbs in short supply (take your own); *Residencial Rivero*, Rivero 420, F, clean, with bath but not always hot water, friendly, helpful, washing facilities; *Crillón Serrano*, Calle Perú 109, G, with bath, hot water a.m., friendly to Germans, mice; *Americano*, Calle Alvarez Tomás (also called Ejercicios on maps), 4 blocks from the plaza, F, hot shower at any time, clean, beautiful geraniums; On San Juan de Dios are *Hostal Royal*, F, hot showers but not enough (some rooms without water), very noisy but clean and friendly; *San Francisco*, F, good, hot showers, washing facilities, clean; and *Hostal Florida*, E (cheaper without bath), clean, modern, good beds, rec. *Hostal Tradicional*, Sucre 113, F, family-run, cheap breakfasts downstairs, order hot water in advance, washing facilities, clothes drying on roof, safe (also for motorcycle), clean, peña in p.m., check bill carefully; *Hostal Sucre*, Sucre 407, G without bath, friendly, clean; *Hostal Fernández*, Quesada 106, E, 10 mins. from centre, beautiful garden with parrot, views of El Misti, family affair, breakfasts, hot water, clean, rec.; *César's*, Consuelo 429, F with bath, clean, good, friendly, safe. *Hostal Cuzco*, Plaza de Armas, G without bath, very basic.

**Restaurants** Many tend to close early—2030 or 2100. *Le París*, Mercaderes 228, good international food and local seafood, quite expensive but good, excellent washrooms; *Central Garden*, San Francisco 127, good food and value; *Astoria*, Calle Santo Domingo, local dishes, good service; *Monza*, Santo Domingo 1½ blocks from Plaza, good set meal and breakfast; *André de París*, Santa Catalina 207, good food, holds peñas twice a week; *El Quinqué*, opp. Santa Catalina, meals and peñas, all week in season, otherwise weekends; *Las Delicias del Carbón*, Villalba 317, near Santa Catalina, good grills, friendly atmosphere; *1900 Pub Pizzería*, behind the cathedral, excellent pizzas; *Balcón Arequipa*, good view over Plaza, popular with locals, good breakfasts and fruit juice (but sangría not rec.), slow service, corner of Merced and Bolognesi; *El Fogón*, Santa Marta 112, good; *Pizzería San Antonio*, Jerusalén y Santa Marta, excellent; *La Rueda* in side street off Jerusalén, US$3 for excellent parrillada; *Bonanza*, Jerusalén 114, one block from Plaza de Armas, excellent fish and local food, but poor service, peña group Fri. evenings; *Bagatelle*, Jerusalén, good snacks and sandwiches, courtyard to eat in; *La Nueva Mundial*, Jerusalén 522, popular, local dishes, band playing; We have received a number of reports of robberies at *El Cerrojo*, Portal de San Agustín 111, Plaza de Armas.

Vegetarian: *Comedor de Gran Fraternidad Universal*, Jerusalén 400, cheap, friendly; *Come y Vive Mejor*, Calle Nueva 410A, cheap and good. *La Zanahoria*, Salaverry 203, not too good; *Secretos y Virtudes de la Naturaleza*, Peral 321, good and cheap; *Mathesis*, Jerusalén 224, a bit more expensive than others; *Rainbow Community Diet System*, San José 1126; *Madre Natura*, Grau 310. Excellent natural yoghurt at Jerusalén 517, US$0.45 per litre.

Rec. café *Monaco*, Calle Mercaderes, cheap and good: *Hospedaje Cuzco*, corner of Plaza, balcony for drinking and watching the world go by, excellent (especially vegetable) tortillas but avoid the *ceviche*; *Harumi* snack bar, San José 216, Chinese, US$1 for set menu. *Dairy Room*, Plaza de Armas, cakes and pastries, very good coffee; cheapest good pisco sours at *Jumbo Jet*, Colon 221. Good ice cream at *Lamborghini* on Pasaje Catedral, behind the Cathedral.

A score of *picanterías* specialize in piquant foods; try one called *El Pato*; *rocoto relleno* (hot stuffed peppers), *cuy chactado* (seared guinea-pig), *papas con ocopa* (boiled potatoes with a hot yellow sauce) and *adobo* (pork stew). Try them at lunchtime in Yanahuara suburb such as the *Sol de Mayo*, Jerusalén, reasonable prices, beautiful garden, open until 1800, also the *Chalet de la Nova*, off Av. Ejército, family run, excellent food in taverna style. Arequipeño food also at San Camilo market. Good cheap places down San Juan de Dios, but dodgy area for tourists, e.g. *Dalmacia* excellent family-run restaurant. *Las Américas* store in same street has good ice cream. A good local speciality is Mejía cheese; try also the *queso helado* (frozen fresh milk mixed with sugar and a sprinkling of cinnamon), the excellent chocolate (*La Ibérica*)—the factory on Jerusalén, NE of Plaza de Armas, gives tours on weekdays only, the toffee (e.g. at *San Antonio Pizzería*), and the fruit drinks called *papayada* and *tumbada*, local specialities in the market and restaurants.

**Current** 220 volts A.C., 50 cycles.

**Clubs** Club Arequipa; International Club; Club Hípico Los Leones (riding club).

**Shopping** *Casa Secchi*, Mercaderes 111, sells good arts, crafts and clothing; also *Artesanías Peruanas*, Puente Bolognesi 147. *Empresa Peruana de Promoción Artesanal (EPPA)*, General Morán 120. The covered market opposite the Teatro Municipal in Calle Mercaderes is rec. for knitted goods, bags, etc. Market around Valdivia and N. de Piérola. Sweaters and woollen goods can be better value than in Juliaca or Puno. Arequipa is noted for its leather work; the street of saddlers and leather workers is Pte. Bolognesi. The handicraft shop in the old prison opposite San Francisco is particularly good for bags. At *Fundo del Fierro* shop 14, on Plaza San Francisco, alpaca-wool handicrafts from Callalli in the Colca canyon are sold. *Lanificio*, La Pampilla, no number, T 225305, the factory for high-quality alpaca cloth at better prices than Lima outlets. At Portal de Flores 134, on eastern side of Plaza de Armas, is the alpaca shop of Arturo Uria Wendorff, good range, helpful owner and good prices. *El Zaguán*, Santa Catalina 120A, good for handicrafts. Three antique shops in Calle Santa Catalina. Supermarkets nr. market sell good bread and yoghurt.

**Photography** Sr. Fernando Delange, N-10 Urbanización Adepa, T 233120, repairs all kinds of electrical equipment as well as cameras. Foto Esperanza S. R. Ltda, Mercaderes 132-2, English spoken, cameras mended.

**Bookshop** *Librerías ABC* has a branch in Calle Santa Catalina 217, between the convent and the Plaza de Armas, *Codersa*, San Francisco 131.

**Laundry** *Lavandería Cayro*, Jerusalén 311 and Ejercícios 442. *Lavendería del Pueblo*, Ejercícios 558.

**Taxi Fares** US$1 a trip, US$2.50 an hr. within the town, US$0.35 minimum; US$2.50 in the country; US$2 airport to city (can be shared). US$1.20 railway station to centre.

**Car Hire** *National*, Bolívar 25; *Avis* (cheaper), Puente Bolognesi nr. plaza.

**Entertainment** Bar *Romie*, Plaza San Francisco, tiny bar with live music rec., Mon., Tues., *autóctono*, Wed.-Sat., *peña*. Excellent *peña El Sillar* in the cloisters of La Compañía church, minimum charge of US$0.50, plus US$1 for the music, 1930-2300; *Peña Waykopac*, Jerusalén 204, good atmosphere, Fri. and Sat. *Peña Chunenea*, Pasaje la Catedral 4. Watch out for the local folk-music group Chachani, said to be one of Peru's best. *Discoteca Casablanca*, Av. Sucre, garage entrance, clean, well-run and safe; downstairs pool room.

**Sports** Two public stadia, a racecourse, several swimming pools, tennis courts. The Arequipa Golf Club (18 holes) welcomes visitors from abroad. Riding is very popular. There are bullfights.
**Climbing** Club de Andinismo de Arequipa. Chanchari Tours, Tristán 224, PO Box 2480, T 213186, hires climbing equipment, can provide guide and transport, rec.; Sr Carlos Zárate,

who also runs a camera repair shop, is a member of the Mountaineering Club of Peru, very helpful with maps and advice.

**Exchange**  Banco Internacional, Mercaderes 217, exchanges Citicorp dollar cheques. **Banco de Crédito** accepts Visa Card and gives good rates, no commission, recommended. Others include Banco Popular, Banco Continental (will not change travellers' cheques) and Banco del Sur del Perú (Calle Jerusalén, close to Post Office, will change travellers' cheques, 2-3% commission, accepts Master Charge). **Lima Tours**, Santa Catalina 120 (American Express agent but will not change any travellers' cheques), **Via Tours**, Santo Domingo 114, good rates. **Diners Club**, San Francisco 112. Parallel market down **Calle Santo Domingo**, Jerusalén near Plaza de Armas, and at Morán y San Juan de Dios.

**Spanish Course**  Silvana Cornejo, 7 de Junio 118, Cerrito Los Alvarez, Cerro Colorado, T 225308, about US$1.50/hour, rec., she speaks German fluently.

**Consulates and Cultural Institutions**  British Consul Mr. Roberts, Calle Quesada 107, Yanahuara, T (054) 211961 **English Library** at Peruvian-North American Cultural Institute, Melgar 109. **Instituto Cultural Peruano-Norte Americano**. **French Consul and Library** Alianza Francesa, Santa Catalina 208. **Chilean Consulate** Mercaderes 212, 4th floor, entrance to lift 30m. down passageway down Mercaderes on left, open 0900-1300, present passport 0900-1100 if you need a visa.

**Post and Telecommunications**  At central Post Office, Moral 118 opposite *Hotel Crismar*. The central Post Office also provides a telex service. Letters can only be posted at the Post Office during opening hours. Telephone and fax: Entel, San Francisco y Valdivia.

**Doctor**  Dr Julio Postigo, Independencia 225; Dr. Jorge A. del Carpio Alvarez, Santo Domingo 123, of 303, T 215483, rec, only Spanish spoken. **Dentist** Dr José Corrales, San Juan de Dios 216.

**Tourist Information**  Foptur, Portal Municipal 112, Plaza de Armas, south side, T 213101. Complaints and suggestions are welcomed, information not always accurate but they try to be helpful, open 0730-1500, free street plans. Another tourist office has opened on Calle Santa Catalina, half a block N of the Plaza, no sign and as yet no reports about it. The Librería at Jerusalén 109 sells maps. Police may be contacted for information by phone: 226549, but not at all hours; Tourist Police, Jerusalén 317, and at the bus station, are also helpful. Touring y Automóvil Club del Perú, Calle Sucre 209.

**Travel Agencies**  *Tony Holley* takes small private groups by 12-seater Land Rover to interesting places in the area such as the Salinas borax lake, Chivay, the slopes of El Misti, cave drawings at Sumbay, the volcanoes Ubinas and Chachani, Caylloma where the Amazon rises, and rural Arequipa. Excursions cost from as little as $20 per person, providing there is a minimum of 6 people on tour. With fewer passengers the cost rises proportionally. Passengers are insured. Mr. Holley's postal address is Casilla 2034, Arequipa, and his home address is Urb. Tahuaycani F-28, Umacollo, Arequipa (T 212525, Mon.-Fri. 0730-1600; 224452 daily after 1700, 24 hrs. Sat., Sun., and feast days.) When not on tour, Mr. Holley's car may be found near Santa Catalina between 0715 and 1230.

*Continental Tours*, Calle Jerusalén 402, good value, English and French-speaking guides. *Conresa Tours*, Jerusalén 409, Casilla 563, T 211847/ 223073/215820, specializes in trips to the Colca Canyon, and to the Toro Muerto petroglyphs (US$20 p.p.), Las Salinas and Mejía lakes, and city tours, *South American Handbook* users welcome. Several agencies offer tours (1 or 2 days) to the Colca Canyon: *Vlado*, Merced 408, cheaper than most; *Expreso Turismo y Confort*, Peral 304; *Cóndor Tours*, on Ugarte across from entrance to Santa Catalina; and *Santa Catalina Tours*, buses with large windows, recommended. *Panambi Tours*, Calle Jerusalén T 241498, run by Marco Rebaza "a big friendly bear", excellent local tours to Colca Canyon and area, reliable transport, not the cheapest but worth it for his expertise. Many agencies, including *Happy Travels*, Santa Catalina 106, offer tours of the city and surrounding area, T 218592; English spoken. Local office of *Lima Tours* reported reliable.

**NB**  Strong warning received of agencies collecting money in advance but not turning up with vehicle for tour. If possible, check that the agency has enough people to run the tour—and only pay a deposit in advance. Alternatively organize your own group.

**Buses**  Most companies have their offices in Calle San Juan de Dios (5-6 blocks from Plaza de Armas) and Calle Victor Lira. To Lima, 1,030 km, colectivos take 19 hrs., rain damage to the road can cause delays; fare US$19 or more. Warning: need to book in advance to and from Lima in Jan.-March holiday season. Buses, de luxe Pullman, air conditioned with hostess, many daily, 16 hours or more: Cruz del Sur, Arequipeño, Tepsa (toilet on board), Ormeño rec.;

Sudamericana is most expensive. Few buses stop at Pisco. Trucks to Lima take 3-4 days. To Puno and Cuzco roads and buses are generally bad; the train is better; buses run only at night to **Puno**, US$6.50, San Cristóbal cheapest, up to 17 hrs., uncomfortable, cold; colectivo, heavily booked, some by day (1000), fare US$13.50. To and from **Cuzco** by bus (680 km.), San Cristóbal, 1600 (18 hrs.) US$12.75; Cruz del Sur, 21 hrs., US$13.50, 1600, Jacantaya at 1800. Colectivo-taxi to Cuzco US$30. Colectivo to **Juliaca** US$13 (office on Calle Salaverry) leaves 0900. Bus to Juliaca 8½-9½ hrs., US$7.75. Bus to **Tacna** (about 20 a day), Cruz del Sur (rec.), Ormeño, US$4.80, 6 hrs.; also Flores Hnos. Colectivo to Tacna, Expreso Tacna, San Juan de Dios 537, T 213281, will collect at hotel, rec., US$7.60, 6 hrs. **Moquegua** by Angelitos Negros, leaves in the morning, US$3.20, interesting journey. Buses must be booked 24 hrs. in advance. Bus to **Nazca**, US$7.20-10, Sudamericana, 3 a day, Ormeño, 7 a day, 10 hours; also with Roggero and Tepsa. Beware, some bus companies to Nazca charge the Lima fare.

**Air** Rodríguez Ballón airport, 7 km. from town. To and from **Lima**, daily air service by Faucett and AeroPerú. No direct flight to Iquitos; all go via Lima. To **Miami** via Lima and Panama; leaves 3 times a week at 1520, arrives Miami 0730 folowing day. To **Cuzco**, US$40, by Faucett and AeroPerú, daily at 1000 (except Sun.); to **Puerto Maldonado** with air force (Grupo 8), usually Friday. To **Juliaca** by AeroPerú daily except Sun. and Faucett, about US$25, 20 mins. (book well ahead). The plainclothes police at the passport desk may arrange a taxi for you (approx. US$2). Buses marked "Zamacola" go to about ½ km. from the airport. The offices of both Faucett and AeroPerú are on the Plaza de Armas. A new airline, Aerochasqui, T 219558/244999, has Boeing 727s flying daily between Arequipa and Lima, and Tacna 3 times a week, but we only have sketchy information so far. Airport tax: US$10.

**Rail** To **Puno**, at 2100, with connections to Cuzco via Juliaca; day train suspended. Fares: 1st class US$7.50, 2nd class US$5. Only the Pullman cars, US$12.50, are heated—important above 4,000 metres—do not wear too much clothing; the doors are locked and therefore it is much safer. If not travelling Pullman, take a blanket. If travelling 2nd class take a cushion as well. Rail trip to Puno and Cuzco is safer in the rainy season than by road. The train arrives in Juliaca after about 7 hrs, there is then a 2 hr. wait; if going to Cuzco you have to change trains here. Fare to Juliaca is US$10 pullman, US$5 first class, US$3.15 second class; to Cuzco, US$20 first class, US$12 second class; best to travel in buffet car, which costs US$20 for tourists; food good. The ticket office is open 0730-1200, 1500-1800, 2000-2100, Sat. 0800-1200, 1500-1800, Sun. 0900-1200, 1500-1800; queue at 0400 for 1st class tickets on day before departure. Sr. Guzmán of *Residencial Guzmán*, Jerusalén 408, may be able to help with tickets, for a fee US$0.35; Continental Tours and others charge US$2 extra to book for you. If you have difficulty buying train tickets, try in the shops opposite the station, or even ask a policeman at the station. Train schedules and ticket office hours change frequently.

If you feel bad on train ask for the oxygen mask at once.

**Warning** On the Arequipa-Juliaca-Puno or Cuzco rail route, beware of thieves at every station, especially at night. Wait until everyone else has left the train and then till everyone else has left the platform, or (at Arequipa) ask at the police office if they will let you out of their exit. If not travelling in the locked "turismo" pullman coach, padlock your bag to the luggage rack, tie all your belongings to you and keep pockets empty. It's best to take only one large bag which cannot be thrown through a window. The lighting may not always work, or may be sabotaged by thieves: take a torch. Latest reports indicate that the least secure part of the trip is the wait at Juliaca, "the theft stop". Police may escort foreigners who have to go to the Juliaca ticket office, but watch your bags all the same.

**Excursions** The hillside suburb of **Cayma**, with delightful 18th century church (open only until 1600). It also has many old buildings associated with Bolívar and Garcilaso de la Vega and is the home of contemporary Arequipeño poet, Manuel Gallegos Sanz. The Candelaria festival on 2 February is colourful. Many local buses marked Cayma. There is a new luxury *Hotel Cayma*. **Yanahuara**, also a suburb, with a 1750 *mestizo*-style church (opens 1500), with magnificent churrigueresque façade, all in *sillar*; the Tiabaya valley; thermal baths of Jesús (½ hour by car, on the slopes of Pichu-Pichu), open 0500-1230. **Yura**, 29 km. from Arequipa (bus every 3 hours from San Juan de Dios, US$0.40) in a small, interesting valley on the W slopes of Chachani (*Yura Tourist Hotel*, D, wth bath, meals, and an unsigned hotel opposite, F, good), has thermal baths open Tues.-Sat., morning only. **Socosani** (1½ hrs. by rail and road), now a spa owned by a mining consortium, can only be visited by appointment, 40 km. from Arequipa, in a beautiful small valley SW of Chachani, with a modern hotel providing meals and Socosani water, sports in Socosani include tennis, bowls. **Tingo**, which has a very small lake and 3 ill-kept swimming pools, should be visited on Sun. (bus 7, US$0.20) for local food; *anticuchos* and *buñuelos*. 3 km. past Tingo on the Huasacanche road is *La*

*Mansión del Fundador*, originally a Jesuit foundation but later a *hacienda*, restored as a museum with original furnishings and paintings, entrance fee US$0.75, with cafeteria and bar; it is beside the Sabandía river. Molino de Sabandía, built 1600, entrance fee US$0.50, swimming bath and countryside, well worth seeing; Yumina (adjoining Sabandía), many Inca terraces which are still in use. The interior of the church at Chiguita is well worth seeing.

Up a passable dirt road running through Cayma, Sumbay (4,150 metres) and Viscachani, between Misti and Chachani, is the village of *Chivay* (regular buses 5 hrs.) lying in the spectacular terraced *Colca Canyon*. If taking a car to Chivay, there is a toll on entering and leaving the village amounting to US$3. Local, very distinctive, costumes still worn by women, and there is a swimming pool 3 km. upstream fed by hot springs (US$0.40, clean, rec.). Water from this river is currently being diverted through a series of tunnels and canals to the desert between Repartición and Camaná, to irrigate the Siguas and Majes pampas. Further down the Colca Canyon, on both sides (bridge—Puente del Inca—at Chivay only) unspoilt Andean villages are to be found, overlooked by the two volcanoes, Hualca-Hualca and Ampato. At one of these, Yanque (good church, where two nuns from the Bronx sell handicrafts), walkers can cross the canyon by a colonial bridge (no vehicles— reached from the main square in Yanque via Av. Santa Rosa) and walk to villages on the other side: Coporaque and Ichupampa (about 2 hrs.), also with good churches; beyond Ichupampa is Lari, also with a fine church. On the opposite side of the river from Lari is Maca, whose church has an interesting interior. Beyond Maca is *Cabanaconde* (2 hrs. walk down, 3 hrs. back up); festivals: 25 May: horseriding, dancing; 14-18 July: bullfighting, dancing. There is a path to the Colca Canyon from the main square, 4 hours' walk; it is possible to cross and go up to Tapay. A longer hike, 4 days, crosses the pass (5,000 m.) and reaches Madrigal through a red walled valley. 10 km. before Cabanaconde, you reach the Cruz del Cóndor viewpoint, spectacular scenery, condors to be seen early a.m. and late p.m. (take 0400 bus from Cabanaconde). If hiking, which is strenuous but worth it, buy food in Arequipa, and maps from the Instituto Geográfico Militar in Lima, take water sterilizer. **N.B.** Robbery in the Colca Canyon has been reported; if hiking seek advice on local conditions.

   The Colca (or Majes) Canyon, said to be twice as deep as the Grand Canyon, was discovered from the air in 1954 by Gonzalo de Reparaz; the first descent was made in 1978 and the first descent by raft and canoe was made in 1981. AeroPerú and Aerocóndor have flights over it. It is possible to visit the canyon in one day, but you will reach Cruz del Cóndor by about 1300, when there will be no condors around, and the return to Arequipa is very long. A short circuit from Arequipa goes via Chivay, Yanque (more thermal baths), Achoma, Maca, Cabanaconde, then on to Huambo and back to Arequipa (private transport only, and rough road). A longer route involves going to Callalli (beautiful alpaca-wool work at Centro Artesanal) from Viscachani, instead of to Chivay, then to Sibayo (possible detour to Cailloma), Tuti, and then to Chivay. This route adds an hour to the circuit, permitting views of fine landscapes with vicuña, Andean duck and llama, and a glance at the churches of Callalli and Tuti.

**Accommodation** Chivay: *Hostal Colca*, Salaverry 307, E, two blocks from square, dormitory rooms and some with private bath, good restaurant, friendly, water infrequent; *Hostal Anita* on plaza, G, clean, friendly, hot shower; *Alojamiento Guillermo*, Bolognesi 816, F, clean and friendly; best food at unnamed restaurant at Calle Siglo 20 107, just off the plaza. The *Aldea Turística de Colca* (rec., E, bungalows for 6 are C) at Achoma, half an hour from Chivay along the Cabanaconde road, offers breakfast US$1.50, other meals US$2.50, only electricity, heating and hot water in valley; book through Receptur in Lima or Arequipa or Ricketts Turismo, Mercaderes 407, Arequipa, T 225-382, open April-Nov. only. In Cabanaconde: *Hotel de la Colca*, F, friendly and clean, good restaurant, hot showers; *Cruz del Cóndor*, basic but clean, good meals, F, horse hire to Cruz del Cóndor, 2-3 hrs. there, 1 back, impressive ride; *Alojamiento Bacilia*, G p.p., unwelcoming; several small restaurants, not particularly good value—look for "cerveza Arequipeña" sign.

**Travel to Colca Canyon** Buses to Cabanaconde from Arequipa via Chivay: Transportes Delgado (rec.), leave Arequipa and Cabanaconde daily, 7½ hours. Transportes El Chasqui Transandino, San Juan de Dios 515, goes as far as Maca. Sur Express, San Juan de Dios 537 goes all the way to Cabanaconde, approx 9 hrs. Via Huambo with Transportes Jacantaya, Víctor Lira 108, T 23258 from Arequipa, and Cabanaconde, but not daily. Generally on this route, buses leave Arequipa early morning, check for times and prices, both of which are erratic. Buses leave Chivay for Cabanaconde at 1100, US$0.60, for views sit on right side of bus, return from Cabanaconde to Chivay 0500. Alternatively a taxi can be hired for a day tour (US$80 for up to 5, make sure no more are carried, too uncomfortable otherwise) at Expreso Chivay (Comité 10), Calle San Juan de Dios (if going by rented car, ask for an extra fuel can; no fuel in Canyon except at Chivay).

Arequipa travel agencies run day tours to the Canyon for about US$17 (avoid agents who overcharge), but the one-day trip (0400-2400) is very tiring and the viewing stops are short. (See under Arequipa Travel Agencies). You can also book in Lima: Coltur, Av. Pardo, Miraflores, Puci Tours, Av. Arequipa, Miraflores, Lima, organize a tour to Chivay with a 2/3 night stop over in Achoma, rec. Canyon best visited April-November, after rainy season, but never travel in mountains after dark. Whether travelling independently or on a tour, always take warm clothing or a blanket.

El Misti volcano may be climbed. Start from the hydroelectric plant (first register with the police there), then you need one day to the Monte Blanco shelter (4,800 metres). Start early (take water) for the 4 hrs. to the top, to get there by 1100 before the mists obscure the view. If you start back at 1200 you will reach the hydroelectric plant by 1800. (Erick and Martine Perruche, of Montargis, who took this route, have left a map in the *Hotel Guzmán* ). Alternatively, buses leave Arequipa for Baños Jesús, then on to Chiguata, where one can walk to the base of El Misti. Be sure to take plenty of food and water, it takes 2 days to reach the crater, guides may be available at Cachamarca.

The world's largest field of petroglyphs (hard to find on your own) at Toro Muerto (off the Majes canyon) can be reached by taking a bus (San Antonio, Lima 119, 0700, returns Arequipa at 1400 and 1700) to Corire, 3 hrs., US$5 return; get out 2 km. before Corire and walk 1 hr. to Toro Muerto (entry US$0.15). Guide for US$3. The higher you go, the more interesting the petroglyphs; take plenty of water and protection against the sun, including sunglasses. There are several restaurants around the Plaza de Armas in Corire; one hotel: *Hostal Willys*, F, clean, good, intermittent water supply.

The railway from Arequipa winds its way up the valley towards Juliaca. Skirting Misti and Chachani the train climbs steadily past Yura, Socosani and Pampa de Arrieros; after another 80 km. it reaches Crucero Alto, the highest point on the line (4,500 metres). Lakes Lagunillas and Saracocha are very pretty lying on opposite sides of the railway, which passes their margins for nearly an hour. As the descent continues streams become more plentiful. The scene changes in a few hours from desolate mountain peaks to a fertile pampa carrying a fairly populous agricultural community. (Since there is no day train at present, much of this scenery is not visible en route.)

The rough road from Arequipa to Juliaca reaches its highest point at Alto de Toroya, 4,693 metres. Train is more comfortable than bus. Arequipa-Juliaca by motorcycle takes about 9 hrs.; if heading for Puno it is better to go via Juliaca than taking the direct branch to Puno. Beautiful scenery, small villages on route, but no gasoline for 350 km.—all the way.

**Juliaca**, 289 km. from Arequipa, at 3,825 metres (cold at night), has a population—mostly Indian—of 100,000. It is reported to be very poor and run down, and therefore lawless; you can buy good alpaca clothing here very cheaply, in the plaza in front of the railway station. When trains pass through Juliaca, there is generally a 1-2 hr. delay, and cheap woolen goods are sold through the train windows. Fleeces can be purchased at about US$2.50 per kilo, but they sell very fast. On the huge Plaza Melgar (good place to meet local students), several blocks from the main part of the town, is an interesting colonial church. Large market in the square on Mondays, reported cheaper than Cuzco and Puno; there is another daily market in the square outside the railway station, which is more tourist oriented. Tupac Amarú market, on Moquegua 7 blocks E of railway line, cheap black market. A first class hospital is run by the Seventh Day Adventists.

**Warning** Beware of pickpockets and thieves, especially at the station, where they get on the train to join those already on board.

**Hotels** *Turistas*, good, D, but water turned off 2300, meals US$3; *Hostal Royal*, San Román 158, E, clean, decent accommodation, rec., restaurant good. *Hostal Perú*, on main square, D, with bath, E, without, clean, comfortable, hot water sometimes; 3 cheap, fairly safe, unnamed hotels around plaza; *Victoria*, F, cold water, clean but simple. *Yasur*, E with bath, F without, clean, safe, friendly, 500 metres from station, rec., small bar and restaurant in evening. *Alojamiento San Antonio*, G, basic but clean. In Juliaca water is available generally only between 0700 and 1900.

**Restaurants** *Ressi*, San Martín, good, but not cheap; *El Comedor del Sur*, adequate; Hole-in-the-wall breakfast parlour at corner of plaza opposite station, good. *El Trebol*, vegetarian restaurant, Pasaje Santa Isabel (off San Ramón, ½ block from station square).

**Transport** **Rail** to **Cuzco**, US$23 "turismo" pullman in buffet car where good, reasonably-priced lunches are served, 1st class, US$12, 2nd class, US$5, ; trains leave Mon.-Fri., 0825, Sat., 1045, 8½ hrs. Ticket office for first class tickets to Cuzco opens at 0630—tickets are hard to get. Trains to **Arequipa** daily at 2155, Tues. Wed. and Thurs. at 0835, Sat. at 1055. See above for warning, under Arequipa **Rail**. Also watch your belongings on the Cuzco line at stations like La Raya and Sicuani.

Jacantaya bus service, which is half the price of other buses, 11 hrs., to **Arequipa**. Bus to **Cuzco**, 3 companies, 12 hrs., US$8.50. **Colectivo to Puno** (from plaza outside rail station), US$2; US$0.65 bus. Taxi to Puno via Sillustani, US$20 per car. Daily bus to Moho, on east side of Lake Titicaca, from where it is possible to hitch into Bolivia. A private car can get to Cuzco in 7 hrs.

**Air** To Lima (US$92), via Arequipa, with Faucett, 2 a day; AeroPerú, daily, US$104, except Sun. 20 mins. to Arequipa. Taxi to airport, US$1.20 (negotiate), to Puno US$14.25, 45 mins. inc. photo stops. Airport tax US$7.

**Excursion** to thermal springs at village of Putina, 90 km. from Puno. Bus from Juliaca, US$0.60. About 32 km. NW of Juliaca (76 km. from Puno) is the unspoiled little colonial town of *Lampa*, known as the "Pink City", with splendid church, la Imaculada, containing a copy of Michelangelo's "Pietà", and Kampac Museo, Ugarte 462, musuem with sculptures and ceramics from Lampa and Juli areas, owner lives next door, interesting. The area also has a chinchilla farm and a grove of *puya* plants. About 114 km. NE of Juliaca is the old town of *Azángaro* with another famous church, La Asunción, filled with *retablos* and paintings of the Cuzco school. Stone monoliths may be seen at Taraco and at Hatuncolla. The sheep farm of San Antonio, between Ayaviri and Chiquibambilla, owned by the Prime family (descendants of British emigrants), may be visited by those with a day to spare.

*Puno*, capital of its Department, altitude 3,855 metres, population 80,000 (with 8,000 at university), on the NW shore of Lake Titicaca, has a fine main square and an interesting, but dirty, lakeside quarter, largely flooded since the rise in the lake's water level. The austere Cathedral was completed in 1657. Puno gets bitterly cold at night: in June-August the temperature at night can fall to -25°C, but generally not below -5°C. Some guerrilla activity; hotels close at midnight, restaurants at 2200. The provinces of Melgar and Azángaro in Puno Department have seen terrorist acitivity; seek advice before visiting them.

**N.B.** The people who invade buses and trains when they arrive seem to have the hotel business sewn up, so don't shrug them off: you may need their help.

**Festival** 1-8 February, the very colourful Fiesta de la Virgen de la Candelaria, bands and dancers from all the local towns compete on the Sunday; better at night on the streets than the official functions in the stadium. Check in advance on actual date because Candelaria may be moved if pre-Lentern carnival coincides with it. 3 May, Invención de la Cruz, exhibition of local art; 29 June, colourful festival of San Pedro, procession at Zepita (**see page 1016**). Also 20 July. 4-5 November, pageant on founding of Puno and emergence of Manco Capac from waters of Lake Titicaca.

**Hotels** *Isla Esteves* (Tourist Hotel), T 724, A, spacious, good views, cold site (you can ask for an electric fire), on an island linked by a causeway 5 km. NE of Puno (taxi US$1.75), is built on a Tiwanaku-period site, with bath, telephone, bar, good restaurant, discotheque, good service, electricity and hot water all day, poor rate of exchange, check bill carefully, camping allowed in car park; *Motel Tambo Titikaka*, B, with half-pension, at Chucuito on the lakeside, 17 km. S of Puno; electricity only between 1800-2300, poor heating, rooms icy after sunset, food indifferent and bill charged in dollars, wonderful view, book in advance (travellers need own transport, local transport is scarce and expensive); *Sillustani*, Jr. Lambayeque 195, T 351881, C, including breakfast and dinner (mixed reports), good service, clean, friendly, cold rooms but hot water. *Ferrocarril*, Av. La Torre 185, T 409, opposite station, is modern, E (reservation may be necessary) usually plenty of hot water, good rooms, but noisy, live folk music from 1915 in restaurant (food overpriced and service poor), central heating adequate, annex (F, not so good) not hot water (accepts many credit cards and changes Bolivian currency); *Don Miguel*, Av. Torre, T 177, D (negotiable), with shower, does not always honour reservations, comfortable, with restaurant, clean, service good, water intermittent;

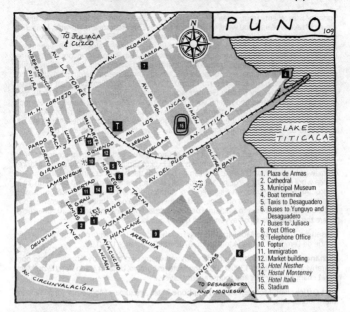

1. Plaza de Armas
2. Cathedral
3. Municipal Museum
4. Boat terminal
5. Taxis to Desaguadero
6. Buses to Yunguyo and Desaguadero
7. Buses to Juliaca
8. Post Office
9. Telephone Office
10. Foptur
11. Immigration
12. Market building
13. Hotel Nesther
14. Hostal Monterrey
15. Hotel Italia
16. Stadium

*Hostal Real*, Av. El Sol (½ block S of Av. Titicaca), E-D, very nice, hot water all day; *Hostal Nesther*, Deústua 268 (T 321), E (also 3-bedded rooms) with bath, hot water, 0730-0900, clean rec., except for safety; *Internacional*, Libertad 161, T 25, D, with shower (extra bed US$1.50), hot water morning and evening (not always reliable), secure, central, reservations not always respected and unhelpfulness reported. *Roma*, La Libertad 115, F, is passable, dirty toilets. *Hostal Embajador*, E, Los Incas 289 (T 592), overpriced, but clean, quiet, hot water, fairly friendly; *Hostal Tumi*, Cajamarca 237, Tel.:147, E (less in low season), negotiable, clean, safe, helpful, hot water limited (1830-2100), noisy from 0600; *Continental*, Alfonso Ugarte 161, F, cold water, dirty, friendly; *Bolognesi*, Bolognesi, E-F, friendly, good; *Hostal Monterrey*, Lima 447A, T 343, F, "gringo hotel", reasonable, some rooms with bath, better than those without, a/c, hot water after 1800, (ask) fairly clean, good restaurant, secure for luggage (has colectivo service to La Paz); *Hostal Lima*, Lima, E, popular, hot water twice a day, mixed reports on cleanliness; *Hostal Arequipa*, Arequipa 153, G, clean, hot water; *Hostal Inti*, Av. La Torre, opp. station, G, clean, basic, hot water sometimes, small. *Hostal Italia*, Teodoro Valcarcel 122 (T 640), E-D (negotiable), with shower and breakfast, good, safe, rec.; hot water except in rooms on ground floor, good food, clean, electric heater, staff helpful, esp. Mario Alvarado, and Rubén, who arranges tours to the Uros islands and Sillustani, US$10 each. *Los Uros*, Alfonso Ugarte (opposite *Hotel Europa*), T 644, F, cheaper without bath, hot water at night, dirty bathrooms, plenty of blankets, breakfast available, quiet, small charge to leave luggage (but reports of armed robbery on hotel received), friendly, often full, close to station and market; *San Carlos*, F, near railway station, no hot water, no bath but nice room; *Europa*, Alfonso Ugarte 112, G, "gringo hotel", luggage may be stored, but don't leave valuables in rooms, hot water in the common bathrooms in the evenings, not too clean, garage space for motorcycles, reports of occasional police drug raids; *Hostal Posada Real*, Av. Titicaca 156, T 738, F, good, central, clean, warm water, rooms overlooking lake are also nearest to disco close by, minibus to station. Hotel rooms are difficult to find after trains arrive as everyone else is also looking. Clean public showers near the football stadium. Puno suffers from power and water shortages.

**Restaurants** Try *Sale Caliente*, Tacna 381, or any of the pollo (chicken) places. *Ambassador*, Lima 347, cheap and varied food, not all dishes of same standard; *Itos*, Plaza de Armas, good food, US$1, rec.; *Café Internacional*, Libertad 161, 2 blocks from Plaza, "gringo", excellent trout, meals huge but not cheap and service variable, thieves around, "take waders if you want to go to the toilet"; *Café Restaurant Dorado*, Lima 361, good lunch, breakfast, quick service; *Peña Hostería*, Lima 453, good music, serves only pizzas, rec. *Club 31* on Moquegua, good cheap café; *Paititi*, Valcarcel 158, vegetarian, excellent; *Las Rocas*, on same street, good but slow; *Samaná*, Puno 334, inconsistent service, sometimes has live folk music from 2100, open fire and snacks and drinks (no minimum charge). *Cafe Tania*, Lima, rec. for good pies, cheap and generous helpings. *Ayllu*, Puno, good sandwiches, pastries; *Cafetería Chimú*, Jr. Lima 517, excellent breakfast and cakes, closed p.m., run by very friendly German lady, highly rec.; *Kimano*, Arequipa y Grau, very good cakes and coffee, good (safe) yoghurt; *Restaurant Monterrey*, behind hotel, good fish, only drink is pisco. *Café Juthma*, Moquegua 153, open 0630, excellent breakfast and nameless café on corner of Libertad and Tacna, good breakfasts and pastries. Above the city is a quinta called *Kantuta* (apparently every taxi driver knows it), good local dishes, open until 1700, rec.

**Shopping** In the covered part of the market (mostly fruit and veg.) there are model reed boats, and attractive carved stone amulets and Ekekos (Bolivian household gods). *Market* on railway between Av. Los Incas and Lampa is one of the best places in Peru for llama and alpaca wool articles, but bargain hard, especially in p.m., many are still hand-made, unlike in Cuzco. *Artesanías Puno*, on Calle Teodoro Valcarcel, has good quality alpaca goods with sizes for large gringos. *Uros* on same road, higher quality alpaca, but more expensive. Food and clothing market next to stadium. For good *artesanías*, take a bus to km. 20, Chinchera, where the *Trenza de Oro* has very good quality goods.

**Museums** The Museo Municipal has been combined with the private museum of Sr. Dreyer, Conde de Lemos 289, open Mon. to Fri. 0700-1800, entrance US$0.50.

**Exchange** Very difficult to use credit cards anywhere: best not to try. Souvenir shop opp. *Hostal Monterrey* (closed 1300-1500). Good rates in *Cambio*, Lima 447, and *Hotel Uros*. Many street changers near bus and tourist agency offices.

**Post Office** Jirón Moquegua 267. **Telephone** Entel, Arequipa y Moquegua, long waits for international calls.

**Bolivian Consulate** Jr. Arequipa between Parque Pino y Jr. Deza; visa on the spot, US$10.

**Laundry** *Lavandería América*, Jr. Moquegua 169; *Lavandería Lava Clin*, Deustua 252, El Sol 431 and Teodoro Valcarcel 132.

**Tourist Information** Government Tourist Office, Foptur, Jr. Arequipa 314, betweeen Lambayeque and Arbulu, T 353804 (above Farmacia Central), open Mon.-Fri., 0830-1300 (has maps). Check for details of village festivals. Touring y Automóvil Club de Perú, Arequipa 457. The booklet by Pedro Sueldo Nava on Puno, Arequipa and La Paz is informative and reasonably priced (includes maps), also available in Cuzco.

**Travel Agencies** *Viajes El Sol*, Jirón Arequipa 401, T 684, Sr. Ronald Zárate; *Puno Travel Service*, Tacna 254, rec. *Cooperativa de Transportes Turísticos Dos de Febrero*, Libertad 111, has received mixed reports. *Turismo Titicaca*, Libertad, rec.; *Kinjyo Travel Service*, Calle Arequipa 401. *Andino Tours*, Teodoro Valcarcel 158, T 35337 (Sr. Eduardo Mamanim), rec. for tours including the Yungas in Bolivia. *Inca Tours*, Av. Los Incas 117 (nr. market) T 353009, Sr. Andrés López, Sra. Paulina Chuspe Aniles, rec. *Cusi Travel* near *Hotel Italia* also rec. for train tickets and trips to Taquile and floating islands. *Turpuno* next to *Hotel Sillustani* on Lambayeque Ave. *Air Travel Services SRL*, Oquendo 250 (Sr. Jorge Oliart García), rec. for travel arrangements. The agency next to *Hotel Ferrocarril* is not rec. Beware of high commissions charged on tours and tickets.

**Railways** There is a 386-km. railway from Puno to Cuzco, via Juliaca. When the Puno-Juliaca section of line is closed, Puno passengers are taken to and from Juliaca by colectivos which leave from Jirón Pardo, 0630, US$1.50 (or by bus, US$0.30), arriving in good time to get Cuzco tickets in Juliaca station. When running, the Puno to Cuzco train leaves 0700 daily, arriving at 2030, tourist coach US$25 (good service, meals and drinks), 1st class US$15, 2nd class, US$5.50. Tickets are on sale only an hour before departure, or you can buy them the day before (which is the only way to get them), after the train to Arequipa has departed (ticket office hours are very irregular—check in advance). Tour companies often buy up all the available tickets and you either have to queue for hours (or ask a young boy to do this for you, paying him half in advance), or pay the companies a premium (from 20% to 100%). A magnificent run, with shopping possibilities at stations. Sit on right side on Puno-Cuzco train for best views. Hotel representatives join train near Cuzco to find customers.

Puno to Arequipa leaves 1900, Mon., Wed., Fri., sometimes withdrawn. Pullman US$12.50 (with blankets, heating, no vendors allowed), lunch, US$3.20, 1st class US$7.50, 2nd class US$5 (no lighting), 8 hrs. Tickets can be booked in advance, get to the station early to queue (0700 for 1000 opening of office); if short of time get them through a travel agent (20% commission, sometimes more). Beware of supposed Turismo class at an exhorbitant price which is actually 1st class.

See **Warning** under Arequipa **Rail**, page 1009.

A good idea in Puno, Juliaca and other Andean towns, when moving about with heavy baggage, is to hire a 3-wheel cycle cart (about US$0.20 per km.)

**Roads and Buses** To Arequipa, road improved: more bridges have been built. Several bus companies leave in the early morning. Transportes San Cristóbal, cheapest, not recommended, 19 hrs. Jacantaya, El Sol 590, opposite the stadium, leaves at 0830, 10-11 hrs., US$6.50. Sur Peruano leaves at 1000, door-to-door service, about a 10-hr. journey by road. Colectivo (Comité 31 rec.; also Comité 3 Juliaca Express, Jirón Tacna), 1000, takes 9 hrs, US$13.50. To Cuzco, 14 hrs., road first 44 km. (to Juliaca) and last 85 km. paved, other 260 km. very bad (the stretch Juliaca-Sicuani is appalling and very demanding for drivers of private cars), again several bus companies cover the route (Ambassador rec.), from US$8, Sur Peruano, Transportes San Cristóbal. Cruz del Sur, El Sol 565, (1730), US$10.50, 11 hrs. Colectivo to Cuzco, US$17.20. To Lima, 35-40 hours, several companies, most buses leave between 1600-1800. To Moquegua, for Chile, San Martín bus, US$8, 1800, 10 hrs., very cold, bad road.

**Excursions from Puno** The walk from Jirón Cornejo following the Stations of the Cross up a nearby hill (with fine views of Lake Titicaca) has been recommended, but be careful, there are dubious characters on the hill. Motorboats charging upwards of US$3.25 p.p. take tourists to the *Uros* "floating islands"; prices should not be over US$6. Pay half before you leave and half on your return. Those furthest from Puno are most worth seeing, but latest indications are that the islands have been totally spoilt by tourism. Boats go about every 1/2 hour from about 0630 till 1000, or whenever there are 10 or more people to fill the boat, and take 3-5 hrs. Local boats may also be hired. Out of season there are no regular boats, either get a group together and pay US$10 for the boat, rent a boat at US$1-2 p.p. or pay an agency US$15-20. (Be careful where you walk on the floating islands.) The Uro Indians on the islands have intermarried with the Aymará and no pure Uros exist. The temptation to move ashore may soon deprive the floating islands of all residents. The present Puno Bay Indians still practise some Uro traditions, but Aymará influence predominates. Many tourists report that though the people are friendly, they are very poor and consequently there are constant requests for money (less persistent out of season). Rather than giving the children money or gifts, buy their little reed boats.

A much more interesting island to visit (quiet and hospitable, except at the height of the tourist season) is *Taquile*, some 45 km. from Puno, on which there are numerous pre-Inca and Inca ruins, and Inca terracing. On the N side of the island is the warmest part of Lake Titicaca. Plentiful accommodation can be found in private houses but best to take warm clothes and a sleeping bag. No previous arrangements can be made; on arrival you walk up a steep path for 30 mins., are greeted by the Indians, pay a US$0.10 fee, sign the guest book and if wishing to stay are "assigned" a family to stay with (F p.p.); some families offer dinner and breakfast for about US$3.50 extra. Boats to Taquile leave daily (get ticket in harbour office 1/2 hr. in advance, 500 metres before boats, tour companies charge extra) at 0800 and 0915 (subject to change), but in low season there is only one a day, at 0830, return 0800, US$3.20 return, 4 hrs. (organized tours can cost double, but ask around), a day return is not recommended if you want to see the island fully, yet 3 hrs. of serenity are still very nice if time is short. Boats usually stop at one of the floating islands on the way to Taquile, for about 20 mins.; if you ask after the boat's started, they won't charge extra. An entire boat can be hired for about US$50 to take 5-7 people to Taquile: 3 hrs. there, 3 back, 3 hrs. on island, so day trip possible this way. A sailing boat can be taken to Taquile for about US$1.50 p.p., departure time depends on the wind. There is a cooperative shop on the square that sells exceptional woollen goods, not cheap but very fine quality (cheaper in the market at Puno). There are several small restaurants on the island (e.g. *El Inca* on main square); fish is plentiful and the island has a trout farm, but meat is rarely available and drinks often run out. Meals are a little more expensive than on the mainland. You are advised to take with you some food, particularly fruit, bread and vegetables, water, plenty of small-value notes, candles and a torch. Take precautions against sunburn. 7 June, mid-July (2 weeks, Fiesta de Santiago), 1 and 2 August are the principal festival days with many dances in between. Ask for Sr. Agustín, a dressmaker, who is very knowledgeable about the island.

Another island supremely well worth visiting, is **Amantaní**. It is very beautiful and peaceful and like Taquile, has 6 villages and ruins on both of the island's peaks, Pacha Tata and Pacha Mama: there are temples and on the shore there is a throne carved out of stone. On both hills, a fiesta is celebrated on 15 January. The Indians make beautiful textiles and sell them quite cheaply at the Artesanía Cooperativa; the people are Quechua speakers, but understand Spanish. There are no hotels but you are assigned to stay with local families, or ask your boat owner where you can stay. Accommodation, inc. 3 meals, is in our G range. Families who have been recommended include: the Borda family, good food, also Benedicto Guli Calsin, nr. the windmill; for an insight into subsistance living, the shy but interesting Amadeus family, just outside the main village, turn left along beach from port, be sure to pay a fair price for their wicker work, they are liable to undercharge. Ricardo Quispe Mamani, who has bar/restaurant on main square has been recommended, F plus food. There is one restaurant, *Samariy*. Boats go to and from the island most days at 0800 (a one day trip is not possible), the cooperatively owned boat *Atún*, will take you for about US$7.50 (4 hours each way). Victoriano Calsín Guispe (Casilla 312, Amantaní) of the cooperative crosses in his boat *Rey Marino*. Also recommended is Benito, who may be found at the docks (establish a price before leaving the dock). The boat *Picaflor* has not received good reports. Buy ticket the day before at the harbour, or on the boat; agencies charge about US$9-15 return, some hotels US$9. Several tour operators in Puno, including the one next to the *Hotel Italia*, now offer 2-day excursions, including meals and accommodation on Amantaní, an afternoon stopover on Taquile, and short stops at the floating islands, US$15 p.p. with negotiating. The festivities in January have been reported as spectacular, very colourful, musical and hard-drinking. There is also a festival the first Sunday in March with brass bands and colourful dancers. Another fiesta is the Aniversario del Consejo (of the local council). If you wish to visit both Taquile and Amantaní, go to Amantaní first, from there a boat goes to Taquile, but it is not possible to take a boat from Taquile to Amantaní.

Near Puno, are the *chullpas* (precolumbian funeral towers) of **Sillustani** (admission, US$0.30) in a beautiful setting on a peninsula in Lake Ayumara, 32 km. (excellent road) from Puno. Highly rec. (Colectivo US$8.50 p.p. for 3 hrs., mini bus from Puno, Tranextur, Jr. Puno 525, Plaza de Armas, 1400, US$4, 1 hr. at site, or bus from any of the agencies on Tacna at 1430; taxi, US$15 wait and return or take morning bus to Juliaca from Corrego y La Torre, get off at Sillustani turn, hitch a ride to Atuncolla, traffic frequent, walk 4 km., return in the afternoon by tourist bus US$1, negotiate. Take water, food and sunscreen.) Museum, reception area and restaurant now built. "Most of the towers date from the period of Inca occupation in the 15th century, but they are burial towers of the Aymará-speaking Colla tribe. The engineering involved in their construction is more complex than anything the Incas built—it is defeating archaeologists' attempts to rebuild the tallest "lizard" *chullpa*. Two are unfinished: one with a ramp still in place to raise blocks; the other with cut stones ready to go onto a very ambitious corbelled false dome. A series of stone circles to the east of the site are now thought to be the bases of domed thatch or peat living huts, rather than having any religious meaning. The quarry near the towers is also worth seeing."—John Hemming. There are local indians at the site, in costume. Take small change or chocolate, matches, pencils etc., as small presents if you wish to photograph the indians. Camera fans will find the afternoon light best; desert country, but impressive. There are Inca ruins at Tancatanca and Caluxo.

## Peru to Bolivia

Anybody interested in religious architecture should go from Puno along the western shore of Lake Titicaca. An Inca sundial may be seen near the village of **Chucuito** (which has an interesting church, La Asunción, a small museum in the church of Santo Domingo, and houses with carved stone doorways); cave paintings at Chichiflope. The best examples are at **Juli**, (*Hostal Téboles*, G, cold, dirty, best not to arrive at night looking for somewhere agreeable to stay) **Pomata** (*Hotel Puma Ata*, on Plaza, no sign, F, water, electricity)and **Zepita**.

Juli has four churches, all are being renovated. San Pedro, now designated as the Cathedral, has been extensively restored; it contains a series of superb screens, some in ungilded mahogany and others taken from other churches; also fine paintings, and a collection of coloured objects in the sacristy. San Juan Bautista has two sets of 17th century paintings of the lives of St. John the Baptist and of St. Teresa, contained in sumptuous gilded frames. San Juan is now a state museum, open a.m. only (US$0.15); it also has intricate *mestizo* carving in pink stone. Santa Cruz is another fine Jesuit church, partly roofless, so that it is easy to photograph the carvings of monkeys, papayas and grapes. The keys to Santa Cruz and San Juan Bautista are kept by the couple who look after San Juan Bautista. The fourth church, La Asunción, now abandoned and its fine bell tower damaged by earthquake or lightning, has an archway and atrium which date from the early 17th century. The Peruvians have established a school of picture restoration at Juli to restore its mass of paintings. The church at Pomata, which is being restored, is spectacular, with beautiful carvings, in Andean *mestizo* baroque, of vases full of tropical plants, flowers and animals in the window frames, lintels and cornices, and a frieze of dancing figures inside the dome (which is unusual in Peru), and alabaster windows (John Hemming). Near Juli is a small colony of flamingoes; many other birds can be seen from the road.

Minibus Puno-Juli, 0800, US$2 (Colectur); bus from Puno market at 1430. A hydrofoil at 0800 from Juli to Bolivia operates most days as part of a Puno-La Paz package tour. Juli-La Paz costs US$115, lunch included, from Transportes El Sol (Sr. Ronald Zárate).

On the road to Juli is **Ilave**, where the road for Tacna branches off. (The Tacna road is unpaved, but in good condition and a worthwhile journey, not only in terms of scenery, but also because road conditions are better than on the alternative Juliaca-Arequipa route to the coast from Lake Titicaca.) Ilave is typical of a gaunt *altiplano* town; has a good Sun. market (woven goods—beware bag slashers). Many buses go there from Puno (US$1.40); Ilave-Tacna, US$10.50, 13 hrs., leaves at 1400 and 1700 (Transportes Ponce, best, and Transportes Gironda).

**To the border** (See also under Bolivia, **Crossing the Peruvian Frontier**.) Small migration tax payable in intis at border.

*By Road*: 1. The most remote route is along east side of Lake via Huancané and Puerto Acosta (Bolivia), rec. only on weekends when there is more traffic; after Puerto Acosta, the road is very bad.

2. The most direct route is the Puno-Desaguadero road (paved) passing through Chucuito, Ilave, Juli and Pomata. Desaguadero is a miserable place (*Alojamiento Internacional*, dirty, F). Many buses to La Paz e.g. Chaski Andina (Sun., 0930). Bus from Titicaca 165 leaves 2000, arrives Desaguadero 0200. Bus from border to La Paz at 1130; advisable to check the day before when buses are running (US$6.50 in total by bus). Puno-Desaguadero by colectivo, US$6.50, leaving between 0600-0730. Colectivo, Juliaca Express, Puno-La Paz, twice daily, US$15. Offices: Puno, Tacna 298; Arequipa, Salaverry 111; **Cuzco, Ruinas 407**; Juliaca, San Román 129. *Ciattur* also run this route, Jr. Tacna 278, T 351045, daily, cheap, rec. tickets also sold at *Hotel Arequipa*. Beware of money "disappearing" at customs checks.

3. Transturin of La Paz runs a costly, luxury service Puno-La Paz, for US$80, including hydrofoil and lunch, leaves Puno 0630, arrives La Paz 1800 on Mon. to Fri. stopping at Copacabana. Transturin has offices in both Puno (Jirón Tacna 201, T 737) and Cuzco (Portal de Panes 109, Of.1, Plaza de Armas, T 222332) where tickets can be booked in advance. There is also a bus-hydrofoil-bus route from Puno to La Paz run by Crillón Tours (the hydrofoil crossing from Juli to Copacabana, calling at the Island of the Sun), leaves Puno 0800, arriving La Paz at 1830. Expensive (US$150, or US$200 with overnight stay and additional sightseeing); all luggage and formalities taken care of.

4. Puno-Yunguyo-Copacabana-La Paz: by far the pleasanter journey. Colectivos, leaving Puno 0800, ply to La Paz via Copacabana for US$12, but often ask you to pay ferry fare, US$0.20, in addition. You can take a bus Puno-Yunguyo (e.g. Cruz del Sur, leaving 0800, arriving 1030, US$1.60, colectivo, US$1.75), then bus (irregular service, US$0.40), truck, colectivo (plenty) or 11 km. walk to Copacabana for Immigration. There are three buses a day Copacabana-La Paz and you must book one or two days in advance (e.g. Pullman, US$2.50, reserve seats at *Hotel Ambassador*). Alternatively local buses and trucks go from Yunguyo to Copacabana, stopping at the frontier, for US$0.40. There are also direct buses from Yunguyo to La Paz, which stop at the border for both authorities to stamp passports. On Sun. there are many trucks carrying people between the markets. **Yunguyo** itself has a privet hedge on main square showing good examples of topiary. *Hotel Amazonas*, G, *Hostal Yunguyo*, also G, clean, but often no water or electricity. Parallel exchange market good in main plaza (the first you come to from Bolivia), better rates than border, and good for changing bolivianos, cash only. In the 2nd plaza are the buses and colectivos for Puno. Passport sometimes stamped at Yunguyo, walk across bridge to Kasami—1 km., where passport must be stamped.

A few agencies in Puno, for example Colectur (Jr. Tacna 232, T 352302/351681), Cosvial Tours (Tacna 257), Tour Latino (Tacna 300), offer minibus services to the Bolivian border, with a lunch stop in Copacabana, stops at all necessary official posts, and at money changers in Yunguyo, with connection to La Paz, for US$12 up (the less expensive do not include lunch, US$2); depart Puno at 0800, arriving in La Paz between 1500 and 1600. It is not uncommon for the service to deteriorate once you have crossed the border (in either direction) and have changed bus in the new country. You may not be dropped at the hotel of your choice. Most agencies make you pay the US$0.20 to the Tiquina crossing. Colectur/Turisbus runs a luxury bus service Puno-La Paz (to *Residencial Rosario*, who give 10% discount for passengers) for US$15; you don't have to change bus, breakdowns not unknown. If you wish you can break your journey in Copacabana (US$3 bus, US$7.50 daily colectivo—you have to change buses at Copacabana regardless) and make a connection to La Paz next day. Coming into Peru at this point you can get an overnight truck to Puno for about US$1.50, though these are cold and uncomfortable. Many colectivos leave from the Laykakota market. La Paz – Copacabana – Yunguyo – Puno is possible in one day as a bus (2 de Febrero company) leaves La Paz at 0800 for Copacabana, leaving you time to catch an onward bus to Yunguyo and bus or colectivo to Puno. The road is unpaved from Yunguyo to Straits of Tiquina.

**N.B.** Delays and consequent expenses have been reported by travellers going from Puno to Bolivia by car. On the **Yunguyo-Copacabana route** immigration, customs and police offices are all at different places on both the Peruvian and Bolivian sides: failure to check in at each usually means several hours wasted. When crossing Peru to Bolivia get an entry stamp in Copacabana (exit stamp in Peru of course). Bolivian authorities may want proof that you have US$10 for each day you intend to spend in Bolivia. There is no need to go to the Bolivian Consul in Yunguyo—he charges US$5 for a 10 day visa, whereas, at the border, a 90 day visa is free. If you go via Desaguadero, there are two Peruvian offices to visit (colectivo drivers know where they are) and three Bolivian—at the frontier. Peruvian customs close from 1200-1400. Tuesday and Friday are bad days to cross because they are days for the peasants on both sides of the border to exchange "national natural produce". Smugglers' paradise: keeps the Customs very busy.

*By Ferry:* 5. In 1985 the passenger ferry service across Lake Titicaca was suspended; in 1991, the ferry and the rail continuation from Guaqui to La Paz were running for freight only.

**Note** Apart from January to April, Peruvian time is one hour behind Bolivian time.

**Puno to Cuzco**  On the way from Puno to Cuzco there is much to see from the train, which runs at an average altitude of 3,500 metres. At the stations, Indians sell food (roast lamb at Ayaviri and stuffed peppers at Sicuani) and local specialities such as pottery bulls at Pucará; fur caps, furs and rugs at Sicuani; knitted alpaca ponchos and pullovers and miniature llamas at Santa Rosa.

There is a research station for high-altitude animals, ten km. after La Raya, the highest spot (164 km. from Juliaca; 4,321 metres—unless staying, do not leave the train here, it stops very briefly; small boys throw snowballs into the train if they can!). It is run by the Universidad de San Marcos, Lima (whose permission is required); llamas, alpaca and vicuña may be seen here, and accommodation is available in the dining room at the research station, US$2.50 p.p. (there is an excellent hot-bath house). Up on the heights breathing may be a little difficult, but the descent along the Río Vilcanota is rapid. Get out of the train at Aguas Calientes, the next station (4 km. from La Raya)— first class fare from Puno, US$5. To the right of Aguas Calientes station are steaming pools of hot water in the middle of the green grass; a startling sight. The temperature of the springs is 40°C, and they show beautiful deposits of red ferro-oxide. At Maranganí, the river is wider, the fields greener, with groves of eucalyptus trees.

**N.B.** If cycling from Juliaca to Cuzco, a suitable path runs beside the railway line for 200 km. from Tirapata; it is preferable to the road, and there is no danger from trains—only one a day in either direction. For drivers, the paved road ends at Juliaca, from where there is a very rough gravel track over La Raya pass up to Tinta, 69 km. south of Urcos, and paved from Tinta all the way to Cuzco.

*Sicuani*, 38 km. beyond the divide (250 km. from Puno—a very tiring road— 137 km. from Cuzco—Oriente Sur bus, US$3), is an important agricultural centre at 3,960 metres, and an excellent place for items of llama and alpaca wool and skins; they sell them on the railway station and at the excellent Sun. morning market.

Also known for its mineral baths at Uyurmiri.

**Hotels** *El Mirador*, E, basic, clean; *Raqchi*, F, basic; *Quispe*, G, basic, no shower, friendly; *Turistas*, D, is cold but best hotel in town (some way from centre), reported renamed *Centro Vacacional*, being modernised, rec. **Restaurants** *Elvis* and *Vilcanota* in centre of town, rec.

On the right, a few kilometres past the San Pedro stop, is the so-called Templo de Viracocha, grandiose, though almost unknown, with Inca baths 180 metres to the E. (For more information about various places between Sicuani and Cuzco, see page 1031.)

Branch roads both S and N of Sicuani lead to a road past the Tintaya mines which forms an alternative route Cuzco-Arequipa. The surface is very bad in places, but it is a spectacular journey. Only one bus a day (Chasqui) passes, usually full. From Sicuani, a pretty lake is passed, then one climbs to a radio-transmission antenna; a few km. from the road is Yauri (primitive accommodation), isolated on a plateau by a canyon; the road leads to the Majes irrigation scheme and on to the Arequipa-Juliaca road.

The Vilcanota plunges into a gorge, but the train winds above it and round the side of the mountain. At Huambutío the railway turns left to follow the Río Huatanay on the final stretch to Cuzco. The Vilcanota here widens into the great Urubamba canyon, flanked on both sides by high cliffs, on its way to join the Ucayali, a tributary of the Amazon.

**Cuzco** stands at 3,310 metres, a little lower than Puno. Its 143,000 inhabitants are mostly Indian, and the city is remarkable for its many colonial churches, monasteries and convents, and for its extensive Inca ruins. Respect the altitude; two or three hours' rest after arriving make a great difference; eat lightly and drink little alcohol, but suck glucose sweets the first day, and remember to walk slowly. To see Cuzco and the surrounding area properly—including Pisac, Ollantaytambo, Chinchero and Machu Picchu—you need 5 days to a week, allowing for slowing down because of altitude.

Almost every central street has remains of Inca walls, arches and doorways. Many streets are lined with perfect Inca stonework, now serving as foundations for more modern dwellings. This stonework is tapered upwards; every wall has a perfect line of inclination towards the centre, from bottom to top. The stones are "battered", with each edge and corner rounded. The circular stonework of the Temple of the Sun, for example, is probably unequalled in the world.

**Inca Society** Cuzco was the capital of the Inca empire—one of the greatest planned societies the world has known—from its rise during the 11th century to its death in the early 16th century. (See John Hemming's *Conquest of the Incas* and B.C.Brundage's *Lords of Cuzco* and *Empire of the Inca*.) It was solidly based on other Peruvian civilizations which had attained great skill in textiles, building, ceramics and working in metal. Immemorially, the political structure of the Andean Indian had been the *ayllu*, the village community; it had its divine ancestor, worshipped household gods, was closely knit by ties of blood to the family and by economic necessity to the land, which was held in common. Submission to the *ayllu* was absolute, because it was only by such discipline that food could be obtained in an unsympathetic environment. All the domestic animals—the llama and alpaca and the dog—had long been tamed, and the great staple crops—maize and potatoes—established. What the Incas did—and it was a magnificent feat—was to conquer enormous territories and impose upon the variety of *ayllus*, through an unchallengeable central government, a willing spiritual and economic submission to the State. The common religion, already developed by the classical Tiahuanaco culture, was worship of the Sun, whose vice-regent on earth was the absolute Sapa Inca. Around him, in the capital, was a religious and secular elite which never froze into a caste because it was open to talent. The elite was often recruited from chieftains defeated by the Incas: an effective way of reconciling local opposition. The mass of the people were subjected to rigorous planning. They were allotted land to work, for their group and for the State; set various tasks—the making of textiles, pottery, weapons, ropes, etc.—from primary materials supplied by the functionaries, or used in enlarging the area of cultivation by building terraces on the hill-sides. Their political organization was simple but effective. The family, and not the individual, was the unit. Families were grouped in units of

10, 100, 500, 1,000, 10,000 and 40,000, each group with a leader responsible to the next largest group. The Sapa Inca crowned the political edifice; his four immediate counsellors were those to whom he allotted responsibility for the northern, southern, eastern and western regions ( *suyos*) of the empire.

Equilibrium between production and consumption, in the absence of a free price mechanism and good transport facilities, must depend heavily upon statistical information. This the Incas raised to a high degree of efficiency by means of their *quipus*: a decimal system of recording numbers by knots in cords. Seasonal variations were guarded against by creating a system of state barns in which provender could be stored during years of plenty, to be used in years of scarcity. Statistical efficiency alone required that no one should be permitted to leave his home or his work. The loss of personal liberty was the price paid by the masses for economic security. In order to obtain information and to transmit orders quickly, the Incas built fine paved pathways along which couriers sped on foot. The whole system of rigorous control was completed by the greatest of all their monarchs, Pachacuti, who also imposed a common language, Quechua, as a further cementing force.

**Churches** (Many are closed to visitors on Sunday.) The heart of the city, as in Inca days, is the Plaza de Armas. Around the square are colonial arcades and four churches. To the N is the **Cathedral** (early 17th century, in baroque style), built on the site of the Palace of Viracocha. The high altar is solid silver; the original altar *retablo* behind it is a masterpiece of native wood carving. In the sacristy are paintings of all the bishops of Cuzco and a painting of Christ attributed to Van Dyck. The choir stalls, by a 17th-century Spanish priest, are a magnificent example of colonial baroque art. The elaborate pulpit and the sacristy are notable. Much venerated is the crucifix of El Señor de las Temblores, the object of many pilgrimages and viewed all over Peru as a guardian against earthquakes. (The Cathedral is open until 1000 for genuine worshippers—Quechua mass 0500-0600, and thereafter 1000-1200, 1500-1800 with the combined entrance ticket—see below). The tourist entrance is through El Triunfo, which has a fine granite altar and a statue of the Virgin of the Descent, reputed to have helped the Spaniards repel Manco Inca when he besieged the city in 1536. It also has a painting of Cuzco during the 1650 earthquake (the earliest surviving painting of the city) in a side chapel. Doors from the Cathedral open into Jesús María.

On the E side of the plaza is the beautiful **La Compañía de Jesús**, built on the site of the Palace of the Serpents (Amaru-cancha) in the late 17th century. Its twin-towered exterior is extremely graceful, and the interior rich in fine murals, paintings and carved altars. The cloister is also noteworthy (closed since 1990).

Three outstanding churches are La Merced, San Francisco, and Belén de los Reyes. **La Merced**, almost opposite the *Tambo Hotel*, first built 1534, rebuilt late 17th century, attached is a very fine monastery with an exquisite cloister; open 0830-1200, 1430-1730 (admission US$0.50, students US$0.35). Inside the church are buried Gonzalo Pizarro, half-brother of Francisco, and the two Almagros, father and son. Their tombs were discovered in 1946. The church is most famous for its jewelled monstrance, on view in the monastery's museum during visiting hours. The superb choir stalls, reached from the upper floor of the cloister, can be seen by men only (but you must persuade a Mercedarian friar to let you see them). **San Francisco** (3 blocks SW of the Plaza de Armas), is an austere church reflecting many Indian influences. Its monastery is being rebuilt (the first of the cloisters is now open to the public 0900-1200, 1500-1700—see the candelabra made from human bones and the wood carving). **Belén de los Reyes** (in the southern outskirts), built by an Indian in the 17th century, has a gorgeous main altar, with silver embellishments at the centre and goldwashed *retablos* at the sides (open 1000-1200, 1500-1700 except Thurs. and Sun.). **Santa Catalina**, on Arequipa, opposite Calle Santa Catalina, is a magnificent building; the church, convent and museum are included on the tourist ticket, closed since 1989. Delicious marzipan is sold next to the museum by the nuns through a revolving wooden door, US$1 for 200 grams. **San Pedro** (in front of the market) was built in 1688, its two towers from stones brought from an Inca ruin (open

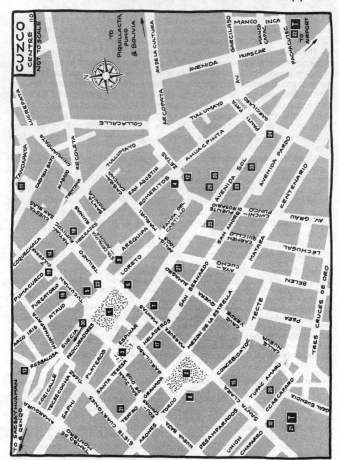

Cuzco : Key to map 1. Plaza de Armas, 2. Plaza San Francisco, 3. Plaza Regocijo, 4. Plaza Santo Domingo, 5. Cathedral, 6. La Compañía, 7. La Merced, 8. San Francisco, 9. Santa Catalina, 10. San Pedro, 11. San Blas, 12. Santo Domingo and Temple of the Sun, 13. San Cristóbal, 14. San Antonio, 15. Santa Clara, 16. Palacio del Almirante, 17. Casa de Garcilaso de la Vega, 18. Museo de Arte Religioso, 19. Plaza de las Nazarenas, 20. Mercado Santa Ana, 21. San Pedro Train Station for Machu Picchu, 22. Train Station for Puno, 23. Tourist Office and PIP Tourist Police (1st floor), 24. Post Office, 25. Entel Telephone Office, 26. American Express, Lima Tours, 27. Banco de la Nación, 28. AeroPerú, 29. Faucett Airlines, 30. Good cafés and camping hire agencies, 31. Customs, 32. Centro Qosqo.

Mon.-Sat. 1000-1200, 1400-1700). The nuns' church of Santa Clara is unique in South America for its decoration, which covers the whole of the interior (but virtually impossible to visit). The smaller and less well-known church of **San Blas** has a fine carved *mestizo* cedar pulpit.

**Santo Domingo** (SE of the main Plaza) was built in the 17th century on the walls of the Temple of the Sun and from its stones; visit the convent to see the ancient walls of the Temple of the Sun, now restored. (Model of the Temple upstairs: ask to see it.) Current excavation is revealing more and more of the five chambers of the Temple of the Sun, which shows the best Inca stonework to be seen in Cuzco. The Temple of the Sun was awarded to Juan Pizarro, the younger brother of Francisco, who willed it to the Dominicans after he had been fatally wounded in the Sacsayhuamán siege. Open 0900-1200, 1500-1700.

The baroque cloister has been gutted to reveal four of the original chambers of the great Inca temple—two on the west partly reconstructed in a good imitation of Inca masonry. The finest stonework is in the celebrated curved wall beneath the west end of Santo Domingo (rebuilt after the 1950 earthquake, at which time a niche that once contained a shrine was found at the inner top of the wall). Below the curved wall was a famous garden of gold and silver replicas of maize and other plants. Excavations now in progress have revealed Inca baths done here, and more Inca retaining walls. The other superb stretch of late Inca stonework is in Calle Ahuacpinta outside the temple, to the east or left as you enter (John Hemming).

Much **Inca stonework** can be seen in the streets and most particularly in the Callejón Loreto, running SE past La Compañía de Jesús from the main plaza: the walls of the House of the Women of the Sun are on one side, and of the Palace of the Serpents on the other. There are ancient remains in Calle San Agustín, to the NE of the plaza. The temples of the Stars and of the Moon are still more or less intact. The famous stone of 12 angles is in Calle Triunfo (Calle Hatun Rumyoc) halfway along 2nd block from the square beside the Cathedral, on the right-hand side going away from the Plaza.

San Sebastián, an interesting church with a baroque façade, is in the little village of San Sebastián, 6½ km. from Cuzco.

**Visitors' Tickets** It is not possible to purchase individual entrance tickets to the churches and ruins in and around Cuzco; one must purchase a combined ticket for US$10 (US$5 for student with identification), said to be payable only in US$ (but try intis—could be cheaper), valid for five days, which allows entry to: the Cathedral, San Blas, Santa Catalina, Santo Domingo-Coricancha, Museo de Arte Religioso and the 3 ruins (Qenqo, Puku Pukara and Tambo Machay—see below) on the way to Pisac, Pisac itself, Chinchero and Ollantaytambo. The tickets can be bought at any of the places mentioned or at the tourist office (0900-1500). Students can pay per individual site, as can others with a lot of insistence (but you may be charged US$5 per site). If time is short, go to Machu Picchu first, stop in Ollantaytambo on the way back and buy your visitors' ticket there before seeing the sites nearer Cuzco. **N.B.** All sites are very crowded on Sun.

**Palaces and Mansions** The **Palacio del Almirante**, just N of the Plaza de Armas, is impressive. Nearby, in a small square, is the colonial house of **San Borja**, where Bolívar stayed after the Battle of Ayacucho. The **Palacio Concha** (on Calle Santa Catalina), with its finely carved balcony, is now used by the Guardia Civil. The **Casona del Marqués de Valleumbroso** (3 blocks SW of the Plaza de Armas) was gutted by fire in 1973 and is being restored. The **Palacio Archiepiscopal** (two blocks NE of Plaza de Armas) was built on the site of the palace occupied in 1400 by the Inca Roca and was formerly the home of the Marqueses de Buena Vista; it contains a the Museo de Arte Religioso (see below). Above Cuzco on the road up to Sacsayhuamán, one finds the church of **San Cristóbal**, built to his patron saint by Cristóbal Paullu Inca and, N of it, the eleven doorway-sized niches of the great Inca wall of the Palacio de Colcampata where Paullu Inca set up home. Further up, to the left, is a private colonial mansion, once the home of the explorer (and murderer) Lope de Aguirre. Also visit the palace called **Casa de los Cuatro Bustos** at San Agustín 400 (which is now the *Libertador-Marriott Hotel*) and the **Convento de las Nazarenas**, Plaza de las Nazarenas (alias Casa de la Sirena). See the Inca-colonial doorway with a mermaid motif.

**Museo Arqueológico** recently moved (1990) into Palacio del Almirante (described above), first-rate precolumbian collection, contains Spanish paintings of imitation Inca royalty dating from the 18th century, as well as an excellent collection of textiles. Visitors should ask to see the forty miniature pre-Inca turquoise figures found at Pikillacta and the golden treasures, all kept under lock and key but on display, US$0.10 entry.

**Museo de Arte Religioso** at old Archbishop's Palace in Calle Hatun Rumyoc (see above), a fine collection of colonial paintings and furniture, including the paintings of a 17th century Corpus Christi procession that used to hang in the church of Santa Ana. Open Mon.-Sat., 0930-1200, 1500-1800. Sun. 1500-1800.

**Museo Histórico Regional**, in the Casa Garcilaso, Jirón Garcilaso y Heladeros tries to show the evolution of the Cuzqueño school of painting. Open Mon.-Fri., 0900-1200, 1500-1800, Sat., 0900-1200. Contains Inca agricultural implements, colonial furniture and paintings and mementos of more recent times. Note the pillar on the balcony over the door, showing a bearded man and a naked woman. Closed after earthquake damage, April 1986.

**Festivals**  24 June; pageant of Inti Raymi (Indians outnumber tourists) enacted at 1300 at the fortress of Sacsayhuamán. (Try to arrive in Cuzco 15 days before Inti Raymi, there are many festivals, and get to Sacsayhuamán at about 1030 as even reserved seats fill up quickly.) Tickets for the stands can be bought a week in advance from the Municipalidad, and cost US$25, but standing places on the ruins are free (but be early and defend your space). Travel agents who try to persuade you to buy a ticket for the right to film or take photos are being dishonest. On Corpus Christi day statues and silver are paraded through the streets; colourful, everyone gets drunk by 1000. The Plaza de Armas is surrounded by tables with Indian women selling *cuy* and a mixed grill called *chiriuchu* (*cuy*, chicken, *tortillas*, fish eggs, water-weeds, maize, cheese and sausage). One week before the Inti Raymi, there is a dance festival in the village of Raqchi (**see also page 1031**). On the Monday before Easter is the procession of El Señor de los Temblores (Lord of the Earthquakes), starting at 1600 outside the Cathedral. A large crucifix is paraded through the streets, returning to the Plaza de Armas around 2000 to bless the tens of thousands of people who have assembled there. On 8 September (day of the Virgin), there is a colourful procession of masked dancers from the church of Alundena, at the SW edge of Cuzco, near Belén, to the Plaza de San Francisco. There is also a splendid fair at Alundena, and a free bull fight on the following day (tourists should be very discreet at these celebrations, as they are not welcome—avoid pickpockets, too). Carnival at Cuzco very basic; flour, water, cacti, bad fruit and animal manure thrown about in streets. **N.B.** Prices shoot up at end-July—Independence celebrations. December 8 is Cuzco day: church and museums close at 1200.

**Warning**  Thieves are numerous and persistent. Do not wear jewellery, watches or carry credit cards, leave valuables with hotel management. Be careful when you change money on the streets. Be especially careful in the railway and bus stations, the bus from the airport, the Santa Ana market (otherwise rec.) and at out-of-the-way ruins. Beware also of cocaine hustlers who will offer you drugs but who, in reality, are setting you up for "fines" from the police (genuine or otherwise). More police patrol the streets and stations than in the past, but one should still be on the lookout.

**Hotels**  Book more expensive hotels well in advance through a good travel agency, particularly for the week or so around 24 June when the Inti Raymi celebrations take place (prices are greatly increased at this time). Prices given are for the high season in June-August. On the Puno-Cuzco train there are many hotel agents for medium-priced hotels; prices can often be negotiated down to F category, but best to pay agent for one day only and then negotiate with hotel. Rooms offered at Cuzco station are usually cheaper than those offered on the train. Agents also provide transport to the hotel, which can be invaluable when arriving at the dimly-lit station and since taxis are not supposed to enter the station yard. It is cold in Cuzco, many hotels do not have heating. It is worth asking for an "estufa", a space heater which some places will provide for an extra charge. The whole city sometimes suffers from water shortages, hotels may only have supplies in the mornings.

A category: The best is *Libertador-Marriott* (5-star), in colonial palace (Casa de los Cuatro Bustos) at Calle San Agustín 400, T 232601/231961, 28% tax, good, especially the service, but in July and August rooms in the older part of the hotel are cold and dark, restaurant poor and overpriced; *Royal Inca I*, Plaza Regocijo 299, T 231067, 3-star, bar, dining room, good service, rec., (its annex, *Royal Inca II* on same street, larger and just as good). *Cusco* Heladeros 150, T 222832/224821, administered by Sociedad de Beneficencia Pública del Cusco, hot water, largest and best known, "old fashioned, not cheap and a little fusty", central; *Alhambra*, Av. Sol 594, T 224076, modern, very good, prices negotiable, but cold, limited hot water, and food disappointing; *Savoy*, Av. El Sol 954, T 224322, group rate B, recently upgraded to Peruvian 5-star, food poor and expensive, no coffee or food served after 2200, disappointing, not a safe area at night; *Marqués de Picoaga* Sta. Teresa, 344, T 232312, 70 rooms, central heating, private bathrooms, dining room, information in Lima T 286 314; *Conquistador*, Santa Catalina Angosta 149, T 233661, clean, safe, good; *San Agustín*, Maruri y San Agustín, T 222322, fine interior, clean, friendly, very hot water, restaurant expensive, rec.

B category: *Espinar*, Portal Espinar 142, (bargain for less in low season), old, not very good value, breakfast OK but dinner poor (except spaghetti), clean and helpful, *Hostal El Dorado*, Av. Sol 365, T 231232, good but can be noisy in a.m., food good but expensive. *Hostal*

*Garcilaso*, Garcilaso de la Vega 233, with bath, in off-season can be negotiated lower (E), safe for luggage, clean, helpful, "historic charm, but service poor", laundry expensive, noisy disco until 0300, overpriced in season, friendly; *Garcilaso III* in same street, C high season, E low, less good (make sure which one you want to go to if dealing with a tout).

**C/D category:** *Hostal Inti Raymi*, Matará 260, T 228401; *Tambo*, Ayacucho 233, D, clean, heating in rooms, laundry facilities, safe for luggage, rec., central, hot water (intermittent), restaurant fair; *Viracocha*, Plaza de Armas, corner of Mantas, C (E low season), clean, hot water, rec., restaurant opens at 0600, good breakfast (Casilla 502), Luis Guillén Pinelo, an employee here, is a good guide; *Hostal Imperial Palace*, formerly *Matheos*, Calle Tecsecocha, 492, T 223324, D, with breakfast, café, bar, restaurant, clean, a bit cold, but well furnished, English spoken, good, friendly; next door, *Hostal Carlos*, Tecsecocha 490, T 223091, C with breakfast, has charm and character, but restaurant poor; *El Inca*, Quera 251, D (F in low season), good, clean, heating, restaurant, breakfast included, Wilbur speaks English, and is helpful; *Colonial Palace*, Quera 270, C-E (negotiable) "has potential", but poor service and independent travel agencies based in forecourt not rec., colonial courtyard; *Samaná*, Nueva Baja 472, D, colonial mansion, good rooms with heaters and private baths, plumbing unreliable, safe for luggage, helpful staff, laundry, restaurant slow but good, breakfast cheap, food must be ordered day before, rec.; *Hostal del Sol*, San Francisco, C in high season, D/E low, clean, rec.

**E/F category:** *Los Marqueses*, Garcilaso 252, E, with bath, heaters extra, early colonial house, very helpful and comfortable, but not well kept, has a masseur, Douglas Chapman, rec., clean and convenient; *Hostal Corihuasi*, Calle Suecia, E, 4-room suites, colonial house, laundry arranged, hot water, quiet, rec.; *Qorichaska*, Nueva Alta 458, close to centre, F, clean, safe, hot water, rec. *Suecia*, Calle Suecia, F, shared rooms, cosy, clean, hot showers, safe, will store luggage, highly rec., can use their bulletin board to arrange groups for the Inca trail; *Suecia* annex, Calle Tecseccocha (blue door, no sign), E without bath, rooms also with, good beds and blankets, clean, same recommendations as for parent hotel, beautiful building; *Huaynapata*, Huaynapata 369, small rooms, F p.p., very safe, family-run, hot water (problematic), stores luggage, friendly. *Trinitarias*, Trinitarias 263, near San Pedro station, E, clean, hot water in shower, friendly, secure for left luggage; *Hispaniola*, Trinitarias, nearby, G, good, safe; also near San Pedro station, *Milán*, Trinitarias 237, F, with unreliable hot water in evening, safe, clean, friendly, a bit noisy; *Imperio*, Calle Chaparro, comfortable new extension, run by Elena and family, also near station, F, hot water, friendly, clean, safe to leave luggage; *Palermo*, San Agustín 287, F, some Inca walls, good breakfast; *Hostal El Arqueólogo*, E (rooms or dormitory), Ladrillos 425 not far from Sacsayhuamán (T 232569), run by a Frenchman, hot water, overpriced, clean, will store luggage, cafeteria (expensive) and kitchen; accommodation in *Convento Santo Domingo* (down an alley, behind the church), G, a sleeping bag p.p. in double rooms, hot showers, clean, friendly, safe to leave bags, must be in by 2200; *Hostal Familiar*, Saphi 661, E, with bath, F without, cold, attractive flower-filled patios, with good rooms around them (other rooms are not as good), can leave luggage here, with café (owner's sister Gloria works with Kantu Tours), rec., but reported casual with reservations. *Hostal San Cristóbal*, Quiscapata 242, near San Cristóbal, G/F, cooking and clothes-washing facilities, baggage deposit, views over city, very nice people, if everywhere full, Sra. Ema de Paredes will let you spread a sleeping bag on the floor, rec.; *Hostal Cáceres*, Plateros 368, 1 block from Plaza de Armas, G, luggage store, mixed reports on all counts, but generally agreement on lack of security, laundry service, can put motorcycle in patio; *Hostal Familiar Las Esmeraldas* (Sra. Vega de Pineda), Av. de la Infancia 433, E, full board available, clean, hot showers, highly rec.; *Hospedaje El Peregrino*, Calle del Medio off Plaza, E with bath, clean, secure, quiet, only a few rooms, no restaurant, but rec. *Hostal Bellavista*, Av. Santiago 100, G, hot water, very friendly, safe (10 mins. walk from centre, not a safe area at night), breakfast available, will store luggage, rec. (particularly, rooms with view towards Estación San Pedro), Carlos here takes guided trips on the Inca Trail, about US$3-4 p.p./day and tents available for hire at good rates; *Hostal Cahuide*, Saphi 845, E, discount for long stay, clean, good laundry service, helpful, café, convenient for centre; *Hostal San Blas*, Cuesta San Blas 526, T 225781, E, basic, a/c, friendly, secure for luggage; *Hostal Sapantiani*, Pumacurco 490, F without bath, hot water sometimes, safe, clean, pleasant, family run, highly rec.; *Mantas*, Calle Mantas 115 (near Plaza de Armas), E, rec., friendly, can leave luggage, has laundry service, good meals; *Posada del Corregidor*, Portal de Panes 151, Plaza de Armas, T 232632, E throughout year, pleasant, clean, central; *Loreto*, Pasaje Loreto 115, Plaza de Armas, E-D (triples available, clean, very friendly, rooms with Inca walls and electric heaters, cheap laundry service, great atmosphere (taxis and other travel can be arranged, Lucio here is a good guide), safe luggage deposit, rec., but dark; *Tambo Real*, Av. Belén, E with bath and hot water, friendly but noisy (not to be confused with *Hotel Tambo*);

*Hotel del Procurador*, F, good beds, clean, hot water, secure, will mind luggage, rec. *Hostal Residencial Rojas*, Tigre 129, F, good value, friendly, safe, clean, hot water, safe luggage store, camping equipment for hire, rec. *Hostal América*, Plateros, G, basi888c but clean, excellent hot showers, friendly; Irma Rodríguez de Alarcón, Zarumilla 2A-101, 15-20 mins'. walk from Plaza de Armas, 2 rooms sleeping 4 people, safe, breakfast, rec.

**Camping**  Not safe anywhere in the Cuzco area, but is permitted on hill above Cuzco museum, about ½ km. past museum on left; also permitted near Sacsayhuamán ruins, but arrive late and leave early so as not to interfere with the sightseeing. Travel agencies (see below) rent equipment (check tents carefully, and some sell camping gaz). If you use a spirit stove, "alcohol para quemar" can be bought in most pharmacies (bring your own bottle).

**Restaurants**  *Mesón de los Espaderos*, Espaderos y Plateros, parrilladas, good; *Roma*, on Plaza de Armas (good food, folk music nightly without extra cost). *Paititi*, Plaza de Armas, live music, fish and also local food, overpriced, complimentary pisco sour; also on the plaza (Portal Panes), is the *Piazza*, rather expensive. For a good meal and décor try *Inti Raymi* in the *Libertador-Marriott*, à la carte dinner for US$13. *El Fogón de las Mestizas*, Ruinas 463, cheap local food, best in the afternoon less good at night, has roast guinea-pig (*cuy*, known in Cuzco as *conejo*—rabbit).

Vegetarian restaurants *Govinda* (Hare Krishna), Espaderos 128, just off W corner of Plaza de Armas, generally good, always busy, you can buy bread here which will keep for days, ideal for Inca Trail (but order a day in advance), also samosas, cheese, ensalada de frutas, etc. *Comedor Vegetariano*, Av. Sol 555, lunch only; *Qhaliama Warí*, Torda, part of a natural health centre. *Cafe Samana*, Plaza de las Nazarenas 199, T 224092, pastries, granola, yoghurt, honey, pancakes (food packs made up for Inca trail, etc.), run by Argentine Cristina, good atmosphere, old foreign magazines available, highly rec., open early for breakfast. *Café Varayoc*, Espaderos 142, good meeting place, Dutch connection (excellent coffee, pizzas and cake, but pricey). *Las Gardenias* is a good juice bar at Sta. Catalina Ancha 427.

On Procuradores, No. 365, *Chez Maggy*, good atmosphere, popular with tourists, music Wed. and Sun., pasta, soups, pizzas freshly baked in wood-burning oven, service sometimes slow; also reasonable restaurants, (e.g. *El Corsario*, No. 350, belongs, and similar to, *Chez Maggy*). *Bar Kukuli* at 392, cheap food (order in advance) and interesting local drinks, slow service, good music, and *Urpi*, good food but expensive and chaotic; *Pizzería America*, on Plateros, cheap and highly rec.; *Pizzería Morengo*, Plaza Regocijo, cheap and good brick-oven pizzas; *Royal Qosco*, Plateros, cheap, good 3-course set meals; *Bilboquet*, Herrajes 171A, French crêperie, good meeting place, rec.; *Tumi*, Playa de Armas, good local dishes; *Ayllu*, Portal de Carnes 208, also on Plaza de Armas, open at 0600, Italian, classical/folk music, good atmosphere, has a superb range of milk products and wonderful apple pastries, try *leche asada*, good breakfast, quick service; *La Yunta*, next door, good pastries, lunches and 40 types of juice; *Lamborghinos*, on Plaza de Armas, nr Plateros, good cheap pastas, garlic bread, rec. for banana split; *Wiracocha*, on Plaza opposite Compañía church, excellent café; *Café Cuzco* on Plaza for breakfast. *Trattoria Adriano*, Calle Mantas y Av. Sol (just off SE corner of Plaza de Armas), tasty Italian food, open for breakfast at 0700, friendly and helpful; *El Truco*, on Plaza del Cabildo (Regocijo 247), excellent stuffed green peppers, good trout, folklore some evenings (at 2030, an extra US$1.20 will be added to your bill), expensive; *Tip-Top*, Palacio 122, good food, reasonable prices; *Café-Restaurant Garcilaso*, Garcilaso 265, rec. for juices and excellent lemon pie, good music and atmosphere in evening; *Hora Antigua*, Garcilaso, log fire, friendly bar, reasonable prices; *Royal Inn*, Plaza San Francisco, good, cheap, enormous cakes; *Focarela*, Saphi 478, good pizzeria, reasonable prices, rec; *Los Candiles*, Calle Plateros near Plaza, mixed reports; *Pucara*, Plateros 309, highly rec., good meals throughout the day, pleasant atmosphere, pottery for sale.; *Café Huaylli* on Plateros, popular meeting place, especially for breakfast, has good snacks and "copa Huaylli"—fruit, muesli, yoghurt, honey and chocolate cake. *Bazar-Cafetín Minka*, Huaynapata 331, craft shop and café (best cheesecake in Cuzco) run to benefit disadvantaged women, has lots of German books and a few English; *Posada*, on Plaza de Armas, good. Several restaurants on Plateros do cheap 3-course set lunches (US$0.50). *Cross Keys Pub*, Plaza de Armas, Portal Confiturias 233, 1st floor (look closely for sign), run by a Mancunian, darts, great atmosphere, a bit exp. but cheap prices in happy hour (US$0.50, 1800-1900); may not be open all year, very popular. You can eat cheaply in the market; a *saltado* (a mixture of meat and vegetables) costs about US$0.25, but be careful. Also cheap juices in Santa Ana market. Street vendors at night on Plaza de Armas sell food: stuffed potatoes (*papas rellenas*) rec. A rec. bakery is *La Nonna Baguetería*, Av. Sol 325, fresh apple turnovers, croissants and various breads.

**Local Specialities**  Roast stuffed guinea pig (*cuy*). Order in advance at one of the *quintas* (inns in the suburbs). *Quinta Zárate*, Calle Tortera Paccha, rec. A good cheap picantería-chichería is *Mi Casa*, on 100 block of Choquechaca. Also *Quintas Eulalia*, Choquechaca 384. Very rich and exotically spiced (US$2 for *cuy*). The yoghurt is excellent. *La Chola*, Calle Palacio, uphill from the Nazarenas, local specialities, atmosphere, good chicha. Also try *Quinta Tejada* and *Quinta Country Club*. Try the *anticuchos* (roast beef hearts) cooked in side streets. The local drinks, herb tea with caña and hot milk with pisco, very warming in the cold evenings.

**Folklore Shows** Regular nightly folklore show at Qosqo Native Art Centre, Av. Sol. 604, at 1830 hours, Amanta Dances, Calle Unión 117, and Qoricancha Dances, San Juan de Dios 285, 1830-2000. *La Taverna* bar on Plaza de Armas has folklore music nightly from 2100-0200, very crowded. Folk-dancing and music in the cellar of *Hotel Ollanta*, Av. Sol, nightly, 1845-2000. Folk dancing at Teatro Central, and at Teatro Inti Raymi, Saphi 605, rec. (nightly 1845, tickets sold by students in Plaza de Armas). Student group Intiraqui plays nightly in Calle Plateros. There are good *peñas* at *Qhatuchay*, Portal Confituría 233 on Plaza, very pleasant (2100), *Peña Do Re Mi*, also on Plaza, opp. La Compañia, and folk music at *Restaurant Roma*, evenings. *Cafir*, Saphi 605, daily 1845, excellent **N.B.** The Centro de Difusión Cultural Wasapay organizes "folklore evenings" in various restaurants which are supposed to be free, but which will be included as 15% extra on the bill—watch out for this if you don't want a more expensive meal.

**Discotheques** *El Muki*, near Tourist office, popular with "local adolescents"; *Kamikaze*, folk and rock music, sometimes live bands, candle-lit cavern atmosphere, many gringos, entrance fee US$1, on San Juan de Dios, nr. Sta Teresa (upstairs), rec. *El Molino Rojo*, Av. de la Cultura; *El Gran Prise*, Av. Antonio Lorena 14. Also, *Las Quenas* in the basement of the *Hotel Savoy*, rec.

**Local Crafts** In the Plaza San Blas and the surrounding area, authentic Cuzco crafts still survive. Wood workers may be seen in almost any street. Leading artisans who welcome visitors include: Hilario Mendivil, Plazoleta San Blas 634 (biblical figures from plaster, wheatflour and potatoes); Edilberta Mérida, Carmen Alto 133 (earthenware figures showing physical and mental anguish of the Indian peasant); Víctor Vivero Holgado, Tandapato 172 (painter of pious subjects); Antonio Olave Palomino, Siete Angelitos 752 (reproductions of precolumbian ceramics and colonial sculptures); Maximiliano Palomino de la Sierra, Triunfo 393 (festive dolls and wood carvings); Santiago Rojas, near San Blas (statuettes). Museo Inca Art Gallery of Amílcar Salomón Zorrilla, Huancaro M-B—L8, T 231232 (P.O. Box 690), telephone between 0900 and 2100, contemporary art.

**Shopping** Market opposite Estación San Pedro (which also has the name Santa Ana) is the best Indian market for a variety of handicrafts, but although less self-conscious and less expensive than Pisac is not very interesting (best value at closing time or in the rain). *Empresa Peruana de Promoción Artesanal (EPPA)*, Plateros 359, and another good market on the corner of San Andrés and Quera. For handicrafts produced by cooperatives, with benefits going to the producers, go to the non-profit organization *Cosart*, Palacio 116 (1 block N of Plaza de Armas); ask for Antonio or Koki for information on local groups and women's committees.

Cuzco is the weaving centre of Peru, and excellent textiles can be found at good value. *Alpaca*, Calle Ruinas, genuine, 100% alpaca goods, but not cheap. *Artesanía La Paloma*, Cuesta San Blas 552 and Plazuela Sta. Catalina 211, good but expensive; *Rafael Salazar Sucesores*, Plateros 305, for good quality alpaca. *Sr. Aller*, Plaza Santo Domingo 261, sells interesting antiques. *Josefina Olivera*, Santa Clara 501, sells old ponchos, without usual haggling. There is a good jewellery store beside the Cathedral in the Plaza de Armas and art shop at *Instituto Americano de Arte*, Av. Sol. Arto Ovaska from Finland and his Peruvian wife Edith have opened *Snow Shop*, Procuradores 347, for *artesanía*, posters, music etc. However, be very careful of buying gold and silver objects and jewellery in and around Cuzco; we have received many reports of sharp practices.

Sacks to cover rucksacks are available in the market by Estación San Pedro for US$0.75.

**Bookshop** Plaza Merced (Mantas 191), a small shop sells used English, French, German and Spanish paperbacks—not cheap, poor selection, but will trade paperbacks 2 for 1. *Librería Studium*, Mesón de la Estrella 144, stocks guide books. *Los Andes*, Portal Comercio 125, Plaza de Armas, large boxes of postcards, low prices.

**Taxis** Large cars parked in Plaza are more expensive. Railway-town, US$0.80; per hour in town, US$2.70, out of town, US$3.65. For many excursions, taxis have a fixed rate; ask the driver for a price list. A rec. taxi driver (also school teacher) is José Cuba, Urb. Santa Rosa, Pasaje R. Gibaja 182, T 226179, who is a guide and can organize tours, accommodation as necessary, he speaks English; he parks at the airport during flight hours, and at the station to await train arrival. Another is Angel Salazar, Saguán del Cielo B-11, T 224597 to leave messages, Cuzco, English speaking, highly rec. helpful, arranges good tours; also José G. Valdivia Díaz, T 222210, not an official guide, but rec. as knowledgeable and helpful; Ferdinand Pinares Cuadros, Yuracpunco 155, Tahuantinsuyo, T 225914, English, French and German spoken, rec., reasonable prices.

**Car Rental** Avis, Av. Sol 900, Volkswagens and Toyotas (poor reports on maintenance). Also, **National Rentacar**, Calle Santa Catalina near main plaza (cheaper). Never leave anything in a hired car, thieves have keys and may strike the same car again and again.

**Exchange** Photocopy of passport sometimes required for changing travellers' cheques. **Banco de Crédito**, Av. del Sol, is good for changing travellers' cheques (same rate as cash). **Banco de los Andes** has the best rates and is quickest for international money transfers. Many travel agencies also change money at favourable rates and remain open during civil disturbances. No bank in Cuzco will give out cash on credit cards and their use is not rec.: surcharges are imposed and your account will be charged at official rate. **Lavamatic laundry** on Procuradores gives good rates as does **Original Travels**, Portal Comercio 141, Plaza de Armas; cash better than travellers' cheques, and **Alpha Tours**, Av. del Sol, in Centro Comercial Ollantaytambo, No. 104, rec. Money changers on **Plaza, or Av. Sol** give a better rate than travel agents. *Casas de cambio* in and around plaza charge about 3-5% commission in changing cheques into intis, 7-10% into dollars. Beware of people watching you when you change money.

**Spanish Classes** Exel, Plaza San Francisco 303, T 235-298, Señorita Sori highly rec.

**Consulates** **US Agent**, Olga Villa García, Apartado 949, Cuzco, T 222183. **German**, Sra Maria-Sophia JÚrgens de Hermoza, San Agustín 307, T 235459, Casilla Postal 1128, Correo Central, Mon., Wed., Fri., 1100-1300, appointments may be made by phone. **French**, Calle Espinar (in a French-run hotel—may let French people leave luggage if going to Machu Picchu).

**Medical** Hospital Regional, Av. de la Cultura, rec. If lab tests needed, Lab. Pasteur, Tullumayo 768 is rec. Dr. Oscar Tejada Ramírez (P.O. Box 425, Cuzco, T 233836 day or night) is a member of the International Association for Medical Assistance to Travellers and is prepared to help any visitor in emergency, 24-hr. attention; he charges according to that organization's scales. Dr Gustavo Garido Juárez, Clínica Paredes, Av. Matará 410, or at home, Av. Pardo 510 T 228613, rec.

**Sauna** corner of San Bernardo and Quera Almagro, dry sauna, Mon.-Sat. 0900-2000, Sun. 0900-1300, US$0.90.

**Laundry** Service at *Lavamatic*, Procuradores 354, min. US$3.50 for 5 kg. (charges per item), 4 hrs. *Lavanderías Splendor*, Suecia 328, just off Plaza de Armas (US$1.50 for 2 kg.), will also dry clean items such as sleeping bags, rucksacks etc. There is one on Plateros, reported cheaper and better. Also *Lavanderías Superchick* (Ana M. Velarde), Pumacurco 435, San Cristóbal, T 235629, US$3 for 5 kg., washed, dried and ironed in 24 hrs.

**Post Office and Telecommunications** Principal one on Av. Sol, hrs.: 0800-1900, 0800-1200 Sun. and festivals. Stamps available and letters can be posted at Procuradores 340, off Plaza de Armas. Telephone, telex and fax at Empresa Nacional de Telecomunicaciones, Av. Sol 386, often long queues and waits for long-distance calls—take a book. To send packages over 2 kg., go first to Customs, Calle Teatro near Plaza San Francisco, open 0900-1200; buy sacking nearby to sew up the package, and then go to main post office. Packages over 2 kg. must be despatched by customs (more expensive).

**Police** Tourist police, Portal de Belén 115, first floor, next to Cathedral on Plaza de Armas (T 221961). If you are robbed and the thief has personal items of no commercial value but important to you, go to **Radio Tawantinsuyo**, Av. Sol 806, and place an *anuncio* offering an unspecified reward for their return. Tell the respondent to go through the radio station; do not reveal your hotel. The *anuncio* costs about US$1 a run and about ten times is standard. They will help you write it; there is a standard etiquette (items are *extraviado*—"strayed" never "stolen"). The local TV station will also broadcast the *anuncio* a few times free; enquire at your hotel or at the Policía de Turismo. If you need a *denuncia*, a crime report for insurance purposes, the Policía de Turismo will tell you what documents to buy (stamped paper) at the Banco de la Nación. The police now investigate your complaint. Stolen cameras often turn up in the local market and can be bought back cheaply; remember the man selling them is not the thief and has got them at about fourth-hand.

**Tourist Office** Foptur (very helpful), Portal Belén 115, Plaza de Armas, T 237364, 0830-1900,

English spoken; at airport (until 1200) and on Av. Sol. Check all train information carefully. Maps available of Cuzco and Inca Trail to Machu Picchu. Gives opening hours of churches in Cuzco. Other good guides to the area are the booklets by Víctor Angles (*Machu Picchu, Ollantaytambo, Sacsayhuamán*) in Spanish and the Uniclam *Machu Picchu* in French. Another office at Tecsecocha 474, 0745-1300 Mon.-Fri. Note that students sell videos of Cuzco and Machu Picchu at inflated prices; cheaper, for example, at airport.

Automóvil Club del Perú, Av. Sol, useful for maps. Motorists beware; many streets end in flights of steps not marked as such. Very few good maps of Cuzco available.

The book *Exploring Cusco*, by Peter Frost, is very good; new edition available in Cuzco bookshops. Also rec. *Cusco Peru Tourist Guide*, published by Lima 2000 at US$3.50. *Apus and Incas*, by Charles Brod, describes cultural walks in and around Cuzco, and treks in the Cordilleras Vilcabamba, Vilcanota and Urubamba, plus the Manu National Park (2nd edition, Inca Expeditions, 2323 SE 46th Avenue, Portland, OR 97215, USA, US$10.95 plus US$1.50 postage, or from bookshops in N. America, Europe and Peru).

**Travel Agencies** Shopping around will always save money. *Lima Tours* at Av. Sol 567, next to Faucett office (American Express agent). *Andean Adventures*, Portal de Panes 137 (T 236201), but may be relocating, friendly, reliable; trips to Tambopata and Manu Reserves, Inca Trail, mountains (Aurelio is highly rec. mountain guide, Raul Medina also rec.) also rent equipment, as do *Walking Tours*, Portal Confituría 257, Plaza de Armas. *The River Rafting Company*, half-way up Saphi, highly rec. for what their name says, ask for Angel who speaks English. *Expediciones Mayoc*, Procuradores 354, Apartado 596, Cuzco, T 232666 organizes river-running and trekking expeditions on the Urubamba, Apurímac, Inanbari rivers, to the National Parks near Cuzco and weekly departures to walk the Inca Trail, also treks to sites round Cuzco on horseback. *Tambo Treks* organize 7-21 day tours in the region (from Paucartambo, Pongo de Mainique, Salcantay, with local weavers) from US$490. For information write to Tambo Treks, Casilla 912, Cuzco. *Aventours*, Av. Pardo 545. T 237307 (see also under Lima Travel Agents), highly rec. for rafting on the Urubamba, US$45 p.p. inc. lunch, ask for Gonzalo or Lucas in Cuzco, who also arrange mountain treks. *Kantu Tours*, Portal Carrizos 258, rec. for local tours, competitive, Gloria Hermosa Tapiá speaks good English. You can pay extra for English-speaking guides. *Sigui Tours*, Portal de Panes 123, rents camping equipment, sells maps, rec. *Snow Tours*, Portal de Panes 109, office 204, run by Arto (Finnish) and Edith Ovaska, local tours, camping equipment hired cheaply (check tents carefully); *Peruvian Andean Treks*, Av. Pardo 705, rec.; *APU Expediciones*, Portal de Carnes 236, P.O. Box 24, T (084) 235408/232743, Fax 241111, Telex 54051 PE, arranges river rafting on the Urubamba, mountaineering expeditions, trips to Manu and the Inca Trail, helpful, English spoken; *SAS Travel*, Plaza de Armas 109, Portal Belén, T 224247/226113, Raúl García is a good guide and Charo is very helpful in the office, efficient and rec.; *Río Bravo*, Almagro 120 (off Av. Sol), white water rafting and alternative routes to Machu Picchu; *Explorandes*, Procuradores, rec., good equipment for hire; *Chincheros Tours* (registered at the Cuzco Tourist office) is recommended for the Pisac-Urubamba- Ollantaytambo-Chinchero round trip; also *Pisac Tours* on Plaza de Armas (US$4 for Sacred Valley tour). *Kique Tours*, T 226627, run by Cesar Silva Guzmán, is a small new agency with one minibus, cheap local excursions, informative guide, highly rec.

Sr. Luis Vargas, Calle Triunfo 374, also is a rec. guide. Srta. Juana Pancorbo, Av. Los Pinos D-2, T 227482, is a guide who speaks English, rec. Marco Bustamante, Casilla 720, T 225391, rec. David Choque, T 224-327, English-speaking, good, but insist on itinerary first. Haydee and Tomás Oblitas, Av. Ramón Castilla J-5, Urbanización Bancopata (15 mins.' walk from centre, or take taxi) have been particularly rec. as guides in and around Cuzco, Tomás speaks English, flexible tours, reasonably priced. Raúl Castelo H., Calle Saphi 877B, Interior No. 6 (flute player at *El Truco*) is a good guide, using his own car. José Huaquina Pacheco, Saphi 635, patio 3, trustworthy guide for the Inca Trail, he has a good tent and stove, highly rec.

**N.B.** Equipment hire prices are often in dollars, so important to agree on exchange rate at time of hire. For river rafting tours, take bathing suit, T-shirt, rain gear, change of clothes and towel; life jackets should be provided.

Minibuses in front of tourist office take tourists to see the "Sacred Valley" (Pisac—make sure driver takes you to the ruins, not just the market, Ollantaytambo and Chinchero), 0800, all-day tour, US$4.20, drivers are competent guides; also Sacsayhuamán, Qenqo and Tambo Machay, 1400, half-day, US$3. Other minibuses to these places, and further afield, from Av. Recoleta.

**Roads and Buses** To Juliaca, Puno, La Paz, road in poor condition especially in the wet season, many parts are unsurfaced. Cruz del Sur, to **Puno**, leave at 1900 US$8, 12 hrs., rec., but very cold (book at least 1 day in advance in busy season). To **Sicuani**, Oriente Sur, Huáscar

244, US$3. Bus to **Juliaca** at 0900, US$8.50. To **Lima** (1,180 km.), road via Abancay, Andahuaylas, Ayacucho, Huancayo and La Oroya is rec. for magnificent scenery and interesting towns, but sometimes closed by guerrilla action. The road is appalling in places and takes from 3 to 6 days by successive buses or colectivos; take a rug for the cold nights, and extra food. Approx. times of journeys from Cuzco: Abancay 8 hrs.; Andahuaylas 14 hrs.; Ayacucho 24 hrs.; Huancayo 36-45 hrs.; Lima 2-3 days. Through fare Cuzco-Lima about US$35. An alternative road to Lima goes SW from Abancay through Puquío and Nazca; this road is narrow, unpaved but spectacular. Ormeño (office at Plaza de Armas 177, depot, Av. Huáscar 128) to Lima via Abancay and Nazca, Mon., Thurs. 0700, to Abancay 7 hrs., Puquío 22 hrs., **Nazca** 27 hrs., US$19, Lima 34-45 hrs. (US$22), also Hidalgo (Tullumayo 826). Señor de Anima, Belén 537, to Lima via Abancay and Nazca, advertised as 13 hrs., more like 40, poor meal stops and often stop at night in Abancay (as do Ormeño), Tues., Wed., Fri., Sun., 0600. By bus to Lima via **Arequipa**, 1,838 km., 3 days non-stop but the stretch Juliaca-Arequipa is poor, passing through a high arid plain at 4,700 metres before descending into Arequipa valley. Cruz del Sur, Av. Tullumayo, daily at 1800 to Lima via Arequipa (fare to Arequipa US$13.50), Señor de Anima, 50-55 hrs., good meal stops; San Cristóbal leave Cuzco at 0900, arrive Juliaca about midnight and depart Juliaca at 1000 for Arequipa next day (fare to Arequipa US$12.75). Ormeño to Arequipa via Tintaya, 18 hrs., Mon. and Thurs. 0800. Better to take a more expensive minibus from one of the companies on the Plaza de Armas (US$30 to Arequipa). For buses to nearby towns and villages, see below under their entries.

No direct buses run from Cuzco to **Ayacucho**, you have to take a bus to **Abancay** (several between 0530 and 1000, at least US$7.75, 7 hrs.), then bus Abancay-Andahuaylas (0630 only, US$6.25, 8 hrs., book seat as soon as possible), and bus Andahuaylas-Ayacucho (1400, US$10.20, 18 hrs. in the dry, forever in the wet, several companies, but don't always run). If taking a truck Andahuaylas-Ayacucho, take a powerful one; the road is terrible after Ocros. Many Guardia checkpoints, and military at Ocros; transport may also be stopped by Sendero Luminoso; because of their activities, the road to Lima via Ayacucho is virtually closed (Feb. '91).

**Rail** To Juliaca and Puno from Av. Sol station, daily, except Sun., at 0800 (though delays common and schedules change) arriving at Juliaca 1735 and Puno 1900, sit on lefthand side. To Juliaca, 1st class, US$12. To Puno, tourist car US$25, 1st, US$15, can be purchased on day before leaving, 2nd, US$5.50, can be booked, tickets on sale before, or from 0630. Meals on train cost US$3, good value, second serving reported better than first. The advantage of the buffet car (if you can get on it: group tours sometimes book the whole car) is that no one is allowed into it without a reserved seat ticket. Usually at stations the attendant keeps out vendors and doors are locked for security, although you are allowed out if you want to buy something. **N.B.** Check ticket very carefully if booking to Puno, or you may find the ticket only covers the train to Juliaca, although paid for to Puno. Beware agents on train offering accommodation in Puno, pay no money.

To **Arequipa**, 0800 daily, 23 hrs., 1st class US$20, 2nd class US$12, heated buffet car, US$20. Train to Sicuani leaves at 1510, arriving at 2120 (US$6). If going to Arequipa but make sure that your carriage does not detach at Juliaca. It is reported that the Juliaca-Puno stretch is sometimes closed; colectivos meet the train at Juliaca. See **Warning** on **page 1009**, under Arequipa **Rail**.

To Anta, Ollantaytambo, Machu Picchu and Quillabamba, **see pages 1034, 1038** and **1040.**

Machu Picchu trains leave from Estación San Pedro, opposite the market. Check all times as they change frequently, and that trains are running.

**Air** A new airport at Quispiquilla is in use. Taxi to airport, US$1.60, bus US$0.15, leaves from Tourist Office on Plaza de Armas (returns from airport to old market, dangerous after dark). To Lima, Faucett has daily flights (1200). AeroPerú also has 2 morning flights. From Lima, AeroPerú flies at 0630 and 0705, and Faucett at 0645, 1 hr. There is a Sat. and sometimes Thurs. military flight to Lima but reliable, ask for next scheduled flight with Grupo Ocho de la Fuerza Aérea; book at airport several days in advance, be at airport at 0830 for 1000/1100 departure, unpredictable in the extreme. Cuzco-Juliaca (for Puno), Fri. AeroPerú and Faucett fly daily to Arequipa, US$40, often delayed. AeroPerú also flies to Iquitos (and on to Miami) Faucett flies to Iquitos, Tues., Thurs., Sat., 0730, calling at Pucallpa, 2½ hrs. N.B. in summer all flights to Iquitos go via Lima. LAB Cuzco-La Paz-Cuzco Wed. and Sat., cheaper from La Paz (US$111 inc. tax, 2-way excursion in 1990, US$149 from La Paz). To Puerto Maldonado: AeroPerú daily; Faucett Tues., Thurs., Sat.; airforce (Grupo 8) Thurs., enquire at office of Grupo Ocho de la Fuerza Aérea in airport. Book return well in advance, especially in the busy season and reconfirm 24 hours before departure. Flights between Lima and Cuzco tend to be heavily booked between 29 July and 11 August because of school holidays. Shop around for seats at travel agencies, especially Lima Tours (ask for Sra. Rossi), if the airlines say they are full. The AeroPerú office is on Av. Sol; Faucett office is at Av. Sol 567. There is no facility for buying tickets at the airport. There is a limited hotel booking service at the airport, which will give you inflated US$-based prices: better to negotiate with hotels yourself. **N.B.** There is no air service between Cuzco and Ayacucho.

**Warning**   Cuzco-Lima, high possibility of cancelled flights during wet season; tourists sometimes stranded for several days. Possible for planes to leave early if bad weather. Sit on right side of aircraft for best view of mountains when flying Cuzco-Lima; it is worth checking in early to get these seats. Both Faucett and AeroPerú are unreliable on bookings: you must reconfirm your tickets personally in the last 24 hrs. (don't trust an agency to do this for you) but even then you cannot be sure of a seat. Baggage is often lost en route. Airport taxes: US$5 security tax; US$2 airport tax.

There is some magnificent walling in the ruined cult centre of **Sacsayhuamán**, on a hill in the northern outskirts, which is within walking distance (about ½ hr. walk, tiring because of the altitude). Take steps to San Cristóbal church (shorter than via Calle Saphi). The Incaic stones are bigger and even more impressive than at Machu Picchu; huge rocks weighing up to 300 tons are fitted together with absolute perfection; three walls run parallel for over 360 metres and there are 21 bastions. Sacsayhuamán was thought for centuries to be a fortress, but the layout and architecture suggest a great sanctuary and temple to the Sun, which rises exactly opposite the place previously believed to be the Inca's throne—which was probably an altar, carved out of the solid rock: broad steps lead to it from either side. The hieratic, rather than the military, hypothesis was supported by the discovery in 1982 of the graves of priests: they would have been unlikely to be buried in a fortress. Zig-zags in the boulders round the "throne" are apparently "*chicha* grooves", channels down which maize beer flowed during festivals. Up the hill is an ancient rock slide for children: the Rodadero; near it are many seats cut perfectly into smooth rock.

The temple and amphitheatre of Qenqo, with excellent examples of Inca stone carving, especially inside the large hollowed-out stone that houses an altar, are along the road from Sacsayhuamán to Pisac, past a radio station. On the same road are the Inca fortress of Puku Pukara and the spring shrine of Tambo Machay, which is in excellent condition; water still flows by a hidden channel out of the masonry wall, straight into a little rock pool traditionally known as the Inca's bath, but he would have had to be a pygmy to have used it as such. It seems much more likely that the site was a centre of a water cult.

The gates are manned from about 0700 but you can get in earlier if you wish and definitely try to get there before midday when the tour groups arrive. Carry your multi-site ticket, there are roving ticket inspectors. After seeing 3 sites you can catch truck back along road, 9 km., for US$0.25. Preferably, take the Pisac bus (from Calle Saphi) to Tambo Machay and walk back (downhill) to Cuzco, or taxi US$0.50 to Tambo Machay (to walk from Cuzco to Tambo Machay takes over an hour, but it's pleasant). If you walk back, don't take short cuts through farmland; you may get chased by packs of dogs. Between Qenqo and Puku Pukara is Cusilluyuioc; caves and Inca tunnels in a hillside (take a torch/flashlight). Taxis to Inca sites outside Cuzco for 3 hrs. cost US$17, not including entry to the sites, and may be hired in the Plaza de Armas. A tour bus to all 4 sites costs US$5. Another good way to see these ruins is on horseback, arranged by travel agents.

Cuzco is at the W end of the gently sloping Cuzco valley, which stretches 32 km. E as far as Huambutío. This valley, and the partly isolated basin of Anta, NW of Cuzco, are densely populated. Also densely populated is the Urubamba valley, stretching from Sicuani (on the railway to Puno) to the gorge of Torontoi, 600 metres lower, to the NW of Cuzco.

There are many interesting villages and ruins in the Cuzco valley itself. **Andahuaylillas** is a village 32 km. S of Cuzco, with a particularly fine early 17th century church; beautiful frescoes, splendid doorway and a gilded main altar (ask for Sr. Eulogio, good guide, Spanish only). Taxis go there as does Oropesa bus (Av. Huáscar, Cuzco) via Tipón, Piquillacta and Rumicolca. (For Piquillacta ask driver to drop you off at the turning or take the bus from Urcos-2 basic lodgings.) There are other unexcavated ruins just beyond Andahuaylillas.

John Streather has most kindly given us information about more places south of Cuzco with interesting Inca remains and colonial buildings:
   **Tipón** ruins, between the villages of Saylla and Oropesa, include baths, terraces and a temple complex, accessible from a path leading from just above the last terrace. **Oropesa** church contains a fine ornately carved pulpit. **Huacarpay**: ruins of the Inca town of Kañaracy, well-preserved, are nearby, reached from a path behind the Albergue. Also nearby are the Huari (pre-Inca) adobe wall ruins of **Piquillacta**, the monkey temple and the wall of Rumicolca. Piquillacta is quite large, with some reconstruction in progress. A colectivo from the street opp. Av. Sol station will drop you at the entrance on the N side of the complex (this is not the official entry); walk through to the official entry and continue to Rumicolca on the other side of the highway. At Lucre, 3 km. from Huacarpay, there is an interesting textile mill, and many unexplored ruins; ask the local history teacher, Sr. Hernán Flores Yávar, for details. About 3 km. from Huacarpay is *El Dorado Inn*, in a converted monastery, some of the rooms in a remarkable style, very good service, but expensive at C. **Tinta**, 23 km. from Sicuani, has a church with brilliant gilded interior and an interesting choir vault. Hotel: *Casa Comunal*, dormitory accommodation, F, clean with good food. Frequent buses and trucks to Cuzco. **Huaro** has a church whose interior is covered entirely with colourful mural painting. **Cusipata**, with an Inca gate and wall, is where the ornate bands for the decoration of ponchos are woven; close by is the Huari hilltop ruin of Llallanmarca.

**Raqchi** is the scene of the region's great folklore festival in mid-June. A special train leaves Cuzco early in the morning, or take a truck, US$1.50, 4 hours. At this festival dancers come to Raqchi from all over Peru; through music and dance they illustrate everything from the ploughing of fields to bull fights, reported to be most enjoyable. John Hemming adds: The Viracocha temple is just visible from the train, looking from the distance like a Roman aqueduct. What remains is the central wall (adobe above, Inca masonry below) of what was probably the largest roofed building ever built by the Incas. On either side of the high wall, great sloping roofs were supported by rows of unusual round pillars, also of masonry topped by adobe. Nearby is a complex of barracks-like buildings and round storehouses. This was the most holy shrine to the creator god Viracocha, being the site of a miracle in which he set fire to the land—hence the lava flow nearby. There are also small Inca baths in the corner of a field beyond the temple and a straight row of ruined houses by a square. The landscape is extraordinary, blighted by huge piles of black volcanic rocks. (San Cristóbal bus to Raqchi from Av. Huáscar, Cuzco every hour, US$2, 4 hrs. Nearest hotel is in Tinta.)

**Pacarijtambo** is a good starting point for the 3-4 hr. walk to the ruins of Mankallajta, which contain good examples of Inca stonework. From there, one can walk to Pumaorco, a high rock carved with steps, seats and a small puma in relief on top; below are more Inca ruins. From Pumaorco walk back to the nearby hamlet of Mollepata (bus from Cuzco, US$1.50) and ask the schoolteacher the way to Pacarijtambo (a 2-3 hr. walk). One may seek lodging for the night in Pacarijtambo at the house of the Villacorta family and leave for Cuzco by truck the next morning. On the way back, one passes the caves of Tambo Toco, where the legend says that the four original Inca brothers emerged into the world.

**Acomayo** is a pretty village (*Pensión Aguirre*), which has a chapel with mural paintings of the fourteen Incas. From Acomayo, one can walk to Huáscar and from there to Pajlia; a climb which leads one through very impressive scenery. The canyons of the upper Apurímac are vast beyond imagination, great cliffs drop thousands of metres into dizzying chasms and huge rocks balance menacingly overhead. The ruins of Huajra Pucará lie near Pajlia; they are small, but in an astonishing position. John Hemming adds that the church at Checacupe is very fine, with good paintings and a handsome carved altar rail.

**Pisac**, 30 km. N of Cuzco, is at the bottom of the Urubamba valley; high above it, on the mountainside, is a superb Inca fortress (admission by combined entrance ticket, **see page 1022**, the ruins close at 1700). The masonry is better than at Machu Picchu, the terraces more extensive and better preserved. When you climb it (a must), remember that there are 3 hill fortifications, but the third is the fortress proper, in which the actual temple is built: so go on to it and get the glorious view from the top. There is a 10-km. motor road up to the level of the ruins, upstream from Pisac town and then up a valley to the S of the spur containing the ruins. From the parking lot, enter along Inca roads and through Inca gates, seeing the fine view of terraces (which can be reached quite easily from the town by a footpath, local boys will guide you US$0.50 per couple). Quite a lot of walking is involved. The central part of the ruins is the Intihuatana group of temples and rock outcrops in the most magnificent Inca masonry. Above on the hilltop reached by a path along a vertiginous cliff are residential groups; there is a large Inca cemetery in caves on the valley opposite to the north; the curving group of houses called Pisallacta below the Intihuatana group; and more buildings, some with curious round towers, others of good Inca adobe, on the steep hillside above the town. It takes about 25 minutes to walk down. There is a path going right round the mountain, behind the main ruins; it has two tunnels. It takes 2½ hours to walk from the parking lot back to Pisac. Taxi to ruins US$2.50.

Pisac has a Sun. morning market, described as touristy and expensive after the arrival of tourist buses around 1000; it starts at 0900 and is usually over by 1500. There are picturesque Indian processions to a Quechua Mass. Pisac has another, less crowded, less expensive market on Thurs. morning. You can take in the market, then take taxi up to ruins, explore them, walk down and get last bus or truck back to Cuzco by 1630. It is reported that transport to the ruins is not always available for those not in a tour group. You can continue the Sun. morning tour to Pisac along the Urubamba to Ollantaytambo, with lunch at the Tourist Hotel in Urubamba but tours from Cuzco usually allow only 1½ hours at Pisac: not enough time to take it in. Splendid scenery. Apart from Sun. when Pisac is crowded, there are very few tourists. An alternative for lunch is the restaurant on the square in **Yukay** , (3 km. east of Urubamba) open-air, good buffet and local dishes. On the N side of the square is the adobe palace built for Sayri Túpac (Manco's son) when he emerged from Vilcabamba in 1558. A pleasant old hotel, the *Alhambra 3*, B, is in Yukay, rather overpriced but very pretty and old. In Yukay monks sell fresh milk, ham, eggs and other dairy produce from their farm on the hillside. The tour by taxi costs US$45-50. Good walks along river to Inca terraces.

**Pisac Hotels** *Albergue Chongo Chico*, F, basic, slightly decayed, electricity and water unreliable, friendly; camping allowed in garden. *Turistas*, E, pleasant, English spoken, meals US$5. The woman who owns the flour mill rents rooms for US$1.30 p.p. *Roma*, near the bridge by the Kodak sign, F, basic, quiet, cold shower, dreadful; camping allowed in its grounds for US$0.45 p.p. Reasonable restaurant on the plaza, but better to take a packed lunch from Cuzco. Fresh bread available from the oven *(el horno)* just off the plaza.

**Buses** Cuzco-Pisac road is paved. Early morning buses (also to Chinchero and Urubamba, US$0.40) on Sunday, every ten min., from 0540 to 0700, 1 hr. (queue early in road opposite Huanchac railway station or catch them on Huáscar, halfway down 1st block on right-hand side looking downhill, before they fill up); several—bus Cuzco-Pisac from Recoleta y Tacna, 1½ hrs, US$0.30. Bus Pisac-Cuzco hourly on weekdays until 1700-1800. Colectivos to Pisac from Cuzco; they return all afternoon until 1715 and are always full, be prepared to return by truck. Fare US$0.84; try and book the previous day if possible. Tourist minibus leaves Cuzco Plaza de Armas outside Cathedral daily for Pisac and Ollantaytambo if there are more than five passengers, US$6 return. Minibus tours also Cuzco, Pisac, Urubamba, Ollantaytambo, US$12, usually market days, Sun., Thur., only; taxi for this route, including Chinchero, US$50. Colectivos to Pisac and Ollantaytambo leave when full from Calle Recoleta, from 0600, Cuzco (past Calle Pumapaccha), to Pisac 45 mins., US$0.75, to Ollantaytambo, 2½ hrs., US$1.20. Return fare by truck, US$0.50, over 1 hr. Taxi fare (return) from Cuzco to the fortress costs US$10 and includes a visit to the market. Two buses daily to Urubamba. Bus stops in Pisac are brief, make sure you get on or off the bus quickly. Try hitching opposite the police checkpoint.

*Calca* is 18 km. beyond Pisac (Hotels: *Alojamiento Grau*, basic; *Alojamiento Alvarez*; Alojamiento Central, F, basic. Restaurants: *Sondar*, *Bolivar*, on Plaza; *Moreñitas* and *Café Calqueñita*, near post office). Mineral baths at Minas Maco (½ hr. walk along the Urubamba) and Machacancha (8 km. E of Calca). If one continues past Minas Maco, one bears right up a small footpath leading by a clump of trees; the first house one comes to after crossing a small stream and climbing a hill is a precolumbian ruin. 3 km. beyond Machacancha are the Inca ruins of Arquasmarca. The ruins of a small Inca town, Huchuy Cuzco, are across the river Vilcanota, and up a stiff climb. There are a two-storey house, paved with flat stones, and a large stone reservoir at Huchuy Cuzco. Bus to Pisac, or to Urubamba, US$0.60; bus to Cuzco, US$0.35. Market day: Sun. It is a two-day hike from Cuzco to Calca, via Sacsayhuamán, Qenqo, Puka Pukará, Tambo Machay and Huchuy Cuzco; there are many places to camp, but take water.

Between Calca and Quillabamba the road is narrow and subject to landslides.

***Zurite*** is a little-known village north of Cuzco; Inca terraces of Patapata are only about an hour's walk from the village's main square. The construction of these terraces represents a Herculean effort as all of the earth is said to have been brought from elsewhere. A canal was built to bring water from the mountains. (John Streather.)

***Chinchero***; with an attractive church built on an Inca temple; recent excavations there have revealed many Inca walls and terraces. (On combined entrance ticket, **see page 1022**.) It has become very tourist-oriented but nonetheless the Sunday market and Indian mass are more authentic than at Pisac (there is a small market on Thurs.). *Hotel Inca*, F, with restaurant; *Albergue Chinchero*, F, basic, clean, friendly. At the market, there is a varied selection of handicrafts, including weaving, pottery and alpaca goods (nothing is cheap). Celebrations are held in Chinchero on 8 September (the day of the Virgin).

A new road Cuzco-Urubamba has been completed, which has cut the travelling time to Chinchero to 40 mins. from Cuzco by bus, leaving about 0700 from Av. Arcopata on Sun. mornings, US$0.30. Also colectivos from Av. Arcopata. Taxi, US$20 for 5-hr. trip. There is also a scenic path from Chinchero to the Urubamba-Calca road: follow the wide trail opposite the terraces in a northerly direction (no chance of getting lost). After 4-5 hrs. you reach the Urubamba river; keep following the road to the left. After 15 mins. there is a bridge over the river.

76 km. from Cuzco on the Abancay road, 2 km. before Limatambo (accommodation in *Albergue*, F; nice restaurant hidden from road by trees), at Hacienda ***Tarahuasi***, a few hundred metres from the road, is a very well-preserved **Inca temple platform**, with 28 tall niches, and a long stretch of fine polygonal masonry. The ruins have grandeur, enhanced by the orange lichen which give the walls a beautiful honey colour. 100 km. from Cuzco along the Abancay road is the exciting descent into the Apurímac canyon, near the former Inca suspension bridge that inspired Thornton Wilder's *The Bridge of San Luis Rey*. Also, 153 km. along the road to Abancay from Cuzco, near Carahuasi (restaurant on main road into town; camping possible on the football pitch, ask police), is the stone of Sahuite, carved with animals, houses, etc., which appears to be a relief map of an Indian village. (Unfortunately, "treasure hunters" have defaced the stone.) There are other interesting carvings in the area around the Sahuite stone.

For US$50 a taxi can be hired for a whole day (ideally Sun.) to take you to Cachimayo, Chinchero, Maras, Urubamba, Ollantaytambo, Calca, Lamay, Coya, Pisac, Tambo Machay, Qenqo and Sacsayhuamán. If you wish to explore this area on your own, Road Map (*Hoja de ruta*) No. 10 from the Automóvil Club del Perú is an excellent guide.

***Urubamba*** is N of Chinchero, on a new direct road from Cuzco via Chinchero; pleasant country surroundings. The Machu Picchu tourist train can be caught at Pachar, about 20 minutes' drive away, at 0830; no fare reduction. Bus Cuzco – Urubamba, US$1.40 from Av. Huáscar 128, 2½ hrs. Urubamba – Ollantaytambo, colectivo, US$0.30, 30-45 mins., 19 km.

**Hotels and restaurants** *Hotel de Turistas*, E, clean, hot water, poor service, bungalows with neglected garden and swimming pool; the *Centro Vacacional Urubamba*, cabins (some with kitchen, must take own stove), sports facilities, 2 pools, E and F, good value restaurant with set menu, though service slow; *Hostal Naranjachayoc*, C, with antique furniture and swimming pool, 20 mins. walk from town, rec., friendly, accommodating, will help with any problems, very clean and well-stocked restaurant and bar, even in low-season, car can be parked in locked patio, *Hotel Urubamba*, F, pleasant; *Hostal Reymada*, F, basic, clean, friendly, outdoor pool, rec.; *Restaurant Quinta los Geranios*, excellent lunch for US$3 with more than enough food; *Comedor Aries* and *Andes*, both on Plaza. *Quinta Galu*, close to Plaza, large, reasonable, friendly, good.

Joanna Codrington writes: 6 km. from Urubamba on the Ollantaytambo road is the village of *Tarabamba*, where a footbridge crosses the Río Vilcanota. If one turns right after the bridge one comes to Piychinjoto, a tumbled-down village built under an overhanging cliff. Also, just over the bridge and to the left of a small, walled cemetery is a salt stream. If one follows this (there is a footpath) one comes to Salinas, a small village below which are a mass of terraced Inca salt pans, still in operation. A very spectacular sight. *Moray* is well worth a visit: there are three "colosseums", used by the Incas as a sort of open-air crop laboratory, known locally as the greenhouses of the Incas. Peter Frost (*Exploring Cuzco*) writes: "There are no great ruined structures here to impress visitors. Moray is more for the contemplative traveller with an affinity for such phenomena as the Nazca Lines, the stone rings of Avebury and the menhirs of Brittany." A remote but beautiful site. Wait for pickup on bridge on Chinchero road. This will take you near to Maras; walk to Maras (½ hr.) and on through it, bearing left a little, and ask directions to Moray (walk 1½ hrs.). Hitching back to Urubamba is quite easy, but there are no hotels at all in the area, so take care not to be stranded.

The Cuzco-Machu Picchu train reaches the heights N of the city by a series of switchbacks and then descends to the floor of the Anta basin, with its herds of cattle. (In **Anta** itself, *Restaurant Dos de Mayo* is good; bus to Anta, US$0.30., felt trilby hats on sale). The railway goes through the Anta canyon (10 km.), and then, at a sharp angle, the Urubamba canyon, and descends along the river valley, flanked by high cliffs and peaks.

The railway and a 53-km. road go on to ***Ollantaytambo***, 70 km., a clean and friendly little town (alt.: 2,800 metres) built on and out of the stones of an Inca town, which is a fine example of Inca *canchas* or corral enclosures, almost entirely intact. The so-called Baño de la Ñusta (bath of the princess) is of grey granite, and is in a small field between the town and the temple fortress. Some 200 metres behind the Baño de la Ñusta along the face of the mountain are some small ruins known as Inca Misancca, believed to have been a small temple or observatory. A series of steps, seats and niches have been carved out of the cliff. There is a complete irrigation system, including a canal at shoulder level, some 6 inches deep, cut out of the sheer rock face. The flights of terraces leading up above the town are superb, and so are the curving terraces following the contours of the rocks overlooking the Urubamba. These terraces were successfully defended by Manco Inca's warriors against Hernando Pizarro in 1536. Manco Inca built the defensive wall above the site and another wall closing the Yucay valley against attack from Cuzco, still visible on either side of the valley. Visitors should also note the Inca masonry channelling the river and the piers of the bridge of Ollantaytambo. Entering Ollantaytambo from Pisac, the road is built along the long wall of 100 niches. Note the inclination of the wall: it leans towards the road. Since it was the Incas' practice to build with the walls leaning towards the interiors of the buildings, it has been deduced that the road, much narrower then, was built inside a succession of buildings. The site opens at 0700.

The temple itself was started by Pachacuti, using Colla Indians from Lake Titicaca—hence the similarities of the monoliths facing the central platform with the Tiahuanaco remains. The Colla are said to have deserted half-way through the work, which explains the many unfinished blocks lying about the site. Admission by combined entrance ticket, which can be bought at the site. If possible arrive very early, 0700, before the tourists. The Sunday following Inti Raymi, there is a colourful festival, the Ollantay-Raymi. The guide book *Ollantaytambo* by Víctor Angles Vargas is available in Cuzco bookshops, and Peter Frost's *Exploring Cusco* is also useful.

**Accommodation** *Parador Turístico*, off main street between Plaza and ruins, for groups by reservation but will sometimes take other groups or couples if not booked up, E-F, good meals at US$2-3; offers travel info. and horseback/walking tours; for reservations write to María S. Martínez, Parador Turístico de Ollantaytambo, Cuzco, Peru or get your Cuzco hotel to phone the Ollantaytambo exchange as the Parador has no phone as yet. Russ Bentley writes: "a veritable oasis of comfort and excellent food (superb Italian cuisine)". *Hostal Miranda*, F with shower, basic, friendly, clean; *Hostal Alcázar*, F with shower, basic, good food, clean; *El Tambo*, also known as *Alojamiento Yavar*, 1½ blocks from main square, G (if full, will let you sleep on the floor free), basic, friendly, has information on riding in the area, horses for hire at US$3 a day; *Hotel Panificadora*, G, tantalizing smell of fresh bread, very hard beds, basic, between main plaza and ruins. *Miramar*, G p.p., clean, basic, hot water available for a fee. Hotel next to station, no sign, door in garden wall, access via footbridge over stream, F p.p., shared amenities, comfortable.

**Camping** possible in eucalyptus grove, ½ km. from town, and along the river between the

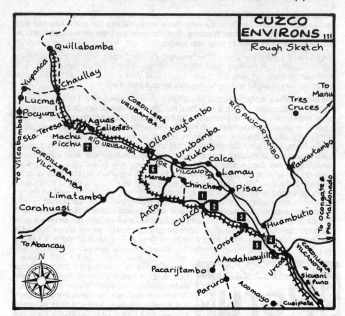

town and the railway station.

Horses can be hired for US$3 per day; a rec. trek is to La Marca, a gentle day's ride along the beautiful river valley; ask in the square for details.

**Restaurants** *Restaurant Ollantay* on Plaza de Armas. *Café Alcázar* opposite *Parador Turístico* good, cheap food, very slow service if full; *El Parador*, in converted barn, down from main square towards ruins, good pasta and garlic bread; *Restaurante Tanta Wasi*, by railway, has two rooms to let, run by Jaime and Pilar Paz. In restaurants, check your bill carefully.

**Transport** For those travelling by car, it is recommended to leave the car in Ollantaytambo (or the station previous on the road from Cuzco) for a day excursion by train to Machu Picchu. Park car in front of the local police station at Ollantaytambo. Much safer there than parked in Cuzco for US$1 a day. Check in advance the time trains pass through here. The tourist train stops here, as do local trains (depending which is running- see **Transport** under Machu Picchu). Station is 10-15 mins. walk from centre. Hourly bus from Av. Húascar 128, Cuzco, 2½ hrs., US$1.40, to Urubamba, then colectivo to Ollantaytambo, also to Pisac. Beware of theft when queuing in Cuzco for the Ormeño bus to Ollantaytambo; if the bus goes down the company's alley to turn, get on there, if it doesn't, either don't rush for a seat, or queue with no valuables or possessions, push on, and reserve 2 seats for yourself and your friend with the gear. Many colectivos to Pisac on Sunday for market from 0600, 70 mins. Bus to Cuzco on Sat. at 0800 and 1200. Tourist minibus from outside Cuzco Cathedral to Pisac, Ollantaytambo, Cuzco, daily if over 5 passengers, US$12 (taxi tour costs US$45.50). Taxi to Cuzco, US$14.50. Bus to Urubamba, US$0.60 (truck US$0.20), from where one can return to Cuzco via Calca.

A major excavation project has been carried out since 1977 under the direction of Ann Kendall in the **Cusichaca** (Qucsichaca) valley, 26 km. from Ollantaytambo (only 9 km. passable by ordinary car) at the intersection of the Inca routes. (The Inca fort, Huillca Raccay, was excavated in 1978-80, and work is now concentrated on Llactapata, a site of domestic buildings).

From Ollantaytambo one can walk to the Inca Trail in about 8 hrs., rec.: follow the railway in the direction of Machu Picchu until you come to a village where you can cross the river; climb up to a path that runs parallel to the river. This is an original Inca trail (still in use) that leads to Llactapata on the Inca Trail. **Warning** Best not to pass a night on this trail: thefts are common because you have to sleep near villages.

Pinculluna, the mountain above Ollantaytambo, can be climbed with no mountaineering experience, although there are some difficult stretches—allow 2-3 hours going up. The path is difficult to make out; best not to go on your own. Walk up the valley to the left of the mountain, very beautiful and impressive, Inca terraces after 4 km.

The *Inca Trail* hike to Machu Picchu, about 33 km., makes a spectacular 3 to 5 day hike (take it slowly to appreciate it fully). It runs from Km. 88, Qoriwayrachi (about 2,600 metres), a point immediately after the first tunnel 22 km. beyond Ollantaytambo station. A sturdy suspension bridge has now been built over the Urubamba River. An entrance ticket (US$13, in Intis only, and no discount for foreign students) for the trail (which also gives entry to Machu Picchu if you get it stamped there) must be bought at Km. 88. The trail is rugged and steep (beware of landslides), at one stage traversing a 4,200-metre high pass, but the magnificent views compensate for any weariness which may be felt. It is cold at night, however, and weather conditions change rapidly, so it is important to take not only strong footwear and warm clothing but also food, water, insect repellant, a supply of plastic bags, coverings, a good sleeping bag, a stove for preparing hot food and drink to ward off the cold at night. A stove using paraffin (kerosene) is preferable, as fuel can be bought in small quantities in markets, whereas camping gas is expensive and scarce. **A tent is essential** (if hiring in Cuzco, check carefully for leaks) because walkers who have not taken adequate equipment have been known to die of exposure; caves marked on some maps are little better than overhangs, and are not sufficient shelter to sleep in. The trail is crowded in July and August. In the wet season (November-March) you don't have to worry about taking drinking water. At Puyopatamarca, on the Trail, there is a "tourist bathroom" where water can be collected (but purify it before drinking). Next place with water is Wiñay-Wayna (where there is a newly-built "tourist complex" with bunk beds (G p.p.), showers and a small restaurant, food and drink expensive, reservations in Cuzco, T 223110/240532), and then none till Machu Picchu, where water supplies are turned off at 1530. A variation to the Trail is to get off the train at Chilca, some 12 km. beyond Ollantaytambo (or you can hire a truck from Ollantaytambo to Chilca for US$5 p.p. approx., or hitch) cross the bridge and walk 10 km. along the Río Urubamba to join the trail at a point above Km. 88. This adds 5 hrs. to the journey, but has the advantage of giving the body an opportunity to acclimatize itself before the very strenuous climb to the top of the first pass (medication for *soroche* may be necessary for some). Camping is possible on the bluff overlooking Llactapata (watch your belongings closely) and Km. 88 and this is an ideal starting point for the climb to the first pass, putting several hours between you and the other hikers who reach Km. 88 by train after 0900. **Warning** We have had a number of reports of armed robbery on the Inca Trail, mostly on the first night, the culprits being variously described as Sendero Luminoso or organized gangsters from Cuzco. For this reason alone, do not go singly or in couples (official advice: no fewer than four—post a guard at night), and if possible stay close to a tour group; avoid the July-August high season and the rainy season from November to March. Camp away from the sites on the main trail, and leave all valuables back in Cuzco.

**Train to Km. 88** Only the local train stops at Km. 88; the tourist train does not stop here. While the

policy exists of deterring tourists from taking the local train (see below), it is difficult to get to the start of the Trail. Unless you can travel on the local train, the simplest method is to go to Ollantaytambo, or Chilca and start walking from there. If you do manage to catch the stopping train, be ready to get out at Km. 88, it's easy to pass it.

All the necessary equipment can be rented; **see page 1028** under **Travel agencies**. Good maps of the Trail and area can be bought from Walking Tours, the tourist office, at the Club Andino, or at Copias Vélez, Plaza San Francisco, Cuzco. Try to get the map prepared by the curator of Machu Picchu Museum; it shows best sleeping places and drinking water. The guide Alberto Miori from Inca Trails is recommended, with many good reports. If you have any doubts about carrying your own pack, reasonably-priced porters/guides are available, most reliably through Cuzco agencies. Remember there are no houses you can rush to if you get into difficulties; check carefully all equipment you hire before starting out.

Susan Whittlesey and Michael Young have prepared an excellent booklet on the Inca civilization and the Inca Trail (including a superb map), which is available for US$4 from Cin Co., 2912 E. 5th Avenue, Denver, Colorado 80206, USA.

The walk to Huayllabamba, following the Cusichaca river, needs about 3 hrs. and isn't too arduous. If planning a 2-4 day trip, carry on past Huayllabamba, which has become notorious for robberies. There is a camping place about an hr. ahead, at Llulluchayoc and another before the ascent to the first pass, Warmiwañuska, about 4 hrs. on in a meadow (highly recommended) 1½-2 hrs. from the summit. From Huayllabamba to the meadows is often discouragingly steep. Following the right path demands intuition more than orienteering knowhow, and the forest is occasionally very thick—but you should emerge towards 1600 hrs.

Leave early next day. The ascent to the first pass (4,200 metres) is the most taxing part of the walk. Afterwards take the path downhill, along left side of valley. You could camp by a stream at the bottom; it is no longer permitted to camp on the way up to the second pass (a much easier climb) at Runkuracay (3,800 metres), an Inca ruin, where there are huts and caves. Magnificent views near the summit in clear weather. Good overnight place is past the Inca ruins at Sayajmarca (3,600 metres), about an hr. on after the top of the second pass.

Muddy jungle terrain leads gently up to the third pass, only about 2-2½ hrs.' walk, the gradient blissfully gentle. Near the top there's a spectacular view of the Urubamba river and the valley to the right. You descend to Inca ruins at Puyopatamarca, well worth a long visit.

From there steps go downhill to Wiñay-Wayna, reached by forking off to the right (it's marked by a sign) near the pylons, 3-4 hrs. or so on from Puyopatamarca. A tourist complex has been built at the fork: there is no road. There is a shop selling drinks, with toilets and comfy chairs and nearby there is a dormitory, F (no electricity). The ruins at Wiñay-Wayna, a village of roofless but otherwise well-preserved Inca houses, are in an impressive location. The path from this point goes more or less level through jungle. You need about 2 hrs. to walk to the Intipunku (3 camping sites on right of track, just before ruins.), where there's a magnificent view of Machu Picchu, especially at dawn, with the sun alternately in and out, clouds sometimes obscuring the ruins, sometimes leaving them clear. Get to Machu Picchu as early as possible, preferably before 0830 for best views but in any case before the tourist train arrives at 1030.

Four days would make a comfortable trip (though much depends on the weather) and you would not find yourself too tired to enjoy what you see. Walking the Trail has the advantage of putting Machu Picchu in its true context: not a "lost city", but an integral part of a heavily populated valley. By the same token Machu Picchu loses some of its uniqueness; the architecture and scenery are often finer at several points along the trail. **N.B** It is not allowed to walk back along the trail, though you may pay US$1.50 at Intipunku to be allowed to walk back as far as Wiñay-Wayna, and you may not take backpacks into Machu Picchu.

It is no longer possible to walk back from Aguas Calientes to Km. 107 and cross the swing bridge to go to Wiñay-Wayna by a switch-back path, thence to Machu Picchu. The terrorist threat to the electricity power station has forced the authorities to close this route.

Littering along the Trail is a serious problem as 5,000 people are now using it each year. The Earth Preservation Fund now sponsors an annual cleanup July-August: volunteers should write to EPF, Inca Trail Project, Box 7545, Ann Arbor, Michigan 48107, USA.

*Machu Picchu*, 42 km. from Ollantaytambo by rail (2,280 metres), is a complete city, set on a saddle of a high mountain with terraced slopes falling away to the Urubamba river rushing in great hairpin bends below. It is in a comparatively good state of preservation because the Spaniards never found it. For centuries it was buried in jungle, until Hiram Bingham stumbled upon it in 1911. It was then explored by an archaeological expedition sent by Yale.

The ruins—staircases, terraces, temples, palaces, towers, fountains, the famous sundial and the Museo de Sitio below the ruins—require at least a day—some say two (take an insect-repellant). The mountain overlooking the site, Huayna Picchu (on which there are also some ruins), has steps to the top for a superlative view of the whole but it is not for those who get giddy (don't leave the path); the walk up takes about 60 minutes but the steps are dangerous after bad weather (it is only possible to walk up in the morning—start early as there is shade then—and you must register at a hut on the trail; guards prevent you after 1300). The other trail to Huayna Picchu, down near the Urubamba, via the Temple of the Moon, in two caves, one above the other, with superb Inca niches inside (sadly blemished by idiots' graffiti), can only be undertaken with a guide to the Temple of the Moon, leaving Machu Picchu at 0900; he will clear the path and kill poisonous snakes. For the trail to the Temple of the Moon: from the path to Huayna Picchu, take the second trail to the left (both are marked "Danger, do not enter"). The danger is in the first 10 minutes, after which it is reasonable, although it descends further than you think it should. After the Temple you may proceed alone to Huayna Picchu; round trip about 4 hours. An almost equally good view can be had from the trail behind the Tourist Hotel. Before doing any trekking around Machu Picchu, check with an official which paths may be used, or which are one way.

From Machu Picchu one can take the Inca Trail, which climbs up behind the Tourist Hotel, back to (2 hours' walk) the Inca settlement of Wiñay-Wayna (see above under the Inca Trail). On the way, you will have to pay US$1.50 for entry to the Trail. About 30 mins. along a well-marked trail on the other side of Machu Picchu ruins is the famous Inca bridge. Both walks give spectacular views of the Urubamba River and the thickly wooded mountains, and the butterflies and flowers are beautiful. When going to the Bridge, "don't dwell on just why the path stays where it does" (Kirk Mayer). The tombs at Chaskapata, near Machu Picchu, have recently been opened.

Gillian Handyside, of Harefield, Mx., tells us that another Inca site was discovered in 1987 opposite Machu Picchu. An archaeologist, Moisés, who works on the project stays in the *Albergue* in Aguas Calientes and sometimes shows slides on the subject.

**Transport N.B.** "Machu Picchu" is the official name for Aguas Calientes station; that for Machu Picchu is "Puente Ruinas". The most convenient way of seeing the ruins is to pay US$95 to Foptur, at the station, or an agency (which may add commission) for a *boleto único*, which includes: transfer hotel-station, return train ride in a locked car, bus to Machu Picchu site, entry and guided tour. There are 2 trips a day, at 0630 and 0800 enabling tourists to arrive at Machu Picchu at about 0945 and 1130, visit the ruins and leave Machu Picchu at 1545 and 1730, arriving in Cuzco about 3½ hrs. later. The tourist trains stop at Ollantaytambo, but not at Aguas Calientes unless requested in advance. The later train out involves going to Ollantaytambo by coach to catch the train; passengers on the early train back are taken from Ollantaytambo to Cuzco by coach. At the San Pedro station you can book a single tourist ticket for US$37, which does not include entry or buses to the ruins. Tickets may be bought one day in advance (returns available); office open 0600-0820, 1000-1100, 1500-1700; make sure you buy a single if staying overnight, or returning on a different type of train.

Local trains from Cuzco, en route to Quillabamba, pass through Ollantaytambo, Aguas Calientes ("Machu Picchu") and Machu Picchu ("Puente Ruinas"). It is imperative to check departure times in advance; they leave Cuzco at 0620, or 1300, or both, arriving at Aguas Calientes at 1030 or 1730, respectively. A tourist Pullman car is sometimes attached to the local train, with a fare of US$10 single. (Ticket office hours: 0800-1200, 1600-1700, Mon.-Fri.; 0500-0600, 1200-1430, Sat.; 1200-1430, Sun.). The local train returns at 0800 and 1600, US$5, but is unreliable and it is already jam-packed by the time it reaches Machu Picchu on its way up from Quillabamba. If the 0530 from Quillabamba is running to Cuzco, it passes Machu Picchu at 0815. Take a drinking mug on the train. **Note**: In the rainy season trains are often delayed by landslides.

Tourists are normally refused tickets for the local trains to "Puente Ruinas", but in low season they may be allowed on at a tourist price (about US$12). Many cannot afford the tourist prices (as opposed to the local fare of about US$1.20 on the "Indian train"), so various alternatives have been worked out by foreigners. None is straightforward. 1) Take a taxi to El Arco, outside Cuzco, where the train stops briefly; the guard may let you on, for a fee. 2)

Go to Ollantaytambo one way or another and buy a tourist ticket (cheaper than in Cuzco), or ask a local to buy a local ticket for you (not possible in Cuzco because identification has to be shown). 3) Persuade station officials that you are going to Quillabamba, not Machu Picchu, then get off at Machu Picchu (which may be difficult). 4) An agent in Cuzco may purchase a local ticket for you, with a hefty mark-up. 5) Buy a single tourist ticket to Machu Picchu from Cuzco, then take the local train back. This is not a problem since residents in Aguas Calientes will help you get a local ticket if you cannot get one yourself (they are angry at tourist prices which discourage independent travellers from going to Machu Picchu.)

Beware of thieves on the local train (bag-slitting is extremely common), particularly at the switch-backs when they can jump on and off the train, and on the Urubamba stretch where there are many short tunnels. Police presence has been stepped up at the stations and on the trains.

Buses from the station to Machu Picchu start at 0700 (0630 buses for workers only) and meet both local and tourist trains, and charge US$4 each way for the 15-minute trip to the ruins and back. There are theoretically enough seats on the buses for all the train passengers, but in practice you will have to wait for a seat (beware of drivers asking inflated prices). Last bus down to station goes at about 1700 (if you wish to stay longer, demand a single bus ticket). You can walk up in 1½ hrs. to 2 hrs., and down in 1 hr., if you have no luggage; there is a short-cut for walkers, the Camino de Herradura, said to take 45 mins. to 1 hr., some of it almost rock climbing (take an extra T-shirt because it can be chilly at the top and, after sweating on the walk up, you may catch cold). Luggage can be deposited safely at the site entrance (for US$0.10, open 0800-1500, there is a self-service restaurant) but not at the station, nor at the museum (on opposite side of river from station, open Tues.-Sun. 1030-1530). **Cost of entry to the ruins**, US$10 in intis, per day (extensions no longer available, but it seems that showing your first day's ticket will get a reduction for a second day), they are open 0630-1700. Only holders of Peruvian student cards get a discount. Post Office at Machu Picchu station has special franking marks.

Permission to enter the ruins before 0630 to watch the sunrise over the Andes, which is a spectacular experience, may be obtained from the Instituto Nacional de Cultura in Colegio San Bernardo, Cuzco (near La Merced), but it is often possible if you talk to the guards at the gate. Sr. Quispe, a guard for many years (and of royal Inca descent), is friendly and informative.

Mon. and Fri. are bad days because there is usually a crowd of people on guided tours who are going or have been to Pisac market on Sun., and too many people all want lunch at the same time. Food is available around the station.

**Camping** Not permitted on the site, nor on Huayna-Picchu; official campsite at Ruinas, US$2 per tent, per night; may be possible on football field downstream of the station, or Aguas Calientes. Beware of thieves.

**Accommodation and Food** In season the Tourist Hotel at the ruins is heavily booked during the week (best rooms for the view are 10, 16, 18, 20, 22); try Sunday night as other tourists find Pisac market a greater attraction. Book well in advance, through a reliable agency, or at the Enturperú office in Lima or Cuzco: in this way you can spend 24 hrs. at the site. Often, however, though reportedly booked up weeks in advance, there are cancellations and you can obtain a room on arrival. Rooms with shower and breakfast (no singles) A, US$10 for meals in poor self-service cafeteria. There is electricity (but rooms are cold at night) and water 24 hours a day. Service and honesty not always good, but as they state in the English version of the rules card: "The grandeur of nature is such, that the conniving of man is overcome."

The Tourist Hotel often does not have intis for exchange, make sure you have enough before setting out for Machu Picchu; but the hotel will accept American Express travellers' cheques at the official rate. Only hotel residents may eat in the restaurant—set lunch US$12; others have to use the expensive self-service counter outside. It is recommended that you take food and soft drinks with you; prices are very high compared with Cuzco

The cheapest options for staying overnight are at *Aguas Calientes*, 1½ km. back along the railway (the town has electricity 24 hrs a day). If you need to phone Aguas Calientes, the number is T 109. The *Albergue Juvenil*, constructed by Copesco, the state tourism agency for the region, has 200 beds in dormitories and private rooms, and dining facilities (US$3 for a poor meal), for travellers and family groups, dirty bathrooms reported, comfortable, noisy with students, laundry, rec., E-F p.p. (no IYHA card needed). *Hostal Caminantes*, with bath, G, basic, but friendly and clean; *Gringo Bill's* (ex-*Qoni Unu*), third house to left of church, F, reasonably clean, relaxed and friendly, cheap, usually has hot water, laundry, money exchange, meals served, offer a US$2 packed lunch to take up to the ruins, luggage stored, new huts built (upstairs rooms better value), very highly rec.; *Hotel Sucre*, F, cheap and dingy; *Hostal Machu Picchu*, F, clean, safe, quiet, friendly (esp. Wilber, owner's son, with travel info.), hot water, nice balcony over the Urubamba, grocery store, rec.; *El Refugio*, cheap, good food, slow service, also *Aiko*, rec.; *Waiki*, good cheap food, breakfast. At the *pizzería*, very slow service, but reasonable food; *El Mirador*, run by Manuel, "the prince of the primus" but bad food, near station, friendly staff and cat, open 0500 for early starters to Machu Picchu, opposite is a fruit stand which will make drinks without water if asked. *Chez Maggi* restaurant here nothing like as good as its namesake in Cuzco; *Huayna Picchu*, good value restaurant beside railway line; *Machu Picchu*, restaurant on hill up to hot baths, good, friendly; cheap, unnamed restaurants at Aguas Calientes station. Despite reports that the standard of food and hygiene has improved, you are warned to be careful about what you eat and if in doubt about your constitution, take your own food. It may be difficult to get a room, so be prepared to sleep on a floor. Two new swimming pools have been built. The thermal baths (a communal pool), a 15-minute walk from the town, are particularly welcome to those who have walked the Inca Trail; officially they open at 0500 and close at 2000 (US$0.80 per bath, bathing suits required, baths murky, but reported cleaner in morning, showers for washing *before* entering baths (take soap and shampoo); bar, beware sandflies.

**Note** Advisable to buy paperback edition of *Lost City of the Incas* by Hiram Bingham, in Lima or Cuzco (more expensive), or *A Walking Tour of Machu Picchu* (rec.) by Pedro Sueldo Nava—in several languages, available in Cuzco and Pisac. The Tourist Hotel also sells guides, although at a rather inflated price. (The South American Explorers' Club in Lima has detailed information on walks here, and so have Hilary Bradt's and Charles Brod's books.)

The railway goes on 79 km. through Chaullay to **Quillabamba** (24,000 people) in the Urubamba Valley at 1,054 metres, where there is a Dominican mission.

The train follows the Río Urubamba much of the way from Machu Picchu, and the improvised station at Quillabamba is right on the river. One crosses a foot bridge put up by the Lions Club and then climbs up a 100-odd flight of stairs to reach the town. Many *heladerías*, much needed in the heat, the best on the northwest corner of the square. Not many attractions for the tourist, but a place to bask in the sun or take a swim in the river, though ask the locals where the safe stretches are, as the current is quite rapid in places. Clean market building, and a football stadium.

**Hotels** *Hostal Alto Urubamba*, F, on Dos de Mayo, clean, good, with or without bath, hot water, restaurant; *Quillabamba* (unmarked entrance next to Autoservicio behind market), roof terrace restaurant, rec., D; other accommodation, F and up, near market, F; *Comercio*, Libertad, D, with bath. The best restaurants are to be found on Plaza de Armas.

**Transport** The morning train from Quillabamba leaves at 0530 and arrives at Machu Picchu about 0815, US$1, giving you 2½ hours at the ruins before the invasion from Cuzco starts with the arrival of the tourist train. If you can get on the 0620 train from Cuzco to Quillabamba, or can catch it at 1030 at Aguas Calientes, you can go down to Quillabamba and return to Aguas Calientes or Cuzco the same day because it is the same train that leaves Quillabamba at 1300, 6½ hrs. to Cuzco. Tickets must be bought one day in advance, from Enafer office off main plaza. Minibus leaves Cuzco a.m. when full, from Calle General Buendía near Machu Picchu station; also trucks go in the daytime, US$2.40. The road between Ollantaytambo and Quillabamba passes through Peña, a place of great beauty with snowy peaks already appearing on either side of the valley (taxis are very reluctant to go there). Once out of Peña, the climb to the pass begins in earnest—on the right is a huge glacier. Soon on the left, Salcantay begins to appear in all its huge and snowy majesty. After endless zig-zags and breathtaking views, one reaches Puerto Málaga (rudimentary *pensión*). The descent to the valley is alarming, highlighted by a series of dangerous curves. The hillsides are covered in lichen and Spanish moss. At Chaullay, the road meets the railway to Quillabamba, Machu Picchu and Cuzco. One can drive from Chaullay to Santa Teresa (hot springs, ask the locals) from where the railway goes to Machu Picchu, and can hike to Lucma and the village of Vilcabamba, from where one can descend to the valley of the Río Concebidayoc where one comes to Espíritu Pampa, the site of the Vilcabamba Vieja ruins, a vast pre-Inca ruin with a neo-Inca overlay in deep jungle at 1,000 metres (the disputed last capital of the Incas); the site is reached on foot or horseback from Pampaconas. From Chaullay, take a truck to Yupanca, Lucma or Pucyura: there rent horses or mules and travel through superb country to Espíritu Pampa. Then continue to Cosireni, from where trucks go to Quillabamba.

A permit from the National Cultural Institute is required to visit this area. Without one, you will be turned back at Pucyura. The Institute is not issuing passes (since Aug. 87) to visit the area between the Ríos Urubamba and Concebidayoc because of guerrilla activity there, but travel to Chaullay, Quillabamba and Kiteni is permitted.

One can also go by boat to Kiteni and then by truck to Quillabamba (at 0400). There are no buses from Quillabamba to Kiteni, but *camiones* leave between 0700-1000, US$3.25, 7-10 hrs. (*Hotel Kiteni*, F, basic, several restaurants). At Kiteni you must register on arrival with the police station. Take torch, no electricity. Irregular boats to the Pongo de Maynique, where the river goes through the mountain with a rock wall of several hundred meters on either side, before descending into jungle, where you can see many varieties of animals, birds, butterflies, snakes etc. 2 days, from Quillabamba to Pongo. This journey is only possible between April and August (too dangerous at other times). Between Kiteni and Pongo, on the river, is the village of Israelitos, whose inhabitants have been convinced by a missionary that they are New Israelites and that the Messiah will arise there. You can stay in a small hut next to the synagogue, but bring food and supplies—also gifts—from Kiteni. From Pongo you can get down through the jungle to Pucallpa if there is the right amount of water in the river; boats can be arranged at Kiteni. Price varies for number of people in the party, beware of overcharging. En route to Pucallpa it is possible to go to Camisea and Sepahua (near where Yaminavak Indians can be visited; they live in constructions made of mud, but have a mini-hotel for passers-through).

*Paucartambo*, on E slope of Andes, is NE of Cuzco by a good road (one way on alternate days). In this remote though now popular tourist town is held the Fiesta of Carmen, usually on 16, 17, 18 July with masked dances. (*Fiesta* dates should be checked in Cuzco.) Hotels: *Quinta Rosa Marina*, near bridge, basic, G; *San Martin*, G, dirty, even more basic. Private car hire for round trip on 16 July: US$30, or the Tourist Office in Cuzco arranges an overnight trip (you sleep in the bus) for US$15. Minibus from Av. Huáscar, Cuzco, every other day, US$4.50, 3-4 hrs. (alternate days Paucartambo-Cuzco).

From Paucartambo, in the dry season, you can go 44 km. to Tres Cruces, along the Pilcopata road, turning left after 25 km.; Sr. Cáceres in Paucartambo will arrange trip. Tres Cruces gives a wonderful view of the sunrise in June and July and private cars leave Paucartambo between 0100 and 0200 to see it; they may give you a lift. One can walk from Paucartambo to the *chullpas* of Machu Cruz in about an hour, or to the *chullpas* of Pijchu (take a guide). You can also visit the Inca fortress of Huatojto, which has admirable doorways and stonework. A car will take you as far as Ayre, from where the fortress is a 2-hour walk.

---

## THE SOUTH-EASTERN JUNGLE (6)

Cooled by winds sweeping down from the Andes but warmed by its jungle blanket, this region contains some of the most important tropical flora and fauna in the world. The frontier town, Puerto Maldonado, only a half-hour flight from Cuzco, is the starting point for expeditions to one of the national parks at Manu, Tambopata or Heath. Besides its natural attractions, the area also harbours gold-diggers, loggers, hunters, drug smugglers and oil-men.

The *Manu National Park* is the biggest nature reserve in Peru, covering 1.5 million hectares of jungle around the river Manu (an area half the size of Switzerland). Charles Munn, a zoologist from Wildlife Conservation International, writes that "No other park on earth can compare with Manu in terms of sheer variety of life forms." Giant otters, alligators, tapirs, jaguars and ocelot, and many other animals and birds may be seen. A gold rush, prospecting for oil and gas on the Park's western borders, and the arrival of colonists all pose a threat to this unique reserve. The dry season runs from April to October; July, August and September are the driest months when animals stay close to the river and are most easily seen. Information is available from Asociación y Conservación para la Selva Sur (ACSS), Av. Sol 627, 3rd floor, Cuzco.

The following companies offer 6-8 day tours: *Manu Expeditions*, Procuradores 372, Cuzco, T 226671, Fax 236706, offers camping trips into Manu; *Manu Nature Tours EIRL*, Av. Sol 627-B, oficina 401, Cuzco, T 231549/234793, Telex 52003/4, which owns *Manu Lodge*, the most remote of the 4 lodges in or near the park; it is highly recommended, both for comfort and as an experience of "pure magic" (it's also expensive). There is also the Amazonia lodge, office in Cuzco at Matará 334, T 231370, US$30 a day p.p., with watchtower for bird spotting, located between Pilcoapata and Salvación on the Madre de Dios, but we have had no reports about this place.

Individual trips can be arranged by the hardy and adventurous. First obtain a permit (free) from the park's office, Calle Laderos, Cuzco, who may send you to Salvación for it (see below). Buy all supplies in Cuzco: camping gear, fishing tackle, food (for the boatmen as well) and gasoline; take finely-woven, long-sleeved and -legged clothing and effective insect repellent (that on sale in Cuzco is no good). On Mon., Wed. and Fri. a truck leaves Calle Huaruropata, Cuzco, supposedly at 0600, for Shintuya, 250 km. through wild scenery, US$8, minimum 30 uncomfortable hours (much longer in the rainy season as there are no bridges; recommended trucks are Augel Riarz, Taodora and Castilla). The priest in Shintuya will let you stay in the dormitory rooms at the mission, or you can camp. One restaurant only.

In Shintuya, hire a boat and guide to go down the Madre Dios river and up the Manu (the 4 Moscose brothers are recommended). A six week trip will cost a minimum of US$350, after bargaining, maximum 10 people, but fewer are better as jungle clearings are small.

At Tres Cruces in the Park there is an empty bungalow that may be used for the night; it has no window-panes, water or electricity. The National Park office at Salvación can also arrange your entry permit and with luck you might catch a lift in with park staff, or they will know of other people going in (*Hostal Salvación*, F, clean, basic bathrooms, swimming pool). Transport to Shintuya infrequent but possible although most boats are already fully laden and rarely carry tourists. *Quinta Erika*, small jungle lodge run by Sra. Gerlach, a German woman who has lived in the jungle since 1951, tranquil, few bugs, good food, animals, boat trips can be arranged with prior notice, transport from Cooperativa landing, 3 km. from Salvación.

From Shintuya, it is 5½ hrs by boat to Boca Manu, then 4½ hrs to Romero where there is a park checkpoint and a park entry fee of US$10 is charged. Three lakes (cochas) can be visited from Romero, Wasi, Otorongo and Salvador. After your trip you can return to Cuzco via Shintuya, or take a colectivo boat from Boca Manu to Colorado (US$6—6 hrs.), then another to Laberinto (US$4—12 hrs.), then to Puerto Maldonado (US$1.50—1½ hrs.).

From Urcos, near Cuzco (bus US$0.60), a spectacular 484-km. road has been constructed over the Eastern Cordillera to Puerto Maldonado in the jungle. No buses, but several trucks do the journey every day. 47 km. after passing the snow-line Hualla-Hualla pass (4,820 metres) the **super-hot thermal baths** (US$0.10) of Marcapata provide a relaxing break. From here the road continues its descent through a tropical rain forest well stocked with orchids. 82 km. from Urcos, at the base of Nevado Ausangate (6,600 metres), is the town of *Ocongate*, which has two hotels on the Plaza de Armas. Beyond Ocongate is Tinqui, the starting point for hikes around Ausangate and in the Cordillera Vilcanota. Trucks leave Cuzco for Tinqui daily between 0600-0900 from beside the railway station, taking 9 rough, cold hours. From Tinqui, you can hire horses for a 3- or 5-day hike passing lakes, ice caves and beautiful scenery. Take tent, food and warm clothing. Guides can also be found in Tinqui.

The air force (FAP) provides a weekly air service from Cuzco and Puerto Maldonado to *Quincemil*, 240 km. from Urcos, a centre for alluvial gold-mining with many banks (*Hotel Toni*, F, friendly, clean, cold shower, good meals); ask the food-carriers to take you to visit the miners washing for gold in the nearby rivers. Quincemil marks the half-way point and the end to the all-weather road. Gasoline is scarce because most road vehicles continue on 70 km. to Masuco, another mining centre, where they fill up with the cheaper gasoline of the jungle region.

Thirty more km. of sloshing mud and cascading waterfalls brings one out of the mountainous jungle and into the flat plains, for the 141 km. straight run to Puerto Maldonado.

Owing to the present gold rush on the Madre de Dios river, there are many trucks from Cuzco to Puerto Maldonado: 50-55 hr. journey; US$12 or so in the back, US$15 up front. As trucks pass each other, watch out for the exchanges of fire with fruit as the ammunition. The road has been widened. Times by truck: Urcos—Ocongate 6 hrs. (US$3.50), Ocongate—Quincemil 12 hrs. (US$8), Quincemil—Masuco—Puerto Maldonado 15-20 hrs. (US$8).

***Puerto Maldonado*** is capital of the jungle Department of Madre de Dios. (Altitude, 250 metres.) Overlooking the confluence of the rivers Tambopata and Madre de Dios, this frontier town is the centre for development of Peru's southern jungle. The Plaza de Armas is very pleasant, and nearby is a new Banco de la Nación built to accommodate (and reflect) the prosperity that gold has brought. However, Puerto Maldonado is an expensive town and because of the gold mining and timber industries, much of the jungle (including most of the mahogany trees) has been destroyed. The temperature normally is between 30°-37°C during the dry season (May to October) and 28°-33°C in the rainy season (November to April); but *friajes* (cold winds that roll northwards along the foothills of the Andes from the South Atlantic region) can send the temperature plummeting, to about 7°C. Insect and reptile activity is greatly reduced; warm-blooded animals survive. Because of this climatic phenomenon, the fauna of the Madre de Dios include many unusual species not found in other jungle areas. Also unique to this area is the *rayo blanco* (white rainbow) seen at sunset on the Río Madre de Dios. According to archaeologist, and loyal correspondent, Helmut Zettl from Austria, near to Puerto Maldonado are the important petroglyphs of Pantiacolla.

Madre de Dios has three superb jungle reserves, among the best in the world: Manu National Park, 1.5 million hectares to the N of the department (**see above 1041**); Río Heath Pampas Sanctuary, 100,000 hectares between the Río Madre de Dios and the Río Heath; Tambopata Wildlife Reserve, 5,500 hectares, 40 km. up the Río Tambopata. The Tambopata Reserve, like Manu, has an incredible diversity of animal, bird, insect and plant life, but, because it is so small, its survival is at risk. Logging rights around the reserve have been sold, settlers are moving in in large numbers, and the government has provided little protection up to now. A pair of binoculars is essential equipment for this area.

**Hotels** *Cuzco Amazonic Lodge* (*Albergue Cuzco Amazónico*), A, 45 mins. by boat down the Madre de Dios River, jungle tours and accommodation for 3 days, 2 nights, good food negotiable out of season; avoid in February when everyone goes on holiday including the mechanic. (Book at Av. Arequipa 4964, Lima, T 462775, or Procuradores 48, Cuzco, T 5047.) *Explorers Inn* (book through Peruvian Safaris,Garcilaso de la Vega 1334, Casilla 10088, T 313047 Lima, or through Peruvian Safaris, Plaza San Francisco 168, T 235342 Cuzco—post to Puerto Maldonado is very bad but local office is Fitzcarrald 136 or Teletours, Antero Aspillaga 240, El Olivar, San Isidro, Lima 27, T 403594, Av. José Pardo 182, piso 2, Miraflores, Lima 18, T 469046/464577), A, located in middle of Tambopata wildlife reserve, 58 km. from Puerto Maldonado: a 4 hr. ride on Tambopata river (2 hours return, in early a.m., so take warm clothes), take food and drink for the journey, one of the best places in Peru for seeing jungle birds (547 species have been recorded here), butterflies (1,100-plus species), dragonflies (over 150 species) as well as tree species and mammals (including a giant otter), but you probably need more than a 2-day tour to benefit fully from the location, guides are biologists and naturalists from around the world who study in the reserve in return for acting as guides, interesting wildlife-treks; US$150 for 3 days, 2 nights (depending on season, 1 day spent actually in the reserve), extra day US$45, flight from Puerto Maldonado not included; naturalists' programme at US$45 a night (minimum 6 nights), comfortable accommodation in thatch-roofed huts with "en suite" bathrooms, lighting by candle but generator for refrigerator with supply of cold beer and soft drinks. *Tambo Lodge*, bungalows 8 km. out on opposite bank of Río Madre de Dios, 2, 3 and 4-day jungle programmes available, book through Cusco-Maldonado Tour, Portal de Panes 109 (T 222-332), Cuzco. *Turistas*, on the bank of the Tambopata River, D( private bath), electricity and water sometimes cut, restaurant quite good.

In town: *Wilson*, D with bath, E without, well run, clean, no hot water, trucks coming from airport stop here; *Rey Port*, F with shower, insecure; *Cross*, clean, generally rec.; *Royal*

*Inn*, F; *Central*, F and *Moderno*, G, (very clean but noisy, safe for luggage, no hot water). *Tambo de Oro*, F. As there are many miners in Maldonado, so rooms can be scarce.

**Restaurants** There are several good restaurants in town. *Rulman*, good Chinese food and large selection of other dishes, rec. apart from poor addition, round the corner from *Hotel Wilson*. *Kalifa*, Piura, some regional specialities, rec. Look for *pensiones* where meals are served at fixed times (lunch is at 1300). *Café Danubio Azul* on Plaza de Armas is good for information.

**Typical Foods** *Castañas* (Brazil nuts), try them, chocolate- or sugar-coated. *Patarashca*, fish barbecued in banana leaves. Try *pescado sudado* as an appetizer. *Mazato*, an alcoholic drink prepared from yuca and drunk by the Indians at their festivals. *Sangre de grado*, a thick deep-red sap collected from trees deep in the jungle which is a highly prized cure-all throughout Peru.

**Bolivian Consulate** is on 2 de Mayo, near Puno; **Peruvian immigration** is on Billinghurst, river end.

**Excursions** Motorcycles can be hired for local trips for US$4 an hour. Bargain for reductions for longer. A very worthwhile one-or two-day excursion by motorcycle is to boat across the Río Madre de Dios and follow the trail towards Iberia (*Hotel Aquino*, F). Along the trail are picturesque *caserios* (settlements) that serve as collecting and processing centres for the Brazil nut. Approximately 70% of the inhabitants in the Madre de Dios are involved in the collection of this prized nut. The beautiful and tranquil Lago Sandoval is a 1-hr. boat ride along the Río Madre de Dios and then a 2-km. walk into the jungle. For fishing Lago Valencia, 60 km. away near the Bolivian border, is unsurpassed (2 days). Many excellent beaches and islands are located within an hour's boat ride; however, make sure you have a ride back at the end of the day. For the adventurous a one-or two-day trip can be planned to visit Indians still relatively unaffected by civilization; the Indians living nearer Puerto Maldonado, like those near Iquitos and Manaus, are strictly tourist Indians. Boats may be hired at the port for about US$30 a day to go to Lago Sandoval or visit the Indians. Bargain hard, and don't pay the full cost in advance. Mosquitoes are voracious. If camping, take food and water. Barbara Fearis from San Francisco and her Peruvian husband, Guillermo, organize interesting trips for photography, bird watching and fishing. They can be contacted at Puerto Tambopata, behind the Tourist Hotel (write to Correo Central, Puerto Maldonado). Tambopata Expeditions offer 2-day tours to Lago Sandoval and longer trips, owner is guide, speaks English and is knowledgeable; take binoculars. A recommended guide is Victor Suárez, Apartado 177, who charges US$25 p.p. per day, all included, and will tailor the trip to his clients' requirements. Contact Sr. Gombringer, who lives beside the plaza (well known) who runs excursions from his house on Lago Victoria, 7 hrs. down river by boat, very good and reasonable, much wildlife. For guides meeting the plane, US$8-10 p.p. per day is a normal fee; they are very pushy. Shop around in Puerto Maldonado, insist on a detailed explanation of the tour offered, if necessary sign a contract and make sure that, once you have paid, the programme is not scaled down. **N.B.** All hunting in Amazonia is illegal.

For those interested in seeing a gold rush, a trip to the town of **Laberinto** (one hotel, several poor restaurants) is recommended. The bus leaves Puerto Maldonado at 0900, 1000 and 1100 and returns in the afternoon daily.

**Transport** It is possible to travel overland from Cuzco (4-5 days). Take a truck from the Parque Zonal, near to Parque Túpac Amaru to Pucapata (lodgings basic), or if possible direct to Shintuya (30 hrs.); boats leave most mornings for Colorado (10 hrs.); next day take a canoe to Laberinto (8-12 hrs.), from where there is a dirt road to Puerto Maldonado (bus US$1.80, 1½ hrs.). Take food. Flying is cheaper and quicker but not so interesting.

Taxi to airport US$2. The airport has a paved runway; flights are often cancelled because of rain. Faucett to and from Lima and Cuzco, Tues., Thurs., Sat., AeroPerú on the other days; AeroPerú may cancel flights in Cuzco if not enough passengers. Once a week to Lima and Cuzco (usually Thursday) there is an air-force flight (Grupo Ocho) that goes in all but the worst conditions via Iberia and Iñapari. A weekly flight Arequipa-Puerto Maldonado is run by the air force, usually Friday, if demand is sufficient. Office of Grupo Ocho is in the airport at Cuzco. Open 0800-1200.

Flight to **Iñapari** (½ hr.) on the Brazilian frontier, Thursday; this is a cargo flight and you must see the captain about a seat on the day of the flight. From the landing field it is 7 km. to the village (one hostel) where you must seek out the police for border formalities. Wade across the river to Brazil, to the village of Assis Brasil. Private boats can be contracted for travel into Bolivia; to Puerto Heath, at the border; to Riberalta (4 days). The trip by boat to Riberalta is very difficult, especially in the dry season. Boats are very few and far between.

Some boats only go as far as Puerto Pardo (a Peruvian military post opposite Puerto Heath). From here one can cross to Puerto Heath, a Bolivian naval post, but boats into Bolivia are just as infrequent here. It should be noted that waiting for sailings in either Puerto Heath or Puerto Maldonado can take a lot of time. In Puerto Pardo you can sleep at the military post, or in empty huts in the village; there is no accommodation in Puerto Heath. Take food with you. It may be possible to take a boat from Puerto Pardo to *garimpeiro* settlements (gold diggers) around Puerto América, 24-hr. journey, but chances depend on whether gold has been found. Planes go from Pto. América to Riberalta (Bolivia).

Before leaving for Bolivia from Puerto Maldonado, one must first get a Bolivian visa (if needed) from the consulate (address above, very helpful), then a Peruvian exit stamp, before one can get a Bolivian entry stamp. Similarly if going to Brazil; if you have not obtained an exit stamp from the P.I.P. in Puerto Maldonado, you will be turned back at either border.

**Books** *An Annotated Check List of Peruvian Birds,* by Theodore A. Parker, Susan Allen Parker and Manuel A. Plenge, published by Buteo Books, Vermillon, South Dakota, is particuarly useful in this area; order through Susan Parker, 2350 E 2nd St, Tucson, AZ 85719, USA. *Birds of Colombia,* by Steven Hilty and William Brown, gives the best coverage of birds in the Peruvian jungle; also *The Birds of Venezuela,* Princeton University, and *The Land Birds of South America,* by John Dunning.

---

## INLAND FROM LIMA (7)

The central Andes are largely bleak and sulphurous, poor mining settlements and restless towns caught up in political agitation and terrorism. When it runs, the train from Lima to La Oroya and Huancayo, provides one of the great spectacles of South America. Despite all the region's troubles, Huancayo is cultivating a revived reputation as a safe and welcoming haven for the adventurous traveller.

The Central Railway reaches its greatest altitude, 4,782 metres, inside the tunnel between Ticlio and Galera, 159 km. from Lima. The ruling grade is about 4½°. Along the whole of its length (335 km. to Huancayo) it traverses 66 tunnels, 59 bridges, and 22 zig-zags where the steep mountainside permits no other way of negotiating it. It is by far the most important railway in the country, and the views during the ascent are beyond compare. **N.B.** If you alight to take photos at Ticlio or Galera, be quick because the train stops for a very short time. This masterpiece was the project of the great American railway engineer, Henry Meiggs, who supervised the construction from 1870 until his death in 1877; it was built by the Pole Ernesto Malinowski, with imported Chinese labour, between 1870 and 1893. Railway buffs may like to know that the last Andes type 2-8-0 steam locomotive No. 206, is still in working order, although usually locked in a shed at Huancayo. It was built specifically for this route in 1953 by Beyer Peacocks of Manchester. The course of the railway is more or less paralleled by that of the Central Highway between Lima and Huancayo.

For a while, beyond Chosica (see page 944), each successive valley seems to be greener, with a greater variety of trees and flowers. At **San Bartolomé** (Km. 57, 1,513 metres), the platform is often crowded with local fruit sellers. The train reverses, then passes through tunnels and over bridges to the next canyon. Sometimes the train seems airborne over the valley and the road far below.

**Matucana**, Km. 84, at 2,390 metres, is set in wild scenery, where there are beautiful walks. At Tamboraque (3,009 metres) is the first of the mountain mines, with its overhead cables and smelter down a gorge. Climbing always, we pass San Mateo (Km. 107, 3,215 metres), where the San Mateo mineral water originates. From San Mateo a spectacular side-road branches off to the Germania mine. Beyond San Mateo is Infiernillo (Little Hell) Canyon, to which car excursions are made from Lima, 100 km. (Hotels: *Ritz*, F, fair, *Grau*, cheap.) Following Infiernillo (only a glimpse seen between tunnels) the train proceeds in rapid zigzags. Between Río Blanco and Chicla (Km. 127, 3,733 metres) the Inca contour-terraces can be seen quite clearly.

*Casapalca* (Km. 139, 4,154 metres) has more mines; its concentrators are at the foot of a deep gorge. A climb to the dizzy heights beyond ends in a glorious view of the highest peaks. Soon we see a large metal flag of Peru at the top of Mount Meiggs, not by any means the highest in the area, but through it runs Galera Tunnel, 1,175 metres long. Ticlio, the highest passenger station in the world (Km. 157, 4,758 metres), at the mouth of the tunnel, is on one side of a crater in which lies a dark, still lake. At Ticlio the line forks, one through the tunnel to La Oroya; the other line goes 14½ km. to Morococha, where there are important mines. The highest point, 4,818 metres, is reached on this latter line at La Cima. A siding off this line reaches 4,829 metres.

Beyond the tunnel zig-zags bring us down to Yauli (4,142 metres). Left is the ugliness inseparable from mining; right are mountainsides and moors with cold, small mountain tarns and herds of sheep, very few llamas. After La Oroya the railway follows the valley of the polluted river Mantaro.

*La Oroya* (Km. 208), the main smelting centre, with its slag heaps is full of vitality and here the train fills up. Population: 36,000. It is at the fork of the Yauli and Mantaro rivers at 3,755 metres, 187 km. from Lima by a road which although officially paved throughout, is in poor condition, particularly between the Anticona Pass at 4,843 metres and La Oroya. (For places to the E and N of La Oroya, **see pages 1053** and **1056** respectively.)

**Hotels** *Hostal San Martín*, F, clean, friendly, no heating but plenty of blankets; *Wilson*, Lima. **Restaurants** *Las Vegas*, rec. *Huánuco*, good, cheap food. *Central*, rec. *El Tambo*, . 2 km. outside La Oroya, good trout and frogs.

**Railway** N to Tambo del Sol and Cerro de Pasco; SE to Jauja and Concepción (**see page 1050**), Huancayo and Huancavelica; SW to Lima and Callao. Train to Cerro de Pasco leaving 1400 and arriving 1740. To Lima at 1005 and Huancayo at 1340. (Local train to Huancayo on Sun.)

**Roads and Buses** SE to Huancayo, Ayacucho, and Cuzco, paved to Huancayo; N to Cerro de Pasco (US$1) and on to Pucallpa; 25 km. north along this road fork E for Tarma (US$1.80 by bus, US$2.20 by colectivo), San Ramón, the Perené colony, and Oxapampa; SW to Lima (6 hrs. by bus, US$4, 5 or less, US$6.50, by colectivo). Take taxi from bus terminal in Lima, which is in a dangerous area.

*Huancayo*, capital of Junín Department, is the main commercial centre for inland central Peru; alt. 3,271 metres; pop. 359,000. The Indians flock in from far and wide with an incredible range of food, and rugs and blankets of llama and alpaca wool, for sale; fleeces can be bought (alpaca, US$2.50 per kilo), but arrive early before 1000, Av. La Marina, 700 block. The Sun. market, Jr. Huancavelica, 3 km. long and 4 stalls wide, sells typical clothes, fruit, vegetables, hardware, handicrafts but especially traditional medicines and goods for witchcraft. Daily market behind railway station also recommended. Huancayo is a good place to buy carved gourds, reputedly the lowest prices in Peru. Very impressive Good Friday processions. The colourful annual fiesta of the Virgin of Cocharcas starts on 8 September at Orcotuna, and there are a big early morning market and an afternoon bullfight on the same day as the parade of the Virgin; the feasting and dancing last a week. Costumes and dances are then at their best. In Huancayo, ponchos and various alpaca woollen goods are quite cheap, but often factory-made; most goods are reported to be cheaper than in Lima, particularly silver jewellery. Displays of folklore at the Coliseo, Calle Real, certain Sundays. For woven alpaca goods and other *artesanías*, much cheaper, go to outlying villages, such as San Jerónimo (for silver filigree), Cochas Chicas (carved gourds), or

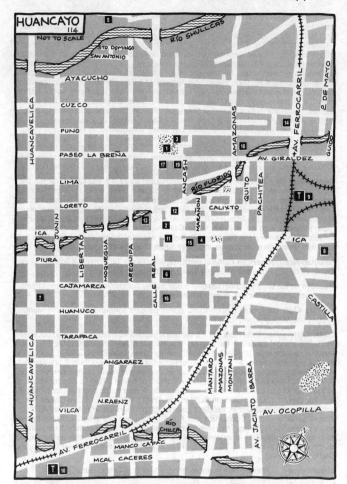

**Huancayo : Key to map** 1. Plaza de la Constitución, 2. Plaza Huamanmarca, 3. Cathedral, 4. La Inmaculada, 5. Museo, Colegio Salesiano, 6. Coliseo Municipal, 7. Sunday Market, 8. Wholesale Market, 9. Train station to Lima, 10. Train station to Huancavelica, 11. Foptur Tourist Office and Municipalidad, 12. Post Office, 13. Entel Telephone Office, 14. Police, 15. *Hotel de Turistas*, 16. *Hotel Presidente*, 17. *Hotel Kiya*, 18. Residencia Baldeón, 19. Restaurante Olímpico

Hualhuas, 11 km. north of Huancayo (2 km. off the Huancayo-Jauja road, try Familia Meza, Jr. 28 de Julio 293); minibus from Huancayo, US$0.20 from Church of the Immaculate Conception (see Excursions below).

**Warning** Huancayo has a bad reputation for thieves, especially in the market and at bus stations, although recent reports suggest that things are safer now (Feb. 91). There is a large military presence owing to terrorist activity. This should not deter visitors, but don't travel at night and on no account go to the jungle areas beyond Huancayo.

**Hotels N.B.** Prices may be raised in Holy Week. *Turistas*, D, with bath, old building, some rooms small, quiet, good meals for US$3.50; *Presidente*, Calle Real 1138, T 231736, D, clean, friendly, helpful, safe, breakfast only, rec.; *Confort*, Calle Ancash 298, F, private bath, basic but clean, good; *Santa Felicidad*, Plaza de Armas, F, good; *El Mesón de Don Jesus*, Giraldez 634, T 226826, F, rec. *Acolla*, corner of Antonio Lobato and Real, Tambo district, F, private toilet, hot shower. *Residencial Inca Wasi*, Federico Villareal 106, clean and friendly, F (owner meets Lima train with car); *Residencia Huancayo*, Av. Giráldez, near railway station, G, all rooms with wash basin, hot showers; *Inca*, Calle Loreto, F, with bath (cold water), clean, but noisy; *Pensión Huanca*, Pasaje San Antonio 113, San Carlos T 223956, small sign (owner's English-speaking daughter meets Lima train—every one, apparently, for the last five years!), F, 8 rooms, very clean, hot water, friendly, breakfast extra, laundry and kitchen facilities, good food, typical Huancayo dishes, rec.; *Residencia Baldeón*, Amazonas 543, G, with European-style breakfast, hot water, friendly; *Kiya*, Giráldez 107, Plaza de Armas (known nowadays as Constitución), E, with bath, hot water, restaurant does not serve breakfast, 'phones in rooms (avoid noisy rooms on Av. Real); *Universal*, opp. railway station, F, reasonable. *Hospedaje Suizo*, Huancas 473, T 231732, G p.p., 10 mins. walk from railway station, comfortable, hot water, family atmosphere, warmly rec. Luis Hurtado (**see page 1049**) has 2 rooms (G including breakfast), with hot water, washing and cooking facilities.

**Restaurants** On Av. Giráldez (Plaza de la Constitución) are *Lalo's*, and *Café Giráldez*, both good; *La Cabaña*, Av. Giraldez 724, excellent pizzas—"best in Peru" (evenings only), sandwiches and home-made ice-cream, rec. (owned by Luis Hurtado—see below); Peruvian dishes at *Olímpico*, Av. Giráldez 199, rec. as the best in town. *Caramba*, good for barbecues. *Marisquería Mar Azul*, Ancash 578, excellent cheap seafood. Street vendors sell delicious apple turnovers, and other delights. On Calle Real are *Santa Rosa*, *La Caravana*, for barbecued chicken and the *Panadería-Pastelería Imperial*, all rec. *Chifa Perú*, Puno 518, good and cheap. Excellent pastries at *Chalet Suizo*, Huancas 473, closed Mon.

**Peruvian-North American Cultural Institute,** Jirón Guido 740. Intensive Spanish courses organized by Luis Hurtado and Beverly Stuart (see below).

**Museum** at the Salesian school has over 5,000 pieces, including a large collection of jungle birds, animals and butterflies, insects, reptiles and fossils.

**Country Club** (very rural) is open to all, in very pleasant surroundings near the Mantaro River, to the north of town.

**Crafts** Craft market, Calle Piura, behind the Municipalidad, open every day, good but smelly, also sellers along Calle Real in the evening. Visit *Kamaq Maki*, "the creating hand", Centro Regional de Artesanías (the best craft centre in the area), Jirón Brasilia 200 in San Carlos, about 2 km. from centre, an artesans' cooperative (formerly the workshop of Sra. Francisca Mayer), selling woven goods, ceramics, carved gourds and much more; open Mon.-Fri., 0800-1200, 1400-1730, Sat.-Sun., 1500-1700 (P.O. Box 609, T 226961). Take minibus 5, 6, 13 to corner of San Carlos with P. Aurora, then walk. Woven goods available from Arequipa 463. For **carved gourds** visit Hermanos Leoncio y Pedro Veli Alfaro, Cochas Chicas, Km. 9, also Florencio Sanabria Osores, excellent quality, high prices, Huancayo (Apartado 402); and Nicanor Sanabria Osores, Cochas Grandes, Km. 10, Huancayo (see under Excursions below). Also visit Izcuchaca, 3-4 hrs. from Huancayo by train or truck to see pottery made. Hotel in main square, F, basic. Back-strap weaving of beautiful *fajas* (belts) can also be seen at Víquez, on the road past Wari-Wilka, 20 mins. S of Huancayo by colectivo from near the Mercado Modelo (go in a.m.)

**Discotheques** *El Molino*, Calle Huancas, good; others in El Tambo district.

**Exchange** Banco de los Andes, near main plaza. For travellers' cheques, Sr. Miguel Velit, Calle Real 552, or Sr. Jung (*Chalet Suizo*, no commission).

**Tourist Information** Foptur information office, Concejo Provincial, 1st floor, Plaza Huamanmarca, very helpful. Huancayo Tours, Calle Real 543, organize tours of the surrounding countryside with English-speaking guides; they handle AeroPerú and Faucett reservations. Emturce, Ancash 475, good service. Touring y Automóvil Club del Perú, Calle Ancash 603. Luis Hurtado (see next page) also gives information; if he's on tour, his New Zealand wife Beverly will help.

**Rail** Train to **Huancavelica** narrow guage 3 ft., daily except Sun. *autovagón* US$9, 3½ hrs. 0700 and 1300, tickets from 0600, make sure to get off at second (smaller) station in Huancavelica (Sub Estación), since it is closer to Plaza; ordinary trains leave every day except Sun. 0730 (6½ hrs.). Both leave from Chilca station, which is not the station for Lima. Train from Huancayo to **Lima** 0700 daily April-October (reduced to Mon., Wed., Sat. Nov.-March)

9-12 hrs., 1st class US$12, 2nd class US$8, lunches in 1st class and buffet (arrive early to ensure getting a seat, best on right hand side), 1st class and buffet are bookable one day in advance for US$0.50 extra; ticket office open 1000-1200, 1430-1700.

**Road Transport**  Bus to Lima, Etucsa—not recommended although their terminal does have a waiting room (several daily, US$8, 10 hrs.) Mariscal Cáceres (US$8, 8 hrs.), and other lines, all leave in evening (very cold, buy a blanket, or wear all the cloths you have). Comité 30 and 22 colectivo to Lima, Av. Loreto 351, five a day, US$14.50, 5-7 hrs. (takes 5 passengers); also Comité 12 (Calle Montevideo 736, T 271283, Lima; Loreto 425, Huancayo), with services to Huanta. N.B. A new road to Lima is under construction, which will shorten the journey time. There is only one morning bus to **Ayacucho** (Empresa Ayacucho, 0700, not every day, US$8.80, 16-19 hrs.); evening buses go via Pampa; they are run by Molina (1700 and 1800, book in advance), Empresa Ayacucho (1800, 1830) and Etucsa (not rec.) Mon., Wed., Fri. 1630, 12 hrs. if weather is good; if not can be 20 hrs., bus waits until daylight to cross pass. Colectivo to Ayacucho, US$30 p.p. (Comité 30). Daily bus with Nor Oriente (Calle Huancavelica) to **Cerro de Pasco** and **Huánuco** at 1500; same company Mon., Wed., Fri., to **Tingo María** and **Pucallpa** at 1600. Ucayali bus company for Huánuco, Loreto 973. Direct buses to **Tarma (see page 1053)**; the departure point for La Merced twice daily, US$3.85. Note: Huancayo and other towns in the area have a *fiesta* in January when it is impossible to get a colectivo to Ayacucho and buses are fully booked. If driving to Ayacucho, be careful with direction. Only three signposts, all to totally unknown villages.

Buses to **Cuzco** can be something of a problem and are not rec. while terrorist activity persists. This road is often closed during wet season or the journey can take up to three days. Book as far ahead as possible, as buses tend to be heavily overbooked. They also frequently break down. Trucks are cheaper and offer better views—but take blankets against the cold on the mountains. The trip gives a fine view of the Sierra; one passes the site of the last battle against the Spaniards, near Ayacucho; some distance before Abancay one passes a bridge built by the Spaniards. The canyon of the Río Tomás is recommended for a visit. Those who have made this journey describe it as one of the most beautiful in Peru, but the road may be closed if guerrillas are active in the Ayacucho area. Do not leave the main road to visit more remote villages, or take photographs.

**Excursions**  W of Huancayo, past Chupaca (good Sat. market) and between Pilcomayo and Huayo is the Geophysical Institute of Huayo on the "Magnetic Equator" (12½° S of the geographical equator). Here meteorological, seismic and cosmic-ray observations are made. Six km. (standard taxi fare US$1.80) S of Huancayo the shrine of Wari-Willka (written "Warivilka" on buses), of the Huanca tribe of Inca times, has been reconstructed in a corner of the main plaza of **Wari** (often written "Huari"). Bus to Wari from Calle Real, US$0.20. Museum in the plaza, of deformed skulls, and modelled and painted pottery of successive Huanca and Inca occupations of the shrine. Open 1000-1200 and 1500-1700, US$0.15 admission. *Hotel Central*, G, good; *Hotel Sol*, G. Take a minibus to Cerrito de la Libertad, walk up hill to Torre Torre to see impressive eroded sandstone towers on the hillside (beware of begging children on the way up). Not far from here is a large park with a depressing zoo but also a beautiful, clean swimming pool (US$0.10, showers and changing rooms).

Another interesting excursion is to Cochas Chicas (beautiful views of Valle de Mantaro) or Cochas Grandes, where gourds are carved, highly recommended. Buses leave Huancayo every ½ hr. from Church of the Immaculate Conception, for 9 km. journey. In the hills beyond Cochas back-strap weaving of *mantas* for carrying babies can be seen. S of Huancayo by colectivo from near the Mercado Modelo. There is a beautiful drive to **Cañete (see page 992)**; the road crosses mountain landscape before following the Cañete river basin with its spectacular gorges (see the Instituto Geográfico Militar map). No bus service, trucks only.

**Lucho (Luis) Hurtado**, Av. Giráldez 724, San Carlos (Apartado Postal 510, Huancayo, T 237063), organizes excursions, using local transport, to Indian villages in the low-lying jungle, or to the mountains, in either case with the possibility of living with the Indians, or to his father's farm near Chanchamayo in the high Selva. Trips cost about US$20 a day. He (from Huancayo, speaks good English) and his wife, Beverly (from New Zealand) own *Pizzería La Cabaña* (see above); you are always welcome for a pizza and information. Students can also study Spanish (14-day course for US$200, including accommodation with local families, and breakfast, rec.), weaving, the pan flute and Peruvian cooking. He has been highly and repeatedly recommended as a guide. Contact him only at his home (impersonators have been operating). Take old tennis shoes or something similar for walking in rivers; no other equipment necessary. He can also be contacted through the South American Explorers Club in Lima.

22 km. NW of Huancayo is the village of **Concepción** (3,251 metres), which has a market on Sun. as well as a colourful bullfight later in the day during the season. Colectivos to Concepción from near *Hotel Turistas*, US$0.60, 30 mins. Other hotels, *El Paisanito*, 9 de Julio 641, G, clean; *Royal*, on Plaza, warm shower, G, pleasant; *Hotel Huaychulo* is near Concepción and a 2 hr. walk from Ingenio where there is a government trout farm; good restaurants, especially for pastries. From Concepción a branch road (5 km.) leads to the **Convent of Santa Rosa de Ocopa**, a Franciscan monastery in beautiful surroundings established in 1724 for training missionaries for the jungle, open 1000-1200 and 1500-1700; closed Tues. Tour costs US$0.65 (students US$0.25). It contains a fine library with over 20,000 volumes and a biological museum with animals and insects from the jungle. The convent has a guesthouse, US$2.50 each, hot water. There is also a good restaurant. Bus from Huancayo (change at Concepción) takes 1½ hrs., US$0.45. Near Concepción is the village of **San Jerónimo**, renowned for the making of silver filigree jewellery (Wednesday market). The work of Sra. Nelly Vásquez, Calle Arequipa, 2 blocks from the Plaza de Armas, is particuarly recommended; opposite is Sra. Porras, who also produces good pieces. Its fiesta is in August. There are ruins 2-3 hrs. walk above San Jerónimo, but the hike is dangerous in places. Buses from Plaza Amazonas, Huancayo, US$0.15. 45 mins'. walk from San Jerónimo is Hualhuas where beautiful tapestries of alpaca and sheeps' wool are made on rustic looms. (Luis Hurtado arranges day tours to these places, US$3 p.p., not incl. transport and food.)

18 km. beyond Concepción, on the road to La Oroya, is the old town of **Jauja** (3,552 metres), Pizarro's provisional capital until the founding of Lima, where an interesting festival (San Fermín and San Fabián) begins on 20 January and lasts several days, enjoyable (but lone tourists should be careful). Also, a very colourful Wed. and Sun. market. Jauja is a friendly, unspoilt town, in the middle of a good area for walking, with ruins near a lake 3½ km. away. It has the best archaeological museum in the Mantaro valley for the Wari culture. A modernised church retains 3 fine 17th-century altars. The Cristo Pobre church is claimed to have been modelled after Notre Dame and is something of a curiosity. On a hill above Jauja there is a fine line of Inca storehouses, and on hills nearby ruins of hundreds of circular stone buildings from the Huanca culture (John Hemming). Bus from Huancayo, US$0.60, many daily, also colectivos (US$1.20). (*Hotel Jauja* and *Hotel Pizarro*, both E; *Hostal Santa Rosa*, on the square, F, some rooms with bath, poor water supply, restaurant, and on north side, *Turistas*, E, near pleasant Laguna de Paca.) Wood carving is practised in the nearby town of Molinas. At Aco, 1½ hrs. walk from Mito on road to Jauja, large ceramic pots are made, take fruit as a gift if you do not intend to buy. The road to Satipo branches off near the Convento de Sta. Rosa de Ocopa; the village of Paca (2 km. further on) is very pleasant; easy to catch a taxi to Jauja; spectacular scenery, snow-capped mountains in the Paso de la Tortuga, followed by a rapid drop to the Caja de Silva in Satipo. (**See page 1055.**)

**Huancavelica**, capital of its Department (altitude, 3,680 metres; population, 37,500), a friendly and attractive town, was founded over 400 years ago by the Spanish to exploit rich deposits of mercury and silver; it is predominantly an Indian town, and is still a major centre for mining. It is possible to visit the old mercury mine on the hill above the town—a stiff walk, or hire a car. There are beautiful mountain walks in the neighbourhood. The cathedral, located on the Plaza de Armas, has an altar considered to be one of the finest examples of colonial art in Peru. Also very impressive are the five other churches in town: the church of San Francisco has no less than 11 altars. (Sadly most of the churches are closed to visitors.) Lectures on precolumbian history and archaeology are given in the museum, 2nd floor.

Bisecting the town is the Río Huancavelica. South of the river is the main commercial centre where fine leather and alpaca products can be purchased (especially on Calle Virrey Toledo). North of the river on the hillside are the thermal baths (US$0.15). There is a daily market. At the Sunday market, the men wear all black, with multicoloured woollen pom-poms dangling from their skull-caps, waists and knees; these are also used to decorate the livestock.

**Warning** The department of Huancavelica has much terrorist activity; do not visit unless you have checked conditions with locals beforehand.

**Hotels and Restaurants** *Turistas*, D, for room with private bath, reasonable, restaurant fair; *Perú*, near railway station, G, clean, good; *Tahuantinsuyo* near Plaza de Armas, F, clean and well maintained. Little water in cheaper hotels in evenings. **Restaurant** *Olímpica*, Virrey Toledo 303, good and cheap. We have no confirmation of which hotels and restaurants are operating.

**Tourist Office** In Correo building on Plaza da Armas, go up stairs from an entrance on the left-hand side of the building.

**Transport** Daily (except Sun.) to **Huancayo** (146 km.) are one train (0730, 7 hrs.) and two *autovagones* (0700 and 1300, 3½ hrs.), and buses (7 hrs. Expreso Huancavelica leaves at 1700, Hidalgo, 0600 and 1500, US$4); sit on the right side for the best views. To **Lima** via Huancayo, US$9.20 (Expreso Huancavelica, 1700). To **Pisco** (267 km.), buses only, daily, US$11, 14 hrs. (Oropesa service leaves at 0600, but be there by 0530 to get a seat, tickets can be bought the day before); route is via Santa Inés (4,020 metres), where there are ten restaurants. Half-an-hour's walk from Santa Inés are Lagunas Choclococha and Orcococha, where llama herds can be seen; beautiful views; be prepared for sub-zero temperatures a.m. as bus passes snowfields, then for temperatures of 25-30°C as bus descends to coast p.m.

Getting to **Ayacucho** (296 km.) is a problem, particularly in the rainy season, and is not recommended while terrorism persists. Take a bus (Oropesa) to Santa Inés, 0600, 4 hrs., US$3.50, then catch the Ormeño bus from Lima (Santa Inés-Ayacucho, 8 hrs., US$4.80). Alternatively catch a pick-up truck to Pilpichaca, via Santa Inés, 1330-1730, US$2.40, then a truck from Pilpichaca to Ayacucho, 2000 to 0500, US$3.20, very cold. The road (very bad) is the highest continuous road in the world, rarely dropping below 4,000 metres for 150 km. Out of Huancavelica one climbs steeply on a road that switchbacks between herds of llamas and alpacas grazing on rocky perches. Around Pucapampa (km. 43) is one of the highest habitable *altiplanos* (4,500 metres), where the rare and highly prized ash-grey alpaca can be seen. 50 km. beyond Santa Inés, the rocks are all colours of the rainbow, and running through this fabulous scenery is a violet river (all caused by oxides). Eleven km. later one encounters Paso Chonta (4,850 metres) and the turnoff to Huachocolpa. By taking the turnoff and continuing for 3 km. one discovers the highest drivable pass (5,059 metres) in the world. Continuing on to Ayacucho one passes some very cold, fish-filled lakes before the road branches to Pisco at km. 77. Seventy km. later the high (4,750 metres) Abra Apachenta is reached, leaving a 98-km. descent into Ayacucho.

*Ayacucho*, capital of its Department, was founded on 9 January 1539. This old colonial city is built round Parque Sucre with the Cathedral, Municipalidad and Palacio de Gobierno facing on to it. The city is famous for its religious processions and its splendid market. There are no less than 33 churches—some long deserted and most closed—and a number of ruined colonial mansions. A week can be spent there and in the surroundings, which include La Quinua, site of the battle of Ayacucho, 9 December 1824, which brought Spanish rule to an end in Peru. Ayacucho has a very active student life. Altitude: 2,440 metres, with gently rolling hills around. A 364-km. road has been built to Pisco on the coast. Population: 75,000.

Visitors are advised to see the 17th century Cathedral (with Museo de Arte Religioso, closed indefinitely) and churches of San Francisco de Asís, La Compañía de Jesús, Santa Clara, Santo Domingo, and Santa Teresa, all with magnificent gold-leafed altars heavily brocaded and carved in the churrigueresque style. There is a small but surprising Museo Histórico Regional, in the Centro Cultural Simón Bolívar, at the outskirts of town, US$0.35 (many Huari artifacts). Tombs of the Huari nobles are being excavated along the road from Ayacucho to Quinua. The University, founded 1677, closed 1886, was reopened in 1958.

**Festivals** Semana Santa begins on the Friday before Holy Week with the procession of the Virgen de los Dolores (very beautiful, but the suffering is "symbolised" by the custom of flinging pebbles from slingshots, aimed mainly at youngsters, but also foreigners). A charming Palm Sunday procession, beginning at 1600, of palm-bearing women and children accompanies a statue of Christ riding on a white donkey. There follows one of the world's finest Holy Week celebrations, with candle-lit nightly processions, floral "paintings" on the streets, daily fairs (the biggest on Easter Saturday), horse races and contests among peoples from all central Peru.

**Warning** Because of guerrilla (Sendero Luminoso) activity in this region, visitors are advised to seek information in advance and check whether a curfew is in force. Entry into the area has on occasion been prohibited for visitors and it is unwise to go outside the city at night.

**Hotels** We have no firm information as to which are operating. *Turistas*, 9 de Diciembre, E, with bath, comfortable (meals, US$3.20, mediocre); *Colmena*, Jirón Cusco 140, just of Plaza de Armas, F, a beautiful building, nice rooms with table, wardrobe, clean, good but no hot water, not secure, noisy, good restaurant below; *Hostelería Santa Rosa*, Jirón Lima 140, F, with bath, hot water mornings and evenings, friendly, car park, restaurant, rec. *Imperio*, Plaza de Armas, F, 4-bedded rooms; *Ayacucho*, just off the Plaza, G, cheap, with shower, basic; *La Sixtina*, Jirón Callao, F, basic but friendly, clean, clothes washing facilities; others near market and bus terminals. It is extremely difficult to find accommodation at Easter.

**Restaurants** *La Fortaleza*, Lima 169, 3 courses for US$1.20, very good coffee, reasonable meals; *Tradicional*, San Martín 406, popular, good variety and value; *San Agustín Café Turístico*, Plaza de Armas, good food and lemon meringue pie; *Tradición*, Vivanco, rec.; *La Casona* behind *Turistas*, rec. Many good small cafés, one inside University buildings. On the Plaza, *Los Portales* is good. The airport offers a good breakfast. Try *mondongo*, a soup made from meat, maize and mint, also *ponche*, a hot drink made of peanuts, coconut and cinnamon.

**Handicrafts** Local crafts include filigree silver, often using *mudéjar* patterns; little painted altars which show the manger scene, carvings in local alabaster, harps, or the pre-Inca tradition of carving dried gourds. The most famous goods are carpets and *retablos* (wooden boxes containing three-dimensional scenes in papier maché). In both weaving and *retablos*, scenes of recent political strife have been added to more traditional motifs. Due to the dramatic decline in tourism in recent years, many craftsmen have left Ayacucho, or are exporting their goods to Lima and Cuzco.

**Exchange** Ayacucho Tours. Try *Hotel de Turistas*, *Hostelería Santa Rosa* (good rates), AeroPerú, Morocucho Tours (Plaza de Armas).

**Tourist Information** Foptur, Portal Municipal 46, on Plaza de Armas next to church, good information, friendly, T 912997. Also available from Ayacucho Tours, San Martín 406, near market, or from the AeroPerú office (Plaza de Armas). Also rec., for information and excursions, Wari Tours. State Tourist Information Office, Asamblea 138, has good free leaflets on Ayacucho. The journalist, Sr. Ylpidio Vargas, Jirón 2 de Mayo 309, T 912987, is very knowledgeable on the department and on recent events there. He is willing to show visitors around in safety.

**Air** To Lima by AeroPerú, 35 minutes, daily at 0720 or 1005; flights Ayacucho-Cuzco with Faucett 4 a week. Much military scrutiny at airport. In the rainy season expect cancellations. Taxi to airport, US$0.80 p.p., buses from 0600 from Plaza de Armas.

**Buses** Bus Ayacucho-**Huancayo**, none by day; via Pampas, Etucsa, 16 hrs., US$8.80, very cold and uncomfortable. Ordinary bus goes at night (1500 and 1800 daily), no wc on board; Ayacucho Transport, Etucsa and Molina, Calle Grau, do the journey. Bus to **Pisco** (and Ica), US$12.50 with Ormeño (Jr. Libertad 257), 12-13 hrs.; and to **Lima** (1300, 1900), US$17, also Hidalgo (San Martín 330), at least once a day. No direct buses between Ayacucho and **Cuzco**, you must take Ayacucho-Andahuaylas bus (Molina, 19 hrs. daily at 0900, US$10.20, beautiful scenery) and change in Andahuaylas for Abancay and again for Cuzco.

**Excursions** Inca ruins at *Vilcashuamán*, to the S, beyond Cangallo; "there is a five-tiered, stepped *usnu* platform faced in fine Inca masonry and topped by a monolithic two-seat throne. The parish church is built in part of the Inca sun temple and rests on stretches of Inca terracing. Vilcashuamán was an important provincial capital, the crossroads where the road from Cuzco to the Pacific met the empire's north-south highway" (John Hemming). Taxi trips can be arranged with Ayacucho Tours and Morocucho Tours, alternatively stay overnight; market day is Wed. A good road going N from Ayacucho (trucks from Calle Salvador Calvero) leads to Wari (**see page 1049 Huari**), dating from the "Middle Horizon", when the Huari culture spread across most of Peru (US$0.80 by public transport). Trips can be arranged by Ayacucho Tours, rec., who do a tour to Wari, La Quinua village and battlefield. **La Quinua** village has a charming cobbled main square and many of the buildings have been restored; there is a small market on Suns. There is a huge obelisk to commemorate the battle of Ayacucho. Handicrafts are recommended, guitars and, especially ceramics; most houses have miniature ceramic churches on the roof. San Pedro Ceramics, at foot of hill leading to monument, and Mamerto Sánchez, Jr. Sucre should be visited. The village's festival is celebrated around 7-8 October, lasting 3 days. Beautiful 18 km. walk downhill from La Quinua to Wari, where trucks leave for Ayacucho until about 1700.

*San Francisco* in the jungle on the Río Apurímac (3 basic hotels, *Suria*, E, the best but dirty) can be reached by bus from Ayacucho (junction of Av. Centenario and Av. Cavero) on Sat. (return Mon.), 10-12 hrs. on a very bad road often impassable in the wet season (very cold at night). Trucks travel daily leaving at about 0700 (wait at police control near airport), US$8 in driver's cabin, US$4.80 on back, or private cars, twice the price, bargain hard. From

San Francisco you can take a morning canoe to **Luisiana**, about 2 hrs. upstream, to stay in Sr. Parodi's *Jungle Hotel*, Centro Vacacional de Luisiana, with swimming pool, C, on his large *hacienda*; trips are organized in the jungle but it is only open for 3 months in the dry season and Sr. Parodi is not always there. There is an airstrip at Luisiana with daily connections to Ayacucho, for over five passengers. Details in the Ayacucho Tourist Office. From San Francisco you can make excursions to nearby villages on cargo canoes, but it is very difficult to find transport all the way to Pucallpa unless you have a large group of people and are willing to pay handsomely.

**From Ayacucho to Cuzco** (Because of guerrilla activity and army counter-measures, public transport is scarcer than it used to be, but travellers will be allowed through if they do not stray from the main road and do not take photographs.) The road to Cuzco goes through **Andahuaylas**, in a fertile, temperate valley of lush meadows, cornfields and groves of eucalyptus, alders and willows. It offers few exotic crafts, no comfortable accommodation (you must register with the army as a condition for getting into a hotel), poor transport, but beautiful, largely undiscovered scenery. Buses (supposedly daily) Ayacucho-Andahuaylas stop between 2100 and 0530 if there is a curfew (very cold on board). From Ayacucho to Ocros, the road is terrible (mudholes and marshes), can take 20 hrs. for 80-100 km. In Ocros is an unfriendly military checkpoint; innumerable Guardia checkpoints thereafter, but the road is not too bad to Andahuaylas. Also be prepared for stoppages by Sendero Luminoso. No direct buses Andahuaylas-Cuzco; you must take the only daily bus or a colectivo to Abancay, then a bus to Cuzco. The road crosses three mountain ranges and is very rough in places but is definitely worthwhile. **Abancay** is first glimpsed when you are 62 km. away by road, nestled between mountains in the upper reaches of a glacial valley (registration with army required, as at Andahuaylas). From Abancay a 470 km. road runs SW through Chalhuanca and Puquío to Nazca on the Pan-American Highway **(see page 1000).**

Trucks and a bus leave Andahuaylas for Abancay at 0630-0700, take 8 hrs., US$6.20. Book at least 2 days in advance for a seat on the bus from Ayacucho to Andahuaylas. Several bus companies from Abancay to Cuzco US$7.75 at least (196 km., 12 hrs.), minibus from near the market takes 7 hours to Cuzco, leaving 1200, colectivos also leave around 0800, arriving 1700, dramatic scenery especially in Apurímac valley, but most of the road between Abancay and Cuzco is very bad. **See page 1033** for sites of interest between Abancay and Cuzco, 10 hrs. Abancay to Machu-Picchu: take a truck to Izcuchaca where the train can be caught to Machu-Picchu.

**Andahuaylas Hotels** *Turistas*, Jirón Dias Bárcenas 500, D with bath (E without), meals US$3 extra (no money exchange or credit cards accepted); *Gran*, Plaza de Armas, G, basic, and *Restaurant Las Palmeras*, meal for US$0.25, is possible; *Hermanos Chipuna*, G, basic, near bus station; *Delicias*, G, hot showers, basic but rec., only 7 rooms, ask for extra blankets, cold at night; *28 de Julio*, cheap, G, adequate.

**Abancay Hotels** Discrimination against foreigners reported. *Turistas*, D, with bath, food good, US$3, comfortable, old-fashioned house, safe car park, camping permitted at US$3; *Gran Hotel*, G, with bath, clean; *Abancay*, F; *El Misti*, G, fair. *Alojamiento Centenario*, F. **Restaurant**: *Elena*, on same street as bus companies, good, plentiful and cheap portions.

Ronald Berg, of Cambridge, Mass., writes: Around Andahuaylas the old road by the river to Talavera offers some pleasant scenery. San Jerónimo is another picturesque town nearby. Most worth seeing is Pacucha, an hour's ride by truck from Andahuaylas. Pick-ups leave from the centre of Andahuaylas daily, most frequently on Sun., which is market day. Pacucha (pop. 2,000) is the largest of six villages on the shores of a large scenic lake, with a view of mountains to the NW. In the plaza, where the trucks stop, women sell bread, coffee and hot lunches, the only food for 16 km. There are dirt roads around the lake and the circumference can be done in an afternoon (but be back in Pacucha before dark to ensure transport back to Andahuaylas). The wildlife includes many types of wild duck and other birds, sometimes including flocks of green parrots and swallows. Opposite Pacucha, some 2km. past the lake, are the ruins of a Chanka fortress called Zondor. The trails into the jungle beyond the lake are not recommended: the area is very desolate. Except for Andahuaylas itself, this is a mainly Quechua-speaking region. It is one of the poorest parts of Peru, but as long as you do not display your wealth or eat in public, the people tend to be friendly to foreigners.

**East of La Oroya** The 60-km. surfaced road to Tarma follows the Cerro de Pasco road for 25 km., then branches off to rejoin the old road quite near Tarma, which is 600 metres lower than La Oroya.

**Tarma**, population 105,200; altitude 3,050 metres, was a nice little flat-roofed town, founded in 1545, with plenty of trees. It is now growing, and there are garish modern buildings, but it still has a lot of charm. Semana Santa celebrations are spectacular, with a very colourful Easter Sunday morning procession in main plaza; Indians make fine flower-carpets. The cathedral is dedicated to Santa Ana; at *Hostal Central*, Calle Huánuco, there is an observatory. The surrounding countryside is beautiful; much terrorist activity here, avoid or check before you go.

**Hotels**  *Turistas*, D, with and without bath, acceptable meals US$3.20, rather run down; medium-priced hotels are on the plaza, e.g. *Tuchu* and *Internacional*, both reasonable; cheaper places around the market, such as *Anchibaya*, *Tarma*, *Central*, and *Córdova*, all basic.

**Restaurants**  *Tradición*, Jr. Moquegua 350, good. *Chavín Café*, beneath *Galaxia* hotel, on square, trout rec; several on Lima, including a vegetarian place. The *manjarblanco* of Tarma is famous; also *pachamanca*, *mondongo* and *picante de cuyes*.

**Tourist Office**  Jr. Dos de Mayo 77, T 2945.

**Bus**  Direct bus service, **Huancayo**-Tarma, twice daily 0600 and 1600, US$3.45. Daily colectivos from Jirón Huánuco 439 run almost hourly to Huancayo, US$3.80, 2½ hrs, bus to **Oroya**, US$2.40, colectivo, US$3; bus to **La Merced**, US$2.65; colectivos often leave for Chanchamayo, US$3.45. Passes over high limestone hills with caves.

Visit the Grutas de Guagapo (*La boca que Llora*: the cave that weeps), 4 km. from town of Polcamayo—bus twice daily from Tarma US$1 (2 hrs). The caves, which are a tourist attraction especially in Easter week, can be entered for about 300 metres. Even without a guide you can penetrate the cave for some way with a torch. Cave guide, Modesto Castro, lives opposite caves and is very informative. His wife cooks trout and potatoes for visitors; you can camp outside his house. The precolumbian ruins of Tarmatamba, Shoguemarca, Yanamarca, Huayipirca, Cachicachi, Pichgamarca and Huancoy also lie nearby.

Eight km. from Tarma (bus US$0.20, or pleasant 2 hrs' walk), the small hillside town of **Acobamba** has the futuristic Santuario de Muruhuay, with a venerated picture painted on the rock behind the altar. It also has fine *tapices* depicting the Crucifixion, made in San Pedro de Cajas. Festivities all May.

**Hotels**  Two *alojamientos* (Doña Norma's near plaza, G, is basic but clean and friendly). Daily buses to Tarma, La Oroya (US$0.60) and Huancayo; 3 buses a week direct to Lima (Coop. San Pedro).

The road from Tarma via Acobamba and Polcamayo, continues from Palcamayo (no buses, 3-hr. walk) to **San Pedro de Cajas**, a large village which used to produce most of the coloured sheep-wool weavings for sale in Lima. Most of the weaving families have now moved to Lima. *Hotel Comercio*, Calle Chanchamayo, G; 2 restaurants; no shops. The road continues on to rejoin the one from La Oroya to Cerro de Pasco below Junín.

Beyond Tarma the road is steep and crooked but there are few places where cars cannot pass one another. In the 80 km. between Tarma and La Merced the road, passing by great overhanging cliffs, drops 2,450 metres and the vegetation changes dramatically from temperate to tropical. A really beautiful run.

Some 11 km. before La Merced is **San Ramón** (population 7,000). Ask at the airport about journey to Pampasilva and Puerto Ubirique (see below).

**Lodging and food**  *Conquistador*, E, with shower, parking, on main street. There is a rec. *chifa* on the main street, and the *Hawaii* is good for juices. *La Estancia*, Tarma 592, local specialities.

*La Merced*, population 10,000, lies in the fertile Chanchamayo valley. Sometimes Campa Indians come to town selling bows and arrows, and there is a small but interesting market selling snake skins, hides, armadillo shells, etc. Festival in the last week of September.

**Hotels**  *Rey* and *Christina*, good, E, with bath; *Cosmos*, opp. police station, E, fair, probably quieter than others; *Hostal Mercedes*, F, with bath, hot water, clean, rec.; *Romero*, Plaza de Armas, T 2106, F, good but noisy and water in evenings only. Best **restaurant** is *Shambari-Campa*, off Plaza de Armas; *Hong Kong*, restaurant; plenty of bars patronized by the coffee workers, who spend 6 months in the mountains each year.

Note that San Ramón and La Merced are collectively referred to as *Chanchamayo*. Many buses, both from **Lima** (e.g. Transportes Chanchamayo, best, Av. Luna Pizarro 453, La Victoria, Lima; Los Andes, Arellano, good, 10 hrs., US$6.40) and from **Tarma** (US$2.35, 3 hrs.). Bus La Merced-**Puerto Bermúdez**, 8 hrs., US$6.40, 1000 (Túpac Amaru). To get to **Pucallpa**, take a launch from Puerto Bermúdez to Laurencia (8 hrs., or more, US$7.20, be prepared for wet luggage), then truck to Constitución, 20 mins., thence colectivo to Zungaro, 1½ hrs., US$3.20. From Zunzaro, colectivos take 4½ hrs., to Pucallpa, US$4.80. Alternatively, you can take a truck from La Merced to Pucallpa, 3 days, but between 0830 and 1400 each day you will probably be drenched by rain.

From La Merced you can take the Carretera Marginal de la Selva (a grandiose edge-of-the-jungle project of the mid-1960s, of which some parts have been built) to the jungle town of *Satipo* (Lobato or Los Andes buses from La Merced US$7.20 at 0800; *Hostal Majestic*, D, with bath, no clothes-washing facilities, electricity 1900-2300 only; *La Residencial*, 4 rooms, F, clean, garden, swimming pool, rec., many smaller hotels, all very basic, the best being *Palmero*, E, with bath, not very clean. Try *Dany's Restaurant*, surprisingly good food for such an out-of-the-way place). A beautiful trip. Halfway between La Merced and Satipo is Pichinaki, which has a good hotel, F, ideal for breaking one's journey (bus La Merced-Pichinaki, US$3.45). There are daily buses direct from Satipo to Huancayo (check whether tunnels are open) and Lima at night, very cold, US$9.50, 12 hrs., Los Andes and Lobato, so no need to return from Satipo via La Merced. Satipo can also be reached from Concepción, following the Santa Rosa de Ocopa road (see page 1050), and from Pucallpa by air.

About 22 km. beyond La Merced is San Luis de Shuaro, but 3 km. before it is reached a road, right, runs up the valley of the Perené river. The Perené colony, a concession of 400,000 hectares, nine-tenths of it still unexplored, has large coffee plantations. The altitude is only 700 metres. Saturday and Sunday are colourful market days for the Indians. Beyond San Luis de Shuaro a branch road runs right to Villa Rica. It is no longer possible to take motorized canoes from Pampasilva on the Río Perené to Puerto Ubirique, since the building of the new road.

The road has been extended from San Luis de Shuaro over an intervening mountain range for 56 km. to *Oxapampa*, 390 km. from Lima, in a fertile plain on the Río Huancabamba, a tributary of the Ucayali. Population, 5,140; altitude, 1,794 metres. Logging, coffee, cattle are local industries, colectivo service from La Merced (taxis leave at 0600, US$2, 4 hrs, very slow-going). A third of the inhabitants are descendants of a German-Austrian community of 70 families which settled in 1859 at *Pozuzo*, 80 km. downstream, and spread later to Oxapampa. There is much livestock farming and coffee is planted on land cleared by the timber trade. 25 km. from Oxapampa is Huancabamba, from where it is 55 km. to Pozuzo; the whole road between La Merced and Pozuzo is very rough, depending on the season, 30 rivers to be crossed. Sr. Luis Orbeza's *mixto* leaves from Oxapampa, opposite *Hotel Bolívar*, to Pozuzo on Mon., Wed., and Fri., early morning, returning 0700, US$4.50, Tues., Thurs., Sat., 6 hrs. on a very rough road. Buses from Lima to Pozuzo with La Victoria, from 28 de Julio 2405, Mon., Thur., Sat., 0800, US$12, about 16 hrs. Downstream 40 km. from Pozuzo is Nuevo Pozuzo (no transport, two-day walk); Padre Pedro has a collection of insects, weapons and stones in his office. There is a family near Padre Pedro's house who welcome guests for dinner (US$1), German spoken. Interesting museum opposite church in town centre.

**Oxapampa Hotels** *Bolívar*, basic, good restaurant; *Hostal Santa Isolina*, Jirón M. Castilla 177, G; *Hostal Liz*, Av. Oxapampa 104, G, clean, rec.; *Hostal Jiménez*, Grau 421, G, basic; *Hostal Vicus*, opp. Bolívar Hotel, G; *Hostal La Cabaña*, on Plaza, G; *Hostal Santo Domingo*, F. **Restaurants**, *Oasis*, highly rec.

**Pozuzo Hotels** *Hostal Tirol*, E, full board, clean, rec.; *Hostal Prusia*, F, clean; *Hostal Maldonado*, F-G, clean, rec.

There is an "air-colectivo" service from La Merced to **Puerto Bermúdez** on the Río Neguachi, 10 kg. baggage allowance, US$5 per kg. of excess luggage. The service continues to Atalaya, Satipo, Puerto Inca (see page 1064) and Pucallpa.

Bus service, La Merced-Puerto Bermúdez (see below). Air-colectivos go to Lima and to most places in the jungle region where there is an airstrip; flights are cheap but irregular, and depend on technical factors, weather and good will. Aero-taxis can be chartered (*viaje especial*) to anywhere for a higher price, maximum five people, you have to pay for the pilot's return to base. In Puerto Bermúdez there is accommodation (*Hostal Tania*, opposite dock where motorized canoes tie up, F, clean), an eating house opposite the airstrip; boat passages possible from passing traders.

**North of La Oroya** A railway (also a paved road) runs 130 km. N from La Oroya to Cerro de Pasco. It runs up the Mantaro valley through narrow canyons to the wet and mournful Junín pampa at over 4,250 metres, one of the world's largest high-altitude plains: an obelisk marks the battlefield where the Peruvians under Bolívar defeated the Spaniards in 1824. Blue peaks line the pampa in a distant wall. The wind-swept sheet of yellow grass is bitterly cold. The only signs of life are the youthful herders with their sheep and llamas. The line follows the E shores of the Lago de Junín. The town of **Junín**, with its picturesque red-tiled roofs, stands beside its lake, whose myriads of water birds have made it famous for its shooting. At Smelter, the coal washing plant, the track branches to Goyllarisquisga, while the main line goes to the long-established mining centre of **Cerro de Pasco** (population 29,810, altitude 4,330 metres), 130 km. from La Oroya by road. It is not a pleasant town, having many beggars and thieves and much unemployment. The nights are bitterly cold. Copper, zinc, lead, gold and silver are mined here, and coal comes from the deep canyon of Goyllarisquisga, the "place where a star fell", the highest coal mine in the world, 42 km. N of Cerro de Pasco. A fine new town—San Juan de Pampa—has been built 1½ km. away (*Gran Hotel*, noisy, no hot water, poor service). A recommended excursion is to the precolumbian funeral towers at Cantamasia, reached on muleback. At Morococha (alight from train at Tuctu) is the Centromín golf course, welcoming to playing visitors, which at 4,400 metres disputes the title of the world's highest with Malasilla, near La Paz, Bolivia.

**Hotels** *Gran Hotel Cerro de Pasco*, Av. Angamos in San Juan suburb, E, shower, little hot water, poor service, noisy; *El Viajero*, on the plaza, F, clean but no hot water; *Santa Rosa*, F, basic, very cold; *Restaurant Los Angeles*, near market, rec. Local specialities, trout and fried frog.

**Train** Through tickets to Cerro de Pasco can no longer be bought at the Desamparados Station in Lima. The train leaves La Oroya for Cerro de Pasco at 1400; it arrives at 1740. The return train for **La Oroya** leaves at 0630 from Cerro de Pasco station, which is 20 min. out of town on foot; on the return journey there should be a connection at La Oroya: the train from Cerro de Pasco arrives there at 0935 and the train for Lima leaves at 1006. The *churrasco* served for breakfast on the train is a welcome defence against the cold.

**Buses** Bus to **Lima**, departs 0830 and 2000, 9 hrs., US$8. To **La Oroya**, bus from Plaza Arenales, 0900 and later, US$1.20; cars go when there are passengers, US$9.50. To **Huancayo**, US$4.75. Colectivos to **Huánuco**, US$6.20, from the central plaza. Buses to Huánuco leave between 0800 and 0900 from Plaza de Armas (5 hrs., US$2). A bus, connecting with the train from Lima, to Huánuco takes 3 hrs., at night.

**Warning** The departments of Junín, Cerro de Pasco and Huánuco are suffering from terrorist activities; do not visit without checking on conditions with locals.

---

## CERRO DE PASCO TO IQUITOS (8)

Gaunt Andean passes plunge down steep valleys into the tropics; this is backwater country. Iquitos, though, combines a frontier feel with many incongruous features: MTV cabled from the USA blares from riverside bars; wrought iron architecture designed by Eiffel hints at

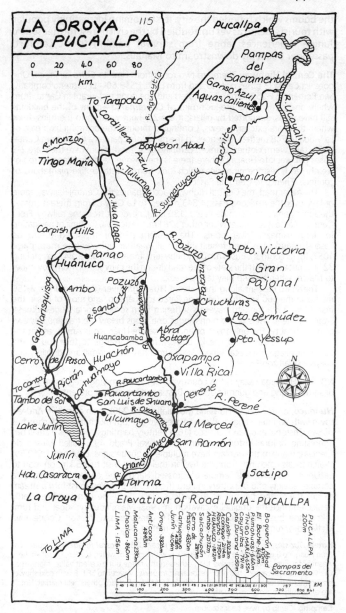

LA OROYA TO PUCALLPA

115

0  20  40  60  80
km.

Pucallpa

Pampas del Sacramento

Ganso Azul
Aguas Calientes

R. Aguaytía

Cordillera Azul

To Tarapoto

R. Monzón

Tingo María

Boquerón Abad.

R. Tulumayo

R. Sungaruyacu

R. Ucayali

R. Pachitea

Pto. Inca

R. Huallaga

Carpish Hills

Panao

Huánuco

R. Pozuzo

Pto. Victoria

Gran Pajonal

Ambo

Pozuzo

R. Santa Cruz

R. Palcazu

Chuchuras

Pto. Bermúdez

Huancabamba

Abra Bottger

Pto. Yessup

Cerro de Pasco

Huachón

Carhuamayo

Oxapampa

Villa Rica

N

Ricrán

Tambo del Sol

R. Paucartambo

Paucartambo
San Luis de Shuaro

R. Oxabamba

Perené

R. Perené

Lake Junín

Ulcumayo

La Merced

Junín

R. Chanchamayo

San Ramón

Hda. Casaracra

Tarma

Satipo

La Oroya

To LIMA

Elevation of Road LIMA–PUCALLPA

PUCALLPA 200m

Boquerón Abad
El Boche 1613m
Pumahuasi 660m
TINGO MARÍA 655m
Cayumba 1435m
Pto Durand 1050m

Carpish 3023m
Acomayo 2114m
Acopayo 1730m
HUÁNUCO 1812m
Ambo 2012m

Cerro de Pasco 2819m
Salcachupán
Carhuamayo
Junín 4106m

Oroya 3723m
Anticona 4843m

Chosica 860m
Matucana 2394m

LIMA 156m

Pampas del Sacramento

40 | 41 | 76 | 45 | 56 | 50 | 44 | 48 | 36 |21|20|19| 45 |34|18|20| 51 | 30 | 87
0        100        200        300        400        500        600        700   800 841

KM

the booms which founded the city. It is becoming increasingly popular with tourists, being as yet untroubled by the civil unrest further south. Jungle experiences range from survival training to a/c comfort; passenger boats ply downstream to Manaus.

**The Central Highway** There are two roads from Lima to Cerro de Pasco. One goes via **Canta** (3 buses daily to and from Lima, US$3.60—El Canteño company, San Román 151-153, Lima). Two hotels and one good restaurant in Canta, from where one can visit the pre-Inca ruins of **Cantamarca**—many of the buildings still have roofs, supported by pillars; it is a 2-3 hour walk up to the ruins, from where there are extensive views. Continuing through the beautiful high pass of La Viuda (4,748 metres), one goes to the mines of Alpamarca (truck from Canta, 0200, take warm clothes, blanket, camping gear, food). From here there are 2-3 buses per week to Huallay, where there is the Bosque de Piedras (an outcrop of weathered limestone pinnacles which look from a distance like plantations of conifers). Thence to Cerro de Pasco.

The other road, the Central Highway, accompanies the Central Railway, more or less, over the Anticona Pass (4,843 metres) to La Oroya. From there it crosses the Junín pampa to Cerro de Pasco (130 km.), never far from the railway. From Cerro de Pasco it continues NE another 528 km. to Pucallpa, the limit of navigation for large Amazon river boats. The western part of this road (Cerro de Pasco-Huánuco) has been rebuilt into an all-weather highway (**see map, page 1057**, for its contour). Buses run daily between Lima and Pucallpa, 847 km., taking 32 hrs., but ask about the state of the road during the rainy season from November to March, when the trip may take a week.

The sharp descent along the nascent **Huallaga River** (the road drops 2,450 metres in the 100 km. from Cerro de Pasco to Huánuco, and most of it is in the first 32 km.) is a tonic to travellers suffering from *soroche*, or altitude sickness. From the bleak vistas of the high ranges one drops below the tree line to views of great beauty. The only town of any size before Huánuco is Ambo; ask at the *dulcería* for Ricardo, who speaks English; he can arrange to take you to the beautiful village of Huacar where Sr. Tiburcio has a water-mill and distillery and keeps a small zoo.

**NB** The Huallaga valley is the country's main coca-growing area; there is both drug-trafficking and guerrilla activity. Best avoid the area at present.

**Huánuco**, on the Upper Huallaga (population: 82,240), is an attractive Andean town with an interesting market and the two old (but much restored) churches of San Cristóbal and San Francisco (16th century paintings). There is a small but interesting natural history museum at General Prado 495, called Museo de Ciencias; many of the displays have multiple language signs. Entrance, US$0.50. Watch locals catch fish from the river in their teeth! Visit ruin 5 km. on road to La Unión: **Kotosh**, the Temple of Crossed Hands, the earliest evidence of a complex society and of pottery in Peru (from 2000 BC). You must ford a stream to get there, and beware of the vicious black flies. The ruin has been sadly neglected since the original excavation in 1963. Main industry: sugar and rum; take Cisne bus from Jirón Ayacucho, 15 mins., in a.m. to visit Cooperativa Vichaycoto, rum for sale. Altitude 1,812 metres.

**Hotels** *Turistas*, D, with bath, no hot water, meals US$6; *Hostal Residencial Huánuco*, Jirón Huánuco (near Plaza de Armas) T 2050, F, with bath, hot water, garden, use of kitchen, washing facilities, more expensive than others in this range but excellent value, highly rec.; *Las Vegas*, on plaza, rec., has good restaurant; *Imperial*, Ayacucho 581, F, with cold shower (intermittent water), reasonable value, clean, quiet; *Kelin*, F, clean; others near market. Hotels are often fully booked; arrive early.

**Camping** Camp by river, near stadium.

**Restaurants** Several on or near the plaza.

**Tourist Information** Foptur, General Prado 714, Plaza de Armas, opp. Post Office, T 522124. Huánuco Tours, Jirón General Prado 691.

**Buses** To Lima, US$11 with León de Huánuco, 10 hrs., 3 a day in early evening, slow; colectivo to Lima, US$20, leaves 0400, arrives 1400; book the night before at General Prado 607, one block from the main square, rec. Etposa also runs to Lima. Daily buses to **Cerro de Pasco**, La Oroya and Huancayo, 0830, 1600, with Nororiente or Ucayali, Constitución 638, 11-12 hrs., US$7.35. "Mixto" Huánuco-Cerro de Pasco, half bus, half truck, departs 0400, 3 hrs., US$3.60; colectivo 1 or 12, US$6.20 at 0500. Frequent buses and colectivos to **Tingo María**, 3 hrs. (colectivo, US$3.20, many start from near river bridge, two blocks from main plaza). Bus to **Pucallpa**, US$11, La Perla del Oriente (Etposa), 0800 and 1600, rec. 10 hrs. plus; buses make stops for meals but some of them are widely spaced; in any case it is wise to take your own food in case of breakdowns. To **Huancayo**, 10 hrs., US$4.80.

**Air** Huancapallac airport, 8 km. from town; AeroPerú (office at the Tourist Hotel) flights to and from Lima, 4 days a week.

To the north-west of Huánuco is *Tantamayo* (3,600 metres), a farming village in the Central Sierra; it is surrounded by precolumbian ruins which can be reached on foot (3-4 hrs., guides available) called Piruru, Susupillu, Japallan, and Castilla de Selinin; pictures and information from Huánaco Post Office. Hotel: *Turística*, where Don Cristián Ocaña and his Swiss wife, Theresa, offer full board, D (F without food), they are very helpful, and Sra. de Ocaña speaks German, French, Italian and English. Bus from Huánuco, US$6.70, 12-14 hrs., departs 1800; returns at night. Tantamayo can also be reached by taking a truck to Tingo Chico, US$2.70, then another to Chavín de Pariarca (US$1.20) where there is a basic hotel (G) and restaurants, then walk. This route, like the walks to the ruins, is arduous; take warm clothing, a hat, suntan lotion.

From Huánuco, a road leads to *La Unión*, capital of Dos de Mayo district a friendly town, but electricity can be a problem (it gets very cold at night); 2 buses daily between 0700 and 1000, including Acosta, 2 blocks from the market, returns to Huánuco about midnight, US$4.80, 8-9 hrs., truck, 10½ hrs., leaves late morning. La Unión-Tingo Chico, US$2.70. *Hostal Turista* and *Hostal Dos de Mayo*, at La Unión (G). Neither safe for left luggage. *Restaurant El Danubio*, near market, good home cooking, lots of garlic.

On the pampa above La Unión are the Inca ruins of *Huánuco Viejo*, a 2½ hr. walk from the town, a great temple-fortress with residential quarters. To get there, take the path starting behind the market and climb towards the cross, which is at the edge of a plateau. Continue straight through the village on the wide path (the locals are friendly, but some of their dogs are nasty); the views of the pampa, surrounded on all sides by mountains, are beautiful. Seemingly at the foot of a mountain, in front and to your right, is a silvery metalic roof of a little chapel, behind which are the ruins (about a 20-min. walk through herds of cattle). Take warm clothing and beware of thunderstorms. (Karin Kubitsch, West Germany).

Bus to Lima daily, crowded. Also possible to get to Callejón de Huaylas by taking 1600 bus to Conococha (US$5.20, 9 hrs.) and waiting there for a truck to Huaraz (2-3 hrs.— **see page 952**). The wait is very cold, at 4,100 metres. La Unión-Huaraz direct is very difficult because most transport does the route La Unión-Chiquián-Lima. You can take a truck from La Unión to Huansalla, then another to Pachacoto (some wait till 0100 for passengers), and from there it's 1 hr. to Huaraz. The San Cristóbal bus to Lima at 1100 goes a few km. S of Catac; from there connections are easy to Huaraz (1 hr.) and Chavín (via Catac). Salazar bus to Lima (3 a week at 1000-more like 1100), takes 9 hrs. To Conococha, US$6.20; this is supposed to connect with a Lima-Huaraz bus at 1900-2000; if you miss it, hitch in the cold and dark (2 hrs., US$2.40 to Huaraz). A night bus from Lima passes at 300, but the restaurant at the Conococha crossroads closes at 2230. Check local political conditions before taking this route.

The journey to Tingo María, 135 km., is very dusty but gives a good view of the jungle. Some 25 km. beyond Huánuco the road begins a sharp climb to the heights of Carpish (3,023 metres). A descent of 58 km. brings it to the Huallaga river again; it continues along the river to Tingo María. (The road is paved from Huánaco to Tingo María, including a tunnel through the Carpish hills, but is reported to be in very bad condition.) Landslides along this section are frequent and construction work causes delays.

*Tingo María* is on the middle Huallaga, in the Ceja de Montaña, or edge of the mountains, isolated for days in rainy season. Climate tropical; annual rainfall 2,642 mm. Population, about 20,560 and very mixed. The altitude (655 metres) prevents the climate from being oppressive. The Cordillera Azul, the front range of the Andes, covered with jungle-like vegetation to its top, separates it from the jungle lowlands to the E. The mountain which can be seen from all over the town is called La Bella Durmiente, the Sleeping Beauty. The meeting here of Sierra and Selva makes the landscape extremely striking. Bananas, sugar cane, cocoa, rubber, tea and coffee are grown. The main crop of the area, though, is coca, grown on the *chacras* (smallholdings) in the countryside, and sold legitimately and otherwise in Tingo María—there have been several shoot-outs between the police and the drug entrepreneurs. As in many other places in Peru, watch out for gangs of thieves around the buses and do not leave luggage on the bus if you get off. Although the town itself is generally safe, it is not permitted to leave it at night (2 U.K. journalists were killed here in June 1990); it is also inadvisable to take a bus through the area at present.

A small university outside the town, beyond the *Hotel Turistas*, has a little museum-cum-zoo, with animals of that zone, and botanical gardens in the town, entrance free but a small tip would help to keep things in order. 6½ km. from Tingo is a fascinating cave, the Cueva de las Lechuzas. There are many nocturnal parrots in the cave and many small parakeets near the entrance. It is reached by car via the new bridge (or colectivo from garage, US$1); take a torch, and do not wear open shoes; also take a tape recorder "for your own private horror-movie soundtracks" when the birds leave the cave. The Cave can be reached by boat when the river is high. 13 km. from Tingo is the small gorge known as Cueva de las Pavas (no caves or turkeys, but good swimming).

**Hotels** *Turistas*, D, with and without bath, restaurant, very good, swimming pool US$0.75, some way out of town; *Viena*, F, good value with private bathrooms, clean, near *Café Rex*; *La Cabaña*, G, the cheapest, tolerably clean, good restaurant. Hotels are often fully-booked. There are a number of cheap hotels, but we have no recent information on which are operating. **Restaurants** (to which the same applies) *Pensión González*, expensive, but nice setting; *Café Rex*, Avenida Raimondi 500, cakes and ice cream, but rather run down; *Gran Chifa Oriental*, Chinese restaurant, on main street, cheap.

**Transport** Flights from Tingo María to Lima. Normally 3 flights a week to Tingo María by AeroPerú, but times often change. 4-seater plane flies to Juanjui, pay extra for every kilo of luggage over 10 kilos. From Tingo María on, several transport services are run; the road is narrow and stony. Landslides and mud can be a problem. Some construction work is going on. Many Lima-Pucallpa buses go via Tingo, for example, Arellano, Av. Raimondi, whose buses leave between 0700 and 0900 (their terminal in Lima is in La Victoria, a very dangerous area). Bus takes 18 hrs. From Tingo to **Pucallpa**, US$8, 8 hrs. Seats are hard to get on buses to Pucallpa; there are 4 booking offices: Huallaga, Tepsa, Arellano, Nororiente. Bus to *Aguaytía*, 3 hrs., US$2.70. León de Huánuco bus Tingo María-**Huánuco** takes 5-6 hrs., 0930, US$2.20; colectivos take 3 hrs. but beware of unauthorized colectivos, which charge the same as authorized ones but are smaller, slower and sometimes get into trouble with the police, US$3.20.

The Río Huallaga winds northwards for 930 km. The Upper Huallaga is a torrent, dropping 15.8 metres per kilometre between its source and Tingo María. The Lower Huallaga moves through an enervation of flatness, with its main port, Yurimaguas, below the last rapids and only 150 metres above the Atlantic ocean, yet distant from that ocean by over a month's voyage. Between the Upper and Lower lies the Middle Huallaga: that third of the river which is downstream from Tingo María, upstream from Yurimaguas. The valleys, ridges and plateaux have been compared with Kenya, but the area is so isolated that less than 100,000 people now live where a million might flourish. The southern part of the Middle Huallaga centres upon Tingo María; down-river, beyond Bellavista, the orientation is towards **Yurimaguas**, which is connected by road with the Pacific coast, via Tarapoto and Moyobamba (**see page 977**). There is a fine church of the Passionist

Fathers, based on the Cathedral of Burgos, Spain, at Yurimaguas; population 25,700. Market from 0600-0800, colourful, full of fruit and animals. Tourist information from Consejo Regional building on main Plaza. Interesting excursions in the area include the gorge of Shanusi and the lakes of Mushuyacu and Sanango. Moped hire US$2.35/hour including fuel. **Warning**: there has been guerrilla activity in the Yurimaguas region; visitors can expect attention from the police.

**Hotels** *Yurimaguas*, E, with shower, toilet and fan, clean, reliable; *Estrella*, F, and shower, rec.; *Floríndez*, E, shower, air conditioning US$1.50 extra; *Camus*, no sign, Manco Capac 201, F, cheap; *Mache*, F, with bath and fan, rec.; *Leo's Palace*, F, Plaza de Armas 104-6, good, friendly, reasonably-priced, restaurant; *Heladería*, round corner from *Estrella*, serves good cheap lunch and dinner.

**Exchange** Interbanc or travel agents; poor rates.

**Air** AeroPerú flies Lima-Trujillo-Yurimaguas-Iquitos Thurs. and Sun. Faucett flies Lima-Tarapoto-Yurimaguas on Wed., and to Yurimaguas on Fri. When Yurimaguas-Tarapoto road is impassable, Grupo Ocho flies for civilians. Flights also to Juanjui. Planes may not land in rain.

**River Travel** Yurimaguas-Iquitos by regular ferry *Jasmin* 60 hrs. (upstream takes longer). *Madreselva* and *Gardenia* are two large ferries to Iquitos, a smaller ferry is the *Oty*, bring your own hammock, takes 2 days and 2 nights, take fruit and drinks, police inspections at each end of the trip; similar is *Vencedor*. Fares usually include meals (1991 rates unknown); cabins cost more. To buy a hammock costs US$10 in Yurimaguas. Ask at the harbour for smaller boats, which can take up to 10 days.

You can break the journey at **Lagunas**, 12 hrs. by boat from Yurimaguas: *Hostal La Sombra*, Jr. Vásquez 1121, G with shared bath, basic, friendly, good food); *Hotel Montalbán*, Plaza de Armas, no sign, 2 clean rooms, friendly owner, Sr. Inga, 20-mins. walk from jetty, also accommodation at the Farmacia. You can ask the local people to take you on a trip into the jungle by canoe; you will see at very close range alligators, monkeys and a variety of birds, but only on trips of 4 days or so. Edinson Saldaña Gutiérrez, Sargento Flores 718 is a good guide; also Hopp and Genaro (ask at *La Sombra*), who include basic food, with fishing and hunting; Juan Huaycama (Jáuregui 689), highly rec., mostly on the river, sleeping in hammocks, fishing. Typical cost for party of 5 for 12 days is US$200, with 2 guides and 2 boats. One person for 5 days with one guide is charged US$45. Take water purifier and mosquito repellant on excursions that involve living off the land. The 45-foot river launch *Constante* plies to Lagunas 2-3 times a week, 12 hrs. downstream from Yurimaguas; from there connections are difficult to Iquitos. A boat, *La Rosita*, runs regularly but stops at every village of any size. *Alfert* has been rec., cabins, good food. Times of boats to Iquitos and Pucallpa very vague (confirm departures the day before by radio). The boats pass by the villages of Castilla and Nauta (*Residencial Olguita*, basic), where the Huallaga joins the Ucayali and becomes the Amazon. You need a hammock, mosquito net, water-purification tablets, extra food and a good book.

At Tulumayo, soon after leaving Tingo María, a road runs N down the Huallaga past La Morada, successfully colonized by people from Lima's slums, to Aucayacu (*Hotel Monte Carlo*, E with bath; one other hotel, both poor) and Tocache (accommodation at *Hostal San Martín*, F; *Hostal Sucre*, F; one other). The road is paved to 20 km. past Aucayacu, thereafter it is good gravel. Colectivos run; Tingo-Tocache US$13 (4½ hrs.) or bus US$9.50 (6 hrs.). The road has been pushed N to join another built S from Tarapoto (Tarapoto-Tocache, US$7.50 by colectivo) and has now been joined at Tarapoto to the Olmos-Bagua-Yurimaguas transandine highway to the coast at Chiclayo. Colectivos and taxis run from Tocache to Yurimaguas (serviceable unpaved road); daily *camioneta* Tarapoto-Yurimaguas, US$7.50, 6 hrs. The Juanjui-Tocache road has five bridges, but the last one across the Huallaga, just before Juanjui, was washed away in 1983 to be replaced by an efficient ferry (US$9.20 per vehicle); Juanjui-Tarapoto by colectivo US$12.50. For the river journey, start early in the morning if you do not wish to spend a night at the river village of Sión. No facilities, but night is not cold. The river runs through marvellous jungle with high cliffs. Boats sometimes run aground in the river near Sión. Take food and water purifier. Many rafts of balsa wood. Also, a small plane flies between Tocache and Juanjui, (25 mins).

From Tingo María to the end of the road at Pucallpa is 288 km., with a climb over the watershed—the Cordillera Azul—between the Huallaga and Ucayali rivers. When the road was being surveyed it was thought that the lowest pass over the Cordillera Azul was over 3,650 metres high, but an old document stating that a Father Abad had found a pass through these mountains in 1757 was rediscovered, and the road now goes through the pass of Father Abad, a gigantic gap 4 km. long and 2,000 metres deep. At the top of the pass is a Peruvian Customs house; the jungle land to the E is a free zone. Coming down from the pass the road bed is along the floor of a magnificent canyon, the Boquerón Abad: luxuriant jungle and ferns and sheer walls of bare rock punctuated by occasional waterfalls into the roaring torrent below. E of the foot of the pass the all-weather road goes over flat pampa with few curves to the village of **Aguaytía** (narcotics police checkpoint; gasoline; *Hostal San Antonio*, F, clean; 2 restaurants). On to Pucallpa (160 km.—5 hrs. by bus, US\$4.35); the last half has no service stations.

**Pucallpa**, a rapidly expanding jungle town, is on the Ucayali River, navigable by vessels of 3,000 tons from Iquitos, 533 nautical miles away. Population has increased to about 90,000 (district 130,000). It is the capital of the new Department of Ucayali. The newer sections have paved streets, sewers and lights, but much of the frontier town atmosphere still exists. Small but attractive zoo at the brewery (tours on Sat. but far out of city). The economy of the area is growing fast; sawmills, plywood factories, a paper mill, oil refinery, fishing and boat building are all thriving; timber is trucked out to the Highlands and the coast. A newly constructed floating dock for freight promises a great expansion in trade. Large discoveries of oil and gas are being explored, and gold mining is underway nearby. The local drugs problem is becoming serious. The Ganso Azul oilfield has a 75-km. pipeline to the Pucallpa refinery. From Tingo María, 286 km. (gravel road); from Lima, 847 km.

All jungle towns are expensive, but bargains can be found. The floating port of La Hoyada and Puerto Italia are worth a visit to see the canoe traffic and open-air markets. Care should be taken when arranging jungle trips from street vendors in Pucallpa or at the ports. The climate is tropical: dry season in July and August, rainy seasons October-November, February-March; the town is hot and dusty between June and November and muddy from December to May. The centre of Pucallpa is now paved, but both the port and new commercial harbour, about 5 km. away, are reached along dirt roads.

**NB** There is much military control because of terrorist and narcotics activity. The city itself is OK to visit, but don't travel at night, or outside the city.

**Hotels** *Turistas*, C with bath (taxes included), swimming pool, good restaurant; *Mercedes*, D, good, but noisy with good bar and restaurant attached, swimming pool; *Inambu*, C, with good value restaurant, a/c; *Komby*, E, comfortable, swimming pool, excellent value; *Sun*, Ucayali, F, without bath, clean, good value next to *Komby*; *Comfort*, E, clean, *Sisley*, E, adequate, both on Coronel Portillo; *Barbtur*, F, Raymondi 670 (T 6377), friendly, clean, central, opp. bus stop, good beds; *Hostal Mori*, Jr. Independencia 1114, G, basic; *Hostal Los Angeles*, on Ucayali, E, clean, communal shower, but noisy; *Tariri*, Raymondi, G, dirty, basic, food cheap and good, Coronel Portillo, near Calle Frederico Basadre. If holidaying, better to stay at Lake Yarinacocha (see below).

**Restaurants** *Chifa Pucallpa* and *Chifa Hongkong*, Raymondi 650. *Jaricho*, under *Hotel Sun*, good; *Escorpión Cebichería*, Jr. Progreso, good, eat in rear garden; *Puerto de Carlos*, best in the downtown area, expensive; *Embutidos La Favorita*, Cnl. Portillo, good, cheap, friendly, US\$1 for all 3 meals; *El Establo*, steak house on road to airport, excellent; *Sandwich Roma*, corner of Portillo and Ucayali, good snack bar. *La Baguette*, good bakery, cheap bottles of pisco. The local beer "San Juan" has been rec.

Small **motorcycles** for hire from Jr. Raymondi 654 and 7 de Junio 864, about US\$1.50 per hour plus gasoline.

**Bookshop** *Librería La Verdad* has a collection of English books on loan; a boon for stranded travellers.

**Exchange** Banco Continental, no commission. Importaciones Gutiérrez Padilla, Jr. Ucayali,

Raymondi 601 (also good ice cream). Try also the owner of the *Barbtur Hotel*, and Textiles Universales, Postillo y Ucayali.

**Tourist Office** Foptur, Saénz Peña 298, T 5008.

**Air** AeroPerú and Aerochasqui to and from Lima at least one flight daily, 1 hr. 3 flights a week to Iquitos with Aerochasqui, twice with AeroPerú, try different agencies for lower price ticket (e.g. Pucallpa Tours, Jr. Coronel Portillo 747, T 6081). Some seats are assigned, you need to arrive early. Departures must be confirmed 24 hrs. in advance. Reconfirmation of tickets can only be done with any certainty at the office in town. Float plane, Aero San Martín, from the airforce base at Yarinacocha, Sat, 0900 to Iquitos (check in Fri., be there at 0700), US$20; will only go if there are enough passengers each end, otherwise one has to pay for additional seats. Grupo Ocho fly to Esperanza, San Ramón, Sepahua, Atalaya, with passengers—office in Pucallpa. The road to Brazil has not yet been opened. For connections by river **see Brazil section 9. Southern Amazonia.** SASA fly to Cruzeiro do Sul, minimum 4 passengers, if plane has no passengers booked for return, you'll have to pay double, very unreliable. Airport to town, bus US$0.25; taxi US$3.60.

**N.B.** Before entering Peru at Pucallpa by air from Cruzeiro do Sul check thoroughly that immigration facilities have been set up at Pucallpa. If you arrive and cannot get a stamp, the PIP in Pucallpa will (or should) send you back to Brazil; if they don't, you'll be in for a lot of hassles further on in Peru, including the possibility of arrest. To leave Peru from Pucallpa, you must get a special exit visa from the PIP in town or at the airport.

**Buses** Much of the Pucallpa-Lima road is now paved (rough stretch for 80 km. E of Tingo María) and there are regular bus services to Lima (check in advance that the road is open and what political conditions are). Huallaga, Arellano, Perla del Oriente and León de Huánuco (at 1730) from **Lima** to Pucallpa (US$16, 24 hrs. in good weather) via **Huánuco** (10 hrs., US$11 with León de Huánuco (slow)—1300 from Pucallpa, US$10.40 with La Perla del Oriente, 1200). From Pucallpa Nororiente goes to **Tingo María**, US$8, 10-11 hours, also Amazonia Express, on Raymondi (controls at Aguaytía and about 40 km. from Tingo María). Advised to take blankets as the crossing of the Cordillera at night is bitterly cold. Try to pick a bus crossing the mountains by day as the views are wonderful. It is also possible to get to Lima by truck.

**Excursions** The Hospital Amazónico Albert Schweitzer, which serves the local Indians, and Summer School of Linguistics (callers by appointment only) for the study of Indian languages are on picturesque Lake **Yarinacocha**, the main tourist attraction of the area. Yarinacocha is 20 mins. by colectivo or bus (line 6) from the market in Pucallpa (US$0.30), 15 mins. by taxi (US$4.30). The Indian market of Moroti-Shobo is a must. *Hotel La Cabaña*, C (by appointment only, price rises in high season), same Swiss owner as *Mercedes* in Pucallpa, good service and food, excellent guide, Isabel, for short expeditions, plane excursions (for instance to Indian villages). Next door to *La Cabaña* is *La Perla* lodge, good and much cheaper, German-Peruvian owned, English and German spoken, homely atmosphere. *Los Delfines*, F, rooms with bath, clean, noisy; *El Pescador*, in Puerto Callao, F, cheap, friendly, restaurant, best buy for budget traveller, but mixed reports recently. Some small houses for rent on weekly basis. Restaurants: *El Cucharón*, good food; *Grande Paraíso*, good view; local specialities include *tamales*, *humitas* (maize patties with meat and herbs), *junies* (rice with chicken and spices), *tacutacu* (banana and sauces).

Here is bathing in clean water, but there is a lot of weed. It is a pleasant change after the mud of Pucallpa and the Amazon; you can camp, though there are no facilities and it is hot and insect-ridden. Motor canoes can be hired for about US$20 a day with guide, but guide not mandatory for lake trips. Trips into the canals and out to the river need a guide (Sr. Antonio has been rec.). Two types of excursions down river, recommended three days, can be arranged from the port in Yarinacocha directly with the boat owners, prices vary but approximately US$20 per boat a day, you buy food and some supplies. Boats hold up to 8 at reduced price. Recommended boats: *Veloz*, *Akito* (of the García family, who also have accommodation, rec., trustworthy), Thierry Giles, good English, has two boats called *Delfín*, rec. Beware, many boats are used for drug-running and tourists have come to grief. Recommended guides Daniel Saavedra (B/M *Progreso*), Roberto C. Cenepo, Jorge Rucoba (navigator), who offer fishing, hunting, walks in the jungle along the rivers Aguaytía, Callena and Ucayali, and rivers and canals (especially the Chanchaguaya region of Contamaná). Also special excursions to Iquitos from Pucallpa. None of them speaks English, but they can be found at Lake Yarinacocha, Puerto Callao, ask for B/M *Progreso*, prices are competitive. Also rec. for tours, Jorge Matos Grijalva of Selva Tours, also an English teacher and bar owner, great local character and most helpful, Coronel Portillo, next to *Hotel Amazonas*. Local guide, Gonzalo Vargas Cárdenas, c/o Aéro San Martín. **Note**: down-river trips visit numerous villages but much of the jungle is cultivated; up-river trips visit fewer villages but mostly virgin jungle.

Certain sections of Lake Yarinacocha have been designated as a reserve. The Botánico Parque Turístico of Francisco Montes-Shuna is worthy of a visit. It is a collection of jungle plants, well-laid out and labelled, by Lake Yarinacocha, including a part of the smaller Lake Ormiga. Sr. Montes Shuna will demonstrate the uses of the plants, is very knowledgeable, and speaks English. To visit is free, but a donation is welcome. To get there take a boat to just past *La Cabaña*, then walk 12 minutes along a path: all details from Francisco Montes-Shuna, Jr. L.M. Sánchez Cerro 465, Pucallpa (turn off Guillermo Sisley Medina, the road from Yarinacocha to central Pucallpa, by Mercado 3), or contact Lenín Mera Rengifa, Elmo Tours, Jr. 7 de Junio 767, T 6798.

**River Service** Bus Line 1 to the port, La Hoyada. In the dry season boats dock 3 km. from the bus stop, along dusty walk, taxi US$3. To **Iquitos**, some better than others; only 3 boats with cabins, but don't count on getting one (hammocks are cooler): *Madre Selva*, clean, friendly, rec.; 6 days. Travellers to Iquitos may need confirmation from the PIP that their documents are in order, this must then be signed by the Capitanía otherwise no passenger can be accepted on a trip leaving Pucallpa. No such clearance is necessary when returning to Pucallpa. Passenger services are in decline owing to competition by air and priority for cargo traffic; it may be better to make journeys in short stages rather than Pucallpa-Iquitos direct. There's a risk of illness on the river, and public transport can be extremely uncomfortable. River water is used for cooking and drinking; tinned food, mosquito netting, hammock and fresh water are necessary purchases, fishing line and hooks advisable. Take lots of insect repellant (local brand, Black Flag, is not effective), water purifier and tummy pills. The smaller boats call often at jungle villages if you want to see them, but otherwise because the river is wide, the shores can only be seen at a distance. Average time: 5 days. Boats leave very irregularly. When conditions are bad they leave in convoy: none may leave afterwards for 4 to 6 weeks. Avoid boats that will be loading en route, this can take up to 6 days. Further down the Ucayali river are Contamaná (with frontier-town atmosphere) and Requena, from which launches sail to Iquitos, taking 12 hrs. Roroboya, a small Shipibo Indian village about 12 hrs. downstream from Pucallpa, should not be missed, as most other villages down to Iquitos are *mestizo*. You can go to Puerto La Hoyada and Puerto Italia (smaller boats) to find a boat going to Iquitos; the Capitanía on the waterfront may give you information about sailings, but this is seldom reliable. Do not pay for your trip before you board the vessel, and only pay the captain. (Captains may allow you to live on board a couple of days before sailing.) Boats going upstream on the Amazon and its tributaries stay closer to the bank than boats going down, which stay in mid-stream.

From Pucallpa to Cruzeiro do Sul overland requires plenty of time and money to organize, and even then is difficult. You can take a boat to Abojao (10 days), then walk to Brasiléia, from where buses go to Rio Branco. Boats and guides are very expensive.

You can take a colectivo from Pucallpa S to Zungaru (US$4.50), where a boat (30 mins.) can be taken to **Puerto Inca** on the Río Pachitea, about 120 km. N by air from Puerto Bermúdez (**see page 1055**) and close to the Carretera Marginal (under construction). It is a gold-rush town, expanding quickly, with two hotels (Don José's *Alojamiento*, G, clean, safe, laundry, big rooms, rec.).

**Iquitos**, capital of the Department of Loreto and chief town of Peru's jungle region, is a fast-developing city of 350,000 people on the W bank of the Amazon, with Padre Isla island (14½ by 3 km.) facing it in midstream. It has paved streets and plenty of vehicles (including taxis) but roads out of the city go only a little way: Iquitos is completely isolated except by air and river. Some 800 km. downstream from Pucallpa and 3,646 km. from the mouth of the Amazon, it has recently taken on a new lease of life as the centre for oil exploration in Peruvian Amazonia. As one might expect from its use by the oil industry and its remoteness, it is an expensive town, but compensates by being a friendly place.

---

**IQUITOS: Key to map**

1. Plaza de Armas; 2. Plaza 28 de Julio; 3. Belén and market; 4. Quistacocha; 5. *Hotel Amazonas*; 6. Capitanía del Puerto; 7. Aduana; 8. Mercado Artesanal. **INSET** 9. Iron House/Casa de Hierro; 10. Casa de Fitzcarrald; 11. Museo Municipal; 12. Foptur Tourist Office; 13. Post Office; 14. Entel Telephone Office; 15. Immigration; 16. AeroPerú; 17. Faucett; 18. *Hotel Turistas*; 19. *Hostal Europa*; 20. Municipalidad. Area of detailed map.::::::::

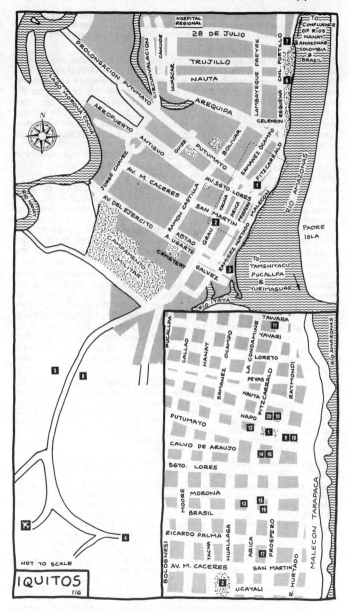

IQUITOS

NOT TO SCALE

116

There is an iron house in the Plaza de Armas, designed by Eiffel for the Paris exhibition of 1898. It is said that the house was transported from Paris by a local rubber baron (the rubber boom lasted until 1912); it is constructed entirely of iron trusses and sheets, bolted together and painted silver.

Belén, the picturesque, friendly waterfront district, is lively, but not safe at night. Most of its huts are built on rafts to cope with the river's 10-metre change of level during floods. *Pasaje Paquito* is a bar with typical local drinks, as is *La China*. The main square has a bandstand made by Eiffel. (Canoes may be hired on the waterfront to visit Belén, US$3 per hour; do not try paddling yourself as the current is very strong.) See in the city the Market, at the end of the Malecón, or riverside walk. Note that the principal street Jirón Lima has been renamed Jirón Próspero. Recommended guide with a good car and two boats is Jorge Chávez, T 231532 or through *Hostal Caravel*.

The University of Amazonia of Loreto (1962) specializes in engineering and agriculture. Of special interest are the older buildings, faced with *azulejos* (glazed tiles). They date from the rubber boom of 1890 to 1920, when the rubber barons imported tiles from Portugal and Italy and ironwork from England to embellish their homes. Werner Herzog's film *Fitzcarraldo* is a *cause célèbre* in the town; Fitzcarraldo's house still stands on the Plaza de Armas, and Herzog's boats are moored in the port.

A short drive S of the city is beautiful Lake **Quistococha** in lush jungle, with a fish hatchery at the lakeside. Recommended is a visit (US$0.60) to the Parque Zoológico de Quistococha (with aquarium) on the lake (closed Mon.). At the entrance are pictures and texts of local legends, the tourist office will supply a map of the zoo. Take bus (tends to be crowded and dirty, and return buses unreliable) from corner of Próspero and Gálves; also a truck (with pink frame, not green) from Abtao and Grau to the zoo and Quistococha, US$0.25; taxi US$3.60 for 4 people, with 2 hrs. wait. We have heard that the animals (and particularly the fish) often depend on food from visitors to survive. The monkeys roam freely, some cages are small, but the zoo attracts mixed reactions (e.g. "The zoo is a disaster. Many animals have died or just disappeared. Not rec. unless one wants to be severely depressed." J. Williams, London, 4/90). See particularly the *paiche*, a huge Amazonian fish whose steaks (*paiche a la loretana*) you can eat in Iquitos' restaurants.

**Warnings** As elsewhere, beware of thieves, especially of handbags, watches, jewellery, etc. Secondly, locals sell necklaces made with red and black rosary peas (Abrus pecatorius), which are extremely poisonous. Do not give them to children. They are illegal in Canada, but not in the U.S.A. If possible, avoid visiting Iquitos around Peruvian Independence Day (27 and 28 July) and Easter as it is very expensive and crowded and excursion facilities are overloaded. Avoid the "headhunters" at the airport who try to steer you to travel agents for a commission (the tourist police at the airport help to avoid this practice): cheaper to go straight to the agents, who are all on Calle Putumayo near the Plaza.

**Festivals** Founding of Iquitos, 5 January; Carnival, February-March; tourist week, third week in June; San Juan, 24 June; Immaculate Conception.

**Hotels** *Amazonas*, previously *Holiday Inn*, on Abelardo Quiñónez, 3 km. out of town (taxi US$1.75), A, plus 19% tax and service, swimming pool (free bus service hourly from airport), designed for air conditioning but not working, a 5-star hotel only in price; *Turistas*, Malecón Tarapacá, C, with bath, meals US$4.50, with many good air-conditioned rooms US$1.50 extra (a few second-hand English books available in reception), does not accept travellers' cheques; *Hostal Caravel*, Próspero, B, a/c, very clean, friendly; *Hostal Acosta*, Ricardo Palma 252, A, hot and cold running water, shower, air conditioning, refrigerator in room, very good café, central, rec.; also *Acosta 2*, C, almost same standard plus good restaurant and swimming pool; *El Dorado*, Napo (½ block from Plaza de Armas), D, swimming pool, cable TV, bar and restaurant quite expensive, credit cards, highly rec.; *Isabel*, Brasil 174, E with bath, very good, clean (but plug the holes in the walls!), secure, often full; *Hostal Safari*, Napo 126, E, a/c, hot showers, restaurant; *Hostal La Pascana*, Pevas 133, F with cold shower, basic, fan, clean, breakfast available, rec.; *Lima*, Próspero 549, F (triple rooms available), with bath and fan, cold water, towel, soap and toilet paper provided, café good, and good breakfast 2 doors to the right; *María Antonia*, Próspero 616, C, clean, air-conditioned, noisy; *Hostal Europa*, Brasil 222, very good, very helpful, D, a/c (cheaper with fan); shower; *Hostal Tacna*, Tacna 516, T 232839, F, basic, clean and cheap, rooms do not have windows and some are noisy; *Hostal Residencial Ambassador*, Pevas 260, C, with shower, a/c and snack-bar, rec.; *Hostal Residencial Loreto*, Jr. Próspero 311, E, with shower and a/c (cheaper without a/c, noisy, poor water supply); *Hostal Karina*, Av. Putumayo 467, F, good value, central, friendly, laundry, cheap food, but poor water supply; *Excelsior* Arica, 3 blocks from Plaza de Armas, F, a/c, cold shower, safe, breakfast extra, friendly. Cheapest: *Alojamiento Moore*, Moore 1164, G, very clean, good water supply, quiet, etc.

**Restaurants**  The best are on or near Plaza Veintiocho (28) de Julio, e.g. *El Dorado Inn*, Calle Huallaga, good value and good menu; *El Tropical*, Av. Quiñónez 39, 1½ km. from centre, owned by Paul Hitschler (German), reasonable, rec.; *El Shupihui*, Calvo de Araujo y Castilla, typical restaurant, highly rec.; *El Mesón*, Jirón Napo 116, fish rec.; *La Terraza*, Maldonado y Napo on waterfront, with frogs hopping between tables, good; *Maloca*, opposite *Hotel Turistas* on riverbank, excellent, average meal US$5, good fish, really good view, highly rec. Chinese restaurants include *Gran Chifa Wai Ming*, San Martín 462/6, good but quite expensive; *Gran Chifa Chung Wa*, on the corner of Arica and San Martín, average. *La Favorita*, Próspero Morona, good ice-cream (try local flavour *aguaje*); *Chicken Broaster*, Próspero, 3 blocks from Plaza de Armas, good for *paiche a la loretana* as well as chicken; *Tucunaré*, Putumayo 157, good for fish (try *paiche*). *Snack Jungle Bar*, Próspero 283, good value. *Olla de Oro*, Calle Calvo de Araujo, close to main indoor market, excellent food, cheaper than riverside area, friendly service, rec.; *La Barca*, Fitzcarrald, near Plaza de Armas, food OK and quite cheap (often open during afternoon siesta when most other places don't serve meals). Pineapples are good and cheap. Try the local drink *chuchuhuasi*, made from the bark of a tree, which is supposed to have aphrodisiac properties, and *jugo de cocona*, and the alcoholic *vete bajando*, *cola de mono*, *rompe colzón* and *siete raices* (aguardiente mixed with the bark of 7 trees and wild honey). You can eat cheaply, especially fish, at the three markets. Palm heart salad (*chonta*); or *a la Loretana* dish on menus excellent; also try *inchicapi* (chicken, corn and peanut soup), *cecina* (fried dried pork) and the *aguaje* palm fruit is an interesting but acquired taste, said to have one of the highest vitamin C concentrations in the world.

**Current**  220 volts, A.C.

**Shopping**  *Artesanías del Perú*, Putumayo 128; Mercado Artesanal de Productores, 4 km. from the centre in San Juan district, take colectivo; *La Cocamita*, Putumayo 120; *Mocahua Juárez*, Arica 1083. All sell handicrafts and un-named shop on Calle Brasil, cuadra 7, sells handicrafts of the Shipibo indians from Pucallpa. Pharmacies: *Tacna*, Tacna 450; *D'Onadio*, Próspero 541; *El Loretano*, Próspero 361-3. Secondhand English books at the travel agent on Próspero 184 (1 for 1 exchange, free).

**Cinemas**  On Plaza 28 de Julio, another on Próspero.

**Discotheques**  The best are said to be *Puma's Club* (*Amazonas Hotel*) or *Tropicana Club*, both in Putumayo. *La Pantera Rosa*, Moore 434; *Pax*, Napo y Condamine; *Acuario*, Napo 1st block; *St Chomas*, Condamine.

**Motorcycle Hire**  US$15 a day, Carlos del Prado Bawer, Brasil 530, T 239147.

**Museum**  Museo Municipal (1st block of Tawara), has a large, old collection of stuffed Amazonian fauna which is rather disappointing. It has been incorporated into the Parque Zoológico.

**Exchange**  Banco Popular cashes travellers' cheques. **Banco de Crédito**, Plaza de Armas, good rates. **Banco Amazónico** changes cheques at the official rate without charging a commission or asking for a copy of your passport. *Importaciones Lima* on Próspero, and shops selling foreign electrical goods offer good rates of exchange. Many money changers on Próspero in the 3 blocks S of Plaza de Armas.

**Consulates**  Brazilian, Sgto. Lores 363; **Colombian**, Plaza de Armas, by Tourist Office; **Spanish**, Moore 249.

**Immigration**  Arica 477, T 235371.

**Medical Services**  Clínica Loreto, Morona 471, T 23-3752, 24-hour attention, recommended, but only Spanish spoken.

**Post Office**  corner of Calle Arica with Morona, near Plaza de Armas. **Entel**, Arica 276.

**Tourist Office**  Foptur, on W side of Plaza de Armas, T 238523; also on Calle Arica 122, T 231688; and at airport: useful town maps, maps of the Quistacocha zoo and literature from the main jungle tour operators. Town map also from Librería Mosquera, Jr. Próspero.

**Travel Agencies**  Good information from Edith (speaks English and French), *Three Roses Travel*, Próspero 246, very helpful. Other agencies recommended for city and surroundings *Belén Viajes y Turismo*, Arica 1233, and *Fénix Viajes*, Pevas 216.

**Jungle Tours**  All agencies are under control of the local office of the Ministry of Tourism, Calle Arica 566: if you think you're being overcharged, ask for Sra. Lastenia Rodríguez, who will show you the operator's file, in which route and price must be recorded. (Not worth while for booking bus or air tickets). They arrange one-day or longer trips to places of interest with guides speaking some English; package tours booked in Lima are much more expensive than those booked in Iquitos. Some agencies are "easy going and that's how they take their responsibilities on an organized trip". Take your time before making a decision, shop around, and don't be bullied by the hustlers at the airport. Get all details of the trip and food arrangements before paying, about US$40 per day. Launches for river trips can be hired by the hour or day (prices are negotiable, about US$10-15 per hour); many tour operators are located on Jirón Putumayo near the Plaza de Armas.

*Explorama Tours* (rec. as the most efficient), new offices by riverside docks (Box 446, Telex 91014, T 51-94-235471, Fax 51-94-234968; in USA, Selective Hotel Reservations, T 800-223-6764, MA (617) 581-0844), has three sites: *Explorama Inn*, 40 km. (1½ hrs.) from Iquitos, hot water, comfortable bungalows in a jungle setting, good food, attractive walks, rec. jungle experience for those who want their creature comforts, US$115 for 2 nights, 1 day, US$60, for additional night (1-2 people); *Explorama Lodge* at Yanamono, 80 km. from Iquitos, US$230 for 3 days/2 nights and US$70 for each additional day; *Explornapo Camp* at Llachapa, 160 km. from Iquitos (better for seeing fauna), US$1,000 for 1 person, 4 nights/5 days, US$90 extra night (all prices include transfers, advance reservations, etc., local rates much lower; flight inclusive packages available from Miami on Faucett Airlines, from US$835 p.p. for 7 days). *Queens Tours*, Arica 297, 4-day trips to Amazon River camp and to Indian village, (guides don't explain much), interesting; good for flights. *Amazon Lodge Safaris*, Putumayo 165, owns the *Amazon Lodge*, clean, excellent food; special tours for fishermen, also a smaller lodge for the more adventurous. *Paseos Amazónicos Ambassador*, Putumayo 124, operates the *Amazon Sinchicuy Lodge*; they also organize visits to Lake Quistacocha and the zoo; *Jungle Amazon Inn*, about 10 km. further downstream from the *Amazon Lodge*, tour operators on ground floor of Eiffel-built house on corner of Plaza de Armas with Putumayo. *Lima Tours* offers 3 day, 2 night tours to Iquitos and the Amazon from Lima for US$250 p.p., flight included. *Amazon River Tamshiyacu Lodge*, S.A., Putumayo 184 or Los Carolinas 121, Miraflores, Lima T 476919, ask for Lucho de Cossio who runs *Tamshiyacu Lodge*, small, friendly, highly rec., swimming, jungle walks, night-time canoe rides, 1-day excursion, with lunch at the *Lodge*, US$19, 5 hrs in all; their trips include the Yarapa River Inn, Tambo Inn and wilderness expeditions; tourists are met at the airport by Sr. Pedro Alava with information. A new ornithological garden is opening at Tamshiyacu Lodge, entrance US$5. *Amazonia Expeditions*, Putumayo 139 (Paul Wright), owns Yarapa river camp near confluence of Marañón and Ucayali 140 km. from Iquitos, warmly rec., experienced guides, strong conservationist inclinations, reductions in low season (make sure sufficient food is provided, but take your own fruit, chocolate and insect repellent). *Amazon Selva Tours*, Putumayo 150, highly rec.; they use *Selva Lodge* on Río Momón, and *Yarapa Lodge*, excellent food and able guides. *Amazon Camp Tourist Service*, Putumayo 196, or 1013 S Central Ave., Glendale, CA 91204, T (818) 246-4816, (800) 423-2791 (outside CA), P.O. Box 39583, Los Angeles, CA 90039, Fax (818) 246-9909, Lodge itineraries to 42-room *Amazon Camp*, or 20-bungalow *Camp Amazonia*, cruises on M/V *Arca*, 2 days/1 night at *Amazon Camp* US$65 p.p., at *Club Amazonia* US$92, cruises start at US$295 single for 3 days, longer stays/cruises available, conscientious and efficient, rec. For those who are tough, *Amazon Adventure Tours*, Sgto. Lores 269, T 237306/237590, now run by Nathaniel Valles who speaks English, organizes survival courses in the jungle and you learn to build your own camp, find your own food etc.; US$60-100 a day for various expeditions of 5-15 days, camping equipment included, rec. but disturbing reports received of alligator hunting—make sure you work out the itinerary in advance. *Amazon Village* was opened in 1981; tours there are operated by Exprinter; for details contact Amazon Village, c/o Amazon Hotel, Iquitos, Miguel Dasso 167A, San Isidro, Lima, T 404-559. It is located on the Río Momón, some hours away from the Amazon itself, so difficult river conditions can easily prevent visits to the Amazon. At the Village there are clean, well-ventilated bungalows and good food. *Amazon Botanical Gardens*, 56 km. from Iquitos on the Amazon (PO Box 105, Jirón Tacna 516, Iquitos, Telex

91003/91002 PBPE IQT, or 4301 Main St., Suite 14, PO Box 10025, Kansas City, Mo. 64111, T 816-931-2840), 3 days, 2 nights, US$175 (or less if more than 1 person), longer stays available. El Sol, Ucayali 276, German-owner, Peter Jenson, has a jungle lodge on the Río Nanay, close to the village of Llanchama, 4 hrs. by boat from Iquitos. Arturo Díaz Ruiz, Sargento Lores 240 (registered guide no. 036) specializes in botanical tours; he is an experienced guide.

It is advisable to take a waterproof coat and shoes or light boots on such trips, and a good torch, as well as *espirales* to ward off the mosquitoes at night—they can be bought from drugstores in Iquitos. The dry season is from July to September and September is the best month to see flowers and butterflies. A recommended tour with a difference is the jungle survival excursion of Moisés Torres Viena, **Expediciones Jungle Amazónica**, Soledad 718—as taught to Peruvian soldiers—not cheap, but you will learn much about jungle botany and how to live off the plants; all the guides used are good, but the pace can be quite quick. Launches may do cruises to Leticia (Amazon Lodge Safaris have a 6-day trip to Leticia on the m/n *Adolfo*).

**Excursions** To the beach at Nanay, white sand, and small boats for hire to see the meeting of the Nanay and Amazon rivers; bus from Jr. Próspero US$0.15, boat US$0.25. By bus to the village of Santo Tomás, about 20 km., a favourite week-end retreat of inhabitants of Iquitos; the village has a good restaurant and canoes may be hired. Launches also leave Iquitos for the village of Indiana; get off at the "Varadero de Mazán" and walk through the banana plantations to the Río Mazán. A trail leads from the village of Mazán through the jungle to Indiana (hotel), about a 2-hr. walk (steamy). Catch the launch back to Iquitos at 1300.

Naturalists should note that the area 50 km. around Iquitos is too inhabited to support much large wildlife; the Napo or Ucayali rivers have more to offer. Similarly the areas around the Lodges; however there is plenty of scope for seeing small fauna and learning about the flora. Trips to see Yagua Indians offer little but a chance to see "a way of life which is not so much in transition as abandoned." (John C. O'Conor, Arlington, Va.)

**Air** International airport, Francisco Secada Vigneta, T 231501, 233094. Taxi to the airport costs US$3 (US$6 at night); *motocarro* (motorcycle with 2 seats), US$1.80; bus, US$0.20, goes to market area, about 12 blocks from Plaza de Armas, taxi from there US$1.80. Automatic 60-day visa given on arrival on international flights. Airport tax on international flights, US$10, plus US$5 security tax and US$2 municipal tax (these two must be paid on local flights). Faucett (Próspero 630, T 239195), AeroPerú (Próspero 248, T 231454) and Aerochasqui between them have at least two daily jet flights to Lima, both Faucett flights direct, one of AeroPerú's via Pucallpa or Tarapoto on alternating days, plus via Yurimaguas and Trujillo on Thur. and Sun. Iquitos-Cuzco via Lima only, No flights Iquitos-Ecuador. Faucett flies Sat. to Miami. TANS offices: Grupo 42 (for Brazil, Colombia), Sargento Lores 127, T 233512; Grupo 8 (for Lima, Trujillo, Yurimaguas and Tarapoto), Castilla 353, nr Plaza Sargento Lores; these flights are less than the cost of the commercial flights. TANS also has a flight to Cabo Pantoja and other villages. TANS to Leticia (Tabatinga), but often booked up 2 months ahead for the aquaplane. Varig/Cruzeiro has one weekly flight on Sat., at 1330, between Iquitos, Leticia (Tabatinga airport), Tefé (see **Northern Brazil**, Section 8) and Manaus. Varig/Cruzeiro office, Arica 273, T 234381; you have to disembark at Tabatinga, pay US$1 tax in cruzeiros, check luggage (which comes off the plane and goes on again), get a new boarding pass and luggage tickets, and then fight for a seat. (Mark your luggage "Iquitos" or it will be unloaded at Tabatinga.) Iquitos flights frequently delayed. (Be sure to reconfirm your flight in Iquitos, as they are often overbooked, especially over the Christmas period.) Peruvian Air Force flies Pucallpa-Iquitos, but unreliable as seats in that plane may be requisitioned at short notice, and Iquitos-Leticia. The Air Force also flies to Andoas, an oil town in the jungle, on the Río Pastaza. TANS hydroplane flies NNW along the river to Peneya, opposite Leguizamo in Colombia, or Gueppi, the military frontier post from where you can get to Puerto Asís (Colombia) by boat. On this flight, locals take precedence.

**Aircraft for Hire** Ask at airport; normal rate US$300 an hour for plane taking 5.

**Shipping** Upstream. River boats to Pucallpa (2 boats a week in rainy season), 7 days, or Yurimaguas, at least 4 days (longer if cargo is being carried, which is usually the case), cheap, but beware of overcharging to gringos; fastest boat to Yurimaguas is *Jasmin*, 4 days or so. Information on boats for Pucallpa obtained on wharves, or at Meneses (Jirón Próspero), Bellavista (Malecón Tarapacá 596), Hurtado (Av. Grau 1223) and Casa Pinto (Sargento Lores 164). Cabins are 4 berth and you have to buy both a first class ticket, which entitles you to food (whether you want it or not) and deck space to sling your hammock, and a cabin ticket if you want the "luxury" of a berth. Adequate washing and toilet facilities, but the food is rice, meat and beans (and whatever can be picked up en route) cooked in river water. Stock up on fruit and tinned food in Iquitos. There is a good cheap bar. Take plenty of prophylactic enteritis tablets; many contract dysentery on the trip. Also take insect repellant; one sold locally, called Black Flag, is not effective.

Downstream. Communications with Manaus by river are unreliable and the journey takes about 15 days (two boats doing this journey are *Clivia*, frequent, good food, and *Almirante Monteiro*, clean, reasonable food). The Hertzog boat, *Juliana*, is the most beautiful; friendly captain. Best go first to Leticia, or Islandia, opposite Tabatinga; Islandia itself is just a mud bank with an exchange shop on the Peruvian side of a narrow creek just a few yards from Benjamin Constant in Brazil. No boats from Iquitos go to Benjamin Constant, but all boats for Manaus start from there and a new hotel (*Benjamin*) has been built. Boats Iquitos-Islandia 36 hrs. (2 days in other direction). On all boats, hang your hammock away from lightbulbs (they aren't switched off at night and attract all sorts of strange insects) and away from the engines, which usually emit noxious fumes.

If a long wait is involved, then Leticia (Colombia) has the best hotels and facilities. Weekly luxury 54-passenger boat, *Río Amazonas*, plies between Iquitos and Leticia, leaves Wed., operated by Amazon Camp, Putumayo 196, Iquitos, T 233931, US$400, US$250 without facilities, for 4 days. Canoes put out from Leticia and will take off passengers from passing boats at another mud bank called Puerto Ancorade, just opposite. There are also ferries from Benjamin Constant to Tabatinga and Leticia, 1½ hrs. The *Huallaga* is highly recommended for river journeys to Leticia or Pucallpa. It is easy to find a boat, but difficult to get it to move, though you can stay on board. Details on exit and entry formalities seem to change frequently, so when leaving Peru, check in Iquitos first (Immigration, Arica 477, office hours 0900-1300); latest indications are that exit stamps are given only at Puerto Alegría, not by the Peruvian Consulate in Leticia (0830-1430—the consul is elusive), while tourist cards for entry into Peru are given at Puerto Alegría, 2 hrs. upstream from Islandia, where the boat stops for police checks. Brazilian entry formalities are in Tabatinga, in town, 2 km. from the pier, or at the airport (taxis from riverfront to airport tend to overcharge). Boats to and across frontiers carry many smugglers and thieves.

## THE INCA ROAD

*We have had great pleasure since 1979 in incorporating an account by Christopher Portway, the explorer and author, of the Andean Inca road. His most interesting book Journey along the Spine of the Andes (Oxford Illustrated Press) was published in 1984. In view of space constraints, we have therefore shortened his account here.*

Basically, there were two great roads in the Inca system. One was the royal road between Cuzco and Quito, progressively extended to take in northern Ecuador, southern Colombia, and southwards, Bolivia and northern Argentina. A mind-boggling 5,230 km. in length, its remains have been best preserved (more through remoteness than any preserving agency) in Peru. Much of the 4,050 km. of the coastal road between Tumbes and the Río Maule in Chile has been built over by the Pan-American Highway.

The standard width of the royal road varied between 5 and 6 metres (as against the 8 metres of the less-obstructed coastal road). It was unpaved, except where there was unavoidable water or when climbing steep hillsides necessitating the use of stone steps.

A good section, bordered by stone, may be seen some 13 km. east of the village of Shelby, served by the railway from La Oroya to Cerro de Pasco. Its course is marked by the lonely ruins of Bonbón, an Inca community centre only recently identified, which in turn lies close to the modern dam holding back the Río Mantaro as it flows out of the northern end of Lago de Junín.

But perhaps the most astounding survival of Inca roads is the long stretch, displaying varied construction over differing terrain, between Yanahuanca and Wari (**see page 1049**).

Yanahuanca is situated in the incredibly beautiful valley of the same name. It is rarely entered by foreigners and thus a visitor has to contend with a retinue of a hundred or more curious inhabitants in his passage through the village. Its amenities include a few bars, a simple restaurant and a community social centre, but no hotel.

Two km. up the Yanahuanca Valley a lesser valley cuts northwards between the towering crags. The road, its paving uneven and disturbed by countless horse and donkey convoys, leads up the smaller valley, its course sometimes shared by a stream, to the village of Huarautambo, a community of some 220 people, about 4 km. distant.

This village is surrounded by many pre-Inca remains and the schoolmaster, Sr. Valentín

Inga Castro, will be only too happy to show visitors the many ruins of the area, as well as the cave-tomb full of deformed skulls only recently discovered by him, a crop of cave paintings and numerous underground chambers.

For more than 150 km. the *Camino Incaico* is not only in almost continuous existence from the Yanahuanca Valley but is actually shown on the map issued by the Instituto Geográfico Militar. From Huarautambo, in company with lesser tracks, it winds up the head of the Huarautambo valley and across rock-scattered grasslands, over escarpments, following valleys, then veering away to utilize more valleys hidden by saddles over which the road triumphs even if the weary 20th-century traveller wilts along the way. At a spot known locally as Incapoyo, superb views of the Cordillera Huayhuash, with peaks soaring to 6,000 metres and more, are to be seen.

While the road fades from sight or has become muddled with present day tracks the route is marked by the ruins of *tampus*—or Inca rest houses—and, occasionally, larger sites. *Tampus* were official and utilitarian. Some of them consisted of a single structure, others had a series of smaller rooms opening on a large corral where the llamas were stabled. Each was maintained by the local *ayllu* as part of its labour tax.

Between Yanahuanca and Wari pre-Inca *tampus* and other remains provide landmarks for the road. Thereafter traces of the road become fainter though short sections can be identified in the hills behind **San Luis, Piscobamba and Pomabamba**. Behind Pomabamba, far up upon the final crest of the mountains to the west, the road is revealed by a chain of old forts older than the highway itself, but it is left to such disintegrating edifices to mark the route to Cajamarca and northwards into Ecuador.

Townships and villages along the way include the following: *Tamboccocha* and *Gashapampa*: One single shop with little to offer enlivens these two remote villages. *Pilcocancha*: A few km. north of the township of Baños, this village is notable only for its hot thermal pools lying a kilometre south. *La Unión* (**see also page 1059**): A "double town" with its main residential section across the Río Vizcarra in the sheer-sided valley of the same name. Several small hotels, simple but adequate at about US$1 per night but no hot water, a farce of a cinema and half a dozen restaurants. On the grass plateau above the town are the spectacular ruins of *Huánuco Viejo* (**see page 1059**). *Pomachaca*: A small village with a couple of shops at a road and river junction. The roads lead to Wari (*Hotel Ideal*, F), San Marcos and Llamellín. *San Luis*: A village in the shadow of the Cordillera Blanca. A few small restaurants and an occasional bus service to *Piscobamba*, with a basic, but clean hotel with friendly owner, and another, both F, and a few shops and small restaurants. The staff of the mayor's office are helpful and from behind the town views across the valley are superb. Occasional buses to *Pomabamba* (**see page 951**), a pleasant enough town. On both sides of the valley in which Pomabamba stands are pre-Inca ruins of considerable interest. *Sihuas*: A small township clinging to a hilltop. No hotel, but a couple of restaurants. *Huamachuco* (**page 967**). *Cajabamba* (**see page 968**), lively little town with a hotel or two and a number of restaurants (not to be confused with the Ecuadorean town of the same name). *Ichocán*: Pleasant village with an interesting church and a few small restaurants. The council do not object to overnight camping in the plaza with its fountain and trees. *San Marcos*: Lively little town with a hotel or two. *Cajamarca* (**page 968**).

**Warning** The Andean Inca road in the north of Peru passes through extremely remote mountain territory. Travellers are advised, therefore, to take full precautions against starvation and exposure. There is, apparently, some danger of attack by cattle rustlers and part of the area has been affected by guerrilla activity.

## INFORMATION FOR VISITORS

**Documents** No visa is necessary for citizens of Western European countries, South American countries (except Chile and Venezuela), Canada, the USA and Japan. Australians and New Zealanders must have visas. A Tourist Card (*Cédula C*, obligatory) is obtained free from the immigration authorities on arrival in Peru for visits up to 90 days (insist on getting the full 90 days, at some borders cards valid for 60, or even only 30 days have been given). It is in duplicate, the original given up on arrival and the copy on departure, and may be renewed (see below). A new tourist card must be obtained for each re-entry or when an extension is given. An International Certificate of Vaccination against smallpox is no longer required. Declaration of foreign currency no longer required. All foreigners should be able to produce on demand some recognizable means of identification, preferably a passport. You must present your passport when reserving tickets for internal, as well as, international travel. Officially, an exit ticket is required for entry into Peru to be allowed. At land frontiers, practices vary; an MCO may not be accepted as an onward ticket. One's best bet is a bus ticket Arequipa-Arica (Tepsa, valid for 6 months, sold as an onward ticket at the Ecuadorean border even though Tepsa have discontinued the route, and more expensive than Arequipa-Tacna, Tacna-Arica bus journeys) which may then be exchanged with persistence. Many travellers have reported that they have not been asked for a ticket at Aguas Verdes, Yunguyo or Desaguadero. If you do not have one on arrival at the border, you may be forced to pay US$15 minimum for an out-going bus ticket. Travellers arriving by air report no onward flight checks at Lima airport.

**N.B.** Tourist visas may be renewed for 60 days at Migraciones, Paseo de la República 585, Lima, 0900-1300 (also, we are told, in PIP offices in certain towns: check). You must present your passport, a valid return ticket to a destination outside Peru, a *solicitud* (written request for an extension) and payment of US$20 or the equivalent in intis. If you wish to extend your entry permit after 90 days have already elapsed since your entry into Peru this is possible at the discretion of the authorities, but on payment of a fine of US$20. The maximum stay in such a case would be 150 days from the first entry. If you are in the Puno area when your visa expires, it is sometimes quicker and easier to cross the border to Bolivia for a day and return with a new visa, often for 90 days, which you would not get in Lima or Cuzco. To obtain a one-year student visa one must have: proof of adequate funds, affiliation to a Peruvian body, a letter of recommendation from your own and a Peruvian Consul, a letter of moral and economic guarantee from a Peruvian citizen and 4 photographs (frontal and profile). One must also have a health check certificate which takes 4 weeks to get and costs US$10. If your tourist card is stolen or lost, apply for a new one also at Migraciones (address above); very helpful.

Students are advised to take an international student card in order to benefit from the student reductions available, especially in and around Cuzco (not as many student concessions are available as there used to be). To be any use in Peru, it must bear the owner's photograph. You can sometimes achieve benefits if "student" is on your tourist card as your occupation, but this can mean hours of haggling.

**Export Ban** No object of archaeological interest may be taken out of Peru.

**Taxes** There is a US$15 airport tax on international flight departures, payable in dollars (unless you have an Aeroflot ticket). There is a 14% tax on economy international flights originating in Peru. For non-Peruvians, there is a security tax of US$5 and an airport tax of US$3-7 (depending on the airport) on domestic flights (if you are working in Peru, carry a letter stating this and insist you are "residente" and pay local tax of US$0.20). Tax should not be charged on an MCO, but 9% often is.

**Air Services from Europe** Direct flights from Frankfurt (Lufthansa), Paris (Air France), Amsterdam (KLM), and Madrid (Iberia). Cheap flights from London; one way is to go via Madrid with Iberia, or standby to Miami, then fly with American, Ecuatoriana or AeroPerú to Lima, or Faucett to Iquitos and Lima. Setours, Jr. Unión 1011, Lima has cheap flights to Brussels fortnightly. Sobelair, the charter subsidiary of Sabena, has flights leaving Brussels Sun., 16 hrs., stopover of 1 hr. in Martinique, return Mon. Tickets available throughout Germany, France, Belgium and Holland. Aeroflot fly to Peru from Moscow via Shannon and Havana, or via Luxembourg and Havana; the flight can be joined either in Moscow, or in Shannon or Luxembourg, but it is *vital* to check that these services are in operation when you want to travel. To avoid paying Peru's 14% tax on international air tickets, take your used outward ticket with you when buying return passage.

**From USA and Canada** Miami is the main gateway to Peru with flights every day with American and AeroPerú, Third Avenue, Miami (T 800-255-7378), Ecuatoriana 3 times a week, and Faucett. Other direct flights from New York (American, Lan Chile), Los Angeles (Aerolíneas Argentinas, Varig) and Toronto (CP Air). Faucett has an office in Toronto. Ecuatoriana from Los Angeles via Quito is more expensive than other carriers, but you don't have to go via Miami (if taking AeroPéru or Faucett), you get 2 free stopovers in Quito, or, if you don't want to spend time in Quito, a free night in the *Hotel Quito*, lunch and a microbus tour of the city. Regular connections can be made from many other North American cities. AeroPerú offers a bargain, US$759 (US$999 1st class) for a round South America air pass, Miami-Miami, 45 days, plus discount flights inside Peru; can be arranged in USA, T 305-591 9420, or 800-327 7080.

**From South America** Regular flights to all South American countries; in most cases, daily. Lloyd Aéreo Boliviano (LAB) is usually the cheapest airline for flights out of Lima but tickets bought in Peru are more expensive. LAB flies twice weekly between La Paz and Cuzco. Aerolíneas Argentinas and AeroPerú fly from Mexico. Beware of buying Viasa tickets in Peru, they often turn out to be forgeries. See above for AeroPerú's "Around South America" pass.

**Trans-Pacific** Flights from Tokyo by Varig. From Australia and New Zealand to Tahiti by Air New Zealand, Qantas or UTA with a Lan-Chile connection to Lima via Santiago (stopover in Easter Island).

**Trans-South Atlantic** From South Africa to Rio de Janeiro by South African Airlines or Varig, with immediate connections.

**Duty-free Imports** 400 cigarettes or 50 cigars or 500 grams of tobacco, 2 litres of alcoholic drinks, new articles for personal use or gifts up to value US$200.

**Internal Air Services** link towns which are often far apart and can only be reached otherwise with difficulty. Virtually all the air traffic is in the hands of the Cía. de Aviación Faucett (who run bingo on board!) and AeroPerú. Aerochasqui is a new airline, based in Arequipa, with flights to and from Lima, with other internal routes to Tacna, and from Lima to Trujillo, Pucallpa, Tarapoto and Iquitos. Tickets are not interchangeable between the companies, but may be permitted in the case of cancelled flights. See under Lima (**page 939**) for towns served, and above for taxes. Internal flights are pegged to the US dollar and have 14% tax added. Faucett offers cheap unlimited travel within Peru; the ticket costs US$180 and is valid for 60 days. You must decide which places you want to go to in advance, but you don't have to go to all of them or fix the date in advance, and you must fly to Peru with Faucett and purchase the ticket outside South America. If you enter Peru with another carrier, a full airpass will cost US$250. It is possible

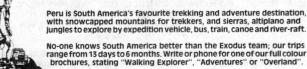

to buy AeroPerú domestic tickets more cheaply outside Peru. A minimum of three tickets costs about US$44 per flight. If you fly to Peru with AeroPerú from Miami, you are given one free internal flight and any other routes for US$50 each. If you have a choice, remember timekeeping tends to be better early a.m. than later. See note on tourist prices, below.

**N.B.** AeroPerú and Faucett are often criticized for frequent cancellations, unannounced route changes, and poor time-keeping (AeroPerú receiving worse reports than Faucett). If possible travel with hand luggage only (48 cm. x 24 cm. x 37 cm.) so there is more chance of you and your baggage arriving at the same destination. The Andean area is dangerous for flying, and unpredictable weather contributes to poor time-keeping, but companies are also criticized for their passenger service, especially as regards information and overbooking. Note that flights into the mountains may well be put forward 1 hr. if there are reports of bad weather. Neither company has enough aircraft and both are in financial difficulties. Flights to jungle regions are also unreliable. See also warning on **page 1030**.

Flights must be reconfirmed 24 hrs. in advance, but 72 hrs. is advised. Twenty mins. before departure, the clerk is allowed by law to let standby passengers board, taking the reserved seats of those who haven't turned up. AeroPerú offers senior citizen discounts (40%) but some offices may not grant them. When buying an internal flight it is better to go direct to the airline rather than use a travel agent (who may not be able to get the flight you want).

**Air Freight** (Internal) Packages must be insured and secure so rucksacks should be enveloped in a flour sack.

**Roads** The Pan-American Highway is open from Lima N along the coast (divided-lane for first 100 km.) to Ecuador (the 1983 flood damage has been almost completely repaired), and S to Arequipa and Chile. It is mostly through desert, with occasional valley oases. The Central Highway from Lima goes through La Oroya NE to Cerro de Pasco, Huánuco, Tingo María and terminates at Pucallpa on the Ucayali River (paved much of the way, but interrupted by mud-slides in the Huallaga valley). From La Oroya a good road goes SE to Huancayo, and on (not good) to Ayacucho, Cuzco, Puno on Lake Titicaca, and into Bolivia. The Puno-Bolivia stretch is now almost entirely paved. The two roads to Cuzco, one by the Central Andes and the other by Arequipa and Puno, make a most spectacular circuit of 2,400 km. possible. Preferably it should be done clockwise: there would be less driving on the outsides of precipices; it would be downhill on the poor stretch between Puno and Arequipa, and the return to Lima would be by a good road. Another road from Lima to the Sierra branches off the Lima-La Oroya highway at Chosica; it goes along the Río Santa Eulalia and joins the road from La Oroya to Cerro de Pasco just beyond Marcapomacocha. (This road is spectacular, but is mainly used for local access; it is not recommended for long-distance driving.) Most of the high Sierra roads are narrow, unsurfaced and liable to landslides; many accidents. Do not drive fast at night; many local vehicles have poor lights. Be sure to check with the Peruvian Touring and Automobile Club regarding road conditions before driving in the Sierra.

Few roads in Peru, except for the Pan-American and Central Highways and the roads connecting Huaraz and Carás with Pativilca, and Pacasmayo with Cajamarca, are paved. Paving of the important Puno-Desaguadero road to Bolivia is now complete. Toll roads in Peru include Aguas Verdes-Tumbes, Pativilca-Huarás, Lima-Pucusana, Ica-Nazca, Lima (highway around city), Variante-Pacasmayo, which vary from US$0.15 (for the roads around Cuzco), to US$0.25 for most others. Landslides are frequent, surfaces are usually very rough, and this makes for slow travel and frequent breakdowns.

**Buses** Services along the coast and to Arequipa (best is Ormeño) are usually quite good; buses in the mountain areas generally are small, old, crowded and offer little comfort; Ormeño and Cruz del Sur thought generally to be the best. For long journey take a water bottle. Blankets and emergency food are a *must* in the mountains. Always possible to buy food on the roadside, as buses stop frequently. If your bus breaks down and you are transferred to another line and have to pay extra, keep your original ticket for refund from the first company. If possible, on country buses avoid the back seats because of the bumpiness, and the left side because of exhaust fumes. Colectivos not always much dearer; trucks not always much cheaper; they charge ¾ bus fare, but wholly unpredictable, not for long hops, and comfort depends on the load: the ideal is a half load of sugar, or a cargo of arguardiente containers (rubber sacks made of old inner tubes—like a waterbed in compartments, with a "happy smell" if they seep, Daniel Morgan). Colectivos go almost anywhere in Peru; most firms have offices. Book one day in advance. They pick you up at your hotel or in main square. Always try to arrive at your destination in daylight: much safer.

**Note** In the preparation of this edition, it has been impossible to verify bus, or other transport schedules with any accuracy. Shortages of spare parts and disruption of services by guerrilla action has resulted in conflicting reports of timetables. While transport prices rose steeply after August 1990, fluctuations owing to exchange rate variations and demand for tickets persist. Consequently, fares may have changed greatly by the time this edition is in use. We hope that travellers will bear with us while unstable conditions exist in Peru.

**Motoring** The Touring y Automóvil Club del Perú, Av. César Vallejo 699, Lince, Lima (T 403270), with offices in most provincial cities, gives news about the roads and hotels along the way (although for the most up-to-date information try the bus and colectivo offices). It sells a very good road map at US$2.25 (Mapa Vial del Perú, 1:3,000,000, Ed. 1980, reliable information about road conditions) and route maps covering most of Peru at US$0.40 (Hoja de Ruta, detail maps 1:1,000,000, very good but no information on road conditions). AAA maps sold at *Lima Times* office. Buy maps separately or in packages of 8. Cuadernos de Viaje are travel notebooks covering all Peru with valuable information and maps, in Spanish. Other maps can be bought from street vendors in Colmena and Plaza San Martín, Lima. "Westermanns Monatshefte; folio Ecuador, Peru, Bolivien" has excellent maps of Peru, especially the archaeological sites. Gasoline is sold as: "extra" (84 octane), and "importada" (95 octane), found in Lima, the coastal towns and Arequipa. Gasoline is cheaper in the Selva. In Lima never trust the green light; Peruvian drivers tend to regard traffic lights as recommendations, at most. When parking remove detachable accessories and screen wipers. No-parking signs are painted at the roadside: illegally parked cars are towed away.

Roads go to very high altitudes in Peru—make sure that the spark is properly adjusted and consider use of smaller carburettor jets if driving much at altitude. Avoid mountain travel between November and April. Take 2 planks of wood in case car gets stuck in soft soil when allowing other vehicles to pass. Never travel off the main roads without being self-sufficient. Always make sure your fuel tank is full when branching off a major highway, fill up whenever possible and make sure you do not receive diesel or kerosene. If you need mechanical assistance in the mountains ask for the nearest mining or road construction camp. If you take your own car you are immediately a symbol of wealth and will be liable to have it broken into. Disadvantages of travelling in your own vehicle include the difficulties of getting insurance, theft, finding guarded parking lots, maintenance on appalling roads and nervous exhaustion, which may outweigh the advantages of mobility and independence.

Imported car spares available and cheaper than in neighbouring countries. Makes with well-established dealerships are easiest to obtain (e.g. Volvo, Peugeot, VW). VW Beetles, Toyota Coronas and Datsun Stanzas are assembled in Peru and therefore easier to get spares and service for. There is also a booming black market in motor parts involving both contraband and stolen parts.

Must have international driving licence—especially with a number. If you don't have a number on your licence, improvise. (It has been reported that a UK driving licence is acceptable.) A 90-day transit permit for vehicles is available at land borders without a *carnet de passages*, contrary to what officials may tell you. The minimum age for renting a car is 25.

**Note for Hitch-Hikers** Hitch-hiking is difficult. Freight traffic has to stop at the police *garitas* outside each town and these are the best places to try (also, toll points, but these are further from towns). Drivers usually ask for money but don't always expect to get it. In mountain and jungle areas you usually have to pay drivers of lorries, vans and even private cars; ask the driver first how much he is going to charge, and then recheck with the locals (the Sierra Indians for whom it is normal method of travel). Private cars are very few and far between. Readers report that mining trucks are especially dirty to travel in, avoid if possible.

**Taxis** In most places taxi fares are fixed before the journey; therefore it is best to ask local advice on average charges before you bargain with taxi drivers. Taxis ordered at hotels are much more expensive than those hailed on the streets.

**Railways** There are passenger services on the following lines, which are often quicker and more comfortable than buses, though it is necessary to watch your belongings: Lima-La Oroya-Huancayo, La Oroya-Cerro de Pasco, Huancayo- Huancavelica, Arequipa-Juliaca-Puno, Puno-Juliaca-Cuzco, and Cuzco-Machu Picchu-Quillabamba. Details of services in the text. Good cheap meals are usually serviced on trains.

**Walking** Serious walkers are advised to get *Backpacking in Peru and Bolivia*, by Hilary Bradt which describes 3-5 day treks in the Cordilleras Blanca, Vilcabamba and Vilcanota (Cuzco region), and in the Cajamarca area. *The Peruvian Andes*, by Philipe Béaud, is a good guide, describing 100 climbs and 40 treks in Spanish, French and English; available at South American Explorers' Club. John Richter's *Yurak Yunka* can be obtained from the South American Explorers' Club or from *Lima 2000* bookshop, J. Bernal 271, Lima. Rob Rachowiecki's *Peru, a Travel Survival Guide*, has been recommended most warmly. For Charles Brod, *Apus and Incas*, see Cuzco, **Tourist Office** section.

When trekking, please do not drop litter; if you have the inclination, pick up that left by others.

**Hotels** The State Tourist Hotels (commonly known as *Hoteles de Turistas*) are run by Enturperú. They vary considerably but frequently offer the best accommodation in town in terms of cleanliness and reliable food. They provide safe garaging for cars at US$0.65 a night. Reservations can be made at Enturperú, Av. Javier Prado-Oeste 1358, San Isidro, P.O. Box 4475, Lima, T 287815, 282742, 274077, Telex: 20394.

Heating in rooms is often unsatisfactory. Good local maps can usually be obtained at the Tourist Hotels; in some of the smaller towns they function as tourist offices. All de luxe, 1st class and State Tourist Hotels charge a high 25% in taxes, which includes service charges; lower category hotels charge 20-23%. Most hotels have this surcharge included in their prices, but best check first. By law all places that offer accommodation now have a plaque outside bearing the letters H (Hotel), Hs (Hostal), HR (Hotel Residencial) or P (Pensión) according to type. A hotel has 51 rooms or more, a hostal 50 or fewer; the categories do not describe quality or facilities. Many hotels have safe parking for motor cycles. Check all bills most carefully. Bargaining is possible outside the peak July-August holiday season; all hotels seem to be crowded at the end of July, Independence celebrations. It should be noted, even in the upper categories, that in general hotel standards are low. Also reception areas may be misleading; it is a good idea to see the room before booking. When booking a hotel from an airport, or station by phone, always talk to the hotel yourself; do not let anyone do it for you (except an accredited hotel booking service). You will be told the hotel of your choice is full and be directed to a more expensive one. Information on youth hostels and student accommodation can be obtained from INTEJ, Av. San Martín 240, Barranco, Lima.

**Note** The Peruvian police seem to be sensitive about finding an unmarried Peruvian woman in a foreigner's hotel room after 1900 hours. They will charge her with prostitution, however innocent your intentions. (Non-Peruvian unmarried couples will not be bothered by the police.)

**Camping** Easy in Peru, especially along the coast. But following a number of attacks in the Andes on campers, it is not wise to camp in lonely places. Camping gas in little blue bottles is available in Lima, see under **Camping** in that section. Those with stoves designed for lead-free gasoline should use *ron de quemar*, available from hardware shops (*ferreterías*). White gas is called *bencina*, also available from hardware stores.

**Food** The high-class hotels and restaurants serve international food and, on demand, some native dishes, but the taverns (*chicherías*) and the local restaurants (*picanterías*) supply the highly seasoned native food at its best. It is generally found that the modest cafés are best value. Soups tend to be very good, and a meal in themselves. In the Lima area the most popular fish dishes are the *cebiche*—raw fish, seasoned with lemons, onions and red peppers (see **Health** below); the *escabeche*—fish with onions, hot green pepper, red peppers, prawns (*langostinos*), cumin, hard eggs, olives, and sprinkled with cheese; and *chupe de camarones*, a shrimp stew made with varying and somewhat surprising ingredients. *Parihuela* is a popular bouillabaisse which includes *yuyo de mar*, a tangy seaweed. *Yacu-chupe*, or green soup, has a basis of potato, with cheese, garlic, coriander leaves, parsley, peppers, eggs, onions, and mint. *Causa* and *carapulca* are two good potato dishes; *causa* is made with yellow potatoes, lemons, pepper, hard-boiled eggs, olives, lettuce, sweet cooked corn, sweet cooked potato, fresh cheese, and served with onion sauce. Favourite meat dishes are *ollucos con charque* (a kind of potato with dried meat), *caucau*, made with tripe, potatoes, peppers, and parsley and served with rice; *anticuchos*, hearts of beef with garlic, peppers, cumin seeds and vinegar; *estofado de carne*, a stew which often contains wine; *carne en adobo*, a cut and seasoned steak; *fritos*, fried pork, usually eaten in the morning; *sancochado*, meat and all kinds of vegetables stewed together and seasoned with ground garlic; *lomo a la huancaína*, beef with egg and cheese sauce; *lomo saltado* is a beef stew with onions, vinegar, ginger, chilli, tomatoes and fried potatoes, served with rice; and *sopa a la criolla* containing thin noodles, beef heart, bits of egg and vegetables and pleasantly spiced. Any dish described as *arequipeño* can be expected to be hot and spicy. *Mondonguito* is a boiled small intestine. The best beef is imported from Argentina and is expensive. Duck is excellent. For snacks, Peruvian *empanadas* are good. *Palta rellena* is avocado filled with chicken salad.

Among the desserts and confections are *cocada al horno*—coconut, with yolk of egg, sesame seed, wine and butter; *picarones*—frittered cassava flour and eggs fried in fat and served with honey; *mazamorra morada*—purple maize, sweet potato starch, lemons, various dried fruits, sticks of ground cinnamon and cloves and perfumed pepper; *manjar blanco*—milk, sugar and eggs; *maná*—an almond paste with eggs, vanilla and milk; *alfajores*—shortbread biscuit with *manjar blanco*, pineapple, peanuts, etc.; *pastellillos*— yucas with sweet potato, sugar and anise fried in fat and powdered with sugar and served hot; and *zango de pasas*, made with maize, syrup, raisins and sugar. *Turrón*, the Lima nougat, is worth trying. *Tejas* are sugar candies wrapped in wax paper; the pecan-flavoured ones are tastiest. The various Peruvian fruits are of good quality: they include bananas, the citrus fruits, pineapples, dates, avocados (*paltas*), eggfruit (*lúcuma*), the custard apple (*chirimoya*) which can be as big as your head, quince, *papaya*, mango, guava, the passion-fruit (*maracuyá*) and the soursop (*guanábana*).

The tea hour starts about 1800 at the good hotels. If asked to a party ask the hostess what time you are *really* expected unless the time is specified on the invitation card as *hora inglesa*—English time; Peruvians tend to ask guests for dinner at 2000, but don't expect them till at least 2130.

A normal lunch or dinner costs US$5-8, but can go up to about US$60 in a first-class restaurant, with drinks and wine included. Lunch is the main meal: dinner in restaurants is normally about 1900 onwards, but choice may be more limited than lunchtime. There are plenty of cheap and good restaurants around the centre of Lima and most offer a "business lunch" called *menú fijo* for US$3 for a 3-course meal. There are many Chinese restaurants (*chifas*) in Peru which serve good food at reasonable prices. For really economically-minded people the *Comedores Nacionales* in most cities of Peru offer a standard 3-course meal US$1.50. Meals at this price, or little more, can be found under name of *menú económico* at many restaurants throughout Peru.

**Drinks** The usual international drinks with several very good local ones: *pisco*, a brandy made in the Ica valley, from which pisco sour is made; *chilcano*, a longer refreshing drink also made with *guinda*, a local cherry brandy; and *algarrobina*, a sweet cocktail made with the syrup from the bark of the carob tree, egg whites, milk, pisco and cinnamon. Wine is acidic and not very good, the best of a poor lot are the Ica wines Tacama and Ocucaje; both come in red, white and rosé, sweet and dry varieties. Tacama blancs de blancs and brut champagne have been recommended, also Gran Tinto Reserva Especial. Viña Santo Tomás, from Chincha, is reasonable and cheap. Casapalca is not recommended. Beer is best in lager and porter types, especially the Cuzco and Arequipa brands (lager) and Trujillo Malta (porter). In Lima only Cristal and Pilsener (not related to true Pilsen) are readily available, others have to be sought out. *Chicha de jora* is a maize beer, usually homemade and not easy to come by, refreshing but strong, and *chicha morada* is a soft drink made with purple maize. Coffee is often brought to the table in a small jug accompanied by a mug of hot water to which you add the coffee essence. If you want coffee with milk, a mug of milk is brought. There are many different kinds of herb tea: the commonest are *manzanilla* and *hierbaluisa*.

**Tips** Hotel 10% in addition to the 10% on the bill. Restaurants: medium to luxury class 5% in addition to bill which includes tax and 10% service unless otherwise stated. Taxi drivers, none (in fact, bargain the price down, then pay extra for good service if you get it). Cloakroom attendants and hairdressers (very high class only), US$0.50-$1. Railway porters, US$0.15 per bag, according to distance carried. Airport porters, US$0.50, or US$1 for 8 bags or more. Note: anyone who as much as touches your bag will expect a tip. Usherettes, none. Car wash boys, US$0.25, car "watch" boys, US$0.10.

**Security** The following notes reflect the many comments we have received on the need to take special precautions when travelling in Peru. This should not hide the fact that the most Peruvians, particularly outside those areas affected by crime or terrorism, are hospitable and helpful.

Thieves are active in markets, streets, hotels, buses and trains, choosing especially tourists as their targets. The most common method of attack is bag-slashing. Take care everywhere, but especially when arriving in or leaving from a town at night by bus or train; in fact, it is better to travel by day whenever possible. For general hints on avoiding crime, please see the **Security** section at the beginning of the book. All the suggestions given there are valid for Peru. Avoid staying in hotels too near to bus companies, as drivers who stay overnight are sometimes in league with thieves; avoid restaurants near bus terminals if you have all your luggage with you, it is hard to keep an eye on all your gear when eating. On trains, one large bag is easier to watch, and lock to a rack, than lots of small ones. If alone, try to avoid walking around in the cities with a big backpack; take a taxi (look on it as an insurance policy). The police presence in Lima, Arequipa, Puno and Cuzco has been greatly stepped up. It is a good idea to inform your Embassy in Lima of your passport data (or leave a photocopy), so that if the passport is stolen delays for replacement are minimized. In general, common sense is the best policy. Keep yourself fully informed, before going and while travelling: seek advice from others at all times (fellow travellers, your consulate, The South American Explorers Club, who issue a pamphlet entitled "How Not to Get Robbed in Peru", Foptur, etc.). Outside the July-August peak holiday period, there is less tension, less risk of crime, and more friendliness. A friendly attitude on your part, smiling even when you've thwarted a thief's attempt, can help you out of trouble. In addition, do not be discourteous to officials.

Although certain illegal drugs are readily available anyone carrying any is almost automatically assumed to be a drug trafficker. If arrested on any charge the wait for trial in prison can take a year and is particularly unpleasant. Unfortunately, we have received reports of drug-planting, or mere accusation of drug-trafficking by the PIP on foreigners in Lima, with US$500 demanded for release. If you are asked by the narcotics police to go to the toilets to have your bags searched, insist on taking a witness. **Drugs use or purchase is punishable by up to 15 years' imprisonment**.

Tricks employed to get foreigners into trouble over drugs include slipping a packet of cocaine into the money you are exchanging, being invited to a party or somewhere involving a taxi ride, or simply being asked on the street if you want to buy cocaine. In all cases, a plain clothes "policeman" will discover the planted cocaine, in your money, at your feet in the taxi, and will ask to see your passport and money. He will then return them, minus a large part of your cash. Do not get into a taxi, do not show your money, and try not to be intimidated.

**Another Warning** The activities of the guerrilla movements, Sendero Luminoso and Túpac Amaru (MRTA), are spreading. Avoid visiting places where they are reported as particularly active: they have no love for foreign tourists. Since Sendero Luminoso has been linked (supposedly) with the drugs trade, police and army searches have increased. Under state of siege legislation, be careful what you photograph. If possible carry an official letter stating your business. At times provinces are under martial law: a curfew (*toque de queda*) may be imposed; remember to make enquiries about this when you arrive in a new place. The following Departments are, or have recently been, under state of emergency: Ancash, Apurímac, Arequipa, Ayacucho, Huancavelica, Huánuco, Junín, Pasco, San Martín and Ucayalí, also the provinces of Lima, Yauyos and Huarochiri in the Department of Lima, the province of Callao, the province of Contamaná in Loreto. Do not enter the slums of any major city, nor of the river valley towns on the coast. As a general rule, do not travel alone and, outside the main centres, go as a group if possible. When travelling on buses in the mountains, there is the likelihood of the transport being stopped, either by guerrillas or by *comités* of villagers who will ask for "donations"; do not refuse to give. For up-to-date information, contact the Tourist Police in Lima (T 714579), the South American Explorers Club (address in Lima and Quito, Ecuador sections), or your Embassy or Consulate. The Country Officer for Peru, Office of Andean Affairs, Dept. of State, Washington D.C. 20520, T 202-632-3360, will inform US citizens on the advisability of travel.

**Police Action** If your belongings are stolen: (1) If the value is over US$20, go to PIP International Police (ask for the *Extranjería* section if you encounter difficulties, the *comandante* or his second-in-command), if under US$20 go to the Guardia Civil. Alternatively, in Lima and other tourist centres, one can go to the Tourist Police. (2) Always make declaration of loss as soon as possible. (3) Obtain *papel sellado* (stamped paper) from the Tourist Police, or buy it from Banco de la Nación, on which to make statement. A small inducement, say US$1, may help them to speed up the documentation process. See also under Cuzco, **page 1027**. If you are robbed on a journey and want to obtain a *denuncia* for insurance purposes and for clearance from the authorities if you have a new passport after the original has been stolen, say you were robbed when the bus or train was moving. If it was standing at a bus stop or station at the time the offence was committed, you will be sent back to that particular place to make the *denuncia*, and that might be very inconvenient.

A *denuncia*—a statement of a theft signed by police—is valid in place of a student card if student card is taken, and is essential for insurance purposes and for clearance from the authorities if you have a new passport after the original has been stolen. If your American Express credit card is stolen apply immediately to American Express in your own country, or to Lima Tours in Lima or Cuzco. For other credit cards, there is now a combined office in Lima, T 461545 (day and night service).

**Health** Following the outbreak of cholera in Peru in 1991, visitors are advised to take precautions while travelling: be very careful with personal hygiene and most cautious over drinking water and food. Don't eat raw fish dishes and ground-growing fruit and vegetables. Seek medical advice before going. Drinking water from the tap is generally not safe in the cities of Peru, but bottled water is available everywhere. Ask for drinks "sin hielo" (without ice) as the ice is likely to be made with ordinary tap water. Salads washed in tap water should be treated with caution on arrival in the country, but once accustomed, you are not likely to get "Inca Quickstep" from salads. Food at better hotels and restaurants is fine, even salads, but watch out for the typical dishes seasoned with highly spiced Peruvian peppers. In cases of diarrhoea, take "Colitina", an effective local remedy. Another recommended anti-diahorrea remedy is Donafan F, available without prescription. There are frequent outbreaks of typhoid in Lima and in many other parts of Peru. Outbreaks of virus hepatitis occur and can be protected against by taking immunoglobulins; be careful when eating in markets. Be careful about buying gamma globulin in Peru as most pharmacists do not keep it under refrigeration, rendering it valueless. Buy a disposable syringe for US$0.25 to obviate risk of hepatitis from the clinic or doctor's needle. In Lima, there is a Centro de Antirabia if you are unfortunate enough to be bitten by a rabid dog; in other cities, hospitals give anti-rabies injections. Because of a TB epidemic, avoid non-pasteurized dairy products.

Altitude is often a problem in the mountain cities. Also, when walking at high altitude, the body needs sugar, which can be carried conveniently in the form of a block of crystallized pure cane sugar, called *chancaca*, and easily found in markets. Tonopan has been recommended for altitude sickness and headaches. (See also **Health Information** at front of book.)

Tampons are very difficult to obtain and when available are expensive.

**Best Time to Visit** The coast is at its most agreeable from December to April inclusive, but this is the period when most rain falls in the Sierra. Business is more active later, but climate does not interfere much with business. During the cooler months, June to November, there is little or no rain but Lima's humidity is from 90 to 98%—and there is little sunshine from Paramonga S to Arica. During this period the temperature rarely falls below 13˚C, or rises above 27˚C. For the high Sierra heavier clothing should be taken—difference between day and night temperatures is great. The jungles beyond are tropical.

**N.B.** Between mid-July and mid-September, a great many Europeans go to Peru on holiday (also, many young Peruvians are on holiday in July and the first half of August), so it is better to avoid the country at this time: prices rise, transport is difficult, and the Peruvians tend to be less friendly.

**Hours of Business** *Shops*: Jan. to March, 0900-1230 and 1600-1900 (0930-1245, 1615-1900 in Lima). Rest of year: 0900-1230, 1530-1900. Some are closed on Sat.; many close later in the evening. *Banks*: Jan. to March, 0830-1130. Rest of year: 0830-1200 (some have introduced afternoon opening). Closed Sat. **N.B.** All banks close on June 30 and December 31 for balancing; if it falls on Sat. or Sun., banks may close one day before or after. *Offices*: Jan. to March, 0830-1130, and 1500-1830. Rest of year: 0830-1230 and 1500-1830. Many now work a through day, 0800-1500, and most close on Sat. *Government Offices*: Jan. to March, 0930-1130, Sat. 0900-1130. Rest of year: 0930-1100, 1500-1700; on Sat. 0930-1130.

British business travellers are strongly advised to get "Hints to Exporters: Peru", from Export Services Division, Department of Trade, Sanctuary Buildings, Great Smith St., London SW1P 3DB.

**Public Holidays** 1 January: New Year. March or April: Maundy Thursday (pm). Good Friday.

1 May: Labour Day. 29 June: Saints Peter and Paul. 28, 29 July: Independence (when all prices go up). 30 August: Santa Rosa de Lima. 8 October: Battle of Angamos. 1 November: All Saints. 8 December: Immaculate Conception. 25 December: Christmas.

**N.B.** Everything closes on New Year's Eve, Christmas Eve, and other holidays designated "family holidays", especially July-August. At these times, expect prices to rise.

**Time Zone** 5 hours behind GMT, except January to April, when GMT -4 (exact date of clock change varies annually).

**Currency** On 1 January 1986, the sol was replaced by the inti (I), worth 1,000 soles. However, the inti itself was due to be replaced by a new sol on 1 July 1991. The inti is divided into 100 céntimos. No coins are in use. Notes are of 5,000, 10,000, 50,000, 100,000, 500,000, 1,00,000 and 5,000,000 intis (a few 10,000 and 50,000 sol notes may still be in circulation).

**Warning** We have been informed that a large number of forged notes (including US$50 and US$100 bills) are in circulation; check the numbers if possible, and hold notes up to the light to inspect the blank white space for silhouette portrait. We have also been told that there is a shortage of change in museums, post offices, railway stations and even shops, while taxi drivers are notorious in this regard—one is simply told "no change".

**Foreign Exchange** Owing to high inflation and devaluation of the inti, it is now recommended to change small amounts of money daily, and ask for smaller denomination notes to avoid the "no change" problem, above. All banks change foreign currency at the official rate. They close Sat., Sun., holidays, and 30 June and 31 December for balancing the books, except that the Jorge Chávez Airport branch is open 24 hrs. every day of the year. Always count your money in the presence of the cashier, particularly the "pre-counted" bundles of notes. It is possible to have US$ or DM sent from your home country. Take the cheque to the Banco de la Nación and ask for a *liquidación por canje de moneda extranjera*. You will be charged 1% commission in US$ or intis. The main hotels and other banks (main branch only in any city) are now allowed to exchange foreign currencies; however, hotels usually only provide this service for their guests, and many commercial banks charge 4% -5% commission. The services of the Banco de Crédito have been repeatedly recommended. US dollars are the most useful currency (take some small bills), but Deutsche marks can be negotiated in all large towns; other currencies carry high commission fees. *Casas de cambio* exchange travellers' cheques for cash dollars, usually at 5% commission, and are the safest places for changing dollars into intis. Banks and *casas de cambio* will change travellers' cheques into intis or dollars, but policies change frequently, so check to see which gives the best rate. Generally a commission of 3-5% is charged on travellers' cheques. For changing small amounts of dollars cash, the street changers give the best rates, but they also employ many ruses to give you a bad deal (check your intis before handing over your dollars, check their calculators, etc., and don't change money in crowded areas). The parallel market rate, now formally illegal but very much alive, is used by street money changers in the main centres, although 10% commission (2-3% in Lima) may be charged on travellers' cheques. With rapid changes in currency exchange rates, there are occasions when the street rate offers little advantage. Street changers usually congregate near an office where the exchange "wholesaler" operates; he will probably be offering better rates than on the street.

The Banco de la Nación at Lima airport, and at large towns near the frontier, will repurchase intis from departing travellers if you can produce official exchange slips; you will not be able to buy dollars at the frontier itself.

American Express state that they will sell travellers' cheques and give out emergency money, but only in Lima. Travel agents are allowed to accept foreign currencies in payment for their services, and to exchange small amounts. Outside Lima, Arequipa and Cuzco changing travellers' cheques can be a long, slow process and a photocopy of your passport may be required. Travellers have reported great difficulty in cashing travellers' cheques in the jungle area, even Iquitos, and other remote areas. Always sign travellers' cheques in blue or black ink or ballpen. There may be shortages of cash for changing travellers' cheques.

**Credit Cards** Visa (most common), Diners Club, and Mastercharge (Access/Eurocard) widely accepted, including at State Tourist Hotels; billed, of course, at the disadvantageous official rate, plus an 8% commission. Visa is accepted at Banco de Crédito, at better rates than for travellers' cheques and cash can be withdrawn—local currency only—at no commission, in most cities. Some shops only accept cards issued in Peru or South America, and we are told that in Puno it is virtually impossible to use any type of credit card.

**Cost of Living** Living costs in the provinces are from 10 to 20% below those of Lima. Since August 1990, when prices were increased steeply by the government, Peru has become expensive for the tourist, especially for those on a tight budget. For low and middle-income Peruvians, prices of many items are beyond their reach. In early 1991 the South American Explorers Club estimated a budget of US$25-30 a day for living comfortably, with US$10-15 a day for travel. Hotel prices compare very favourably with those in other Latin American countries, ranging from US$3 to US$50. For meal prices, see **Food** above.

**Tourist Prices** In 1989, in response to declining tourist numbers, taxes on tourism were increased so that foreigners had to pay far more than Peruvians for internal flights, museums and archaeological sites. This unpopular move led visitors to boycott some places, for instance Machu Picchu. Only foreigners working in Peru, and in possession of a Green Card/work permit were able to get reductions in hotels, etc., and (with some brazenness) on flights. Still true in 1990, with a few complaints, but more people sympathize with the mass of Peruvians who cannot even afford the local prices.

The **metric system** of weights and measures is compulsory.

**Electric Current** 220 volts A.C., 60 cycles throughout the country, except Arequipa (50 cycles).

**Mail** Sending parcels abroad must be done at Centro de Clasificación de Correos, Tomás Valle, block 600, Lima (take bus 128, direction San Germán). Staff in the post office help with all checking and then sew parcels into sacks for US$1. To avoid paying a tax of US$0.20 per kg. on parcels sent abroad, take your passport and onward ticket, plus a photocopy of each to the post office. Better still, take your parcels to another country for mailing home; it will almost certainly be cheaper. Try not to have articles sent by post to Peru; pilfering is very serious. Strikes are also very common. For US$0.50 extra letters can be sent "con certificado", which is recommended.

**Telephones** Overseas calls cost on average US$6 per minute. Collect calls can now be made (most of the time) to North America and Europe (but not Switzerland or Denmark) at the Entel offices. The best place to try is Lima. A *rin* (token/*ficha*) for an international call costs US$5 and lasts for about 35 seconds; it can only be bought at an Entel office. Similarly, a *rin* for a long-distance domestic call costs US$0.50, for 1½ mins., only at an Entel office. Public phone boxes are for local calls only; a *rin* costs US$0.10 from street vendors. Telephone directories found in most hotel rooms have a useful map of Lima and show itineraries of the buses. Fax and telex abroad can be sent from major Entel offices, US$6 per page, per minute.

**The Press** Lima has 8 morning papers: *La Prensa, El Comercio* (good international news), *La República* (liberal-left) *La Crónica, Expreso, Ojo, El Diario, La Actualidad* . There is a weekly paper in English, the *Lima Times*, and a monthly economic and political report, the *Andean Report*. The main provincial cities have at least one newspaper each.

**Sports** Association football is the most popular. Basketball and other sports are also played on the coast, particularly around Lima and Callao. Golf clubs and racecourses are mentioned in the text. Riding is a favourite recreation in the Sierra, where horses can be hired at reasonable rates. Cricket is played at the Lima Cricket Club. Bullfights and cockfights are held in Lima. There is excellent deep-sea fishing off Ancón, N of Lima, and at the small port of Cabo Blanco, N of Talara (see text). In that part of the Andes easily reached from La Oroya, the lakes and streams have been stocked with trout, and fly fishing is quite good.

For details about the best rainbow trout fishing in Peru (near Juliaca and in Lakes Arapa and Titicaca) write to Sr. José Bernal Paredes, Casilla 874, Arequipa.

**Swimming** Between December and April the entire coast of Peru offers good bathing, but during the rest of the year only the northern beaches near Tumbes provide pleasantly warm water.There are many bathing resorts near Lima (do not swim at, or even visit, these beaches alone).

**Language** Spanish. Quechua, the language of the Inca empire, has been given some official status; it is spoken by millions of Sierra Indians who have little or no knowledge of Spanish. Another important Indian language is Aymará, used in the area around Lake Titicaca.

**Tourist Information** The Fondo de Promoción Turística (Foptur), at Av. Andrés Reyes 320, San Isidro, Lima, T 70 0781, has offices in the main cities of tourist interest: details in text. See also information under Lima, **page 936.** A new book of photographs of Peru was published by Aston Publications in May 1990.

We are deeply grateful to Huw Clough and Kate Hennessy for updating this chapter. For new information on Peru we should like to thank Petra Schepens (South American Explorers Club, Lima), James Vreeland (Indiana Tours, Chichlayo), and the following residents and travellers: Ace and Laurie (Salem, O.R., U.S.A.), Ralph Arnold (Vegreville, Canada), Arno Michael Auer (Ottobrunn), Steven Avgort and Carol Seger (California), Tobias Banaschewski, Anne Heintel and Klaus Knobel (Marburg, Germany) Petra Bell and Hans-Georg Henle (Schwaigern, Germany), Matthew Bell (Market Lavington, Wiltshire), Riemer De Boer (Netherlands) Andreas Böttner and Annette Drinkuth (Otterstedt, Germany), Klaus Brandl (Rio de Janeiro, Brazil), Paul Carter (Hamilton, New Zealand) and Vivienne Mitchell (Coleraine, N. Ireland), Pamela Caunt and Bob Brass (London N1), Tim Cobb (Dorking) and Caroline Wren (Conisbrough), Andrew Craig (Arlington, East Sussex), Bryan Crawford (Invernesshire, Scotland), Andrea Cujnik (München, Germany), Alastair and Ann Cuthbert (Broome, W. Australia), Stewart Dallos (Fremantle, W. Australia), Dr. Tony Daniels (Coton, Salop), Christian Deutsch (Gümligen, Switzerland), Gerd Diehl (Lima), Louise Dionne (St. John's, Newfoundland), Nelle Driessen (Maastricht, Netherlands), Holger Eberhardt (Wesel, Germany), Wolfgang Eder (München, Germany), Kirsten Eichhorn (München, Germany), Dr Brian Elce (London WC1), Richard Everson and Jo Penty (West Wickham, Kent), Daniel Ezekiel (Vancouver, BC), Paul Francescutti (CKCO-TV, Kitchener, Ontario), Nicholas J. Gardner (Loughborough, UK), Walter Gebhardt (Erlangen), Yves Genier (Louay, Switzerland), Gerhard J. (Santiago), Theodor A. Gevert (São Paulo), Michael S. Gonin (Canberra), Pilou Grenié (Antibes), Eric Hamovitch (Montréal, Canada), Ulrich Harlan (Berlin), Martin Hautkappe (München, Germany), Peter Hazdra (Vienna), Nell Henderson (Lima, Peru), Ian Henderson (London SW16), Ulrich Herbert (Stuttgart), Gert Jan Hof and Yvonne Evers (Huissen, Neth), Sabine Imhoff (Germany), Helma Jansen (Apeldoorn, Holland), Anne Toft Johnsen (Frederiksberg, Denmark), B.D. Jones (London SW14), A. P. Kirk (Middlesbrough), Ursula Kohlendorfer (Gunskirchen, Austria), Ulrike Krauss (Edinburgh), Andreas Kühn (Germany), Lena and Lars Kylberg (Lidingö, Sweden), Dr. Judith Kuriansky (New York), Christina Kuseffsky (Stockholm), Christina Kusoffsky (Stockholm, Sweden), John Lewis (London NW2), Reni Lindauer and Hugo Wey (São Paulo), Judith Locher (Switzerland), Markus Maier and Gitte Wiedmann (Zürich), Susan Marfield (Long Beach, California), Julianne McCabe, Maggie Widow, Jean O'Leary and Bill Shaffer (San Anselmo, C.A.), Gemma McGrath (London N8), Mariann Metzer and Andrea Stark (Germany), Patrick Meyer (Ammerschwihr, France), Alison Milner and Keith Doyle (Manchester), Charles B. Motley (Orlando, FL), Monica Napper (Eastbourne, UK), Asbjørn Nielsen (Denmark) Roland and Kerstin Nilsson (Södra Sandby, Sweden), Vital Pajarola and Eva Grunder (Zurich), Drs Sabine and Athanasios Papageorgiou (Mutlangen, Germmany), Jeff Perk (Carbondale, Illinois), Thomas Pichler (Berlin 65), John Pomfret (Woking, Surrey), Arthur Poyner (Chiloe), Bernd Proissl (Wernau), John Raspey (Argentina), Mariann Rehn (Enskede, Sweden), Jamie Rein (Boston, Mass), Carol Sue Richardson (San Francisco), Wendy Richardson (London SW19), Hilda Riedler (Ismaning, Germany), Bryan and Charmaine Roche (Cape Town), Ann Rodzai and Doug Hanaver (Ithaca, NY), Ms Alex Rossi (Norwich, Norfolk), Kalle Ruokolainen and Hanna Tuomisto (Turku, Finland), Bob Ryziuk (Summerland, BC), Nick Saunders and Sarah Jaggs (London W1), Martin Schafer (Aarau, Switzerland), Ronald Schaulin and Christina Brand (Reinach, Switz), Bettina Schmeiduch and family (Böblingen, Germany), Florian Schulz (Berlin), Florian and Erdbeere Schulz (Berlin 27), Roland and Brigitte Schwarz-Aaschbacher (Rüderswil, Switz), Michael Scott-Watson (Roxburghshire, Scotland), James Siever (Wiesbaden, Germany), Trevor and Lynn Stacey (Windhoek, Namibia), Maree Stenberg (Remuera, New Zealand), Fredi Suter (Goldau) and Claudia Räber (Oberkirch), Christoph Theis (Wiesloch, Germany), Åse Totland and Jarle Unneland (Ålesund, Norway), Ian Trontz (Brooklyn, NY), Michael Turner (Burnham-On-Sea), Mark Van Den Boer (Tilberg, Netherlands), E.A.N. Vauderkuip-Zilvold (Cuenca), Ric Verwer (Santa Barbara, C.A.), Béatrice Völkle (Gampelen, Switz.), Peter and Miek Vullings (Panningen, Netherlands), Joanna Watts and Shaun Pinchbeck (Bath), Thorsten Weiland (Leichlingen, Germany), Urs Wickli (Neu St. Johann, Switzerland), Ben Wiggersfeldt (Vildbjerg, Denmark), Robert Wilkinson (Berkeley, California), Jacqueline P M Williams (London SW1), Peter Woods and Wendy Thompson (Christchurch, New Zealand), Julian Woodhouse (London NW3), Helmut Zettl (Ebergassing, Austria), and Bart Zwart (Eindhoven, Netherlands).

# URUGUAY

## INTRODUCTION

URUGUAY (area 186,926 square km.) is the smallest Hispanic country in South America; its official name is República Oriental del Uruguay. It has Brazil to the north, the Río Uruguay between it and Argentina to the west, and the wide estuary of the Río de la Plata to the south. The Atlantic Ocean washes its shores on the east.

Apart from a narrow plain which fringes most of the coast (but not near Montevideo), and an alluvial flood plain stretching N from Colonia to Fray Bentos, the general character of the land is undulating, with little forest except on the banks of its rivers and streams. The long grass slopes rise gently to far-off hills, but none of these is higher than 600 metres. Five rivers flow westwards across the country to drain into the Río Uruguay, including the Río Negro, which rises in Brazil and on which a number of dams have been built, creating a series of large, artificial lakes across the centre of the country.

**Climate** Temperate, if somewhat damp and windy, and summer heat is tempered by Atlantic breezes, but there are occasional large variations. In winter (June-September), when the average temperature is 10° to 16°C, the temperature can fall now and then to well below freezing. It is generally humid and hardly ever snows. Summer (December-March), with an average temperature of 21° to 27°C, has irregular dry periods. There is always some wind and for the most part the nights are relatively cool. There are normally 120 sunny days in the year. The rainfall, with prolonged wet periods in July and August, averages about 1,200 mm at Montevideo and some 250 more in the N, but the amount of rain varies markedly from year to year.

**History** The Spanish explorer, Juan Díaz de Solís, sailed up the Río de la Plata in 1516 and landed E of the site of Montevideo, near what is now Maldonado. His second landing was in the present Department of Colonia, where he was killed by the Charrúa Indians. There was no gold or silver in Uruguay, and it was only after about 1580 that the Spaniards showed any interest in it. Military expeditions against the Indians were unsuccessful, but Jesuit and Franciscan missionaries, landing in 1624, founded a settlement on Vizcaíno Island. It is said that cattle were first introduced during an unsuccessful expedition by Hernando Arias in 1607; they were successfully established between 1611 and 1620.

By 1680, the Portuguese in Brazil had pushed S to the Plata and founded Colonia as a rival to Buenos Aires, on the opposite shore. It was the Portuguese

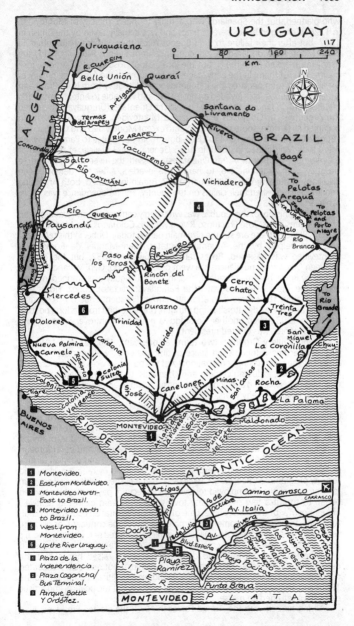

URUGUAY
117

1 Montevideo.
2 East from Montevideo.
3 Montevideo North-East to Brazil.
4 Montevideo North to Brazil.
5 West from Montevideo.
6 Up the River Uruguay.

1 Plaza de la Independencia.
2 Plaza Cagancha/Bus Terminal.
3 Parque Battle Y Ordóñez.

MONTEVIDEO

who planned, but the Spaniards who actually founded, the city of Montevideo in 1726. It changed hands several times and was actually taken by the British in 1807, but after their failure to hold Buenos Aires, they withdrew altogether. In 1808 Montevideo declared its independence from Buenos Aires. In 1811, the Brazilians attacked from the N, but the local patriot, José Gervasio Artigas, rose in arms against them. In the early stages he had some of the Argentine provinces for allies, but soon declared the independence of Uruguay from both Brazil and Argentina. Buenos Aires invaded again in 1812 and was able to enter Montevideo in June 1814. In January the following year the Orientales (Uruguayans) defeated the Argentines at Guayabos and regained Montevideo. The Portuguese then occupied all territory south of the Río Negro except Montevideo and Colonia. The struggle continued from 1814 to 1820, but Artigas had to flee to Paraguay when Brazil took Montevideo in 1820. In 1825 General Juan Lavalleja, at the head of 33 patriots (the Treinta y Tres Orientales), crossed the river and returned to Uruguay, with Argentine aid, to harass the invaders. After the defeat of the Brazilians at Ituzaingó on 20 February 1827, Britain intervened, both Argentina and Brazil relinquished their claims on the country, and independence was finally achieved in 1828.

The early history of the republic was wretchedly confused by civil war between two rival presidents, José Fructuoso Rivera with his Colorados and Manuel Oribe with his Blancos; these are still the two main parties today. Oribe, in this ten years' war, was helped by the Argentine dictator, Juan Manuel de Rosas, and Montevideo was besieged. Rosas fell from power in 1852, but the contest between Colorados and Blancos still went on. A Colorado, Gen. Venancio Flores, helped by Brazil, became president, and, in 1865, Uruguay was dragged into the war of the Triple Alliance against the Paraguayan dictator, López. Flores was assassinated in 1868 three days after his term as President ended. The country, wracked by civil war, dictatorship and intrigue, only emerged from its long political turmoil in 1903, when another Colorado, a great but controversial man, José Batlle y Ordóñez, was elected president.

During Batlle y Ordóñez' two terms as president, 1903-07 and 1911-15, Uruguay became within a short space of time the only "welfare state" in Latin America. The state has not only nationalized the public services but also controls many industries, including cement and chemicals. Its workers' charter provides free medical service, old age and service pensions and unemployment pay. Divorce has been legal for many years; illegitimate children have status and the right to inherit, and the investigation of paternity is obligatory. Education is free and compulsory, capital punishment abolished, and the church disestablished.

However, as the country's former prosperity has ebbed away since the 1960s, the welfare state has become increasingly fictitious. In 1973 the military promised to reduce the massive bureaucracy, spend more on the poor and development, and generally get the country moving again after the social and political turmoil of 1968-1973. In practice they expanded state spending by raising military and security programmes. Real wages fell to less than half their 1968 level. Less than ten per cent of the unemployed received social security payments. Montevideo began to sprout a few small shanty towns, once unheard of in this relatively affluent corner of the hemisphere. One of the most egalitarian countries in Latin America has increasingly come to resemble the rest of the continent, as only the very wealthy benefited from the military regime's attempted neo-liberal economic policies. Nevertheless, the country's middle class remains very large, if impoverished, and the return to democracy in 1985 raised hopes that the deterioration in the social structure would be halted, if not reversed. Almost ten per cent of the population emigrated for economic or political reasons during the 1960s and 1970s: the unemployed continue to leave, but the political and artistic exiles have returned *en masse*.

Allying himself with the Armed Forces in 1973, the elected President, Juan

M. Bordaberry, decreed the closure of Parliament, and stayed on to rule as the military's figurehead until 1976. Scheduled elections were cancelled in that year, and a serious wave of political and trade union repression instituted. Unable to convince the population to vote for a new authoritarian constitution in 1980, the military became increasingly anxious to hand back power to conservative politicians. However, moderate politicians refused to accept the harsh conditions the military continued to try and impose. Finally, in August 1984 agreement was reached on the legalization of most of the banned leftist parties and elections were held in November. The euphoria was spoiled by the fact that the strongest opponent of the regime was not allowed to stand. The new moderate government of Julio María Sanguinetti (of the Colorado party) was inaugurated in March 1985 for a five year term of office. The process of national reconstruction and healing of political wounds began with a widespread political amnesty (endorsed by referendum in April 1989), but no new radical economic policies. The moderate conservative Partido Nacional (Blancos) won November 1989 presidential and congressional elections with only 38% of the vote, thereby failing to secure a working majority in either house. President Luis Alberto Lacalle took office on 1 March 1990 and secured the support of the Colorados in return for four cabinet posts. The Blancos hold 39 seats in the 99-seat House of Representatives, compared with 30 for the Colorados, 21 for the left wing Frente Amplio and 9 for Nuevo Espacio. Frente Amplio holds the powerful post of mayor of Montevideo.

**Settlement** There was little Spanish settlement in the early years and, for a long time, cattle were responsible for the social structure of Uruguay. Groups of nomadic *gauchos* trailed after the herds, killing them for food and selling their hides only. Organized commerce began with the arrival of cattle buyers from Buenos Aires who found it profitable to hire herdsmen to look after cattle in defined areas around their headquarters. By about 1800 most of the land had been parcelled out into large *estancias*. The only commercial farming was around Montevideo, where small *chacras* grew vegetables, wheat and maize for the near-by town.

It was only after independence in 1828 that immigration began on any scale. Montevideo was then a small town of 20,000 inhabitants. Between 1836 and 1926 about 648,000 immigrants arrived in Uruguay, mostly from Italy and Spain, some into the towns, some to grow crops and vegetables round Montevideo. The native Uruguayans never took to agriculture: they remained pastoralists, leaving commercial farming to the immigrants. More recent immigrants, however, Jewish, Armenian, Lebanese and others have chosen to enter the retail trades, textiles and leather production rather than farming.

**The Uruguayan People** The population was 3.08m by mid-1989; just under half live in Greater Montevideo. Only some 15% are rural, and the drift to the towns is 1.6% per year. The natural population increase is low for Latin America: 0.6% per annum. So is infant mortality, 37.6 per thousand; the death rate is 9.8 per thousand. Uruguayans are virtually all European, mostly of Spanish and Italian stock. A small percentage in parts of Montevideo and near the Brazilian border are of mixed African and European descent. Less than 10% are *mestizos*. About 95% are literate.

**The Economy** Although accounting for only 11% of gdp (less than either manufacturing or commerce and catering), agriculture is the dominant sector of the economy, as a supplier and a consumer. It employs 17% of the workforce. 90% of the land area is suitable for farming, and only about 3% of that is unused. With a black soil, rich in potash, producing grasses superior even to those in Argentina, over three-quarters of the land is given over to livestock rearing, the rest for crop production.

Uruguay used to be second only to Argentina as a meat and meat-product exporter, but in the early 1980s, the beef-cattle sector suffered from low world prices and high interest rates, with the result that much of the herd was slaughtered. Slaughtering, domestic consumption and exports all declined in the 1983-85 period, but picked up thereafter, exports particularly in response to increased Brazilian demand in 1986. The number of sheep rose in the 1980s, despite increased demand for exports of live and slaughtered animals. This reflects the lower prices for meat than for wool, of which Uruguay accounts for about 3% of total world production. Livestock and its manufactures contribute the major proportion of exports: in 1988, raw wool and manufactures' share was 25%, beef 10%, and hides and skins 7%. The only cereal exported is rice, accounting for 6% of the total. Others grown are maize and wheat. Also important are oilseeds (sunflower and linseed) and citrus fruits, of which oranges and tangerines are the main crops. The fishing industry expanded in the 1970s and 1980s, but catches and exports fluctuated.

Manufacturing, which contributes 24% to gdp and employs 23% of the workforce, is concerned largely with agroindustrial activities. The most important of these are meat packing, drinks, tobacco, textiles, clothing and footwear. There are also some medium-technology industries such as oil refining, plastics, rubber products, electrical appliances and motor vehicle assembly. Import substitution behind tariff barriers encouraged growth until the 1960s, to be followed by stagnation until more export-oriented policies were introduced in the late 1970s. Various factors contributed to mixed results in the 1980s, not the least of which were economic problems in Argentina and Brazil. Construction accounts for 3% of gdp and 6% of employment. In the late 1970s, it benefited from Argentine investment, which was curtailed as the Uruguayan peso appreciated against its Argentine counterpart. The financial sector's fortunes also fluctuate according to the economic health of Argentina and Brazil. Uruguay has been called the Switzerland of Latin America, and is the repository of much of the region's flight capital.

Uruguay has no major mining industry, apart from the extraction of marble and various construction materials. It also has no known reserves of oil or natural gas. Its coal deposits are of poor quality and are not suitable for commercial mining. Almost 100% of electricity generation comes from hydroelectric plants, of which there are four. The combined installed capacity of their 14 turbines is 1,890 MW.

Like many Latin American debtors, Uruguay became unable to service its debts normally in the 1980s and had to reschedule its loans to commercial bank and government creditors in the context of an IMF stabilization programme. IMF targets were successfully met and when the agreement expired in 1987, it was replaced by enhanced surveillance. By the late 1980s Uruguay's external position had strengthened and net new borrowing from multilateral and commercial creditors took place on a voluntary basis, raising total external debt from US$4bn in 1985 to US$6.6bn in 1989. Nevertheless, debt servicing absorbed over half of all exports of goods and services and in 1990 the Government secured a debt reduction agreement from commercial banks, supported by another IMF programme and structural adjustment loans from other multilateral and bilateral lenders.

**Government** Uruguay is a republic with a bicameral legislature: a Senate with 31 seats and a Chamber of Representatives with 99 seats. The president, who is head of state and of the government, holds office for 5 years. The country is divided into 19 provinces.

**Music** Uruguay is a small and particularly Europeanized country, whose native tribes were totally eliminated over 150 years ago, so there is no Amerindian influence in the music. The folk songs and dances are very closely related to those of Argentina pampas, except in the north, where they are shared with the neighbouring Brazilian state of Rio Grande do Sul. The major song genres are the Estilo, Cifra, Milonga and Vidalita, whilst the "national" dance is the stately Pericón for six or more couples. The Milonga is also danced, as are the Tango, Cielito, Media Caña and Ranchera. The guitar is the instrument that accompanies most country music and as in Argentina, the gauchos like to engage in Payadas de Contrapunto, where two singers vie with each other, alternating improvised verses. Nineteenth century Europe introduced other popular dances into Uruguay, such as the polca, waltz, chotis and mazurca, all of which were given a local touch.

In the northern departments a number of dances are shared with Brazil, such as the Chimarrita, Carangueijo and Tirana, which are also sung, either in Spanish or Portuguese or a mixture of both.

There were many black slaves in the Río de la Plata during colonial times and the African ritual of the Candombe was practised in Montevideo until late in the 19th century. Now less than 3% of the population is black and the only musical remains of African origin are to be found in the presence during carnival of the Morenada groups of up to 50 Candomberos, who take part in the procession, playing their *tamboril* drums, while smaller groups take part in these so-called "Llamadas" from December through to Holy Week. There are four sizes of drums - *chico*, *repique*, *piano* and *bajo* - and the complex polyrhythms produced by the mass of drummers advancing down the street is both unexpected and impressive in otherwise somewhat staid Montevideo.

---

## MONTEVIDEO (1)

*Montevideo*, the capital and the only large city in the country, was founded in 1726. Population, in and near: 1,760,000 (1990). The original site on a promontory between the Río de la Plata and an inner bay, though the fortifications have been destroyed, still retains a certain colonial atmosphere. The city not only dominates the country's commerce and culture—almost 90% of all the imports and exports pass through it—but is also a summer resort and the point of departure for a string of seaside resorts along the coastline to the E.

In the Ciudad Vieja (the old town) is the oldest square in Montevideo: the Plaza Constitución, also known as the Plaza Matriz. Here on one side is the Cathedral (1790-1804), with the historic Cabildo (1808) opposite. Still further west along Calle Rincón is the small Plaza Zabala, with a monument to Zabala, founder of the city. N of this Plaza are four buildings well worth seeing: the Banco de la República (Cerrito y Zabala), the Aduana (Rambla 25 de Agosto), and the houses of Generals Rivera (Rincón 437, see **Museums** below) and Lavalleja (Zabala 1469, see **Museums**). Together, the latter two buildings form part of the Museo Histórico Nacional.

Set between the Ciudad Vieja and the new city is the grandest of Montevideo's squares, Plaza Independencia, a short distance east of Plaza Constitución, with the impressive black marble mausoleum of Artigas in the middle. On three sides it is surrounded by colonnades, and there are three pavement cafés at the eastern end. Also at the eastern end is the Palacio Salvo, a major landmark now residential, but in a poor state of repair. The western end has been spoiled by rebuilding, as has the southern side around the Casa de Gobierno Histórico (Palacio Estévez). The long unfinished modern block to the west of the Casa de Gobierno was originally intended to be the Palace of Justice, then presidential offices, but its future use is in doubt. The Casa de Gobierno itself is now used for ceremonial purposes only as the executive offices have been moved to the Edificio Libertad, far from the centre. Just off the plaza to the west is the splendid Solís Theatre, in a wing of which is the Museo de Historia Natural (closed).

The Avenida 18 de Julio, whose pavements are always thronged, begins at Plaza Independencia. Along this avenue, between Julio Herrera and Río Negro, is the Plaza del Entrevero (with a statue of a group of *gauchos* engaged in battle) a very pleasant place to sit; and the Plaza Cagancha (or Plaza Libertad), with a statue of Liberty and the main tourist office. The Palacio Municipal (La Intendencia) is on the south side of Av. 18 de Julio, just before it bends N, at the statue of the local equivalent of a cowboy (*El Gaucho*). From the top of the Palacio Municipal is the best view of the city; external glass elevators take you up to a *mirador* (glass-fronted terrace) on the 23rd floor, where there is a *confitería*, and an

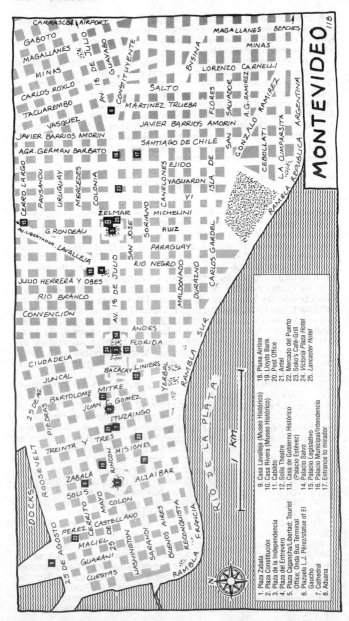

MONTEVIDEO

1. Plaza Zabala
2. Plaza Constitución
3. Plaza de la Independencia
4. Plaza del Entrevero
5. Plaza Capancha/Libertad; Tourist Office; Onda Bus Terminal
6. Plazuela L.J. Pérez/statue of El Gaucho
7. Cathedral
8. Aduana
9. Casa Lavalleja (Museo Histórico)
10. Casa Rivera (Museo Histórico)
11. Cabildo
12. Solis Theatre
13. Casa de Gobierno Histórico (Palacio Estévez)
14. Palacio Salvo
15. Palacio Legislativo
16. Palacio Municipal/Intendencia
17. Entrance to mirador
18. Pluna Airline
19. Lloyds Bank
20. Post Office
21. Antel
22. Mercado del Puerto
23. Soko's Café-Grill
24. Victoria Plaza Hotel
25. Lancaster Hotel

expensive restaurant, *La Panorámica* (24th floor). Entrance at the back of the building on Soriano, between Ejido and Santiago de Chile; open 1230-2300, US$0.10. In front of the Palacio Municipal is a plaza with a copy of Michelangelo's David in one corner. Inside the Palacio Municipal, entered around the corner in Ejido, is the Museo de Historia de Arte (see below). The road which forks S from the *Gaucho* is Constituyente, and leads to the fashionable beachside community of Pocitos.

Further along Av. 18 de Julio is the University, and nearby are the Biblioteca Nacional, the French *lycée*, and the Ministry of Health. The avenue ends at an intersection with Bulevar General Artigas. Here is an obelisk commemorating the makers of the 1830 Constitution, by José Luis Zorrilla de San Martín (born 1891). In Parque Batlle y Ordóñez (reached by a continuation eastwards of Av. 18 de Julio), are several statues: the most interesting group is the very well-known "La Carreta" monument, by José Belloni, showing three yoke of oxen drawing a waggon. In the grounds is the Estadio Centenario, the national football stadium with a seating capacity of 70,000 and a football museum, a field for athletics and a bicycle race-track (buses 177, from Av. 18 de Julio, 107 or Trolleybus 64). The Jardín Zoológico and adjacent Planetrium are SE of this park at Av. Gral. Rivera 3254 (buses 141, 142 or 144 from San José). The zoo is open Wed.-Sen. 0900-1900, entry US$0.15; the planetarium (free) gives good, 40-minute shows on Thur. at 1730, Sat. and Sun. at 1630 and 1730. There is also a drive-in zoo in the Parque Lecoq, a few km. out of town on road to Colonia del Sacramento (entrance US$0.10 per car, closed Mon. and Tues.).

The immense Palacio Legislativo, built of local marble, is reached from Plaza Fabini along Av. del Libertador Brig. Gen. Juan Lavalleja (normally known as Av. Libertador), 5 blocks E of Plaza Independencia (buses 150, 173, 175 from Calle Mercedes). From the Palacio Legislativo, Av. Agraciada runs northwest to Parque Prado.

Of the many parks, Parque Prado (about 5 km. from Av. 18 de Julio, along Av. Agraciada, bus 125 and others) is the oldest. Among fine lawns, trees and lakes is a rose garden planted with 850 varieties, the monument of La Diligencia (the stage coach), the Círculo de Tenís and the Sociedad Rural premises. Here, during August, an annual farm show (Feria Ganadería) is held. The adjacent Jardín Botánico is reached via Av. 19 de Abril (bus 582 from Yaguarón), or via Av. Dr. L.A. de Herrera (bus 147 from Paysandú). The largest and most popular park is Parque Rodó, on Rambla Presidente Wilson. Here are an open-air theatre, an amusement park, and a boating lake studded with islands. The Museo Nacional de Artes Visuales (see **Museums**) is at the eastern end.

At the western end of the bay is the Cerro, or hill, 118 metres high (from which Montevideo gets its name), with an old fort on the top, now the Museo Militar (see **Museums**). The Cerro is surmounted by the oldest lighthouse in the country (1804). Bus from centre to Cerro: 125 "Cerro" from Mercedes, and others. In the port (which one can visit on Sat. from 1300 till sunset and on Sun. from 0800 till sunset), opposite the Port Administrative Building, the ship's bell of HMS *Ajax* has been set up to commemorate the scuttling of the *Graf Spee*. The anchor of the *Graf Spee* was set up inside the port area in 1964 to commemorate the 25th anniversary of the battle; the wreck itself lies about 3 km. offshore, but is no longer visible as it was dismantled some years ago. However, plates from its bulkheads have been used in the construction of the city stadium.

**The Beaches** (See inset map, page 1090) Nine sandy bathing beaches extend along almost the whole of the metropolitan water front, extending from Playa Ramírez in the W to Playa Carrasco at the eastern extension of the city. Along the whole waterfront runs the Rambla Naciones Unidas, named along its several stretches in honour of various nations. Bus 104 from Aduana, which goes along Av. 18 de Julio, gives a pleasant ride (further inland in winter) past Pocitos, Punta

Gorda and all the beaches to Playa Miramar, beyond Carrasco. The express bus DI leaves from Plaza España every ½ hour and stops at special yellow bus stops on Av. 18 de Julio; by using this service, which costs slightly more (US$0.40) about 30 minutes are saved on the journey time to Carrasco. The town beaches are reported still to be polluted, despite a major clean-up programme.

Among the main seaside residential areas are Pocitos, well supplied with hotels, restaurants and night-clubs (*boites*), variously compared to Copacabana, Brighton, or Wembley Stadium after a Cup Final for the amount of plastic debris; and Carrasco, a delightful semi-rural place behind the beach of the same name at the end of the Rambla Sur, backed by a thick forest which has partly been turned into a national park. The international airport is nearby. E along the coast is a string of resorts, with much less polluted beaches, which are dealt with later in **East from Montevideo**.

**Festivals** Easter week is also Tourist Week (Fiesta Gaucha), with rodeo-type competitions held in the Parque Prado (US$1.50 entry—bus 185 from Pocitos, or 522 from Yaguarón) horse-breaking and handicrafts, music (mostly folk). Large barbecues are held in the open air. Christmas Eve and New Year's Eve are celebrated with drummers and firecrackers in the streets. During carnival week and a few days after there are many live shows; especially recommended is the traditional *candombe* singing and dancing in the Barrio Sur.

**Note** Some streets have changed name in recent years but this fact may not be marked on all maps: Michelini was Cuareim; Hector Gutiérrez Ruiz was Ibicuy; Convención was Latorre.

**Hotels** During the tourist season, 15 Dec.—15 March hotels should be booked in advance. At the beaches many hotels offer full board only during the season. After 1 April prices are greatly reduced and some hotel dining rooms shut down. For Carnival week, on the other hand, prices are raised by 20%. Throughout the year many hotels increase prices at weekends, ask in advance. In general it is best to pay daily to avoid price hikes.

The tourist office on Plaza Cagancha (Libertad) has information only on more expensive hotels. **Hint**: cheap hotel rooms in Uruguay are invariably gloomy. Bring your own 220V Edison-screw bulbs and hope they don't put too much strain on the wiring. When not included, breakfast (*café completo*) usually costs US$2 in 1/2-star hotels, US$3 in more expensive places. There is a 22% value-added tax on hotel bills.

*Hostería del Lago*, Arizona 9637, L, reported best in Montevideo area.

In the vicinity of the Onda bus terminal/Plaza Cagancha, and west towards Plaza Independencia are: *Internacional*, Colonia 823, A-L, rec. for business visits, however, no telex; *Victoria Plaza*, Plaza Independencia, A, a/c, excellent restaurant (rooftop, fine views), some dishes good value, friendly staff, faded old world charm which may be affected by development of large new extension; *Crillón*, Andes 1318, B, a/c, including breakfast, shabby, gloomy but clean; *London Palace*, Río Negro 1278, T 920024, B with breakfast (15% discount for Argentine ACA members), central, garage, parking. *Columbia*, Rambla Rep. de Francia 473, T 960001, Fax 960192, B-A, first class accommodation with breakfast, restaurant, sauna; *California*, San José 1237, T 920408, B with breakfast, a/c, garage, rec; *Lancaster*, B, a/c, incl. breakfast and bath, across plaza from bus terminal; *Oxford*, near Tourist Office, clean, good breakfast, B; *King's*, Andes 1491 casi Uruguay, N of Plaza Indpendencia, B with breakfast, rec.; *Los Angeles*, Av. 18 de Julio 974, B, private bath, clean, old-style, friendly, rec., (reductions for stays of over 3 days); *Alvear*, Yí 1372, B, good service, friendly, rec. for business travellers.

*Aramaya*, Av. 18 de Julio 1103, C-D with bathroom, old, clean, comfortable; *Río de la Plata*, Av. 18 de Julio 937, D, clean, hot water; *Americana*, Av. 18 de Julio 1212, D with breakfast; *Balfer*, Cuareim 1328, one block off 18 de Julio, C, good, safe deposit, excellent breakfast. *Montevideo*, Yaguarón 1309, C, no breakfast but good rooms, rec., small garage. Several hotels in D range on Uruguay.

Many on Soriano: *Royal*, No. 1120, D, dark rooms, hot showers, clean, friendly, rec.; *Hospedaje del Centro*, T 901419, E with bath, cooking facilities, clean, friendly, rec.; *Nueva Pensión Ideal*, 1073, D, excellent washing facilities, friendly, no breakfast; *Pensión del Este*, 1137, D, dark, run down, friendly; *Libertad*, Gutiérrez Ruiz 1223, D, clean, quiet, laundry facilities and food available.

*Cifre*, D, (10% discount on stays of over 2 weeks) Mercedes 1166, clean. *Claridge*, Mercedes 942, clean, friendly, E with bath, rec.; *Torremolinos*, San José 774, E, clean, friendly; *Casablanca*, San José 1039, D, friendly, with bath; *Itá*, San José 1160, next to Onda terminal, E, clean and quiet; *Pensión Trinidad*, San José 1220, D, dark and not too clean, though friendly. *Arapey*, Uruguay 925, T 907032, D with bath, E without, good value.

Several along Colonia: *Ateneo*, No. 1147, D with bath, clean,, friendly; *Hospedaje Ideal*, 914, E, clean, friendly; *Windsor*, Michelini 1260, clean, pleasant, E with bath, rec.; *Hospedaje Diagonal 2*, Convención 1326 entre Av. 18 de Julio y San José, E, clean, friendly (not to be confused with *Diagonal 1*, Colonia 1168, which is red light).

Plenty of hotels in and near the Ciudad Vieja, e.g. *Lavalle*, Bartolomé Mitre 1314, T 962887, E, clean, basic; *Palacio*, Bartolomé Mitre 1364, T 963612, D, friendly, clean, safe, rec.; and *Matriz*, Ituzaingó 1327, clean and friendly, though run down; next door, No. 1339, is *Gran Hotel Pyrámides*, better looking. *City*, Buenos Aires 462 (opp. Correos), E, good value.

East of Plaza Cagancha: *Balmoral*, Plaza Libertad 1126, A+, excellent; *Parque*, Playa Ramírez, B inc. breakfast; *Ermitage*, Juan B. Blanco 779-83, Playa Pocitos, B. At Carrasco: *Cottage*, Miraflores 1360, B, friendly, no restaurant; *Casino Carrasco*, Rambla República de México, B with breakfast, good, "ancient splendour, reasonable service"; *Bristol*, Rambla México 6095, D, built in 1926 in Louis XV style, must be seen, pleasant; *Oceania*, Mar Artico 1227, Punta Gorda, B, pleasant view, good restaurant and night club, highly rec. *Maracana*, Rambla Rep. de Chile 4667, Malvin Beach, D with bath single, clean, rec., take bus 60 from near Onda terminal.

**Youth Hostel**  The headquarters of the Association are at Pablo de María 1583, 8th floor, T 404245, open 1300-1900 Mon.-Fri. Hostel (members only) is at Canelones 935, T 981324, open all year. US$2.70 p.p. (with seasonal variations), probably the best bargain, but doors locked at 2400, friendly, clean, dormitory style, closed Sat. and Sun. 1000-1700.

**Camping**  Information on camping from Camping Club del Uruguay, Agraciada 3096. Parque Roosevelt, near Carrasco, about US$2 p.p., free, hot showers, safe, no electricity, 15 km. from centre, open all year. For vans and caravans only at Punta Ramírez on Rambla República Argentina, free for stays under 48 hrs, central, basic facilities, 24 hr security.

**Restaurants**  Dinner in "top class" establishments is taken between 2000-0100. (Less formal restaurants serve from 1930 onwards.) First-class restaurants at the centre are *Aguila*, Buenos Aires 694, next to the Solís Theatre; *Morini*, Ciudadela 1229, serves excellent steaks, simple but not cheap. *Panorámico*, 24th floor of Intendencia, pricey but worth it for the service and view. Don't miss eating at the Mercado del Puerto, opposite the Aduana, on Calle Piedras, between Maciel and Castellanas (take "Aduana" bus), closed Sun., grills cooked on huge charcoal grates (menus are limited to meat); colourful atmosphere and friendly; *El Rincón del Pescado* and *Cabana Verónica* have been particularly rec.; several are open at night, e.g. *El Palenque*, *La Posada del Puerto* (seafood), *La Tasca del Puerto* (plus dance show) and *La Marina Café-Bar*. Other good grill rooms (*parrilladas*) include *Forte di Makale*, Requena García y Wilson, *Las Tejas*, Av. Brasil 3098, *Del Ferrocarril*, Río Negro 1748, in former railway station, excellent at US$10 p.p.; *Otto*, Río Negro 1301, good, rec.

In the central Plaza Cagancha/bus terminal district: *La Genovesa* (Spanish), San José 1242, excellent, *marisquería* and *parrillada* (about US$15 with wine); *Las Brasas*, San José 909, good typical food; *Viejo Sancho*, San José 1229, excellent, popular, complimentary sherry or vermouth to early arrivals, tearoom by day; *Ruffino* (Italian), San José 1166, expensive, but pastas good value; *Gran César*, Gutiérrez Ruiz 1285, similar, rec.; *El Chivito de Oro*, 18 de Julio 1251, quick, good, rec; *Mesón del Club Español*, 18 de Julio 1332, seafood, rec. A good cheap place for lunch is restaurant on 6th floor of YMCA building, Colonia 1870, US$2 (two courses) and plentiful with good views too; ask for the Asociación Cristiana de Jóvenes; cheap lunches also at *Comedor Universitaria*, Michelini y Canelones. *Centro Residentes de Artigas*, San José 885, cheap, clean and friendly; *Anticuario*, Maldonado 1602, expensive *parrillada*, atmospheric. In the Barrio Sur, *Bellini*, San Salvador y Minas, Italian, expensive, with piano music and singing. *Bungalow Suizo*, Carrasco 150, new location, very good.

Oriental: Several, including *Shanghai*, San Jozé 1216, authentic Chinese menu, good food and value, most dishes about US$3-4.

Vegetarian: *Vegetariana*, Yí 1334, esq. Av. 18 de Julio, also San José 1056 and Av. Brasil 3086, Pocitos, excellent, self-service buffet; *Cocina Vegetariana*, Rivera 208, good value; for weekday lunches try *Natura*, Ituzaingó 1478, *Sabor Integral*, F. Crespo 1531, or *Vida Natural*, San José 1184.

A good place for lunch is the *Golf Club*, Artigas 379, good food, international cuisine, smart, expensive, excellent surroundings and grand view.

Many good restaurants on seafront in Pocitos, including *Doña Flor*, Artigas 1034, classy French restaurant, limited menu but superb, moves to Punta del Este in summer, US$25 p.p.; *Anzuelo*, Carlos Berg, 2550, nr. Parque Rodó, for fish; *Entrevero*, 21 de Setiembre 2774, popular with Americans. In Malvín, *Beiramar*, Almeria 4703, behind Rambla Chile, open 24 hrs., good, inexpensive, rec.

**Confiterías** A *confitería* is an informal eating/drinking place which serves meals at any time, as opposed to a *restaurante*, which serves meals at set times. A *confitería* may describe itself as a *cafetería, bar, repostería, cervecería, coctelería, sandwichería, grill, pizzería, salón de té* or *whiskería*. Many serve *preparación*, a collection of hors d'oeuvres. The following have been recommended: on Av. 18 de Julio, *La Pasiva*, No. 1763 (esq. Ejido), also at Sarandí 600 (Ciudad Vieja) and other branches, fast food; *Los Chivitos*, No. 949 (esq. Río Branco); *Puerta del Sol*, No. 850; *The Manchester*, No. 899; *Lusitano*, esq. Paraguay; *Bar del Rex*, No. 1006; *Lion d'Or*, No. 1981; *Soko's*, 18 de Julio e Yí, popular, good if expensive food, good coffee, open till 0100, 0400 on Sat. *Café Brasilero*, Ituzaingó 1477, founded 1877, closed Sun.; *Oro de Rhin*, Convención 1403, open 0830-2100, good cakes; *Alvear*, Sarandí 550 and Río Branco 1325; *Nuevo Metro*, San José 1200, friendly, good and cheap; *Café Sorocabana*, Yí 1377, good coffee and ice cream, another branch at 25 de Mayo 435, Ciudad Vieja. *Cake's*, 21 de Septiembre (Villa Biarritz) at Punta Carretas and Dr. A. Schroeder 6536, Carrasco; *Café de la Paix*, Rambla República del Perú y Bulevar España, Pocitos, pleasant, on seafront; *Virgilio's Café*, Rambla México, next to *Hotel Oceania*, Punta Gorda, open from 1700, nice location, light meals, no alcohol.

**Heladerías** Ice-cream parlours produce very good, unusual ice creams in the summer, and draw large crowds. Try *La Cigale*, R. Graseras 845 (Pocitos), Ejido 1368 and several other locations; *Karlia*, Canalones 952; *Papito*, 18 de Julio 1060.

**Shopping** The main shopping area is Av. 18 de Julio, good for men's business suits. Suede and leather are good buys; styling is more traditional than in Buenos Aires; try *Casa Mario*, Piedras 641 (expensive); shops and workshops around Plaza Independencia may be a better bet. Amethysts, topazes, agate and quartz are mined and polished in Uruguay and are also good buys: recommended is *Benito Sityá*, Sarandí 650 (Ciudad Vieja). For woollen wall hangings see *Manos del Uruguay*, which sells floor cushions, crafts, high quality woollen goods, etc. at Reconquista 616, and at San José 1111, and in the shopping centre in Carrasco near the Rambla. Other good craftwork (cheaper) in daily covered craft market on Plaza Cagancha, and Sat. a.m. craft fair in Villa Biarritz (Parque San Martín), behind Rambla Gandhi, Playa Pocitos. Ciudad Vieja is an excellent district in which to buy antiques, especially antique jewellery; go to Bartolomé Mitre: at No. 1368 is *Portobello Road*; next door, No 1366, is *Mariano*, a wig-maker. Many galleries here, and in Maldonado and Punta del Este, selling contemporary paintings. On Sunday morning there is a large, crowded street market on Tristán Narvaja (good for silver and copper, and all sorts of collectibles) opposite Facultad de Derecho on 18 de Julio. On Sats. there is a market at Pocitos for fruit, leather and woollen handicrafts. The Montevideo Shopping Center on the E edge of Pocitos (Herrera y Galanza, 1 block S of Rivera) has wide range of shops including Manos del Uruguay as well as others selling leather goods (bus 141 or 142 from San José).

**Cameras and Film** Best place for developing films is **Photo Martín**, Av. Libertador and Uruguay; **Delucchi**, on Herrera y Obés, good for developing slides; **Foto Tecnifilm**, Av. 18 de Julio 1202, helpful, English spoken; camera repairs by **Fotocámara**, on Cuareim between Mercedes and Colonia. Film developing and equipment are quite expensive in Uruguay; better to bring film from abroad.

**Bookshops** English and American books: **Librería Barreiro y Ramos**, 25 de Mayo y J.C. Gómez; *Ibana*, International Book and News Agency, Convención 1479, specializes in foreign publications. *Librería Inglesa*, Sarandí 580, specializes in language and children's books. Others include *Librería Mosca Hermanos*, Av. 18 de Julio 1578; *Feria del Libro*, Av. 18 de Julio 1308; *Paseo del Lector*, Av. 18 de Julio y Michelini; *Librería Papacito*, Av. 18 de Julio 1415 and *Heritage Internacional*, Soriano 1610. *Ruben*, Tristán Narvaja 1736. *Librería Oriente Occidente*, Cerrito 477 and *Librería El Aleph*, Bartolomé Mitre 1358, both sell used and rare books (former has English books, also book exchange).

**Taxis** US$0.45 for first 600 metres, and US$0.10 for each 140 metres afterwards; an additional 20% from midnight to 0600, charge for each hour of waiting, US$3.30. There is a small charge for each piece of luggage. Taxis can be hired, by agreement, by the hour within city limits.

**City Transport** Buses and trolley buses US$0.20 (pay the conductor on board). There are many buses to all parts from 18 de Julio; from other parts to the centre or old city, look for those marked "Aduana". For Pocitos from city centre take bus No. 121 from San José behind the Onda station.

**Car Hire** without chauffeur, US$40-100 per 24 hrs (insurance included)., plus extra per kilometre if only hiring for the day; guarantee of US$800 required. Hire for 3-day weekend is US$130 (rates are much lower out of season and vary according to size of vehicle). Cheaper weekly rates available. Colision damage waiver, US$13 per day. With chauffeur, US$35 per 8-hr. day plus US$0.12 per kilometre, and payment for a chauffeur's lunch or supper. **Rogelio Martinelli**, Canelones 1450; **Luis Moro e Hijos**, Camino Ariel 4737; **Empresa Salhon**, Av. 8 de Octubre 4199; **F. Miramonte**, Magallanes 1446; **ARI**, 18 de Julio 2142; **Hertz**, Calle Colonia 183 near Plaza Independencia; **National**, Ciudadela 1397; **Snappy**, Andes 1363; **Punta Car**, Yaguarón 1523/27, T 902772/920726, telex Rencar UY 26313, also at Aeropuerto Carrasco. **Budget**, Mercedes 935; **Sudancar**, Piedras 533; and **Avis** at airport and México 633; many others.

**Casinos** *Parque Hotel*, Rambla Presidente Wilson, entry US$2; *Hotel Carrasco*, Rambla República de México, entry free.

**Boliches** (Café-Concerts/Peñas/Folk-Pubs, offering the most typical local night-life) *Clave de Fu*, 26 de Marzo 125, Pocitos, Wed.-Sun. from 2200, best local folk-rock groups live at weekends; *Amadeus Café Concert*, Atlántico 1716, Malvín, from 2100 nightly, Latin American folk-rock; *TK*, Bulevar Artigas 1081, from 2200 nightly, the place to hear *candombe*; *Vieja Viola*, Pampas 1995 esq. Venezuela, 2400 onwards, folk songs, *candombe*, tango; *Amarcord*, Yaguarón 1234, Wed.-Sun. 2200 onwards, traditional pop music; *Templo del Sol*, Constituyente y P. de María, Latino-Tropical music.

**Tanguerías** *La Vieja Cumparsita*, C. Gardel 1811, nightly 2330-0500, no singles admitted, also has *candombe* shows, book ahead; *Tanguería del 40*, in *Hotel Columbia*, Rambla República de Francia 473, Sat. 2300-0400, book in advance; *La Tasca del Buho*, 18 de Julio y Martínez, Fri.-Sat. from 2230.

**Discos** (*Boites* are the more expensive discos which provide live music for dancing.) *Caras y Caretas*, Friburgo 5817, Punta Gorda, Thur.-Sat. 2200-0600, live music, chic; *Zum Zum*, Rambla Armenia 1647, from 2200 nightly, rock, live music weekends; *Ton-Ton*, Arizona 9635, Carrasco, nightly till 0530, live music—these three are expensive and you need to book ahead. *Kiel Disco Pub*, Mercedes 1820, Thur.-Sat. 2300 onwards, acid house etc., rock videos, live music weekends, good fun; *Hard Rock*, Bulevar España 2721, Fri., Sat. 2400 onwards, rock 'n' roll, open air terrace is a nice retreat from the heat, noise and lasers; *Too Much*, Río Negro 1382, Fri.-Sun. from 2400; *Freedom*, Pimienta y Cavia, Pocitos, nightly from 2300. Cheaper discos include *San Telmo*, Maldonado 1194, live music, always full and *Chant Clair*, Soriano 1338.

**Night Clubs** (*Clubes Nocturnos*) These all-night clubs, of which there are many, provide strip-tease, music and willing sexual partners; all expensive.

**Sports** There are two good 18-hole municipal links. There are several lawn tennis clubs, and two for polo. Horse races at Las Piedras (**see page 1105**).

**Museums** Museo Nacional de Antropología, Av. de las Instrucciones 948, open Tues.-Fri. 1300-1900, Sun. 1400-1800, ex-Quinta de Mendilaharsu, a modest but well-presented anthropological collection in the hall of a superb, late 19th century mansion (see, among other things, the Music Room with its huge, Chinese silk tapestry), bus 149 from Ejido. Museo Zoológico, Rambla República de Chile 4215, Buceo, Tues.-Sun. 1500-1900, free, well-displayed and arranged, rec., great for children too (bus 104 from 18 de Julio); Museo Casa Lavalleja, Zabala 1469, Ciudad Vieja, Tues.-Fri. 1300-1900, Sun. 1400-1800, free, historical mementos, furniture, etc., vast panoramic painting of the Battle of Sarandí by Juan Manuel Blanes; Museo Casa Rivera, Rincón 437, closed for renovation, due open again in 1991. The Panteón Nacional, Av. Gonzalo Ramírez y Yaguarón, houses the burial monuments of local families, many with sculptured façades and inscriptions.

Museo Juan Manuel Blanes, Millán 4015, Tues.-Sun. 1400-1800, free, ex-Quinta Raffo (late 19th century mansion) dedicated to the work of the artist Blanes (1830-1901), plus a room of the works of Pedro Figari (1861-1938), a lawyer who painted strange, naive pictures of peasant life and negro ceremonies, also work by other Uruguayan artists; has a room with paintings by Courbet, Vlaminck, Utrillo, Dufy, etchings by Orozco and engravings by Goya; temporary exhibitions, admission free (buses 146, 148, 149, 150 from Mercedes). Museo Nacional de Artes Visuales, Parque Rodó, Tues.-Sun. 1500-1900, free, fine collection of contemporary plastic arts, plus a room devoted to Blanes, rec. Museo de Historia de Arte, at Palacio Municipal (Ejido), closed for renovation, due to reopen March 1991; Centro de Exposiciones, Palacio Municipal (Soriano entrance), Mon.-Sat. 1600-2000, temporary exhibitions of contemporary art. Salón Municipal de Exposiciones, Plaza del Entrevero (underground), open daily 1700-2100, free, temporary exhibitions of contemporary art, photography, etc.

**Museo del Gaucho y de la Moneda**, Av. 18 de Julio 998, Edificio Banco de la República, open Tues.-Fri. 0930-1230, 1530-1900, Sat.-Sun. 1530-1900, free: Museo de la Moneda has a survey of Uruguayan currency and a collection of Roman coins; Museo del Gaucho is a fascinating history of the Uruguayan gaucho, rec.; also temporary exhibitions. **Museo Militar**, at Fortaleza Gral. Artigas, Cerro, Thur.-Sun. 1400-1900, free, historical mementos, documentation of War of Independence (bus 125 from Mercedes goes near). **Museo Naval**, Rambla Costanera, near Marina del Buceo, 0800-1200, 1400-1800, closed Thur., free, naval history from War of Independence onwards, documentation on Battle of the River Plate and sinking of the **Graf Spee**, and on the sailing ship **Capitán Miranda**, which circumnavigated the globe in 1937-8 and is now in the Puerto (can be visited Sat. and Sun.), bus 104 from 18 de Julio. **Museo Aeronáutico**, Plaza de la Aviación, open Sat., Sun. and holidays, 1600-2000, entry US$0.15 (bus 71, 79 from Mercedes), collection of vintage planes; **Museo del Automóvil**, in Automóvil Club del Uruguay building, 6th floor, Yí y Colonia, Tues.-Fri. 1700-2100, Sat.-Sun. 1500-2100, free, superb collection of about 40 classic and vintage cars.

**Theatres** Solís, Buenos Aires 678, two auditoria, home of the Comedia Nacional. El Galpón, Av. 18 de Julio 1618; Circular, Av. Rondeau 1388; del Notariado, Av. 18 de Julio 1730; de la Candela, 21 de Septiembre y Ellauri; del Centro, Plaza Cagancha; Stella d'Italia, Mercedes y Narvaja; La Máscara, Río Negro 1180: the above present professional productions. Sala Verdi, Soriano 914, presents semi-professional and amateur theatre, concerts, etc. Teatro Millington-Drake at the Anglo (see **Cultural Institutions**) puts on occasional productions, as do the theatres of the Alianza Uruguay-Estados Unidos and the Alianza Francesa. Opera and ballet at Auditorio del Sodre, Sala Brunet, Av. 18 de Julio, 900 block (a new Sodre Cultural Complex is under construction at Mercedes y Andes). Many theatres close during January and February.

**Cinema** is very popular. Price is almost the same in all cinemas, at US$2.75 (US$1 Tues. and Wed.). Classic and serious films at Cinemateca film club (3 separate cinemas—at L. Carnelli 1311, Soriano 1227 and A. Chucarro 1036), monthly membership US$6, and Ciné Universitaria (2 halls, Lumière and Chaplin, Canelones 1280). Films are released quite soon after the UK and USA, and often before they get to Buenos Aires. Details in *Guía del Ocio* and monthly *Cinemateca Uruguaya* (free). At least half Montevideo's cinemas show blue films—marked *sexo explícito*.

**Music** Pop concerts are held in Centenario stadium and Parque Rodó. During the two weeks around Carnival there is a music and dance competition, in the Parque Rodó amphitheatre, in "Murga", a form of satirical revue, 4 hrs. every night, US$0.50 entry, starting at 2100. See also under **Tanguerías**, etc. and **Theatres**, above.

**Exchange** Lloyds Bank, Calle Zabala 1500, and 11 city agencies; **Citibank**, Cerrito 455 (corner Misiones), no commission on own cheques; **Banco Holandés Unido**, 25 de Mayo 501, reported as cheapest bank to have money sent; **Banco Comercial**, Cerrito 400 and Av. Libertador (up to US$1,000 available on Access or Visa, commission 3½% for deutschemark cheques); and **Banco Panamericano Uruguayo** on Plaza Cajón. Only **Banco de la República** deals in US personal cheques for collection: 30 working days, high charge and not always reliable. **American Express Bank**, Rincón 473, T 960092/961162, no commission on travellers' cheques to dollars (open 1300-1700 Mon.-Fri.—see Turisport under **Travel Agents**). Cash available on Mastercard from **Banco Pan de Azúcar**, Sarandí y Zabala, and some other banks. There are exchange houses, especially along 18 de Julio (many open till 2300 on Sat.), e.g. **Gales** at 1048, **La Favorita** at 1459, but do shop around for best rates (rates for cash are better than for travellers' cheques). **Exprinter** on Plaza Independencia and **Cambio Indumese**, Cagancha y 18 de Julio, have been recommended. No restriction on foreign exchange transactions (i.e. an excellent place to stock up with US$ bills, though American Express and some banks refuse to do this for credit cards; most places charge 3% commission for such transactions). Airport bank open every day 0900-2200; so are Banco de la República exchange office (good rates for cash and travellers' cheques, will accept torn dollar bills) and several exchange houses on Plaza Cagancha. Note that rates for Brazilian currency are poor.

**Embassies and Consulates** Argentine Consulate, Río Branco 1281, T 900897, open 1400-1900, visa US$15, one day wait, English spoken. **Brazilian Consulate**, Convención 1343, T 912024/921703 (service for visas is quicker and less complicated in Buenos Aires), Embassy is at Andes 1365, Torre Independencia, 6 piso, T 905043. **Paraguayan Consulate**, Blvd. Artigas 1191, T 485810, open 0900-1200 summer, 1400-1730 winter. **Chilean Embassy**, Andes 1365, T 982223, open 0900-1400, visa US$5, same day.

US Embassy and Consulate, Dr. H. Abadie S. 808, T 236276/236061. Canadian Consulate, Gómez 1348, T 958583.

British Embassy, Marco Bruto 1073, T 623597/623581. Spanish Consulate, Libertad 2750, T 780048. Swedish Embassy, Av. Brasil 3079, piso 6, Pocitos, T 780088. Swiss Embassy, Ing. Frederico Abadie 2934-40, T 704315. German Embassy, La Cumparsita 1417-35, T 904958 (open 0930-1230). Belgian Embassy, Leyenda Patria 2880, T 701265. French Embassy, Uruguay 853, T 904377. Israeli Embassy, Blvd Gral Artigas 1585, T 404164. Italian Embassy, J.B. Lamas 2857, T 780542. Austrian Consulate-General, Maldonado 1193, 914000. Netherlands Embassy, Leyenda Patria 2880, T 701631. Portuguese Embassy, Av. Dr F. Soca 1128, T 96456, USSR Embassy, Blvd. España 2741, T 782171.

**Chambers of Commerce and Cultural Institutions** American Chamber of Commerce, Bartolomé Mitre 1337, esq. 108. T 959048. Alianza Cultural Uruguaya-Estados Unidos, Paraguay 1217, T 915234, library open Mon.-Fri., 1400-2000 Mon.-Fri., US publications and books (excellent selection), theatre, art gallery. British Chamber of Commerce, Av. Libertador 1641, piso 2, of 201. T 900936. Instituto Cultural Anglo-Uruguayo (known as the "Anglo"), San José 1426, T 908468 (theatre, rec., library open Mon.-Fri. 0930-1200, 1430-1930). The British Hospital, Av. Italia 2420, T 409011. The English Club, Treinta y Tres 1309, T 951212. Alliance Française, Soriano 1180, T 911979 (theatre, concerts, exhibitions in French and Spanish, library, excellent bookshop). Goethe Institut, Canelones 1524, T 405813/404432 (open Mon., Thur. 1600-2000, Tues., Fri. 0930-1230, closed Wed.). Casa Cultural Uruguaya-Suecia, Ejido 1444, T 900067. Instituto Italiano de Cultura, Paraguay 1177, T 903354. Instituto de Cultura Uruguayo-Brasileño, Av. 18 de Julio 994, T 986531.

**Schools** The British School at Carrasco and some 4 others, 1 French, 1 German, and the Crandon Institute, an American school for children up to 17. All have good scholastic ratings.

**Health and Fitness** Suomi, Dr. José Scocería 2909 (Pocitos).

**Laundry** at Michelini 1238, US$2 for 3 kg; Andes 1205, US$2, rec.

**Places of Worship** The Roman Catholic Cathedral is known locally as the Iglesia San Juan. Anglican Church (Holy Trinity), Reconquista 522 (a national monument) T 721630 (English Service 0945 Sunday). Methodist services at Christ Church, Carrasco. Holy Trinity Episcopal (British), and the Emanuel Methodist Church (American), hold regular services in English. The German Evangelical Church holds services in German at Calle J M Blanco 2. There is a synagogue.

**Post Office** Misiones 1328 y Buenos Aires; 0800 (0730 in summer)-1845 Mon.-Fri., 0800-1245 Sat. and holidays (0730-1145 in summer); philatelic bureau on top floor sells back issues. *Poste restante* at main post office will keep mail for 1 month, 2 if authorized in advance by administrator. Next to Pluna office at Plaza del Entrevero, and under Intendencia at corner of Av. 18 de Julio and Ejido. Closer to tourist area, there is one at Mercedes 929, at Convención.

**Telecommunications** Antel, Sarandí 472 (headquarters); public offices at Telecentro Antel round corner at Rincón y Treinta y Tres (Ciudad Vieja), for international phone calls (inc. USA Direct Express), telex, fax, cables, etc., open 0800-2000 daily; also Telecentro Plaza, San José 1102, open 24 hrs. for all services. Centres also at Av. Italia y B. Foresti (Hospital de Clínicas), F. Crespo y Colonia (Sede Central) and San Martín 2677 (Agueda), all 0800-2000.

**Travel Agents** *Mustelli*, Yaguarón 1344 bis, *J.P. Santos*, Colonia 951, and *Jetmar*, Plaza Independencia 725-7, all helpful. *Wagon-Lits* (Thomas Cook agents), Av. Gral. Rondeau 1392; *Exprinter*, Sarandí 700; *Turisport Ltda*, Mercedes 942 (American Express for travel and mail services, good; sells Amex dollar travellers' cheques on Amex card and personal cheque at 1% commission); *Golden Tours*, Colonia 1221, T 90 7500, English spoken. *Viajes y Turismo*, Convención 1343 y 18 de Julio, 4th floor, T 916461, very helpful, English spoken. *Turinter*, Río Negro 1358, very helpful. *Sur Bus* does good US$10 day trip to Punta del Este, 0900-1800, with transfers from and to your hotel. *Pasaporte*, Galería El País, Plaza Cagancha, T 921539, friendly and helpful; *Environs Viajes*, 18 de Julio 1302, T 916647 and *Freeway*, 18 de Julio 843, T 908931, both run tours of Montevideo, US$7.

**Tourist Information** Information Centre is on Plaza Cagancha, T 905216; open every day (but a.m. only Sat. and Sun.), friendly though little English spoken, free maps, sells bus tours of the city and elsewhere, limited information. Also at Carrasco international airport.

**Information** Dial "214" ("124" inland) for the Antel information office for details on the weather, pharmacies on night duty, automobile service stations, airline arrivals and departures (Montevideo), long-distance bus schedules, shipping movements, in Spanish. Dial "6" for exact time. The *Guía del Ocio*, a weekly guide, US$0.70 from newsstands, gives information on museums, cultural events, nightlife and entertainment, including addresses, rec.

**Maps** Best street maps of Montevideo are at the beginning of the Guía Telefónica (both white and yellow page volumes). *Eureka Guía De Montevideo* is rec. for streets, sector by sector, with index and bus routes (US$4.75 from bookshops).

**Airport** The main airport is at Carrasco, 21 km. outside the city, modernized in 1990 with coffee shop and children's play area in departure lounge; left luggage about US$1 per day per item; if exchange facilities closed, buses will accept dollars for fares to town. To Montevideo 30 mins by taxi (US$13-15), or about 50 mins by bus No. 209 to Plaza del Entrevero (US$1.50), tell the driver where you want to get off. Onda and COT bus services to and from Punta del Este also call at the airport.

**Buses within Uruguay** Good services to most towns. During the summer holiday season buses are booked heavily; it is recommended to book in advance (also for Fri. and weekend travel all year round). Fares and journey times from the capital are given under destinations. Bus terminus under construction near Plaza de la Bandera, but buses leave from bus company offices around Plaza Cagancha (check exact departure point when booking). Those to the east make a compulsory stop at Dante 1945/9; others at Terminal Goes, Av. General Flores y Domingo Aramburu. Onda runs services all over the country (the office is just off Av. 18 de Julio). The smaller competing services are just as fast and may be less expensive. Services along Route 7 to Tala and San Jacinto are operated by Cita and leave from their office at Av. Libertador 1446. Arco office for buses to Colonia on Plaza Cagancha.

**To Paraguay, Brazil, Chile** To Asunción, Paraguay: twice a week (Wed. and Sat. 1500) by COIT US$51, twice a week by Brújula bus, US$45 Tues. Fri., plus Sun. in Summer, 0800 and by Lynsa bus (18 hrs. US$30); alternatively take bus to **Santa Fe**, Argentina, via Paysandú bridge, for easy access to Asunción. The through bus route is via Paysandú, Salto, Bella Unión, Uruguaiana, Paso de los Libros, Posadas, Encarnación, to Asunción (there are no passport or customs formalities except passport checks at Bella Unión and at Encarnación). There are very comfortable buses to **Porto Alegre** (US$21, 12 hrs.) and **São Paulo** (US$41 daily, 32 hours) at 2200 with Onda or TTL (Plaza Cagancha, 1385, T 908419/915482), with drinks service on the *coche cama* luxury service at 2100, 10 hrs. to Porto Alegre, US$66: often booked very early. A cheaper alternative route (which also avoids the risk of being stranded at the border by through-bus drivers) is to Chuy (US$7-9, 6 hrs.), then catch an onward bus to Porto Alegre (7½ hrs., US$5.50), either direct or via Pelotas. To **Santiago** (Empresa Gen. Artigas) via Buenos Aires and Mendoza, US$70, 28 hrs., departs Mon. 0800. Round trips to Argentina, Chile or Brazil by bus or plane, booked at travel agents are reported to be good value.

    **N.B.** One needs a passport when buying international tickets.

**To Argentina: Ferries** (Argentine immigration officer on ferries.) **Direct to Buenos Aires**, overnight services, 3 companies: **Ferry turismo**, Río Negro y 18 de Julio, alternate evenings at 2100, 11 hrs., US$45 without sleeper or breakfast, about double for sleeper, restaurant, bar, disco; cars about US$100. **Buquebus**, Río Negro 1400, T 920670, Tues., Thur., Sun. at 2000, 11 hrs., similar accommodation and fares. **Tamul** also has regular services, tourist class and cabins. **Services via Colonia**: bus/ferry services by Buquebus (three crossings a day, 2 on Sunday) and Ferryturismo (2 a day). 6-7½ hours, combined bus/ferry ticket about US$32, ferry also takes cars (**see also under Colonia**, page 1106); more expensive is bus/hydrofoil service by Aliscafos (Plaza Cagancha 1124, T 904608) 4 services a day between 0700 and 1700 from Rinconada de Plaza Libertad, 4 hours, book in advance (break of journey in Colonia is allowed). Services **via Carmelo and Tigre** (interesting trip): bus/motor launch service by Deltanave, Plaza Cagancha 1340, T 917277, 7 hours, 0745 and 2400 daily (tell driver where you want to go in Buenos Aires). Bus/motor launch service by Cacciola at 0700 (arr. Carmelo 1100, Tigre 1400, Bs. As. 1500) and 1330 (arr. Bs. As. 2100), US$30. Bus service **via Fray Bentos** (Bus de la Carrera): joint service by Onda, CIT and COT at 1000, 2200 and 2300 daily, US$14, 8 hrs. Bus service to Córdoba, via Paysandú and Paraná, ONDA, Mon. and Fri., 15 hrs, US$30, snacks served. Advanced booking is advisable on all services at busy periods.

---

## EAST FROM MONTEVIDEO (2)

320 km. of beautiful coast, consisting of an endless succession of small bays, beaches and promontories, set among hills and woods. Punta

del Este, 139 km. from Montevideo is a major international resort. From Punta del Este to the Brazilian frontier is much less developed; good bird watching in the coastal lagoons. The beach season is from December to end February.

Two roads, both paved, go to Punta del Este. The northern branch (no tolls) via Pando and Soca, is Route 8; at Km. 75 Route 8 continues NE towards Minas (**see page** 1104), while Route 9 branches off to San Carlos (14½ km. N of Maldonado or 19 km. N of Punta del Este) through beautiful rolling country with views of the Laguna del Sauce. The "Interbalnearia", runs largely along the coast, with short branches to some of the resorts, and is the one described in the text. There are toll posts (US$0.75) at Arroyo Pando and at Arroyo Solís Grande. For the first 15 km. or so out of Montevideo an alternative road to the Interbalnearia route runs parallel between it and the coast—its use is recommended during heavy traffic periods due to the frequency of dangerous road junctions.

Route 9 runs from San Carlos through the towns of Rocha and Castillos to Chuy. A spur of the road turns south to La Paloma and there are secondary roads to some of the resorts further along the coast. The area's past as a frontier zone between Spanish and Portuguese colonial rule is indicated by fortresses Santa Teresa (near Rocha) and San Miguel (near Chuy). There is a series of well-equipped, modern campsites along the coast.

The resort of **Atlántida** (*Rex*, C, is main hotel; *Munday*, C, is clean and friendly; many good *residenciales* charging E off season; campsite *El Ensueño* at Km. 46; some good restaurants), 45 km. from Montevideo, is ringed by fir forest and has a good country club. A short distance beyond, in groves of eucalyptus and pine, is the small and intimate beach of Las Toscas, followed by Parque del Plata, on the Solís Chico river. An *asado* on the beach (with wine) costs about US$12. Shortly before Atlántida, in an old fortress set in pine woods, is *El Fortín de Santa Rosa* hotel and restaurant, 2 mins from a lovely sandy beach. Small zoo not far off.

At Km. 64.5 on the Interbalnearia is Sr. Garabedian's **campsite**. For bookings, telephone Sr. Garabedian at Montevideo 561230.

Crossing by a (toll) bridge we come to **La Floresta** (*Oriental*, highly rec.), surrounded by woods. The chalets are pretty, reminiscent of the villages of the Landes, near Biarritz. About 35 km. on, over a toll bridge, is **Solís**, at the mouth of the Río Solís. It has a very long beach, good fishing, delightful river and hill scenery. About 8 km. beyond Solís lies the small village of Las Flores, with a better beach than that at Solís. Accommodation is available at *Hostería del Mar*, T Solís 99 or Montevideo 786657, B bed and breakfast, clean, well-run, open all year, and Edén Camping with room at US$3 p.p. or camping at km. 91 site. *Restaurant Charma*, rec.

**Piriápolis** (pop 6,000), the next resort, 16 km. from Solís, 101 from Montevideo, may be reached either by turning south at the end of the Interbalnearia, and coming through Solís and then along the very beautiful R10, or by taking the original access road (R37) from Pan de Azúcar, which crosses the R93. It has a fine casino hotel and some 50 others, a good beach, a yacht harbour, a country club, a golf course, a motor-racing track and is particularly popular with Argentines. The town, set among hills, is laid out with an abundance of shade trees, and the district is rich in pine, eucalyptus and acacia woods. There are medicinal springs. Six km. to the N is Cerro Pan de Azúcar (Sugar Loaf), crowned by a tall cross with a circular stairway inside, fine coastal views; there is only a steep path up to the cross. Just outside Piriápolis on the side road to Pan de Azúcar (town) by the entrance to the municipal park is a good zoo, containing among other things live specimens of all snakes and most animals native to Uruguay including endangered pampas deer. The bus from Piriápolis to Pan de Azúcar passes the gates. In the municipal park (La Cascada) is the Museo Castillo de Piriá, open 1300-1700, Fri., Sat., Sun. and holidays. The shortest route from Piriápolis to Punta de Este is by the Camino de las Bases which runs parallel to the R37 and joins the R93 some 4 km. east of the R37 junction.

**Hotels** Most close end-Feb. until mid-Dec. *Argentino*, B, with casino, medicinal springs, ice rink and dirty pool open to public for US$3.50, also sauna; *City*, D (closed in winter), with bath, ocean view, clean, friendly, rec.; *Riva Davia*, next to Onda bus terminal, open all year, E (D in summer) with bath, hot water, clean; *Luján*, C in season, E out of it, rec; many others in our price ranges D and up. The Centro de Hoteles y Anexos de Piriápolis runs a reservation office at Edificio Piriá on Rambla de los Argentinos. House and apartments for hire, Aloia—Colmegna Ltda, on Edif. Claramar on Rambla rec., English spoken.

**Youth Hostel** Close to beach, behind *Hotel Argentino*, at Simón del Pino 1136, T 0432-2157, US$1.50 p.p. (open all year), mostly double bedrooms, hot showers, cooking facilities. Student cards accepted. There is also an international YMCA camp on the slope of Cerro del Toro, double rooms in bungalows, and tents.

**Camping** Site at Misiones y Niza, T 2306.

**Restaurants** *Don Quijote*, rec. for paella, cheap and good; many small restaurants near the harbour, e.g. *Don Anselmo* (shellfish, excellent, overlooking sea) and *Naútico*, both rec.

**Bus** to/from Montevideo, US$2, 1½ hrs. Buses also to Rocha and Gen. José Artigas bridge (Argentina), US$17.

**Tourist Information** Asociación de Fomento y Turismo, Rambla de los Argentinos 1348.

R93 runs between the coast and the Laguna del Sauce to **Portezuelo** , which has good beaches. The Arboreto Lussich (open 1030-1630) on the west slope of the Sierra de la Ballena (north of R93) contains a unique set of native and exotic trees. From Portezuelo it is possible to drive north towards the R9 by way of the R12 which then continues, unpaved, to Minas. At *Punta Ballena* there is a wide crescent beach, calm water and very clean sand. The *Solana del Mar Hotel* (opens mid-December, payment in dollars cash is demanded unless you protest) modern, is on the beach, A with full board. Campsite near Arboreto Lussich. The place is a residential resort but is still quiet. Casa Pueblo, the house and gallery of Uruguayan artist Carlos Páez Villaro, is built in a Spanish-Moroccan style on a cliff over the sea; the gallery can be visited (US$0.80), there are paintings, collages and ceramics on display, and for sale; season: Nov. 1 to April 1. At the top of Punta Ballena there is a panoramic road 2½ km. long with remarkable views of the coast.

**Maldonado** (pop. 33,000), capital of Maldonado Department, 140 km. from Montevideo. This peaceful town, sacked by the British in 1806, is now a dormitory suburb of Punta del Este, but it has many colonial remains: the parish church, El Vigia watch tower, and fortifications on Gorriti Island in the semi-circular bay. Gorriti Island, densely wooded and with superb beaches, is an ideal spot for campers. See also the Cathedral (completed 1895), the Mazzoni Regional Museum (Ituzaingó 787, Tues.-Sat. 1200-1900, Sun. 1400-1900); San Fernando de Maldonado Museum (Sarandí y Rafael Pérez del Puerto, Tues.-Sat. 1300-2000); Museo de Arte Americano de Maldonado (José Dodera 648 y Treinta y Tres, private museum, interesting); the windmill, the Cuartel de Dragones exhibition centre and the Cachimba del Rey (an old well—local legend claims that those who drink from the well will never leave Maldonado)

**Hotels** *Maldonado*, quiet, clean, C; *Hospedaje Isla de Gorriti*, Calle Isla de Gorriti 884, C, rec.; *Celta*, Ituzaingó 839, T 30139, friendly and helpful, E and up, rec., Irish owner, No. 7 bus stop outside; *Le Petit Hotel*, Gral. Marco de los Reyes (1st floor), T 23044, shower, a/c, B, dirty, short stay.

**Camping** Two sites: one free, in Parque El Placer, T 70034; the other charges.

**Restaurants** *Matias Módena*, 3 de Febrero 642, good fish and meat, US$14 p.p.; *Cantina del Italiano*, Sarandí 642, pizzería, old building, good value.

**Information** on concerts and exhibitions in summer T 22276. Tourist information at bus station, T 25701.

**Bus** to/from Montevideo, US$3.25; to Minas, Coom, 2 hrs., 5 a day, US$2.50.

*San Carlos*, on Route 9, 14½ km. N of Maldonado, is a charming old town of 20,000 people. Buses run from Plaza Artigas to Maldonado every 15 mins; it is a good point for connections to La Paloma, and Chuy on the Brazilian border. Of interest are the church, dating from 1722, heavily reconstructed, an excellent zoo, and a historical museum opposite *Hotel Reyes* (Olivera y Carlos Reyes, D, friendly, "immaculate"); other hotels: *Residencial Plaza*, Treinta y Tres, opposite plaza (similar range) and *El Amanecer*, Treinta y Tres 634. Free camping, with facilities, in lovely municipal park. 2 *cambios* which exchange travellers' cheques. *Benítez*, Treinta y Tres y Maldonado, for good leather items.

**Punta del Este** Seven km. from Maldonado and 139 km. from Montevideo, facing the bay on one side and the open waters of the Atlantic on the other, lies the largest and best known of the resorts, Punta del Este, which is particularly popular among Argentines. The narrow peninsula of Punta del Este has been entirely built over (a "concrete jungle"); it has excellent bathing beaches, the calm *playa mansa* on the bay side, the rough *playa brava* on the ocean side. There are an excellent yacht marina, yacht and fishing clubs, and many beautiful holiday houses. There is good fishing both at sea and in three near-by lakes and the river Maldonado (which the main road crosses at Manantiales by a unique inverted-W-shaped bridge). The rest of the area consists of sand dunes covered with pines. On Isla de Lobos, which is a government reserve within sight of the town, there is a huge sea-lion colony; excursions to it every morning at 0800 if demand is sufficient, return at 1115, US$7 p.p.; ticket should be bought at the harbour the day before. Direct daily Boeing 737 flights from Buenos Aires to Punta del Este airport during the high season. On the land side, Punta del Este is flanked by large planted forests of eucalyptus, pine and mimosa. There are a golf course and two casinos. After the Easter vacation the place is all your own and on sunny days it is still warm enough to swim (even between 10 March and Easter it is quiet). Many of the best hotels and restaurants close after the end of the season in March. Streets have names and numbers on the peninsula; lowest numbers at the tip.

**Hotels** Very many, but expensive: *Palace*, Gorlero y 11, T 41418, A+ (A in March, closed in winter), breakfast only (expensive restaurant, *La Stampa*, in the hotel), lovely courtyard, colonial style, well kept; *Amsterdam*, El Foque (Calle 14) 759, T 42682, L, ocean view; *Embajador*, by new bus terminal at Parada 1, T 81008, A-A+, good; *Iberia*, Calle 24, No. 685, T 40405/6, 43348, about centre-peninsula, A, pleasant, open all year, covered garage opposite; *Florinda*, Calle 27/24, A (C off season), T 40003, with bath, helpful, clean, central, friendly; *Playa Brava*, Calle 27 esq. 24, D off season, T 41618, similar good standard. *Charrúa*, Calle 27, No. 617, T 41406, about 5 blocks from bus station. *Puerto*, Calle 7 y Calle 10, C, clean and friendly, English spoken; *Milano*, Calle 24, No. 880, T 40039, C (closed out of season), family run, excellent, highly rec.; *Dollar*, Sta Teresa y Amazonas, Parade 2, T 82233, B and C, open Dec.-Easter, English and German spoken, friendly; *L'Auberge*, near golf course, T 82601, L-A, own transport essential, air-conditioned, "lo más refinado", open all year, special weekend offers, good restaurant. *Cantegril* country club lets cottages and hotel apartments at a high price, or one may hire from an "Inmobiliaria". Hotel rates are as much as halved in the winter months. In the high season (Dec-March), cheapest doubles cost about US$18; it is better to find a hotel in Maldonado and commute, or look for a hotel that is rebuilding, so that you can negotiate on prices. To stay at a hotel in the woods you will need a car; no public transport to beach or town.

**Restaurants** *La Lutèce*, Los Sauces casi Pedragosa Sierra, French cuisine. *Bleu Blanc Rouge*, Calle 6 y 12, very good, US$25 p.p.; *Mariskonea*, Calle 26, No. 650, one of the oldest establishments, US$25 p.p., good quality; *Doña Flor*, Deauville y Niza, French food, rec.; *Bungalow Suizo*, Av. Roosevelt y Parada 8, excellent, US$25 p.p., must book; *El Mastil*, Av. de las Palmeras esq. 8 (behind port), charming atmosphere, open all year; *La Pomme*, Calle 11 esq. 12, Belgian-run, good food, US$15 p.p.; *El Ciclista*, Calle 20 801, one of the oldest restaurants, Italian food, US$10 p.p.; *Los Caracoles*, Calle 20 y 28, excellent food at good prices; *Viejo Marin*, Las Palmeras, fish restaurant, very busy so go early, US$12 p.p.; *Forte di Makalle*, Calle 8-828 y 11, US$17.50, rec.; *Stromboli*, Gorlero y 17, excellent seafood, US$18 p.p., rec.; *Andrés* on a terrace at the Edificio Vanguardia, US$13 p.p.; *da Carmela*, Gorlero 635 y Rambla Gen. Artigas, pizza and pasta, US$10 p.p., pleasant; *Blue Cheese*, Calle 20, No. 717, overlooking yacht harbour, for steaks and unlimited salads; *Yacht Club Uruguayo* (not to be confused with the exclusive Yacht Club), Gral. Artigas y 8, simple, friendly, views over the port, US$9 p.p.; *El Metejón*, Gorlero y 17, US$20, good food but overpriced. On the main street, *La Fragata*, Gorlero 800, open 24 hours all year, a good meeting place. Many enticing ice-cream parlours in Gorlero.

**Discotheques** often don't begin till 0200. *New Faces*, Calle 20; *Caras y Caretas*, near yacht club, not expensive.

**Crafts** *Manos del Uruguay* in front of the Casino Nogaró. Best sweaters from *San Carlos*.

**Museum** Foundation museum of Contempory Latin American Art, Barrio Beverly Hills, T 83476, open Dec. to end of Holy Week, Tues.-Sun. 1000-1400. Worth a visit but car needed to get there.

**Car Hire** Punta-Car, Cont. Gorlero, *Hotel Playa*, T 82112/82761 telex Punt-Car UY 28105; Serracar, T 88855.

**Exchange** Both Amex and Diner's Club have offices. Best rates of exchange from Banco de la República, which opens earlier and closes later than the other banks. Also *casas de cambio*.

**Telephone, telex and fax** on Calle 24 at Calle 25, by the square.

**Tourist Information** Liga de Fomento, Parada 1, T 44069, Terminal de Omnibus Playa Brava, or Onda at Av. Gorlero and Calle 27, T 40023.

**Buses** New terminal at Av. Gorlero, Blvd. Artigas and C.32 (served by local bus No. 7). To/from Montevideo, COT, Sur Bus or Onda (rec.) buses, US$3.50, less than 2 hrs., plenty of buses in the summer; to Piriápolis, US$1.50. To San Carlos (US$1.50) for connections to Porto Alegre (US$30), Rocha, La Paloma, Chuy. Direct to **Chuy**, 4 hrs., US$5. To Gen. José Artigas bridge (Argentina) US$20. Local bus fare about US$0.20.

**Airport** El Jagüel (full customs facilities) as well as the airport on the southern shore of the Laguna del Sauce, Capitán Curbelo, which handles the Pluna and Aerolíneas Argentinas flights to Buenos Aires, US$110. Pluna to Porto Alegre and São Paulo. Airport tax US$2.50 and bus to town US$1.50. Exchange facilities, but no tax-free shopping yet. Buses to/from Montevideo call at the airport.

Near Punta del Este, to the E, **Playa San Rafael**, where there is an 18-hole golf course, is growing rapidly. (*Casino San Rafael*, L high season (20/12-1/3), B low season, closed after Easter, no credit cards, no a/c or balconies, much used for conferences, Telex 28035, T 042-82161; *San Marcos*, B, very pleasant; *La Capilla*, next to the church, behind the *San Marcos*, reported good; *Hotel Porto Bari* (A+). Further E, across the "ondulating" bridge is La Barra, with *Hotel Posta del Cangrejo*, L, and restaurants *San Jorge*, just across the bridge, speciality *torta de mariscos*; *Neuhausen*, pleasant, not too expensive; *Lo de Miguel*, Ruta 10 y C. 7, good, small, noisy, booking essential. Barra's beaches, and those further north (Manantiales, Montoya) are gaining in popularity. 30 km. from Punta del Este is the quiet fishing village of Faro José Ignacio, with lighthouse and the well-known restaurant *Parador Santa Teresita*, where seaweed omelette is a speciality. *Parador Renner* at Balneario José Ignacio, rooms A with breakfast, good dining room. Further E are Punta del Diablo, with a beautiful beach, camping and a picturesque fishing village, and Cabo Polonio, which may be reached by horse-drawn carriage (look for signs on the road), or by bus from La Paloma and 1¾ hrs. walk.

**Rocha** (pop. 24,000) is 211 km. from Montevideo and 28 km. from the sea at La Paloma. Two casinos located at *Costas del Mar* and *Cabo Santa María* hotels. Groves of palms dotted about the fields give the area an unusual beauty.

**Accommodation and Food** Among others, *Municipal*, very good and cheap; *Hospedaje Plaza* on the plaza, budget, D/E (3 rooms only). **Youth Hostel** at Barra de Valizas, open 1 December to 30 March. Cheap food at *Las Vegas* on Ramírez.

**Camping** Sites at Parque Andresito, Rocha, and Rancho Pucará.

**La Paloma** is a good port for yachts as it is protected by two islands. It has an oil refinery and a fishmeal plant which can smell bad but there is attractive scenery and good freshwater and sea fishing. Buses run to and from Rocha, and to and from the capital (US$4). Bike rental opposite the casino, US$2 a day; horses can be hired. Tourist office in Av. Solari, T 6088.

**Hotels** *Bahía*, B, rec.; *Embeleco*, friendly, English spoken, B, rec.; *La Tuna* (T 0473-6083), C, rec.; *Parque*, clean, E. **Youth Hostel** at Parque Andresito, F, small, clean, friendly, good meals available, kitchen facilities, open 1 November to 30 March, book at Montevideo office. Also thatched cabins in the woods for rent, US$13-21 a day with maid and kitchen, sleep 4-6. **Camping Sites** in Parque Andresito and at Los Delfines. **Restaurant** *Trattoria di Luigi*, highly rec., superb views.

From La Paloma, Route 10, the coastal road, runs northeast to Aguas Dulces. At Km. 10 is **La Pedrera**, a beautiful village with sandy beaches and a campsite. (*Hotel La Pedrera*, D; swimming pool, tennis, comfortable rooms, rec.; *Hotel San Michel*, D; *Restaurant Costa Brava*, overlooking the sea.) North of La Pedrera the road runs through pleasant fishing villages which are rapidly being developed with holiday homes and where basic accommodation is available (Youth Hostel at Barra de Valizas, open summer only, check in Montevideo first, camping nearby). Visits to the islands of Castillos and Wolf can be arranged; look out for sea lions and penguins along the coast, for instance at Cabo Polonia. From Aguas Dulces (campsite) the road runs inland to Castillos (from where buses run to Chuy).

About 100 km. from Rocha, 308 km. from Montevideo lies the colonial fortress of Santa Teresa, begun by the Portuguese in 1762 and seized by the Spanish in 1793. It is set in the Parque de Santa Teresa, with avenues of palms, a bird sanctuary, fresh-water pools to bathe in, a campsite and cottages to let in the summer. There is a small supermarket, a butcher's and a bar in the commercial area where campers are expected to register. The fortress is very impressive and houses a museum of artefacts from the Wars of Indpendence. Open 1000-1700 except Mon. (restricted hours in winter), entry US$0.30, tickets from restaurant opposite, recommended. Nine km. beyond and 20 km. S of Chuy is the bathing resort of **La Coronilla** with a campsite, excellent ocean fishing for sharks, skate and black *corvina* from the rocks: there is an annual competition in January. Tour by taxi or Onda bus (US$9, daily) from La Coronilla to the Santa Teresa fortress and the strange and gloomy Laguna Negra, and the collection of native and exotic plants under glass. The beach stretches for many km., but there are too many waves for swimming. Practically every amenity is closed off-season.

**Hotels** *Gure-Etxe*, B, on beach, small and very pleasant; *Costas del Mar*, C, on beach, rec., swimming pool; *Oceanía* (seems to be only one open all year), C (highly rec.), family runs restaurant close by; *Las Palmas*, D with shower (electric), clean, helpful, restaurant; both *Rivamar* and *Las Cholgas* (T 33, B with bath, restaurant) claim to have heating.

**Restaurants** *La Ruta*, open all year, rec; at entrance to town a *parrillada* is open off-season.

**Bus** To/from Montevideo, US$6.25, 5 hrs.

At **Chuy**, a run-down town (pop. 9,000), the frontier runs along the main street. Tourists may freely cross the border in either direction.

There are many duty free shops in Chuy and tourists from Uruguay may buy limited amounts of manufactured goods on the Brazilian side without formalities (but see below).

There is a tourist office caravan opposite the casino.

**Hotels and Restaurants** All are open the year round. *Hotel Chuy*, D, casino; *Hotel Plaza*, D; *International*, D (incl. own bath); *Hospedaje Vitoria*, 4 blocks E of *Hotel Chuy*, F, basic, clean, friendly, rec. *Restaurant Jesús*, ½ block from Onda, good, cheap, friendly.

**Exchange** at *Hotel Chuy* (open until 0300), and at 3 places opposite (open until 1830), giving slightly better rates. No exchange facilities on Sundays. Buy Brazilian currency here as the black market is difficult to find until São Paulo. Banks won't change travellers cheques.

The Uruguayan passport control is 2½ km. before the frontier on the road into Chuy. If travelling by bus, make sure the driver knows you want to stop at Uruguayan immigration. The Brazilian immigration is 2 km. from Chuy on the road to Pelotas (Brazilian Consul is at Tito Fernández s/n y Laguna Merín, T 49). Buses from Chuy to Santa Vitoria or Pelotas stop at Brazilian customs; alternatively take a taxi. The office for the Pelotas bus is one block inside Brazil, near the *Hotel Quarain*. Make sure your passport is stamped or you may have difficulties leaving Brazil. Similarly, on entering Uruguay, get an entry stamp otherwise you will not be permitted to proceed (e.g. at the customs post between Chuy and San Miguel fortress). Taking a car into Brazil is no trouble, especially if the car is not registered in Brazil or Uruguay.

**Excursions from Chuy**: on the Uruguyan side, overlooking the Laguna Merín, stands the restored fortress of **San Miguel**, dating from 1752 and surrounded by a moat. It is set in a park in which many plants and animals are kept. (Bus from Chuy US$0.35, entry US$0.20, open Thurs.-Sun. only.) A casino nearby is open until 0400. From Chuy buses run every two hours to the Barra del Chuy; campsite, good bathing, many birds. The hotel nearby, the

*Parador San Miguel*, is excellent. Onda runs daily excursion buses from La Coronilla to Barra del Chuy beach and from Chuy to San Miguel fort, US$9.

**Transport**  Uruguayan taxis are allowed 25 km. beyond the frontier and vice versa. Buses: to *Rio Grande* (Rodoviaria) at 0700 and 1500, 4 hrs., with stop at immigration; to *Porto Alegre*, 7½ hrs., US$5.50; to *Montevideo* (Onda or Cita) US$9, also by Ruta del Sol US$7, 6 hrs., frequent stops; to *Maldonado* US$5; to *La Paloma* US$3, 3¾ hrs.

---

## MONTEVIDEO NORTH-EAST TO BRAZIL (3)

**Two roads run towards Melo, heart of cattle-ranching country: Route 8 and Route 7, the latter running for most of its length through the Cuchilla Grande, a range of hills with fine views.**

Route 8 is the more important of these two roads to the border. It is paved to about 150 km. from Montevideo; beyond it is all-weather.

The first main town is *Minas*, (pop 34,000). It is a picturesque small town 120 km. N of Montevideo, set in the beautiful wooded hills, which supply granite, marble and other minerals. Juan Lavalleja, the leader of the Thirty-Three who brought independence to the country, was born here (equestrian statue), and there is an equestrian statue to Artigas, said to be the largest such in the world, on the Cerro Artigas just out of town. The church's portico and towers, some caves in the neighbourhood, and the countryside around are worth seeing. In March and April you can buy *butea* palm fruit, which is grape size, orange and tastes bitter-sweet. Good confectionery is made in Minas; the largest firm, opposite *Hotel Verdun*, shows tourists round its premises. Museum in the Casa de la Cultura.

**Hotels**  *Verdun*, main plaza, clean, E; *Ramos*, 18 de Julio near bus station, basic, clean, E (discount for IYHA members); *Residencia Minas*, 25 de Mayo 502 on main plaza, clean, E.

**Camping**  Camping Areguita, beautiful surroundings, US$2.

**Youth Hostel**  Route 8, Km. 145, in small village of Villa Serrana, US$1.80 a night (open all year), 28 km. beyond Minas on road to Treinta y Tres; most attractive, but take plenty of food and drink as there is no shop. Direct bus from Montevideo or Minas, ask driver to set you down and walk 3 km. to Villa Serrana; essential to book through Montevideo office.

**Restaurants**  *San Francisco*, 25 de Mayo 586, is recommended as is *El Portal*, Aníbal del Campo 743, for *parrillada*. The best pastry shop is *Irisarri*, Calle Treinta y Tres 618, known for *yemas* (egg candy) and *damasquitos* (apricot sweets).

**Exchange**  Lloyds Bank and national banks, open 1300-1700 Monday-Friday.

**Tourist Office**  at the bus station.

**Air Service**  Daily flight by Tamu from Montevideo.

**Bus**  To Montevideo, US$2.25, COT (4 a day) and many others, 2½ hrs. To Maldonado, Coom, US$2.50, 5 a day, 2 hrs.

**Excursions**  The Parque Salus, on the slopes of Sierras de las Animas, is 8 km. to the S and very attractive; take the town bus marked "Cervecería Salus" from plaza to the Salus brewery, then walk 2 km. to the mineral spring and bottling plant (*Parador Salus*, C p.p. full board, acceptable; reasonable set lunch.) The Cascada de Agua del Penitente waterfall, about 11 km. out of town, off the Minas-Aigue road, is interesting and you may see wild rheas (protected) nearby. It is difficult to get to the falls in the off-season.

The next centre of any importance, 286 km. from Montevideo, is *Treinta y Tres*, (pop. 28,000), picturesquely placed a little way from the Río Olimar. Free camping and swimming at Municipal Park at Río Olimar. Main plaza has all the main restaurants and grills.

**Hotel**  *Central*, and pensions *Jorgito* or *Mota*.

**Air Service**  Daily by Tamu from Montevideo.

Some 20 km. from Treinta y Tres on Route 8, a dirt road, left, runs 19 km. among and over hills to a rocky region with small streams—the **Quebrada de los Cuervos**—now a beautiful and quite unspoilt national park.

Route 8 continues north through **Melo** (pop. 42,000), 113 km. from Treinta y Tres (*Hotel Internacional*, acceptable) to the Brazilian frontier near Aceguá (Brazilian Consul in Melo at Av. Aparicio Saravia 711, T 2084). From Melo Route 26 runs south-east for 88 km. to the border town of **Río Branco**, founded in 1914, on the Río Yaguarón (Río Branco is also reached from Treinta y Tres direct on Route 18). The 1½ km.-long Mauá bridge across the river leads to the Brazilian town of Jaguarão (Brazilian Consul, Lavalleja y Palomeque, T 3).

**Hotel** *Italiano*, D, with bath. **Youth Hostel** Av. Artigas 279, open all year (reservations in Montevideo).

**Restaurant** *Oasis*, good, *pollo a la brasa*.

This is where most international traffic used to cross the frontier; now the road via Chuy is better. Customs officials are at the international bridge, passport officials at the police station at Jaguarão. From Jaguarão buses run several times daily to Pelotas and Porto Alegre. There is usually a better rate of exchange at Melo than at the frontier.

---

## MONTEVIDEO NORTH TO BRAZIL (4)

Dams on the Río Negro have created an extensive network of lakes near Paso de los Toros, with camping and sports facilities. South of the Río Negro is gently rolling cattle country, vineyards, orchards, orange, lemon and olive groves. North is hilly countryside with steep river valleys and cattle ranching.

Route 5, the 509 km. road from Montevideo to the border town of Rivera runs almost due north, bypassing Canelones before passing through Florinda, Durazno and Tacuarembó. The road is dual carriageway as far as Canelones; there is a toll 67.8 km. north of Montevideo.

**Las Piedras** (pop. 58,000), 24 km. from Montevideo, in vineyard country, has a Gothic Chapel of the Salesians. Race meetings (pari-mutuel betting) Tues., Thurs., Sat. and Sun, entry US$0.50, take bus 102 from Río Branco y 18 de Julio in Montevideo.

**Exchange** Lloyds Bank, Calle General Artigas 652. Open 1300-1700, Mon.-Fri.

**Canelones**, 45 km. from the capital, is a typical small town (pop. 17,000) in a grain growing area. It was the seat of Artigas' first government in 1813 (in what is now the Police station). 52 km. further north is the pleasant country town of **Florida**, (pop. 28,000), where the Act of Uruguayan Independence was signed in 1825. This is celebrated by a folklore festival on Independence Day (25 Aug.) each year. (*Hotel Español*, José Rodó 360, D with bath, E without; camp site; *Restaurant Negro el 8*, Italian food.)

**Durazno**, (pop. 28,000), 182 km. from Montevideo on the Río Yí, is a friendly provincial town with tree-lined avenues and an airport. There is a good view of the river from the western bridge. (*Hotel Central*, Manuel Cribe y Mons Arrospiede, D; **Youth Hostel**, Campus Municipal, T 2835 between 1300 and 1900, open all year.)

**Paso de los Toros** (pop. 13,000) is close to the huge lake created by the Rincón del Bonete dam on the Río Negro (*Hotel Onda*, F, not very clean; beautiful camping by the river, tourist information at Parador Municipal, Durazno s/n, T 2074); E of Paso de los Toros (1½ hrs. by Onda bus at 1700) is San Gregorio, cheap camping and bathing in Río Negro. Bus returns to Paso de los Toros 0245.

***Tacuarembó***, 390 km. north of Montevideo, is a major route centre (pop. 40,000) Museo del Indio y del Gaucho at Flores y Artigas (*Hotel Tacuarembó*, 18 de Julio 133, T 2945, E with bath, breakfast, clean, central; campsite 1 km. out of town).

***Rivera*** (pop. 55,400), is on the Brazilian frontier. It is divided by a street from the Brazilian town of Santa Ana do Livramento, which has a good golf course, and a daily bus to Porto Alegre. Points of interest are the park, the Plaza Internacional, and the dam of Cañapirú. There are an airport and a casino, and many duty-free shops. Tourist Information at Dr. Analles 328, T 3083. Brazilian consul, Ceballos 1159, T 3278/4470; Argentine consul, Ituzaingó 524, T 3257.

**Hotels** *Casablanca*, Sarandí 484, T 3221, E, shower, breakfast, a/c, clean, pleasant. *Mabé* (near station); *Casino*. **Camping** in Municipal site near AFE station, and in the Parque Gran Bretaña 7 km. south along Route 27.

**Bus** to/from **Montevideo**, US$10 or less, to **Fray Bentos** and **Durazno**; to **Paysandú**, by Onda 0400 and 1700, or take 1000 service to **Tacuarembó** and change.

**Excursion** To Minas de Corrales (pop. 3,000), in an area of abandoned goldmines, including long tunnels which run under the town. Daily bus from Rivera, 2 hrs. (rec. by Kirsten Bruun and Jesper Rasmussen, Copenhagen).

---

## WEST FROM MONTEVIDEO (5)

This is the route from the capital to Colonia del Sacramento, with its colonial quarter and connections for Argentina.

Route 1, part of the Pan-American Highway, runs W from Montevideo (toll at the Santa Lucía bridge, Km. 22.5) for 177 km. to Colonia del Sacramento. Route 3, the road to Paysandú and Salto, turns off at Km. 67. Route 2, for Mercedes and Fray Bentos, leads off at Km. 128 (no tolls on Routes 2 and 3). Route 1 is lined with ribbon development for much of the way to Libertad (Km. 51). Roads lead off to several beaches, notably Playa Pascual at Km. 34, Kiyú (campsite) at Km. 76 and Boca del Cufre (campsite) at Km. 101.

At Km. 121 from Montevideo the road passes **Colonia Valdense** , a colony of Waldensians who still cling to some of the old customs of the Piedmontese Alps. (**Hotels** *Brisas del Plata*; *Parador Los Ceibos*.) A road branches off here to **Colonia Suiza** , a zone of Swiss settlement centred around the town of Nueva Helvecia (pop. 9,000). (**Hotels** *Nirvana*, T 0522-4052, A, restaurant, sports facilities, run down but good; *Granja Hotel Suiza*; *Central*; *Del Prado*—Youth Hostel—open all year, T 0522-4169). The area is famous for its cheeses and other dairy produce. The Swiss national day is celebrated with great enthusiasm.

**Buses** Onda and COT: **Montevideo—Colonia Valdense**, frequent, 2 hrs, US$3; to **Colonia del Sacramento**, frequent, 1 hr, US$1.20; local services between Colonia Valdense and Nueva Helvecia connect with Montevideo/Colonia del Sacramento buses.

***Rosario*** , 5 km. along Route 2 from the junction with Route 1, is a typical agricultural town given over to dairying and grain production (pop. 8,000). It has 2 fishing clubs and the Club Cyssa, a social, cultural and sports club. (**Hotels** *Ricardi* and *Riviera*, E, good).

***Colonia*** (del Sacramento), a charming small town (pop. 22,000) with an interesting historic section jutting into the Río de la Plata, was founded by Portuguese settlers from Brazil in 1680. The Barrio Histórico, with its narrow streets (see the Calle de los Suspiros), colonial buildings and reconstructed city walls, is particularly interesting because there are few such examples in this part of the continent. The Plaza Mayor is especially picturesque. Grouped around it are the Museo Municipal in the former house of Almirante Brown, the Casa del Virrey and the Museo Portugués. Also worth a visit are the Faro (lighthouse), the Santísimo Sacramento church near the Plaza de Armas, and the house of Gen. Mitre, now housing the Museo Español. (All museums open 1130-1830.) At Real de San Carlos just out of town (take blue bus from the centre) there is an unusual tourist complex, built by Nicolás Mihanovic between 1903-1912, which includes a racecourse (Hipódromo), a disused casino and an elegant bull-ring. The best beach is Playa Ferrando, 2 km. to the east. In the third week of January, festivities are held marking the founding of Colonia. Ferries connect with Buenos Aires, only 50 km. away.

**Hotels** *Posada del Gobernador*, 18 de Julio 205, A+, with breakfast, charming, rec.; *El Mirador*, Av. Roosevelt, Km. 176½, T 2004, A+, a/c, casino, sports facilities; *Royal*, General Flores 340, C with breakfast, comfortable, good restaurant, pool, rec.; *Beltrán*, Gral. Flores 311, D, shared bath; *Rincón del Río*, D, shower but no breakfast, clean, friendly; *Natal John*, Gral. Flores 394, C; *Los Angeles*, Roosevelt 203, D, small rooms, no restaurant, but clean and friendly, English spoken; *Leoncia*, Rivera 214, C, modern, good; *Esperanza*, Gral. Flores 237, D, clean, charming. *Posada de la Ciudadela*, Washington Barbot 164, E, clean, pleasant, a/c, simple; *Italiano*, Ituzaingó y De La Peña, E without bath, friendly, clean, English spoken, good restaurant, rec. The municipal sports complex has 2 dormitories with 80 beds, which are sometimes available—ask at the tourist office.

**Camping**   Municipal site at Real de San Carlos, US$1 a day, excellent, rec.; also at Playa Ferrando.

**Restaurant**   *Esperanza* (at hotel) and *Yacht Club* (at harbour) are good; *Mercado del Túnel*, Flores 227, good meat dishes; *Suizo*, Flores y, Ituzaingó, rec.; *Parrillada El Portón*, Flores 338. Several good *parrilladas* along 18 de Julio. *Los Faroles*, rec., friendly, on plaza in colonial zone, also *La Casona*, good cakes; unnamed *parrillada*, Rivadavia y Rivera, good value.

**Exchange**   Cambio Viaggio, Flores y Suárez, open every day 0900-1200, 1300-1800. Several exchange houses at the ferry port.

**Argentine Consulate**   Flores 215, open weekdays 1200-1700.

**Telephones**   Antelco, Rivadavia 420, open till 2300. **Post Office** on main square.

**Tourist Office**   Flores y Rivera, open Mon.-Fri. 0800-1830, Sat. and Sun. 0900-2200, good maps of the barrio histórico; also at passenger terminal at the dock.

**Buses**   to/from **Montevideo**, 2½ hrs, Onda and COT, frequent service, US$4; to **Carmelo**, 1½ hrs, Onda and Tauriño, 4 a day each, US$1.50; to **Salto**, 8 hrs, Chadre, at 0555 and 1430, US$10.

**To Buenos Aires**   By ferry, 3 hrs. crossing, US$18 one way with Buquebus, 3 sailings a day, and Ferryturismo, 2 sailings a day. By hydrofoil (Aliscafo) 1 hr. crossing, US$24 one way, 4 a day, more in summer. The company runs buses to the port from Punta del Este, Piriápolis, *Carrasco Hotel* (Carrasco), and Montevideo (Plaza Libertad).

**By Air**   Lapa and Aero Uruguay both fly to Aeroparque, Buenos Aires 2 times a day, US$35 and run connecting bus services to/from Montevideo. This is generally quicker than hydrofoil. The airport is 17 km. out of town along Route 1. **N.B.** Book in advance for all sailings and flights in summer, especially at weekends.

**Excursion**   To Conchillas, 45 km north, pop. 700, an unusual village of attractive one-storey terraced houses, abandoned quarry and mill, all built in 1890s by H.J. Walker & Co to extract stone to build the port facilities of Buenos Aires. From Colonia take Tauriño bus for Carmelo, changing to connecting service at Radial Conchillas, 6 km. from the village, bus waits in Conchillas 1 hr. before returning. About 6 km. further is Puerto Conchillas, with similar stone houses, disused port facilities and camping site.

---

## UP THE RIVER URUGUAY (6)

The Río Uruguay marks the frontier with Argentina (international crossings at Fray Bentos, Paysandú and Salto). On the Uruguayan side are rolling hills crossed by a network of rivers. At all the major towns on the Uruguay are beaches and campsites and there are thermal springs at Guaviyú, Daymán and Arapey.

Route 21 swings N and NW to reach the sleepy resort town of **Carmelo**, (pop. 15,000), 74 km. from Colonia, on the shores of Las Vacas river. Across the bridge is a white restaurant on the left-hand side of the road: friendly, recommended. The port harbours several hundred yachts during the season. There is a free zone at the port. There are 2 companies with a launch service to Tigre, across the delta, a most interesting ride past innumerable islands (Cacciola, twice a day, 3 hrs., and Delta Nave daily at 1200 and 0415, 3 hrs, US$9.75, Movilan SA, Constituyentes 263, T 418). You can pay at the Onda bus station in Montevideo for both bus and launch, US$18. Bus to Montevideo, 1210, 2240, US$8.15; to Fray Bentos, Salto, from main square 0710, 1540; to Colonia, Onda and Tauriño, 4 a day each, 1½ hrs, US$1.50.

**Accomodation and Services** *Casino Carmelo;* Rodó s/n; *La Unión*, Uruguay 368, E, very good value; *Centro*, next door, E; *Rambla*, Uruguay y 12 de Febrero; *Nuevo Carmelo*, Sarandí 308; *Bertoletti*, Uruguay 171. **Camping** Site near the bridge (T 2058). The **bank** will only exchange bills and not travellers' cheques.

**Argentine Consulate** F.D. Roosevelt 318, T 266.

Some 30 km. north, by road, is **Nueva Palmira** (pop. 7,000), a popular yachting resort with a free zone and campsite. Worth visiting in the vicinity are the Pirámide of Solís dating from 1888 (8 km. out of town), the Calera de las Huérfanas, a Jesuit chapel built in 1750, the Camacho, the Capilla de Narbona (1732) and the Convento de la Reducción Jesuítica (1780—both in poor condition, 12 km. from town, and 3 km. off the road).

Some 20 km. further north is the historic beach of La Agraciada, famous for the landing of the Thirty-Three patriots on 19 April 1825, which led to Uruguayan independence. On the beach is a statue to General Juan Lavalleja, leader of the Treinta y Tres. A festival is held on each anniversary.

The road continues north through the small river port of **Dolores** (pop. 13,000), 32 km. up-river from the confluence of the Río San Salvador with the Río Uruguay, to **Mercedes**, a livestock centre and resort on the Río Negro best reached by Route 2 from the main Colonia-Montevideo highway. Founded in 1788, this pleasant town (pop. 37,000) is a yachting and fishing centre during the season. Its charm (it is known as "the city of flowers") derives from its Spanish-colonial appearance, though it is not as old as the older parts of Colonia. There is a pleasant *costanera* (riverside drive). Seven km. west of town is the Parque Mauá, dating from 1757, with a castle and Museum of Palaeontology and Natural Sciences.

**Accommodation and Food** *Brisas del Hum*, C; *Himalaya*, D, with bath; *Universal*, D, rec. *Hospedaje Hotelcito*, Giménez 703, E. Cheap *hospedaje* (no name), Giménez 848, G; *Club de Remeros*, on riverside, G. Good food at *La Brasa*, Calle Castro y Careaga, and at *Círculo Policial*, Calle 25 de Mayo.

**Camping** Site at Mercedes, beside Ríos Negro and Uruguay (US$0.45 p.p.).

**Exchange** Cambio Fagalde, Giménez 709.

**Tourist Office** Artigas 215, T 2733.

**Bus** to Paysandú, 2½ hrs., US$4.

**Excursions** To the islands in the Río Negro—the largest has an inn. To the small town of **Santo Domingo** (Soriano), first town to be founded in Uruguay, to see a fine colonial church and an old house. Difficult to do this trip easily in one day. 70 km. inland from Mercedes is La Palmar, hydro-electric power station and tourist complex with motels, camping sites, fishing and sports facilities.

Route 2 continues westwards (34 km.) to **Fray Bentos** (pop. 22,000), a port on the Río Uruguay, 193 km. above Buenos Aires, famous for its meat-packing plant (now closed). Free port planned. There are beaches to the northeast and southwest and also at Las Canas, 8 km. away (where there is a tourist complex including motels, E, campsite, sports facilities and services). Nine km. upriver from the town is the San Martín International Bridge, the most popular overland route with Argentina, toll US$2.10 per car (tourist office). All customs formalities (including the Argentine) are on the Uruguayan side. Bicycles are treated as vehicles (but not at the bridge toll); bicycles are not allowed to cross, but officials will give you a lift if there is no other traffic. Argentine Consulate in Fray Bentos at Sarandí 3195.

**Hotels** *Gran Hotel Fray Bentos*, Paraguay y 18 de Julio, overlooking river, casino; *Colonial*, 25 de Mayo 3293, E; *Plaza*, Plaza Constitución next to Onda offices, D, clean, comfortable. **Camping** at the *Club de Remeros*, near the river.

**Restaurants** *Enramada*, España y 25 de Agosto, the best; several cafés and pizzerias on 18 de Julio near Plaza Constitución.

**Museum** The meat packing plant, known as El Anglo, is now an industrial museum, very interesting, details from the tourist office or the Intendencia.

**Exchange** Cambio Fagalde, Plaza Constitución, open Mon.-Fri. 0800-1900, Sat. 0800-1230.

**Buses** Bus station, 18 de Julio y Blanes, with tourist office, but buses also leave from bus company offices around Plaza Constitución. To/from **Montevideo**, Onda and ETA, 4½ hrs, 6 a day, US$6; to Mercedes, Onda and ETA, frequent, ½ hr; to **Paysandú**, Onda, 1 a day, US$3, to **Gualeguayachú** (Argentina), ETA, 4 a day, 2 on Sun. 1 hr, US$3.

*Paysandú*, on the E bank of the Río Uruguay, 122 km. north of Fray Bentos along Route 24; and 480 along Route 3 from Montevideo via Trinidad, has a population of about 80,000. Temperatures in summer can rise as high as 42°C. There is a golf club, and a rowing club which holds regattas. The cathedral is 19th century; the attached Salesian college has an interesting museum, opens 1700. The cemetery on the outskirts is worth a look. Also worth a visit is the Museo de la Tradición, with *gaucho* articles, a bus-ride north of town at the Balneario Municipal beach. A historical museum can be found at Florida 930. The José Artigas international bridge connects with Colón, Argentina, (toll US$2 per car), about 8 km. away. Airport with daily Tamu flights to Montevideo (US$12). Local fiesta during Holy Week (book hotels in advance).

**Hotels** *Gran Hotel Paysandú*, D, 18 de Julio y 19 de Abril, T 3400, a/c, best; *Onda*, D, "super suites", good restaurant (one can reserve through Onda in Montevideo), rec.; *Pensión Popular*, E, with shower; *Concordia*, 18 de Julio 984, E, clean; *Rafaela*, 18 de Julio 1181, E, large rooms, modern and friendly, electric showers, no food but surrounded by cafés; *Lobato*, Leandro Gómez 1415, E, good. A good hotel, but not in the centre, is *Bulevar* at Bulevar Artigas and República Argentina. *Victoria*, 18 de Julio 979, F, highly rec., cheapest, very friendly.

**Youth Hostel** Liga Departamental de Fútbol, Gran Bretaña 872, T 4247, US$1 p.p., neither clean nor well-maintained. Cabins for 5 or more people.

**Camping** in a municipal park by the river, no facilities.

**Restaurant** *Artemio*, Plaza de Constitución, 18 de Julio, "best food in town", but closed in winter. *Parrillada de Asturias*, good and cheap. *Don Diego's*, 19 de Abril, serves cheap *parrillada*, good value. *Pipan*, 2 blocks S of Cathedral, good and cheap.

**Exchange** Cambio Fagalde, 18 de Julio 1004,.

**Consulates** Argentina, Leandro Gómez 1034, T 2253; Brazil, Dr. L.A. de Herrera 932, T 2723.

**Tourist Office** Plaza de Constitución, 18 de Julio 1226; also at the International Bridge.

**Travel Agency** Viñar Turismo, Artigas 1163, helpful.

**Bus** to/from **Montevideo**, 5½-7½ hrs., US$9.50, by Onda, four buses daily. Other lines (Chadre, Agencia Central) are just as good. To **Salto** US$3. To **Paso de los Toros** 1430 (return 0430), US$4, or by Alonso bus to **Guichón** at 0600,1100, 1430 and change. To **Colonia** by Chadre, 1700, 6 hrs, US$5.

**Excursions** To the waterfalls of the Río Quequay, a few km. to the N; the Termas del Guaviyú thermal springs 50 km. north (1½ hrs. by bus, 4 a day) with excellent cheap camping facilities, and to the Meseta de Artigas, 90 km. N of Paysandú, 13 km. off the highway to Salto. The Meseta, where General Artigas lived (statue), is 45 metres above the Uruguay river, which here narrows and forms whirlpools at the rapids of El Hervidero. A terrace commands a fine view, but the rapids are not visible from the Meseta. The statue, with the general's head topping a tall shaft, is very original. There are some pleasant, somewhat primitive, chalets available from Erwin Frey, 90 Estación Chapieny, Dept. Paysandú. Early booking recommended. Bus to Km. 462 on Paysandú-Salto road.

*Salto*, (pop. 80,000), 120 km. by paved road N of Paysandú, is a centre for cultivating and processing oranges and other citrus fruit. See the beautiful park of Solari; the Parque Harriague with an open air theatre and a well-kept zoo (closed Mon., US$0.15—7 blocks from centre, feeding time 1400-1500); the fine-arts museum in the donated mansion, French style, of a rich *estanciero*, Uruguay 1067, opens at 1700, well worth a visit; and the promenade along the Río Uruguay. North of the town there is an international bridge to Concordia, Argentina. Ferries still run, 2 companies, twice a day, US$5. Sometimes the river is low enough to walk across.

**Festival** Shrove Tuesday carnival.

**Hotels** *Gran Hotel Salto*, Plaza Artigas, best, good restaurant, reasonably priced; *Los Cedros*, a/c, D, Uruguay 657 (T 3989); *Plaza*, Plaza Treinta y Tres, near the river, simple, clean, good food, E. *Pensión 33*, Treinta y Tres 269, F, basic, central. *Concordia*, Uruguay 749, E, shower, a/c, central, clean, friendly; *Pensión Santa Catalina*, Brasil 1633 or *Pensión Las Tres Fronteras*, General Rivera 1155, cheaper, basic, E; *Artigas Plaza*, Artigas 446, Plaza 18 de Julio next to Onda bus station, E with bath, F without, hot water, very clean, log fire in winter, friendly (T4824), rec.

**Youth Hostels** Club de Remeros Salto, Rambla Gutiérrez y Belén (by the river) T 0732-3418, open all year, or Club de Leones, Uruguay 1626, if you can find a student to sign you in.

**Camping** At the Club de Remeros and at several sites along the river both north and south.

**Restaurants** *Chef Restaurant*, Uruguay 639; *Pizzería Los Mil y Una*, Uruguay 906, popular, good atmosphere; *Club de Remeros de Salto. Club de Uruguay*, Uruguay, good breakfast and good value meals; *Club Bancario*, Brasil 765, lunch US$2, good.

**Exchange** Lloyds Bank, two agencies: Uruguay 585 and Blandengues y 8 de Octubre, open Mon.-Fri. 0800-1200 (cashes Amex cheques). Banco de Galicia y Buenos Aires, Uruguay 532, does not change cheques. Several exchange houses in Calle Uruguay, best rates nearest the river. Cambio Pensotti has been recommended as helpful. The *cambio* at Uruguay 800 is open until 2000, Mon.-Sat.

**Argentine consul** Artigas 1112, T 2931.

**Anglican Church** Calle República de Argentina, close to Calle Uruguay.

**Tourist Office** Calle Uruguay 1052, T 4096, free map.

**Bus** to/from Montevideo, 7½ hrs., 4 a day, US$12.50 (Onda); to **Termas del Arapey**, 2 hrs., daily, US$3.50. *Paysandús* US$3.65, four a day. To *Rivera*, US$8.50. To *Colonia* by Chadre, 0555, 8 hrs., US$10.

**Air Service** Mon., Wed., Sat. to and from Montevideo via Paysandú, by Tamu, US$35 single. To Buenos Aires.

**Excursions** One excursion from Salto is by launch to the Salto Chico (uninteresting); another is to Salto Grande, where a ranch-style guest house for anglers is run by the Tourist Commission. Nearby is the resort *Hotel Horacio Quiroga*, A, sports facilities, staffed by nearby catering school. The most popular tourist site in the area is the large **Salto Grande** dam and hydroelectric plant 20 km. from Salto, built jointly by Argentina and Uruguay; a 2-hr. free tour can be arranged with the CTM (office on corner of *Hotel Gran Salto*). A road runs along the top of the dam. Medicinal springs at Fuente Salto, 6 km. N of the city. Ten km. outside Salto, reached by bus No. 4 every hour from Calle Artigas (US$0.15) is **Termas de Daymán**, beautifully laid out with 8 swimming pools (entrance US$0.35, towel US$0.50, locker US$0.10; it is cheaper to buy combined bus/entrance ticket in Salto). **Youth Hostel** on Route 3, Km. 490, T 0732-4361 (open all year, book well in advance during holiday season), restaurant, souvenir shop, capsite (poor facilities).

The road to **Termas del Arapey** branches off the partially paved Route 3 to Bella Unión, at

61 km. N of Salto, and then runs 35 km. first E and then S. Pampa birds, rheas and metre-long lizards much in evidence. Termas del Arapey is on the Arapey river S of Isla Cabellos (Baltazar Brum). The waters at these famous thermal baths (five pools) contain bicarbonated salts, calcium and magnesium. There is a new hotel with pool (*Hotel Termas del Arapey*, A), 2 motels, both C (very small bungalows with kitchens, no sheets provided), a nice swimming pool, a very simple *parador* (meals only) and a good Onda restaurant. Book ahead at tourist offices in Salto or Montevideo. Camping US$2 p.p. (beware of theft at campsite and take food as local markets very expensive).

Route 3 runs N to the little town of **Bella Unión**, (pop. 12,000), on the Río Cuaraim, 144 km. north of Salto (campsite in the Parque Fructuaso Rivera, insect repellant needed), near the Brazilian frontier which is crossed by the Barra del Cuaraim bridge. Brazilian consul at Lirio Moraes 62, T 54. (If entering from Brazil by car take plenty of fuel as there are few service stations on the roads south).

From near Bella Unión Route 30 runs east to **Artigas** (pop. 34,000), a frontier town in a cattle raising and agricultural area (excellent swimming upstream from the bridge). There is a bridge across the Río Cuaraim to the Brazilian town of Quaraí opposite. Brazilian Consul at Lecueder 432, T 2504.

**Accommodation** *Concordia; Oriental, Pensión Uruguay* and *Hawaii*, basic but clean.

**Camping** at Paseo 7 de Setiembre (by river), US$0.25 p.p. a day, or at Agua Corriente—chance of camping at the yacht club on the river. **Youth Hostel** Club Deportivo Artigas, Pte. Berreta and L.A. de Herrera, T 0642-3015, open all year.

**Restaurants** *Maricarmen*, Calle Lecueder 302, and *Municipal*, Lecueder y Berreta.

**Bus** service to Salto, 225 km. **Airport** at Bella Unión

---

## INFORMATION FOR VISITORS

**Documents** A passport is necessary for entry except for nationals of other American countries, who can get in with national identity documents. Visas (about US$10) are not required by nationals of American and Western European countries, Israel and Japan. Tourist cards (obligatory for all tourists, obtainable on entry) are valid for 3 months, extendable for a similar period. For extensions (small fee) go to Migraciones office, Calle Misiones 1513, T 960471/961094.

The Ministry of Tourism sells a "tarjeta turística" at points of entry, US$20 (blue), US$26 (red). Both cover medical and dental assistance, free transport back to country of origin in case of sickness/accident, legal assistance, shopping discounts; the red card also covers car insurance.

**Airport Tax** of US$4.50 on all air travellers leaving Uruguay for South American republics or Mexico (US$2.50 to Aeroparque, Buenos Aires); US$7 for all other countries, and a tax of 3% on all tickets issued and paid for in Uruguay.

**Flights from Europe** By air: direct flights by Pluna (Madrid), Iberia, KLM, and Lufthansa. Flying by other carriers, a change must be made at Rio or Buenos Aires.

**From North America** Pan Am (2 a week from New York), and LanChile (from Montreal and/or New York), and (as far as Buenos Aires) by Canadian Pacific Airlines (from Toronto), Ecuatoriana (Los Angeles) and Aerolíneas Argentinas.

**From Argentina** Ferry services (Montevideo and Colonia to Buenos Aires), hydrofoil services (Colonia to Buenos Aires) and launch services (Carmelo to Tigre) are given in the text. Aerolíneas Argentinas and Pluna have several flights a day between Aeroparque in Buenos Aires and Carrasco Airport. Service intensified during holiday period (US$90 single). Also frequent flights to Punta del Este from Buenos Aires, US$110. Lapa and AeroUruguay fly between Colonia and Buenos Aires; US$35 single. From Colonia there is a fast bus service by Onda to Montevideo. Foreign airlines connect Carrasco with the Buenos Aires international airport at Ezeiza. Buses run across the Paysandú and Fray Bentos bridges. Direct bus between Buenos Aires and Montevideo by one of these routes takes about 10 hours. Ferries cross the Río Uruguay between Salto and Concordia.

**From Brazil**   Direct connection between Brazil and Uruguay by all the international airlines landing at Montevideo. Varig flies daily from Rio de Janeiro to Montevideo, via Buenos Aires. Cruzeiro do Sul has two flights a week São Paulo, Porto Alegre and Montevideo. Pluna also flies from Rio, São Paulo and Porto Alegre to Montevideo. By road: the Pan-American Highway runs 2,880 km. from Rio de Janeiro to Montevideo and on to Colonia. It is poorly surfaced in parts. There are several bus services.

**From Chile**   KLM (once), Pluna (twice) and LanChile three times a week to Santiago. LanChile flies between Santiago, Buenos Aires and Montevideo and between Montevideo and Lima. **NB** Tamu, the military airline, has flights to Santiago and Rio de Janeiro every other week; civilians are taken for US$35 but service is unreliable (ask at Pluna office in Montevideo or at Uruguayan consulates in Rio or Santiago).

**From Paraguay**   Once a week each by Pluna, and Líneas Aéreas Paraguayas (LAP). Twice-weekly buses Asunción-Montevideo.

**Customs**   Duties are not usually charged on a reasonable quantity of goods (such as tobacco and spirits), brought in obviously for the traveller's own use: 400 cigarettes or 50 cigars or 250 grammes of tobacco are admitted duty-free; so are 2 litres of alcoholic drink, 3 little bottles of perfume and gifts up to the value of US$5.

**Local Air Services**   Internal flights are very cheap, e.g. US$15 to Salto, and to the Brazilian border at Rivera. Pluna will accept credit cards only at its office in Plaza del Entrevero, Montevideo. Tamu, the military airline, offers considerably reduced fares on many internal flights; tickets from Colonia 1021, Montevideo. Provincial airports are given in the text.

**Roads**   There are 45,000 km. of roads, 80% of them paved or all-weather. The Comisión Nacional de Turismo will help to plan itineraries by car.

**Bus Travel**   Onda buses radiate into the interior from Montevideo, using comfortable American (they even use the Greyhound logo) long-distance coaches; other companies do not run the same extensive network, but are often cheaper and as fast. All hotels display Onda timetables. Owing to financial problems, Onda's services were reported to be less efficient in 1990-91.

**Hitch-hiking**   is fairly easy, along the coast, but difficult in the interior because the population is sparse; it is reportedly fairly safe for women to hitch alone.

**Motoring**   Vehicles do not stop, nor is there a right of way, at uncontrolled intersections. Traffic is slow because there are so many ancient cars (1920s and 1930s models are called *cachilas* and skilled mechanics keep them on the road) outside Montevideo there is little traffic and few gas stations (many close at weekends). Care is needed at night since vehicle lights do not always work. Insurance is not required by law. Uruguay is said to be much better than Argentina or Brazil to ship a car to, but vehicles are admitted for 6 months only, with the possibility of a further 3 months extension.Gasoline prices are US$0.90/litre; gas/oil is US$0.40/litre. Automóvil Club del Uruguay has a fuel and service station for its members only at Yí y Colonia, Montevideo (head office is Av. Libertador General Lavalleja 1532).

Car spares are expensive. The area around Galicia and Yí in Montevideo is recommended for new parts. Warnes, Minas y Cerro Largo, have been rec. for second-hand parts. Land-Rover garage in Montevideo at Cuareim 2082, near old railway station.

**Railways**   All passenger services were withdrawn in January 1988.

**Youth Hostels**   Asociación de Alberguistas del Uruguay, Calle Pablo de María 1583 (open 1300-1900), Montevideo (T 404245) operates hostels (IYHA members only) at Montevideo (Canelones 935), Artigas, Paysandú, Piriápolis, Salto, La Paloma, Colonia Suiza, Villa Serrana (near Minas), Barra de Valizas (between La Pedrera and Aguas Dulces), Durazno and Río Branco. A 10% rebate is available on Lapa plane tickets between Colonia and Buenos Aires—obtainable at the Onda terminal in Montevideo, and rebates have also been reported (10-20%) for bus fares and hotel prices.

**Camping**   Lots of sites. Most towns have municipal sites (quality varies). Many sites along the Ruta Interbalnearia, but most of these close off season. The Tourist Office in Plaza Cagancha issues a good guide to campsites and youth hostels; see references in main text.

**Food and Drink** Beef is eaten at almost all meals. The majority of restaurants are *parrilladas* (grills) where the staple is beef. *Asado* (barbecued beef) is popular; the main cuts are *asado de tira* (ribs); *pulpa* (no bones), *lomo* (fillet steak) and entrecote. To get a lean piece of *asado*, ask for *asado flaco*. *Costilla* (chop) and *milanesa* (veal cutlet) are also popular; usually eaten with mixed salad or chips. *Chivitos* are Uruguayan steak burgers; *chivitos canadienses* are sandwiches filled with slices of meat, lettuce, tomato, egg, etc. (normally over US$2—very filling). Two other good local dishes are *puchero* (beef with vegetables, bacon, beans and sausages) and the local varieties of pizza, fast becoming a staple. Other specialities are barbecued pork, grilled chicken in wine, *cazuela* (or stew) usually with *mondongo* (tripe) or sea foods (e.g. squid, shark—*cazón*, mussels—*mejillones*). The sausages are very good and spicy (*chorizos, morcillas, salchichas*). *Morcilla dulce*, a sweet black sausage, made from blood, orange peel and walnuts, has been highly praised; so has the *morcilla salada*, which is savoury. For snacks, *media lunas mixtas* are a type of croissant filled with ham and cheese, either hot or cold; toasted sandwiches are readily available; *panchos* are hot dogs, *húngaros* are spicy sausage hot dogs. *Preparación* is a selection of crisps, nuts, vol-au-vent, etc. An excellent dessert is *chajá*, a type of sponge-cake ball with cream and jam inside—very sweet; others are *messini* (a cream sponge) and the common lemon pie. Pastries are very good indeed, and crystallized egg-yolks, known as *yemas*, are popular sweets. Ice cream is excellent everywhere.

The dinner hour is usually from 2000 to 0100. Note that restaurants generally charge *cubierto* (bread), which ranges from US$0.30 to US$1 in Punta del Este.

The local wines are very varied: the following have been recommended by various correspondents: Santa Rosa Cabernet red and Santa Rosa Anticuario del Museo (light, claret type); Castel Pujol Cabernet Sauvignon and Chardonnay, and Castel Pujol Tannat del Museo (Burgundy-type) and white Pinot del Museo. Simon Watson Taylor recommends the following rosés: Irurtia Cabernet Rosado and Franciacorta Ca'del Sacramento Rosado. N.B. "del museo" indicates the bodega's vintage reserve. The beers are good. Imported drinks are freely available in Montevideo, e.g. whisky, US$2.50-3 and Chilean wines. *Mate* is a favourite drink between meal hours. The local spirits are *caña* and *grappa*; some find the locally-made whisky and gin acceptable. In the Mercado del Puerto, Montevideo, a *medio medio* is half still white wine, half sparkling white (a must! Elsewhere a *medio medio* is half *caña* and half whisky). *Espillinar* is a cross between whisky and rum. Try the *clérico*, a tasty mixture of wine, fruit juices and fruits. Coffee is good: a *cortado* is a strong, white coffee, *café con leche* is milk with a little coffee. Milk is available, in bottles or plastic sacs.

**Tipping** Normally all hotel and restaurant bills include a percentage service charge plus 20% value-added tax, but an additional small tip is expected. In other cases give 10% of the total bill. Porters at the airport expect about US$0.20 per piece of luggage; although there is an official rate of tips for porters at seaports, the actual charges are mostly higher. Taxi drivers are tipped 10% of the fare. Tips at cafés are about 10%. Cinema ushers get a small tip, as do cloakroom attendants and hairdressers (10%-15%).

**Shopping Bargains** See under Montevideo, page 1094.

**Security** Personal security offers few problems in Uruguay to travellers who are reasonably prudent.

**Health** Milk and tap water can be drunk and fresh salads eaten fairly freely throughout the country. Medical services are reported to be expensive. Under the Clínica Panamericana Plan, if you pay US$6 a month, a visit to a specialist costs US$0.60 plus free laboratory and emergency care. Many reports of hepatitis from injections and visits to the dentist. The British Hospital in Montevideo is recommended.

**Best times for visiting** Most tourists visit during the summer (December-mid March), though hotels have to be booked in advance. Business visits can be paid throughout the year, but it is best to avoid the tourist months.

**British business travellers** are strongly advised to read "Hints to Exporters: Uruguay", obtainable from the Department of Trade, Sanctuary Buildings, 16-20 Great Smith Street, London SW1.

**Hours of Business** Most department stores generally are open 0900 to 1200 (or 1230), 1400 (or 1430) to 1900, but 0900 to 1230 on Sat. Business houses vary but most work from 0830 to 1200, 1430 to 1830 or 1900, according to whether they open on Sat. Banking hours are 1300 to 1700 in Montevideo; there are special summer hours (1 Dec.-15 March) in Montevideo (1330-1730), in the interior (0800-1200) and in Punta del Este, Maldonado and other resorts (1600-2000); banks are closed on Sat. Government departments, mid-March to mid-November, 1300 to 1830 from Mon. to Fri.; rest of the year, 0700 to 1230 (not Sat).

**Holidays** 1, 6 Jan.; Carnival (see below); Easter week; 19 April; 1, 18 May; 19 June; 18 July; 25 August; 12 October; 2 November; 25 December. (8 Dec. is a religious holiday which also marks the official start of the summer holiday.)

**Carnival Week** is officially the Monday and Tuesday immediately preceding Ash Wednesday, but a great many firms close for the whole of the week.

Business comes to a standstill also during Holy Week, which coincides with La Semana Criolla (horse-breaking, stunt riding by cowboys, dances and song, many Argentine visitors). Department stores close only from Good Friday. Banks and offices close Thursday-Sunday. Easter Monday is not a holiday.

**Currency** Bank notes issued are for 50, 100, 200, 500, 1,000, 2,000, 5,000, 10,000, 20,000 and 50,000 new pesos, and coins for 5, 10, 50, 100, 200 and 500 new pesos (notes of 50 to 500 NP are being withdrawn). Any amount of currency can be taken in or out.

**Exchange** Rates change frequently because of a floating exchange rate and inflation differentials against the US dollar; see the "Latest Exchange and Inflation Rates" table near end of book. Many banks and exchange houses (casas de cambio) will give you US$ cash for US$ travellers' cheques with no commission charged (but at about 2-3% poorer rates than for cash). Obtaining US$ cash against a credit card is difficult; try the Banco Comercio Exterior and Caja Obrera. Dollars cash can be purchased when leaving the country. Exchanges from Brazilian and Argentine currency receive much worse rates than straightforward deals between dollars and pesos.

**Credit Cards** Argencard is a member of the Mastercard organization, so one may use Access at outlets displaying their sign. Many shopkeepers are unaware of this but a phone call will confirm it. Also American Express, Diners Club and Visa. Most hotels outside Montevideo do not accept credit cards. There is a 10% charge on the use of credit cards.

**Cost of Living** Several recent travellers have reported Uruguay as being very expensive, although comparisons with Argentina and Brazil will depend on the financial regimes in force in those countries. Prices vary considerably between summer and winter, Punta del Este being particularly expensive.

**Weights and Measures** Metric units alone are legal. Odd fact: the timber trade still uses inches for the cross section of lengths of timber.

**Electric Power** 220 volts 50 cycles AC.

**Postal services** are very unreliable; all items should be registered and sent by air mail to avoid delay (probably better to go direct to airport, avoiding chaos of the sorting office). Rates are low, e.g. US$0.25 for postcard, US$0.30 for a letter to Europe; US$8 by air for up to 500 g., US$10 for 500-1,000 g. US$21 up to 3 kg.; by sea US$7 for 1 kg., US$11 for 3 kg. (but best not to send parcels at all—if they do arrive they will probably have been opened).

**Telecommunications** Provided by Antel (see under Montevideo). The telephone service still has a poor reputation. Direct dialling abroad is straightforward. Collect calls available to most countries (collect calls are the cheapest way of phoning USA and Canada). Cost: to USA about US$4 a minute; to Europe US$4.50; to New Zealand, US$5. Phone calls are cheaper by 20% between 2200 and 0700.

**Media** Of the 20 colour-TV stations, 4 transmit from Montevideo (channel 12 is the most popular). There are also 35 radio stations (8 private FM) in Montevideo and 65 in the rest of the country.

There are 6 Montevideo newspapers: El País, El Día, La República, La Mañana and La Hora Popular, and El Diario and Ultimas Noticias which come out in the evening. Búsqueda is published weekly. The town of Paysandú has the Telégrafo. At about 1000 the main Buenos Aires papers, including the Buenos Aires Herald, can be had in Montevideo.

**Sport** The beach is more popular than the water. Uruguay has three important yacht clubs, the Uruguayo, the Nautilus and the Punta del Este. Fishing. Association football is played intensively. Rugby football is also played, and there is a yearly championship.

**Local Information Centres** The Comisión Nacional de Turismo information office, at Plaza Cagancha, Montevideo, issues tourist literature. It has built a number of good guest houses at the various resorts and gives information about them at the Information Office. There is a good information kiosk at Montevideo's main bus station. The local papers publish "what's on" columns on Friday evenings and on Saturdays. See also Montevideo, **Information**.

**Maps** Automóvil Club del Uruguay, Av. Libertador General Lavalleja 1532, Montevideo, publishes road maps of the city and the country at large, and so do Esso and Ancap at about US$2 each. Official maps are issued by Instituto Geográfico Militar, Abreu y 8 de Octubre, open 0800-1230, T 816868.

We should like to thank Charlie Nurse, who visited Uruguay in August, 1990, for updating this chapter. We are also grateful to Sonya Ayling of Montevideo for valuable assistance, to Simon Watson Taylor for thorough and detailed corrections of the Montevideo section and to the following travellers: Jackie Annesley (Australia) and Suzie James (Scotland), Frank Bakker and Nike Darley (Amsterdam), Monique Belleau (Quebec), Erik Bernesson (Båstad, Sweden), Gianmarco Broggini (Milan), Elizabeth Buettner (Ann Arbor, M.I.) and Alexander Protopapas (Pasadena, California), Daniel Ezekiel (Vancouver, BC), Tim Farnworth (Market Harborough, Leicestershire), Theodor A. Gevert (São Paulo), Michael Gonin (Canberra, Australia), Loukas Grafakos (Papagou, Greece), Pilou Grenié (Antibes), Lucy Harper, Gert Jan Hof and Yvonne Evers (Huissen, Neth), Ralf Hönsch and Martin Stark (Switzerland), Barry Isaac (Miami Beach, Florida), Eliana S. and Prof. Jeff H. Lesser (Connecticut, U.S.A.), Herbert Levi (Buenos Aires), Hans Liechti and Veronica Araneda de Liechti (Grenchen, Switzerland), Philipp Magura (Reutlingen, Germany), Bernard Milward (Salvador), Steve Newman and Wendy Chilcott (Horsham, West Sussex), Nikolaus Nolden (Berlin), Arthur Poyner (Chiloe), John Raspey (Argentina), Ken Sattell (Boulder, C.O.), Nick Saunders and Sarah Jaggs (London W1), Uwe Schluter (Hannover, Germany), Michael Scott-Watson (Roxburghshire, Scotland), Christoph Theis (Wiesloch, Germany), Jeremy Thorp (London SW1), Ian Trontz (Brooklyn, NY), Jarle Unneland (Alesund, Norway), Mark Van Den Boer (Tilberg, Netherlands), Dirk Vandersypen (Managua), Joanna Watts and Shaun Pinchbeck (Bath), Allan Wearden (Blackburn, Lancs), A. J. Wearden (Blackburn, Lancs.), Dr Volker Weinmann (São Paulo, Brazil), Trish and Tony Wheeler (Southport, Queensland), Urs Wickli (Neu St. Johann, Switzerland), Manfred Wolfensberger (Uster, Switzerland), Meg Worley (Knoxville, Tennessee) and Peter Grover (Montreal, Canada.

# WILL YOU HELP US?

We do all we can to get our facts right in **The South American Handbook.** Each chapter is thoroughly revised each year, but the territory covers a vast area, and our eyes cannot be everywhere. A new highway or airport is built; a hotel, a restaurant, a cabaret dies; another, a good one is born; a building we describe is pulled down, a street renamed. Names and addresses of good hotels and restaurants for "budget-minded" travellers are always very welcome. We would especially like to receive diagrams of walks, national parks and other interesting areas.

*Your information may be far more up-to-date than ours. If your letter reaches us early enough in the year it will be used in the next edition, but write whenever you want to, for all your letters are used sooner or later.*

Thank you very much indeed for your help.

Trade & Travel Publications Limited
6 Riverside Court, Lower Bristol Road, Bath BA2 3DZ. England

# VENEZUELA

## INTRODUCTION

WHEN the Spaniards landed in Venezuela in 1498, in the course of Columbus' third voyage, they found a poor country sparsely populated by Indians who had created no distinctive culture. Four hundred years later it was still poor, almost exclusively agrarian, exporting little, importing less. The miracle year which changed all that was 1914, when oil was discovered near Maracaibo. Today, Venezuela is said to be the richest country in Latin America and is one of the largest producers and exporters of oil in the world. The oil revenues have been used to rebuild Caracas and Maracaibo and other cities, and to create the best network of roads on the continent. In view of recent new discoveries and the cutback of production, at the present rate of extraction oil reserves will last for at least 40 years. Vast investments have been poured into state industry and agrarian reform and into tackling the problems of education, housing and unemployment.

Venezuela has 2,800 km. of coastline on the Caribbean Sea, and 72 islands. To the east is Guyana, to the south Brazil, and to the west Colombia. Its area is 912,050 square km., and its population exceeds 18 million. It was given its name— "Little Venice"—by the Spanish navigators, who saw in the Indian pile dwellings on the Lago de Maracaibo a dim reminder of the buildings along Venetian waterways.

The country falls into four very different regions: the Venezuelan Highlands to the west and along the coast; the Maracaibo Lowlands around the fresh water lake of Maracaibo; the vast central plain of the Llanos of the Orinoco; and the Guayana Highlands, which take up over half the country.

The Venezuelan Highlands are an offshoot of the Andes. From the Colombian border they trend, at first, towards the NE to enfold the Maracaibo Lowlands. This section is known as the Sierra Nevada de Mérida. Beyond they broaden out into the Segovia Highlands N of Barquisimeto, and then turn E in parallel ridges along the coast to form the Central Highlands, dipping into the Caribbean Sea

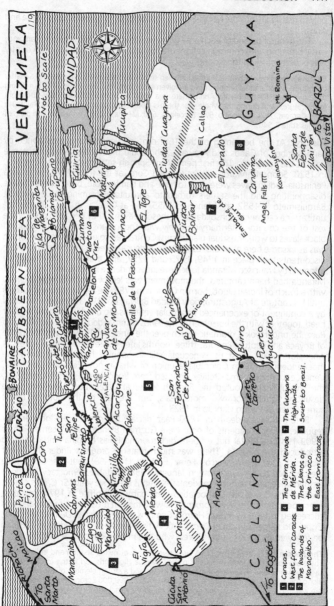

VENEZUELA

Not to Scale

CARIBBEAN SEA

TRINIDAD

GUYANA

COLOMBIA

BRAZIL

1 Caracas.
2 West from Caracas.
3 The lowlands of Maracaibo.
4 The Sierra Nevada de Mérida.
5 The Llanos of the Orinoco.
6 East from Caracas.
7 The Guayana Highlands.
8 South to Brazil.

only to rise again into the North-Eastern Highlands of the peninsulas of Paria and Araya.

The general outline of each area will reveal that natural obstacles to farming, cattle breeding, and communications are formidable. It explains why the country was poverty-stricken for so long.

**Climate** is tropical, with little change between season and season. Temperature is a matter of altitude. Mean annual temperatures are given in the text. At Caracas it is 20°C, but during the dry season (December to April), there is a great difference between day and night temperatures, and during the whole year there is a burst of heat around mid-day. Rainfall in mm.: Caracas, 762; Maracaibo, 573; Barcelona, 660; Mérida, 1,295; Amazonas and parts of Barinas state 2,540.

**History** At the beginning of the 16th century, Venezuela was inhabited by various tribes of Caribs and Arawaks, who could make no effective resistance against the Spaniards. The first permanent Spanish settlement was at Cumaná, in 1520. Soon afterwards settlers reached Coro, at the foot of the Paraguaná Peninsula. Indian slaves were used to mine and pan for gold, but the results were disappointing and the settlers turned to agriculture, forming settlements at Barquisimeto in 1552, at Valencia in 1555, and at Caracas in 1567. It was not until after a century of consolidation in these areas that they began to occupy the rest of the country, intermarrying freely with the Indians and later introducing black slaves to work the sugar plantations. Centralized colonial control from Spain was as irksome here as in the rest of Latin America: three risings reflecting these discontents took place in 1749, 1775 and 1797, and there were two abortive attempts by Francisco Miranda to achieve independence in 1806 and 1811. After Miranda had been captured, the movement was led by Simón Bolívar, a *criollo* with a touch of Indian blood, born in Caracas in 1783. He met with mixed success until his capture of Angostura, now Ciudad Bolívar, in 1817. There he was joined by a contingent of experienced Peninsular veterans recruited in London. At their head, together with the horsemen of the *llanos* commanded by Gen. José Antonio Páez, he undertook a dramatic march over the Andes in 1819 to win the battle of Boyacá and capture Bogotá. Three months later, the revolutionary congress at Angostura—with most of Venezuela still in Spanish hands— declared the independence of Gran Colombia, a union of what is now Ecuador, Colombia, Venezuela, and Panama. Bolívar returned from Bogotá, and on 24 June 1821, the revolutionaries routed the Spanish forces at Carabobo. There was some desultory fighting for two more years, but the last of the Spanish forces surrendered at Puerto Cabello in 1823.

Before Bolívar's death in 1830 Páez declared Venezuela an independent republic. Other presidents of note were Guzmán Blanco, Juan Vicente Gómez (1909-1935), a brutal but efficient dictator, and Isaías Medina Angarita, who introduced the oil laws. There was much material progress under the 6-year dictatorship of Gen. Marcos Pérez Jiménez (1952-58), but his Gómez-like methods led to his overthrow in January 1958. A stable democracy has been created since, with regular presidential elections every five years. Sr. Carlos Andrés Pérez of the centre-left Democratic Action party took office in 1974, presiding over a period of rapid development following the first great oil-price rise, and was succeeded in 1979 by Sr. Luis Herrera Campins of the Christian Democratic party, Copei. Dr. Jaime Lusinchi of Democratic Action was elected president in 1983, to be followed by Carlos Andrés Pérez, who began his second term in 1989.

**The People** 53% are under 18. A large number are of mixed Spanish and Indian origin. There are some pure Indians, mostly in the Guayana Highlands and in the forests west of Lago de Maracaibo. There are some pure Africans and a strong element of African descent along the coast, particularly at the ports. The arrival of 800,000 European immigrants since the war, mostly in the 1950s, has greatly modified the racial make-up in Venezuela. One in 6 of all Venezuelans is foreign born. Total population was 19,735,000 in 1990.

About 84% of the population is urban. Annual growth: 2.8%; urban growth: 3.3%.

Birth-rate (1988) 27.9; mortality per 1,000 inhabitants: 4.3; infant mortality 21.5 per 1,000 live births; expectation of life, 70 years.

Venezuela, despite its wealth, still faces serious social problems. About 12% are unemployed; about 10% are illiterate. Many rural dwellers have drifted to the cities; one result of this exodus is that Venezuelan farmers do not provide all the food the nation needs and imports of foodstuffs are necessary, even for items such as beans and rice.

**The Economy** Venezuela's economy has been dominated by petroleum, despite its contributing only 8% to gdp. Oil exports have inflated foreign exchange receipts and government fiscal revenues. Oil revenues have shaped the rest of the productive sector, even though employment creation has been minimal, and inter-industry links have been relatively underdeveloped. High earnings from oil have in the past overvalued the exchange rate, which has discouraged export-based production and hindered import substitution. Non-oil industry and agriculture are now being targeted for expansion as oil's role has diminished since the early 1980s.

Venezuela has vast natural resources, and is especially rich in energy, possessing 55.52 bn barrels of proved oil reserves. Apart from proved and exploitable reserves, there are another 1.2 trillion barrels in potential reserves of very heavy oil in the as yet unexploited Orinoco belt. There are 2.65 trillion cubic metres of natural gas reserves (plus 5 trillion probable), and 500 m tonnes of coal (9 bn estimated) in the provinces of Zulia and Táchira. There is believed to be a hydroelectricity potential (HEP) of 80,000 MW. The new hydroelectric generating capacity around Ciudad Guayana in the east is designed to act as the hub of economic growth. It includes the 10,300 MW Guri dam project, the second largest HEP station in the world after Itaipú, and which in July 1986 provided just over half the country's generating capacity.

Venezuela is Opec's third largest oil producer, with a capacity of 2.6 m barrels a day. Oil production is concentrated in three major sedimentary basins: the Maracaibo, the eastern, and the Apure-Barinas basins. Petróleos de Venezuela (PDVSA), the state-owned oil company created out of the nationalization of oil companies in 1976, has been relatively successful in keeping its market share because of its forward-looking marketing strategy based on forming partnerships with refineries and marketing chains in Europe and the USA.

The mining sector has been probably the most buoyant part of the economy since 1984, and is likely to continue in this vein with important mining ventures in bauxite, iron ore, gold and coal. Venezuela could become the world's leading aluminium producer by the end of the century.

Only about 20% of the land surface is devoted to agriculture, and about three-quarters of this is pasture. Like mining, it is a small sector of the economy, accounting for 8% of gdp and employing 15% of the workforce. The main grain staples are maize and sorghum, while sugar and rice are also important. The main export crop is coffee, with other cash crops being cocoa and cotton.

Venezuela is Latin America's fourth largest debtor, and despite huge foreign reserves of over US$20 bn accumulated by the mid-1980s from oil wealth, the country became unable to service its external debt normally from 1982 because of a bunching of maturities. A US$21 bn debt rescheduling agreement was signed with commercial banks in 1986 but was almost immediately renegotiated, with longer repayment terms and lower interest rates, as falling oil prices that year caused unexpected foreign exchange constraints; oil revenues fell by 44% in 1986. The government avoided taking adjustment measures and chose instead to spend reserves until by end-1988 liquid foreign exchange reserves were exhausted. In 1989 the new administration turned to the IMF and World Bank for support for a comprehensive macroeconomic adjustment programme to rebuild reserves, encourage domestic savings and cut the public sector deficit. Previous policies were reversed with the freeing of interest rates and the exchange rate. The initial impact was a severe recession and gdp fell by 8.1% in 1989, accompanied by a burst of inflation and higher unemployment. Nevertheless, in 1990 the economy rebounded with a growth of 4.4%, strengthened by the reforms, a higher level of investment and windfall oil revenues during the Gulf war. A debt restructuring package was implemented in 1990 which allowed banks to choose from a menu of options including debt reduction, debt service reduction or new loans.

**Government** Venezuela is a federal republic of 20 states, a Federal District, and two territories. There are two legislative houses, a Senate with 49 seats and a Chamber of Deputies with 201 seats. The current Constitution is dated 23 January 1961. Voting is now compulsory for all over 18.

**Education** Elementary schools are free, and education is compulsory from the age of 7 to the completion of the primary grade.

**National Parks** Venezuela has 35 national parks and 15 smaller national monuments, some of which are mentioned in the text. A full list is published by the Instituto Nacional de Parques (Inparques), Avenida Rómulo Gallegos, Parque del Este (opp. *Restaurante Carreta*), T 284-1956, Caracas. Each park has a regional director and its own guards (*guardaparques*). Permits (free) are required to stay in the parks, although this is not usually necessary for those visited frequently. For further information on the National Parks system, visit the Ministerio del Ambiente y de los Recursos Naturales Renovables (MARNR) at Parque del Este in Caracas. The book: *Guía de los Parques Nacionales y Monumentos Naturales de Venezuela*, is obtainable in Audubon headquarters, 0900-1230 and 1430-1800, Las Mercedes shopping centre, Las Mercedes, Caracas in the La Cuadra sector next to the car parking area (it is difficult to find), T 913813. The society will plan itineraries and make reservations.

**Music and Dance** Venezuelan music is more homogenous than that of some of the other republics. Its highly distinctive sound is based on an instrumental combination of harp, *cuatro* (a small, four stringed guitar) and *maracas*. Many of the rhythms have a very fast, almost headlong pace to them, stimulating both to the senses and to the feet, music here being almost inseparable from dance. The recipe for Venezuelan music is a classic European/African/Amerindian mix. The country's national dance is the Joropo, a name deriving from the Arab "Xarop", meaning syrup and which originally meant a country dance. This is a dance for couples with several sequences, such as the Valseao, Zapatiao, Escobillao and Toriao. Closely related to the Joropo are the Corrido, with a ballad content, Galerón (slow for singing or fast for dancing), Pasaje (lyrical, very popular in the Llanos) and Golpe, from the State of Lara, to all of which styles the Joropo may be danced in different parts of the country. Note that the little *cuatro* is normally referred to as "guitarra", while the Spanish guitar is called the "guitarra grande". Some of the dance rhythms have been imported from abroad or are shared with neighbouring countries, such as the urban Merengue (introduced into Caracas in the 1920s), the Jota and Malagueña of Anzoátegui State, the Pasillo (shared with Colombia and Ecuador), the Polo of the Oriente and Isla Margarita and the Bambuco, found in Lara and Táchira states near the border with Colombia.

There is a wealth of dances and musical forms found in particular towns or states at religious festivities. Outstanding among these is the Tamunangue of Lara State, danced in the second fortnight of June to the accompaniment of drums and small guitars and made up of seven individual dances, varying from the "Batalla", where men battle with sticks, to the "Bella", a flirtatious dance for couples. Corpus Cristi is the time to visit San Francisco de Yare in Miranda State and see the 80 or so male "Diablos" of all ages, dressed entirely in red and wearing large horned masks, who dance in the streets to the sound of their own drums and rattles. The Bailes de Tambor take place among the largely black people of the Barlovento coast during the feasts of San Juan and San Pedro and at Christmas. This is brilliant polyrhythm on huge drums (*cumacos*, *minas* and *curvetas*) held between the legs. Also in Barlovento, but in May, can be heard the Fulias, chant-and-response songs addressed to a venerated saint or cross, to the accompaniment of *cuatro*, *tambora* drum and *maracas*. Christmas is a great period for music from the Gaitas of Zulia to the ubiquitous Aguinaldos, both in Merengue rhythm, with solo verses responded to by a chorus and varied instrumental accompaniment. Notable in the eastern states are the folk theatre dances of the Pájaro Guarandol (hunter shoots large bird that is brought back to life), Carite (from Margarita, using a large model fish), Chiriguare (a monster that is duly despatched) and Burriquita (a hobby horse). More surprising is to find the Calipso, played on steel bands by the black inhabitants of El Callao in the Orinoco region, whose ancestors came from Trinidad and who also perform the Limbo.

Venezuelans enjoy Salsa as much as other Hispanic peoples around the Caribbean, but they are also very keen on their own music, whether rustic "folk" or urban "popular". The virtuoso harpist Juan Vicente Torrealba has performed with his group Los Torrealberos for more than three decades, usually with Mario Suárez as vocal soloist. Another famous singer is Simón Díaz. Outstanding among the folk groups who strive for authenticity are Un Solo Pueblo, Grupo Vera and Grupo Convenezuela. Choral and contrapuntal singing of native music in a more sophisticated style has also been perfected by Quinteto Contrapunto and Serenata Guayanesa.

## CARACAS (1)

**The capital and nearby excursions including to mountain towns, the Monte Avila National Park, beaches and Los Roques, a beautiful Caribbean atoll.**

The capital, Caracas, and the cities of Valencia and Maracay are in the Central Highlands, the most important upland area in Venezuela. The mountains here rise abruptly from a lush green coast to heights of from two to three thousand metres. Caracas, lies in a small basin, a rift in the thickly forested mountains which runs some 24 km. east and west. This historic colonial town has been transformed into one of the most astonishing modern cities in Latin America.

**Caracas**, founded in 1567, now has a population of around 4 million (the city proper 1.3 million). It lies at 960 metres, but the southern parts of the city are 160 metres higher. Temperatures are moderate (a maximum of 32°C in July and August, and an occasional minimum of 9°C in January and February) and it is always cool at night.

A comparatively low pass (1,040 metres) in the mountains gives Caracas access by road to its port, La Guaira, and its international and domestic airports nearby at Maiquetía. The distance by a magnificently engineered road is 28 km. or 30 mins. by car (toll US$0.10 when going up; going down is free). Much longer should be allowed, however, for anyone with a plane to catch, as there are often delays arising from heavy traffic.

The proportionate growth of Caracas since the war has been greater than that of any other Latin American capital. Colonial buildings have given way to modern multi-storeyed edifices, many of which are architecturally impressive. Excellent examples are the Ciudad Universitaria, the twin towers of the Parque Central (containing a Ministry of Transport exhibition, open Mon.-Fri. 0900-1530), the Centro Simón Bolívar, and the Círculo Militar.

Starting in Catia, an industrial area in the W where both roads from La Guaira enter, Avenida Sucre goes past the 23 de Enero workers' flats to join Av. Urdaneta between Palacio Miraflores and the Palacio Blanco, housing government offices. Later come the Post Office and Santa Capilla Church, looking like a wedding cake by a Parisian master pastrycook. Turn right here for Plaza Bolívar and the Capitolio Nacional (the National Congress, do not take photographs in the vicinity or you may be arrested), or carry straight on down the Av. Urdaneta to San Bernardino (Museo de Arte Colonial). Here, we enter Av. Andrés Bello, which passes just

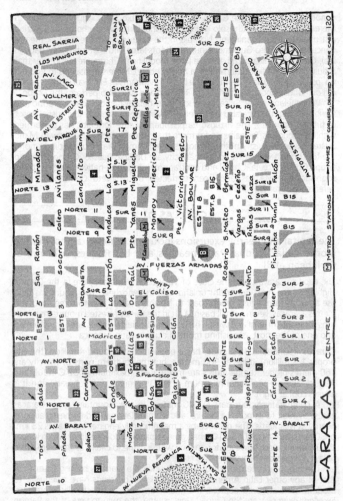

## Caracas: Key to map

1. Plaza Bolívar; 2. Parque Carabobo; 3. Parque Los Caobos; 4. Plaza Candelaria; 5. Plaza O'Leary; 6. Plaza Miranda; 7. Plaza La Concordia; 8. Parque Central, Museo de Arte Contemporáneo, Museo de los Niños; Tourist Office; 9. Centro Simón Bolívar, CANTV; 10. Cathedral; 11. Capitolio Nacional; 12. San Francisco; 13. Santa Capilla; 14. Santa Teresa; 15. Casa y Museo de Bolívar; 16. Museo de Bellos Artes; 17. Museo de Ciencias Naturales; 18. Biblioteca Nacional; 19. Jardín Botánico; 20. Post Office; 21. Consejo Municipal; 22. Banco Central; 23. Bus to Airport; 24. *Hotel Caracas Hilton*; 25. Road to Quinta Anauco and San Bernardino; 26. Road to Ciudad Universitaria; 27. Palacio Miraflores.

below the cable railway station to join Av. Libertador to the Country Club and the E, or we can turn down the Av. La Salle to the eastern end of Los Caobos park, with the fine mahoganies which give it its popular name. From the Plaza Venezuela intersection at the eastern end of the park, the Avenida Abraham Lincoln leads E through Sabana Grande and continues as the Avenida Francisco Miranda to the residential section of Altamira, with its fine plaza and obelisk. Sabana Grande, a modern shopping, hotel and business centre, is now a pedestrian mall closed to vehicular traffic: a very popular place to take a stroll.

Alternatively, forking right out of Avenida Sucre and crossing the viaduct, we reach El Silencio, and thence pass through the Centro Simón Bolívar, with its twin skyscrapers, underground parking and shopping centre (with an interesting mosaic at the lowest level), and finally along the Avenida Bolívar past Nuevo Circo bullring towards Ciudad Universitaria, the Sports Stadium, the *Tamanaco Hotel* and La Casona, residence of the President. S of the Nuevo Circo is the Helicoide, planned as a commercial centre under the Pérez Jiménez regime but left uncompleted at his fall in 1958. From the viaduct, we can also take Av. Universidad past the Biblioteca Nacional (former University), Capitol and San Francisco church. Two corners later, we glimpse, left, Bolívar's birthplace, before continuing to the Museo de Bellas Artes and on round Los Caobos park, or by the Av. Libertador, to the east.

Another west-east route is along the Avenida Boyacá from Avenida Baralt in the west to Petare in the east, connecting with the main road east to Barcelona (Route 9), which skirts the Cordillera de la Costa, including Monte Avila, and gives fine views along the length of the city. Towards the E end is a monument commemorating the battle of Boyacá, and a viaduct strides majestically over the recently remodelled park in Los Chorros suburb, to which access is signposted.

To the SW from El Silencio the Avenida San Martín leads towards the factories of Antímano. This area can also be reached direct from Catia by the Planicie tunnel. In the SW is also the older residential section of El Paraíso.

The shady Plaza Bolívar, with its fine equestrian statue of the Liberator and pleasant colonial cathedral, is still the official centre of the city, though no longer geographically so. There are squirrels in the trees (quite tame) and sloths (harder to see) in the plaza. In fact, several centres (Plaza Bolívar, Plaza Venezuela, Sabana Grande, Chacaíto, La Floresta, Boleíta) are strung along the valley with residential areas between.

**Parks** Jardín Botánico, near Plaza Venezuela, entrance by Ciudad Universitaria (free), is quite small and disorganized. **Parque Los Caobos** is being extended; it is peaceful and has a cafetería in the middle. By the entrance in Av. México is the cultural centre, Ateneo de Caracas, with a theatre, art gallery, concert rooms, bookshop and the imposing Teresa Carreño theatre complex. **Parque Nacional del Este** (renamed the Parque Rómulo Betancourt in 1989) is a popular place to relax, especially at weekends, entrance US$0.05, closed Mon., otherwise opens 0530 for joggers, 0800 for mere mortals, till 1730 (reached from Parque del Este metro station). There is a boating lake, a replica of Columbus' *Santa María* (being renovated in 1991), the Humboldt Planetarium (weekend shows), a number of different sunken lakes featuring caiman and turtles, monkeys, two frustratingly caged jaguars, many types of water birds, a terrarium (open Sat.-Sun.). Although the zoo is well cared for, some find it disappointing. The **Parque Caricuao** is at the end of the Metro line, quite heavily wooded; it has the city's main zoo, open 0900-1700 weekends, check if open Tues.-Fri. (the metro station is called Zoológico). **Parque El Pinar** also has a large zoo (Av. José Antonio Páez, El Pinar). The **Parque Los Chorros** at the foot of the mountain has impressive waterfalls, also recommended; **El Calvario**, west of Plaza O'Leary, recently renovated and with the Federation Arch at the entrance is quiet and pleasant with a good view of Centro Simón Bolívar. It has a small zoo, botanical gardens and a picturesque chapel. A new park, **Parque Vargas**, is eventually to replace the Nuevo Circo bus station; similar in concept to the Champs Elysées, some is already in place. A model of the area, as it is planned, is on display in the Galería de Arte Nacional. See below for Paseo de los Próceres, and page 1134 for El Avila National Park.

## National Monuments

**Panteón Nacional** Open Tues.-Sun., 0900-1300 and 1400-1700. This was designed as the resting place of Simón Bolívar, the Liberator, and Francisco Miranda, the Precursor of Independence. The remains of Bolívar lie there, but the tomb of Miranda, who died in a Spanish prison, has been left open to await the return of his body, likewise the tomb of Antonio José de Sucre, who was assassinated in Colombia. Every 25 years the President opens Bolívar's casket to verify that the remains are still there. Daniel O'Leary, Bolívar's Irish aide-de camp, is buried alongside. The building was originally Santísima Trinidad church with ceiling paintings by Tito Sales (1874). There is a small military ceremony at 1515 daily.

**Capitolio Nacional** Open to visitors Tues.-Sun., 0900-1200 and 1500-1800, passport must be shown. The Elliptical Salon has some impressive paintings by the Venezuelan artist Martín Tovar y Tovar and a bronze urn containing the 1811 Declaration of Independence. One of the paintings on the ceiling shows a British regiment fighting in the Battle of Carabobo, and the names of the officers appear on the wall; in acknowledgement of this assistance Bolívar granted the British armed forces the right to march through any city in Gran Colombia (Colombia, Ecuador, Panama and Venezuela) with bayonets fixed, drums beating and flags flying.

## Museums

**Museo de Bellas Artes**, Plaza Morelos in Parque Los Caobos, the oldest museum in Caracas, designed by Carlos Raúl Villanueva: open Tues.-Fri., 0900-1200, 1500-1730, weekend 1000-1700. Pictures include an El Greco among works by mainly Venezuelan artists. Adjacent is the Galería de Arte Nacional, T 571-0176, same opening hours, which also houses the Cinemateca Nacional (Tues.-Sun. 1830 and 2130, Sun. 1100 for children's films).

**Museo de Ciencias Naturales**, also in Plaza Morelos in Parque Los Caobos; open Tues.-Fri., 0900-1200, 1500-1730, weekend 1000-1700: archaeological, particularly precolumbian, zoological and botanical exhibits.

**Museo de Arte Colonial**, Quinta Anauco, Av. Panteón, San Bernardino: open Tues.-Sat., 0900-1200, 1400-1700, Sun., 1000-1730. Guided tour in Spanish available. A delightful house built in 1720, the residence of the Marqués del Toro. Chamber concerts most Saturdays at 1800. The beautiful suburb of San Bernardino glories in tropical flowers and whole avenues of forest trees, smothered in blossom in season.

**Casa Natal del Libertador** Open Tues.-Fri., 0900-1200 and 1430-1700, Sun. and holidays, 1000-1700. The present house is a reconstruction of the house where Bolívar was born (on 24 July 1783). The first, of adobe, was destroyed by an earthquake. The second became a stable, and was later pulled down. The present building of stone was built by order of Gómez (whose birthday was the same as Bolívar's) in the early 1920s; it was recently completely refurbished and contains interesting pictures and furniture. **The Museo Bolivariano** is alongside the Casa Natal and contains the Liberator's war relics.

    **Cuadra Bolívar** Bárcenas y Las Piedras, 8 blocks S of Plaza Bolívar; "El Palmar", the Bolívar family's summer home, now an historical museum, a beautifully preserved colonial country estate: walled gardens, stables, Bolívar memorabilia, well worth a visit. Open Tues.-Sat., 0900-1300, 1430-1700; Sun. and holidays 0900-1700.

**House of Arturo Michelena**, La Pastora y Puente Miraflores, four blocks north of Miraflores palace, in the La Pastora section, is a typical 19th century home, now a museum. Open 0900-1200 and 1500-1700 (closed Mon. and Fri.).

**Museo de Transporte**, Parque Nacional del Este (to which it is connected by a pedestrian overpass), includes a large collection of locomotives and old cars, as well as a fascinating series of scale models of Caracas a century ago. Open Wed., Sat., Sun., 0900-1600. Admission US$0.10 adults (Bs. 1 for children).

In the Parque Central, between Av. Lecuna (E end) and the elevated section of Av. Bolívar there are four museums in a complex which includes 2 octagonal towers (56 floors each) and four large apartment buildings with shopping below.

**Museo de Arte Contemporáneo**, Parque Central, Cuadra Bolívar, entrance beside *Anauco*

*Hilton*, very good, European and Venezuelan painters represented. The museum is in two sections, the larger of which is downstairs and is easily missed; reference library, gift shop. Open Tues.-Sun. 1000-1800.

**Museo de los Niños**, Parque Central, next to East Tower, is open to the public Wed.-Sun. and holidays, 0900-1200, 1400-1700, otherwise is for school visits; a highly sophisticated modern science museum, well worth a visit and extremely popular, US$0.75 (adults). Book a day or so in advance in school holidays or August. Also in the Parque Central complex, **Museo Audiovisual**, Tues.-Fri., 0900-1700, US$1, includes a library of Venezuelan television programmes, a practice TV studio, and **Museo del Teclado** (keyboard instruments).

**Museo Histórico Militar**, near Metro Gato Negro.

**The Ministry of Foreign Relations** contains pictures mostly of national heroes and historical events.

**The Concejo Municipal** (City Hall) on Plaza Bolívar contains three museums: a collection of the paintings of Emilio Boggio, a Venezuelan painter; the Raúl Santana Museum of the Creole Way of Life, a collection of miniature figures in costumes and poses characteristic of Venezuelan life, all handmade by Raúl Santana and extremely realistic; Francisco Pizarro's battle standard, presented by him to Sucre after the battle of Ayacucho and then given to Bolívar is shown here; and the Sala de Arqueología Gaspar Marcano, exhibiting ceramics, mostly discovered on the coast. All three open Tues.-Fri., 0930-1200, 1500-1800; Sat. and Sun., 0930-1800. Informative guides are available.

Those with a deeper interest in archaeology might like to contact the Junta Nacional Protectora y Conservadora del Patrimonio Histórico y Artístico de la Nación, Palacio de Miraflores, Av. Urdaneta.

**Museo Criminológico**, Edificio Tajamar, level, room 118, weapons, forgeries, forensic exhibits, etc.; grim but fascinating.

**Churches** The present **Cathedral** building dates from 1674 and should be seen for its beautiful façade, its gilded altar, the Bolívar family chapel and pictures including Michelena, Murillo and an alleged Rubens "Resurrection". **San Francisco**, Av. Universidad y San Francisco (1 block SW of Plaza Bolívar), should be seen for its colonial altars and Murillo's "San Agustín" (oldest church in Caracas, rebuilt 1641). **Santa Teresa**, between La Palma and Santa Teresa, just SE of the Centro Simón Bolívar, has good interior chapels and a supposedly miraculous portrait of Nazareno de San Pablo (popular and solemn devotions on Good Friday).

**N.B.** Check museum schedules in *El Universal, El Nacional* or the *Daily Journal* (which also have details of events for children). Many museums and most religious buildings will refuse entry to anybody wearing shorts.

**Modern Caracas** Visitors should see the Paseo de los Próceres with its twin monoliths and other monuments to the heroes of independence (it also has flowers and gardens); the magnificent Officers' Club on the same avenue; and the University City, an enormous and coherent complex of great buildings in which paintings, sculpture and stained glass are completely integrated with the architecture (which is now showing signs of wear).

**N.B.** In the centre of Caracas, each street corner has a name, and addresses are generally given as, for example, "Santa Capilla a Mijares", rather than the official "Calle Norte 2, No. 26". On some maps Av. Luis Rocha is still shown as Av. España (Altamira). For maps see **Tourist Information**, below, and **Maps** in Information for Visitors.

**Festivals** 3 May, Velorio de la Cruz de Mayo still celebrated with dances and parties in some districts. Carnival and Holy Week are not widely celebrated in Caracas as many people leave town. 18-25 Dec. Yuletide masses at different churches leading up to Christmas; young people go roller-skating after the masses. Traditional creole dishes served at breakfasts.

**Warning** It is advisable not to arrive in Caracas at night and not to walk down narrow streets after dark. Avoid certain areas such as all suburbs from the El Silencio monument to Propatria, other than main roads, the area around the *teleférico*, Chapellín near the Country Club, and Petare. If you have problems try contacting Detective Robert Pechi at Interpil, Parque Carabobo, who speaks English, Italian, Spanish and Portuguese. Police searches are common, especially in airports; if you have entered overland from Colombia, you can expect thorough investigation (once you've left the border, better to say you flew in). Car theft is common.

**Hotels** Cheap *pensiones* are usually full of long-stay residents and have very few rooms available for travellers. Hotels tend to be particularly full at weekends and in July and August. In the centre all cheap hotels take only short stay customers on Fri. p.m. Better hotels often try to give you a suite instead of a double room. Hotel prices do not include 10% tax. Hotels marked with an asterisk (*) are bookable through Fairmont International (see next page).

Recommended hotels not in the centre: The *Tamanaco*\* is the best hotel in Caracas, but it is difficult to get rooms as it is normally fully booked, changes travellers' cheques for guests only (poor rate), L (US$165d, rooms are priced in dollars). *Hotel Paseo de las Mercedes*, A, Las Mercedes is almost next door to the *Tamanaco*. The *Caracas Hilton*\*, L (US$135-185d, priced in dollars), is more central but noisy (traffic and air conditioning) and although the rooms are excellent and clean, the service has been criticized; connected with the *Hilton* are the *Residencias Anauco Hilton*\*, Parque Central, an "apartotel", A-A+; another apartment hotel is the *CCT Venantur*\* in the Centro Ciudad Comercial Tamanaco, luxury, A; also *Lincoln Suites Venantur*, Av. Fco. Solano, entre Los Jabillos y San Jerónimo, Sabana Grande, T 712727, Fax 728579, A, a/c, TV, restaurant, bar, fax, drugstore, etc.; *Crillón*\*, Av. Libertador, corner of Las Acacias (2 blocks N of Plaza Venezuela metro), T 71-4411/6912, C for room with TV, sitting room, a/c, fridge, good value for longer stays, *El Chalet* Swiss restaurant downstairs. The *Ávila*\* is on Av. Jorge Washington in San Bernardino on the higher levels of the city (T 515128/515173, Telex: 21637 Avila), set in park-like gardens and very pleasant, A, good service, most of staff speak English and German, backpackers frowned upon, rooms vary, avoid top floor, no a/c in rooms, noisy, pool, Metrobus nearby, good restaurant, María José Mendes at the Camar Tours desk helpful; *Aventura*\*, Av. Fco. Fajardo, San Bernardino, A, clean, modern, large rooms, pool, restaurant; *Waldorf*, Av. Industria, San Bernardino, Bellas Artes metro, T 571-4733, D, shower, restaurant, English spoken, good value, under new management and in course of refurbishment; Banco Consolidado next door for exchange (the airport tourist office often recommends this hotel). *La Floresta*\*, Av. Avila, Sur Plaza Altamira, T 2844111, D, clean, friendly, helpful, but restaurant not very good. *Centro Uslar*, 2a Av., Calles 1 y 2, Sector B, Urb. Montalbán, C, good but a long way from centre; *El Paseo*, Av. Los Ilustres, Urb. Los Chaguaramos, T 661-3438/3547/3315, D, good, clean. In the E of the city, *El Marqués*, Av. El Samán esq. Yaruari, El Marqués, medium-priced, comfortable, quiet, good restaurant.

Cheapest hotels can be found around the Nuevo Circo bus terminal, many of them on Av. Lecuna: e.g. *ABC*, F, with shower, very noisy (less so on higher floors, which are good value); *Center Park*, No. 20, T 5418619, E, helpful, safe; *Ber Mar*, Arismendi a Pichincha 100, 200m from bus terminal, E-F, a/c, safe, used by businessmen, need to book in advance at weekends, rec.; *Urupagua*, Limón and Río Bravo, F, but this area is unpleasant and unsafe for women. Better to go several blocks WSW to a quieter area, e.g. *Pensión San Marcos*, Hoyo a Santa Rosalía, T 5453723, G, quiet, clean, basic; *Avenida*, Calle Sur 4 (nr. Capitolio), T 426440, E, hot water, a/c, safe, rec.; *La Neve*, Pilita a Glorieta No. 126—Sur 4, nr. Metro Capitolio, E, a/c or fan, bath, good, clean, safe, quiet, good restaurant, rec.; *Hospedaje Fidelina*, Sur 4 No. 120, E, clean, safe, fan, TV, shared bath/toilet. *Líder*, Baralt y Crespo, D, modern, a/c, friendly, rec.; *Hispano—Venezolano*, Sur 4 (Reducto a Glorieta), T 422553, D, a/c, good value. *Santa Mónica*, Av. Baralt between Av. Lecuna and Oestel 12, F, clean, fan; *Limón*, Av. Lecuna "behind the tall buildings if coming from Parque Central", E with shower, TV, clean, safe, parking. For other cheap hotels look on Calle Sur 2.

In the downtown area: *Inter*\*, Animas a Calero on corner of Av. Urdaneta, T 562-0333, D, very clean, shower and toilet with each room, friendly, English spoken, very popular so be sure to make a reservation, the queues for rooms begin before 0700 and the hotel is full by 0800, poor restaurant; *Ausonia*, Bolero a Pineda, D, with bath, hot-water, TV, central, clean; *Cervantes*, Av. Urdaneta, Norte 5, F, cheap but spartan, safe, very noisy. *Plaza Catedral*\*, Blvd. Plaza Bolívar, next to Cathedral, D, a/c, TV, phone, some English spoken, clean, central but a bit noisy, stays limited to 2 nights; *Caroní*, 2 blocks from Capitolio, near Cathedral, E, popular, good value, safe but a bit noisy; *Hospedaje Torreiro*, San Agustín, Sur 11 Bolívar, E, clean, friendly, safe, rec.; *Grand Galaxie*\*, Truco a Caja de Agua, between Av. Baralt and Norte 4 on Salas Sta. Bárbara, T 83-90-11/83-90-44, C, deluxe, a/c, TV, phone, restaurant, central, comfortable; *Palais*, Norte 4 (Pilita a Glorieta), E, modern, clean, a/c, friendly, luggage stored, excellent restaurant.

If you arrive in Caracas in doubt, ask a taxi driver to take you to Las Acacias in Sabana Grande, where you can choose a hotel from the very large number in that area. There are various grades all close together so you can walk from one to another until you find one suitable. However, many of the numerous small hotels on Av. Las Acacias do not cater for singles or for couples staying more than a few hours. If not using a taxi, take metro to Sabana Grande (for example). On Av. Las Acacias are *Bruno*\*, D, TV, air conditioning, fair, Peruvian restaurant with live entertainment, unremarkable; *Everest*, D; *Myriam*, E, few single rooms, off-street parking, clean but noisy; *Embassy*, T 782-7821, E with bath, hot water negotiable, a/c, rec., expensive bar downstairs, *Restaurant Las Acacias* opp. is good value; *Tanausú\**, E; *Mirage*, D, clean, friendly, good restaurant. On Av. Casanova are *Luna\**, D, clean, friendly, rec. (with Calle El Colegio); *Capri-Casanova*, F-E; *Broadway\**, No. 4, convenient for Chacaíto metro station, D, private bathroom, TV, friendly, clean, a bit noisy, Italian specialities in restaurant. Others in Sabana Grande include *Karibik*, 2da Av. de las Delicias, entre Av. Fco. Solano y Av. Libertador, T 729961, Fax 725549, from B to A+, not inc. tax, very pleasant; *El Cóndor\** (3a Av. Las Delicias), C, TV, air conditioning, businessmen on their own need to take suites because single rooms have no desks; *Coliseo*, D, rec., *Plaza Palace*, Av. Los Mangos, Las Delicias, very good, friendly, good atmosphere, B; *Las Américas\**, Los Cerritos, end of Casanova, C, classic 50's style, safe, helpful, English spoken, warm water, food passable but unexciting; *City\** (Av. Bolivia, Los Caobos), D, all rooms have TV and private bath; *Ritz*, Av. Las Palmas y Av. Libertador, D, with bath, a/c, secure free parking; *Madrid*, D, Av. Chacaíto, small, hot water, showers in all rooms, short stay; *Capri*, E, Calle Las Flores, clean; *The King's Inn Hotel\**, D, Calle Olimpo, near Av. Lincoln; *Tampa\**, Av. Francisco Solano López, B; *Savoy\**, Av. Francisco Solano López, Las Delicias, C, good food, good, efficient, clean, secure vehicle park. *Mari*, Av. Casanova Bellomonte, near metro station, E, clean, safe, rec.; *Plaza Venezuela*, Av. La Salle, D, clean, friendly, noisy; *Cristal*, Plaza Venezuela, Av. Colegio, E, a/c, convenient, basic, comfortable, safe, good value, disco at weekends, good cheap Chilean food; *Nuestro Hotel*, Calle del Colegio, F, clean. Elena and Enrique Ganteaume (T 334276) rent out a colonial style villa and can arrange tours.

**Hotel Reservations** Fairmont International, Torre Capriles, Planta Baja, Plaza Venezuela, Caracas, T 782 8433, Telex 21232 SNRHO, Fax 782 4407, will book hotel rooms in Caracas and also in 102 hotels in the rest of the country. "Packages" organised by Fairmont International are reported to be much more expensive than hotel bookings. The airport tourist office is very helpful and will book hotel rooms. Finding a hotel, particularly in the middle-price range, is always difficult. If you book from abroad (e.g. Thomas Cook in England) make sure you receive confirmation before beginning your journey or you may turn up and find yourself without a room. **Economy tip:** most hotel rooms have a TV set for which you will be charged; if you don't want it, ask for it to be removed. For apartment rental, consult *El Universal* daily paper, small ads. columns.

**Restaurants** There is such a profusion of eating places in Caracas that we give the following general advice, with a mention of just a few places currently reported reliable, rather than attempt the impossible task of keeping up to date with all the changes. Guides to eating are published in the *VAAUW Guide to Caracas* and the magazine "Ve Venezuela". Also "Gourmet Dining out in Caracas", available at travel agencies and good hotels. Advertisements appear in the "Daily Journal" and the Yellow Pages of the telephone directory. Don't be shy about asking the price before you order in a bar as beer in one will cost three times as much as in another, and a modest portion of manchego cheese will cost more than a good steak. Food on display in a bar is free with your drink if they offer it as a *pasapalo*, but will be charged for if offered as a *ración*. You can save on the service charge by eating at the bar and not at a table. By decree, restaurants must put up a list of prices on or near the front door, and are prohibited from charging for place settings (*cubiertos*) or bread, butter, condiments etc. (*guarnición*).

For dining out, there is a selection of good restaurants around Avenida Urdaneta (*Mesón de Cervantes*—friendly multilingual manager, Nelson, *Marinero de Oriente* for seafood), La Castellana, Plaza Altamira, Las Mercedes (*Mr Ribs*, Av. Valle Arriba, barbecued ribs etc., very fashionable; *Era de Acuario*, vegetarian, open for dinner; Lebanese food: *Kibbe*, Calle Madrid, Las Mercedes, T 910519; good take away at CCCT shopping centre, Nivel C-2; *El Granjero del Este*, Rio de Janeiro, T 916619, traditional barbecues, excellent arepas), El Rosal and Sabana Grande (see below). There are plenty of eating places around Plaza Bolívar. The arty/theatre crowd lunch at *Café Rajatabla*, US$1.50, between Teatro Teresa Carreño and the cinema, Paseo Colón; sea food at *Las Vegas* near *Hotel Plaza Catedral*. *Tarzilandia*, 10th Transversal Altamira, San Juan Bosco, international food. Very good Mexican/Peruvian dishes at *El Tizón*, CC Bello Campo, Sótano Local 80, T 316715/2613485. Excellent pastries and cheese from *Panadería y Pastelería Madona*, Av. Sur, near corner with Camejo (0800-2300).

Although it is not practicable to cover the whole of Caracas, the following description of the Sabana Grande area will give an idea of what is available. Breakfast in your hotel is likely to be poor (poor bread or none, insipid coffee and orange juice which is half artificial). It is better and cheaper in a *fuente de soda*—once you have purchased your ticket you will find there is little sense of queuing, shout your order to the staff like the locals, and cheaper still in a *pastelería* or *arepería*. Tables in the open air on the boulevard, however, are expensive. (The boulevard waiters overcharge. Check prices on the displayed list.) Mid-day is the most economical time to eat the main meal of the day and about the only opportunity to find fresh vegetables. Particularly good value is the "menú ejecutivo" or "cubierto", which is a three-course meal for US$2-3, e.g. at *Ventas de Madrid* on San Gerónimo, *O' Gran Sol* on Villa Flor between Casanova and Sabana Grande (excellent paella, reasonable prices), *Rincón de Bucanero*, on Casanova (also has music in the evenings), *Pizzería Adelia*, near Plaza Venezuela and *Gran Pizzería*, on Gran Bulevar.

Good, economical meals in the evening at *Sorrentino* and *Jabillos* on Francisco Solano, *Coraveña* (next to *La Bússola*, one block east of Torre La Previsora), *La Soledad* (next block south on Casanova), *Tívoli* (El Colegio between Lincoln and Casanova, home made pasta) and *Tropical Room* (two blocks east on Casanova). For business and similar occasions: *La Bússola* (see above—try carpaccio), *Rugantino* in *Hotel Tampa* (speciality cartuccio), *El Chicote* behind La Previsora, and *Villa D'Este* in *Hotel Cóndor*. For variety: *Floridita* in La Previsora and *Esquina de Tejas* in *Hotel Kursaal* (both Cuban), *Le Coq d'Or*, Av. Los Mangos (French), *Hotel Bruno* (Peruvian), *Mario's* on Casanova (Brazilian—noisy), *Tasca, Tacos y Algo Más* on Casanova (Mexican), *Dragón Verde*, Ciné París, Av. Maturín (Chinese), *Le Chalet*, in *Hotel Crillón* (Swiss), good selection, highly rec., and *Buffet Vegetariano*, Av. Los Jardines. Other vegetarian restaurants are *El Acuarino*, Truco a Caja de Agua; *Super Bueno*, esq. Chorro a Dr Paúl, Edif. Plaza El Venozolano and in front of El Conde Hotel, US$2, highly rec.; *Chalet Naturista*, nr. Sabana Grande metro station; these four are not open for dinner. Also *El Exquisito Menú Vegetariano*, near Metro Parque Carabobo rec. for buffet, US$2, friendly, and *Almuerzo*, Hoyo a Sta Rosalía, good and cheap. Roast lamb at *La Taberna*, Torre Capriles, Plaza Venezuela. *Shorthorn*, Av. Libertador, El Bosque, very good, US$18. Fast foods: there is a plethora of burger and pizza places, as well as the ubiquitous hot dog stalls of doubtful hygiene (when the police don't close them down). *Arturo's*, is a chain of clean, modern, chicken-and-chips style restaurants in various locations, e.g. next to Centro Plaza complex, Miranda y Andrés Bello, also on Av. Lincoln pedestrian mall, 1 block E of Sabana Grande metro.

**Clubs** There are 3 country clubs in Caracas, all of which have excellent restaurants. The Country Club in the eastern part has an 18-hole golf course. The Social Centre of the British Commonwealth Association, Quinta Alborada, Avenida 7 with Transversal 9, Altamira, Caracas, with bar and swimming pool; British and Commonwealth visitors only; entry fee according to length of stay; T 261-30-60. Membership of the better clubs is by the purchase of a share, which can run to thousands of dollars. An exception is the sports club run by the *Tamanaco Hotel*, open to non-guests and suitable for people staying a short time. The Military Club (Círculo de las Fuerzas Armadas) is well worth seeing and, if the visitors are soberly dressed, permission to view the premises is often granted. Flying Club, at La Carlota, near *Tamanaco Hotel*, mixed reports. Robert and Daisy Kunstaetter of Richmond Hill, Ontario (call sign VE300G) tell us the Radio Club Venezolano is a very welcoming, efficient organization of amateur radio operators which is eager to meet amateurs from around the world (address: P.O.Box 2285, Caracas 1010-A, T 781-4878, 781-8303—Av. Lima, Los Caobos; branches around the country).

**Shopping** For gems and fine jewellery, visit the *H. Stern* shops at the Hotels *Hilton* and *Tamanaco* and at the International Airport; try also *Labady*, Sabana Grande 98, beautifully-made gold jewellery, English spoken. *Pro-Venezuela Exposición y Venta de Arte Popular*, Gran Avenida at Calle Olimpo, between Plaza Venezuela and beginning of Av. Casanova (opp. Torre La Previsora), sells Venezuelan crafts, very crowded, no prices, bargain hard. Indian and Andean crafts can be found in Las Mercedes shopping centre, Paseo Las Mercedes opp. *Tamanaco*. The **CCCT shopping centre** is worth a visit. Large-size shoes (up to 47) at Catedral Sur 4 y Mercaderes. From Chacaíto, along Av. Abraham Lincoln, Sabana Grande, to Plaza Venezuela, is a pedestrian precinct, with good shops, handicrafts for sale, street traders and cafés.

**Bookshops** English language ones include: *English Bookshop*, Concresa, Prados del Este, will exchange nearly new books; *Lectura*, Centro Comercial Chacaíto. The *American Bookshop*, Av. San Juan Bosco, Edif. Belveder, T 331140, near Altamira metro has a good selection of secondhand English books; also available in bookstalls in the street. *Librería del Este*, Av. Francisco de Miranda 52, Edif. Galipán, *Librería Multilingua*, Concresa, and *Librería Unica*, Centro Capriles, ground floor local 13N, Plaza Venezuela, all have foreign language books. *Librería Washington*, La Torre a Veroes No. 25, good service. A French bookshop is *Librería La France*, Centro Comercial Chacaíto, Italian bookshop, *El Libro Italiano*, Pasaje La Concordia (between Sabana Grande pedestrian street and Av. Fco. Solano López), and for German books, *Librería Alemana* (Oscar Todtmann), Centro El Bosque, Avenida Libertador.

**City Buses** Starting from the bus station at Nuevo Circo, there are many buses, overcrowded in the rush hours, urban fare usually US$0.07 (the correct fare helps to speed things up). On the longer runs these buses are probably more comfortable for those with luggage than a *por puesto*. Midibuses are known as *carmelitas*. *Por puesto* minibuses running on regular routes charge between US$0.08 and US$0.15 depending on the distance travelled within the city; fares rise to US$1.40 for journeys outside. Many *por puesto* services start in Silencio.

**Taxis** are required by law to instal and use taxi-meters, but they never use them, if they have not already been removed. Fares must be negotiated in advance. Most city trips are US$1.50-3 during the day, US$2-3.50 at night. Taxi drivers are authorized to charge an extra 20% on night trips after 1800, on Sun. and all holidays, and US$0.45 for answering telephone calls. After 1800 drivers are selective about where they want to go. Beware of taxi drivers trying to renegotiate fixed rates because your destination is in "a difficult area". The sign on the roof of a taxi reads "Libre". There are pirates, however, with possibly a taxi sign, but without yellow licence plates/registration-number plate, which are to be avoided. Several radio taxi firms operate; see yellow pages.

**The Metro**, opened in 1983, operates 0530-2300. It is air-conditioned, clean, well-patrolled, safe and more comfortable and quicker than any other form of city transport; no smoking, no large bags. There are 2 lines which are continually being extended: Line 1 (W-E) from Propatria to Palos Verdes; Line 2 (N-S), Capitolio/El Silencio connecting station to Zoológico. Tickets vary in price from Bs. 7-10 according to number of stations travelled. Ten-journey tickets, known as Multi Abono, are available (saves queuing): US$1.20 for up to 5 stations, US$1.40 for 6-8 stations, US$1.60 over 8 stations. Student discounts are available, an ISTC card should suffice. Metrobuses (feeder buses) connect with the Metro system: get transfer tickets (*boleto integrado*) for services to southern districts, route maps displayed at stations—retain ticket after exit turnstile. Guide: *La Practiguía del Metro*, published by Practiguía Azul. Public relations T 208-2740.

**Driving** Self-drive cars (Hertz, National, Avis, Volkswagen, Budget) are available at the airport and in town. They are cheaper than guided excursions for less than full loads. Driver's licence from home country accepted. Major credit card or US$210 cash deposit required. Category A, e.g. Fiat Uno, Hertz US$20, Avis US$10, both US$0.10 per km. National Car Rental offers 10-15% discount with Amex cedit cards. Auto and personal insurance (about US$4 per day) strongly recommended as you will be lucky to survive two or three days as a newcomer to Caracas traffic without a dent or a scrape.

**Motorcycles** may not be ridden in Caracas between 2300 and 0500. Also see **Motoring**.

**Garage** Yota-Box, 3a Transversal Mis Encantos, Quinta Morava, No. 1 15, Chacao, T 313772/331035, owner Gerardo Ayala, rec., especially for Toyota.

**Night Clubs** Caracas is a lively city by night, and there are many and varied discotheques and night clubs. Caraqueños dine at home around 2000, and in restaurants from 2100 to 2300, so night clubs don't usually come to life until after 2300, and then go on to all hours of the morning. *Naiguatá* (*Hotel Tamanaco*), expensive; best show in town. *Un Solo Pueblo*, typical Venezuelan music, 3rd Transversal, Altamira (there are many small clubs, restaurants and bars on Plaza Altamira Sur). The "Noches Caraqueñas" show put on by the *Hilton* each Mon. evening makes a pleasant introduction to Caracas night-life. Opposite, the *Café Rajatabla*, in the Ateneo cultural complex, draws the young crowd and often has live music. *Weekends*, San Juan Bosco, and *Café L'Attico*, both Altamira, are hard rock cafés, no cover charge. *City Rock Café*, Chacaíto, looks like a shopping centre but is good for dancing. *La Padrona*, Calle Humboldt, Chaguaramos, Brazilian music. *Cervecería Nueva Esparta*, Av. los Marquitos (Sabana Grande) is cheap, provides good music, but is another couples-only venue.

**Discotheques** A great many; recent recommendations: *Pida Pizza*, Sabana Grande; *Weekend*, Las Mercedes; *Palladium*. Couples only seems to be the norm.

**Sports and Recreations** Golf, tennis, riding, fishing, horse-racing every Sat. and Sun. at La Rinconada (a truly magnificent grandstand; betting is by a tote system, the sport is widely followed), bull fights (in season; go to the *Bar-Restaurant Los Cuchilleros* on Av. Urdaneta next to Plaza Candelaria to meet bullfighters and *aficionados*; tickets sold there on bullfight Sunday mornings, ticket sales end 1400, bar closes 1530, bullfight starts 1600), baseball (October-January), football, swimming, etc. Horse-racing commences at 1300, admission price to grandstand US$1.10. Several buses go to La Rinconada. Wildlife Park at Caricuao, west of the city, along the autopista Francisco Fajardo, T 431 9166. For flying try Halcón, Centro Comercial San Luis, T 987 1834. To hire fishing boats contact Ani Villanueva, T 740862. The recreational event of the year is the two days of Carnival.

**Cultural Events**  There are frequent Sun. morning concerts in the Teatro Municipal, 1100, usually US$2.25. Concerts, ballet, theatre and film festivals at the Ateneo de Caracas, Paseo Colón, Plaza Morelos; and similar events, including foreign artists, at the Complejo Cultural Teresa Carreño, on Paseo Colón, just E of *Caracas Hilton* (an interesting building, too). There are numerous **cinemas**, normally four showings a day (US$1-half price Mon.). For details of these and other events, see the newspapers, *El Universal*, *El Nacional* and *Daily Journal*, and the Sunday issue of *El Diario de Caracas*.

**Exchange**  Citibank will exchange Citicorp cheques; Banco Unión for **Visa** transactions. For cash advances on **Mastercard**, go to Credimático for a voucher then to Banco Mercantil for the cash from a side office, up to US$250 a day. For **Thomas Cook** cheques try Banco Internacional or Banco Mercantil. For **exchange** go to Italcambio offices: esquina Veroes and Urdaneta (or Visesta C.A. opposite), Av. Casanova (Sabana Grande), Av. L. Roche (Altamira Sur) Simón Bolívar Airport (may limit transaction to US$100, open public holidays); La Moneda, Centro Financiero Latino, Urdaneta, Piso 8; Infesa, Av. Libertador, between Negrín and Jabillos; Confinanzas, Centro Comercial Paseo Las Mercedes, Local PA-CI, open 0800-1200, 1400-1700. Commission of US$0.04 charged per US$1 changed in travellers' cheques. **American Express** cheques, Banco Consolidado, Av. San Francisco, Edif. Torre California, piso 9, Urb. Colinas de La California, until 1100 only; **AmEx rep** is Turisol, Centro Comercial Tamanaco, level C-2, Chuao suburb, T 927922, also in *Hotel Tamanaco*.

**Cultural Institutions**  British Council, Edificio Torre la Noria, 6th floor, Las Mercedes; English classes and modest library oriented towards English teaching, literature and fiction; Centro Venezolano-Americano, Av. Las Mercedes, good free library of books in English, and free concerts; also Spanish courses, US$195 for 2 months; Asociación Cultural Humboldt (Goethe Institut), Av. Juan Germán Roscio, San Bernardino, T 527634, library, lectures, films, concerts, Spanish courses.

**Spanish and English Courses**  Technical English Workshop, T 752 3218/752 2861, and English Speaking Skills, Edif. Anauco, 2nd floor, Parque Central.

**Embassies and Consulates**  **Colombian Consulate**, Guaicaipuro, Sector Chacaíto, Urb. El Rosal, T 951-3631; open Mon.-Fri. 0800-1400 for visas, photo and US$10 (maybe free), can take anything from 10 minutes to one day; **Mexican Embassy** (visa section), Edif. Parque Cristal, Torre Este, piso 14 (Mon.-Fri. 0900-1300), next to Parque del Este metro, tourist cards issued on the spot, free; **Brazilian Consulate**, Ed. Cen., Gerencial Mohedano, Av. Mohedano, near Metro Chacao, T 261-3459; 0900-1200, visas returned next day; **Cuban Consulate**, Av. 3/2, Campo Alegre, behind Clínica Sanatriz, 0900-1300; **Guyanese Embassy**, Quinta Roraima, Av. El Paseo, Prados del Este, T 771158, 9732781 (visa Mon., Wed., Fri., 0830-1200, same day if early, US$3, 2 application forms, 2 photos required); **Suriname Embassy**, 4a Avenida, between 7a and 8a Transversal, Urb. Altamira, T 324490; **Trinidadian Embassy**, Edif. Roraima, Av. El Paseo, Prados del Este, 2 blocks E of Chacaíto metro, opp. Torre Europa, T 261-5796 (visa US$17, 2 photos, up to 1 week).

   **USA Embassy and Consulate**, Av. Francisco Miranda, La Floresta (almost opp. Centro Comercial Centro Plaza, between metros Altamira and Parque del Este), T 285-3111/2222; **Canadian Embassy**, Edificio Torre Europa, piso 7, Av. Francisco de Miranda, corner of Av. Escuela, 2 blocks E of Chacaíto metro (T 951-6166); **Australian Embassy**, Luis Rocha between 6 and 7 Transversal, T 263-4033; 4 blocks N of Metro Altamira.

   **British Embassy and Consulate**, Torre Las Mercedes, 3rd floor, Av. La Estancia, Chuao (T 751-1022/1166/1966), Apartado 1246 for letters; **Danish Embassy**, Ed. EASO, 17th floor, Av. Francisco Miranda, nr. Chacaíto metro station, T 9514618/5606; **Finnish Embassy**, Torre C, piso 14, Centro Plaza, Av. Francisco de Miranda, T 284 5013; **French Embassy**, Ed. Las Frailes, La Guairita, T 910-0333/0324; **German Embassy**, Edificio Panavén, piso 2, Av. San Juan Bosco, Altamira, T 261-0181/1205; **Israeli Embassy**, Av. Francisco de Miranda, Centro Empresario Miranda, piso 4; **Netherlands Consulate**, Edif. San Juan, piso 9, San Juan Bosco y Av. Transversal 2, Altamira; **Spanish Embassy**, Ed. Banco Unión, Sabana Grande, piso 1; **Swedish Embassy**, Edificio Panavén, piso 5, Av. San Juan Bosco con Tercera Transversal, Altamira, T 2620176; **Swiss Embassy**, Torre Europa, piso 6, Av. Francisco de Miranda, corner of Av. Escuela, 2 blocks E of Chacaíto metro (T 951-4064). **Austrian Embassy**, Torre Las Mercedes, Chuao, T 91-3863.

**Diex**  for visa renewal, Av. Baralt, El Silencio.

**YMCA**  Edificio YMCA, Av. Guaicaipuro, San Bernardino, T 52-0291.

**Places of Worship** (with times of services in English): San Ignacio College, Calle Santa Teresa, La Castellana, Sunday mass 0915. Protestant: The United Christian Church, Av. Arboleda, El

Bosque, Sun. 1000; St. Mary's Anglican and Episcopal, Calle Chivacoa, San Román, Sun. 1030; Shalom Temple, Av. Jorge Washington, San Bernardino, Sat. 0900 and 1600.

**Telecommunications** are operated by the state company, CANTV, in south building, Centro Simón Bolívar (facing Plaza Caracas), T 41-8644; on mezzanine of Centro Plaza on Francisco Miranda in the east (corner of Andrés Bello between metros Parque del Este and Altamira), open 0800-2100, T 284-7932, phone cards sold here. Public telex at Centro Simón Bolivar and *nivel* C-I, Centro Ciudad Comercial Tamanaco. Few public phones, use those in metro stations.

**Post Office** Central at Urdaneta y Norte 4, close to Plaza Bolívar. *Lista de correos* costs US$0.04, Mon.-Fri. only. Philatelic collection at Correos on corner of Av. Baralt, near Plaza Bolívar.

**Hospitals** Hospital de Clínicas, Av. Panteón y Av. Alameda, San Bernardino, T 574-2011. Instituto Médico La Floresta, near US Embassy, T 284-8111.

**Laundry** *Lavandería Parque Central*, Av. Lecuna. **Dry Cleaning** Tintorería Tulipán, Las Acacias Sur, next to *Hotel Colón*; nearby is a same-day launderette called De-Blan-Ro.

**Tourist Information** Corpoturismo main office on floors 35-37, Torre Oeste, Parque Central (metro Bellas Artes is closest). T 507-8726/8814/8815. No maps but wonderful view. There is a smaller office at the airport (see below). The best selection of maps and guides is at the *Hilton Hotel* bookshop. **See page 1196** for **Maps** and further recommended reading.

**Travel Agents** *Maso Internacional*, Plaza Altamira Sur, Av. San Juan Bosco, T 313577, reps. for Thomas Cook, generally good reports of tours. *Wagons Lit*, Av. Urdaneta y Calle 5, helpful. *Turven Tropical Travel*, Real Edificio Unión, local 13, Sabana Grande, PO Box 60622, Caracas 1050, T 9511032, varied tours. *Lost World Adventures*, Edificio 3-H, Piso 6, Oficina 62, Boulevar de Sabana Grande, Caracas 1050. Specialised tours and expeditions. Venezuelan Travel Advisers, Venezuela, Edif. Policlínica Americana, Local D-PB, El Rosal, T 9514922. *Candes Turismo*, office in lobby of *Hilton*, T 571 0987 and Edif. Celeste, Boulevard Sabana Grande, helpful, English spoken; *Servicios Colectivos Especiales* in lobby of *Tamanaco*, T 283 6506, trips more varied and slightly cheaper. *Ideal Tours*, Centro Capriles,

Plaza Venezuela, for trips to Cuba: 4 days US$366 (rec.), 8 days US$488 (flight only US$295). *Manatec Tours*, Torre Banvenez, Av. Francisco Miranda y Calle Pascual Navarro, Sabana Grande, rec. particularly for ecological tours. Also rec: *Paradise Expeditions*, Lacal 7, Ed. Unión 71, Chacaíto, T 9517741; *Airone*, Torre Lincoln, Sabana Grande con Las Acacias, T 781 2512; *Madrid Caracas*, Urdaneta 73 between Norte 9 and 11, rec. for flights.

**Airport** 28 km. from Caracas, near the port of La Guaira: Maiquetía, for national flights, Simón Bolívar for international flights, adjacent to each other (5 mins.' walk—taxis take a circular route, fare US$1.15; Viasa and Avensa have shuttle buses). The Tourist Office at the international airport is very helpful; English spoken, open 0600-2400, 2-5 star hotel bookings can be made there, T 55-1060, passenger assistance T 55-2424; police T 55-2498. 3 *casas de cambio* open 24 hrs. (Italcambio, good rates for cash, outside duty-free area). Check your change. Pharmacy, bookshops, basement café (good value meals and snacks, open 0500-2400, hard to find); no seating in main terminal until you pass through security and check in. No official left luggage; ask for Paulo at the mini bar on the 1st floor of international terminal. Look after your belongings in both terminals. At Simón Bolívar, the airline offices are in the basement, hard to find: Viasa information and ticket desk open 0500-2400 daily, others at flight times. In Caracas, Viasa, Esquina La Marrón, 2 blocks E of Plaza Bolívar; Avensa, Esquina El Conde, 1 block W of Plaza Bolívar; Aerolíneas Argentinas, Torre la Previsora (Mezzanine) at Plaza Venezuela metro.

Always allow plenty of time when going to the airport, whatever means of transport you are using: the route can be very congested and check-in procedures are very slow (2 hrs. in daytime, but only ½ hr. at 0430). Allow at least 2 hrs. checking-in time before your flight, especially if flying Viasa. Taxi fares from airport to Caracas cost on average US$8-12, depending on part of city but overcharging is rife (fare in early a.m. about US$14). Fares are supposedly controlled: the taxi office in the airport issues you with a card with the official fare. Give this to the driver after you have checked the fare. After 2200 and at weekends a surcharge of 20% is included on the card. Drivers may only surcharge you for luggage (US$0.50 per large bag). If you think the taxi driver is overcharging you, make a complaint to Corpoturismo or tell him you will report him to the Departamento de Protección del Consumidor. The airport shuttle bus (blue and white with "Aeropuerto Internacional" on the side) leaves from E end of terminal, left out of exit for the city terminal (under the flyover at Bolívar and Av. Sur 17, 250 m. from Bellas Artes metro, poorly lit at night), regular service from 0600 to 0030, bus leaves when there are enough passengers and may not stop at international terminal if no flights due; go to start of route at national terminal, fare US$2. The bus is usually crowded so first time visitors may find a taxi good value. *Por puesto* airport—Caracas also US$2; from Caracas they are marked "Caracas Litoral", asked to be dropped off. When checking in, keep 10 bolívar bills handy to pay departure tax levied at most large airports (**see page 1190**).

**Long Distance Buses** The somewhat chaotic Nuevo Circo bus station in the city centre is due to be replaced in the mid 1990s. Hoyada metro station is nearest. Give yourself plenty of time to find the bus you need. Long-distance bus travel varies a lot in quality. However, buses from Caracas to Maracaibo, Mérida and San Cristóbal are usually in excellent condition; buses to Guayana are of poorer quality. Frequent service to Maracay, Valencia and Barquisimeto, but buses are often in bad shape; the Panamericana route is not recommended because it takes the old road on which there are many accidents. Aerobuses maintain regular services by air-conditioned coaches with reclining seats between Caracas and the main towns in eastern and western Venezuela, and also to Cúcuta, in Colombia. The fares of other good companies are a third less. The best lines are: to Maracaibo, Expresos los Llanos; to Guayana, Rápidos de Guayana. Buses stop frequently but there will not always be a toilet at the stop; always take your own toilet paper. Long distance *por puesto* services are twice as expensive as buses, but generally faster. On public holidays buses are usually fully booked leaving Caracas and drivers often make long journeys without stopping. Sat. and Sun. morning are also bad for travel into/out of Caracas, so buy ticket in advance (tickets only go on sale the day before travel—seats cannot be reserved). Always take identification when booking a long-distance journey; half-price tickets are available for those with a student card but you may need to provide a photocopy, and only Venezuelan cards may be accepted. There is a left luggage store at the bus station. To avoid theft it is advisable not to sleep on the buses. Arrive early, buses may start before time. Times and fares of buses are given under destinations.

Tepsa agents in Caracas: Rayco, Av. Olimpo, Edif. Anuncia, San Antonio, Sabana Grande, T 782-8276, reported to be very helpful and friendly.

**Excursions** The cable railway (*teleférico*) up Mount Avila from Av. Perimetral de Maripérez,

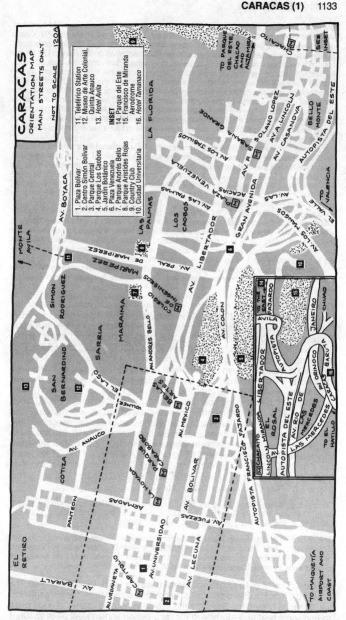

CARACAS
ORIENTATION MAP
MAIN STREETS ONLY
NOT TO SCALE

1. Plaza Bolívar
2. Centro Simón Bolívar
3. Parque Central
4. Parque Los Caobos
5. Jardín Botánico
6. Plaza Venezuela
7. Parque Andrés Bello
8. Parque Arístides Rojas
9. Country Club
10. Ciudad Universitaria
11. Teleférico Station
12. Museo de Arte Colonial, Quinta Anauco
13. Hotel Ávila

INSET
14. Parque del Este
15. Francisco de Miranda Aerodrome
16. Hotel Tamanaco

giving a stupendous view of the city (especially at night) and the coast, seems to be out of action for more time than it works; it was closed for "maintenance" in March 1991. Check details beforehand (when in operation reservations are necessary 4 hrs. in advance; on Sundays queues are very long). The future of the *Humboldt Hotel* on the summit (2,159 m.) has still not been decided. It has been refurbished, but only the ground floor bar/restaurant/disco operates at weekends. Camping is possible with permission. At the summit there is a restaurant, horseriding and an ice rink. Look out for 15 cm. moths with wood or leaf camouflage, trapped in corridor up to restaurant. A dirt road runs from La Puerta section of San Bernardino to the summit, 45 mins. in 4WD vehicle, 3 hrs. on foot. A recommended trip, when the cable railway is operating, is to ride up and hike back down (note that it is cold at the summit, average temperature 13°C). However, areas near the *teleférico* are notorious for armed robbery, probably wise to take a taxi and ask for it to wait. The *Tamanaco* offers jeep with driver US$50 p.p.

Good hiking: the three principal entrances to the **Avila National Park** are (a) 100 metres W of the restaurant *Tarzilandia* in Altamira (the easiest walk up); (b) the car park on the N side of Av. Boyacá above Urbanización Los Chorros (where there is a crude map)—8 hrs. to Pico Oriental, 2,650 metres; and (c) the entrance to Av. Boyacá from El Marqués (this route well signposted)—7 hrs. to Pico Naiguatá, 2,750 metres. (b) and (c) are in the east of Caracas, note that Av. Boyacá is closed to traffic on Sundays. A map of the paths (and entrance permit— US$2.85) is available from the Instituto Nacional de Parques, Av. Rómulo Gallegos, Parque del Este, Caracas, T 284-1956, price US$1. Try the city's hiking club, Centro Excursionista de Caracas, Calle Chivacoa, San Román, T 417067, director Marac Papajian, who meet Wed. 2030. They arrange day and weekend hikes. A description of the park is included in *No Frills Guide to Venezuela*, published by Bradt Publications. Essential to carry your own drinking water and food, and to set out early. Serious danger of bush fires in the dry season January-April, so be careful with cigarettes, etc.

Another excursion is to the village of El Hatillo, ½ hr. from the city centre by car, where colonial style housing has been well preserved. On the square is a tearoom serving good cakes.

***La Guaira*** is Venezuela's main port, only 20 mins. by road from Caracas (traffic permitting). Population: 22,500. Mean temperature: 29°C. Dating back to 1567, La Guaira achieved its greatest importance in the 18th century when the Basque Guipuzcoana Company held the royal trading monopoly; many British export-import companies flourished here in the 1800s. The old town, l km. E of the port, remains intact (much restoration work in progress), with delightful colonial houses along steep narrow streets leading up to the forts of El Vigía and La Pólvora; a short bus ride up to the lighthouse affords a fine view of the port and its surroundings. See the imposing Casa Guipuzcoana, on coast road (1734), original HQ of the company, now restored and used as government offices), open Tue.-Sun. 0800-1800. Many other mansions and churches, inc. the Casa José María España, home of the first 'martyr' in the War of Independence, and the beautifully-kept Museo Fundación John Boulton (Calle Bolívar18-13), housed in the home of the British merchant who arrived in 1828 and built a still-active business. Informative museum of La Guaira's colourful history; T 031-25921, open Tue.-Fri. 0930-1300, 1500-1800; Sat.-Sun. 0900-1300. The old Camino Real leads upwards from the restored Fuerte San Carlos and can be hiked to Caracas (see Bradt's *No Frills Guide* for hiking details).

The town of ***Maiquetía***, US$9 by taxi from Caracas is not spoilt by proximity to the airport. *Hotel Ovetense*, Ranco a Autopista, T 21527, F, basic, friendly; *Hotel Senador*, Plaza Los Maestros, F. The *Avila* is a good restaurant, near Los Maestros.

The coast E of Maiquetía-La Guaira has a string of popular seaside resorts and residential districts with a total population of about 75,000. The Avenida Soublette sweeps eastwards to Macuto, El Caribe, Naiguatá and so on to **Los Caracas**. All these places can be reached quite cheaply by most 'Litoral' buses from the W end of Nuevo Circo in Caracas.

***Macuto***, 5 km. E of La Guaira, is a pleasant seaside town, founded in 1740. The coastal promenade (Paseo del Mar) is lined with seagrape trees; there is a splendid yacht marina behind the *Sheraton* and a 'pigeon housing estate'. A good place to find some heat and sunshine in the rainy season and an ideal place to stay if 'stopping over' between flights. From the Plaza de las Palomas (lots of pigeons) can be seen La Guzmanía, the coastal residence of the President, built by Guzmán Blanco, complete with guards in colonial uniforms. Opposite is the presidential residence built in 1888 for Joaquín Crespo; the initials J and C can be seen over the entrance (for Joaquín and Jacinta Crespo). The building is now a college but can be visited by arrangement. The Castillete de las Quince Letras is the only building on the beach facing the sea, built by Armando Julio Reveron, whose paintings are on display in the Galería Nacional del Arte in the capital. The terminal for the Teleférico de Macuto from Pico Avila is here (see Caracas **Excursions**); its future is uncertain. Macuto's fine beaches tend to be overcrowded at weekends, go midweek if possible. There are no exchange facilities.

**Hotels** The posher area of Caraballeda is 5 km. E of Macuto: *Macuto Sheraton\**, on public beach, Apatado 65 La Guaira, T 944-300, Fax 944-318, A+, 3 restaurants (good food and value) and all 5-star facilities (although humidity problems from a/c). *Meliá Caribe\**, on beach just E of *Sheraton*, T 031-94-5555, A+, 3 restaurants (good), pool, disco, car rental, free tennis, expensive gym. *Royal Atlantic*, C/D, on seafront promenade, two blocks from beach, pool, restaurant with seafood specialities, T 031-94-1350. *Fioremar*, D, near *Meliá Caribe* and beach, T 031-92478, solarium, in good restaurant area. *Posada del Hidalgo*, D, Av. La Playa, close to *Macuto Sheraton*, Spanish-style hacienda, well-maintained, restaurant, warmly rec. *Sierra Nevada*, D, near *Sheraton*, small pool, bar/restaurant, pleasant. *Mar y Cel*, D/E, Av. La Costanera y El Palmar Oeste, T031-94-2174, reasonable value. Quite a few aparthotels in the area, up to US$100 a day without meals.

*Macuto\**, Av. La Playa y Calle 3, Urb. Alamo, T 031-44561/2/3, 3-star, D with bath, a/c, hot water, 5 min. walk to beach, comfortable but poorly maintained, swimming pool, safe parking, good restaurant. *Riviera*, Blvd. Caraballeda y Calle San Bartolomé, T 44313, D, clean, good food (French); *Las Quince Letras\**, B, Av. La Playa, good restaurant, pool; *Alamo*, Av. La Playa, E (possible to bargain), with shower and fan, clean, good value, good restaurant on the shore, not cheap; *La Choza de Santiago*, Av. La Playa, T (031) 44214/44118, E with bath, good restaurant, and next door *Posada del Hidalgo*, E, good; *Diana*, D-F, Boulevard Caraballeda (T 031-44278), on the beach, bath, clean, a/c, helpful, noisy on ground floor especially, safe for motorcycles; *Bahía del Mar*, La Playa y La Costanera, Los Corales, D, 100 m. from beach, restaurant; *Bahía*, Paseo Macuto, E, friendly, clean; *Plazamar*, E, Plaza Las Palomas, near La Guzmanía; *Colonial*, Paseo del Mar, E, good value, bath, a/c, smart, clean, good restaurant and service; *Isabel*, Isabel la Católica y Calle 3, 2 mins. from sea, F, small, quiet, good; *Pensión Guanchez*, Calle Guzmania, F with fan, shower and toilet, breakfast US$1, no sign outside, noisy, friendly.

**Restaurants** In Caraballeda, along Av. Principal are *Neptuno*, good seafood, rec.; *El Bodegón del Lino*, Spanish-style; *El Portón del Timotes*, seafood, good service. Good cheap Arab food at *La Barra de Nelson*; *La Esquina*, near *Hotel Alamo*, good, on Av. La Playa; on same ave. *Los Roques*;. many more on Paseo del Mar, e.g. *Criolla II Castilleto*, on Perimetral, for seafood. *Panadería* Apolo. 8, on Alamo, good.

**Transport** *Por puesto* from Caracas US$2, about 1 hr.; *por puesto* to airport, domestic terminal, US$0.65, 15 mins., or take Catia La Mar bus. The taxi fare from the airport is US$7 (plus US$0.50 for a large suitcase or rucksack); to the *Macuto Sheraton*, US$11. Anyone wanting to get on a *por puesto* back to Caracas at rush hour (weekend afternoons, etc.) is advised to walk back to one of the early stops such as the *Macuto Sheraton*. Bus from Caracas is caught one street down from Universidad.

**Beaches** Fishing (boats for hire at *Macuto-Sheraton* marina) just N of La Guaira (mostly marlin).

To the W of the airport is Catia La Mar, not recommended because it is industrial, very littered and the sea is heavily polluted, but it is very convenient for Maiquetía airport, taxi, US$2.10-2.35 depending on time of day. (Hotel Del Sur, D; *Scorpio*, F, clean, modern, but cockroaches; *Aeropuerto*, E, shower, a/c, OK; *Balneario Camuri Chico*, 3 good beaches, restaurant, showers, water fairly clean, rec.)

E of Caraballeda are a series of small resorts, most with their own walled-in public beaches (strong undertows)—Tanaguarena, Puerto Azul, Uria, etc.—until the cliff-hugging road arrives at *Naiguatá*, an old village in the shadow of the Avila National Park's highest peak (Fiesta of San Juan, 24 June, and Corpus Christi, costumed devil dancers, etc.). There are lovely views of rocky coast and surf from the corniche road to *Los Caracas* (50 km. from La Guaira), a holiday resort subsidised by the government for low-income workers; there is a beautiful white sandy beach and many cheap hotels, cabins (US$5) and apartments to rent. *Hotel Guai Camacuto*, D, restaurant, pool, T 541-6487 (INCRET—Worker's Training & Recreation Institute) for reservations.

It is possible to continue on along the Barlovento coast to Higuerote and return to Caracas on paved roads via Caucagua and Guatire, a round trip of about 300 km. Beyond Los Caracas (last gas until Carenero), the road is unimproved and carries little traffic (4WD vehicle rec.). It does not hug the coast as before but links many tiny fishing settlements. Near Osma (10 km.) is the Granja Osmán, which has some cottages for rent (B, inc. meals and water sports equipment); in Todasana (22 km.) is the German-run *Egua* hotel and restaurant, E, rooms with fans, modest. The road continues on through La Sabana and Chuspa to Chirimena (68 km. from Los Caracas), where the highway paving begins again, and thence 14 km. to Higuerote (see page 1162).

**Los Roques islands** lie 150 km. due N of Caracas; the atoll, of about 340 islets and reefs, constitutes one of Venezuela's loveliest National Parks. There are long stretches of white beaches (beware of sunburn as there is little shade), miles of coral reef with crystal-clear water ideal for snorkelling, and many bird nesting sites (e.g. the huge gull colonies on Cayo Francés and the pelicans, boobies and frigates on Selenqui). Small lizards, chameleons and iguanas, and cactus vegetation on some islets also add to the atoll's variety. Many of the islands' names seem strange because they are contractions of earlier names: e.g. 'Sarky' comes from Sister Key, 'Dos Mosquices' from Domus Key—where there is a Marine Biology Centre researching the coral reef and its ecology. For more information write to La Fundación Científica Los Roques, Apartado No. 1, Av. Carmelitas, Caracas 1010, T 32-6771.

Gran Roque is the main and only inhabited island; here flights land near the scattered fishing village (pop. 900) which is Park Headquarters; average temp. 27°C with coolish nights. Private accommodation is available for US$6-9 inc. meals, and you can negotiate with local fishermen for transport to other islands: you will need to take your own tent, food and (especially) water. There are some tiny beach houses on Cayo Rasqui, and Cayo Francés has an abandoned house and enough vegetation to provide shaded hammock sites, but otherwise there are no facilities. For solitude, Los Roques are a "must" midweek: Venezuelans swarm here on long weekends and at school holidays. Tiny but irritating biting insects in the calmer months can make camping miserable.

It is sometimes possible to find a boat from La Guaira to Los Roques (6-8 hours); the more usual way is a 35-minute ride with Helicópteros del Caribe at Maiquetía (return fare US$135-175; be prepared to wait at airport—ask for Rudi González who speaks English) or with Aereotuy (T 02-262-1966), who fly to Gran Roque from Maiquetía, Porlamar and Barcelona daily except Mondays. Day excursion fare of US$100 inc. food. boat ride, insurance—and mask and snorkel! Good value. Another possibility is to hitchhike a lift from Aeroclub at La Carlota airport (often difficult). Best to go in the morning or weekends; several planes leave then and often have spare places if you ask. T Caracas 952-1840/1/2 for flights at US$36 return.

**Other Excursions** Further afield, in San Francisco de *Yare*, a celebration is held at Corpus Christi (early June; the dance before the church of the enormously masked red devils, and of most of the villagers. It lasts the whole day (see **Music and Dance** section). Yare is about 90 km. from Caracas; the road to it is through Petare and down the Río Guaira as far as Santa Teresa, and then up the Río Tuy. From Santa Teresa make a detour to the beautiful and little frequented **Guatopo National Park** on the road to Altagracia de Orituco, but you must return to Santa Teresa to continue your journey to Yare.

At the Parque Guatopo are various convenient places to picnic on the route through the forest. Take insect repellant. To stay the night in the park a permit must be obtained. There are a number of good nature trails in the park, for instance a 3-km. trail from Santa Crucita Recreation Area (well-signposted).

Another excursion is into the mountains to **Colonia Tovar** (1,890 m), a village founded in 1843 by German immigrants enticed by the government's promise of free land and little interference. They retained their customs and isolation until a paved road reached the settlement in 1953. It is now a favourite of Caraqueños and has become very touristy, but the blond hair, blue eyes and Schwarzwald-accented German of the inhabitants are still much in evidence; *tovarenses* still make their unsurpassed bread, blackberry jam and bratwurst, and grow strawberries, coffee, garlic, rhubarb and flowers for the Caracas market. A tour of Colonia Tovar encompasses delightful landscapes, mild climate, old architecture (see the Scandinavian-style ceramics) and dignified hospitality. Ask in the village for the nearby *petroglifos* (rock paintings).

The 1½-hr. drive up from Caracas is easy during the week, but murder on weekends—long traffic jams, difficult to find picnic spots or accommodation, definitely not rec. The road leaves the capital at Antímano and climbs gently for l9 km. to the market town of *El Junquito*, another town heavily frequented by Caraqueños at weekends; roadside stalls sell souvenirs, fruit and barbequed *chorizos* (pork sausages). The road then winds another 19 km. to a paved turnoff, where several roads lead down to the coast (see below). To the south of the road is the **Parque Nacional Macarao**, small but attractive; from one point on this road Caracas can be seen to the E and the Caribbean to the N. Just before the coast turnoff is an arch over the road marking the Aragua state border; just beyond is the *Charcutería Tovar*, a good place to stock up on picnic supplies, and (Km. 43) the *Parador Castilla*.

**Hotels** *Alta-Baviera*, T 51-483, 0.8km above village on La Victoria road (Prolongación Calle Codazzi), heated, private bath, good view from restaurant terrace; *Bergland*, T 51-229, on same road, some cabins, beautiful views, good cheap breakfasts; *Drei-Tannen*, T51-246. private road on right just before entering village from east, 7 rooms, 2 heated apartments, parking, owner Señora Klemperer; *Edelweiss*, T 51-139, just past the *Alta Baviera*, highest hotel in town!—superb vistas, 8 rooms, 3 cabins, parking; *Freiburg*, T 51-313, cross river at "El Molino" sign in village and continue along hillside until signs to hotel, rooms and cabins, heated, restaurant; *Kaiserstuhl*, T 51-132, Calle Bolívar in centre, parking, good views, two restaurants; *Selva Negra\**, T 51-072, in centre near church, some cabins, heated, children's park, popular restaurant, parking. All are B and are normally full at weekends; room rates inc. good, German-style food. Other rec. **restaurants**: *El Codazzi*, in centre on Calle Codazzi, goulash and traditional German dishes, strudel and biscuits; *El Molino*, on Molino next to the historic old mill (worth a visit), wide selection of German dishes; *Perolón*, Calle Codazzi, open weekends and holidays, homemade vegetable soup a speciality; *Café Munstall*, opposite the church, interesting location in oldest house in Colonia Tovar, pastry and coffee at weekends; also *Bogedón La Bruja* and *La Montaña*.

There is said to be a good spot for camping just below the town's cemetery, if you don't mind the company!

It is generally easy to get a lift if there are no buses. Taxi fare for the round trip from Caracas to Colonia Tovar (driver will wait) is about US$10. Bus from Av. Sur 9 y El Rosario, next to Nuevo Circo, to El Junquito (1 hr.), then change for Colonia Tovar (1 hr.). *Por puesto* from Plaza Catia or O'Leary (more frequently), Caracas, 1 hr., US$0.75. Alternatively, take a *por puesto* from Plaza Capuchino to El Junquito, then one from there to Colonia Tovar, US$0.70. If changing *por puesto*, make sure the driver stops at the right place.

The road which leaves the Colonia Tovar-Caracas road (Highway 4) 8 km. before Tovar divides soon after into three paved roads which wind down the mountains through beautiful scenery to Puerto Cruz, Chichiriviche and Carayaca respectively. It is 43 km. to Puerto Cruz, a tiny harbour with a good beach. Boats can be hired here for a 14-km. trip W to the even smaller settlement (pop. 200) of Puerto Maya, on a beautiful bay and accessible only by boat; the villagers are mostly descended from African slaves. The second road leads down the valley to Chichiriviche (40 km. from Tovar -not to be confused with the resort W of Puerto Cabello), a neat little town with no accommodation; potholes in the last section of the road make a high-clearance vehicle useful. (A new coastal jeep track now links Chichiriviche with Puerto Cruz, not yet suitable for conventional cars.) The paved coast road begins at Chichiriviche and runs E to Catia La Mar and Maiquetía. First resort is Oricao with its lovely palm-rimmed but private beach, then comes Puerto Carayaca, where the third paved road down from Tovar reaches the coast. At Pto. Carayaca is *Casa Francisco*, hotel and restaurant, D, attractive setting. A few km. inland are the small towns of Tarma and Carayaca (only other gas station in the area apart from Colonia Tovar), where yet another paved road runs from the Tovar-El Junquito road to the coast (at Arrecifes). Many of the coves along this coast are good for swimming and renowned for sport fishing; the vegetation covering the mountainsides is lush and attractive: ferns, orchids, bromeliads, etc.

From Colonia Tovar, Highway 4 continues (well-paved but hair-raising) S down the slopes for 34 km. to La Victoria on the Caracas—Valencia Highway (see below); four buses a day; glorious scenery.

## WEST FROM CARACAS (2)

A varied region, through which run the Central Highlands; north of the highlands is the Caribbean, with secluded coves and popular resorts. Two coastal national parks are Morrocoy, offshore, and the dunes around the old city of Coro. Straddling the mountains is the birders' paradise of Henri Pittier National Park. South of the Highlands are Lake Valencia and the agricultural and industrial centres of Maracay and Valencia.

A hundred km. W of Caracas is the great basin in which lies the Lago de Valencia and the towns of Maracay and Valencia. The basin, which is only 450 metres above sea-level, receives plenty of rain and is one of the most important agricultural areas in the country; sugar, cotton, maize, beans and rice are the main crops. In the other valleys and depressions in the Central Highlands are also grown manioc, bananas, cocoa and the superb local coffee.

The Pan-American Highway, which links Caracas by road with the other capitals of South America, follows closely the route of Gómez' Great Andean Highway as far as the Lago de Maracaibo, though many sections have been widened and straightened. At the start, there is the choice of a direct toll motorway to Valencia (with exit to Maracay), toll US$0.60, or the old road called, familiarly, "La Pan-americana" and known for its dangerous bends. It leaves La Rinconada race course to its left, passes the park of Las Colinas de Carrizal (collections of local fish and birds, and pleasant paths), and climbs steadily but easily for 25 km. to **Los Teques**, capital of Miranda state (pop.: 85,000; alt. 1,180 m., founded 1703). The city is a mixture of skyscrapers and colonial buildings, with several attractive parks (Parque Gustavo Kloop down-town, Plaza Altamira, Parque El Encanto in the mountains nearby, reached by special tram). Hotels: *Alemán*, Plaza Miranda, E, friendly, good food; *Gran Casino*, Calle Boyacá, E, central, noisy; many motels on the old highway from Caracas. A little way E, in picturesque countryside between the old and new highways, are the quiet residential towns of San Diego and San José de los Altos. (25 km. S of Caracas, 10 km. E of the toll motorway a new international airport is being built at La Lagunita.) Twenty-four km. beyond Los Teques on the way down into the fertile valleys of Aragua, we can either join the Caracas-Valencia tollway or take the older road through several attractive little towns such as La Victoria (named for the 1814 battle between Spanish troops and Venezuelan students; pop. 14,600). The Quinta de Bolívar is at San Mateo, between La Victoria and Maracay. A little nearer Maracay, a good road leads off to **San Juan de Los Morros (see page 1159)**.

The Panamericana to Maracay should be taken at least once, for views and local colour, but winding up and down the mountains behind slow, smelly trucks is not much fun. The toll road also offers good views.

The new highway avoids city centres, so all that is seen of Maracay, Valencia and Barquisimeto are factories plus the huge concrete Barquisimeto Fourth Centenary Monument. Beyond Barquisimeto there are mountains like slag heaps, until we reach the green of the Andes.

**Maracay**, capital of Aragua State, has a population of 538,620 (altitude 445 metres). In its heyday it was the favourite city of General Gómez and some of his most fantastic whims are still there: the former *Hotel Jardín* (now a Government centre) with its beautiful zoo, park and fountain, built for his revels; the striking, modern opera house opposite; his modest little house for personal use, and the bull ring, an exact replica of the one at Seville. The Gómez mausoleum, built in his honour, has a huge triumphal arch. See also the Cathedral, dating back almost to the city's foundation in 1697. There is an interesting collection of prehispanic artefacts in the museums of the Instituto de Antropología e Historia on the S side of the plaza; they reveal how densely-populated the shores of Lago de Valencia once were. Maracay is an attractive, peaceful city; it is the centre of an important agricultural area, and the school and experimental stations of the Ministry of Agriculture are worth visiting; it is also important industrially and militarily.

**Hotels** *Byblos*\*, C, Av. Las Delicias, high standard; *Maracay*\*, Las Delicias, B, swimming pool, gymnasium, night club; *San Luis*, Carabobo Sur 13, off the main shopping street, E, clean, showers, friendly; *Caroní*, Ayacucho Norte 197, Bolívar, E, a/c, comfortable, rec.; *Bolívar*, Av. Bolívar Este, E, adequate; *Wladimir*, F, Av. Bolívar Este 27, friendly, good restaurant at reasonable prices; *Pipo*\*, D, Av. Principal, El Castaño, swimming pool, discotheque, friendly, rec. restaurant (parrillas a speciality), in hills above the city; *Pensión Libertad*, Calle Libertad 32, between Av. Paez and Av. Miranda, F with bath, clean, safe; (\*-bookable through Fairmont International).

**Restaurants** *Napoli*, near Plaza Central, good selection, reasonably priced; many reliable Chinese restaurants.

**Exchange** Banco Consolidado (American Express), Av. Bolívar y Fuerzas Aéreas.

**Tourist Office** Ed. Fundaragua, La Soledad, friendly.

The **FAV (Fuerza Aérea Venezolana) Museum** in Maracay is open on Sun. from 0800 to 1800. About two dozen aircraft are displayed, including Second World War fighters and bombers, later jets and earlier aircraft from between the wars.

**Buses** To Maracaibo Expresos los Llanos, US$6; **Valencia**, US$0.50, 1 hr.; **Caracas**, US$1.10, 2 hrs., *por puesto* US$2.20.

**Excursions** Lago de Valencia; to Las Delicias, Gómez' crumbling country house, where he died, with its adjoining zoo. Take an Ocumare bus from the terminal. Stretching N from Maracay to the Caribbean is the 1,000-hectare **Henri Pittier National Park**, the country's first (established 1937), said to be host to 500 species of birds. Sept.-Oct. is probably the best time for viewing migrants. Take a coat, it is cold in the cloud forest at night; it is also wet, 92% humidity is not uncommon. Two paved roads cut down through the Park to the coastal towns of Turiamo (naval base), *Ocumare de la Costa*, 48 km. from Maracay, 2-2½ hrs. by bus US$0.50, several hotels and **Cata**, once the most beautiful beach in Venezuela, now overdeveloped, basic cabins for rent on beach (E), good fish restaurant, run by Pepe (in low season, May-June, restaurants close 1530), *por puesto* from Ocumare US$0.50. Cuyagua beach, unspoilt, is 22 km. further on at the end of the road.

The Ocumare road climbs to the 1130-m. high Portachuelo pass, guarded by twin peaks (38 km. from Maracay); this is the main gateway for migrating birds and insects. The road was built by Gómez as an escape route if things grew too hot for him. At the pass is Rancho Grande, the uncompleted palace/hotel Gómez was building when he died; it is in the shape of a question mark and is worth visiting. The Rancho Grande Biological Station has been built on the ruins, from which several trails lead off into the forest; birdwatching is best in the early morning and late afternoon, and peccaries and agoutis may also be seen in the vicinity. Permission to stay should be sought from Dr. Alberto Fernández Badillo at the Escuela de Agronomía. Bring warm sleeping bag, candles and food; nearest supplies at El Limón, 20 km. before Rancho Grande. A taxi can be hired at Maracay for a day's outing in the park for about US$20 (bargain hard). The nearby town of **Victoria** has the oldest bullring in Venezuela and an interesting old hotel, *Hotel El Recreo*, D, originally a colonial house built in 1724 (also *Omni*, B). In the hills nearby is the *Hacienda San Mateo* formerly occupied by Simón Bolívar and now a museum. There is also a museum of sugar cane.

The second road through the Henri Pittier National Park (spectacular but not for timid drivers), goes over a more easterly pass (1,830 metres), to Santa Clara de **Choroní**, a beautiful colonial town (beautiful journey by bus from Maracay, US$1.20, 2½ hrs., 2 or 3 a day). *Hotel Club Cotoperix*, B p.p. for accommodation, T 573 5241, English spoken, full board and drinks in 3 colonial houses converted into guest houses, price also includes boat trips to otherwise inaccessible beaches, recommended; *Hotel Alemania*, D with small breakfast, simple rooms, not very friendly; *Hotel Bahía*, E near bridge to beach, safe, clean, good restaurant, fan or a/c, friendly; *Hospedaje La Montañita*, E. About 10 km. before Choroní are 2 waterfalls known as El Dique, where one can bathe; ask for directions, they are not easy to find. There is also an electricity museum. Just beyond the town is the dazzling white beach of Puerto Colombia (*Posada Alfonso*, E, clean; camping possible on the beach, dirty at weekends), from where launches (US$10) may be taken to the otherwise inaccessible colonial village of Chuao, famous in the past for its cocoa; the bay is very pleasant with a couple of bars.

Fifty km. to the west of Maracay the road reaches Valencia, through low hills thickly planted with citrus, coffee and sugar.

**Valencia** (population, 955,000; alt. 480 m.), the capital of Carabobo State, was founded in 1555. It stands on the W bank of the Cabriales river, 15 km. before it empties into the Lago de Valencia (the second largest in the country, with 22 islands but no outlet, consequently it is polluted). Valencia is Venezuela's third largest city, the centre of its most developed agricultural region, and the most industrialized. Annual mean temperature 24°C, but the valley is generally hot and humid; rainfall, 914 mm. a year. The atmosphere of the older and narrower streets is that of old Spain. The Cathedral, built in 1580 yet remodelled to retain its original style is on the central Plaza Bolívar (open 0630-1130, 1500-1830 daily, 0630-1200, 1500-1900 Sun.). The statue of the Virgen del Socorro in the left transept is the most valued treasure; on the second Sunday in November (during the Valencia Fair) it is paraded with a richly jewelled crown. See also El Capitolio (Páez, between Díaz Moreno y Montes de Oca), the Teatro Municipal (Colombia y Av. Carabobo), the old Carabobo University building and the handsome Plaza de Toros (Av. Las Ferias, S of city) which is the secondmost important in South America; it seats 26,500 spectators and features renowned international matadors during the November Valencia Fair. At Páez y Boyacá is the magnificent former residence of General Páez (hero of the Carabobo battle), now a museum where annual painting competitions take place in the Michelena Salon, open Mon.-Fri., free admittance. Equally attractive is the Casa de Célis (1766), which houses the Museo de Arte e Historia including precolumbian exhibits; Calle 98 and Av. 104 (open Tue.-Sat. 0800-1200, 1400-1730). San Francisco church dates back to the 16th century but was rebuilt in 1857. The Giradot Monument commemorates Atanácio Giradot, one of Bolívar's warriors. There are also several pleasant parks: Parques Cristóbal Mendoza, Andrés Eloy Blanco and Metropolitano have fountains, nicely-tended flower gardens and leisure activities. Most interesting, perhaps, is the Aquarium, at the W end of Calle 107 beyond the *autopista*, which displays a wide selection of Latin American fish and features a dolphin show at 1600 (open Tues.-Sun., 0930-1800, admission US$0.50). There is a small, unremarkable zoo behind the aquarium. Like its Spanish namesake, Valencia is famous for its oranges. There is a nice country club and a celebrated race track. (**N.B.** Most of the interesting sights are closed on Sundays.)

**Festivals** Late March, Valencia Week; mid-Nov., Valencia Fair (1 week).

**Hotels** *Intercontinental Valencia\**, A+, Av. Juan Uslar, T (041) 210-133, swimming pool, night club; *Canaima*, Av. Lara con Branger, D, clean, TV, rec.; *Continental*, Av. Boyacá 101-70, T 83014, D, restaurant, good value; *Hotel 400* and *Le Paris*, both on Av. Bolívar (Nos. 113-63 and 125-92), a/c, latter with restaurant, D; *Carabobo*, on Plaza Bolívar, central,C; *Don Pelayo\**, E, in 2town centre, Av. Díaz Moreno, rec., good restaurant; *Palermo*, Calle Colombia, F, clean and friendly with laundry, other *residencias* on same street for the same price (\*-bookable through Fairmont International).

**Restaurants** *Sorrento*, Av. Bolívar, rec.; *Fego*, Av. Bolívar 102-75, rec.

**British Vice-Consul** (Hon.): Corporación Mercantil Venezolana, Calle Silva No. 100-70, Edif. Comersa, T 50411/7.

**Exchange** Banco Consolidado (American Express), Av. Bolívar, Edif. Exterior; Turisol (also Amex); Italcambio, Av. Bolívar, Edif. Talia, Loc. 2.

**Buses** Bus terminus 3 km. from centre. To **Caracas**, US$1.50, *por puesto* US$3; to **San Cristóbal**, 10 hrs., US$7; **Barquisimeto**, US$2.25, 3 hrs; **Maracay**, 1 hr., US$0.50. *Tucacas*, US$2.

**Excursions** Valencia is a useful jumping-off point for the western and central states; there are also many interesting places to visit in the immediate vicinity. There is a petroglyph cave at Vigirima, 28 km. NE, reached by turning off the tollway at Guacara (14 km. E of Valencia); this is only one of many precolumbian sites scattered throughout the valley, there are other gloomy caves to the south of the Lake near Belém and Gualamaya. 30 km. SW of Valencia on the highway to San Carlos is the site of the Carabobo battlefield, an impressive historical monument surrounded by splendid gardens. Two battles were fought here: although Bolívar won the first in 1814, his forces were subsequently routed by the *llaneros* of Tomás Boves ('The Butcher') and Bolívar had to flee the country. Seven years later came the famous battle which established Venezuelan independence; on this occasion, Bolívar was greatly assisted by Páez's lancers and by the British legionnaires who had joined him at Ciudad Bolívar (they are particularly realistically represented in the bronze bas-reliefs on the monument). The view over the field from the *mirador* where the Liberator directed the battle is impressive. Buses to Carabobo leave from La Sanidad (Health Centre) in Valencia, US$0.25, 1 hr.

Just before the battlefield is the Safari Carabobo Reserva Animal, an Africa-shaped recreation and safari park where 600 exotic animals—including black bears, Bengal tigers and African species—roam freely in well-planned and spacious natural surroundings. Cars with roof racks are not permitted to enter.

Near the S shore of Lago de Valencia, about 34 km. E of Valencia, is the sleepy town of Güigüe; nearby, at the village of La Taimata extensive ancient petroglyphs have been discovered. Other sites can be found on the W shore of the Lake, and near the Hacienda Cariaprima, reached by paved road from Highway 11 at La Mona, 50 km. W of Valencia.

The Caracas-Valencia motorway (Highway 1 to Puerto Cabello) continues down the mountains, reaching the sea near El Palito (refinery and pier). Here we turn right to Puerto Cabello. 18 km. from Valencia, the road passes Las Trincheras, a decaying spa with the second sulphur hottest springs in the world (98°C); there are three baths (hot, hotter, very hot), a mud bath and a Turkish bath. Entrance US$1. Hotel* C, good restaurant.

*Puerto Cabello*, 96 km. W of La Guaira, is the port for Valencia, 55 km. away by modern freeway; it is an industrial city, the second most important Venezuelan port, with an excellent harbour, a lighthouse and a shipyard with dry dock. Average temperature, 28°C; population approaching 90,000. Little of the town's history as a smugglers' port and gateway for an illicit cacao trade with Curaçao is now evident. The Museo de Historia is housed in one of the few remaining colonial houses on Calle Los Lanceros, in the tangle of small streets, near the seafront. The forts of San Felipe (1741, also called the Castillo del Libertador) and Solano (1750) recall Spain's strength in the Caribbean. Solano is in a military zone and it is difficult to get permission to enter; the Navy, however, runs free launches across the channel to San Felipe, which was a prison until the death of Gómez in 1935. El Aguila monument in the colonial section marks the site where North American mercenaries (in the pay of Francisco de Miranda) were executed by the Royalists in 1806 during the War of Independence. A standard-gauge 175-km. railway runs to Barquisimeto (under which, below, details given).

**Festival** Shrove Tuesday, carnival festivities including "hammock dances".

**Hotels** *Balneario Caribe*, Urbina Palma Sol, on beach front, T (052) 71395, C, cold showers; *Miramar*, at El Palito, T 3853, E, on own beach.

**Exchange** Banco Italo de Venezuela.

One can hike on the old, cobbled Camino Real from Valencia to the village of San Esteban, 8 km. inland from Puerto Cabello, rec. (Bradt's *No Frills Guide* has full details).

A paved road runs 18 km. E through the picturesque village of Borburata (pilgrimages during Holy Week) to Patanemo, both within the **Parque Nacional San Esteban** (or Miguel J. Sanz), 44,000 ha. abutting the Henri Pittier Park on the E and stretching almost to Puerto Cabello.

About half an hour E on this road is a beautiful horseshoe-shaped beach shaded by palms called La Bahía. It has a refreshment stand, changing rooms, toilets and lifeguards, but take your own lunch. You can buy oysters from boys who open them for you and douse them with lemon juice.

There are 2 other attractive sandy beaches, Quizandal, with a coral reef, near the naval base (difficult to find, take a taxi, US$4, but you may find it hard to get one on the way back), and Patanemo. Offshore is Isla Larga, where sunken ships make for ideal snorkelling; *lanchas* from Quizandal, US$1, 15 mins. All these beaches are very crowded and noisy at weekends. **N.B.** The beach to the W of Puerto Cabello is not so attractive; be careful of going beyond the bathing area as the beach is notorious for armed robbery.

Twenty-four km. W of Puerto Cabello, at the junction of the Pan-American Highway and the road to Tucacas, is **Morón**, where there is a state-owned petrochemical plant.

Quite near Morón is the lovely beach of **Palma Sola**, 16 km. long and deserted save at Easter time when Venezuelans camp out there in crowds. The water can be dangerous but the sands and palms are superb. There are hotels, many closed in the off season (*Balneario Canaima*, C, children's swimming pool; *Balneario Caribe*, C), restaurants and changing rooms. A road has been built from Morón to Coro via Tucacas, an hour from Puerto Cabello.

**Tucacas** is a small town where bananas and other fruit are loaded for Curaçao and Aruba, but offshore is the **National Park of Morrocoy**, where there are hundreds of coral reefs, palm-studded islets, small cosy beaches and calm water for water-skiing, snorkelling, and skin-diving. The Park is reached on foot from Tucacas; camping allowed, no facilities, take food and drink, very crowded at weekends (no alcohol for sale in the park). With appropriate footwear it is possible to walk between some of the islands. The largest, cleanest and most popular of the islands is Cayo Sombrero; even so it has some deserted beaches, with trees to sling hammock. Boats are for hire (US$10-20 to Cayo Sombrero, per boat, US$5.25 to nearer islands; they will pick you up for the return journey; Pepe has been recommended). Venezuelan skin-diving clubs come here for their contests. Scuba diving equipment can be hired from near the harbour for US$5 a day, but the diving is reported not very interesting. Try American-owned Submatur, run by Belgian André, for equipment hire, scuba courses (US$350) and trips. This is one of the two main fishing grounds of Venezuela; the other is off Puerto La Cruz.

**Tucacas accommodation and services** Hotel *Manaure-Tucacas*, C, Av. Silva, a/c, hot water, clean, restaurant; *Hotel Said*, at entrance, E, swimming pool, good; *Greta*, D, a/c, clean, friendly, rec.; *La Suerte* on main street, E, but bargain, dirty; seek out Carlos, who provides accommodation in his unnamed hotel, E, safe, friendly. Restaurant *Fruti Mar*, very good; *Cervecería Tito*, good food; many good bakeries. Camping gas available in Tucacas or Puerto Cabello for camping in the Park. Bicycles can be hired in town. Banco Unión for exchange.

A few km. beyond, towards Coro, is the favourite, and hence expensive, beach resort of **Chichiriviche**; the town is filthy but offshore are numerous lovely islands and coral reefs. Crowded at holidays and long weekends. It is possible to hire a boat to any one of the islands; recommended for a weekend away from Caracas (note that prices posted onboard or on the jetty are per boat, not per person, about US$5.25—take a snorkel, no hire facilities). All day cruises, stopping at 3 islands, cost US$60 per boat. There is no direct bus, but frequent *por puestos* from Puerto Cabello, US$1, but direct buses from Valencia to Chichiriviche turnoff. You may camp on the islands, but there are no facilities or fresh water (good lunches on some of the beaches) and you may require a permit from Inparques (National Parks). Take precautions against rats. Nearby is a vast nesting area for scarlet ibis, flamingoes and herons.

**Hotels** Hotel *Mario**, B including 3 meals, swimming pool, rec.; *La Garza**, C (including 3 meals, but poor food and service) or D, pool; *Vaya*, C, small, clean, restaurant; *Náutico*, D with breakfast and dinner, friendly, clean, good meals, fans but no a/c; *Villa Marina*, aparthotel, E p.p., good, clean, safe, pool; *Balatón*, E, fan; *Capri*, near docks, E (bargain), shower and a/c, clean, pleasant Italian owned, good restaurant and supermarket; bakery opposite has rooms, E, fan, shared bathroom. Restaurants (both near *Capri*), *Fregata*, expensive, rec.; *Falcón*, good, cheap, good coffee and juices.

From Tucacas it is 177 km. to **Coro** (population 96,000, founded 1527, mean annual temperature 28°C), capital of the State of Falcón, a charming town, very quiet on Sundays, with interesting colonial buildings (the town is a national monument), surrounded by sand dunes (*médanos*, themselves a **National Park**: take bus, US$0.30, to Parque Ferial and walk). Worth seeing are the Cathedral, a national monument, begun in 1583; San Clemente church, built in the shape of a cross with arms pointing to the cardinal points, the wooden cross in the square in front of the church is said to mark the site of the first mass said in Venezuela and is believed to be the country's oldest such monument. The Museo Diocesano, Calle Zamora is opposite plaza San Clemente (open Tues. and Sun. 0900-1200, Wed.-Fri., 1600-1900, very interesting, entry US$0.60), Museo de Cerámica, Calle Zamora 98 (open Tues., 0900-1200, Wed.-Fri., 1600-1900, Sat. 1000-1300 and 1600-1900, Sun., 1000-1300, entry US$0.40). There are several interesting colonial houses, Los Arcaya, Zamora y Federación, one of the best examples of 18th century architecture; Los Senior, Talavera y Hernández, where Bolívar stayed in 1827; Las Ventanas de Hierro, Zamora y Colón, architecture and furniture, opp. is the Casa del Obispo (Museo del Tesoro) with a collection of colonial objects housed in the building where the town's rich hid their treasures during the War of Independence. The Jewish cemetery, on Calle 43-B y Zamora, is the oldest on the continent. Note that many historical sites in Falcón state close for a siesta; many open only at weekends. Near the village of La Vela along the Morón road the local handicraft is the production of rocking chairs of all sizes made from cactus wood.

**Festivals** 26 July, Coro Week; 9-12 Oct., state fair; 24-25 Dec., *Tambor Coriano* and *Parranda de San Benito* (Coro, La Vela and Puerto Cumarebo).

**Hotels at Coro** *Miranda\**, Av. Josefa Camejo, opposite old airport, T 51-0587, A, restaurant, swimming pool (very dirty, but non-residents can pay to use it); *Arenas*, opp. bus terminal, D, restaurant; *Caracas*, E, Calle Toledo 17, T 51-2465, old, very good, charming, a/c; *Coro*, E, Av. Independencia, friendly, run down; *Venezia*, T 068 511811, Av. Manacure entre Zamora y Urdaneta, D, expensive food, but renovated and good, often request Bs. 1000 deposit on arrival; *Valencia*, D with private shower, a/c, clean; *Los Médanos*, Av. Esteban Smith, T 55-4434, D with a/c, some cabins, restaurant, safe parking; *Capri*, very basic but friendly, large selection of rooms and facilities reflected in prices, poorly maintained; and nearby is *Hotel Colonial*. The *Bella Nápoli* is good, F, cheap, but run down; the *Pedregal*, F, is cheaper, with bath, fan, friendly, patio, basic, cockroaches; *Roma*, Calle 14 (20 de Febrero) close to plaza, F, good; *Hotel Martín*, next door is similar. At Av. 3 y Calle 95, *Coruña*, G, fan, and *Santa Ana*. 1 hr. S of Coro at scenic Curimagua is *Falcones*, E, good food, rec.

**Restaurant** *Don Camilo*, by *Hotel Miranda* and airport, reasonable prices. *Cafetería El Indio*, Independencia, nr. statue, very good breakfast. *La Tasca Española*; *Cervecería Alhambra*, Calle Zamora, good, cheap.

**Exchange** Banco Consolidado, Calle Federación con Buchivacoa (for American Express). Banco Venezuela (unfriendly) also takes Thomas Cook or Master Card.

**Tourist Office** On Plaza Alameda, English spoken, helpful.

**Transport and Roads** Airport (good restaurant on 1st floor, 10 mins. walk from centre); flights to Caracas and Barquisimeto. Buses to **Caracas** US$5.15; **Maracaibo**, US$3, 4½ hrs., *por puesto* US$5; **Tucacas**, US$2.25. From Coro, there is a good but uninteresting road to Maracaibo and another paved road along the isthmus leading to the Paraguaná Peninsula, along whose beaches men fish, 15 to 20 a net.

There is a ferry service (Ferrys del Caribe, unhelpful) from La Vela de Coro to Aruba via Curaçao, once a week. The schedules are continually being changed, so apply to the company's offices. Buy tickets on morning of departure. The journey usually takes 4-6 hrs., but the bureaucracy can lengthen this period to 8-12 hrs. Fare to Curaçao US$25 (cabin extra, to Aruba US$30). It is necessary to have ticket out of Curaçao and Aruba before entering, even if you are Dutch. It is advisable to arrive at the terminal at least 4 hours in advance, because the immigration officers often leave their posts before the boat departs. The tourist office can provide more information. The office for the boat in Coro is at Av. Independencia, beside Supermercado Victoria; there are also offices in Caracas at Av. Urdaneta esq. Ibárrez, Edificio Riera. *Por puesto* between La Vela de Coro and Coro itself costs US$1 per seat, bus costs US$0.25; taxi from La Vela to the ferry dock (3 km.) is US$2.75; *por puesto* from Maracaibo to ferry terminal, US$9. As an alternative to the ferry, there are flights from Las Piedras (see below) to Curaçao, daily with Servivensa (you must purchase a return ticket out of Curaçao and Aruba), daily with Air Aruba, US$40.

The **Paraguaná Peninsula** is connected by pipelines with the oilfields of Lago de Maracaibo. The Maravén (ex-Shell) and Lagovén (ex-Esso) groups have refineries, the former at Cardón, and the latter at Amuay. The airport, which has services to Maracaibo (30 min.), Coro, Maiquetía, Curaçao and Aruba (see above, Air Aruba, T 069-51605) is known as **Las Piedras**, the town itself as *Punto Fijo* (Hotels: *Jardín\**, D, Centro Comercial Judibana; *Caribe\**, E, Calle Comercio 21-112; *Safri*, Av. Colombia 78-15, clean, cheap, central; *Miami*, Calle Falcón No. 21-196; *Fuente de Soda-Restaurant Maracaibo*, Av. Bolívar, good, cheap). Taxi from Punto Fijo to Las Piedras, US$7. There is said to be good hiking from Punto Fijo through various vegetation zones up the Cerro Santa Ana. The beaches are at least 30 minutes away. There is a seaport, Las Piedras-Paraguaná, between Amuay and Cardón, which also serves the town of Coro. The villages on the peninsula have interesting colonial churches, notably that of Santa Ana. There are many beaches accessible by car, few visitors, good for camping but no shade or facilities. Adicora is a quiet little resort where you can rent a house by the week (no snorkelling); good seafood restaurants. *Hotel Montecano*, F, Italian-owned, friendly, clean, meals, rec. Bus to Coro, 0915, US$1, 2 hrs.

The Segovia Highlands, lying N of Barquisimeto, suffer from droughts, and are only sparsely settled along the river valleys. From Morón the Pan-American Highway strikes up into the hills, reaching 550 metres at *San Felipe* (population 30,750), capital of Yaracuy State. Festivals: 2 April, *día patronal*; 3 May, Velorio de la Cruz de Mayo; 23 June, San Juan. (Hotels: *Hostería Colonial\**, E, Av. La Paz, pool; *El Fuerte\**, E, Av. La Patria; *La Fuente*, E, Av. La Fuente; *La Patria*, G, 6A Avenida; *Comercio*, F, 6A Avenida; *Cabaiguan*, F, Calle 14).

If you do not want to go to Puerto Cabello and the coast, a newer section of the Highway from Valencia via Carabobo to just beyond San Felipe is 56 km. shorter.

**Barquisimeto**, capital of Lara State, has a population of 723,000. Altitude 565 metres, mean temperature 25°C. It stands on one of the alluvial fans so frequent in the Andes, and is Venezuela's fourth largest city, with the University of Lara. The Cathedral, on Calle 30 and Carrera 26 (Venezuela), a modern structure of reinforced concrete and glass, is interesting. The Palacio Municipal at Carrera 17 with Calle 25 is an attractive modern building. Across the street is a large well-shaded plaza with a bronze equestrian statue of Bolívar. There is a local museum 2 blocks away, free entry. On Carrera 15 (Av. Francisco de Miranda) between Calles 41-43 there is a charming park, resplendent with lush vegetation, paths, fountains and another bronze statue of Bolívar. There is a road from Barquisimeto to Acarigua (see page 1158) on the alternative route from Caracas to Mérida.

**Festival** 6 Jan., La Divina Pastora.

**Hotels** The *Motel El Parador*, A, excellent, near El Obelisco, a great roundabout in the northern suburbs of the town in the middle of which stands a tower; *Hilton\**, A, Carrera 5, Nueva Segovia; *Príncipe*, Carrera 19 y Calle 23, C, clean, pool, gourmet restaurant, highly rec.; *Gran Hotel Barquisimeto\**, D, Av. Pedro León Torres, pool; *Del Centro*, F, Av. 20, between Calles 26-27, good value; *La Casona*, E, Carrera 17 con Calle 27 near Plaza Bolívar (T 051-315311/317151), a/c, clean, hot water, excellent, parking, restaurant; *Yacambú*, E, Av. Vargas, between Carreras 19-20, swimming pool. *Avenida*, F, Av. Vargas, No. 21-124, 2nd floor, clean, economical. Many small cheap hotels near the bus terminal e.g. *Yaguara*, G, basic; *Miami Vice*, F, Calle 44.

**Exchange** Banco Consolidado, Av. Vargas entre Calles 20 y 21, also Turisol (T 516743), both American Express.

**Transport** Railway to Puerto Cabello (Sat., Sun. and holidays 0600 and 1600 in each direction, 2¾ hr. journey; daily trains run from Yaritagua en route to/from Acarigua for Puerto Cabello). Airport; no buses, only taxis. There is a single bus terminal on the edge of the city at Carrera 25 and Calle 44. Bus to Mérida, only one a day, leaves at 0315, 8 hrs. via Agua Viva and El Vigía, US$5; to Acarigua, 1 hr., US$1.20; to Valera *por puesto*, 3½ hrs., US$3.50. To Tucacas every 2 hours; to Coro every 2 hours, 7 hrs. Bus to **Caracas**, US$3.60. For renting cars (Volkswagen best), Av. Pedro León Torres y Calle 56, or agency in lobby of *Hotel Curumato*, Calle 34 with Av. 20, also at airport.

West of Barquisimeto, about half an hour's drive, is *El Tocuyo* with a good hotel in a delightful colonial setting, *La Posada Colonial*, D, with moderately priced restaurant. Between Barquisimeto and El Tocuyo is the main grape-growing area.

About 24 km. SW of Barquisimeto is the small town of **Quíbor** (*Hotel Duque*, F; outside the town is the *Posadas Turísticas de Sahare**, E). Festivals on 18 Jan. (N.S. de Altagracia) and 12 June (San Antonio de Padua). There is an interesting museum, Centro Antropológico de Quíbor, with exhibits of the Indians who used to live in the region. Stop in the plaza for a *chicha de maíz* or *arroz*, a refreshing traditional drink of the local Indians. Turn right a few km. before Quíbor to get to a tiny *rancho* in the village of Tintorero where "blankets" are made from local wool. These are in bright coloured stripes or plaids and serve well as colourful rugs, but not as what we call blankets. They are very good value. About 18 km. from Quíbor is the mountain village of Cubiro (two hotels) which stands at 1,600 metres, ideal for walking. Direct buses from Barquisimeto or change at Quíbor.

About 60 km. east of Barquisimeto is the little town of **Chivacoa**. Passing sugar-cane fields you reach the mountain of Sorte which is the holy region for the María-Lionza cult (similar to Voodoo) practised throughout Venezuela. Celebrations are held there mostly at weekends with 12 October (Día de la Raza) being the most important day. It is interesting to walk up the mountain when the pilgrims are camping beside the river and waterfalls, but do not go unless you are prepared to take it seriously, and use only the parking lot to park your car; other places are unsafe because of robbery. There is a Catholic festival, La Inmaculada Concepción, from 8-14 Dec.

Another pleasant excursion from Barquisimeto by bus or car is to **Río Claro**, about 28 km. inland, "where the Andes begin". You follow a lush river valley through the mountains. There are banana plantations in the area and many dirt trails you can follow on horseback or in a 4-wheel drive vehicle. From Río Claro a gravel road (dry season only) goes to Buena Vista and on to Quíbor; good views and pleasant villages.

Some 75 km. past Barquisimeto the Lara-Zulia motorway to Maracaibo forks off to the right (Caracas-Maracaibo 660 km.), through **Carora** (several hotels and restaurants).

---

## THE LOWLANDS OF MARACAIBO (3)

**Venezuela's main oil producing zone has the city of Maracaibo as its centre, on the western shore of the entrance to the Lago de Maracaibo. North of the city is the border crossing to Colombia on the Guajira Peninsula. The whole region is very hot.**

The Lowlands of Maracaibo, lying in the encircling arms of the mountains, are more or less windless and extremely humid. Average annual temperature is higher than anywhere else in Latin America. Rainfall decreases steadily from the foothills of the Sierra Nevada to the coast. In these lowlands is the semi-salt Lago de Maracaibo, of about 12,800 square km., 155 km. long and in places over 120 km. wide. It is joined to the sea by a waterway, 3 to 11 km. wide and 55 km. long, at the mouth of which is the bar of Maracaibo.

The area was once dependent on fishing and the transport of coffee across the lake from the Sierra. Since the discovery there of one of the world's greatest oilfields in 1914, there has been a great transformation, both in appearance (a forest of oil derricks covers the shore swamps and some of the lake), and in prosperity. The Lara-Zulia motorway reaches Maracaibo by the beautiful 8-km. long General Rafael Urdaneta bridge, which has the longest pre-stressed concrete span in the world.

**Maracaibo**, on the north-western shore of Lago de Maracaibo, capital of the State of Zulia, is Venezuela's oil capital: 70% of the nation's output comes from the Lake area. Maracaibo, which is 55 mins. by jet from Caracas, is the country's second largest city. Population: 1.2 million. The airport is at La Chinita. The bus terminal is on the edge of the city.

The climate is damp and hot, but healthy. The hottest months are July, August and September, but there is usually a sea breeze from 1500 until morning. The mean temperature of 28°C and average humidity of 78% are most felt at sea level. The new part of the city round Bella Vista and towards the University is in vivid contrast with the old town near the docks; this, with narrow streets and colonial style adobe houses, is hardly changed from the last century (parts, especially around Santa Lucía church—blue and white, facing Parque Urdaneta, have been well-restored). A trip across the lake through the oil derricks is difficult to organize as the oilfields are a long way from Maracaibo. The zone begins at Cabimas (*Cabimas Internacional**, B, luxury, pool, discotheque) on the E shore of the lake and you can get a good view of the oil rigs from there (*por puesto*, US$1.25, 40 mins., semi-legal trip in fishing boat among the derricks, US$3-5, ask behind the market) and from other towns further down, such as Lagunillas (*Hotel Lagunillas**, E, pool)—though don't take pictures without asking permission. A tourist taxi from *Hotel del Lago* to see the oil wells costs US$25.

From the port, you can take a ferry to Altagracia for US$0.40, the first at 0645, 25 mins.: exchange facilities at the terminal. Return the same way or take a minibus (US$0.55), travelling through exotic scenery for almost an hour and crossing the General Urdaneta bridge.

**Festivals around the Lake** at Cabimas, *gaitas* (see **Music and Dance**) 1-6 Jan.; Virgen del Rosario, 5 Oct. At Lagunillas, San Isidro processions and games, 15 May.

**Hotels** It is difficult to obtain rooms without making reservations well in advance. *Hotel del Lago Intercontinental**, El Milagro, Av. 2, T 912167/911868, A+, plastic atmosphere, pool open to non-residents; *Gran Hotel Delicias**, Av. 15 esq. Calle 70, C, swimming pool, night club; *Aparthotel Presidente**, C, Av. 11, 68-50, pool; *Maruma Internacional**, Circunvalación No.2, A, old and new sections, hot water, a/c, TV, reasonable restaurant; *Roma*, D, Calle 86, 3F-76, T 220868, a/c, popular with Italians, car parking, food is very good; *Kristoff**, B, Av. 8 (Santa Rita), swimming pool open to non-residents US$6, night club, poor exchange rates offered, poor breakfast, self service launderette adjacent to hotel; *San José**, D, Av. 3Y (San Martín) 82-29, a/c, bath, good beds, friendly, Italian restaurant, rec.; several others nearby, e.g. *Caribe*, Av. 7, F, good value, a/c and shower; *Yacambú*, F, Av. Libertador, a/c, central, restaurant; *Aurora*, F, Calle 96, near waterfront, spacious, friendly. *Victoria*, Av. 6, Calle 99, in picturesque old part of town, F, rec.; *Novedades*, Calle 78 (antes Dr. Portillo) No. 9-43, Bella Vista, T 75766, E, a/c, shower, rec., safe, Italian owner Francesco Scherra; other hotels in Bella Vista include *Montevideo* (E), *Falcón* and *Mary* (both F), a US$0.50 taxi ride from bus terminal. *Santa Ana* is the cheapest, G, poor but friendly, near main banking area on Av. 3, between Ciencias and Venezuela; nearby is *Pensión Familiar*, same price (beside *Restaurant La Friulana*).

**Restaurants** Most are closed on Sunday. *El Chicote* (seafood), Av. Bellavista (Av. 4), corner with Calle 70; *Pizzería Napoletana*, Calle 77 near Av. 4, excellent, closed Tues.; *El Jardín*, Centro Comercial Costa Verde, Av. 4, good lunches; in port district, *Café Comercio*, off Av. 4 and corner of Av. Libertador, good, "Bogart style". *ABC*, Av. Bella Vista near Calle 78, good Chinese, small, clean, open till 2100, closed Sun. *La Habana*, Av. Bella Vista (Av. 4) near Calle 76, good salads and milkshakes. *La Friulana*, Calle 95, Av. 3. for good cheap meal at less than US$2, repeatedly rec. (closes 1900). For confectionery, *Café Samemrum*, Av. 5 de Julio between Avs. 10 and 11, and *Kabuki*, Av. 5 de Julio opp. Banco de Maracaibo, more fashionable. Health food store, *Larga Vida*, Av. 13A between Calles 75 and 76.

**Taxis** US$1 fixed fare, in theory.

**Bookshops** *Librería Universal*, Av. 5 de Julio y Av. 4, maps, stationery, Caracas newspapers; *Librería Italiana*, Av. 5 de Julio, Ed. Centro América, post cards and foreign publication (inc US). *Librería Europa* has English publications. Staff at the public library, Av. 2, are helpful to tourists.

**Shopping** *Fin de Siglo* department stores sell handicrafts, records, tapes, posters of local sights. The outdoor market, **Las Pulgas**, is enormous, take any bus S down Av. 4 (Bella Vista). **Centro Comercial Costa Verde**, Av. 4 (antes Bella Vista), good new shopping complex.

**Exchange** Banco Consolidado, Av. Bella Vista con Calle 67 (American Express, also **Turisol** Amex rep., T 70611); **Citibank** (Banco de Venezuela and local banks offer no exchange facilities). All banks shut at 1630 sharp, exchange in morning only. All Thomas Cook transactions have to be verified in Caracas. *Cambio* at bus terminal will change Colombian pesos into bolívares at a poor rate.

**Consualtes** Colombian, Av. 3Y (San Martín) 70-16 nr. Av. 4/Bella Vista (T 72232), 10 km.

from centre, take bus or *por puesto* (Bellavista) out of town on Av. 4 to Calle 70; open Mon.-Fri., 0700-1300 prompt, 60-day visa in 5 hrs., no questions, no tickets required (better than Caracas). **Spanish**, Av. 15, No. 84-41, Delicias, T 526513. **British Vice-Consul**, Av. 9B con Calle 66A, No. 66-146, T 78642/82794. **Danish**, Av. 15, No. 88-78, Las Delicias, aptdo 301, T (61) 513077, open 0800-1200, 1400-1800.

**Anglican Church**  Christ Church, Av. 8 (Santa Rita) a Calle 74.

**Laundry**  *Lavandería Laza*, Calle 72 near Av. 3H, Bella Vista, rec.

**Post Office**, Av. Libertador y Av. 3. **Telecommunications**  Servicio de Telecomunicaciones de Venezuela, Calle 99, esq. Av. 3. CANTV, Calle 76 near Av. 3E, Bella Vista, open 0700-2330, inc. Sunday.

**Doctors**  Dr. García, Hospital Coromoto, Av. 3C and Calle 72, T 912222, speaks English, as does Dr. Carlos Febres, a dentist, Av. 8, No. 84-129, Mon.-Fri. 0900-1200, 1500-1800, T 221504.

**Air Services**  to Maiquetía, Mérida, Valencia, Barquisimeto, Las Piedras (for Amuay and Cardón), San Antonio (be early to guarantee seat) and other towns. Other airlines connect Maracaibo with Barranquilla (daily), Curaçao, Aruba, Miami and New York. (Pan Am Office, Centro Comercial Tamacuary, Av. 22 y Calle 72. T 529826/513199.) The airport is 14 km. S of the town. Taxis have a set fare of about US$3.50, there are no *por puestos*.

**Buses**  Bus station is 15 mins. walk from centre, 1 km. S of the old town. There are several fast and comfortable buses daily to **Valencia** (US$5.55 by Expresos del Lago), **San Cristóbal** (US$5.40, 8 hrs., *por puesto*, US$10.80), **Barquisimeto**, 5½ hrs. including police stops and searches (US$3.55), Coro US$3, 4 hrs., and **Caracas** (US$8, 10 hrs., *por puesto* US$15.60). Bus lines, other than Aerobuses de Venezuela, rec. are Occidente and Alianza, whose fares are cheaper. To **Mérida**, 5 hrs. (US$5), or take bus to El Vigía and change.

On the W side of the lake, between the rivers Santa Ana and Catatumbo, a large area of swampland is crossed by the road to La Fría. The swamp is inhabited by the Motilones, who, until 1960, refused to have dealings either with white men or other Indians. The southern border of the Motilones' territory, the Río Catatumbo, is famed for its almost nightly display of lightning for which there is, as yet, no accepted explanation and which caused it to be known in the old days as "The Lighthouse of Maracaibo". There are various missions you can visit: the easiest to reach is Los Angeles del Tocuco, 51 km. from Machiques (*por puesto* US$0.80, 1 hr. 15 mins.), where they welcome visitors; it helps to take a present, such as dried milk. There is a priest at the mission who was attacked, and they now preserve in their museum the arrow head they took from his body. Shop-cum-restaurant, family-run, simple, filling food, accommodation F. From here you can do a 5-day trek to Picci Cacao, through beautiful scenery to meet Yuspa Indians. Take them rice and blankets if you can carry them. Ask the padre for a guide and mules, take your own food and camping equipment. *Machiques* is on a fast road from San Cristóbal (Expreso Los Llanos good) via La Fría to Maracaibo, and has the good *Motel Tukuko*, E; *Hotel Italo Zuliano*, F. Machiques celebrates the Fiesta de San José on 19 March, and the Feria de Virgen del Carmen, with agricultural shows, on 14-18 July.

The best sightseeing trip is north about 1 hr. to the Río Limón (it has another local name). Take a bus (US$0.40) to El Moján, riding with the Guajira Indians as they return to their homes on the peninsula. Another bus or taxi (US$1.75) can be taken to the river. Alternatively, take a Sinamaica bus (e.g. Autobus Especial to Puerto Mara) from the new station, US$0.60 (*por puesto*, US$1.20, shorter delays from police searches make this worthwhile), then a colectivo to Puerto Cuervito, a small port on the Sinamaica lagoon, US$0.25. Hire a boat (bargaining rec. as the price is around US$30 for a boat holding 10 people; fix price, duration and route in advance to ensure full value, or pay US$7-10 p.p. for a round trip), and go up the river for an hour to La Boquita (2,500 inhabitants) to see Indians living in houses made of woven reed mats built on stilts: the only place where they can be seen. Return by *por puesto* Sinamaica-El Moján (US$0.40), thence to Maracaibo (US$1.75). Excursions by boat to the Sinamaica lagoon from Maracaibo charge about US$10 for 1½ hrs., but if you think you are being overcharged, ask for *el libro de reclamaciones* which should give the maximum official price. Sinamaica has an agricultural show on 15-21 August. The tension of the border area and the problem of *infiltraciones* suggests 1600 as the time limit to be in this area.

By crossing the bridge over the river you come, in the north, to a paved road that leads to Riohacha, in Colombia, where border formalities are quick and easy, a recommended route, but the Colombian border town, Maicao, has a most unsavoury reputation; best not to stop there. If you enter Venezuela from Colombia at Maicao, you can expect very rigorous searches both at the border and on the way to Maracaibo (6 police checks in all). Buses Maracaibo-Maicao, with Expreso Maicao or Expreso Gran Colombia, US$3-4, risk of ambush by bandits/guerrillas. Taxi fare US$24 per car (takes 5). It is reported that a visa is essential despite what may be said by Venezuelan Consulates.

Along the way you see Guajira Indians, the men with bare legs, on horseback; the women with long, black, tent-shaped dresses and painted faces, wearing the sandals with big wool pom-poms which they make and sell for US$2, as against the US$7-10 in the tourist shops. The men do nothing: women do all the work, tending sheep and goats, selling slippers and raising very little on the dry, hot, scrubby Guajira Peninsula. If you don't do this trip, you can see these Indians in the Ziruma district of Maracaibo. There is an interesting Guajira market at Los Filuos, a mile beyond Paraguaipoa, where you can buy the local tent-dress (*manta*) for about US$5-10, depending on the quality, but much cheaper than in Maracaibo.

Those who wish to go on to the Sierra Nevada de Mérida or the State of Trujillo should return over the lake and turn sharp right through Cabimas, Lagunillas, Bachaquero and Mene Grande, all unattractive oil towns, to rejoin the Pan-American Highway at Agua Viva. For the Colombian frontier or San Cristóbal we follow the Pan-American Highway.

The Pan-American Highway from Agua Viva is a splendid asphalt speed track, but devoid of much scenic or historical attraction. It runs along the foot of the Andes through rolling country planted with sugar or bananas, or park-like cattle land. At Sabana de Mendoza, 24 km. S of Agua Viva, is a possible stopover—*Hotel Panamérica* (good; air-conditioned). This road has plenty of restaurants, hotels and filling-stations, especially at Caja Seca and El Vigía, both rather new and raw looking towns. At *El Vigía* (*Hotel Gran Sasso*, E; *Hostería El Vigía*, E; *La Suiza*, Av. 15, opposite bus terminal, F, rec.; restaurant, *Armarilla*, try armarilla asado), where the road from Mérida to Santa Bárbara (Zulia) crosses the Río Chama, there is a fine bridge over 1 km. long. Santa Bárbara (56 km. NW) is a milk, meat and plantain producing centre, with air and boat services to Maracaibo and an important annual cattle show.

From El Vigía, the road continues fairly flat until *La Fría*, with a large natural-gas fuelled power station, where it is joined by the road along the west side of Lago de Maracaibo and begins to climb to San Cristóbal. La Fría has two hotels; the family-run *Hotel Turística*, F, on main square, basic but clean, is rec.

## THE SIERRA NEVADA DE MERIDA (4)

Venezuela's high Andes offer hiking and mountaineering, and fishing in lakes and rivers. The main tourist centre is Mérida, but there are many interesting villages, often with colonial churches. The Pan-American Highway runs through the Sierra entering Colombia at the decidedly dubious town of Cúcuta.

The *Sierra Nevada de Mérida*, running from S of Maracaibo to the Colombian frontier, is the only range in Venezuela where snow lies permanently on the higher peaks. Near Mérida itself there are five such snowcaps of almost 5,000 metres. Several basins lying between the mountains are actively cultivated; the inhabitants are concentrated mainly in valleys and basins at between 800 and 1,300 metres above sea level. The three towns of Mérida, Valera and San Cristóbal are in this zone. There are two distinct rainy and dry seasons in the year. Two crops of the staple food, maize, can be harvested annually up to an elevation of about 2,000 metres.

Those who wish to visit the Sierra Nevada should turn left at Agua Viva to *Valera*, the most important town in the State of Trujillo, with a population of 117,000 and an airport with connections to Caracas and La Fría. The bus terminal is on the edge of the town. The Banco Consolidado, Av. Bolívar, changes Amex cheques. The US$3-5 trip by *por puesto* to Mérida across the Pico del Aguila pass (5½ hrs.) is well worth taking. Agricultural and industrial fair in August.

**Hotels** *Motel Valera*\*, Urb. La Plata, E, clean, a/c; *Pensión Lara*, Av. 13, Calle 8, G, clean, good, friendly. *Aurora*, Edif. Rangel on Av. 7 (Bolívar), E; *Albergue Turístico*,E, good value;

*Camino Real*, nearby, E; *Hidrotermal San Rafael*, 4 km. off road between Valera and Motatán, notable for its hot water springs and the thermal bath.

**Restaurants** *La Terraza Café*, Av. Bolívar, good, cheap, live music; *Italio* opp. *Motel Valera*, rec.; *Vegetariano Tihuani*, in front of La Clínica María.

**Bus** To **Boconó**, US$1.50, 3 hrs.; to **Caracas**, 9 hrs. (Aerobuses), US$6.10.

From Valera a visit can be made to the state capital, **Trujillo** (43,000 people), at 805 metres; a *por puesto* from Valera costs US$0.55. This politically important town is losing ground commercially to Valera. Trujillo runs up and down hill; at the top, across from the university, is a park (sadly rundown) with waterfalls and paths. The Centro de Historia de Trujillo is a restored colonial house, now a museum. Bolívar lived there and signed the "proclamation of war to the death" in the house. A monument to the Virgen de la Paz was built by the wife of President Herrera Campins in 1983; it stands on a mountain, at 1,608 m., 2½ hrs. walk from town; open 0900-1700, good views. On the road to Valera is the restored colonial village of La Plazuela. (*Hotel Turística*, Av. Independencia 5-65, F with bath and hot water, highly rec.; *Hotel Roma*, F, good, clean, owner's daughter speaks English; *Restaurant Alfa*, Av. Independencia, friendly, reasonable.) Exchange for AmEx travellers' cheques, Banco Regional, Av. Independencia.

From Trujillo there is a high, winding, spectacular paved road to **Boconó** (pop. 35,000), a town built on steep mountain sides. It is a craft centre with demonstrations of weaving in the Casa Artesanal de Boconó and pottery in the Briceño family workshop. Festival of Romería de los Pastores de San Miguel is on 4-7 Jan.; that of San Isidro El Labrador on 15 May. From there you can continue down to Guanare (bus US$1.50, 3½ hrs.) in the *llanos* via Biscucuy (where a very difficult road through Guárico leads to Barquisimeto). Bus to Caracas, 8 hrs.

**Hotels** *Hotel Vega del Río\**, F, offers most services and food and is clean; *Colonial*, F, Av. Miranda; *Colina*, near the river at bottom of town, E, motel-style, clean, comfortable, restaurant; *Italia*, F, Calle Jáuregui.

**Restaurants** *Turística La Casa Vieja*, despite its name, good food, good value, lots of old photos of the area; *El Paisano*, popular restaurant with locals.

The small town of **Niquitao** (pop. 2000) is 1 hr. by public transport from Boconó. It is still relatively unspoilt, colonial-style, celebrating many festivals, particularly Holy Week, when paper is rolled out in the streets for children to create a giant painted mural. Entertainment is rustic, concentrated in the bars round the main square. *Posada Turística de Niquitao*, E, T (072) 53111/31448 and *Na Delia*, E, T (072) 52113/52522, on a hill ½ km. out of town, both have restaurants. Excursions can be made to the Teta de Niquitao (4,007 m.) 2 hrs. by jeep, the waterfalls and pools known as Las Pailas, and a nearby lake.

We are now in the Sierra Nevada de Mérida, the Western Andes of Venezuela. The people are friendly, and very colourful in their red and navy blue ruanas. Forty km. beyond Trujillo on a good paved road we come to **Timotes** (hotels: *Las Truchas*, D, very nice, good food; *Carabay*, family run, clean, good rooms, excellent restaurant; *Posada Caribe*, F, good value; restaurant), a mountainous little place set high in the cold grain zone. Near Timotes are La Mesa de Esnujaque (*Hotel Tibisay\**, E; *Miraflores*, F) and La Puerta (*Guadalupe\**, D, a fine hotel; *Chiquinquirá*, E, Av. Bolívar 34; *Valeralta*, F, on road to Timotes; *Los Andes*, F, Av. Bolívar), both places hill resorts for Maracaibo and district. The road now climbs through increasingly wild, barren and rugged country and through the windy pass of *Pico El Aguila* (4,115 metres, best seen early in the morning, frequently in the clouds). This is the way Bolívar went when crossing the Andes to liberate Colombia, and on the peak is the statue of an eagle. In the pass is the tourist *Restaurant Páramo Aguila* in chalet style. Behind it there is a three lane road leading up to the antenna and down towards the village of Piñango where there is trout fishing. Horses can be hired for treks to the Virgen del Carmen shrine and to the lake. The breath-taking scenery and the old village are worth the hardship of the 40 km. road; 4-wheel drive vehicles rec. if the road is wet.

The road then dips rapidly through **Apartaderos**, 12 km. away (*Hotel Parque Turístico*, E, clean, beautiful house, pricey restaurant; *Posada Viejo Apartaderos*, E, pool, fires, friendly, warmly rec.; *Hotel y Restaurant Mifiafi*, beautiful, several rooms to let, gardener will give you seeds from his flowers); over the centuries the Indians have piled up stones from the rocky mountainside into walls and enclosures, hence the name. On Sunday they all stand and watch the tourists, their potential income (there is a certain amount of high pressure selling); the children sell flowers and fat puppies called *mucuchíes* (a variant of the Grand Pyrené) after a near-by town. Only 3 km. from Apartaderos is Laguna Mucubají, and a 1-hour walk takes you to Laguna Negra in the **Parque Nacional Sierra Nevada** for trout fishing; there is a campsite near the lake, restaurant and shop by the turn-off from the main road. A further 1½-hr. walk from Laguna Negra is the Laguna Los Patos (very beautiful if the weather is fine). Horses can be hired. Guides (not absolutely necessary) can be found at Laguna Mucubají or at the hotels in Santo Domingo, a centre for fishing. This quaint little hamlet lies a few km. away on the road which leads off to Barinas in the *llanos* and then on to Valencia (bus Barinas-Santo Domingo US$1.80). Take the cobbled path that leads to a hillock overlooking the village and surrounding countryside. Good handicraft shops.

**Hotels** The beautiful *Hotel Moruco*, alt. 2,300 m., D, food very good, bar expensive, reservations can be made through *Hotel Río Prado* in Mérida; *Brisas Del Páramo*, E; *Hotel La Trucha Azul*, E, open fireplace, views, rec.; *Cabañas Halcon de Oro*, C for small groups, or *Las Cabañas*, B; *Santo Domingo*, E, hot water, clean, good restaurant but beware of overcharging; rooms for rent opp. *Restaurante Familia*, F; *Restaurant Brisas de la Sierra*, highly rec.

Between Santo Domingo and Laguna Mucubají is the former monastery, *Hotel Los Frailes*\*, alt. 3,000 m., B, said to be one of the best in Venezuela, excellent food, international menus, expensive wines. Book well ahead through Avensa (Av. Universidad, Edif. El Chorro, piso 13, T 564-0098/562-3022, Fax 562-3196, Aptdo Postal 943, Caracas), but don't pay in advance as Avensa will not reimburse you in case of transport problems. *Mucubají* restaurant, at the highest point of the road that passes Laguna Mucubají, is very good for trout.

Rene Erhardt and Lorena Ibáñez suggest a trip to Páramo El Tisure where Féliz Sánchez and Epifania Gil have built a stone house and church and offer free accommodation; take your own food and bedding. From Mérida take the bus to Puente de la Mucuchachi, US$1, 2 hrs., at 3,500 m. the highest settlement in Venezuela, then walk for 10-12 hours, or hire a mule (6 hours) from Juan Serpa. The trail rises to 4,200 m.

From Apartaderos the road to Mérida takes 3-4 hours, a pleasant drive. It leads up to San Rafael de Mucuchíes, at 3,140 metres (Sra. Crys, a French artist, will provide meals if you book in advance; *Hotel El Rosal*, F, hot water, clean, good), from where you can walk up to a high valley where Indians tend cows and sheep (beware of the dogs that protect the houses), then down to **Mucuchíes** (*Hotel Los Andes*, F, old house above plaza, 4 rooms, clean hot water, shared bathrooms, good creole food, excellent; *Hotel Faro*), where there is a trout farm. At Moconoque, to the NW there is a hot spring. An old colonial trail, El Camino Real, can be taken from Apartaderos to Mucuchíes (3-4 hrs.), sometimes joining the main road, sometimes passing through small villages; below San Rafael is an old flour mill still in operation. **Tabay**, 10 km. from Mérida, has a pleasant main square, look out for humming birds. Hotels: *Las Cumbres*, *El Castaño*; restaurant *Cancha de Bolas*. Gasoline here. There are two hot springs. From Plaza Bolívar in Tabay, a jeep can be taken to Aguas Calientes and the cloud forest at La Mucuy. We descend through striated zones of timber, grain, coffee and tropical products to reach level land at last and the city of Mérida. All through this part of the country you see a plant with curious felt-like leaves of pale grey-green, the *frailejón* (or great friar), which blooms with yellow flowers from September to December.

The patron saint of Mucuchíes is San Benito; his festival on 29 December is celebrated by participants wearing flower-decorated hats and firing blunderbusses continuously.

**Mérida** (173 km. from Valera and 674 km. from Caracas), founded 1558, is the capital of Mérida State. Its white towers are visible from far along the road, and it stands at 1,640 metres (mean temperature 19° C) on an alluvial terrace 15 km. long, 2½ km. wide, surrounded by cliffs and plantations and within sight of Pico Bolívar, the highest in Venezuela (5,007 metres), crowned with a bust of Bolívar. In January-February, the coldest months, and August-September, it rains almost every late afternoon (in the latter often throughout the night, too). Mérida still retains some colonial buildings which contrast with the fine modern buildings, such as those of the University of the Andes (founded 1785), which has 37,000 students from all over South America and the Caribbean. The main square with rebuilt Cathedral is pleasant, but is no longer colonial.  Population: 132,000, including students.

Mérida is known for its many parks (thirty three, some very small) and statues: the Parque de las Cinco Repúblicas (Calle 13, between Avs. 4 and 5), beside the barracks, had the first monument in the world to Bolívar (1842, replaced in 1988) and contains soil from each of the five countries he liberated (photography strictly prohibited). It is reported poorly maintained at present. Bolívar is venerated in Venezuela and it is not permitted to cross a square containing his statue, if unsuitably dressed or carrying large bundles. The peaks known as the Five White Eagles (Bolívar, 5,007 m., Humboldt, 4,942 m., Bompland, 4,882 m., Toro, 4,755 m., León, 4,740 m.) can be clearly seen from here. There is a local legend that five Indian girls were transformed into mountains when they refused to submit to the Conquistadores. In the Plaza Beethoven, a different melody from Beethoven's works is chimed every hour—not working Nov. 90 (*por puestos* run along Av. 5, marked "Santa María" or "Chorro de Milla", US$0.10). The Parque Los Chorros de Milla has a zoo (some cages disgracefully small) in a hilly setting with a waterfall, closed Mon., it is some distance from the centre (minibus, US$0.35). Plenty of handicraft shops near the zoo. On the way, there is a new chapel, built on the site where the Pope said mass in 1985. The Parque La Isla contains orchids, basketball and tennis courts, an amphitheatre and fountains; Jardín Acuario, besides the aquarium, is an exhibition centre, mainly devoted to the way of life and the crafts of the Andean peasants, admission US$0.10, open 0800-1200, 1400-2000 (*por puestos* leave from Av. 4 y Calle 25, US$0.10, passing airport). There is fishing and mountaineering in the neighbouring Sierra Nevada. Kite flying is very popular; enthusiasts meet at the Viaducto bridge.

**Festivals** The week of 4 December; hotels will only let for the whole week. Mérida is well known for its Feria del Sol, held on the week preceding Ash Wednesday. Also 1-2 Jan., Paradura del Niño; and 15 May, San Isidro.

**Hotels** *Prado Río\**, D, Cruz Verde 1, private bath, swimming pool, main building and individual cabins; *Pedregosa\**, B, Av. Panamericana on the edge of town, pool, restaurant, rec., National car hire office; *Belensate\**, D, Urb. La Hacienda, La Punta; *Park Hotel\**, Parque Glorias Patrias, C, but out of high season (i.e not Easter, August, Christmas or carnival) D, with discounts offered on car hire, noisy, but clean, good service, rec.; *La Terrazza\**, Los Chorros de Milla, D, modern, on outskirts, good view, friendly service, warmly rec.; *Caribay\**, Final Av. 2, noisy, D, good restaurant but poor service throughout. *Hostal Madrid*, F, Calle 23, Av. 7-8, basic, good value, good restaurant; *La Sierra*, E, Calle 23, No. 2-31, private bath, friendly, clean, good value; *Luxemburgo*, Calle 24 (Rangel), between Avs. 6-7, E, private bath, excellent breakfast, friendly, rec.; *El Andinito*, Plaza Bolívar, clean and friendly, E, good restaurant; *Montecarlo*, Av. 7 with Calles 24 and 25, T 52-66-88, E, clean, safe, parking, hot water, good but restaurant poor (located between teleférico station and Plaza Bolívar); *Mintoy*, Calle 26 (Ayacucho), No. 8-130, T 520340/523545, rec., except for breakfast, D-E, new, very clean, good value, but noisy, friendly, next to *Teleférico*, beside teleférico station, E, noisy, clean, hot water, good bar and restaurant. *Chama*, D, Av. 4 con Calle 29, private bath, pleasant, friendly, restaurant, noisy disco, guarded car parking; nearly opp. is *Hotel Prince*; *Posada La Merideña*, Av. 4 y Calle 16, clean, quiet, charming, E; *Italia*, Calle 19

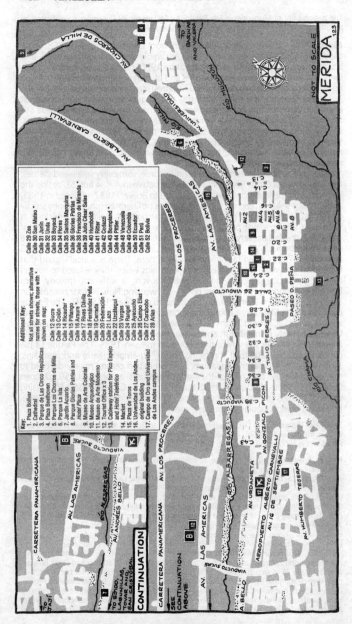

MERIDA

NOT TO SCALE

123

**Key:**
1. Plaza Bolívar
2. Cathedral
3. Parque de Las Cinco Repúblicas
4. Plaza Bolívar
5. Parque Los Chorros de Milla
6. Parque La Isla
7. Jardín Acuario
8. Parque Glorias Patrias and Hotel Plaza
9. Museo de Arte Colonial
10. Museo Arqueológico
11. Tourist Office
12. Cableway station for Pico Espejo and Hotel Teleférico
13. Railway station, original building
14. Market
15. Plaza de Toros
16. Universidad de Los Andes, original building
17. Campo de Oro and Universidad de Los Andes campus

**Additional Key:**
Not all streets shown; alternative names for streets, those with * shown on map:

Calle 12 Sucre
Calle 13 Colón
Calle 14 Ricaurte *
Calle 15 Piñango
Calle 16 Araure *
Calle 17 Rivas Dávila
Calle 18 Fernández Peña
Calle 19 Cerrada
Calle 20 Federación *
Calle 21 Lazo
Calle 22 Uzcátegui *
Calle 23 Vargas
Calle 24 Rangel
Calle 25 Ayacucho
Calle 26 Campo Elías
Calle 27 Carabobo
Calle 28 Arias

Calle 29 Zea
Calle 30 San Mateo *
Calle 31 Junín
Calle 32 Ejido
Calle 33 Boyacá
Calle 34 Flores *
Calle 35 Santos Marquina
Calle 36 Glorias Patrias
Calle 38 Francisco de Miranda *
Calle 39 Julio César Salas
Calle 40 Humboldt
Calle 41 Ritter
Calle 42 Orozzi
Calle 43 Bompland *
Calle 44 Pittier
Calle 48 Venezuela
Calle 49 Colombia
Calle 50 Ecuador
Calle 51 Perú
Calle 52 Bolivia

between Avs. 2 and 3, F, with bath, hot water (cheaper, smaller rooms available), clean, friendly but beware theft (even from safe) and scorpions, noisy TV; *Residencias San Pedro*, Calle 19, No. 6-36, T 522735, F, brand new, family run, fully equipped, clean, friendly, hot water, highly rec.; *Posada Luz Caraballo*, Plaza Mérida, F, small, clean, friendly, restaurant; *Encanto*, Av. Lora 25-30, entre Calles 25/26, F, friendly, take own lock, clean, popular, cheapest; *Posada Las Heroínas*, F, Calle 24, No. 8-95, clean, rec.; *De Paz* (formerly *Roje's*), Av. 2, Calles 24/25, F with bath, clean, good value, English spoken, friendly; *Regent*, Av. 2, F, clean, safe, hot water, friendly; several hotels on Av. 2 between Calles 17 and 20. *Don Cándido*, Av. 2, between Calles 17 y 18, G, good but noisy TV; also on Av. 2, *Mari* at Calle 25, F, good; *Bella Vista*, at Calles 21/22, F; and *Royal*, at No. 22/36, rec. On Av. 3, *Panamá*, at Calles 18/19, F, nice; *Budapest*, same block, G; *Tinjaca*, at Calles 20/21, F; *Turística Milla*, Calles 13/14, F. It is difficult to get rooms during school holidays and the Feria del Sol. Recommended to book in advance.

**Restaurants** *El Pub*, Av. 5, Calles 24/23, good Italian food; *Bimbo's*, Calle 23 near Plaza Bolívar, good; *Zaguán de Milla*, Av. 2, Calles 13/14, very good service. *Pekín*, Av. 3 y Calle 28, good set meal for US$3; *Hong Kong*, Av. 5 y Calle 25, good Chinese, reasonable prices; *Onde Jaime*, near Plaza Bolívar, Colombian food, very good;

Vegetarian restaurants: *Comida Vegetariana*, Calle 24, No. 8-205, opp. Parque Las Heroínas, lunch time only; *Fonda Vegetariana*, Calle 29/Av. 4, rec.; *Gran Fraternidad*, Av. 4, Calle 26; *Anfora de Acuario*, Av. 2, Calles 24 and 23, good set lunches. *La Mamma*, Av. 4 and Calle 19, very nice, good pizza, pasta and set lunches, popular in the evening; *Merengades La Sabrosita*, Calle 25, Av. 6/7, for *batidos* and good hamburgers; *Chipilino*, Av. 3 y Calle 19, popular with locals, open 24 hrs., rec. and *Restaurante Estudiantil Cuarta Avenida*, Av. 4 between C. 18 and 19. *El Puntal*, Calle 19, Av. 3/4, good atmosphere, English spoken, book exchange, Arab food; in same building in the courtyard, *Café Arabe*, especially for vegetarian food. *El Lano*, Av. 3, Calles 28-9, excellent breakfast; *El Palacio*, Calle 23, good *batidos*; *Café Santa Rosa*, Av. 4 y Calle 23, good coffee; *Tía Nicota*, inside Galerías 1890 on Av. 3, Calle 26, excellent cakes and coffee; good tea shop on Av. 23 between Calle 25 and 26. The *Heladería La Coromoto*, Av. 3 y Calle 29, offers 292 flavours, 88 choices of ice cream each day, e.g., trout, cornflakes, garlic, spaghetti. Local specialities, trout, *pastelitos* (savoury); sweetmeats include *dulces abrillantados, higo relleno, mantecado de maiz*; also try the local drink, *calentado*. Cheeses at the shop at Calle 14 and Av. 1.

**Shopping** Handicraft market on the Viaducto over Av. Urdaneta. **Films** One-day service, CA, Calle 23 between 5 y 6, T 527981.

**Disco** *La Viuda Negra*, on the road to Parroquía; and *El Fin del Mundo*.

**Museums** Museo de Arte Colonial, Av. 3 No. 18-48, three blocks from Plaza Bolívar (open Tues.-Fri., 0900-1200, 1500-1800, Sat. 1500-1800, and Sun., 1000-1200, 1500-1800). More interesting is the small **Museo Arqueológico** on the main square. **Museo de Arte Moderno**, Plaza Beethoven. Instituto Municipal de Cultura, Av. 4, half block from Parque Bolívar, stages poetry readings, art shows etc.

**Taxis** Journeys in town cost about US$1.50.

**Car Hire** Several companies at the airport. For motorcycle hire try Buggy's Bikes, Av. Miranda, Quinta Sajomi 3-83, T 639145, US$12 per day.

**Exchange** Most banks now accept travellers' cheques, and do not appear to restrict exchange to specific periods. Banco Internacional, corner Calle 31 y Av. 3; **Banco Mercantil** for Thomas Cook; **Banco Unido** accepts Visa and Mastercard. Cheques accepted by the *Casa de Cambio* in Centro Comercial Las Tapias, Av. Andrés Bello and in airport arrivals, and by hotels. Turisol, Amex representative, T 631085. On Saturday, try the Latin Travel Agency by the *Park Hotel*.

**Language Schools** Several schools including Instituto Europa, rec. Try also Mailer Mattíc, Av. 7 between Calle 25 and 26, rec.

**Colombian Consulate** Calle 9, T 636543, 2 blocks from C.C. Las Tapias, visas take 10 mins.

**Post Office and Telephones** CANTV, Calle 21 and Av. 14.

**Bullfights** Mérida is a famous centre; the Feria del Sol in February is the peak time.

**Tourist Offices** Near the airport (good map, US$0.15) and near *Hotel Mucubaji*. At Terminal Sur, helpful, map, hotel list, useful addresses and guide to events. At Oficina de Turismo Aeropuerto, Manuel, is very informative about excursions in the mountains, T 639330. The helpful Tourist Offices are probably a better bet than the police if you need to register a theft report for insurance purposes. **Inparques** (National Parks) office at end of Calle 51, turn right, map of Sierra Nevada national park (mediocre) US$1.

**Travel Agencies** *Club de Turismo*, Calle 24, No. 8-107 (opp. Teleférico), good advice on excursions, ask for Fanny. *Occidente Turismo y Viajes*, Av. 4 between Calles 18 and 19 for all flight bookings. *Montaña* offers climbing holidays (US$75-125 per day, including transport and equipment), horseriding, birdwatching, hang gliding, mountain biking, trout fishing, trips to Roraima and down the Río Caura to Para Falls, and a 21-day tour of Venezuela, English-speaking guides, trips graded according to difficulty. Ed. Las Américas P.B., Av. Las Américas, Mérida, T (074) 631740, Apartado Postal 645, Fax (5874) 631740; *Sierra Tours, Park Hotel*, T 630879, can book teleférico and has a range of excursions. It is cheaper to take a taxi for a day trip, *Línea Tibisay*, outside *Park Hotel*, T 637930, rec. *Mountain Tours*, Calle 24, No. 8-107, T 074-526402, offer a wide range of climbing tours and trips to the jungle. *Nevada Tours* at the airport offer interesting trips. They will take non-climbers up the Pico Bolívar, but owing to the altitude and weather conditions, this can be dangerous. Check all equipment carefully. Camilo Trujillo Medina, Parque Las Américas, Edificio M, T 637677, and Alan Highton, T 635332/637677, both offer tours of Mérida, speak English and have been recommended.

**Air Services** Airport is on the main highway, *por puesto* into town US$0.10, taxi US$1.25. Aeropostal and Avensa. To Caracas 4 flights daily, 1 hr., also to San Antonio at 1730. In the rainy season, especially on afternoon flights, planes may be diverted to San Antonio (if they aren't, it's a hair-raising approach). Avensa pay for overnight accommodation or for *por puestos* to Mérida, 3-5 hrs. on winding roads where landslides are common. Sit on left side of plane from Caracas for views. A new airport is being built at El Vigía, 1 hr. from Mérida; much safer as it is on a plain.

**Buses** The bus terminal is about 3 km. out of town on the W side of the valley, connected by frequent minibus service. Bus from city centre to bus terminal from Calle 25, Av. 2/3. An exit tax of US$0.10 has recently been imposed, make sure you pay, officials check buses before departure. Essential to book in advance at least the day before. To **Caracas**, US$7 (11-15 hrs.), *por puesto*, US$14 (from Caracas there are night buses with Alianza and others, either via Panamericana or Los Llanos, continuing to San Cristóbal); daily bus to **Maracaibo**, US$5, or *por puesto* service US$10, by Unión de Conductores, T 24364. Many buses to **San Cristóbal**, US$3-5, 6 hrs. Expresos Unidos not rec.; *por puesto* US$6-10. Buses to **Barinas**, US$2, 6 hrs. *Por puesto* to **Apartaderos**, US$2.50, bus US$1.25. Those hitchhiking east from Mérida should take a minibus to Tabay (US$0.30) and try from there. *Por puesto* to Valera, US$3-5 (3½ hrs.), sit on the right side for best views, alternatively take Transporte Barinas bus, US$2, pay on board.

The world's alleged highest and longest aerial cableway runs to *Pico Espejo* (4,765 metres) in four stages; it was built by the French in 1958. The trip up and down takes three hours and costs US$7.50, children US$3.75; it runs Tuesday (Wednesday in low season) to Sunday, except holidays, starting up at 0730 (supposedly), last trip up at 1200, last trip down at 1345 (only 2 rucksacks are allowed in each cabin, children are affected by the thin air, which makes them vomit). Check beforehand that the cable car is operating as it is periodically closed for maintenance and is subject to power cuts when in operation. There is a quota of 200 people per hour and it is very popular at weekends and holiday periods. Book several days in advance from the ticket office on Calle 25 (T 074-525080), or at the airport, or other travel agencies (US$8 charge). At busy periods queues start at 0600 or earlier. This is a "must", best done early in the morning (before 0830 ideally), before the clouds spoil the view, and from November to June. In summer the summit, with its statue to Nuestra Señora de las Nieves (Our Lady of the Snows, patron saint of mountaineers), is clouded and covered with snow and there is no view. In the station in Mérida one can buy or or hire warm jackets, gloves, caps, and climbing equipment, although there is a café at the top which you don't have to leave if you feel the cold—temperatures can be as low as 0°C. August is the coldest month on the peaks. The glacier on Pico Bolívar can be seen clearly; so can Picos Humboldt and Bompland, forming the Corona, and to the E, on a clear day, the blue haze of the *llanos*. Electric storms in the mountains are not uncommon. There is a restaurant at La Montaña, 2,442 m.

If the peak is slightly clouded when you start, stop at the Loma Redonda station (4,045 metres) the last station but one. From this station there is a path to Los Nevados (2,711 metres), a pretty little hamlet, plentiful accommodation G (e.g. Doña Rosa, or Señor Castillo), guest house has food (5 or more hours' walking down, not recommended for the inexperienced, 7 hours up to the cableway; breathtaking views; be prepared for cold rain in the afternoon, start very early and rest before walking because of the sudden ascent in the cable car). Take water. Mules do the journey Tues.-Sun., 5 hrs., in Los Nevados ask for Jorge, bargain hard, US$2 for mule, US$2 for guide. From Los Nevados you can continue to El Morro (7½ hours, very steep) or take a jeep to Mérida (2½ hrs., very rough, US$2.50). It is possible to get a room to stay overnight (*Posada Abel Gámez*, run by Adriana Dugerte, friendly, meals, rec.; *Hospedaje Nerios*, G, friendly, meals, rec.). Sr. Oviller Ruiz provides information on the history of the church and Indian cemetery. From here it is 47 km. to Mérida, jeep 3 hrs., US$3, do not attempt to walk before discovering if any facilities are available en route. There is also an ice cave with dazzling crystal ice stalactites two hours' rough walk from the last station. Only those in good heart can make this high trip. Jeep back to Mérida US$4, 2 hrs. At La Aguada station you can see the *fraílejón* plant and throughout the area there is a great variety and quantity of flora. From La Aguada it is possible to trek on foot for 1 hr. to Laguna La Fría, and on foot or by mule to the village of Los Aleros (see below), at 2,700 metres, 5 hours. From here you can continue to El Morro, 6 hours (beware of snakes on the path). The walk from La Aguada to the next station down is 2½ hrs. From the penultimate station on the way down is a ½-hr. walk to Los Calderones' farm, accommodation and horses for hire. A description of the Sierra Nevada is included in *No Frills Guide to Venezuela* published by Bradt Publications.

**Note** Because this is a national park, you need a permit to leave the station area at the summit, or to walk this mountain range. It must be obtained from the Inparques (National Parks) office in Mérida (see above). Permits are not given to single hikers: a minimum of 2 people is required. Have your passport available. Camping gas may be bought in Mérida from a Remate Panamá, Calle 23 y Av. 2, near *Hotel Playa*. If camping, remember that the area is between 3,500 and 4,200 metres so acclimatization is necessary as is warm clothing for nighttime. Water purification is also recommended.

**Mountain Guides** The Andean Club in Mérida organizes trips to the top and guides will provide all equipment; enquire at the *teleférico* station at the end of Calle 24, beyond Av. 8. Carlos Rodríguez C., can be contacted at the vegetarian restaurant of María Guerrero next to the *teleférico* (home address Av. Universidad, Edificio María Gracia, Piso 2, Apto. 5); he offers 1 to 7 day trips around Mérida, inc. in the price transportation, equipment and food. Carlos Torres, Av. 2, No. 9-81, or through *Hotel Italia*, rec., US$30 per day for two. Yanesha Expediciones, Av. 3, T 523291/636932, offer climbing, hiking, as well as normal tourist excursions, novices catered for, English spoken. Guides can often be found at *Café París* in the centre.

**Excursions** 40 km. NW is the Centro de Investigaciones en Astronomía (CIDA), responsible for the national observatory. Open daily 1030, 1400, 1530, 1900, 2200, but confirm by T 74-922660/791202. There is a library, Mon.-Fri. 0900-1200, 1530-1730, T 791893, 791988. Visits to other resorts near Mérida: to Laguna de Mucubají, Laguna Negra or Pico El Aguila (**see page 1149**—*por puesto* to Pico El Aguila, US$3). Just outside Mérida is Los Aleros, a model of a 1930s Andean village; examples of traditional skills, fascinating collection of old cameras and photographs; a ride in an open-sided bus and other events; very touristy (however, no Coca Cola, only traditional refreshments), rec. as a "must" (*Hospedaje Florencia*, G, and other *pensiones*). *Antano* is a good nearby restaurant. *Jají*, 43 km. (good picnic spot en route overlooking Mérida), *por puesto* (US$1, sit on the left, or Taxis Teleférico, ask for Luis Sosa, US$16 return for 4 hr. trip), famous for its colonial architecture, including a nice main square. On the way is La Mesa de Ejido village (*Posada Turística Papá Miguel*, E, rec., good food). Tourists can get advice from the Club Andino (P.O. Box 66) or Casa del Turista, La Compalla; T 3391. Recommended hotel and restaurant *Posada de Jají*, good food; *Restaurant El Zaguán*. Continuing for 62 km.—narrow, but mostly paved—beyond Jají, the Panamericana is reached (several gas stations on the way). From La Azulita, between Jají and the Panamericana, one can visit La Cueva del Pirata. Through splendid scenery to Lagunilla, with pleasant lakeside restaurant; San Juan de Lagunillas, believed to be the first site of Mérida, has a striking church and is noted for its craftwork especially weaving. Fiestas from Christmas to Candlemas (2 Feb., also in Bailadores—see below), 3 weeks in May (14 and 15 the highpoint) and in July. Thirty mins. beyond Lagunilla lies the little church of Estanques (seldom open except on Christmas Day) with a stupendous gold colonial altar. Near Estanques is the colonial village of Chiguará with mineral springs (*Posada Colonial Cantarranos*, F, friendly, try *El Merendero* for local delicacies), visited by exchange students; *por puesto* from Mérida, US$0.85. At El Pedregal there are botanical gardens and a good view over the town. Giant cacti in the area are said to be 300 years old.

After Mérida the road passes on through the Chama valley to Lagunilla. Ninety-six km. beyond Mérida comes **Tovar** (population 19,000; *Hostería Sabaneta*, E, private bath; *Pensión Ideal*, G, clean, basic, laundry facilities, friendly; *Hospedaje Tovar*, G; *Restaurant Kek Duna*, Hungarian owner speaks 6 languages and serves interesting food), a nice little town with pleasant excursions, whence we can rejoin the Panamericana via Zea, itself a pleasant village, or tackle the wild and beautiful old mountain road over La Negra to San Cristóbal. 15 km. from Tovar is **Bailadores** (*Hotel La Cascada*, C, modern— Wilfredo plays electric organ in the bar on Sat. night, and at Mass on Sun. in the beautiful church, entertaining on both occasions; *Hospedaje Villa*, F); beautiful walk to the waterfall with strawberries and cream half-way at La Capellería; *por puesto* to San Cristóbal US$3.60. Las Tapias, 2 km. away, has a hot spring. From Bailadores the road climbs up into the mountains. The *Hotel de Montaña*, C, private bath, T 077-82401/2, is rec., 7 km. before La Grita on the road from Mérida. Buses twice daily (0900 and 1530) between Tovar and La Grita on the old road. **La Grita** is a pleasant town, still not entirely Americanized, good Sunday market, festival 6 Aug.; Hotels: *La Casona*, F, Carrera 2A, No. 6-69, clean, friendly; *Capri*, F, Carrera 3, good value, bargain; good pizza restaurant next door. San Pedro del Río is a well preserved colonial village (*Posada Valparaíso*, beautiful garden, rec.).

**San Cristóbal**, capital of Táchira State, is on a plateau 55 km. from the Colombian border, at 830 metres. Average temperature 22°C, population 230,000. The city is on three levels, running N-S: a 112 km. wide level zone along the Torbes river, which flows S into the Orinoco basin, and two terraces, one of them 200 metres above the river, and 5°C cooler. This, and the La Concordia sector to the S, are the "select" suburbs. The city was founded in 1561, and the Spanish colonial appearance—the appearance only—is preserved. The Cathedral, finished in 1908, had its towers and façade rebuilt in colonial style for the 400th anniversary of the foundation. There is a good road over the mountains, with beautiful Andean views, to San Antonio. Short or day trips can be made to Rubio and Delicias, both with accommodation.

**Festival** 20-30 January.

**Hotels** *De Ferias El Tamá**, C, Av. 19 de Abril, overlooking the town, has an Olympic-size swimming pool, very good; *Korinu*, D, Carrera 6 bis, rec., with restaurant; *Círculo Militar*, Av. 19 de Abril, D, all services including swimming pool and gymnasium; *Machirí*, E, Calle 7 No. 4-30, bath, hot water, central, "bizarre owners"; *Hospedaje El Almendro*, opp. old bus station, F, cheap and homely, near to *El Amparo* restaurant; *Motel Las Lomas**, E, Av. Libertador; *Ejecutivo*, Calle 6, No. 3-45, F, old and basic but clean and central; *Cariongi*, near bus terminal, F, basic but convenient; *Tropicana*, F, clean, spacious, just across the street behind the old bus terminal (billiard hall next door). There are several cheap hotels on Avenida 6A, just off the central plaza, in F category; *Residencia Hilton*, clean and friendly, is probably the most expensive; opposite is *Internacional*, F, cheaper and better; but neither are as grand as they sound. *Alba*, G, next to barracks.

**Restaurants** *Fung Wah*, on lower of 2 main thoroughfares, Chinese, expensive but good.

**Exchange** **Banco Consolidado** (American Express), 5a Av., Edif. Torre E.

**Post Office** Palacio Municipal, next to Cathedral.

**Launderette** in Cada shopping centre next to *Hotel El Tamá*, open 0800-1200, 1400-1800.

**Airports** for San Cristóbal: at San Antonio (1 hr.) and La Fría (90 mins.).

**By Road** To Maracaibo, 8 hrs., US$5.40, *por puesto*, US$10.80. To Mérida, US$6-10 by *por puesto* or bus, US$3-5. To Caracas, US$7.50-8.10, 12 hrs. by Llanos and Panamericana routes respectively; similarly to **Valencia**, US$6.10-7. To San Antonio, 2½ hrs. by bus, US$0.40, or *por puesto*, which continues to Cúcuta, US$1.50, stopping at Immigration in both countries, runs every 20 mins. By taxi to Cúcuta: US$11 to San Antonio, US$5 to wait at border, then US$6 to Cúcuta.

**San Antonio**, the frontier town (not a tourist attraction, although there is an attractive colonial cathedral, also some pleasant parks), is connected by international bridge with Cúcuta, Colombia, distant about 16 km. (bus

US$0.80—in bolívares or pesos—to international bridge), whence you can continue by road or air to Bogotá. Be sure to get your Venezuelan exit stamp in San Antonio as facilities are no longer available at the bridge. *Por puesto* drivers may say its not required and refuse to wait. Colombian officials will send you back if you have no exit stamp (unless you are only visiting Cúcuta; officials do not seem overly concerned about day visitors). Once you are in Colombia go straight to the DAS office in Cúcuta or the airport to complete formalities there (**see Colombia Section 2**). Entry charge, US$1.50. Entering Venezuela from Cúcuta, there is no point in buying a bus ticket to San Cristóbal before going through formalities. Go to DIEX on the other side of San Antonio, 3 blocks down from Carrera 9. If travelling on a Cúcuta-San Cristóbal bus, the driver should wait for you to go through formalities. 5 km. after San Antonio is a customs post; be prepared to be strip-searched, and then for further searches between San Cristóbal and Mérida. **N.B.** Venezuelan customs is often closed at weekends; it is therefore impossible to cross from Colombia at these times. Be prepared for long queues on the international bridge after 1500. Beware of all sorts of sharp practices at Cúcuta bus station (theft, contricks, selling tickets for buses that do not exist). Entering Venezuela in your own car presents no problems as long as you have obtained a visa in advance. You must visit Immigration in town, pay US$0.20 for a form on which to pay exit tax and have your passport photocopied. Once in Venezuela, you may find that local police are ignorant of documentation required for foreign cars. Thirteen km. N on the Venezuelan side lies the spa of Ureña, with natural hot springs (*Hotel Aguas Calientes*\*, C, private thermal bath, swimming pool).

**Festivals** San Antonio, 13-20 May; Ureña, 3-12 December.

**Hotels** At San Antonio: *Don Jorge,* F, a/c dining room expensive; *Terepaima*, Carrera 8, No. 1-37, F, clean, friendly; *Táchira*, E, with bath, rec.; *Neveri*, E, Calle 3, No. 3-11, esq. Carrera 3, private bath, parking nearby, by border; *La Residencial Colonial*, Carrera 11, No. 251, F, clean, cheap restaurant, rec.; many hotels near town centre.

**Exchange** at the Banco de Venezuela on main square. *Casas de cambio* near the international bridge will not all change cheques and some will only change Colombian pesos, not even US dollars cash. The exchange rate for changing bolívares to pesos is better in San Antonio than in Cúcuta; change sufficient if going to anywhere other than Bucaramanga or Bogotá.

**Colombian Consulate** Carrera 6, No. 3-29, for visas, open until 0200.

**Bus** Cúcuta to **Caracas** US$9 (coming from the capital buses to the border stop for exit stamps in San Antonio); bus Caracas-**San Antonio** US$8.10.

**Airport** has exchange facilities. Taxis run to DIEX (emigration) in town, and on to Cúcuta airport, US$6. *Por puesto* to airport, US$0.15. Internal flights, Avensa, to Maiquetía, Mérida, Barquisimeto, Maracay, Maracaibo and Valencia.

---

## THE LLANOS OF THE ORINOCO (5)

A spectacular route descends from the Sierra Nevada to the flat *llanos*, perhaps one of the best places in the world to see birds. South of these cattle lands stretch the forests through which flow the Orinoco and its tributaries; out of the lowlands rise strange, flat-topped *tepuyes*. The area is excellent for "nature tourism".

This area of flat grasslands, 1,000 km. by 320 km., lies between the Andes and the Río Orinoco. It is veined by numerous slow running rivers, forested along their banks. The vast flatland is only varied here and there by *mesas*, or slight upthrusts of the land. About 5 million of the country's 6.4 million cattle, many of the Zebu type from Brazil and India, are in the *llanos*, 30% of the country's area, but holding no more than 13% of the population. When the whole plain is periodically under water, the *llaneros* drive their cattle into the hills or through the flood from one *mesa* to another. When the plain is parched by the sun and the savanna grasses become uneatable they herd the cattle down to the damper region of the Apure and Orinoco. Finally they drive them into the valley of Valencia to be fattened for slaughter.

Parts of the area are coming under cultivation. The Guárico dam has created thousands of hectares of fertile land by controlling flood and drought. The *llanos* State of Portuguesa has now the largest cultivated area of any: rice and cotton are now produced.

## Alternative route from Caracas to Mérida

There is a splendid road to the western *llanos* of Barinas, from Valencia through **San Carlos**, capital of Cojedes State (uninteresting, *Hotel Central*, D, clean, safe, a/c, good bar and restaurant, and secure offstreet parking; *Hotel Italo*, F, Av. Carabobo, a/c, private bath; festivals 18 Jan. and 2-5 Nov.—San Carlos Borromeo), **Acarigua**, a thriving agricultural centre (*Motel Payara\**, D, on road to Guanare, pool, a/c; *Hotel Parigua*, D, Calle 31, a/c, bath, secure parking; *Campeste*, 1 minute from bus terminal; *San Carlos*, E, good restaurant, not too safe; *Kety* for cakes) and **Guanare**, a national place of pilgrimage with an old parish church containing the much venerated relic of the Virgin of Coromoto, Patron of Venezuela. Population 32,500 (*Hotel Italia*, D, Carrera 5, No. 19-60, the most expensive, clean, a/c, bar and restaurant, offstreet parking; others, all E, include *Coromoto*—out of town, swimming pool; *Motel Portuguesa*, a/c, hot water, clean, good restaurant, pool; *Hotel Los Angeles*; *Restaurant Don Quixote*, near *Hotel Italia*, good atmosphere but expensive).

After the first appearance of the Virgin, Chief Coromoto failed to be baptized, though he did hedge by getting other members of the tribe baptized. When the Virgin reappeared he made a grab at her and told her gruffly to be gone, but she vanished leaving in his hand a likeness of herself on the inner surface of a split stone now on display in the church. For years little attention was paid to the image, and it was only in 1946 that this Virgin was declared the Patron of Venezuela.

**Festivals in Portuguesa State** Pilgrimages to Coromoto, 2 Jan. and 8 Sept.; Candlemas in Guanare, 1 Feb.; Virgen de la Corteza in Acarigua, 11 Feb. (bull-baiting, dancing).

The road continues to **Barinas** (population 92,000), the capital of the cattle-raising and oil-rich State of Barinas. The shady Parque Universitario has a botanical gardens and a zoo open at weekends. The tourist office is on the Plaza Bolívar. There are two museums. Fishing and game-watching excursions into the *llanos*. The rivers are full of *caribes* (*piranha*) and many kinds of fish good to eat. The local music at *Hotel Venezuela* (no rooms!) near the bus terminal has been rec.; harp *cuatro*, singing, informal and very good.

**Hotels** *Motel El Cacique*, D, good, noisy a/c, out of centre, good restaurant, swimming pool; *Bristol\**, Av. 23 de Enero, C; *Comercio\**, D, Av. Marqués del Pumar, cooking facilities; **Plaza**, E, a/c, shower, restaurant not rec.; *Motel La Media Avenida*, Av. 23 de Enero, E, cold showers, bar, restaurant, parking, clean, rec.; opposite bus terminal are: *Lisboa*, F, good, rec.; *Motel San Marino*, F and El Palacio, F, clean, a/c.

*Restaurant Gladismar*, Av. 7, good evening meals; *Adán y Eva*, Av. Sucre, *criollo* restaurant, good; *Heladeria Metro*, Av. 7, good patisserie opposite the bus terminal; *Cantarana Bar*, near bus terminal, good, cheap.

**Exchange** Banco Consolidado (American Express), Av. Libertador con Calle Camejo.

**Buses** 4 a day for **Mérida**, US$2, magnificent ride through the mountains, 6-8 hrs. (sit on right for best views); *por puesto*, US$4. Bus to **Caracas**, US$5.50, 8 hrs; to **San Antonio**, US$3.35. To **Acarigua**, US$2, 3 hrs; **San Cristóbal**, US$1.20, 4½ hrs; **Maracay**, US$2, 8 hrs. The bus terminal is on the edge of the town.

**Airport** with local services and to Caracas (3 a day, 2 Sun., US$38).

From Barinas there is a beautifully scenic road to Apartaderos, in the Sierra Nevada de Mérida **(see page 1150)**.

Motorists travelling East from Mérida to Ciudad Bolívar can either go across the *llanos* or via San Carlos, El Sombrero, Valle de la Pascua and El Tigre, which route requires no ferry crossings and has more places with accommodation. In the *llanos*, near El Baúl (turn off main road E of San Carlos), is a safari-type lodge at the working ranch of Hato Piñero, including all meals, free drinks, good room, and guide for excellent bird- and animal-watching trips, highly rec.; address: Hato Piñero, Edif. General de Seguros, Piso 6, Ofic. 6B, Av. La Estancia, Chuao, Caracas 1060, T (2) 912011—contact Ani Villanueva. From Caracas the direct route is 6 hrs., the expensive alternative is to use the airstrip.

Sixteen km. E of Maracay, a good road leads off to **San Juan de los Morros** where a cock-fighting tournament is held each year (Hotels: *Motel Santa Mónica*, E; *Gran Hotel Los Morros*, E, on Carretera Nacional towards Villa de Cura; *Excelsior*, E, Calle Marino; *Ana*, F). It has natural hot springs. Nearby are mountains with vertical cliffs, on which several climbing routes have been opened. The road divides later: S to the Guárico dam, the *llanos* and San Fernando de Apure, and E to Valle de la Pascua (*Hotel Venezuela*, E, Plaza Bolívar; *San Marcos*, E, Carretera Nacional towards El Socorro; *Gran Hotel Monte Carlo*, opp. bus station, F, a/c, shower) and El Tigre.

Going S, keep an eye open for egrets, which were almost exterminated early in the century for their feathers, once a valuable export. Crossing the bridge over the Río Apure at Puerto Miranda we come to **San Fernando de Apure**, the capital of the western *llanos*. (Bus to Caracas, US$4.50; to Barinas 2 buses a day, 9 hrs.)

**Hotels** *Hotel Plaza*, D, two blocks from the bus terminal, good; *La Fuente*, Av. Miranda, E, a/c, good; others on Av. Miranda and Paseo Libertador in E range with a/c, water spasmodic. *Hospedaje Central*; *Hotel-Restaurant Apure*, good steaks, accommodation E; *Mister Pollo*, Av. Carabobo, good value chicken.

**Exchange** Banco Consolidado for American Express, Av. Miranda, Res. 19 de Abril.

Manfred W. Frischeisen recommends a detour from the Guárico dam: San Fernando road, turn left at Calabozo (*Motel Tiuna*, a/c and good restaurant) along a gravel road (being paved) to Paso del Caballo (81 km.). A little trail goes on to Cazorla (85 km.); on the swamps one can see egrets, parrots, alligators, monkeys (and hear howlers). Turn left in Cazorla to Guayabal, back on the main road, 21 km. from San Fernando (there is also a road to the right to Guayabal, very bad, only passable with 4-wheel-drive or a trail bike with effort).

From San Fernando you can drive W towards Barinas, the road is beautiful between Mantecal and Bruzual. In the early morning, many animals and birds can be seen, and in the wet season alligators cross the road. Lars Anderssen suggests Mantecal as a base for wildlife tourism. Accommodation: *Hospedaje Centro Llano*, G, fair, friendly. Two other hotels and many places to eat. About 30 mins. by bus is *Hato Turístico Cedral*, where hunting is banned, visits arranged only through Turismo Aventura, Caracas, T 935696. To view the waterbirds from the road be there before sunrise. *Fiesta* in Mantecal, 23-26 February. At Bruzual, just S of Puente Nutrias over the Apure river, there are 3 primitive inns (e.g. *Los Llaneros*, F, you eat with the family). A few km. to the N is the *Turist Center El Gaban*, recently opened, rec. A fair, interesting road heads W after Mantecal at La Ye junction and goes over Guasdualito to San Cristóbal (take spare gasoline). Peter Straub recommends taking the bus from San Cristóbal to Guasdualito, then the mail plane to San Fernando, continuing to Ciudad Bolívar. Most travel agents do not know of this method: insist on seeing the timetables.

From San Fernando you can travel east to Ciudad Bolívar either by taking a boat (expensive and unreliable and not possible in the dry season) from opposite the airport to Caicara (see below), or by taking a bus to El Sombrero and catching the Ciudad Bolívar bus at 1700.

Due S of San Fernando is Puerto Páez at the confluence of the Meta and Orinoco rivers; here there are crossings to Puerto Carreño in Colombia, see below, and to El Burro W of the Caicara-Puerto Ayacucho road. A road is being built from San Fernando to Puerto Páez; for 134 km. it is paved, then from the Río Capanaparo it is dirt, passable only in the dry season by 4WD vehicles or buses (2 a day San Fernando-Pto. Páez, dry season). Between the Capanaparo and Cinaruco rivers is the **Parque Nacional Santos Luzardo**, reached only from this road.

There is a route across the *llanos* to Ciudad Bolívar: from Chaguaramas on the road to Valle de la Pascua, turn S through Las Mercedes and flat cattle land to **Cabruta**, 179 km., daily bus to Caracas, US$4.75, there is no ferry to Puerto Ayacucho, but you can try to take a barge, US$10, 3-day trip, fix price with boat captain. There is a small hotel, infested with rats and cockroaches, but better accommodation in *Caicara*—ferry from Cabruta, about 1 hr., US$2 for car, passengers US$0.35, or *lanchas* which leave when full every half hour or so, costing US$0.40 for the 25 minute journey. Hotels: *Tres Ríos*, E, a/c, parking, clean; *La Fortuna*, F, run by blind family, friendly; *Central*, F; *Italia*, F; *Buenos Aires*, F; *Miami*, E; *Venezuela*, F; *Bella Guayana*, F. By bus from Caicara to Ciudad Bolívar, 6 hrs., US$4; to Puerto Ayacucho six a day, 4-5 hours US$3.50. There are two flights a week (Wed. and Sat.) to Puerto Ayacucho. Cargo boats take three days to Puerto Ayacucho but are unwilling to take passengers; might be better from Cabruta (see above).

**Roads** From Caicara a brand new, paved road runs 370 km. SW to Puerto Ayacucho, passing scruffy settlements and bauxite—mining towns like Maniapure, Los Pijiguaos and Parguaza; the turn off to El Burro, where the boat crosses the Orinoco to Puerto Páez is 88 km. N of Puerto Ayacucho (*por puesto* Buro-Pto. Ayacucho, 1 hr.).

Another newly-paved road leaves the above 11 km. out of Caicara and winds S through forested hills to mining settlements like Las Flores, Guaniamo and Barrial Largo (160 km., end of the pavement); a deteriorating track continues S from Guaniamo almost to the Río Ventuari at San Juan de Manapiare (as far as one can go by road into Amazonas). Near the Río Ventuari is Camani Camp, reached by plane from Puerto Ayacucho or Ciudad Bolívar (2 hrs.). Jungle activities, 3 day/2 night package, all lodging, meals, excursions, horseriding, airtaxi to camp but excluding airfare to and from Puerto Ayacucho US$290 p.p. (double room). *Campamento Camani*, Centro Plaza, Torre C, piso 19, Caracas, T 284-2804.

**Puerto Ayacucho** is the capital of the Federal Territory of Amazonas, which has an area of 175,000 square kilometres and a population of 80,000, three quarters of whom live in Puerto Ayacucho. At the end of the dry season (April), it is very hot and sticky. It is 800 km. up the Orinoco from Ciudad Bolívar, deep in the wild, but no direct boats do the five day journey up river. Museo Etnológico del Territorio Federal Amazonas, opp. church, open Tues.-Sat., US$0.80, has a library and collection of regional exhibits, good.

**Hotels** *La Ventana*, resort ranch by the Orinoco, L+ inc. use of extensive facilities, meals, horses, sporting and fishing equipment, tours, etc. (in USA T 305-771 2283); *Gran Hotel Amazonas\**, D, dilapidated but new section has a/c rooms and bar, pool, restaurant expensive, food supply sometimes limited; *Hotel El Tobogán*, Orinoco, T (048) 21320, E, popular, clean, a/c, reasonable value; *Comercial*, E, seen better days; *Italia*, E, with fan, very run down, unfriendly; *Residencia Internacional*, Av. Aguerrevere 18, T 21242, F, clean, safe, friendly, laundry, warmly rec.; *Residencia Río Siapa*, Av. Orinoco, T 21138, E, modern, clean, friendly, hard to find; *Maguari*, F, friendly, will store luggage, rec. **Restaurants** *Gran Sarola*, opp. gas station, clean; *El Angoleño*, one block from *Hotel Amazonas*, Portuguese owner-cook Ignacio very friendly.

In the Mercado de Artesanía you can buy hammocks and other useful equipment (best early Fri. a.m.). A great many tourist souvenirs are on offer and Vicente Barletta, of *Típico El Casique*, Urb. Andrés Eloy Blanco, has a good collection of masks (free).

**Exchange** Banco Unión, for Visa and American Express; Banco de Venezuela.

**Transport** Ferry across the Orinoco, US$0.50. Boat to Caicara, 1½ days, US$15 including food, but bargain; repellant and hammock required. Bus to Caicara, 0500, 0800, 1400 daily, 6 hrs; bus to Maracay and Caracas (11 hrs.) leaves from the "ferry town", 1630. Scheduled flights to Caracas, 2 a day via San Fernando de Apure; others to Caicara and to Ciudad Bolívar.

**Crossing to Colombia** 88 km. N of Puerto Ayacucho a paved branch road leads W to El Burro, from where a ferry-barge crosses to Puerto Páez. On the S bank of the Meta opposite (ferry, US$0.75) is Puerto Carreño in Colombia, which is connected to Bogotá by twice-weekly SATENA flights and a more-or-less passable road; there is a DAS office and Venezuelan consulate.

*Bongos* and ferries run regularly across the river from Puerto Ayacucho to Casuarino (Colombia), which has quite good shopping, locals make these excursions without formalities, and many gringo travellers have experienced no problems crossing for a few hours (ferries leave from the Guardia Nacional post on the northern edge of town). On the other hand, some difficulty with the local authorities is not uncommon, both here and at Puerto Carreño. You may be asked how much money you have and where you are going; some travellers have had to obtain Colombian visas when only a passport and ticket out of the country were strictly necessary. From Ayacucho there is a cargo boat to Puerto Páez, 4 hrs. Check with Guardia Nacional and insist on exit stamp if crossing to Colombia (they are strangely reluctant).

**Excursions** Tobogán Tours, Av. Río Negro 44, Puerto Ayacucho (T (48)21700), owner Pepe Jaimes, arranges trips on the Orinoco, to Indian villages and to the Paraguena river through waterfalls, untouched jungle with fascinating wildlife, mixed reports (US$40-45 per day). Turismo de la Selva also run a variety of tours, poor reports. Autana Aventura, Av. Amazonas 91, owned by Julián Jaramillo, friendly and fluent English; Amazonia Tours, owned by Cruz and Alejandro, both run reasonable 3-day tours, US$120-140. Some companies run tours for as little as US$25 a day. For tours of the Territorio Federal Amazonas, S of Puerto Ayacucho, a rec. guide is Yamal A. Nasser, Calle Crisanto Mato Coba 33, Barrio Virgen del Valle, Ciudad Bolívar, T 085-48969 (he may be contacted through the Tourist Office in Ciudad Bolívar). Pedro Lucchini, T (048) 21156, in *artesanía* shop to left of Tobogán Tours will advise and arranges some trips. Other rec. guides include Fernando Escobar, Av. Constitución, T 048-21946, very knowledgeable, speaks English; and Abid Seguias, T 048-24028, who organizes plane trips to villages. A recommended guide is Dr. Virgilio Limpiar, of Turismo Yutajé, Monte Bello 31, T (048) 21664, various packages at about US$200 p.p. per week from Caracas; he will meet you at the airport for boat trips off the beaten track, sleeping in hammocks or Indian huts, he and another guide do all the cooking (profits go towards buying vaccines for villages that get no other care). In the low season, May-June, it may be difficult to organize tours for only a few days. If planning to travel south from Puerto Ayacucho you need a permit from the Bureau of Indian Affairs (Orai) in Caracas, or Puerto Ayacucho: several copies of photograph and description page in your passport will be needed. Near Puerto Ayacucho is *Jungle Camp Calypso*, run by Calypso Tours, La Guaira (T 031-24683), US$150 p.p. for 2 days including food, cabin accommodation, highly rec., excursions in canoes. Also *Jungle Lodge Camturama* (T 048-22574), 20 minutes by vehicle south of town, C, a/c, pool, buffet meals US$4-7, full day tours US$10, highly rec.

For trips anywhere from Puerto Ayacucho check at the central service station. Other recommended trips are to the small village of Pintado (l2 km. S), where petroglyphs described by Humboldt can be seen on the huge rock called Cerro Pintado; this the most easily accessible petroglyph site of the hundreds scattered throughout Amazonas. 35 km. S on the road to Samariapo is the Parque Tobogán de la Selva, a pleasant picnic area with tables and refreshments centred around a steeply inclined, smooth rock over which the Río Maripures cascades—a 'water slide' to delight children and the young-at-heart in the wet season. Nearby, also by paved road, is Coromoto colony, founded by the Salesian Fathers to protect and evangalize the "howling Guaharibos" (as early explorers called this nomadic tribe).

The well-paved road from Puerto Ayacucho to Samariapo (63 km) was built to bypass the rapids which here interrupt the Orinoco, dividing it into "Upper" and "Lower"; the powerful Maripures Rapids are very impressive. The road (gravel) continues for 17 km. to Morganito, from where smaller launches continue on up river. Boats run from Samariapo to Isla de Ratón and Santa Rosa.

On the Río Negro, towards Brazil, is **San Carlos de Río Negro**. Hotel at customs post. Flights to Puerto Ayacucho Wed. and Sat.; military flights occasionally, if you pay for at least 7 passengers there will be an extra flight. It is possible to take a cargo boat from San Carlos up the Río Casiquiare and down the Orinoco (following Humboldt's route); it takes 8 days to Puerto Ayacucho. You can also rent a canoe to Santa Lucía on the Brazilian border on the Río Negro (US$20, 5 hrs. Santa Lucía-San Carlos); no hotel, food at the customs post.

Much of Amazonas Territory is stunningly beautiful and untouched, but access is only by river. Do not travel alone. By ascending the Autana or Sipapo rivers, for example, one can see Autana-tepuí, a 1200 m.-high soaring mass of rock resembling a petrified tree trunk, riddled with massive caves; it was first explored in 1971 by Charles Brewer Carias, who descended by helicopter (an Anglo-American expedition parachuted onto the summit in 1986—no-one has yet climbed from the base). There are other *tepuís* throughout the region, including the great mass of the Sierra de la Neblina on the Brazilian border, but the difficulties of organizing expeditions are formidable: permits are needed from the Gobernación in Puerto Ayacucho and the Indian Bureau in Caracas (great patience required), and possibly also from the Catholic *Vicariato* which administers many of the missions along the rivers. Some of these missions provide rough accommodation (e.g. at La Esmeralda and Platanal, about 130 km. further up the Orinoco, US$35-45 per night: "Jungle" Rudy Truffino can make arrangements, **see page 1181**), otherwise it is a matter of slinging hammocks in any available shelter. There are a number of private river camps on the upper Orinoco but they do not solicit casual guests; the most welcoming is *Yutajé Camp*, located on a tributary of the Río Manapiare due E of Puerto Ayacucho. This can theoretically be reached from the track running S from Guaniamo via

Sabana de Cardona to San Juan de Manapiare, but a very tough jeep indeed would be required. The camp accommodates 30, with restaurant and bar, L with meals, fishing, canoes, horses, airboats, excursions to Indian villages, spectacular falls in the vicinity, much wildlife.

In 1955/56 two Americans successfully canoed to Argentina, continuing from the Amazon by way of the Tapajós, Paraguay and Paraná. The trip took about one year. The journey up the Amazon to the Casiquiare and Orinoco has also been successfully negotiated by a hovercraft with a British crew.

---

## EAST FROM CARACAS (6)

Some of Venezuela's most interesting coast, not just for its beautiful beaches, islands and forested slopes, but also for its historical links, from Columbus' landfall to Spanish colonial rule and the War of Independence. It is also an industrial coast, shipping coal, cocoa and serving the oil industry inland. If you're lucky you can cross to Trinidad by boat, unlike the frequent crossings to Isla Margarita (next section).

The eastern part of the North-Eastern Highlands, with summits rising to 2,000 metres, has abundant rainfall in its tropical forest. The western part, which is comparatively dry, has most of the inhabitants and the two main cities, Cumaná and Barcelona.

Eastern Venezuela, with the Highlands in the NE, the great *llanos* of the Orinoco to the south, and south of the Orinoco again the range of Guayana Highlands, was until quite recently not of much account in the Venezuelan economy. Some coffee and cacao are grown on the eastern slopes of the north-eastern highlands in the tropical forest, but the western slopes are subject to drought. Cattle roam the *llanos*, and the Guayana Highlands produce gold and diamonds. The picture has now been changed, as about 30% of Venezuelan oil now comes from this area. South of the Orinoco vast iron ore deposits are mined.

It is now only five hours from Caracas to Barcelona by road through Caucagua, from which there is a 58-km. road NE to **Higuerote** (pop. 4,300). Surrounded by sandy beaches and currently the focus of large-scale tourist projects. Higuerote remains quite tranquil but is expensive, especially during the festival of the Tambores de San Juan (23-26 June, see **Music and Dance**).

**Hotels** *Sol Mar*, D, clean, modest rooms, beachfront; *Barlovento*, beachfront, E, colonial style, fan, clean, safe, small pool, restaurant.

Higuerote and nearby villages (e.g. Caruao. rebuilt in old style—population almost entirely black, friendly, good beach, one hotel—ask for Josefa, who cooks delicious seafood—the sports club has a wild beach party each Sat. p.m.) can also be reached along the partly paved coastal road from Los Caracas (**see page 1135**), beautiful views, many beaches. Tankers loading at Buche Refinery near Higuerote sometimes tar the coves around Carenero at the head of the bay (6 km. N). Near Caruao is the Pozo del Cura, a waterfall and pool, good swimming.

14 km. before Higuerote on the road from Caucagua is Tacarigua de Mamporal, where you can turn off to the **Laguna de Tacarigua National Park**. The road passes a Tunnel of Vegetation (almost 3 km. long), cocoa plantations, the towns of San José and Río Chico (*Hotel Italia*, E, a/c; excellent natural fruit icecream). In the fishing village of Tacarigua de la Laguna (rooms to rent), you can eat delicious *lebranche* fish; an unmotorized ferry crosses the lagoon, which has many water birds (including flamingoes, usually involving a day-long boat trip to see them), to the beach on the Caribbean.

Highway 8 (Caracas-Barcelona) parallels the coast after Tacarigua, passing through the fishing villages of Boca de Uchire and El Hatillo and the small inland town of Clarines, with its faithfully restored colonial church, before reaching the twin towns of Píritu and Puerto Píritu (3 km-apart): worth seeing in Píritu is the 18th century Franciscan church of Nuestra Señora de la Concepción (well restored); Puerto Píritu has a modern beach resort with all facilities, safe swimming in calm waters (*Casacoima Puerto Píritu*\*, D). Nearby, but not obtrusive, is Criogénico de Oriente, the biggest gas refining complex in Latin America. Local delicacies include *queso de mano* (a soft cheese) and *arepitas* (corn bread pasties filled with goat cheese!)

**Barcelona**, population 116,000, mean temperature, 27°C, founded 1671, capital of Anzoátegui State, is on the W bank of the Río Neveri, 5 km. from the sea. The state is named after General Anzoátegui, a hero of the Battle of Boyacá, whose statue stands in the main Plaza Boyacá. Near Plaza Bolívar (with obligatory statue) is the Cathedral (1748, rebuilt 1773 after an earthquake). W of Plaza Bolívar are the ruins of the Casa Fuerte, where 1600 of Bolívar's followers were massacred in 1817. Teatro Cajigal is a replica of the Teatro Municipal in Caracas. Museo de la Tradición, Calle Juncal, in a building once the centre of the slave trade, houses a wide collection of indigenous and Spanish religious art. Opposite the bus station on Av. San Carlos is the Mercado Libre, for just about anything.

**Hotels** *Barcelona\**, Av. 5 de Julio, 1 block from Cathedral, T 77-1065, D, TV, parking, 6th floor restaurant (good fish and views); *Neveri*, Av. Miranda, T 77-2376, similar, good restaurant *Castillo del Oriente*; *Nacional*, Zamora, D-E; *Venezia*, Bolívar 42, E, a/c, parking, restaurant; *Venus*, Av. Intercomunal y Lecherías, T 77-4202, E, a/c. There is a wide variety of restaurants in town.

**Transport** Airport 9 km. SW, services to Caracas; Oficambio exchange facilities; taxi to Puerto La Cruz US$5. Bus to Caracas, 6½ hrs., 315 km. The port for Barcelona and Puerto La Cruz is **Guanta**, which ships out coal from the nearby Naricual field. Vessels from La Guaira call here.

Barcelona has been surpassed touristically and commercially by Puerto La Cruz, 12 km. away by 4-lane highway (Av. Intercomunal) skirting the pleasant residential resort of Lechería (minibus US$0.10, then walk or *por puesto* to the beach; several good restaurants).

Off the highway is the Polideportivo sports stadium seating 10,000 people: covered gymnasium, velodrome, basket-ball courts, 2 pools, etc. Soon after Barcelona is El Morro Tourist Complex, with hotels, cultural centres, condos with access from the street or from a new system of canals, and the Club Náutico Marino; this is the first of many such projects.

**Puerto La Cruz**, pop. 220,000, originally a fishing village, has emerged since the 1980s as an enormously popular destination for North Americans and Venezuelans. The lack of tourists is compensated by the fine avenues and modern hotels and restaurants. All types of watersport are well catered for and tourist facilities are above average. Most (craft shops, *cambios*, discos, etc.) can be found on Av. 5 de Julio and Paseo Colón. The latter has excellent views of the Bahía de Pozuelas and the islands of the Mochima National Park (see below). The evening *paseo* along Colón is a relaxing, cheerful end to the day.

**Festival** 3 May, Santa Cruz.

**Hotels** at Puerto La Cruz tend to be fully booked with package tours. *Meliá\**, A+, on Paseo Colón, luxury hotel with all services and facilities; *Doral Beach\**, C, swimming pool, beach, nearer Barcelona than Puerto La Cruz; *Europa*, Calle Sucre, esq. Plaza Bolívar, D, good, clean, a/c. On Maneiro, *Comercio*, T 23465, E, TV, phones; *Gaeta City*, in centre, 10 mins. from beach, T 691242, TV, fridge, snack bar, parking. On Paseo Colón: *Neptuno\**, D, a/c, good restaurant; next door is *Margelina*, E with bath, a/c, safe, clean, very good; *Regis*, Paseo Colón 73, F, with fan in old part, E with a/c in new; *Gaeta*, No. 9, T 691816, a/c, D/E, good location, restaurant; *Miramar*, T 21160, E, a/c, restaurant, good value; *Riviera*, No. 33, T 22039, TV, phone, bar/restaurant, water sports, good location; *La Sirena*, F, clean. *Senador*, Miranda y Bolívar, T 22035, D, a/c, TV, phone, restaurant, parking, highly rec.; *Puerto La Cruz*, Av. 5 de Julio, T 21698, D-E, phone, rec.; *Sorrento*, Av. 5 de Julio, E, shower, comfortable. *Colón*, Libertad, E with a/c, TV, English spoken, friendly, 2 blocks from beach; *Mi Hotel*, Calle Libertad, D, a/c, showers, comfortable, clean, rec.; *Noray*, Av. Libertad, E with a/c, good, friendly; *Marina*, at the new ferry terminal, D, a/c, good views, expensive waterside restaurant, rec., parking for those using the Margarita ferry; *Wimar*, Providencia y Venezuela, E, a/c, TV, good budget hotel; *La Llovizna*, Av. Municipal 27, T 667408, D, restaurant, a/c, kitchens, parking; *Guayana*, Plaza Bolívar, F, fan, clean.

**Restaurants** On Paseo Colón: *El Parador*, excellent food and service; *Da Luigi*, Italian, good; *Bonasera* (Italian), *O Sole Mio* (No. 115), *Las Tinajas* (No. 55, Spanish); *Big Garden*, delicious sea food; *El Dragón* (No. 121) and *Tong Sing*, both Chinese; *Reale*, No. 69, pizzería, good bacon and eggs for breakfast; *Pastelería Fornos* for breakfast; plenty of others. *Nature*, vegetarian, Constitución 70, lunch and dinner. *Rincón Criollo*, Av. Libertad, popular with locals. *Swing* night club, 13 km. from Puerto La Cruz, US$3.30 one way by taxi, free entry, good music.

**Shopping** Vendors of paintings, jewellery, leather, etc. on Paseo Colón in evenings. Good hammocks may be bought, US$6-12. *Perfectfoto SA*, Carabobo, Fuente Torre Oriente, T 22821 for film processing; also *Fotolisto*, Paseo Colón, US$1.70 per film without mounts.

**Laundry** *Lavandería Margarita*, Bolívar 160.

**Exchange** Banco Consolidado (American Express), Av. 5 de Julio, Local No. 43; **Turisol**, Am Ex rep., T 662161/669910. Banco Royal Venezolano. *Casa de Cambio*: Oficambio Oriente, Calle Maneiro 17, Edif. Latina; also *cambio* in *Hotel Riviera*.

**Post Office and Telecommunications** Freitas y Bolívar, one block from Paseo Colón.

**Travel Agency** *Viajes Ven-Mex*, Av. Alberto Ravell 15, recommended. *Venezuelan Travel Advisers*, Municipal esq. Freitas, Edif. Montalero, T (081) 660113/669204.

**Airlines** Avensa, Av. Municipal y Pepsi, and at Barcelona airport; Viasa, Av. Municipal y Gran Parada; Aeropostal, Paseo Colón, opp. *Hotel Gaeta*; Alitalia at *Meliá*; Dominicana, Independencia 124, Chapurín Central.

**Buses** to Caracas, 5 hrs., US$4, Expresos San Remo, Sol de Margarita (rec.), *por puesto* US$8; to Ciudad Bolívar US$3, but often full since service starts at Cumaná.

**Excursions** To the Chimana La Plata and Borracha islands in Mochima National Park for swimming and snorkelling: take minibus or *por puesto* (US$0.20) to Guanta, then boat, or *por puesto* to Pamatacualito then walk 10 mins. to harbour, bargain with boat owners and fishermen (US$4-14 return regardless of number of passengers, pay on return). Take hat and sunscreen. Fishing boats can be hired on Paseo Colón beach to the beaches E of Puerto La Cruz (about US$12). At E end of beachfront boulevard is Centro Vacacional del Consejo del Niño for underprivileged children.

**The Coastal Zone** Starting east from Puerto La Cruz is the Costa Azul, with a seemingly endless series of beaches backed by some of Venezuela's most beautiful scenery, and offshore the islands of the **Mochima National Park**; near Los Altos is a *mirador* with a superb view of this lovely coast. Highway 9 follows the shore for much of the 85 km. to Cumaná. It passes the small Playa Blanca, by boat US$5 return from Puerto La Cruz, excellent snorkelling, take own equipment. The locals cook and sell fish. Further along past Playa Arapito (restaurant, parking US$0.35, camping possible), where boats can be hired to the lovely, little La Piscina beach for good snorkelling, is the popular but dirtier beach of Playa Colorada (Km. 32) with red sands and palm trees (*por puesto* from Mercado Municipal in Puerto La Cruz or hitch). Here accommodation is available (*Villas Turísticas Playa Colorada*, B, clean pool, also trailers for 4 US$28 per day; pool, restaurant, run by Sra. Baumgartner who is very helpful, Apartado 61355, Caracas 1060-A. Sra Mónica lets rooms, D, while Seniorca, who runs a beach bar, hires tents, US$8 per night), camping is permitted for a small fee and there is a restaurant. Nearby are Playas Vallecito (free camping, car US$0.80, bar with good food, plenty of palm trees for hammock-slinging) and Santa Cruz (buy fresh seafood from the fishermen's huts). Next comes Playa Los Hicacos, which is a beach club for the Universidad del Oriente, Cumaná; it has a lovely coral reef.

40 km. from Puerto La Cruz, in Sucre state is *Santa Fe*, a good place to relax, not (yet) a tourist town, though plenty of loud music, golf course on the dark red, sandy beach, market Sat. (*Hotel Cochaima*, run by Margot, E, rec.; *Hotel/restaurant Chomena*, Av. Principal, F, family run.) Gasoline is available; *por puesto* and bus to Cumaná and Puerto La Cruz. It is sometimes difficult to get the bus from Puerto La Cruz to stop at Santa Fe, *por puesto* may be a better bet. The village of Mochima, beyond Santa Fe, is 4 km. off the main road, hitching difficult, bus to Cumaná, 1400, US$0.80; here Sra Cellita Día and Doña Luisa both

let out rooms, F; houses to rent from US$12 per day depending on length of stay; eat at *Los Mochimeros*, good and friendly (try the *empanadas* with ice cold coconut milk), or *Don Quijote*, Av. Bermúdez, very good. Boats to nearby beaches, such as Playa Marita and Playa Blanca, and around the islands, fares negotiable, about US$10 to one island, US$20 for a 2-hr. trip round the islands (up to 6 people). **N.B.** At holiday times this coast is very busy.

*Cumaná* (pop. 172,000) capital of Sucre state, straddles both banks of the Río Manzanares, its economy based on coffee, sugar and cacao, supplemented by fishing, tourism and salt from the mines on the Araya Peninsula. Average temperature 27°C. It is possibly the oldest Hispanic city on the South American mainland, founded 1521 to exploit the nearby pearl fisheries; from here the strategies for conquest and colonization of the new continent were planned. Because of a succession of devastating earthquakes (the last in 1929), only a few historic sites remain. Los Uveros on the Ensenada de Manzanillo is the largest public beach in Venezuela, there are two restaurants and camping allowed on the 3-km. long clean, sandy stretch just W of the airport. San Luís is a short local bus ride away, rec. but the water is dirtier than Los Uveros. Cumaná is generally a pleasant place with its mixture of old and new, but the port area (1½ km.) is not safe at night.

The newer sections of the city near the airport are barren and uninteresting; the older sections flow around the base of the hill dominated by the Castillo de San Antonio. There are walks along the treelined river (beware mosquitoes), which has the Parque Ayacucho and markets on both sides (food and craftwork, good for hammocks). The Castle of San Antonio de la Eminencia, affords a wide view of the town, Araya Peninsula and coast; it was built in 1686 as a defence against pirates, with 16 mounted cannon, drawbridge and dungeons (Páez was held captive here 1849-50) from which there are said to be underground tunnels leading to the Santa Inés church. Restored in 1975, it is flood-lit at night. The Castillo de Santa María de la Cabeza (1669) is a rectangular fortress with a panoramic view of San Antonio and the elegant homes below. San Francisco Monastery, the original Capuchin mission of 1514, was the first school on the continent; its remains are on the Plaza Badaracco Bermúdez facing the beach. The Church of Santa Inés (1637) was the base of the Franciscan missionaries; earthquakes have caused it to be rebuilt five times. A tiny 400-year-old statue of the Vírgen de Candelaria is in the garden. The home of Andrés Eloy Blanco (1896-1955: one of Venezuela's greatest poets and politicians), near the cathedral, has been nicely restored to its turn-of-the-century elegance: photographs, poetry recordings, political notes and personal effects of the owner. Beside the Cathedral on Plaza Sucre is the Government Office around a courtyard lined by cannon from Santa María de la Cabeza, note the gargoyles and other colonial features. The Sucre Museum (Museo Gran Mariscal de Ayacucho) was set up in the old City Hall in Parque Ayacucho in 1974 to commemorate the 150th anniversary of the battle of Ayacucho: mainly portraits, relics and letters of Bolívar and José Antonio Sucre (born 1795, Bolívar's first lieutenant, President of Peru in 1826, assassinated in Colombia in 1828). There is also a maritime museum (Museo del Mar) with good exhibits of tropical marine life, at the old airport, Av. Universidad with Av. Industrial, open Tues.-Sun. 0830-1130, 1430-1630, US$0.60: take San Luis minibus from outside the cathedral. In the suburb of Chaima a bronze monument marks the 450th anniversary of the city's founding: it depicts in bas-relief the more martial encounters between Spaniards and natives; a Capuchin friar and a Cumanagoto Indian top the 16 m. column.

**Festivals** 22 Jan., Santa Inés; pre-Lenten carnival throughout the state of Sucre; 2 Nov., Santos y Fideles Difuntos at El Tacal.

**Hotels** *Cumanagoto**, C, Av. Universidad, poor food and service, excellent swimming pool and beach, travel agency for trips to Angel Falls, etc., trailer park with all facilities, US$5 p.p.

*Los Bordones*, B, Final Av. Universidad, 8 km. from the bus station, rec., beautifully situated on a good beach with excellent food and a swimming pool; *Villa Mar*, D, Av. Universidad, clean, comfortable, restaurant; these three are a long way from the centre of town. *Gran Hotel\**, D, Av. Universidad, beach, mid-way between *Cumanagoto* and town centre; *Caribe*, on San Luis beach, E with bath and a/c, clean, basic, English spoken, no restaurant. *Minerva\**, E, clean, modern, Av. Cristóbal Colón, US$1 taxi ride from centre; *Turismo Guaiqueri*, Av. Bermúdez 26 T (093) 24230/663444, D, comfortable, clean, a/c, bath, friendly, no restaurant; *El Río*, E, Av. Bermúdez, a/c, bath, phone, reasonable restaurant; *Residencias Trevi*, E, with bath and fan, on Av. Universidad, 2 km. from San Luis beach. *Regina*, Av. Arismendi, E with bath, a/c, restaurant, good value; *Mariño*, D, near centre on Av. Mariño with fan, private bath, a/c, not very clean; *Europa*, E, Mariño, clean, friendly, restaurant. Cheaper hotels can be found across the river from those above, around Plaza Ayacucho, especially on Calle Sucre: *Hospedaje La Gloria*, Sucre 31, opposite Sta. Inés church, G with fan and bath, basic, clean; on same street *Astoria*, F with bath, clean and friendly; *Italia*, F with fan, or a/c with bath, good (around the corner is *Madrid* bar, good cheap food, music); *Macuto*, *Cumaná*, *Colón*, all reasonably priced. Private accommodation at Bolívar 8, G, clean, fan.

**Restaurants** Good food at *El Colmao* restaurant in the centre; *Sand Hills* and *Los Montones*, near *Caribe Hotel*, San Luis beach, rec. *Italia*, Sucre, cheap and good; *Jardín de Sport*, only outdoor café, good food, rec. *Rancho E. Morris*, good food and service, reasonable, open late. *Helados Bariloche*, Plaza Ayacucho. All central restaurants close Sun. lunchtime.

**Exchange** Banco Consolidado, Av. Bermúdez y Perimetral, Edif. Ajounián, unfriendly; Banco Provincial, Calle Mariño y Av. Perimetral, Visa and Mastercard. Exchange at Oficambio, Calle Mariño, Edificio Funcal, poor rates.

**Panamanian Consulate** in a one-way street, next to Grupo Escolar José Silvero Córdova in Parcelamiento Miranda Sector D, T 663525; take a taxi.

**Travel Agent** *Happy Tour*, Centro Comercial, La Banca, P.B., Local No. 6, T 24592; also at *Hotel Cumanagoto*, T 653111.

**Bus** Bus terminal some distance from city centre, buses are often fully booked. *Por puesto* to **Puerto La Cruz**, US$4, bus US$2, 2 hrs. To **Güiria (see page 1167)**, US$2.60, *por puesto* US$5.20 (5 hrs.), often stop in Carúpano. To **Caripe**, 1200, 4 hrs. To **Caracas**, US$4.55 upwards depending on company (7 hrs.), frequent service; many daily to **Ciudad Guayana** and **Ciudad Bolívar**, US$4, 6 hrs.

**Air** New airport 10 km. from centre (taxi fare US$2.50). To Caracas, US$20 with Aeropostal or Avensa; from Caracas only Aeropostal 1805.

**Excursions** A paved road runs S down the Manzanares to Cumanacoa (56 km.), a traditional creole town in a rich agricultural area (2 hotels, E-F). At the Casa de Cultura, Calle Motedano 20, authentic folk music is performed by "Los Carrizas Precolombinos", a band of local musicians and members of the Turimiquire tribe. Near the town is the Cuchivano grotto from which flares a jet of natural gas.

To the Araya Peninsula with its desert landscapes and purple salt lakes, either by Cumaná-Araya boat (return boats haphazard and difficult to get on as more cars than spaces) or by road from Cariaco, 78 km. E on the Cumaná-Carúpano highway. The peninsula road out to Araya is now paved (95 km.). Araya is the main settlement on the peninsula (pop. 3,300), it has an airport, a ferry dock and the *Hospedaje San José*, G. The major sight is the Castillo de Santiago (or Fuerte Araya), built by Spain in 1625 to protect the salt mines, where in colonial times wretched miners laboured naked on the shimmering salt flats (naked because salt rapidly destroyed clothing). So important was salt in the preservation of food that the authorities spent three years constructing the fortress, one of the best preserved in the Caribbean, bringing all materials, food and water in by sea. It is considered one of the most important historical sites on the continent; certainly it was Spain's most expensive project to that time in the New World. Today the mines are exploited by a Government-owned corporation; annual production has almost reached 500,000 tonnes.

The highway from Cumaná goes on to the port of Carúpano, on the Paría Peninsula (135 km.). The coastal route as far as Villa Frontado is beautiful, running along the Golfo de Cariaco past a succession of attractive beaches and small villages: even the larger places along this stretch—Marigüitar and San Antonio del Golfo—are very quiet and have little accommodation (*Balneario Cachamaure*),

44 km. from Cumaná, beautiful beach, cabins US$18, barbecue equipment, US$2. After Cariaco (gas/petrol) the road winds inland over the Paría Ridge to **Carúpano**, a well-preserved colonial town of 84,000, from which 70% of Venezuela's cocoa is shipped. Its narrow streets, beautifully wooded parks and graceful buildings date back to 1647, when the wealthy cocoa plantations were worked by African slaves (here in 1816 Bolívar freed the blacks, thus acquiring new allies). The town sits between the Ríos Revilla and Candoroso; its beach is wide and desolate but the waterfront boulevard is beautifully-landscaped. A Conferry service crosses each morning to Margarita (passengers only; cars must use the ferry from Cumaná). Carúpano is famous throughout Venezuela as the last place still celebrating a traditional pre-Lenten Carnival: days of dancing, rum drinking, completely masked women in black (*negritas*), etc. The area becomes a focus for tourists at this time (February), so book accommodation ahead.

**Festivals**  3 May, Velorios de la Cruz (street dances); 15 Aug., Asunción de la Virgen.

**Hotels**  *San Francisco*, D-E, Av. Juncal 87A (good food, try the mussels); *Bologna*, Av. Independencia, E, a/c, owner speaks German, rec.; *El Yunque*, Av. Perimetral, E, dirty, beach, good seafood restaurant; *Lilma*, E, Av. Independencia 161, good restaurant; *Victoria\**, D, Av. Perimetral, seen better days but good, swimming pool, restaurant. *Playa Copey*, on beach at nearby Santa Catalina, E, airy rooms, pool.

**Transport**  Bus to **Caracas**, Responsable de Venezuela, US$5.80, 8 hrs.; to **Cumaná**, US$1.50, 2 hrs., sit on right for sea views, *por puesto* US$3; **Güiria** US$1.20, 3 hrs., *por puesto* US$4, 2 hrs. (from airport). Airport with flights to Porlamar (Isla Margarita).

There is an alternative road between Cariaco and Carúpano which reaches the coast after 17 km, and runs E by the Caribbean a further 38 km. to Carúpano. The beaches on this coast are covered with shells which make swimming less attractive, but good sand can be found at Saucedo and the Balneario Costa Azul (2 km. E of Guaca; restaurant). Escondido is a deep calm bay surrounded by sand dunes. On this drive are Cereza, famed for its basket-making, and Guaca, where clams packed with peppers are sold.

**The Paría Peninsula**  Highway 9 continues a further 160 km. E along the Peninsula to Güiria. The coast is left behind until Irapa, as the main highway climbs over the central spine through luxuriant forests of bamboo and Spanish moss to the village of El Pilar (33 km.), where there are a number of hot springs (El Hervidero and Cueva del Pato) and the river bathing resort of Sabacual. E of El Pilar is Guaraúnos (40 mins. from Carúpano), the base of Claus Müller (Calle Bolívar 8, T 094-69052) who has worked with Indian communities and in conservation for 25 years. His trips in the peninsula, to the cloud forest, and the delta are highly rec., US$60 per day for 4 wheel drive, food and lodging, money ploughed back into the local community. A second road which joins the highway beyond El Pilar follows the coast E of Carúpano to the fishing village of El Morro de Puerto Santo (15 km.), sited on a sandspit between the coast and a rocky offshore island, then to the lovely town of Río Caribe, whose old pastel-hued houses testify to the former prosperity of the place when it was the chief cacao-exporting port. The paved road then crosses the mountains and joins Highway 9 at Bohordal, a distance of 55 km. from Carúpano.

Irapa (117 km.) is a fishing town surrounded by a grove of coconut palms; it is said to be here that Papillon came ashore after his last escape from Devil's Island in 1945; hotel and restaurant, G with bath, clean (*fiesta* 19 March). Across the Gulf of Paría are the dismal swamps of the Orinoco Delta. The climate is dry and very hot but the coast E of Irapa is a string of coves, palms and rich vegetation—Columbus was so impressed he named the region "Los Jardines". The well-surfaced highway continues on 42 km. to *Güiria*, a hot, rundown fishing town with poorly-maintained streets and a quiet, pleasant beach (where you can camp; plenty of firewood washed up, buy fish from locals). *Feria de la Pesca*, 14 July. Roads end here, but there are fuel supplies for the return journey. Airport: flights to Caracas, Margarita, Tucupita, Anaco.

**Accommodation** *Hotel Fortuna*, E, with restaurant, best of a bad lot, rec.; *Hotel Plaza*, F, basic, ring the buzzer high up on the wall; *Hotel Nayade*, F; *Pensión Raúl Leoni*, G, clean, opp. bus terminal; a number of other cheap hostels. There are a couple of basic eateries on the main square: *Heladería Güiria* or *Exprex*, rec., but not much else.

A good excursion from Güiria is to *Macuro*, a quiet town of 1,500 on the tip of the Peninsula. It is accessible only by boat, being surrounded on its landward sides by jungle. Boats leave Güiria daily at 1000 (US$2.50, take protection against sun, and plastic sheeting in case of rough seas—ask for Don Pedro), returning 0530, taking 3 hrs., passing dense jungle which laps against deserted, palm-fringed beaches. It was in one of these coves—perhaps Yacúa, there is no record—that Spaniards of Columbus' crew made the first recorded European landing on the continent on 5 August 1498, before taking formal possession in the estuary at Güiria the next day (locals like to believe the landing took place at Macuro, and the town's official new name is Puerto Colón).

Macuro is friendly, with a good beach, a few understocked shops, one restaurant, one hotel (F) and rooms to let (easy to camp or sling your hammock somewhere). Eduardo is a bar-owner who also manages the little history museum; he is knowledgeable about the immediate area and can advise on hiking on the Peninsula, the National Park which covers the north side of Paría, and boats to Trinidad (usually on Mondays if there are sufficient passengers, US$6.50 p.p.) to the Orinoco Delta, and through the Bocas del Dragón to the miniscule settlement of Patao (3 hrs.), where one can hire a guide for a trek across the Peninsula or an ascent of Cerro Patas, climbing up from cacao and banana plantations into cool montane forest. Fishing boats can often be hired to take you to many small villages, making for a hot but relaxed holiday in one of Venezuela's less-visited corners. Also helpful for boats to Trinidad, or for excursions, is Adrian Winter-Roach, a Trinidadian: Calle Carabobo, Casa s/n, Macuro, or Vereda Paracanomie 37, Banco Obrero, Güiria. The waters of the Gulf are murky from the output of the Orinoco, but snorkelling on the Caribbean coast is excellent. Few boat owners seem willing to cross to Trinidad; if you are leaving Venezuela, remember to get an exit stamp, probably in Macuro, but check in advance.

You can visit the Orinoco delta from Güiria; there are occasional motor boats trading between Güiria and *Pedernales* in the delta. The trip takes about 5 hrs., check for boats at the harbour or the *Hotel Fortuna* (not always open). Pedernales is a small village only a few km. from the south-western point of Trinidad. It is only accessible by boat from Güiria (ask for Andrecito, who lives on N side of small plaza nearest harbour entrance, or ask owner of *Hotel Plaza*—boats are very hard to find), or from Tucupita (much easier—**page 1183**), or boats from Trinidad costing about US$30-60, the more official, the more expensive. Sisiliano Bottini is a shipping agent. (Some cheap boats carry contraband and unless you avoid Trinidadian or Venezuelan immigration controls you will find this method both difficult and very risky: the Trinidadian authorities are reluctant to let even legal boats in for fear of drug smuggling.) Only one hotel, *Gran Arturo*, F, very basic, bar and restaurant, take your own hammock; the store on the riverbank also has rooms with cooking facilities, F. For a shower, ask Jesús, who runs a fish-freezing business. Only Indians live in the northern part of the village. Travel out of Pedernales is often difficult—to Tucupita by fishing boat, US$25, rec. as the boat stops in some of the Indian villages, where you can buy the best hammocks (*chinchorros*) and some beautiful carved animal figures made of balsa wood (**see also page 1183**).

From Puerto La Cruz a toll road goes inland, skirting Barcelona. At Km. 52 (where there is a restaurant) a road forks left to (near) Santa Bárbara (airport) and goes on to Jusepín, Quiriquire, and Caripito, all Lagovén oil camps.

In Santa Bárbara can be bought the native *chinchorros*, hammocks made by hand of woven *moriche* palm leaves, decorated with coloured yarn. They can also be found in Tucupita (**see page 1183**). They "give" when you lie on them and do not absorb moisture when used on the beach. Very good for camping.

*Maturín*, capital of Monagas State, an important commercial centre, is 16 km. beyond Jusepín. Population 152,000.

**Hotels** *El Cacique*, D, Av. Bolívar; *Pensión El Nacional* and *Latino*, both F, are rec. as simple and clean. *Friuli*, E, Carrera 9 with Calle 30; *Trinidad*, F, clean, English speaking, rec.; *Europa*, F, rec. as being as good as the *Trinidad* but with larger rooms; *Manolo*, Av. Bolívar, F, pleasant, restaurant with good food, bar; *Tamanaco*, F, is reasonable; *Mallorca*, F, Calle Mariño, reasonable with good food; *Comercio*, F with bath, not too clean, English spoken, central; *Asturias*, F, with cheap restaurant which serves excellent rice pudding. All hotel rooms have private bathroom and a/c.

**Exchange** Banco Consolidado (American Express), Av.Raúl Leoni, Edif. D'Amico; **Banco de Venezuela**, Av. Bolívar.

**Transport** Air services to Caracas, Margarita and Puerto Ordaz (Aeropostal, 25 mins.). Buses leave three times a day for **Caracas** from the central bus terminal, 2030, 2200 and 2245 hrs. (US$5.40, 8 hrs., *por puesto* US$10.80); buses for **Ciudad Guayana** (US$2.10) and **El Dorado** leave from the terminus near the airport. To **Puerto La Cruz** or **Barcelona**, take a *por puesto* to Cumaná and change, 2 hrs., US$4.20. Bus only to **Ciudad Bolívar**, US$3.30. Bus to **Carúpano**, US$2, 3 hrs.; *por puesto* to Caripe, US$2.50. Travelling between the airport and town: *por puesto* Nos. 1,5,6 (US$0.25), or bus from main road outside airport (US$0.10). Taxis from the Reponsable de Venezuela office will try to charge much more.

There are no exchange facilities in the airport except at the Aeropostal desk or the bar in the departure lounge, and they give a very bad rate.

Just beyond Jusepín an unpaved 32-km. road, left, joins the Maturín-Cumaná road (212 km., all paved but twisty; beautiful tropical mountain scenery). At San Francisco on this road is a branch road running 22½ km. NE to *Caripe*, a small town set in a mountain valley. There is a huge *samán* tree in purple glory when the orchids which cover it bloom in May. There is also a paved road between Carúpano and Caripe via Santa Cruz and Santa María, 2 hrs.

**Festivals** 2-12 Aug., *Feria de las Flores*; 10-12 Oct., N.S. del Pilar.

**Hotels** *Samán\**, Enrique Charner 29, D, excellent value and atmosphere, restaurant; *Caripe*, F, restaurant; *San Francisco*, F with bath, hot water, clean, rec., good restaurant; *Las Chaimas*, F, T 51141. *Venezia*, E, with excellent **Coba Longa** restaurant, owner speaks English. *Humboldt Cabañas*, between Teresén and Caripe, good, clean, sleep 4 for C, full cooking facilities, little hot water. *Hacienda Campo Claro*, Teresén, T (092) 51994, E-F, managed by Francisco Belancourt, rents cabins, can provide meals, horseriding. *Lonchería Arabe*, rec.

12 km. from Caripe is the remarkable **Cueva del Guácharo** National Monument; open 0830-1700, entrance US$1, tour with guide, 2 hrs. Also a caving museum, US$0.15, with a good range of publications for sale and a cafeteria; *Hotel Guácgaro* nearby. A bus from Cumaná to Caripe—0730, returns 1300—takes 4 hrs. and costs US$2.70, or take the *por puesto*, 2 hrs., US$5, buses stop 3 km. from caves; if staying in Caripe, take a *por puesto* at 0800, see the caves and waterfall and catch the Cumaná bus which goes past the caves between 1200 and 1230. Taxis from Caripe US$1.50, hitching difficult. The cave was discovered by Humboldt, and has since been penetrated 10½ km. along a small, crystal-clear stream. First come the caves in which live about 30,000 *guácharos* (oil birds) with an in-built radar system for sightless flight. Their presence supports a variety of wildlife in the cave: blind mice, fish and crabs in the stream, yellow-green plants, crickets, ants, etc. For two hours at dusk (about 1900) the birds pour out of the cave's mouth, continously making the clicking sounds of their echo-location system, coming back at dawn with their crops full of the oily fruit of certain local palms. Through a very narrow entrance is the *Cueva del Silencio* (Cave of Silence), where you can hear a pin drop. About 2 km. in is the *Pozo del Viento* (Well of the Wind). No backpacks allowed in the caves (leave them at the ticket office); tape recorders are permitted, check if cameras, torches/flashlights are allowed. Guides are compulsory (included in entry price—Jesus speaks English, rec.); to go further than 1½ km. into the caves, permits from Inparques in Caracas and special equipment are needed . The streams are now bridged, but there is still quite a lot of water around; wear old clothes, stout shoes and be prepared to take off your shoes and socks. In the wet season it is very slippery with mud and guano (bird droppings); tours into the cave may be shortened. Opposite the road is a path to Salto Paila, a 25-metre waterfall, about 30 minutes' walk, not easy to find, guides available; orange and other fruit trees along the way. Other routes are suggested at the cave.

Continuing straight on from Km. 52, the road passes W of **Anaco** (*Motel Bowling Anaco*, E; *Motel Canaima*, Av. Aeropuerto, D, good; *Internacional*, Av. Miranda, E; *Dragón Oriental* on same street nearby, E, clean, central; *Mand's Club*, Av. Venezuela, E, restaurant, bar, a bit noisy; *Muñiz*, Sucre, F, basic; *Viento Fresco*, F, some fans, dark rooms, poor security). It has an airport, is an important centre for oil-well service contracting companies. Beyond Anaco a branch road leads to the oilfields of San Joaquín and San Roque.

The main road passes near Cantaura, a market town, and goes on to **El Tigre**, a busy city of 105,000 on the edge of the Guanipa Plateau. It too is a centre for petroleum, but also for large peanut plantations. El Tigre and its neighbour, El Tigrito (10 km. E), are well-served by highways to all parts of the country. The local airport is at San Tomé, 5 km. from El Tigrito (regular bus to El Tigre US$2.50). In San Tomé, the eastern headquarters of Menevén, the former Mene Grande oil company, the public relations office (Calle Guico) is happy to arrange tours to nearby wells.

**Hotels** *Internacional Gran Hotel*, Av. Intercomunal, D, swimming pool, night club, best but not central; *Tamanaco*, Av. España, D, opp. bus terminal, a/c, good; also on Av. España, *La Fuente* and *Caribe*, both E, near main plaza, and *Santa Cruz* and *Arichuna* both F, clean and basic. *Orinoco*, Guayana, D-E, best of cheaper places, cafetería; *Milelvi*, F with bath, good, clean, parking in courtyard. Chilean restaurant serves excellent Chilean food and salads, on Av. España. In El Tigrito is *Hotel Rancho Grande*, D, acceptable; services better in El Tigre.
**Warning** Pickpockets work the city buses, usually in pairs.

From El Tigre, well-paved Highway 15 leads off to Caracas (via Valle de Pascua, Camatagua and Cua—550 km.); the one we are following leads, straight and flat, 130 km. over the *llanos* to the Angostura bridge across the Orinoco to Ciudad Bolívar (298 km. from Puerto La Cruz—*por puesto* US$2, 1½ hrs.).

---

## ISLA DE MARGARITA

Margarita is the country's main Caribbean holiday destination; some parts are crowded and trippery, but there are undeveloped beaches, villages with pretty churches, colonial La Asunción and several national parks including the fascinating Restinga lagoon.

Isla de Margarita and two close neighbours, Coche and Cubagua, form the state of Nueva Esparta.

*Isla de Margarita* is in fact one island whose two sections are tenuously linked by the 18 kilometre sandspit which separates the sea from the Restinga lagoon. At its largest, Margarita is about 32 kilometres from north to south and 67 kilometres from east to west. Most of its people live in the developed eastern part, which has some wooded areas and fertile valleys. The western part, the Peninsula de Macanao, is hotter and more barren, with scrub, sand dunes and marshes. Wild deer, goats and hares roam the interior, but four-wheel drive vehicles are needed to penetrate it. The entrance to the Peninsula de Macanao is a pair of hills known as Las Tetas de María Guevara, a national monument covering 1,670 hectares.

The climate is exceptionally good, but rain is scant. Water is piped from the mainland. The roads are good, and a bridge connects the two parts. Nueva Esparta's population is over 200,000, of whom about 20,000 live in the main city, Porlamar (which is not the capital, that is La Asunción).

The island has enjoyed a boom since 1983, largely as a result of the fall in the value of the bolívar and the consequent tendency of Venezuelans to spend their holidays at home. Margarita's status as a duty-free zone also helps. Venezuelan shoppers go in droves for clothing, electronic goods and other consumer items. Gold and gems are good value, but many things are not. There has been extensive building in Porlamar, with new shopping areas and Miami-style hotels going up. A number of beaches are also being developed. The island now has little to offer budget travellers, who would be better advised to stay on the mainland for the beaches and islands around Puerto La Cruz. However, its popularity means that various packages are on offer, sometimes at good value.

Local industries are fishing and fibre work, such as hammocks and straw hats. Weaving, pottery and sweets are being pushed as handicraft items for the tourists. An exhibition centre has been opened at El Cercado, near Santa Ana, on Calle Principal, near the church.

Despite the property boom and frenetic building on much of the coast and in Porlamar, much of the island has been given over to natural parks. Of these the most striking is the **Laguna La Restinga**. Launches provide lengthy runs around the mangrove swamps, but they create a lot of wash and noise. The

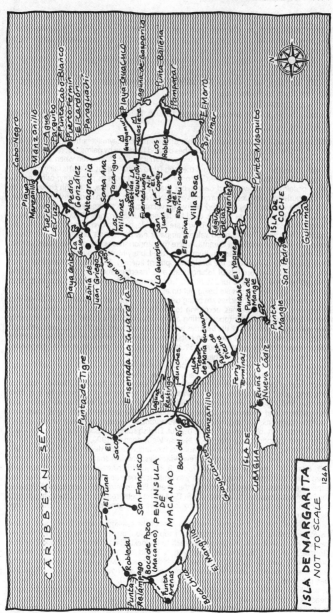

**ISLA DE MARGARITA**
NOT TO SCALE
124A

mangroves are fascinating, with shellfish clinging to the roots. The launch will leave you on a shingle and shell beach (don't forget to arrange with your boatman to collect you), and you can rummage for shellfish in the shallows (protection against the sun essential—see below for prices, etc.). Flamingos live in the lagoon.

There are mangroves also in the **Laguna de las Marites** natural monument, west of Porlamar. Other parks are **Las Tetas de María Guevara, Cerro el Copey**, 7,130 hectares, and **Cerro Matasiete y Guayamurí**, 1,672 hectares (both reached from La Asunción).

By boat from Porlamar you can go to the Isla de los Pájaros, or Morro Blanco, for both bird-spotting and underwater fishing. In Boca del Río there is a Museum of the Sea.

**Beaches** Apart from the shopping, what attracts the holidaymakers from Venezuela and abroad are the beaches: long white stretches of sand bordered by palms, but rather hot, with little shade (sunscreen essential—local wisdom is that you can burn even when sitting in the shade). Topless bathing is not seen, but the tanga (*hilo dental*—dental floss) is fairly common.

In Porlamar, the beach by the *Concorde* hotel suffers from its popularity: calm shallow water, pedalos for hire, windsurf classes; but that by the *Bella Vista*, although crowded with foreign tourists, is kept clean. For a more Venezuelan atmosphere go northwest to **Pampatar**, which is set around a bay favoured by foreign yachtsmen as a summer anchorage. A scale model of Columbus' *Santa María* is used for taking tourists on trips. (*Residencial Don Juan*, E with bath and fan; apartments sleeping 6 are available, bargain over price; beach restaurant *Antonio's*, rec.; also *Trimar*, good value) Pampatar has the island's largest fort, San Carlos Borromeo, and the smaller La Caranta, where the cannon show signs of having been spiked. Visit also the church of Cristo del Buen Viaje, the Library/Museum and the customs house (now the offices of Fondene, the local development agency). The beach at Pampatar is not very good, but there are lots of fishing boats and fishermen mending their nets. A fishing boat can be hired for US$12 for 2½ hours, 4-6 passengers; shop around for best price, good fun and fishing. New hotels are being put up along this stretch.

A number of good beaches are being developed on the eastern side. These are divided into ocean and calm beaches, according to their location in relation to the open sea. The former tend to be rougher (good surfing and windsurfing) and colder. Water is uniformly clear and unpolluted. Not all the beaches have local services yet, such as restaurants, though these, *churuatas* (bars built like Indian huts), sunshades and deckchairs are becoming more widespread. (Hire charges are about US$1.30 per item.) It is still possible, even in high season, to find practically deserted beaches.

On the eastern coast go Playa Guacuco, reached from La Asunción by a road through the Guayamurí reserve: a lot of surf, fairly shallow, palm trees, restaurant and parking lot, liquor shop at La Sabana sells ice by the bucket, cheap, 1 km. before the beach; Parguito: long and Paraguachí: some *churuatas*; Playa del Agua: 45 minutes by bus from Porlamar, US$0.30, sea very rough for children, but fairly shallow, the fashionable part is at the southern end (interesting range of vendors on the beach—quail's eggs, caipirinha cocktails, coconuts, *cachapa* maize buns; *Restaurant El Paradiso*, rents out cabins, US$12, small but comfortable; *Kiosko El Agua*, helpful, English spoken; *Posada Shangri-Lá*, rec., and many other seafood restaurants, such as *Casa Vieja*, open till 1900, most are pricey but *La Dorada* rec. as good value; beach restaurants hire umbrella and deckchair for about US$3); the northern end is less touristy, has fewer facilities, and less shade. (*Residencias Mirama*, E-D, clean, rec.; and the small *Casa Trudel*, B, no young children.) Manzanillo: water gets deep rather suddenly, fishing huts, fish sold on beach, new apartments under construction, expensive restaurant, Playa Escondida at the far end; Puerto Fermín/El Tirano (Lope de Aguirre, the infamous conquistador, landed here in 1561 on his flight from Peru), El Caserío handicrafts museum is nearby; Punta Cabo Blanco: attractive limestone outcrop; El Cardón: some development.

The coast road is interesting, with glimpses of the sea and beaches to one side, inland vistas on the other. There are a number of clifftop look-out points. The road improves radically beyond Manzanillo, winding from one beach to the next. Playa Puerto la Cruz adjoins Pedro González, another fashionable spot with a broad sweeping beach, running from a promontory (easy to climb) to scrub and brush that reach down almost to the water's edge (ask for Antonietta Luciani at *Restaurant Pedrogonzález*, she has an apartment to rent, US$40 per day, sleeps 6, well-equiped, rec. as her restaurant). The next bay is accessible by scrambling over rocks (major building work under way). One advantage of Pedro González beach is that there is a large lagoon on the other side of the coast road, so it will be impossible to spoil the bay with speculative building. There are a lot of pelicans and sea urchins (harmless).

Further west is **Juan Griego** bay and town, famous for its sunsets (tours go to see them). The town is marred by a number of cheap clothing bazaars and the beach has little sand. The bays to the north, however, are worth the walk. (*Hotel La Galera*, rec.; several others; also cabins for 5 with cooking facilities US$20. *Restaurant Mi Isla* is rec., also the Lebanese restaurant on the beach.) Playas Caribe and Galera are less spoilt. Fortín La Galera is worth a visit for the view of Juan Griego and Galera bays; children will breathlessly recite the epic siege fought here during the wars of independence.

South of Juan Griego, the road goes inland to San Juan, then to Punta de Piedra (a pleasant stretch through cultivated land and farms at regular intervals). Near San Juan is Fuentedueño park which has special walks. A branch goes northwest to La Guardia at the eastern end of La Restinga. The dyke of broken seashells stretches to the Peninsula de Macanao: on its right a spotlessly clean beach, on its left the lagoon. At the far end is a cluster of fishermen's huts with landing stages from which the launches make trips into the labyrinth of canals in the lagoon (US$7 per boat taking 5 passengers; bus from Porlamar harbourfront US$0.80, ask driver to drop you off).

The Peninsula de Macanao is quite underdeveloped, although it is hardly an untouched paradise. Construction companies are extracting large amounts of ballast for the building boom in Porlamar, while urban waste is simply being dumped in large quantities along the roadside. Some of the beaches, however, are highly regarded: Manzanilla, Guayaconcito, Boca de Pozo, Macanao, Punta Arenas and El Mangillo. Harbour at Chacachacare.

**Festivals on Margarita** 6-13 Jan. at Altagracia; 20-27 Jan. at Tacarigua; 16-26 March at Paraguachí (*Feria de San José*); 3-10 May at Los Robles; 24-30 May at La Guardia; 6 June at Tacarigua; 25-26 July at Santa Ana; 27 July at Punta de Piedras; 31 July (Batalla de Matasiete) and 14-15 Aug. (Asunción de la Virgen) at La Asunción; 30 Aug.-8 Sept. at Villa Rosa; 8-15 Sept. at El Valle; 11-12 and 28 Oct. at Los Robles; 4-11 Nov. at Boca del Río, 4-30 Nov. at Boca del Pozo; 5-6 Dec. at Porlamar; 15 Dec. at San Francisco de Macanao; 27 Dec.-3 Jan. at Juan Griego. See map for locations.

The capital, **La Asunción** (population 8,000), is a few kilometres inland from Porlamar. It has several colonial buildings, a cathedral, and the fort of Santa Rosa, with a famous bottle dungeon (open Monday 0800-1500, other days 0800-1800). There is a museum in the Casa Capitular, and a local market, good for handicrafts. Nearby are the Cerro Matasiete historical site and the Félix Gómez look-out in the Sierra Copuy.

Between La Asunción and Porlamar are the Parque Francisco Fajardo, beside the Universidad de Oriente, and El Valle del Espíritu Santo. Here is the church of the Virgen del Valle, a picturesque building with twin towers, painted white and pink. The Madonna is richly dressed (one dress has pearls, the other diamonds); the adjoining museum opens at 1400, it displays costumes and presents for the Virgin, including the "milagro de la pierna de perla", a leg-shaped pearl. A pilgrimage is held in early September. Proper dress is requested to enter the church.

Throughout the island, the churches are attractive: fairly small, with baroque towers and adornments and, in many cases, painted pink.

Most of the hotels are at **Porlamar**, 11 kilometres from the airport and about 28 kilometres from Punta de Piedra, where most of the ferries dock. It has a magnificent cathedral. At Igualdad y Díaz is the Museo de Arte Francisco Narváez. The main, and most expensive, shopping area is Avenida Santiago Mariño; better bargains and a wider range of shops are to be found on Gómez and Guevara. At night everything closes by 2300; women alone should avoid the centre after dark.

Ferries go to the Isla de Coche (11 kilometres by 6), which has over 5,000 inhabitants and one of the richest salt mines in the country. They also go, on hire only, to Isla de Cubagua, which is totally deserted, but you can visit the ruins of Nueva Cádiz (which have been excavated).

**N.B.** August and September are the vacation months when flights and hotels are fully booked.

**N.B.** also, there is both a Calle Mariño and Av. Santiago Mariño in the centre.

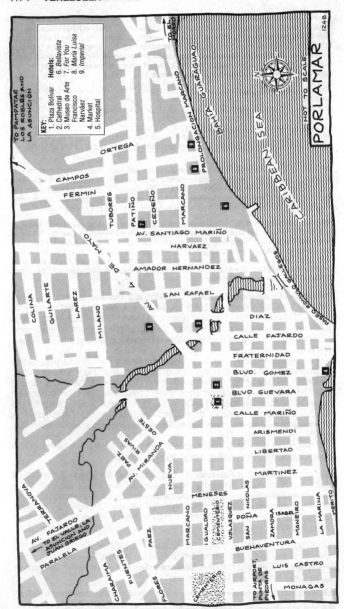

KEY:
1. Plaza Bolívar
2. Cathedral
3. Museo de Arte Francisco Narváez
4. Market
5. Hospital

Hotels:
6. Bellavista
7. For You
8. María Luisa
9. Imperial

PORLAMAR

NOT TO SCALE

CARIBBEAN SEA

BAHÍA GUARAGUAO

TO PAMPATAR LOS ROBLES AND LA ASUNCIÓN

TO EL MORRO

ORTEGA
CAMPOS
FERMIN
PROLONGACION MARCANO
TUBORES
PATIÑO
CEDEÑO
MARCANO
AV. SANTIAGO MARIÑO
NARVAEZ
AMADOR HERNANDEZ
SAN RAFAEL
DIAZ
CALLE FAJARDO
FRATERNIDAD
BLVD. GOMEZ
BLVD. GUEVARA
CALLE MARIÑO
ARISMENDI
LIBERTAD
MARTINEZ
COLINA
GUILARTE
LAREZ
MILANO
AV. DE MAIO
OESTE
RIVAS
PAEZ
AV. MIRANDA
NUEVA
MENESES
IGUALDAD
MARCANO
VELAZQUEZ
DOÑA SAN NICOLAS
ZAMORA
ISABEL
MANEIRO
LA MARINA
MERITO
BUENAVENTURA
LUIS CASTRO
MONAGAS
PAEZ
FUENTES
CHARAIMA
PARALELA
FLORES
CEMENTERIO
CEMENTERIO
PASEO RÓMULO GALLEGOS

AV. FAJARDO
TO EL VALLE, LA ASUNCION AND JUAN GRIEGO

TO AIRPORT, PUNTA DE PIEDRAS

TERRANOVA

124B

**Hotels at Porlamar** *Hilton*, L-A+ (+10% tax), new, sailing dinghies for hire; other top class establishments, *Concorde*, Bahía de El Morro, and *Bella Vista\**, Av. Santiago, A-A+, swimming pool, beach; *Cardón*, B, opposite old airport at Playa Cardón, peaceful, good rooms and restaurant, swimming pool, diving and snorkelling trips organized; *For You\**, Patiño y Av. Santiago Mariño, B, good breakfast, rec.; *Venus*, T (095) 23722, Calle Milano y San Rafael, C, clean, a/c, safe; *Caribbean*, Vía El Morro, D, pool, beach; *Vista Mar*, D, Urb. Bella Vista, on the way to El Morro, beach; *Agila Inn*, Narváez, D, clean, swimming pool, restaurant, rec.; *Colibrí*, Av. Santiago Mariño, T 616346, D, rec.; *Dos Primos*, Calle Mariño entre Zamora y San Nicolás, E, clean and modern, rec.; on the Boulevard, *Italia*, San Nicolás, D with bath, cold water, a/c, clean, safe, rec., but district is a bit rough; *Brasilia*, San Nicolás, F, quiet, clean, nice new rooms at back; *María Luisa\** (under reconstruction), Vía El Morro, E, beach; *Evdama*, Bella Vista y Campos, E, helpful, also holiday flats with parking; opposite is *Imperial*, C, clean, comfortable, safe, English spoken, rec., but restaurant only average; *Tamá*, E (more with a/c, hot water, TV, etc.), very nice, excellent restaurant and atmosphere, highly rec., Vía El Morro, beach; opposite is *Chez David*, E, a/c, on beach, modern; *Garland*, E, Av. Miranda, good restaurant, convenient for *pos puestos*; *Porlamar*, Igualdad y Fajardo, E, clean, good restaurant, a/c or fan, friendly; opposite is *Canadá*, E, rec. *Chez Toni*, San Nicolás 14-56, E, English spoken, cheap restaurant, rec; *La Opera*, Igualdad y Fraternidad, E with bath (just off plaza); *Residencia Paraíso*, near main square, F, basic but clean, fan; *Residencia Don Francisco*, Igualdad, 2 blocks from plaza, F with bath, quiet, good; *Hotel España*, Marino 6-35, E, hot shower, very clean, friendly, rec; better value is *Rioja*, F with fan and bath, clean, safe. Many others round Plaza Bolívar. Cheaper places on Maneiro, e.g. *Res. Javi*, G, very basic, but friendly. *Cabañas Turísticas*, Vía La Isleta, US$35 for a cabin, sleeps 4, pool, restaurant. For longer stays, Enrique and Elena Ganteaume rent apartments in Porlamar, Juan Griego and La Asunción (Av. Principal 41, Urb. Santa Lucía, La Asunción, T 095-610467, friendly, English spoken).

**Restaurants** *El Peñero*, vía El Morro, service slow but good food; *Vecchia Marina*, Vía El Morro, good but more expensive; *Bahía* bar-restaurant, Av. Raúl Leoni y Vía El Morro, excellent value, live music; good breakfast at *Panadería*, Av. 4 de Mayo y Fermín; *Martín Pescador*, Av. 4 de Mayo, lobsters and other seafood, friendly, rec.; *Cheers*, 4 de Mayo, good bar, popular, rec.; *Flamingo*, 4 de Mayo (in hotel), cheap, good, but small portions; *El Yate*, next to *Hotel For You* main entrance, highly rec. for food and service, steaks superb, US$20-25 for 2, but wine can double the bill; *Café de París*, outside *Hotel For You*, croissants and enormous ice creams, a good meeting place; also *París Croissant* on Blvd. Santiago Mariño; *Los 3 Delfines*, Cedeño 26-9, seafood, rec.; *Guanaguanare*, pedestrian boulevard by sea, good food and service, reasonable prices. *La Isla*, Mariño y Cedeño, 8 fast food counters ranging from hamburgers to sausages from around the world. *La Cotorrera*, Av. Santiago Mariño, steaks, rec., closed Sunday; *Kiosco La Nena*, Av. Raúl Leoni, Italian and local dishes, highly rec. for food and value if not atmosphere, try *pabellón margariteño* (white fish, rice, black beans, fried plantains—add sugar and chilli sauce to taste). *Jardín de Italo*, Calle Campos, French, classy, little atmosphere; *Centro Vegetariano Mariuxu*, Fermín 12-79, yellow and green house, no sign, lunch only, rec.

**Entertainment** *Mosquito Coast Club*, behind *Bella Vista Hotel*, disco with genuine Venezuelan feel, good *merengue* and rock music, bar outside discotheque for singles, *Village Club*, Av. Santiago Mariño.

**Shopping** Besides all the duty-free shops, *Del Bellorín*, Cedeño, near Santiago Mariño, is good for handicrafts. Good selection of jewellery at *Sonia Gems*, on Cedeño; *Ivan Joyería* and *Inter Gold*, both on 4 de Mayo (latter is between *Ivan* and *Hotel Flamingo*); many other places on the main street are overpriced. When purchasing jewellery, bargain hard, don't pay by credit card (surcharges are imposed), get a detailed guarantee of the item and, if unsure, get another jeweller to check its validity.

**Exchange** Banco Consolidado (American Express), Guevara y San Nicolás; banks generally slow with poor rates; best at Banco Construcción, Guevara or at *Hotel Contemporáneo* next to Banco Consolidado. *Casa de cambio* at Igualdad y Av. Santiago Mariño. Banks and Amex office closed on Monday. There are often long queues. Most shops accept credit cards.

**Post Office** Calle Arismendi. **Phones** CANTV, Bolívar, between Fajardo and Fraternidad.

**Information** Tourist Office, Miranda, near cathedral, free city map. An English-language newspaper, *Mira*, is published on the island; the editor/publisher acts also as an inexpensive tour guide; Av. Santiago Mariño, Ed. Carcaleo Suites, Apartamento 2-A, Porlamar (T 095-613351). The best map is available from Corpoven.

**Travel Agents** *Turisol*, Calle Hernández, friendly and helpful; *Supertours*, Calle Larez, Quinta Thaid, T 618781, Fax 617061, tours of the island and elsewhere; *Zuluoga Tours*, very helpful; *Tourismo Guaiquerí*, Santiago Mariño y Marcano, English spoken, mixed reports.

**Car Hire** An economic proposition for any number above one and probably the best way of getting around the island, about US$27 a day, several competing offices at the airport, and at *Hotel Bella Vista* (inc. Avis, poor service), others also on Av. Santiago Mariño. **Lizmar** is the cheapest, US$23 per day unlimited mileage, insurance included (excess US$300), but cars are in poor condition. In all cases, check the brakes. Scooters can also be hired for about US$14 a day from **Diversion Rentals**, Calle Amador Hernández, **Maruba Motor Rentals**, La Marina (English spoken, good maps, highly rec.) or **Auto Camping Margarita** (boats and bicycles also for rent). Motor cycles may not be ridden between 2000 and 0500; although this (apparently) should not apply to tourists, police officers have been known to confiscate tourists' machines and impose heavy fines. **N.B.** Remember to keep an eye on the fuel gauge; there are service stations in towns, but air conditioning is heavy on fuel. Driving on Isla Margarita: the roads are generally good and most are paved. Sign posts are often poorly-positioned (behind bushes, round corners), which adds to the night time hazard of vehicles with badly-adjusted lights. It is best not to drive outside Porlamar after dark.

**Public Transport** *Por Puestos* serve most of the island, leaving mainly from the corners of Plaza Bolívar in Porlamar. Fares: to Punta de Piedra, US$0.85; to La Asunción, US$0.25; to Pampatar, US$0.40; to La Restinga (from La Marina y Mariño), US$0.85, El Agua, US$0.40; Juan Griego, US$0.40.

**Communications** There are 18 **flights** a day from **Caracas**, with Avensa and Aeropostal, 45 mins. flight; tickets are much cheaper if purchased in Venezuela in local currency (about US$30 one way). Daily Avensa flight to **Ciudad Guyana**, about US$21, 1710, also Aeropostal at 1815, and daily Aereotuy to **Ciudad Bolívar**. Daily flight from **Cumaná** at 0700, Aeropostal, and 2020, Avensa. Viasa, Av. 4 de Mayo, Edif. Banco Royal, Porlamar (T 32273, airport 691137); Avensa and Aeropostal are both on Calle Fajardo, Porlamar, opposite each other (Aeropostal hours 0800-1200, 1400-1800, T 617064, airport 691128; Avensa T 617111, airport 691021). (Airport: General Santiago Mariño, between Porlamar and Punta de Piedras; taxi US$6.)

    **Ferries** (very busy at weekends): from **Puerto La Cruz**, Turismo Margarita, Los Boqueticos, T 87-683, Pto. La Cruz to Margarita 0700 and 1300, 4 hrs. (5-6 inc., check-in), depart Margarita (Punta de Piedra) 1000 and 1800; Conferries, Los Cocos terminal, T 66-0468, and *Meliá Hotel*, Pto. La Cruz to Margarita, 6 a day between 0300 and 2400 each way, 3½ hrs., passengers US$6 1st class, US$4.20 2nd, vehicles about US$10. From **Cumaná**, vehicle ferries of Conferry and Naviarca at 0700 and 1600 daily, 3 hrs., cars US$5, passengers US$2.50, ferry terminal is almost at mouth of the river. Faster launch, *Gran Cacique I* (Turismo Margarita) twice daily to Punta de Piedra, 6½ hrs., US$3.50. Several bus companies in Caracas sell through tickets (US$17.50) from Caracas to Porlamar, arriving about midday. By car from Caracas, it takes about 4 hrs., but will be reduced to 2½ when the Sucre motorway is opened.

    A ferry sails from Mercado Viejo to Chacopata on the mainland at 1000 and 1200, US$1.20, also takes cars. A ferry to Grenada, *The Eastward*, sails once a month. Go to the Puerto de Pescadores, El Guamache, near Punta de Piedra, and ask boat captains about taking a boat to the Leeward or Windward Islands; e.g. US$50 p.p. to Martinique (very difficult to find boats willing to take passengers).

---

## THE GUAYANA HIGHLANDS (7)

The historic Ciudad Bolívar on the Río Orinoco, besides being worth a visit in itself (not least for the sunsets on the river), is a good starting place for the superb landscapes further south, notably the table-top mountains and waterfalls around Canaima. The most spectacular of all is Angel Falls. Man-made features include the huge hydroelectric scheme at Guri and the industries at Ciudad Guyana, from where the Orinoco Delta can be reached.

These uplands, lying S of the Orinoco River, constitute half of Venezuela. They rise, in rounded forested hills and narrow valleys, to flat topped tablelands on the borders of Brazil. These lands with savannas interspersed with semi-deciduous forest are very sparsely populated. So far, communications have been the main difficulty, but a road has now been opened to Santa Elena de Uairén on the Brazilian frontier (**see page 1187**). This road can be followed to Manaus, and thence, by a suitable vehicle, to Brasília and southern Brazil. The area is Venezuela's largest gold and diamond source, but its immense reserves of iron ore, manganese and bauxite are of far greater economic importance.

**Ciudad Bolívar**, on the S bank of the Orinoco, is 400 km. from its delta and 640 by road from Caracas. Average temperature 29°C, but a cool and refreshing breeze usually springs up in the evening. It still has much colonial building, some under restoration, but is growing rapidly. Population 115,000. It stands by the narrows of the Orinoco, with its Cathedral (completed 1840), on a small hill, and the Zanuro hill fort (1902), on another hill in the centre, dominating the city.

The narrows, not more than 300 metres wide, gave the town its old name of Angostura. It was here that Bolívar came after defeat to reorganize his forces, and the British Legionnaires joined him; it was at Angostura that he was declared President of that Gran Colombia which he had yet to build, and which was to fragment before his death. At the Congress of Angostura, 15 February 1819, the representatives of the present day Venezuela, Colombia and Ecuador met to proclaim Gran Colombia. The building, on Plaza Bolivar, houses a museum (Casa del Congreso de Angostura). Also on this historic square is the Cathedral, the Casa de Los Gobernadores de la Colonia, the Real Intendencia, and the Casa de la Cultura. When the town was still known as Angostura a physician invented the famous bitters there in 1824; the factory moved to Port of Spain in 1875.

There is a floating pontoon dock where ocean-going cargo boats can discharge, but the harbour is now naval. A walk along the river bank is rec. at dusk when the sun is setting. Launches take passengers across the river (US$0.25), but there are no other passenger boat services.

You can buy baskets and items made by the Indians, and good hammocks. It is also the best place in Venezuela for anything made of gold. There are beautiful hand-made charms for charm bracelets and, most typical of all, the Venezuelan orchid, made by hand, of red, yellow and green gold. The gold orchid pin or earrings, or a gold nugget (known as *cochano*), are the best souvenirs of Venezuela. There are many jewellers on Pasaje Guayana, which runs off Paseo Orinoco. Gold shops also in Pasaje Gran Hotel Bolívar: for nuggets, Irma Lapeña has the most beautiful and the most expensive—bargain for a good price. A feature is the netting of *sapoara*, a delicious fish 30 to 35 cm. long which pours from the inlets when the river begins to swell in late June at the start of the rainy season and swims up stream to spawn. During its short season this is the favourite dish of the town.

**Festival** 5-8 Sept., fair and exhibition.

**Hotels** *Orinoco*, on outskirts, overlooking river, B, pool, tourist agency; *Don Salo**, Av. Bolívar, nr. Av. Táchira, D, seen better days, disappointing restaurant; difficult to find, though quite near the airport; also *Valentina*, Av. Maracay 55, D, pleasant part of town; *Laja Real**, opp. airport, D, swimming pool open to non-residents for US$5 per day, excellent restaurant; *Florida*, Av. Táchira y Mario Briceñol, T 27942, E, a/c, clean, friendly, good restaurant, near airport; *Canaima*, Av. Upata (far from centre), E, bath, a/c, clean, noisy; *La Cumbre*, Av. 5 de Julio, good view of town but rather run down, E, without food; *Hotel del Sur*, Plaza las Banderas, far from centre, T 206241, E, clean, a/c, rec.

On or near Paseo Orinoco: *Gran Hotel Bolívar*, closed for refurbishment in 1990; *Mimo*, E, on the corner of Paseo Orinoco and Calle Amazonas, not rec. except for superb views of the river, suspension bridge and sunsets; *El Silenico*, F, just off Paseo Orinoco, good, clean, friendly, highly rec.; *Sicilia*, Paseo Orinoco y Dalla Costa, E, clean, friendly, modern, Italian and German spoken; *Caracas*, Paseo Orinoco, E, friendly, safe, balcony overlooking river; *Italia*, Paseo Orinoco, F, very friendly, a/c and bath, a few single rooms with fan, no bath, restaurant; nearby *Hospedaje Tropicana*, F, fan; *Unión*, Calle Urica, also nr. *Italia*, F with a/c (cheaper with fan), clean, safe, good value, rec., good restaurant; *Residencias Delicias*, Venezuela, F, clean, highly rec.; *Pensión Panamericana*, Calle Rocía 5, F, shower, fan, safe, laundry facilities. *Terminal y Adriana*, E, Av. Moreno de Mendoza, near bus terminal, friendly; similar location, *Universo*, D, rec. It is often difficult to find rooms in hotels here. For the cheaper hotels, take a red bus from the airport to Paseo Orinoco; at the eastern end there are many to choose from.

**Restaurants** *Alfonso*, Av. Maracay, for criollo parrilla; *Da Gino*, next to *Hotel Laja Real*, rec. *Savoy*, Venezuela y Dalla Costa, good value breakfast and lunch; good restaurant at Venezuela y Igualdad; *Mi Casa*, Venezuela, open air, good value; *Brazil*, Calle Venezuela, good, cheap. Chinese restaurant on Av. Upata, opp. *Hotel Canaima*, good, open late. *Bonbonería Exquisito*, near airport, pizzas, cakes, milkshakes and coffee. Cheap food at the market at the east end of Paseo Orinoco, need to bargain. The *Cervezeria* at No. 36 serves tasty *sopa de chipichipi*.

**Museum** The **Museo Soto**, Av. Germania, on the outskirts of the town has works by Venezuela's José Rafael Soto and other artists, open Tues.-Sun. 1000-1800, good. Museum at **Casa del Correo del Orinoco**, Paseo Orinoco y Carabobo, modern art and some exhibits of history of the city, and a fat precolumbian goddess, including the printing press of the newspaper which spread the cause of independence; Tues.-Sat. 0900-1200, 1500-1800, Sun. 0900-1200. Has free town map (poor) and booklet on Ciudad Bolívar. **Museo Geológico y Minero** at the School of Mines in the University of the East (UDO), Av. Principal, La Sabanita. **Museo Regional de la Guayana**, housed in the former prison, 2 blocks from Cathedral on Paseo Orinoco. Many other museums in the city, such as **Museo Casa San Isidro**, Av. Táchira (Tues.-Sat. 0900-1200, 1430-1700, Sun. 0900-1200) a mansion where Simón Bolívar stayed.

**Taxis** Under US$1 to virtually anywhere in town.

**Exchange** **Banco Consolidado** (American Express), Edif. Pinemar, Av. Andrés Bello, Centro Comercial Canaima; **Banco Royal Venezolano** (Calle Orinoco 38) and **Banco Mercantil y Agrícola** (Av. Jesús Soto) will change dollars cash. **Banco Internacional**, Paseo Orinoco. **Banco Unión** or **Filanbanco** handle Visa transactions. Travellers' cheques accepted by **Banco Consolidado** near airport.

**Brazilian Consulate** near Paseo Orinoco. **Danish Consulate**, Av. Táchira, Quinta Maninata 50, of. 319, T (85) 23490, 0800-1200, 1500-1700.

**Post Offices** Av. Táchira, 15 mins' walk from centre.

**Tourist Offices** On Dalla Costa, provides free map of state and city, but otherwise little information. The small offices in the airport car park and the bus station in particular are very friendly and helpful. You will need a map: the town has a rather confusing layout.

**Travel Agencies** *Venezolano Internacional de Turismo*, Av. Andrés Bello and at the airport, rec. for tours to Canaima and Gran Sabana, English spoken; *Agencia de Viajes Auyantepuy*, Av. Bolívar, Ed. Roque, Centro No. 8, English and French spoken. Rafael Urbina at *SASTA*, T (085) 126931, has been recommended.

**Airport** Minibuses and buses (Ruta 2) marked Terminal to town centre. Taxi to Paseo Orinoco US$1.75. Served by Aeropostal which flies twice daily to Caracas (US$45) and Maturín. (Reserve well in advance at the Aeropostal counter at the airport.) Also flights to Tucupita, and to Porlamar (Isla de Margarita—Aereotuy daily). Aereotuy also to Santa Elena de Uairén and villages near the Brazilian border. Charter airline, Utaca, is rec.; ask for Jorge, and verify all prices.

**Buses** To get to the bus station take a bus marked Terminal going W along the Paseo Orinoco. Several daily to **Caracas** 8 hrs., US$6 (from the capital all buses overnight, *por puesto* US$12), and to the coast: to **Puerto La Cruz**, US$3, 4½ hrs.; to **Cumaná**, US$4; to Maracay US$3, 10 hrs.; Valencia, via Maracay, US$7. Tumeremo US$3.90; Tumeremo bus through to El Dorado US$4.10, 3 daily. To Santa Elena de Uairén direct with Línea Orinoco, Transportes Mundial or Expreso Rápidos de Güiria leave at 0500, 0800 and 1900, spectacular views of the Gran Sabana at sunset (book in advance), US$8-11, 11-14 hours. To **Boa Vista** with Transportes Mundial, Mon and Thurs at 2000, US$25, 20 hrs. To **Ciudad Guayana** hourly from 0700 by Expresos Guayanera, US$1.80, 1½ hrs., *por puesto*, US$3.60, 1½ hrs. Terminal at junction of Av. República and Av. Sucre. Bus to Caicara, 7½ hrs., including 2 ferry crossings.

---

### Ciudad Bolívar: Key to map

1. Plaza Bolívar; 2. Plaza de las Banderas; 3. Cerro El Zamuro and Fort; 4. Cathedral; 5. Casa del Congreso de Angostura; 6. Casa de los Gobernadores de la Colonia; 7. Real Intendencia/Palacio de Gobierno; 8. Casa de la Cultura; 9. Casa del Correo del Orinoco; 10. Museo Soto; 11. Museo Geológico y Minero/Universidad del Oriente; 12. Archivo Histórico y Museo Etnográfico de Guayana/Carcel Viejo; 13. Market; 14. Post Office; 15. *Gran Hotel Bolívar*. ⌐⌐⌐⌐⌐⌐⌐⌐ area of detailed map.

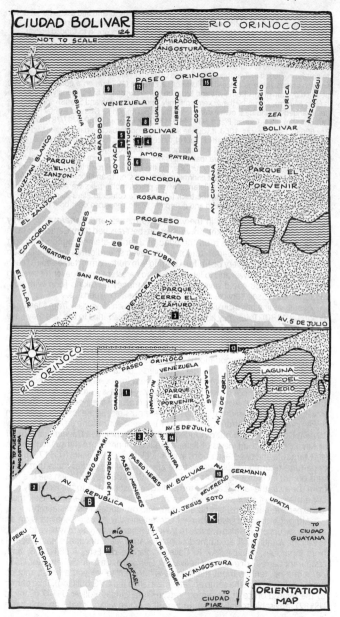

CIUDAD BOLIVAR
124
NOT TO SCALE

RIO ORINOCO

MIRADOR
ANGOSTURA

PASEO ORINOCO

BABILONIA

VENEZUELA

GUZMAN BLANCO

PARQUE
EL
ZANJON

EL ZANJON

CONCORDIA

PURGATORIO

EL PILAR

CARABOBO

BOYACA

CONSTITUCION

MERCEDES

SAN ROMAN

IGUALDAD

LIBERTAD

DALLA COSTA

PIAR

ROSCIO

URICA

ANZOATEGUI

ZEA

BOLIVAR

BOLIVAR

AMOR PATRIA

CONCORDIA

ROSARIO

PROGRESO

LEZAMA

28 DE OCTUBRE

DEMOCRACIA

AV. CUMANA

PARQUE EL
PORVENIR

PARQUE
CERRO EL
ZAMURO

AV. 5 DE JULIO

RIO ORINOCO

PASEO ORINOCO

VENEZUELA

CARABOBO

AV. CUMANA

CARACAS

Parque EL
PORVENIR

AV. 1° DE ABRIL

LAGUNA
DEL
MEDIO

AV. 5 DE JULIO

PASEO GASPARI

MORENO

PASEO MENESES

PASEO HERES

AV. TACHIRA

AV. BOLIVAR

GERMANIA

AV.

AV. REPUBLICA

AV.
RIO
SAN

PERU

AV. ESPAÑA

AV. 17 DE DICIEMBRE

AV. JESUS SOTO

REVEREND

UPATA

TO
CIUDAD
GUAYANA

RIO
SAN RAFAEL

AV. ANGOSTURA

AV. LA PARAGUA

TO
CIUDAD PIAR

ORIENTATION
MAP

For an excursion to see gold mining at Río Claro, take a bus to Guri and ask to be set down at the gate to Río Claro. Minibuses run to the mines, where the people are very friendly and will take visitors by boat to the workings. Return with workers going to Ciudad Bolívar.

73 km. E of Ciudad Bolívar is La Encrucijada (junction). To the left is the freeway to Ciudad Guayana (37 km.); straight on is the road to Upata via the Paso Carnachi (Caroní ferry); to the right is the road to Ciudad Piar (97 km.) and the iron ore mountain (Cerro Bolívar—cheaper to visit from Ciudad Bolívar than from Ciudad Guayana). Following this route through typical Guayana landscape you reach the village of La Paragua (107 km. on a good, paved road) peopled by immigrants from Syria and Lebanon (*Hotel Guyana*, F, basic, friendly). In this area is *Hato El Burro*, A, run by the Ackerman family, English, German and Spanish spoken. Trips are arranged around their own extensive ranch, Guri dam, Angel Falls etc. Contact at Vía La Paragua, Km. 434, Ciudad Piar, T 938148/931395, or Caracas T 782-0797/781-8778, P.O. Box 60636, Este Caracas, 1060. If you like adventure and untouched nature, take two ferries crossing the Río Paragua, towards El Paúl (4-wheel drive vehicles Dec.-May). There is usually transport available. From El Paúl you can get a ride towards the nearest river to Canaima, which you can cross on a *curiara* (passengers only), and from there hike about 15 km. to Canaima. Alternatively, from La Encrucijada, on the right hand road (in the direction of La Paragua) turn left after 8 km., past enormous black rocks, on to an almost hidden trail. After a further 2 km. is the Cueva del Elefante, where precolumbian relics were found and rock paintings can be seen. Following the track (10 km.) one comes to Playa Blanca on the Río Caroní, where miners dive for gold and diamonds. Mario Venarusso does boat trips.

Angel Falls, the highest fall in the world (979 metres) and **Canaima**, a nearby tourist lodge and hotel, 70 km. down-river, are best reached from Caracas or from Ciudad Bolívar. The lodge is on the edge of a tannin-stained lagoon with soft beige beaches; the Río Carrao tumbles over seven splendid falls into the lagoon below. The country is very beautiful. Lodging is in quite comfortable cabins; each is complete with shower and toilet; there are no hardships whatsoever. If travelling independently, you could save yourself some money by taking food with you. Meals are basic, self-service, no choice; drinks are also expensive.

Avensa airline has inclusive charges for tours which leave daily from Maiquetía airport (at 1130). Tours may also start at Ciudad Bolívar. Trips to the falls may have to be booked weeks in advance in the holiday season. From Caracas the return flight, two nights' accommodation, six meals and a free boat trip around the lagoon costs about US$325 (Nov. 1990); from Ciudad Bolívar the return flight with two nights' accommodation is about US$170 (half those prices for one night and 3 meals). Attempts to get travellers to take longer stays through "non-availability" of preferred return date seem frequent. All arrangements are made through Avensa, direct (best in Caracas—address as for *Los Frailes*, **page 1150;** Ciudad Bolívar Avensa office is closed for most of the weekend) or through travel agencies. One-night trips (US$108) are possible, as are longer stays (open flights can be booked from Ciudad Bolívar). Aereotuy runs one day excursions by 19-seat Dornier aircraft out of Ciudad Bolívar one landing at Canaima, the other at Kavac; giving good views of Falls, there is a connecting Aereotuy flight from Isla Margarita and direct excursions from Barcelona and Margarita (US$175, 0730, departure, returning 1800). Reductions are available for parties (note that these trips do not include a visit to Angel Falls, and that you may not even see the falls from the air in the rainy season—the additional cost of a trip to the Falls may well bring the cost of your journey up to that of a package). At Canaima itself there are expensive gift shops, but no alternative accommodation or restaurant.

Although the quickest and most convenient way to visit Canaima is on an Avensa excursion, it is also possible to travel independently (you may have to insist, the airline wants to sell accommodation) and camp near Canaima: obtain a permit from Inparques, Caracas, Av. R. Gallegos, Parque del Este, T 284-1956, opp. restaurant *Carreta*, or in Ciudad Bolívar, Av. Germania, Casa de Gobernador, US$1 per night inc. tent (without this Avensa will try not to sell you a ticket, though permits are issued at the camp at Canaima itself in the CVG building). Take permit to the Avensa office at the airport: return flight Ciudad Bolívar US$47 (Caracas US$82), advisable to take food, though the Indian village near Canaima has a small store selling mainly canned foods; also souvenir shop in airport, and the *fuente de sodo* overlooking the lagoon; some families in the village also offer basic accommodation, but expensive, e.g. US$40 for hammock outdoors under cover has been known, but usually US$15. Ask for details at the information desk at the camp. Alternatively camp for free; fires are permitted and plenty of wood is available. Try hanging your hammock at the home where Canaima Tours guides live (ask for Raúl or María García). Do not forget swimming costumes, insect repellant and sun cream; waterproof clothing may be advisable.

Many travel agencies, especially in Caracas, Isla Margarita and Ciudad Bolívar, book one-day excursions on Cessna planes (Saeta; Aerobol, 5 seaters; Aereotuy, 9 seaters), from Caracas US$200, from Ciudad Bolívar US$170, includes guide, flight over falls, lunch at Canaima, boat tour of the lagoon, swimming. The cheapest way to fly over the falls is on scheduled flights from Ciudad Bolívar with Aereotuy to Kavanayen or Icaburú, or to Santa Elena de Uairén, calling at either of these villages, about US$24 single, sit on right-hand side.

There are various excursions from Canaima, which are all worthwhile (and usually crowded): upriver to the **Angel Falls** costs up to US$150 (June 1990); 5 operators organize this trip at short notice, including Isidoro Sandoval of Excursiones Churun-Vena S.R.L. (rec., he has a video of a Japanese expedition which climbed the Falls in 1980), and **"Jungle" Rudy Truffino**, the most expensive (he has his own hotel, US$80 with 3 meals, at Campamento Ucaima, just above the Hacha Falls, 2 hrs. walk from Canaima). All *curiaras* (dug-outs) must have 2 motors, by law, and carry first aid, life jackets, etc. Take wet weather gear, swimwear, mosquito net for hammock and insect repellant. Trips by boat to the Falls only go June-November (sometimes September depending on water level), leaving usually in the afternoon, staying the first night at Isla Orquídea, continuing to the Falls next day. Depending on the river, the trip takes on average 3 days (best to go Mon.-Wed. as everything is fully booked at weekends). Alternatively there are 12 hour day trips, US$90 p.p. which are hard going. The flat-topped Auyan-Tepuy, from which spring the Angel Falls, was the setting for W. H. Hudson's *Green Mansions*. The sheer rock face of the Falls, named after Jimmy Angel, the US airman who discovered them in 1937, was climbed in 1971 by three Americans and an Englishman, David Nott, who recounted the ten-day adventure in his book *Angels Four* (Prentice-Hall).

You can also make walking expeditions into the jungle to Indian villages with a guide (e.g. Tomás, Matherson or Clifford), but bargain hard on the price. Recommended Indian guide is Canaima Jones, ask for him at the camp or Canaima airport. A highly recommended flight by Cessna 5-seater costs US$90 p.p., takes 45 mins. and does some circuits over and alongside the falls; there are also 20-min. flights at 0930 for US$55-60 which return in time for the 1315 Avensa flight out of Canaima (better than organized flights is to go to the airstrip and ask around the pilots waiting there on business if they will fly over the Falls for the same price as a tour). Other excursions to Mayupa (US$45, half day), to Yuri Falls (US$30, half day); to Isla Orquídea (US$50, full day, good boat ride, island may disappoint); to Salto de Sapo, 2 hrs., US$4.

Auyan-Tepuy can also be reached by a 2-3-day hike from the village of **Kamarata**, reached only by air from Ciudad Bolívar (with Aereotuy or Utaca, 2½ hrs., book at least a week ahead in Ciudad Bolívar or Caracas, flights once a week, US$40). In the dry season you can take a 3-4 day excursion to Kamarata from Canaima by boat (see also under Kavanayén, below). A friendly village with no hotels or restaurants, but rooms to let, about US$2 p.p.; camping also possible (mosquito nets necessary); take food, though locals may sell you dinner. Several good day-long hiking trips; guides to Auyan-Tepuy, waterfalls and the Cuevas de Kavac, US$10.

In Caracas contact *Hotel Tamanaco*, T 914555, or Caribex Tours, T 728271/2, for trips to Falls. Excursiones Canaima (Hermanos Jiménez) at Maiquetía (T 55-2462) run a number of well-organized trips from Canaima, e.g. to Mayupa Falls, inc. canoe ride on Río Carrao; Yuri falls—jeep/boat; Isla Orquídea (with beach barbecue); 4 day/3 night trip to Angel Falls (native guides, camp fire meals, on foot and by boat, US$200 p.p. inclusive, minimum 6 people); very experienced company. Italcambio, T 820611, organizes camping trips up the Río Paragua for parties of four at a cost of US$220 for three days, or US$325 four days. The travel agency at the *Caracas Hilton* has also been recommended; also Edgar Belser, Caracas T 978 1628, fax 978 1508, friendly, who also runs the *Diamante Inn* at La Paragua near the river; 3 day package from Caracas including Falls, Kavac, and Canaima, US$600. Tours can usually be booked on the spot, with no reservation problems.

**N.B.** Travellers' cheques can be cashed, but at a poor rate.

**Warning** Necklaces of poisonous red and black seeds (rosary peas) are on sale here.

In an area rich in natural resources 105 km. down-river from Ciudad Bolívar an entirely new metropolis, known as *Ciudad Guayana*, is still being built. It is forging into one the four separate centres of San Félix, Palúa, Puerto Ordaz and Matanzas. Its population is already approaching half of the planned million, on the south bank of the Orinoco and both sides of the Caroní river before it spills into the Orinoco. The mixing of the rivers' waters is like "pouring cream into coffee". East of the Caroní are the commercial port of *San Félix* (extensive work in progress to make a riverside walk and park) and the Palúa iron-ore terminal of the railway from El Pao. Crossing the Caroní by the 470-metre concrete bridge we come to *Puerto Ordaz* (airport), the iron-ore loading port connected by rail with the famous Cerro Bolívar open-cast iron mine (see below). The iron-tinted waterfall, which looks like a beerfall, in the pretty Parque Cachamay is worth a visit. To the west are the government-owned Siderúrgica del Orinoco whose production is being raised to 4.8m tonnes of steel a year, and an aluminium plant, Venalum. About 3 km. away, across bare savanna, is an area reserved for smaller industries. The Casa Machupicchu, Calle Guasipati, sells a city map for US$0.70.

Just up the Caroní is the Macagua hydroelectric plant (with a second phase under construction); there are some truly beautiful cataracts called Salto Llovizna as you enter the grounds (known as Parque La Llovizna, reached by bus from San Félix most of the way, then hitch). Higher up the river is the massive Guri dam and hydroelectric undertaking, **see page 1119.** The trip to Guri takes 90 minutes by taxi; the plant is open daily 0900-1030, 1415-1515, for a conducted tour (4 daily, 1 hr.) phone Edelca, Puerto Ordaz 20-80-66 (Relaciones Institucionales del Guri); the area gets very full during holidays, Easter or carnival. You can also visit the rest of the complex including the hotel, D, a/c, comfortable; camping possible outside the entrance with permission. *Por puesto* from Ciudad Bolívar, Route 70, US$12.50 one way; for return, ask at Alcabala Río Claro (gatehouse) if they can get you a free lift.

**Hotels** *Intercontinental Guayana\**, Parque Punta Vista, A+, all facilities, swimming pool, food and service poor; nearby is *Habana Cuba*, Av. Américas, E, cheapest in Puerto Ordaz, a/c, clean, unfriendly; *Dos Ríos*, México esq. Ecuador, C, shower, a/c, clean, swimming pool; *El Rasil*, A, Centro Cívico, with all comforts, swimming pool, overpriced, rooms good but food and service poor; tour agency organises trips to Orinoco delta, rec.; *Tepuy\**, F, a/c, Carrera Upata, Edif. Arichuna; *La Guayana\**, F, Av. Las Américas, clean, a/c, no hot water; *Turista*, F, Av. Caracas, basic, friendly. Many cheaper hotels in San Félix, the historical town, have been removed or closed down in the restoration works. Only *Aguila* (E) and *Yoli* (F, no hot water, otherwise OK) in San Félix have decent restaurants. It is difficult to find hotels because of the influx of workers, who live in them for lack of other housing.

**Local speciality** *Parahifa* is an interesting local drink of passion fruit and orange.

**Bookshop** *Librería Orinoco*, Centro Cívico Puerto Ordaz, international magazines and English paperbacks.

**Car Hire** 18 different operators at the airport, Puma cars rec.; Hertz, Puerto Ordaz, rents 4-wheel drive vehicles. A car is very useful in this area, especially for visiting the Cerro Bolívar mine and Guri dam.

**Exchange** Banco Consolidado (American Express), Calle Urbana, Edif. Don Andrés, Banco Royal Venezolano and Banco Provincial at Puerto Ordaz. Banco Mercantil. Banco Unión for Visa. Very difficult to change travellers' cheques. Hotels give poor rates.

**Brazilian Consulate** Av. Las Américas, nr. CANTV, T (086) 227246, 0900-1700, can issue visas but there is delay and a charge for authorisation. Information on roads in Boa Vista area.

**Buses** Bus station at San Félix (can be a dangerous place), frequent minibuses to centre. Bus 0500, 0800, 1900 from Ciudad Guayana to **Santa Elena de Uairén**, US$8.50 with Líneas Orinoco, 0700 at least 12 hrs. (or overnight bus 9 hrs.), via El Callao, **Tumeremo** (US$2.50), El Dorado and Km. 88; book a day in advance. *Por puesto* to **Ciudad Bolívar** US$3.60 (bus US$1.80); to **Maturín** US$3.50, 2½ hrs., 0800 every day (bus US$2.10); to **Caracas**, US$7.20, 10½ hrs. To **Barcelona** and **Puerto La Cruz**, 8 a day; to **Cumaná**, 4 a day. Minibuses in town are fast, frequent and cheap; fare San Félix-Puerto Ordaz, US$0.20-0.30; buses run until about 2100. Taxis San Félix—Puerto Ordaz US$1, Puerto Ordaz—airport US$1.50, airport—bus station US$2.20.

**Air Transport** Airport, with daily flights to Caracas, and twice weekly to Boa Vista, walk 600 metres to main road for buses to San Félix or Puerto Ordaz.

**Excursions**  To Cerro Bolívar mine, take a *por puesto* (US$5.60) or hitchhike to Ciudad Piar, or go with guided tour organized by Ferrominera Orinoco at their headquarters building in Ciudad Guayana. Tours are free, and leave Ciudad Piar at 0900 and 1400. To visit industries in the area, ask at the Corporación Venezolana de Guayana, Departmento de Relaciones Públicas. Boat trips from *Intercontinental*, US$32 for boat (say 12 passengers), or US$8.50 p.p.

From San Félix or Puerto Ordaz go down the Orinoco to Los Castillos (either by *por puesto*, 1 hr., US$1.50, or by bus to Aceiles, US$0.35, ask to be let off where pick-up goes to Los Castillos 0700, 1130, 1530, returns 0830, 1300 and 1700, US$1; difficult to get there by boat). It is possible to camp on the beach. Candes Tours run an excursion from Puerto Ordaz but only if there are four people. There are two old forts here: one on a huge rock near the water, the other on top of a hill and both in good condition. A tiny village lies at their feet. It is said to have been here that Sir Walter Raleigh's son was killed in battle while searching for El Dorado. From Los Barrancos, on the N bank of the Orinoco, opposite San Félix, *curiaras* and other boats can be taken to the delta; settle prices before setting out, take hammock, mosquito net and repellant, and canned food (in the rainy season, take a raincoat).

A most interesting side trip along asphalted roads can be made to the small town of **Tucupita**, with an interesting cathedral, on the Orinoco delta. The climate is very humid and Tucupita often suffers from flooding and subsequent loss of electricity. The cafés on the edge of the plaza are rec. and are said to be "especially interesting at night, without electricity, with your feet virtually awash in the Orinoco." Travellers' cheques only accepted in the Banco Unión.

**Hotels**  *Gran Hotel Amacuro*, Calle Bolívar 23, E, a/c, very good; *Delta*, F, Calle Pativilca 28, a/c, basic; *Victoria*, near Cathedral, F with a/c, cheaper with fan, reasonable; *Pequeño*, Calle La Paz, F, clean, safe, good value; and a few cheaper *hospedajes*. *Pequeña Venezia* campsite, 20 km. from Tucupita, good, with showers; will arrange river trips. Also 1 star hotel and restaurant beside river.

**Restaurants**: *Tucupita*, Calle Bolívar, good; *El Río*, rec.; *Refresquería La Cascada*, Monomo 25, English spoken; *Rincón Criollo*, cheap; *Latinaja*, large portions.

**Transport**  Bus from **San Félix** at 0600 and 1400, *por puesto* 2 hrs., US$3. Flights are also available from Caracas, Anaco, Porlamar and Güiria (US$7) with Aeropostal. Taxi from airport to village US$3. *Por puesto* from **Maturín** or **Ciudad Guayana** about US$6, 2-3 hrs. Tucupita-**Caracas** by bus, 10 hrs., 2000, US$7.20; for **Puerto La Cruz** at 1530, US$4.80, 6 hrs.

For a 3-4 day trip to see the delta, its fauna and the Indians, boats may be arranged by asking for help at the information office near Plaza Bolívar, or contact Juan Carrión (all the taxi drivers know him, but he is very expensive), but they are not easy to come by and are expensive except for large groups. The only recognized tours of the delta are run by Delta Sur, about which poor reports received, US$20 p.p. (it is possible to negotiate). Some boat owners visit hotels in the evenings looking for clients and may negotiate a price, about US$30 per day minimum. Delta trips can be arranged in Puerto Ordaz at Happy Tours, *Hotel Intercontinental*, T (086) 223257/227748, up-market but good. For shorter excursions by boat, ask at gas station (*bomba*) by the river. Excursions often only travel on the main river, not in the *caños* where wildlife can be seen. To avoid disappointment, check all details before committing yourself. Alternatively, take a *por puesto* from Plaza Bolívar to the village of La Horqueta (US$0.50), where it is easier to get a boat and where there are many Indians. Be warned, if the river level rises after a downpour, arrangements may be cancelled. Take enough food for yourselves, the guide and the Indians, and plenty of water. Hammocks and mosquito repellants are essential. . You can buy hammocks and local handicrafts.

An interesting dead-end village is **Barrancas** (2 hotels) on the Orinoco, reached by road from Tucupita, 63 km. (*por puesto* to San Félix US$4) or from Maturín. From Barrancas you can take a boat to Curiapo (Indian village) and Amacuro (near Guyana border), check at the harbour. It is also possible to go to Georgetown from here; ask for boats to Amacuro and then on to Mabaruma (only for the adventurous) or check with the lady at the *librería* on the river at the bottom of the village, she is from Georgetown and travels there occasionally.

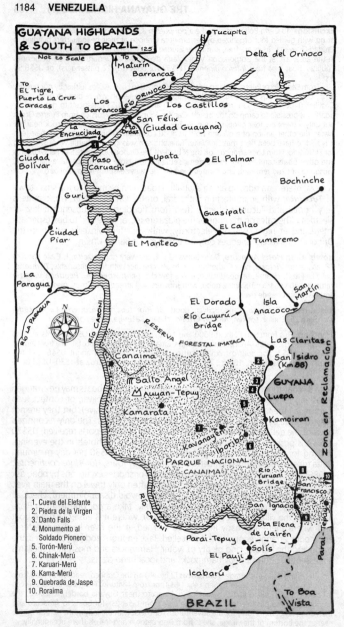

GUAYANA HIGHLANDS
& SOUTH TO BRAZIL
Not to Scale

1. Cueva del Elefante
2. Piedra de la Virgen
3. Danto Falls
4. Monumento al
   Soldado Pionero
5. Torón-Merú
6. Chinak-Merú
7. Karuari-Merú
8. Kama-Merú
9. Quebrada de Jaspe
10. Roraima

Tucupita
Delta del Orinoco
To Maturín
Barrancas
To El Tigre, Puerto La Cruz Caracas
río ORINOCO
Los Barrancos
Los Castillos
San Félix (Ciudad Guayana)
La Encrucijada
Río Ordaz
Ciudad Bolívar
Paso Caruachi
Upata
El Palmar
Bochinche
Guri
Guasipati
El Callao
Ciudad Piar
El Manteco
Tumeremo
La Paragua
RÍO LA PARAGUA
RÍO CARONÍ
N
El Dorado
Río Cuyurú Bridge
Isla Anacoco
San Martín
RESERVA FORESTAL IMATACA
Las Claritas
San Isidro (Km 88)
Canaima
Salto Angel
Auyan-Tepuy
Kamarata
GUAYANA
Luepa
Kamoiran
Zona en Reclamación
Kavanayén
Iboribó
PARQUE NACIONAL CANAIMA
Río Yuruani Bridge
San Francisco
Río Caroní
San Ignacio
Sta Elena de Uairén
Parai-Tepuy
Solís
El Pauji
Icabarú
Parai-Tepuy
To Boa Vista
BRAZIL

## SOUTH TO BRAZIL (8)

The land route to Boa Vista, Brazil, passes over the beautiful Gran Sabana plateau, an ancient land of flat-topped mountains and waterfalls. The road is not difficult until you get to Brazil, or make excursions off it. The trek to Roraima, perhaps Conan Doyle's "Lost World", begins at a point on the highway south.

Travelling South from Ciudad Guayana to the Brazilian border is becoming an increasingly popular excursion for Venezuelan tourists, as well as for overland travellers heading for Manaus and the Amazon. It is no longer an arduous trip; the road to the border at Santa Elena de Uairén is now paved for all but the last 20 km., with all bridges in place. Four-wheel drive is only necessary if one wanders off the main road, particularly in the rainy season. It is forbidden to travel beyond Km. 88 or off the main road without a spare 20 litres of gasoline (spare tanks are available there, but better and cheaper to get one earlier); all petrol pumps have fuel, but not all octane levels. It is also advisable to carry extra water and plenty of food. Camping is possible but a tent with good waterproofing is essential. There are police checks at the Río Cuyuní and at Km. 126, and a military check at San Ignacio de Yuruaní all driving permits, car registration papers, and identification must be shown.

South from Ciudad Guayana Highway 10 is a 4-lane *autopista* as far as Upata (Hotels: *Andrea*\*, E, credit cards accepted, restaurant, good; *Yocoima*, *Adriático*, F, good; *La Palma*, which also has a restaurant; *Comercio*, Calle Ayacucho, F, excellent restaurant; water is rationed in Upata and hot water in hotels is rare S of Ciudad Guayana). From Upata to Km. 88 the road is resurfaced and widened with broad hard shoulders. The rolling savannas become thick lowland forest. 18 km. beyond Guasipati (*Hotel La Reina*, D, a/c, good) is **El Callao** on the S bank of the Río Yuruari, off the highway, surrounded by jungle. It is a small, clean, bright town whose Trinidadian inhabitants add a touch of calypso to its pre-Lenten carnival. A plant reprocesses the old gold mine tailings from El Perú, 8 km. away, but the centre of gold mining has moved to Km. 88 and Las Claritas (see below). Hotels: *Ritz*, F; *Italia*, F, 10 rooms, central, no phone; one restaurant serving beer and greasy chicken.

On another 41 km. is **Tumeremo** (Hotels: *Leocar*, 3 blocks from plaza, F, fair, with shower and toilet, fan, restaurant rec.; *Central*, near plaza, fan, good (but may be "full", try again later); bakery and snackbar, clean, F; *Florida*, E, not too good; restaurant *El Esturión*, good, friendly, Calle El Dorado, Edificio Bolívar; *Restaurante Turístico* expensive but OK, does not serve yucca with everything). There is a chronic water shortage, check when it is available in your hotel. Tumeremo is recommended as the best place to buy provisions, there is Banco de la Unión (Visa), Banco de Orinoco (AmEx, after 1500 US\$5 commission per transaction), and gasoline (all grades) at a normal price (better than El Dorado). 5 km. from Tumeremo towards the Fuerte Tarabay is the beautiful artificial lake of San Pedro with an attractive campsite.

**Bus** to Santa Elena, US\$6.25 (8-10 hrs., Líneas Orinoco, 1100, 2 blocks from plaza near *Leocar*); **El Dorado**, US\$0.80, 1½ hrs.; bus to **Ciudad Bolívar**, US\$3.90, 6 a day, 6½ hrs. or *por puesto* (via San Félix and Puerto Ordaz); bus to San Félix (Ciudad Guayana), US\$2.50, *por puesto* US\$5; bus Tumeremo-Caracas, US\$8.10.

From Tumeremo you can go to the Isla Anacoco, on the Río Venamo which forms the border with Guyana. A paved road runs through the jungle to San Martín (one military and one police post en route), where you can arrange a visit to the island. Much English spoken in San Martín; in a house opposite the water tank are some stuffed animals.

278 km. from Ciudad Guayana and 76 km. from Tumeremo is **El Dorado**, 7 km.

off the road on the Río Cuyuni, a hot, dusty miners' supply centre in dense forest. On an island in the river stands the regional prison made famous by Papillon's stay there in 1945 (take a taxi, can't get in without a car, though even this does not guarantee entry, US$5 for an hour, arrange price with official, not driver, or see if you can travel with soldiers crossing the river to the base). Since the closure of the prison and the exhaustion of the gold seams, El Dorado has relied for its existence mainly on its gas station (open 0800-1900, daily). Exchange at El Dorado is possible with the gold buyer on the main street; cash only, poor rates. Bus from Caracas to El Dorado, Expresos del Oriente, at 1830 daily, US$8.40, 14½ hrs., return at 1400 (925 km.). The Orinoco bus line connects with Ciudad Bolívar (6 hrs.) and Santa Elena, as does Transmundial (better buses, leaving 1100). 4 hrs. to Ciudad Guayana. Boat trips can be taken—12 km. up river to a gold camp, US$15.

**Hotels** *San Antonio*, Edif. Ceferino, next to bus stop, E, fan, clean; *El Dorado, Hotel and Tourist Camp*, at confluence of Chicanán and Cuyuni rivers, run by Richard Sidney Coles (speaks English and German), 6 rooms, E-F, on own beach, basic, may be persuaded to arrange river journeys for groups; *Mirador*, F, basic, clean; *Alfonso*, quite good, will make excursions to the mines; *San Agostino*, main plaza; *Hospedaje Portugal*, F, only six rooms, the Portuguese owner also runs the store next door. **Restaurants**: *El Minero*; *La Brasa*, good.

6 km. south of the turnoff to El Dorado, is the Río Cuyuni: distances further south are measured from the bridge. From here it is possible to take boat trips to the gold mines, e.g. Payapal 1 hr. 40 mins. each way, US$6. At Km. 67 there is said to be a trail that leads to Guyana. The forest again gives way to scrub; the roadside is dotted with tiny Indian villages—San Miguel de Betania, Araimatepui—and subsistence level farms. At Km. 83, is Barquilla de Fresa, where tropical fish are bred (Henry Cleve speaks English and German, accommodation in bunk beds, plus food, US$40 per day, trails for hiking). From Km. 85 it's a ½-hr. drive (US$3 by jeep) to the nearest gold-digging village, Las Claritas (small hotel, restaurant; big market for food and gold; safe parking at Las Hermanitas de las Pobres Convent), which can be better reached by the track from Km. 88. This, and other settlements like it, is built out of oil cans and other rubbish, but complete with hotels, restaurants, small shops, hairdressers, brothels, etc. The miners guard their claims and diggings jealously, best to go with a guide or friendly local.

At Km. 88 (also called San Isidro), there is gasoline (rarely 92 octane—the last before Santa Elena), a garage, a number of eating places and hotels: *La Pilonera*, opp. Vargas store, F with fan, some rooms with bath, restaurant with good fruit drinks, very friendly; *El Parador del Vía*, with restaurant, O.K. Everything is expensive. Gold is sold here; ask Francisco Vargas at the grocery store and restaurant. Bus Km. 88-Caracas, US$7.50. Frequent *por puestos* from El Dorado to Km. 88, 1 hr., US$2. The only reliable public transport out of Km. 88 is the bus from Ciudad Bolívar, which stops at Vargas store at 1400 daily, 6 hrs. to Santa Elena, US$3.25; the alternative is to get a ride with passing jeeps and trucks (very little passes after 1030). The wall of the Gran Sabana looms above Km. 88 and the highway climbs steeply in sharp curves for 40 km. before reaching the top; much of this must be done in first gear, but the road is in very good condition and presents no problem for conventional cars. 4WD may be better in the wet season (May-Oct.). At Km. 100 the huge, black Piedra de la Virgen is passed before the steepest climb (La Escalera) enters the beautiful **Canaima National Park** (30,000 sq km.) one of the six largest parks in the world—to venture off the highway into the park, a permit must be obtained from Inparques. Good views 100 m. W of the road at Km. 102.

Characteristic of this area are the large abrupt *tepuis* (flattopped mountains or *mesas*), hundreds of waterfalls, and the silence of one of the oldest plateaus on earth. The landscape is essentially savanna, with clusters of trees, moriche palms and bromeliads; there is plenty of firewood and few terrors should you wish to spend a night under the stars, but nights are very cool. At Km. 123 a short trail leads to the 40-metre Danto ('Tapir') Falls, a powerful fall wreathed in mosses and mist. If you are paying for your ride, try to persuade the driver to make a short stop; the falls are close to the road (about 5 mins. slippery walk), but not visible from it. On the E is Cerro Venamo, a cornerstone of the Guyana border only a short distance away. Further fine views at Km. 133. The Monumento al Soldado Pionero (Km. 141) commemorates the army engineers who built the road up from the lowlands, finally opened in 1973. 4 km. beyond is Luepa, whose fort is the HQ of the 'General Mario Montilla' Jungle Batallion (who maintain the road); all travellers must stop at the *ciudadela* (military checkpoint) a little way S. There is a popular camping place at Luepa, on the right going S: ask permission

at the fort.
    At Km. 102 to the west of the road, about 100 m., are fine views across the country.

8 km. beyond Luepa, a graded gravel road leads 70 km. W to **Kavanayén** (little traffic, best to have your own vehicle, preferably 4WD). Off this road after 25 km. are the falls of Torón Merú (17 km.) and, further on, a left turn to the falls of Chinak-Merú, 100 metres high and very impressive (take the trail to the Río Aponguao and the Pemón Indian village of Iboribó, tip someone to ferry you across the river and walk 30 mins. to the falls; 30-min. boat trips to the falls cost US$15; this trip is reported not to be possible by normal car, take great care near the falls. 18 km. before Kavanayén is a rough road to the *Hotel Chivaton*, E, good beds but icy water, no food, very isolated. Kavanayén is the site of a Franciscan mission, founded in 1943, accommodation at the mission G, no food but one of the two grocery stores will prepare food. Medical post near the airstrip (bargain with pilots to fly you over the Gran Sabana). The settlement is surrounded by *tepuis*. Beyond Kavanayén a beautiful but risky trail (18 km., 5 hrs. walk) leads along flat-topped mountains to the Karuari-Merú Falls (good swimming in the pool below). Ask in the mission for information on boat trips and the trail W to Kamarata (see under Angel Falls, above). Although considered impassable for vehicles, there are a few 4 x 4s in Kamarata.

For the remaining 180 km. to Santa Elena de Uairén few people and only a handful of Pemón Indian villages are to be seen. Kampirán, Kamoirán (Km. 176, restaurant, rooms to let, gasoline) and Oriwarai are passed. The impressive falls at the Kama river should not be missed (Km. 211); there is also a small lake, possible to camp, Indian handicrafts for sale. At Km. 249 is the Río Yuruaní (ferry crossing free 0600-1800) in the Quebrada Pacheco, full of splendid waterfalls; a 15-minute hike to the Yuruaní waterfall leaves the main road 250 metres after the crossing, turn left. Then comes the Pemón village of San Francisco de Yuruaní **(see page 1189)**, followed, 9 km. of bends later, by the larger village of San Ignacio de Yuruaní (military checkpoint; excellent regional food). As the highway crosses a wide plain, Kukenaam and Roraima (the more southerly of the two) may be seen to the E on a clear day. A trail at Km. 289 leads to the Quebrada de Jaspe where a river cuts through striated cliffs and pieces of jasper glitter on the banks (don't take them home to glitter on your shelf). About 30 km. from San Francisco the highway begins to descend until, at the Río Cuquenen, it leaves Canaima National Park and runs the last few km. to Santa Elena, 642 km. from Ciudad Guayana.

**Santa Elena de Uairén** is a growing, pleasant frontier town, established by Capuchin monks in 1931. The festival of Santa Elena, 9-19 August, features music, dance and handicrafts. If the service station is dry, ask for Sr. Lucca who sells gasoline out of barrels. Grocery store: *Tienda Mixta El Gordito*, English and French spoken. Passports and car documents must be stamped here if leaving or entering the country; the immigration office is on the north edge of the town on a hill opposite the Corpovén gas station (open 0700-1700 except Sun., and holidays). If shut, go to No. 26, uphill from gas station and ask for help. CANTV phone office for international calls, but not all day (closed for repair Dec. 90).

**Hotels and Restaurants**  Accommodation is often difficult to find because of visiting mine workers and Brazilian shoppers. *Fronteras\**, E with bath, clean, quiet, comfortable, rec., good restaurant; *Hospedaje Uairén*, E, good, clean, rec.; *Hospedaje Roraima*, noisy, mosquitoes, not rec.; new *Luz*, E, bath, clean, friendly, rec., if hotel's full owner will help to find a room in a private home; *Cantaima*, on outskirts, new, clean, spacious rooms, rec.; *Tres Naciones*, F; *Cabañas Familiares Friedeman*, English and German spoken; *Yarimá*, F, rec., good food; *Aurantepuy*, opp. Ciudad Bolívar bus stop, F with bath (cheaper rooms available), basic, not rec.; *Mini Hospedaje*, F, 2 blocks from *Fronteras*, clean, basic, friendly, some rooms with private shower; *Hospedaje La Rica*, F, very clean, hot water, good value; *Tropical*, E, hot water, modern, good restaurant next door, five minutes' walk from town. Opposite airport, rooms to let at Sergio's *granja*, friendly, cheap. 2 good restaurants on S side of town, *3 Vs* and a *Lonchería*, within a block of each other; *La Perla*, good grill; *Roraima*, good. Rooms are difficult to find during the fiesta (if stuck, ask for Charlie at the *Hotel Fronteras*, he may be able to find you somewhere else to stay, or hang your hammock in one of the *hospedajes* for US$2-3).

**Exchange** The bank does not change money—instead try the shops in the centre, e.g. the gold shop S of main plaza, which changes travellers' cheques, the grocery store *El Gordito*, *Hotel Fronteras*, or *Hotel Tres Naciones*. Generally the rates are poor (check with travellers going in opposite direction what rates should be); to obtain better rates you must wait until Ciudad Guayana, or Boa Vista if going to Brazil (change some money into cruzeiros before the bus leaves).

For excursions into the Gran Sabana contact Willy or Carol at *Hospedaje Uairén*; take food, water, warm clothing and insect repellant. Alternatively, ask for Frank, or Runge and Irene. The owner of the *Luz Hotel*, Roberto Fuenmayor Quintero, arranges 2-day tours in his own vehicle, max. 8 passengers, costing US$100 per day, or US$50 p.p. inc. food, drink and accommodation, highly rec., also arranges tours to Roraima.

An office nr. *Hotel Uairén* dispenses malaria tablets during office hours, Mon.-Fri. Yellow fever inoculations are not available.

**Mechanic** Antonio Mejías, good, cheap, a miracle-worker.

Leaving by private car may involve a bit of a run-around, up to 2 hrs. **N.B.** If you need a visa for Brazil (check Brazil **Information for Visitors**), don't leave it until Santa Elena, it can take 2 weeks to get there. The new road to Brazil links Caracas with Manaus in three days if you drive hard. The Brazilian section has been described as "that rutted track which has no business being called a road." Be prepared.

**Transport to and from Santa Elena** All regular transport appears to call at the Immigration office when leaving Santa Elena. There is a daily bus to **Boa Vista** (Brazil) at about 0700 (Sunday 1330) from *Hotel Fronteras*, 6 hrs., US$12 (cheaper in cruzeiros; money changers on buses). From **Caracas** it is best to go to **Ciudad Bolívar** and take either the Expreso Brazil-Venezuela bus direct to Boa Vista, or the Línea Orinoco bus straight through to Santa Elena, US$8-11, 11-14 hrs., returns from Santa Elena at 1600, take food. Alternatively take a daily bus to Tumeremo or El Dorado; Transmundial runs from **Tumeremo** to Santa Elena (US$6.25) and from **El Dorado** (US$4, 6 hrs.), returning from Santa Elena at 0830. From Tumeremo you can get a bus to San Félix (Ciudad Guayana), 4 hrs., or colectivo to Maturín, 2 hrs., but Líneas Orinoco go direct, day and night, Santa Elena-**Ciudad Guayana** (US$8.50, 12-13 hrs.), or Expreso Maturín goes to Ciudad Guayana and Maturín daily. Aereotuy has daily flights by Twin Otter, 1000, US$52, to Ciudad Bolívar, standby basis only on Sundays; sometimes stops at Indian villages. On Wednesdays there is an interesting flight available to Tumeremo via Icabarú and the Indian villages of Uriman, Wonkin, and Kamarata. Book a week in advance. Airport, 10 km. from town. It is possible to take a day trip into Brazil if you leave your passport at the border post, but nothing much to see.

120 km. W of Santa Elena is Icabarú, a diamond-producing centre with few facilities, where prices are understandably high. The road leaves the highway 8 km. S of Santa Elena and after passing through a tunnel of jungle vegetation emerges onto rolling savannas dotted with *tepuis*. The road is in terrible condition: conventional cars and pick-ups will get no more than 30 km., 4WD only as far as El Pauji. Flying is the only alternative. At Km. 58 is a Guardia Nacional checkpoint at Paraitepuí, with a waterfall nearby. At Km. 68 is Shailili-ko camp, English, Italian and French spoken, rec. 17 km. further is *El Pauji*, an agricultural settlement with a number of foreign residents (US$10 by jeep—if full, if not, cost increased—from Santa Elena, 0600, 3 hrs.; ask in Santa Elena for possibility of a lift with families returning after buying supplies). Ask for Luigi, an Italian at El Cajón mine (he speaks English). It is in a lovely area, with good walking and bird-watching. A good walk is to the small hill, 2 km. from El Pauji beyond the airfield; views from the crest into El Abismo, a huge valley.
  In El Pauji, Danielle operates *El Caminante* tourist camp, just after the bridge, coming from Santa Elena, F p.p., helpful and friendly, camping, trips arranged, restaurant; in the village is the *hospedaje* of Mariella, near the airstrip and small store, cabins E, bath, clean; *Hospedaje Karaware*, run by Nelson and Elizabeth, F, helpful, friendly; *Alojamiento Weimore*, on the other side of the bridge from Danielle's camp, F, has owner-designed space-age accommodation, peaceful, good food, natural pool; *Hospedaje Chimahtá*; just before the bridge is *El Merendero* restaurant. At *La Bodega* general store, Victoriano has information on guides for tourists. Jeep hire in El Pauji, US$50 per day. 15 km. from El Pauji, at Solís, Arquimedes and Philippe have a tourist camp; they organize tours. 25 km. from the town is the *Canta Rana* tourist camp with basic accommodation (owners, Alfonso and Barbara Borrero, speak German, English and Spanish); waterfall and lovely surroundings; they have a private plane that collects people from Puerto Ordaz (T 086-22-68-51 or 22-07-09, Sr. Haissan Al Atrache). Flight El Pauji to Ciudad Bolívar, US$50.

*Mount Roraima* An exciting trip is to walk to Mt. Roraima (2,810 metres), which it has been suggested was the **"Lost World"** made famous by Arthur Conan Doyle's novel (although conflicting evidence points to the Brazilian Serra Ricardo Franco near the Bolivian border west of Cuiabá as the site). Supplies for a week or more should be bought in Santa Elena or San Francisco de Yuruaní, but cheaper and better to bring food from Ciudad Bolívar on the way up to the Gran Sabana. The jumping-off point is the concrete and corrugated iron Indian village of *San Francisco de Yuruaní*, 60 km. N of Santa Elena and 9 km. N of the San Ignacio military checkpoint (at which you are required to register—one report says that Roraima is officially closed, so don't state it as your destination). Buses from Santa Elena will let you off here; jeeps may be negotiated with prices varying between US$2.50 and US$5.50. Meals are available, the grocery store sells canned goods and Coca Cola. Guides in San Francisco charge about US$15-19 a day, more if they carry your supplies: Basílio is highly rec. though Carmelo is also good. The track to Paraitepuí, the nearest village to the mountain, leaves the highway a kilometre S of San Francisco; it is unsigned but easily seen. The badly eroded road winds across open savanna with patches of forest in the river valleys; bear right at the major fork, the other track goes to Chirimata (jeep San Francisco-Paraitepuí US$31, set rate; the 25 km. can be walked in 7 hrs). In Paraitepuí, the *cacique* greets visitors; he may provide a hut and will try to insist on providing guides; decline politely or, if requiring one, bring extra food for him; there are few supplies available here. The Ayuso brothers are the best-known guides (about US$55 for 5 days). The villagers speak Tauripen, the local dialect, but not Spanish.

The foot trail winds back and forth on a more direct line than the little-used jeep track; it is comparatively straightforward and adequately marked descending from the heights just past Paraitepuí across rolling hills and numerous clear streams. The goal, Roraima, is the mountain on the right, the other massive outcrop on the left is Mata Hui (known as Kukenaam after the river which rises within it). If leaving the village early enough in the day, you may reach the Río Cuquenan crossing early afternoon; this river floods quickly after rain, the bottom is slippery and the current swift; take a 50m. rope if not going with a party and be prepared to get wet (good camping here, you can swim in the many pools). Three hours' walk brings you to a lovely bird-filled meadow below the foothills of the massif, another perfect camping spot known as *campamento abajo*. The footpath now climbs steadily upwards through the cloud forest at the mountain's base and becomes an unpleasant scramble over tree trunks and damp rocks until the cliff is reached. From here it is possible to ascend to the plateau along the "easy" rock ledge which is the only route to the top. It is quite broad and supports much vegetation; it manoeuvres around three spurs, drops sharply in places, and passes under an icy waterfall before heading steeply and directly to the summit. Walkers in good health should take about 4 hrs. from the meadow to the top. The vistas across the Gran Sabana are magnificent, and the summit is an eerie world of stone and water, difficult to move around easily. There are not many good spots to camp; best is *El Hotel*—a sandy patch under an overhanging ledge—to which red painted arrows lead the way to the right after reaching the summit. From *El Hotel* a marked track leads to the survey pillar near the E cliff where Guyana, Brazil and Venezuela meet; allow a day as the track is very rough. Full camping equipment including stove is essential (an igloo-type tent is best for the summit), wear thick socks and boots to protect legs from snakes, also essential are warm clothes for the summit (much mist, rain squalls and lightning at night: beware) and effective insect repellant—biting *plaga* infest the grasslands. The whole trip can take anywhere between five days and two weeks; if you don't wish to camp on the summit, a trip to the top and return can be done in a day, but keep an eye on weather conditions. A cloud belt usually wells up around the massif after dawn and often remains all day to blot out Roraima, even though the summit may remain clear. Litter is beginning to appear along the trail; please take care of the environment.

**N.B.** The dry season for trekking is Dec.-Feb. **Note also** that the National Guard requires you to have a guide beyond Paratepuí. There seems to be no enforcement of this and while some feel a guide is unnecessary, others have found them of great assistance for the hike's final stages and for showing dry cliff overhangs.

---

## INFORMATION FOR VISITORS

**Documents** Entry is by passport and visa (normally valid for 3 entries), or by passport and tourist card. Tourist cards (*tarjetas de ingreso*) are valid only for those entering by air and are issued by most airlines to visitors from 25 countries including the USA, Canada, Japan and all Western European countries except

Spain and Portugal. They are valid for 60 days with, theoretically, 2 extensions of 30 days each permissible, at a cost of US$40 each. DIEX offices in many cities do not offer extensions—best to go to DIEX in Caracas, take passport, photograph and return ticket. If you enter the country overland, you will be required to obtain a visa from a Venezuelan consulate prior to arrival. Visas cost US$10 (£6 in UK), but US$3 to US citizens; you will need your passport, return ticket and letter of reference from your employer and bank. You must fill in an application form and the visa will take about three working days to come through, sometimes longer if authorization has to come from Venezuela. It appears that you cannot get a visa in advance in the USA or Canada, so to apply for an overland visa in Colombia or Brazil you need: passport, one photo and an onward ticket. A tourist card issued by Viasa in Bogotá is only valid for arriving in Caracas by air from Bogotá, not if you travel overland. To extend a visa for one month, in any city, costs about US$25 (passport photo needed); it is best to leave the country (e.g. to Curaçao) and get a new one free. To change a tourist visa to a business visa, to obtain or to extend the latter, costs US$50 (£31 in UK). Tourist visas are multiple entry within their specified period. Transit passengers to another country can stay only 72 hrs.

**N.B.** Carry your passport with you all the time you are in Venezuela as the police are increasing spot checks and anyone found without identification is immediately detained (carrying a certified copy for greater safety is permissible, though not always accepted by officials). A press card as identification is reported to work wonders. Border searches are very thorough.

Information for business visitors is given in "Hints to Exporters: Venezuela", issued by the Export Services Division, Dept. of Trade, Sanctuary Buildings, 16-20 Great Smith Street, London SW1. Businessmen on short visits are strongly advised to enter the country as tourists, otherwise they will have to obtain a tax clearance certificate (*solvencia*) before they can leave.

**Taxes**  All non-tourists leaving the country, except nationals of Denmark and transit passengers, must pay US$10 (approx.), Bs. 500 at the airport or port of embarkation (payable in bolívares only). At Caracas airport this procedure is split between two desks; the form, or parts of it, may be required for up to 3 separate checks. Minors under 12 years of age do not pay the exit tax. There is also an airport tax of US$0.80 for those passengers on internal flights. Exit stamps for overland travellers, US$0.60.

**Travel by Air from UK and Europe**  British Airways and Viasa fly from London to Simón Bolívar, the international airport for Caracas, the former twice a week direct. Viasa fly via Paris, and Paris and Porlamar. Viasa also serves Amsterdam, Frankfurt, Madrid, Milan, Porto, Rome, Santiago de Compostela and Zurich. The cheapest route from Europe is with Air Portugal from Lisbon to Caracas. There are also services from Europe by Air France, KLM, Iberia, Alitalia, Lufthansa, Swissair and Avianca. Iberia has a weekly service to Tenerife, Canary Islands, from where connections can be made to various North and West African countries.

**From North America**  By air, passengers may reach Venezuela by Pan American, (Miami, New York, San Francisco), American Airlines (New York, Orlando, Miami), Viasa (Houston, Miami, New York), and Avensa (Miami, New York, also). Viasa and Air Canada fly to Toronto; there are also many charters at holiday times.

**From Colombia**  There are direct flights by Viasa and Avianca.

**From Argentina, Brazil and Bolivia**  There are direct air services by Viasa, LAB, Aerolíneas Argentinas and Varig.

**Others**  Lacsa flies from San José (Costa Rica), Panama and Barranquilla (Colombia) to Caracas. Aeropostal has services to Port of Spain (5 times a week from Caracas). BWIA flies the same route 2 times a week, and Pan Am daily. **Difficulties have been reported in entering Trinidad** unless with a UK, US or Canadian passport. LIAT (once a week) and Aeropostal (twice) fly to Bridgetown,

Barbados; Aeropostal also to Martinique and Guadeloupe; Viasa and Aeropostal twice a week each to Havana (Viasa's outward flights London-Caracas connect with this service—see also Ideal Tours, Caracas **Travel Agents**); Aeropostal twice a week to Havana. There is direct air service from Chile (Viasa and LAN Chile both have 2 weekly flights; connections can also be made via Bogotá on Avianca), Peru (Aero Perú and Viasa—Viasa tickets purchased in Peru should be checked most carefully), Ecuador (Ecuatoriana and Viasa—to Quito and Guayaquil), Santo Domingo (Viasa, Avensa), Puerto Rico (American, Aeropostal), Curaçao (ALM, Air Aruba, Aeropostal, Servivensa), Aruba (Air Aruba, Avensa, Aeropostal and Viasa; Air Aruba flights cheaper from Las Piedras, **see page 1144** than from Caracas).

International **road** connections are given in the text. **Shipping** routes are given in the Introduction and Hints, apart from those with Curaçao and Aruba, which can be found in the text under Coro.

**Shipping a car from the USA** From Miami to Maracaibo: Venezuelan Line (agent Oceanic Steamship Co.—rec.) and Delta Line, fare is less Maracaibo-Miami; no passengers. From New Orleans: Delta Line, passengers carried, but very expensive. Alternatively, agent Hansen and Tiedemann charges same price as Delta for vehicle, but you can accompany it at much lower cost (5 days, including meals). Also recommended: Coordinadora del Caribe Transmodal C.A. (CCT) Calle Veracruz, Ed. Torreón, Piso 7, Las Mercedes, Caracas, T 92-71-33. Also Seaboard Marine, agent in Venezuela, Conavén; their route is advertised as La Guaira-Miami, but actually goes to West Palm Beach, 80 miles North of Miami; almost impossible to travel with your vehicle. Vencaribe (shipping) agent is Taurel y cía, Edif. Taurel, Calle Cují a Romualdo No. 69, Apto. de Correos 1592, Caracas; representative is Sonigar on 3rd floor, but Paul Paulheim on 1st floor is helpful. In port of La Guaira Taurel is on main street, just ask; Johnny Hilahl is the representative, but Wendy the receptionist and Bobby Momighan are also helpful, all speak English. Taurel's shipping department is called "vapores". A recommended agent for importing a vehicle is Sr. Freddy Diz, T (031) 22028; for unpacking a containerized vehicle, Sr. Gustavo Contreras V., Transporte Gusconval, T (Radio) 02-661-9222, or (031) 943901.

**Shipping a vehicle from Europe** Harms Hamburg of Bremerhaven ship a car in a container for US$4,100 plus port handling to Venezuela.

On arrival in Venezuela (La Guaira), you must go to the Tourism Department at Simón Bolívar airport where you must obtain a document identifying your car (take photocopies of driving licence, passport, car documents and bill of lading). With this you can get your car out of the port: a shipping agent is not necessary, though knowledge of Spanish is useful. Go then to Aduanas Marítimas at the port with your bill of lading, ownership documents and passport, and 5 hours to spare. They stop for lunch 1200-1300 and close at weekends.

**Customs** You may bring into Venezuela, free of duty, 25 cigars and 200 cigarettes, 2 litres of alcoholic drinks, 4 small bottles of perfume, and gifts at the inspector's discretion.

**Air Services** Most places of importance are served by Avensa (private) and/or Aeropostal (government-owned, both heavily overbooked always). Aeropostal and Avensa also have international service (Viasa does not have domestic services). Both internal airlines offer special family discounts and student discount but practice is variable, photocopies of ISTC card are useful as it allows officials to staple one to the ticket. Beware of overbooking during holiday time, especially at Caracas airport; it is recommended that you check in two hours before departure, particularly at Easter. Internal night-time flights are scarce, and there is no late hour discount. If you travel with Viasa or any other airline for which Viasa is agent, it is possible to check in the day before flying out of Caracas by taking baggage, ticket and passport to their office at Centro Comercial Tamanaco, Nivel C.2, "Predespacho", between 1500 and 2100 (cost US$0.40); take bus from Chacaíto. To avoid overbooking the Government now obliges airlines to post a passenger list, but it is important to obtain clear instructions from the travel agent regarding confirmation of your flight and checking-in time. Passengers leaving Caracas on international flights must reconfirm their reservations not less than 72 hours in advance; it is safer to do so in person than by telephone; not less than 24 hours for national flights (if you fail to do this, you lose all rights to free accommodation, food, transport, etc. if your flight is cancelled and may lose your seat if the plane is fully booked). Beware of counterfeit tickets; buy only from agencies. If told by an agent that a flight is fully booked, try at the airport anyway. International passengers must check in two hours before departure or they may lose their seat to someone on a waiting list. Read carefully any notice you see posted with the relevant instructions. Handling charge for your luggage US$0.50. All flights are subject to delays or cancellation. Avensa operates an air-pass system, open only to non-residents and purchasable only outside Venezuela: unlimited travel for 21 days for US$139. Passengers are issued with an MCO (Miscellaneous Charges Order) in the country of purchase, this is exchanged in Caracas at Pasajes Avensa, Esq. El Conde, 1 block W of Plaza Bolívar. At the same time ask for a timetable of all Avensa flights. (In view of the cheapness of internal flights and the good bus services, the pass may not be worth buying). For independent charter flights try Rudi González at Carlota airport.

**Motoring** A tourist can bring in his/her car without paying duty, and the only documentation required is a visa for overland entry (this is necessary despite what Consulates may tell you). An entry permit for a car costs US$10 and requires one photograph (takes 24 hrs.); ask for a permit for 6 months, or unspecified time. **See also page 1157.** For vehicles with Venezuelan registration leaving Venezuela the following documents are required: an Automóvil passport book from the Touring y Automóvil Club de Venezuela, Apartado 68102, Centro Integral Santa Rosa, Locales 11 y 12, Calle A, Av. Principal, Santa Rosa de Lima, Caracas, T 914879; the original car papers; the registration document; a police *revisión* obtained from the Policía Técnica Judicial; and a temporary import/export licence for a vehicle obtainable from the Ministerio de Hacienda, Caracas, or from a customs agent in San Antonio de Táchira (border town) for about US$100. The export/import licence and the passport book must be signed and stamped by the Customs Administrator. In the border area with Colombia, police checks are frequent; make sure you have all your papers. If possible, check all details on bringing in/taking out a car in advance. For third party insurance contact Sra. Joaqui I. de Castaneda (Corredor de Seguros), Av. Andrés Bello y Av. El Parque. Edif. Oficentro, piso 6, San Bernardino, Caracas, T (02) 575-2522/574-6111.

All visitors to Venezuela can drive if they are over 18 and have a valid driving licence from their own country. It is a good idea to hire a car (**see page 1129**); many of the best places are off the beaten track. Some companies such as National have a wide network of offices in towns and airports allowing a fly-drive approach to travel, using a number of different vehicles. Car hire with insurance around US$300 per week. Deals are often available—try asking for the oil company personnel price list. If planning to hire a car for any length of time it is worth the trouble to obtain a *licencia temporal para conducir*; for this you require a medical certificate (eye examination, blood pressure, US$2, issued by an authorised medical centre, try Torre Phelps, Plaza Venezuela, Caracas), photocopy of your home driver's licence and two black-and-white passport photos which must be presented at the Ministerio de Transporte y Comunicaciones, Torre Este, Parque Central, Dep. Licencias. If you have an accident and someone is injured, you will be detained as a matter of routine, even if you are not at fault. Do not drive at night if you can help it (if you do have to, don't drive fast). Carry insect spray if you do; if you stop and get out, the car will fill with biting insects. Self drive tours are now being marketed.

In 1982 a nationwide speed limit of 80 k.p.h. was imposed. The roads in Venezuela are very good, all major routes are fully paved and even the dirt and gravel roads are reliable. Motoring restrictions in Caracas include a ban on parking in front of a bank; motorcycles may not be driven at night; pillion passengers may not be carried on motorcycles if of the same sex as the driver. You are more likely to be penalized for infringing these rules than for driving through a red light; they are designed to improve security for banks and pedestrians. In addition, motorcyclists are obliged to wear a crash helmet but it must not be of a type which obscures the face.

There are 5 grades of gasoline: "normal", 83 octane (Bs.2.70 a litre); 87 octane (Bs.2.62 a litre); 89 octane (Bs.2.65 a litre); 91 octane (Bs.2.83 a litre); and "alta", 95 octane (Bs.3 a litre). Diesel is hard to find, for example only one station in Caracas sells it; ask around. Service stations are open 0500-2100, Mon.-Sat., except those on highways which are open longer hours. Only those designated to handle emergencies are open on Sun. In the event of breakdown, Venezuelans are usually very helpful. There are many garages, even in rural areas; service charges are not high, but being able to speak Spanish will greatly assist in sorting out problems. Carry spare battery water, fan belts, the obligatory breakdown triangle, a jack and spanners. Some cars have a security device to prevent the engine being started and this is recommended. **Warning** There is an automatic US$20 fine for running out of fuel. See **Tourist Information** under Caracas, and **Maps**, below.

**Road Transport** There are excellent (but slow) bus services between the major cities, but the colectivo taxis and minibuses, known in Venezuela as *por puesto*, seem to monopolize transport to and from smaller towns and villages. They may be reluctant to take luggage and the ill-kempt. Outside Caracas, town taxis are relatively expensive. If possible check the bus before getting a ticket. At peak periods *revendedores* (touts) will try to sell tickets at 2-3 times face value.

**Railways** The only passenger traffic of any importance is on the Barquisimeto to Puerto Cabello line. The 110-km. Yaritagua-Acarigua-Turén electric railway line was opened at the beginning of 1983, intended mostly to transport agricultural products. It appears that passengers are now being carried on the Acarigua-Yaritagua stretch.

**Rivers** In Amazonia wait at the police posts where boats are obliged to report.

**Hitch-Hiking** (*Cola*) is not very easy but the Venezuelans are usually friendly and helpful if you know some Spanish. The best places to try are Guardia Nacional posts outside cities (may get free bus rides from them). It is illegal on toll roads and, theoretically, for non-family members in the back of pick up trucks.

**Hotel Reservations** Fairmont International (**see page 1127**) will book hotel rooms both in Caracas and in other towns, where they have 102 hotels on their books, not all of which are mentioned in these pages. Hotels marked with an asterisk (*) are bookable through Fairmont. Officially controlled prices exist for one-star and two star hotels. In 1988 a 10% tourist tax was added to hotel prices, not for the benefit of hoteliers but for the construction and maintenance of tourist amenities.

**Camping** Equipment, perhaps not of the highest standard, is available at sports-goods shops in Caracas. It is impossible, in fact illegal, to refill portable gas cylinders. Cylinders are sold at Deportes el Llanero, Caracas, T 545 1634. Camping in Venezuela is a popular recreation, for spending a weekend at the beach, on the islands, in the *llanos* and in the mountains. (People pitch their tents on Monte Avila, overlooking Caracas.) Camping is not however used by travellers as a substitute for hotels on the main highways, and no special camp sites are yet provided for this purpose. Wild camping is much easier with a car than with just a tent. If camping on the beach, for the sake of security, pitch your tent close to others, even though they play their radios loud. For information on hiking, climbing and relevant equipment, telephone Alexander on (02)573-00-56 (Spanish only).

**Food** Both in Caracas and to a lesser extent in Maracaibo there are excellent restaurants specializing in foreign regional cuisines. There is excellent local fish (we recommend *pargo* or red snapper), crayfish, small oysters and prawns, though sole, trout and large oysters are imported. Sometimes there is turtle, though it is a protected species. For those without a conservationist conscience, turtle may appear on menus in the Peninsula de Paraguaná as *ropa especial*. The *Tarzilandia* restaurant in Caracas also serves it. Of true Venezuelan food there is *sancocho* (a stew of vegetables, especially yuca, with meat, chicken or fish); *arepas*, a kind of white maize bread, very bland in flavour; toasted *arepas* served with a wide selection of relishes, fillings or the local somewhat salty white cheese are cheap, filling and nutritious; *cachapas*, a maize pancake (soft, not hard like Mexican *tortillas*) wrapped around white cheese; *pabellón*, made of shredded meat, beans, rice and fried plantains; and *empanadas*, maize-flour pies containing cheese, meat or fish. At Christmas only there are *hallacas*, maize pancakes stuffed with chicken, pork, olives, etc. boiled in a plantain leaf (but don't eat the leaf). The nearest thing to a boiled egg in most places is a *huevo tibio*. It comes without the shell because there are no eggcups. A *muchacho* (boy) on the menu is not a sign of cannibalism; it is a cut of beef. *Ganso* is also not goose but beef. *Solomo* and *lomito* are other cuts of beef. *Hervido* is chicken or beef with vegetables. *Contorno* with a meat or fish dish is a choice of fried chips, boiled potatoes, rice or yuca. *Caraotas* are beans; *cachitos* are *croissants* of bread. *Pasticho* is what the Venezuelans call Italian *lasagne*. The main fruits are bananas, oranges, grapefruit, mangoes, pineapple and pawpaws. N.B. Some Venezuelan variants of names for fruit: *lechosa* is papaya, *patilla* water melon, *parchita* passion fruit, and *cambur* a small banana. Excellent strawberries are grown at Colonia Tovar, 90 minutes from Caracas. A delicious sweet is *huevos chimbos*—egg yolk boiled and bottled in sugar syrup. The Caracas *Daily Journal* (in English) lists many reliable restaurants in Caracas and Maracaibo. Venezuelans dine late.

**Drink** There is no good local wine though some foreign wines are bottled locally. Local wine is used only in cooking or in *sangría*. Liqueurs are cheap, try the local *ponche crema*. There are four good local beers: Polar (the most popular), Regional (with a strong flavour of hops), Cardenal and Nacional (a *lisa* is a glass of keg beer; for a bottle of beer ask for a *tercio*), mineral waters, gin and excellent rum. The coffee is very good (*café con leche* has a lot of milk, *café marrón* much less, *cafe negro* for black coffee, which, though obvious, is not common in the rest of Latin America); visitors should also try a *merengada*, a delicious drink made from fruit pulp, ice, milk and sugar; a *batido* is the same but with water, not milk. A *plus-café* is an after-dinner liqueur. Water is free in all restaurants even if no food is bought. Bottled water in *cervecerías* is often from the tap; no deception is intended, bottles are simply used as convenient jugs. Insist on seeing the bottle opened if you do not want a mouthful of chlorine with your whisky. *Chicha de arroz* is a sweet drink made of milk, rice starch, sugar and vanilla; fruit juices are very good. Gin and rum at about US$2 and coffee beans at US$1.50 per kilo are good buys.

**Tipping** Taxi drivers are tipped if the taxi has a meter (hardly anywhere), but not if you have agreed the fare in advance. Usherettes are not tipped. Hotel porters, Bs.2; airport porters Bs.2 per piece of baggage. Restaurants, between 5 and 10% of bill.

**Shopping** Goods in shops bear a label "PVP" followed by the price. This is the maximum authorized price; you may be able to negotiate a discount but should never pay more than the PVP price.

**Security** In the cities, take the usual precautions to protect your valuables and belongings, but in addition, carry handbags, cameras etc. on the side away from the street as motor-cycle purse-snatchers are notorious, especially in Caracas. Hotel thefts are becoming more frequent.

**Health** Conditions are good. Water in all main towns is heavily chlorinated, so safe to drink, although most people drink bottled water. Medical attention is good. State health care is free and said to be good (the Clínica Metropolitana in Caracas has been recommended). Some rivers are infected with bilharzia and in some areas there are warning signs; check before bathing. Inoculation against typhoid and yellow fever, and protection against malaria, is recommended for the Orinoco and other swampy or forest regions. Malaria tablets may be obtained in Caracas from Hospital Padre Machado (left-hand building as you face it), T

61-8211, no charge; or Ministerio de Sanidad y Asistencia Social (MSAS), Torre del Silencio (SW corner of Plaza Caracas), División de Malariología, free, English spoken and at Alarialogía, Calle El Degredo y Av. Roosevelt, free; alternatively, bring malaria tablets with you. It is as well to carry some remedy in case of gastric upsets. Factor 15 sun-tan cream is widely available. On the coast from Cumaná eastwards precautions against vampire bat bite are warranted since they can be rabies-carriers. Lights over hatches and windows are used by local fishermen to deter bats from entering boats and shore cabins. If bitten seek medical advice.

**Clothing** Tropical weight in normal city colours is best for business in Caracas, otherwise clothing is less formal, but smart jackets and ties are required in the most exclusive restaurants and clubs. In Maracaibo and the hot, humid coastal and low-lying areas, regular washable tropical clothing is used. For women: blouse and trousers (shorts quite acceptable on the coast); cotton dresses, with a wrap for cool evenings, and for air-conditioned restaurants and cinemas. Shoes are very good value. Cinemas may not admit men in shorts or anyone in flip-flops.

**Hours of Business** Banks are open from 0830 to 1130 and 1400 to 1630. Mon. to Fri., but are no longer open on Sat. Government office hours vary, but 0800-1200 are usual morning hours. Government officials have fixed hours, usually 0900-1000 or 1500-1600, for receiving visitors. Business firms generally start work about 0800 and some continue until about 1800 with a midday break. Shops, 0900-1300, 1500-1900, Mon.-Sat. Generally speaking, Venezuelans start work early, and by seven in the morning everything is in full swing. Most firms and offices close on Sat.

**Holidays** There are two sorts of holidays, those enjoyed by everybody and those taken by employees of banks and insurance companies. Holidays applying to all businesses include: 1 January, Carnival on the Monday and Tuesday before Ash Wednesday, Thursday-Saturday of Holy Week, 19 April, 1 May, 24 June, 5, 24 July, 12 October, 25 December. Holidays for banks and insurance companies only include all the above and also: 19 March and the nearest Monday to 6 January, Ascension Day, 29 June, 15 August, 1 November and 8 December. There are also holidays applying to certain occupations such as Doctor's Day or Traffic Policeman's Day. On New Year's Eve, everything closes and does not open for a least a day; public transport runs, but booking offices are not open. Queues for tickets, and traffic jams, are long. Business travellers should not visit during Holy week or Carnival.

Local: La Guaira: 10 March. Maracaibo: 24 October, 18 November.

**Official Time** in Venezuela is 4 hrs. behind GMT, 1 hour ahead of EST.

**Currency** The unit of currency is the bolívar, which is divided into 100 céntimos. There are nickel alloy coins for 25 and 50 céntimos and 1, 2 and 5 bolívares, and notes for 1, 2, 5, 10, 20, 50, 100 and 500 bolívares. The 1,000-bolívares note no longer circulates, because of extensive counterfeiting. There is a shortage of small coinage: many shops round up prices unless you have small change and bars may refuse to serve you unless you produce the correct change. In 1989, the official and free rates of exchange were unified. Change travellers' cheques or US dollar notes in a *casa de cambio* for optimum rates (if travelling off the beaten track consider changing a considerable amount); of the banks, Banco Unión and Banco de Venezuela change cheques and cash, but the latter usually only change money after 1500. The majority of banks do not cash travellers' cheques; in major towns, one or two banks may, but this varies from branch to branch. American Express cheques are widely accepted as is the Visa card (Banco Consolidado is affiliated with American Express, no commission, some branches cash personal cheques from abroad on an Amex card; Banco Unión handles Visa transactions and Banco Mercantil handle Mastercard). When changing dollars cash in banks, it is best to go in the morning. If changing money in hotels, do not take sterling or any other European currencies. It is impossible to change sterling in Ciudad Guayana or Ciudad Bolívar. Have money sent to you by telex and not by post, which can take weeks. Rates of exchange in hotels are generally poor.

Popular names for coins: Fuerte. Bs.5; Real, Bs.0.50; Medio, 0.25; Puya or Centavo, 0.05.

**Weights and Measures** are metric.

**Voltage** 110 volts, 60 cycles, throughout the country.

**Postal Services** The postal service is extremely slow, unreliable and expensive. Air mail letters to the USA or Europe can take from one to four weeks and registered mail is no quicker. Internal mail also travels slowly, especially if there is no P.O. Box number. As in other Latin countries removing stamps from letters occurs, Trish and Tony Wheeler suggest that you insist on seeing your letters franked because you are a collector. If you want money sent to you from abroad, have it sent by telex. Avoid the mail boxes in pharmacies as some no longer have collections.

**Telephone Service**  All international and long distance calls are operated by CANTV. Most major cities are now linked by direct dialling (*Discado Directo*), with a 3-figure prefix for each town in Venezuela. Otherwise CANTV offices deal with most long-distance and international calls in the cities outside Caracas. Collect calls are possible to some countries, at least from Caracas, though staff in offices may not be sure of this. Calls out of Venezuela are more expensive than calls into it and are subject to long delays. Local calls are troublesome and the connection is often cut in the middle of your conversation; calls are best made from hotels or CANTV offices, rather than from booths. Many public phones operate with phonecards (*tarjetas*), available for many different values up to US$10 equivalent, though many small shops impose a 25% handling charge and *tarjetas* may be out of stock. International calls are cheaper with a *tarjeta*. Rate to Europe about US$5.50 for 3 minutes.

**Note**  Telephone, fax or telex are far preferable to cables. Ask your hotel for use of its telex or fax machine.

**Press**:  Caracas: *El Universal, El Nacional* and *El Diario de Caracas, La Religión, Ultimas Noticias. The Daily Journal* (English), *El Mundo* and *2001* (evening), *Número* (weekly), *Resumen* (weekly), *Elite* (weekly), *Momento* (weekly), *Venezuela Gráfica* (weekly), *Páginas* (weekly), *Semana* (weekly), *Ve Venezuela*, tourist bi-monthly. Maracaibo: *Panorama, La Crítica*. Puerto La Cruz: *El Tiempo*.

**Maps**  The official mapping agency is the Ministerio del Ambiente y de los Recursos Naturales Renovables, Dirección de Cartografía Nacional, although its office is not in the same building as the Ministry's other departments (Centro Simón Bolívar). The exact address is not known, but it does sell 1:50,000 and 1:250,000 sheets covering most of Venezuela N of the Orinoco, plus some state maps and a 1:500,000 series. Apart from the *Guide to Venezuela* (see below), there is the *Guía Progreso* (published by Seguros Progreso S.A., available at the company's offices and elsewhere), which is very detailed, but not very accurate S of the Orinoco. The best road map is published by Lagoven, available from most service stations (not just Lagoven's), latest edition 1989. Kiosks in Caracas sell poor maps of the country.

**Tourist Information** may be obtained from Corpoturismo, Apartado 50.200, Caracas, main office for information in floors 35-7, Torre Oeste, Parque Central. The *Guide to Venezuela* (1981), by Janice Bauman, Leni Young and others, in English (freely available in Caracas) is a mine of information and maps (US$8). Bradt Publications of 41 Nortoft Road, Chalfont St. Peter, Bucks, SL9 0LA, UK, publish *No Frills Guide to Venezuela*, by Hilary Dunsterville Branch and others, containing information on hikes and excursions and on Caracas. There are many fine coffee-table books on the various regions of Venezuela, for example Charles Brewer-Carías' books on Roraima and Venezuela as a whole.

We should like to thank John Hale for doing the updating, and the following travellers for help in revising the Venezuelan section: Janine Allimann (Zurich), Lars Andersson (Halmstad, Sweden), Michael Auer (Ottobrunn), Frank Bakker and Nike Darley (Amsterdam), Jamie Banford, Marita Baulesch (Ludwigsburg, Germany), Erik Bernesson (Båstad, Sweden), Salik B. Biais (Montmorency), Riemer De Boer (Netherlands) Dr. J. Boersma, Andreas Böttner and Annette Drinkuth (Otterstedt, Germany), Binka Le Breton (Muriaé, Minas Gerais), R. J. Brooks (Northolt, Middlesex, UK), Go Bruëns (Utrecht, Netherlands), Elizabeth Buettner (Ann Arbor, M.I.) and Alexander Protopapas (Pasadena, California), Rubén Chapp and Diego Puls (Amsterdam), Erez Chimovits (Tel Aviv), Trina Cholewick (Montréal, Canada), Andrew Clarke (Bucaramanga, Colombia), Mary D'Ambrosio (Caracas), Hans van Dijk (Hilversum), Gavin Dispain (Adelaide), Carolyn Dougall and Howard Johnson (Edinburgh), Joanna Dyer (Neuss) and Nico Meyden (Sauerlach, Germany), Dee, Coralle Edwards (New Zealand) and Joy Gregory (London N1), C. and R. Eicher (Bulach, Switzerland), Kirsten Eichhorn (München, Germany), René Erhardt and Lorena Ibáñez (Berlin and Caracas), Tim Farnworth (Market Harborough, Leicestershire), Mrs. P.L. Fearon (London E6), Arnon Friedman (Tel Aviv, Israel), Glyn Fry and Trui Anseeuw (Hyde, Cheshire), May-Lill Garly and Palle Valentiner-Branth (Copenhagen), Paul Geerits (Gent, Belgium), Yves Genier (Louay, Switzerland), Theodor A. Gevert (São Paulo), David Graves (Brooklyn, N.Y.), Jacqueline Greig (Cuckfield, East Sussex), Michael Günther (Albstadt, Germany), Paul Gurn and Eileen Synnott (Waterburg, Conn), H. M. Hare (King's Lynn, Norfolk), Eckhart Harm (Tornesch, Germany), Luc Haven and Margaret Mulcahy (Vilvoorde, Belgium), Kevin Healey (Melbourne, Australia) for many additions and corrections to the text, Ulla Henning (München 70), Ulrich Herbert (Stuttgart), Sarah Hill (Kenilworth,

Warwickshire), Werner Höfler (Alzenau), Cathy and Chris Holman (Sale, Cheshire), Sabine Imhoff (Germany), Paul James and Deborah Scattergood (Walsall), Glenna Kalen (Caracas), Diane Karper (St Vincent, WI), Nicola Keirren (Melba, Australia), Anke Kessler (Berlin), Peter Kloosterman (Gouda, Netherlands), Torsten Knebusch (Lauenburg, Germany), Stuart and Wendy Knill (Kidderminster, Worcs), Andy Kuendig and Rosi Nueesch (Zuerich), Andreas Kühn (Germany), Daniel Küng (Wohlen, Switzerland), Christina Kusoffsky (Stockholm, Sweden), Jürgen Langer (Leitershofen, Germany), Henrik K. Larsen (V. Skeringe) and Mai Britt Noerskvu (Svendberg, Denmark), Steffen Layer (Frankfurt 1), Herbert Levi (Buenos Aires), Patrick Liebau (Freiburg, Germany), Ileike Liebers (Berlin), Judith Locher (Switzerland), Matt Long (Bogotá), Irvine Low (Kelowna, BC), Heidi Mangei (Tübingen, Germany), Richard and Sonia Maycock (Marlborough, UK), Heidi and Peter Merdian (Weinstadt, Germany), Greg Merrell (Boston, Mass.) and Kevin Merrell (New York), Willem and Kitty Meyburg (Hoofddorp, Netherlands), Catherine Morris-Adams (West Derby), Asbjørn Nielsen (Denmark) Alice Owen and Ian Davie (Newton Abbot, Devon), Anki Peters (Aruba), Donald Peterson (Albuquerque, U.S.A.), Thomas Pfister (Birchwil, Switzerland), Prof. M. Picardello (Rome), Shauna Picard and Grant Findlay (Melbourne, Australia), Melanie and David Poley (England), Josef Rama Souto (Recklinhausen, Germany), John Raspey (Argentina), Maria and Harvey Reeder (Northridge, CA, U.S.A.), Mariann Rehn (Enskede, Sweden), Klaus Reuter (München, Germany), Dä Roz Us Kölle, Yasmina Rüegg (Orbe, Switz.), Uwe Schluter (Hannover, Germany), Chris Sharpe (Leeds), Tony Silard (Washington, D.C.), Fredi Suter (Goldau) and Claudia Räber (Oberkirch), Kristina Swenningsson and Stefan (Sweden), Hans-Günther Tappe and Kathrin von Saretzky (Leinstücken, Germany), Birgitte Thale (Denmark), Alan P.M. Thompson (Sevenoaks, Kent), Åse Totland and Jarle Unneland (Ålesund, Norway), Béatrice Völkle (Gampelen, Switz.), H.M. Wams (Amsterdam), Allan Wearden (Blackburn, Lancs), Brigitte Weber and Rita Huber (Duisburg), Trish and Tony Wheeler (Southport, Queensland), Heinz Wind (Caracas, Venezuela), Meg Worley (Maryville, Tennessee), and Helmut Zettl (Ebergassing, Austria).

# WILL YOU HELP US?

We do all we can to get our facts right in **The South American Handbook.** Each chapter is thoroughly revised each year, but the territory covers a vast area, and our eyes cannot be everywhere. A new highway or airport is built; a hotel, a restaurant, a cabaret dies; another, a good one is born; a building we describe is pulled down, a street renamed. Names and addresses of good hotels and restaurants for "budget-minded" travellers are always very welcome. We would especially like to receive diagrams of walks, national parks and other interesting areas.

*Your information may be far more up-to-date than ours. If your letter reaches us early enough in the year it will be used in the next edition, but write whenever you want to, for all your letters are used sooner or later.*

Thank you very much indeed for your help.

**Trade & Travel Publications Limited
6 Riverside Court
Lower Bristol Road
Bath BA2 3DZ. England**

# THE GUIANAS

LIKE the West Indians, the people of the three Guianas, Guyana (formerly British Guiana), Suriname (formerly Dutch Guiana) and French Guyane, are not regarded as belonging to Latin America. The explanation of these three non-Iberian countries on the South American continent goes back to the early days of the Spanish conquest of the New World. There was no gold or any other apparent source of wealth to attract the attention of the Spanish discoverers. This part of the coast, which Columbus had first sighted in 1498, seemed to them not only barren but scantily populated and seemingly uninhabitable. The English, the French and the Dutch, anxious to establish a foothold in this part of the world, were not so fastidious.

All three countries are geographically very similar: along the coast runs a belt of narrow, flat marshy land, at its widest in Suriname. This coastland carries almost all the crops and most of the population. Behind lies a belt of crystalline upland, heavily gouged and weathered. The bauxite, gold and diamonds are in this area. Behind this again is the massif of the Guiana Highlands. They reach a height of 3,000 feet (915 metres), in the Tumuc-Humac range, the divide between French Guyane and Suriname, and Brazil, and 9,219 feet (2,810 metres) at flat-topped Mount Roraima (**see Venezuela, South to Brazil**), where Guyana, Venezuela and Brazil all meet.

**N.B.** You need to have your own shoe-cleaning equipment; there seem to be no shoeshine boys in any of the Guianas.

Thanks and acknowledgements for help with the Guianas sections will be found at the end of the chapter on French Guyane.

# GUYANA

GUYANA has an area of 83,000 square miles, nearly the size of Britain, but only about 0.5% (or 280,000 acres) is cultivated. The population numbers some 754,000, of whom about 96% are literate. There has been considerable emigration to the USA, Canada and Britain.

About 90% of the population lives on the narrow coastal plain, most of which is below sea level. A sea wall keeps out the Atlantic and the fertile clay soil is drained by a system of dykes. Sluice gates are opened to let out water at low tide; and separate irrigation channels are used to bring water back to the fields in dry weather. In several places fresh water is supplied by reservoirs, known as conservancies. Most of the western third of the coastal plain is undrained and uninhabited. Most people live either in Georgetown, the capital, or in villages which are strung along the main road running from Charity in the west to the Suriname border. Large wooden houses stand on stilts above the damp soil. The strange cultural mix—Dutch place names and drainage techniques, Hindu temples, mosques, coconut palms and calypso music—reflect the chequered history of the country. The rich agricultural land of this area is used for producing rice and sugar and for raising cattle. Coffee, fruit and vegetables are also grown.

Four major rivers cross the coastal plain—(from west to east) the Essequibo, the Demerara, the Berbice, and the Courantyne (which forms the frontier with Suriname). Only the Demerara is crossed by a bridge. Elsewhere ferries must be used. In the mouth of the Essequibo river are islands the size of Barbados. The lower reaches of these rivers are navigable; but waterfalls and rapids prevent them being used by large boats to reach the interior.

Inland from the coastal plain most of the country is covered by thick rain forest, although in the east there is a large area of grassland. Although some timber has been extracted, the main economic activity is mining: bauxite is extracted at Linden, Ituni and Kwakwani; gold and diamonds are sifted from the sand and gravel of the river beds by small teams of miners using mercury (at considerable environmental cost). Large areas of rain forest are still undisturbed, however, and even the more accessible areas have varied and spectacular wildlife, including brightly-plumaged birds. Towards the Venezuelan border the rain forest rises in a series of steep escarpments, with spectacular waterfalls, the highest and best-known of which are the Kaieteur Falls on the Potero river.

In the south west of the country is the Rupununi Savanna, an area of open grassland more easily reached from Brazil than from Georgetown.

The area west of the Essequibo river—about 70% of the national territory—is claimed by Venezuela. Another area in the south east, between the Koeroeni and New rivers, is claimed by Suriname.

The **climate**, although hot, is not unhealthy. Mean shade temperature throughout the year is 80°F; the mean maximum is about 87°F and the mean minimum 75°F. The heat is greatly tempered by cooling breezes from the sea and is most felt from August to October. There are two wet seasons, from the middle of April to the middle of August, and from the middle of November to the end of January. Rainfall averages 91 inches a year in Georgetown.

**History** The country was first partially settled between 1616 and 1621 by the Dutch West India Company, who erected a fort and depot at Fort Kyk-over-al (County of Essequibo). The first English attempt at settlement was made by Captain Leigh on the Oiapoque River (now French Guyane) in 1604, but it failed to establish a permanent settlement. Lord Willoughby, famous in the early history of Barbados, founded a settlement in 1663 at Suriname, which was captured by the Dutch in 1667 and ceded to them at the Peace of Breda in exchange for New York. The Dutch held the three colonies till 1796 when they were captured by a British fleet. The territory was restored to the Dutch in 1802, but in the following year was retaken by Great Britain, which finally gained it in 1814, when the three counties of Essequibo, Berbice and Demerara were merged to form British Guiana.

During the 17th century the Dutch and English settlers established posts up-river, in the hills, mostly as trading points with the Amerindian natives. Plantations were laid out and worked by slaves from Africa. Poor soil defeated this venture, and the settlers retreated with their slaves to the coastal area in mid-18th century: the old plantation sites can still be detected from the air. Coffee and cotton were the main crops up to the end of the 18th century, but sugar had become the dominant crop by 1820. In 1834 slavery was abolished. Many of the slaves scattered as small landholders, and the plantation owners had to look for another source of labour. It was found in indentured workers from India, a few Chinese, and some Portuguese labourers from the Azores and Madeira. About 240,000 had come from India alone by 1914. At the end of their indentures many settled in Guyana.

The end of the colonial period was politically turbulent, with rioting between the mainly East Indian People's Progressive Party (PPP), led by Dr. Cheddi Jagan, and the mainly African People's National Congress (PNC), under Mr. Forbes

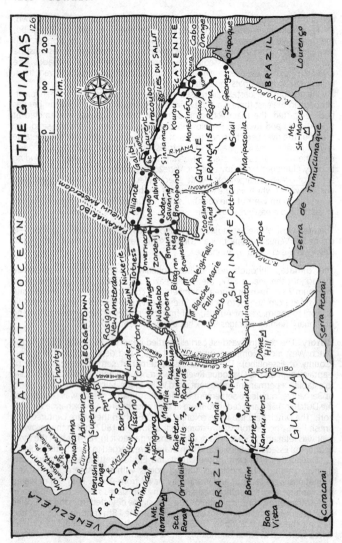

Burnham. The PNC, favoured over the PPP by the colonial authorities, formed a government in 1964 and has retained office since.

On 26 May 1966 Guyana gained independence, and on 23 February 1970 it became a cooperative republic within the Commonwealth, adopting a new constitution. Another new constitution was adopted in 1980; this declared Guyana to be in transition from capitalism to socialism. Many industries, including bauxite and sugar, were nationalised in the 1970s and close relations with the USSR and Eastern Europe were developed. Following the death of President Forbes Burnham in August 1985, Mr Desmond Hoyte became President. Since then, overseas investors have been invited back and relations with the United States have improved.

Elections to the National Assembly and to the Presidency have been held regularly since independence, but have been widely criticised as fraudulent. The main opposition parties are the PPP, still led by Dr. Jagan, and the Working People's Alliance, which attracts support from both East Indian and African communities. Elections, due to be held by May 1991, were postponed until a new electoral register had been drawn up.

**The People** Until the 1920s there was little natural increase in population, but the eradication of malaria and other diseases has since led to a rapid growth in population, particularly among the East Indians (Asian), who, according to most estimates comprise over 50% of the population. The results of the 1980 census have still not been published, possibly because of embarrassment over the high level of emigration, but more likely because of the extreme sensitivity of the racial balance between the East Indian and African (black) communities. Descendants of the original Amerindian inhabitants form a very small minority who have rapidly lost their isolation and moved to the urban areas.

**The Economy** Apart from instant, temporary prosperity brought about by the brief non-oil commodities boom in the mid-1970s, which raised gdp growth to 10.4% in 1975, Guyana's economy has been in almost permanent recession in the last two decades, despite considerable, unexploited potential in hydroelectric power, minerals and forestry. While Venezuela's long standing claim to the Essequibo region, within which most of these resources are situated, has discouraged investment, other factors are more to blame. Inefficient management in the dominant state sector covering vital sugar and bauxite industries, an investment climate discouraging both domestic and foreign savings, and an acute foreign exchange shortage, have resulted in poor performances from the key agricultural and mining sectors, and a largely moribund manufacturing sector.

Most agriculture is concentrated on the coastal plain, and many sugar plantations are below sea level, necessitating an extensive system of dams, dykes, canals and pumps to prevent inundation. Sugar is the main crop, and has vied with bauxite and alumina as the most important source of export earnings. Rice is the second most important crop, and a useful foreign exchange earner, though significant quantities of rice production are bartered or export proceeds are undeclared through trade with South American neighbours, especially Suriname and Brazil.

Guyana is the world's largest producer of calcined bauxite, the highest grade of the mineral, and currently has roughly half the world market, though competition from China is becoming stronger. Production is currently concentrated at Linden, on the Demarara river, and at Kwakwani in Berbice county. No alumina (refined bauxite) has been exported since 1982 because the Linden refinery still awaits investment for refurbishment.

A series of devaluations of the Guyana dollar between January 1987 and February 1991 culminated in the alignment of the official exchange rate with that of licensed exchange houses. These and other adjustment measures proved beneficial both for the current account and for government finances but the economy remained depressed. The Government struggled to come to terms with the IMF, which declared Guyana ineligible for further assistance in May 1985 because of payment arrears. It was rewarded in June 1990 when the Bank for International Settlements and a group of donor countries provided funds to clear the country's arrears to the IMF and other creditors. This opened the way for lending from a variety of sources, but the government experienced difficulties in meeting targets set by the IMF in a programme which began on 1 July 1990.

Guyana has suffered from serious economic problems for over 15 years; some estimates now put per capita income below that of Haiti. Wages are very low and many people depend on overseas remittances or "parallel market" activities to survive. There are frequent shortages of many basic items including some foodstuffs, gasoline and spare parts. The country's infrastructure is seriously run down. There are frequent electricity blackouts—sometimes lasting over 12 hours—and during these no water is available, except in larger hotels and businesses which have emergency generators and water pumps.

**Government** A Prime Minister and cabinet are responsible to the National Assembly, which has 65 members elected for a maximum term of 5 years. The President is Head of State. The country is divided into ten administrative regions.

*Georgetown*, the capital, and the chief town and port, is on the right bank of the River Demerara, at its mouth. Its population is roughly 200,000. The climate is tropical, with a mean temperature of 27°C, but the trade winds often provide welcome relief. The city is built on a grid plan, with wide tree-lined streets and drainage canals following the layout of the old sugar estates. Despite being located on the Atlantic coast, Georgetown is known as the "Garden City of the Caribbean". Parts of the city are very attractive, with white-painted wooden nineteenth century houses raised on stilts and a profusion of flowering trees. Lying, like most of the coastal area, below sea level, the city is protected from the ocean by a sea wall; in the evening this is crowded with strollers and at Easter it is a mass of colourful paper kites. Although part of the old city centre was destroyed by fire in 1945, there are some fine nineteenth century buildings, particularly on or near the Avenue of the Republic. The Gothic-style City Hall dates from 1887. St George's Anglican Cathedral, which dates from 1889, is 44 metres (143 feet) high and is reputed to be the tallest wooden building in the world. The Public Buildings, which house Parliament, are an imposing neo-classical structure built in 1839. Much of the city centre is dominated by the imposing tower above Stabroek market (1880). At the head of Brickdam, one of the main streets, is an aluminium arch commemorating independence. Nearby is a monument to the 1763 slave rebellion, surmounted by an impressive statue of Cuffy, its best-known leader. Near the Pegasus Hotel on High Street is the Umana Yana, a conical thatched structure built by a group of Wai Wai Amerindians using traditional techniques for the 1972 conference of the Non-Aligned Movement.

The National Museum, opposite the post office, houses an idiosyncratic collection of exhibits from Guayana and elsewhere, including a model of Georgetown before the 1945 fire. The Walter Roth Museum of Anthropology has a good collection of Amerindian artefacts.

The Botanical Gardens (entry free), covering 120 acres (50 hectares), are beautifully laid out, with Victorian bridges and pavilions, palms and lily-ponds (reported dilapidated in 1991). Near the south west corner is the residence of the President and there is also a large mausoleum containing the remains of the former president, Forbes Burnham, which is decorated with reliefs depicting scenes from his political career. Look out for the rare cannonball tree (Couroupita Guianensis), named after the appearance of its poisonous fruit. The zoo has a fine collection of local animals and the manatees in the ponds will eat grass from your hand. The police band gives a free concert on Thursdays, 1730-1830. There are also beautiful tropical plants in the Promenade Gardens on Middle Street and in the National Park on Carifesta Avenue.

---

**Georgetown: Key to map**

1. Independence Park; 2. Promenade Gardens; 3. St George's Anglican Cathedral; 4. Roman Catholic Cathedral; 5. City Hall; 6. Parliament; 7. Stabroek Market; 8. National Museum; 9. Post Office; 10. Bank of Guyana; 11. Frandec Travel; 12. Money Market; 13. *Pegasus Hotel* (off map); 14. *Park Hotel*; 15. *Tower Hotel*; 16. *Woodbine Hotel*; 17. *Rima Guest House*; 18. UK High Commission; 19. US Embassy.

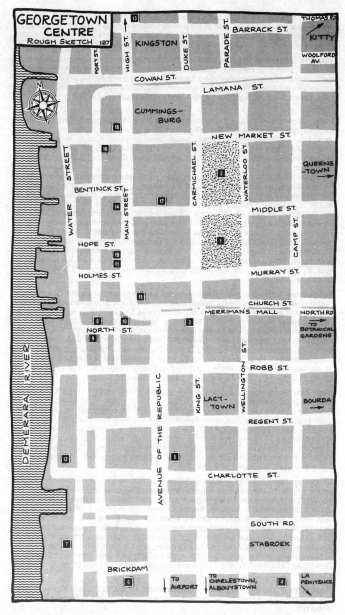

The Georgetown Cricket Club at Bourda has one of the finest cricket grounds in the tropics. Near the south east corner of the Botanic Gardens is a well-equipped National Sports Centre. Nearby is the Cultural Centre, an impressive air-conditioned theatre with a large stage. Performances are also given at the Playhouse Theatre in Parade Street.

**Warning**  Georgetown is a dangerous city at night, especially during blackouts and periods of reduced electricity. There are frequent "choke and rob" attacks. Don't walk the streets at night; taxis are cheap and easy to find. Most areas are fairly safe by day, provided the usual precautions are taken. Particular care is required around the Stabroek Market area and on Main Street. Avoid Albouystown (south of the centre) and Tiger Bay (along the Demerara River).

**Hotels**  In the following large hotels foreigners have to pay in foreign currency (US, Canadian, East Caribbean, Barbadian or British): *Pegasus*, High St., L, a/c, pool, restaurant, small rooms; *Park*, Main St., A (some rooms C), a/c, secure, beautiful Victorian ballroom (worth a visit); *Tower*, Main St., A, a/c, recently renovated, lively bar, restaurant, pool open to public, rec; *Woodbine*, New Market St., T 59430, a/c, rec; *Campala*, Camp St., T 52951, modern, a/c, near prison.

There are also many smaller, cheaper hotels which take payment in Guyanese dollars. Recommended are: *Demico*, near Stabroek Market, T 56372, D with a/c, E without; *Waterchris*, Water St., T 71980, E, a/c, good restaurant, friendly; *Rima Guest House*, 92 Middle St., T 57401, F, modernised, well-run, good value; *Van Ross*, North Road and Camp St., G, same management, very basic. Others include: *Belvedere*, Camp St., D, noisy; opposite is *Alpha Guest House*, E, 2nd floor with shower and mosquito net (no fan), 1st floor cheaper but usually short stay, bar downstairs; *Trio La Chalet*, D, corner of Camp St. and Hadfield St.; *Le Grille*, 176 Middle St, T 57493, D, repeated reports of theft from rooms; *Roma*, Main St., D, used by short-stay clients; *Elizabeth Guest House*, Wellington St. Many small hotels and guest houses are full of long-stay residents, while some are rented by the hour. Try to book in advance. If in doubt, go to a larger hotel for first night and look around next day in daylight.

**Restaurants**  Eating out is very cheap at present because of the favourable exchange rate. Best in town are *Del Casa* and *Caribbean Rose*, both on Middle St.; also rec. are *Palm Court*, Main St., and the *Tower Hotel* restaurant, and *Arawak Steak House*, in roof garden above *Demico Hotel*. Buffet breakfast at *Woodbine Hotel*, cheaper breakfast at *Waterchris*. Good lunches for around US$2 at the *Rice Bowl* and *Country Pride*, both in Robb St., the *Coalpot* in New Town and *Hack's Hallal* (all of these close in the evening). Many Chinese restaurants (all pretty rough), including *Double Dragon*, Av. of the Republic; and *Diamond Food House*, 9 Camp St. For late night eating there are several Chinese restaurants on Sheriff St. inc. *Double Happiness*. For fast food, try *Red Rooster*, Regent St.; *Arapaima*, Main St.; *Idaho*, Brickdam; *Forest Hills*, Camp St.; *Calypso*, Regent St.

**Night Life**  Georgetown is surprisingly lively at night, mainly with gold miners, traders and overseas Guyanese throwing US$ around. Liveliest disco is *Hollywood*, Camp St., (but it's expensive and they are said to water the drinks) though *The Library*, also on Camp St., *The Cave*, Regent St. and *The Dark*, in the *Park Hotel*, are also lively. *Palm Court Bar*, Main Street; *Mingles*, Crown St., is a good bar with live music and dancing (entrance US$0.40). Near the Kitty Market are *Jazzy Jacks*, Alexander St., and *We Place*, Lamaha St, but this area is unsafe unless you go with locals. Sheriff St., is some way from the centre but is "the street that never sleeps" full of late night Chinese restaurants and has some good bars inc. *Tennessee Lounge*, *Burns Beat*, *Halloween Bar* and *Shuttle Club*.

**Shopping**  Normal shopping hours are 0900-1700 (Sat. 0900-1300). The main shopping area is Regent St. The two main department stores are *Guyana Stores* in Church St., and *Fogarty's*, but neither has a wide range of goods. Most Guyanese do their regular shopping at the four big markets—Stabroek, Bourda, La Penitence and Kitty. Craft items are a good buy; Amerindian basketwork, hammocks, wood carvings, pottery, and small figures made out of Balata, a rubbery substance tapped from trees in the interior. *Houseproud*, on Avenue of the Republic has a good selection of craftwork, but there are many other craft shops inc. *Creations*, near *Fogarty's*. Gold is also sold widely, often at good prices but make sure you know what you are buying. Imported goods are available for foreign currency at *Sijan Plaza*. Developing film takes time and is not always reliable—*Risans* on Main St. rec. as quick and efficient.

**Bookshops**  Some interesting books in *Houseproud*. Try also *GNTC* on Water St., *Argosy* and *Kharg* both on Regent St., *Dimension* on Cummings St., as well as *Guyana Stores* and *Fogarty's*.

**Local Transport** Car hire is virtually impossible. **Minibuses** run regularly to most parts of the city, mostly from Stabroek market or Avenue of the Republic, standard fare US$0.20, very crowded. It is difficult to get a seat during rush hours. **Taxis** charge US$1.20 for short journeys, US$2.20 for longer runs, with higher rates at night and outside the city limits.

**Exchange** National Bank of Industry and Commerce; Guyana Bank of Trade and Industry; Bank of Baroda; Bank of Nova Scotia. Bank hours are 0800-1230 Mon.-Fri., plus 1500-1700 on Fri. **Exchange houses** (*cambios*) in shops may be open longer hours.

**Embassies and Consulates** There are a surprisingly large number of embassies, including: **British High Commission** (44 Main St., P.O. Box 10849); **Canadian High Commission** (Young St.) and the Embassies of the **United States** (31 Main St, T 54900), **Venezuela** (Thomas St.), **Brazil** (Church St.), **Cuba** (Main St.) and **Suriname** (Bourda).

**Post Office** Main one on Avenue of the Republic, slow service.

**Churches** Anglican: St. Georges Cathedral, Christ Church, Waterloo Street; St. Andrews (Presbyterian), Avenue of the Republic; Roman Catholic Cathedral, Brickdam.

**Travel Agencies** Try Mr. Mendoza at *Frandec Travel Service*, Main St., repeatedly rec.; *M and Ms Tour Service*, 76 First Av., Subryanville, T 62860/6529. Barbara Sansculotte at *Pisces Services Limited*, 9 Croal St., T 59259/69107, P.O Box 10902. *Wonderland Tours* at *Tower Hotel*. *Rainbow River Safari*, 54 Lamaha Gardens, T 71746.

**Bus Services** There are regular services by minibuses and collective taxis to most coastal towns from the Stabroek Market. To **Rosignol** (for New Amsterdam, Springlands and Suriname), 1½ hrs, US$1.50; to **Parika** US$2; to **Linden** US$2.

**Airport** The international airport is at Timehri, 25 miles south of Georgetown. Minibus No. 42 to Georgetown US$0.80, taxi US$10. There is a small duty-free shop where local goods are reportedly slightly cheaper than in the capital and an exchange house, usually open at times of incoming flights; if not, plenty of parallel traders outside (find out from fellow passengers what the rate is). (For internal flights see **Information for Visitors**).

**Linden** (pop. 30,000), the second-largest town in Guyana, is a bauxite mining town 70 miles south of Georgetown on the Demerara river. A good (toll) road connects the two towns. On the west bank of the river, Linden is a company mining town with an executive area and golf course. Across the river (bridge or ferry) are the poorer suburbs of Wismar and Christianburg. The town is dominated by a disused alumina plant and scarred by old bauxite pits. Accommodation is scarce (*Mackenzie Hotel*, pleasantly situated on the river, T 04-2183, D; *Hotel Star Bonnett*, clean, good lunches).

From Linden rough roads suitable for four-wheel drive vehicles run south to the bauxite mining towns of Ituni and Kwakwani; south to the logging centre at Mabura Hill and on to Kurupukari; and west to Rockstone ferry on the Essequibo river. From Rockstone very bad roads run north to Bartica and south to Issano. The first stage of a road from Kurupukari south to Annai, Lethem and Boa Vista was completed in early 1991, suitable only for 4WD vehicles.

**New Amsterdam** (pop. 20,000) is 65 miles south-east of Georgetown on the east bank of the Berbice river, near its mouth. From Georgetown, take a minibus or collective taxi to Rosignol on the west bank of the Berbice, then cross the river by launch rather than the slow, smelly ferry (US$0.10; also takes vehicles). The town is run-down but picturesque.

**Hotels** *Penguin*, T 03-2012, a/c, D; *Church View Guest House*, D, inc. meals; *Hotel Embassy*, at Rose Hall.

**Banks** National Bank of Industry and Commerce; Guyana National Commercial Bank; Bank of Baroda.

From New Amsterdam, it is sometimes possible to get a lift on a bauxite barge up the Berbice river to the small mining town of Kwakwani.

The road continues east from New Amsterdam (minibus, US$1), to **Springlands** and Skeldon at the mouth of the Courantyne river. The two towns are officially known as **Corriverton** (Courantyne River Town).

**Hotels** In Springlands: *Ambassador*, near point for ferry to Nieuw Nickerie; *Swiss Hotel*, Pakistani run, rough but helpful. In Skeldon: *Mahogony*, F, fan, clean, friendly, rec.; *Parapak*, E, no fan, no mosquito net, poor value; *Arawak*, G, rough, avoid. Several good Chinese restaurants within a few blocks of Springlands town centre.

**Exchange** National Bank of Industry and Commerce; Guyana National Commercial Bank. *Cambio* (National Bank of Industry and Commerce) at Skeldon for arriving ferry passengers.

**Transport** To Georgetown by minibus to New Amsterdam, ferry to **Rosignol** and minibus from Rosignol, US$2.50.

## Crossing to Suriname

Before you leave Georgetown, check with the Suriname embassy whether you need a visa. From Springlands there is a daily ferry (not Sunday or national holidays of either country) to Nieuw Nickerie (foot passengers only). Queue at the booking office near the jetty from 0700, office opens 0800, booking fee US$0.25, all passports must be presented when booking, tickets are sold later on the ferry, Sf15 one way, payable in Suriname guilders only. Immigration and customs formalities (very slow and thorough) take place from 0900, ferry sails from 1100 depending on tides and weather, crossing time normally 2 hours. Change money at the stelling (ferry pier) before you travel. If you have Georgetown at 0300 you should catch the ferry and reach Paramaribo by late p.m. (A new ferry, partly paid for by the EEC, was due to replace this service in 1990).

Travelling west from Georgetown, the road crosses the Demerara bridge (toll) and continues to *Parika*, a small town on the east bank of the Essequibo river (minibus US$0.50). If you need accommodation, there are two small brothels where you can stay fairly safely. From here ferries cross the river to Adventure on the west bank at 1700 daily and 0830 Wed. and Fri., returning at 0300 daily and 1330 Wed. and Fri. (See *Three Singles to Adventure* by Gerald Durrell). There are also three ferries a day to Leguan Island (½ hr, US$0.25); accommodation available at the *Hotel President*.

From Parika there is also a ferry up the Essequibo river to Bartica on Tues. and Fri. at 0700, Sat. 1330, returning on Mon. and Thurs. at 0930, Sat. 0815, US$1 one way. The 36 mile journey takes 6 hours, stopping at Fort Island where you can buy sweetcorn and pastries; small boats come out from riverside settlements to load up with fruit. Local people generally prefer to take a speedboat, US$5 p.p., 1-2 hours, depending on horsepower.

**Bartica**, at the junction of the Essequibo and Mazaruni rivers, is the "take-off" town for the gold and diamond fields, Kaieteur Falls, and the interior generally. Here an Amazon-like mass of waters meets, but with an effect vastly more beautiful, for they are coloured the "glossy copper" of all Guyanese rivers and not the dull mud-brown of most of the Amazon. Swimming very good. There is a direct weekly ferry connection with Georgetown.

**Hotels** *Marin*; *The Nest* on Fifth Avenue, E, unsafe, very noisy, meals to be had from disco after 1730, or "Robbie's". *Modern*, near ferry, good food, noisy disco. Book ahead if possible. Mrs Payne, near Hospital, basic, clean.

The Essequibo is navigable to large boats for some miles above Bartica. The Cuyuni flows into the Mazaruni 3 miles above Bartica, and above this confluence the Mazaruni is impeded for 120 miles by thousands of islands, rapids and waterfalls. To avoid this stretch of treacherous river a road has been built from Bartica to Issano, where boats can be taken up the more tranquil upper Mazaruni.

The *Kaieteur Falls*, on the Potaro river, rank with the Niagara, Victoria, and Iguazú Falls in majesty and beauty, but have the added attraction of being surrounded by unspoilt forest. The Falls, nearly five times the height of Niagara, with a sheer drop of 228 metres, are nearly 100 metres wide. They are unspoilt because of their isolation. M and Ms Tour Service and Pisces, both in Georgetown, sometimes arrange tours depending on demand for about US$100 p.p. or you can charter a small plane in Georgetown. Mrs. Chan-A-Sue in Georgetown, T 65298, organises day trips by plane which include the Oronduik Falls, US$150 p.p., including lunch.

The overland route to the falls takes 7-10 days. In Bartica ask around for trucks (which can be hired for around US$200), or for gold prospectors going to the Mahdia area. The journey to Kangaruma (government rest house, F, reservations can be made by radio from Georgetown) is 113 miles, via Garraway Stream with its fine suspension bridge over the Potaro, along a very poor jungle road which is often impassable especially during the rainy season and can take over 7 hours. From Kangaruma take a boat up the river (with portages around the Amatuk and Waratuk Falls) to Tukeit (government rest house, F, take your own food). The climb to the top of the Kaieteur Falls takes at least two hours but is worth it to watch the blue, white and brown water tumbling into a stupendous gorge. The rest house at the top of the Falls is closed. It is also possible to walk to the Falls from Mahdia—allow 4-6 days each way. Avoid April and October, which are the dry months when the flow of the falls is reduced, and June, which is the height of the wet season when the route is impassable.

The Kaieteur Falls lie within the **Kaieteur National Park**, where there is a variety of wildlife—tapirs, ocelots, monkeys, armadillos, anteaters, and jungle and river birds. The Pakaraima Mountains stretch from Kaieteur westwards to include the highest peak in Guyana, Mt. Roraima, the possible inspiration for Conan Doyle's *Lost World* (**see Venezuela, South to Brazil**). Roraima is very difficult to climb from the Guyanese side.

There are several other spectacular waterfalls in the interior, including Imbaimadai and Oronduik, but none is very easy to reach.

**Precautions** Permits are required for travelling in many parts of the interior—obtainable from the Department of the Interior, Water Street, Georgetown. Detailed planning and a guide are essential. Take adequate supplies of food and drink, a sleeping bag, a sheet and blanket, a mosquito net, and kerosene for Tilley lamps.

The north-western coastal area is mainly accessible by boat only. From **Adventure** on the west bank of the Essequibo a road runs north through Anna Regina. Nearby is Lake Mainstay, a small resort (due for renovation), reached by taxi; it is also known as the hot and cold lake because it varies in temperature from one place to another. Then goes on to **Charity**, a pleasant little town with two small hotels and a lively market on Mondays.

Near the border with Venezuela is the small port of **Morawhanna** (Morajuana to the Venezuelans), which may be reached by an unreliable ferry from Georgetown. The journey is surprisingly rough and "you will have to fight for hammock space and watch your possessions like a hawk". From Morawhanna boats sail up the river to Port Kaituma, 40 miles inland, from where a small passenger railway connects with the isolated settlement of Matthews Ridge (more easily reached by chartered aircraft from Georgetown). The site of the Jonestown mass-suicide is nearby.

The **Rupununi Savanna** in the south west is an extensive area of dry grassland with scattered trees, termite mounds and wooded hills. The freshwater creeks, lined with Ite palms, are good for swimming. The region is scattered with occasional Amerindian villages and a few large cattle ranches which date from the late nineteenth century: the descendants of some of the Scots settlers still live here. Between the 1920s and 1950s a rough cattle trail led to the coastal region, but this has since reverted to bush. Balata, a rubbery substance bled from trees, was once a source of income but it no longer has commercial value, having been replaced by synthetic substances; craft items are still made from it. Most of the airstrips used to transport balata are now closed. Links with Brazil are much closer than with the Guyanese coast; many people speak Portuguese and most trade, both legal and illegal, is with Brazil.

Avoid visiting the Rupununi in the wet season (May to August) as much of the Savanna is flooded and malaria mosquitoes widespread.

**Lethem**, a small but scattered town on the Brazilian frontier, is the service centre for the Rupununi and for trade with Brazil. There are a few stores, a small hospital, a police station and government offices which have radio telephone links with Georgetown. About 1½ miles south of town at St Ignatius there is a Jesuit mission dating from 1911.

A road link between Lethem and the Guyanese coast via Kurupakari and Linden was opened in early 1991, but was suitable only for 4WD vehicles in "pioneering conditions". Regular charter planes link the town with Georgetown, about US$60 one way. Chartering an 8 seater plane from Georgetown to Lethem costs about US$800 round trip—pay extra for a detour over the Kaieteur Falls en route. Seats on private charter flights are often available for US$0.50 per pound bodyweight and luggage—travel light and don't eat breakfast.

Transport around the Rupununi is difficult; there are a few four-wheel drive vehicles, but ox-carts and bicycles are more common on the rough roads. From Lethem trucks can be hired for day-trips to the Moco-Moco Falls and the Kamu Falls and to the Kanuku Mountains. Trucks may also be hired to visit Aishalton, 70 miles south along a very bad road, 6 hour journey, US$260; and to Annai, 60 miles north east along a better road, 3 hour journey, US$110. An interesting trip is to the Amerindian village of Yukupari, where the Alan Knight Training Centre, a theological college training Amerindians for the Anglican priesthood, is always happy to see visitors and can, on occasion, provide accommodation for stranded travellers. Truck-hire and tours can be arranged through Don and Shirley Melville, who run a bar near the air-strip in Lethem.

To visit Amerindian villages, a special permit must be obtained from the District Council in Revolution Square, Lethem.

An extraordinary account of an overland journey from Georgetown to the Rupununi and on to Boa Vista in the 1930s is to be found in *Ninety-Two Days* by Evelyn Waugh.

**Hotels in the Rupununi** In Lethem: *Takutu Hotel*, near airfield, C, full board, run down, reports of theft; *Cacique Guesthouse*, F, full board also available, clean, highly rec.; try also the government rest house next to Guyana Stores, F, good meals, clean, efficient, rec. The *Manari Ranch Hotel*, 7 miles north of Lethem, D p.p. inc. meals, creek for swimming, rec. Duane and Sandy de Freitas at the *Dadanawa Ranch*, 50 miles south of Lethem, takes guests and organises tours, US$30 p.p., per day, as does Diane McTurk at *Karanambo Ranch*, 50 miles north-east of Lethem, US$100 p.p., per day; they can both be contacted via Peter Seabra in the offices of the Rupununi Livestock Producers' Association, above Gapoor's shop, America Street, Georgetown, or Johnette Gonsalves, T 65759.

**Exchange** Mr Jardin, the Portuguese shopkeeper, may exchange travellers' cheques (technically illegal), at a poor rate; Mr Mahoney gives better rates for cash. Changing money is much better on the Brazilian side of the frontier.

**Crossing to Brazil** Formalities are generally reported to be very lax on both sides of the border, but it is important to observe them as there are reports of people being refused entry to Guyana for not having the correct papers, including visa. In Lethem all procedures are dealt with at the police station; report there also with a visa if arriving from Brazil. The Takutu river, the frontier between the two countries, is about 1 mile north of Lethem (taxis available). There are small boats for foot passengers and a pontoon for vehicles. Just over the river is a shop and the Brazilian customs post. From here it is 1½ mile walk to the village of Bom Fim, from where a bus leaves for Boa Vista at 0800 (from Boa Vista to Bom Fim at 1600), 3½ hours, US$10. (Note that Brazilian time is one hour behind Guyanese time).

---

## INFORMATION FOR VISITORS

**Documents** All visitors require passports and all, apart from nationals of Caribbean Community countries, require visas, obtainable from Embassies, High Commissions and Consulates in London, Washington, Port of Spain, Bridgetown, Caracas, Brasília, Paramaribo and elsewhere. To obtain a visa, two photos, an onward ticket and yellow fever certificate are required. Visas are charged strictly on a reciprocal basis, so that they are free for US citizens since visas for the USA cost nothing, but UK citizens have to pay £20, and so on. Visitors arriving without visas are refused entry.

A permit from the Department of the Interior, Water St., Georgetown, is required for visiting the interior. This may take some time to obtain.

**Taxes** There is an exit tax of G$1,000, payable in Guyanese dollars, and a 10% tax on international airline tickets bought in the country. Exit tax can be paid when reconfirming your outward flight.

**International Air Services** There are no direct flights to Guyana from Europe; from North America BWIA flies 5 times a week from New York, Guyana Airways 3 times a week from New York, once from Miami. BWIA flies to Guyana from Trinidad daily (some days twice), LIAT flies from Barbados daily, BWIA 5 times week and Cubana from Cuba and Barbados fortnightly. There are also twice weekly flights from Caracas by Aeropostal and once a week from Boa Vista and Manaus by Cruzeiro do Sul. Suriname Airways flies 5 times a week from Paramaribo, but these flights are difficult to book from outside the Guianas.

Flights are often booked weeks in advance, especially at Christmas when overseas Guyanese return to visit relatives. Flights are frequently overbooked, so it is essential to reconfirm your outward flight, which can take some time, and difficult to change your travel plans at the last minute. Foreigners must pay for airline tickets in US$ or other specified currencies. Luggage should be securely locked as theft from checked-in baggage is common.

**Customs** Baggage examination is very thorough. Jewellery and foreign currency must be declared on arrival or else you will not be allowed to take them out of the country. Duties are high on goods imported in commercial quantities.

**Internal Air Services** There are no scheduled internal services. There are several charter companies, including Mazerally, Air Service, Correia and Sankar. Surplus seats on privately chartered flights are sometimes available and are advertised in the press.

**Road Transport** Most coastal towns are linked by a good 185 mile road from Springlands in the east to Charity in the west; the Berbice and Essequibo rivers are crossed by ferries, the Demerara by a toll bridge near Georgetown (in poor condition, 3 spans collapsed in April 1991). Apart from a good road connecting Georgetown and Bartica, most other roads in the interior are very poor. Car hire is virtually impossible. There are shortages of car spares. Gasoline costs about US$1.75 a gallon but is subject to periodic shortages. Traffic drives on the left. Minibuses and collective taxis run between Georgetown and most towns in the coastal belt.

**River Transport** There are over 600 miles of navigable river, which provide an important means of communication. Ferries and river boats are referred to in the text, but for further details contact the Transport and Harbours Department, Water St., Georgetown. Note that there is no vehicle ferry across the Courantyne to Suriname.

**Accommodation** The largest hotels in Georgetown have their own emergency electricity generators and water pumps to deal with the frequent interruptions in supply. Other hotels usually provide a bucket of water in your room—fill this up when water is available. When booking an air-conditioned room, make sure it also has natural ventilation.

**Food and Drink** The blend of different national influences—Indian, African, Chinese, Creole, English, Portuguese, Amerindian, North American—gives a distinctive flavour to Guyanese cuisine. One well-known dish, traditional at Christmas, is pepper-pot, meat cooked in bitter cassava juice with peppers and herbs. Seafood is plentiful and varied, as is the wide variety of tropical fruits and vegetables. Staple foods are rice and long thin bora beans. The food shortages and import ban of the early 1980s have ended, but they did have the positive effect of encouraging experimentation with local ingredients, sometimes with interesting results. In the interior wild meat is often available—try wild cow, or else labba (a small rodent).

Rum is the most popular drink. There is a wide variety of brands, all cheap, including the best which are very good and cost less than US$2 a bottle. High wine is a strong local rum. There is also local brandy and whisky (Diamond Club), which are worth trying. The local beer, Banks, made partly from rice is acceptable and cheap. There is a wide variety of fruit juices.

**Health**   There is a high risk of both types of malaria in the interior, especially in the wet season. Recommended prophylaxis is chloroquine 500 mg weekly plus paludrine 200 mg daily. Reports of chloroquine-resistant malaria in the interior (seek advice before going). If travelling to the interior for long periods carry drugs for treatment as these may not be available. Sleep under a mosquito net. Although there are plenty of mosquitoes on the coast, they are not malarial.

There is some risk of typhoid and water-borne diseases owing to low water pressure. Purification tablets are a good idea. Tapwater is usually brown and contains sediment, but this is not a cause for concern. The Georgetown Hospital is run down, understaffed and lacking equipment, but there are a number of well-equipped private hospitals, including St Joseph's on Parade St., Kingston; Prasad's on Thomas St.; and the Davis Memorial Hospital on Lodge Backlands. Charges are US$2 to US$8 per day and medical consultations cost US$2 to US$4. If admitted to hospital you are expected to provide your own sheets and food (St. Joseph's provides all these).

Travellers should examine shower pipes, bedding, shoes and clothing for snakes in the interior.

**Public Holidays**   1 January, New Years' Day; 23 February, Republic Day and Mashramani festival; Good Friday, Easter Monday; Labour Day, 1 May; Caricom Day, first Monday in July; Freedom Day, first Monday in August; Christmas Day, 25 December, and Boxing Day, 26 December.

The following public holidays are for Hindu and Muslim festivals; they follow a lunar calender, and dates should be checked as required: Phagwah, usually March; Eid el Fitr, end of Ramadan; Eid el Azah; Youm un Nabi; Deepavali, usually November.

Note that the Republic Day celebrations last about a week: during this time hotels in Georgetown are very full.

**Official Time**   3 hrs behind GMT; one hour ahead of neighbouring regions of Brazil, Venezuela and Trinidad.

**Currency**   The unit is the Guyanese dollar. There are notes for 1, 5, 10, 20 and 100 dollars, though devaluation and inflation mean that even the largest of these is worth very little. Coins for amounts under a dollar exist but are of little practical use.

The devaluation of the Guyanese dollar in February 1991 aligned the official exchange rate with that offered by licensed exchange houses (known as *cambios*). Since that date the exchange rate was to be adjusted weekly in line with the market rate. In June 1991, this stood at G$125 = US$1. At present *cambios* only buy US or Canadian dollars and pounds sterling. Most *cambios* accept drafts (subject to verification), travellers' cheques and telegraphic transfers, but not credit cards. Rates vary slightly between *cambios* and from day to day and some *cambios* offer better rates for changing over US$100. Note that to sell Guyanese dollars on leaving the country, you will need to produce your *cambio* receipt. The illegal black market on America St. ("Wall Street") in Georgetown still operates, but the rates offered are not significantly better than the *cambio* rate and there is a strong risk of being robbed or cheated. The black market also operates in Springlands, the entry point from Suriname.

**Cost of Living**   The devaluation to the *cambio* rate means that, for foreigners, prices are low at present. Even imported goods may be cheaper than elsewhere and locally produced goods such as fruit are very cheap. For Guyanese dependent on local salaries, the country is expensive and becoming more so with rising inflation.

**Weights and Measures** Although Guyana went metric in 1982, imperial measures are still widely used.

**Voltage** 100 v in Georgetown; 220 v in most other places, including some Georgetown suburbs.

**Postal and Telephone Services** Overseas postal and telephone charges are very low. There are no public telephones. Some businesses and hotels may allow you to use their phone for local calls if you are buying something—usual charge about US$0.05. Overseas calls can be made from the Guyana Telephone and Telegraph Company office in the Bank of Guyana building (arrive early and be prepared for a long wait), or from the *Tower Hotel* (more expensive but more comfortable). Travel agencies may allow you to make overseas collect calls when buying tickets. International calls from private houses and from outside Georgetown are practically impossible.

**Press** *The Chronicle*, daily, government-run; *The Mirror*, weekly, opposition PPP-run; *The Stabroek News*, weekdays, independent; *The Catholic Standard*, weekly, well-respected and widely read. Street vendors charge more than the cover price—this is normal and helps them make a living.

**Broadcasting** There are two TV channels, mainly broadcasting programmes from US satellite television. GBC Radio is government-run and is often difficult to receive.

**Things to Take** Take a good supply of small gift items (e.g. imported cigarettes, batteries, good quality toiletries); these won't be asked for but will be well received. A good torch/flashlight (for the electricity cuts) is essential.

# SURINAME

SURINAME has a coast line on the Atlantic to the N; it is bounded on the W by Guyana and on the E by French Guyane; Brazil is to the S. Its area is 163,820 sq. km.

The principal rivers in the country are the Marowijne in the E, the Corantijn in the W, and the Suriname, Commewijne (with its tributary, the Cottica), Coppename, Saramacca and Nickerie. The country is divided into topographically quite diverse natural regions: lowland, savanna, and highland.

The northern part of the country consists of lowland, with a width in the E of 25 km., and in the W of about 80 km. The soil (clay) is covered with swamps with a layer of humus under them. Marks of the old sea-shores can be seen in the shell and sand ridges, overgrown with tall trees.

There follows a region, 5-6 km. wide, of a loamy and very white sandy soil, then a slightly undulating region, about 30 km. wide. It is mainly savanna, mostly covered with quartz sand, and overgrown with grass and shrubs.

South of this lies the interior highland, almost entirely overgrown with dense tropical forest and intersected by streams. At the southern boundary with Brazil there are again savannas. These, however, differ in soil and vegetation from the northern ones. A large area in the SW is in dispute between Guyana and Suriname. There is a less serious border dispute with Guyane in the SE.

**Climate** Tropical and moist, but not very hot, since the north-east trade wind makes itself felt during the whole year. In the coastal area the temperature varies on an average from 23° to 31°C, during the day; the annual mean is 27°C, and the monthly mean ranges from 26° to 28°C, only. The mean annual rainfall is about 2,340 mm. for Paramaribo and 1,930 mm for the western division. The seasons are: minor rainy season, November-February; minor dry season, February-April; main rainy season, April-August; main dry season, August-November. None of these seasons is, however, usually either very dry or very wet. The degree of cloudiness is fairly high and the average humidity is 82%. The climate of the interior is similar but with higher rainfall.

**History** Although Amsterdam merchants had been trading with the "wild coast" of Guiana as early as 1613 (the name Parmurbo-Paramaribo was already known) it was not until 1630 that 60 English settlers came to Suriname under Captain Marshall and planted tobacco. The real founder of the colony was Baron Willoughby of Parham, governor of Barbados, who sent an expedition to Suriname in 1651 under Anthony Rowse to find a suitable place for settlement. Willoughbyland became an agricultural colony with 500 little sugar plantations, 1,000 white inhabitants and 2,000 African slaves. Jews from Holland and Italy joined them, as well as Dutch Jews ejected from Brazil after 1654. On 27 February 1667, Admiral Crynssen conquered the colony for the states of Zeeland and Willoughbyfort became the present Fort Zeelandia. By the Peace of Breda—31 July 1667—it was agreed that Suriname should remain with the Netherlands, while Nieuw Amsterdam (New York) should be given to England. The colony was conquered by the British in 1799, and not until the Treaty of Paris in 1814 was it finally restored to the Netherlands. Slavery was forbidden in 1818 and formally abolished in 1863. Indentured labour from China and the East Indies took its place.

On 25 November 1975, the country became an independent republic, which signed a treaty with the Netherlands for an economic aid programme worth US$1.5bn until 1985. A military coup on 25 February 1980 overthrew the elected government. A state of emergency was declared, with censorship for press, radio and TV. The military leader, Col. Desi Bouterse, and his associates came under pressure from the Dutch and the USA as a result of dictatorial tendencies. After the execution of 15 opposition leaders on 8 December 1982, the Netherlands broke off relations and suspended its aid programme, although bridging finance was restored in 1988.

The ban on political parties was lifted in late 1985 and a new constitution was drafted. In 1986 guerrilla rebels (the Jungle Commando), led by a former bodyguard of Col. Bouterse, Ronny Brunswijk, mounted a campaign to overthrow the government, disrupting both plans for political change, and the economy. Nevertheless, elections for the National Assembly were held in November 1987. A three-party coalition (the Front for Democracy and Development) gained a landslide victory over the military, winning 40 of the 51 seats. In January 1988, a former agriculture minister, Mr Ramsewak Shankar, was elected President by the Assembly for a 5-year term. Conflicts between President Shankar and Col. Bouterse led to the deposition of the government in a bloodless coup on 24 December 1990 (the "telephone coup"). A military-backed government under the presidency of Johan Kraag was installed and elections for a new national assembly were held on 25 May 1991. The New Front of four traditional parties won 30 National Assembly seats. Twelve went to the army-backed National Democratic Party and nine to the Democratic Alternative, which favours closer links with The Netherlands. Both the Netherlands and the USA suspended aid after the coup, but the Dutch said they would reconsider relations after the elections. Although a basis for peace was drawn up in mid-1989 (the Kourou Accord), it was not until March 1991 that Col. Bouterse and Brunswijk stated publicly that hostilities had ceased (Brunswijk had declared an end to his campaign in June 1990). No formal ceasefire had been signed at the time of going to press. The relationships between the different groups, government, army, Jungle Commando, bush blacks and Amerindians, were complex, with the added dimension of involvement by some groups in the cocaine trade undermining efforts to end the civil war.

**Population** The 1980 census showed that the population had declined to 352,041, because of heavy emigration to the Netherlands. By 1989 it was estimated to have grown to 405,000. The 1983 population consisted of East Indians (known locally as Hindustanis), 37%; Creoles (European-African and other descent), 31%; Indonesians, 14%; Chinese, 3%; Amerindians, 3%, and Bush Blacks (retribalized descendants of slaves who escaped in the 17th century, living on the upper Saramacca, Suriname and Marowijne rivers), 8.5%; Europeans and others, 3%. About 90% of the existing population live in or around Paramaribo or in the coastal towns; the remainder, mostly Carib and Arawak Indians and Bush Blacks, are widely scattered. Life expectancy 68 years; birth rate, 25.9 per 1,000; death rate, 6.1 per 1,000; infant mortality 27.6 per thousand; literacy, 79.2%.

The Asian people originally entered the country as contracted estate labourers, and settled in agriculture or commerce after completion of their term. They dominate the countryside, whereas Paramaribo is a predominantly Creole city. One of Suriname's main problems is the racial tension between Creoles and East

Indians.

The official language is Dutch. The native dialect, called negro English (Sranan Tongo or Taki-Taki) originally the speech of the Creoles, is now a *lingua franca* understood by all groups, and standard English is widely spoken and understood. The Asians still speak their own languages among themselves.

**The Economy**  Agriculture is restricted to some districts of the alluvial coastal zone, covering about 0.8m hectares and employing about 16.7% of the labour force. At least two-thirds of permanent crop and arable land is under irrigation. Farming accounts for 9.4% of gdp and 10% of exports. The main crops are rice (the staple), sugar cane and citrus fruits, all of which are exported to Europe, along with small quantities of coffee and bananas. Apart from rice, Suriname is a net importer of food; priority is being given to rice and livestock. Between 1981 and 1983, the sector registered annual declines in output, but after 1984, positive growth was restored with the rice and shrimp sectors receiving new incentives. Suriname has vast timber resources, but exports account for only 1.1% of the total and development has been hampered by a lack of investment. There is a small fishing industry, the chief catch being shrimps.

Manufacturing's contribution to gdp is 16.0%, employing 10.6% of the workforce. Import substitution, using both imported goods and local raw materials, is the main activity, with food processing accounting for 60% of the total.

Suriname is the world's sixth largest producer of bauxite, with reserves estimated at 1.9% of the world's total. The country has the capability to process the extracted ore into alumina and aluminium ingot. The bauxite/aluminium industry accounts for 80% of exports, while the mining sector as a whole contributes 6.6% of gdp and employs 4.0% of the workforce. Two companies control the industry, the Suriname Aluminium Company (Suralco), a subsidiary of Alcoa, and Billiton Maatschappij, part of Royal Dutch Shell. Their progressive merging of operations to improve competitiveness on world markets began to yield positive results in 1986 until the industry was severely disrupted by the civil war which started in that year.

Oil production from the Tambaredjo heavy oil deposit, operated by the state oil company, Staatsolie, is about 2,000 bpd. Exploratory wells in the Saramacca district have also yielded oil. Installed electricity generating capacity is 415 MW, of which 54% is thermal, 46% hydroelectric.

After 5 years of decline and a fall in gdp of 8.1% in 1987 alone, the economy began to recover, helped by resumption of activity in the bauxite industry, the attenuation of the domestic insurgency and the resumption of aid from the Dutch Government. Consistent improvement was not maintained and The Netherlands, the IMF and World Bank urged Suriname to unify the official and parallel exchange rates, reduce state involvement in the economy and cut the huge budget deficit to attract overseas investment.

**Government**  There is one legislative house, the National Assembly, which has 51 members. The President is both head of state and government. Suriname is divided into ten districts, of which the capital is one.

**Warning**:  Those caught taking pictures of Fort Zeelandia, the People's Palace, police stations, military installations etc. face confiscation of their film, at least. Be careful also when taking pictures from ferries.

As a result of the civil war which began in 1986, large sections of the interior are under guerrilla control and travellers are advised not to go there. The coastal route from Guyane through Paramaribo to Nieuw Nickerie was however open. We retain our information on other places in the hope that the situation will improve (peace had not been restored by June 1991).

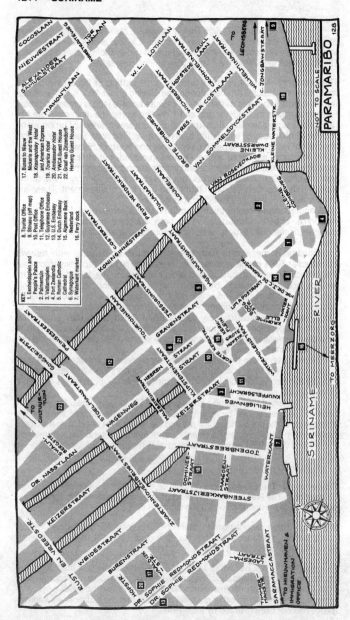

## PARAMARIBO

NOT TO SCALE

128

KEY:
1. Eenheidsplein and People's Palace
2. Palmentuin
3. Vaillantsplein
4. Fort Zeelandia
5. Roman Catholic Cathedral
6. Synagogue
7. Waterkant market

8. Tourist Office
9. Stinasu (off map)
10. Post Office
11. Telephone Office
12. Guyanese Embassy
13. U.S. Embassy
14. Dutch Embassy
15. Algemene Bank Nederland
16. Ferry dock

17. Buses to Nieuw Nickerie and the West
18. *Krasnopolsky Hotel*
19. *Torarica Hotel*
20. *Ambassador Hotel*
21. *YWCA Guest House*
22. *Graaf van Zinzendorff Herberg Guest House*

*Paramaribo*, the capital and chief port, lies on the Suriname river, 12 km. from the sea. It has a population of about 192,000, mainly Creoles. There are many attractive colonial buildings.

The People's Palace (the old Governor's Mansion) is on Eenheidsplein (formerly Onafhankelijkheidsplein, and before that, Oranjeplein) and many beautiful 18th and 19th century buildings in Dutch (neo-Normanic) style are in the same area. The restored Fort Zeelandia used to house the Suriname Museum, but the fort has been repossessed by the military (the whole area is fenced off); very few exhibits remain in the old museum in the residential suburb of Zorg-en-Hoop, Commewijnestraat, 0700-1300. Look for Mr. F. Lim-A-Po-straat if you wish to see what Paramaribo looked like only a comparatively short time ago. The nineteenth-century Roman Catholic Peter and Paul cathedral (1885), said to be the largest wooden building in the Americas, is built entirely of wood and is well worth a visit. Much of the old town and its churches have been restored, and date only from the nineteenth century. Other things to see are the colourful market and the waterfront, Hindu temples in Koningstraat, the Caribbean's largest mosque at Keizerstraat and the Synagogue (1854) at Heerenstraat (under renovation and closed since 1989). A new harbour has been constructed about 1½ km. upstream. Two pleasant parks are the Palmentuin and the Cultuurtuin (with zoo, US$1.20, busy on Sun.)—but the latter is quite a distance from the town and there are no buses to it. National dress is normally only worn by the Asians on national holidays and at wedding parties, but some Javanese women still go about in sarong and klambi. A university was opened in 1968. There is one public swimming pool at Weidestraat, US$0.60 p.p. There is an exotic Asian flavour to the market and nearby streets. Cinemas show US, Indian and Chinese movies, with subtitles.

**Hotels** Prices are at official rate unless stated otherwise. *Krasnapolsky* Domineestraat 39, T 75050, Fax 78524, L+ at official rate, at parallel, ugly, swimming pool and shops, good breakfast, launderette on 1st floor, and bank (open until 1430); much nicer is *Torarica*, A at parallel rate, very pleasant, book ahead, swimming pool, casino, nightclub, tropical gardens, fully air conditioned, central, superb breakfast US$6-12 (T 71500, Fax 11682); *Ambassador*, (T 77555, Fax 77903), Sophie-Redmondstraat, prices as *Krasnapolsky*, quality as poor; *Riverclub*, at Leonsberg (8 km. from city), T 51959, Fax 52981, same prices, many very-short-stay customers, swimming pool. Service charge at hotels is 10-15%.

For budget travellers, best is still the recently refurbished *YWCA Guesthouse* at Heerenstraat 14-16, T 76981, D (at official exchange rate, G parallel), cheaper weekly rates, clean, full of permanent residents, essential to book in advance (office open 0800-1400); if it's full try the *Graaf Van Zinzendorff-Herberg* at Gravenstraat 100, the same price as the YWCA. Advance booking advisable. Otherwise, try *Continental Inn*, E; *Fanna*, Princessestraat 31, T 76789, D (official), G (parallel), safe, clean, friendly; *Au Soleil Levant*; E. *La Vida* on the way in from the airport is "cheap but nice". *Blue Moon*, Prinsesesstraat, D, overpriced, fleas; *Lisa's Guest House*, Buren Straat. *Balden*, Kwathweg 183, 2 km. from centre on the road to Nickerie is probably the cheapest available accommodation; its Chinese restaurant serves cheap meals. Beware: many cheap hotels not listed above are "hot pillow" establishments. The *Salvation Army* will give the hard up a bed for Sf4.50 a night (Saramaccastraat).

**Restaurants** Main meals cost Sf60-100 p.p. There are some good restaurants, mainly Indonesian and Chinese dishes. Try a *rijsttafel* in an Indonesian restaurant, e.g. *Sarinah* (open-air dining), Verlengde Gemenelandsweg 187. *La Bastille*, Kleine Waterstraat, opp. *Tocarica*, good, T 73991; also *Golden Dragon*, Anamoestraat 22, *New Korean*, Mahonylaan, *Golden Crown*, David Simmonstraat and *New China*, Verlengde Gemenelandsweg. *Fa Tai*, Maagdstraat 64, air conditioned; for the best Chinese food, but not cheap, try *Iwan's*, Grote Hofstraat. Many other Chinese restaurants: *Chi Wan* for its *egg foo yung* and *won ton soup*, Keizerstraat and Zwartenhovenbrugstraat 16. The *YWCA Cafeteria* is quite good. Cheap lunches and light meals at *Hofje*, Wagenwegstraat, and *Chalet Swiss*, Heerenstraat (more Chinese than Swiss.) Meat and noodles from stalls in the market costs Sf3.00. Javanese foodstalls on Waterkant are excellent and varied, lit at night by candles. Try *bami* (spicy noodles) for Sf1 and *petjil* (vegetables) for Sf0.50. Especially rec. on Sundays when the area is busiest. In restaurants a dish to try is *gadogado*, an Indonesian vegetable and peanut concoction, available for about Sf5. Good places for lunch include *Hola's Terrace*, Domineestraat. For breakfast, try *Klein Maar Fijn*, Watermolenstraat. The ice-cream parlour in Keizerstraat has been rec. as selling the best ice-cream in the Guianas.

**Shopping** *Arts & Crafts*, Neumanpad 13a. Amerindian goods, batik prints, carvings, basket work, drums are attractive. *Cultuurwinkel*, Anton de Kom Straat, bushnegro carvings, also available at *Hotel Torarica*. Carvings are better value at the workshops on Nieuwe Dominee Straat and the Neumanpad. Old Dutch bottles US$10-25.

**Bookshops** The two main bookshops are *Vaco* and *Kersten*, both on Domineestraat, and both sell English-language books. Also *Hoeksteen* (Gravenstraat 17) and the kiosk in *Krasnapolsky Hotel*. *Boekhandel Univers N.V.*, Gravenstraat 61, is recommended for nature, linguistic and scholarly books on Suriname. Second hand books, English and Dutch, are bought and sold in the market. Most bookshops sell a large map of Paramaribo, price US$7.

**Local Transport** Buses run regularly to most parts of the city; most services leave from Waterkant or Dr. Sophie Redmondstraat. There are also privately run "wild buses", also known as "numbered buses" which run on fixed routes around the city.

**Taxis** generally have no meters. The price should be agreed on beforehand to avoid trouble. A trip inside the city costs about Sf15. Rec. is Ally's Taxi service, T 79434, English spoken.

**Self-Drive Cars** City Taxi, Purperhart, Kariem, Intercar, and other agencies. Kentax (T 72078) is open 24 hours a day. All driving licences accepted, but you need a stamp from the local police and a deposit of US$140-420. Gasoline/petrol is sold as "regular", or "extra" (more expensive).

**Bicycles** Can be bought for about US$100 from A. Seymonson, Rijwielhersteller, Rust en Vredestraat (cheaper in Guyana). Recommended rides include to Nieuw Amsterdam, Marienburg, Alkmaar and back via Tamanredjo in the Javanese Commewijne district or from Rust en Werk to Spieringshoek to Reijnsdorp (3½ hours) and return to Leonsberg via ferry, whence it is a 30 minute ride to Paramaribo.

**Exchange** Algemene Bank Nederland (Kerkplein 1), Surinaamse Bank and Hakrin Bank, 0700-1400. Surinaamse branch in *Hotel Krasnapolsky* open 0700-1430; 0800-1200 Sat., Amex agents, charges Sf1.30 flat rate commission on each travellers cheque exchanged. Black market (illegal) around Waterkant market (see **Currency** in Information for Visitors).

**Church** The Anglican Church is St. Bridget's, Hoogestraat 44 (Sunday 0900 service in English).

**Golf Club** Introduction from a member required.

**Tourist Bureau** On waterfront, Waterkant 8, T 71163/78421 (P.O.Box 656). Has useful handouts on lodgings in town and rural areas as well as restaurants. Free city map. English spoken, friendly and helpful; organizes tours (4 days at Sf275) and bus journeys.

**Tourist Agencies** *Stinasu*, the Foundation for Nature Preservation in Suriname, Jongbawstraat 14, T 75845/71856, P.O. Box 436, Paramaribo, offers reasonably priced accommodation and provide tour guides on the extensive nature reserves throughout the country. One can see "true wilderness and wildlife" with them. (**See page 1218.**) Mrs. W. J. Robles-Cornelissen, *Independent Tours*, Rosenveltkade 20, T 74770, organizes excursions to the interior. *Ram's Tours*, Neumandplaan 30 Ben, T 76011/76223. *Does Travel Service*, Domineestraat. *Saramaccan Jungle Safaris* (John Ligeon), P.O. Box 676, Zwartenhovenbrugstraat 19, Paramaribo, has been recommended for visits by canoe to Saramaccan Bush Black villages and wildlife tours. *Suriname Safari Tours*.

**Bus Services** To **Nickerie** from Dr. Sophie Redmondstraat, last usually at 1200, Sf20 (extra for large bag). Other westbound services from Waaldijkstraat; to **Totness** at 1300. To **Afobaka** via Brokopondo, leaves from Saramaccastraat, at 0700. To **Brownsberg** at 0930. In 1990/91 there were no services eastwards to Albina via Moengo. For full details enquire at the tourist office.

**Local Shipping** The three ferries across the main rivers operate only in daytime (the Paramaribo-Meerzorg ferry until 2200). Two bridges have been built. The Suriname Navigation Co. (SMS) has a daily service, leaving 0700, on the Commewijne river (a nice four-hour trip; one can get off—see below—at *De Nieuwe Grond*, a plantation owned by an English couple, and stay overnight). The SMS has a daily service to Reynsdorp, leaving Paramaribo early in the morning. SMS also has infrequent services on other rivers (Wayombo and Cottica). The coastal service to Nieuw Nickerie has been discontinued, but there is a weekly (Mon.) 36-hour run there over inland waterways (**see page 1218**).

**Airports** The international airport is Zanderij, 45 km. S. of Paramaribo. Minibus or shared taxi to town costs Sf75; ordinary taxi, Sf150, regular minibus, marked PZB or POZ, which leaves from the service station 15 minutes' walk from the centre on the south highway, US$0.30, daytime only. De Paarl minibus rec. as cheaper (T 79600).

Money exchange facilities, Hakrin Bank between Customs and Immigration (closed Sundays). There is a new guest house near Zanderij airport.

Internal flights leave from Zorg-en-Hoop airfield in a suburb of Paramaribo; since 1988, local flights have been restricted to two destinations: Nieuw Nickerie and Apoera.

**Note** It is advisable to check the weather conditions and probabilities of returning on schedule before you set out on a trip to the interior. Heavy rains can make it impossible for planes to land in some jungle areas; little or no provision is made for such delays and it can be a long and hungry wait for better conditions. Check also that entry to the area you wish to visit is permitted.

**Excursions** Powaka, about 90 minutes outside the capital, is a primitive village of thatched huts but with electric light and a small church. In the surrounding forest one can pick mangoes and other exotic fruit. An interesting half, or full day excursion is to take Minibus 4, 0800, or taxi, to Leonsberg on the Suriname river, then ferry to **Nieuw Amsterdam**, the capital of the predominantly Javanese district of Commewijne. There is an open-air museum inside the old fortress (open only in mornings except Fri. 1700-1900, Sf15), which guarded the confluence of the Suriname and Commewijne rivers. There are some old plantation mansions left in the Commewijne district which are of interest; Mariënburg is the last sugar estate in operation in Suriname. The return trip can be made by bus to Meerzorg on the river, taking the vehicle ferry back to Paramaribo.

By private car to **Jodensavanne** (Jews' Savanna, established 1639), S of Paramaribo on the opposite bank of the Suriname river, where part of one of the oldest synagogues in the Western Hemisphere has been restored. It has a small museum. There are interesting Amerindian villages nearby. You need permission from the Forestry Department (LBB), in Jongbawstraat, to use the ferry to Jodensavanne. There is a new guesthouse, D (with six rooms), at Blakkawatra, nearby. Accommodation is available through Stinasu (see above) and camping is possible. Some 4 km. from Zanderij Airport there is a resort called Cola Creek, so named for the colour of the water, but good swimming.

By bus or car to **Afobakka**, where there is a large hydro-electric dam on the Suriname river. There is a government guesthouse, C (including 3 meals a day) in nearby **Brokopondo**. Victoria is an oil-palm plantation in the same area. The Brownsberg National Park is one hour by car from here.

The narrow-gauge railway, originally built for the Lawa goldfields, between Onverwacht (½ hour from Paramaribo by bus, Sf1, route PBO) and Brownsweg (87 km.) is no longer in operation. There is no hotel at Brownsweg, but transport (14 km. up hill) to **Brownsberg**, where there is accommodation, can be arranged, US$20 (T 75845, Ext 34). The return bus is supposed to leave at 1100. Guest house, C. A bus to Paramaribo leaves Brownsweg every morning (price doubles between low and high seasons—see page 1221).

Stinasu arranges trips to the Brownsberg Park (entry US$1) as well as the Raleigh Falls/Voltzberg Nature Reserve on the Coppename river (good swimming), the Wia-Wia reserve on the northeast coast where giant sea-turtles nest, and the Galibi reserve on the Marowijne river, another nesting place for turtles. There is accommodation of sorts in all these places. Soft drinks are generally available from Park offices. See below for more details on Nature Reserves.

Suriname Airways (SLM) has organized tours to **Stoelmanseiland** on the Lawa River (guest house with full board, C, including meals) in the interior, and to the Bush Black villages and rapids in that area. Price US$150 p.p. for 3 days (5 persons, minimum). SLM and other airlines (Gonini, GumAir) organize occasional charters to Tepoe, up the Tapanahony river in the S, where one can visit the Trio and Wayana Indians.

**Nature Reserves** N.B. In 1989 all reserves except Matapica were closed due to the civil war; it is not known what facilities exist (or will exist when reopened) for the visitor. **Raleighvallen/Voltzberg Nature Reserve** (57,000 hectares) is rain-forest park, including Foengoe Island and Voltzberg peak; climbing the mountain at sunrise is unforgettable.

The **Coppename Estuary** is also a national park, protecting many bird colonies.

Only two or three hours by car from Paramaribo is the **Brownsberg Nature Park** (6,000 hectares). In this tropical rain-forest park live giant toads, communal spiders, monkeys, jaguars, peccaries, agoutis, and a variety of birds. Hiking maps are available at the Park office, and a guidebook to the birds of Brownsberg can be purchased in the **Stinasu office** in Paramaribo. A useful contact is Lesley Hattun (English speaking) Stinasu, P.O.B. 436, Paramaribo. T 75845/71856, who is the organization tour organizer.

Two reserves are located on the northeast coast of Suriname. Known primarily as a major nesting site for sea turtles—five species including the huge leatherback turtle come ashore to lay their eggs—**Wia-Wia Nature Reserve** (36,000 hectares), also has nesting grounds for some magnificent birds. The nesting activity of sea turtles is best observed February-July. Since the beaches and consequently the turtles have shifted westwards out of the reserve, accommodation is now at **Matapica** beach, not in the reserve itself. (After a visit to the reserves please send any comments to Hilde Viane at Stinasu. Your support is needed to keep the reserve functioning.) There may also be mosquitoes and sandflies, depending on the season. A riverboat leaves Paramaribo daily at 0700 (buy ticket on board) and arrives in Alliance by way of the Commewijne River at 1100. You then transfer to a Stinasu motorboat for a one-hour ride to Matapica. The motorboat costs US$50 for 4 people, round trip. Suitable waterproof clothing should be worn. The beach hut accommodates 18 people in 4 rooms, and costs US$4 p.p. Take your own bedding/food. Cooking facilities provided. Book the hut and boat through Stinasu and keep your receipts or you will be refused entry. Early booking is essential as the closure of the other reserves has made Matapica very popular.

The **Galibi Nature Reserve**, where there are more turtle-nesting places, is near the mouth of the Marowijne River. There are Carib Indian villages. From Albina it is a 3-hour (incl. ½ hr. on the open sea) boat trip to Galibi.

**Nieuw Nickerie**, on the S bank of the Nickerie River 5 km. from its mouth, opposite Guyana is the main town and port of the Nickerie district and is distinguished for its ricefields and for the number and voraciousness of its mosquitoes. The town has a population of more than 8,000, the district of 35,000, mostly East Indian. Paramaribo is 237 km. away by road. Buses leave hourly or when full, Sf20 (extra for large bag) and take less time (5 hrs.) with the opening of the bridge than they did before. A special, late afternoon bus connecting with the ferry from Guyana may cost Sf40. Sit on the left-hand side of the bus to get the best views of the bird-life in the swamps. SLM has two daily flights to the capital (Sf60), often cancelled at short notice. The coastal ferry service has been discontinued, but once a week the SMS company makes an interesting water trip, using inland waterways, to Nieuw Nickerie taking 36 hours; it leaves Paramaribo on Mondays at 0800, departs Nieuw Nickerie 1200 Wednesday (times subject to 2 hrs variation due to tides), no cabins, only slatted seats, but there is hammock space; take food and drink; lots of mosquitoes.

**Hotels** *Blue Hawaii*, E, central, reported to overcharge foreigners; *Dorien*, T 031352, C, bed and breakfast; *Ameerali*, G.G. Maynardstraat, T 0316427/031212, fax 031066, near ferry, clean, A (official rate), E (parallel); *De-Vesting*, similar quality, but B/E prices, Balatastraat near ferry, T 031265. On Gouverneurstraat are *Tropical, President* and *Luxor*, E-F, among the cheapest.

**Restaurant** *Moksie Patoe*, Gouverneurstraat 115, run by Frenchman, Jean Amar, provides European and Indian dishes with items rarely found elsewhere in friendly atmosphere. *Ella*, Javanese food. *Tokyo*, rather basic. Good food at the Asanredjo foodstand (unmarked), ask to be directed, two blocks east of *Ajai*, on Oranjenassaustraat. Cheap filling meals can be obtained on the street for as little as US$1.50.

**Banks** Algemene Bank Nederland, Hakrin Bank, Post Office Savings Bank, People's Credit Bank, Surinaamse Bank. The bank at the immigration office is reported to close at 1500 Mon.-Fri., whether or not the ferry has arrived.

**Ferry to Springlands, Guyana**, Sf15, one way, 2 hrs., no service Sun. or national holidays of either country, foot passengers only. Best to book 24 hrs. in advance, though you can book on day of departure. Book for same day departures by handing in your passport at the Immigration Office, 200 metres below ferry point, opens 0700, be there 0630. After booking, go to the stelling (ferry pier) and pass quite quickly through outgoing customs inspection and immigration. Book in advance either at Immigration Office or at military police station, corner of Maynardstraat and Bataviastraat, Mon.-Fri. 0900-1200, Sat. 0900-1100. Guyanese entry and currency forms available on ferry, US$0.50. For entry to Guyana a return ferry ticket will suffice as an onward ticket: without one you can be sent back on the next ferry. You will reach Springlands at 1000; take a minibus immediately to New Amsterdam, then launch, then minibus from Rossignol to get to Georgetown by 1400. Whole journey time 26 hrs., overall cost US$5 (ex parallel rates).

The EEC has approved a grant of ECU 12m to finance the provision of a new ferry service to Guyana; a new terminal for the ferry is to be constructed 25 km. up river from Nieuw Nickerie; it had not been brought into service by June 1991.

**Totness** is the largest village in the Coronie district, along the coast between Paramaribo and Nieuw Nickerie. There is a good government guesthouse, E. The road (bad, liable to flooding) leads through an extensive forest of coconut palms. Bus to Paramaribo at 0600.

**Wageningen** is a modern little town, the centre of the Suriname rice-growing area. The road from Nickerie has recently been renewed. One of the largest fully mechanized rice farms in the world is found here. (*Hotel de Wereld*, C.) The Bigi-Pan area of mangroves is a bird-watchers' paradise; boats may be hired from local fishermen.

Vast reserves of bauxite have been discovered in the Bakhuis Mountains, in the northern part of Nickerie District. A road has been built from Zanderij to Apoera, but the laterite roads to the Bakhuis Mountains and on to the Kabalebo River, where a large hydro-electric station is planned are now overgrown and almost impassable. Gasoline available at Apoera only. **Apoera** is on the Corantijn and can also be reached by sea-going vessels. **Blanche Marie Falls**, 320 km. from Paramaribo on the Apoera road, is a popular destination. There is a guesthouse, *Dubois*, B, contact Eldoradolaan 22, Paramaribo T 76904/2. Camping is Sf30 tent/day. There is a good guesthouse at Apoera (C, with 3 meals, advance booking from Paramaribo advisable). **Washabo** near Apoera, which has an airstrip, is an Amerindian village. There is no public transport from Paramaribo to the Apoera-Bakhuis area, but many private cars and trucks go there and there are frequent charter flights to the Washabo airstrip. Irregular small boats go from Apoera to Nieuw Nickerie and to Springlands (Guyana). Try to rent a canoe to visit the Amerindian settlement of Orealla in Guyana or Kaboeri creek, 12 km. downstream, where giant river otters may possibly be seen in October or March.

**Moengo**, 160 km. up the Cottica River from Paramaribo, is a bauxite mining and loading centre for the Suriname Aluminium Company (Suralco) a subsidiary of Alcoa. (*Government Guesthouse*, B, annex D.) Paranam, another loading centre for the Company, is on the left bank of the Suriname River. It can be reached by medium draught ships and by cars. Near Paranam is Smalkalden, where bauxite is loaded by the Billiton company on the road to Paramaribo.

**Albina**, the eastern frontier village, is 140 km. from Paramaribo, 29 km. from the mouth of the Marowijne River—the boundary with French Guyane. In normal times Albina is the centre for trips by powered dugouts to Amerindian and Bush Black villages on the Marowijne, Tapanahoni and Lawa rivers (about Sf50 plus). It takes 1½-2 days to get to the beautiful Stoelmanseiland (**see Excursions, page 1217**). There is a park along the Marowijne river (about 15 minutes walk from the town centre) called Het Park with free hammock places. Opposite Albina, in French Guyane, is St.-Laurent (**see page 1227**), with good restaurants and the old penal settlement to see.

The border crossing to Guyane was reopened in 1991. It is essential to get correct entry stamps from Immigration, not the police. If you do not, you will have real problems on departure.

---

## INFORMATION FOR VISITORS

**Documents** Visitors must have a valid passport (issued by any government other than those of the communist countries or Hong Kong), a visa, or tourist card. Visas cost US$20 and must be obtained in advance (up to 4 weeks wait not unusual) by citizens of all countries except Great Britain, Japan, Israel, The Gambia, South Korea, Denmark, Finland, Sweden, Switzerland, Netherlands Antilles, Brazil, Ecuador, Canada, Chile and Guyana (these require a tourist card, obtainable at the airport, US$14). There are consulates in Caracas, Brasília, Georgetown and Cayenne. Even with a visa you may on arrival be given only an eight day entry permit, but extensions may be obtained by reporting to the Immigration Office, van't Hogerhuystraat, Nieuwe Haven, Paramaribo, as soon as possible after arrival, with two passport-size photos (extension costs US$6).

**Airport Tax** There is an exit tax of US$15 (Sf30).

**Air Services** Zanderij airport is served by SLM (Suriname Airways), KLM, Air France, ALM and Cruzeiro do Sul. SLM flies to Miami (once a week—May 1991), Amsterdam (4 a week), Belém, Curaçao, once a week each, Cayenne (twice a week), and Georgetown (4 times a week). KLM flies from Amsterdam twice a week, once via Port of Spain; Air France flies from Cayenne Pointe à Pitre (Guadeloupe) once a week, and ALM from Curaçao once a week. Cruzeiro do Sul flies to Cayenne and Belém on Mondays. Many people go to Cayenne to take advantage of cheap Air France tickets to Europe as well as increased seat availability. Internal services are maintained by SLM and two small air charter firms.

**Travelling to Guyana and Guyane** The ferry crossing to Guyana is covered in the text. There is no overland crossing to Guyane owing to the war in eastern Suriname, but note that GUM-Air flies to St.-Laurent du Maroni in western Guyane from the Zorg-en-Hoop airfield near Paramaribo.

**Visa for Guyana** Nearly everyone now needs a visa to enter Guyana. The application form costs US$0.50, visa US$3, from the Guyanese Embassy at 82 Gravenstraat, open Mon., Wed., Fri., 0800-1300. Same day service if you make an early application. Take three passport photos and onward ticket from Guyana.

**Embassies** USA (Dr. Sophie Redmondstraat 129, P.O. Box 1821, T 72900), Netherlands, Belgium, Brazil, Cuba, France, Mexico, Venezuela, South Korea, India, Indonesia, Guyana, India, Japan, China (People's Republic), USSR.

**Consulates** There are consuls-general, vice-consuls or consular agents for Canada, Denmark, Dominican Republic, Ecuador, Finland, Germany, Haiti, UK, Mexico, Norway, Spain, and Sweden—all in Paramaribo. British Honorary Consul, Mr. James Healy, T 72870 office/74764 house, is very helpful.

**Customs** Duty-free imports include (if declared) 400 cigarettes or 100 cigars or ½ kg. of tobacco, 2 litres of spirits and 4 litres of wine, 50 grams of perfume and 1 litre of toilet water, 8 rolls of still film and 60 metres of cinefilm, 100 metres of recording tape, and other goods up to a value of Sf40. Personal baggage is free of duty. Customs examination of baggage can be very thorough.

**Communications** There are 2,500 km of main roads, of which 850 km are paved. The main east-west road, 390 km in length, links Albina (inaccessible in 1991) with Nieuw Nickerie. Driving is on the left. Most settlements have an airstrip, but internal air services are limited. Internal bus services are poor.

**Tourism** Points of interest are: some colonial architecture, especially in and around Paramaribo; and the tropical flora and fauna in this very sparsely populated country. There are no beaches to speak of; the sea and the rivers in the coastal area are muddy, and mosquitoes can be a worry in places. Hotels and restaurants are rare outside the capital, and you usually have to bring your own hammock and mosquito net, and food. A tent is less useful in this climate. Hitchhiking is not common, but it is possible. The **high seasons**, when everything is more expensive, are 15 March-15 May, July-September and 15 December-15 January. Travelling is only cheap if you can change cash dollars on the black market, but taking your own hammock and food will reduce costs. Note that travel has been limited within Suriname since 1986, especially eastward to Albina and French Guyane.

**Health** No special precautions necessary except for a trip to the malarial interior; for free malaria prophylaxis contact the Public Health Department (BOG). Chloroquine-resistant malaria in the interior. Mosquito nets should be used at night over beds in rooms not air-conditioned or screened. Outside Paramaribo drinking water should still be boiled despite protestations. In some coastal districts there is a risk of bilharzia (schistosomiasis). Vaccinations: yellow fever and tetanus advisable, typhoid only for trips into the interior. Swim only in running water because of poisonous fish. There is good swimming on the Marowijne river and at Matapica beach and on the Coppename river. There are 5 hospitals in Paramaribo, best is St. Vincentius.

**Clothing** Except for official meetings, informal tropical clothing is worn, but not shorts. An umbrella or plastic raincoat is very useful.

**Hours of Business** Shops and Businesses: Mon.-Thurs 0730-1630, Fri. 0730-1300 and 1700-2000, Sat. 0730-1300. Government departments: Mon.-Thur. 0700-1500, Fri. 0700-1430. Banks are open Mon.-Fri. 0730-1400. The airport bank is open at flight arrival and departure times.

**Public Holidays** 1 January, New Year; Holi Phagwa (1 day in March); Good Friday; Easter (2 days); 1 May (Labour Day); 1 July (National Unity); 25 November (Independence Day); Christmas (2 days). For Moslem holidays see note under Guyana (**page 1210**).

**Time** is 3 hrs. behind GMT.

**Currency** The unit of currency is the Suriname guilder (Sf) divided into 100 cents. There are notes for 5, 10, 25, 100 and 500 guilders. Since end-1982 only notes showing the revolutionary symbol have been legal tender: do not accept the old ones. Coins are for 1 guilder and 5, 10, 25 (the 25-cent coin is usually known as a *kwartje*) and 50 cents. Suriname's monetary system is quite independent of Holland's; the Suriname guilder is valued officially against the US dollar at US$1 = Sf1.78 (fixed), which makes Suriname one of the most expensive in the world, but at the parallel rate of about Sf16=US$1 (June 1991), it is one of the cheapest. Parallel trading is illegal. The easiest place to change is on the stelling (ferry pier) at Springlands (Guyana), where it's not against the law. In Paramaribo visit the market; traders will approach you. Find out the day's rate and go elsewhere to change money, e.g. a discreet shopkeeper or other contact (rates will be slightly worse).

The **metric** system is in general use.

**Electricity Supply** 127 volts AC, 60 cycles. Plug fittings are usually 2-pin round (European continental type). Lamp fittings are screw type.

**Post, Telegraph, Telephone** Telegrams can be sent from 0700 until 2200 and from Government Telegraph Service, Gravenstraat, in urgent cases.
There is a telephone and telegraph office on Vaillantplein. Book and pay in advance, very time-consuming. Calls can be made to the US and UK via satellite. The office is open 0700-2000; calls booked before 2000 can be made up till midnight. Censorship is reported to be in operation on telephones and mail. Best way to communicate abroad is by Fax at TeleSur, which can receive faxes for the public as well as send; number is 10555.

**Newspapers** in Dutch, *De Ware Tijd* and *DeWest* (evening).

**Broadcasting** There are several stations in Paramaribo and in the districts, broadcasting in Dutch, Hindi, Negro English and Javanese. There is also one state-controlled television station called Surinaamse Televisie Stichting (STVS), transmitting for 4 hours daily in colour on channel 8 (in Dutch), and a second channel, ATV.

**Information** about Suriname can be had from: the Suriname Embassy, Alex. Gogelweg 2, The Hague, Netherlands (T 070-65-08-44) or the Tourist Board, Waterkant 8, P.O.B. 656 (T 71163/78421; telex 292 Surair SN), Paramaribo, or Stinasu, Cornelis Jongbawstraat 14, P.O.B. 436 (T 75845). Also from embassies.

The *Surinam Planatlas* is available from the National Planning office on Dr. Sophie Redmondstraat, Sf100; maps with natural environment and economic development topics, each with commentary in Dutch and English. Beautifully prepared and a real bargain.

# GUYANE

GUYANE, an Overseas Department of France, has its eastern frontier with Brazil formed partly by the River Oiapoque (Oyapoc in French) and its southern, also with Brazil, formed by the Tumuc-Humac mountains. The western frontier with Suriname is along the River Maroni-Itani. To the north is the Atlantic coastline of 320 km. The area is estimated at 89,941 square km., or one-sixth that of France. The land rises gradually from a coastal strip some 15-40 km. wide to the higher slopes and plains or savannas, about 80 km. inland. Forests cover some 8 million hectares of the hills and valleys of the interior, and timber production is increasing rapidly.

The territory is well watered, for over twenty rivers run to the Atlantic. Besides those named above, there are the Mana, Cayenne, Sinnamarie (with its tributary the Coureibo), Maroni, Oyack, and Approuage. Smaller rivers are the Inini, Ardoua, and Camopi.

The only mountain range of importance is the Tumuc-Humac. Among the higher peaks are Mounts Mitarka, Temorairem, Leblond, and Timotakem; this last in the extreme S on the Brazilian frontier. The mountains reach a height of 800 metres.

**Climate** is tropical with a very heavy rainfall. Average temperature at sea-level is 27°C, and fairly constant at that. Night and day temperatures vary more in the highlands. The rainy season is from November to July, with (sometimes) a short dry interruption in February and March. The great rains begin in May. The dry season is from July to mid-November.

**History**   Awarded to France by the Peace of Breda in 1667, Guyane was twice attacked, first by the British in 1654 and later by the Dutch in 1676. In the same year the French retook possession and remained undisturbed until 1809. In that year a combined Anglo-Portuguese naval force captured the colony, which was handed over to the Portuguese (Brazilians). Though the land was restored to France by the Treaty of Paris in 1814, the Portuguese remained until 1817. Gold was discovered in 1853, and disputes arose about the frontiers of the colony with Suriname and Brazil. These were settled by arbitration in 1891, 1899, and 1915. By the law of 19 March, 1946, the Colony of Cayenne, or Guyane Française, became the Department of Guyane, with the same laws, regulations, and administration as a department in metropolitan France. The seat of the Prefect and of the principal courts is at Cayenne. The colony was used as a prison for French convicts with camps scattered throughout the country; Saint-Laurent was the port of entry. After serving prison terms convicts spent an equal number of years in exile and were usually unable to earn their return passage to France. Those interested should read *Papillon* by Henri Charrière. Majority opinion seems to be in favour of greater autonomy: about 5% of the population are thought to favour independence.

**The People**   The total population is estimated 97,000, the work force 38,000. The basic population 95,000 consists of Creoles, who, by the widest measure, account for 72% of the population; bush negroes, 6.4%; Amerindians, 4.2%; Asians, Europeans and others (including Brazilians), 17.1%. There are an estimated 15,000 migrant workers from Haiti and nearby countries. Their presence has contributed to a rise in the school age population from 13,215 in 1973 to 21,660 by 1987/88; the literacy rate is 82%.

**Note** The Amerindian villages in the Haut-Maroni and Haut-Oyapoc areas may only be visited with permission from the Préfecture in Cayenne *before* departure to Guyane.

**The Economy** Guyane has renewable natural riches in its timber forests (about 80,000 sq km.) with 15 sawmills and mineral resources. Farming employs only 13% of the population and the country is very sparsely populated. An estimated 42 million tons of extractable bauxite have been located in the Kaw mountains to the SE of Cayenne by Alcoa and Pechiney. Some 40m tonnes of kaolin have been located at St.-Laurent du Maroni and gold is again being mined.

Guyane imports most of its foodstuffs and manufactured goods, of which about 50% come from France. The value of exports, mainly shrimps, rum, essence of rosewood, hardwoods and gold, is very low; France buys just over 20% and the USA about 50%.

At end-1982 the French Government announced plans to step up the Department's development in consultation with local parties: the so-called Green Plan (Plan Vert), backed by the Société Financière de Développement de la Guyane. Under the plan local production of basic foodstuffs, such as meat and eggs, was to be raised, and areas of timber plantations doubled to 22,000 hectares. In recent years new building has taken place and facilities for visitors have been much improved.

**Government** The head of state is the President of France; the local heads of government are a Commissioner of the Republic, for France, and the Presidents of the local General and Regional Councils. The General Council (19 seats) and the Regional Council (31 seats) are the two legislative houses. Guyane is divided into two *arrondissements*, Cayenne and St. Laurent du Maroni.

**Cayenne**, the capital and the chief port, is on the island of Cayenne at the mouth of the Cayenne River. It is 645 km. from Georgetown (Guyana) and 420 km. from Paramaribo (Suriname) by sea. Population 42,000. There is an interesting museum in Rue de Remire, near the Place de Palmistes, which includes paintings of convict life on the Iles du Salut (open Tues.-Sat. 0800-1300, Sun. 0900-1200, Mon. 1000-1300, Tues. and Fri. 1600-1830; free admission). Also worth a visit are Crique, the colourful but dangerous area around the Canal Laussat (built by Malouet in 1777); the Jesuit-built residence (circa 1890) of the Prefect (L'Hôtel-de-Ville) in the Place de Grenoble; the Place des Amandiers (also known as the Place Auguste-Horth) by the sea; the Place des Palmistes, with assorted palms; a swimming pool; a municipal library and five cinemas. There are bathing beaches (water rather muddy) around the island, the best is Montjoly (no bus), but watch out for sharks.

**Hotels** *Novotel Cayenne*, T 303888, on beach, A+, restaurant, a/c, very good; *Amazonia*, Av. Gen. de Gaulle, A, good, friendly, a/c, luggage stored, central location, T 30-03-02; *Guyane Studios*, 16 rue Mole, T 30-25-11, A; *Ajoupa*, T 30-33-08, Route Camp de Tigre, 2 km. From town, A-B, helpful; *Le Baduel*, T 30-51-58, A; *Central Hotel*, corner rue Mole and rue Becker, T 31-30-00, A; *Phigarita Studios*, 47 bis, rue F. Arago, T 30-66-00, A+, friendly, helpful, breakfast 40F; *Chez Mathilde*, Av. Gen. de Gaulle 42, D-C, hammock space, friendly, clean, noisy, not safe for left luggage, always full; *Neptima*, Rue F. Eboué 21, T 30-11-15 (15 rooms), C, best value, a/c, clean, friendly. *Madeleine*, T 30-17-36, B, a/c, basic, clean, breakfast, will book Raffinel bus to St.-Laurent, 1 km. out of town, friendly (good Surinamese snackbar nearby). Cheapest in town is *Foyer Paul VI*, Rue Yasim, T 30-04-16, E, cheap meals. About 9 km. from Cayenne is the *Beauregard*, A. Also *Hotel M*, a motel with air conditioned rooms and a small swimming pool; the owner hires out small cars, rec. for businessmen, breakfast, T 35-41-00, Telex 010 310. Mme. Izeros, T 31-06-55, lets out rooms, D, without breakfast. Most hotels do not add tax and service to their bill, but stick to prices

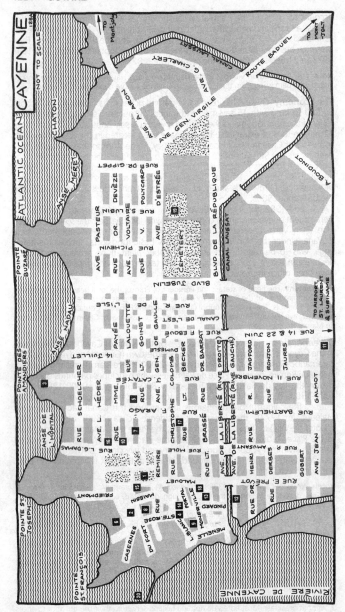

CAYENNE

NOT TO SCALE

ATLANTIC OCEAN

posted outside or at the desk. Hotel rooms are expensive—at the end of 1990 none cost less than 150F a night double. Bed and breakfast accommodation is available for about US$20-30 a night—contact the tourist office for details. Amex cards often not accepted but Visa OK.

**Restaurants and Bars** Main hotels. *L'Auberge des Amandiers*, Place Auguste-Horth, excellent, good value; *Armand Ti A Hing*, Place des Palmistes, French, excellent, 180F p.p.; *Cap St. Jacques*, Rue Docteur E. Gippet, excellent Vietnamese food, reasonable. *Maxim'um*, Av. Estrée. *La Croix du Sud*, 80, Av. de Gaulle; *Le Snack Créole*, 17 Rue Eboué; *Palmiste*, 12 Av. de Gaulle, central and spacious; *Frégate*, Av. de Gaulle; *Le Traiteur de la Fôret*, Blvd. Jubelin, friendly, good; *Marveen Snack Bar*, Rue Ch. Colombe, near Canal de L'Est, food and staff pleasant, the patrons are very helpful regarding air travel and excursions (the elder of the two is a pilot for the Guyane Flying Club). *Ko Fei*, 18, Rue Lalouette, T 312888, good Chinese; *Apsara*, 95 Rue Colombe, Chinese, good value. Along the Canal Laussant there are Javanese snack bars; try *bami* (spicy noodles) or *saté* (barbecued meat in a spicy peanut sauce). Vans around Place des Palmistes in evenings sell cheap, filling sandwiches. *Bar Cayenne Palace*, 45 Av. de Gaulle, disco 80F with first drink. *Delifrance*, Av. de Gaulle, hot chocolate and croissants; *Epi D'or*, Av. Jubelin, good sweets and cakes, rec. Food is expensive, probably 30% more than in metropolitan France.

**Bookshops** *Librairie AJC*, 31 Boulevard Jubelin, has some stock in English. Also old maps and prints. Current map sold at *Librairie Alain* Pion, Av. de Gaulle and in most bookshops.

**Car Hire** 15 companies incuding both Hertz and Avis at airport. Full list available from ARDTLG (see **Tourist Office** below). An international driving licence is required. **Bicycle Hire** Rue J. Catayee, 50 F per day, 300F per week.

**Bank** Banque Nacional de Paris-Guyane, 2 Place Schoelcher; no exchange facilities on Sat. Banque Française Commerciale, 2 Place des Palmistes; Crédit Populaire Guyanais, 93 Rue Lalouette. Cambios give slightly better rates for US$ than banks. There are no exchange facilities at the airport; if in extreme need on Sat. you may be able to change money at Air France office in Place des Palmistes. Central drugstore may help when banks closed. Buy francs before arrival if possible.

**Laundromat** Corner of Rue Lalouette and Rue Eboué, US$5 load all in.

**Post Office** 2 km. out from town (15F by taxi or 20 minutes on foot). Poste Restante letters are only kept for 2 weeks maximum. Post Office annex opp. Préfecture open a.m. (Place Grenoble).

**Tourist Office** Agence Régionale de Développement du Tourisme et des Loisirs de la Guyane (ARDTLG), 12 Rue Lalouette (T 30-09-00). Free map and tourist guide (Guyane Poche). The SLM manager is reported to be very helpful with advice.

**Travel Agent** *Takari Tour*, Colline du Montabo, T 31-19-60 (BP 513). *Somarig*, Place L. Heder, T 31-29-80, is reported to be good for South American and European airline tickets. It also sells boat tickets to Ile Royale as well as meal tickets for the Auberge which are recommended. *JAL Voyages*, T 38-23-70 and *Guyane Excursions*, Centre Commercial Simarouba, T 32-05-41, both organise a varied programme of tours. *Agence Sainte-Claire*, 8 rue de Rémire, T 30-00-38; *Havas*, 2 place du Marché, T 31-26-22; *Minerve*, 65 rue Justin Catayéc, T 31-89-00.

**Bus** Only westbound bus is run by Ruffinel & Cie, Av. Galmot, T 31-26-68 (Kourou 60F, St Laurent 150F) leaves 0515; will pick up at hotel if ticket bought day before. Service to **Mana** Monday and Thursday only. Otherwise transport is by shared taxis (collectifs), which leave from Av. de la Liberté, near the fish market early in the morning (Kourou 60F, St. Laurent 150F).

**International Airport** Cayenne-Rochambeau is 16 km. from Cayenne, 20 mins. by taxi. (**See** Air Routes to Guyane, page 1228.) Air France, Place des Palmistes, T 30-27-40; Air Guyane, 2 rue Lalouette, T 31-72-00/35-65-55; Suriname Airways, 2 place Schoelcher, T 31-72-98. Local air services: Air Guyane to all main centres. No public transport; only taxis

---

**Cayenne: Key to map**
1. Place des Palmistes; 2. Place de Grenoble; 3. Place des Amandiers/Auguste Horth; 4. Place Victor Schoelcher; 5. Cathedral; 6. Préfecture; 7. Tourist Office (ARDTLG); 8. Post Office; 9. Somarig Agency; 10. Air France; 11. Ruffinel Buses to the West; 12. Fish Market; 13. Covered Market; 14. Banque Nationale de Paris Guyane; 15. Banque Française Commerciale; 16. Brazilian Consulate; 17. Suriname Consulate; 18. British Consulate; 19. Stadium; 20. Port.

(100F daytime, 150F night, but you can probably bargain or share). No exchange facilities. Cheaper taxi: Richard Lugret, T 31-29-89. Cheapest method of return to airport is by collective taxi from corner of Av. de la Liberté and Rue Malouet to Matoury (10 km.) for 12F, then hitch or walk.

**Excursions**  Trips by motor-canoe (*pirogue*) up-river into the jungle can be arranged. Six-and-a-half km. outside Cayenne is a restaurant with paintings of prison life by Huguet, an ex-convict, whose work can also be seen in the church at Iracoubo, between Kourou and St.-Laurent. Ten km. out, near the bridge to the mainland, is an American shrimp-packing plant.

Forty km. away is Ile Connétable, a small offshore island with large frigate-bird colonies; although a restricted area for tourists, some tour operators may take you.

*Kourou*, 56 km. W of Cayenne, where the main French space centre (Centre Spatial Guyanais), used for the European Space Agency's Ariane programme, is located, is referred to by the Guyanais as "white city" because of the number of metropolitan French families living there; its population is about 6,450. It has two excellent hotels and a number of good restaurants, but the project and population have been substantially reduced. Tourist attractions include bathing, fishing, sporting and aero club, and a variety of organized excursions. The space centre occupies an area of about 4 km. deep along some 30 km. of coast, bisected by the Kourou river. It is open to the public on Tues., Weds., and Thur. 0800-1130. Phone 33-49-19 to reserve a place on a tour of the centre (in French only, max 40), often booked up days ahead; closed during Carnival. Kourou has its own port facilities, 4 km. out of town. One can sometimes hitch a lift with the Space Centre bus to the cross roads 1 km. from the port. *Taxis collectifs* leave for Cayenne at 0600 and 1400 from Shell petrol station. Ruffinel bus stop is at the supermarket one block from *Studio Sodexho*. Taxi from Cayenne or from airport, 300F.

**Hotels**  *Relais de Guyane* (*Hotel des Roches*), Les Roches (T 32-00-66), A+, pool, beach, good restaurants; *Hotel Manguiers*, A+ (T 32-00-66). *Diamant*, (T 32-10-90) A; *Auberge des Iles du Salut* (T 32-11-00), A-B, see below; *Studio Sodexho*, Place Newton (T 32-06-11); *Centre D'Accueil*, de Gaulle, D, basic, clean, friendly.

**Restaurants**  Many, esp. on de Gaulle inc. *Le Catouri*, *Cachiri*, *Auberge de Père Jean* (all Creole), *Vieux Montmartre* and *L'Aubrevoir* (French). Cheapest in town is *La Légion*, very good value. Snack Bars: *La Cage*, Av. Les Roches; *Felicio*, Allée des Tamanoirs; **Night Clubs**: *Bellevue* and *Club des Roches*, Les Roches, *Le Vieux Montmartre*, de Gaulle.

**Exchange**  Banque National de Paris Guyane, Place Newton; Banque Française Commerciale, Place Jeanne d'Arc; Crédit Populaire Guyanais, de Gaulle.

**Suriname Consulate**  38 Rue Christophe Colomb.

**Travel Agency**  *Guyane Excursions*, T 32-05-41. *Floreal Tours*, T 32-17-00; *Havas Voyages Kourou*.

The **Iles du Salut** islands (many visitors at weekends), opposite Kourou, include the Ile Royale, the Ile Saint-Joseph, and the Ile du Diable. They were the scene of the notorious convict settlement built in 1852; the last prisoners left in 1953. The Ile du Diable ("Devil's Island"), a rocky palm-covered islet almost inaccessible from the sea, was where political prisoners, including Alfred Dreyfus, were held. There is a 60-bed hotel on Ile Royale, *Auberge Iles du Salut* (address Sothis, 97310 Kourou, T 32-11-00), A; former guard's bungalow, main meals (excellent), minimum 180F, breakfast 40F (ex-mess hall for warders, with good food; bottled water sold). Camping is possible, but suitable sites are limited, the strong-hearted may try the old prison barracks; take food and water (you can also sling a hammock in the open); bread and water (check bottle is sealed) can be bought from the somewhat unfriendly hotel stall. You can see agoutis, turtles, humming birds and macaws, and there are many un-owned coconut palms. Beware the many open wells. Take a torch for visiting the ruins. Paintings of prison life are on show in the tiny church. Points of interest include the children's graveyard, hospital, mental asylum and death cells. Boat from next to *Hotel des Roches*, Kourou 150F return, leaves 0830, returns from island at 1600, 1 hr. each way. Tickets may be obtained from Somarig Voyager, Place Heder, Cayenne and from other tour agencies. Also boat from port at Kourou 4 km. out of town, or try hitching a lift at the yacht club. Four daily crossings (40F return) by small boat from Ile Royale to Ile Saint-Joseph, which is wilder and more beautiful, with a small beach (this island had solitary-confinement cells and the warders' graveyard). Surfing and swimming are possible between Ile Royale and Ile du Diable; strong currents at high tide. Boat owners are very reluctant to visit Devil's Island except around July-August when the sea is calmer.

Between Kourou and Iracoubo, on the road W to St.-Laurent, is **Sinnamary**, where Galibi Indians at a mission make artifical flowers from feathers, for sale to tourists ( Hotels *Sinnarive*, T 34-55-55, A, and *Eldo Grill*, A-A+, T 34-51-41, or contact M. Derain, T 34-53-09, who lets out rooms, D p.p.). Scarlet ibis can be seen in numbers on the Sinnamary estuary. A hydroelectric project is under construction on the Sinnamary River.

**St.-Laurent du Maroni**, population 5,000, formerly a penal transportation camp, is now a quiet colonial town 250 km. from Cayenne on the River Maroni, bordering Suriname. (Nearby is St.-Jean du Maroni, an Indian village.) There are three acceptable hotels and several restaurants. *Hotel Toucan*, Boulevard de General de Gaulle, B, unfriendly, poor value. *Hotel Bacadel*, Avenue Felix Eboué, above *Le Saramarca* restaurant, E, airy; the owner, Mme. Bacadel, is friendly. *Star Hotel*, Rue Thiers, T 34-10-84, A, a/c, friendly, rec. Restaurants *Vietnam* and *Le Point d'Intérrogation* have been rec. The old Camp de Transportation (the original penal centre but now full of squatters) can be wandered round at will (an absolute must if visiting the country), though if you want to see the cells you will have to apply to the local *gendarmerie*. The bank in St.-Laurent does not offer exchange facilities. Bus to Cayenne, 150F, 0500 daily; *taxis collectifs* to and from Cayenne, 140F a head, 3½-hr. trip.

The frontier with Suriname was reopened in 1991; make sure you obtain proper entry stamps from immigration, not the police, to avoid problems when leaving. *Pirogues* cross the river to Suriname. GUM airways fly from St-Laurent to Paramaribo, enquire at the *Star Hotel*.

40 km north of St.-Laurent du Maroni is **Mana**, a delightful town with rustic architecture near the coast (*Gite d'Etape*, rooms OK, filthy kitchen, mosquitoes, disco next door; or contact Mme. Hidair, T 34-80-62, who has rooms, C). 16 km west of Mana following the river along a single track access road is Les Hattes (*Gite Rureau*, B, clean) an Amerindian village (ask M. Daniel for permission to stay in the church); 4 km. further on is Les Hattes beach where leatherback-turtles lay their eggs at night; season April-August with its peak in June-July. No public transport to Les Hattes and its beach; take food and water and mosquito repellant. The fresh water of the Maroni and Mana rivers makes sea bathing very pleasant. Very quiet during the week.

**Aouara**, an Amerindian village with hammock places, is a few kilometres south east of Les Hattes. It also has a beach where the leatherback turtles lay their eggs; they take about three hours over it. Take mosquito nets, hammock and insect repellant.

There are daily flights from Cayenne to **Maripasoula** (*Auberge Chez Dedè*) up the Maroni from St.-Laurent (2-4 day journey up river in *pirogue*). There may be freight canoes which take passengers (200F) or private boats (750F) which leave from St.-Laurent; 5-day tour with Takari Tour US$450 p.p. If going up the Maroni, take malaria prophylaxis.

Jef D. Boeke of Boston, Mass., has recommended a visit to **Saül**, a remote gold-mining settlement in the "central massif". The main attractions are for the nature-loving tourist—beautiful undisturbed tropical forests are accessible by a very well-maintained system of 90 km. of marked trails, including several circular routes. The place has running water, a radiotelephone, and electricity. Ten-day expeditions are run by Christian Ball, "Vie Sauvage", 97314 Saül, 350F (30% in advance) per day with meals, maps of local trails provided, own hammock and bedding useful but not essential. It can be cold at night. In spite of the dryish climate Mana is a malaria region. *Restaurant Chez Joseph*. Air service Mon., Wed., Fri. with

Air Guyane from Cayenne (330F one way, 620F return) or via Maripasoula; try at airport even if flight said to be full. By *pirogue* from Mana up Mana River, 9-12 days, then one day's walk to Saül, or from St-Laurent via Maripasoula along Moroni and Inini Rivers, 15 days and one day's walk to Saül, both routes expensive.

South-East of Cayenne is the small town of **Roura** (*Hotel La Pirogue*, B, clean, good views), which has an interesting church; an excursion may be made to the Fourgassier Falls several km. away. From Cayenne take a minibus to Stoupan, then catch the ferry across the River Comte (departs every hour 0730-1830). From Roura an unpaved road runs south-east towards the village of Kaw. At Km. 36 from Cayenne is the *Hotel Relais de Patawa* (T 31-93-95), C, or sling your hammock for 30F, cheaper rates for longer stays, highly rec. The owners, M and Mme Baloué, who are entomologists, will show you their collection, take you on guided tours of local sights and introduce you to their pet anaconda and boa constrictors. At Km. 80 is Cacao, where Hmong refugees from Laos are settled; they are farmers and produce fine traditional handicrafts. **Kaw**, at Km. 83, is on an island amid swamps which are home to much rare wildlife including caymans. The village is reached by dugout either from the Cayenne road or from Régina; basic accommodation available (Mme Musron, T 31-88-15), take insect repellant. South-West of Kaw on the River Approuague is Régina, linked with Cayenne by an unpaved road.

***St.-Georges de l'Oyapoc*** is 15 min. down river from Oiapoque (Brazil) US$2 p.p. (canoe), *Hotel Damas*, *Hotel Modestina*, E, restaurant, also *Theofila*, lunch US$3, other restaurants and a night club. Several duty-free shops with French specialities. Immigration (*gendarmerie*) some 200m. from the town hall, ½ km. from docks—French and Spanish spoken. There is nowhere to change dollars into francs; if entering the country here, you must change money before arriving in St.-Georges. There is a beautiful 19 metre waterfall one day's journey up the Oyapoc River at Saut Maripa.

Air Guyane (office opposite Post Office) has daily flights to Régina and regular flights to and from St.-Georges, usually booked up a week in advance, but go to the airport if they say the flight is full). If the Air Guyane flights to St.-Georges are fully booked, it is probably cheaper not to wait for a standby (and pay Cayenne prices), but to find 2 or 4 others and take a Cessna from the Guyane Flying Club for US$90 (price includes baggage), 50 minute flight, recommended. The police check that those boarding flights who have arrived from Brazil have obtained their entry stamp.

About once a week a small vessel, the *Sao Pedro*, sails to Cayenne, deck passengers 100F one way.

Camopi is an Indian village 2-3 days up the Oyapoc from St.-Georges (*pirogue*, 600F); to go beyond Saut-Maripa requires a special permit from the Préfecture in Cayenne, which takes 6 weeks and is usually granted only to scientists. Tours from Cayenne, 4,800F p.p. for 6 days.

## INFORMATION FOR VISITORS

**Documents**   Passport not required by nationals of France and most French-speaking African countries carrying identity cards. No visa (45F) required for most nationalities (except for those of Guyana, Australia, the communist bloc and Asian—not Japan—and other African countries) for a stay of up to 3 months, but an exit ticket out of the country is essential (a ticket out of one of the other Guianas is not sufficient); a deposit is required otherwise. If one stays more than three months, income tax clearance is required before leaving the country. Inoculation against yellow-fever officially required only for those staying in Guyane longer than 2 weeks, but advisable for all. Travel to certain Amerindian villages is restricted (**see page 1223**).

**Air Routes to Guyane**   Air France flies 3 times a week direct to Guyane from

Paris 11 times a week from Pointe-à-Pitre (Guadeloupe) and 10 times a week from Fort-de-France (Martinique). Cheapest flight from Europe is reported to be with Minerve (Paris T 45-22-08-50), once a week from Paris. Cruzeiro do Sul fly to Belém on Tues. and Fri. (return Mon. and Fri.), with a further flight on Thur. operated by Air France, and to/from Paramaribo on Mon. (Brazilian leg often booked 4-6 weeks in advance). Suriname Airways fly to Paramaribo twice a week; for Georgetown you have to change in Paramaribo. **NB** Do not accept verbal confirmation of flights from Air France in Cayenne: insist on a time/date stamped confirmation to avoid later misunderstandings.

**Surface Transport to Guyane** The Compagnie Général Maritime runs a passenger service to France once a month via Martinique and a freight service every 3 months. Boat connections with Suriname recommended in 1991. To Brazil by motorized dugout from St. Georges to Oiapoque, no custom or immigration post but foreigners are still sometimes returned to Guyane if their papers are not in order. Make sure you get an exit stamp from Gendarmerie in St-Georges. This journey is possible in reverse.

**Internal Transport** There are no railways, and about 1,000 km. of road (65% asphalted). The main road, narrow but now paved, runs for 130 km. from Pointe Macouris, on the roadstead of Cayenne, to Iracoubo. Another 117 km. takes it to Mana and St.-Laurent. One-to three-ton boats which can be hauled over the rapids are used by the gold-seekers, the forest workers, and the rosewood establishments. There is a twice-a-month shipping service which calls at nearly all the coastal towns of Guyane. Ferries are free. Internal air services by Air Guyane. These flights are always heavily booked, so be prepared to wait or write or telephone Air Guyane in Cayenne (T 317200). There are regular connections with Maripasoula, daily at 0930, 900F return; St-Georges, daily at 0745 and Mon. Tues., Thur., and Fri., at 1500, 560F return; Saül on Mon., Tues., Thur., and Fri., at 0930, 620F return; Régina, daily at 0745, 300F return. No services on Sun.

**Road Transport** There is a lack of public transport; car hire can be a great convenience (there are 15 agencies in Cayenne); Renault 4s perform well on the rough roads. Gasoline/petrol costs 5.50F a litre.

**Accommodation** Details of hotels are given in the text. For information on *Gîtes* and *Chambres chez l'habitant* write to Agence Régionale de Développement du Tourisme et des Loisirs de la Guyane (ARDTLG), 12, rue Lalouette, 97338, Cayenne Cedex, T 30-09-00, Telex 910364 FG; also, for *Gîtes*, Association pour le Tourisme Vert en Guyane, 27, rue Justin Cataye, 97300 Cayenne, T 31-10-11.

**Food** Most is imported, except seafood; it is of very high quality but expensive.

**Health** Tropical diseases, dysentery, malaria, etc., occur, but the country is fairly healthy. Malaria prophylaxis recommended. In 1987 there were 5 hospitals with 861 beds and 237 physicians.

**The best months to visit** are between August and November, which are the usual months for trips to the jungle.

**Public Holidays** In addition to the feasts of the Church: 1 January, New Year's Day and 14 July, Fête Nationale. Moslem holidays are observed, but the dates vary because of the shorter Moslem year; see note under Guyana, **page 1210**.

**Time Zone** 3 hours behind GMT.

**Currency** The currency is the French franc. Try to take francs with you as the exchange rate for dollars is low, many banks do not offer exchange facilities and most places demand cash. A better rate can be obtained by using Visa cards to withdraw cash from the Banque Nacionale de Paris Guyana, Place Victor Schoelcher, Cayenne.

**Weights and Measures** The metric system is in use.

**Telecommunications** There is telephone communication throughout the territory. International telephone calls via STD to Europe and French Antilles. Foreign telegraph communication is via Paramaribo or Fort-de-France, from the TSF station at Cayenne.

**Consulates** British (Honorary), 16 Av. Monnerville (B.P. 664, Cayenne 97300, T 31-10-34/30-42-42, Fax 30-40-94); Brazilian, 12 Rue L. Héder, at corner of Place des Palmistes, near Air France offices (closed Sats. T 30-04-67). Suriname, 38 rue Christophe Colomb (T 30-04-61).

**General** The language is French, with officials not usually speaking anything else. The religion is predominantly Roman Catholic.

**Media** *La Presse de la Guyane* is the daily paper (circ. 1,500). *France-Guyane-Antilles* is a weekly newspaper with a good information page for the tourist.

**Tourist Information** The French Government tourist offices generally have leaflets on Guyane; there is a special office in Paris, L'Office du Tourisme des Antilles et de la Guyane, 12 rue Auber, 75009 Paris, T 268-11-07. The Cayenne offices are at 12, rue Lalouette, Cayenne (Telex 910356, T 300900); Délégation Régionale, 10, rue L.-Heder, 97307 Cayenne, T 31-84-91; Syndicat d'initiative de Cayenne, Jardin Botanique, P.O. Box 702, 97338 Cayenne, T 31-29-19; St.-Laurent du Maroni, 16, rue du Colonel Chandon, T 34-10-86; Syndicat d'Initiative Rémire-Montjoly, Mairie de Rémire, 97305 Rémire, T 35-41-10.

We are most grateful to John Hale for updating the Guianas section, to Daniel Morgan (Wellington, NZ for the basic map of Georgetown, Trevor Petch (*Caribbean Insight*, London), and to the following travellers: Dr Carlo Andreis (Monza, Italy), Tom Bergan (Oslo, Norway), Erik Bernesson (Båstad, Sweden), Graham R. Cox (Port Pirie, S. Australia), Henk van Dyk Theodor A. Gevert (São Paulo), Eva and Ulrich Hellinger (Munich 40), Marian Janssen (Rosmalen, Netherlands), Andreas Kühn (Germany), John Raspey (Argentina), R. T. Shannon (Auckland, New Zealand), Georg Sütterlin (Rapperswil, Switz), and Mark Wilson (Nassau).

---

# WILL YOU HELP US?

We do all we can to get our facts right in **The South American Handbook.** Each chapter is thoroughly revised each year, but the territory covers a vast area, and our eyes cannot be everywhere. A new highway or airport is built; a hotel, a restaurant, a cabaret dies; another, a good one is born; a building we describe is pulled down, a street renamed. Names and addresses of good hotels and restaurants for "budget-minded" travellers are always very welcome. We would especially like to receive diagrams of walks, national parks and other interesting areas.

*Your information may be far more up-to-date than ours. If your letter reaches us early enough in the year it will be used in the next edition, but write whenever you want to, for all your letters are used sooner or later.*

Thank you very much indeed for your help.

 **Trade & Travel Publications Limited**
**6 Riverside Court**
**Lower Bristol Road**
**Bath BA2 3DZ. England**

# FALKLAND ISLANDS
# ISLAS MALVINAS

*(In accordance with the practice suggested by the UN, we are calling the Islands by both their English and Spanish names.)*

The Falkland Islands (Malvinas) comprise two groups: East Falkland (Isla Soledad) with its adjacent islands, about 2,600 square miles; and West Falkland (Gran Malvina), with its islands, about 2,100 square miles. Approximately 480 miles northeast of Cape Horn, the Islands lie between latitudes 51° and 53° S and between longitudes 57° and 62° W. Nearly all land combat during the 1982 war was confined to the northern half of East Falkland; its southern peninsula of Lafonia, and West Falkland were little affected. According to the 1986 census, two-thirds of the 1,916 residents are Falklands-born; another quarter were born in the United Kingdom. Slightly more than one-third live and work on sheep farms. During the past decade, land reform through sale and subdivision of traditional large stations has resulted in more broadly based local ownership of pastoral land.

**Early History** Records of early voyages are ambiguous, but Dutchman Sebald de Weert made the first universally acknowledged sighting in 1598. The Englishman Strong landed in 1690 and named the Falkland Sound for a British peer; this name was later applied to the entire group. The Islands acquired their French appellation, Iles Malouines, from 17th century seafarers from the channel port of St Malo. This in turn became the Spanish Islas Malvinas.

In 1764 France established a small colony of Acadians at Port Louis under Bougainville. Two years later France ceded the settlement to Spain, under which it became a military garrison and penal colony. At about the same time as France, Britain had built an outpost at Saunders Island, West Falkland, whose occupants Spain discovered and expelled in 1770. Restored in the following year after threat of war, the post was abandoned in 1774.

Deserted by Spain in 1811, during the South American wars of independence, the Islands lacked formal authority until 1820, when the United Provinces of the River Plate (later Argentina) raised their flag at Port Louis (Soledad). In 1831, an American warship destroyed a promising colonization project under the auspices of a German-born merchant from Buenos Aires, who had arrested and imprisoned American sealers operating in the area. After British warships expelled a token Argentine force in 1833, the Islands experienced nearly 150 years of stability until April 1982, when Argentina invaded and occupied. Britain's counter-invasion recaptured the Islands by June of that year.

**Administration** The Islands' Constitution provides for a Governor, appointed from London, an Executive Council composed of appointed and elected members, and an elected Legislative Council. **Education** A Junior and Senior School in Stanley cater to the needs of town children and rural children who board in the School Hostel. Instruction to GCSE Level is available locally (compulsory to the age of 15), but higher education requires overseas travel, usually to Britain. Rural children receive attention from settlement instructors or travelling teachers. Radio is used to keep in contact with the more isolated farms.

**Climate** Although the *Sunday Express* once referred to a mutton freezer in the Falklands as a "Colonial Development project near the South Pole" (8 March 1953), the Islands are in the

same latitude South as London is North. Mean monthly temperatures are lower than in London, but London experiences greater extremes. Normal temperature range is 20°F to 70°F, with an annual mean of 42°F. Though not always inclement, weather is very changeable. Persistent westerlies, blowing at an annual average of 14 knots, are the most trying aspect of the climate. Calm is more common in winter than summer. Stanley's annual rainfall of about 26 inches is slightly higher than London's. In the drier camp, outside Stanley, summer drought sometimes threatens local water supplies. Spring, autumn and winter clothing, as used in the United Kingdom, is suitable.

**Stanley**, the capital, is the major population centre on East Falkland. Its 1,232 residents live mostly in brightly-painted houses, many of which have corrugated iron roofs. Stanley Harbour, surrounded by rolling moorland, resembles parts of the Hebrides. The outer harbour of Port William is larger but less protected. East Cove, 30 miles southeast of the capital, is the principal port for the new military installations at Mount Pleasant.

**Accommodation and Food** *Upland Goose Hotel*, Ross Road, T 21455, Fax 21520, from £35.75 bed and breakfast, evening meal £12; *Emma's Guest House*, Ross Road, T 21056, Fax 21573, from £25 bed and breakfast; *Malvina House Hotel*, 3 Ross Road, T 21355, Fax 21357, from £35.50 bed and breakfast. Prices subject to change. Full meals at all three, with reservations recommended at *Upland Goose* and *Malvina*. *Fenton Guest House*, 7 Fitzroy Road, T 21282, from £20 bed and breakfast; *Beauchene Guest House*, John Street, T 21252, from £30 bed and breakfast; *Sparrowhawk House*, Drury Street, T 21568, £18.50 bed and breakfast. Fish and chips and pizza at *Woodbine Cafe*, 29 Fitzroy Road, closed Sun. and Mon. *Monty's* bistro, bar snacks on John Street, includes vegetarian menu, closed Sun.; *Boathouse Café*, Ross Road, lunch only, Sun.-Thur.; *Penguin Snacks*, John St., opp. Goodwin's, Mon.-Fri., 1030-1700; *Home Cookin'*, 3 Drury St., 1830-2130 except Wed. and Fri.; *Sandy's Bakery*, T 21273, Mon.-Fri., 1000-1530.

On Sea Lion Island: *Sea Lion Lodge*, T 32004, £47 full board; at Port Howard, *Port Howard Lodge*, T 42150, £47 full board; on Pebble Island, *Pebble Island Lodge*, T 41097, £47 full board. Each lodge has a long wheelbase Land Rover for transport to the airstrip and points of interest nearby. The comfortable tourist lodges at Sea Lion Island, the most southerly inhabited island of the group (35 minutes flight fom Port Stanley), and Pebble Island (40 minutes flight) are good bases to view wildlife. Also on Pebble Island *Marble Mountain Shanty*, T 41098, Mr R. Evans, self-catering, £45 per night, £7 per family, £245 per week, £40 per family; room for up to 4. It is 12 miles from the rest of the population so is peaceful with plenty of wildlife (3 types of penguin within 1/2 hrs. walk). Bring food and bedding, all else provided. Scenic Port Howard's lodge on West Falkland, offers excellent trout fishing, a small but interesting war museum, and an opportunity to see the operations of a traditional large sheep station. *Blue Beach Lodge*, San Carlos East Falkland, opened Feb. 91, fishing camp to be built, £47 full board. Self catering at *Dunbar Cottage*, T 41103, Mr and Mrs Barnes, Dunbar Farm, £20 per night; and *Carcass Island Cottages*, Mr and Mrs McGill, T 41106, £25 per night per cottage, both on West Falkland. Further self-catering at Fox Bay Village and Fox Bay West, prices from £7.50 p.p. per night to £25 per group per night.

Fred Clark's *Great Britain Hotel*, on the highway near Fitzroy, serves alcoholic beverages and snacks during normal licensing hours. Accommodation is limited on the islands but most farms help if they can.

**Camping** is not encouraged on the islands; there is a very real risk of fire and of disturbance to wildlife.

Stanley has an excellent new civilian-military hospital, replacing the one damaged by fire early in 1984. Dental services are also available. Post Office, Philatelic Bureau, library and some other Government services are in Town Hall, Ross Road. Other Government offices are in the nearby Secretariat. Cable and Wireless, Ross Road, operate overseas telephone, fax, telegraph and telex services. The islands' telephone system has been completely replaced, with direct dialling worldwide. There are some fairly well-stocked stores, open mainly Monday to Friday. The few pubs, the *Globe* near the public jetty, the *Rose*, on Dury St. the *Victory* on Philomel Hill, and *Deanos* on Dean St. are popular meeting places during drinking hours (Mon.-Sat. 1000-1300, 1730-2200; Sundays only from 1200 to 1300, the "Glory Hour").

The new Museum at Britannia House, Ross Road West, merits a visit (Tues.-Fri., 1000-1200, 1400-1600, also Wed., 1800-2000, Sun., 1000-1200). Mr John Smith, Sparrow Hawk House, Allardyce Street, is knowledgeable on the Islands' maritime history. Government House, the Anglican Cathedral (most southerly in the world, built in 1890), and monuments commemorating the naval battle of 1914 and the 1982 liberation are also worth seeing. During the December holidays, the annual sports meeting at the race course attracts visitors from all over the Islands. The equally popular West Falkland sports, at the end of the shearing season in February or March, rotate among various settlements.

**National Tourism Bureau** Falkland Islands Tourist Board (FITB), Graham Bound, Managing Director, 56 John Street, Port Stanley, T (010500) 22215/6, Telex 2433 FITOURISM FK, Fax 22619, will provide all information on holidays on the islands. Bookings for lodgings and for fishing, riding, etc. are handled by Stanley Services Ltd., Port Stanley, T 22624, Fax 22623, Telex 2438. See below under communications for the Falklands Islands Tourist Board's London Office.

**Rentals** The Falkland Islands Company, Stanley, rents Fiat Strada 4 x 4 cars for about £125 per week, for road use only. Dave Eynon, South Atlantic Marine Services, P.O. Box 140, Stanley, T 21145/22667, Telex 2413, hires out a Land Rover and his dinghy *Zodiac* with diving equipment, also arranges diving and fishing trips. Ian Bury on Davis Street rents Land Rovers for £50 a day. Insurance is extra from the Falkland Islands Company. Dave Clarke, T 21300, and the *Malvina House Hotel*, T 21355, offer overland Land Rover excursions from Stanley. For boat hire for trips to Kidney Island and Narrows Island (50 ft. *Beaulie*) contact the owners, Jimmy and Owen Smith, T 31399. Boat trips are also available in the motor launch *Warrah*.

**Tourists** For wildlife enthusiasts, especially birders, the Islands are an exceptional destination. Best months to visit are October to March. Make allowance for unpredictable weather. Outside Stanley, the only major road is that to the new airport at Mount Pleasant; elsewhere, tracks require Land Rovers or motorbikes. Remember to phone farms in the camp for permission to drive across private land. Off-road driving in the boggy terrain is a skill not easily learned by short-term visitors. Near Stanley and a few farm settlements there are still unexploded mines, but hazardous areas are clearly marked and fenced. Visitors should *never* enter these areas, and should report suspicious objects to the police or military authorities in Stanley. Free minefield maps are available from the Bomb Disposal Office, Ross Road, Stanley. Ordnance Survey maps of the Islands are available from the Secretariat, £2 each for the 1:50,000 sheets; there is also a two-sheet, 1:250,000 map suitable for most purposes.

Travel outside the vicinity of Stanley is mainly by air. The Falkland Islands Government Air Service (FIGAS) operates three Islander aircraft to farm settlements and settled outer islands according to bookings, seat availability, and weather. To book a seat, visitors should telephone FIGAS no later than the morning of the day before travelling; flight schedules are announced that evening on local radio (airfares are about £1 per minute for non-islanders, luggage limit 14 kg/30 lbs). FIGAS tickets are also available from FITB, 56 John Street, Stanley, T 22215. Regular service operates 7 days a week. Flights leave from Stanley Airport, three miles east of town on the Cape Pembroke peninsula; Stanley Bus Service carries passengers for £1.50.

**Points of interest** Sparrow Cove, Kidney Cove, and adjacent areas, only a short distance across Stanley Harbour by boat and out into Port William, are good areas to see penguins and other wildlife; dolphins often follow in the wake of your boat near The Narrows. Gypsy Cove, walking distance from Stanley, features a colony of burrowing Magellanic penguins and other shorebirds. Observe minefield fences which prevent close inspection of the penguins. At Cape Pembroke, around the old airport and lighthouse one can see Gentoo penguins and ground-nesting birds such as dotterels, snipe, and Upland geese.

Kidney Island, a very small island densely covered with tussock grass, is a Nature Reserve. By arrangement in Stanley, it is possible for hardy and dedicated bird lovers to stay in the basic shanty. Rockhopper penguins, King cormorants and many other species nest here. Kidney Island is accessible by boat, 1½ hours from Stanley. Permission to visit must be obtained from the government Lands Officer. Trips—all day—are organized occasionally by Falklands Island Tourist Board.

Of particular interest are the hulls of old sailing ships at Stanley and Darwin. Examples at Stanley are the *Jhelum* (built in 1839 for the East India Company) near Government House, the *Charles Cooper* (the last US sailing packet to sail out of New York Harbour; in the Islands since 1866), and the iron-built *Lady Elizabeth* at the far end of the harbour (228 ft long, with three masts still standing). *Snow Squall*, one of the last American clipper ships, was removed by a team of marine archaeologists from Harvard University in 1987. A Maritime History Trail has been set up in Stanley (self-guided with interpretive panels at key points, and guide book available at FITB). At Darwin are the *Vicar of Bray* (last survivor of the California Gold Rush fleet), and another old iron ship, the *Garland*. Some of these hulls are still used for storage. There are interesting old French buildings and ruins at Port Louis.

Volunteer Point, north of Stanley, is a wildlife sanctuary. Permission to visit must be obtained from the owner, Mr Osmond Smith, at Johnson's Harbour; he charges £5 to visit—the fee goes towards the time used receiving the aircraft and looking after the penguins. By arrangement with Mr Smith it is possible to camp at the shepherd's house at Volunteer Point (you must take your own food and sleeping bag—don't drink the stream water, it is polluted by the penguins). Falklands Islands Tourist Board occasionally arranges tours; a 15-minute flight to Johnson's Harbour, then a 1½ hr. Land Rover trip across the camp. On other occasions, the farmer will drive you to the point if he is not busy; otherwise it is a 10 mile walk. Volunteer contains the only substantial nesting colony of King penguins in the Falklands. Gentoo penguins, Magellanic penguins, geese, ducks, and elephant seals are very tame and easily photographed. An exceptional wildlife hike is along the north coast of East Falkland, from Seal Bay to Volunteer Point. Ask permission of the manager of Port Louis as well, and allow three to four days.

Battlefield tours, to some of the sites associated with the 1982 conflict, can be arranged.

The smaller islands off West Falkland, such as West Point, Carcass and New Island, are the most spectacular and attractive for wildlife and scenery. New Island, on the extreme west of the archipelago, is run as a nature reserve. Enquiries should be addressed to Tony Chater, The Pink Shop, Stanley, or to Ian or Maria Strange, T 42017. The Island has large colonies of rockhopper penguins, black-browed albatrosses, Gentoo and Magellanic penguins, King and Rock cormorants and many other birds, as well as a fur-seal colony. Carcass can be visited more easily and has two self-catering cottages (see above). Saunders Island, besides a representative sample of wildlife, contains the ruins of the 18th-century British outpost at Port Egmont. At nearby Keppel Island are ruins of the South American Missionary Society, which used the site to catechize Indians from Tierra del Fuego during the latter half of the 19th century.

## Economy

Since the declaration of a 150-mile fisheries protection zone in 1986, the economy has been transformed. License fees from Asian and European fleets exploiting the Islands' squid, hake, and whiting have quadrupled Government revenue, to about £30 million a year. Much of this revenue is being used to fund overdue improvement in education and infrastructure, as well as social expenditures for increased pensions. A new telephone system has been installed and a new secondary school is being built. The housing stock has doubled since the 1982 war, roads have been improved and there are many more vehicles in use. A new swimming pool has been constructed in Stanley.

Most of the camp, as the countryside is known locally, is covered with grass and low heath. Almost all land outside Stanley is devoted to sheep grazing. There are some 600,000 sheep, all of whose wool is exported to the United Kingdom. Native tussock grass, the most valuable fodder, grows to seven feet or more and also shelters wildlife. It has disappeared from East and West Falkland because of grazing pressure, but still abounds on some smaller islands. There are only a few trees, introduced and carefully cultivated at settlements such as Hill Cove.

**Entry requirements** All travellers must have full passports. Generally, visa requirements are the same as for the UK, but at present Argentine citizens are not permitted to visit.

The new **airport** at Mount Pleasant, 30 miles from Stanley, is built to international specifications. Bob Stewart's Stanley Bus Service, St Mary's Walk, Stanley, T 21191, transports passengers and luggage to and from the capital for £10 single. Departing passengers should make reservations. Also, J's Taxi Service, 2 Harbour View Road, T 21105, for transport between Stanley and the airport, and within Stanley (Mon.-Fri., 0800-2000).

## Communications

The RAF presently operates two Tri-Star flights a week from Brize Norton, Oxfordshire, to the new airport at Mount Pleasant (Thursday and Monday, returning to UK Saturday and Wednesday). Standard fare is £1,900 return or £1,180 return on 28-day advance purchase; Falkland Islands residents receive a discount. Enquiries about passages can be addressed to Ms. Carol

Stewart, Falkland Islands Government London Office, Falkland House, 14 Broadway, Westminster, London SW1H 0BH, T 071-222 5852, Telex 8950476 FIGLON, Fax 222 2375. Enquiries about the islands themselves can be addressed to Ms Victoria Poland, Falklands Islands Tourist Board, at the same address, T 071-222 2542. This office can also be contacted for information on organized tours from the UK, other European countries and the USA.

It is hoped that scheduled airline service to the South American continent may begin soon. Aerovías DAP of Chile began charter flights between Punta Arenas and Port Stanley in April 1990; they fly on demand, which is not very frequent. It is occasionally possible to obtain passage to Montevideo on European fishing boats, but this requires some patience and is undependable.

**Cost of living** is about the same as in Britain. Freight adds to the price of imported groceries. Since the construction of a hydroponic market garden near Stanley, fresh produce such as lettuce, tomatoes and aubergines are available year-round. Potatoes and other vegetables are grown in gardens and conservatories for household use, but are not readily purchased.

There is no value-added tax; only tobacco, wine, spirits and beer pay import duty. Small luxury goods on which freight is correspondingly low are sometimes cheaper than in the UK. Colour slide film, which can be scarce, should be brought from Britain.

**Currency** The local £ is on a par with sterling. Local notes and coins. UK notes and coins also legal tender. Currency from Ascension Island, where the RAF Tri-Star stops for refueling, is not accepted, nor are Falklands notes or coins legal in the United Kingdom. Foreign currency may be changed at Standard Chartered Bank, Ross Road, Stanley.

**Mails** Since the opening of Mount Pleasant, there is direct and dependable air mail service from the United Kingdom. Heavy parcels come by sea from the UK four or five times a year. Inter-island mail service is carried out by FIGAS and by the vessels *Monsunen* and *Forrest*.

## SOUTH GEORGIA

South Georgia, in latitude 54½° S and longitude 36° to 38° W, has an area of about 1,450 square miles, and a small transient population of soldiers and British Antarctic Survey scientists. During the summer months, tourists may book a passage on the merchant supply vessel *Sir Bedivere* at Stanley for £400 return, but weather conditions sometimes prevent passengers from going ashore. Intending visitors must submit a request through the Government Secretary, Stanley. The Island was occupied by Argentina in April-May 1982.

South Georgia is a mass of high, snow-covered mountains and glaciers. Between 1951 and 1980 at King Edward Point, at sea level, snow fell an average of nearly 200 days per annum, but the coastal area is free from snow and partially covered by vegetation in summer. Wildlife consists of most of the same species found in the Falklands, but in much larger numbers. Reindeer, introduced by Norwegian whalers at the turn of the century, have flourished. Other points of interest are several abandoned whaling stations, the little white church, and many sailing-ship hulks.

We are deeply grateful to Victoria Poland, Falkland Islands Government London Office, Graham Bound of Falkland Islands Tourist Board, Wayne Bernhardson (Oakland, CA), Rüdiger Schultz (St. Gallen, Switzerland) and T. Stephensmith (Warlingham, Surrey) for valuable new information.

# CLIMATIC TABLES

*The following tables have been very kindly furnished by Mr. R. K. Headland. Each weather station is given with its altitude in metres (m.). Temperatures (Centigrade) are given as averages for each month; the first line is the maximum and the second the minimum. The third line is the average number of wet days encountered in each month.*

## SOUTH AMERICA

| | Jan. | Feb. | Mar. | Apr. | May | June | July | Aug. | Sept. | Oct. | Nov. | Dec. |
|---|---|---|---|---|---|---|---|---|---|---|---|---|
| **Arica, Chile** | 26 | 26 | 25 | 23 | 21 | 19 | 19 | 18 | 19 | 21 | 22 | 24 |
| 29m. | 18 | 18 | 17 | 16 | 14 | 14 | 12 | 13 | 13 | 14 | 16 | 17 |
| | 0 | 0 | 0 | 0 | 0 | 0 | 0 | 0 | 0 | 0 | 0 | 0 |
| **Asunción, Par.** | 34 | 34 | 33 | 28 | 25 | 22 | 24 | 25 | 27 | 29 | 31 | 33 |
| 64m. | 22 | 22 | 21 | 18 | 14 | 13 | 14 | 14 | 16 | 17 | 19 | 21 |
| | 7 | 6 | 9 | 7 | 5 | 4 | 4 | 4 | 6 | 5 | 6 | 7 |
| **Bariloche, Arg.** | 21 | 21 | 18 | 14 | 10 | 7 | 6 | 8 | 10 | 11 | 16 | 18 |
| 825m. | 8 | 8 | 6 | 4 | 2 | 1 | 0 | 0 | 1 | 3 | 5 | 6 |
| | 2 | 3 | 5 | 7 | 11 | 13 | 11 | 11 | 8 | 6 | 4 | 4 |
| **Barranquilla, Col.** | 31 | 31 | 32 | 33 | 34 | 33 | 33 | 33 | 33 | 32 | 32 | 30 |
| 12m. | 22 | 22 | 23 | 24 | 25 | 25 | 25 | 25 | 25 | 24 | 24 | 23 |
| | 0 | 0 | 0 | 1 | 4 | 8 | 5 | 6 | 8 | 11 | 6 | 4 |
| **Belém, Braz.** | 31 | 30 | 30 | 31 | 31 | 32 | 32 | 32 | 32 | 32 | 32 | 32 |
| 24m. | 23 | 23 | 23 | 23 | 23 | 23 | 22 | 22 | 22 | 22 | 22 | 22 |
| | 24 | 26 | 25 | 22 | 24 | 15 | 14 | 15 | 13 | 10 | 11 | 14 |
| **Belo Horizonte** | 27 | 27 | 27 | 27 | 25 | 24 | 24 | 25 | 27 | 27 | 27 | 26 |
| 857m. | 18 | 18 | 17 | 16 | 12 | 10 | 10 | 12 | 14 | 16 | 17 | 18 |
| | 15 | 13 | 9 | 4 | 4 | 2 | 2 | 1 | 2 | 10 | 12 | 14 |
| **Bogotá** | 21 | 21 | 21 | 20 | 20 | 19 | 19 | 19 | 20 | 20 | 20 | 21 |
| 2560m. | 7 | 7 | 9 | 10 | 10 | 9 | 8 | 8 | 8 | 9 | 8 | 7 |
| | 9 | 7 | 10 | 18 | 16 | 10 | 16 | 10 | 13 | 18 | 16 | 13 |
| **Brasília** | 27 | 28 | 28 | 28 | 27 | 26 | 26 | 28 | 30 | 29 | 27 | 27 |
| 912m. | 18 | 18 | 18 | 17 | 15 | 13 | 13 | 14 | 16 | 18 | 18 | 18 |
| | 19 | 16 | 15 | 9 | 3 | 1 | 0 | 2 | 4 | 11 | 15 | 20 |
| **Buenos Aires** | 30 | 29 | 26 | 22 | 18 | 15 | 15 | 16 | 18 | 21 | 25 | 29 |
| 25m. | 18 | 17 | 15 | 12 | 9 | 6 | 6 | 6 | 8 | 11 | 13 | 16 |
| | 5 | 5 | 6 | 6 | 4 | 4 | 5 | 6 | 5 | 7 | 7 | 7 |
| **Caracas** | 26 | 26 | 28 | 28 | 28 | 27 | 26 | 27 | 28 | 27 | 27 | 26 |
| 1035m. | 15 | 15 | 16 | 17 | 18 | 18 | 17 | 17 | 17 | 17 | 17 | 16 |
| | 4 | 3 | 2 | 4 | 8 | 13 | 13 | 11 | 11 | 11 | 8 | 6 |
| **Córdoba, Arg.** | 32 | 31 | 28 | 25 | 21 | 19 | 19 | 20 | 23 | 26 | 28 | 31 |
| 425m. | 17 | 16 | 14 | 11 | 7 | 4 | 4 | 5 | 8 | 11 | 13 | 16 |
| | 8 | 9 | 9 | 6 | 4 | 2 | 2 | 1 | 3 | 7 | 9 | 10 |
| **Cuzco** | 20 | 21 | 21 | 22 | 21 | 21 | 21 | 21 | 22 | 22 | 23 | 22 |
| 3310m. | 7 | 7 | 7 | 4 | 2 | 1 | -1 | 1 | 4 | 6 | 6 | 7 |
| | 18 | 13 | 11 | 8 | 3 | 2 | 2 | 2 | 7 | 8 | 12 | 16 |
| **Guayaquil** | 31 | 31 | 32 | 31 | 31 | 29 | 28 | 29 | 30 | 29 | 30 | 31 |
| 6m. | 22 | 22 | 23 | 23 | 22 | 21 | 20 | 20 | 20 | 21 | 21 | 22 |
| | 12 | 13 | 15 | 10 | 4 | 1 | 0 | 0 | 0 | 1 | 0 | 2 |
| **La Paz, Bol.** | 18 | 18 | 18 | 19 | 17 | 17 | 17 | 17 | 18 | 19 | 19 | 19 |
| 3632m. | 6 | 6 | 6 | 5 | 3 | 2 | 1 | 2 | 3 | 5 | 6 | 6 |
| | 21 | 18 | 16 | 9 | 5 | 2 | 2 | 4 | 9 | 9 | 11 | 18 |
| **Lima** | 25 | 26 | 26 | 24 | 21 | 19 | 17 | 17 | 17 | 19 | 20 | 23 |
| 137m. | 19 | 20 | 19 | 18 | 16 | 15 | 14 | 13 | 13 | 14 | 16 | 17 |
| | 1 | 0 | 0 | 0 | 1 | 1 | 1 | 1 | 2 | 1 | 0 | 0 |
| **Manaus** | 30 | 30 | 30 | 30 | 31 | 31 | 32 | 33 | 33 | 33 | 32 | 31 |
| 48m. | 23 | 23 | 23 | 23 | 24 | 23 | 23 | 24 | 24 | 24 | 24 | 24 |
| | 20 | 18 | 21 | 20 | 18 | 12 | 12 | 5 | 7 | 4 | 12 | 16 |
| **Montevideo** | 28 | 28 | 26 | 22 | 18 | 15 | 14 | 15 | 17 | 20 | 23 | 26 |
| 22m. | 17 | 16 | 15 | 12 | 9 | 6 | 6 | 6 | 8 | 9 | 12 | 15 |
| | 6 | 5 | 5 | 6 | 6 | 5 | 6 | 7 | 6 | 6 | 6 | 7 |

## SOUTH AMERICA (Cont.)

| | Jan. | Feb. | Mar. | Apr. | May | June | July | Aug. | Sept. | Oct. | Nov. | Dec. |
|---|---|---|---|---|---|---|---|---|---|---|---|---|
| **Porto Alegre, Braz.** | 31 | 30 | 29 | 25 | 22 | 20 | 20 | 21 | 22 | 24 | 27 | 29 |
| 10m. | 20 | 20 | 19 | 16 | 13 | 11 | 10 | 11 | 13 | 15 | 17 | 18 |
| | 9 | 10 | 10 | 6 | 6 | 8 | 8 | 8 | 11 | 10 | 8 | 8 |
| **Punta Arenas,** | 15 | 14 | 13 | 9 | 6 | 4 | 3 | 4 | 7 | 10 | 12 | 14 |
| **Chile** | 7 | 7 | 6 | 4 | 2 | 1 | 1 | 1 | 2 | 3 | 4 | 6 |
| 28m. | 6 | 5 | 7 | 9 | 6 | 8 | 6 | 5 | 5 | 5 | 5 | 8 |
| **Quito** | 21 | 21 | 21 | 21 | 21 | 21 | 21 | 22 | 22 | 21 | 21 | 21 |
| 2818m. | 8 | 8 | 8 | 8 | 8 | 7 | 7 | 7 | 7 | 8 | 8 | 8 |
| | 9 | 11 | 11 | 15 | 10 | 9 | 3 | 3 | 8 | 13 | 13 | 7 |
| **Recife, Braz.** | 30 | 30 | 30 | 30 | 29 | 28 | 27 | 27 | 28 | 29 | 30 | 30 |
| 56m. | 24 | 25 | 24 | 23 | 23 | 22 | 21 | 21 | 22 | 23 | 24 | 24 |
| | 7 | 8 | 10 | 11 | 17 | 16 | 17 | 14 | 7 | 3 | 4 | 4 |
| **Rio de Janeiro** | 30 | 30 | 29 | 27 | 26 | 25 | 25 | 25 | 25 | 26 | 28 | 28 |
| 30m. | 23 | 23 | 23 | 21 | 20 | 18 | 18 | 18 | 19 | 20 | 20 | 22 |
| | 13 | 11 | 9 | 9 | 6 | 5 | 5 | 4 | 5 | 11 | 10 | 12 |
| **Salvador (Bahia)** | 29 | 29 | 29 | 28 | 27 | 26 | 26 | 26 | 27 | 28 | 28 | 29 |
| 8m. | 23 | 23 | 24 | 23 | 22 | 21 | 21 | 21 | 21 | 22 | 23 | 23 |
| | 6 | 9 | 17 | 19 | 22 | 23 | 18 | 15 | 10 | 8 | 9 | 11 |
| **Santa Cruz, Bol.** | 30 | 31 | 30 | 28 | 25 | 23 | 24 | 28 | 29 | 30 | 31 | 31 |
| 437m. | 21 | 21 | 20 | 19 | 16 | 15 | 15 | 16 | 19 | 20 | 20 | 21 |
| | 14 | 10 | 12 | 9 | 11 | 8 | 5 | 4 | 5 | 7 | 8 | 11 |
| **Santiago de Chile** | 29 | 29 | 27 | 23 | 18 | 14 | 15 | 17 | 19 | 22 | 26 | 28 |
| 520m. | 12 | 11 | 9 | 7 | 5 | 3 | 3 | 4 | 6 | 7 | 9 | 11 |
| | 0 | 0 | 1 | 1 | 5 | 6 | 6 | 5 | 3 | 3 | 1 | 0 |
| **São Paulo** | 28 | 28 | 27 | 25 | 23 | 22 | 21 | 23 | 25 | 25 | 25 | 26 |
| 792m. | 18 | 18 | 17 | 15 | 13 | 11 | 10 | 11 | 13 | 14 | 15 | 16 |
| | 15 | 13 | 12 | 6 | 3 | 4 | 4 | 3 | 5 | 12 | 11 | 14 |

*Sources:*—H.M.S.O. Meteorological Reports
K.L.M. Climatic Data Publication

# TEMPERATURES CONVERSION TABLE

| °C | °F | °C | °F | °C | °F | °C | °F |
|---|---|---|---|---|---|---|---|
| 1 | 34 | 11 | 52 | 21 | 70 | 31 | 88 |
| 2 | 36 | 12 | 54 | 22 | 72 | 32 | 90 |
| 3 | 38 | 13 | 56 | 23 | 74 | 33 | 92 |
| 4 | 39 | 14 | 57 | 24 | 75 | 34 | 93 |
| 5 | 41 | 15 | 59 | 25 | 77 | 35 | 95 |
| 6 | 43 | 16 | 61 | 26 | 79 | 36 | 97 |
| 7 | 45 | 17 | 63 | 27 | 81 | 37 | 99 |
| 8 | 46 | 18 | 64 | 28 | 82 | 38 | 100 |
| 9 | 48 | 19 | 66 | 29 | 84 | 39 | 102 |
| 10 | 50 | 20 | 68 | 30 | 86 | 40 | 104 |

The formula for converting °C to °F is: $°C \times 9 \div 5 + 32 = °F$.

# STANDARD TIME ZONES

| | | | |
|---|---|---|---|
| Argentina | 3 | Paraguay | 4(3†) |
| Falkland Islands | 4 | Peru | 5 |
| Bolivia | 4 | Uruguay | 3 |
| Brazil | 3*(2*1) | Venezuela | 4 |
| Chile | 4(3†) | Guyana | 3¾ |
| Colombia | 5 | Suriname | 3½ |
| Ecuador | 5 | Guyane | 3 |

* Standard time, except for Fernando de Noronha (2); Amazonia W of the Jari and Xingu rivers and E of the Tabatinga-Porto Acre line, and the States of Mato Grosso and Mato Grosso do Sul (4); and Amazonia W of the Tabatinga-Porto Acre line (5).    † Summer time, October-March.

# ECONOMIC INDICATORS

| COUNTRY | US$ GNP per head (1989)† | % change pa (1980-89)† | Annual Inflation* | Exchange rate/US$ | Parallel rate/US$ |
|---|---|---|---|---|---|
| ARGENTINA | 2,160 | -1.6% | 267.0%(4) | 9,833 | |
| BOLIVIA | 600 | -3.5% | 16.4%(2) | 3.54 | |
| BRAZIL | 2,550 | 0.9% | 414.0%(3) | 268 | 300 |
| CHILE | 1,770 | 1.0% | 22.9%(3) | 355 | 338 |
| COLOMBIA | 1,190 | 0.9% | 31.7%(2) | 611 | |
| ECUADOR | 1,040 | -0.5% | 49.0%(3) | 993 | 1,088 |
| PARAGUAY | 1,030 | -1.5% | 37.1%(3) | 1,323 | |
| PERU | 1,090 | -1.6% | 4,688.0%(3) | 0.76 | |
| URUGUAY | 2,620 | -0.8% | 111.6%(4) | 1,888 | |
| VENEZUELA | 2,450 | -2.3% | 36.0%(3) | 55.2 | |

† Source: World Bank
* 1991 latest month in brackets
Exchange rates at 10 May 1991

## WEIGHTS AND MEASURES

### Metric

*Weight:*
1 kilogram (kg.) = 2,205 pounds
1 metric ton = 1.102 short tons
= 0.984 long ton

*Length:*
1 millimetre (mm.) = 0.03937 inch
1 metre = 3.281 feet
1 kilometre (km.) = 0.621 mile

*Area:*
1 hectare = 2.471 acres
1 square km. (km²) = 0.386 sq. mile

*Capacity:*
1 litre = 0.220 Imperial gallon
= 0.264 U.S. gallon
(5 Imperial gallons are approximately equal to 6 U.S. gallons)

*Volume:*
1 cubic metre (m³) = 35.31 cubic feet
= 1.31 cubic yards

### British and U.S.

1 pound (lb.) = 454 grams
1 short ton (2,000 lb.) = 0.907 metric ton
1 long ton (2,240 lb.) = 1.016 metric tons

1 inch = 25.417 millimetres
1 foot (ft.) = 0.305 metre
1 mile = 1.609 kilometres

1 acre = 0.405 hectare
1 square mile (sq. mile) = 2,590 km²

1 Imperial gallon = 4.546 litres
1 U.S. gallon = 3.785 litres

1 cubic foot (cu. ft) = 0.028 m³
1 cubic yard (cu. yd.) = 0.765 m³

**N.B.** The *manzana*, used in Central America, is about 0.7 hectare (1.73 acres).

# INDEX TO PLACES

1245

# TOWN AND REGIONAL MAPS

# INDEX TO ADVERTISERS